ZONDERVAN CLASSIC REFERENCE SERIES

Zondervan's Pictorial Bible Dictionary

MERRILL C. TENNEY, GENERAL EDITOR

The Famous Wailing Wall
at Jerusalem. © MPS

ZONDERVAN CLASSIC REFERENCE SERIES

Zondervan's Pictorial Bible Dictionary

MERRILL C. TENNEY, GENERAL EDITOR

GRAND RAPIDS, MICHIGAN 49530

About the Author

The late Dr. Merrill C. Tenney, general editor, was professor of theological studies, Graduate School of Theology, Wheaton College, and the author of several scholarly books on the Bible and theology.

ZONDERVAN™

Zondervan's Pictorial Bible Dictionary
Copyright © 1963, 1964, 1967 by Zondervan

Requests for information should be addressed to:

Zondervan, *Grand Rapids, Michigan 49530*

ISBN: 0-310-23560-X

Published in association with Alive Communications, Inc., 7680 Goddard Street, Suite 200, Colorado Springs, CO 80920

Printed in the United States of America

16 17 18 19 /DCI/ 80 79 78 77 76 75 74 73

Preface

Robert A. Millikan, American physicist and Nobel prizewinner, once said that a knowledge of the Bible is an indispensable qualification of a well-educated man. No other single book in the history of literature has been so widely distributed or read, or has exercised so powerful an influence upon civilization. It is the fountainhead of Western culture, and is the sole source of spiritual life and revelation for all Christians. For the development of Christian experience and for the propagation of faith, a study of the Scriptures is absolutely necessary. The history, laws, prophecies, sermons and letters which they contain provide God's estimate of man and His disclosure of Himself through the historic process of revelation culminating in the person of His Son, Jesus Christ.

Understanding the Bible is often difficult for the average reader because of the unfamiliar names of persons, places and objects to which it alludes. The historical and cultural backgrounds are alien to those of the modern day, and presuppose knowledge that is not easily attainable. The function of a Bible dictionary is to render accessible a body of information which will enable one to comprehend the meaning of the text he is reading, and to obtain ready and complete data concerning any related subject.

Within recent years, the need for a new, up-to-date reference work has become increasingly urgent. Fresh discoveries in archaeology, better understanding of the history and geography of the Middle East, and the fruit of multiplied research have provided new insights and interpretations. The advance of the graphic arts has improved greatly the effectiveness of photography, so that the artifacts and inscriptions of the past can be reproduced vividly for public exhibition. Realizing the opportunity for a fresh venture in this field, the Zondervan Publishing House, inspired by the interest and foresight of Mr. Peter deVisser, Director of Publications, has undertaken the task of creating a totally new dictionary, enlisting the cooperation of sixty-five competent scholars in every field from archaeology to zoology. The content includes more than five thousand entries, among which may be found a number of important monographs on Biblical and theological topics. In addition, the dictionary contains an extensive series of articles on Christian doctrines.

Zondervan's Pictorial Bible Dictionary is a completely new, fully illustrated one-volume work. It is designed to provide quick access to explanatory data, both by the verbal exposition of biographical, chronological, geographical and historical aspects of the Bible, and by the illustrations related to them. The pictures have been selected for their relevance to the subject matter, for their historical value, and also with an eye to human interest.

The scope of a one-volume dictionary is necessarily limited. The articles are not intended to be exhaustive, nor are they planned primarily for professional scholars. They are gauged for the use of pastors, Sunday-school teachers, Bible class leaders and students who desire concise and accurate information on questions raised by ordinary reading. For intensive research, a more detailed and critical work is recommended.

Although the articles are written from a conservative viewpoint, each writer has been free to express his own opinions and is responsible for the material that appears over his signature. There may be minor disagreements between statements by different persons; in such instances there is room for debate, and the contributors have liberty to differ. Uncertainty still exists in some fields, since sufficient data are not available for final conclusions.

While the writers are indebted to many sources, no previously published work has been incorporated in these pages. The pictures have been taken chiefly from recent photographs, and are not old reprints. No expense has been spared to prepare the best possible aid for the Bible student.

In the matter of illustrations, special thanks are due Mr. and Mrs. G. Eric Matson of the Matson Photo Service, Los Angeles, formerly of the American Colony in Jerusalem, for placing at our disposal their vast and unsurpassed collection of photographs gathered in a lifetime career of professional photography in the Bible lands. We wish herewith also to thank all organizations and individuals who have extended their help in supplying photos and illustrations, including: the Oriental Institute of the University of Chicago; the British Museum of London; the University Museum of Pennsylvania; the Radio Times Hulton Picture Library of London; Dr. Edward F. Campbell, Jr., Editor of *The Biblical Archaeologist*; the American Schools of Oriental Research; the University of Michigan Library; Dr. John F. Walvoord and Dr. Merrill F. Unger of Dallas Theological Seminary; Dr. and Mrs. Henry H.

Halley of Chicago; Dr. Siegfried H. Horn of Andrews University, and others.

A complete bibliography of all sources of information would obviously be impossible. Selected references have been appended to major articles in order to afford opportunity for further research.

Names of persons and places, for the most part, have been taken from the King James Version, which is still more widely read than any other, but variants occurring in the American Standard Version and in the Revised Standard Version have been noted. Pronunciation follows the practice of the unabridged second edition of Webster's *New International Dictionary of the English Language*. All Hebrew and Greek names, as well as other names and terms, are followed by their English pronunciations in parentheses. Transliterated Hebrew and Greek words appear in italics, with their meaning when it can be identified. A list of symbols and abbreviations appears on pages xiii and xiv.

Special acknowledgments are due to Dr. Steven Barabas, Associate Editor, who collaborated in preparing articles for publication, and who contributed many himself; to Dr. E. M. Blaiklock, Professor Wick Broomall, Dr. Howard Z. Cleveland, the Rev. Charles Cook, Dr. Carl DeVries, the Rev. Arthur B. Fowler, the Rev. J. P. Freeman, Dr. Guy B. Funderburk, the Rev. Clyde E. Harrington, Dr. D. Edmund Hiebert, the Rev. John G. Johansson, the Rev. Brewster Porcella, Professor Arthur M. Ross, Dr. Emmet Russell, and Dr. Walter Wessel, who, in addition to the initialed articles published under their names contributed many of the unsigned articles; to Miss Verda Bloomhuff and the Rev. Briggs P. Dingman, who assisted in correction of copy and proof; and to Mrs. Carol Currie and Mrs. Alice Holmes for invaluable secretarial service. The General Editor wishes to express his gratitude to all those scholars named in the list of contributors who have lent their time and counsel to the production of this book.

Wheaton, Illinois
February, 1963

MERRILL C. TENNEY

Picture Sources

As stated on the copyright page, the photos and illustrations included in this Zondervan Pictorial Bible Dictionary are used by special arrangement with the copyright owners of these materials, and are not to be reproduced without special permission from the original sources. These sources are indicated by initials at the close of descriptive cutlines with each picture:

ABA, APD	American Baptist Assembly, Green Lake, Wisconsin, and A. Paul Davis, St. Louis, Mo., designer and author of *Aaron's Breastplate*
AMO	Ashmolean Museum of Antiquities, Oxford, England
ASOR	American Schools of Oriental Research, Jerusalem and Baghdad; c/o Yale Station, New Haven, Conn.
AU	Andrews University, Berrien Springs, Michigan
BA	*Biblical Archaeologist, The;* c/o ASOR above
BFBS	British and Foreign Bible Society, London
BM	British Museum, London; courtesy of the Trustees of the British Museum
BrM	Brooklyn Museum, Department of Ancient Art, Brooklyn, New York
CE	Comstock's *Introduction to Entomology*, Cornell University Press
CM	Cairo Museum (Egyptian National Museum), Cairo, Egypt
CNHM	Chicago Natural History Museum, Chicago
CS	Cooper Square Facsimile Edition of the Gutenberg Bible, Cooper Square Publishers, New York
CWC	Dr. Charles W. Carter, Marion, Indiana; map from *Evangelical Commentary on Acts*
DV	J. DeVries' drawings from *Bijbels Beeld Woordenboek*, published by J. H. Kok, N.V., Kampen, Holland
EG	Ewing Galloway (photo agency), New York
EGH	E. G. Howland, Troy, Ohio, builder of Howland-Garber models of the Temple (with Dr. Paul L. Garber, Agnes Scott College, Decatur, Georgia)
FK	Fahim Kouchakji, New York; from *The Great Chalice of Antioch*, by G. A. Eisen, © 1933
FRC	*Everyday Life in Ancient Rome*, © by F. R. Cowell; drawings by D. Stredder Bist, published by B. T. Batsford, Ltd., London
GHR	Elder Gwang Hyuk Rhee, Seoul, Korea
GL	Georgios Lykides (photo agency), Thessaloniki, Greece
HAR	H. Armstrong Roberts (photo agency), Philadelphia
HML	Harold M. Lamberts (photo agency), Philadelphia
JFW	Dr. John F. Walvoord, Dallas Theological Seminary

JG	John and J. B. E. Garstang, from *The Story of Jericho*, Marshall, Morgan & Scott, Ltd., London
JHK	J. H. Kok, N.V., publishers: *De Antieke Wereld en Het Nieuwe Testament*, by A. Sizoo; Kampen, Holland
JPF	Dr. Joseph P. Free, Wheaton, Illinois (from *The Bible and Archaeology*, Scripture Press)
KB	Kriebel & Bates, Inc., Indianapolis, Indiana
KC, FC	Kreigh Collins' drawings, from *Bible Days*, by Meindert DeJong, © Fideler Company, Grand Rapids, Michigan
KPA	Keystone Press Agency, Inc., New York
LMP	Louvre Museum, Paris (Musée du Louvre, Paris; Ministère D'État Affaires Culturelles)
LO	Mrs. Lowell Orth
MM	Metropolitan Museum of Art, New York
MPS	Matson Photo Service, Mr. and Mrs. G. Eric Matson, Los Angeles, California
NPG	National Portrait Gallery, London
OIUC	Oriental Institute of the University of Chicago
PAM	Palestine Archaeological Museum, Jerusalem
PB	Dr. Paul Bauman, Winona Lake, Indiana
PEF	Palestine Exploration Fund, Jerusalem
PG	Philip Gendreau (photo agency), New York
RHP	Robert H. Pfeiffer, *Ancient Alphabets*, Semitic Museum, Harvard University, Cambridge, Mass., 1947
ROL	Rijksmuseum van Oudheden, Leiden, Holland
RTHPL	Radio Times Hulton Picture Library, British Broadcasting Corporation, London
SB	Shrine of the Book, Jerusalem
SD	*Stitt's Diagnosis, Prevention and Treatment of Tropical Diseases*, by R. P. Strong, © Blakiston Co. (McGraw-Hill), Philadelphia, 1944
SHH	Dr. S. H. Horn, Andrews University, Berrien Springs, Michigan
SMB	State Museum of Berlin
SPF	Standard Publishing Foundation, Cincinnati, Ohio. Drawings by Wilbur G. Adam from *Life and Customs in Jesus' Time*, by Joseph L. Gift, © 1957 SPF
UANT	Unger's *Archaeology and the New Testament*; drawings by Alan Marshall and Robert Ramey, courtesy Dr. Merrill F. Unger, Dallas Theological Seminary
UAOT	Unger's *Archaeology and the Old Testament*
UML	University of Michigan Library, Rare Book Department, Ann Arbor, Michigan
UMP	University Museum of the University of Pennsylvania, Philadelphia

Frontispiece: The famous Wailing Wall, or Wailing Place, at Jerusalem, where Jews gather each year to mourn the lost glory of ancient Israel and to observe the destruction of the Temple. Solomon's Temple was destroyed by the Babylonians in 586 B.C. and Herod's Temple by the Romans in 70 A.D. This wall is a section of the west wall of the Dome of the Rock, the mosque that now stands on the temple site, and which wall is believed to be composed of stones taken from the ruins of Herod's Temple when the mosque was built. The wall is also sometimes called Solomon's Wall, because traditionally these same stones are thought to have been part of the original Temple of Solomon. © MPS

Contributors

Initials at left, used at close of articles, designate authorship of major articles in this work.

P.E.A. **PAUL E. ADOLPH**
M.D. (School of Medicine, University of Pennsylvania). Deceased. Former Medical Director, Chicago Missionary Medical Office. F.A.C.S., 1944. Author: *Health Shall Spring Forth; Triumphant Living; Missionary Health Manual; Physical and Emotional Stress of Missionary Work.*

O.T.A. **OSWALD T. ALLIS**
B.D. (Princeton Theological Seminary), Ph.D. (University of Berlin). Deceased. Former Professor Emeritus of Old Testament, Westminster Theological Seminary, Philadelphia. Author: *The Five Books of Moses; Prophecy and the Church.*

G.L.A. **GLEASON L. ARCHER, JR.**
Ph.D. (Harvard University). B.D. (Princeton Theological Seminary). Professor of Old Testament and Chairman of Division, Trinity Evangelical Divinity School. Author: *In the Shadow of the Cross; The Study Manual of the Epistle to the Hebrews.*

S.B. **STEVEN BARABAS**
Th.D. (Princeton Theological Seminary), Professor of Theology, Wheaton College. Author: *So Great Salvation.*

C.B.B. **CLARENCE B. BASS**
B.A., M.A. (Wheaton College), Th.D. (University of Edinburgh). Professor of Systematic Theology, Bethel Seminary, St. Paul, Minn. Author: *Dispensationalism.*

E.M.B. **E. M. BLAIKLOCK**
Litt.D., Professor of Classics, University of Auckland, New Zealand, Emeritus. Author: *The Acts of the Apostles (Tyndale Commentary); The Seven Churches; Out of the Earth; The Christian in Pagan Society; The Century of the New Testament.*

D.C.B. **DONALD CHAPIN BOARDMAN**
B.S. (Wheaton College), M.S. (Iowa), Ph.D. (Wisconsin). Professor of Geology, Department Chairman, Wheaton College, Wheaton, Illinois. Co-Author with John DeVries: *Essentials of Physical Science.*

G.W.B. **G. W. BROMILEY**
Ph.D., D.Litt.,D.D. (University of Edinburgh). Professor of Church History and Historical Theology, Fuller Theological Seminary. Author: *Baptism and the Anglican Reformers; Thomas Cranmer, Theologian; Sacramental Teaching and Practice of the Reformation Churches.*

W.B. **WICK BROOMALL**
Th.M. (Princeton Theological Seminary), M.A. (Princeton University). Deceased. Former Pastor, Westminster Presbyterian Church, Augusta, Georgia. Author: *The Holy Spirit; Biblical Criticism.*

F.F.B. **F. F. BRUCE**
M.A., D.D. (Aberdeen University). Rylands Professor of Biblical Criticism and Exegesis, University of Manchester, England. Editor, *The Evangelical Quarterly* and *The Palestine Exploration Quarterly.* Author: *The Books and the Parchments; The Spreading Flame; The Book of the Acts; The English Bible; Second Thoughts on the Dead Sea Scrolls; Israel and the Nations.*

J.O.B. **JAMES OLIVER BUSWELL, JR.**
B.D. (McCormick Theological Seminary), M.A. (University of Chicago), Ph.D. (New York University). Dean of the Graduate Faculty, Covenant College and Seminary, St. Louis. Author: *Problems in the Prayer Life; The Lamb of God Series; Sin and Atonement; A Christian View of Being and Knowing; Systematic Theology.*

H.Z.C. **HOWARD Z. CLEVELAND**
Th.D. (Dallas Theological Seminary). Chairman, Departments of Theology and Greek, Oak Hills Bible Institute. Contributor to *Dictionary of Theology* (Ed., Everett Harrison).

C.E.C. **CHARLES E. COOK**
Th.M. (Westminster Theological Seminary). Pastor, First Baptist Church, Concord, New Hampshire. Instructor, Barrington College.

C.E.D. **CARL E. DeVRIES**
B.D. (Wheaton College), Ph.D. (University of Chicago). Research Associate (Associate Professor), The Oriental Institute, University of Chicago. Member University of Chicago Oriental Institute Nubian Expedition, 1963-64.

B.P.D. **BRIGGS P. DINGMAN**
A.B. (Southwestern Bible College), Moody Bible Institute, Dickinson College, Xenia Theological Seminary. Deceased. Former instructor, Modern Languages and History, Elim Bible Institute, Lima, New York.

R.E. **RALPH EARLE**
M.A. (Boston U.), Th.D. (Gordon Divinity School). Professor of New Testament, Nazarene Theological Seminary, Kansas City. Author: *The Story of the New Testament; Meet the Minor Prophets; Meet the Major Prophets; Meet the Early Church; Revelation; The Gospel According to Mark.*

A.B.F. **ARTHUR B. FOWLER**
B.A. (Princeton University), B.D. (Princeton Theological Seminary). Dean Emeritus, Buffalo Bible Institute.

J.P.F. **JOSEPH P. FREE**
Ph.D. (Princeton University). Professor of Archaeology and History, Bemidji State College, Minnesota. Author: *Archaeology and Bible History.*

J.D.F. **JOHN D. FREEMAN**
Th.M. (Southern Baptist Seminary), LH.D. (University of Arkansas). Editor, *Baptist and Reflector* of Tennessee and *Western Recorder* of Kentucky.

G.B.F. **GUY B. FUNDERBURK**
Ph.D. (Southern Baptist Theological Seminary). Retired. Former Chairman, Department of Religion and Philosophy, Salem College, West Virginia.

J.F.G. **JOHN F. GATES**
S.T.D. (Temple University School of Theology). Professor of Bible and Philosophy, Saint Paul Bible College, St. Paul, Minnesota. Author: *Adventures in the History of Philosophy.* Contributor, *Wycliffe Bible Commentary.*

B.L.G. **BURTON L. GODDARD**
Th.D. (Harvard University). Professor of Biblical Languages and Exegesis, Gordon Divinity School, Beverly Farms, Mass. Contributor, *Dictionary of Theology, Wycliffe Bible Commentary, The Biblical Expositor, Encyclopedia of Christianity.*

J.B.G. **JOHN B. GRAYBILL**
Ph.D. (Brandeis University), B.D. (Faith Theological Seminary), Barrington Presbyterian Church, Barrington, R. I. Contributor, *Wycliffe Commentary.*

J.H.G. **J. HAROLD GREENLEE**
Ph.D. (Harvard University). Missionary of O.M.S. International and Professor, United Biblical Seminary of Columbia. Author: *The Gospel Text of Cyril of Jerusalem; A Concise Exegetical Grammar of New Testament Greek; Introduction to New Testament Textual Criticism.*

V.C.G. **VERNON C. GROUNDS**
B.D. (Faith Theological Seminary), Ph.D. (Drew University). President, Conservative Baptist Theological Seminary, Denver, Colo. Author: *The Reason for Our Hope.*

C.E.H. **CLYDE E. HARRINGTON**
B.D. (Faith Theological Seminary), Ph.D. (Dropsie College). Former instructor, Lancaster School of the Bible. Editorial Assistant, American Sunday School Union, Philadelphia.

R.L.H. **R. LAIRD HARRIS**
Ph.D. (Dropsie College), Th.M. (Westminster Theological Seminary). Professor of Old Testament and Dean of the Faculty, Covenant Theological Seminary, St. Louis. Author: *Introductory Hebrew Grammar; Inspiration and Canonicity of the Bible;* Contributor, *Inspiration and Interpretation* (Ed., John F. Walvoord); *The Wycliffe Commentary.*

E.F.H. **EVERETT F. HARRISON**
Th.D. (Dallas Theological Seminary), Ph.D. (University of Pennsylvania). Professor of New Testament, Fuller Theological Seminary. Author: *The Son of God Among the Sons of Men;* reviser, *Alford's Greek New Testament;* editor, *A Dictionary of Theology.*

R.K.H. **ROLAND KENNETH HARRISON**
M.Th. (London University), Ph.D. (University of London), D.D. (Huron College), Professor of Old Testament, Wycliffe College, University of Toronto. Author: *Teach Yourself Hebrew; A History of Old Testament Times; The Dead Sea Scrolls; The Psalms for Today; The Archaeology of the Old Testament.*

H.H.H. **H. HAROLD HARTZLER**
Ph.D. (Rutgers University). Professor of Physics, Mankato State College, Minn.

W.H. **WILLIAM HENDRIKSEN**
Th.D. (Princeton Theological Seminary). Pastor, Creston Christian Reformed Church, Grand Rapids, Michigan. Author: *More Than Conquerors; Bible Survey.* Contributor, *New Testament Commentary.* Translator, H. Bavinck's, *The Doctrine of God.*

D.E.H. **D. EDMOND HIEBERT**
Th.D. (Southern Baptist Theological Seminary). Professor of Greek and New Testament, Mennonite Brethren Biblical Seminary. Author: *Titus and Philemon; I Timothy and II Timothy.*

H.P.H. **H. PAUL HOLDRIDGE**
Tarleton College, Southern Methodist University; B.A. Central Pilgrim College. Pastor and editor, Bartlesville, Oklahoma.

J.G.J. **JOHN G. JOHANSSON**
A.B. (Methodist Theological School), Uppsala, Sweden. Production Manager, *Christianity Today,* Washington, D. C.

L.A.K. **LLOYD A. KALLAND**
A.B. in Th., (Gordon College), B.D. (Theological Seminary of the Reformed Episcopal Church), M.A. (University of Pennsylvania), Th.M. (Westminster Theological Seminary), Th.D. (Northern Baptist Theological Seminary). Professor of Philosophy of Religion, Gordon Divinity School.

K.S.K. **KENNETH S. KANTZER**
S.T.M. (Faith Theological Seminary), Ph.D. (Harvard University). Chairman, Division of Biblical Education and Philosophy, Wheaton College, Wheaton, Illinois. Contributor, *Inspiration and Interpretation* and *Religions of the World.*

M.G.K. **MEREDITH G. KLINE**
Th.B., Th.M., Ph.D. (Dropsie College). Professor of Old Testament, Westminster Theological Seminary, Philadelphia; Contributor, *Wycliffe Bible Commentary; New Bible Dictionary.*

G.E.L. **GEORGE E. LADD**
B.D. (Gordon Divinity School), Ph.D. (Harvard University). Professor of Biblical Theology, Fuller Theological Seminary. Author: *Crucial Questions About the Kingdom of God; The Blessed Hope; The Gospel of the Kingdom.*

W.S.L.S. **WILLIAM SANFORD LaSOR**
Ph.D. (Dropsie College), Th.D. (University of Southern California). Professor of Old Testament, Fuller Theological Seminary. Author: *Amazing Dead Sea Scrolls and the Christian Faith; Great Personalities of the Old Testament; Historical Geography of the Bible Lands; Great Personalities of the New Testament.* Bibliography Editor, *Revue de Qumran.*

J.L.L. **JOHN L. LEEDY**
Ph.D. (University of Minnesota). Professor of Botany, Wheaton College, Wheaton, Illinois.

C.M. **CLINTON MACK**
Ph.D. (Western Reserve). Professor of Biology, Wheaton College, Wheaton, Illinois.

A.A.M. **ALLAN A. MacRAE**
Th.B. (Princeton Theological Seminary), Ph.D. (University of Pennsylvania). President and Professor of Old Testament, Biblical School of Theology, Hatfield, Pennsylvania, Contributor, *New Bible Dictionary.*

A.B.M. **A. BERKELEY MICKELSEN**
B.D. (Wheaton), Ph.D. (University of Chicago). Professor of Bible and Theology, Wheaton College Graduate School of Theology. Contributor, *The Biblical Expositor; Wycliffe Bible Commentary.*

G.R.M. **GLEN R. MILLER**
Ph.D. (State University of Iowa). Chairman, Science Division, and Chairman, Chemistry Department, Goshen College, Goshen, Indiana.

R.L.M. **RUSSELL L. MIXTER**
Ph.D. (University of Illinois). Professor of Zoology, Wheaton College. Editor, *Evolution and Christian Thought Today.*

L.G.O. **LEE G. OLSON**
S.M.D. (Union Theological Seminary). Chairman, Division of Sacred Music, Nyack Missionary College, Nyack, New York. Editorial Advisor and Coordinator for *Hymns of the Christian Life,* 1962.

G.F.O. **G. FREDERICK OWEN**
A.B., M.A., B.D. (Vanderbilt University). Retired. Former Professor of Archaeology, Pasadena College, Carver Foundation Lecturer; Member, Society of Oriental Research. Author: *Abraham to Armageddon; The Shepherd Psalm of Palestine; Archaeology and the Bible.*

J.B.P. **J. BARTON PAYNE**
Th.D. (Princeton Theological Seminary). Professor of Old Testament, Covenant Theological Seminary. Author: *An Outline of Hebrew History; Hebrew Vocabularies; Theology of the Older Testament; The Imminent Appearing of Christ.*

L.M.P. **LORMAN M. PETERSEN**
Th.M. (Concordia Seminary). Professor of New Testament Interpretation; Academic Dean, Concordia Theological Seminary, Springfield, Ill.

C.F.P. **CHARLES F. PFEIFFER**
B.D. (Theological Seminary of the Reformed Episcopal Church), Ph.D. (Dropsie College). Professor of Ancient Literature, Central Michigan University. Author: *The Dead Sea Scrolls; The Book of Leviticus; The Book of Genesis; Between the Testaments.*

B.P. **BREWSTER PORCELLA**
B.D., A.M. (Wheaton College). Pastor, Twin City Bible Church, Urbana, Illinois.

J.R. **JOHN REA**
Th.D. (Grace Theological Seminary).
Managing Editor of *Wycliffe Bible Commentary; New Bible Dictionary.*

A.M.R. **ARTHUR M. ROSS**
B.S., B.D., A.M. (Wheaton). Dean of
College-Credit Instruction, Correspondence School, Moody Bible Institute.

E.R. **EMMET RUSSELL**
S.T.D. (Gordon College of Theology
and Missions). Retired. Former pastor
of Short Beach United Church, Short
Beach, Conn.

A.C.S. **ARNOLD C. SCHULTZ**
Th.D. (Northern Baptist Theological
Seminary). Lecturer in Archaeology,
Roosevelt University.

S.J.S. **SAMUEL J. SCHULTZ**
A.B., B.D., S.T.M., Th.D. (Harvard
University). Chairman, Division of Biblical Studies, Wheaton College and
Wheaton Graduate School. Author: *The
Old Testament Speaks.*

D.H.S. **DWIGHT H. SMALL**
B.D. (San Francisco Theological Seminary). Pastor, Peninsula Covenant
Church, Redwood City, Calif. Author:
Design for Christian Marriage; The Biblical Basis for Infant Baptism.

W.M.S. **WILBUR M. SMITH**
Emeritus Professor of English Bible,
Trinity Evangelical Divinity School,
Deerfield, Ill. Editor, *Peloubet's Select
Notes* on the International Sunday School
Lessons. Author: *Profitable Bible Study;
Chats from a Minister's Library,* etc.

M.C.T. **MERRILL C. TENNEY**
Ph.D. (Harvard University). J. P. Williston Professor of Bible and Theology,
Graduate School of Theology, Wheaton
College. Author: *John, the Gospel of
Belief; New Testament Survey; The
Genius of the Gospels; Galatians, The
Charter of Christian Liberty; Interpreting Revelation.*

E.R.T. **EDWIN R. THIELE**
Ph.D. (University of Chicago). Chairman, Department of Religion, Andrews
University, Berrien Springs, Mich. Author: *The Mysterious Numbers of Hebrew Kings.*

M.F.U. **MERRILL F. UNGER**
Ph.D. (Johns Hopkins University), Th.D.
(Dallas Theological Seminary). Professor of Old Testament and Chairman, Old
Testament and Semitics, Dallas Theological Seminary. Author: *Introductory
Guide to the Old Testament; Archaeology and the New Testament; Biblical Demonology; Archaeology and the Old
Testament; Israel and the Aramaeans of
Damascus.* Editor, *Unger's Bible Dictionary.*

W.W. **WINNIFRED WALKER**
Fellow, Linnean Society, gold medallist;
Artist to Royal Horticultural Society,
1929, 1939; appointed artist to University of California, 1943; Instructor of
Art, University of California at Los Angeles, 1947. Author: "Flowers of Shakespeare," "Plants of the Holy Bible,"
"Flowers of London's Bombed Areas" in
*Illustrated London News; All the Plants
of the Bible.*

J.F.W. **JOHN F. WALVOORD**
A.M. (Texas Christian University),
Th.D. (Dallas Theological Seminary).
President and Professor of Systematic
Theology, Dallas Theological Seminary.
Author: *The Holy Spirit; The Return of
the Lord; The Thessalonian Epistles; The
Rapture Question; The Millennial Kingdom; To Live Is Christ; Israel in Prophecy; The Church in Prophecy;* Editor,
Truth for Today.

W.M.W. **W. M. WHITWELL**
B.S., B.D. Pastor, Evangel Baptist
Church, Portland, Oregon.

W.W.W. **WALTER W. WESSEL**
Ph.D. (University of Edinburgh). Associate Professor of Biblical Literature,
Bethel College, St. Paul, Minn. Contributor, *Dictionary of Theology; The
New Bible Dictionary; The Biblical Expositor; The Wycliffe Bible Commentary.*

J.C.W. **JOHN C. WHITCOMB, JR.**
Th.D. (Grace Theological Seminary).
Professor of Theology and Old Testament; Director of Post Graduate Studies,
Grace Theological Seminary, Winona
Lake, Indiana. Author: *The Genesis
Flood; Darius the Mede.* Contributor,
*I.V.F. Bible Dictionary; Encyclopedia of
Christianity; Wycliffe Bible Commentary.*

E.J.Y. **EDWARD J. YOUNG**
Th.M. (Westminster Theological Seminary), Ph.D. (Dropsie College). Professor of Old Testament, Westminster Theological Seminary, Philadelphia. Editor,
Tyndale Old Testament Commentaries.
Author: *Introduction to the Old Testament; The Prophecy of Daniel; Studies
in Isaiah; Arabic for Beginners.*

Abbreviations

The following is a standard list of abbreviations for periodicals, reference works, and dictionaries, used in this work:

A-S	Abbott-Smith, *Manual Greek Lexicon of the NT*	JBR	*Journal of Bible and Religion*
Alf	Alford's Greek Testament	JNES	*Journal of Near Eastern Studies*
Arndt	Arndt-Gingrich, *Greek-English Lexicon*	Jos	Josephus, *Antiquities of the Jews*, etc.
ARAB	*Ancient Records of Assyria and Babylonia* (D. D. Luckenbill, 1926)	JQR	*Jewish Quarterly Review*
		JTS	*Journal of Theological Studies*
ARC	*Archaeology*	KD	Keil and Delitzsch, *Commentary on the OT*
ASV	American Standard Version (occasionally designated ARV) (1901)	KJV	King James (Authorized) Version
AThR	Anglican Theological Review	LSJ	Liddell, Scott, Jones, *Greek-English Lexicon*
AV	Authorized (King James) Version; see KJV	LXX	Septuagint
BA	*Biblical Archeologist*	MM	Moulton and Milligan, *The Vocabulary of the Gr. Test.*
BASOR	*Bulletin of American Schools of Oriental Research*	MNT	*Moffatt's New Testament Commentary*
Beng	Bengel's *Gnomon*	MSt	McClintock and Strong, *Cyclopaedia of Biblical, Theological and Ecclesiastical Literature*
Blunt	Blunt's *Dictionary of Doctrinal and Historical Theology*		
BS	*Bibliotheca Sacra*	NT	New Testament
BTh	*Biblical Theology*	Nestle	Nestle (ed) *Novum Testamentum Graece*
CBQ	*Catholic Biblical Quarterly*		
ChT	*Christianity Today*	NovTest	*Novum Testamentum*
Corp Herm	*Corpus Hermeticum*	NTS	*New Testament Studies*
Crem	Cremer's *Biblico-Theological Lexicon of NT Greek*	OT	Old Testament
		PTR	*Princeton Theological Review*
DeissBS	Deissmann, *Bible Studies*	RB	*Révue Biblique*
DeissLAE	Deissmann, *Light from the Ancient East*	RGG	*Die Religion in Geschichte und Gegenwart*
EQ	*Evangelical Quarterly*	R-V	Revised Version (see ERV)
ERV	English Revised Version (1881), occasionally designated RV	RSV	Revised Standard Version, 1952
		RTWB	*Richardson's Theological Word Book*
ETh	*Evangelische Theologie*	SBK	*Kommentar zum Neuen Testament aus Talmud und Midrasch* (Strack and Billerbeck)
EXP	*The Expositor*		
EB	*The Expositor's Bible*		
EGT	*The Expositor's Greek Testament*	SHERK	*The New Schaff-Herzog Encyclopedia of Religious Knowledge*
ExpT	*The Expository Times*		
GR	*Gordon Review*	ST	*Studia Theologica*
HDAC	Hastings' *Dictionary of the Apostolic Church*	TCERK	*The Twentieth Century Encyclopedia of Religious Knowledge*
HDB	Hastings' *Dictionary of the Bible*	ThLZ	*Theologische Literaturzeitung*
HDCG	Hastings' *Dictionary of Christ and the Gospels*	ThR	*Theologische Rundschau*
		ThT	*Theology Today*
HERE	Hastings' *Encyclopaedia of Religion and Ethics*	Trench	*Trench's Synonyms of the New Testament*
HJ	*Hibbert Journal*	TWNT	*Theologisches Worterbuch zum Neuen Testament* (Kittel)
HR	Hatch and Redpath, *Concordance to the LXX*		
		VT	*Vetus Testamentum*
HTR	*Harvard Theological Review*	Wett	Wettstein's *Novum Testamentum Graecum*
HZNT	*Handbuch zum Neuen Testament* (Lietzmann)		
IB	*Interpreter's Bible*	WC	Westminster Commentaries
ICC	*International Critical Commentary*	WH	Westcott and Hort, *Text of the Greek NT*
INT	*Interpretation*		
ISBE	*International Standard Bible Encyclopaedia*	WTJ	*Westminster Theological Journal*
		ZAW	*Zeitschrift fur die alttestamentliche Wissenschaft*
JewEnc	*Jewish Encyclopaedia*		
JBL	*Journal of Biblical Literature*	ZNW	*Zeitschrift fur die neutestamentliche Wissenschaft*

The following abbreviations are used for books of the Bible when mentioned in parenthetical references. When the name of the Bible book is in the text of an article, it is ordinarily not abbreviated.

OLD TESTAMENT

Gen.	Prov.
Exod.	Eccl.
Lev.	S. of Sol.
Num.	Isa.
Deut.	Jer.
Josh.	Lam.
Judg.	Ezek.
Ruth	Dan.
I Sam.	Hos.
II Sam.	Joel
I Kings	Amos
II Kings	Obad.
I Chron.	Jonah
II Chron.	Mic.
Ezra	Nah.
Neh.	Hab.
Esth.	Zeph.
Job	Hag.
Ps. (Pss.)	Zech.
	Mal.

NEW TESTAMENT

Matt.	II Thess.
Mark	I Tim.
Luke	II Tim.
John	Titus
Acts	Philem.
Rom.	Heb.
I Cor.	James
II Cor.	I Pet.
Gal.	II Pet.
Eph.	I John
Phil.	II John
Col.	III John
I Thess.	Jude
	Rev.

ENGLISH PRONUNCIATION

VOWELS

ā as in tāme, hāte, chā'ŏs, dāte
ă as in hăt, ăsk, glăss, ădd, lăp
â as in câre, bâre, râre
à as in àh, àrm, fà'thêr, sō'fà

ē as in ēve, hēre, ēvĕnt', mēēt
ĕ as in ĕnd, sī'lĕnt, pĕt, ēvĕnt
êr as in mākêr, ōvêr, ŭndêr, fàthêr, êrr

ī as in īce, bīte, mīle, fīne
ĭ as in ĭll, hĭt, hĭm, chârĭty
î as in bîrth, mîrth

ō as in ōld, ōbey, gō, tōne, bōwl
ŏ as in ŏn, ŏdd, cŏnnĕct, lŏt, tŏp
ô as in ôrb, sôft, hôrn, fôrk, nôr

ōō as in fōōd, lōōt, trōōp
ŏŏ as in fŏŏt, bŏŏk, hŏŏk

ū as in tūne, rūde, ūnīte', ūse, cūte
ŭ as in ŭs, ŭp, bŭt
û as in ûrn, tûrn, fûr

CONSONANTS

b bed, dub
d did, had
f fall, off
g get, dog
h he, ahead
j joy, jump
k kill, bake
l let, ball
m met, trim
n not, ton
p put, tap
r red, dear
s sell, pass
t top, hat
v vat, have
w will, always
y yet, yard
z zebra, haze

ch chin, arch
n ring, drink
sh she, dash
th thin, truth
th then, father
zh azure, leisure

For other variations, also double vowels and consonants, we use simplified and phonetic spelling to indicate pronunciation:

â for e in where, there, etc.
â for ei, ai, ea in their, fair, bear, etc.
ā for ai in hail, pail, etc.
aw for au, ou in ought, caught, etc.
ē for ee, ea, in heed, meat, meal, dear, etc.
ē for i in machine, etc.
ē for y in belly, fully, charity, etc.
ī for ei in heil, etc.
ī for y in type, why, etc.
ĭ for y in typical, hypnosis, etc.

oi for oy, oi, in boy, boil, oil, foil
ow for ou in about, shout
ū for eu in neuter, etc.
egs for x in example, etc.
j for soft g in giant, etc.
k for hard ch in character, etc.
s for soft c in celestial, etc.
sh for s in adhesion, etc.
shun for tion in attention, etc.
z for soft s in his, etc.

Zondervan's
Pictorial
Bible
Dictionary

MERRILL C. TENNEY, GENERAL EDITOR

Jethro's Pass in the
Valley of Mount Sinai
© MPS

A

AARON (âr'ŭn, Heb. *'ahărôn,* meaning undetermined), the oldest son of Amram and Jochebed, of the tribe of Levi, and brother of Moses and Miriam (Num. 26:59, Exod. 6:20). He was born during the captivity in Egypt, before Pharaoh's edict that all male infants should be destroyed, and was three years older than Moses (Exod. 7:7). His name first appears in God's commission to Moses (Exod. 4:14). When Moses objected that he did not possess sufficient ability in public speaking to undertake the mission to Pharaoh, God replied: "Is not Aaron the Levite thy brother? I know that he can speak well.... And thou shalt speak unto him, and put words in his mouth: and I will be with thy mouth, and with his mouth, and will teach you what ye shall do. And he shall be thy spokesman unto the people: and he shall be, even he shall be to thee instead of a mouth, and thou shalt be to him instead of God" (Exod. 4:14-16). In accordance with this command he met Moses in "the mount of God" after forty years' separation, and took him back to the family home in Goshen. Aaron introduced him to the elders of the people, and persuaded them to accept him as their leader. Together Moses and Aaron proceeded to Pharaoh's court, where they carried on the negotiations that finally brought the end of the oppression of the Israelites and the exodus from Egypt.

During Moses' forty years in the wilderness Aaron had married Elisheba or Elizabeth, daughter of Amminadab, and sister of Naashon, a prince of the tribe of Judah (Exod. 6:23, I Chron. 2:10). They had four sons: Nadab, Abihu, Eleazar, and Ithamar.

Upon leaving Egypt, Aaron assisted his brother during the wandering in the wilderness. On the way to Sinai, in the battle with Amalek, Aaron and Hur held up Moses' hands (Exod. 17:9-13) in which the rod of God, and Israel consequently won the battle. With the establishment of the tabernacle, Aaron became high priest in charge of the national worship, and the head of the hereditary priesthood.

In character he was weak and occasionally jealous. He and Miriam criticized Moses for having married an Ethiopian (Cushite) woman, outside the nation of Israel, and complained that Moses was not God's sole spokesman (Num. 12:1,2). When Moses went up onto Mt. Sinai to receive the tables of the law from God, Aaron acceded to the people's demand for a visible god that they could worship. Taking their personal jewelry, he melted it in a furnace and made a golden calf similar to the familiar bull-god of Egypt. The people hailed this image as the god who had brought them out of Egypt. Aaron did not remonstrate with them, but built an altar and proclaimed a feast to Jehovah on the morrow, which the people celebrated with revelry and debauchery (Exod. 32:1-6). When Moses returned from the mountain and rebuked Aaron for aiding this abuse, he made the naive answer: "They gave it (the gold) to me, and I threw it into the fire, and there came out this calf" (Exod. 32:24). It may be that Aaron meant to restrain the people by a compromise, but he was wholly unsuccessful.

The "Hill of Aaron" in Sinai, close to Jebel Mousa, Mount Sinai. © Matson Photo

When the revelation of the pattern for worship in the Tabernacle was completed two months later, Aaron and his sons were consecrated to the priesthood (Lev. 8:1 — 9:22). The consecration involved three offerings: a sin-offering to express cleansing and reconciliation; a burnt-offering of consecration to God; and a meat-offering or food-offering without blood, consisting of flour, salt, oil, and frankincense, representing the giving of worship and thanks to God. Aaron was invested with the clothes of his office: the robes "for glory and for beauty," breastplate, ephod, robe, embroidered coat, mitre (or turban), and girdle or sash, and linen drawers (Exod. 28). The final act of the ceremony was anointing him with holy oil, as a symbol of the grace and Spirit of God, equipping him with special power. Aaron immediately offered sacrifice and blessed the people, and the divine acceptance of his ministry was marked by fire from the Lord which consumed the offering laid upon the altar.

At the end of the wilderness wandering Aaron was warned of his impending death. He and Moses went up onto Mt. Hor, where he was stripped of his priestly robes, which passed in succession to his son, Eleazar. He died at the age of 123, and was buried in the mountain (Num. 20:22-29, 33:38, Deut. 10:6, 32:50). The people mourned for him thirty days.

The Psalms speak of the priestly line as the "house of Aaron" (Pss. 115:10,12, 118:3, 135:19), and he is mentioned in the book of Hebrews as a

The Tomb of Aaron on Mount Hor, near Petra. © MPS

type of Christ who was "called of God as was Aaron" (Heb. 5:4,5), though the eternal priesthood of Christ is stated explicitly to be patterned on the order of Melchizedek and not on that of Aaron (Heb. 7:11).   S.B.

AARONITES (âr'ŭn-īts), descendants of Aaron who fought with David against Saul (I Chron. 12:27). They were distinguished from the general tribe of Levites (I Chron. 27:17).

AB (ăb), the fifth month of the Hebrew year, coinciding approximately with early August (Num. 33:38).

ABADDON (à-băd'ŭn, Heb. 'ăvaddôv, ruin, perdition, destruction), occurs six times in the OT (Job 26:6; 28:22; 31:12; Prov. 15:11; 27:20; Ps. 88:11). In Job 31:12 it has the general meaning of "ruin," "destruction." In three instances (Job 26:6; Prov. 15:11; 27:20) the word is parallel with Sheol, the abode of the dead. In Job 28:22 it means "death." In Ps. 88:11 it is synonymous with the grave. The word is found once in the New Testament (Rev. 9:11), where its Greek equivalent is Apollyon, the angel who reigns over the infernal regions. The Prince of Darkness is known under the name of Apollyon in Bunyan's *Pilgrim's Progress*.

ABAGTHA (à-băg'thà, Heb. 'ăvaghethă'), one of the seven eunuchs who served King Ahasuerus as chamberlains (Esth. 1:10). The king had the eunuchs bring Queen Vashti before him. Oriental kings customarily had eunuchs to supervise their harems.

ABANA (à-băn'à, Heb. 'ăvānâ, KJV, ASV Abanah, m. Amanah, RSV Abana, m. Amana), the name of a river that flows through Damascus. Mentioned in the Bible only in II Kings 5:12, where Naaman says, "Are not Abana and Pharpar, rivers of Damascus, better than all the waters of Israel?" It was called by the Greeks the Chrysorrhoas ("golden stream"), and is the same as the modern Barada. Beginning about twenty-three miles NW of Damascus, in the Anti-Lebanon Mountains, it flows through Damascus, making the city, though bordering on a desert, one of the loveliest and most fertile on earth. It divides into nine or ten branches, and spreads out like an open fan into the plain east of Damascus.

ABARIM (ăb'à-rĭm, Heb. 'avārîm, those beyond, or on the other side), either the region east of the Jordan or the name of a mountain range NW of Moab. The Israelites encamped here just before crossing the Jordan, and from one of its peaks Moses saw the Promised Land (Num. 27:12).

ABBA (ăb'à, Heb. 'abbā'), Aramaic word for *father*, transliterated into Greek and thence into English. The corresponding Hebrew word is Ab. Found three times in the NT (Mark 14:36; Rom. 8:15; Gal. 4:6).

ABDA (ăb'dà, Heb. 'avdā', probably *servant of God*). 1. the father of Adoniram (I Kings 4:6); 2. a Levite, the son of Shammua (Neh. 11:17), called "Obadiah the son of Shemaiah" (I Chron. 9:16).

ABDEEL (ăb'dē-ĕl, Heb. 'avde'ēl, *servant of God*), the father of Shelemiah, ordered by King Jehoiakim to arrest Jeremiah the prophet and his scribe Baruch (Jer. 36:26).

ABDI (ăb'dī, Heb. 'avdî, probably *servant of Jehovah*). 1. A Levite, father of Kishi or Kish; the grandfather of David's singer Ethan (I Chron. 6:44). It is uncertain whether the Abdi of II Chron. 29:12 is the same man. 2. One of the sons of Elam who in Ezra's time had married foreign wives (Ezra 10:26).

ABDIEL (ăb'dī-ĕl, Heb. 'avdi'ēl, *servant of God*), a Gadite who lived in Gilead (I Chron. 5:15).

ABDON (ăb'dŏn, Heb. 'avdôn, meaning uncertain; may be *servant, service*, or *servile*). 1. One of the judges of Israel — the eleventh one mentioned. Nothing is said about his rule except that he judged Israel for eight years (Judg. 12:13-15). Josephus says (*Ant.* V 7, 15) that his reign was a peaceful one, and therefore "he had no occasion to perform glorious actions." 2. One of the sons of Shashak, a Benjamite, living in Jerusalem (I Chron. 8:23, 28). 3. The son of Jeiel of Gibeon (I Chron. 8:30; 9:35, 36). 4. An official of King Josiah, sent by him to Huldah the prophetess (II Chron. 34:20; called Achbor in II Kings 22:12).

ABDON (City), one of four Levitical cities in the tribe Asher (Josh. 21:30; I Chron. 6:74). It may

The Abana River (El Barada) flowing through Damascus. © Matson Photo

be the same as "Hebron" in Joshua 19:28. Now called Abdeh, near the Mediterranean and about 15 miles S of Tyre.

ABEDNEGO (à-bĕd′nē-gō, Heb. *'ăvēdhneghô', servant of Nego*), one of the three Hebrews (Shadrach, Meshach and Abednego) whom Daniel requested be appointed over the affairs of the province of Babylon. The three were later saved from the fiery furnace (Dan. 1:7; 3:12-30).

ABEL (ā′bĕl, Heb. *hevel*, etymology uncertain; several meanings have been suggested: *breath, transitoriness*, suggestive of his brief life; *shepherd, herdman*, and *son*). Adam's second son, murdered by his brother Cain (Gen. 4). "Abel was a keeper of sheep, but Cain was a tiller of ground" (Gen. 4:2). Here are represented the two basic pursuits of civilized life, the agricultural and the pastoral. Abel is described as a righteous man (Matt. 23:35). He offered to God a lamb from his flock, which was accepted; while Cain's offer of the fruit of the ground was rejected. The reason for the divine preference is not given. The Scriptures do not say specifically that it was because of a difference in the material of the sacrifice. Hebrew law and custom allowed for both kinds. It may be that God had made known that a sacrifice involving the shedding of blood would alone be acceptable to Him and that Cain had defiantly decided to disregard God's will. On the other hand, it may have been the disposition of the offerer, not the outward offering, that God regarded. We read that Cain's "works were evil, and his brother's righteous" (I John 3:12). S.B.

ABEL (ā′bĕl, Heb. *'āvēl, a meadow*). 1. The name of a city involved in the rebellion of Sheba (II Sam. 20:14, 18); the same as Abel-beth-maacah (II Sam. 20:15).

2. In I Samuel 6:18 KJV, "the great stone of Abel" should probably be "stone."

ABEL-BETH-MAACHA (ā′bĕl-bĕth-mā′à-kà, Heb. *'āvēl bêth ma'ăkhâh*), and *Abel of Beth-Maacah*, in KJV written "Maachah"; Abel, i.e. meadow, near Beth-maacah. A town in the extreme north of Palestine, probably about twelve miles north of Lake Huleh, in the tribe of Naphtali (II Sam. 20:15; I Kings 15:20). Sheba, son of Bichri, fled to it when his revolt against David failed. The town was saved from assault by Joab when, with its proverbial shrewdness, it followed the advice of a "wise woman" that it sacrifice Sheba (II Sam. 20:14-22). About 80 years later it was seized by Benhadad (I Kings 15:20), and in 734 B.C. by Tiglath-pileser, who captured it and carried off its inhabitants to Assyria (II Kings 15:29).

ABEL-CHERAMIM (ā′bĕl-kĕr-à-mĭm, Heb. *'āvēl-kerāmîm, meadow of vineyards*), a place in Ammon, east of the Jordan, to which Jephthah pursued the Ammonites (Judg. 11:33).

ABEL-MAIM (ā′bĕl-mā′ĭm, Heb. *'āvēl mayim, meadow of waters*), a variant of Abel-beth-maacah (II Chron. 16:4).

ABEL-MEHOLAH (ā′bĕl-mē-hō′là, *meadow of dancing*), a town, not exactly identifiable, but probably in the Jordan valley, where Elisha was born and lived. The Midianites routed by Gideon fled to its environs (Judg. 7:22).

ABEL-MIZRAIM (ā′bĕl-mĭz′rā-ĭm, Heb. *'āvēl-mitsrayim, meadow* or *mourning of Egypt*), a place east of the Jordan at which the funeral cortege of Jacob stopped to mourn for seven days before entering Canaan to bury the patriarch (Gen. 50:11). It had been called the "threshing floor of Atad," but the Canaanites now called it the "mourning of Egypt," or the "funeral from Egypt," very likely because the princes and chief men of Egypt, with their chariots and horsemen, took part in the funeral rites.

ABEL-SHITTIM (ā′bĕl-shĭt′ĭm, Heb. *'āvēl ha-shittîm, acacia-meadow*), a locality in the plains of Moab where Israel rested for the last time before crossing the Jordan (Num. 33:49).

ABEL THE GREAT. In I Samuel 6:18 the Hebrew text has "Abel," and is so translated by the KJV. The LXX reads *Eben*, meaning "stone," which is followed by the ASV and the RSV.

ABEZ (ā′bĕz). Used in KJV for Ebez. A town, mentioned in Joshua 19:20, found in Issachar.

ABI (ā′bī, Heb. *'ăvî*), the mother of King Hezekiah, spoken of also as the daughter of Zechariah. The name is a contraction of Abijah (II Kings 18:2; II Chron. 29:1).

ABIA (à-bī′à), a variant for Abijah.

ABIASAPH (à-bī′ă-săf, Heb. *'ăvî'āsāph, the father gathers*, or *adds*), a descendant of Levi through Korah (Exod. 6:24).

ABIATHAR (à-bī′ă-thàr, Heb. *'eviāthār, father of abundance*), the son of Ahimelech, the high priest, who with 84 priests was slain by Saul at Nob, on Doeg's telling the king that Ahimelech had inquired of the Lord for David and had given him the shewbread and the sword of Goliath (I Sam. 22). Abiathar escaped, bringing the ephod with him, and joined David (I Sam. 22:20-23). Abiathar and Zadok apparently shared the high priesthood between them when David ordered the ark to be brought to Jerusalem (I Chron. 15:11). It may be that Saul had appointed Zadok high priest after the murder of Abimelech. The two men are mentioned together as high priests a number of times in the story of the rebellion of Absalom (II Sam. 15:24ff.).

Abiathar rendered David loyal service during Absalom's rebellion (II Sam. 15; 17:15; 19:11), but he joined Adonijah when the latter sought to seize the throne from Solomon (I Kings 1:7).

After Solomon's accession to the throne Abiathar again favored Adonijah, and for this the king deprived him of the high priesthood and banished him to his estate at Anathoth. Zadok became sole high priest (I Kings 2:26, 35). I Kings 4:4 still refers to Abiathar as being priest with Zadok, but this may refer to the period just before he was deposed. With the deposition of Abiathar, the rule of the house of Eli came to an end, as had been foretold 150 years before (I Sam. 2:31-35). Jesus refers to Abiathar in Mark 2:26. S.B.

ABIB (ā′bĭb, Heb. *'āvîv, an ear of corn*), the preexilic name for the first month of the year (Exod. 13:4; 23:15; 34:18). After the exile the name was changed to Nisan. It fell about the time of our March and early April.

ABIDA (à-bī′dà, Heb. *'ăvîdhā', the father knows*), appears as Abidah in KJV (Gen. 25:4). A son of Midian and grandson of Abraham and Keturah Gen. 25:4; I Chron. 1:33).

ABIDAN (à-bī′dăn, Heb. *'ăvîdhān, the father is judge*), a prince of the tribe of Benjamin chosen to represent his tribe at the census in the wilderness of Sinai (Num. 1:11; 2:22). He was present at the dedication of the tabernacle, making an offering as one of the heads of Israel (Num. 7:60, 65).

ABIEL (ā′bī-ĕl, Heb. *'ăvî'ēl, the father is God*, or *God is father*). 1. The grandfather of Saul and Abner (I Sam. 9:1; 14:51).

2. One of David's mighty men (I Chron. 11: 32), also called Abi-Albon (II Sam. 23:31).

ABIEZER (ā'bĭ-ē'zêr, Heb. *'avî'ezer, father of help,* or *father is help*). 1. A descendant of Joseph the son of Jacob who became head of one of the families of Manasseh. The judge Gideon belonged to this family (Judg. 6:11f; 8:2, 32). In Numbers 26:30 the form is Iezer (in KJV Jeezer).

2. One of David's mighty men (II Sam. 23:27; I Chron. 11:28; 27:12).

ABIGAIL (ăb'ĭ-gāl, Heb. *'avîghayil, father is rejoicing*). 1. The wife of Nabal, and, after his death, of David (I Sam. 25:3, 14-44; 27:3; II Sam. 3:3), to whom she bore his second son, Chileab (II Sam. 3:3, or Daniel, as in I Chron. 3:1).

2. A sister of David, daughter of Nahash, and mother of Amasa, commander of David's army (I Chron. 2:16).

ABIHAIL (ăb'ĭ-hāl, Heb. *'avîhayil, the father is strength*). 1. A Levite, the father of Zuriel, who in the wilderness was the head of the house of Merari (Num. 3:25).

2. The wife of Abishur, of the tribe of Judah (I Chron. 2:29).

3. A Gadite who lived in Gilead of Bashan (I Chron. 5:14).

4. The wife of Rehoboam, king of Judah. She was a daughter of Eliab, David's eldest brother (II Chron. 11:18).

5. The father of Queen Esther (Esther 2:15, 9:29).

ABIHU (à-bī'hū, Heb. *'avîhû', the father is he*), second son of Aaron (Exod. 6:23). With Aaron, Nadab his brother, and the 70 elders he went with Moses up Sinai for a limited distance (Exod. 24: 1). He and Nadab were slain by Jehovah when they offered strange fire (Lev. 10).

ABIHUD (à-bī'hŭd, Heb. *'avîhûdh, the father is majesty*), the son of Bela, the eldest son of Benjamin (I Chron. 8:3).

ABIJAH (à-bī'jà, Heb. *'avîyâh or 'avîyāhû, Jehovah is Father*). 1. The wife of Judah's grandson Hezron (I Chron. 2:24).

2. The seventh son of Becher the son of Benjamin (I Chron. 7:8).

3. The second son of the prophet Samuel. Appointed a judge by his father; he became corrupt (I Sam. 8:2; I Chron. 6:28).

4. A descendant of Aaron. The ancestral head of the eighth of the 24 groups into which David had divided the priests (I Chron. 24:10). The father of John the Baptist belonged to this group (Luke 1:5).

5. A son of Jeroboam I of Israel (I Kings 14: 1-18). He died from illness when still a child, in fulfillment of a prediction by the prophet Ahijah, to whom the queen had gone in disguise to inquire the issue of the child's illness. The death was a judgment for the apostasy of Jeroboam.

6. King of Judah, the son and successor of Rehoboam. He made war on Jeroboam in an effort to recover the ten tribes of Israel. In a speech before an important battle, in which his army was greatly outnumbered, he appealed to Jeroboam not to oppose the God of Israel, for God had given the kingdom to David and his sons forever. Abijah gained a decisive victory. Prosperity tempted him to multiply wives and to follow the evil ways of his father. He reigned three years. (II Chron. 12: 16; 13; 14:1.)

7. A priest of Nehemiah's time (Neh. 10:7; 12:4,17).

8. The mother of Hezekiah (II Chron. 29:1), called Abi in II Kings 18:2.

9. A chief of the priests who returned from Babylon with Zerubbabel (Neh. 12:4,7).

ABILENE (ăb'ĭ-lēn, Gr. *Abilené*, probably from Heb., *meadow*), a tetrarchy near Anti-Lebanon. Luke 3:1 mentions it as the tetrarchy of Lysanias when John the Baptist began his ministry. Its capital Abela was about 18 miles NW of Damascus. In 37 A.D. the tetrarchy, with other territories, was given to Agrippa, and when he died in 44 A.D. it was administered by procurators until 53 A.D., when the emperor of Rome conferred it upon Agrippa II; and upon his death, toward the end of the century, it was made a part of the province of Syria.

ABIMAEL (à-bĭm'ā-ĕl, Heb. *'avîmā'ēl, God is Father*), the ninth of the 13 sons or descendants of Joktan, who was descended from Shem (Gen. 10:28; I Chron. 1:22).

ABIMELECH (à-bĭm'ĕ-lĕk, Heb. *'avîmelekh*, probably either *the father is king* or *the father of a king*). 1. A Philistine king of Gerar, near Gaza. It was at his court that Abraham tried to pass off Sarah as his sister. Struck by her beauty, Abimelech married her, but returned her to Abraham when he was warned by God in a dream (Gen. 20:1-18). Later, the two men made a covenant, when their servants contended over a well (Gen. 21:22-34).

2. A second king of Gerar, probably the son of the one mentioned in 1, at whose court Isaac tried to pass off his wife Rebekah as his sister (Gen. 26: 1-11). He upbraided Isaac when the falsehood was detected. Later, their servants quarreled and a covenant was made between them, as had been done between Abraham and the first Abimelech.

3. The son of Gideon by a concubine (Judg. 8: 31,9:1-57). After the death of his father, aspiring to be king, he slew 70 sons of his father. Only one son, Jotham, escaped. He was then made king of Shechem. After a reign of three years, an insurrection broke out against him. He captured and completely destroyed the city. Later, at the siege of Thekez, into which the defeated rebels from Shechem had fled, he was severely wounded by a mill-stone dropped from a wall on his head by a woman, and ordered his armorbearer to kill him with his sword, lest it be said to his shame that he was killed by a woman.

4. A Philistine king mentioned in the title of Psalm 34, who very likely is the same as Achish, king of Gath (I Sam. 21:10-22:1), with whom David sought refuge when he fled from Saul. It is possible that Abimelech was a royal title of Philistine kings, and not a personal name.

5. A priest in the days of David, a son of Abiathar (I Chron. 18:16); also called Ahimelech (LXX and in I Chron. 24:6). S.B.

ABINADAB (à-bĭn'à-dăb, Heb. *'avînādhāv, the father is generous*). 1. A man living in Kiriath-jearim to whose home the ark was brought from the land of the Philistines. About a century later David removed the ark to Jerusalem (I Sam. 7: 1,2; II Sam. 6:3; I Chron. 13:7).

2. The second of the eight sons of Jesse. He was in Saul's army when Goliath gave his challenge (I Sam. 16:8; 17:13; I Chron. 2:13).

3. A son of Saul, killed with his father by the Philistines at Mt. Gilboa (I Sam. 17:13; 31:2; I Chron. 8:33; 9:39; 10:2).

4. The father of a son-in-law of Solomon (I Kings 4:11).

ABINOAM (à-bĭn'o-ăm, Heb. *'ăvînō'am, the father is pleasantness*), the father of Barak (Judg. 4:6; 5:12).

ABIRAM (à-bī'răm, Heb. *'ăvîrām, the father is exalted*). 1. A Reubenite who with his brothers Dathan and Korah conspired against Moses and was destroyed by God (Num. 16).

2. The eldest son of Hiel the Bethelite, who rebuilt Jericho (I Kings 16:34).

ABISHAG (ăb'ĭ-shăg, Heb. *'ăvîshagh, the father wanders,* or *errs*). A Shunamite woman who nursed David in his old age (I Kings 1:3,15). Adonijah's request to marry her after David's death caused Solomon to put him to death (I Kings 2:17ff.).

ABISHAI (à-bĭsh'ā-ī, Heb. *'ăvîshay,* meaning is doubtful). Son of David's sister Zeruiah, and brother of Joab and Asahel. He was impetuous and courageous, cruel and hard to his foes; but always intensely loyal to David. He counselled David to kill the sleeping Saul (I Sam. 26:6-9). He aided Joab in the murder of Abner, an act of revenge for the slaying of their brother Asahel (II Sam. 3:30). He was loyal to David when Absalom and Sheba revolted (II Sam. 16:9). He defeated a large army of Edomites (I Chron. 18:12,13). Late in David's life he rescued the king in the fight with Ishbibenob, the Philistine giant (II Sam. 21:17).

ABISHALOM (à-bĭsh'à-lŏm), a variant of Absalom.

ABISHUA (à-bĭsh'ū-à, Heb. *'ăvîshûa', perhaps the father is salvation* or *noble*). 1. The son of Phinehas the priest (I Chron. 6:4,5,50; Ezra 7:5).

2. A Benjamite of the family of Bela (I Chron. 8:4).

ABISHUR (à-bī'shêr, Heb. *'ăvîshûr, the father is a wall*), a man of Judah, the son of Shammai (I Chron. 2:28,29).

ABITAL (à-bī'tăl, Heb. *'ăvîtāl, the father is dew*), one of the wives of David (II Sam. 3:4; I Chron. 3:3).

ABITUB (à-bī'tŭb, Heb. *'ăvîtûv, the father is goodness*), a Benjamite, son of Shaharaim and Hushim (I Chron. 8:8-11).

ABIUD (à-bī-ŭd, Gr. *Abioúd,* probably the Greek form of Abihud), the son of Zerubbabel. Mentioned only in the genealogy of Jesus (Matt. 1:13).

ABLUTION (See Washing)

ABNER (ăb'nêr, Heb. *'avnēr, the father is a lamp*). The son of Ner, who was the brother of Kish, the father of King Saul. Abner and Saul were therefore cousins. During the reign of Saul, Abner was the commander-in-chief of his army (I Sam. 14:50). It was Abner who brought David to Saul following the slaying of Goliath (I Sam. 17:55-58). He accompanied Saul in his pursuit of David (I Sam. 26:5ff), and was rebuked by David for his failure to keep better watch over his master (I Sam. 15).

At Saul's death Abner espoused the cause of Saul's house and had Ishbosheth, Saul's son, made king over Israel (II Sam. 2:8). Abner and his men met David's servants in combat by the pool of Gibeon and were defeated with great slaughter. During the retreat from this battle, Abner was pursued by Asahel, Joab's brother, and in self-defense, slew him (II Sam. 2:12-32).

Soon after, Abner and Ishbosheth had a quarrel over Saul's concubine. This resulted in Abner's entering upon negotiations with David to go to his side, and he promised to bring all Israel with him. David graciously received him; but he was not gone for long when Joab heard of the affair, and

believing or pretending to believe that Abner had come as a spy, Joab invited him to a friendly conversation and murdered him "for the blood of Asahel his brother."

David sincerely mourned the death of Abner. "Know ye not," he said, "that there is a prince and a great man fallen this day in Israel?" He left it to his successor to avenge Abner's death (I Kings 2:5). S.B.

ABOMINATION OF DESOLATION, meaning *the abomination that desolates or appalls.* When Daniel, in prophecy, tried to describe an abomination so abhorrent and loathsome to all moral and religious decency as to leave its abode desolate, he used this term (Dan. 9:27; 11:31; 12:11).

The Jews thought that Daniel 11:31 was fulfilled in 186 B.C., when Antiochus Epiphanes the king of Syria erected an idolatrous altar on the altar of the Temple in Jerusalem and sacrificed a pig thereon to the heathen god Jupiter Olympus (I Macc. 1:54; 6:7; II Macc. 6:2; Jos. *Antiq.* 12:5,4; 7,6).

Many scholars hold that Jesus' prophecy that His followers would see the abomination of desolation, spoken of by Daniel the prophet, standing in the Holy Place (Matt. 24:15) was fulfilled when Jerusalem was destroyed in the year 70 A.D., when the Temple was desecrated by Roman soldiers and by Jewish Zealots. Other scholars, however, see in the prophecies of Daniel and of Jesus an eschatological reference, interpreting them to refer to the "man of sin" Paul speaks of in II Thessalonians 2. S.B.

ABRAHAM (ā'brà-hăm, Heb. *'avrāhām, the father is high*). The son of Terah, and founder of the Hebrew nation. His family, descended from Shem, settled in Ur of the Chaldees. It appears that Terah was an idolater, for Joshua says of him that he "served other gods" (Josh. 24:2). He had three sons—Abraham, Nahor, and Haran.

Abraham was married to his half sister, Sarah. After the death of his brother Nahor, Abraham

Ancient Oak of Mamre. Although now almost extinct, this specimen of historic grove still lives. Here, near Hebron, Abram pitched his tent (Gen. 13:18). © Matson Photo

Cenotaph (tomb) of Abraham (above) in the Mosque of Machpelah (below) built over the Cave of Machpelah in Hebron. © MPS

and his family, including his nephew Lot and his father Terah, left Ur to go to the land of Canaan (Gen. 11:27-31). We are not told the reason for the migration. Stephen, however, says that God had appeared to Abraham before he dwelt in Haran and had told him to leave his country for another land (Acts 7:2-4).

After staying some time in Haran, Abraham, now 75 years old, departed for Canaan, probably by way of Damascus. Not more than a year later he arrived in Canaan, where the Lord assured him in a vision that this was the land his seed would inherit.

A period of wandering, lasting about ten years, followed his entrance into Canaan. Successive stages of the journey are indicated by the mention of Shechem, Bethel, and the Negeb. During a time of famine Abraham went to Egypt, where he was hospitably received by the Pharaoh. Fearful for his life, he represented Sarah as his sister, but was

compelled to leave when the Pharaoh learned the truth. In Canaan he and Lot separated because their herdsmen quarrelled. Lot selfishly chose the fertile plain of the Jordan, while Abraham pitched his tent among the oak groves of Mamre, in the hill country near Hebron.

Abraham lived in the hill country at least 15 years. He strengthened his position with the local Amoritish chieftains by uniting with them in the rescue of Lot from an Elamite king. On his return he was blessed by Melchizedek, the priest-king of Salem, to whom he gave a tithe of his spoils.

God now renewed His promise of an heir to Abraham; but when no son came, his wife, despairing of having children of her own, suggested that he take as his concubine her maid Hagar. In the eighty-sixth year of his life Hagar bore him Ishmael (Gen. 16). Thirteen years later (Gen. 17:1), God revealed to him that the son of Sarah, and not Ishmael, should be his heir. God now appointed the rite of circumcision as a sign of the covenant made between Him and Abraham. Through the intercession of Abraham, Lot and his family were delivered from the impending destruction of Sodom.

Abraham then moved to the south country (Gen. 20:1), where he lived in a succession of places, for a while among the Philistines in Gerar, with whose king, Abimelech, he and Sarah had an experience similar to an earlier one with the Pharaoh of Egypt.

When Abraham was 100 years old, Isaac was born, an event soon followed by the expulsion of Ishmael (Gen. 21:1-21). Abraham and Abimelech concluded a treaty at Beersheba. Abraham's faith in God's promise met one last severe test when God commanded him to sacrifice his only son. He was saved from doing so by God's gracious substitution of a ram (Gen. 22).

After the death of Sarah, when Abraham was 140 years old, he obtained a wife for Isaac from his own people in Haran; and he married Keturah, by whom he had 6 children. Isaac, however, was left his sole heir. At the age of 175 years he died and was buried beside Sarah (Gen. 25:7-10) in the Cave of Machpelah he had purchased from Ephon (Gen. 23).

Abraham is a significant figure throughout the Bible. He is the progenitor of the people of Israel and the founder of Judaism. He stands out prominently in the Old Testament. In the New Testament there is a wealth of references to him. Paul calls him not only the father of the Jews but of all who believe (Rom. 4:11). He is thus the type of the Christian believer. Repeatedly he is held up as an example of faith at its best.   S.B.

ABRAHAM'S BOSOM (Luke 16:22,23), represents *blessedness after death*. The figure is derived either from the Roman custom of reclining on the left side at meals, Lazarus being in the place of honor at Abraham's right, leaning on his breast; or from its appropriateness as expressing closest fellowship (John 1:18, 13:23). Because Abraham was the founder of the Hebrew nation, to be honored with his intimacy was the highest bliss.

ABRAM (See Abraham)

ABRECH (ăb'rĕk; Gen. 41:43) ASV margin, RSV margin, with note, "*Abrek*, probably an Egyptian word, similar in sound to the Hebrew word meaning *to kneel*"; KJV "bow the knee." It was the cry with which Joseph was announced when he appeared in public as second to Pharaoh. The word may have been imported from Assyria by the

Hyksos kings, in which case it would be a title like "grand vizier." It is a vivid touch, in which we hear the very shout of the heralds honoring Joseph.

ABRONAH, KJV Ebronah (à-brō′nà, Heb. 'avrōnâ). A camping place of the Israelites in the wilderness, one march before Eziongeber on the Gulf of Aqabah (Num. 33:34,35). Exact location uncertain. Possible meaning, *crossing, ford*.

ABSALOM (ăb′sà-lŏm, Heb. 'avshālôm, *father (is) peace*, written Abishalom in I Kings 15:2,10, meaning *my father (is) peace*). Third son of David, by Maacah, daughter of Talmai, king of Geshur, a small district NE of Lake Galilee (II Sam. 3:3; I Chron. 3:2). David's eldest son, Absalom's half-brother Amnon, ravished Absalom's sister Tamar (II Sam. 13:1-19), which greatly angered David, but Amnon was not punished (13:21). Absalom nursed his hatred for two years, then treacherously procured Amnon's assassination (13:22-29). Absalom fled to his grandfather and remained with him three years (13:37-39), while David "longed to go forth unto Absalom: for he was comforted concerning Amnon, seeing he was dead." At the end of that time Joab by stratagem induced David to recall Absalom, but David would not see him for two years more (14:1-24). Then Absalom by a trick of his own moved Joab to intercede with the king, and Absalom was restored to favor (14:28, 33).

Meanwhile, "in all Israel there was none to be so much praised as Absalom for his beauty," and for the abundance of his hair (14:25-27). He had three sons and a daughter, whom he named Tamar after his sister. Absalom now began to act like a candidate for the kingship (15:1-6), parading a great retinue, and subtly indicating how he would improve the administration of justice in the interests of the people. In the fortieth year of David's reign, or after forty years (or four, according to the LXX and Syriac versions) Absalom made pretence of a proper motive for visiting Hebron, the former capital of Judah when David began his reign, and Absalom's birthplace (II Sam. 3:2,3). There Absalom proclaimed himself king, and attracted the disaffected to his standard (II Sam. 15:7-14). David at once realized the seriousness of the rebellion and made hasty plans for immediate departure from Jerusalem (15:13-18). It was a sad as well as a hurried flight, marked by partings from friends, the defection of valued counselors such as Ahithophel, and the intense loyalty of men like Zadok and Abiathar the priests, whom David sent back to the capital, that with their sons as messengers they might keep David informed of events. Hushai the Archite also was asked to return and feign loyalty to Absalom, that he might "defeat the counsel of Ahithophel" (15:20-37).

Ahithophel advised Absalom to attack David at once, before he could gather a large following (17:1-4). Hushai advised delay until all the military power of the realm could be gathered under command of Absalom himself, to make sure of having a large enough force to defeat the warlike David and his loyal soldiers (17:5-14). Absalom actually followed a compromise plan. The armies met in the wood of Ephraim, where Absalom's men were disastrously defeated (18:1-8). Absalom, riding on a mule, was caught by his head in the branches of an oak, and the mule going on left him dangling helpless there, where Joab and his men killed him, though David had, in the hear-

The so-called Tomb of Absalom outside the southeast corner of the Jerusalem city wall, in the Kidron Valley. © MPS

ing of the whole army, forbidden anyone to harm his son Absalom. It is thought that his luxuriant hair contributed to his downfall, by becoming entangled in the oak branches. Absalom was buried in a pit, covered with a heap of stones, in the wood where he fell (18:9-17). David's excessive grief over the death of this ungrateful son nearly cost him the loyalty of his subjects (18:33-19:8). Because all his three sons had died, Absalom had raised a "pillar" or monument to himself "in the king's dale." This pillar cannot be identified with the more recent building known as Absalom's tomb, in the valley of the Kidron. The title of Psalm 3 states that David wrote this psalm "when he fled from Absalom his son." The psalm breathes strong trust in God, to whom is ascribed the overthrow of David's enemies. There is no note of vindictiveness, but a sense of sorrow and resignation.   E.R.

ABSTINENCE (ăb′stĭ-nĕns). The noun occurs once in KJV (Greek *asitía*) (Acts 27:21), and means *abstinence from food*. The verb "abstain" (Greek *apéchomai*) occurs six times, and means "hold oneself away from." The decree of the Jerusalem council (Acts 15:20,29) commanded abstinence from "meats offered to idols, and from blood, and from things strangled, and from fornication," practices abhorrent to Jewish Christians. Paul (I Thess. 4:3) connects abstaining from fornication with sanctification. In I Thessalonians 5:22 he exhorts to abstain from all appearance of evil. In I Timothy 4:3 he refers to false teachers commanding "to abstain from meats, which God hath created to be received with thanksgiving of them which believe and know the truth." In I Peter 2:11, Peter exhorts, "Dearly beloved, I beseech you as strangers and pilgrims, abstain from fleshly lusts, which war against the soul."

Abstinence from eating blood antedates the Mosaic law (Gen. 9:4). The life was held to reside in the blood (Lev. 17:11). Israel abstained voluntarily from eating the sinew on the thigh for the reason given in Genesis 32:32. Leviticus 11 defined what animals the children of Israel might not eat, "to make a difference between the unclean and the clean" (v. 47), and to keep Israel separate from other nations. The priests were forbidden to drink wine while they were ministering (Lev. 10:8,9). The Nazarites were to abstain from the fruit of the vine absolutely. The Rechabites took such a vow in deference to their ancestor Jonadab (Jer. 35). God's people are to abstain from participation in idol feasts (Exod. 34:15, Ps. 106:28, I Cor. 8:4-13, Rom. 14:21).

The injunctions regarding drunkenness and sobriety (Eph. 5:18, I Tim. 3:3,8, Tit. 2:2-4, I Cor. 5:11, 6:9,10, etc.) point to the wisdom of total abstinence from alcoholic beverages if one would be at his best for the Lord. They are reënforced by the fact that the believer's body is the temple of of the Holy Spirit (I Cor. 6:19, II Cor. 6:16), and by such words as Colossians 3:17. Paul's advice to Timothy (I Tim. 5:23) sanctions no more than medicinal use of wine mixed with water.

Abstinence is not a virtue in itself, but a means to make virtue possible.   E.R.

ABYSS (à-bĭs', Greek *ábyssos*) means, in the NT, *the nether world, prison of disobedient spirits* (Luke 8:31, Rev. 9:1,2,11, 11:17, 17:8, 20:1-3), or *the world of the dead* (Rom. 10:7). Abyss does not occur in KJV, but is translated "deep" in Luke 8:31 and Romans 10:7, "the bottomless pit" elsewhere. ASV has uniformly *abyss,* and RSV has *abyss* in Luke 8:31 and Romans 10:7, "the bottomless pit" in Revelation, except 20:3, where "the pit" alone appears.

In classical Greek *ábyssos* was an adjective meaning "bottomless," applied to the primeval deep of ancient cosmogonies, an ocean surrounding and under the earth. In the LXX it translates Heb. *tehôm* meaning the primal waters of Genesis 1:2; once the world of the dead (Ps. 71:20). In later Judaism it means also the interior depths of the earth, and the prison of evil spirits.

The use of abyss in Romans 10:7 is parallel with the use of "the lower parts of the earth" in Ephesians 4:9 (see Ps. 106:28). In both, a contrast between the highest heaven and the lowest depth is intended. In Luke 8:31 the demons fear the primal prison deep more than the known depth of the Lake of Galilee. In Revelation the horror of infinite deeps is intensified.   E.R.

ACCAD (ăk'ăd, Heb. *'akkadh*), one of the cities or districts of Nimrod's kingdom, with Babel, Erech, and Calneh. Babel and Erech are located on or near the lower Euphrates, Erech not far from what was then the head of the Persian Gulf. Calneh, formerly identified with Nippur between Babel and Erech, is now generally thought to be not the name of a city, but a word meaning "all of them," referring to the first three cities. This would leave the capital, Babel, and the chief cities of the northern (Accad) and southern (Erech) districts of Babylonia. The location of Accad is uncertain, though it is thought to be identical with Agade, chief city of a district of the same name in northern Babylonia, which Sargon I, the Semitic conqueror of the Sumerian Accadians, made his capital in 2475 B.C. The kingdom called Nimrod's had evidently fallen into disorder, and Sargon united the warring city-states under his firm rule. With the help of invaders first from the northeast and then from the northwest, Accadian civilization flourished sporadically and precariously until Semitic Amorites from the west founded a dynasty at Babylon about 1894 B.C., whose most illustrious ruler was Hammurabi (1792-1750 B.C.). Sumerian or Accadian civilization now finally came to an end. As Nimrod cannot be certainly identified with any person otherwise known, so Accad remains a shadowy city or region (Gen. 10:10).

ACCHO (ăk'ō, Heb. *'akkô*, Judg. 1:31 KJV, in ASV and RSV Acco). The name occurs in some manuscripts and versions of Joshua 19:30. In the NT, Ptolemais; modern Arabic, 'Akka; English, Acre. A seaport, eight miles N of Mt. Carmel,

30 miles south of Tyre. The river Belus flows into the Mediterranean Sea close to the town. Accho was in the portion assigned to the tribe of Asher, but the Hebrews did not drive out the original inhabitants (Judg. 1:31). It received the name Ptolemais from the ˉPtolemies of Egypt, from whom it was wrested by the Romans. Paul stayed here a day with Christian brethren on his way from Tyre to Caesarea (Acts 21:7). The Crusaders occupied the town and named it St. Jean d'Acre. In modern times it was part of the Turkish Empire, except for a time when it was occupied by Egypt, being restored to the Turks with British help. Today it is in the nation of Israel, opposite the larger city of Haifa.

ACELDAMA (à-sĕl'dà-mà) KJV, Akeldama (à-kĕl'-dà-mà) ASV and RSV (Gr. *Akeldamá*). The field purchased with the money Judas received for betraying Christ (Acts 1:18,19). In Matthew 27: 3-10 is a fuller account of the purchase, in which it is said that the priests bought it "to bury strangers in." Acts 1:18,19 is a parenthesis, not part of Peter's speech, but an explanation by Luke. These verses say that Judas "purchased a field with the reward of iniquity." The priests may have bought it in Judas' name, the money being his. The field was called "the place of blood" in Aramaic. Some think the Aramaic word means "field of sleep," or "cemetery," but the meaning "field of blood" is preferable, and appropriate because of Judas' death as described in Acts 1:18 in gruesome detail.

Aceldama, the Potters Field now known as the Field of Blood, on the southern slope of the Hinnom Valley.
© MPS

ACHAIA (à-kā'yà, Gr. *Achaiá*). In NT times, a Roman province including the Peloponnesus and northern Greece south of Illyricum, Epirus and Thessaly, which were districts of Macedonia. Macedonia and Achaia generally mean all Greece (Acts 19:21, Rom. 15:26, II Cor. 1:1, I Thess. 1:7,8). In Acts 18:12 Gallio is accurately called "proconsul" (RSV) of Achaia; "deputy" in the KJV; for Claudius had just made Achaia a senatorial province, and the governors of such provinces were called proconsuls, while the governors of imperial provinces were called procurators. Corinth was the capital. In Acts 20:2 "Greece" refers to Achaia. In Romans 16:15 RSV has "Asia" instead of "Achaia," following the best Greek text. Other NT references to Achaia are II Corinthians 9:2 and 11:10.

ACHAICUS (à-kā'ĭ-kŭs, Gr. *Achaikós*). A Corinthian Christian, named for his country of origin, who accompanied Stephanas and Fortunatus to bring supplies to Paul at Ephesus (I Cor. 16:17-19).

ACHAN (ā'kăn, Heb. *'ākhān*), an Israelite whose story is told in Joshua 7. Achan took a garment, silver and gold, part of the spoil of Jericho. Joshua had devoted the metals to God (Josh. 6:17-19). All else was to be destroyed. Because of one man's disobedience Israel was defeated at Ai. God revealed the reason to Joshua. By a process of elimination Achan was found out. He confessed, and he and his family and possessions were brought down to the valley of Achor. The LXX reads, "and all Israel stoned him with stones. And they raised over him a great heap of stones," omitting the destruction of family and goods (Josh. 7:25,26). From this and the confusion of pronouns in the Hebrew text, sometimes "him," sometimes "them," some think that the command in Joshua 7:15 was not fully carried out. But the situation called for complete obedience. Achan is called Achar in I Chronicles 2:7. The Hebrew root of Achan has no known meaning. That of Achar means *trouble*. Joshua 7:26 says "wherefore the name of that place was called Achor (troubling) unto this day." The chronicler may have changed Achan's name to Achar because of the events of Joshua 7.   E.R.

ACHAR (ā'kàr, Heb. *'ākhār, trouble*). The same as Achan (I Chron. 2:7).

ACHAZ (ā'kăz, Gr. *Áchaz*). The same as Ahaz.

ACHBOR (ăk'bôr, Heb. *'akhbôr, mouse*). 1. Father of a king of Edom (Gen. 36:38,39, I Chron. 1:49).
2. A messenger sent by king Josiah to inquire of the Lord concerning the book found by Hilkiah (II Kings 22:12,14; called Abdon in II Chron. 34:20); father of Elnathan (Jer. 26:22; 36:12).

ACHIM (ā'kĭm, Gr. *Acheím*, from Heb. meaning *Jehovah will establish*). A descendant of Zerubbabel (Matt. 1:14). One of the ancestors of Christ, after the Babylonian captivity.

ACHISH (ā'kĭsh, Heb. *'ākhîsh*). King of Gath, to whom David fled for protection (I Sam. 21:10-15). David becoming fearful, pretended insanity. Achish repulsed him, and David fled. David again seeking refuge with Achish, so behaved as to win his confidence (I Sam. 27:1-12). David consented to join Achish against Israel, but the Philistine lords objected; so Achish sent David away (I Sam. 29:1-11). He may be the same Achish to whom Shimei's servant fled (I Kings 2:39,40).

ACHMETHA (ăk'mē-thà, Heb. *'akhmethā'*), ancient Ecbatana, modern Hamadân, capital of Media, where, in the reign of Darius, was found the decree

The Valley of Achor, near Jericho, the depression running through the Jericho Plain toward the Jordan, where Achan was stoned. © MPS

of Cyrus authorizing the rebuilding of the Temple at Jerusalem (Ezra 6:2).

ACHOR (ā'kôr, Heb. *'ākhôr, trouble*). Valley (Josh. 15:7) where Achan was stoned (Josh. 7:24-26); subject of promises in Isaiah 65:10, Hosea 2:15.

ACHSA (See Achsah)

ACHSAH (ăk'sà, Heb. *'akhsâ, anklet*), daughter of Caleb the son of Jephunneh, who was given in marriage to Othniel, son of Kenaz, Caleb's younger brother, in performance of a promise Caleb had made to give his daughter to him "that taketh Kirjath-sepher." The bride moved her husband to ask her father for a field. It was given him, but Achsah was not satisfied. Out riding one day, she met Caleb, and dismounting, she asked Caleb for springs to water the field. Caleb gave her both the upper and the lower springs. The story is told in charming and picturesque detail in both Joshua 15:16-19 and Judges 1:12-15.

ACHSHAPH (ăk'shăf, Heb. *'akhshāph*), a city (Josh. 11:1) which Joshua captured with its king (Josh. 12:7,20). It is named as being on the border of the lot assigned to Asher (Josh. 19:24,25). Achshaph is now tentatively identified with Tell Keisân, a few miles southeast of Accho (Acre; Ptolemais) and NE of Mt. Carmel.

ACHZIB (ăk'zĭb, Heb. *'akhzîv, a lie*). 1. A city of Judah (Josh. 15:44) perhaps Tell el-Beidâ, southwest of Adullam. Called Chezib (Gen. 38:5) and Chozeba (I Chron. 4:22). See Micah 1:14.
2. A town in Asher (Judg. 1:31, Josh. 19:29) on the coast north of Accho. The Hebrews did not drive out the earlier inhabitants. In NT times Ecdippa, modern ez-Zib.

ACRE (ā'kêr). In Isaiah 5:10, Heb. *tsemedh*, a pair; the amount of land a yoke of oxen could plow in a day. In I Samuel 14:14, Heb. *ma'ănâh*, a field for plowing by a yoke of oxen (*tsemedh*).

The Acropolis, civic center of ancient Athens, crowned by the spectacular Parthenon and other temples. At its base are the ruins of the Odeon (music hall) of Herod Atticus. EG

ACROPOLIS (à-krŏp′ō-lĭs, Gr. *akrópolis,* from *ákros, highest,* and *pŏlis, city*), the upper or higher city, citadel or castle of a Greek municipality; especially the citadel of Athens, where the treasury was. Athens' crowning glory is the Parthenon, the finest exemplar of Greek architecture. During Paul's stay in Athens (Acts 17:15-18:1), "his spirit was stirred in him, when he saw the city wholly given to idolatry." The images of gods and of heroes worshiped as gods filled Athens, and were inescapably conspicuous on the Acropolis. As Paul stood on Mars Hill, before the court of the Areopagus, he could see the temples on the Acropolis directly to the east, and the Agora (market place) below it.

Other NT cities — Corinth, Philippi, Samaria, etc. — each had its own Acropolis, which served as the town's civic and religious center, while the Agora constituted the central shopping plaza of thaᵗ time.

ACROSTIC (à-krôs′tĭc, Gr. *akrostichís,* from *ákros, topmost,* and *stíchos, a line of poetry*). In tne form of acrostic found in OT poetry, each line or stanza begins with a letter of the Heb. alphabet in order. This literary device aided the memory. It is difficult to render in English. Monsignor Knox, *The OT in English,* (New York, Sheed and Ward, 1950), has tried to, in the passages cited below. English readers who would feel the effect of the Heb. acrostic may consult his translation. Psalms 25, 34, 37, 111, 112, 145, Proverbs 31:10-31, Lamentations 1, 2, 4 are nearly regular acrostics. Psalm 119 has 22 sections of 8 verses, each section headed with a letter of the Heb. alphabet. Within the sections, each verse begins with the same letter. Lamentations 3 has groups of 3 lines, each beginning with the same letter. In chapter 5 the poet burst the bonds of the acrostic form, composing freely. Traces of acrostic are in Psalms 9 and 10, which Knox translates as such; possibly Nenemiah 1:2-10, etc. The imperfections of OT acrostics may be due to textual corruptions, or the poet's not adhering strictly to the acrostic form.   E.R.

ACTS OF THE APOSTLES (à-pŏs″lz), the New Testament book which gives the history of early Christianity from the ascension of Christ to the end of two years of Paul's imprisonment in Rome.

I. Title of the book. An early MS has the title "Acts" (Greek *práxeis,* doings, transactions, achievements). Other early titles are "Acts of Apostles," "The Acts of the Apostles," "Acts of the Holy Apostles," etc. Acts narrates doings and speeches chiefly of Peter and Paul. There is some information about Judas (1:16-20), and the man chosen to succeed him (1:21-26); about John (3:1-4:31, 8:14-17); and James (12:12). The Twelve, except the betrayer, are listed in 1:13. Acts is not a history of all apostles, but a selection from the deeds and words of some who illustrate the progress of first century Christianity in those phases which interested the author, as he was moved by the Holy Spirit. The title "Acts of the Holy Spirit" has often been suggested, and the contents of the book bear out the appropriateness of such a title.

II. Author. Not until A.D. 160-200 do we have positive statements as to the authorship of Acts. From that time onward all who mention the subject agree that the author of the two books dedicated to Theophilus, the Gospel according to Luke, and the Acts of the Apostles, are by "Luke the beloved physician." Only in modern times have there been attempts to ascribe both books to Titus or some other author.

The author indicates that he was a companion of Paul, by writing "we" instead of "they" in recounting events when he was present. Luke joined Paul, Silas, and Timothy at Troas during the second missionary journey and accompanied them to Philippi, but did not go with them when they left there (16:10-17). Luke is next mentioned as being at Philippi toward the end of the third missionary journey, when Paul is about to sail for Palestine with the contributions of the Gentile churches for the poor at Jerusalem (20:4ff., Rom. 15:25ff.). We do not know whether Luke spent all the interval at Philippi. From this point Luke accompanied Paul to Jerusalem (Acts 20:5-21:18). Nor do we know how Luke spent the two years during which Paul was imprisoned at Caesarea, but Luke enters the narrative again "when it was determined that we should sail into Italy" (27:1), and continues with him, giving us a vivid account of the voyage to Rome. Acts breaks off abruptly (28:31), at the end of Paul's two years of ministry in the relative freedom of "his own hired house," where he "received all that came unto him, preaching the kingdom of God, and teaching those things which concern the Lord Jesus Christ, with all confidence, no man forbidding him." If a later writer had incorporated these "we" sections, he would have named their author to enhance their authority. But the style of the "we" passages cannot be distinguished from the style of the rest of Acts, nor from that of the Gospel according to Luke. The author of Luke and Acts is the author of the "we" sections of Acts, and a companion of Paul.

The question remains: Which of the companions of Paul is the author? He cannot be one of those named in the "we" sections as distinct from the author. He is not likely to have been one of those named in Paul's epistles written at times other than those included in the "we" sections. Of those named in Paul's letters written when the "we" author might have been with Paul, early Christian writers chose "Luke, the beloved physician" (Col. 4:14). Luke is not otherwise prominent in the NT. Why should he have been chosen, unless he was the right one? The medical language in Acts is not sufficient to prove that the author was a physician, but it is sufficient to confirm other evidence to that effect. Luke was with Paul shortly before his expected death (II Tim. 4:11).

Luke cannot be certainly identified with Lucius of Acts 13:1 or with Lucius of Romans 16:21. There is wide and ancient support for connecting Luke with Antioch in Syria. It is not probable that he was from Philippi. The tradition that he was a painter cannot be traced earlier than the tenth century. From II Corinthians 8:18 it is possible that Titus was Luke's brother, and that Luke

was "the brother, whose praise is in the gospel throughout all the churches." Titus and Luke are named together in II Timothy 4:10,11. The conjecture that Luke was the "man of Macedonia" of Paul's vision (Acts 16:9) is attractive and inherently possible, but not certain.

III. Place. The place where Acts was written is not named, though the sudden ending of the book, while Paul is residing at Rome awaiting trial, makes Rome an appropriate place. The question of place is tied in with that of Luke's purpose in writing, and with the occasion for the publication of the book.

IV. Date. Allusions to the book in the Apostolic Fathers are too indefinite to compel the setting of a date much before the end of the first century A.D. If Acts is dependent on Josephus for information, it cannot be earlier than A.D. 93. But such dependence is not proved, and is highly unlikely. Acts must have been finished after the latest date mentioned in the book, in 28:30. The abrupt close indicates that it was written at that time, c. A.D. 61 or 62. Luke's Gospel has an appropriate ending; Acts does not. We are not told how the trial of Paul came out. There is no hint of Paul's release or of his death. The attitude toward Roman officials is friendly, which would not have been the case after the persecution under Nero set in, A.D. 64. The Jewish War of A.D. 66-70 and the destruction of Jerusalem are not referred to. Chapters 1-15 picture accurately conditions in Jerusalem before its destruction. It would be attractive to think that Luke's two books were written to inform and influence well-disposed Roman officials in their disposal of Paul's case.

V. The speeches in Acts. Do the speeches report what was actually said? We do not expect stenographic reporting, but Luke is a careful writer, as a comparison of his Gospel with Mark and Matthew shows. The style of the speeches in Acts is not Luke's, but that which is appropriate to each speaker, Peter, Stephen, Paul; even minor characters such as Gamaliel (5:25ff.), the Ephesian town

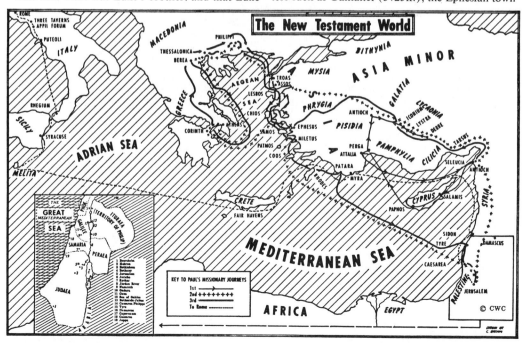

clerk (19:35ff.), Tertullus (24:2ff.). Similarities between the speeches of Peter and Paul are explained by the fact that Paul explicitly preached the same Gospel as Peter. Speeches by the same person are varied in type, each suited to the occasion.

VI. Summary of the contents. Introduction, a. Summary of ground covered by the "former treatise," especially the resurrection ministry of Jesus, 1:1-11. b. The period of waiting; a ten days' prayer meeting in the upper room, 1:12-14. c. The choice of a successor to the betrayer as one of the Twelve, 1:15-26.

1. Pentecost, the birthday of the Church. a. the occasion and the event, 2:1-13. b. Peter's sermon, 2:14-36. c. The result: the beginning of the Church, 2:37-47.

2. Pictures of the first church in Jerusalem. a. A lame man healed, 3:1-11. b. Peter's sermon on this occasion, 3:12-26. c. Attempted suppression of the new church met by prayer-power, 4:1-30. d. A contrast in givers, 4:31-5:11: Barnabas, the generous giver, 4:31-37; Ananias and Sapphira, the grudging givers, 5:1-11. e. Growth of the healing ministry of the church, 5:12-16. f. Another attempt at suppression of the church met by obedience to God, 5:17-42. g. An administrative problem solved leads to further advance, 6:1-8. h. The attempt of the Council (Sanhedrin) to suppress the new leader, Stephen, 6:9-15. i. Stephen's defense, 7:1-53. j. Stephen's martyrdom, 7:54-60.

3. The Gospel spread to all Judea and Samaria, 8:1-25. a. The stimulus to expansion: Saul as persecutor, 8:1-4. b. Problems in Samaria, 8:5-25.

4. Three "continental" conversions. a. From the continent of Africa: the Ethiopian eunuch, 8:26-40. b. From Asia: Saul of Tarsus, 9:1-31. (Interlude: Peter in western Palestine, 9:32-43). c. From Europe: Cornelius of Italy, 10:1-48.

5. The Judean church accepts the mission to the Gentiles, 11:1-30. a. Peter convinces the Jewish Christians, 11:1-18. b. The extent of the early mission to the Gentiles, 11:19-21. c. Barnabas and Saul minister in Antioch of Syria, 11:22-26. "And the disciples were called Christians first in Antioch," 11:26. d. Response of the church in Antioch to need in Judea, 11:27-30. e. A further attempt to suppress the Christian movement frustrated by the miraculous escape of Peter from prison, 12:1-19. (Note: The death of Herod, 12:20-23).

6. Paul's first missionary journey. a. The church at Antioch commissions Barnabas and Saul as missionaries to the Gentiles, 12:34-13:3. b. The mission to Cyprus, 13:4-12. c. The mission to Antioch in Pisidia, 13:13-50. d. The mission to Iconium, 13:51-14:5. e. The mission to Lystra, 14:6-20. f. The mission to Derbe, 14:20, 21. g. Return through the cities visited, formally establishing churches, 14:21-25. h. Furlough in Antioch, 14:26-28.

7. The Church Council at Jerusalem: terms of admission of Gentile believers settled, 15:1-29.

8. Paul's second missionary journey. a. Completion of furlough in Antioch: reporting the proceedings of the Council, 15:30-35. b. Paul and Barnabas part, Barnabas to Cyprus, Paul to Cilicia, 15:36-41. c. The journey to Troas, 16:1-8. d. Invitation to Europe accepted, 16:9-11. e. The mission to Philippi, 16:12-40. f. The mission to Thessalonica, 17:1-9. g. The mission to Berea, 17:10-14. h. The mission to Athens, 17:15-34. i. The mission to Corinth, 18:1-18. j. Beginning of the mission to Ephesus, and journey to Jerusalem and Antioch, 18:18-23.

9. Paul's third missionary journey. a. Confirming the disciples in Galatia and Phrygia, 18:23. b. Apollos at Ephesus, 18:24-28. c. The mission to Ephesus, 19:1-20:1. d. Journeyings through Greece and Macedonia to Troas, 20:1-6. e. The mission to Troas, 20:6-12. f. The journey to Jerusalem, 20:13-21:16.

10. Paul's arrest and voyage to Rome, a. Paul in Jerusalem, 21:17-23:30. b. Paul in Caesarea, 23:31-26:32. c. The voyage to Rome, 27:1-28:15. Paul in Rome, 28:16-31. E.R.

ADADAH (ă-dā'dà, Heb. *'adh'ādhâh*), a city in Judah (Josh. 15:22), not surely identified.

ADAH (ā'dà, Heb. *'ādhâh, ornament* or *morning*). 1. One of Lamech's two wives (Gen. 4:19, 20, 23), mother of Jabal and Jubal. Lamech spoke a poem in praise of himself to his wives.

2. One of Esau's wives (Gen. 36:2, 4, 10, 12, 16), daughter of Elon the Hittite. In Genesis 26:34 Esau marries Bashemath, daughter of Elon the Hittite, either another name for Adah, or her sister. Adah's son is Eliphaz (Gen. 36:10) and his sons are called hers (Gen. 36:12, 16).

ADAIAH (à-dā'yà, Heb. *'ădhāyâh, Jehovah hath adorned,* or *pleasing to Jehovah*). 1. A man of Boscath, father of Josiah's mother (II Kings 22:1).

2. A Levite descended from Gershom (I Chron. 6:41-43).

3. A son of Shimshi the Benjamite (I Chron. 8:1, 21).

4. A Levite of the family of Aaron, head of a family living in Jerusalem (I Chron. 9:10-12).

5. The father of Captain Maaseiah who helped Jehoiada put Joash on the throne of Judah (II Chron. 23:1).

6. A son of Bani who married a foreign wife during the exile (Ezra 10:29).

7. Another of a different Bani family who did the same (Ezra 10:34).

8. A descendant of Judah by Perez (Neh. 11:5).

9. A Levite of the family of Aaron. Most likely the same as 4 (Neh. 11:12).

ADALIA (ad-â-lī'à, Heb. *'ădhalyā'*), the fifth of Haman's sons, all of whom were hanged with their father (Esth. 9:8).

ADAM (ăd'ăm, Heb. *'ādhām,* Greek *Adám, of the ground* or *taken out of the red earth*), the first human son of God (Luke 3:38, I Tim. 2:13-14, Jude 14), and God's masterpiece and crowning work of creation. The word occurs about 560 times in the OT, meaning *man* or *mankind,* sometimes clearly as a proper name (e.g., I Chron. 1:1), oftener as a common noun. In some cases it is hard to tell which the writer meant (e.g., Deut. 32:8; KJV "sons of Adam" ASV "children of men;" RSV "sons of men."

The man God made. All men should be interested in the history of the first man who ever breathed, man's great ancestor, the head of the human family, the first human being who trod the earth. What a beautiful world Adam found himself in with everything to make him happy, a world without sin and without sorrow! God first made, as it were, the great house of the world, then brought His tenant to occupy it. And it was not an empty house, but furnished with everything needed to make life content. There was not a single need God had not satisfied.

The Bible does not tell us how long Adam's state of blessedness and innocence lasted. But Paradise was lost through Eve's listening to the voice of the tempter. Relieved of his occupation as gardener, Adam was condemned to make his living by tilling the stubborn ground, and to eat his bread in the sweat of his brow.

I. Adam was a necessary complement to the divine plan. "There was not a man to till the ground" (Gen. 2:5). The accomplishment of God's plan required human instrumentality. God made the earth for man, and then the man for the earth.

II. Adam was fashioned a creature of God, bearing the image of God and possessing God-like faculties (Gen. 1:27; Ps. 8:6; Eccl. 7:29).

III. Adam was created a tripartite being, having a spirit, soul and body (Gen. 2:7; I Thess. 5:23).

IV. Adam was alone and needed companionship to satisfy his created instincts (Gen. 2:18), thus Eve was formed.

V. Adam was enticed and sinned (Gen. 3:6). After the satanic tempter there came the human tempter, and the act of taking the forbidden fruit offered by Eve ruined Adam and made him our federal head in sin and death. "In Adam all die."

VI. Adam received the promise of the Saviour. The first promise and prophecy of One able to deal with sin and Satan was given, not to Adam, but to the one responsible for Adam's transgression (Gen. 3:15), and in the coats of skins God provided to cover the discovered nakedness of Adam and Eve we have a type of the sacrifice of the Cross. In Adam we die, but in Christ we can be made alive. The first man Adam was of the earth, earthly, but the Second Man, the last Adam, was from heaven and kept His first estate of sinless perfection.

Hence we are led to consider Adam, a type of Christ: Christ, the Second Adam. In two key NT passages Paul takes Adam as a type of Christ. In Romans 5:12-21, Adam is the head of a race doomed by sin to death; Christ is the beginning of a people made righteous by His death. Paul is here concerned with the justification of sinners before a holy God. Adam, the first sinner, is an ap-propriate type of all who have followed in his path of disobedience to God. More than that, his sin is the source of their misery, for "by one man's offence death reigned." Paul not only thus compares Christ with Adam, but contrasts the two, in that while "by one man's disobedience many were made sinners, so by the obedience of one shall many be made righteous" (Rom. 5:19).

In I Corinthians 15, after having proved that Christ has risen from the dead, Paul introduces an argument which really continues that in Romans 5:12-21: "For since by man came death, by man came also the resurrection of the dead. For as in Adam all die, even so in Christ shall all be made alive" (I Cor. 15:21-22). All who are in Adam (the whole human race) are here contrasted with all who are in Christ (those human beings who have received Him as Saviour). The destiny of the former is death; the destiny of the latter, resurrection life. For (I Cor. 15:45), "the first man Adam was made a living soul; the last Adam (Christ) was made a quickening (life-giving) spirit."

The study of the life of Adam (Gen. 1:26-5:5) shows us the natural man in his original and intended glory, in the extremity of his fall, and in the possibilities which yet remain to him as man. The NT passages cited open before us the infinitely rich and eternal destiny awaiting and available to us through the perfect obedience unto death of the Second Adam, our Lord Jesus Christ. E.R.

ADAM (ăd'ăm, Heb. *'ādhām, red,* or *made*), a city in the Jordan valley near Zaretan, where the waters of the river were backed up so that the Israelites crossed on dry ground when they entered the promised land from east of Jordan (Josh. 3:16). The exact location is in dispute.

The flow of the Jordan River temporarily blocked by earthquake-caused landslides near the ancient town of Adam, or Adamah, on July 11, 1927. This is thought to be near the spot of the Israelite crossing of Joshua 3:16. © MPS

ADAMAH (ăd'à-mà, Heb. *'ădhāmâh, red ground*), a fenced city of Naphtali (Josh. 19:36). Location disputed.

ADAMANT (ăd'à-mănt, Heb. *shāmîr*), a stone harder than flint (Ezek. 3:9, Zech. 7:12). The Heb. word is translated "diamond" in Jeremiah 17:1, "briers" in Isaiah 5:6, 7:23-25, 9:18, 10:17, 27:4, 32:13.

ADAMI (ăd'ă-mî, Heb. *'ădhāmî, earthy*), a place on the border of Naphtali (Josh. 19:33), united with "Nekeb" and forming "Adami-nekeb," in ASV and RSV.

ADAR (ā'dàr, Heb. *'ăddār*), a place on the south border of Judah (Josh. 15:3 KJV). In ASV and RSV, Addar.

ADAR (à-dàr', ā'dàr, Heb. *'ădhār*), the 12th month of the Babylonian calendar; used by the Hebrews after the exile (Ezra 6:15, Esth. 3:7, 13, 8:12, 9:1, 15, 17, 19, 21).

ADBEEL (ăd'bē-ĕl, Heb. *'adhbe'ēl, languishing for God*), the third son of Ishmael and grandson of Abraham (Gen. 25:13, I Chron. 1:29).

ADDAN (ăd'ăn, Heb. *'addān*, Ezra 2:59; *'addôn* in Neh. 7:61), one of the places in Babylonia from which the people named in Ezra 2:60-63 and Nehemiah 7:62-65 returned to Jerusalem after the exile, whose names could not be found in the genealogy of those entitled to be priests.

ADDAR (ăd'àr, Heb. *'addār, threshing floor*). 1. Son of Bela, grandson of Benjamin (I Chron. 8:3). Called Ard in Genesis 46:21 and Numbers 26:40; counted as a son of Benjamin and head of a family in the tribe.
2. In ASV and RSV for Adar of KJV.

ADDER (See Animals—Reptiles)

ADDI (ăd'ī, Gr. *Addí, Addeí, my witness,* or *adorned*), an ancestor of Joseph, the husband of Mary, our Lord's mother (Luke 3:28).

ADDON (ăd'ŏn), the same place as Addan (Neh. 7:61; compare Ezra 2:59).

ADER (ā'dêr, Heb. *'adher, a flock*), a son of Beriah, grandson of Shaharaim, a Benjaminite (I Chrcn. 8:15).

ADIEL (ā'dĭ-ĕl, Heb. *'ădhiēl, ornament of God*).
1. A descendant of Simeon (I Chron. 4:36).
2. A priest, son of Jahzerah (I Chron. 9:12).
3. Father of Azmaveth, who was supervisor of David's treasuries (I Chron. 27:25). Perhaps the same as No. 2.

ADIN (ā'dĭn, Heb. *'ădhîn, delicate,* or *ornament*).
1. One whose family returned from exile with Zerubbabel (Ezra 2:15, Neh. 7:20).
2. One whose posterity came back with Ezra (Ezra 8:6).
3. The name of a family sealing the covenant (Neh. 10:16). These are all thought to be the same family. The list in Ezra 2 appears to include both exiles who returned with Zerubbabel and some who returned later. The family included "chiefs of the people" (Neh. 10:14).

ADINA (ăd'ĭ-nà, Heb. *'ădhînā', ornament*), a Reubenite and one of David's military officers (I Chron. 11:42).

ADINO (ăd'ĭ-nō, à-dī'nō, Heb. *'ădhînô, his adorned one*). "The Tachmonite that sat in the seat, chief among the captains; the same was Adino the Eznite; he lift up his spear against eight hundred, whom he slew at one time" (I Sam. 23:8 KJV). ASV and RSV have the proper name Josheb-bassebeth instead of "that sat in the seat," and RSV

omits the name of Adino the Eznite. I Chronicles 11:11 has "Jashobeam, an Hachmonite," with the same title and exploit.

ADITHAIM (ăd-ĭ-thā'ĭm, Heb. *'ădhîthayim, double ornaments*), one of "the uttermost cities of. . . Judah" (KJV), "in the extreme South, toward the border of Edom" (RSV; Josh. 15:21), in the "lowland" or Shephelah (Josh. 15:33 ASV, RSV), and named in Joshua 15:36.

ADJURATION (ăj-ōō-rā'shŭn). The noun does not occur in the Bible, but the verb "adjure" (à-jōōr') is found. In I Samuel 14:24 it translates a form of Heb. *'ālâh* meaning *cause to take an oath,* rendered *laid an oath on the people* in RSV. In Joshua 6:26 it translates the Heb. *shāva'* in a form with the same meaning, which RSV renders "laid an oath on them." A curse for disobedience to the command is meant. The same Heb. word occurs in I Kings 22:16 and II Chronicles 18:15 with the meaning "charge, bind or command solemnly as if under penalty of a curse." While the actual taking of an oath is not involved, the circumstances are as solemn as if one were exacted. In Matthew 26:63 adjure translates Greek *exorkizo* where a charge of like solemnity is meant. In Mark 5:7 the Greek is *horkizo*, the simple verb without a strengthening preposition, and it is the appeal of a demoniac. In Acts 19:13 exorcists attempt to command demons in the name of Jesus. In I Thessalonians 5:27 Paul says "I charge you" (Greek *horkizo*) where ASV and RSV have "adjure." In every case, an appeal in the most impressive manner, an earnest entreaty, is meant; a solemn appeal. E.R.

ADLAI (ăd'lā-ī, Heb. *'adhlay, justice of Jehovah,* or *weary*), father of Shaphat, who was overseer of David's cattle in the lowlands (I Chron. 27:29).

ADMAH (ăd'mà, Heb. *'adhmâh, red earth*), a city near Gomorrah and Zeboiim (Gen. 10:19) with a king (Gen. 14:2, 8), destroyed with Sodom and Gomorrah (Deut. 29:23 with Gen. 19:24-28; see Hos. 11:8).

ADMATHA (ăd'mà-thà, Heb. *'adhmāthā', unrestrained*), a prince of Persia and Media (Esth. 1:14).

ADNA (ăd'nà, Heb. *'adhnā, pleasure*). 1. A son of Pahath-moab who had married a foreign wife during the exile (Ezra 10:30).
2. A priest, head of his father's house in the days of Joiakim (Neh. 12:12-15).

ADNAH (ăd'nà, Heb. *'adhnāh, pleasure*). 1. A Manassite who joined David at Ziklag (I Chron. 12:20).
2. A man of Judah who held high military rank under Jehoshaphat (II Chron. 17:14).

ADONI-BEZEK (à-dō'nī-bē'zĕk, Heb. *'ădhōnî-vezeq, lord of lightning,* or *of the city of Bezek*), a king of Bezek, captured by the men of Judah and Simeon and taken to Jerusalem, where he was mutilated. The cutting off of his thumbs and great toes not only rendered him harmless but reminded him that man reaps what he sows (Judg. 1:5-7; Gal. 6:5).

ADONIJAH (ăd'ō-nī'jà, Heb. *'ădhōnîyāhû, my Lord is Jehovah*), the fourth son of David, by Haggith, born at Hebron (II Sam. 3:2-4, I Chron. 3:2). Amnon and Absalom, David's first and third sons, had died; the second, Chileab, had not been mentioned since his birth, and might have died also. Adonijah, as the eldest living son, aspired to the throne. The story of his attempt and failure to seize the crown is told in I Kings 1:5-2:25.

He was a spoiled, handsome lad (1:6), and now he "prepared him chariots and horsemen, and fifty men to run before him (1:5). He won over Joab, also Abiathar the priest, but failed to gain Zadok the priest and Nathan the prophet. Moreover, "the mighty men which belonged to David, were not with Adonijah" (1:7,8). He held a great feast at En-rogel, to which he invited "all his brethren the king's sons, and all the men of Judah the king's servants," but he did not invite "Nathan the prophet, and Benaiah, and the mighty men, and Solomon his brother" (1:9,10). Nathan spoke to Bathsheba, Solomon's mother, and together they warned David of what Adonijah was doing. David, roused to action, had Solomon proclaimed king at Gihon (1:11-40). Adonijah and his guests heard the shout and the sound of the trumpet (1:41). Immediately Jonathan, the son of Abiathar, brought a full account of what had happened (1:42-48). The guests fled, and Adonijah sought refuge at the altar (1:49,50). Solomon pardoned him, and he returned home (1:51;53).

But after the death of David, Adonijah emboldened himself to ask Bathsheba to persuade king Solomon to give him Abishag, David's nurse in his last illness, for a wife (2:13-18). This revived Solomon's suspicions, and he had him killed (2:19-25).

2. A Levite, sent by Jehoshaphat to teach the law (II Chron. 17:8).

3. A chieftain who with Nehemiah sealed the covenant (Neh. 10:14-16). E.R.

ADONIKAM (ăd-ō-nī'kăm, Heb. *'ădhōnîqām, my Lord has arisen*), the ancestor of a family, 666 of whom returned from exile with Zerubbabel (Ezra 2:13). Among the chiefs of the people who returned with Ezra are three sons and 60 males of this family (Ezra 8:13). In the list of exiles whose genealogy proved them Israelites are 667 of this family (Neh. 7:18). The Adonijah of Nehemiah 10:16, because of his position among those who sealed the covenant, is thought to be the same as Adonikam.

ADONIRAM (ăd-ō-nī'răm, Heb. *'ădhōnîrām, my Lord is exalted*), first appears by the name Adoram as an officer of David "over the tribute" (II Sam. 20:24). He continues under Solomon (I Kings 4:6); "over the levy" of laborers in Lebanon (I Kings 5:14). Rehoboam sends Adoram to compel the obedience of the rebels, but "all Israel stoned him . . . that he died" (I Kings 12:18). Both Adoram and Hadoram (II Chron. 10:18) are shortened forms of Adoniram.

ADONI-ZEDEK, ADONI-ZEDEC (KJV) (à-dō'nī-zē'dĕk, Heb. *'ădhōnîtsedheq, lord of righteousness*, or, *my lord is righteous*), Amorite king of Jerusalem (Josh. 10:1-27). Having heard how Joshua destroyed Ai and Jericho, and how Gibeon made peace with Israel, Adoni-zedek invited four other Amorite kings to join him in attacking Gibeon. Joshua came to the aid of Gibeon. God discomfited the kings, both in battle and with great hailstones. This was the day when Joshua called on the sun and moon to stand still until the people had avenged themselves upon their enemies. The kings hid in a cave, which Joshua sealed with great stones. Victory complete, Joshua ordered the kings brought out and slew them, and hanged them on trees until sunset, when they were cut down and buried in the cave where they had hidden. An earlier king of Jerusalem (Salem) bore a name, Melchizedek, meaning "king of righteousness" (Gen. 14:18-20).

ADOPTION (à-dŏp'shŭn). The word occurs five times in the NT (Gr. *huiothesía*). The practice of adoption is exemplified in the OT: Pharaoh's daughter adopted Moses (Exod. 2:10) as her son. Hadad the Edomite married the sister of the Egyptian queen, and their son Genubath was brought up "among the sons of Pharaoh," whether formally adopted or not (I Kings 11:20). Esther was adopted by Mordecai (Esth. 2:7,15). These cases were outside Palestine, in Egypt or Persia. Whether adoption was practiced in the Hebrews' own land is not clear. Abram thinks of Eliezer of Damascus as his heir, but God tells him this shall not be (Gen. 15:2-4). Sarai gave her maid Hagar to Abram that he might obtain children by her (Gen. 16:1-3). Rachel (Gen. 30:1-5) and Leah (Gen. 30:9-12) gave Jacob their maids for a like purpose, a kind of adoption by the mother but not by the father. Jacob adopted his grandsons Manasseh and Ephraim to be as Reuben and Simeon (Gen. 48:5). The case of Jair (I Chron. 2:21,22) is one of inheritance rather than adoption. Whether Mary the mother of Jesus, or Joseph her husband, or both, were adopted, is a matter of inference incapable of direct proof (Luke 3:23, Matt. 1:16). Levirate marriage (Deut. 25:5,6) involved a sort of posthumous adoption of a brother's later-born son.

But none of the OT instances have a direct bearing on the NT usage of the term. Paul is the only writer to employ it, and with him it is a metaphor derived from Hellenistic usage and Roman law. The legal situation of a son in early Roman times was little better than that of a slave, though in practice its rigor would vary with the disposition of the father. The son was the property of his father, who was entitled to his earnings; who could transfer ownership of him by adoption or by a true sale; who could, under certain circumstances, even put him to death. An adopted son was considered like a son born in the family. He could no longer inherit from his natural father. He was no longer liable for old debts (a loophole eventually closed). So far as his former family was concerned, he was dead. Modifications of the rigor of sonship were at intervals introduced into Roman law, and a more liberal Hellenistic view was doubtless in the mind of Paul.

In Galatians 4:1-3 Paul states accurately the Roman law of sonship. In verse 4 he says that God sent His Son to be born into the human condition under law, and in verse 5 the purpose of God in so doing: "to redeem them that were under the law, that we might receive the adoption of sons." We were not merely children who needed to grow up; we had become slaves of sin who needed to be redeemed, bought out of our bondage, that we might enter the new family which Christ brought into being by His death and resurrection. Adoption expresses both the redemption and the new relation of trust and love, for "because ye are sons, God hath sent forth the Spirit of His Son into your hearts, crying, Abba, Father" (verse 6). The adoption brought us from slavery to sonship and heirship (verse 7).

The same thought appears in Romans 8:15. Verses 1-14 demonstrate that the adoption is more than a matter of position or status; when God adopted us, He put His Spirit within us, and we became subject to His control. This involves chastisement (Heb. 12:5-11) as well as inheritance (Rom. 8:16-18).

In Romans 8:23 "the adoption" is spoken of as future, in the sense that its full effects are to be consummated at the time of "the redemption of our body." This "redemption" is not the "buying out" of Galatians 4:5, but a word (Gr. *apolytrosis*) emphasizing the release, the loosing from all restraints which the limitation of a mortal body imposes. We are part of a suffering creation (verse 22). The spiritual body, the resurrection body, pictured in vivid terms of I Corinthians 15:35-57, is the object of Paul's longing (Phil. 3:21, II Cor. 5:1-8). The present effects of God's adoption of us as sons are marvelous, yet they are only an earnest (II Cor. 1:22, 5:5, Eph. 1:13,14) of what the adoption will mean when we come into our inheritance in heaven.

In Romans 9:4 Paul begins with enumeration of the privileges of Israelites with "the adoption." Though God said, "Israel is my son, my first-born" (Exod. 4:22); and, "When Israel was a child, then I loved him, and called my child out of Egypt" (Hos. 11:1); and Moses expressed the relationship, "Ye are the children of the Lord your God" (Deut. 14:1); yet Israel's sonship was not the natural relationship by creation, but a peculiar one by a covenant of promise, a spiritual relationship by faith, under the sovereign grace of God, as Paul goes on to explain in Romans 9-11. Thus a clear distinction is drawn between the "offspring" of God by creation (Acts 17:28) and the children of God by adoption into the obedience of faith.

With utmost compression of language Paul expresses, in Ephesians 1:4, 5, God's action which resulted in His adoption of us; and enumerates its effects in verses 6-12. This action began with God's election; "He hath chosen us in Him before the foundation of the world," using predestination as the mode, ("having predestinated us"); Christ is the agent (by Jesus Christ); and He Himself is the adopting parent (to Himself). God's sovereign act is stressed by the concluding phrase of verse 5: "according to the good pleasure of His will." That adoption is not a mere matter of position is made plain in the statement of the purpose of election: "that we should be holy and without blame before Him in love" (verse 4).

Adoption is a serious matter under any system of law. As a figure of speech expressing spiritual truth it emphasizes the sovereign and gracious character of the act of God in our salvation; our solemn obligation as adopted sons of our adopting Parent; the newness of the family relationship established; its climate of intimate trust and love; and the immensity of an inheritance which eternity alone can reveal to us.   E. R.

ADORAIM (ăd′ō-rām, Heb. *'ădhōrayim*), a fortress built by Rehoboam in Judah (II Chron. 11:9). Probably now Dûra, a large village on rising ground W of Hebron.

ADORAM (à-dō′răm), the same as Adoniram.

ADORATION (ăd-ō-rā′shŭn), "to kiss the hand with the mouth" in homage (Job 31:26,27: "If I behold the sun ... or the moon ... and my mouth hath kissed my hand"), the earliest idolatry, that of the sun, moon, and stars. Laying the hand on the mouth expressed deep reverence and submission (Job 40:4). So "kiss the Son," i.e. adore Him (Ps. 2:12). Falling down prostrate was the worship paid to Babylonian idols (Dan. 3:5,6). Worship is due to God only, and was rejected by angels and saints when offered to them (Luke 4:8, Acts 10:25,26, Rev. 19:10; 22:8,9). "The adoration of the Magi" is the name given to the visit of the wise men to the infant Jesus (Matt. 2:11), and to paintings of the scene.

ADORE (See Adoration)

At the Caves of Adullam, near Bethlehem, where David took refuge from Saul. © MPS

ADRAMMELECH (ăd-răm′ĕ-lĕk, Heb. *'adhramme-lekh, Adar is king*). 1. The name which the author of II Kings 17:31 gives to Adar, the god the Sepharvites brought to Samaria when the king of Assyria settled them there, and in the worship of whom children were burnt in fire. It was a time of syncretism, when Israelites and Assyrian colonists both paid service to God and to heathen deities alike (II Kings 17:24-41).

2. A son of Sennacherib, who, with his brother Sharezer, slew their father in the temple of Nisroch (II Kings 19:37, Isa. 37-38).

ADRAMYTTIUM (ăd′rà-mĭt′ĭ-ŭm), an old port city of Mysia, in the Roman province of Asia, near Edremit. Paul sailed in a ship of Adramyttium along the coast from Caesarea in Palestine to Myra in Lycia, where an Alexandrian ship bound for Italy took him on board (Acts 27:2-6).

ADRIA (ā′drĭ-à), originally that part of the gulf between Italy and the Dalmatian coast near the mouth of the Po River, named for the town of Adria. Later, it was extended to include what is now the Adriatic Sea; and, in NT times, also that part of the Mediterranean between Crete and the Peloponnesus on the east and Sicily and Malta on the west. This extended meaning appears in Acts 27:27, where Paul's ship is "driven up and down in Adria." "The shipmen deemed that they drew near to some country," and that land proved to be Malta (Acts 28:1 RSV; Melita in KJV).

ADRIEL (ā′drĭ-ăl, Heb. *'adhrîēl, honor* or *flock* or *help of God*), son of Barzillai the Meholathite, to whom Merab, Saul's daughter, was given in marriage, when she had been promised to David (I Sam. 18:19, II Sam. 21:8). In II Samuel 21:8 "the five sons of Michal the daughter of Saul, whom she brought up for Adriel," are spoken of. "Michal" is here thought to be a copyist's error for Merab. The expression is peculiar, and so may the relationship have been. Adriel probably came from Abel-Meholah, which was either in West Manasseh or in Issachar.

ADULLAM (à-dŭl'ăm, Heb. *'ădhullām, retreat, refuge*), a city in the Shephelah or low country, between the hill country of Judah and the sea, 13 miles SW of Bethlehem; very ancient (Gen. 38:1,12,20; Josh. 15:35); the seat of one of the 31 petty kings smitten by Joshua (Josh. 12:15). Fortified by Rehoboam (II Chron. 11:7). Called for its beauty "the glory of Israel" (Mic. 1:15). Reoccupied on the return from the Babylonian exile (Neh. 11:30).

David hid in one of the many limestone caves near the city, with his family and about 400 men (I Sam. 22:1,2) at times when Saul sought his life. While David was here, three of his "mighty men" risked their lives to fulfil his expressed desire for water from the well of Bethlehem, but David refused to drink it because it was obtained at the risk of life (II Sam. 23:13-17, I Chron. 11:15-19). Adullam was indeed a "refuge" for David.

ADULLAMITE (à-dŭl'ăm-īt, *belonging to Adullam*), used of Hirah, Judah's friend (Gen. 38:1, 12,20).

ADULTERY (à-dŭl'tĕr-ē). In the OT, sexual intercourse, usually of a man, married or unmarried, always with the wife of another. One of the Ten Commandments forbids it (Exod. 20:14, Deut. 5:18). The punishment for both man and woman was death (Lev. 20:20, 18:20), probably by stoning (Deut. 22:22-24, John 8:3-7). Adultery and related words translate derivatives of the Heb. root *n'ph* (*nā'aph*), conveying the one plain meaning. The simple stem (*Qal*) of the verb is used, in addition to the foregoing, of the literal deed or doer (Prov. 6:32, Jer. 5:7, 7:9, 23:14, Hos. 4:2, Job 24:15); the intensive stem (*Piel*), suited to intense, emotionally charged speech (Jer. 29:23, Ezek. 23:37, Jer. 9:2, 23:10, Hos. 7:4, Mal. 3:5, Ps. 50:18). Instances where the woman is the doer are: in the simple verb stem, of literal action (Lev. 20:10, Ezek. 16:38 "as women that break wedlock," Ezek. 23:45): in the intensive stem (Hos. 4:13,14, 3:1, Prov. 30:20, Ezek. 16:32).

The OT also uses adultery as a figure for idolatrous worship. The simple verb stem occurs in this sense in Jeremiah 3:9; the intensive stem in Ezekiel 23:37, Jeremiah 3:8, and Isaiah 57:3. Plural nouns (adulteries) occur: Heb. *ni'uphîm* (Ezek. 23:43, Jer. 13:27); *na'ăphûphîm* (Hos. 2:4; all of idolatrous worship).

While fornication (the wider term for sexual offenses) is frequently and severely condemned in the OT, special solemnity attaches to the reproof of adultery, either in the relations of individual men and women, or figuratively, in the relations of the covenant people Israel, conceived of as a wife, with God, their spiritual husband. Isaiah, Jeremiah and Ezekiel use the figure (see references above). Hosea develops from personal experience with an adulterous wife an allegory of God's love for His unfaithful people. Adultery in the marriage relation is reprehensible: how much more infidelity in the behavior of human beings toward a God who loves us with a love which can well be expressed as that of a husband for his wife? Thus the figurative use enhances the literal sense, emphasizing the divine institution and nature of marriage.

In the NT, "adultery" translates Greek *moicheúo* and related words, which the LXX had already used for Heb. *nā'aph*. The meaning throughout the Bible widens and deepens, first with the prophets, then with Jesus and His apostles.

Jesus quotes the commandment (Matt. 5:27-30, 19:18, Mark 10:19, Luke 18:20), broadening its application to include the lustful look which betrays an adulterous heart. He teaches that such evils as adultery come from the heart (Matt. 15:19, Mark 7:21). Dealing with divorce, Jesus declares remarriage of a divorced man or woman to be adultery (Matt. 5:31,32, 19:3-9, Mark 10:2-12, Luke 16:18), with one exception (Matt. 5:32, 19:9), the interpretation of which by various interpreters differs. The Pharisee in a parable rejoices that he is not an adulterer (Luke 18:11). Jesus uses the term figuratively of a people unfaithful to God (Matt. 12:39, 16:4, Mark 8:38). In John 8:2-11 the account of a woman taken in adultery reveals Jesus' insistence on the equal guilt of the man. Without belittling the seriousness of adultery, Jesus exercises the sovereign pardoning power of the grace of God, coupled with a solemn injunction against future offenses. Jesus' attitude toward adultery springs from His conception of marriage as God intended it, and as it must be in the new Christian society.

Paul names adultery as one of the tests of obedience to the law (Rom. 2:22), quotes the commandment (Rom. 13:9), uses adultery as an analogy of our relation to God (Rom 7:3), says that adulterers "shall not inherit the kingdom of God" (I Cor. 6:9), and lists adultery among works of the flesh (Gal. 5:19). The sanctity of marriage is the point stressed in Hebrews 13:4. James 2:1 uses adultery and murder as examples of the equal obligation of all the commandments of God. In James 4:4 adultery is a figure of speech for unfaithfulness to God. Revelation 2:20-23 condemns spiritual adultery.

The NT treatment of adultery, following the implications of the OT concept, supports marriage as a lifelong monogamous union. Adultery is a special and aggravated case of fornication. In the teaching of Jesus and the apostles in the NT, all sexual impurity is sin against God, against self, and against others. Spiritual adultery (unfaithfulness to God) violates the union between Christ and His own.   E.R.

ADUMMIM (à-dŭm'ĭm, Heb. *'ădhummîm*, perhaps *red spots*), a pass, "the going up to Adummim" (Josh. 15:7, 18:17), the ascent of Adummim on the road between Jerusalem and Jericho. It was on the north border of Judah and the south border of Benjamin. Convincingly held to be the scene of Jesus' parable of the Good Samaritan (Luke 10:30-35).

ADVENT (See Eschatology)

ADVERSARY (ăd'vêr-sâr'ē), an enemy, personal, national, or supernatural. In the OT, *adversary* translates a number of Heb. words meaning "show hostility to" (Exod. 23:22); "to bind, restrict" (Deut. 32:27); "straitness" (I Sam. 1:6); "to straiten, distress" (Exod. 23:22); "to strive, plead," (I Sam. 2:10); "accuser, opponent" (Num. 22:22); "to accuse, oppose" (Ps. 71:13); "owner of a judgment" (Isa. 50:8); "a man of strife" (Job 32:35). In the NT "adversary" translates *antídikos* (Matt. 5:25 etc.); *antíkeimai*, "be opposed to" (Luke 13:17 etc); *hypenantíos,* "opposed to" (Heb. 10:27). *Antídikos* refers to Satan in I Peter 5:8 and I Timothy 5:14.

ADVOCATE (ăd'vō-kāt, Gr. *parákletos, advocate, supporter, backer, helper, Paraclete*), Jesus Christ (I John 2:1). Also Jesus speaks of the Holy Spirit as "another Comforter" (John 14:16), using the same Greek word, thereby implying that He Himself is a "Comforter." The Holy Spirit is the Advocate of the Father with us, therefore our Comforter (John 14:16,26, 15:26, 16:7, where RSV translates "Counselor"). As applied to the Holy

Spirit, the Greek word is so rich in meaning that adequate translation by any one English word is impossible. Comforter is as satisfactory as any, if it is taken in the fullest sense of one who not only consoles but strengthens, helps, counsels, with such authority as a legal advocate has for his client. As applied to Christ, the meaning is narrowed to that of Advocate with the Father (I John 2:1,2).

AENEAS (ē-nē'ăs), a paralytic, healed at Lydda by Peter (Acts 9:32-35).

AENON (ē'nŏn; in Aramaic means *springs*), a place near Salim, where John the Baptist was baptizing at the time Jesus was baptizing in Judea (John 3:22,23). The site of Aenon is unknown. Two possibilities are suggested for Salim; one east of Mt. Gerizim, the other 6 miles S of Scythopolis. There are springs near both places. It would have been unnecessary to mention "much water" (John 3:23) if Aenon had been close to the Jordan River. John seems to have moved from "Bethabara beyond Jordan" where we find him in John 1:28.

AEON (ē'ŏn, Greek *aión*). The word "aeon" does not occur in the English Bible, but is variously translated. Its original meaning is "relative time duration, limited or unlimited," i.e., a period of time, or eternity. A common translation in the NT is "world" (RSV often "age"). Frequently it occurs in phrases meaning "forever" (e.g., Matt. 6:13). KJV has "ages" twice (Eph. 2:7, Col. 1:26). When aeon is the word translated "world," its duration in time is involved, though aeon is sometimes synonymous with Greek *kósmos,* world-order (e.g., Mark 4:19, I Cor. 1:20, 2:6, 3:19). Good examples of aeon meaning a period of time are Hebrews 9:26, where "the end of the world" is the period ushered in by the first coming of Christ; and Matthew 24:3, 28:20, where "the end of the world" is its culmination at His second coming. We live during the period between (I Cor. 10:11). "This present age (time)" and "the age (world) to come" are distinguished (e.g., Mark 10:30, Matt. 12:32). "This (present) age (world)" (e.g., Rom. 12:2, II Tim. 4:10, Titus 2:12) implies the existence of another world. In Ephesians 1:21 "this world" precedes "that which is to come." Hebrews 6:5 speaks of "the powers of the world (RSV "age") to come," which believers already experience. The Gnostic concept of aeons as beings emanating from, and standing between God and the world, is foreign to the NT.   E.R.

AGABUS (ăg'à-bŭs), one of the prophets from Jerusalem who came to Antioch and prophesied a famine "throughout all the world" (inhabited world: the Roman Empire). This "came to pass in the days of Claudius Caesar." The prophecy led Christians at Antioch "to send relief unto . . . Judea . . . by . . . Barnabas and Saul" (Acts 11:27-30). Years later, a "certain prophet, named Agabus" came down from Jerusalem to Caesarea, and by a dramatic action warned Paul that he would be put in bonds if he persisted in going to Jerusalem (Acts 21:10,11). Though we cannot prove that the two prophets are one and the same man, there is no reason to doubt it.

AGAG (ā'găg, Heb. *'ăghāgh,* perhaps meaning *violent*). 1. An important king of Amalek (Num. 24:7), of whom Balaam prophesied that a king of Jacob (Israel) would surpass him.

2. The king of the Amalekites, whom Saul captured alive, though God had through the prophet Samuel ordered him to destroy them entirely (I Sam. 15:8,9). When Samuel reproached him, Saul excused himself (I Sam. 15:22 ff.), but Samuel was not satisfied. When Samuel had Agag brought

The "Tree of Agony" in the Garden of Gethsemane. © MPS

in for judgment, Agag concluded, "Surely the bitterness of death is past." But Samuel, as judge, pronounced sentence of death upon him for all his cruel deeds, "and Samuel hewed Agag in pieces before the Lord" (I Sam. 15:32,33).

AGAGITE (ăg'à-gīt, ā'găg-īt), an epithet applied to Haman as enemy of the Jews (Esth. 3:1,10, 8:5, 9:24).

AGAPE (ăg'à-pā, Gr. *agápe*), the more frequent of two NT words for love, connoting the preciousness or worthiness of the one loved. It is used in Jude 12 (KJV "feasts of charity," ASV, RSV "lovefeasts") of common meals which bore that name because they cultivated brotherly love among Christians. II Peter 2:13, I Corinthians 11:21,22, 33,34, Acts 20:11 may refer to them. In Acts 2:46 "breaking bread" refers to the Lord's Supper (cf. v. 42), but "eat their meat (food)" requires a full meal. I Corinthians 11:20-34 rebukes abuses which had crept into the love-feasts, and which marred the Lord's Supper. The Lord's Supper properly followed, but was distinct from the love-feast.

AGAR (ā'gàr), the Greek name of Sarai's handmaid (Gal. 4:24,25).

AGATE (See Minerals)

AGE (See Aeon)

AGE, OLD, called the reward of filial obedience, according to the commandment (Exod. 20:12). The Mosaic legislation spelled out the respect to be shown the aged (Lev. 19:32). Younger men waited till they had spoken (Job 32:4). God promised Abraham "a good old age" (Gen. 15:15). When Pharaoh received him, Jacob lamented that he had not lived as long as his ancestors (Gen. 47:7-9). There are many Heb. words relating to old age in the OT, showing the honor in which the aged were usually held; yet the gray hairs which were so much respected had also their sorrows (Gen. 44:29-31). Official position went to older men (elders, e.g., Exod 3:16, Matt. 21:23). Elders were ordained·for the early Christian churches (e.g., Acts 14:23). Aged men and women are given sound advice in Titus 2:2-5. There is a fine picture of old age in Ecclesiastes 12:1-7. Jesus Christ is portrayed with the white hair of old age in Revelation 1:14.

AGONY (ă'gō-nē, Gr. *agonía, agony, anguish*). Occurs only in Luke 22:44, of Jesus' agony in Gethsemane. The word is derived from the Gr. *agōn*, "contest," "struggle," and depicts severe conflict and pain. Luke tells us that Christ's agony was such that "His sweat was as it were great drops of blood falling down to the ground." (See also Matt. 26:36-46, Mark 14:32-42, Heb. 5:7,8.) While Luke alone records the bloody sweat and the appearance of an angel from heaven strengthening Him, Matthew and Mark speak of the change in His countenance and manner, and record His words expressing overwhelming sorrow even unto death. The passage in Hebrews is the only clear reference in the New Testament apart from the Gospels to this agonizing crisis. His struggle was in part with the powers of darkness, which were then returning with double force, having retreated after Satan's defeat at the Temptation (Luke 4:13) "for a season" (Gr. *until* the season," viz. in Gethsemane, Luke 22:53). Chiefly, however, His agony was caused by the prospect of the darkness on Calvary, when He was to experience a horror never known before, the hiding of the Father's face, the climax of His vicarious suffering for our sins. The one who knew no sin was to be made sin for mankind. The hour was before Him when He would cry out in wretchedness of soul, "My God, My God, why hast Thou forsaken me?" The prospect of this dreadful cup was that which caused the struggle in the Garden. In this supreme spiritual conflict, the Captain of our salvation emerged triumphantly victorious, as is evident in the language of final victory of faith over the sinless infirmity of His flesh: "The cup which My Father hath given Me, shall I not drink it?" (John 18:11). B.P.

AGORA (ă'gō-rà, Gr. *agorá, market place*). In ancient cities the town meeting place, where the public met for the exchange of merchandise, information and ideas. As centers where people congregated, the agorae of Galilee and Judea were the scenes for many of the healing miracles of Christ (Mark 6:56). Here the village idlers, as well as those seeking work, would gather (Matt. 20:3). Here the vain and the proud could parade in order to gain public recognition (Matt. 23:7; Mark 12:38; Luke 11:43; 20:46). Here also the children would gather for play (Matt. 11:16,17, Luke 7:32). In Gentile cities, the agorae served also as forums and tribunals. The agora of Philippi was the scene of the trial of Paul and Silas following the deliverance of a "damsel possessed with a spirit of divination" (Acts 16:16ff). In Athens, Paul's daily disputations in the agora led directly to his famed message before the Areopagus (Acts 17:17ff), which court met on Mars Hill, north of the Acropolis.

AGRAPHA (ăg'rà-fà, Gr. *ágrapha, unwritten things*). These are units of tradition concerning Christ, mostly sayings ascribed to Him, transmitted to us outside of the canonical Gospels. The entire collection of *agrapha,* gathered from all sources, is not large; and when what is obviously apocryphal or spurious is eliminated, the small remainder is of very little value.

Several sources of the agrapha may be noted. The best authenticated are those found in the NT outside of the Gospels: four in the Acts of the Apostles (1:f; 1:7f; 11:16; 20:35); two in the epistles of Paul (I Cor. 11:24f; I Thess. 4:15ff); and one in the Epistle of James (1:12). A second source of agrapha is found in ancient manuscripts of the New Testament. For the most part, sayings preserved in such manuscripts are of the nature of textual variations: parallel forms or expansions or combinations of sayings found in the canonical Gospels. A few, however, cannot be fitted into this category, as, for example, the following, which is found after Luke 6:5 in Codex Bezae: "On the same day, seeing someone working on the Sabbath, he [Jesus] said to him, 'Man, if indeed you know what you are doing, you are blessed; but if you do not know, you are cursed and a transgressor of the Law.'" A third source of *ágrapha* is patristic literature. Papias, bishop of Hierapolis (c. 80-c. 155), was the first of the Church Fathers to make a collection of the sayings of Jesus not recorded in the Gospels, but very little of his work survives. Agrapha are found in the works of Justin Martyr, Clement of Alexandria, Origen, and a few others. In Origen, for example, we have this: "I have read somewhere that the Saviour said ... 'He that is near me is near the fire; he that is far from me is far from the kingdom.'" Still another source of agrapha is the papyri which have been discovered in Egypt during the past century, especially those found by Grenfell and Hunt at Oxyrhynchus. In some of these papyri one *ágraphon* follows another without context, introduced by the simple formula, "Jesus says," as in the following one: "Jesus says; Wheresoever there are two, they are not without God, and where there is one alone, I say, I am with him. Lift up the stone, and there shalt thou find me; cleave the wood, and I am there." Agrapha are found also in the apocryphal gospels, like the gospel according to the Hebrews and the gospel according to the Egyptians, but few, if any, of these can be regarded as genuine. The recently-discovered (1945 or 1946) Gnostic Coptic Gospel of Thomas, found near Nag Hamadi in Upper Egypt, which is dated around A.D. 150, consists of more than 100 short sayings of Jesus, the majority of which begin with the words "Jesus said," or they give a reply by Jesus when asked by His disciples to instruct them on a doubtful point. Many sayings ascribed to Jesus are found in Mohammedan sources, but these traditions are for the most part of no value. Although the number of *agrapha* collected by scholars seems imposing, only a very

The Agora (market place) at Corinth. © EG

few have anything like a strong claim to acceptance on the ground of early and reliable source and internal character. Some scholars reject the *agrapha in toto*; others think that they are the remains of a considerable body of extra-canonical sayings which circulated in early Christian circles, and that a few of them, at least, may be genuine. See THOMAS, GOSPEL OF.   S.B.

AGRICULTURE (ăg′rĭ-kŭl-chûr). Not a Bible word; husbandry and husbandman are used for the activity and the man who practices it. In the form of horticulture, it is as old as Adam (Gen. 2:5, 8-15). Caring for the garden of Eden became labor after the curse (Gen. 3:17-19). Nomad and farmer began to differentiate with Abel and Cain (Gen. 4:2-4), with the herdsman gaining favor with God. As animal husbandry took its place along with tillage as part of the agricultural economy, the farmer gained in social status. Yet as late as shortly before the Babylonian exile, nomads still felt a sense of superiority over the settled agricultural people (Jer. 35:1-11, the Rechabites). "Noah began to be an husbandman, and he planted a vineyard" (Gen. 9:20). Abraham and his descendants were nomad herdsmen in Canaan, though Isaac and Jacob at times tilled the soil (Gen. 26:12, 37:7). Recurrent famines and the sojourn in Egypt taught the Israelites to depend more on agriculture, so that the report of the spies regarding the lush growth in Canaan interested them (Num. 13:23, Deut. 8:8). Agriculture became the basis of the Mosaic commonwealth, whose land legislation is suited to an agricultural rather than a pastoral economy. The soil is fertile, wherever water can be applied abundantly. The Hauran (Peraea) is productive. The soil of Gaza is dark and rich, though light, and retains rain: olive trees abound. The Israelites cleared most of the wood which they found in Canaan (Josh. 17:18). Wood became scarce; dung and hay heated their ovens (Ezek. 4:12-15, Matt. 6:30). The water supply was from rain, rills from the hills, and the Jordan. Irrigation was effected by ducts from cisterns hewn out of rock. As population increased, the more difficult cultivation of the hills was resorted to, and yielded abundance. Terraces were cut, one above another, faced with low stone walls. The rain is chiefly in autumn and winter, November and December, rare after March, almost never as late as May. The "early" rain fell from about the September equinox to sowing time in November or December, the "latter" rain in January and February (Joel 2:23, Jas. 5:7). Drought two or three months before harvest meant famine (Amos 4:7,8). Wheat, barley and rye (millet rarely), were the staple cereals. "Corn," according to British usage, refers to any grain, not specifically to maize. The barley harvest was earlier than the wheat harvest. By the plague of hail in Egypt, "the flax and the barley were smitten, for the barley was in the ear, and the flax was bolled (i.e., in blossom) but the wheat and the rye were not smitten, for they were not grown up" (Exod. 9:31,32). Accordingly, at the Passover, the barley was just fit for the sickle, and the wave sheaf was offered. At the Pentecost feast, fifty days later, the wheat was ripe for cutting, and the first fruit loaves were offered. The vine, olive, and fig abounded, and traces everywhere remain of wine and olive presses. Cummin (including the black "fitches" (Isa. 28:27), peas, beans, lentils, lettuce, endive, leek, garlic, onion, cucumber and cabbage also were cultivated.

The Passover in the month Nisan answered to the green stage of produce; the feast of weeks in Sivan, to the ripe; and the feast of Tabernacles in Tisri, to the harvest home. The six months from Tisri to Nisan were occupied with cultivation; the six months from Nisan to Tisri, with gathering fruits. Rain from the equinox in Tisri to Nisan is pretty continuous, but is more decidedly marked at the beginning (the early rain) and the end (the latter rain). Rain in harvest was almost unknown (Prov. 26:1).

Viticulture is pictured in Isaiah 5:1-7, and Matthew 21:33-41. Some farming procedures are described in Isaiah 28:24-28. The plough was light, and drawn by yokes of oxen (I Kings 19:19). Fallow ground was broken and cleared early in the year (Jer. 4:3, Hos. 10:12). Seed was scattered broadcast, as in the parable of the sower (Matt. 13:1-8), and ploughed in afterward, the stubble of the preceding crop becoming manure by decay. In irrigated fields the seed was trodden in by cattle (Isa. 32:20). The contrast between the exclusive

A peasant plowing with a primitive plow, drawn by a yoke of cattle, in the hill country of olive groves and vineyards. © MPS

A shepherd and his flock in the Shepherds Fields near Bethlehem, the city visible on the distant hills.
© MPS

dependence on irrigation in Egypt and the larger dependence on rain in Palestine is drawn in Deuteronomy 11:10-12. To sow among thorns was deemed bad husbandry (Job 5:5, Prov. 24:30-32). Hoeing and weeding were seldom needed in their fine tilth. Seventy days sufficed between barley sowing and the offering of the wave sheaf of ripe grain at Passover. Oxen were urged on with a spearlike goad, which could double as a deadly weapon (Jud. 3:31). Harvesting and harvest customs in the time of the Judges are described in Ruth 2 and 3. Sowing varied seed in a field was forbidden (Deut. 22:9). Oxen, unmuzzled (Deut. 25:4), five abreast, trod out the grain on a threshing floor of hard beaten earth, to separate the grain from chaff and straw. Flails were used for small quantities and lighter grains (Isa. 28:27). A threshing sledge (Isa. 41:15) was also employed, probably like the Egyptian sledge still in use; a stage with three rollers ridged with iron, which cut the straw for fodder, while crushing out the grain. The shovel and fan winnowed the grain afterward by help of the evening breeze (Isa. 30:24, Ruth 3:2); lastly it was shaken in a sieve (Amos 9:9, Luke 22:31). The fruit of newly planted trees was not to be eaten for the first three years. In the fourth it was offered as firstfruits. In the fifth year it might be eaten freely (Lev. 19:23-25).

We have glimpses of the relations of farm laborers, steward (manager or overseer) and owner, in the book of Ruth, in Matthew 20:1-16, and Luke 17:7-9.

Agriculture was beset with pests: locust, cankerworm, caterpillar and palmerworm (Joel 2:25): God calls them "my great army," as destructive as an invasion by human enemies. Haggai speaks (2:17) of blasting, mildew and hail. Development of agriculture under the British mandate, and since the establishment of the State of Israel, and parallel but lesser development in the country of Jordan are restoring the coastal plain, the plains of Esdraelon and of Dothan, the Shephelah, the Negev and the Hauran to their ancient prosperity. See FARMING, OCCUPATIONS.   E.R.

An Arab peasant girl picking figs in the orchards near ancient Ephraim. © MPS

AGRIPPA I (à-grĭp′à), known in history as King Herod Agrippa I, and in the NT, where he is mentioned in Acts 12, as Herod. He was the son of Aristobulus and Bernice and grandson of Herod the Great. Through friendship with the emperors Caligula and Claudius he gained the rulership first of Iturea and Trachonitis, then of Galilee and Perea, and ultimately of Judea and Samaria. He ruled over the thus reunited domain of Herod the Great from A.D. 40 until his death in A.D. 44 at the age of 54. While owing his position to the favor of Rome, he recognized the importance of exercising great tact in his contacts with the Jews. Thus it was that his natural humanity gave way to expediency in the severe conflict between Judaism and the growing Christian movement. He slew James "to please the Jews" and imprisoned Peter with the intention of bringing him before the people for execution after the passover (Acts 12:2-4). Agrippa's sudden death shortly thereafter, noted in Acts 12:20-23, is fully recorded by Josephus (*Ant.* XIX, 8). On the second day of a festival held in Caesarea in honor of Claudius, Agrippa put on a silver garment of "wonderful" texture and entered the amphitheater early in the morning. When the sun's rays shone upon his garment, the brilliant glare caused his flatterers to cry out that he was a god. Josephus adds that "the king did neither rebuke them nor reject their impious flattery." Almost immediately a severe pain arose in his abdomen; five days later he died in great agony. See also Herod.

AGRIPPA II (à-grĭp′à), known in history as King Herod Agrippa II and in the NT, where he is mentioned only in Acts 25 and 26, as Agrippa. He was the son of Agrippa I. Being only 17 at the death of his father, he was thought too young to succeed to the throne. Six years later (A.D. 50), he was placed over the kingdom of Chalcis, which included the right to appoint the high priest of the temple in Jerusalem. In A.D. 53 he was transferred to the tetrarchies formerly held by Philip (Iturea and Trachonitis) and Lysanias (Abilene) and given the title, "king." After the death of Claudius in A.D. 54, Nero added to his realm several cities of Galilee and Perea. When Festus became procurator of Judea, Agrippa, accompanied by his sister (and consort) Bernice, went to Caesarea to pay his respects. It was at this time that Paul appeared before him, as recorded in Acts 25:23-26:32. In the final revolt of the Jews against Rome, Agrippa sided with the Romans in the destruction of his nation in the same cynical spirit with which he met the impassioned appeal of the apostle. Following the fall of Jerusalem in A.D. 70, he retired with Bernice to Rome, where he died in A.D. 100.

AGUE (See Diseases, Malaria)

AGUR (ā-gûr, Heb. *'āghûr, gatherer*), the author or "collector" of the wise sayings in Proverbs 30. He is named as the son of Jakeh (Prov. 30:1). His words are called "the prophecy," but better "the weighty utterance" (Heb. massa'). Cf. ASV mg. which reads, "Jakeh, of Massa." If this is the true reading, a connection might possibly be made between Agur and the tribe of Ishmael (Gen. 25:14).

AHAB (ā′hăb, Heb. *'ah'āv, father's brother*). 1. Son of Omri and seventh king of the northern kingdom of Israel. He reigned 22 years, 873-851 B.C. Politically, Ahab was one of the strongest of the kings of Israel. In his days Israel was at peace with Judah and maintained her dominion over Moab, which paid a considerable tribute (II Kings 3:4). He went into battle on three different occasions in later years against Ben-hadad, king of Syria. While he had great success in the first two campaigns, he was defeated and mortally wounded in the third. Not mentioned in the Bible is Ahab's participation in the Battle of Karkar in 854 B.C. The "Monolith Inscription" of the Assyrian king Shalmanezer III contains a description of this battle which the Assyrians fought against a Syrian coalition of twelve kings. Of these, "Hadad-ezer," king of Damascus, is named first. Irhuleni of Hamath follows and in third place is "Ahab, the Israelite." The inscription states that Ahab commanded 2,000 chariots and 10,000 men. The number of his chariots was far greater than the number credited to any other king. Successful as he might have been politically, however, Ahab owes his prominence in the OT to the religious apostasy which occurred in Israel during his reign. Of him it is said, he "did evil in the sight of the Lord above all that were before him" (I Kings 16:30). His marriage to Jezebel, daughter of the king of the Zidonians, while politically advantageous, was religiously disastrous. Jezebel introduced the idolatrous worship of Baal into Israel as well as the licentious orgies of the goddess Ashtoreth. She also instituted a severe persecution against the followers of Jehovah and killed all the prophets of the Lord with the sword, except the one hundred who were hidden by Obadiah (I Kings 18:4; cf. 19:14). At this critical period in the history of Israel, God raised up Elijah, whose faithful ministry culminated in the conflict with the prophets of Baal on Mount Carmel (I Kings 18). Ahab's religious corruption was equaled by his love of material wealth and display. He was well known, e.g., for his elaborately ornamented ivory palace (I Kings 22:39). Not content with what he had, however, he coveted the vineyard of Naboth, which adjoined his palace at Jezreel. Naboth refused to sell the land and Ahab was utterly cast down in dejection. Seeing his state, Jezebel asked him to remember who was king in Israel and proceeded unscrupulously to charge Naboth with blasphemy, doing so in the name of the king, who weakly maintained silence. False witnesses testified against Naboth and he was stoned to death, following which Ahab took possession of the vineyard. This crime sealed the doom not only of Ahab, but of his family as well. The judgment of the Lord was that all of his posterity would be cut off (I Kings 21:21), even as had been the case with the two previous dynasties, those of Jeroboam and Baasha. The ringing condemnatory sentence given by Elijah, "In the place where dogs licked Naboth's blood, shall dogs lick thy blood," was fulfilled to the letter on Joram, his son (II Kings 9:24-26), and in part on Ahab himself (I Kings 22:38). Execution of this sentence was delayed owing to Ahab's partial and temporary repentance (I Kings 21:27-29). Ahab sinned also in failing to kill Ben-hadad, king of Syria, in their second battle (I Kings 20:20-43). This disobedience, as Saul's in the case of Agag, king of the Amalekites, was prompted by practical considerations which took precedence in Ahab's mind over God's will. For this sin, Ahab, as Saul before him, was told that he would pay with his life. Three years later he went into battle accompanied by Jehoshaphat, king of Judah, in the attempt to recover Ramoth-Gilead from the Syrians. He was mortally wounded by an arrow shot by one who "drew a bow at a venture" (I Kings 22:34). Ahab's character is succinctly summarized by the historian: "There was none like unto Ahab, which did sell himself to work wickedness in the sight of the Lord, whom Jezebel his wife stirred up" (I Kings 21:25).

A busy scene at Ahab's Well near Jezreel. © MPS

2. A false prophet who deceived the Jews in Babylon. Joining with Zedekiah, another false prophet, Ahab predicted an early return to Jerusalem. For this sin and for their immoral conduct, Jeremiah prophesied that they would be burned to death by the king of Babylon and that their names would become a byword (Jer. 29:21-23).   B.P.

AHARAH (à-hâr'àh, Heb. *'ahrah*), the third son of Benjamin, probably the founder of a family (I Chron. 8:1).

AHARHEL (à-hàr'hĕl, Heb. *'ăharhēl*), a son of Harum, founder of a family enrolled in the tribe of Judah (I Chron. 4:8).

AHASAI (à-hā'sī, Heb. *'ahzay, my protector*), a priest who lived in Jerusalem (Neh. 11:13).

AHASBAI (à-hăs'bī, Heb. *'ăhasbay*), the father of Eliphelet, one of David's heroes (II Sam. 23:34).

AHASUERUS (à-hăz'û-ê'rŭs, Heb. *'ăhashwērôsh*, representing the Persian *Khshayârshā*, which in Gr. became *Xerxes*). 1. The father of Darius the Mede. Mentioned in Daniel 9:1.

2. King of Persia, mentioned in the book of Esther. There seems to be little doubt that he is to be identified with the well-known Xerxes, who reigned from 486 to 465 B.C. The main support for this identification is to be found in the linguistic equivalence of the names, as noted below. In addition, a close similarity has been noted between the character of Xerxes and the character of the king of the Persians portrayed in the book of Esther. There are also historical correlations. Thus, the feast which was held in the third year of the reign of Ahasuerus at Shushan (Esth. 1:3) corresponds to an assembly held by Xerxes in his third year in preparation for the invasion of Greece. Herodotus states that Xerxes, following his defeat at Salamis and Plataea, consoled himself in his seventh year with the pleasures of the harem (Herodotus IX, 108). This parallels the biblical account which relates that Ahasuerus replaced Vashti by marrying Esther in his seventh year (Esth. 2:16) after gathering all the fair young virgins to Shushan. The Ahasuerus of Ezra 4:6, to whom were written accusations against the Jews of Jerusalem, is in all probability this same Xerxes, although sometimes identified with Cambyses, son of Cyrus.

AHAVA (à-hā'và, Heb. *'ahăwā'*), a river in Babylonia named after a place by which it flowed Ezra 8:15, 21), where Ezra assembled the Jewish exiles to seek God's guidance and protection for the long and dangerous journey to Jerusalem.

AHAZ (ā'hăz, Heb. *'āhāz, he has grasped*). 1. The 12th king of Judah in the divided monarchy; son of Jotham. He ruled from 735 to 715 B.C. Ahaz ascended the throne at the age of 20 (II Kings 16:2), ruling as co-regent with his father for four years and as sole monarch for 16 (Edwin R. Thiele, *The Mysterious Numbers of the Hebrew Kings,* Chicago: The University of Chicago Press, 1951, pp. 116-120). The critical period of his reign began when Rezin, king of Damascus, and Pekah, king of Israel, made a league against Judah. As the moment of attack approached, the prophet Isaiah was sent by God to deliver a comforting message to Ahaz, whose heart was overwhelmed with fear (Isa. 7:1-9). After having promised that God would spare the city, Isaiah told Ahaz to ask a sign of God. Ahaz hypocritically refused to "tempt the Lord" by asking one, whereupon Isaiah cried out, "The Lord himself shall give you a sign: Behold, a virgin shall conceive and bear a son and shall call his name Immanuel" (Isa. 7:14). In the invasion, Pekah slew 120,000 men of Judah in one day; Zichri of Ephraim slew the king's son, Maaseiah, as well as Azrikam, the governor of his house, and Elkanah, who was second to the king. The Israelites carried 200,000 men, women and children captive to Samaria along with much spoil. Oded, the prophet, however, persuaded them to release the captives (II Chron. 28:6-15). Rezin also took many captives (II Chron. 28:5) and captured Elath (II Kings 16:6). Following this disastrous defeat, Judah was invaded by the Edomites from the E and the Philistines from the S and W (II Chron. 28:17,18). In his distress, Ahaz asked assistance of Tiglath-pileser, king of Assyria, sending treasure from the temple and palace as tribute (II Kings 16:8). Tiglath-pileser did come against the Syrians, whom he conquered (II Kings 16:9), but otherwise added to the difficulties of Ahaz. For "Tiglath-pileser king of Assyria came unto him, and distressed him, but strengthened him not" (II Chron. 28:20). The contact with Tiglath-pileser confirmed Ahaz in his religious apostasy. Early in his reign "he walked in the way of the kings of Israel, yea and made his son to pass through the fire, according to the abominations of the heathen, whom the Lord cast out from before the children of Israel. And he sacrificed and burnt incense in the high places, and on the hills, and under every green tree" (II Kings 16:3,4). Following his meeting with Tiglath-pileser in Damascus, Ahaz "sacrificed unto the gods of Damascus which smote him, and he said because the gods of the kings of Syria help them, therefore will I sacrifice to them, that they may help me. But they were the ruin of him and of all Israel" (II Chron. 28:23). He cut the temple vessels in pieces, closed the doors of the temple, made altars in every corner of Jerusalem, and made high places to burn incense to other gods in the cities of Judah (II Chron. 28:24,25). After the death of Ahaz, his body was "not brought into the sepulchres of the kings" (II Chron. 28:27) because of his great wickedness.

2. A great-grandson of Jonathan, son of King Saul; one of four sons of Micah and the father of Jehoadah (I Chron. 8:35,36).   B.P.

AHAZIAH (ā'hà-zī'à, Heb. *'ahazyâh, Jehovah hath grasped*). 1. Son of Ahab and Jezebel; eighth king of Israel. He reigned only briefly, 851-850 B.C.

Ahaziah was a worshiper of Jeroboam's calves and of his mother's idols, Baal and Ashtoreth. The most notable event of his reign was the revolt of the Moabites, who had been giving a yearly tribute of 100,000 lambs and 100,000 rams (II Kings 1:1; 3:4,5). Ahaziah was prevented from trying to put down the revolt by a fall through a lattice in his palace at Samaria. Injured severely, he sent messengers to inquire of Baalzebub, god of Ekron, whether he would recover. Elijah the prophet was sent by God to intercept the messengers and proclaimed to them that Ahaziah would die. The king in anger tried to capture the prophet, but two groups of 50 men were consumed by fire from heaven in making the attempt. A third contingent was sent to seize the prophet but instead prayed Elijah to deliver them from the fate of their predecessors (II Kings 1:13,14). Elijah then went down to Samaria and gave the message directly to the king, who died shortly afterwards. He was succeeded by his brother Jehoram (II Kings 1:17; cf. 8:16).

2. Son of Jehoram of Judah, and Athaliah; thus grandson of Jehoshaphat and Ahab, and nephew of Ahaziah of Israel. He was the sixth king of Judah in the divided monarchy and reigned only one year (II Chron. 22:2), 843 B.C. His name appears also as Jehoahaz (II Chron. 21:17; 25:23), thus representing a simple transposition of the component parts of the compound name. The name Azariah, which is given him in II Chronicles 22:6, is probably the result of a scribal error. According to II Kings 8:26, Ahaziah was 22 years old when he began to reign. There is undoubtedly a scribal error in II Chronicles 22:2, where it is stated that he was 42 years old when he ascended to the throne; for his father, Jehoram, was only 40 when he died (II Chron. 21:20). Ahaziah walked in all the idolatries of the house of Ahab, his mother being his counselor to do wickedly (II Chron. 22:3,4). He sinned also in allying himself with Jehoram of Israel against Hazael of Syria, going into battle at Ramoth-Gilead (II Chron. 22:5). Jehoram was wounded and Ahaziah went to see him at Jezreel. Here judgment came upon him through the hand of Jehu, who fell upon Jehoram and all the house of Ahab. Ahaziah, seeing the slaughter, fled "by the way of the garden house," but was smitten in his chariot at the going up to Gur by Ibleam. He fled to Megiddo and died there (II Kings 9:27). The account given in Chronicles presents different though not irreconcilable details of his death (II Chron. 22:6-9). Ahaziah was buried with his fathers in Jerusalem (II Kings 9:28), Jehu allowing this honorable burial because Ahaziah was the grandson of Jehoshaphat, who sought the Lord with all his heart (II Chron. 22:9). Following the death of Ahaziah, Athaliah seized the throne and killed all the seed royal of the house of Judah except Joash, Ahaziah's son, who was hidden by Jehoshabeath, sister of Ahaziah and wife of Jehoiada the high priest (II Chron. 22:10-12).

AHBAN (a-băn, Heb. *'ahbān*), a man of Judah, of the house of Jerahmeel (I Chron. 2:29).

AHER (ā-hêr, Heb. *'ahēr*), a Benjamite (I Chron. 7:12).

AHI (ā'hī, Heb. *'ăhi*). 1. Chief of the Gadites in Gilead (I Chron. 5:15).

2. A man of Asher, son of Shamer (I Chron. 7:34).

AHIAH (See Ahijah)

AHIAM (ā-hī'ăm, Heb. *'ăhi'ām, mother's brother*), one of David's 30 heroes (II Sam. 23:33).

AHIAN (à-hī'ăn, Heb. *'Ahyān*), a Manassite of the family of Shemida (I Chron. 7:19).

AHIEZER (ā-hī-ē'zêr, Heb. *'ăhi'ezer*). 1. The head of the tribe of Dan in the wilderness (Num. 1:12; 2:25; 7:66).

2. A Gibeonite who joined David at Ziklag (I Chron. 12:3).

AHIHUD (à-hī'hŭd, Heb. *'ăhihûdh, brother is majesty*). 1. Prince of the tribe of Asher; selected by Moses to help divide the land of Canaan (Num. 34:27).

2. A son of Ehud (I Chron. 8:7).

AHIJAH (à-hī'jà, Heb. *'ăhiyâ, brother of Jehovah*). 1. One of the sons of Jerahmeel, a great-grandson of Judah and brother of Caleb (I Chron. 2:25).

2. A descendant of Benjamin, mentioned in connection with an intra-family conflict (I Chron. 8:7).

3. Son of Ahitub, the brother of Ichabod and son of Phinehas, the son of Eli. He served as priest in Shiloh, "wearing an ephod," in the days of Saul (I Sam. 14:3). In the midst of a Philistine-Israelite battle, "Saul said unto Ahijah, Bring hither the ark of God. For the ark of God was at that time with the children of Israel" (I Sam. 14:18). This statement is often held to be in conflict with I Chronicles 13:3, where David says, "Let us bring again the ark of our God to us; for we inquired not at it in the days of Saul." Saul's order to Ahijah is thought also to imply that the ark was at Shiloh, whereas I Samuel 7:1 and I Chronicles 13:5-7 indicate that it was in Kirjath-jearim during the entire reign of Saul. The contradictions are only apparent ones. The definite statement concerning Ahijah as priest is that he wore an ephod, *not* that the ark was under his care at Shiloh. At a critical moment, Saul, contrary to his normal lack of interest in the ark, called upon Ahijah to bring it up to the scene of the battle. The text states, however, that even while Saul was talking to Ahijah, the sound of the battle in which Jonathan was engaged reached his ears (I Sam. 14:19). The ark was promptly forgotten for the time, and, as the battle was won by the Israelites, for the remainder of Saul's reign as well. It is felt by many that Ahijah is the same as Ahimelech, the son of Ahitub who, as priest at Nob, befriended David when he fled from Saul, following which Saul exacted terrible revenge by slaying Ahimelech and all the inhabitants of the city. Others suggest that Ahijah was the father or brother of Ahimelech.

4. The Pelonite, one of the valiant men of David's armies (I Chron. 11:36).

5. A Levite who was in charge of the treasures of the house of God in David's reign (I Chron. 26:20).

6. Son of Shisha and brother of Elihoreph. He was a scribe of Solomon (I Kings 4:3).

7. A prophet of Shiloh who met Jeroboam as he was going out of Jerusalem and foretold the transfer of ten tribes to him from Solomon by the symbolic action of rending his garment into twelve pieces, ten of which he gave to Jeroboam. He told him further that God would build him a "sure house" such as He had built for David if Jeroboam would walk in God's ways (I Kings 11:29-39). His other recorded prophecy was given to Jeroboam's wife, who in disguise consulted him as to her son Abijah's recovery. The prophet foretold not only the death of the son but also the extermination of the house of Jeroboam because he "had done evil above all that were before" him in making idols and in provoking God to anger (I Kings 14:1-16). Reference to his prophecy as one of the records of

Solomon's reign is made in II Chronicles 9:29.

8. The father of Baasha, King of Israel, of the tribe of Issachar (I Kings 15:27).

9. One of the men who set their seal to the covenant drawn up before the Lord in the days of Nehemiah (Neh. 10:26).   B.P.

AHIKAM (à-hī'kăm, Heb. *'ăhîqām, my brother has risen up*), son of Shaphan the scribe, and sent by Josiah to ask the meaning of the Book of the Law that was found (II Kings 22:12). Later, he successfully pleaded before the princes and elders that Jeremiah should not be put to death for his warnings of impending doom (Jer. 26:24). After the deportation to Babylon, Ahikam's son Gedaliah became governor over the remnant who remained in the cities of Judah (II Kings 25:22; Jer. 40:5).

AHILUD (à-hī'lŭd, Heb. *'ăhîlûdh, a child's brother*), father of Jehoshaphat the recorder (II Sam. 8:16; 20:24; I Kings 4:3; I Chron. 18:15).

AHIMAAZ (à-hīm'ā-ăz, Heb. *'ăhîma'ats, brother of anger*). 1. The father of Ahinoam, wife of King Saul (I Sam. 14:50).

2. Son of Zadok the high priest (I Chron. 6:8). With Jonathan, son of Abiathar, he served as messenger in Absalom's rebellion, carrying tidings from Hushai, David's counselor and spy. Zadok and Abiathar, who took back the ark to Jerusalem at David's request, were to tell them while they were hiding outside the city whatever Hushai directed. They told David the counsel of Ahithophel for an immediate attack, Hushai warning that David should cross the Jordan at once (II Sam. 15:24-27; 17:15-22). David's estimate of Ahimaaz appears in his remark at his approach after the battle: "He is a good man, and cometh with good tidings" (II Sam. 18:27). Ahimaaz announced the victory but evaded the question concerning Absalom's fate, wishing to spare the feelings of the king. While he was still in David's presence the Cushite arrived and unfeelingly broke the news concerning the death of the king's son. Comparing I Kings 4:2 with I Chronicles 6:8-10, some infer that Ahimaaz died before he attained the priesthood and before his father Zadok, who was succeeded by Ahimaaz's son, Azariah.

3. One of Solomon's 12 commissary officers (I Kings 4:15). He married Basmath, the daughter of Solomon. Some suggest that he should be identified with the son of Zadok.

AHIMAN (à-hī'măn, Heb. *'ăhîman, my brother is a gift*). 1. One of the three giant sons of Anak seen in Mount Hebron by the spies (Num. 13:22). The Anakim race was cut off from the land of Israel and Judah by Joshua (11:21,22). The three sons, Sheshai, Ahiman, and Talmai, were driven by Caleb from Hebron (Josh. 15:14) and killed (Judg. 1:10).

2. A Levite gatekeeper (I Chron. 9:17).

AHIMELECH (à-hīm'-ĕ-lĕk, Heb. *'ăhîmelekh, brother of a king*). 1. Saul's high priest who helped David by giving him the shewbread and Goliath's sword. Upon hearing this, Saul ordered the death of Ahimelech and the other priests with him (I Sam. 21-22). Abiathar, son of Ahimelech, escaped.

2. Son of Abiathar and grandson of Ahimelech (II Sam. 8:17; I Chron. 18:16; 24:6).

3. A Hittite who, with Abishai, was asked to accompany David to Saul's camp (I Sam. 26:6).

AHIMOTH (à-hī'-moth, Heb. *'ăhîmôth, brother of death*), son of Elkanah (I Chron. 6:25), descendant of Kohath and a Levite.

AHINADAB (à-hĭn'-à-dăb, Heb. *'ăhînādhāv*), a commissary officer of Solomon (I Kings 4:14).

AHINOAM (à-hĭn'-ō-ăm, Heb. *'ăhînō'am, my brother is delight*). 1. Wife of King Saul (I Sam.14:50).

2. One of David's wives, a Jezreelitess (I Sam. 25:43), who lived with him at Gath (27:3). She and Abigail were captured by the Amalekites at Ziklag (30:5), but rescued by David (30:18). They were with David in Hebron (II Sam. 2:2), where Ahinoam bore Amnon, his first son (3:2).

AHIO (à-hī'ō, Heb. *'ahyô, brotherly*). 1. Son of Abinadab. He and his brother Uzzah accompanied the ark of God from Gibeah on David's first attempt to remove it to Jerusalem (II Sam. 6:1-11; I Chron. 13:1-14). Ahio walked before, guiding the oxen that drew the cart, while Uzzah walked alongside.

2. A Benjamite (I Chron. 8:14).

3. A Gibeonite, son of Jehiel (I Chron. 8:31; 9:37).

AHIRA (à-hī'rà, Heb. *'ăhîra', brother of evil*), prince captain of the tribe of Naphtali (Num. 1:15, 2:29, 7:78,83, 10:27).

AHIRAM (à-hī'răm, Heb. *'ăhîrām, brother of height, exalted brother*), son of Benjamin (Num. 26:38). While his name does not appear in the list of Benjamin's sons given in Genesis 46:21, it is thought that Ehi is perhaps a shortened form of Ahiram. In the list of five sons given in I Chronicles 8:1,2 the name of Aharah, expressly mentioned as "the third" son, is thought to be a variant of Ahiram or a different name for the same person (cf. Num. 26:38,39, where Ahiram is the third name in a list of five).

AHIRAMITE (à-hī'-rà-mīt, Heb. *'ăhîrāmî, of the family of Ahiram*), Num. 26:38.

AHISAMACH (à-hĭs'-à-măk, Heb. *'ăhîsāmākh. my brother supports*), a Danite, the father of Aholiab (Exod. 31:6, 35:34, 38:23).

AHISHAHAR (à-hĭsh'à-hàr, Heb. *'ăhîshahar, brother of dawn*), a descendant of Benjamin through Jediael and Bilhan (I Chron. 7:10).

AHISHAR (à-hī'shàr, Heb. *'ăhîshār, my brother has sung*), an official over Solomon's household (I Kings 4:6).

AHITHOPHEL (à-hĭth'ō-fĕl, Heb. *'ăhîthōphel, brother of folly*), David's counselor who joined the conspiracy of Absalom. His oracular wisdom was proverbial (II Sam. 16:23), and it seems clear that he was a mainspring of the rebellion (II Sam. 15:12). Some suggest, in looking for motivation for his treachery, that he was the grandfather of Bathsheba, for she was the daughter of Eliam (II Sam. 11:3), and an Eliam, the son of Ahithophel the Gilonite, is listed as one of David's valiant men (II Sam. 23:34). Thus it is suggested that Ahithophel had a certain bitterness toward David, the murderer of his grandson by marriage and the corrupter of his granddaughter. Others note, however, that the time element seems insufficiently long for Ahithophel to have a married granddaughter at the time of David's great sin, and that it seems easier to believe that there were two men in Israel named Eliam. Furthermore, it seems unlikely that a man such as Ahithophel would conspire against the interests of his granddaughter and her son. His main motivation would appear to be ambition for personal power. His proposal to Absalom that he pursue David immediately with 12,000 men, smiting the king while he was still weary and under-protected, indicates his wisdom and boldness. David's prayer turned his counsel into foolishness (II Sam. 15:31), as Absalom deferred to Hushai's advice that they take time to muster all Israel against such a mighty man of war as David. Ahithophel, seeing his counsel rejected, realized that the cause of Absalom was lost, and went to his home and hanged himself (II Sam. 17:1-23). B.P.

AHITUB (à-hī'tŭb, Heb. *'ăhîtûv, brother of goodness*). 1. The brother of Ichabod and son of Phinehas the son of Eli; father of Ahiah (I Sam. 14:3) and Ahimelech (22:9,11,20). Though he is a son and father of priests, nothing is said of his own priestly office.

2. Son of Amariah and father of Zadok the high priest (II Sam. 8:17; I Chron. 6:7,8). He appears as grandfather of Zadok in I Chronicles 9:11; Nehemiah 11:11. A descendant of Aaron through Eleazar, he is to be distinguished from Ahitub 1. who descended through Ithamar (I Chron. 24).

3. Son of another Amariah and father of another Zadok (I Chron. 6:11,12). Cf. list in Ezra 7:1-5. Due to compression of names or copyist's error, 3. may be the same as 2.

AHLAB (à'lăb, Heb. *'ahlāv, fat or fruitful*), a town of Asher from which the Israelites were not able to drive the inhabitants. Some identify Ahlab with Gush Chaleb or Giscala, in the hills NW of the Sea of Galilee, home of John of Giscala.

AHLAI (à'lī, Heb. *'ahlay, O would that!*). 1. The father of Zabad, one of David's soldiers (I Chron. 11:41).

2. A daughter of Sheshan who married her father's Egyptian slave Jarha. They had a son Attai (I Chron. 2:31-35).

AHOAH (à-hō'à, Heb. *'ăhôah, brotherly*), a son of Bela (I Chron. 8:4), from whom is derived the term "Ahohite" (II Sam. 23:9,28; I Chron. 11:12).

AHOHITE (à-hō'hīt, Heb. *'ăhôhî*), a patronymic given to the descendants of Ahoah: Dodo (II Sam. 23:9), Zalmon (23:28), and Ilai (I Chron. 11:29).

AHOLA (See Aholah)

AHOLAH (à-hō'-là, Heb. *'ăhŏlâh, tent-woman*). In God's parable to Ezekiel (Ezek. 23) is a woman who represents Samaria, capital of the Northern Kingdom, whose worship ("tabernacle") was self-devised (John 4:9,20-22). Her sister Aholibah (*my tent is in her*) is a symbol of Jerusalem (v. 4), capital of Judah whose worship was appointed by God. These "women" had been unfaithful to Jehovah their true husband (Isa. 54:5) by their lewdness with Egypt in their youth (i.e. adopting the ways of the world). Later, Aholah (Israel) was spiritually adulterous by her coalition with Egypt and Assyria and by imitating their luxury and idolatry. For these "whoredoms" God punished her with captivity by the very agent of her sin (Ezek. 23:9,10). Instead of being warned by the awful fate of Samaria, Aholibah (Judah) yielded to Babylonian culture (vv. 11-22). For this alienation from Him, God promised her a similar captivity by the very agent of her sin (vv. 22-49).

AHOLIAB (à-hō'-lǐ-ăb, Heb. *'ăhŏlîāv, father's tent*), a man who was divinely endowed with artistic skill to construct the tabernacle (Exod. 31:6).

AHOLIBAH (See Aholah)

AHOLIBAMAH (à-hŏl'ĭ-bā'mà, Heb. *'ăhŏlîvāmâh, tent of the high place*). 1. One of Esau's three wives, daughter of Anah the Hivite (Gen. 36:2,18, 25). She is also called Judith the daughter of Beeri (Gen. 26:34). Judith may have been her personal name and Aholibamah her married name, taken from the district in Edom near Mount Hor and Petra. Each of her three sons, Jeush, Jaalam, and Korah, became head of a tribe of Edomites

occupying Mount Seir. The Edomites were always troublesome to the descendants of Jacob (Num. 20:14-21). They were the ancestral stock of the Idumeans, of whom was Herod the Great.

2. An Edomite duke (Gen. 36:41, I Chron. 1:52), probably so named from the district of his possession.

AHUMAI (à-hŭ'mī, Heb. *'ăhûmay*), a descendant of Judah (I Chron. 4:2).

AHURA MAZDA (à'hōō-rà măzdà), the all wise spirit in the dualistic system of Zoroastrianism. Darius the Great, Xerxes (the Biblical Ahasuerus), and Artaxerxes were zealous worshipers of Ahura Mazda, held to be the creator of the worlds, greatest of the gods and source of all good.

AHUZAM (à-hŭ-zăm, Heb. *'ăhuzzām, possessor*), a man of the tribe of Judah, one of four sons born to Ashur by his wife Naarah (I Chron. 4:6).

AHUZZATH (à-hŭz'ăth, Heb. *'ăhuzzath, possession*), a "friend" of Abimelech. These men and Phicol, chief of the Philistine army, made a peace treaty with Isaac at Beersheba after they saw that the Lord had blessed him (Gen. 26:23-33). The ending *-ath* is in other Philistine names as Gath, Goliath.

AI (ā'ī, Heb. *'ay, ruin*). 1. A city of central Palestine, E of Bethel. Abraham pitched his tent between Ai and Bethel when he arrived in Canaan (Gen. 12:8). Ai figures most prominently in the account of the conquest of the land; it was the second Canaanite city taken by the forces under Joshua (Josh. 7,8). Having conquered Jericho, the Israelites felt that a portion of the armies would be sufficient to conquer the much smaller Ai. The Israelite contingent was routed, however. It was then disclosed that Achan had sinned in taking articles from the consecrated spoil of Jericho. After the sin had been confessed and punishment meted out to Achan and his family, the Israelites made a second attack, which resulted in the total destruction of the city and the annihilation of all its inhabitants, 12,000 people. The city, the site of which belonged to the tribe of Benjamin following the partition of the land, had not been rebuilt when the book of Joshua was written (Josh. 8:28). It was, however, rebuilt in later days, for men of Ai returned from Babylon with Zerubbabel (Ezra 2:28; Neh. 7:32). Recent archaeological excavations at the site commonly identified with Ai indicate that the city was destroyed about 2350 B.C. and lay in ruins at the time of the Israelite conquest. In order to bring Scripture into harmony with this fact some suggest that the city was merely an outpost of Bethel under the control of a military captain. Thus there would have been a lack of substantial buildings, which would account for the absence of tangible remains of the period. Others suggest that the true site of Ai is yet to be found.

2. A city of Ammon, near Heshbon (Jer. 49:3).

AIAH (ā'yà, Heb. *'ayyâh, falcon*). 1. A Horite (Gen. 36:24; I Chron. 1:40).

2. The father of Rizpah, Saul's concubine (II Sam. 3:7, 21:8).

AIATH (ā'yăth, Heb. *'ayyāth*), feminine form of the city Ai (Isa. 10:28).

AIJA (ā-ī'-jà, Heb. *'ayyā'*), another form of the city Ai (Neh. 11:31).

AIJALON (See Ajalon)

AIJELETH SHAHAR (ā'-jĕ-lĕth shā'hàr, Heb. *'ayyeleth hash-Shahar, the hind of the morning*), title of Psalm 22. Some explain it as the name of a hunting tune to which the psalm was sung. More likely it alludes to its subject, the lovely and innocent hind symbolizing one who is persecuted unjustly (vss. 12,13,16). "The morning" may represent joy and deliverance after affliction. It suggests Messiah, whose deep sorrow (vss. 1-21) turns to triumphant joy (vss. 22-31).

AIN (à'ēn, Heb. *'ayin, eye, fountain*). From the basic meaning, "eye," is derived, by the vivid imagery of the East, the word, "fountain"; for the spring flashes in the landscape like a gleaming eye. It differs from *beer,* which is used of a dug well. Generally it is found in compounds, as En-gedi, En-dor, etc.

1. A landmark on the eastern border of the Promised Land; west of Riblah (Num. 34:11). It is usually thought to be the modern *Ain el 'Azy,* the main source of the Orontes river.

2. A southern city of Judah (Josh. 15:32), afterwards of Simeon (Josh. 19:7), then assigned to the priests (Josh. 21:16).

AIN FESHKA, oasis on the western side of the Dead Sea, south of Khirbet Qumran. Remains of buildings found in 1956 suggest that this was another center of the Qumran community; it provided a place for their work as farmers.

AIN KAREM (Heb. *bekarmēy 'ên gedhî*), a Hebrew phrase found in the Song of Solomon 1:14, meaning "the vineyards of Engedi." Engedi was a town on the W coast of the Dead Sea, about 35 miles from Jerusalem. In it was a copious fountain, which has created an oasis, rich with palms, vineyards, and balsam.

AIN KAREM (à'ēn kâr'ĭm), a village in the hill country of Judea, five miles W of Jerusalem, and the traditional home of Zacharias and Elizabeth, parents of John the Baptist, who was born here. Mary came here from Nazareth to visit her cousin Elizabeth. The church in the town is dedicated to John the Baptist.

AIR. In the OT and Gospels found usually in expressions speaking of the birds or fowl of the air (Job 41:16 is the only exception) and representing words normally rendered by "heaven." Elsewhere in the NT it stands for *aér,* the atmosphere. Ineffective Christian living is pictured as a boxer "beating the air" (I Cor. 9:26). "Speaking into the air" describes unintelligible utterance (I Cor. 14:9). Satan is called "the prince of the power of the air" (Eph. 2:2), i.e. the ruler of the demonic beings which fill the air. The rapture of the church shall culminate in her meeting her Lord the Saviour, Jesus Christ "in the air" (I Thess. 4:17).

AJAH (ā'-jà, Heb. *'ayyâh, falcon*), a Horite (Gen. 36:24).

AJALON, AIJALON (ā'jà-lŏn, Heb. *'ayyālôn, place of gazelles*). 1. A city of Dan (Josh. 19:42), assigned to the Levite sons of Kohath (I Chron. 6:69). It is mentioned most notably in the memorable words of Joshua, "Sun, stand thou still upon Gibeon, and thou moon, in the valley of Ajalon" (Josh. 10:12). It is identified with the modern Yalo, 14 miles from Jerusalem, north of the Jaffa road.

2. The burial place of the judge Elon, in Zebulun (Judg. 12:12).

AKAN (ā'-kăn, Heb. *'ăqān, twisted*), a descendant or branch of the Horites of Mount Seir (Gen. 36:27).

AKELDAMA (See Aceldama)

AKHENATON (à'kĕn-à't'n, *he who is beneficial to Aton*), the name chosen by Amenhotep IV (1377-1360 B.C.), ruler in the Eighteenth Dynasty of Egypt, when he changed the religion of his country, demanding that all worship only the sun god

The village of Ain Karim, in the hill country of Judea, the birthplace of John the Baptist. © MPS

under the name Aton. Politically, his reign was disastrous. Internal disorders prevailed, and Egypt's Asian possessions began to slip away. His external troubles are illustrated by clay tablets found at *Tell el-Amarna,* the site of Akhetaton, the capital which he established. Hundreds of letters from vassal governors in Syria and Palestine speak of invasions and intrigue, and make appeal for help. Many of these tablets refer to invaders called the Habiru. Some feel that this name designates the Hebrews; others that it speaks of a non-Semitic people. Akhenaton is credited by many as being the first monotheist and, indeed, the inspiration for the monotheism of Moses. He clearly, however, worshiped the sun itself and not that Holy One who created the sun and all else in the universe.

The Valley of Ajalon and the Shephelah hills, bordering the Plain of Sharon, in the area once called Philistia. © MPS

AKKAD (See Accad)

AKKUB (ăk'-ŭb, Heb. *'aqqûv, pursuer*). 1. Son of Elioenai (I Chron. 3:24).

2. A Levite who founded a family of Temple porters (I Chron. 9:17).

3. The head of a family of the Nethinim (Ezra 2:45).

4. A Levite who helped expound the Law (Neh. 8:7).

AKRABBIM (ăk-răb'ĭm, Heb. *'aqrabbîm, scorpions*), always found with *Ma'āleh* (Mā'-a-la), meaning "the going up to," "ascent of," or "pass." So the "ascent of the Scorpions," rising between the SW corner of the Dead Sea and Zin, was the southern boundary between Judah and Edom (Num. 34:4, Josh. 15:3), and was the boundary of the Amorites (Judg. 1:36). It was the scene of Judas Maccabeus' victory over the Edomites. Now identified as the pass Es-Sufah.

ALABASTER (ăl'-à-băs'têr, Gr. *alábastron*), not today's softer gypsum or sulphate of lime often called alabaster, but the harder oriental alabaster, a carbonate of lime. Its stalagmitic formation often gave to it streaks of varying shades and colors, which led to its being called onyx or onyx marble. Alabaster was popular for making perfume vases and boxes for precious ointments. This usage is referred to three times in the NT (Matt. 26:7, Mark 14:3, and Luke 7:37).

ALAMETH (ăl'-ă-měth, Heb. *'ālāmeth, concealment*). 1. A son of Becher and grandson of Benjamin (I Chron. 7:8).

2. Variant of Alemeth (KJV, ASV), son of Jehoadah or Jarah (I Chron. 8:36, 9:42).

ALAMMELECH (à-lăm'-ĕ-lĕk, Heb. *'allammelekh, oak of a king*), a town of Asher (Josh. 19:26).

ALAMOTH (ăl'à-mŏth, Heb. *'ālāmôth, maidens, virgins*), a musical term (Ps. 46:1; I Chron. 15:20) the meaning of which is uncertain. It may indicate a women's choir, musical instruments set in a high pitch, or instruments played by virgins.

ALCIMUS (ăl'sĭ-mŭs, Heb. *'elyāqûm, God will rise*; Gr. *Álkimos, valiant*), a wicked high priest who was opposed by the Maccabees (I Macc. 7; 9).

ALEMETH or **ALMON** (ăl'-ĕ-mĕth, ăl'mŏn, *hidden*), a priests' city (I Chron. 6:60, Josh. 21:18). Now modern Almit.

ALEPH (á'lĕf, *ox*), first letter of the Hebrew alphabet (**א**). Although a consonant, it is the forerunner of the Gr. *alpha* and our English "a."

ALEXANDER, THE GREAT (ăl'ĕg-zăn'dêr, Gr. *'Aléxandros, man-defending*), son of Philip, King of Macedon, and Olympias, an Epirote princess; born 356 B.C. Although not named in the Bible, he is described prophetically in Daniel, the "he goat" from the West with a notable horn between his eyes. He came against the ram with two horns which was standing before the river, defeated the ram, and became very great until the great horn was broken and four notable ones came up from it (Dan. 8:5-8). The prophecy identifies the ram as the kings of Media and Persia, the goat as the king of Greece, the great horn being the first king. When he fell, four kings arose in his place (Dan. 8:18-22). The historical fulfillment is striking: Alexander led the Greek armies across the Hellespont into Asia Minor in 334 B.C. and defeated the Persian forces at the river Granicus. Moving with amazing rapidity (the he goat "touched not the ground," Dan. 8:5), he again met and defeated the Persians at Issus. Turning south, he moved down the Syrian coast, advancing to Egypt, which fell to him without a blow. Turning again to the East, he met the armies of Darius for the last time, defeating them in the battle of Arbela, E of the Tigris River. Rapidly he occupied Babylon, then Susa and Persepolis, the capitals of Persia. The next years were spent in consolidating the new empire. Alexander took Persians into his army, encouraged his soldiers to marry Asians and began to Hellenize Asia through the establishment of Greek cities in the Eastern Empire. He marched his armies eastward as far as India where they won a

Bust of Alexander the Great, in the Capitoline Museum at Rome, and his route of conquest. RTHPL

ALEXANDER'S ROUTE OF CONQUEST

great battle at the Hydaspes River. The army, however, refused to advance farther, and Alexander was forced to return to Persepolis. While still making plans for further conquests, he contracted a fever. Weakened by the strenuous campaign and increasing dissipation, he was unable to throw off the fever and died in Babylon in 323 B.C. at the age of 32. His empire was then divided among four of his generals. While Alexander was outstanding as a conqueror, his notable contributions to civilization came via his Hellenizing efforts. The fact that Greek became the language of literature and commerce throughout the "inhabited world," for example, was of inestimable importance to the spread of the Gospel.   B.P.

ALEXANDRA (ăl-ĕg-zăn′drà, Gr. *Aléxandra*), wife of Aristobulus, King of the Jews (105-104 B.C.). Upon his death, she made her brother-in-law, Jannaeus Alexander king, and married him. After he died, Alexandra ruled from 78-69 B.C. John Hyrcanus II and Aristobulus II were her sons.

ALEXANDRIA (ăl′ĕg-zăn′drĭ-à, Gr. *he Alexándreia*), founded by Alexander the Great, 332 B.C.; successively the Ptolemaic, Roman and Christian capital of Lower Egypt. Its harbors, formed by the island Pharos and the headland Lochias, were suitable alike for commerce and war. It was the chief grain port for Rome. Its merchant ships, the largest and finest of the day, usually sailed directly to Puteoli, but at times, because of the severity of the weather, sailed under the coast of Asia Minor, as did the vessel which carried Paul (Acts 27:6). Alexandria was also an important cultural center, boasting an excellent university. This was patterned after the great school at Athens but soon outstripped its model. It was especially noted for the study of mathematics, astronomy, medicine and poetry. Literature and art also flourished. The library of Alexandria became the largest and best known in the world. In different eras it was reported as possessing from 400,000 to 900,000 books and rolls. The population of Alexandria had three prominent elements: Jews, Greeks and Egyptians. The Jews enjoyed equal privileges with the Greeks, so that they became fixed there. While they continued to regard Jerusalem as "the holy city," they looked upon Alexandria as the metropolis of the Jews throughout the world. It was here that the translation of the Old Testament into Greek, known as the Septuagint, was made in the third century before Christ. This became the popular Bible of the Jews of the Dispersion and was generally used by the writers of the New Testament. At Alexandria the OT revelation was brought into contact with Greek philosophy. The consequent synthesis became of great importance in subsequent religious thought. The influence of Alexandrian philosophy on the thought of the writers of the NT is debatable, but its impact on later theological and Biblical studies in the Christian church was great. According to tradition, Mark the evangelist first carried the Gospel to Alexandria and established the first church there. From this city, Christianity reached out into all Egypt and the surrounding countries. A theological school flourished here as early as the second century. Among its great teachers were Clement and Origen, pioneers in Biblical scholarship and Christian philosophy.   B.P.

ALGUM (See Plants of the Bible)

ALIAH (See Alvah)

ALIAN (See Alvan)

ALLEGORY (Gr. *allegoreúein,* from *állos, other,* and *agoreúein, to speak in the assembly*). Used but once (Gal. 4:24), in reference to Hagar and Sarah,

Two views of Alexandria, Egypt's second city, port and fashionable resort on the Mediterranean. Above, the seafront. Below, the harbor. © MPS

and Ishmael and Isaac; although the literary device is used extensively in Scripture, for example in Isaiah 5:1-7 and in the Song of Songs. To speak allegorically is to set forth one thing in the image of another, the principal subject being inferred from the figure rather than by direct statement. Clarity of inference differentiates between allegory and parable, because the latter usually requires an interpretation for the teaching which it parallels. Allegorizing (to be distinguished from the drawing out of spiritual truths from factual presentations) has had broad application in Bible teaching. Alexandrian Jews spiritualized Scripture, and in this they were followed by the Church Fathers, who reached an extreme in the school of Origen, where spiritualization reached great heights in mystical and moral meanings. In Galatians 4:24 Isaac, the child of promise, typifies the Christian who, justified in Christ, is free to love and serve his Father; while Ishmael, the child of contrivance, typifies the legalist who, under the law, is bound to serve and to seek justification in obedience.   C.E.C.

ALLELUIA (ăl-lĕ-lū′yà, Heb. *halellû-yāh;* Gr. alle-louiá, praise ye Jehovah*), a word used by the writers of various psalms to invite all to join them in praising God (104:35; 105:45; 106:1,48; 111:1; 112:1; 113:1,9; 115:18; 116:19; 117:2; 135:1,21; first and last vs. of Psalms 146 to 150). The term Alleluia in Revelation 19:1,3,4,6 is borrowed from these psalms.

ALLIANCES. Bible: *affinity, confederacy, conspiracy, covenant, join, testament.* In this article *covenant* and *testament* (Heb. *berîth*, Gr. *diatheké*) are omitted when associated with God. In Genesis 21:27-32 Abraham and Abimelech "made a covenant" (Heb. *kārath běrîth, cut a covenant*). To *cut a covenant* is a formal term basic to alliance and covenant making. The cutting up and arranging the pieces of the sacrificial victim in pact-making was common among nations of antiquity and a regular practice of the Israelites. Jeremiah 34:18-20 refers to the practice of contracting parties passing between the pieces of flesh. Such cutting up and arrangement is understood variously: threat of similar treatment to covenant-breakers, animals representative of contracting parties, new unity by contractors passing between the pieces, association of divine witness in consecration of the sacrifice. "Cutting a covenant" is involved in pacts between individuals (I Kings 20:34), nations (Hos. 12:1), with death (Isa. 28:15,18), in agreements (II Kings 11:4), friendships (I Sam. 18:3), marriages (Mal. 2:14). Certain alliances were forbidden, as with Canaanites (Deut. 7:2), yet an agreement even on false premises was binding (Josh. 9:15,19). Sometimes a pillar was set up (Gen. 31:45-52), and presents given (I Kings 15:18). In the NT *diatheké* is a "covenant" or "testament," between men (Gal. 3:15), or with God.

ALLON (ăl'ŏn, Heb. *'allôn, oak*). 1. A prince of Simeon (I Chron. 4:37).

2. Or Elon (Heb. *'ēlôn*), a town, or *"the oak in Zaanannim,"* a southern boundary point in Naphtali (Josh. 19:33 cf. Judg. 4:11).

3. *Allon Bachuth,* "the oak of weeping," a tree marking the burial place of Deborah, the nurse of Rebekah (Gen. 35:8).

ALLON BACHUTH (See Allon 3)

ALMIGHTY (awl-mīt'ē, Heb. *shadday,* meaning uncertain). LXX *pantokrátor, all powerful.* Used 57 times with *'ēl, Kúrios, Theós,* for identification (Gen. 17:1), invocation (Gen. 28:3), description (Ezek. 10:5), praise (Rev. 4:8).

ALMODAD (ăl-mō'-dăd, Heb. *'almôdhādh, the beloved*), first-mentioned of Joktan's 13 sons (Gen. 10:26, I Chron. 1:20). This Arabian name is preserved in El-Mudad, famous in Arabian history as reputed father of Ishmael's Arab wife and as chief of Jurham, a Joktanite tribe.

ALMON (ăl'mŏn, Heb. *'almôn, hidden*), a Levitical city in Benjamin (Josh. 21:18). The same as "Alemeth" KJV and "Allemeth" ASV (I Chron. 6:60).

ALMON - DIBLATHAIM (ăl'mŏn-dĭb-là-thā'ĭm, Heb. *'almōn divlāthayim, Almon of two cakes of figs*), one of the last stops of the Israelites on their journey from Egypt to the Jordan. Lying between Dibon-gad and the mountains of Abarim (Num. 33:46,47), it is probably the same as Beth-Diblathaim of Moab (Jer. 48:22), which King Mesha boasts in the famous Moabite stone as "built" by him.

ALMOND TREE (See Plants)

ALMS (ähms), kind deeds arising out of compassion, mercy, pity for the unfortunate. Word found 14 times, in Matthew, Luke and Acts only, although practice is of Mosaic legislation and epistolary injunction. Greek *eleemosýne,* also in LXX for *tsedhāqâh,* "righteousness," and *hesedh,* "kindness." Matthew 6:1 has *dikaiosyné,* "alms"; and in Acts 9:36 *eleemosýne* is translated "almsdeeds." Frequently the verb *poiein,* "to do," "perform" is used with the noun as periphrasis for simple verb of *doing* (Matt. 6:1,2,3; Acts 9:36; 10:2 = "gave alms"; 24:17 = "to bring alms"). In the OT the Law prescribes gleanings from the harvest, the vineyards, and the grain in the corners of the field for the poor (Lev. 19:9-10). Deuteronomy 24:10-22 stipulates further gleanings from the orchards and olive groves, and protects the rights of the poor and unfortunate concerning wages and working conditions, especially as to pledges, lest the poor be deprived of necessary garments, or be otherwise inconvenienced. Almsgiving is set forth in Deuteronomy 15:11, "For the poor shall never cease out of the land: therefore I command thee, saying, Thou shalt open thine hand wide unto thy brother, to thy poor, and to thy needy, in thy land."

In later Judaism the righteousness of almsgiving becomes somewhat legalistic and professional. The lame man at the Gate Beautiful exemplifies professional begging in that daily he "sat for alms," and would "ask for alms," being well known to the people (Acts 3:1ff.). Perversion in receiving alms is seen in a beggar's cry couching the idea of "bless yourself by giving to me," while perversion in giving alms is seen in benefactors who "sound the trumpet," probably to be taken figuratively, and "to be seen" of men, involving the word from which we derive "theatre" (Matt. 6:1f). Almsgiving was of two kinds: "alms of the dish," food and money received daily for distribution; and "alms of the chest," coins received on the sabbath for widows, orphans, strangers and the poor. Practice of the NT Church is foreshadowed in the admonition of Jesus, "give alms of such things as ye have" (Luke 11:41, cf. I Cor. 16:2); and, "sell that ye have, and give alms" (Luke 12:33, cf. II Cor. 8:3). Alms in the NT Church, not named as such, are seen in the church of Macedonia in "their deep poverty . . . beyond their power . . . willing of themselves . . . ministering to the saints" (II Cor. 8:1-5). True purpose and spirit is shown in, "now at this time your abundance may be a supply for their want, that their abundance also may be a supply for your want" (II Cor. 8:14). The full measure of ministry, blessings and ability to give by God's grace is delineated in II Corinthians 8 and 9, to be done liberally, prayerfully, and cheerfully. See also James 2:15-16, and I John 3:17. A primary function of deacons was to distribute alms (Acts 6).

C.E.C.

ALMUG (See Plants of the Bible)

ALOE (See Plants of the Bible)

ALOTH (ā'-lŏth, Heb. *'ālôth*), a town or district mentioned with Asher and of which Baanah was Solomon's commissary (I Kings 4:16). ASV has Bealoth.

ALPHA (ăl'-fà), first letter of the Gr. alphabet, (A). ALPHABET, a list of elementary sounds in any language, comes from the first two Gr. letters, Alpha and Beta. In contrast is Omega, the last letter of the Gr. alphabet. Combined with Alpha, it signifies completeness, as "from A to Z" in modern usage. So God is the Alpha and Omega, the First and the Last, the Beginning and the End (Rev. 1:8), as is also Christ (Rev. 21:6, 22:13). Compare Isaiah 41:4, 44:6.

ALPHABET (See Writing)

ALPHAEUS (ăl-fē'-ŭs, Gr. *Alphaíos*). 1. Father of Levi (Mark 2:14).

2. Father of James the apostle (Matt. 10:3, Mark 3:18, Luke 6:15, Acts 1:13) and named with him to distinguish from James the brother of John.

3. Possibly Cleophas, husband of the Mary at the cross (John 19:25 cf. Mark 15:40), as *Cleo-*

phas (Gr. *Klōpas*) and *Alphaeus* are of Semitic derivation. Unlikely the Cleopas of the Emmaus road (Luke 24:18) since *Cleopas* was a common Greek name.

ALTAR (awl'têr, Heb. *mizbēah,* meaning *place of slaughter,* Gr. *bomós,* in Acts only, and *thusiastérion*). Altars in Old Testament times were many and varied. Their importance is seen in that the word "altar" is used 433 times in the Bible (KJV).

Some of the early ones were crude elevations, usually of earth or stone, though other materials were sometimes employed. The shape and size varied with the kind of materials used. For instance, in I Kings 18:31 one is noted that was simply a pile of stones, while another was made of one single stone (I Sam. 14:33-35). Later on, altars were made of a great variety of materials such as bronze, horns, ashes, wood, marble, brick and alabaster. Some were very simple; others, elaborate. Cobern tells of a triangular altar found in an ancient Roman temple (Camden Cobern, *The New Archeological Discoveries,* New York: Funk and Wagnalls, 1921, p. 505). The usual custom of the heathen was to have their altars face the east. Sometimes upon them was carved the name of a deity or its appropriate symbol. These heathen altars varied in height depending on the kind of gods worshiped, celestial or terrestrial.

The first Hebrew altar we read about (Gen. 8: 20) was the one erected by Noah after leaving the ark. Subsequently altars are spoken of as being built by Abraham (Gen. 12:7-8; 13:4,18; 22:9), Isaac (Gen. 26:25), Jacob (Gen. 35:1-7), Moses (Exod. 17:15), and Joshua (Josh. 8:30-31). Some of these must have been very simple in structure as the context of Genesis 22:9 would indicate. Most of the altars were built for sacrificial purposes, but some seem to have been largely memorial in character (Exod. 17:15-16; Josh. 22:26-27). Sometimes God stated just how the altar was to be built and of what materials.

With the erection of the tabernacle, altars were constructed by the Hebrews for two chief purposes, the offering of sacrifices and the burning of incense. Moses was commanded to make the altar of burnt offering for the tabernacle exactly as God had commanded him (Exod. 25:9). It was to be made of shittim (acacia) wood, which was to be overlaid with brass, or, as is more probable, copper. The shape was a square of five cubits which was to be three cubits high. A horn was to be made at each of the four corners. The purpose of these is uncertain. Apparently fugitives could hold to the horns for protection (I Kings 1:50-51), and sacrificial victims were bound to them (Ps. 118:27). A brass grating was placed in the center of the altar which projected through the opening on two sides.

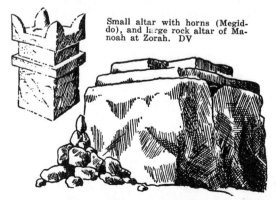

Small altar with horns (Megiddo), and large rock altar of Manoah at Zorah. DV

The Great High Place of Sacrifice of the Nabateans at Petra. © MPS

Four rings were fastened to it in which two poles of the same material as the altar were to be placed to carry the altar. Steps leading up to the altar were forbidden (Exod. 20:26). "A septad of sacrifices were to be made 'an atonement for it' — apparently to sanctify it for the uses to which it was to be devoted (Exod. 29:37); and it was to be 'reconciled' or 'cleansed' on the Day of Atonement after the presentation of sin offerings for the high priest and the nation (Lev. 16:19,20), as if contact with the sin offering had defiled its sanctity." (W. S. Martin and A. Marshall, *Tabernacle Types and Teaching,* London: Pickering & Inglis, n.d., p. 34).

Certain brass utensils were made in connection with the altar. There were pans to hold the ashes, shovels for removing the ashes, basins to receive the blood and to convey it to the varied places for sprinkling, three-pronged flesh hooks with which to remove the flesh, and censers for carrying coals from the altar (Exod. 27:3). Once the fire on this altar was kindled, it was required that it burn continually (Lev. 6:13).

The altar of burnt offering was also in Solomon's temple, the second temple, and in the temple built by Herod. Its form was altered to fit into the varying sizes of these structures. Solomon made his altar of copper twenty cubits square and twenty cubits high (II Chron. 4:1). After its construction it had a very interesting history. Because idols had polluted it, King Asa had it rededicated (II Chron. 15:8). Later on Uriah had it removed from its regular place, in order, it seems, to make room for another one that he had patterned after the one Ahaz had seen in Damascus (II Kings 16: 11-14). The terrible pollution of spiritual things in the reign of Ahaz led Hezekiah to cleanse the altar (II Chron. 29:12-18). Finally it was repaired and restored to its place by Manasseh (II Chron. 33:16).

In Zerubbabel's temple the altar was built first (Ezra 3:2), on the exact spot where it stood previously (Jos. *Ant.,* 11:4, 1). After it had been desecrated by Antiochus Epiphanes, it was rebuilt, apparently with unhewn stone, by Judas Maccabeus (I Macc. 4:47).

In addition to the altar for sacrifice, Moses was also commanded by God to make "an altar of incense" (Exod. 30:1), sometimes called a "golden altar" (Exod. 39:38; Num. 4:11). It was to be a cubit square and two cubits high (Exod. 30:2) with horns at each corner. It was made of shittim wood overlaid with pure gold. Around the top of this structure a crown of gold was placed beneath

A rough altar of stones, for votive offerings, with Sinai in the distance. © MPS

which were fixed two golden rings, one on each side. Staves of the same construction as the altar were placed through these rings to carry it (Exod. 30:1-5).

This altar was to be located before the veil that separated the holy place from the holy of holies, midway between the walls (Exod. 30:6; 40:5). Because of its special location, it was referred to as "the altar before the Lord" (Lev. 16:12). Elsewhere in the Bible it is referred to as "the whole altar that was by the oracle" (I Kings 6:22) and "the golden altar which is before the throne" (Rev. 8:3). Incense was burnt upon this altar twice each day (Exod. 30:7-8) and upon it was sprinkled the blood of the atonement (Exod. 30:10). The burning of incense on this altar symbolized the offering up of the believers' prayers (Rev. 8:3). It was while officiating at this altar that the angel appeared to Zacharias (Luke 1:10).

There are no altars recognized in the New Testament Church. While Hebrews 13:10 is sometimes used to prove the contrary, a careful study of this passage in its context is fatal to this idea. The idea in this passage is that Jesus Christ is the true altar of each believer. Paul mentions in Acts 17:23 the inscription "the altar to the unknown God," that had been placed over the altar erected in Athens. Such inscriptions were common in heathendom and are referred to by a number of early writers (see Augustine, *The City of God* 3:12).

The great Canaanite altar at Megiddo. OIUC

There is good reason to feel that the need for altars was revealed to man very early as basic in approaching God. It played a leading role in all OT worship of the true God, and is seen both in and outside the Bible as playing a prominent part in most heathen religions. A careful study of the use of this article of furniture in Israel's worship furnishes us with many spiritual lessons today. It was the place of sacrifice where God was propitiated and where man was pardoned and sanctified. It looked to the great sacrifice that the Son of God was to make on the cross. The altar of sacrifice, being the first thing visible as one approached the tabernacle, spoke loudly to man that without the shedding of blood there would be no access to God and no forgiveness of sin (Heb. 9:9, 22). Most writers feel the brass or copper speaks of divine judgment.   H.Z.C.

ALTASCHITH (ăl-tăs'chĭth, Heb. *'al tashēth, destroy not*), a title notation in Psalms 57, 58, 59, 75. Significance uncertain. Same form found in prayer of Moses, "O Lord God, *destroy not* thy people" (Deut. 9:26).

ALUSH (ā'lŭsh, Heb. *'ālûsh*), a desert campsite of the Israelites between Dophkah and Rephidim (Num. 33:13,14). Meaning: "crowding" (Rabbis).

ALVAH, ALIAH (ăl'vȧ, Heb. *'alwâh*), a duke of Edom (Gen. 36:40) called "Aliah" in I Chron. 1:51.

ALVAN, ALIAN (ăl'văn, Heb. *'alwān, tall*), a son of Shobal the Horite (Gen. 36:23, I Chron. 1:40).

AMAD (ā'măd, Heb. *'am'ādh*), a town of the tribe of Asher (Josh. 19:26).

AMAL (ā'măl, Heb. *'āmāl*), an Asherite (I Chron. 7:35).

AMALEK (ăm'ȧ-lĕk, Heb. *'āmālēq*), son of Eliphaz (eldest son of Esau) by his concubine Timna (Gen. 36:12, I Chron. 1:36). Duke of Edom (Gen. 36:16).

AMALEKITES (ȧ-măl'ĕk-īts, ăm'ȧ-lĕk-īts; Heb. *'āmālēqî*), an ancient and nomadic marauding people dwelling mainly in the Negeb from the times of Abraham to Hezekiah, c. 2000-700 B.C.

HISTORY: First mention is among those smitten by Chedorlaomer in days of Abraham (Gen. 14:7). Moses felt their fury in the unprovoked attack upon the Israelites at Rephidim, for which God decreed continual war and ultimate obliteration (Exod. 17:8ff.). Joshua and the spies encountered them in Canaan and they and the Canaanites repulsed the Israelites at Hormah (Num. 14:45). During the period of the Judges they sided with the Ammonites and Moabites against the Israelites in the days of Ehud (Judg. 3:13), with the Midianites and the children of the East against Gideon (Judg. 6:3,33); and Abdon was buried "in the mount of the Amalekites" (Judg. 12:15). Saul was commissioned to destroy them utterly, but failed to do so and spared Agag (I Sam. 15:8ff.), and was himself slain by an Amalekite (II Sam. 1:8ff.). David invaded the Amalekites and other ancient inhabitants of the land from Shur to Egypt (I Sam. 27:8), and smote them severely in recovering his wives and property stolen during the raid upon Ziklag (I Sam. 30:18). They are numbered among nations subdued by him (II Sam. 8:12, I Chron. 18:11). Simeonites during the time of Hezekiah finally exterminated them (I Chron. 4:43).

DISTRIBUTION: Primarily in the Negeb SW of the Dead Sea, but also in the Sinai Peninsula from Rephidim (Exod. 17:8) to the border of Egypt (I Sam. 27:8); northward at Jezreel (Judg. 6:33), Pirathon (Judg. 12:15) and at or near Jericho

(Judg. 3:13); and eastward to Mount Seir (I Chron. 4:42). See also Numbers 13:29.

ORIGIN: Unknown unless note in Genesis 14:7 is proleptic and Amalek is grandson of Esau (Gen. 36:12). Accordingly, "first of the nations" in Numbers 24:20 can be first in time, first in preeminence, or first to molest liberated Israel (at Rephidim). Arab traditions, late and conflicting, make the Amalekites stem from Ham.

CHARACTER: Warlike, usually confederate with Canaanites (Num. 14:45) or Moabites (Judg. 3: 13), but sometimes alone, as at Rephidim (Exod. 17:8) and Ziklag (I Sam. 30:1). They "smote the hindmost . . . all that were feeble . . . and . . . feared not God" (Deut. 25:18), destroyed crops (Judg. 6:4). Agag likely a royal title, as Pharaoh in Egypt.

DESTINY: At Rephidim the Lord said, "I will utterly put out the remembrance of Amalek from under heaven," and about Balaam, "his latter end shall be that he perish for ever" (Num. 24:20). Saul failed to destroy them, but David reduced them to inactivity, and the Simeonites at Mount Seir "smote the rest of the Amalekites that were escaped" (I Chron. 4:43). Archaeology has produced no evidence of them thus far.   C.E.C.

AMAM (ā'-măm, Heb. *'āmām*), an unidentified southern town belonging to Judah (Josh. 15:26).

AMANA, AMANAH (See Abana)

AMANA (à-mā'nà, Heb. *'āmānâh, constant* (?)), a mountain near Lebanon (S of Sol. 4:8), whence flow the Amana springs (II Kings 5:12, marg.).

AMARANTHINE (ăm-à-răn'-thĭne, *fadeth not away*), an inheritance (I Pet. 1:4), glory (I Pet. 5:4). From *amaranth*. a flower which when picked does not wither; the unfading flower of the poets.

AMARIAH (ăm'à-rī'àh). 1. Levite, and ancestor of Ezra (I Chron. 6:7,11,52; Ezra 7:3).

2. Levite serving in house of the Lord under David (I Chron. 23:19; 24:23).

3. Chief priest under Jehoshaphat (II Chron. 19:11).

4. Levite under Hezekiah (II Chron. 31:15).

5. One guilty of intermarrying (Ezra 10:42).

6. Covenant signer (Neh. 10:3).

7. Levite under Zerubbabel (Neh. 12:2).

8. Son of Hezekiah and great-grandfather of Zephaniah (Zeph. 1:1). See also Nehemiah 11: 4 and 12:13.

AMARNA, TELL EL (à-màr'nà, tĕll ĕl, *the hill amarna*), a name used to describe a mound of ruins in Egypt, halfway between Memphis and Luxor. It is the modern name for the ancient capital of Amenhotep IV (c. 1387-1366 B.C.). In 1887 a peasant woman, seeking the dust from ancient buildings with which to fertilize her garden, was digging in the ruins of Tell El Amarna. She found some clay tablets which she pulverized and took to her home. Finally an American missionary stationed at Luxor, Chauncey Murch, heard of this and notified some cuneiform scholars. After the site producing these tablets had been identified, it was excavated by Sir Flinders Petrie.

The excavation yielded 320 clay tablets of varying sizes with cuneiform writing upon both sides. Eighty-two are now in the British Museum; 160 in Berlin; 60 at Gizeh Museum, and the rest in private hands. They contain the private correspondence between the ruling Egyptian Pharaohs at that time and the political leaders in Palestine. It is believed they reflect the prevailing conditions that existed during the time Joshua carried on his campaigns in Palestine. Aside from confirming certain Biblical

El-Amarna letter (clay tablet) from Egypt, with Cuneiform writing. BM

facts, they reveal the plan of Egyptian houses, thus throwing light on the early activities of Joseph in Egypt. These tablets have also provided valuable aid to scholars in establishing the Egyptian vocalic system.

AMASA (ă-mā'sà, Heb. *'āmāsā'*). 1. Captain of the rebel forces under Absalom. According to II Samuel 17:25, his father was Ithra the Israelite, while Jether the Ishmeelite is given in I Chronicles 2: 17. In either case, Abigail, sister of Zeruiah and David, was his mother, making him nephew to David and cousin to Absalom. Following the defeat of the rebels under Amasa and the death of Absalom by Joab in the wood of Ephraim (II Sam. 18:6ff), David made Amasa captain of the host in the place of Joab (II Sam. 19:13). When Sheba and the men of Israel rebelled, David set three days for Amasa to assemble the men of Judah (II Sam. 20:4). Amasa delayed beyond the set time, so David sent Abishai, brother of Joab, and a body of armed men after Sheba. Amasa joined forces with Abishai at "the great stone which is in Gibeon," where Joab, in feigned greeting, "took Amasa by the beard with the right hand to kiss him," and ran him through with his sword (II Sam. 20:8-10).

2. A prince of Ephraim, son of Hadlai, among those who sided with the prophet Oded in opposition to the intentions of Pekah of Israel to hold as slaves Jews taken in an attack upon Ahaz of Judah (II Chron. 28:12f).

AMASAI (à-măs'ā-ī). 1. Chief of the captains and spokesman for some men of Benjamin and Judah met by David as they came out to him at Ziklag. The Spirit came upon Amasai and he assured David of their loyalty to him (I Chron. 12:18).

2. A trumpeter among the priests in the procession bringing the ark to Jerusalem during the reign of David (I Chron. 15:24).

3. Father of Mahath, one of several Levites who sanctified themselves for the repairing of the temple during the time of Hezekiah (II Chron. 29:12). Possibly identified with "Mahath, the son of *Amasai*, the son of Elkanah" in I Chronicles 6:35, 36, which would make him a Levite in the line of Kohath, and progenitor of Samuel. See also I Chronicles 6:25.

AMASHAI (à-măsh'ā-ī), a priest of the house of God at Jerusalem under Nehemiah (Neh. 11:13).

AMASIAH, Heb. *'amasyâh, Yahwe bears*), son of Zichri who offered himself to the Lord as a captain under Jehoshaphat (II Chron. 17:16).

AMAZIAH (ăm-à-zī'à, Heb. *'āmatsyâh, whom Jehovah strengthens*). 1. The ninth king of Judah (including Athaliah), lineage of David through Rehoboam (I Chron. 3:12), succeeding his father Joash who had been murdered by conspirators (II Kings 12:21). Seemingly co-regent with his father who was sick, for we read concerning Joash that the departing Syrians "left him in great diseases," and the conspirators subsequently "slew him on his bed" (II Chron. 24:25). Jehoash of Israel came to the throne in the 37th year of Joash of Judah (II Kings 13:10). Amaziah began to rule in the second year of Jehoash of Israel, which would be the 39th year of Joash of Judah (II Kings 14:1). Since Joash ruled for 40 years (II Chron. 24:1), there must have been a co-regency for at least a year.

The account of Amaziah is found chiefly in II Kings 14, with a parallel and supplementary account in II Chronicles 25. Amaziah came to the throne when 25 years old and ruled for 29 years, doing right as did his father, "but not with a perfect heart," for the high places were not taken away and the people continued to offer sacrifices and to burn incense. His first act was to slay his father's murderers, though he spared their children, as Moses had ruled in Deuteronomy 24:16. He then assembled an army of 300,000 men, appointed captains over thousands and hundreds (II Chron. 25: 5-6), and an additional 100,000 men of Israel, hired for 100 talents of silver. Warned by a man of God against using the Israelitish mercenaries, Amaziah protested the loss of his 100 talents, but, assured that "the Lord is able to give thee much more than this," he dismissed the Israelites, who returning home in anger, sacked certain cities of Judah along the way, taking away much spoil (II Chron. 25:13).

In the meantime, Amaziah went against Edom, took Selah (II Kings 14:7), possibly the rock-city now identified as Petra, slew 10,000 Edomites in battle, and slew another 10,000 captives by hurling them to death from the "top of the rock" (II Chron. 25:11-12). He brought back the gods of the Edomites and bowed down to them, offering incense, for which his destruction was foretold (II Chron. 25: 14-16). Amaziah then challenged Jehoash of Israel to war. In replying, Jehoash likened Amaziah to a "thistle" making demands of a "cedar," and advised him to be content with his victory over Edom. Amaziah persisted, so they joined in battle at Bethshemesh. The men of Judah were routed; Amaziah was captured and returned to Jerusalem, where 400 cubits of the wall facing Israel was broken down, after which Jehoash returned to Samaria, taking along hostages and treasures from the house of God and the house of the king. Fifteen years later a conspiracy made Amaziah flee to Lachish, but he was followed and killed, and his body brought back to Jerusalem.

2. A priest of Bethel, during the reign of Jeroboam II, who complained about the prophet Amos and advised him to go back to Judah, whereupon Amos prophesied his death in a foreign land and the tragic end of his wife and family (Amos 7: 10-17).

3. A Simeonite, whose son Joshah was among those who smote the remnant of Amalekites who had fled to Mount Seir (I Chron. 4:34, 43).

4. A Levite in the ancestry of the Ethan who served in the tabernacle about the time of David (I Chron. 6:45, 48).   C.E.C.

AMBASSADOR, an envoy or messenger: OT Heb. *tsîr*, "ambassador," as in Isaiah 18:2, but "messenger," as Isaiah 57:9; *mal'ākh*, "ambassador," as in II Chronicles 35:21, but "messenger" in Numbers 20:14; *lîts*, "ambassador" as in II Chronicles 32:31, but "interpreter" in Genesis 42:23. Earliest instance is in the case of Edom and the Amorites (Num. 20:14; 21:21). Usually men of high rank, as Sennacherib's field-marshal, Tartan; chief eunuch, Rabsaris; and chief officer, Rabshakeh, met by Hezekiah's house-master, scribe and recorder (II Kings 18:17f). Note: Joshua 9:4, ". . . made as if they had been ambassadors . . ." may be read ". . . supplied themselves with provisions . . ." "We are ambassadors for Christ" (II Cor. 5: 20) and, "I am an ambassador in bonds" (Eph. 6:20), are both from *presbeuein*, "to be, work or travel as an envoy or ambassador." The concept of ambassador as personal representative of sovereign and state, in foreign residence, is likely foreign to the Biblical concept of messenger as ambassador.

AMBER (ăm' bêr, Heb. *hash-mal, meaning unknown*), only in description of color of divine glory (Ezek. 1:4, 27; 8:2). LXX *eléktron*, allied with *eléktor*, "the beaming sun," designating a compound of silver and gold.

AMEN (ā-mĕn, Heb. *'āmēn*, Gr. *amén*), English and Greek both transliterations of Hebrew, from root meaning "confirm" or "support". LXX translates by *génoito*="may it become", KJV "verily." In NT as assent of congregation to utterances of leader (I Cor. 14:16); also equated with certainty of promises of God (II Cor. 1:20). General sense "so let it be," "truly," "indeed." OT: with doxologies (I Chron. 16:36, Neh. 8:6 and in the Psalms as 41:13); assent by congregation to laws (Num. 5:22, Deut. 27:15-26); oaths (Neh. 5:13); appointments (I Kings 1:36); title of God (Isa. 65:16) but KJV translates "God of truth" which suggests different Hebrew pointing; call to divine witness (Jer. 28:6). NT: To introduce a solemn saying of Jesus, always as, "Verily I say . . . ," doubled always and only in John (but sometimes in OT, as Ps. 41:13 etc.); following a doxology (Rom. 11:36 etc.); following a benediction (Rom. 15:33 etc.); concluding particle at end of a writing, as frequently the Greek *télos* and Arabic *tamm*, both meaning "completion" (all but Acts, James and III John end with "Amen," with 15 benedictions, 3 doxologies and 6 unrelated); assent to forebodings (Rev. 1:7; 22:20); reverence to God (Rom. 1:25; 9:5, Rev. 1:18); title of God (Rev. 3:14 cf. Isa. 65:16).

AMETHYST (See Minerals)

AMI or **AMON** (ā'mî, Heb. *'āmî*), a servant of Solomon (Ezra 2:57), called Amon in Neh. 7:59.

AMINADAB (See Amminidab)

AMITTAI (à-mĭt'î, Heb. *'āmittay, faithful*), father of Jonah (II Kings 14:25, Jonah 1:1).

AMMAH (ăm'à, Heb. *'ammâh, mother, or beginning*), a hill facing Giah by way of the wilderness of Gibeon, where Joab and Abishai stopped at sundown in their pursuit of Abner after Asahel's death (II Sam. 2:24).

AMMAN (see Rabbah)

AMMI (ăm'î, Heb. *'ammî, my people*), a symbolic name given to Israel (Hos. 2:1) predictive of God's reconciliation to them, in contrast to sinful Israel represented by Hosea's son Lo-ammi, "not my people" (Hos. 1:9). See Rom. 9:25,26.

AMMIEL (ăm'ĭ-ĕl, Heb. *'ammî'ēl, my kinsman is God*). 1. The son of Gemalli and spy of the tribe of Dan sent out by Moses (Num. 13:12).

2. The father of Machir, of Lo-debar (II Sam. 9:4,5; 17:27).

3. The father of Bath-sheba, one of David's wives (I Chron. 3:5).

4. The sixth son of Obed-edom who, with his family, was associated with the Tabernacle porters (I Chron. 26:5).

AMMIHUD (ă-mī'hŭd, Heb. *'ammîhûdh, my kinsman is glorious*). 1. The father of Elishama, chief of Ephraim (Num. 1:10, 2:18, 7:48,53).

2. A man of Simeon and father of Shemuel (Num. 34:20).

3. A Naphtalite whose son, Pedahel, also assisted in the division of the land (Num. 34:28).

4. Father of Talmai and king of Geshur. Absalom fled to Talmai after he slew his brother Amnon (II Sam. 13:37).

5. Son of Omri, father of Uthai (I Chron. 9:4).

AMMINADAB (ă-mĭn'a-dăb, Heb. *'ammînādhāv, my people is willing* or *my kinsman is generous*).

1. A Levite. Aaron's father-in-law (Exod. 6:23).

2. A prince of Judah (Num. 1:7, 2:3, 7:12,17, 10:14, Ruth 4:19,20, I Chron. 2:10).

3. A son of Kohath, son of Levi (I Chron. 6:22). Perhaps the same as No. 1.

4. A Kohathite who assisted in the return of the Ark from the house of Obed-edom (I Chron. 15:10,11).

AMMISHADDAI (ăm-ĭ-shăd'ī, *an ally is the Almighty*), father of Abiezer, captain of the tribe of Dan in Moses' time (Num. 1:12, 2:25, 7:66,71, 10:25).

AMMIZABAD (à-mĭz'a-băd, Heb. *'ammîzāvādh, my kinsman hath endowed,* made a present), son of Benaiah, third of David's captains (I Chron. 27:6).

AMMON (ăm'ŏn, Heb. *'ammôn, a people*). Ammon or Ben-ammi is the name of one of the sons of Lot born to him by his youngest daughter in the neighborhood of Zoar (Gen. 19:38). He was the father of the Ammonites, who occupied an area of land E of the Dead Sea in the land of Gilead.

AMMONITES (ăm'ŏn-īts, Heb. *'ammônîm*), the name given to the descendants of Ben-ammi or Ammon (Gen. 19:38). They were related to the Moabites by ancestry (Gen. 19:38) and often appear in the Scriptures in united effort. Because by ancestry they were related to Israel, reflected in the name by which they are often called in the OT, Ben-ammi "children of my people," the Israelites were told by the Lord not to enter into the battle with them as they journeyed towards the land of Canaan (Deut. 2:19). Lot fled from the destruction of the cities of Sodom and Gomorrah, and dwelt in the mountains to the E of the Dead Sea. In this area God gave a tract of land for the Ammonites (Deut. 2:19), who occupied the land just east of Moab. It stretched to the N as far as the Jabbok River and on the S to the hills of Edom. Many years later the Ammonites made war with Israel in order to extend their borders farther west. However, though this land never really belonged to the Ammonites, they claimed it, and gave this as a reason for their aggression (Judg. 11:13).

Unable to expand westward and not desiring the desert tract of land on the E the Ammonites were confined to a small area. Although they were a nomadic people, they did have a few cities, their capital, Rabbath-Ammon, being the more famous.

The people were fierce in nature, rebellious against Israel and idolatrous in their religious prac-

A view of present-day Amman, capital of Trans-Jordan, showing the old Roman theater at right, and the modern city in foreground. In ancient times it was Rabbath-Ammon, capital of the Ammonites. © MPS

tices. They threatened to thrust out the right eye of all in Jabesh Gilead (I Sam. 11:2). They were given to brutish murder (Jer. 40:14; 41:5-7; Amos 1:14). Though related to Israel, they refused to help them when asked (Deut. 23:4) and then joined with Moab in securing Balaam to curse them (Deut. 23:3-4). Later on in Israel's history they united with Sanballat to oppose the work of Nehemiah in restoring the walls of Jerusalem (Neh. 2:10,19). In religion they were a degraded, idolatrous people. Their chief idol was Molech, to whom they were guilty of offering human sacrifices (I Kings 11:7).

Because of their sins and especially because they constantly opposed Israel, Ezekiel predicted their complete destruction (Ezek. 25:1-7). Their last stand seems to have been against Judas Maccabeus (I Macc. 5:6).   H.Z.C.

AMNON (ăm'nŏn). 1. Son of David by Ahinoam. By contrivance, he forced his half-sister Tamar as she tended him during a pretended sickness. For this he was later murdered by Tamar's brother Absalom.

2. A son of Shimon, of Judah (I Chron. 4:20).

AMOK (ā'mŏk, Heb. *'āmōq*), chief of priests who returned with Zerubbabel from exile (Neh. 12:7, 20).

AMON (ā'mŏn, Heb. *'āmôn*), the successor and son of king Manasseh and the father of the illustrious king Josiah. Since this name was identical with that of the Egyptian deity, it is thought that perhaps Manasseh named him while he was still in idolatry. He was an evil king and after two years of reign was slain by officials of his household (II Kings 21:19-26; II Chron. 33:21-25).

2. The governor of Samaria to whom Micaiah the prophet was committed by Ahab the king of Israel because he had predicted the king's death (I Kings 22:15-28).

3. One of Solomon's servants (Neh. 7:57-59), though sometimes he is called Ami (Ezra 2:57).

AMON (ā′mon, Heb. ′āmôn), a city thought by most scholars to be the same as No (Jer. 46:25; Ezek. 30:14-15,16; Nah. 3:8), and as No-Amon. The word "sea" in Nahum 3:8 has given rise to some difficulty as to the location of this ancient city. However, the Nile is called "the sea" because of its appearance at the time of its flood stage, or this designation is used of the Nile in a poetic fashion (Job 41:31; Isa. 18:2). Therefore, this city in the days of Nahum, Jeremiah, and Ezekiel is today identified as Thebes.

Thebes is the Greek name of this old capital of Upper Egypt. It was called "No Amon" meaning "city of Amon," because this was the name of its chief deity. It was an obscure city in the old kingdom, but it became the capital of the middle kingdom commonly known as the Theban. This included the 11th through the 14th dynasties. It lessened in importance during period of the Hyksos, but with their expulsion it again became the capital. It was in this period that the city rose to the height of its fame. It has a number of famous temples and tombs. Perhaps the most famous tomb, discovered in 1922, was the tomb of Tutankhamen, with all of its equipment still intact.

AMORITE (ăm′ō-rīt, Heb. ′ĕmōrî, mountain dwellers). Although this word in the Hebrew is always in the singular, it is used collectively of that tribe of people who, according to Genesis 10:16, descended from Canaan. They probably were east Semites and while not Akkadians, were very closely akin to them.

They were a very prominent people in pre-Israelitish days, for it is believed that at one time their kingdom occupied the larger part of Mesopotamia and Syria, with their capital at Haran. The Mari tablets throw a flood of light on them, and it is now thought that Amraphel, king of Shinar (Gen. 14:1), was one of their kings. People from the north drove them from this region, causing them to settle in Babylonia, where they brought the entire area under their control, giving to Babylonia one of the richest periods in her history. When, after several hundred years, they were defeated by the Hitties, they settled throughout a large portion of Canaan and may even have ruled in Egypt for a time.

We do know that during their supremacy in Canaan they marched on the kingdom of Moab and under the leadership of king Sihon subdued a large portion of this land, in which they settled (Num. 21:13, 26-31). Joshua speaks of their land as E of the Jordan (Josh. 24:8), but Moses tells of their abode as being on the western shore of the Dead Sea (Gen. 14:7), on the plain Mamre (Gen. 14:13) and around Mount Hermon (Deut. 3:8). They were apparently a very wicked people, for God told Abraham that his descendants would mete out His vengeance on this people when their iniquity was full (Gen. 15:16). Under Moses' leadership this judgment was dealt to Og, king of Bashan, and to Sihon, king of Heshbon, the kings of the Amorites east of the Jordan. Their territory was subdued and given to Reuben, which he held for 500 years until it fell to Moab. This was a very rich land, being attractive to both farmers and herdsmen. Joshua met these people in battle in the united campaign of the five Amoritish kings of Jerusalem, Hebron, Jarmuth, Lachish and Eglon

(Josh. 10:1-43). These battles (Josh. 11:1-14), fought by Joshua under divine leadership, ended forever Amorite hostilities against Israel (I Sam. 7:14 and I Kings 9:20-21). H.Z.C.

AMOS (ā′mŏs, Heb. ′āmôs, Gr. Amós, burden-bearer), was one of the colorful personalities in an era which saw the rise of several towering prophetic figures. His ministry occurred in the reign of Jeroboam II (c. 786-746 B.C.), the son of king Jehoash of the Jehu dynasty. Due to the removal of Benhadad III of Syria as a military threat, the northern kingdom had been able to consolidate its hold on Damascus and extend its borders northwards to the pass of Hamath. To the south and east its territorial acquisitions equaled those of the early kingdom period under David and Solomon. While Assyria was becoming an increasingly serious political threat, its military might under Tiglath-pileser III was still a distant prospect when Jeroboam II began to rule Israel.

His forty-year reign was one of great prosperity for the northern kingdom, approaching in character the "golden age" of David and Solomon. With the threat of war removed, a cultural, social and economic revival took place. The expansion of trade and commerce resulted in a steady drift from country to city, and the small towns in the northern kingdom gradually became overcrowded. But prosperity was accompanied by an almost unprecedented degree of social corruption (Amos 2:6-8; 5:11-12) caused principally by the demoralizing influence of Canaanite Baal worship, which had been fostered at the local shrines from the time when the northern kingdom had assumed a separate existence.

Archaeological discoveries in Palestine have furnished a dramatic picture of the extent to which this depraved, immoral religion exerted its corrupting influences over the Israelites. Characteristic of the ritual observances were drunkenness, violence, gross sensuality and idolatrous worship. The effect of this demoralizing religion upon Hebrew society was seen in the corruption of justice, in wanton and luxurious living, and in the decay of social unity. The rich manifested no sense of responsibility towards the poor, and instead of relieving their economic distress, seemed bent upon devising new means of depriving them of their property.

To this perilous situation Amos brought a message of stern denunciation. Although he was not an inhabitant of the northern kingdom he was painfully aware of its moral, social and religious shortcomings. Amos lived in the small mountain village of Tekoa, which lay to the south of Jerusalem on the borders of the extensive upland pastures of Judah. By trade he was a herdsman of sheep and goats (7:14), and was also engaged in dressing the sycamore-fig tree, whose fruit needs to be incised about four days before the harvest to hasten the ripening process. His background was of a strictly agricultural nature, and his work afforded him ample time for meditating upon God's laws and their meaning for wayward Israel.

On receiving his call, Amos protested vigorously against the luxurious and careless living characteristic of Samaria, castigated the elaborate offerings made at the shrines of Beersheba and Gilgal, and stated flatly that ritual could never form an acceptable substitute for righteousness. He asserted the moral jurisdiction of God over all nations (1:3,6,9,11; 2:1,4,6) and warned the Israelites that unless they repented of their idolatry, and following a renewed spiritual relationship with God, commenced to redress social inequalities, they would fall victim to the invader from the East. So great

Ruins of Tekoah, the birthplace of the prophet Amos.
© MPS

was the impact of this vigorous personality that Amos was accused of sedition by Amaziah, the idolatrous high priest of Bethel (7:10 seq.). In reply Amos pointed out that he had no connection with any prophetic order, nor was he linked in any way politically with the house of David. Instead he was called by God to prophesy the captivity of an unrepentant Israel.

The style of his book, though simple, is picturesque, being marked by striking illustrations taken from his rural surroundings. His work as a herdsman was clearly not incompatible either with a knowledge of history (9:7) or with an ability to assess the significance of contemporary political and religious trends. The integrity of his book has suffered little at the hands of modern critical scholars.
Analysis:

1-2. The indictment of foreign nations including Judah and Israel.

3.1-5.17. The condemnation of wicked Samaria.

5.18-6.14. False security exposed; judgment foretold.

7.1-9.10. Five visions illustrate Divine forbearance and justice; Amos' reception at Bethel (7.10-17).

9.11-15. Epilogue promising restoration and prosperity.

Bibliography. E. J. Young. *An Introduction to the Old Testament.* (1953) pp. 250-252.
R.K.H.

AMOZ (ā'mŏz, Heb. *'āmôts*), the father of the prophet Isaiah (II Kings 19:2,20, Isa. 1:1, etc.).

AMPHIPOLIS (ăm-fĭp'ō-lĭs, Gr. *Amphípolis, a city pressed on all sides*), a city of Macedonia, situated on a bend of the river Strýmon, founded by the Athenians in the fifth century B.C. and under the Romans, the capital of one of the four districts into which Macedonia was divided. It was a military post on the Via Egnatia, 33 miles SW of Philippi. Paul passed through it on the way from Philippi to Thessalonica (Acts 17:1).

AMPLIAS (ăm'plĭ-ăs, Gr. *Ampliás*), ASV, RSV, Ampliatus (ăm'plĭ-ā'tŭs), a Christian to whom Paul sent a greeting (Rom. 16:8).

AMRAM (ăm'răm, Heb. *'amrām, people exalted*).
1. A descendant of Levi and of Kohath, and father of Aaron, Moses and Miriam (Exod. 6:18,20, Num. 26:59, I Chron. 6:3).
2. A son of Bani, who married a foreign wife during the exile (Ezra 10:34).
3. A son of Dishon, descendant of Anah (I Chron. 1:41). ASV, RSV have Hamran.

AMRAPHEL (ăm'rà-fĕl, Heb. *'amrāphel*), king of Shinar, one of four kings, led by Chedorlaomer, king of Elam, who invaded Palestine to crush a rebellion (Gen. 14). After pillaging Sodom and Gomorrah, they took Lot and his goods and departed. Amraphel has been identified with Hammurabi, king of Babylon, whose reign has been variously dated from 1760 to 2100 B.C., but leading Babylonologists doubt whether there is any connection.

AMULET (ăm'ŭ-lĕt,), occurs once in ASV, RSV, Isa. 3:20), never in KJV. It translates the plural of Heb. *lāhash,* meaning "serpent-charmer" as shown by KJV of Jeremiah 8:17, and ASV, RSV of Ecclesiastes 10:11, Isaiah 3:3, etc. Amulets have been worn from earliest times to ward off harm from snake-bites, diseases and other dangers. They were commonly stones, gems, or clay figurines, representing animals or gods, or scrolls inscribed with sacred words and were worn usually suspended from the neck.

AMUN (See Amon)

AMZI (ăm'zī, Heb. *'amtsî*). 1. A descendant of Merari and of Levi, and progenitor of Ethan, whom David set over the service of song (I Chron. 6:44-46).
2. Ancestor of Adaiah, a priest in the second Temple (Neh. 11:12).

ANAB (ā'năb, Heb. *'ānāv, grapes*), a city of the Anakim, taken by Joshua (Josh. 11:21). It fell to Judah (Josh. 15:50). SE of Debir, SW of Hebron, it retains its ancient name.

ANAH (ā'nà, Heb. *'ănâh*). 1. Daughter of Zibeon and mother of Aholibamah, Esau's wife (Gen. 36:2,14,25).
2. Son of Seir, duke of Edom (Gen. 36:20,29, I Chron. 1:38).
3. Son of Zibeon (Gen. 36:24, I Chron. 1:40, 41).

Taking the names as names of individuals, the above is what the text gives us, except that in Genesis 36:14 "son" may be a better reading than "daughter." Taking the names as clan-names, there may be confusion as to the origin and relationships of kindred groups.

ANAHARATH (à-nā'hà-răth, Heb. *'anāhărāth*), a town in the territory of Issachar, in the valley of Jezreel, near Shunem, Nain, and Endor. Modern en-Naura (Josh. 19:19).

ANAIAH (à-nī'àh, Heb. *'ănāyâh, Jehovah has answered*). 1. A prince or priest who assisted in the reading of the law to the people (Neh. 8:4).
2. A Jew who, with Nehemiah, sealed the covenant (Neh. 10:22). Nos. 1 and 2 may be the same person.

ANAK (ā'năk, Heb. *'ănāq, long necked*), descendant of Arba (Josh. 15:13) and ancestor of the Anakim (Num. 13:22,28,33).

ANAKIM (ăn'à-kĭm, Heb. *'ănāqîm*), also called "sons (children) of Anak" or "of the Anakim." The spies compared them to the giants of Genesis 6:4

(ASV, RSV, Nephilim); also they were reckoned among the Rephaim (Deut. 2:11, ASV, RSV). Three chiefs of the Anakim were in Hebron (Num. 13:22) from the time of the spies till Caleb took it (Josh. 15:13,14). Remnants of them remained in Gaza, Gath and Ashdod (Josh. 11:21, 22).

ANAMIM (ăn'à-mĭm, Heb. *'ănāmîm*), a people descended from Mizraim (Gen. 10:13, I Chron. 1:11) of whom nothing further is known.

ANAMMELECH (à-năm'ĕ-lĕk, Heb. *'ănammelekh*), one of the gods of Sepharvaim, worshiped by colonists from that city settled in Samaria by order of the king of Assyria. The identity and location of Sepharvaim and the character of Anammelech are disputed (II Kings 17:31).

ANAN (ā'năn, Heb. *'ānān, cloud*), a returned exile who sealed the covenant with Nehemiah (Neh. 10:26).

ANANI (à-nā'nī, Heb. *'ănānî*), a son of Elioenai, of the family of David (I Chron. 3:24).

ANANIAH (ăn'à-nī'àh, Heb. *'ănanyâh, Jehovah is a protector*). 1. The father of Maaseiah and grandfather of Azariah (Neh. 3:23).
   2. A town of Benjamin (Neh. 11:32).

ANANIAS (ăn'à-nī'ăs, Gr. form of Heb. *hănan-yâh, Jehovah has been gracious*). 1. Husband of Sapphira (Acts 5:1-11). He and his wife pretended to give to the church all they received from a sale of property, but kept back part. When Peter denounced his deceit, Ananias fell down dead. The generosity of others (Acts 4:32-37) accentuates the meanness of Ananias. Yet lying to the Holy Spirit, rather than greed, was the sin for which he was punished. That his was the first gross act of disobedience within the church justifies the severity of the punishment. Peter rather prophesied than decreed his death, which was a penalty God inflicted.
   2. A disciple of Damascus, who, obeying a vision, was the means of healing the sight of Saul of Tarsus, and of introducing him to the Christians of Damascus (Acts 9:10-19). In Acts 22:12-16, Paul recalls Ananias' part in his conversion, and speaks of him as "a devout man according to the law, having a good report of all the Jews which dwelt" in Damascus.
   3. A high priest before whom Paul was tried in Jerusalem (Acts 23:1-5). Paul, whether because of poor eyesight, or momentary forgetfulness, or Ananias' unpriestly behavior, reviled him, and promptly apologized. Ananias came down to Caesarea in person to accuse Paul before the Roman governor Felix (Acts 24:1).   E.R.

ANAT (ā'năt) or *Anu,* Babylonian-Assyrian god of the sky, first named in a triad with Bel and Ea.

ANATH (ā'năth, Heb. *'ănāth*), father of Shamgar, third judge after Joshua (Judg. 3:31; 5:6).

ANATHEMA (à-năth'ĕ-mà, Gr. *anáthema,* the rendering in the LXX and in the NT of the Hebrew *herem; anything devoted*). A thing devoted to God becomes His and is therefore irrevocably withdrawn from common use. A person so devoted is doomed to death — a death implying moral worthlessness (Lev. 27:28,29; I Cor. 12:3; 16:22; Gal. 1:9; Rom. 9:3).

ANATHEMA MARANATHA (à-năth'ĕ-mà mâr'-à-năth'à). The words were formerly interpreted as a double imprecation, but are now believed to have no necessary connection. Maranatha is a distinct sentence made up of two Aramaic words, either *Maran atha,* "Our Lord is come or comes," or

Air view of the village of Anathoth, the home of the prophet Jeremiah. © MPS

Marana tha, "Our Lord, come," and was probably a widely-used expression among early Christians to indicate their fervent hope in the speedy return of Christ (I Cor. 16:22).

ANATHOTH (ăn'à-thŏth, Heb. *'ănāthôth,* probably the plural of "Anath," a *goddess*). 1. A city of Benjamin assigned to the priests (Josh. 21:18), the native place of Abiathar the high priest (I Kings 2:26) and Jeremiah the prophet (Jer. 1:1). Two of David's distinguished soldiers, Abiezer (II Sam. 23:27) and Jehu (I Chron. 12:3), also lived there.
   2. A Benjamite, the son of Becher (I Chron. 7:8).
   3. A leader of the men of Anathoth who sealed the covenant to worship Jehovah (Neh. 10:19).

ANCHOR (Gr. *ángkyra*). In ancient times every ship carried several anchors. In successive periods they were made of stone, iron, lead, and perhaps other metals. Each had two flukes, and was held by a cable or a chain. The word is used only in Acts 27:29,30,40 and Hebrews 6:19: in Acts, in connection with Paul's journey to Rome, and in Hebrews, in a figurative sense.

ANCIENT OF DAYS. In Daniel 7:9,13,22, God, as He appeared in a vision to the Prophet. Compare "the likeness as the appearance of a man" in Ezekiel 1:26, where "the voice of the Almighty" has been heard (Ezek. 1:24); also the appearance of Christ in Revelation 1:12-16.

ANCIENTS (ān'shĕnts). This word (except in one instance — I Sam. 24:13) renders a Hebrew word which should always be translated "old men" or "elders"— men of age and experience.

ANDREW (ăn'drōō, Gr. *Andréas, manly*), the brother of Simon Peter, and son of Jonas, of Bethsaida on the Sea of Galilee (John 1:44). He was a fisherman, like his brother, with whom he lived at Capernaum (Mark 1:29). John the Baptist, whose disciple he was, directed him to Jesus as the Lamb of God. Convinced that Jesus was the Messiah, he forthwith brought his brother to Jesus (John 1:25-42). Subsequently Jesus called the two brothers to abandon their fishing and take up permanent fellowship with Him (Matt. 4:18,19); and later Jesus appointed him an apostle (Matt. 10:2; Mark 3:18; Luke 6:14; Acts 1:13). In the lists of the apostles his name always appears next to that of Philip, who was also from Bethsaida, and with whom he is associated at the feeding of the 5,000, where he expressed doubt that the multitude could be fed with the lad's five loaves and two fishes (John 6:6-9), and also at the request of the Greeks to see Jesus (John 12:22). Andrew was one of the four who asked Jesus about the destruction of the Temple and the time of the Second Advent. After Acts 1:13 he is never mentioned again. According to tradition, he preached in Scythia and suffered martyrdom in Achaia, being crucified on an X-shaped cross, now called a St. Andrew's cross.

ANDRONICUS (ăn'drō-nī'kŭs, Gr. *Andrónikos*), a Jewish believer, once a fellow-prisoner of Paul, to whom the apostle sent a greeting (Rom. 16:7).

ANEM (ā'něm, Heb. *'ānēm*), a city of Issachar, set aside for the Levites (I Chron. 6:73). Omitted in the parallel list in Joshua 21:29.

ANER (ā'nêr, Heb. *'ānēr*). 1. A brother of Mamre the Amorite, Abraham's ally in battle (Gen. 14:13,24).
2. A Levitical city in Manasseh (I Chron. 6:70).

ANGEL (Gr. *ángelos, messenger*), a supernatural or heavenly being a little higher in dignity than man. Angels are created beings (Ps. 148:2-5, Col. 1:16). Scripture does not tell us the time of their creation, but it was certainly before the creation of man (Job 38:7). They are described as "spirits" (Heb. 1:14). Although without a bodily organism, they have often revealed themselves in bodily form to man. Jesus said that they do not marry and do not die (Luke 20:34-36). They therefore constitute a company, not a race developed from one original pair. Scripture describes them as personal beings, not mere personifications of abstract good and evil. Although possessed of superhuman intelligence, they are not omniscient (Matt. 24:36; I Peter 1:12); and although stronger than men, they are not omnipotent (Ps. 103:20; II Peter 2:11; II Thess. 1:7). They are not glorified human beings, but are distinct from man (I Cor. 6:3; Heb. 1:14). There is a vast multitude of them. John said, "I heard the voice of many angels . . . and the number of them was ten thousand times ten thousand, and thousands of thousands" (Rev. 5:11). They are of various ranks and endowments (Col. 1:16), but only one — Michael — is expressly called an archangel in Scripture (Jude 9). This great host of angels, both good and bad, is highly organized (Rom. 8:38; Eph. 1:21; 3:10; Col. 1:16; 2:15).

Angels were created holy (Gen. 1:31; Jude 6), but after a period of probation some fell from their state of innocence (II Peter 2:4; Jude 6). Scripture is silent regarding the time and cause of their fall, but it is clear that it occurred before the fall of man (for Satan deceived Eve in the Garden of Eden) and that it was due to a deliberate, self-determined rebellion against God, as a result of which they lost their original holiness, became corrupt, and were confirmed in evil. Some were "cast down to hell," where they are held in chains until the day of judgment (II Peter 2:4); while others were left free, and they oppose the work of God.

The work of the angels is varied. Good angels stand in the presence of God and worship Him (Matt. 18:10; Rev. 5:11; Heb. 1:6). They assist,

Fishermen on the Sea of Galilee, reminiscent of Andrew and his brother, Simon Peter. © MPS

protect, and deliver God's people (Gen. 19:11; Ps. 91:11; Dan. 3:28; 6:22; Acts 5:19). The author of Hebrews says (1:14), "Are they not all ministering spirits, sent forth to minister for them who shall be heirs of salvation?" They sometimes guide God's children, as when one told Philip to go into the desert near Gaza (Acts 8:26), and they bring encouragement, as when one spoke encouragingly to Paul in Corinth (Acts 27:23,24). Sometimes they interpret God's will to men (Dan. 7:16; 10:5,11; Zech. 1:9,13,14,19). They execute God's will towards individuals and nations (Acts 12:23; Gen. 19:12,13; II Sam. 24:16; Ezek. 9:2, 5,7). The affairs of nations are guided by them (Dan. 10:12,13,20). God uses them to punish His enemies (II Kings 19:35; Acts 12:23).

Angels had a large place in the life and ministry of Christ. They made their appearance in connection with His birth to Mary, Joseph, and the shepherds. After the wilderness temptation of Christ they ministered to Him (Matt. 4:11); an angel strengthened Him in the Garden (Luke 22:43); an angel rolled away the stone from the tomb (Matt. 28:2-7); and angels were with Him at the ascension (Acts 1:11).

As for the evil angels, it is clear that their principal purpose is to oppose God and to try to defeat His will and frustrate His plans. The word "Satan" means adversary, and Scripture shows him to be the adversary of both God and man. All of his many other names show his nefarious character. Evil angels endeavor to separate believers from God (Rom. 8:38). They oppose good angels in their work (Dan. 10:12,13). They hinder man's temporal and eternal welfare by a limited control over natural phenomena (Job. 1:12,13,19; 2:7), by inflicting disease (Luke 13:11,16; Acts 10:38; II Cor. 12:7), by tempting man to sin (Matt. 4:3; John 13:27; I Peter 5:8), and by spreading false doctrine (I Kings 22:21-23; II Thess. 2:2; I Tim. 4:1). They cannot, however, exercise over men any moral power independent of the human will, and whatever power they have is limited by the permissive will of God.

Scripture shows that good angels will continue in the service of God in the future age, while evil angels will have their part in the lake of fire (Matt. 25:41). S.B.

ANGEL OF THE LORD. In the OT we find the oft-recurring phrase, "the angel of the Lord," in which, in almost every case, this messenger is regarded as deity and yet is distinguished from Jehovah (Gen. 16:7-14; Gen. 22:11-18; Gen. 31:11,13; Exod. 3:2-5; Num. 22:22-35; Judg. 6:11-23, 13:2-25; I Chron. 21:15-17; I Kings 19:5-7). There is good reason for thinking that He is the pre-incarnate Logos, his appearance in angelic or human form foreshadowing His coming in the flesh.

ANGER, used of both the anger of man and of God, but oftener of the latter. The early Hebrews, observing that when a man is angry his nose swells and his nostrils quiver, sometimes used the expression "his nose burned" for "he became angry" (Gen. 30:2; Exod. 4:14). God's anger differs from man's in that it is a holy wrath, directed against sin.

ANIAM (à-nī′ăm, Heb. *'ănî'ām, lament of the people*), a son of Shemidah, a Manassehite (I Chron. 7:19).

ANIM (ā′nĭm, Heb. *'ānîm*), a city in the southern hill country of Judah (Josh. 15:50), probably the ruins of el-Ghuwein S of Eshtemoa.

ANIMALS OF THE BIBLE. As there are far more references to mammals in the Bible than to any other animal forms, with the possible exceptions of insects and birds, the first part of this section treats of mammals, listing them alphabetically. Non-mammalian animals included here are dealt with separately. These include sponges, corals, mollusks, and three other classes of vertebrates besides mammals, viz., fishes, amphibians and reptiles.

Instead of discussing such forms as ox, bull, bullock, calf, cow, and heifer under separate headings, they have been included under the heading of "Cattle." Similarly, under "Horses" are included colt, foal, and ass; and under "Sheep" will be found lamb, ram and ewe.

Comparisons of the names given to the different animals were made as they occur in the Revised Standard Version, the American Standard Version, and the King James Version. An attempt has been made to include all of these mentioned in the last-named version.

Apes. King Solomon sent ships once every three years to Tarshish to obtain gold, silver, apes and other treasures. Although the identity of Tarshish is uncertain, it seems probable that the rhesus monkey of India, the one so popular in present-day zoos, was the animal meant. The term ape is now more restricted in meaning than formerly and would exclude the monkey.

Ass. More than 150 verses in the Bible refer to the ass. Along with zebras and horses they constitute the horse family, *Equidae*. The domesticated ass or donkey has served man for thousands of years, and is believed to have been derived from the still-existing Abyssinian or Somali Wild Ass. The ass is better at carrying loads, and is more sure-footed on mountain trails than the horse.

Abraham is believed to have owned asses that he took into Egypt, and Egyptians used them in monument building in 3000 B.C. White asses were more highly esteemed and commanded a higher price. The number of asses an Old Testament worthy owned was an indication of his wealth. Heavy farm work was done by them and they were also used as saddle animals, being preferred by rulers and great men for peaceful journeys. Horses were reserved for war. Jesus entered Jerusalem on the colt of an ass. Balaam rode a she-ass

A donkey colt, "the foal of an ass" (Matt. 21:2, 7). © MPS

that was given the power of speech by the Lord in order to rebuke him. Samson used the jawbone of an ass to slay a thousand Philistines. Israelites were commanded neither to covet an ass nor to plow with an ox and an ass together. On one occasion they captured 61,000 asses from the Midianites.

Badger. Where references in Exodus and Numbers in the KJV mention "Badgers' skins," the RSV uses "goatskins." The badger as we know it is not found in Bible lands. European badgers have a wide distribution but are fierce fighters and hardly seem to satisfy the requirements for the dozen references found in the Scriptures. To have constructed a covering seventy-five feet by forty-five feet for the tabernacle from their skins would have required a considerable number of animals. It seems much more probable that goats both domesticated and available in numbers would have been used to provide the skins. Some have suggested that badgers' skins were made from a seal or cetacean.

Bats. Although bats are mammals they are named along with birds in the Scriptures. The bats of Palestine according to Wiley are mostly insectivorous but this statement has been questioned by one who has more recently lived for a considerable period in the Bible Lands. Among the approximately two thousand kinds throughout the world are fruit, meat, fish, nectar, and blood eaters. All are equipped with a natural "radar" system; most are social and nocturnal. The Bible classified them as unclean.

Bears. Fourteen references to bears occur. The "Syrian Brown Bear," *Ursus syriacus,* is the bear of the Old Testament. After Elisha's bald head (an unusual spectacle among the Hebrews) had drawn the mistreatment of the forty-two youths, two she bears appeared and tore them. On another occasion David fought and killed a bear while guarding his flocks. If, as some believe, Palestine was once much more heavily wooded, such encounters would appear more likely. The prophets Isaiah, Daniel, and John all had visions in which the bear figured prominently.

Behemoth. The hippopotamus is thought by some to be the animal Job had in mind. Known as the "River horses of Africa," they are bulky, ungainly, short-legged creatures weighing up to four tons. They sleep by day, blow and snort at night, and can swim, float, or sink and run along on the bottom.

The elephant has also been named as the animal meant by "Behemoth." The fact that the Arabs traded extensively in ivory, that the elephant has a larger tail than a hippo's, and the manner of visibly taking copious draughts of water, all are presented as evidence that the animal that "moveth his tail like a cedar" and "drinketh up a river, and hasteth not" was surely an elephant (Job 40:17,23).

Boar. In Psalm 80:13 the wild "boar from the forest" is said to destroy the vine, but other references imply domesticated swine. Although the meat of swine was forbidden as food for the Israelites, in one instance a herd of two thousand was found in the country of the Gadarenes (Mark 5:11-13). The prodigal's degradation led to the feeding of swine (Luke 15:15,16). Warning was given not to cast pearls before swine.

Wild pigs are very fierce, courageous, and swift, and have been hunted as game animals for hundreds of years. Domestication by the Chinese occurred at a very early time. Pigs reproduce prolifically and are a good source of meat that can be easily preserved owing to the readiness with which it absorbs salt.

A mother camel and her foal. © MPS

Camel. The Bible is reported to contain sixty-six references to the camel. These animals are very hardy, can endure privation, can withstand temperature extremes very well, and have a life span of forty to fifty years. They are cud-chewing vegetarians with a three-chambered stomach that can store a three days' water supply. In their hump a reserve supply of food is stored in the form of fat.

Camel's hair is used in cloth making. Their flesh and milk are esteemed by natives in certain areas. As beasts of burden the two-humped Bactrian camel can carry about four hundred pounds and in caravans covers about thirty miles per day. The one-humped camel or dromedary has longer legs, travels faster, and in a twenty-four hour day may cover more than 150 miles, and more often is the one used for riding and for carrying mail.

Job had three thousand camels and after prosperity returned to him he had six thousand. Abraham was rich in camels. In Matthew 19:24 the difficulty of a camel passing through the eye of a needle is mentioned. Oriental cities had small gates called "needle's eyes" for admitting late travelers, after the main gates had closed. To pass, the camel had to kneel down, be unloaded, work its way through on its knees.

1. Dromedary (one hump). 2. Camel (two humps). 3. Gazelle. 4. Ibex, or wild goat. 5. Onager, or wild ass. DV

Cattle. Cattle of today are descendants of wild forms such as the Aurochs, or Urus, *Bos taurus primigenius,* that occurred in parts of Europe and Northern Africa. These, like other members of the family *Bovidae,* are true ruminants with cloven hoofs and hence a very important item of food. As ruminants they have the four-chambered stomach enabling them to masticate their food leisurely and thoroughly.

Part of the loot in a battle between the Israelites and the Midianites consisted of seventy-two thousand beeves (Num. 31:33). A portion of Jacob's wealth consisted of forty kine and ten bulls (Gen. 32:15). Calves were valued for food, sacrifice, and idolatrous worship. It was a calf that was prepared upon the prodigal son's return. Calf-worship like that practiced by the Egyptians, was indulged in under the leadership of Aaron and of Jeroboam. Prophets Isaiah, Ezekiel, and John had visions in which the calf had a part. Bullocks were extensively used, particularly in the consecration of the Levites, the sacrificing of the priests, and in making sin offerings for the congregation. During the revivals under a number of Old Testament leaders, great numbers of bullocks along with rams and lambs were sacrificed. When Solomon built the temple he included in it a molten sea of brass supported by twelve brazen bulls (I Kings 7:25). David's distress when hunted by Saul was stated thus, "Many bulls have compassed me; strong bulls of Bashan have beset me round" (Ps. 22:12).

Cattle are mentioned in the first chapter of the Bible and constituted much of the wealth of Abraham and his descendants. Cattle figure prominently in the account of Joseph, Pharaoh, and the Egyptians. While wandering forty years the Israelites killed very few animals for food and consequently lusted for flesh. Heavy judgments upon the Egyptians in the time of Moses, and upon the Israelites in later times included the destruction or loss of their cattle.

The products which gave cattle much of their value are milk, butter, cheese, and leather. To describe Canaan as a place of prosperity it was called "a land flowing with milk and honey." While milk and butter are nourishing, Paul was distressed that the Corinthians had need of milk rather than of strong meat.

Oxen provided not only food and animals for sacrifice, but they also were important as draft animals. A number of commands were given pertaining to the care of these animals, and property rights associated therewith. When Elijah found him, Elisha was plowing with twenty-four oxen. They were partly responsible for Saul's decline when he spared the oxen after routing the Amalekites. Nebuchadnezzar was reduced to eating grass as the oxen. Ezekiel's vision of four creatures included the ox.

Chamois. In Deuteronomy 14:4-6 the chamois is listed among those animals that could be eaten. "Mountain sheep" is the name used in the RSV. It was probably the mountain sheep of Egypt and Arabia known as the Barbary Sheep or Aoudad.

Coney. The coney is similar to a rabbit except for its short legs and ears, and the absence of a tail. They are also called "little cousins of the elephant" and "drassies." As rock dwellers they are timid but very active. Conies occur from Africa north through Arabia to Asia. Their feet are four-toed like an elephant's; they are vegetarians with teeth like those of the rhinoceros, and their jaw action resembles cud-chewing although they lack the type of stomach for rumination.

Dogs. Dogs were possibly the first animal domesticated, being derived from wolf stock of Europe and Asia. Job spoke of the dogs that guarded his flocks (Job 30:1). In Bible times they were generally despised outcasts known for their ravenous and ruthless nature, and given to prowling and filthy habits (Prov. 26:11). The Syrophenician woman spoke of dogs that ate the children's crumbs (Matt. 15:26,27). Approximately forty Bible references are made to these unclean animals.

Dragons. Thirty-five references to "dragons" appear in the KJV. In those instances where the word is derived from the Hebrew word "tannin" a long serpent-like, symbolical animal is meant. Examples of this sort are found in Psalm 74:13, Ezekiel 32:2, and the Revelation. John uses the word "dragon" for Satan. Where "tannim," the plural of the Hebrew "tan" occurs, literal animals are understood. In some of these instances the crocodile is meant and elsewhere jackals were intended.

1. Mule. 2. Goat. 3. Fat-tailed sheep. 4. Hyrax, or coney. DV

Dromedary. See Camel.

Elephant. In the RSV the word "behemoth" is rendered "hippopotamus" in the footnote, whereas it is given as "elephant" in the margin of KJV (Job 40:15). Repeated references to elephants being used in warfare occur in the first and second books of Maccabees.

In a dozen or more instances ivory is mentioned in the Bible. For example, Solomon overlaid his ivory throne with gold thereby giving an indication of the relative values of these materials (I Kings 10:18). Where the doom of Tyre and Babylon is foretold reference is made to the extensive use they had made of ivory. King Ahab had houses and beds of ivory. Dr. Reisner's expedition from Harvard in 1931, reported that Ahab's palace covered between seven and eight acres, and that lavish use of ivory had been made there.

Fallow Deer. This term is changed to roebuck, q.v., the male of the roe deer, in the RSV (Deut. 14:5; I Kings 4:22,23). The term fallow deer is used today of a smaller deer that is found in forests and mountains across Europe and northern Asia. Along with the wild boar it is about the only wild game remaining in Europe.

Fox. In nine verses this animal is named, where it refers to the common fox of Palestine, *Vulpes vulgaris*, that resembles the common fox of Europe and the red fox of America. It is a member of the dog family, and in a number of ways resembles the dog. They are carnivorous, wary, quick-sensed, and swift. It is believed that the word fox in Scripture referred to jackals, for example, "that spoiled the vines." Samson could have more readily secured jackals in such numbers so that three hundred could be used in burning the fields of the Philistines (Judg. 15:14). It is thought that the animals were tied in pairs with a firebrand connected by a cord to their tails, thereby spreading fire far and wide as they raced away in terror.

The fox's craftiness was attested to by the fact that Jesus likened Herod's conduct to that of a fox.

Gazelle. The RSV employs the term "gazelle" in a dozen or more verses. They are small, swift antelopes found in hot, arid, barren wilderness areas of the Old World. Arabs train falcons to overtake, swoop down and stun gazelles with a blow on the head enabling hunters on fast horses to overtake them. In Asia hunters also use greyhounds, sometimes with the falcon, to effect their capture. There are sixty or more kinds of gazelles in Southern

Asia and Northern Africa. A small form, the Dorcas Gazelle, is found in hot and barren areas of Syria and Palestine. As many as a hundred have been observed in a single herd. In Libya during World War II army trucks were used to chase them. Records of forty-five miles per hour for six or seven miles were reported.

Goats. Goats and sheep in the wild are inhabitants of the mountains. Both are cud-chewing, have hairy coats, and hollow horns. Wild goats are more surefooted and adventurous. Both sheep and goats were domesticated as early as 3000 B.C. Milk, butter, cheese, and meat are obtained from goats. In Palestine goats were driven to the doors of customers where they were milked. They were much used for sacrifice and for feasts. Their hair was made into clothing. Containers for water and wine were made from goatskins in Bible times. The Bible has more than 130 references to goats and approximately fifty references to kids.

Greyhound. Proverbs 30:31 lists the "greyhound" among those things that Solomon said are "comely in going." An alternate translation given in the footnote of the ASV is "war-horse," whereas it is translated "strutting cock" in the RSV. Early Egyptian monuments carry pictures of this ancient breed of dog that is known to attain speeds up to forty miles per hour.

Hare. Baby hares are born with a good coat of hair and good eyesight whereas rabbits are born naked and blind. No native rabbits occur in Palestine but at least two species of hares are numerous. Hares are classified as unclean because they lack the divided hoof. Their jaw action resembles cud-chewing but they lack the ruminant's stomach.

In two instances where hares are mentioned in the Bible they are named by Moses (Lev. 11:4,6; Deut. 14:7).

Hart. Harts were apparently rather plentiful since they are mentioned as part of the daily fare at Solomon's table. These may have been either the red deer of Europe and Asia, *Cervus elephus* or the Syrian deer, *C. barbatus*. The former is similar to the American elk but somewhat smaller. Harts are stags or male deer whereas hinds are female deer. A single hart may weigh as much as three hundred pounds. Their six-pronged antlers are shed annually. The habitat of the hart differs from that of the gazelle as the former must have more water. This requirement is alluded to in Psalm 42:1, where the hart is said to long for flowing streams and its need of pasture is implied in Lamentations 1:6. The leaping of the hart is referred to in Isaiah 35:6.

Hind. See Hart. These female red deer are mentioned a number of times in the poetical books of the KJV, but are not listed as an item of food. Their fleetness is referred to by both Habakkuk and David who, almost four hundred years apart, used very similar expressions, "He maketh my feet like hinds'" in speaking of swiftly escaping their enemies (Ps. 18:33, Hab. 3:19).

Horse. At least four thousand years ago in central Asia some type of wild horse was tamed and domesticated. Only one species of truly wild horse remains today known as Prjevalsky's Wild Horse of Mongolia. Babylonians began using them to draw war chariots around 1700 B.C. Without horses, conquests on a large scale would have been impossible for Alexander the Great and for Genghis Khan. Herodotus reported the use of swift horses by the Persians for their postal system at least three thousand years ago.

The first of more than 150 verses referring to horses is found in Genesis 47:17 where Joseph in

A flock of goats at the River Kishon, Mt. Carmel in the distance. © MPS

Egypt bought horses by giving bread to the people during a famine. Upon the death of Jacob, Joseph and an escort of horsemen and chariots carried him back to Canaan for burial. One of the ten plagues that befell the Egyptians in the the time of Moses led to a heavy loss of horses. Later, to overtake the fleeing Israelites, horses and chariots were used by the Egyptians.

Under Moses, God warned the people not to multiply horses. Saul was later killed in a battle with the Amalekites who were outfitted with chariots and horses. David captured chariots from the Syrians and destroyed most of them but reserved a hundred chariots. In so doing he disobeyed God and introduced their use in Israel. Solomon greatly increased their numbers and depended heavily on them as he strengthened the defenses of his land.

In most instances horses were employed in warfare; however, Isaiah connected them with agriculture (Isa. 28:24-29). They were also used in idolatrous processions (II Kings 23:11). Their use for riding is mentioned in II Kings 9:14-37 and Esther 6:8,10,11. In prophecy horses play a role as in Joel 2:4,5, and Revelation 9:7,9 and 6:1-8, where four horses of different colors are associated with singular disasters.

Hyena. Curiously, the word for hyena does not occur in the Bible although hyenas were abundant in Palestine. The word "Zeboim" in I Samuel 13:17-18 comes from a Hebrew word that is generally considered to refer to hyenas, and basically the same word is translated "speckled bird" in Jeremiah 12:7-9.

Ibex. See Pygarg.

Jackal. In both the ASV and RSV the word "jackals" in Job 30:29, is substituted for the word "dragons" of the KJV. The same change has been made in Psalm 44:19 and Isaiah 13:22; 34:13. In other instances where the word "dragon" is applied literally, that is, to mammals inhabiting desert places, one finds "jackals" in the newer versions.

Jackals are the wild dogs of warmer parts of the Old World. They hunt in small packs in a stealthy manner at night, and their role as scavengers is important. Abandoned buildings and desolate spots are frequented. The Gray or Yellow Jackal, *Thos aureus* is probably the species of the Bible Lands. See Fox.

Lamb. See Sheep.

Leopard. The word "leopard" is used in the same eight verses in the RSV as in the KJV. A leopard (panther) is more savage and malevolent than a lion. It possesses great fighting ability and is wary, treacherous, highly intelligent and subtle. It does not ordinarily attack human beings, although it is fearless. In Solomon's time leopards lived in parts of Palestine and in mountainous regions of Lebanon in Syria. Isaiah suggested the improbable by referring to a leopard lying down with a kid; Jeremiah spoke of the impossibility of the leopard changing its spots; Daniel and John used it in a figurative sense.

Leviathan. Both the ASV and RSV employ "leviathan" in Job 41:1. In footnotes for this verse both versions give the crocodile as an alternative meaning; however crocodiles are not caught with fishhooks. Some fabulous creature may be meant in Job 41:1 and also in Psalm 74:14 where breaking or crushing "the heads of Leviathan" is mentioned. It has been suggested that the latter reference was telling of the removing of the crocodiles so that the Israelites could safely cross the Red Sea. Sperm whales have been observed in the Mediterranean Sea and may have been intended in Psalm 104:26. Its use in Isaiah 27:1 may have been to symbolize Israel's enemies that were to experience God's judgment.

Lion. Lions by their size and majestic bearing have won the title, "King of Beasts." Usually they are friendly, travel in small groups, share prey peaceably, and kill only what they intend to consume. Few are man-killers. However, once a lion eats a man it is a threat thereafter. While lions are on their honeymoon they are particularly dangerous. During the construction of the Uganda Railway in East Africa two lions killed and ate twenty-eight Indian coolies as well as scores of natives.

India, Turkey, Iraq, Iran, Greece, Asia Minor and Syria all had lions in early times. Today, few remain outside of Africa and possibly India.

The Hebrew people were very familiar with lions and many books in the Bible mention them. The lion's strength is often referred to in the Scriptures. The Lord Jesus Christ is called the Lion of the tribe of Judah. The traits of lions are used to foreshadow those of the "King of Kings." Jacob compared three of his sons, Judah, Dan, and Gad, to lions. Throughout the Bible lions are either treated as natural animals or they are used as symbols of might.

Daniel's experience in the lions' den illustrates the use Oriental monarchs made of them as executioners. A number of instances are mentioned where a man killed a lion in a single-handed encounter (Judg. 14:5-18 and I Sam. 17:36,37).

God's judgment was visited upon the disobedient by the actual use of lions, and its severity predicted by likening the character of attacking nations to the ferocity of a lion.

Symbolically, Daniel described Babylon as a winged lion. Peter represented the devil as a destroying lion.

Mouse. Mice came from the Old World and accompanied man as he migrated all over the world. The terms "mouse" and "mice" occur in both the RSV and KJV in references found in Leviticus, I Samuel, and Isaiah, and probably include a number of small rodents. Evidently the Jews had followed heathen practices of eating swine's flesh and mice, and perhaps even hamsters, rats and jerboas, as the Arabs and Syrians did. After taking the ark from the Israelites, the Philistines were ravaged by a scourge of mice.

Mole. Where "mole" occurs in Leviticus 11:29,30 in the KJV, it is rendered "chameleon" in the RSV. Isaiah (Isa. 2:20) probably meant the blind rat or mole rat of Southeastern Europe rather than our true mole of America.

Monster. In place of "sea monsters" the ASV and RSV use "jackals' in Lamentations 4:3. From the facts that monsters are usually large, powerful animals, and that in this instance no difficulty was experienced in nursing their young during a time of severe famine, it seems probable that whales are meant. Where the KJV in Genesis 1:21 speaks of "great whale," the RSV uses "Sea monsters."

Mule. A mule is a cross between a male donkey and a female horse. Mules have been bred since earliest times and are almost always sterile. Breeding them was forbidden to Israelites (Lev. 19:19), but they were imported into Palestine. The finest were used by kings and officers, King David apparently having initiated their use for riding purposes. All of his sons rode on mules (II Sam. 13:29) and it was one of these that deserted Absalom (II Sam. 18:9).

Pygarg. The word "pygarg" means white-rumped and hence has been said to apply to some antelope such as the addax, one species of which is a native of desert regions of Northern Africa and the Egyptian Sudan.

The RSV translates it ibex, meaning a type of bearded wild goat. The Nubian Ibex occurs in Palestine as well as in Egypt and Arabia.

Roe. This word is used in nearly a dozen verses in the KJV but does not appear in the RSV. In most instances, both the RSV and ASV use the word "gazelle." Like the hind, a gazelle was not to be eaten. As the hart could be eaten so could the roebuck or male of the female roe.

Satyr. Both the KJV and RSV use "satyr" in Isaiah 13:21 and 34:14, but the ASV used "wild goat." Monsters supposedly half man and half goat were worshiped in both Egypt and Greece. The same word is translated "devils" in Leviticus 17:7 and II Chronicles 11:15, where idolatrous practices are denounced.

Sheep. If sheep ever existed in the wild state they were certainly domesticated before 3000 B.C., and probably before cattle. Sheep receive more attention in the Bible than any other animal. They were important in the domestic, civic, and religious life of the Israelites. Even today the Arabs depend heavily upon them. Earliest mention of sheep is in Genesis 4:2 where it is said that "Abel was a keeper of sheep."

Both Hebrew and Arab shepherds had to move to new locations whenever pasturage gave out. This led to a nomadic existence and to using tents as habitations. Water requirements meant that the shepherd must know where streams or wells could be found, and his movements with the flock were governed accordingly. Watering was always done at noon. The shepherd's care was beautifully portrayed in Psalm 23. Continuous care of sheep eventually led the shepherd to know each by name. Sheep were always led, never driven. Occasionally shepherdesses cared for sheep as in the case of the seven daughters of the priest of Midian whom Moses assisted. Wells became important meeting places of a tribe. Both good and poor shepherds are mentioned, and during the latter parts of Israel's history their leaders were denounced as being bad shepherds. Figures of speech concerning shepherding were used repeatedly as God warned them of their shortcomings. Jesus Christ came as the Good Shepherd and His arrival was announced to shepherds.

Sheep were kept for their milk more than for their flesh. The common breed could store a vast amount of fat in the tail and this was used as food. They also provided wool, and horns, used either for carrying oil or wine, or as trumpets for summoning the people and in religious rites. The skins of rams were used in making the covering of the tabernacle.

The fat-tailed sheep of Palestine. © MPS

The reason why so much attention is given to sheep in the Bible is doubtless because they were used so much in sacrifice. Offerings consisted not only of lambs but also of ewes and rams. Where a prescribed service was intended, the type of animal was usually named. The ultimate and final sacrifice was the Lamb of God who in many respects was foreshadowed by the way in which lambs had served as sacrifices.

Swine. Although the names of "hog" and "pig" are not named in the Bible, "swine" are referred to a number of times. Members of the family Suidae, swine are unclean although they have the divided hoof. Solomon declared that "a beautiful woman without discretion" is "like a gold ring in a swine's snout" (Prov. 11:22, RSV). Through Isaiah, God rebuked the Israelites for eating swine's flesh (Isa. 65:2, 3, 4). Jesus warned against casting pearls before swine (Matt. 7:6). Peter spoke of a washed sow wallowing in mire (II Pet. 2:22). All of the Gospel writers except John told of the man freed of a legion of devils which entered a herd of two thousand swine that then dashed into the water and were drowned. It was odd that they should have been in Palestine, unless owned by Gentiles. The prodigal son was degraded to the place where he was forced to feed swine.

Unicorn. Wiley enumerates characteristics of this creature which may be pieced together from the eight passages where it is mentioned: it is exceptionally powerful, a voracious eater, has a pair of strong horns, was well known to people of Old Testament lands, was untamable, impossible to use for agriculture, very active while young, and fit for sacrifice. Instead of "unicorn" the ASV and RSV use "wild ox." This was possibly the auroch that stood six feet at the shoulder and was once plentiful in Palestine. Seen in profile it appeared to have but a single horn, hence the name unicorn.

Weasel. The weasel is listed along with the mouse and tortoise as an unclean animal (Lev. 11:29). These important rodent killers seem to kill for the sake of killing, and are found in almost all parts of the world.

Whale. "Whale" is retained in the RSV in the account found in Matthew 12:40. In Jonah 1:17 the RSV uses "great fish," and in Genesis 1:21 and Job 7:12 it is rendered "sea monsters" or "sea monster." Goodwin maintains that among whales, only the sperm whale has a throat structure capable of swallowing a man. Such whales have been seen in the Mediterranean. He relates an incident told by Sir Francis Fox of a sailor, who in 1891 fell overboard, was swallowed by a sperm whale and after twenty-four hours was rescued by his shipmates when they opened up the whale. After being mentally deranged for two weeks, he is said to have recovered. Sir Francis got this story from the ship's captain and crew.

Wolf. Wolves, dogs, and jackals are members of a family of carnivores. Wolves were very widely distributed across Europe and North America. Unprovoked attacks upon man are questioned unless the animal is famished. They are mentioned twelve times. Benjamin, a tribe, was likened to a wolf. Jesus repeatedly likened false prophets and teachers to wolves. Isaiah foretold that the wolf and lamb will feed together in the Messianic Kingdom (Isa. 11:6; 65:25).

Non-Mammalian Animals

Sponges. Sponges have served many purposes since earliest times. Ancient Greeks used them for padding their shields and armor as well as for bathing and scrubbing floors and furniture. They were used as mops and paint brushes by the Romans, and at one time were used as drinking cups, the user squeezing their contents into his upturned mouth.

At the crucifixion a bystander used a sponge fastened to a reed to lift vinegar to the lips of Jesus.

Corals. The central and western Mediterranean has a red coral, *Corallium nobile,* that has varied greatly in commercial value through the years. Slender twigs from its branching colonies are extensively used in making jewelry. Coral is mentioned by both Job and Ezekiel (Job 28:18; Ezek. 27:16).

Mollusks. The occurrence of mollusks is implied by numerous Old Testament references to the use of purple cloth. A dye, "Tyrian purple," was obtained from a glandular fluid secreted by several members of the genera Murex and Purpura.

Pearls are mentioned in several instances in the New Testament. They are produced by certain bivalve mollusks such as the clam and oyster and have always been highly esteemed. Jesus warned against casting pearls before swine in Matthew 7:6, and in Matthew 13:45,46. He likened the kingdom of heaven to "one pearl of great price" for which a merchant was willing to give his all.

Fishes. A goodly number of references to fish occur in both Old and New Testaments, but in no instance is a particular species implied in any way. They are mentioned in all five books of the Pentateuch.

Among kinds certainly known in Bible times as a food fish is the striped mullet, *Mugil cephalus,* found in the Mediterranean and numerous other waters. Another variety that was likely known was the barbel which is represented by various species, from England eastward to the East Indies.

One of the disasters meted out to the Egyptians was the destruction of the fish, and the fact that

The chameleon of Palestine. © MPS

later on the Israelites lusted for the fish they had eaten while in Egypt signifies their importance as food. Several references to a fish gate imply the existence of a fish market. The use of line and hook is referred to in the Old Testament and the use of the net is mentioned in both Old and New Testaments. The numerous references to fish and to fishing in the Gospels give clear indication of their commercial importance in Palestine.

Amphibians. Two species of frogs and three of toads are reported from Egypt. One frog, *Rana esculenta,* is found all over Europe, in Syria and in Palestine, as well as in Egypt. One of the plagues visited on Pharaoh was a horde of frogs. Unclean spirits are likened to them in Revelation 16:13.

Reptiles. The Northern Viper or Adder, *Vipera berus,* is common in Europe and members of the same genus are found in Africa. In any case, the context in which the word "adder" occurs clearly implies a poisonous reptile. Because this English word is used for several different Hebrew words it is difficult to determine present-day species to which it applied.

Asp. Four times the word "asp" is used in such a manner as to indicate a poisonous reptile. There is general agreement that the Egyptian Cobra, *Naja haje,* is meant. This reptile was used by Pharaoh Tutankamen as his imperial symbol. It attains a length of at least eight and a half feet, prefers warm, dry regions with water available, and is found along the north and east coasts of Africa. A subspecies occurs in part of the Arabian Peninsula.

Chameleon. A family of large lizards, the Varanidae, are represented by species in Africa and Asia. The Nile Monitor, *Varanus niloticus* is the largest four-footed reptile in Africa with the exception of the crocodile, and attains a length of six feet. Nile monitors eat a wide variety of food, and deposit their eggs in termite nests.

The RSV uses "chameleon" rather than "mole" in Leviticus 11:30.

Cockatrice. Some dreaded reptile is evidently meant in Isaiah 11:8 and 59:5, and Jeremiah 8:17. Although basilisks have been suggested, they are harmless despite myths to the contrary.

Gecko. The word "ferret" of Leviticus 11:30 is translated "gecko" in the RSV and ASV. The one intended may be *Ptyodactylus lobatus,* although any of a number of species of three generally-nocturnal lizards may have been meant.

Lizard. Mentioned once in the Bible (Lev. 11:30), this animal may refer to the commonest lizard of Palestine, the *Agama stellio,* belonging to a family of dragon-lizards. These animals are diurnal, possess crests and dewlaps, and somewhat resemble the iguanids.

Serpent. The Bible has many references to serpents which imply poisonous qualities. No single species can be identified with certainty. The serpent is commonly used as a symbol of evil and Satan was called a serpent. Snakes do not use legs for locomotion, and are evidently meant rather than lizards.

Tortoise. This unclean animal of Leviticus 11:29 is rendered "great lizard" in the RSV. The Arabian thorny-tailed, color-changing lizard (*Uromastix spinipes*) is common in Egypt, and members of the same genus occur in Syria and Arabia.

Viper. Poisonous serpents of several varieties are probably meant where this term is used. C.M.

ANISE (See Plants of the Bible)

ANKLET, an ornament for the ankles, consisting of metal or glass spangles, worn by women. Sometimes anklets were linked together by an ankle chain. See DRESS.

ANNA (ăn'à, Gr. form of *Hannah, grace*), daughter of Phanuel of the tribe of Asher. Widowed after seven years of marriage, she became a prophetess, and at the age of 84, when the infant Jesus was brought into the Temple to be dedicated, she recognized and proclaimed Him as the Messiah (Luke 2:36-38).

ANNAS (ăn'ăs, Gr. for Hanan, contraction for Hananiah, *merciful, gracious;* called "Ananos" by Josephus). In his 37th year, about A.D. 6, he was appointed high priest by Quirinius, governor of Syria, and was deposed about A.D. 15 by Valerius Gratus, governor of Judea. His five sons became high priests, and he was father-in-law of Caiaphas, the high priest (Jos. *Antiq.* XVIII. 2,1 and 2; John 18:13). He and Caiaphas are described as the high priests when John the Baptist began his public ministry (Luke 3:2), perhaps because as head of the family Annas was the most influential priest and still bore the title. That may explain why when Jesus was arrested He was first led to Annas (John 18:13), and after a preliminary hearing was sent bound to Caiaphas (John 18:24). That may also be the reason why Annas is called the high priest in Acts 4:6, when Peter and John were arrested, although Caiaphas was very probably the actual high priest.

ANOINT, to apply oil to a person or thing, a practice common in the East. Anointing was of three kinds: ordinary, sacred, and medical. Ordinary anointing with scented oils was a common toilet operation (Ruth 3:3; Ps. 104:15; Prov. 27:9). It was discontinued during a time of mourning (II Sam. 14:2; Dan. 10:3; Matt. 6:17). Guests were anointed as a mark of respect (Luke 7:46; Ps. 23:5). The dead were prepared for burial by anointing (Mark 14:8; 16:1). The leather of shields was rubbed with oil to keep it from cracking (Isa. 21:5).

Sacred anointing had as its purpose the dedicating of things or persons to God. Jacob anointed the stone he had used for a pillow at Bethel (Gen. 28:18). The Tabernacle and its furniture were anointed (Exod. 30:22-29). Prophets (I Kings 19:16; I Chron. 16:22), priests (Exod. 28:41; 29:7; Lev. 8:12,30), and kings (Saul—I Sam. 9:16; 10:1;

David—I Sam. 16:1,12,13; II Sam. 2:7; Solomon —I Kings 1:34; Jehu—I Kings 19:16; among others) were anointed, the oil symbolizing the Holy Spirit, and they were thus set apart and empowered for a particular work in the service of God. "The Lord's anointed" was the common term for a theocratic king (I Sam. 12:3; Lam. 4:20).

Messiah, from the Hebrew word *mashah,* and Christ, from the Greek *chrein,* means "the anointed one." The word is twice used of the coming Redeemer in the OT (Ps. 2:2; Dan. 9:25,26). Jesus was anointed with the Holy Spirit at His baptism (John 1:32,33), marking Him as the Messiah of the OT (Luke 4:18,21; Acts 9:22; 17:2,3; 18:5, 28). His disciples, through union with Him, are anointed with the Holy Spirit, too (II Cor. 1:21; I John 2:20).

Medical anointing, not necessarily with oil, was customary for the sick and wounded (Isa. 1:6; Luke 10:34). Mark 6:13 and James 5:14 speak of the use of anointing oil by disciples of Jesus.   S.B.

ANTELOPE (See Animals, Gazelles)

ANTICHRIST (Gr. *antíchristos, against* or *instead of Christ*). The word antichrist may mean either an enemy of Christ or one who usurps Christ's name and rights. The word is found only in I John 2:18,22; 4:3; II John 7, but the idea conveyed by the word appears throughout Scripture. It is evident from the way John and Paul refer to the Antichrist that they took for granted a tradition well known at the time (I John 4:3 "ye have heard," II Thess. 2:6 "ye know").

The OT gives evidence of a general Jewish belief in a hostile person or power who in the end time would bring an attack against God's people — an attack which would be crushed by Jehovah or His Messiah. Psalm 2 gives a picture of the rebellion of the world kingdoms "against the Lord and against his anointed." The same sort of contest is described in Ezekiel 38,39 and in Zechariah 12-14. In the Book of Daniel there are vivid descriptions of the Antichrist which find their echo in the writings of the apostles (cf., e.g., II Thess. 2:4 with Daniel 11:36f, and Rev. 13:1-8 with Daniel 7:8, 20f, 8:24, 11:28,30).

In His eschatological discourse Christ warns against "the false Christs" and "the false prophets" who would lead astray, if possible, even the elect (Matt. 24:24; Mark 13:22). In Matthew 24:15 He refers to "the abomination of desolation" spoken of by Daniel.

Paul gives us, in II Thessalonians 2:1-12, a very full description of the working of Antichrist, under the name of the "man of sin," in which he draws on the language and imagery of the OT. The Thessalonian Christians seem to have been under the erroneous impression that the "day of Christ" was at hand, and Paul tells them that before that day could come two things would have to take place, an apostasy and the revelation of the man of sin, the son of perdition. The "mystery of iniquity," ne says, is already at work, but is held in check by some restraining person or power. With the removal of this restraining force, the man of sin is revealed. He will oppose and exalt himself above God and will actually sit in the temple of God and claim to be God. With Satanic power he will perform signs and lying wonders, bringing great deception to men who reject God's truth. In spite of his extraordinary power, however, the Lord Jesus at His parousia will slay him with the breath of His mouth.

In I John 2:18 John shows that the coming of the Antichrist was an event generally expected by the Church. It is apparent, however, that he is more concerned about directing the attention of Christians to antichristian forces already at work ("even now are there many antichrists"). He says that teachers of erroneous views of the person of Christ (evidently Gnostic and Ebonite) are antichrists (I John 2:22; 4:3; II John 7).

In the Book of Revelation the Beast of Revelation 17:8 recalls the horned Beast of Daniel 7,8. He claims and is accorded divine homage, and makes war on God's people. For a period of three and one half years he rules over the earth, and is finally destroyed by the Lord in a great battle. With his defeat the contest of good and evil comes to its final decision.   S.B.

ANTI-LEBANON (See Lebanon)

ANTIOCH (ăn'tĭ-ŏk, Gr. *Antiócheia*). 1. Antioch in Syria, the capital of Syria, built in 301 B.C. by Seleucus Nicator, the founder of the Seleucid Empire, which had been the Asiatic part of the vast empire of Alexander the Great. It was the greatest of 16 Antiochs he founded in honor of his father, Antiochus. Situated on the left bank of the Orontes, about 15 miles from the Mediterranean, with Seleucia as its port, the river being navigable up to the city, it was a great commercial center, with caravan roads converging upon it from the East. The city was set in a broad and fertile valley, shielded by majestic snow-covered mountains, and was called Antioch "the Beautiful and the Golden." In 65 B.C. the Romans took the city and made it the capital of the Roman province of Syria. Seleucid kings and early Roman emperors extended and adorned the city until it became the third largest in the Roman Empire (after Rome and Alexandria), with a population, in the first century A.D., of about 500,000. A cosmopolitan city from its

Antioch on the Orontes River, at the foot of Mount Silpius, in Syria. © MPS

In 1916 announcement was made of the finding of what has come to be known as "The Chalice of Antioch," found by Arabs in or near Antioch. It is a plain silver cup surrounded by an outer shell decorated with vines and the figures of Christ and the Apostles, and is set on a solid silver base. The cup was vigorously claimed to be the Holy Grail, used by Jesus at the Last Supper, and the figures on the shell were interpreted as first century portraits, but the authenticity of the chalice has been called in question. Serious scholars have, however, virtually proved that the most that can be said is that it may be a piece of early Christian silver from the fourth or fifth century, and had nothing to do with the Last Supper in Jerusalem. (For a careful study of this matter, see esp. H. H. Arnason, "The History of the Chalice of Antioch," BA, Vol. IV, No. 4 (Dec. 1941) and Vol. V, No. 1 (Feb. 1942).   S.B.

2. Antioch near Pisidia, a town in southern Asia Minor, founded by Seleucus Nicator, and named in honor of his father, Antiochus. It was situated in Phrygia, not far from Pisidia, and was therefore called Antioch toward Pisidia and Pisidian Antioch to distinguish it from the other cities of the same name. In 25 B.C. it became a part of the Roman province of Galatia. Soon after, it became the capital of southern Galatia and was made a Roman colony. The Romans made it a strong garrison center to hold down the surrounding wild tribes. Paul and Barnabas preached in the synagogue there on their first missionary journey, but the Jews, jealous of the many Gentile converts that were made, drove the missionaries from the city to Iconium, and followed them even to Lystra (Acts 13:14-14:19). On Paul's return journey he revisited Antioch to establish the disciples. He must have visited Antioch on his second journey (Acts 16:6), and on his third (Acts 18:23).   S.B.

The famous Chalice of Antioch. © F K

foundation, its inhabitants included many Jews, who were given privileges similar to those of the Greeks. Its citizens were a vigorous, aggressive race, famous for their commercial aptitude, their licentiousness, and the scurrility of their wit.

Antioch has an important place in the early history of Christianity. One of the original deacons of the Apostolic church was Nicolas, a proselyte of Antioch (Acts 6:5). The first Gentile church, the mother of all the others, was founded there. Many fugitive Christians scattered at the death of Stephen went to Antioch, where they inaugurated a new era by preaching not only to Hellenist Jews but to "the Greeks also" (Acts 11:20). The Jerusalem church sent Barnabas to assist in the work, and he, after laboring there for a while, summoned Paul from Tarsus to assist him. After working there for a year, they were sent with relief to the famine-stricken saints in Jerusalem. The disciples were called Christians first in Antioch (Acts 11:19-26), a designation probably coming from the populace, who were well-known for their invention of nicknames. The church at Antioch sent Paul and his companions out on his three missionary journeys Acts 13:1ff; 15:36ff; 18:23), and he reported to it on his return from the first two (Acts 14:26ff; 18:22). It submitted the question of the circumcision of Gentile converts to a council at Jerusalem (Acts 15), winning for the church at large a great victory over Judean narrowness.

Antioch gave rise to a school of thought distinguished by literal interpretation of the Scriptures. Between 252 and 380 ten Councils were held there. The city was taken and destroyed in A.D. 538 by the Persians, rebuilt by the Roman emperor Justinian shortly afterward, and in A.D. 635 was taken by the Moslems, by whom it has since, except for a brief period, been held. The place, now called Antakiyeh, is today unimportant, with a population of about 42,000.

Coin from Antioch in Pisidia (Asia Minor). Right, Antiochus III the Great.

ANTIOCHUS (ăn-tī'ŏkŭs, Gr. *withstander*). 1. Antiochus III, the Great (223-187 B.C.), king of Syria and sixth ruler of the Seleucid dynasty. By his victory over the Egyptians in 198 B.C. Syria gained control of Palestine. He was decisively defeated by the Romans in 190 and thereby lost control over Asia Minor. He was murdered by a mob while plundering a temple.

2. Antiochus IV (Epiphanes), son of Antiochus III and eighth ruler of the Seleucid dynasty, 175-163 B.C. (I Macc. 1:10; 6:16). In his attempt to Hellenize the Jews he had a pig sacrificed on the altar in Jerusalem, forbade circumcision, and destroyed all the OT books he could find. These outrages involved him in the Maccabean war in which the Syrian armies were repeatedly defeated by the brilliant Judas Maccabeus.

3. Antiochus V (Eupator), son of the above. He reigned as a minor for two years and then was slain.

ANTIPAS (ăn'tĭ pàs, Gr. *Antípas*), a contraction of Antipater. 1. An early Christian martyr of Pergamum, described as "my faithful martyr" (Rev. 2:13).

2. Herod Antipas, son of Herod the Great, and brother of Philip the tetrarch and of Archelaus, both, like him, rulers of parts of Palestine. See Herod.

ANTIPATER (See Herod)

ANTIPATRIS (ăn-tĭp'à-trĭs, Gr. *Antípatris, belonging to Antipater*), a city built (or rebuilt) by Herod the Great, and named after his father Antipater. It lay on the road between Jerusalem and Caesarea. There is only one reference to it in Scripture, in connection with Paul's being taken, following his arrest in Jerusalem, from that city to Caesarea (Acts 23:31). It marked the NW limit of Judea.

ANTITYPE. By a type, in a Biblical sense, is meant a picture or object lesson by which God taught His people concerning His grace and redemptive power. An antitype is that which is represented by the type.

The castle Tower of Antonia in Jerusalem. © MPS

ANTONIA, TOWER OF, a castle connected with the Temple at Jerusalem, rebuilt by Herod the Great and named by him in honor of Mark Anthony, his patron. A Roman legion was stationed in the castle to guard against excesses on the part of the people. When Paul was seized in the Temple by the Jews, he was carried to this castle, from the stairs of which he addressed the people (Acts 21:30ff).

ANTOTHIJAH (ăn'tō-thī'jà, Heb. *'anthōthîyâh*), a son of Shashak, a Benjamite (I Chron. 8:24,25).

ANTOTHITE (ăn'tŏth-ĭt), inhabitant of Anathoth; ASV, "Anathothite"; RSV, "of Anathoth" (I Chron. 11:28; 12:3).

ANTS (See Insects)

ANUB (ā'nŭb, Heb. *'ānûv*), a son of Coz, descendant of Judah (I Chron. 4:8).

ANVIL (ăn'vĭl). The Heb. *pa'am* originally meant strike, hit. The word occurs in several senses in the OT; only once with the meaning "anvil," Isaiah 41:7, in a passage concerning the encouragement given by one workman to another.

APELLES (à-pĕl'ēz, Gr. *Apellés*), an approved Christian at Rome to whom Paul sent a greeting (Rom. 16:10).

APES (See Animals)

APHARSATHCHITES (ăf'àr-săth'kĭts), Ezra 4:9; *Apharsakites* (à-fàr'săk-ĭts), Ezra 5:6; 6:6, people in Samaria who protested to Darius against the rebuilding of the Temple in Jerusalem. RSV translates "governors," considering the word as the name of a class of officials rather than of a tribe.

APHARSITES (à-fàr'sĭts), Ezra 4:9, people in Samaria who protested against the rebuilding of the Temple in Jerusalem. RSV translates "Persians."

APHEK (ā'fĕk, Heb. *'āpēk, strength, fortress*). 1. A city NE of Beirut, identified with Afqa (Josh. 13:4).

2. A city in the territory of Asher, never wrested from its Canaanite inhabitants (Josh.19:30; Judges 1:31).

3. A town in the Plain of Sharon (Josh. 12:18), probably within 25 miles of Shiloh (I Sam. 4:1,12). The Philistines may have encamped here before the first battle with Israel at Ebenezer.

4. A town W of the Jordan in the Plain of Jezreel. The Philistines used it as a base in two important campaigns against Israel (I Sam. 1:4, 29:1). It may also have been the town where a wall fell and killed 27,000 of Benhadad's soldiers (I Kings 20:26-30), and where, according to prophecy, the Syrians were to be destroyed (II Kings 13:14-19).

APHEKAH (à-fē'kà, Heb. *'āphēqâh*), a city in the hill country of Judah (Josh. 15:53) whose location is unknown.

APHIAH (à-fī'à, Heb. *ăphîah*), one of Saul's ancestors (I Sam. 9:1).

APHIK (See Aphek)

APHRAH (ăf'rà). "The house of Aphrah" is named in parallelism with Gath in Micah 1:10. ASV, RSV have "Beth-le-aphrah."

APHSES (ăf'sēz), a Levite chief of the 18th of the 24 courses in the service of the Temple (I Chron. 24:15). ASV, RSV, Happizzez.

APOCALYPSE (See Apocalyptic Literature)

APOCALYPTIC LITERATURE, a type of Jewish and Christian religious writing which developed between the testaments and had its roots in Old Testament prophecy. The word "apocalyptic," derived from the Greek word *apokalypsis* in Revelation 1:1, means "revelation" or "unveiling," and is applied to these writings because they contain alleged revelations of the secret purposes of God, the end of the world, and the establishment of God's Kingdom on earth.

After the days of the post-exilic prophets, God no longer spoke to Israel through the living voice of inspired prophecy. The prophetic forecasts of the coming of God's Kingdom and the salvation of Israel had not been fulfilled. Instead of God's Kingdom, a succession of evil kingdoms ruled over Israel: Medo-Persia, Greece, and finally Rome. Evil reigned supreme. The hope of God's Kingdom grew dim. God no longered offered words of comfort and salvation to His people.

The apocalypses were written to meet this religious need. Following the pattern of canonical Daniel, various unknown authors wrote alleged revelations of God's purposes which explained present evils, comforted Israel in her sufferings and afflictions, and gave fresh assurances that God's Kingdom would shortly appear. Many modern critics place Daniel in these times, but there are valid reasons for an earlier date.

The outstanding apocalypses are *I Enoch* or *Ethiopic Enoch*, a composite book written during the first two centuries B.C., which is notable for its description of the heavenly Son of Man; *Jubilees*, an alleged revelation to Moses of the history of the world from creation to the end, written in the second century B.C.; the *Assumption of Moses*, late first century B.C.; *Fourth Ezra* or *Second Esdras* and the *Apocalypse of Baruch*, both written after the fall of Jerusalem in A.D. 70, and reflecting upon the tragic fall of God's people; *Second Enoch* or *Slavonic Enoch*, date uncertain. Other writings have been discovered among the so-called Dead Sea Scrolls which have not yet been made available for study.

A number of other writings are usually included in the discussion of apocalyptic literature, although they are not, properly speaking, apocalypses. *The Testaments of the Twelve Patriarchs*, written in the second century B.C., imitating Old Testament predictive prophecy rather than apocalyptic, contains important eschatological materials. The 17th and 18th *Psalms of Solomon*, first century B.C., portray the hope of the coming of the Lord's Anointed to establish God's Kingdom. The *Sibylline Oracles*, which follows the pattern of Greek oracular literature, also contain eschatological passages.

Certain characteristics mark these apocalypses. 1. *Revelation*. They describe alleged revelations of God's purposes given through the media of dreams, visions, or journeys to heaven by which the seer learns the secrets of God's world and the future. 2. *Imitation*. These writings seldom embody any genuine subjective visionary experiences. Their "revelations" have become a literary form imitating the visions of the prophets in a thinly veiled literary fiction. 3. *Pseudonymity*. These books, although actually written close to New Testament times, are usually attributed to some Old Testament saint who lived long ago. Pseudonymity was employed as a means of validating the message of these authors to their own generation. Since God was no longer speaking through the spirit of prophecy, no man could speak in his own name or directly in the name of the Lord. Instead, the apocalyptists placed their "revelations" in the mouths of Old Testament saints. 4. *Symbolism*. These works employ an elaborate symbolism similar to that appearing in Daniel as a means of conveying their predictions of the future. 5. *Pseudo-predictive*. The authors take their stand in the distant past and rewrite history under the guise of prophecy down to their own day when the end of the world and the Kingdom of God were expected shortly to come.

There are distinct similarities, but also even more important differences between canonical and noncanonical apocalypses. The visions of Daniel provide the archetype which the later apocalypses imitate, and the Revelation of John records visions given to the apostle in similar symbolic forms. Both Daniel and the Revelation contain revelations conveyed through symbolism; but they differ from non-canonical apocalypses in that they are genuine experiences rather than imitative literary works, are not pseudonymous, and do not rewrite history under the guise of prophecy.

The importance of these apocalyptic writings is that they reveal to us first century Jewish ideas about God, evil, and history, and disclose Jewish hopes for the future and the coming of God's Kingdom. They show us what such terms as the Kingdom of God, Messiah, the Son of Man, etc., meant to first century Jews to whom our Lord addressed his Gospel of the Kingdom.   G.E.L.

APOCRYPHA. Interspersed among the canonical books of the Old Testament in the old Latin Vulgate Bible are certain additional books and chapters. It is to these that Protestant usage generally assigns the term "Apocrypha." In English versions the Apocrypha are usually presented as 15 separate books. (See below for individual treatment of these.)

At the Council of Trent (1546) the Roman Catholic Church received as canonical all the additional materials in the Vulgate, except for I and II Esdras and the Prayer of Manasseh. That decision was taken, in contradiction of the best tradition of even the Roman Church, by way of reaction to the Reformers, who recognized as divinely inspired and, therefore, as their infallible rule of faith and practice only those books which were in the canon of the Jews (cf. esp., Josephus, *Contra Apionem* 1:8), the canon sanctioned by the Lord Jesus Christ.

I Esdras: It is called III Esdras in post-Trentian editions of the Vulgate, where the canonical Ezra and Nehemiah are called I and II Esdras ("Esdras" being the Greek form of Ezra). Except for the story of the wisdom contest (3:1-5:6), the contents are a version of the history narrated in II Chronicles 35-36:23, Ezra, and Nehemiah 7:73-8:12, embracing the period from the Josianic Passover to Ezra's reformation. Nothing is known of the author (or translator) of the LXX form except that he produced it some time before Josephus, who in his *Antiquities* strangely prefers it to the canonical record.

II Esdras: The Vulgate designation is IV Esdras. Some call it Apocalyptic Esdras because the central kernel (chapters 3-14) presents seven revelations allegedly given to Ezra in exile, several in visionary form and of largely eschatological import. To this original, composed by an unknown Jew, probably near the end of the first century A.D., and later translated into Greek Christian authors subsequently added in Greek, chapters 1, 2, 15, and 16. The Jewish original offers its apocalyptic prospects as an answer to the theodicy problem, acutely posed for Judaism by the fall of Jerusalem in A.D. 70. The Christian addition assigns the casting off of Israel in favor of the Gentiles to Israel's apostasy.

Tobit: This romantic tale with religious didactic purpose was composed at least as early as the second century B.C. It is named after its hero, who is pictured as an eighth century B.C. Naphtalite carried into exile to Nineveh. His story becomes entwined with that of his kinswoman Sarah, exiled in Ecbatana. The tragedies of both are remedied through the adventures of Tobit's son Tobias, whom Sarah marries, and all under the angel Raphael's supervision. Prayer, fasting, and almsgiving are stressed but unfortunately in a context of auto-soterism.

Judith: Judith, like Tobit, is Jewish historical fiction with a religious moral. The historical setting is an anachronistic amalgam, including elements from two centuries (seventh to fifth) of Israelite fortunes. Using Jael-like tactics, Judith, a beautiful Jewess, saves besieged "Bethulia" by slaying Holofernes, the enemy commander. Possibly the grotesque anachronisms are intentional; Luther interpreted it as an allegory of Israel's triumphing, under God, over her enemies. The book evidences appreciation of Israel's peculiar theocratic privileges but magnifies a ceremonial piety which would exceed the requirements of Moses. Some think it was composed to inspire zeal during the Maccabean revolt in the 2nd century B.C.

Additions to the Book of Esther: The canonical Hebrew text of Esther has 163 verses; the Greek version has 270, the additional material being divided into seven sections and distributed at the appropriate points throughout the narrative, thus: A. before 1:1; B. after 3:13; C. and D. after 4:17; E. after 8:12; F. after 10:3. Inasmuch as genuine Esther contains explicit references to neither God nor traditional Jewish religious practices other than fasting, it is significant that prayers of Mordecai and Esther are included in the additions and also frequent mention of God. The Greek additions contradict details of canonical Esther and contain other obviously fictional elements. They appeared as an appendix to Esther in the Vulgate and this fusion of disconnected fragments constitutes a "book" in our Apocrypha.

The Wisdom of Solomon: The LXX uses this title; the Vulgate, *Liber Sapientiae.* The author, who identifies himself with the figure of Solomon, apparently was an Alexandrian Jew writing in Greek in the first century B.C. or A.D. (some, however, judge the book of composite authorship). The influence of Greek philosophy is evidenced by the dependence on *logos* speculations in the treatment of personified Wisdom and by the acceptance of various pagan teachings: the creation of the world out of pre-existent matter; the pre-existence of souls; the impedimentary character of the body; perhaps too, the doctrine of emanation. In tracing Wisdom's government of history from Adam to Moses, numerous fanciful and false embellishments of the biblical record are intruded.

Ecclesiasticus: This second representative of the wisdom genre of literature among the Apocrypha is also called after its author The Wisdom of Jesus ben Sira. Written in Hebrew, 180 B.C. or earlier, it was translated into Greek for the Alexandrian Jews by the author's grandson, c. 130 B.C. Ben Sira, apparently a professional scribe and teacher, patterned his *magnum opus* after the style of Proverbs. In it he expounds the nature of Wisdom, applying its counsel to all areas of social and religious life. Though often reflecting sentiments of the canonical books, Ben Sira also echoes the ethical motivations of pagan wisdom literature. Moreover, he contradicts biblical soteriology by teaching that almsgiving makes atonement for sin.

Baruch: This pseudepigraphic book is evidently composite. The first part (1:1-3:8), dated by some as early as the 3rd century B.C., was probably written in Hebrew, as was possibly also the remainder, which is of later origin. 1:1-3:8, composed in a prophetic prose, purports to have been produced by Jeremiah's secretary in Babylonian exile and sent to Jerusalem. It is a confession of national sin (in imitation of Daniel's) petitioning for removal of divine favor. Actually Baruch went to Egypt with Jeremiah and there is no evidence that he was ever in Babylonia. From 3:9 the book is poetry. 3:9-4:4 recalls Israel to wisdom. In 4:5-5:9 Jerusalem laments her exiled children, but assurances of restoration are offered.

Epistle to Jeremiah: In some Greek and Syriac manuscripts this "epistle" is found after Lamentations; in others and in the Vulgate it is attached to Baruch and hence appears as a 6th chapter of Ba-

ruch in most English editions. A superscription describes it as an epistle sent by Jeremiah to certain captives about to be led into Babylon. Cf. Jeremiah 29:1ff. The true author is unknown and the original language uncertain. A baffling reference to "seven generations" of exile (contrast Jer. 29:10) has figured in speculation as to its date which was no later than the second century B.C. It ridicules the inanity of idol worship as represented by the Bel cult and so served as warning to Jews and polemic against Gentiles.

The Prayer of Azariah and the Song of the Three Young Men. This is one of three sections (see also Susanna and Bel and the Dragon) added to the canonical Daniel in the "Septuagint" translation (whether from the first, i.e., probably by the early second century B.C., or in a later edition is not known) and afterwards in Theodotion's Greek Version. From the latter Jerome translated the additions into Latin, commenting that they did not exist in manuscripts of the Hebrew-Aramaic original of Daniel.

Between 3:23 and 3:24 of canonical Daniel both Greek and Latin Versions insert: a. a prayer of national confession with supplication for deliverance which Daniel's friend Azariah (cf. Dan. 1:7) offers while he and his two companions are in the fiery furnace; b. a psalm of praise (dependent on Pss. 148 and 136), uttered by the three; and c. a narrative framework, containing details not warranted by the genuine Daniel. This section is itself perhaps of composite authorship and was probably written in Hebrew.

Susanna: In the Vulgate, Susanna follows canonical Daniel as chapter 13; in Greek manuscripts it is prefixed to chapter 1. Two crucial puns at the climax of the tale suggest it was composed in Greek but there is no consensus. Its provenance and date are unknown; Alexandria about 100 B.C. is one theory. The story relates how two Israelite elders in Babylon, their salacious advances having been resisted by Susanna, falsely accuse her of adultery. But young Daniel effects Susanna's deliverance and the elders' doom by ensnaring them in contradictory testimony.

Bel and the Dragon: These fables ridiculing heathenism appear as Chapter 13 of Daniel in Greek and as chapter 14 in the Vulgate. They date from the first or second century B.C.; their original language is uncertain. Daniel plays detective to expose to Cyrus the fraud of the priests who clandestinely consumed the food-offerings of Bel (Baal, i.e., Marduk). After destroying Bel, Daniel concocts a recipe that explodes a sacred dragon. Consigned to a den of lions Daniel is miraculously fed and delivered.

The Prayer of Manasseh: According to II Chronicles 33:11ff, when the wicked king Manasseh had been carried into exile he repented and God restored him to Jerusalem. Verses 18, 19 refer to sources which contained Manasseh's prayer of repentance. The origin of the Apocryphal book which purports to be that prayer is unknown; possibly it was produced in Palestine a century or two before Christ. It contains confession of sin and petition for forgiveness. The view is expressed that certain sinless men need no repentance. In Greek manuscripts the Prayer appears in the Odes attached to the Psalter. In the old Vulgate it came to be placed after II Chronicles.

The First Book of the Maccabees: Beginning with the accession of Antiochus Epiphanes (176 B.C.), the history of the Jewish struggle for religous-political liberation is traced to the death of

Simon (136 B.C.) in this, our most valuable source for that period. It narrates the exploits of the priest Mattathias and of his sons, Judas, Jonathan, and Simon, who successively led the Hasidim to remarkable victories. To Judas was given the surname "Maccabee," afterwards applied to his brothers, and four books (I-IV Maccabees). The author wrote in Hebrew and was a contemporary of John Hyrcanus, son and successor of Simon. According to one theory the last three chapters were added and the whole re-edited after the destruction of the Temple.

The Second Book of the Maccabees: Independent of I Maccabees, this history partly overlaps it, extending from the last year of Seleucus IV (176 B.C.) to the defeat of Nicanor by Judas (161 B.C.). The author states that he has epitomized the (now lost) five-volume history of Jason of Cyrene (2:23). Both Jason and the Epitomist wrote in Greek. Suggested dates for II Maccabees vary from c. 120 B.C. to the early first century A.D. Two introductory letters (1:1-2:18) were perhaps lacking in the first edition. While there are various errors in I Maccabees, legendary exaggeration is characteristic of the moralizing II Maccabees. It also inculcates doctrinal errors like the propriety of prayers for the dead. M.G.K.

APOLLONIA (ăp′ŏ-lō′nĭ-à, Gr. *Apollonía, pertaining to Apollo*), a town of Macedonia on the celebrated Egnatian Way, 28 miles W of Amphipolis and 38 miles E of Thessalonica (Acts 17:1).

APOLLOS (à-pŏl′ŏs, Gr. *Apollós,* the short form of Apollonius), an Alexandrian Jew, described in Acts 18:24,25 as a man mighty in the Scriptures, eloquent, fervent in the spirit, and instructed in the way of the Lord, but knowing only the baptism of John. He came to Ephesus after Paul had visited that city on his second missionary journey and there met Aquila and Priscilla, who had been left there to labor pending the apostle's return. They heard him speak boldly in the synagogue, and observing that he was deficient in his knowledge of the Gospel, they "expounded unto him the way of God more perfectly" (Acts 18:26). It is not easy to determine from the brief account in Acts the precise character of his religious knowledge. Before long he went to Achaia with letters of recommendation from the Ephesian brethren. When he arrived in Corinth he "helped them much which had believed through grace: For he mightily convinced the Jews, and that publicly, shewing by the Scriptures that Jesus was Christ" (Acts 18:27, 28).

Apollos' gifts and methods of presenting the Gospel were undoubtedly different from those of Paul, and he put the impress of his own mode of thinking upon many who heard him. Before long a party arose in the Corinthian church with the watch-word "I am of Apollos" (I Cor. 3:4). There does not, however, appear to have been any feeling of rivalry between Paul and Apollos. Paul urged Apollos to revisit Corinth (I Cor. 16:12), and he also asked Titus to help Apollos, apparently then in or on his way to Crete (Titus 3:13).

Luther suggested the theory, since accepted by many scholars, that Apollos was the writer of the Epistle to the Hebrews. S.B.

APOLLYON (See Abaddon)

APOSTASY (à-pŏs′tà-sē, Gr. *apostasía, a falling away, a withdrawal, a defection*). The Greek word is twice found in the NT, but in neither case is it rendered "apostasy" in the English Version. In Acts 21:21 Paul is falsely accused of teaching the Jews "to forsake Moses" (lit. "apostasy from Moses"). In II Thess. 2:3 Paul assures the Thessalonian Christians that the day of the Lord shall not come except the falling away (lit. "the apostasy") come first, and the man of sin be revealed. Apostasy, not in name but in fact, is often referred to in both testaments. OT Jews are rebuked for it. It is condemned in the Epistle of Jude. Biblical examples of it are Saul (I Sam. 15:11); Hymenaeus and Alexander (I Tim. 1:19,20); Demas (II Tim. 4:10).

APOSTLE (à-pŏs′l, Gr. *apóstolos; one sent forth, a messenger*), one chosen and sent with a special commission as the fully authorized representative of the sender.

In the NT the word appears in a twofold sense, as the official name of those 12 disciples whom Jesus chose to be with Him during the course of His ministry on earth, to see Him after His resurrection, and to lay the foundations of His Church; and in a broader, non-official sense, to designate Christian messengers commissioned by a community — like Barnabas, who was sent forth as a missionary by the church at Antioch (Acts 13:3). Once in the NT Jesus is called an apostle (Heb. 3:1), obviously in the sense referred to by Him in John 17:18. The Twelve were chosen by Jesus early in His Galilean ministry. Some had previously been disciples of John the Baptist (John 1:35-42). Four, at least, were fishermen (Luke 5:1-11); and one, a tax-collector (Matt. 9:9-13). Their names are given by each of the Synoptists (Matt. 10:2-4; Mark 3:14-19; Luke 6:13-16) and by the author of Acts (1:13).

In the Gospels they are usually called disciples, because as long as Jesus was with them they were still learners; after that, they are invariably referred to as apostles. Jesus gave much attention to their spiritual training; yet to the time of His resurrection, they failed to understand His mission, thinking that He was going to set up a temporal kingdom (Matt. 20:20-28; Mark 10:35-45). More than once they quarreled as to which of them should be greatest in that kingdom. It appears that, after the feeding of the 5,000, they fell in with the purpose of the multitude to make Jesus king by force (John 6:15). Though they accepted Jesus' Messianic claims, they could not understand the necessity of His death. All were on an equal footing, although three of them — Peter, James the son of Zebedee, and John — seem to have been somewhat closer to Jesus than the others; and Peter, by force of personal character, usually took the place of leadership. Peter, however, is nowhere in Scripture accorded a position of superiority or primacy. John is called the disciple whom Jesus loved (John 19:26; 20:2; 21:7,20). Judas betrayed the Lord into the hands of His enemies and then committed suicide. His place was later taken by Matthias (Acts 1:15-26). The apostles accompanied Jesus on His various preaching tours, went with Him to the Jewish feasts in Jerusalem, saw His wonderful works, and were privately instructed by Him. In spite of all this, when finally they saw Him arrested and crucified, as He had often foretold He would be, they all forsook Him and fled (Matt. 26:56). It is plain that they did not expect His resurrection, which Jesus had also frequently foretold, and that they were convinced of it only by the very plainest proofs furnished by Himself. It was only when this became undeniable, that light entered their minds and they saw Him for what He is, the Saviour of the world. Between the resurrection and the ascension Jesus spent much time opening their minds to understand the Scriptures (Luke 24:45; Acts 1:2).

The experience of Pentecost, ten days after the Lord's ascension, made them altogether different men, so that henceforth they fearlessly gave witness with power to the life, death, and resurrection of Jesus. At first, the preaching of the Gospel was confined to Jerusalem, with Peter and John taking the lead. Their first mission outside of Jerusalem was to Samaria, where many believed (Acts 8:5-25). Persecution, arrest, and even murder of one of their number by the Jewish religious leaders only caused them to increase their efforts.

The number of the Twelve was increased when Paul, the chief persecutor of the Christians, was miraculously converted and called to be an apostle. With the transfer of the center of church activity to Antioch, where an active church consisting of Jews and Gentiles was built up, Paul became the leading figure in the Church, and most of the remaining narrative of the Acts is occupied with his missionary journey to the Gentiles. When we leave him a prisoner in Rome, the Gospel witness has spread through all the Mediterranean world.

Of the missionary work of the other apostles we know almost nothing from Scripture. Tradition tells us a little, but not much that is trustworthy. The majority, it seems, died martyrs' deaths. In the early Church they consistently claimed to possess and exercised a unique authority, given them by Christ, to lay the foundations of the Church. They spoke, wrote, and acted with a consciousness that they were specially commissioned to represent their Lord and to give to needy men the message of redemption. Their office was not, and could not be, passed on to others. It was unique.   S.B.

APOSTOLIC AGE, the period in the history of the Christian Church when the Apostles were alive, beginning with the Day of Pentecost and ending with the death of the Apostle John near the end of the first century. Our only source for the period is the NT, especially Acts and the Epistles.

APOTHECARY (à-pŏth′ĕ-kâ-rē), a word found in Exodus 30:25,35; 37:29; II Chronicles 16:14; Nehemiah 3:8; Ecclesiastes 10:1 in the KJV, although the Hebrew word it renders is more accurately translated "perfumer," as it usually is in the RV; for the reference is not to the selling of drugs, but to the making of perfumes.

APPAIM (ăp′ā-ĭm, Heb. *'appayim*), son of Nadab, of the family of Hezron (I Chron. 2:30, 31).

APPAREL (See Dress)

APPEAL (à-pēl′). No provision is made in the OT for the reconsideration from a lower to a higher court of a case already tried. Exodus 18:26 shows, however, that Moses provided for lower and higher courts: "The hard cases they brought unto Moses, but every small matter they judged themselves." In Deuteronomy 17:8-13 provision is made for a lower court, under certain conditions, to seek instructions as to procedure from a higher court; but the decision itself belonged to the lower court.

In NT times the Roman government allowed each synagogue to exercise discipline over Jews, but only the Romans had the power of life and death. A Roman citizen, could, however, claim exemption from trial by the Jews and appeal to be tried by a Roman court. Paul did this when he said, "I appeal unto Caesar" (Acts 25:11).

APPEARING (See Eschatology)

APPELLATIO (ăp′ĕ-là′tĭō), the judicial process to which Paul resorted in Festus' court (Acts 25:1-12), was the act by which a litigant disputes a judgment, with the effect that the matter in dispute is automatically referred to a higher magistrate, nor-

Ruins along the Appian Way in Rome. The road is now surfaced for modern travel. © MPS

mally the one who appointed the magistrate from whose judgment appeal is made. Hence, in Paul's case, the appeal to Caesar. The litigant either pronounced the word *appello* as Paul did (Acts 25:11), or submitted the appeal in writing. In either case the presiding magistrate was under obligation to transmit the file, together with a personal report (*litterae dimissoriae*) to the competent higher magistrate.

APPHIA (ăf′ĭ-à, ăp′fĭ-à, Gr. *Apphía*), called "our beloved" in KJV, "our sister" in ASV, RSV, following a different text. A Christian of Colossae, by many believed to be the wife of Philemon and mother of Archippus (Philem. 2).

APPIAN WAY (ăp′ĭ-ăn), oldest of Roman roads, begun in 312 B.C. which originally ran from Rome to Capua and was later extended to Brundisium. Parts of the road are still in use. Paul must have traveled by it from Puteoli to Rome (Acts 28:13-16).

APPII FORUM (ăp′ĭ-ī fō′rŭm), a town on the Appian Way, a day's journey for sturdy travelers, 43 Roman (39½ English) miles from Rome toward Naples, where Paul was met by Christian brethren from Rome (Acts 28:15).

APPIUS, MARKET OF (See Appii Forum)

APPLE (See Plants)

"APPLE OF THE EYE" (Heb. *'ishôn, little man*, Deut. 32:10, Ps. 17:8, Prov. 7:2; *babhâh, gate*, Zech. 2:8; *bath ayin, daughter of the eye*, Lam. 2:18), the eyeball, or the pupil in its center, protected by the eyelids automatically closing when anything approaches too near. A symbol of that which is precious and protected.

APRON (See Dress)

AQABAH, GULF OF (à′kà-bà), the eastern arm of the Red Sea, between the Sinai Peninsula on the W and Midian on the E. Solomon's seaport of Eziongeber is located at its head, where the Wadi Arabah empties into it (I Kings 9:26).

An arm of the Gulf of Aqabah, looking toward the mountains of Midian. © MPS

Ruins of ancient aqueduct to Caesarea. JFW

AQUEDUCT (ăk'wĕ-dŭkt), a channel, covered or open, cut in the rock; or built of stone and sometimes faced with smooth cement; or carried on stone arches across depressions; to convey water from reservoirs, pools, cisterns or springs to the places where the water is to be used. The word does not occur in the Bible, but aqueducts may have existed even in pre-Israelite times, and were probably developed until the excellent work of the Nabatean period (100 B.C. to A.D. 100). The Roman period shows many fine examples. Hezekiah excavated the Siloam tunnel (conduit) to bring water into Jerusalem by a way which could not be stopped up in time of siege (II Kings 20:20, II Chron. 32:30), and this served the purpose of an aqueduct.

AQUILA (ăk'wĭ-là, Gr. *Akýlos;* Latin for "eagle"), a Jew whom Paul found at Corinth on his arrival from Athens (Acts 18:2,18,26; Rom. 16:3,4; I Cor. 16:19; II Tim. 4:19). A characteristic feature of Aquila and his wife Priscilla is that their names are always mentioned together. One in their interest in Christ, all that they accomplished was the result of that unity of spiritual nature and purpose. Having been expelled from Rome, they opened a tent-making business in Corinth. Because Paul followed the same trade, he was attracted to them. Being in full sympathy with Paul, they hospitably received him into their home, where he remained for a year and a half. Their willingness to "lay down their necks" for him earned the gratitude of all the churches. By their spiritual insight Apollos and many others were helped. Aquila and Priscilla had a "church in their house." Priscilla is usually named first: whether because she became a Christian first, or was more active, or for some other reason, is a matter of conjecture.

AR (àr, Heb. *'ār*), a city or district of Moab, referred to in a song quoted in Numbers 21:15, named in Deuteronomy 2:9,18,29 and in a prophecy of Isaiah (15:1).

ARA (ā'rà, Heb. *'ărā'*), son of Jether, of the tribe of Asher (I Chron. 7:38).

ARAB (ăr'ăb, Heb. *'ărāv*), a city in the hill country of Judah, probably er-Râbiyeh, south of Hebron (Josh. 15:52).

ARABAH (ăr'à-bà, Heb. *hā-ărāvâh, desert plain, steppe*), El-Ghor (the Jordan Valley) N of the Dead Sea; Wadi el-Arabah S of it. The remarkable rift running from Mt. Hermon to the Gulf of Aqabah. Its northern portion drains into the Dead Sea, and from above the Sea of Chinnereth (Gennesaret) is below sea level. South of the Dead Sea it is higher, and drains into the Gulf of Aqabah at Ezion-geber. The name is transliterated in KJV only in Joshua 18:18, but everywhere in ASV and RSV; where KJV usually has "plain," sometimes "desert," or "wilderness," once "champaign." The southern portion is referred to in Deuteronomy 1:1, 2:8. It is connected with the Dead Sea and the Sea of Galilee in Deuteronomy 3:17, 4:49, Joshua 3:16, 12:3, II Kings 14:25. It was used in the most extended sense, as appears from Deuter-

onomy 11:30, Joshua 8:14, 12:1, 18:18, II Samuel 2:29, 4:7, II Kings 25:4, Jeremiah 39:4, 52:7. The Arabah represents one of the major natural divisions of Palestine in Joshua 11:16, 12:8. It is a narrow valley of varying breadth; the productivity of various sections depends on availability of water; populated intermittently from early ages, it lay in the path of caravan traffic between the Arabian and Sinai deserts and Canaan to the N. The Israelites made stops here in their wilderness wanderings. Solomon got iron and copper from the mines of the Arabah, which was part of the extended kingdom of David and Solomon, when they ruled over Edom.

Typical desert scene in the Arabah. © MPS

ARABIA (à-rā'bĭ-à, Heb. *ha'erev, 'ărav, 'ărāv, steppe*), the large peninsula, consisting of Arabia Petraea, including Petra and the peninsula of Sinai; Arabia Deserta, the Syrian desert, between the Jordan Valley and the Euphrates; Arabia Felix, the S; bounded E, S and W by the Persian Gulf, Indian Ocean and Red Sea; N by the Fertile Crescent. Arabia is an arid steppe, rocky tableland with enough rainfall in the interior and south to support considerable population, yet its resources are so meager as to encourage emigration. With water barriers on three sides, expansion was toward the more fertile lands northward, in successive waves of Canaanites, Israelites, Amorites, Babylonians, Assyrians, Aramaeans (called Syrians in the Bible), Idumaeans and Nabataeans, all Semitic peoples, who collided with Indo-Europeans pressing down from Asia Minor and Iran. The proximity of Arabia, with a border ill-defined and difficult of defense, and with a "have-not" population ready to plunder, was a major factor conditioning the history of Israel.

The first mention of Arabia in the Bible by name is in the reign of Solomon, when its kings brought gold and spices, either as tribute or in trade (I Kings 10:15, II Chron. 9:14). Arabians brought tribute to Jehoshaphat (II Chron. 17:11). They joined the Philistines against Jehoram, defeating him disastrously (II Chron. 21:16-22:1). At desolate Babylon not even the Arabian nomad will pitch his tent (Isa. 13:20). Isaiah 21:13-17 lays a burden upon Arabia and her "forests" (thickets, RSV). Moral depravity is indicated in Jeremiah 3:2. The kings of Arabia are involved in judgment on the nations after the Babylonian captivity (Jer. 25:24). Arabia sold cattle to Tyre (Ezek. 27:21). Arabians gave Nehemiah trouble when he was rebuilding the walls of Jerusalem

(Neh. 2:19, 4:7, 6:1). Arabians were among those present at Pentecost (Acts 2:11). Paul "went into Arabia" (Gal. 1:17). Belief that he went to Mt. Sinai is based on the experiences of Moses and Elijah there, and on Paul's mention of "mount Sinai in Arabia" in the same letter (4:25).   E.R.

ARAD (ā'răd, Heb. *'ărādh*). 1. A descendant of Benjamin, (I Chron. 8:15).

2. A city in the Negev, about 17 miles south of Hebron. In Numbers 21:1,33; 40 KJV has "king Arad the Canaanite" where ASV, RSV have "the Canaanite, the king of Arad." He attacked Israel in the wilderness, and is listed as one of the kings conquered by the Israelites (Josh. 12:14). Arad is named in locating the settlement of the Kenites (Judg. 1:16).

ARAH (ā'rà, Heb. *'ārah, wayfarer*). 1. A son of Ulla, an Asherite (I Chron. 7:39).

2. The father of a family that returned from exile (Ezra 2:5; Neh. 7:10). Perhaps the same as No. 1.

3. A Jew whose granddaughter became the wife of Tobiah the Ammonite (Neh. 6:18).

ARAM (ā'răm, Heb. *'ărām*). 1. A son of Shem (Gen. 10:22,23, I. Chron. 1:17).

2. Son of Kemuel, Abraham's nephew (Gen. 22:21).

3. Son of Shamer, of the tribe of Asher (I Chron. 7:34).

4. In KJV, for the Greek form of Ram (Matt. 1: 3,4, ASV, RSV), called Arni in ASV, RSV of Luke 3:33.

5. A district of the hill country belonging to Gilead (I Chron. 2:23).

6. The name of Syria (Num. 23:7) and of its people, and usually so translated (II Sam. 8:5, I Kings 20:20, Amos 1:5). The land of Mesopotamia is Aram-naharaim, Aram between the two rivers (Gen. 24:10 etc.). The title of Psalm 60 refers to David's wars with two districts of Syria, Aram-naharaim and Aram-zobah. Isaac's wife was "the daughter of Bethuel the Syrian of Padan-aram, the sister of Laban the Syrian" (Gen. 25:20), Aramaean in RSV. The Aramaeans of Damascus play a significant role in the history of the Hebrew people from the time of Abraham (Gen. 15:2). Conquered by David, the Aramaean kingdom of Damascus became a rival of the northern kingdom of Israel, and after long conflict, its master, but fell to Assyria in the last days of Israel.

Aram was thus a broad term designating the lands of the Fertile Crescent from Mesopotamia to Phoenicia. Its people came out of the same Arabian reservoir of Semitic peoples as the Hebrews, and were closely related to Israel, with whom their history was intertwined, sometimes in alliance, often in conflict.   E.R.

ARAMAIC (âr'à-mā'ĭk, Heb. *'ārāmîth*), a West Semitic language, closely related to Hebrew, which developed various dialects. Genesis 31:47 calls attention to Laban's use of Aramaic in contrast to Jacob's use of Hebrew. That Aramaic had become the language of Assyrian diplomacy is clear from II Kings 18:26, Isaiah 36:11 (see RSV); also that Aramaic and Hebrew were so different that the people of Jerusalem did not understand the former. Jeremiah 10:11 is in Aramaic, an answer by the Jews to their Aramaic-speaking conquerors who would seduce them to worship idols. Daniel 2:4-7:28 is in Aramaic, also Ezra 4:8-6:18 and 7:12-26. It is not surprising that men in government circles in their period of history should write Aramaic, but why these particular parts of their books should be in Aramaic is not clear. Some Aramaic place and personal names occur in the OT,

Arabian scenes. Above, ascending the Wady Hebron in Sinai. Below, a caravan on the march during a dust storm. © MPS

as Tabrimmon and Hazael. There are several Aramaic words and phrases in the NT, such as *Talitha cumi* (Mark 5:41); *Ephphatha*, (Mark 7:34); *Eloi, Eloi, lama sabachthani* (Mark 15:34, Matt. 27:46); *Maranatha* (I Cor. 16:22); *Abba,* Father (Mark 14:36, Rom. 8:15, Gal. 4:6), and many other words and names. It has been generally assumed as proven that Aramaic was the colloquial language of Palestine from the time of the return of the exiles from Babylon. But some believe that Hebrew was spoken in Galilee in NT times. It is probably safe to assert that our Lord habitually spoke Aramaic and occasionally Greek, and read and could speak Hebrew.

ARAN (ā'răn, Heb. *'ărān*), one of the two sons of Dishan, and grandson of Seir the Horite (Gen. 26:28; I. Chron. 1:42).

Mount Ararat, in eastern Armenia, now Turkey.
RTHPL

ARARAT (âr'à-răt, Heb. *'ărārāt*), a country in eastern Armenia, a mountainous tableland from which flow the Tigris, Euphrates, Aras (Araxes) and Choruk rivers. Near its center lies Lake Van, which, like the Dead Sea, has no outlet. Its general elevation is about 6,000 feet, above which rise mountains to as much as 17,000 feet, the height of the extinct volcano which in modern times is called Mt. Ararat, and on which the ark is supposed to have rested, though Genesis 8:4 is indefinite: "upon the mountains of Ararat" (plural). Thither the sons of Sennacherib fled, after murdering their father (II Kings 19:37; Isa. 37:38, where the land is correctly called Armenia in KJV, following the LXX of Isa. 37:38). Jeremiah 51:27 associates the kingdoms of Ararat, Minni and Ashkenaz with the kings of the Medes as prophesied conquerors of Babylonia. The region is now part of Turkey. The Babylonian name was Urartu, having the same consonants as Heb. *'ărārāt*, and its meaning cannot be determined with certainty.

ARATUS (âr'à-tŭs), Greek poet from Paul's native province, Cilicia. Flourished about 270 B.C. From his *Phaenomena* Paul quotes (Acts 17:28).

ARAUNAH (à-rô'nà, Heb. *'ărawnâh*), the Jebusite who owned a threshing floor on Mount Moriah, which David purchased in order to erect an altar. Because of David's sin in numbering the people, the land was smitten with a plague. When the plague was stayed, David presented a costly offering to the Lord (II Sam. 24:15-25). Called Ornan in I Chronicles 21:18-28.

ARBA (âr'bà, Heb. *'arba'*), the father of Anak, founder of the city which bore his name, Kirjath-arba or Hebron.

ARBATHITE (âr'bà-thīt, Heb. *ha-'arvāthî*), one of David's 30 heroes, a native of the Arabah or of Beth-arabah, called Abi-albon in II Samuel 23:31, Abiel in I Chronicles 11:32.

ARBITE (âr'bīt, Heb. *ha-'ārbî*), one of David's mighty men, in II Samuel 23:35, Parai. In his place in I Chronicles 11:37 we have Naarai the son of Ezbai.

ARCH (See Architecture)

ARCHAEOLOGY

I. The Nature, Scope, and Functions of Biblical Archaeology.

A. The Nature of Archaeology. Archaeology is concerned with all phases of man's activity in the past, and investigates the varied aspects of human endeavor by excavating ancient buried cities, and by examining the houses, implements, and other artifacts, by deciphering inscriptions, and by evaluating the language, literature, monuments, art, architecture, and other components of human life and achievement.

B. The Scope of Biblical Archaeology. In Biblical Archaeology, all the results of Near Eastern Archaeology which bear directly or indirectly on the Biblical record are brought into focus in order to help us to understand the Scriptures better, to evaluate critical questions, to solve exegetical problems, and to gain a fuller appreciation of the ancient world in which the Bible was written and which forms its background. The following paragraphs illustrate these functions.

C. The Functions of Biblical Archaeology.

1. Archaeology and the Understanding of the Bible. At countless points archaeological discoveries furnish a fuller understanding of the Bible, and in this role the discoveries serve as a gigantic commentary. To illustrate: in the patriarchal record, we read of Jacob's leaving the home of Laban in northern Mesopotamia (Gen. 31:20-21). Laban pursued after Jacob and his family to recover the family images which Rachel had stolen, and finally overtook them. Failing to find the family images, Laban pointed to his grandchildren (Jacob's children), and announced with the air of one achieving a psychological victory, "These children are my children" (Gen. 31:43). One is perplexed at this indication of a grandfather claiming control over his grandchildren, for it is quite universally understood that parents, not grandparents, have such control. Specific archaeological light, which helps to understand this passage came in the discovery of the Nuzi Tablets in 1925 in northern Iraq, near

One of the Nuzi adoption tablets. OIUC

Kirkuk. These tablets date from the 15th century B.C., the latter part of the Patriarchal Period (2000-1500 B.C.), and illuminate many aspects of patriarchal life and customs. In relation to Laban's statement concerning his grandchildren, the Nuzi Tablets are significant, for they show that in ancient Assyria, when a man, as Laban, adopts a son, which he evidently did with respect to Jacob, then the grandfather did exercise control not only over his adopted children, but also over their children, his grandchildren. Thus the Nuzi Tablets enable us to understand the implications of Laban's statement, "These children are my children." Furthermore, the Nuzi Tablets show that these events portrayed in the lives of the Patriarchs fit into the early period when the Bible indicates the Patriarchs lived, and not into the later period of the supposed J and E documents. Others aspects of the archaeological illumination of the Patriarchal Period are dealt with in the later section of this article on that era.

2. Archaeology and Critical Questions. At numerous points, subjective critical views of the Bible are elucidated objectively by specific archaeological discoveries. Such a case is the dating of the Song of Miriam (Exod. 15) in the record of the Exodus from Egypt, which by implication of its contents would date back to the period of Moses, c. 1400 B.C. Certain liberal critics have dated it to the days of the building of Solomon's Temple (c. 970 B.C.) and some as late as the Exile (600-500 B.C.). One of the chief reasons for such a late date is the reference to "the mountain of thine inheritance, O Jehovah" (Exod. 15:17). This was assumed to refer to Mount Zion and the Temple, necessitating a date at least as late as 970 B.C., and according to some, as late as the period 600-500 B.C. Striking light on the question came from the Ras Shamra Tablets, discovered on the coast of Syria in 1929, and dating back to 1400 B.C. One of these tablets has the very same expression, "The mountain of thine inheritance," in the Baal Epic where Baal speaks of the mountain to the north. W. F. Albright commented in this connection, "It now becomes absurd to use the verse as an argument for such an improbable late date of the Song of Miriam. This beautiful triumphal hymn, which may rightfully be termed the national anthem of ancient Israel, must now be pushed back to Israelite beginnings" ("The Bible After Twenty Years of Archaeology," *Religion in Life*, 21:4:543, Oct. 1952). Again and again archaeological evidence shows that late-dating and many other aspects of liberal higher criticism are now unsupported.

3. Archaeology and Higher Criticism. It is sometimes stated that archaeological discoveries have had little if any bearing on higher criticism, as in the observation of A. W. F. Blunt, Bishop of Bradford: "It is unfortunate that . . . we have been treated to such statements as that 'archaeology has disproved the higher criticism.' " (Introduction to Caiger's *Bible and Spade*). On the contrary, an examination of archaeological evidence shows just the reverse. Higher criticism cannot remain aloof in its ivory towers, oblivious to the vast amount of light cast on a multitude of problems by archaeological evidence. Beginning with the book of Genesis and the record of the Patriarchs, we find that the view of the late background of the Pentateuch is not supported by the evidence of the Nuzi Tablets. The implications of the broader phases as well as the small details of the Patriarchal record show that the background of the Patriarchal accounts fits into the earlier part of the second

One of the Ras Shamra tablets from Ugarit. LM

millennium B.C. (Cf. Laban's statement, "These children are my children" earlier in this article). Space prevents detailed consideration of other illustrations of the way in which archaeology bears on higher criticism, and we give merely the summary at the end of an article by the writer on "Archaeology and Higher Criticism" (*Bib. Sac.*, Jan., 1957):

Israelite monotheism cannot be denied to the day of Moses, for either monotheism or an approach to it is found revealed in the archaelogical records of the Near East at that time.

The documentary theory cannot remain aloof, for even the Babylonian flood account, discovered in the excavation of ancient Nineveh, fails to support the idea of two separate documents being fused to form the biblical flood record. Supposed early and late words have been held in the past to point to early and late documents in the Bible, but when objective factual light is brought to bear, as the discovery of the two words for "I" in the Ras Shamra Tablets from the period of 1400 B.C., we see that a convenient theory has to give way to potent fact.

Nor is the sacrificial system a late development, as shown by the Ras Shamra Tablets. Judges is acknowledged in the light of topographical and archaeological light to reflect "remarkable accuracy," and Daniel's Belshazzar in the light of the archaeological discoveries is no longer an unhistorical person and an item of evidence for dating the book late.

Archaeological discoveries do not support the idea of late material in the last twelve chapters of Joshua, to be assigned to a late writer designated by "P." The word "javelin" (*sword,* Joel 2:8) is not a late word supporting the late dating of Joel, but is early, as shown by the Ras Shamra Tablets, and the internal evidence of both Psalms and Job

One of the "Creation Tablets" from Nineveh. BM

show, in the light of archaeology, reason for the long-accepted early dates for both. The chronicler knew whereof he spoke in referring to the drachma, a Greek coin, and the Aramaic of Ezra is not late, as shown by the Elephantine Papyri, but is contemporary with the century of Ezra.

In conclusion, we see that rationalistic higher criticism, far from maintaining itself in a lofty position on an untouchable pedestal, finds itself not only modified at almost every point but definitely weighed in the balance and found wanting in respect to many of its most crucial tenets.

4. Archaeology and the Study of the Biblical Text. At times Biblical students are puzzled when seeking to get the exact meaning of a Biblical text. In the account of the childhood of Samuel, the Bible records that when Hannah brought Samuel to the tabernacle, she also brought three bullocks, or as the Hebrew text read originally, "bullock three." Then, we are told, she offered a bullock; here the Hebrew text actually reads, "*the* bullock." The words, "*the* bullock" imply that she brought one bullock. Is one to explain the passage as indicating that she brought one or three? Specific light on this question concerning this biblical text came from the ancient Assyrian clay tablets, excavated in Iraq, which show that in referring to the age of animals, the number follows the name of the animal and the word "year" is understood but not written. Thus the phrase "bullock three" is an elliptical expression for the fuller phrase "a bullock of three years." In the light of the archaeological evidence, Hannah did not bring three bullocks and then offer "the bullock," but she brought one bullock of three years and sacrificed the bullock. Light on word construction, vocabulary, and many other phases of the biblical text has come from the ancient clay tablets, which for the most part

are written in Semitic languages related to the Biblical Hebrew.

5. Archaeology and the Appreciation of the Ancient World. In earlier years, scholars could sit at their desks in London or Philadelphia and imagine what life was like in Bible times. Today, thanks to archaeology, we no longer imagine — we can reconstruct much of ancient life. We illustrate from the days of Elisha, nearly 3000 years ago (850 B.C.): Houses in that day often had two stories, and underground drains kept the interior of the city relatively dry. The houses were provided with plaster-lined cisterns (abundantly illustrated in the writer's excavation of Dothan), and Israelite women no longer needed to depend on water from the nearest spring.

The workman had iron tools of every kind — iron axes and adzes to cut trees, thin iron saws set in frames; sledge hammers as well as chisels and gouges. The farmer had iron sickles to harvest his grain. With the potter's wheel, which had already been in use for nearly 2000 years, there developed a type of mass-production in turning out a great deal of everyday pottery which was functional, rather than decorative as it had been in earlier centuries. Jewelry, cosmetic palettes, pendants of bone and ivory appear in every excavation of this period. Clothing, as pictured in the Assyrian monuments depicting Israelites, consisted of long fringed tunics for men, over which they wore fringed mantles, while on their feet they wore high boots turned up at the toes. (Cf. Albright, "The Time of Elijah," in *Archaeology of Palestine,* pp. 208-212). Every phase of ancient life is illuminated by archaeological discoveries.

II. Archaeological Light on the Main Periods of Biblical History.
  A. The Early Chapters of Genesis.
    1. Creation Tablets (Gen. 1 and 2).
    a. *Subject of the Tablets.* Archaeological excavation in the region of ancient Mesopotamia in the 19th century brought forth tablets which give the text of the so-called Babylonian Creation Account. It tells of a plot of the gods of the lower world led by the goddess Tiamat against the great gods of Babylonia. The great gods chose a champion, Marduk, who fought against Tiamat, and cut her in half, using one half to form the heavens. Imbedded within this myth is a reference to the creation of man and the world. It is not primarily a pagan account of creation, but rather an epic in praise of Marduk, as pointed out by the late Professor Heidel at the University of Chicago (*Babylonian Genesis,* p. 3).
    b. *Comparison with the Biblical Record.* The majesty and authority of the biblical record of creation stands in sharp contrast to the polytheism and crassness of the Marduk-Tiamat myth in the Babylonian account.
    c. *The Bible and Pan-Babylonianism.* At the beginning of the twentieth century, Fredrich Delitzsch of Berlin set forth the radical idea that much of the early part of Genesis was a reworking and "purifying" of Babylonian myths and legends. At first glance the Hebrew word for deep, *tehom,* does bear a resemblance to the name Tiamat, the Babylonian goddess. A careful examination of the two words, however, shows that the Babylonian word Tiamat cannot yield the word *tehom.* A significant analysis of the question was given by Alexander Heidel in his *Babylonian Genesis.* He concluded: "To derive *tehom* from *tiamat* is grammatically impossible because the former has a masculine, the latter a feminine ending. Moreover, it would have no h . . . ." (*Ibid.,* p. 85).

2. *Archaeology and Eden* (Gen. 1-2). The clay tablets and inscriptions of ancient Mesopotamia tell of an early sacred garden in which there was a tree of life. This sacred tree appears often on the seals of important people of ancient Babylon, as well as in the reliefs on decoration of the palaces (Ira Maurice Price, *The Monuments and the Old Testament,* Philadelphia: Judson Press, 1958, p. 111).

3. *The Fall of Man* (Gen. 3): *The Adapa Story.* The Story of Adapa, on ancient Babylonian tablets, tells that Adapa was brought before the gods because he broke the wing of the south wind. Food was placed before him, but he did not eat it and failed to gain eternal life (*Ancient Near Eastern Texts Relating to the Old Testament,* edited by James B. Pritchard, Princeton University Press, 1955, pp. 101-102). In both the biblical record and the Adapa story, eating is involved in relation to eternal life. One must leave open the question whether this is a coincidental parallel or whether the Adapa story does represent a handing down of some knowledge of the events in Eden.

4. *The Long-Lived Patriarchs* (Gen. 5). A parallel to the long-lived patriarchs in the early chapters of Genesis is found in the Sumerian King List. The figures given for the kings listed here are beyond imagination: "Alalgar ruled 36,000 years . . . Dumuzi, a shepherd, ruled 36,000 years . . ." (*Ibid.,* p. 265).

5. *The Flood* (Gen. 6-8). One of the striking archaeological discoveries of the last century was that of the Babylonian tablets giving the account of a great flood. The text of these tablets appears to date back to the early second millennium B.C. and is paralleled by fragments even earlier. It tells that the great god Ea warned a man named Utnapishtim: "Build a ship . . . aboard the ship take thou the seed of all living things (*Ibid.,* p. 93). The flood waters came upon the land, then subsided, and the craft landed on a mountain. A dove was sent forth, then a swallow, and finally a raven. The many parallels between the biblical account and the Babylonian are evidence of an early knowledge of the flood. Throughout the world are records, traditions, and legends of a great flood. According to Johannes Riehm, there are a total of 268, all implying a universal knowledge of a great flood.

6. *The Table of the Nations* (Gen. 10). Many of the names of peoples and countries given in the Table of Nations in Genesis 10 were unknown outside of the Bible until discovered in the archaeological monuments. These would include *Ashkenaz,* the *Ashkunz* of the monuments; *Togarmah-Tegarama*; *Elishah-Alashi*; *Tarshish-Tarsisi* (pronounced in Assyrian *Tarshish*); *Accad-Akkadu,* and many others. W. F. Albright had commented on this chapter: "The Table of Nations remains an astonishingly accurate document" ("Recent Discoveries in Bible Lands," Supplement to *Young's Concordance,* published separately by The Biblical Colloquium, 1955, p. 71).

B. The Patriarchal Period (Gen. 12-36) (2000-1800 B.C.).

1. *Patriarchal Palestine.* Archaeological documents give us a graphic picture of Palestine in the early second millennium B.C. Shortly after 2000 B.C., an Egyptian nobleman named Sinuhe fled from Egypt, because of the political situation, and came to Canaan, where he lived for an extended period. He tells that it was "a goodly land . . . there were figs in it and vines . . . copious was its honey, plenteous its oil; all fruits were upon its

Fragment of a clay tablet from the library of Ashurbanipal at Nineveh, with Assyrian version of the Flood Story. BM

trees. Barley was there and spelt" (Price, *Monuments and the Old Testament,* 1958, p. 148).

2. *The Battle of the Kings* (Gen. 14). In earlier years the record of the invasion of the four kings in the days of Abraham was rejected as unhistorical by many critics. The discovery in the archaeological records of names paralleling Arioch (Eri-aku) and Tidal, the two words forming Chedorlaomer (Gen. 14:1), has taken the account out of the realm of legend. The very term for "retainers" (Gen. 14:14) is found in a cuneiform tablet from 15th century Palestine (Albright, "Recent Discoveries in Bible Lands," p. 76). Evidence of extended travel, as implied in this expedition, and the discovery of some of the very place names in Palestine (such as Ham, Gen. 14) show the historical background of the account. "Such early accounts can no longer be regarded as mythical or prehistoric" (Price, *Monuments and the Old Testament,* 1958, p. 145).

3. *The Nuzi Tablets and the Patriarchal Accounts* (Gen. 15:35). A whole series of events in the lives of Abraham, Isaac, and Jacob has become clearer as a result of the discovery of the Nuzi Tablets from ancient Assyria, datable to the 15th century B.C.

a. *Adoption.* The Nuzi Tablets show the practice of adopting a son in patriarchal times, if one had no natural son. This clarifies the relationship between Abraham and Eliezer and explains Abraham's statement: "One born in my house is my heir" (Gen. 15:13).

b. *Oral Blessing.* When Isaac blessed Jacob, thinking it was Esau, it might be expected that upon discovery of the deception, he would merely repeat the blessing and apply it to Esau. But this he did not do. Light on the question also came from the Nuzi Tablets, which show the binding nature of an oral promise, and that it had validity even in a law court. This is demonstrated in the case of a young man named Tarmiya, recorded in the Nuzi Tablets, who sought to marry a young woman, Zululishtar. His brothers, however, tried to prevent him. Tarmiya won legal permission in the law court case which followed, by invoking his father's oral promise that he could take Zululishtar to wife.

c. *Family Images* (Gen. 31). Rachel's theft of the family images (Gen. 31:19) and Laban's great concern to recover them has puzzled Bible commentators. The Nuzi Tablets show, however, that the possession of the family images indicated right of inheritance. Laban did not want Jacob to inherit his estate. Many other aspects of customs and practices in the patriarchal period are graphically illuminated by the Nuzi Tablets (Cf. Laban's statement, "These children are my children," in this article, I, C, 1.).

C. Egypt and the Wilderness (Gen. 37-Deut. 34) (1800-1400 B.C.).

1. *Joseph in Egypt.* The turning point in Joseph's career came when he went to Dothan in northern Palestine to find his brothers. The site of this ancient city has been excavated in a series of campaigns by the writer and Mrs. Free and their excavation staff. These discoveries show that it was a thriving city in the days of Joseph (Gen. 37:17) and in the time of Elisha (c. 850 B.C.; II Kings 6: 13), the two periods in which it is mentioned in the Biblical narrative. Sold by his brothers to a passing camel caravan of traders, he was brought to Egypt, where the background of his life is abundantly illuminated by Egyptian archaeological discoveries.

a. *Rise to Power* (Gen. 41, 42). It has been objected that a Hebrew slave could never rise to power in a powerful foreign state. Archaeological discoveries show, on the contrary, that a Canaanite by the name of Dudu rose to high favor in the Egyptian court; another Canaanite, Meri-Ra, became armor-bearer to Pharaoh; and Yankhamu, also a Canaanite, acted as deputy for Pharaoh of Egypt in the grain growing district of Egypt (J. P. Free, *Archaeology and Bible History*, Wheaton, Illinois: Scripture Press, 5th ed., 1956, p. 77).

b. *Joseph's Titles* (Gen. 45:8). Joseph is designated as "Father to Pharaoh," "Lord of all his house," and "Ruler throughout all the land of Egypt" (*Ibid.*, p. 78). Egyptian archaeological texts illustrate the various governmental posts which Joseph likely held as the important official under the king (William A. Ward, "Egyptian Titles in Genesis 39-50," BS, Jan., 1957, pp. 40-59).

c. *Egyptian Names.* Some scholars have completely rejected the historicity of the sojourn of

Dr. Free pointing to a layer of ashes at Jericho. Joshua 6 says that Jericho was burned after capture.

Israel in Egypt. This view, however, is contradicted by many lines of evidence, including the discovery that many Israelite names were of Egyptian origin. According to W. F. Albright instances of Israelite names include Moses, Hophni, Phinehas, perhaps Merari, and others. ("Recent Discoveries in Bible Lands," 1955, p. 84). More recent research has also made it possible to be reasonably confident of the location of many sites referred to in Exodus, including Ramses, Pithon, Succoth, and Baal-zephion (*Ibid.*, p. 84).

d. *Joseph's Era and Biblical Criticism.* There are many bits of Egyptian coloring in the account of Joseph in Egypt which have been beautifully illustrated by Egyptian archaeological discoveries (*Ibid.*, p. 78). R. H. Pfeiffer, late Professor of Old Testament at Harvard, acknowledges a definite knowledge of Egypt on the part of the author of the Pentateuch.

2. *The Exodus:* The Song of Miriam (Exod. 15). The Song of Miriam, composed at the time of the Exodus from Egypt, has been dated hundreds of years later by certain liberal scholars, chiefly because the reference to the "Mountain of thine inheritance" was held to be a reference to Mt. Zion and the Temple. As noted at the beginning of this article, the discovery of the Ras Shamra tablets yielding a text with the same phrase from 1400 B.C. showed that such a phrase occurs early and is not evidence of a late date (this article, I, C, 2.).

Illustration of the occupational levels (strata) of a mound (Tell). This is Tell Beisan, ancient fortress city of Bethshan (I Sam. 31:10), which guarded the eastern approaches to the Valley of Esdraelon. From Free, **Archaeology and Bible History.**

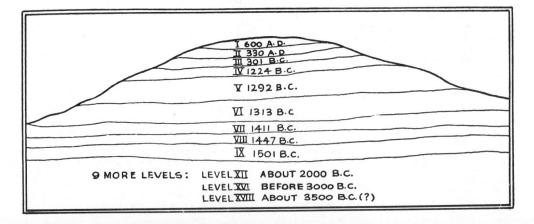

I 600 A.D.
II 330 A.D
III 301 B.C.
IV 1224 B.C.
V 1292 B.C.
VI 1313 B.C
VII 1411 B.C.
VIII 1447 B.C.
IX 1501 B.C.

9 MORE LEVELS:　LEVEL XII　ABOUT 2000 B.C.
　　　　　　　　　LEVEL XVI　BEFORE 3000 B.C.
　　　　　　　　　LEVEL XVIII　ABOUT 3500 B.C.(?)

D. The Conquest and Judges (Joshua, Judges) (1400-1050 B.C.).

1. *Evidence of the Conquest.* A number of sites excavated in Palestine show evidence of violent destruction in the period between 1400 and 1200 B.C. They are very definitely to be connected with the conquest under Joshua and the further conquests in the period of the Judges. In this period, Bethel (Judges 1:22) was destroyed by a great fire which left a solid mass of burned brick (Jack Finegan, *Light from the Ancient Past,* Princeton University Press, Second Edition, 1959, p. 160). At Lachish the burned remains of a city from the 13th century B.C. was discovered (*Ibid.,* p. 162). At Kirjathsepher (Josh. 10:38; Judg. 1:11-13), there is at the end of the Late Bronze Period (1600-1200 B.C.) a great burned layer and above it an Israelite city (*Ibid.,* p. 163). At Hazor (Josh. 11:10-13), Garstang found evidence of destruction about 1400 B.C. and subsequent excavations by Yiga'el Yadin showed similar destruction at the end of the Late Bronze Period (*Ibid.,* p. 165).

2. *Jericho* (Josh. 6). From 1930 to 1936 Jericho was excavated by John Garstang of the University of Liverpool. He found the fallen walls of Jericho and reported that they "fell outward so completely that the attackers would be able to clamber up and over the ruins into the city" (John Garstang, *Joshua-Judges,* London, Constable, 1931, p. 146; cf. Free, *op. cit.,* p. 130). Further excavation 1952-1958 by the British School of Archaeology found some Late Bronze Age pottery (1600-1200 B.C.) but not as much as they expected. Miss Kathleen Kenyon, the director, concluded that much of the city of Joshua's day had been eroded away. It should also be pointed out that Garstang had already dug there for seven years and had removed much of it.

3. *The Record of the Book of Judges.* Some critical scholars have held that the book of Judges is made up of stories which were not written until about 550 B.C., more than half a millennium after the time portrayed in the accounts. John Garstang, however, in his book *Joshua-Judges,* points out: "We find no reason to doubt that the historical narrative contained in the books of Joshua and Judges, so far as it was derived from the old sources . . . was founded upon fact" (p. 141). At many points archaeological evidence has been found which illuminates and confirms the book of Judges:

a. *Names.* Names in the book of Judges, such as Ahiman and Talmai (Judg. 1:10), appear in the Ras Shamra Tablets, showing that these names fit into that early period (Free, *op. cit.,* p. 141).

b. *Cities.* Jerusalem was not captured in this period according to Joshua and Judges. This is confirmed by the evidence of the Amarna Tablets, which show that the king of Jerusalem remained loyal to the Pharaoh of Egypt. Hazor's destruction is evidence in the archaeological discoveries (For other evidence concerning the book of Judges, see Free, *op. cit.,* pp. 142-145).

E. The Monarchy (I Sam.-Dan.) (1050-600 B.C.).

1. *The Rise of the Monarchy in Israel.* The archaeological monuments and records show that the two great powers on either side of Israel — Assyria and Egypt — were at a low ebb in the eleventh and tenth centuries B.C. (1100-900 B.C.), when the monarchy in Israel began and developed under Saul, David, and Solomon. God's sovereignty in restraining nations is here evidenced.

Remains of the city walls of ancient Jericho. © MPS

2. *Light on the Reign of Saul* (c. 1025 B.C.). Saul ruled Israel from the town of Gibeah, about two miles N of Jerusalem. Excavations there by W. F. Albright revealed seven levels, from 100 B.C. to A.D. 70. The fortress of the second town, with walls six feet thick and a massive stair case, is likely the castle of Saul. The archaeological evidence showed that it was destroyed shortly after his death (*Bulletin of American Schools of Oriental Research,* No. 52).

3. *The Period of David* (II Sam.; I Chron. 11-29) (1010-971 B.C.). In the earlier years of the 20th century, critical theory denied to the age of David the musical development and musical organizations described in the Bible (I Chron. 23:5-6). Archaeological discoveries show, on the contrary, that music was well developed long before the days of David.

a. *Objects of Art.* Tomb paintings dated about 1900 B.C. show Asiatic Semites coming into Egypt, one carrying a lyre. Tomb paintings at Thebes (1400 B.C.) portray a girl with a lyre, another with an oboe. The name of David's guild musician, Calcol (I Chron. 2:26) is paralleled on inscriptions on the Megiddo ivories, and Than and Haman (I Chron. 2:6), in the Ras Shamra Tablets. W. F. Albright observes that such discoveries prove the correctness of the biblical indication of early musical guilds in the days of David (W. F. Albright, *Archaeology and the Religion of Israel,* Baltimore: the Johns Hopkins Press, 1942, p. 127; cf. Free, *op. cit.,* p. 151).

b. *Davidic Psalms.* Many Psalms attributable to David from their internal evidence have been dated hundreds of years later by critics of the 19th and 20th centuries. Archaeological discoveries throw specific light on several aspects of this problem: the spelling used in the Gezar Calendar and in contemporary archaeological inscriptions help us fix a date in the tenth century B.C. for Psalm 18 (Albright, *Archaeology of Palestine,* p. 220). Also, in the light of the Ras Shamra Tablets (Ugaritic Texts) many of the Psalms once downdated to the late period must be put back into early Israelite times, not later than the tenth century B.C. Albright comments, "There is no longer any reason to refuse a Davidic date for such Psalms" (*Ibid.*, pp. 226-227).

c. *David's Reign.* Details of David's reign are highlighted by archaeological discoveries. The low ebb of both Egypt and Assyria in the eleventh and tenth centuries B.C. explains why, under God's direction, the Kingdom could develop and expand (See E, 1. above). The power of the Philistines in the time of Saul and David is explained by the Egyptian monuments showing the attempt of the Philistines to enter Egypt. They were repulsed, then landed in Palestine to add to the troubles of Saul and David.

4. *Solomon's Reign* (I Kings 1-11) (971-931 B.C.). Many details of Solomon's reign are illuminated by archaeological discoveries:

Shishak's Relief, at the Temple of Karnak in Egypt, recording his victory over Rehoboam. © MPS

Ruins of Solomon's Stables at Megiddo. OIUC

a. *Solomon's Stables* (I Kings 9:19). Extensive stables dating to the tenth century B.C. and used by following generations were uncovered by the University of Chicago at Megiddo, a city specifically mentioned as the scene of Solomon's extensive building operations (I Kings 9:15). One section uncovered would have housed nearly 500 horses; similar stables have been found at Hazor and Tell el Hesi. Some archaeologists have suggested that these stables date to the time of Ahab, rather than Solomon, and a similar view was set forth in the spring of 1960 by Yiga'el Yadin, Israelie archaeologist. However, as W. F. Albright observed in earlier years, the stables were built by Solomon, and used by succeeding generations down into the time of Ahab.

b. *Trade Activities.* Solomon's relations with the land of Sheba (I Kings 10:ff) are illuminated by discoveries showing that the latter country was a thriving kingdom earlier than had been previously supposed. Tarshish (I Kings 10:22) is now shown by archaeological inscriptions to be the Island of Sardinia, and Ophir is mentioned in an inscription from Tell Qasileh (near Jaffa and the modern city of Tel-Aviv; Albright, "Recent Discoveries in Bible Lands," pp. 93-94).

c. *Building Styles.* While nothing remains of Solomon's temple, details of construction are illuminated by archaeological discoveries. The proto-Ionic or proto-Aeolic pilaster capital for columns was extensively used, as shown by archaeological discoveries at Megiddo, Samaria, Shechem in Moab, and near Jerusalem, dating from the tenth to the eighth centuries B.C. It was likely used in some of the Solomonic buildings (*Ibid.*, p. 93).

d. *Solomon's Seaport* (I Kings 9:26). The biblical reference to Solomon's seaport on the Red Sea was strikingly illuminated by the excavation of Nelson Glueck (1938-40) which uncovered this important copper smelting center in the Solomonic period. Solomon's workmen utilized the principle of the forced draft in refining copper (Cf. Free, *op. cit.*, pp. 171-2).

5. *Over Forty Kings of Scripture.* Earlier in the 20th century, Robert Dick Wilson pointed out that 41 kings of the Bible are to be found in the ancient archaeological records. Of these there are 26 foreign kings, including five kings of Egypt (Shishak, Tirhakah, *et al.*), five Assyrian kings, five Babylonian, and kings of several other countries. Six kings of Israel and four of Judah were found in archaeological inscriptions by Dr. Wilson, and since his death in 1930, the names of two more Judean kings have been discovered: Jehoiachin on tablets found near the Ishtar Gate in Babylon and brought to the attention of scholars in the early 1940's, and Ahaz on a carnelian seal published in 1940 by C. C. Torrey (BASOR, 79, pp. 27-28; cf. G. Ernest Wright, *Biblical Archaeology*, Philadelphia: Westminster Press, 1957, p. 162; also Edward J. Young's revision of Robert Dick Wilson, *A Scientific Investigation of the Old Testament*, Chicago: Moody Press, 1959, p. 71). Wilson pointed out that these archaeological monuments containing the names of more than 40 biblical kings show that "the text of the proper names in the Hebrew Bible has been transmitted with the most minute accuracy" (*Ibid.*, p. 71).

6. *Rehoboam's Reign.* The Bible records that shortly after the division of the kingdom, in the reign of Rehoboam, the Egyptian King Shishak invaded Palestine (I Kings 14:25). This is illuminated by the archaeological inscriptions on the walls of the temple of Karnak in southern Egypt, which portray Shishak, tell of his invasion into Palestine, and enumerate 156 place names in Palestine which he claimed to have taken. These included Ajalon, Gaza, Gibeon, and Taanach (Price, *op. cit.*, p. 233).

7. *Ahab* (874-853 B.C.) *and other kings of the Northern Kingdom.* Ahab is listed in the Assyrian royal inscriptions as one of those combating Shalmaneser III of Assyria. The archaeological monument known as the Black Obelisk of Shalmaneser records and portrays the tribute paid to the same king by Jehu a few years later. The invasion of Moab in the days of Omri and Ahab is illuminated by the Moabite stone, which gives details paralleling the record in II Kings 3-4-7. In another inscription Tiglath-pileser refers to the payment of tribute by Menahem. In inscriptions

A section of the Moabite Stone.

written by the scribes of Sargon II, he tells of the capture of Samaria and the carrying away of 27,-290 Israelite captives. Some of the captives, as recorded in II Kings 17:6, were settled in the valley of the Habor, the river of Gozan. Excavation by von Oppenheim at Halaf in northern Mesopotamia established the location of Gozan, the capital of the upper Khabur district (Albright, *Recent Discoveries in Bible Lands*, p. 95).

8. *Light on Samaria and the end of the Northern Kingdom.* The excavation of Samaria by Harvard University revealed the buildings of the days of Omri and Ahab (ninth century B.C.). In the level following their time, nearly 70 ostraca (potsherds bearing writing) were found listing payments of oil and wine as revenue or taxes sent to

Ruins of Ahab's Palace in Samaria. © MPS

The Black Obelisk of Shalmaneser III, King of Assyria, views of front (left) and one side. The panels record and portray King Jehu and Israelites bringing tribute. BA BM

the storerooms of the royal palace (Free, *op. cit.*, pp. 182-3). Many of the names on these ostraca are formed with the word *Baal* — Abi-baal, Meribaal —, giving archaeological light on the impact of Baal worship, as implied in the Bible (I Kings 16:31-32). Baal worship had made such inroads that people were giving names to their children which included the name *Baal*. The Samaria excavations also brought forth many ivory plaques, panels, small boxes, and furniture decorations, confirming the biblical reference to Ahab's "ivory house" (I Kings 22:39). The fall of Samaria (722-21 B.C.) is described in the archaeological records of Sargon, king of Samaria, and the biblical record is given in II Kings 17:5-6.

9. *The Last Days of the Southern Kingdom* (II Kings 22-25; II Chron. 34-36; Jeremiah) (640-586 B.C.). Striking archaeological light on the last days of the Southern Kingdom (just before and after 600 B.C.) came in the discovery of a group of clay tablets found near the Ishtar Gate in Babylon (cf. this aritcle, II, E, 5.). These tablets record the rations given by the king of Babylon to the captive King Jehoiachin, confirming the biblical

One of the Lachish Letters. PAM

record that Jehoiachin, the next to the last king of Judah, was taken captive by the Babylonians and later given a daily allowance by the Babylonian king (II Kings 25:27-30). As the Babylonian army closed in on the Kingdom of Judah in the period of 588-87 B.C., the Bible indicates that the cities of Lachish and Azekah had not yet fallen (Jer. 34:7). Most significant archaeological light on these two cities comes from the discovery in the excavation at Lachish of ostraca which proved to be military dispatches. One of these letters (No. 4), written by the army officer at a military outpost to his superior officer at Lachish, says, "We are watching for the signals of Lachish, according to all indications which my lord hath given, for we cannot see Azekah." This letter not only shows that the Babylonian army of Nebuchadnezzar was tightening its net around the land of Judah, but mentions the very two cities, Azekah and Lachish, which the Bible indicates fell at the end of the war, shortly before Jerusalem. Much other important light is brought to bear on this period by the Lachish Letters (For details, cf. Free, *op. cit.,* pp. 579-600).

F. The Exile and Return from Captivity (II Kings 25-Malachi) (c. 600 B.C.-425 B.C.).

1. *The Desolation of Palestine in the Days of the Exile* (sixth century B.C.). The biblical record of the destruction of many towns (Jer. 34:7) at the beginning of the Exile and the desolation of Jerusalem and much of the land (II Kings 25:10-12) has been doubted by certain scholars. C. C. Torrey of Yale considered the account of the restoration given in Ezra as "quite apocryphal" (Albright, *Archaeology of Palestine,* p. 141). The excavations have shown, on the contrary, that many of the cities of Judah were destroyed and not rebuilt, and others were destroyed and reoccupied after a long period of abandonment. There is not a single known case where a town of Judah itself was occupied continuously throughout the period of the Exile (*Ibid.,* p. 142). This strikingly illustrates the Biblical indication of the desolation of the land, and fails to support Torrey's theory that the biblical writers exaggerated the destruction of Nebuchadnezzar's army.

2. *Evidence of the Exiles in Babylonia and Egypt.* Archaeological evidence of the Jews who were taken to Babylonia (II Kings 25:11) was found in tablets excavated at Nippur, which come from this period and contain many typically Jewish names. In Egypt, the Elephantine Papyri, found on an island in the Nile, gives us light on the Jews living there who stemmed from the group that went down at the beginning of the Exile in the days of Jeremiah (Jer. 43:6-7). These papyrus letters were actually written by these Jews in the fifth century B.C. (cf. J. P. Free, *op. cit.,* p. 231).

3. *The Edict of Cyrus and the Return from Exile.* The Bible records that when King Cyrus gained control of Babylon (539 B.C.), he allowed the Jews to return to their native land (Ezra 1:1-4). Archaeological light on this action of Cyrus came in the discovery of a clay cylinder on which Cyrus' edict is recorded concerning his sending displaced and captive people back to their original homes: "I gathered together all their populations and restored them to their dwelling places" (Price, *op. cit.,* p. 314; cf. *Ancient Near Eastern Texts,* edited by Pritchard, p. 316).

G. The Intertestamental Period (400 B.C. to the Time of Christ).

1. *Spread of Greek Culture.* Archaeology has illuminated the general background from the close of the Old Testament (425-400 B.C.) to New Testament times. The spread of Greek culture following the days of Alexander the Great (333 B.C.) is illustrated in the discovery of Greek inscriptions, coins and objects of art in practically every excavation of this period.

2. *The Zeno Papyri.* The Zeno Papyri, excavated in Egypt, contain a letter from Tobias, the governor of Ammon (c. 250 B.C.) in eastern Palestine, stating that he was sending horses, dogs, and camels to the king of Egypt. This Tobias is a later descendant of the Tobiah (Greek, Tobias) who troubled Nehemiah in the days of rebuilding the walls of Jerusalem (Neh. 2:10; cf. Free, *op. cit.,* p. 249). Much other light has been shed on the Intertestamental period, but the limits of this article preclude further discussion. Useful material will be found in Finegan, *Light from the Ancient Past,* pp. 244-253; Free, *Archaeology and Bible History,* pp. 255-282; and John A. Thompson, *Archaeology and the Pre-Christian Centuries,* Grand Rapids: Eerdmans, 1958.

H. Archaeology and the New Testament.

1. *The Language of the New Testament.* Up until the turn of the last century, many Bible students believed that the New Testament was written in a special Greek, quite different from classical Greek, and sometimes characterized as "Biblical" Greek. At the end of the 19th century, a young German scholar, Adolph Deissmann, realized that the ancient everyday Greek documents being excavated in Egypt were written in a Greek very similar to that of the New Testament. This revolutionary discovery showed that the New Testament was written in the Greek of everyday life, a language that would be meaningful and bring home the mes-

A section of the Cylinder of Cyrus. BM

sage of Scripture to every man who used Greek as his means of communication, and not merely to those who understood so-called "Biblical" Greek. The archaeological discoveries have shown that one New Testament word after another is not some special invented term, but a word that would have immediate and full meaning to those who lived 2,000 years ago. The word "daily" for example, was found in one of the papyrus documents at the head of a shopping list, and has the specific meaning of food just "for the day."

2. *The Dead Sea Scrolls and the New Testament.*

a. *New Testament Vocabulary.* The Dead Sea Scrolls, first brought to the attention of the world in 1948 after being discovered in a cave at the north end of the Dead Sea, contain a number of manuscripts of a Jewish sect which was flourishing between 100 B.C. and A.D. 100. Here we find light on the religious vocabulary of the New Testament period, for words parallel to "fellowship," "congregation," and "church" appear in the Dead Sea Scroll documents (Finegan, *op. cit.,* p. 289). It should be emphasized that the Dead Sea Scrolls were not the source for the words of Christ. This is forcefully pointed out by Millar Burrows, who states that the differences between the Dead Sea Scrolls and the words of Christ are more striking than the similarities (Millar Burrows, *Dead Sea Scrolls,* New York: Viking Press, 1955, p. 331). The scrolls do, however, give us specific light on the "religious vocabulary" of the first century A.D.

b. *The Religious Background of the New Testament.* From the Gospels we know of several Jewish religious groups, including the Pharisees, the Sadducees, and the Herodians. Now the Dead Sea Scrolls give us additional insight into another group, who may be the Essenes, described by the Jewish historian Josephus. They were a religious community which could be joined by those who adhered to the laws and regulations set down in their "Manual of Discipline."

c. *The Scrolls and the Work of Christ.* The scrolls tell of a teacher of righteousness, who has been identified by some as Dupont-Sommer, as a Messianic parallel to Christ. Again, competent scholars, as Burrows, have pointed out that the

Ruins of the Essene community buildings at Qumran. © MPS

divergences are great, and one cannot maintain the teacher of righteousness of the scrolls to be a source of things stated concerning Christ (Burrows, *op. cit.,* pp. 330-31).

d. *The Scrolls and the Evangelical View of the Bible).* The evangelical view of the Bible, that it is divinely inspired, is not challenged by the material in the Dead Sea Scrolls. In view of the fact that some writers have implied that the Dead Sea Scrolls were the origin of ideas in the New Testament, and that conservative theologians have much to dread from the Dead Sea Scroll material, one should note W. F. Albright's forcible statement that he "doubts whether any conservative theologian is in the least apprehensive as to what the scrolls may bring forth, but he does know a number of liberals who are seriously worried about the fate of their pet hypotheses" (Review of Edmund Wilson's book, *The Scrolls from the Dead Sea,* New York *Herald Tribune* Book Review section).

For further study, out of the multitude of books on the Dead Sea Scrolls, two of the most useful are Millar Burrows, *Dead Sea Scrolls,* 1955, mentioned above in section (a). Though Burrows by his own acknowledgment holds the liberal position, there is a wealth of useful objective material in this book; it is supplemented by his second volume, *More Light on the Dead Sea Scrolls,* New York: Viking Press, 1958. A shorter very useful book by an evangelical scholar is F. F. Bruce's *Second Thoughts on the Dead Sea Scrolls,* Grand Rapids, Eerdmans, 1956.

3. *Archaeological Confirmation of the New Testament.* While the New Testament, in contrast to the Old Testament, was written over a span of much less than one hundred years, there are a number of specific confirmations, including the evidence of the accuracy of Luke's reference to the enrollment of Cyrenius in Luke 2:1-3, and the confirmation of the accuracy of the geographical references concerning Iconium, Lystra, and Derbe in Acts 14:6. (For further summaries of specific confirmation and illumination of the New Testament, see the writer's *Archaeology and Bible History,* pp. 282-340.)

For further study in New Testament archaeology, though written many years ago, Camden M. Cobern's *The New Archaeological Discoveries and Their Bearing upon the New Testament,* (New York, Funk and Wagnalls, 9th ed., 1929) still has a great amount of useful material not found in more recent books. It can be supplemented by Finegan's, *Light from the Ancient Past,* 2nd ed., 1959, pp. 247-551, which has very useful and up-to-date material. See also Merrill F. Unger's recent volume, *Archaeology and the New Testament,* Grand Rapids: Zondervan, 1962.   J.P.F.

Section of one of the Dead Sea Scrolls. © SB MPS

ARCHANGEL (See Angel)

ARCHELAUS (àr'kě-lā'ŭs), son of Herod the Great, who succeeded his father as ruler of Idumea, Samaria and Judea in 4 B.C. He was deposed by the Roman government in A.D. 6 (Matt. 2:22).

ARCHERS (ar'chẽrz), bowmen, hunters or warriors with bow and arrow. Ishmael is the first man so named in the Bible (Gen. 21:20). Joseph is represented as victor in a battle of archery (Gen. 49:23,24). RSV has "sound of musicians" instead of KJV "noise of archers" (Jud. 5:11), which makes better sense, archers not being noted for noise. Archery plays a part in a crisis in the relations of David and Jonathan (I Sam. 20:17-42). Philistine archers mortally wounded Saul (I Sam. 31:3, I Chron. 10:3). The sons of Ulam, Benjamites, "were mighty men of valor, archers" (I Chron. 8:40). Josiah was killed by archers (II Chron. 35:23). Job compares his troubles to being surrounded by archers (Job 16:13). Archers are mentioned in Isaiah 21:17, 22:3; Jeremiah 50:29. Light-armed, mobile, effective at a distance, archers were valuable in any army, and their skill was no less useful in hunting.

ARCHEVITES (ar'kē-vĭts), colonists in Samaria who complained to Artaxerxes about the Jews' rebuilding Jerusalem (Ezra 4:9). Identified in RSV as "the men of Erech" in Babylonia.

ARCHI (àr'kī), probably not the name of a place but of a clan which possessed Ataroth in Ephraim, perhaps modern Tell es-Nasbeh, a few miles S of Bethel. In Joshua 16:2, where KJV has "and passed along until the borders of Archi to Ataroth," ASV renders, "and passed along unto the border of the Archites to Ataroth," and RSV, "it passes along to Ataroth, the territory of the Archites."

ARCHIPPUS (àr-kĭp'ŭs, *master of the horse*), a Christian at Colossae, conspicuous as a champion of the Gospel, a close friend (or perhaps son) of Philemon, an office-bearer in the Church (Col. 4:17, Philem. 2). Because of the spiritual atmosphere at Colossae (like Laodicea, Rev. 3:14-19), it is not surprising to find Paul exhorting his fellow-soldier to maintain his zeal and fidelity.

ARCHITE (àr'kīt), a member of the clan of Ataroth in Ephraim (Josh. 16:2). Hushai, David's friend (I Chron. 27:33), acted as his secret agent in the rebellion of Absalom, to defeat the counsel of Ahithophel (II Sam. 15:31-17:23).

ARCHITECTURE, may be defined as the art or science of building. As a form of art (*q.v.*), architecture is the effort to make a building aesthetically pleasing as well as useful. It must be classified as an abstract art, for it is the least representational of all the arts. For example, an artist who wished to portray the Madonna and Child could hardly use architecture as his medium; modern architects do indeed attempt to employ symbolism in order to make it representational, but even this is greatly limited. Architecture could further be described as the most social of the arts, since a building is usually designed for more than one person, whether it is a church, a railroad station, or a home. The sole exception probably would be the monument or tomb which is intended simply to contain the remains of a single individual.

The materials of architecture in antiquity were wood, clay, brick (formed of clay, whether sun-baked or kiln-fired), and stone — in general, local availability was the determining factor in the choice of material used. It is well known that wooden beams were exported from Lebanon (the famed "cedars of Lebanon") to practically all parts of the ancient Middle East; likewise the beautiful and distinctive rose granite was exported from the quarries at Aswan in Upper Egypt to many lands to be used for columns and statues, but these are notable exceptions.

One of the earliest materials for building is known as "wattle and daub," formed by driving stakes into the ground and interlacing reeds or withes to form the framework, and then covering both sides with plastic clay. When the clay had dried in the sun it was quite permanent and required only a periodic coat of plaster to preserve it. Wattle-and-daub walls have been found dating back to the earliest period of building, namely the late Neolithic period. Buildings of this material can be included under the subject of architecture only in the broadest sense of the word, however, for there is little indication of an aesthetic quality.

Clay bricks seem to have been invented by the Obeid people in Persia before they descended to the Mesopotamian plain early in the fourth millennium B.C. The temple at Abu Shahrein (known in ancient times as Eridu) in southern Mesopotamia, and that at Tepe Gawra in northern Mesopotamia (both from the early part of the fourth millennium) can clearly be described as architectural buildings, incorporating several features which became characteristic of Mesopotamian architecture, of which we shall mention only the use of the buttress, designed not so much to strengthen the construction as to break up the monotonous expanse of a clay-brick wall.

In Egypt, early builders not only experimented with clay and brick, but also with wood, and then they made a remarkable transition to stone masonry. The genius traditionally connected with this new building technique was Imhotep, the designer and builder of the Step Pyramid at Saqqara in the

Two views, distant and close-up, of the famous Step Pyramid at Saqqara in Egypt. © MPS

time of Zoser (or Djoser) of the Third Dynasty (c. 2780 B.C.). From an examination of the remains at Saqqara there seems to be little doubt that the builders were seeking to imitate wood through the medium of stone, for we find simulated hinges and boards carved in stone doors that obviously could not function and other features that would be useful in wood but only ornamental in stone.

In the same building compound at Saqqara are found such remarkable features as the Proto-Doric column (which seems to have been formed in stone after the pattern of papyrus bundles), the cornice, corner posts, and other tectonic elements. The columns, it should be added, are not free-standing but are an integral part of the stone building; yet they cannot properly be identified as pilasters since they have all of the other features of the column. Fluting is not only concave in the customary Doric manner but also convex, and the capitals appear to be papyrus and palm leaves, which compare to the acanthus leaves of the Corinthian columns of Greek architecture of a much later period. If the columns were free-standing, the fluting would number from 14 to 20 around the circumference of the column, which compares to 20 flutes in the classical Doric order.

One of the early problems to be faced in building was the construction of the roof, and the solutions led to two main forms of architecture: trabeated and arcuated. The trabeated form is designed and constructed using horizontal beams supported by vertical posts, commonly called "post and lintel." The arcuated form makes use of various modifications of the arch. In the trabeated form the length of span between vertical supports is limited by the strength of the material used for the lintel. If, for example, the lintels were constructed of stone, as in ancient Egypt, it was only by using stone of great thickness that a span of any reasonable length could be obtained, and as a result the space between columns in Egyptian temples is not much greater than the diameter of the columns. Wooden beams, on the other hand, permitted more useful space between the uprights. With the modern invention of structural steel and reinforced concrete, the span reaches probably its greatest limit.

An attempt to solve this problem resulted in the development of the arch. The first step was probably the corbelled vault, which is formed by stepping out successive courses of brick or stone beyond the supporting wall or column, to meet similar corbelling from the adjacent vertical support. Corbelled vaults can be found at Ur in Mesopotamia as early as the Early Dynastic Period (c. 3000-2340 B.C.), and in Egypt as early as the tombs of the Third Dynasty (c. 2780-2680 B.C.) at Reqaqnah and Beit Khallaf. To judge from predynastic drawings from Egypt, the true arch may have developed from the practice of bending reeds which had been erected vertically to form side walls, so they would join overhead to form a roof. The arch, which is but a refinement of corbelling to effect a curved line rather than a step-like appearance, is found also in some of the buildings of Ur. The use of the arch in large buildings, however, does not seem to have been used successfully until the Roman period, and is generally attributed to the Etruscans. A modification of the corbelled vault, in which the stones form the sides of a triangle coming to an apex overhead, is found in Mycenaean tombs at Mycenae and Ugarit, dating from the 15th or 14th century B.C.

Model of Mesopotamian ziggurat.   OIUC

Unusual styles of architecture include the pyramid-shaped building. The ziggurat in Mesopotamia is generally believed to be the representative of a mountain; it was built of clay brick with exterior staircases or a sloping ramp, and probably a shrine at the top. One of the best preserved has recently been excavated at Choga Zambil, 20 miles SE of Susa, in Iran. The pyramids in Egypt were built as tombs and were constructed of stone, having an inner room or rooms. The Egyptians developed great precision in squaring and orienting their pyramids.

The Levant was very poor architecturally in the early second millennium B.C., and what little there is of quality can be traced to external origins. Original architecture does, however, seem to have developed in northern Syria, the most characteristic being the *bît hilani,* a temple or palace compound in which there are a portico and a throne room with their long axis parallel to the façade, and behind which are small rooms, probably bedrooms and a storeroom. This pattern developed in the second millennium but became characteristic of the early first millennium B.C. One feature of north Syrian architecture that should be mentioned is the use of a zoomorphic base to support a column, and often a human figure for the column.

The Arch of Titus at Rome.   UANT

Among the Israelites, architecture does not seem to have been developed as an art or a skill; rather, Phoenician craftsmen were brought in to build Solomon's palace and temple. Phoenician elements seem to be present also in the building of subsequent Israelite periods; it is difficult to classify these, however, for the Phoenicians seem to have made use of many techniques and styles, some of which can be traced to Cyprus and Egypt. Their use of metalwork in architecture, (e.g., the columns in front of Solomon's temple) was possibly derived from Asia Minor.

The Hittites made use of stone foundations, often using large stones, at first rough but later dressed, and characteristically with the first course set with the long dimension vertically. The upper portions of their buildings were frequently built of sun-dried brick strengthened by wooden beams — a type of architecture which can be found in the same areas in Asia Minor to the present time.

Late Assyrian architecture is perhaps best understood through the excavations of the palace of Sargon II at Khorsabad (720-704 B.C.). Regularity and a notable use of symmetry in the buildings are characteristic. Much of the work was still of clay brick, with the use of glazed bricks (a technique which had been imported by the Mitanni from Crete) to protect the exterior or exposed surfaces, as well as to lend decorative elements.

Reconstruction of the Palace of Sargon II, King of Assyria (721-705 B.C.), at Khorsabad. OIUC

Persian architecture seems to have developed the use of the cyclopean foundation, which may have come from the Urartians in the region of Lake Van. This use of huge stones, sometimes with drafting around the edges, is comparable to the well-known Herodian use of large stones; this is particularly true of Taht-i-Sulayman, north of Pasargadae in Iran, where the foundation stones could easily be mistaken for those at Râmat el-Khalîl near Hebron built by Herod several centuries later. The Persians seem to have brought in the Ionic column from the Greek world and to have developed and used it widely. The base of Persian columns is characteristically Ionic with fluting; the double volute at the capital is likewise Ionic; the columns, however, are more slender and graceful. Some idea of the gracefulness of Persian columns may be gained from the fact that the ratio of the height to the diameter, which in Egyptian columns is rarely more than six to one and which attained a maximum of ten to one in the Corinthian order, is twelve to one in the Hall of Xerxes at Persepolis. Likewise the distance between the columns, which in Egypt is rarely much more than one diameter, and in Greek architecture from one to slightly less

The Parthenon on the Acropolis at Athens. © MPS

than three diameters, in Persian buildings is between three and a half and six, and even seven, diameters. This gave the halls a sense of spaciousness not found in other large buildings of antiquity. One feature of the capital of the Persian column seems to be unique, namely the use of a stylized bull with a head at either end, the heads serving to support the longitudinal beams, while the hollow of the back supported the transverse beams.

The supreme achievement in architecture is admittedly the Periclean architecture of Greece (460-400 B.C.). This is the Doric order characterized by simplicity and symmetry. There are certain optical refinements, among which may be mentioned the use of entasis (a slight convexity in columns to avoid the impression of hollowness that straight lines would give), similarly a slight convexity of long horizontal lines (to avoid the appearance of sagging), deviation from perpendicular at the corners of the building and from exact intervals of spacing between the columns (to avoid the appearance that the end columns are leaning outward and the central columns are too close together). We can clearly see the developments of the Doric order if we consult first of all the Temple of Apollo at Corinth (about the sixth century B.C.), then the great temple of Poseidon at Paestum in Italy (early fifth century B.C.), which is in the transition stage, and finally the Parthenon at Athens (middle fifth century B.C.). The Ionic order achieved its classical form during this same period, having originated along the Asiatic coast of the Aegean Sea. The Corinthian order developed toward the end of the fifth and the beginning of the fourth century B.C., and reached its zenith in the Greco-Roman period a few centuries later.

Columns of the Doric Temple of Apollo at Corinth. © MPS

Remains of an arch at Corinth. JFW

A view of Athens from Areopagus Hill (Mars Hill), as Paul must have seen it. JFW

Roman architecture owed much to the Greeks but adopted some elements from the Etruscans; among the latter is principally the arch. In general we may say that Roman is not as subtle as Greek architecture but at the same time it is more utilitarian. The Greeks had developed the skill of masonry to a high degree of perfection and fit marble blocks together with remarkable accuracy without mortar or cement. The Romans, on the other hand, developed the use of pozzolana, a volcanic earth which was mixed with lime to make a hydraulic cement. Using this as mortar, they were able to bond courses of stone without exact precision in masonry, increase the span in arches, and build two-story structures. Roman architecture even more so than Greek included memorial arches and columns, amphitheaters, theaters, the forum (or market place), and many other forms familiar to us from the numerous remains of the Roman world to be found all over the Middle East.

W.S.L.S.

ARD (àrd), listed as a son of Benjamin in Genesis 46:21, but as a son of Bela, son of Benjamin, in Numbers 26:40; called Addar (with the consonants transposed) in I Chronicles 8:3.

ARDITE (àr′dīt), a descendant of Ard (Num. 26: 40).

ARDON (ar′dŏn), a son of Caleb (I Chron. 2:18).

ARELI (à-rē′lī), a son of Gad and founder of the tribal family, the Arelites (Gen. 46:16, Num. 26: 17).

AREOPAGITE (âr′ē-ŏp′a-jīt, -gīt), Dionysius, (Acts 17:34), a member of the court of Areopagus which had jurisdiction of manners, morals and teaching in Athens.

AREOPAGUS (âr′ē-ŏp′a-gŭs, Gr. *Áreios págos*), the rocky hill of the god Ares, or Mars. A spur jutting out from the western side of the Acropolis at Athens, separated from it by a short saddle. To the N, directly below, was the Agora or marketplace.

Areopagus is also the name of the council which met on Mars' hill, a court dating back to legendary times, in NT days still charged with questions of morals and the rights of teachers who lectured in public. Its importance was enhanced under the Romans. Paul was brought to the Areopagus (Acts 17:19) to be examined regarding his teaching. KJV says that "Paul stood in the midst of Mars hill," where ASV and RSV have "in the midst

(middle) of the Areopagus," referring to the court, not the hill, which is clearly the meaning (Acts 17: 22). Before these "solid citizens," the bulwark of civic and religious conservatism, Paul met the mocking taunts of adherents of the two most popular philosophies, Epicureanism and Stoicism, in an address more widely read today than any of the writings of the philosophers, and by which almost alone the Council of Areopagus is remembered. There were numerically scant results of Paul's mission in Athens, and the founding of no church is recorded, but Dionysius the Areopagite, one of the members of this honorable court, "clave unto him, and believed" (Acts 17:34). E.R.

ARETAS (ār′ē-tăs, *pleasing* or *virtuous*), a Nabatean king, father-in-law of Herod the tetrarch, whose deputy sought to apprehend Paul at Damascus (II Cor. 11:32, see Acts 9:24).

ARGOB (àr′gŏb, Heb. *'argōv, heap,* or *region of clods*). 1. A well-defined region of Bashan, identified with the kingdom of Og in Deuteronomy 3:4, 13, 14, and I Kings 4:13. This land of 60 strong, fortified cities was taken by the Israelites under Moses (Deut. 3:4), and was given to the half-tribe of Manasseh (Deut. 3:13), because Jair of this tribe conquered the region. He gave it his own name, Bashan-havoth-jair (Deut. 3:14). In Solomon's reign, one of his princes, the son of Geber, held Argob, which still had 60 "great cities with walls and brasen bars" (I Kings 4:13).

2. II Kings 15:25 refers to either a place or a person. If a place, it would appear to be where one of the king's houses was located. If a person, he may have been either a follower of Pekahiah, killed with him; or a follower of Pekah who took part in the murder of Pekahiah. The Heb. text is uncertain. RSV omits mention of Argob altogether.

ARIDAI (à-rĭd′ā-ī, à-rĭd′ī), one of Haman's ten sons, killed by the Jews (Esth. 9:9).

ARIDATHA (à-rĭd′à-thà, ăr-ĭ-dā′thà), a son of Haman, killed by the Jews (Esth. 9:8).

ARIEH (à-rī′ĕ, ār′ĭ-ĕ), named with Argob in II Kings 15:25 KJV, ASV, either as places or as persons. Omitted in RSV. The Heb. text is uncertain.

ARIEL (âr′ĭ-ĕl, Heb. *'arî′ēl, lion of God*). 1. One of an embassy sent by Ezra to bring "ministers for the house of our God" to the returning exiles from Babylonia (Ezra 8:16,17).

2. In II Samuel 23:20 and I Chronicles 11:22, where KJV has "two lionlike men of Moab," ASV conjectures "two sons of Ariel of Moab," and RSV

"two ariels of Moab," explaining in the margin, "the meaning of the word *ariel* is unknown." But in view of the context, the KJV translation is still acceptable.

3. A poetic name, "lioness of God," given to Jerusalem (Isa. 29:1, 2, 7).

ARIMATHEA (âr'ĭ-må-thē'å), the city of the Joseph who buried the body of Jesus in his own new tomb near Jerusalem (Matt. 27:57, Mark 15:43, Luke 23:51, John 19:38). The location of Arimathea is in doubt, but is conjectured to be Ramathaim-zophim, the Ramah of Samuel's residence, in the hill-country of Ephraim, about 20 miles NW of Jerusalem and six miles SE of Antipatris.

ARIOCH (ăr'ĭ-ŏk). 1. The king of Ellasar in Syria and confederate with Chedorlaomer (Gen. 14:1, 4, 9).

2. Captain of the king's guard at Babylon under Nebuchadnezzar (Dan. 2:14-25).

ARISAI (à-rĭs'ā-ī, ăr'ĭ-sī), a son of Haman who was killed by the Jews (Esth. 9:9).

ARISTARCHUS (ăr'ĭs-tär'kŭs, *the best ruler*), a Macedonian of Thessalonica, one of Paul's travel-companions. This convert from Judaism is spoken of as Paul's "fellow-prisoner," implying imprisonment for the Gospel's sake (Acts 19:29, 20:4, 27:2, Col. 4:10, Philem. 24).

ARISTOBULUS (à-rĭs'tō-bū'lŭs, *the best counselor*), a Christian in Rome, whose household Paul greeted. There is a tradition that he was one of the 70 disciples, and that he preached in Britain (Rom. 16:10).

ARK (àrk) of Noah; Heb. *tēvâh*, meaning 1. *a chest*; 2. *a vessel to float*; in the Bible, always the second meaning. It is used of the vessel which God directed Noah to build (Gen. 6:14-16). God told Noah what to bring into it (Gen. 6:18-21), and Noah obeyed (Gen. 6:22-7:10). The ark floated during the Flood (Gen. 7:11-8:3), then came to rest "upon the mountains of Ararat (Gen. 8:4). After Noah abandoned the ark (Gen. 8:18, 19), what happened to it is unknown. There are traditions, and there have been expeditions, with claims of finding remains, but nothing conclusive. We do not even know on which peak of the mountains in the land of Ararat the ark grounded.

The ark of Noah is referred to in Matthew 24:38, Luke 17:27 in a warning of coming judgment; in Hebrews 11:7 as an example of faith; and in I Peter 3:20 "the days of Noah, while the ark was in preparation," are held up as an example of "the long-suffering of God," followed by disaster for the "disobedient," salvation for the few who entered the ark. The same Hebrew word is used of the basket of bulrushes in which Moses was cast out to float upon the Nile (Exod. 2:2-5).

ARK, *of the covenant* or *of the testimony*; Heb. *'ărôn ha-berîth, chest of the covenant.* The word *'ărôn* is used of the coffin (mummy-case) of Joseph (Gen. 50:26); elsewhere of the chest containing the tables of the law, resting in the tabernacle or in the temple. God directed Moses (Exod. 25:10-22, Deut. 10:2-5) to make it of shittim (acacia) wood, of precise dimensions, and to overlay it with pure gold within and without, with a crown of gold about it. There were to be rings of gold at the corners, and staves covered with gold to put through the rings to carry the ark. Within was to be placed "the testimony which I shall give thee." A mercy seat of gold, with two winged cherubim of gold, was to be placed on top of the ark. There God promised to meet and talk with

Relief showing structure on wheels, representing the Ark of the Covenant, found in the ruins at Capernaum. © MPS

Moses. The ark was made after the golden calf was destroyed (Deut. 10:1, "At that time"), and was set up in the tabernacle (Exod. 40:20).

The ark went before Israel in the wilderness journeys "to search out a resting-place for them" (Num. 10:33). The ark was instrumental in the crossing of Jordan on dry land under Joshua (Josh. 3), and in the capture of Jericho (Josh. 4:7-11). Joshua prayed before the ark after the defeat at Ai (Josh. 7:6) and after the subsequent victory, at Mt. Ebal, the ark being present (Josh. 8:33). In the days of Eli the ark was in the tabernacle at Shiloh (I Sam. 3:3). It was taken into battle against the Philistines, and captured by them. "The glory is departed from Israel, for the ark of God is taken" (I Sam. 4:3-22). It was held by the Philistines until a plague convinced them that the ark was too dangerous to keep, and it was ceremoniously sent back (I Sam. 5:1-6:15) to Beth-shemesh. The men of this place also suffered a plague for looking into the ark, and it was removed to Kirjath-jearim (I Sam. 6:19-21). Here it was treated with due respect, being kept in the house of Abinadab under the care of his son Eleazar (I Sam. 7:1, 2).

David brought the ark to Jerusalem, after some misadventures (II Sam. 6, I Chron. 13 and 15). When Uriah said to David, "The ark, and Israel, and Judah, abide in tents" (II Sam. 11:11), he may have meant that the ark had been taken away by the army into the field, or merely that the ark was in a tent (the tabernacle) just as the armies of Israel and Judah were in tents. At the time of Absalom's rebellion, Zadok and the Levites carried the ark out of Jerusalem, but David had them take it back (II Sam. 15:24-29). The priests brought the ark into Solomon's temple (I Kings 8:3-9). There was nothing in it at this time "save the two tables of stone, which Moses put there at Horeb."

Before the ark was made, Moses directed that a pot of manna be laid up before the Lord (Exod. 16:32-34) and Hebrews 9:4 says that "the golden pot that had manna, and Aaron's rod that budded, and the tables of the covenant" were in the ark (at some time;.not necessarily throughout its existence). Jeremiah, writing after the destruction of Jerusalem by Nebuchadnezzar, prophesies that in time to come the ark will no longer be of significance for worship (Jer. 3:16). Psalm 132:8 speaks of the ark poetically as representing the strength of the Lord, whether the ark was in existence at the time this psalm was written or not. Hebrews 9 uses the tabernacle and all its furnishings, including the ark, in explaining by analogy salvation by the high-priesthood of Christ. After the destruction of the first temple, there is no evidence as to what happened to the ark, but only highly speculative tradition and conjecture. Synagogues, from our earliest knowledge of them to the present, have had arks in the side wall toward Jerusalem; therein the scrolls of the Law are stored behind a curtain. E.R.

ARKITES (är'kīts, Heb. 'areqî), people of Arka, a Phoenician town a few miles NE of Tripoli, and near but not on the sea. The Arkites are named among descendants of Canaan (Gen. 10:17, I Chron. 1:15).

ARM, used as a figure for might, of God (Isa. 53:1). "Break the arm," i.e., the power (Ezek. 30:25). "Stretched out arm," image from a warrior with spear or sword thrust forth (see Josh. 8:26).

ARMAGEDDON (är-mà-gĕd'ŏn, Gr. Armageddón, from Heb.; Mount Megiddo; ASV, Har-Magedon), a word found only in Revelation 16:16, for the final battleground between the forces of good and evil. The Valley of Jezreel and the Plain of Esdraelon at the foot of Mount Megiddo were the scene of many decisive battles in the history of Israel: the victory sung by Deborah and Barak (Judg. 5:19, 20); Gideon's defeat of Midian (Judg. 6: 33); Saul's death at the hands of the Philistines (I Sam. 31, see II Sam. 4:4); where Josiah was slain in battle with Pharaoh-nechoh (II Kings 23: 29, 30); Ahaziah fled and was killed there (II Kings 9:27). The town of Megiddo guarded the pass which formed the easiest caravan route between the Plain of Sharon and the Valley of Jezreel, and the low mountains around were silent witnesses of perhaps more bloody encounters than any other spot on earth, continuing down to recent times. Hence the appropriateness of this place for the vast conflict pictured in Revelation 16.

ARMENIA (är-mē'nĭ-à), occurs only in KJV of II Kings 19:37 and Isaiah 37:38, where it is said that the two sons of Sennacherib, king of Assyria, "escaped into the land of Armenia" after murdering their father. ASV and RSV, and KJV elsewhere (e.g. Gen. 8:4, Jer. 51:27) have Ararat, following the Heb. and LXX. The same mountainous country, north of Assyria, is meant by both names.

ARMLET, BRACELET (ärm'lĕt; -lĭt; brās'lĕt; -lĭt), an ornament usually for the upper arm, worn by both men and women. "Armlet" appears in ASV, RSV of Exodus 35:22, Numbers 31:50, in RSV of II Samuel 1:10, Isaiah 3:20. KJV usually has "bracelet" here, and in other places (e.g., Gen. 24: 22, 38:25, Ezek. 16:11, 23:42). The Heb. original uses several different words, the precise meaning of none of which is certain. Archaeological finds illustrate possible objects to be designated armlets.

ARMONI (är-mō'nī, belonging to the palace), a son of Saul by his concubine Rizpah. He was slain by the Gibeonites to satisfy justice (II Sam. 21:8-11).

ARMOR-BEARER, bearer of weapons. Abimelech (Judg. 9:54), Saul (I Sam. 31:4), Jonathan (I Sam. 14:12) and Joab (II Sam. 23:37) had one. Cf. Goliath (I Sam. 17:7,41).

ARMORY. Three Hebrew words: ('ôtsār, Jer. 50: 25) figurative for the "Lord's means of judgment"; rendered also "treasure," "treasury," "store-house"; (nesheq, Neh. 3:19) "store-house for valuables and arms"; (talpîyôth, S. of Sol. 4:4) used figuratively for "beauty."

ARMS, ARMOR (ärms, är'mêr), mentioned often in the Bible, both literally and as illustrative of spiritual conflicts. Here only hand weapons and body armor are considered, not chariots or machines used in sieges.

A. Offensive weapons. 1. Sword is the first mentioned in the Bible; "a flaming sword which turned every way, to keep the way of the tree of life" (Gen. 3:24). Heb. hereb, a weapon for smiting, is the common sword (Gen. 27:40; Exod. 17:13); a sword for punishment is ascribed to God (Exod. 5:3, 22:24). Figurative and literal are united in "the sword of the Lord and of Gideon" (Judg. 7:20). Gideon's men were executing the judgment of God. In NT Greek the commoner word is máchaira, short sword, dagger, or saber (Matt. 26:47-53, Rom. 8:35, 13:4); figuratively "the sword of the Spirit" (Eph. 6:17). Once, in Luke 2:35, and six times in the Book of Revelation (1: 16, etc.), rhomphaía, a large, broad sword, occurs, with symbolic meaning. 2. Rod, a stick loaded at one end, which could be for reassurance (Ps. 23:4); used to count sheep (Lev. 27:32), or a weapon (Ps. 2:9). 3. Sling, a band of leather, wide in the middle to receive a stone. With the ends held together, it was swung around the head, then one end was released that the stone might fly to its mark (I Sam. 17:40, 49, Judg. 20:16, II Kings 3:25). 4. Bow, sometimes of steel (II Sam. 22:35, Job 20:24, Ps. 18:34) and arrows. First mentioned (Gen. 27:3) as used in hunting, except the "bow in the cloud" (Gen. 9:13-16, rainbow). The practice of archery is described in I Samuel 20:20-22, 35-40. The bow is mentioned but once in the NT (Rev. 6:2). 5. Spear, lance, javelin or dart, sharp-pointed

Israelites in armor. Left, heavily armed, with shield, spear and helmet; right, lightly armed with sling, bow and quiver. DV

Roman and Greek soldiers in armor.

instruments to be thrust or thrown (Josh. 8:18, Judg. 5:8, I Sam. 17:7, 18:11, Ps. 68:30, different Heb. words). Spearmen are mentioned in Acts 23: 23, and a Roman lance pierced the body of Jesus on the cross (John 19:34). Flame-tipped darts were used (Eph. 6:16).

B. Defensive armor. 1. *Shields* were either large, Heb. *tsinnâh,* (I Sam. 17:7, 41), and sometimes for display (II Chron. 9:16), called *thyreós,* "like a door" in Greek (Eph. 6:16); or small, round, Heb. *māghēn* (Gen 15:1, Judg. 5:8). 2. *Helmet,* (I Sam. 17:5, Isa. 59:17), sometimes of brass (I Sam. 17:38), surrounding the head (Eph. 6:17, I Thess. 5:8). 3. *Coat of mail,* only in I Samuel 17:5, 38, called "breastplate" in Isaiah 59:17. In the NT, Greek *thórax* (Eph. 6:14, I Thess. 5:8, figuratively; Rev. 9:9, 17, symbolic). 4. *Greaves,* for the legs, only in I Samuel 17:6. 5. *Girdle,* or belt from which the sword hung (II Sam. 20:8). Ephesians 6:14 implies it as part of a heavy-armed soldier's equipment, the description of which in Ephesians 6:11-18 is evidently drawn from Paul's intimate contact, as a prisoner, with Roman guards. "The whole armor," Greek *panoplía,* is a technical term for such armament. Note also the detailed description of the armor of Goliath (I Sam. 17:4-7).
E.R.

ARMY, a collection of men armed and organized for warfare. Of the several words used for army, *gedhûdh* is used 32 times and generally means a band of light troops foraging (I Sam. 30:8, II Sam. 22:30, etc.), though in the time of Amaziah (ninth century B.C.) it was used (II Chron. 25) of his great army of 300,000 chosen men of Judah and Benjamin with, at first, 100,000 mercenaries from the northern kingdom. These were drafted and put under colonels and captains ("captains of thousands and captains of hundreds"). The armies of Israel, when directed of God and led by Him, were uniformly successful (Josh. 1:3, 5:14), but when like Amaziah (II Chron. 25:14) and, earlier, Saul (I Sam. 15) the king refused to listen to God, defeat and death followed. *Hayil,* used 231 times and translated "army" 54 times, implies might, valor or wealth (Exod. 14:9: "all the horses and chariots of Pharaoh, and his horsemen and his army"). "Army" here implies infantry, which in most times has been the backbone of the army. For some reason, God did not want Israel to use or to depend upon cavalry. (Deut. 17:16, 20:1, Isa. 13:1) *mahăneh,* used over 200 times, generally means "encampment," but is rendered "army" three times, referring to the Philistine forces, and hinting at their methodical warfare.

The word *ma'ărākhâh,* used 20 times is generally rendered "army" and implies ordered arrangement or battle array (I Sam. 17:21). The word *tsāvā'* properly means "host," e.g., "Lord God of Sabaoth" (Isa. 22:15, etc.) means "Lord God of hosts." It is used nearly 500 times and is rendered "army" 29 times. The word emphasizes the vast number of the soldiers. When used of God's army, the "soldiers" may be people (Ex. 7:4), angels (Ps. 103:21) and by implication locusts (Joel 2). The corresponding Greek word *stratia* is used of angels (Luke 2:13) and of stars and planets (Acts 7:42).

God's arrangement for His people and His army in the wilderness journey made for perfect order. They encamped with the tabernacle at the center (Num. 2), the three families of the Levites and the priests closely surrounding it, then the other 12 tribes at a slightly greater distance. Three tribes were grouped on each side of the tabernacle under the banners of the leading tribes: Judah eastward, with Issachar and Zebulun; Reuben southward, with Simeon and Gad; Ephraim, westward, with Manasseh and Benjamin; and Dan to the north, with Asher and Naphtali. When they marched, the Levites, carrying the tabernacle, occupied the center of the line, and the high command was there.

In the days of the judges, God raised up from time to time men of special ability to save Israel when she had suffered for her apostasies and had been brought to repentance. These judges saved Israel from her foreign oppressors, and they varied greatly in character, from the godly Deborah (Judg. 4,5) to the rather erratic champion, Samson (Judg. 14-16). Israel's armies down to Solomon's time were composed mostly of footmen, armed with swords, spears, bows and arrows and slings, and protected by small shields, with a judge, general or king at the head.

Numbers 1 contains a military census of Israel at Sinai just after the exodus, and Numbers 26 a second census taken 40 years later in the plains of Moab. According to the plain sense of the English versions, the number of military men was immense: over 603,000 at the exodus and nearly as many at the Jordan, and these figures imply a total population of something like three million men, women, and children, accompanied by herds and flocks. It is hard to picture them drinking at a common spring, even a large one. The Hebrew word *eleph* means either a thousand or a family, and by reading "families" in the censuses, some would make the numbers more comprehensible. E.g., Numbers 1:21 could read "forty-six families, five hundred men." This would not only make the story more easy to understand, but it would explain the very remarkable numerical phenomenon in censuses. In all the twenty-four numbers recorded, in the hundreds' digits we have not a single "zero," "one," "eight" or "nine" and only one "two" in the whole list. The trouble with this theory, however, lies in the totals: if *eleph* here means family, the total in Numbers 1:46 would become 598 families, 5,500 men instead of 603,550 men, for we could not "carry over" the hundreds' digit.

Israel, on condition of obedience (Deut. 28:1-7) could have become the paramount power of the earth, but when she had gone into hopeless apostasy, God began to raise up great universal world powers (Dan. 2) and to overturn (Ezek. 21:27) Israel, preparing for the coming of our Lord. The Babylonians with their hordes were overthrown by the Persians, originally a hardy race whose armies were mostly cavalry; but when Xerxes, the "Ahasuerus" of Esther 1, attempted to invade

Europe, he was defeated. Esther 1 tells of his great "feast" of six months, which was really a military council preparing for his invasion of Greece in 480 B.C. The eastern army was defeated by the Greeks with their phalanxes of heavy armed infantry, arranged closely in ranks and files. The Greek armies, in turn, were conquered by the Romans. The Romans had a genius for government and for military organization, and the various NT references mention their "chief captains" (Acts 21:31), whom we would call colonels, their centurions (Acts 10:1), etc., implying their organization into legions and armies. Our Lord (Matt. 26:53) hints at a possible angelic army divided like the Roman into legions. The smallest group of soldiers mentioned in the Bible is the quaternion (Acts 12:4), composed of only four soldiers.   A.B.F.

ARNAN (ȧr'năn), head of a noble Jewish family about 500 B.C. (I Chron. 3:21).

ARNON (ȧr'nŏn), the swift "roaring stream" and the valley of the same name which empty into the E side of the Dead Sea a little N of its center. It arises in the hills of northern Arabia and flows a little W of N and then turns westward to descend precipitately into the Sea, emptying at about the lowest point on the earth's surface. It is now a "wadi," implying that it is dry through most of the year. It is first mentioned (Num. 21:13) as the boundary between the Moabites and the Amorites in the time of Moses, and Israel encamped upon its N side so as not to invade Moab. In Judges 11:18-26 Jephthah tells the Ammonites how Israel had held the land N of the Arnon for 300 years previous to his time (c. 1560-1260 B.C.). For all those years, and for a long time after, the Arnon was the southern boundary of the tribe of Reuben. It now flows through the kingdom of Jordan. In the days of Jehu, (ninth century B.C.) Hazael, king of Syria smote Israel E of the Jordan as far as Arnon (II Kings 10:32,33).

AROD (ā'rŏd), a son of Gad (Gen. 46:16), where he is called Arodi, head of the family of Arodites in the time of Moses (Num. 26:17).

AROER (ȧ-rō'ẽr, Heb. *poor, naked, helpless*). The same word is rendered "heath" in Jeremiah 17:6, 48:6. 1. A town on a branch of the brook Jabbok, fortified early by the tribe of Gad (Num. 32:34), having been taken from Sihon, king of the Amorites (cf. Josh. 13:25). A camping place of Joab (II Sam. 24:5) when taking a census in the days of David. Isaiah speaks of it (Isa. 17:2) as being deserted in his time.
2. A town about 35 miles south of 1, located on the N bank of the Arnon, and so in the tribe of Reuben and just across from Moab. Moses took this also from Sihon (Deut. 2:36), and gave it to Reuben (Josh. 13:9). Hazael, king of Syria, took it from Israel in the days of Jehu (II Kings 10:33). Jeremiah scoffs at its inhabitants (Jer. 48:19).
3. A town in the southern part of Judah (I Sam. 30:28).

ARPAD (ȧr'păd), a town and its surrounding region in the northern part of Syria near Hamath (modern Hamah), with which it is associated in all six biblical references. Rabshakeh, representing Sennacherib before the Jews of Jerusalem, 701 B.C., boasts that the gods of Arpad could not stand before his master, therefore neither could the God of the Jews. In Jeremiah's time (c. 580 B.C.) Arpad had melted away (Jer. 49:23).

ARPHAXAD (ȧr-făk'săd, Heb. and ASV, *Arpachshad*), third son of Shem, c. 2479 B.C., the first birth recorded after the Flood. He lived 438 years, and was the ancestor of Hebrews and of many

Gorge of the River Arnon where it enters the Dead Sea. © MPS

Arab tribes; in fact, of all Semites except Assyrians, Elamites, Lydians and Syrians (Gen. 10:22-11:13). Also possibly a region of Assyria.

ARROW (See Arms)

ART, the application of human skills to produce a pleasing effect. The word is also used in a broader sense with reference to the good and the useful, but the narrower meaning, referring to the beautiful, is more common. The six major arts are music, the dance, architecture, sculpture, painting, and literature.

It is difficult to date the beginning of art. If some human being found pleasure in the shape of a stone axe or flint sickle, this might be described as the beginning of art. By any definition, the line drawings in the cave of La Madelaine from the Old Stone Age would seem to be art. Architecture (*q.v.*) might be traced to the first building of a house, although some effort at an aesthetic quality should be added to the utilitarian value in order for the building to qualify as "art." Artistic attempts can be found in the early temples in Mesopotamia from the fourth millennium B.C. and in Egypt only slightly later. Sculpture is found in Mesopotamia and Egypt as early as the beginning of the third millennium. Literature must be placed before the time of writing, for the folk stories and legends had already taken on forms that gave pleasure to the hearers in the preliterary period — again toward the end of the fourth millennium B.C. To judge from wall paintings in Egypt, music and the dance must go back to about the same time. Hence it seems reasonable to date the beginning of art in historical cultures to some time in the fourth millennium B.C. The origin of the arts may be intended in Genesis 4:21-22, where Jubal and Tubal-Cain are mentioned.

The arts can be classified as spatial (architecture, sculpture, painting) and temporal (music, literature), with the dance extending over both categories. Spatial art can be seen as a whole before the parts become meaningful; temporal art on the other hand must be seen or heard in the parts before the whole is comprehended. The temporal forms therefore require a greater use of the memory on the part of the observer, and a certain amount of repetition and interpretation on the part of the artist. Music, and in many cases, literature, might be called aural arts, whereas the others are visual arts.

In each of the arts, categories of matter, form, and content can be distinguished. By matter is meant all the material available to the artist which he can select, arrange, and use for his purpose; by form is meant all the ways in which he can organize the material; and by content, what is actually expressed when he has finished. The artist's innate ability is discernible in his selection of matter and form; it would be ludicrous if an artist were to attempt to present a sunset at sea by sculpturing in marble, or a thunderstorm by a piccolo solo.

It becomes increasingly apparent, as we think on the subject of art, that something of the image of God as Creator is to be found in man as artist. The artist creates. In fact, some authors claim that there is no art in nature and no art without the creativity of the artist.

Each art has limitations imposed upon it in the extent of its message. Music and the dance can convey certain emotional messages, but in spite of the saying that "music is the universal language," it is seriously limited in the intellectual message it can convey. Sculpture and painting can convey messages from the visible world, but are more limited in conveying ideas or emotions. Literature is by far the most communicative of all the arts and can be used to convey conceptual, emotional, and other ideas. In keeping with this fact is the presentation of the revelation of God through the medium of literature.

In Israel, probably because of the commandment against representational art (Exod. 20:4), there were no great contributions to the arts of painting or sculpturing. The major architectural works in Israel seem to have been done by Phoenician craftsmen. References to the dance in the Old Testament are extremely limited, and afford no information on the form or content. The development of music in Israel, on the other hand, is noteworthy, and to judge from the titles, we may assume that many of the Psalms, if not all, were sung to music and accompanied by musical instruments. Literature, however, was the most thoroughly developed art in Israel and reached a level not surpassed in all antiquity.   W.S.L.S.

ARTAXERXES (är-tà zûrk'sēz), a proper name or possibly title, like *Pharaoh, Caesar, etc.* for several kings of Persia. The name is variously derived by scholars but perhaps "strong king" (Gesenius) is as good as any. Herodotus made it mean "great warrior." The name or title of three Persian kings in the OT. 1. The pseudo-Smerdis of Ezra 4:7-23, a Magian usurper who claimed to be Smerdis, a son of Cyrus who had died. This false Smerdis took the title Artaxerxes and reigned about seven months in 522, 521 B.C. He was opposed to the liberal policies of Cyrus and Cambyses (called Ahasuerus in Ezra 4:6) and so was glad to prohibit the Jews from building the temple.
2. A Persian king (Ezra 7:1-8:1, Neh. 2:1, 5:14, 13:6) nicknamed "Longimanus" or "Long-handed" because of a deformity of his right hand. He granted the requests of Ezra (7:6) in 457 B.C. and of Nehemiah (Neh. 2:1-8) in 444 B.C. to go to Jerusalem and gave them power, supplies, and authority.
3. Possibly another king who must have reigned before 516 B.C. (Ezra 6:14).

ARTEMAS (är'tĕ-măs), a companion of Paul at Nicopolis whom Paul expected to send to Crete. Mentioned only in Titus 3:12. In tradition, a bishop of Lystra.

Above, reconstruction of the Temple of Artemis (Diana) at Ephesus. Below, the site as it appears today. UANT © MPS

ARTEMIS (är'tĕ-mĭs), the Greek goddess of hunting, corresponding to the Roman Diana. She had many temples, but the greatest was at Ephesus where she was deeply venerated, but her worship there was more like the impure worship of Ashtaroth of Phoenicia (Acts 19:23-41). Her temple at Ephesus was counted as one of the wonders of the world.

ARTIFICER (See Occupations)

ARTILLERY (är-til'êr-ē), a word which in the KJV is used only in I Samuel 20:40, where it refers to Jonathan's bow and arrows. The RV has "weapons."

ARUBOTH (à-rŭb'ŏth), a region of the Shephelah in Judah assigned to Ben-hesed to provide food for Solomon's court (I Kings 4:10).

ARUMAH (à-rōō'mà), a place near Shechem in Ephraim where Abimelech dwelt (Judg. 9:41). Variously placed NE or S of modern Nablus.

ARVAD (är'văd), a small island, containing a city of the same name, off the coast of Syria about 40 miles north of Tripoli. Its people are mentioned with Sidonians as rowers of Tyre (Ezek. 27:8,11). They were descendants of Ham through Canaan (Gen. 10:18). The name seems to mean "a place of fugitives," and it is said to have been first built by fugitives from Sidon. Later called "Ruad" from the same root. There are remains of the sea-walls with immense stones 12 feet long and 10 feet high, indented with deep grooves, perhaps for tying up boats.

ASA (ā'sà, Heb. *'āsā', healer*). 1. Third king of Judah, reigning from 964-923 B.C. (I Kings 15:9-24, II Chron. 14-16). He was the first of the five kings of Judah (Asa, Jehoshaphat, Joash, Hezekiah, Josiah) who were outstanding for godliness, and he deserves special credit considering his idolatrous ancestors. He was the son of Abijam and grandson of Rehoboam. The grandmother of Asa was Maacah, a daughter of Absalom, a confirmed idolatress who greatly influenced Judah toward idolatry. She is spoken of as "mother" of both her son (I Kings 15:2) and her grandson (15:10). Asa began his reign by deposing his wicked and powerful grandmother and by destroying a fearful, impure image that she had set up. He then drove out the Sodomites, and destroyed idols that his fathers had worshiped (15:12), commanding Judah to seek the Lord God of their fathers (II Chron. 14:4).

In the early peaceful days of his reign, he gathered into the house of the Lord the dedicated things which his father and he had vowed to the Lord (I Kings 15:15). Then c. 953 B.C. Zerah the Ethiopian (probably Osorkon II of Egypt's dynasty XXII) came against him with an immense force which the Lord helped Judah defeat at Mareshah in the west-central part of Judah, because Asa trusted the Lord (II Chron. 14:9-15). In II Chronicles 15:1-13 we see how the Lord approved and encouraged Asa in his faith and in his work of reformation. Later, in 948 B.C., (the 36th year of the kingdom, not the reign) of Asa, Baasha of the northern kingdom made war against Judah; and this time, Judah did not put her whole trust in the Lord, but Asa bribed Ben-hadad of Syria to break his league with Baasha so as to draw off the forces of Israel. This Ben-hadad did, but the Lord, through his prophet Hanani rebuked Asa for trusting in politics rather than in God (I Kings 15:16-22, II Chron. 16:1-10). In the 39th year of his reign Asa was taken with a severe disease of the feet, and because he trusted his physicians rather than the Lord, he died (II Chron. 16:11-14).

2. A Levite among those who had returned from captivity (I Chron. 9:16).

ASADIAH (ă-sà-dī'à), the son of Chelcias and father of Sedecias, in the ancestry of Baruch, according to the apocryphal book that bears his name (Baruch 1:1).

ASAHEL (ăs'à-hĕl, *whom God made*). 1. Youngest son of Zeruiah, David's sister; and brother of Joab and Abishai. These three were among the mighty men of David; and Asahel was over 24,000 men (I Chron. 27:7). Very fleet of foot, he pursued Abner, Saul's former general (II Sam. 2:18-23), who slew him.

2. A teaching Levite in the reign of Jehoshaphat (II Chron. 17:8).

3. A Levite in Hezekiah's reign, who oversaw the offerings (II Chron. 31:13).

4. Father of a certain Jonathan (Ezra 10:15).

ASAHIAH (ăs'à-hī'à, *whom Jehovah made*, ASV Asaiah), one of Josiah's officers whom he sent to inquire of the Lord concerning the words of the law which Shaphan had read to the king (II Kings 22:12-14).

ASAIAH (à-sā'yà, *whom Jehovah made*). 1. A Simeonite, c. 800 B.C. (I Chron. 4:36).

2. A Levite of the family of Merari in the time of David (I Chron. 6:30).

3. A Shilonite, one of the first after the captivity to dwell in Jerusalem (I Chron. 9:5).

4. One of the chief Levites of the family of Merari in David's day (I Chron. 15:6,11). This

may be the same as 2 above. He seems to have been the leader of about 220 Levites who assisted in bringing the ark from the house of Obed-edom to Jerusalem.

ASAPH (ā'săf), a Levite of the Gershonite family, appointed over the service of praise in the time of David and Solomon (I Chron. 16:5, II Chron. 5:12). He led the singing and sounded cymbals before the ark, and apparently set up a school of music (Neh. 7:44). There are 12 psalms credited to Asaph (50, 73-83); and it seems as though there must have been two Asaphs, centuries apart, who wrote psalms. Psalms 50, 73, 76, 78 certainly, and perhaps 75, 77, 82, could have been written in David's time; but 74, 79, and perhaps 83 belong to the Captivity. On the other hand, all these seem to have been written by a man, or men, of deep, spiritual contemplative nature, easily distinguished from David and the other psalmists.

2. Father of Hezekiah's recorder (II Kings 18:18).

3. An official under Artaxerxes Longimanus, king of Persia (Neh. 2:8).

4. In I Chronicles 26:1 read Ebiasaph (cf. ch. 9:19).

ASAREEL (à-sā'rē-ĕl, ASV Asarel), a descendant of Judah and a son of Jehallelel (I Chron. 4:16).

ASARELAH (ăs'à-rē'là, ASV Asharelah), a Levite singer of the sons of Asaph in David's time (I Chron. 25:2). Called Jesharelah in v. 14.

ASCENSION OF CHRIST (See Acts 1:6-11, Mark 16:19, Luke 24:50-52). The ascension of our Lord Jesus Christ necessarily came between His earthly and His heavenly ministry. He came to die for our sins, and to rise for our justification (Rom. 4:25). then He entered heaven to sit at the right hand of the Father (Acts 2:32-35) and to act as our Mediator (I Tim. 2:5) when we come to the Father in prayer, and as our Advocate (I John 2:1) when we fail to come. It occurred publicly and visibly, partly to convince His disciples of the reality of the event, and partly to build a strong hope for His equally visible return (Acts 1:11). His ascension was predicted in the OT (Ps. 68:18, cf. Eph. 4:8) and by our Lord Himself (John 20:17), and has been accepted as a central doctrine by all Christians since Pentecost. It is included in the Apostles' Creed: "He ascended into heaven and sitteth at the right hand of God." His going was a necessary preliminary to the Holy Spirit's coming (John 16:7).

ASENATH (ăs'ĕn-ăth), a daughter of Poti-pherah, priest of On, the modern Heliopolis, near Cairo, Egypt. Pharaoh gave her to Joseph as wife (Gen. 41:45-50), and she bore to him Manasseh ("causing to forget") and Ephraim ("doubly fruitful") before the famine began.

ASER (ā'sêr), the Greek form of Asher (*q.v.*).

ASHAN (ā'shăn), a town in the tribe of Judah, later given to Simeon because Judah's territory was too large; then made a city of refuge and given to the priests (Josh. 15:42, 19:7, I Chron. 4:32, 6:59). This was one of about a dozen towns mentioned in the lists of Judah and Simeon, as the boundary was indistinct and the territories overlapped.

ASHBEA (ăsh'bē-à), head of a family in Judah which worked in fine linen (I Chron. 4:21). He was a descendant of Shelah.

ASHBEL (ăsh'bĕl), the second son of Benjamin, son of Jacob. (I Chron. 8:1). The Ashbelites (Num. 26:38) descended from him.

ASHCHENAZ (See Ashkenaz)

At left, the ruins of Ashdod, and, at right, the village today. © MPS

ASHDOD (ăsh'dŏd, *stronghold, fortress*), one of the five chief cities of the Philistines: Ashdod, Gaza, Ashkelon, Gath and Ekron (Josh. 13:3). They were assigned to Judah, but Judah failed to dispossess the inhabitants "because they had chariots of iron" (Judg. 1:19). Ashdod was a center of Dagon (fish-god) worship, but when the Philistines thought to honor the ark of the Lord by placing it in the house of Dagon (I Sam. 5:1-7), God cast down and destroyed their idol. The Philistines found by careful testing that their plagues (see I Sam. 5,6) were from God and so they sent back the ark, with a trespass-offering. Uzziah, king of Judah early in the eighth century B.C., conquered the city (II Chron. 26:6). Amos predicted Ashdod's destruction (1:8). C. 700 B.C. Sargon II of Assyria took it (Isa. 20:1). In Jeremiah's prophecy (25:15-29) Ashdod was to drink with the nations "the cup of wrath" from the hand of the Lord. Zephaniah prophesied the destruction of the Philistines (Zeph. 2:4), and Zechariah said that "a bastard" (probably a foreign race) would dwell there (Zech 9:6). In Nehemiah's time (c. 444 B.C.) the men of Ashdod combined with others to hinder the Jews (Neh. 4:7-9), and, failing, they tried intermarrying with them (Neh. 13:23,24) so as to produce a mongrel race, but Nehemiah foiled them. In the LXX and in NT Ashdod is "Azotus." Philip, the evangelist, found himself there after the Holy Spirit had taken him away from the Ethiopian eunuch.

ASHDODITES (See Ashdod)

ASHDOTH PISGAH (ăsh'dŏth-pĭz'gà), the slopes or the springs of Pisgah, a mountain range just E of the northern end of the Dead Sea, belonging to the high, rugged mountains of Abarim which reach from the Arnon to the Jabbok. E of Jordan (Deut. 3:17, 4:49, Josh. 12:3, 13:20).

ASHER, or **ASER** (ăsh'êr, ă'sêr, *happy,* Aser in KJV of NT). 1. The second son of Zilpah, the hand-maid whom Laban gave to Leah his daughter and whom she gave to Jacob; and named "Happy" by Leah in her happiness at his birth. Born at Padan-Aram (in the plain of Mesopotamia) during Jacob's service with Laban (Gen. 30:13). We know little of his personal history, except the names of his five children (Gen. 46:17).

2. The tribe. descended from Asher (Josh. 19:24-31) was given the territory along the Mediterranean in the NW corner of Palestine, but failed to drive out the inhabitants of Sidon, Accho (modern Acre) and other Canaanite towns, and settled down to dwell among them. By David's time Asher seems to have become insignificant, for this tribe is omitted in the list of David's chief rulers (I Chron. 27:16-22). In NT and LXX "Aser" (*q.v.*).

ASHERAH (à-shē'rà), wrongly translated "grove" in KJV, 1. A goddess of the Phoenicians and Syrians, taken over by Israelites when they fell into idolatry.

2. The images supposed to represent this goddess. Her worship was lewd and associated with that of Baal (Ex. 34:13, I Kings 16:29-33).

ASHES. The expression "dust and ashes" (Gen. 18:27, etc.), is a play on words (*"aphar"* and *"epher"*) and signifies man's origin, as to his body, from the ordinary chemical elements. It contrasts the lowliness of man with the dignity of God. Ashes were sprinkled over a person, or a person sat among ashes, as a sign of mourning (II Sam. 13:19, Job 2:8); and so the word is often united with "sackcloth" to express mourning (Jer. 6:26).

The lovely expression "beauty for ashes" (Isa. 61:3) is also a play on words. Another word for ashes, *deshen,* is used for the remains of the burnt offering (Lev. 6:10,11, etc.).

ASHIMA (à-shī'mà), a god of the Hamathites, whose worship was brought to Samaria at its repopulation by the king of Assyria c. 715 B.C. (II Kings 17:30).

ASHKELON, ASKELON, ASCALON (ăsh'kĕ-lŏn, ăs'kĕ-lŏn), one of the five chief cities of the Philistines, located on the sea-coast about 12 miles N,NE of Gaza. It was taken by the tribe of Judah shortly after the death of Joshua (Judg. 1:18), but was retaken by the Philistines and was in their hands through much of the OT period. In the eighth century B.C. it was denounced by Amos for its complicity with Phoenicia and Edom in their warfare upon Israel (Amos 1:6-8). Zephaniah, writing in the dark days before the captivity of Judah (Zeph. 2:4,7) and looking far into the future, saw the restoration of Judah, and the Jews occupying the desolate ruins of Ashkelon; and Zechariah, writing about 518 B.C., prophesied, first, that Ashkelon would see the destruction of Tyre, and, second, that Ashkelon itself would be destroyed (Zech. 9:5). Apparently it was rebuilt, for Herod the Great was born there, and Roman ruins have been found. During the crusades, it came to life again and Richard Coeur-de-Lion held court there. Later the town reverted to the Saracens.

ASHKENAS (See Ashkenaz)

ASHKENAZ (ăsh'kĕ-năz). 1. Great grandson of Noah through Japheth and Gomer (Gen. 10:3, cf. I. Chron. 1:6).

2. A tribe or nation mentioned once (Jer. 51:27) and associated with Ararat and Minni as an instrument of wrath in the hands of God against Babylon.

ASHNAH (ăsh'nà), the name of two villages of Judah: 1. in the lowland W of Jerusalem and near the tribe of Dan (Josh. 15:33), and 2. about 27 miles SW of Jerusalem (Josh. 15:43).

ASHPENAZ (ăsh'pĕ-năz), prince of the eunuchs in the court of Nebuchadnezzar. It was he who gave to Daniel and his companions their new heathen names: Belteshazzar, etc. (Dan. 1:3,7).

ASHTAROTH OR ASTAROTH (ăsh'tà-rŏth), an ancient city in Bashan, where king Og dwelt. Probably so named from its having a temple to the goddess Ashtoreth (q.v.). It is generally mentioned with Edrei (q.v.), and the two were given to Machir of the tribe of Manasseh when Moses divided the territory east of the Jordan before his death (Deut. 1:4, Josh. 9:10, 13:31, etc.). It was given in Joshua's time to the children of Gershon, of the tribe of Levi (Josh. 21:27 — here called "Beeshterah"). Its site is now known as Tell-Ashtarah, in the fertile plain of Hauran, S of Damascus and E of the Sea of Galilee. Uzzia (I Chron. 11:44) one of David's mighty men, came from this town.

ASHTAROTH (ăsh'tà-rŏth), **ASTARTE** (ăs-tàr'tĕ). Ashtaroth is plural of Ashtoreth, name of any of the fertility goddesses of the ancient Near East; Babylonian *Ishtar*, Greek *Astarte*; in Canaan a consort of El (Baal) (Judg. 2:13, I Kings 11:5, 33, II Kings 23:13). The plural Ashtaroth refers to the many local goddesses (Judg. 10:13, I Sam. 7:3,4, 12:10, 31:10); also to the city of Og, king of Bashan, (Deut. 1:4, Josh. 9:10, 12:4, 13:12, 31), which became a Levitical city in Manasseh E of Lake Galilee (I Chron. 6:71), called Ashtaroth-Karnaim in Genesis 14:5. Modern Tell 'Ashtaroth.

ASHTEROTH-KARNAIM (ăsh'tĕ-rŏth-kàr-nā'ĭm), a town or region of the Rephaim in Abram's time smitten by four kings of the East (Gen. 14:5). It is located by some E of the Jordan and identified with the Ashtaroth of Bashan (Deut. 1:4). Exact site unknown.

ASHTORETH (ăsh'tō-rĕth), a goddess of the Canaanites, worshiped all along the seacoast from Ras Shamra (Ugarit) southward through Phoenicia and Philistia. The plural Ashtaroth is found commonly and refers to the idols representing her. Her male consort was apparently Baal, and the two were worshiped with lewd rites. In Judges 2:11-23 we are told that Israel forsook their God, and served Baal and Ashtaroth. The prophet Samuel brought about a great revival, but before Israel could be saved from the Philistines, they had to give up Ashtoreth and turn to Jehovah (I Sam. 7:3,4). Israel kept fairly close to the Lord through the times of Samuel, Saul and David and the early days of Solomon, until that "wise" man lost his wisdom by marrying various heathen women for political reasons. They succeeded in turning his heart from the Lord to the worship of the Ashtaroth and other idols (I Kings 11:4-8). These idols remained more than three and a half centuries till Josiah defiled and demolished them (II Kings 23:13,14). Gesenius related the name Ashtoreth to the Persian word "sitarah" or "star" and connects it with Venus, the goddess of love.

Ivory carving from Nimrud, of the "woman at the window," possibly the goddess Ashtoreth, or Astarte. BM

ASHUR (ăsh'ēr), great grandson of Judah through Pharez and Hezron (I Chron. 2:24, 4:5).

ASHURBANIPAL (ă-shoor-bă'nĕ-păl, *Ashur creates a son*), king of Assyria. He was grandson of the famous Sennacherib (q.v.) who reigned from 704 to 681 B.C. and son of Esar-Haddon, who reigned from 681-668 B.C. Ashurbanipal, or, as he was known to the Greeks, Sardanapalus, reigned from 668-626 B.C., and therefore was contemporary with Manasseh of Judah in the last half of his reign, Jotham his son, and the godly Josiah during the first twelve years of his reign. Modern scholars have reason to be grateful to Ashurbanipal because he was a lover of learning and collected a great library of cuneiform tablets (over 22,000 in number) which have given to us most of what we know of Babylonian and Assyrian literature.

ASHURITES (ăsh'ûr-īts) a tribe mentioned as a part of the realm of Ishbosheth, son of Saul (II Sam. 2:9). Possibly the same as the Asherites or men of Asher (Judg. 1:32). Possibly the "Asshurim" of Genesis 25:3, mentioned among the Arabian descendants of Abraham through Keturah, are the same. In KJV (Ezek. 27:6) we find the expression "the company of the Ashurites" but in ASV the very different rendering "inlaid in boxwood." The literal reading of the Hebrew is "daughter of Ashurites," but with a slightly different pointing the same letters yield "in boxwood."

ASHURNASIRPAL II (ă-shoor-năs' ĭr-păl), ruthless and mighty king of Assyria late in the tenth or early in the ninth century B.C. when she was rising by constant warfare to her greatest power. During the reigns of his grandfather Adadnirari II and his father Tukulti-Ninurta, the power of Assyria had been centralized and strengthened and the army had been highly organized and well armed. Assyria was seeking always to expand — her strength lay in constant conquest — and so this ruler subjugated all Mesopotamia, and defeated Babylon, which had challenged his power.

ASHVATH (ăsh'văth), an early descendant of Asher (I Chron. 7:33).

ASIA (ā'zhà). 1. The great continent E of Europe and Africa.

2. Asia Minor, otherwise Anatolia, the great western promontory of Asia, partially bounded by the three seas, Black, Aegean and Mediterranean, and the site of much of Paul's missionary work.

3. Proconsular Asia, the Roman province in NT times, which contained the SW part of Asia Minor, and in particular "the seven churches of Asia" addressed in the first three chapters of Revelation. In the NT the word occurs 21 times and always refers to this division, not the first two mentioned above. Its capital was Ephesus, where both Paul and John labored. Most of its cities have disappeared; but Smyrna (Rev. 2:8-11) remains a great city even now; and Philadelphia endured till the Middle Ages.

ASIARCHS (ā'shĭ-àrk, "chief of Asia"), found once in ASV as a transliteration of the Greek title, but is rendered "chief of Asia" (Acts 19:31) in KJV. Civil and priestly officials of the province of Asia chosen yearly to preside over the national games and theatrical displays. These patriotic pageants were financed by the Asiarchs, and so only rich men could afford to enjoy the honor. The meaning of the word in Greek is "rulers of" (or chief of) Asia and is a purely honorary title. It is to the real honor of those mentioned in Ephesus that they showed themselves friends to Paul.

ASIEL (ā'sĭ-ĕl, *God is maker*), a Simeonite, mentioned only in I Chronicles 4:35, as a prince in his family.

ASNAH (ăs'nà), head of a family of temple servants ("Nethinim") who returned from the captivity with Zerubbabel, 536 B.C. (Ezra 2:50).

ASNAPPER (ăs-năp'êr), mentioned only in Ezra 4:10 as "the great and noble Asnapper" who had brought over and set in Samaria people of various nations previous to the time of Zerubbabel. His name is not mentioned in the Assyrian annals, but it has been proved, almost to a certainty, that this name is an Aramaean corruption of Ashurbanipal. It was he who colonized Samaria and other regions by wholesale deportations of conquered peoples.

ASP (See Animals)

ASPATHA (ăs-pā'thà), third son of Haman, enemy of the Jews. (Esth. 9:7).

ASRIEL (ăs'rĭ-ĕl). KJV once *Ashriel*. 1. Grandson of Manasseh and son of Gilead, and head of the family as Asrielites. (Num. 26:31, Josh. 17:2).

2. A son of Manasseh by his Aramaean concubine (I Chron. 7:14).

ASS (See Animals)

ASSIR (ăs'êr, *captive*). 1. A cousin once removed of Moses (Exod. 6:24).

2. Great grandson of the former (I Chron. 6:23).

3. In KJV apparently a son of Jeconiah (I Chron. 3:17), but it should read "Jeconiah the captive." Cf. ASV.

ASSOS (ăs'ŏs), modern Behramkoy, seaport of Mysia in Asia Minor, on the N coast of the gulf of Adramyttium, seven miles from the island of Lesbos to the S near Methymna, 20 miles S of Troas (Acts 20:13,14). The ship, with Luke and others, sailed from Troas around Cape Lectum, while Paul walked the shorter way (20 Roman miles) overland to Assos, where he reached the ship in time for her to arrive that evening at Mitylene, a port on the SE coast of Lesbos.

ASSUR, ASSHUR (ăs'ûr, ăsh'ûr, Heb. *'ashshûr*), the god of the Assyrians; their reputed human founder; the ancient capital of the country; often the nation Assyria. Asshur is the builder of Nineveh and nearby cities (Gen. 10:11). He comes from the kingdom of Nimrod, a descendant of Ham, and may not be of his race, for in Genesis 10:22 and I Chronicles 1:17 Asshur is a descendant of Shem. ASV, RSV render Genesis 10:11 to read that Nimrod went into Assyria, a descendant and founded Nineveh. In Balaam's prophecy (Num. 24:22,24) Asshur appears to be Assyria. Assur in Ezra 4:2 is translated Assyria in ASV, RSV. In Psalm 83:8, in a list of enemies of Israel, RSV retains Assur, ASV has Assyria. In Ezekiel 27:23 in a list of nations with whom Israel traded, and 32:22, in a list of nations to be destroyed, ASV retains Asshur, RSV has Assyria. In Hosea 14:3 ASV, RSV translate Assyria. For most occurrences of the Heb. word, KJV has Assyria, which is the probable meaning in every instance.

ASSURANCE (ă-shoor'ăns) and related words render two Heb. words, *'āman,* "confirm," "support," also translated by words meaning "to be faithful," "believe," etc.; and *bātah,* "trust," also translated by words meaning "confidence," etc.; and once *qûm,* "rise" (Lev. 27:19). Isaiah 32:17 says that in the reign of Messiah (verse 1), "the work of righteousness shall be peace, and the effect of righteousness quietness and assurance (*bâtah*) forever." OT teaching clearly is that such assurance, though under other names, is open to those who are righteous before God in any age (Ps. 37:1-7,25, Prov. 3:5,6). In the NT, *pístis,* "faith," occurs once (Acts 17:31) and *peítho,* "persuade," once (I John 3:19), for "assurance." Elsewhere the word is *plerophoría,* "the supreme fulness," "certainty." In I Thessalonians 1:5, "in much assurance" is contrasted with "in word only," but is parallel with "in power, and in the Holy Ghost," which shows that assurance is not a formal acceptance of doctrine, but a vital certainty incorporated into the Christian life. Colossians 2:2 speaks of "full assurance of understanding"; Hebrews 6:11 of "full assurance of hope"; and Hebrews 10:22 of "full assurance of faith." As in the OT, much NT teaching fosters assurance without using the word (John 14-17, I John 5:13,20). Interpretations by theologians of the nature and extent of assurance differ widely from one confessional group to another. The Biblical basis remains for the Christian to explore and appropriate.   E.R.

ASSYRIA (à-sĭr'ĭ-à, Heb. *'ashshûr*), originally a land between the upper Tigris and Zab rivers, with its capital first at Assur, later at Nineveh. Assyria was taken over in the third millennium B.C. by Semites from Arabia. First mentioned in the Bible in Genesis 2:14. Assyria and the Assyrians are frequently named, sometimes as Asshur or Assur. By 1900 B.C. Assyrian traders had a colony in Hittite territory, at Kanish in Asia Minor. In the 13th century B.C., Assyrian military expeditions crossed the Euphrates, and by 1100 B.C. they reached the Mediterranean. Assyria was not strong enough to maintain this advance. By 1000 B.C. the Aramean kingdom of Zobah reached the Euphrates, but David, by conquering Zobah, stopped its invasion of Assyria, and by the irony of history, enabled Assyria to become strong. In the tenth century began a century of powerful and systematic advance. Assyria rounded out its borders N and E, conquered Babylonia, and advanced westward through Aramean territory to the Mediterranean. Under Shalmaneser III, the Assyrians turned toward Pal-

As symbolic of Assyria as the Sphinx is of Egypt, this great human-headed winged bull, 10 ft. high, guarded the gateway to the palace of Ashurnasirpal II, at Nimrud. BM

Mounds covering the site of ancient Nineveh, capital of Assyria. © MPS

estine, and in 853 were defeated at Karkar, but claimed a victory over Ben-hadad of Damascus and a coalition including Ahab, king of Israel. They failed to follow up their effort.

After the religious revival under Elijah and Elisha, the coalition of Israel with Syria broke up, at the accession of Jehu as king (II Kings 9,10). Shalmaneser III seized the opportunity to claim tribute from Jehu and to weaken Damascus. Internal difficulties kept Assyria from further Palestinian inroads for nearly a century, when, shortly after the middle of the eighth century B.C., Tiglath-pileser III invaded the West, divided the territory into subject provinces, and exchanged populations on a large scale, to make rebellion more difficult. In 733-732 B.C. he conquered Galilee, the plain of Sharon and Gilead from Israel, and made Israel and Judah pay tribute (II Kings 15:29, 16:9). Isaiah prophesied that this attempt to subjugate Judah would eventually fail. Shalmaneser V besieged Samaria for three years. He died during the siege, and his successor Sargon II (now called Sargon III) took the city in 721 B.C. and carried its more prosperous citizens into exile, replacing them with colonists from other provinces of his empire (II Kings 17:6-41).

For nearly a century thereafter, Assyria was troubled from all sides, from Babylon, Elam, the Medes, Phrygia and Egypt. Yet Sennacherib nearly captured Jerusalem in 701-700 B.C. (II Kings 18:13-19:37, Isaiah 36,37), the danger ending only when "the angel of the Lord went out and smote in the camp of the Assyrians" 185,000, followed by the assassination of Sennacherib. Manasseh, king of Judah, paid tribute, except during a short rebellion for which he was carried to Babylon, but released after he sought the Lord (II Chron. 33:11-13). The last quarter of the seventh century B.C. saw the fall and decline of the Assyrian empire and

its subjugation by the Chaldean conquerors of Babylonia, with the Medes. Nineveh was taken in 612 B.C. For a short time Babylonia replaced Assyria as the great power. The prophets Elijah, Elisha and Isaiah are largely concerned with Assyria, and several other prophets, Jeremiah, Ezekiel, Hosea, Micah, Nahum, Zephaniah and Zechariah refer to it. Jonah was actually sent to prophesy to Nineveh, and the revival he unwillingly promoted saved the city from destruction for a long period of time.

Assyrian kings who reigned during the centuries of closest contact with Israel and Judah, with approximate dates from the list found at Khorsabad in Mesopotamia (all B.C.):

Shalmaneser III	858-824	Sennacherib	704-681
Shamshi-Adad V	823-811	Esarhaddon	680-669
Adad-Nirari III	810-783	Ashurbanipal	668-633
Shalmaneser IV	782-773	Ashur-eti-ilani	632-629
Ashur-dan III	772-755	Sin-shum-lishir	———
Ashur-Nirari V	754-745		
Tiglath-pileser III	744-727	Sin-shar-ishkum	623-612
Shalmaneser V	726-722	Ashur-uballit	611-608
Sargon III	721-705		

(formerly called Sargon II).

Assyrian art, architecture, and technology were successively influenced by Sumerians, Akkadians and Babylonians, and early attained high levels, exciting the admiration and imitation of Ahaz king of Judah (II Kings 16:10-13). Literature was largely utilitarian: legal, historical, commercial, scientific, pseudo-scientific and religious, but exists in abundance, notably the recently discovered library of Ashurbanipal, consisting of thousands of clay tablets. The Assyrians early added to their worship of the primitive national god Asshur the Babylonian deities with their cultic apparatus. Wherever they influenced Israel and Judah, the effect was demoralizing, as the historical books of the Bible and the prophets bear abundant witness.

E.R.

ASTARTE (See Ashtaroth, Ashtoreth)

ASTROLOGERS (ăs-trŏl'ō-jêrz, Heb. *'ashshāph*), in Daniel 2:10, 27, 4:7, 5:7, 11, 15, singular; 1:20, 2:22, plural; means "conjurer, necromancer." RSV translates uniformly "enchanter," but has "astrologer" for KJV "soothsayer," Heb. *gezar*, "divider, determiner of fate" in these passages. In Isaiah 47:13, "the astrologers, the star-gazers" of KJV are "those who divide the heavens, who gaze at the stars" in RSV. "Astrologers" here is Heb. *hāvar shāmayîm*, "they that divide the heavens, distinguish the signs of zodiac." It is difficult to distinguish the various sorts of practicers of magical arts. Seeking information from the stars was widely practiced from earliest times, but with all other forms of superstition was forbidden to the Chosen People, who were to seek their God directly.

ASTROLOGY (ăs-trŏl'ō-jē), the art practiced by astrologers.

The great Milky Way — "stars without number." EG

ASTRONOMY. While the word astronomy is not found in the Bible, there are many passages in the Scriptures which refer to some aspect of the subject. God is recognized as the maker of the stars (Gen. 1:16) as well as the one who knows their number and names (Ps. 147:4). In the 19th Psalm there is a beautiful poem telling how the heavenly bodies (referring to the stars) show forth the glory of their Creator. Here there is reference made to the sun as another of the heavenly bodies.

In the Bible there are hundreds of references to stars, sun, moon, and planets. Evidently the early Bible writers were much better acquainted with the subject of astronomy than are many modern people. When God wished to tell Abraham how numerous his descendants would be, he took him out and showed him the stars. Then God said, "Look toward heaven and number the stars, if you are able to number them" (Gen. 15:5). Later on God compared the number of Abraham's descendants not only with the stars, but also with the sand on the seashore (Gen. 22:17). For many years it was not clear that this was a fair comparison. Before the invention of the astronomical telescope it was not at all certain that the number of stars was as great as the number of grains of sand on the seashore. Modern discoveries, however, have proved that the Bible was right. The total number of stars is approximately equal to the number of grains of sand which are on the seashore. This number is so large that it is very difficult to comprehend. The Bible refers in a most striking manner to the height of the stars; that is, to their distance from the earth: "Is not God high in the heavens? See the highest stars, how lofty they are!" (Job 22:12).

The true distances to the stars were not known until 1838 when Bessel first computed the distance to a star. Before that time astronomers had little idea how distant stars were from the earth. Now the distances to many stars have been measured, and it turns out that these distances are more than one hundred thousand times the diameter of our solar system.

Another reference to the great height of the stars is found in Isaiah 14:13. Here Satan says, "I will ascend to heaven above the stars of God." The inference here is that it must be a very great distance to the stars. This is exactly what astronomers have found to be the case, though for many years scientists did not know this fact.

It appears that the biblical writers were aware that the stars differ greatly from each other. Paul, writing to the church at Corinth, says, "There is one glory of the sun, and another glory of the moon, and another glory of the stars; for star differs from star in glory" (I Cor. 15:41). This has been verified by the astronomers. Not only do stars have different colors, but they also differ widely in size, in density, in temperature, and in total amount of light emitted. The sun, about which the earth revolves, is an average star. While it is over one million times as large as the earth, there are some stars which are one million times as large as the sun. On the other hand, there are other stars smaller than the planet Mercury.

One of the many sins of the children of Israel was that of worshiping idols. They wanted to worship also the sun, the moon, and the stars. In Deuteronomy 4:19 they were warned not to indulge in such worship. In spite of such warnings, sun-worship prevailed many times. Asa and Josiah, kings of Judah, found it necessary to take away the sun images which had been kept at the entrance to the temple.

A number of individual stars and constellations are mentioned in the Old Testament. *Kesil* (Orion) is mentioned in Isaiah 13:10, Amos 5:8, and Job 9:9. *Ash* or *Ayish* occurs in Job 9:9; 38:32, and refers to the Great Bear or possibly the Hyades or Pleiades. Also in Job 38:32 is found *Mazzarot*, which may possibly be the Northern or Southern Crown.

While there is little evidence in the Bible that the Hebrew people had indulged very much in the study of astronomy, yet it is abundantly clear that they recognized a sublime order in the movements of the heavenly bodies. They observed carefully the daily rising of the sun, its majestic movement across the meridian, and its final setting in the west. This is vividly portrayed in the story of the battle with the Amorites as recorded in the tenth chapter of Joshua. Here it is recorded that the sun stood still in the midst of the heaven. This expression undoubtedly refers to the meridian, the great arc connecting the zenith with the north and south points.

Many theories have been proposed in an attempt to give a scientific explanation to this "long day of Joshua." None is completely satisfactory and they will not be discussed here. It is sufficient to add that this is one of many miracles recorded in the Bible given to us to show that God is the ruler and sustainer of the universe.

More remarkable than the long day of Joshua when the sun apparently stood still, is the story of the return of the shadow on the sundial of Ahaz. In this case the Lord gave the King Hezekiah a sign saying, "Behold, I will make the shadow cast by the declining on the dial of Ahaz turn back ten steps" (Isa. 38:8). This is, indeed, a very remarkable miracle. If taken literally, this means not only that the earth stopped rotating on its axis, but that it reversed its direction of rotation for a short time. Again the scientists have no answer to explain such an event.

There are a number of allusions in the Bible to eclipses of the sun and of the moon. In Isaiah 13:10 it is stated that, "the sun will be dark at its rising," while in Joel 2:31 we have the statement, "the sun shall be turned to darkness, and the moon to blood." These two descriptions accord quite well with observations of eclipses of the sun and of the moon. As the shadow of the moon sweeps across the face of the sun it appears that the sun is turned to darkness. When the earth comes directly between the sun and the moon, there is an eclipse of the moon. When the eclipse is complete, it is still possible to see the surface of the moon, due to the fact that the atmosphere of the earth bends the light rays from their straight line path. Thus sunlight is bent somewhat as it passes the earth, is then reflected by the moon and returns again to the earth. Just as the sun appears to be red when it is setting, due to the passage of the light through more atmosphere, so the eclipsed moon appears orange in color. The Bible uses the apt expression, "turned to blood" to describe this astronomical phenomenon.

Calculated eclipses of the sun which occurred during Old Testament times are as follows: July 31, 1063 B.C.; Aug. 15, 831 B.C.; June 15, 763 B.C.; May 18, 603 B.C.; May 28, 585 B.C. Very likely the prophets Amos and Joel witnessed the eclipse of Aug. 15, 831 B.C. Such an eclipse is vividly described by Amos, "I will make the sun go down at noon, and darken the earth in broad daylight" (Amos 8:9).

The subject of astrology has been connected with astronomy since early times. The reference in Judges 5:20 no doubt refers to the influence of the stars in the lives of men. The writer states, "From heaven fought the stars, from their courses they fought against Sisera." However, the Hebrew people seemed to have had little to do with the subject. In the book of Daniel there are repeated statements made concerning the astrologers. It is to be noted that Daniel and his three friends, though closely associated with astrologers, are always mentioned as keeping themselves separate and undefiled. Again and again when the magicians and the astrologers were unable to perform a task, it was

Daniel who was able to do important things for the king. Thus it is apparent that the Bible condemns the pseudo-science of astrology.

Probably the most fascinating part of biblical astronomy concerns the star of Bethlehem. This story is told in the second chapter of Matthew. When the wise men from the east came to Jerusalem they asked, "Where is he who has been born king of the Jews? For we have seen his star in the east and have come to worship him" (Matt. 2:2). Even the king was greatly disturbed over the news, for he inquired of them diligently at what time the star appeared. This star seemed to be their ever present guide, for it is stated that "the star which they had seen in the east went before them; till it came to rest over the place where the child was" (Matt. 2:9).

The question before us is this: What kind of a star can continually guide men to a definite point on the earth? Many answers have been proposed. One is that this was an unusual conjunction of bright planets. A conjunction is the coming together on the same meridian at the same time of two or more celestial objects. It is known that in the year 6 B.C. there was a conjunction of Mars, Jupiter, and Saturn. However, this conjunction would not have been visible to the wise men for it was too near the sun. Another difficulty is that 6 B.C. is two years too early for the birth of Christ.

Another theory is that this star was a nova. A nova is a star that suddenly becomes very bright. Ordinarily such a star is too dim to be seen by the unaided eye. Very quickly such a star increases its brightness greatly and becomes as bright or brighter than the brightest star in the sky. Many novae have been discovered and studied. The problem in this case is to explain how such a bright star could serve as a guide to the wise men.

Still another theory proposed to explain the star of Bethlehem is that this was the planet Venus at its greatest brilliance. It is true that this planet does appear at times as a very bright object in the winter sky. However, these wise men knew the movements of the planets, and, therefore, the bright appearance of Venus would hardly have served as a guide to lead them to the Christ child.

Evidently we have here another of the many Bible miracles which modern science is unable to explain. Undoubtedly this miraculous appearance, which is called a star, aroused the curiosity of the wise men to such an extent that they followed it for many miles until finally it pointed out the exact place where they wished to go.

Solar corona, photographed during total eclipse of the sun. HAR

In the last book of the Bible and in the last chapter of that book, the Lord Jesus is called "the bright and morning star" (Rev. 22:16). Evidently the writer, the apostle John, had frequently waited for the morning light and had watched for the bright morning star, which is usually a planet. Its beauty had greatly inspired him, so he uses this apt figure by referring to the Lord Jesus Christ as the bright morning star. May Christians watch for His coming as men of old have watched for the morning and have seen the bright stars of the morning!   H.H.H.

ASUPPIM (à-sŭp'ĭm), a Heb. word meaning "collectors," left untranslated in KJV (I Chron. 26:15, 17); in ASV, RSV, "storehouses." The same word (Neh. 12:25) in KJV is "thresholds," ASV, RSV, "storehouses." They were at the S gate of the Temple.

ASYNCRITUS (à-sĭng'krĭ-tŭs, *incomparable*), a Christian in Rome to whom Paul sends a salutation (Rom. 16:14).

ATAD (ā'tăd, Heb. *'ātādh, thorn*), name of a place, "the threshing floor of Atad," E of Jordan, where the Children of Israel mourned for Joseph. The Canaanites called the place Abelmizraim (Gen. 50-11).

ATARAH (ăt'à-rà), a wife of Jerahmeel and mother of Onam (I Chron. 2:26).

ATAROTH (ăt'à-rŏth, -rŏth, *crowns*). 1 Modern Khirbet-at-tārûs, E of Jordan in the territory of Reuben, but fortified by Gad (Num. 32:3, 34).
2. On the border between Ephraim and Benjamin, to the W (Josh. 16:2), probably the same as Ataroth-addar (Josh. 16:5, 18:13).
3. On the eastern border of Ephraim (Josh. 16:7).
4. Near Bethlehem (I Chron. 2:54). The locations of the last three are uncertain.

ATER (ā'têr). 1. The ancestor of an exiled family (Ezra 2:16; Neh. 7:21).
2. Ancestor of a family of gatekeepers who returned from exile with Zerubbabel (Ezra 2:42; Neh. 7:45).
3. The chief of the people who, with Nehemiah, sealed the covenant (Neh. 10:17).

ATHACH (ā'thăk), a city of Judah, probably near Ziklag. David sent to it from Ziklag some of the spoil taken from the Amalekites (I Sam. 30:30).

ATHAIAH (à-thī'à, *Jehovah is helper*), the son of Uzziah a Judahite in Nehemiah's time (Neh. 11:4).

ATHALIAH (ăth'à-lī'à). 1. The only woman who ever reigned over Judah. Her story is told in II Kings 8:18, 25-28; 11:1-20, and in fuller detail in II Chronicles 22:1-23:21, 24:7. She was the daughter of Ahab king of Israel and Jezebel the devotee of Baal, the granddaughter of Omri king of Israel, and the wife of Jehoram king of Judah. After the death of their son Ahaziah, Athaliah reigned for six years. She put to death all Ahaziah's sons except Joash, whom Jehosheba, sister of Ahaziah and wife of Jehoida the priest hid until the seventh year. Then Jehoida conspired to put Joash on the throne. Coming into the Temple to see what the excitement meant, Athaliah found that the coronation had already taken place. She was allowed to leave the Temple, that it might not be defiled with her blood, but was killed as she went out the door.
2. A son of Jeroham, a Benjamite (I Chron. 8:26).
3. The father of Jeshiah, a returned exile (Ezra 8:7).

Above, nebula of stars in Cassiopeia. HAR
Below, the star cluster of the Pleiades. HML

There is abundant evidence in the Bible that many of the constellations were known to the writers. The Lord asked Job many questions. Among these is the following: "Can you bind the chains of the Pleiades, or loose the cords of Orion?" (Job 38:31). One constellation has a special significance to the Christian. It is Cygnus, the flying swan or the Northern Cross. It really has the appearance of a huge cross in the summer sky. Six bright stars form a Roman Cross. It is about the size of the Big Dipper.

This cross may be said to be the evening's call to worship. It reminds us of the passage from Luke, "Look up and raise your heads, because your redemption is drawing near" (Luke 21:28). This constellation sinks westward in the sky until at Christmas time it stands upright just above the horizon in the northwest. There is rich symbolism here in the fact that the star, Deneb, at the top of the cross, where the head of Christ was, is a supergiant, while the one at the bottom, Albireo, where his feet were, is a telescopic double. It is really very beautiful with one star being yellow and the other blue.

Athens, ancient and modern. Top, two views overlooking the city from the Acropolis. At left are the well-preserved remains of the ancient Temple of Erechtheum, with its beautifully sculptured marble columns. Below, left, a downtown street scene in modern Athens. At right, a view of the city from Mars Hill, with the Temple of Theseus visible in left center. JFW

ATHENS (ăth'ĕnz, Gr. *Athénai*), in ancient times the famous capital of Attica, one of the Greek states, now the capital of Greece. The city was named after its patron goddess Athene. It centered around a rocky hill called Acropolis, and was 4½ miles from the sea. Two walls, 250 feet apart, connected the city with its harbor (Peiraeus). According to tradition, the city was founded by Cecrops, who came from Egypt about 1556 B.C.; it sent 50 ships to the Trojan War; and it was ruled by kings until about 1068 B.C. After that it was ruled by archons. Two of the most famous archons were Draco, who c. 620 B.C. issued laws "written in blood," and Solon, who in 594 B.C. gave the state a constitution. The Athenians defeated the Persians at Marathon in 490, and again in 480 at Salamis. They then built a small empire, with a powerful fleet for its support. The period of Athens' greatest glory was during the rule of Pericles (459-431), who erected many beautiful public buildings in the city and under whose administration literature and art flourished. The Peloponnesian War (431-404) ended with the submission of Athens to Sparta. Later wars sapped the strength of Athens. Philip of Macedon crushed the city in 338 B.C. In 146 B.C. the Romans made it a part of the province of Achaea. The Roman general Sulla sacked the city in 86 B.C. It subsequently came into the hands of the Goths, the Byzantines, and other peoples. The Turks ruled it from A.D. 1458 until the emancipation of Greece in 1833.

In ancient times Athens had a population of at least a quarter of a million. It was the seat of Greek art, science and philosophy, and was the most important university city in the ancient world, even under Roman sway. Although politically conquered, it conquered its conquerors with its learning and culture.

Paul visited the city on his second missionary journey, and spoke to an interested but somewhat disdainful audience on Mars Hill (Acts 17). He called their attention to an altar "to an Unknown God" he had seen in the city, and declared that he could tell them about this God. He made some converts in the city, but there is no record of his establishing a church there or of his returning on any later occasion. From Athens he went to Corinth, where he remained for a year and a half and established a strong church.   S.B.

ATHLAI (ăth'lā-ī), a man of Israel who in the days of Ezra (c. 456 B.C.) divorced his foreign wife (Ezra 10:28).

ATONEMENT (ă-tōn'ment), root meaning in English, "at-one-ment": i.e. the bringing together of two who have been enemies into a relationship of peace and friendship. The word belongs primarily to the OT, as it occurs only once in the NT (Rom. 5:11) and there the ASV properly renders it "reconciliation." "For if, while we were enemies, we were reconciled to God through the death of his Son, much more being reconciled, we shall be saved by his life; and not only so, but we also rejoice in God through our Lord Jesus Christ, through whom we have now received the reconciliation."

The words "atonement," "make atonement," "appease," "pacify," etc. from the Hebrew root *kaphar* occur about 110 times in the OT, principally in Leviticus and Numbers, and the root idea is "to cover." The primitive verb and its noun occur in Gen. 6:14, "*pitch* it within and without with pitch." Just as the pitch covered the ark and protected its inmates, so the shed blood of sacrifice stands between man and the outraged law of a holy God.

On the Day of Atonement, the high priest had first to make atonement for himself and his house (Lev. 16:16), then for the tabernacle itself because it was fouled by the sins of Israel, then for the people. Their sins were ceremonially dealt with by the use of two goats: the first goat died as a sin offering (16:15), even as our Lord died for us on the cross; then the high priest confessed the iniquities and transgressions of Israel over the scapegoat (16:21,22), which was then released and bore "upon him all their sins into a solitary land." And so we read in Psalm 103:12 "As far as the east is from the west, so far hath he removed our transgressions from us"; in Micah 7:19, "thou wilt cast all their sins into the depths of the sea" (of God's forgetfulness) and in Isaiah 38:17, "For thou hast cast all my sins behind thy back." The beautiful word "mercy-seat" for the covering of the ark of the covenant comes from the same word, and has been rendered by some just "covering," but the beauty of the meaning is thus lost. The sprinkling of the blood upon the mercy-seat (Lev. 16:14) was the divine way of picturing the merciful covering of our sins.

In Christian theology, atonement is the central doctrine of our faith and can properly include all that our Lord accomplished for us on the cross. It was a vicarious (i.e. substitutionary) atonement. On the Day of Atonement, perhaps the goat which was substituted was in some sense not as valuable as a man, though the goat had never sinned: but God in His matchless grace provided a Substitute who was infinitely better than the sinner, absolutely sinless and holy, and dearer to the Father than all creation. "The wages of sin is death" (Rom. 6:23a), and "Him who knew no sin, he made to be sin on our behalf: that we might become the righteousness of God in Him" (II Cor. 5:21).

There are two opposite facts that the ingenuity of the theologians could not have reconciled without God's solution: first, that God is holy and He hates sin, and that by His holy law sin is a capital crime; and second, that "God is love" (I John 4:8); and so the problem was "How can God be just and at the same time justify the sinner?" (cf. Rom. 3:26). John 3:16 tells us that God so loved that He gave — but our blessed Lord was not just a means to an end — He was not a martyr to a cause. In the eternal counsels of the Trinity, He offered Himself to bear our sins (Rev. 13:8), and so, voluntarily, He emptied Himself of the divine trappings of omnipotence, omniscience, and glory (Phil. 2:5-8), that He might be truly human, became the Babe of Bethlehem. For about 33 years He perfectly fulfilled the law on our behalf (Matt. 5:18) and then paid the penalty for our sins in His death for us upon the cross. Our Lord's work of atonement looks in three directions: looking toward sin and Satan, He redeemed us with His precious blood (I Pet. 1:18, 19: "Ye know that ye were not redeemed with corruptible things, as silver and gold — but with the precious blood of Christ, as of a lamb without blemish and without spot"); looking toward us, He reconciled a world of sinners with God (Rom. 5:6-11: "For if when we were enemies we were reconciled to God by the death of his Son, much more, being reconciled, we shall be saved by his life"—); and looking toward the Holy Father, He propitiated divine justice (I John 2:2: "And he is the propitiation for our sins: and not for ours only, but for the sins of the whole world").

It seems strange that theologians have invented so many theories of the atonement when the teaching expressed above seems to be clear and simple. A partial answer lies in the difficulty of putting into philosophical language the mysteries of the faith; but a larger explanation is that the truth cannot be explained adequately by those who have not experienced it.   A.B.F.

ATONEMENT, DAY OF. Theologically and spiritually, the center of Leviticus, "the book of holiness," is the 16th chapter, which gives the law for the day of atonement; and the divinely inspired commentary on this chapter is found in Hebrews 9:1-10:25. Israel practically had two beginnings for its years, six months apart. In the first month, the 14th day, they ate the Passover as a memorial of the events leading to the exodus from Egypt; and half a year later, in the seventh month, and the tenth day (Lev. 16:29) they afflicted their souls and the priest made atonement for them. Nowadays, the Jews celebrate their New Year's day (*rosh hash-shanah*) on the first day of the "seventh" month, and the day of atonement (*yom kippur*) properly *yom hakkippurim* on the tenth. The purpose of the day of atonement seems to have been at least four-fold: first to show God's hatred of sin, that the "wages of sin is death" (Rom. 6:23), and that "without the shedding of blood there is no remission" of sin (Heb. 9:22); second, to show the contagious nature of sin, for even the Holy place had to be cleansed (Lev. 16: 16) "because of the uncleanness of the children of Israel, and because of their transgressions in all their sins"; third, to point forward by three types to the death of "the Lamb of God," our blessed Saviour; and fourth, by its repetition year after year to signify that the way into the very presence of God had not been made manifest before the death of Christ (Heb. 9:7-9). When our Lord offered Himself on Calvary, the veil of the temple was rent (Mark 15:38), and God signified that from that moment on, we were under a new covenant — a covenant of grace, not of law. "For the law was given by Moses, but grace and truth came by Jesus Christ" (John 1:17). The OT ceremonies were but symbols and types and shadows: the NT records the realities; in OT times, God was teaching His people by "kindergarten" methods — godliness brought health, long life, and prosperity; and sin brought quick, visible, corporeal punishment. Today, under grace, we look back to Calvary, when the great Day of Atonement took place once for all.

ATROTH (ăt′rŏth). Properly "Atroth-shophan," a town built and fortified by the tribe of Gad, E of Jordan (Num. 32:35). KJV reads Atroth, Shophan, as though two towns are named.

ATTAI (ăt′á-ī). Half-Egyptian member of the tribe of Judah (I Chron. 2:35,36).

2. Mighty man of Gad who joined David (I Chron. 12:11).

3. Younger brother of Abijah, king of Judah (II Chron. 11:20).

ATTALIA (ăt′á-lī′á), a seaport of Pamphylia near Perga, mentioned in Acts 14:25. On Paul's first missionary journey, he landed at Perga, several miles inland, but on his return he and Barnabas sailed for Antioch in Syria from Attalia, the main seaport on the Gulf of "Adalia" as it is spelled today. The city was founded by and named for Attalus Philadelphus, king of Pergamum from 159-138 B.C.

ATTIRE (See Dress)

AUGUSTUS CAESAR (ô-gŭs′tŭs sē′zêr). Gaius Octavius, whose male ancestors for four generations had the same name, was born in Rome, Sept. 23, 63 B.C. and early became influential through his great-uncle, Julius Caesar. He was studying quietly in Illyria when he heard of Caesar's murder, March 15, 44 B.C. and then, hastening to Italy he learned that Caesar had adopted him and made him his heir. Thus, in his early manhood, by skillful manipulation of his friends he conquered his rival, Antony, at Actium. The beginning of the Roman Empire may be reckoned from this date, Sept. 2, 31 B.C. By his adoption he had become "Caesar," and now, in 31 B.C., the Roman senate added the title "Augustus." Although he preserved the forms of a republic, he gradually got all the power into his hands. He reigned till A.D. 14. Some of the secular histories omit the most important event in his reign — a Babe was born at Bethlehem! In the NT, Augustus Caesar is mentioned just once (Luke 2:1).

AUL (ôl), an obsolete variant of awl. A sharp, piercing tool (Exod. 21:6, Deut. 15:17).

AUTHORIZED VERSION (See Bible. Translations of)

AVA (ā'và), ASV Avva, a region in Assyria from which Sargon brought men to populate devastated Samaria (II Kings 17:24); thought by some to be the Ivah (ASV Ivvah) of II Kings 18:34. These men worshiped the gods Nibhaz and Tartak (II Kings 17:31).

AVEN (ā'vĕn; Heb. '*āwen, vanity*). 1. The Egyptian city "On" (Gen. 41:45), dedicated to the sun, and still existing as "Heliopolis" or "City of the Sun," about eight miles from Cairo (Ezek. 30:17). Some think that Ezekiel deliberately mispronounced On to show his contempt for its idol worship.

   2. Hosea (10:5,8) contemptuously calls the places of the heathen calves of Bethel, the "high places of Aven."

   3. Evidently a valley in Syria, dedicated to heathen worship (Amos 1:5), and thought by some to be Baalbek.

AVENGER (a-vĕn'jêr). In the Mosaic law, and in primitive societies quite commonly the law was "life for life," and so if a man was killed, his nearest of kin was made the avenger of blood (Num. 35:11-34). A distinct difference was made between murder and manslaughter. The same Hebrew word is rendered "kinsman" (Ruth 4:1) and "redeemer" (Job 19:25).

AVIM, AVIMS, AVITES (ā'vĭm, ā'vĭmz, ā'vīts). 1. An ancient people who dwelt in the region of Gaza before the time of Moses (Deut. 2:23). In the time of Joshua's old age, these people still were not rooted out (Josh. 13:3).

   2. A city in the tribe of Benjamin (Josh. 18:23), perhaps populated by the remains of this ancient tribe.

AVITH (ā'vĭth), name of a town or city, which was the capital of Hadad, the fourth king of Edom, before there were any kings of Israel (Gen. 36:35).

AWL (See Aul)

AX, the well-known chopping instrument, represented by a number of Heb. and Gr. words (I Kings 6:7, Ps. 74:6, II Sam. 12:31, Jer. 10:3, Matt. 3:10).

AYIN (ā'yĕn), in KJV, Ain, Heb. '*ayin*, "an eye," "a spring or fountain." 1. The 16th letter of the Hebrew alphabet, probably so named because originally in outline an eye.

   2. A place on the N boundary line of Palestine (Num. 34:11).

   3. A town in Judah near Rimmon (Josh. 15:32; I Chron. 4:32).

AZAL (See Azel)

AZALIAH (ăz'à-lī'à, Heb. '*ătsalyâhû*, probably *Jehovah has set aside*, or *Jehovah has shown himself distinguished*), a son of Meshullam and father of Shaphan the scribe (II Kings 22:3).

Augustus Caesar. JHK

AZANIAH (ăz'à-nī'à, Heb. '*ăzanyâh, Jehovah has set aside*, or *Jehovah has given ear*), a son of Jeshua, a Levite who signed the covenant (Neh. 10:9).

AZAREEL, AZARAEL (à-zā're-ĕl, Heb. '*ăzar'ĕl. God is helper*; AV reads *Azareel* in Nos. 1-5, *Azarael* in No. 6). 1. A Levite who entered the army of David at Ziklag (I Chron. 12:6).

   2. A musician in the temple in David's time (I Chron. 25:18).

   3. A captain in the service of David (I Chron. 27:22).

   4. A man Ezra persuaded to divorce his foreign wife (Ezra 10:41).

   5. A priest who lived in Jerusalem after the exile (Neh. 11:13).

   6. A musician who played in the procession when the wall was dedicated (Neh. 12:36).

AZAREL (Same as Azareel)

AZARIAH (ăz'à-rī'à, Heb. '*ăzaryāhu, Jehovah hath helped*). 1. King of Judah. See Uzziah.

   2. A man of Judah of the house of Ethan the Wise (I Chron. 2:8).

   3. The son of Jehu, descended from an Egyptian through the daughter of Sheshan (I Chron. 2:38).

   4. A son of Ahimaaz (I Chron. 6:9).

   5. A Levite of the family of Kohath (I Chron. 6:36).

   6. A son of Zadok the high priest, under Solomon (I Kings 4:2).

   7. A high priest and son of Johanan (I Chron. 6:10).

   8. Son of Nathan, an officer at Solomon's court (I Kings 4:5).

   9. A prophet, son of Obed, in the reign of King Asa (II Chron. 15:1-8).

   10. Two sons of King Jehoshaphat; probably half brothers.

11. A son of Jehoram (II Chron. 22:6, called Ahaziah in verse 1).

12. Son of Jeroham, who helped to overthrow Athaliah (II Chron. 23:1).

13. Son of Johanan who helped in getting the captives of Judah released (II Chron. 28:12).

14. A Levite who assisted in purifying the Temple in Hezekiah's reign (II Chron. 29:12).

15. A high priest who rebuked Uzziah's attempt to assume priestly functions (II Chron. 26:16-20).

16. A son of Hilkiah; a high priest not long before the Exile (I Chron. 6:13,14).

17. A man of Judah who bitterly opposed Jeremiah (Jer. 43:2).

18. One of the captives taken to Babylon, whose name was changed to Abed-nego (Daniel 1:7).

19. The son of Maaseiah, who helped repair the walls of Jerusalem (Neh. 3:23 f).

20. A Levite who assisted Ezra in explaining the Law (Neh. 8:7).

21. A priest who sealed the covenant (Neh. 10:2).

22. A prince of Judah who marched in the procession at the dedication of the wall of Jerusalem (Neh. 12:32,33).

AZAZ (ā'zăz, Heb. *'āzāz, strong*), a Reubenite, the son of Shema or Shemaiah (I Chron. 5:8).

AZAZEL (à-zā'zĕl, Heb. *'ăzā'zēl;* KJV *scapegoat,* RV *removal*), a name used in connection with one of the goats chosen for the service of the Day of Atonement. The word occurs in one passage only (Lev. 16:8, 10, 26). The meaning of the word is very uncertain. Many interpretations have been proposed, none completely satisfactory. The word has been interpreted both personally and impersonally:

1. It has been regarded as the name of an evil spirit living in the wilderness to whom the goat laden with the sins of the people was sent.

2. Some consider the word as an abstraction meaning "removal." One of the two goats was for the Lord; the other, for removal.

3. The word is regarded as an epithet of the devil. The goat laden with sin belongs to the devil.

Whatever the exact meaning of the word, it is clear that the aim of this part of the ritual of the Day of Atonement was to provide the people with a visible token of the removal of their sins. It was a symbolical declaration that the land and people were purged from guilt.

AZAZIAH (ăz'à-zī'à, Heb. *'ăzazyāhû, Jehovah is strong*). 1. A harper during the reign of David (I Chron. 15:21).

2. The father of the prince of Ephraim in the reign of David (I Chron. 27:20).

3. A Levite overseer of the Temple in the reign of Hezekiah (II Chron. 31:13).

AZBUK (ăz'bŭk), father of a certain Nehemiah who lived at the same time, but was not the same as the famous governor of that name (Neh. 3:16).

AZEKAH (à-zē'kà), a town in NW Judah. It is mentioned as a place to which Joshua pursued the kings at the battle of Gibeon (Josh. 10:10,11). Other places where it is mentioned are Joshua 15:35; I Samuel 17:1; II Chronicles 11:9; Jeremiah 34:7; Nehemiah 11:30.

AZEL (ā'zĕl). 1. A descendant of Jonathan, son of Saul (I Chron. 8:37 f., 9:43 f.).

2. A place near Jerusalem (Zech. 14:5).

AZGAD (ăz'găd, Heb. *'azgādh, Gad is strong,* or *fate is hard*), the ancestral head of a family of postexilic Jews (Ezra 2:12, 8:12; Neh. 7:17, 10:15).

AZIEL (ē'zĭ-ĕl, Heb. *'ăzī'ēl, God is my strength*), a Levite musician (I Chron. 15:20, Jaaziel in verse 18, and Jeiel in 16:5).

AZIZA (à-zī'zà, Heb. *'ăzîzā', strong*), a man in the time of Ezra who divorced his foreign wife (Ezra 10:27).

AZMAVETH (ăz-mā'vĕth, Heb. *'azmāweth, death is strong.* 1. One of David's heroes (II Sam. 23:31).

2. A Benjamite, one of whose sons followed David (I Chron. 12:3).

3. A man in charge of David's treasures (I Chron. 27:25).

4. A descendant of Jonathan, Saul's son (I Chron. 8:36).

5. A place north of Anathoth to which some exiles returned (Ezra 2:24; Neh. 12:29; also called Beth-azmaveth [Neh. 7:28]).

AZMON (ăz'mŏn, Heb. *'atsmôn, strong*), a town on the south border of Judah (Num. 34:4,5; Josh. 15:4, RV). Site unknown.

AZNOTH-TABOR (ăz'nŏth-tā'bôr, Heb. *'aznôth tāvōr, the ears,* i.e., slopes of Tabor), a place near Mt. Tabor on the border of Naphtali (Josh. 19:34).

AZOR (ā'zôr), a post-exilic ancestor of Christ (Matt. 1:13,14).

AZOTUS (See Ashdod)

AZRIEL (ăz'rĭ-ĕl, Heb. *'azrî'ēl, God is help*). 1. A chieftain of the half tribe of Manasseh E of the Jordan (I Chron. 5:24).

2. A Naphtalite of David's time (I Chron. 27:19).

3. The father of Seraiah of Jeremiah's time (Jer. 36:26).

AZRIKAM (ăz'rĭ-kăm, Heb. *'azrîqām, my help has arisen.* 1. A son of Neariah (I Chron. 3:23).

2. A descendant of Saul (I Chron. 8:38; 9:44).

3. A Levite, descended from Merari (I Chron. 9:14).

4. An officer of Ahaz (II Chron. 28:7).

AZUBAH (à-zū'bà, *forsaken*). 1. A wife of Caleb (I Chron. 2:18,19).

2. The mother of Jehoshaphat (I Kings 22:42).

AZUR (See Azzur)

AZZAH (See Gaza)

AZZAN (ăz'ăn, *strong*), the father of Paltiel, prince of Issachar in the days of Moses (Num. 34:26).

AZZUR (ăz'êr, Heb. *'azzur, helped,* in KJV twice *Azur*). 1. Father of Hananiah the false prophet (Jer. 28:1).

2. Father of Jaazaniah (Ezek. 11:1).

3. One of the signers of the covenant in the days of Nehemiah (Neh. 10:17).

A typical house and courtyard in Ashdod, showing decorative coloring of the mud wall and thatched roofing. © MPS

B

BAAL (bā'ăl, Heb. *ba'al, lord, possessor, husband*).
1. The word Baal appears in the OT with a variety
of meanings. Originally it was not a proper noun,
but later it came to be so used. Sometimes it is
used in the primary sense of "master" or "owner,"
as in Exodus 21:28,34; Judges 19:22; Isaiah 16:8.
Since the Hebrew husband was regarded as the
literal owner of his wife, Baal was the common
term for husband, as in Exodus 21:3; II Samuel
11:26; Hosea 2:16. Most often, however, the
word refers to the Semitic deity or deities called
Baal. Baal is not the name of one god, but the
name of the presiding deity of any given locality.
Because the worship of Baal was much the same
everywhere in Canaan, in time Baal came to represent the idea of one god. The Baalim were the
gods of the land, owning and controlling it, and
the increase of crops, fruits, and cattle was under
their control. The farmer was completely dependent upon the Baalim. Some Baals were greater
than others. Some were in control of cities, as Mel-
kart of Tyre. The name Baal occurs as early as the
Hyksos period (c. 1700 B.C.). The Amarna letters
and the Ras Shamra texts (c. 1400 B.C.) make
Baal a prominent Semitic deity, and in the latter
the name is not only applied to local gods, but is
also used as the name of a distinct god Baal.

Baal was worshiped on high places in Moab in
the time of Balaam and Balak (Num. 22:41). In
the period of the Judges there were altars to him in
Palestine (Judg. 2:13; 6:28-32); and in the time
of Ahab and Jezebel, the daughter of the heathen
king of the Sidonians, the worship of Jehovah was
almost supplanted by that of Baal. The struggle

The six great pillars of the Temple of the Sun at
Baalbek (in Lebanon). © MPS

Front and rear views of a statuette of Baal, the
weather god, brandishing a thunderbolt. Bronze, with
helmet of polished stone; from Ras Shamra (Ugarit),
about 1400 B.C. ASOR

between Baalism and Judaism came to a head on
Mount Carmel when the Prophet Elijah met the
priests of Baal and slew 450 of them (I Kings 16:
32; 18:17-40). The cult quickly recuperated, however, and prospered until crushed by Jehu (II Kings
10:18-28). Jezebel's daughter, Athaliah, the wife
of Jehoram, gave the worship of Baal a new impulse (II Chron. 17:3; 21:6; 22:2). When she was
overthrown, the temple of Baal at Jerusalem was
destroyed and the chief priest killed before the
altar (II Kings 11:18). Before long, however, there
was another revival of the worship of Baal (II
Chron. 28:2; II Kings 21:3). Josiah again destroyed the temple of Baal at Jerusalem, and
caused the public worship of the god to cease for
a time (II Kings 23:4,5). Prophets of Israel, especially Jeremiah, often denounced Baal worship
(Jer. 19:4,5).

In the worship of Baal, incense and burnt sacrifices were offered to him (Jer. 7:9), and on extraordinary occasions the victims were children offered by their parents (Jer. 19:5). Lascivious rites
accompanied the worship (I Kings 14:23,24).
Sometimes priests, dancing around the altar in a
state of frenzy, slashed themselves with knives (I
Kings 18:26,28). At first the name Baal was used
by the Jews for their God without discrimination,
but as the struggle between the two religions developed, the name Baal was given up in Judaism
as a thing of shame, and even names like Jerubbaal
were changed into Jerubbesheth.

Remains of the Temple of Bacchus at Baalbek. (To judge size, note human figures in right foreground among fragments of fallen pillars.) © MPS

2. A descendant of Reuben, the first-born son of Jacob (I Chron. 5:5).

3. A Benjamite (I Chron. 8:30).

4. A town somewhere on the border of Simeon (I Chron. 4:33).

5. In composition it is often the name of a man and not of Baal, e.g. Baal-hanan, a king of Edom (Gen. 36:38; I Chron. 1:49).   S.B.

BAALBEK (bāl'bĕk, *city of Baal*), a city of Coele-Syria, about 40 miles NW of Damascus, celebrated for its magnificence in the first centuries of the Christian era, and famous since then for its ruins. Early identified with the worship of Baal, the sun god, the Greeks named it Heliopolis, "City of the Sun." It cannot be identified with any Bible locality. It became a place of importance only after it was made a Roman colony. Chief of the ruins is the great Temple of the Sun, 290 ft. x 160 ft., built of incredibly huge stones from near-by quarries. The city was completely destroyed by earthquake in 1759. The Prussian government undertook its excavation in 1902.

BAALE OF JUDAH (bā'ăl-jōo'dà), a town on the N border of Judah, the same as Baalah and Kiriath-baal and Kiriath-jearim (II Sam. 6:2; I Chron. 13:6).

BAAL-GAD (bā'ăl-găd, *Gad is Baal*), a place in the valley of Lebanon, at the foot of Mount Hermon, which marked the N limit of Israel's conquest of Canaan (Josh. 11:17; 12:7; 13:5). Its site is uncertain.

BAAL-HAMON (bá'ăl-hā'mŏn, *Baal of Hamon*), a place where Solomon had a vineyard (S. of Sol. 8:11). Its location is unknown.

BAAL-HANAN (bā'ăl-hā'năn, *Baal is gracious*).
1. The son of Achbor and king of Edom (Gen. 36:38; I Chron. 1:49).
2. An official under David (I Chron. 27:28).

BAAL-HAZOR (bā'ăl-hā'zôr, *Baal of Hazor*), a place beside Ephraim where Absalom had a sheep-range and where he brought about the death of Amnon in revenge for the outrage upon his sister (II Sam. 13:23).

BAAL-HERMON (bā'ăl-hûr'mŏn, *Baal of Hermon*), a town or place near Mt. Hermon marking the NW limit of the half tribe of Manasseh E of the Jordan (Judg. 3:3; I Chron. 5:23).

BAALI (bā'ă-lĭ, *my lord, my master*). After the conquest of Canaan it was the common practice of the Israelites to use the name "Baal," the common name for all local gods, as well as "Jehovah." Hosea demands that this degradation cease and that Jehovah be no longer called "my Baal," but "Ishi" (my husband) (Hos. 2:16) The Israelites later abandoned the use of "Baal" for "Jehovah."

BAALIS (bā'ă-lĭs, Heb. *ba'alîs*), a king of the Ammonites who reigned soon after Nebuchadnezzar's capture of Jerusalem. He instigated the murder of Gedaliah (Jer. 40:14).

BAAL-MEON (bā'ăl-mē'ŏn, Heb. *ba'al me'ôn, Baal of Meon*), an old city on the frontiers of Moab, assigned to Reuben (Num. 32:38). It is called Beth-meon in Jeremiah 48:23 and Beon in Numbers 32:3.

BAAL-PEOR (bā'ăl-pē'ôr, Heb. *ba'al pe'ôr, Baal of Peor*), a Moabite deity, probably Chemosh, the national deity of the Moabites, worshiped on the top of Mount Peor. The Israelites, when encamped at Shittim, were induced by Moabite women to the worship of this deity, and were severely punished by God as a result (Num. 25:1-9; Ps. 106:28; Hos. 9:10).

BAAL-PERAZIM (bā'ăl-pē-rā'zĭm, Heb. *ba'al pe-rātsîm, Baal of the breaking through*), a place near the valley of Rephaim where David obtained a great victory over the Philistines (II Sam. 5:18-20; I Chron. 14:9-11).

BAAL-SHALISHA (bā'ăl-shăl'ĭ-shà, Heb. *ba'al shālīshâh, Baal of Shalisha*), a place in Ephraim from which bread and corn were brought to Elisha when he was at Gilgal (II Kings 4:42-44).

BAAL-TAMAR (bā'ăl-tā'mȧr, Heb. *ba'al tāmār, Baal of the palm tree*), a place in Benjamin, near Gibeah and Bethel (Judg. 20:33).

BAAL-ZEBUB (bā'ăl-zē'bŭb, Heb. *ba'al zevûv, Baal, or lord of flies*), the name under which Baal was worshiped by the Philistines of Ekron (II Kings 1:2,3,6,16). Ahaziah consulted him to find out whether he should recover from his illness, and was therefore rebuked by Elijah. There can be little doubt that Beelzebub is the same name as Baalzebub. The Greek text, however, has Beelzebul. Just how these changes in spelling took place is a matter of conjecture. Beelzebub is the prince of the demons (Matt. 10:25; 12:24; Mark 3:22; Luke 11:15,18,19). Jesus identifies him with Satan (Matt. 12:26; Mark 3:23; Luke 11:18). Beelzebul signifies "lord of the dwelling"; this is pertinent to the argument in Matthew 10:25; 12:29; Mark 3:27.

Ruins of the so-called Tower of Babel at Birs-Nimrud in Babylonia. © MPS

BAAL-ZEPHON (bā'ăl-zē'fŏn, Heb. *ba'al tsephôn, lord of the north*), a place near which the Israelites encamped just before they crossed the Red Sea (Exod. 14:2,9; Num. 33:7). The site is unknown.

BAANA (bā'à-nà, Heb. *ba'ănā', son of oppression*). 1. Two officers in the service of Solomon (I Kings 4:12; 4:16; A.V. "Baanah").
2. The father of Zadok, one of those who helped in rebuilding the wall in Nehemiah's time (Neh. 3:4).

BAANAH (bā'à-nà, Heb. *ba'ănâh, son of oppression*). 1. A captain in the army of Ish-bosheth who with his brother murdered Ish-bosheth and thus assisted in turning the kingdom to David, who, however, had them put to death as criminals (II Sam. 4).
2. The father of Heleb, one of David's warriors (II Sam. 23:29; I Chron. 11:30).
3. A Jew who returned from Babylon with Zerubbabel and was one of those who sealed the covenant (Ezra 2:2; Neh. 7:7; 10:27).

BAARA (bā'à-rà, Heb. *ba'ărā', the burning one*), a wife of Shaharaim, a Benjamite (I Chron. 8:8).

BAASEIAH (bā'à-sē'yà, Heb. *ba'ăsēyâh, the Lord is bold*), an ancestor of Asaph, the musician (I Chron. 6:40).

BAASHA (bā'à-shà, Heb. *ba'shā', boldness*), the son of Ahijah, of the tribe of Issachar. He became the third king of Israel by assassinating Nadab, the son of Jeroboam, in the second year of his reign, when the latter was directing the siege of Gibbethon in the land of the Philistines. He exterminated the house of Jeroboam, and made Tirzah his capital. He ascended the throne in the third year of Asa, king of Judah (I Kings 15,16). He carried on a long war with Asa. About the 16th year of Asa, Baasha began to fortify Ramah, five miles N of Jerusalem, in order to blockade the N frontier of Judah, but was prevented from completing this work by Ben-hadad, king of Damascus, whom Asa hired (I Kings 15:16-21; II Chron. 16:1-6). Asa then tore down Baasha's defences, and for his own protection built up the bulwarks of Geba (between Ramah and Jerusalem). Baasha continued the calf worship begun by Jeroboam, and the Prophet Jehu threatened him and his house with a worse fate than Jeroboam's. After a reign of 24 years he died a natural death and was succeeded by his son, Elah, who was killed, along with every member of the house of Baasha, by Zimri (I Kings 15,16). **S.B.**

BABEL, TOWER OF (bā'bĕl, *gate of God*), an expression is not found in the OT, but it is used popularly for the structure built in the plain of Shinar, as the story is told in Genesis 11:1-9. The men of Shinar intended to build a tower "whose top may reach unto heaven," but Jehovah frustrated them by confusing their tongues. The author of Genesis assumes that before this the whole human species was a single tribe moving from place to place and speaking one language. The event took place not very long after the Deluge.

At the sites of many ancient cities in Mesopotamia there are found the remains of large towers called "ziggurats." These were sacred temple-towers, built in stages, steplike, of brick and asphalt, at the top of which there was usually a shrine. The Tower of Babel was, however, not a temple-tower, but simply a tower, apparently the first one ever attempted. The ziggurats were very likely to an extent imitations of this tower.

It is not known for certain whether the ruins of the Tower of Babel are still extant. There are rival claimants for the honor. **S.B.**

BABYLON (Băb'ĭ-lŏn), the Greek form of the Hebrew word *bâvel*, which was closely allied to, and probably derived from, the Akkadian *babilu* or "gate of God." The name referred not only to the city itself but also to the country of which it was the capital. Though not the oldest city in Babylonia it soon became the most important both from the standpoint of size and influence.

Babylon was situated in central Mesopotamia on the river Euphrates, some fifty miles south of modern Baghdad, capital of Iraq. A huge plantation of palm trees added to the beauty of the ancient city, and a permanent water supply assured fertility for the surrounding areas. It was within easy reach of the Persian Gulf, and being situated on an important caravan-trade route was in contact with all the most important cultural centers of the ancient Near East.

The date of its foundation is still disputed. The connection between Akkad, Calneh, Erech and Babylon (Gen. 10:10) indicates a period at least as early as 3000 B.C. Babylon may have been founded originally by the Sumerians, and an early tablet recorded that Sargon of Akkad (c. 2400 B.C.) destroyed Babylon and took some of its sacred earth to his own capital city, Akkad. This is probably a reference to the hallowing of the spot by the Tower of Babel (Gen. 11) which the ancient Mesopotamians had constructed in the apparent hope that the deity could be persuaded to descend from heaven and dwell among men. Whatever the date of its foundation, the earliest archaeological levels of the mound which once was stately Babylon come from the first dynasty period, i.e. the nineteenth to sixteenth centuries B.C.

The history of Babylon is complicated by the fact that it was governed by rulers from several lands, who were successively engaged in struggles for its capture and retention. It was the scene of many a decisive battle, its magnificent buildings being plundered in various periods and its walls and temples leveled from time to time. Yet this apparently indestructible city rose from its ruins on each occasion more splendid than before, until during the reign of Nebuchadnezzar II (c. 605-562 B.C.) it was probably the largest and most elaborate city in the ancient world. All that now remains of its former glory is a series of mounds some five miles in extent, lying mostly on the left bank of the Euphrates.

The political history of Babylon was bound up with that of Babylonia and Assyria, though from the beginning of the eighteenth century B.C. (about the period of Terah's migration from Ur, Gen. 11: 31) until the time of the Assyrian regime (ninth to sixth centuries B.C.), Babylon was the dominant influence in Mesopotamia. Under Hammurabi (c. 1704-1662 B.C.), the last great king of the first dynasty, the Babylonian empire stretched from the Persian Gulf to the middle Euphrates and upper Tigris regions. Archaeological discoveries have brought to light many of the achievements of this remarkable scholar-statesman, the most interesting of which is his celebrated legal code. His attempts to unify and organize social life led him to collect and expand existing minor law codes. The resulting legislation was of a most comprehensive nature, and Hammurabi ordered it to be incised on a basalt column and placed in the temple of Shamash, god of justice, for all to see. This column is in every sense a monument of ancient jurisprudence. It was carried away as a trophy by invading Elamites in a surprise raid during the twelfth century B.C., and was unearthed only in 1901 at Susa (Biblical Shushan) by J. de Morgan.

The first dynasty of Babylon fell about 1596 B.C. when the Hittite king Mursilis I (c. 1600 B.C.) advanced from modern Anatolia (modern Turkey) with an army and sacked the city. For about three hundred years Babylon was at the mercy of the Kassites who lived to the north, the Elamites, and other warlike nomadic peoples. An early Assyrian monarch Tukulti-Ninurta I (c. 1250 B.C.) occupied Babylon and took the sacred statue of Marduk, patron deity of the city, to Ashur. From the end of the tenth century B.C. Babylon became a vassal of Assyria, being controlled by the kings of Nineveh. Occasionally the vassal ruler revolted and attempted to form a new dynasty in Babylon, but by the time of Tiglath-pileser III of Assyria (c. 745-727 B.C.) Babylon was completely under Assyrian control. This redoubtable monarch, known as Pul in II Kings 15:19 and I Chronicles 5: 26, attacked the northern kingdom of Israel, carried away captives from Gilead, Galilee and Naphtali (II Kings 15:29), demanded booty and reduced Israel to a series of provinces.

One of the more vigorous vassal rulers of Babylon who revolted against Assyria was Marduk-apal-iddin (c. 722-711 B.C.), the Merodach-Baladan of II Kings 20:12f., and Isaiah 39:1. He endeavored to organize a coalition against his overlord Sargon II (c. 722-705 B.C.), and sought the

Babylon, at the Ishtar Gate. © MPS

kingdom of Judah as an ally. Isaiah dissuaded Hezekiah from such a course on the ground that it would be futile. A small stone tablet was unearthed in Babylonia which depicted Merodach-Baladan as a stout man with the long curled hair and beard typical of Babylonia. He held a sceptre in his left hand, and on his head he wore a conical helmet quite unlike the usual Assyrian crown. Merodach-Baladan's schemes were ended by Sargon, who subdued him with difficulty and occupied the throne of Babylon.

Sargon was succeeded by his son Sennacherib (c. 705-681 B.C.), who employed vassal princes to keep Babylon in subjugation. When this device failed he attacked the city and sacked it in 689 B.C., removing the statues of its gods to Assyria. It was left to his son Esarhaddon (c. 681-669 B.C.) to repair the damage and restore the city, perhaps at the instigation of his mother, who was apparently of Aramean descent. When Esarhaddon died his kingdom was divided between his two sons. Ashurbanipal (c. 669-626 B.C.), the last great Assyrian ruler, reigned in Nineveh while his brother Shamash-Shumukin occupied the throne of Babylon. They quarreled bitterly, and in 651 B.C. Ashurbanipal attacked and burned Babylon. His brother was killed and a vassal was appointed to succeed him. Towards the end of Ashurbanipal's life this man became increasingly rebellious, and from 631-612 B.C. the influence of Babylon increased to the point where Nabopolassar founded an independent dynasty in 626 B.C., known as the neo-Babylonian or Chaldean regime.

Among the ruins of the great palaces of Babylon. © MPS

Under Nabopolassar (c. 626-605 B.C.) and his son Nebuchadnezzar II (c. 605-562 B.C.), ancient Babylon attained to the height of its splendor. While both men were notable military strategists they were also individuals of cultural interests, and they set about rebuilding the old Babylonian empire so as to make it the most splendid and notable of all time. Military expeditions brought numbers of captive peoples to Babylonia, and these were employed as artisans and craftsmen on the vast reconstruction projects. As a result of the energy and imagination of Nabopolassar and his son, the influence of Babylon far outstripped that of Nineveh, and in 616 B.C. the Babylonians began a military campaign against the middle Euphrates region which ended in the destruction of the Assyrian empire.

Nabopolassar first marched to the Balikh river and sacked a number of towns, but returned to Babylon the same year. In 615 B.C. he set out to attack Ashur, and after a year's siege the city capitulated. A revolt in the central Euphrates region delayed a further attack on Assyria, but in 612 B.C. a combined force of Babylonians and Medes marched against Nineveh, captured it and burned it to the ground. The remnant of the Assyrian forces fled to Haran in northwestern Mesopotamia, and despite their attempts to ally with Egypt they were decisively defeated in 610 B.C., ending the power of the Assyrian regime.

A battle at Carchemish in 605 B.C. against the Egyptians gave the Babylonian forces a decided military advantage, and Nabopolassar decided to occupy southern Palestine, probably with the intention of using it as an advance base for a subsequent attack upon Egypt. Nebuchadnezzar directed the operation on the death of Nabopolassar in 605 B.C., and in 597 B.C. the first attack upon Judah took place. This was followed by others in 586 and 581 B.C., the result of which was to send several thousand inhabitants of Judah to Babylon as captives. This group joined other previously-enslaved peoples, supplementing the already large labor force employed on the gigantic tasks of reconstruction and expansion current in the empire.

Once Nebuchadnezzar felt reasonably secure he devoted an increasing amount of attention to the expansion of cultural interests in imperial territory, and more particularly in Babylon. His objective was to make his capital the most notable city in the world, and to this end he constructed new canals and navigable waterways, erected magnificent buildings and laid out extensive parks. A number of travelers who visited Babylon at this time have left their impressions of the city. The description furnished by Herodotus in particular clearly indicates his amazement at its great size and splendor.

According to this notable historian of antiquity the city occupied an area of about 200 square miles, and was built on both sides of the Euphrates. It was protected by a double defensive brick wall reinforced with towers. To the outside of this wall, about twenty yards distant, was an additional de-

Babylon, the ruins of the famous "hanging gardens," from a point on the Great Procession Street just south of the Ishtar Gate. OIUC

fensive wall of burnt bricks set in bitumen. The outer portion of the twin walls extended over seventeen miles and was constructed under Nebuchadnezzar, while his predecessors were responsible for other parts of the fortification. Excavations at the mound have shown that the earliest attempt at constructing a defensive system goes back to the nineteenth century B.C.

According to cuneiform sources, access to the city was gained by eight gates, four of which have been excavated. Probably the most impressive of these is the Ishtar gate, located at the northern end of the mound. To reach it one passed down part of the great stone-paved processional street which was about 1000 yards in length. It was decorated on either side with figures of lions *passant* in enameled brick. Assyrian art was at its height at this period, and the draftmanship and execution of these animals indicates an advanced degree of artistic skill. The Ishtar gate was also decorated with animals, consisting of about a dozen rows of bulls and mythological dragons placed alternately. The decor was executed predominantly in blue and brown enamel, and was done in the time of Nebuchadnezzar.

When the city was at the height of its influence there were more than fifty temples in Babylon. When some of these were excavated they were found to be in a reasonably good state of preservation. The temple of Ninmah, goddess of the underworld, was built by Ashurbanipal near the Ishtar gate. The ground plan indicated that when approached from the north a vestibule led into a larger courtyard, the south end of which was decorated with pillars. Beyond these was an antechapel while to the south of this area was the shrine of the deity, containing among other structures an elevated platform designed to support a statue of the goddess. In addition there were living quarters for the priests, and stairways which gave access to other parts of the building. A great number of terra cotta figurines were uncovered at the site, but proved to be of little importance.

The southern citadel which was adjacent to the processional street comprised a huge complex of buildings whose main sections were the work of Nabopolassar and Nebuchadnezzar. Several blocks of buildings and courtyards finally led to the royal palace, many of whose rooms were ornately decorated with blue enameled bricks incorporating motifs similar to those used in Greece at a later time. The living quarters provided for the royal family, the court officers and the retinue of servants displayed the grandeur and pomp characteristic of an eastern court.

In this complex was situated one of the seven wonders of the world, the celebrated "hanging gardens" of Babylon. They actually consisted of terraces supported on huge masonry arches, on which carefully tended gardens had been laid out at different levels. Most probably they were designed and executed under Nebuchadnezzar, who had married a Median princess and intended the raised gardens to be a comforting reminder of her mountainous homeland. They included many species of Babylonian and Persian plants in addition to the palm trees which were a characteristic feature of Babylonia at that time. The interesting feature of these raised gardens was the fact that they were visible above the tops of the buildings, and provided a welcome contrast of greenery against an otherwise unrelieved background of white roofs or an expanse of sky. A number of mechanical hoists provided the means by which water was raised to these elevated terraces.

In an enclosed area southwest of the Ishtar gate was the huge *ziggurat* of Babylon, which was closely linked with the temple of Marduk lying immediately to the south. A *ziggurat* was properly a staged or terraced tower crowned with a small shrine dedicated to a particular deity. The structure was generally erected upon a mound or artificial brick platform, presumably to serve as a protection against floodwaters. Sometimes the term *ziggurat* is used to include the platform as well as the tower itself. This great staged tower of Babylon may have been the original Tower of Babel (Gen. 11: 1-9), modified by subsequent reconstruction and additions. From archaeological and other sources it would appear that it was a seven-story building of sun-dried mud brick faced with kiln-dried brick. An eighth story probably consisted of a small shrine dedicated to Marduk, and in the time of Nebuchadnezzar it was faced with blue enameled bricks. Access to the various levels was gained by means of stairways or ramps. The ground plan of the *ziggurat* was approximately 300 feet square, and the structure as it stood in the sixth century B.C. exceeded 300 feet in height.

The associated temple of Marduk consisted of an annex leading to the principal building. In the latter were a number of chapels devoted to deities other than Marduk, but his shrine was by far the most ornate, being richly decorated with gold, alabaster, cedar-wood panelling, lapis lazuli, obsidian and other semi-precious stones. Much of this work was done in the sixth century B.C.

Nebuchadnezzar died in 562 B.C., and during the next five years three kings, one of whom was the Evil-Merodach of II Kings 25:27, occupied the throne until Nabonidus came to power in 556 B.C. He was a mystic who had antiquarian interests, and after a short rule made his son Bel-shar-usur (Belshazzar) regent while he retired to Teima in Arabia. After nine years he returned to Babylon only to witness the overthrow of the city by Cyrus in 539 B.C. This conqueror did not pillage Babylon, however, but acted respectfully towards the shrines and deities of the land. Enslaved populations were liberated, including the captive Hebrews, and Cyrus, "king of Babylon," set about building up his vast Persian empire.

Darius I (c. 521-485 B.C.) continued the political tendencies begun by Cyrus, but in later years the center of influence of the Achaemenid regime moved from Babylon to Persepolis and Ecbatana. When the Persian empire fell to Alexander the Great in 330 B.C., Babylon was destroyed. Alexander intended to reconstruct the great *ziggurat*, and ordered the rubble removed from the site, but his death in 323 B.C. saw the task unfinished.

Although remaining as an inhabited site, Babylon declined still further in importance under the Parthians (c. 125 B.C.), and was last mentioned on a Babylonian clay tablet dated about 10 B.C. At the present time the Baghdad to Bassorah railway line passes within a few yards of the mound that was once the most splendid city of the world.

R.K.H.

On the ruins of the Via Sacra, the "Pennsylvania Avenue" of ancient Babylon, the scene of many victory parades. © MPS

BACA (bā'kà, Heb. *bākhā, a balsam tree*), in KJV in Psalm 84:6, where RV has "the Valley of weeping," with a marginal variant, "the valley of the balsam-trees." The tree is called a weeper probably because it exudes tears of gum. There is nô trace of a real tree with this name. The phrase refers figuratively to an experience of sorrow turned into joy.

BACHRITES (băk'rīts), a family of Ephraim, called Becherites in ASV, RSV (Num. 26:35), descendants of Becher (called Bered in I Chron. 7:20).

BADGER (See Animals)

BAG, various kinds are mentioned in the Bible. 1. Heb. *kelî;* Gr. *péra.* This was a kind of haversack, made of skin, for the carrying of one or more days' provisions. This is the "scrip for the journey" mentioned in Matthew 10:10.

2. Heb. *kîs,* a bag for merchant's weights such as is mentioned in Deuteronomy 25:13: "Thou shalt not have in thy bag divers weights, a great and a small."

3. Gr. *ballántion,* a more finished leather pouch which served as a "purse": "Carry neither purse, nor scrip" (Luke 10:4).

4. Heb. *hărît,* a large bag, one large enough to hold a talent of silver (II Kings 5:23).

5. Heb. *tserôr,* this was a bag that could be tied with a string, and was a favorite receptacle for valuables. It is translated "bundle" in Genesis 42:35. In the NT this bag is expressed by *zone* in Greek (Matt. 3:4; 10:9; Acts 21:11; Rev. 1:13; 15:6).

BAHURIM (bà-hū'rĭm, Heb. *bahurîm*), a place in Benjamin which lay on the road from Jerusalem to Jericho, not far from the Mount of Olives. It is frequently mentioned in the history of David. It was the home of Shimei, who cursed David on his flight from Absalom (II Sam. 16:5; 19:16; I Kings 2:8). Jonathan and Ahimaaz hid in a well there when acting as David's spies (II Sam. 17:18).

BAJITH (bā'jĭth, Heb. *bayith, house*), found only in Isaiah 15:2. *Bayith* may be textual error for *bath,* "daughter," in which case we should read "The daughter of Dibon is gone up to the high places." Some think that the RVm reading, "Bayith and Dibon are gone up to the high places to weep," is the proper rendering.

BAKBAKKAR (băk-băk'êr, Heb. *baqbaqqar, investigator*), a Levite (I Chron. 9:15).

BAKBUK (băk-bŭk, Heb. *baqbûq, bottle*), the founder of a family of Nethinim who returned from the Captivity with Zerubbabel (Ezra 2:51; Neh. 7:53).

BAKBUKIAH (băk'bū-kī'à, Heb. *buqbuqyâh, flask,* or perhaps, *the Lord pours out*), a name occurring three times in Nehemiah (11:17, 12:9,25), all the references being to one person, a Levite in high office in Jerusalem right after the Exile.

BAKER (See Occupations and Professions)

BALAAM (bā'lăm, Heb. *bil'ām,* perhaps *devouring* or *devourer*), the son of Beor from the city of Pethor on the Euphrates, a diviner whose remarkable history may be found in Numbers 22:2-24:25; 31:8,16; Deuteronomy 23:4; Joshua 33:22; 24:9; Nehemiah 13:2; Micah 6:5; II Peter 2:15; Jude 11; Revelation 2:14.

When the Israelites pitched their tents in the plains of Moab, immediately after their victory over Sihon and Og, Balak, the king of the Moabites, sent an embassy of elders of Moab and Midian to Balaam, offering to reward him if he would curse the Israelites. After looking to God about the matter, he replied that God had forbidden him to comply with the request. Balak then sent some messengers of a higher rank with more alluring promises. This time God permitted him to go, cautioning him, however, to give only the message God gave him. On his way to Balak this command was strongly impressed on Balaam's mind by the strange behavior of his ass and his encounter with the angel of the Lord.

Balak took him to the high places of Baal from which a part of the camp of the Israelites could be seen. To Balak's disappointment, Balaam pronounced upon the Israelites a blessing instead of a curse. Surprised and incensed at the words of the diviner, Balak thought that a fuller view of the camp of Israel might change his disposition, and took him to the top of Mt. Pisgah, but the only result was further blessing instead of cursing. The children of Israel are compared to a lion who will not lie down until he has eaten his prey. In his despair Balak now suggested that the issue be tried from a third locality. They went to the top of Peor, and there the Spirit of God came upon Balaam and caused him to declare not only that God would bless Israel, but that he who blessed her would be blessed, and he who cursed her would be cursed. In his bitter disappointment, Balak now broke forth in angry reproaches, and ordered Balaam to go home, but without the promised reward. Before he left, Balaam reminded the king that at the very beginning he had said that no amount of money could make him give anything other than the commandment of the Lord. He then uttered a last prophecy — the most remarkable he had given so far — in which he foretold the coming of a Star from Jacob and a scepter out of Israel which would smite Israel's enemies, including Moab.

Nothing else is said of Balaam until Numbers 31. There the seer who had sought to turn away Jehovah from His people, and failed, tried before long to turn the people from Jehovah. He knew that if he succeeded in this, the consequences to Israel would be such as Balak had desired, God's curse upon Israel. By his advice the Israelites were seduced into idolatry and all the vile abominations connected with it. In the judgment that followed, no fewer than 24,000 Israelites perished, until it was evident that the nation abhorred idolatry as a great crime against Jehovah. By God's command Israel meted out vengeance upon her seducers the Midianites; and in the universal slaughter, Balaam also perished.

In the NT Balaam is several times held up as an example of the pernicious influence of hypocritical teachers who attempt to lead God's people astray. No Bible character is more severely excoriated.					S.B.

BALAH (bā'là, Heb. *bālâh*), a town in SW Palestine (Josh. 19:3), Bilhah in I Chronicles 4:29. Site unknown. It may be the same as Baalah in Judah (Josh. 15:29).

BALAK (bā'lăk, Heb. *bālāq, devastator*), a king of Moab in Moses' day who hired Balaam, a diviner from the Euphrates, to pronounce a curse on the Israelites (Num. 22-24; Judg. 11:25; Micah 6:5; Rev. 2:14). Frightened by the story of Israel's victory over Sihon and Og, he evidently thought that the favor of Jehovah could be turned from Israel to his own nation. Instead of cursings, he heard blessings; but he achieved his end in an indirect way when he followed Balaam's advice to seduce men of Israel to idolatry, as a result of which sin God brought heavy judgment on the chosen people.

BALANCE (băl'ăns), the English word is from the Latin *bilanx* and means "having two scales." It is used to translate three Hebrew words: *mo'znayim, kaneh,* and *peles.* The balances of the Hebrews consisted of a horizontal bar, either suspended from a cord that was held in the hand, or pivoted on a perpendicular rod. Scales were suspended from the ends of the bar, one for the object to be weighed, the other for the weight. At first the weights were of stone. Weighing with such balances could be accurately done, but the system was liable to fraud, so that in the OT there is much denunciation of "wicked balances" (Micah 6:11).

BALD LOCUST (See Insects)

BALDNESS (bôld'nĕs). Natural baldness is seldom mentioned in the Bible. It was believed to result from hard work (Ezek. 29:18) or disease (Isa. 3:17,24). Baldness produced by shaving the head, however, is frequently referred to. It was done as a mark of mourning for the dead (Lev. 21:5; Isa. 15: 2; 22:12; Micah 1:16). Shaving the head as a sacrifice to the deity was the custom of the people in the land, and the Israelites were strictly forbidden to practice it (Lev. 21:5; Deut. 14:1). The custom among neighboring nations of shaving all but a small patch in the center of the head was also forbidden (Lev. 19:27; 21:5). When a Nazarite completed his vow, the shaven hair was offered as a sacrifice to Jehovah (Num. 6:18; cf. Acts 18:18; 21:24).

BALM (bäm, Heb. *tsŏrî*), an odoriferous resin perhaps obtained in Gilead (Gen. 37:25; Jer. 8:22; 46:11), and exported from Palestine. It was used as an ointment for healing wounds (Jer. 51:8). It came from a small tree not now found in Gilead, and perhaps it never grew there. See PLANTS.

BAMAH (bà'mà, Heb. *bāmâh, high place*). Ezekiel (Ezek. 20:29) plays upon the two syllables *ba* (go) and *mah* (what), with evident contempt for the high place to which the word refers.

BAMOTH-BAAL (bā'mŏth-bā'ăl, Heb. *bāmôth ba'al, high places of Baal*), a place N of the Arnon, in the tribe of Reuben, to which Balak took Balaam (Num. 21:19; 22:41).

BANDS. In English the word has two common meanings: that which holds together or binds, and a company of men. Both meanings are found in Scripture. In the NT reference is made to the "Italian Band," a cohort of Roman soldiers stationed at Caesarea (Acts 10:1), and the "Augustan Band," a cohort to which the Roman centurion Julius, who had charge of Paul on his voyage to Rome, belonged (Acts 27:1).

BANI (bā'nī, Heb. *bānî, posterity*). 1. A Gadite, one of David's heroes (II Sam. 23:36).
2. A Levite whose son served in the tabernacle in David's time (I Chron. 6:46).
3. A descendant of Judah whose son lived in Jerusalem after the Captivity (I Chron. 9:4).
4. A Levite and builder (Neh. 3:17).
5. A Levite (Neh. 9:4).
6. A Levite who lived before the return from exile (Neh. 11:22).
7. A Levite who sealed the covenant (Neh. 10: 13).
8. A leader who also signed the covenant (Neh. 10:14).
9. Founder of a family some of whom returned from Babylonia with Zerubbabel (Ezra 2:10). Some took foreign wives (Ezra 10:29).
10. Founder of a house (Ezra 10:34), a descendant of whom was also named Bani (Ezra 10: 38).

BANK (băngk). In its modern form, banking is of recent origin (17th century), but banking of a primitive kind was known in ancient times, among both Jews and Gentiles. Money was received on deposit, loaned out, exchanged for smaller denominations or for foreign money. Israelites could not charge each other interest (Exod. 22:25), but could lend on interest to Gentiles (Deut. 23:20).

BANNER (băn'êr, Heb. *nēs, deghel, banner, ensign, standard*). Banners were used in ancient times for military, national, and ecclesiastical purposes very much as they are today. In connection with Israel's wilderness journey we read, "The children of Israel shall encamp every man by his own standard, with the ensigns of their fathers' houses" (Num. 2:2). The word occurs frequently in the figurative sense of a rallying point for God's people (Isa. 5:26; 11:10; Jer. 4:21).

BANQUET (băng'kwĕt). The Hebrews, like other peoples of the ancient East, were very fond of social feasting. At the three great religious feasts, which all males were expected to attend, the family had its feast. Sacrifices were accompanied by a feast (Exod. 34:15; Judg. 16:23-25). There were feasts on birthdays (Gen. 40:20; Job 1:4; Matt. 14:6), marriages (Gen. 29:22; Matt. 22:2), funerals (II Sam. 3:35; Jer. 16:7), laying of foundations (Prov. 9:1-5), vintage (Judg. 9:27), sheep-shearing (I Sam. 25:2,36), and on other occasions. A banquet always included wine-drinking; it was not simply a feast in our sense. At a large banquet a second invitation was often sent on the day of the feast, or a servant brought the guests to the feast (Luke 14:17; Matt. 22:2ff). The host provided

A Roman banquet table,

for reclining at meals. UANT

robes for the guests, and they were worn in his honor and were a token of his regard. Guests were welcomed by the host with a kiss (Luke 7:45), and their feet were washed because of the dusty roads (Gen. 18:4; Judg. 19:21; Luke 7:44). The head was anointed (Ps. 23:5; Luke 7:46), and sometimes the beard, the feet, and the clothes. The head was decorated with garlands (Isa. 28:1). The guests were seated according to their respective rank (I Sam. 9:22; Luke 14:8), the hands were washed (II Kings 3:11), and grace was said (I Sam. 9:13; Matt. 15:35; Luke 22:17). The Pharisees made hand washing and the saying of grace burdensome rituals. The feast was put under the superintendence of a "govĕrnor of the feast," usually one of the guests, whose task it was to taste the food and the drinks and to settle about the toasts and amusements. The most honored guests received either larger or more choice portions than the rest (Gen. 43:34; I Sam. 9:23f). Portions were sometimes sent to friends not attending the feast (II Sam. 11:8; Neh. 8:10). Often the meal was enlivened with music, singing, and dancing (II Sam. 19:35; Luke 15:25), or with riddles (Judg. 14:12). A great banquet sometimes lasted seven days, but excess in eating and drinking was condemned by the sacred writers (Eccl. 10:16f; Isa. 5:11f).   S.B.

BAPTISM (băp'tĭzm), a term derived from the Greek *báptisma* (antecedent, *baptízo*); the etymological significance of the word often has been obscured by a lack of exegetical clarity and by forced interpretation. Its true meaning can be found only in its usage and its theological significance. Its *antecedent meaning* involves its Judaic usage in the OT times, and its practice by John the Baptist. Its *incipient meaning* lies in Christ's baptism and His interpretation of it. Its *formal meaning* is to be found in its apostolic interpretation, particularly Pauline.

The use of the word *baptízo* in Jewish usage first appears in the Mosaic laws of purification (Exod. 30:17-21; Lev. 11:25; 15:8; 17:15; Num. 19:17, 18; 31:22,23) where it undeniably means a mere "washing" or "cleansing." In the Septuagint version of the OT, translated into the Hellenistic idiom of the New Testament, the word is used but three times: II Kings 5:14 and Ecclesiasticus 34:25, where the meaning again is that of cleansing, and Isaiah 21:4, where its meaning is obscured. It is clear, however, that later Judaism incorporated this primary connotation of cleansing and purification into its idea of the New Covenant relation and used it as a rite of initiation, as reflected in the practices of the Qumran sect and the Dead Sea Scroll communities.

While late Judaism certainly attached a deeply pietistic significance to the cleansing act, John the Baptist, who followed in this tradition, infused into the ritual act of initiation and purification an ethical quality which it had not had before. His was a moral community of penitent souls seeking personal righteousness, and he associated with the act of baptism the imperative necessity for a thorough change in the condition of the soul, manifested in a remission of sins through repentance. His fervent exhortation to "repent and flee from the wrath to come" (Matt. 3:7,8) was not a mere invitation to a religious ceremony, but was, rather, symptomatic of the change in the act of baptism itself. The meaning of the act was deepened, therefore, by its transformation from a rite to which one submitted himself to a positive moral act initiated by the individual as a decisive commitment to personal piety.

John's baptism was, nevertheless, only transitory — his baptism of *repentance* was but preparatory to a baptism of identification. The meaning and efficacy of baptism can be understood only in the light of the redemptive death and resurrection of Christ. Christ referred to his death in the words "I have a baptism to be baptized with" (Luke 12:59) and, "Can you drink of the cup that I drink of? and be baptized with the baptism that I am baptized with?" (Mark 10:38; Matt. 20:22). Here the word *báptisma*, which indicates the state or condition, is used instead of *baptismos,* which applies to Jewish rites and refers only to the act itself. *Baptisma,* used only in the NT and in Christian writings, never refers to the act alone, but always incorporates into its meaning the entire scope of the redemptive significance of the incarnate person of Christ.

The baptism of Jesus, therefore, relates the act of baptism to the meaning of the salvation events through His own person and work. When Jesus submitted to the baptism of John He conjoined the act of water baptism with the efficacy of His redemptive work, making them inter-related and vital to each other. To this act of water baptism He added the promise of the baptism with the Spirit, the means by which His redemptive work for man became efficacious (Mark 1:8; Matt. 3:11; Luke 3:16; Acts 1:4ff; 11:16). Through this baptism, entry into Christ's redemptive work is gained. Utilizing the initiatory and purificatory connotations found in water baptism, Christ made spiritual baptism (by the Holy Spirit) synonymous with the actual application of the virtues of His death and resurrection to sinful man.

The Apostolic writers, particularly Paul, enlarged the concept of the spiritual aspect of baptism by relating it to the whole of the redemptive act. To the generic symbolism of cleansing, Paul attributed to its spiritual significance the quality of entry into the righteousness of Christ through an identification with Christ Himself. *Spiritual baptism* is the means by which the redeemed sinner is incorporated into the spiritual body of Christ, not merely as an act of initiation, but as a state or condition of personal righteousness. It is, therefore, the only access to *identification* with the redeeming Christ.

Baptism may, therefore, he regarded from two perspectives: its *subjective significance,* as the baptism of the Holy Spirit in which the believer is brought into positive relationship to God; and its *symbolic significance,* as the objective manifestation of the believer's acquiescence to that relationship. Its subjective significance lies in its nature as spiritual baptism, while its objective form relates to its symbolic significance.

Its subjective significance is represented in the NT by many analogies. It is regarded as the means of *participation in the death and resurrection* of Christ. In Romans 6:3-5, Paul relates the actual spiritual condition of his readers to such a participation in the death and resurrection through baptism. "Do you not know that all of us who have been baptized into Christ Jesus were baptized into his death? We were buried therefore with him *by baptism* into death, so that as Christ was raised from the dead by the glory of the Father, we too might walk in newness of life." This identification is not merely to the death of Christ, in which the believer has also died to sin, but to the resurrection of Christ, in which the believer has found "newness of life." Spiritual baptism is therefore an *entry into the new life in Christ* — a passage from the old creation into the new creation. This involves not merely forgiveness of sins, but an impartation of the life and righteousness of Christ to the believer (II Peter 1:4). The believer is "in Christ," and Christ is in the believer. Moreover, this identification, effected through spiritual baptism, *cleanses the believer through the blood of Christ* (Titus 3:5f). True baptism is, therefore, the incorporation of the believer into Christ's righteousness and an infusion of that righteousness into the believer.

Its symbolic significance is depicted in its objective form. While much debate has focused on the varying interpretations of the forms of baptism, each form (immersion, sprinkling or pouring) is clearly associated with the concept of cleansing and identification, which are, as reflected in its spiritual significance, its two integral parts. Immersion, however, depicts more clearly the symbolic aspect of baptism since its three steps of *im*mersion — going into the water, *sub*mersion — going under the water, and *e*mersion — coming out of the water, more closely parallel the concept of entering into the death of Christ, experiencing the forgiveness of sins, and rising to walk in the newness of Christ's resurrected life (Rom. 6:4).

The genius of Christian baptism, however, is to be found not merely in its symbolic significance, but in its actual effect in the life of the believer. True baptism must always be vitally related to faith. Only through responsive faith to the regenerative work of Christ can the soul participate in spiritual baptism, and subsequently in the symbolic form of the act itself. Through faith, as a commitment to the person of Christ, the believer is brought into an actual relation to God through the radical change of nature which is inherent in spiritual baptism. Faith is a "surrender-in-response" relationship to the Holy Spirit, who, through spiritual baptism, brings man into vital union with God.

While much emphasis in recent evangelical use has been placed on the "symbol only" concept of baptism, and, while the NT pointedly abstains from ascribing a sacramental value to the act itself, a renewed emphasis upon the spiritual significance of baptism will restore to its proper place a much neglected aspect of this doctrine. No statement of the doctrine can be a truly Biblical one if it fails to emphasize that beyond the symbolic and commemorative act performed by man there is also the inward operation of the Holy Spirit, bringing man into a redemptive relationship through his participation in and identification with the death, burial, and resurrection of Christ, and the subsequent infusion of the merits of that death and resurrection into the life of the believer, by which he may live as one dead to sin, but alive to God (Rom. 6:11).   C.B.B.

BAR- (bàr), an Aramaic word for the Hebrew *bēn*, "son." In the NT it is used as a prefix to the names of persons, e.g., Bar-Jonah, "son of Jonah" (Matt. 16:17); Barabbas; Bar-Jesus; Barnabas; Barsabbas; Bartholomew; Bartimaeus.

BARABBAS (bàr-ăb'ăs, Gr. *Barabbás*, for Aramaic Bar-abba, *son of the father,* or *teacher*), a criminal chosen by the Jerusalem mob, at the instigation of the chief priests, in preference to Christ, to be released by Pilate on the feast of the Passover. Matthew calls him a notorious prisoner, and the other evangelists say he was arrested with others for robbery, sedition, and murder (Matt. 27:16; Mark 15:15; Luke 23:18; John 18:40). The custom here mentioned of releasing a prisoner on the Passover is otherwise unknown. The reading "Jesus

A baptism scene at the River Jordan, the Epiphany ceremony. © MPS

Barabbas" for his full name in Matthew 27:16f, was found by Origen in many MSS., and is still to be found in some early versions and a few cursives. It is probably due to a scribe's error in transcription.

BARACHEL (băr'à-kĕl, Heb. *bārakh'ēl, God blesses*), a Buzite, whose son Elihu was the last of Job's friends to reason with him (Job 32:2,6).

BARACHIAS (băr'à-kĭ'ăs, Gr. *Barachías*), the father of Zachariah, who was slain between the Temple and the altar (Matt. 23:35).

BARAK (băr'ăk, Heb. *bārāq, lightning*), the son of Abinoam of Kedesh, a refuge city in Mt. Naphtali. He was summoned by Deborah the judge and prophetess to lead the Israelites to war against the Canaanites under the leadership of Sisera, the commander in chief of Jaban, king of Canaan. For 20 years Israel had been oppressed by the Canaanites. The farm lands were plundered; traffic almost ceased; and the fighting men of Israel were disarmed, so that not a shield nor a spear was to be seen among them. Barak raised an army of 10,000 men, mostly from a few faithful tribes, which encamped on Mt. Tabor, the wooded slopes of which protected them against the chariots of the Canaanites. The army of Israel routed Jabin's 800 iron chariots and heavily-armed host in the plain of Jezreel (Esdraelon). A heavy rainfall caused the alluvial plain to become a morass in which the Canaanite army found it impossible to move, and assisted in the discomfiture. Sisera abandoned his chariot and ran away on foot. Barak pursued him and found him slain by Jael in her tent. A peace of 40 years was secured (Judg. 4,5). In Hebrews 11:32 Barak's name appears among those who achieved great things through faith.

BARBARIAN (bàr-bâr'ĭ-ăn), originally anyone who did not speak Greek. Paul uses it in this strict sense in Romans 1:14, where Greeks and barbarians means the whole human race. Romans and Jews did not mind being called barbarians in this sense. In I Corinthians 14:11 Paul uses the word to describe one who spoke an unintelligible foreign tongue; and so also in Acts 28:2,4, where the inhabitants of Melita are called barbarians (they spoke a Punic dialect). In Colossians 3:11 the word refers to those who did not belong to the cultivated Greek race.

BARBER (See Occupations and Professions)

BAR-JESUS (bàr'jē'sŭs, Gr. *Bariesoús, son of Jesus*), a Jewish magician and false prophet in the court of Sergius Paulus when the latter was proconsul of Cyprus. He was struck blind for interfering with Paul's work (Acts 13:6-12).

BAR-JONA (bàr'jō'nà, Gr. *Bar-iōnás,* probably *son of Jonah,* or *son of John*), a surname of the Apostle Peter (Matt. 16:17).

BARKOS (bàr'kŏs, Heb. *barqôs*), one of the Nethinim who founded a family some members of which returned with Zerubbabel to Jerusalem (Ezra 2:53; Neh. 7:55).

BARLEY (See Plants)

BARNABAS (bàr'nà-bàs, Gr. *Barnábas,* explained in Acts 4:36 to mean *son of exhortation* or *consolation*), the surname of Joseph, a Levite from Cyprus, who was an early convert to Christianity. He sold a field and gave the proceeds to the support of the poorer members of the church in Jerusalem (Acts 4:36ff). In Acts 11:24 he is described as "a good man, and full of the Holy Ghost and of faith," traits which early brought him into leadership. When the church in Jerusalem hesitated to receive Paul into their fellowship, Barnabas removed their fears by speaking in the apostle's behalf (Acts 9:27).

After the start of the work at Antioch, the church in Jerusalem sent Barnabas there to give the work direction; and he, after laboring there for some time, went to Tarsus and brought back Paul as his associate (Acts 11:22-26). At the end of a year the two men were sent to carry alms from the infant church to their brethren at Jerusalem, who were suffering from famine (Acts 11:27-30). Returning with John Mark from Jerusalem, they were ordained as missionaries and proceeded on a mission to the Gentiles (Acts 13:2,3). Barnabas as well as Paul is called an "apostle" (Acts 14:14) Together the two men labored at Cyprus, Antioch in Pisidia, Iconium, Lystra, and Derbe. Up to Acts 13:43, the leadership is ascribed to Barnabas; after that, Paul takes the precedence. At Lystra, after a cripple was healed, the inhabitants worshiped Barnabas as Jupiter, and Paul, the chief speaker, as Mercury (Acts 13:3-14:28). After their return to Antioch, the church sent them to the council at Jerusalem (Acts 15:2). They were commissioned to carry the decrees of the council to the churches in Syria and Asia Minor (Acts 15:22-35).

The beginning of a difference between the two men is suggested by Paul in Galatians 2:13, where he says that Barnabas went along with Peter in the latter's inconsistent course. This was followed by a more serious break when, after Paul had suggested a second missionary journey, he refused to take along Mark, the cousin of Barnabas, on the ground that he had left them on their first journey. The two men separated, Barnabas going with Mark to Cyprus, while Paul went to Asia Minor (Acts 15:36-41). The mutual affection of the two evangelists did not, however, cease. Paul's allusions to Barnabas in his epistles shows that he continued to hold his former associate in high esteem (I Cor. 9:6; Gal. 2,1,9,13; Col. 4:10). Some early church leaders attributed the authorship of the Epistle to the Hebrews to Barnabas.   S.B.

BARREL (bǎr'ĕl), the KJV rendering of *kadh* in I Kings 17:12-16, 18:33. A large earthenware water jar is meant. Such a jar is still used in Palestine.

BARSABAS (bàr-sàb'ăs, Gr. from Aram., *son of Sabbas,* or perhaps, *son of,* i.e., *born on, the Sabbath*). 1. The surname of the Joseph who with Matthias was nominated by the apostles as the successor of Judas (Acts 1:23).

2. The surname of Judas, a prophet of the Jerusalem church, sent with Silas to Antioch with the decree of the Jerusalem council, and afterward returned to Jerusalem (Acts 15:22). Nothing further is recorded of him.

BARTHOLOMEW (bàr-thŏl'ō-mū, Gr. from Aram., *son of Tolmai* or *Talmai,* Gr. *Bartholomaíos*), one of the twelve apostles. He is mentioned in all four of the lists of the apostles in the NT (Mark 3:18; Matt. 10:3; Luke 6:14; Acts 1:13). There is no further reference to him in the NT, and the traditions concerning him are not trustworthy. Some scholars think that Bartholomew is the surname of Nathanael, who was led to Christ by Philip (John 1:45,46). The reason for this is that in the list of the apostles in the Gospels the name of Bartholomew immediately follows that of Philip, and the Synoptic Gospels never mention Nathanael, while John never mentions Bartholomew. This view has, however, not been conclusively established.

BARTIMAEUS (bàr'tĭ-mē'ŭs, Gr. *Bartímaios, son of Timaeus*), a blind man healed by Jesus as He went out from Jericho on His way to Jerusalem shortly before Passion Week (Mark 10:46-52). A very similar account is given by Luke (18:35-43), except that the miracle occurred as Jesus drew near to Jericho, and the blind man's name is not given. Matthew (20:29-34) tells of Jesus healing *two* blind men on the way out of Jericho. On the surface the stories seem irreconcilable, but there is no doubt that if we knew some slight circumstance not mentioned the difficulty would be cleared up. Various explanations, which may be found in the standard commentaries, have been suggested.

BARUCH (bâr'ŭk, Heb. *bārûkh, blessed*). 1. Son of Neriah and brother of Seraiah (Jer. 36:32), of a princely family. He was the trusted friend (Jer. 32:12) and amanuensis (Jer. 36:4ff) of the prophet Jeremiah. A man of unusual acquirements, he might have risen to a high position if he had not thrown in his lot with Jeremiah (Jer. 45:5). Jeremiah dictated his prophecies to Baruch, who read them to the people (Jer. 36). King Jehoiakim, on hearing the opening sentences of the prophecy, became greatly angered, and burned the roll. He ordered the arrest of Baruch and Jeremiah, but they escaped. Baruch rewrote the prophet's oracles with additions (Jer. 36:27-32). In the reign of Zedekiah, during the final siege of Jerusalem, Jeremiah bought his ancestral estate in Anathoth, and since he was at that time a prisoner, placed the deed in Baruch's hands, and testified that Israel would again possess the land (Jer. 32). Josephus (*Ant.* X,ix,1) says that Baruch continued to live with Jeremiah at Mizpah after the fall of Jerusalem. After the murder of Gedaliah, the leaders accused him of unduly influencing Jeremiah when the latter urged the people to remain in Judah (Jer. 43:3), a fact which shows how great Baruch's influence was thought to be over his master. He was taken to Egypt with Jeremiah (Jer. 43:6). After that, all reliable records about him cease. Jerome preserves a tradition that he died in Egypt soon after reaching there. Other traditions say that he was taken by Nebuchadnezzar to Babylon after this king conquered Egypt, and that he died there twelve years later. The high regard in which Baruch was held is shown by the large number of spurious writings that were attributed to him, among them *The Apocalypse of Baruch*, the *Book of Baruch; the Rest of the Words of Baruch*; the *Gnostic Book of Baruch*, and others.

2. A man who helped Nehemiah in rebuilding the walls of Jerusalem (Neh. 3:20).

3. A priest who signed the covenant with Nehemiah (Neh. 10:6).

4. The son of Colhozeh, a descendant of Perez (Neh. 11:5).　　S.B.

BARUCH, BOOK OF, one of the Apocryphal books, standing between Jeremiah and Lamentations in the LXX. It is based on the tradition which represents Baruch, the son of Neriah, as spending his last years in Babylon. Although some modern Roman Catholic scholars hold that it is the work of Jeremiah's friend and amanuensis, the book in its present form is usually thought to belong to the latter half of the first century of our era. The book purports to be a treatise by Baruch to the exiles, and is made up of an introduction and three sections. The first section contains a confession of sin and a prayer for the return of God's favor. In the second section wisdom is praised in words recalling Job 28 and 29 and the Book of Proverbs. In the third section words of encouragement are addressed to the exiles similar to those in the second part of Isaiah.

BARZILLAI (bär-zĭl'ā-ī, Heb. *bārzillay, made of iron*). 1. A wealthy Gileadite of Rogelim, E of the Jordan, who brought provisions to David and his army when the king fled from Absalom (II Sam. 17:27-29). When David was returning to Jerusalem, after Absalom's defeat, David invited Barzillai to come to live in the capital, but Barzillai, who was then 80, refused because of his age, and therefore arranged that his son Chinham should go in his stead (II Sam. 19:31-40). David before his death charged Solomon to "show kindness unto the sons of Barzillai" (I Kings 2:7).

2. One of the returning exiles living in Ezra's time. He took "a wife of the daughters of Barzillai the Gileadite" and adopted his wife's family name (Ezra 2:61,62).

3. A Meholathite, whose son Adriel married Saul's daughter, either Michal (II Sam. 21:8) or Merab (I Sam. 18:19).

BASEMATH (băs'ĕ-măth, Heb. *basmath, fragrant*), see Bashemath.

BASHAN (bā'shăn, Heb. *bāshān, smooth, fertile land*), the broad, fertile region E of the Sea of Galilee, extending, roughly, from Gilead on the S to Mt. Hermon on the N. Josephus identifies Bashan with Gaulonitis and Batanea (cf. Jos. *Antiq.* iv. 5,3 with I Kings 4:13; and *Antiq.* ix. 8,1 with II Kings 10:33). In the days of Abraham it was occupied by a people called the Rephaim (Gen. 14:5). Og, the last king of the race, was defeated and slain by the Israelites at Edrei in the time of Moses (Num. 21:33-35; Deut. 3:1-7). The whole district was assigned to the half tribe of Manasseh (Deut. 3:13). Edrei, Ashtaroth, Golan, and Salecah were its chief cities (Deut. 1:4; 3:1,10; 4:43). Solomon taxed the land (I Kings 4:13). It was lost to Israel in the Syrian wars (I Kings 22: 3ff; II Kings 8:28; 10:32,35). Tiglath-pileser incorporated it in the Assyrian empire (II Kings 15: 29). The Nabataeans held it in the second century B.C. It was included in the kingdom of Herod the Great, and then belonged to Philip, Herod's son.

It was celebrated for its cattle (Ps. 22:12), its breed of sheep (Deut. 32:14), and for its oak trees (Isa. 2:13; Ezek. 27:6).　　S.B.

BASHAN-HAVOTH-JAIR (bā'shăn-hă'vŏth-jā'ĭr, Heb. *bashan-hawwōth-ya'ir, encampments of Jair in Bashan*), a group of unwalled towns in the NW part of Bashan (Deut. 3:14). They were conquered by the Manassite clan Jair (Num. 32:41) when Reuben and Gad requested to have the eastern Jordanic region, immediately after Israel's conquest of Og and Sihon. There were 60 of these towns (Josh. 13:30).

BASHEMATH (băsh'ē-măth, Heb. *bāsmath, fragrant,* "Basemath" in RV). 1. One of Esau's wives, daughter of the Hittite Elon (Gen. 26:34). She is called Adah in the genealogy of Edom (Gen. 36:2,3).

2. Ishmael's daughter and sister of Nebaioth, the last of Esau's three wives, according to the genealogy in Genesis 36:3,4,13,17. In Genesis 28:9 she is called Mahalath.

3. Solomon's daughter, married to Ahimaaz, Solomon's tax collector for Naphtali (I Kings 4: 15).

BASIN (bā'sĭn, the ARV has "basin," the KJV and ERV "bason"), a wide hollow vessel for holding water for washing and other purposes (John 13:5). The word is used for various kinds of bowls and dishes: 1. a small vessel used for wine and other liquids (Exod. 24:6).

2. A shallow vessel used to receive the blood of sacrifices in the Temple (Exod. 12:22) and for domestic purposes.

3. A large bowl used in the Temple for various purposes, especially at the great altar (Zech. 9:15).

BASKET (băs'kĕt), four kinds of baskets mentioned in the OT, but we cannot tell from their names their differences in size, shape and use. They were made of various materials — leaves, reeds, rushes, twigs, or ropes; and they had various shapes and sizes. Some were small enough to be carried in the hands; others had to be carried on the shoulder or head or borne upon a pole between two men. They were used for a variety of purposes: for carrying fruit (Deut. 26:2); for carrying bread, cake, and flesh (Gen. 40:17; Exod. 29:2,3); for carrying clay to make bricks, and earth for embankments (Ps. 81:6). In the NT two kinds of

Basket carriers working at an archaeological excavation project at Bethel. © MPS

baskets are referred to. The *kóphinos* (Matt. 14:20; Mark 6:43; John 6:13) was a relatively small basket that could be carried on the back to hold provisions. Twelve of these baskets were used to gather the food that remained after the feeding of the 5,000. The *spurís* was considerably larger, as we may be sure from its being used in letting Paul down from the wall at Damascus (Acts 9:25). Seven of these were used to gather the food that was left after the feeding of the 4,000 (Matt. 16:9,10).   S.B.

BASMATH (băs'măth), in the KJV, with this spelling, appears only in I Kings 4:15. Elsewhere it is spelled Bashemath. See BASHEMATH.

BASTARD (băs'têrd, Heb. *mamzēr*, Gr. *nóthos, bastard,* specifically, *child of incest*), appears only three times in Scripture, twice in the OT, once in the NT. In Deuteronomy 23:2 it probably means a "child of incest," not simply an illegitimate child. There it says that a bastard and his descendants to the tenth generation are excluded from the assembly of the Lord. Jephthah, the son of a strange woman, was called to be a judge of Israel (Judg. 11:1,2). In Zechariah 9:6 we read, "And a bastard shall dwell in Ashdod, and I will cut off the pride of the Philistines." The RVm has "a bastard race." Brown, Driver, and Briggs suggest this means a "mixed population." In Hebrews 12:8 the word is used in its proper sense of "born out of wedlock." Bastards had no claim to paternal care or the usual privileges and discipline of legitimate children.

BAT (See Animals)

BATH (See Weights and Measures)

BATH, BATHING, BATHE. Bathing in the ordinary, non-religious sense, whether for physical cleanliness or refreshment, is not often met with in the Scriptures. The average Hebrew had neither the water nor the inclination for bathing. In most cases where "bathe" occurs in the KJV, partial washing is meant. Public baths of the Greek type were unknown among the Hebrews until Greek culture invaded Palestine under Antiochus Epiphanes (c. 168 B.C.). The dusty roads of Palestine made frequent washing of the feet necessary, and this was always done when tarrying at a house (Gen. 18:4; 19:2; John 13:10). Bathing in the Bible stands chiefly for ritual acts — purification from ceremonial defilement because of contact with the dead, defiled persons or things, or things under the ban. Priests washed their hands and feet before entering the sanctuary or making an offering on the altar (Exod. 30:19-21). The high priest bathed on the day of the atonement before each act of expiation (Lev. 16:4,24). In the time of Christ, the Jews washed their hands before eating (Mark 7:3,4). According to Josephus, the Essenes practiced daily bathing for ceremonial reasons.   S.B.

BATHRABBIM (băth'răb'ĭm, Heb. *bath-rabbîm, daughter of multitudes*), the name of a gate of Heshbon (S. of Sol. 7:4). Near it were two pools which are compared to the Shulammite's eyes.

BATH-SHEBA (băth-shē'bà, Heb. *bath-sheva', daughter of Sheba*), the daughter of Eliam (II Sam. 11:3) or Ammiel (I Chron. 3:5); both names have the same meaning. She was the wife of Uriah the Hittite, a soldier in David's army, during whose absence in the wars David forced her to commit adultery with him (II Sam. 11). Uriah was then treacherously killed by the order of David (II Sam. 11:6ff). She became David's wife and lived with him in the palace. Four sons, including Solomon, were the result of this marriage (II Sam.

5:14; I Chron. 3:5), after the first child had died (II Sam. 12:14ff). With the help of the prophet Nathan she defeated the plot of Adonijah to usurp the kingdom, and succeeded in having David choose Solomon as his successor. Adonijah was ultimately put to death. She was a woman of resourcefulness and energy and retained her influence over David until his death. Her sons Nathan and Solomon were both ancestors of Jesus Christ (Matt. 1:6; Luke 3:31).

BATH-SHUA (băth'shōoà, Heb. *bath-shûa', daughter of opulence,* or *daughter of Shua*). 1. In Genesis 38:2 and I Chronicles 2:3, where the name is translated "Shua's daughter," the wife of Judah.

2. In I Chronicles 3:5, the mother of Solomon. It is probably a misreading of Bath-sheba, due to a scribal error. The LXX has Bath-sheba.

BATTERING RAM (See War, Warfare)

BATTLE. In ancient times a trumpet-signal by the commander opened each battle (Judg. 7:18), and, when it was over, called the soldiers away from the fight (II Sam. 2:28; 18:16). Priests accompanied the army into war to ascertain the Divine will (I Sam. 14:8ff; Judg. 6:36ff). To make Jehovah's help in battle more certain, the Ark was taken along. When the army drew nigh unto battle, a priest or the commander encouraged the soldiers by reminding them of God's presence and help. The faint-hearted were exempted (Deut. 20:8). Military science was relatively simple. A force was usually divided into two attacking divisions, the one in the rear serving as a reserve or as a means of escape for the leader, in case of defeat. Spearmen probably formed the first line, bowmen or archers the second, and slingers the third. Horses and chariots were not used by Israel until quite late. Most of the fighting was done by footmen. Sometimes the battle was preceded by duels between individuals, and these on occasion determined the outcome of the battle (I Sam. 17:3ff; II Sam. 2:14ff). Night attacks and ambushments were often resorted to (Judg. 7:16ff; Josh. 8:2).   S.B.

BATTLE-AX (See Arms and Armor)

BATTLE-BOW (See Arms and Armor)

BATTLEMENT, a term applied to parapets with open spaces, surmounting ancient fortified buildings and city walls. From the openings, stones, lances, and arrows were hurled upon attacking soldiers below. In Deuteronomy 22:8 we read that battlements should be provided for the roofs of houses to keep people from falling from them, since roofs were much used for evening recreation.

BAVIA (băv'â-ī, Heb. *bawway*), a son of Henadad, who helped in the rebuilding of the wall of Jerusalem (Neh. 3:18).

BAYTREE (See Plants)

BAZLITH (băz'lĭth, Heb. *batslîth, stripping*), the ancestor of a family of Nethinim, members of which returned from captivity (Ezra 2:52; Neh. 7:54).

BAZLUTH (băz'lŭth, Heb. *batslûth*), the same as Bazlith, see above. Spelled Bazluth in Ezra 2:52 and Bazlith in Nehemiah 7:54.

BDELLIUM (dĕl'ĭ-ŭm, Heb. *bedhōlah*), a substance mentioned in Genesis 2:12 and Numbers 11:7, variously taken to be a gum or resin, a precious stone, or a pearl. It was of the same color as manna, and found like gold and the onyx stone or the beryl in the land of Havilah. The Greeks gave the name bdellium to a gum obtained from a tree growing in Arabia, Babylonia, India, and Media. The LXX translates it in Genesis 2:12 as "ruby," and in Numbers 11:7 as "rock crystal."

BEALIAH (bē'à-lī'à, Heb. *be'alyâh, Jehovah is Lord*), a Benjamite soldier who joined David at Ziklag (I Chron. 12:5).

BEALOTH (bē'à-lŏth, Heb. *be'ālôth*). 1. A town in the south of Judah (Josh. 15:24).

2. A locality in north Israel (I Kings 4:16, Aloth KJV). The text is uncertain.

BEAM (bēm), used in the OT to refer to beams used in constructing the upper floors and roofs of buildings (I Kings 7:3) and to the beam of a weaver's loom (Judg. 16:14). Jesus uses the term in a figurative sense in Matthew 7:3 and Luke 6:41 in contrast to a mote in order to show how inconsistent it is to criticize minor faults in others when ours are so much greater.

BEAN (See Plants)

BEAR (See Animals)

BEARD (bērd), with Asiatics a badge of manly dignity, in contrast to the Egyptians, who usually shaved the head and the face. As a sign of mourning, it was the custom to pluck it out or cut it off. The Israelites were forbidden to shave off the corners of their beards, probably because it was regarded as a heathenish sign (Lev. 19:27). To compel a man to cut off his beard was to inflict upon him a shameful disgrace (II Sam. 10:4f).

BEAST (bēst). 1. A mammal, not man, distinguished from birds and fishes, and sometimes also from reptiles (Gen. 1:29,30).

2. A wild, as distinguished from a domesticated animal (Lev. 26:22; Isa. 13:21,22; 34:14; Mark 1:13).

3. Any of the inferior animals, as distinguished from man (Ps. 147:9; Eccl. 3:19; Acts 28:5). The Mosaic law made a distinction between beasts that were ceremonially clean or unclean.

4. An apocalyptic symbol of brute force—sensual, lawless, and God-opposing. In Daniel 7 four successive empires are thus symbolized: Babylon, Media-Persia, Greece, and Rome. In Revelation 13:1-10 a superman rises out of the sea, manifests great power, and demands worship as if he were God. Revelation 13:11-18 tells of another beast, who comes out of the earth; he is often identified with the Antichrist. The beasts of Revelation 4:6-9 of the KJV are in the RV very properly called "living creatures."

BEATITUDES (bē-ăt'ĭ-tūds, Lat. *beatitudo, blessedness*). The word "beatitude" is not found in the English Bible. It means either (1) the joys of heaven, or (2) a declaration of blessedness, especially as made by Christ. Beatitudes occur frequently in the OT (Pss. 32:1,2; 41:1; 65:4, etc.). The Gospels contain isolated beatitudes by Christ (Matt. 11:6; 13:16; 16:17; 24:46, with the Lukan parallels; John 13:17; 20:29). But the word is most commonly used of the declarations of blessedness made by Christ in the discourses recorded by Matthew (5:3-11) and (Luke 6:20-22) which are called the "Sermon on the Mount" and the "Sermon on the Plain." Scholars are not agreed whether we have here two different records of the same discourse or records of two different but similar discourses.

The Beatitudes do not describe separate types of Christian character, but set forth qualities and experiences that are combined in the ideal character as conceived by Christ. In Matthew there are eight beatitudes and no woes; in Luke, four beatitudes and four corresponding woes. In Matthew all the sayings except the last are in the third person; in Luke they are in the second. In Matthew all the blessings except the last are attached to spiritual qualities; in Luke, to outward conditions of pov-

The traditional Mount of Beatitudes (Hattin), probably the scene of the Sermon on the Mount. © MPS

erty and suffering. The general declarations in Matthew require the spiritual conditions; while the special declarations in Luke, since they are addressed to disciples, do not. Luke omits the third, fifth, sixth, and seventh beatitudes of Matthew. Some scholars profess to find a gradation in the order in which they are recorded. Much has been written on the grouping of the beatitudes, but no grouping is generally accepted.　　S.B.

BEBAI (bē'bā-ī, Heb. *bēvay*). 1. The ancestral head of a family that returned from the captivity (Ezra 2:11; 8:11; Neh. 7:16; 10:15).

2. One of this family.

BECHER (bē'kêr, Heb. *bekher, first born*, or *young camel*). 1. The second son of Benjamin (Gen. 46:21; I Chron. 7:6). His descendants find no place in the registry of families (Num. 26:38; I Chron. 8:1-6), probably because they were too few in the beginning to form a tribal family. Becher's nine sons ultimately had 20,200 male descendants (I Chron. 7:8,9). They lived in Anathoth and other places in the territory of Benjamin.

2. A son of Ephraim, and founder of a family (Num. 26:35, Bachrites in KJV). But in I Chronicles 7:20 we read "Bered," which may be the correct form.

BECHORATH bē-kō'răth, Heb. *bekhôrath, the first birth*), an ancestor of Saul of the tribe of Benjamin (I Sam. 9:1).

BED. In the East, in ancient times, as now, the very poor as a rule slept on the ground, their outer garments serving as both mattress and blanket. The law, therefore, forbade such a garment to be kept in pledge after sunset, lest the man should be with-

Bedtime in a Palestinian home of Bible times. © SPF

out covering (Deut. 24:13). In more advanced conditions a rug or a mat was used as a bed. At first it was laid on the floor, usually near a wall; later it was put on an elevation, either a raised part of the floor or a bedstead, which gave rise to the expression "go up into my bed" (Ps. 132:3). Beds on raised platforms along the walls of a room were covered with cushions and used as a sofa during the day. Such beds were rolled up and put away in a closet or another room for the day. The bedchamber where Joash was hidden was not a chamber for sleeping, but a storeroom in which bedding was kept (II Kings 11:2). Still later, in some cases, a mattress took the place of the mat, and a pillow was also used, along with a blanket of some kind. Bedsteads must have been used occasionally, for the giant Og had one made of iron, a marvel in those days (Deut. 3:11). The very wealthy had more elaborate and ornamented bedsteads. Amos speaks of "beds of ivory" (6:4; 3:15), and in Esther 1:6 we read of "beds . . . of gold and silver." Such bedsteads were sometimes further furnished with pillars and a canopy (S. of Sol. 3:10), and they had on them silken cushions (Amos 3:12 RV) and rich coverings (Prov. 7:16).   S.B.

BEDAD (bē'dăd, Heb. *bedhadh, alone*), the father of Hadad, king of Edom (Gen. 36:35; I Chron. 1:46).

BEDAN (bē'dăn, Heb. *bedhān,* perhaps *son of judgment*). 1. A Hebrew judge who with Jerubbaal, Jephthan, and Samuel is mentioned as a deliverer of the nation (I Sam. 12:11). The Book of Judges does not mention him. It is thought that "Bedan" is a misreading for "Abdon" (Judg. 12:13) or for "Barak," which is found in the LXX and the Syriac.
2. A son of Ulam of the house of Manasseh (I Chron. 7:17).

BEDEIAH (bē-dē'yà, Heb. *bēdheyâh, servant of Jehovah*), a son of Bani who had taken a foreign wife (Ezra 10:35).

BEE (See Insects)

BEELIADA (bē'ē-lī'à-dà, Heb. *be'elyādhā', the Lord knows*), a son of King David (I Chron. 14:7); called Eliada in II Samuel 5:16 and I Chronicles 3:8.

BEELZEBUB (See Baalzebub)

BEELZEBUL (See Baalzebub)

BEER (bē'êr, Heb. *be'ēr, a well*). 1. A place where the Israelites stopped during their wilderness journey (Num. 21:16), possibly the same as Beer-elim (Isa. 15:8).
2. A place to which Jotham fled from his brother Abimelech (Judg. 9:21). Site unknown.

BEERA (bē-ê'rà, Heb. *be'ērā', a well*), a descendant of Asher (I Chron. 7:37).

BEERAH (bē-ê'rà, Heb. *be'ērâh, a well*), a Reubenite prince whom Tiglath-pileser carried away captive (I Chron. 5:6).

BEER-ELIM (bē'êr-ē'lĭm, Heb. *be'ēr 'ēlĭm, well of Elim*), a village of Moab (Isa. 15:8). See Beer 1.

BEERI (bē-ê'rī, Heb. *be'ērî, belonging to the well*). 1. A Hittite, father of Judith, one of Esau's wives (Gen. 26:34).
2. The father of the prophet Hosea (Hos. 1:1).

BEER-LA-HAI-ROI (bē'êr-là-hī'roi, Heb. *be'ēr lahay rō'î, the well of the living one who sees me*), a well, probably near Kadesh, where the Lord appeared to Hagar (Gen. 16:7,14) and where Isaac lived for some time (Gen. 24:62; 25:11).

BEEROTH (bē-ê'rŏth, Heb. *be'ērôth, wells*), a Canaanite town whose inhabitants succeeded in deceiving Israel by making a covenant with them (Josh. 9:3ff). When the deceit was discovered, they were made slaves by the Israelites (Josh. 9). Apparently they were Hivites (Josh. 9:7). It was in the territory assigned to Benjamin (Josh. 18:25; II Sam. 4:2). The murderers of Ish-bosheth (II Sam. 4:2), and Naharai, Joab's armor-bearer (II Sam. 23:37), came from Beeroth; and Beerothites returned from Babylon after the Exile (Ezra 2:25).

Village of Beeroth, known today as El Bireh. © MPS

Beersheba, near the southern boundary of Judah. © MPS

BEERSHEBA (bē'êr shē'bà, Heb. *be'ēr shēva'*, Gr. *Bersabée, well of seven,* or *the seventh well*).

Location: The most southerly town in the kingdom of Judah; hence, its practical boundary line, with only the Wady el Arish (the river of Egypt, Gen. 15:18) some 60 miles below the city, to the S. In the days of the conquest of Canaan, allotted to the tribe of Simeon (Josh. 19:2). The familiar expression "from Dan to Beersheba" is employed to designate the northern and southern extremities of the nation of Israel (II Sam. 3:10; 17:11; 24:2, et. al).

Etymology: The most probable meaning of the appellation "Beersheba" is the "Well of seven," or "the seventh well." In Hebrew the verb "to swear" and the numeral "seven" are almost identical; therefore, by inference, Beersheba has been styled the "well of the oath" (Gen. 21:31).

The religious and historical background: Hagar wandered in the wilderness of Beersheba as she fled from before her mistress, Sarah (Gen. 21:14). Abraham made the covenant with the Philistine princes here (Gen. 21:32). The patriarch made this his residence after the "offering up" of Isaac (Gen. 22:19). God appeared to Jacob on his way down into Egypt to be reunited to his son Joseph, after their years of separation, promising His continued presence (Gen. 46:1). Elijah, the prophet, sought refuge in Beersheba in seeking to escape from the terror of the wicked Queen Jezebel, wife of Ahab, of Israel (I Kings 19:3). The prophet Amos was constrained to rebuke the idolatrous tendencies which he saw infiltrating into the religious life of Beersheba from Bethel and from Dan (Amos 8:14). The town receives no mention in the New Testament. The modern name of Beersheba is Bir Es Seba. J.F.G.

BEETLE (See Insects)

BEGGAR (bĕg'àr, *one who lives off the charity of others*). The beggar, as a professional class, was unknown during Mosaic times. The law of Moses made ample provision for the poor of the land. In imprecatory fashion, Psalm 109:10 sets forth begging as the fate and punishment of the children of the wicked. As cities developed, begging became more prevalent. In the New Testament, beggars appear with some frequency: the blind beggar (John 9:8,9), blind Bartimaeus (Mark 10:46-52), the beggar by the "Beautiful" gate of the Temple (Acts 3:1-11) and, perhaps, most famous of all, Lazarus, the godly beggar who stands in opposition to the ungodly rich man (Luke 16:19-31).

BEHEMOTH (See Animals)

BEKAH (See Weights & Measures)

BEL (Bāl, Heb. *bēl*), the Baal of the Babylonians. The Babylonian Hymn to Bel translated from the cuneiform script reveals him as the supreme ruler, the life-giver, the god of justice, he who holds society together, controller of the elements, particularly fire. Isaiah 46:1; Jeremiah 50:2; 51:44. See Baal.

BELA (bē'là, Heb. *bela', destruction*), a neighboring city of Sodom and Gomorrah, in the vicinity of the Dead Sea; spared, through the intercession of Lot (Gen. 19:23-30), from the fiery holocaust which overtook the cities of the plain, later known as Zoar. According to Deutermonomy 34:3, Moses is said to have viewed the southern sector of the Promised Land from Jericho, the city of palm trees, unto Zoar. For all practical purposes this places its situation at the S end of the Dead Sea. On the basis of the LXX reading of Isaiah 15:5 and Jeremiah 48:34, it would appear as if the Dead Sea extended farther than at the present time. The name Zoar implies "little one."

BELAH (bē'là, Heb. *bēlay*). 1. The son of Beor, an Edomite king, previous to the kings of Israel (Gen. 36:32ff; I Chron. 1:43).

2. First-born son of Benjamin (I Chron. 7:6; 8:1). Head of the family of the Belaites (Num. 26:40).

3. Son of Azaz, a Reubenite, an exceptionally wealthy man (I Chron. 5:8,9). His possessions extended from Nebo to the Euphrates.

BELIAL (bē'lĭ-ăl, Heb. *belîya'al*, Gr. *Belíar*), an epithet of scorn and disdain that appears frequently throughout the OT, either as such or in its associate variation, "Sons of Belial" (Deut. 13:13; Judg. 19:22; I Sam. 2:12, etc.). The term implied "reckless," "lawless." The word also came to be used as a synonym for "vain fellow" or "fool," a "good for nothing." Nabal (I Sam. 25:25) receives such a description from the lips of Abigail, his wife. Cf. Raca (Matt. 5:22). The Apostle Paul employs the term once (II Cor. 6:15) where Belial (Beliar) stands as opposed to Christ, thus approaching the diabolical status of Antichrist. In this later usage, it is frequently employed by Jewish Apocalyptic writers for both Satan and Antichrist.

BELL (Heb. *metsillôth, pa'ămôn*). The latter of these terms rendered bell is found in Exodus 28:33ff, 39:25,26. These bells were attached to the hem of the sacerdotal robes worn by Aaron and his descendants as they performed priestly service in the Tabernacle. The tinkling of the bells gave assurance to the worshipers without that the high priest had not incurred divine retribution but remained alive as their intercessor. The other Hebrew term is employed just once, in Zechariah 14:20, where the bells bear the inscription "Holy unto the Lord." These "bells" are more like our cymbals than bells so understood. The bell was not used in biblical times for the purpose of religious convocation as today. The use of the bell to summon the worshipers is a distinctively Christian practice dating back to the end of the fourth century, A.D. Its usage seems to have been introduced by Bishop Paulinus who lived during that time. Miniature bells, however, are frequently used to the present time to fasten to the necks of goats and sheep, thus facilitating the shepherd's task of knowing their whereabouts.   J.F.G.

BELLOWS (bĕl'ōs), an ancient device employed to fan the flames of the fires of the smelting furnace. The Egyptian type of bellows was operated by the feet, alternately treading upon two inflated skins. This created a forced draft by means of reed tubes, tipped with iron, as the air thus jettisoned into the glowing fire, caused the flames to burn more brilliantly and hotly. As each skin was exhausted of its supply of air, the workman would raise it by a cord attached for that purpose and inflate the skin again. This process was then repeated as many times as deemed necessary. See Jeremiah 6:29.

BELSHAZZAR (bĕl-shăz'àr, Heb. *bēlsha'tstsar, may Bel protect the king*). For many years regarded as a fictitious literary creation of a post-captivity author assuming the *nom de plume* of Daniel (c. 165 B.C.), it is now well-authenticated through archaeological studies that Belshazzar was an historic personage. In the fifth chapter of Daniel, he is referred to as the "Son of Nebuchadnezzar 5:2,11,13, 18,22). This is in conformity to general Semitic usage where one's descendant is frequently referred to as his "son." Nebuchadnezzar died in 562 B.C., after a forty-two year reign, and was followed in quick succession by Amel-Marduk (562-560 B.C.), the Evil-Merodach of Jeremiah 52:31 and II Kings

25:27. He was replaced by Nergal-Shar-usar (Neriglissar) who reigned 560-556 B.C. He was succeeded by Labashi-Marduk, his weak son, who reigned but a few months, and then was overthrown by revolution.

One of the conspirators Nabonidus (Nabonaid) now ascended the throne. Though a revolutionary, he was still a man of culture and religious zeal for the gods of Babylon. He is sometimes styled the "World's first archaeologist." Nabonidus is thus the last true king of Babylon, and the father of Belshazzar whom he constituted co-regent with him as he himself retired to Arabia, presumably to consolidate the weakening empire. The Nabonidus chronicle was written after the capture of Babylon in 539 B.C. Cyrus of Persia declares how he was able to take the city without a struggle, and, describing his leniency towards the population, regards himself as an "Enlightened Despot" and executioner of the will of the gods. His estimation of the character of Belshazzar is exceedingly low, not at all out of harmony with that represented by the biblical account.

In regards to the scriptural account, Belshazzar's miserable doom came about at the end of, and largely as a consequence of, a drunken orgy, held October 29, 539 B.C. (cf. the "Feast of Belshazzar"). Suddenly the fingers of a man's hand appeared, writing in fiery letters a message which Belshazzar could not decipher, but which he still recognized as ominous. Following the failure of his advisers to decipher the "cryptogram," upon the suggestion of the Queen-Mother the venerable Hebrew prophet Daniel was summoned. He, after verbally castigating Belshazzar, interpreted the message ("Thou art weighed in the balances, and art found wanting," etc.). The judgment was swift and inevitable. Babylon fell to the Medo-Persians; Belshazzar was slain; and Darius in the name of Cyrus, took the throne.   J.F.G.

BELTESHAZZAR (bĕl'tĕ-shăz-àr, Heb. *bēltsha'-tstsar, may Bel protect his life*). The name given to the Hebrew Prophet Daniel by Nebuchadnezzar's steward (Dan. 1:7; 2:26; 4:8; 5:12). Not to be confused with Belshazzar (Dan. 5:1ff).

BEN (Heb. *ben*). 1. In Semite usage, a term employed to designate a male descendant, without being limited to the paternal-filial association of the west. Thus, Uzziah (Azariah) can be represented as Joram's son, despite the intervening generations (Matt. 1:8). The term Ben is also employed in connection with a clan; in plural only, as in the children of (sons of) Israel; children of (sons of) Ammon, etc. It is also used in prefixes of proper names, as BENjamin, BENhadad, etc. It is likewise used to connote a class, as "Sons of the prophets" (II Kings 2:15).

2. A Levite appointed by David to serve in a musical capacity before the Ark of the Lord (I Chron. 15:18). The text is doubtful, because Ben is not mentioned in vs. 20, and receives no reference at all in the LXX.

BENAIAH (bē-nā'yà, Heb. *benāyâh, Jehovah has built*), according to I Chron. 27:5, the son of Jehoiada, the priest, and so of the tribe of Levi; probably from the village of Kabzeel in the S of Judah (II Sam. 23:30). He was appointed over David's personal body-guard, the Cherethites and the Pelethites (I Kings 1:38). He was a man of exceptional prowess and bravery. He earned this reputation by slaying two "lion-like" men of Moab, and also killing a lion trapped in a pit in a snowstorm. Although outstanding for these achievements, Benaiah never gained the status of David's "original three," of whom Joab was the chief (II Sam. 23:8), but is always listed as being next in order of rank. One of the special duties imposed upon Benaiah by the rapidly failing monarch was the oversight of the coronation of his son Solomon (I Kings 1:38f). Benaiah played no part in the rebellion of Adonijah, but remained faithful to the cause of Solomon. He thus succeeded Joab as captain of the host (I Kings 2:35; 4:4).

Some 12 men bear this designation. 1. One of David's "valiant 30," the Pirathonite, tribe of Ephraim (II Sam. 23:30).

2. A prince from the tribe of Simeon, who drove the Amalekites from the pastureland of Gedor (I Chron. 4:39f).

3. A Levite who played with the psaltery "upon alamoth" at the return of the Ark to Jerusalem (I Chron. 15:18).

4. A priest appointed to blow the trumpet upon the same occasion (I Chron. 15:24).

5. Ancestor of Jahaziel the prophet who prophesied for Moab and Ammon in the days of Jehoshaphat, the good king (II Chron. 20:14).

6. One of the overseers for the offerings in the Temple in the days of Hezekiah (II Chron. 31:13).

7. A man who had taken a foreign wife in the time of Ezra (Ezra 10:25). Four different men are called Benaiah in Ezra (Ezra 10:25,30,35,43).

8. Father of Pelatiah who died as a judgment for teaching falsity in the days of Ezekiel (Ezek. 11:13). J.F.G.

BEN-AMMI (běn'ăm'ī, Heb. *ben 'ammî, son of my people*), son of the younger daughter of Lot (Gen. 19:38) whom she conceived through her own father following the destruction of Sodom. The progenitor of the Ammonites. Moab shares a like origin through the older sister (Gen. 19:37).

BENE-BERAK (běn'ě-bē'răk, Heb. *benê beraq,* Gr. *Banebarak, sons of lightning*), a town allotted to the tribe of Dan (Josh. 19:45). Its modern counterpart is represented by Ibn Ibrak, a few miles SE of Jaffa.

BENE-JAAKAN (běn'ě-jā'ă'kăn, Heb. *benê ya'aqān*), a desert encampment of the Israelites on their journey, placed immediately before Mosera, the site of Aaron's demise in Deuteronomy 10:6. The Bene-jaakans are sometimes identified with the Horites.

BENEVOLENCE, DUE (běn-ěv'ō-lěns, Gr. *ophelé*), so rendered by the KJV, I Corinthians 7:3. The more modern translations simply render the term Ophele as "due." Paul uses it to refer to obligation in the marriage bed. A euphemism for sex relations.

BENHADAD (běn-hā'dăd, Heb. *ben hădhadh,* Gr. *huios Hader*), the name is titular, as opposed to a proper name. As the rulers in Egypt bore the title Pharaoh, so the rulers of Syria bore the designation Benhadad, "son of (the god) Hadad." The Syrians believed their rulers were lineal descendants of the Syrian god Hadad, the deity of storm and thunder, to be identified with Rimmon (II Kings 5:18). There are three individuals in the OT called Benhadad: Benhadad I, Benhadad II, Benhadad III.

Benhadad I was a contemporary with Asa, king of Judah (I Kings 15:18). It is plausible that he is to be identified with Rezon, the founder of the kingdom of Damascus (I Kings 11:23-25). At the request of Asa of Judah, Benhadad severed his alliance with Baasha of Israel and aligned himself with the southern kingdom (I Kings 15:16ff). Though his assistance was of temporary value, the price which Asa was obliged to pay for such aid was tremendous, as Benhadad not only gained con-trol of the treasures of Asa's kingdom, but was able through his alliance to extend his territory into the Hebrew kingdoms themselves. Asa was sternly reprimanded for this unfortunate alliance by the prophet, Hanani (II Chron. 16:7ff).

Benhadad II was in all probability the son of Benhadad I. He is the Hadadezer of the monuments. He was contemporary with Ahab of Israel, against whom he waged war, laying siege to the newly constructed capital, Samaria. Because of the ungracious terms of surrender demanded by Benhadad, Ahab refused to capitulate. With divine aid, Ahab was able utterly to rout the Syrian army at the battle of Aphek (I Kings 20:26ff). Ahab spared the life of Benhadad, thus never fully realizing the victory which otherwise would have been his.

Benhadad III was son of the usurper Hazael, hence not in direct line. His name was adopted from the illustrious name before him. He was a contemporary of Amaziah, king of Judah, and Jehoahaz of Israel. He reduced the fighting personnel of the nation till it was like the dust of the threshing (II Kings 13:7). It was at this time that God raised up to Israel a deliverer, most likely Ramman-Mirari III, as shown from an inscription. Joash was able to defeat Benhadad on three different occasions and to recover the cities of Israel (II Kings 13:25). Under Jeroboam II the northern kingdom restored its prestige, but Amos had already prophesied of the time when Israel and Samaria would go into captivity beyond Damascus (Amos 1:4ff and 5:27). J.F.G.

BENHAIL (běn'hā'ĭl, Heb. *ben-hayil, son of strength*), one of the princes sent out by Jehoshaphat on a "teaching-mission" to the cities of Judah (II Chron. 17:7).

BEN-HANAN (běn'hā'năn, Heb. *ben-hānān, son of grace*), a son of Shimon of the tribe of Judah (I Chron. 4:20).

BENINU (bě-nī'nū, Heb. *benînû, our son*), a Levite in post-exilic days, one of the co-signers of the covenant with Nehemiah (Neh. 10:13).

BENJAMIN (Běn'jà-mĭn, Heb. *binyāmîn, son of my right hand,* Gen. 35:17ff), the youngest son of the patriarch Jacob whom his wife Rachel bore to him in her dying agony; named Benoni ("son of my sorrow") by Rachel, his mother, but renamed Benjamin ("son of my right hand") by his father Jacob. Of all the children of Jacob, he alone was born in Palestine, between Ephrathah and Bethel. Together with his elder brother, Joseph, he appears as a special object of parental love and devotion, no doubt due in part at least to the sad circumstances surrounding his birth. He seems to have played no part in the sale of Joseph into Egypt. The intercession on the part of Judah in the behalf of Benjamin (Gen. 44:18-34) is one of the most moving speeches in all of literature. No doubt, the brothers had been softened in their attitude as they had observed the continued suffering of their father over the fate of Joseph whom he believed irrevocably lost.

2. A great-grandson of Benjamin, son of Jacob (I Chron. 7:10).

3. One of those who had married a foreign wife (Ezra 10:32).

BENJAMIN, TRIBE OF, named for Jacob's youngest son. On the basis of the first census taken after the exodus, the tribe numbered 35,400; at the second census, it numbered 45,600 (Num. 1:37; 26:41).

In the division of territory by Joshua among the 12 tribes, the portion for the tribe of Benjamin was assigned between Judah on the S and Ephraim on the N (Josh. 11:18ff). Benjamin thus occupied a strategic position commercially and militarily. Benjamin loyally participated in Deborah's rebellion against Sisera (Judg. 5:14). The civil war with Benjamin constitutes a sad and strange story (Judg. 19,20).

Saul, son of Kish, came from this tribe (I Sam. 9:1ff). After the death of Saul, there was tension and actual fighting between the forces of David and the men of Benjamin. Ishbosheth, Saul's weak son, was set up as David's rival (II Sam. 2:8). Shemei, of Bahurim, who cursed David, was a Benjamite (II Sam. 16:5,11). At the time of the schism, after the death of Solomon, however, the Benjamites threw in their lot with the tribe of Judah, and followed the Davidic house as represented by Rehoboam, as against Jeroboam, the son of Nebat, to the north. Benjamin was included in the restoration. Saul of Tarsus (Paul) was a member of the tribe of Benjamin (Phil. 3:5). J.F.G.

BENO (bē′nō, Heb. *benô, his son*), a Levite, the son of Jaaziah (I Chron. 24:26,27).

BEN-ONI (bĕn′ō′nī, Heb. *ben-'ônî, son of my sorrow*), the other name given to Benjamin by his expiring mother Rachel (Gen. 35:18). See BENJAMIN.

BEN-ZOHETH (bĕn′zō′hĕth, Heb. *ben-zôhĕth*, probably *to be strong*), son (or perhaps grandson) of Ishi of the tribe of Judah (I Chron. 4:20).

BEON (bē′ŏn, Num. 32:3, known also as Baal-Meon), a town built by the tribe of Reuben, which chose to remain on the E side of the Jordan. Under its new name it was allotted to the Reubenites after the conquest of Canaan (Josh. 13:17). See BAAL-MEON.

BEOR (See Balaam)

BERA (bē′rà, Heb. *bera', gift*), king of Sodom, defeated by Chedorlaomer in the days of Abraham at the battle of Siddim (Gen. 14:2,8).

BERACHAH (bêr′à-kà, *a blessing*), one of the 30 volunteers who came to the aid of David at Ziklag when he fled from Saul. These men were known for their ability as archers (I Chron. 12:3).

BERACHAH, VALLEY OF (bêr′à-kà, *valley of blessing*), the location where Jehoshaphat assembled his forces to offer praise to God for victory over the Ammonites and Moabites (II Chron. 20:26). It lies between Bethlehem and Hebron, not far from En-Gedi.

BERACHIAH (bêr-à kī′à, Heb. *berekhyâh, Iehovah blesses*), sometimes Berechiah. 1. One of David's descendants (I Chron. 3:20).
2. Father of Asaph, the singer (I Chron. 6:39).
3. A Levite dwelling in Jerusalem (I Chron. 9:16).
4. A custodian of the Ark (I Chron. 15:23).
5. An Ephraimite who protested the sale of Hebrews to their fellows (II Chron. 28:12).
6. The father of Meshullam, a builder during the days of Nehemiah (Neh. 3:4,30; 6:18).
7. The father of Zechariah, a prophet of the restoration (Zech. 1:1,7).

BERAIAH (bêr′à-ī′à), a son of Shimei of the house of Benjamin (I Chron. 8:21).

BEREA or **BEROEA** (bêr-ē′à, Gr. *Béroia*), a city in SW Macedonia (Acts 17:10-15; 20:4). Lying at the foot of Mt. Bermius, situated on a tributary of the Haliacmon, its origins appear lost in the mists of time. The Berea mentioned by Thucydides in all likelihood refers to another place. However, it is twice mentioned by Polybius (xxviii:8, xxvii:

8). Following the battle of Pynda in 168 B.C., it surrendered to the Romans and was counted in the third of the four divisions of the empire of Alexander the Great. In the NT Paul and his party visited there on the second missionary journey. Here they found some open-minded people who were willing to study the teachings of Paul in the light of the Scripture. This happy situation was disrupted, however, when Jews from Thessalonica arrived, turning the Bereans against the message, thus forcing Paul to flee to Athens. Silas and Timothy remained there for a brief while, instructing the true believers.

BERED (bē′red, Heb. *beredh, to be cold*). Between Kadesh and Bered was the well-known well, Beer-la-hai-roi (Gen. 16:14). The various Targums render Bered as Shur, thus placing it in the vicinity of Kadesh-Barnea. That Bered is to be located in the region of the Negeb cannot be doubted. It was called Elusa by Ptolemy. It formed a connecting link between Palestine, Kadesh and Sinai.

BERI (bē′rī, Heb. *bērî, wisdom*), a descendant of Asher (I Chron. 7:36).

BERIAH (bē-rī′à, Heb. *berî'âh, meaning uncertain, perhaps gift or evil*). 1. This name is given to a son of Asher the father of Heber and Malchiel (Gen. 46:17; I Chron. 7:30). The Beriites were descended from him (Num. 26:44).
2. Ephraim called one of his sons Beriah "because it went evil with his house" (I Chron. 7:23). Men of Gath had slain a number of men in the land in connection with a raid they had made on the cattle there. If Beriah means "a gift" he was thus named because in the face of Ephraim's losses, this son is regarded as a gift from the Lord.
3. One of the descendants of Benjamin (I Chron. 8:13,16). He with his brother "drove away the inhabitants of Gath." Apparently from him and Shema, his brother, were descended the people of Aijalon (I Chron. 8:13).
4. A Levite, the son of Shimei of the Gershonites. His children, being few, were counted with those of his brother, Jeush (I Chron. 23:7-11).

BERIITES (bē-rī′īts, Heb. *berî'îm*), a people mentioned only once in the Bible (Num. 26:44). It descended from Beriah, who, in turn, was from the tribe of Asher (Gen. 46:17).

BERITES (bē′rīts, Heb. *bērîm, choice young men*), mentioned only in II Samuel 20:14. During the revolt of Sheba, responding to his call, these people followed him.

BERNICE (bêr-nī′sē, Gr. *Bernīke, victorious*). Three times in the book of Acts reference is made to Bernice (Acts 25:13,23; 26:30), Herod Agrippa's eldest daughter (Acts 12:1), a very wicked woman who lived an incestuous life. According to Josepus, she was first married to Marcus. After his death she became the wife of Herod of Chalcis, her own uncle (Josephus, *Ant.* 19:5,1; 20:7,1-3). After Herod's death she had evil relations with Agrippa, her own brother, and with him listened to Paul's noble defense at Caesarea. Later she was married to King Ptolemy of Sicily. This marriage was of short duration, as she returned to Agrippa. She was later the mistress of Vespasian and Titus, who finally cast her aside.

BERODACH-BALADAN (bē-rō′dăk-băl′a-dăn, *Marduk has given a son*), a king of Babylon, called also Merodach-baladan, and referred to in Isaiah 39:1 as sending a letter and a present to king Hezekiah. Scripture records that this was done to congratulate him for his physical recovery. Archaeology reveals that this present was designed to urge him to rebel against Assyria.

BEROTHAH, BEROTHAI (bē-rō'thà, bē-rō'thī, Heb. *běrôthāh, well* or *wells*), a town situated between Hamath and Damascus (Ezek. 47:16). Probably the same as a city of Hadadezer which David took (II Sam. 8:8). It has now been identified as Bereitan N of Damascus.

BERYL (bêr'ĭl, Heb. *tarshîsh, yellow jasper,* Gr. *bēryllos*), a stone mentioned several times in the OT and once in the NT (Rev. 21:20). Brown, Driver and Briggs feel this was a yellow or gold-covered stone. The Latin and Greek words used to translate this indicate uncertainty about the true nature of this stone. Fletcher's article in I.S.B.E. reflects the same uncertainty. It was one of the precious stones in the high priest's breastplate (Exod. 28:20; 39:13). Daniel uses it to describe the man in his vision (Dan. 10:6). Our modern beryl is beryllium aluminum silicate, but of the true nature of this ancient stone, little is known.

BESAI (bē'sī, Heb. *bēsay, down-trodden*), the founder of a family which returned to Jerusalem from Babylon under the leadership of Zerubbabel (Ezra 2:49; Neh. 7:52).

BESODEIAH (běs'ō-dē'yà, Heb. *besòdheyâh, in the counsel of Jehovah*), the father of Meshullam, a builder under Nehemiah (Neh. 3:6).

BESOM (bē'zŭm, Heb. *mat'ătē', broom*), a word signifying the punishment that was to be meted out to Babylon (Isa. 14:23). It is an eastern metaphor for utter destruction.

BESOR (bē'sôr, Heb. *besôr*), a brook five miles S of Gaza where David left 200 of his men who were too faint to assist in pursuing the Amalekites (I Sam. 30:9,10,21). Some identify this as Wady en Sheriah, while others think it is Wady Ghazzah.

BETAH (bē'tà, *confidence*), a city of Syria which David captured and from which he took much brass, later used by Solomon in making furnishings for the temple (II Sam. 8:8). It is called "Tibhath" in I Chronicles 18:8. The site is unknown.

BETEN (bē'těn, Heb. *beten, hollow*), a city on Asher's border (Josh. 19:25). Its location is uncertain.

BETH (běth, *house*), the name by which the second letter of the Hebrew alphabet is known. The Hebrew uses it also for the number two. It is the most common OT word for house. It designates a more permanent dwelling than tent. It is used often in connection with other words to form proper names, the most common of which is Bethlehem.

BETHABARA (běth'ăb'à-rà, *house of the ford*), a place on the E bank of the Jordan where John baptized (John 1:28). The later and more reliable Greek manuscripts have rendered this word "Bethany." Care must be taken, however, not to confuse this with the city of the same name near Jerusalem, the home of Mary, Martha and Lazarus. Its exact location is uncertain. Some identify it with Beth-barah (Judg. 7:24).

BETHANATH (běth'ā'năth, *the temple of Anath*), a city near Naphtali (Josh. 19:38; Judg. 1:33) identified with the modern el-Baneh.

BETH-ANOTH (běth'à'nŏth, *house of Anoth*), a town in the hill country of Judea (Josh. 15:59). It derives its name from Anoth, the goddess of the Canaanites.

BETHANY (běth'à-nē, Gr. *Bethania, house of unripe dates or figs*). 1. Bethabara of John 1:28 (KJV) is in the best MSS. rendered "Bethany." From the best authorities we learn that nothing certain is known of its location except that it is beyond the Jordan where John was accomplishing his work (John 1:28).

Village of Bethany in the springtime, with almond trees in blossom. © MPS

2. Another city of this name, the home of Mary, Martha and Lazarus, situated about two miles SE of Jerusalem (John 11:18) on the eastern slope of Mount Olivet. Some refer to this as the Judean home of Jesus. It was here He raised Lazarus (John 11) and attended the feast at Simon's house (Matt. 26, Mark 14, and Luke 7). In the region of this city the ascension took place (Luke 24:50-51). It

Ruins of the home of Mary and Martha in Bethany. © MPS

General view of the ruins of the village of Bethany, with the minaret in the center marking the site of the tomb of Lazarus. The ruins of the two towers on the right are thought to be those of the house of Simon the Leper. © MPS

is known today as El-Azariyeh. The modern city contains the supposed tomb of Lazarus and house of Simon the leper.

BETH-ARABAH (bĕth'är'à-bà, *house of the desert*), a town known also as Arabah (Josh. 18: 18), probably located at the northern end of the Dead Sea. It was one of the six cities of Judah on the northern border of that tribe's territory.

BETHARAM (bĕth'ä'răm), a town belonging to Gad, E of the Jordan (Josh. 13:27). It is called also "Bethharam" (Num. 32:36), which some think is the more correct spelling.

BETHARBEL (bĕth'är'bĕl, *house of Arbel*), probably a town in the tribe Naphtali, mentioned in Hosea 10:14 as the scene of a horrible destruction brought about by Shalmaneser. The event is used as illustrative of the disaster to come upon Ephraim. It hardly seems possible that this name is used here of the well-known city by this name on the Euphrates. It is the modern Irbid, located a few miles NW of Tiberias.

BETHAVEN (bĕth'ä'vĕn, Heb. *bēth'āwen, house of vanity*), a town located on the northern mountains of Benjamin (Josh. 18:12), beside Ai, E of Bethel (Josh. 7:2) and W of Michmash (I Sam. 13:5; 14:23). The name, though not the place mentioned by Amos (4:4; 5:5), is used by Hosea (4:15; 10:5, 8) to reveal the fallen condition of Bethel due to the idolatry introduced by King Jeroboam. The house of God (Bethel) had become the house of vanity and idolatry (Bethaven).

BETHAZMAVETH (bĕth'ăz-mä'vĕth, *house of the strong one of death*), a village belonging to Benjamin mentioned in Nehemiah 7:28. Forty-two former inhabitants of this city accompanied Zerubbabel from Babylon on his return to Jerusalem.

BETH BAAL MEON (bĕth bā'ál mē'ŏn, Heb. *bêth ba'al me'ôn, house of Baal-meon*), a place in the territory assigned to Reuben, E of the Jordan (Josh. 13:17). This is the same as Baal-meon (Num. 32: 38) and Beon (Num. 32:3). Jeremiah speaks of it as belonging to Moab (Jer. 48:23), and this is confirmed by the appearance of this name on the Moabite Stone. It is identified today with the ruins of Ma'in in N Moab.

BETHBARAH (bĕth'bâr'à, Heb. *bêthbārâh, house of the ford*), one of the important fords across the Jordan. It has never been identified, though some identify it with Bethabarah. The Midianites were expected to use this as they escaped from Gideon. This is the reason for Gideon's instruction to his messengers to "take before them the waters unto Beth-barah" (Judg. 7:24). Here Jephtha slew the Ephraimites (Judg. 12:4) and perhaps it is the place where Jacob crossed (Gen. 32:22).

BETH-BIREI (bĕth' bĭr'ī, *house of my creator*), a town of Simeon (I Chron. 4:31) in the southern part of Judah. Joshua refers to this place as Bethlebaoth "abode of lions" (Josh. 19:6) and as Lebaoth (Josh. 15:32). It has not yet been identified.

BETHCAR (bĕth′kàr, *house of sheep*), a place W of Mizpah to which Israel pursued the Philistines. They "smote them, until they came under Bethcar" (I Sam. 7:11). It has never been identified. In this area the stone was set up called Ebenezer (I Sam. 7:12).

BETH DAGON (bĕth′dā′gŏn, *house of Dagon*), a town located in the shephelah of Judah. Mentioned in Joshua 15:41. It was five miles from Lydda and has been identified as Khirbet Dajun. The name suggests the worship of Dagon the god of the Philistines, revealing how far this worship had been extended beyond Philistine territory. This name was also used of a town on the border of Asher (Josh. 19:27).

BETH-DIBLATHAIM (bĕth′ dĭb′là-thā′ĭm, *house of a double cake of figs*), a Moabitish town known also as Almondiblathaim (Num. 33:46) and Diblath (Ezek. 6:14). Jeremiah speaks of it (Jer. 48:22) and it is mentioned on the Moabite Stone. It is not certainly identified.

BETHEL (bĕth′ĕl, Heb. *bêth-'ĕl, house of God*). 1. A town originally known as "Luz," located 12 miles N of Jerusalem (Gen. 28:19), W of Ai. It was near this spot that Abraham stopped on his way to the Negeb and offered a sacrifice (Gen. 12:8; 13:3). Jacob called Luz "Bethel" (Gen. 28:10-22), since it was here that God met him and confirmed the Abrahamic covenant to him. Jacob revisited this town when he returned from Padan-aram in response to the command of God (Gen. 35:1). Here he built an altar and worshiped, calling the place "El-bethel" (Gen. 35:7). Here Jacob buried Deborah, the nurse of Rebekah who had died (Gen. 35:8). It was a logical stopping place, for it lay on a well-known route running from the Plain of Esdraelon to Beersheba.

Bethel seems to have been a Canaanite city originally, and after the conquest by Joshua was given to the tribe of Benjamin (Josh. 18:21-22). Joseph's descendants, under the guidance of the Lord, went up against Bethel and took it (Judg. 1:22-26). It remained on the southern border of Ephraim. During the period of the Judges, because of the wickedness of the tribe of Ephraim, the Israelites marched against them. They stopped at Bethel to ascertain God's will (Judg. 20:18). The ark abode there at this time (Judg. 20:26-28). To this city Samuel went from time to time to conduct business and to worship (I Sam. 7:16; 10:3).

At a later period when the kingdom was divided, Jeroboam, in order to nullify the influence of Jerusalem as the center of religious activity for the people, chose Bethel as one of the two centers in which he set up golden calves (I Kings 12:26-30). Here he sacrificed to the calves and placed priests to minister in the high places (I Kings 12:32). Because of these and other sins, Amos cried out against this city (Amos 3:14; 4:4-6). Hosea too pronounced judgment on this city, even calling it "Bethaven," "the house of idols" (Hos. 4:15). Here the Assyrian priest dwelt that he might teach the people whom Assyria had placed in the land (II Kings 17:27-28). It was not until Josiah became king that this idolatry was removed from Bethel and the true worship of Jehovah established (II Kings 23:15-23). When the Jews returned from the Babylonian captivity, Ezra and Nehemiah both record that some returned to Bethel (Ezra 2:28; Neh. 7:32) and, as one might suppose, they are listed as Benjamites (Neh. 11:31).

Bethel is mentioned in the apocryphal books as being fortified by Bacchides (I Macc. 9:50).

Village of Bethel. © MPS

Bethel has now been identified as Beitin. The ruins cover several acres on a low hill between two wadies which unite and descend into Suweinit towards the SE. Abundant stones are still seen in the area not unlike those Jacob set up in this city for his pillow. Albright has done extensive excavation on this site and writes of many archaeological confirmations of the Biblical history of this place.

2. Another city mentioned in southern Judah (I Sam. 30:27) is also called Bethel. Joshua refers to it as "Bethul" (Josh. 19:4). It is noted again as "Bethuel" (I Chron. 4:30). This site has not yet been identified.   H.Z.C.

Excavations of the ruins of ancient Bethel of Joshua's time. © MPS

The Pool of Bethesda. © MPS

BETHEMEK (běth'ē'měk, *house of the valley*), a city mentioned in Joshua 19:27 in the valley of Jiphthahel on the edge of Asher's territory. It is not yet identified.

BETHER (bē'thêr, Heb. *bether, separation*), a range of mountains mentioned in the Song of Solomon (2:17). The RSV renders this "rugged mountains," indicating that a proper name was not intended. Perhaps the "mountains of spices" (8:14) is a reference to the same place.

BETHESDA (bě-thěs'dà, Gr. *Bethesda, house of grace*), a spring-fed pool at Jerusalem, surrounded by five porches (John 5:1-16). Sick folk waited to step down into these waters which were thought to have healing properties. The fourth verse of the KJV, mentioning a regular troubling of the waters by the descent of an angel, is omitted in the RV, since evidence from the best texts does not support this statement. Here Jesus healed a man who had been sick for 38 years.

In 1888, while the church of St. Anne in NE Jerusalem was being repaired, a reservoir was discovered. On the wall is a faded fresco which depicts an angel troubling the water. It is thought, therefore, that this best fits the description in the New Testament. The reservoir is cut from the rock and is rain-filled. It is about 55 feet in length and 12 feet in width. It is approached by a flight of steps both steep and winding.

BETHEZEL (běth'ē'zěl, *a house adjoining*), a town in southern Judea in the Philistine plain (Mic. 1:11). For a time this was thought to be the same as Azel (Zech. 14:5), but now has been identified with Deir el-Asal.

BETHGADER (běth'gā'dêr, *house of the wall*), a place in the tribe of Judah (I Chron. 2:51), probably to be identified with Geder (Josh. 12:13).

BETHGAMUL (běth'gā'mŭl, *house of recompense*), a Moabitish city (Jer. 48:23). It is now identified with Khirbet Jemeil. It has been cited as a good example of an unwalled town.

BETH-GILGAL (běth'gĭl'găl, Heb. *bêth hagilgal, house of Gilgal*), a place from which singers came to the dedication of the Jerusalem wall. It is probably to be identified with Gilgal (Neh. 12:27-29).

BETHHACCEREM (běth'hă-kē'rěm, *house of the vineyard*), a Judean town (Neh. 3:14), ruled by Malchiah. Jeremiah notes it as a vantage site for signaling in time of danger (Jer. 6:1). It is now identified with a place on top of Jebel 'Ali called 'Ain Karim. On top of this hill are cairns which are thought to have been used for beacons.

BETH-HARAN (běth'hā'răn, *house of the mountaineer*), a fenced city built by the Gadites E of the Jordan (Num. 32:36). It is the same as Beth-haram.

BETH-HOGLAH (běth'hŏg'là, *house of a partridge*), a place belonging to Benjamin lying between Jericho and the Jordan (Josh. 15:6; 18:19, 21). It is identified now with Ain Hajlah.

BETHHORON (běth'hō'rŏn, Heb. *bêth-hôrōn, place of a hollow*), two towns, the upper and the lower (Josh. 16:3,5; I Chron. 7:24; II Chron. 8:5), separated by a few miles. Beit Ur el foka ("the upper") is 800 ft. higher than Beit Ur el tahta ("the lower"). Built by Sherah, a granddaughter of Ephraim (I Chron. 7:24), Bethhoron lay on the boundary line between Benjamin and Ephraim (Josh. 16:3,5), on the road from Gibeon to Azekah (Josh. 10:10,11). It was assigned to Ephraim and given to the Kohathites (Josh. 21:22).

For centuries a strategic route into the heart of Judea went up from Joppa (modern Jaffa) on the coast through the Valley of Ajalon (modern Yalo), ascending through the two Bethhorons to Gibeon (four miles distant) on its way to Jerusalem. It was in this valley that Joshua commanded the sun and moon to stand still while he discomfited the Amorite kings in his defense of the Gibeonites. These five kings he chased over the pass to Bethhoron (Josh. 10:10-13). Along this route the Philistines fled after they had been defeated at Michmash (I Sam. 14:31), and it was there that Judas Maccabeus overthrew the army of Seron, a prince of Syria (I Macc. 3:13-24). The importance of the Bethhoron pass as a key route into Palestine explains the fortification of its towns by Solomon (II Chron. 8:5). It is no longer important, but great foundation stones can be seen there yet today.

Bethhoron, the upper and lower towns. © MPS

A view of Bethlehem from the southwest. © MPS

Typical street scene in old Bethlehem. © MPS

BETH-LE-APHRAH (bĕth'lē-ăf'rȧ, Heb. *bêth-le'-aphrâh, house of dust*), a town, site unknown; "In the house of Aphrah roll thyself in the dust" (Mic. 1:10).

BETHLEBAOTH (bĕth'lē-bā'ŏth, Heb. *bêth levā'-ôth, house of lionesses*), a town of Simeon (Josh. 19:6), called Beth-birei in I Chronicles 4:31.

BETHLEHEM (bĕth'lē-hĕm, Heb. *bêth-lehem, house of bread*). 1. A town five miles SW of Jerusalem, 2550 ft. above sea level, in the hill country of Judea, on the main highway to Hebron and Egypt. In Jacob's time it was called Ephrath ("fruitful") and was the burial place of Rachel (Gen. 35:16,19; 48:7). After the conquest of Canaan it was called Bethlehem-judah (Ruth 1:1) to distinguish it from Bethlehem 2 (see below). It was the home of Ibzan, the tenth judge (Judg. 12:8-10); of Elimelech, father-in-law of Ruth (Ruth 1:1,2), as well as her husband Boaz (2:1,4). Here their great-grandson David kept his father's sheep and was anointed king by Samuel (I Sam. 16:13, 15). Hence, it was known as "the city of David" (Luke 2:4,11). It was once occupied by a Philistine garrison (II Sam. 23:14-16), later fortified by Rehoboam (II Chron. 11:6).

In Jeremiah's time (41:17) the caravan inn of Chimham (see II Sam. 19:37-40) near Bethlehem was the usual starting-place for Egypt. The inn mentioned in Luke 2 was a similar one and may have been the same. Here the Messiah was born

Church of the Nativity in Bethlehem, the oldest church in Christendom, exterior and interior views. © MPS

(Matt. 2:1, Luke 2), for which this town that was "little among the thousands of Judah" (Mic. 5:2) achieved its great fame. Its male children under two years of age were slain in Herod's attempt to kill the King of the Jews (Matt. 2:16).

Justin Martyr, second century, said that our Lord's birth took place in a cave close to the village. Over this traditional manger-site the emperor Constantine (330 A.D.) and Helena his mother built the Church of the Nativity. Rebuilt more sumptuously by Justinian in the sixth century, part of the original structure still stands, and it is a popular attraction for tourists today. The grotto of the nativity is beneath a crypt, 39 ft. long, 11 wide, and 9 high, hewn out of the rock and lined with marble. A rich altar is over the supposed site of the Saviour's birth. In a part of this cave Jerome, the Latin scholar, spent thirty years translating the Bible into Latin.

Modern Bethlehem is a village of less than ten thousand inhabitants. The slopes abound in figs, vines, almonds, and olives. The shepherds' fields are still seen to the NE.

2. A town of Zebulun (Josh. 19:15), now the village of Beit Lahm, seven miles NW of Nazareth.

BETH-LEHEM-JUDAH (See Bethlehem)

BETH-LE-JESHIMOTH or **BETHJESIMOTH** (bĕth'jĕsh'ĭ-mŏth, Heb. *bĕth ha-yeshīmōth, place of deserts*), a town E of the mouth of the Jordan, next to the last camp of the Israelites (Num. 33:49). It was assigned to Reuben (Josh. 13:20).

BETH-MAACHAH (bĕth'mā'à-kà, Heb. *bêth ma'-akhâh*), a town to which Joab pursued Sheba (II Sam. 20:14,15).

BETHMARCABOTH (bĕth'màr'kà-bŏth, Heb. *bĕth hamarkāvōth, the house of chariots*), a town of Simeon in the extreme S of Judah (Josh. 19:5; I Chron. 4:31). Possibly one of the cities which Solomon built for his chariots (I Kings 9:19).

BETH-MEON (bĕth'mē'ŏn), a city of Moab (Jer. 48:23), same as Beth-baal-meon (Josh. 13:17).

BETHNIMRAH (bĕth'nĭm'rà, Heb. *bêth nimrâh, house of leopard*), a fenced city of Gad E of the Jordan (Num. 32:3,36). The LXX reading, "Beth-anabra," in Joshua 13:27 has led some to identify this with Bethabara in the NT, whose abundant waters were the scene of John's baptizing (John 1:28).

BETHPALET or **BETH-PHELET** (bĕth'pā'lĕt or bĕth'fĕ'lĕt, Heb. *bêth pelet, house of escape*), a town in the S of Judah (Josh. 15:27; Neh. 11:26).

BETHPAZZEZ (bĕth'pàz'ĕz), a town of Issachar (Josh. 19:21).

BETHPEOR (bĕth'pē'ôr, Heb. *bêth pe'ôr, house of Peor*), one of Israel's last camp sites (Deut. 3:29; 4:46). Here Moses was buried (Deut. 34:6). A possession of Reuben (Josh. 13:20).

BETHPHAGE (bĕth'fà-jē, Heb. *bêth paghâh, house of unripe figs*), a village on the mount of Olives, on the road going E from Jerusalem to Jericho. The traditional site is NW of Bethany, which the NT mentions twice (Mark 11:1-11; Luke 19:28-40). Here the colt was obtained for the Palm Sunday entry into Jerusalem (Matt. 21:1-11). It was in the vicinity of Bethphage that Jesus cursed the fruitless fig tree (Matt. 21:18-20; Mark 11:12-14,20-21).

BETHRAPHA (bĕth'rà'fà, Heb. *bêth rāphā*), son of Eshton in the genealogy of Judah (I Chron. 4:12).

BETHREHOB (bĕth'rē'hŏb, Heb. *bêth rehôv, house of Rechob*), an Aramean town and district near the valley containing the town Laish or Dan (Judg. 18:28). Probably identical with Rehob (Num. 13:21), the northern limit of the spies' search, it is thought to be the modern Hunin, site of a Crusaders' castle-fortress commanding the Huleh plain. The Ammonites, having needlessly provoked David, hired the men of Bethrehob in a futile defense against David's attack (II Sam. 10).

Bethphage, in middle foreground, with Bethany behind it, in center of picture. In the distance are the Jordan River and Dead Sea, with the mountains of Moab on horizon. This view taken from summit of Mount of Olives. © MPS

Ruins of old Byzantine church at Bethsaida on the shore of the Sea of Galilee. © MPS

Fishing boats on Sea of Galilee at Bethsaida. © MPS

BETHSAIDA (bĕth'sā'ĭ-dȧ, Gr. *Bethsaidá, house of fishing*). 1. A village close to the W side of the sea of Tiberias, in the land of Gennesaret, where Jesus sent His disciples by boat after He had fed the 5000 (Mark 6:45-53). John says that they headed for Capernaum (6:17), but when they were blown off their course they landed in Gennesaret and then went to Capernaum. Possibly, therefore, this Bethsaida was close to Capernaum and may have been its fishing district next to the lake. This would explain how Peter and Andrew are said to be of Bethsaida (John 1:44; 12:21), whereas Mark mentions their house close to the synagogue in Capernaum (1:29). Along with Chorazin and Capernaum, Jesus upbraided Bethsaida for unbelief (Matt. 11:20-23; Luke 10:13-15).

2. Another Bethsaida, NE of the sea of Tiberias and scene of the feeding of the 5000 (Luke 9:10). Jesus restored sight to a blind man in Bethsaida (Mark 8:22), which is on the E side of the lake, since Jesus had just come from Dalmanutha (same as Magdala, Matt. 15:39) on the W side (Mark 8:10-13). This Bethsaida was a village in Gaulonitis (now Jaulan) and enlarged to be the capital by Philip the tetrarch who called it Julias, after Julia, the daughter of Emperor Augustus. Its site is uncertain, but some identify it with et Tel, E of the Jordan and a mile from the sea of Tiberias, from which it rises to a height of 100 feet.

BETHSHAN or **BETHSHEAN** (bĕth'shăn or bĕth'-shē'ăn, Heb. *bêth-shan* or *bêth-sheān, house of quiet*), a city of Manasseh in the territory of Issachar, but one out of which the Canaanites could not be driven (Josh. 17:11,12; Judg. 1:27). It lay 14 miles S of the Sea of Galilee, overlooking the plain of Esdraelon in the valley of Jezreel. After Saul died in Mount Gilboa, the Philistines fastened his body to the wall of Bethshan and put his armor in the temple of Ashtaroth as trophies of their victory (I Sam. 31:8-12). Later, the men of Jabesh-gilead stole the bones of Saul and his sons from the street of Bethshan, but David recovered them and gave them a proper burial (II Sam. 21:12-14).

Today the site of the city is a mound, called Tell el-Husn ("Mound of the Fortress"), located near the Arab village of Beisan (note the similarity to Bethshan). Excavations by the University of Pennsylvania, 1921-33, have yielded rich finds, dating the history of the city from 3500 B.C. to the Christian era. A stratification of 18 levels of debris and ruined houses can be seen as evidence of repeated destructions and eras of rebuilding. Because of its commanding location, it was fortified with double walls and was a strong Egyptian outpost from the 15th to the 12th century B.C. Temples and monument-inscriptions by three Pharaohs were discovered which date back to this time. The excavators have shown that Bethshan was destroyed between 1050 and 1000 B.C., the approximate time of King David, who may have destroyed it. Four Canaanite temples were unearthed at the site, one of which has been identified with the "house of Ashtaroth" (I Sam. 31:10), and another with the temple of Dagon where the Philistines fastened Saul's head (I Chron. 10:10). In Solomon's reign, Bethshan was included in one of his commissary districts (I Kings 4:12).   A.M.R.

Village of Bethshan, Mount Gilboa in distance. © MPS

Bethshemesh, near the Philistine border. Zorah on extreme right horizon. © MPS

BETHSHEMESH (běth'shē'měsh, Heb. *bêth-she-mesh, house of the sun*). 1. A town of NW Judah near the Philistine border (Josh. 15:10; I Sam. 6: 12). It was a priests' city given by Judah to the Levites (Josh. 21:16; I Chron. 6:59). The Philistines had been plagued for their seizure of the ark of God. Anxious to be rid of it, they put the ark on a cart pulled by two milking cows and tied their calves at home (I Sam. 6). They expected the cows to return instinctively to their young, but if they left them behind, this would be a sure sign of guidance by Israel's God and of His influence on the Philistines' misery. The animals left Ekron and headed for Bethshemesh seven miles away, not turning aside until they came to the field of Joshua the Beth-shemite where the ark was received and a sacrifice made to the Lord. Here, too, many died for their irreverence toward the ark; but perhaps only 70 were smitten instead of 50,070 (I Sam. 6:19); the latter figure may be due to an error in later texts (see Keil & Delitzsch, *Biblical Commentary on the Books of Samuel*, p. 68).

Bethshemesh was in a commissary district of Solomon (I Kings 4:9). Here Joash king of Israel encountered Amaziah of Judah and took him prisoner (II Kings 14:11-13; II Chron. 25:21-23). Ir-shemesh ("city of the sun," Josh. 19:41) may be the same city. Today the name is preserved as Ain Shems, SE of Gezer. Implements of the late Canaanite and early Israelite period have been discovered here such as pottery, weapons, and jewelry. Quantities of pottery suggest a later Philistine occupancy (II Chron. 28:18).

2. A city of Issachar (Josh. 19:22).

3. A city of Naphtali (Josh. 19:38; Judg. 1:33) from which the Canaanites were not driven.

4. An idol city in Egypt (Jer. 43:13), the Egyptian city On, the Greek Heliopolis. So many cities of the same name show how widespread was sun worship. A.M.R.

BETHSHITTA (běth'shǐt'à, Heb. *bêth ha-shittâh, house of the acacia*), a town in Zererath near Jordan to which the Midianites fled after their overthrow by Gideon (Judg. 7:22).

BETHTAPPUA (běth'tăp'ū-à, Heb. *bêth-tappûah, house of apples*), a town in the hill part of Judah (Josh. 15:53). Tappuah was a son of Hebron (I Chron. 2:43). Now Taffuh, five miles W of Hebron, surrounded by fruitful terraces.

BETHUEL or **BETHUL** (bē-thū'ĕl or běth'ŭl, Heb. *bethû'ēl* or *bethûl, abode of God.*). 1. Son of Nahor and Milcah, nephew of Abraham, and

father of Rebekah and Laban (Gen. 22:22,23; 24: 15,24,47; 28:2). His significance in the arrangements for his daughter's marriage is conspicuous. When Abraham's servant asked Rebekah if there was room at her *father's* house, she ran and told those in her *mother's* house (Gen. 24:28). Her *brother* invited him in, not Bethuel, the natural one to do so. Laban and Bethuel (the son mentioned first) acknowledged his mission to be from the Lord. Presents were given to Rebekah, and to her mother and brother, not her father; and when the bride left home, it was not as a daughter but as a "sister" (24:55-60). These many references make Bethuel seem incapable, whether from age or imbecility, to manage his own affairs.

2. A town in the S of Simeon (Josh. 19:4; I Chron. 4:30) and same as Chesil (Josh. 15:30).

BETHUL (See Bethuel)

BETHZUR (běth'zûr, Heb. *bêth-tsûr, house of rock*), one of Judea's strongest natural fortresses in the mountains of Judah, near Halhul and Gedor (Josh. 15:58). It was fortified by Rehoboam (II Chron. 11:7). Nehemiah, son of Azbuk and ruler of half of Beth-zur, helped to repair the wall of Jerusalem (Neh. 3:16). Known as Bethsura in Maccabean times, it was an important military stronghold, where Judas Maccabeus defeated the Greek army under Lysias (I Macc. 4:28-34). It is now Beit Sur, four miles N of Hebron, near the main road from Hebron to Jerusalem.

BETONIM (bět'ō-nĭm, Heb. *betōnîm*), a town of Gad, E of the Jordan (Josh. 13:26).

BEULAH (bwū'là, Heb. *be'ûlâh, married*), a poetic name for the land of Israel in its future restored condition (Isa. 62:4). The word is the feminine passive participle from the verb *ba'al* ("to be a lord," or "to marry"), and hence could almost be rendered "lorded" (cf. I Pet. 3:6; Isa. 54:4-6).

BEZAI (bē'zā-ī). 1. Head of a family of 323 men who returned with Zerubbabel (Ezra 2:17; Neh. 7:23).

2. Probably a member of the same family a century later (Neh. 10:18).

BEZALEEL (bē-zăl'ē-ĕl, *in the shadow of God*). 1. Son of Uri, son of Hur of the tribe of Judah, whom the Lord called by name (Exod. 31:2; 35:30) and by his Spirit empowered to work in metals, wood, and stone for the tabernacle. He had as a helper Aholiab (ASV Oholiab) of the tribe of Dan, whom God similarly empowered for the work in textiles.

2. A descendant of Pahath-moab, an official of Moab, who in the days of Ezra and Nehemiah was compelled to give up his foreign wife (Ezra 10:30).

BEZEK (bē'zĕk, *scattering, sowing*). 1. A town in the territory of Judah taken for Israel under Joshua from the Canaanites and Perizzites of whom more than 10,000 had congregated there. Its king had either the name or more probably the title "Adoni-bezek" (i.e. lord of Bezek). The ruin *Bezkah*, about 20 miles NW of Jerusalem, may mark the spot (Judg. 1:4,5).

2. The place where Saul numbered his forces before going to relieve Jabesh-gilead (I Sam. 11: 8), about 14 miles NE of Samaria.

BEZER (bē'zêr, Heb. *betser, strong*). 1. A city in the wilderness plateau E of the Dead Sea and in the tribe of Reuben, set apart as a city of refuge (Deut. 4:43) and as a home for Merarites of the tribe of Levi (Josh. 21:36). Mesha, king of Moab, on the Moabite stone, claims that he fortified it.

2. One of the mighty men of the tribe of Asher, known only as a son of Zophah (I Chron. 7:37).

BIBLE. The collection of books recognized and used by the Christian church as the inspired record of God's revelation of Himself and of His will to mankind.

1. Names. The word "Bible" is from Gr. *biblia,* pl. of *biblion,* diminutive of *biblos* (book), from *byblos* (papyrus). In ancient times papyrus was used in making the paper from which books were manufactured. The words *biblion* and *biblia* are used in the OT (LXX) and the Apocrypha for the Scriptures (Dan. 9:2; I Macc. 1:56; 3:48; 12:9). By about the fifth century the Greek Church Fathers applied the term *biblia* to the whole Christian Scriptures. Later the word passed into the western church, and although it is really a plural neuter noun, it came to be used in the Latin as a feminine singular. Thus "The Books" became by common consent "The Book."

In the NT the OT is usually referred to as "the scriptures" (Matt. 21:42; 22:29; Luke 24:32; John 5:39; Acts 18:24). Other terms used are "scripture" (Acts 8:32; Gal. 3:22), the "holy scriptures" (Rom. 1:2; II Tim. 3:15, KJV), and "sacred writings" (II Tim. 3:15, RV).

The plural term *biblia* stresses the fact that the Bible is a collection of books; that the word came to be used in the singular emphasizes the fact that behind these many books there lies a wonderful unity; that no qualifying adjective stands before it points to the uniqueness of this book.

The names "Old" and "New Testament" have been used since the close of the second century to distinguish the Jewish and Christian Scriptures. "Testament" is used in the NT (KJV) to render the Greek word *diatheke* (Latin *testamentum*), which in classical usage meant "a will," but in the LXX and in the NT was used to translate the Hebrew word *berith,* "a covenant." Strictly, therefore, "Old" and "New Testament" mean "Old" and "New Covenant," the reference being to the covenants God made with His elect people in the two dispensations. The name *Novum Testamentum* occurs first in Tertullian (A.D. 190-220).

2. Languages. Most of the OT is written in Hebrew, the language spoken by the Israelites in Canaan before the Babylonian Captivity, but after the "Return" giving way to Aramaic, a related dialect generally spoken throughout SW Asia. A few parts of the OT are in Aramaic (Ezra 4:8-7:18; 7:12-26; Jer. 10:11; Dan. 2:4-7:28). The ancient Hebrew text consisted only of consonants, since the Hebrew alphabet had no written vowels. Vowel signs were invented by the Jewish Masoretic scholars in the sixth century and later.

Except for a few words and sentences, the NT was composed in Greek, the language of ordinary intercourse in the Hellenistic world. The difference of NT Greek from classical Greek and the Greek of the LXX used to be a cause of bewilderment to scholars, but the discovery, since the 1890's, of many thousands of papyri documents in the sands of Egypt has shown that the Greek of the NT is identical with the Greek generally spoken in the Mediterranean world in the first century. The papyri have thrown a great deal of light upon the meaning of many NT words.

3. Compass and Divisions. The Protestant Bible in general use today contains 66 books, 39 in the OT and 27 in the NT. The 39 OT books are the same as those recognized by the Palestinian Jews in NT times. The Greek-speaking Jews of this period, on the other hand, recognized as Scripture a larger number of books, and the Greek OT (LXX) which passed from them to the early Christian Church contained, in addition to the 39 books of the Hebrew canon, a number of others, of which seven — Tobit, Judith, Wisdom, Ecclesiasticus, Baruch, I and II Maccabees, plus the two so-called additions to Esther and Daniel — are regarded as canonical by the Roman Catholic Church, which therefore has a canon of 46 books. Jews today consider canonical only the 39 books accepted by Protestants.

In the Hebrew Bible the books are arranged in three groups, the Law, the Prophets, and the Writings. The Law comprises the Pentateuch. The Prophets include the Former Prophets: Joshua, Judges, Samuel, and Kings; and the Latter Prophets: Isaiah, Jeremiah, Ezekiel, and the Minor Prophets. The Writings take in the remaining books: Psalms, Proverbs, Job, Canticles, Ruth, Lamentations, Ecclesiastes, Esther, Daniel, Ezra-Nehemiah, and Chronicles. The total is traditionally reckoned as 24, but these correspond to the Protestant 39, since in the latter reckoning the minor prophets are counted as 12 books, and Samuel, Kings, Chronicles, and Ezra-Nehemiah as two each. In ancient times there were also other enumerations, notably one by Josephus, who held 22 books as canonical (after the number of letters in the Hebrew alphabet), but his 22 are the same as the 24 in the traditional reckoning.

In the LXX both the number of books and the arrangement of them differ from the Hebrew Bible. It is evident that the NT writers were familiar with the LXX, which contained the Apocrypha, but no quotation from any book of the Apocrypha is found in their pages. The books of the Apocrypha are all late in date and are in Greek, though at least one (Sirach) had a Hebrew origin. The more scholarly of the Church Fathers (Melito, Origen, Athanasius, Jerome, etc.) did not regard the Apocrypha as canonical, although they permitted their use for edification.

The Protestant OT does not follow the grouping of either the Hebrew canon or the LXX. It has, first, the five books of the Pentateuch; then the 11 historical books, beginning with Joshua and ending with Esther; after that what are often called the poetical books: Job, Psalms, Proverbs, Ecclesiastes, and the Song of Solomon; and finally the prophets, first the major and then the minor.

All branches of the Christian Church are agreed on the NT canon. The grouping of the books is a natural one: first the four Gospels; then the one historical book of the NT, the Acts of the Apostles; after that the Epistles, first the Epistles of Paul and then the General Epistles; and finally the Revelation.

4. Text. Although the Bible was written over a period of approximately 1,400 years, from the time of Moses to the end of the first century A.D., its text has come to us in a remarkable state of preservation. It is of course not identical with the text that left the hands of the original writers. Scribal errors have necessarily crept in. Until the invention of printing in the middle of the 15th century, all copies of the Scriptures were made by hand. There is evidence that the ancient Jewish scribes copied the books of the OT with extreme care. The recently discovered Dead Sea Scrolls, some going as far back as the second and third centuries B.C., contain either whole books or fragments of all but one (Esther) of the OT books; and they bear witness to a text remarkably like the Hebrew text left by the Masoretes. The Greek translation of the OT, the Septuagint, begun about 250 B.C. and completed about 100 years later, although it differs

Reproduction of an illuminated page from the Gutenberg Bible, the first major book in the Western world to be printed from movable type, c. 1455. This page is from the Book of Proverbs. CS

in places from the Hebrew text current today, is also a valuable witness to the accuracy of the OT text.

In the NT the evidence for the reliability of the text is almost embarrassingly large, and includes about 4500 Greek manuscripts, dating from about A.D. 125 to the invention of printing; versions, the Old Latin and Syriac going back to about A.D. 150; and quotations of Scripture in the writings of the Church Fathers, beginning with the end of ιe first century. The superabundance of textual vidence for the NT may be appreciated when it s realized that very few manuscripts of ancient Greek and Latin classical authors have survived, and these are all late in date. Among the oldest manuscripts of the Greek NT that have come down to us are the John Rylands fragment of the Gospel of John (c. 125); Papyrus Bodmer II, a manuscript of the Gospel of John dating c. 200; the Chester Beatty Papyri, consisting of three codices containing the Gospels and Acts, most of the Pauline Epistles, and the Revelation, dating from c. 200; and Codices Vaticanus and Sinaiticus, both written about 350.

5. Chapters and Verses. The books of the Bible originally had no chapters or verses. For convenience of reference, Jews of pre-Talmudic times divided the OT into sections corresponding to our chapters and verses. The chapter divisions we use today were made by Stephen Langton, archbishop of Canterbury, who died in 1228. The division of the NT into its present verses is found for the first time in an edition of the Greek NT published in 1551 by the Paris printer, Robert Stephens, who also, in 1555, brought out an edition of the Vulgate which was the first edition of the Bible to appear with our present chapters and verses. The first English Bible to be so divided was the Genevan edition of 1560.

6: Translations. The Old and New Testaments appeared very early in translations. The OT was translated into Greek (the LXX) between 250-150 B.C., and other translations in Greek appeared soon after the beginning of the Christian era. Parts, at least, of the OT were rendered into Syriac as early as the first century; and a Coptic translation appeared probably in the third century. The NT was translated into Latin and Syriac c. 150 and into Coptic c. 200. In subsequent centuries versions appeared in the Armenian, Gothic, Ethiopic, Georgian, Arabic, Persian, and Slavonic languages. The Bible, in whole or in part, is now available in more than 1100 different languages and dialects. Many languages have been reduced to writing in order that the Bible might be translated into them in written form; and this work still goes on in many lands.

7. Message. Although the Bible consists of many different books written over a long period of time by a great variety of writers, most of whom did not know one another, it has an organic unity that can be explained only by assuming, as the book itself claims, that its writers were inspired by the Holy Spirit to give God's message to man. The theme of this message is the same in both Testaments, the redemption of man. The OT tells about the origin of man's sin and the preparation God made for the solution of this problem through His own Son the Messiah. The NT describes the fulfilment of God's redemptive plan; the four Gospels telling about the Messiah's coming, the Acts of the Apostles describing the origin and growth of the Church, God's redeemed people; the Epistles giving the meaning and implication of the Incarnation; and the Revelation showing how some day all of history will be consummated in Christ. The two Testaments form two volumes of one work. The first is incomplete without the second; and the second cannot be understood without the first. Together they are God's revelation to man of the provision He has made for his salvation.

See also: TEXTS AND VERSIONS, OLD TESTAMENT, NEW TESTAMENT. S.B.

The place in the Church of the Nativity at Bethlehem marking the site of the cell where St. Jerome translated the Bible into Latin. © MPS

BIBLE, ENGLISH VERSIONS. In the earliest days of English Christianity the only known Bible was the Latin Vulgate, made by Jerome between A.D. 383 and 405. This could be read only by the clergy and by monks, who alone were familiar with the language. In A.D. 670 Caedmon, a monk at Whitby, produced in Old English a metrical version of some of the more interesting narratives of the OT. The first straightforward translation of any part of the Bible into the language of the people was the Psalter, made c. A.D. 700 by Aldhelm, first bishop of Sherborne in Dorset. Some parts of the NT were translated into English by Bede, the learned monk of Jarrow, author of the famous *Ecclesiastical History of the English Nation.* According to a letter of his disciple Cuthbert, Bede was engaged in translating the Gospel of John into English on his deathbed. It is not certain whether he completed it, but, unfortunately, his translation has not survived. King Alfred (871-901) produced during his reign English versions of parts of the Old and New Testaments, including a part of the Psalter. Some Latin Gospels which survive from this period have written between the lines what are known as "glosses," a word-for-word translation of the text into English, without regard to the idiom and usage of the vernacular. From the same period as these glosses come what are known as the Wessex Gospels, the first independent Old English version of the Gospels. Towards the end of the tenth century Aelfric, archbishop of Canterbury, translated parts of the first seven books of the OT, as well as parts of other OT books.

For nearly three centuries after the Norman conquest in 1066 the uncertain conditions of the language prevented any real literary progress, but some manuscripts survive of translations of parts of the Bible into Anglo-Norman French. About the beginning of the 13th century an Augustinian monk named Orm or Ormin produced a poetical version of the Gospels and the Acts of the Apostles called the *Ormulum*. From the first half of the 14th century there survive two prose translations of the Psalter, done in two different dialects; and from the end of the 14th century, a version of the principal NT epistles, apparently made, however, not for the use of the common people, but for monks and nuns. There was no thought as yet of providing ordinary layfolk with the Bible in their own tongue. It was Wycliffe who first entertained this revolutionary idea. And it was Wycliffe who first made the whole Bible available in English.

John Wycliffe. Born in Yorkshire about the year 1320, Wycliffe stands out as one of the most illustrious figures of the 14th century. This was a period of transition, neither the Middle Ages nor the Reformation — a kind of middle ground between the two. The old order was struggling with the new. Throughout the whole of this century the prestige of the Roman Catholic Church was very low. The "Babylonian captivity" of the popes at Avignon (1309-1378) was followed by the "Great Schism," when for 40 years there were two rival popes, one at Rome and the other at Avignon. In the struggle between the papacy and the English parliament over the papal tribute, Wycliffe sided with the parliament. The outstanding Oxford theologian of his day and an ardent ecclesiastical reformer, he is called the "Morning-star of the Reformation." He was convinced that the surest way of defeating Rome was to put the Bible into the hands of the common people, and therefore decided to make such a translation available. Under his auspices, the NT came out in 1380, and the OT two years later. It is uncertain exactly how much of the translation was done by Wycliffe himself. A number of scholars worked with him on the project, one of them, Nicholas Hereford, doing the greater part of the OT. The translation was made from the Latin, not from the original languages. Since printing was not known until the next century, copies were made by hand, and were naturally very expensive. About 170 are at present in existence. It was never really printed until 1850, when the Oxford Press brought it out. The original manuscript in the handwriting of at least five different men is preserved in the Bodleian Library at Oxford. To help him in his efforts for reform, Wycliffe organized a kind of religious order of poor preachers, called Lollards, whom he sent abroad through England to preach his doctrines and to read the Scriptures to all who wished to hear. Foxe reports that the people were so eager to read it that they would give a whole load of hay for the use of the NT for one day. There was opposition to Wycliffe on the part of the Church, but contrary to his own expectations, he was permitted to retire to his rectory at Lutterworth, where he quietly died in 1384. Twelve years later, however, his bones were disinterred and burned, and the ashes scattered over the river that flows through Lutterworth. His translation has indelibly stamped itself on our present-day Bible. Some of the expressions that are first found in his version are: "strait gate," "make whole," "compass land and sea," "son of perdition," "enter thou into the joy of thy Lord."

Four years after Wycliffe's death his secretary, John Purvey, issued a careful revision of his translation, introduced with an interesting prologue and accompanied by notes. The Church, however, did not approve of the new Bible. In 1408 a decree, known as the "Constitutions of Oxford," was issued forbidding anyone to translate or read any part of the Bible in the vernacular without the approval of his bishop or of a provincial council. Six years

The Gospell

folowe hím:foʒ they knowe his voyce. A ſtraunger they wil not folowe,but wyll flye from him : foʒ they knowe not the voyce of ſtraungers. This ſimilitude ſpake Jeſus vnto the. But they vnderſtode not what thinges they were whyche he ſpake vnto them. Then ſayde Jeſus vnto them agayne: Uerely,verely J ſaye vnto you, J am the doʒe of the ſhepe. All,euen as many as came before me,are theues and robbers,but the ſhepe did not heare them. J am the doʒe,by me if any man enter in,he ſhalbe ſafe,and ſhall go in and out,and fynde paſture. The thefe commeth not but foʒ to ſteale, kyll and deſtroy. J am come that they might haue life, and haue it moʒe aboundantly.

J am that good ſhepeherde. A good ſhepehearde geueth his life foʒ the ſhepe. And hired ſeruaunt,and he which is not the ſhepeherde (nether the ſhepe are his owne) ſeeth the wolfe comming,and leueth the ſhepe,and flyeth, and the wolfe catcheth them,and ſcattereth the ſhepe. The hired ſeruaunt flieth,becauſe he is an hyʒed ſeruaunt,and careth not foʒ the ſhepe. J am that good ſhepehearde,and know myne, and am knowen of myne. As my father knoweth me : euen ſo know J my father. And J geue my life foʒ the ſhepe : and other ſhepe J haue, whiche are not of this folde. Them alſo muſte

A page from Tyndale's Illustrated New Testament, with a portion of John 10, probably printed in 1553. BM

later a law was enacted that all persons who should read the Scriptures in the mother tongue should "forfeit land, catel, life, and goods from their heyres for ever." Nicholas Hereford and John Purvey were imprisoned. The public demand for the Bible continued, however, in spite of the severe penalties attached to its circulation.

The 15th century was one of the great epochs of human history. In that century there lived such men as Columbus, Galileo, Francis Bacon, Kepler, Marco Polo, and the inventor of printing, Gutenberg, who in 1454 brought out in Germany the first dated printed work, a Latin Psalter, and two years later the famous Gutenberg Bible in the Vulgate. After the capture of Constantinople in 1453, Christian scholars were compelled to leave the capital of the Eastern Empire, where for a thousand years Greek learning had flourished. They brought with them to Western Europe many Greek manuscripts. This led to a revival of interest in Biblical studies and made it possible for Erasmus to issue in 1516 the first printed edition of the Greek New Testament. At the beginning of the 16th century Greek was for the first time introduced as a subject of study in the universities of Oxford and Cambridge. By 1500 most of the countries of Europe had the Scriptures in the vernacular. England, however, had only scattered copies of the Wycliffe manuscript version, the language of which had by then become obsolete. The Constitutions of Oxford were still in force. England was ready for a new translation of the Bible, from the original languages.

William Tyndale translating the Bible (painting by Alexander Johnstone). © RTHPL

William Tyndale. William Tyndale, the next great figure in the history of the English Bible, was born about the year 1494, and spent ten years studying at Oxford and Cambridge. Soon after leaving Cambridge, while working as a chaplain and tutor, he said in a controversy with a clergyman, "If God spare my life, ere many years I will cause a boy that driveth a plough to know more of the Scripture than thou dost." This became the fixed resolve of his life. In his projected translation he tried to get the support of the Bishop of London, but without success. A wealthy London cloth-merchant finally came to his support, but after six months, in 1524, Tyndale left for the Continent because, he said, he "understood at the last not only that there was no room in my lord of London's palace to translate the New Testament, but also that there was no place to do it in all England, as experience doth now openly declare." He was never able to return to England. He seems to have visited Luther at Wittenberg, and then went to Cologne, where he found a printer for his New Testament. A priest discovered his plan, and Tyndale was obliged to flee. In Worms he found another printer, and there, in 1525, 3000 copies of the first printed English NT were published. By 1530 six editions, numbering about 15,000 copies, were published. They were all smuggled into England — hidden in bales of cotton, sacks of flour, and bundles of flax.

As soon as Tyndale's NT reached England, there was a great demand for it: by the laity, that they might read it, and by the ecclesiastical authorities, that they might destroy it! A decree was issued for its destruction. Bishops bought up whole editions to consign to the flames. As a result, only a few imperfect copies survive. Tyndale's English NT began a new epoch in the history of the English Bible. It was not a translation from the Latin, as Wycliffe's had been, but was rendered from the original Greek, the text published by Erasmus. With each successive edition, Tyndale made cor-

rections and improvements. So well did Tyndale do his work that the KJV reproduces about 90 per cent of Tyndale in the NT. After the completion of the NT, Tyndale started to bring out a translation of the OT from the Hebrew text, but he lived only to complete the Pentateuch, Jonah, and probably the historical books from Joshua to II Chronicles. After ten years on the Continent, mostly in hiding, he was betrayed in Antwerp by an English Roman Catholic, and was condemned to death for being a heretic. He was strangled, and his body burned at the stake. His last words were a prayer, "Lord, open the King of England's eyes." But Tyndale won his battle. Although his NT was burned in large quantities by the Church, it contributed greatly towards creating an appetite for the Bible in English. The government, moreover, began to see the wisdom and necessity of providing the Bible in English for common use. The break with the papacy in 1534 helped greatly in this.

Miles Coverdale. While Tyndale was incarcerated in Belgium, an English Bible suddenly appeared in England. This was in 1535. It had come from the Continent. The title-page stated that it had been translated out of the German and Latin into English. This Bible was the rendering of Miles Coverdale, although in the NT and in those parts of the OT done by Tyndale, it was no more than a slight revision of the latter's work. It was the first complete printed Bible in the English language. It was not made from the Hebrew and Greek, for in the dedication (to Henry VIII) Coverdale says that he used the work of five different translators. His version of the Psalms still appears in the Book of Common Prayer, used daily in the ritual of the Church of England. Two new editions of Coverdale's Bible appeared in 1537, with the significant words on the title page, "Set forth with the King's most gracious license." So within a year of Tyndale's death, the entire Bible was translated, printed, and distributed, apparently with royal approval.

First page of Coverdale's Bible, dated 1536, probably printed in Switzerland. The second edition, in 1537, was the first complete English Bible to be printed in England. BFBS

Thomas Matthew. In 1537 another Bible appeared in England, this one by Thomas Matthew (a pen-name for John Rogers, a former associate of Tyndale's) who was burned at the stake by Queen Mary in 1555. The whole of the NT and about half of the OT are Tyndale's, while the remainder is Coverdale's. It bore on its title-page the words, "Set forth with the king's most gracious license." This Bible has the distinction of being the first edition of the whole English Bible actually to be printed in England. So now two versions of the English Bible circulated in England with the king's permission, Coverdale's and Matthew's, both of them heavily dependent upon Tyndale.

The Great Bible. The next Bible to appear was a revision of the Matthew Bible, by Coverdale. The printing of this was begun in Paris, but the Inquisition stepped in and the work was completed in England. It appeared in 1539 and was called the Great Bible because of its large size and sumptuousness. In his revision Coverdale made considerable use of the Hebrew and Greek texts then available. Subsequent editions were called Cranmer's Bible because of a preface he wrote for it in which he commended the widespread reading of the Scriptures and declared that they were the sufficient rule of faith and life. At the foot of the title-page were the words, "This is the Bible appointed to the use of the churches." This makes explicit an order that was issued in 1538, while this Bible was being printed, that a copy of it was to be placed in every church in the land. The people cordially welcomed the Great Bible, but its size and cost limited it largely to use in churches.

The later years of Henry VIII were marked by a serious reaction against the Reforming movement. In 1543 Parliament passed an act to ban the use of Tyndale's NT, made it a crime for an unlicensed person to read or expound the Bible publicly to others, and restricted even the private reading of the Bible to the upper classes. Three years later Parliament prohibited the use of everything but the Great Bible. In London large quantities of Tyndale's NT and Coverdale's Bible were burned at St. Paul's Cross.

In the brief reign of Edward VI, who succeeded his father Henry VIII on the latter's death in 1547, no new translation work was done, but great encouragement was given to the reading of the Bible and to the printing of existing versions, and injunctions were repromulgated that a copy of the Great Bible be placed in every parish church.

The Genevan Bible. With the accession of Mary in 1553, hundreds of Protestants lost their lives, among them some men closely associated with Bible translation, like John Rogers and Thomas Cranmer. Coverdale escaped martyrdom by fleeing to the Continent. Some of the English Reformers escaped to Geneva, where the leading figure was John Calvin. One of their number, William Wittingham, who had married Calvin's sister, produced in 1557 a revision of the English NT. This was the first English NT printed in roman type and with the text divided into verses. He and his associates then undertook the revision of the whole Bible. This appeared in 1560 and is known as the Genevan Bible, or more familiarly as the Breeches Bible from its rendering of Genesis 3:7, "They sewed fig-tree leaves together, and made themselves breeches." It enjoyed a long popularity, going through 160 editions, 60 of them during the reign of Queen Elizabeth alone, and continued to be printed even after the publication of the KJV in 1611.

The Bishops' Bible. Queen Elizabeth, who succeeded Mary Tudor after the latter's three years and nine months' reign, restored the arrangements of Edward VI. The Great Bible was again placed in every church, and people were encouraged to read the Scriptures. The excellence of the Genevan Bible made obvious the deficiencies of the Great Bible, but some of its renderings and the marginal notes made it unacceptable to many of the clergy. Archbishop Parker, aided by eight bishops and some other scholars, therefore made a revision of the Great Bible, which was completed and published in 1568 and came to be known as the Bishops' Bible. It gained considerable circulation, but the Genevan Bible was far more popular and was used more widely.

Rheims and Douai Version. This came from the Church of Rome, and is the work of Gregory Martin, who with a number of other English Romanists left England at the beginning of Elizabeth's reign and settled in the NE of France, where in 1568 they founded a college. The NT was published in 1582, and was done while the college was at Rheims, and hence is known as the Rheims New Testament, but the OT was not published until 1609-10, after the college had moved to Douai, and hence it is called the Douai Old Testament. The Preface warned readers against the then existing "profane" translations and blames Protestants for casting what was holy to dogs. Like Wycliffe's version, this one was made not from the original languages but from Latin, and is therefore only a secondary translation. The main objection to the version is its too close adherence to the words of the

The opening verses of the book of Genesis from the first edition of the Authorized (King James) Version, 1611. BM

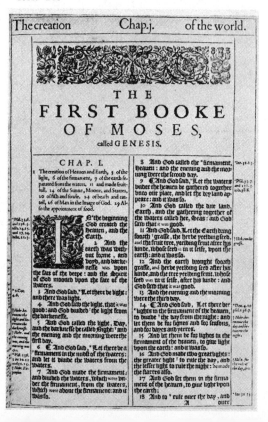

Sir George Harvey's historic painting of the first reading from the Chained Bible in the crypt of old St. Paul's church in London, 1540. © RTHPL

original Latin and the too great Latinizing of the English. It included the Apocrypha, and contained a large number of notes, most of them to interpret the sacred text in conformity with Roman Catholic teaching and to reply to the arguments of the Reformers. The Rheims-Douay Bible in use today is not the same as the one made by Gregory Martin, but is a thorough revision made of it between 1749 and 1763 by Bishop Richard Challoner. It was first authorized for use by American Roman Catholics in 1810.

King James Version. When Elizabeth died, in 1603, the crown passed to James I, who had been king of Scotland for 37 years as James VI. Several months after he ascended the throne of England he called a conference of bishops and Puritan clergy to harmonize the differences that existed in the Church. At this conference Dr. John Reynolds, President of Corpus Christi College, Oxford, a leader of the Puritan party in the Church of England, suggested that a new translation of the Bible be made to replace the Bishops' Bible, which many people found unacceptable. The proposal pleased the king, who violently disliked the Genevan Bible, and a resolution was passed to produce a new translation of the Bible from the original Hebrew and Greek, without any marginal notes, for the use of all the churches in England.

Without delay, King James nominated 54 of the best Hebrew and Greek scholars of the day. Only 47 actually took part in the work, which did not begin until 1607. They were divided into six groups: three for the OT, two for the New, and one for the Apocrypha. Two of the groups met at Ox-

ford, two at Cambridge, and two at Westminster. Elaborate rules were laid down for their guidance. When a group had completed its task, its work was submitted to 12 men, two from each panel. Final differences of opinion were settled at a general meeting of each company. In cases of special difficulty, learned men outside the board of revisers were consulted. Marginal notes were used only to explain Hebrew and Greek words and to draw attention to parallel passages. Italics were used for words not found in the original but necessary to complete the sense.

The revisers, who received no financial remuneration for their work, completed their task in two years; and nine more months were devoted to a revision of their work by a special committee consisting of two members from each group. In 1611 the new version was published. Although the title-page described it as "newly translated out of the original tongues" and as "appointed to be read in churches," neither statement is entirely in accord with the facts. The work was actually a revision of the Bishops' Bible on the basis of the Hebrew and Greek; and it was never officially sanctioned by King, Parliament, or the Church. It did not win immediate universal acceptance, taking almost 50 years to displace the Genevan Bible in popular favor. In the course of time slight alterations were made, especially in spelling, to conform to changing usage, but these were all done piecemeal by private enterprise. Its excellence is shown by the fact that after 350 years it is still used in preference to any other version in the English-speaking Protestant world, for both public and private use.

passages in the OT as poetry and in grouping verses into paragraphs according to sense-units.

The NT was published in 1881, and the OT in 1885. The work occupied the NT company for about 40 days each year for ten years; while the OT company was occupied for 792 days over a period of 14 years. The revisers gave their time and labor without charge. When they completed their work, they disbanded. Although the new version received acceptance unprecedented in the history of the Bible, so that three million copies were sold within the first year, it did not meet with immediate approval, nor has it in the years since then won for itself a place of undisputed supremacy. There is no doubt of its superior accuracy as a translation, but sacred associations clinging to the KJV have caused many people to turn from it.

American Standard Version. The American scholars who cooperated with the English revisers on the ERV were not entirely satisfied with it. For one thing, the suggested changes printed in the Appendix represented only a part of the changes they wanted made; and for another thing, the English revisers retained a large number of words and phrases whose meanings and spellings were regarded as antiquated, and words that are English but not American in meaning. For these and other reasons they did not disband when the ERV was published, but their revision of the ERV was not published until 1901. It is regarded as being on the whole superior to the ERV, at least for American uses, but it has its defects, as, for example, the substitution of "Jehovah" for "Lord," especially in the Psalter.

Other Twentieth Century Versions. The discovery, at the end of the 19th century, of many thousands of Greek papyri in the sands of Egypt, all written in the everyday Greek language of the people, had a revolutionary influence upon the study of the Greek of the NT. NT Greek had hitherto presented a vexing problem, since it is neither classical Greek nor the Greek of the Septuagint. Now it was shown to be the Greek of the papyri, and therefore the colloquial language of Greek-speaking people in the first century. It was felt that the NT should be translated into the everyday speech of the common man, and not in stilted and antiquated English. These developments created a keen interest in bringing out fresh translations of the NT in the spoken English of today; and in the next 45 years a number of new modern-speech versions came out, most of them by individuals, but a few by groups of scholars.

The first of these to appear was *The Twentieth Century New Testament: A Translation into Modern English Made from the Original Greek. (Westcott & Hort's Text).* This was published in 1902 (reprinted 1961) and was the work of about 20 translators whose names were not given. In 1903 R. F. Weymouth brought out *The New Testament in Modern Speech;* it was thoroughly revised in 1924 by J. A. Robertson. James Moffatt, the well-known Scottish NT scholar, brought out *The Bible: A New Translation* in 1913,14. The American counterpart of Moffatt is *The Complete Bible: An American Translation* (1927, revised 1935). The NT part first appeared in 1923 and was the work of E. J. Goodspeed; while four scholars, headed by J. M. Powis Smith, did the OT. *The New Testament. A Translation in the Language of the People,* by C. B. Williams, came out in 1937. *The New Testament in Modern English* (1958), by J. B. Phillips, is one of the most readable of the modern-speech translations. *The Amplified New Testament* (1958), which gives variant

King James I, under whose authority was prepared the King James, or Authorized, Version of the English Bible issued in 1611. NPG

English Revised Version. This version was made necessary for a number of reasons: in the course of time the language of the KJV had become obsolete; a number of Greek manuscripts were discovered that were far superior to those available to the KJV translators; and improvement in the knowledge of Hebrew made possible a more accurate rendering of the OT. It had its origin in 1870 with the Convocation of Canterbury of the Church of England when a committee was appointed to invite outstanding Hebrew and Greek scholars, irrespective of religious denomination, to join in the revision of the KJV. Eventually two companies were formed, each of 27 men, one for the OT, the other for the NT. American scholars were also invited to cooperate, and they formed two companies corresponding to the British. It was agreed that American suggestions not accepted by the British revisers were to be recorded in an appendix to the published volume, and that the American revisers were to give their moral support to the new Bible and were not to issue an edition of their own for a term of 14 years. The revisers were guided by a number of rules, the most important being that they were to make as few alterations as possible into the text of the KJV consistently with faithfulness.

Altogether, the Greek text underlying the revised NT differed from that used by the KJV translators in 5,788 readings, only about one fourth of these making any material difference in the substance of the text, although none so seriously as to affect the doctrines of the faith. In the English text of the NT there are about 36,000 changes. The new Bible differed from its predecessors in printing poetical

shades of meaning in the original, was followed in 1961 by *The Amplified Old Testament.* Part Two (Job-Malachi), balance of OT to follow in 1964. It is the work of Frances E. Siewert and unnamed assistants. *The Holy Bible: The Berkeley Version in Modern English* (1959) is the work of Gerrit Verkuyl in the NT and of 20 American scholars in the OT. Kenneth Wuest's *The New Testament — An Expanded Translation* appeared complete in 1961. Also in 1961 appeared *The Simplified New Testament,* a new translation by Olaf M. Norlie.

During this period the Roman Catholic Church brought out a number of new versions: *The New Testament of Our Lord and Savior Jesus Christ* (1941), a revision of the Rheims-Challoner NT sponsored by the Episcopal Committee of the Confraternity of Christian Doctrine; the *Westminster Version of the Sacred Scriptures,* under the general editorship of Cuthbert Lattey, of which only the NT (1935) and parts of the OT have thus far appeared; and the translation from the Latin Vulgate made by Ronald A. Knox, the NT in 1945 and the OT in 1949.

Revised Standard Version. This is a revision of the ASV (1901), the NT appearing in 1946 and the OT in 1952. It was sponsored by the International Council of Religious Education, and is the work of 32 American scholars who worked in two sections, one dealing with the OT, the other with the NT. It was designed for use in public and private worship. In this version the language is modernized; direct speech is regularly indicated by the use of quotation marks; and the policy is followed (as in the KJV) of using a variety of synonyms to translate the Greek words where it is thought to be advisable.

New English Bible. This is a completely new translation, not a revision of previously existing versions. The first suggestion for this version came from the General Assembly of the Church of Scotland; but it is the joint effort of all the major religious denominations and organizations in the British Isles. C. H. Dodd is the General Director of the whole translation. The first requirement put on the translators is to produce a genuinely new translation, in which an attempt should be made consistently to use the idiom of contemporary English to convey the meaning of the original languages. Assisting the translators is a panel of advisors on literary and stylistic questions. Only the NT (1961) has come out thus far. As in the case of all previous translations, this one has been greeted with a mixture of praise and criticism. It is expected that the OT will be published in a few years. S.B.

BICHRI (bĭk'rī, *first-born*), mentioned in II Samuel 20:1 as the father of Sheba, who made insurrection against David.

BIDKAR (bĭd'kȧr), a military officer of Israel who joined Jehu in his revolt and was made his captain (II Kings 9:25). He cast the body of Joram, king of Israel, into the plot of Naboth's vineyard, after Jehu had slain him.

BIGTHA (bĭg'thȧ), one of the seven chamberlains of Ahasuerus, i.e. Xerxes (Esth. 1:10).

BIGTHAN or **BIGTHANA** (bĭg'thăn or bĭg'thā'nȧ), one of the chamberlains of king Ahasuerus, i.e. Xerxes, who with another, Teresh, had plotted to slay the king. Mordecai heard of the plot, and through Esther warned the king, who had the two men hanged (Esth. 2:21-23; 6:2).

BIGVAI (bĭg'vā-ī, *fortunate*). 1. One of the 11 or 12 chief men who returned from captivity by permission of Cyrus in 536 B.C. (Ezra 2:2; Neh. 7).

2. The ancestor of a family of over 2,000 who returned with Zerubbabel from captivity (Ezra 2:14; Neh. 7:19). Some think that the slight difference of numbers in the two verses quoted is due to the possibility that Ezra's was a list made in Babylon before starting, and Nehemiah's at Jerusalem after arriving. Some few have dropped out and a few added during the migration.

3. Probably the same as 2. The ancestor of a family of which 72 men returned with Ezra in 457 B.C. (Ezra 8:14).

BILDAD (bĭl'dăd), one of Job's three "comforters" (cf. Job 2:11-13 with 42:7-10). He was evidently a descendant of Shuah (Gen. 25:2), a son of Abraham by Keturah, who became patriarch of an Arab tribe. Bildad made three speeches (Job 8,18,25), and his distinctive character as a "traditionalist" can best be seen in 8:8-10.

BILEAM (bĭl'ē-ăm), a town in the western half of the tribe of Manasseh given in Joshua's time to the Levites of the Kohathite family who were not priests (I Chron. 6:70). Perhaps the same as the Ibleam of Joshua 17:11; Judges 1:27, and II Kings 9:27.

BILGAH (bĭl'gȧ, *cheerfulness*). 1. Head of the 15th course of priests in David's time (I Chron. 24:14).

2. A priest who returned with Zerubbabel in 536 B.C. (Neh. 12:5).

BILGAI (bĭl'gā-ī), a priest in Nehemiah's time, 444 B.C. (Neh. 10:8).

BILHAH (bĭl'hȧ, *foolish*). 1. Maid-servant of Rachel, Jacob's beloved wife, and later given to Jacob by Rachel that she might bear children who would be credited to Rachel (Gen. 29:29; 30:1-8). She became ancestress of the two tribes, Dan and Naphtali. In the polygamous system of early Israel, she would be ranked higher than a mere concubine, but not as high as her free-born mistress.

2. A town in the tribe of Simeon. Spelled "Balah" in Joshua 19:3.

BILHAN (bĭl'hăn, *foolish*). 1. A son of Ezer, son of Seir the Horite (Gen. 36:27; I Chron. 1:42). Etymologically, the name is the same as *Bilhah,* but with the Horite ending.

2. An early Benjamite; son of Jediael, son of Benjamin (I Chron. 7:10). He had seven sons who were mighty men and heads of large families.

BILSHAN (bĭl'shăn), one of the 11 or 12 leaders of the Jews who returned from captivity in 536 B.C. (Ezra 2:2; Neh. 7:7).

BIMHAL (bĭm'hăl), one of the three sons of Japhlet of the tribe of Asher (I Chron. 7:33).

BINDING AND LOOSING. The carrying of a key or keys was a symbol of the delegated power of opening and closing. In Matthew 16:19, our Lord gave the "power of the keys" to Peter, and Peter's use of the keys is narrated in what may be called the "three stages of Pentecost." On the day of Pentecost (Acts 2:14-40) Peter preached the first Christian sermon and opened "the kingdom of heaven" to what became a Hebrew-Christian church; then with John he went to Samaria (Acts 8:14-17) and opened the same "kingdom" to the Samaritans; and still later in the house of Cornelius (Acts 10:44-48) he opened it to the Gentiles; so that the Church could become universal. The medieval teaching about Peter standing at the gate of heaven to receive or reject souls of men has no basis in the Bible teaching.

BINNUI (bĭn'ū-ī, *built*). 1. A Levite, whose son was partly in charge of the silver and gold at Ezra's return (Ezra 8:33).

2. One of the sons of Pahath-moab who had married foreign wives (Ezra 10:30).

3. A son of Bani who had been similarly guilty (Ezra 10:38).

4. One of the rebuilders of Jerusalem in 444 B.C. who also became a covenanter under Nehemiah (Neh. 3:24; 10:9).

5. Alternate spelling of Bani (cf. Ezra 2:10; Neh. 7:15) whose family returned with Zerubbabel.

6. A Levite who returned with Zerubbabel (Neh. 12:8).

BIRDS of 360 to 400 different kinds occur in Palestine, and of these, 26 are found only there. The Bible mentions about 50, using Hebrew or Greek names which can sometimes be identified with particular species of the present. Birds are mentioned in all but 21 books of the Bible and 19 times in the apocryphal books. The following birds are specifically mentioned.

Bittern, a heron-like bird of marshy environment with a mournful call. It was prophesied that it would live in a waste land which replaced the cursed Edom (Isa. 34:11). Translated as "porcupine" in ARV and RSV.

Chicken, the common domesticated barn yard fowl, descended from the wild red jungle fowl of India, Burma, and Malaya. Mentioned as the young of a hen which shows consideration for her offspring, as Christ would have comforted Jerusalem (Matt. 23:37). Perhaps the "fatted fowl" of I Kings 4: 22-23. See "hen."

Cock, the male of the domestic chicken. Used as a symbol of the early part of the day because of its morning crowing (Mark 13:35), a reminder of Jesus' word to Peter that he would deny his Lord (Matt. 26:74). There is a church in Jerusalem today named Gallicante, after the cock which Peter heard.

Cormorant, a swimmer and diver with webs between all four toes. It can pursue and catch fish under water. Some orientals use it to capture fish for them. A dweller in waste places, hence a sign of a curse on land formerly inhabited, such as Edom and Nineveh. Included in list of unclean birds in Leviticus 11, probably because it is a flesh eater. Since the flesh contained blood, and Israelites were forbidden to eat blood, they were also prohibited from eating birds which were carnivorous. In Isaiah 34:11 it is "pelican" in ARV, and "hawk" in RSV. Zephaniah 2:14 replaces "cormorant" with "pelican" in ARV and "vulture" in RSV.

Crane, a long-necked, long-legged wading bird whose voice is a croak or a honk heard for several miles. Hezekiah's lament over his sickness is compared to that of a crane (Isa. 38:14). Its time of migration is well known, so that its faithful return is contrasted to Israel's faithlessness (Jer. 8:7).

Crow. No specimen is mentioned in the Bible, but the word is the symbol of the voice of the cock and other birds.

Cuckoo, an unclean bird of Leviticus 11 and Deuteronomy 14. The RSV translates this "sea gull," the ARV "sea mew," and G. R. Driver "long-eared owl." The gull and owl are flesh eaters, hence condemned for human food.

Cuckow, the KJV name for cuckoo. See cuckoo.

Dove. Probably the rock pigeon or the rock dove similar to our domestic pigeon, common in flocks in parks and around buildings. It was sent from the ark after the flood, but found no land, so returned, but did not go out until after a fortnight when firm footing was available (Gen. 8:8-12). It flies rapidly on high, as the Psalmist wishes his prayers also could. The dove is a promise of a blessed future for those in humble circumstances; for though one has lain among the pots, yet he shall be as the wings of doves covered with silver and feathers covered with gold (Ps. 68:13). The "pots" may be ash grates, as in some translations. This, then, becomes a source of the phrase, "Beauty for ashes." The dove appropriately becomes a symbol of a lover in the Song of Solomon for its soft cooing voice was well known. However, Hezekiah compares his mourning over his illness to the voice of a dove (Isa. 38:14) and both Isaiah and Ezekiel felt that sinful Israel would mourn like a dove. Like the swift flight of doves (Isa. 59:11; Ezek. 7: 16) so would help come from Zion (Isa. 60:8). Their nests "in the clefts of the rock, in the covert of a cliff" (S. of Sol. 2:14 RSV) or "in the sides of the mouth of a gorge" (Jer. 48:28 RSV) suggest peaceful retreats for lovers or from threat of judgment. Doves are among the less intelligent of birds, hence foolish Ephraim is compared to a "silly dove." Their harmlessness is mentioned in Matthew 10:16. The Spirit of God descends "like a dove" (Matt. 3:16). Doves were sold in the Temple for the rites of purification, but Jesus cast out the sellers (Matt. 21:12).

Eagle, a large, hawk-like bird having powerful beak, talons, and wings, with a spread of over four feet. Israel was carried from Egypt by Jehovah on eagles' wings (Exod. 19:4; Deut. 32:11). The Lord renews the youth of the soul like the eagle (Ps. 103:5) so that it mounts up with wings as eagles (Isa. 40:31). The woman of Revelation 12 escapes the serpent by using the gift of "two wings of a great eagle." Israel will be chastised by a nation "as swift as the eagle flieth" (Deut. 28:49; Jer. 4: 13). Even though Edom should be as inaccessible as an eagle's high nest, it will be destroyed (Jer. 49:16; Obad. 4). Eagles will eat the eyes of mockers (Prov. 30:17; Matt. 24:28). In these verses the KJV and ARV use the term "young eagles," while the RSV prefers "vultures." Several symbolic creatures have eagles' features (Ezek. 1:10; Ezek. 17: 3). Nebuchadnezzar's kingdom was compared to a lion with eagle's wings (Dan. 7:4). In their death Saul and Jonathan were "swifter than eagles" (II Sam. 1:23), and Job's days passed away as fast as an eagle hastening to the prey (Job 9:26). Riches are not to be desired, for they fly away as eagles toward heaven (Prov. 23:5). The eagle is among the unclean birds of Leviticus 11.

Falcon, a hawk with long-pointed wings and long tail. It is an unclean bird in Leviticus 11 (KJV), translated "kite" by RSV.

A Bedouin hunter with his trained falcons. © MPS

Fowl, used of all flying birds (Gen. 1:20) and even includes the bat (Lev. 11:13,19) which is a mammal. Mentioned as sacrifices (Lev. 1:14), food (Deut. 14:20) and scavengers of perished sinners (Ezek. 29:5). They are wise (Job 35:11) but God possesses greater wisdom (Job 28:7). Men are worth more than many fowls (Luke 12:24).

Gier Eagle, a KJV term; called "vulture" in RSV and ARV and "osprey" by G. R. Driver. See "ospray."

Glede, a kind of vulture or hawk. An unclean bird of Deuteronomy 14:13.

Great Owl, an unclean bird of Leviticus 11. Listed as "Ibis" in RSV. See "owl."

Hawk, a fast-flying, sharp-tongued, curved-beaked predator, considered unclean in Leviticus 11 and Deuteronomy 14. It is similar to the eagle and the flight of both is mentioned as God given in Job 39:26-27.

Hen, the female of the domestic chicken, which is solicitous for its young, even as Jesus wishes to be for Jerusalem (Matt. 23:37).

Heron, a long-legged, marsh-inhabiting wading bird. Unclean in Leviticus 11 and Deuteronomy 14.

Hoopoe, see "lapwing."

Kite, see "falcon" as it is translated in ARV and RSV.

Lapwing, perhaps the woodcock, a long-billed bird living on worms. RSV and ARV translate this term "hoopoe" as does Driver. The hoopoe has a prominent crest and curved bill pictured in an Egyptian fowling scene 3800 years ago. "It probes in filth for insects and worms and this habit doubtlessly earned for it an 'unclean' classification." (Parmalee)

Little Owl, see "owl." An unclean bird of Leviticus 11.

Nighthawk, called the same in KJV and RSV but "short-eared owl" by Driver and "owl, swallow, cuckoo" by Young's *Analytical Concordance.* Nighthawks and whip-poor-wills are similar small-beaked, strong-flying insect-eating birds. The nighthawk is listed as unclean in Leviticus 11.

Ospray, spelled "osprey" in modern English, as in RSV. A fish-eating hawk which has roughened pads on its feet to help hold slippery fish. An unclean bird of Leviticus 11.

Ossifrage, the "bearded vulture" in Driver's dictionary account. An unclean bird of Leviticus 11. See "vulture." (Called "gier eagle" in ARV.)

Ostrich, the largest living bird, whose habits are accurately described in Job 39:13-18. With "a bounding stride of 15 feet or more, ostriches can indeed 'scour the plain,' running 40 miles an hour and easily out-distancing the fastest horse" (Parmalee). The author of Lamentations considered them cruel (4:3). Job felt that his sad state made him like a companion of the reticent ostrich (Job 30:29 ARV).

Owl, a nocturnal bird of prey, hunting rodents and other small animals. They reminded the Israelites of desolate and ruined cities (Isa. 34:15). The "great owl" is similar to the American great-horned owl, twenty-two inches long, and the "little owl" is the most common owl in Palestine. All were considered unclean (Lev. 11 where ARV and RSV have "ostrich"). All owls have mournful voices, resembling a discouraged prayer (Ps. 102:6).

Partridge, a member of the order of birds to which chickens belong. Because of their swift and sneaky running, they are excellent game birds. David com-

Above, the hawk of Palestine, and below, the owl of Palestine. © MPS

pared himself to a partridge when Saul was hunting him (I Sam. 26:20). It was supposed that partridges robbed eggs from others and hatched them, a symbol of getting riches unfairly (Jer. 17:11).

Peacock, the beautiful birds brought for Solomon's courtyard, probably from India and Ceylon. The peacocks mentioned in Job 39:13 (KJV) are probably ostrich hens (ARV).

Pelican. Dr. Driver thinks the pelican in the list of unclean birds of Leviticus 11 is the scops owl, only eight inches long. Pelicans, like cormorants, have webs between all four toes, which enable them to pursue the fish they eat. Whether the Hebrew *qaath* means owl or pelican, it refers to an unclean bird on account of its flesh eating habit.

Pigeon, the common rock dove (see dove). Because pigeons do not migrate and are numerous, their young were easily obtained by the poor for sacrifice (Gen. 15:9; Luke 2:24).

Quail, a ground dweller, scratching for food and having strong flying muscles for rapid flight of short duration. Its flesh is good for food (Exod. 16:13; Ps. 105:40). Quail migrate in enormous flocks only a few feet above the ground, "two cubits high" (Num. 11:31).

Raven, similar to a large crow, with larger head and shoulders, and an omnivorous eater, hence condemned in Leviticus 11. It could live on dead bodies, so did not return when Noah sent it from the ark. Ravens fed Elijah (I Kings 17:4) and are fed by God (Job 38:41), dwell in places formerly inhabited (Isa. 34:11) and will pick out the eye of a mocker (Prov. 30:17).

Screech Owl, a small owl with penetrating voice. Parmalee mentions that many owls are found "in the rock tombs of Petra, chief city of ancient Edom," which may point to a fulfillment of Isaiah 34:13,14, although the creature mentioned here may be the ostrich (ARV).

Sea Mew, see "cuckoo."

Sparrow, a small, seed-eating bird closely akin to the American house sparrow. Noisy, active and prolific. It was protected in the Temple (Ps. 84:3). This name may also include wrens like our house wren. Sparrows were so cheap that when four were purchased a fifth was added free, but all are noticed by the heavenly Father, "Fear ye not, therefore . . ." (Matt. 10:31). Sparrows live in groups, so a sparrow "alone on a housetop" (Ps. 102:7) is an unusual sight. The Hebrew word *tsippor* in this verse may better be translated rock thrush, which haunts lonely places.

Stork, a long-legged, heron-like bird feeding in marshes but nesting in trees (Ps. 104:17). It has a regular migration time, more faithful than God's people (Jer. 8:7). Their powerful wings are referred to in Zechariah 5:9.

Swallow, probably the swift, with dashing flight and piercing repeated call. Appropriate to Hezekiah's chattering in his illness (Isa. 38:14).

Swan, member of duck and goose family but with longer neck. Called "swan" in KJV, but "water hen" in RSV, "horned owl" in ARV, and "little owl" by Driver, and Young's *Analytical Concordance.* Because it is included in the list of unclean birds it is more than likely the meat-eating owl rather than the vegetarian swan.

Turtledove, a wild pigeon of migratory habits, similar to our mourning dove, singing frequently early in the spring (S. of Sol. 2:12), abundant for sacrifices (Gen. 15:9), so that they were a godsend to the poor (Luke 2:24).

Vulture, a hawk-like bird feeding on dead animals, and the slain of Isaiah 34:15 (called "kite" in ARV). Included among unclean birds of Leviticus 11 and Deuteronomy 14. Wide ranging in its soaring, but God knows a path the vulture has not seen (Job 28:7, ARV has "falcon" here).   R.L.M.

BIRSHA (bîr'shà), king of Gomorrah who was defeated by Chedorlaomer (Gen. 14:2,10).

BIRTH, the bringing into existence of a separate life. Although this is accompanied by rending pain, there is no evidence that such pain would have occurred had not sin entered the human race. (See Genesis 3:16 where pain in child-bearing is a part of the curse upon Eve for her sin.) This pain is so uniquely severe that in nine-tenths of the forty-odd uses of the word "travail" in Scripture ("as of a woman in travail") it is used as a figure for intense suffering (Jer. 13:21; Rom. 8:22; Gal. 4:19, etc.) Apparently the ancient Hebrew women went through travail more easily than the Egyptians (Exod. 1:19).

The day of one's birth is, in a sense, the most important day of his life, for without it, he would not have been; and so the celebration of birthdays goes back into very ancient times (Gen. 40:20; Matt. 14:6, etc.). The Hebrew ceremonies connected with childbirth are given in Leviticus 12. The permission to the poor to offer "a pair of turtledoves or two young pigeons" in place of a lamb (Luke 2:24) gives touching testimony to the comparative poverty of Mary, the mother of Jesus. Our Lord, in John 3:3-6, makes a clear distinction between the first and second births of a regenerate person; and when this distinction is applied, it seems so to divide men as almost to make two different species; the once-born and the regenerate. The former are depraved, and unless they repent they are destined for judgment (Heb. 9:27; 10:31); while the latter are being made partakers in the divine nature (II Peter 1:4, etc.) and are destined for glory.   A.B.F.

BIRTHRIGHT. From time immemorial a man's firstborn son has been given privileges above those of his younger brothers. This is illustrated today by the order of succession to the throne (in Britain for instance). Among the Israelites God had a special claim on the firstborn, at least from the time of Exodus, when He destroyed the firstborn of Egypt, and claimed those of Israel by right of redemption (Exod. 13:2,12-16). The birthright included a double portion of the inheritance (Deut. 21:15-17), and the privilege of priesthood; but in Israel God later set apart the tribe of Levi instead of the firstborn for that service. (Note Numbers 3:38-51, where the Levites are about the same in number as the firstborn of Israel). Esau lost his birthright by selling it to Jacob for a mess of pottage, and no regret could undo the loss he had brought upon himself. (See Gen. 25:27-34, Heb. 12:16 and compare the destinies of Israel and of Edom, Obad. 17,18). In Israel, Reuben lost his birthright through sin, and his next brothers Simeon and Levi lost theirs through violence; and so the blessing came to Judah (Gen. 49:3-10).

BIRZAVITH (bîr-zā'vĭth), either a son of Malchiel of the tribe of Asher (I Chron. 7:31), or a village whose people were descendants of Malchiel.

BISHLAM (bĭsh'lăm), an officer of Cambyses ("Artaxerxes") who opposed the rebuilding of the temple (Ezra 4:7).

BISHOP (bĭsh'ŭp, Gr. *epískopos, overseer*), originally the principal officer of the local church, the other being the deacon or deacons (I Tim. 3: 1-7). The title "elder" or "presbyter" generally applied to the same man; "elder" referring to his age and dignity, and "bishop" to his work of superintendence. As the churches multiplied, the bishop of a larger church would often be given special honor, and so gradually there grew up a hierarchy, all the way from presiding elders to bishops (over groups of churches), then archbishops.

BITHIAH (bĭ-thī'à, *daughter of Jehovah*), the name suggests that she was a convert to Judaism, though she is called a daughter of Pharaoh. Mentioned only in I Chronicles 4:18 as wife of Mered of the tribe of Judah.

BITHRON (bĭth'rŏn, *rough country*), a region in the tribe of Gad between the Jordan and Mahanaim. Mentioned only in II Samuel 2:29.

BITHYNIA (bĭ-thĭn'ĭ-à, Gr. *Bithunía*), a region along the northern edge of Asia Minor fronting on the Black Sea, the Bosphorus and the Sea of Marmora. Paul and his companions desired to enter Bithynia with the Gospel (Acts 16:6-10) but the Holy Spirit was leading toward Europe, and so they could not enter. However, there were Christians there in the first century (I Pet. 1:1). The Roman governor Pliny the Younger complained to Trajan concerning the Christians and at the beginning of the second century asked how to deal with them.

Bithynia was settled very early, and its known history goes back past the sixth century B.C., when Croesus made it a part of his kingdom. A king of Bithynia in the third century B.C. invited the Gauls into Asia, so originating "Galatia." From the 13th century on, it has been Turkish, or at least ruled by the Turks.

BITTER HERBS. At the passover, the Israelites were to eat roast lamb (a lamb whose blood had been sprinkled for their salvation) with unleavened bread (because of the haste of their departure), and bitter herbs (as symbolic of the bitterness of their servitude, Exod. 12:8; Num. 9:11). Perhaps horse-radish is the nearest equivalent in our diet. See PLANTS.

BITTERN (See Birds)

BITUMEN (bī-tū'měn), a mineral pitch widely scattered over the earth, and one of the best waterproofing substances known. It was used with slime (or perhaps as "slime and pitch") to cover the ark of bulrushes (Exod. 2:3) and to waterproof Noah's ark (Gen. 6:14), for mortar in the tower of Babel (Gen. 11:3), and as a curse upon Edom (Isa. 34:9). There were great deposits near the Dead Sea, and at different places in Mesopotamia. The principal modern source is a great lake of pitch on the island of Trinidad.

BIZJOTHJAH (bĭz-jŏth'jà, *contempt of Jehovah*, ASV Biziothiah), a town in the south of Judah in Joshua's time (Josh. 15:28).

BIZTHAH (bĭz'thà), one of the seven chamberlains in the court of Xerxes ("Ahasuerus") who were commanded to bring out Queen Vashti for exhibition.

BLAINS (See Diseases)

BLASPHEMY (blăs'fē-mē, Gr. *blasphémia*). To reproach or to bring a railing accusation against any one is bad enough (Jude 9), but to speak lightly or carelessly of God is a mortal sin. In Israel the punishment of blasphemy was death by stoning (see Lev. 24:10-16). The third commandment, "Thou shalt not take the name of Jehovah thy God in vain" (Exod. 20:7) was observed so meticulously by the Jews that they would not speak the sacred Jehovah name at all, and so no one knows today for certain how it was pronounced. In the Hebrew Bible the consonants of the "sacred tetragrammaton" YHWH occur more than 6,000 times, but always with the vowels for the word "LORD." As a result of this superstitious reverence, the word Jehovah is found only half a dozen times in the KJV, and the word LORD is used instead. Naboth, at Jezebel's instigation, was falsely charged with

blasphemy (I Kings 21:10-13), as were our Lord (Matt. 9:3, etc.) and Stephen (Acts 6:11). What our Lord said would have been blasphemy were it not true. The Jews, with a peculiar sense of humor, sometimes used the word "to bless" meaning "to curse" or "to blaspheme" (I Kings 21:10,13; Job 1:5,11, 2:5,9).

BLASTUS (blăs'tŭs, Gr. *Blástos*), a chamberlain of King Agrippa (Acts 12:20) who apparently was easily bribed. The men of Tyre and Sidon used him in approaching the king.

BLESS, BLESSING (Heb. *bārakh*). 1. God blesses nature (Gen. 1:22), mankind (Gen. 1:28), the Sabbath (Gen. 2:3), nations (Ps. 33:12), classes of men (Ps. 1:1-3) and individuals (Gen. 24:1, etc.).

2. Godly men should "bless" God; i.e. they should adore him, worship him and praise him (Ps. 103:1,2, etc.),

3. Godly men by words and actions can bestow blessings on their fellows (Matt. 5:44; I Pet. 3:9).

4. In Bible times, godly men under inspiration bestowed prophetic blessings on their progeny, e.g. Noah blessing Japheth and Shem (Gen. 9:26,27), Isaac blessing Jacob and Esau (Gen. 27:27-29,39, 40), Jacob blessing the tribes of Israel (Gen. 49), and Moses also blessing them (Deut. 33).

5. We can bless things when we set them apart for sacred use e.g. the "communion cup" (I Cor. 10:16).

BLESSING, THE CUP OF. In the "communion" service, the church (i.e. the assembly of believers) blesses the cup when it is set apart for the Lord's Supper (I Cor. 10:16).

BLINDNESS (See Diseases)

BLOOD, the well-known fluid pumped by the heart all through the body of animals and of men. The word occurs over 400 times in the Scriptures, being especially frequent in Leviticus, which deals with Hebrew worship and the way to holiness; in Ezekiel, which has much to say about God's judgments; and in the letter to the Hebrews, which is the divine commentary on Leviticus. In 24 of the Bible books, the word does not occur, not because it is unimportant but because these books deal with other subjects.

The blood contains the vital principle or the essence of animal and human life (Gen. 9:4 — "But flesh with the life thereof which is the blood thereof, shall ye not eat"). Because of the sacredness of life, that energy which only God can give, the Israelites were enjoined from eating the blood, or even flesh from which the blood had not carefully been removed. This prohibition is at the basis of the Jewish usages referred to as "kosher," which prevents the orthodox Jews from buying or eating meat which has not been slaughtered and drained of blood under the supervision of a rabbi. Not only was the eating of blood forbidden to Israel, but also to the strangers who lived with Israel (Lev. 17:10-14), and the penalty for the breaking of this law was that the sinner should be "cut off from among his people." This meant at least exclusion from fellowship and probably death as well.

The book of Leviticus speaks of the blood nearly one hundred times. It is mentioned especially in chapter 17, which deals with the eating of flesh. In the various offerings (Lev. 1-7), except for the meal offering of chapter 2, the blood was to be sprinkled upon the altar, indicating the substitution of the victim's blood for that of the sinner.

Because of the sacredness of God's law and of His demand of holiness in His creature, man, from the beginning this principle has held — that "the wages of sin is death" (Rom. 6:23a); but "God is love," and so, in His infinite wisdom, He has provided an escape for the sinner. Though it is true that "without the shedding of blood, there is no remission" (Heb. 9:22), He has been pleased to accept the blood of our Lord Jesus Christ in lieu of ours, but only on condition of our belief in him. "Christ was once offered to bear the sins of many" (Heb. 9:28) and this could take place only once, and so the Old Testament offerings were provided, not to take away sin, but to point forward to the supreme sacrifice upon Calvary.

The prohibition of eating blood with the flesh, like the rest of the law, was no doubt "nailed to the cross" when our Lord's death fulfilled the demands of the law (Col. 2:14).   A.B.F.

BLOOD, AVENGER or **REVENGER OF.** Genesis 9:6, "Whoso sheddeth man's blood, by man shall his blood be shed," is the basis for capital punishment. In Israel of old, and among the Arabs and other primitive peoples of today, when murder or manslaughter was committed, the nearest of kin of the slain person took it upon himself to execute vengeance. In the law of Moses, it was recognized that the avenger would pursue a killer, and so cities of refuge were provided for those guilty of manslaughter, but not of murder (Num. 35:6). The Hebrew word for "avenger" is *go'el* and this word means also "kinsman" and "redeemer." This indicates that the executioner would ordinarily be a kinsman. In the book of Ruth, Boaz was the kinsman, who also performed the duty of a redeemer in Ruth's behalf (Ruth 4:1-8; Deut. 25:5-10). The word *go'el* had a twofold application to Boaz, who was both kinsman and redeemer to Ruth, but in the case of our Lord it is threefold. As Son of man he is our kinsman, he was our Redeemer (I Pet. 1:18, 19); and he will be the Avenger of blood (Isa. 63:1-6; Rev. 14:14-20; 19:11-21).   A.B.F.

BLOOD, ISSUE OF (See Diseases)

BLOODY SWEAT (See Diseases)

BOANERGES (bō'à-nûr'jēz, *sons of thunder*), a title bestowed by our Lord upon the two brothers James and John, the sons of Zebedee (Mark 3:17), probably because of their temperamental violence (cf. Luke 9:54-56).

BOAR (See Animals)

BOAZ (bō'ăz, Heb. *bō'az*), a well-to-do Bethlehemite in the days of the judges who became an ancestor of our Lord by marrying Ruth, the Moabitess, widow of one of the sons of Elimelech, his kinsman (Ruth 2,3,4). This was in accordance with the levirate law of Deuteronomy 25:5-10; Boaz could marry Ruth only after the nearer kinsman (Ruth 3:12; 4:1-8) had refused the privilege, or the duty. The other refused because if he had married Ruth and had had a son, a portion of his property would have gone to the credit of Elimelech's posterity, instead of his own by a former marriage. It is impossible to date Boaz exactly, because the genealogy of Ruth 4:18-22 (given in Matt. 1:4-6) is almost certainly a partial list, giving ten names to cover 800 years. The list in Matthew 1 is demonstrably schematic, as it omits four names of kings, and this one in Ruth is almost as surely so. They are both true, but, like most genealogies, partial. Salmah (or Salmon) given here as the father of Boaz, lived at the time of the Conquest, for he married Rahab, but the general setting of the story is that of a later period of settled life.

Harvesting in the fields of Boaz near Bethlehem. Scene reminiscent of Ruth 2:5. © MPS

BOAZ AND JACHIN (See Temple)

BOCHERU (bō′kĕ-rōō), a distant descendant of
Saul, at the time of the return from captivity (I
Chron. 8:38). One of the six sons of Azel.

BOCHIM (bō′kĭm, *weepers*), a name given to the
place where the Angel of Jehovah appeared and
rebuked the children of Israel because of their
failure to drive out the heathen and to destroy
their places of worship (Judg. 2:1-5).

BOHAN (bō′hăn), a descendant of Reuben after
whom a stone was named (Josh. 15:6; 18:17).
The stone was on the boundary between the tribes
of Judah and Benjamin, and was NW of the northern end of the Dead Sea and NE of Jerusalem.

BOIL (See Diseases)

BOLSTER, a head-rest, or pillow (Gen. 28:11,18;
I Sam. 19:13; 26:11,16).

BONDMAID, BONDMAN (See Occupations)

BONE. In the living body, bones form the strong
framework, and the connotation is one of strength.
"Bone of my bones and flesh of my flesh" (Gen.
2:23) was spoken in a literal sense of Eve; but
almost the same words (Gen. 29:14), spoken by
Laban to Jacob, are figurative and show only kinship. Strong chastening is thought of as a bone-
breaking experience (Ps. 51:8), and the terrible
writhing on the cross of Calvary literally threw
bones out of joint (Ps. 22:14). Dry bones form a
picture of hopeless death (Ezek. 37:1-12). The
paschal lamb, without a broken bone (Exod. 12:
46) was a type of the Lamb of God (John 19:36).

BOOK, generally a literary production having more
or less unity of purpose. Books may be classified
by their forms or subjects, but more particularly
by the nature and quality of the written material
within. In ancient Assyria and Babylonia much of
the writing which was thought to be of value was
done in wedge-shaped characters on soft clay which
was then baked, and the "libraries" were, in form,
almost like piles of brick.

In ancient Egypt, men early learned to press
and glue thin sheets of the papyrus plant into
sheets of "paper"; the writing was in narrow columns upon sheets of regular size which were then
glued together and wound around two sticks, thus
forming a "volumen" or roll. Still later, men
learned to bind the sheets together into a "codex"
very similar to our modern books. "Book" in the
Bible always refers to a roll, which word occurs
14 times in Jeremiah 36. In Pergamum, in the
second century B.C., due to the scarcity of paper,
men learned to dress the skin of calves and of kids.
This new substance was named "parchment" in
honor of its origin, and almost displaced papyrus
in many regions.

In ancient books made of papyrus or of parchment, the writing was generally upon one side of
each sheet, but occasionally, owing to afterthoughts,
material was written also on the backside (see Rev.
5:1). When a book was sealed, the contents were
made secret, and when unsealed they were open
(cf. Dan. 12:4,9 and Rev. 5:1-4 on the one hand,
with Rev. 5:5; 22:10 on the other). Only the Son
of God was found worthy to open the seals of
the book of the future which had been locked in
the hands of "him that sat on the throne."

Judaism, Christianity and Islam are all "book-
ish" religions and their main books have greatly
changed the history of the human race.

The Bible is *the* book, God's word, and it differs
from all other books in that it alone is inspired
(God-breathed). The Bible originally had 63 books,
as the division of Samuel, Kings and Chronicles

Ancient Hebrew scrolls in a synagogue in the old
city of Jerusalem. © MPS

into "First" and "Second" was not originally intended. The larger books were generally written
upon separate rolls (see Luke 4:17) but sometimes
the "megilloth" (Ruth, Esther, Lamentations, Song
of Solomon and Ecclesiastes) were bound together,
as were also "The Twelve" i.e. the Minor Prophets.
Many books which have been lost are mentioned
in the Bible: e.g. "the book of Jasher" (Josh. 10:
13), "the Acts of Solomon" (I Kings 11:41) etc.
The word "book" is also used figuratively as in
"the Lamb's book of life" (Rev. 21:27). A.B.F.

Famous library of the Monastery of St. Katherine at
Sinai. © MPS

BOOTH, a simple, temporary shelter generally constructed of tree-branches with the leaves left on. It was used by the guardian of a vineyard or vegetable garden when the fruit was fit to be stolen. Sometimes used for a larger enclosure (Gen. 33:17) such as Jacob built for his cattle. (Cf. Isa. 1:8 ARV)

BOOTY, that which is taken from a defeated enemy. In the law, as given through Moses, very different arrangements were made for varying circumstances. In the case of some very wicked heathen cities, everything was to be "devoted" to the Lord; i.e. to be destroyed absolutely so as not to be used by any man, except for some metallic vessels which could be sterilized by fire (Josh. 6:18-21). Persons who were taken as prey could sometimes be enslaved (Deut. 20:14), but in other cases must be utterly destroyed (Deut. 20:16-18). The purpose here was to prevent the heathen from teaching their abominations to God's people, Israel. Cf. I Samuel 15, where Saul's hypocritical half-obedience brought ruin upon himself and his house.

The very practical question as to the division of the booty was solved partly by custom, as when Abram freely devoted a tenth of the spoil to the Lord by giving it to Melchizedek (Gen. 14:20), and partly by legislation, as when David ordered that booty be shared equally by those who because of weariness could not continue in battle (I Sam. 30:21-25).

BOOZ (See Boaz)

BORROW, BORROWING. The Semitic peoples, as a general thing, have "an eye to business," and it seems quite natural when leaving a place of service, whether as a hireling or a slave, to ask for a gift. In Exodus 3:22, 11:2, 12:35 the KJV unfortunately translates the Hebrew verb *shā'al* ("ask") by the verb "borrow," and so gives the wrong impression that the Israelites cheated the Egyptians, and worse still that the Lord encouraged this "borrowing." The fact is that the Egyptians, thoroughly cowed by the rigors of the ten plagues, were willing to give largely in order to get rid of their troublesome "guests"; and God, in His providence, allowed Israel to despoil the Egyptians (Exod. 12:36), in order to provide gold and silver for the tabernacle which was to be constructed. "Surely the wrath of man shall praise thee" (Ps. 76:10).

The law of Moses gives careful directions concerning the responsibility of those who borrow, or who hold property in trust, or who are criminally careless in regard to the property of another (Exod. 22:1-15). Among the blessings promised Israel on condition of obedience is that they would be lenders and not borrowers (Deut. 28:12).

BOSCATH (See Bozkath)

BOSOM (boōz'ŭm). Although in English the word means the part of the body between the arms, in Scripture it is generally used in an affectionate sense, e.g. "the Son, who is in the bosom of the Father" (John 1:18), carrying the lambs in his bosom (Isa. 40:11), John leaning on the bosom of Jesus (John 13:23), or Lazarus in Abraham's bosom (Luke 16:22,23). It can be almost synonymous with "heart" as the center of one's life, as in Ecclesiastes 7:9, "anger resteth in the bosom of fools," or Psalm 35:13, "my prayer returned unto mine own bosom." Quite commonly, of course, it refers to conjugal love, as in Micah 7:5, "her that lieth in thy bosom." We read also of the bosom as a place of hiding money (Prov. 17:23).

BOSOR (Same as Beor, See Balaam)

BOSSES, the convex projection in the center of a shield (Job 15:26).

BOTCH (See Diseases)

BOTTLE. 1. Container made of goat-skin, sewed up with the hair outside and used for carrying water (Gen. 21:14-19), for storing wine (Josh. 9:4,13), for fermenting milk into "leben" or "yogurt" (Judg. 4:19, etc.). The fact that fermenting wine expands and stretches its container is used by our Lord in His discourse about putting new wine into old bottles (Luke 5:37,38). A new skin bottle would be elastic enough to stretch with the pressure of the fermenting wine, whereas an old stiff wine-skin would burst. Our Lord's teaching here is that Christianity cannot be contained in Judaism, nor can grace be confined in the bonds of the law. This meaning of "bottles" is used figuratively by Elihu in Job 32:19 as indicating his feeling that he must relieve himself by speaking.

2. Container made of baked clay, and hence very fragile (Jer. 19:1-11). As Jeremiah broke the bottle, so God would deal in fury with Israel.

3. Beautifully designed glass bottles, often found in Egyptian tombs, were used originally for burying some of the tears of the mourners with the deceased. See Psalm 56:8: "Put thou my tears into thy bottle."

4. The word rendered "bottles" in Hosea 7:5 could better be translated "heat" or "fury."

5. Figuratively, the clouds as the source of rain (Job 38:37).

6. Psalm 119:83, "I am become like a bottle in the smoke" does not refer, as some think, "to a custom," but rather to careless housekeeping. In the smoke of a kitchen without windows or chimney, a leather vessel which hung there would soon become brittle and dry. A.B.F.

Water carriers using goatskin "bottles." © MPS

BOTTOMLESS PIT (See Abyss)

BOUNDARY STONES. Our God is a God of order and not of confusion; and so in the matter of property, He not only set careful bounds to the land of His people (Josh. 13-21), but provided a curse for those who remove their neighbors' landmarks (Deut. 27:17; cf. 19:14). Figuratively, this implies a decent regard for ancient institutions (Prov. 22:28; 23:10).

BOW (See Arms and Armor)

BOW (See Rainbow)

BOWELS, in the KJV occurs 36 times, and in three principal senses: 1. Literally (II Chron. 21:15-19; Acts 1:18).

2. As the generative parts of our bodies whether male or female (Gen. 15:4; Ps. 71:6).

3. The seat of the emotions, as we use the word "heart." (See Lam. 1:20 [ASV "heart"]; Phil. 1:8 [ASV "tender mercies"]).

BOWL (bōl). There are a number of Heb. and Gr. words rendered "bowl" in the RV. 1. *sēphel,* a large, flat earthenware dish for holding something like milk (Judg. 5:25).

2. *mizrāq,* sometimes also rendered "basin", large costly bowls, like the silver bowls presented by the princes of the congregation (Num. 7:13f).

3. *gāvia',* rendered "pot" by the KJV in Jeremiah 35:5; a large silver bowl like the kind used at banquets to replenish drinking cups.

4. *gullâh,* the receptacle for oil in the candlestick of Zechariah's vision (Zech. 4:3), and the bowl-shaped capitals of Jachin and Boaz (I Kings 7:41,42; II Chron. 4:12,13).

5. *kubba'ath kôs,* RV "bowl of the cup"; KJV "dregs of the cup" (Isa. 51:41,42).

6. *phiále,* RV "bowl," KJV "vial" (Rev. 5:8, etc.).

BOX, BOX TREE (See Plants)

BOZEZ (bō'zĕz), a rocky crag near Gibeah (I Sam. 14:4). Because one of General Allenby's officers read this account, the British followed the route of Jonathan and attacked the Turks here in 1918, conquering them even as Jonathan and his armorbearer defeated the Philistines.

BOZKATH or **BOSCATH** (bŏz'kăth), a city of Judah (Josh. 15:39), the home of the maternal grandfather of king Josiah (II Kings 22:1).

BOZRAH (bŏz'rà, Heb. *bŏtsrâh, sheepfold*). 1. An important city of Edom, the residence of Jobab, one of Edom's early kings (Gen. 36:33). In Jeremiah 49:13,22, where the approaching doom of Edom is given, Bozrah is especially mentioned, and in Amos 1:12 we read of its palaces. The place is identified as the modern village of "el-Busaireh" i.e. "the little Bozrah," a few miles SE of the Dead Sea near the road toward Petra. In Micah 2:12 the word is probably "Bozrah," though it can be read as a common noun, i.e. "a sheepfold."

2. In Jeremiah 48:24 the word refers to a town in Moab. It lies about 75 miles S of Damascus, and was enlarged and beautified (c. A.D. 106) by the emperor Trajan who made it the capital of the province of Arabia.

BRACELET, properly a circlet for the wrist, but the word translates in the KJV five different Hebrew nouns. In II Samuel 1:10 the word probably means "armlet" as a mark of royalty; in Exodus 35:22 it could be "brooches," as in ASV, or "clasps"; in Genesis 38:18,25 it represents the cords about the neck from which the signet ring was suspended (see ASV in loc); in Genesis 24: 22, etc., it is properly 'bracelet," from the root

Boundary stone of Nebuchadnezzar I, picturing many gods and goddesses. BM

meaning, "something bound on," and so in Ezekiel 16:11 and 23:42, and in Isaiah 3:19, in the interesting inventory of 21 items of feminine adornment, it could be rendered "twisted chains." Bracelets and other rather showy adornments (anklets, nose-rings, armlets, etc.) were much admired in ancient days. See DRESS.

BRAMBLE (See Plants)

BRANCH, a word representing 18 different Hebrew and four Greek words in the Bible. The most interesting use of it is as a title applied to the Messiah as the offspring of David (Jer. 23:5; 33:15; Zech. 3:8; 6:12).

BRASS, next to silver and gold, the most frequently mentioned metal in Scripture. Today, brass is an alloy of copper and zinc, whereas bronze is an alloy of copper with tin; but the OT uses one word (or rather four words from one root) for copper (Job 28:2), bronze (II Sam. 22:35 probably), and brass (Dan. 10:6, cf. Rev. 1:15). Copper and its alloys were among the earliest metals worked by man; Tubal-cain (Gen. 4:22) being the first man mentioned as a worker in brass and iron. Most of the vessels for the courts of the tabernacle and of the temple were of "brass." In Nebuchadnezzar's vision (Dan. 2:31-39) the "belly and thighs of brass" signified the then future dominion of Greece, whose soldiers were notable for their brazen shields and weapons. The brazen cooking vessels of today in the East are mostly of copper, prevented from poisoning the food by a thin plating of tin which needs frequently to be restored by a process similar to soldering.

BRAY. 1. The ass brays when hungry (Job 6:5), and some low-grade people are described contemptuously as braying (Job 30:7).

2. To pound or "bray" as in a mortar (Prov. 27:22). This word, related to the verb "to break," is rare both in English and in Hebrew, but is easily understood by the context.

BRAZEN SEA. In II Kings 25:13, I Chronicles 18:8, and Jeremiah 52:17, we read of the great "sea of brass," a rather exaggerated figure for the immense laver which Solomon placed in front of the temple for washing the sacrifices and the bodies of the priests.

BRAZEN SERPENT. Numbers 21:4-9 records how the people of Israel complained against Moses and against God, who in judgment sent fiery serpents against them. When the people confessed their sin, Moses made a "serpent of brass," set it upon a pole and in effect said, "Look and live"; and whosoever looked recovered. This brazen serpent later was worshiped, but Hezekiah contemptuously called it "a piece of brass" (II Kings 18:4) and destroyed it. This brazen serpent was a type of our Lord bearing our sins on the cross (John 3:14-16).

BREAD, the "staff of life," generally baked from dough made of wheat flour which has been leavened (raised by means of fermenting yeast) and made into loaves of various shapes and sizes. At the time of the Passover (Exod. 12), the Israelites ate unleavened bread because of their haste, and ever afterward they memorialized this in their annual feast of unleavened bread (Exod. 12:15-20). In times of distress and of famine, barley was used

Grinding meal and baking bread. © SPF

instead of wheat. It was used by the poorer classes as a general thing. In Judges 7:13, the Midianite's dream of a barley loaf, which was interpreted as "the sword of Gideon," perhaps hinted at the poverty of Israel under Midianite oppression; and in John 6:9 the boy's store of five barley loaves would suggest that he came from a family or a region which could not afford the more delicious and nutritious wheat bread.

In the more primitive parts of Syria today, there are several sorts of wheat bread. In some villages, a barrel-shaped hole in the ground is used as an oven and the women adroitly knead the bread into large thin sheets which they lay on cushions and slap against the hot wall of the oven. Though dried dung mixed with straw is used as fuel, the taste is not impaired. Ezekiel 4:9-17 gives a vivid picture of baking in famine times. In other villages of Syria, a convex sheet of iron is placed over an open fire and the bread is similarly baked; but in the larger towns and cities there are bakeries to which the people bring their loaves for baking. The long stone oven is heated for hours, then the raised loaves, about eight to ten inches in diameter and one-fourth inch thick, are placed inside by means of a long wooden paddle. The heat quickly bakes the surface, and gas forming inside splits the loaves; then they are turned and soon removed (Hos. 7:8).

"Bread," as the most universal solid food, is often used figuratively for food in general. Genesis 3:19, "in the sweat of thy face shalt thou eat bread," Matthew 6:11, "Give us this day our daily bread," and similar passages refer to all sustenance. The word "bread" is used by the Lord in a mystical, but very true and precious sense in His discourse on "the bread of life" in John 6:43-59. As important as is solid food ("bread") to our bodies, so necessary is the Lord to spiritual life. And so, in the "breaking of bread" at our "communion" services, some partake in a very real way of Christ, while others, not discerning the body, eat and drink condemnation to themselves. In the tabernacle and in the Temple, the loaves of shew-bread indicated the presence of the Lord, the "Bread of life" among His people.   A.B.F.

BREAD, SHEW (See Bread)
BREECHES (See Dress; Inner Tunic)
BRICK, building material made of clay dried in the sun. The word for "brick" in the Hebrew is derived from the verb "to be white" and is almost identical with "Lebanon," so-named for its snow-clad mountain tops. The very name would lead us to expect the oriental bricks to be whitish in color, rather than red like our more common brick. The earliest mention of brick in the Bible (Gen. 11:3) shows that the molding of clay into brick and its thorough burning were known when the tower of Babel was built, not more than a century after the Flood; and the finding of potsherds *under* the Flood deposits at Ur and Kish shows that the allied art of making clay into pottery was known before the Flood.

Owing to the prevalence of stone in Egypt, and its comparative rarity in lower Mesopotamia, the use of brick for building was much more common in Chaldea than in Egypt, though the sad record of the bondage of Israel in Egypt (Exod. 1:11-14; 5:7-19) shows that at least some cities in Egypt were built of brick rather than of stone. In fact, the ruins of Pithom have been found with the three grades of brick *in situ*: bricks with binding material of straw at the bottom; above them, brick made of stubble; and at the top, bricks of pure clay with no binding material at all. The ancient

Making bricks of clay. © SPF

bricks were generally square instead of oblong, and were much larger than ours; something like 13 x 13 x 3½ inches, and often were stamped before baking with the name of the monarch: e.g. Sargon or Nebuchadnezzar. Much of the ancient brick-work was of bricks merely baked in the sun, especially in Egypt, but at Babylon the bricks were thoroughly burned. In Jeremiah 43:9 (KJV) we read of a "brick kiln" in Egypt in the sixth century B.C. The ASV renders the word "brickwork," but II Samuel 12:31 clearly speaks of a brick kiln back in David's time, and Nahum, taunting the Ninevites four centuries later (Nah. 3:14) tells them to "make strong the brick kiln." In Isaiah 9:10 the "pride and stoutness of heart" of the Israelites is rebuked because they intended to replace the thrown-down bricks with stone, even as many a modern city has been rebuilt after a catastrophe. The sin was not in their desire for improvement, but in their impious and profane pride.   A.B.F.

BRIDE, BRIDEGROOM (See Wedding)

BRIDECHAMBER (See Wedding)

BRIDGE. The word "bridge" is not found in the English Bible. The idea of a bridge must have been suggested early, perhaps by a plank or fallen tree across a small stream, but Israelites seem to have been more talented commercially (Deut. 8: 17,18) than as engineers; and so they generally crossed a stream by a ford (Gen. 32:22; Josh. 2:7; Judg. 3:28) or in some cases by a ferry-boat (II Sam. 19:18). Although the principle of the arch was early known, as seen in two stones leaning against each other to bridge a small gap in Mycenaean ruins, it was not till the time of the Roman Empire that the magnificent arches, bridges and and aqueducts appeared and that the bridge may be said to have come into its own.

BRIDLE, the part of a harness that surrounds the head of the beast and connects the bit with the reins. It occurs properly, seven times in the OT and represents two words: one used in Proverbs 26:3, "a bridle for the ass," and the other in Psalm 32:9, "with bit and bridle." In Psalm 39:1 the word should be "muzzle." In the NT the word occurs once (Rev. 14:20) and the corresponding verb

twice (James 1:26; 3:2). The ancient Assyrians sometimes bridled their captives. In Isaiah 37:29 God is represented as about to bridle the Assyrians in a similar way, but, of course, figuratively.

BRIER (See Plants)

BRIMSTONE, properly sulphur. The Hebrew word is related to "*gopher*," a resinous wood which was used in the construction of the ark; and so its root meaning is "resinous" or "highly combustible." It is generally connected with judgment, as when the Lord rained brimstone and fire upon Sodom and Gomorrah (Gen. 19:24; cf. Ps. 11:6), or as when the dust of Edom shall be turned into brimstone (Isa. 34:9), and in the NT, where "fire and brimstone" are principal elements in the punishment of the wicked in Gehenna, or the "lake of fire" (Rev. 20:10; 21:8). In Revelation 9:17, "fire, jacinth, brimstone" refer to colors — red, blue, yellow.

BRONZE, an alloy of copper with tin. The word is not found in Scripture, but probably the "steel" used as a material for making metallic bows (II Sam. 22:35; Job 20:24; Ps. 18:34) was really bronze. Bronze is much more elastic than brass, and so is more suitable for bows and for bells than the other alloy. Since there are so many varying proportions in which copper can be alloyed with tin, it is difficult to describe accurately "copper" (Ezra 8:27), and "brass" (Exod. 35:5, et seq.), and to be sure whether or not bronze is intended.

BROOK, a small stream. One of "the sweet words of Scripture," because the Bible was written in lands near the desert, and by men who therefore appreciated water. Many brooks are named in the Bible: Kidron (II Sam. 15:23), Besor (I Sam. 30: 9) et al. In Isaiah 19:6-8 the word rendered "brooks" in the KJV seems to refer to the Nile or its irrigating streams (see ASV). In Psalm 42: 1 the word rendered "brooks" seems to mean "channels" and is generally rendered "rivers" (S. of Sol. 5:12; Ezek. 36:4,6, etc.). The word *nahal*, rendered "brook" over 40 times in the KJV, often means "a wadi"; i.e. a torrent in winter and spring, which dries up in summer.

BROTHER. 1. A male person related to another person or other persons by having the same parents (Gen. 27:6), or the same father (Gen. 28:2), or the same mother (Judg. 8:19).

2. A man of the same country (Exod. 2:11; Acts 3:22).

3. A member of the same tribe (II Sam. 19:12).

4. An ally (Amos 1:9).

5. One of a kindred people (Num. 20:14).

6. A co-religionist (Acts 9:17; I Cor. 6:6); often, Christian disciples (Matt. 23:8; Rom. 1:13).

7. A fellow office-bearer (Ezra 3:2).

8. Someone of equal rank or office (I Kings 9: 13).

9. Any member of the human race (Matt. 7: 3-5; Heb. 2:17). Someone spiritually akin (Matt. 12:50).

BROTHERS OF OUR LORD. Were it not for the prevalence of the false doctrine of "the perpetual virginity of the blessed Virgin" this subject would hardly have seemed worthy of the long discussions which have been written about it. The expression in Matthew 1:25, "and knew her not till she had brought forth her first-born son; and he called his name Jesus," testifies not only to the fact of the virgin birth of our Lord, but also to the other items, well-known later, that she bore to Joseph several children while Jesus was growing up. Mark 6:3, "Is not this the carpenter, the son of Mary, the brother of James, and Joses, and of Juda and Simon? and are not his sisters here with us?" testifies that when Jesus was a little more than 30 years of age he had at least six uterine brothers and sisters. If, as some have ingeniously argued, these had been sons of Joseph by a previous marriage, the whole argument of this passage would have lost its force.

John 7:1-10 states that the brothers of Jesus, in the midst of His ministry did not believe in Him, though it is almost a certainty that James was not only the human leader of the first church at Jerusalem by 50 A.D. (Acts 15:13, 21:18) but the writer of the epistle that bears his name; and that Jude, the author of the epistle, was the "Juda" (ASV "Judas") of Mark 6:3. The fact of their not claiming to be his brethren in the headings of their respective epistles is beautiful evidence of their Christian humility and of their reverence for His position as their Lord.

Of Joses (Tischendorf "Joseph") and of Simon, there is no further record. One would hardly expect four sons of a carpenter to have had prominent places in the early church.

The genealogists work out with much detail a list of the "kinsmen" of our Lord, making James and John His first cousins, Joseph of Arimathea the uncle of His mother, etc.; whereas the only hint of Christ's human relation in the Bible is where Elisabeth, mother of John the Baptist, is called "cousin" (ASV "kinswoman") of Mary (Luke 1:36). A.B.F.

BUCKET or **PAIL,** a vessel for drawing or holding water, found only in two verses of Scripture. In Isaiah 40:15 all the nations, compared with God, are but as the last drop in a bucket which has just been emptied. In Numbers 24:7 the reference is to a numerous posterity.

BUKKI (bŭk'ī). 1. A prince of the tribe of Dan chosen to help Joshua divide the land (Num. 34:22).

2. Son of Abishua, and high priest of Israel (I Chron. 6:5,51; Ezra 7:4).

BUKKIAH (bŭ-kī'à), one of the sons of Heman (I Chron. 25:4,13), who were appointed over the service of song in the time of David. Bukkiah had in his group at least 11 of his "sons and his brethren."

BUL (bool), the eighth month of the Jewish ecclesiastical year (I Kings 6:38), fitting into November and/or December of our calendar.

BULL (See Animals: Cattle)

BULLOCK (See Animals: Cattle)

BULRUSH (See Plants)

BUNAH (bū'nà), a great-great-grandson of Judah (I Chron. 2:25) in the early days of the judges.

BUNNI (bŭn'ī), three Levites mentioned in Nehemiah had this name. 1. A helper of Ezra (Neh. 9:4).

2. An early dweller in Jerusalem in the fifth century B.C. (Neh. 11:15).

3. One of the chief covenanters with Nehemiah (Neh. 10:15).

BURDEN, that which is laid upon one in order to be carried. The word translates eight different words in the OT and three in the NT. When it is literally used, it is easily understood and needs no special comment. Figuratively, it is used in the sense of "responsibility" (Num. 11:11; Matt. 11:30) or of a "sorrow" (Ps. 55:22), but by far the most frequent use in the OT is "oracle" (Isa. 15:1; 19:1; 22:1, etc.). These are generally "dooms," though in Zechariah 12:1 and in Malachi 1:1 the word is used simply for a "message."

Mummy of Amenophis II in royal tomb at Thebes, Egypt. © MPS

BURIAL, the act of placing a dead body in a tomb, in the earth or in the sea, generally with appropriate ceremonies; as opposed to exposure to the beasts, or abandonment or burning. Various peoples, notably the Egyptians, who believed that their dead would live and practice ordinary human occupations in "the land of the dead," often went to great lengths to preserve the bodies of their departed loved ones. They sometimes placed with the mummy tools or instruments or weapons, and occasionally slew and buried a wife or a servant to accompany the one whom they had buried.

Partly because of God's word, "Dust thou art and to dust thou shalt return" (Gen. 3:19), the people of Israel almost always buried their dead; and because the land of Canaan had so many caves, these places were very frequently used as places of burial. Probably the prevailing motive for our respect for the dead, and even for the place of burial is the sense of decency, and our feeling of love for the person, often without regarding the fact that the real person has gone and that only his former "residence" remains.

The story of the treatment of the bodies of Saul and of his sons sheds light on the whole subject. The Philistines beheaded the bodies, exhibiting the heads throughout their land and fastening Saul's body to the wall of Bethshan (I Sam. 31:8-13). The men of Israel rescued the bodies, burned them, and reverently buried the bones under a tree and mourned seven days.

It is remarkable that although God had given to Abraham the deed of the land of Canaan (Gen. 15:18-21), the only land which the patriarchs possessed before Joshua's time was the burial places for the original family: a cave at Hebron, and a field at Shechem (cf. Gen. 23 — the burial of Sarah, Gen. 49:29-32 — Jacob's final request, and Josh. 25:32,33 — the burial of the mummy of Joseph and the body of Eleazar). In Canaan, in ancient times, and in the more primitive parts of the land even today, there was (and is) no embalmment in most cases, but immediate burial to avoid unpleasant odors (Acts 5:5-10) and ceremonial uncleanness (Num. 19:11-22). In the time of Christ, men's bodies were wrapped in clean linen (Matt. 27:57-60) and spices and ointments were prepared (Luke 23:56).

The strange story of the dead Moabite reviving when he touched the bones of Elisha (II Kings 13: 20,21), shows not only the speedy decomposition of a body, but the informality of burials in the time of war or necessity; and the still stranger story of the disobedient prophet (I Kings 13) shows how a heathen altar could be defiled by the burning of bones upon it (13:1-3) and the desire of a prophet to be buried near another whom he honored (13:30,31). In several cases of sinful rulers, ordinary burial was denied to their bodies: the dogs ate Jezebel (II Kings 9:10); Jehoram of Judah, who died with incurable diseases, was not buried with the kings (II Chron. 21:18-20); Uzziah was buried in a field, not in the tombs of the kings (II Chron. 26:23); and Jehoiakim was buried with the burial of an ass (Jer. 22:18,19).

BURNING. God's judgments have often been accompanied with fire, e.g. Sodom and Gomorrah (Gen. 19:24-28), Nadab and Abihu (Lev. 10:1-6), the 250 rebels in the wilderness (Num. 16:2,35). The final dissolution of this present evil world is to be with fierce fire (II Pet. 3:7-10,12).

BURNING BUSH, a thorny bush which Moses saw burning and from which he heard Jehovah speak (Exod. 3:2,3; Deut. 33:16; Mark 12:26). Many attempts have been made to identify the bush, but without success. There are varied interpretations of the exact meaning of the incident as a method of revelation. There are three other theophanies with fire in the Bible: Exodus 13:21; 19:18; II Thess. 1:8 KJV (yet to be fulfilled).

BURNT OFFERING (See Offerings)

BUSH (See Plants)

BUSHEL (See Weights & Measures)

BUSINESS (See Trade and Travel)

BUTLER (See Occupations and Professions)

BUTTER. After the milk has been churned and the "butter" (in our sense of the word) produced, it is boiled and the curds separated from the almost pure oil; this is poured into a goatskin and kept until slightly rancid (to western taste) and then is used with food, but more generally for frying eggs or vegetables. It is mentioned eleven times in the OT, of which three are figurative uses: (Job 20:17, "the brooks of honey and butter"; 29:6, "when I washed my steps with butter"; and Psalm 55:21, "the words of his mouth were smoother than butter, but war was in his heart"). In the other cases, where the word is used literally, e.g. Gen. 18:8, it implies good eating.

BUZ (bŭz). 1. A nephew of Abraham, second son of Nahor (Gen. 22:21) whose family apparently settled in Arabia. See Jeremiah 25:23, where Buz is mentioned with various districts of Arabia. The word means "contempt" and probably illustrates an eastern superstition of giving a baby an unpleasant name so as "to avert the evil eye." One belonging to this region was a "Buzite" (see Job 32:2,6). 2. Head of a family in the tribe of Gad (I Chron. 5:14) otherwise unknown.

BUZI (bū'zī), Ezekiel's father (Ezek. 1:3).

BYBLOS (See Gebal)

BYWAYS, literally "crooked paths." The word occurs only in Judges 5:6. On account of the oppression of the enemies of Israel (Philistines and Canaanites), people dared not walk on the highways, but kept out of sight by using little-known crooked paths.

C

CAB (căb, *a hollow vessel,* ASV "kab"), a measure of capacity, a little less than two quarts; mentioned only in II Kings 6:25.

CABBON (kăb'ŏn), a town in Judah, taken by Israel from the Amorites (Josh. 15:40). It may be the same as Machbena (I Chron. 2:49).

CABUL (kā'bŭl). 1. A city of Galilee, mentioned in Joshua 19:27 as a border city of the tribe of Asher in the NE of Palestine. It lies between the hills about nine miles SE of Acre and is still inhabited. 2. A name given by Hiram of Tyre to a district in N Galilee, including twenty cities, which Solomon ceded to him (I Kings 9:13) and which probably included the original Cabul. It seems from II Chronicles 8:2 that Hiram (Huram) returned these cities and that Solomon rebuilt them.

CAESAR (sē'zêr). 1. The name of a Roman family prominent from the third century B.C., of whom Caius Julius Caesar (c. 102-—Mar. 15,44 B.C.) was by far the most prominent. 2. The title taken by each of the Roman emperors: e.g. Augustus Caesar who reigned when our Lord was born (Luke 2:1); his successor Tiberius Caesar who reigned 14-37 A.D. (Luke 3:1); Claudius Caesar, 41-54 (Acts 11:28; 18:2). Nero, under whom Peter and Paul were martyred, 54-68 (Philip. 4:22). Domitian was "Caesar" from 81-96 and it was under him that John was exiled to Patmos. "Caesar" is mentioned by our Lord (Luke 20:22-25) both literally as referring to Tiberius, and figuratively as meaning any earthly ruler. The name Caesar came to be used as a symbol of the state in general, and is often used in this sense in the NT (Matt. 22:17,21; Mark 12:14,16,17; Luke 20:22,24,25).

CAESAREA (sĕs'à-rē'à), a city built between 25-13 B.C. by Herod "the Great" at a vast cost and named in honor of his patron Augustus Caesar. It lay on the coast of the Mediterranean about 25 miles NW of Samaria which Herod had rebuilt and renamed "Sebaste," also in honor of Augusta. Herod intended it as the port of his capital, and

Caesarea on the Mediterranean. Ruins of the ancient seafront from which Paul set sail for Rome and where Peter preached to Cornelius. © MPS

a splendid harbor was constructed. Great stone blocks were used to top the reefs that helped to form the harbor. Being military headquarters for the Roman forces, and the residence of the procurators, it was the home of Cornelius in whose house Peter first preached to the Gentiles (Acts 10). It was the place of residence of Philip, the evangelist, with his four unmarried prophesying daughters (Acts 8:40; 21:8,9), who entertained Paul and Luke and their party on their return from the third missionary journey. Later it was the enforced residence of Paul while he was a prisoner for two years, and there Paul preached before King Agrippa (Acts 23:31-26:32). The Jewish war which Josephus described with such power and pathos, and which culminated in the destruction of Jerusalem, had its origin in a riot in Caesarea. Here Vespasian was proclaimed emperor of Rome in the year 69, while he was engaged in the Jewish war. In church history it was the birthplace of Eusebius (c. 260 A.D.) and the seat of his bishopric. Caesarea is still called Kaysārīyeh.

CAESAREA PHILIPPI (sĕs'à-rē'à fĭ-lĭp'ī, *Caesarea of Philip*), a town at the extreme northern boundary of Palestine, about 30 miles inland from Tyre and 50 miles SW of Damascus. It lies in the beautiful hill country on the southern slopes of Mt. Hermon, and was probably very near the scene of our Lord's transfiguration. (Cf. Matt. 16:13-17: 8; Mark 8:27-9:8). The town was very ancient, being perhaps the Baal-gad of Joshua 12:7, 13:5, and for centuries it was a center of worship of the heathen god "Pan," whence it was known as "Paneas" and whence the modern name Banias (because there is no "p" in the Arabic alphabet).

Augustus Caesar presented it, with the surrounding country, to Herod the Great, who built a temple there in honor of the emperor. Herod's son, Philip the tetrarch, enlarged the town and named it Caesarea Philippi to distinguish it from the other Caesarea. It lies at the easternmost of the four sources of the Jordan, and near here these streams unite to form the main river. It was at a secluded spot near here that the Lord began to prepare His disciples for His approaching sufferings and death and resurrection, and that Peter made his famous confession (Matt. 16:13-17).

CAGE, so-called when used by the fowler to keep his live birds, but "basket" when used for fruit (Jer. 5:27; Amos 8:1,2). Cf. Revelation 18:2 KJV.

CAIAPHAS, JOSEPH (kā'yà-făs). In the century from 168 B.C. when Antiochus Epiphanes desecrated the temple, to 66 B.C. when the Romans took over, the high-priesthood was almost a political office, the priests still coming from the descendants of Aaron but being generally appointed for worldly considerations.

From 66 B.C. the Roman rulers appointed not only the civil officers (e.g. Herod) but the high-priests as well with the result that the office declined spiritually. Annas, the father-in-law of Caiaphas (John 18:13) had been high-priest by appointment of the Roman governor from 7 A.D. to 14 (see Luke 3:2) and though three of his sons succeeded for a short period, Caiaphas held the office from A.D. 18-36, with Annas still a sort of "high-priest emeritus." After our Lord had raised Lazarus from the dead (John 11) many of the Jews believed in Him (11:45,46), but some

View of Caesarea Philippi on slopes of Mount Hermon, the scene of Peter's historic confession of Christ's divinity. The village is now known as Benaias. © MPS

through jealousy reported the matter to the Pharisees, who with the chief priests gathered a council, fearing, or pretending to fear, that if Jesus were let alone many would accept Him, and the Romans would destroy what was left of Jewish autonomy. Then Caiaphas (John 11:41-53) declared that it would be better for Jesus to die than that the nation be destroyed. When, a little later, our Lord was betrayed into the hands of His enemies, the Roman soldiers and the Jewish officers took Him first to the house of Annas, where by night He was given the pretense of a trial (John 18:12-23). Then Annas sent Him bound to Caiaphas before whom the "trial" continued (John 18:24-27). Thence He was delivered to Pilate, because the Jews could not legally execute Him.   A.B.F.

CAIN (kān). 1. The first son of Adam and Eve, and a farmer by occupation. As an offering to God, he brought some of the fruits of the ground, while his brother brought an animal sacrifice. Angry that his offering was not received (Heb. 11:4 shows that this was because of the lack of a right disposition toward Jehovah), he slew his brother. He added to his guilt before God by denying his guilt and giving no evidence of repentance. He fled to the land of Nod and there built a city, becoming the ancestor of a line which included Jabal, forefather of tent-dwelling cattle-keepers; Jubal, forefather of musicians; Tubal-cain, forefather of smiths; and Lamech, a man of violence. His wife must have been one of his own sisters — not an impropriety in those days.

2. The progenitor of the Kenites (Josh. 15:57).
3. A village in Judah (Josh. 15:57).

CAINAN (kā-ī'năn). 1. In ASV "Kenan," the fourth from Adam in the Messianic line (Gen. 5:12-14; I Chron. 1:2; Luke 3:37).

2. A son of Arphaxad (Luke 3:36), omitted in Genesis 10:24; 11:12, but found in the LXX, from which Luke quotes.

CALAH (kā'là), a very ancient city of Assyria on the upper reaches of the Tigris, built originally by Nimrod, who is listed in Genesis 10:6-12 as a grandson of Ham, son of Noah. According to KJV, the builder was "Asshur" an eponym for Assyria, but cf. ASV. The city was apparently rebuilt by Shalmanezer I (reigned c. 1456-1436 B.C.), then later abandoned for many centuries till Ashurnasir-pal who is pictured as "Ruthlessness Incarnate" (reigned c. 926-902 B.C.) restored it. Aside from the Bible mention, the city is famous for having been the site of immense statuary in the form of winged lions and winged bulls some of which can be seen in the British Museum today. Several great palaces have been excavated there, and the place is now known as "Nimrud."

CALCOL (See Chalcol)

CALDRON, a large pot or vessel in which meat is to be boiled (Jer. 52:18,19 [ASV "pots"]; Ezek. 11:3,7,11). In Job 41:20 it is probably a mistranslation.

CALEB (kā'lĕb, *dog*). 1. The son of Jephunneh, the Kenezite; the prince of Judah who represented his tribe among the twelve chief men whom Moses sent from the wilderness to Paran to spy out the land (Num. 13:6). Most of the spies brought back a pessimistic report. Their names are almost forgotten, but two heroes of faith, Caleb and Joshua, who encouraged the people to go up and take the land are still remembered. Because Israel in cowardice adopted the majority report, God imposed upon them forty years "wandering" in the wilderness till that generation should die out. Caleb was

House of Caiaphas on Mount Zion, Jerusalem. Above, the approach; below, courtyard interior. © MPS

40 years old when the spies were sent (Josh. 14:7). At the age of 85, at the distribution of the land of Canaan, he asked for Hebron and the hill country where lived the fearful Anakim who had terrorized ten of the spies, and Joshua gave it to him. Later he became father-in-law of Othniel, the first of the "judges," by giving him Achsah his daughter (Judg. 1:12-15,20).

2. A son of Hezron, son of Judah (I Chron. 2:18,19,42) probably the same as the "Chelubai" of I Chronicles 2:9.

CALEB-EPHRATAH (kā'lĕb-ĕf'rà-tà), named in I Chronicles 2:24 as the place where Hezron died. The Hebrew and LXX texts differ here; and many scholars prefer the LXX reading, "after the death of Hezron, Caleb came unto Ephrath, the wife of Hezron, his father." When a son took his father's wife, it signified that he was claiming his father's possessions.

CALENDAR (kăl'ĕn-dàr). Calendars are devised as a trustworthy means for recording history and determining dates in advance for social, civic and religious anniversaries, and for economic planning. Comparatively little is known of the calendar of the early Israelites from the patriarchs to the Exile, but a critical study of the Biblical records and archaeological discoveries is rewarding.

During the Bible period, time was reckoned solely on astronomical observations. The early Chaldean and Egyptian astrologers became quite learned in the movements of astronomical bodies. Their discoveries, as well as those of other Near Eastern neighbors, made their impact on the Jewish calendar. From earliest times the sun and moon were determinants of periodicity, days, months and years.

I. Days in the Biblical record of time begins with the account of creation. Various reckonings and measurements were derived from these early records. The order of the Jewish day, beginning in the evening, was based on the repeated phrase, "and there was evening, and there was morning" (Gen. 1:5b). While the Babylonian day, like that of most Near Easterners, began at sunrise, the Jewish day began at sunset (Deut. 23:11). Actually the demarcation between the end of one day and the beginning of another as observed by the ancient Israelites was that moment when three stars of the second magnitude became visible. This is confirmed in Nehemiah (4:21) "so we labored at the work, and half of them held the spears from the break of dawn till the stars came out."

Days of the week were not named by the Jews, but were designated by ordinal numbers. The term "sabbath" was not the name of the seventh day but a sacred designation.

Days were also subdivided in a manner set forth in the Creation account. And God said, "Let there be lights in the firmament of the heaven to separate the day from the night . . . the greater light to rule the day" (Gen. 1:14-16; see also Num. 9:16; Ruth 3:13).

Days were further subdivided into hours and watches. The day, as distinguished from the night, showed no exact divisions into parts in early Biblical records. It was, however, divided into periods of indefinite lengths designated by the terms "evening," "morning," "mid-day," and "the day declines" (Judg. 19:8). Dividing the day into hours was probably a later adoption. The Hebrew word for hour, *sha'ah* variously translated, is Aramaic (Dan. 3:6; 4:33), but Babylonians and Egyptians had hour-marking devices long before Daniel, and apparently Israel did, too. Babylonians divided the day by sun-watches into twelve equal parts, which were subdivided by the sexagenary system into minutes and seconds. The Egyptians divided the day plus the night into twenty-four hours, for which they had at least two calibrated measuring devices. One was a shadow clock, comprised of a horizontal piece of wood with markings to which was attached at one end a short T-like piece, set toward the E in the morning and toward the W in the afternoon. A specimen, dating about 1400 B.C., is now in the Berlin Museum. Another Egyptian timepiece was the water-clock, clepsydra, the oldest known specimen of which dates from the reign of Amenhotep III, c. 1400 B.C. It is of alabaster, shaped like a flower-pot, with calibrated marks inside and a small aperture near the bottom through which the water gradually flowed out. Whether borrowed or devised the Jews had sundials as early as the reign of Hezekiah, king of Judah, c. 715-687 B.C. When he was deathly sick,

"Isaiah the prophet cried to the Lord; and he brought the shadow back ten steps, by which the sun had declined on the dial of Ahaz" (II Kings 20:11; Isa. 38:8). In the New Testament, John 11:9) records the rhetorical question of Jesus, "Are there not twelve hours in the day?" — as distinguished from night. This kind of daily reckoning is also seen in the crucifixion account which mentions the third, sixth and ninth hours (Mark 15:25; 33f), referring to 9 A.M., noon, and 3 P.M. respectively.

Early Hebrews divided the nights into three watches: "the morning watch" (Exod. 14:24); "the middle watch" (Judg. 7:19); and "at the beginning of the watches" (Lam. 2:19). The Romans divided the night into four watches, from which Jesus drew an analogy in his eschatological warning of unpredictable time — ". . . in the evening, or at midnight, or at cockcrow, or in the morning" (Mark 13:35).

II. Weeks constituted special and significant periodicity units for the "chosen people." The seven-day week is of Semitic origin, but reckoned from various reference points. The Babylonians and Assyrians bound their weeks to the lunar cycle, corresponding with the four phases, and began anew with each new moon. The Jewish week had its origin in the Creation account of seven days' duration, and ran consecutively in a free week system irrespective of lunar or solar cycles. This was out of the high esteem held for the sabbath. Conversely, the Egyptian week had ten days.

Astronomical bodies were divinely ordained in creation to be timemarkers. Days and years were measured by the sun; months by the moon; and cycles by sun, moon and stars. The week alone was not controlled by celestial bodies, but originated by divine command for man's economic, physical and spiritual welfare.

Though God placed special emphasis on the seventh day at the time of creation (Gen. 1:2f), the records are silent as to its observance during the long intervening interlude between then and Moses' day. If those of the pre-flood era or of the patriarchal period observed a "sabbath," there are no Biblical records of it. However, since it was kept alive in tradition until recorded in Genesis, it is a reasonable conjecture that it was preserved in practice also. Anyway, it was either revived or given special emphasis by Moses. The first recorded instance of the observance of "a day of solemn rest, a holy sabbath to the Lord" (Exod. 16:23) was when the Israelites were gathering manna in the wilderness. Subsequently, the sabbath became the most holy, as well as the most frequent of all the sacred days observed by the Jews.

When the fourth commandment in the Decalogue, "Remember the sabbath day, to keep it holy" (Exod. 20:8), was transmitted to Israel by Moses, it was designated as a perpetual memorial sign of the covenant between God and His chosen people. "And the Lord said to Moses, 'Say to the people of Israel, You shall keep my sabbaths, for this is a sign between me and you throughout your generations, that you may know that I, the Lord, sanctify you" (Exod. 31:13). Thereafter it became a distinctive Jewish day, with successive injunctions to observe it, describing the manner of doing so, and the penalties for its desecration (Exod. 23:12; 35:2f). Emphasis on keeping "His holy sabbath" is seen in the Habakkuk (1:5) commentary of the Dead Sea Scrolls and the bitter accusations hurled at Jesus on this point (Mark 2:24). However superficial might have been the observance by some of Jesus' contemporaries, He confirmed

Synchronized Jewish Calendar

Nos.		Names of Months		Farm Seasons
1	(7)	Nisan	(Mar-Apr)	Begin barley harvest
2	(8)	Iyyar	(Apr-May)	Barley harvest
3	(9)	Sivan	(May-Jun)	Wheat harvest
4	(10)	Tammuz	(Jun-Jul)	
5	(11)	Ab	(Jul-Aug)	Grape, fig, olive ripe
6	(12)	Elul	(Aug-Sep)	Vintage begins
7	(1)	Tishri	(Sep-Oct)	Early rains; plowing
8	(2)	Heshvan	(Oct-Nov)	Wheat, barley sowing
9	(3)	Kislev	(Nov-Dec)	
10	(4)	Tebeth	(Dec-Jan)	Rainy winter months
11	(5)	Shebat	(Jan-Feb)	New Year for trees
12	(6)	Adar	(Feb-Mar)	Almonds blooming
13		Adar Sheni		Intercalary month

The Synchronized Jewish Calendar. The first column indicates the numerical order of months in the sacred calendar, while the column in parentheses shows the civic year beginning with Tishri.

its divine authenticity by going "to the synagogue, as his custom was," on the sabbath day to teach, preach and heal (Luke 4:16). Early Christian Jews made a habit of assembling on the first day of the week to commemorate Jesus' resurrection on that day (Luke 24:1); hence the last day became the first for worship and rest in Christendom.

III. Months, in effect, is a synonym for moons. Ancient people seemingly universally worshiped the moon and measured time by it, probably because of its conspicuousness and regular occurrence. The Arabic word for moon means "the measurer," and the Egyptian moon god, Thoth, was the god of measure. Even apostate Jews at times worshiped the moon along with other heavenly bodies (II Kings 23:5; Jer. 8:2).

"Moon" was synonymous with "month" in common parlance in Moses' day (Exod. 19:1). Later, when the responsibility of making the calendar was vested in the Sanhedrin, three of their number, including the chief, were entrusted as watchmen to report the first appearance of the new moon. A declaration of the beginning of a new month was then quickly dispatched over the country by fire signals, and later by messengers. The patriarch Hillel probably introduced the constant calendar.

The early Israelites designated their months by names which they borrowed from the Canaanites or Phoenicians. These names had seasonal connotations as implied in the four which have survived in the early Biblical records. Abib (Exod. 13:4; Deut. 16:1), corresponding to Nisan in the later calendar, means "month of the ripening ears." Ziv (I Kings 6:1), corresponding to Iyyar, means "month of flowers." Ethanim (I Kings 8:2), corresponding to Tishri, means "month of perennial streams." Bul (I Kings 6:38), corresponding to Marchesvan, means "rain or showers," being the first month in the rainy season.

About the end of the kingdom period the calendar was reformed, replacing the old names of the months with ordinal numerals, and changing the beginning of the year to spring. This is illustrated in I Kings (6:1 and 8:2), where the writer explicitly correlated the numeral month with older names, as "the month of Ziv, which is the second month." On the other hand the writer of Haggai (1:1; 2:1,10), about 520 B.C., at the time of the rebuilding of the temple, uses the numeral designation of months without any explanatory references. Yet Zechariah, a contemporary work, relates the numeral month to the Babylonian names, which came into popular use after the Exile. This is illustrated in the seventh verse of the first chapter in the expression "the eleventh month which is the month Shebat," and in chapter seven, verse one, "the ninth month, which is Chislev."

The post-exilic names of months were, as confirmed by the Talmud, adopted from the Babylonian calendar, but not used for civil and historical purposes. These, like the early Canaanite names, had their origin close to nature, as is seen from their derivations. Nisan — "move," "start," being the first month of the ecclesiastical year as well as of the vernal equinox; Iyyar — "to be bright," "flower"; Sivan — "appoint," "mark"; Tammuz—name of an ancient Akkadian god identified with vegetation; Ab — "hostile" heat, "bulrushes" growing; Elul — "to shout for joy" at vintage; Tishri — "begin" civil year, "dedicate" to the sun-god by Babylonians, and to which the Jews might have associated the Creation and the Day of Judgment; Marchesvan — "drop," "rainy season"; Kislev — (derivation uncertain); Tebeth — "to sink," "dip"; Shebat — (unknown); Adar — "to be dark."

The Gezer Calendar, dated in the tenth century B.C., gives an interesting glimpse into the agricultural life in Palestine at that early date. This archaeological find by Macalister is a limestone plaque bearing a Hebrew inscription enumerating farm operations for eight months, mentioning sowing, flax harvest, barley harvest, and vine pruning.

IV. Years. The Jewish calendar contained two concurrent years, the sacred year, beginning in the spring with the month Nisan, and the civil year, beginning in the fall with Tishri. The sacred year was instituted by Moses following the Exodus, and consists of 12 or 13 lunar months of 29½ days each. The civil year claims a more remote antiquity, reckoning from the Creation, which traditionally took place in autumn (3760 B.C.). It came into popular use in the third century of the Christian Era. That this order of the year was kept by the ancient Hebrews is supported by the Mosaic command, "You shall keep the feast of ingathering at the end of the year, when you gather in from the field the fruit of your labor" (Exod. 23:16).

The Babylonians and Egyptians devised the intercalary month in order to reconcile the lunar and solar years. The Jewish leap years in their Metonic cycle of 19 years were fixed, adding an intercalary month to the 3rd, 6th, 9th, 11th, 14th, 17th, and 19th years. If, on the 16th of the month Nisan, the sun had not reached the vernal equinox, the month was declared to be the second Adhar and the following one Nisan.

In 46 B.C. a great advance over contemporary calendars was made by Julius Caesar, whose calendar year contained 365¼ days. It had a discrepancy of 11 minutes in excess of the solar year, and so was superseded by the Gregorian calendar in A.D. 1582, which was adopted by England in 1752. It has the infinitesimal error of gaining one day in 3,325 years.

Josephus (*Ant.* I, iii, 3) said that Moses ordered that the year of holy days and religious festivals begin with Nisan, the month in which the Exodus transpired, but that he retained the old order of year for buying and selling and secular affairs. This observation has been confirmed by critical study and subsequent Jewish custom of keeping both a sacred and a civil year.

Feasts and fasts were intricately woven into the lunar-solar sacred year. Three great historic feasts were instituted by Moses: "the feast of unleavened bread"; "the feast of harvest"; and "the feast of ingathering" (Exod. 23:14-17), corresponding roughly to Passover, Pentecost, and Thanksgiving. There were also numerous minor feasts.

Beginning in the month Nisan or Abib (Neh. 2:1; Exod. 23:15) the sacred holidays of feasts and fasts came in the following order. On the 14th of Nisan, the first month, the Passover (Exod. 12:18f; 13:3-10) was observed in preparation for the following week's festival and in eating the paschal supper (see Matt. 26:17-29). The 15th to 21st was the Feast of Unleavened Bread (Lev. 23:6) which included, on the 15th, a sabbath, a day of holy convocation; on the 16th, Omer or presenting the first sheafs of harvest; and on the 21st another holy convocation. This is also the month of latter or spring rains when the Jordan was in flood (Josh. 3:15).

Christian Easter, fulfilling the Passover, is reckoned on solar-lunar cycles, coming on the first full moon on or after the vernal equinox (March 21).

The name of the second month, Iyyar, known formerly as Ziv (I Kings 6:1,37), does not occur in the Bible, as is also true with Tammuz, Ab, and Marchesvan. The Jews fasted on the 10th in commemoration of the death of Elijah; the 14th was the Second or Little Passover for those who could not keep the regular one (Num. 9:10,11); and on the 16th was a fast for the death of Samuel.

Pentecost or Feast of Weeks, or of Harvest, or of Firstfruits, when loaves as firstfruits of the gathered harvest were presented (Exod. 23:16; 34:22; Lev. 23:17,20; Num. 28:26; Deut. 16:9f) was celebrated on the sixth or seventh of Sivan (Esth. 8:9). (Cf. Acts 2:1.) This was the first of the two great agricultural feasts, coming at the end of seven weeks after the beginning of barley harvest, or 50 days after the Passover.

Next in annual order was the Jewish New Year (*Rosh Hashanah*), one of the most important and probably the oldest feast, observed on the first day of the civil year, in the month, Tishri, the former Ethanim or seventh month (I Kings 8:2). It was called the Feast of Trumpets, a precursor of one emblem of modern New Year's celebration. It was a day of holy convocation, of reading the law (Neh. 8:1-8), of blowing trumpets, of burnt offerings, of cereal offerings, and of profound solemnity, introducing "Ten Days of Repentance" (Num. 29: 1-16; Ezra 3:4-6). This protracted feast culminated in the Day of Atonement (*Yom Kippur*), Tishri 10th, one of the most holy days for the Jews. This is strictly a fast day and the only one commanded by law (Lev. 16:26-34; 23:27-32), called "the fast" in Acts 27:9. The Jewish Calendar makes "provision that neither *Rosh Hashanah* nor *Yom Kippur* may fall on the day before or the day after the sabbath, or the seventh day of Tabernacles on a sabbath." From the 15th to 21st of Tishri the Jews held the Feast of Ingatherings or Tabernacles or Booths (recalling the wilderness wandering), when the Firstfruits of wine and oil were offered (Exod. 23:16; Lev. 23:34-42; Deut. 16:13). It was a day of soul-searching and expiation of sins and of deep gratitude to God. It was the third of the three great feasts commanded by Moses, and the second of the two great agricultural feasts, corresponding to our modern Thanksgiving.

Winter holy days were few, though one of significance is mentioned in the Gospel of John (10: 22f): "It was the Feast of the Dedication at Jerusalem; it was winter, and Jesus was walking in the temple." Dedication of the Temple was instituted by Judas Maccabaeus in 164 B.C. This feast was held on the 25th of Chislev (Zech. 7:1), which month was followed by the tenth month, Tebeth (Esth. 2:16), and the eleventh month, Shebat (Zech. 1:7).

Besides the one divinely ordained fast, the Day of Atonement, there were minor fasts, some temporary (Ezra 9:5; Neh. 1:4) and some annual. One fast in memory of the destruction of Jerusalem by Nebuchadnezzar (II Kings 25:1-7), instituted after the Exile, was observed on the ninth of Ab. Another, the fast of Esther, was observed on the 13th of Adar and followed the next two days by the Feast of Purim.

The lunar-solar year of Jewish feasts, fasts, and farming was fortified between the divine order of heavenly bodies "for signs and for seasons and for days and years" (Gen. 1:14), and the divine promise after the Flood that "While the earth remains, seedtime and harvest, cold and heat, summer and winter, day and night shall not cease" (Gen. 8:22).

V. Cycles. Inspired by God's hallowing the seventh day in creation, the Jews derived a special sacredness for the number seven. Religious convocations and festivals were highly regarded on the seventh day, seventh week, seventh month, seventh year, and seven times seven years.

Hence, the epitome of the sabbatical feasts, of which the perennial ones have been mentioned, may thus appear. The sabbath of seven days; Pentecost, at the end of seven weeks after Passover; the Feast of Trumpets, introducing the sacred seventh month, were all "appointed assemblies" (*mo'adhim*) of the Lord.

The sabbatical year was one of solemn rest for landlords, slaves, beasts of burden, and land, and freedom for Hebrew slaves. The volunteer produce of farm and vineyard was to be gathered and consumed by the poor alone (Exod. 23:10f; Lev. 25:20-22). The sabbatical and jubilee years were synchronized with the civil or agricultural year, beginning in autumn.

The Jubilee, every 50th year, following "seven weeks of years," was a hallowed year whose observance included family reunions, canceled mortgages, and return of lands to original owners (Lev. 25:8-17).

VI. Eras in the Bible calendar comprise the whole span of time from the Creation of the world to the consummation of the ages. Great events are terminal markers. These mountain peaks of time, in chronological sequence, are Creation, Flood, Abraham, Exodus, Exile and Birth of Jesus. Consequently the eras may be designated Antediluvian, Post-diluvian, Patriarchal, Israelite, Judean, and Christian. (Cf. Matt. 1:2-17; Luke 3: 23-37.)

Astronomically, that phenomenal star which guided the Magi divided human history. It is the pivotal point from which all history is dated, terminating the old order and initiating the new. It stands as the signal reference point of all time, the pre-eminent red-letter date in the Bible calendar. In the Jewish calendar it separates the history "Before the Christian Era" (B.C.E.) from that of the "Christian Era" (C.E.). In the Christian calendar it separates all "Before Christ" (B.C.) from that in *"Anno Domini"* (A.D.), "year of our Lord."   G.B.F.

CALF, a young bull or cow. Calves were used for food and for sacrifice. Calves used for sacrifice were usually males a year old.

CALF, GOLDEN (See Calf Worship)

CALF WORSHIP was a part of the religious worship of almost all ancient Semitic peoples. At least as early as the Exodus, living bulls were worshiped in Egypt. The Babylonians looked upon the bull as the symbol of their greatest gods. The bull was a sacred animal in Phoenicia and Syria. Among the Semitic Canaanites the bull was the symbol of Baal. It appears that the bull was in some way connected with the reproductive processes of plants and animals and with the sun. It symbolized strength, vigor, and endurance.

The bronze bull-calf of the god Apis of Egypt.

Aaron made a golden image of a male calf in order that the people might worship Jehovah under this form (Exod. 32:4). It is very unlikely that the Golden Calf was a representation of an Egyptian deity. The feast held in connection with this worship was a "feast of Jehovah" (Exod. 32:5).

After the division of the kingdom, Jeroboam set up two golden calves in his kingdom, one at Bethel and one at Dan (I Kings 12:28,29) because he feared that his people might desert him if they continued to worship in Jerusalem. He was not trying to make heathenism the state religion, for the bull images were erroneously supposed to represent Jehovah. In time, these images, at first recognized as symbols, came to be regarded as common idols (I Kings 12:30; Hos. 13:2).   S.B.

CALKER, one who makes a boat waterproof whether in building or repairing (Ezek. 27:9,27). The men of Gebal (modern Jebail) were calkers for Tyre.

CALL (Gr. *klésis, calling*), one of the most common verbs in the Bible, representing over 20 words in the Hebrew and Greek text; but principally with one or another of four different meanings: 1. To speak out in the way of prayer — "Call unto me, and I will answer thee" (Jer. 33:3).

2. To summon or appoint — "I will call all the families of the kingdoms of the earth (Jer. 1:15).

3. To name a person or thing —"and God called the light Day" (Gen. 1:5).

4. To invite men to accept salvation through Christ. This last is a call by God through the Holy Spirit, and is heavenly (Heb. 3:1) and holy (II

Tim. 1:9). I Corinthians 1:26 and 7:20 use the word in a peculiar sense, as referring to that condition of life in which men were when they became Christians.

CALNEH (kăl'nĕ), one of the four cities, including also Babel, Erech (whence "Iraq"), and Akkad which were founded by Nimrod in the third generation after the Flood (Gen. 10:10). It was in the land of Shinar in the southern part of Mesopotamia. It is not identified, but Kulunu and Nippur have been suggested.

CALNO (kăl'nō), a city named in Isaiah 10:9 in a list of the Assyrians' victories. Almost certainly the same as *Calneh q.v.*

CALVARY (kăl'và-rē, Lat. *calvaria, skull*), a place not far from the walls of Jerusalem where Christ was crucified and near which He was buried (Luke 23:33). The Latin *calvaria* is a rendering of the Greek *kranion,* skull, which renders the Hebrew *Gulgoleth* and the Aramaic *Gulgulta.* The common explanation is that the name was due to the cranial shape of the hill.

The exact site of Calvary is a matter of dispute. Two sites contend for acceptance, the Church of the Holy Sepulchre, which is within the walls of the modern city; and the Green Hill, or Gordon's Calvary, in which is Jeremiah's Grotto, a few hundred feet NE of the Damascus Gate. The first is supported by ancient tradition, while the second was suggested for the first time in 1849, although much is to be said in its favor.

CAMEL, the well-known "ship of the desert" because of its ability to go long without water and to pad safely through soft sand; and to the Arabs a prized possession. The fact that the word for "camel" is practically identical in Hebrew and in Arabic tells us that the patriarchs knew and used camels long before they used horses. They are mentioned prominently in the inventories of Abraham (Gen. 12:16), Jacob (Gen. 30:43) and of Job (Job 1:3 cf. 42:12). Though the camel was reckoned as unclean to the Hebrews (Lev. 11:4) its milk was used (Gen. 32:15). The "dromedaries" of I Kings 4:28 were probably swift horses (cf. ASV). Though some writers have described them as "docile," "stupid" would be a better word. They obey in a grumbling way and growl as loudly while being unloaded as when being loaded. Not dangerous except for a month in winter; but their bite is dangerous because of their filthy teeth. See also ANIMALS.

Camel caravan crossing the Palestine hill country. © MPS

Above, site of Gordon's Calvary; below, Church of the Holy Sepulchre, in Jerusalem. © MPS

CAMEL'S HAIR, mentioned only in Matthew 3:4 and Mark 1:6, where we are told that John the Baptist wore a garment of camel's hair. It is probable, however, that this was not a garment made of the relatively expensive woven camel's hair, but of dressed camel's skin. Such garments are still used in the Near East. Some think that Elijah's mantle was made of camel's hair (II Kings 1:8; cf. Zech. 13:4).

CAMON or **KAMON** (kā'mŏn), a town in Gilead mentioned in Judges 10:5 as the burial place of the judge Jair.

CAMP, ENCAMPMENT (Heb. *mahăneh*), a group of tents intended for traveling or for temporary residence as in case of war — contrasted with village, town or city which are composed of houses and other more or less permanent buildings. The word *mahaneh* occurs over 200 times and is properly rendered by "camp," but 61 times it is translated "host" and four times "army," indicating the military purpose of the encampment. In Genesis 32:1,2, when the angels of God met Jacob, he exclaimed "This is God's host" (literally "camp") and he named the place "Mahanaim" or "Two Camps," referring to God's host and his own. Israel in the wilderness was given precise instructions as to the order and arrangements of its camp, both at rest and in traveling (Num. 2,3). The tabernacle in the center indicated the centrality of God in their life and worship. It was surrounded rather closely by the priests and Levites; and then further back were the 12 tribes, grouped in threes and led by Judah on the E, Reuben on the S, Ephraim on the W, and Dan on the N. In Deuteronomy 23:9-14 are given the sanitary and ceremonial observances which were used to keep the camp clean and wholesome.   A.B.F.

CAMPHIRE (kăm'fīr, Heb. *kōpher*), an Asiatic thorny shrub with fragrant white flowers (S. of Sol. 1:14; 4:13). "Henna-flowers" in ASV.

CANA of Galilee (kā'nȧ of găl'ĭ-lē), mentioned four times in the Gospel of John (2:1-11; 4:36-54; 21:2) and nowhere else in Scripture. It was in the highlands of Galilee, as one had to go *down* from there to Capernaum; but opinions differ as to its exact location. It may have been at "Kefr Kenna" about five miles NE of Nazareth, or at "Kana-el-Jelil" a little further N. Here Jesus performed His first miracle, graciously relieving the embarrassment caused by the shortage of wine at a marriage feast. It was here too (John 4:46) that he announced to the nobleman from Capernaum the healing of his apparently dying son; and Nathanael was of Cana (John 21:2).

CANAAN, CANAANITES (kā'năn, kā'năn-īts). 1. Canaan was the son of Ham in the genealogical lists in Genesis 9,10. His descendants occupied Canaan and took their name from that country (Gen. 9:18,22; 10:6).

2. Canaan was one of the old names for Palestine, the land of the Canaanites dispossessed by the Israelites. The etymology of the name is unknown, as is also the earliest history of the name; but Egyptian inscriptions of c. 1800 B.C. use it for the coastland between Egypt and Asia Minor. In the Amarna letters of c. 1400 B.C. the name is applied to the Phoenician coast. According to Judges 1:9,10, Canaanites dwelt throughout the land. In Genesis 12:6; 24:3,37; Joshua 3:10 the Canaanites include the whole pre-Israelite population, even E of the Jordan. The language of Canaan (Isa. 19:18) refers to the group of West Semitic languages of which Hebrew, Phoenician, and Moabite were dialects. The Canaanites were of Semitic stock, and were part of a large migration of Semites (Phoenicians, Amorites, Canaanites) from NE Arabia in the third millennium B.C. They came under Egyptian control c. 1500 B.C. The Israelites were never able completely to exterminate them. Many were undoubtedly absorbed by their conquerors. The continued presence rendered the religious problem of the Israelites serious and difficult.   S.B.

CANAANITE, SIMON THE, so-called in Matthew 10:4 KJV, but in ASV "the Cananaean" (margin "or Zealot"); one of the original twelve apostles. He bore the epithet "Canaanite" to distinguish him from Simon Peter.

CANANAEAN (kā'nȧ-nē'ăn), the description of Simon "the Zealot" in Matthew 10:4 ASV, but "Canaanite" by mistake in KJV. Probably "zealot" (Luke 6:15) from an Aramaic word is the correct description.

CANDACE (kăn'dȧ-sē, Gr. *Kandáke*), the Queen of Ethiopia mentioned only in Acts 8:27. The name seems to have been a general designation of Ethiopian queens (like "Pharaoh" for Egyptian kings,

Cana of Galilee, with nearby gardens. © MPS

and "Caesar" for Roman emperors). Her chief treasurer, a eunuch went to Jerusalem to worship and was led by Philip the evangelist to faith in Christ.

CANDLE. In a way, the word "candle" should not appear in the English Bible at all. The Hebrew word *nēr,* occurring 43 times, is rendered in KJV "lamp" 33 times (and this should be its rendering every time), "candle" nine times, and "light" once.

The simple fact is that in Elizabethan days in England people used candles and not lamps, whereas in ancient times in the warm climate, where the Word of God was given, men used little olive-oil lamps. Wax or tallow candles would have melted in the wilderness heat, even if they had been invented. It was the custom of the ancients to keep a house lamp burning day and night. A perennially burning lamp was a symbol of prosperity (Job 29:3; Ps. 18:28), a lamp put out, of judgment (Prov. 24:20; Jer. 25:10; Rev. 2:5).

CANDLESTICK. The Hebrew word *menôrâh,* always rendered "candlestick" in KJV, occurs 43 times in the OT, but could more accurately be rendered "lampstand," because the "lights" were not candles at all, but olive-oil lamps. The Aramaic word *nebrashta,* occurring only in Daniel 5:5, would better have been rendered "chandelier" and the Greek word *luchnia* would better be understood "lampstand." Matthew 5:15 KJV has "candle" and "candlestick," but ASV more correctly "lamp" and "stand." In the tabernacle, as constructed in the wilderness, the lampstand (described

Seven-branched candlestick, or lampstand.

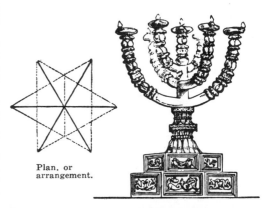

Plan, or arrangement.

in Exod. 25:31-40) with its seven branches holding the seven lamps of gold, stood at the left as the priests entered the Holy place. In the temple that Solomon built, there were ten lampstands of gold (II Chron. 4:7), but they were placed in front of the Holy of Holies (I Kings 7:49; II Chron. 4:7). A.B.F.

CANDY, a word that does not occur in the Bible, but the Jews had "confections" (Exod. 30:35) and the children chewed sugar cane when they could.

CANE, probably the sweet calamus (in KJV Isa. 43:24, Jer. 6:20 only; but cf. Exod. 30:23, where it is listed among the "chief spices").

CANKER (kăn′kêr, Gr. *gággraina, gangrene*), a word that occurs once in Scripture, II Timothy 2: 17. It may mean cancer. See DISEASES.

CANKERWORM (Heb. *yeleq*), the name given to a larval stage of the locust (Joel 1:4; 2:25; Nah. 3:15,16). It was very voracious (Nah. 3:15). See INSECTS.

CANNEH (kăn′ē), mentioned only in Ezekiel 27: 23 among the towns and regions with which Tyre traded. Some identify it with Calneh, *q.v.*

CANONICITY (kăn-ŏn-ĭc′ĭtē). The word "canon" originally meant "measuring rule," hence "standard." In theology its chief application is to those books received as authoritative and making up our Bible. The Protestant canon includes 39 books in the Old Testament, 27 in the New. The Roman Catholic Canon adds seven books and some additional pieces to the Old Testament (see Apocrypha). The Jews receive as authoritative the same 39 books as do Protestants.

It is commonly said that the Protestant test of canonicity is inspiration. That is, Protestants receive into their canon those books which they believe to be immediately inspired of God and therefore true, infallible, inerrant, the very Word of God. Creeds of the Reformation age often listed the books received as inspired, but the Protestant churches have received these books not because of the decision of a Church or Council, but because the books themselves were recognized as true and inspired, having God for their author. The history of the acceptance of these books and the study of the principles on which this reception occurred is an important phase of Bible introduction.

The Old Testament Canon

The Jewish Talmud of about 400 A.D. names the books of the Jewish canon in approximately the order found in our Hebrew Bibles today. By combining the 12 Minor Prophets, counting the books of Samuel, Kings, and Chronicles each as one book, etc., they arrive at the number of 24 books, divided into 5 of law, 8 of prophets, and 11 books of writings (Psalms, Proverbs, Job, Song of Solomon, Ruth, Lamentations, Ecclesiastes, Esther, Daniel, Ezra-Nehemiah, Chronicles). In earlier days they combined Ruth with Judges, Lamentations with Jeremiah and thus made 22 books equivalent to the 22 letters in the Hebrew alphabet. Origen, the Christian scholar of about A.D. 250, lists 22 OT books, but not in the order of the Talmud. Earlier, Melito of Sardis about A.D. 170 tells us that he went to Palestine to ascertain accurately the number of Old Testament books. He lists the five books of the Law first, then the others following in an order rather similar to that of our English Bible.

Before Melito, we have the vital witness of the Jewish historian Josephus. About A.D. 90 he wrote his work against Apion. In it, (i.8), he says that

the Jews receive 22 books—5 of the Law of Moses, 13 of prophecy, and 4 of hymns to God and precepts for life. These books, he says, the pious Jew would rather die than to alter or deny. He says these books were written by Moses and the succeeding prophets from that time to the days of Artaxerxes (around 400 B.C.) and that their other later books, not being by prophets, were not thus regarded. It is obvious that the Talmudic order and classification of the books had not yet arisen in Josephus' day.

About A.D. 90 the Jews held the Council of Jamnia. We have only the later Talmudic reports concerning it, but apparently the canonicity of certain books was discussed, Ecclesiastes, Proverbs, etc. It should be made emphatic that this was not the time of original canonization of any book, as Josephus' witness assures us. Doubters arise in any age. But that Proverbs was already considered as canonical in the second century B.C. we can now prove by the reference in the Zadokite Documents xi. 20.

Earlier evidence on the OT canon gives us no listing, but considerable valuable information. Philo, the Egyptian Jew of the first century A.D., evidently received the 22 Hebrew books, for he quotes from many of them and from them only, as authoritative. The NT evidence is in accord. Most of the OT books are quoted and the seven apocryphal books are not. The NT gives no positive evidence on the order of the books, but it reveals in general a twofold division of the OT such as is found in Melito rather than the threefold. A dozen times the OT is referred to as the "Law and the prophets" or "Moses and the prophets," etc. As is evident from NT usage, this twofold category included all 22 books. Only once does it adopt the threefold classification, Moses and the prophets and the Psalms (Luke 24:44; but cf. vs. 27).

Pre-Christian evidence has been greatly augmented by the discovery of the Dead Sea scrolls. Previously, only the apocryphal books and other Jewish writings were available. These sources occasionally quoted books of the OT, but not with great frequency. Of special importance was the prologue to Ecclesiasticus, dated in 132 B.C. Three times it refers to the "law, and the prophets, and the other books of our fathers." One time it refers to these as already translated into Greek—the LXX. Because of the antiquity of this witness, the threefold canon was formerly held to be original. The twofold canon of the NT was not then explained. The Dead Sea Scrolls now, however, give four places (Zadokite Documents v. 21; vii. 15ff; Manual of Discipline 1,3; viii. 13ff) where the OT is referred to in two categories, the law and the prophets, as is usual in the NT. That this twofold canon included all our present books seems obvious from the fact that the Qumran Community quoted from most of the OT books, including those later classified in the third division of "writings," and has left manuscripts of all the Biblical books, except Esther. Thus the twofold canon is as early or earlier than the threefold. In line with this evidence is the fact that the LXX translation, at least in later copies, accords with the twofold, but not the threefold division.

From the above outline of evidence it is easily seen that the apocryphal books of Tobit, Judith, Wisdom, Ecclesiasticus, Baruch, I and II Maccabees, and certain additions to Esther and Daniel, have no ancient authority and were not received by Christ, the apostles, or the Jewish people. Only in the Roman Catholic Council of Trent of about

A.D. 1545 were they canonized and then it was likely a result of the reaction against the Reformers.

It also appears that the critical development theory that the law was canonized in 400 B.C., the prophets in 200 B.C. and the writings in A.D. 90 is opposed to the facts. Some of the books concerning which the Council at Jamnia at A.D. 90 had questions were already accepted in the Qumran texts (Proverbs, in the Zadokite Documents xi,20) or were in A.D. 90 actually counted among the prophets by Josephus. The view is that Daniel was not classed among the prophets because it was not written until 165 B.C. after the canon of the prophets had closed. But now it is admitted that Ecclesiastes, also among the writings in our Hebrew Bibles, was composed before 250 B.C. Josephus' testimony is also clear. Daniel *was* among the prophets in the early days.

The view of the conservative W. H. Green also is in error. He said the third division was composed by men who did not have the office of a prophet (Daniel, he claims, had the *gift* but not the *office*). But Daniel *was* among the prophets in antiquity. So were Ezra, Nehemiah, Chronicles, Ruth, etc. Furthermore, how does Green know that the author of Judges, now in the second division, was a prophet, and that the author of Chronicles, now in the third division, was not?

The fact is that those who spoke the word of God to Israel were called prophets. There is no record of any group who were inspired without being prophets. Most of the OT books were clearly written by prophets. The authors of some others, like Joshua and Proverbs, Song of Solomon, most of the Psalms, etc., were also prophets—at least they received revelations from God (Num. 12:6). For several books information on authorship is lacking, but even Green admits that Joshua, Judges, Samuel, and Kings were written by prophets. One has as much right to hold that Ruth, Job, Esther, Chronicles, etc., were by prophets as to say that Judges was. Certainly these books are included under the designation "prophets" in the Qumran scrolls and in the NT. If books of prophetic origin were to be received by Israel, this is a practical test that would check on the authority of written teaching as well as oral (cf. Deut. 13:1-5; 18:15-22). On this basis it can be explained how it was that the writings of prophets were accorded prompt acceptance by the faithful (cf. Josh. 1:7,8; Jer. 36:8-16; 26:18; Dan. 9:2, etc.). Hebrews 1:1 sums up the whole matter, "God . . . spake . . . by the prophets."

The New Testament Canon

Information on the early use of the NT books has been augmented in recent years both by the discovery of old portions of the NT and of early books quoting it.

There has been no question among the Christian churches since early times as to which books belong in the NT. All branches of Christendom have accepted as authoritative and inspired the current 27 books. They are accepted as authoritative because they are held to be true and immediately inspired of God.

Copies of the NT date from an early age. Already in the last century two remarkable old manuscripts had come to light—Sinaiticus and Vaticanus —from about AD. 325. Since then, the discovery of the Chester Beatty papyri has given portions from the previous century which cover parts of the Gospels and Acts, most of the Pauline Epistles and about half of Revelation. In 1935 an even more remarkable fragment was published. Though small —parts of five verses of John 18—it is precious as being the earliest. This Rylands papyrus is dated to the first half of the second century, or around A.D. 125. When skeptical scholars of the last century dated the fourth Gospel around 170, little did they know that there existed a piece of it coming from within 30 years of John's lifetime!

Recently the sands of Egypt have yielded new treasures. The Bodmer papyrus of John, dating from about A.D. 200, is almost complete. Another Bodmer papyrus coming from the early 200's includes I and II Peter and Jude along with a portion of the Psalms. Thus some actual NT manuscripts are now not too far removed from the days of the apostles themselves.

There was early a general agreement as to the books which the church at large accepted as canonical, but early evidence is not complete in detail for every book. Several books were accepted in some quarters but not in others. Contrary to statements sometimes made, no other books beside these 27 were ever given significant or general acceptance. The history of this acceptance of books is given very carefully by Westcott in his work on the *Canon* and the details for individual books are extensively presented in Zahn's monumental *Introduction to the NT*. One must not, however, confuse the acceptance of the books with the establishment of the canon. In a sense, the canon was established at once as soon as there were inspired books, for the NT books claim authority and recognize the authority of one another. Some churches had some of the books early, but it took time for all of the books to be distributed and for the evidence of their genuineness to be given to all and accepted by all. Fortunately for us, the early Christians were not gullible; they had learned to try the spirits. Furthermore, the Gnostic heresy rather soon began to multiply spurious writings and this made people cautious. It took time to convince everybody of every book. The history of the collection of the books traces this process.

The Period of A.D. 170

In brief survey, we may take three early periods for analysis. At about 170 the Muratorian Canon listed those books acknowledged to be apostolic and to be read in the churches. It includes the Gospels and Acts, mentions 13 Pauline epistles, warning against some forgeries, refers to two epistles of John—probably in addition to the first epistle which is quoted—and names Jude and the Revelation of John. It mentions an apocalypse of Peter "though some amongst us will not have this latter read in the churches." We now know it was a spurious writing. The Shepherd of Hermas is rejected as non-apostolic. Thus all our books are listed except Hebrews, James, I and II Peter which are not mentioned at all. Westcott thinks this was due to a break in the manuscript's archetype, for all these had been accepted earlier.

The Period of A.D. 140

This is the age of Justin Martyr who tells us how the Gospels (all four) are read in the church services along with the OT. He quotes several other books including Hebrews. From this period we now have new evidence in the "Gospel of Truth" discovered recently in Egypt. This book, written by the Gnostic Valentinus, was referred to by Irenaeus in 170 and dates from about 150. It weaves into its pantheistic composition all our NT books except James, II Peter, II, III John and Jude. Hebrews and Revelation are definitely included. One student, W. C. van Unnik, concludes that "round about 140-150 a collection of writings was known at Rome and accepted as authoritative which was virtually identical with our NT ("The Gospel of

Truth and the NT," *The Jung Codex,* trans. and ed. by F. L. Cross, New York: Morehouse-Gorham, 1955, p. 124).

The Period from 95 to 118

Omitting many details, we may turn to the three great witnesses of the earliest age. Clement of Rome, Ignatius, and Polycarp all wrote between A.D. 95 and about 118. They show by quotation or clear allusion, that they knew and used all our NT books except Luke, Revelation, Colossians, Philemon, II Peter, II and III John and Jude. (See the evidence in Westcott, *General Survey of the History of the Canon of the New Testament,* pp. 22-48, and the author's *Inspiration and Canonicity of the Bible,* pp. 202-206). Moreover, these authors held the apostles in such high repute that their writings would obviously be treasured and accepted. Clement rather clearly ascribes inspiration to Paul. Actually, the omission of some of the books was not significant. Revelation and II and III John were possibly not yet written when Clement wrote in A.D. 95.

Later Problems

Although our books were accepted at an early date, yet the history of their use is discontinuous. The Gospels were never challenged until a later group of heretics questioned all the Johannine writings, claiming that they were spurious. Note that here, as usual, denial of apostolicity involved denial of authority. The book of Hebrews was continuously and from early days received and accepted as Pauline in Egypt. In Rome it was used by Clement, Justin, and Valentinus. The witness of Irenaeus (170) and Tertullian (about 200) is hardly clear. Then for a while its apostolicity was questioned and therefore its authority. Finally the views of Egypt and Palestine prevailed and it was fully accepted. II Peter had least external testimony, but here fortunately, the internal testimony is strong. Jude, which is in the Muratorian Canon and was accepted as apostolic by Tertullian, clearly quotes from II Peter 3:3. Also, if II Peter is not genuine, it is the basest of forgeries.

The New Testament Witness

And we must not forget the vital witness of the NT itself. Paul claims the authority of an apostle (I Cor. 9:1; II Cor. 12:11,12, etc.) and declares his letters are to be accepted (I Cor. 14:37; II Thess. 3:14). John in Revelation does the same (Rev. 1:3; 22:18,19). Peter insists that Paul's writings are Scripture (II Pet. 3:15; cf. 3:2). Jude quotes Peter as apostolic (Jude 18). It seems probable that I Timothy 5:18 quotes Luke 10:7 as Scripture. The fact is, as the early Church knew, that Christ had promised His apostles a special work of the Spirit, inspiring them as teachers of His revelation (John 14:26; 16:13). It is true that a few, a very few of the books were actually written by those not themselves apostles. But it is clear that the apostles used helpers in their writing (Rom. 16:22; I Pet. 5:12). The early church fathers called such men as Mark, Luke, and the author of Hebrews helpers or disciples of the apostles and accepted their work as that of the apostles with whom they labored. At least the books were all written and apparently were all accepted within the period of the apostles.

Other indications combine to teach us that these 27 books are rightly in our canon. The Holy Spirit has witnessed through the generations to the saving truth therein contained. These books have brought untold blessing where they have been received and obeyed. The church with one voice finds them to be the very word of God.   R.L.H.

CANTICLES (See Solomon, Song of)

Above, Capernaum as viewed from the Sea of Galilee; below, ruins of the ancient synagogue at Capernaum. © MPS

CAPERNAUM (kȧ-pûr′nā-ŭm, Gr. *Kapernaóum,* from Heb. *Kaphar-Nahum, village of Nahum*), a town on the NW shore of the Sea of Galilee where Jesus made His headquarters during His ministry in Galilee (Matt. 4:13; Mark 2:1). In Scripture it is mentioned only in the Gospels, and perhaps did not arise until after the Captivity. That it was a town of considerable size in the days of Christ is shown by a number of facts: a tax-collector had his office there (Mark 2:14); a high officer of the king (Herod Antipas) had his residence there and built a synagogue for the people there (Matt. 8:5-13; Luke 7:1-10). Jesus performed many striking miracles there, among them the healing of the centurion's palsied servant (Matt. 8:5-13), the man sick of the palsy borne by four (Mark 2:1-13), and a nobleman's son (John 4:46-54). It was there that He called Matthew to the apostleship as he was sitting at the receipt of custom (Matt. 9:9-13). The discourse on the Bread of Life, which followed the feeding of the 5,000, and many other addresses were delivered there (Mark 9:33-50). In spite of Jesus' striking works and teachings, the people did not repent, and Jesus predicted the complete ruin of the place (Matt. 11:23,24; Luke 10:15). His prophecy was so completely fulfilled that the town has disappeared and its very site is a matter of debate. There are two main claimants, about 2½ miles apart, for the honor of being the site: Tell Hum, which is about 2½ miles SW of the mouth of the Jordan; and Khan Minyeh, which is SW of Tell Hum. The present trend of opinion is in favor of Tell Hum.   S.B.

CAPH (kȧf), the 11th letter of the Hebrew alphabet corresponding to our "k." As a numeral it is eleven.

CAPHTOR (kăf'tôr, Heb. *kaphtôr*), the place from which the Philistines originally came (Amos 9:7). Jeremiah (47:4) calls it an island. There are a number of theories regarding the matter, but the one that is most widely accepted is that they came from the Isle of Crete in the Mediterranean. There is evidence of ancient connection between Crete and Philistia (Ezek. 25:16; Zeph. 2:5, where the LXX renders Cherethites "Cretans"); and the Philistines are called Cherethites, which may mean Cretans. It is possible that Caphtor includes with Crete also the other islands in the vicinity, including Caria and Lycia.

CAPPADOCIA (kăp'à-dō'shĭ-à), a large inland region of Asia Minor which apparently was given this name by the Persians though its people were called "Syrians" by the Greeks. In the latter time of the Persian empire the region was divided into two territories of which the more northerly was later named Pontus and the southerly Cappadocia, which name it retained in New Testament times. It was bounded on the N by Pontus, on the E by Syria and Armenia, on the S by Cilicia and on the W by Lycaonia. The Romans built roads through the "Cilician gates" in the Taurus range so that Cappadocia could readily be entered from the S. The Cappadocians were Aryans. Jews from Cappadocia (Acts 2:9) were among the hearers of the first Christian sermon along with men from other Anatolian provinces; and Peter directed his first epistle (I Pet. 1:1) in part to "the elect—of the Diaspora"—dwelling in various provinces in the N. It is almost certain that many of these Cappadocian Jews were converted on the day of Pentecost and so have the honor of being among the very earliest Christians.   A.B.F.

CAPTAIN, a word that in KJV translates 16 different words in the original text (12 Hebrew, one Aramaic, three Greek), but by far the most frequent is *sar* which occurs 419 times in the OT and is rendered "prince" 208 times (cf. "Sarah" for "princess"), "captain" 126 times, "chief" and "ruler" each 33 times. Most of them are terms expressing leadership, and do not refer to specific grades or ranks in a military organization. The meaning is obvious. In the NT Christ is called "captain of their (our) salvation" (Heb. 2:10). "*Chiliarchos*" or "leader of a thousand" (John 18: 12) could be translated "colonel," while the "captain of the temple" (Acts 4:1, etc.) was not a military officer at all, though he had soldiers under his authority. Though the general intent is clear, the meaning is not technically definite.

CAPTIVITY. The term Captivity, when used of Israel, has reference not to the long series of oppressions and captivities of the Israelites by hostile peoples, beginning with the bondage in Egypt and ending with the domination of Rome, but to the captivity of the Ten Tribes in 722 B.C. and the captivity of Judah in 586 B.C. The practice of making wholesale deportations of people as a punishment for rebellion was introduced by Assyria, but other nations adopted it.

1. *The Captivity of the Northern Kingdom.* Assyria first made contact with the Northern Kingdom when Shalmaneser II (860-825 B.C.) routed in the battle of Karkar (854 B.C.) the combined forces of Damascus, Hamath, Israel, and other states who had united to stop his westward progress. In another campaign Shalmaneser received tribute from Jehu, king of Israel. Not many years later, Rimmon-nirari III (810-781) compelled Syria to let go her hold of Israel. Tiglath-pileser III (745-727 B.C.), one of the greatest monarchs of antiquity, after capturing Samaria, put on the throne as his vassal Hoshea, who had slain Pekah, king of Israel. With the death of Tiglath-pileser III, Hoshea decided to strike a blow for independence. Help was promised by the king of Egypt, but it did not come. Hoshea was made a prisoner, and the capital doomed to destruction, as the prophets had foretold (Hos. 10:7,8; Isa. 28:1; Mic. 1:5,6). It was, however, only after a three years' siege that the city was captured. Before it fell, Shalmaneser had abdicated or died, and Sargon, who succeeded him, completed the conquest of the city and deported the inhabitants to Assyria (II Kings 17:6,7; 18:11,12). Some time later, Sargon's grandson Esarhaddon, and his great-grandson Ashur-banipal, imported to the region of Samaria some conquered peoples from the East (Ezra 4:2,10). Not all of the inhabitants of the Northern Kingdom were taken into captivity. The very poor, who could cause no trouble in the future, were left (II Kings 25:12). Intermarriage with the imported peoples resulted in the hybrid stock later known as the Samaritans. The Ten Tribes taken into captivity, sometimes called the Lost Tribes of Israel, must not be thought of as being absorbed by the peoples among whom they settled. Some undoubtedly were, but many others retained their Israelitish religion and traditions. Some became part of the Jewish dispersion, and others very likely returned with the exiles of Judah who had been carried off by Nebuchadnezzar in 536 B.C.

2. *The Captivity of the Southern Kingdom.* The captivity of Judah was predicted 150 years before it occurred (Isa. 6:11,12; 11:12). Isaiah (11:11; 39:6) and Micah (4:10) foretold that the place of the captivity was to be Babylon; and Jeremiah announced that it would be for 70 years (Jer. 25: 1,11,12). The Southern Kingdom rested on a firmer religious foundation than the Northern Kingdom, and was therefore able to survive longer, but it too had in it the seeds of moral and spiritual decay that caused its eventual disintegration.

Sargon was followed by a number of brilliant rulers, but by 625 B.C. the hold of Assyria over its tributary peoples had greatly slackened. Revolts broke out everywhere, and bands of Scythians swept through the empire as far as Egypt. Nineveh fell to the Babylonians in 606 B.C., never to rise again. A great new Babylonian empire was built up by Nebuchadnezar (604-562 B.C.). Judah became a vassal of Nebuchadnezzar, but Jehoiakim the king, although warned by the Prophet Jeremiah, turned and rebelled against him. Nebuchadnezzar thereupon came into Jerusalem in 605 B.C. and carried off to Babylon the vessels of the house of God and members of the nobility of Judah, among them Daniel the prophet (II Chron. 36:2-7; Jer. 45:1; Dan. 1:1-3). Jehoiakim was taken in chains to Babylon (II Chron. 36:6). In 597 B.C. Nebuchadnezzar carried off Jehoiachin, his mother, his wives, 3,000 princes, 7,000 men of might, and 1,000 artisans (II Kings 24:14-16). Among them was the prophet Ezekiel. This was the first large-scale deportation of the Southern Kingdom into Babylonia. Eleven years later (586) Nebuchadnezzar burned the temple, destroyed the city of Jerusalem, and deported into Babylonia all but the poorest of the land (II Kings 25:2-21). A third group was taken into Babylonia five years after the destruction of the city (Jer. 52:30).

The exiled Jews were not heavily oppressed by their conquerors. They engaged in business, built houses (Jer. 29:5-7; Ezra 2:65), and even held high positions in the state (Dan. 2:48; Neh. 1:11). They could not continue their system of sacrifices, but they had with them their priests and teachers

(Jer. 29:1; Ezra 1:5); and Ezekiel gave them constant encouragement (Ezek. 1:1). In 539 B.C. Babylon fell to Cyrus king of Persia, who issued a decree permitting the return of the Jews to Jerusalem to rebuild the temple (Ezra 1:1-4). The next year about 43,000 returned with Zerubbabel (Ezra 2:64), the rest preferring to remain in Mesopotamia (Zech. 6:10). In 458 B.C. 1,800 returned with Ezra.   S.B.

CARAVAN, a group of travelers united together for a common purpose or for mutual protection and generally equipped for a long journey, especially in desert country, or through foreign and presumably hostile territory. Jacob's "company" (Gen. 32,33) is a good example of a caravan organized to carry a clan to a new home; and the host of the Amalekites whom David destroyed (I Sam. 30:1-20) is another caravan, organized for raiding purposes. In the trackless desert where oases are few and far between and where savage beasts and more savage men are found, it was essential to go in caravans for protection's sake. The word does not occur in KJV, but "company" and "troop" could often have been "caravan."

CARBUNCLE, a word occurring four times in KJV but rendering three different Hebrew words, all representing something bright and glittering. Both ruby and emerald have been suggested as equivalents. Used in the high priest's breastplate (Exod. 28:17; 39:10). See MINERALS.

CARCAS (kär'kăs), a eunuch in the service of Xerxes ("Ahasuerus"). (Esth. 1:10.)

CARCASE (ASV and modern English, *carcass*), the dead body of a man or beast. The word is a translation of six different words in Scripture with root ideas of something fallen, faded, exhausted; or just the bare idea of body, as in Judges 14:8,9. The law of Moses, probably partly for sanitary reasons, required that carcasses of "unclean" beasts should be considered abominable. Read Leviticus 11:8-40.

CARCHEMISH (kär'kē-mĭsh), an ancient city of the Hittites located on the W bank of the Euphrates 63 miles NE of Aleppo. It was important commercially and militarily. For many years it paid tribute to the kings of Assyria. When Sargon captured it in 717 B.C., the Hittite empire fell with it (Isa. 10:9). It was the scene of a great victory by Nebuchadnezzar over Pharaoh Necho in 605 B.C. (Jer. 46:2; II Chron. 35:20). Its site is called Jerabis or Jerablus.

CAREAH (kà-rē'à), or generally and more properly Kareah. The father of Johanan and Jonathan who tried to save Gedaliah from assassination (Jer. 40:8-43:7), but later wickedly went to Egypt to dwell there.

CARMEL (kär'mĕl, *garden*). 1. The mountainous promontory jutting into the Mediterranean Sea just S of the modern city Haifa and straight W of the Sea of Galilee. On the map of Palestine, it forms the principal deviation from a comparatively straight coastline, and it forms the southern wall of the magnificent bay (or gulf) of Acre, the best natural harbor south of Beirut. When the word occurs with the definite article it generally refers to Mt. Carmel and is often used as an illustration of a beautiful and fruitful place (Isa. 35:2; but contrast 33:9, which pictures God's judgment). South of Carmel lies the fruitful plain of Sharon and NE of it flows the river Kishon through the plain of Esdraelon. At Carmel Elijah stood against 850 heathen prophets and defeated them (I Kings 18). Carmel was visited by Elisha (II Kings 2:25; 4:25).

Typical caravan of Bedouin nomads crossing the desert, reminiscent of "Jacob's company." © MPS

2. A very ancient town of Judah about seven miles nearly S of Hebron. First mentioned in Joshua 15:55, it is best known as the residence of the very churlish Nabal who refused kindness to David (I Sam. 25:2-40) and whose life was saved by the tact of his beautiful wife Abigail, who later became a wife of David.

CARMELITE (kär'mĕl-īt), a native of Judaean Carmel: applied to David's wife Abigail who had first married Nabal (I Sam. 27:3, etc.) and to Hezro, one of David's mighty men (I Chron. 11:37, etc.).

CARMI (kär'mē). 1. One of the sons of Reuben, eldest son of Jacob; and head of the family of the "Carmites" (Gen. 46:9; Num. 26:6, etc.).

2. An early descendant of Judah (probably great-grandson) and father of Achan (Josh. 7:1), mentioned in I Chronicles 4:1 as "son" i.e. descendant of Judah.

CARNAL (kär'năl). Fleshly, of or pertaining to the body as the seat of the desires and appetites; usually employed in Scripture in the bad sense, as opposed to spiritual. In I Corinthians 2:14-3:4, Paul first divides mankind practically into two classes—the natural and the spiritual. This corresponds to the classification of men as once-born and twice-born. Then he classifies Christians as "carnal" and "spiritual" and lists the marks of carnality as "envying, strife, divisions" (KJV) and undue emphasis of personalities: "I am of Paul— I am of Apollos." "Carnal" does not necessarily imply active and conscious sin, but is opposed to "spiritual" (Rom. 7:14; II Cor. 10:4; Heb. 7:16;

Sunset scene at Mount Carmel on Mediterranean coast. © MPS

9:10, etc.), the dominance of the lower side of man as apart from the divine influence.

The Old Testament uses the expression "lying carnally" to describe adultery (Lev. 18:20) and fornication (Lev. 19:20), but these ugly words are used far more often figuratively and refer to idolatry. To take the love that belongs to husband or wife and give it to another is adultery; and to take the love that belongs to God and give it to another is idolatry (Hos. 1-3; Rev. 17:18). A.B.F.

CARPENTER (See Occupations, Professions)

CARPUS (kär'pŭs), a Christian brother living at Troas mentioned only in II Timothy 4:13. He had evidently been the host of Paul while he was in Troas.

CARRIAGE, occurs five times in the KJV and in each case refers to that which is carried; baggage (I Sam. 17:22; Isa. 10:28).

CARSHENA (kär'shē-nà), one of the seven princes of the Medo-Persian kingdom in the days of the great Xerxes, husband of Vashti, and later of Esther (Esth. 1:14).

CARTS, and wagons, are very ancient. In Genesis 45:19-21 Pharaoh provided carts for the wives and children of Jacob at the descent into Egypt. In the days of Eli the Philistines took the ark of God, and finding it a most unwelcome guest, they put it upon a cart and let it go back to Israel (I Sam. 6); but when David later desired to bring the same ark to his city, he used a cart, and the result was disastrous (See II Sam. 6:1-11).

CASIPHIA (kà-sĭf'ĭ-à), a place near the river Ahava, a tributary of the Euphrates, twice mentioned in Ezra 8:17 as a place where exiled Levites lived.

CASLUHIM (kăs'lū-hĭm), one of the seven tribes listed in Genesis 10:13,14 and its parallel passage I Chronicles 1:11,12 as descended from "Mizraim," which is the name for Egypt. The Philistines are said to have come out from this tribe.

CASSIA (See Plants)

CASTLE, a large fortified building or set of buildings, as that of a prince or nobleman. David took the Jebusite castle in Jerusalem and made it into his residence (I Chron. 11:5,7). Castles were built in the cities of Judah by Jehoshaphat (II Chron. 17:12) and in its forests by Jotham (II Chron. 27:4). Where the KJV uses "castles," the RV sometimes, more correctly, uses encampments (I Chron. 6:54). Nehemiah erected a castle in Jerusalem which later became the Tower of Antonia, where Paul was confined.

The famous ancient Crusader's Castle, the Krak de Chevaliers, in Lebanon. © MPS

CASTOR AND POLLUX (kàs'têr, pŏl'ŭks; Gr. *Dióskuroi, sons of Zeus*). In Greek mythology, they were sons of Zeus by Leda, one of his numerous mistresses. Castor was a horseman, and Pollux an adept boxer. They were later put in the sky in the constellation known as "Gemini," "the Twins," and were considered as tutelary deities favorable to sailors, which explains why the ship mentioned in Acts 28:11, in which Paul sailed, was named in their honor. St. Elmo's fire used to be credited to Castor and Pollux.

Room lined with skulls in the Capuchin cemetery in the Catacombs at Rome. © RTHPL

CATACOMBS are subterranean burial places used by the early Church. The principal catacombs are outside Rome, where the galleries in the tufa rock extend for six hundred miles, according to one estimate, and so surround the city that they even act as a cushion against earthquake shocks. The lowest estimate of the graves contained in the catacombs is 1,750,000, the highest 4,000,000, covering ten generations. This permits minimum and maximum estimates of 175,000 and 400,000 Christians in each generation, not allowing for the upward curve in the numbers of those connected with the Church over the period named. Since the population of Rome was about 1,000,000 it will be seen that the catacomb figures make nonsense of Gibbon's once accepted estimates of the Christian population of the capital. Family burial places in the catacombs provide striking evidence for the vertical spread of the faith.

CATERPILLAR (See Insects)

CATHOLIC EPISTLES, a term applied to the Epistles of James, Peter, John, and Jude. It goes back to the early church Fathers, but how it arose is unknown. The most commonly accepted explanation is that the Epistles were addressed not to individual churches or persons, but to a number of churches. They were addressed to the Church at large, i.e., the universal Church. The seeming exceptions, II and III John, were probably included as properly belonging with I John and of value to the general reader.

CATTLE (See Animals)

CAUDA (kow'dà), a small island lying about 25 miles to the S of Crete (Acts 27:16 in KJV "Clauda") and now called Gavdo. Here Paul and his companions were almost wrecked on their journey toward Rome.

CAUL. 1. The chief meaning is a deep fold above the liver, the omentum which is loaded with fat and which with the kidneys was used in several of the Levitical offerings (Lev. 3:4; 4:9, etc.).

2. The pericardium or the breast as a whole (Hos. 13:8).

3. Bag or purse (Isa. 3:18). See also DRESS.

A mother and baby at entrance to their cave dwelling in Petra region. © MPS

CAVE, a hollowed-out place in the earth, whether formed by nature or by man. In a mountainous land such as Palestine, where there is much limestone, caves are likely to be quite numerous. Caves were often used for regular human habitation, for hiding from the law or from enemies in warfare, for securing precious treasure (such as the recently discovered Dead Sea scrolls), for storehouses and cisterns, for stables for cattle, and for burial (Gen. 19:30; I Kings 19:9, etc.).

CEDAR (See Plants)

CEDRON (sē'drŏn, in ASV more properly "Kidron"), a ravine which in winter contains the brook of the same name, flowing southward between Jerusalem and Mt. of Olives on the E of the city. It is mentioned by this name only in John 18:1. It is loved for the sacred memories connected with it and the Garden of Gethsemane which lay beside it.

CEILING (KJV and ERV "cieling"), appears only in I Kings 6:15, where it says that Solomon built the walls of the ceiling with cedar. The reference here is not to the upper surface of a room, but to the inner walls. The word "ceiled" appears several times, but it usually means to panel the walls of a building.

CELLAR, a place for storage of wine (I Chron. 27:27) or oil (v. 28). The root idea here is not that of a room under a house, but that of a place of storage.

CENCHREA (sĕn'krē-à, Cenchreae in ASV), the eastern harbor of Corinth, and the little town on the harbor. Paul in Romans 16:1 commends to the Roman church, Phoebe, a deaconess of the church

at Cenchrea, which Paul may have founded on his second missionary journey. Paul stopped here to have his head shaved in fulfillment of a vow (Acts 18:18).

CENSER, a vessel, probably shaped like a saucepan, for holding incense while it is being burned (Num. 16:6,7,39). The Hebrew word rendered "censer" is generally translated "censer," sometimes "firepan," and in three cases "snuffdish" (Exod. 25:38; 37:23; Num. 4:9).

CENSUS, a numbering and registration of a people. The OT tells of three different occasions when a formal census was taken. The first was at Mount Sinai, soon after the Israelites left Egypt (Num. 1). The second was taken at Shittim near the end of the 40 years' wilderness wandering. The third was made by David. The exiles who returned from Babylonia with Zerubbabel were also numbered (Ezra 2). Shortly before the birth of Christ, the Emperor Augustus ordered an enrollment in his empire (Luke 2:1).

CENTURION (cĕn-tū'rĭ-ŏn, Lat. centum, 100), a commander of a hundred soldiers in the Roman army. The word, of course, does not appear in the OT. The one first mentioned is the centurion of Capernaum whose beloved servant was sick unto death (Matt. 8:5-13; Luke 7:2-10). This officer had gone so far as to build a synagogue for the Jews, so that the Jews appreciated him and begged Jesus to heal the servant. The centurion showed real reverence to Jesus when he said "I am not worthy that thou shouldest come under my roof," and Jesus said "I have not found so great faith, no, not in Israel." The next is Cornelius (Acts 10) "a devout man, and one that feared God with all his house." It was to him that Peter was sent, and going almost unwillingly, Peter "used the keys" to open up salvation to the Gentiles, as he had at Jerusalem for the Jews (Acts 2) and at Samaria for its people (Acts 8:14-17). Another was Julius, of the Augustan band (Acts 27:1-43) whose duty it was to take Paul to Rome. He saved Paul's life when the soldiers wished to kill all the prisoners, and Paul, by his presence and counsel, saved the centurion with all the ship's company. Other centurions are mentioned elsewhere (Matt. 27:54; Acts 22:25; 23:17). A.B.F.

CEPHAS (sē'fás, Gr. Kephás, from Aram. Kepha, rock, or stone). A name given by Jesus to the Apostle Peter (John 1:42). See PETER.

CHAFF, the refuse of the grain which has been threshed and winnowed. This is partly dust and dirt, but the real chaff is the hard and inedible coat of the grain. By threshing, most of this is separated, and then on a windy day the grain is tossed into the air and the chaff and the shorter pieces of straw are blown away. In Isaiah 5:24 and 33:11 the word properly means "dry hay" fit for burning. The more common word (Heb. mots) is generally used as a figure for worthless or godless men (Ps. 1:4; "The ungodly are not so: but are like the chaff which the wind driveth away"). It is used also for godless nations (Isa. 17:13). The evanescence of the wicked is likened in Hosea 13:3 to the morning cloud, the early dew, the chaff driven by the whirlwind, and the smoke out of the window (KJV "chimney"!). In Daniel 2:35, the Aramaic word rendered chaff signifies the small chaff that can get into the eye and irritate it. The word in Jeremiah 23:28 means the broken straw. In the preaching of John the Baptist (Matt. 3:12; Luke 3:17) our Lord is to save the righteous (gather the wheat into His garner) but the wicked ("the chaff") He will burn with unquenchable fire.

CHAIN. The English word represents many Hebrew words, meaning *chain, necklace, band, bracelet, clasp, hook, ring* and *rope.* All OT references are given without distinguishing the Hebrew originals. Chains were used: 1. As marks of distinction, in the case of Joseph (Gen. 41:42), and Daniel (Dan. 5:7,16,29).

2. For ornaments (Exod. 28:14,22; 39:15,17, 18) in the tabernacle. Chains were among the atonement offerings (Num. 31:50). Some had lunettes attached, such as the Midianites used to adorn their camels' necks (Judg. 8:21,26). Wreaths of chain work ornamented the tops of the pillars (I Kings 7:17; II Chron. 3:16) and elsewhere in Solomon's Temple (I Kings 6:21; II Chron. 3:5). As jewelry, chains are referred to in Psalm 73:6; Proverbs 1:9; Song of Solomon 1:10; 4:9; Isaiah 3:19; 40:19 (idols); Ezekiel 16:11.

3. For fetters (Ps. 68:6; 149:8; Isa. 45:14; Jer. 39:7; 40:1; 52:11; Lam. 3:7; Ezek. 7:23; 19:4, 9; Nah. 3:10). In the NT most of the references represent the Greek *hálusis, chain.* In Mark 5:3,4; Luke 8:29, chains are used to bind a demoniac; in Acts 12:6,7, Peter in prison was bound with two chains to the guards who slept on either side of him; in Acts 21:33, Paul was bound with two chains, but quickly released; in Acts 28:20, Paul was bound by a chain on his right hand to a soldier's left; to which he refers also in II Timothy 1:16; a circumstance which offers one explanation of why Paul dictated his letters to an amanuensis. An angel binds Satan with a chain (Rev. 20:1). In Jude 6 chain translates *desmós,* anything for tying or fastening; in II Peter 2:4, *seirá, cord, rope.* See also DRESS.   E.R.

CHALCEDONY (kăl-sĕd′ō-nē, kăl-sĕ-dō′nē, Gr. *chalkedón*), the precious stone adorning the third foundation of the New Jerusalem (Rev. 21:19). The modern meaning of the term cannot be traced earlier than the 15th century A.D. Pliny writes of a Chalcedonian emerald, also of a Chalcedonian jasper. Chalcedon, modern Kadikoy near Scutari on the Bosporus opposite Istanbul, was probably the place of origin. RSV translates "agate" without explanation.

CHALCOL (kăl′kŏl), a son (or descendant) of Mahol (I Kings 4:31). Solomon was wiser than he. Calcol, a son (or descendant) of Zerah (I Chron. 2:6). Since four of the same names occur in both passages as brothers, Chalcol and Calcol are probably the same person. ASV, RSV have Calcol in both places.

CHALDAEA or **CHALDEA** (kăl-dē′à), the country of which Babylon was the capital, and which conquered Judah and carried its inhabitants into captivity. The name occurs in KJV only in Jeremiah 50:10; 51:24,35; Ezekiel 11:24; 16:29; 23:15,16.

CHALDEAN (kăl-dē′ăn), an adjective referring to things pertaining to Chaldaea; or a noun referring to a man of Chaldaea.

CHALDEAN ASTROLOGERS (See Wise Men)

CHALDEES (kăl-dēz, kăl′dēz), the people of Chaldea; the Chaldeans.

CHAMBERING (chăm′bêr-ĭng), repeated or habitual acts of illicit intercourse (Rom. 13:13).

CHAMBERLAIN (chăm′bêr-lĭn). In the OT the eunuch in charge of a king's harem, especially in Persia (Esth. 1:10,12,15; 2:3,14,15,21; 4:4,5; 6:2,14; 7:9), called "eunuch" in RSV. In II Kings 23:11 RSV retains "chamberlain" for the same Hebrew word. In Acts 12:20 the chamberlain is "one who is over the king's bedchamber," an intimate and confidential position. In Romans 16:23

the word used is often translated "steward." ASV, RSV have "treasurer," which is accurate in this connection.

CHAMBERS OF IMAGERY, rooms in the temple where seventy elders of Israel worshiped idols with incense. RSV has "room of pictures" (Ezek. 8:12). Verse 10 indicates what the pictures or images represented.

CHAMELEON (See Animals)

CHAMOIS (See Animals)

CHANAAN (See Canaan)

CHANCELLOR (chăn′sĕ-lêr, RSV *commander*), a Persian official in Palestine (Ezra 4:8,9,17).

A Jewish money-changer in Jerusalem. © MPS

CHANGERS OF MONEY, men who exchanged one currency for another at a premium. Coins issued by many governments circulated in Palestine; also Jews must convert their currency into shekels for the temple-tax. It was not the trade but the place where they plied it which led Christ to drive them out of the temple court (Matt. 21:12; Mark 11:15; John 2:14,15). All three Gospels use the Greek *kollybistés, a changer of small coins.* John 2:14 has *kermatistés,* with identical meaning. "Exchangers" (Matt. 25:27) translates *trapezítes,* better rendered (RSV) "banker," lender of money at interest. Both used tables (*trapezas*) and often combined the two functions.

CHAPMAN (chăp′măn), a traveling trader or merchant (II Chron. 9:14).

CHARASHIM (kăr′ă-shĭm, Heb. *hărāshîm, craftsmen*), Valley of, E of Joppa between Ono to the N and Lod (Lydda) to the S; settled by one Joab, apparently of Judah (I Chron. 4:14). It received its name because artificers or craftsmen dwelt there (Neh. 11:35).

CHARCHEMISH, CARCHEMISH (kàr'kē-mǐsh, kàr-kē'mǐsh), Hittite capital on the Euphrates, focus for invasions between Egypt, Assyria and Europe. See CARCHEMISH.

CHARGER, a dish or platter given as an offering for the tabernacle (Num. 7:13-85); called "dishes" in Exodus 25:29; 37:16. Another word (Ezra 1:9) refers to baskets or dishes belonging to the temple service. The NT word means a wooden dish or platter (Matt. 14:8,11; Mark 6:25,28).

CHARIOT (chăr'ĭ-ŭt, Heb. *rekhev* and derivatives, from a root meaning *mount and ride*), a two-wheeled vehicle drawn by two horses. In Egypt, Joseph rides in Pharaoh's second chariot (Gen. 41: 43). Chariots were in Jacob's funeral procession (Gen. 50:9). Pharaoh pursued the children of Israel into the Red Sea with chariots (Exod. 14:7-15:19).

King Tutankhamen's chariot in the Cairo museum.

The Canaanites used chariots studded with iron, or covered with plates of iron, which kept the Israelites from conquering the plains (Judg. 1:19). The Philistines mustered mighty hosts of chariots against Israel (I Sam. 13:5). David hocked the chariot-horses of his enemies (II Sam. 8:4). Adonijah prepared chariots when he plotted to overthrow his father David (I Kings 1:5). Solomon built establishments to house many chariots (I Kings 9: 19). He imported chariots from Egypt at 600 shekels each (I Kings 10:28,29). Both divided kingdoms used chariots in war (I Kings 16:9; 22: 34; II Kings 23:30). Some parts of a chariot are referred to in I Kings 7:33. There was a pole to which the two horses were yoked; an axle; wheels with six or eight spokes; and a body fastened to the axle and pole.

Often only two men rode in the chariot; a driver and a warrior (I Kings 22:34), but sometimes the Hittite practice of adding a shield-bearer was followed. The Assyrian chariot was heavier than the Egyptian or Hebrew, and carried three or four men. Nahum 2:3,4 is a vivid picture of such chariots. Elijah was honored by being escorted up to heaven by a chariot of fire (II Kings 2:11), and his manner of going became a proverb (II Kings 2:12; 13:14). God is represented as having thousands of chariots, showing His power (Ps. 68:17). Trust in chariots is vain compared with trust in God (Ps. 20:7). Habakkuk 3:8 sees God riding upon the chariots of salvation. The chariots of the sun (II Kings 23:11) were used in sun-worship (verse 5). Chariots were used for riding (S. of Sol. 1:9; 6:12), especially by royalty. Other Hebrew words are used for chariot: in Song of Solomon 3:9,10, a

litter is meant; in Ezekiel 23:24 a *war-chariot*; Psalm 46:9, *a wheeled vehicle*. In the NT, Greek *hárma,* a *war-chariot* (Rev. 9:9) drawn by horses, used also for riding (Acts 8:28,29,38). In Revelation 18:13 the word is *rhéda,* a Gallic wagon with four wheels.   E.R.

CHARITY (chăr'ĭ-tē), the KJV rendering of Greek *agápe* in 28 places. *Agápe* is translated "love" in 87 places; "dear," once (Col. 1:13). Charity represents Latin *caritas,* but *caritas* also stands in the Vulgate in passages where KJV has "love." Charity in the Bible never means giving to the poor, but always a God-inspired love which includes respect for, and concern for the welfare of the loved one. The inspired description is found in I Cor.13.

CHARRAN (See Haran)

CHASTE, CHASTITY (chāst, chăs'tĭ-tē, Gr. *hagnós*), originally meaning *pure* in a ritual sense, *tabu, consecrated*; it developed a moral sense as the Greeks gained higher conceptions of deity. In the Bible, where the highest conception of God always prevailed, the moral and the religious are never separated. *Hagnós* is translated "chaste" in I Peter 3:2, Titus 2:5, regarding Christian women; II Corinthians 11:2, referring to the Corinthian Christians as a "chaste virgin" bride for Christ. It is translated "clear" (II Cor. 7:11), "pure" (I John 3:3; Phil. 4:8, etc.). Derivatives are translated "pure," "pureness," "purity," "purify," "purification," "sincerely," and in the LXX they are used for Heb. words of kindred meanings. Chastity in the relations of men and women is the NT norm; the standard for all forms of purity.

CHASTISEMENT (chăs'tīz-měnt, Heb. *mûsār,* from verb *yāsar, discipline* [the moral nature], *chasten, admonish, correct*; Gr. *paideía, child-training, the formation of manhood*). Both are translated by many English words, exhibiting shades of meaning derived from the central concept: the widest sense (Deut. 11:2); *punishment* (Jer. 30:14); *discipline* (Heb. 12:8); in Isaiah 53:5 the whole range of meaning is exhibited in the substitution of the sinless Servant of Jehovah for His guilty people. When *mûsār* is translated "chastening," discipline rather than punishment is meant (Job 5:17; Prov. 3:11,12, whence Heb. 12:5-11 is drawn; Isa. 26:16); *retribution* (Lev. 26:28); *instruction in wisdom* is prominent in Proverbs; *unjust chastisement* (I Kings 12:11); the prayer of Psalm 6:1 is answered (Ps. 94:12). The Greek word in Acts 7:22; 22:3; II Timothy 3:16 (*learn, teach, instruction*) refers to education. Heb. *yākah* occurs of child-training (II Sam. 7:14); of the meaning and value of suffering (Job 33:19; Ps. 73:14). Daniel has chastened himself by humility (Dan. 10:12, Heb. *'ānâh*). Chastisement is the process by which God provides a Substitute to bear our sins, brings men to put their trust in Him, trains those whom He has received till they reach maturity.   E.R.

CHEBAR (kē'bàr), a river or canal beside which Ezekiel saw visions (Ezek. 1:1; 3:23; 10:15,20,22; 43:3); in Babylonia ("the land of the Chaldeans," Ezek. 1:3); at Tel-abib (Ezek. 3:15); not yet identified.

CHECKER WORK (chěk'êr-wûrk), ornamentation for the capitals of two pillars in Solomon's temple (I Kings 7:17). ASV, RSV have "coats of checker work" in Exodus 28:4. The root means "interweave."

CHEDORLAOMER (kěd'ŏr-lā-ō'mûr), king (Gen. 14:1,4,5,9,17) of Elam, S of Media and E of Babylonia; named by Semites (Gen. 10:22), but inhabited chiefly by Indo-Europeans; later part of Persia, modern Iran. Chedorlaomer, with Amraphel king of Shinar (Babylonia), Arioch king of Ellasar and Tidal king of nations or of Goiim (so ASV, RSV), made war with Bera king of Sodom, Birsha king of Gomorrah, Shinab king of Admah, Shemeber king of Zeboiim, and the king of Bela or Zoar, all near the Dead or Salt Sea. Chedorlaomer held sway over the five cities for 12 years. In the 13th year they rebelled. In the 14th year Chedorlaomer and his allies conquered the country they traversed, and met the king of Sodom and his allies on the same battleground (the vale of Siddim or the Salt Sea) where Chedorlaomer had defeated them 14 years earlier. The bitumen pits of the region were the undoing of the local defenders. But Abram the Hebrew in a swift night raid with 318 retainers recovered the spoil of Sodom, and pursued the invaders to a point near Damascus. The story is told fully (Gen. 14) because it involved Abram and his brother's son Lot.

CHEESE, once Heb. *gevînâh* (Job 10:10) *curd, cheese,* from a root meaning "coagulate"; once Heb. *shâphâh* (II Sam. 17:29) *cream,* because skimmed off; once Heb. *hǎrîtsî hehālāv* (I Sam. 17:18) *cuts of milk, i.e., cheese.* Milk of kine, goats or sheep was stored in skins. In a warm climate, without refrigeration, it would soon curdle. The process of cheese-making employed can only be guessed from the practices current in the Near East today.

CHELAL (kē′lăl), a man of Palath-moab who put away his foreign wife (Ezra 10:30).

CHELLUH (kĕl′ū), one of the sons of Bani who married a foreign wife (Ezra 10:35).

CHELUB (kē′lŭb, Heb. *kelûv,* another form of *Caleb*). 1. A brother of Shuah, a Judahite (I Chron. 4:11).
2. Father of Ezri, and superintendent of the tillers of the ground in David's time (I Chron. 27:26).

CHELUBAI (kē-lōō′bī), son of Hezron, elsewhere called Caleb (I Chron. 2:9).

CHEMARIM (kĕm′à-rĭm, Heb. *kemārîm*), probably from a root meaning "prostrate oneself" (Zeph. 1:4). The Heb. word occurs also in II Kings 23:5; Hosea 10:5, and always refers to idolatrous priests.

CHEMOSH (kē′mŏsh), the god of Moab, so named in an ancient Israelite song (Num. 21:29, alluded to in Jer. 48:7,13,46). Jephthah refers to Chemosh as god of the Ammonites (Judg. 11:24), either by mistake or because Ammon also worshiped Chemosh in addition to Molech. Solomon introduced the worship of Chemosh into Jerusalem to please a foreign wife, though thereby he displeased his God (I Kings 11:7,33). Josiah defiled this high place of Chemosh (II Kings 23:13), putting an end to its use as a place of worship. Mesha, king of Moab, suffered a great disaster in his rebellion against Israel, in consequence of which he offered his son, the heir to the throne of Moab, as a burnt offering (II Kings 3:4-27). The inscription on the Moabite stone shows that this sacrifice was made to Chemosh, and describes (in terms whose similarity in style to the terms employed by the Israelites of the true God only accentuates the contrast between the two) the help which Mesha believed Chemosh had given his people in war, and the chastisement which Chemosh meted out to them when they were unfaithful.

CHENAANAH (kē-nā′à-nà). 1. The father of the false prophet Zedekiah who smote Micaiah (I Kings 22:11,24; II Chron. 18:10,23).

2. The brother of Ehud, son of Bilham, a Benjamite (I Chron. 7:10).

CHENANI (kē-nā′nī, kĕn′à-nī), a Levite who helped bring the returned exiles into agreement about the covenant worship of God (Neh. 9:4).

CHENANIAH (kĕn′à-nī′à). 1. A chief Levite when David brought up the ark from the house of Obed-edom (I Chron. 15:22,27).
2. An Izharite, an officer of David's (I Chron. 26:29). Some identify the two as one.

CHEPHAR-HAAMMONI (kē′fàr-hă-ăm′ō-nī, ASV, RSV Chephar-ammoni, Josh. 18:24), an Ammonite town in the territory of Benjamin, site unknown.

CHEPHIRAH (kē-fī′rà), a Hivite town which, with Gibeon, by deceit gained the protection of the Israelites (Josh. 9:17); in the territory of Benjamin (Josh. 18:26); some of whose citizens returned after the Exile (Ezra 2:25; Neh. 7:29); modern Tell Kefireh between Aijalon and Gibeon.

CHERAN (kē′răn), son of Dishon, the son of Seir the Horite (Gen. 36:26; I Chron. 1:41).

CHERETHIM, CHERETHITES (kĕr′ĕ-thĭm, kĕr′ĕ-thīts), a Philistine tribe in southern Palestine (I Sam. 30:14; Ezek. 25:16; Zeph. 2:5), from whom David drew his bodyguard, commanded by Benaiah (II Sam. 8:18; 15:18; 20:7,23; I Kings 1:38,44; I Chron. 18:17). The Heb. name may be from a root *kareth, to cut down,* indicating that the Cherethite guards were executioners, or at least swordsmen. Twice LXX translates "Cretans" (Ezek. 25:16; Zeph. 2:5), indicating their belief that the Cherethites came from Crete; and indeed the Philistines originated there. Elsewhere LXX has *Cheleththi* or *Chereththi* (except I Sam. 30:14, *Cholthi*). David's guard was probably recruited from foreign mercenaries.

CHERITH (kē′rĭth), the brook where, at God's command, Elijah hid himself during the first part of the famine he had predicted (I Kings 17:1-5). It was "before Jordan," a Heb. expression (*'al-penê*), which means "toward the face of"; of location, "in front of"; usually "east of" (so RSV); but not always so; hence is no conclusive help in identifying the brook. Perhaps it was as obscure in Elijah's day as now; therefore a secure hiding place.

CHERUB (chĕr′ŭb), pl., **CHERUBIM** (chĕr′ū-bĭm), which KJV treats as singular, with a plural, cherubims. In other than Biblical usage, the English plural is cherubs. The cherubim and a flaming sword were placed at the E of Eden to keep the way of the tree of life, after Adam and Eve were expelled from the garden (Gen. 3:24). God directs Moses to place two cherubim of beaten gold on the mercy seat above the ark, where God would commune with Moses in the tabernacle (Exod. 25:18-22; 37:7-9). The curtains of the tabernacle were embroidered with cherubim (Exod. 26:1). God dwelt between the cherubim (Num. 7:89; I Sam. 4:4; II Sam. 6:2; II Kings 19:15; Ps. 80:1; 99:1; Isa. 37:16), both in the tabernacle and the temple. The cherubim in the temple were huge figures newly made for the purpose (I Kings 6:23-28; II Chron. 3:10-13; 5:7,8). Carved cherubim also ornamented the walls of the house (I Kings 6:29). Hebrews 9:5 mentions the cherubim in the tabernacle. David sings of God riding on a cherub (II Sam. 22:11; Ps. 18:10). Psalm 18 pictures a storm, God riding upon and speaking from the clouds. His glory rested between the cherubim above the mercy seat in the tabernacle.

That the cherubim were more than clouds or statues is plain from the description Ezekiel gives (Ezek. 10:1-22; 9:3), which shows that they are the "living creatures" of the first chapter. They were winged creatures with features both animal and human. Each had four faces; of a man, a lion on the right side; of an ox on the left side; also of an eagle (Ezek. 1:10). In Ezekiel 10:14 the faces are of a cherub, a man, a lion and an eagle, wherein "cherub" substitutes for "ox." The etymology is doubtful; possibly from Heb. root *karah*, *give a feast*. A connection with Greek *glyps*, *griffin*, is not established. There is no corresponding word for similar winged animal-human representations in Assyria or Egypt. The Heb. conception is original.

Primarily the cherubim are the living chariot or carriers of God when appearing to men; His throne or the bearers of it. Their earliest recorded employment was as guardians of Eden. Figures of these living beings were used symbolically in both tabernacle and temple. In the new temple of Ezekiel's vision the only cherubim are those decorating the walls (Ezek. 41:17-25); and those show two faces; of a man and a young lion.

The seraphim of Isaiah 6:2-8 are similar beings. Four constellations of the zodiac were given the same names as the four faces of the cherubim, and in ancient times they marked the solstices and the equinoxes. Rabbinical tradition assigns them to the standards of the divisions in the camp of Israel; the lion, Judah, on the E; the ox, Ephraim, W; a man, Reuben, S; the eagle, Dan, N. Thus the standards, leading the Israelites, would indicate Israel as the earthly counterpart of the heavenly host, led by the cherubim. Early church fathers equated the four faces with the four Evangelists; Matthew, the lion; Mark, the ox; Luke, the man; John, the eagle. In Revelation 4:6-9; 5:6-14; 6:1-8; 7-11; 14:3; 15:7; 19:4 are four "beasts" (Greek *zōa, living creatures*; so ASV, RSV; to be distinguished from the beasts, Greek *thería*, wild beasts mentioned in Rev. 13:1, etc.). They are described in terms identifying them with Ezekiel's living creatures or cherubim. The first living creature was like a lion; the second like a calf; the third had a face as a man; the fourth was like a flying eagle (Rev. 4:7). They are the bearers of the judgments which follow the breaking of the first four seals.

To sum up: the cherubim are living heavenly creatures, servants of God in theophany and judgment, appearing in winged human-animal form with the faces of lion, ox, man, and eagle. Their representations in tabernacle and temple as statues and in embroidery and carving are not a breach of the commandment (Exod. 20:4). They are significant in prophecy (Ezek.), and in the Apocalypse (Rev.). Their service is rendered immediately to God. They never come closer to man than when one took fire in his hand and gave it into the hands of "the man clothed with linen" (Ezek. 10:7). Yet it is "between the cherubim" that lay the mercy seat on which the blood of atonement was sprinkled: nothing can more nearly touch our salvation. In the OT sanctuary, where everything was done and taught by visible, tangible types and symbols, physical representations of the living heavenly cherubim were essential. In Ezekiel's new temple, and in the heavenly sanctuary of Hebrews and Revelation, they are no longer needed, for redeemed man there stands in the presence of the living cherubim themselves. The carvings in Ezekiel 41:18 are memorial only.   E.R.

CHERUB (kē'rŭb), an unidentified place in Babylonian territory whence exiles returned to Judea (Ezra 2:59; Neh. 7:61).

CHESALON (kĕs'à-lŏn), a place identified (Josh. 15:10) with Mount Jearim. It lay on the northern border of Judah, W of Jerusalem, NE of Beth-shemesh. Modern Kesla.

CHESED (kē'sĕd, kĕs'ĕd), the fourth son of Nahor, and nephew of Abraham (Gen. 22:22).

CHESIL (kē'sĭl, kĕs'ĭl), a town in the S of Judah, near Hormah and Ziklag (Josh. 15:30). Its place in the lists is taken by Bethul in Joshua 19:4; by Bethuel in I Chronicles 4:30.

CHEST. 1. Receptacles for money to repair the temple (II Kings 12:9,10; II Chron. 24:8,10,11). Heb. *'ārôn* is translated "coffin" once (Gen. 50:26); elsewhere the "ark" in tabernacle and temple.
2. "Chests of rich apparel, bound with cords, and made of cedar," of the merchandise of Tyre (Ezek. 27:24). RSV, on no better lexical authority, translates "carpets of colored stuff, bound with cords and made secure." Heb. *genāzîm* is rendered "treasuries" in Esther 3:9; 4:7.

CHESTNUT TREE (See Plants)

CHESULLOTH (kē-sŭl'ŏth), a town in Issachar (Josh. 19:18). In NT times Exaloth or Xaloth, modern Iksâl, SE of Nazareth.

CHEZIB (kē'zĭb), the town where Shelah was born to Judah and Shuah (Gen. 38:5). It may be the same as Achzib 1.

CHICKEN (See Birds)

CHIDON (kī'dŏn), threshing floor of, (I Chron. 13:9), where Uzza died for touching the ark. Called Nachon's in II Samuel 6:6. Near Jerusalem; site unknown.

CHILD, CHILDREN (chīld, chīl'drĕn). Among the people of the Bible, both OT and NT, as in most other cultures, children, especially male, were greatly desired (Gen. 15:2; 30:1; I Sam. 1:11,20; Ps. 127:3; 128:3; Luke 1:7,28). Among the Hebrews all the firstborn belonged to God and must be redeemed (Num. 3:40-51). Children were sometimes dedicated to God for special service (Judg. 13:2-7; I Sam. 1:11; Luke 1:13-17,76-79). Male descendants of Abraham were circumcised on the eighth day (Gen. 17:12; 21:4; Luke 1:59; 2:21), when the name was given. Weaning often was delayed, and celebrated (Gen. 21:8) with a feast. Education was primarily in the home and was the duty of parents (Exod. 12:26,27; Deut. 6:7; Josh. 4:21-24; Prov. 22:6; Eph. 6:4; Col. 3:21; II Tim. 3:15). Discipline was to be firm, with corporal punishment (Prov. 22:15; 23:13; 29:15). Much was expected of children (Prov. 20:11). Obedience and respect to parents were commanded (Exod. 21:17; Eph. 6:1-3; Col. 3:20; I Tim. 3:4,12; Tit. 1:6). Favoritism was sometimes shown (Gen. 25:28; 37:3). Affection for children is strikingly portrayed in many instances, as in David's love for a child who died (II Sam. 12:15-23); and in the raising of children to life by Elijah (I Kings 17:17-24), by Elisha (II Kings 4:18-37) and by Jesus (Matt. 9:23-26; Mark 5:35-43; Luke 8:49-56). Jesus' love and concern for children is seen in Matthew 18:1-14; 19:13-15; Mark 9:35-37; 10:13-16; Luke 9:46-48; 18:15-17. Jesus recognized children's play (Matt. 11:16). Many attractive pictures of childhood occur; e.g. Moses (Exod. 2:1-10), Samuel (I Sam. 1:20-3:19), Jesus (Luke 2:7-40), Timothy (II Tim. 1:5; 3:14,15).

"Children" is an affectionate address, as in I John, of an old man to adults, who are, nevertheless, expected to act their age (I Cor. 13:11; 14:20). The attention given to the childhood of the Messiah in prophecy (Isa. 7:14; 9:6) prepares us for the infancy narratives in Matthew 2 and Luke 2. The Savior came as a helpless babe, and grew up through a normal childhood. A return to child-like receptiveness and trust is required of those who would enter the kingdom of heaven (Matt. 18: 1-14; 19:13-15; Mark 9:35-37; 10:13-16; Luke 9: 46-48; 18:15-17). E.R.

CHILDBEARING. The word occurs (I Tim. 2:15) in a passage relating to the proper sphere and conduct of woman. "She shall be saved in childbearing" cannot refer to salvation from sin, which is by grace through faith, but to safe-keeping through the pain which became incident to childbirth through the Fall (Gen. 3:16). Hebrew mothers had the assistance of midwives (Exod. 1:15-21). Newborn babies had the navel cut, were washed with water, salted and wrapped in swaddling clothes (Ezek. 16:4; Luke 2:7,12). Purification rites were prescribed after childbirth (Lev. 12; Luke 2:22-24).

CHILDREN OF GOD, or sons and daughters of God. 1. Angelic beings (Gen. 6:1-4; Job 1:6; 2:1; 38:7), though at least the first of these may be godly men.
2. Men, by creation (Luke 3:38; Isa. 64:8; "his offspring" Acts 17:28).
3. Israel in covenant relation to God (Exod. 4: 22; though rebellious Isa. 1:2-4).
4. Individual Israelites (Hos. 1:10).
5. The inclusion of Gentiles is intimated (Isa. 19:25).
6. Jesus (Matt. 3:17; 17:5; Luke 1:35).
7. Through Jesus men may become redeemed children of God (John 1:12; 14:6; by a new birth, John 3:3) in full moral and spiritual sonship (Rom. 8:14-17; Phil. 2:15; I John 3:10) with final likeness to God (I John 3:1-3).

CHILDREN OF ISRAEL (See Israel)

CHILEAB (kĭl'ē-ăb), the second son of David (the first by Abigail) born at Hebron (II Sam. 3:3). Called Daniel in I Chronicles 3:1.

CHILION (kĭl'ĭ-ŏn), one of the two sons of Elimelech and Naomi, who married Orpah in Moab and died there (Ruth 1:2-5; 4:9,10).

CHILMAD (kĭl'măd), a place which traded with Tyre; associated with Asshur (Ezek. 27:23); site unknown, perhaps modern Kalwâdha near Bagdad. Other readings of the text give "all Media," or "Asshur was as thine apprentice in trading."

CHIMHAM (kĭm'hăm), presumably a son of Barzillai the Gileadite, whom David took to Jerusalem in his service at the request of Barzillai and in his place (II Sam. 19:37-40). "The habitation of Chimham" (Jer. 41:17) retained his name for centuries after his time.

CHINNERETH, CHINNEROTH (kĭn'ē-rĕth, -rŏth). 1. A fortified city on the NW shore of the Sea of Galilee (Josh. 19:35)); modern Tel Oreimeh, meaning *Harp Hill.* Chinnereth means "harp," and the hill on which it stood is harpshaped.
2. A district in Galilee; "All Chinnereth, with all the land of Naphtali" (I Kings 15:20).
3. The sea later known as Gennesaret or Galilee (Num. 34:11; Deut. 3:17; Josh. 11:2; 12:3; 13:27). The sea also is harpshaped.

CHIOS (kī'ŏs), an island in the Mediterranean Sea 12 miles W of Smyrna, past which (between Mitylene and Samos) Paul sailed on his voyage to Rome (Acts 20:15).

CHISLEV (kĭz'lĕv, KJV Chisleu), the ninth month of the Hebrew ritual year (Neh. 1:1; Zech. 7:1).

CHISLON (kĭz'lŏn), the father of Elidad, the prince of Benjamin in Moses' time who assisted in the division of the land (Num. 34:21).

CHISLOTH-TABOR (kĭs'lŏth-tā'bêr), the same place as Chesulloth (Josh. 19:12).

CHITTIM, KITTIM (kĭt'ĭm), descendants of Javan (Gen. 10:4; I Chron. 1:7, Kittim); Cyprus and its inhabitants. Balaam prophesies that ships from Chittim (KJV), Kittim (ASV, RSV) will afflict Asher (Num. 24:24). In Isaiah 23:1,12; Jeremiah 2:10; Ezekiel 27:6, KJV has Chittim, ASV Kittim, RSV Cyprus. In Daniel 11:30 KJV has Chittim, ASV, RSV Kittim. The Heb. *kittîm* came to apply not only to Cyprus, but also to the islands and coasts of the Mediterranean.

CHIUN (kī'ŭn), Saturn as a god (Amos 5:26). KJV has, "the tabernacle of your Molech and Chiun your images, the star of your god"; ASV, "the tabernacle of your king and the shrine of your images, the star of your god"; RSV, "Sakkuth your king, and Kaiwan your star-god, your images."

CHLOE (klō'ē), a woman whose people informed Paul of contentions in the Corinthian church. Where she lived and how her people gained their information is not told. She was well-known to the Corinthian Christians by her personal name.

CHORASHAN (kŏr'ăsh'ăn), a place in the S of Judah to which David sent some of the spoil of the Philistines (I Sam. 30:30). ASV, RSV Borashan. The same as Ashan.

Ruins of Chorazin, north of Capernaum. © MPS

CHORAZIN (kō-rā'zĭn), modern *Khirbet Kerâzeh,* ruins about two miles N of *Tell Hûm,* the site of Capernaum. Chorazin is mentioned only in the woes Christ pronounced upon it (Matt. 11:21; Luke 10:13). His condemnation of it, in conjunction with Bethsaida and Capernaum, indicates that Chorazin must have been an important city. It ceased to be inhabited by the time of Eusebius (latter half of the third century). Only a few carved stones remain today.

CHOZEBA (kō-zē'ba), a town of Judah; ASV, RSV, Cozeba (I Chron. 4:22). "Then men of Chozeba" are notable, among others, because "the records are ancient" (ASV, RSV).

CHRIST, JESUS (krīst, jē′zŭs, Gr. *Iesoús*, for Heb. *Jeshua, Jehoshua, Joshua, Jehovah is salvation*; Heb. *māshîah*, Gr. *Christós, anointed*).

I. Comprehensive Life and Work. Though the life of Christ, as ordinarily understood, embraces the years our Lord spent on this earth, as described in the four Gospels, His full career spans the ages and invites reflection on its several aspects. Fundamental to the various "I Am" sayings of Jesus is His assertion of absolute existence (John 8:58). Therefore it is reasonable to think of Him as belonging to eternity. Scripture, in fact, affirms His *pre-existence*, and does so in terms of fellowship with the Father (John 1:1); glory (John 17:5) and designation in advance as the Saviour of the world (I Pet. 1:20). His more immediate relation to the realm of men and things belongs to His activity in *creation*. All things came into being through Him (John 1:3; I Cor. 8:6; Heb. 1:2) and in Him continue to have their cohesive principle (Col. 1:17). Evidence is not lacking for His presence, too, in the OT. The manifestations of God in this period are apparently connected with the pre-incarnate Christ. When Isaiah glimpsed the glory of God he was seeing Christ (John 12:41). Moses and the prophets spoke of Him (John 5: 46; Luke 24:27,44) with special reference to His sufferings and the glories that should follow (I Pet. 1:11). Some of the more important passages of a predictive nature are Genesis 3:15; Deuteronomy 18:15,18; Psalms 2,16,22,110; Isaiah 7:14; 9:6-7; 11; 42:1-4; 52:13-53:12; 61:1-2; Jeremiah 23:5-6; Micah 5:2. In addition there are covenantal statements which do not speak of the Messiah directly and personally, but which involve Him in crucial ways (Gen. 12:3; II Sam. 7:12-16). As though in anticipation of the incarnation, the Son of God showed Himself at times to the faithful in visible form as the Angel of the Lord or the Angel of the covenant (Gen. 18:1-19:1; Judg. 13). Before His Advent Christ had thoroughly identified Himself with His people, so that when He came, He came unto His own (John 1:11).

By the *incarnation*, the Christ of God took on Himself human nature in order to reveal God to men in a way they could grasp (John 1:14,18), to become their Saviour by ransoming them from their sins (Mark 10:45) and to deal sympathetically with their needs (Heb. 2:17-18). Today, in glory, He is still the God-man. The incarnation persists.

The *present ministry* of Christ is being carried on in heaven, where He represents the saints before the throne of God (I John 2:1; Heb. 7:25). By the successful completion of His work on earth He is exalted to be the head of the church (Eph. 1:22; 4:15), and by the Spirit directs the life and service of His saints on earth (Matt. 28:20).

One purpose of the incarnation was not achieved during the earthly ministry of our Lord, but is reserved for His *second coming*. His kingly rule will then be introduced following His work as judge (Matt. 25:31-34). This future coming is one of the major truths set forth in the Epistles (Phil. 3:20-21; II Thess. 1:7-10) and is the leading theme of the Book of Revelation. After the millennial kingdom, Christ will enter with His people upon the blessedness of the *eternal state* which will be unmarred by the inroads of sin or death.

II. The Earthly Ministry. The long-heralded Christ came in the fulness of time (Gal. 4:4). God providentially supplied the proper *background* for His appearing and mission. The world had become to a great extent homogeneous through the spread of the Greek language and culture and through the organizing genius of Rome. The means were thus provided for the spread of the gospel once it had been forged out in the career of the Son of God. His Advent occurred at a point in human history when the law of Moses had done its work of demonstrating the sinfulness of man and the impossibility of achieving righteousness by human effort. Men here and there were looking with longing for spiritual deliverance.

Entirely in keeping with this divine control of the circumstances surrounding the incarnation is the careful selection of the Virgin Mary as the mother of Jesus. The *birth* of the Saviour was natural, but His conception was supernatural, by the power of the Holy Spirit (Matt. 1:18; Luke 1:35). Augustus, too, was drawn into the circle of the instruments chosen of God, when he was constrained to order a universal enrollment for taxation, not realizing that thereby he would make possible the birth of Jesus in the place appointed by prophetic announcement (Luke 2:1-7; Mic. 5:2). The shepherds, by their readiness to seek out the babe in the manger and by their joy at seeing Him, became prototypes of the humble souls in Jewry who in coming days would recognize in Jesus their Saviour. An intimation of Gentile desire to participate in the Christ may be seen in the coming of the Magi from the East. In darker perspective appears the figure of Herod, emblematic of the hatred and opposition which would meet Jesus of Nazareth and work for His death. In the scribes who are conversant with the Scriptures but apathetic about seeking the One who fulfilled them we see the shape of things to come—the leaders of a nation receiving Him not when He came unto His own.

In more theological terms the Christ-event is an incarnation. God was manifest in flesh. The one who was in the form of God took the form of a servant and was made in the likeness of men (Phil. 2:6-7). Therefore, when the Scriptures assert from time to time that God sent His Son into the world, this affirmation is not to be treated as though Christ is merely a messenger of God such as the prophets of old. Rather, He is the eternal Son of God now clothing Himself with human nature to accomplish the salvation of men. Though the expression God-man is not found in the sacred records, it faithfully expresses the truth regarding the person of Jesus Christ. God did not appropriate a man who already existed and make of him an automaton for the working out of the divine pur-

Bethlehem in Judea. © MPS

poses. He took what is common to us all, our human nature, yet free from any taint of sin, and combined it with deity to become an actual person with His own individuality. This is the mystery of the incarnation. The gulf between the Creator and the creature is bridged, first by the person and then by the mediatorial work of Christ.

The *boyhood* of Jesus should be approached from the standpoint of the truth revealed about the incarnation. Deity did not eclipse humanity so as to render the process of learning unnecessary. Christ grew in body and advanced in knowledge and in the wisdom which enabled Him to make proper use of what He knew. He did not command His parents but rather obeyed them, fulfilling the law in this matter as in all others. The scriptural accounts have none of the fanciful extravagances of the Apocryphal Gospels which present the boy Jesus as a worker of wonders during His early years. They emphasize His progress in the understanding of the OT and affirm His consciousness of a special relation to His Father in heaven (Luke 2:49).

At His *baptism* Jesus received divine confirmation of the mission now opening out before Him and also the anointing of the Holy Spirit for the fulfillment of it. The days of preparation were definitely at an end, so that retirement was put aside and contact begun with His people Israel. By the baptism He was fulfilling all righteousness (Matt. 3:15) in the sense that He was identifying Himself with those He came to redeem.

Closely related to the baptism is the *temptation,* for it partakes likewise of this representative character. The first man Adam failed when put to the test; the last Adam succeeded, though weakened by hunger and harried by the desolation of the wilderness. In essence, the temptation was the effort of Satan to break Christ's dependence on the Father, so that He would desert the standpoint of man and rely upon special consideration as the Son of God. But Christ refused to be moved from His determined place of chosen identification with the race. "Man shall not live by bread alone . . ." is His first line of defense, and He maintains it in the two following episodes, quoting the obligation of Israel in relation to God as His own reason for refusing to be moved from a place of trustful dependence upon the Almighty (Matt. 4:7,10).

Only when equipped by the baptism and seasoned by the ordeal of temptation was Jesus ready for His life work. No word of teaching and no work of power is attributed to Him prior to these events, but immediately thereafter He began moving in the power of the Spirit to undertake the work the Father had given Him to do (Luke 4:14).

The public ministry of Jesus was brief. Its length has to be estimated from the materials recorded in the Gospels. John gives more information on this point than the other Evangelists. Judging from the number of Passovers mentioned there (John 2:23; 5:1 [?]; 6:4; 13:1) the period was at least somewhat in excess of two years and possibly more than three.

John supplements the Synoptic Gospels also in the description of the place of ministry, for whereas they lay chief stress upon Galilee, plus notices of a visit to the regions of Tyre and Sidon (Matt. 15:21-28); Caesarea-Philippi (Matt. 16:13ff); the Gentile cities of the Decapolis (Mark 7:31; cf. also Mark 5:1-20); Samaria (Luke 9:51-56; 17:11); and the region east of the Jordan River known as Perea (Mark 10:1), John reports several visits to Jerusalem. In fact, most of his record is taken up with accounts of Jesus' ministry in Judea. The

Nazareth, a view from ancient road leading east to the Lake of Galilee. © MPS

Synoptists hint at such a ministry (e.g., Matt. 23:37; Luke 10:38-42), but give little information.

For the conduct of His Galilean mission, Jesus made the city of Capernaum His headquarters. From this center He went forth, usually in the company of His disciples, to challenge the people in city and town and village with His message. Several such tours are indicated in the sacred text (Mark 1:38; 6:6; Luke 8:1). A part of His ministry consisted in healings and exorcisms, for many had diseases of various sorts and many were afflicted with demon possession. These miracles were not only tokens of divine compassion but also signs that in the person of Jesus of Nazareth the Promised One had come (cf. Matt. 11:2-6; Luke 4:16-19). They were revelations of the mercy and power of God at work in God's Anointed. Jesus found fault with the cities of Galilee for rejecting Him despite the occurrence of so many mighty works in their midst (Matt. 11:20-24).

The message proclaimed by Jesus during these itinerating journeys was epitomized in the phrase, "the kingdom of God." Fundamentally, this means

Traditional Mount of Temptation. (The building on hillside is a Greek monastery.) © MPS

the rule of God in human life and history. The phrase may have a more concrete significance at times, for Jesus speaks now and again about entering into the kingdom. In certain passages He makes the kingdom to be future (Matt. 25:31ff) but in others it is present (Luke 11:20). This last reference is of special importance, for it connects the kingdom with the activity of Jesus in casting out demons. To the degree that Jesus invades the kingdom of Satan in this fashion, to that degree the kingdom of God has already come. But in the more spiritual and positive aspects of kingdom teaching, where the individual life is concerned, the emphasis does not fall upon invasion of personality or compulsive surrender to the power of God. The laws of discipleship are demanding indeed, but for their application they await the consent of the individual. No disciple is a monument to force but rather to the persuasive power of love and grace.

If we inquire more definitely into the relation of Jesus Himself to the kingdom, we are obliged to conclude that He not only introduces the kingdom (in a sense John the Baptist did that also) but was its perfect embodiment. The appropriate response to the preaching of the kingdom is committal to the will of God (Matt. 6:10), and it is crystal clear that the doing of the will of God was the mainspring of Jesus' ministry (Matt. 12:50; John 4:34; Mark 14:36). It is evident, of course, that Jesus will also inaugurate the final phase of the kingdom when He comes again in power and glory. Entrance into the present aspect of the kingdom comes through faith in the Son of God and the successful completion of His mission. This could be done during His earthly ministry by anticipation of His redeeming work and thereafter by acceptance of the Gospel message.

Much of our Lord's teaching was conveyed through the instrumentality of parables. These were usually comparisons taken from various phases of nature or human life. "The kingdom of

A familiar· subject: "Jesus Blesses the Children," by Plockhurst. MPS

God is like . . ." This method of teaching preserved the interest of the hearers until the spiritual application could be made. If the truth so taught was somewhat veiled by this method, this served to seal the spiritual blindness of the unrepentant and at the same time created a wholesome curiosity on the part of those who were disposed to believe, so that they could be led on to firm faith by more direct teaching.

The ministry of the Saviour was predominantly to the multitudes during its earlier phase, as He sought out the people where they were, whether in the synagogue or on the city street or by the lakeside. "He went about doing good" is the way Peter described it later on (Acts 10:38). But much of the last year of ministry was given over to instruction of the twelve disciples whom He had chosen (for the two phases see Matt. 4:17 and 16:21). This shift of emphasis was not due primarily to the lack of response on the part of the multitudes, although His following faded at times (John 6:15,66), but principally to His desire to instruct His disciples concerning Himself and His mission. These men, nearly all Galileans and many of them fishermen, had been able to learn much through hearing Jesus address the crowds and through watching Him heal the sick and relieve the distressed, and especially through being sent out by Him to minister in His name (Luke 9:1-6), but they needed more direct teaching to prepare them for the part they would play in the life of the church after the ascension.

What they saw and heard during those early days confirmed them in their understanding of the person of Jesus as the Messiah and the Son of God (Matt. 16:16), but they were quite unprepared to receive His teaching on the issue of His earthly life as involving suffering and death (Matt. 16:21-23). Although this prospect was a "must" for Jesus (vs. 21), for Peter it was something that the Lord could dismiss from consideration if He would (vs. 22). If the most prominent one of the apostolic circle felt this way about it, no doubt the others were of the same mind. Their thoughts were so taken up with the prospect of a kingdom of external power and glory that they were perplexed and disturbed to find that their Master anticipated quite a different experience. His prediction of a rising again from the dead fell on deaf ears, for the blow of the announcement about the forthcoming death had been too heavy. Even the lessons of the transfiguration scene, where the death was the theme under discussion and the glory beyond was presented to their sight, did not completely effect the orientation of the disciples to the teaching of Jesus. He had to repeat it more than once (Mark 10:34-45). Their sorrow in the garden of Gethsemane shows that they had reluctantly adjusted to it but could not look beyond it to resurrection nor could they realize how much that death itself could mean to their spiritual welfare. After the resurrection they were much more open to the Lord's instruction, and He used the occasion of His appearances to them for enlightenment from the OT as to the divine purpose pre-written there concerning Himself (Luke 24:26-27,44).

Christ's investment of time and patience with these men was well rewarded, for when the Spirit took up the work of instruction begun by Him and gave them His own power for witness, they became effective instruments for the declaring of the Word of God and for the leadership of the Christian Church. The record of the Book of Acts vindicates the wisdom of Christ and His understanding of the future.

Standing over against the Twelve in their attitude to Jesus are the scribes and Pharisees. The former were experts in the law and the traditions which had grown up around it, and the latter were men dedicated to a meticulous devotion to this heritage of Judaism. These groups usually worked together, and they collided with Jesus on many occasions over many issues. It was shocking to them that He would declare men's sins forgiven and claim a special relation to God as Son which others did not have. They resented His rejection of the traditions which they kept so carefully, and stood aghast at His willingness to break the sabbath (in their way of thinking) by doing deeds of mercy on that day. It was tragic that men who held to the Scriptures as God's Word should fail to see in Jesus Christ the One of whom that Word spoke. They refused to put their trust in Him despite all His miracles and the matchless perfection of His personal life. Because tradition meant more to them than truth, they stumbled in their apprehension of the Christ of God. In the end they made common cause with their opponents, the Sadducees, in order to do away with Jesus.

Even as Christ was engaged in teaching His disciples, from the days of the transfiguration on, He was ever moving toward Jerusalem to fulfill His course at the cross (Luke 9:51). In those latter days some stirring events were unfolded—the triumphal entry into Jerusalem, the cleansing of the temple, the institution of the Lord's Supper, the soul conflict in the garden of Gethsemane, the arrest and trial, the crucifixion, the resurrection, the appearances, the ascension into heaven. In all of them Jesus remains the central figure. In all of them He receives testimony to Himself or gives it. Nothing is unimportant. All contribute to the working out of the plan of God. The cross is man's decision respecting Christ, but it had already been His own decision and that of the Father. It underscored the sins of some men even as it removed the sins of others. In the cross man's day erupted in violence and blasphemy. In the resurrection God's day began to dawn. It was His answer to the world and to the powers of darkness. In it Christ was justified and His claims illuminated.

III. Names, Titles and Offices. Considerable help in understanding the person and work of Christ may be gleaned from a consideration of the terms used to designate Him, especially as these are employed by Himself and His close associates. *Jesus* is used mostly in the narratives of the Gospels, and only rarely does it appear in direct address. It means Saviour (Matt. 1:21), being related philologically to the Hebrew name Joshua. In the KJV of Hebrews 4:8, Jesus actually stands in the text instead of Joshua. For the most part the name Jesus is joined with other terms when used in the Epistles, but occasionally it stands alone, especially in Hebrews, and doubtless for the purpose of emphasizing His humanity as a continuing element of His being. Therefore it is legitimate for us today to use the simple name in unadorned fashion, but to do so exclusively could indicate a lack of appreciation of the rounded presentation which the Scriptures give of Him.

Christ, meaning "anointed one," is the Greek equivalent of the Hebrew word *Messiah*. Its function as a title is emphasized by the fact that often it occurs with the definite article, which gives it the force of "the promised Christ," the one who fulfills the concept of Messiah as set forth in the Old Testament Scriptures. Our Lord uses it thus of Himself in Luke 24:46, for example: "And he said to them, Thus it stands written that the Christ

A miniature of a unique portrait of Christ, made up entirely of all the words of the New Testament, hand-lettered in 902 lines, a total of 181,259 words, 838,380 characters. Done by a Korean pastor, Gwang Hyuk Rhee of Seoul. © GHR

should suffer and rise from the dead the third day." By extension of meaning the same form is used by Paul as a synonym for the Church (I Cor. 12: 12), thus emphasizing the intimate bond between Christ and His people. Of special interest is the development which led to the use of Christ as a personal name. It must have taken place early in the life of the Church, for we find it reflected, for example, in the opening verse of Mark's Gospel— "The beginning of the gospel of Jesus Christ, the Son of God." Possibly our Lord Himself is responsible for this usage (John 17:3). In the Epistles there are numerous occurrences of Christ alone as a name (I Cor. 15:3, e.g.).

A circumstance which may strike the reader of the Gospels as odd is the prohibition against making Jesus known as the Christ during the days of His ministry. He imposed this restriction on the disciples (Matt. 16:20) and somewhat similarly choked off any possible testimony from demons (Luke 4:41). If this title should be used freely of Him among the Jews, it would excite the populace to expect in Him a political Messiah who would gain for them their national freedom and many accompanying benefits. Since this was not the purpose of Jesus, He did what He could do to suppress the use of the term Messiah with regard to Himself, though He welcomed it in the circle of the apostles (Matt. 16:16).

Only once does the name *Emmanuel* occur, and then in connection with the conception of Jesus (Matt. 1:23). It is a Hebrew word meaning "God with us," and is peculiarly appropriate as an explanation of the significance of the birth of Jesus as involving the incarnation. For some reason the name did not gain currency in the Church, perhaps because it was crowded out by Jesus and Christ.

Among the ancients it was common to distinguish a man not only by name but also by place of residence. Consequently Jesus was often called the Nazarene because of his years spent in the village of Nazareth (Luke 24:19). As used of Jesus' followers by the Jews the term took on an element of reproach which it did not possess in any recognizable way during His life on earth.

When Jesus referred to Himself His most usual method of identification was to use the title *Son of Man*. It was more than a means of identification, however, for it linked Him to a conception of majesty which had gathered around the term since its use in Daniel 7:13. Although it is possible that occasionally the title stresses Jesus' humanity, in the main it serves to point to His transcendence as a heavenly figure. Certainly the widespread notion that Son of Man expresses the humanity of Jesus, as Son of God expresses His deity, is quite misleading (cf. Luke 22:69-70). By using this title publicly rather than Messiah, Jesus was able to avoid suggesting that His mission was political in nature, and instead could put into the title by His own use of it the content which He wanted to give to it. The Church recognized the Lord's right to exclusive use of the term and did not employ it, out of deference to Him (the one exception is Stephen in Acts 7:56).

One of the most familiar designations for Jesus is *Son of God*. Only in John's Gospel does He use it of Himself (John 5:25; 10:36; 11:4). But elsewhere He uses its equivalent, the Son (Matt. 11:27), which is especially appropriate when used opposite the Father, and which in such a passage clearly sets off the uniqueness of this particular Son. In the Synoptic Gospels considerable care is needed in order to impute to the term Son of God the exact nuance of meaning proper to its every occurrence. Geerhardus Vos discerned four meanings· the nativistic, which stresses the divine origination of the person of Jesus as a human figure; the ethico-religious, which points to the filial relation which Christ sustained to the Father within the context of His human life, similar to that which any child of God has; the Messianic, which has to do with His appointment as the anointed of God to execute His mission as the one sent of the Father, in fulfillment of OT prophecy; the trinitarian or ontological, in which the unique relation of Christ to the Father as the only Son is expressed. This latter, of course, represents the highest level of sonship (see G. Vos, *The Self-Disclosure of Jesus*, pp. 141ff).

Rather frequently in the course of His ministry Jesus was addressed as *Son of David* (Matt. 21:9; Luke 18:38), which is distinctly a Messianic title pointing to Him as the one who fulfilled the Davidic covenant, the one who was expected to establish the kingdom and bring Israel to freedom, peace, and glory (cf. Matt. 1:1; Luke 1:32-33).

A few passages proclaim outright that Jesus is *God* (John 1:1 in a pre-incarnate setting; John 1:18 according to the strongest manuscript evidence; John 20:28; Rom. 9:5 according to the most natural construction of the verse; Titus 2:13; Heb. 1:8). That the passages are relatively few in number is probably due to the fact that Jesus Christ, as known to men, was in a position of subordination to the heavenly Father, His deity veiled by His humanity, so that it was much more natural to assign to Him the predicates of deity than to refer to Him directly as God. Semitic monotheism as the background for the early Hebrew Christians doubtlessly exercised a restraining influence also. Some moderns about whose orthodoxy there is no question have nevertheless confessed to a feeling of restraint in referring to Jesus as God, though they do not doubt His essential deity (e.g., James Denney in a letter to W. Robertson Nicoll included in the life of Nicoll by T. H. Darlow, New York: Doran Co., 1925, p. 361).

No term is more expressive of the faith of early believers in Jesus than *Lord* (Acts 2:36; 10:36; Rom. 10:9; I Cor. 8:6; 12:3; Phil. 2:11). It denotes the sovereignty of Christ, His headship over the individual believer, the church as a body, and all things. For those who were strangers, it was merely a title of respect (John 4:11), but for those who were deeply attached to the Saviour it had the highest import, calling alike for homage and obedience (John 20:28; Acts 22:10). Used sparingly during the period of the earthly ministry prior to the resurrection, it takes on an increased use and heightened significance as a result of that tremendous event.

Some titles pertain to the mission of Christ more than to His person. One of these is *Word* (John 1:1,14; I John 1:1). As such Christ is essentially the revealer of God, the one who opens to the understanding of men the nature and purposes of the Almighty and discloses that higher wisdom which stands in contrast to the wisdom of men. In keeping with such a title is the designation *Teacher*, by which our Lord was customarily addressed in the days of His flesh. This attests the impact of His instruction and the authority which lay behind it. Despite the fact that Jesus lacked rabbinic training, He could not be denied the recognition of the wisdom which shone through His spoken word.

The classic designation of Christ as *Servant* is given by Paul in Philippians 2:7, but it was widely recognized in the early church that our Lord fulfilled the Servant of Jehovah role in Himself (see Matt. 12:17-21). That it dominated the thinking of Christ Himself may be safely affirmed in the light of such a passage as Mark 10:45.

Central to the mission of Christ was His work as *Saviour*. We have already seen that the name Jesus has this meaning, the name suggesting the reason for His coming into the world. Luke 2:11 and John 4:42 are among the passages which herald Christ under the aspect of His Saviourhood. The idea in the word is not merely deliverance from sin and all the other woes which afflict man, but the provision of a state of wholeness and blessedness in which man realizes the purpose of God for him. In reports of the healings of Jesus, the verb form denotes the state of soundness which results from the healing touch of the Saviour.

Jesus' saving mission is declared also in the expression, *Lamb of God* (John 1:29,36; cf. Rev. 5:6). Peter likewise uses the word "lamb" of Jesus, with special reference to His qualification of sinlessness (I Pet. 1:19).

The reference to Jesus as *High Priest* is confined to the Epistle to the Hebrews, where it occurs some ten times, His work being described as taking place in the heavenly sanctuary, in the presence of God, where the fruits of His death for sinners on the earth are conserved in His work of intercession (Heb. 9:11-12).

More general is the characterization of our Lord as the *Mediator* between God and men (I Tim. 2:5). This term takes account of the barrier which sin erected between the Creator and the creature, which Christ alone was qualified to remove. For the concept in the OT, see Job 9:33.

Paul uses the title *Last Adam* (I Cor. 15:45) in contrast to the first Adam, suggesting the undoing of the consequences of sin brought on by Adam's transgression (cf. Rom. 5:12-21), and the realization of new creation life which is to be communicated to all believers in resurrection glory even as it is already their portion in Christ in a spiritual sense.

This list of names and titles of Christ is not exhaustive. The resources of languages are taxed in the sacred record to set forth the full excellence and worth of the Son of God. When His work is considered in its broad sweep, the most satisfying analysis divides it in accordance with the offices which He fulfills—*prophet, priest* and *king*. The prophetic ministry relates especially to the testimony borne in the days of His flesh as He heralded the kingdom of God, warned of coming judgment, and encouraged the people of God. He is still the faithful and true witness as He speaks to the church through the Spirit. As priest our Lord made the one sacrifice of Himself which brought to an end animal sacrifices and put away sin for ever (Heb. 9:26). Faithful and merciful, He ministers before God on behalf of His people who are compassed by sin and infirmity (Heb. 2:17; 4:15-16). The term *king* relates especially to the future activity of our Lord as He comes again to supplant the kingdom of the world with His own gracious and sovereign rule (Rev. 11:15). He shall be no ordinary ruler, but King of kings, without a peer.

IV. Character. "What manner of man is this?" Such was the amazed observation of the disciples of Jesus as they beheld Him in action and felt the strength and mystery of His personality as they companied with Him. Certain ingredients of character deserve special mention, but it cannot be said that He was noted for some things above others, for this would involve disproportion and would reflect upon the perfection of His being. He had *integrity*. After all, this is the kernel of character. The Gospel appeal consisting in the challenge to lodge faith in Christ would be impossible if He were not trustworthy. No taint of duplicity marred His dealings with others, for there was no mixture of motives within His heart. He could not deceive, for He was Truth incarnate. The claims of Jesus in areas where we have no means of testing them can be cordially received for the reason that in areas where His affirmations can be judged they stand the test.

Christ had *courage*. When Aristotle advanced his famous doctrine of the mean, he illustrated it by courage, which lies midway between cowardice and recklessness. Judged by this standard, the character of Jesus appears in a most favorable light, for in Him one can detect no wild instability even in the most intense activity, nor any supineness in His passivity. Christ had physical courage. Without it He could never have cleared the temple singlehandedly. He had the courage of conviction. Peter was probably His boldest disciple, yet he denied his Lord under pressure, whereas Jesus confessed His own person and mission before the Sanhedrin even though it meant His death. The stamina of men is often attributable, at least in part, to the help and sympathy of their fellows, but Jesus stood alone as He faced His final ordeal.

Our Lord showed great *compassion* as He dealt with people. This is the word used in the Gospels. In the Epistles it is called love. The sight of multitudes forlorn and forsaken by those who should have been their spiritual shepherds stirred Christ to the depths of His being. Out of His compassion He ministered to their physical need for food and health, and went on to tell them the secrets of the life of true godliness. Compassion was more than an emotion with Jesus. It was a call to

Warner Sallman's "Head of Christ," which is perhaps the most popular contemporary representation of the Saviour in sacred art. © Kriebel & Bates, Inc. Used by permission.

action, to selfless ministry on behalf of the needy. He gave Himself to one with the same intensity that He showed in dealing with the many. Virtue went out of Him and He did not regret the loss, for it is the nature of love to give. To love the loveless and love them to the end and to the uttermost — this is the love that Paul describes as passing knowledge (Eph. 3:19). It is a love that proved itself through death—He loved me and gave Himself for me (Gal. 2:20), and yet remains deathless.

Jesus clothed Himself with *humility*. He could talk about this as His own possession without affectation (Matt. 11:29). Christ wrought a revolution in ethics by dignifying humility in a world which despised it as weakness. Though the universe was His creation and though He was equal with the Father, though every knee would one day bow before Him, yet He was not lifted up with pride because of these things. The mind of Christ is that which takes every reason for exaltation and transmutes it into a reason for selfless service. In essence His humility was His refusal to please Himself. He came not to be ministered unto but to minister.

Our Lord's character is crowned with perfection or *sinlessness*. This perfection was not simply the absence of sin, but the infusion of a heavenly holiness into all that He said and did. It may be objected that when Jesus gave way to anger and spoke out in bitter denunciation of the Pharisees (Matt. 23) that He revealed at least a trace of imperfection. But a character without the power of righteous indignation would be faulty. If Jesus had failed to expose these men He would not have done His full duty as the exponent of truth. He is the image of the Father, and God is angry with the wicked every day.

V. Influence. A life so brief, so confined in its geographical orbit, so little noticed by the world in His own time, has yet become the most potent force for good in all of human history. This is seen in the *Scriptures* of the NT. In every single book which goes to make up this collection, Jesus Christ is the inevitable point of reference. Even so brief and personal a writing as Philemon owes its inspiration to the Son of God who came to make men free. The Gospels picture Him in the flesh; the Epistles present Him in the Spirit. The Acts of the Apostles depicts the victories of His grace in the extension of His Church; the Revelation sets forth the triumph of His glory through His personal presence once more in history.

His influence upon the *saints* is so radical and comprehensive that nothing can describe it better than the assertion that Christ is their life. They were not truly living until they came to know Him by faith. Until He comes into the heart, self rules supreme. When He comes, He creates a new point of reference and a new set of values. To be Christ-centered is simply normal Christian experience.

What Christ can do in transforming a life may be seen to good advantage in the case of Saul of Tarsus. Apart from Christ the world might never have heard of him. Because in Christ he died to self and lived in the energy of the risen Christ to glorify God, his is a household name wherever Christians are found.

It is inevitable that *sinners* should feel the touch of Christ and never be the same afterward. Regarding the self-righteous leaders of His own time Jesus could say, "If I had not come and spoken unto them, they had not had sin; but now they have no cloke for their sin" (John 15:22). Christ is the conscience of the world. Because He is the light of the world, when men stand in that light then turn from it, they walk in deeper darkness and are without hope.

In a more general sense, Christ has mightily affected *society* in its organized state. He has taught the world the dignity of human life, the worth of the soul, the preciousness of personality. Because of this the status of women has steadily been improved under Christian influence, slavery has been abolished, and children, instead of being exposed as infants and neglected in formative years, are recognized as a primary responsibility for the lavishing of love and care. Human life, when weak or deformed or diseased, is no longer regarded as forfeiting a right to a place in society, but rather entitled to help. The fact that governments and scientific groups are now engaged in social service on a large scale ought not to disguise the fact that the impulse for these works of mercy has been the Christian church acting in the name and spirit of Christ. The arts owe their sublimest achievements to the desire to honor the Son of God. Beethoven called Handel the greatest composer of all time, a man who could not complete his oratorio *The Messiah* without being moved repeatedly to tears as he thought upon the incarnation. Every cathedral spire that pierces the sky throughout Christendom bears its silent testimony to the loving outreach toward God that is induced through the knowledge of Christ the Lord. Moralists and philosophers, even when they lack faith in Him for the saving of the soul, nevertheless are often found acknowledging wistfully that they wish they had a personal inheritance in Him as they commend Him to others as the one great hope for mankind. E.F.H.

BIBLIOGRAPHY: Eric F. F. Bishop, *Jesus of Palestine*, London: Lutterworth Press, 1955; Otto Borch-ert, *The Original Jesus*, London: Lutterworth Press, 1933; E. Digges La Touche, *The Person of Christ in Modern Thought*, London: James Clarke and Co., 1912; T. W. Manson, *The Servant-Messiah*, Cambridge: The University Press, 1953; A. E. J. Rawlinson, *Christ in the Gospels*, London: Oxford University Press, 1944; Wilbur Moorehead Smith, *The Supernaturalness of Christ*, Boston: W. A. Wilde Co., 1943; Maisie Spens, *Concerning Himself*, London: Hodder and Stoughton, 1937; James S. Stewart, *The Life and Teaching of Jesus Christ*, London: SCM Press Limited, 1933; Vincent Taylor, *The Names of Jesus*, London: Macmillan and Co., 1953.

CHRISTIAN (krĭs'chăn, krĭst'yăn, Gr. *Christianós*). The Biblical meaning is "adherent of Christ." The disciples were formally called Christians first in Antioch (Acts 11:26). Agrippa recognized that to believe what Paul preached would make him a Christian (Acts 26:28). Peter accepted the name as in itself basis for persecution (I Pet. 4:16). Thus gradually a name imposed by Gentiles was adopted by the disciples of Jesus. Some Jews had referred to them as "the sect of the Nazarenes" (Acts 24:5); and Paul, when a persecutor, as those "of the Way" (Acts 9:2). The Latin termination *ianós*, widely used throughout the empire, often designated the slaves of the one with whose name it was compounded. This implication occurs in the NT (e.g., Rom. 6:22; I Pet. 2:16). The apostles wrote of themselves as servants (slaves) of Christ (Rom. 1:1; James 1:1; II Pet. 1:1; Jude 1:1; Rev. 1:1). The NT calls the followers of Christ *brethren* (Acts 14:2); *disciples* (Acts 6:1,2); *saints* (Acts 9:13; Rom. 1:7; I Cor. 1:2); *believers* (I Tim. 4:12); *the church of God* (Acts 20:28); *those that call upon the name of the Lord* (Acts 9:14; Rom. 10:12,13); etc. To the first Christians, their own name mattered not at all: their concern was with the one Name of Jesus Christ (Acts 3:16; 4:10,12; 5:28). Inevitably, the name which they invoked was given to them: Christians, Christ's men. Its NT meaning is alone adequate for us. E.R.

CHRISTIANITY (krĭs'chĭ-ăn'ĭtē, krĭs'tĭ-ăn'ĭ-tē). The word does not occur in the Bible. Greek *Christianismós*, "Christianism," Christianity, was first used by Ignatius (*Ad Magnes* 10). Latin *Christianismus* occurs in Tertullian, *Against Marcion* 4, 33; in Augustine, *The City of God*, 19, 21, 1; and Jerome, on Galatians 6:4. Latin *Christianitas*, whence our word Christianity, occurs first in the *Codex Theodosianus* 16, 7, 7 and 12, 1, 112; and by metonymy for the Christian clergy, 12, 1, 123. The name was made by Christians to designate all that which Jesus Christ brought to them of faith, life and salvation. Its character is summed up in the words of Jesus, "I am the way, the truth, and the life: no man cometh unto the Father but by me" (John 14:6); "I am come that they might have life, and that they might have it more abundantly" (John 10:10). The classic summary of its doctrines is in the words of Paul in I Corinthians 15:1-4. It is all "according to the scriptures": OT and NT together form the authoritative revelation of what Christianity is. The resurrection of Jesus was the final proof to His disciples that He is the Messiah and Redeemer of men (Acts 2:22-36).

CHRISTMAS (krĭs'măs, krĭst'măs), the anniversary of the birth of Christ, and its observance; celebrated by most Protestants and by Roman Catholics on December 25; by Eastern Orthodox churches on January 6; and by the Armenian church on January 19. The first mention of its observance on December 25 is in the time of Constantine, about A.D. 325. The date of the birth of Christ is not known. The word Christmas is formed of Christ + Mass, meaning a mass of religious service in commemoration of the birth of Christ. Whether the early Christians thought of or observed Christmas is not clear. Once introduced, the observance spread throughout Christendom. Some Christian bodies disapprove of the festival. Many customs of pagan origin have become part of Christmas, e.g., the Christmas tree; but most of these no longer have a heathen connotation, but have acquired a Christian meaning (e.g., the Christmas tree points upward to God and reminds us of His gifts). A commemoration of the birth of Christ in harmonious keeping with the events surrounding that birth (Luke 2:1-20; Matt. 1:18-2:12) is a natural and normal expression of love and reverence for Jesus Christ.   E.R.

CHRONICLES, I and II, are called in Hebrew, *diverê ha-yāmîm,* "The words (affairs) of the days," meaning "The annals" (cf. I Chron. 27:24). Similar annals, now lost, are mentioned in I and II Kings (for example, I Kings 14:19,29); they cannot, however, consist of our present books, which were not written until a century later. The church father Jerome (A.D. 400) first entitled them, "Chronicles." Originally, they formed a single composition, but were divided into I and II Chronicles in the LXX, about 150 B.C. In the Hebrew, they stand as the last books of the OT canon. Christ (Luke 11:51) thus spoke of all the martyrs from Abel, in the first book (Gen. 4), to Zechariah, in the last (II Chron. 24).

Chronicles contains no statements about its own authorship or date. The last event it records is the decree of Cyrus in 538 B.C., which permitted the Jews to return from their Babylonian captivity (II Chron. 36:22); and its genealogies extend to approximately 500 B.C., as far, that is, as to Pelatiah and Jeshaiah (I Chron. 3:21), two grandsons of Zerubbabel, the prince who led in the return from exile. The language, however, and the contents of Chronicles closely parallel that of the book of Ezra, which continues the history of the Jews from the decree of Cyrus down to 457 B.C. Both documents are marked by lists and genealogies, by an interest in priestly ritual, and by devotion to the law of Moses. The closing verses, moreover, of Chronicles (II 36:22-23) are repeated as the opening verses of Ezra (1:1-3a). Ancient Hebrew tradition and the modern scholarship of Wm. F. Albright (JBL 40 [1921], pp. 104-124) therefore unite in suggesting that Ezra may have been the author of both volumes. His complete work would then have been finished some time around 450 B.C. (See CYRUS)

Ezra's position as a "scribe" (Ezra 7:6) may also explain the care that Chronicles shows in acknowledging its written source materials. These include such records as those of Samuel (I Chron. 29:29) and Isaiah (II Chron. 32:32) and a number of other prophets (II 9:29; 12:15; 20:34; 33: 19) and, above all else, "The book of the kings of Judah and Israel" (16:11; 25:26; etc.). This latter work cannot be equated with our present-day I-II Kings, for verses such as I Chronicles 9:1 and II 27:7 refer to "The book of the kings" for further details on matters about which I-II Kings is silent. The author's source must have been a larger court record, now lost, from which both Kings and Chronicles subsequently drew much of their information.

The occasion for the writing of Chronicles appears to be that of Ezra's crusade to bring postexilic Judah back into conformity with the law of Moses (Ezra 7:10). From 458 B.C. and onward, Ezra sought to restore the temple worship (7:19-23,27; 8:33-34), to eliminate the mixed marriages of Jews with their pagan neighbors (9-10), and to strengthen Jerusalem by rebuilding its walls (4:8-16). Chronicles, accordingly, consists of these four parts: genealogies, to enable the Jews to establish their lines of family descent (I Chron. 1-9); the kingdom of David, as a pattern for the ideal theocratic state (I Chron. 10-29); the glory of Solomon, with an emphasis upon the temple and its worship (II Chron. 1-9); and the history of the southern kingdom, stressing in particular the religious reforms and military victories of Judah's more pious rulers (II Chron. 10-36).

As compared with the parallel histories in Samuel and Kings, the priestly annals of Chronicles lay a greater emphasis upon the structure of the temple (I Chron. 22) and upon Israel's ark, the Levites, and the singers (I Chron. 13, 15-16). They omit, however, certain individualistic, moral acts of the kings (II Sam. 9; I Kings 3:16-28), as well as detailed biographies of the prophets (I Kings 17-22:28; II Kings 1-8:15), features which account for the incorporation of Chronicles into the third (non-prophetic) section of the Hebrew canon, as distinguished from the location of the more homiletical books of Samuel and Kings in the second (prophetic) division. Finally, the chronicler foregoes discussion of David's disputed inauguration and later shame (II Sam. 1-4, 11-21), of Solomon's failures (I Kings 11), and of the whole inglorious history of Saul (I Sam. 8-30, except his death, 31) and of the northern kingdom of Israel: the disillusioned, impoverished Jews of 450 B.C. knew enough of sin and defeat; but they needed an encouraging reminder of their former, God-given victories (as II Chron. 13,14,20,25).

Because of these emphases, many modern critics have rejected Chronicles as being Levitical propaganda, a fiction of "what ought to have happened" (IB, III:341), with extensive (and conflicting) revisions as late as 250 B.C. (so Adam C. Welch, Robert F. Pfeiffer, and W. A. L. Elmslie). The book's high numeric totals (such as the 1,000,000 invading Ethiopians, II Chron. 14:9) are subject to particular ridicule, despite the elucidations that have been presented by believing scholars (see Edward J. Young, *An Introduction to the Old Testament,* Grand Rapids: Eerdmans, 1949, pp. 388-390). Liberal writers, however, with their prior repudiation of the Mosaic origin of OT religion, are simply unable to evaluate Chronicles in an objective fashion: its repeated validations of the ceremonies of the Pentateuch leave them no alternative but to deny its historicity. Yet excavations at Ugarit, a Canaanitish city of Moses' day, have confirmed the authenticity of just such religious practices (see J. W. Jack, *The Ras Shamra Tablets: their Bearings on the Old Testament,* Edinburgh: T. & T. Clark, 1935, p. 29ff); and Albright observes that the reliability of many of the historical statements that are found only in Chronicles has been established by recent archaeological discovery (BASOR 100 [1945], p. 18). Furthermore, though Chronicles does stress the bright side of Hebrew history, it does not deny the defeats (cf. I Chron. 29:22 on the successful *second* anointing of Solomon and II Chron. 17:3 on the more exemplary *first* ways of David). The prophetic judgments of Kings and the priestly hopes of Chronicles are both true, and both are necessary. The morality of the former is invaluable, but the redemption of the latter constitutes the more distinctive feature of Christian faith.   J.B.P.

CHRONOLOGY, NEW TESTAMENT, the science of determining the dates of the NT books and the historical events mentioned therein. The subject is beset with serious difficulty since sufficient data are often lacking and the computations must be based upon ancient documents which did not record historical events under precise calendar dates like modern historical records. Neither sacred nor secular historians of that time were accustomed to record history under exact dates but felt that all demands were satisfied when some specific event was related to a well-known period, as, the reign of a noted ruler, or the time of some famous contemporary. Luke's method of dating the beginning of the ministry of John the Baptist (Luke 3:1,2) is typical of the historian's method of that day. Further, the use of different local chronologies and different ways of computing years often leave the results tentative. NT chronology naturally falls into two parts: the life of Christ, and the apostolic age.

Life of Christ. The erection of a chronology of the life of Christ turns around three points: His birth, baptism, and crucifixion. Luke's statement of the age of Jesus at His baptism (Luke 3:23) links the first two, while the problem of the length of the ministry links the second and third.

The Christian Era, now used almost exclusively in the Western World for civil chronology, was introduced at Rome by Abbot Dionysius Exiguus in the sixth century. It is now generally agreed that the beginning of the era should have been fixed at least four years earlier.

According to the Gospels Jesus was born some time before the death of Herod the Great. Josephus, the Jewish historian, who was born A.D. 37, affirms (*Ant.* XVII,6,4) that Herod died shortly after an eclipse of the moon, which is astronomically fixed at March 12-13, 4 B.C. His death occurred shortly before Passover, which that year fell on April 4. His death in 4 B.C. is also confirmed from the known commencement of the rule of his three sons in that year. The age of Jesus at Herod's death is not certain. The "two years" for the age of the children slain at Bethlehem (Matt. 2:16) offers no sure indication, since Herod would allow a liberal margin for safety, and since part of a year might be counted as a year. It does show that Jesus was born at least some months before Herod's death. Christ's presentation in the temple after He was 40 days old (Luke 2:22-24; Lev. 12:1-8) makes it certain that the wise men came at least six weeks after His birth. The time spent in Egypt is uncertain, but may have been several months. Thus the birth of Jesus should be placed in the latter part of the year 5 B.C.

Luke's statement (3:1,2) that Jesus was born in connection with the "first enrollment" when "Quirinius was governor of Syria" (ASV) was once fiercely assailed as erroneous, since Cyrenius (AV), or Quirinius, was known to be governor in connection with the census of A.D. 6. But it is now known that he was also connected with the Syrian government at some previous time. Papyrus evidence shows that Augustus inaugurated a periodic census every 14 years, from 8 B.C. onward. Herod's war with the king of Arabia, his troubles with Augustus, as well as the problem of the method of taking the census among the Jews, may have delayed the actual census in Palestine for several years, bringing it down to the year 5 B.C.

Luke gives the age of Jesus at His baptism as "about thirty years" (3:23). Although the statement of age is not specific, it naturally implies that His age was just about 30, a few months under or over. Born in the latter part of 5 B.C., His baptism then occurred near the close of A.D. 26 or the beginning of 27. The 40-day period of the temptation, plus the events recorded in John 1:19-2:12 seem to require that the baptism occurred at least three months before the first Passover of His public ministry (John 2:13-22). Since Herod began the reconstruction of the temple in 20 B.C., the "forty and six years" mentioned by the Jews during this Passover, using the inclusive Jewish count, again brings us to A.D. 27 for this first Passover.

Apparently John began his ministry some six months before the baptism of Jesus. Luke dates that beginning as "in the fifteenth year of the reign of Tiberius Caesar" (3:1). Augustus died in August of A.D. 14, but 15 years added to that would be two years too late for our previous dates. Since Tiberius had been reigning jointly with Augustus in the provinces for two years before his death, it seems only natural that Luke would follow the provincial point of view and count the 15 years from the time of Tiberius' actual assumption of authority in the provinces. Thus counted, the date is in harmony with our other dates. The ministry of John, begun about six months before the baptism of Jesus, commenced about the middle of A.D. 26.

The time of the crucifixion will be determined by the length of the ministry of Jesus. Mark's Gospel seems to require at least two years: the plucking of the ears of grain (April-June) marks a first spring; the feeding of the 5,000 when the grass was fresh green (March-April), a second; the Passover of the crucifixion, a third. John's Gospel explicitly mentions three Passovers (2:23; 6:4; 11:55). If the feast of 5:1 is also a Passover, as seems probable, a view having the traditional backing of Irenaeus, then the length of the ministry of Jesus was full three years and a little over. This places the crucifixion at the Passover of A.D. 30.

Apostolic Age. Due to the uncertainties connected with the limited data for an apostolic chronology, authorities have arrived at varied dates. The Book of Acts with its many notes of time, mostly indefinite, offers but few points for the establishment of even relatively fixed dates. Even Paul's apparently precise chronological notes in Galatians 1:18 and 2:1 leave us in doubt as to whether "after three years" and "after the space of fourteen years" are to be regarded as consecutive or as both counting from his conversion. The death of Herod Agrippa I (Acts 12:23) and the proconsulship of Gallio (Acts 18:12) are important for the chronology of the period.

The death of Herod Agrippa I, one of the fixed dates of the New Testament, is known to have taken place in A.D. 44. It establishes the year of Peter's arrest and miraculous escape from prison. The proconsulship of Gallio is also strongly relied upon for an apostolic chronology. A fragmentary inscription found at Delphi associates his proconsulship with the 26th acclamation of Claudius as Imperator. This would place his proconsulship between May 51 and 52, or May 52 and 53. The latter date is more probable since Gallio would assume office in May and not in midsummer as some advocates of the earlier date assumed. Since apparently Paul had already been at Corinth a year and a half when Gallio arrived, his ministry at Corinth began in the latter part of A.D. 50. Efforts to determine the time of the accession of Festus as governor, under whom Paul was sent to Rome, have not resulted in agreement. From the inconclusive data advocates have argued for a date as early as A.D. 55 and as late as 60 or 61. The balance of the arguments seems to point to 60, or perhaps 59. If the latter, the suggested dates should be adjusted accordingly.

Chronological Table. The dates for many NT events must remain tentative, but as indicated by Luke (3:1,2), they have a definite correlation with secular history. (See the accompanying diagram). The following chronological table is regarded as approximately correct. The dates for the NT literature assume a conservative viewpoint.

Birth of Jesus	5 B.C.
Baptism of Jesus	late A.D. 26 or early 27
First Passover of Ministry	27
Crucifixion of Jesus	30
Conversion of Saul	34 or 35
Death of Herod Agrippa I	44
Epistle of James	before 50
First Missionary journey	48-49
Jerusalem Conference	49 or 50
Second Missionary journey	begun spring 50
Paul at Corinth	50-52
I and II Thessalonians from Corinth	51
Galatians from Corinth (?)	early 52
Arrival of Gallio as Proconsul	May 52
Third Missionary journey	begun 54
Paul at Ephesus	54-57
I Corinthians from Ephesus	spring 57
II Corinthians from Macedonia	fall 57
Romans from Corinth	winter 57-58
Paul's arrest at Jerusalem	Pentecost 58
Imprisonment at Caesarea	58-60
On Island of Malta	winter 60-61
Arrival at Rome	spring 61
Roman Imprisonment	61-63
Colossians, Philemon, Ephesians	summer 62
Philippians	spring 63
Paul's release and further work	63-65
I Timothy and Titus	63
Epistle to the Hebrews	64
Synoptic Gospels and Acts	before 67
I and II Peter from Rome	64-65
Peter's death at Rome	65
Paul's second Roman imprisonment	66
II Timothy	66
Death at Rome	late 66 or early 67
Epistle of Jude	67-68
Writings of John	before 100
Death of John	98-100

D.E.H.

Chronological Chart of the New Testament

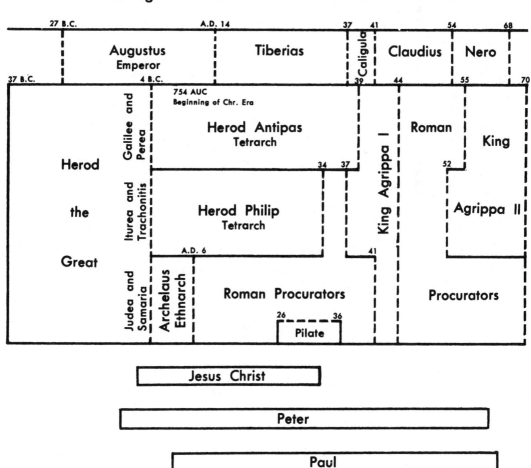

CHRONOLOGY, OLD TESTAMENT. The chronology of the Old Testament presents many complex and difficult problems. The data are not always adequate or clear, and at times are almost completely lacking. Because of insufficient data many of the problems are at present beyond solution. Even where the data are abundant the exact meaning is often not immediately apparent, leaving scope for considerable difference of opinion and giving rise to many variant chronological reconstructions. The chronological problem is thus one of the availability of evidence, of the correct evaluation and interpretation of that evidence, and of its proper application. Only the most careful study of all the data, both Biblical and extra-Biblical, can hope to provide a satisfactory solution.

FROM THE CREATION TO THE DELUGE. From the creation to the deluge the only Biblical data are the ages of the patriarchs in the genealogical tables of Genesis 5 and 7:11. The Masoretic text gives 1,656 years from Adam to the deluge; the Samaritan Pentateuch gives 1,307 years, and the Septuagint, 2,242. The numbers of the MT are in agreement with the Samaritan except in the cases of Jared, Methuselah, and Lamech, where the numbers of the MT are higher by 100 years, 120, and 129 respectively. For the eight patriarchs from Adam to Methuselah, the numbers of the LXX are a century higher in each instance than those of the Samaritan, while for Lamech the number is 135 years higher.

Extra-Biblical sources for this period are almost completely lacking. The early Sumerian king list names eight kings with a total of 241,200 years from the time when "the kingship was lowered from heaven" to the time when "the Flood swept" over the land and once more "the kingship was lowered from heaven." (Thorkild Jacobsen, *The Sumerian King List,* Chicago: The University of Chicago Press, 1939, pp. 71, 77). Such a statement, however, makes no practical contribution to the solution of this phase of OT chronology. Nor is modern science in a position to supply a detailed and final solution.

The Deluge to Abraham. For the period from the deluge to Abraham we are again dependent upon the genealogical data in the Greek and Hebrew texts, and the Samaritan Pentateuch. Reckoning the age of Terah at the birth of Abraham as 70 (Gen. 11:26), the years from the deluge to Abraham would be 292 according to the MT, 942 according to the Samaritan Pentateuch, and 1172 according to the LXX. But if the age of Terah at Abraham's birth is reckoned as 130 years (on the basis of Gen. 11:32; 12:4; and Acts 7:4), the above totals would be raised by 60 years. On this basis the Hebrew text would give 352 years from the deluge to Abraham, and the Greek, 1232.

In this area the testimony of the MT stands alone against the LXX and the Samaritan Pentateuch, where the numbers are 100 years higher than those of the MT for Arphaxad, Salah, Eber, Peleg, Reu, and Serug, while for Nahor, the grandfather of Abraham, the Samaritan is 50 years higher and LXX 150, than the MT.

Serious chronological difficulties are thus encountered in the period immediately beyond Abraham. Abraham was 86 years old at the birth of Ishmael (Gen. 16:16), and 100 at the birth of Isaac (Gen. 21:5). But how old was Terah at the birth of Abraham, 70, 130, or some number not revealed? And how old was Nahor at the birth of Terah, 29, 79, or 179? If Terah was 130 years old at the birth of Abraham, as seems to be indicated by the Biblical evidence, it must be admitted that

the numbers of the Septuagint for this period (135, 130,130,134,130,132,130,179,130), are much more consistent with each other than the numbers of the Hebrew (35,30,34,30,32,30,29,130). But it will be noticed that in the case of nine patriarchs in the Septuagint, five of them were 130 years old when their sons were born, while in the Hebrew three out of eight were 30, one was 130, while the others were all in their thirties with the exception of Nahor who was 29—one year from 30. And if Terah was 130 years old when Abraham was born, why should it have been regarded as so very unusual for Abraham to have a son at the age of 100 (Gen. 17:17; 18:11; 21:2,5)?

An endeavor to assess the relative values of the three sources involved accomplishes little, for the indications are that none is altogether complete. Certainly the LXX had great weight in NT times, for in Luke's table of the ancestors of Christ, there is listed a second Cainan, son of Arphaxad (Luke 3:36), in harmony with the LXX of Gen. 11:12,13 —a name not found in the MT. If the LXX is here to be followed rather than the MT, another 130 years should be added to the years of the deluge and creation, for that is the age of Cainan in the LXX at the time of the birth of Salah.

The omission of the names of known individuals is frequent in Biblical genealogical records. Thus Matthew's table of the ancestors of Christ omits the names of three Judean kings—Ahaziah, Joash, and Amaziah—with the statement that "Joram begat Ozias" (Matt. 1:8), whereas Uzziah was actually the great-great-grandson of Joram. A comparison of Ezra 7:1-5 with I Chronicles 6:4-15 shows a block of six names missing in Ezra's tabulation.

Extra-Biblical materials from the deluge to Abraham are of little assistance in the establishment of an absolute chronology for this period, but there is sufficient evidence to show that the time involved is much greater than that indicated by the genealogical data of the MT. No exact synchronisms exist between Biblical and secular chronology of this period, and the exact chronology of Mesopotamia and Egypt has not yet been established.

Because of the difficulties involved, it must be admitted that the construction of an absolute chronology from Adam to Abraham is not now possible on the basis of the available data.

Abraham to Moses. From Abraham to Joseph the detailed patriarchal narratives provide more data than are available for the preceding periods, and we have the certainty that there are no missing links. There are, also, a number of correlations with later and better known periods. Since Abraham was 75 years old at the time of his entrance into Canaan (Gen. 12:4), and since he was 100 at the birth of Isaac (Gen. 21:5), there were 25 years from the entry into Canaan to Isaac. Isaac was 60 at the birth of Jacob (Gen. 25:26), and Jacob was 130 at his entrance into Egypt (Gen. 47:9,28), making 215 years from the beginning of the sojourn in Canaan to the beginning of the sojourn in Egypt. The total length of the sojourn was 430 years (Exod. 12:40). Did this involve only the sojourn in Egypt or did it include also the sojourn in Canaan? If Israel was in Egypt 430 years, there were 645 years from the entrance into Canaan to the Exodus. Otherwise there were 430 years from Abraham's entry into Canaan to Moses' departure from Egypt, and the length of the Egyptian sojourn would have been only 215 years.

According to I Kings 6:1 the temple was founded in the 480th year after the Exodus, which was the fourth year of Solomon's reign. On the basis of a 40-year reign for Solomon (I Kings 11:42) and in accord with the established chronology of the kings, that was 966 B.C. This would provide 1445 as the date of the Exodus and 1525 as the year of Moses' birth (Exod. 7:7). If the 430-year sojourn involved only the period in Egypt, Abraham entered Canaan in 2090. If it included the years in Canaan, the date was 1875. The answer depends on the meaning of the prophecy of Genesis 15:13-16 and the reconstruction of the details from Abraham to Moses. From Abraham to Joseph the details are known, but from Joseph to Moses there is only genealogical evidence.

Due to omissions, repetitions, and other variations in the genealogical lists, the endeavor to establish times by the evidence of such lists must be regarded as highly precarious. Compare, for instance, the line of descent of Samuel and his sons from Levi and Kohath as recorded in I Chronicles 6:22-28 and in verses 33-38, and see I Samuel 8:2 for the names of these sons. Compare also the various lists of the sons of Benjamin and their descendants as found in Genesis 46:21; Numbers 26:38-40; I Chronicles 7:6-12; and 8:1-40. The variations in existence here and in many other lists indicate the dangers involved in dogmatic reconstructions based only on genealogical evidence.

The ancestry of Moses from Jacob through Levi, Kohath, and Amram is repeatedly given (Num. 3:17-19; 26:57-59; I Chron. 6:1-3; 23:6, 12,13), including the ages of these patriarchs at the time of death (Exod. 6:16,18,20), but the ages at the time of their sons' births are not recorded. Jochebed, the wife of Amram and mother of Moses, is said to have been the sister of Kohath, son of Levi and father of Moses (Exod. 6: 16,18,20), and to have been born to Levi in Egypt (Num. 26:59). This might appear to be conclusive evidence of a comparatively brief period in Egypt and to make a sojourn there of 430 years impossible. But there are difficulties. While four to five generations from Jacob to Moses may be indicated in the above line of descent, 11 generations may be counted from Jacob to Joshua (I Chron. 7:20-27). And that some considerable period was involved is clear from the fact that Joseph before his death saw the children of the third generation of both his sons (Gen. 50:23), and that at the time of the Exodus Amram and his brothers were already regarded as founders of clans (Num. 3:27).

Levi was the elder brother of Joseph and must have been born not more than ten years before Joseph (Gen. 29:30-34; 30:22-43; 31:41). Since Joseph was 30 when he stood before Pharaoh (Gen. 41:46), and since seven years of plenty and two years of famine had passed at the time of Jacob's entry into Egypt (Gen. 41:47,53; 45:6), Joseph would have been 39 when Jacob was 130 (Gen. 47:9,28), and would thus have been born when Jacob was 91. That, however, would have made Jacob an old man of about 80 at the time of his marriage and the birth of his firstborn. That is possible but hardly probable. In view of the frequency of the numbers of 30 or 130 in age lists of Biblical patriarchs, and in view of the significance of the number 30 in connection with the Sed Festival in Egypt honoring a ruler on the 30th anniversary of his appointment as heir to the crown, the question might well be raised as to whether 130 as the age of Jacob is employed in an absolute sense. If not, the chronological reckonings based upon it are only approximate and not absolute.

It should also be noticed that if the sojourn in Egypt was 215 years and if there were only four generations from Jacob to Moses, then Levi must have been about 100 at the birth of Jochebed, and Jochebed 84 at the birth of Moses. Since the birth of Isaac to Sarah when she was 90 and to Abraham when he was 100 was regarded as in the nature of a miracle (Gen. 17:17; 18:11-14; Rom. 4:19), these ages are hardly probable.

On the basis of the Old Testament data it is impossible to give a categorical answer as to exactly what was involved in the 430-year sojourn, nor is it possible to give an absolute date for Abraham's entry into Canaan. Paul regarded the 430 years as beginning at the time when the promises were made to Abraham (Gen. 12:1-4) and terminating with the giving of the law at Sinai (Gal. 3:16,17). On this basis the date of the entry into Canaan and the beginning of the sojourn was 1875.

An Exodus date of 1445 calls for 1405 as the beginning of the conquest (Num. 33:38; Deut. 1:3; Josh. 5:6). According to these dates the Exodus took place during the reigns of the famous rulers of Egypt's Eighteenth Dynasty, c. 1570-1325. This fits in well with the Habiru inroads of the Amarna period and with the evidence of Israel's presence in Palestine during the Nineteenth Dynasty, c. 1325-1200. In view of recent evidence of a sedentary occupation of Trans-Jordan from the end of the Middle Bronze Age, c. 1550 B.C., to the end of the Late Bronze Age, c. 1250 (see G. Lankester Harding, "Recent Discoveries in Jordan," *Palestine Exploration Quarterly*, Jan.-June, 1958, pp. 10-12), the view that non-occupation of that area from the 18th to the 13th centuries B.C. makes a 15th century date for the Exodus impossible, is no longer tenable.

The Conquest to the Kingdom. The establishment of absolute dates from Moses through Joshua and the judges to the setting up of the monarchy is again not possible with the available data. With the date 1405 for the beginning of the conquest, we secure 1399 as the year when Caleb received his inheritance, since he was 40 when he was sent as a spy from Kadesh-barnea (Josh. 14:7) in the second year after the departure from Egypt (Num. 10:11,12; Deut. 2:14), and he was 85 when he received his inheritance 45 years later (Josh. 14: 10). The date of Joshua's death can not be given, for we do not know how old he was when he was sent as a spy, although he was 110 when he died (Josh. 24:29).

Many attempts have been made to set dates for the judges, but with the data now available an accurate chronology for this period is at present impossible. The data are as follows:

	Reference	Years
Oppression under Cushan-rishathaim	Judg. 3:8	8
Deliverance under Othniel; rest	Judg. 3:11	40
Oppression under Eglon of Moab	Judg. 3:14	18
Deliverance by Ehud; rest	Judg. 3:30	80
Oppression under Jabin of Hazor	Judg. 4:3	20
Deliverance under Deborah; rest	Judg. 5:31	40
Oppression under Midian	Judg. 6:1	7
Deliverance under Gideon; rest	Judg. 8:28	40
Reign of Abimelech	Judg. 9:22	3
Judgeship of Tola	Judg. 10:2	23
Judgeship of Jair	Judg. 10:3	22
Oppression of Gilead by Ammon	Judg. 10:8	18

Judgeship of Jephthah	Judg. 12:7	6
Judgeship of Ibzan	Judg. 12:9	7
Judgeship of Elon	Judg. 12:11	10
Judgeship of Abdon	Judg. 12:14	8
Oppression under the Philistines	Judg. 13:1	40
Judgeship of Samson	Judg. 15:20; 16:31	20
Judgeship of Eli	I Sam. 4:18	40

The sum of the above numbers is 450 years. But there is no evidence that that is the actual length of the judges' period. The judgeship of Samuel is not included in the above total because the years are not given. That these terms of judgeships and oppressions should be regarded as consecutive is mere conjecture. A number of the judges were unquestionably local rulers, exercising control over limited areas while others held office in other parts of the land. This was the case with Jephthah who ruled over Gilead (Judg. 10:18; 11:5-11; 12:4). Judgeships and oppressions at times overlapped as with Samson who "judged Israel in the days of the Philistines twenty years" (Judg. 15:20). Two oppressions might have been simultaneous in different parts of the land, as with the Ammonites in the NE and the Philistines in the SW (Judg. 10:6,7). The numerous 40's or multiples and submultiples of 40 (40,80,20,40,40,10,40,20,40) are no doubt to be taken as round rather than absolute numbers. Jephthah's 300 years after the conquest (Judg. 11:26) is almost certainly merely approximate. Due to the above uncertainties no detailed chronology of this period can be given with confidence.

The United Monarchy. Due to a number of uncertainties the absolute date for the establishment of the United Monarchy can not be given. The OT does not give the length of the reign of Saul, but Paul in a sermon at Antioch refers to it as 40 years (Acts 13:21). If Saul reigned a full 40 years, David was not born until ten years after Saul began his reign, for he was 30 when he took the throne (II Sam. 5:4). The battle with the Philistines at Michmash, with Jonathan in command of a large part of the army, presumably took place early in Saul's reign, perhaps even in his second year (I Sam. 13:1,2). In such a case Jonathan would have been well advanced in years when David was a mere youth, which is out of harmony with the picture in the Biblical record. Other difficulties are also involved, all making it clear that Saul either did not reign a full 40 years, or that he must have been very young when he took the throne.

The reign of David, on the other hand, may be regarded as a full 40 years for he reigned seven years in Hebron and 33 in Jerusalem (II Sam. 5:4,5; I Kings 2:11; I Chron. 3:4), and one event is dated in the 40th year (I Chron. 26:31).

Solomon began his reign before the death of David (I Kings 1:32-48), but how long is not recorded. Presumably it was only a short time, but the indefiniteness of this period must be taken into consideration in any endeavor to establish an absolute chronology. And the 40 years of his reign (I Kings 11:42) might have been intended as a round number. Going back to the Exodus the recorded periods are as follows: 40,8,40,18,80,20,40, 7,40,3,23,22,18,6,7,10,8,40,20,40,40,40,40. Unless we can be certain that all these numbers are absolute, we cannot be certain of an absolute chronology for the periods involved.

The Divided Monarchy. For the period of the Divided Monarchy an entirely different situation is found. Here there are an abundance of data which may be checked against each other, and which are no longer round. Four Biblical yardsticks are here provided—the lengths of reign of the rulers of Judah and those of Israel, and the synchronisms of Judah with Israel and of Israel with Judah. Furthermore, a number of synchronisms with the fixed years of contemporary Assyria make possible a check with an exact chronological yardstick, and make possible the establishment of absolute years B.C. for the period of the kings.

Various methods were employed in the ancient East for reckoning the official years of kings. When Solomon's kingdom was first divided, Judah followed those nations where the year when a ruler took the throne was termed his "accession year." Israel, on the other hand, followed those nations where a king termed his initial year his "first year." According to this latter method the year when a king began to reign was always counted twice—as the last year of his predecessor and as his own first official year. Thus reigns reckoned according to this method were always one year longer in official length than those reckoned according to the former method, and there was always a gain of one year for every reign over absolute time. The following graphs will make these two methods of reckoning clear, and will show how the totals of Israel for this period increase by one year for every reign over those of Judah:

	Old king		New king					
Accession-year reckoning	last year	accession year	1st year				2nd year	3rd year
Non-accession-year reckoning	last year	1st year	2nd year				3rd year	4th year
JUDAH, official years:	22	23	46	47	58	61	78	79
Rehoboam 17 Abijam 3 Asa	2nd	3rd	26th	27th	38th	41	Jehoshaphat 17th	18th
Jeroboam	22	Nadab 2 Baasha 24		Elah 2	Omri 12 / Zimri	Ahab 4th	22	Ahaziah 2 Jehoram
ISRAEL, official years:	22	24	48	50	62	66	84	86
Excess years for Israel	0	1	2	3	4	5	6	7

The following table shows how the totals of both nations from the disruption to the death of Ahaziah in Israel in the 18th year of Jehoshaphat in Judah (omitting the seven-day reign of Zimri) are identical and perfectly correct when correctly understood:

ISRAEL			JUDAH	
King	Official years	Actual years	King	Years
Jeroboam	22	21	Rehoboam	17
Nadab	2	1	Abijam	3
Baasha	24	23	Asa	41
Elah	2	1	Jehoshaphat	18
Omri	12	11		
Ahab	22	21		
Ahaziah	2	1		
Total	86	79		79

The following are the conditions that make possible the construction of a chronological pattern of the kings based on the Biblical data which possess internal harmony and are in accord with the years of contemporary Assyria and Babylon: Tishri regnal years for Judah and Nisan years for Israel; accession-year reckoning for Judah except for Jehoram, Ahaziah, Athaliah, and Joash, who followed the non-accession-year system then employed in Israel; non-accession-year reckoning in Israel for the early period, and from Jehoash to the end, accession-year reckoning; synchronisms of each nation in accord with its own current system of reckoning; a number of co-regencies or of overlapping reigns when rival rulers exercised control; a double chronological pattern for both Israel and Judah involving the closing years of Israel's history.

The years of the kings based on the above principles are as follows:

ISRAEL			JUDAH		
Ruler	Overlapping Reign	Reign	Ruler	Overlapping Reign	Reign
Jeroboam I		931/30-910/9	Rehoboam		931/30-913
			Abijam		913 -911/10
Nadab		910/9 -909/8	Asa		911/10-870/69
Baasha		909/8 -886/85	Jehoshaphat	873/72-870/69	870/69-848
Elah		886/85-885/84	Jehoram	853 -848	848 -841
Zimri		885/84	Ahaziah		841
Tibni		885/84-880	Athaliah		841 -835
Omri	885/84-880	880 -874/73	Joash		835 -796
Ahab		874/73-853	Amaziah		796 -767
Ahaziah		853 -852	Azariah (Uzziah)	792/91-767	767 -740/39
Joram		852 -841			
Jehu		841 -814/13			
Jehoahaz		814/13-798	Jotham	750 -740/39	740/39-732/31
Jehoash		798 -782/81			
Jeroboam II	793/92-782/81	782/81-753	Ahaz	735 -732/31	732/31-716/15
Zachariah		753 -752			
Shallum		752	Hezekiah		716/15-687/86
Menahem		752 -742/41	Manasseh	697/96-687/86	687/86-643/42
Pekahiah		742/41-740/39	Amon		643/42-641/40
Pekah	752 -740/39	740/39-732/31	Josiah		641/40-609
Hoshea		732/31-723/22	Jehoahaz		609
			Jehoiakim		609 -598
			Jehoiachin		598 -597
			Zedekiah		597 -586

THE EXILE AND RETURN. The book of Kings closes with the notice of the release of Jehoiachin from capitvity on the 27th day of the 12th month, in the 37th year of his captivity and the accession year of Amel-Marduk (II Kings 25:27). That was April 2, 561 B.C.

Babylon fell to the Persians Oct.12, 539 B.C., and Cyrus in the first year of his reign issued a decree permitting the Jews to return and rebuild the temple (II Chron. 36:22; Ezra 1:1). On the basis of Nisan regnal years this would have been 538 B.C. However, Nehemiah 1:1; 2:1 gives evidence that the author of Nehemiah reckoned the years of the Persian kings not from Nisan as was the Persian custom, but from Tishri, in accord with the Jewish custom. The Aramaic papyri from Elephantine in

Egypt give evidence that the same custom was employed by the Jewish colony there in the fifth century B.C. (See S. H. Horn and L. H. Wood, "The Fifth-Century Jewish Calendar at Elephantine," *Journal of Near Eastern Studies*, XIII (January, 1954), pp. 1-20.) Inasmuch as Chronicles-Ezra-Nehemiah were originally one and came from the same author, the indications are that the first year of Cyrus referred to in Ezra 1:1 was reckoned on a Tishri basis, and that it was, therefore, in 537 that Cyrus issued his decree.

Haggai began his ministry on the first day of the sixth month in the second year of Darius (Hag. 1:1), Aug. 29, 520, and Zechariah commenced his work in the eighth month of the same year (Zech. 1:1), in October or November, 520. The temple was completed on the third of Adar, the sixth year of Darius (Ezra 6:15), March 12, 515

The return of Ezra from Babylon was begun the first day of the first month, in the seventh year of Artaxerxes (Ezra 7:7,9). Artaxerxes came to the throne in December, 465, which would bring the first of Nisan of his seventh year on April 8, 458, according to Persian reckoning, but on March 27, 457, according to Judean years. The evidence that this was the custom then employed has already been given above.

Word was brought to Nehemiah of the sad state of affairs at Jerusalem in the month Kislev of the 20th year of Artaxerxes (Neh. 1:1), and in Nisan of that same 20th year Nehemiah stood before the king and received permission to return to Jerusalem to rebuild the city (Neh. 2:1-8). That was April, 444. With Nehemiah's return to Babylon in the 32nd year of Artaxerxes (Neh. 13:6), 433/32, the chronology of the Old Testament proper comes to a close.   E.R.T.

BIBLIOGRAPHY
W. F. Albright, "The Chronology of the Divided Monarchy of Israel," *Bulletin of the American Schools of Oriental Research*, No. 100 (December, 1945), pp. 16-22.
S. H. Horn and L. H. Wood, "The Fifth-Century Jewish Calendar at Elephantine," *Journal of Near Eastern Studies*, XIII (January, 1954), pp. 1-20.
A. Malamat, "A New Record of Nebuchadnezzar's Palestinian Campaigns," *Israel Exploration Journal*, Vol. 6, No. 4 (1956), pp. 246-256; "The Kingdom of David & Solomon in its Contact with Egypt and Aram Naharaim," *The Biblical Archaeologist*, XXI (December, 1958), pp. 96-102.
P. Van der Meer, *The Ancient Chronology of Western Asia and Egypt*, Leiden: E. J. Brill, 1955.
James A. Montgomery, Henry Snyder Gehman (ed.), *A Critical and Exegetical Commentary on the Books of Kings*, "The International Critical Commentary," New York: Charles Scribner's Sons, 1951, pp. 45-64.
Richard A. Parker and Waldo H. Dubberstein, *Babylonian Chronology 626 B.C.-A.D. 75*, Providence: Brown University Press, 1956.
John Rea, *The Historical Setting of the Exodus and the Conquest*, Winona Lake, Indiana: Grace Theological Seminary, 1959, (mimeographed).
Hayim Tadmor, "Chronology of the Last Kings of Judah," *Journal of Near Eastern Studies*, XV (October, 1956), pp. 226-230; "The Campaigns of Sargon II of Assur; A Chronological-Historical Study," *Journal of Cuneiform Studies*, XII, 1 (1958), pp. 22-42.
Edwin R. Thiele, "A Comparison of the Chronological Data of Israel and Judah," *Vetus Testamentum*, IV (April, 1954), pp. 185-195; "New Evidence on the Chronology of the Last Kings of Judah," *Bulletin of the American Schools of Oriental Research*, No. 143 (October, 1956), pp. 22-27; "The Chronology of the Kings of Judah and Israel," *Journal of Near Eastern Studies*, III (July, 1944), pp. 137-186; *The Mysterious Numbers of the Hebrew Kings*, Chicago: The University of Chicago Press, 1955; "The Question of Coregencies Among the Hebrew Kings," *A Stubborn Faith*, ed. Edward C. Hobbs, Dallas: Southern Methodist University Press, 1956, pp. 39-52.
John C. Whitcomb, Jr., *Bible Chronology, 640-400 B.C.*, Winona Lake, Indiana: Grace Theological Seminary, 1958, (mimeographed).

CHUB (kŭb, Heb. *kûv*), a land mentioned with Ethiopia, Libya, and Lydia in Ezekiel 30:5. The Hebrew text may here be corrupt. The LXX has *Lud*.

CHUN (kŭn, Heb. *kûv*), an Aramean city taken by David (I Chron. 18:8). In II Samuel 8:8 *Berothai* is given as the name of the city. The identification is uncertain.

CHURCH. The English "church" derives from the Greek *kuriakós* (belonging to the Lord), but it stands for another Greek word *ekklesía* (whence "ecclesiastical"), denoting an assembly. This is used in its general sense in Acts 19:32, but had already been applied in the LXX as an equivalent for the "congregation" of the Old Testament. Stephen's speech makes this equation (Acts 7:38), and in this sense it is adopted to describe the new gathering or congregation of the disciples of Jesus Christ.

In the Gospels the term is found only in Matthew 16:18 and 18:17. This paucity is perhaps explained by the fact that both these verses seem to envisage a situation still future. Only after the saving work of Christ is effected will the Old Testament Church be reconstituted as that of the New. Yet the verses show that Christ has this reconstitution in view, that the Church thus reconstituted will rest on the apostolic confession, and that it will take up the ministry of reconciliation.

When we turn to Acts, the situation changes. The saving work has been fulfilled, and the New Testament form of the Church can thus have its birthday at Pentecost. The term is now used regularly to describe local groups of believers. Thus we read of the churches at Jerusalem in Acts 5:11, Antioch in 13:1, and Caesarea in 18:22. At the same time the word is used for all believers in universal fellowship, as is possibly the case in 9:31. From the outset the Church has both a local and a general significance, denoting both the individual assembly and the world-wide community.

This twofold usage is also seen in Paul. He addresses his epistles to specific churches, e.g., Corinth (I Cor. 1:2) or Thessalonica (I Thess. 1:1). Indeed, he seems sometimes to localize further by referring to specific groups within the local community as churches, as though sending greetings to congregations within the one city (cf. Rom. 16: 5). Yet Paul also develops more fully the conception of a Church of all believers embracing the local churches, as in I Corinthians 10:32 and I Timothy 3:15, and with an even grander sweep in Colossians 1:18 and especially Ephesians. The other New Testament books give us mostly examples of the local usage, as in III John 9 and Revelation 1:4; 2:1, etc.

A point to be emphasized is that there is no tension between the local and the universal sense. Each church or congregation is the Church in its own setting, and each a manifestation or concretion of the whole church. This means that there is scope for great flexibility in organization and structure according to particular and varying needs. At the world-wide level it is unlikely that there can ever be more than the loosest practical interconnection. Varying degrees of integration are possible at national, provincial or municipal levels. But the basic unity is always the local church, not in isolation or as a parochially-minded body, but as a concretion of the universal fellowship with a strong sense of belonging to it.

This leads us to the further consideration that the Church is not primarily a human structure like a political, social or economic organism. It is basically the church of Jesus Christ ("my church" Matt. 16:18), or of the living God (I Tim. 3:15). The various Biblical descriptions all emphasize this. It is a building of which Jesus Christ is the chief corner-stone or foundation, "an holy temple in the Lord," "an habitation of God through the Spirit" (Eph. 2:20f). It is the fellowship of saints or people of God (cf. I Pet. 2:9). It is the bride of Jesus Christ, saved and sanctified by Him for union with Himself (Eph. 5:25f). Indeed, it is the body of Jesus Christ, He being the head or whole body, and Christians the members (Rom. 12:5; I Cor. 12:12f; Eph. 4:4,12,16f). As the body, it is the fulness of Christ, who Himself fills all in all (Eph. 1:23).

It is to be noted, as opposed to many commentators, that the Bible does not call this being of the Church as Christ's temple, bride or body, its ideal or mystical reality. While there is an element of imagery in the terms, this is its true reality as the company of those who believe in Christ, and are thus dead, buried and raised in Him as the Saviour-substitute. True, this reality is not the visible one of earthly organization. The various local concretions in this sinful age do not conform to their new and true reality any more than does the believer to what he now is in Christ. In its real life the Church is known only in faith. It is thus hidden, and in the old phrase may be styled invisible. The visible life which it must also have, and which should be conformed to its true reality, may fall far short of it. Indeed, in visible organization even the membership cannot be fully identical with that of the true Church (cf. Simon Magus). Yet the Church invisible is not just ideal or mystical, but the real fact of the Church is in Christ, as the new man of faith is the real fact of the believer. In every manifestation, there should thus be the aim, not of conformity to the world, but of transformation by renewal into the likeness of Him in whom it has its true life (cf. Rom. 12:2).

In this connection appears the relevance of the traditional marks or "notes" of the Church. It is one (Eph. 4:4), for Jesus Christ has only one temple, bride and body, and all divisions are overcome in death and resurrection with Him, and by endowment of His Spirit. In all its legitimate multiformity, the visible Church should thus seek a unity corresponding to this reality. It is holy, for it is set apart and sanctified by Himself (Gal. 1:4; Eph. 5:26). Even in its pilgrimage in the world, it is thus to attest its consecration by the manner of its life and the nature of its service (cf. I Pet. 1:15). It is catholic, constituted from among all men of all races, places and ages (Eph. 2:14; Col. 1:6; 3: 11; Rev. 5:9). For all its diversity of membership and form, it is thus to maintain its universality of outreach, yet also its identity and relevance in every age and place. It is apostolic, for it rests on the foundation of the apostles and prophets (Eph. 2: 20), the apostles being raised up as the first authoritative witnesses (Acts 1:8) whose testimony is basic and by whose teaching it is called, instructed and directed. In all its activity it is thus to "continue steadfastly in the apostles' doctrine and fellowship" (Acts 2:42), not finding apostolicity in mere externals, but in conformity to apostolic teaching and practice as divinely perpetuated in Holy Scripture.

This brings us to the means of the Church's life, and its continuing function. It draws its life from Jesus Christ by the Holy Spirit, but it does so through the Word of which it is begotten (James 1:18), and by which it is nourished and sanctified (Eph. 5:26; I Pet. 2:2). Receiving life by the Word, it also receives its function, namely, to pass on the Word that others may also be quickened and cleansed. It is to preach the Gospel (Mark 16:15), to take up the ministry of reconciliation (II Cor. 5:19), to dispense the mysteries of God (I Cor.

4:1). Necessarily, therefore, it is the Church of the divine Word and sacraments first received by believers and then passed on to others; hence the Reformation insistence that the marks of the visible Church are preaching of the Word and administration of the Gospel sacraments.

The ministry of the Church arises in this connection. The apostles were first commissioned, and they ordained others, yet no rigid form of ministry arises in the New Testament. Rather, we have patterns, notably of speech, action and rule as historically focused in the elders, deacons and overseers or bishops. If it is essential that there should be the threefold pattern, there seems no Biblical prescription for its discharge in a fixed order, nor for non-interchangeability of function, nor for the sharp isolation of an official ministry from the so-called laity or "mere" people of God. The Bible's concern is that there should be real ministry, i.e., service, not in self-assertion and pride, but in humility, obedience and self-offering conformable to the example of Him who was among us as one who serves (cf. Matt. 23:11f; Phil. 2:5f; I Pet. 5:1f).

Finally, the Church's work is not merely for men's salvation, but to the praise of God's glory (Eph. 1:6; 2:7). Hence neither the Church nor its function ceases with the completion of its earthly task. There is ground, therefore, for the old distinction between the Church triumphant and the Church militant. All the Church is triumphant in its true reality. But the warring and wayfaring church is still engaged in conflict between the old reality and the new. Its destiny, however, is to be brought into full conformity to the Lord (I John 3:2) with all the saints. Towards this it moves hesitantly yet expectantly, confident in its future glory when it will be wholly the Church triumphant as graphically depicted in Revelation 7:9ff, enjoying its full reality as the bride and body of the Lord.   G.W.B.

CHUSHAN RISHATHAIM (kū'shăn rĭsh'á-thā'ĭm), a Mesopotamian king who held the Israelites in bondage for eight years. Othniel, Caleb's younger brother, put an end to his rule (Judg. 3:5-11).

CHUZA (kū'zà, Gr. *Chouzás*), the steward of Herod Antipas. In Luke 8:3 we read that his wife Joanna, "and Susanna, and many others," ministered to Christ and His disciples of their substance. He was undoubtedly a man of rank and means.

CILICIA (sǐ-lǐsh'ǐ-à, Gr. *Kilikía*), a country in SE Asia Minor, bounded on the N and W by the Taurus range, on the E by the Amanus range, and on the S by the Mediterranean. It had two parts, the western one called the Rugged; the eastern one, the Plain Cilicia, the chief city of which was Tarsus, the birthplace of Paul (Acts 21:39; 22:3; 23:34). The early inhabitants must have been Hittites. Later, Syrians and Phoenicians settled there. It

The Adana River near Tarsus in Cilicia (now part of Turkey). © MPS

came under Persian sway. After Alexander, Seleucid rulers governed it from Antioch. It became a Roman province in 100 B.C., and was reorganized by Pompey, 66 B.C. One of its governors was Cicero, the orator (51-50 B.C.). Cilicia is accessible by land only by way of its two famous mountain passes, the Cilician Gates and the Syrian Gates. Jews from Cilicia disputed with Stephen (Acts 6:9). The Gospel reached it early (Acts 15:23), probably through Paul (Acts 9:30; Gal. 1:21). On Paul's second missionary journey he confirmed the churches which had been established there (Acts 15:41), and on his way to Rome as a prisoner he sailed over the sea of Cilicia (Acts 27:5). S.B.

CINNAMON (See Plants)

CIRCUMCISION (sĭr kŭm sĭ shŭn, Lat., *a cutting around*), the cutting off of the foreskin, a custom that has prevailed, and still prevails, among many peoples in different parts of the world — in Asia, Africa, America, and Australia. In ancient times it was practiced among the western Semites — Hebrews, Arabians, Moabites, Ammonites, Edomites, and Egyptians, but not among the Babylonians, Assyrians, Canaanites, and Philistines. Various theories are held regarding the origin and original significance of circumcision, but there can be no doubt that it was at first a religious act.

Among the Hebrews the rite was instituted by God as the sign of the covenant between Him and Abraham, shortly after the latter's sojourn in Egypt. God ordained that it be performed on Abraham, on his posterity and slaves, and on foreigners joining themselves to the Hebrew nation (Gen. 17:12). Every male child was to be circumcised on the eighth day. Originally the father performed the rite, but in exceptional cases a woman could do it (Exod. 4:25). In later times a Hebrew surgeon was called in. The child is named at the ceremony. Nowadays the rite is performed either in the home of the parents or in a synagogue. In former times flint or glass knives were preferred, but now steel is usually used.

According to the terms of the covenant symbolized by circumcision, Jehovah undertook to be the God of Abraham and His descendants, and they were to belong to Him, worshiping and obeying only Him. The rite effects admission to the fellowship of the covenant people, and secures to the individual as a member of the nation his share in the promises God makes to the nation as a whole. Circumcision reminded the Israelites of God's promises to them and of the duties they had assumed. The prophets often reminded them that the outward rite, to have any significance, must be accompanied by a "circumcision of the heart" (Deut. 30:6; Lev. 26:41; Ezek. 44:7; Jer. 9:25, 26). Jeremiah says that his countrymen are no better than the heathen, for they are uncircumcised in heart. Paul uses the word *concision* for this outward circumcision not accompanied by a spiritual change. In the early history of the Christian church Judaizing Christians argued for the necessity of circumcising Gentiles who came into the Church, over against Paul, who held that Christ made an end of all Jewish rites. The Apostolic Council took up the problem and decided against them (Acts 15). S.B.

CISTERN (sĭs'têrn, Heb. *bō'r* or *bôr*), an artificial tank or reservoir dug in the earth or rock for the collection and storage of rain-water, or, sometimes, of spring water brought from a distance by a conduit. A cistern is distinguished from a pool by being always covered. Cisterns were very numerous in Palestine. The long, dry, rainless summers, lasting from May to September, and the small

A covered well, or cistern, near the entrance to the Church of the Nativity in Bethlehem. © MPS

annual precipitation, together with a lack of natural springs, made the people largely dependent upon rain water. Cisterns were fed from surface and roof drainage by gutters and pipes. The hilly character of the land allowed little rain to penetrate the soil. Most of it flowed down the steep hillsides through the many ravines and water-courses, and it was easily brought by conduits to pools and cisterns. Cisterns in Palestine varied in size and character. Some were cut wholly in the rock, often in the form of a bottle-shaped tank, with a long stairway leading to the surface of the ground. They were frequently of great depth, some more than a hundred feet deep. Very large ones were supported by rock pillars. The Temple area in Jerusalem had at least 37 great cisterns, one of them holding between two and three million gallons. Public rock-cut cisterns were made within the city walls so that the inhabitants could hold out in time of siege.

Where the substratum of the soil was earth and not rock, cisterns of masonry were built. Some of these were large and had vaulted roofs supported by pillars. Besides the large public cisterns, there were many smaller private ones. Ancient sites are honeycombed with them. All cisterns had one or more openings for drawing water to the surface. They needed periodic cleaning because of the impurities washed in from the outside. Empty cisterns were sometimes used as prisons. Joseph was cast into one (Gen. 37:22), and Jeremiah the prophet was let down into one with a miry bottom (Jer. 38:6). Zechariah 9:11 alludes to the custom of confining prisoners in an empty cistern. S.B.

CITIES OF REFUGE, six cities, three on each side of the Jordan, set apart by Moses and Joshua as places of asylum for those who had accidentally committed manslaughter. Those E of the Jordan were Bezer in Reuben, Ramoth-Gilead in Gad, and Golan in Manasseh (Deut. 4:41-43); those W of the Jordan were Hebron in Judah, Shechem in Ephraim, and Kedesh in Naphtali (Josh. 20:7,8). To aid the killer in escaping the pursuit of the avenger of blood, provision was made that the principal roads leading to these cities should always be kept open. No part of Palestine was more than 30 miles away from a city of refuge — a distance that could easily be covered in one day.

In Semitic lands, if a man were slain it was regarded as the duty of his nearest relative to avenge him. Only in that way could justice be satisfied. Almost no distinction was made between intentional and unintentional killing. Many a man was therefore killed in revenge for what was an accident. Cities of refuge were provided to protect a man until his case could be properly adjudged. The right of asylum was only for those who had taken life unintentionally. Wilful murderers were put to death at once.

The regulations concerning these cities of refuge are found in Numbers 35, Deuteronomy 19:1-13, and Joshua 20. If a manslayer reached a city of refuge before the avenger of blood could slay him, he was given asylum until a fair trial could be held. The trial took place where the accused had lived. If proved innocent of wilful murder, he was brought back to the city of refuge. There he had to stay until the death of the high priest. After that he was free to return to his own home. But if during that period he passed beyond the limits of the city of refuge, the avenger of blood could slay him without blame. The temple at Jerusalem could also be used as a place of refuge.   S.B.

CITIES OF THE PLAIN (Heb. *kikkar ha-yardēn, circle of the Jordan*), cities near the Dead Sea, including Sodom, Gomorrah, Admah, Zeboiim, and Zoar; first referred to in Genesis 13:10-12, where Lot, after Abraham had given him the choice of where he wanted to live, decided to dwell in the cities of the plain, and pitched his tent toward Sodom. In Genesis 14 it says that they were royal cities, each with its own king, and that Abraham delivered Lot when the cities were attacked and Lot taken captive. The story of the destruction of the cities because of their wickedness is given in Genesis 19. It is thought that God may have accomplished this by causing an eruption of gases and petroleum to ignite. Only Lot and his two daughters were spared. The exact site of the cities is unknown; but although there are weighty arguments for believing that they were at the N end of the Dead Sea, scholars favor the S end, especially since asphalt in large quantities has been found only at the S. It is believed that the sea covers the site. In the Bible, Sodom and Gomorrah are often used as a warning example of sin and divine punishment (Deut. 29:23; Isa. 1:9, 3:9; Jer. 50:40; Ezek. 16:46; Matt. 10:15; Rom. 9:29, etc.). S.B.

CITIZENSHIP (Gr. *politeuma, commonwealth*). In the NT the word for citizen often means nothing more than the inhabitant of a country (Luke 15:15; 19:14). Among the ancient Jews emphasis was placed on Israel as a religious organization, not upon relationship to city and state. The good citizen was the good Israelite. Non-Israelites had the same protection of the law as native Israelites, but they were required not to perform acts hurting the religious feelings of the people. The advantage of a Jew over a Gentile was thus strictly spiritual. He was a member of the theocracy.

Among the Romans, citizenship brought the right to be considered as equal to natives of the city of Rome. Emperors sometimes granted it to whole provinces and cities, and also to single individuals, for services rendered to the state or to the imperial family, or even for a certain sum of money. Roman citizens were exempted from shameful punishments, such as scourging and crucifixion, and they had the right of appeal to the emperor with certain limitations.

Paul says he had become a Roman citizen by birth. Either his father or some other ancestor had acquired the right and had transmitted it to his son. He was proud of his Roman citizenship, and, when occasion demanded, availed himself of his rights. When writing to the Philippians, who were members of a Roman colony, and therefore Roman citizens, Paul brings out that Christians are citizens of a heavenly commonwealth, and ought to live accordingly (Phil. 1:27; 3:20).   S.B.

Southern end of the Dead Sea, the site of the Cities of the Plain of Genesis. © MPS

CITY. In ancient times cities owed their origin not to organized manufacture, but to agriculture. When men left the pastoral life and settled down to the cultivation of the soil, they often found their cattle and crops endangered by wandering tribes of the desert; and it was to protect themselves from such enemies that they created first the village and then the city. Cities were built in areas where agriculture could be carried on, usually on the side of a mountain or the top of a hill, and where a sufficient supply of water was assured. The names of cities often indicate the feature that was determinative in the selection of the site. For example, the prefixes Beer, meaning "well," and *En*, meaning "spring," in such names as Beer-sheba and En-gedi, show that it was a local well or spring that determined the building of the city. Names like Ramah, Mizpah, and Gibeah (all from roots indicating height), which were very common in Palestine, indicate that a site on an elevation was preferred for a city. A ruling family sometimes gave its name to a city (*Beth*, meaning "house of").

Ancient farmers did not have their own farmsteads. At the end of a day's work they retired for the night to the village or city. Smaller villages sought the protection of nearby cities. That is the meaning of the expression "cities and their villages" and "cities and their daughters," in Numbers 21:25; 32:42; Josusha 15 and 19. In return for the protection offered against nomadic depredations, the cities received payment in service and produce. Sometimes a city was protected by a feudal lord around or near whose fortress the city was built. Often it depended entirely upon the strength of its walls and the bravery of its men.

The chief feature distinguishing a city from a village was that it had a wall (Lev. 25:29f). Walls 20 and 30 feet thick were not unusual. Sometimes it was also surrounded by a moat (Dan. 9:25, "wall" in KJV), and even by a second smaller wall acting as a rampart (II Sam. 20:15, "trench" in KJV). The wall had one or more gates which were closed during the night (Josh. 2:5,7), and in later times on the sabbath (Neh. 13:19). The gates were strengthened with iron or bronze bars and bolts (Deut. 3:5; Judg. 16:3), and had rooms overhead (II Sam. 18:24). From the roof of the wall or from a tower by the gate, a watchman was on the lookout for approaching danger (Jer. 6:17). The gates were approached by narrow roads easy to defend. From a distance, usually all that could

A typical street market in a Palestinian city. This scene is in the older part of Bethlehem. © MPS

be seen of a city was its walls, except possibly its inner stronghold.

Within the walls, the important features of a city were the Tower or Stronghold, the High Place, the Broad Place by the Gate, and the streets. The Tower was an inner fort protected by a garrison to which the inhabitants could flee when the outer walls were taken by an enemy. The people of Shechem tried unsuccessfully to hold out against Abimelech in such a tower (Judg. 9:49), and the king was afterwards killed by a stone thrown by a woman from the tower within the city of Thebez (Judg. 9:53). When David captured the stronghold of Zion, the whole city came into his possession (II Sam. 5:7). Sometimes towers abutted against the inside of the city wall.

The High Place was an important part of every Canaanite city and retained its place in Palestine to the time of Solomon's reign (I Sam. 9:12 ff). There sacrifices were offered and feasts held. Originally they were on an elevation, but the term became the general one for any local sanctuary even when it was on level ground.

The Broad Place was an open area — not a square, but only a widening of the street, just inside the city gate, serving the purpose of social intercourse in general. It was the center of communal life. Here justice was administered, deliberative assemblies were held, news was exchanged, and business was transacted. Strangers in the city passed the night there if they had no friends in the city. It had a defensive value in time of war, as it permitted the concentration of forces in front of the city gate.

The streets in ancient cities were not laid out on any fixed plan. They were narrow, winding, unpaved alleys. The streets of Jerusalem were not paved until the time of Herod Agrippa II. Cities built on steep hillsides had streets on the roofs of houses. Streets were rarely cleaned and were unlighted. Certain streets were allocated to particular trades and guilds—for bakers, cheese-makers, gold smiths, etc.

Little is known about the way city government was administered. In Deuteronomy 16:18 and 19:12 mention is made of elders and judges. Samaria had a governor (I Kings 22:26). Jerusalem must have had several high officials (II Kings 23:8). S. B.

CITY OF DAVID. 1. The Jebusite stronghold of Zion captured by David, and named by him the city of David. It stood on a ridge near the later site of the temple. David made it his royal residence.

2. Bethlehem, the home of David (Luke 2:4).

CLAUDA (klô'dà), a small, unimportant island off the SW coast of Crete. Paul's ship was driven under its lee by a storm on his way to Rome (Acts 27:16).

CLAUDIA (klô'dĭ-à), a member of the Christian church at Rome, who, along with other members of that church, joined with Paul in sending Timothy greetings (II Tim. 4:21).

CLAUDIUS (klô'dĭ-ŭs), the fourth Roman emperor (41-54). He was nephew of Tiberius, the second Roman emperor. A weak, vacillating man, he was under the influence of unprincipled favorites and his wife Messalina. His second wife, Agrippina, poisoned him in 54. Herod Agrippa I, the grandson of Herod the Great, had assisted him much in his advancement of the throne, and in consequence was given the whole of Palestine. Claudius also gave to the Jews throughout the empire the right of religious worship, but later he banished all Jews from Rome (Acts 18:2; cf. Suet. *Claud.* 25). The famine foretold by Agabus took place in the reign of Claudius (Acts 11:28). Ancient writers say that from various causes his reign was a period of distress over the whole Mediterranean world.

The Emperor Claudius

CLAUDIUS LYSIAS (klô'dĭ-ŭs lĭs'ĭ-ăs), a chief captain who rescued Paul from fanatical Jewish rioters at Jerusalem (Acts 21:31; 24:22). He was a chiliarch (i.e. leader of 1,000 men), in charge of the Roman garrison at Jerusalem, stationed in the Castle of Antonia, adjoining the temple. When Paul informed him that he was a Roman citizen, and therefore could not legally be scourged, he told Paul that he had purchased his Roman citizenship with a great price. To protect Paul, he soon afterward sent him to Caesarea, to Felix, the Roman governor.

CLAY, a word that renders a number of different Hebrew words and one Greek word, and is frequently used in the Bible in a literal or metaphorical sense, in the latter sense meaning *dust* or *flesh* (as made from earth). Clay was widely used in OT times for the making of brick, mortar, and pottery, and, in some countries, for the making of tablets on which inscriptions were impressed. Mud bricks were not always made of true clay, but of mud mixed with straw. True clay was variable in composition, giving variety to quality and color, and thus was suited for different uses. As a building material, clay has been used from very ancient times. Babylon was made wholly of brick, either baked or dried in the sun. Nineveh, the capital of Assyria, was made mostly of brick. The villages of Egypt were constructed of sun-dried clay.

CLAY TABLETS. In ancient times writing was done on papyrus, parchment, potsherds, and clay tablets. Clay tablets were made of clean-washed, smooth clay. While still wet, the clay had wedge-shaped letters (now called "cuneiform" from the Latin *cuneus,* meaning "wedge") imprinted on it with a stylus, and then there was kiln-fired or sun-dried. Tablets were made of various shapes — cone-shaped, drum-shaped, and flat. They were often placed in a clay envelope. Vast quantities have been excavated in the Near East. It is estimated that of those that have been found, about a half million are yet to be read, and that 99 per cent of the Babylonian tablets have yet to be dug. The oldest ones go back to 3,000 B.C. They are practically imperishable; fire only hardens them the more. Personal and business letters, legal documents, books, communications between rulers are represented. One of the most famous is the Code of Hammurabi, a Babylonian king who lived long before the time of Moses. They reveal intimate details of everyday life in the Near East and shed light on many obscure customs mentioned in the Old Testament. Some tell the story of the Creation, the Fall, and the Deluge. They do much to verify the truthfulness of the Biblical record.   S.B.

CLEANTHES (klē-ăn'thēz), son of Phanius of Assos and head of the Stoic school from 263 to 232 B.C. He infused religious fervor into Zeno's Stoicism. He taught that the universe was a living being and God its soul. He taught disinterestedness in ethics, maintaining that doing good to gain advantage was like feeding cattle for meat. He taught, too, that evil thoughts were worse than evil deeds. His *Hymn to Zeus,* a surviving poem, contains the words quoted by Paul in Athens (Acts 17:28).

CLEMENT (klĕm'ĕnt), a Christian who labored with Paul at Philippi (Phil. 4:3). It is uncertain whether he was in Philippi when Paul wrote. Origen (Comm., John 1:29) identifies him with the church father who afterwards became bishop of Rome and wrote an epistle to the Corinthian church, but if he is right, Clement must have lived to an extreme old age.

Clay tablet from near Kish, c. 3100 B.C. BM

CLEOPAS (klē'ō-păs), one of the two disciples to whom the Lord appeared on the afternoon of the resurrection day. They walked with Him from Jerusalem to Emmaus, about seven miles away (Luke 24:18). Nothing more is known about him. He is not to be confused with the Cleophas mentioned in John 19:25, although some Christian fathers assumed that the two were identical.

CLEOPHAS (klē'ō-făs), mentioned in John 19:25 as the husband of Mary, one of the women who stood beside the cross, and is described as a sister of the mother of Jesus. He is not the same as the Cleopas who walked with Jesus to Emmaus (Luke 24:18).

CLERK (See Occupations, Professions)

CLOAK (See Dress)

CLOSET (Gr. *tameíon*), found in Matthew 6:6 and Luke 12:3, and referring most probably to a special store closet in which bedding was stored during the day. If required, it could also be used as a sleeping-room or for private conference. Our Lord advised that it be used for private prayer.

CLOTH, CLOTHES, CLOTHING (See Dress)

CLOUD. There are few references in the Bible to clouds having to do with actual weather conditions, the reason for this being that the weather in Palestine is not very varied. There were two recognized seasons, a rainy one from October to April, and one of sunshine from May to September. The Hebrews were not much given to making comments upon the weather. In Scripture there are, however, many references to clouds in a metaphoric and figurative sense. They symbolize transitoriness. God says Judah's goodness is like a morning cloud (Hosea 6:4), and Job compares his prosperity to the passing clouds (Job 30:15). Sometimes they are used as a type of refreshment, for they bring shade from the oppressive sun and give promise of rain. Clouds without water, therefore, symbolize a man who promises much but does not perform (Prov. 16:15; 25:14; Jude 12). The darkness of clouds is the symbol of mystery, especially that of creation (Job 3:5; 38:9; Ps. 97:2). Their distance from the earth is made to typify the unattainable (Isa.:14:14; Job 20:6; Ps. 147:8). One of the most frequent and suggestive uses of the figure is in connection with the presence of God. Clouds both veil and reveal the divine presence. Jehovah rides upon the cloud (Isa. 19:1; Nah. 1:3); He is present in the cloud (Exod. 19:9; 24:16; 34:5). The pillar of cloud symbolized God's presence and guidance to the children of Israel in their wilderness journeys

(Exod. 40:36; Ps. 78: 14). The cloud appears at our Lord's transfiguration (Matt. 17:5) and at His ascension (Acts 1:9), and it has a place in His prediction of His coming again (Matt. 24:30; 26:64).   S.B.

CLOUD, PILLAR OF, was a symbol of the presence and guidance of God in the 40 years wilderness journey of the Israelites from Egypt to Canaan (Exod. 13:21,22). At night it became fire. When God wanted Israel to rest in any place, the cloud rested on the tabernacle above the mercy seat (Exod. 29:42,43) or at the door of the tabernacle (Exod. 33:9,10; Num. 12:5), or covered the tabernacle (Exod. 40:34-38).

CLOUT (See Dress)

CNIDUS (nī'dŭs), a city of Caria, at the SW corner of Asia Minor, past which Paul sailed on his journey to Rome (Acts 27:7). It was situated at the end of a long, narrow peninsula projecting between the islands Cos and Rhodes, and had two excellent harbors. It had the rank of a free city. Jews lived there as early as the second century B.C. Only ruins are left of a once flourishing city, especially noted for its temple of Venus and a statue of the goddess by Praxiteles.

COAL, often found in the English Bible, but it never has reference to true mineral coal, which has not been found in Palestine proper, where the geological formation as a whole is recent. Coal of a poor quality has been found at Sidon, and for a time some was mined at Lebanon. The half dozen Hebrew and Greek words rendered "coal" refer either to charcoal or to live embers of any kind. Charcoal was used by the Hebrews to provide warmth in winter (Isa. 47:14; John 18:18), for cooking (Isa. 44:19; John 21:9), and by the smith (Isa. 44:12; 54:16). It was made by covering a carefully stacked pile of wood with leaves and earth and then setting fire to it. After several days of burning and smoldering, the wood was converted into charcoal and the pile was opened.

In Psalm 120:4 there is mention of "coals of juniper," doubtless a kind of broom abundant in Judaea. In Isaiah 6:6 and I Kings 19:6 the Hebrew word denotes a hot stone (RVm). Frequently the word is used metaphorically. "As coals are to burning coals . . . so is a contentious man to kindle strife" (Prov. 26:21), means that quarrelsome men add fuel to a flame. In Proverbs 25:22 and Romans 12:20, where we are told to give to an enemy good in return for evil, for so coals of fire will be heaped upon his head, the coals of fire are not meant to suggest the pain of punishment to the guilty, but the softening of his heart as he thinks with burning shame of his unworthy hatred. Love will melt and purify. In Lamentations 4:8 the literal meaning of the Hebrew word translated "coal" is "blackness" (RVm).   S.B.

COAT (See Dress)

COCK (See Birds)

COCKATRICE (See Animals)

COCK CROWING, when referring to time, is the third of the four watches into which the Romans divided the night: evening, midnight, cock crowing, morning. Cock crowing was between 12 and 3 a.m. (Matt. 26:34; Mark 13:35).

COCKLE (See Plants)

COELE SYRIA (sēl'ē-sēr'ĭ-à), in KJV Celosyria, Gr. Koíle Syría, hollow Syria), the name for that part of Syria that lay between the Lebanon and Anti-Lebanon Mountains, but it was often used to cover all the Syrian possessions as far S as

Egypt and as for E as the Euphrates. The term frequently occurs in the OT Apocrypha.

COFFER (kŏf'ēr), a word occurring only in I Samuel 6:8,11,15, and probably referring to a small box in which the Philistines put their golden mice and other offerings when they returned the Ark. The exact meaning of the term is obscure.

COFFIN, used only in Genesis 50:26. The literal meaning of the Hebrew word is "chest" or "box," but in this case may mean "mummy-case." Coffins were unknown among the Israelites, who were carried to the grave upon a bier, a simple flat board with two or three staves. In Egypt, where Joseph died, the dead were embalmed and put in a mummy-case.

COIN (See Money)

COL-HOZEH (kŏl-hō'zĕ, all-seeing one), a Judahite of Nehemiah's day whose son Shallum rebuilt the fountain gate of Jerusalem (Neh. 3:15; 11:5).

COLLAR (See Dress: 4,Cloak, Mantle, Robe)

COLLEGE, a mistranslation of the Hebrew mishneh in the KJV of II Kings 22:14 and II Chronicles 34:22. The Hebrew word also appears in Zephaniah 1:10, where it is correctly rendered "the second," and denotes the second quarter of the city of Jerusalem, which was not far from the Fish-Gate.

COLLOP (kŏl'ŭp, Heb. pîmâh), an old English word meaning a slice of meat or fat. It is used only in Job 15:27, where the wicked man is said to gather fat upon his loins.

COLONY (Gr. kolonía, a transliteration of the Latin colonus, farmer), in the only occurrence of the word in the NT, Acts 16:12, it says that Philippi was a colony. A colony was a settlement of Roman citizens, authorized by the government, in conquered territory. The settlers were usually retired Roman soldiers, settled in places where they could keep enemies of the empire in check. They were the aristocracy of the provincial towns where they lived. Such colonies had the rights of Italian cities: municipal self-government and exemption from poll and land taxes.

COLOSSAE (kŏ-lŏs'ē, Gr. Kolossaí), an ancient city of Phrygia, situated on the S bank of the Lycus river. It was about 11 miles from Laodicea and 13 from Hierapolis. Colossae stood on the most important trade route from Ephesus to the Euphrates, and was a place of great importance from early times. Xerxes visited it in 481 B.C., and Cyrus the Younger in 401 B.C. The city was particularly renowned for a peculiar wool, probably purple in color (colossinus). The church at Colossae was established on Paul's third missionary journey, during his three years in Ephesus, not by Paul himself (Col. 2:1), but by Epaphras (Col. 1: 7,12,13). Archippus also exercised a fruitful ministry there (Col. 4:17; Philem. 2). Philemon was an active member of this church, and also Onesimus (Col. 4:9). During Paul's first Roman imprisonment Epaphras brought to him a report of the religious views and practices in Colossae which called forth his epistle, in which he rebuked the church for its errors. Colossae lost its importance by the change of the road-system. Laodicea became the greater city. During the seventh and eighth centuries its openness exposed it to the terrible raids of the Saracens, and the people moved to Chonae (now called Chonas), a fortress upon the slope of Mt. Cadmus, about three miles farther south. In the 12th century the Turks destroyed the city. Archaeologists have unearthed ruins of the ancient church.   S.B.

COLOSSIANS, BOOK OF (kŏ-lŏsh'ănz), an epistle
written by the Apostle Paul when he was a prisoner
(Col. 4:3,10,18), about the year 62, probably during his first imprisonment in Rome (Acts 28:30,
31), although Caesarea (Acts 23:35; 24:27) and
Ephesus have also been suggested. The external
and internal evidence for its genuineness is all
that can be desired. The church was very likely
founded during Paul's three year stay in Ephesus
on his third missionary journey. It appears from
Colossians 2:1 that Paul himself had never
preached in Colossae. Epaphras, a native of Colossae (Col. 4:12), was probably converted under
Paul's ministry at Ephesus, and was then sent by
the apostle to preach in his native city (Col. 1:7).
He also appears to have evangelized the nearby
cities of Laodicea and Hierapolis (Col. 4:13). At
the time Paul wrote this epistle, the minister of
the church at Colossae was Archippus (Col. 4:17),
who may have been Philemon's son (Philem. 2).
Epaphras had recently come to Paul with a disturbing report of the condition of the church and
this led Paul to the writing of the letter. The bearer
of the letter was Tychicus (Col. 4:7,8), to whom
Paul also intrusted the epistle to the Ephesians
(Eph. 6:21), which was probably written at the
same time. With him went Onesimus (Col. 4:9),
a runaway slave converted by Paul, bearing Paul's
letter to Philemon, a resident of Colossae, who
was also one of Paul's converts, perhaps made at
Ephesus.

In the few years since Paul had been in the
province of Asia an insidious error had crept into
the church at Colossae. Who the false teachers
were we do not know; but it is clear that the
trouble was different from that faced by Paul at
Galatia, where Judaizers had tried to undermine
his work. The teaching attacked by Paul is described in 2:8,16-23. It was, at least in part, Judaistic, as is seen in his reference to circumcision
(2:11; 3:11), ordinances (2:14), meats and
drinks, feast days, new moons, and sabbaths
(2:16). There was also in it a strong ascetic element. Special self-denying rules were given (2:16,
20,21) which had as their purpose the mortifica-
tion of the body (2:23). Some sort of worship of
angels was practiced — a worship which continued for several centuries, as we know from the
fact that in the fourth century the Council of
Laodicea in one of its canons condemned it, and
in the fifth century Theodoret said that the archangel Michael was worshiped in the area. This
heresy claimed to be a philosophy, and made
much of wisdom and knowledge (2:8). Plainly,
the Colossians were beguiled by this religious syncretism and even took pride in it (2:8). The exact
origin of this false teaching is unknown. Some find
it in Essenism; others in incipient Gnosticism or
in contemporary Judaism with a syncretistic admixture of local Phrygian ideas.

Paul met these errors, not by controversy of
personal authority, but by presenting the counter
truth that Jesus Christ is the image of the invisible
God (1:15), in whom are hid all the treasures of
wisdom and knowledge and in whom the fulness
of the divine perfections find their perfect embodiment (1:19). He is the creator of all, and all power
is from Him. On the cross He revealed the im-
potence of all the powers that had tried to work
His purposes (2:15). Freedom from the corruption of human nature is found in the newness of
life which the death and resurrection of Christ
provide. The epistle may be divided into four
parts: 1. The salutation and thanksgiving (1:1-8);
2. The doctrinal section (1:9-2:5); 3. Practical

Colossae in Phrygia (Asia Minor). SHH

exhortations (2:6-4:6); 4. Concluding salutations
4:7-18). Towards the end of the epistle (4:16),
Paul asks that the Colossian church exchange
epistles with the church at Laodicea, to which he
has also written. It is likely that this letter to the
Laodiceans is our epistle to the Ephesians, sent as
a circular letter to various churches in the Roman
province of Asia.   S.B.

COLT (See Animals; Ass)

COMFORTER, THE (See Holy Spirit)

COMMANDMENT, used in the English Bible to
translate a number of Hebrew and Greek words
meaning law, ordinance, statute, word, judgment,
precept, saying, charge, etc. The idea of authority
conveyed by these words comes from the fact that
God as sovereign Lord has a right to be obeyed.
The instruction of Jesus is full of ethical teachings which have the force of divine commandments. What He says is as authoritative as what
was said by Jehovah in OT times. That is true even
when He does not use the word "commandment"
or its equivalents, as He often does. But what is
said of Jehovah and Jesus Christ is also true of the
apostles. Paul, for example, does not hesitate to
say, "the things that I write unto you are the commandments of the Lord" (I Cor. 14:37). The
Bible makes it abundantly clear that God is not
satisfied with mere external compliance with His
commandments, but expects willing and joyful
obedience, coming from the heart.

COMMANDMENTS, TEN The OT is distinctly a
religion of law, with creed, cult, and conduct prescribed minutely by Jehovah. Judaism glories in
the Torah (Rom. 9:4), the revelational instruction
which has come to the elect nation as a gift of
grace and which has come to it invested with divine
authority and sanction. Torah is revered because
it embodies the will and wisdom of the Creator.
Expressing God's own nature, it demands of the
creature only what the Creator's holiness necessi-
tates for fellowship with Himself. The apex and
quintessence of Torah is the Decalogue, the Code
of the Ten Words, received by Moses on Mt. Sinai.
That it is unique among the several Codes found
in the OT can scarcely be disputed. Originally
spoken by God in a context calculated to produce
unforgettable awe (Exod. 19:9-25), it was afterward inscribed by His finger on two tables of
stone (Exod. 31:18); in fact, it was inscribed by
Him a second time after Moses in anger had
shattered the first two tables (Deut. 10:1-4). It
was placed in the Ark of the Covenant (Exod.
25:21) and thus enshrined at the very center of
Israel's worship. All of its precepts, with the exception of sabbath-keeping, are repeated in the
NT. Hence the Code of the Ten Words is indeed
sui generis, a statement which gives the distillation
of religion and morality: these principles, so

The Plain of the Law, Wady Er-Raha, at the foot of Mount Sinai. © MPS

simply phrased, are remarkably comprehensive and universally valid. Mt. Sinai, therefore, was the scene of an epochal event in human history; from a religious standpoint, only Mt. Calvary surpasses it.

Before examining this Code in any detail we must answer several questions concerning it. First, How explain the two somewhat dissimilar versions of it which the Pentateuch contains, one in Exodus 20:1-17, the other in Deuteronomy 5:6-21? In the Exodus version the Fourth Commandment grounds sabbath-keeping in God's sabbath-rest after His six days of creation; in the Deuteronomic version, however, sabbath-keeping is grounded in the Egyptian deliverance. Moreover, the two versions do not agree with respect to the Tenth Commandment, which forbids covetousness; different verbs are used and the order of clauses varies. But surely these are trivia which fade into nothingness when we remember that the Deuteronomic version is part of an address Moses delivered. In an oral recital one scarcely expects notarial precision. Not only so: Moses, because of the Spirit's guidance, was free to introduce new elements and slight changes.

Second, How are the Ten Words to be numbered? W. S. Bruce helpfully clears away the complexities of this question. "These commandments are not numbered by Moses, and consequently different schemes of arrangement have been common. The most ancient of these is that found in Josephus and in the writings of Philo. It is accepted by the Greek Church and by the Reformed Churches, and is that most commonly known among English-speaking communities. In it the preface is not made a commandment or part of one: but the first commandment simply forbids the worship of false deities, and the second prohibits the use of idols; while all the prohibitions of covetousness are included under the last commandment. Among the Fathers this division is supported by Origen. The Jews, on grounds that do not appear to be very trustworthy, regard the first commandment as containing only Exodus xx.2: 'I am the Lord thy God, which have brought thee out of the land of Egypt.' This they interpret as a command to believe in Jehovah as their God, because of His gracious deliveries of their forefathers from bondage. Then, to preserve the number ten, they include in one our first and second commandments; and they justify this by regarding the prohibition of images as an extension of the idea of the unity of God. On the other hand, the Roman and the Lutheran Churches reverse this order and include the first and second commandments in one; while to preserve the number ten, they divide the last commandment into two, thus combining two separate and dividing two

similar things" (*The Ethics of the Old Testament,* Edinburgh: T. & T. Clark, 1909, pp. 101-102).

Third, How are the Ten Words to be divided between the two tables? The Roman Catholic Church puts three commandments on the first table, seven on the second. The Reformed Church adheres to a four and six classification. Josephus, however, gives the traditional five and five arrangement, the first table dealing, as he says, with piety, the second with probity. Taking Josephus as his guide, C. E. Luthardt in his *History of Christian Ethics* gives what seems to be the most satisfactory division:

FIRST TABLE
1. No other gods.
2. No image of God.
3. No dishonouring of God's name.
4. No desecration of God's day.
5. No dishonouring of God's representatives (parents).

SECOND TABLE
1. No taking away of a neighbour's life.
2. No taking away of his wife — his home — his dearest good.
3. No taking away of his goods.
4. No taking away of his good name.
5. Nor even coveting of his good or his goods. (Quoted in Bruce, *op. cit.,* pp. 103-104).

Fourth, Is there any significance to the fact that the Ten Words are inscribed on two tables rather than one? Apparently so. The first table is devoted to the worship of God, the second to the service of man. We gather, accordingly that in OT thought a right relationship with God is essential for a right relationship with man. In other words, religion is the basis and dynamic of morality. Our Lord Jesus in His master-simplification of Torah (Matt. 22:37-40) teaches that love to God and love to man are the two all-inclusive imperatives; actually, love is the sole imperative since neighbor-love is derived from and sustained by our love for God.

Fifth, Is this Code merely negative or does it have a positive aspect as well? Admittedly, the only commandment couched in positive terms is the Fifth Law which enjoins respect for one's parents. But the seeming negativism of the Ten Words is only superficial. Whenever an evil is forbidden, the opposite good is implicitly demanded. Here we have far more than a forbidding: we have a requiring as well. So, as we have noticed, when Jesus interprets and epitomizes this Code, He reduces it to the positive virtue of love. Paul does exactly the same thing in Romans 13:8-10. This Law cannot be fulfilled only by concern and care; it calls for loving obedience to God and loving service to man.

Sixth, Is this Code really to be viewed as "a yoke of bondage" (Gal. 5:1) or as a wise provision which God graciously made for His people? Undeniably in the course of the centuries rabbinic traditionalism perverted Torah into a grievous legalism; undeniably, too, the Law as a whole had a pedagogic function, revealing as it did — and still does — man's need of Jesus Christ (Rom. 7:7; Gal. 3:24). Yet the primary purpose of the Ten Words was to enable the Israelites, as Jehovah's redeemed and peculiar treasure, to enter into a life of joyful fellowship with their Redeemer. This Code issued from God's sovereign and saving relationship with His elect nation. It was imposed at His initiative and as the result of His covenantal activity. Passages like Exodus 20:2 and Deuteronomy 4:32-40 show that Israel's Saviour was Israel's Legislator. This Law, then, was designed to bring Jehovah's saving deed to its fulfillment by creating a holy community, a community reflecting His own nature, a community in which He could dwell and by which He could be magnified (Lev. 11:44; 20:8). Hence, used lawfully (I Tim. 1:8), this Code, which guided life rather than gave it, was a source of beatitude (Ps. 19:8-9; 119:54).

With these six questions answered, let us now analyze briefly each of the Ten Words. The First Commandment (Exod. 20:3) enjoins a confession of Jehovah's singularity, His absolute and exclusive deity. It predicates faith in Him as the one and only God. Though not expressly teaching monotheism, it inferentially denounces polytheism as treason and unbelief. It demonstrates that God is not a class term but a proper Name.

The Second Commandment (Exod. 20:4-6) enjoins the adoration of Jehovah's spirituality. Forbidding His worship by any false means, it rebukes the gross idolatry which surrounded Israel. It shows that because of His very Being (John 4:24) no visible or material representation of true Deity is possible. Thus it prevents wrong concepts of God from taking root in man's mind (Rom. 1:21-23).

The Third Commandment (Exod. 20-7) enjoins the reverence of Jehovah's Name. Since in the OT name and person are equivalent, with the name practically a reification of the person, this Law prohibits blasphemy and profanity. It also interdicts immorality, any conduct which causes God's honour to suffer defilement by the sinner who bears His Name (Rom. 2:24-25). With respect to the sacredness and significance of God's Name, Malachi 3:16-17 is instructive.

The Fourth Commandment (Exod. 20:8-11) enjoins the observance of Jehovah's day. For both humanitarian (Amos 8:5-6) and religious (Isa. 58:13-14) reasons, one day of rest in every seven is a blessed necessity. A sabbath — whether on Saturday as commemorating a finished creation or on Sunday as commemorating a finished redemption — serves man's physical and spiritual welfare simultaneously (Mark 2:27).

The Fifth Commandment (Exod. 20:12) enjoins the honor of God's surrogates, parents to whom He grants a kind of co-creatorship in the begetting of children and to whom He grants a kind of co-rulership in the governing of children. Let any nation abandon respect for the mystery, dignity, and authority of parenthood, and before long the moral fibre and social fabric of that nation are bound to disintegrate. That is why the OT statutes on this score are so severe (Exod. 21:15; Deut. 27:16; Prov. 20:20).

The Sixth Commandment (Exod. 20:13) is a prohibition of murder. A man's life is, patently, his one utterly indispensable possession; but, more

The Nash Papyrus, from the first century B.C., contains the Ten Commandments as presented in Deuteronomy 5. Until discovery of the Dead Sea Scrolls, this was the earliest Hebrew document containing any portion of the Bible. BA

than that, man is God's image-bearer, and murder wantonly destroy's God's image. Hence capital punishment is the penalty affixed to a breaking of this law (Gen. 9:5-6).

The Seventh Commandment (Exod. 20:14) is a prohibition of adultery, a stringent prohibition which safeguards the sanctity of marriage and throws a bulwark around the home. In our day we are beginning to see what happens when the home is undermined by marital infidelity.

The Eighth Commandment (Exod. 20:15) is a prohibition of theft in any and all forms. Property is essentially an extension of a man's personality, and thus this law indicates that the rights and achievements of one's neighbor must not be ignored.

The Ninth Commandment (Exod. 20:16) is a prohibition of falsehood in its many varieties, whether perjury, slander, or defamation. Truth is the cement of community, the sine qua non of enduring interpersonal relationships on every level. Consequently, the OT like the NT stresses the need for a sanctified tongue (Ps. 5:9; 15:1-4; Prov. 18:21; Jer. 9:1-5).

The Tenth Commandment (Exod. 20:17) is a prohibition of covetousness, and as such reveals that the Ten Words are not simply a civil code, but form a moral and spiritual code which strikes beneath the surface of the overt act (and the overt act is the exclusive province of civil law), tracing evil conduct to evil desire, probing the hidden motives of men (and motive is the province of morality and religion, God's province). This Tenth Commandment, therefore, highlights the pivotal importance of wrong appetites and intentions; it agrees with Paul that covetousness is idolatry (Col. 3:5), since inordinate craving means that man's ego has become man's god.

Except as the NT deepens and extends its principles, the Decalogue represents the high-water level of morality. V.C.G.

COMPEL, in English, suggests the idea of force, though not necessarily physical. When Jesus, in Luke 14:23, says "compel them to come in," He means that Christians should use the utmost zeal and moral urgency to get people to enter the kingdom of God.

CONANIAH (kŏn′á-nī′á, Heb. *kônanyāhû, Jehovah has founded*, in KJV twice *Cononiah*. 1. A Levite in charge of tithes and offerings in the reign of Hezekiah (II Chron. 31:12,13).
   2. A Levite in Josiah's reign (II Chron. 35:9).

CONCISION (kŏn-sĭzh′ŭn, Gr. *katatomé, mutilation, cutting*), a term used only once in the Bible, in Philippians 3:2, to designate circumcision that is wholly ceremonial and without regard for its spiritual significance. Paul distinguishes it from true circumcision (verse 3).

CONCUBINE, in the Bible, not a paramour, but a woman lawfully united in marriage to a man in a relation inferior to that of the regular wife. No moral stigma was attached to being a concubine. It was a natural part of a polygamous social system. Concubinage is assumed and provided for in the law of Moses, which tried to prevent its excesses and abuses (Exod. 21:7-11; Deut. 21:10-14). Concubines were commonly taken from among Hebrew or foreign slave girls, or Gentile captives taken in war, although free Hebrew women might also become concubines. They enjoyed no other right but lawful cohabitation. They had no authority in the family or in household affairs. Their husbands could send them away with a small present, and their children could, by means of small presents, be excluded from the heritage (Gen. 25:6). The children were regarded as legitimate, although the children of the first wife were preferred in the distribution of the inheritance. In patriarchal times, at least, the immediate cause of concubinage was the barrenness of the lawful wife, who herself suggested that her husband have children by her maid-servant (Gen. 16 and 30). Prominent OT figures who had concubines were Nahor (Gen. 22:24), Abraham (Gen. 25:6), Jacob (Gen. 35:22), Eliphaz (Gen. 36:12), Gideon (Judg. 8:31), Saul (II Sam. 3:7), David (II Sam. 5:13; 15:16; 16:21), Solomon (I Kings 11:3), Caleb (I Chron. 2:46), Manasseh (I Chron. 7:14), Rehoboam (II Chron. 11:21), Abijah (II Chron. 13:21), and Belshazzar (Dan. 5:2).   S.B.

CONCUPISCENCE (kŏn-kū′pĭ-sĕns, Gr. *epithumía*), a word meaning intense longing or yearning for what God would not have us to have or be. It does not refer to sexual desire only. (Rom. 7:8; Col. 3:5; I Thess. 4:5).

CONDUIT (kŏn′dū ĭt), a channel, either cut out of solid rock or made of masonry, for conveying water from its source to the place where it was delivered. It was covered with stones to keep the water pure and cool. Conduits were used to deliver water to towns or for purposes of irrigation. One of the oldest in Palestine was about 13½ miles long and brought water from the Pools of Solomon, beyond Bethlehem, to the temple in Jerusalem. Tradition ascribes its construction to Solomon. Hezekiah constructed a conduit in anticipation of Sennacherib's invasion (II Kings 20:20). Other conduits mentioned in the Bible are one where Isaiah was commanded to meet Ahaz (Isa. 7:3), and beside which the messengers of Sennacherib stood when they spoke to the people on the wall (II Kings 18:17; Isa. 36:2), and another referred to in II Chronicles 32:30.

CONEY (See Animals)

CONFECTION, found only in Exodus 30:35, it refers to a compound of perfume or medicine, not sweetmeats.

CONFECTIONARY, a perfumer; found only in I Samuel 8:13. RVm has "perfumers."

CONFECTIONER (See Occupations, Professions)

CONFESSION (Heb. *yādhâh*, Gr. *homológeo*, and their derivatives). Both the Hebrew and Greek words are capable of the same twofold meaning as the English. To confess is openly to acknowledge one's faith in anything, as in the existence and authority of God, or the sins of which one has been guilty. Occasionally it also means to concede or allow (John 1:20; Acts 24:14; Heb. 11:13), or to praise God by thankfully acknowledging Him (Rom. 14:11; Heb. 13:15). In the Bible confession of sin before God is recognized as a condition of forgiveness. Christ taught the necessity of confessing offenses committed against other men (Matt. 5:24; Luke 17:4). The Bible gives no instruction about the mode of confession or the person to receive it, but no authority is found in it for the auricular confession practiced in the Roman church.

CONGREGATION (Heb. *′ēdhâh* and *qāhāl*, Gr. *ekklesía* and *sunagogé*), a word used in Scripture mainly to refer to the Hebrew people; in its collective capacity regarded as God's people, or as an assembly of the people summoned for a definite purpose (I Kings 8:65) or met on a festal occasion (Deut. 23:1). Sometimes it refers to an assembly of the whole people; sometimes, to any part of the people who might be present on a given occasion. Occasionally it conveys the idea of "horde." Every circumcised Hebrew was a member of the congregation and took part in its proceedings probably from the time he bore arms. He had, however, no political rights as an individual, but only as a member of a house, a family, or a tribe, which was usually represented by its head, known as an elder or a prince. The elders, summoned by the supreme governor or the high priest, represented the whole congregation, served as a national parliament, and had legislative and judicial powers. They sat as a court to deal with capital offenses (Num. 15:32, 33), declared war, made peace, and concluded treaties (Josh. 9:15). The people were strictly bound by their acts, whether they approved of them or not (Josh. 9:18). Occasionally the whole body of people was assembled for some solemn religious occasion (Exod. 12:47; Num. 25:6; Joel 2:15) or to receive some new commandments (Exod. 19:7,8; Lev. 8:4). After the conquest of Canaan, the congregation was assembled only to consider very important matters.   S.B.

CONIAH (kō-nī′a, Heb. *konyāhû, Jehovah is creating*). A form of the name Jehoiachin, found in Jeremiah 22:24,28; 37:1. See JEHOIACHIN.

CONSCIENCE (Gr. *syneídesis*), a word is not found in the OT, but the idea frequently appears, as when Adam and Eve hide from God (Gen. 3:8) and Joseph's brothers confess their guilt regarding him (Gen. 42:21). In ancient religion and philosophy the word seldom appeared in its modern meaning of the moral sense of the individual applied to his conduct, but it was never thought of as having any religious connection. Jesus never used the word.

In the NT outside of Paul's epistles, where it is found with fair frequency, it is used only in Acts (in speeches by Paul) and in Hebrews and I Peter. Nowhere in the NT is there a clearly defined doctrine of conscience, or even a description of it.

The most illuminating passage in the NT on the nature of conscience is Romans 2:14,15, where Paul declares that all men, both Gentiles and Jews, are responsible for their actions before God, because all have a revelation of God's moral law as their standard for right living, the Jews in the law of Moses, and the Gentiles in the law written on their hearts. Heathen Gentiles, moreover, know that they ought to obey it, for their conscience tells them to. I Corinthians 8-10 is the passage where "conscience" occurs most often. There Paul says that the Christian whose conscience allows him to eat meat offered to idols has no right to disregard the conscience of a less well-instructed Christian brother who thinks it wrong to eat it (I Cor. 8:7,12), or the ignorant conscience of a heathen (I Cor. 10:27). In II Corinthians 4:2 and 5:11 he applies the word "conscience" to the approval of his conduct by others. Repeatedly, Paul, Peter, and the author of Hebrews stress the need of having a good conscience toward God. Hebrews, which emphasizes the effects of the atonement on the individual, declares that the OT sacrifices did not produce a conscience free from the sense of guilt, because only the blood of Christ can do that.   S.B.

CONSECRATION, an act by which a person or thing is dedicated to the service and worship of God. It is the translation of several Hebrew and Greek words of different meanings. 1. Heb. *hāram*, "devote"; "I will consecrate ("devote") their gain unto the Lord" (Micah 4:13). 2. Heb. *nāzar*, *nēzer*, "separate" (Num. 6:7,9,12). 3. Heb. *qādhēsh*, "to be set apart," i.e., set apart from that which is common or unclean (Exod. 28:3; 30:30; Josh. 6:19; II Chron. 26:18; 29:33; 31:6; Ezra 3:5). 4. Heb. *mille' yadh*, lit. "to fill the hand," a peculiar idiom usually used for the installation of a priest into his office or of the installation offerings put into his hands (Exod. 28:41; 29:9; 29:29; Lev. 8:33). 5. Gr. *teleióo*, "to make perfect" Heb. 10:20).

CONVERSATION, a word often used in the KJV to render various terms signifying conduct or manner of life, especially with respect to morals. The Greek words rendered "conversation" in Philippians 1:27 and 3:20 refer to "civil life" or "citizenship." Paul means that we should live like citizens of heaven.

CONVERSION (kŏn-vêr'zhŭn, Heb. *shûv*, Gr. *epistrophé*), occurs only once in the Bible (Acts 15:3). The words commonly used in the English Bible as equivalent with the Hebrew and Greek words are "turn," "return," and "turn back," "turn again." Thus "conversion" is synonymous with "turning." The turning may be in a literal or in a figurative, ethical or religious, sense, either from God, or, more frequently, to God. It is to be noted that when the turning refers to a definite spiritual change, it almost invariably denotes an act of man: "Turn ye, turn ye from your evil ways (Ezek. 33:11); "Except ye turn" (Matt. 18:3). Since the word implies both a turning *from* and a turning *to* something, it is not surprising that in the NT it is sometimes associated with repentance (Acts 3:19; 26:20) and faith (Acts 11:21). That is, conversion on its negative side is turning from sin, and on its positive side is faith in Christ, "Repentance toward God, and faith toward our Lord Jesus Christ" (Acts 20:21) expresses the content of the idea, although the word turning is not found in the verse. Although conversion is an act of man, Scripture makes clear that it has a divine ground. The turning of sinful man is done by the

power of God (Acts 3:26). In the process of salvation, conversion is the first step in the transition from sin to God. It is brought about by the Holy Spirit operating upon the human mind and will, so that the course of man's life is changed. It is not the same as justification and regeneration, which are purely divine acts. It may come as a sudden crisis or as a process more or less prolonged.

CONVICTION (kŏn-vĭk'shŭn, Gr. *elégcho, to convince* or *prove guilty*). Conviction is the first stage of repentance, experienced when in some way the evil nature of sin has been brought home to the penitent, and it has been proved to him that he is guilty of it. Although the word "conviction" is never used in the KJV, both Testaments give many illustrations of the experience. In the OT one of the most notable is found in Psalm 51, where David, realizing he has sinned against God, is overwhelmed with sorrow for his transgression and cries out to God for forgiveness and cleansing. In the NT the central passage bearing on this theme is John 16:7-11, where Jesus says that when the Holy Spirit comes "He will reprove the world of sin, and of righteousness, and of judgment." Here the word "reprove" means "convince" or "prove guilty." The thought is that the Holy Spirit addresses the heart of the guilty and shows how inadequate ordinary standards of righteousness are. The purpose of conviction is to lead to godly repentance.   S.B.

CONVOCATION (kŏn-vō-kā'shŭn, Heb. *mikrā'*), used in the expression "Holy Convocation," but it is sometimes used alone (Num. 10:2; Isa. 1:13; 4:5). A convocation was a religious festival during which no work could be done. The holy convocations were the sabbath days (Lev. 23:1-3), Pentecost (Lev. 23:15-21), the first and seventh days of the feast of unleavened bread (Exod. 12:16; Lev. 23:6,7), the first and tenth days of the seventh month, the latter being the great day of atonement (Lev. 23:24-28), and the first and eighth days of the Feast of Tabernacles (Lev. 23:34-36). The phrase "solemn assembly" is applied only to the concluding festivals at the end of Passover and Tabernacles.

COOS (Kō'ôs, Gr. *Kós, summit*), a long, narrow island off the coast of Caria in S Asia Minor, mentioned in connection with Paul's third missionary journey in Acts 21:1. It was the birthplace of Hippocrates (the father of medicine), and famous painter Appelles, and Ptolemy Philadelphus.

COPING (kōp'ĭng), a word used only in I Kings 7:9 and probably referring to the customary parapets on Oriental house roofs, which were always flat.

COPPERSMITH (kōp'êr-smĭth, Gr. *chalkeús*), found in the NT only in II Timothy 4:14: "Alexander the coppersmith did me much evil." The word should be rendered "worker in brass."

COR (See Weights & Measures)

CORAL (kôr'ăl, Heb. *rā'môth*), the Hebrew word, the meaning of which is not entirely certain, is twice rendered "coral" (Job. 28:18; Ezek. 27:16), and, once, "too high" (Prov. 24:7). Red coral, which is the calcareous skeleton of a branching colony of polyps, was highly prized in ancient times, and was obtained in the Mediterranean and Adriatic seas at various depths down to about 100 fathoms. It differs much from the white coral which forms coral reefs. It was made into beads and charms.

CORBAN (kôr'băn, Heb. *qorbān, an offering*), occurs in the Hebrew text of the OT and refers to an offering or sacrifice, whether bloody or unbloody, made to God (Lev. 1:2,3; 2:1; 3:1; Num. 7:12-17). It is found in the NT in Mark 7:11, where it has reference to money dedicated to God. The Talmud says that the Jews were much given to making rash vows to God, without any intention of carrying them out. By Christ's time the reprehensible practice arose of children avoiding the responsibility of looking after their parents' material needs by telling them that their money was dedicated to God and that it would be wrong to divert it from this sacred purpose. This could be done by simply pronouncing the votive word "Corban." Ideally, the money thereafter belonged to God, but actually the one who made the vow might keep it in his possession. By referring to this custom Christ demonstrated the sophistry of tradition which enabled the Jews to disregard plain commandments of God, like the one requiring children to honor their parents.

CORD (kôrd, Heb. *hevel, yether, mêthār*, Gr. *schoinion*). Throughout the East in ancient times ropes and cords were made of goat's or camel's hair spun into threads and then plaited or twisted into the larger and stronger form. Sometimes they were made of strips of skin from goats and cows twisted together. Ropes for temporary fastenings were sometimes made from vines twisted together, and also from the bark of the branches of the mulberry tree. Frequently the word is used in a figurative sense in the Bible. Thus Job speaks of being "holden in cords of affliction" (Job 36:8), and Solomon says that the wicked "shall be holden with the cords of his sins" (Prov. 5:22). Other illustrations of this figurative use are Psalm 2:3; 129:4; 140:5; Ecclesiastes 4:12; Isaiah 5:18; 54:2.

CORIANDER (See Plants)

CORINTH (kôr'ĭnth, Gr. *Kórinthos, ornament*), a city of Greece on the narrow isthmus between the Peloponnesus and the mainland. Under the Romans, Athens was still the educational center of Greece, but Corinth was the capital of the Roman province called by them Achaia, and the most important city in the country. Land traffic between the N and S of Achaia had to pass the city, and much of the commerce between Rome and the East was brought to its harbors.

Corinth occupied a strategic geographical position. It was situated at the southern extremity of the isthmus, at the northern foot of the lofty (2000 ft.) and impregnable Acrocorinthus, which commands a wonderful view over the Saronic Gulf on the E and the Corinthian Gulf on the W, as well as over central Greece and the Peloponnesus. From the Acrocorinthus it is possible on a clear day to see the Acropolis of Athens 40 miles away. Corinth had three harbors: Lecheam, 1½ miles to the W, Cenchreae, 8½ miles to the E, and Schoenus, also to the E, but much less used than Cenchrea. Lechaeum was connected with Corinth by a double row of walls. Because of its highly-favored commercial position, in ancient times the city was known as "two-sea'd Corinth."

Ancient sailors dreaded making the voyage round the southern capes of the Peloponnesus, and this, as well as the saving of time effected, caused many of the smaller ships and their cargoes to be hauled across the narrow isthmus on a track. Sometimes the cargo of large ships was removed at the harbor, carried across the isthmus, and then loaded on another ship on the other side. Several attempts were made in ancient times to

Canal across the Isthmus of Corinth, in Greece. **JFW**

cut a ship-canal across the isthmus, notably one by Nero about A.D. 66, but none was successful. One was opened in 1893, and is now in use.

Corinth had an ancient and very interesting history. Phoenician settlers were early attracted to it. They introduced many profitable manufactures and established the impure worship of the Phoenician deities. Later, Greeks from Attica became supreme. They probably changed the name of the city to Corinth, and glorified the games held there in honor of Poseidon, the god of the sea. About 1074 B.C. the Dorians conquered the city. After the invention of triremes, about 585 B.C., a series of important colonies was founded, and Corinth became a strong maritime force. The city was lukewarm in the Persian wars, and opposed Athens in the Peloponnesian war. Except for a brief period, the Macedonians held the city from 335-197 B.C. The Romans declared Greece and Corinth free in 196 B.C., but in 146 B.C., in consequence of a rebellion against Rome, the city was totally destroyed by the Roman consul Mummius, and its famous art treasures taken as spoil to Rome. Julius Caesar rebuilt it as a Roman colony and made it the capital of Achaia in 46 B.C., and after that it rapidly came into prominence again. The Goths raided it in the third and fourth centuries; the Normans sacked it in 1147; the Venetians and Turks held it in the Middle Ages; from 1715 until 1822 it remained with the Turks. A severe earthquake in 1858 caused the abandonment of the city and the building of a new town a few miles from the ancient site. Modern Corinth has a population of about 9000 people. Until, in recent times, archaeologists began excavating the ancient city, nothing marked its site except seven columns of an old Doric temple.

Ruins of the Forum at Corinth, with pillars of the Temple of Apollo in background. **SHH**

In Roman times Corinth was a city of wealth, luxury, and immorality. It had no rivals as a city of vice. "To live like a Corinthian" meant to live a life of profligacy and debauchery. It was customary in a stage play for a Corinthian to come on the scene drunk. The inhabitants were naturally devoted to the worship of Poseidon, since they drew so much of their wealth from the sea, but their greatest devotion was given to Aphrodite, the goddess of love. Her temple on the Acrocorinthus had more than a thousand *hierodouloi*—priestesses of vice not found in other shrines of Greece, and she attracted worshipers from all over the ancient world. Besides drawing vast revenues from the sea, Corinth had many important industries, its pottery and brass, especially, being famous all over the world. The Isthmian games, held every two years, made Corinth a great center of Hellenic life.

At the height of its power, Corinth probably had a free population of 200,000, plus a half million slaves. Its residents consisted of the descendants of the Roman colonists who were established there in 46 B.C., many Romans who came for business, a large Greek population, and many strangers of different nationalities attracted to the city for various reasons. In the last group was a considerable body of Jews, and also some Gentiles brought under the influence of Judaism because of its monotheism and lofty morality.

Paul visited Corinth for the first time on his second missionary journey (Acts 18). He had just come from Athens, where he had not been well-received, and he began his work in Corinth with a sense of weakness, fear, and trembling (I Cor. 2:3). A special revelation from the Lord in a night vision altered his plans to return to Thessalonica (Acts 18:9,10; I Thess. 2:17,18), and he was told to speak freely and boldly in the city. At his first arrival, he became acquainted with Aquila and Priscilla, fellow Christians and, like himself, tent-makers. During his stay of a year and a half he resided in their home. He labored with his own hands, so that his motives as a preacher would be above suspicion. Soon after his arrival, Silas and Timothy rejoined him, Timothy bringing news from the church at Thessalonica (I Thess. 3:6).

Every sabbath Paul preached in the synagogue, but before long he met with strong opposition from the Jews, so that he turned from them and for the rest of his stay in Corinth gave his attention to the Gentiles (Acts 18:6). He was then offered the use of the house of Titus Justus, a God-fearing Gentile, who lived next door to the synagogue. Many turned to Christ and were baptized as a result of Paul's preaching, among them Crispus, the ruler of the synagogue, and all his house. None of the baptisms in Corinth were performed by Paul himself, except those of Crispus, Gaius (Paul's host on his later visit (Rom. 16:23), and the household of Stephanas, who were Paul's first converts (I Cor. 16:15).

During Paul's stay in Corinth, Gallio, the elder brother of the Roman philosopher, Seneca, came to govern Achaia as proconsul. This was about the year 51, as an inscription found at Delphi in 1908 shows. The Jews brought an accusation before him against Paul, charging that he was preaching a religion contrary to Roman law. Gallio, however, refused to admit the case to trial and dismissed them. It is evident that he looked upon Christianity as being only an obscure variety of Judaism and that to him the quarrel between the Jews and Paul had its origin in nothing more

Ruins of Lechaeum Road at Corinth. JFW

than differing interpretations of the Jewish law. Following Gallio's decision, the Greek bystanders vented their animus against the Jews by seizing and beating Sosthenes, the ruler of the synagogue, and Gallio paid no attention to them. Gallio's action was highly important, for it practically amounted to an authoritative decision by a highly-placed Roman official that Paul's preaching could not be interpreted as an offense against Roman law; and from this experience Paul gained a new idea of the protection the Roman law afforded him as a preacher of the Gospel. After many days, Paul left Corinth to go to Jerusalem and Antioch, on his way stopping off briefly at Ephesus.

Luke tells little of the subsequent history of the church at Corinth. Apollos, a convert of Aquila and Priscilla at Ephesus, was sent from Ephesus with a letter of recommendation, and he exercised an influential ministry in Corinth (Acts 18:27,28; I Cor. 1:12). There is evidence that during Paul's stay in Ephesus on his third missionary journey he paid a brief visit to Corinth (II Cor. 12:14; 13:1), although some hold that he did this later from Macedonia. While at Ephesus he wrote a letter to Corinth which has not been preserved (I Cor. 5:9). A reply to this, asking advice on important problems facing the church, and an oral report brought to him that all was not well in the church, led to his writing I Corinthians. This was probably sent by the hands of Titus: at least he was sent to Corinth by Paul about this time (II Cor. 7:13). Timothy was also sent to Corinth on some mission (I Cor. 4:17). After the silversmiths' riot at Ephesus, Paul went to Troas, hoping to meet Titus there with news from Corinth, but he was disappointed and went on to Macedonia, where he did meet him. On getting a largely favorable report, Paul wrote II Corinthians, and probably sent Titus to deliver it. After some time in Macedonia, Paul went to Greece, spending three months there (Acts 20:2,3), chiefly, no doubt, in Corinth. On Paul's third missionary journey he had been much occupied with getting offerings of money for the poor Christians in Jerusalem from the various churches he had founded. The Corinthian church responded to this appeal generously (II Cor. 9:2-5). It was during this visit to Corinth that Paul wrote his Epistle to the Romans (Rom. 16:23). Whether he ever returned to the city is unknown.

About the year 97, Clement of Rome wrote an epistle, which survives, to the church at Corinth. It shows that in his time the Christians there were still vexed by divisions.   S.B.

CORINTHIANS (kô-rĭn′thĭ-ănz), First and Second Epistles. The First Epistle to the Corinthians was written by the Apostle Paul in Ephesus on his third missionary journey (Acts 19; I Cor. 16:8,19), probably in 56 or 57. He had previously written a letter to the Corinthians which has not come down to us, in which he had warned against associating with immoral persons (I Cor. 5:9); and in reply had received a letter, (alluded to several times in I Corinthians 5:10; 7:1; 8:1), in which they declared it was impossible to follow his advice without going out of the world altogether, and submitted to him a number of problems on which they asked his opinion. This letter from Corinth was probably brought by three of their number, Stephanas, Fortunatus, and Achaícus (I Cor. 16:17), who came to visit Paul at Ephesus, and undoubtedly told him about the condition of the church. Meanwhile, Paul had heard of factions in the church from the servants of Chloe (1:11), probably from Corinth, and this news caused him much pain and anxiety. It was these various circumstances that led to the writing of I Corinthians.

The following are the subjects discussed in the epistle, after the introductory salutation (I Cor. 1:1-9):

1. In the first four chapters the apostle takes up the reported factionalism in the church, and points out the danger and scandal of party spirit. He reminds them that Christ alone is their Master, their Christian teachers being only servants of Christ and fellow-workers with God.

2. In chapter 5 the apostle deals with a case of incestuous marriage, and prescribes that the offender be put out of the church so that his soul may be saved.

3. In chapter 6 Paul comes to their practice of bringing disputes between themselves before heathen judges for litigation, and shows that this is morally wrong and out of harmony with the spirit of love by which they as Christians should be animated.

4. Various phases of the subject of marriage are considered in chapter 7. While commending a celibate life, Paul holds marriage to be wise and honorable. He forbids divorce between Christians and separation of Christians married to heathen partners.

5. The eating of meat offered to idols was a problem of conscience to many Christians, and ch. 8-10 are devoted to it. Paul points out (ch. 8) that while there is nothing inherently wrong in a Christian's eating such food, the law of love requires that it be avoided if it will offend another who regards the eating of it as sin. In ch. 9 he illustrates this principle of self-control in his own life; lest his motives in preaching the Gospel be misunderstood, he refuses to exercise his undoubted right of looking for material aid from the church. In ch. 10 he warns against a spirit of self-confidence and urges them to be careful not to seem to countenance idolatry.

6. Paul next takes up certain abuses in public worship: first, the matter of appropriate head apparel for women in their assemblies (11:2-16), and then the proper observance of the Lord's Supper (11:17-34), in the administration of which there had been serious abuses.

7. There then follows a long discussion of the use and abuse of spiritual gifts, especially speaking in tongues (chs. 12-14), and the apostle, while commending the careful exercise of all the gifts, bids them cultivate above all God's greatest gift, love (chs. 13).

8. In ch. 15 Paul turns to a consideration of one of the most important of their troubles — the resurrection of the dead, which some were inclined to doubt. He meets the objections raised against the doctrine by showing that it is necessitated by the resurrection of Christ and that their salvation is inseparably connected with it.

9. The epistle concludes with directions about the collections being made for the saints in Jerusalem, the Mother-Church, and with comments about Paul's plans and personal messages to various of his friends.

The Second Epistle to the Corinthians was written by Paul on his third missionary journey somewhere in Macedonia, where he had just met Titus, who had brought him a report concerning the church at Corinth.

The epistle reveals that Judaising teachers — perhaps recently arrived from Jerusalem — had sought to discredit the apostle, and had succeeded in turning the church as a whole against him. Paul was denounced as no minister of Christ at all. This revolt caused Paul to make a brief visit to Corinth in order to restore his authority (II Cor. 12:14; 13:1,2), but the visit did not have its expected effect.

The report Titus brought Paul was, on the whole, most encouraging. The majority had repented of their treatment of Paul and had cast out of the church the man who had led the attack on him. Paul's authority was acknowledged once more. Titus seems to have helped greatly in bringing about this happy change. It was the report of Titus that chiefly occasioned the writing of this epistle.

Paul's mention of a severe letter which had caused him great sorrow of heart to write (2:3,4, 9; 7:8-12) has naturally caused scholars to wonder what he had in mind. Some think he refers to I Corinthians; others hold that this letter, like the one referred to in I Corinthians 5:9, is wholly lost; while still others believe that it is preserved in II Corinthians 10-13, which, they say, was written by Paul at Ephesus sometime after the writing of I Corinthians.

II Corinthians is the least methodical and the most personal of Paul's epistles. It is very autobiographical, and falls naturally into three main divisions:

1. In chs. 1-7 Paul, after giving thanks to God for his goodness to him in trial (1:1-11), gives some thoughts on the crisis through which the church has just passed. 2. In chs. 8 and 9 he treats of the collection for the poor in Jerusalem. 3. Chs. 10-13 are a defense of Paul's ministry against the attacks of his enemies and a vindication of his apostleship.   S.B.

CORMORANT (See Birds)

CORN (See Plants, Wheat)

CORNELIUS (kôr-nēl'yŭs, Gr. *Kornélios, of a horn*), a name of ancient and honorable standing among the Romans. Before the NT age, it was borne by such distinguished families as the Scipios and Sulla. He was a centurion of the Italian cohort. While being stationed at Caesarea, in obedience to instructions received in a vision, he sent for Simon Peter, who was staying at Joppa, to learn from him the message whereby he and his household should be saved (Acts 11:14).

As to his moral character, he is described as *díkaios kaì phoboúmenos*, "upright and god-fearing." His exact religious status prior to Peter's visit is ambiguous, but the likelihood is that Cornelius was a pious Roman, who, disillusioned by polytheism and disappointed by philosophy, had gravitated spiritually towards Judaism, and was now a "proselyte of the Gate" (Acts 11:2). Any doubts that Peter was acting improperly by sharing the message with this first Gentile convert are obviated by the twofold consideration of Peter's preparatory vision (10:9-16) and the subsequent outpouring of the Holy Spirit upon Cornelius' household (Acts 10:44-47). On these grounds, Peter defended his conduct before his critics at Jerusalem (Acts 11:1-18). J.F.G.

CORNERSTONE (Heb. *pinnâh, akrogoniaíos*), a term that has both a literal and figurative use in Scripture but is usually used figuratively (Ps. 118: 22; Job 38:6; Isa. 28:16; Zech. 10:4, etc.). Among the Canaanites, before the conquest of the land of Joshua, the laying of the foundation stone was accompanied by the dreadful rite of human sacrifice. Numerous skeletons have been unearthed, especially those of tiny babies in earthen jars.

Jar burial of an infant, from Megiddo. OIUC

Following rabbinical practice, which understood the term "cornerstone" in a Messianic context, the Synoptics validate the claim of Jesus of Nazareth to Messiahship by citation of Psalm 118:22 (Matt. 21:42; Mark 12:10; Luke 20-17). In a similar fashion must be understood the Pauline and Petrine usage of the word (see Rom. 9:33, quoting Isa. 28:16 and 8:14, following LXX; also Eph. 2:20 et. al., I Peter 2:6, etc.). J.F.G.

CORNET (Heb. *shôphār, qeren*). The musical instruments mentioned in the OT fall into three groups: the stringed, the percussion, and the wind. The instrument known as the "cornet" is to be found in the last class. It was a curved horn, the sound being a dull monotone. Some translators have understood the term to imply a musical instrument akin to the bagpipe or oboe (I Chron. 15:28; Ps. 98:6; Dan. 3:5,10,15; Hos. 5:8).

COS, COOS (kŏs, KJV Cŏ ŏs), an island off the coast of Asia Minor, one of the Sporades; mountainous in terrain, especially in the southern sector. The birthplace of Hippocrates, the father of medicine and of Ptolemy Philadelphus. The name of its capital is also Cos. A large Jewish settlement was located here. It is mentioned in connection with Paul's third missionary journey (Acts 21:1).

COSAM (kō'săm), an ancestor of Christ (Luke 3:28).

COSMETICS, any of the various preparations used for beautifying the hair and skin. Such practices are regarded with disfavor by the writers of Holy Writ. Jezebel, Ahab's wicked queen, painted her face immediately prior to her slaying by Jehu, son of Nimshi (II Kings 9:30). The practice of painting the eyes is referred to by Ezekiel in an uncomplimentary vein in the parable of Aholah and Aholibah (Ezek. 23:40b). The "painted stare" is referred to by Jeremiah (Jer. 4:30). See Perfume.

COTTON (Per., *karpas*), originally designated muslin or calico. Its use was gradually extended to include linen. The plant was imported to Palestine shortly after the Captivity. Cotton was spun into cloth by weavers in Egypt. The mummies of Egypt were wrapped in this material. It is mentioned but once in the Bible (Esth. 1:5,6), where the word "green" should be rendered "cotton," as in the RSV. See Plants.

COUCH, a piece of furniture for reclining. The couch became so ornate that Amos rebuked the rich for the costly display of their couches (Amos 6:4). Sometimes, however, the couch was no more than a rolled-up mat which could be easily transported (Matthew 9:6). See Bed.

COULTER (kōl'têr), a plowshare (I Sam. 13:19-21). The plows used in eastern lands today are very similar to those used in ancient times. At first, a plow was nothing more than a sturdy branch of a tree; later it was improved so that a pair of oxen could be attached to it. The sharp end of the plow scratched rather than turned over the soil so that the seed might be sown. In later times, the plowman steered the plow with one hand, while guiding the oxen with the other. See Plow.

COUNCIL (koun'sĕl, Heb. *rigmâh*, Gr. *sumboúlion, sunédrion*), a Jewish governing body, more or less informally held. David speaks of "the princes of Judah and their council" (Ps. 68:27); but he does not mean the Sanhedrin, which did not come into existence until after the Captivity. Except for Matthew 12:14 and Acts 25:12, the word "council" in the KJV always refers to the Sanhedrin, as the Greek shows.

COUNSELLOR (koun'sĕ-lêr). The modern English spelling, "counselor," is not found in the KJV. The word refers to one who gives counsel. It is found in both Testaments. A counsellor (Gr. *bouletes*) was a member of the Sanhedrin. The word is applied to Joseph of Arimathea (Mark 15:43; Luke 23:50).

COURSE OF PRIESTS AND LEVITES. David divided the priests and Levites into 24 groups, called courses in Luke 1:8, each with its own head (I Chron. 24:1 ff). These courses officiated for a week at a time, the change being made on the sabbath before evening sacrifice.

COURT. At the advice of Jethro, Moses instituted a system of jurisprudence for the Israelites. He appointed judges over tens, fifties, hundreds, and thousands; and finally a Supreme Court under himself and his successors. There was no opportunity of appeal to a higher court (Exod. 18:25, 26). The office of judge was an elective one (Deut. 1:13). Eventually judges were usually chosen from among the Levites, although this was not necessary. They were held in very high regard. In time, the profession of law developed among the Hebrews, its members being called "Lawyers," "Scribes," or "Doctors of the Law" (Luke 2:46). These men studied and interpreted the law, decided questions of the law, and taught Hebrew boys the law.

Technical knowledge of the law was not a prerequisite to become a judge. Under the Romans the supreme legislative and judicial body was the Sanhedrin. Its judgment was final except in cases involving capital punishment, when the consent of the procurator had to be secured. The Sanhedrin met in Jerusalem.

COVENANT, translates the Hebrew noun *berîth*. The verbal root of *berîth* means either "to fetter" or "eat with," which would signify mutual obligation, or "to allot" (I Sam. 17:8), which would signify a gracious disposition: compare the Hittite "suzerainty covenant," in which a vassal swore fealty to his king, out of gratitude for favors received (E. J. Young, *The Study of Old Testament Theology Today,* London: J. Clarke, 1958, p. 62).

In the OT, *berîth* identifies three differing types of legal relationships. 1. A two-sided covenant between human parties, both of which voluntarily accept the terms of the agreement (for friendship, I Sam. 18:3-4; marriage, Mal. 2:14; or political alliance, Josh. 9:15, Obad. 7). God, however, never "enters in" to such a covenant of equality with men. The closest approximation is the "covenant of redemption" between Jehovah and Christ (mentioned in certain of the Psalms, 2:7-8; 40: 6-8), under which the Son agrees to undertake man's salvation. But the actual term *berîth* is not employed. 2. A one-sided disposition imposed by a superior party (Ezek. 17:13-14). God the Lord thus "commands" a *berîth* which man, the servant, is to "obey" (Josh. 23:16). In the original "covenant of works" (Hos. 6:7 ASV), He placed Adam on probation, bestowing life, should he prove faithful (Gen. 2:17). Humanity failed; but Christ, the last Adam (I Cor. 15:45), did fulfill all righteousness (Matt. 3:15, Gal. 4:4), thereby earning restoration for all who are His. 3. God's self-imposed obligation, for the reconciliation of sinners to Himself (Deut. 7:6-8, Ps. 89:3-4). As He stated to Abraham, "I will establish My covenant between Me and thee . . . to be a God unto thee and to thy seed after thee" (Gen. 17:7).

The LXX avoided the usual Greek term for covenant, *synthéke* (Meaning a thing mutually "put together"), as unsuitable for the activity of the sovereign God, and substituted *diathéke* (a thing, literally, "put through"), the primary meaning of which is "a disposition of property by a will." The LXX even used *diathéke* for the human-agreement type of *berîth*. NT revelation, however, makes clear the wonderful appropriateness of *diathéke,* testament, for describing the instrument of God's redemptive love: "For, where a testament is, there must of necessity be the death of him that made it . . . [Christ's] death, for the redemption of the transgressions that were under the first covenant" (Heb. 9:16). "Testament," indeed, signifies a specific form of covenant, the bequest; and it well describes God's OT *berîth,* because apart from the death of Christ the OT saints "should not be made perfect" (11:40; see J. B. Payne, *An Outline of Hebrew History,* Grand Rapids: Baker, 1954, pp. 220-228).

The covenant then constitutes the heart of all God's special revelation: when put into writing, "the book of the covenant" becomes the objective source for man's religious hope (Exod. 24:7); and, as E. J. Young has summarized it, "The subject matter with which [Biblical] theology is concerned is that covenant which God has made with man for man's salvation" (*op. cit.,* p. 61). Scripture consists of "the Old Testament" and "the New Testament." For while there can be but one testament, corresponding to the one death of Christ ("My blood of *the* testament," according to the better MSS of Matt. 26:28), revelation yet organizes itself under the older testament, with its anticipatory symbols of Christ's coming (Jer. 31-32, II Cor. 3:14), and the newer testament, commemorative of His accomplished redemption (Jer. 31:31, II Cor. 3:6).

The following aspects compose the testamentary arrangements: the testator, God the Son, "the mediator" (Heb. 9:15); the heirs, "the called" ones (9:15); the objective method of effectuation, a gracious bequest (9:16); the subjective conditions by which the heir qualifies for the gift, namely, commitment (9:28: it is "to them that wait for Him"); and the inheritance of reconciliation, "eternal salvation" (9:15,28). Certain specific features then characterize this covenant. Its objective effectuation is always marked by a monergism, "one worker," God exercising pure grace (*cf.* Gen. 15:18, Exod. 19:4), unassisted by man's works (Eph. 2:8-9); b. the death of the testator (Exod. 24:8, Heb. 9:18-22); c. the promise, "I will be their God, and they shall be My people" (Gen. 17:7 to Rev. 21:3); d. the eternity of the inheritance (Ps. 105:8-10. Num. 18:19 thus mentions "a covenant of salt"; compare Lev. 2:13, "the salt [eternal preservation] of the testament of thy God"); and e. a confirmatory sign, such as the rainbow to Noah (Gen. 9:12-13), the exodus to Moses (Exod. 20:2), or Christ's resurrection to us (Rom. 1:4). Subjective appropriation of the covenant is likewise marked by unchangeable features of human response: a. faith (Gen. 15:6, Deut. 6:5; Heb. 11:6) and b. obedience, both moral (Gen. 17:1, Matt. 7:24, Eph. 2:10) and ceremonial (Gen. 17:10-14, Acts 22-16, I Cor. 11:24); for genuine faith must be demonstrated by works (James 2:14-26).

Yet God's revelations of His covenant also exhibit historical progression (covenants, plu., Rom. 9:4). Under the older testament appear 1. the Edenic (Gen. 3:15), God's earliest promise of redemption, though at the cost of the "bruising of the heel of the seed of woman"; 2. the Noachian (9:9), for the preservation of the seed; 3. the Abrahamic (15:18), granting blessing through Abram's family; 4. the Sinaitic (Exod. 19:5-6), designating Israel as God's chosen people; 5. the Levitical (Num. 25:12-13), making reconciliation through priestly atonement; and 6. the Davidic (II Sam. 23:5), with Messianic salvation promised through David's dynasty. Each of these covenants anticipated the same redemptive death; yet differences appear, particularly in their ceremonial response. A "dispensation" may thus be defined as a covenantal period during which faith in Christ is manifested by a distinct form of ceremonial obedience. Even our own, newer testament thus exhibits two stages: 7. the present new covenant in Christ, which is internal, "in their heart"; reconciling (as always, "I will be their God"); direct, "They shall all know Me"; and with finished atonement, "For I will forgive their iniquity" (Jer. 31:33-34, Heb. 8:6-13). But its ceremony, the Lord's Supper, possesses a dispensational limit, exhibiting "the Lord's death *till He come*" (I Cor. 11: 26). For Ezekiel speaks of 8. the future covenant of peace, when our internal salvation will reach out to embrace external nature (Ezek. 34:25), when direct spiritual communion will become "face to face" (20:35; 37:27), and when divine forgiveness will achieve the goal of peace among all nations (34:28). J.B.P.

COVERING THE HEAD, mentioned only in I Corinthians 11:15, where Paul says that a woman's hair is given her for a covering. In the preceding verses he says that women should have their heads covered in public worship. At that time in Greece only immoral women were seen with their heads uncovered. Paul means that Christian women cannot afford to disregard social convention; it would hurt their testimony. In giving them long hair, a natural veil, nature teaches the lesson that women should not be unveiled in public assemblies.

COVETOUSNESS, (kŭv'ĕt-ŭs-nĕs), has various shades of meaning, among the most important the following: 1. The desire to have something (I Cor. 12:31; 14:39). 2. The inordinate desire to have something (Luke 12:15 ff; Eph. 5:5; Col. 3:5). 3. Excessive desire of what belongs to another (Exod. 20:17; Rom. 7:7). A great deal of OT law was intended to counteract the spirit of covetousness. Outstanding examples of covetousness are: Achan (Josh. 7); Saul (1 Sam. 15:9,19); Ananias and Sapphira (Acts 5:1-11).

COW (See Animals: Cattle)

COZ (kōz), a man of the tribe of Judah (I Chron. 4:8).

COZBI (kŏz'bī), a Midianite woman slain by Phineas, Aaron's grandson, because through her the plague had come upon Israel in the wilderness (Numbers 25:16-18).

CRACKNEL, cakes cooked in a pan, corresponding to our pancakes (I Kings 14:3).

CRAFT, CRAFTSMAN (See Occupations, Professions)

CRAFTINESS, CRAFTY, ability that stops short of nothing, however bad, to attain its purpose; guile; cunning (Dan. 8:25; Luke 20:23).

CRANE (See Birds)

CREATION, does not occupy a great deal of space in the Bible, but is clearly presented in Genesis 1-2, and in Hebrews 11:3, and is emphasized in Isaiah 40-51 and in the latter part of Job. The Bible clearly teaches that the universe, and all matter, had a beginning, and came into existence through the Will of the eternal God. In Genesis 1:1, the words "the heaven and the earth" summarize all the various materials of the universe. This verse has been interpreted in various ways, but all agree in its essential significance. This is true even of the new interpretation that takes it as a mere introduction to what follows, rendering it: "When God began to create heaven and earth," for even on this interpretation v.2 would describe the situation that came into existence shortly after God began to create, rather than to contradict Hebrews 11:3 by implying that there was pre-existing matter.

Some hold that there is a long gap between verses 1 and 2, in which God's perfect creation came into chaos through a great catastrophe. Hebrew syntax permits such a view but does not require it.

The length of the creative days of Genesis 1 is not stated in the Bible. The Hebrew word "day" may mean a period of light between two periods of darkness, a period of light together with the preceding period of darkness, or a long period of time. All three usages occur frequently in the Bible, including Genesis 1-2. No one of them is exactly 24 hours, though the second one is near it. There is no indication as to which of the three is meant, though the type of expression used in the third, fifth and sixth days seems to suggest a long period. The Bible gives no information as to how long ago the original creation of matter occurred, or the first day of creation began, or the sixth day ended.

On the seventh day (Gen. 2:2-3) God ceased from His labors. This is given as an example for man in his life of six days of labor followed by one day of rest (cf. Exod. 20:11). No end to the seventh day is mentioned. As far as the Bible tells us, the cessation of God's creative activity still continues.

There is much discussion about the question of "evolution" in relation to creation, but the word "evolution" is used in many different ways. If taken in its historic sense, to indicate the theory that everything now existing has come into its present condition as a result of natural development, all of it having proceeded by natural causes from one rudimentary beginning, such a theory is sharply contradicted by the divine facts revealed in Genesis 1-2. These chapters indicate a number of specific divine commands bringing new factors into existence. God's activity is indicated throughout the entire creation. It is explicitly stated several times that plants and animals are to reproduce "after their kind." Moses nowhere states how large a "kind" is, and there is no ground for equating it with any particular modern definition of "species." Yet it is clear that Genesis teaches that there are a number (perhaps a large number) of "kinds" of plants and of animals, which cannot reproduce in such a way as to evolve from one into the other. Nothing in the Bible denies the possibility of change and development within the limits of a particular "kind."

Moreover, the creation of man is sharply distinguished from the other parts of the creation, and the creation of woman is described as a distinct act of God. Genesis 2:7 (in the Hebrew) clearly teaches that man did not exist as an animate being before he was a man, created after the image of God.

It is sometimes said that the Bible begins with two contradictory accounts of creation. To say that it begins with two creation accounts is like saying that an atlas begins with two maps. A map of the world and a map of the United States would overlap. The first would include a great deal of territory not included in the second. The second would include a great deal of detail not mentioned in the first. This is exactly the relation between the two creation accounts. Genesis 1 describes the creation of the universe as a whole. Genesis 2:4-25 gives a more detailed account of the creation of man and says nothing about the creation of matter, of light, of the heavenly bodies, or of plants and animals, except to refer to the creation of animals as having taken place at an earlier time.

It is sometimes said that the creation story of Genesis 1 begins with a watery chaos and that of Genesis 2 with a dry earth. There is no contradiction in this because the two begin at different places in the whole series of creative events.

It is sometimes alleged that Genesis 2 gives a different order of events of creation from Genesis 1. Actually, however, only two creative acts are involved in Genesis 2: the creation of man and that of woman. There is no contradiction between the order in which they are described and that of Genesis 1.

Genesis 2 does not describe the creation of vegetation, as some interpreters allege, but simply mentions that God planted a garden. Even this act took place before the creation of man. Only by reading extremely primitive concepts into Genesis 2 could one insist on interpreting it as meaning that God created man and then laid him on the shelf for a few years while the garden that He proceeded to plant should grow large enough to be a satisfactory place for man to live. The verbs in Genesis 2:8,9 must be interpreted, in normal fashion, as implying an English pluperfect.

The same is true of v.19 where creation of the animals is specifically referred to. God, looking for a companion for man, brought before him the animals that He had previously created, to show him the need of a different sort of helper. Genesis 2 does not contradict Gen. 1 in any way, but adds to our understanding of the details of an important portion of God's creative activity.   A.A.M.

CREATURE (Gr. *ktísis*), in the NT the word denotes that which has been created (Rom. 1:25; 8:39; Heb. 4:13). Sometimes used with adjective *kaine* in the sense of the new creation (II Cor. 5: 17) or in contrast to the old man versus the new man (Gal. 6:15).

CREATURE, LIVING (Heb. *hayyâh*, Gr. *zóon*) a symbolical figure presented first in Ezekiel's vision (Ezek. 1:5ff), and again in Revelation 4: 6-9; 5:6,8,11; 6:1,3,5-7. In Ezekiel's vision there are four living creatures. They had the general appearance of a man, but each had four faces and four wings, and the feet of an ox. Under their wings they had human hands. The front face was that of a man; to the right and left of this were the faces of a lion and of an ox, and in the back was the face of an eagle. Fire gleamed from their midst. Later they are called "cherubim" (Ezek. 10:1ff). The living creatures in Revelation are somewhat modified from those in Ezekiel's vision.

CREED (Lat. *credo*, "I believe"), a rule of faith, a symbol, a public confession or declaration of Christian doctrine or belief. The creeds of Christendom group themselves into five more or less distinct groups. First are the ecumenical or earlier creeds, which include the Apostles' Creed (n.d.), the Nicene Creed (A.D. 325), the Chalcedonian Creed (A.D. 451), the Athanasian Creed, commonly ascribed to Athanasius (d. A.D. 333). The second larger division deals with the creeds of the Greek Church, embracing the confessions of Gennadius (A.D. 1453), the "Orthodox Confession of Peter Mogilas" (A.D. 1643), the Decrees of the Synod of Jerusalem (A.D. 1672), etc. In addition, the Greek Church tenaciously holds to the above-mentioned ecumenical creeds. The third division is that of the Roman Catholic Church, which in addition to the basic ecumenical creeds, holds to the Canons and Decrees of the Council of Trent (A.D. 1563-64), the Profession of the Tridentine Faith (A.D. 1564), the Papal Definition of the Immaculate Conception of the Virgin Mary (A.D. 1854), the Vatican Decrees of 1870, upholding the dogma of Papal Infallibilty, the Ecumenical Council summoned by the late Pius XII, where the dogma of the bodily assumption of the Virgin Mary was adopted (A.D. 1950). Within the Councils of the Roman Catholic church in the 1960's some modifications of the more stringent laws of said church seem to be taking place, such as the abolition of the "Sacred Latin" tongue for the modern languages, and the abrogation of "Extreme Unction" for simply "Praying for the Sick."

The fourth division contains the Lutheran Confessional Statements, which include the Augsburg Confession, (A.D. 1530) for which Luther himself produced the doctrinal sections, a mild conciliatory decree, the Articles of Smalcald (A.D. 1537), the Formula of Concord (A.D. 1577).

The fifth and final division embraces the Reformed and Evangelical Church Creeds. These include the Swiss or Zwinglian Confessions (A.D. 1536-66), the Belgic Confession (A.D. 1561), the Decrees of the Synod of Dort (A.D. 1604-1619), the Remonstrance (A.D. 1610), the Canons of Dort (A.D. 1619), the Westminster Confession (1643-48). This confession consisted at first of the revision of the thirty-nine Articles of the Church of England, which was followed by a strong affirmation of the Nicene Creed. The Westminster Confession was likewise given a strong Puritanical or Calvinistic orientation.

Baptistic groups and Quakers doubt the advisability of creeds, having as a motto: "No creed, but Christ." Nevertheless, despite rancor, abuses and excesses, it seems that the Holy Spirit has been pleased in general to use the various creeds as an instrument to insure the doctrinal purity of the Church at large.   J.F.G.

CREEK (Gr. *kólpos*). Modern translations utilize the word "bay" as a substitution for the KJV "creek," identified as the traditional "St. Paul's Bay" about eight miles NW of the town of Zaletta on the island of Malta (Melita) (Acts 27:39).

CREEPING THING (See Animals, Insects)

CRESCENS (Gr. *Kréskes, increasing*), the companion of the apostle Paul at Rome who had departed for Galatia (II Tim. 4:10).

CRETE, CRETAN (krēt, krē'tăn, Gr. *Kréte, Krétes*, Acts 2:11, Titus 1:12), an island in the Mediterranean Sea with Cythera on the NW and Rhodes on the NE, forming a natural bridge between Europe and Asia Minor. Crete is about 156 miles long and from seven to 30 miles wide. Despite its enviable geographical position, Crete has never attained a prominent place in history, partly because of internal dissensions and, in more modern times, because of its acceptance of Turkish rule and the Islamic faith. In mythology Mt. Ida is the legendary birthplace of Zeus, the head of the Greek Pantheon. King Minos, the half historical, half mythological character, alleged son of Zeus, was an early ruler. Both Thucydides and Aristotle accepted the existence of King Minos and claimed that he established maritime supremacy for Crete by putting down piracy. Aristotle compares the institutions of Crete to those of Sparta. Crete is said to have been colonized by the Dorians from Peloponnesus. The most important cities of Crete are Cnossos, excavated by Arthur Evans; Gortyna near the gulf of Messara; and Cydonia. Around 140 B.C. the Jews established a large enough colony on this island to be able to appeal successfully to the protection of Rome.

CRETE IN THE OT — The Cherethites (I Sam. 30:14; Ezek. 25:16) held to be a group of Philistines, are identified as Cretans.

CRETE IN THE NT — A number of Cretans are represented as being present upon the Day of Pentecost. Paul visited Crete and left his assistant Titus in charge. In the opinion of the Apostle Paul, even the Christians in Crete were not of high moral character: "Cretans are always liars . . ." (Titus 1:12). The first words of this quotation are to be found in the hymn to Zeus by Callimachus. The particular lie of which the Cretans were always guilty was that they said the tomb of Zeus, a non-existent personage, was located on their island. Laziness and gluttony also characterized them. Titus is charged sharply to rebuke them (Titus 1:13). A storm on his journey to Rome forced Paul's ship into the port of Cnidus (Acts 27:17). The narrative does not specifically indicate that Paul actually landed on the island.

CRIB (Job 39:9, Prov. 14:4, Isaiah 1:3), a rack constructed for the feeding of domestic livestock. A manger (Luke 2:7). Isaiah complains that "the ox knoweth his master and the ass his master's crib" (Isaiah 1.3).

CRIMSON (Heb. *karmîl, tôlā'*), refers to the brilliant red dye obtained from a bug. The word is applied to garments (II Chron. 2:7,14; Jer. 4:30 KJV). The best known citation is doubtless the prophet's assurance in Isaiah 1:18.

CRISPING PIN (Heb. *hărîtîm*, Isaiah 3:22 KJV), pins for crisping or curling the hair. The term has also been translated as bags (II Kings 5:23), girdles, veils, and turbans. See DRESS.

CRISPUS (krĭs'pŭs, Gr. *Kríspos,* "curled," Acts 18,7, 8; I Cor. 1:14), formerly the ruler of the Jewish synagogue at Corinth; converted under the preaching of Paul and subsequently baptized by him.

CROP (Lev. 1:16), the enlargement of the gullet of a bird where food is partly macerated, removed by the priest for sacrificial purposes.

CROSS (Gr. *staurós*). There are three Biblical uses of the term: first, the cross in its literal aspect; secondly, the Cross as a symbolic representation of redemption; thirdly, death upon the cross, i.e., crucifixion. Our English word is derived from the Latin *Crux*. The cross existed in four different forms: 1, the *crux immissa*, the type usually presented in art in which the upright beam extends above the cross beam, traditionally held to be the cross upon which the Redeemer suffered and died; 2, the *crux commissa*, or "Saint Anthony's Cross" in the form of the letter "T"; 3, the Greek cross in which the cross beams are of equal length; 4, the *crux decussata*, or "Saint Andrew's Cross," in the shape of the letter "X." Antedating these forms, the Assyrians impaled the body with a crude pointed stick. "I marched from the Orontes . . . I conquered their cities . . . I caused great slaughter . . . I took their warriors prisoner, and impaled them on stakes before their cities . . ." (From the report of Ashurbanipal), Keller, Werner: THE BIBLE AS HISTORY; New York: Wm. Morrow and Co., 1954: pp. 229-30.

Because of the sacrificial death of the Saviour upon the cross, the cross rapidly became interwoven into the theological construction of religious thinking, especially Paul's. In I Corinthians 1:17, the "preaching" (*kerugma*) of the Cross is set forth as the "divine folly" in sharp contrast to earthly wisdom. In Ephesians 2:16, it is presented as the medium of reconciliation. In Colossians 1:20, peace has been effected through the Cross. In Colossians 2:14, the penalties of the law have been removed from the believer by the Cross. How Paul as a pious Hebrew, to whom one hanged was accursed, and as a Roman to whom one crucified was an object of scorn (Gal. 3:13), came to glory in the Cross would be one of the absurdities of history, were it not for the fact that the apostle held the Crucified as the Christ of God. (Gal. 2:20). Crucifixion was one of the most cruel and barbarous forms of death known to man. It was practiced, especially in times of war, by the Phoenicians, Carthaginians, Egyptians, and later by the Romans. So dreaded was it that even in the pre-Christian era, the cares and troubles of life were often compared to a cross.

The details of the crucifixion of Christ are passed over, the evangelists resting content with the simple statement "They crucified him" (Matt. 27:35; Mark 15:24). Following His trial before

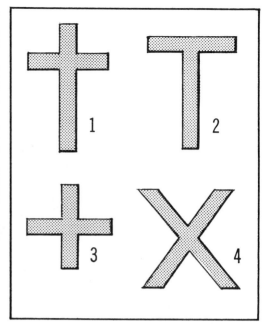

Four forms of the Cross.

the Jewish and Roman authorities, He was led forth for crucifixion. Preparatory to the actual ordeal itself, He was scourged. The prisoner was bent over, tied to a post, while the Roman lictor applied blow upon blow upon His bared back with a lash intertwined with pieces of bone or steel. This in itself was frequently sufficient to cause death.

The agony of the crucified victim was brought about by a number of factors. First, the painful but non-serious character of the wounds inflicted. Although there were two distinctive methods of affixing a living victim to a cross, tying or nailing, it is well established that Christ underwent the horror of the latter, or possibly both. The second factor causing great suffering was the abnormal position of the body. The slightest movement would be accompanied with additional torture. The third factor would be the traumatic fever induced by hanging for such a long period of time.

What was the physical reason for Christ's death? Recent medical studies have sought an answer to the question. When a person is suspended by his two hands, the blood sinks rapidly into the lower extremities of the body. Within six to twelve minutes blood pressure has dropped to 50 per cent, while the rate of the pulse has doubled. The heart is deprived of blood and fainting follows. This leads to an orthorastic collapse through insufficient circulation. Death by crucifixion is due to heart failure. Victims of crucifixion did not generally succumb for two or three days. Death was hastened by the "crucifragium" or the breaking of the legs. "When they came to Jesus and saw that He was dead already, they brake not his legs" (John 19:33). Sometimes, a fire was built beneath the cross that its fumes might suffocate the sufferer.

Among the Jews, a stupefying potion was prepared by the merciful women of Jerusalem, a drink which Christ refused (Mark 15:23). To such a death, the one who was co-equal with God descended (Phil. 2:5). J.F.G.

CROW (See Birds)

CROWN, a band encircling the head to designate honor; there are three principal types of crowns: the royal crown, the priestly crown, and the crown of the victor. Some of the terms employed for "crown" in the OT are: Heb. *qodhqôth*, a part of the human anatomy, the *"crown" of the head, the pate* (Deut. 28:35, II Sam. 14:25, etc.); Heb. *zēr, that which encircles the head,* viz. *a garland of fllowers* (Exod. 25:11); Heb. *nezer, that which is a symbol of dedication to the priesthood, the priestly crown;* Heb. *'ătārâh,* the customary term (I Chron. 20:2, Prov. 4:9). In the NT (Gr., *stéphanos* and *diádema* are used. The first refers to a garland or chaplet such as was worn by a victorious athlete. This type of crown is employed figuratively by Paul and John as a symbol of Christian triumph (II Tim. 4:8, Rev. 2:10). The diadem was a symbol of the power to rule.

Of particular interest is the crown of thorns which Jesus wore (Gr. *akánthinos stéphanos,* Matt. 27:29, Mark 15:17, John 19:2). The particular variety of thorns from which this crown was woven is impossible to determine, as there are about 22 words in the Bible used for the thorny plants, and the Greek word is a generic, not a specific term.   J.F.G.

CROWN OF THORNS (See Crown)

CRUCIFIXION (See Cross)

CRUSE (*krōos*), a small, porous, earthen vessel for the purpose of holding liquids (I Sam. 26:11, 12, 16; I Kings 19:6). In the NT *alabástron* as the alabaster cruse or flask for holding ointment — not a box as in KJV (Matt. 26:7, Mark 14:3, Luke 7:37).

CRYSTAL. Both Hebrew and Greek terms can be rendered "ice"; more likely it means rock crystal or crystallized quartz. The reason for the selection of the word "ice" is that the ancients believed that crystal was formed by the process of intense cold (Job 28:17; Rev. 4:6, 21:11, 22:1). See METALS and MINERALS.

CUBIT (See Weights and Measures)

CUCKOO (See Birds)

CUCKOW (See Birds)

CUCUMBER (See Plants)

CUMMIN (See Plants)

CUNEIFORM (*kū-nē'ĭ-fôrm*), a system of writing by symbolic characters used chiefly in the Mesopotamian area in ancient times. The system is regarded as the forerunner of the alphabet. The cuneiform characters were developed by the Sumerians, who recorded them upon clay tablets which they baked firm in the oven. The term refers to the wedged-shaped characters of the script. At the time of the discovery of the personal library of Ashurbanipal of Nineveh (ruled 668-626 B.C.) by Layard and Rassam (1850-1854) literally multitudes of these clay tablets were unearthed, among them the Babylonian versions of creation and of the flood, which show striking similarities with the accounts in the OT. According to Olmsted of the Oriental Institute of the University of Chicago, more than half a million of these tablets are yet to be deciphered.

The Tel-El-Amarna Letters (1400-1350 B.C.), found in Egypt in 1887, consisting of 300 clay tablets are written in the Akkadian form of the cuneiform script. The Akkadian was the "Lingua Franca" of that day, i.e., the language of trade and diplomacy used between Syria and Egypt. (See AMARNA, TELL-EL).Of still greater importance was the discovery between 1929 and 1939

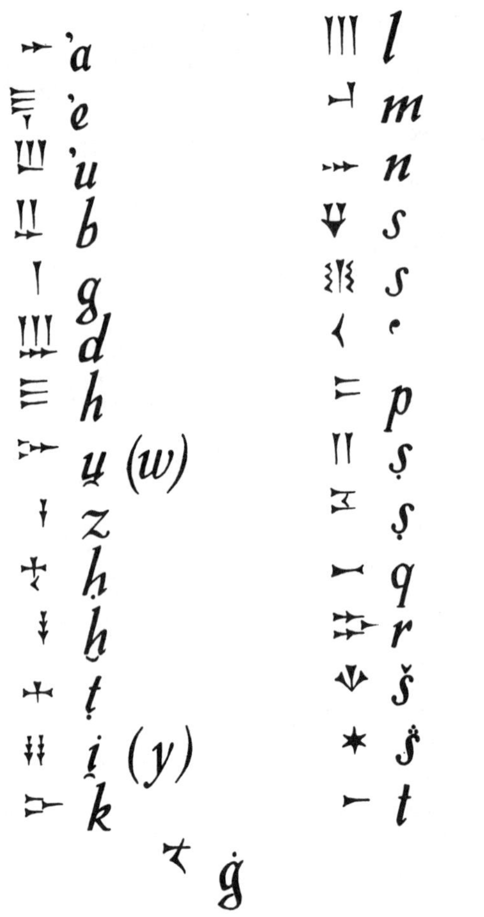

Cuneiform alphabet from Ras Shamra (after Pfeiffer).

at Ras Shamra in the NW of Syria of the Ugaritic literature. This was written in a Canaanite dialect closely related to proto-Hebrew. The Ras Shamra literature, dating closely c. 1400 B.C., gives us much information on Canaanite religion and presents many parallels to the OT in vocabulary and poetic style.   J.F.G.

CUP (Heb. *kôs,* Gr. *potérion*), a term used in a literal and figurative sense. Cups were of various forms and designs, and made of a variety of materials: gold, silver, earthenware, copper, bronze, etc. The cups of the Hebrews, whether metal or porcelain, often carried designs borrowed from Phoenicia and Egypt. All of Solomon's drinking vessels were of gold (I Kings 10:21). The cups mentioned in the NT were, beyond much doubt, of Roman style.

The word *cup* may also signify a laver (Exod. 24:6) or goblet (S. of Sol. 7:2; I Chron. 28:17). The cup is used as a symbol of prosperity or of Jehovah's blessing and, in reverse, of Jehovah's malediction upon the wicked (Ps. 11:6; 16:5; 23:5). The cup also represents drunkenness and other illicit pleasures (Prov. 23:31; 51:7; Rev. 17:4; 18:6). "Cup of consolation" (Jer. 16:7) stems from the oriental custom of sending to bereaved friends food and drink for their mourning feast. "Cup of salvation" (Ps. 116:13), "Cup of blessing" (I Cor. 10:16), or "Cup of the Lord" (verse 21). Paul here refers to the communion cup, over which the blessing is said prior to the feast which commemorates the Lord's death and burial. The cup from ancient times signifies fellowship. Thus, when the believer takes the cup of the Lord, he enters into fellowship with Him. The "cup of demons" (I Cor. 10:21) mentioned in opposition to the cup of the Lord can best be understood in this context. The apostle is saying in a figurative way that we cannot have fellowship with Christ and with the forces of darkness at one and the same time. At heathen feasts the cup was sacred to the name of the god in whose name the feast was being held. Thus at the communion service, the cup is sacred to the name of the Redeemer who instituted its practice (Matt. 26:27; Mark 14:23, 24; Luke 22:20). The "cup of trembling" literally, cup of intoxication (Isa. 51:17, 22; Zach. 12:2); "Cup of astonishment, desolation" (Ezek. 23:33); "Cup of fury" (Isa. 51:17-22); "Cup of indignation" (Rev. 14:10).

CUPBEARER (Heb. *mashqeh, one giving drink),* a palace official who served wine at a king's table. Cupbearers were men of confidence and trust. They are mentioned in Genesis 40:1ff; I Kings 10:5; II Chronicles 9:4; Nehemiah 1:11.

CURSE (Heb. *'ālāh, me'ērâh, qelālâh;* Gr. katápa), the reverse of "to bless." On the human level, to wish harm or catastrophe. On the divine, to impose judgment. In the oriental mind the curse carried with it its own power of execution. A curse was imposed upon the serpent (Gen. 3:14). Noah cursed Ham (Gen. 9:25). The curse of Balaam, the pseudo-prophet, turned to a blessing. (Num. 24:10). A curse was placed upon Mount Ebal for disobedience to the law of Moses (Deut. 27:1-9). The cursing of one's parents is sternly prohibited by Mosaic regulations. Christ commanded those who would be His disciples to bless and curse not (Luke 6:28). When Peter, at Christ's trial, denied that he knew Him, he invited a curse upon himself (Matt. 26:74). This passage is often misunderstood by Western readers. Paul represents the curse of the law as borne by Christ upon the cross for the believer (Gal. 3:13). The modern Western practice of cursing, i.e., using profane language, is never referred to in the Scriptures. See BLASPHEMY.

CURTAINS (Heb. *yerî'âh*). 1. The curtains of fine linen and goats' hair which covered the tabernacle (Exod. 26:1ff; 38:9ff). Gradually, the "curtains" gave their name to the entire structure.

2. Employed figuratively by Isaiah (40:22), referring to the heavens. He uses the word *dōq,* lit. "gauze."

CUSH (kūsh, Heb. *kûsh*). 1. The oldest son of Ham, one of the three sons of Noah. (Gen. 10:6-8, I Chron. 1:8-10). Among the descendants were Seba, Havilah, Sabta, Raamah, and Sabtecha. They were mostly located in Arabia. Nimrod is likewise said to be the son of Cush, but the word "son" probably means "descendant."

2. "Cush, the Benjamite," the title for Psalm 7, viewed as referring to King Saul, the Benjamite. Since Cush and Kish are similar in sound, they are held to be one. Saul's father's name was Kish. 3. Cush, the country. The name of the territory through which the Gihon flowed (Gen. 2:13), translated Ethiopia by KJV, but in view of the distance of Ethiopia in relation to the Red Sea, the site is probably in SE Babylon or Chaldea. The wife of Moses is referred to as a Cushite, making her a target of criticism by Miriam and Aaron (Num. 12:1). If this be Zipporah, the wife of Moses, mentioned earlier, her origin was that of the land of Midian. The earlier passages seem to indicate Cush as African, the latter as Asian. The precise identification of either the woman or the country constitutes an unsolved problem.

CUSHI (kū'shī), a member of the Cushite people. 1. The man sent by Joab to inform David that Absalom's rebellion was quelled and that the time was ripe for him to return to his throne. (II Sam. 18:21-32).

2. A contemporary of Jeremiah, the great-grandfather of Jehudi (Jer. 36:14).

3. The father of the Prophet Zephaniah (Zeph. 1:1).

CUSTOM, when not referring to a tax, usually means "manner," "way," or "statute" (Gen. 31:35; Judg. 11:39; Jer. 32:11). Heathen religious practice is referred to in Leviticus 18:30 and Jeremiah 10:3. In the NT it means "manner," "usage" (Luke 1:9; Acts 6:14) and "religious practices."

CUSTOM, RECEIPT OF (RV "place of toll"), from which Matthew (Levi) was called to follow Christ (Matt. 9:9). In post-exilic days the tribute was usually in terms of a road toll. The Romans imposed tribute or tax upon the Jews as upon all their subjects for the maintenance of their provincial government. Tax collectors or publicans were despised because of their notorious dishonesty and willingness to work for a foreign power.

CUTHA or **CUTH** (kū'thà, kŭth), the longer form preferable, one of the cities from which Sargon, king of Assyria, brought immigrants to repopulate the area of Samaria which he had sacked in 720 B.C. (II Kings 17:24-30). Because of their numerical predominance, the inhabitants of Samaria were henceforth referred to as Cutheans. As a result of mixture, a synthesis between Mosaism and heathenism arose. This is one of the explanations for the deep antipathy existing between the Jews and the Samaritans down into the days of the NT (John 4:9). *The ruins and temples of Cutha.* From the contract tablets found by Rassam at Tel-Ibrahim it now appears that the ancient name of Cutha was Gudua or Kuta. This city of high culture and commerce lay NE of Babylon and was one of its most important centers. Rassam describes its almost perfect ruins as being about 3,000 feet in circumference and 280 feet high. In it was a sanctuary dedicated to Ibrahim (Abraham). Both city and its great temple, the latter dedicated to Nergal, appear to date back to Sumerian times.

CUTTINGS (cuttings in the flesh), a heathen practice, usually done in mourning for the dead, which was forbidden to the children of Israel (Lev. 19:28). This cruel practice, extending from the cutting of the hair or beard to self-mutilation, was widespread among the heathen nations. Homer refers to it in the *Iliad* where, in place of human sacrifice, the people cut themselves in mourning for the deceased Achilles. Besides being indicative of excessive grief, these cuttings were supposed to propitiate the idols of the heathen. They included tattooings, gashes, castrations, etc. In Elijah's day, the priests of Baal cut themselves till the blood ran in a vain attempt to make Baal answer (I Kings 18:28). Tattooing as a mark of allegiance to a deity, or as soldiers to their commander was also explicitly forbidden (Lev. 19:28). This practice was forbidden on humanitarian grounds and because most of it was performed as a religious rite to some local heathen deity. Solon forbade the women of Athens of his day to beat themselves till the blood ran. The holiness code of Israel reads, "Ye are the children of the Lord your God: ye shall not cut yourselves" (Deut. 14:1). The LXX adds the phrase, "in your flesh for the dead." The only cutting in the flesh allowed in Israel is that of circumcision at the command of God (Gen. 21:4).

J.F.G.

CYLINDER SEALS, a cylindrical disc measuring from 1½ to 3 inches long — sometimes made of terra cotta, other times of precious stones. On it were printed for publication insignia of different descriptions.

CYPRESS (see Plants)

CYPRUS (sī'prŭs, Gr. *kúpros*, "copper"), an island in the eastern part of the Mediterranean directly off the coast of Syria and Cilicia, 148 miles long and about 40 miles across. In mythology, it is famous as the birthplace of Zeus. Historically, its roots are deep in the past. The OT refers to it as the "Isles of Chittim" (*Kittim*, RSV, Ezek. 27:6).

days of Esarhaddon. The demise of the Assyrian Empire appears to have brought it relative freedom, until it was annexed to Egypt in 540 B.C. With the rise of Cambyses (526 B.C.), Cyprus passed under Persian rule until the time of Alexander the Great, to whom it surrendered voluntarily and helped with the siege of Tyre. During the late inter-testamental period it fell into the hands of the Romans (cf. I Macc. 10:13). A number of the ill-famed guard of Antiochus Epiphanes were Cypriots. In 58 B.C. Cyprus was accorded provincial status by the Romans. In 22 B.C. it was made the direct charge of the Senate. Roman coins of this particular period are rather numerous.

It was at Paphos in Cyprus that Elymas, the sorcerer, attempted to dissuade the deputy from becoming a Christian, and was punished by being deprived of his sight (Acts 3:11).

J.F.G.

A scene on the island of Cyprus. © MPS

The island is rich in copper deposits, hence, its name. In the pre-Christian era, a large colony of Jews settled there, who later formed the nucleus of the Christian church ministered to by Paul and company. During the Roman rule, the Jews were expelled from Cyprus in the days of Hadrian.

Barnabas, who accompanied Paul on his first missionary journey, was a native of the island (Acts 4:36), and with John Mark returned to evangelize Cyprus after they had left Paul's company (Acts 15:36-39). The Apostolic party passed through the island from Salamis to Paphos. At Paphos, Sergius Paulus, the imperial deputy of the island believed in Christ (Acts 13:12).

Cyprus has known various conquerors, in addition to the Assyrians who had been attracted by its rich resources. The Egyptians, the Hittites, the Phoenicians, the Greeks, Romans, Turks, and British have all taken advantage of its attractive character.

The aboriginal inhabitants of Cyprus seem to have been of Minoan stock. After the breakup of the Minoan civilization, the dark ages settled down upon the island. The curtain rose again when Hellenistic settlers from the Greek mainland reached it. Sargon in 709 B.C., made himself ruler of Cyprus and it paid tribute to Assyria until the

CYRENE, CYRENIAN (sīrē'nĭ, Gr. *Kyréne, wall*), a Libyan city in N. Africa, W of Egypt from which it was separated by a part of the Libyan Desert. It was situated some 2,000 feet above the Mediterranean from which it was ten miles distant. The coastline afforded a natural shelter from the heat of the Sahara. It is protected by steps of descending ranges about 80 miles to the S. The fertility and climate of the city are delightful and productive.

Cyrene, originally a Greek colony, was founded by Battus in 603 B.C. This veritable "oasis in the desert" attracted travelers and commerce from early times. Among its distinguished citizens was Carneacles, the founder of the new Academy at Athens. Aristippus, the Epicurean philosopher and friend of Socrates, also came from this city. Ptolemy Euregetes I incorporated Cyrene as a part of Egypt in 231 B.C. It later passed into the hands of the Romans, being willed to them by the last Ptolemy.

Cyrene is not mentioned in the OT but becomes important in the NT. A native of Cyrene, Simon by name, was impressed by the Roman soldiers into carrying the cross of Jesus (Luke 23:26). Thus Simon immortalized his city. There were also representatives of this city present in Jerusalem upon the day of Pentecost (Acts 2:10). Its Jewish

The Cylinder of Cyrus, telling of his capture of Babylon and his liberation of captive peoples. BM

population warranted a synagogue (Acts 6:9). Lucius of Cyrene receives mention in Acts 11:19, 20. Archaeology has shown that it was the Greek plan to make Cyrene the "Athens of Africa." The most interesting remains are a great system of tombs cut out of solid rock into the cliff. Architecture and paintings adorn these tombs.

CYRENIUS (sĭ-rē'nĭ-ŭs, KJV, better Quirinius, RV), mentioned but once in the NT (Luke 2:2). (See Quirinius)

CYRUS (sī'rŭs, Heb. *Kôresh*), the son of Cambyses, king of Anshan. With the rise of Cyrus began the renowned Persian Empire which was to continue until the coming of Alexander the Great. Seven years subsequent to the demise of Nebuchadnezzar, Nabonidus ascended the throne of Babylon, in 555 B.C. He was destined to be the last ruling sovereign of the neo-Babylonian Empire, for in the highlands of Iran another kingdom was forging out of its own program of conquest. With the defeat of the Medes, when Astyages, king of the Medes, was vanquished by Cyrus, the realm of Persia commenced to assume threatening proportions. Cyrus himself announced his genealogy: "I am Cyrus, king of the hosts, the great king, king of Babylon, king of Sumer and Akkad ... son of Cambyses, the king, king of Anshan; the grandson of Cyrus ... the great-grandson of Teispes ... king of Anshan ..." In this same inscription, Cyrus proceeds to relate how the city of Babylon opened its gates to him without resistance, thus confirming the Biblical account recorded in Daniel 5 when Darius, acting as vice-regent for Cyrus, took the city of Babylon in the name of Cyrus the Great. The neo-Babylonian empire was in no condition to resist the advance of Cyrus, and fell easy prey into the hands of the Persians. The OT sets the framework of reference against the backdrop of Belshazzar's impious feast (Daniel 5:1-30).

Cyrus entered Babylon on October 29, 539 B.C. and presented himself in the role of the liberator of the people. He allowed the images of the gods to be transported back to their original cities, and instituted a kindly policy of repatriation for captive peoples. His policies of moderation naturally extended to the Hebrews, whom he encouraged to return to Judea to rebuild their temple (II Chron. 36:22, 23; Ezra 1:1-6; etc.). Isaiah refers to Cyrus as the "Anointed One" (Isa. 44:27, 28; 45:1-5).   J.F.G.

The Tomb of Cyrus at Pasargadae, in Iran. SHH

D

DABAREH (dăb'à-rě), erroneous spelling of Daberath (Josh. 21:28).

DABBASHETH (dăb'à-shĕth), hill town of uncertain location, but adjoining the heritage of Zebulun (Josh. 19:10).

DABERATH (dăb'ĕ-răth), an ancient town near the western side of Mt. Tabor; part of the heritage of Issachar given to the Levites (Josh. 19:12; I Chron. 6:72). A strategic location, the probable site of the defeat of Sisera by Barak. (Judg. 4:14-22).

DAGON (dā'gŏn, Heb. *dāghôn*, probably *fish*), chief god of the Philistines. Originally worshiped by Canaanites before Philistine invasion of Canaan, as indicated by place names such as Beth-dagon in Judah (Josh. 15:41), and in Asher (Josh. 19:27). Either a fish god or the god of agriculture, from *Dag*, "fish," or *Dagan*, "grain." On a wall of a palace in Babylon he is shown as half fish. That he was god of agriculture is supported by the tribute which priests and diviners bade the rulers to send when the ark was returned to Israel. Five golden mice and five golden emerods (*tumors*, ASV) were votive offerings expressing gratitude for Dagon's freeing their fields of mice and their bodies of tumors. Saul's head was placed in a temple of Dagon (I Chron. 10:10). Samson destroyed the temple of Dagon in Gaza (Judg. 16:30).   J.D.F.

DALAIAH (dăl'ā-ī'à). 1. Descendant of David (I Chron. 3:1-24).

2. A priest of Aaron's line (I Chron. 24:18).

3. A prince who pleaded with King Jehoiakim not to destroy the roll containing the prophecies of Jeremiah (Jer. 36:12,25).

4. The founder of a post-exilic family whose genealogy was lost (Ezra 2:60; Neh. 7:62).

5. The father of Shemaiah (Nah. 6:10).

DALE, THE KINGS. 1. Where Abram met Melchizedek (Gen. 14:17).

2. Absalom's memorial (II Sam. 18:18).

DALMANUTHA (dăl-mà-nū'thà), a village on the W coast of the Sea of Galilee, adjoining Magdala (Matt. 15:39). Landing place of Jesus after feeding the multitude (Mark 8:10). It is mentioned only in the NT. Considerable ruins near modern Mejdel (Magdala) are considered the location.

DALMATIA (dăl-mā'shà, Gr. *Dalmatía, deceitful*), a mountainous province on the E shore of the Adriatic Sea. Christianity, implanted under Titus, (II Tim. 4:10), continues until today. It was ruled by Rome as early as 160 A.D. Paul may have visited in the province (Rom. 15:19); in his time it was regarded as part of Illyricum.

DALPHON (dăl'fŏn), one of Haman's sons who were slain and hanged after Esther became queen (Esth. 9:6-13).

DAMARIS (dăm'à-rĭs, Gr. *dámaris*), a convert of Paul at Mars Hill (Acts 17:34).

DAMASCUS (dà-măs'kŭs, Gr. *Damaskós*), for more than four thousand years the capital of one government after another, a prize for which

Damascus in Syria. Above, gateway to Straight Street. Below, the "Street called Straight." © MPS

nation after nation went to war, a city whose boast for centuries has been, "The world began at Damascus, and the world will end there." It is a modern focal point between the Christian and the Mohammedan worlds, center of tourist interest and of international unrest.

It was founded some 2,200 years before Christ by Uz, a grandson of Shem (Josh. 1:6; 4). It is the

City of Damascus, viewed from the east. © MPS

capital of Syria, a small region of unique geological formation, lying between Mt. Hermon and the Syrian Desert. It is watered by the Barada and the Wady Awaj, Abana and Pharpar of the OT (II Kings 5:12). A 2,000 foot elevation gives it a delightful climate. Its gardens and olive groves still flourish after millennia of cultivation. By the time of Abraham it was well-enough known to be a landmark (Gen. 14:15). Caravan routes from the E, W, and S crossed in the city, carrying treasures of silks, perfumes, carpets, and foods.

Damascus and Syria played an important part in Biblical history. En route from Ur, Abraham found in Syria a steward, Eliezer, who was his heir presumptive until Isaac came (Gen. 15:2,3). From the days when Abram liberated Lot (Gen. 14:13-16), there were repeated periods of peace and war among his descendants, many of them involving Damascus. Abraham secured a wife for Isaac from Syria, hence Israel is of Syrian ancestry (Gen. 24; Deut. 26:5). Jacob labored long in Syria for Rachel (Gen. 29). Damascus was once a rich city whose fairs were far-famed (Ezek. 27:16). According to Josephus, Hadad was the first king (*Ant.* VII:5; 2). David subjugated and ruled the city for a season (II Sam. 8:5,6; I Chron. 18:3-6). Rezon, a deserter, slew King Hadadezer whom David had defeated, and made himself king. He hated Israel and harassed Solomon "during all the days of his life" (I Kings 11:23-25). Solomon had made extensive purchases from Syria (I Kings 10:29). Asa, king of Judah, bribed Ben-hadad, grandson of Rezon of Syria, to aid him against Israel, paying him with temple treasures (I Kings 15:16-21). Elijah, acting upon instructions from God, anointed Hazael to be king of Syria and Jehu to rule Israel, to the end that Judah might be punished (I Kings 19:15-17). Elah succeeded Baasha in Israel (I Kings 16:6) and while drunk was slain by Zimri who usurped the throne and destroyed the house of Baasha (I Kings 16:10-14). Zimri killed himself (I Kings 16:18); his son

Omri succeeded him, and was followed by Ahab (I Kings 16:29). Ben-hadad attacked Ahab with a great force, but during a drunken orgy was overwhelmed. Ahab foolishly allowed him to return to his throne (I Kings 20:1-34). Later, becoming ill, he sent Hazael to consult Elisha who made a prophecy that led Hazael to assassinate Ben-hadad and usurp the throne for which Elijah had anointed him (I Kings 19:15; II Kings 8:7-15). Hazael overcame Ahaziah and Joram (II Kings 8:28), ravaged Reuben and Manasseh, and Israel (II Kings 10:32-33; 13:3).

A strong kingdom was developed under Ahab, with merchants in Samaria (I Kings 20:34). Syrians defeated Joash after he failed in a test before Elisha (II Kings 13:14-22). Ben-hadad II succeeded Hazael, and Israel recovered her lost possessions (II Kings 13:24,25). Under Jeroboam Damascus was retaken by Israel (II Kings 14:28). Ahaz, in order to save his kingdom from Syria, made an alliance with Tiglath-Pileser (Pul) who destroyed Damascus and ended Syria's power for many decades (II Kings 16:7-9). The city remained of little importance until 333 B.C. when an army of Alexander the Great captured it. Then followed two centuries of rise and fall. In 63 B.C. Syria became a province of the Roman Empire (Jos. *Wars* I:6;2).

During New Testament days Damascus was an important center, ruled by Arabia under Aretas (II Cor. 11:32). A strong Christian community had developed by Paul's day. While en route there to arrest the believers, Saul was converted (Acts 9:1-18). He escaped his Jewish enemies of the city by being let down from a wall in a basket (Acts 9:25; II Cor. 11:33). After a checkered history under Rome, Damascus was captured by Moslems in 635 A.D. and made the seat of the Mohammedan world. It remained the center of the Moslem faith until 1918 when it was put under French mandate after World War I. In 1946 it became a free state.　　　　　　　J.D.F.

DAMNATION (Heb. *rasha, to hold guilty*, Deut. 25:1; Isa. 50:9; 54:17, etc.; Gr. *kríno, to put under condemnation*, John 3:17,18; Rom. 14:22; *katakrino, to hold to be unpardonable*, Matt. 12:41; 20:18; Rom. 8:1,3,34; Heb. 11:7; *kríma* and *krísis, judgment, eternal punishment*, Matt. 23:33; Mark 12:40; John 5:29; Rom. 3:8; 5:16; 13:2; I Cor. 11:29,34; *apóleia, destruction, damnation*, II Pet. 2:3). The penalty for unbelief (II Thess. 2:12); for adulterous relations (I Tim. 5:11,12); for hypocrisy (Matt. 23:14); for treason (Rom. 13:2). When referring to the future, the words mean primarily eternal separation from God with accompanying awful punishment (see Ps. 88:10-12; Isa. 38:18); being cast into Gehenna (Matt. 5:29; 10:28; 23:33; 24:51; Mark 9:43, etc.). The severity of the punishment is determined by the degree of sin (Luke 12:36-48), and it is eternal (Mark 3:29; II Thess. 1:9; Isa. 66:24; Jude 6,7).
J.D.F.

DAN (CITY), northernmost city of Palestine. Originally Leshem (Josh. 19:47; Judg. 18:29). Captured by Danites and renamed Dan (Judg. 18). It was a commercial center at one time (Ezek. 27:19). Here Jeroboam I set up the golden calf (I Kings 12). The city marked the northern limit of Israel in the common phrase "from Dan to Beersheba" (Judg. 20:1; I Sam. 3:20, etc.).

DAN (TRIBE OF), the tribe to which Dan the fifth son of Jacob gave origin, and, the territory allotted it in Canaan. One son is mentioned among those who migrated to Egypt (Gen. 46:8,23). By the time of the Exodus his offspring had increased to a total of 62,700 men (Num. 1:39). The tribe acted as rear guard during the Exodus (Num. 10:25). They were given a fertile area lying between Judah and the Mediterranean Sea, occupied by the Philistines whose lands extended from Egypt to the coast W of Shechem (Josh. 13:3). Failure to conquer Philistia made the Danites move northward where, by a bit of strategy, they conquered Leshem (Laish of Judg. 18:29), and renamed it Dan (Josh. 19:47; Judg. 18:1-29).

The heritage of Dan, though small, was productive and, with the acquisition of extra lands, provided for growth. Aholiab and Samson were Danites (Exod. 31:6; Judg. 13:2, 24). Jeroboam, Solomon's servant, set up a golden calf in Dan and put high places throughout Israel (I Kings 12:25-33). Menahem stayed Pul (Tiglath-Pileser) by bribery (II Kings 15:14-20), but eventually Pul returned, overran Israel and took many Danites into captivity (I Chron. 5:26). Little is known of the tribe from that time.   J.D.F.

DANCING has formed a part of religious rites and has been associated with war and hunting, with marriage, birth, and other occasions since the records of man began to be written. It grew out of three basic human reactions: 1, the desire to imitate movements of beasts, birds, even the sun and moon; 2, the desire to express emotions by gestures; 3, gregarious impulses.

Throughout past ages dancing has been associated with worship. Closely related to religious praises was the sacramental dance in which worshipers sought to express through bodily movements praise or penitence, worship or prayer. Out of the primitive dances the esthetic dance of civilized ancient nations slowly developed. In these the primary concern of the dancers was to reveal grace, speed, and rhythm, often to appeal to the carnal nature of both participants and spectators. Vashti refused to expose herself to this end (Esth. 1:12). Priests of all pagan religions cultivated

Region of Dan (Tell El-Kabi), one of the sources of the Jordan River, near Caesarea Philippi. © MPS

dancing, but at times found it the source of dissipation and harm. For ages it has been accompanied by clapping of the hands. Percussion and other noise-making instruments seem to be native to the dance (Judg. 11:34; Ps. 68:25).

The Hebrew people developed their own type of dancing, associated in the main with worship. Basically, it was more like modern religious shouting by individuals, or processions of exuberant groups. Three things characterized it: 1, the sexes never intermingled in it, except where pagan influences had crept in (cf. Exod. 32:19); 2, usually dancing was done by women, with one leading, as in the case of Miriam (Exod. 15:20,21). In this incident, as well as on other occasions, a form of antiphonal singing was used. 3. Dancing usually took place out of doors. For women dancers, see Exodus 15:20; Judges 21:19ff; I Samuel 18:6; Psalm 68:25. Men danced solo, as in the case of David before the Ark (II Sam. 6:14-16), and in groups, as when Israel celebrated the victory over the Amalekites (I Sam. 30:16). The time for dancing was recognized by the writer of Ecclesiastes (3:4). Job complained against the rich because of their ability to dance (Job 21:11). Jeremiah bemoaned the tragedy that made singing and dancing out of place (Lam. 5:15). The redemption of Israel was to be celebrated by dancing, both virgins, and men and boys having part (Jer. 31:13). The Romans introduced the Greek dance to Palestine. Primitive Christian churches allowed the dance, but it soon caused degeneracy and was banned, as is indicated by many of the early Christian writers.   J.D.F.

DANIEL (dănyĕl, Heb. *dānîyē'l* or *dāni'ĕl, God is my judge*). 1. David's second son (I Chron. 3:1;—Chileab, II Sam. 3:3).

2. A post-exilic priest (Ezra 8:2; Neh. 10:6).

3. The exilic seer of the book of Daniel. The prophet was born into an unidentified family of Judean nobility at the time of Josiah's reformation (621 B.C.); for he was among the select, youthful hostages of the first Jewish deportation,

taken to Babylon by Nebuchadnezzar in 605 B.C., the third year of king Jehoiakim (Dan. 1:1,3). The reliability of this date and, indeed, of the whole account has been consistently attacked by hostile criticism. Daniel's dating, however, simply follows the customary Babylonian practice of numbering the years of a king's reign *after* his accession-year (contrast Jer. 46:2 which speaks of this date as Jehoiakim's fourth year). The publication, moreover, of D. J. Wiseman's Nebuchadnezzar tablets demonstrates that after the Babylonian defeat of Egypt at Carchemish in 605 B.C. Nebuchadnezzar did "conquer the whole area of Hatti" (Syria and Palestine) and "take away the heavy tribute of Hatti to Babylon" (*Chronicles of Chaldean Kings (626-556 B.C.*, London: Trustees of the British Museum, 1956, pp. 26,29), just as claimed in Daniel 1:2 (cf. II Chron. 36:6-7 and J. B. Payne, "The Uneasy Conscience of Modern Liberal Exegesis," *Bulletin of the Evangelical Theological Society*, I:1 (Winter, 1958), pp. 14-18).

For three years Daniel was trained in all the wisdom of the Chaldeans (Dan. 1:4-5) and was assigned the Babylonian name Belteshazzar, "Protect his life!", thereby invoking a pagan deity (4:8). Daniel and his companions, however, remained true to their ancestral faith, courteously refusing "the king's dainties" (1:8, tainted with idolatry and contrary to the Levitical purity-laws). God rewarded them with unsurpassed learning (1:20), qualifying them as official "wise-men" (cf. 2:13). Upon Daniel, moreover, He bestowed the gift of visions and of interpreting dreams (1:17; cf. Daniel's wisdom in the Apocryphal stories of *Susanna* and *Bel and the Dragon*).

Near the close of his second year (602 B.C.) Nebuchadnezzar required his fellow-Chaldeans, who as the ruling strata in society had assumed the position of priestly diviners (2:2; cf. Herodotus, I:191), to identify and interpret an undisclosed dream that had troubled him the preceding evening (2:5,8, ASVmg). The hoax of spiritism and astrology was duly exposed, but when judgment was pronounced upon the enchanters Daniel and his companions were included under the death-sentence. But the "God in heaven that revealeth secrets" (2:28, cf. 2:11) answered Daniel's prayer for illumination (2:18-19). Daniel revealed both the dream, depicting a fourfold image, and its import of four world empires (Babylon, Persia, Greece, and Rome) that should introduce God's Messianic kingdom (2:44; see DANIEL, BOOK OF). Nebuchadnezzar forthwith elevated him to be chief over the wise-men (2:48 does not, however, state that he became a pagan priest, as inferred by those who would discredit Daniel's historicity). He further offered him the governorship of the province of Babylon, though Daniel committed this latter appointment to his three friends (2:49; see SHADRACH, FURNACE).

In the latter years of Nebuchadnezzar's reign (604-562 B.C.), Daniel's courage was demonstrated (4:19, cf. 4:7) when he interpreted the king's dream of the fallen tree. Tactfully informing his despotic master that for seven "times" (months? cf. 4:33) pride would reduce him to beast-like madness, he reiterated "that the Most High ruleth in the kingdom of men" (4:24-25; cf. its historical fulfillment twelve months later, 4:28-33).

In 552 B.C., after the retirement of king Nabonidus to Arabian Teima and the accession of his son Belshazzar to the royal dignity (ICC, p. 67), Daniel was granted his vision of the four great beasts (Dan. 7), which parallels Nebuchadnezzar's earlier dream of the composite image.

The Lion Monument in the ruins of Babylon, supposedly marking the site of Daniel's den of lions. © MPS

Then in 550, at the time of Cyrus' amalgamation of the Median and Persian states and of the growing eclipse of Babylon, Daniel received the prophecy of the ram and the he-goat, concerning Persia and Greece (8:20-21) down to Antiochus IV (8:25). On Oct. 12, 539 B.C., Cyrus' general Gobryas, after having routed the Chaldean armies, occupied the city of Babylon. During the profane revelries of Belshazzar's court that immediately preceded the end, Daniel was summoned to interpret God's "handwriting on the wall"; and the prophet fearlessly condemned the desperate prince (5:22-23). He predicted Medo-Persian victory (v. 28), and that very night the citadel fell and Belshazzar was slain.

When Darius the Mede (presumably Gobryas, or another official of similar name, cf. John C. Whitcomb, *Darius the Mede,* Grand Rapids: Eerdmans, 1959, pp. 17-24) was made king of Babylon by Cyrus (5:31; 9:1), he at once sought out Daniel as one of his three "presidents" (6:2; cf. Whitcomb, *op. cit.*, p. 17, on the established historicity of such appointments), because of his excellency, and was considering him for the post of chief administrator (6:3). Daniel's jealous colleagues, failing to uncover valid charges of corruption (6:4), proceeded to contrive his downfall through a royal edict prohibiting for thirty days all prayers or petitions, save to Darius himself. Daniel was promptly apprehended in prayer to God; and Darius had no recourse but to cast him into a den of lions, as had been prescribed. God, however, intervened on behalf of His faithful servant (cf. 6:16) and shut the lions' mouths, though they subsequently devoured his accusers, when condemned to a similar fate. It was in this same first year of Darius, as the seventy years of Babylonian exile drew to a close, that the angel Gabriel answered Daniel's prayers and confessions with a revelation of the "seventy weeks" of years (490 yrs., Dan. 9:24-27), from the decree for rebuilding Jerusalem (under Ezra (?), 7:18,25; cf. 4:12-16) to the Messiah, His death, and the confirming of the Gospel to Israel (458 B.C. through A.D. 33). "So Daniel prospered into the reign of Cyrus the Persian" (Dan. 6:28; 1:21).

The last known event in the life of Daniel took place in the third year of Cyrus (536 B.C.), when he was granted an overpowering vision of the archangel Michael contending with the demonic powers of pagan society (10:10-11:1); of the course of world history, through the persecutions of Antiochus IV (11:2-39); and of the eschatological antichrist, the resurrections, and God's final judgment (11:40-12:4). The vision concluded with the assurance that though Daniel would come to his grave prior to these events he would yet receive his appointed reward in the consummation (12:13). Thus in his mid-eighties, after completing his inspired autobiography and apocalyptic oracles, he finished his honored course.

The historicity of Daniel the prophet is confirmed, both by the words of Christ (Matt. 24:15) and by references to his righteousness and wisdom, as witnessed by his prophetic contemporary Ezekiel (14:14,20 and 28:3, in 591 and 586 B.C., respectively), though modern critics have attempted to relate the latter passages to a mythological Daniel of Ugaritic legend. Those, however, who stand committed to the truth of Scripture, find in Daniel a timeless demonstration of separation from impurity, or courage against compromise, of efficaciousness in prayer, and of dedication to Him whose "kingdom is from generation to generation" (Dan. 4:34).   J.B.P.

DANIEL, BOOK OF, although standing as the last of the major prophets in the English Bible, it appears in the Hebrew OT (which consists of "the law, prophets, and writings") as one of the "writings." For though Christ spoke of Daniel's *function* as prophetic (Matt. 24:15), his *position* was that of governmental official and inspired writer, rather than ministering prophet (cf. Acts 2:29-30).

The first half of the book (chapters 1-6) consists of six narratives on the life of Daniel and his friends: their education (605-602 B.C.), Daniel's revelation of Nebuchadnezzar's dream-image, the trial by fiery furnace, his prediction of Nebuchadnezzar's madness, his interpretation of the handwriting on the wall (539 B.C., the fall of Babylon), and his ordeal in the lions' den (see DANIEL, SHADRACH). The second half consists of four apocalyptic visions, predicting the course of world history. Their scope may be outlined as follows:

Daniel 7 envisions the rise of four beasts, explained as representing successive kings (kingdoms, 7:23). The description parallels that of the image in chap. 2. The first empire must therefore be contemporary Babylon (2:38); and the fourth, Rome, in which God's Messianic kingdom was set up (2:44). Between lie Persia and Greece. The vision further describes the disintegration of Rome into a tenfold balance of power (2:42; 7:24; Rev. 17:12,16), the eventual rise of antichrist for an indefinite period of "times" (Dan. 7:8,25), and his destruction when a "Son of man" comes with the clouds of heaven (7:13). This last figure symbolizes the saints of the Most High (7:22), epitomized in Jesus Christ, the "last Adam" (Mark 14:62; I Cor. 15:45). For though His kingdom was "set up" at His first coming, it will "consume [earth's pagan] kingdoms" at His glorious second advent (Dan. 2:44) and millennial reign ("a season," 7:12).

Chapters 2:4b-7:28 are composed in the international language of Aramaic. But with chapter 8, Daniel resumes his use of Hebrew, probably because of the more Jewish orientation of the remaining three visions. That of the ram and the he-goat depicts the coming victory of Greece (331 B.C.) over the amalgamated empire of Media and Persia (8:20-21) and the subsequent persecution of Judah by Antiochus IV (168-165 B.C., 8:9-14,23-26). Chapter 9, on the 70 weeks, then illuminates Christ's first coming, 69 "weeks" of years (= 483 yrs.) after the decree for Jerusalem's rebuilding, presumably to Ezra in 458 B.C. (Ezra 7:18,25; cf. his results, 4:12-16). With God-inspired accuracy, Daniel thus inaugurates the 70th week in A.D. 26, with the baptismal anointing of Christ (Dan. 9:25; Luke 3:21-22; 4:18). In the midst of this week the Anointed One is to be cut off (Dan. 9:26), thereby making reconciliation for iniquity (9:24) and causing Old Testament sacrifice to cease (9:27; see Matt. 27:51; Heb. 9:8-12). Yet for an additional three and one-half years, God's redemptive covenant will be confirmed to Israel (cf. Rev. 12:6,14), after which Jerusalem will be rendered desolate (A.D. 70, Dan. 9:26-27; Matt. 24:15). Other evangelical interpreters terminate the 69th week with Christ's death and commence the 70th week with a covenant of antichrist, before His second coming. Chaps 10-12, after

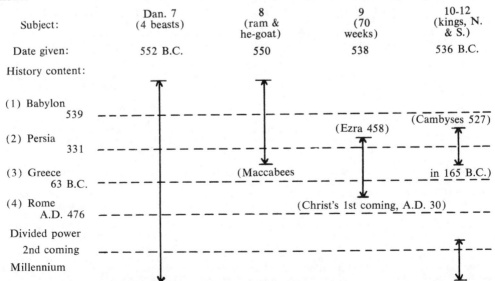

Subject:	Dan. 7 (4 beasts)	8 (ram & he-goat)	9 (70 weeks)	10-12 (kings, N. & S.)
Date given:	552 B.C.	550	538	536 B.C.
History content:				
(1) Babylon 539				(Cambyses 527)
			(Ezra 458)	
(2) Persia 331				
(3) Greece 63 B.C.		(Maccabees		in 165 B.C.)
(4) Rome A.D. 476			(Christ's 1st coming, A.D. 30)	
Divided power				
2nd coming				
Millennium				

elaborating on the succession of Persian and Greek rulers through Antiochus, then moves on to "the time of the end," foretelling Antichrist's tribulation (Dan. 11:40-12:1), the resurrections of the saved and the lost (12:2, cf. Rev. 20:4-6,12), and the final judgment (Dan. 12:2).

The authorship of the book of Daniel is nowhere expressly defined, but is indicated by the autobiographical, first-person composition from 7:2 onward. Unity of style and content (as admitted by Driver, Rowley, and Pfeiffer), plus God's commitment of "the book" to Daniel (Dan. 12:4), implies the latter's authorship, shortly after his last vision, in 536 B.C. (10:1).

Modern criticism, however, overwhelmingly denies the authenticity of Daniel as a product of the sixth century B.C. Indeed, as early as A.D. 275 the neo-Platonic philosopher Porphyry had categorically repudiated the possibility of Daniel's miraculous predictions. Anti-supernaturalism must bring the "prophecy" down to a time after the events described (especially after Antiochus' sacrilege of 168 B.C.); or, if the latest possible date has been reached, it must then reinterpret the predictions to apply to other, already-accomplished events. Consequently, since Daniel was extensively quoted (and misunderstood) as early as 140 B.C. (Sibylline Oracles 3:381-400), rationalists have no alternative but to apply the supposed coming of the Messiah and the fulfillment of the 70 weeks to Maccabean times, rather than Christ's, even though this requires "surmising a chronological miscalculation on the part of the writer" (ICC, p.393). Dating Daniel in the second century is thus the result, fundamentally, of presuppositions of skepticism and is opposed to the actual evidence and testimony: for it makes the book's record of itself a deception and a fraud; and Jesus Christ, who believed that "Daniel the prophet" did predict Roman imperialism (Matt. 24:15), it charges with falsehood based on ignorance.

The surface arguments of current negative criticism may be classified as historical, literary, and theological. A number of specific censures have been advanced against Daniel's historical authenticity. These may, however, be dismissed, either as arguments from silence or as answered by recent archaeology (see DANIEL). More generally, it is asserted that Daniel conceived of a fictitious Median empire, existing as a separate kingdom between Babylon and Persia (thus allowing Daniel's fourth empire to be identified with Greece rather than Rome, as required by liberalism's presuppositions). But the very passage adduced (5:31-6:1) speaks of unified Medo-Persia (6:8,12 cf. 5:28); and Daniel elsewhere identifies his second empire as the dual kingdom of Media *and* Persia (7:5, cf. 8:3,20) and his third, as the fourfold Greek (7:6, 8:8,22). Again, the fact that the apocryphal book of Ecclesiasticus, written about 180, omits Daniel from its survey of Scripture proves little other than the Sadducaic prejudice of its writer; for he likewise disregards the book of Ezra, whose high theology parallels that of Daniel. Fragments of Daniel have, moreover, been discovered among the Dead Sea scrolls of Qumran, datable to the very second century B.C., in which the book's fraudulent composition is commonly claimed.

On literary grounds Daniel has been questioned because of its utilization of certain terms of Persian or Greek origin. The book itself, however, was not written until the Persian period; and its Greek words are limited to the names of musical instruments, as "psaltery" (3:5), that may early

have been imported into Babylon. Among the apocryphal literature from Qumran, there has been recovered a "Prayer of Nabonidus" (RB 63:3 July, 1956), pp. 507-415) that closely parallels Daniel's record of Nebuchadnezzar's madness (Dan. 4). Far, however, from proving Daniel to be a corruption of this third century work, the Qumranic legend, though garbled, serves to suggest the essential historicity of Daniel's account. As to the so-called "late" Aramaic and Hebrew languages of Daniel, Edward J. Young has concluded that "There is nothing in them which in itself necessarily precludes authorship by Daniel in the sixth century B.C." (*An Introduction to the Old Testament*, rev. ed.; Grand Rapids: Eerdmans, 1958, p. 392).

Lastly, the theology of Daniel, with its apocalyptic eschatology, Biblicism, and developed angelology, is said to prohibit exilic origin. Yet Isaiah had composed an apocalypse, describing the resurrection in terms similar to Daniel's, as early as 711 B.C. (Isa. 26:19 — negative critics deny its authenticity, too!); when Daniel in 538 B.C. devoted himself to the inspired "books" (Dan. 9:2), the Old Testament canon was complete, except for three minor prophets, the last two books of Psalms and Chronicles — Esther (see CANON); and Daniel's angels, both in name and in function, stand naturally in the Hebraic religious development. His book was designed to inspire Jewish exiles with confidence in the Most High (4:34-37), and those of God's people today who will approach this book in faith believing will discover therein victorious supernaturalism that overcomes the world. J.B.P.

DAN-JAAN (dăn′jā′ăn), a town covered by David's census (II Sam. 24:6). Hebrew *dān ya'an*, "Dan played a pipe," indicates it was a suburb of Dan. It was on the road to Ijon or Sidon (I Kings 15:20; II Chron. 16:4).

DANNAH (dăn′à), a mountain town given by Caleb as part of the heritage of Judah (Josh. 15:49). Its location is uncertain but not far from Hebron. Some authorities make it modern Idnah.

DARA, DARDA (dăr′à, dàr′dă), a member of a noted family of wise men. He was either a son of Mahol (I Kings 4:31) or son of Zerah (I Chron. 2:6).

DARIC (dăr′ĭk), a Persian gold coin used in Palestine after the return from captivity (Ezra 2:69; Neh. 7:70-72 ASV). It was worth about $5.00. See MONEY.

DARIUS (dă-rī′ŭs, Heb. *dāryāwesh*, Gr. *Dareíos*), a common name for Medo-Persian rulers. Numerous cuneiform tablets contain references to them, especially to Darius Hystaspes. Darius, the Mede, seems to have been the same as Gubaru who was an officer in the army of Cyrus, probably governor of a Persian province N of Babylon. His name is possibly a translation of "Darius." He was the son of Ahasuerus, hence a Mede (Dan. 9:1). Belshazzar's notable feast (Dan. 5) ended in the destruction of the Chaldean Empire, and Darius the Mede (Gubaru) became ruler of the province by appointment of Cyrus at the age of 62. Daniel tells us that Darius the Mede was not heir to the throne, but nevertheless was made king (Dan. 5:31). He seems to have exercised authority contemporaneously with Cyrus.

Cuneiform records list Nabonidus as the last king of the Medes; so Belshazzar, his son, was ruling in Babylon while his father was away

The beginning of the inscription of DARIUS, King of Persia (521-486 B.C.), on the rock of Behistun.

Translation of part of an inscription of Darius in ancient Persian (after Pfeiffer).

Tombs of Darius I, Artaxerxes I and Darius II hewn in the rocks at Naqsh-I-Rustan in Iran. OIUC

at war. Darius reorganized the government and gave Daniel a high place (Dan. 6:1-3). Evil princes set out to destroy him (6:4-9). Jehovah rescued Daniel from the lions and thus advanced his cause before the king (6:10-23). Darius the Mede seems to have ruled for only a brief time (10:1; 11:1).

Darius Hystaspes was the greatest of the Persian rulers. Cambyses, the son of Cyrus, continued the conquests which his noted father had started. He did not, however, recognize the claims of the Jews (Jos. *Ant.* XI:1:2). In one of his campaigns he was defeated by the Egyptians, and on his way home committed suicide. Taking advantage of the king's defeat, a pretender named Smerdis was made king by zealots of the Magian religious sect and he ruled one year (Jos. XI:3;1), until slain by Darius and other princes, Darius having had himself made king. He was a collateral descendant of Cyrus who, according to tradition, had selected Darius to succeed him. Between the reign of Cyrus and that of Darius, the Jews had been mistreated, and work on rebuilding Jerusalem and the temple stopped (Ezra 4:1-6). An appeal was made to Darius who made search and discovered the original decree of Cyrus favoring the Jews. Under his lenient reign, they restored the walls of the city and rebuilt the temple (Ezra 6:1-15). Darius was beset by rebellious subjects and spent much time in putting these down. He reorganized the government and extended its boundaries. He conducted many magnificent building enterprises and encouraged men of letters, especially the historians who extolled his prowess (Josephus, *Ant.* XI:1:3). The Greeks never yielded to him, however, and after some futile campaigns, his forces were overwhelmed in the battle at Marathon 490 B. C. Darius planned another campaign against the Greeks, but rebellion in Egypt interfered, and death in 486 B. C. ended his career. He was succeeded by Xerxes, a grandson of Cyrus the Great.

Darius, the Persian (Neh. 12:22). There is uncertainty among scholars as to whether this was Darius Nothus or Darius Codomannus, but evidence favors the claim that he was the latter, whose kingdom was destroyed by Alexander the Great in 330 B.C. Following a disastrous defeat near Arbela the Persian Empire crumbled, Darius the Persian being its last king. J.D.F.

DARKNESS (Heb. *hōshekh, the dark,* Gr. *skótos, darkness*), used in the Old and in the New Testaments both in a literal and in a figurative sense. For ages mankind has associated it with evil, danger, crime; it has also been the metaphor whereby mystery is described and the place of eternal punishment has been pictured. Several uses of the term are found in the Scriptures: 1. To denote the absence of light (Gen. 1:2,3; Isa. 45:7; Job 34:22).

2. To depict the mysterious (Exod. 20:21; I Kings 8:12; Ps. 97:2; Isa. 8:22; II Sam. 22:10; Matt. 10:27).

3. As ignorance, especially about God (Job 37:19; Prov. 2:13; Eccl. 2:14; John 12:35; I Thess. 5:1-8).

4. To describe the seat of evil (Prov. 4:19; Matt. 6:23; Luke 11:34; 22:53; John 8:12; Rom. 13:12; I Cor. 4:5; Eph. 5:11).

5. Presenting supernatural events (Gen. 15:12; Exod. 10:21; Matt. 27:45; Rev. 8:12; 16:10).

6. A sign of the Lord's return (Joel 2:2; Amos 5:8; Isa. 60:2; Matt. 24:29).

7. An agency of eternal punishment (Matt. 22:13; II Pet. 2:4,17; Jude 6,7; see also Job 2:1-5; 20:20).

8. It describes spiritual blindness (Isa. 9:2; John 1:5; I John 1:5; 2:8; Eph. 5:8), sorrow and distress (Isa. 8:22; 13:10; Ps. 23:4). It never holds sway where the Redeemer has come to shed His light (Col. 1:13).

DARKON (dȧr'kŏn), a descendant of Solomon's servant, Jaala, who returned with Zerubbabel from exile (Ezra 2:56).

DATHAN (dā'thăn), a great-grandson of Reuben (Num. 16:1). He, with his brothers, Abiram and Korah, rebelled against Moses (Num. 16:1-15), for which sin they were swallowed by the earth (Num. 16:31-35; see also Num. 26).

DAUGHTER (dô'têr), is a word of various uses in the Bible. It refers to both persons and things, often without regard to kinship or sex. There is the familiar usage of child to parent (Gen. 6:1; 20:12; 24:23; Judg. 11:34; Matt. 15:28). Not prized as highly as sons they were sometimes sold into slavery (Exod. 21:7). The word is used to indicate a remoter relationship, as when Rebekah is called "my master's brother's daughter" (Gen. 24:48) although she was the speaker's granddaughter (Gen. 24:15,24). It often refers to any female descendant, regardless of the nearness of relations (Luke 1:5), Jacob's sons called their sister a daughter (Gen. 34:13-17; see Ps. 45:13; 144:12). It represents women in general (Gen. 28:6; Num. 25:1). It was often used in the figurative sense, referring to offspring (Isa. 22:4; Jer. 9:1; Lam. 4:10); to those who worshiped the true God (Ps. 45:10; S. of Sol. 1:5; 3:11; Isa. 62:11; Zech. 9:9; Matt. 21:5; John 12:15). Physical means of making music, the mouth, ears, etc., were called daughters of music (Eccl. 12:4).

DAVID (dā'vĭd, Heb. *Dāwîdh, beloved* or, as in ancient Mari, *chieftain,* BA 11 1948, p. 17), Israel's greatest king, described in I Samuel 16 through I Kings 2:11 (I Chron. 11-29), plus many of the Psalms, he ranks with Moses as one of the most commanding figures in the Old Testament.

David was born in 1040 B.C. (II Sam. 5:4), the youngest son of Jesse of Bethlehem (I Sam. 16:10-11), and developed in strength, courage, and attractiveness while caring for his father's sheep (16:12, 17:34-36). When God rejected Saul, the prophet Samuel sought out David and secretly anointed him as Israel's next king; and the youth became correspondingly filled with God's Spirit (16:13). Saul, meanwhile, summoned David to periodic appearances at court, to soothe his own demon-possessed mind by skillful harp-playing (16:18, 17:15). While still in his teens, David gained national renown and the friendship of Saul's son Jonathan (18:1-3; cf. 20:12-16, 23: 16-17) through his faith-inspired victory over the Philistine champion Goliath (17:45-47). Saul's growing jealousy and four insidious attempts on David's life served only to increase the latter's popularity (cf. 18:13-16,27). At length, urged on by David's rivals (cf. Ps. 59:12), Saul openly sought his destruction; and, though frustrated by Samuel and the priests at Nob, he did succeed in driving David into a life of outlawry (I Sam. 19: 11, 21:9).

David fled to Philistine Gath, but his motives became suspect. Only by a stratagem and by God's grace (I Sam. 21:12, Ps. 56:3, 34:6-8) did he reach the wilderness cave of Adullam in Judah (Ps. 142:6). Here David was joined by the priest Abiathar, who had escaped Saul's retaliatory attack upon Nob (cf. Ps. 52:1), and by a variety of malcontents [I Sam. 22:2]. On three separate occasions Saul attempted to seize David: when fellow-Judeans from Ziph betrayed his presence, after his deliverance of Keilah (I Sam. 23, Ps. 54: 3); at the cave of En-gedi by the Dead Sea, where Saul was caught in his own trap (I Sam. 24, Ps. 7: 4, 57:6); and upon David's return to Ziphite territory, when he again spared his pursuer's life (I Sam. 26). Near the end of 1012 B.C., however (27:7), David in despair sought asylum in Gath, feigning vassalage (27:8-12; 28).

Upon the destruction of Saul at Mt. Gilboa in 1010 B.C. and the Philistine domination of Israel from Beth-shan (cf. the demonstrated abandonment of Gibeah, Saul's capital, G. Ernest Wright, *Biblical Archaeology,* Philadelphia: Westminster, 1957, pp. 122-123), David composed his moving lament of "The Bow" (II Sam. 1:19-27),

A "modern David," a shepherd boy with sling. © MPS

Bethlehem, the City of David, with a shepherd and his flock, illustrative of David's younger life. © MPS

the authenticity of which is unquestionable (R. H. Pfeiffer, *Introduction to the Old Testament,* New York: Harper, 1941, p. 351). Shortly thereafter, David's forces advanced inland to Hebron, where he was declared king over Judah. His appeal, however, to the northern and eastern tribes elicited no response (II Sam. 2:7); and for five years most of Israel lay under Philistine control.

In 1005 B.C. Saul's general, Abner, enthroned Ish-bosheth, a son of the former monarch; but in the conflict that followed David's arms gained ascendancy. Abner himself eventually transferred his support to David, only to be treacherously slain by David's vengeful commander, Joab (II Sam. 3); But after the death of Ish-bosheth (II Sam. 4) all Israel acclaimed David king, 1003 B.C. (II Sam. 5:1-5; I Chron. 11:10, 12:38).

Realizing that their "vassal" had gotten out of hand, the Philistines undertook an all-out attack upon reunited Israel. David, however, after an initial retreat to Adullam (II Sam. 5:17, 23:13-17), expelled the enemy in two divinely-directed campaigns (5:18-25; cf. the archaeological confirmation of his reoccupation of Beth-shan, Wm. F. Albright, *The Archaeology of Palestine and the Bible,* New York: Revell, 1932, pp. 40-44). He next established a new capital by capturing the Jebusite stronghold of Jerusalem. This strategic site on the Benjamite border served not only as an incomparable fortress, vulnerable only to the "scaling hooks" of Joab (II Sam. 5:8; Merrill F. Unger, *Archaeology and the Old Testament,* Grand Rapids: Zondervan, 1954, pp. 206-208), but also as a neutral location between the rival tribes of N and S. David then constructed "Millo," a fortification (?) that "filled up" Jerusalem's breached northern wall (R. A. S. Macalister, *A Century of Excavation in Palestine,* New York: Revell, 1925, pp. 104-106). Actually, because of Maccabean demolitions on the hill Ophel (David's City of Zion), no ruins survive that may be assigned him with confidence, though Davidic fortifications have been uncovered at Debir and Bethshemesh. Joab, for his bravery was confirmed as commander (I Chron. 11:6). Under him were organized twelve corps of militia, each with 24,000 men, on periods of one-month duty annually (I Chron. 27). David's military organization also included the professional Cherethites and Pelethites (Cretans and Philistines) and certain elite groups: "the 600" mighty men (II Sam. 15:18; cf. I Sam. 27:2), "the 30" heroes, and "the 3" most distinguished (II Sam. 23; I Chron. 11).

David also elevated Jerusalem into his religious capital by installing Moses' ark of the covenant in a tent on Zion (Ps. 24; II Sam. 6; cf. Num. 4:15 on the death of Uzzah). He honored it, both with a dedicatory psalm (I Chron. 16, from Pss. 96, 105, 106) and with a permanent ministry of Levitical singers under Asaph (I Chron. 25; 16:5,37, 42). Once criticized as post-exilic fiction, these regular *shārîm* have been authenticated by even earlier Canaanitish parallels from Ugarit (Unger, *op. cit.*, pp. 215-218; cf. BA 4 (1941), pp. 33-47). Eventually David organized 38,000 Levites under hereditary leaders, appointing them as doorkeepers, treasurers, or even district judges (I Chron. 23-26). The Aaronic priests he divided into 24 rotating courses, which were continued into NT times (I Chron. 24:10; Luke 1:5).

From 1002 to about 995 B.C., David expanded his kingdom on all sides: W against Philistia, taking Gath, one of its five ruling cities (II Sam. 8:1); E against Moab, (8:2); N against Syria, in two campaigns (10:13 and 18, cf. 8:3), to the Euphrates River; and S against stubborn Edom (I Kings 11:15; Ps. 60:10). An alliance with Hiram of Tyre enabled David to construct a palace in Jerusalem (II Sam. 5:11). David's political organization shows analogies with Egypt's, his "cabinet" (8:15-18) including such officers as the recorder (public relations official), the scribe (secretary of state; Albright, *Archaeology and the Re-*

The structure known as David's Tower, near the Joppa Gate, at Jerusalem. © MPS

ligion of Israel, Baltimore: Johns Hopkins, 1953, p. 120), and other later additions (20:23-26). Over all, however, whether tribal princes (I Chron. 27:16-24) or royal officials (27:25-31), David reigned supreme.

Rest ensued (II Sam. 7:1; 22:1-51 = Ps. 18), and David proposed a permanent temple for Jehovah in Jerusalem. But while the Prophet Nathan denied David the privilege of building God's house (because of excessive bloodshed, I Chron. 22:8; 28:3), he revealed that God would build David's "house," raising up his son to construct the temple (II Sam. 7:13a) and establishing his dynasty (7:13b), to culminate in the incarnation of God's eternal Son (7:14). This "Davidic covenant" (Ps. 89:3; 132:12) mediates Christian salvation for all (Isa. 55:3; Rev. 22:16), climaxing God's promises, begun in Genesis 3:15 and accomplished in the new testament of Jesus Christ. God's Spirit then inspired David to compose Messianic psalms, depicting the deity of Jehovah's anointed Son (Ps. 2), His eternal priesthood (Ps. 110), His atoning death (Ps. 22), and His resurrection, ascension, and coming kingdom (Pss. 2, 16, 68). Some of David's greatest achievements lie in this literary sphere. Of the 150 canonical psalms, 73 possess titles asserting Davidic authorship. These references, moreover, appear in the oldest MSS and warrant full acceptance (Robert Dick Wilson, PTR 24 (1926), pp. 353-395). David also composed some of the titleless psalms (cf. Pss. 2, 95; Acts 4:25; Heb. 4:7); he stimulated Asaph and his associates to the inscripturation of others; and the king personally compiled the first book of the Psalter (Pss. 1-41; cf. his closing doxology in 41:13). One of the world's best loved compositions is David's heart-affirmation, "The Lord is my shepherd . . ." (Ps. 23).

Yet soon after this, David lapsed into a series of failures (Mephibosheth's appearance [II Sam. 9] could not have preceded 995 B.C. [9:12, 4:4], nor could Solomon's birth [12:24] have been long subsequent). He slew seven innocent descendants of Saul (but not Mephibosheth, 21:7) to enforce a promise rashly made to pagan Gibeonites (contrast Num. 35:33). He committed adultery with Bath-sheba and murdered her husband to conceal his crime (II Sam. 10-11). When exposed by Nathan, he humbly confessed his sin (the great penitential psalms 32 and 51); but the testimony of God's people had suffered compromise, and Nathan condemned the king to corresponding punishments (II Sam. 12:10-14). David also became guilty of ineffective control over his sons. Thus in about 990 B.C. Amnon, following his father's shameful example (13:1-14), raped his sister Tamar; and two years later Absalom avenged Tamar by murdering Amnon (13:23-29). Until about 983 B.C. (13:38; 14:28) David shunned Absalom's presence; and four years later (15:7 ASVmg) Absalom revolted, driving his father from Jerusalem (cf. Pss. 3, 63) and specifically fulfilling Nathan's curses (II Sam. 16:20-22). Through fatal delay, Absalom was defeated and slain by Joab, though only the latter's stern rebuke could shake David from irresponsible grief over the death of his son (18:33-19:8). Even after David's restoration to Jerusalem, inter-tribal jealousies led Sheba of Benjamin to prolong the disorder (II Sam. 20).

David's last years (975-970 B.C.) were occupied with Philistine wars (21:15-22) and with a military census, motivated by David's pride in his armed forces (24:3,9; Ps. 30:6). Plague resulted. But when the destroying angel halted at Araunah's threshing floor on Mt. Moriah, just N of Jerusalem

(II Chron. 3:1), this area became marked as
David's place of sacrifice and the very house of
God (I Chron. 22:1; Ps. 30 title). David subsequently undertook massive preparations for the
temple (I Chron. 22); he received in writing from
God's Spirit the plans for its construction (28:12,
19); and he solemnly charged Solomon and the
princes with their execution (I Chron. 22, 28-29).
As David became increasingly incapacitated by
age, his oldest surviving son, Adonijah, attempted
to usurp the throne from Solomon, the divinely
designated heir. Nathan, however, aroused David
to proclaim Solomon's coronation (I Kings 1).
Thus in 970 B.C., after a final charge to his son
(2:2-9), David died. His last words were a prophecy of the future Davidic Messiah and of his own
salvation, springing from this covenant (II Sam.
23:5).   J.B.P.

DAVID, CITY OF, a part of the Jerusalem plateau,
2500 feet above sea-level. This plateau is bounded
on the E by the Kidron Valley and on the W
and S by the Hinnom, which show a 500 ft. drop
to their southeastern junction. It is connected on
the N with the central ridge of Palestine and is
bisected by a smaller valley, the Tyropoeon. Western Jerusalem, the "Upper City," is larger and
higher and, since the fourth Christian century, has
been designated (erroneously) the City of David.
The eastern half, however, the peak of which is
called Ophel or Zion (I Kings 8:1; II Chron. 33:
14), possesses Jerusalem's chief water-supply (the
Gihon spring, in the Kidron Valley) and marks
the true City of David (II Chron. 32:30).

Mixed Canaanite settlement on Zion (Ezek. 16:
3) dates back to the third millennium. The area
occupied was small, about 1250 x 400 ft.; but a
Jebusite wall, 27 feet in width, rendered the natural
cliffs almost impregnable (cf. the "descent" noted
in Neh. 3:15-16; 12:37). David, however, scaled
the stronghold in 1003 B.C., made it his capitol,
and called it and the surrounding town the "City
of David" (II Sam. 5:9, 6:10; I Chron. 11:7).
He is known to have constructed fortifications, palaces and other government houses, and a tent for
God's ark (II Sam. 5:11; I Kings 3:1, 9:24; I
Chron. 11:8, 15:1,29; II Chron. 8:11); but no certainly Davidic structures have been recovered.
David and his successors were buried in the City
of David (I Kings 2:10, 11:43; 15:8; II Chron.
16:14, 21:20, 24:16, etc.).

Solomon enlarged Jerusalem beyond the City of
David to include Mt. Moriah, for the temple and
other buildings, on the N (I Kings 8:1) and probably part of the western plateau opposite Ophel.
In the eighth century, Hezekiah seems to have extended the City of David southward to include the
new Pool of Siloam, for his water tunnel from
Gihon (II Chron. 32:4-5,30; II Kings 20:20; Isa.
22:9-11). By the time of Josiah, 621 B.C., Jerusalem also included the *mishneh* or "second quarter,"
W of the temple (?) (Zeph. 1:10; II Kings 22:
14); but it was the old City of David which the
Greeks chose to fortify as their citadel during the
Maccabean wars (I Macc. 1:33, 7:32). Simon reoccupied this "Lower City" in 139 B.C. (14:36-
37). He partially leveled the ridge so that it should
not rival Moriah to the north (Jos. *Ant.* XIII,
vi,7), and the name Ophel (Ophlas) was shifted
to the area between the old City and the temple.
After A.D. 70 the original City of David was
abandoned and now lies outside the walls of Jerusalem.

In Luke 2:11, the Christmas angels identified
David's native town of Bethlehem as "the city of
David."   J.B.P.

Above, site of the City of David at Jerusalem, the
walls of Zion and the Citadel, viewed from the market
place at the Pool of Gihon. Below, the Mosque marking the Tomb of David on Mount Zion. © MPS

DAY (Heb. *yôm,* Gr. *heméra*), a word often misinterpreted because of its various uses in the Bible.
It often denotes time from sunrise to sunset (Gen.
1:5; Ps. 74:16). At an early date it was divided
into three parts—morning, noon, and evening
(Ps. 55:17; Dan. 6:10). Probably due to Medo-
Persian influence after the Exile, it was divided
into 12 hours (John 11:9). Early morning was the
first hour; the sixth hour was noon. Time could
not be determined by clocks, so the length of an
hour depended upon the time of the year. The
word also refers to time in general (Judg. 18:30;
Obad. 12; Job 18:20). It is also used figuratively,
referring to the day of judgment (Isa. 2:12; Joel
1:15; Amos 5:18; Rom. 13:12), the length of life
(Gen. 5:4), the time of opportunity (John 9:4),
and any time (Prov. 12:16 ASV, note 3). J.D.F.

DAY OF ATONEMENT (Heb. *yŏm hakkipūrîm*), the annual day of atonement when the high priest offered sacrifices for the sins of the nation (Lev. 23:27; 25:9). It was the only fast period required by Mosaic law (Lev. 16:29; 23:31). It came in August and was preceded by special sabbaths (Lev. 23:24). Instituted in recognition of man's inability to offer full atonement for his sins (Heb. 10:1-10), it was a day of great solemnity and strictest conformity to the law. The elaborate ritual, given in Leviticus 16, was as follows: 1. The high priest sanctified himself by a ceremonial bath and putting on white garments (v. 4). 2. He made atonement for himself and the other priests by sacrificing a bullock (Num. 29:8). 3. A goat was chosen by lot for a sin offering and sacrificed before the congregation (Lev. 16:8,9); blood from the bullock first and then the goat, was sprinkled on and about the mercy seat after the Holy of Holies had been sanctified by incense (vv. 12,14,15); a scapegoat was sent into the wilderness, the anti-type of the promised "Sin-bearer" (vv. 20-22); the high priest changed his garments, after a second ceremonial bath, and made the final offering (vv. 23-28).

J.D.F.

Sketch of the High Priest in the Holy of Holies on the Day of Atonement, after DeVries. JHK

DAY OF CHRIST, a term used in the NT to indicate the redemptive ministry of Jesus, both while in the flesh and upon His return. Sometimes it is called "that day" (Matt. 7:22) and "the day" (I Cor. 3:13). It refers to the return of Jesus for his own and for the judgment of unbelievers (I Cor. 1:8; 5:5; II Cor. 1:14; Phil. 1:6,10; 2:16; II Thess. 2:2,3). It is for the completion of the redemptive work (II Thess. 2:1,13). It is the day of triumph (Phil. 2:9-11). Paul's epistles, especially, are suffused with the longing for the day of Christ when He will manifest Himself in glory and establish His kingdom.

DAY OF THE LORD, an eschatological term referring to the consummation of God's kingdom and triumph over His foes and deliverance of His people. It begins at the second coming and will include the final judgment. It will remove class distinction (Isa. 2:12-21), abolish sins (II Pet. 3:11-13) and will be accompanied by social calamities and physical cataclysms (Matt. 24; Luke 21:7-33). It will include the millennial judgment (Rev. 4:1-19:6) and culminate in the new heaven and the new earth (Isa. 65:17; 66:22; Rev. 21:1).

DAYSMAN (dāz'măn, Heb. *yākhah, to act as umpire*), a mediator or arbitrator—one who has set a day for hearing a dispute. As used in Job 9:33, the word means an umpire or referee who hears two parties in a dispute and decides the merits of the case. In eastern lands it was the custom for the judge to put his hands upon the heads of the two parties in disagreement to show his authority and desire to render an unbiased verdict. Job means that no human being is worthy of acting as a judge of God.

DAYSPRING (dā'sprĭng, Heb. *shahar, to break forth*), a poetic name for dawn (Job 38:12). It describes the advent of Messiah (Luke 1:78).

DAYSTAR (Gr. *phosphóros, light-giving*), the planet Venus, seen as a morning star, heralding the dawn. The prophet compared the splendor of the king of Babylon to Lucifer, son of the morning (Isa. 14:12; in RV daystar). Jesus calls Himself "the bright and morning star" (Rev. 22:16). In II Peter 1:19 the word daystar is applied to Christ.

DEACON, DEACONESS (dē'kŭn, dē'kŭn-ĕs, Gr. *diákonos, servant*). Paul called himself a deacon (I Cor. 3:5; Eph. 3:7). Jesus was declared to be a deacon of the circumcision (Rom. 15:8). He said, "If anyone will serve me" (*Emoí tis diakoné*) . . . "where I am, there shall also my servant (*diákonos*) be" (John 12:26). Household servants were *diakónoi* (Matt. 22:13). Paul told Timothy how to be a good *diákonos* (I Tim. 4:6). The diaconate, as a church office, is based by inference upon Acts 6:1-8, but at least two of the seven men were evangelists. Ignatius, a contemporary of the Apostle John, declared that the deacons were not mere servers of meat and drink. But they did serve (*diakonein*) tables, so that the apostles could give themselves to the ministry (*diakonía*) of the Word. Their successors came to be recognized as church officers. Qualifications given in I Timothy 3 show that they were not considered ordinary lay members of the church. Paul's mention of deacons in connection with bishops (Phil. 1:1) supports the view. Clement of Rome based the office upon the two classes of synagogue workers given in Isaiah (60:17,LXX translation) where pastors and helpers are named. *Deaconess* is from the same Greek word. Phebe was named by Paul as a deaconess (Rom. 16:1). Certain women ministered (*diekónoun*) unto Jesus (Luke 8:2,3). It does not appear from the Scripture or early church literature that deaconesses were ever church officers. J.D.F.

DEAD SEA, called in Scripture the Salt Sea (Gen. 14:3), Sea of the Arabah ("plain," Deut. 3:17), or East(ern) Sea (Joel 2:20; Zech. 14:8 ASV). It has the earth's lowest surface, 1290 ft. below sea-level. Occupying a geologic fault that extends from Syria through the Red Sea into Africa, it measures 47 x 10 miles (approximately 300 sq. mi.). Cliffs rise 1500-2500 ft. on either shore. North of Lisan, "the tongue" (Josh 15:2 ASVmg), the water's depth attains 1300 ft., though southward it averages less than ten. The Sea is slowly expanding, as the muddy Jordan extends its northern delta. Salt concentration reaches 25%, four times that of ocean water. Magnesium bromide prevents organic life; the climate is arid, and the heat extreme.

Though man's historical access to the Dead Sea has been slight, five streams S of Lisan recommended the Plain of Siddim to Lot as a "well-watered garden," 2090 B.C. (Gen. 13:10). Yet writing some 600 yrs. later Moses explained, "The same is the Salt Sea" (14:3 ASV), a fact suggested by the known growth of the Sea (once crossable at Lisan), by his mention of "slime pits" (bitumen, 14:10 ASVmg) now active on the Sea's floor (cf. Josephus' name, "Lake Asphaltites," *Ant.* i, 9,1), and by contemporaneous ruins discovered on Lisan (BA 5, May 1942). God's destruction of Sodom in 2067 B.C. may thus reflect the area's combustibleness (19:24,28); and Jebel Usdùm, "mountain of Sodom," still identifies an extensive rock-salt formation opposite Zoar (cf. 19:26; Luke 17:32).

The Dead Sea constituted Israel's eastern border (Num. 34:12; Ezek. 47:18). At En-gedi, which terminates the principal descent from Judah, a spring provided refuge for David, 1015 B.C. (I Sam. 24:1). The Valley of Salt, S of the Sea, witnessed the victories of David and of Amaziah, 790 B.C., over Edom (I Chron. 18:12; II Kings 14: 7) and countermarches in the days of Jehoshaphat (II Chron. 20:1-2; II Kings 3:8-9; the "Moabite Stone"). On the E shore above the Arnon, the springs of Callirhoe served Herod the Great during his final illness (4 B.C.); and at Machaerus his son Herod Antipas imprisoned John the Baptist (Mark 1:14; 6:17). On the W shore, above En-gedi lies Khirbet Qumran, site of the NT Essene community with its famous scrolls; and opposite Lisan rises Masada, Palestine's finest natural fortress, the refuge of Herod against Parthians in 42 B.C., and the last stand of Jerusalem's zealots in A.D. 70 (Jos. *Wars* VII, x,1). In modern times the Dead Sea has produced potash; but Ezekiel predicts a healing of its waters, granting abundant life in God's kingdom-age (47:8-10).

J.B.P.

DEAD SEA SCROLLS, discovered, probably in 1947, by Arabic Bedouin and brought to the attention of the scholarly world late that year and early in 1948. The discoveries were made in caves located in the marly cliffs, a mile or so W of the northwestern corner of the Dead Sea, at a place known by the modern Arabic name of Qumran, which is near a copious spring of fresh water known as Ain Feshkha. This location is at the eastern edge of the Wilderness of Judah. Accordingly, alternate names for the discoveries including "Qumran," "Ain Feshkha," or "Wilderness of Judah" are sometimes used.

The scrolls were seen by several scholars in the latter part of 1947, some of whom have admitted that they passed them up as forgeries. One of the scholars who recognized the antiquity of the scrolls was the late Professor Eleazar L. Sukenik of Hebrew University, who was subsequently successful in purchasing some of them. Other scrolls were taken to the American School of Oriental Research in Jerusalem, where the Acting Director *pro tempore,* Dr. John C. Trever, convinced of their value, arranged to photograph the portions which were brought to him. One of his photographs was sent to Professor William F. Albright, who promptly declared that this was *"the most important discovery ever made* in Old Testament manuscripts."

The scrolls which were purchased by the Hebrew University included *the Hebrew University*

Above, colossal salt slabs in the cliffs of Jebel Usdum (the Hill of Sodom) at the southern end of the Dead Sea. Below, the vast salt pans and mud flats where the Jordan enters the Dead Sea at the north; this view is looking southeast, with the mountains of Moab in the distance. © MPS

Isaiah Scroll (1QIs^b), which is a partial scroll of the book, the *Order of Warfare,* also known as the *War of the Sons of Light against the Sons of Darkness* (1QM), and the *Thanksgiving Hymns* or *Hodayot* (1QH). The scrolls purchased by the Syrian archbishop and published by the American Schools of Oriental Research included the *St. Mark's Isaiah Scroll* (1QIs^a) which is a complete scroll of the book, the *Habakkuk Commentary* (1QpHab) which contains the text of chapters one and two of Habakkuk with a running commentary, and the *Manual of Discipline* (1QS), which contains the rules for the members of the Qumran community. These all have subsequently come into the possession of the State of Israel and are housed in a shrine in the Hebrew University, Jerusalem.

The ruins and excavations at Qumran, less than a mile from the northwestern shore of the Dead Sea. These are the remains of the monastery of the Essene Community of the first century B.C. © MPS

Israel. They have been published in numerous editions and translated into many languages, and are readily available for anyone who wishes to study them either in translation or in facsimile.

Following the discovery of these important scrolls, which are now all but unanimously accepted as having come from the last century B.C. and the first century A.D., the region from which they came was systematically explored. Numerous caves were found, and so far eleven caves have yielded materials from the same period as the original scrolls. Most of these materials have come from the fourth cave explored (known as Cave Four or 4Q); others of significance come from Cave Two, Five, and Six. According to recent reports the most significant discoveries are those from Cave Eleven (11Q).

At least 382 manuscripts are represented by the fragments of Cave Four alone, about 100 of which are Biblical manuscripts. These include fragments of every book of the Hebrew Bible except Esther. Some of the books are represented in many copies: e.g., 14 different manuscripts of Deuteronomy, 12 manuscripts of Isaiah, and 10 manuscripts of Psalms are represented in Cave Four; other fragments of these same books have been found in other caves. Almost complete scrolls of Psalms and Leviticus have been found in Cave Eleven, but these have not yet been published. One of the significant finds, which may turn out to have important bearing on the theories of date and authorship, concerns the Book of Daniel, fragments of which have been found with the change from He-

brew to Aramaic in Daniel 2:4 and from Aramaic to Hebrew in 7:28-8:1, exactly as in our modern texts of Daniel.

In addition to Biblical books, fragments of Deuterocanonical writings have been found, specifically Tobit and Ecclesiasticus, as well as fragments of several noncanonical writings. Some of these latter were already known, such as Jubilees, Enoch, the Testament of Levi, etc.; others were not previously known, such as the peculiarly Qumranian documents: the Thanksgiving Psalms, the Book of Warfare, the commentaries on portions of Scripture, etc. These last give us insights into the nature and beliefs of the community at Qumran.

Near the cliffs on an alluvial plateau overlooking the shore of the Dead Sea is the site of an ancient building complex often referred to as the "Monastery." This was thoroughly excavated over several seasons, and has yielded important data about the nature, size, and date of the Qumran community. From coins found there, together with other remains, the community has been dated within the limits of 140 B.C. and A.D. 67. The members were almost all male, although the literature contains provisions for the admission of women and children. The number of living there at any one time was in the neighborhood of two to four hundred. A mile or so S at Ain Feshkha were found the remains of other buildings, the nature of which is not exactly clear. The fresh water of the spring probably was used for the growing of crops and other needs of the community.

The Qumran caves, where the Dead Sea Scrolls were discovered. In foreground is cave No. 4, where the main library of the Essenes was found. © MPS

From the sect's literature we know that the people of Qumran were Jews who had split off from the Jerusalem or main stream of Judaism, and indeed were quite critical of and even hostile toward the priests at Jerusalem. The fact that they used the name, "The Sons of Zadok" has suggested to some scholars that they should be connected with the Zadokites or Sadducees; other scholars believe that they are rather to be identified with the Essenes, a third sect of Judaism described by Josephus and Philo. It is not impossible that elements of truth are to be found in both of these theories and that there was originally a split in the priestly or Sadducean line which first joined the movement known as the Hasidim, the forerunners of the Pharisees, ultimately to split again and form a narrow separatist group part of which located at Qumran. We must await further discoveries before we attempt to give a final answer to this entire problem.

The community devoted itself to the study of the Bible. The life of the community was largely ascetic, and their practices included ritual bathing, sometimes referred to as baptism. This has been understood by some to be the origin of the baptism of John the Baptist. A study of John's baptism alongside that of the Qumranians shows, however, that the two practices were quite distinct; hence, if John did come from this community (which is not yet proven and may never be), he must have developed important distinctions in his own doctrine and practice of baptism.

Some scholars believe that Zoroastrian elements are to be found in the Qumran writings, particularly with reference to dualism and angelology. The problem is extremely complex. Zoroastrian dualism developed greatly in post-Christian times, and therefore it is precarious to assume that the Zoroastrian beliefs as we know them represent the beliefs a century or two before the time of Christ.

The discoveries at Qumran are important for Biblical studies in general. The matter of the canon is not necessarily affected, since the group at Qumran was a schismatic group in the first place, and, moreover, the absence of Esther does not necessarily imply that they rejected this book from the canon. In the matter of the text of the Old Testament, however, the Dead Sea Scrolls are of great importance. The text of the Greek Old Testament (or the Septuagint), as well as the quotations of the Old Testament in the New, indicate that there were other texts beside the one that has come down to us (the Masoretic Text). The study of the Dead Sea Scrolls makes it clear that at the time of their production, which would be about the time of the production of the Scriptures used by the New Testament authors, there were at least three texts in existence: one we might call the ancestor of the Masoretic Text; the second was a text closely related to that used by the translators of the Septuagint; the third was a text differing from both of these other texts. The differences are not great and at no point do they involve doctrinal matters; but for careful textual study of the Old Testament it is important that we free ourselves from the notion that the Masoretic Text is the only authentic

Fragment of the Dead Sea scroll of the Habakkuk commentary, found in cave No. 4 at Qumran. MPS ©SB

text. As a matter of fact, the quotations of the Old found in the New Testament rather imply that it was not the Masoretic Text which was most commonly in use by New Testament authors. These statements should be qualified by pointing out that the quality of the text varies from book to book in the Old Testament, and that there is much more uniformity in the text of the Pentateuch than in some of the other portions of the Hebrew Bible. The Dead Sea Scrolls have particularly made great contributions to the study of the text of Samuel.

In relation to the New Testament, the Dead Sea Scrolls are likewise of importance. There are no New Testament texts in the discoveries at Qumran, obviously, since the earliest book of the New Testament had been written only very shortly be-

Close-up view of the Dead Sea scroll entitled "The War of the Sons of Light against the Sons of Darkness." MPS © SB

fore the destruction of the Qumran community. Moreover, there was no reason why any of the New Testament writings should have reached Qumran. On the other hand, there are certain references and presuppositions found in the New Testament, particularly in the preaching of John the Baptist and Jesus Christ, and in the writings of Paul and John, which are placed against a background now recognizably similar to that furnished by the documents from Qumran. Thus, for example, the Gnostic background found in certain Pauline writings and formerly thought to be second century Greek Gnosticism—thus requiring a late date for the composition of Colossians—is now recognized as a Jewish Gnosticism of the first century or earlier. Similarly the Fourth Gospel is shown to be Palestinian and not Hellenistic.

A great deal has been written concerning the relationship of Jesus Christ to the Qumran community. There is no evidence in the Qumran documents that Jesus was a member of the sect, and nothing in the New Testament requires such a position. Rather, the outlook of Jesus with reference to the world and particularly toward His own people is diametrically opposite that of Qumran, and it can be safely asserted that He was not a member of that group at any time. He may have had some disciples who had come out of that background, particularly those who were formerly disciples of John the Baptist—though this is far from proven. The attempt to show that the Qumran Teacher of Righteousness was the pattern for the Gospel portrayal of Jesus cannot be established on the basis of the Dead Sea Scrolls. The Teacher of Righteousness was a fine young man with high ideals who died untimely; there is, however, no clear statement that he was put to death, certainly

Looking out of the mouth of cave No. 4, with remains of the Essene Monastery in the distance. © MPS

no indication that he was crucified or rose from the dead or that the Qumranians expected him to return. The difference between Jesus and the Teacher of Righteousness stands out clearly at several points: the Teacher of Righteousness was never referred to as the Son of God or God Incarnate; his death was not sacrificial in its nature; the sacramental meal (if such it was indeed) was not viewed as a memorial of his death or a pledge of his return in any way connected with the forgiveness of sin. Obviously in the case of Jesus Christ, all of these things are clearly asserted, not once but repeatedly in the New Testament, and indeed form a necessary basis without which there is no Christian faith.   W.S.L.S.

BIBLIOGRAPHY: F. F. Bruce, *Second Thoughts on the Dead Sea Scrolls.* Millar Burrows, *The Dead Sea Scrolls; More Light on the Dead Sea Scrolls.* William Sanford LaSor, *Amazing Dead Sea Scrolls and the Christian Faith; A Bibliography of the Dead Sea Scrolls, 1948-1957.*

DEATH. In the Bible the word is used in various senses.

It refers to cessation of natural life: Abraham (Gen. 25:11), Aaron's wicked sons (Lev. 16:1), Moses (Deut. 34:5), a woman in travail (1 Sam. 4:20), a father (Matt. 8:22), David's child (II Sam. 12:23), a thief (Mark 15:27), even the son of Man (Mark 15:37), from every age and class death takes its victims. It is pictured as the departure of the spirit from the body (II Tim. 4:6), as being inevitable (Josh. 23:14), as laying aside the body (II Cor. 5:1), as the return to the former natural state (Eccl. 3:20; 12:7). It is pictured as a sleep (Jer. 51:39; Dan. 12:2; John 11:11; Acts 7:60). It is a state in which God is not seen (Isa. 38:11; Job 35:14), nor praised (Ps. 6:5; Isa. 38:18). It is the result of sin (Gen. 2:17; Rom. 5:21; 6:23; I Cor. 15:56; Heb. 2:14; James 1:15). In the spiritual sense death is a separation from God, or spiritual night (Luke 1:79; I John 3:14; Rom. 5:12, 6:23; John 3:36; Eph. 2:1,5; Rev. 2:11). The righteous and wicked go on forever, the righteous to everlasting good (Isa. 35:10, 45:17; Dan. 7:14, 12:2; Rev. 7:17), the evil to eternal torment (Jer. 20:11; Dan. 12:2; Matt. 25:46; Mark 3:29; II Thess. 1:9; Jude 7).

Confusion has arisen in some minds regarding the meaning of passages which seem to teach total destruction of man, whether good or bad. David's plaint over the death of his child (II Sam. 12:21, 22) is cited, but that David knew that death was not the end of rational existence is attested by numerous expressions such as Psalm 23; 62:2,7; 89:26; 116:14, etc. Job's question (14:14) is readily answered by himself (Job 19:25-27). Matthew 10:28 must be interpreted in the light of the discourse which it contains. Such passages as Job 7:9,10; and Psalm 6:5 must be interpreted in the light of other statements by their authors, none of which teaches that sin ultimately annihilates the wicked. Death to the righteous is a glorious experience (Num. 23:10; Ps. 116:15; Rev. 14:13). Jesus has conquered death and removed from it the awful sting (Isa. 25:8, 26:19; Hos. 13:14; John 5:24; I Cor. 15:53-57; I John 5:12; Rev. 1:18).

The second death has been misinterpreted by many, yet the revelation regarding it is plain. It is definitely final separation from God. God's law of the wages of sin included the penalty of death (Gen. 2:17). While physical death was involved, the special penalty was spiritual death, or separation from fellowship with the Creator. Expulsion from Eden typified this. So spiritual death is at

Tell Beit Mirsim, ruins of Debir, ancient Kirjath-sepher in southern Palestine. © MPS

first broken fellowship with Jehovah, with its consequent penalties. Paul so interpreted it (I Cor. 15:21-23). They who are victorious in their faith will not be hurt by the second death (Rev. 2:11), because He who has power over it will never forsake his inheritance (Ps. 94:14). Consummation of the judgment ushers in the second death, eternal and absolute separation from God in the lake of fire and brimstone (Rev. 20:6,14).   J.D.F.

DEBIR (dē'bêr), a city of Judah, once a center of culture for the Canaanite people. Probably it took its name from the pagan temple in which the oracle occupied the holy place (see I Kings 6:5, where *Debhir* is translated "oracle" — Holy of Holies in margin). It is called *Kirjath-sepher*, or "town of books" (Josh. 15:15). It could have been "town of scribes" (*sopher*). In Joshua 15:49 it is called *Kirjath-sannah*. It was SW of Jerusalem, some ten miles west of Hebron and was occupied by the Anakim (Josh. 11:21; 15:14). It was captured by Joshua (10:38,39), evidently retaken by the Canaanites, and captured a second time under Caleb, who gave his daughter as reward to its captor, Othniel being the winner (Josh. 15:13-17). It later became a priestly possession (Josh. 21:15; I Chron. 6:58).

2. *Debir*, a king of Eglon, who made an alliance with the king of Jerusalem against Joshua and was defeated at Gibeon (10:1-11).

3. *Debir*, a town on the border of Gad near Mahanaine (Josh. 13:24-26).

4. A town on the border between Judah and Benjamin (Josh. 15:7), on the road between Jerusalem and Jericho.

DEBORAH (dĕb'ō-rà, Heb. *devôrâh, bee*). 1. Rebekah's beloved wet-nurse (Gen. 24:59, 35:8), who accompanied her former nursling to Palestine — she became attached to Jacob's household and died at great age (c. 2065-1909 B.C.; cf. Gen. 25:20, 35:8) near Bethel, the tree under which she was buried being called '*Allôn-bākhûth* (oak of weeping).

2. The fourth and greatest (with Gideon) of Israel's judges, a prophetess, a wife of Lappidoth (Judg. 4-5). She resided near the border of Benjamin and Ephraim, probably belonging to the latter tribe, and administered justice under "the palm-tree of Deborah" (4:4-5). Like most Hebrew "judges," however, Deborah served primarily as a divinely-appointed deliverer and executive leader of Israel.

After the death of Ehud, God's people had lapsed into apostasy, with the result that He subjected them to the Canaanitish king Jabin II of

Hazor, whose commander, Sisera, "had 900 chariots of iron; and 20 years he mightily oppressed Israel" (4:2-3; cf. James B. Pritchard, *Ancient Near Eastern Texts*, Princeton Univ. Press, 1950, p. 237). This period (c. 1240-1220 B.C.) coincides with the unrest that followed upon Hittite collapse and the death of Egypt's Rameses II, the treaties between which had preserved order in Palestine since the days of Seti I, 80 years before (3:30; cf. John Garstang, *Joshua-Judges*, London: Constable, 1931, pp. 278-283). Rameses' successor, however, was the elderly Merneptah. Despite his claim to have pacified both Canaanites and Israelites (cf. his famous "Israel-stela," Pritchard, *op. cit.*, pp. 376-378), disorder became rampant: "The highways were unoccupied, and . . . was there a shield seen in Israel?" (5:6-8)

Then arose Deborah, "a mother in Israel," (5: 7). Summoning Barak of Naphtali, she prophesied that an offensive from Mt. Tabor at the northeastern limit of Esdraelon would lure Sisera and Jabin's army to annihilation on the plains below (4:6-7). Barak agreed, provided Deborah's inspiring presence should accompany the troops, though Deborah predicted Sisera's death by a woman (4:8-9). Barak and Deborah then scouted Esdraelon around Kedesh (Tell Abu Kudeis, E of Megiddo? Garstang, *op. cit.*, p. 301); they mustered 10,000 men of Naphtali and Zebulun; and, together with princes of Issachar (5:15), they occupied Tabor (4:12). Deborah also summoned Dan and Asher in the N (cut off by Hazor) and Reuben and Gad in Transjordan, who failed to respond (5:16-17; Simeon and Judah in the far S remain unmentioned). But Benjamin, Ephraim, and Machir (Manasseh) answered the call (5:14), probably massing at Jenin at the southeastern edge of Esdraelon (*Ibid.*, pp. 299-300). Deborah thus accomplished Israel's first united action since the conquest, 175 years before.

Sisera, meanwhile, advanced from Harosheth in western Esdraelon, forded the Kishon southward to marshal the Canaanite kings from Jokneam, Megiddo, and Taanach (5:19), and pressed inland along its southern bank. But God in heaven's courses fought against Sisera (5:20). A providential storm (cf. 5:4), which turned the plain into a morass, rendered Sisera's chariotry unmaneuverable, and they were cut to pieces by Israel's wildly charging foot-soldiers. The routed Canaanites, cornered at the Kishon ford, were then swept away by a flash-flood (5:21). Sisera was slain in single flight, by the woman Jael at Kedesh (4:11,17-22); Jabin was destroyed (4:24); and the land rested 40 years (5:31), corresponding to the reign of Rameses III, the last great Pharaoh of Egypt's XXth dynasty. After the battle, Deborah and Barak sang Deborah's song of victory (5:2-31, cf. v. 7), the contemporaneous authenticity of which is universally recognized from its archaic language, vivid descriptions, and ringing faith (v. 31).

Yet Deborah's record has occasioned manifold criticism against Scripture. 1. Textually, her song's admitted antiquity has been used to discredit the reliability of Scripture's earlier prose narratives (ICC, p. 110). But while poetry does tend to preserve archaic forms, the "modernized" Hebrew of the Pentateuch need not affect true Mosaic authorship (cf. R. Laird Harris, "On a Possible Revision of the Biblical Text During the Monarchy," Evangelical Theological Society, *Annual Papers*, 1953, pp. 18-24).

2. Confusion, futhermore, is alleged between Joshua II and Judges 4-5, as two garbled accounts

of one actual battle against Jabin (IB II:683, 712). Yet Joshua's opponent, in 1400 B.C., may have been a predecessor of Deborah's; or "Jabin," a hereditary title in Hazor.

3. Contradictions are discovered between the prose and the poem: fewer tribes fighting in chapter 4, and Sisera killed in his sleep (ICC, pp. 107-108). But the poetry intentionally singles out the tribes; and Sisera's sleeping, in 5:26, is apparently understood; and his "bowing and falling," in 5:27, simply describes his subsequent death-agonies.

4. Within the prose, a conflation is surmised between a King-Jabin story in Kedesh-Naphtali and a King-Sisera story in Esdraelon (ICC, pp. 108-109). Yet the Kedesh of 4:9-11 fits Esdraelon, not Naphtali; and Scripture never designates Sisera "king," only "captain" (an Aegean or Hittite mercenary-adventurer?) of Jabin.

5. The Biblical date of Deborah is lowered a full century by Albright to 1125 B.C. (BASOR 62 (1936), p. 29), but only because of his theory that no Philistines (cf. 5:6, 3:31) could reach Palestine before the 1100's; yet see Genesis 21:34, 26:1!

6. Morally, the charge that the scriptural account of Jael is "reprehensible . . . cannot be justified" (IB II:716). But while we question this Gentile's treacherous methods, Deborah's insight into her fearless and unsolicited devotion to God's people renders her "blessed above women" (5:24).

J.B.P.

DEBT (Heb. *neshî*, Gr. *opheílema, a sum owed, an obligation*). Under Mosaic law Jews were not allowed to exact interest (usury) from other Jews (Exod. 22:25). Special laws protected the poor against usurers (Exod. 22:25-27; Deut. 24:12,13). After the Exile cruel practices arose in collecting debts (II Kings 4:1-7; Isa. 50:1). A debtor had to make good his obligation, so land that was pledged (mortgaged) could be seized, but had to be restored during the Jubilee year (Lev. 25:28). A house so pledged could be sold, or held in perpetuity if not redeemed during a year, unless it was an unwalled town (Lev. 25:29,30). In NT times the Mosaic code was disregarded. We read of bankers, money-changers, interest, usury (Matt. 25:16-27; John 2:13-17). Debtors were often thrown into prison (Matt. 18:21-26). Jesus taught compassion towards those in debt (Matt. 18:23-35). The prayer of Jesus, "forgive us our debts," implies guilt from unpaid moral obligations to God (Matt. 6:12). J.D.F.

DECALOGUE (dĕk'à-lŏg, Gr. *déka, ten* and *logós, word*), the basic laws of the Hebrew state. They were given by God to Moses at Mt. Sinai (Exod. 20). The laws were inscribed on tablets of stone (Deut. 4:13) and were afterwards carried in the ark of the covenant (Deut. 10:2). There is a slight difference between the record in Exodus 20:1-17 and that in Deuteronomy 5:6-21. Catholics and Lutherans unite 1 and 2 and divide 10; Eastern (Greek) Catholics and most Protestants accept the order given in the KJV. Jesus approved the law (Matt. 5:18; 22:40), fulfilled it (Matt. 5:27-48; 23:23), and became the end of the law for righteousness to all who believe (Rom. 10:4; 8:1-4).

DECAPOLIS (dē-kăp'ô-lĭs, Greek *déka, ten, and pólis, city*), a region E of Jordan that had been given to the tribe of Manasseh (Num. 32:33-42). A league of ten cities, consisting of Greeks who had come in the wake of Alexander's conquests, was established after the Romans occupied the area (65 B.C.). According to Ptolemy, the num-

Ruins of Gerasa (modern Jerash), one of the principal cities of the Decapolis, showing the Forum, above, and a general view of the ruins below. © MPS

ber was later increased to 18. They had their own coinage, courts, and army (Jos. XIV:4:4). Ruins of temples, theaters and other buildings tell of the high degree of culture which developed in these cities. Jesus drove the demons into swine near Gadara, one of these cities (Mark 5:1-20), and became popular in the Decapolis (Matt. 4:24,25; Mark 7:31-37).

DECISION, VALLEY OF, where God will some day gather all nations for judgment (Joel 3:2,12). It is called the Valley of Jehoshaphat (*Jehovah judges*), and has been identified by some with the valley of Kidron, but this is only conjecture. Perhaps no particular valley is intended, and the name may be only a symbol of the event.

DECREE, an official ruling or law. It translates various words in the OT such as *'ēsār, interdict* (Dan. 6:7); *gezērāh, decision* (Dan. 4:17); *dāth, law* (Dan. 2:9), In general it refers to any fiat of an official nature. In Esther 1:20, Daniel 3:10, Jonah 3:7, the word refers to laws governing special occasions. In Acts 16:4 the Greek *dogma* means rules for Christian living. God's decree is His settled plan and purpose (Ps. 2:7-10; Dan. 4:24; see also Exod. 32:32; Rev. 13:8).

DEDAN (dē'dăn), an Arabian people descended directly from Noah (Gen. 10:6,7). They established themselves in the region about the northwestern end of the Persian Gulf. They were also related to Abraham by his concubine Keturah (Gen. 25:3). Mention of these people occurs frequently in the Chaldean and Assyrian tablets. Israelites of later generations considered them kinsmen. Dedanites were warned by Jeremiah to flee to the back country (Jer. 49:7,8). They were an important commercial people. Isaiah called

the Dedanites traveling tradesmen (21:13). Ezekiel wrote of their connection with Tyre (27:3,15, 20), and foretold that the destruction of the Dedanim was to accompany that of the Edomites (Ezek. 25:13).   J.D.F.

DEDICATION (Heb. *kādhēsh, to sanctify, hănuk-kâh, to consecrate*), an expression denoting dedication to holy ends. Often used of the consecration of persons, but usually of the setting apart of things for God's use. Consecration of the tabernacle (Num. 7) was an elaborate ceremony, as was that of the temple (I Kings 8). Among various dedicated things were: the city wall (Neh. 12:27), private dwellings (Deut. 20:5), the temple treasure (I Chron. 28:12), the child (Exod. 13:2), people (Exod. 19:14; I Sam. 16:5), and booty of war (II Sam. 8:10,11). The dedication of Nebuchadnezzar's image (Dan. 3:2,3), and of Herod's temple (Jos. XV:11:6), were elaborate occasions.

DEDICATION, FEAST OF, an annual festival of the Jews held throughout the country for eight days, celebrating the restoration of the temple following its desecration at the hands of the Syrians under Antiochus Epiphanes (I Macc. IV: 52-59; II Macc. X:5), of which Josephus gives a graphic picture (Ant. XII:5:4). The feast came on the 25th of Kislev (December). Josephus called it the "Feast of Lights." Like the Feast of Tabernacles, it was a time of pageantry and joy. It was at this feast that Jesus delivered in the temple the discourse recorded in John 10:22ff, at Jerusalem.   J.D.F.

DEEP, a translation of Hebrew and Greek words of varying meaning. Hebrew: *metsûlâh, the ocean* (Neh. 9:11; Job 41:31; Ps. 107:24; Isa. 44:27); *metsôlâh, torment* (Ps. 88:6); *tehôm, chaos* (Gen. 1:2; 7:11); *subterranean water* (Gen. 49:25; Deut. 33:13); *ămîq, mysterious* (Dan. 2:22); *āmōq, depth,* or *power* (Lev. 13:4,31; Job 11:8). Greek: *báthos,* of *water* or *condition* (Luke 5:4; John 4:11; Acts 20:9; II Cor. 8:2); *buthós, sea* (II Cor. 11:25) or *abyss* (Luke 8:31; Rev. 9:1, 11:7).

DEFILE (dē-fīl'). There are a number of Hebrew and Greek words which in general mean *to profane, pollute, render unclean*. In the OT, defilement was physical (S. of Sol. 5:3), sexual (Lev. 18:20), ethical (Isa. 59:3; Ezek. 37:23), ceremonial (Lev. 11:24; 17:15; etc.), and religious (Num. 35:33; Jer. 3:1). In the NT it is ethical or religious (Mark 7:19; Acts 10:15; Rom. 14:20). In the NT the idea of ceremonial or ritual defilement does not exist. In OT times God's purpose in issuing laws regarding ceremonial defilement was clearly an educative one—to impress the Israelites with His holiness and the necessity of their living separate and holy lives.

DEGREE (dē-grē, Heb. *ma'ălāh, a going up* or *ascent,* Gr. *tapeinós, low*). The word *degrees* occurs in the titles of 15 psalms, Psalms 120 to 134, which are called Songs of Degrees. The common opinion regarding the meaning is that they were sung by the pilgrims as they went up to Jerusalem (cf. I Sam. 1:3; Ps. 42:4; 122:4; Isa. 30:29). The word is also used in II Kings 20:9,10, where Hezekiah is told that the sign that the Lord would heal him would be that his sundial would go back ten degrees, and in a secondary sense of rank or order (I Chron. 15:18; 17:17; Ps. 62:9; Luke 1:52; James 1:9).

DEGREES, SONGS OF, the title given Psalms 120-134. Uncertainty exists as to the origin of the title. Some Jewish authorities attributed it to the use made of fifteen steps leading from the court of men to the court of women in the temple. The Levitical musicians performed with these steps as the stage. It is possible that originally the songs were part of a ritual which required the Levities to advance up the steps as they played or sang. Some scholars attribute the title to the way in which the thought advances from step to step, as seen in 121:4,5; 124:1,2,3,4, but all these songs do not do this. Because Ezra (7:9) used the word *hammă'lâh, a going up from Babylon,* some have thought that the title originated when exiles were returning to Jerusalem during the reign of Artaxerxes in Babylon. The most logical explanation is that the title was given the series of hymns because they were used by pilgrims during the annual journeys to the three required feasts in Jerusalem. One tradition has it that Solomon wrote Psalm 132 and the others were written later. They are songs of penitence (120,131), praise (121,128,133, 134), and praise and prayer (122,123,129,132).

J.D.F.

DEKAR (dĕ'kàr), the father of one of Solomon's twelve purveyors (I Kings 4:7-9).

DELAIAH (dē-lā'yà, *raised* or *freed by Jehovah*).
1. A descendant of David (I Chron. 3:1,24).
2. A priest of David's time and leader of the 23rd course of temple service (I Chron. 24:18).
3. A prince who besought Baruch not to burn the sacred roll containing the prophecy of Jeremiah (Jer. 36:12,25).
4. Head of a tribe that returned under Zerubbabel from captivity (Ezra 2:60; Neh. 7:62).
5. The father of Shemaiah who advised Nehemiah to flee (Neh. 6:10).

DELILAH (dē-lī'là, *dainty one*), a Philistine woman from the valley of Sorek, which extends from near Jerusalem to the Mediterranean. By her seductive wiles she learned the secret of Samson's strength and brought him to his ruin (Judg. 16:4-20).

DELUGE (See Flood)

DEMAS (dē'măs, Gr. *Demás, popular*), a faithful helper of Paul during his imprisonment in Rome (Col. 4:14). Paul called him a "fellow laborer" (Philem. 24). He was probably a citizen of Thessalonica to which place he went upon deserting Paul (II Tim. 4:10).

DEMETRIUS (dē-mē'trĭ-ŭs, Gr. *Demétrios, belonging to Demeter*). 1. The disciple whom John praised in his letter to Gaius (III John 12).
2. The jeweler of Ephesus who raised a mob against Paul because his preaching had resulted in damage to his lucrative business of making silver images of the goddess Diana (Acts 19:23-27). The name of one Demetrius, a warden of the Ephesian temple, has been found by modern explorers; he probably was the silversmith. Three kings of Syria bore the name: Demetrius Soter or Saviour (Jos. *Ant.* XII:10;1-4); D. Nikator, or Conqueror (*ibid.* XIII:5,2,3,11); D. Eukarios, the fortunate, (*ibid.* XIII:13;3 and XIV:1;3).

DEMONS (Gr. *daimónion*), evil spirits (Matt. 8: 16, Luke 10:17,20; Matt. 17:18 compare with Mark 9:25). The immaterial and incorporeal nature of both Satan and his demon hosts is graphically set forth by the Apostle Paul in describing the believer's intense conflict as being "not against flesh and blood," but against "principalities," "powers," "world-rulers of this darkness," and "spiritual hosts of wickedness in the heavenly places" (Eph. 6:12). Again the non-material and incorporeal character of demons is hinted in the expression "The prince of the powers of the air,

the spirits that are now at work in the hearts of the sons of disobedience" (Eph. 2:2, Weymouth).

The Apostle John likewise stresses the incorporeality of demons in his reference to the three unclean spirits issuing out of the mouth of the dragon, the beast, and the false prophet as the "spirits of demons" (*pneúmata daimoníon,* Rev. 16:14). The construction is patently a genitive of apposition, more particularly defining the general term "spirits," which may be either good or bad, as in this case, bad, or "demon-spirits."

As purely spiritual beings or personalities, demons operate above the laws of the natural realm and are invisible and incorporeal. The Bible presents them as such, and thus free from magical rites and exorcistic rigmarole, which contaminate ethnic and rabbinic demonology. The Word of God however, does recognize the principle of miracle where natural law may be temporarily transcended and denizens of the spirit world glimpsed (II Kings 6:17; 2:11). On this principle John in apocalyptic vision *saw* the awful last-day eruption of locust-demons from the abyss (Rev. 9:1-12), as well as the three hideous frog-like spirits which emanate from the Satanic trinity (the dragon, the beast and the false prophet) in the Tribulation to muster the world's armies to their predestined doom at Armageddon (Rev. 16: 13-16).

As spirit personalities demons have an intellectual nature through which they possess superhuman knowledge. Plato's etymology of *daimon* from an adjective meaning "knowledge" or "intelligent" (*Cratylus* I, 389) points to intelligence or knowledge as the basic characteristic of demonic nature. Scripture features the perspicacity of demons. They know Jesus (Mark 1:24), bow to Him (Mark 5:6), describe Him as "the Son of the Most High God" (Mark 5:7), entreat Him (Luke 8: 31), obey Him (Matt. 8:16), vitiate sound doctrine (I Tim. 4:1-5), conceal the truth of Christ's incarnate deity and sole Saviourhood (I John 4: 1-3) and comprehend prophecy and their inevitable doom (Matt. 8:29).

Because of their superphysical knowledge, demons are consulted in spiritistic oracles through spiritistic mediums, who allow themselves to get under the control of evil spirits for oracular purposes (I Sam. 28:1-25; Acts 16:16), as is seen in both ancient and modern spiritism, erroneously called "spiritualism."

In their moral nature all demons (as fallen angels) are evil and depraved, in distinction to the good spirits (the unfallen angels), who are sinless. The moral turpitude of demons is everywhere evidenced in Scripture by the harmful effects they produce in their victims, deranging them mentally, morally, physically and spiritually, and by the frequent epithet of "unclean," which often describes them (Matt. 10:1; Mark 1:27; Luke 4:36; Acts 8:7; Rev. 16:13). Fleshly uncleanness and base sensual gratification are the result of demon control of the human personality (Luke 8:27). Demons figure in the moral collapse of a people who yield to gross carnality and sexual sin, so rampant in the world today (II Tim. 3:1-9; Rev. 9:21,22).

In addition to their superhuman intelligence and moral turpitude, demons possess terrible strength, imparting it to the human body (Luke 8:29), and binding their victims as with chains and with physical defects and deformities (Luke 13:11-17), such as blindness (Matt. 12:22), insanity (Luke 8:26-36), dumbness (Matt. 9:32,33) and suicidal mania (Mark 9:22).

An Assyrian demon, Pazuzu, front and rear views of a bronze representation. "The ancient Semitic world was thought of as populated with these creatures, who caused every conceivable kind of trouble. Cuneiform literature abounds with omens, charms and incantations against these evil spirits. This bronze charm was made to insure the efficacy of a charm or incantation uttered against his baneful activity as evil spirit of the southwest wind." OIUC (from Unger, **Archaeology and the Old Testament**)

Demons under the leadership of Satan seek to oppose God's purposes and to hinder man's welfare. So intimately bound up are they with their prince leader that their work and his are identified rather than differentiated. Thus the earthly life of our Lord is said to have consisted in going about "doing good, and healing all that were oppressed of the devil" (Acts 10:38). Certainly much of this so-called oppression by the devil was the work of Satan's minions, the demons, as a cursory examination of the Gospel records will show.

Demons are of two classes — those who are free with the earth and the air as their abode (Cor. 1:13; Eph. 2:2; Eph. 6:11-12) and those who are imprisoned in the abyss (Luke 8:31; Rev. 9:1-11; Rev. 20:1-3). The abyss is only the temporary prison house of evil spirits, which must surrender its doleful inhabitants to Gehenna or the "lake of fire" (Matt. 25:41), the eternal abode of Satan, demons, and unsaved men.   M.F.U.

DENARIUS (See Money)

DEPRAVITY (dē-prăv′ĭ-tē), a theological term not found in Scripture, although the reality expressed by the word is certainly there. Negatively, it means that man, as a result of the fall, has lost his original righteousness and love for God. Positively, it means that man's moral nature has become corrupted, and that he has an irresistible bias toward evil. The corruption extends to every part of his nature and every faculty of his being. In his depraved state man can do nothing perfectly pleasing to God. This does not mean that he has no qualities pleasing to men, that he is as bad as he can be, or that he is as opposed to God as he can possibly be. The image of God in which he was created has not been completely obliterated; some vestiges of it remain. He cannot, however, no matter how hard he tries, love God with all his heart or his neighbor as himself; nor can he change his supreme pre-

ference for himself, or so radically transform his character that he can live according to God's law. Arminian and Calvinistic theologians differ on the extent of depravity, but they are agreed that without the saving grace of God no salvation is possible.   S.B.

DEPUTY (dĕp′ū-tē, Heb. *nitstsāv,* Gr. *anthúpatos*), one appointed to rule under a higher authority, as a regent in place of a king (I Kings 22:47) or a Roman consul or proconsul (Acts 13:7; 18:12; 19:38). Roman proconsuls were appointed by the Roman senate to govern senatorial provinces, usually for one year. They exercised judicial as well as military power in their province. During their term of office their power was absolute, but when it expired they were accountable for what they had done.

DERBE (dûr′bē, Gr. *Dérbe*), a city in the SE corner of Lycaonia, in Asia Minor. In Acts 14:20 it is called *Dérbe*; in 20:4, *Derbaíos.* Paul visited it on the first journey after being stoned at Lystra (Acts 14:20), also on his second tour (Acts 16:1), and probably on the third. Gaius, who accompanied Paul to Jerusalem, was from there (Acts 20:4). It was about three miles NW of Zasta and 45 miles S of Konia (Iconium).

DESERT, a rendering of a number of Hebrew and Greek words. 1. Heb. *midbar* and Gr. *éremos, a wilderness,* yet capable of pasturing flocks (Gen. 16:7; 21:20; I Sam. 17:28; Matt. 3:1; Mark 1:13).

2. Heb. *'ārāvâh, an arid region.* When used with the definite article, it denotes the plain of the Jordan and Dead Sea (Ezek. 47:8; II Sam. 2:29).

3. Heb. *yeshîmôn, a waste.* With the definite article, it is rendered as a proper name, Jeshimon (Num. 21:20).

4. Heb. *hārbâh, waste, desolate place* (Isa. 48:21; Ezek. 13:4). It must not be thought that the deserts known to the Israelites were merely wastes of sand, like the Sahara. They were mostly latently fertile lands, needing only rain to make them fruitful.

DESIRE OF ALL NATIONS, a phrase occurring only in Haggai 2:7. The ERV has *desirable things;* and the KJVm, *things desired.* When the temple was erected in Ezra's time, the prophet was directed to encourage the older men who had seen the more magnificent Temple of Solomon and were disappointed with what they now saw, by assuring them that God was with them, and in a little while He would shake the heavens, the earth, the sea, the dry land, and the nations, and "the desire of all nations" would come to fill the house with His glory. Many expositors refer the prophecy to Christ's first advent, and others to the second advent; while still others deny a Messianic application altogether, translating "the desire of all nations" by "the desirable things of all nations," i.e. their precious gifts (cf. Isa. 60:5,11; 61:6).

DESOLATION, ABOMINATION OF (See Abomination of Desolation)

DEUEL (dū′ĕl), a Gadite, father of Eliasaph, prince of Gad in the wilderness just after the Exodus from Egypt (Num. 1:14, 7:47, 10:20). In Num. 2:14 the name is Reuel. It is uncertain which form of the name is correct.

DEUTERONOMY (dū′têr-on′ō-mē, Gr. *Deuteronómion, second law*). In sight of the Canaan he may not enter, Moses gathers the hosts of Israel about him as would a father his children for his farewell addresses. These, set within the historical framework of several brief narrative passages, constitute the book of Deuteronomy. Since the occasion of

A small portion of the Nash Papyrus fragment of Deuteronomy 5. BA

Moses' farewell was also the occasion of the renewal of the covenant made earlier at Sinai, the appropriate documentary pattern for covenant ratification supplied the pattern for Moses' speeches and thus for the book.

The English title is unfortunate, being based on the LXX's mistranslation of the phrase, "a copy of this law" (17:18), as *to deuteronomion touto*, "this second law." The Jewish name, *devârîm*, "words," derives from the opening expression, "These are the words which Moses spake" (1:1a). This title is felicitous because it focuses attention on a clue to the peculiar literary character of the book; for with such an expression began the treaties imposed by ancient imperial lords upon their vassals. Deuteronomy is the text or "words" of a suzerainty covenant made by the Lord of heaven through the mediatorship of Moses with the servant people Israel beyond the Jordan.

The claims of Deuteronomy concerning its own authorship are thus plain. It purports to consist almost entirely of the farewell speeches of Moses addressed to the new generation which had grown to manhood in the wilderness. The speeches are dated in the last month of the 40 years of wandering (1:3) and it is stated that Moses wrote as well as spoke them (31:9,24; cf. 31:22). There is the confirmatory witness of Jesus who affirmed the Mosaic authorship of the Law, i.e., the Pentateuch (cf. esp. Mark 10:5; 12:26; John 5:46,47; 7:19). Modern orthodox Christian scholars, therefore, join older Jewish and Christian tradition in maintaining the Mosaic authorship of Deuteronomy as well as of the first four books of the Pentateuch. Almost all such scholars recognize that the account of Moses' death (Deut. 34) is exceptional and some would attribute to a compiler (perhaps the unknown author of Deut. 34) much of the narrative framework of Deuteronomy. Whether or not the Biblical testimony allows the latter latitude,

even that variety of the conservative position stands in clear opposition to modern negative theories of the origin of Deuteronomy.

According to the Development Hypothesis which won the day among 19th century negative critics, Deuteronomy was a product of the seventh century B.C., and provided the program for the reform of Josiah (cf. II Kings 22:3-23:25), allegedly introducing the concept of a centralized cultus into Israelite religion at that late date. But unless a wholesale critical rewriting of the historical sources be undertaken, it is manifest that the concept of the central altar was normative during the entire life of Israel in Canaan. Moreover, it is equally apparent that, taken at their face value, the covenant stipulations propounded in Deuteronomy are directed to a unified young nation about to enter upon a program of conquest to secure its inheritance, not to the diminishing remnant of the divided kingdom. Indeed, many of those stipulations would be completely incongruous in a document produced in the seventh century B.C. That dating, though still dominant, is being increasingly challenged even from the side of negative criticism. While some have suggested a post-exilic origin, more have favored a pre-Josianic date. There is a growing tendency to trace the sources of the deuteronomic legislation back to the early monarchy — if not earlier. The view that these traditions were preserved at a northern cult center, being shaped according to ritual patterns, is widespread. Some would detach Deuteronomy from the Pentateuch and treat Deuteronomy — II Kings as a unit representing the historical-theological perspective of a distinctive "school," i.e., the "deuteronomic."

The unity, antiquity, and authenticity of Deuteronomy are evidenced by the conformity of its total structure to the pattern of Near Eastern suzerainty treaties dating from the second millennium B.C. The classic covenantal pattern consisted of the following sections: preamble, historical prologue, stipulations, curses and blessings, invocation of oath deities, directions for deposit of duplicate treaty documents in sanctuaries and periodic proclamation of the treaty to the vassal people.

Such substantially is the outline of Deuteronomy:

I. Preamble: Covenant Mediator (1:1-5)
II. Historical Prologue: Covenant History (1:6-4:49)
III. Stipulations: Covenant Life (5-26)
IV. Curses and Blessings: Covenant Ratification (27-30)
V. Succession Arrangements: Covenant Continuity (31-34)

(1:1-5): Here the speaker is identified, viz., Moses as the Lord's representative. (1:6-4:49): A rehearsal of God's past covenantal dealings with Israel from Horeb to Moab serves to awaken reverence and gratitude as motives for renewed consecration. (5-26): When covenants were renewed the former obligations were repeated and brought up to date. Thus chapters 5-11 republish the decalogue with its primary obligation of fidelity to Yahweh, while chapters 12-26 in considerable measure renew the stipulations of the Book of the Covenant (Exod. 21-23) and other earlier Sinaitic legislation, adapting where necessary to the new conditions awaiting Israel on the threshold of Canaan. (27-30): Directions are first given for the future and final act in this covenant renewal to be conducted by Joshua in Canaan (27). Blessings and curses are then pronounced by Moses as the sanctions for Israel's immediate ratification of the covenant, but also as a prophecy of Israel's future down to its ultimate exile and restoration (28-30). (31-34): Here the necessary preparations are made for the continuity of leadership through the succession of Joshua and for the continuing confrontation of Israel with the way of the covenant by periodic reading of the covenant document, which was to be deposited in the sanctuary, and by a prophetic song of covenant witness (31,32). Then there are the final blessings and the death of Moses, by which the "dynastic" provisions became operative (33,34).

Stylistically, the adoption of the documentary pattern of the international suzerainty treaties is the most noteworthy fact. Next in importance is the preponderantly oratorical nature of the contents. There is general acknowledgement of the homogeneity of style, which is a fluent prose (chapters 32,33 are poetry) marked by majestic periods, warmly impressive eloquence, and the reiteration and exhortation of the earnest preacher for decision.

Deuteronomy is the Bible's full-scale exposition of the covenant concept and demonstrates that, far from being a contract between two parties, God's covenant with His people is a proclamation of His sovereignty and an instrument for binding His elect to Himself in a commitment of absolute allegiance.

Israel is confronted with the demands of God's governmental omnipotence, redemptive grace, and consuming jealousy. Consecration to the Lord is to be manifested in obedience to the programmatic mandate of establishing His kingdom in His land. That involves on the one hand the execution of the commission of conquest, by which divine judgment would be visited on the devotees of alien gods in God's land, and on the other hand the creation of a community of brotherly love in the bonds of common service to the Lord within the possessed inheritance. This covenant calling was not an unconditioned license to national privilege and prosperity. By the covenant oath Israel came under both the curses and the blessings which were to be meted out according to God's righteous judgment. The covenant relation bestowed, called still to responsible decision: "I call heaven and earth to witness against you this day, that I have set before you life and death, blessing and curse; therefore choose life, that both you and your seed may live: that you may love the Lord your God ... for that is your life" (30:19,20a).

M.G.K.

DEVIL (Gr. *diábolos, slanderer*), one of the principal titles of Satan, the arch-enemy of God and of man. Thirty-five times in the NT the word refers to Satan; but unfortunately in KJV the same word is used about 60 times to render the Greek *daimonion* which is properly translated "demon" in ASV. Three times in the NT the word *diabolos* is used for ill-natured persons, or "slanderers" (I Tim. 3:11, II Tim. 3:3, and Titus 2:3, but in KJV the last two of these are "false accusers"). The word "devil" occurs only four times in the OT (KJV), twice representing *sa'îrim* which means "he-goats" (Lev. 17:7, II Chron. 11:15) and twice translating *shēdim* or "demons" (Deut. 32:17, Ps. 106:37. (Cf. ASV for these four renderings.) The LXX renders "Satan" in the OT as *"diábolos,"* i.e., "devil," but the Vulgate and the English versions rightly employ "Satan" as the proper name. In Numbers 22:22, the Angel of the Lord stood in the way as an adversary (Hebrew *Satan*) to the mad prophet Balaam, but generally the word is used in the bad sense.

How did Satan originate? "God is love," and God is holy. Because love is His predominating characteristic, God desired to surround His throne with creatures whom He might love, and by whom He might be loved. Because of His holiness, these creatures must also be holy; and by logical necessity love and holiness cannot be forced. Compulsory love or holiness would not be either love or holiness, and could not satisfy the all-wise Creator. Therefore these loving and holy creatures must be endowed with the ability to choose whether "to glorify God and to enjoy Him forever" or to reject Him and suffer the consequences. The story of the beginning of sin is nowhere related explicitly in the Word; but certain passages seem to hint so strongly, that the following theory has long been held to explain them. [If this theory is not true, we have not the slightest inkling as to the origin of sin. Isaiah 14:12-20 is apparently directed to "the king of Babylon" and Ezekiel 28:12-19 similarly to "the prince of Tyre" but in each case the prophet uses language which could not truly and literally refer to any mere man.]

Apparently God first peopled the universe, or at least our part of it, with a hierarchy of holy angels, of whom one of the highest orders was (or contained) the cherubim. One of them, perhaps the highest of all, was "the anointed cherub that covereth," who was created beautiful and perfect in his ways. This cherub knew that he was beautiful (this required only intelligence), but pride entered his heart and the first sin in the whole history of eternity occurred. Pride led to self-will (Isa. 14:13,14) and self-will to rebellion. This great cherub became the adversary ("Satan") of God, and apparently led other angels into rebellion. (Cf. Jude 6, II Pet. 2:4, etc.). God then created man in His own image (innocent but with the possibility of becoming holy on condition of obedience. Because Satan already hated God, he hated man whom God loved, and tried to destroy him. It is evident that God could have destroyed Satan at the moment that he became "Satan," but God has tolerated him these many centuries, and has used him for testing man until the days of testing shall be over. Then Satan and all the other enemies of God will be cast into the "lake of fire", (Rev. 20:10-15). In the age-long (though not eternal) conflict between good and evil, it sometimes seems as though God has given Satan every advantage. Even so, God's victory is certain.

Among the devil's characterizations are "the god of this world" (or "age") (II Cor. 4:4), "the prince of the powers of the air" (Eph. 2:2), and "the devil and his angels" (Matt. 25:41). All these point to his immense power. In Ephesians 6:12 it is stated that our wrestling is "not against flesh and blood, but against principalities — powers — the rulers of the darkness of this world (or "age") — against spiritual wickedness in high places." Our enemy is a murderer and a liar (John 8:44). On the other hand, he is a coward (James 4:7), and he can be defeated (Matt. 4:1-11) by "the sword of the Spirit, which is the word of God" (Eph. 6:17). His principal method of attack is that of temptation (Matt. 4:3), and his leading temptations can be grouped under "the lust of the flesh, and the lust of the eyes, and the pride of life" (I John 2:16). These three he used effectively on Eve (Gen. 3;6) and on her descendants, but ineffectively on our Lord (Matt. 4:1-11). He is called "Abaddon" and "Apollyon" (i.e. "Destroyer") in Revelation 9:11, "Beelzebub, the prince of the devils" in Matthew 12:24 and "the accuser of our brethren" (Rev. 12:7-12), where he is also characterized as "the great dragon," "the old serpent" and "the deceiver of the whole world." Satan clearly showed his brazen shamelessness when, as recorded in Job 1,2, he came before God with "the sons of God" and misrepresented the character and the purposes of Job. His end and our victory are sure (Rev. 20). A.B.F.

DEVOTED THING, that which is set apart unto the Lord, and therefore belongs no longer to the former owner, nor may it be used for sacrifice. A sacrifice or offering is a voluntary gift from the owner, and can at any time previous to the ceremony be recalled, but not so a devoted thing. Achan's sin at Jericho (Josh. 6:17-19) was considered far more serious than mere stealing, for he had taken of the devoted thing. Nations, cities or men who were "devoted" were utterly to be destroyed; e.g. the Amalekites (I Sam. 15).

DEW, the moisture which forms in drops during a still, cloudless night upon the earth or any body which rapidly radiates heat, under air which is saturated with water vapor. In Syria and most of Palestine, these conditions are fulfilled through the cloudless summer and early autumn, and the dew is a great blessing to the fruits of the land. The word (Hebrew and Aramaic *tal)* occurs 35 times and almost always with pleasant connotation. Dew is often used in Scripture as a symbol of blessing (Gen. 27:28; Micah 5:7) and of refreshment (Deut. 32:2; Job 29:19; Ps. 133:3; Isa. 18:4).

DIADEM (Gr. *diádema*), properly an emblem of royalty, but in the OT, the Hebrew word is generally rendered "mitre" and refers to the turban of the chief priest (Zech. 3:5), a royal diadem (Isa. 62:3), or a turban (Job 29:14). In the NT, the word does not occur in the KJV but is used three times in Rev. (12:3,13:1,19:12) as an emblem of absolute power, and is sharply to be distinguished from the crown (Gr. *stéphanos*) which is used elsewhere in the NT. The *stéphanos* was given to victorious athletes, to generals and to the early emperors of Rome, until Diocletian (c. 284-305) transformed the empire into an Oriental absolutism, and adopted the diadem as a symbol of his autocracy. Our Lord, too, will wear the diadem (Rev. 19:12).

DIAL, properly a graduated arc intended to mark the time of day by the shadow of a style or gnomon falling upon it. In modern times the style is generally (and properly) parallel to the axis of the earth. The word occurs only twice in the Bible (II Kings 20:11, Isa. 38:8) referring to the "sun-dial of Ahaz" which he may have introduced from Babylonia, where it was used as early as the eighth century B.C. The Hebrew *ma'ălâh* here rendered "dial" is generally "degrees" or steps, from the root meaning "to go up". It would seem from this that the time of day was found by the men of Hezekiah's time by the shadow of a pillar as it ascended or descended the steps leading to the palace. The miracle recorded in connection with the dial can be compared with the "long day" in Joshua's time (Josh. 10:12-14) and is equally inexplicable on natural grounds.

DIANA (dī-ăn'à, Lat. *Diana,* Gr. *Ártemis*), the Roman goddess of the moon. A daughter of Jupiter, she was a twin sister of Apollo, who was associated with the sun, as she was with the moon. She was represented as a virgin huntress and was widely worshiped. When the Greek worship penetrated Italy about 400 B.C. the Italians identified Diana with Artemis, her Greek counterpart. Her worship was pure as compared with the sensual worship of eastern gods and goddesses.

Diana of the Ephesians (Artemis). **JHK**

"Diana of the Ephesians," mentioned only in Acts 19:24-35, is *Artemis* in the Greek, and her myths were of a very different sort. Her silver "shrines" (Acts 19:24) were little "temples" containing an image of Artemis as imagined by the Asiatics, a combination of the Greek virgin goddess with the many-breasted and lewd Semitic moon goddess Ashtoreth. For the Ephesians, Artemis was the great Asiatic nursing mother of gods, men, animals, and plants, and was the patroness of the sexual instinct. Her images, instead of being artistically beautiful like those of the Greeks, were ugly, more like the lascivious images of India and Tyre and Sidon. Her special worship was centered in the great temple at Ephesus. The reason for the location there was probably the finding of a very interesting aerolite which supposedly fell from heaven (Acts 19:35). The feasts of Diana "whom all Asia and the world worshippeth" (19:27) were commercialized, and there was a large industry among the silversmiths of making shrines and idols to this goddess. The preaching of Paul interfered with this commerce, and aroused violent opposition. It seems that Paul and his companions had preached the Gospel from the positive side instead of directly attacking, for the townclerk testified that they "were neither robbers of temples nor blasphemers of our goddess (19:37). A.B.F.

DIASPORA (dī-ăs′pô-rà, Gr. *diasporá, that which is sown)*, the name applied to the Jews living outside of Palestine and maintaining their religious faith among the Gentiles. God had warned the Jews through Moses that dispersion among other nations would be their lot if they departed from the Mosaic Law (Deut. 4:27; 28:64-68). These prophecies were largely fulfilled in the two captivities, by Assyria and Babylonia, but there were other captivities by the rulers of Egypt and Syria, and by Pompey, which helped scatter the Israelites. Especially from the time of Alexander the Great, many thousands of Jews emigrated for purposes of trade and commerce into the neighboring countries, particularly the chief cities. By the time of Christ the diaspora must have been several times the population of Palestine. As early as 525 B.C. there had been a temple of Jehovah in Elephantine, in the early years of the Maccabean struggle. The synagogues in every part of the known world helped greatly in the spread of Christianity, for Paul invariably repaired to them in every city he visited. S.B.

DIBLAIM (dĭb-lā′ĭm), father-in-law of Hosea, the prophet (Hos. 1:3).

DIBLATH (dĭb′lăth) occurs in Ezekiel 6:14; in the RV it is "Diblah," which seems to have been an early copyist's error for Riblah, *q.v.* It was a town about 50 miles S of Hamath. In Ezekiel, this place was the northern limit of God's judgments which were to fall upon Palestine for its odious idolatry.

DIBON, DIBON-GAD (dī′bŏn). 1. A place in the high plain of Moab about ten miles E of the Dead Sea. It was one of the stations of Israel in its journey toward the Promised Land (Num. 33:45, 46). It belonged to Sihon, king of the Amorites (Num. 21:21-31) who was conquered by Israel under Moses. The city was rebuilt by the tribe of Gad (Num. 32:34). Moses apparently gave it to Reuben (Josh. 13-17). It was later taken by Moab under King Mesha, who rebelled against Israel after the death of Ahab c. 906 B.C. (II Kings 1:1, 3:4,5). According to Scripture (II Kings 3), Israel badly defeated Mesha at the ensuing battle, but Mesha set up a stele at Dibon (the famous "Moabite stone") boasting of his defeating Ahab.

(2). A town in Judah, occupied by some of the Jews who returned with Zerubbabel (Neh. 11:25).

DIBRI (dĭb′rē), a Danite, whose grandson fought with an Israelite in the camp, cursed, and then was stoned for his blasphemy (Lev. 24:11-16).

DIDRACHMA (See Money)

DIDYMUS (dĭd′ĭ-mŭs, *a twin)*, surname of Thomas (John 11:16, 20:24, 21:2).

DIKLAH (dĭk là), son of Joktan, and his descendants who probably lived in Arabia (Gen. 10:27; I Chron. 1:21).

DILEAN (dĭl′ē-ăn), a town in the lowlands of Judah (Josh. 15:38).

DIMNAH (dĭm′nà), a town in Zebulun, bestowed upon the Merarite Levites (Josh. 21:35). Rimmon (I Chron. 6:77) may be the same place.

DIMON (dīmŏn), a town in Moab, generally called "Dibon" (*q.v.)*, but in Isaiah 15:9 twice written Dimon, about four miles N of Aroer.

DIMONAH (dī-mŏ′nà), a town in the S of Judah (Josh. 15:22), probably the same as the "Dibon" of Nehemiah 11:25.

DINAH (dī′nà), a daughter of Jacob and Leah (Gen. 30:21), and so far as is recorded, his only daughter. While sightseeing (Gen. 34) at the city near which Israel encamped, Shechem, the prince, violated her, for which crime Levi and Simeon, her brothers, destroyed the city.

DINAITE (dī′nà-īt), a member of the tribe of Dinaites whom Ashurbanipal had brought from Assyria to colonize Samaria (cf. II Kings 17:24 with Ezra 4:7-10).

DINHABAH (dĭn′hà-bà), the city of Bela, the first known king of Edom (Gen. 36:32).

DIONYSIUS, THE AREOPAGITE (dī-ŏnĭsh′ĭ-ŭs, the ăr′ē-ŏp′à-gīt), a member of the Areopagus, the Athenian supreme court; mentioned as one of Paul's converts at Athens (Acts 17:34).

DIOSCURI (dī-ŏs′kŭ-rē, Gr. *Dióskouroi, sons of Zeus)*. In mythology, they were twin sons of Zeus by Leda, named Castor and Pollux (Acts 28:11), and were regarded by sailors as guardian deities.

DIOTREPHES (dī-ŏt′rĕ-fēz, Gr. *Diotrephés, nurtured by Zeus)*, a leading member, perhaps the bishop, of the church to which Gaius belonged, to whom John the beloved apostle wrote his third epistle. Few facts are known about him. His domineering attitude made him an obstacle to the progress of the church. The facts, though sad, have been a great blessing and comfort to many a minister who has had to serve a "one-man church." Pride and love of pre-eminence are of the devil and are exactly opposite to that unselfish humility that the Holy Spirit demands (Phil. 2: 3-8).

DISCERNING OF SPIRITS, the ability which the Holy Spirit gives to some Christians to discern between those who spoke by the Spirit of God and those who were moved by false spirits. The phrase occurs in I Corinthians 12:10 as one of the gifts of the Spirit.

DISCIPLE (Gr. *mathetés, a learner)*, a pupil of some teacher. The word implies the acceptance in mind and life of the views and practices of the teacher. In the NT it means, in the widest sense, those who accept the teachings of anyone — like the disciples of John the Baptist (Matt. 9:14) the Pharisees (Matt. 22:16), Moses (John 9:28). Usually, however, it refers to the adherents of Jesus. Sometimes it refers to the Twelve Apostles (Matt. 10:1; 11:1; etc.); but, more often, simply to Christians (Acts 6:1,2,7; 9:36). Followers of Jesus were not called "Christians" until the founding of the church at Antioch (Acts 11:26).

DISEASES to which the Bible refers appear largely to have been well-known disease entities, identical with those that now exist. Inaccurate translation and archaic nomenclature for the descriptions and names of diseases in the KJV, and only patchy improvement in the ASV, have produced much confusion in understanding these diseases.

I. Diseases with Primary Manifestations in Skin. The hygienic measures outlined in Leviticus are in agreement with modern concepts of communicable disease control, especially as regards availability of running water and isolation of the patient. Two kinds of skin disease are recognized in Leviticus: a) those classified as (Heb.) *tsāra′ath* (so-called leprosy in KJV) which were believed to require isolation, and b) those not requiring isolation. Leviticus 13 gives clear diagnostic distinctions and procedural guides based upon the developmental characteristics of the various diseases. Spinka believes that human *tsāra′ath* diseases include leprosy, syphilis, smallpox, boils, scabies, fungus infections (e.g. favus, tinea, actinomycosis), all of which are of known contagious potentiality, and also pemphigus, dermatitis herpetiformis, and skin cancer, which are doubtfully contagious. In addition there are classified as *tsāra'ath* certain mold and fungus growths in houses and cloth, conditions assuming importance from the standpoint of human allergy, often with manifestations in the form of asthma.

A. *Tsāra'ath* diseases.

1. **Leprosy,** also known as Hansen's disease, as defined today, is the name for disease processes caused by the microorganism *Mycobacterium leprae*. There are two types: a. The lepromatous type begins with brownish-red spots on the face, ears, forearms, thighs and/or buttocks which later become thickened nodules and, losing their skin covering, become ulcers ("sores") with subsequent loss of tissue and then contraction and deformity. It was apparently the lepromatous type that was chiefly in view in the Biblical cases of true leprosy. b. The tuberculoid type is characterized by numbness of an affected area of skin and deformity such as fingers like claws resulting from paralysis and consequent muscle wasting (atrophy). The advanced forms of leprosy are not described in Leviticus 13, presumably because this chapter is concerned with early diagnosis. Advanced leprosy would only be seen in isolation outside the camp.

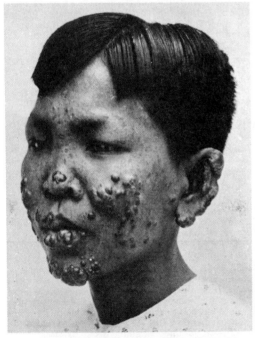

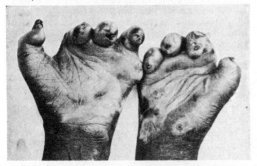

Above, Lepromatus Leprosy (from **Stitt's Diagnosis**). Below, mutilation of the hands in leprosy. SD

2. **Syphilis** is regarded by Spinka as probably the disease called the "botch of Egypt" in Deut. 28:27. It is a disease which from time to time throughout the ages has burst forth in virulent form with high mortality, e.g, Israel in Num. 25:9, and Europe after the discovery of America'. It is chiefly spread by sexual intercourse and is often associated with gonorrhea (cf. *tsāra'ath* associated with "running issue" in Lev. 22:4). Starting with a hard ulcer on the privates, after some weeks raised spots (papular eruptions) appear on the torso and extremities (almost never on the face) devoid of itching. Years later syphilis of the vital organs such as heart, liver or brain may become evident, often with fatal outcome. This late type of syphilis seems to be in view in Prov. 7:22,23 where, referring to a harlot, it says, "He goeth after her straightway, as an ox goeth to the slaughter . . .till a dart strike through his liver; as a bird hasteth to the snare, and knoweth not that it is for his life." Syphilis may also be present from birth and give rise to abnormalities such as "flat nose" (Lev. 21:18) in which the septal cartilage of the nose is largely destroyed.

3. **Smallpox,** uncontrolled, is a serious scourge of mankind. It consists of red spots which turn rapidly into blister-like pustules over the entire body including the face. Short suggest that Job's so-called boils (Heb. *shehîn*) were smallpox, true boils not occurring in such profusion. The Heb. *shehîn* refers to several types of diseased skin, today referred to as a. papule (a raised red spot), b. vesicle (a small blister containing yellow fluid) called "blain" in KJV and ASV, an archaic word that is found in the 1868 but not the 1957 medical dictionary, c. pustule (a small blister containing pus), d. boil (a deep, broad inflammation about a hair root resulting in death of the tissues in its center with pus formation about this core, the pus discharging through an external opening), e. carbuncle (a large boil with multiple openings), and f. malignant pustule (anthrax).

4. Hezekiah's so-called "boil," which was almost fatal, may well have been a true boil or carbuncle. Another suggestion is that it was anthrax. The locai application of a poultice of figs has been recognized therapy for gumboils in comparatively recent times. Its use by Hezekiah at the command of God's prophet (II Kings 20:7) has often been cited as divine approval of the utilization of medicinal means of therapy.

5. Speculation regarding the "boil breaking forth with blains" (Heb. *shehîn*) upon man and beast in Exod. 9:9 (the sixth plague) has suggested two alternative explanations. a. Both man and beast were infected with virtually the same disease called smallpox in man and cowpox in cattle, the germ of cowpox being originally utilized for vaccination against smallpox. b. The "murrain" of domestic animals of Exod. 9:3 (the fifth plague) was anthrax of animals later transmitted to man as malignant pustule (anthrax). Anthrax, untreated, is a fatal infectious disease, chiefly of cattle and sheep, characterized by the formation of hard lumps and ulcers and symptoms of collapse. In man without modern therapy it is also often fatal.

6. **Scabies** is called "the itch, whereof thou canst not be healed" (Deut. 28:27). It is caused by a tiny insect allied to spiders which burrows under the skin. The itching is intense. Infection is spread to others through close bodily contact. The ancients knew no cure for it, but it readily responds to modern medicines.

B. Skin diseases not requiring isolation. Non-tsāra'ath skin diseases (Heb. gārāv and yallepheth) are called "scab," "scall" and "scurvy" in the KJV, and probably include what today are known as eczema, psoriasis and impetigo. Of these only impetigo is very contagious, it being of very superficial character without system manifestations. The scurvy of modern medicine, which is cured by citrus fruits by virtue of their vitamin C content, obviously is a different disease from the scurvy of the KJV. Modern scurvy could not occur amongst the fruit and vegetable-eating Israelites and is not a skin disease.

Inflammation is present in wounds, bruises and sores, and is aggravated by accompanying infection when the skin is broken. *Wounds* are usually due to external violence and when the skin is unbroken are called *bruises*. A *sore*, more properly called an *ulcer*, is a wound in which the skin and underlying tissues are laid open, almost invariably becoming infected, e.g. Heb. yabbāl (Lev. 22:22) which Gesenius defines as a running suppurating sore, but is mistranslated *"wen"* in both the KJV and ASV, both old and new medical dictionaries failing to give such meaning to the word *wen*. A wen is properly defined as a sebaceous cyst formed by a hair root which has failed to discharge its oily secretion.

II. Diseases With Primary Internal Manifestations.

A. **Plague** evidently played a large rôle in OT history. It begins with fever and chills which are followed by prostration, delirium, headache, vomiting and diarrhea. Caused by the germ *Pasteurella pestis*, two forms of plague occur: a. bubonic and b. pneumonic, both forms being sudden in onset and very serious.

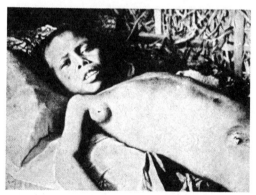

Plague bubo of the right armpit. SD

1. **Bubonic Plague** apparently broke out among the Philistines when they placed the captured ark of God in an idol temple (I Sam. 5). This disease is transmitted by rats through infected fleas which they carry on their bodies, the fleas transferring to man for livelihood after the rat host dies of the disease. The disease causes the lymph nodes of the groin and armpits to enlarge to the size of walnuts. These enlarged nodes are known as buboes (Heb. 'ŏphālīm, meaning *mounds*), wrongly called "emerods," i.e., hemorrhoids, in the KJV. This outbreak of bubonic plague was attributed to "mice that mar the land" (I Sam. 6:5 KJV). The Septuagint more vividly says: "In the midst of the land thereof mice were brought forth, and there was a great and deadly destruction in the city . . . and the land swarmed with mice." As

does the Chinese word *lao-shu* today, the Heb. 'akhbār doubtless means rat as well as mouse, no other word for rat occurring in the Bible, although rats are known to have existed in the land since rat skeletons have been found there by archeologists. The recognition of plague breaking out in dwellings (cf. Ps. 91:10), following lines of communication, and its transmission by rats is noteworthy.

2. **Pneumonic Plague** is transmitted by droplet spray from the mouth. The first case in an epidemic apparently arises from a case of bubonic plague that has been complicated by plague pneumonia. Untreated pneumonic plague is always fatal. The victim goes to bed apparently well and is found dead by morning. It appears very likely that it was either bubonic or pneumonic plague or both that destroyed Sennacherib's army (II Kings 19:35) when 185,000 men were "all dead corpses" by early morning.

B. **Consumption** (Heb. shahepheth, "wasting disease") doubtless included tuberculosis, malaria, typhoid fever, typhus fever, dysentery, chronic diarrhea, and cholera. These diseases are contagious and are sometimes referred to as *pestilences*, being especially prevalent under circumstances of impaired nutrition and crowding such as are encountered in the siege of a city, e.g. Jeremiah 21:6,7,9; Deuteronomy 28:21,22.

1. **Tuberculosis** occurs in acute or chronic form, more commonly the latter. Under the living conditions of OT days, it probably not only attacked the lungs (common form in America today), but also the bones and joints (common in underdeveloped lands today). *Crookback*, i.e. extreme hunchback of Leviticus 21:20 may result from tuberculosis of the spinal vertebrae, and less commonly from severe back injury. Tuberculosis anywhere in the body may produce fever, defective nutrition with underweight, or discharge of infectious pus (referred to as an *"issue"* in Leviticus). The disease may produce chronic invalidism or death if the disease process is not arrested.

2. **Typhoid Fever** and **Typhus Fever** both give rise to similar symptoms of steady fever and delirium lasting for a matter of weeks, frequently being fatal. Typhoid fever is transmitted through contaminated water, and flies carrying contamination to food and drink. Typhus fever is transmitted to humans by lice which have fed on infected human beings.

3. **Malaria** is believed to be the great fever with which Peter's mother-in-law was stricken. The burning ague of Leviticus 26:16 and the extreme burning of Deuteronomy 28:22 were probably malaria. Transmitted by certain species of mosquito, malaria is responsible for much chronic illness. A chill followed by fever often subsides in a few hours only to recur more severely some hours later, continuing intermittently thereafter. Death may ensue if untreated.

4. **Diarrhea, Dysentery** and **Cholera**, caused by microorganisms taken into the body in contaminated food or drink, were doubtless prevalent in OT times. They are characterized by frequent watery bowel movements, often by vomiting and fever, and, if protracted, by weakness and prostration. Publius' fever and "bloody flux" (Acts 28:8) was probably dysentery, a diarrhea associated with painful spasms of the bowel, ulceration, and infection, either amoebic or bacillary, giving rise to blood and pus in the excreta. As to cholera, it is fatal in half of the cases when modern treatment is not utilized.

III. Diseases Caused By Worms and Snakes.

1. **Intestinal Roundworm Infection** (*Ascariasis*) is a common disease today in lands where sanitation is poor, and is believed to have been responsible for Herod Agrippa I's death (Acts 12:21-23). The pinkish yellow roundworm, *Ascaris lumbricoides,* is about 10 to 16 inches long and 1/5 inch in diameter. Aggregated worms sometimes form a tight ball with their interlocking bodies so as to obstruct the intestine, producing severe pain and copious vomiting of worms. If the obstruction is not promptly relieved by surgery, death may ensue. The roundworm does not chew and devour, but feeds on the nutrient fluids in the bowel and may work its way through diseased portions of the bowel as though it had eaten a hole through it. This writer, when in China, encountered such a worm emerging through a perforation in an inflamed appendix which he was removing surgically. Josephus' account of Herod's death is highly suggestive of intestinal obstruction as produced by these worms.

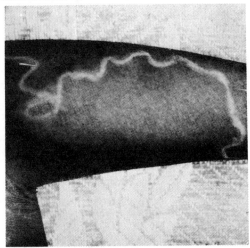

Female guinea worm lying under the skin of the forearm. SD

2. The **Guinea Worm,** *Dracunculus medinensis,* formerly called the serpent or dragon worm, has probably been known longer than any other human parasite. It is still found in interior Arabia and the adjacent Red Sea coast. Some regard it as the fiery serpent of Numbers 21. The infection enters the human body through drinking water containing *Cyclops* (a water insect 1/50 inch long) infected with tiny Guinea worm larvae. In about one year the female worm attains a length of 3 feet, being 1/15th inch in diameter, usually maturing under the skin of the leg or arm. A blister is raised in the skin through which a huge brood of tiny larvae are extruded. This area itches and burns intensely. Death may result from internal complications or severe secondary infection, particularly if the worm becomes broken. The ancient and modern treatment consists in hastening the extrusion of larvae with cold water followed by gradual extraction of the worm. This is done by winding the worm around a stick of wood without breaking it, taking a turn or two of the stick each day. Complete removal takes about 3 weeks. The implication is that Moses with his brass model of the Guinea worm twisted around a wooden stick taught the Israelites how to extract the worm.

3. The **Snake-bite** which Paul received was doubtless inflicted by a venomous snake of the pit-viper type. Experts today stress that the bite of a venomous snake is not poisonous unless it is accompanied by envenomation, the latter failing to take place if the contents of the poison sac located at the base of the snake's hollow fangs have just previously been completely squeezed out, or if the sac is ineffectively squeezed when the snake strikes. Note envenomation apparently did not take place in Acts 28:3,6, the snake, enraged by the fire, having doubtless repeatedly struck at surrounding objects whereby it exhausted all its venom. At any rate, in a life-saving effort it evidently fastened itself to Paul's hand without squeezing any venom out of its poison sac. This is a frequent occurrence and makes for difficulty in assessing degree of envenomation and evaluating the efficacy of one snake-bite treatment as compared with another. When envenomation with pit-viper venom takes place the tissues may swell to three or four times their normal size in the region of the bite in a few minutes.

IV. Diseases of the Eyes.

1. **Epidemic Blindness** described in II Kings 6:18, when a whole army was struck with blindness, is not the rarity that some may imagine. The writer, while a missionary in China, was in close contact with an army contingent which was decimated with blindness in a few days. Gonorrhea of the sexual organs had been occurring sporadically. Suddenly this same gonorrhea germ in the midst of unsanitary conditions changed its propensities to produce acute blinding inflammation of the eyes in violent epidemic form, spreading from eye to eye like wildfire, which is one of the recognized potentialities of this germ. Many of the soldiers were permanently blinded. The army troops which had been the most feared for their cruel depredations were suddenly rendered powerless and the condition of the men was pitiful as one saw them trying to grope their way about, the totally blind being led about by the partially blinded.

2. **Infirmity** (Gal. 4:13) of the Apostle Paul, referred to as his "thorn in the flesh" (II Cor. 12:7), is considered by many authorities to have been *trachoma,* an infectious eye disease. Early in the disease there is often acute inflammation of the eyelids with sago-like elevations which make the lids feel like sandpaper. This frequently spreads on to the bulb of the eye, especially the cornea, the transparent part of the bulb, which becomes red and inflamed. At this stage, infection with other germs is often added. Copious purulent secretion is poured out over the lid margins, forming a tough, crusting scab as the secretion dries and unites with the greasy secretion of the glands of the lid margin.

It is possible that Paul's blindness encountered on the Damascus road was of this type. For three days the secretion was evidently so severe that it formed incrustations at the lid margins

Guinea worm rolled on stick for gradual extraction. SD

such as to glue and mat together the lashes of the lids, so that the eyelids could not be parted. At the end of this time we are told he saw again after scabs (Gr. *lepídes,* which Hobart says is the medical term for particles or scaly substance thrown off from the body) fell (Gr. *apepesan* which Hobart points out was used by Hippocrates with reference to "the falling off of the scab, caused by burning in a medical operation, from the eyelid") from his eyes. Subsequently Paul seemingly was afflicted with chronic trachoma as might well be expected. a. He failed to recognize the high priest (Acts 23:2-5). b. The Galatians proffered their good eyes for his (Gal. 4:13-15). c. He wrote with "large letters" (Gal. 6:11 ASV). d. He used amanuenses.

Severe chronic trachoma commonly produces scarring of the eyelids with incurving of the cartilage of the eyelid called entropion which makes the lashes poke into and rub back and forth on the cornea, resulting in a frosted appearance, impaired vision, and blindness if unrelieved. This condition comprises a literal thorn in the flesh of the eye. It is frequently encountered by medical missionaries in underdeveloped lands today. Modern surgery performed on these eyelids produces outcurving of the lids and either transplants or removes the offending eyelashes. Without surgery the only recourse is to pluck out the lashes one by one, but this only affords transient relief since the lash soon reappears as a sharp, stiff stubble which even more effectively sticks into the cornea like a thorn.

V. Nervous and Mental Diseases.

While terminology and explanations of causation regarding emotional and mental diseases have varied greatly through the centuries, there is clear insight in the Scriptures concerning the relationship between the emotional state and physical disease (psychosomatic medicine). This is exemplified in Proverbs 17:22: "A merry heart doeth good like a medicine: but a broken spirit drieth the bones." Here the merry heart might well imply the resolution of excessive emotional tensions in a manner superior to that of any tranquilizer. In contrast, some forms of arthritis occur on an emotional basis, the outcome of a "broken spirit," whereby the bones are seemingly dried of joint lubrication.

Both Elijah and Jonah were men who lapsed into states of extreme nervous exhaustion, often referred to as *neurasthenia,"* a common condition amid the tension of modern days. God's method of dealing with this condition as outlined in the Scriptures in I Kings 19 and in Jonah is a model for modern psychiatric therapy for this condition. In the case of Epaphroditus (Phil. 2:25-30) there is clear recognition then as today of the rôle played by *pressure* of work and *anxiety* as he endeavored to accomplish a colossal task unaided by those who should have been his helpers. Doubtless there was physical illness superimposed upon the emotional tension symptoms in his case, as is often encountered in modern times. In addition there are mental diseases which are recognized as disease entities just as distinctive as appendicitis or pneumonia. The general term used in the KJV for those so afflicted is *lunatic,* although formerly this term referred to epilepsy as well as insanity because of supposed relationship to the phases of the moon. As today, legal responsibility for actions was regarded as tempered by proof of mental incompetence. Hence we find David escaping from Achish by pretending "madness" (I Sam. 21:13-15). Perhaps he was even imitating some

of Saul's actions as observed during Saul's state of what the modern psychiatrist would diagnose as *manic-depressive insanity,* with its periods of black melancholy, flashes of homicidal violence, and deeply rooted delusion that people were plotting against him which characteristically ended in Saul's suicide. Nebuchadnezzar is considered by Short to have been a victim of paranoia, a delusional form of insanity well known to medical science.

VI. Miscellaneous Medical Disorders and Therapy.

1. The woman's *issue of blood* of 12 years' duration (Luke 8:43,44) was doubtless excessive menstrual flow, a fairly common condition. In its severe form, it is commonly due to fibroid tumor in the womb encroaching upon the lining of the womb. Flooding flow of blood with large clots occurs, depleting the body of blood so as to cause severe anemia. The modern remedy usually employed in this condition is removal of the tumor from the womb or removal of the womb (hysterectomy). This surgery obviously was not available in NT times so that it is quite understandable that all this woman's living was spent on unavailing medical care.

2. In connection with Jesus' agony in Gethsemane, we read that "His sweat was *as it were great drops of blood* falling down to the ground" (Luke 22:44 — italics ours). Some have thought that this refers to actual blood-tinged sweat. Short tends to take this point of view despite his confession that this phenomenon must be very rare and is not well authenticated. Rather it seems that the emphasis here is to be put upon the phrase "as it were," referring to the size and weight of the drops of sweat. It should be recalled that this occurred at night. Jesus' enemies carried lanterns and torches, but evidently He had neither. The color of the sweat was therefore unobservable. In the quietude of the garden the heavy drip of large drops of sweat was probably heard and not seen by the disciples, particularly as Jesus came to them to arouse them from sleep. The word drops (Gr. *thromboi*) when used in connection with blood usually means "clots." It may be that the simile here includes that idea, i.e. the drops of sweat sounded like blood clots falling on the ground.

3. Timothy was admonished to shun profane babblings on the basis that "their word will eat as doth a *canker"* (II Tim. 2:17 KJV — *italics* ours). The word canker is more appropriately rendered *gangrene* in the ASV, the Greek word being *ganggraina.* Gangrene means local death of the tissues. Common forms of gangrene are: (a) gas gangrene, a rapidly fatal type caused by a spreading gas-forming germ in muscles after recent injury; (b) diabetic gangrene a "dry" gangrene which spreads less rapidly, caused by circulatory impairment associated with uncontrolled diabetes; (c) septic gangrene which spreads from the edges of infected ulcers.

4. *Dropsy* (Luke 14:2), in modern medical language called edema, is a condition in which the tissues retain too much fluid. It may be caused by heart disease, kidney disease, or local infection, and may terminate fatally.

5. *Dumbness,* i.e. inability to speak, may arise from deafness since difficulty naturally is encountered in reproducing unheard sounds. It also may arise from hemorrhage (*apoplexy*) or thrombosis (*clotting*) in relation to the blood vessels of one or more of the speech centers of the brain. Often

a marked degree of recovery takes place in these instances of so-called stroke as the clotted blood is gradually absorbed from the affected area. Such may have happened to Zacharias (Luke 1:20-22, 64), whereas Nabal (I Sam. 25:36-38) evidently experienced a fatal stroke.

6. Of similar nature to stroke of the brain is coronary occlusion (of an artery of the heart), commonly referred to as a *heart attack,* such as apparently took place when David's heart smote him (II Sam. 24:10).

7. A *dwarf* such as is referred to in Leviticus 21:20 may have been dwarfed through tuberculosis or injury of the spine, but deficiency of thyroid function such as is found in cretinism is also a likely cause. In the latter condition there is also usually mental deficiency which comprises added reason for not permitting such an individual to participate in priestly service. Cretinism today responds well to thyroid extract therapy if administered early in life.

8. As to orthopedic conditions, reference is made to the *maimed* (those whose bodies are deprived of a part) and the *halt* (those who limp in walking because of *lameness* from a disabled lower extremity). The latter may be due to a fracture which has healed in an unfavorable position or it may be due to atrophy (wasting) of the muscles. Atrophy of a hand is referred to as a *withered* hand in Luke 6:6. Atrophy usually results from *palsy* or *paralysis* (synonymous terms), a condition characterized by loss of control of movement of muscles through disease or destruction of nerves or nervous tissue.

9. Frequent instances of unspecified sickness occur throughout the Biblical record. It is noteworthy that some of these cases of sickness did not experience divine healing. For example, Paul informs us, "Trophimus have I left at Miletum sick" (II Tim. 4:20). Also Paul tells us concerning himself that his thrice-repeated prayer for the removal of his thorn in the flesh was answered not by removal of his infirmity but by the bestowal of more grace (II Cor. 12:8-10). It therefore does not follow that the Bible teaches that all Christians are entitled to divine healing by virtue of being Christians.

James exhorts that the church elders be called to pray for the sick. He also directs "anointing with oil in the name of the Lord" (James 5:14). The latter has perhaps wrongfully been assumed to refer to a church ritual. Bauer's Greek Lexicon states that the Greek verb *aleipho,* used for "anointing," commonly referred to rubbing oil on the skin as a household remedy, corresponding to the modern household remedy of rubbing camphorated oil on the skin. It would seem to be James' meaning that the sick one is not only to be prayed for but the commonly accepted remedies are also to be applied as an indication of compassionate concern so that all that can be done to help the sick is done. Jesus' disciples made similar use of the application of oil to the sick (Mark 6:13). P.E.A.

Bibliography: Short, A.R. *The Bible and Modern Medicine.* Paternoster Press, London, 1953; Strong, R.P. *Stitt's Diagnosis, Prevention and Treatment of Tropical Diseases.* 7th Edition. Blakiston Co., Philadelphia, 1944; Spinka, H.M. "Leprosy in Ancient Hebraic Times," *Journal of the American Scientific Affiliation* 11: 17-20 (March) 1959; Hobart, W.K. *Medical Language of Luke.* Baker Book House, Grand Rapids, Mich., 1954

DISH, a receptacle for food, generally made of baked clay, or else of metal. The "chargers" of Numbers 7 were large flat dishes of beaten silver; but most of the dishes in Scripture were pottery. "Bosom" in Proverbs 19:24, 26:15 should be "dish." Orientals ate from a central platter or dish, generally using a thin piece of bread for a spoon and handling the food quite daintily (Matt. 26:23). A special courtesy consisted in picking out a good piece of meat from the central dish and handing it to a guest. See POTTERY.

DISHAN (dī'shăn), the seventh son of Seir, the Horite. (Gen. 36:21, etc.).

DISHON (dī'shŏn). 1. A chief among the Horites (Gen. 36:21).

2. A great-grandson of Seir the Horite (Gen. 36:25). The two may, however, be the same.

DISPENSATION (dĭspĕn-sā'shŭn, Gr. *oikonomía, law or arrangement of a house*), a word that appears in the Bible four times, all of them in the NT: I Corinthians 9:17; Ephesians 1:10, 3:2; Colossians 1:25. In the first two and the fourth it means "stewardship," "office," "commission" — words involving the idea of administration. Thus Paul says in I Corinthians 9:17, "I have been entrusted with a commission"; in Ephesians 3:2, "you have heard of the stewardship of God's grace that was granted to me for you; and in Colossians 1:25, "according to the divine office which has been granted to me for you." In Ephesians 1:10, a linguistically difficult passage, the word dispensation refers to God's plan of salvation which He is bringing to reality through Christ, in the fulness of times. The idea of administration is involved here, too, but it is considered from the divine side. The stewardship, or arrangement, for man's redemption, is God's. The NT therefore uses the word in a twofold sense: with respect to one in authority, it means an arrangement or plan; with respect to one under authority, it means a stewardship or administration.

The modern theological use of the term as a "period of time during which man is tested in respect to obedience to some specific revelation of the will of God" (Scofield Reference Bible, p.5) is not found in Scripture. Scofield divides the whole of time from the creation to the judgment into seven dispensations. The Scriptures do indeed make a distinction between the way God manifested His grace in what may be called the "Old Covenant" and the way His grace has been manifested since the death of Christ in what may be called the "New Covenant." It is this that Paul has in mind when he speaks of God's dispensations in Ephesians and Colossians. In God's redemptive plan the era of law prepared the way, by types and shadows, for the new era of salvation through Christ, which in the NT is regarded as the climax of history (Heb. 1:2). S.B.

DISPERSION (See Diaspora)

DIVES (dī'vēz, Lat. *rich*), a name applied to the rich man in the parable of the rich man and Lazarus (Luke 16:19-31) in the Vulgate. It renders the Greek word *ploúsios.*

DIVINATION (dĭv'ĭ-nā'shŭn), the attempt to obtain secret knowledge, especially of the future, either by inspiration (Acts 16:16) or by the reading and interpreting of certain signs called omens. Those who practice divination assume that the gods or spirits are in possession of secret knowledge desired by men and that they can be induced to impart it. Divination was highly developed by all ancient peoples — the Babylonians, Egyptians, Greeks, Romans, etc. — and even the Hebrews

Clay model of the liver, inscribed with magical formulae, for use of diviners, from Megiddo. DV

practiced it, although it was severely condemned by Moses and the prophets. Deuteronomy 18:10f is the classical passage on this subject. There were various modes of divination: by reading omens, dreams, both involuntary and those induced by what is called "incubation," i.e. by sleeping in some sacred place where the god revealed his secrets to the sleeper; the use of the lot; hydromancy or foretelling from the appearance of water; astrology or the determination of the supposed influence of the heavenly bodies on the destiny of a person or nation; rhabdomancy, or the use of the divining rod (Hosea 4:12; Ezek. 8:17); hepatoscopy, or divination by an examination of the liver of animals; necromancy, or consulting the dead; and the sacrifice of children by burning.

S.B.

DIZAHAB (dī'zà-hăb), a place located in the region of Sinai, or possibly farther north where Moses gave his farewell address to the Israelites (Deut. 1:1).

DOCTOR (Gr. *didáskalos, teacher*). The word *didáskalos* appears many times in the NT, but is rendered *doctor* only in Luke 2:46. It is usually rendered *master* or *teacher,* whether referring to Jesus or other teachers.

DODAI (dō'dī), David's captain over 24,000 men whose service culminated in the second month of each year. (I Chron. 27:4).

DODANIM (dō'dà-nĭm), the fourth son of Javan, the son of Japheth (Gen. 10:4). In the LXX, the Samaritan Pentateuch, and in the Hebrew text of I Chron. 1:7 it is written "Rodanim."

DODAVAH (dō'dà-và), father of Eliezer, who prophesied against Jehoshaphat (II Chron. 20:37).

DODO (dō'dō). 1. A man of Issachar, grandfather of the judge Tola. (Judg. 10:1).

2. A son of Ahohi, and father of Eleazar the second of David's mighty men (II Sam. 23:9).

3. A man of Bethlehem whose son Elhanan was one of David's mighty men (II Sam. 23:24).

DOEG (dō'ĕg), an Edomite whom Saul had made chief of his herdsmen. When David, fleeing from Saul, came to Nob, Doeg was being detained "before the Lord" for some reason. He reported to Saul about Ahimelech, the priest helping David

(I Sam. 21:1-9). In revenge, Saul gathered all the house of Ahimelech and Doeg slew them, 85 priests, all the women and children of the village, and killed even the cattle. (I Sam. 22:11-23).

DOG (See Animals)

DOOR (Heb. *pethah, opening, doorway, deleth, door* — the swinging part, Gr. *thúra.* Doors in ancient times turned on pivots turning in sockets above and below, and were frequently two-leaved. The word is often used in the NT in a figurative sense, many times referring to Christ (John 10:1,2,7; Rev. 3:20); but also to opportunity (Matt. 25:10; Acts 14:27; I Cor. 16:9), and freedom and power (Col. 4:3).

DOORKEEPER. Public buildings, temples and walled cities had special officers to keep the doors; see Psalm 84:10: "I had rather be a doorkeeper"; John 18:16,17, "the maid that kept the door," etc. Generally in the English Bible the word is "porter," e.g. II Sam. 18:26, "the watchman called unto the porter."

DOPHKAH (dŏf'kà), a station of the Israelites, between the Red Sea and Sinai (Num. 33:12), about 25 miles NW of Mt. Sinai.

DOR (dôr), a very ancient Canaanite city on the coast of Palestine, about eight miles north of Caesarea. In Joshua 11:12 for "borders of Dor" read "heights of Dor" and similarly for "coast of Dor" in Joshua 12:23. Its ruler fought against Joshua, but he conquered Dor (Josh. 11:1-8). In Judges 1:27 it is mentioned as one of the towns not occupied by the Israelites. Its place is now occupied by the village of Tantura.

DORCAS (dôr'kăs, Gr. *Dorkàs,* a *gazelle),* an early Christian disciple living at Joppa, who was well known for her works of charity. When she died, Peter was sent for. He prayed and she was raised from the dead. As a result, many believed (Acts 9:36-43).

DOTHAN (dō'thăn, Heb. *dōthán,* possibly *two wells),* a place in the boundaries between the tribes of Manasseh and Issachar, about 13 miles N of Shechem. Gesenius says its name derives from the Chaldaic *"Dothain,"* i.e., "two wells," and if that is correct, it adds interest to the story of Joseph's brethren casting him into a dry well-pit there (Gen. 37:24). Nearly a millennium after Joseph's experience, the prophet Elisha (II Kings 6:13) was dwelling at Dothan when the king of Syria tried to capture him with an army, for he had learned that Elisha was able to tell his plans to the king of Israel, Joram. When Elisha's servant informed him that a great host surrounded Dothan, Elisha prayed that the Lord would open his servant's eyes, and the servant saw angelic hosts defending his master. A.B.F.

The Hill of Dothan. © MPS

Arab women on the way to the spring for water. © MPS

DOUGH, the soft mass of moistened flour or meal which after baking becomes bread or cake. The word may apply before the mass has been raised by yeast as in Exod. 12:34,39, but generally after raising, as in Jeremiah 7:18 and Hosea 7:4.

DOVE (See Birds)

DOVE COTE, referring to the openings of pigeon-houses, is not found in the KJV, ERV, ASV, or RSV. It is found in the Moffatt translation. Isaiah 60:8, "Who are these that fly as a cloud, and as the doves to their windows?" is the only Biblical reference to dove cotes. In ancient times pigeon-houses had many openings. Pigeons were kept for food, for sport, and for their dung.

DOVE'S DUNG, mentioned only in II Kings 6:25 as a food to which the famished people of Samaria were reduced. See PLANTS.

DOWRY (dou′rē), the price paid by the suitor to the parents of the prospective bride; also the portion which the bride brought to her husband. Genesis 30:20, 34:12, Exodus 22:17, and I Samuel 18:25 illustrate various uses of the word.

DRACHMA (See Money)

DRAGON. The Hebrew word *tannîn* is variously translated "dragon," "whale," "serpent," or "sea-monster." It referred to an imaginary creature of great size and frightening aspect. A number of passages in the KJV rendered "dragon" are more correctly translated "jackal" in the RV (Job 30:29; Ps. 44:19; Isa. 13:22; etc.) In the NT, Satan is portrayed in the Book of Revelation by means of dragon imagery (12:9; 20:2).

DRAM (See Weights and Measures)

DRAUGHT HOUSE, a privy or water-closet. In some Oriental cities unspeakably filthy, and so Jehu (II Kings 10:27) gave the utmost disgrace to the temple of Baal, whose worship he extirpated. See Mark 7:19.

DRAWER OF WATER. Bringing water from a well or a spring to the house was generally relegated to the servants, and was heavy work (Deut. 29:11; Josh. 9:23-27). Sometimes the girls did it. (Gen. 24:19-25).

DREAM. In early patriarchal times, God often appeared in theophany to godly men but from the time of Jacob and onward His revelations were more often in dreams. (Contrast for instance the experience of Abraham in Genesis 18 with that of Jacob in Genesis 28:10-17). He could reveal His will in dreams today, but the written Word of God, and the indwelling Holy Spirit have made dreams of this sort unnecessary. (Contrast Num. 12:6 with Jude 8). Frequently in ancient times God spoke in dreams to persons outside the chosen family, e.g. to Abimelech of Gerar (Gen. 20:3), to Laban (Gen. 31:24), to the butler and baker of Pharaoh (Gen. 40:8-19), to Pharaoh himself (Gen. 41:1-36) then much later to Nebuchadnezzar (Dan. 2:1-45, 4:5-33) etc. In these dreams, the meaning was clear enough to need no interpretation, as in those of Abimelech and Laban, or else God caused one of his servants to interpret the meaning, as in the latter cases. One principle of interpretation seems quite evident: when the symbol is in the natural realm, the interpretation is in the human realm; e.g. when Joseph dreamed of the sun, moon and eleven stars bowing to him, his brethren immediately knew the meaning as referring to his father, mother and brethren (Gen. 37:9-11). When the symbol is in the human realm, as in Daniel 7:8, "eyes like the eyes of a man and a mouth speaking great things," the interpretation is in the spiritual realm. Dreams may lead men astray, but God's Word tells how to deal with this situation (Deut. 13:1-3; cf. I John 4:1-6), Jeremiah 23:25-32 and other passages speak of lying prophets, perhaps akin to spiritists and other deceivers of today. Notice the contrast between Mary, to whom God spake directly by the Angel Gabriel (Luke 1:26-35), and Joseph, to whom the angel appeared in a dream (Matt. 1:20-24).   A.B.F.

DRESS. Our knowledge of the kind of clothing worn by the people of Biblical times comes from Scriptural statements; from representations of the people and their clothing we find on monuments, reliefs, seals, plaques, and tomb-paintings; and from graves and tomb remains.

All these, coupled with the traditions and usages extant among the present Bedouin Arab tribes, lead us to the conclusion that at a very early period of man's existence he learned the art of spinning and weaving cloth of hair, wool, cotton, flax, and eventually silk (Gen. 14:23; Gen. 31:18,19; 37:3; 38:28; Job 7:6; Ezek. 16:10,13), and from these established certain simple styles which were continued from generation to generation, then carried by Esau and Ishmael and their descendants into Arabia, where the Arab continued them through the centuries — always with a feeling that it was decidedly wrong to change.

When the Arabs overran the larger part of the Bible lands in the sixth century A.D., they returned with these patterns of clothing, and in general have so nearly continued the basic forms that in unspoiled areas much the same garments will be worn today as were worn by Jacob of OT times, and by Jesus of NT times.

The clothing worn by the Hebrew people of Biblical times was graceful, modest, and exceedingly significant. They were considered so much a part of those who wore them that they not only told who and what they were, but were intended as external symbols of the individual's innermost feelings and deepest desires, and his moral urge to represent God aright. With certain kinds of cloth and with astonishingly vivid colors of white, purple, scarlet, blue, yellow, and black, they represented the state of their minds and emotions. When joyful and ready to enter into festive occasions, they donned their clothing of brightest array, and when they mourned or humbled themselves, they put on sackcloth — literally cloth from which sacks were made — which was considered the very poorest kind of dress, and quite indicative of their lowly feelings (I Kings 20:31,32; Job 16:15; Isa. 15:3; Jer. 4:8; 6:26; Lam. 2:10; Ezek. 7:18; Dan. 9:3; Joel 1:8).

When a person's heart was torn by grief, the inner emotions were given expression by "rending" or tearing the garments (Mark 14:63; Acts 11:14). To confirm an oath, or seal a contract, a man plucked off his shoe and gave it to his neighbor. When Jonathan made a covenant with David, he went even farther, and gave him his own garments.

There was variety in clothing such as characterized the people from the various lands adjacent to Palestine, and within the narrow confines of the country itself there was a distinctive clothing that set off the Canaanite from the Philistine. Among the Hebrews there were slight differences in dress as characterized ranks, trades, and professions. Yet it was little less than amazing how similar were the general patterns worn. The variety for the most part was in quality and in decoration. Clothing was colored red, brown, yellow, etc., but white was much preferred. It denoted purity, cleanliness, and joy. Princes, priests, and kings of near eastern countries wore purple, except on special occasions when they often dressed in white garments. Others sometimes wore white on the occasions of joy and gladness. But in general the people wore darker colors, yet they tended toward the brighter side.

The basic garments in general used among the men of Biblical times, seem to have consisted of the inner-tunic, the tunic-coat, the girdle, and the

Arab peasant types, who still wear clothing very similar to that worn in Bible days. © MPS

cloak. Added to this was the head-dress, and the shoes or sandals.

1. The *inner-tunic* or *undershirt,* which in cooler weather the male members of the oriental family wore next to the body, was usually made of a long piece of plain cotton or linen cloth made into a short shirt-like under-garment. At times it was little more than a loin-cloth in length, and at other times it reached below the knees, or even just above the ankles. It was not usually worn when the weather was warm. The KJV refers to such under-garments worn by priests as "breeches" (Exod. 28:42).

2. The *tunic-coat* or *Ketonet* was a close-fitting shirt-like garment which was the most frequently worn garment in the home and on the street. In ancient times it was frequently of one solid color, but at the present it is more often made of a gaily-colored striped cotton material which among the Arabs is often called "the cloth of seven colors" because of the narrow vertical stripes of green, red, yellow, blue, and white which alternate. It was lined with a white cotton material, and worn over the undershirts when it was cool, but next to the body when the weather was warm. This garment usually had long sleeves, and extended down to the ankles when worn as a dress coat, and was held in place by a girdle. Hard-working men, slaves, and prisoners wore them more abbreviated — sometimes even to their knees, and without sleeves — as shown on the Behistun inscription. On Sennacherib's Lachish relief (701 B.C.), the elders and important men of the city are shown wearing long dress-like white tunics which came well down near the ankles. These garments were pure white, with no decorations, and no girdle to hold them. In this and other reliefs, however, the Hebrews had just been taken captive and were prisoners of war, therefore could well have been divested of all but their basic garments.

3. The *girdle* was either a cloth or a leather *belt,* which was worn over the loose coat-like *skirt* or *shirt.* The *cloth girdle,* ordinarily worn

Clothing worn by men and women was similar in appearance in many respects, but with important differences. KC © FC

by village and townspeople, was a square yard of woolen, linen, or even silk cloth first made into a triangle, then folded into a sash-like belt about five to eight inches wide and some 36 inches long. When drawn about the waist, and the tapering ends tied in the back, it not only girded the loins but its folds formed a pocket in which was carried a variety of articles such as nuts, loose change, and other small objects or treasures. It was worn by both men and women and the model woman of Proverbs 31 made them to sell to the merchants. The girdle is not only a picturesque article of dress, but also may indicate the position and office of the wearer. It is sometimes used to signify power and strength (II Sam. 22:40; Isa. 11:5; Jer. 13:1; Eph. 6:14).

The *leather girdle* or belt was from two to six inches wide, and was frequently studded with iron, silver, or gold. It was worn by soldiers, by men of the desert, and by countrymen who tended cattle or engaged in the rougher pursuits of life. This type of girdle was sometimes supported by a shoulder strap, and provided a means whereby various articles such as a scrip (a small bag or wallet for carrying small articles), sword, dagger, or other valuables could be carried. It was the kind of girdle worn by Elijah (II Kings 1:8) and by John the Baptist (Matt. 3:4). Today the laborer and the poorer classes use rawhide or rope for a girdle; the better classes use some woolen or camel's hair sashes of different widths. The women wear long garments reaching to the feet, and a girdle of silk or wool, usually having all the colors of the rainbow, and with fringe hanging from the waist nearly to the ankles.

The girdle, whether made of cloth or leather, was a very useful article of clothing in that it so frequently entered into so many activities of everyday life. When one was to walk, or run, or enter into any type of service he "girded himself" for the journey or for the task at hand. Thus it was that girded loins were a symbol of readiness for service or endeavor. Isaiah said of the Messiah that righteousness should be "the girdle of his waist and faithfulness the girdle of his loins" (Isa. 11:5), and Paul spoke of the faithful Christian as having his "loins girt about with truth" (Eph. 6:14).

4. The *cloak, mantle,* or *robe* was a large, loose-fitting garment, which for warmth and appearance was worn over all other articles of clothing as a completion of male attire. It was distinguished by its greater size and by the absence of the girdle. It existed in two varieties, which were usually known as the "me-il," and the "simlah."

The *me-il* was a long, loose-sleeved robe or public dress which was worn chiefly by men of official position and by ministers, educators, and the wealthy. It was the robe of the professions (I Sam. 2:18,19), a dress of dignity, culture, and distinction — the mark of high rank and station (I Sam. 24:11; I Chron. 15:27). It was rich in appearance and could well have been the "coat of many colors" which Jacob gave to Joseph, or the like of which Hannah made and brought to Samuel from year to year as he ministered before the Lord at Shiloh (I Sam. 2:18,19). In its finest form, it must have been the high priests' "robe of the ephod with its fringes of bells and pomegranates swaying and swinging and tinkling" as he walked (Exod. 28:31-38). It is generally understood that there were two kinds of ephods — one with its rich and elaborate insignia and paraphernalia peculiar to the office of high priest, and by the other a more simple "linen ephod" worn by leaders of distinction other than the high priests (II Sam. 6:14).

The *simlah* was the large, loose-fitting sleeveless cloak or mantle which, in general pattern, corresponds to the long and flowing garment which the Arab shepherd and peasant call an *abba* or *abayeh*. They wear it by day, and wrap themselves in it by night, therefore it was not to be taken in pledge unless it was returned by sundown (Exod. 22:26).

These simple yet picturesque garments were usually made of wool, goat-hair, or camel-hair. Men of distinction frequently wore more colorful cloaks called "robes," which were made of linen, wool, velvet, or silk, elaborately bordered and lined with fur.

This long outer garment or top-coat was, in all probability, the "mantle" worn by Elijah and Elisha (II Kings 2:8-14). It was the camel's-hair garment worn by John the Baptist (Matt. 3:4). It is frequently made of alternate strips of white, red, and brown, or is formed by sewing together two lengths of cloth so that the only seams required were those along the top of the shoulders. In unusual cases, however, the cloak is woven of one broad width, with no seam. Such, many believe, was the garment, wrongly translated "coat," which Christ wore, and over which, at the crucifixion, the Roman soldiers "cast lots" rather than "rend" it, for it "was without seam, woven from the top throughout" (John 19:23).

On Shalmaneser's Black Obelisk (ninth century B.C.), the artist shows Israelite men wearing long cloaks or mantles with elaborate fringed borders both on the cutaway fronts and along the bottom. These were in keeping with the Mosaic injunction to make them blue "fringes in the borders of their garments" that they might remember to do all the commandments and be holy unto God (Num. 15:38-40; Deut. 22:12).

The word "skirt," found a number of times in the Bible (KJV), usually refers to an article of male, not female, clothing, and has a number of meanings: (1) "extremity" (Ruth 3:9, (2) "corner" (I Sam. 24:4ff), (3) "hem" (Exod. 28:33), (4) "collar" (Ps. 133:2).

5. The *headdress* was chiefly worn as a protection against the sun and a finish to a completed

costume. It varied from time to time according to rank, sex, and nationality. In the main, however, there were three known types that were worn by the male members of the Hebrew and surrounding nations; the *cap*, the *turban*, and the *head-scarf*.

The ordinary brimless cotton or woolen cap, corresponding somewhat to our skull-cap, was sometimes worn by men of poorer circumstances. Captives are seen wearing these as they are depicted on the Behistun Rock. The turban (hood, RV in Isa. 3:23) was made of thick linen material and formed by winding a scarf or sash about the head in artistic style and neatly concealing the ends. That of the high priest was called a *mitre* (Exod. 28).

The head-scarf, known among the Arabs as the *kaffiyeh*, is usually made up of a square yard of white or colored cotton, wool, or silk cloth folded into a triangle and draped about the head. The apex of the triangle falls directly down the back, forming a V point, while the tapering ends are thrown back over the shoulders, or in cold weather they are wrapped about the neck. This graceful head-scarf is held in position by an *ajhal*, which is made of several soft woolen or silk twists bound by ornamental threads, and worn in coils about the head. An ornamental tassel falls to the side or down the back. When Ben-hadad's shattered Syrian army realized the serious loss it had suffered, some of his men suggested to him that they "put sackcloth on their loins and ropes upon their heads" and go to the king of Israel, hoping he would save their lives (I Kings 20:31,32).

Shoes and *sandals* were considered the lowliest articles that went to make up the wearing apparel of the people of Bible Lands (Mark 1:7). In the Bible, and in secular sources, they were mentioned at a very early period, and are seen in considerable variety on the Egyptian, Babylonian, Assyrian, and Persian monuments. A pair of terra cotta shoes, of the modern snow-shoe variety, were found in an Athenian grave of about 900 B.C.

Making clothing in the home. © SPF

Shoes were of soft leather, while sandals were of a harder leather. The sandals were worn for rougher wear. According to some authorities, the sole was of wood, cane, or sometimes bark of the palm tree and was fastened to the leather by nails. They were tied about the feet with thongs, or *shoe-latchets* (Gen. 14:23; Neh. 1:7). It was customary to have two pairs, especially on a journey.

Shoes were usually removed at the doorway before entering a home, on approaching God (Exod. 3:5), and during mourning (II Sam. 15:30). Property rights were secured by the seller pulling off his shoe and giving it to the purchaser (Ruth 4:7). The "clouts" referred to in Josh. 9:5 are patched shoes.

Women's Dress. Among the Hebrews neither sex was permitted by Mosaic law to wear the same form of clothing as was used by the other (Deut. 22:5). A few articles of female clothing carried somewhat the same name and basic pattern, yet there was always sufficient difference in embossing, embroidery, and needlework so that in appearance the line of demarcation between men and women could be readily detected.

The women wore long garments reaching almost to the feet, with a girdle of silk or wool, many times having all the colors of the rainbow. Often such a garment would have a fringe hanging from the waist nearly to the ankles.

The ladies' head-dress, for example, usually included some kind of a *kaffiyeh* or cloth for covering the head, yet the material that was in that covering was of a different quality, kind, or color from that worn by the men. And, also, it was frequently pinned over some kind of a cap made of stiff material and set with pearls, silver, gold, or spangled ornaments common to that day. If a woman was married, these or other more significant coins covered the entire front of her cap and constituted her dowry. Her under garments would be made of material such as cotton, linen, or silk, as might befit her wealth or station in life. She would probably wear a long skirt with long, pointed sleeves. Over this was a small rather tightly-fitting jacket or "petticoat" — meaning little coat. The small jacket would be made of "scarlet" or other good material and was a thing of exquisite beauty because of its being covered with "tapestry" or fine needlework, wrought with multi-colored threads. A woman of even moderate circumstances could have beautiful clothing, for it was "the fruit of her own hands" (Prov. 31:19).

In the OT many articles of women's clothing are mentioned which cannot be exactly identified. Ezekiel 13:18,21 refers to a "kerchief" (Heb. *mispahah),* a head-covering or veil of some sort, the exact nature of which is unknown. Isa. 3:16-24 speaks of "mufflers," probably two-piece veils, one part covering the face below the eyes; the other, the head, down over the neck; "wimples," rendered "shawls" in the RV; "stomachers," which in the English means that part of a woman's dress which covered the breast and the pit of the stomach — usually much ornamented, but the meaning of the Hebrew is unknown; also "crisping-pins," and "cauls" (RV), which cannot be identified.

Women often added to their adornment by an elaborate "plaiting" of the hair. I Peter 3:3 finds it necessary to warn Christian women against relying upon such adorning to make themselves attractive. In the OT there are a number of references to painting the eyes in order to enhance their beauty, but it is always spoken of as a mere-

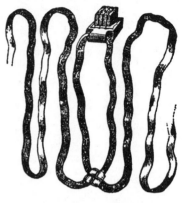

Beginning about the second century B.C., all male Jews were expected to wear at morning prayers, except on sabbaths, and festivals two *phylacteries,* one on the forehead, called a *frontlet,* the other on the left arm. They consisted of small leather cases containing four passages of Scripture from the OT; Exodus 13:1-10, 11-16; Deuteronomy 6:4-9; 11:13-21.   G.F.O. & S.B.

A phylactery, or frontlet — Scriptures contained in a small box made of parchment, painted black, with strips of leather to bind to the head or arm. DV

Women's hair styles in the Greek and Roman world of Paul's day. UANT

tricious device, unworthy of good women. Jezebel painted her eyes (II Kings 9:30).

In ancient times women especially were much given to various kinds of ornaments. Earrings and nose-rings were especially common. On account of their drop-like shape, earrings are called "pendants" (Isa. 3:19), "chains" (Isa. 3:19 KJV), and "collars" (Judg. 8:26). Men also wore such earrings (Gen. 35:4; Judg. 8:24). The nose-ring, or nose-jewel made necessary the piercing of the nostrils. Rings were worn by both men and women. All ancient Israelites wore signet-rings (Gen. 38:18). Rings were often worn on the toes; anklets (spangles) on the ankles (Isa. 3:18); bracelets on the arms and wrists (Gen. 24:22; Ezek. 16:11).

Below, prayer time in the home. Note phylacteries on the men's arms and foreheads. © SPF

A woman wearing many ornaments, while at work sifting archaeological findings. © MPS

DRINK. The most common beverage of the Jews was water. This was procured chiefly in two ways, by means of cisterns, which were possessed by every well-appointed house (II Sam. 17:18; Jer. 38:6) and by means of wells, which were rare and were usually the possession of a clan or community.

Wine was also widely used, both in the form of new wine, called must, and fermented wine. In the heat of harvest frequent use was made of a sour drink consisting of a mixture of water and wine, and of a strong drink, called *shekhar,* the method of preparing which is unknown. Wine was sometimes spiced to improve its taste. Wine was also made from pomegranates, and possibly also from ripe dates and barley. The Mishna also speaks of honey-wine and cider.

Next to bread and vegetables the most important food was milk, both of larger and smaller cattle, especially goat's milk. This was usually kept in skins. Because of the hot climate, fresh milk soon became sour, but it was very effective for quenching thirst. S.B.

DRINK OFFERING, an offering of oil and wine made to God as a part of the Levitical worship. Such offerings accompanied many of the sacrifices (Exod. 29:40,41). They were presented at all set feasts (Lev. 23:13,18,37). The heathen also made drink offerings to their gods (Deut. 32:38). See OFFERINGS.

DROMEDARY (See Animals)

DROPSY (See Diseases)

DROSS, the refuse in impure metals which is generally separated by melting, when the dross rises to the top and may be skimmed off. Used figuratively of what is worthless (Isa. 1:22,25; Ezek. 22:18,19; Ps. 119:119).

DRUNKENNESS. The Scriptures show that drunkenness was one of the major vices of antiquity, even among the Hebrews. Among the better-known cases of intoxication are the following: Noah (Gen. 9:21), Lot (Gen. 19:33,35), Nabal (I Sam. 25:36), Uriah (II Sam. 11:13), Amnon (II Sam. 13:28), Elah, king of Israel (I Kings 16:9), and Benhadad, king of Syria (I Kings 20:16). The prophets frequently denounce drunkenness as a great social evil of the wealthy. Even the women were guilty (Amos 4:1). The symptoms and effects of strong drink are vividly pictured in the Bible (Job 12:25; Ps. 107:27; Isa. 28:7; Hosea 4:11; etc.). While the writers of Scripture condemn intemperance in the strongest terms, they do not prescribe total abstinence as a formal and universal rule. Nevertheless, the principles laid down point in that direction. In ancient times the poor could not afford to drink to excess. The cheapening of alcoholic drinks has made drunkenness a much greater social problem in modern times. The following passages state principles which point to voluntary abstinence from all intoxicants: Matt. 16:24f; Mark 9:42f; Rom. 14:13-21; I Cor. 8:8-13. Drunkenness is sometimes used figuratively (Isa. 29:9). S.B.

DRUSILLA (drōō-sĭl′à, Gr. *Droúsilla*), the youngest of the three daughters of Herod Agrippa I, her sisters being Bernice and Mariamne. At the age of 14 she married Azizus, king of Emesa, but left him for Felix, procurator of Judea, who was captivated by her beauty and employed a Cyprian sorcerer to gain her for his wife. They had one son, Agrippa, who died in an eruption of Mount Vesuvius. When Paul unsparingly preached before Felix and Drusilla of righteousness, temperance, and judgment. Felix trembled (Acts 24:24,25). See HEROD.

DUKE (Heb. *'allûph* and *nāsîkh*). These Hebrew words are sometimes rendered "duke" (especially when used of the leaders of the Edomites), "princes," "principal men," and "governor." In general, they mean a leader of a clan or a tribal chief. See Genesis 36:15ff; Exodus 15:15; I Chronicles 1:5lff; Joshua 13:21.

DUMAH (dū′mà, Heb. *dûmâh, silence*). 1. One of the twelve sons of Ishmael (Gen. 25:14-16) and apparently head of one of the twelve tribes of Ishmaelites in Arabia.

2. A place (unknown) but connected with Seir or Edom (Isa. 21:11-12). The designation may be symbolic, applying to all Edom and indicating its coming destruction. (Cf. Obad. 1:15,16).

3. A village in the S of Judah and associated with Hebron in Joshua 15:52-54.

DUMBNESS (See Diseases)

DUNG, the excrement of man or beast. In several of the offerings, under the Levitical priesthood the blood and the fat and the flesh were used, but the skins and the dung were discarded or burnt outside the camp (Exod. 29:14; Lev. 8:17). The ultimate disgrace was to have one's carcass treated as dung (II Kings 9:37). Dry dung was (and is) often used as fuel (See Ezek. 4:12-15). Paul counted his natural advantages as dung (ASV "refuse") compared with his blessings in Christ.

DUNG GATE, one of the eleven gates of the Jerusalem of Nehemiah's time (See Neh. 3, especially v. 14). It was located near the SW corner of the wall, and was used for the disposal of rubbish, garbage and dung. It led out to the valley of Hinnom.

DURA (dū′rà), a plain in the province of Babylon where Nebuchadnezzar set up his great image of gold to be worshipped (Dan. 3:1).

DWARF (Heb. *daq, thin, small, withered*), an abnormally small person, but in Leviticus 21:20 one of those twelve sorts of unfortunate people who could not officiate at the altar, but who with their brethren, the Levites, could eat the bread of their God. See DISEASES.

DYERS, DYEING (See Occupations)

The Dung Gate in the Jerusalem City Wall. © MPS

E

EAR (Heb. *'ōzen, Gr. oús, otíon, the physical organ of hearing*). In Biblical times people spoke to each other's ears; instead of listening they "inclined their ears." When they prayed, God "bowed down His ear" to hear them. The ear had a significant part in some Jewish ceremonies. It was sanctified by blood in the consecration of Aaron and his sons to the priesthood. (Exod. 29:20; Lev. 8:24) and at the cleansing of a leper (Lev. 14:14). The piercing of the ear of a slave denoted permanent servitude (Exod. 21:6; Deut. 15:17).

EARING (ēr'ing, Heb. *hārîsh, ploughing time*), translated "earing" in KJV, the RV rendering is *plowing* (Gen 45:6; Exod. 34:21).

EARNEST (êr'něst, Gr. *arrábon*), a legal term in English law denoting the payment of a sum of money to make a contract binding, guaranteeing a further payment to fulfill the contract. Thus the significance of the apostle Paul's use of this word in regard to the Holy Spirit in three passages may be understood (II Cor. 1:22; 5:5; Eph. 1:14). The gift of the Holy Spirit to believers is the assurance that their redemption will be fully carried out.

EARRING (ēr'rĭng, Heb. *nezem, 'āghîl, hoop*). The ancient Hebrews had no specific word for earrings; these jewels were just rings or hoops made of gold (though sometimes the metal is not specified). They were worn by men and women either on the nose or on the ears: a nose-ring in the following passages (Gen. 24:47; Isa. 3:21; Ezek. 16: 12), and earrings in these references (Gen. 35:4; Exod. 32:2,3; Ezek. 16:12). In the rest of the passages where such rings or hoops are mentioned they may be either nose rings or earrings (Exod. 35:22; Num. 31:50; Judg. 8:24-26; Job 42:11; Prov. 11:22; 25:12; Hosea 2:13). When worn as earrings the ring was passed through a hole pierced in the lobe of the ear. Probably pendants were suspended from them. In Isaiah 3:20 the Hebrew term *lachash* is translated *earring*s in KJV, but this word actually means an amulet.

EARTH (Heb. *'ādhāmâh, ground, 'erets, earth*, Gr. *gē, earth, oikouméne, inhabited earth; kósmos, orderly arrangement*). *'ādhāmâh* most commonly means the tilled reddish soil of Palestine. But it is also used to denote a piece of real estate property (Gen. 47:18ff1); earth as a material substance (Gen. 2:7); a territory (Gen. 28:15); the whole earth (Gen. 12:3; Deut. 14:2).

'Erets denotes commonly the earth as opposed to the sky (Gen. 1:1; Josh. 2:11); also very frequently it means *land* in the sense of a country (Gen. 13:10; 45:18). In the New Testament *gē* means *ground*, arable and otherwise (Matt. 5:18; John 8:6); *the earth* as opposed to the heavens (Matt. 6:10; Acts 2:19); *territory* or *region* (Luke 4:25; John 3:22). *Oikouméne* carries the meaning of the inhabited earth or the *world* (Luke 4:5; Matt. 24:14), the Roman Empire (Luke 2:1), all the inhabitants of the earth (Acts 17:6; Rev. 3: 10). *Kósmos* in a derived sense is used to denote the earth, though it is always translated *world* in our Bibles. It has more to do with the inhabitants of the earth than with the actual planet.

Sometimes it is difficult to tell whether the earth or the land is meant, particularly in the prophetic books. For example, in Isaiah 24:1,3, 4,5, the word "earth" may mean "land" instead. The ancient Hebrew had no idea of the shape or size of the earth, or that it was a planet. The earth was simply the area where men lived, moved and had their being. But Job 26:7 is a scientifically correct statement, "He stretcheth out the north over empty space, and hangeth the earth upon nothing."

EARTHQUAKE (ûrth'kwāk, Heb. *ra'ash, quaking*, Gr. *seimos, earthquake*). There are four actual earthquakes recorded in Scripture: the one which occurred at Mt. Horeb for Elijah's benefit (I Kings 19:11); that referred to by Amos (1:1) and Zechariah (14:5) as occurring in the reign of Uzziah, king of Judah; the one which happened at the resurrection of Christ (Matt. 28:2); and the one which freed Paul and Silas from prison (Acts 16:26). An earthquake is mentioned in Isaiah 29:6 as a form of judgment from the Lord on the enemies of His people.

The earth has been plagued with quakes all through its history. The book of Revelation predicts more for the future (8:5; 11:13,19; 16:18).

In most of the cases of the mention of an earthquake in the Bible, God caused them for a specific purpose. But earthquakes have occurred in Palestine in modern times as they did.in ancient times. This land is situated on the edge of one of the main earthquake belts of the planet, which extends from Spain eastward through the Mediterranean area and the Himalaya mountains to the East Indies.
C.E.H.

EAST (Heb. *qedem* and other forms of this root, *front, aforetime, east; mizrâh, place of the sunrise, east*, Gr. *anatolé, rising, east*). East was a significant direction for the Hebrews. The gate of the tabernacle was on the east side (Exod. 38:13; 14). In the wilderness, Moses and Aaron encamped on the east side of the Tabernacle and this area was barred to strangers (Num. 3:38). Judah encamped on the east side of the camp (Num. 2:3). This same tribe was first in the line of march (Num. 10:14). On the analogy of the Tabernacle many scholars think the chief entrance to Solomon's temple was on the east side. In Herod's temple the "door of the temple which is called Beautiful" (Acts 3:2) was the east gate (Alfred Edersheim *The Life and Times of Jesus the Messiah*, Vol. I, New York: Longmans, Green, and Co., 1899, p. 245). Ezekiel saw the glory of the Lord leave the doomed temple by the east gate (Ezek. 10: 19; 11:23). In this prophet's description of the Lord's temple, Ezekiel saw the glory of the Lord coming from the East and entering the temple by the east gate (Ezek. 43:2,4).

The phrase "children of the East" occurs frequently in the OT. It refers to the inhabitants of the lands E of Palestine, on the edge of the desert. Job was such a one (Job 1:3). The Wise Men came from the East, and said they had seen the star of the King of the Jews in the East (Matt. 2:1,2).
C.E.H.

EASTER (Gr. *páscha, passover*), rendered *Easter* in Acts 12:4 KJV, but correctly translated *Passover* in ASV. The day on which the Church celebrates the resurrection of Jesus Christ.

There is no celebration of the Resurrection in the NT. The Jewish Christians linked it with the Passover, and so observed it on the 14th day of Nisan regardless of the day of the week. But Gentile believers celebrated the Resurrection on the Lord's day, Sunday. This difference was settled by the Council of Nicea in 325 A.D. which ruled that Easter should be celebrated on the first Sunday after the full moon following the vernal equinox. This is the system followed today, the date of Easter varying between March 22 and April 25.

EAST SEA, or the Dead Sea, formed part of the eastern boundary of Canaan proper, being the southern section of the great valley of the Jordan river. In the division of the tribes this sea became the eastern boundary of Judah (Josh. 15:5).

EAST WIND (Heb. *qādîm*). Winds of the E came to Palestine over the desert; therefore it was a hot, dry, wind in the wilderness (Jer. 4:11). An E wind brought the plague of locusts on Egypt (Exod. 10:13), and dried up the sea so the Israelites could cross over on dry land (Exod. 14:21). Many references mention the destructive results of the E wind; thin and blasted ears of corn (Gen. 41:6), broken ships (Ps. 48:7; Ezek. 27:26); withered plants (Ezek. 17:10); dried fountains (Hosea 13:15); Jonah smitten (Jonah 4:8). The E wind was used as a means of judgment by God (Isa. 27:8; Jer. 18:17).

EBAL (ē'bǎl, Heb. *'ēvāl,* meaning uncertain). 1. A son of Shobal (Gen. 36:23; I Chron. 1:40).

2. A mountain 3077 feet high, one of the highest points in the land of Samaria. It stood opposite Mt. Gerizim, across a valley through which ran an important route of travel. At its foot was Jacob's well (see John 4:20: "on this mountain"), and the city of Shechem was located near by. When the Israelites first entered the land, Moses commanded them to erect on Mt. Ebal a monument of stones on which the law was inscribed, and a stone altar for burnt offerings and peace offerings. The law, with its blessings and curses was recited by the people antiphonally, the blessings from Mt. Gerizim, and the curses from Mt. Ebal (Deut. 27:4-26). Joshua renewed this procedure after the conquest of Ai (Josh. 8:30-35). The central location of this mountain and its height made it valuable for military purposes. A ruined fortress is still visible on its summit.

3. One of the sons of Joktan (I Chron. 1:22).

EBED (ē'bĕd, Heb. *'evedh, servant*). 1. Father of Gaal, the adversary of Ahimelech who unsuccessfully rebelled against this ruler in Shechem (Judg. 9:26-45).

2. Son of Jonathan, one of the 50 men of the family of Adin that came from Babylon under Ezra (Ezra 8:6).

EBED-MELECH (ē'bĕd-mē-lĕk, Heb. *'evedh melekh, servant of the king*), an Ethiopian eunuch who, when he heard about Jeremiah's being cast into a miry dungeon, was moved to go to the king and ask for permission to pull the prophet out. The king granted him 30 men, and with cords of rags and worn-out garments they drew Jeremiah up out of that dungeon (Jer. 38:7-13). The Lord gave Jeremiah a message for Ebed-Melech, assuring him of safety and protection in the coming destruction of the city (Jer. 39:15-18).

EBEN-EZER (ĕb'ĕn-ē'zĕr, Heb. *'even-'ezer, stone of help*). 1. A town of Ephraim near Aphek by which the Israelites encamped before fighting a losing battle with the Philistines (I Sam. 4:1). The ark of God was captured by these enemies of Israel, and they brought it from Eben-ezer to their city, Ashdod (I Sam. 5:1).

2. Later God gave them victory over the Philistines. Samuel then took a stone and set it up as a memorial of the occasion calling it *Eben-ezer,* "the stone of help," saying, "Hitherto hath the Lord helped us" (I Sam. 7:12).

Mount Ebal, as viewed from Jacob's Well. © MPS

EBER (ē'bêr, Heb. *'ēver*). This word means "a region across or beyond." It may be the eponym of the Hebrews, as its form is the same as the word *'iberi* (Hebrew) without the gentilic ending. The Hebrews were a people who came from a region beyond the Euphrates river. 1. The son of Shelah, a grandson of Shem (Gen. 10:24; 11:14; I Chron. 1:18). He was the father of Peleg and Joktan (Gen. 10:25; 11:16; I Chron. 1:19-25).

2. The head of a family in the tribe of Gad (I Chron. 5:13).

3. The oldest son of Elpaal, a Benjamite (I Chron. 8:12).

4. A son of Shemei, a Benjamite (I Chron. 8:22).

5. Head of a priestly family that came from Babylon under Zerubbabel (Neh. 12:20).

EBIASAPH (ē-bī'à-sǎph, Heb. *'avî'āsāph* and *'ĕvî'āsāph, my father has gathered*), a son of Elkanah, a descendant of Kohath, son of Levi (Exod. 6:24; I Chron. 6:23; 9:19).

EBRONAH (ē-brō'nàh, Heb. *'avrōnâh,* the ASV has *Abronah*), the encampment of the Hebrews just before they arrived at Ezion-geber at the gulf of Aqabah (Num. 33:34). The site is uncertain.

ECBATANA (ĕk-bǎt'-à-nà, Heb. *'ahmethā'*), the capital of Media and the summer residence of the Persian kings. It is found in the Behistun inscription of Darius I. It is mentioned in an inscription of Tiglath-Pileser I at a much earlier time. It was later the Parthian capital also. In Greek the name of this city became *Hagbatana* (Herodotus) or *Ecbatana* (II Maccabees). It is mentioned in the Bible only in Ezra 6:2 as *Achmethā,* denoting the location of the palace in which the decree of Cyrus authorizing the building of the Jewish temple was found. According to Herodotus, this city was founded by Deioces, a Median king. Cyrus captured it in 550 B.C., and Alexander the Great took it from the Persians in 330 B.C. The modern city of Hamadan is located on or near the same site. Very little remains of the ancient city.

ECCLESIASTES (ĕ-klē-zĭ-ăs'-tēz, Gr. *Ekklesiatés,* Heb. *qōheleth,* meaning, probably, *an official speaker in an assembly—the Preacher*). This is one of the most perplexing books in the Bible. The

Solomonic authorship, now generally rejected, can still be maintained on the following grounds: 1. The one who calls himself "the Preacher" is described as David's son and as king in Jerusalem (1:1,12).

2. This same person designates himself as a collector of proverbs (12:9), a description that obviously fits Solomon (cf. I Kings 4:32).

3. The reference to the author's great wisdom (1:16; 2:9) accords with Solomon's ability (cf. I Kings 4:30f).

4. The author's description of the splendor of Jerusalem during his reign (2:4-9) points unmistakably to Solomon (cf. I Chron. 29:25).

5. Several rather subtle references to characteristics of his life (e.g., 4:13; 7:26,28; 10:6,16) point plainly to Solomon.

6. The close parallel between this book and Proverbs is best explained by unity of authorship.

Some have considered Ecclesiastes as unworthy of a place in the sacred canon because of its rather apparent skepticism and pessimism. In order, however, to understand the nature and purpose of this book one must weigh carefully the import of such features as the following: 1. The exclusive use of Elohim (rather than Jehovah) as the divine name tacitly reminds us that the author is dealing with man's relationship to God as Creator rather than as Redeemer.

2. The oft-repeated "under the sun" designation confirms the supposition that the author is speaking from the viewpoint of general rather than supernatural revelation.

3. The ubiquitous "vanity" that resounds like a doleful refrain adds further weight to the view that the author is dealing with life apart from the light of special revelation.

4. Finally, the denial that anything can be "new" (1:9f) cogently enforces the idea that the author's thoughts are within the circle of the old covenant rather than the new covenant (cf. Isa. 42:9; 43: 18f; 65:17; Jer. 31:31).

In this book, therefore, we find the basic elements of general revelation: 1. God's existence (3: 14; 5:2).

2. God's sovereignty and power (6:2; 7:13; 9:1).

3. God's justice (5:8; 8:12f).

4. man's sinfulness (7:20; 9:3).

5. man's finiteness and limitations (8:8,17).

6. man's duty and responsibility (9:7-10; 12: 13).

7. man's immortality (3:11; 12:7).

8. punishment and rewards (2:26; 3:17; 8:12; 11:9; 12:14).

Thus this book, properly understood, is a negative preparation for the Gospel; for, using a man especially endowed with knowledge and experience, the Spirit of God shows in this book how far such a man can go "under the sun." Here we have natural revelation at its best; for, let us note, there is nothing in this book that contradicts the rest of Scripture. In fact, the author's final conclusion (12:1,13) leads him to the very door of the kingdom of God. As the law was designed to lead men to Christ, so this book was written to lead those "under the sun" to the Son (cf. Heb. 1:1). W.B.

ECUMENICISM (ĕcū-mĕn'ĭ-cĭsm), derives from the Greek *oikouméne*, the whole inhabited world. An older adjectival derivative is *ecumenical*. Thus the first world-wide councils from Nicea (A.D. 325) were described as ecumenical, and the patriarch of Constantinople claimed to be the ecumenical bishop in virtue of his assumed primacy. Neither the adjective nor the noun is used in the Bible in any special sense.

More recently, the term ecumenical has come into Protestant usage through missionary conferences aimed to bring the Gospel to the whole inhabited globe (New York, A.D. 1900). It was adopted by Archbishop Soderblom of Sweden when, after the First World War, he convened a conference to study the role of the church in reconstruction (Stockholm, A.D. 1925). Since then, the efforts of the churches to work together and to try to achieve closer unity have been commonly styled the Ecumenical Movement, and ecumenicism or ecumenism has been coined to express concern for, participation in, or the fulfillment of this or similar movements.

While not a Biblical term, ecumenicism may claim a Biblical basis. From the missionary angle, Christians are committed to a world-wide task. From that of inter-relationships, the churches of various localities cannot be isolated units. They share a common faith, common tasks and common interests. Where matters of general importance arise, they should be considered on a global and not just a parochial or national level (cf. Acts 15:6ff). In its basic significance, ecumenicism as concern for the faith, work and welfare of the whole church is something which none would wish to hamper or ignore.

Yet there are aspects of contemporary ecumenicism which demand care and caution. In some quarters there is the tendency to think of it more strictly in ecclesiastical terms. This may find expression in the unbiblical and undesirable hope of ultimately constructing a single world-church under central control; or it may emerge in the notion that only churches linked with and participating in the movement should be regarded as Christian bodies, e.g., for negotiation with the state. Such hierarchical attitudes negate true ecumenicism, yet form a tempting substitute.

Moreover, there is the danger of the desire for ecumenicity taking precedence of Christian confession in the strict sense. That is, attempted comprehension may lead to the recognition of all groups which in some sense claim to follow Jesus Christ. Fortunately, the World Council has thus far clung to a minimal confession of Jesus Christ as Saviour and God, but many local supporters would prefer to weaken this in order to include, e.g., Unitarians. Once more, the result would be fatal to true ecumenicism, and true Christians alienated might well be greater than the peripheral groups included.

Again, it is hard to see how there can be real ecumenicism without agreement in basic Scriptural doctrine. To cooperate in missionary or social work is not enough, nor is it always possible if there is no agreement on the Gospel to be preached nor the basis and goal of the action undertaken, nor is discussion adequate, though obviously useful. Nor is there any value in formulae which merely hide disagreement. The Ecumenical Movement realizes this, but without acceptance of Scripture as the supreme rule of faith and conduct ecumenicism must surely be unattainable or fictitious.

Finally, there is the danger of confusing unity and uniformity. Churches may confess a common faith, but with variations of statement and emphasis, and minor disagreements on some issues. They may engage in basic acts of worship and ministry, yet in very different outward forms. To achieve world-wide fellowship, it is not necessary that the same forms or practices should be accepted by or enforced on all. Thus far, the Ecumenical Movement has hardly seen uniformity as a desirable or practicable end, but groups within it are prepared to insist on at least some specific forms, e.g., of baptism or the ministry, as essentials of true ecumenical recognition. Such demands negate real ecumenicism, and submission to them can only destroy rather than promote it.

More positively, the requirements of a genuinely Biblical ecumenicism may be briefly stated. It may be agreed that all Christians should be concerned for their world-wide fellowship. But the basis of this fellowship is not found in shared interests, the sense of unity or fellowship, or a common structure. It is found in Jesus Christ as the One in whom all are one. Ecumenicism arises where He is given preeminence as Saviour and Lord. Without this, there can be no common missionary program, social task or doctrinal conversation. With it, ecumenicism is already achieved. The rest is only expression and application in varying needs and situations. In a word, ecumenicism has not to be built up by human construction; it is already given in the Lord Himself.

Yet this is not quite so simple as it sounds. The Jesus Christ confessed must be the real Jesus Christ, not our idea of Him. He must be the Jesus Christ of the Old and New Testaments. Any other is an illusory Christ with an illusory message. Hence, ecumenicism centered in Christ is centered in Him as preached in Scripture. It is thus Bible-centered. Problems arise in this connection, e.g., of the canon and interpretation. Discussion and even disagreement may arise. This does not destroy real ecumenicism, however, so long as there is common loyalty to the Biblical testimony. Outside that, there neither is nor can be true unity.

Again, confession of Jesus Christ implies affirmations concerning Him, concerning God as revealed in Him, and concerning His saving work. Now ultimately all that is sure and essential is found in the Bible. Yet this needs to be stated for confession and instruction. Thus difficulties arise, and in areas of less importance these need not be resolved for true unity. But it is essential that there should be material agreement on the great and basic affirmations, e.g., as reached at the first ecumenical councils, or as brought out at the Reformation. Ecumenicism is not destroyed by isolated or private errors, e.g., on the part of some leaders. But even these can be disruptive, and public disavowal by churches of the cardinal Biblical articles makes ecumenicism impossible, since it involves basic repudiation of Christ Himself.

Finally, faith in Jesus Christ means ministry of word and action, and therefore evangelism and practical service in obedience and discipleship. Evangelism is the preaching of the evangelical word and the administering of the evangelical sacraments or ordinances. Service is the relief of the needy in the name of Jesus Christ. It is to be noted that mere attachment to a common cause, or acceptance of a common form, theory or method, gives only a spurious or incomplete unity in these fields. True ecumenicism demands obedience to the command of Jesus as Lord and conformity to the pattern of Jesus as Servant. Where these are present, cooperation and even in some cases integration as well as more concentrated action may be expected among contiguous and even more separated churches, not from without or in terms of uniformity, but from within in deep and enduring unity. Naturally and spontaneously, therefore, ecumenicity will find practical expression as on the New Testament scene.   G.W.B.

EDAR (ē'där, ASV Eder, Heb. *'ēdher, flock*), a tower near which Jacob encamped on his way back to Canaan (Gen. 35:21).

EDEN (ē'd'n, Heb. *'ēden, delight*). 1. The district in which the Lord God planted a garden in which He put the newly-created man, Adam. In it grew every tree that was pleasant to see and good for food, including the tree of life and the tree of the knowledge of good and evil. A river flowed out of Eden and divided into four heads or streams; the Pishon which went around the land of Havilah, where gold was found; the Gihon which flowed around the whole land Cush; the Hiddekel (or Tigris) which flowed in front of Assyria; and the Euphrates (Gen. 2:8-14). Adam and Eve lived there until they sinned by eating the forbidden fruit and were expelled from it (Gen. chapters 2 & 3). Later Scripture writers mention Eden as an illustration of a delightful place (Isa. 51:3; Ezek. 28:13; 31:9,16,18; 36:35; Joel 2:3).

The location of Eden has been much investigated in both ancient and modern times. Actually the data given in Genesis are not sufficient to fix its site because two of the rivers, the Pishon and Gihon, were unknown even to the ancients and still are to modern scholars. Attempts have been made to locate Eden in the mountains of Armenia in the area where the Tigris and Euphrates and several other rivers rise. But the sources of all these streams are not together but are separated by mountain ranges. Mesopotamia, where the Tigris and Euphrates rivers flow, is also within the Fertile Crescent where archaeology has found the oldest civilization. Some scholars suggest the district at the head of the Persian Gulf as the likely location. It has been widely believed that the silt brought down by the rivers has added over a hundred miles of land to the head of the gulf since 3000 B.C. But recent geological examination of this land has indicated that it may not have changed much during the ages. At the site of Eridu, situated near what was considered to be the ancient shore line, clay tablets have been found which tell of a garden in the neighborhood in which grew a sacred palm tree. Further upstream, a short distance N of ancient Babylon, the Tigris and Euphrates flow close together so that canals connect them. Delitzsch considered this area to be the proper location of Eden.

2. An Eden mentioned by the Assyrians as conquered by them along with Gozan Haran and Rezeph (II Kings 19:12; Isa. 37:12). Ezekiel 27:23 also mentions this region. It is believed to be the *Bit-adini* of the Assyrian inscriptions located on the Euphrates. The house of Eden, or Beth-Eden (Amos 1:5), was probably near Damascus, since it is mentioned in a Syrian context, but some scholars think it was the same place as *Bit-adini*.

3. A Gershonite who lived in Hezekiah's time and served under Kore, the porter of the E gate of the temple, in distributing the holy oblations (II Chron. 29:12; 31:15).   C.E.H.

EDER (ē'dêr, Heb. *'edher, floods*). 1. A city in S Judah near Edom (Josh. 15:21), possibly the same as Adar. Site unknown.

2. A son of Mushi, the son of Merari (I Chron. 23:23; 24:30).

EDOM, EDOMITES (ē'dŏm, ē'dŏmīts, Heb. *'ĕdhōm, 'ădhōmîm,* from *'ĕdhōm, red*), the nation and its people who were the descendants of Esau. He founded the country, so his name is equated with Edom (Gen. 25:30; 36:1,8). The country was also called Seir, or Mt. Seir, which was the name of the territory in which the Edomites lived, the

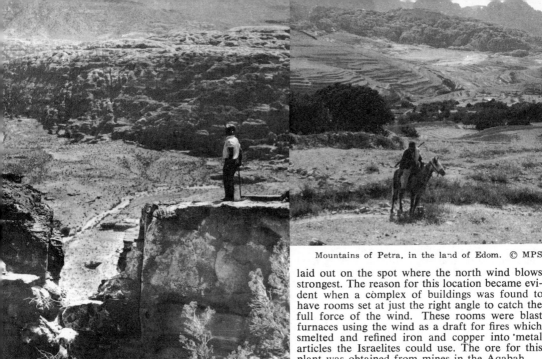

Mountains of Petra, in the land of Edom. © MPS

A view in Edom — the Valley of Petra, the Khubta Ridge, and the desert plateau. © MPS

mountain and plateau area between the Dead Sea and the Gulf of Aqabah about 100 miles long and up to 40 miles wide. The original inhabitants of this land were the Horites, or "cave dwellers" (Gen. 14:6). When Esau departed from Canaan to find room for his cattle and came to Mt. Seir (Gen. 46:5-8), the Horites had some tribal chiefs reigning in the land (Gen. 36:29,30). Esau took the daughter of one of these chiefs for a wife, Oholibamah, daughter of chief Anah (Gen. 36:2, 25). Esau's sons and grandsons were also tribal chiefs (Gen. 36:15-19,40-43). Probably the Edomites gradually absorbed the Horites, until they disappeared (Deut. 2:12,22).

The kingdom of Edom was founded during the 13th century B.C., according to archaeological evidence. In the process of about four centuries the government of Edom changed from one under tribal chiefs to a monarchy. Eight of these kings reigned over Edom before the Israelites had any such ruler (Gen. 36:31-39). One of these kings was on the throne at the time of Moses and refused to permit the Israelites to pass through his country (Num. 20:14-21). Other evidence of ancient Edom is the Papyrus Anastasi VI of Egypt, dated late 13th century B.C., which mentions the passage of shepherd tribes from Edom to the richer pasture land of the Nile delta. The El Amarna letter No. 256, from about 1400 B.C., mentions Edom, in the form *Udumu,* as one of the enemies of a Jordan valley prince.

Saul fought against the Edomites (I Sam. 14:47), but David conquered them and put garrisons throughout the whole land (II Sam. 8:14). The Israelite army spent six months cutting off all the men of the kingdom (I Kings 11:15,16). Solomon made Ezion-geber and Eloth, on the Gulf of Aqabah, seaports from which his ships sailed to Ophir (II Chron. 8:17,18). Archaeologists investigating the site of Ezion-geber discovered that this city had been carefully planned by Solomon. It was laid out on the spot where the north wind blows strongest. The reason for this location became evident when a complex of buildings was found to have rooms set at just the right angle to catch the full force of the wind. These rooms were blast furnaces using the wind as a draft for fires which smelted and refined iron and copper into 'metal articles the Israelites could use. The ore for this plant was obtained from mines in the Aqabah.

Judah lost Edom in the reign of Jehoram when she revolted against him about 847 B.C. (II Kings 8:20,22). About 50 years later Amaziah, king of Judah, inflicted a severe defeat on the Edomites (II Kings 14:7). About 735 B.C. Rezin, king of Syria, at war with Judah, captured Eloth and drove the Jews out (II Kings 16:6). When Jerusalem was destroyed and Judah depopulated by the Babylonians in 586 B.C., the Edomites rejoiced over the affliction of the Judeans and began to take over the southern part of Palestine. Eventually they penetrated as far N as Hebron. This action intensified the already smoldering hatred between the Jews and Edomites (see Ps. 137:7; Ezek. 25:12-14; Amos 1:11; Obadiah 10-14).

The Edomites were also subject to Babylon. Under the Persian Empire Edom became a province called Idumea, the Greek form of Edom. In 325 B.C. an Arab tribe known as the Nabateans conquered the eastern part of Edom's territory. In Maccabean times, John Hyrcanus subdued the Idumeans and forced them to accept Judaism. When the Romans took over Palestine the Edomites also were included. From Idumea came Antipater, the father of Herod the Great. He became procurator of Judea. After the destruction of Jerusalem by the Romans in 70 A.D. the Idumeans disappeared from history. Thus the rather mournful career of the Edomites came to an end. Only in the early centuries of their kingdom, before the Israelites became powerful, did they enjoy freedom to any great extent.

The Assyrians came in contact with Edom as early as the seventh century B.C. When her kings began to penetrate as far south as Palestine, Edom, along with Judah, and her other neighbors, paid tribute to Assyria for many years. She is mentioned many times in the inscription of the kings of Assyria beginning with Adad-Nirari III 800 B.C. to Ashurbanipal (686-633).

Edom figures prominently in the prophetic Scriptures as the scene of great future judgments (see notably Isa. 34:5,6; 63:1). She is the only neighbor of the Israelites who was not given any promise of mercy from God.　　　　C.E.H.

EDREI (ĕd'-rē-ī, Heb. *'edhre'î, strong*). 1. One of the chief sites of Og, king of Bashan (Deut. 1:4; Josh. 12:4) where he fought with the Israelites (Num. 21:33; Deut. 3:1). They defeated him and took his country with its cities, including Edrei (Deut. 3:10). This town was assigned to the half-tribe of Manasseh (Josh. 13:12,31). It was located near the southern source of the Yarmuk river, about ten miles NE of Ramoth-Gilead, and about 30 miles E and a little S of the Sea of Galilee. In the temple of Ammon in Karnak, Egypt, is a list of the cities which Thutmose III (1490-1936 B.C.) claimed he conquered or exercised dominion over in Upper Retenu (Syria and Palestine). Ederi appears on this list. Its modern name is *Der'aa,* a town of about 5,000 inhabitants in southern Syria.

2. A fortified city of Naphtali, location unknown (Josh. 19:37).

EDUCATION (See Schools)

EGG (Heb. *bêtsâ, whiteness*), appears only in the plural form *bêtsîm.* Birds' eggs (Deut. 22:6); ostrich eggs (Job 39:14); any kind of eggs (Isa. 10:14); snake eggs (Isa. 59:5). Another word, *hallāmût* (Job 6:6) is translated "egg" in KJV and ASV, but in the margin ASV has "purslain," a plant whose juice had an insipid taste.

EGLAH (ĕg'-lȧh, Heb. *'eglâh, heifer*), the name of one of David's wives who was the mother of his sixth son, Ithream (II Sam. 3:5; I Chron. 3:3).

EGLAIM (ĕg'-lā-ĭm, Heb. *'eglayim*), a place in Moab (Isa. 15:8). Site unknown.

EGLON (ĕg-lŏn, Heb. *'eghlôn*). 1. A city of Canaan located between Gaza and Lachish, whose king joined four others against Gibeon because this city had made a covenant with Joshua. Gibeon appealed to Joshua, who came with the Israelites, defeated, and destroyed the five kings (Josh. 10: 3,5,23). Later Joshua captured the city (10:36,37; 12:12). It was assigned to Judah (Josh. 15:39). Its modern site is believed to be *'Aglan* north of *Tell el Hesey.* Archaeologists have ascertained that it was destroyed by fire in the 13th century B.C. thus confirming Joshua's conquest of it. Remains of Solomon's building program have also been found there.

2. A king of Moab who, with the help of the Ammonites and Amalekites, captured Jericho, the city of palm trees (Judg. 3:12,13). The Israelites served him for 18 years (3:14). Then he was killed by Ehud, whom the Lord had raised up to save the children of Israel (3:21).

EGYPT, LAND OF (ē'jĭpt, Gr. *Aígyptos*). "Egypt is the gift of the Nile." This classic statement of Hecateus, echoed by Herodotus, is a reflection of actual circumstances and of the Egyptian appreciation of the great river. The Nile, which courses like a living tube through the desiccated hills and deserts of NE Africa, laid down the black alluvium of the delta and the entire river valley. In view of the almost complete absence of rain, the annual overflow of the Nile was of great importance to the land, for it watered the soil and provided it with new alluvium and some organic fertilizer. Its waters were used for drinking (Exod. 7:18,21,24; Ps. 78:44), for bathing (Exod. 2:5), and for irrigation (Deut. 11:10). Its stream (Heb. *ye'or*) was the main channel of commerce and travel, with a prevailing north wind to favor southbound sailing vessels against the current.

The regularity of the inundation afforded a practical agricultural calendar and the coincidence of the rise of the Nile and the appearance of the Dog Star (Sirius; e.g., Sothis) on the horizon at daybreak around July 19 was the basis for a chron-

The Sphinx and the Pyramids are the great symbols of Egypt. © MPS

ological unit of 1460 years, which is termed a Sothic cycle. Since the Egyptian calendar of 365 days was one-fourth day short of the true year, the Egyptian New Year's Day worked its way through the calendar until it again coincided with the rising of Sothis and the inundation (365 x 4 = 1460). The recognition of this cycle and several references to it in dates of historical records make some helpful checkpoints in Egyptian chronology.

The awareness of the dependence of land and people on the resources of the Nile led to the deification of the river. The longest river in the world, the Nile covers some 4000 miles from its sources in equatorial Africa to its divided mouths which open into the Mediterranean. The White Nile is the principal stream, with tributaries joining it from the E, from their points of origin in the Ethiopian hills. The Blue Nile enters at Khartoum. Farther N the Atbara, the last consequential affluent, empties its periodic flow into the northbound stream. From this junction the Nile continues some 1500 miles without tributary to the sea. Numbered from Aswan S, in order of their discovery by modern explorers, are six cataracts,

Egypt is the Nile, and the Nile is Egypt. This is the river at ancient Cairo, showing the typical sailboats, the **felucca.** © MPS

Typical village scene in Egypt. © MPS

areas in which hard rock resisted the erosive action of the rushing stream. To varying degrees these hindered river travel and served as barriers to military movement. From Aswan to Cairo is a stretch of somewhat less than 600 miles. Below Cairo spreads the fan of the delta, c. 125 miles long and 115 miles wide.

The division of the land into Upper and Lower Egypt predates the union into one nation. Lower Egypt included the delta and a short section of the valley southward; the balance of the valley to Aswan was Upper Egypt. These areas were subdivided into administrative units which in Greek times were called "nomes," 20 in Lower Egypt and 22 in its southern counterpart. With the cataracts and the Nubian desert to the S and SE, the Libyan desert and the Sahara to the W, and the Arabian desert on the E, the valley was not subject to the frequent invasions which characterize less defensible lands. The biggest threat from outside was on the delta edges; even here the passage of armies was handicapped by terrain and climate. On the NE border, fronting Asia, the Egyptians made early use of fortress and other checkpoints to control ingress from this direction. With such protection, the country was free to develop its culture in comparative security and still to retain a free exchange of goods and ideas with other peoples.

The climate of the land, along with the particular beliefs of the people, has been of great advantage to archaeology, so that it may be said that Egypt is the archaeological area par excellence. Lack of rain and frost, plenty of dry sand to form a protective cover over remains, and abundant use of stone for monumental building are helpful environmental factors. The burial customs have been of much help to the cultural historian, for the relief sculpture, tomb furniture, models, and inscriptions tell much of the daily life of antiquity.

Its Name. To the Israelites, Egypt was Mizraim (Heb. *mitsraim*), a term of which the form and derivation are unknown. The Egyptians themselves had a number of names they used for their country; usually it was called "the Two Lands," which has reference to the origin of the nation in the union of Upper and Lower Egypt, just as the name "the United States of America" has historical derivation. Egypt was also Kemet, "the Black Land," the rich alluvial soil of the valley, as opposed to Desheret, "the Red Land," the barren waste of the desert.

Religion. The religion of ancient Egypt is a vast and labyrinthine subject. Much of the religious literature appears as a hodgepodge of heterogeneous conflicting statements to the modern Western reader, to whom many of the allusions must remain obscure. In general, the religion may be described as a complex polytheism, with many local deities of varying importance. A list of these divinities would be impractical, but seven may be singled out: Osiris and Isis, who are well-known from their later adoption by the mystery religions of Greece and Rome; Ra (Re), a sun-god, who came into prominence in Dynasty 5; Horus, another sun-god, the son of Osiris and Isis; Set, the rival of Osiris and Horus; Amon-Re, who became the god of empire; Ptah, the god of Memphis; Khnum, the god of Elephantine. The attempt of Akhenaton (Amenhotep IV) to reorient Egyptian religion with a primary emphasis on Aton, the sun-disc, has been widely discussed as a tendency toward monotheism. There is no evidence of possible Israelite influence on his beliefs. His innovations did not long survive him and the priests of Amon at Thebes scored a theological-political victory. Much of the religious literature has a mortuary interest; this preoccupation with death was a futile gesture to transfer earthly life to an eternal dimension. There are no reflections of the Egyptian concept in the Bible, and the absence of any large body of OT teaching concerning life beyond the grave may be a divine avoidance of a possible snare to the Israelites. The influence of Egyptian religion on Israelite religious practice was largely negative. In several

The great Temple of Amon at Karnak. © MPS

The Obelisk of King Thutmose III, now in Central Park, New York.

instances the Israelites were led into apostasy to worship Egyptian gods (see below), but even these occasions were rare.

Its History. Preceding the historical or dynastic period are a number of prehistoric cultures which are known in general outline. In the late predynastic epoch there is interesting evidence of cultural influence from Mesopotamia. The rudiments of hieroglyphic writings also appear about this time and usher in the historical period. The materials for writing the political history of Egypt are lists of kings (such as those inscribed in temples of Abydos and Karnak, that of a tomb at Sakkarah, the Turin Papyrus, and the Palermo Stone) and numerous historical records, both of kings and of lesser persons active in history-making. The dynastic scheme is a historiographical convenience inherited from the priest-historian Manetho, who divided Egyptian history from Menes to Alexander into 31 dynasties. Egyptologists have used a somewhat standard arrangement of these dynasties into historical periods. A highly condensed outline follows: *Protodynastic Period* (Dyn. 1-2; 3100-2700 B.C.). According to the tradition of Manetho, the first king of united Egypt was Menes, who came from Thinis in Upper Egypt, united the Two Lands, and established his capital at Memphis, in about 3200-3100 B.C. Some scholars equate Menes with Narmer and/or Aha. Royal tombs of this period have been found at Sakkarah and Abydos. *Old Kingdom* (Dyn. 3-6; 2700-2200). This is a high point in Egyptian history. The canons of art were firmly established in this period and perhaps the bases of the applied sciences were also laid. In Dyn.3 the step

pyramid of Djoser, "the world's first monumental architecture in stone," was built at Sakkarah. Its architect, Imhotep, was also famed in other fields of accomplishment. Dyn.4 was the time of the pyramid-builders par excellence: the pyramids of Khufu(Cheops), Khafre(Chephren), and Menkaure(Mycerinos) were constructed at Giza. Kings of Dyn.5-6 had their pyramids at Sakkarah; in these were inscribed the religious writings known as the Pyramid Texts. The proverbs of Ptahhotep, a vizier of Dyn.5, are well-known. *First Intermediate Period*(Dyn.7-11; 2200-2050). This was a period of weakness and confusion; Dyn.7-8 were at Memphis; 9-10, at Herakleopolis; 11, at Thebes. The literature is an outgrowth of the pessimism of the times; it includes the writing of Ipuwer, the Dialogue of a Man Weary of Life; the Song of the Harper. *Middle Kingdom*(Dyn.12; 2050-1800) was another peak in Egyptian history. Art and architecture flourished. This is the time of the Eloquent Peasant and of the adventures of the courtier Sinuhe. In religious literature the Coffin Texts are found. There is a trend toward democratization of royal privileges, along with an emphasis on *ma'at,* "justice, right." The king is heralded as "the shepherd" of the people. The *Second Intermediate Period* (Dyn.13-17; 1800-1580) was another dark age for Egypt. Insignificant rulers made up Dyn.13-14; Dyn.15-16 are the Hyksos dynasties, which may be of greater importance than brief, derogatory Egyptian references lead us to think. Dyn.17 was made up of Theban rulers who began the movement to expel the Hyksos. The *New Kingdom or Empire*(Dyn.18-20; 1580-1090) marked the height of Egyptian imperialistic ambitions, with some fluctuations. Outstanding rulers include: in the Eighteenth Dynasty, Hatshepsut, the woman-king, who sponsored a voyage to Punt and built a fine mortuary temple at Deir el Bahri; Thutmose III, the energetic warrior and capable administrator; Amenhotep III, the Magnificent, a lavish spender who neg-

Columns of the great Hypostyle Hall at Karnak. MPS

lected the empire and with his successor, Akhenaton, the religious innovator, ignored the pleas for help from Palestine-Syria (Amarna Tablets). In the Nineteenth Dynasty the outstanding figure is Rameses II, the builder, renovator, and chiseler; in the Twentieth it is Rameses III, who defeated the Sea Peoples. The *Post-Empire Period* or *Period of Decline*(Dyn.21-25; 1150-663) finds Egypt a "broken reed." There was a short restoration in the *Saite Period*(Dyn.26; 663-525), which includes Necho and Apries (Biblical Hophra, Jer. 44:30). Conquered earlier by the Assyrians, Egypt was subject to Persian domination(Dyn.27-30; 525-332). With Alexander the Great came the end of the dynasties and of native rule. After the death of Alexander(323), Egypt was governed by the Ptolemies until the Romans made it a province in 31 B.C.

Egypt and the Bible: To the Israelites, Egypt was somewhat of an enigma, a land of contrasts, a country which they hated but respected. When a Psalmist looked back to the days of the Exodus, he referred to the Egyptians as a "people of strange language" (Ps. 114:1), a description to which even many moderns may assent. Egypt was the iron furnace of affliction during the bondage, but Israelites were so impressed with the might of the Pharaonic kingdom that there were elements in Judah that looked to Egypt for help even after Egypt had become the broken reed of Assyrian contempt (cf. II Kings 18:21: Isa. 36:6). An unreliable ally, Egypt was also a sanctuary for some of Israel's individual enemies. From Egypt, too, came some of the worst occasions for apostasy in Israel. Egypt appears in the Bible as a type of the ephemeral, earthbound system called "the world"; in one instance it is an allegorical synonym for Sodom and for rebellious Jerusalem (Rev. 11:8). Nevertheless, it was an abundant Near Eastern breadbasket and

The Temple of Rameses III at Karnak. © MPS

was for centuries the ranking world power. It afforded food for many a hungry Palestinian, and heat-smitten wandering tribes were permitted to cross its borders to graze their animals in the delta. Joseph realized that God's providence was in his being sold into Egypt (Gen. 45:5-9), and Jacob was instructed by the Lord to go to Egypt (Gen. 46:3-4).

Egypt appears early in Biblical references, since Mizraim (Egypt) is found in the Table of Nations as a son of Ham (Gen. 10:6). Abram's sojourn in Egypt is a well-known incident. It is evident from Genesis 12:10 that Egypt was the place to which Palestinians naturally looked in time of famine. The famous scene from the wall-paintings of the tomb of Khnumhotep II at Beni Hasan shows a group of Asiatics in Middle Egypt for purposes of trade and illustrates several facets of Abram's descent into Egypt. The fears of Abram concerning the king's interest in Sarai were real and perhaps well-founded, but there is no certain evidence for such royal behavior in Egyptian literature. The oft-cited Tale of Two Brothers relates a quite different sort of situation, for there the wife is anxious to be rid of her husband so that she may become a wife of Pharaoh. The closest Egyptian-Biblical relationships may be seen in the narrative of Joseph and the account of Israelite life in Egypt to the time of their Exodus (Gen. 37, 39-50; Exod. 1-15). A listing of some of the most intriguing elements includes: Joseph's coat (Gen. 37); Potiphar, "an Egyptian" (Gen. 39); Potiphar's wife (39:6-18), with interesting parallels in the Tale of Two Brothers, a not uncommon episode in many cultures; the prison for political offenders (39:20); the duties of butler and baker; dreams in Egypt; Egyptian viticulture (Gen. 40); cattle and the Nile; grain-growing (Gen. 41); shaving (41:14); east wind (41:27); taxes (41:34); the gold (41:42); chariots (41:43); the priest of On (Heliopolis) (41:45); Egyptian names; Egypt as a source of food (41:57); divination (44:5); the land of Goshen (Gen. 47); the Egyptian priesthood (47:22); embalming, mummification, and burial rites (Gen. 50). In Exodus 1 there are references to brick-making, field work, and obstetrical practices which are particularly Egyptian. In Chapter 2 the references to the Nile are of interest. The account of the signs and the plagues shows an intimate knowledge of Egyptian life and provides a study in the relationship of natural and miraculous phenomena. In Exodus 11:2 the asking for jewelry of silver and gold is a reflection of the expert Egyptian work in metals. The Egyptian pursuit of the fleeing Israelites (Exod. 14:10,23) finds pictured parallels in the battle reliefs of Egypt's chief monarchs. The ironic mention of graves in Egypt (14:11) reminds us of the vast necropolis that marks the desert fringe. Well into the wilderness, the refugees were outside of Egyptian concern and out of its effective reach; but, barely escaped from slavery, the Israelites were soon engrossed in worshiping the golden calf (Exod. 32), a descendant of the bovine worship of Memphis and other Egyptian cities. There were also fond recollections of good eating in Egypt, with its fish, cucumbers, leeks, onions, and garlic, which the Israelites regarded as strength-giving fare (Num. 11:5-6). During the period of the Judges, the hill-country of Palestine saw little likelihood of antagonistic Egyptian interference. Egyptian power had declined; in about 1100 B.C. the royal emissary, Wen-Amon, found little respect for the might of Egypt along the Mediterranean coast.

A list of slaves, including Hebrews, from Egypt, about the time of Joseph, c. 1700 B.C. Brooklyn Papyrus.

With this weakness, the time was ripening for the rapid growth of a young and vigorous nation in the former Asiatic empire of Egypt. When the Israelite monarchy came into existence, neither Saul nor David had recorded immediate dealings with the land of the Nile. Solomon, however, married a daughter of the current Pharaoh, who captured and destroyed Gezer and presented it to his daughter as dowry (I Kings 9:16). It is stated that Solomon's wisdom excelled that of Egypt (I Kings 4:30) and we are informed of his commercial relations with Egypt (II Chron. 1:16-17). Late in Solomon's reign, an Edomite enemy, Hadad, who as a child had found asylum in Egypt after a raid by David into Edomite territory, left Egypt to become an active adversary of Solomon. Jeroboam, the son of Nebat, fled to Egypt to escape Solomon; as first king of the northern tribes, this Jeroboam, "who made Israel to sin," set up calf-images at Dan and Bethel (I Kings 12:26-33), a religious importation influenced by his Nilotic exile. In the fifth year of Rehoboam (926 B.C.) the Egyptian king Sheshonk (Biblical Shishak) carried out an expedition into Palestine which saw the temple stripped of its treasures to meet his demands (I Kings 14:25-26; II Chron. 12:1-9).

Egypt was a strong influence in Judean politics in the days of Isaiah and Jeremiah, who were aware of the weakness of Egypt against the Assyrian threat. When the Assyrian remnant was making its dying stand and Egypt marched to aid them against the rampaging Babylonians, the Judean Josiah made a fatal effort to stop the Egyptian forces at Megiddo (II Kings 23:29-30; II Chron. 35:20-27). After the fall of Jerusalem in 586 B.C. and the subsequent murder of Gedaliah, the Judeans again looked to Egypt as a place of refuge in spite of the prophet's warning. Here they were scattered about, with a group as far S as Elephantine maintaining a temple and keeping up correspondence with Palestine, as revealed by the Aramaic papyri found at Elephantine. In the NT most of the references to Egypt have to do with Israel's past. One important mention had current meaning, for Joseph was divinely directed to take the infant Jesus and Mary to Egypt to escape the wrath of Herod (Matt. 2:13-15; cf. Hosea 11:1; Exod. 4:22).

Significance and future. It is remarkable that Egypt so often was a place of refuge or a means of sustaining life. Though it is regarded by typological extremists as an invariable epitome of "the world," Egypt has the scriptural prediction of

a wonderful future: "In that day Israel will be the third with Egypt and Assyria, a blessing in the midst of the earth, whom the Lord of hosts has blessed, saying, 'Blessed be Egypt my people, and Assyria the work of my hands, and Israel my heritage'" (Isa. 19:24-25 RSV; cf. 19:18-23).

C.E.D.

EGYPT, RIVER OF, the dividing line between Canaan and Egypt (Gen. 15:18; Num. 34:5), the southern boundary of Judah (Josh. 15:4,47). In the other four occurrences it is coupled with the Euphrates river (Gen. 15:18; I Kings 8:65; II Kings 24:7; II Chron. 7:8) as marking the N and S limits of the land given to the Israelites. It is not really an Egyptian river at all, but a *wady* (a stream and its valley) of the desert near the border of Egypt. It is identified as the *Wady el-Arish*.

EHI (e'hī, Heb. *'ēhî*), a son of Benjamin (Gen. 46:21); in Numbers 26:38, spelled Ahram; in I Chronicles 8:1, Ahara.

EHUD (ē'hŭd, Heb. *'ēhûdh*, union). 1. A descendant of Benjamin (I Chron. 7:10; 8:6).

2. A judge of the Israelites, a Benjamite, the son of Gera. The people were in distress because of the heavy hand of Eglon, the king of Moab, who had captured Jericho and extracted tribute from Israel from there. Ehud, a left-handed man, made a double-edged dagger which he carried on his right thigh. After he had delivered the tribute, he secured an opportunity to commune with Eglon, the king, in private. He drew his dagger, thrust it through the king's body, and locked the doors of the room when he went out. The king's servants hesitated to disturb him too quickly. During the delay, Ehud escaped. Back home he rallied the Israelites from Benjamin and Ephraim and led them against the Moabites. They utterly subdued these enemies. The land had peace for 80 years until Ehud died (Judg. 3:15-30).

EKER (ē'kêr, Heb. *'ēqer*, root), a son of Ram descendant of Judah (I Chron. 2:27).

EKRON (ĕk'rŏn, Heb. *'eqrôn, eradication*), the most northern of the five chief cities of the Philistines (see I Sam. 6:17). It was located on the boundary between Judah and Dan (Josh. 15:11; 19:43), but was assigned to Judah (Josh. 15:45). After the captured ark of God was sent by the Philistines from Ekron to escape the wrath of God (I Sam. chap 6), the Israelites regained possession of Ekron and other cities (1 Sam. 7:14). Following David's victory over Goliath the Israelites drove the Philistines back to Ekron (I Sam. 17:52). The god of this city was Baal-zebub (II Kings 1:3). The prophets mention Ekron along with other Philistine cities (Jer. 25:20; Amos 1-8; Zeph. 2:4; Zech. 9:5,7).

In the Assyrian inscriptions Ekron appears as *amquarruna*. Sennacherib assaulted it and killed its officials because they had been disloyal to Assyria *(Ancient Near Eastern Texts* pp. 287, 288). Esarhaddon called upon 22 cities which paid tribute to him (Ekron being one of them) to help transport building supplies for his palace *(ibid.* p. 291). Ashurbanipal included Ekron in the list of cities which paid tribute to him *(ibid.* p. 294). The Greek form of Ekron, *Accaron*, appears once in the Apocrypha (I Macc. 10:89) and in the accounts of the Crusades. Its modern site is *'Aqir* or *Catrah*, both on the Wady *Surar*.

C.E.H.

EL (Heb. *'ēl, God*), the primitive, generic word for God in the Semitic languages: Aramaic *elah*, Arabic *ilah*, Akkadian *ilu* (the *u* is the ending for the nominative case). In the OT *el* is used over

200 times for "God." In the prose books it often has a modifying term with it, but in the poetic books, Job and Psalms, it occurs alone many times. The name of the chief god of the Canaanites was El, as the Ras Shamra texts demonstrate. The Hebrews borrowed this word from the Canaanites. *El* has a plural *elim,* occasionally *elhm,* in Ugaritic; but the Hebrews needed no plural, though a plural term, *'elohim,* was their regular name for God.

The root from which *'ēl* was derived has been much discussed. Gesenius held that *'ēl* was from *'wl,* "to be strong," and many have accepted this view. Noldeke derived it from the Arabic root *'ul,* "to be in front of" as a leader. Ewald suggested a Hebrew root *'lh* to which both *'el* and *'elohim* belonged, with the meaning "strong." Kittel viewed the preposition *el,* "to be in front of," in combination with the root *'alah,* to which *'el* belonged, giving it the meaning "the end of all human seeking." Lagarde, using the same preposition, put forth the idea of God as the goal for which all men seek. Gesenius' view seems the most likely. But a truly satisfactory theory is impossible because *'el* and the other terms for God, *'elohim* and *'eloha,* are all prehistoric in origin.

The Canaanite god El was the father of men and of gods. He was called *ab adm,* "father of mankind" (Krt. 37,151); ab *snnm,* "father of years" (text) 49: 1:8; 51:IV:24; 2 Aqht: VI:49). He was an immoral and debased character. It is a tribute to the high quality of the character of the God of Israel that when the Hebrews took over this name and applied it to Him, it lost all its evil connotations.   C.E.H.

ELA (ē'là, KJV Elah, Heb. *'ēlā', terebinth*), the father of Solomon's commissary officer stationed in the tribe of Benjamin (I Kings 4:18).

ELADAH (ĕl'-à-dàh, Heb. *'el'ādhâh, God has adorned*), ASV Eleadah, a descendant of Ephraim (I Chron. 7:20).

ELAH (ē-'làh, Heb. *'ēlâh, terebinth*). 1. A descendant of Esau, who was a chief of Edom (Gen. 36:41).

2. The valley in which David killed Goliath (I Sam. 17:2,19; 21:9).

3. A king of Israel, the son of Baasha. He reigned two years and was slain by Zimri, a captain in his army, who destroyed all the rest of Baasha's descendants, thus fulfilling the prediction of Jehu, the prophet, made in I Kings 16:1-4 (I Kings 16:6-14).

4. The father of Hoshea, the last king of Israel (II Kings 15:30; 17:1; 18:1,9).

5. A son of Caleb, the son of Jephunneh (I Chron. 4:15).

6. A Benjamite, one of the people who returned to Jerusalem from Babylon (I Chron. 9:8).

The Valley of Elah. © MPS

ELAM (ē'lăm, Heb. *'êlām*). 1. A son of Shem, thus making the nation, Elam, to be Semitic. The Hebrews looked at them as such, but neither in custom nor language were they Semitic (Gen. 10:22; I Chron. 1:17).

2. A son of Shashach, a descendant of Benjamin (I Chron. 8:24).

3. The fifth son of Meshelemiah, a doorkeeper of the Korahites (I Chron. 26:3).

4. The progenitor of a family of 1254 members which returned from exile under Zerubbabel (Ezra 2:7; Neh. 7:12).

5. Another forefather of a returned family with the same number of members (Ezra 2:31; Neh. 7:34).

6. The father of two sons who returned from exile with Ezra (Ezra 8:7).

7. An ancestor of a man who confessed marriage to a foreign woman. Evidently this ancestor was either No. 4, 5, or 6 (Ezra 10:2,26).

8. A chief who sealed the covenant with Nehemiah (Neh. 10:14).

9. One of the priests who took part in the dedication of the wall (Neh. 12:42).

ELAM (ē'lăm, Heb. *'êlām*), a country situated on the E side of the Tigris river opposite Babylonia in a mountainous region. Its population was made up of a variety of tribes. Their language, different from the Sumerian, Semitic, and Indo-European tongues, was written in cuneiform script. It has not yet been deciphered to any great extent. Elam was one of the earliest civilizations. In Sumerian inscriptions it was called *Numma* (high mountain people), which term became *Elamtu* in Akkadian texts; in classical literature it was known as *Susiana,* the Greek name for Susa, the capital city of Elam.

Sargon I (2350 B.C.) claimed conquest of Elam in his day. Later on, about 2280 B.C., an Elamite king invaded Babylonia and took back much spoil. Gudea, a ruler of the city of Lagash, about 2100 B.C., mentions that the Elamites collected some of the timbers which he used in constructing the temple of Ningirsu, the god of Lagash. Hammurabi (1728-1686 B.C.) subdued the Elamites. In the time of Abraham, according to Genesis 14:1 ff., an Elamite king, Chedorlaomer, made a raid on Palestine.

Elam figures prominently in Babylonian and Assyrian texts because it was situated so close to them. When Babylon became active against Assyrian supremacy, Elam became her chief ally. Assyria was not able to subdue Elam completely until the time of Ashurbanipal (668-626 B.C.), who sacked the country thoroughly in 640 B.C. This catastrophe practically finished Elam as a nation, but part of the country was not much affected by these intrusions of Semitic powers. This district called *Anzan* was, next to the capital at Susa, the most important part of the nation. From that area Cyrus, the conqueror of Babylon, arose.

Isaiah cites Elam as one of the nations going up with Cyrus against Babylon (Isa. 21:2) and joining the Assyrian army against Judah (Isa. 22:6). Elam was one of the nations forced to drink the cup of God's wrath (Jer. 25:25), and doomed to judgment (Jer. 49:34-39). Ezra 4:9,10 refers to Elamites as among the peoples brought over to Samaria by the Assyrians. Acts 2:9 includes Elamite as one of the tongues being spoken by visitors at Jerusalem.   C.E.H.

ELASAH (ĕl'à-sàh, Heb. *'el'āsâh, God has made*).
1. One of the sons of Pashur who was guilty of marrying foreign women (Ezra 10:22).

2. Son of Shaphan, one of the men by whom Jeremiah sent from Jerusalem a message of advice to the exiles in Babylon (Jer. 29:3).

ELATH, ELOTH (ē'lăth, ēlŏth, Heb. *'êlâth,* or *'êlôth, lofty trees*), a town situated at the head of the Gulf of Aqabah in Edom. It was located very near to Ezion-geber, Solomon's seaport (I Kings 9:26). The Israelites passed the area on the way to the promised land (Deut. 2:8). Azariah (767-740 B.C.) built it up, probably for use as a seaport, when he took it from Edom (II Kings 14:22; II Chron. 26:2). During the reign of Ahaz over Judah (736-716 B.C.) Rezin, king of Syria, joined with Pekah, king of Israel, and threatened Jerusalem. Rezin captured Elath, and the Syrians (or more likely, the reading should be Edomites) occupied it (II Kings 16:5,6). The Romans called it *Aelana* and made it a military post. After the Moslems conquered the Middle East a castle was erected there to protect the pilgrims going to Mecca from that port. In the tenth century, according to reports, Elath was a great port of Palestine. Later it fell into decay. Turkey and Egypt both controlled it; after 1917 the Arabs took it over. Aqaba, or Eilar (its modern name) was in the territory allotted to the Jews in 1949. They have made it a port to bring in oil.   C.E.H.

EL-BETHEL (ĕl-bĕth'ĕl, Heb. *'ēl bêth-'ēl, the God of the house of God*), the name Jacob gave to Luz because there God revealed Himself to him (Gen. 35:7).

ELDAAH (ĕl-dā'ah, Heb. *'eldā'â, God has called*), a son of Midian (Gen. 25:4).

ELDAD (ĕl'dăd, Heb. *'eldādh, God has loved*), a man who, along with another man, Medad, remained in camp when the 70 elders selected by Moses were gathered around the Tabernacle to receive the gift of prophecy. The spirit of prophecy came to Eldad and Medad in camp and they prophesied there. The news of this fact excited Joshua and he begged Moses to forbid them. But Moses said he wished that all God's people were prophets (Num. 11:24-29).

ELDER (ĕld'êr, Heb. *zāqēn,* Gr. *presbúteros*). In ancient times the older men of a community were known as the elders. They governed the community and made all major decisions. Moses called the elders of Israel together to announce that the Lord had heard their cries for help and had appointed him to lead them out of Egypt (Exod. 4:29). Later he called them out to institute the Passover (Exod. 12:21). At Sinai 70 of the elders went up the mountain with Moses and saw the God of Israel (Exod. 24:9). In the wilderness, to relieve Moses, 70 elders shared his divine anointing (Num. 11:25). After the Israelites had settled in Canaan and had a king over them, the elders still functioned. They were a separate group from the heads of the tribes and the princes of the fathers' houses (I Kings 8:1). Each town had its group of elders, as Bethlehem did (I Sam. 16:4), "the elders of every city" (Ezra 10:14). After the return from exile the elders made up the Sanhedrin, the governing council of the Jews.

This type of society continued into New Testament times. The elders joined the priests and scribes against Jesus (Matt. 27:12). When churches came into being, elders were appointed for each congregation (Acts 14:23). The terms "elders" and "bishops" are used interchangeably in the NT. The "elders" of Acts 20:17 are called "bishops" in verse 28. In Titus 1:5, "elders" in the Cretan churches are mentioned. In listing

qualifications for such an office, Paul calls them "bishops" in verse 7. These men were required to be blameless in their lives and obedient to the truth in their faith (I Tim. 3:1-7; Titus 1:6-9). Their duties involved spiritual oversight of the congregation and teaching the Word. Those who ruled well and had done teaching were worthy of honor on both these aspects of their work (I Tim. 5:17). Before the first century A.D. had elapsed, the term "bishop" had taken on a special meaning, denoting the one leader of a church. This situation is illustrated both in the book of Acts and in Paul's epistles in the person of James, the brother of Jesus, who was obviously the head man in the Jerusalem church.

The 24 elders in heaven around the throne of God as depicted in the book of Revelation probably represent the heavenly priesthood of the church associated with Christ, the Great High Priest.   C.E.H.

ELEAD (ĕ'lē-ăd, Heb. *'el'ādh, God has testified*), an Ephraimite slain by men of Gath while making a raid to steal cattle (I Chron. 7:21).

ELEADAH (See Eladah)

ELEALEH (ē'lē-ā'lĕ, Heb. *'el'ālēh, God doth ascend*), a town always mentioned with Heshon, being located about a mile N of that place, in the tribe of Reuben (Num. 32:3,37). Isaiah and Jeremiah mention it in prophecies against Moab (Isa. 15:4; 16:9; Jer. 48:34). The modern site is marked by ruins and is called El Āh.

ELEASAH (ĕ'-lē-ā-săh, Heb. *'el'āsâh, God has made*). 1. A Hezronite (I Chron. 2:39,40).
2. A Benjamite, a descendant of Saul (I Chron. 8:37; 9:43).

ELEAZAR (ĕ-lē-ā'-zàr, Heb. *'el'āzār, God has helped*). 1. The third son of Aaron (Exod. 6:23). After the death of the two elder sons, Nadab and Abihu (Lev. 10:1,2), Eleazar was designated to be chief priest (Num. 3:32). He ministered before the Lord with Ithamar, his brother, helping his father. But the Lord assigned special tasks to Eleazar: gathering up the 250 censers offered to the Lord by rebellious men, and beating them out for a covering for the altar (Num. 16:36-39); and taking the lead in the ceremony with the red heifer (Num. 19:3,4). When Aaron died Eleazar became the chief priest (Num. 20:28). He assisted Moses in numbering the people (Num. 26:1,2); in dividing the spoil from the slaughter of the Midianites (Num. 31:13-54); and in assigning to the 2½ tribes land E of the Jordan river (Num. 32:28). He was divinely appointed to help Joshua divide the promised land among the tribes (Num. 34:17), and carried out this task (Josh. 14:1; 19:51). His only son was Phineas (I Chron. 6:4). Eleazar died soon after Joshua's death (Josh. 24:33).
2. The son of Abinadab who was sanctified to keep the ark after it had been brought to his father's house (I Sam. 7:1).
3. Son of Dodai, one of the three mightiest men of David who wrought a great victory over the Philistines (II Sam. 23:9,10; I Chron. 11:12-14).
4. A childless son of Mahli (I Chron. 23:21,22; 24:28).
5. Son of Phineas, a Levite, one of the group to which Ezra delivered the temple treasures for tabulating and keeping for the temple (Ezra 8:32-34).
6. A priest who took part in the service dedicating the wall (Neh. 12:42).
7. An ancestor of Joseph, the husband of Mary (Matt. 1:15).

ELECT (ē-lĕct', Heb. *bāhîr*, Gr. *eklektós, chosen*), as used in Scripture, both words mean "chosen" or "elected" by God. In the OT Moses is called "the chosen of God" (Ps. 106:23). The nation of Israel is six times noted as God's chosen people (I Chron. 16:13; Ps. 105:6,43; 106:5; Isa. 43:20; 45:4). King Saul is once so designated (II Sam. 21:6). David is once called God's chosen one (Ps. 89:3). In prophecy Christ is set forth as God's "elect one" (Isa. 42:1). The redeemed Israelites of the future will be "God's elect" (Isa. 65:9,15,22).

In the NT those who have received Christ as Saviour are called "the elect" 20 times. Twice Jesus is designated as "God's chosen" (Luke 9:35; 23:35). Once angels are called "elect" (I Tim. 5:21).

C.E.H.

ELECTION (Gr. *eklogé, choice, selection*). Since the whole of humanity is fallen in sin from which it cannot extricate itself, none will be saved apart from the redeeming grace of God. The decree, as a sovereign choice of God, as to who may receive this grace is the basis of election.

Election is God's eternal and immutable decree to choose from depraved men, who because of their sin deserve condemnation, those whom He will save, providing the source of their salvation in grace through Christ, and the means through the instrumentality of the Holy Spirit's regenerative work. Biblical usage of the word centers primarily in *eklektos*, as an adjective signifying "the chosen," and in *eklogē*, as a noun, signifying "that which is chosen," the object of the choice. In its larger context, it is applied in a variety of ways. In the OT this concept is often used of the election of Israel to be the people of covenant privilege (Deut. 4:37; 7:6,7; I Kings 3:8; Isa. 44:1,2). In both Testaments it is applied to Christ as the Messiah (Isa. 42:1 and I Peter 2:4,6). While *eklektos* is used of Christ (Luke 23:35) and of angels (I Tim. 5:21) it is most often used of individual believers (Mark 13:20,22,27; Rom. 8:33; Col. 3:12; II Tim. 2:10; I Pet. 1:1; II John 1:13). *Eklage* is used almost invariably in the NT to individuals. In its more restricted sense, it refers to the election of men to salvation.

The sovereign decree of God to *choose out* (*ek*, from *lego*, to pick out) is the basic idea in election. This concept is applied in at least five ways: to elect those who are to be saved, to elect the means of their salvation in Christ, to elect the means in the redeeming activity of the Holy Spirit, to elect the results in the implantation of Christ's righteous nature to those who are saved, and to elect the destiny of eternal fellowship with God.

The source of election is in God alone (John 6:37,44; Eph. 1:4). The very nature of election restricts its source to God, without regard to anything external to Himself. All men are depraved: none will be saved apart from God's divine intervention in grace; whom He chooses to be saved lies within His own sovereign will (Rom. 9:11,16, 18; Eph. 1:5,11).

The cause of election is at least twofold: God's compassionate mercy extended toward men in Christ (without which no man would be saved), and His own glory. No ground can be delineated for God's mercy: it can be understood only in His love (John 3:16); nor can any ground be determined for God electing to salvation men who have spurned His moral demands, other than His freely-electing, sovereignly-determined compassion Election is, however, set within the context of His glory, which is to be seen displayed magnificently in the redeemed soul of man (Rom. 9:23; 11:33; Eph. 1:6).

While election is an immutable decree of the one Godhead, administratively it may be viewed as: the decree of the Father by which He gave to the Son those whom He elected to salvation in the Son, the decree of the Son to receive those to be redeemed and to assume the human nature to accomplish their redemption, and the decree of the Spirit to accomplish in them by regenerative activity the total ends of the decree.

Much attention has been given to the relation between God's sovereign choice in election and the foreknowledge of God, since the two concepts are related in Romans 8:27-30, and I Peter 1:1,2. Erroneous interpretations have implied that election was based on a foreknowledge by God of the choice which man would make, using foreknowledge "prior" knowledge. This interpretation not only contradicts the idea of sovereignty, but ignores the basic meaning of the word foreknow.

In Hebraistic use, *proginosko* does not mean mere knowledge beforehand, but connotes the idea of "regard with favor," or "to make an object of care" as in Exodus 2:25 and Romans 11:2 where "know" carries the additional idea of approval. While it is certain that God had a prior knowledge of man's actions, it does not follow that any such actions were to be the basis of God's choice of them. Prior knowledge arose out of prior choice — God's unconditioned choice. Foreknowledge implies not knowledge alone, but an act of God's will to accomplish that which He knows. His knowledge cannot be separated from His will, nor can His will be conditioned by mere prior knowledge of an event. Foreknow is synonymous with forelove. Foreseen faith or foreseen holiness is not the cause of election. A man is not elected because he is going to believe; he believes because he is elect (Acts 13:48). The sole grounds of election rests in the divine counsel.

When election refers to salvation, its objects are individual men. The concept of universal election is foreign to Scriptures; rather, particular election only is taught (Matt. 22:14; John 15:19; Rom. 8:29; 9:13,15,18,22; I Thess. 5:9). At the same time election is not to a general conformity to the redeemed life, but to a specific regeneration of nature and indwelling of the life-force of Christ's righteousness. Election assures that the redemptive grace of God will draw the depraved and rebellious heart of man into loving fellowship and responsive obedience to God.

C.B.B.

Bibliography: G. C. Berkouwer, *The Providence of God.* (Grand Rapids: Eerdmans) 1952; *Divine Election* (Grand Rapids: Eerdmans) 1957; C. H. Hodge, *Commentary on Romans*; Pierre Maury, *Predestination and other Papers* (Richmond: John Knox) 1960; John Murray, *Redemption: Accomplished and Applied* (Grand Rapids: Eerdmans) 1955; B. B. Warfield, *Biblical Studies.*

EL-ELOHE-ISRAEL (ĕl'ē-lō'hĕ-ĭz'rà-ĕl), an altar erected by Jacob when he settled near Shechem. The name means "God, the God of Israel," and reflects the revelation of God and of his own name, received at Peniel (Gen. 33:20).

ELEMENTS (ĕl'ē-mĕnts, Gr. *stoicheía, rows, series, alphabet, first principles of a science, physical elements, primary constituents of the universe, heavenly bodies, planets, personal cosmic powers*). In Hebrews 5:12 *first principles* is clearly the meaning, as shown by Greek *arché, principles*, in Hebrews 6:1. Galatians 4:3,9 refer to heathen deities and practices. Colossians 2:8,20, translated *rudiments*, indicate a more philosophical concept of the elements. II Peter 3:10,12 refer to heavenly bodies or physical elements.

ELEPH (ē'lĕf), a place in the lot of Benjamin, near Jerusalem (Josh. 18:28). RSV, Ha-eleph. Perhaps the name should be read with the preceding word, Zelah-eleph. Site uncertain.

ELEPHANT (See Animals)

ELEUSIS (ĕl'ū-sĭs), today an industrial suburb of Athens where the ruins of a considerable temple and precinct are found. This was the shrine of Demeter, or the Earth-Goddess, into whose "mystery cult" freeborn Athenians were annually initiated. The ceremonies were elaborate, aiming at the stirring of emotion and promoting a conviction of regeneration. Little is known about the ceremony, for the initiates generally kept their vows of secrecy; but it seems clear that part of the ritual was the elevation of an ear of corn (wheat), the symbol of death and re-birth. This is perhaps the explanation of the imagery of Christ's remark at John 12:24. A sheaf of corn may be seen on a plinth lying among the ruins today.

ELEVEN, THE, the eleven apostles (Acts 1:26) or disciples (Matt. 28:16) remaining after the death of Judas (Mark 16:14; Luke 24:9,33; Acts 2:14).

ELHANAN (ĕl-hā'năn). 1. A son of Jaare-oregim (called also Jair), a Bethlehemite who slew Lahmi, the brother of Goliath (II Sam. 21:19; I Chron. 20:5).
2. A son of Dodo of Bethlehem and one of David's 30 heroes (II Sam. 23:24; I Chron. 11:26).

ELI (ē'lī, Heb. *ēlī*), of the family of Ithamar, fourth son of Aaron, who acted as both judge and high priest in Israel. He lived at Shiloh in a dwelling adjoining the Tabernacle (I Sam. 1-4; 14:3; I Kings 2:27). Little is known about him until he was well advanced in age, when Hannah came to pray for a son. The conduct of Eli's sons, Phinehas and Hophni, who, although lacking their father's character, were put into the priest's office, brought sorrow upon his declining years. Their conduct so shocked the people that they "abhorred the offering of the Lord." While Eli warned them of their shameful ways, he did not rebuke with the severity their deeds merited. Instead, Eli mildly reasoned with his sons, saying, "Why do ye such things?" But the sons no longer heeded their father, and he "restrained them not." An old man of ninety, almost blind, Eli waited to hear the result of the battle between the Israelites and the Philistines. When the messenger came with the news of the slaughter of his sons and of the taking of the ark, Eli fell off his seat and died of a broken neck. A good and pure man, Eli was weak and indecisive.

ELI, ELI, LAMA SABACHTHANI (ā'lēē, ā'lēē, làmà sàbach'thànēē, Gr. *eloi, eloi, lama sabach-thani*), the English transliteration of a Greek phrase (Matt. 27:46; Mark 15:34), which in turn is a transliteration of either the Hebrew or an Aramaic version of Psalm 22:1. The phrase as it appears in the best text of Matthew is closer to Aramaic; in Mark it is closer to Hebrew. The words are the central one of the seven cries of Jesus from the cross, as gathered from all four Gospels. The fact that in both instances the words are first transliterated shows the deep impression they made on some of the hearers. Both evangelists then translated them for the benefit of readers unfamiliar with either Hebrew or Aramaic, and their translation is authoritative as to what Jesus meant when He uttered them, since during His resurrection ministry He explained to them the meaning of all that concerned His death (Luke 24:45,46). Conjecture has been made which would connect *sabachthani* with an Aramaic verb meaning "de-liverer," which would permit a rendering, "for this hast thou spared me," which is inconsistent with the evangelists' translation. Christ was forsaken by the Father when He bore our sins.   E.R.

ELIAB (ē-lī'ăb, Heb. *ĕlī'āv*). 1. A son of Helon and leader of the tribe of Zebulun when the census was taken in the wilderness (Num. 1:9; 2:7; 7:24, 29; 10:16).
2. A son of Pallu or Phallu, a Reubenite, and father of Nathan and Abiram (Num. 16:1,12; 26: 8,9; Deut. 11:6).
3. The eldest son of Jesse and brother of David (I Sam. 16:6; 17:13,28). Once called Elihu (I Chron. 27:18). Of commanding appearance, when he was serving with Saul's army at the time it was menaced by Goliath, Eliab resented his younger brother's interference. Eliab's daughter Abihail became one of Rehoboam's wives (II Chron. 11:18).
4. A Levite in David's time who was a tabernacle porter and musician (I Chron. 15:18,20; 16:5).
5. A Gadite warrior who with others came over to David when David was hiding in the wilderness (I Chron. 12:9).
6. An ancestor of Samuel the prophet; a Kohathite Levite (I Chron. 6:27). Called Elihu (I Sam. 1:1) and Eliel (I Chron. 6:34).

ELIADA (ē-lī'á-dà, Heb. *elyādhā'*). 1. One of David's sons (II Sam. 5:16; I Chron. 3:8).
2. A Benjamite, a mighty warrior who led 200,-000 of his tribe to the army of Jehoshaphat (II Chron. 17:17).
3. KJV, Eliadah; ASV, RSV, Eliada. The father of Rezon, the captain of a roving band that annoyed Solomon (I Kings 11:23).

ELIAH (ē-lī'á). 1. A son of Jeroham, the Benjamite who was head of his tribe (I Chron. 8:27).
2. One of the sons of Elam who married a foreign wife (Ezra 10:26).

ELIAHBA (ē-lī'á-bà), a Shaalbonite, and one of David's famous guard (II Sam. 23:32; I Chron. 11:33).

ELIAKIM (ē-lī'á-kĭm, Heb. *elyāqîm, God sets up*). 1. A son of Hilkiah, successor of Shebna as the master of Hezekiah's household. The manner of his displacing Shebna, and the reasons for it, together with the responsibilities and honors of his office, are set forth in Isaiah 22:15-25. He was spokesman for the delegation from Hezekiah, king of Judah, which attempted to negotiate with the representatives of Sennacherib, king of Assyria who was besieging Jerusalem (II Kings 18:17-37; Isa. 36:1-22). Upon the failure of these negotiations, Eliakim headed the delegation sent to implore the help of Isaiah the prophet (II Kings 19:2; Isa. 37:2).
2. The original name of king Jehoiakim (II Kings 23:34; II Chron. 36:4).
3. A priest who helped in the dedication of the rebuilt wall in Nehemiah's time (Neh. 12:41).
4. A grandson of Zerubbabel and ancestor of Jesus (Matt. 1:13).
5. Another and earlier ancestor of Jesus (Luke 3:30).

ELIAM (ē-lī'ăm). 1. The father of Bathsheba, wife of David (II Sam. 11:3). Called Ammiel in I Chronicles 3:5.
2. The son of Ahithophel the Gilonite (II Sam. 23:34).

ELIAS (ē-lī'ăs), the Greek form of the name of the Prophet Elijah, used in KJV in all occurrences in the NT. ASV, RSV have Elijah. See ELIJAH.

ELIASAPH (ē-lī'á-săf). 1. The son of Deuel and

head of the Gadites in the sojournings in the wilderness (Num. 1:14; 2:14; 7:42,47; 10:20).

2. A son of Lael, a Levite and prince of the Gershonites during the wilderness wanderings (Num. 3:24).

ELIASHIB (ē-lī'à-shĭb, Heb. *'elyāshîv, God restores*). 1. A priest in David's time from whom the 11th priestly course took its name (I Chron. 24:12).

2. A son of Elioenai, descendant of Zerubbabel, a Judahite (I Chron. 3:24).

3. The high priest at the time of the rebuilding of the city wall (Neh. 3:1,20,21; 13:4,7,28).

4. A Levite and singer who put away his foreign wife (Ezra 10:24).

5. A son of Zattu who married a foreign wife (Ezra 10:27).

6. A son of Bani who also married a foreign wife (Ezra 10:36).

7. An ancestor of Johanan who helped Ezra in gathering together the foreign wives, and other matters during the reign of Darius the Persian (Ezra 10:6; Neh. 12:10,22,23).

ELIATHAH (ē-lī'à-thà), a son of Heman and a musician in David's reign (I Chron. 25:4,27).

ELIDAD (ē-lī'dăd), a prince of the tribe of Benjamin and a member of the commission in the division of Canaan (Num. 34:21).

ELIEL (ē'lĭ-ĕl, ē-lī'ĕl, Heb. *'elî'ēl, God is God*). 1. A Levite of the family of Kohath and an ancestor of Samuel the prophet (I Chron. 6:34). Called Eliab in 6:27.

2. A chief man of the half tribe of Manasseh in Bashan (I Chron. 5:24).

3. A son of Shimhi the Benjamite (I Chron. 8:20).

4. A son of Shashak, a Benjamite (I Chron. 8:22).

5. A Mahavite and a captain in David's army (I Chron. 11:46).

6. Another of David's heroes (I Chron. 11:47).

7. The seventh Gadite who joined David at Ziklag (I Chron. 12:11). Perhaps the same person as No. 5 or 6.

8. A chief of Judah, a man of Hebron, in David's time (I Chron. 15:9). Perhaps the same man as No. 5.

9. A chief Levite who helped in the return of the ark from the house of Obed-edom (I Chron. 15:11).

10. A Levite overseer of tithes and offerings in Hezekiah's reign (II Chron. 31:13).

ELIENAI (ĕl'ĭ-ē'nī), a son of Shimhi, a Benjamite (I Chron. 8:20).

ELIEZER (ĕl'ĭ-ē'zêr, Heb. *'elî'ezer, God is help*). 1. Abraham's chief servant, and "son of his house," that is, one of his large household. He is named "Eliezer of Damascus" probably to distinguish him from others of the same name (Gen. 15:2). Probably he is the unnamed servant Abraham sent to his own country and kindred to secure a bride for Isaac, his son of promise (Gen. 24).

2. The second son of Moses and Zipporah to whom his father gave this name ("God is my help") as a memento of his gratitude to God (Exod. 18:4; I Chron. 23:15,17; 26:25).

3. A son of Becher and grandson of Benjamin (I Chron. 7:8).

4. A priest who assisted, by blowing a trumpet, in the return of the ark to Jerusalem (I Chron. 15:24).

5. Son of Zichri, a Reubenite ruler in David's time (I Chron. 27:16).

6. The prophet who rebuked Jehoshaphat for his alliance with Ahaziah in the expedition to Tarshish (II Chron. 20:37).

7. A chieftain sent with others to induce many of the Israelites to return with Ezra to Jerusalem (Ezra 8:16).

8. A priest who put away his foreign wife (Ezra 10:18).

9. A Levite who had done the same (Ezra 10:23).

10. One of the sons of Harim who had done likewise (Ezra 10:31).

11. An ancestor of Jesus in the inter-testamental period (Luke 3:29).

ELIHOENAI (ĕl'ĭ-hō-ē'nī, *to Jehovah are my eyes*. See also Elioenai). 1. A descendant of Pahath Moab who returned with Ezra in Artaxerxes' time (Ezra 8:4). In ASV, RSV, Eliehoenai.

2. Perhaps also the seventh son of Meshelemiah the son of Kore of the sons of Asaph, a Korahite doorkeeper of the tabernacle in David's reign (I Chron. 26:3). In KJV, Elioenai; ASV, RSV, Eliehoenai.

ELIHOREPH (ĕl'ĭ-hō'rĕf), one of king Solomon's scribes (I Kings 4:3).

ELIHU (ē-lī'hū, Heb. *'elîhû, He is my God*). 1. The father of Jeroham and great-grandfather of Samuel the prophet (I Sam. 1:1). Called also Eliel in I Chronicles 6:34.

2. A man of Manasseh who joined David at Ziklag (I Chron. 12:20).

3. A Kohathite of the family of Korah, and a tabernacle porter in David's time (I Chron. 26:7).

4. A brother of David, who became ruler over Judah (I Chron. 27:18). Also known as Eliab.

5. The youngest of Job's friends, the son of Barachel, a Buzite, that is, an Aramean (Job 32: 2-6; 34:1; 35:1; 36:1).

ELIJAH (ē-lī'jà, Heb. *'ēlîyāhû, Jehovah is God*). See also Elias. The name is borne by four men in the Bible, of whom three are mentioned but once each: 1. A Benjamite and son of Jeroham, resident at Jerusalem (I Chron. 8:27 ASV, RSV; called Eliah in KJV).

2. A son of Harim, who married a foreign wife during the exile (Ezra 10:21).

3. An Israelite induced to put away his foreign wife (Ezra 10:26 ASV, RSV; called Eliah in KJV).

4. The well-known prophet. The story of his life begins at I Kings 17:1, where he is said to be, according to the received text, born at Tishbeh. This might possibly be Lisdib, in the territory of Naphtali, W of the Jordan. But Elijah is strongly identified with the region E of the Jordan, and Nelson Glueck (*The River Jordan*, Philadelphia: The Westminster Press, 1946, pp. 169-174) accepts a correction of the text of I Kings 17:1 to read "Elijah the Jabeshite, from Jabesh-gilead." This would make Elijah a native of Gilead, and not a mere sojourner there. This fits well with what we know of the prophet, but the traditional view is also possible. Wherever he was born, Elijah has been living in Gilead for some time when he enters the Biblical narrative.

The story opens dramatically, Elijah confronting Ahab with a prophecy of drought (17:1), to be broken only "by my word," says the prophet. God directs Elijah to go eastward to the brook Cherith and to hide there (17:2-7). The location of this brook is uncertain. It has been identified with wady Kelt, W of the Jordan. Glueck (*op. cit.* p. 170) maintains that it is E of the Jordan, because "east" is the usual meaning of "before" in topographical indications. He suggests a branch

of the River Jabesh. The interest centers not in
the location, but in what happened there; the
ravens brought food to Elijah morning and evening till the brook dried up, and God directed
Elijah to Zarephath, where a widow would sustain
him (17:8-16). Zarephath is outside Israel in
Phoenician territory, a circumstance to which
Jesus Christ refers in His first sermon at Nazareth
(Luke 4:25-26). The widow is in extremely
straitened circumstances, and her reward for entertaining the prophet is that her supply of meal
and oil is miraculously multiplied as long as Elijah
is with her. Her son becomes so ill "that there was
no breath left in him." Elijah prayed, and stretched
himself upon him three times and prayed again,
and the sick child revived (17:17-24).

Three years pass, and it is time for the drought
to be broken (18:1-16). King Ahab in person, and
his steward Obadiah go out through the land of
Israel to find grass for the horses and mules.
Obadiah is a faithful believer in God, who has
supported a hundred young prophets in hiding.
Elijah meets Obadiah, and asks him to warn Ahab
that he is coming to meet him. Obadiah demurs,
but is reassured, and obeys. Ahab and Elijah meet,
and Elijah proposes a test as to whether the
Canaanite Baal or the Israelite God is the true God
(18:17-40). Four hundred fifty prophets of Baal
and 400 prophets of the groves (sacred to the
Baals) are to be on one side; Elijah alone on the
other. The meeting takes place on Mt. Carmel, in
the sight of a vast multitude of the people. Elijah
challenges the people to accept the verdict of fire
from heaven. Elijah directs the whole proceeding,
the preparations made by the prophets of Baal,
and later his own. While the Baal worshipers call
frantically on their gods in orgiastic dances, Elijah
jeers at them and at their gods. When they retire,
it is time for the evening oblation in the temple
at Jerusalem. Elijah directs the building of an altar
of rough stones. The sacrificial animal is prepared
and laid upon the wood. A trench is dug about the
altar, and water poured in to fill it and to drench
the sacrifice. With simple, majestic directness Elijah prays, and fire from heaven falls, burning up
sacrifice and altar and dust, licking up the water
in the trench. Convinced, the people cry, "The
Lord, He is God; the Lord, He is God!" On the
orders of Elijah, the prophets of Baal are taken
down to the brook Kishon at the foot of Mt. Carmel, and there slain. Elijah curtly orders Ahab,
"Get thee up, eat and drink; for there is a sound
of abundance of rain" (18:41-46). Whatever his
feelings in the matter, whether meekly or sullenly,
Ahab goes to attend to his eating and drinking.
Elijah has other business to occupy him. He
climbs Mt. Carmel once more, with a servant,
whom he sends to a lookout point to scan the skies
for rain clouds, while Elijah prays. At the seventh
look, there is a cloud "like a man's hand." Elijah
sends his servant to warn Ahab to hasten "that the
rain stop thee not." As Ahab rode to Jezreel, Elijah
girded up his long gown in his belt and ran before
Ahab's chariot to Jezreel. When Ahab told Jezebel
all that Elijah had done, she vowed vengeance
on the prophet (19:1-8). Elijah fled for his life, a
day's journey beyond Beersheba into the wilderness, and sat down under a juniper tree, despondent. But an angel had baked a cake on coals, and
set a cruse of water at Elijah's head, so Elijah
ate and drank, rested and ate again, and went in
the strength of that food 40 days and 40 nights to
Horeb the mount of God (19:9-21). There, where
Moses had received the Law, Elijah experienced
mighty wind, earthquake and fire, before he heard

The rock where Elijah rested between Jerusalem and
Bethlehem. © MPS

the still, small voice of the Lord. He received a
commission to anoint Hazael king over Syria in
Damascus, and Jehu to be king over Israel, and
Elisha to be his own successor as prophet. Elijah
is assured that there are yet 7,000 in Israel who
have not bowed the knee to Baal. To this Paul
refers in Romans 11:2-4. Elijah first finds Elisha,
and calls him to his side.

In the ensuing wars between Ahab and Ben-
hadad king of Syria, Elijah does not appear (I
Kings 20). But when Jezebel takes Naboth's vineyard for Ahab, and has Naboth murdered, Elijah
meets the king in the vineyard to rebuke him for
the act (21:1-24). Ahab repented, and Elijah
brought him word from the Lord that the prophesied ruin should not come in his days, but in his
son's (21:27-29). Elijah does not appear again
during the lifetime of Ahab, but in his son Ahaziah's days, Elijah sends him a message of impending death (II Kings 1). Ahaziah sends a captain with 50 men to take Elijah, but Elijah calls

Traditional site of Elijah's victorious sacrifice on Mt.
Carmel. © MPS

down fire from heaven, which destroys them. A second company of 50 meet the same fate. When the third captain with his 50 approaches Elijah, he begs for mercy, and the angel of God directs Elijah to go with this captain without fear. So Elijah repeats his message of impending death to Ahaziah, who shortly dies. In the reign of Ahaziah's son Jehoram, Elijah is taken up to heaven in a whirlwind (II Kings 2:1-15). Elisha insists on following him all the way to Bethel, then to Jericho, and at each place the sons of the prophets warn Elisha of his master's being taken away. They go on to Jordan, where Elijah wrapped his mantle together and with it struck the water, and the waters were divided so that Elijah and Elisha went over on dry ground. Elijah invited Elisha to make one last request, and Elisha asks for "a double portion of thy spirit." Elijah says that this is a hard request, which will be granted only if Elisha sees Elijah when he is taken from him. As they walked along and talked, a chariot and horses of fire parted them, and Elijah went up by a whirlwind into heaven. Elisha saw it, cried, "My father, my father, the chariot of Israel, and the horsemen thereof!" Elisha rent his own clothes in two, took up the mantle of Elijah that fell from him as he ascended, and went back to Jordan. Smiting the waters with the mantle of Elijah, he cried "Where is the Lord God of Elijah?" and the waters parted as before. The prophets of Jericho recognized that the spirit of Elijah rested on Elisha.

The fulfillment of Elijah's prophecy concerning Jezebel is recorded in II Kings 9:36; regarding the house of Ahab in II Kings 10:10,17. Jehoram receives "a writing" from Elijah (II Chron. 21:12-15), the only reference we have to any writing by the prophet. An old man at this time, it is natural that he should write rather than journey to the court in person.

In Malachi 4:5,6, God promises "Behold, I will send you Elijah the prophet before the coming of the great and dreadful day of the Lord. And he shall turn the heart of the fathers to the children, and the heart of the children to their fathers, lest I come and smite the earth with a curse." This expectation of the return of Elijah appears frequently in the NT, as John the Baptist (Matt. 11:14; 17:10-13; Mark 9:13; Luke 1:17; John 1:21, 25); and Jesus (Matt. 16:13; 14; Mark 6:15; 8:28; Luke 9:8,19). Elijah appears to Jesus on the Mount of Transfiguration (Matt. 17:3,4; Mark 9:4,5; Luke 9:30-33). James and John are reminded of how Elijah called down fire from heaven (Luke 9:54). Some thought Jesus called for Elijah to rescue Him from the cross (Matt. 27:47,49; Mark 15:35,36). The epistle of James uses Elijah as an example of a man who prevailed in prayer (James 5:17,18). Whether Elijah is one of the two witnesses, together with Enoch, in Revelation 11, is a matter of interpretation, resting on the fact that Enoch and Elijah are the only two men recorded as being taken up to heaven without dying. E.R.

ELIKA (ē-lī'kà), a Harodite, one of David's mighty men (II Sam. 23:25).

ELIM (ē'lĭm, Heb. *'êlîm, terebinths*), the second stopping-place of the Israelites after they crossed the Red Sea on their exodus from Egypt. It is on the W side of the Sinaitic peninsula, on the caravan route to the copper and turquoise mines of Sinai. In spite of its advantages, 12 springs of water and 70 palm trees, the Israelites seem not to have stayed there long, preferring to put a greater distance between themselves and the land of their bondage (Exod. 15:27; 16:1; Num. 33:9,10).

ELIMELECH (ē-lĭm'ĕ-lĕk, Heb. *'ĕlîmelekh, my God is king*), a man of Bethlehem-judah who emigrated to Moab during a famine in Judah in the time of the Judges (Ruth 1:2,3; 2:1,3; 4:3,9). He and his sons died in Moab. He is remembered because his daughter-in-law Ruth was faithful to his widow Naomi.

ELIOENAI (ĕl'ĭ-ō-ē'nī, *to Jehovah are my eyes*). See also Elihoenai. 1. A son of Neariah of the family of David (I Chron. 3:23,24).
2. The head of a family of Simeon (I Chron. 4:36).
3. The head of one of the families of the sons of Becher, son of Benjamin (I Chron. 7:8).
4. A son of Pashur, a priest who put away his foreign wife (Ezra 10:22). Perhaps the same person as the one mentioned in Nehemiah 12:41.
5. A son of Zattu who married a foreign wife (Ezra 10:27).
6. A priest, perhaps the same person as No. 4 (Neh. 12:41).

ELIPHAL (ē-lī'făl, ĕl'ī-făl, Heb. *'ĕlîphāl, God has judged*), son of Ur, one of David's mighty men (I Chron. 11:35). Eliphal and Ur are thought to be Eliphelet and Ahasbai of II Samuel 23:34, for textual reasons.

ELIPHALET (ē-lĭf'ă-lĕt), the last of David's sons born at Jerusalem (II Sam. 5:16; I Chron. 14:7; called Eliphelet in I Chron. 3:8 KJV and in all places in ASV, RSV). See ELIPHELET.

ELIPHAZ (ĕl'ĭ-făz, Heb. *'ĕlîphaz, possibly God is fine gold*). 1. A son of Esau by Adah, daughter of Elon (Gen. 36:4-16; I Chron. 1:35,36).
2. The chief of Job's three friends (Job 2:11); from Teman, traditionally famous for its wise men (Jer. 49:7). Eliphaz' speeches show clearer reasoning than those of the other two friends. In his first speech (Job 4,5) Eliphaz traces all affliction to sin, through the natural operation of cause and effect, and admonishes Job to make his peace with God. In his second address (Job 15) Eliphaz shows irritation at Job's sarcasm, reiterates his arguments, and depicts strongly the fate of the wicked. In his third address (Job 22) Eliphaz definitely charges Job with sin and points out to him the path of restoration. In Job 42:7-9 God addresses Eliphaz as the chief of Job's friends, and commands him to make sacrifice in expiation of their fault in wrongly accusing Job, saying that Job will pray for them and they will be forgiven.

View of ancient Elim, an oasis in the Sinai Peninsula. © MPS

ELIPHELEH (ē-lĭf′ĕ-lĕh), a Levite singer and harpist who had charge of the choral service when the ark was returned (I Chron. 15:18,21). Called Eliphelehu in ASV, RSV.

ELIPHELET (ē-lĭf′ĕ-lĕt). 1. The last of David's sons (I Chron. 3:8). See ELIPHALET.

2. Another son of David born in Jerusalem (I Chron. 3:6; called Elpalet I Chron. 14:5 KJV, Elpelet ASV, RSV).

3. A son of Ahasbai, one of David's heroes (II Sam. 23:34).

4. A son of Eshek and descendant of Saul, a Benjamite (I Chron. 8:39).

5. A leader of the sons of Adonikam who returned from exile with Ezra (Ezra 8:13).

6. A son of Hashum who put away his foreign wife (Ezra 10:33).

ELISABETH (See Elizabeth)

ELISHA (ē-lī′shà, called *Eliseus,* the Gr. form of Heb. *'ĕlîshā',* in Luke 4:27 KJV, Elisha in ASV, RSV). At Horeb God directed Elijah to anoint Elisha as his successor (I King 19:16-21), who was to aid Hazael, king of Syria, and Jehu, king of Israel in taking vengeance on the enemies of God. Elijah left Horeb and on his way north found Elisha the son of Shaphat of Abelmeholah (I Kings 19:16) plowing with the last of 12 yoke of oxen. The number of oxen indicates the wealth of the family. Elijah cast his mantle upon Elisha, who understood the significance of the act as the choice of himself to succeed the older prophet. Elisha ran after Elijah, who had not tarried to explain his action, and begged for permission to kiss his parents farewell. Elijah's reply, "Go back again; for what have I done to thee?" led Elisha to go home and make his own decision to accept the prophetic call. Elisha next appeared in connection with the translation of Elijah (II Kings 2). He persisted in following Elijah till the latter was carried up to heaven. Because he saw him go, a double portion of Elijah's spirit was given him. Taking the mantle of Elijah, he used it to make a dry path over Jordan, as his master had done, and tried to dissuade the sons of the prophets from a fruitless search for the body of Elijah. Elisha healed the waters of a spring at Jericho with salt. When children of the city made fun of his baldness, Elisha cursed them in the name of the Lord. Two she-bears came out of the wood and "tare" 42 of them. It is not said that they were killed; the bears clawed them.

Elisha had a long ministry during the reigns of Jehoram, Jehu, Jehoahaz and Joash, kings of Israel. After the death of Ahab (II Kings 3), Moab rebelled against his son Jehoram. When Jehoram secured the king of Edom and Jehoshaphat, king of Judah, as allies, Jehoshaphat insisted on consulting Elisha. Elisha referred Jehoram to the prophets of his parents, but out of regard to Jehoshaphat, counseled them to dig trenches to channel water from Edom to relieve their army, and predicted victory over the Moabites. Elisha saved a poor widow from financial distress by miraculous multiplication of her oil supply (II Kings 4:1-7). He visited the home of a "great woman" and her husband in Shunem so often that she had a room built for him (II Kings 4:8-37). Elisha sent his servant Gehazi to ask the woman what she would like to have him do for her in return for her hospitality. She asked a son, and a son was given her. When the lad was old enough to go to the fields with his father, he suffered a fatal sunstroke. His mother herself went for Elisha, who, after sending Gehazi, whose efforts were fruitless, himself came, and after great effort the child came back to life. At Gilgal during a famine (II Kings 4:38-41), Elisha saved a school of the prophets from death because of eating poisonous vegetables. When a present of food was given him, Elisha set it before 100 men, and the Lord increased the supply to satisfy them (II Kings 4:42-44). Elisha healed the Syrian captain Naaman of leprosy (II Kings 5); Gehazi proved himself an unworthy servant. Elisha rescued a young prophet's borrowed ax-head (II Kings 6:1-7). He gave timely warning, repeatedly saving Israel from defeat by the Syrians (II Kings 6:8-23). The Syrians came to Dothan, where Elisha was living with a servant, whom Elisha showed the armies of God protecting the city. The Syrians were stricken with blindness, and Elisha led them to Samaria, and persuaded the king of Israel to feed them and release them. The Syrians invaded Israel no more for a time. When Syria finally besieged Samaria and the city was reduced to terrible straits, the king of Israel blamed Elisha (II Kings 6:24-7:20). Elisha predicted relief the next day. Four lepers, considering their case hopeless, visited the Syrian camp, found it deserted, and reported. The spoils of the Syrians relieved the inhabitants of Samaria. Elisha advised the "great woman" to escape a coming famine by going to Philistia (II Kings 8:1-6). When she returned and sought restoration of her property, Gehazi, who had just been telling the king the deeds of Elisha, was the means of the woman's securing restitution.

Elisha visited Damascus and had an innocent part in Hazael's succeeding Ben-hadad as king of Syria. Elisha sent a young prophet to anoint Jehu king of Israel (II Kings 9:1). Before Elisha died (II Kings 13:14-21), Joash, king of Israel, came to visit him and received an object lesson by means of arrows, with regard to his war against the Syrians. A man being hastily buried in Elisha's sepulchre touched Elisha's bones and revived. Elisha's ministry was filled with miracles, many relieving private needs, some related to affairs of state. Elisha's prophetic insight and wise counsel made him a valuable though not always appreciated adviser to kings. He finished the work of Elijah, destroying the system of Baal worship, completed the tasks assigned to Elijah of anointing Hazael and Jehu, and saw the final ruin of the house of Ahab and Jezebel. The mention of the cleansing of Naaman, the Syrian, from leprosy in Luke 4:27 perhaps indicates this as the crowning achievement of his career, giving Elisha an influence with the Syrian king which enabled him to help Israel. Elisha's story is told with vigor and vivid detail, making him live as few OT characters do. The incidents are not all told in chronological order; but they bear the marks of historical truth in the simplicity of their narration.   E.R.

ELISHAH (ē-lī′shà, Heb. *'ĕlîshâh, God saves*), the eldest son of Javan, grandson of Noah and founder of a tribal family (Gen. 10:4; I Chron. 1:7). The land from which Tyre got its purple dye (Ezek. 27:7); somewhere around the Mediterranean; South Italy, North Africa or Greece, perhaps; not yet identifiable.

ELISHAMA (ē-lĭsh′àmà, Heb. *'ĕlîshāmā', God has heard*). 1. Grandfather of Joshua and son of Ammihud and prince of the Ephraimites at the outset of the wilderness sojourn (Num. 1:10; 2:18; 7:48, 53; 10:22; I Chron. 7:26).

2. A son of David born in Jerusalem (II Sam. 5:16; I Chron. 3:8).

3. Another son of David, who is also called

Elishua (I Chron. 3:6; cf. II Sam. 5:15).

4. A son of Jekaniah, a Judahite (I Chron. 2:41).

5. Father of Nethaniah and grandfather of Ishmael "of the seed royal" who lived at the time of the Exile (II Kings 25:25; Jer. 41:1). Nos. 4 and 5 may be the same person.

6. A scribe or secretary to Jehoiakim (Jer. 36: 12,20,21).

7. A priest sent by Jehoshaphat to teach the people the law (II Chron. 17:8).

ELISHAPHAT (ē-lĭsh'a-făt), one of the "captains of hundreds" who supported Jehoiada in the revolt against Athaliah (II Chron. 23:1).

ELISHEBA (ē-lĭsh'ēba), Amminadab's daughter, sister of Nahshon, captain of Judah (Num. 2:3). By marrying Aaron (Exod. 6:23) she connected the royal and priestly tribes.

ELISHUA (ĕl'ĭ-shū'a, ē-lĭsh'wa), a son of David born in Jerusalem (II Sam. 5:15; I Chron. 14:5). Likewise called Elishama in I Chronicles 3:6.

ELIUD (ē-lī'ŭd), the son of Ashim and father of Eleazar and ancestor of Christ (Matt. 1:14,15).

ELIZABETH (ē-lĭz'a-bĕth. Gr. *Elisábet, God is [my] oath,* KJV Elisabeth), the wife of a priest Zacharias, herself of the lineage of Aaron (Luke 1:5-57). In fulfillment of God's promise, she in her old age bore a son, John the Baptist. Her kinswoman (cousin) Mary of Nazareth in Galilee, having learned that she was to be the virgin mother of Jesus, visited Elizabeth in the hill country of Judea. Elizabeth's Spirit-filled greeting prompted Mary to reply in a song called *Magnificat.* After Mary returned home, Elizabeth's son was born. She was a woman of unusual piety, faith, and spiritual gifts, whose witness to Mary must have been an incomparable encouragement. Luke, who alone tells the story, appreciated the significant role of women in the history of redemption, and emphasized the agency of the Holy Spirit in the life of Elizabeth.

ELIZAPHAN (ĕl'ĭ-zā'făn, ē-lĭz'afăn, Heb. *'ĕlîtsāphān, God has concealed*). 1. The son of Uzziel, chief ruler of the Kohathites when the census was taken in Sinai (Num. 3:30; I Chron. 15:8; II Chron. 29:13), called Elzaphan in Exodus 6:22 and Leviticus 10:4. In Chronicles his Levitical class is treated as co-equal with the Kohathites.

2. The son of Parnach, prince of the tribe of Zebulun in the wilderness (Num. 34:25).

ELIZUR (ē-lī'zēr), the son of Shedeur, and prince of the Reubenites, who helped in the census Moses took (Num. 1:5; 2:10; 7:30-35; 10:18).

ELKANAH (ĕl-kā'na, Heb. *'elqānâh, God has possessed*). 1. The father of Samuel, the prophet (I Sam. 1:1-2:21). His tender solicitude for his favorite wife Hannah and for their first son appears in the story. He is called an Ephraimite from Ramathaim-zophim, in the hill country of Ephraim, but he appears to have been a Levite, descendant of Kohath (I Chron. 6:22,23,27,33,34), though the genealogical data are not clear.

2. A son of Korah, a Levite, descendant of Kohath (Exod. 6:23,24; I Chron. 6:24). The sons of Korah did not die with their father, who perished for rebellion against Moses and Aaron (Num. 26: 11).

3. The second to king Ahaz, killed by Pekah, king of Israel, when he invaded Judah (II Chron. 28:7).

4. One of the ambidextrous warriors who came to David at Ziklag (I Chron. 12:6).

5. In addition, several Levites bear the name Elkanah (I Chron. 6:22-28; 33-38; 9:16). It is

impossible to distinguish them with certainty from one another. Elkanah was a favorite name in the Kohathite line.

ELKOSH (ĕl'kŏsh), *Nahum* 1:1, the place of origin of Nahum. (KJV, ASV, the Elkoshite; RSV, of Elkosh). Jerome says that a town in Galilee was shown him as Elkosh. The Nestorians locate it and the tomb of the prophet near the Tigris, N of Mosul. Another tradition places Elkosh "beyond Jordan," but emendation of that text and other considerations lead some to believe that Elkosh was in the S of Judah. "Unknown" is the safest conclusion.

ELLASAR (ĕl-lā'sar, Heb. *'ellāsār*), one of the city-states whose king, Arioch (Eri-aku), invaded Palestine in the time of Abraham (Gen. 14:1,9). It is the ancient Babylonian Larsa (with the last three letters transposed in Heb.), modern Senkereh, SE of Babylon, between Erech and Ur. At first independent, it became subject to Hammurabi (Amraphel of Gen. 14:1,9) or to his successor. Ellasar was at this period a city of a high degree of civilization, a center of sun-god worship, with a temple-tower (Ziggurat) called "House of Light," which was a seat of mathematical, astronomical and other learning. Ruins of city walls and of houses remain. Thus the four kings with whom Abraham fought (Gen. 14:13-16) were no petty chieftains, but sovereigns of flourishing and cultured cities, from one of which Abraham himself had recently emigrated.

ELMODAM (ĕl-mō'dăm), Elmadam in ASV, RSV), the son of Er, and ancestor of Joseph, Mary's husband (Luke 3:28).

ELNAAM (ĕl-nā'ăm), the father of David's guard, Jeribai and Joshaviah (I Chron. 11:46).

ELNATHAN (ĕl-nā'thăn, Heb. *'elnāthān, God has given*). 1. Father of Nehushta, the mother of Jehoiachin (II Kings 24:8).

2. The son of Achbor, sent to Egypt by king Jehoiakim to bring back the Prophet Uriah (Jer. 26:22). He was one of those who urged king Jehoiakim not to burn the roll which Jeremiah had written (Jer. 36:12,25). (He may be the same person as No. 1.)

3. Name of two "leading men" and one man "of insight," Levites, sent on an embassy by Ezra (Ezra 8:16).

ELOHIM (ĕ-lō'hĭm), the most frequent Hebrew word for God (over 2,500 times in the OT). Several theories of the origin of the word have been proposed, some connecting it with Heb. *'ēl* or *'ĕlôah,* others distinguishing them from *'ĕlōhîm.* The origin is prehistoric and therefore incapable of direct proof. Elohim is plural in form, but is singular in construction (used with a singular verb or adjective). When applied to the one true God, the plural is due to the Hebrew idiom of a plural of magnitude or majesty. (Gen. 1:1, etc). When used of heathen gods (Exod. 18:11; 20:3; Gen. 35:2; Josh. 24:20, etc.) or of angels (Ps. 8:5; 97:7; Job 1:6, etc.) or judges (Exod. 21:6; I Sam. 2:25, etc.) as representatives of God, Elohim is plural in sense as well as form. Elohim is the earliest name of God in the OT and persists along with other names to the latest period. Whatever its etymology, the most likely roots mean either "be strong," or "be in front," suiting the power and preëminence of God. Jesus is quoted as using a form of the name from the cross (Matt. 27:46, Eli; Mark 15:34, Eloi). See articles *Eli, Eli, lama sabachthani.* E.R.

ELOI (See Elohim)

ELON (ē'lŏn). 1. Hittite whose daughter Bashemath (Gen. 26:34) or Adah (Gen. 36:2) Esau married.

2. The second of Zebulon's three sons (Gen. 46:14; Num. 26:26).

3. The Zebulonite who judged Israel ten years (Judg. 12:11,12).

ELON (place). 1. A town in the territory of Dan (Josh. 19:43), location unidentified.

2. Elon-beth-hanan, a town in one of the districts which furnished provisions for Solomon's household (I Kings 4:9).

ELPAAL (ĕl-pā'ăl), son of Shahuraim, a Benjamite and head of his father's house (I Chron. 8:11,12,18).

ELPALET (ĕl-pā'lĕt, ĕl'pa-lĕt; ASV, RSV Elpelet), a son of David (I Chron. 14:5). See ELIPHALET (I Chron. 3:6).

EL SHADDAI (ĕl shăd'à-ī, -shăd'ī), the name of God by which, according to Exodus 6:3, He appeared to Abraham, Isaac, and Jacob. As to Abraham, this is borne out by Genesis 17:1; as to Jacob, by Genesis 28:3; 35:11; 43:14; 48:3; translated "God Almighty." Often "the Almighty" (*Shaddai* without *El*) is used as a name of God (Gen. 49:25; Num. 24:4,16, in Balaam's prophecies; Ruth 1:20,21; Ps. 68:14; 91:1; 30 times by Job and his friends, from Job 5:17 to 37:23; once God refers to Himself as "the Almighty," Job 40:2). The name is rare in the prophets (Isa. 13:6; Ezek. 1:24; 10:5; Joel 1:15). "Almighty" appears in the NT as a designation of God, translating Greek *pantokrátor,* all-powerful (II Cor. 6:18; 8 times in Rev., once, 19:6, translated "omnipotent"). Thus this name for God which was a favorite of the patriarchs, especially Jacob and Job, becomes prominent in the songs of heaven. The etymology of El Shaddai is in dispute, "Almighty God" being the widely accepted meaning, while some who would derive the Hebrew religion from pagan cults favor "mountain god."   E.R.

ELTEKEH (ĕl'tē-kē), a city in the territory given to Dan, on its southern border with Judah (Josh. 19:44). With its suburbs (KJV, ASV) or pasture lands (RSV) it was given to the Kohathite Levites (Josh. 21:23, ASV, RSV Elteke). Probably Khirbet el-Muqenna, E of Ekron.

ELTEKON (ĕl'tē-kŏn), one of six cities in the hill country of Judah (Josh. 15:59); site unknown; perhaps near Hebron because named next to Bethanoth which is in that vicinity.

ELTOLAD (ĕl-tō'lăd), a city in the Negeb of Judah toward Edom (Josh. 15:30), but assigned to Simeon (Josh. 19:4). Also (I Chron. 4:29) called Tolad.

ELUL (ĕ-lōol'), the sixth month of the Hebrew year, approximately August-September (Neh. 6:15). See CALENDAR.

ELUZAI (ē-lū'zā-ī), a Benjamite who joined David at Ziklag (I Chron. 12:5).

ELYMAS (ĕl'ĭmăs, Gr. *Elýmas*), a Jew, Bar-jesus (meaning *son of Jesus* or *Joshua*), a sorcerer who was with Sergius Paulus, the proconsul of Cyprus. He became blind following Paul's curse, in consequence of which the proconsul believed in the Lord (Acts 13:4-13). His name, Elymas, is Greek in form, but is not a Greek translation of Bar-jesus or of "sorcerer" (Greek *mágos*), but may be the transliteration of an Aramaic or Arabic root meaning "wise," and equivalent to *mágos*: hence the phrase, "Elymas the sorcerer (for so is his name by interpretation") (Acts 13:8).

ELZABAD (ĕl-zā'băd, ĕl'za-băd). 1. A Gadite who joined David at Ziklag (I Chron. 12:12).

2. The son of Shemaiah and a Korhite Levite (I Chron. 26:7).

A fine example of Egyptian embalming, the mummy of the woman Katebet, at Thebes. BM

EMBALM (ĕm-bàm), to prepare a dead body with oil and spices to preserve it from decay. Embalming was of Egyptian origin. The only clear instances of it in the Bible were in the cases of Jacob and Joseph. Joseph ordered his slaves, the physicians, to embalm his father (Gen. 50:2,3; a process which took 40 days); and later Joseph himself was embalmed (Gen. 50:26). The purpose of the Egyptians in embalming was to preserve the body for the use of the soul in a future life: the purpose of the Hebrews was to preserve the bodies of Jacob and Joseph for a long journey to their resting place with Abraham (Gen. 50:13). In the case of Joseph, centuries elapsed before burial in the ancestral tomb (Exod. 13:19; Josh 24:32). The process of embalming is not described in the Bible. Body cavities were filled with asphalt, cedar oil or spices, or all three. The body was wrapped tightly in linen cloths, the more perishable parts being stuffed with rolls of linen to maintain the shape of the human form. The Hebrew word for "embalm," *hānat,* means "to spice, to make spicy." The body of Asa is said to have been buried with spices, but is not said to have been embalmed (II Chron. 16:14). Jesus comments on the use of spices in burying (Matt. 26:12; Mark 14:8; John

12:7); and His body was buried with 100 pounds of myrrh and spices, wrapped in a linen cloth (John 19:39,40). The women who watched the burial considered this inadequate, for they prepared and brought to the sepulchre more spices (Mark 16:1; Luke 23:35,36; 24:1). Martha thought the body of Lazarus was decaying, hence clearly he had not been embalmed (John 11:39); but he was so bound that he had to be loosened (John 11:44). The widow's son at Nain was simply being carried out for burial (Luke 7:11-17): Ananias (and presumably Sapphira) were merely wrapped up (Acts 5:6,10). The Biblical concept of the future life made embalming unnecessary. E.R.

EMBROIDERY (ĕm-broi'dêr-ē), appears once in KJV as verb *embroider* (Exod. 28:39), translating Hebrew *shāvats*, referring probably to a checkered weaving (ASV, RSV) or plaiting of the coat with colored threads. The noun "embroider" occurs twice (Exod. 35:35; 38:23), Hebrew *rāqam, to variegate, weave in colored threads.* "Broidered" translates Hebrew *riqmâh,* variegated Ezek. 16:10,13,18; 26:16; 27:7,16,24: RSV *embroidered*), and renders Hebrew *tashebēts,* ASV, RSV *checkerwork* (Exod. 28:4) and Greek *plégma, twined, twisted, plaited;* of hair (I Tim. 2:9, KJV broided, ASV, RSV braided). *Riqmâh* is also translated "divers colors" (I Chron. 29:2, RSV colored stones; Ezek. 17:3, of bird plumage); "needlework" (Judg. 5:30, ASV, RSV embroidered with a design on both sides); and Psalm 45:14, ASV broidered work, RSV many-colored. Aside from the use of the Hebrew terms for the colors of gems and of feathers, they seem to have meant to weave into the cloth or draw in with a needle, or appliqué colored threads to make checkered designs, or other, for hangings of the tabernacle, for the coats, girdles and ephod of the priests, for royal garments, and for clothing of private persons. The details of such work given in the Bible impress us with the rich and gorgeously colorful character of needlework which may be called embroidery but furnish no exact idea of its appearance or method of manufacture. E.R.

EMIM (ē'mĭm, Heb. *'êmîm,* KJV Emim), the original inhabitants of Moab (Deut. 2:10,11). They were a great people, that is, powerful and of advanced civilization; numerous; and tall of stature, so that they were, like the Anakim, called giants. Out of harsh experience, the Moabites čalled them "Terrors," such being the meaning of Hebrew *'êmîm.* In the time of Abraham they were defeated by the Mesopotamian invaders in Shaveh Kiriathaim (Gen. 14:5), a plain E of the Dead Sea.

EMMANUEL (ĕ-măn'ū-ĕl), or *Immanuel,* the name meaning "with us is God," given by Isaiah to a child whose birth and childhood are a sign to Ahaz (Isa. 7:14; 8:8,10), and whose later life, sufferings and glory are the theme of his book. Micah 5:2 takes Immanuel to be the Messiah, whom Matthew 1:23 identifies as Jesus.

EMMAUS (ĕ-mā'ŭs), the village to which two disciples were going on the day of Jesus' resurrection, when He met and was recognized by them as He broke the bread at supper (Luke 24:7-35). It was about 60 furlongs or stadia (RSV, seven miles) from Jerusalem, in what direction is not stated. From early centuries several possibilities to the NW have been advocated. One site, 'Amwâs, is 20 miles (some manuscripts read 160 stadia) from the city, too far to suit Luke's narrative. Kubeibeh, Kuloniych and other sites have their partisans.

EMMOR (ĕm'êr), the father of Sychem (Acts 7: 16). Same as Hamor.

ENAM (ē'năm, Heb. *'ênayim, place of a fountain*), one of 14 cities "in the valley," lowland or Shephelah of Judah, near Jarmuth, Azekah, Bethshemesh, and Socoh. It is thought to be the same as Enaim, between Adullam and Timnah in the same region of the Negev (Gen. 38:14,21 ASV, RSV: in KJV "an open place," "openly"). This name means "two fountains." It has not yet been identified.

ENAN (ē'năn), the father of Ahira, of the tribe of Naphtali, who assisted in the Sinai census (Num. 1:15; 2:29; 7:78,83; 10:27).

ENCAMPMENT (ĕn-kămp'mĕnt). The children of Israel encamped at many places on their way from Egypt to Canaan (Exod. 13:20; 14:2,9; 15:27; Num. 33:10-46; Josh. 4:19; 5:10). Hebrew *hānât,* usually translated "encamp," is also rendered "abide in tents, pitch, rest intent," etc. Often the stay at an encampment was brief, sometimes long (Exod. 18:5). God gave instructions for the camp and its movements (Num. 1:50-2:34; 10:1-28, 33-36). Though men, women and children camped together, arrangements were military. References to encampments of soldiers, of Israel or of other nations, assembled for war, occur (Josh. 10:5, 31, 34; Judg. 6:4; 9:50; 10:17; 20:19; 1 Sam. 11:1; 13:16; II Sam. 11:11; 12:28; I Kings 16:15,16; I Chron. 11:15; II Chron. 32:1). Job 19:12 uses the word figuratively. Psalm 34:7 applies it to an angel; Zechariah 9:8, to God. It is literal in Psalms 27:3 and 53:5.

ENCHANTMENT (ĕn-chànt'mĕnt), the use of any form of magic, including divination. Several Hebrew and Greek words, variously translated, occur. All forms of enchantment were forbidden God's people (Deut. 18:10; Acts 8:9,11; 13:8,10; 19:19).

The village of Emmaus. © MPS

ENDOR (ĕn'dôr, Heb. *'ên dor, spring of habitation*), a village about seven miles SE of Nazareth, in Manasseh's territory, in western Palestine, and the home town of the "witch of Endor," the spiritist medium Saul visited before his last battle with the Philistines (I Sam. 28:8-25).

EN-EGLAIM (ĕn-ĕg'lā-ĭm), a place by the Dead Sea, between which and En-gedi Ezekiel prophesied that fishers would one day spread their nets (Ezek. 47:10). Site unknown.

EN-GANNIM (ĕn-găn'ĭm, Heb. *'ên gannîm, fountain, spring of gardens*). 1. A town in the lowland, valley or Shephelah of Judah, mentioned with Eshtaol and Zanoah (Josh. 15:34).

2. A town in the territory of Issachar, assigned to the Gershonite Levites (Josh. 19:21; 21:29). The modern *Jenīn*, SW of Mt. Gilboa, at the southern edge of the plain of Esdraelon, on the main road through Samaria to Jerusalem; with beautiful gardens and fruitful orchards, well watered by local springs.

EN-GEDI (ĕn-gē'dī, Heb. *'ên gedhî, spring or fountain of the kid or wild goat*), an oasis on the W coast of the Dead Sea about midway of its length, in the territory of Judah (Josh. 15:62). Here David fortified a refuge from Saul (I Sam. 23:29; 24:1). Jehoshaphat defeated the Ammonites, Moabites, and Edomites from Mt. Seir when they attacked by the narrow paths up the steep cliffs from the shore (II Chron. 20:2). En-gedi is there identified with Hazazon-tamar, occupied by Ammorites, which Chedorlaomer invaded in the days of Abraham (Gen. 14:7). Its luxurious verdure, due to warm springs, was famous in the days of Solomon (S. of Sol. 1:14). Ezekiel prophesied that fishers would stand here, in the restored land (Ezek. 47:10). Known then as Engaddi, it continued to be prominent through the NT period and until the time of Eusebius. It is the modern Ain Jidi, and the OT site is Tell ej-Jurn.

ENGRAVER. The OT and archaeology reveal a knowledge of engraving or carving among the Israelites, although developed neither to the extent nor skill as among neighboring countries. This may have been due to the warnings against "graven images" (Exod. 20:4). Signet rings, engraved with a man's seal or sign, were common (Gen. 38:18, Esth. 3:12, Jer. 22:24). Each of the two onyx stones on the high priest's shoulders was engraved with the names of six tribes, and his breastplate bore 12 stones, each engraved with the name of a tribe (Exod. 28:9-21). Bezaleel and Aholiab were craftsmen in gold, silver, brass, stones, and wood (Exod. 31:1-9, 38:22,23), gifted by God to make the furnishings of the tabernacle. Not only did they carve and engrave, but they taught these skills to others (Exod. 35:30-35). See also OCCUPATIONS.   A.M.R.

EN-HADDAH (ĕn-hăd'à, Heb. *'ên haddâh, swift fountain*), a town on the border of Issachar (Josh. 19:21).

EN-HAKKORE (ĕn-hăk'-ō-rē, Heb. *'ên ha-kôrē', fountain of him who cried*), a spring which burst out from Ramath-lehi ("hill of the jawbone") at Samson's cry, when he thirsted after slaying a thousand Philistines with a jawbone (Judg. 15:19).

EN-HAZOR (ĕn-hā'zôr, Heb. *'ên hātsòr, fountain of the village*), a fenced city in Naphtali named with Kedesh and Edrei (Josh. 19:37). Probably modern Hasireh, W of Kadesh.

The village of Endor, typical Palestinian peasant village. © MPS

EN-MISHPAT (ĕn-mĭsh'-păt, *fountain of judgment*), the older name for Kadesh (Gen. 14:7).

ENOCH (ē'nŭk, Heb. *hănôkh, consecrated, Gr. Henóch*). 1. Cain's eldest son, for whom the first city was named (Gen. 4:17,18).

2. Son of Jared (Gen. 5:18) and father of Methuselah (Gen. 5:21-22, Luke 3:37). Abram walked "before God" (Gen. 17:1), but of Enoch and Noah alone it is written that they walked *"with God"* (Gen. 5:24, 6:9). Walking with God is a relic of the first paradise when men walked and talked with God in holy familiarity, and it anticipates a new paradise (Rev. 21:3, 22:3,4). The secret of his walk with God was "faith";

Upper spring of En-gedi, a place where David found refuge from Saul. © MPS

The well at En-Rogel, called "Job's Well," south of Jerusalem. © MPS

faith was the ground of his "pleasing God"; his pleasing God was the ground of his being "translated that he should not see death" (Heb. 11:5,6). After the monotonous repetition of the patriarchs who "lived . . . begat . . . and died" (Gen. 5), the account of Enoch's walk with God and translation without death stands forth in bright relief. He, too, begat sons and daughters, yet family ties were no hindrance to his walking with God. Indeed, it was not until after he was 65 years old, when he begat Methuselah, that it is written, "Enoch walked with God." He typifies the saints living at Christ's coming who will be removed from mortality to immortality without passing through death (I Cor. 15:51,52). His translation out of a wicked world was an appropriate testimony to the truth ascribed to him in Jude 14,15, "Behold, the Lord cometh . . . to execute judgment."

ENOCH, BOOKS OF, a collection of apocalyptic literature written by various authors and circulated under the name of Enoch. I Enoch is an Ethiopic version made through the Greek from the original Hebrew text that was written by the Chasidim or by the Pharisees between 163-63 B.C. It is the best source for the development of Jewish doctrine in the last two pre-Christian centuries. Jude 14, 15 may be an explicit quotation from it. II Enoch was written A.D. 1-50.

ENOS (ē'nŏs, Heb. 'ĕnôsh, mortal, Gr. Enós), son of Seth and grandson of Adam (Gen. 4:26, 5:6-11, Luke 3:38). Attached to his birth is an implication of godly fear (see Gen. 4:26, marg.). He lived 905 years.

ENOSH (ē'nŏsh, Heb. 'ĕnôsh, mortal), a more acceptable way of Anglicizing the name of Seth's son (I Chron. 1:1; ERV Gen. 4:26, 5:6-11, Luke 3:38).

EN-RIMMON (ĕn-rĭm'ŏn, Heb. 'ēn-rimmôn, fountain of a pomegranate), a place S of Jerusalem (Zech. 14:10), 11 miles NE of Beersheba. "Ain and Rimmon" (Josh. 15:32; Josh. 19:7; I Chron. 4:32). Reinhabited after the Captivity (Neh. 11:29).

EN-ROGEL (ĕn-rō'gel, Heb. 'ēn rōghēl, fountain of feet), so-called because fullers trod their cloth with their feet there. It was on the border between Benjamin and Judah (Josh. 15:7, 18:16), below Jerusalem near the junction of the valley of Hinnom and the valley of Jehoshaphat. Here Jonathan and Ahimaaz hid to receive intelligence for David from within the walls (II Sam. 17:17). Here also Adonijah held his sacrificial feast, expecting to seize the throne (I Kings 1:9). Today it is a well 125 ft. deep called Bir Aiyub or "well of Job." En-rogel is often mistaken to be Gihon Spring (I Kings 1:38) or "The Virgin's Fount," but this is too close to Jerusalem to be a hiding place (II Sam. 17:17).

ENTAPPUAH (ĕn-tăp'ū-à, Heb. 'ēn tappûah, spring of apple), a town on the eastern border of Manasseh in the land of Tappuah (Josh. 17:7,8).

EPAENETUS (ĕp-ē'nē-tŭs, Gr. Epaínetos, praised), a Christian at Rome greeted by Paul as "my well-beloved, who is the firstfruits of Asia (better MS reading) unto Christ" (Rom. 16:5). This is all that is known of him.

EPAPHRAS (ĕp'à-frăs, Gr. Epaphrás), a contraction of Epaphroditus, but not the same NT character. He was Paul's "dear fellowservant" and minister to the church at Colosse, perhaps its founder (Col. 1:7). He brought to Paul a report of their state (1:4,8) and sent back greetings to them from Rome (4:12). Commended by Paul for his ministry of intercession, he desired their perfect and complete stand in all the will of God. Here is true pastoral concern which extended to other churches in the Lycus River valley as well (4:13). Paul also called him "my fellow-prisoner." This may mean that he voluntarily shared the apostle's imprisonment; or he may have been apprehended for his zeal in the Gospel.

EPAPHRODITUS (ē-păf-rō-dī'tŭs, Gr. Epaphróditos, lovely), the messenger delegated by the church at Philippi to bring their gifts to Paul while he was in prison. This the apostle gratefully received as a sweet-smelling sacrifice to God (Phil. 4:18). Epaphroditus contracted a serious illness. On recovery, he longed to return to his flock and relieve their anxiety on his behalf. Paul held him in high esteem as "brother, companion in labor, and fellowsoldier," and sent him back to Philippi bearing his epistle (2:25-30).

EPHAI (ē'fī, Heb. 'ĕphay, gloomy), the Netophathite whose sons were among the captains of the forces left in Judah after the deportation to Babylon (Jer. 40:8). They served under Gedaliah, the governor appointed by the Babylonians. After their warning of the plot against Gedaliah went unheeded (40:13-16), they were slain with him by Ishmael, son of Nethaniah (41:3).

EPHER (ē'fēr, Heb. 'ēpher, calf). 1. Son of Midian and grandson of Abraham (Gen. 25:4, I Chron. 1:33).
   2. Son of Ezra of the tribe of Judah (1 Chron. 4:17).
   3. A family head in the half-tribe of Manasseh E of Jordan (I Chron. 5:23,24).

EPHESDAMMIM (ē-fĕs-dăm'ĭm, Heb. 'ephes dammîm, boundary of blood), a place so-called from the bloody battles fought there between Israel and the Philistines. Lying between Shocoh and Azekah in Judah, it was the Philistine encampment when David slew Goliath (I Sam. 17:1). Called Pas-dammim in I Chronicles 11:13. Modern Beit Fased ("house of bloodshed") may be over the ancient site.

EPHESIANS, EPISTLE TO THE, generally acknowledged to be one of the richest and most profound of the NT epistles. The depth and grandeur of its concepts, the richness and fullness of its message, and the majesty and dignity of its contents have made it precious to believers in all ages and in all places. Its profound truths and vivid imagery have deeply penetrated into the thought and literature of the Christian Church.

Ephesians explicitly claims Pauline authorship (1:1; 3:1) and its entire tenor is eminently Pauline. The early Christian Church uniformly received and treasured it as from Paul. Only within the modern era have liberal critics raised doubts as to its Pauline origin. The attacks are based solely on internal arguments drawn from the style, vocabulary, and theology of the epistle. These arguments are subjective and inconclusive and offer no compelling reasons for rejecting the undeviating evidence of text and tradition. If the Pauline authorship is rejected, the epistle must be ascribed to someone who was fully Paul's equal, but the literature of the first two centuries reveals no traces of anyone capable of producing such a writing.

Ephesians was written while Paul was a prisoner (3:1; 4:1; 6:20). The prevailing view has been that it was written from Rome during Paul's first Roman imprisonment (Acts 28:30-31). Some attempts have been made to shift the place of composition to Caesarea (Acts 24:27), or even to Ephesus during an unrecorded imprisonment there (II Cor. 11:23; Acts 19:10; 20:18-21,31), but the traditional Roman origin firmly holds the field.

The letter was transmitted to its destination by Tychicus (6:21-22), being dispatched together with Colossians and Philemon (Col. 4:7-8; Philem. 9,13,17). Thus all three were sent to the Roman province of Asia, but there is much scholarly disagreement as to the precise destination of Ephesians. The uncertainty arises from the fact that the words "at Ephesus" (*en Ephesō*) in 1:1 are not found in three very ancient copies (the Chester Beatty papyrus, the Uncials *Aleph* and *B*). Passages in the writings of Origen and Basil indicate that they also knew the enigmatical reading produced by the omission of "at Ephesus." But the words are found in all other manuscripts in their uncorrected form and in all ancient versions. With the exception of the heretical Marcion, whom Tertullian accused of tampering with the title, ecclesiastical tradition uniformly designates it as "to the Ephesians."

How are the phenomena to be accounted for? One widely accepted view is that the epistle was really an encyclical sent to the various churches of Provincial Asia, of whom Ephesus was the most important. It is often further assumed that originally a blank was left for the insertion of the local place name. The impersonal tone and contents of the epistle are urged as confirmation.

The view is plausible but it has its difficulties. If it was originally directed to a group of churches, would not Paul, in accordance with his known practice of making a direct address, rather have written "in Asia," or "in the churches of Asia"? In all other places where Paul uses the words "to those who are" he adds a local place name. Then how is the uniform tradition of its Ephesian destination to be accounted for? Those who insist it was for Ephesus alone are confronted with the encyclical nature of its contents. A fair solution would seem to be that the epistle was originally addressed to the saints "at Ephesus" but was intentionally cast into a form that would make it suitable to

Ruins of the great theater at Ephesus. © MPS

meet the needs of the Asian churches. As transcriptions of the original to the mother church were circulated, the place of designation might be omitted, although uniformly recognized as the epistle originally addressed to the Ephesians.

Its contents offer no clear indication as to the occasion for the writing of Ephesians. Its affinity to Colossians in time of origin and contents suggests an occasion closely related to the writing of that epistle. Ephesians seems to be the after-effect of the controversy that caused the writing of Colossians. Colossians has in it the intensity, rush, and roar of the battle field, while Ephesians has a calm atmosphere suggestive of a survey of the field after the victory. With the theme of Colossians still fresh in mind Paul felt it desirable to set forth the positive significance of the great truths set forth in refuting the Colossian heresy. A firm grasp of the truths here set forth would provide an effective antidote to such philosophical speculations.

Ephesians sets forth the wealth of the believer in union with Christ. It portrays the glories of our salvation and emphasizes the nature of the Church as the Body of Christ. As indicated by the doxology in 3:20-21, its contents fall into two parts, the first doctrinal (1-3), the second practical and hortatory (4-6). An outline may suggest some of its riches.

THE SALUTATION. 1:1-2
  I. DOCTRINAL: The Believer's Standing in Christ. 1:3-3:21
    1. The thanksgiving for our redemption. 1:3-14
    2. The prayer for spiritual illumination. 1:15-23
    3. The power of God manifested in our salvation. 2:1-10
    4. The union of Jew and Gentile in one Body in Christ. 2:11-22
    5. The apostle as the messenger of this mystery. 3:1-13
    6. The prayer for the realization of these blessings. 3:14-19
    7. The doxology of praise. 3:20-21

Remains of the great marble street of the Arkadiane at Ephesus, which ran from the theater to the harbor. © MPS Below, an artist's reconstruction. UANT

II. PRACTICAL: The Believers' Life in Christ. 4:1-6:20
   1. Their walk as God's saints. 4:1-5:21
      a. The worthy walk, in inward realization of Christian unity. 4:1-16
      b. The different walk, in outward manifestation of a changed position. 4:17-32
      c. The loving walk, in upward imitation of our Father. 5:1-17
      d. The summary of the Spirit-filled life. 5:18-21
   2. Their duties as God's family. 5:22-6:9
   3. Their warfare as God's soldiers. 6:10-20

THE CONCLUSION. 6:21-24.   D.E.H.

EPHESUS (ĕf'ĕ-sŭs, Gr. *Éphesos, desirable*), an old Ionian foundation at the mouth of the Cayster. Greek colonies which surround the Mediterranean and Black Sea were primarily trading-posts. Migrant communities of Greeks did not seek to dominate the hinterlands, but to secure an *emporion* or "way in," a bridgehead for commerce, and enough surrounding coast and territory to support the community. Great cities grew from such foundations from Marseilles to Alexandria, some of them royal capitals. And in all cases colonies became centers or outposts of Hellenism, distinctive, and civilizing.

Ephesus displaced Miletus as a trading port, but when its harbor, like that of Miletus, in turn silted up, Smyrna replaced both as the outlet and *emporion* of the Maeander valley trade-route. In the heyday of Asia Minor 230 separate communities, each proud of its individuality and wealth, issued their own coinage and managed their own affairs. The dominance of Persian despotism, wide deforestation, and the ravage of war in a natural bridge and highway between the continents slowly sapped this prosperity, but in early Roman times, as in the days of its Ionian independence, Ephesus was a proud, rich, busy port, the rival of Alexandria and Syrian Antioch.

Built near the shrine of an old Anatolian fertility goddess, Ephesus became the seat of an oriental cult. The Anatolian deity had been taken over by the Greeks under the name of Artemis, the Diana of the Romans. Grotesquely represented with turreted head and many breasts, the goddess and her cult found expression in the famous temple, served, like that of Aphrodite at Corinth, by a host of priestess courtesans.

Round the cult clustered much trade. Ephesus became a place of pilgrimage for tourist-worshipers, all eager to carry away talisman and souvenir, hence the prosperous guild of the silversmiths whose livelihood was the manufacture of silver shrines and images of the meteoric stone which was said to be Diana's image "fallen from heaven." Ephesus leaned more and more on the trade which followed the cult as commerce declined in her silting harbor. Twenty miles of reedy marshland now separate the old harbor works from the sea and even in Paul's day the process was under way. Tacitus tells us that an attempt was made to improve the seaway in A.D. 65, but the task proved too great. Ephesus in the first century was a dying city, given to parasite pursuits, living, like Athens, on a reputation, a curious meeting place of old and new religions, of East and West. Acts 19 gives a peculiarly vivid picture of her unnatural life. The "lampstand" has gone from its place, for Ephesus' decline was mortal sickness, and it is possible to detect in the letter to Ephesus in the Apocalypse a touch of the lassitude which was abroad in the effete and declining community. The temple and part of the city have been extensively excavated.   E.M.B.

EPHLAL (ĕf'lăl, Heb. *'ephlāl, judge*), son of Zabad of the tribe of Judah (I Chron. 2:37).

EPHOD (ēf'-ŏd, Heb. *'ēphōdh*). 1. A sacred vestment originally worn by the high priest and made of "gold, blue, purple, scarlet, and fine twined linen, with cunning work" (Exod. 28:4ff; 39:2ff). It was held together front and back by two shoulder pieces at the top and a girdle band around the waist. On each shoulderpiece was an onyx stone engraved with six names of the tribes of Israel. Attached to the ephod by chains of pure gold was a breastplate containing 12 precious stones. Beneath the ephod was worn the blue robe of the ephod, having a hole for the head and extending to the feet with a hem alternating with gold bells and pomegranates of blue, purple, and scarlet (Exod. 28:31-35; 39:22-26).

A village in Ephraim. © MPS

The High Priest clothed in the Ephod. DV

Later, persons other than the high priest wore ephods. Samuel wore a linen ephod while ministering before the Lord (I Sam. 2:18) which was characteristic of the ordinary priests (2:28; 14:3; 22:18). David wore a linen ephod while he danced before the Lord after bringing the ark to Jerusalem (II Sam. 6:14). Abiathar carried off from Nob an ephod which represented to David the divine presence, for of it he inquired the will of the Lord (I Sam. 23:6,9; 30:7,8).

The ephod was misused as an object of idolatrous worship by Gideon (Judg. 8:27) and associated with images by Micah (Judg. 17:5; 18:14).

2. Father of Hanniel who was the prince of the children of Manasseh (Num. 34:23).   A.M.R.

EPHPHATHA (ĕf'ȧ-thȧ, Gr. *Ephphathá* from Aram. *'etpătah,* passive imper. of the verb *petah, be thou opened*), occurs only in Mark 7:34. Uttered by Jesus as He was healing a deaf man.

EPHRAIM (ē'frâ-ĭm, Heb. *'ephrayim, double fruit*), the younger of two sons of Joseph and his Egyptian wife Asenath (Gen. 41:50-52). The aged Jacob, when he blessed his grandsons Manasseh and Ephraim, adopted them as his own sons. Despite Joseph's protest, Jacob gave the preferential blessing (signified by the right hand) to Ephraim (Gen. 48:1-22). When Jacob blessed his own sons, he did not mention Ephraim and Manasseh, but gave a special blessing to their father Joseph (Gen. 49: 22-26).

Ephraim was the progenitor of the tribe called by his name, as was also Manasseh. This brought the number of the Hebrew tribes to 13, but the original number 12 (derived from the 12 sons of Jacob, of whom Joseph was one) continued to be referred to. The separation of the tribe of Levi from the others for the Tabernacle service, and its failure to receive a separate territory in which to live, helped to perpetuate the concept of "The Twelve Tribes of Israel."

Ephraim together with Manasseh and Benjamin camped on the W side of the Tabernacle in the wilderness (Num. 2:18-24). Joshua (Hoshea) the son of Nun, one of the spies and Moses' successor, was an Ephraimite (Num. 13:8). Ephraim and Manasseh were mentioned as making up the Joseph group in Moses' blessing (Deut. 33:13-17).

At the division of the land among the tribes the children of Joseph (except half of Manasseh which settled E of the Jordan, Num. 32:33; 39-42) received the central hill country of Palestine, sometimes called Mt. Ephraim. This area is bounded on the N by the Valley of Jezreel, on the E by the Jordan River, on the S by a "zone of movement" (a series of valleys which invite travel across Palestine) which runs from Joppa to Jericho, and on the W it stretches to the Mediterranean. The Joseph tribes were not able to occupy this land completely for a long time, being forced up into the heavily wooded hill country (Josh. 17:14-18) by the Canaanites and Philistines who occupied the good bottom lands and who by their superior civilization and power (Judg. 1:27-29) kept the Hebrews subservient until the time of David. Ephraim and Manasseh seem to have been bitter rivals (Isa. 9:20,21), Manasseh being the larger group (Gen. 49:22) but Ephraim asserting the more vigorous leadership. Although they seem to have held their land in common for a time (Josh. 17:14-18) it was presently divided between them. Ephraim's portion was well defined and very fruitful, its soil fertile and its rainfall more plentiful than Judah's to the S (Deut. 33:13-16).

Ephraim's inheritance is described in Joshua 16:5-10. The territory was bounded on the S by the northern borders of Benjamin and Dan. Bethel was just across the line in Benjamin, the two Beth-horons were just in Ephraim, as was Gezer toward the sea. The western boundary seems ideally to have been the Mediterranean. On the N, the brook Kanah separated Ephraim from the half of Manasseh, as did the towns of Shechem (in Manasseh) and Taanath-shiloh. Then the line seems to have turned abruptly southward, through Ataroth, passing near Jericho and thence to the Jordan. References to the towns for Ephraimites within Manasseh (Josh. 16:9; 17:9) suggest that the rivalry between these two tribes had resulted in some boundary changes.

At Shiloh, in the territory of Ephraim, the Tabernacle was pitched by Joshua (Josh. 18:1) and this town remained a religious center for the Hebrews (Josh. 22:12; Judg. 18:31; 21:19; I Sam. 1:3,9,24; 2:14; 3:21) until it was destroyed by the Philistines after the battle of Ebenezer (I Sam. 4:1-11). Samuel was an Ephraimite (I Sam. 1:1). The Ephraimites contributed their share of the hatred and strife which divided the Hebrew tribes during the dark days of the judges (Judg. 8:1-3; 12:1-6).

It would appear that Ephraim, in common with the rest of the central and northern tribes, was never completely reconciled to the rule of Judah which the Davidic dynasty brought (II Sam. 2:8, 9; I Kings 12:16). When Jeroboam I, an Ephraimite (I Kings 11:26), rebelled against Solomon's son Rehoboam, no doubt his own tribe supported him completely. Ephraim became such a leader in the new northern Hebrew kingdom that in addition to its more common name Israel, the kingdom is also called Ephraim (Isa. 7:2,5,9,17; Hos. 9:3-16). From this time on the tribe's history is merged with that of this kingdom.

Ephraim is also the name of a city N of Jerusalem, mentioned in II Sam. 13:23 and John 11:54. It has been identified with modern Et-Taiyibeh, a few miles NE of Bethel. The forest of Ephraim (II Sam. 18:6) was probably located in Transjordan near Mahanaim.   J.B.G.

EPHRAIM, MOUNT OF (ē'frā-ĭm, Heb. *har 'ephrayim*), the mountainous part of the territory of the tribe of Ephraim (Josh. 17:15, etc., ASV) or "hill-country," which phrase is not accurate, as all the hills are part of the same mountain range which runs through central Palestine.

EPHRAIM, WOODS OF (Heb. *ya'ar 'ephrayim*), occurs only in II Samuel 18:6 where it denotes the place of the decisive battle in which the soldiers of David defeated the forces of Absalom. The context indicates that this fighting took place in the land of Gilead E of the Jordan. The site has not been identified.

EPHRAIMITE (ē'frā-ĭm-īt, Heb. *'ephrayim*, always occurs in this plural form), a member of the tribe of Ephraim (Josh. 16:10 and Judg. 12).

EPHRAIN (ē'frā-ĭn, Heb. *'ephrôn, fawn*), the name of one of the towns which, along with Bethel, Abijah took from Jeroboam (II Chron. 13:19). ASV has Ephron in this verse with Ephrain in the margin. May be same as Ophrah (Josh. 18:23). Modern *Taiyibeh*.

EPHRATH (ĕf'răth, Heb. *'ephrāth, fruitful land*), a shorter form of Ephrathah, KJV Ephratah, the place where Rachel was buried. (Gen. 35:16).

2. Second wife of Caleb, son of Hezron. She was the mother of Hur (I Chron. 2:19,20).

3. The ancient name of Bethlehem or the district around it. This name is attached to that of Bethlehem in the great prophecy of the place of the birth of Christ (Mic. 5:2).

EPHRON (ē'frôn, Heb. *'ephrôn, fawn*), a Hittite, the son of Zohar, of the children of Heth in Hebron, from whom Abraham purchased, for four hundred shekels of silver, the field of Machpelah which contained a cave in which he buried Sarah, his wife (Gen. 23:8,9).

2. A mountain on the N border of Judah located about six miles NW of Jerusalem (Josh. 15:9).

3. A city taken from Jeroboam by Ahijah (II Chron. 13:19). Perhaps identical with Ephrain or Ophrah.

EPICUREANS (ĕp-ĭ-kū-rē'ănz, Gr. *Epikoúreioi*), the followers of Epicurus, the Greek philosopher who lived 341-270 B.C. He taught that nature rather than reason is the true reality; nothing exists but atoms and void, that is, matter and space. The chief purpose of man is to achieve happiness. He has free will to plan and live a life of pleasure. Epicurus gave the widest scope to this matter of pleasure, interpreting it as avoidance of pain, so that the mere enjoyment of good health would be pleasure. Such stress on the good things of life, while very practical, is also very dangerous. For the philosopher the highest joy is found in mental and intellectual pursuits, but for lesser souls lower goals of sensual satisfaction fulfill the greatest pleasure. Thus the high standards of the founder were not maintained and the philosophy gained a bad reputation. Since such teaching appealed to the common man, this natural philosophy became widespread. It was widely held at the time of Christ. Paul met it at Athens when he encountered the philosophers of that city (Acts 17:16-33). They were not impressed by his teaching of creation, judgment and resurrection, since all these doctrines were denied by the Epicurean philosophy.   C.E.H.

The Hill Country of Ephraim. © MPS

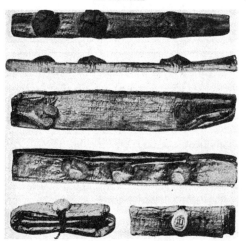

Sealed letters, or epistles, sheets of papyrus rolled, tied and sealed, to be delivered by messenger.   JHK

EPISTLE (ē-pis'l, Gr. *epistolé, letter, epistle*). Written correspondence, whether personal or official, has been common to all ages. The OT abounds with evidences of widespread written letters, among the best known being David's letter to Joab concerning Uriah (II Sam. 11:14,15), Jezebel's letter regarding Naboth (I Kings 21:8,9), Sennacherib's letter to Hezekiah (II Kings 19:14); as does also the NT (Acts 9:2; Rom. 16:1ff; I Cor. 7:1).

The term is, however, almost a technical one, referring particularly to the 21 epistles of the NT. The NT epistles were written by 4 (possibly 5) writers: Peter, Paul, John, Jude, and the author of Hebrews. Paul wrote 13 (or 14, if Hebrews is by him); Peter, 2; John, 3; and Jude 1. According to the custom of the time, they usually begin with the name or title of the writer and that of the addressee or addressees; then follow words of greeting, the message of the epistle; and at the end the author usually gives his name. It was Paul's usual practice to employ an amanuensis to write from dictation. The epistles were written to individual churches or groups of churches (almost always given by name) and to individuals. Seven are called General Epistles, because they were written to the church at large.

The epistles are not disguised doctrinal treatises. They were written in the way of ordinary correspondence, and deal with situations, whether doctrinal or practical, needing immediate attention. They were written in reply to letters or as the result of other information otherwise obtained. It is very apparent that the writers realized that what they wrote was authoritative and came from God. They all deal with some aspect of the redemptive message and experience. Although written to deal with specific local situations, they set forth fundamental principles applicable to the individual and collective life of all believers. They were received from the beginning with the OT Scriptures (II Peter 3:15,16).

The influence of the NT Epistles on the literature of Christianity is seen in the writings of the next century, which were mostly epistolary in form. Indeed, heretics wrote epistles in the name of the apostles.

It is not to be supposed that all of the epistles of the apostles have survived. Paul in I Corinthians 5:9 refers to a letter he had written to the Corinthians prior to our I Corinthians; and in Colossians 4:6 he speaks of an epistle to the Laodicean church.   S.B.

ER (ûr, Heb. *'ēr, watchful*), eldest son of Judah by the daughter of Shua, the Canaanite. Judah took a wife for him named Tamar. He was so wicked the Lord slew him (Gen. 38:3,6,7).

2. The third son of Shelah, the son of Judah (I Chron. 4:21).

3. An ancestor of Jesus in the maternal line (Luke 3:28).

ERAN (ē'răn, Heb. *'ērān, watcher*), the son of Shuthelah who was the oldest son of Ephraim. His descendants were the Eranites (Num. 26:36).

ERASTUS (ē-răs'tŭs, Gr. *Érastos, beloved*), a name which occurs three times, each time denoting a friend of Paul: 1. Acts 19:22 "And having sent into Macedonia two of them that ministered under him, Timothy and Erastus," Paul stayed in Asia.

2. The treasurer of the city of Corinth whom Paul mentions as saluting the Christians at Rome (Rom. 16:23).

3. Probably the same man is designated in II Timothy 4:20 as remaining at Corinth.

ERECH (ē'rĕk, Heb. *'erekh*), a city of ancient Babylonia mentioned in Genesis 10:10 as the second city founded by Nimrod. The Babylonian form of the name is *Uruk*. The modern site is called *Warka,* and is located near the Euphrates river, 40 miles NW of Ur. This city was mentioned much in ancient Mesopotamian literature. Erech was the home of Gilgamesh, the hero of the great Akkadian epic.

Archaeology has found that this city was one of the oldest of Babylonia, being founded before 4000 B.C., and continued to flourish until after 300 B.C. One of the early dynasties of the Sumerians ruled from Erech. Culturally, it boasted the first ziggurat, or tower, and began the use of clay cylinder seals.

ERI (ē'rī, Heb. *'erî, my watcher*), the fifth son of Gad (Gen. 46:16).

ESAIAS (See Isaiah)

ESAR-HADDON (ē'sàr-hăd'ŏn, *Ashur has given a brother*), a younger son of Sennacherib, who upon the murder of his father by his older brother (II Kings 19:36,37; II Chron. 32:21; Isa. 37:37,38) obtained the throne of Assyria. His reign (681-669 B.C.) brought important political developments. He restored the city of Babylon which his father had destroyed, and fought campaigns against the Cimmerians and other barbaric hordes from beyond the Caucasus. His greatest accomplishment was the conquest of Egypt, Assyria's competitor for world domination.

In preparation for his Egyptian campaign, Esarhaddon subdued the Westlands. Sidon was destroyed, its inhabitants deported, its king beheaded, and a new city erected on its site. According to Ezra 4:2, Esar-haddon brought deportees into Samaria, which had already been colonized with pagans by Sargon when he destroyed it in 722 B.C. After Sidon's fall, 12 kings along the Mediterranean seacoast submitted to the Assyrians, and were forced to supply wood and stone for the king's palace in Nineveh. Among these was "Manasi king of Yaudi," the Manasseh of the Bible. Manasseh had little choice. The Assyrian empire had now reached its greatest power and it appears that most of the Judean citizenry preferred peaceful submission, even with the Assyrian pagan influences now imposed upon them, to constant abortive rebellion. Manasseh's summons to appear before an Assyrian king, mentioned in II Chronicles 33:11-13, probably took place in the reign of Esar-haddon's successor, Assurbanipal.

In 671 Egypt fell to Esar-haddon when he occupied Memphis and organized Egypt into districts under princes responsible to Assyrian governors. A later Egyptian rebellion necessitated a second Assyrian campaign there, during which Esar-haddon died and Assurbanipal his son succeeded him.

ESAU (ē'saw, Heb. *'ēsāw, hairy*), the firstborn of the twin brothers, Esau and Jacob, sons of Isaac and Rebecca (Gen. 25:24,25). Before their birth God had told their mother that the elder should serve the younger (Gen. 25:23). Esau became a man of the fields. He apparently lived only for the present. This characteristic was demonstrated when he let Jacob have his birthright for a mess of pottage because he was hungry (Gen. 25:30-34).

At the age of 40 he married two Hittite women (Gen. 26:34). When the time came for Isaac to give his blessing to his son, he wanted to confer it on Esau, but, through trickery, Jacob obtained the blessing instead. This loss grieved Esau very much. He begged for another blessing and when he received it he hated it because it made him the servant of his brother. He hated Jacob for cheating him and intended to kill him (Gen. 27).

When Esau saw Jacob sent away to obtain a wife from his mother's relatives he understood that Canaanite wives did not please his father so he went out and took for himself two additional wives of the Ishmaelites (Gen. 28:6-9).

Years later when he was living in Mt. Seir, Esau heard that Jacob was returning to Canaan (Gen. 32:3-5). With 400 men he set out to meet his brother. But the provisions Jacob made to placate him caused him to greet his brother warmly (Gen. 32:7-33:15). They soon parted company and Esau went back to Mt. Seir (Gen. 33:16).

In the providence of God Esau was made subservient to Jacob. In Hebrews 12:16,17 he is described as a profane person. Long after his death the Lord declared he had loved Jacob and hated Esau (Mal. 1:2,3). The apostle Paul used this passage to illustrate how God carries out His purposes (Rom. 9:10-13).

Sometimes in Scripture Esau is used as the name of the land of Edom in which his descendants lived (Gen. 36:8). C.E.H.

ESCHATOLOGY (ĕs-kà-tŏl'ō-gē, Gr. *éschatos, last* and *lógos, ordered statement*), a division of systematic theology dealing with the doctrine of last things such as death, resurrection, the second coming of Christ, the end of the age, divine judgment, and the future state. It properly includes all that was prophetic of future events when recorded in Scripture.

PRESUPPOSITIONS. Among theological conservatives it is generally agreed that Biblical prophecies will be fulfilled and such events as resurrection from the dead, reward of the saints, punishment of the wicked, and the continued conscious existence of all human souls throughout eternity will eventuate. Biblical eschatology assumes that the Scriptures predict future events with infallible accuracy and constitute a divine disclosure of the future.

Contemporary liberalism has questioned the predictive character of Biblical prophecy by denying that it is possible to know the details of future events in advance. Schweitzer in his *The Mystery of the Kingdom of God* (translated from the German, 1925) introduced the liberal teaching that eschatology was the center of apostolic teaching and that Christ Himself erroneously taught the imminent end of the age, dying on the cross when He realized He was mistaken. The contemporary

emphasis in interpretation of eschatology has been further developed by C. H. Dodd, O. Cullmann, and others, in their definition of "realized eschatology" as divine purpose being fulfilled today. The contemporary experience of eschatology is also characteristic of the neo-orthodox and crisis theologians such as Karl Barth, Emil Brunner, and Reinhold Niebuhr, though the concept of a future consummation at the end of the age is also allowed. Only the conservative point of view does full justice to predictive Scripture as actually foretelling future events.

PRINCIPLES OF INTERPRETATION. Though conservatives agree on essential doctrines, three types of interpretations have arisen. The early church adopted the point of view of premillennialism or chiliasm, anticipating a literal return of Christ to the earth, the establishment of His kingdom on the earth for one thousand years, and the beginning of the eternal state thereafter. The Alexandrian school of theology (third century), interpreting prophecy in a nonliteral or allegorical way, viewed the millennial kingdom as having already begun with the first coming of Christ, to be consummated in His second coming, and to be followed immediately by the eternal state. This view was championed by Augustine (354-430) and was adopted by the Roman Catholic Church and the Protestant Reformers such as Calvin and Luther. A variation of amillennialism known as postmillennialism was introduced by Daniel Whitby (1638-1725) who taught that the last one thousand years of the present age would fulfill promises of peace and righteousness on earth and be a crowning triumph of the Gospel. The world conflicts of the first half of the 20th century and a realistic appraisal of the world situation have caused a general abandonment of postmillennialism and a return to either Augustinian amillennialism or premillennialism.

Differing interpretations of eschatology result from the literal or nonliteral interpretation of prophecy, the more literal leading to premillennialism, the less literal to the amillennial view. Approaches also vary on the question of the central purpose of God in eschatology. Amillennialism tends to emphasize soteriology or the salvation of the elect as the dominating factor, whereas premillennialism usually adopts the principle that the manifestation of the glory of God is the supreme purpose in divine dealing with men in successive ages, and distinguishes God's program in eschatology for Israel from that of His program for the world as a whole or His program for the church.

ESCHATOLOGY IN THE OLD TESTAMENT. Though eschatology is not the main theme of the early books of the OT, eschatological considerations are constantly applied. God is presented as the Creator and Ruler who in divine providence directs the progress of history. Man is introduced as created in the image and likeness of God, and human life is declared to be purposeful and consummated in the life after death. The major burden of OT prophecy deals with life on earth and events of future human history, but belief in life after death, the resurrection of the body, and divine rewards and punishments in the life to come permeate the OT as they do the New. Job, probably a contemporary of Abraham, anticipated a coming Redeemer and the resurrection of his body (Job 19:25-26). Abraham, according to Hebrews 11:14-16, anticipated dwelling in a heavenly city after death. The OT abode of the dead called "Sheol," though often merely a reference to the grave, in some instances refers to the intermediate state (Deut. 32:22; Ps. 16:10; 139:8). The saint is promised deliverance from death by resurrection (Isa. 25: 6-9; 26:19; Dan. 12:2-3).

Individual eschatology, concerned with life, death, resurrection, and reward or punishment, is set in a context of general eschatology or prediction of the movement of history. In the OT this concerns principally the nation Israel, beginning with Genesis 12 and the divine covenant with Abraham. Abraham was promised not only personal reward, but that his seed should possess the Holy Land as a perpetual possession and that through his posterity blessing should come to all nations of the earth. David was promised that his kingdom and throne should continue forever. The prophets in the midst of the captivity and the apostasy of Israel connected the fulfillment of these prophecies with the coming of the Messiah and the establishment of His kingdom in the earth. Amillenarians and postmillenarians interpret these prophecies as largely fulfilled in the Church, and have not attempted literal explanation of the details. Many premillenarians assert the promise of future possession of the Holy Land to Israel as valid and to be fulfilled literally in the coming millennial kingdom of Christ on earth following His second advent. Promises given to Israel are distinguished from promises addressed to saints in general or to the Church in the present age.

The OT abounds also in prophecies relating to Gentiles or those outside the seed of Abraham. Many predictions were given of individual judgments, already largely fulfilled. To Daniel was revealed the larger picture of the divine program for the nations of the world as embodied in the four empires of his vision (Dan. 2,7). Daniel predicted that there would be four major movements in Gentile history, beginning with the Babylonian Empire, followed by the Medio-Persian Empire, the Macedonian Empire of Alexander the Great, and to be concluded with the Roman Empire. Many consider the last stages of the Roman Empire to be still future and to be fulfilled in the world conflict immediately preceding the second advent. The eschatology of the OT, therefore, while dealing with individual hope, is largely concerned with the major movement of divine providence as it relates to Israel and the Gentiles. Of great importance is the line of prophecy relating to the coming of the Redeemer, the Son of David, who was to be the Saviour of the World.

NEW TESTAMENT ESCHATOLOGY. Though sometimes distinguished sharply from OT eschatology, it is reasonable to assume that the NT continues, interprets, enlarges, and completes the OT eschatology. The fulfillment of prophecies in the NT which are related to the first advent of Christ, involving hundreds of OT Scriptures, is obvious proof of the principle that prophecy will have actual fulfillment in specific events. Looming large in eschatology are the teachings of Christ related to the kingdom of God. Some have considered this primarily a reference to the spiritual government of God as embracing all saints. Others have recognized the added factor of further teachings concerning the spiritual qualities which will enter into His future millennial kingdom. From the lips of Christ Himself is given a comprehensive prophetic picture presenting moral and spiritual aspects of the kingdom of God in the Sermon on the Mount (Matt. 5-7), the character of divine spiritual government in the present age (Matt. 13), and the consummating events climaxing in the second advent of Christ to set up His earthly king-

dom (Matt. 24-25). In recognition of the age between the first and second advents, Christ gave extensive teaching on the spiritual qualities of the present age (John 13-16). This is subsequently enlarged in the epistles and recorded in part historically in Acts. The present age is characterized as a time in which the church is formed, composed of Jew and Gentile alike, who believe in Christ. Premillenarians find also in the NT, and especially in Revelation 20, anticipation of a future mediatorial kingdom of Christ in which He reigns over the entire earth for one thousand years.

Though liberal theologians tend to interpret the second advent as a spiritual experience occurring contemporaneously, conservatives are agreed that the second advent is a future event in which Christ personally and bodily returns to the earth. Differences arise as to details relating to the coming great tribulation and time of trouble preceding the second advent. Pretribulationists anticipate a coming of Christ for the saints before the time of trouble (I Cor. 15:51-52; I Thess. 4:13-18). The translated and resurrected saints will return with Christ from heaven to the earth when He comes to establish His earthly kingdom. Post-tribulationists view both events as occurring after the tribulation.

The NT adds considerably to scriptural testimony concerning individual eschatology. Extensive treatment is given to the subject of resurrection (I Cor. 15), and many details are supplied such as the character of the judgment seat of Christ (II Cor. 5:10-11), the description of the lake of fire (Rev. 20:14-15), and the hope of the imminent return of Christ (Titus 2:13). Amillenarians find fulfillment of both reward and punishment at the time of the second advent. Premillenarians postpone the resurrection of the wicked until after the millennial kingdom has been completed (Rev. 20: 11-15). The NT also gives further light on the intermediate state, describing it as a time of consciousness either in bliss or suffering (Luke 16: 19-31; Phil. 1:23).

New Testament eschatology concludes with the picture of the eternal state in Revelation 21-22. The New Jerusalem, represented as a city 1350 miles square and a similar distance in height, whether interpreted literally or figuratively, presents the glorious hope of an eternal home in the presence of God. Biblical eschatology does not dwell on the details of the eternal state, but rather emphasizes the application of eschatology to contemporary decisions. Eschatology is not designed to satisfy curiosity but to provide an intelligent comprehension of the future as a guide for a present program, and a sure ground for hope. The superlative and distinctive character of Biblical eschatology becomes immediately apparent when compared to the fragmentary and fantastic eschatologies offered in heathen religions. J.F.W

ESDRAELON (ĕs′drā-ē′lŏn, a Gr. modification of *Jezreel;* does not occur in Heb.; is Gr. in form; found only in Revelation), the great plain which breaks the central range of Palestine in two. In the OT it is known as the plain, or valley, of Jezreel. It affords a direct connection between the maritime plain and the Jordan valley. It lies between Galilee on the N and Samaria on the S.

This plain is triangular in shape, and is 15 by 15 by 20 miles in size. Several passes enter into it making it easy of access and important commercially and in military operations. Many cities were situated in it, one of the most important being Megiddo, which guarded one of the main en-

The Plain of Esdraelon, viewed from the Nazareth Hills. © MPS

trances. The Canaanites were strongly established in this region before the Israelites came into Palestine. The tribes of Issachar and Zebulun were assigned to this area, but the Israelites never gained complete control of it until the time of David.

Esdraelon was the scene of some of the most important battles in Bible history: the victory of Barak over Sisera (Judg. 4) and of the Philistines over Saul and his sons (I Sam. 31). Here the Egyptians mortally wounded Josiah, king of Judah, when he went out to intercept the army of Pharaoh Necho (II Kings 23:29).

This valley has always been very fertile. Today Jewish colonists find it a prosperous farming region. A great future conflict seems indicated for this area, according to Revelation 16:16. C.E.H.

ESDRAS, BOOKS OF (See Apocrypha)

ESEK (ē′sĕk, Heb. *'ēseq, contention*), the name which Isaac gave to a well which his servants dug in the valley of Gerar and which the herdsmen of Gerar struggled for, claiming it belonged to them (Gen. 26:20).

ESH-BAAL (ĕsh′bā′ăl, Heb. *'esha'al, man of Baal*), the fourth son of Saul (I Chron. 8:33 and 9:39). The same man is called Ishbosheth in II Samuel 2:8,10,12, etc. He was made king of Gilead by Abner after Saul's death. A few years later he was murdered.

ESHBAN (ĕsh′băn, Heb. *'eshvān, man of understanding*), a descendant of Seir, the Horite (Gen. 36:26; I Chron. 1:41).

ESHCOL (ĕsh′kŏl, Heb. *'eshkōl, cluster*). 1. An Amorite who lived in Hebron and who helped Abram defeat king Chedorlaomer and his forces and bring back Lot and his family (Gen. 14:13,24).

2. A valley near Hebron in which the men sent by Moses to spy out the land found a cluster of grapes which they carried back to the people (Num. 13:23,24).

ESHEAN (ĕsh′ē-ăn, Heb. *'esh'ān*), a city in the territory assigned to the tribe of Judah (Josh. 15:52). In ASV Eshan. It was located in the Hebron area.

ESHEK (ē′shĕk, Heb. *'ēsheq, oppression*), a descendant of Jonathan, son of Saul, and brother of Azel. His grandsons were mighty men of valor in the tribe of Benjamin (I Chron. 8:38-40).

ESHTAOL (ĕsh′tā-ŏl, Heb. *'eshtā'ôl*), a town in the lowlands of Judah on its border with Dan (Josh.

15:33; 19:41). In the book of Judges it is always mentioned with Zorah. Samson, as he grew up, began to be moved by the Spirit of the Lord at times in the camp of Dan between Zorah and Eshtaol (3:25). He was buried there (16:31). The Danites sent out five brave men from Zorah and Eshtaol to look for an area where the tribe could have additional living space. After discovering the city of Laish they returned to these cities and gave a favorable report. Then 600 armed men set forth out of Zorah and Eshtaol to go and conquer Laish (Judg. 18:2,8,11).

ESHTEMOA (ĕsh′tē-mō-à, Heb. *eshte môa'*). 1. A city assigned to the Levites (Josh. 21:14). It was located eight miles S of Hebron. This city, among others, received from David a share of the spoil of his victory over the Amalekites (I Sam. 30:28). The modern name of the site is *Es Semu*.

2. The son of Ishbah (I Chron. 4:17).

3. A Maacathite, a son of Hodiah (I Chron. 4:19).

ESHTEMOH (ĕsh′tē-mō), a city located in the hill country of Judah (Josh. 15:50). The same as Eshtemoa above.

The Valley of Eschol, near Hebron. © MPS

ESHTON (ĕsh'tŏn, Heb. *'eshtôn*, perhaps *effeminate*), a descendant of Judah (I Chron. 4:11,12).

ESLI (ĕs'lī, Gr. *Eslí*), an ancestor of Christ (Luke 3:25).

ESROM (ĕs'rŏm, Gr. *Esróm*), the son of Perez, an ancestor of Christ (Matt. 1:3; Luke 3:33). KJV Esrom, RV Hezron.

ESSENES (ĕ-sēnz', Gr. *Essenoí* or *Essaíoi*). The meaning of the name is much debated; possibly it denotes "holy ones." They constituted a sect of the Jews in Palestine during the time of Christ, but are not mentioned in the NT. Our principal sources of information regarding them are Josephus and Philo (first century) and Pliny the Elder and Hippolytus (second century).

The Essenes lived a simple life of sharing everything in common. They practiced strict rules of conduct. They were mostly unmarried. They were reported to number 4,000. The majority of them lived together in settlements, but some resided in the cities of the Jews. Apparently they kept their ranks filled by the adoption of other people's children. They did not participate in the temple worship, but had their own purification rites. They observed the sabbath day very strictly and greatly venerated Moses. They would take no oaths; but new members, after going through a three-year probationary period, were required to swear a series of strong oaths that they would co-operate in every way with the organization and would never reveal to outsiders any of the affairs or beliefs of the sect.

The Essenes have come into public attention in late years because of the study of the Dead Sea scrolls, and the excavation of the monastery called Khirbet Qumran where the scrolls were written. This literature and building give evidence of an organization very similar to what is known about the Essenes. The structure was occupied from the end of the second century B.C. to 135 A.D. The Essenes are known to have flourished in this period. Also, the location of the building fits the description of the elder Pliny. The literature reveals that the people of Qumran Community were avid students of the Jewish Scriptures. Many scholars believe them to be the Essenes; but so many religious groups were in existence during the last century B.C. that certainty in the matter has not yet been achieved.

Many of the Essenes perished in the wars against the Romans. Many of the survivors probably became Christians. C.E.H.

ESTHER (ĕs'têr, Heb. *'estēr,* which may come from Akkad. *Ishtar* (Venus), Gr. *astér, star*), a Jewish orphan maiden in the city of Shushan, who became Queen of Persia. Her Hebrew name was Hadassah (myrtle). Her cousin, Mordecai, who was a minor official of the palace, reared her as his own daughter. Xerxes, the Persian king, had divorced his wife, and when he sought a new queen from among the maidens of the realm he chose Esther. When the Jews in the empire were faced with destruction she was able to save them. In honor to her the book which bears her name is read every year at the Feast of Purim.

ESTHER, BOOK OF, the last of the historical books of the OT. It was written after the death of King Ahasuerus (Esth. 10:2). Most scholars agree that Ahasuerus was Xerxes who reigned 485 B.C. to 465 B.C. Probably the book was written about 400 B.C. The author is unknown, but it is evident from the details of the story that he was well acquainted with the Persian court life. The book of Esther has always been accepted as canonical by the Jews.

Ruins of the monastery of the Essene Community at Qumran, near the Dead Sea. JFW

External proof of the career of Mordecai has been found in an undated cuneiform text which mentions a certain Mordecai (Marduka) who was a high official at the Persian court of Shushan during the reign of Xerxes and even before that under Darius I. This text came from Borsippa and is the first reference to Mordecai outside the Bible.

Outstanding peculiarities of the book are the complete absence of the name of God; the lack of any direct religious teaching; and no mention of prayer. These remarkable features can have occurred only by deliberate design. Probably the book was written for the Jews in the Persian empire as a story which could be circulated without danger of offending the people of that land who ruled over many Jews.

The story contains many dramatic elements. King Ahasuerus gave a great feast to all the officials of his realm. Queen Vashti offended him when she refused to appear before the company at the command of the king. As a result he divorced her (Ch. 1). Later, in order to procure another queen, he ordered all the beautiful maidens of the land brought together. Among them was Hadassah, who had been reared by her cousin Mordecai. Her name was changed to Esther by the Persians. This maiden was chosen by the king to be his queen. Mordecai discovered a plot against the king's life (Ch. 2). The king made Haman his chief minister. Everybody bowed down to him but Mordecai refused to do so. This disrespect infuriated the high official. Knowing Mordecai was a Jew, Haman decided to destroy all the Jews in revenge for his hurt feelings. Lots, called *Pur*, were cast to find an auspicious day for the destruction. The consent of the king was obtained, and an official decree was written and publicized throughout the empire setting the date for the slaughter of the Jews (Ch. 3). Mordecai sent word to Esther that she must plead for her people before the king (Ch. 4). At the risk of her life she went in before the king. He received her favorably. Instead of pleading with him at once she invited him and Haman to a banquet. There the king asked her to state her request, but she put it off and invited them to another banquet. Haman, rejoicing in his good fortune, but incensed at Mordecai, had a gallows constructed on which to hang him (Ch. 5). That night, unable to sleep, the king was listening to the reading of the royal chronicles. When the account of Mordecai's discovery of the assassination plot was read, the king asked what reward had been given him, and was told none at all.

It was early morning and Haman had come to ask permission to hang Mordecai. But the king asked him what should be done to a man he wished to honor. Being convinced that the king could have only him in mind, Haman suggested the greatest of honors he could imagine. At the king's command he was obliged to bestow those honors on Mordecai (Ch. 6). At the second banquet Esther told the king about the scheme to destroy her people and named Haman as the one responsible for it. The king became very angry and ordered Haman to be hanged on the gallows he had made (Ch. 7). Another decree was sent out which enabled the Jews to save themselves (Ch. 8). In two days of fighting they were victorious everywhere. Esther and Mordecai wrote letters to the Jews instituting the commemoration of these two days in an annual Feast of Purim (Ch. 9). Mordecai, being next to the king, brought blessing to the people (Ch. 10).

In the Septuagint the book of Esther contains several interpolations scattered through the story.

C.E.H.

ETAM (ē'tăm). 1. A town and clan in Judah between Bethlehem and Tekoa (I Chron. 4:3), Khirbet el-Khôkh, rebuilt by Rehoboam (II Chron. 11: 6); also named in LXX of Joshua 15:59a.

2. A village near En-rimmon in Simeon (I Chron. 4:32).

3. The rock where Samson lived after a slaughter of Philistines (Judg. 15:8,11). Maybe same as 1.

ETERNAL LIFE (ē-tûr'năl, -n'l, līf, Gr. zoé aiónios). Zoé is the usual NT word for life in a general sense; the opposite of death. Aiónios is the usual word for eternal, everlasting. Literally it means age-long. Since an age is the longest time which the human mind can conceive clearly, aiónios came to be used for infinity of time, whether conceived as unending duration, or as existence in which past and future are always present. Eternal life, therefore, is not merely age-long, after which it ceases to be. It is endless in duration, having its beginning in the mind of the eternal God (Eph. 1:4), and eternal in quality, that is, like the life of God as revealed in His Son Jesus Christ (I John 5:11,12). Though our eternal life thus has an eternal past in the purposes of God, our experience of it begins with the new birth (John 3; Tit. 3:4-7), when we believe in Jesus who truly is our eternal life (John 17:2,3; Gal. 2:20). Eternal or everlasting life is most prominent in John's Gospel (3:15,16, 36; 4:14,36; 5:24,39; 6:27,40,47,54,68; 10:28; 12: 25,50; 17:2,3) and in I John (1:2; 2:25; 3:15; 5:11,13,20) but is not absent from the Synoptics (Matt. 19:16,29; 25:46; Mark 10:17,30; Luke 10: 25; 18:18,30), nor from Acts (13:46,48) or the Epistles (Rom. 2:7; 5:21; 6:22,23; Gal. 6:8; I Tim. 1:16; 6:12; Tit. 1:2; Jude 21). John 3 describes the beginning of eternal life; John 6 its continuance; I John 1:1-4 its rootage in Christ. The references in the Synoptic Gospels show that eternal life was a concept independent of, though related to, the kingdom of God; not peculiarly Johannine. "Eternal" defines the "life" which believers receive "in Christ"; the word "eternal" stresses the endless character of that life, freed from the fear and the fact of death by the hope of the resurrection (John 11:25,26). E.R.

ETERNITY (ē-tûr'nĭ-tē), occurs but once in KJV (Isa. 57:15); for Heb. 'adh, perpetuity, advancing time; usually translated "ever"; also "everlasting, evermore, (of) old, perpetually." ASV, RSV replace KJV "world" in Ecclesiastes 3:11 with "eternity" (Heb. 'ôlām, age, long duration, antiquity, futurity, duration of the world). The adjective eternal renders Heb. 'ôlām (Isa. 60:15;

RSV for ever); qedhem, before (Deut. 33:27); Gr. aídios, everlasting (Rom. 1:20); aión, age (Eph. 3:11; I Tim. 1:17 RSV of ages); elsewhere aiónios, age-long, eternal, everlasting; mostly in the phrase "eternal life." The Biblical concept of eternity and the eternal refers to the endless past, the unending future, or to God's present experience of all time.

ETHAM (ē'thăm, Heb. 'ēthām), an uncertain site on the journey of Israel out of Egypt, which they reached after leaving Succoth and before turning back to Pihahiroth. After crossing the Red Sea they traveled three days in the wilderness of Etham to reach Marah (Exod. 13:20; Num. 33:6-8). Thus Etham appears to have been a wilderness district on both sides of the N end of the Red Sea.

ETHAN (ē'thăn, Heb. 'êthan). 1. An Ezrahite of Solomon's time, renowned for his wisdom (I Kings 4:31; Ps. 89 title).

2. A son of Zerah, son of Judah (I Chron. 2:6, 8).

3. A descendant of Gershon, son of Levi (I Chron. 6:39-43).

4. A singer, descendant of Marari, son of Levi (I Chron. 6:44; 15:17,19)

ETHBAAL (ĕth'bā'ăl, Heb. 'ethbaal), a king of Sidon whose daughter Jezebel became the wife of Ahab, king of Israel (I Kings 16:31).

ETHER (ē'thêr, Heb. 'ether), a town in Judah named between Libnah and Ashan (Josh. 15:42); Khirbet 'Ater; perhaps the same assigned to Simeon named between En-rimmon and Ashan (Josh. 19:7,9).

ETHIOPIA (ē'thĭ-ō'pĭ-à, Heb. kûsh, Gr. Aithiopía), a country extending S of Egypt from the first cataract of the Nile indefinitely, including Nubia, Sudan and northern if not southern modern Ethiopia. Heb. Kûsh, Cush, son of Ham (Gen. 10:6-8; I Chron. 1:8-10), from whom descended the most southern peoples known to the Hebrews, in Arabia and N Africa. Ethiopia (Gen. 2:13 ASV, RSV Cush) may be anywhere in this general direction. Job 28:19 mentions the topaz of Ethiopia. Moses married an Ethiopian woman (Num. 12:1 RSV Cushite). In the reign of Rehoboam, Ethiopians came against Judah with the king of Egypt (II Chron. 12:3); and in the reign of Asa (II Chron. 14:9-13; 16:7-9) Zerah, the Ethiopian with a million men, was defeated in Judah. "The Arabians, that were near the Ethiopians" (II Chron. 21:16) indicates the lands on both sides of the Red Sea, in the Arabian peninsula and in Africa, sometimes under the same rule.

The Ethiopians had skin of different appearance (Jer. 13:23); the Greek name Aithíops, burntface, shows the color to have been dark. Pictures on monuments show that they were a mixed race, some Negro, some Semitic, some Caucasian. Ethiopia enters Bible history most prominently when Tirhakah, an Ethiopian king of a dynasty which had conquered Egypt, came against Judah in the days of Hezekiah, and was only driven away by the superior force of Assyria (II Kings 19:9; Isa. 37:9). Henceforth the ultimate ruin of Ethiopia is a theme of prophecy (Isa. 11:11; 18:1; 20:3-5; 43:3; 45:14; Jer. 46:9; Ezek. 29:10; 30:4, 5; 38:5; Zeph. 3:10; Nah. 3:9). The English versions vary between "Ethiopia" and "Cush." Echoes are in Psalms 68:31; 87:4. Ethiopia is the western limit of the Persian empire of Ahasuerus (Esth. 1:1; 8:9). Ethiopia in NT times was ruled by a queen whose name or title was Candace (Acts 8:27). Ethiopia was a sparsely populated land traversed by the Blue and White Nile and their tributaries, a reservoir of hardy manpower for ambitious rulers (Isa. 18:1; 2 ASV, RSV).

E.R.

ETHIOPIAN EUNUCH (ē'thĭ-ō'pĭ-ăn ū'nŭk), treasurer of Candace, queen of the Ethiopians (Acts 8:26-39). He was a mighty man (Gr. *dynástes*) or nobleman. As a eunuch he could not be a full member of the Jewish community (Deut. 23:1), but he had been worshiping in Jerusalem and was reading aloud the book of Isaiah when Philip, sent by the Holy Spirit from Samaria to help him, met his chariot. From Isaiah 53, Philip led the African to faith in Christ, so that he asked for and received baptism and went on his way toward Gaza rejoicing.

ETHNAN (ēth'năn), a son of Helah, wife of Ashur, a Judahite (I Chron. 4:7).

ETHNI (ĕth'nī), a Gershonite Levite and an ancestor of Asaph whom David set over the service of song (I Chron. 6:41). Likely the same person named Jeaterai in I Chronicles 6:21.

EUBULUS (ū-bū'lŭs), a Christian disciple at Rome who, with others, saluted Timothy (II Tim. 4:21).

EUERGETES (ū-ûr'jē-tēz), "benefactors," a title of honor often voted by Greek states to public men. Our Lord alludes to the title (Luke 22:25).

EUNICE (ū'nĭs, ū-nī'sē, Gr. *Euníke*), the Jewish wife of a Greek; daughter of Lois and mother of Timothy (Acts 16:1; II Tim. 1:5). They lived at Lystra, where the two women and Timothy were converted, probably on Paul's first visit (Acts 14:6-20), since Timothy knew of Paul's persecution there (II Tim. 3:11). She brought up her son to know the OT Scriptures (II Tim. 3:15).

EUNUCH (ū'nŭk, Heb. *sārîs*, Gr. *spádon, eunoúchos*), a castrated male. From the employment of such men as custodians of royal harems the term came to designate an officer, whether physically a eunuch or not. Heb. *sārîs* is translated *officer* 12 times (e.g., Gen. 37:36; 39:1, *a married man*); *chamberlain* 13 times (e.g., II Kings 23:11); *eunuch* 17 times (II Kings 9:32, Jezebel's attendants; Jer. 29:2; 34:19; 38:7; 41:16; in 52:25 ASV, RSV *Officer*, of the last kings of Judah; II Kings 20:18; Isa. 39:7; Dan. 1:3-18, in the service of heathen kings). The Mosaic law forbade those blemished by castration to enter the congregation (Deut. 23:1), but Isaiah prophesied of a day when this disability would be removed and their loss compensated (Isa. 56:3-5). Eng. eunuch is a transliteration of Greek *eunoûchos*. The Ethiopian (Acts 8:27-39) was a queen's treasurer in whom Isaiah's prophecy may well have encouraged a new hope. Our Lord uses the term and its cognate verb four times in Matthew 19:12; those born eunuchs and those made eunuchs by men are physically incapable of begetting children; those who "have made themselves eunuchs for the kingdom of heaven's sake" are they whom continence has kept chaste and celibate that they may concentrate their lives on promoting the kingdom of heaven. Jesus Himself was the prime example. Such are the men referred to as "virgins" (RSV chaste) in Revelation 14:4. The eminent though erratic Christian scholar Origen, late in life regretted having taken Matthew 19:12 literally.

EUODIAS, properly *Euodia* (ŭ-ō'dĭ-à, Gr. *Euodía, prosperous journey* or *fragrance*), a Christian woman at Philippi. She is mentioned in Philippians 4:2 where Paul beseeches Euodia and Syntyche that they be of the same mind in the Lord.

Above, Euphrates River scene near ancient Babylon. Below, air view of Euphrates River, showing its great circuitous, treeless course. © MPS

EUPHRATES (ū-frā'tēz, Heb. *perāth*, from a root meaning *"to break forth,"* Gr. *Euphrátes*), the longest and most important river of Western Asia, frequently in the OT called "the river," "the great river," as being the largest with which Israel was acquainted, in contrast to the soon drying up torrents of Palestine (Isa. 8:7; Gen. 15:18; Deut. 1:7). It rises from two sources in the Armenian mountains whose branches join after having run 400 and 270 miles, respectively. The united river runs SW and S through the Taurus mountains towards the Mediterranean; but the ranges N of Lebanon prevent its reaching that sea; it turns SE and flows 1000 miles to the Persian Gulf. The whole course is 1780 miles; for 1200 it is navigable for small vessels. The melting of the snows in the Armenian mountains causes the river to flood each spring. Nebuchadnezzar controlled the floods by turning the water through sluices into channels for distribution over the whole country. The promise to Abraham that his seed's inheritance should reach the Euphrates (Gen. 15:18; Deut. 1:7; Josh. 1:4) received a partial fulfillment in Reuben's pastoral possessions (I Chron. 5:9,10); a fuller accomplishment under David and Solomon, when an annual tribute was paid by subject petty kingdoms in that area (I Chron. 18:3; II Sam. 8:3-8; I Kings 4:21; II Chron. 9:26). The Euphrates was the boundary between Assyria and the Hittite country after Solomon's time, according to inscriptions.

B.P.

EUROCLYDON (ū-rŏk'lĭ-dŏn, Gr. *Euroklýdon,* from *eúros,* the east wind, and *klýdon,* a wave; thus *an east wind raising mighty waves*), found only in Acts 27:14. RV has Euraquilo. Euraquilo thus is an ENE wind, just that which is best suited to the facts. It came down from the island of Crete, S of which Paul was sailing. It would be extremely dangerous to a ship with large sails, threatening either to capsize her or to drive her onto the quicksands (vs. 17).

EUTYCHUS (ū'tĭ-kŭs, Gr. *Eútychos, fortunate*), a young man of Troas mentioned in Acts 20:9 who, while listening to Paul preach, was overcome with sleep and fell out of the third story window to his death. Paul then went down and restored him to life.

EVANGELIST (ē-văn'jĕ-lĭst, Gr. *euangelistés, one who announces good news)*, used in a general sense of anyone who proclaims the Gospel of Jesus Christ. Sometimes in the NT, however, it designates a particular class of ministry, as in Ephesians 4:11: "And he (Christ) gave some, apostles; and some, prophets; and some, evangelists; and some, pastors, and teachers..." The *evangelist* founded the church; the *pastor-teacher* built it up in the faith. The evangelist was not confined in service to one spot, but moved about in different localities, preaching the good news concerning Jesus Christ to those who had not heard the message before. Once such had put their trust in the Lord, then the work of the pastor-teacher began. He would remain with them, training them further in the things pertaining to Christ and building them up in the faith. Apostles (Acts 8:25; 14:7; I Cor. 1:17) did the work of an evangelist, as did also bishops (II Tim. 4:2-5). Philip, who had been set apart as one of the seven deacons (Acts 6:5) was also called "the evangelist" (Acts 21:8). Thus it can be seen that the word refers to a *work* rather than to an *order*. The evangelist was not necessarily an apostle, bishop-elder, or deacon, but might be any of these. Evangelist in the sense of "inspired writer of one of the four Gospels," was a later usage. B.P.

EVE (Heb. *hawwâh, life, living)*, the first woman, formed by God out of Adam's side. Adam designated her (Gen. 2:23) as woman (Heb. *'ishshâh)* for she was taken out of man (Heb. *'ish)*. In these words there is suggested the close relationship between man and woman; a relationship which the first man was unable to find in the animal creation. Both the way in which Eve was created and the designation "woman" serve to emphasize also the intimacy, sacredness and inseparability of the marital state, transcending even that relationship which exists between children and parents (Gen. 2:24). The name "Eve" was given to her after the fall and implies both her being the mother of all living and her being the mother of the promised Seed who should give life to the human race now subjected to death. While the Scriptures uniformly trace the fall of the race to the sin of Adam, the part which Eve played in this tragedy is vividly portrayed in Genesis 3. Her greater weakness and susceptibility to temptation are juxtaposed with Adam's willful act of disobedience. Deceived by Satan, she ate of the fruit. Enamored of his wife, Adam chose to leave God for the one He had given him. Paul twice refers to her in his epistles (II Cor. 11:3; I Tim. 2:13). B.P.

EVENING SACRIFICE, one of the two daily offerings prescribed in the Mosaic ritual (Exod. 29:38-42; Num. 28:3-8). Every evening (as also every morning) a yearling lamb was sacrificed as a continual burnt offering. With each lamb there was offered a tenth deal of flour, mingled with oil, for a meal offering and the fourth part of a hin of wine for a drink offering.

EVI (ē'vī, Heb. *'ĕwî)*, one of the five kings of Midian slain by the Israelites during their encampment in the plains of Moab (Num. 31:8). His land was allotted to Reuben (Josh. 13:21).

EVIL (ē'vĭl, Heb. *ra', *Gr. *ponērós, kakós)*, a term designating that which is not in harmony with the divine order. In the Bible evil is clearly depicted under two distinct aspects: moral and physical. The reconciliation of the existence of evil with the goodness and holiness of a God infinite in His wisdom and power is one of the great problems of theism. The Scriptures indicate that evil has been permitted by God in order that His justice might be manifested in its punishment and His grace in its forgiveness (Rom. 9:22,23). Thus the existence of evil is a reminder of the fact that the universe is designed not for the production of happiness among rational creatures but for the manifestation of the manifold perfections of God. Moral evil, or sin, is any lack of conformity to the moral law of God. According to the Bible, it is the cause of the existence of physical or natural evil in this world. Adam and Eve, the first humans, enjoyed perfect fellowship with God in the garden of Eden. In the day that they partook of the fruit of the tree which was in the midst of the garden, thus disobeying God, they fell under God's condemnation and were banished from the garden. The ground was then cursed for man's sake, and from that time forward man has been forced to gain his sustenance through arduous, sorrowful toil, even as woman has borne children only through suffering and labor (Gen. 3:16-19). In the NT the relationship between moral and natural evil is indicated by Paul in Romans 8:18-22. B.P.

EVIL-MERODACH (ē'vil-mĕ-rō'dăk), a king of Babylon who reigned two years (562-560 B.C.). His name *(Amelu-Marduk* is the Babylonian form) means "Man of Marduk." This is a theophorous name, Marduk being the chief god of Babylon (cf. Ishbosheth, Ishbaal). The son and successor of Nebuchadnezzar, Evil-Merodach was murdered by his brother-in-law, Neriglissar (the Nergal-Sharezer of Jer. 39:3), a prince who usurped the throne. References to him as lawless and indecent indicate the probable reasons for the coup which cut short his reign.

Evil-Merodach released Jehoiachin, king of Judah, from his 37-year Babylonian imprisonment, and gave him a position of prominence among the captive kings and daily allowance of food for the rest of his life (II Kings 25:27-30; Jer. 52:31-34); but he was not permitted to return home to Judah. Cuneiform tablets recovered from Babylon, dated from the reign of Nebuchadnezzar, refer to provisions which were supplied to Jehoiachin and other royal prisoners. The latest of these tablets is at least eight years earlier than the time of Jehoiachin's release referred to in Scripture. It would seem that Evil-Merodach increased the king's allowance from the small amount mentioned in these tablets. J.B.G.

EVIL SPIRITS (See Demons)

EWE (ū), a female sheep. Several Hebrew words *(rāhēl, 'ûl, seh, cavsâh)* are represented in translation by this term.

EXCOMMUNICATION, disciplinary exclusion from church fellowship. The Jews had two forms of excommunication, apparently alluded to in Luke 6:22 by Christ: "Blessed are ye when men . . . shall separate you from their company [the Jewish *middûy,* for 30, 60 or 90 days], and shall reproach you, and cast out your name as evil [the Jewish *hĕrem,* a formally pronounced, perpetual cutting off from the community; cf. John 9:34,35, marg.], for the Son of man's sake." Christian excommunication is commanded by Christ (Matt. 18:15-18), and apostolic practice (I Tim. 1:20) and precept (I Cor. 5:11; Titus 3:10) are in agreement. "Delivering unto Satan" (I Cor. 5:5; I Tim. 1:20) seems to mean casting out of the church, Christ's kingdom of light, into the world that lies in the power of the wicked one (Eph. 6:12; I John 5:19). The object of excommunication is the good of the offender (I Cor. 5:5) and the moral well-being of the sound members (II Tim. 2:17). Its subjects are those guilty of heresy or great immorality (I Tim. 1:20; I Cor. 5:1-5). It is inflicted by the church (Matt. 18:18) and its representative ministers (Titus 3:10; I Cor. 5:1,3,4). Paul's infallible authority when inspired gives no warrant for uninspired ministers claiming the same right to direct the church to excommunicate as they will (II Cor. 2:7-9). B.P.

EXECUTIONER, an officer of high rank in the East; commander of the bodyguard who executed the king's sentence. Potiphar (Gen. 37:36, marg.) was the "chief of the executioners." Nebuzaradan (Jer. 39:9, marg.) and Arioch (Dan. 2:14, marg.) held this office. In the Gospel record we are told that King Herod sent an executioner (Gr. *spekouattōr,* originally a military watch or scout) i.e. one of his bodyguard, to behead John the Baptist (Mark 6:27).

EXILE usually refers to the period of time during which the Southern Kingdom (Judah) was forcibly detained in Babylon. It began with a series of deportations during the reigns of the Judaean kings, Jehoiakim (609-598 B.C.), Jehoiakim (598 B.C.), and Zedekiah (598-587 B.C.). After the destruction of Jerusalem by Nebuchadnezzar (587 B.C.) the kingdom of Judah ceased to exist as a political entity. Although there were settlements in Egypt, it was the exiles in Babylon who maintained the historic Jewish faith and provided the nucleus which returned to Judea subsequent to the Decree of Cyrus (536 B.C.). The Northern Kingdom (Israel) was earlier exiled to Assyria (722 B.C.). It was the policy of the Assyrian conquerors to move the populations of captured cities, with the result that Israelites were scattered in various parts of the empire, and other captives were brought to the region around Samaria (II Kings 17:24). Subsequent history knows these people as the Samaritans. Although men from the Northern Kingdom doubtless returned with the Judaean exiles, no organized return took place from the Assyrian captivity.

Causes. Both theological and political causes are mentioned in the Biblical accounts of the exile. The prophets note the tendency of both Israel and Judah to forsake the Lord and adopt the customs of their heathen neighbors. These include the licentious worship associated with the Baal fertility cult and the Molech worship which required the offering of human beings in sacrifice to a heathen deity. Politically the exile was the result of an anti-Babylonian policy adopted by the later kings of Judah. Egypt, the rival of Babylon, urged the Judaean kings to refuse to pay tribute to Nebuchadnezzar. Although Jeremiah denounced this pro-Egyptian policy it was adopted with disastrous results. Egypt proved to be a

Babylonian chronicle for 605-594 B.C., describing the removal of King Jehoiachin and other Jewish prisoners to exile in Babylonia. BM

"broken reed" and the kingdom of Judah was rendered impotent before the Babylonian armies. After a siege of eighteen months Nebuchadnezzar entered Jerusalem, destroyed the temple, and took captive the inhabitants of the city.

SOCIAL AND ECONOMIC CONDITIONS. The exile worked great hardships on a people who were forcibly removed from their homeland and settled in new territory. The Psalmist pictures the exiles weeping in Babylon, unable to sing the songs of Zion in a strange land (Ps. 137:4). The exiles who had been deported with Jehoiakim and Jehoiachin prior to the destruction of Jerusalem hoped that they would soon be able to return home. False prophets placed a two-year limit on the period of exile (Jer. 28:11). Jeremiah, however, urged the exiles to settle down, build houses, marry, and pray for the peace of the land in which they lived. He stated that it would be 70 years before they would be back in Judaea (Jer. 29:4-14). The Babylonians permitted the Jews to congregate in their own settlements. One of these, known as Tel Abib, was the scene of Ezekiel's prophetic ministry. Tel Abib was located near Nippur on the River Chebar, also known as the Grand Canal.

Religious Conditions. The Prophets Ezekiel and Daniel ministered in Babylon during the exile. Jeremiah, who had urged Zedekiah to make peace with Nebuchadnezzar, was permitted to remain in Judah after the destruction of Jerusalem. The murder of Gedaliah, appointed by Nebuchadnezzar as governor of Judah, precipitated a move on the part of the remaining Jews to migrate to Egypt. Although tradition suggests that he subsequently went to Babylon, Jeremiah's actual prophetic ministry ends among the Jews in Egypt.

Ezekiel was taken to Babylon at the time of the deportation of Jehoiachin. He prophesied to the Jews at Tel Abib, warning them of the impending destruction of Jerusalem. Subsequent to the fall of the city, Ezekiel held forth the hope of a return from exile and the re-establishment of Jewish worship in Palestine.

Daniel was one of the youths selected to be taken to Babylon at the time of the first deportation (under Jehoiakim). God-given abilities and a spirit of faithfulness enabled Daniel to rise to a

A ration list for Jewish prisoners in Babylon, including King Jehoiachin and his sons. SMB

position of influence in the Babylonian court — a position which he maintained through varying political regimes to the time of Cyrus the Persian, conqueror of Babylon. Like Ezekiel, Daniel spoke of the exile as temporary in duration. He also depicted a succession of world powers, culminating in the reign of the Messiah as the goal of history.

Within pre-exilic Judaism, the center of worship was the Jerusalem Temple where sacrifices were offered daily and where annual festive occasions were observed. With the destruction of the temple a new spiritual orientation took place. Jews came together for the purpose of prayer and the study of Scripture in gatherings which later were called synagogues. The emergence of the synagogue made possible the continuance of Jewish religious life during the period of absence from the temple. The synagogue persisted after the building of the second temple (516 B.C.), and is still an important factor in Jewish life.

The sacred books of the Jews assumed great importance during the period of the exile. The law, which had been lost prior to Josiah's reign (II Kings 22:8), became the subject of careful study. By the time of the return from Babylon, the institution of the scribe was established. Scribes not only made copies of the law, but they also served as interpreters. Ezra is regarded as the first scribe (Neh. 8:1 ff). The sabbath, a part of the Mosaic law, assumed a new meaning to the displaced Jews of the exile. It served as a weekly reminder of the fact that they had a definite covenant relationship to God, and became a marker to distinguish the Jew from his Babylonian neighbor. When Nehemiah led a group back to Palestine he insisted that the sabbath be scrupulously observed (Neh. 13:15-22).

Political Conditions. The exile began during the reign of the Neo-Babylonian king, Nebuchadnezzar, and ended with the decree of the Persian king, Cyrus. Nebuchadnezzar defeated an Egyptian army which had joined forces with the Assyrians, who were retreating before the Babylonians, at Carchemish on the upper Euphrates (605 B.C.). The campaign against Egypt was deferred when Nebuchadnezzar, on receiving news of the death of his father, Nabopolassar, returned home to insure his succession to the kingdom. Judah was among the states of western Asia which Nebuchadnezzar claimed as heir to the Assyrians whom he had defeated in battle. Babylonian armies occupied Judah during the reign of Jehoiakim (c. 603 B.C.) and took captive a number of its leading citizens, leaving only "the poorest of the people" in the land. Jehoiakim was allowed to retain his throne until he rebelled (II Kings 24:12-16). In 598 B.C. the Babylonian king called upon the vassal states (including Moab, Syria, and Ammon) to support his power in Judah by force of arms (II Kings 24:2). When Jehoiakim was killed in battle his eighteen year old son, Jehoiachin, succeeded him. After a reign of but three months, Jehoiakin was deported to Babylon with 10,000 Jews, including Ezekiel. Jehoiachin's uncle, Zedekiah, the third son of Josiah, was made a puppet king in Jerusalem (II Kings 24:17-19). In spite of the warnings of Jeremiah, Zedekiah yielded to the pro-Egyptian party and refused to pay tribute to Babylon. Thereupon Nebuchadnezzar laid siege to Jerusalem and, after one and one-half years, entered the city, destroyed its temple, and deported its citizens (587 B.C.) Following the murder of Gedaliah, the governor appointed by Nebuchadnezzar to handle Judaean affairs after the destruction of Jerusalem, the final deportation took place (c. 581 B.C.) (II Kings 25:22).

Nebuchadnezzar reigned for more than 40 years, but he left no able successor. Jehoiachin was given a place of honor among the exiles in Babylon by Evil-Merodach (561-560 B.C.), son and successor of Nebuchadnezzar. Neriglissar (559-556 B.C.) and Labashi-Marduk (556 B.C.) had brief, non-significant reigns. Nabonidus (Nabu-Na'id), with his son Belshazzar, served as the last ruler of the Neo-Babylonian Empire 556-539) B.C.). Nabonidus had an interest in archaeology and religion, but was inefficient as a ruler. He repaired the *ziggurat* to the moon god Sin at Ur where one of his daughters served as priestess. Another daughter is said to have maintained a small museum of archaeological finds. His diversified interests caused Nabonidus to name Belshazzar, his eldest son, as prince regent. It was during the reign of Belshazzar that the Neo-Babylonian Empire came to an end. Cyrus had made rapid conquests after his succession to the throne of the small Persian principality of Anshan (559 B.C.) Successively unifying the Persians, conquering the neighboring Medes and the distant Lydians of Asia

Minor, Cyrus marched against Babylon, which he defeated (539 B.C.) The governor of Babylon, Gubaru, is doubtless to be identified with "Darius the Mede" mentioned in Daniel 5 and 6. Cyrus issued the decree which permitted Jews to return to Jerusalem to rebuild the temple (Ezra 1:1-4). This may be regarded as the end of the exile, although many Jews chose to remain in Babylon.

Results. Although the exile ended the political independence of Judaea, it served to emphasize the fact that God was in no sense confined to Palestine. He accompanied His people to Babylon and providentially cared for them there. In an idolatrous environment, the Jew stressed his monotheistic faith, having seen the errors of idolatry which brought on the exile. Although many Jews returned to their homeland following the decree of Cyrus, others remained in the Persian Empire with the result that Judaism became international in scope. C.F.P.

EXODUS (ĕk'sō-dŭs, Gr. *a going out),* the event which terminated the sojourn of Israel in Egypt. The family of Jacob (Israel) voluntarily entered Egypt during a time of severe famine in Canaan. Joseph, who had been sold into slavery by jealous brothers, was then vizier of Egypt and his Israelite brethren were assigned suitable land in the northeastern section of Egypt known as Goshen. When a new dynasty arose "which knew not Joseph," i.e., forgot what he had done for Egypt, the Israelites were reduced to the status of slaves. Fearful lest they should prove sympathetic with foreign invaders, Pharaoh ordered the male children destroyed. The infant Moses, however, was placed in an ark of bulrushes where he was seen by Pharaoh's daughter who ordered that he be rescued. Raised in the royal court, Moses chose to turn his back on the possibilities of advancement in Egypt in order to lead his oppressed people into freedom.

Date of the Exodus. There has been no unanimity among Bible students concerning the date of the Exodus, or the identity of the pharaohs who took part in the oppression of Israel. Later pharaohs are sometimes mentioned by name (e.g. Pharaoh Hophra, Pharaoh Necho), but the title, "Pharaoh," is given only in the Exodus account. Some Biblical scholars consider that I Kings 6:1 is decisive in furnishing the date of the Exodus. We are told that Solomon began to build the temple "in the 480th year after the children of Israel were come up out of the land of Egypt." Since we know the approximate dates of Solomon's reign, this information can be used in calculating the date of the Exodus. The date suggested by this method of computation, about 1441 B.C., falls within the reign of Amenhotep II, son of Thutmose III, one of the great empire builders of New Kingdom Egypt. Paintings from the tomb of Rekhmire, vizier of Thutmose III, depict Semites working as slave laborers on building projects.

Adherents of the "early date" of the Exodus (1441 B.C.) also find support for their position from the Amarna Letters (1400-1366 B.C.). These cuneiform tablets, discovered at the site of Akhnaton's capital, contain correspondence from the kings of the city-states in Canaan who ask the help of the pharaoh against a people known as Habiru. This, it is suggested, is a description of the battles fought subsequent to the Exodus by the armies of Israel in seeking to accomplish the conquest of Canaan. There are, however, serious difficulties in the matter of accepting the early date. During the Eighteenth Dynasty of Egyptian history (when the early date would fall), the capital of Egypt was

Statue of Rameses II at Temple of Luxor. He may have been either the pharaoh of the oppression, or of the exodus. © MPS

at Thebes S of the delta, and the building operations of Thutmose III seem to have been centered there. Subsequently, however, (during the time of the Rameses) the pharaohs resided in the delta where they engaged in extensive building activity. It is specifically in the delta region, adjacent to Goshen, where Moses met with Pharaoh, and it was in the city of Rameses (also known as Avaris and Tanis) in the eastern delta where the Israelites are reported to have labored (Exod. 1:11). Advocates of the early date suggest that the name Rameses is a modernization of an older name.

Because of these problems in dating the Exodus as early as 1441 B.C., an increasing number of Biblical scholars have come to accept a date in the 13th century. Explorations in Transjordan by the archaeologist, Nelson Glueck, indicate a gap in the sedentary population of that region from about 1900 to 1300 B.C. The Bible, however, indicates that Israel met formidable opposition from Sihon and Og, kings in the East-Jordan country and that the Moabite king sought to bring a curse on Israel to prevent their progress into Canaan. The earlier suggestion of evidence that Jericho fell about 1400 B.C.—put forth by Garstang—has been questioned by recent expeditions there, under the direction of Dr. Kathleen Kenyon. The excavations at Hazor by Yigael Yadin also tend to point toward a 13th century date for the Exodus, as

The famous "Israel Tablet" of Pharaoh Merneptah, found at Thebes, mentioning the departure of the Israelites from Egypt. CM

did earlier excavations at Lachish and Debir. The Stele of Merneptah (c. 1229 B.C.) provides the first reference to Israel in the Egyptian monuments. Merneptah claims a decisive victory over the Israelite people. It may be significant that the ideogram for "nation" is not used. In any event we know that Israelites were fighting in Canaan during the reign of Merneptah. The predecessor of Merneptah was Rameses II who reigned for 67 years from his capital at Tanis (or Rameses) in the delta. Some Biblical scholars suggest that Sethi I, father of Rameses, began the oppression, which was continued under Rameses, during whose reign the Exodus took place. Those who hold to this 13th century date for the Exodus suggest that the 480 years of I Kings 6:1 be taken as a round number signifying 12 generations. Since generations are frequently much less than 40 years apart, there may be a smaller time span between the Exodus and the building of Solomon's temple. This view is accepted by many who hold to the full inspiration of the text of Scripture. In view of the fact that the non-Israelite characters in the story of the Exodus are not identified in Scripture, it is wise to avoid a dogmatic approach to the question. The evidence for the historicity of the Exodus account is decisive, but the evidence for specific dates is still inconclusive.

Route. The Biblical record (Exod. 13:17) states that Israel did not take the direct route

through the Philistine country to Canaan. Had she done so Israel would have had to pass the Egyptian wall (Biblical Shur) which protected the northeastern highways out of Egypt. This wall was guarded and could be passed only with great difficulty. If she successfully crossed the border, further opposition could be anticipated from the Philistines. The discipline of the wilderness was a part of God's preparation for His people before they were to come into open conflict with formidable foes. Leaving Rameses (Exod. 12:37), in the eastern delta, the Israelites journeyed southeastward to Succoth (*Tell el-Mashkutah*). They then moved on to Etham "in the edge of the wilderness" where they were conscious of God's guidance in the pillar of cloud and pillar of fire (Exod. 13: 21-22). The word Etham is derived from an Egyptian word meaning "wall" and was probably part of the series of fortifications built by the Egyptians to keep out the Asiatic nomads. From Etham they turned back and encamped before Pi-hahiroth, described as "between Migdol and the sea over against Baal-zephon." The location of these sites is not known with certainty. Pi-hahiroth is possibly an Egyptian word meaning "house of the marshes." Baal-zephon is the name of a Semitic deity who was worshiped in Egypt, doubtless at a shrine located at the town which bore his name. After passing Pi-hahiroth, Israel arrived at the body of water designated in the English versions as the Red Sea, the *Yam Suph* of the Hebrew text. The geography of the Exodus suggests that this *Yam Suph,* or Sea of Reeds, formed a natural barrier between Egypt and the Sinai Peninsula, the ultimate destination of the Israelites. The topography of this region has been altered since the construction of the Suez Canal, but the *Yam Suph* was probably N of Lake Timsah. An Egyptian document from the 13th century B.C. mentions a Papyrus Lake not far from Tanis. Wright and Filson (in *Westminster Historical Atlas to the Bible,* Philadelphia: Westminster Press, 1956) suggest a location at the southern extension of the present Lake Menzaleh. The Exodus from Egypt through the *Yam Suph* was made possible by the direct intervention of God, who "caused the sea to go back by a strong east wind" (Exod. 14:21). Israel was thus able to cross from Egypt to the Sinai Peninsula. When the armies of Pharaoh attempted to pursue the Israelites, the Egyptians were destroyed by the waters which returned to their normal course.

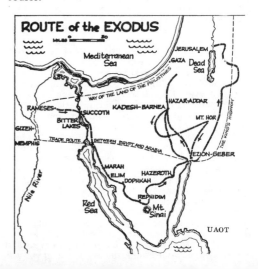

ROUTE of the EXODUS

Number of Israelites. The Bible states that 600,000 men took part in the Exodus (Exod. 12:37). A year later the number of male Israelites over the age of 20 was 603,550 (Num. 1:46). During the years of Israel's sojourn in Egypt, the population multiplied to the point where Pharaoh was alarmed lest Israel side with an enemy in the event of war (Exod. 1:7-10). It was this very fear that brought about the oppression.

Miracles. The Exodus period was one of the great epochs of Biblical miracles. The first nine plagues may have been related to the natural phenomena of Egypt, but their timing and intensification were clearly supernatural. The last plague—the death of the firstborn—signaled the beginning of the Exodus. Israel ate the Passover meal in haste, ready to depart from Egypt. The opening of the Red Sea by the "strong east wind" was the means by which God brought His people out of Egypt into the wilderness where, for period of 40 years, they were miraculously sustained. C.F.P.

EXODUS, BOOK OF, the second book of the Bible. The name is a transliteration of the Greek word meaning "a going out," referring to the departure of Israel from Egypt. The Hebrews called the book "and these are the names," which are the opening words of 1:1. The book may be conveniently divided into three main sections:

1. **Israel in Egypt** (1:1-12:36), describing the multiplication of Israel and their sufferings; the birth, preparation, and commission of Moses; the ministry of Moses and Aaron to Israel and to Pharaoh; and the ten plagues upon the Egyptians, climaxed by the Passover and the death of the firstborn.

2. **The Journey to Sinai** (12:37-19:2), which tells of the hasty flight of Israel from Egypt; the importance of the Passover and the consecration of the firstborn; the destruction of Pharaoh's army; the Song of Moses and Miriam; the waters of Marah; the miracle of the quails and the manna; the waters of Massah and Meribah; the war with Amalek; and the counsel of Jethro.

3. **Israel at Sinai** (19:3-40:38 deals with Jehovah's manifestation at Mount Sinai: the Ten Commandments; the civil law; instructions for building the tabernacle and its furniture and for making the priests' garments; sacrifices for the consecration of Aaron and his sons; the episode of the golden calf; the renewing of the two tables; the shining of Moses' face; the construction of the tabernacle; and the filling of the tabernacle with the glory of Jehovah.

Whereas the Book of Genesis sets forth the origin of the nation of Israel, the Book of Exodus describes the process whereby God molded it into a full-grown theocratic nation, redeemed and set apart for His purposes in the earth. In this book is recorded the fulfillment of three great prophecies of Genesis: 1. that Israel would become a great nation in Egypt (Gen. 46:3); 2. that they would be afflicted there 400 years (Gen. 15:13); and 3. that God would finally judge Egypt and bring Israel out with great substance (Gen. 15:14). Joseph emphasized the hope of Exodus on his deathbed (Gen. 50:24-25), and during the centuries that followed, this promise must have served as "a more sure word of prophecy . . . a light that shineth in a dark place" (II Pet. 1:19).

The actual date of the Exodus, though a difficult problem, is also an important one for understanding the background of the book. Critical scholars usually date the Exodus around 1280 B.C. in the reign of Rameses II. But the chronology of the Book of Judges, plus the explicit statement of I Kings 6:1, calls for 1447 B.C. as the correct date. Biblical chronology dates the arrival of Joseph in Egypt as a slave around 1900 B.C., during the height of the Middle Kingdom. He died about 1806 B.C., and the new king "who knew not Joseph" (1:8) must have been the first Hyksos invader of Egypt (about 1730 B.C.). These Hyksos invaders were less numerous than the Hebrews at that time, and had cause to fear that they might ally themselves with the native Egyptians. After the Hyksos were driven out (c. 1580 B.C.), the Egyptians of the powerful Eighteenth Dynasty continued to oppress the Hebrews. Moses was born in 1527 B.C. and was raised by Hatshepsut, daughter of Thutmosis I and later a Pharaoh-Queen (1501-1480). Thutmosis III (1480-1447), the mighty "Napoleon of Egypt," was the Pharaoh of the Oppression, and his son Amenhotep II (1447-1425) was the Pharaoh of the Exodus. Not only do the Biblical events fit perfectly into this portion of Egyptian history, but also it must be said that the Biblical account cannot be harmonized with the view that the Exodus occurred around 1280 B.C. The main argument in support of this view is that the store city of Raamses (1:11) could only have been built during the reign of Raamses (or Rameses) II (1290-1224 B.C.). But if this be so, then the birth of Moses must be dated later than this to allow for the lengthy events of 1:12-22, and the Exodus could not be dated until 80 years after that (7:7). This would allow less than a century between the Exodus and the reign of Saul! Such a view is utterly unnecessary, however, for evidence has been discovered that pharaohs of the Nineteenth Dynasty used names employed by the Hyksos, and even worshiped gods honored by the Hyksos, so that Hyksos kings could have built a city named Raamses. Also, it has been shown that although the capital of the Eighteenth Dynasty pharaohs was located far to the S of the land of Goshen at Thebes, both Thutmosis III and Amenhotep II built extensively in the delta and thus could have had a palace and court in the vicinity of the land of Goshen (cf. John Rea, "The Date of the Exodus," *Bulletin of the Evangelical Theological Society,* Summer, 1960). J.C.W.

EXORCISM (ĕk'sôr-sĭzm, Gr. *exorkízo, to adjure*), the expelling of demons by means of magic charms, spells, and incantations. It was a common practice among ancient heathen. In Acts 19:13-16, the profane use of Jesus' name as a mere spell was punished by the demon's turning on the would-be exorcists; these "vagabond Jews" were pretenders. Christ, however, implies that some Jews actually cast out demons (Matt. 12:27), probably by demoniacal help; others, in the name of Jesus, without saving faith in Him (Matt. 7:22). He gave power to the twelve, the seventy, and to the other disciples after His ascension (Matt. 10:8; Luke 10:17-19; Mark 16:17; Acts 16:18). The term "exorcise" is never applied in Scripture to the Christian casting out of demons.

EXPIATION (ĕx'pĭ-ā'shŭn), the act or means of making amends or reparation for sin. The word is to be distinguished from its correlative term, "propitiation." From the Bible viewpoint sin is looked upon as a failure to meet obligations, a failure for which satisfaction must be provided. "Expiation" speaks of this satisfaction. Sin is also looked upon as that which awakens on the part of God a righteous anger which must be set aside before He can and will deal with the sinner without imposing judgment upon him. "Propitiation" views satisfaction as appeasing the wrath of God. The sinner's guilt, then, is expiated by satisfaction (i.e. by a vicarious punishment). God is thereby rendered propitious; i.e. He is now able to pardon and bless the sinner. See PROPITIATION.

EYE (Heb. *'ayin,* Gr. *ophthalmós*), the organ of sight. The literal sense is that which is most frequently found in the Scriptures, where the eye is recognized as among the most valued of the members of the body. In the Mosaic legislation, if a man should smite a slave's eye so that it was blinded, the slave was to be released on account of the eye (Exod. 21:26). One of the most cruel customs of the heathen nations was that of putting out the eyes of a defeated enemy (II Kings 25:7). The word is also used often in figurative expressions. Frequently "eye" speaks of spiritual perception and understanding. Thus the Word of God enlightens the eyes (Ps. 19:8). Growth in spiritual knowledge comes through the eyes of the understanding being enlightened (Eph. 1:18). Other expressions speak of the eye as indicative of character. The good man has a "bountiful eye (Prov. 22:9). High or lofty eyes (Ps. 131:1) describe the proud man. The envious man is one with an evil eye (Matt. 20:15).

EYES, PAINTING OF, referring to the ancient practice of painting the eyelids in order to enhance the beauty of the feminine face (Jer. 4:30, marg.; Ezek. 23:40). Thus Jezebel "put her eyes in painting" (II Kings 9:30, marg.). To this day Oriental women paint the eyelids with antimony or *kohl* (a black powder made of the smoke black from the burning of frankincense) to make them look full and sparkling, the blackened margin contrasting with the white of the eye.

EYESALVE (Gr. *kolloúrion*), a preparation compounded of various ingredients used either by simple application or by reduction to a powder to be smeared on the eye (Rev. 3:18). When used figuratively, it refers to the restoration of spiritual vision.

EZBAI (ĕz'bā-ī), the father of Naari, one of David's valiant men (I Chron. 11:37).

EZBON (ĕz'bŏn). 1. One of the sons of Gad (Gen. 46:16), also called Ozni (Num. 26:16).

2. The first named son of Bela, a son of Benjamin (I Chron. 7:7).

EZEKIEL (ē-zēk'yĕl, Heb. *yehezqē'l, God strengthens*), a Hebrew prophet of the Exile. A play is made on this name in connection with the prophet's call (3:7,8,14). Of a priestly family (1:3), Ezekiel grew up in Judea during the last years of Hebrew independence and was deported to Babylon with Jehoiachin in 597 B.C., probably early in life. He was thus a younger contemporary of the Prophet Jeremiah and of Daniel, who, also as a young man was taken to Babylon in 605 B.C. Ezekiel lived with the Jewish exiles by the irrigation canal Chebar (1:1,3; 3:15) which connected the Tigris River with the Euphrates above Babylon; Daniel carried out his quite different work in the Babylonian court. We know little more about Ezekiel, except that he was married (24:18).

Ezekiel was called to be a prophet in the fifth year of his captivity (1:1,2); the last date mentioned is the 27th year (29:17); his ministry therefore lasted at least 22 years, from about 593-571 B.C.

The "captivity" of the Jews consisted in their deportation to a foreign land. Once arrived in Babylon, however, the exiles seem to have been completely free to settle and live their lives as they pleased. At Nippur, located on the Chebar canal, have been found many records of a Jewish business house, the Murashu Sons, indicating the possibilities open to the exiles. Many of the Jews

Conical tower over Ezekiel's Tomb in Kifl, Babylonia. © MPS

became so settled in their adopted land that they refused to leave it at the end of the Exile, and from that time to this the majority of the Hebrews have lived outside of Palestine.

When Jerusalem was finally destroyed, some ten years after he arrived in Babylon, Ezekiel entered into the sufferings of his people. On the day on which the final siege began, the prophet's wife became suddenly sick and died. In this he became a sign to the people and was not allowed to go through the customary period of mourning, doubtless to emphasize to them the greater sorrow now coming upon the nation.

In recent years a good deal of interest has been awakened in the unusual states of the prophets during the reception of their revelations. Some have diagnosed Ezekiel's condition as catalepsy, but the passages adduced (3:14,15,26,27; 4:4,5; 24:27) hardly support such a theory. Rather it would seem that the occasional silence of the prophet and his lying on the ground were signs to gain the attention of the people and to act out his message.

Ezekiel was a powerful preacher. Possessing a deeply introspective and religious nature, he used allegory, vivid figures and symbolic actions to clothe his message. His favorite expression to denote the divine inspiration, "The hand of the Lord was upon me" (1:3; 3:14,22, *et al.*) shows how strongly he felt impelled to communicate the message given him. His preaching was directed to his Jewish brethren in exile, and, like Jeremiah's, was often resented, for it held out little hope for the immediate future. No doubt his message was ultimately received, for the Exile became a time of religious purgation. In Babylon the Jews were cured permanently of their idolatry, and Ezekiel, their major religious leader, must be given much credit for that.

The prophet's ministry was divided into two periods. The first ends with the siege of Jerusalem in 587 B.C. (24:1,27). It was a message of approaching destruction for Jerusalem and of condemnation of her sin. The second period begins with the reception of the news of Jerusalem's fall, some two years later (33:21,22). Now the prophet's message emphasized comfort and looked forward to the coming of the Kingdom of God. It would appear that during the two years between, Ezekiel ceased all public ministry.

Frequently in this book (87 times), Ezekiel is referred to as "son of man." The term means a mortal, as in Psalm 8:4 and is used here to emphasize the prophet's weakness and need of dependence upon God for his success. Later the term came to be a messianic designation.   J.B.G.

EZEKIEL, BOOK OF, until quite recently universally accepted as written by the author whose name the book bears. Recent radical critics have denied the unity of the book and have attributed all or parts of it to later writers. There has been no agreement among these critics, however. The arguments for both the unity of the book and its origin with Ezekiel are very strong. The book is autobiographical, Ezekiel frequently using the first person singular pronoun. The arrangement of the book shows its unity—all the parts fit together and, indeed, need each other to make the whole.

The locality of Ezekiel's ministry was Babylon to which he had been deported in 597 B.C. Chapters 8-11 contain a unique vision of events which were transpiring in Jerusalem, made possible when "the spirit lifted me up . . . and brought me in the visions of God to Jerusalem" (8:3). Elsewhere in the book an intimate knowledge of events in far away Jerusalem is implied (e.g., 24:1,2). It appears impossible that Ezekiel in Babylon could have known in such detail events in Jerusalem except by divine inspiration. Therefore many modern scholars are of the opinion that Ezekiel really prophesied in Jerusalem until the city fell. The clear statements of the book, however, indicate his presence with the Jews in Babylon when he "saw" (8:6,9,10) the Jerusalem events, and a serious attempt to understand the visions must grapple with these statements rather than deny them.

The book is divided into three parts: 1. Denunciation of Judah and Israel, 1-24, dated 593-588 B.C.

2. Oracles against foreign nations, 25-32, dated 587-571 B.C.

3. The future restoration of Israel, 33-48, dated 585-573 B.C.

The prophecies of the first section (1-24) were uttered before the fall of Jerusalem. Ezekiel's call to the prophetic work is described in chapters 1-3. Here occurs his vision of the divine glory—God's throne borne by an unearthly chariot of cherubim and wheels (1:4-21). The prophet eats the scroll upon which his sad message is written (2:8-3:3) and he is commanded to be the Lord's watchman, his own life to be forfeit if he does not cry the alarm (3:16-21; cf. 33:1-9). Ezekiel then predicts the destruction of Jerusalem by symbolic acts (4-7), such as laying siege to a replica of the city (4:1-8) and by rationing food and drink (4:9-17). Next follows the famous vision of Jerusalem's iniquity, for which Ezekiel is raptured in spirit to Jerusalem (8-11), and sees all kinds of loathsome

idolatry being practiced in the temple courts. While he watches the desecration of the House of the Lord, he beholds the divine glory which had been manifested in the holy of holies (8:4) leave the temple and city (9:3; 10:4,19; 11:22,23) symbolizing God's abandonment of His apostate people. At that moment Ezekiel returns in spirit to Babylon. The rest of the first section (12-24) records symbolic actions and sermons of the prophet predicting the fall of Jerusalem. He enacts the departure into exile (12:1-7), preaches against false prophets (13) and in two deeply moving oracles (16,23) depicts the ungrateful people's apostasy. His statement of the individual's responsibility before God (18) is famous. Finally he announces the beginning of the siege of Jerusalem, and in the evening of the same day his wife dies and he becomes dumb until the fall of the city (24).

After the prophecies of judgment against foreign nations (25-32) comes the climax of the prophet's vision, written after the fall of Jerusalem—the restoration of Israel (33-48). God will bring back the people to their land, send the Son of David to reign over them, and give them a new heart (34,36). The vision of the valley of dry bones (37) is a figurative statement of this regathering of the nation. Then follows Israel's defeat of the Gentile powers, Gog and Magog (38,39). Finally a great restored temple is pictured (40-43), its holy services (44-46), the river of life running from it (47) and the people of Israel living in their places around the city called "The Lord is there" (48) to which the glory of the Lord has returned (43:2,4,5; 44:4).   J.B.G.

EZEL (ē'zĕl, Heb. *hā'āzel, departure*), the stone near Saul's house which marked the final meeting place of David and Jonathan (I Sam. 20:19).

EZEM (ē'zĕm, in AV twice Azem, *mighty*), a town near Edom assigned to Simeon (Josh. 15:29; 19:3; I Chron. 4:29).

EZER (ē'zêr, Heb. *'ēzer, help*). 1. One of the sons of Seir and a chief of the Horites (Gen. 36:21; I Chron. 1:38).

2. Descendant of Hur, of the tribe of Judah, and the father of Hushah (I Chron. 4:4).

3. An Ephraimite who was slain by men of Gath (I Chron. 7:21).

4. The first of the Gadite men of might who joined David in Ziglag when he was a fugitive from Saul (I Chron. 12:9).

5. The son of Jeshua, ruler of Mizpah. Under Nehemiah, Ezer repaired a section of the wall of Jerusalem (Neh. 3:19).

6. One of the Levitical singers who participated in the dedication of the rebuilt walls of Jerusalem under Nehemiah (Neh. 12:42).

EZION-GEBER (ē'zĭ-ŏn-gē'bêr, Heb. *'etsyôn gever*), a city near Elath on the Gulf of Aqabah. It was the last stopping place of the Israelites in their wilderness wanderings before Kadesh (Num. 33:35,36). The city's period of greatest prosperity was in the time of Solomon, who there built a fleet of ships which sailed between Ezion-Geber and Ophir, a source of gold (I Kings 9:26ff; II Chron. 8:17,18). Jehoshaphat joined with Ahaziah in making ships at Ezion-Geber which were designed to sail to Ophir, but the fleet was destroyed before leaving port (II Chron. 20:35,36; I Kings 22:48, 49). The site of Ezion-Geber has been located at Tell Kheleifeh, and extensive excavations have been carried on under the direction of Nelson Glueck. The city was located between the hills of Edom on the E and the hills of Palestine on the W, where N winds blow strongly and steadily down the center of the Wadi el-Arabah. The location was chosen to take advantage of these winds, for the city was an industrial center as well as a seaport. The excavation uncovered an extensive industrial complex centered on the smelting and refining of copper (chiefly) and iron. The furnace rooms were so placed that they received the full benefit of the prevailing winds from the N which were used to furnish the draft for the fires. Nearby mines were worked extensively in Solomon's day to supply the ore for these smelters. These operations were an important source of Solomon's wealth.   B.P.

EZNITE (ĕz'nīt, Heb. *'etsnî*), designation of Adino, one of David's chief captains (II Sam. 23:8). The parallel passage (I Chron. 11:11) speaks of Jashobeam, a Hachmonite, who "lifted up his spear." It has been conjectured that the words of II Samuel "the same [was] Adino the Eznite" are a corruption for the Heb. "he lifted up his spear."

EZRA (ĕz'rà, Heb. *'ezrā', help*). 1. A man of Judah, mentioned in I Chronicles 4:17.
2. A leading priest who returned from Babylon to Jerusalem with Zerubbabel (Neh. 12:1). In Nehemiah 10:2 the name is spelled in its full form, Azariah.
3. The famous Jewish priest and scribe who is the main character of the Book of Ezra and the co-worker of Nehemiah.

Ezra was a lineal descendant from Eleazar, the son of Aaron, the high priest, and from Seraiah, the chief priest put to death at Riblah by order of Nebuchadnezzar (II Kings 25:18-21). All that is really known of Ezra is what is told in Ezra 7-10 and Nehemiah 8-10. There are various traditions about him in Josephus, II Esdras, and the Talmud, but they are discrepant, and consequently no reliance can be put on anything they say unless it is also found in the canonical Scriptures.

In the seventh year of the reign of Artaxerxes Longimanus, king of Persia (458 B.C.), Ezra received permission from the king to return to Jerusalem to carry out a religious reform. Following the return from the Babylonian captivity, the temple had been rebuilt in 516 B.C., in spite of much powerful and vexatious opposition from the Samaritans; but after a brief period of religious zeal, the nation drifted into apostasy once more. Many of the Jews intermarried with their heathen neighbors (Mal. 2:11); the temple services and sacrifices were neglected (Mal. 1:6-14) and oppression and immorality were prevalent (Mal. 3:5). Just how Ezra acquired his influence over the king does not appear, but he received a royal edict granting him authority to carry out his purpose. He was given permission to take with him as many Israelites as cared to go; he was authorized to take from the king and the Jews offerings made for the temple; to draw upon the royal treasury in Syria for further necessary supplies; to purchase animals for sacrifice; to exempt the priests, Levites, and other workers in the temple from the Persian tax; to appoint magistrates in Judaea to enforce the law of God, with power of life and death over all offenders. Eighteen hundred Jews left Babylon with him. Nine days later, they halted at a place called Ahava, and when it was found that no Levites were in the caravan, 38 were persuaded to join them. After fasting and praying three days for a safe journey, they set out. Four months later they reached the Holy City, having made a journey of 900 miles. The treasures were delivered into the custody of the Levites, burnt-offerings were offered to the Lord, the king's commissions were handed to the governors and viceroys, and help

was given to the people and the ministers of the temple.

When he had discharged the various trusts committed to him, Ezra entered on his great work of reform. The princes of the Jews came to him with the complaint that the Jewish people generally, and also the priests and Levites, but especially the rulers and princes, had not kept themselves religiously separate from the heathen around them, and had even married heathen wives. On hearing this report, he evinced his horror and deep affliction of soul by rending his garment and tearing his hair. Those who still feared God and dreaded His wrath for the sin of the returned exiles gathered around him. At the evening sacrifice that day he made public prayer and confession of sin, entreating God that they might not lose His favor by reason of their awful guilt. The assembled congregation wept bitterly, and amid the general grief, Shechaniah, one of the company, came forward to propose a covenant to put away their foreign wives and children. A proclamation was issued that all Jews were to assemble in Jerusalem three days later, under pain of excommunication and forfeiture of goods. At the time appointed, the people assembled, trembling on account of their sin and promising obedience. They requested that, since the rain fell heavily (it was at the time of the winter rains in Palestine) and the number of transgressors was great, Ezra would appoint times for the guilty to come, accompanied by the judges and elders of each city, and have each case dealt with. A divorce court, consisting of Ezra and some others, was set up to attend to the matter; and after three months, in spite of some opposition, the work of the court was finished and the strange wives were put away.

The Book of Ezra ends with this important transaction, and nothing more is heard of Ezra till 13 years later, in the 20th year of Artaxerxes (446 B.C.), he appears again at Jerusalem, when Nehemiah, a Babylonian Jew and the favored cupbearer of Artaxerxes, returned to Jerusalem as governor of Palestine with the king's permission to repair the ruined walls of the city. It is uncertain whether Ezra remained in Jerusalem after he had effected the above-named reformation, or whether he had returned to the king of Persia and now came back with Nehemiah, or perhaps shortly after the arrival of the latter. Since he is not mentioned in Nehemiah's narrative till after the completion of the wall (Neh. 8:1), it is probable that Nehemiah sent for him to aid in his work. Under Nehemiah's government his functions were entirely of a priestly and ecclesiastical character. He read and interpreted the law of Moses before the assembled congregation during the eight days of the feast of Tabernacles, assisted at the dedication of the wall, and helped Nehemiah in bringing about a religious reformation. In all this he took a chief place. His name is repeatedly coupled with Nehemiah's, while the high priest is not mentioned as taking any part in the reformation at all. Ezra is not again mentioned after Nehemiah's departure for Babylon. It may be that he had himself returned to Babylon before that year.

Evidence points to Ezra's ministry taking place during the reign of Artaxerxes I (465-424 B.C.); but there are some modern critics who put Ezra after Nehemiah, holding that the sections dealing with them in the two books that bear their names have been transposed and that the chronicler (the supposed author of the two books and of I and II Chronicles) blundered in the few passages which associate the two.

According to Jewish tradition, Ezra is the author of the Book of Ezra and of I and II Chronicles. Many modern scholars hold that he wrote the Book of Nehemiah as well. I Esdras, a part of the OT Apocrypha, reproduces the substance of the end of II Chronicles, the whole of Ezra, and a part of Nehemiah, and was written somewhere near the beginning of the first century, A.D. There is also an apocalyptic book known as II Esdras, written about 100 A.D., describing some visions granted to Ezra in the Babylonian exile.

Ezra made a lasting impression upon the Jewish people. His influence shaped Jewish life and thought in a way from which they never altogether departed.   S.B.

EZRA, BOOK OF, so named because Ezra is the principal person mentioned in it; possibly also because he may be its author. It does not in its entirety claim to be the work of Ezra, but Jewish tradition says it is by him. Supporting this view is the fact that chs. 7-10 are written in the first person singular, while events in which he did not take part are described in the third person. The trustworthiness of the book does not, however, depend on the hypothesis that Ezra is the author. The majority of modern critics believe that the two books of Chronicles, Ezra, and Nehemiah constitute one large work, compiled and edited by someone designated the Chronicler, who has been dated from 400 to 300 B.C. Ezra's ministry is to be placed during the reign of Artaxerxes I (465-424 B.C.).

The Book of Ezra continues the narrative after Chronicles, and tells the story of the return from Babylon and the rebuilding of the temple. The purpose of the author is to show how God fulfilled His promise given through prophets to restore His exiled people to their own land through heathen monarchs, and raised up such great men as Zerubbabel, Haggai, Zechariah, and Ezra to rebuild the temple, re-establish the old forms of worship, and put a stop to compromise with heathenism. All material which does not contribute to his purpose he stringently excludes.

As sources for the writing of the book, the author used genealogical lists, letters, royal edicts, memoirs, and chronicles. Some of these were official documents found in public records. This diversity of material accounts for the varied character of the style and for the fact that it is written in both Hebrew and Aramaic.

The order of the Persians kings of the period is Cyrus (538-529 B.C.), Darius (521-486), Xerxes (486-464), and Artaxerxes I (464-424). In view of this succession, 4:7-23 departs from the chronological order of events. The reason for this is probably that the author regarded a sequence of content more important than a chronological order. He brings together in one passage the successful attempts of the Samaritans to hinder the building of the temple and the city walls.

The period covered is from 536 B.C., when the Jews returned to Jerusalem, to 458 B.C., when Ezra came to Jerusalem to carry out his religious reforms. It thus covers a period of about 78 years, although the 15 years between 535 and 520 and the 58 years between 516 and 458 are practically a blank; so that we have a description of selected incidents, and not a continuous record of the period.

For an understanding and appreciation of the book a few historical facts must be kept in mind. There is an interval of 50 years between the last events in the previous historical writings and the

The Behistun Rock, northeast of Babylon, dated 516 B.C., engraved by order of Darius the Great, under whose authority the temple at Jerusalem was rebuilt, as recounted by Ezra.   UMP

events of Ezra. Both Kings and Chronicles close with the destruction of Jerusalem by Nebuchadnezzar and the deportation of many of its inhabitants into Babylonia. There they were settled in colonies, and were not mistreated as long as they were quiet subjects. Many of them prospered so well that when, later, they had an opportunity to return to their home land, they chose not to do so. Since the temple was destroyed, they could not carry on their sacrificial system; but they continued such religious ordinances as the sabbath and circumcision, and gave great attention to the study of the Law.

The Exile was brought to a close when the Babylonian Empire fell before Cyrus, king of Persia, in 538 B.C. The way in which the expectations of the Jews respecting Cyrus were fulfilled is told in the opening narrative of the book of Ezra. The return from exile did not bring with it political freedom for the Jews. They remained subjects of the Persian Empire. Jerusalem and the surrounding districts were under the control of a governor, who sometimes was a Jew, but usually was not. Persian rule was in general not oppressive; but tribute was exacted for the royal treasury and the local governor. The hostile population surrounding them, especially the Samaritans, did all they could to make life miserable for them, especially by trying to bring them into disfavor with the Persian authorities. There were a few differences in the religious life of the Jews before and after the Exile. Idolatry no longer tempted them—and never did again. The external features distinctive of Jewish worship and the ceremonial requirements of the Laws were stressed. Prophecy became less important, scribes gradually taking the place of the prophets.

The Book of Ezra consists of two parts. The first (chs. 1-6) is a narrative of the return of the Jews from Babylonia under Zerubbabel and the restoration of worship in the rebuilt temple; while the second (7-10), tells the story of a second group of exiles returning with Ezra, and of Ezra's religious reforms.   S.B.

EZRAHITE (ĕz'rà-hīt, Heb. *'ezrāhî, designation* of Ethan and Heman (I Kings 4:31; titles of Pss. 88,89).

EZRI (ĕz'rī, Heb. *'ezrî, my help*), son of Chelub and overseer for David of those who tilled the ground (I Chron. 27:26).

F

FABLE, usually defined as a narrative in which animals and inanimate objects of nature are made to act and speak as if they were human beings. The word "fable" is not found in the OT, but the OT has two fables: Judges 9:7-15 and II Kings 14:9. In the NT "fable" is found as the translation of *múthos* ("myth") in I Timothy 1:4; 4:7; II Timothy 4:4; Titus 1:14; II Peter 1:16. In II Peter 1:16 it has the general meaning of *fiction,* that is, a story having no connection with reality. The exact nature of the fables referred to in the pastoral epistles is beyond our knowledge, but they may have to do with some form of Jewish-Gnostic speculation.

FACE, in the OT, the translation of three Hebrew words: 1. *'ayin, eye;* 2. *'aph, nose;* 3. *pānîm, face;* and in the NT, of the Greek *prósopon, face.* The word is used literally, figuratively and idiomatically. Often "my face" is nothing more than an oriental idiomatic way of saying "I." Sometimes it means *presence,* and sometimes *favor.* The averted face was the equivalent of disapproval or rejection (Ps. 13:1; 27:9). To spit in the face was an expression of contempt and aversion (Num. 12:14). To harden the face means to harden one's self against any sort of appeal (Prov. 21:29). To have the face covered by another was a sign of doom (Esth. 7:8). Falling on the face symbolized prostration before man or God (Gen. 50:18). Setting the face signified determination (Luke 9:51). To cover the face expressed mourning (Exod. 3:6).

FAIR, a word translating more than a dozen Hebrew and Greek words, none of which have the modern sense of blond or fair-skinned. It has the meaning of beautiful, attractive (Acts 7:20); unspotted, free of defilement (Zech. 3:5); plausible, persuasive (Prov. 7:21); making a fine display (Gal. 6:12); good (of weather) (Job 37:22).

FAIR HAVENS (Gr. *Kaloí Liménes*), a small bay on the S coast of Crete, about 5 miles E of Cape Matala. Paul stayed there for a time on his way to Rome (Acts 27:8-12). The harbor was not suitable to spend the winter in, so it was decided to sail from there, with the hope of reaching Phoenix, a more secure harbor, also on the S coast of Crete.

FAIRS (Heb. *'izzāvôn*), a word found in KJV only in Ezekiel (27:12,14,16,19,27). The RV more accurately renders it "wares," the commodities bartered in Oriental markets. The KJV so translates the Hebrew word in Ezekiel 5:33.

FAITH (Heb. *'ēmûn,* Gr. *pístis*), has a twofold sense in the Bible, an active and a passive one; in the former, meaning "fidelity," "trustworthiness"; in the latter, "trust," "reliance." An example of the first is found in Romans 3:3, where "the faith of God" means His fidelity to promise. In the overwhelming majority of cases it has the meaning of reliance and trust.

In the OT (KJV) the word "faith" occurs only twice (Deut. 32:20; Hab. 2:4), and even the verb form, "to believe," is far from common, appearing less than 30 times. What we find in the OT is not so much a doctrine of faith, as examples of it. It sets forth the life of the servants of God as a life of faith. That which differentiates their lives from others is their self-commitment to God, implicitly involving unwavering trust in and obedience to Him. The foundation of Israel's faith was the revelation that God had made to the fathers and to Moses, the covenant He had made with them at Sinai, and the conviction that the covenant promises would some day be fulfilled. The observance of the Law and a life of faith were not for them incompatible. Faith lay behind the keeping of the Law as its presupposition. The Law was a mode of life incumbent upon those whose trust was in Jehovah. OT faith is never mere assent to a set of doctrines or outward acceptance of the Law, but utter confidence in the faithfulness of God and a consequent loving obedience to His will.

When used with a religious application, faith, in the OT, is sometimes in a specific word or work of God (Lam. 4:12; Hab. 1:5), or the fact of God's revelation (Exod. 4:5; Job 9:16), or the words or commandments of God in general (Ps. 119:66); or in God Himself (Gen. 15:6). Faith is put in the word of God's prophets because they speak for Him, and He is absolutely trustworthy (Exod. 19:9; II Chron. 20:20). NT writers, especially Paul and the author of Hebrews, show that the faith manifested by OT saints was not different in kind from that expected of Christians.

In contrast with the extreme rarity with which the terms "faith" and "believe" are used in the OT, they occur with great frequency in the NT — almost 500 times. A principal reason for this is that the NT makes the claim that the promised Messiah had finally come, and, to the bewilderment of many, the form of the fulfilment did not obviously correspond to the Messianic promise. It required a real act of faith to believe that Jesus of Nazareth was the promised Messiah. It was not long before "to believe" meant to become a Christian. In the NT, faith therefore becomes supreme of all human acts and experiences.

In His miracles and teaching Jesus aimed at creating in His disciples a complete trust in Himself as the Messiah and Saviour of men. Everywhere He offered Himself as the object of faith, and made it plain that faith in Him is necessary for eternal life, that it is the certain outcome of faith in the OT Scriptures that God requires it of men, and that refusal to accept His claims will bring eternal ruin. His primary concern with His own disciples was to build up their faith in Him.

The record in Acts shows that the first Christians called themselves "the believers" (Acts 2:44, etc.) and that they went everywhere persuading men and bringing them unto obedience to the faith that is in Jesus (Acts 6:7; 17:4; 28:24). Before long, as communities of believers arose in various parts of the Mediterranean world, the meaning and implications of the Christian faith had to be taught them in considerable fullness by the apostolic leaders, and so the NT books appeared.

It is in Paul's epistles that the meaning of faith is most clearly and fully set forth. Faith is trust in the person of Jesus, the truth of His teaching, and the redemptive work He accomplished at Calvary, and, as a result, a total submission to Him and His message, which are accepted as from God. Faith in His person is faith in Him as the eternal Son of God, the God-man, the second man Adam, who died in man's stead, making possible justification with God, adoption into His family, sanctification, and, ultimately, glorification. His death brings redemption from sin in all its aspects. The truth of His claims is attested by God's raising Him from the dead. Some day He will judge the quick and the dead. Faith is not to be confused with a mere intellectual assent to the doctrinal teachings of Christianity, though that is obviously necessary. It includes a radical and total commitment to Him as the Lord of one's life.

Unbelief, or lack of faith in the Christian Gospel, appears everywhere in the NT as the supreme evil. Not to make a decisive response to God's offer in Christ means that the individual remains in his sin and is eternally lost. Faith alone can save Him.   S.B.

FAITHFULNESS (Heb. *ĕmûnâh*), an attribute or quality applied in the Bible to both God and man. When used of God, it has in the OT a twofold emphasis, referring first to His absolute reliability, firm constancy, and complete freedom from arbitrariness or fickleness, and also to His steadfast, loyal love toward His people and His loyalty. God is constant and true in contrast to all that is not God. He is faithful in keeping His promises, and is therefore worthy of trust. He is unchangeable in His ethical nature. God's faithfulness is usually connected with His gracious promises of salvation. Faithful men are dependable in fulfilling their responsibilities and in carrying out their word. In the NT there are frequent exhortations to faithfulness. It is one of the fruits of the Spirit in Galatians 5:22.

FALCON (See Birds)

FALL, THE. The fall of man is narrated in Genesis 3 as a historical fact, not as a myth. It stands in a context of historical facts. Though not alluded to again in the OT, it is regarded as historical in the Apocrypha (Wis. 2:24) and in the NT (Rom. 5:12 f.; I Cor. 15:22). Some philosophers and theologians think the story is an allegory describing the awakening of man from a brute state of self-consciousness and personality — a fall upward, rather than downward, but such an explanation conflicts radically with Biblical teaching. There is no doubt that Paul takes the story literally and sees in the fall the origin of sin in the human race. The Scriptural view of sin and of redemption takes the fall for granted.

A denial of the fall requires that sin be made a necessity, with its origin in the Creation or in the Creator, and thus sin loses its character as sin; it becomes everlasting and indefeasible. If there has been no fall into sin, no redemption from sin is possible. Sin, moreover, becomes an inexterminable trait of man's nature. The Scriptures, however, teach us that man was created in God's own image, with a rational and moral nature like God's, with no inner impulse or drive to sin, and with a will perfectly free to do His will. There was nothing, moreover, in his environment to compel him to sin or to make sin excusable. God made him responsive to His call of love, and responsible for maintaining that responsivity. There was, indeed, outward solicitation to sin, on the part of the serpent, but there was no need to yield to the temptation.

The question Adam faced was whether ultimate happiness and fulfilment for him lay in theonomy or in autonomy, in the doing of God's will in love or in conducting his life in the way he chose, apart from the will of God.

The effect of the fall, as the rest of the Bible explicitly and implicitly brings out, was not merely immediate alienation from God for Adam and Eve, but guilt and depravity for all their posterity and the cursing of the earth.

Redemption from the effects of the fall is accomplished through the second man Adam, Jesus Christ (Rom. 5:12-21; I Cor. 15:21,22, 45-49).
                    S.B.

FALLOW DEER. (See Animals)

FALLOW GROUND (Heb. *nîr*, *untilled*), twice found in the OT (Jer. 4:3; Hos. 10:12), is used in the sense of untilled ground.

FALSE CHRISTS (Gr. *pseudó-christoi, false Christs*). On Tuesday of Passion Week, Jesus warned His disciples that false Christs and false prophets would arise and that they would with great signs and wonders try to lead astray even the elect (Matt. 24:5,11, 23:25; Mark 13:6,21-23; Luke 21:8).

FALSE PROPHET, THE, is referred to only in the book of Revelation (16:13; 19:20; 20:10), but is usually identified with the two-horned beast of Revelation 13:11-18, who deceived the peoples of the earth with his lying wonders and killed those who refused to worship the image of the seven-headed beast (Rev. 13:1-10). The two beasts are clearly tools and instruments of Satan. In some way, the two-horned beast is a minister of the seven-headed one. In Revelation 16:13 we are told that three unclean spirits like frogs came out of the mouths of the dragon, beast, and false prophet. In Revelation 19:20 the beast (apparently the one with seven heads) and the false prophet, who is described as having performed deceiving miracles and killed those who refused to worship the image of the beast, are cast into a lake burning with brimstone. The devil is cast into that same lake of fire where the beast and the false prophet are (Rev. 20:10). Christian opinion is divided upon the interpretation of the two-horned beast.   S.B.

FAMILIAR SPIRIT (Heb. *'ôv*, etymology and exact meaning unknown). The term is generally used to refer to the spirit of a dead person which professed mediums claimed they could summon for consultation (Deut. 18:11). The word "familiar" has in this phrase the sense of the Latin *familiaris*, belonging to one's family, and hence ready to serve one as a servant. Such a spirit was thought to be able to reveal the future (Isa. 8:19; I Sam. 28:7). Since the voice seemed to come in a whisper from the ground, the medium was very likely a ventriloquist. Israelites were forbidden by Jehovah to consult familiar spirits (Lev. 19:31; Isa. 8:19). This was regarded as apostasy so serious that those who consulted them were put to death (Lev. 20:6). Saul put away mediums early in his reign, but consulted the witch of Endor, who "had a familiar spirit," when he became apostate just before his death (I Sam. 28:3-25; I Chron. 10:13). Manasseh dealt with familiar spirits (II Kings 21:6; II Chron. 33:6), but his grandson Josiah carried out the enactment of the Mosaic Law against them (II Kings 23:24). The practice of consulting them probably prevailed more or less to the time of the exile (Isa. 8:19; 19:3).
                    S.B.

FAMILY (Heb. *mishpahah, bayith, house, family;* Gr. *patriá, clan*). The OT has no term corresponding exactly to the English "family." The Hebrew family unit was larger than families today, and included some or all of the following: the father or master, the supreme head of the household; his mother, if she was living with him after the death of his father; his wives and concubines and their children; his children by other women; daughters-in-law and sons-in-law living on the paternal estate; other free Israelite friends and relatives; foreigners living under his protection; and male and female slaves. Since in primitive times the family assumed many of the responsibilities of modern government, like protection of life and property, large families were necessary.

Marriage was arranged not by the young people involved, but by the man (or his father) and the family of the bride, for whom a dowry, or purchase money, was paid to her father. In spite of this commercial aspect of the marriage contract, there is evidence that the love of the young people for each other often had an important part in the preliminaries of the marriage (Gen. 29; I Sam. 18:20). The wife was regarded as the property of the husband. He could divorce her, but she could not divorce him. Not only were polygamy and concubinage permitted, but no disgrace was attached to them. Wives, however, usually enjoyed more consideration than concubines.

Within his own domain, the authority of the head of the family was almost absolute. He could sell his children as slaves, and had power of life and death over them (Lev. 18:21; 20:2-5; II Kings 23:10). To dishonor a parent was a crime punishable with death (Exod. 21:15,17). He was also the chief religious functionary of the house, offering sacrifices to Jehovah on behalf of his family. Upon him rested the responsibility of training them in the ancient traditions.

While a wife was bought and paid for, her actual position was usually far from being a mere chattel. Her own family stood ready to avenge her in case she was mistreated by her husband. She had the chief place in the sub-family formed by her and her children in a polygamous household. The early training of the children was given mostly by her.

A large family was regarded as a great blessing. To be without children was a disgrace.

In the NT, Paul has much to say about family life. He stresses the need of bringing all family relationships under the principle of Christian love.
                                        S.B.

FAMINE (Heb. *rā'āv*, hunger, famine, Gr. *limós*, want of food). In ancient times, in Palestine and Egypt, famines were not infrequent. They were produced by (1) want of rainfall in due season, (2) destructive hail storms and rain out of season, (3) destruction of crops by locusts and caterpillars, and (4) the cutting off of food supplies by a siege. Pestilence often followed, and the suffering was great. Famines which were the result of natural causes are recorded in the time of Abraham, who left Canaan and sojourned in Egypt (Gen. 12:10); in the time of Joseph, when the famine "was over all the face of the earth" (Gen. 41:56); in the time of the Judges (Ruth 1:1), of David, for three years (II Sam. 21:1), of Ahab and Elijah (I Kings 17:1; 18:2, and of Elisha (II Kings 4:38). Famines produced by sieges are mentioned in II Kings 6:25 — the siege of Jerusalem by Nebuchadnezzar. Nehemiah 5:3 tells of a "dearth" after the return from the Babylonian Captivity. The NT tells of a famine "throughout all the world" in the time of Claudius (Acts 11:28). In His Olivet discourse Jesus predicted famines in various places (Matt. 24:7), a prophecy believed to be partly fulfilled in the siege of Jerusalem by Titus, which is described with harrowing detail by Josephus, who says that "neither did any other city ever suffer such miseries" (*Wars*, V.x.5). Famines are sometimes said to be sent as punishments, and sometimes they are threatened as such (Lev. 26:19 f; Deut. 28: 49-51; II Kings 8:1; Isa. 14:30; 51:19; Jer. 14:12,

15; Ezek. 5:16). A special mark of God's favor and power is to be preserved in time of famine (Job 5:20; Ps. 33:19; 37:19). Sometimes the word "famine" is used in a figurative sense, as when Amos says that God will send a famine, not of bread and water, "but of hearing the words of the Lord" (Amos 8:11).   S.B.

FAN (Heb. *mizreh*, winnowing fan), a fork with two or more prongs used to throw grain into the air after it had been threshed, so that the chaff might be blown away. The work was done toward evening and at night when a wind came in from the sea and carried away the light chaff. Sometimes a shovel was used for the same purpose.

FARMING. The Israelites in the time of the patriarchs were a nomadic people. They first learned agriculture in Palestine, after the conquest of Canaan. After that a large proportion of the people were engaged in agrarian pursuits. The pages of the Bible have much to say about agricultural occupations.

Agriculture was the background for all the legislation of Israel. At the time of the conquest every family probably received a piece of land, marked off by stones that could not be removed lawfully (Deut. 19:14; 27:17; Hos. 5:10). The soil of Palestine was generally fertile. Fertilizing was almost unknown. To maintain the fertility of the land, the law required that farms, vineyards, and olive orchards were to lie fallow in the seventh year (Exod. 23:10). On the year of jubilee those who had lost their ancestral estates recovered possession of them. Terracing was necessary to make use of soil on the hillsides. Irrigation was not required, since there was usually sufficient rainfall.

Plowing to prepare the land for sowing was done in autumn, when the early rains softened the ground that had become stone-hard in the summer sun. This was done with a crude wooden plough drawn by oxen; or, if the soil was thin, with a mattock. With such implements the surface of the ground was hardly more than scratched — perhaps three or four inches. Little harrowing was done, and was probably unknown in Palestine in early times.

Palestine peasant plowing with primitive plow, in a field before the Hill of Samaria. © MPS

"The Reapers" in the barley fields before Mount Scopus, north of Jerusalem. © MPS

The summer grain was sown between the end of January and the end of February. Usually the seed was scattered broadcast from a basket, but careful farmers put it in furrows in rows (Isa. 28:25). Between sowing and reaping the crops were exposed to several dangers: the failure of the latter rain, which came in March and April; the hot, drying easterly winds that often came in March and April (Gen. 41:6); hailstorms (Hag. 2:17); various kinds of pestiferous weeds like tares and thorns (Jer. 12: 13; Matt. 13:7, 25); injurious insects, especially the palmer-worm, the canker-worm, the caterpillar, and the locust (Amos 7:2); the thefts of crows and sparrows (Matt. 13:4); and fungus diseases, especially mildew (Deut. 28:22). As the harvest season approached, particularly valuable crops were protected by watchmen (Jer. 4:17); but the law permitted a hungry person to pick grain in passing by (Deut. 23:25; Matt. 12:1).

The time of harvest varied somewhat according to the climatic condition of each region, but usually began about the middle of April with the coming of the dry season. Barley was the first grain to be cut, and this was followed a few weeks later with wheat. The grain harvest generally lasted about seven weeks, from Passover to Pentecost. Whole families moved out of their village homes to live in the fields until the harvest was over. The grain was cut with a sickle and laid in swaths behind the reaper. It was then bound into sheaves and gathered into shocks (Exod. 22:6). In the interests of the poor, the law forbade a field to be harvested to its limits.

The grain was threshed in the open air, a custom made possible because the harvest season was free

Traditional method of sowing seed.   © SPF

Threshing grain on a threshing floor at the village of Sepphoris, north of Nazareth. © MPS

Winnowing on the threshing floor. © MPS

from rain (I Sam. 21:16 ff.). During the threshing-time the grain was guarded by harvesters who spent the nights upon the threshing floor (Ruth 3:6). The threshing floor was constructed in an exposed position in the fields, preferably on a slight elevation, so as to get the full benefit of the winds. It consisted of a circular area 25 or 40 feet in diameter, sloping slightly upward at the edges, and was usually surrounded with a border of stones so as to keep in the grain. The floor was level and rolled hard. The sheaves of grain, brought in from the fields on the backs of men and animals, were heaped in the center. From this heap, sheaves were spread out on the floor, and then either several animals tied abreast were driven round and round the floor, or two oxen were yoked together to a threshing-machine, which they dragged in a circular path over the grain until the kernels of grain were separated from the stalks. The threshing machines were of two kinds, a board with the bottom studded with small stones or nails, or a kind of threshing wagon. While this was going on, the partly threshed grain was turned over with a fork. After that the grain was winnowed by tossing the grain and chaff into the air with a wooden fork or shovel so that the wind might blow away the chaff. This was usually done at night, to take advantage of the night breezes. The chaff was either burned or left to be scattered by the winds. The grain was then sifted with a sieve to remove stones and other impurities, and collected into pits or barns (Luke 12:18).

Of the large number of crops the Israelites cultivated, wheat and barley were the most important. Among other crops they raised were rye, millet, flax, and a variety of vegetables. See also AGRICULTURE.   S.B.

FARTHING (See Money)

FASTING (Heb. *tsûm*, Gr. *nesteía, néstis*), meaning abstinence from food and drink for a longer or shorter period, is frequently mentioned in the Scriptures. Sometimes, instead of the single word "fast" the descriptive phrase "to afflict the soul" is used, the reference being to physical fasting rather than to spiritual humiliation. This term is used in various parts of the OT, but is the only one used to denote the religious observance of fasting in the Pentateuch (Lev. 16:29-31; 23:27; Num. 30:13; Ps. 35:13; Isa. 58:3,5,10).

The only fast required by Moses was that of the Day of Atonement. Before the Babylonian Captivity it was the one regular fast (Lev. 16:29,31; 23:27-32; Num. 29:7; Jer. 36:6). During this period there are many examples of fasts on special occasions, held because of transgression or to ward off present or impending calamity. Samuel called for such a fast (I Sam. 7:6); Jehoiakim and the princess proclaimed a fast after Baruch had read the condemnatory word of the Lord given through Jeremiah (Jer. 36:9); Jezebel hypocritically enjoined a fast when she sought to secure Naboth's vineyard (I Kings 21:9,12). We read of individuals who were moved to fast — for example, David, when his child became ill (II Sam. 12:16, 21-23), and Ahab on hearing his doom (I Kings 21:27).

After the Captivity four annual fasts were held in memory of the national calamities through which the nation had passed. They are mentioned only in Zechariah 7:1-7; 8:19). These fasts, established during the Captivity, were held on the fourth, fifth, seventh, and tenth months. The Mishna (*Taarith*, iv,6) and St. Jerome (in *Zachariam*, viii) give information on the historical events which these fasts were intended to commemorate. By the time of Christ they had fallen into disuse, and were not revived until after the destruction of Jerusalem by the Romans. In Rabbinic times the Feast of Purim, the origin of which is explained in Esther (9:31,32), was accompanied by a fast in commemoration of the fast of Esther, Mordecai and the Jews (Esther 4:1-3, 15-17). The OT gives a number of instances of other fasts in which the whole people joined (Ezra 8:21-23; Neh. 9:1). Examples of fasts by individuals are given in Nehemiah 1:4 and Daniel 9:3. A fast of great strictness was proclaimed by the heathen king of Nineveh to avert the destruction threatened by Jehovah through Jonah (Jonah 3:5).

Fasting among the Israelites was either partial or total, depending upon the length of the fast. When Daniel mourned three full weeks, he ate no "pleasant bread, neither came flesh nor wine in his mouth" (Dan. 10:2,3). The fast on the Day of Atonement was "from even till even" (Lev. 23:32); and no food or drink was taken. Other daylong fasts were from morning till evening. Longer fasts are mentioned in Nehemiah 1:4 and Daniel 10:2,3. The fasts of Moses and Elijah for forty days were exceptional (Exod. 34:28; I Kings 19:8).

Religious fasting was observed as a sign of mourning for sin, with the object of deprecating divine wrath or winning divine compassion. The prophets often condemn the abuse of the custom, for Israelites superstitiously thought that it had value even when dissevered from purity and righteousness of life (Isa. 58:3-7; Jer. 14:10-12; Zech. 7,8). Fasts were not necessarily religious in nature. They were commonplace when someone near and dear died, as when the inhabitants of Jabesh fasted after they had buried Saul and Jonathan (I Sam. 31:13), and after the death of Abner (II Sam. 1:12).

There are few references to fasting in the Gospels, but what is said shows that frequent fasts were customary with those Jews who desired to lead a specially religious life. We are told that Anna "served God with fastings and prayers night and day" (Luke 2:37). Again, the Pharisee in the parable says, "I fast twice in the week" (Luke 18:12). Jesus fasted for forty days in the wilderness, but it is not clear whether this fast was voluntary or not. There is no reason to doubt that He observed the usual prescribed public fasts, but neither by practice nor by precept did He stress fasting. He was so unascetic in His ordinary mode of life that He was reproached with being "a gluttonous man and a wine-bibber" (Matt. 11:19; Luke 7:34). In all His teaching He spoke of fasting only twice. The passages are as follows:

Matthew 6:16-18. In this passage voluntary fasting is presupposed as a religious exercise, but Jesus warns against making it an occasion for a parade of piety. The important thing is purity and honesty of intention. Fasting should be to God, not to impress men. Jesus approves of fasting if it is an expression of inner contrition and devotion. The externalism of the Pharisees has its own reward.

Matthew 9:14-17; Mark 2:18-22; Luke 5:33-39. Here, the disciples of John and of the Pharisees ask Jesus, "Why do we and the Pharisees fast oft, but thy disciples fast not?" Jesus replies that fasting, which is a sign of mourning, would be inconsistent with the joy which should characterize those who know that the Messiah has finally come and is now with them. The time will come, however, when He will be taken away, and then His disciples will mourn. It is obvious that the reference to His being taken away is to His crucifixion, not His ascension, for the ascension, signifying the completion of His redemptive work, is no occasion for mourning. Jesus here sanctions fasting, as He does in the Sermon on the Mount; but He refuses to enjoin it on His disciples. In the parables of the Old Wineskins and the Old Garment He shows that fasting belongs to the body of old observances and customs and is not congruous with the liberty of the Gospel. The new era that He inaugurates must have new forms of its own.

The references to fasting in Matthew 17:21 and Mark 9:29 are regarded by textual scholars as corruptions of the text.

The Acts of the Apostles has a few direct references to fasting. The church at Antioch fasted and prayed before sending out Paul and Barnabas as missionaries (Acts 13:2,3). On Paul's first missionary journey, elders were appointed in every church, with prayer and fasting (Acts 14:23). The reference to the fasting of Cornelius, in Acts 10: 30, is an interpolation. The only other direct references to fasting in the NT are found in II Corinthians 6:5 and 11:27, where Paul describes his sufferings for Christ; and here, most likely, he has in mind involuntary fasting.

There are, therefore, in the NT only four indisputable references to voluntary fasting for religious purposes, two by our Lord in the Gospels, and two in the Acts of the Apostles. Jesus does not disapprove of the practice, but says nothing to commend it. The apostolic church practiced it, but perhaps only as a carry-over from Judaism, since most of the early disciples were Jews.

S.B.

FAT (Heb. *hēlev, helev*). 1. The subcutaneous layer of fat around the kidneys and other viscera, which, like the blood, was forbidden by the Mosaic law to be used for food, but was burned as an offering to Jehovah, for a sweet savor unto Him (Lev. 4:31). This had to be done on the very day the animal was slain, apparently to remove temptation (Exod. 23:18). The purpose of the law was to teach the Israelite that his best belonged to God. Long before the Mosaic law was given, Abel brought the fat of the firstlings of his flock to Jehovah; and we read that the Lord had respect unto Abel and to his offering. (Gen. 4:4).

2. Sometimes used in the KJV to refer to a wine vat, a receptable into which the grape juice flowed from the "press" above (Joel 2:24; Isa. 63:2).

FATHER (Heb. *'āv*, Gr. *patér*), has various meanings in the Bible. 1. Immediate male progenitor (Gen. 42:13). In the Hebrew family the father had absolute rights over his children. He could sell them into slavery and have them put to death. Reverence and obedience by children is prescribed from the earliest times (Exod. 20:12; Lev. 19:3; Deut. 5:16, etc.). The Scriptures many times set forth the character and duties of an ideal father.

2. Ancestor, immediate or remote. Abraham is called Jacob's father (Gen. 28:13), and God tells him he will be the "father of many nations" (Gen. 17:4). The founders of the Hebrew race, the patriarchs, are referred to as its fathers (Rom. 9:5); so also heads of clans (Exod. 6:14; I Chron. 27:1).

3. The word has many figurative and derived uses. A spiritual ancestor, whether good or bad, as Abraham, "the father of all them that believe" (Rom. 4:11); and the devil, "Ye are of your father the devil" (John 8:44). The originator of a mode of life ("Jabal: he was the father of such as dwell in tents, and of such as have cattle" (Gen. 4:20). One who exhibits paternal kindness and wisdom to another: "be unto me a father and a priest" (Judg. 17:10). A revered superior, especially a prophet and an elderly and venerable man (I Sam. 10:12; I John 2:13). Royal advisors and prime ministers: "God hath made me a father to Pharaoh" (Gen. 45:8). Early Christians who have died: "since the fathers fell asleep" (II Peter 3:4). A source: "Hath the rain a father?" (Job 38:28).

4. God is Father: as Creator of the universe, "the Father of lights" (James 1:17); as Creator of the human race, "Have we not all one father? hath not one God created us?" (Mal. 2:10); as one who begets and takes care of his spiritual children, "Ye have received the Spirit of adoption, whereby we cry, Abba, Father" (Rom. 8:15). In a special and unique sense, God is the Father of Jesus Christ (Matt. 11:26; Mark 14:36; Luke 22:42).

S.B.

FATHOM (See Weights and Measures)

FATLING. One of the clean animals (calf, lamb, kid, etc.) fattened for offering to God. See Psalm 66:15, II Samuel 6:13, etc.

FEAR (Heb. *yir'âh*, Gr. *phóbos*). This word in English has two principal meanings: first, that apprehension of evil which normally leads one either to flee or to fight; and second, that awe and reverence which a man of sense feels in the presence of God, and to a less extent in the presence of a king or other dread authority. A child feels the first of these in the presence of a cruel parent, and the second before one who is good, but who must also be just. There are 15 different Hebrew nouns which are rendered "fear" in KJV, but in the NT the Greek *phóbos* is used in both senses; i.g., in Matthew 14:26 the disciples cried out for fear, thinking that they saw a ghost; whereas in Romans 3:18, "There is no fear of God before their eyes," the second meaning is implied. The word "reverend" which occurs only in Psalm 111:9 means literally "to be feared," and is used only for God. For the two senses in the OT, contrast Psalm 31:13, "fear was upon every side," with Proverbs 9:10, "the fear of the Lord is the beginning of wisdom."

A.B.F.

(Lev. 23:5-8). This combined feast was one of the three feasts the Mosaic Law enjoined to be attended by all male Jews who were physically able and ceremonially clean (Exod. 23:17; Deut. 16:16), the other two being the Feast of Weeks, or Pentecost, and the Feast of Tabernacles. These were known as the pilgrimage festivals; and on all of them special sacrifices were offered, varying according to the character of the festival (Num. 28,29).

3. The Feast of Pentecost. Other names for this are the Feast of Weeks, the Day of the First-fruits, and the Feast of Harvests. It was celebrated on the sixth day of the month of Sivan (our June), seven weeks after the offering of the wave sheaf after the Passover. The name "Pentecost," meaning "50th," originated from the fact that there was an interval of 50 days between the two. The feast lasted a single day (Deut. 16:9-12), and marked the completion of the wheat harvest. The characteristic ritual of this feast was the offering and waving of two loaves of leavened bread, made from the ripe grain which had just been harvested. This was done by the priest in the name of the congregation. In addition to these wave offerings, the people were enjoined to give the Lord an offering of the first fruits of their produce. The amount of the offering was not designated.

4. The Feast of Trumpets, or New Moon. This was held on the first day of the seventh month, Tishri (our October), which began the civil year of the Jews. It corresponded to our New Year's day, and on it, from morning to evening, horns and trumpets were blown. After the exile the day was observed by the public reading of the Law and by general rejoicing.

5. The Feast of the Day of Atonement. This was observed on the 10th day of Tishri. It was really less a feast than a fast, as the distinctive character and purpose of the day was to bring the collective sin of the whole year to remembrance, so that it might earnestly be dealt with and atoned for. On this day the high priest made confession of all the sins of the community, and entered on their behalf into the most holy place with the blood of reconciliation. It was a solemn occasion, when God's people through godly sorrow and atonement for sin entered into the rest of God's mercy and favor, so that as the partakers of His forgiveness they might rejoice before Him and carry out His commandments.

6. The Feast of Tabernacles, or Booths, or Ingathering. This was the last of the sacred festivals under the old covenant, in pre-exilic times. It began five days after the day of atonement (Lev. 23:34; Deut. 16:13), and lasted seven days. It marked the completion of the harvest, and historically commemorated the wanderings in the wilderness. During this festival people lived in booths and tents in Jerusalem to remind themselves of how their forefathers wandered in the wilderness and lived in booths. The sacrifices of this feast were more numerous than at any other. The last day of the feast marked the conclusion of the ecclesiastical year. The whole feast was popular and joyous in nature.

Besides the above feasts, which were all pre-exilic and instituted by Jehovah, the Jews after the Captivity added two others, the Feast of Lights, or Dedication, and the Feast of Purim.

The Feast of Lights was observed for eight days beginning on the 25th day of Kislev (our December). It was instituted by Judas Maccabeus in 164

A Samaritan chief priest exposing the Scroll of the Law before the congregation on Mount Gerizim during the Passover celebration. © MPS

FEASTS (Heb. *mô'ēdh, an assembling; hagh, dance, or pilgrimage*). The feasts, or sacred festivals, held an important place in Jewish religion. They were religious services accompanied by demonstrations of joy and gladness. In Leviticus 23, where they are described most fully, they are called "holy convocations." Their times, except for the two instituted after the exile, were fixed by divine appointment. Their purpose was to promote spiritual interests of the community. The people met in holy fellowship for acts and purposes of sacred worship. They met before God in holy assemblies.

1. The Feast of the Weekly Sabbath. This stood at the head of the sacred seasons. The holy convocations by which the sabbaths were distinguished were quite local. Families and other small groups assembled under the guidance of Levites or elders among them and engaged in some common acts of devotion, the forms and manner of which were not prescribed. Little is known of where or how the people met before the Captivity, but after it they met in synagogues and were led in worship by teachers learned in the law.

2. The Passover, or the Feast of Unleavened Bread. The Passover was the first in point or time of all the annual feasts, and historically and religiously it was the most important of all. It was called both the Feast of the Passover and the Feast of Unleavened Bread, the two really forming a double festival. It was celebrated on the first month of the religious year, on the 14th of Nisan (our April), and commemorated the deliverance of the Jews from Egypt and the establishment of Israel as a nation by God's redemptive act. The Feast of Unleavened Bread began on the day after the Passover and lasted seven days

THE JEWISH SACRED YEAR

MONTH		SPECIAL DAYS
Nisan	(April)	14 — Passover
		15 — Unleavened Bread
		21 — Close of Passover
Iyar	(May)	
Sivan	(June)	6 — Feast of Pentecost — seven weeks after the Passover (Anniversary of the giving of the law on Mt. Sinai)
Tammuz	(July)	
Ab	(August)	
Elul	(September)	
Tishri	(October)	1 & 2 — The Feast of Trumpets *Rosh Hashanah,* beginning of the civil year
		10 — Day of Atonement
		15-21 — Feast of Tabernacles
Marchesvan	(November)	
Kislev	(December)	25 — Feast of Lights, Dedication, *Hanukkah*
Tebeth	(January)	
Shebet	(February)	
Adar	(March)	14 — The Feast of Purim

B.C. when the Temple which had been defiled by Antiochus Epiphanes, king of Syria, was cleansed and rededicated to the service of Jehovah. During these days the Israelites met in their synagogues, carrying branches of trees in their hands, and held jubilant services. The children were told the brave and stirring deeds of the Maccabees to rouse them to noble emulation.

The Feast of Purim was kept on the 14th and 15th days of Adar (our March), the last month of the religious year. It is said to have been instituted by Mordecai to commemorate the failure of Haman's plots against the Jews. The word Purim means "lots." On the evening of the 13th the whole book of Esther was read publicly in the synagogue. It was a joyous occasion.   S.B.

A Yemenite Jewish family at Jerusalem celebrating the ceremony of eating the Passover. © MPS

FELIX fē'lĭks, Gr. *Phélix, happy*), born Antonius Claudius, a Greek subject, was made a freedman by Claudius, the emperor from A.D. 41 to 54, and given the surname Felix (i.e. *Happy*) probably in congratulation. He and his brother Pallas were favorites of Claudius and later of Nero (A.D. 54-68), and so Felix evidently thought that he could do as he pleased. Tacitus said of him that "he revelled in cruelty and lust, and wielded the power of a king with the mind of a slave." His very title of "procurator" hints at his fiscal duties of procuring funds for Rome, which he seems to have accomplished with all sorts of tyranny. He began his career as procurator of Judea by seducing Drusilla, the sister of Agrippa II, and wife of the king of Emesa (modern Homs), and marrying her. Because she was Jewish (at least on one side) he learned much of Jewish life and customs.

Felix appears in the Biblical account only in Acts 23:24 - 25:14. He was susceptible to flattery, as the speech of Tertullus shows, and also to conviction of sin, as is shown by his terror when Paul reasoned before him of "righteousness, temperance and judgment to come." His conviction faded; he procrastinated; and then held Paul for about two years (c. 58 - 60), hoping that Paul would buy his freedom. He was then replaced by Festus, a far better man.

FELLOES (fĕl'ōz), the exterior parts of the rim of a wheel which unite the outer ends of the spokes. The word occurs only in I Kings 7:33.

FELLOW (Heb. *rē'a*, Gr. *hetaíros*), a word which in English has two diverse meanings: 1. A person, but usually implying a certain amount of contempt as in Judges 18:25, "lest angry fellows run upon thee," and I Samuel 29:4, "Make this fellow return," where AVS has, "Make the man return," which is technically correct but lacks the feeling of KJV.

2. A friend, companion, associate or partner, as in Hebrews 1:9: "God hath anointed thee . . . above thy fellows." In denying the Christian doctrine of the Trinity, the Koran says of "Allah," "He does not beget, nor is he begotten, and he has no fellow." In Judges 11:37 (KJV) the word occurs once in the feminine, but ASV has "companion."

FELLOWSHIP (Gr. *koinonía, that which is in common*). 1. Partnership or union with others in the bonds of a business partnership, a social or fraternal organization, or just propinquity. Christians are told not to be unequally yoked together with unbelievers (II Cor. 6:14-18) because such a union, either in marriage, business or society, is incompatible with that fellowship with Christians and with God.

2. Membership in a local Christian church or in *the* Church. From the very beginning of the Church at Pentecost, "they continued stedfastly in the apostles' doctrine and fellowship, and in breaking of bread, and in prayers" (Acts 2:42).

3. Partnership in the support of the Gospel and in the charitable work of the Church (II Cor. 8:4).

4. That heavenly love which fills (or should fill) the hearts of believers one for another and for God. For this love and fellowship, the Scriptures employ a word *"agape"* which scarcely appears in classical Greek. This fellowship is deeper and more satisfying than any mere human love whether social, parental, conjugal or other.

FENCED CITY. All of the six Hebrew words which are used for fenced cities are from the one root,

bātsar, which means *to restrain, withhold,* or *to make inaccessible.* Owing to the usual insecurity in the East, most of the towns and even many of the small villages are enclosed in walls. It seems strange to ride through two or three miles of fields without a single building, and then to enter the gate of a little village and find the houses packed together with hardly a place to breathe. In the description of the kingdom of Bashan in the days of Moses (Deut. 3:5) we read of cities "fenced with high walls, gates, and bars," but the Israelites utterly destroyed them. The Edomite city of Bozrah (Mic. 2:12) gets its name from the same root. Figuratively, the word is used to show God's protection of Jeremiah — "I will make thee unto this people a fenced brazen wall . . . for I am with thee to save thee and to deliver thee, saith the Lord" (Jer. 15:20).

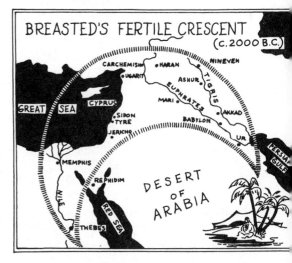

FERTILE CRESCENT, does not occur in Scripture but is a modern description of the territory which may roughly be described as reaching NW from the Persian Gulf through Mesopotamia, then W to the N of Syria, then SW through Syria and Palestine. In this crescent the land is mostly rich and fertile, and is watered by the Tigris, the Euphrates, the Orontes and the Jordan, besides numerous rivers descending the west side of Lebanon, and in most of the region irrigation has long been employed. Various grains like wheat and barley, and fruits such as grapes, olives, figs, oranges, lemons, pomegranates abound. If one attempts to cross in a straight line from one end of the crescent to the other he will find himself most of the way in the great Syrian desert, with only an occasional oasis. This configuration of the land explains much of Bible history.

FESTIVALS (See Feasts)

FESTUS, PORCIUS (Gr. *Pórkios Phéstos, festal, joyful*), the Roman governor who succeeded Felix in the province of Judea (Acts 24:27). The date of his accession in uncertain. Of the life of Festus before his appointment of Nero as procurator of Judea almost nothing is known, and he appears in the Bible (Acts 24:27 - 26:32) principally in his relationship with his prisoner, the apostle Paul. Festus was apparently a far better and more efficient man than his predecessor. At the very beginning of his rule, he took up the case of Paul, and as king Agrippa said, Paul "might have been set at liberty if he had not appealed unto Caesar." Paul had made this appeal when Festus, at the instance of the Jews, was considering bringing Paul to Jerusalem for trial. Festus evidently knew that Paul was a good man (Acts 25:25), but he was unable to understand Paul's reasoning with king Agrippa, and thought that Paul had gone mad with much study. (Acts 26:24). Festus died at his post, and was followed, c. A.D. 62, by Albinus.

FETTERS, bonds, chains or shackles, generally for the feet of prisoners and made of brass or of iron (Judg. 16:21; Ps. 105:18; 149:8). The NT word (Mark 5:4, Luke 8:29) indicates that the fetters were for the feet.

FEVER (See Diseases)

FIELD. The Biblical "field" was generally not enclosed, but was marked off from its neighbors by stone markers at the corners, and sometimes one or two along the sides. Because they were unenclosed, and because of the usually unsettled conditions, a watchman was ordinarily employed, especially when the crop was nearing maturity. Besides the danger of human intruders, there was sometimes danger from straying cattle or even of cattle driven by thieving men (Exod. 22:5), and of fire if a Samson (Judg. 15:5) or an angry Absalom (II Sam. 14:30) were about. The word is used also in a larger sense for "territory," as in Genesis 36:35, where "the field of Moab" is any place in Moabite territory; and as in the parable of the tares (Matt. 13:38), where "the field is the world." Many of the ancient "fields" were the habitat of wild animals (Ps. 80:13).

FIG (See Plants)

FILLET. In the description of the tabernacle in Exodus 27:10,11 and 38:10-19 the "fillets" were the rods between the columns that supported the hangings of the court. In Jeremiah 52:21 the word means a cord for measuring. Cf. ASV in loco.

FINING-POT, found only in Proverbs 17:3 and 27:21 and means the crucible in which silver or gold is melted to be purified from dross.

FIR (See Plants)

FIRE (Heb. 'ēsh, Gr. pýr), probably one of the earliest discoveries of man; perhaps first seen as a result of lightning, but man soon invented ways to use it and found it a most useful servant as well as a cruel master. The first use of the word "fire" in Scripture is in Genesis 19:24, which says that "fire from the Lord out of heaven" destroyed the cities of the plain; but the use of fire was far more ancient. Before the Flood, Tubal-Cain (Gen. 4:22) was the father of smiths, in the account of the Abrahamic covenant (Gen. 15:17) one reads of a smoking furnace and a flaming torch. Many students believe that God showed His acceptance of Abel's offering (Gen. 4:4) by sending fire to consume it. In the institution of the Aaronic priestly ceremonies, God sent fire from heaven to consume the first offering (Lev. 9:24) to show His acceptance. This fire was to be kept burning continually (Lev. 6:9). When the two sons of Aaron, Nadab and Abihu, offered "strange fire," probably when intoxicated (Lev. 10:1,9,10), God's fiery judgment descended upon them and slew them. The final destiny of the wicked out of God is the "lake of fire" (Rev. 19:20; 20:10,14). This world will some day be consumed by fire (II Pet. 3:7-12).

God uses "fire" not only for judgment but also for testing, and so we learn that the works of all believers will be tested as by fire (I Cor. 3:12-15). God's glory is accompanied by fire (Ezek. 1:27),

the seraphim are fiery creatures (Isa. 6:2), as were the "fiery serpents" of Numbers 21:6 (from the same Hebrew verb saraph "to burn"), and our Lord is pictured with eyes as a flame of fire, hinting at his work of judgment (Rev. 1:14). Fire is used to refine gold and to cleanse us (Mal. 3:2).

FIREBRAND, from three Hebrew words: (1) a stick for stirring fire (Isa. 7:4, Amos 4:11), (2) brands, sparks (Prov. 26:18), and (3) a torch, as in Judges 15:4 and Judges 7:16. Job 12:5 has the same word, meaning a lamp that is burnt out.

FIREPAN (Heb. mahtâh), a vessel used for carrying live coals, as in Exodus 27:3. The Hebrew word is rendered "censer" 15 times, as in Leviticus 10:1, and "snuff dish" three times, as in Exodus 25:38. The meaning is evident from the context.

FIRKIN (See Weights and Measures)

FIRMAMENT (fîr'mà-měnt, Heb. raqîa'), the expanse of sky surrounding the earth, made by God on the second day of creation to "divide the waters from the waters" (Gen. 1:6). The Hebrews thought of the "firmament" as the apparent void above in which the clouds float and the lights of heaven are set by God. The Hebrew word suggests something stretched or spread out like a curtain (Isa. 40:22). It corresponds to the "empty space" of Job 26:7. The translators of the LXX rendered the Hebrew word raqîa' as steréoma, which has the meaning of a firm and solid structure — something beaten out, like brass. This fitted in with the Alexandrian conception of the universe as being a succession of spheres, each carrying a planet; but it is not in accord with the real meaning of the Hebrew word. St. Jerome, in the Vulgate, made c. A.D. 400, translated the word steréoma as firmamentum, which also suggests something solid or firm. Our English word "firmament" does not correctly suggest the real meaning of the Hebrew word. S.B.

FIRST-BEGOTTEN (Gr. protótokos), a term applied to the Lord Jesus Christ in Hebrews 1:6 and in Revelation 1:5, the former referring to "the eternal generation of the Son of God" and the latter to his resurrection. ASV has "firstborn" in both places.

FIRSTBORN (Heb. bekhôr, Gr. protótokos). The Hebrew word is used chiefly in men, but is used also of animals (Exod. 11:5). It appears that man early felt that God has the first claim on animals (Gen. 4:4). Among the ancestors of the Hebrews there was a sacrifice to the deity of the firstborn offspring of men and animals. Because the firstborn of the Israelites were preserved at the time of the first Passover, every firstborn male of man and beast became consecrated to Jehovah (Exod. 13:2; 34:19). The beasts were sacrificed, while the men were redeemed (Exod. 13:13,15; 34:20; cf. Lev. 27:6). At Sinai the Levites were substituted for the Israelite firstborn (Num. 3:12,41,46; 8:13-19). On the 30th day after birth the father brought his firstborn to the priest and paid five shekels to redeem him from service in the temple (cf. Luke 2:27).

Among the Israelites the firstborn son possessed special privileges. He succeeded his father as the head of the house and received as his share of the inheritance a double portion. Israel was Jehovah's firstborn (Exod. 4:22) and was thus entitled to special privileges, as compared with other peoples. Jesus Christ is described as the firstborn (Rom. 8:29; Col. 1:15; Heb. 1:6), an application of the term that may be traced back to Psalm 89:27, where the Messiah is referred to as the first-born of Jehovah. S.B.

FIRST DAY OF THE WEEK (See Sunday)

FIRST FRUITS (Heb. *rē'shîth*, *bikkûrîm*, Gr. *aparché*). In acknowledgement of the fact that all the products of the land came from God, and thankfulness for His goodness, Israelites brought as an offering to Him a portion of the fruits that ripened first, these being looked upon as an earnest of the coming harvest. Such an offering was made both on behalf of the nation (Lev. 23:10,17) and by individuals (Exod. 23:19; Deut. 26:1-11). These first fruits went for the support of the priesthood.

FISH (See Animals)

FISH GATE, an ancient gate on the E side of the wall of Jerusalem, just W of Gihon, where in the days of Nehemiah, men of Tyre congregated to sell fish and various wares on the sabbath (II Chron. 33:14; Neh. 13:16). It is probably identical with the "Middle Gate" of Jeremiah 39:3.

FISHING (See Occupations and Professions)

FISHHOOK, not only the means of catching fish as is done today, but also of keeping them, at least for a time (cf. Amos 4:2 with Job 41:1,2). Peter generally used a net, but see Matthew 17:27, where the Lord told him to cast a hook.

FISH POOL (Heb. *berēkhôth*, pool), in KJV occurs only in Song of Solomon 7:4, but the word should be rendered "pool," as it is in the RV.

FITCH (See Plants)

FLAG (See Plants)

FLAGON, a large container for wine. The word *nevel* is rendered "flagon" in Isaiah 22:24, elsewhere "bottle." The word *'ăshîshâh* rendered "flagon" in II Samuel 6:19 and other places in KJV should be "cakes of raisins" as in ASV.

FLAX (See Plants)

FLEAS (See Insects)

FLEECE, the shorn wool of a sheep. The first of the shearing was to be given to the priesthood, as a part of their means of support (Deut. 18:4). Gideon's experience (Judg. 6:37-40) has given rise to the custom of "putting out a fleece" in seeking God's guidance.

FLESH (Heb. *bāsār*, *shē'er*, Gr. *sárx*). 1. Literally, the soft part of the bodies of men and animals.

2. By metonymy, all animals, as in Genesis 6: 19.

3. Again by metonymy, mankind in general, as in Numbers 16:22, "the God of the spirits of all flesh."

4. Our ordinary human constitution as opposed to our mental and moral qualities as in Matthew 26:41, "the spirit indeed is willing but the flesh is weak."

5. Human nature deprived of the Spirit of God and dominated by sin (Rom. 7:14; I Cor. 3:1,3; Col. 2:18; I John 2:16).

FLESH-HOOK (Heb. *mazlēgh*), a metal implement with one or more teeth, used for handling large pieces of flesh, especially around the sacrificial altar. In the tabernacle it was made of brass (Exod. 27:3; 38:3), but in the temple it was made of gold (I Chron. 28:17). In Samuel's time it was used to remove the priests' share of the meat offering (I Sam. 2:13,14).

FLIES (See Insects)

FLINT (See Minerals)

FLOCK, a collection of sheep under the care of a shepherd, sometimes including goats as well (Gen. 27:9). The larger animals such as cattle, camels, asses, etc. were counted as herds, not flocks. Israel lived in OT times in a pastoral civilization and a man's flocks made up most of his wealth, providing clothing, food, milk and animals for sacrifice. Figuratively both Israel and the Church are counted as flocks, and God is the Good Shepherd (Isa. 40: 11; Matt. 26:31; Luke 12:32; I Pet. 5:2,3).

FLOOD, DELUGE.

I. Historical Background of Flood Interpretations. The Noahic flood has been a subject for discussion among scientists and theologians for many centuries.

During the middle ages the Church was the authority in all areas of thought. Science as we know it today did not exist, for with its theological orientation the Church looked with disfavor upon observations which did not have theological explanations. It was only natural then that when the early geologists observed many thousands of feet of sedimentary rocks (those formed from particles of previously existing rock or chemically precipitated from solution) in the mountains of Europe and the British Isles, they should turn to the Church for an explanation. The easiest answer for the layers of sediments was that they were laid down by the Noahic Flood. As the sedimentary layers were studied further, problems arose when it was discovered that not all the layers were contemporaneous. It was also readily observed that some sediments had been deposited, hardened into rock, folded into mountain ranges, eroded off and then covered with new sediments. At some places the sedimentary rock layers were cut by formerly molten rock material which indicated volcanic activity after the sediments were deposited. Sixteenth and seventeenth century scientists attempted to harmonize the interpretation of field observations with church tradition.

As a result, many interpretations of the meaning and physical characteristics of the Flood have been suggested, modified, abandoned, and sometimes reproposed. These interpretations have produced some highly improbable explanations of the events of the deluge which have so confused the issue that it is difficult to separate intelligent exegesis of the Biblical accounts from fanciful eisegesis of the same passages. The reality of the Flood can hardly be questioned, however, because of the many references to it in both the Old and New Testament. Among these are chapters 6, 7, and 8 of Genesis, Genesis 9:11, 28; 10:1, 32; Matt. 24:38, 39; Luke 17:27; II Peter 2:5.

II. The Purpose of the Flood. An important aspect of the deluge is that God preserved some men, for Noah and his family were saved from destruction by going into an ark which Noah made according to God's specifications, and in which he gathered animals and birds preserved to replenish the earth.

It is apparent from Gen. 6:5-7 and other passages such as II Peter 2:5, 6 that the Flood was brought upon the earth as a judgment on the sins of the people. Man had become so sinful that "it repented the Lord that He had made man on the earth" (Gen. 6:6 KJV). In Scripture the reference to the Flood is linked with the judgment at the second coming of the Lord (Matt. 24:39). It is also mentioned in relation to the destruction of Sodom and Gomorrah (Luke 17:27-29; II Peter 2:5, 6).

The purpose of God as stated in Genesis 6:7 indicates that His judgment was not against the inanimate rocks or against plants, but against "man and beast, and the creeping things and the fowls of the air."

Annipadda's Foundation Tablet, a marble slab found by Dr. Woolley in a cornerstone of a temple near Ur. This is one of the oldest historical documents ever found, dating back to soon after the Flood. UMP

III. The Phenomena of the Flood. In the following passage, however (Gen. 6:11-13), the earth is included in the judgment. There is again difference of opinion as to the meaning of Gen. 6:13 in which God said, "The end of all flesh is come before me: for the earth is filled with violence through them; and, behold I will destroy them with the earth" (KJV). That the earth was not utterly destroyed as it will be in the last times (II Peter 2:10) is apparent. Some writers would interpret Gen. 6:13 to mean that great geologic catastrophes overwhelmed the earth's surface, while others point out that Gen. 6:6, 7, 12, and 13 all stress that it was the sin of living things ("flesh") that was to be punished and that the effect upon the inanimate rocks of the world is only incidental to punishing man.

Despite all attempts at scientific explanation of the minute details of the Flood, there seems to be no doubt that God worked a miracle in causing the Flood. In II Peter 3:5, 6 the Flood is compared with the creation of the world and is a miracle of the same order. In the same passage, II Peter 3:7ff, the final destruction of the world is given the same miraculous explanation as the Noahic Flood.

IV. The Source of the Flood. The Biblical account of the accumulation and dispersal of the waters of the Flood is very brief. In Gen. 7:11 the source of the water is explained ". . . all the fountains of the great deep were broken up and the windows of heaven were opened."

The Hebrew word *Tehom*, translated *great deep* in the KJV, is the same used in Gen. 1:2. That this does not necessarily include all the oceans is shown by its use in Isaiah 51:10 when it refers to the escape of the Israelites through "the depths of the sea" (the Red Sea). The word "fountain" (Hebrew *ma'yan*) means literally *place of a spring*. This could mean that water rose from the ocean or from fresh water springs on the earth or both.

V. Suggested Causes of the Flood. Some would prefer to believe that the expression "fountains of the great deep were broken up" indicates that the ocean (actually the Persian Gulf, an arm of the ocean) invaded the land. Others have assumed this implies volcanic activity and that some of the water of the Flood is "juvenile water" which is formed from the oxygen and hydrogen which may occur as separate elements in the molten rock deep in the earth's crust. This school of thought would also attribute a great deal of diastrophism (movements of the solid crust which result in a relative change of position of the rock formations concerned) to this verse. This could account for the subsidence of the mountains of the earth so that they could be covered more easily by the waters of the deluge.

To attribute volcanic activity to Gen. 7:11 is highly speculative, for at no place in the Genesis account of the Flood is any more specific description of conditions given. The fact that igneous rock (rock formed by the cooling of molten rock material) is found between or cutting sedimentary rock layers is not good evidence for volcanic activity at the time of the Flood. Sediments which have been laid down during historic time have been cut by lava coming up to present day volcanoes. It has also been observed that the oldest layers are also cut by igneous rocks. It seems apparent, therefore, that volcanic activity has gone on throughout the world's history. It is not possible to designate any particular rock body as being coincident with the Flood.

"The windows of heaven were opened" has been accepted as a description of rain. Some have seen this as a torrential downpour greater than normally experienced on the earth today. A hypothesis has been proposed that the earth from the time of Creation (or at least man's creation) was surrounded by a canopy of water in some form until the time of the Flood. The canopy was suggested as being water vapor, ice or liquid water. If such a canopy existed, it is proposed that its transfer from around the earth to the earth as water would cause a rain for many days.

The canopy idea, although firmly entrenched in literature, has doubtful Biblical authority. The language of Ezekiel, "the likeness of the firmament upon the heads of the living creature was as the colour of the terrible crystal stretched forth over their heads above" (Ezek. 1:22), has been cited as authority, with "the terrible crystal" referring to an ice canopy. This theory seems highly speculative. Again it should be noted that if a miraculous explanation for the Flood is accepted, physical explanations are not necessary.

VI. The Duration of the Flood. The length of the Flood is generally agreed upon within a few days. The Hebrews used a solar calendar in contrast to the Babylonian lunar month and the Egyptian arbitrary 365-day year. Most authorities would put the number of days from the time the rain started (Genesis 7:11) to the time Noah left the ark (Genesis 8:14) between 371 and 376 days.

VII. Traditions of the Flood. Traditions regarding a disastrous flood which occurred long ago are handed down by many peoples. Isolated tribes in all parts of the world have been found to have such traditions. This is not surprising when the destruction caused by present day floods as well as hurricanes and tornadoes accompanied by great rains is considered. A tribe occupying a limited area could be destroyed completely by one storm. If there were survivors they would date their civilization from such an event. Some traditional floods have been dated as having occurred within the last few hundred years by archaeological evidence.

The Hebrews, Assyrians and Babylonians, who lived within the area of the Tigris-Euphrates basin, all had traditions of a great flood. These narratives stated the purpose of the flood to be punishment because the world was full of violence, but the Hebrew story remained simple and credible, whereas the other accounts became complex and fanciful. Only the Biblical account retained a monotheistic viewpoint. Although it is not possible to affirm dogmatically that all of these three histories had a common origin, it seems probable that they did.

VIII. The Universality of the Flood. One of the great differences of opinion in describing the Flood concerns its extent. Traditionally most Biblical interpreters considered the submergence to be universal; that is, that it covered the entire globe including the highest mountains. The reasons proposed to defend this viewpoint include the fact that in the Gen. account universal terms are used. "*All* the high hills that were under the whole heaven were covered" (Gen. 7:19) and "*all* flesh died" (Gen. 7:21). It has been pointed out that if the Flood were local there would be no need for an ark to preserve Noah, for God could have directed him to move with the animals to an area that was not to be submerged.

The fact that many civilizations have flood traditions has been cited as an evidence for a universal flood. The same evidence could be used to argue for a local flood because the accounts of floods in other parts of the world are less like the Hebrew tradition than those of the Assyrians and Babylonians who lived in the same areas as the Hebrews.

Today many conservative scholars defend a local flood. The crux of their argument seems to center in the covenant relation of God to man. He deals with certain groups, such as the children of Israel. The reasoning in regard to Noah is that Noah was not a preacher of righteousness to peoples of other areas but was concerned with the culture from which Abraham eventually came. Physical arguments have also been raised against a universal flood: origin and disposal of the amount of water necessary to make a layer six miles thick over the whole world, the effect upon plant life by being covered for a year, the effect upon fresh water life of a sea which contained salt from the ocean, and the fact that many topographic features of the earth such as cinder cones which show no evidence of erosion by a flood and which are much older than the flood could possibly be. It seems, therefore, that a person can advocate either a local or a universal concept of the Flood and find evidence to support his view.

IX. Chronology of the Flood. Although Ussher in his chronology placed the flood at 2348 B.C., most scholars recognize a much earlier date.

Scholars who have advocated that the earth has developed to its present condition by a series of major calamities have been called catastrophists. These consider the Noahic Flood as the greatest of these catastrophes and believe that the Pleistocene ice age was related to the Flood. If, as the catastrophists believe, the Flood was associated in some way with the end of the Pleistocene ice age, a date of at least 10,000 B.C. would have to be accepted. Archaeological and anthropological evidence has caused some scholars to put the origin of man back more than 100,000 years so that there is not any general agreement among conservative scholars concerning the actual date of the deluge. The lack of consensus with regard to the details of the Flood should make all aware of the danger of placing so much importance on the interpretation of this important event that the other lessons of the Bible are missed.

Suggested References:

Geikie, Sir Archibald, *The Founders of Geology,* London: Macmillan, 1905, pp. 42-72.

Gillespie, Charles Coulston, *Genesis and Geology,* New York: Harper, 1959, pp. 41-72.

Ramm, Bernard, *The Christian View of Science and Scripture,* Grand Rapids: Eerdmans, 1954, pp. 229-253.

Whitcomb, John C. and Morris, Henry M., *The Genesis Flood,* Philadelphia: Presbyterian and Reformed Publishing Co., 1961. D.B.

Tabulated Chronology of the Flood

1. The making of the ark (Gen. 6:14)	
2. Collection of the animals (Gen. 7:9)	7 days before the rain started
3. Fountains of the great deep were broken up and the windows of heaven were opened	Second month, 17th day in Noah's 600th year
4. Rain (Gen. 7:12)	40 days and 40 nights
5. All the high hills covered (Gen. 7:19)	
6. Water prevailed upon the earth (Gen. 7:24)	150 days
7. Water returned from off the earth (Gen. 8:3)	150 days
8. Ark rested upon the mountains of Ararat (Gen. 8:4)	Seventh month, 17th day
9. Waters decreased (Gen. 8:4)	
10. Tops of mountains seen (Gen. 8:5)	Tenth month, 1st day
11. Noah waited (Gen. 8:6)	40 days
12. Noah sent forth raven and a dove; dove returned (Gen. 8:7-9)	
13. Noah waited (Gen. 8:10)	7 days
14. Noah sent forth dove again (Gen. 8:10); dove returned with olive branch (Gen. 8:11)	7 days
15. Noah waited (Gen. 8:12)	7 days
16. Noah sent forth dove which did not return (Gen. 8:12)	7 days
17. Noah removed covering; face of the ground was dry (Gen. 8:13)	1st month, 1st day, Noah's 601st year
18. Earth dried; Noah left ark (Gen. 8:14)	2nd month, 27th day

FLOUR, fine-crushed and sifted grain, generally wheat or rye or barley (Judg. 7:13). Eastern flour was not quite as fine or as white as ours, and as a result, the bread was more wholesome. The "meat" offerings, were of flour. "Meat" here should be "meal." (Cf. Lev. 6:15 in KJV and ASV.)

FLOWER (See Plants)

FLUTE (See Music)

FLY (See Insects)

FOAL (See Animals)

FODDER, the mixed food of cattle, generally from several kinds of grain sown together (Job 6:5; Job 24:6 "corn" in ASV; Isa. 30:24).

FOOD, nutritive material taken into a living organism to sustain life, to promote growth and the repair of the tissues, and to give energy for the vital processes. The Bible says little about food for animals. Bible animals for the most part are herbivorous, though carnivorous ones are mentioned. Some omnivorous animals, like swine, are mentioned, but almost always in a contemptuous way (Matt. 7:6) and swine were forbidden as food (Isa. 65:4).

At the very beginning of human history, Adam's food for his first day was probably some ripe fruit near him as he awoke to consciousness, and when he began to hunger, his nose as well as his eyes directed him to his first meal. Food and water would of course be necessary from that first day. Before sin had entered into human history, God apparently prescribed a vegetarian diet, both for man and beast (Gen. 1:29,30), but one must not build too much on silence here as regarding the content of diet. By the time that Noah built the ark, there was a distinction between clean and unclean beasts (Gen. 7:2,3) and when God made his covenant with Noah after the flood (Gen. 9:3,4) flesh was permitted as food. Blood was forbidden, and it seems that the reason for this prohibition was as much theological as sanitary for "the life (Hebrew *nephesh* or soul) is in the blood" (cf. Lev. 17:11). Coming down now to the time of Moses, fat was also prohibited as food (Lev. 3:16,17) and again, the reason given is religious but not hygienic. In the time of the Restoration (Neh. 8:10) Nehemiah encouraged the people to "eat the fat" while celebrating a national "Thanksgiving day." One might imagine here that Nehemiah had forgotten that "all the fat is the Lord's" (Lev. 3:16) until one notices that the Hebrew word for "fat" here is not the one used in Leviticus. The word in Nehemiah could just as well be rendered "dainties" and refers probably to the various rich confections of which Eastern people are so fond.

The animals most frequently mentioned in the Bible are the domestic herbivorous animals, and these are divided sharply into two classes; the clean and the unclean. (See Lev. 11) The clean animals were to be used for food and for sacrifice and the four-footed ones were distinguished by their hoofs and by their chewing the cud. The camel chews the cud but does not part the hoof and so was considered unclean, though its milk was and is greatly used by desert-dwellers. Swine part the hoof but do not chew the cud, and so were ceremonially unclean. They were perhaps prohibited as food because of the mischievous *trichina spiralis*, a worm which has long infested swine, and from half-roasted pork can enter the human body and create great harm. Of the seafood which was reckoned unclean the principal ones were oysters and shrimps. One can easily realize how dangerous they would be in a land where climate was hot

Cooking in a peasant home. Note the pottery cooking pot and the fire of thorns (cf. Psalm 58:9). © MPS

and there was no refrigeration. In other words, most of the distinctions between "clean" and "unclean" foods were clearly based upon sanitary reasons.

In Palestine and Syria, fresh fruit can be obtained throughout the year. Oranges last in the spring till the very short season of apricots arrives. After the apricots come the plums, figs, pomegranates, etc., which last until the grapes appear, and they in turn remain until the oranges and lemons are again in season.

The preparation of food differs from Western custom. Generally meat is eaten not in steaks and roasts, but cut up and served with rice, and often imbedded in "coosa" (a kind of squash) or wrapped in cabbage or grape leaves. The bread is not as white and fine as is ours, but is far more healthful. A common laborer often takes as his lunch two hollow loaves of bread, one filled with cheese and the other with olives. There were several sorts of sweets, of which dried figs boiled in grape molasses (Gen. 43:11) was one of the best known. Near the sea, fish were very commonly eaten. Various kinds of vegetables were used: beans, lentils, millet, melons, onions, gourds; also spices: cummin, mint, mustard, and salt; and honey.

Food is a figure of spiritual sustenance. Peter tells his readers to "desire earnestly the sincere [unadulterated] milk of the Word, that ye may grow thereby." Peter was writing to young Christians (I Pet. 2:1-3) but Paul clearly distinguishes between Scripture which can be likened to "milk for babes" and that which can be compared with "strong meat," or solid food.   A.B.F.

FOOL, in modern usage, a dolt or a simpleton, but in Scripture generally impiety or lack of moral good sense is implied as well. "The fool hath said in his heart, There is no God" (Ps. 14:1; 53:1). Solomon in his writings, Proverbs and Ecclesiastes, makes about 80 statements about fools, showing their emptiness, their conceit and pride, their boasting and self-confidence, and in four cases in Ecclesiastes, their thick-headedness and their wordiness (Eccl. 2:19; 10:3,14). In Matthew 23:17 we read how the Lord called the scribes and Pharisees fools; not implying intellectual stupidity, but spiritual blindness. Men can be clever in mind, but at the same time fools in spiritual matters.

FOOT, the part of the body on which men and animals walk, or that part of furniture on which it stands. As regards furniture, the base of the laver just outside the tabernacle is several times called its foot (Exod. 30:18; 35:16, etc.). The foot of man, because in contact with the earth, is thought to be less honorable than the hand or the head, but in the Christian church "the foot" (i.e. the lowest member) should not suffer a feeling of inferiority or of envy, and say "Because I am not the hand, I am not of the body" (I Cor. 12:15) nor should the more prominent directing member ("the head") say to the foot, "I have no need of thee." In the East, shoes are ordinarily removed when entering a house. On entering a house, the lowest servant is detailed to wash the feet of the visitor. So the priests, before entering the tabernacle in divine service, must wash their feet as well as their hands at the laver, just outside, so that no trace of defilement would accompany their service. (For spiritual application, see John 13:10, Heb. 10:22). In lands where irrigation is practiced, men use shovels to move the earth for the larger channels, but a foot will suffice for a small channel to water a furrow (Deut. 11:10). To humiliate an enemy utterly, one sometimes put his foot upon the captives' necks as Joshua's captains did (Josh. 10:24).

FOOTMAN. 1. A member of the infantry as distinguished from the cavalry—horsemen and charioteers. The bulk of ancient armies consisted of footmen.

2. A runner, one of the king's bodyguard (I Sam. 22:17).

FOOTSTOOL (Heb. *keves*, Gr. *hypopódion*), a word is used in Scripture both literally (II Chron. 9:18; James 2:3) and figuratively: of the earth Isa. 66:1; Matt. 5:35), of the Temple (Lam. 2:1), of the Ark (Ps. 99:5), and of subjection, especially of heathen enemies by the Messianic king (Ps. 110:1; Matt. 22:44; Acts 2:35).

FORD (Heb. *ma'var*), a shallow place in a stream where men and animals can cross on foot. In the small streams of Palestine and Syria, fording places are quite frequent and can easily be found simply by following the main roads which in many cases are mere bridle paths. Such probably were the fords of the Jabbok (Gen. 32:22) where Jacob halted, and of the Arnon (Isa. 16:2). The Jordan, however, is a strong and rapid stream, and its fording places are few and far between. When Israel crossed, God miraculously stopped the waters upstream by a landslide. John the Baptist baptized at Bethabara (John 1:28 KJV), which name indicates that a ford was there. Joshua's spies (Josh. 2:7) evidently forded the Jordan, and Ehud (Judg. 3:28) took the same place to prevent Moabites from crossing there. Farther up the river and about two hundred years after Ehud, Jephthah (Judg. 12:5,6) made his famous "Shibboleth test" at a ford of the Jordan.

FOREHEAD, that part of the face which is above the eyes. Because it is so prominent, its appearance often determines our opinion of the person. In Ezekiel 16:12 KJV reads "I put a jewel on thy forehead," but ASV (more correctly) has, "I put a ring upon thy nose." The forehead is used as a very dishonorable word where we read of a "harlot's forehead" (Jer. 3:3) indicating utter shamelessness, and at the same time it stands for courage, as when God told Ezekiel (Ezek. 3:9) that he had made the prophet's forehead harder than flint against the foreheads of the people. The forehead is also the place for the front of a crown or mitre (Exod. 28:38), where the emblem of holiness on Aaron's forehead would make the gifts of the people acceptable before the Lord. A mark was put upon the foreheads of the men of Jerusalem who

mourned for its wickedness, and they were spared in a time of terrible judgment (Ezek. 9:4). Similarly in Revelation 7 God's servants were sealed by an angel; and it seems that this seal not only saved the elect ones but it showed forth their godly character. In the ages of glory that are to come, the name of God will be marked on the foreheads of his own people (Rev. 22:4).   A.B.F.

FOREIGNER (Heb. *nokhrî, stranger*; Gr. *póroikos, sojourner*). The Jewish people divided all humanity into two groups, of which they belonged in the smaller and more select group; namely, Jews and Gentiles. "Lo, it is a people that dwelleth alone, and shall not be reckoned among the nations" (Num. 23:9b ASV). With the Greeks, the division was Greeks and Barbarians (Rom. 1:14). The common word for foreigner (Hebrew, *nokri*) is generally translated "stranger" and seems generally to be used with a slightly contemptuous meaning. "Are we not accounted of him strangers?" (Gen. 31:15). It generally implies also a heathen religion, as in I Kings 11:1 where "Solomon loved many strange women."

Foreigners were debarred from a number of privileges accorded only to Israelites: eating the passover (Exod. 12:43), entering the sanctuary (Ezek. 44:9), becoming king (Deut. 17:15). Israelites were forbidden to enter into covenant relations with them (Exod. 23:32), or to intermarry with them on equal terms (Exod. 34:12,16). They could be sold the flesh of animals that had died, which Israelites were forbidden to eat (Deut. 14:21); they could be loaned money with interest (Deut. 23:20); and debts could be collected from them even in the year of release (Deut. 15:3). In NT times the Jews even refrained from eating and drinking with Gentiles (Acts 11:3; Gal. 2:12). Foreigners, could, however, always become Israelites by fully accepting the Law and its requirements.   A.B.F.

The ford of the Jabbok (Zerka) River, near where Jacob wrestled with the angel. © MPS

FOREKNOWLEDGE (See Election)

FOREORDINATION (See Election)

FORERUNNER (Gr. *pródromos*). Rulers, intending a visit, often send advance agents to prepare the way for their reception; so John the Baptist was the forerunner of our Lord (Isa. 40:3; Luke 3:4-6). The word "forerunner" is used of Jesus, who has preceded us into the visible presence of God to insure our personal access to God (Heb. 6:20).

FORESKIN (Heb. *'orlâh,* Gr. *akrobustía*), the fold of skin which is cut off in the operation of circumcision. Just as the American Indians used scalps of enemies as signs of their prowess, so David presented two hundred foreskins of the Philistines (I Sam. 18:25-27). In Deuteronomy 10:16 the word is used figuratively meaning submission to God's law. In Habakkuk 2:16 it refers to the indecent exhibitionism of a drunken man.

FOREST (Heb. *ya'ar, sevakh, āvîm*), a piece of land covered with trees naturally planted, as distinguished from a park where man's hand is more evident. In ancient times, most of the highlands of Canaan and Syria except the tops of the high mountains were covered with forests. Several forests are mentioned by name, those of Lebanon the most often, for these were famous for the cedar and the fir trees. From the forest of Lebanon, Hiram of Tyre (I Kings 5:8-10) brought down cedar and fir trees to the sea and floated them southward to the port which Solomon had constructed, from which his servants could transport the timbers to Jerusalem. Solomon's "house of the forest of Lebanon" (I Kings 7:2, etc.) was apparently his own house, and was so named because of the prevalence of cedar in its structure. KJV names the "forest of his Carmel" in II Kings 19:23 and Isaiah 37:24, but ASV renders it more truly the "forest of his fruitful field" without attempting to locate it. "The forest of Arabia" (Isa. 21:13) is also incapable of location upon a map. It was in a wood or forest in Ephraim that the crucial battle of Absalom's rebellion was fought (II Sam. 18) and "the wood devoured more people than the sword devoured" (v. 8).

FORGIVENESS (Heb. *kāphar, nāsā', sālah;* Gr. *apolúein, charízesthai, áphesis, páresis*). In the OT, *pardon,* and in the NT, *remission,* are often used as the equivalents of *forgiveness.* The idea of forgiveness is found in either religious or social relations, and means the giving up of resentment or claim to requital on account of an offense. The offense may be a deprivation of a person's property, rights, or honor; or it may be a violation of moral law.

The normal conditions of forgiveness are repentance and the willingness to make reparation, or atonement; and the effect of forgiveness is the restoration of both parties to the former state of relationship. Christ taught that forgiveness is a duty, and that no limit should be set to the extent of forgiveness (Luke 17:4). An unforgiving spirit is one of the most serious of sins (Matt. 18:34,35; Luke 15:28-30). The ground of forgiveness by God of man's sins is the atoning death of Christ. Jesus taught that the offended party is, when necessary, to go to the offender and try to bring him to repentance (Luke 17:3). God's forgiveness is conditional upon man's forgiveness of the wrongs done him (Matt. 5:23,24; 6:12; Col. 1:14; 3:13). Those forgiven by God before the Incarnation were forgiven because of Christ, whose death was foreordained from eternity. Christ's atonement was retroactive in its effect (Heb. 11:40). God's for-

giveness seems, however, to be limited. Christ speaks of the unpardonable sin (Matt. 12:31,32), and John speaks of the sin unto death (I John 5:16). The deity of Christ is evidenced by His claim to the power to forgive sins (Mark 2:7; Luke 5:21; 7:49). S.B.

FORK, mentioned only in I Samuel 13:21 as the translation of two words which could be rendered "a three-tined gatherer." It probably was the ancient type of our modern pitchfork.

FORNICATION (Heb. *zānâh,* Gr. *porneía*), unlawful sexual intercourse of an unwed person. It is to be distinguished from adultery which has to do with unfaithfulness on the part of a married person, and from rape which is a crime of violence and without the consent of the person sinned against. When these sins are mentioned in the Bible, they are often figurative of disloyalty. Idolatry is practically adultery from God. This ugly sin ought not even to be a subject of conversation among Christians (Eph. 5:3,4) and is commonly associated with the obscene worship of the heathen. For the spiritualizing of this sin, see Jeremiah 2:20-36, Ezekiel 16, and Hosea 1-3, where it applied to Israel; and Revelation 17, where it applies to Rome.

Ancient fortifications at Lachish. © MPS

FORT, FORTRESS. Every city in ancient times was fortified by a wall and its citadel. The KJV often speaks of such cities as "fenced," and other terms are also used by the KJV and the RV. Even before the Israelites entered Canaan, they were terrified by the reports of cities "great and fortified up to heaven" (Num. 13:ff; Deut. 1:28). These cities were not necessarily large; they were usually, indeed, quite small. Jerusalem was so well fortified that it was not until the time of David that the city was captured from the Jebusites. Usually the city was built on a hill, and the fortifications followed the natural contour of the hill. Many times there was both an inner and an outer wall. The walls were built of brick and stone, and were many feet thick. After the Israelites entered the land, they too built fenced cities (Deut. 28:52; II Sam. 20:6).

FORTUNATUS (fôr-tū-nā'tŭs, Gr. *Phortounátos, blessed, fortunate*), a Christian who came with two others to bring gifts from the Corinthian church to Paul when he was about to leave Ephesus in A.D. 59 (I Cor. 16:17).

FORUM APPII, rendered Appii Forum in KJV (Acts 28:15), but more correctly in ASV as "The Market of Appius," a place 43 miles SE of Rome, where Paul was met by the brethren. It was a station on the famous Appian Way to Naples.

FOUNDATION (Heb. *yāsadh, to found;* Gr. *katabolé, themélios*), that upon which a building stands, or else the first layer of the actual structure; its walls. The word is often used figuratively. A temporal use of the word is found at least nine times in the NT, referring to the time of the foundation of the world. Some other figurative uses: as when the Church is built upon "the foundation of the apostles and prophets" (Eph. 2:20), or when simple Christian teaching is based upon "the foundation of repentance from dead works" (Heb. 6:1), or as when Jesus Christ is spoken of as the foundation of Christian theology (I Cor. 3:10,11).

FOUNTAIN, a spring of water issuing from the earth. In a country near the desert, springs, pools, pits, cisterns and fountains are of great importance and many towns and other locations are named from the springs at their sites: e.g., Enaim, "two springs" (Gen. 38:21 ASV); Enam, with the same meaning (Josh. 15:34); En-gedi, i.e., "the fountain of the kid" (Josh. 15:62); and a dozen others, like the English Springfield, or the French Fontainebleau. In the story of the Flood "the fountains of the great deep" were broken up, referring to great convulsions of the earth's surface (Gen. 7:11) which, with the rain, caused the Flood; and in the preparation of the earth for man, the Son of God (Wisdom personified) was with the Father before there were any "fountains abounding with water" (Prov. 8:24). The word is used both literally and figuratively, both pleasantly and unpleasantly. Figuratively, it refers to the source of hemorrhages (Lev. 20:18; Mark 5:29). In Proverbs, compare "a troubled fountain and a corrupt spring" (25:26) with "a fountain of life" (13:14;

The Virgin's Fountain at Nazareth. © MPS

14:27). In the Bridegroom's praise of his pure bride (S. of Sol. 4:12,15) she is first "a fountain sealed" then "a fountain of gardens." In the curse of Ephraim (Hos. 13:15), "his fountain shall be dried up" as a terrible punishment; but on the pleasant side, David speaks (Ps. 36:9) of "the fountain of life" as being with the Lord. In the Lord's conversation with the woman at the well (John 4:14), He told her of "a well of water springing up into everlasting life." Among the delights of heaven, will be "the fountain of the water of life" (Rev. 21:6).   A.B.F.

FOUNTAIN GATE, the gate at the SE corner of the walls of ancient Jerusalem, mentioned only in Nehemiah (2:14; 3:15; 12:37).

FOWL (See Birds)

FOWLER (Heb. *yōkēsh*), a bird-catcher. Because fowlers used snares, gins, bird-lime, etc. and caught their prey by trickery, "fowler" is used to describe those who try to ensnare the unwary and bring them to ruin (Ps. 91:3; 124:7; Hos. 9:8).

FOX (See Animals)

FRANKINCENSE (Heb. *levōnâh,* from root meaning *whiteness*), a resinous substance obtained from certain trees of the *Boswellia* genus and the family of balsams. To obtain the frankincense, an incision is made through the bark of the tree deep into the trunk, and a strip of bark is peeled off. As the whitish juice exudes, it hardens in the atmosphere and is gathered after about three months' exposure in the summer. When sold, the frankincense is in the form of "tears" or of irregular lumps, and has been used as a perfume, as a medicine, and by Egyptians and Hebrews in their religious rites. It is spoken of as coming from Arabia (Isa. 60:6; Jer. 6:20) and perhaps from Palestine (S. of Sol. 4:6,14). It was an ingredient of the perfume for the most holy place (Exod. 30:34-38) which was exclusively reserved for this particular use. Frankincense was mingled with the flour in the meal-offering (Lev. 2:1,15,16) but was rigidly excluded from the sin-offering (Lev. 5:11) which was far from being an offering of a sweet savor. Soon after the birth of Jesus, the wise men presented to Him gifts of gold, of frankincense and myrrh; and these precious gifts, presented in worship may well have helped to finance His sojourn in Egypt (Matt. 2:11,15). See PLANTS.

FREEMAN, a rendering of two slightly different Gr. words, *apeleútheros,* found in I Corinthians 7:22, where it refers to a slave who has received his freedom, although in this verse the reference is to one who has received spiritual freedom from the Lord, and *eleútheros,* found in Galatians 4:22,23, 30, Revelation 6:15, where it means a free man as opposed to a slave.

FREEWILL OFFERING (See Offerings)

FRET (Heb. *hārâh, mā'ar*). 1. To fret is to be vexed, chafed, irritated, or to be angry; and the godly man is not to fret himself (Ps. 37:1,7,8). By contrast, one should have his mind stayed on the Lord (Isa. 26:3).

    2. A fretting leprosy (Lev. 13:51,52) is a sharp, bitter, painful leprosy.

FRINGE (Heb. *tsîtsith, tassel, lock*), the tassel of twisted cords fastened to the outer garments of Israelites to remind them of their obligations as Israelites to be loyal to Jehovah (Num. 15:38, 39; Deut. 22:12). Later they became distinct badges of Judaism (cf. Zech. 8:23). They were common in NT times (Matt. 9:20; 14:36; 23:5).

FROG (See Plagues)

FRONTLET (Heb. *tôtāphôth,* from *tûph, to bind*), anything bound on the forehead, particularly phylacteries, which were worn on the forehead and on the arms. Phylacteries were prayer bands consisting of the following passages from the Law of Moses: Exodus 13:1-10; 11-16; Deuteronomy 6: 4-9; 11:13-21, which were put in small leather cases and fastened to the forehead and the left arm. They were worn by all male Jews during the time of morning prayer, except on the sabbath and festivals.

FROST, (Heb. *kephōr, hănāmāl*), usual in winter on the hills and high plains in Bible lands. Frosts in the late spring do great damage to fruit. The manna in the wilderness is compared to hoar-frost (Exod. 16:14). Frost is an evidence of God's power (Job 37:10; 38:29).

FRUIT (Heb. *perî,* Gr. *karpós*). The fruits most often mentioned in Scripture are the grape, pomegranate, fig, olive, apple; all of which are grown today; but the lemon, orange, plum and apricot were unknown or at least unmentioned. The word "fruit" is often used metaphorically: "the fruit of thy womb" (Deut. 7:13, cf. 28:11), "the fruit of their own way" (Prov. 1:31), "fruit unto life eternal" (John 4:36) etc. The fruit of the Holy Spirit consists of all the Christian virtues (Gal. 5:22,23).

FRYING PAN (Heb. *marhesheth*), properly a pot or saucepan in which things are boiled or baked. The word occurs only in Leviticus 2:7 and 7:9 and no frying is intended or implied.

FUEL (Heb. *'ōkhlâh,* or *ma'ăkhōleth, food*). In ancient times wood, charcoal, various kinds of thorn bushes, dried grass, and the dung of camels and cattle was used as fuel. There is no evidence that coal was used by the Hebrews as fuel; their houses had no chimneys (Isa. 9:5,19; Ezek. 4:12, 15; 15:4,6; 21:32).

FULLER (See Occupations and Professions)

FULLER'S FIELD (Heb. *sedhēh khôvēs*), a field, just outside of Jerusalem, where fullers washed the cloth material they were processing. A highway and a conduit for water passed through it (Isa. 7:3; 36:2). It was so near the city that the Assyrian Rabshakeh (*q.v.*), standing and speaking in the field, could be heard by those on the city wall (II Kings 18:17). Its exact site is in dispute.

FULLER'S SOAP, an alkali prepared from the ashes of certain plants and used for cleansing and fulling new cloth. The word is used figuratively in Malachi 3:2.

FUNERAL, the ceremonies used in disposing of a dead human body; whether by burying, cremation, or otherwise. The word does not occur in the Bible. The rites differed with the place, the religion, and the times; except for royal burials in Egypt, the elaborate ceremonies that are used with us today were not held.

In Palestine, as a general thing, there was no embalmment and the body was buried a few hours after death; sometimes in a tomb, but more often in a cave. Coffins were unknown. The body was washed and often anointed with aromatic spices (John 12:7; 19:39). The procession of mourners, made up of relatives and friends of the deceased, were led by professional mourning women, whose shrieks and lamentations pierced the air. It was an insult to a man's reputation to be refused proper burial (Jer. 22:19). The "Tombs of the kings" on the E side of Jerusalem, and the "Garden tomb," where our Lord's body was laid, are evidences of the two types of burial. In Egypt, the bodies were embalmed so skillfully that many of them are recognizable today after the lapse of thousands of years.

FURLONG (See Weights and Measures)

FURNACE (Heb. *kivshān, kûr, attûn, 'ălîl, tannûr;* Gr. *káminos*). Furnaces for central heating are not mentioned in the Bible nor are they much used today in Bible lands. The burning fiery furnace of Daniel 3 was probably a smelting furnace and used only incidentally for the punishment of men. The most common word "tannur" could be and often is more properly rendered oven (cf. Gen. 15: 17 with Lev. 2:4; Hos. 7:4-7). Furnaces were used for melting gold (Prov. 17:3), silver (Ezek. 22: 22), brass or bronze (Ezek. 22:18) and including also tin, iron and lead and for baking bread (Neh. 3:11; Isa. 31:9). The word is often used figuratively, as in Deuteronomy 4:20 where it means Egypt and in Matthew 13:42, which refers to the punishment of the wicked at the end of the world. Quite recently, Solomon's ingenious smelting furnaces near Elath on the Gulf of Akaba have been found, arranged so that the constant north wind furnished a natural draft for melting the brass or copper. After being prepared there, the metal was taken to the plain of the Jordan for casting (I Kings 7:46).

FURNITURE (Heb. *kār, kēlîm;* Gr. *skevé*). In the Bible the principal reference to furniture is in the articles in and about the tabernacle and the temple. The main items were the large altar and the laver, outside; then the table of showbread (KJV "shewbread"), the lamp-stand, or "candlestick" and the altar of incense in the holy place, then in the holy of holies the ark of the covenant (Exod. 25-40). Generally beds were mats, spread upon the floor, and rolled up during the day, though Og of Bashan is said to have had a bedstead (Deut. 3:11). The tables in OT times were generally very low and people sat upon the floor to eat. Royal tables were often higher (Judg. 1:7), as were those in NT times (Mark 7:28).

FUTURE LIFE (See Immortality, Eschatology)

A funeral procession in Bible days. © SPF

G

GAAL (gā'ăl, Heb. *ga'al, loathing*), a son of Ebed (Judg. 9:26-41), captain of a band of freebooters who incited the Shechemites to rebel against the rule of Abimelech. After the death of his father, Gideon, Abimelech murdered all but one of his 70 brothers so that he might become king of Shechem. After gaining the confidence of the men of Shechem, Gaal boasted under intoxication that he could overcome Abimelech if made leader of the Shechemites. Zebul, the prefect of Shechem, jealous of Gaal, secretly relayed this information to Abimelech who set up an ambush by night with four companies against Shechem. In the morning when Gaal went out and stood in the gate of the city, Abimelech and his army rose up out of hiding and chased Gaal and his company into the city, but Zebul thrust them out. Whereupon, Abimelech fought against the rebels and killed them and destroyed their city and sowed it with salt. Nothing more is known of Gaal, but clearly his weakness was foolhardy boasting which he failed to make good in action.

GAASH (gā'ăsh, Heb. *ga'ash, quaking*), a hill near Mount Ephraim. On its N side was Timnath-serah, the city given to Joshua (Josh. 19:49,50), where also he was buried (Judg. 2:9). The "brooks of Gaash" was the native place of Hiddai (II Sam. 23).

GABA (gā'-bà, Heb. *gāva'*), a Benjamite city (Josh. 18:24). Same as Geba (21:17; I Kings 15:22).

GABBAI (găb'-ā-ī, Heb. *gabbay, collector*), a chief of Benjamin after the captivity (Neh. 11:8).

GABBATHA (găb'à-thà, Aram. *gabbetha', height, ridge*), the place called the "Pavement" (John 19:13). Here Pilate sat on the Bema, or judgment seat, and sentenced Jesus before the people. Josephus (*Ant.* xv. 8, 5) states that the temple was near the castle of Antonia, and implies that Herod's palace was near the castle (xv. 11, 5). Therefore, if Pilate was residing in Herod's palace at Passover time in order to keep a watchful eye on the Jews, his residence was near the castle. An early pavement has been excavated near here consisting of slabs of stones three feet square and a foot or more thick. This may well have been the pavement where Jesus was brought forth from the judgment hall for sentencing.

The Gabbatha, or Pavement, before Pilate's judgment hall, the Praetorium, showing marks of games cut in the flagstones, for the amusement of the Roman soldiers. © MPS

GABRIEL (gā'brĭ-ĕl, Heb. *gavrî'ēl, man of God,* Gr. *Gabriél*), an angel mentioned four times in Scripture, each time bearing a momentous message. He interpreted to Daniel the vision of the ram and the he-goat (Dan. 8:16f). In Daniel 9:21f he explained the vision of the 70 Weeks. Gabriel announced to Zacharias the birth of John, forerunner of the Messiah (Luke 1:11-20), and he was sent to Mary with the unique message of Jesus' birth (Luke 1:26-38). His preparation is the ideal for every messenger of God: "I am Gabriel, that stand in the presence of God; and am sent to speak unto thee" (Luke 1:19). The Bible does not define his angel-status, but he appears in the Book of Enoch (chs. 9,20,40) as an archangel.

GAD (găd, Heb. *gādh, fortune*). 1. Jacob's seventh son; firstborn of Zilpah, Leah's handmaid (Gen. 30:9-11). Of his personal life nothing is known except that he had seven sons at the time of the descent into Egypt (46:16).

The Gadites numbered 45,650 adult males (Num. 1:24,25), but at the second census their number had fallen to 40,500 (26:18). Their position on march was S of the tabernacle next to Reuben. These two tribes and the half-tribe of Manasseh remained shepherds like their forefathers, and because of their "great multitude of cattle" they requested of Moses the rich pasture lands E of Jordan for their possession (Num. 32). This was granted (Josh. 18:7) on the condition that they accept their responsibility by accompanying the nine and a half tribes across Jordan in warfare against the Canaanites. The warriors of these two and a half tribes took the lead in the conquest of western Palestine (Josh. 1:12-18; 4:12) and returned to their families with Joshua's blessing (22:1-9). Fearing that the Jordan would alienate their children from the fellowship and faith of the western tribes, they erected a huge altar called Ed ("witness") as evidence of their unity in race and faith (Josh. 22:10-34). A satisfactory explanation removed the thought of war which seemed inevitable at first over a schismatic religion.

The territory of Gad, difficult to define, was formerly ruled by Sihon, king of the Amorites. It lay chiefly in the center of the land E of Jordan, with the half-tribe of Manasseh on the N and Reuben to the S. The northern border reached as far as the Sea of Chinnereth (Josh. 13:27); the southern border seems to have been just above Heshbon (13:26), although cities below this were built by Gad (Num. 32:34). One of these is Dibon, where the famous Moabite stone was found.

Genesis 49:19 seems to describe the military prowess of the Gadites: "Gad, a troop shall overcome him: but he shall overcome at the last" ("press upon their heel," ASV) meaning that they would put their enemies to retreat. Moses said of Gad: "Blessed is he that enlargeth Gad: he dwelleth as a lioness and teareth the arm, yea, the crown of the head," etc. (Deut. 33:20,21). Because they trusted in the Lord and cried to Him for help, they utterly defeated the Hagarites (I Chron. 5:18-22). It was natural for men of such faith and ability to extend their borders as far as Gilead (5:16). Of the Gadites who joined themselves to David it is said that they were "men of might, and men of war fit for the battle, that could handle shield and buckler," etc. (I Chron. 12:8,14,15). Other famous men of Gilead or Gad were Barzillai (II Sam. 17:27; 19:31-40) and Elijah. The land of Gad was long the battlefield between Syria and Israel (II Kings 10:33). Gad finally was carried captive by Assyria (II Kings 15:29; I Chron. 5:26) and Ammon seized their land and cities (Jer. 49:1).

2. The seer or prophet of King David. He advised David to get out of "the hold" and flee from Saul into Judah (I Sam. 22:5). Later, he gave David his choice of punishment from the Lord for his sin in numbering the children of Israel (II Sam. 24:11-17; I Chron. 21:9-17) and told him to build an altar to the Lord in the threshingfloor of Araunah (II Sam. 24:18). Gad assisted in arranging the musical services of the temple (II Chron. 29:25) and recorded the acts of David in a book (I Chron. 29:29).

3. A Canaanite god of fortune, seen in compound names such as Baal-gad (Josh. 11:17; 12:7; 13:5) and Migdal-gad (Josh. 15:37). In Isaiah 45: 11f there is a curse against idolaters. "That troop" (Gad) is the Babylonian or Syrian deity *Fortune* and "that number" (Meni) is the deity *Destiny* (see ASV). A.M.R.

with rock-caves suitable for tombs does meet the narrative description of the Gospels. In Roman times Gadara was the best fortified city in Peraea, and its remains are impressive still. A Roman street can be seen with its colonnades prostrate on either side. A.M.R.

GADDI (găd′ī, Heb. *gaddî*), Manasseh's representative among the twelve spies (Num. 13:11).

GADDIEL (găd′ĭ-ĕl, Heb. *gaddî′al*), Zebulun's representative among the twelve spies (Num. 13:10).

GADI (gā′dī), father of Menahem who usurped the throne of Israel from Shallum (II Kings 15:14-20).

GAHAM (gā′-hăm), a son of Nahor, brother of Abraham, by his concubine Reumah (Gen. 22:24).

GAHAR (gā′hàr), a family of the Nethinim who returned with Zerubbabel to Jerusalem (Ezra 2: 47).

The country of the Gadarenes as viewed from the Lake of Galilee. © MPS

GADARA, GADARENES (găd′à-rà, găd-à-rēnz′, Gr. *Gádara, Gadarenón*). Gadara was a member of the Decapolis and is associated with "the country of the Gadarenes" in the Gospels (Mark 5:1; Luke 8:26,37; Matt. 8:28, Gr. text). Its ruins are identified with Um Keis today on a steep hill five miles SE of the Sea of Galilee and three miles S of the Hieromax or Yarmuk River. At the foot of the hill to the N were hot springs and baths. When Christ came across the lake from Capernaum, He landed at the SE corner where the steep bank descends from the eastern highlands into the Jordan valley. Two demoniacs met Him, and out of them Jesus cast many demons. There were swine feeding nearby, and when Jesus allowed the demons to enter them they ran headlong down the steep slope into the lake and were drowned. In the cliffs around Gadara, or Um Keis, tombs have been excavated out of the limestone, some measuring 20 feet square, with side recesses for bodies. Like the demoniacs, people still dwell in them today. Nearby there is a field of several acres strewn from stone coffins and their lids. This description would hardly fit Gerasa, a town some 50 miles S of the Sea of Galilee, although it might be appropriate to refer generally to it as the "country of the Gerasenes," which is the reading of an important manuscript in Mark and Luke. Some texts of Matthew and Luke read "country of the Gergesenes," which is identified with the present Khersa farther N on the eastern shore of the lake. This might not be improper if the town were under the jurisdiction of the larger Gadara. Khersa's steep hill rising from the water's edge

GAIUS (gā′yŭs, Gr. *Gaíos*). 1. A Macedonian who traveled with Paul on his third missionary journey and was seized in the riot at Ephesus (Acts 19:29).

2. A man of Derbe who was one of those accompanying Paul from Macedonia to Asia (Acts 20:4).

3. A Corinthian whom Paul baptized (I Cor. 1: 14). Since Paul wrote the Epistle to the Romans from Corinth, this may be the same Gaius who was his host and "of the whole church" (either in whose house the Christians assembled or were given lodging Rom. 16:23).

4. The addressee of III John. A convert of John, he is spoken of as "the wellbeloved" (III John 1) and is commended for his love and hospitality to traveling preachers of the Gospel (III John 5-8).

GALAL (gā′lăl), the name of two Levites: 1. I Chronicles 9:15.

2. I Chronicles 9:16; Nehemiah 11:17.

GALATIA (gà-lā′shǐ-à), the designation in NT times of a territory in north-central Asia Minor, also a Roman province in central Asia Minor The name was derived from the people called Galatians (*Galatai*), a Greek modification of their original name *Keltoi* or *Keltai*, Celtic tribes from ancient Gaul. After having invaded Macedonia and Greece about 280 B.C., they crossed into Asia Minor on the invitation of Nikomedes I, king of Bithynia, to aid him in a civil war. After ravaging far and wide, they were finally confined to the north-central part of Asia Minor, where they settled as conquerors, giving their name to the territory. Their chief city-centers were Ancyra, Pessinus, and Tavium. In

189 B.C. the Galatians were subjugated by Rome and continued as a subject kingdom under their own chiefs, and after 63 B.C. under kings. Upon the death of King Amyntas in 25 B.C., the Galatian kingdom was converted into a Roman province called Galatia. The province included not only the area inhabited by the Galatians but also parts of Phrygia, Pisidia, Lycaonia, and Isauria. The terms *Galatia* and *Galatians* henceforth carried a double connotation: geographically, to designate the territory inhabitated by the Galatians, politically to denote the entire Roman province. That the cities of Antioch, Iconium, Lystra, and Derbe, evangelized by Paul on his first missionary journey, were in the province of Galatia is now recognized by all scholars.

The name *Galatia* occurs in I Corinthians 16:1; Galatians 1:2; II Timothy 4:10; and I Peter 1:1. In the last passage some scholars think the reference may be to the European Gaul. In Acts 16:6, 18:23 the name is an adjective (*Galatikē chōra*), the *Galatian country* or region. Luke apparently means the district, not the province, since in Acts, when speaking of Asia Minor, he employs the old ethnographic designations. The context in I Peter 1:1 seems clearly to indicate that the province is meant. Paul's general practice of employing political designations would point to that usage also in Galatians 1:1 and I Corinthians 16:1.

If *Galatia* in Galatians 1:1 means the Roman province, then the churches addressed were those founded on the first missionary journey (Acts 13-14); if it means the old ethnographic territory of Galatia, then the churches were established on the second missionary journey (Acts 16:6).

D.E.H.

GALATIANS, EPISTLE TO THE, a short but very important letter of Paul, containing his passionate polemic against the perversion or contamination of the Gospel of God's grace. It has aptly been described as "the Magna Charta of spiritual emancipation" and it remains as the abiding monument of the liberation of Christianity from the trammels of legalism.

The contents of the epistle so unmistakably reveal the traces of Paul's mind and style that its genuineness has never been seriously questioned even by the most radical NT critics. The testimony of the early church to its integrity and Pauline origin is strong and unambiguous.

Written to "the churches of Galatia," it is the only Pauline epistle that is specifically addressed to a group of churches. They were all founded by Paul (1:8,11; 4:19-20), were all the fruit of a single mission (3:1-3; 4:13-14), and were all affected by the same disturbance (1:6-7; 5:7-9). Paul had preached among them the Gospel of the free grace of God through the death of Christ (1:6; 3:1-14). The reception of Paul and his message by the Galatians had been warm and affectionate (4:12-15). The converts willingly endured persecution for their faith (3:4) and "were running well" when Paul left them (5:7).

The startling information received by Paul that a sudden and drastic change in attitude toward him and his Gospel was taking place in the Galatian churches caused the writing of the epistle. The change was being induced by the propaganda of certain Jewish teachers who professed to be Christians, acknowledged Jesus as Messiah, but overlaid and obscured the simplicity of the Gospel of free grace by their insistence that to faith in Christ must be added circumcision and obedience to the Mosaic law (2:16; 3:2-3; 4:10,21; 5:2-4; 6:12). Paul realized clearly that this teaching neutralized

the truth of Christ's all-sufficiency for salvation and destroyed the message of justification by faith. From this fatal mixing of law and grace Paul sought to save his converts by means of this epistle.

Due to the geographical and the political connotation of *Galatia* in NT times, two views concerning the location of the Galatian churches are advocated. The *North-Galatian* theory, which interprets the term in its old ethnographic sense to denote the territory inhabited by the Galatian tribes, locates the churches in north-central Asia Minor, holding that they were founded during Acts 16:6. The *South-Galatian* theory identifies these churches with those founded on the first missionary journey (Acts 13-14), located in the southern part of the province of Galatia. The former was the unanimous view of the Church Fathers. They naturally adopted that meaning since in the second century the province was again restricted to ethnic Galatia and the double meaning of the term disappeared. The majority of the modern commentators support the latter view. Supporting this view is the known practice of Paul of using provincial names in addressing his converts; it best explains the familiar reference to Barnabas in the epistle; Acts 16:6 gives no hint of such a protracted mission as the older view demands; the older view cannot explain why the Judaizers would bypass the important churches in South Galatia; known conditions in these churches fit the picture in the epistle.

Views concerning the place and date of composition are even more diverse. Advocates of the *North-Galatian* theory generally assign the epistle to Ephesus during the third missionary journey, near the time of Romans. *South-Galatian* advocates vary considerably; some place it before the Jerusalem Conference, while others place it as late as the third missionary journey. Advocates of the pre-Conference date place it at Syrian Antioch. Others place it on the second missionary journey, perhaps during the ministry at Corinth. The effort to date it before the Jerusalem Conference faces definite chronological difficulties. This early dating is not demanded by the silence of the epistle concerning the Conference decrees. The decrees were already known to the Galatians (Acts 16:4), while in writing the epistle Paul would desire to establish his position on grounds independent of the Jerusalem Church. Since apparently he had already twice visited the churches (4:13; 1:9), a date after Paul's second visit to the south-Galatian churches seems most probable (c. A.D. 52). During that second visit Paul had sought by warning and instructions to fortify his converts against the danger (1:9; 4:16; 5:3). The impact of the Judaizers upon the Galatians threatened to destroy his work. The result was this bristling letter.

The contents of Galatians make evident Paul's purpose in writing. The first two chapters show that he was compelled to vindicate his apostolic authority. The Judaizers, in order to establish their own position which contradicted Paul's teaching, had attempted to discredit his authority. Having vindicated his apostolic call and authority, Paul next sets forth the doctrine of justification in refutation of the teaching of the Judaizers. A reasoned, comprehensive exposition of the doctrine of justification by faith exposed the errors of legalism. Since the Judaizers asserted that to remove the believer from under the law opened the floodgates to immorality, Paul concluded his presentation with an elaboration of the true effect of liberty upon the Christian life, showing that the truth of justification by faith logically leads to a life of good works. The epistle may be outlined as follows:

THE INTRODUCTION. 1:1-10
   1. The salutation. 1-5
   2. The rebuke. 6-10
I. The Vindication of his Apostolic Authority. 1:11-2:21
   1. The reception of his Gospel by revelation. 1:11-24
   2. The confirmation of his Gospel by the apostles at Jerusalem. 2:1-10
   3. The illustration of his independence. 2:11-21
II. The Exposition of Justification by Faith. 3:1-4:31
   1. The elaboration of the doctrine. 3:1-4:7
     a. The nature of justification by faith. 3:1-14
     b. The limitations of the law and its relations to faith. 3:15-4:7
   2. The appeal to drop all legalism. 4:8-31
III. The Nature of the Life of Christian Liberty. 5:1-6:10
   1. The call to maintain their liberty. 5:1
   2. The peril of Christian liberty. 5:2-12
   3. The life of liberty. 5:13-6:10
THE CONCLUSION. 6:11-17
THE BENEDICTION. 6:18

D.E.H.

GALBANUM (găl′bà-nŭm), a gum resin from two Persian plants of the carrot family. It has a pungent, disagreeable odor and was mixed with other ingredients in the sacred incense to increase and retain its fragrance longer. (Exod. 30:34).

GALEED (găl′ē-ĕd, Heb. *gal′ēdh, a heap of witnesses*), the name given by Jacob to the heap of stones which he and Laban raised on Mount Gilead as a memorial of their brotherly covenant (Gen. 31:47,48). Sealing their compact of friendship with a common meal, Laban called the place *Jegarsahadutha,* the Aramaic or Chaldee equivalent, meaning "the heap of testimony."

GALILEAN (găl′ĭ-lē′ăn), a native or resident of Galilee (Matt. 26:69; John 4:45; Acts 1:11, 5:37) and detected as such by his dialect (Mark 14:70).

GALILEE (găl′ĭ-lē, Heb. *hā-gālîl, the ring or circuit,* Gr. *he Galilaía*), the most northerly of the three provinces of Palestine (Galilee, Samaria, Judea). Measuring approximately 50 miles N to S and 30 miles E to W, it was bounded on the W by the plain of Akka to the foot of Mt. Carmel. The Jordan, the Sea of Galilee, Lake Huleh, and the spring at Dan marked off the eastern border. Its northern boundary went eastward from Phoenicia to Dan. The southern border was in a southeasterly direction from the base of Mt. Carmel and the Samaritan hills along the Valley of Jezreel (Plain of Esdraelon) to Mt. Gilboa and Scythopolis (Bethshean) to the Jordan. The Valley of Jezreel was a vital communications link between the coastal plain and the center of Palestine. For this reason, decisive battles were often fought here for possession of this desirable pass. The city of Megiddo was important for the control of the valley and lends its name to *Har-Magedon,* the Hill of Megiddo, or Armageddon, where the conflict between Christ and the armies of the Antichrist is predicted to occur (Rev. 16:16).

An imaginary line from the plain of Akka to the N end of the Sea of Galilee divided the country into Upper and Lower Galilee. "Galilee of the Gentiles" refers chiefly to Upper Galilee, which is separated from Lebanon by the Leontes River. It was the territory of Asher and Naphtali. Here

View of Mount Gilboa across the Plain of Esdraelon.
© MPS

lie the ruins of Kedesh Naphtali, one of the cities of refuge (Josh. 20:7; 21-32). In this region lay the twenty towns given by Solomon to Hiram, King of Tyre, in payment for timber from Lebanon (I Kings 9:11). The land was luxurious and productive, a rugged mountainous country of oaks and terebinths interrupted by fertile plains. It was said of Asher, in the west, that he would eat fat for bread and yield royal dainties and dip his feet in oil (Gen. 49:20; Deut. 33:24,25). The olive oil of Galilee has long been esteemed as of the highest quality. Lower Galilee was largely the heritage of Zebulun and Issachar. Less hilly and of a milder climate than Upper Galilee, it included the rich plain of Esdraelon (or Jezreel) and was a "pleasant" land (Gen. 49:15) that would yield "treasures in the sand" (Deut. 33:19) The sand of these coasts was especially valuable for making glass. Important caravan trade routes carried their busy traffic through Galilee from Egypt and southern Palestine to Damascus in the NE as well as E and W from the Mediterranean to the Far East.

The northern part of Naphtali was inhabited by a mixed race of Jews and heathen (Judg. 1:33). Its Israelite population was carried away captive to Assyria to Tiglath-pileser and replaced by a colony of heathen immigrants (II Kings 15:29; 17:24), hence called "Galilee of the nations" or "Gentiles" (Isa. 9:1; Matt. 4:13,15,16). During and after the captivity, the predominant mixture of Gentile races impoverished the worship of Judaism. For the same reason the Galilean accent and dialect were noticeably peculiar (Matt. 26:73). This caused the southern Jews of purer blood and orthodox tradition to despise them (John 7:52). Nathanael asked, rather contemptuously, "Can there any good thing come out of Nazareth?" (John 1:46). Yet its very darkness was the Lord's reason for granting it more of the light of His presence and ministry than to self-satisfied and privileged Judea. He was sent "for a light of the Gentiles" (Isa. 42:6) as well as to the "lost sheep of the house of Israel" (Matt. 15:24). Wherever He found faith and repentance, He bestowed His blessing, whereas unbelief often hindered His activity (Matt. 13:58). He preached His first public sermon in the synagogue at Nazareth, in Lower Galilee, where He had been brought up (Luke 4:16-30). His disciples came from Galilee (Matt. 4:18; John 1:43,44; Acts 1:11, 2:7); in Cana of Galilee He performed His first miracle (John 2:11). Capernaum in Galilee, the home of His manhood (Matt. 4:13; 9:1), is where the first three

Gospels present His major ministry. Galilee's debasement made some of its people feel their need of the Saviour. This and its comparative freedom from priestly and pharisaical prejudice may have been additional reasons for receiving the larger share of the Lord's ministry.

After the death of Herod the Great in 4 B.C., Herod Antipas governed the tetrarchy of Galilee (Luke 3:1) until A.D. 39. Jesus referred to him as "that fox" (Luke 13:32). Sepphoris was his capital at first, three miles N of Nazareth, but about A.D. 20 he built a new capital on the shore of the Sea of Galilee and named it Tiberias, after the reigning emperor. Succeeding him was Herod Agrippa I with the title of "king." Upon his death in A.D. 44 (Acts 12:23), Galilee was joined for a while to the Roman province of Syria, after which it was given to Agrippa II. It became the land of Zealots and patriots who, in their hatred of foreign rule and in their longing for the Messiah, incited the populace to rebellion, which led Rome to destroy Jerusalem in A.D. 70. After the fall of Jerusalem, Galilee became famous for its rabbins and schools of Jewish learning. The Sanhedrin or Great Council was moved to Sepphoris and then to Tiberias on the western shore of the Sea of Galilee. This is most interesting in light of the fact that when Herod Antipas built his capital and residence on top of a cemetery, strict Jews utterly abhorred the place. Here the Mishna was compiled, to which the Gemara was added subsequently, forming the Palestinian Talmud. The remains of splendid synagogues in Galilee, such as those at Capernaum and Chorazin, still attest to the prosperity of the Jews there from the second to the seventh century.

In 1925 the famous "Galilee skull" was found in a cave near the Sea of Galilee; and in 1932, in a cave near Mt. Carmel, Dr. Theodore D. McCown discovered a Paleolithic skeleton resembling primitive Neanderthal man.   A.M.R.

GALILEE, SEA OF, so-called from its washing the E side of Galilee. It is also known by other names. It is called "the Sea of Gennesaret" (Luke 5:1), since the fertile Plain of Gennesaret lies on the NW (Matt. 14:34). The OT calls it "the Sea of Chinnereth (Heb. "harp-shaped," the shape of the sea, Num. 34:11; Deut. 3:17; Josh. 13:27) or "Chinneroth" (Josh. 12:3; I Kings 15:20), from the town so named on its shore (Josh. 19:35), of which Gennesaret is probably the corruption. "The Sea of Tiberias" is another designation (John 6: 1; 21:1), associated with the capital of Herod Antipas. All its names were derived from places on the western shore. Its present name is *Bahr Tabariyeh.*

North end of the Sea of Galilee, showing inflow of the Jordan River and the mountains beyond, looking eastward. © MPS

Sunrise on the Sea of Galilee. © MPS

Located some 60 miles N of Jerusalem, its bed is but a lower depression of the Jordan valley. The water's surface is 685 feet below the level of the Mediterranean and it varies in depth up to 150 feet. As the Jordan River plunges southward on its course from Mt. Hermon to the Dead Sea, it enters the Sea of Galilee at its northern end and flows out of its southern end, a distance of thirteen miles. Its greatest width is eight miles, at Magdala. The view from Nazareth road to Tiberias is beautiful. The bare hills on the W, except at Khan Minyeh (present Capernaum) where there is a small cliff, are recessed from the shore. From the eastern side, the western hills appear to rise out of the water to a height of 2000 feet, while far to the N can be seen snowy Mt. Hermon. The eastern hills rise from a coast of half a mile in width and are flat along the summit. The whole basin betrays its volcanic origin, which accounts for the cliffs of hard porous basalt and the hot springs at Tiberias, famous for their medicinal value. The warm climate produces tropical vegetation — the lotus thorn, palms, and indigo. The Plain of Gennesaret on the NW abounds with walnuts, figs, olives, grapes, and assorted wild flowers. Josephus called it "the ambition of nature which forces those plants that are natural enemies to one another to agree together" (Josephus iii. *Wars,* x.8). The fresh water is sweet, sparkling, and transparent, with fish in abundance. Smith paints an idyllic picture of the whole scene: "In that torrid basin, approached through such sterile surroundings, the lake feeds every sense of the body with life. Sweet water, full of fish, a surface of sparkling blue, tempting down breezes from above, bringing forth breezes of her own, the Lake of Galilee is at once food, drink and air, a rest to the eye, coolness in the heat, an escape from the crowd, and a facility of travel very welcome in so exhausting a climate. Even those who do not share her memories of Christ feel enthusiasm for her. The Rabbis said: 'Jehovah hath created seven seas, but the Sea of Gennesaret is His delight.' " (George Adam Smith, *The Historical Geography of the Holy Land,* New York: A. C. Armstrong and Son, 1908, p.

Fishing on the Sea of Galilee, drawing in the nets. © MPS

442). The Gospel accounts picture fishing as a prosperous industry here in Biblical times, but today, instead of fleets of fishing vessels, only a boat or two is seen. On these shores Jesus called His first disciples, four of whom were fishermen, and made of them fishers of men (Matt. 4:18; Luke 5:1-11).

The Sea of Galilee is noted for its sudden and violent storms caused by cold air sweeping down from the vast naked plateaus of Gaulanitis, the Hauran and Mt. Hermon through the ravines and gorges and converging at the head of the lake where it meets warm air. It was just such a storm that Jesus rebuked with His "Peace, be still" (Mark 4:39). Another time, the disciples were trying to reach Bethsaida when "a great wind" turned the water into huge waves, preventing any headway. Then Jesus appeared, walking toward them on the tempestuous water. As soon as they took Him into the boat they reached their desired haven (Matt. 14:22-34; Mark 6:45-53; John 6:15-21). So impressed were the disciples that they worshiped Him saying, "Of a truth Thou art the Son of God."

The Sea of Galilee was the focus of Galilee's wealth. Nine cities of 15,000 or more stood on its shores. To the NW was Capernaum, the home of Peter and Andrew (Mark 1:29) and where Matthew sat at custom (Matt. 9:9). It was the scene of much of Jesus' Galilean ministry. Below this, on the western side, was Magdala (present Mejdal), the home of Mary Magdalene, and three miles S of here was Tiberias, the magnificent capi-

Sudden storm on the Sea of Galilee. © MPS

tal of Galilee. On the NE corner was Bethsaida Julias, the native place of Philip, Andrew and Peter (John 1:44), and one-time capital of Philip the tetrarch. Gergesa lay S of here. The sites of Capernaum, Chorazin (modern Kerazeh) to the N of it, and Bethsaida have long been in dispute. Whatever their locations may have been, their near obliteration accords with their condemnation by the Saviour for their unbelief (Matt. 11:20-24). Of these towns, once thriving with dyeing, tanning, boat building, fishing, and fish-curing, two are now inhabited, namely Magdala, consisting of a few mud huts, and Tiberias.   A.M.R.

GALL. 1. From a Heb. root meaning *bitter,* the human gall (Job 16:13; 20:25); the poison of serpents (20:14).

2. Heb. *rō'sh, head.* A bitter and poisonous herb, perhaps the poppy (Deut. 29:18; Jer. 8:14, 9:15; Hos. 10:4, "hemlock"). Criminals were given a potion before crucifixion to deaden pain. Thus, opium would suit well the drink given to the Lord: "vinegar (wine, ASV) mingled with gall" (Gr. *cholé,* Matt. 27:34, cf. Ps. 69:21). Mark says "with myrrh" (15:23). But Jesus chose to bear the full agony of death.

GALLERY, three terraced passageways or balconies running round the chambers in the temple of Ezekiel's vision (Ezek. 41:16; 42:3,5,6). The upper two stories were shorter due to the absence of supporting pillars.

GALLEY (See Ship)

GALLIM (găl'ĭm, Heb. *gallîm, heaps*), a town of Benjamin enumerated with Laish and Anathoth (Isa. 10:30). By "daughter of Gallim" is meant the inhabitants. It was the home of Phalti the son of Laish (I Sam. 25:44). Site uncertain.

GALLIO (găl'ĭ-ō, Gr. *Gallíon*), Junius Annaeus Gallio, the Roman proconsul (AV, "deputy") of Achaia when Paul was in Corinth (A.D. 51). Luke accurately calls him "proconsul," for Achaia had been an imperial province administered by a legate, but in A.D. 44 Claudius gave it to the Senate whose provinces alone were under the rule of proconsuls.

Born in Cordova, Spain, as Marcus Annaeus Novatus, he was adopted into the family of Lucius Junius Gallio, the rhetorician, whose name he took. Of his amiable character Seneca said, "No mortal was ever so sweet to one as Gallio was to all," and, his brother adds, "to love him to the utmost was to love all too little." How exactly and undesignedly this independent testimony coincides

Gallio's judgment seat, the Bema, among the ruins of the Forum at Corinth. SHH

with Acts 18:12-17! Alarmed over the inroads that the Gospel was making, the Jews in Corinth brought Paul before the judgment seat of Gallio. The charge: "persuading men to worship God contrary to the law." But which law? Meaning their own, they hoped to convince Gallio that Paul was guilty of an offense against a lawful religion and hence against the Roman Government itself; but he was not impressed. "If it were a matter of wrong or wicked lewdness, O ye Jews, reason would that I should bear with you," said he. "But since (Gr.) it is a question of words and names and your law, look ye to it; for I will be no judge of such matters. And he drave them from the judgment seat." The Greeks then beat the chief ruler of the synagogue, but Gallio remained indifferent to the incident. A governor more stern might have arrested the violence at once, but in the providence of God Gallio's action amounted to an authoritative decision that Paul's preaching was not subversive against Rome. This gave Paul the protection he needed to continue his preaching there. Had Gallio become a Christian, he might not have committed suicide later.

GALLOWS, a pole for executing and exhibiting a victim by impalement. Made 75 feet high by Haman for Mordecai (Esth. 5:14; 6:4).

GAMALIEL (gȧ-māʹlĭ-ĕl, Heb. *gamlîʹēl, reward of God,* Gr. *Gamaliél*). 1. Son of Pedahzur and chief of the tribe of Manasseh (Num. 1:10; 2:20; 7:54, 59; 10:23). He assisted Moses in numbering the people.

2. A Pharisee and eminent doctor of the law; grandson of Hillel and first of only seven rabbis to be given the title of Rabban. Paul was one of his pupils (Acts 22:3). When the enraged Sanhedrin sought to slay the Apostles for their bold testimony to Christ, Gamaliel stood up in the council and urged judicious caution on the ground that if the new doctrine were of God they could not overthrow it, and if it were of man it would perish of itself (Acts 5:34-39). Held in esteem by all the people, his counsel was heeded, and God used it to give a needed respite to the infant Church. Inasmuch as Gamaliel believed in God's sovereign control, his advice was sound; but also underlying it was the premise of pragmatism that what succeeds is good and what fails is evil. Contrarily, the Scriptures point out that the wicked do prosper (Ps. 73:12) and the godly are often destitute (Ps. 109:22-26). Truth must be tested by the standard of God's word. The tradition that he afterward became a Christian is incongruous with the high

esteem accorded him in the Talmud: "Since Rabban Gamaliel died, the glory of the Law has ceased."

GAMES. Not much is known concerning the amusements of the ancient Israelites, partly because the earnestness of the Hebrew character did not give them prominence. Instead of public games, the great religious feasts supplied them with their anniversary occasions of national gatherings. There are references to dancing (Ps. 30:11; Jer. 31:13; Luke 15:25). The dance led by Jephthah's daughter (Judg. 11:34) and the dances of the Israelitish women (I Sam. 18:6; 21:11; 29:5) were public dances of rejoicing to celebrate a warrior's victory. Religious dancing was engaged in by Miriam and the women of Israel at the Red Sea (Exod. 15:20); by the Israelites around the golden calf at Sinai (32:19); and by David before the ark (II Sam. 6:14,16). (See also Ps. 149:3; 150:4). Of course, children of every race have their games. Zechariah prophesied that "the city shall be full of boys and girls playing in the streets thereof" (8:5). "He will . . . toss thee like a ball into a large country," warned Isaiah (22:18). In the NT the only children's game mentioned is that of mimicking the wedding dance and funeral wail to the music of the flute (Matt. 11:16,17; Luke 7:32).

Jason's introduction of Greek games and a gymnasium, frequented by the priests, was among the corrupting influences which broke down the fence of Judaism against Hellenism and threw it open to the sacrilegious assaults of King Antiochus Epiphanes, c. 175 B.C. (I Macc. 1:14; II Macc. 4:12-14). Herod erected a theater and amphitheater at Jerusalem and Caesarea where contests in gymnastics, chariot races, music, and wild beasts were held every five years in honor of Caesar, much to the annoyance of the faithful Jews (Josephus, *Ant.,* XV, viii,1; ix,6).

The public games of Greece and Rome were common knowledge among Christians and non-Christians of the first century, providing the NT writers with rich source material from which to illustrate spiritual truths. Condemned criminals were thrown to lions in the arena as punishment and for sport. In I Corinthians 15:32 Paul alludes to fighting with beasts at Ephesus (though *his* frays were with beastlike men—Demetrius and his craftsmen—not with literal beasts, from which his Roman citizenship exempted him). When a Roman general returned home victorious, he led his army in a triumphal procession, at the end of which trailed the captives who were condemned to fight with beasts. Paul felt that in contrast to the proud Corinthians, God had *set forth* (exhibited prior to execution) the Apostles last as captives doomed to die, because they were made a spectacle to be gazed at and made sport of in the arena of the world (I Cor. 4:9). Nero used to clothe the Christians in beast skins when he exposed them to wild beasts. Cf. II Timothy 4:17, "I was delivered out of the mouth of the lion" (viz. from Satan's snare, I Pet. 5:8).

In I Corinthians 9:24,25 the Isthmian games, celebrated every two years on the isthmus of Corinth, are vividly alluded to. Held in honor of the Greek gods, the festival consisted of foot races, horse races, chariot contests, jumping, wrestling, boxing, and throwing of the discus and javelin. To the Greeks they were a subject of patriotic pride, a passion rather than a pastime, and thus made a suitable image of earnestness in the Christian race: "Know ye not that they which run in a race run all, but one receiveth the prize? So run, that ye may obtain. And every man that striveth for the mastery is temperate in all things. Now they do it to obtain a corruptible crown; but we an incorruptible." The coveted crown was a garland made of laurel, olives leaves, or pine needles; our crown is incorruptible (I Pet. 1:4) and therefore demands greater fidelity. The competitor had to "strive lawfully" or else he was not crowned (II Tim. 2:5), i.e. he had to observe the conditions of the contest, keeping to the bounds of the course, having previously trained himself for ten months with chastity, abstemious diet, enduring cold, heat, and severe exercise. As in boxing, so in the Christian race, Paul beat his body and brought it under subjection, lest that by any means when he had preached ("heralded"; the herald announced the name and country of each contestant and displayed the prizes) to others, he should be rejected by the judge, not as to salvation but to the winner's crown of victory (James 1:12). In view of the reward, Paul denied himself, being servant of all in order to win more souls to Jesus Christ. The Christian does not beat the air, missing his opponent, but he fights certainly, with telling blows upon the enemy (I Cor. 9:18-27). As the runner looks intently at the goal and casts away every encumbrance, so the Christian runs, casting aside not only sinful lusts but even harmless and otherwise useful things which would retard him. He must run with *enduring perseverance* the race set before him, *looking off* unto Jesus who is the Captain and Finisher of our faith (Heb. 12:1,2). Paul used the same figure in addressing the Ephesian elders (Acts 20:24) and the Philippians (3:12-14). The Colossians were urged to let the peace of God *rule as umpire* in their hearts and thus restrain wrong passions that they might attain the prize to which they were called (3:15). Other allusions to the language of games are in Ephesians 6:12, "We wrestle not against flesh and blood" and II Timothy 4:7, "I have fought the good fight, I have finished the course" (Gr. *I have struggled the good contest,* not merely a fight). See also I Timothy 6:12 and Revelation 2:10.   A.M.R.

GAMMADIM (găm′a-dĭm, Heb. *gammādhîm*), occurs in Ezekiel 27:11 only as "gammadims" (KJV), but in ASV translated "valorous men." Foreigners would hardly be trusted to watch in the towers of Tyre. Variously interpreted, the ASV rendering seems most fitting as an epithet of the warriors of Tyre.

GAMUL (gā′-mŭl, Heb. *gāmûl*), the head of the twenty-second course of priests (I Chron. 24:17).

GARDEN (Heb. *gan, gannâh, a covered or hidden place,* Gr. *kéros*), a cultivated piece of ground, usually in the suburbs, planted with flowers, vegetables, shrubs, or trees, fenced with a mud or stone wall (Prov. 24:31) or thorny hedges (Isa. 5:5) and *guarded* (whence "garden") by a watchman in a lodge (Isa. 1:8) or tower (Mark 12:1) to drive away wild beasts and robbers.

The quince, citron, almond and other fruits, herbs, and various vegetables and spices are mentioned as growing in gardens. A reservoir cistern, or still better a fountain of water, was essential to a good garden. See Song of Solomon 4:15, "a fountain of gardens," i.e. a fountain sufficient to water many gardens.

The occurrence of no less than 250 botanical terms in the OT shows the Israelite fondness for flowers, fruits, and pleasant grounds. These are still a delight to the Oriental who lives in a hot, dry country. Every house court or area generally had its shade tree. The vine wound round the trel-

lis or outside staircase, the emblem of the loving and fruitful wife and happy home (Ps. 128:3). The "orchards" (Heb. *paradises*) were larger gardens specially for fruit trees. Solomon's gardens and fruit orchards with pools of water for irrigation (Eccl. 2:4-6) very likely suggested the imagery of Song of Solomon 4:12-15. The "king's garden" (II Kings 25:4; Neh. 3:15; Jer. 39:4; 52:7) was near the pool of Siloam.

The Hebrews used gardens as burial places. The field of Machpelah, Abraham's burial ground, was a garden with trees in and around it (Gen. 23:17). Manasseh and Amon were buried in Uzza's garden (II Kings 21:18,26). The garden of Gethsemane was a favorite resort of Jesus for meditation and prayer (Matt. 26:36; John 18:1,2). In idolatrous periods, gardens were made the scene of superstition and image worship, the awful counterpart of the primitive Eden (Isa. 1:29; 65:3; 66:17). The new Paradise regained by the people of God (Rev. 22:1-5) suggests in a fuller way the old paradise planted by God but lost through sin (Gen. 2:8).

Spiritually, the believer is a garden watered by the Holy Spirit (Jer. 2:13; 17:7,8; John 4:13,14; 7:37-39). The righteous "shall be like a tree planted by the rivers of water, that bringeth forth his fruit in his season" (Ps. 1:3). "A well watered garden" expresses abundant happiness and prosperity (Isa. 58:11; Jer. 31:12) just as "a garden that hath no water" (Isa. 1:30) expresses spiritual, national and individual barrenness and misery.
                 A.M.R.

GARDENER (See Occupations & Professions)

A view of a corner of the Garden of Gethsemane. © MPS

GAREB (gā'rĕb, Heb. *gārēv, scabby*). 1. An Ithrite, a member of one of the families of Kirjathjearim (I Chron. 2:53) and one of David's mighty men (II Sam. 23:38; I Chron. 11:40).

2. A hill near Jerusalem to which the city would expand, as foreseen by the prophet Jeremiah (31:39). The site is unknown.

GARLICK, GARLIC (See Plants)

GARMENTS (See Dress)

GARMITE (gar'mīt, Heb. *garmî*), a name applied to Keilah (I Chron. 4:19). Meaning is obscure.

GARNER (gar'nêr, Heb. *māzû*), a *barn* or *storehouse* (Ps. 144:13); Heb. *'ōtsār,* a storehouse for precious items (II Chron. 32:27) and for food (Joel 1:17). Gr. *apothéke,* a barn used as a granary (Matt. 3:12; 6:26; Luke 3:17; 12:18,24).

GARRISON (Heb. *matstsāv* and *netsîv, placed*), a fortress manned by soldiers (II Chron. 17:2). Its primary reference is that of a military post for the occupation of a conquered country such as the Philistines had when they held the land of Israel (I Sam. 10:5; 13:3; 14:1,6). David put garrisons in Syria and Edom when he subjugated those people (II Sam. 8:6,14). In Ezekiel 26:11, "thy strong garrisons" is a wrong rendering of *matstsēvâh.* It refers to the pillars or obelisks in honor of the gods of Tyre which would totter before the conquering Nebuchadnezzar.

GASHMU (găsh'mū, Heb. *gashmû,* Neh. 6:6), a form of Geshem (2:19; 6:1,2), an Arabian who opposed Nehemiah's building of the wall of Jerusalem.

GATAM (gā'tăm, Heb. *ga'tām*), grandson of Esau; an Edomite chief (Gen. 36:11,16; I Chron. 1:36).

GATE (Heb. usually *sha'ar, opening,* Gr. *púle*), the entrance to enclosed buildings, grounds, or cities. The gates of a city were the place where the Oriental resorted for legal business, conversation, bargaining, and news. The usual gateway consisted of double doors plated with metal (Ps. 107:16; Isa. 45:2). Wooden doors without iron plating were easily set on fire (Judg. 9:52; Neh. 2:3,17). Some gates were made out of brass, as was "the Beautiful Gate" of Herod's temple (Acts 3:2), more costly than nine others of the outer court that had been poured over with gold and silver (Joseph, *Wars of the Jews,* V,v,3). Still others were of solid stones (Isa. 54:12; Rev. 21:21). Massive stone doors are found in ancient towns of Syria, single slabs several inches thick and ten feet high, turning on pivots above and below. Gates ordinarily swung on projections that fitted into sockets on the post and were secured with bars of wood (Nah. 3:13) or of metal (I Kings 4:13; Ps. 107:16; Isa. 45:2).

Being the weakest points in a city's walls, the gates were frequently the object of a foe's attack (Judg. 5:8; I Sam. 23:7; Ezek. 21:15,22) and therefore flanked by towers (II Sam. 18:24,33; II Chron. 14:7; 26:9). To "possess the gates" was to possess the city (Gen. 22:17; 24:60). They were shut at nightfall and opened again in the morning (Deut. 3:5; Josh. 2:5,7).

Markets were held at the gate, and the main item sold there gave its name to the gate ("sheep gate," Neh. 3:1; "fish gate," Neh. 3:3; "horse gate," Neh. 3:28). The gate was the place where people met to hear an important announcement (II Chron. 32:6; Jer. 7:2; 17:19-27) or the reading of the law (Neh. 8:1,3) or where the elders transacted legal business (Deut. 16:18; 21:18-20; Josh. 20:4; Ruth 4:1,2,11). "Neither oppress the afflicted in the gate" meant to mete out impartial justice

Typical scene at a city gate. © SPF

(Prov. 22:22). Psalm 69:12, "They that sit in the gate speak against me, and I was the song of the drunkards"; i.e., not only among the drunken revellers, but in the grave deliberations of the judges in the place of justice was he an object of abusive language. Amos 5:12, "they turn aside the poor in the gate"; i.e., they refuse them their right; vs. 10, "they hate him that rebuketh in the gate," viz. the judge who condemns them (Zech. 8:16). Isaiah 29:21, "They lay a snare for him that reproveth in the gate"; i.e., they try by bribes and misrepresentations to ensnare into a false decision the judge who in public court would reprove them for their iniquity, or to ensnare the prophet who publicly reproves them. "The Sublime Porte," the title for the Sultan of Turkey, was derived from the eastern usage of dispensing law in the gateway. It was also the king's or chief's place of audience (II Sam. 19:8; I Kings 22:10). Daniel sat in the gate of King Nebuchadnezzar as "ruler over the whole province of Babylon" (Dan. 2:48,49). Regarded as specially sacred, the threshold in Assyrian palaces bore cuneiform inscriptions and was guarded by human-headed bulls with eagles' wings. In Israel, sentences from the Law were inscribed on and above the posts and gates of private houses (Deut. 6:9). Josiah destroyed the high places near the gates that were used for heathen sacrifices (II Kings 23:8).

Figuratively, gates refer to the glory of a city (Isa. 3:26; 14:31; Jer. 14:2) or to the city itself (Ps. 87:2; 122:2). In Matthew 16:18, the "gates of Hades" not prevailing against the Church may refer to infernal powers assaulting the Church or to the Church's greater power in retaining her members than the grave has for its victims.

A.M.R.

GATH (găth, Heb. *gath, winepress*), one of the five great Philistine cities (Ashdod, Gaza, Askelon, Gath, and Ekron, Josh. 13:3; I Sam. 6:17). Its people were the Gittites, of whom were Goliath (I Sam. 17:4) and other giants (II Sam. 21:19-22). In harmony with this fact is the record of the Anakims' presence in Gath after Joshua had destroyed the neighboring territory (Josh. 11:22). It was one of the five cities to which the Philistines carried the ark of God and thereby brought on the people God's heavy visitation with tumors (I Sam. 5:8,9). David fled from Saul to Gath where he feigned madness to save his life (I Sam. 21:10-15). The second time he visited Gath, King Achish assigned him Ziklag as a residence (I Sam. 27:2-6). During his sixteen months here, he won the confidence of the king through subterfuge and intrigue (27:7-29:11). Some of David's six hundred followers were Gittites, one of whom was his loyal friend Ittai. They may have attached themselves to him at this time or when he smote and subdued the Philistines (II Sam. 8:1; 15:18-21). Though tributary to Israel after David conquered it (I Chron. 18:1), Gath retained its own king (I Kings 2:39). Rehoboam, Solomon's son, rebuilt and fortified the town (II Chron. 11:8). Later, Hazael, king of Syria, captured Gath from Jehoash, king of Judah (II Kings 12:17), but Uzziah won it back (II Chron. 26:6). From the fall of this walled city Amos sounds a warning lesson to those at ease in Zion (6:1,2). The omission of Gath from the list of the five cities (Amos 1:6,8; Zeph. 2:4,5; Zech. 9:5,6) indicates it had lost its place among them by that time. Its site today is uncertain. Gath lay on the border between Judah and Philistia, between Shocoh and Ekron (I Sam. 17:1,52). Tell es-Safiyeh favors this description, lying on a hill at the foot of Judah's mountains, ten miles E of Ashdod and ten SE of Ekron.

GATH-HEPHER (găth-hē′fêr, Heb. *gath ha-hēpher, winepress of the well*), a town on Zebulun's border (Josh. 19:12,13, ASV). Birthplace of Jonah the prophet (II Kings 14:25). Now el Meshhed, where his supposed tomb is still shown, on a hill two miles from Nazareth in Galilee.

GATH-RIMMON (găth-rĭm′ŭn, Heb. *gath rimmôn, winepress of Rimmon* or *pomegranates*). 1. A city of Dan on the Philistine plain, given to the Levites (Josh. 19:45; 21:24; I Chron. 6:69).

2. A town of Manasseh, W of Jordan, assigned to the Levites (Josh. 21:25). In I Chronicles 6:70 this is called Bileam, which is probably the true reading in Joshua 21:25, an error due to a copyist's eye catching "Gath-rimmon" in the previous verse.

GAULANITIS (gôl-ăn-ī′-tís), a province NE of the Sea of Galilee ruled by Herod Antipas. The name is derived from Golan, a city of Manasseh in Bashan and one of three cities of refuge E of the Jordan (Deut. 4:43; Josh. 20:8; 21:27).

GAZA (gā′-zà, Heb. *'azzâh, strong,* Gr. *Gáza*), one of the five chief Philistine cities and the most southwesterly toward Egypt. Originally a seaport, the town moved to a hill three miles inland on the great caravan route between Syria and Egypt. Here it became an important rest stop on the edge of the desert and a popular trading center. Its position and *strength* (as its name means) made it the key of this line of communications. It is called by its Hebrew name *Azzah* (Deut. 2:23; I Kings 4:24; Jer. 25:20).

Originally a Canaanite city (Gen. 10:19), Gaza was assigned by Joshua to Judah (Josh. 15:47) but was not occupied till after Judah had taken it (Judg. 1:18), as the Anakims were still present

The city of Gaza as seen from the west. © MPS

(Josh 11:22; 13:3). The Philistines soon recovered it (Judg. 13:1) and there Samson perished while destroying his captors (16:1,21). Solomon ruled over it (I Kings 4:24), but it was Hezekiah who gave the decisive blow to the Philistines (II Kings 18:8). God through Amos threatened Gaza with destruction by fire for her transgressions (Amos 1:6). This was fulfilled by one of the pharaohs of Egypt (Jer. 47:1). The predictions that Gaza would be forsaken (Zeph. 2:4) and that its king should perish (Zech. 9:5, i.e., its Persian satrap, or petty king subordinate to the great king of Persia) were fulfilled by Alexander the Great who took the city in 332 B.C., after it had resisted his siege for two months. He bound Betis the satrap to a chariot, dragging him round the city, and slew 10,000 of its inhabitants, selling the rest as slaves. It was desolated again by fire and sword by the Maccabees in 96 B.C. In turn, Gaza passed under the control of Syria and Rome.

Philip met the Ethiopian eunuch "S unto the way that goeth down from Jerusalem unto Gaza which is desert" (Acts 8:26). Once Gaza was the seat of a Christian church and bishop in the midst of Greek culture and temples, but it turned Moslem in A.D. 634. Now, of its 20,000 inhabitants, only a few hundred are Christians, the rest Moslems.

Modern Ghuzzeh is the metropolis of the Gaza Strip which is crowded with Arab refugees today. N of Ghuzzeh lies an extensive olive grove from the fruit of which soap is made. Its trade in corn is considerable, and there can still be heard the grinding of corn by millstones such as Samson was forced to work with in his prison house at Gaza (Judg. 16:21). The Tel el Muntar or "hill of the watchman" (II Kings 18:8), SE of Gaza, is the hill up which Samson carried the gates of the city (Judg. 16:3).   A.M.R.

GAZELLE (See Animals)

GAZER (See Gezer)

GAZEZ (gā'zĕz). 1. Son of Ephah.
2. Grandson of Ephah, Caleb's concubine (I Chron. 2:46).

GAZZAM (găz'ăm), one of the Nethinim, whose posterity returned from exile (Ezra 2:48; Neh. 7:51).

GEBA (gē'ba, gā'ba, Heb. *geva' hill*), a town in the territory of Benjamin (Josh. 18:24 ASV, RSV; Gaba in KJV), assigned to the Levites (Josh. 21:17; I Chron. 6:60; 8:6). Jonathan defeated the Philistines at Geba (I Sam. 13:3). Saul and Jonathan then remained in Geba (I Sam. 13:16 ASV, RSV; KJV translates Gibeah, also in 14:5; see Judg. 20:10,33). Geba is SW of Wady Suweinît, opposite Michmash (I Sam. 14:5), where Jonathan and his armor-bearer, by a bold stratagem won a signal victory. Geba should be Gibeon in II Samuel 5:25 (ASV margin has Gibeon), as in the parallel passage (I Chron. 14:16). Asa fortified Geba with stones and timber which Baasha had gathered to build Ramah (I Kings 15:22). In the time of Hezekiah Geba was the northernmost city of the kingdom of Judah, as Beersheba its southernmost (II Kings 23:8; II Chron. 16:6). The Assyrians, marching toward Jerusalem, stored their baggage at Michmash, crossed the pass to Geba and camped for a night (Isaiah 10:28,29). Men from Geba returned after the exile (Ezra 2:26; Neh. 7:30 ASV, RSV; Gaba in KJV). Levites from Geba helped in the rebuilding of Jerusalem (Neh. 11:31; 12:29). Zechariah 14:10 prophesied that the land will be made a plain from Geba to Rimmon, except for lofty Jerusalem.

GEBAL (gē'băl, Heb. *geval, border*, Gr. *Búblos, Bíblos*). 1. A seaport of Phoenicia, between Sidon and Tripolis; modern Jebeil, 25 miles N of Beirut. In the 15th century B.C. it was subject to Egypt. Its political history included periods of independence alternating with subjection to successive empires. In Greek and Roman times it was called Byblos, from the manufacture of papyrus there. Joshua 13:5,6 refers to the land of the Giblites or Gebalites, the land of Lebanon at the foot of Mt. Hermon, as part of the land God gave to the children of Israel; God promised to drive out its inhabitants if Joshua would divide it by lot to the Israelites; but we have no record of Joshua accepting the offer, and the Israelites never controlled Gebal. In I Kings 5:17,18, ASV, RSV replaces "stonesquarers" of KJV with "Gebalites" or "men of Gebal." Expert stonemasonry was among the industries of Gebal. Shipbuilding was another, for Ezekiel 27:9 tells us that caulkers from Gebal

The village of Geba. © MPS

worked on ships at Tyre. Skilled technologies, paper-making, fine stonework and seaworthy shipbuilding distinguished Gebal, rather than the extraction of raw materials or mass production alone.
2. A land between the Dead Sea and Petra; modern Jibâl, in northeastern Edom; allied with enemies of Israel, including Edom and Assyria (Ps. 83:6-8).

GEBER (gē'bêr). 1. One of Solomon's twelve purveyors for Southern Gilead (I Kings 4:13).
2. The son of Uri, who was over great pasture lands east of Jordan (I Kings 4:19). The two Gebers are sometimes identified as the same person.

GEBIM (gē'bĭm), a place near Anathoth and Nob, whose inhabitants fled at the approach of the Assyrian invaders (Isa. 10:31).

GECKO (See Animals)

GEDALIAH (gĕd'á-lī'á, Heb. *gedhalyâh*). 1. A son of Shaphan, king Josiah's secretary and Governor of Mizpah (II Kings 25:22-25; Jer. 39:14; 40:5-16; 41:1-18; 43:6). This Judean of high rank was the one who protected Jeremiah, whose views he shared, from the anti-Chaldeans. Nebuchadnezzar made him governor over "the poor people left in the land." He ruled, however, for only two months. The anniversary of his treacherous murder is observed as one of the four Jewish feasts (Zech. 7:5; 8:19).
2. A priest, of the sons of Jeshua, who had taken a strange wife during the exile (Ezra 10:18).
3. Grandfather of the prophet Zephaniah (Zeph. 1:1).
4. One of the six sons of Jeduthun, a harper and head of the second of twenty-four companies, his consisting of twelve musicians (I Chron. 25:8,9).
5. A son of Pashur and the prince who caused Jeremiah to be imprisoned (Jer. 38:1-6).

GEDER (gē'dêr, Heb. *gedher*), Canaanite royal city near Debir, taken by Joshua (Josh. 12:13); perhaps Beth-gader (I Chron. 2:51) and the birthplace of Baal-hamon the Gederite (I Chron. 27:28).

GEDERAH (gĕ-dē'ra, Heb. *gedhērâh, wall*), a town on the heights between the valleys of Sorek and Aijalon in the Shephelah of Judah (Josh. 15:36,41) named with Gedorothaim (two walls) and Gederoth (walls). Modern Jedîreh. Jozabad (I Chron. 12:4) was a Gederathite. For KJV "those that dwelt among plants and hedges" ASV, RSV have "the inhabitants of Netaim and Gederah."

GEDOR (gē'dôr, Heb. *gedhôr, wall*). 1. A city in the hill country of Judah (Josh. 15:58); now Khirbet Jedûr, a few miles north of Hebron.
2. The town where Jeroham lived, whose sons were among the Benjamites who came to David at Ziklag (I Chron. 12:7); location unknown.

General view of ruins at Gebal (Byblos). © MPS

3. A descendant of Benjamin, who, with his father Jehiel and brothers, dwelt at Gibeon (I Chron. 8:31; 9:37).

4. Among the descendants of Judah, Penuel (I Chron. 4:4) and Jered (I Chron. 4:18) are both named as the "father" of Gedor: since the genealogical tables in which the names occur are different, two persons named Gedor must be meant.

5. In the time of Hezekiah, princes of Simeon went to Gedor to find pasture for their flocks, and finding it so good, they drove out the inhabitants and settled there.

GEHAZI (gē-hā′zī, Heb. *gêhăzî, valley of vision*), the servant of Elisha. He first appears when Elisha sought to reward the Shunamite woman for her hospitality (II Kings 4:8-37). When she declined to ask any reward, Gehazi answered, "Verily she hath no child, and her husband is old." Elisha promised her that she should bear a child, which came to pass. "When the child was grown," he died of sunstroke. The woman went with her sorrow to Elisha. He sent Gehazi with instructions to lay Elisha's staff upon the face of the child; but "the child is not awaked." Elisha then came himself and restored the child to life. Elisha had Gehazi call the woman to receive her son. Gehazi next appears when Naaman is healed (II Kings 5: 1-27). Elisha refused any reward. After Naaman left, Gehazi determined to run after Naaman and ask something. Naaman gave him more than he asked. Gehazi hid his booty before he reached home, but Elisha knew what had happened, and rebuked Gehazi by invoking upon him the leprosy of which Naaman had been cured. Gehazi is last met with, talking with the king of "all the great things that Elisha hath done" (II Kings 8:4-6). As Gehazi was telling of the Shunamite woman's son being restored to life, the woman herself appeared, to ask the king to restore to her the property which she abandoned upon the advice of Elisha during a seven years' famine. The king ordered her fully compensated. Because Gehazi appears in the court of the king, it has been inferred that he had repented and been healed of his leprosy, though II Kings 5:27 renders this doubtful. He shows no resentment against Elisha. Gehazi was an efficient servant, but weak enough to yield to avarice. He lacked his master's clear moral insight and stamina, and he bore no such relations to Elisha as Elisha bore to Elijah.

GEHENNA (gē-hĕn′à, Gr. *geénna*, a transliteration of the Aramaic form of Heb. *gê-ben-hinnôm, valley of the son of Hinnom*), a valley on the W and SW of Jerusalem, which formed part of the border between Judah and Benjamin (comparing Josh. 15:8 with 18:16); still recognized as the border after the exile (Neh. 11:30,31); modern Wadî errabâbi. Here Ahaz (II Chron. 28:3; see II Kings 16:3) and Manasseh (II Chron. 33:6; see II Kings 21:6) sacrificed their sons to Molech (Jer. 32:35). For this reason Josiah defiled the place (II Kings 23:10). After referring to the idolatrous barbarities (Jer. 7:31,32) Jeremiah prophesies a great slaughter of the people there, and in the siege of Jerusalem (Jer. 19:1-13). After the OT period, Jewish apocalyptic writers began to call the Valley of Hinnom the entrance to hell, later hell itself. In Jewish usage of the first century A.D., Gehenna referred to the intermediate state of the godless dead, but there is no trace of this sense in the NT. The NT distinguishes sharply between Hades, the intermediate, bodiless state, and Gehenna, the state of final punishment after the resurrection of the body. Gehenna existed before the judgment

(Matt. 25;41). The word occurs 12 times in the NT, always translated "hell" ASV, RSV margin "Gehenna." Eleven times it is on the lips of Jesus; as the final punishment for calling one's brother a fool (Matt. 5:22); for adultery, when the severest measures have not been taken to prevent commission of this offense (Matt. 5:29,30); and others (Matt. 18:9; Mark 9:43,45,47); in a warning as to whom to fear (Matt. 10:28; Luke 12:5). A hypocrite is called a "son of hell" (Matt. 23:15) who cannot "escape the damnation of hell" (Matt. 23:33). James 3:6 speaks of the "tongue" as "a fire," being "set on fire of hell." A fire was kept burning in the Valley of Hinnom to consume the offal deposited there. Terms parallel to Gehenna include "furnace of fire" (Matt. 13:42,50); "lake of fire" (Rev. 19:20; 20:10 14,15); "eternal fire" (Jude 7); "cast down to hell" (II Pet. 2:4), where the Greek verb means "cast down to Tartaros," a Greek name for the place of punishment of the wicked dead. Its use by our Saviour Jesus Christ warns us of the destiny which even the love of God does not avert from those who finally refuse His forgiveness. See HADES, HELL E.R.

Gehenna, the Valley of Hinnom, which was a place for dumping and burning refuse. The village of Siloam and the Hill of Offence are shown beyond. © MPS

GELILOTH (gē-lī′lŏth—lŏth, Josh. 18:17), the name of a place on the border of Benjamin with Judah, E of Jerusalem; perhaps the same as the Gilgal of Joshua 15:7, whose name has a similar meaning (circuit). It cannot be the Gilgal near Jericho in the Jordan Valley.

GEMALLI (gē-măl′ī, *camel owner* or *rider*), the father of Ammiel, ruler of the tribe of Dan, and one of the twelve spies sent out to explore the land (Num. 13:12).

GEMARIAH (gĕm′à-rī′à, *Jehovah hath fulfilled* or *accomplishment of the Lord*). 1. A prince, son of Shaphan the scribe and brother of Ahikam (Jer. 36:10-25). This scribe with others sought in vain to keep king Jehoiakim from burning the roll which Baruch had written at the dictation of Jeremiah.

2. A son of Hilkiah, sent by King Zedekiah as ambassador to Nebuchadnezzar at Babylon. He also carried a letter from Jeremiah to the captive Jews (Jer. 29:3).

GENEALOGY (jĕn'ē-ăl'ō-jē, Heb. *yahas,* Gr. *genea-logía*), a list of ancestors or descendants; or descent from an ancestor; or the study of lines of descent. Genealogies are compiled to show biological descent, the right of inheritance, succession to an office, or ethnological and geographical relationships. The word occurs several times in the English Bible (I Chron. 4:33; 5:1,7; 7:5,7,9,40; 9:22; II Chron. 12:15; 31:16-19; Ezra 2:62; 8:1; Neh. 7:5, 64; I Tim. 1:4; Tit. 3:9), but most Bible genealogies are introduced by other words, such as "the book of the generations of," or "these are the generations of," or are given without titles. Bible genealogies are not primarily concerned with mere biological descent. The earliest (Gen. 4:1, 2,17-22), by its emphasis on occupations (Abel, shepherd; Cain, farmer and city-builder; Jabal, cattleman; Jubal, musician; Tubal-cain, metal worker), in a family register of Cain's descendants, shows when new features of the culture were introduced. The genealogy of the line of Seth (Gen. 4:25,26; 5:1-32), a list of long-lived individuals, contrasts with the genealogy in Genesis 10:1-32, which is clearly a table of nations descended from the three families of Shem, Ham, and Japheth. Many of the names are Heb. plurals in "-im," signifying nations, tribes, cities or towns rather than individuals. The scope of Biblical genealogies narrows to the Chosen People and their close relatives (Gen. 11:10-22, Shem to Abraham; 22:20-24, Abraham's near kin). Next are the children of Abraham by Hagar (Gen. 16:15; 25:12-18); by Sarah (21:1-3; 25:19-28) and by Keturah (25:1-4); then the children of Jacob (Gen. 29:31-30:24; 35:16-26); and of his brother Esau (Gen. 36) for many generations in Edom. Jacob's posterity who came into Egypt are carefully enumerated (Gen. 46:8-27); part of them again (Exod. 6:14-27) to bring the genealogy down to Moses and Aaron; the inclusion of brief mention of the sons of Reuben and Simeon before the fuller genealogy of the Levites may be due to this list being taken from an earlier one. Numbers 26:1-56 is a census on genealogical principles, for the purpose of equitable division of the land. The military organization of the Israelites for the wilderness journey was by genealogy (Num. 1-3), and this included the priests and Levites (3:11-39), and provided for a tax and offerings (7:11-89) for the support of religion (3:40-51), as well as the order of march in peace or war (10). Many other references to persons must be taken into account in attempting a complete genealogy. Ruth 4:17-22 picks up the genealogy of Judah from his son Pharez, to carry it down to David, whose children are listed: those born in Hebron (II Sam. 3:2-5) and in Jerusalem (5:13-16). David's "mighty men" are named, with brief notices of their descent (II Sam. 23:8-39). Solomon's princes and providers of food are likewise treated (II Kings 4:1-19).

The major genealogical tables of the OT are in I Chronicles 1-9. They use most of the earlier genealogical material, but show differences which at a distance of time are puzzling. Satisfactory solutions are not available for many of these. Mistakes in copying would account for some; differences in the purpose of the recorders for others. The books of Kings and Chronicles contain information about the family relationships of the kings of Judah and of Israel. Ezra 2:1-63; 8:1-20 and Nehemiah 7:7-63 name by families those who returned with Zerubbabel from Babylonian captivity, including many whose descent could not be traced. Ezra 7:1-6 gives Ezra's own line of descent from Aaron. Ezra 10:18:44 names those

who had married foreign women. Nehemiah 3 names those who helped rebuild the walls of Jerusalem. There follow lists of those who helped Ezra proclaim the law of God (Neh. 8:1-8); of those who sealed the covenant to keep the law (Neh. 10:1-27); of the leading inhabitants in Jerusalem (Neh. 11:1-10), in nearby Judah (11:20-24), and in more remote villages of Judah and Benjamin (11:25-36). Nehemiah 12 deals with the priests who accompanied Zerubbabel (1-9); the succession of high priests from Jeshua to Jaddua (10,11); the "priests, the chief of the fathers," in the days of Joiakim (12-21); Levites in this period (22-26); princes and priests who took part in the dedication of the wall of Jerusalem (31-42). The prophets usually begin their books with some indication of their genealogy (Isa. 1:1; Jer. 1:1; Ezek. 1:3; Hos. 1:1; Joel 1:1; Jonah 1:1; Zeph. 1:1; Zech. 1:1).

The genealogies of Jesus Christ will be dealt with in a separate article. Other NT persons generally appear without indication of their descent. Occasionally the father is named (e.g., James and John, the sons of Zebedee, Luke 5:10, etc.). Paul cherishes his pure Heb. descent (Phil. 3:4,5). I Timothy 1:4 and Titus 3:9 are sometimes thought to refer to pagan Gnostic series of beings intermediate between God and the created earth, but it is more likely that the rabbinic over-concern with human genealogies is meant, because the false teachers seem to be Jewish, and the term "genealogies" is not used by heathen authors of the pagan Gnostic series. Since the two genealogies of Jesus Christ in Matthew and Luke are known to have caused controversy a century or so later, it may not be improper to surmise that this difficulty was already troubling the churches.

It is certain that the NT shows far less concern for the genealogy of human beings than does the OT. In the OT, God was bringing forth a Chosen People who should be a nation peculiarly devoted to preserving the revelation of Him until in the fulness of time God sent forth His Son, Who should draw to Himself a new people, united not by descent from a common human ancestor, but by a genealogy of one generation only: a child of God by a new and spiritual birth.   E.R.

GENEALOGY OF JESUS CHRIST (jĕn'ē-ăl'ō-jē). Two genealogies are given in the NT: in Matthew 1:17, and in Luke 3:23-38. Matthew traces the descent of Jesus from Abraham and David, and divides it into three sets of fourteen generations each, probably to aid memorization. There are fourteen names from Abraham to and including David. From David to and including Josiah, and counting David a second time, there are fourteen names. (David is named twice in Matt. 1, v. 17). From Jechoniah to Jesus we have fourteen names. Matthew omits three generations after Joram, namely Ahaziah, Joash and Amaziah (I Chron. 3:11,12). Such an omission in Heb. genealogies is not peculiar to Matthew. He names Zerah as well as Perez, and mentions the brethren of Judah and of Jechoniah, which is unusual. Contrary to Heb. practice, he names five women: Tamar, Rahab, Ruth, Bathsheba (the wife of Uriah), and Mary, each name evoking associations, dark or bright, with the history of the chosen people. Matthew carefully excludes the physical paternity of Joseph by saying "Joseph the husband of Mary, of whom" (feminine singular in Greek) "was born Jesus" (1:16). The sense of "begat" in Heb. genealogies was not exact: it indicated immediate or remote descent, an adoptive relation, or legal heirship, as well as procreation.

Luke's genealogy moves from Jesus to Adam. Between Abraham and Adam it is the same as in I Chronicles 1:1-7,24-28, or the more detailed genealogies in Genesis; making allowance for the different spelling of names in transliteration from Heb. or Greek. From David to Abraham Luke agrees with OT genealogies and with Matthew. Between Jesus and David Luke's list differs from Matthew's, and there is no OT record to compare with Luke's, except for Nathan being one of David's sons, and for the names of Salathiel (Shealtil) and Zorobabel (Zerubbabel). At this point the two genealogies crossed, through adoption or otherwise.

As Matthew gave the line of the kings from David to Jechoniah, it is probable that from Salathiel to Joseph he named those who were heirs to the Davidic throne. Luke's record then would be that of physical descent, though crossing the royal line at one point. In Luke 3:23 there is a question as to how much should be considered parenthetical. Some would include "of Joseph" in the parenthesis: "(as was supposed of Joseph)," making Heli in some sense the father of Jesus, perhaps his maternal grandfather. This construction is awkward. Another supposition is that Joseph is really the son-in-law of Heli, through his marriage to Mary, thought to be Heli's daughter. If both genealogies are those of Joseph, his relationship to Heli must be different from his relationship to Jacob. Scholars have wrestled with the problems of the two genealogies from the second century, when pagan critics raised the difficulty. Many explanations have been more ingenious than convincing, involving complicated and uncertain inferences.

A relatively simple solution is given by A. T. Robertson in his *A Harmony of the Gospels for Students of the Life of Christ*, New York: George H. Doran and Co., 1922, pp. 259-262. In this view, widely accepted, Matthew gives the legal descent of heirship to the throne of David, through Joseph, while Luke gives the physical descent of Jesus through Mary. Matthew is concerned with the kingship of Jesus, Luke with His humanity. Both make plain His Virgin Birth, and therefore His Deity. In the light of these salient facts, on which the agreement of Matthew and Luke is obvious, their differences only accentuate their value as independent witnesses, in whose testimony the Holy Spirit did not see fit to cause them to collaborate. The question is fully discussed in J. G. Machen, *The Virgin Birth of Christ*, New York: Harper and Brothers, 1930, pp. 202-209, and in ISBE, vol. 2, pp. 1196-1199. Matthew's genealogy establishes the legal claim to the throne of David through his foster-father Joseph; Luke's establishes His actual descent from David through Mary. Luke 1:32 says that Mary's child "shall be called the Son of the Highest: and the Lord God shall give unto Him the throne of his father David." Romans 1:3,4 agrees with this: Jesus "was made of the seed of David according to the flesh," which could only be through Mary; "and declared to be the Son of God . . . by the resurrection from the dead." II Timothy 2:8 echoes this. Isaiah 11:1 indicates that Messiah is to be physically a descendant of David's father Jesse. The genealogies must be seen in the light of this fact. (Compare Matt. 22:41-46 and parallels with the answer in Rom. 1:4). E.R.

GENERATION (jĕn'ẽr-ā'shŭn), in the OT, the translation of two Heb. words: (1) *tôledhôth*, from a root *yalad*, to beget, used always in the plural, refers to lines of descent from an ancestor, and occurs in the phrase "these are the generations of,"

introducing each of eleven sections of Genesis, from 2:4 to 37:2 (also elsewhere in Gen., Exod., Num., I Chron., and Ruth 4:18); (2 *dôr, a period of time* (e.g., Deut. 32:7, past; Exod. 3:15, future; Ps. 102:24, both); *all the men living in a given period* (e.g., Gen. 7:1; Judg. 3:2); *a class of men characterized by a certain quality* (e.g., Deut. 32:5; Ps. 14:5); *a dwelling place or habitation* (Isa. 58:12; Ps. 49:19).

In the NT, *generation* translates four Greek words, all having reference to descent: (1) *geneá*, most frequent in the synoptic Gospels; for *lines of descent from an ancestor* (e.g., Matt. 1:17); or *all the men living in a given period* (e.g., Matt. 11:16); or *a class of men characterized by a certain quality* (e.g., Matt. 12:39); also, *a period of time* (Acts 13:36; Col. 1:26). (2) *génesis*, in Matthew 1:1, in a heading to verses 2:17, used to mean "genealogy"; (3) *génnema*, in the phrase "generation of vipers" (Matt. 3:7; 12:34; 23:33; Luke 3:7; ASV "offspring"; RSV "brood"); *génos*, race (I Pet. 2:9; ASV, RSV "race"); (4) Matthew 24:34 and parallels Mark 13:30 and Luke 21:32 present a special problem. If "this generation" (*geneá*) refers to the people then living, these verses, despite their position, must relate to the destruction of Jerusalem and not to the Second Coming of Christ. But the meaning may be that the generation which sees the beginning of the special signs of the Second Coming will see the end of them. Another interpretation is that "generation" here refers to the Jewish nation. *Geneá* may bear the sense of *nation* or *race*. E.R.

GENESIS (jĕn'ĕ-sĭs), the first book of the Bible. The name is derived from a Greek word meaning "origin" or "beginning," which is the title given to the book in the Septuagint. The Hebrew name for the book is *berēshîth*, from Genesis 1:1 ("in the beginning"). The special phrase, "These are the generations of" divides the book into eleven sections (2:4, 5:1, 6:9, 10:1, 11:10, 11:27, 25:12, 25:19, 36:1, and 37:2), and serves as a superscription to the section that follows it. These sections do not describe the origin of the person mentioned in the superscription (or of "the heavens and earth" in the case of 2:4), but rather the further history of the one whose origin has already been described, plus that of his immediate offspring. A broader outline divides the book into two unequal sections. Genesis 1:1 through 11:26 describes the creation of the heavens, the earth, plants, animals, and man; the Fall and the Edenic curse; the antediluvian age and the great Flood; and the descendants of Noah down to Terah. Genesis 11:27 through 50:26 traces the history of Abraham and Lot; Ishmael and Isaac; Jacob and Esau; and Joseph and his brethren in Egypt.

GENESIS 1-11 AND UNIFORMITARIAN SCIENCE. Evangelical scholars have differed widely in their reaction to the claims of uniformitarian and evolutionary science that the earth has existed for billions of years, that animals preceded man by millions of years, that man has been on earth for hundreds of thousands of years, and that the Flood could have covered only a small part of the earth. Various attempts to harmonize Genesis with uniformitarian theories have gained wide acceptance among evangelicals, but such harmonizations reveal fatal inconsistencies and concessions which render them Biblically untenable. The Scriptural doctrine of a geographically universal and geologically significant Flood actually undermines the entire superstructure of uniformitarianism; for such a catastrophe, continuing for an entire year and covering all the high mountains of the antediluvian earth, must, of absolute necessity, have accomplished a vast amount of geologic work in a relatively short period (cf. H. C. Leupold, *Exposition of Genesis,* Columbus: The Wartburg Press, 1942, pp. 201, 296, 301; and J. C. Whitcomb and H. M. Morris, *The Genesis Flood,* Nutley, N. J.: The Presbyterian and Reformed Pub. Co., 1961, pp. 76, 123, 265-72). See FLOOD OR DELUGE.

It is difficult to find room in Genesis 1-11 for the vast periods of time which are demanded by uniformitarians. The Scriptures reveal that the heavens, the earth, the sea, "and all that in them is" were created within six days, and therefore that man should labor for six days (Exod. 20:9-11). This is not the only indication that the days of creation were literal 24-hour days. (1) Although the word "day" sometimes refers to a period of undetermined length (cf. Joel 1:15), it always refers to a 24-hour period when a numerical adjective accompanies it, as it does six times in the first chapter of Genesis. (2) The phrase "evening and morning" is a technical Hebrew phrase meaning 24 hours (cf. Dan. 8:14 ASV). (3) Plants (created the third day) could hardly have survived a geologic age without sunlight (created the fourth day). If Moses had wanted to express the idea that the sun was simply made visible on the fourth day he could have used such a term as "appear" (verse 9). All attempts to make the days of creation correspond to the geologic ages have failed. For example, the Bible states that fruit trees were created two days before marine organisms; but paleontologists of the uniformitarian school insist that marine life existed millions of years before fruit trees. Other harmonization efforts, such as the revelatory view and the framework hypothesis, are contradicted by the plain reading of the text (cf. Paul A. Zimmerman, ed., *Darwin, Evolution, and Creation,* St. Louis: Concordia Pub. House, 1959, pp. 57-64).

The basic incompatibility of Genesis and uniformitarianism is seen further in the fact that Adam is said to have had dominion over the entire animal kingdom and that the diet of both man and beast was vegetarian (1:26-30; cf. Isa. 11:6-9). This could hardly have been the case if animals had been dying, devouring each other, and in many cases whole species becoming extinct millions of years before Adam's creation. Romans 8: 20-22 teaches that "the whole creation groaneth and travaileth in pain" under "the bondage of corruption" as a consequence of Adam's fall. To postulate a "reign of tooth and claw" during vast ages before Adam would be to undermine the force of this passage. In contradiction to uniformitarian hypotheses, Genesis reveals that God created the heavens and the earth as a dynamic, functioning entity. Thus, even as Adam was created instantly as a grown man, so also the earth and its living creatures were created fully "grown" within six days, with the oceans already containing the salts and chemicals necessary for sustaining marine life (1:2,10,20), the dry land equipped with a mantle of soil for plants and trees (1:11), the light rays from distant stars already performing their God-intended function of shining upon the earth (1:14-19), and the animals and plants created after their kinds (1:11,12,20-25). The "grown creation" doctrine is simply the Biblical doctrine of creation rightly understood, and is illustrated in the NT by the miracle of the changing of water to wine (John 2:1-11). The presuppositions which underlie the various age-determination methods of modern geology may be properly challenged, therefore, by those who accept the Biblical

Fragment of a Creation Tablet, from Nineveh, with Assyrian account of creation. BM

doctrine of creation (cf. John W. Klotz, *Genes, Genesis, and Evolution,* St. Louis: Concordia Pub. House, 1955, pp. 86-96).

GENESIS 12-50 AND ARCHAEOLOGICAL DISCOVERY. In spite of a century and a half of attacks by scholars of the critical school, the unity and Mosaic authorship of Genesis have been successfully defended by orthodox scholars, and the documentary hypothesis has been shown to rest upon false presuppositions (cf. O. T. Allis, *The Five Books of Moses,* Nutley, N. J.: The Presbyterian & Reformed Pub. Co., 1943). Furthermore, the entire field of OT studies has been revolutionized in recent decades by the discovery of vast numbers of clay tablets which shed important light upon ancient Near Eastern history and customs. Over 100,000 of these tablets date to the early second millennium B.C., and therefore fall within the patriarchal period (cf. D. J. Wiseman, *Illustrations From Biblical Archaeology,* Grand Rapids: Wm. B. Eerdmans Pub. Co., 1958, p. 25). Only a few of the discoveries which shed light on Genesis can be listed here.

The "Adam and Eve Seal" found near Nineveh in 1932 by Dr. E. A. Speiser, who dated it about 3500 B.C. UMP

Abraham's choice of Eliezer of Damascus to be his heir (15:2-4) corresponds to ancient Semitic and Hurrian custom, which provided that the adopted heir yield his rights in case a natural son should be born (Wiseman, *op. cit.,* p. 25). Sarah was only following the ways of her contemporaries when she gave Hagar to Abraham to bear a child for him (16:1-3), and Abraham was understandably grieved when Sarah later insisted on driving out both Hagar and Ishmael (21:11), for a Nuzi legal document (c. 1500 B.C.) states that "if Kelim-ninu (the bride) does not bear, Kelim-ninu shall acquire a woman of the land of Lullu (a slave) as wife for Shennima (the bridegroom), and Kelim-ninu may not send the offspring away" (James B. Pritchard, ed., *Ancient Near Eastern Texts,* Princeton University Press, 1950, p. 220). Furthermore, Nuzi sale-adoption documents have shed light on Jacob's relationship to Laban. We thus discover that possession of the household gods marked a person as the legitimate heir, and that the adopted son forfeited his inheritance if he took another wife outside of the family. This explains Rachel's theft of Laban's teraphim (31:19) and Laban's warning that Jacob should take no other wives besides his daughters (31:50) (Pritchard, *op. cit.,* pp. 219-220). We have also learned that personal names like Abraham, Isaac, and Jacob were current in those days; that Shechem, Ai, Bethel, and Dothan were thriving cities around 2000 B.C.; that the Negev region and the Jordan valley were also thickly populated; and that Sodom and Gomorrah were destroyed about that time and their ruins lie under the waters of the Dead Sea (Wiseman, *op. cit.,* pp. 29-30).

With regard to the patriarchs in Egypt, important archaeological discoveries have also been made (see EXODUS). For example, it is now recognized that Abraham could have had camels in Egypt (12:16) (cf. Joseph P. Free, "Abraham's Camels," JNES, July, 1944, pp. 187-93), and that groups of Semites migrated into Egypt as early as 2000 B.C. (tomb paintings at Beni Hassan). A recently published papyrus dating to about 1800 B.C. "lists seventy-nine servants in an Egyptian household, forty-five of whom are 'Asiatics', probably sold into Egypt as slaves . . . Some of them bear good Hebrew names like Shiphrah and Menahem" (Wiseman, *op. cit.,* p. 39). A great many examples of authentic Egyptian coloring in the patriarchal narrative of Genesis 39-50 have now been fully illustrated by archaeological discoveries (cf. M. F. Unger, *Archaeology and the Old Testament,* Grand Rapids: Zondervan Pub. House, 1954, pp. 132-34). In the words of the eminent archaeologist William Foxwell Albright, "So many corroborations of details have been discovered in recent years that most competent scholars have given up the old critical theory according to which stories of the Patriarchs are mostly retrojections from the time of the Dual Monarchy (9th-8th centuries B.C.)." (*From the Stone Age to Christianity,* 2nd ed., New York: Doubleday & Co., 1957, p. 241.) J.C.W.

GENNESARET (gĕ-nĕs'à-rĕt). 1. "The land of Gennesaret" (Matt. 14:34; Mark 6:53), a plain stretching about three miles along the northwest shore of the Sea of Galilee, extending about a mile inland: the modern el-Ghuweir. With a rich, loamy, well-watered soil, today as in Bible times it is extraordinarily fertile; the only easily tillable land bordering the Sea of Galilee. The fig, olive, palm and walnut trees, which ordinarily require diverse conditions, all grow well here.

2. "The Lake of Gennesaret" (Luke 5:1), elsewhere in Luke simply "the lake" (5:2; 8:22,23,33); the same as the Sea of Galilee (Matt. 4:18; 15:29; Mark 1:16; 7:31; John 6:1); or the OT "Sea of Chinnereth."

GENTILES (jĕn'tīlz, Heb. *gôy,* plural *gôyîm, nation, people*), translated "Gentiles" in KJV of the OT 30 times, "people" 11 times, "heathen" 142 times, "nation" 373 times, "nation" being the usual translation in ASV, RSV. Sometimes *gôy* refers to Israel (Gen. 12:2; Deut. 32:28; Josh. 3:17; 4:1; 10:13; II Sam. 7:23; Isa. 1:4; Zeph. 2:9; translated "nation" or "people" in KJV as well as ASV, RSV). But *'âm* is the ordinary term for Israel. *Gôy* usually means a non-Israelite people. In the NT, Greek *éthnos* renders *gôy,* while *laós, people,* corresponds to Heb. *'âm. Éthnos* is translated "Gentiles" in the NT in KJV, ASV and RSV. *Héllenes, Greeks,* is translated "Gentiles" in KJV, "Greeks" in ASV, RSV (John 7:35; Rom. 2:9,10; 3:9; I Cor. 10:32; 12:13).

Under conditions of peace, considerate treatment was accorded Gentiles under OT law (e.g., Deut. 10:19; 24:14,15; Num. 35:15; Ezek. 47:22). Men of Israel often married Gentile women, of whom Rahab, Ruth and Bathsheba are notable examples, but the practice was frowned upon after the return from exile (Ezra 9:12; 10:2-44; Neh. 10:30; 13:23-31). Separation between Jew and Gentile became more strict, until in the NT period the hostility is complete. Persecution embittered the Jew, and he retaliated by hatred of everything Gentile, and by avoidance, so far as was possible, of contact with Gentiles. The intensity of this feeling varied, and gave way before unusual kindness (Luke 7:4,5).

While the teachings of Jesus ultimately broke down "the middle wall of partition" between Jew and Gentile, as is seen in the writings of Paul (Rom. 1:16; I Cor. 1:24; Gal. 3:28; Eph. 2:14; Col. 3:11) and in Acts, yet Jesus limited His ministry to Jews, with rare exceptions (the half-Jewish Samaritans, John 4:1-42, the Syrophoenician woman, Matt. 15:21-28; Mark 7:24-30; the Greeks in John 12:20-36). He instructed His twelve disciples, "Go not into the way of the Gentiles, and into any city of the Samaritans enter ye not" (Matt. 10:5); but did not repeat this injunction when He sent out the Seventy (Luke 10:1-16). Jesus' mission was first to "his own" (John 1:11), the Chosen People of God; but ultimately to "as many as received him" (John 1:12). Limitations of time held His ministry on earth within the bounds of Israel; reaching the Gentiles was left to the activity of the Holy Spirit working through His disciples.

In Acts, from the appointment of Paul as the apostle to the Gentiles (9:15), the Gentiles become increasingly prominent. Even the letters ad-

The Plain of Gennesaret and the Sea of Galilee, as viewed from Bethsaida. © MPS

dressed particularly to Jewish Christians (James; I Pet.; Heb.; Rom. 9-11) are relevant to Gentiles also. The division of all mankind into two classes, Jew and Gentile, emphasizes the importance of the Jews as the people through whom God made salvation available to all people.   E.R.

GENTILES, COURT OF THE, the outer part of the temple, which Gentiles might enter. See TEMPLE.

GENUBATH (gē-nū′băth, Heb. *genuvath, theft*), a son of Hadad the Edomite, the fugitive prince, by the sister of Queen Tahpenes, the wife of the pharaoh who governed Egypt toward the end of David's reign (I Kings 11:20).

GERA (gē′rà, Heb. *gērā′, grain*), a name common in the tribe of Benjamin. 1. A son of Benjamin (Gen. 46:21).

2. A son of Bela and grandson of Benjamin (I Chron. 8:3,5).

3. Father of Ehud (Judg. 3:15).

4. A son of Ehud (I Chron. 8:7).

5. Father of Shimei (II Sam. 16:5; 19:16,18; I Kings 2:8). Some of these are thought to be the same person, taking "father" to mean a remote ancestor, and "son" a remote descendant.

GERAH (See Weights and Measures)

GERAR (gē′rär, Heb. *gerār, circle, region*), a town in the Negev, near but not on the Mediterranean coast south of Gaza, in a valley running northwest and southeast, and on a protected inland caravan route from Palestine to Egypt (Gen. 10:19). Here Abraham sojourned with its king, Abimelech (Gen. 20:1,2); and later Isaac (Gen. 26:1-33) had similar and more extended experiences with the king and people of the region. Here Asa and his army defeated the Ethiopians, and plundered Gerar and the cities round about (II Chron. 14: 13,14). Its site is thought to be the modern Tell ej-Jemmeh, which has been excavated, uncovering levels of occupation from the Late Bronze Age to the Byzantine period.

GERASA (gē-rà′sà), a city E of the Jordan midway between the Sea of Galilee and the Dead Sea, in the Decapolis at the eastern edge of the Peraea; partially excavated; the modern Jerash. The name does not occur in the Bible, but the adjective Gerasenes occurs in Mark 5:1 ASV, RSV, and the margin of Matthew 8:28 RSV and Luke 8:26,37 RSV. The MSS vary in all these passages between Gadarenes, Gerasenes and Gergesenes; and all the above occurrences relate to the region where Jesus healed a demoniac and permitted the demons which possessed the man to rush down a steep slope into the Sea of Galilee, hence this incident must have occurred on the shore. A possible location is at Kursi (Gergesa) on the eastern shore of the lake. Gadara (Muqeis) is SE of Lake Galilee. The place where the Gospel incident occurred may have been referred to sometimes as the country of the Gergesenes, a purely local name; or of the Gadarenes, from the nearest city; or of the Gerasenes, from the most important city of the district. See GADARA.

GERGESA (gûr-gē′sà), a place probably midway of the eastern shore of Lake Galilee, where the bank is steep. The adjective Gergesenes occurs in Matthew 8:28 KJV and RSV margin; Mark 5:1 RSV margin; and Luke 8:26,37 ASV, RSV margins. See GADARA.

GERIZIM (gĕ-rī′zĭm, gĕr′ĭ-zĭm), a mountain of Samaria, Jebel et-Tôr, 2,849 feet high, SW of Mt. Ebal. Through the valley between runs a main N-S road of Palestine, so that this pass is of strategic military importance. Moses commanded that when the Israelites came into the Promised Land, the blessing for keeping the law should be spoken from Mt. Gerizim, and the curse for not obeying it from Mt. Ebal (Deut. 11:29; 27:4-26), six tribes standing on the slopes of either peak (Deut. 27: 11-14). It is conjectured that Mt. Gerizim was selected for the blessing and Mt. Ebal for the curse, from the point of view of one looking eastward, to whom Mt. Gerizim would be on the right or "fortunate" side. From the top of Mt. Gerizim Jotham shouted his parable of the trees to the men of Shechem in the valley below, reminding them of all that his father Gideon had done for them (Judg. 9: 7-21). After the Israelites, returning from Babylonian exile, refused to let the mixed races of Samaria

Mount Gerizim, towering above the ruins of the ancient ramparts of Shechem. © MPS

Remains of the ancient ramparts of Gerar. © MPS

Roman ruins at ancient Gerasa, modern Jerash, showing the theater and the forum. The present village of Jerash lies beyond the ruins. Gerasa was one of the leading cities of the Decapolis. © MPS

help rebuild Jerusalem (Ezra 4:1-4; Neh. 2:19,20; 13:28), the Samaritans built themselves a temple on Mt. Gerizim. "This mountain" referred to in John 4:20,21, is Gerizim, where the Samaritans worshiped in the open, after their temple was destroyed by the Maccabees. The small Samaritan community of Nablus still celebrates the Passover on Mt. Gerizim. Samaritan tradition maintains that Abraham attempted to sacrifice Isaac on this mountain (Gen. 22:1-19); that at a nearby Salem he met Melchizedek (Gen. 14:17-20); and that Jacob's dream (Gen. 28:10-17) occurred at Khirbet Lanzah on Mt. Gerizim. The ruins of a fortress built by the Emperor Justinian in 533 A.D. remain. A rock with a cup-shaped hollow which could have been used for libations, is the traditional altar of the Samaritan temple. The Nablus community also possesses an important MS of the Pentateuch.

GERSHOM (gûr'shŏm, from Heb. *gārash, to cast out,* but in popular etymology explained as from *gēr, stranger,* Exod. 2:22; 18:3). 1. The first-born son of Moses and Zipporah. He was born in Midian (Exod. 2:22; 18:3; I Chron. 23:15,16; 26:24). The unusual circumstances of his circumcision are told in Exodus 4:21-28.

2. The eldest son of Levi, according to I Chronicles 6:16,17,20,43,62,71; 15:7). Elsewhere called Gershon. See Gershon.

3. One of the family of Phinehas, and one of the "heads of houses" who returned with Ezra from Babylon (Ezra 8:2).

4. Father of Jonathan, the Levite who became priest to the Danites who settled in Laish (Judg. 18:30). KJV calls him "son of Manasseh," but ASV, RSV have "sons of Moses," since the "n" in

the Heb. text which converts the consonants of Moses into Manasseh is thought to have been inserted to disguise the fact that Moses had such a graceless descendant as this Jonathan.

GERSHON (gûr'shŏn, Heb. *gēreshôn*), firstborn of the three sons of Levi (Gen. 46:11; Exod. 6:16, 17; Num. 3:17,18,21,25; 4:22,28,38; 7:7; 10:17; 26:57; Josh. 21:6; I Chron. 6:1; 23:6). His descendants are also called Gershonites (Num. 3:21, 23,24; 4:24,27; Josh. 21:33; I Chron. 23:7; 26:21; 29:8; II Chron. 29:12). The functions of the Gershonites during the wilderness wanderings are described in Numbers 3:23-25; 4:21-28; for which functions two wagons and four oxen were deemed sufficient (Num. 7:7). They continued prominent in the service of the Temple of Solomon, and in that of Zerubbabel, especially as singers. See also GERSHOM 2.

GERZITES (gûr'zīts), **GIZRITES** (gĭz'rīts), or **GERIZZITES** (gĕ-rĭz'īts, gĕr'ĭ-zīts), a tribe named between the Geshurites and the Amalekites (I Sam. 27:8), KJV Gezrites; ASV Girzites, margin Gizrites; RSV Girzites. They are called the ancient inhabitants of the land, on the way to Shur, toward Egypt; that is, in the S or Negev of Judah; not certainly connected with Gezer. If originally of Gezer, they may have been driven S by invading Israelites or Philistines.

GESHAM (gē'shăm), a son of Jahdai and descendant of Caleb (I Chron. 2:47). KJV Gesham; ASV, RSV Geshan, also the 1611 edition of KJV.

GESHEM (gē'shĕm), the Arabian who along with Sanballat and Tobiah, sought to oppose the building of the wall by Nehemiah (Neh. 2:19; 6:1,2). The same as Gashmu (Neh. 6:6).

GESHUR (gē′shûr, Heb. *geshûr, bridge*). 1. A country in Syria (II Sam. 15:8; ASV margin and RSV, Aram) on the western border of Og's kingdom of Bashan E of the Jordan (Josh. 12:5). Jair of Manasseh conquered Bashan up to Geshur (Deut. 3:14). Although in the territory of Israel, the Geshurites were not driven out (Josh. 13: 11,13) but "dwelt in the midst of Israel." In fact, Geshur and Aram took from Jair sixty towns (I Chron. 2:23 ASV, RSV) though KJV makes it appear that Jair took the cities from Gilead. David made alliance with their king Talmai by marrying his daughter Maacah (II Sam. 3:3; I Chron. 3:2). Her son Absalom, after he murdered Amnon, sought refuge with her father (II Sam. 13:37,38), whence Joab brought Absalom back (II Sam. 14: 23,32; 15:8).

2. A district between southern Palestine and Sinai, near Philistine territory (Josh. 13:2), unconquered at the close of Joshua's career; against which David made a raid when he was taking refuge from Saul among the Philistines (I Sam. 27:8). Whether these Geshurites were a branch of the same people as 1, is undetermined.

GETHER (gē′thêr), third of Aram's sons (Gen. 10:23; I Chron. 1:17). The latter reference reckons him among the sons of Shem.

GETHSEMANE (gĕth-sĕm′à-nē, probably from the Aramaic for "oil-press"), the place of Jesus' agony and arrest (Matt. 26:36-56; Mark 14:32-52; Luke 22:39-54; John 18:1-12—John tells of the arrest only). In Matthew 26:36; Mark 14:32 it is called "a place"; Luke does not give the name, says that the place was one to which Jesus customarily resorted, and that it was on the Mount of Olives; John 18:1, also without naming it, explains that it was a garden across the Cedron (Kidron) valley from Jerusalem. The traditional site, cared for by the Franciscans, is not far from the road, near the bridge over the Kidron, and is laid out in neat gardens. Within are eight large olive trees. If the Emperor Titus destroyed all the trees around Jerusalem during the siege of 70 A.D., as Josephus asserts, these trees cannot be so old as the time of Jesus, but they are certainly ancient, and they add to the atmosphere of a place where Christian devotion centers. Armenian, Greek and Russian churches claim other olive groves nearby as the correct site. It is certainly in the vicinity. The sufferings of Christ as His hour approached, portrayed by Matthew, Mark and Luke, and the humiliation of His arrest, told by all four evangelists, concentrate the reverent thought and feeling of believers, so that the very name Gethsemane evokes the love and adoration due to the Saviour who prayed here.   E.R.

GEUEL (gē-ū′ĕl), a son of Machi, a prince of Gad and the representative of the Gadite tribe sent out to explore Canaan (Num. 13:15).

GEZER (gē′zêr, Heb. *gezer, portion*), a fortified place, Tell-Jezer, 18 miles NW of Jerusalem, between the valley of Sorek and the valley of Aijalon. It lies S of the main road from Jerusalem to Jaffa (Haifa), and E of the railroad. The site was

General view of the Garden of Gethsemane, lying beneath the east city wall of Jerusalem, below the Golden Gate. © MPS

identified by M. Clermont-Ganneau in 1873, and excavated by R. A. S. Macalister in 1904-7. Prehistoric inhabitants occupied caves on the rocky heights. Its military importance, overlooking main routes through the country, has led to its occupation in many periods of history. The Egyptians captured Gezer about 1500 B.C., but their power decreased a century or so later. When Israel entered the land, Horam king of Gezer came to help Lachish, after their king had been killed following the battle of the day on which the sun stood still (Josh. 10:1-34). Horam and "his people," that is, his army, were destroyed completely, but Gezer was not taken. The king of Gezer is listed (Josh. 12:12) among those whom Joshua smote (defeated). Gezer is on the southern boundary of Ephraim, near the Bethhorons (Josh. 16:3-10; I Chron. 7:28). The inhabitants of Gezer were not driven out (Josh. 16:10; Judg. 1:29) but later became slave-labor. Gezer was one of the cities given to the Kohathite Levites (Josh. 21:21; I Chron. 6:67). David smote the Philistines as far as Gezer (I Chron. 20:4; also Gazer, KJV, Gezer in ASV, RSV, in II Sam. 5:25; I Chron. 14:16), but it remained for Solomon to reduce the people of Gezer to forced labor, and to rebuild the city, which the pharaoh of Egypt had taken and burnt and given to Solomon as a dowry with his daughter (I Kings 9:15-17). Gezer was occupied in the Greek period. Though not mentioned in the NT, it was known in NT times as Gazara. The Crusaders fortified Gezer, and it has undergone several changes of owners since then. Archaeological remains illustrate the life of the people fully.
E.R.

GHOR, THE (gôr), the upper level of the Jordan valley, about 150 feet above the Zor or jungle through which the river channel winds.

GHOST (gōst), the human spirit as distinguished from the body. Ghost translates Heb. *nephesh, breath* (of life) in KJV, ASV of Job 11:20 (RSV, *breathe their last*), and Jeremiah 15:9 (RSV, *swooned away*). Heb. *gāwa', gasp out, expire,* is used of Abraham (Gen. 25:8), Ishmael (Gen. 25:17), Isaac (Gen. 35:29) and Jacob (Gen. 49:33); in all which cases RSV has "breathed his last." For *gāwa'* in Job 3:11; 10:18; 13:19; 14:10, RSV uses varied expressions. In the NT, "ghost" renders Greek *pneúma, breath, spirit,* in Matthew 27:50; John 19:30 KJV: ASV, RSV have "spirit." Gr. *ekpnéo, breathe out,* appears in Mark 15:37,39; Luke 23:46 KJV, ASV: RSV has "breathed his last." These four Gospel references all relate to Jesus. In Acts 5:5 (Ananias); 5:10 (Sapphira); 12:23 (Herod), RSV has "died" for Greek *ekpsýcho, lose consciousness, expire.* "Holy Ghost" in KJV is translated "Holy Spirit" in ASV, RSV.

GIAH (gī'à), an unknown place near Gibeon, where Joab overtook Abner (II Sam. 2:24).

GIANTS. The first mention of giants in the Bible is in Genesis 6:4, where ASV, RSV have *Nephilim,* a Heb. word of uncertain etymology. Nephilim were found in Canaan when the spies went through the land (Num. 13:33; KJV giants). Beside their huge stature the spies felt like grasshoppers. Once (Job 16:14) "giant" translates Heb. *gibbôr,* which RSV text renders "warrior," ASV margin "mighty man," its usual meaning. The other Heb. words translated "giant" are *rāphā', rāphâh,* and the plural *rephāîm,* of uncertain etymology. The giants whom the Israelites met when they attempted to enter Canaan through Moab (Deut. 2:11,20), are called Rephaim in ASV, RSV. They resembled the Anakim, and the Moabites called

them Emims, while the Ammonites called them Zamzummims. They were tall, large-framed and powerful. The last of this race was Og, king of Bashan, whose iron bedstead, nine cubits long, was famous (Deut. 2:11; Josh. 12:4; 13:12). The giant Rephaim were a vanishing race when the Israelites came out of Egypt. The land of the giants (Rephaim) is referred to in Joshua 17:15; the valley of the giants or Rephaim, located southwest of Jerusalem, in Joshua 15:8; 18:16. The Rephaim are named in Genesis 14:5; 15:20; the valley of Rephaim in II Samuel 5:18,22; 23:13; I Chronicles 11:15; 14:9; Isaiah 17:5. So the memory of this fearsome race persisted in their ancient haunts. II Samuel 21:15-22 records encounters of some of David's mighty men with descendants of the giant (Raphah). But the best known giant of all, Goliath of Gath, champion of the Philistines, whom David as a youth slew (I Sam. 17), though described as of a huge stature and great strength, is not called a giant on that account. It was not necessary to name the obvious. Thus giants terrorized the Israelites from their entry into Canaan until the time of David. Tall men like Saul were admired (I Sam. 10:23); the Lord had to remind Samuel not to consider height when choosing the next king (I Sam. 16:7). Isaiah 45:14 notes that the Sabeans were tall. The question, How tall is a giant? can be answered only in terms of the average height of the race which is using the term. Giants were abnormally strong, yet they had their weak points, as David's victory over Goliath proved.

GIBBAR (gĭb'är), a man whose children returned from captivity with Zerubbabel (Ezra 2:20). Perhaps the Gibeon of Nehemiah 7:25.

GIBBETHON (gĭb'ē-thŏn), Tell el-Melât, W of Gezer in the territory of Dan (Josh. 19:44), allotted to the Kohathite Levites (Josh. 21:23). Baasha killed King Nadab at Gibbethon while Israel was besieging the city, which was now in the hands of the Philistines (I Kings 15:27). A quarter century later Israel again besieged Gibbethon, and Omri was made king there by the army, upon receiving news that Zimri had killed Baasha (I Kings 16:15-17), whereupon the army abandoned the siege of Gibbethon.

GIBEA (gĭb'ē-à), a son of Sheva, and grandson of Caleb (I Chron. 2:49).

GIBEAH (gĭb'ē-à). 1. A city in the hill country of Judah, site unknown (Josh. 15:57).
2. A city of Benjamin (Josh. 18:28), modern Tell el-Fûl, in NT times Gabath Saul; on the E side of the N-S road a few miles north of Jerusalem and on a height commanding a view of the latter; Gibeah of Saul, where excavation has uncovered the rustic but strong fortress-palace from which Saul ruled Israel. Here in the time of the

Gibeah of Saul. © MPS

The village of Gibeon, northwest of Mizpah. © MPS

Judges took place the abuse of a Levite's concubine, which brought on war between Benjamin and the rest of Israel (Judg. 19,20). The transactions at Gibeah during the reign of Saul are recorded in I Samuel 10:26; 11:4; 13:2,15,16; 14: 2, (ASV, RSV have Geba); 14:16; 15:34; 22:6; 23:19; 26:1. Also ASV margin has Gibeah instead of "the hill," referring to the place where stood the house of Abinadab to which the ark of God was brought when it was returned by the Philistines (I Sam. 7:1), and whence David brought it into Jerusalem (II Sam. 6:3). Here seven of Saul's descendants were hanged to satisfy the vengeance of the Gibeonites (II Sam. 21:6; RSV has Gibeon). One of David's mighty men was from Gibeah of Benjamin (II Sam. 23:29; I Chron. 11:31). The people of Gibeah fled when the Assyrians marched toward them (Isa. 10:29). Hosea calls for a warning (Hos. 5:8) at Gibeah because of the sins Israel has committed "from the days of Gibeah" (Hos. 9:9; 10:9); the sins of Saul's reign had been remembered for centuries.

GIBEATH (gĭb'ē-ăth, Josh. 18:28), probably the same as Gibeah of Saul, which see. RSV text has Gibeah; margin Heb. Gibeath.

GIBEON (gĭb'ē-ŏn, Heb. *giv'ôn, pertaining to a hill*), a city of Benjamin (Josh. 18:25) NW of Jerusalem; in NT times Gabao; modern ej-Jib. It was given to the priests (Josh. 21:17). At the time of the Conquest, Joshua, without consulting the Lord, was deceived by the ambassadors of Gibeon into making a treaty with them (Josh. 9) whereby he promised not to destroy them. Upon discovering the deception, though their lives were spared, they were made woodcutters and water-carriers. A coalition of Canaanite kings attacked Gibeon because they had made peace with Joshua (Josh. 10), whereupon Joshua came to the aid of Gibeon, and the battle was fought in which Joshua called upon the sun to stand still to give him time for more fighting (alluded to in Isa. 28:21). No other city made peace with Israel (Josh. 11:19). Gibeon was the chief of four Hivite cities (Josh. 9:17). Abner representing Israel, and Joab representing David, met at a pool, the remains of which may still be seen, at Gibeon; and here, after an indecisive contest between two groups of twelve men each, a disastrous battle was fought (II Sam. 2:1-28; 3:30), following which Abner and Joab agreed to a cessation of the fighting. At a great stone in Gibeon Joab slew Amasa (II Sam. 20:8). David smote the Philistines from Gibeon on the north to Gezer on the south (I Chron. 14:16). Zadok the priest was assigned to minister at the high place in Gibeon (I Chron. 16:39,40; 21:29). Solomon, at the outset of his reign, came to Gibeon to sacrifice, and to dream — to good purpose (I Kings 3:3-15; II Chron. 1:2-13). Again Solomon received a message from the Lord here (I Kings 9:1-9). In I Chronicles 8:29; 9:35 we read of the father of Gibeon, husband of Maachah, dwelling there. People from Gibeon returned to Jerusalem from the captivity and helped build the walls (Neh. 3:7; 7:25). Jeremiah confronted a false prophet from Gibeon in the temple (Jer. 28:1). Gibeon is the scene of a rescue of Israelites during the Assyrian occupation (Jer. 41:11-16).   E.R.

GIBEONITES (gĭb'ē-ŏn-īts), the inhabitants of Gibeon; Hivites (Josh. 9:3,7), Hurrians or Horites (Gen. 36:20; Deut. 2:12) who had formerly lived in Edom. Because of the deceitful manner in which they gained the favor of Joshua, they were made slave-laborers for menial tasks such as chopping wood and drawing water (Josh. 9). They were the peasants of the Mittannian empire which in 1500 B.C. reached from Media to the Mediterranean. Its rulers were Indo-Aryans, its peasants of another but non-Semitic race. The Gibeonites and their allies, at the time of the Conquest by Joshua, controlled a tetrapolis of four cities — Beeroth, Chephirah, Kirjath-baal and Gibeon. Because of a prolonged famine, David inquired of the Lord and learned that the cause was blood-guilt because Saul had massacred the Gibeonites; wherefore David delivered up seven descendants of Saul to their vengeance (II Sam. 21:1-9). A Gibeonite was leader of David's thirty mighty men (I Chron. 12:4). Gibeonites helped repair the walls of Jerusalem (Neh. 3:7).

GIBLITES (gĭb'lĭts), the inhabitants of Gebal or Byblos (Josh. 13:5; ASV, RSV Gebalites). The Gebalites (ASV) or men of Gebal (RSV) are called stonesquarers in KJV of I Kings 5:18. See GEBAL.

GIDDALTI (gĭ-dăl'tī), a son of Heman, and one of the heads of music (I Chron. 25:4,29).

GIDDEL (gĭd'ĕl). 1. A member of the family of Nethinims who returned from exile with Zerubbabel (Ezra 2:47; Neh. 7:49).

2. Sons of Giddel; descendants of Solomon's servants who also came up to Jerusalem from exile (Ezra 2:56; Neh. 7:58).

GIDEON (gĭd'ē-ŏn, Heb. *gidh'ôn, feller* or *hewer*), the son of Joash, an Abiezrite (Judg. 6:11), who lived in Ophrah, not far from Mt. Gerizim, not the Ophrah of Benjamin (Josh. 18:23). The record about Gideon is found in Judges 6:1-9:6. When he is first mentioned he was a mature man. His first-born, Jether, was a youth (8:20). Gideon had already become a noted warrior (6:12), perhaps by waging "underground" warfare against the marauding Midianites. The extent to which the people had been enslaved is shown by the fact that Gideon had to hide in a winepress to do the threshing (6:11). That the messenger who called Gideon to lead Israel was from God was attested to by supernatural fire which consumed a sacrifice which he had placed upon a rock (6:17-23).

Gideon responded to the call and, with the help of some friends, overthrew the altar of Baal and cut down the sacred grove around it. He erected instead a new altar, naming it Jahveh-Shalom, *Jehovah gives peace* (6:24). For his daring feat the followers of Baal wanted to slay him, but his father intervened. Instead of death he was given a new name, Jerubbaal, or "Contender with Baal" (6:28-32). Later the name was changed to Jerub-besheth, "Contender with the Idol," evidently to eliminate any recognition of Baal (II Sam. 11:21). Gideon then issued a call to adjoining tribesmen to war against the Midianites. Having gathered a formidable host, he sought to know the surety of his faith and so put forth the famous test of the fleece (6:36-40). As further assurance, he was instructed to slip into the enemy's camp, and there he overhead one soldier tell another of a dream and interpret it as meaning that Gideon's smaller army would win the battle (7:9-14). To prevent human boasting over victory, God instructed Gideon to reduce his force to 300 picked men by (1) letting the faint-hearted go home; and (2) by choosing only such men as were cautious enough to dip their drinking water while passing over a stream (7:1-8). Thus came the famous army of 300.

By a piece of strategy, involving psychological warfare, Gideon's small band surprised the enemy by a night attack. Three groups of 100 each attacked from three directions. At the proper time a signal was given, shields for the lights were removed, and trumpets blared forth. The sleeping Midianites were terrified. So complete was their rout that they slew one another in the mad flight (7:15-22). Gideon then called upon his allies to join in the chase. Ephraim captured two of the kings (8:1-3). Gideon pursued the other two northward and captured them near the confluence of the Sea of Galilee and the Jordan (8:4-21). Thus the country was delivered all the way to the Jordan (7:22,23; 8:1-21). When his people would have made him king, Gideon refused and instead called for an offering of the golden trinkets which had been captured from the Midianites. With these he made an ephod, either an image of Jehovah, or a sacred vestment worn by a priest in the sanctuary. Because of its worth and beauty, it later became an object of worship (8:24-27). Gideon's ability and statesmanship are shown in his long and fruitful ministry of forty years as judge (8:28). During his life he begat 71 sons, one, Abimelech, by a concubine of Shechem. After Gideon's death idolatry returned (8:32-35), Abimelech seized an opportune time, engaged mercenaries, invaded the land of Gideon, and destroyed all the seventy sons except Jotham who escaped by a bit of strategy (9:1-6).   J.D.F.

GIDEONI (gǐd'ē-ō'nī, *cutter down*), a prince of Benjamin's tribe (Num. 7:60) whose son ruled them (10:24).

GIDOM (gī'dŏm, Heb. *gidh'ōm, desolation*), mentioned only in Judges 20:45. An isolated place east of Bethel, to which the routed Benjamites fled from angry brethren.

GIER EAGLE (See Birds)

GIFT, GIVING. Giving played a great part in the social life of Bible times. At least eleven words in the Bible are used for it: *eshkār*, a reward (Ps. 72:10); *minhâh*, an offering to a superior (Judg. 3:15); *mattān*, that given to gain a favor (Gen. 34:12), or as an act of submission (Ps. 68:29); *mattenā'* and *mattānâh*, an offering (Gen. 25:6; Dan. 2:6); *shōhadh*, a bribe (Deut. 16:19). In the NT, *dósis* and *dóron*, anything given (Luke 21:1; James 1:17); *dóma*, a present (Matt. 7:11); *cháris*,

At the well of Ain Harod, known as Gideon's Fountain, at the foot of the Mountains of Gilboa. © MPS

and *chárisma*, special enduement (Rom. 1:11; I Tim. 4:14); to be cherished (I Cor. 12:31).

GIFTS, SPIRITUAL (Gr. *charísmata*), a theological term meaning any endowment that comes through the grace of God (Rom. 1:11). They make possible good works (Eph. 2:10). Paul discussed at length in I Corinthians 12 the enduements for special tasks in and through the churches (Rom. 6:23; II Cor. 1:11; I Pet. 4:10). They are found in ability to speak an unlearned tongue (I Cor. 14:1-33); power to drive out evil spirits (Matt. 8:16; Acts 13:7-12); special ability in healing the sick (I Cor. 12:9); prophecy (Rom. 12:6); keenness of discernment (wisdom) and knowledge (I Cor. 12:4-8). These gifts are to be sought diligently (I Cor. 12:31), but never at the risk of neglecting the "more excellent way" of pursuing faith, hope and love, of which love is the greatest gift (I Cor. 13:13). Fruits of the Spirit are given in Galatians 5:22-23.

Everyone is accountable for any gift bestowed upon him (I Pet. 4:10; I Cor. 4:7). Claims of having such gifts are to be tested by doctrine (I Cor. 12:2,3) and on moral grounds (Matt. 7:15; Rom. 8:9). Ability in preaching is a spiritual gift (I Cor. 2:4; II Tim. 1:6). To know the deep things of God requires spiritual insight (I Cor. 2:11-16). The gifts are distributed by the Holy Ghost (Heb. 2:4).   J.D.F.

GIHON (gī'hŏn, Heb. *gîhôn, burst forth*). 1. One of the four rivers in Eden (Gen. 2:8-14). The name indicates that it arose either from some large spring or a cataract. Since it "encompasseth the whole land of Ethiopia" it is supposed to be the Nile whose origin from lakes Albert and Victoria would account for the name. However, Ethiopia was the name given to the land occupied by the descendants of Cush, and covered a vast area. Isaiah called it the land of Cush (11:11). Cushan appears in Habakkuk 3:7. Since Eden was probably in the Tigris-Euphrates Valley, it is possible that Gihon was a small stream in that region. Reliable evidence confirms the claim of some scholars that Cush refers to an area in northwest India. *Kassi* (Cush) appears in some ancient records of the region.

In the land of Gilead, southeast of the Sea of Galilee, showing the Yarmuk River and the road to Damascus. © MPS

2. Gihon is also the name of a noted spring near Jerusalem. Solomon was anointed there to succeed David (I Kings 1:32-40). That the spring provided a goodly supply of water is shown by the fact that Hezekiah, during his prosperous reign, had its water diverted by a tunnel to serve the growing population of Jerusalem (II Chron. 32:27-30). Recent discoveries show that this tunnel was that connected with the Pool of Siloam, so-called because it fed that watering place in the city. Remains of an ancient canal have been found through which the water once entered and it may be of this that Isaiah wrote (8:6). This spring was originally controlled by the Jebusites (II Sam. 5:6) who cut a tunnel to bring it near enough to the wall for it to be drawn without exposure of their women to raiders.　　　　　　　　　　　　J.D.F.

GILALAI (gĭl'à-lī), a member of a band of musicians who under Ezra's direction had part in the dedication of the wall of Jerusalem (Neh. 12:36).

GILBOA (gĭl-bō'à, Heb. *gĭlbō'a, bubbling*). It has been identified as Jabel Fuku'a, a range of barren hills on the eastern side of the Plain of Esdraelon, named from a noted spring. The mean elevation of the hills is about 1,600 feet. Ain Jalud on the northern slope of the range has been identified as the location of the spring. Saul gathered his forces here to await an attack by the Philistines. Fear drove him to consult the Witch of Endor (I Sam. 28:4-7). During the battle he was wounded; his forces were routed; and he committed suicide (I Chron. 10:1-8).

GILEAD (gĭl'ē-ăd, Heb. *gil'ādh, rugged*). The name is used to indicate Israel's possession E of the Jordan River. Josephus so understood it (*Ant.* XII; 8:3). It extended from the lower end of the Sea of Galilee to the northern end of the Dead Sea, and from the Jordan eastward to the desert, a plateau of some 2,000 feet elevation. At the time of Moses it was a lush region with goodly forests,

rich grazing lands, and abundant moisture. A scenic gorge of the noted brook, Jabbok, running into the Jordan, divided it. Jacob camped at Gilead when fleeing from Laban (Gen. 31:7-43). Overtaken at that place, he made a covenant with Laban which was confirmed by a pile of stones which Jacob named *Galeed,* "Heap of Witness" (Gen. 31:47 marg.). During succeeding years it came to be applied to the entire region which included Mount Gilead (Gen. 31:25), the land of Gilead (Num. 32:1), and Gilead (Gen. 37:25).

When Canaan was allocated to the Israelites, Gilead fell to the Reubenites, Gadites and to half the tribe of Manasseh (Deut. 3:13). An account of the conquest of the region is found in Deuteronomy 2 and 3. Moses was permitted to see the goodly plain before his death (Deut. 34:1). After the land was conquered a great altar was erected beside the Jordan that true worship might not be forgotten (Josh. 22:10).

Gilead became famous because of some of its products. Balm was exported to Tyre (Ezek. 27:17); Jeremiah knew of its curative power (8:22; 46:11; 51:8). The Ishmaelites who bought Joseph carried balm to Egypt (Gen. 37:25). Beside the Jabbok Jacob had his reconciliation with Esau (Gen. 32:22-33:15). Jair, a Gileadite, served for twenty years as judge over Israel (Judg. 10:3). Jephthah, a great grandson of Manasseh, was also a judge. Being the son of a concubine, he was banished by his brothers, but when Gilead was in dire distress, he was recalled by the elders (Judg. 11:1-3). He defeated the Ephraimites and prevented fugitives from crossing the Jordan by resorting to the noted password, Shibboleth (Judg. 12:1-7). Absalom gathered his forces in Gilead when he rebelled against David (II Sam. 15:13-23). The Gileadites finally fell into gross idolatry (Hos. 6:8; 12:11), were overcome by Hazael (II Kings 10:32-34), and led into captivity by Tiglath-pileser (II Kings 15:27-29).　　　　　　　J.D.F.

GILGAL (gĭl'găl, Heb. *Gilgāl, circle of stones*), the first camp of Israel after crossing the Jordan (Josh. 4:19,20). While encamped there Joshua restored the Hebrew rite of circumcision in response to God's promise to "roll away the reproach of Egypt" (Josh. 5:2-9). The town which grew up was near the northern border of Judah (Josh. 15:7). Most authorities agree that this is the town included in the judicial circuit of Samuel (I Sam. 7:16). And it is certain that the altar-memorial of stones erected there became a pagan shrine of later years against which Hosea (4:15) and Amos (4:4) warned the people. According to Josephus, Gilgal was about ten miles from the Jordan and two miles or more from Jericho.

Site of ancient Gilgal, one of the first camping sites of Joshua's army in the Promised Land. © MPS

It was to Gilgal that Saul was sent by Samuel to be confirmed as king over Israel (I Sam. 11: 15). There Saul later grew restless because of the delay in the coming of Samuel and offended Jehovah by presuming to act as priest and make his own sacrifice (I Sam. 13:1-10). Judah gathered at Gilgal to meet David when he returned from defeating the rebels under Absalom (II Sam. 19).

Gilgal is not mentioned in the NT and its location is not known. The town from which Elijah ascended was not this Gilgal (II Kings 2:1). Gilgal furnished singers who had part in the dedication of the wall of Jerusalem (Neh. 12:27-43). A large pool has been located at modern Jiljuliyeh, which may mark the site. Some authorities disagree with the idea that Gilgal near Jericho was the city in Samuel's circuit, and others claim that the Gilgal mentioned by Hosea and Amos was another city near Shechem. J.D.F.

GILOH (gī'lō), home of Ahithophel, one of David's counsellors who rebelled with Absalom (II Sam. 15:12), also a town of Judah (Josh. 15:51).

GIMZO (gĭm'zō, *place of lush sycamores*), a town some three miles southwest of Lydda, off the Jerusalem highway, captured by Philistines during the reign of Ahaz (II Chron. 28:18). Jimza is no doubt its present location.

GIN, a trap to ensnare game (Amos 3:5) or to deceive and destroy (Ps. 140:5; 141:9); a pitfall (Job 18:9) or an offense (Isa. 8:14).

GINATH (gī'năth, *protector*), the father of Tibni, a contender for the throne of Israel (I Kings 16: 21).

GINNETHO (See Ginnethon)

GINNETHON (gĭn'ē-thon), a priest who returned to Jerusalem with Zerubbabel (Neh. 12:4) and signed the Levitical covenant (Neh. 10:6. Gennetho in KJV).

GIRDLE (See Dress)

GIRGASHITES (gûr'gà-shītes), one of seven Canaanite tribes conquered by Joshua (Deut. 7:1). They were descendants of Ham (Gen. 10:15,16). Their land was promised to Abram (Gen. 15:21) and to Israel (Josh. 3:10). Tradition says they fled to Africa.

GISPA (gĭs'pà, *listener*), an overseer of the Nethinims, in Nehemiah's time (Neh. 11:21).

GITTAH-HEPHER (See Gath-hepher)

GITTAIM (gĭt'à-ĭm, Heb. *gittayim*, perhaps *two wine presses*), a town of Benjamin to which the Beerothites fled (Neh. 11:31,33), probably at the time of Saul's cruelty (II Sam. 4:3), and lived as protected strangers. Exact site unknown.

GITTITES (gĭt'īt, *of Gath*), natives of Gath, unconquered at the time of Joshua's death (Josh. 13: 1-3). The Ark was deposited in a Gittite home (II Sam. 6:8-11). David's guard included 600 men of Gath (I Sam. 15:18). Goliath was a Gittite (II Sam. 21:19).

GITTITH (gĭt'īth, Heb. *gittîth*), a word found in the titles of Psalms 8, 81, 84. Its meaning is uncertain. It may denote some musical instrument made in Gath, or a melody or march popular in Gath.

GIZONITE (gī'zō-nīt). Hashem, one of David's valiant men, was described as a Gizonite (I Chron. 11:34). Probably an error for Gunite. He was probably the same as Jashen the Gunite (II Sam. 23:32).

GLASS, although a product known and used by man for ages, where its manufacture first arose is unknown. Pliny attributed it to the Phoenicians, but it was made in Egypt at least 2,500 years before Christ. It is supposed to have been discovered from lumps of glass found where large shocks of straw had burned, or through glaze appearing on pottery that was burned where sand and soda were present. By 1500 B.C. glass trinkets, as well as vessels, had come into general use in Egypt. No doubt Egyptian artisans introduced it to Nineveh, Phoenicia and other lands. As early as 750 B.C. Assyrians were making it, and Phoenicians had developed into a paying industry the making of glass beads.

The fact that glass does not seem to have been used to any degree by the Hebrews may be accounted for by their hatred of Egyptian products (Lev. 18:3), or else it was cheaper for them to produce pottery. Mirrors (Exod. 38:8) were made of polished bronze. The only direct reference in the OT to glass is Job 28:17, where gold and crystal (glass RSV) are compared with wisdom. The Hebrew word is *zekukith,* and may be translated *mirror,* hence the claim of some scholars that even this passage does not refer to glass. The glass mentioned by Paul (II Cor. 3:18), and that to which James referred (1:23,24) was evidently the customary mirror of polished bronze, as the Gr. word used, meant such. By the time of Christ the people of Palestine were familiar with glass. The figurative expressions, revealing the transparent nature of the Holy City, pictured by John in Revelation 21:18,21, refer to crystal glass. J.D.F.

GLEAN (Heb. *lāqat, 'ālal*), the Hebrew custom of allowing the poor to follow the reapers and gather the grain that was left behind or the grapes which remained after the vintage (Judg. 8:2; Ruth 2:2, 16; Isa. 17:6). This custom was backed by one of the agricultural laws of Moses (Lev. 19:9; 23: 22; Deut. 24:19-21). The word is also used figuratively to describe the utter destruction of Israel (Jer. 6:9; 49:9,10).

GLEDE (See Birds)

GLORY, the exhibition of the excellence of the subject to which it is ascribed. Concerning God, it is the display of His divine attributes and perfections. Concerning man, it is the manifestation of his commendable qualities, such as wisdom, righteousness, self-control, ability, etc. A connotation of splendor is included, such as "the glory of the moon and the stars" (I Cor. 15:41). In both Testaments there are references to the Shekinah glory of God, although not by name, for the word occurs in the Targums, not in the Bible. To avoid anthropomorphisms (ascription of physical characteristics to God) which might lead to erroneous doctrine, the Targum writers spoke of the glory of the Shekinah. This was actually the physical manifestation of the presence of God, as seen in the pillars of cloud and fire. NT references to the Shekinah glory are seen in John 1:4 and Romans 9:4. Glory is both physical and spiritual, as is seen in Luke 2:9 ("the glory of the Lord shone round about them") and John 17:22, where it refers to the glory of the Father, which Jesus gave to His disciples. As for the saints, glory culminates in the changing of their bodies to the likeness of their glorified Lord (Phil. 3:20).

GNASH (năsh, Heb. *hāraq,* Gr. *brugmós*). In the OT the expression "to gnash with the teeth" represents for the most part rage, anger, or hatred (Job 16:9; Pss. 35:16; 37:12; 112:10). In the NT it expresses disappointment rather than anger (Matt. 8:12; 13:42,50; 22:13; 24:51; 25:30; Luke 13:28).

GNAT (See Insects: Flies)

GOAD (gōd, Heb. *dŏrevān, malmādh,* Gr. *kéntron*), an eight-foot wooden pole, shod at one end with a spade used for removing mud from the plow and at the other with a sharp point for prodding oxen. It was a formidable weapon in the hands of Shamgar (Judg. 3:31). To "kick against the pricks" pictures oxen kicking against the goads — a figure of useless resistance to a greater power.

GOAT (See Animals)

GOATH (gō'āth, Heb. *gō'âh*), a place (RV has *Goah*) the site of which is unknown, but apparently W of Jerusalem. Mentioned only once, in Jeremiah 31:39, in connection with prophecy concerning the restoration of Jerusalem. Referred to by Josephus as "the camp of the Assyrians."

GOB (gŏb, Heb. *gôv,* pit, cistern), a place mentioned in II Samuel 21:18 as the scene of two of David's battles with the Philistines. Here the brother of Goliath defied Israel but was slain by Jonathan, son of Shimei. The Septuagint calls it Gath, which is probably correct.

GOD (Heb. *'ĕlōhîm, ēl, 'elyôn, shaddāy, yahweh;* Gr. *theós*). Although the Bible does not contain a formal definition of the word "God," yet His being and attributes are displayed on every page. The greatest definition of the word in the history of Christendom, that is, in the culture in which the Bible has been a prevailing influence, is the definition found in the Westminster Shorter Catechism (Q.4): "God is a Spirit, infinite, eternal, and unchangeable, in his being, wisdom, power, holiness, justice, goodness, and truth." It is fair to say that this definition faithfully sets forth what the Bible constantly assumes and declares concerning God.

God is a Spirit. These words mean that God is a non-material personal being, self-conscious and self-determining.

In the differentia of the definition we have three adjectives each modifying seven nouns. The descriptive units in which these words are combined are not logically separable, but are inextricably woven together, so as to delineate the unity and the integrated complexity of God's attributes. The analysis cannot be exhaustive, but only descriptive.

Infinite. The infinity of God is not an independent attribute. If we were to say, "God is the infinite," without specification, the meaning would be pantheistic, equal to saying, "God is everything." In using the word "infinite" we must always be specific.

Infinite in His being. This doctrine is intended to teach that God is everywhere. The omnipresence of God is vividly brought out in such scriptures as Psalm 139. God is not physically, relatively, or measurably big. The word "immensity" is used by good theologians, but it conveys to some minds a false impression, as though God were partly here and partly there, like a giant, or an amorphous mass, or a fluid. The omnipresence of God means that wherever we are, even though we be like fleeing Jacob at Bethel (Gen. 28:16), God *Himself* is there.

It is easier to conceive of God's omnipresence by saying, "Everything everywhere is immediately in His presence." Finite creatures can act instantaneously in a limited area. Everything within one's reach or sight is immediately in His presence, in the sense that distance is no problem. So in an absolutely perfect sense, everything in the universe is immediately in the presence of God.

Infinite in His wisdom. This phrase designates God's omniscience. The Bible throughout regards His omniscience as all-inclusive, and not dependent upon discursive processes. God's knowledge does not increase or diminish as He knows when the temporal events of his redemptive program take place. He eternally knows what He has known in the past and what He will know in the future.

The words **Infinite in His power** point to His omnipotence, His ability to do with power all that power can do, His controlling all the power that is or can be.

Infinite in His holiness, justice and goodness. These words signify God's moral attributes. *Holiness* is regarded in the Bible as His central ethical character. Basic ethical principles are revealed by the will of God, and derived from and based upon the character of God. "Ye shall be holy for I am holy" (Lev. 11:44f. *et passim*). *Justice* refers to His administration of rewards and punishments among the personal beings of the universe. *Goodness* in this context indicates His love, His common grace toward all, and His special grace in saving sinners.

Infinite in His truth. This is the attribute which designates the basis of all logic and rationality. The axioms of logic and mathematics, and all the laws of reason, are not laws apart from God, to which God must be subject. They are attributes of His own character. When the Bible says that "it is impossible for God to lie" (Heb. 6:18; Titus 1:2) there is no contradiction of omnipotence. How much power would it take to make two times two equal five? Truth is not an object of power.

There is no mere tautology in the Bible, as though the multiplication tables were true by mere divine fiat. As in ethics, so in rationality, the Biblical writers constantly appeal to the truth of God's immutable character. "He cannot deny himself" (II Tim. 2:13).

Just as the adjective "infinite," in the definition we are considering, applies to all the specified attributes, so the words "eternal" and "unchangeable" similarly apply to all.

Eternal in the Bible means, without temporal beginning or ending; or in a figurative sense, "eternal" may designate (as in the words "eternal life") a quality of being suitable for eternity.

That God existed eternally before the creation of the finite universe does not imply a personal subject with no object, for God is triune. (See TRINITY.)

The idea that eternity means timelessness is nowhere suggested in the Bible. This false notion doubtless came into Christian theology under the influence of Aristotle's "Unmoved Mover" (see Aristotle's *Physics,* book *Theta,* Ch. 6, 258b, 1.12, and *Metaphysics,* book *Lambda,* Ch. 7 *et passim*), the influence of which is strong in Thomas Aquinas.

That the Bible does not teach that God is timeless, is an objective, verifiable fact. The evidence is well set forth by Oscar Cullmann. See his *Christ and Time.*

Unchangeable, in Bible language, points the perfect self-consistency of God's character throughout all eternity. This is not a static concept, but dynamic, in all His relations with His creatures. That God brings to pass, in time, the events of his redemptive program is not contradictory. The notion that God's immutability is static immobility (as in Thomism) is like the notion of timelessness, and is contrary to the Biblical view. The God of the Bible is intimately and actively concerned in all the actions of all His creatures.

God is known by His acts. Supremely, "God has spoken in his Son" (Heb. 1:1ff). Further, His "invisible" being, that is, His "eternal power and divine character [*theiotes* as distinguished from *theotes*]" are "known" and "clearly seen" by "the things he has made" (Rom. 1:20). "The heavens declare the glory of God" (Ps. 19; Rom. 10:18). It is customary to distinguish between "natural revelation" and "special revelation," the Bible being identical with the latter.

God is known in fellowship. That by faith God is known, beyond the mere cognitive sense, in fellowship with His people, is one of the most prominent themes throughout the Bible. Moses, leading His people in the exodus, was assured, "My presence shall go with thee, and I will give thee rest." And Moses replied, "If thy presence go not with me, carry us not up hence" (Exod. 33:14f). The Bible abounds in invitations to seek and find fellowship with God. See Psalm 27, Isaiah 55, and many similar gracious invitations.

Other gods are referred to in the Bible as false gods (Judg. 6:31; I Kings 18:27; I Cor. 8:4-6), or as demonic (I Cor. 10:19-22).   J.O.B.

GODLINESS (Gr. *eusébeia, theosébeia*), the piety toward God and rectitude of conduct which springs from a proper relationship with Him. It is not belief in itself, but the devotion toward God and love toward man which result from that belief. Religious faith is empty without godliness, for it is then but an empty form (II Tim. 3:5). The Gr. *eusébeia* is found fifteen times in the NT; it is translated fourteen times as *godliness* and once as *holiness*. It is the sum total of religious character and actions, and produces both a present and future state of happiness. It is not right action which is done from a sense of duty, but is that spontaneous virtue that comes from the indwelling Christ, and which reflects Him.   B.P.D.

GOLAN (gō'lăn, Heb. *gôlān*), a city in the territory of the half tribe of Manasseh in Bashan, E of the Jordan. It was one of the three cities of refuge, and assigned to the Gershonite Levites (Deut. 4:43). Probably an important city in its day, it was destroyed by Alexander Janneus after his army had been ambushed there. The site cannot definitely be identified, but the archaeologist Schumacher believes it was seventeen miles E of the Sea of Galilee, in present Syria, located in Gaulanitis, one of the four provinces into which Bashan was divided after the Babylonian captivity. It is a fertile plateau, 1000-3000 feet in elevation.

GOLD (See Minerals)

GOLDSMITH (See Occupations & Professions: Artificer)

GOLGOTHA (gŏl'gō-thà, Gr. *Golgothá,* from Aram. *gulgaltā', skull*), the place of our Lord's crucifixion. From the Heb. *gulgoleth,* which implies a *bald, round, skull-like mound* or *hillock.* The Latin name, *Calvarius (bald skull)* has been retained in the form *Calvary* (Luke 23:33). In the RV, it is simply, "the skull." Two explanations of the name are found: (1) It was a place of execution, and therefore abounded in skulls; (2) The place had the appearance of a skull when viewed from a short distance. The Gospels and tradition do not agree as to its location. Both Matthew (27:33) and Mark (15:22) locate it outside the city, but close to it (John 19:20) on the public highway, which was the type of location usually chosen by the Romans for executions. Tradition locates it within the present city.   B.P.D.

GOLIATH (gō-lī'ăth, Heb. *golyāth,* Gr. *Goliáth, exile*), a gigantic warrior of the Philistine army, probably one of the Anakim (Num. 13:33; Josh. 11:22). Goliath's size was extraordinary. If a cubit is 21 inches, he was over eleven feet in height; if about 18 inches, he was over nine feet. The only mention made of Goliath is his appearance as a champion of the Philistines (I Sam. 17). The Philistines had ventured on another inroad into Israel's territory, and had taken a firm position on the slope of a hill, with Israel encamped on a hill opposite. From the Philistine camp Goliath made daily challenges to personal combat, but after forty days no one had accepted. David had been sent to his brothers with provisions. When he heard Goliath's challenge, he inquired its meaning. Upon being told, he went to face Goliath, armed only with a sling and five stones. Hit in the forehead, Goliath fell, and David cut off his head. When the Philistines saw that their champion was dead, they fled, pursued by victorious Israel. The Goliath of II Samuel 21:19 was probably the son of the giant whom David killed. He was slain by Elhanan, one of David's men. A discrepancy has been imagined, and some have thought that it was Elhanan who slew the giant.   B.P.D.

GOMORRAH (gō-mŏr'à, Heb. *'ămōrâh,* Gr. *Gomórra, submersion*), one of the five "cities of the plain" located in the Vale of Siddim at the S end of the Dead Sea. Zoar alone escaped the destruction by fire from heaven in the time of Abraham and Lot. The district where the five cities were located was exceedingly productive and well-peopled, but today traces of the punitive catastrophe abound. There are great quantities of salt, with deposits of bitumen, sulphur and nitre on the shores of the Dead Sea. The location was long a contention, but it definitely was established in 1924 by an archaeological expedition led by the late eminent archaeologist, Dr. Melvin Grove Kyle. "The Lisan is a kind of promontory that juts out from the eastern shore toward the western mountains and almost cuts the sea in two. Anciently, it manifestly separated the sea to the north of it from the low plain to the south of it. Thirty-five years ago, when I first saw the Dead Sea, it was so much lower than now that there was a beautiful island at the north end. Today, as we approach the Port of Jericho, we pass over the region of that island in several feet of water. The cities are clearly shown to have stood in front of Jebel Usdum, where they lie under the waters today. This region was found by geologists to be a burned-out area of oil and asphalt, of which there has been an accumulation which is now being exploited. Where these conditions exist, there is an accumulation of gases. Geologists admit that at some past

Traditional site of Golgotha, called Gordon's Calvary. JFW

time there was a great explosion, with first an upheaval and then a subsidence of strata. Salt, mixed with sulphur, was carried up into the heavens white hot and so rained down upon the cities of the plain, exactly as the Scriptures describe the rain of fire and brimstone from heaven" (Kyle, *Explorations at Sodom*, pp. 67,130,137-38).   B.P.D.

GOPHER WOOD (gō'fẽr wŏŏd, Heb. *'ătsê ghōpher*), the wood from which Noah's ark was made (Gen. 6:14). The word "gopher" is unknown elsewhere in Hebrew or allied languages. It may refer to some resinous wood, like pine, cedar, or cypress; or the reference may be to boats made cf interwoven willow branches and palm leaves, coated on the outside with bitumen.

GOSPEL (gŏs'pĕl, Gr. *euaggélion, good news*). The English word Gospel is derived from the Anglo-Saxon *godspell,* which meant "good tidings" and, later, the "story concerning God." As now used, the word describes the message of Christianity and the books in which the story of Christ's life and teaching is found. This message is the good news that God has provided a way of redemption through His Son Jesus Christ. The Holy Spirit works through the Gospel for the salvation of men (Rom. 1:15,16). In the NT the word Gospel never means a book (one of the four Gospels), but always the good tidings which Christ and the apostles announced. It is called "the gospel of God" (Rom. 1:1; I Thess. 2:2,9); "the gospel

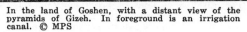

In the land of Goshen, with a distant view of the pyramids of Gizeh. In foreground is an irrigation canal. © MPS

Plowing with water buffaloes in the land of Goshen. © MPS

GOSHEN (gō'shĕn, Heb. *gōshen,* probably *mound of earth*). 1. The NE section of the Nile delta region is usually termed "the land of Goshen." Here the Israelites under Jacob settled, while Joseph was prime minister (Gen. 46). The district is not large, having an area of some 900 square miles, but because of irrigation is considered some of the best land of Egypt, excellent for grazing and for certain types of agriculture. The district had two principal cities, both built for the Pharaohs by the Hebrews. The one of greater importance had, at various times, at least three and possibly four names. Zoan, Avaris and Tanis were certainly its names, and archaeologists do not agree as to whether it also bore the name of Raamses. Some indicate a different location for Raamses. Under the name of Avaris, it was for 500 years the capital of the Hyksos. The other city, Pithom, is particularly interesting to the student of Biblical archeology because here is found a proof of Exodus 5:7-13, where the labor overseers were told to refuse the Hebrew workmen straw for making bricks, yet with no diminution of the assigned quota. In a building at Pithon are found three types of bricks, beginning at its foundation where straw was used. After the refusal of straw, the Hebrews desperately gathered all bits of straw and stubble they could find, and such bricks are found higher in the building. It was completed with bricks devoid of straw.

2. A district of S Palestine, lying between Gaza and Gibeon, its name probably given in remembrance of Egypt (Josh. 10:41).

3. A town mentioned with Debir, Socoh and others, in the SW part of the mountains of Judah (Josh. 15:51).   B.P.D.

of Christ" (Mark 1:1; Rom. 1:16; 15:19); "the gospel of the grace of God" (Acts 20:24); "the gospel of peace" (Eph. 6:15); "the gospel of your salvation" (Eph. 1:13; and "the glorious gospel" (II Cor. 4:4). The Gospel has to do entirely with Christ. It was preached by Him (Matt. 4:23; 11:5), by the apostles (Acts 16:10; Rom. 1:15), and by the evangelists (Acts 8:25). It was not until c. A.D. 150 that the word Gospel was applied to the writings concerning the message of Christ. Each of the four records was called a Gospel, and likewise the four together.   S.B.

GOSPEL, THE FOUR GOSPELS. The word *Gospel* is derived from the Anglo-Saxon *gōd spell*, or *good tidings,* and is a literal translation of the Greek *euaggélion,* which meant originally a reward for bringing good news, and finally the good news itself. In the NT the term is applied to the revelation of God's plan for reconciling man to Himself by forgiving his sin and by transforming his character. The Gospel is the story of God's gift of salvation through the person and work of Christ which the church has been commissioned to proclaim (Mark 16:15; Acts 20:24; Eph. 1: 13). The impact of the life, death, and resurrection of Christ compelled His disciples to present His message to the public. By repeating the significant features of His ministry and His accompanying precepts, following the general order of His biography, they formulated a body of teaching which may have varied in detail with each recital, but which maintained the same general content.

The existence of this standardized message is confirmed by the NT itself. Paul, in the Epistle to the Galatians, mentioning a visit to Jerusalem which took place before A.D. 50, said: ". . . I laid before them the gospel which I preach among the Gentiles" (Gal. 2:2). In another passage he defined it clearly: ". . . the gospel which I preached unto you, which ye also received, wherein also ye stand, by which also ye are saved . . . For I delivered unto you first of all that which I also received: that Christ died for our sins according to the scriptures: and that he was buried; and that he hath been raised on the third day according to the scriptures; and that he appeared to Cephas . . ." (I Cor. 15:1-5). A similar presentation is afforded by the report of Peter's address in the house of Cornelius, the Gentile centurion. After sketching the baptism, life, death, and resurrection of Jesus, Peter concluded: "He [God] charged us to preach unto the people, and to testify that this is he who is ordained of God to be the judge of the living and the dead. To him bear all the prophets witness that through his name every one that believeth shall have remission of sins" (Acts 10: 42,43).

From these samples of apostolic preaching one may conclude that the facts of Jesus' life constituted the Gospel, which was interpreted and applied to suit the occasion on which it was preached.

This Gospel, which was initially proclaimed in oral form, has been transmitted through the writings which are consequently called the "Gospels." Although Matthew, Mark, Luke, and John differ considerably in detail, they agree on the general outline of Jesus' career, on the supernatural character of His life, and on the high quality of His moral precepts. From the earliest period of the church they have been accepted as authoritative accounts of His life and teachings.

Character: Reduced to writing, the Gospel message constitutes a new type of literature. Although it is framed in history, it is not pure history, for the allusions to contemporary events are incidental, and the Gospels do not attempt to develop them. They contain biographical material, but they cannot be called biography in the modern sense of the word, since they do not present a complete summary of the life of Jesus. The Gospels are not sufficiently didactic to be called essays; they conceal rather than reveal the direct opinions of their writers. The chief purpose of the Gospels is to create faith in Christ on the part of their readers, who may or may not be believers. Nothing exactly like them can be found either in the OT, to which their writers referred frequently, nor in the Hellenic and Roman literature contemporary with them.

Of the numerous accounts and fragments that were composed to perpetuate the ministry and teaching of Jesus, only four are accorded a place in the NT: Matthew, written by Jesus' disciple Matthew Levi, the tax-gatherer; Mark, from the pen of John Mark, an inhabitant of Jerusalem and a companion of Barnabas and Paul; Luke, the first half of a history of Christianity in two volumes by an associate of Paul; and John, a collection of select memoirs by John, the son of Zebedee. Although the authorship of all of these Gospels has been disputed, there has been an increasing tendency to revert to the traditional views stated above. Other Gospels, such as the Gospel of Peter, or the Gospel of Thomas, are later productions of the second and third centuries, and usually represent the peculiar theological prejudices of some minor sect.

Origin of the Gospels: The existence of the oral Gospel is attested by Papias, one of the earliest of the church fathers, who lived at the close of the first century. A quotation from the preface to his "Interpretation of our Lord's Declarations" preserved in Eusebius indicates that he still depended on the transmission of the Gospel content by the living voice. "But if I met with any one who had been a follower of the elders anywhere, I made it a point to inquire what were the declarations of the elders . . . for I do not think that I derived so much benefit from books as from the living voice of those that are still surviving" (quoted in Eusebius: *Historia Ecclesiae,* III. 39). In Papias' time not more than two or three of the original band of Jesus' disciples would still be living, and he would be compelled to obtain his information from those who had heard the apostles. Nevertheless, he preferred the oral testimony to written record. Irrespective of the value of Papias' judgment, his words indicate that the content of the apostolic preaching was independently transmitted by word of mouth two generations after the crucifixion, simultaneously with the use of whatever written records existed.

A clue to the transition from oral preaching to written record is provided by explanatory statements in the Gospels of Luke and John. In the introduction to his Gospel, Luke asserts that he was undertaking to confirm by manuscript what his friend Theophilus had already learned by word of mouth (Luke 1:1-4). He spoke of facts which were taken for granted among believers, and indicated that there had already been numerous attempts to arrange them in orderly narratives. Since his use of the word "narrative" (Gr. *diēgēsis*) implies an extended account, there must have been a number of "gospels" in circulation which he considered to be either inaccessible or else unsatisfactory. If his use of language permits deduction by contrast, these rival gospels were the opposite of his own. They were partial in content, drawn from secondary sources, and perhaps were not organized by any consecutive line of thought. They may have been random collections of sayings or events which had no central theme, or they may not have contained enough biographical material to afford an adequate understanding of Jesus' life.

Luke affirmed on the contrary that he had derived his facts from those who "from the beginning were eye-witnesses and ministers of the word" (1:2). Not only had his informants shared in the events of which they spoke, but also they had been so affected that they became propagandists of the new faith. Luke had been a contemporary of these witnesses, and had investigated personally the truth of their claims, that he might produce an orderly and accurate record of the work of Christ.

John also committed his Gospel to writing that he might inculcate faith in Christ as the Son of God (John 20:30,31). He did not profess to give an exhaustive account of Jesus' activities, but took for granted that many of them would be familiar to his readers. The selective process that he employed was determined by his evangelistic purpose and theological viewpoint.

Although Matthew and Mark are less explicit concerning their origins, the same general principles obtain. The introduction of Matthew, "The book of the generation of Jesus Christ, the son of David, the son of Abraham" (Matt. 1:1), duplicates the phraseology of Genesis (Gen. 5:1) to convey the impression that, like Genesis, it is giving a significant chapter in the history of God's dealing with man. Mark's terse opening line, "The beginning of the Gospel of Jesus Christ, the Son of God," is a title, labeling the following text as a summary of current preaching. Neither of these two offers any reason for its publication, but one may deduce fairly that all of the Gospels began in an attempt to preserve for posterity what had hitherto existed in the minds of the primitive witnesses and in their public addressses.

There has been some question whether the Gospels were first published in Aramaic, the language of Palestine, where the church began, or in Greek. Eusebius quoted Papias' statement that Matthew composed his history in the Hebrew dialect and everyone translated it as he was able (Eusebius, *Historia Ecclesiae,* III, 39). Without the original context, these words are ambiguous. Papias does not make clear whether "Hebrew" was the speech of the OT, or whether he really meant Aramaic. He does not specify whether Matthew's contribution was simply collected notes from which others composed a Gospel, or whether he had already formed an organized narrative that was translated. He does imply that before the Gentile expansion had made the literature of the church Greek, there was a body of material written in Hebrew or Aramaic.

Papias' statement has aroused a great deal of controversy. There are Aramaisms in the Gospels such as *Ephphatha* (Mark 7:34), *Talitha cumi* (Mark 5:41), and the cry from the cross, *Eloi, Eloi, lama sabachthani* (Mark 15:34), which reflect Jesus' use of His mother tongue and the perpetuation of His language in the memoirs of His followers. These, however, do not necessitate that the Gospels were written originally in Aramaic. C. C. Torrey (*Our Translated Gospels.* New York, Harper, 1936) contended that all four Gospels were translations, but there is no agreement on the evidence. If they were translations, they must have been composed prior to the middle of the first century, when the churches were predominantly Palestinian. It is more likely that the Gospels originated in the evangelistic preaching to the Gentile world, and that they were written in Greek, although they contained an Aramaic background.

Composition of the Gospels: The personal reminiscences of the apostolic band, plus the fixed content of their preaching constituted the materials from which the Gospels were constructed, and the purpose of the individual writers provided the method of organization. Both Luke (1:1-4) and John (20:30,31) pledge accuracy of historical fact before they proceed with interpretation, and the same may safely be predicated of Matthew and Mark. All the Gospels were composed for use in the growing movement of the Church; they were not written solely for literary effect. Matthew obviously wished to identify Jesus with the Messiah of the Old Testament by pointing out that He was the fulfilment of prophecy and that He was intimately related to the manifestation of the kingdom. Mark, by his terse descriptive paragraphs, depicted the Son of God in action among men. Luke employed a smoother literary style and a larger stock of parabolic stories to interest a cultured and perhaps humanistic audience. John selected episodes and discourses which others had not used in order to promote belief in Jesus as the Son of God.

The Publication of the Gospels: Where and when these documents were first given to the public is uncertain. The earliest quotations from the Gospel material appear in the letters of Ignatius, in the *Epistle of Barnabas,* the *Teaching of the Twelve Apostles,* and the *Epistle of Polycarp.* All of these are related to Antioch of Syria, and their quotations or allusions bear a stronger resemblance to the text of Matthew than to that of any

other Gospel. If, as Papias said, Matthew was first written for the Hebrew or Aramaic church in Jerusalem, it may have been the basis for a Greek edition issued from Antioch during the development of the Gentile church in that city. It would, therefore, have been put into circulation some time after A.D. 50, and before the destruction of Jerusalem in A.D. 70.

Clement of Alexandria (A.D. 200) described the writing of the Gospel of Mark: "When Peter had proclaimed the word publicly at Rome, and declared the gospel under the influence of the Spirit; as there was a great number present, they requested Mark, who had followed him from afar, and remembered well what he had said, to reduce these things to writing, and that after composing the Gospel he gave it to those who requested it of him. Which, when Peter understood, he directly neither hindered nor encouraged it." (Eusebius, *Historia Ecclesiae,* VI, 14.) Irenaeus (c. A.D. 100), Clement's contemporary, confirmed this tradition, adding that Mark handed down Peter's preaching in writing after his death. If the second Gospel represents the memoirs of Peter, it is possible that its content did not become fixed in literary form until A.D. 65 or later.

The Gospel of Luke may have been a private document, sent first of all to Luke's friend and patron, Theophilus. The adjective "most excellent" (Luke 1:3) implies that he probably belonged to the aristocracy, and that the dual work which Luke wrote was calculated to remove any lingering doubts that he may have entertained concerning the historical and spiritual verities of Christian faith. It can hardly have been written later than A.D. 62, since it must have preceded Acts, which was written about the end of Paul's first imprisonment.

The last chapter of John's Gospel attempts to correct a rumor that he would never die. Obviously the rumor would have no basis unless he had attained an advanced age at the time when the concluding chapter was written. It is possible that it can be dated before A.D. 50, but most conservative scholars place it about A.D. 85. Traditionally it has been ascribed to the apostle John, who ministered at Ephesus in the closing years of the first century.

Synoptic Problem: The three Gospels of Matthew, Mark, and Luke are called *synoptic* from the Greek word *synoptikos,* which means "to see the whole together, to take a comprehensive view." They present similar views of the career and teaching of Christ, and resemble each other closely in content and in phraseology.

The numerous agreements between these Gospels have raised the question whether the relationship between them can be traced to common literary sources. Almost the entire content of the Gospel of Mark can be found in both Matthew and Luke, while much material not found in Mark is common to the other two Gospels. On the other hand, each Gospel has a different emphasis and organization. The "Synoptic Problem," as it is called, may be stated as follows: If the three Gospels are absolutely independent of each other, how can one account for the minute verbal agreements in their text? If they are copied from each other, or compiled freely from common sources, how can they be original and authoritative? Are they, then, truly the product of inspired writers, or are they merely combinations of anecdotes which may or may not be true?

Numerous theories have been propounded to account for these phenomena. The most popular in recent years has been the documentary theory, which assumes that the Gospels were derived from Mark and a hypothetical document called "Q" (from the German *Quelle,* meaning *source*), containing chiefly sayings of Jesus. According to this theory Matthew and Luke were composed independently by combining these two sources. Canon B. H. Streeter (*The Four Gospels,* New York, Macmillan, 1936) suggested also the addition of two special sources, *M* for Matthew and *L* for Luke, embodying the private knowledge or research of the two writers.

While this hypothesis seemingly solves the problem of the verbal resemblances, it is not entirely satisfactory. The existence of "Q" is at best only a probability; no copy of it has ever been found. R. M. Grant has pointed out that extant collections of the "Sayings of Jesus" dating from the second and third centuries should probably be assigned to the Gnostics, who, in turn, were dependent either on oral tradition or upon the canonical Gospels for their text (R. M. Grant, *The Secret Sayings of Jesus,* New York, Doubleday, 1960, pp. 29,40-61). These documents which have been considered analogous to "Q," and therefore as justifying the hypothesis of its existence, are themselves secondary. It is more likely that the coincident didactic passages of Matthew and Luke are drawn from utterances that Jesus repeated until they became fixed in the minds of His disciples, and were reproduced later in the Gospels.

In recent years the school of historical criticism, called *Formgeschichte,* has advanced another alternative. In an attempt to penetrate the development of the Gospel story before the Gospels, it has suggested that they were composed out of individual reminiscences of Jesus' deeds and bits of His teaching that were first preserved and circulated by His followers. Through repetition and selection these stories took permanent shape, and were incorporated into a general sequence that constituted the Gospel narratives. Advocates of *Formgeschichte* have separated the unitary sections of the Gospels into various classes: the *Passion story* of Jesus' last days; the *Paradigms,* stories of Jesus' deeds that illustrate the message; *Tales* of miraculous occurrences told to interest the public; *Legends* of saintly persons that are morally edifying; *Sayings* of Jesus that preserve His collected teachings in speeches or in parables.

This modification of oral tradition injects a greater uncertainty into the process of literary history. If the Synoptic Gospels are merely different arrangements of independent blocks of text, the problem of origins is multiplied. While sections of the Gospels may have been used for illustrative purposes, and while certain parts of them, like the Sermon on the Mount, might have once been a separate collection of sayings (or deeds, as the case may be), the fact that they were composed in the first century by trustworthy disciples of Jesus precludes fraud or unreliability.

Perhaps the best solution of the Synoptic Problem is the fact that all three Gospels are dealing with the life of the same Person, whose deeds and utterances were being continually preached as a public message. Constant repetition and frequent contact between the preachers tended toward fixing the content of the message. From the day of Pentecost the "teaching of the apostles" possessed some definite form, for it was used in instructing inquirers (Acts 2:42). As the church expanded, the written accounts were created to meet the demand for instruction, and they reproduced the phraseology and content of the oral teaching.

Each Gospel, however, was shaped to its own purpose and audience, so that the variations in wording reflected the differences of interest and environment. Matthew was written for Christians with a Jewish background; Mark for active Gentiles, probably Romans; Luke for a cultured and literary Greek. All three, however, bear united witness to the supernatural character and saving purpose of Jesus Christ.

The Johannine Problem: The Fourth Gospel differs markedly in character and in content from the Synoptics. Excluding the feeding of the five thousand and the Passion narrative, there are few points of agreement with the others. So radical are the differences that the veracity of the Gospel has been challenged on the grounds that if it is historical, it should coincide more nearly with the Synoptics.

For this reason some have held that the Fourth Gospel was written in the second century as the church's reflection on the person of Christ, phrased in terms of the Greek *Logos* doctrine. The discovery of the Rylands Fragment, a small scrap of papyrus on which a few verses of John were written, demonstrated that by the beginning of the second century the Gospel of John was circulated as far as southern Egypt. Since the handwriting of the fragment can be dated about 125 A.D., the Gospel must have been written earlier. It could not have been a late product of church tradition.

The language of the Gospel does not necessitate a Hellenistic origin. The existence of the concepts of light and of darkness, truth and falsehood, living waters, and others in the Dead Sea Scrolls show that John need not have drawn his vocabulary from Hellenism, but that many of his terms were a part of contemporary Judaism (Wiliiam LaSor, *The Amazing Dead Sea Scrolls,* Chicago, Moody Press, 1953, pp. 211-214). The Gospel of John is the account of an eye-witness, writing in his later years and interpreting the person of Christ in the perspective of his Christian experience.

Canonicity: The Gospels were among the first writings to be quoted as sacred and authoritative. There are quotations or allusions from individual passages in Ignatius of Antioch (c. A.D. 116), the *Epistle of Barnabas,* and the *Shepherd of Hermas,* which were written in the early part of the second century. Justin Martyr (c. A.D. 140) mentions the Gospels explicitly, calling them "Memoirs of the Apostles" (*First Apology,* LXVI). Marcion of Sinope (c. A.D. 100), a Gnostic, edited a compilation of Scriptures in which he included a mutilated Gospel of Luke. Tatian, (c. A.D. 150) an Assyrian who was converted in Rome under the ministry of Justin, and later became a Gnostic, produced the first harmony of the Gospels, called the *Diatessaron.* It included only the familiar four, weaving their text together into one continuous narrative. Only a few traces of the *Diatessaron* are still available in translations or in commentaries, but its existence proves that Matthew, Mark, Luke, and John were already the chief sources of information concerning the life and works of Jesus in the first half of the second century.

Growing intercommunication between the churches and the need for strengthening their defenses against heresy and the attacks of pagan critics promoted their interest in a canon of the Gospels. By A.D. 170 the four Gospels were securely established as the sole authorities. According to Irenaeus' contention, "It is not possible that the Gospels can be either more or fewer in number than they are. For since there are four zones of the world in which we live and four principal winds . . . it is fitting that she [the church] should have four pillars, breathing out immortality on every side . . ." (*Against Heresies,* III, xi, 8). Irenaeus' reasons are not very cogent, but the fact that he acknowledged only four indicates the sentiment of his times. The Muratorian Canon, a fragmentary manuscript of the seventh or eighth century containing a list of accepted books earlier than A.D. 200, included in its original form the four Gospels; and they were used by Tertullian of Carthage (c. A.D. 200), Clement of Alexandria (c. A.D. 200), Origen of Alexandria (c. A.D. 250), Cyprian of Carthage (c. A.D. 250); and they appear in the manuscript texts of the Chester Beatty Papyri and of the Old Latin version, both of which were in existence before A.D. 300. Eusebius (c. A.D. 350) and the fathers following him exclude all other Gospels from their official list, leaving these four the undisputed supreme authorities for knowledge of the life and work of Jesus Christ. See MATTHEW, Gospel of; MARK, Gospel of; LUKE, Gospel of; JOHN, Gospel of; CANON, N.T.   M.C.T.

BIBLIOGRAPHY:

Bruce, F.F. *Are the New Testament Documents Reliable?* London: The Inter-Varsity Fellowship of Evangelical Unions, 1943.
Grant, R.M., *The Secret Sayings of Jesus.* Garden City, New York: Doubleday & Co., Inc., 1960.
Nineham, D.E., Ed. *Studies in the Gospels.* Oxford: Basil Blackwell, 1955.
Redlich, Edwin Basil. *Form Criticism: Its Value and Limitations.* New York: Charles Scribner's Sons. 1939.
Scroggie, W. Graham. *A Guide to the Gospels.* London: Pickering and Inglis, Ltd.. 1948.
Stonehouse, Ned B. *Origins of the Synoptic Gospels.* Grand Rapids, Mich.; Wm. B. Eerdmans Pub. Co., 1963.
Streeter, Burnet H. *The Four Gospels.* Fifth Impression, Revised. London: Macmillan & Co., Ltd., 1936.
Zahn, Theodor. *Introduction to the New Testament.* Ed. M.W. Jacobus. Three volumes. Edinburgh: T. & T. Clark, 1909. See II, pp. 307-617; III, pp. 1-354.

GOURD (See Plants)

GOVERNOR (gŭv′ẽr-nôr), one who governs a land for a supreme ruler to whom he is subordinate. The word governor in the ERV is the rendering of a large variety of Hebrew and Greek words, and is used to represent men holding a number of official governmental positions. For example, Joseph, the prime minister of Egypt, was called its governor (Gen. 42:6; 45:26); Gedaliah, left in Judah to rule the conquered Jews after the destruction of Jerusalem, was called governor (Jer. 40:5; 41:2). In the NT the term occurs chiefly in reference to the Roman procurators of Judea — Pilate, Felix, and Festus. In the 1st century A.D., Roman provinces were of two kinds: imperial and senatorial. The first were ruled by procurators appointed by the emperor; the second, by proconsuls appointed by the senate. Judea was an imperial province. Pontius Pilate was the fifth of the governors of Judea; Felix, the eleventh; and Festus the twelfth. Procurators were directly responsible to the emperor for their actions, and ruled for as long as he willed.

GOZAN (gō′zăn, Heb. *gôzān*), a city located in NE Mesopotamia, on the Habor River, a tributary of the Euphrates. Here the Israelites were deported by the Assyrians following the fall of Samaria, the capital of the northern kingdom, (II Kings 17:6; 18:11; 19:12; I Chron. 5:26). The Assyrians called the city Guzanu, (the Guzanitis of Ptolemy). In 1911 Baron Von Oppenheim discovered a new culture at Tell Halaf, the modern name for Gozan. The relics of pottery are thought to date back to as far as 4000 B.C.

GRACE (Heb. *hēn*, Gr. *cháris*), a term employed by the Biblical writers with a considerable variety of meaning: (1) Properly speaking, that which affords joy, pleasure, delight, charm, sweetness, loveliness; (2) Good will, loving-kindness, mercy, etc; (3) the kindness of a master toward a slave. Thus by analogy, it has come to signify the kindness of God to man (Luke 1:30). The NT writers, at the end of their various epistles, frequently invoke God's gracious favor upon their readers (Rom. 16:20, 24; Phil. 4:23; Col. 1:19; I Thess. 5:28; *et. al.*). In addition, the word "grace" is frequently used to express the concept of kindness bestowed upon someone undeserving thereof. Hence, undeserved favor, especially that kind or degree of favor bestowed upon sinners through Jesus Christ. "For God who is rich in mercy for his great love wherewith he loved us, even when we were dead in sins hath quickened us together in Christ — by grace we are saved" (Eph. 2:4,5). Grace, therefore, is that unmerited favor of God towards fallen man, whereby, for the sake of Christ — who is the only begotten of the Father, full of grace and truth—(John 1:14) He has provided for man's redemption. He has from all eternity determined to extend favor towards all who exercise faith in Christ as Lord and Saviour.

The relationship between law and grace is one of the major themes of the Pauline writings (Rom. 5:1; 15-17; 8:1,2; Eph. 2:8,9; Gal. 5:4,5). Grace is likewise without equivocation identified as the medium or instrument through which God has effected the salvation of all believers (Titus 2:11). Grace is also regarded as the sustaining influence enabling the believer to persevere in the Christian life (Acts 11:23; 20:32; II Cor. 9:14). Thus, it is not merely the initiatory act of God in grace which secures the believers' eternal salvation, but also that which maintains it throughout the entirety of the Christian life. It is also used as a token or proof of salvation (II Cor. 1:5, RV "benefit"). A special gift of grace is imparted to the humble (I Pet. 5:5; James 4:6). Grace can also refer to the capacity for the reception of divine life (I Pet. 1:10). There are likewise several secondary senses in which "grace" is used: a gift of knowledge (I Cor. 1:4); thanksgiving or gratitude expressed for favor (I Cor. 10:30; I Tim. 1:1,2). Grace is employed at least once in the sense of "reward or recompense" (Luke 6:32), for which Matthew substitutes the term *misthos,* or *wages* (Matt. 5:46).

GRAFF, GRAFT, a horticultural process by which the branches of the wild olive tree in eastern lands are cut back so that branches from a cultivated olive may be inserted and grafting take place. Paul makes use of this practice in reverse (Rom. 11:17-24) where the opposite process is envisioned as happening; *i.e.,* the wild branches, the Gentiles, are thought of as "grafted in" to the good stock of the parent tree, the children of Israel. This deliberate inversion, certainly not a foolish mistake, heightens rather than mitigates the picturesque figure of speech conveying the eternal truth of the rejection of Israel and the status of the church.

GRAIN (See Plants)

GRANARY (grăn′ẽrē, Heb. *māzû,* Gr. *apothéke,* derived from a Hebrew word meaning *to gather* (Ps. 144:13), or Heb. *ôtzār, storehouse* (Joel 1:17). In the NT the term is sometimes rendered *barn,* and sometimes *garner* (Matt. 3:12; Luke 3:17). The Egyptians had storehouses for grain, liquor, armor, provisions, jewels, etc. Joseph, during the years of famine in Egypt, had authority over the storehouses (Gen. 41:56).

GRAPE (See Plants)

GRASS. There are a great many species of true grasses in Palestine, but actual turf is virtually unknown. The word "grass" is used in a somewhat comprehensive sense in the English version and is the rendering of a number of Hebrew terms and one Greek term. Genesis 1:11,12 divides the vegetable kingdom into three great classes: grass, herbs, and trees. The word is used in a figurative sense, too, as when man's brief exile is compared to grass (Ps. 103:15,16; Matt. 6:30; Luke 12:28).

GRASSHOPPER (See Insects)

GRATE (Heb. *resheth*), a copper network, moved by a copper ring at each corner and placed under the top of the great altar (Exod. 27:4; 35:16; 38: 4,5). It reached halfway up the altar and was doubtless to catch the ashes from the burning sacrifices.

GRAVE (Heb. *qĕvĕr, she'ôl,* Gr. *mnemeíon*), a place for the interment of the dead; a tomb, a sepulchre. Graves and accompanying burial customs differed in Biblical times from country to country. The pyramids were used for burial of members of the royal house. The Egyptians were meticulous in the construction of their graves because of their ardent belief in a future life. The rich were buried in a *mastaba,* or a rectangular structure of brick placed above the grave itself. In the neighborhood of Gizeh near the pyramids and at Saqqarah a number of these mastabas have been discovered. The very poor were interred clothesless and coffinless in the dry, sandy soil of Egypt. In later centuries, the rock tomb was substituted for the mastaba. Examples of these are the rock-hewn tombs of Thotmes III and Tutankhamon. Tutankhamon's tomb consisted of a passage cut into a hill of rock leading to a hall supported by columns where the sarcophagus of the pharaoh lay. Bas-reliefs in bright colors were frequently depicted on the walls of these tombs. Sumerian practice demanded that the royal dead be accompanied by the living, human beings and animals, forming a ghastly entourage. Queen Shu-ad of Ur, Abraham's city, was interred in this style with her husband. Three of the great kings of Persia cut their tombs out of the rocks near Perse-

Excavation of the royal tombs at Ur, in Babylonia. UMP

One of the Tombs of the Kings in Jerusalem, showing a rolling stone at the opening. © MPS

Roman sarcophagi at Antioch, along the Orontes River bank. © MPS

polis. Among the Hebrews, graves were sometimes mere holes in the earth (Gen. 35:8; I Sam. 31:13); natural caves or grottos; or artificial tombs hewn out of the rock (Luke 7:12, John 11: 30). In such a sepulchre, provided through the kindness of Joseph of Arimathea, the body of Jesus was laid. Flat stones were placed upon the graves as markers to warn passers-by that they should not contract ceremonial defilement by unwittingly trespassing. These stones were whitewashed annually in the month of Adar. This was the underlying figure of speech behind Jesus' stinging rebuke of the Pharisees, "Ye are like unto whited sepulchres" (Matt. 23:27). There were some traces still extant in the days of Christ (Matt. 8:28) of the idea that tombs were the dwelling places of demons.   J.F.G.

GRAVE CLOTHES (Gr. *keiría, winding sheet*). Preparatory to burial, the body was washed, and frequently anointed with spices, then stretched out on a bier until it was ready to be buried (Acts 5:7). After the washing and anointing, the corpse was wrapped in a linen winding sheet, the hands and feet were bound with grave-bands, and the face covered with a napkin (John 11:44; 19:40).

GRAVEN IMAGE, an image of wood, stone, or metal, shaped with a sharp cutting instrument as distinguished from one cast in a mold (Isa. 20:22; 44:16,17; 45:20). Images were, however, sometimes cast and then finished by the graver (Isa. 40:19). Such images were used by the Canaanites (Deut. 7:5), by the Babylonians, and by others (Jer. 50:38; 51:47,52). The Israelites were forbidden by the Decalogue to make them (Exod. 20:4).

GREAT OWL (See Birds)

GREAVES (See Arms, Armor)

GRECIA, GRECIANS. Grecia is Greece, the home of the Hellenes. Greeks and Grecians, however, are to be distinguished. Greeks are generally those of Hellenic race (e.g. Acts 16:1; 18:4 and probably John 12:20), but the word may be used to indicate non-Jews, foreigners and aliens (Rom. 1: 16). Grecians were Greek-speaking Jews, folk of the Dispersion, from areas predominantly Greek (Acts 6:1; 9:29). Greece and its associated island groups form the SE end of southern Europe's mountain system, a rugged peninsula and archipelago, not rich in fertile or arable land, which was the terminus of the southward movement of the Indo-European-speaking tribes who became the Greek people. These tribes, or their predecessors, had established ordered life in the peninsula and islands by the twelfth century before Christ. Their civilization vanished before the end of the second millennium, in a dark age of destruction and invasion occasioned by further waves of wandering tribes, just as Celt, Roman, Saxon, Dane, Norman, ripples of the same folk-movement of related peoples, made a succession of construction and destruction in Britain. Out of four centuries of chaos emerged the complex of peoples on island and mainland who are called the Greeks. Their own generic name was Hellenes, but Graecia was a portion of the land which, lying in the NW, naturally came first into the ken of Rome. After the common fashion of popular nomenclature (see under 'Palestine'), the name of the part which first claimed attention was extended to include the whole. Mediated through Rome, the term Greece was applied to all Hellas, and all Hellenes were called Greeks by western Europe. Geography, as always, played a part in the history of the people. The city state was a natural consequence of the isolated plain or river valley ringed by precipitous terrain. So was sea-faring. And from sea-faring and the dearth of fertile land in a rugged peninsula, sprang colonization, and the spread of Greek colonies which marked the first half of the pre-Christian millennium. As early as the eighth century before Christ, Greek ports and

trading posts were scattered from the Crimea to Cadiz. In these same centuries began the first flowering of Greek thought and poetry. In Ionia, the foundations of scientific and philosophical thought were laid. On Lesbos, in those same years, Sappho and Alcaeus wrote supreme lyric poetry. In short, the active, inquisitive, brilliant, inventive Greek race was visible in full promise round the eastern end of the Mediterranean before the bright flowering of fifth-century Athens. That century was one of the great golden ages of man. Greece, interpreted by the dynamic people of Attica, in one brief noon-tide of the human spirit, made immortal contributions to literature, art, philosophy and political thought. Everything Greek in all future centuries was deepened and colored by Athens' achievement. Hellenism, which had centuries of dynamic life ahead of it, was shaped by Athens in the short years of its spiritual supremacy. Athens' glory faded, and her strength was sapped in lamentable war with the dour and uncreative autocracy of Sparta. On the ruins of a Greece fatally weakened by internecine strife, Philip of Macedon, in the mid-fourth century before Christ, built his empire. His son Alexander, in one of the strangest acts of conquest in all history, took that empire to India, swept the vast state of Persia out of existence, and, as his father had unified Greece, brought under his single rule the great complex of states and kingdoms which lay between the Dardanelles and the Indus, the Caspian and the Nile. When Alexander died in Babylon at the age of thirty-three in 323 B.C., his generals divided the world (vid. sub *Seleucids*, Ptolemy), and out of the division arose the Oriental kingdoms which the Romans conquered when their empire rounded the Mediterranean Sea. The Greek language, Greek thought, Greek culture, in the wake of Alexander, provided a unifying element in all the Middle East. Without the vast flow

Ruins of the theater and the Temple of Apollo at Delphi, a cultural center of ancient Greece near Mount Parnassus. © MPS

of the Greek tide eastwards, the NT could not have been born. Greek provided its language and fashion of thought. Hellenism was a stimulus to the human mind. To reason, question, speculate, was a habit with the Greeks. Hence the logical mind of Greek-speaking Paul of Tarsus, heir of both Hellenism and Judaism. Hence the 'Grecians' of the NT, Stephen, for example, and Philip, who sweep fresh, bold, and vigorous into the story of the early Church, ready to reform, and to re-think old concepts. Paul needed his Greek education, as he needed the Judaism of Gamaliel. Paul's synthesis of the covenants, so compelling in its logic, so fundamental in Christian theology, was the work of a Greek Jew. It was thought trained in the Hellenism of Tarsus which solved the problem of the Testaments, and brought out from the stores of Judaism the wares which Christians could recognize and use. E.M.B.

GREEK LANGUAGE

GREEK LANGUAGE was a major branch of the Indo-European language which is the presumed parent of all the languages of Europe except Basque, Finnish and Hungarian, and of Sanskrit and the languages which derive from the Sanskrit stock in India. From Ireland to Pakistan this linguistic kinship can be demonstrated from vocabulary, morphology, and syntax. No monuments of the original Indo-European language exist, but the wide diffusion of demonstrably related tongues is strong argument for some form of early unity. The pattern of folk-wandering, which spread the Indo-European languages so widely, was a longer and more complex process than was imagined in the nineteenth century. This century has demonstrated the Indo-European basis of Hittite, and in 1953 Michael Ventris showed that the language of the Pylos tablets was a primitive Greek, thus proving that the language was spoken in the Peloponnesus several centuries before the time once favored for the arrival in the area of the Hellenic tribes. The piecemeal nature of their southward infiltration, and the firm geographical subdivisions of the area they occupied, led to the survival into literary times of several dialects, *Attic-Ionic,* spoken in Attica, and the Ionic areas of Asia Minor, with associated islands; *Achaean,* which included the Aeolic of Lesbos, and the dialects of Thessaly and Boeotia, together with the undocumented dialect of the Arcado-Cyprian; and thirdly what L. R. Palmer calls *West Greek,* including under that name the dialects of Phocis, Locris, Elis, and Aetolia, together with the Doric of the Peloponnesus, the Peloponnesian colonies, and Magna Graecia. Of these dialects, Attic achieved the supreme position because of the worth and greatness of the incomparable literature in which it found its expression. Attic Greek was one of the major achievements of the human mind. The richness and subtlety of its syntax, its flexibility, the delicacy of its particles, these and other linguistic features make Attic the most expressive medium ever developed for human thought. The dialects passed with the city states and the unification of Greece, and were followed by a basic Greek which developed in the form of a simplified Attic. This, spread by Alexander's conquests throughout the eastern end of the Mediterranean, was called the *Koine* or Common Dialect. It was the speech of the LXX and the NT, and the major influence in bringing the contributions of Palestine, Greece, and Rome into that partnership which determined the form and shape of the NT, the global Gospel of Paul of Tarsus, the Christian Church, and modern Europe. E.M.B.

An excerpt from the Septuagint, a fragment of the Sinaitic manuscript, photographed from one of the scraps found by Dr. Tischendorf at Mount Sinai. © MPS

GREEK VERSIONS. 1. The first and most famous of the Greek Versions of the OT, and the only one to survive in its entirety, is the Septuagint or "Version of the Seventy." This is the version most frequently quoted in the NT, for it became the Bible of the Hellenistic Jews, as the Vulgate became the Bible of the Latin world. The Vulgate was, in fact, in direct succession, being a translation of the Septuagint. Legend has gathered around so remarkable an achievement of translation, but it is possible to disengage some essential facts. It seems certain that the Septuagint was published in the time of Ptolemy II Philadelphus (295-247 B.C.), the Golden Age of Greek Alexandria. The city was always remarkable for its large colony of Jews, and the Greek Version of the Scriptures was probably a nationalistic gesture, designed to demonstrate, in what was becoming the world's second language, the worth of Jewish literature. It is doubtful whether the suggestion emanated from the king himself, interested though he was in all literature . The story of the 72 elders sent from Jerusalem, and the 72 days taken to complete the work, is legend. The Septuagint is written in the common dialect, but tinged by Hebraisms. The quality of the language and style varies, but on the whole the Greek is odd and undistinguished. It prompts knotty questions of criticism, to the solution of which the Dead Sea Scrolls have provided a little material. They have demonstrated, for example, that the Septuagint followed an older Hebrew text than that which survived in the traditional OT.

2. The acceptance of the Septuagint as the Bible of Greek-speaking Christianity, prompted orthodox Jewry to produce its own version distinct from it. Hence the version of Aquila of Hadrian's day (A.D. 117-138). The version of which only fragments exist, was in the worst "translation Greek," which followed slavishly the Hebrew forms and syntax.

3. Theodotian, an Ephesian of the second century, and an Ebionite Christian, produced a version which could be described as a RV of the Septuagint. It found favor with the Christian community. It was a freer translation than that of Aquila.

4. Symmachus, of unknown date, produced, perhaps at the end of the second century, a Greek version which appears to have been the best of all the translations, a rendering into idiomatic Greek. E.M.B.

GREYHOUND (See Animals)

GRIND (Heb. *tāhan*, Gr. *alétho*, *grind with a hand mill*), the grinding of grain into flour when pulverized between two heavy stones, a domestic art usually performed by women; hence, the import of Christ's parable: "Two women shall be grinding at the mill . . ." (Matt. 24:41; Luke 17:35).

GROVE (Heb. *ăshērâh*, Gr. *álsos*, mistranslated *grove* in the KJV following the LXX and the Vulgate). Although one gains a rather confused picture from the mere reading of the Scripture, the sum total of information affords a rather full and horrible panorama of iniquitous idolatry. The equipment for such worship, presumptively Phoenician in origin, were the "high places," (Heb. *bāmôth*), the altars crowning them, the standing pillars and the images of the Ashera. The worship was interwoven with the concept of the fertility of the land, and so became a fertility cult. The chosen symbol of the cult was the trunk of a tree. This explains the prohibition against the planting of trees by the altar of Jehovah (Deut. 16:21; Judg. 6:25,28,31). The goddess of the cult was Asherah, who also appears as mistress of the sea. A long risqué poem describes the journey of Lady Asherah to obtain permission from El to erect a temple (see Pritchard: *Archaeology and the Old Testament*, pp. 112f). The prophets of Israel roundly condemn the worship of Asherah and congratulate those kings who destroyed them (I Kings 15:13f; II Kings 17:10; 21:3; 23:4). Allied with the idea of fertility, Asherah has her counterpart in the Babylonian Ishtar, the goddess of love, and as such the goddess of human productivity.

GUARD, the rendering of a number of Heb. and Gr. words: 1. *tabbāh*, *slaughterer*, used of Potiphar (Gen. 37:36, etc.), Nebuzaradan (II Kings 25:8, etc.; Jer. 39:9, etc.), and Arioch (Dan. 2:14). The term may refer to a member of the king's bodyguard, who also had the duty of "slaughtering" anyone who tried to harm the king. 2. *rûts*, *runner*, trusted foot soldiers of a king, who performed various functions (I Kings 14:27,28; II Kings 10:25). 3. *mishmār*, *watch* (Neh. 4:22). 4. *mishma'ath*, *guard* (II Sam. 23:23). 5. *spekoulátor*, *guard, a spy* (Mark 6:27). 6. *koustodía*, *watch* (Matt. 27:65).

GUDGODAH (gŭd-gō'dà, Heb. *gudgōdhâh*, *cleft*, *division*), a place in the wilderness journeys of the children of Israel (Deut. 10:7), corresponding to Hor-haggidgag of Numbers 33:32. Identification still uncertain.

GUEST CHAMBER (Heb. *lishkâh*, in I Sam. 9:22 of KJV "parlor", *katáluma*, *inn, room in which to eat*). The *lishkâh* may have been a room in which the sacrificial feasts were held. *Katáluma* often means "inn," but in Mark 14:14 and Luke 22:11 it means a room in which to eat.

GUILT is the deserving of punishment because of the violation of a law or a breach of conduct. In the OT law the conception of guilt is largely ritualistic and legalistic. A person could be guilty as the result of unwitting sin (Lev. 5:17). Israel, moreover, is viewed as an organic whole, so that what one does affects all. There is collective responsibility for sin, as when Achan sinned and all Israel suffered. With the prophets, the ethical and personal aspects of sin and of guilt are stressed. God is less interested in ritual correctness than in moral obedience.

In the NT Jesus stressed the importance of right heart attitude as over against outwardly correct acts, and taught that there are degrees of guilt, depending upon a person's knowledge and motive (Luke 11:29-32; 12:47,48; 23:34). Paul also recognized differences of degree in guilt (Acts 17:30; Eph. 4:18). Theologians differ as to whether Paul in Romans 5:12-21 teaches that Adam's guilt was imputed to all his posterity; and if it was, just how it was done.　　　　S.B.

GUNI (gū'nī). 1. The name of a family clan of the tribe of Naphtali (Gen. 46:24; Num. 26:48; I Chron. 7:13).
2. The head of a Gadite family (I Chron. 5:15).

GUNITE (gū'nīt), the family of Guni, son of Naphtali (Num. 26:48).

GUR (gûr), a rising ground, not definitely identified, but thought to be near Jenin; roughly, about 12 or 13 miles NE of Samaria. The place where Ahaziah received his mortal wound while fleeing from Jehu, after the slaughter of Joram (II Kings 9:27).

GUR-BAAL (gûr'bā'ăl, *sojourn of Baal*), a small colony town of Arabs, against whom Uzziah of Judah was given divine aid (II Chron. 26:7); perhaps in the desert S of Beer-sheba.

GUTTER (gŭt'têr, Heb. *tsinnôr*, *pipe, spout, conduit*), the channel or tunnel (AV Gutter) through which David's soldiers are inferred to have marched to wrest the city of Jerusalem from Jebusite rule (II Sam. 5:8), at the fountain of Gihon (q.v.), site of the later tunnel which Hezekiah constructed (II Kings 20:20) connecting the spring at Gihon with the pool of Siloam. It was 1800 ft. long and 6 ft. high. It was dug out as a far sighted measure so that the city's water supply would not be imperiled during the impending siege at the hands of Sennacherib of Assyria.

A view in the Siloam Tunnel, built by King Hezekiah in the eighth century B.C., and also known as Hezekiah's Tunnel or the Gutter. The famous Siloam Tunnel inscription was cut out from the wall near this point. © MPS

H

HAAHASHTARI, HAASHTARI (hā′à-hăsh′tà-rī, hā-ăsh′tà-rī, *the Ahashtarite*), a man of Judah, mentioned in I Chronicles 4:6. Probably a muleteer, son of Naarah.

HABAIAH (hà-bā′yà, *Jehovah has hidden*), ancestor of some priests in Zerubbabel's time (Ezra 2: 61); called Hobaiah in Nehemiah 7:63 RV.

HABAKKUK (hà-băk′ŭk, Heb. *hăvaqqûq, embrace*), the name of a prophet and of the eighth book of the Minor Prophets, which is entitled "The oracle which Habakkuk the prophet saw" (1:1). Of the man Habakkuk nothing is known outside of the book which bears his name. Legendary references to him (in the apocryphal *Bel and the Dragon* and elsewhere) appear to have no historical value. The musical references in Chapter 3 have led some to believe that he was a member of a Levitical musical guild; even this is uncertain.

Most traditional scholars believe the book to be a unity, the work of Habakkuk, produced in Judah during the Chaldean period. The reasons for this view are found in the book itself. The temple still stands (2:20; 3:19) and the rise of the Chaldean power is predicted (1:5,6). The argument here depends upon the understanding of the Hebrew word *kasdîm,* translated Chaldeans. Some recent scholars emend the word to *kittîm,* meaning Cypriots, and understand it to refer to the Macedonian Greeks under Alexander the Great. They therefore date the book to this much later period. There is no good reason to make this emendation. *Kasdîm* clearly means Chaldeans.

The Neo-Babylonian or Chaldean empire first came to prominence when the Babylonian king Nebuchadnezzar defeated the Egyptians at the battle of Carchemish in 605 B.C., and re-established Babylon as the seat of world power. The prophecy of Habakkuk could hardly have been given before 605 B.C. Jerusalem fell to Nebuchadnezzar in 587 B.C. The book must be placed somewhere between these dates, probably during the reign of the Judean king Jehoiakim. Some date the book earlier, believing that the Chaldeans were known to Judah before Carchemish and emphasizing the unexpectedness of the attack mentioned by Habakkuk (1: 5). Still, a date soon after 605 B.C. seems to be preferred.

A fragment of the Habakkuk Commentary from the Dead Sea Scrolls. © Shrine of the Book, Jerusalem. MPS

In modern times the unity of the book has been questioned. The psalm of Chapter 3 is certainly somewhat different in style from the rest of the book, but this is hardly sufficient reason to deny it to Habakkuk. The theory that all psalms were post-Exilic in Israel is now discredited. The theme of the prose part (chs. 1,2) is the same as that of the psalm. And there are real similarities of language. Chapter 3 is specifically ascribed to Habakkuk (3:1), and there seems to be no good internal indication that he was not its author.

Chapters 1 and 2 set forth Habakkuk's prophetic oracle or burden. Twice the prophet is perplexed and asks divine enlightenment; twice he is answered. First he is concerned over the violence and sin of his people, the Judeans. Why are these wicked men not punished (1:2-4)? God answers that He is about to send the Chaldeans to judge Judah (1:5-11). This answer plunges Habakkuk into a greater perplexity: How can a righteous God use the wicked Chaldeans to punish Judah, which, although it has become apostate, is still better than the Chaldeans (1:12-17)? God's answer is that the proud conquerors will themselves be punished (2:1-20). The Chaldeans are puffed up with self-sufficient pride, but in this hour of national calamity the righteous will live by His faithfulness, i.e., by His constancy, abiding in God although all of the helps given to the OT believers (the nation, the temple and its ritual) are swept away (2:4). This statement naturally becomes important to the NT writers and is quoted in Romans 1:17, Galatians 3:11, and Hebrews 10:38. The second answer to Habakkuk concludes with a series of woes against the Chaldeans (2:5-20).

Chapter 3 is called "a prayer of Habakkuk the prophet" (3:1). In a moving lyric poem the prophet records his final response to God's message of judgment. He describes the divine revelation in terms of a stormy theophany (3:2-15), but concludes that no matter what comes he will trust in God (3:16-19).

The commentary on Chapters 1 and 2 recently found at Qumran near the Dead Sea casts little light on the meaning of these chapters, although it enables us to know how the Essene community there in the first century B.C. understood the book.
                                                    J.B.G.

HABAZINIAH (hab′à-zĭ-nī′à), ancestor of the Rechabites of the time of Jeremiah. Mentioned only in Jeremiah 35:3.

HABERGEON (hăb′êr-jŭn, Heb. *tahărā′*), a jacket of mail to defend the breast and neck (II Chron. 26:14; Neh. 4:16). Job 41:26 has "pointed shaft," with "coat of mail" in the margin. Habergeon is also used to render a different Heb. word of uncertain meaning in Exodus 28:32; 39:23.

HABIRU (hà-bī′rū), the name of a people first made known in the Amarna letters (15th century B.C.), where they are mentioned among those who are intruders of Palestine. Since then the name has appeared in Babylonian texts and documents from Mari (18th century B.C.), the Hittite records from Boghaz-keui and the Hurrian texts from Nuzi (14th century B.C.). The same name appears in Egyptian records as "Apiriu" as late as the 12th century B.C. Abraham is the first person in the Bible to bear the name Hebrew, *'Ibri* (Gen. 14: 13). Some scholars philologically equate the names Habiru and 'Ibri. The fundamental meaning of Habiru seems to be "wanderers." It is not an ethnic designation, for the Habiru of these various texts are of mixed racial origin, including both Semites and non-Semites. The name Habiru therefore has a wider connotation than the people known as Hebrews, although it became associated with them particularly. The patriarchal movements of Genesis appear to be parts of a larger movement of peoples known as the Habiru, with the Hebrew conquest of Canaan as only one of these. The connection, if any, of the Hebrews with the Habiru still remains obscure.　　　　　　　　　S.B.

HABOR (hā'bôr, Heb. *hāvōr*), a river of Gozan, the region in the northern part of Mesopotamia to which Shalmanezer, king of Assyria, banished the northern tribes of Israel after Hoshea, the last king, had rebelled against him (II Kings 17:6; 18: 11). To this same region, Tiglath-pilezer (Tilgath-pilneser) had carried the tribes E of Jordan (I Chron. 5:26).

HACHALIAH (hăk'à-lī'à, in ASV, *Hacaliah*), the father of Nehemiah, governor of the Jews (Neh. 1:1; 10:1).

HACHILAH (hà-kī'là), a hill in the wilderness SE of Hebron, near Ziph and Maon (I Sam. 23:19; 26:1,3)). Here David hid from Saul, but was discovered, and here Saul encamped, seeking David.

HACHMONI (hăk'mō-nī, Heb. *hakhmônî, wise*), the father of Jehiel, an associate of David's sons (I Chron. 27:32) and of Jashobeam, one of David's mighty men (I Chron. 11:11). Cf. "Tachmonite" in II Samuel 23:8. The text is obscure.

HADAD (hā'dăd, *sharpness, fierceness*). 1. A grandson of Abraham through Ishmael (Gen. 25: 15; Hadar in KJV; I Chron. 1:30).

2. An early king of Edom, whose capital was at Pau or Pai (I Chron. 1:50). In Genesis 36:39 he is called "Hadar."

3. An earlier king of Edom, a son of Bedad, who smote Midian in the field of Moab (Gen. 36: 35; I Chron. 1:46).

4. An Edomite of royal descent whose life had been saved in his early childhood by flight from David's devastating attacks. Hadad went to Egypt, where Pharaoh received him and his men, gave him a house, and highly favored him. Hadad became brother-in-law to Tahpenes, queen of Egypt, but later when he learned that Joab had died, he went back to Edom and became an adversary to Solomon (I Kings 11:14-25).

5. The supreme God of Syria, whose name is found in proper names like Ben-hadad and Hadadezer. In Assyrian inscriptions he is identified with their air-god Ramman, i.e., Rimmon.

HADADEZER, HADAREZER (hăd'ăd-ē'zêr, hăd'-ăr-ē'zêr, *Hadad is a help*), a king of Zobah, twice defeated in battle by David, king of Israel (II Sam. 8:3ff; 10:15-19; I Chron. 18:3ff). Zobah was a kingdom lying NE of Damascus and between the valleys of the Orontes and the Euphrates.

HADAD-RIMMON (hā'dăd-rĭm'ŏn, *Hadad and Rimmon, two Syrian divinities*), a place in the valley of Megiddo, where Josiah, king of Judah, was mortally wounded (II Kings 23:29,30), and where later there was a memorable mourning for him as recorded in Zechariah 12:11. It is now called Rummaneh, i.e. "place of pomegranates."

HADAR (hā'dàr). 1. According to Genesis 25:15 in KJV a son of Ishmael, but the Hebrew and ASV unite in calling him Hadad and I Chronicles 1:30 supports Hadad.

2. The last of the ancient kings of Edom (Gen. 36:39) but in I Chronicles 1:50,51 he also is called Hadad. "Hadar" and "Hadad" are easily confused in Hebrew.

HADASHAH (hà-dăsh'à, *new*), a town of Judah in the low plain in Joshua's time (Josh. 15:37).

HADASSAH (hà-dăs'à, *a myrtle*), daughter of Abihail, who became Esther, queen of Xerxes, i.e. Ahasuerus (Esth. 2:7,15).

HADATTAH (hà-dăt'à, *new*), a town in the S of Judah. In Joshua 15:25 KJV makes it seem to be a separate town, but the Hebrew and ASV make it clear that "Hadattah" is simply a description of Hazor. It may be that there were an old and a new Hazor.

HADES (hā'dēz, Gr. *Haídes, not to be seen*), the place or state of the dead, as contrasted with the final punishment of the wicked. In the NT Greek, the word occurs ten times and is uniformly rendered "hell" in KJV. In the TR from which KJV was translated, the word occurs also in I Corinthians 15:55 and is rendered "grave," but in the better texts the Greek has *thanate* and ASV "death," which is correct. The NT word is taken over from the Greek mythology, where *Hades* was the god of the lower regions. Although the word was taken from heathen myths, the concept is from the OT word *Sheol*. *Sheol* occurs 65 times in the Hebrew OT and is rendered in KJV as "hell" 31 times, "the grave" 31 times, and "the pit" three times; but in ASV it is uniformly transliterated *Sheol*, even as *Hades* in the ASV is a transliteration rather than an attempt to translate the Greek. The word "hell" in English always has an unpleasant connotation and is properly thought of as the final destiny of the wicked when it translates *geenna*, which occurs 12 times and is always rendered "hell."

For the most part, the NT does not give very definite light on Hades. In Matthew 11:23 (cf. Luke 10:15) our Lord says that Capernaum will go down into Hades. The preposition "down" points to the OT teaching that Sheol is inside the earth (Amos 9:2; Ps. 139:8, etc.) and the following verse (Matt. 11:24) puts the day of judgment for both Sodom and Capernaum later than the stay in Hades. In Matthew 16:18, "the gates of hell" seem to be a reference to Satan's headquarters, as the great enemy of the Christian Church. In the parable of the rich man and Lazarus (Luke 16:19-31) the rich man is pictured as being tormented in Hades, but able to see in the distance Abraham with Lazarus in his bosom. He asks for a drop of water to cool his tongue and for a message to be sent to his five brethren who are still alive on earth, and in each case his request is denied. In the first Christian sermon Peter quotes (Acts 2:25-31) from Psalm 16:8-11 proving from it that our Lord arose from the dead and was not left in Hades. In Revelation "death and Hades" are four times associated (1:18; 6:8; 20:13,14), being attested as almost synonymous terms. In the last verse mentioned, death and Hades are to be cast into the lake of fire, i.e. doomed to utter destruction. See GEHENNA.　　　　　　　　A.B.F.

HADID (hā'dĭd, Heb. *hādhîdh, sharp*), a village in Benjamin named with Lod (Ezra 2:33; Neh. 7:37; 11:34). It was located about three miles E of Lydda.

HADLAI (hăd'lī, *ceasing, forbearing*), the father of Amasa, an Ephraimite chief, mentioned only in II Chronicles 28:12.

HADORAM (hà-dō'răm, Heb. *hădhōrăm*). 1. A son of Joktan (Gen. 10:27; I Chron. 1:21) and probably an Arab tribe of that name in Arabia Felix.

2. Son of the king of Hamath whom his father sent to congratulate David on his victory over Hadadezer (I Chron. 18:9-11). In II Samuel 8:9, 10 the name is written as Joram.

3. Rehoboam's superintendent of the men under taskwork (II Chron. 10:18). The children of Israel stoned him when Rehoboam sent him to them, presumably to collect taxes or to raise a levy of workers. (Perhaps the same as Adoniram of I Kings 4:6.)

HADRACH (hā'drăk, Heb. *hadhrākh*), a country associated with Damascus and Hamath and mentioned only in Zechariah 9:1. Gesenius guesses that it lay E of Damascus.

HAGAB (hā'găb, Heb. *hāghāv, locust*), ancestor of some temple servants who returned with Zerubbabel (Ezra 2:46).

HAGAR (hā'gàr, Heb. *hāghār, emigration, flight*), an Egyptian handmaid to Sarai, wife of Abram (Gen. 12:10-20). God had promised to him a son who would be his heir (Gen. 15:4), but Sarai was barren, and so, following the marital customs of the times, she gave Hagar to her husband as her substitute (Gen. 16:1-16). Nuzi documents which have been discovered stipulate that if a wife is barren, she must furnish her husband with a slave wife.) When Hagar saw that she had conceived, she despised her mistress, causing trouble in the household. Hagar was driven out, but the angel of the Lord appeared to her and sent her back to her mistress (Gen. 16:7-14). When Ishmael, her son, was 14 years old, his father 100 and Sarah 90, Isaac was born. At a great feast held in connection with Isaac's weaning, Ishmael scoffed at the proceedings (Gen. 21:9), and as a result Sarah insisted that Hagar and her son be cast out, which Abraham unwillingly did. God told Abraham that Ishmael's descendants would become a nation. Hagar is last seen taking for her son a wife out of the land of Egypt, her own land (Gen. 21:1-21). Paul made the story of Hagar an allegory of the difference between law and grace (Gal. 4:21-5:1).

HAGARENES, HAGARITES (hā'gàr-ēnz, hā'gàr-īts, in ASV "Hagrites"), an Arab people with whom in the days of King Saul, the tribe of Reuben made war (I Chron. 5:19,20). The Hagarites were so strong that Reuben won the victory only by crying to God in the battle. Psalm 83 tells how the Hagarenes were leagued not only with Moab and the Ammonites E of the Jordan, Edom, the Ishmaelites and Amalek to the S, but also with Gebal, Tyre and Philistia along the coast against Israel, and Asaph prays that God for His own name's sake will defeat them utterly.

HAGGAI (hăg'ā-ī, Heb. *haggay, festal*), prophet of the Lord to the Jews in 520 B.C. Little is known of his personal history. He lived soon after the Captivity, and was contemporary with Zechariah (cf. Hag. 1:1 with Zech. 1:1).

After the return from the Captivity the Israelites set up the altar upon its base, established daily worship, and laid the foundation for the second temple; then they were compelled to cease building for some years. However, though times were hard they were able to build fine ceiled houses for themselves (Hag. 1:4). Meanwhile kings succeeded one another in Persia. Cyrus, favored of God and friend of the Jews (Isa. 44:28; II Chron. 36:22) passed away in 529 B.C.; then his son Cambyses (the "Ahasuerus" of Ezra 4:6) reigned 529-522 B.C., followed for only seven months in 522 by the Pseudo-Smerdis (a usurper); then arose Darius Hystaspes (Ezra 4-6; Hag., Zech. 1-6), who helped and encouraged the Jews to go ahead, and who commanded the hinderers to desist. In the second year of Darius (520 B.C.) Haggai fulfilled his brilliant mission of rebuking and encouraging the Jews. The five short messages which make up

The Lahai-Roi spring at Mount Seir, pointed out as the spot where Hagar and her son Ishmael obtained water. © MPS

his books are all dated, occupying only three months and 23 days; and in those few weeks the whole situation changed from defeat and discouragement to victory. Zechariah assisted Haggai in the last month of his recorded ministry (Zech. 1:1-6).

In order to make the dates clearer to modern readers, we shall give the months their approximately equivalent names in our calendar. On "Sept." 1, 520 B.C. the Lord spoke through Haggai, and instead of addressing the people at large, the prophet went straight to "headquarters," i.e., to Zerubbabel the prince and to Joshua, the high priest. The people stopped building the Lord's house though they were quite able to build their own, and God's message was "Consider your ways." The punishment for their neglect had been futility; they labored much but produced little; and so God used "weather judgments" to bring them to their senses. The leaders heeded the message and with the best of the people, they began immediately to build and on "Sept." 24 God's short message was "I am with you" (Hag. 1:13). A month later, they were tempted to be discouraged when they contrasted their present effort with the former magnificent temple and so God told them that "the glory of this house shall be greater than the former" (2:9). This message was delivered on "Oct." 21 and it contained the notable statement, that "the silver is mine, and the gold is mine." The fourth and fifth messages came in one day "Dec." 24, 520 B.C. In the fourth, Haggai said that holiness is not contagious, though evil is, and Israel's change in attitude would cause God to change chastening into blessing. In the last message (2:20-23) God predicts a shaking of the nations but at the same time a great reward to Zerubbabel. One wonders if this is connected with the fact of Zerubbabel's becoming an ancestor of our Lord in both the royal line (Matt. 1:13) and the Lucan line (Luke 3:27). A.B.F.

HAGGERI (hăg'ē-rī, *wanderer*), the father of Mibhar, one of David's heroes (I Chron. 11:38), ASV "Hagri."

HAGGI (hăg'ī, *festal*), a son of Gad, and grandson of Jacob (Gen. 46:16); patriarch of the Haggites (Num. 26:15).

HAGGIAH (hă-gī'à, *a festival of Jehovah*), a Levite of the family of Merari, mentioned only in I Chronicles 6:30.

HAGGITH (hăg'ĭth, *festal*), wife of David (II Sam. 3:4) and mother of Adonijah (I Kings 1:5-31).

HAGIOGRAPHA (hăg'ĭ-ŏg'rà-fà, *holy writings*), a name applied to the third division of the OT by the Jews, the other two being the Law and the Prophets. Sometimes they were called the "Writings." They comprise 11 books, in the following order: Psalms, Proverbs, Job, Song of Solomon, Ruth Lamentations, Ecclesiastes, Esther, Daniel, Ezra, Nehemiah, I and II Chronicles.

HAI (hā'ī, *the heap*). 1. A town E of Bethel and near Beth-aven (Gen. 12:8; 13:3). Because of the sin of Achan, the Israelite attack on it failed; but after he was punished, it was taken (Josh. 7,8). In Joshua the name is spelled Ai in the KJV.
2. A city of the Ammonites (Jer. 49:3).

HAIL. 1. Hail storms sometimes take place in the Near East in the spring and summer and do considerable damage to crops, sometimes even injuring property and endangering life. Plagues of hail are mentioned in Exodus 9:23,24 and Joshua 10:11. The prophets speak of hail as a means of punishing the wicked (Isa. 28:2; Ezek. 38:22; Rev. 8:7; 11:19).
2. An interjection found only in the Gospels as a translation of *chaíre*, used as a greeting or salutation.

HAIR, the natural head-covering common to man and to most mammals. It varies in length, color and structure among the different races and seems to be intended of God for protection, for beauty and for identification. The peoples of the Bible lands were generally black-haired, though red-haired individuals are fairly common among the people of Israel. Hebrews and Arabs (cf. Rev. 9: 8) wore their beards long as a mark of dignity but the Egyptians were clean-shaven (Gen. 41:14).

The quick-whitening of hair was one of the symptoms of leprosy (Lev. 13:3,10), but if the leprosy and the white hairs covered the body and there was no raw flesh, the leprosy was no longer contagious (Lev. 13:13). Thin yellow hair appearing in the head or beard was a symptom of scall or scurf, related to leprosy (Lev. 13:29-37).

The men of Israel were not to mar the corners of the beard (Lev. 19:27) and this prohibition explains the "prayer-locks" in front of the ears of Jewish men today. The word "hair" is used in several figurative senses: e.g., in marksmanship some Benjamites could "sling stones at a hair-breadth and not miss" (Judg. 20:16); or in meaning complete safety — "there shall not one hair of his head fall to the ground" (I Sam. 14:45); or to indicate multiplicity — "my iniquities are more than the hairs of my head" (Ps. 40:12); or to show age or dignity — "the hair of his head like pure wool" (Dan. 7:9). Hair was a mark of beauty and sometimes of pride. Absalom's hair (II Sam. 14:26; 18:9), of which he was inordinately proud, caused his death. In Samson's case, his uncut hair was a symbol of his Naziritic dedication, and when he lost his hair, his strength went with it (Judg. 13:7; 16:17-20). In NT times the length of hair was one mark of distinction between the sexes (I Cor. 11:14-16).   A.B.F.

HAKKATAN (hăk'à-tăn, *the little one*), father of Johanan who returned with Ezra (Ezra 8:12).

HAKKOZ (hăk'ŏz, *the nimble,* KJV sometimes has Koz, once Coz). 1. A descendant of Aaron whose descendants returned with Zerubbabel from the captivity (I Chron. 24:10; Ezra 2:61; Neh. 3:4,21).
2. A man of Judah (I Chron. 4:8).

HAKUPHA (hà-kū'fà, *bent, bowed*), father of some of the Nethinim who returned with Zerubbabel from Babylon (Ezra 2:51; Neh. 7:53).

HALAH (hā'là), a district in Media to which many of the captive Israelites were taken by Shalmanezer and by Tiglath-pilezer (II Kings 17:6; 18:11; I Chron. 5:26). It is about 80 miles W by N of the famous Behistun rock.

HALAK (hā'lăk, *smooth*), a mountain that marked the southern limit of the conquests of Joshua; perhaps the chalk cliffs crossing the Arabah about six miles S of the Dead Sea (Josh. 11:17; 12:7).

HALHUL (hăl'hŭl), a town in the hill country of Judah (Josh. 15:58) about four miles N of Hebron. It retains its ancient name, and contains a mosque dedicated to the Prophet Jonah.

HALI (hā'lī, *ornament*), a town on the southern boundary of the tribe of Asher (Josh. 19:25).

HALL, in the KJV denotes: (1) the court of the high priest's palace (Luke 22:55); (2) the official residence of a Roman provincial governor. It was called the praetorium (Matt. 27:27; Mark 15:16).

HALLEL (hă-lāl, *praise*). Psalms 113-118, which were read on Passover day, were called the "Egyptian Hallel"; Psalm 136 is an antiphonal Psalm of praise and is sometimes called "the Hallel." Psalms 120-136 are often called the "Great Hallel."

HALLELUJAH (hăl'ē-lōō'yà, Heb. *hallelû-yâh, praise ye Jehovah*), a word which is found in most of the languages into which the Bible has been translated. Like "Amen," it is nearly a universal word. It is found dozens of times, principally in the Psalms, often at the beginning and the end, as in Psalm 150:1,6.

HALLOHESH (hă-lō'hĕsh, *the whisperer*), in Nehemiah 3:12, father of Shallum, a ruler, and in Nehemiah 10:24 one of the covenanters, perhaps the same man.

HALLOW (hăl'ō, *to render or treat as holy*). The prime idea in this as in the kindred words "holy," "sanctify," etc., is the setting apart of a person or a thing for sacred use; to hold sacred; reverence as holy.

HAM (hăm, Heb. *hām*, perhaps *hot*). 1. The youngest son of Noah, born probably about 96 years before the Flood; and one of the eight persons to live through the Flood. He became the progenitor of the dark races; not the Negroes, but the Egyptians, Ethiopians, Libyans and Canaanites (Gen. 10:6-20). His indecency, when his father lay drunken, brought a curse upon Canaan (Gen. 9: 20-27).
2. A city of the Zuzim, E of the Jordan (Gen. 14:5). This is not the same word as the son of Noah.
3. The descendants of the original Ham (Ps. 78:51; 105:23; 106:22). In these passages "Ham" is used as another name for Egypt as representing Ham's principal descendants.

HAMAN (hā'măn, Heb. *hāmān*), the great enemy of the Jews in the days of Esther. He is called "the Agagite," undoubtedly because he came from Agag, a territory adjacent to Media. "Ahasuerus" or Xerxes, as he is known in secular history, had promoted Haman to a high position in the court, but Mordecai, the noble Jew, refused to do him obeisance, and so Haman plotted to destroy the

Jewish race, but God intervened. Esther foiled Haman's plot (Esth. 7) and Haman died on the gallows he had made for Mordecai.

HAMATH (hā′măth, Heb. *hămāth, fortification*), one of the most ancient surviving cities on this earth, located in upper Syria on the Orontes river from which it derives its water by means of immense undershot water wheels driven by the current. The "entrance of Hamath" (Num. 34:8) was to be the northern limit of Israel, but God left some of the Hivites in that neighborhood to be a test to the faithfulness of Israel (Judg. 3:3). In the days of David, Hamath had a king of its own (II Sam. 8:9). Jeroboam II, the last powerful king of the northern tribes (II Kings 14:23-28), recovered Hamath to Israel. It has had for thousands of years a checkered history. For a time it was under the power of Assyria (II Kings 18:34), later under Babylonia (Jer. 39:5); and still later Antiochus Epiphanes of Syria (c. 175-164 B.C.) renamed it Epiphaneia after himself. Today it is largely Moslem, but with a large admixture of Christians. The city is dominated by its citadel hill which no doubt contains layers of many different civilizations.

HAMATH-ZOBAH (hā′măth-zō′bà), mentioned in II Chronicles 8:3, but the reference is uncertain. It could mean the neighbor kingdoms of Hamath and Zobah, or some place called Hamath, belonging to the kingdom of Zobah; or, to avoid confusion with the Zobah in the Hauran (II Sam. 23:36), Hamath may have been mentioned in connection with it.

HAMMATH (hăm′ăth, *hot spring*). 1. One of the fortified cities assigned by lot to the tribe of Naphtali in the division of the land under Joshua (Josh. 19:35). It lay close to the shore of the Sea of Galilee, only a mile or so S of the city of Tiberias, and even today three of these hot springs send up sulphurous water at the southern extremity of the ancient ruins. Gesenius thinks that it is probably the same as the Hammoth-dor of Joshua 21:32, and Hammon of I Chronicles 6:76.
2. The founder of the house of Rechab (I Chron. 2:55). Hemath in KJV.

HAMMEDATHA (hăm′ē-dā-thà), father of Haman the Agagite, the villain in the book of Esther (Esth. 3:1, etc.).

HAMMELECH (hăm′ē-lĕk, *the king*), father of Jerahmeel and Malchiah (Jer. 36:26; 38:6). The KJV wrongly translates it as a proper name; it should be rendered "the king," as in ARV.

HAMMER. There are two chief words for "hammer" in the OT, *pattîsh,* a tool for smoothing metals and for breaking rocks (Isa. 41:7; Jer. 23:29), and *maqqeveth,* a mallet to drive tent-pins into the ground (Judg. 4:21; I Kings 6:7), for building and for making idols (Isa. 44:12; Jer. 10:4). The word "hammer" is sometimes used figuratively for any crushing power, as Babylon (Jer. 50:23) or God's word (Jer. 23:29).

HAMMOLEKETH (hă-mŏl′ē-keth, *the queen*), a sister of Gilead (I Chron. 7:18). "Hammolecheth" in KJV.

HAMMON (hăm′ŏn, *hot spring*). 1. A place in Asher about 10 miles S of Tyre (Josh. 19:28).
2. A city of Naphtali (I Chron. 6:76). See Hammath, which may be the same place (Josh. 19:35).

HAMMOTH-DOR (hăm′ŏth-dôr, *warm springs of Dor*), a city in Naphtali, appointed as a city of refuge (Josh. 21:32). See Hammath.

Portrait of Hammurabi, King of Babylon, carved on a limestone tablet. BM

HAMMURABI (hàm′ōō-rà′bē), the king of the city of Babylon who brought that city to its century-and-a-half rule over southern Mesopotamia known as the Old Babylonian Kingdom. He was an Amorite, the name given to a Semitic group which invaded the Fertile Crescent about 2000 B.C., destroying its civilization and establishing their own Semitic culture. There has been considerable difference of opinion about the date of his reign, recent scholars favoring 1728-1686 B.C.

Hammurabi made Babylon one of the great cities of the ancient world. Archaeologists have discovered that in his city the streets were laid out in straight lines which intersect approximately at right angles, an innovation which bears witness to city planning and strong central government, little known in Babylon before this time. Marduk, the god of Babylon, now became the head of the pantheon and his temple, Etemenanki, one of the wonders of the ancient world. Many letters written by Hammurabi have been found. These show his close attention to the details of his realm, and enable us to call him an energetic and benevolent ruler.

Hammurabi began the first golden age of Babylon — the second being that of Nebuchadnezzar, over a thousand years later. He systematically unified all of the old world of Sumer and Akkad (southern Mesopotamia) under his strongly centralized government. The prologue to his famous law code describes his administration: "Anu and Enlil (the sky and storm gods) named me to promote the welfare of the people, me, Hammurabi, the devout, god-fearing prince, to cause justice to prevail in the land, to destroy the wicked and the evil, that the strong might not oppress the weak, to rise like the sun over the black-headed (people), and to light up the land. Hammurabi the shepherd, called by Enlil, am I; the one who makes affluence and plenty abound . . . the one revived Uruk, who supplied water in abundance to its people; the one who brings joy to Borsippa; . . . who stores up grain for mighty Urash; . . . the savior of his people from distress, who establishes in security their portion in the midst of Babylon . . . that justice might be dealt the orphan and the widow . . . I established law and justice in the language of the land, thereby promoting the welfare of the people."

The famous Code of Hammurabi, 282 laws engraved on a stone stele eight feet high. At the top, Hammurabi is shown receiving the symbols of authority from the god Marduk. © LMP

By far his most famous claim to fame is Hammurabi's law code. It is inscribed on a magnificent stele of black diorite, eight feet high, found at Susa in 1902. Formerly it had stood in Babylon, but the Elamites carried it off when they conquered Babylon in the 12th century B.C. It is now in the Louvre in Paris. At the top of the stele is a finely sculptured scene showing Hammurabi standing before the sun god Shamash (the patron of law and justice) who is seated and is giving to Hammurabi the laws. Beneath in 51 columns of text are the laws, in beautiful cuneiform characters.

It is now known that Hammurabi's was not the first attempt to systematize the laws of Babylonia. Fragments of several previous law codes have been found. Ur-nammu of Ur and Lipit-Ishtar of Isin both promulgated earlier codes and another was known in Eshnunna. But Hammurabi's is the most complete expression of early Babylonian law, and undoubtedly incorporates many laws and customs which go back to far earlier times. Hammurabi did not invent these laws; he codified them.

The monument contains not only the code, but Hammurabi added a prologue and epilogue, which narrated his glory (a portion was quoted above) and that of the gods whom he worshiped, blessed those who should respect his inscription and cursed future vandals who should deface it. The whole inscription is translated in *Ancient Near Eastern Texts Relating to the OT* (edited by James B. Pritchard, Princeton, Princeton University Press, 1950, pp. 163-180) and should be read by students interested in the subject.

The law code itself included nearly 300 paragraphs of legal provisions touching commercial, social, domestic and moral life. There are regulations governing such matters as liability for (and exemption from) military service, control of trade in alcoholic drinks, banking and usury, the responsibility of a man toward his wife and children, including the liability of a husband for the payment of his wife's debts. Hammurabi's code was harsher on upper-class offenders than on a commoner committing the same offense. Death was the penalty not only for homicide, but for theft, adultery, and bearing false witness in cases involving the accused's life. But the graded penalties show a great advance on primitive laws, and contemporary legal texts show that the harsher penalties were rarely exacted.

Women's rights were safeguarded. A neglected wife could obtain a divorce. A concubine who had become a mother was entitled to the restitution of whatever she had brought with her, or a pecuniary indemnity appropriate to her social position. If a house fell on its owner, or a doctor injured his patient, the man who built the house, or treated the patient, might suffer death, mutilation, or at least a heavy fine.

Students of the Bible are especially interested in the comparison of Hammurabi's code with the Mosaic legislation of the Bible. There are many similarities. In both a false witness is to be punished with the penalty he had thought to bring upon the other man. Kidnapping and house-breaking were capital offenses in both. The Biblical law of divorce permits a man to put away his wife, but does not extend to her the same right as did Hammurabi. Both codes agree in prescribing the death penalty for adultery. The principle of retaliation upon which a number of Hammurabi's laws were based is vividly stated in Exodus 21:23-25.

How are these similarities to be explained? It is obvious that Hammurabi's could not have borrowed from Moses, for the Hebrew lawgiver lived several centuries after the Babylonian. Direct borrowing in the other direction also seems very unlikely. Most scholars today agree that the similarities are to be explained by the common background of the Hebrews and Babylonians. Both were Semitic peoples inheriting their customs and laws from their common ancestors. At first this explanation would seem to run counter to the Biblical claim that Moses' law was given to the legislator by divine revelation. A closer examination of the Pentateuch will show that the Hebrews before they came to Sinai followed many of the regulations set forth in the law (e.g. penalties against murder, adultery, fornication, Gen. 9:6; 38:24; the levirate law, Gen. 38:8; clean and unclean animals, Gen. 8:20; Sabbath, Gen. 2:3; Exod. 16:23,25-29). Moses' law consists of things both old and new. What was old (the customs the Hebrews received from their ancient Semitic ancestors) was here formally incorporated into the nation's constitution. Much is new, especially the high view of the nature of Jehovah and the idea that law is an expression of this nature (Lev. 19:2).

Formerly many scholars identified the Amraphel, king of Shinar, whose invasion of Transjordan is described in Genesis 14:1-12 with Hammurabi king of Babylon. Recently this identification has generally been given up. The two names are not the same and the chronological problems raised by the new low date for Hammurabi makes their equivalence very unlikely. J.B.G

HAMONAH (hà-mō′nà, *multitude*), prophetic name of a city near the future burial place of Gog (Ezek. 39:16).

HAMON-GOG, VALLEY OF (hā′mŏn-gŏg, *multitude of Gog*), a place E of the Dead Sea which will be set apart for the burial of the "multitude of Gog" (Ezek. 39:11-15), after God's destruction of the northern host which will invade Israel in "the latter years" (Ezek. 38:8).

HAMOR (hā′môr, Heb. *hămôr, an ass*), father of Shechem who criminally assaulted Dinah, a daughter of Jacob, as a result of which both father and son were killed in revenge by her brothers Simeon and Levi (Gen. 34:1-31).

HAMUEL (hăm′ū-ĕl, *warmth of God*), a Simeonite mentioned only in I Chronicles 4:26. In ASV more properly Hammuel.

HAMUL (hā′mŭl, *pitied, spared*), a grandson of Judah, and son of Perez (Gen. 46:12), head of the family of Hamulites.

HAMUTAL (hà-mū′tal, *father-in-law is dew*), mother of two kings of Judah, Jehoahaz (II Kings 23:31) and Zedekiah (24:18).

HANAMEEL (hăn′à-mĕl), mentioned only in Jeremiah 32:7-12, was a cousin of J e r e m i a h the prophet, who while in prison bought from Hanameel a field, when real estate values were low because of the Chaldean invasion, to encourage the Jews to believe that the captivity would not be permanent and that restoration was certain. In ASV, Hanamel.

HANAN (hā′năn, Heb. *hănān, gracious*). 1. A Benjamite of Jerusalem (I Chron. 8:23).

2. A son of Azel, a descendant of Jonathan (I Chron. 9:44).

3. One of David's mighty men, son of Maachah (I Chron. 11:43).

4. One of the Nethinim, or temple-servants who returned with Zerubbabel (Ezra 2:46; Neh. 7:49).

5. An interpreter of the Law (Neh. 8:7).

6. Three covenanters with Nehemiah (Neh. 10: 10,22,26).

7. An influential Jew in Jerusalem (Jer. 35:4).

HANANEEL (hà-năn′ē-ĕl, Heb. *hănan'ēl, God is gracious*), a tower in the wall of Jerusalem (Jer. 31:38; Zech. 14:10) on the N side between the sheep gate and the fish gate (Neh. 3:1; 12:39).

HANANI (hà-nā′nī, Heb. *hănānî, gracious*). 1. A son of Heman, David's seer who served in music (I Chron. 25:4,25).

2. Seer in Asa's time who rebuked Asa and was imprisoned (II Chron. 16:7-10).

3. A priest who had married a foreigner (Ezra 10:20).

4. Brother of the great Nehemiah. (Neh. 1:2; 7:2). It was he who brought to Nehemiah in Shushan, the news of Jerusalem's sad state, and Nehemiah later gave to him and to Hananiah, governor of the castle, authority over Jerusalem.

5. One of the musical priests whom Nehemiah appointed for the celebration at the dedication of the wall of Jerusalem (Neh. 12:36). Ezra was the leader of this band.

HANANIAH (hăn′à-nī′à, Heb. *hănanyâh, Jehovah is gracious*). 1. A son of Heman, David's seer (I Chron. 25:4,23) who headed the 16th course of musical Levites.

2. A captain of Uzziah's army (II Chron. 26: 11).

3. Father of Zedekiah, who was one of Jehoiakim's princes (Jer. 36:12).

4. The grandfather of Irijah who arrested Jeremiah for alleged treason (Jer. 37:13).

5. Father of a Benjamite household, who dwelt at Jerusalem (I Chron. 8:24).

6. The Heb. name of Shadrach, one of the three who survived the furnace of fire (Dan. 1: 6,7).

7. A son of Zerubbabel (I Chron. 3:19,21).

8. A returner with Ezra (Ezra 10:28) who married a foreign woman.

9. A perfumer in the time of Nehemiah (Neh. 3:8).

10. Another repairer of the wall (Neh. 3:30).

11. A governor of the castle in Jerusalem, a faithful man who feared God (Neh. 7:2).

12. One of the chief covenanters, perhaps the same as the preceding (Neh. 10:23).

13. Head of a priestly house in the days of the high priest Joiakim (Neh. 12:12,41).

14. A false prophet of Gibeon in the tribe of Benjamin in the days of Zedekiah, the last king of Judah (Jer. 28). In the year 594 B.C. he stood up against Jeremiah, God's prophet who had been pronouncing the doom of Judah and Jerusalem, and prophesied that within two years Nebuchadnezzar would bring back the vessels of the temple, would restore to power Jehoiachin who had reigned for three months in 597 B.C., and would bring back the Jewish captives. Jeremiah rebuked him. Jeremiah had been wearing a yoke of wood to symbolize the coming captivity. Hananiah broke it off and he was told that a yoke of iron would take its place. The Lord slew him that year.

HAND, one of the most frequently used words in Scripture, occurring over 1,600 times. Besides its literal use, it occurs in many figurative senses as well. It very often stands for power, as in Genesis 9:2,5. "Into your hand are they delivered" would make nonsense if taken literally; and "at the hand of every beast will I require it" does not prove that beasts have hands. To "put one's hand under the thigh" as in Genesis 24:2,9; 47:29 meant to take a solemn oath; to "put one's hand upon the head" meant blessing, as in Genesis 48:14, and signifies ordination, as in I Timothy 4:14 and II Timothy 1:6. To "kiss one's own hand" can be a mark of adoration, as in Job 31:27; while to kiss the hand of another is one of the usual marks of respect in the East, though this custom is not mentioned in Scripture.

The Hebrew expression "to consecrate" would be literally "to fill the hand," thus intimating that without consecration we have little or nothing to offer to God. God, being a spirit, neither has nor needs hands, yet we read of the "hand of God" in several connections, all of which are easily understood. "The hand of God was very heavy there" (I Sam. 5:11) refers to a plague which the Philistines suffered. "By stretching forth thy hand to heal" (Acts 4:30) shows God's powerful mercy. "No man is able to pluck them out of my Father's hand" (John 10:29) indicates God's omnipotent protection of His own. To be placed at the right hand of royalty is a high honor and, of course, at "the right hand" of Deity is incomparably higher. "Jehovah said to my Lord, Sit thou at my right hand —" (Ps. 110:1) shows the supreme position of the Son of God. When He judges the nations (Matt. 25:31-46), separating the "sheep" from the "goats," "he shall set the sheep on his right hand, but the goats on the left," showing that the left hand is equally the place of dishonor. The Hebrew word for "north" is the same as for "the left hand" and for "south" the same as for the right hand. In a trial, the accuser stood at the right hand of the accused, as is shown in Zechariah 3:1, where Satan is the accuser; but our Advocate stands also at our right hand to defend us (Ps. 109:31; 16:8).

A.B.F.

HANDICRAFT, a trade requiring manual skill, the art of using one's hands gainfully. Among some rich and decadent nations, the crafts and trades were left to slaves, but the Jews trained every boy to a trade; so Paul was a tent-maker (Acts 18:3) and even our Lord learned the art of carpentry (Mark 6:3). Some handicrafts go back to extreme antiquity; e.g. the making of musical instruments and smithery to antediluvian days (Gen. 4:21, 22). Bezalel was called of God to his trade (Exod. 31:2).

HANDKERCHIEF. The Gr. *soudárion* is a transliteration of the Latin word *sudarium,* which was a cloth intended to wipe sweat from the face. Handkerchiefs were brought from Paul's body for healing purposes (Acts 19:12); the wicked servant (Luke 19:20-23) kept his lord's money in a napkin; the face of dead Lazarus was enclosed in a napkin — the same word —(John 11:44), as was also the face of our Lord (John 20:7).

HANDLE, found only in Song of Solomon 5:5 referring to the door knob. The Hebrew word has over a dozen meanings.

HANDMAID or HANDMAIDEN, a female slave or servant. When used of one's self, it indicates humility, as Ruth, speaking to Boaz (Ruth 3:9); Hannah praying to the Lord (I Sam. 1:11) and speaking to Eli (1:16); Mary speaking to Gabriel (Luke 1:38) and singing (Luke 1:48).

HANDS, IMPOSITION OF, a ceremony, the idea behind which varies, but the fundamental sense seems to be that of transference, but sometimes accompanied by the ideas of identification and of devotion to God. It appears in the ritual of sacrifice (Exod. 29:10,15,19, etc.), in the act of blessing(Gen. 48:14) and of witness-bearing in capital offenses (Lev. 24:14).

On the great day of atonement (Lev. 16:21) Aaron was to lay all the sins of Israel upon the head of the scape-goat who would carry them away. Jacob put his hands of blessing upon both the sons of Joseph (Gen. 48:13-20); Peter and John laid hands on the Samaritan Christians who then received the Holy Spirit (Acts 8:14-17); Paul ordained Timothy (II Tim. 1:6) who also received a gift through ordination by the presbytery (I Tim. 4:14). The act was accompanied by prayer (Acts 6:6).

HANDSTAFF, a rod carried in the hand, mentioned only in Ezekiel 39:9. Probably a weapon.

HANES (hā'nēz), a place in Egypt mentioned only in Isaiah 30:4. From its association with Zoan, and the context, it would seem to have been in the Delta, though some associate it with Heracleopolis Magna, W of the Nile and far up the river.

HANGING, or death by strangulation, was not a form of capital punishment employed in Bible times. Where the word is used in Scripture, except in the two cases of suicide by hanging (Ahithophel, II Sam. 17:23; Judas, Matt. 27:5), it refers to the suspension of a body from a tree or post after the criminal had been put to death. This was practiced in Egypt (Gen. 40:19,22), by the Israelites (Deut. 21:22), and by the Persians. Hanging added to the disgrace. The body was buried before nightfall (Deut. 21:23, Josh. 8:29).

HANGINGS (Heb. *kelā'îm, māsākh*), those parts of the tabernacle and its court which were so hung as to preserve the privacy and the sacredness of that which was within. Some were more or less permanent, but others could be removed to permit passage of a person. Of the first class were the 280 cubits of fine twined linen, five cubits wide which enclosed the court (Exod. 27:9-19) and the curtains of the tent itself (Exod. 26:1-14); and of the second class the screen of the court (Exod 27:14-16), the hanging screen at the door of the tent (Exod. 26:36), and the veil which shut out from vulgar view the most holy place (Exod. 26:31-35). It was the veil corresponding to this that was rent of God from top to bottom at the crucifixion of our Lord (Matt. 27:51, Heb. 9:8, 10:19,20).

HANIEL (hăn'ĭ-ĕl, Heb. *hannî'ēl, grace of God,* ASV Hanniel). 1. A prince of Manasseh who helped in dividing the land among the tribes (I Chron. 34:23).

2. An Asherite, son of Ulla (I Chron. 7:39).

HANNAH (hăn'à, Heb. *hannâh, grace, favor*), one of the two wives of Elkanah, a Levite who lived at Ramathaim-zophim, a village of Ephraim. It was otherwise known as Ramah (cf. I Sam. 1:1 with 1:19). Peninnah, the other wife of Elkanah (I Sam 1:2), had children, but Hannah was for a long time barren, and as is common in polygamous households, "her rival provoked her sore" (1:6). The fact that Elkanah loved Hannah and gave her a double portion (1:5) only increased the hatred and jealousy in Peninnah's heart. But Hannah was a godly woman and she prayed for a son and vowed to give him to the Lord as a perpetual Nazirite. Eli saw Hannah's lips moving in silent prayer, and rebuked her for what he thought was drunkenness. She replied very humbly and Eli apologized; the family returned home; she conceived and became the mother of Samuel the great prophet of Israel and the last of the judges. Hannah's praise (2:1-10) shows that she was a deeply spiritual woman. Her song resembles Mary's song, "the Magnificat" (Luke 1:46:55) when she, too, was expecting a baby in miraculous circumstances.

Each woman rejoiced in the Lord, and each gave in marvelous fashion God's way of dealing with the proud and with the humble. Cf. 1:8 with Luke 1:52,53 and Ps. 113:7-9.) A.B.F.

HANNATHON (hăn'nà-thŏn, Heb. *hannāthôn, gracious*), a city on the northern boundary of Zebulon (Josh. 19:14). It is mentioned in the Amarna Letters.

HANNIEL (han'ĭ-ĕl, Heb. *hannî'ēl, the favor of God*). 1. Son of Ephod, the prince of the tribe of Manasseh, appointed by Moses to help in dividing the land (Num. 34:23).
2. Son of Ulla, and a descendant of Asher (I Chron. 7:39).

HANOCK (hăn'nŏk, Heb. *hănôkh, initiation*). 1. A grandson of Abraham by Keturah through their son, Midian (Gen. 25:4, I Chron. 1:33; KJV has *Henoch*).
2. Eldest son of Reuben (Gen. 46:9; Exod. 6:14, I Chron. 5:3), he was the head of the family of the Hanockites (Num. 26:5).

HANUN (hā'nŭn, Heb. *hānûn, favored*). 1. King of Ammon who, having mistaken David's friendly servants for spies, mistreated them, thus bringing on a war in which the Ammonites lost their independence (II Sam. 10; and I Chron. 19).
2. A man who, with the help of the inhabitants of Zanoah, built the valley gate setting up the doors, locks and bars of it in the wall of Jerusalem (Neh. 3:13).
3. Son of Zalaph, who helped repair the wall of Jerusalem (Neh. 3:30).

HAPHRAIM (hăph-rā'ĭm, ASV Hapharaim, Heb. *hăphāraîyim, two pits*), a city located near Shumem in Issachar (Josh. 19:19). Modern *Et-Taiyibeh*.

HARA (ha'rà, Heb. *hārā', mountain country*, a place named in I Chronicles 5:26, along with Halah, Habor and the river Gozan, as the destinations of the tribes of Reuben and Gad and the half-tribe of Manasseh when they were carried away by the Assyrians. But such a place as Hara is unknown. The LXX omits it in this verse, as also do II Kings 17:6 and 18:11 in naming the destinations of the captive nation, Israel. Both these latter references add the phrase "in the cities of the Medes"; LXX has "mountains of the Medes". Some scholars think Hara should read Haran; others believe the text is corrupt.

HARADAH (hàr-ā'dâ, Heb. *hărādhâh, terror*), one of Israel's encampments in the wilderness wanderings at which they tarried after leaving Mount Shepher (Num. 33:24). The site is unknown, but its name suggests it was a mountain.

HARAN (hā'răn, Heb. *hārān, mountaineer*). 1. Youngest brother of Abram and father of Lot, Abram's nephew. He died in Ur before his father, Terah, departed with his family from that city (Gen. 11:27,28).
2. A son of Caleb by his concubine, Ephah. This Haran had a son named Gazez (I Chron. 2:46).
3. A Gershonite Levite who lived in the time of David, he was the son of Shimei (I Chron. 23:9).

HARAN or **CHARRAN** (hā'răn, chär'răn, Heb. *hārān*, Gr. *charhrán*), a city located in northern Mesopotamia, on the Balikh river, a branch of the Euphrates, to which Terah, the father of Abram, emigrated with his family (Gen. 11:31). After his father's death Abram departed from this city to go into the land of Canaan (Gen. 12:4). His brother Nahor remained there. Abraham later sent his servant to find a wife for his son Isaac among his relatives there (Gen. 24:4). After that Jacob,

at the request of his father, Isaac, came to this same area in search of a wife (Gen. 29:4,5). In the time of Hezekiah, Rabshakeh, an officer of Sennacherib, when delivering a propaganda lecture to the people of Jerusalem, mentioned Haran, along with other cities in the same area, as conquered by Assyria (II Kings 19:12; and Isa. 37:12). Ezekiel mentions this city as one of those which carried on trade with Tyre (Ezek. 27:23).

Haran is frequently referred to in Assyrian and Babylonian records under the form of *harranu*, Anglicized as Harran. This term means *road*, probably because this city was located at the intersection of the trade routes from Damascus in the S and that going E and W between Carchemish and Nineveh. A center of worship of the moon-god, Sin, was established there in very early times. The city and temple were wrecked in the wars of the Assyrian kings. After the fall of Nineveh in 612 B.C., some Assyrian refugees fled to Harran and held out there until 610 B.C. Nabonidus, king of Babylon, who delighted in restoring old temples, rebuilt the city and temple and reinstated the worship of the moon-god there about 75 years later. This city is mentioned in Mari documents in the form of Nakhur, probably from Nahor, Abram's brother. The Romans knew it as Carrhae, famous as the place where the Parthians defeated Crassus in 53 B.C. It is still in existence as Harran, near the original site in southern Turkey. The present day Moslems who live in the area have many traditions concerning Abraham. C.E.H.

HARARITE (hā'rà-rīte, Heb. *hărārî, mountain dweller*), an area in the hill country of either Judah or Ephraim. This term occurs only in the catalog of David's mighty men. Shammah, the son of Agee, a Hararite (II Sam. 23:11,33); Jonathan, the son of Shagee the Hararite (I Chron. 11:34); Ahiam, the son of Sacar the Hararite (I Chron. 11:35).

HARBONA, HARBONAH (hàr-bō'nà, hâr-bō'nà, Heb. *harevônā',. harevônâh, ass driver*), one of the seven chamberlains of Ahasuerus, king of Persia (Esth. 1:10; 7:9).

HARE (See Animals)

HAREPH (hā'rĕf, Heb. *hārēph, scornful*), son of Caleb, and father of Bethgader (I Chron. 2:51).

HARETH, HERETH (hā'rĕth KJV, Hē'rĕth ASV, Heb. *hereth*), occurs only in I Samuel 22:5 as the name of a forest in Judah where David stayed.

HARHAIAH (hàr-hā'ja, Heb. *harhāyâh*, meaning unknown), father of Uzziel, a goldsmith, who repaired a portion of the wall of Jerusalem (Neh. 3:8).

HARHAS (hàr'hăs, Heb. *harhas*, meaning uncertain), grandfather of Shallum, husband of Hulda the prophetess (II Kings 22:14). In II Chronicles 34:22 this name is Hasrah.

HARHUR (hàr'hûr, Heb. *harhūr, fever*), head of one of the families which returned from exile with Zerubbabel (Ezra. 2:51, Neh. 7:53).

HARIM (hā'rĭm, Heb. *hărim, consecrated or slit-nosed*). 1. A priest assigned to the third course in David's time (I Chron. 24:8).
2. A family which returned from Babylon with Zerubbabel (Ezra 2:32, Neh. 7:35).
3. A family of priests which returned from exile with Zerubbabel (Ezra 2:39, Neh. 7:42; 12:15). Members of this family married foreign wives (Ezra 10:21).
4. Another family who married foreign wives (Ezra 10:31).

5. Father of Malchijah, a worker on the wall (Neh. 3:11). This man may have been the same one who entered into a covenant with the Lord under Nehemiah (Neh. 10:5).

6. Another man who covenanted with the Lord under Nehemiah (Neh. 10:27).

HARIPH (hā'rĭf, Heb. *harîph, autumn*), a family which returned to Judah from Babylon with Zerubbabel (Neh. 7:24). (The corresponding place, Ezra 2:18, has Jorah). A man of this name was among those sealed in the covenant with God (Neh. 10:19).

HARLOT, a prostitute, which kind of woman is designated by four terms in the OT: (1) *zônâh,* the regular word for harlot and the most frequently used; (2) *qedēshâh,* a special kind of harlot, a religious prostitute, that is, a priestess of a heathen religion in which fornication was part of the worship. Mentioned only four times, but three of those references are early (Gen. 38:21,22, and Deut. 23:17; (3) *'ishshâh zārâh,* or *zārah* alone, a "strange woman," occurs only in the Book of Proverbs, and the way it is used there shows that a harlot is meant; (4) *nokhrîyâh,* a foreign (or strange) woman, found, in this form, also only in the Book of Proverbs, and it obviously means harlot.

The first two of the above terms were sometimes translated *whore,* other times *harlot* in the KJV. In ASV *zônâh* is consistently rendered *harlot* and *qedēshâh, prostitute.*

The NT word for harlot is *pórnē,* which in KJV is inconsistently sometimes *whore* and sometimes *harlot,* but in ASV is always *harlot.*

Some legal measures were in force concerning harlots. Parents were not to force their daughters to become harlots (Lev. 19:29; 21:7,14), priests were not to marry harlots (Lev. 19:29), the wages of harlotry were not to be brought into the temple to pay a vow (Deut. 23:18). These prohibitions were necessary to keep the worship of the Lord free from the impurities of the sin of harlotry.

The actual punishment of harlots was severe when enforced. In Genesis 38:24 Judah ordered Tamar to be burned for being a harlot. Leviticus 21:9 commanded burning for a priest's daughter who became a harlot. Deuteronomy 22:21 ordered stoning for a bride found to have played the harlot.

Such a common sin needed to be guarded against. It is not surprising to find that the Book of Proverbs, which mentions every term for harlot except *qedēshâh,* teaches about and warns against harlots by admonitions and illustrations. The situation in the Corinthian Church was such that the Apostle Paul had to give the Christians there special warnings against fornication with harlots (I Cor. 6:15,16).

The words harlot and harlotry are used very often, especially in the prophetic books, to describe idolatry. This figurative use was evidently based on the idea that the Lord was the husband of the nation of Israel (see Jer. 3:20). When the people took their allegiance from Jehovah and gave it to idols instead, He called it "going a whoring after other gods" (KJV) or "playing the harlot with other gods" (ASV). This expression occurs rather frequently in the prophetic books, and a few times in other books. Also, this spiritual harlotry is mentioned several times in the Book of Revelation, chapter 17. C.E.H.

HARNEPHER (hàr'nĕ-fêr, Heb. *harnepher*), a son of Zophal in the tribe of Asher (I Chron. 7:36).

HAROD (hā'rŏd, Heb. *hârôdh, trembling*), a spring, or well, beside which Gideon and his men encamped one morning. The Lord reduced his army there to 300 men with whom he routed the Midianites that night (Judg. 7:1). It was located in the Mount Gilboa area about four miles SE of the city of Jezreel. The modern name of the spring is *Ain Jalud.*

HARODITE (hā'rŏd-īt, Heb. *hărōdî, belonging to Herod*), patronymic of two of David's mighty men, Shammah and Elika (II Sam. 23:25). In the parallel place in I Chronicles 11:27 this name is given as "Harorite", a scribal error for "Harodite".

HAROEH (hà-rō'ĕ, Heb. *hārō'eh, the seer*), a son of Shobal, and grandson of Caleb, son of Hur (I Chron. 2:52).

HAROSHETH OF THE GENTILES (hā-rō'shĕth, Heb. *hărōsheth haggôyim*), a town near the Kishon river in N Palestine. It was the home of Sisera, the captain of the army of Jabin, king of Canaan (Judg. 4:2,13,16). The significance of the phrase "of the Gentiles" is unknown but suggests mixed races lived there. It has been identified with modern Teil 'Amr in the Mt. Carmel Kishon area.

HARP (See Music)

HARROW (hă'rō, Heb. *sādhādh*), occurs three times, always as a verb. Job 39:10 translated "harrow." In Isaiah 28:24 and Hosea 10:11 it is rendered "break up the clods." From the root meaning of the word it seems to mean dragging or leveling off a field.

HARROWS (Heb. *hārîts*), a sharp instrument made of iron with which David cut conquered peoples (II Sam. 12:31, I Chron. 20:3). It has no connection with the verb rendered "harrow."

HARSHA (hàr'shà, Heb. *harshā', dumb, silent*), the head of family of the Nethinim which returned under Zerubbabel from exile (Ezra 2:52, Neh. 7:54).

HART (See Animals)

HARUM (hā'rŭm, Heb. *hārum, made high*), a descendant of Judah mentioned as the father of Aharhel (I Chron. 4:8).

HARUMAPH (hà-rōō'maf, Heb. *hărûmaph,* perhaps *slit-nosed*), the father of Jedaiah, a worker helping to repair the wall (Neh. 3:10).

HARUPHITE (hà-rōō'fît, Heb. *harûphî, or hărî-phî*). Shephatiah, one of the men who joined David's forces in Ziglag, was called the Haruphite or the Hariphite (I Chron. 12:5). If this latter form is the correct one, then this man may be connected with the Hariph clan (Neh. 7:24).

HARUZ (hā'rŭz, Heb. *hārûts, diligent*), father-in-law of Manasseh, king of Judah (II Kings 21:19).

HARVEST (hàr-vĕst, Heb. *qātsîr,* Gr. *therismós*). The economy of the Israelites was strictly agricultural. Harvest time was a very significant event for them. They had three each year. The barley reaping (Ruth 1:22) came in April-May; the wheat harvest (Gen. 30:14) was about six weeks later in June-July, and the ingathering of the fruits of tree or vine took place in September-October.

Grain crops were reaped with sickles, and the cut stalks were laid in bunches which were carried to the threshing-floor. Some laws governed these simple harvest operations. The corners of the fields were not to be reaped, and the scatterings of the cut grain were not to be picked up. The part of the crop thus left was for the poor people to use (Lev. 23:22). The owner was required each year to present the first-fruits of the crop as an offering to God before he could take any of it for his own use (Lev. 23:10,14). Stalks of grain which grew up without being sown could not be harvested (Lev. 25:5). With a new orchard or vineyard the fruit could not be gathered for three years, and the fourth year's crop had to be given entirely to the Lord. So the owner had to wait until the fifth year to get any fruit for himself (Lev. 19:23-25).

The Lord fitted the three main religious feasts which He prescribed for the people into this agricultural economy. The Passover came in the season of the barley harvest (Exod. 23:16). Seven weeks later at time of the wheat harvest occurred the feast of Pentecost (Exod. 34:22). The feast of Tabernacles was observed the seventh month, which was the period of the fruit harvest (Exod. 34:22).

In the New Testament, most of the time the term harvest is used figuratively for the gathering in of the redeemed saints at the end of the age (Matt. 13:39). C.E.H.

A busy summer harvesting scene on the threshing floors at the ancient village of Sepphoris. © MPS

HASADIAH (hă-à-dī'à, Heb. *hăsadhyâh, Jehovah is kind*), a son of Zerubbabel (I Chron. 3:20).

HASENUAH (hăs-ē-nū'à, Heb. *hassenu'âh*, the word is *senuah* with the definite article prefixed, meaning *the hated one*). 1. An ancestor of Sallu, a Benjamite who returned from exile (I Chron. 9:7). In ASV "Hassenuah."

2. The father of Judah, the assistant overseer of Jerusalem in Nehemiah's time (Neh. 11:9). In KJV Senuah (q.v.).

HASHABIAH (hăsh-à-bī'à, Heb. *hăshavyâh, whom Jehovah esteems*). 1. An ancestor of Ethan, a Levite and temple singer in David's time (I Chron. 6:45).

2. An ancestor of Shemaiah, a Levite, who returned from Babylon (I Chron. 9:14) and lived in Jerusalem (Neh. 11:15).

3. A son of Jeduthun, a musician in David's time (I Chron. 25:3).

4. A civil official in David's time (I Chron. 26:30).

5. Overseer of the tribe of Levi in David's time. (I Chron. 27:17).

6. A chief of the Levites in Josiah's time (II Chron. 35:9).

7. A Levite teacher whom Ezra brought with him (Ezra 8:19).

8. A chief priest in Ezra's company (Ezra 8:24).

9. Ruler of the half tribe of Keilah, a worker on the wall (Neh. 3:17).

10. A priest, head of the family of Hilkiak (Neh. 12:21).

11. An ancestor of Uzzi, the overseer of the Levites at Jerusalem in Nehemiah's time (Neh. 11:22).

12. A chief of the Levites who sealed the covenant (Neh. 3:17) and was appointed to praise God (Neh. 12:24).

HASHABNAH (hà-shăb'nàh, Heb. *hăshavnâh*), one of those who sealed the covenant with Nehemiah (Neh. 10:25).

HASHABNIAH (hăsh'àb-nē-ī'à, Heb. *hăshavneyâh*). 1. The father of Hattush, a worker on the wall (Neh. 3:10). ASV Hashabneiah.

2. One of the Levites who prayed at the confession of sin (Neh. 9:5). ASV Hashabneiah.

HASHBADANA (hăsh-băd'à-nà, Heb. *hashbaddānâh*), a man who stood on the left of Ezra as he read the law to the people (Neh. 8:4).

HASHEM (hā'-shĕm, Heb. *hāshēm*), a man whose sons were among David's mighty men (I Chron. 11:34). The parallel passage (II Sam. 23:32) has Jashen.

HASHMANNIM (hăsh'-măn-nĭm, Heb. *hashman-nîm*, meaning unknown), a Hebrew word that occurs only in Psalm 68:33 and is translated *heaven of heavens*. But it may be a textual error for *bashmannim*, which means "with oils or ointment."

HASHMONAH (hăsh-mō'nà, Heb. *hashmōnâh*), a station where the Israelites encamped in the wilderness (Num. 33:29,30). The site is unknown.

HASHUB (See Hasshub)

HASHUBAH (hà-shoō'bà, Heb. *hăshuvâh, consideration*), a son of Zerubbabel (I Chron. 3:20).

HASHUM (hā'-shŭm, Heb. *hāshum*). 1. A family that returned from exile under Zerubbabel (Ezra 2:19; 10:33; Neh. 7:22).

2. A priest who stood at the left of Ezra as he read the law to the people (Neh. 8:4).

3. A chief of the people who sealed the covenant (Neh. 10:18). Maybe the same as 2.

HASHUPHA (hà-shoō'fà, Heb. *hăsūphā'*), a family that returned from exile under Zerubbabel (Ezra 2:43; Neh. 7:46), ASV Hasupha.

HASMONAEANS (See Maccabees)

HASRAH (hăs'-rà, Heb. *hasrâh*, meaning uncertain), grandfather of Shallum, the husband of Hulda the prophetess (II Chron. 34:22). In the parallel place (II Kings 22:14) this name is given as Harhas.

HASSENAAH (hăs-ē-nā'-à, Heb. *hassenā'âh*, the word is *sena'ah* (q.v.) with the definite article prefixed, meaning *the hated one*). Father of the sons who built the fish gate in the wall of Jerusalem (Neh. 3:3).

HASSHUB (hăsh'ŭb, Heb. *hashshûv, considerate*). 1. The father of Shemaiah, a Levite who returned from exile (I Chron. 9:14). He dwelt in Jerusalem (Neh. 11:15. KJV Hashub.

2. A worker on the wall of Jerusalem (Neh. 3:11).

3. Another worker on the wall (Neh. 3:23). KJV Hashub.

4. One who sealed the covenant (Neh. 10:23). KJV Hashub. May be identical with 2 or 3.

HASUPHA (See Hashupha)

HAT (See Dress)

HATACH (hā'tăk, Heb. *hăthākh*, meaning uncertain), a chamberlain of the king of Persia appointed to attend upon Esther (Esth. 4:5-10).

HATHATH (hā'-thăth, Heb. *hăthath, terror*), a son of Othniel, the first judge of Israel (I Chron. 4:13).

HATIPHA (hȧ-tī'fȧ, Heb. *hătîphā'*, meaning uncertain), head of family of the Nethinim which returned from exile under Zerubbabel (Ezra 2:54; Neh. 7:56).

HATITA (hȧ-tī'tȧ, Heb. *hătîtā'*, *exploring*), an ancestor of a family of Levitical porters which returned from exile under Zerubbabel (Ezra 2:42; Neh. 7:45).

HATSI HAM MENUCHOTH (hȧ-tsī-hăm-měn-ū'-kōth, Heb. *hătsî hammenûhôth, half of the Menuhoth*), a marginal reading on I Chronicles 2: 54 in KJV which is eliminated in ASV.

HATTIL (hăt'-ĭl, Heb. *hattîl, waving*), a family which returned from exile under Zerubbabel (Ezra 2:57; Neh. 7:59).

HATTIN, HORNS OF (hăt'tēn, *hollows*), a peculiar form of a hill near the village of Hattin, which tradition dating from the 13th century holds as the scene of Christ's Sermon on the Mount. The crater-like top of this hill has a grassy knoll about 60 feet high on each end of it; these are called the Horns of Hattin. This phrase is not mentioned in the Bible but it may denote the "mountain" of Matthew 5:1.

HATTUSH (hăt'-ŭsh, Heb. *hattûsh,* meaning unknown). 1. A descendant in the royal line of Judah in the fifth generation from Zerubbabel (I Chron. 3:22).

2. A descendant of David who returned from Babylon with Ezra (Ezra 8:2).

3. A worker on the wall (Neh. 3:10), may be the same as 2.

4. One of those who sealed the covenant (Neh. 10:4), may be the same as 2 or 3.

5. A priest who returned with Zerubabbel (Neh. 12:2).

HAURAN (hȧ'ōō-rȧn, Heb. *hawrān,* probably *black* or *black land*), the modern name of a great plain situated on a plateau 2000 feet high E of the Jordan river and N of the land of Gilead. In ancient times it was called Bashan. Its soil is of volcanic origin and is very rich, making the region famous for its wheat crops. The name Hauran is mentioned only by Ezekiel in his description of the boundaries of the land of Israel in the Millennial age (47: 16,18).

The Israelites never had a very great hold on this area. Its openness to the E made it a frequent prey to robbers from the desert. Under the Romans, Herod ruled over it as part of his realm, and he greatly encouraged settlement by stopping the robber raids. It was then known as Auranitis. Christianity flourished there from the second century A.D. until the seventh century, when it was overthrown by the Moslems. Today Hauran is an integral part of Syria.

HAVILAH (hăv'-ĭ-lȧ, Heb. *hăwîlâh, sand-land*). 1. A son of Cush, a descendant of Ham (Gen. 10:7; I Chron. 1:9).

2. A son of Joktan, a descendant of Shem (Gen. 10:29; I Chron. 1:23). These names are generally taken to mean tribes or nations. If both references refer to the same area, it pertained to both Hamitic and Semitic peoples. It is generally thought to have been located in southern Arabia.

3. A land encompassed by the river Pishon which flowed from a source in the Garden of Eden; it contained gold and other minerals (Gen. 2:11, 12). Probably located in Armenia or Mesopotamia, although actual location is uncertain.

4. A land mentioned as one of the boundaries of the dwelling of the Ishmaelites "from Havilah unto Shur that is before Egypt." This Havilah is probably the same as 2 in southern Arabia (Gen. 25:18). Saul conquered the Amalekites in this same area "from Havilah as thou goest to Shur that is before Egypt" (I Sam. 15:7).

HAVOTH-JAIR (hā-vŏth-jā'-îr, Heb. *hawwōth-yā'îr,* [ASV Havvoth-jair] *villages of Jair*), a group of villages which Jair, son of Manasseh, took (Num. 32:41). The word *hawwah* means a village of tents; it is used only in connection with these towns of Jair. This group consisted of 30 villages (Judg. 10:4; I Chron. 2:22,23). Jair captured both Gilead and Bashan, this latter district evidently contained 30 more towns (Deut. 3:14; Josh. 13:30; I Kings 4:13; I Chron. 2:23). The phrase Havoth-jair applied only to the villages in Gilead.

HAWK (See Birds)

HAZAEL (hăz'-ā-ĕl, Heb. *hăzā'ēl, God sees*), a high official of Benhadad, king of Syria, whom, when the king was sick, he sent to inquire of the prophet Elisha concerning his recovery from this illness. Elisha told Hazael the king would certainly recover, but he would surely die. Previously God had instructed Elijah to anoint Hazael king of Syria (I Kings 19:15). Hazael pretended to be surprised by Elisha's statement that he would become king. He returned and suffocated Benhadad, and seized the throne for himself (II Kings 8: 7-15).

This usurpation is confirmed by an inscription of Shalmaneser III which states that Hadadezer of Damascus (that is, Benhadad) perished and Hazael, a son of nobody, seized the throne. This phrase "a son of nobody" means he was not in the royal line of descent.

The date of Hazael's reign can be ascertained as at least 43 years in length (841-798 B.C.); very likely it was a few years longer. Ahaziah, king of Judah, reigned only one year (II Kings 8:26). That year was 841. During that year he fought with Joram, king of Israel against Hazael (II Kings 8:28). In the annals of Shalmaneser III, king of Assyria (858-824), for his 14th year (844), he recorded a battle against Hadadezer (Benhadad) of Damascus. In his 18th year (840) Shalmaneser said he encountered Hazael at Damascus. So Hazael usurped the throne during the period (844-841). He reigned at least until 798, the date of the death of Jehoahaz, king of Israel, for Hazael oppressed Israel all the days of this king (II Kings 13:22.) He died shortly afterwards (II Kings 13: 24).

Hazael greatly punished Israel, as Elisha had foreseen (II Kings 8:12). He wounded Jehoram, son of Ahab, at Ramoth-gilead (II Kings 8:29). During the reign of Jehu, Hazael took all the territory E of the Jordan valley from Israel (II Kings 10:32). While Joash was ruling in Judah, Hazael captured Gath and threatened Jerusalem, but Joash induced him to retire by paying tribute (II Kings 12:17,18). He continually raided Israel during the reign of Jehoahaz (II Kings 13:3). As previously mentioned, he oppressed Israel all the days of this king (II Kings 13:22). Shalmaneser III records two attacks on Hazael in which the Assyrian king claims great victories with severe damage to the Syrian countryside. C.E.H.

HAZAIAH (hȧ-zā'yȧ, *Jehovah sees*), member of a family of Shiloh whose great-grandson lived in Jerusalem 444 B.C. (Neh. 11:5).

HAZAR (hā'zȧr, Heb. *hătsar, a settlement*), often the first element in Heb. place names.

HAZAR-ADDAR (hā'zȧr-ăd'ȧr), a place on the southern boundary of Judah, W of Kadesh-barnea and E of Azmon (Num. 34:4). In Joshua 15:3 it is called simply Addar (KJV Adar).

HAZAR-ENAN (hā'zàr-ē'năn, *village of fountains*), the NE corner of the land of Canaan as promised of the Lord to the people of Israel (Num. 34:9,10; cf. Ezek. 47:17).

HAZAR-GADDAH (hā'zàr-găd'à, *village of good fortune*), a town in the south of Judah, very close to the boundary of Simeon (Josh. 15:27).

HAZAR-HATTICON (hā'zàr-hăt'ĭ-kŏn, *middle-village*), mentioned only in Ezekiel 47:16 as being near Damascus and on the border of Hauran. Exact location uncertain.

HAZARMAVETH (hā'zàr-mā'věth, *village of death*), found in the "Table of the nations" (Gen. 10:26 and I Chron. 1:20); apparently a son of Joktan, but probably representing the people or the district of modern Hadramut.

HAZAR-SHUAL (hā'zàr-shōō'ăl, *village of the jackal*), a town in the south of Judah (Josh. 15: 28) later bestowed upon Simeon (Josh. 19:3). After the captivity held by Simeonites (I Chron. 4: 28) and Judah (Neh. 11:27).

HAZAR-SUSAH (hā'zàr-sū'sà, *village of a mare*), a town given to Simeon out of Judah (Josh. 19:5), but called "Hazar-susim," i.e. "village of horses" in I Chronicles 4:31. Site uncertain.

HAZAZON-TAMAR (hăz'à-zŏn-tā'mēr, *Hazazon of the palm trees*), ancient name of a town on the W coast of the Dead Sea, occupied in Abraham's time by the Amorites (Gen. 14:7), but smitten by the four great kings of the East. KJV Hazezon-tamar.

HAZEL (hā'z'l), found in Genesis 30:37, KJV, where it renders the Heb. *luz,* which the RV better translates "almond tree."

HAZELELPONI, ZELELPONI (hăz'ĕ-lĕl-pō'nī, zĕlĕl-pō'nī, ASV Hazzelelponi), a Jewish woman mentioned only in I Chronicles 4:3.

HAZERIM (hà-zē'rĭm, *villages*), the ancient homes of the Avvim near Gaza in southern Palestine (Deut. 2:23). RV properly translates "villages."

HAZEROTH (hà-zē'rŏth, *courts* or *villages*), a station on Israel's journeys in the wilderness, about 40-45 miles from Mt. Sinai, northeastward toward the Gulf of Akabah. The people seem to have stayed there for some time after the terrible plague at Kibroth-hattaavah (Num. 11:35). It was here that Aaron and Miriam made their rebellion against Moses (Num. 12). The identification of the place is uncertain.

HAZEZON-TAMAR (hăz'ĕ-zŏn-tā'mēr), another spelling for Hazazon-tamar, *q.v.*

HAZIEL (hā'zĭ-ĕl, *God sees*), a Gershonite Levite in the latter days of David (I Chron. 23:9).

HAZO (hā'zō), a son of Nahor and uncle of Laban and Rebekah (Gen. 22:22).

HAZOR (hā'zôr, Heb. *hātsôr, an enclosed place*), the name of at least five towns mentioned in the Bible: 1. An important town in northern Palestine, ruled in the days of Joshua by Jabin (Josh. 11:1, 10). Palestine at the time was a conglomeration of little city-states or kingdoms, and of various groups united by tribal ties. For the former, see Joshua 11:1, and for the latter Joshua 11:3. This Hazor was reckoned as "the head of all those kingdoms" in Joshua's day, and Jabin led them against Joshua, who almost annihilated them. Nearly two centuries later, another Jabin (Judg. 4) reigning at Hazor was reckoned as king of Canaan, but God, using Deborah and Barak, subdued and destroyed

The site of Hazor, which was the chief city of Canaan. © MPS

him. Hazor, having a strategic location in the hills, about five miles W of the waters of Merom, was fortified by Solomon (I Kings 9:15). Its Israelite inhabitants were carried away into captivity (II Kings 15:29) in Assyria by Tiglath-pileser about the middle of the eighth century B.C.

2. A town in the extreme south of Judah, mentioned only in Josh. 15:23.

3. Another town in the south of Judah (Josh. 15:25). Its name "Hazor-hadattah" means simply "new Hazor" and indicates that some of the inhabitants of Hazor (2) had removed to a new location. KJV in Joshua 15:25 makes it seem that Hazor and Hadattah were separate places but cf. ASV.

4. A town N of Jerusalem, inhabited by Benjamites in the restoration (Neh. 11:33).

5. A region in the south of Arabia against which Jeremiah pronounced a "doom" (Jer. 49:28-33).

HAZOR-HADATTAH (hā'zôr-hà-dăt'à, *new Hazor*), see No. 3 in the article on Hazor. Joshua 15:25 in KJV makes it seem like the names of two villages.

HE (hā), the fifth letter of the Hebrew alphabet, pronounced like English *h*. It was also used for the number 5.

HEAD (hĕd, Heb. *rō'sh,* Gr. *kephalé*). The word "head" occurs about 433 times in Scripture and the Hebrew word for "head" occurs 592 times, being translated "head" 349 times, "chief" 90 times, "top" 75 times, "company" 12 times, "beginning" 14 times, "captain" 10 times, "chapiter" 4 times, etc. There are many figurative uses: "the hoary head" (Prov. 16:31), expressing old age; "heads over the people" (Exod. 18:25); "round the corners of your heads" (Lev. 19:27, referring to a heathen custom of trimming the beard); "heads of the people" (Num. 25:4, probably meaning "chiefs"; cf. ASV); "his blood shall be upon his head" (Josh. 2:19, meaning "we shall not be responsible for his life"); keeper of mine head" (I Sam. 28:2 i.e. "my protector"); "Am I a dog's head" (II Sam. 3:8 i.e. "Am I utterly contemptible?"); "yet will I not lift up my head" (Job 10:15, i.e. "yet will I not be self-assertive"); "his head reached unto the clouds" (Job 20:6, i.e "he be highly exalted"), etc.

HEADBAND, HEADDRESS (See Dress)

HEAD OF THE CHURCH. In the NT Christ is described as "the head of the church" (Eph. 1:22; 5:23), and "head of the body, the church" (Col. 1:18; cf. Eph. 4:15). This figure speaks of the preeminence of Christ, His authority, and the complete dependence of the church upon Christ. It must not be pressed to mean that Christ is the intellectual center of His people, through whom the members are passively governed, for to the Jewish mind, the heart, not the head, was the seat of the intellect. In Colossians 1:18 the headship of Christ over the body denotes His priority of rank.

HEADSTONE (See Cornerstone)

HEART (Heb. *lēv, lēvāv,* Gr. *kardía*). Although the word occurs more than 900 times in Scripture, it is almost never used in a literal sense, the principal exception being in Exodus 28:29,30, which speaks of the breastplate of judgment upon the heart of Aaron. Commonly the "heart" is regarded as being the seat of the intellect, the feelings and the will; e.g., "every imagination of the thoughts of his heart" (Gen. 6:5) would imply intellect; "comfort ye your hearts" (Gen. 18:5; or "strengthen your heart" as in ASV) would imply feeling; while "that seeking him with the whole heart" (Ps. 119:2) means the will. It is often used to signify the innermost being, i.e., "It grieved him at his heart" (Gen. 6:6). In modern usage, "heart" is used to imply affection, as "I have you in my heart," as found in Psalm 62:10, "If riches increase, set not your heart upon them" and in scores of other passages.

Both in ancient times and today, different parts of the body are used figuratively as the seat of different functions of the soul; and the ancient usage often differs from the modern. In expressing sympathy, we might say "This touches my heart," where the ancient might say "my bowels were moved for him" (S. of Sol. 5:4). Psalm 7:9 in KJV has "the righteous God trieth the hearts and reins," whereas ASV has "the minds and hearts." Here ancient "hearts" is equated with modern "minds" and ancient "reins," i.e., "kidneys" with modern "hearts." This is not a question of truth and error as between ancient and modern psychology, but reflects a difference in common figurative usage. The NT was written mostly by Jews and so is colored by Hebrew thinking and usage; e.g. "They do always err in their heart" means "They are wrong in their thinking" though probably the affections are included as well. Often the word "heart" implies the whole moral nature of fallen man, e.g. "The heart is deceitful above all things, and desperately wicked" (Jer. 17:9) whereas the next verse in KJV has "search the heart, try the reins" but in ASV "search the mind, try the heart."   A.B.F.

HEARTH. In ancient times homes were heated very differently from today. In the poorer houses the hearth consisted of a depression in the floor of a room in which a fire was kindled for cooking or for warmth. Chimneys were unknown: smoke escaped from the house as it could, or through a latticed opening for the purpose. The better class of houses were heated by means of a brazier of burning coals. This was a wide, shallow pan which could also be used for cooking. (See Gen. 18:6; Ps. 102:3; Isa. 30:14; Hosea 13:3; Jer. 36:22,23; Zech. 12:6.)

HEATH, a shrub with very small, narrow, rigid leaves. The species *Erica verticillata* grows on the W slopes of Lebanon. (See Jer. 17:6; 48:6).

HEATHEN (hēē'th'n, Heb. *gôy,* pl. *gôyim,* Gr. *éthnos, people, nation*). [Anglo-Saxon, *dweller on the heath.*] In the OT *gôy* is rendered "Gentiles," "heathen," and "nation," but it is usually used for a non-Israelitish people, and thus has the meaning of "Gentiles." Sometimes, however, it refers to the Israelites, as in Genesis 12:2; Deuteronomy 32: 28, but the word ordinarily used for the people of God is *'ām.* In the NT *Éthnos* is the equivalent of *gôy* in the OT, while *laós* corresponds to *'ām.* Sometimes in the KJV the Gr. *Héllenes* renders "Gentiles" (John 7:35; Rom. 2:9,10).

The differentiation between Israelites and Gentiles was more sharply accentuated in NT times than in OT times, the reason for this being chiefly that the Jews had suffered so much from Gentile hands. Gentiles were looked upon with aversion and hatred. This is evident in the NT (John 18: 28; Acts 10:28; 11:3).

God's interest in and concern for the heathen is seen in the OT, especially in the Book of Jonah. In the NT Jesus commanded the apostles to preach the Gospel to all the world; and we find them proclaiming it to Gentile nations throughout the Mediterranean world.   S.B.

HEAVEN (Heb. *shāmayim,* Gr. *ouranós*). 1. Cosmologically, one of the two great divisions of the universe, the earth and the heavens (Gen. 1:1; 14:19; etc.); or one of the three — heaven, earth, and the waters under the earth (Exod. 20:4). In the visible heavens are the stars and planets (Gen. 1:14-17; Ezek. 32:7,8). Later Jews divided the heavens into seven strata, but there is no evidence for this in the Bible, although Paul spoke of being caught up into the third heaven (II Cor. 12:2). The term, "heaven of heavens" (Deut. 10:14; I Kings 8:27; Ps. 148:4) probably means the "height of heaven."

2. The abode of God (Gen. 28:17; Ps. 80:14; Isa. 66:1; Matt. 5:12) and of the good angels (Matt. 24:36); where the redeemed shall some day be (Matt. 5:12; 6:20; Eph. 3:15); where the Redeemer has gone and intercedes for the saints, and from which He will some day come for His own (I Thess. 4:16).

3. The inhabitants of heaven (Luke 15:18; Rev. 18:20).   S.B.

HEAVE OFFERING (See Offerings)

HEAVE SHOULDER (See Offerings)

HEAVING AND WAVING (See Offerings)

HEBER (hē'bēr, *associate*). 1. A great-grandson of Jacob through Asher and Beriah (Gen. 46:17).

2. The Kenite whose wife Jael killed Sisera (Judg. 4:11-21). He had been friendly with the Canaanites who had been oppressing Israel.

3. A son of Ezrah (KJV "Ezra") of the tribe of Judah and probably of the family of Caleb, the good spy (I Chron. 4:18).

4. A man of the tribe of Benjamin, and son of Elpaal (I Chron. 8:17). In KJV the name of these other men, whose name should be Eber as in ASV.

5. The head of a family in the tribe of Gad (I Chron. 5:13).

6. A Benjamite, son of Shashak, mentioned only in I Chronicles 8:22.

7. One mentioned in Christ's genealogy (Luke 3:35 KJV), father of Peleg and Joktan. He is properly called "Eber" elsewhere (e.g. Gen. 10:24, 25; Gen. 11:12-16). See EBER, HEBREWS.

HEBREW OF THE HEBREWS. When Paul in Philippians 3:4-6 so described himself, he meant that he was a pure-blooded Hebrew who had retained the language and customs of his fathers, in contrast to other Jews who had adopted Greek language and customs.

HEBREWS, EPISTLE TO THE. Authorship. The writer of Hebrews does not attach his name to his letter. I John is the only other epistle in the NT to which a name is not attached. Because of this fact, there has been much discussion since the first century as to who wrote Hebrews.

Early Christians held various opinions. Those on the eastern shore of the Mediterranean and around Alexandria associated the book with Paul. Origen (185-254 A.D.) held that the thoughts of the book were Paul's, but the language and composition were someone else's. In North Africa, Tertullian (155-225 A.D.) thought that Barnabas wrote Hebrews. Although the epistle was first known in Rome and the W (I Clement, dated around 95 A.D. cites Hebrews frequently), for 200 years Christians in Rome and the W were unanimous in their opinion that Paul did not write Hebrews. Who did write Hebrews these early Christians did not say.

Present day Christians should hardly be dogmatic about an issue which from the very beginning of the church was surrounded with uncertainty. A careful study of the epistle in the Greek text discloses some important things about the author: 1. The letter has a polished Greek style, like that of a master rhetorician. The continuous use of this style is unlike Paul who frequently picks up a new stream of thought before he finishes the one he is treating. 2. The vocabulary, figures of speech, and manner of argument show an Alexandrian and Philonic influence (Philo, 20 B.C. to 50 or 60 A.D.). Paul, having come from Tarsus and having been educated in Jerusalem, did not have such a background. 3. Both Paul and the writer of Hebrews quote the Old Testament frequently. But the way they introduce their quotations is quite different. Paul's formulas — "just as it has been written" (19 times), "it has been written" (10 times), "the Scripture says" (6 times), "the Scripture proclaims good tidings beforehand" (1 time) — never occur in Hebrews. Paul's manner of introducing quotations puts the reader's attention on the content quoted. The writer of Hebrews, as an orator, puts the stress on the one who speaks. For him God, Christ, or the Holy Spirit is speaking.

Along with many present day scholars, this author favors Apollos as the possible writer of Hebrews. He was a Jew, born in Alexandria (Acts 18:24), a learned and cultured man. He was well-versed in the Scriptures (Acts 18:24). Being orally taught the way of the Lord, Apollos was teaching about Jesus even when he knew only John's baptism (Acts 18:25). He was a man of enthusiasm. Priscilla and Aquila, Paul's friends, led Apollos to a full knowledge of Christ (Acts 18:26). After he received this fuller knowledge, he was a man of courage. He left Ephesus for Achaia to help the believers there (Acts 18:27). He consistently used the Scriptures in his public preaching (Acts 18: 25). Paul testifies to Apollos' capability in I Corinthians chapters 1-4. His polished rhetorical style may have been a contributing cause to the Apollos party which was found in Corinth (I Cor. 3:4,5,6). Apollos' modesty and desire to avoid friction are seen in I Corinthians 16:12. He was still an active co-worker of Paul late in Paul's ministry (see Titus 3:13). In Apollos one can explain all of Hebrews' similarities with Paul as well as the distinct differences from Paul.

Assuming Apollos to be the author, one can best date the letter between 68-70 A.D.

Beginning of the Epistle to the Hebrews (with ending of Romans), on a leaf from the Michigan Papyri (Beatty-Michigan MS.), in the University of Michigan Library. UML

Original Readers. The letter was first known in Rome and the West. Its first readers were Jewish Christians who spoke and wrote Greek. The brief statement: "They from Italy salute you" (Heb. 13: 24) certainly favors the readers' being located in Italy. If the writer had been in Italy, he would have named the precise place. A letter from any city in the United States would not say: "Those from the United States send greetings." But if the letter came from an interior city of India or Brazil, such a greeting would be appropriate. Hence, it appears there were Italian Christians with the writer somewhere outside of Italy as he penned this letter. The writer knows the readers well. He refers to their spiritual dullness (5:11-14), their faithful ministering to the saints (6:9-10), their experiences after their conversion (10:32-36). The term used for their spiritual leaders or rulers is *hoi hēgoumenoi* (13:7,17,24), a technical term found nowhere else in the New Testament, but other writings coming from Rome and the West have this same term (cf. I Clement 1:3; 21:6; Shepherd of Hermas II, 2:6, 9:7 [*proegoumenoi*]). Their first leaders seem to have died (13:7), while their present leaders are continually engaged in the task of watching over the flock (13:17). To these the writer sends greetings (13:24).

Although absolute certainty cannot be reached, it seems best to regard the original readers as being located somewhere in Italy. Many roads led to Rome. These believers may have been in one of the cities nearer or farther from the capital. Paul himself spent seven days with the brothers in Puteoli (Acts 28:13-14). They could have been in Rome or its suburbs. As the writer pens this letter, Timothy has departed [from him] and is absent (perfect tense) — very likely on some tour of churches. As soon as he appears (or if he comes soon), the writer and Timothy together will visit the readers (Heb. 13:23).

Outline and Summary of Content — An outline shows the centrality of Jesus Christ in the book of Hebrews.

PROLOGUE: COURSE AND CLIMAX OF DIVINE REVELATION (1:1-3)

I. PRE-EMINENCE OF CHRIST HIMSELF (1:4-4:13)
   A. Superiority of Christ to Angels (1:4-14)
   B. Warning: Peril of Indifference to These Truths (2:1-14)
   C. Reason Christ Became Human (2:5-18)
   D. Christ's Position is Greater than That of Moses (3:1-6)
   E. Warning: Unbelief Brings Temporal and Eternal Effects (3:7-4:13)

II. PRIESTHOOD OF JESUS CHRIST (4:14-10:18)
   A. Importance of His Priesthood for a Believer's Conduct (4:14-16)
   B. Qualifications of a High Priest (5:1-10)
   C. Warning: Immaturity and Apostasy are Conquered Only by Faith, Longsuffering, and Hope (5:11-6:20a)
   D. Melchizedek's Eternal Successor (6:20b-7:28)
   E. Heavenly Sanctuary and New Covenant (8:1-13)
   F. Priestly Service under the Old Covenant and the New (9:1-28)
   G. Inadequacy of the Sacrifices under the Law contrasted with the Efficacy and Finality of Christ's Sacrifice (10:1-18)

III. PERSEVERANCE OF CHRISTIANS (10:19-12:29)
   A. Attitudes to be Sought and Attitudes to be Shunned (10:19-38)
   B. Faith in Action—Illustrious Examples from the Past (11:1-40)
   C. Incentives for Action in the Present Scene and in the Future Goal (12:1-29)

POSTSCRIPT: EXHORTATIONS, PERSONAL CONCERNS, BENEDICTION (13:1-25)

Although God spoke to the fathers by the prophets, He has now spoken by His Son. In the prologue we see the distinctiveness of the Son. He is before history, in history, above history, the goal of history, and the agent who brings about a cleansing of men from sins committed in history. He shares the essence of Deity and radiates the glory of Deity. He is the supreme revelation of God (1:1-3).

The writer's first main task is to make clear the pre-eminence of Christ (1:4-4:13). He is superior to angels. They assist those who will be heirs of salvation. Christ, by virtue of who He is, of God's appointment, and of what He has done, stands exalted far above them. It would be tragic to be careless of the great salvation which He proclaimed. He will achieve for man the promise that all things will be in harmonious subjection to man. He can do this because He is fully man and has provided the expiation for sins. He is superior to Moses, for Moses was a servant among the people of God, while Christ is a son over the people of God. It would be tragic to cease trusting Him. Unbelief kept one entire generation of Israelites from Canaan. Christians are warned of such unbelief. Faith is emphasized as well as zeal to enter into the eternal rest of God. Both the Gospel of God and God Himself scrutinize men.

The second major emphasis in the letter falls upon the priesthood of Christ (4:14-10:18). Qualifications, conditions, and experiences of the Aaronic priesthood are listed in comparison to Christ as a priest. Before further developing this theme, the writer warns his readers of their unpreparedness for advanced teaching. Only earnest diligence in things of God will bring them out of immaturity. Christ as a priest, like Melchizedek, is superior to the Levitical priesthood because His life is indestructible. He was both priest and sacrifice. His priesthood is eternal. His sanctuary is in heaven and His blood establishes the validity of the New Covenant which is also an eternal covenant. His one offering on behalf of sins is final; i.e., it is for all time. Likewise He has made perfect for all time those who are in the process of being sanctified.

The last main section of Hebrews deals with the response of Christians. Perseverance on the part of Christians springs out of fellowship with God, activity for God, faith in God, and a consciousness of what lies ahead (10:19-12:29).

In concluding the letter the writer puts stress on the cross as the Christian altar and the resurrection of the Shepherd of the sheep as the basis for God's action. Such redemptive-historical events move the believer to action (13:1-25).

Teaching. Although more space is devoted to Christ, the letter has a fully developed set of teachings about God the Father.

Much is said about Christ. He is fully God and fully man. He is active in creation. The atonement of Christ, as both priest and sacrificial victim, is developed in detail. In the role of a priest, He is a leader and guide. He also is the revealer of God. Great depth is achieved in all of these teachings about Christ's person and work.

Very little is said about the Holy Spirit in Hebrews. The Spirit is mentioned only seven times: three times in reference to the inspiration of the OT, once in regard to the work of Christ, once in regard to the apostate's rejection of Christianity, and twice in regard to the believer.

The Old and New Covenants are compared and reasons for the superiority of the New or Eternal Covenant are given.

The doctrine of sin in Hebrews focuses attention on unbelief and the failure to go on with God to the eternal city.

Shadow and reality are carefully contrasted. Heaven is the scene of reality. Earth is concerned both with shadow and reality. Christ is the bridge between the temporary and the eternal.

The people of God are looked upon as migrating from a transitory setting to an abiding city. This migration involves God's Word, the matter of testing, discipline or punishment, faithfulness, and God's activity in sanctifying or making holy. The Christian life is developed in the framework of this heavenly pilgrimage.

Eschatology or last things involves the obtaining of eternal rest, a final shaking of heaven and earth, the personal return of Christ, and glory belonging to God for ever and ever.   A.B.M.

HEBREW, HEBREWS, traditionally considered designations for Abraham and his descendants, especially through Jacob, the equivalent of Israelite(s). I Samuel 14:21 may suggest that the terms are to be equated. Jews quite uniformly have used "Israel" and "the children of Israel" (later "Jews") in referring to themselves, finding in such terminology treasured religious and national associations. Foreigners thought of them as "Hebrews" (Exod. 1:16; 2:6), and they so identified themselves in speaking to non-Jews (Gen. 40:15; Exod. 10:3; Jonah 1:9). Also, in contexts involving contrasts between Israelites and those of other nations, the same phenomenon appears (Gen. 43:32; Exod. 1:15; 2:11; I Sam. 13:3; 14:21).

One must reckon, however, with the possibility that in OT times the names "Hebrews," "Habiru," "Khapiru," " 'Apiru," and 'pr were forms of the same word, (equivalent to the Akkadian SA.GAZ), a designation without national significance. Rather, they indicated wandering peoples greatly restricted as regards financial means and without citizenship and social status. Ancient records show "Habiru" to be scattered over western Asia for centuries until about 1100 B.C. Nomadic peoples, mostly Semitic — sometimes raiders, sometimes skilled artisans — they frequently offered themselves as mercenaries and slaves, with individuals occasionally rising to prominence. In Egypt, the Israelites were reduced to a lowly position and later moved about in the wilderness. Conceivably they could, therefore, have been known as "Hebrews." Interestingly enough, in taking oaths the Habiru swore by "the gods of the Habiru," whereas identical phraseology, "The God of the Hebrews," is found in Exodus 3:18; 5:3; 7:16. "Hebrews" and "Habiru" were terms employed prior to the name "Israel," and both were discontinued generally about the time of the Judges.

NT "Hebrew" references contrast people (Acts 6:1) and language (John 5:2; 19:13,17,20; 20:16) to differentiate between the Greeks and Hellenistic culture on the one hand and Jews and their traditional life and speech on the other. What is called "Hebrew language" may in John's Gospel refer to Aramaic, but in the Apocalypse to Hebrew proper (Rev. 9:11; 16:16).

Etymologically, it has been debated whether "Hebrew" is to be traced to Eber, the father of Peleg and Joktan (Gen. 10:24,25; 11:12-16) or is derived from the Hebrew root "to pass over" and has reference to "a land on the other side," as the dweller E of the Euphrates might think of Canaan. However, the possible equating of the Hebrews and the Habiru might suggest that the Hebrews were "those who crossed over" in the sense of trespassing, i.e. "trespassers."   B.L.G.

HEBREW LANGUAGE. With the exception of Aramaic in Ezra 4:8-6:18; 7:12-26; Daniel 2:4-7; 28 and Jeremiah 10:11, Hebrew is the language of the OT. The term "Hebrew" was first used as a

The Gezer Calendar, the earliest extant written document of ancient Israel. It is a school exercise tablet from the time of Solomon. OIUC

designation for individuals or a people and only later denoted a language. The OT refers to the language not as "Hebrew" but as "the language of Canaan" (Isa. 19:18) or "the Jews' language" (II Kings 18:26,28 and parallel passages; also Neh. 13:24). Josephus, Ecclesiasticus and the NT (Rev. 9:11; 16:16), however, speak of it as "Hebrew." With close affinity to Ugaritic, Phoenician, Moabitic and the Canaanite dialects, Hebrew represents the northwest branch of the Semitic language family. Its sister languages include Arabic, Akkadian and Aramaic. With few exceptions, extant texts of Ancient Hebrew are those of the OT and certain of the apocryphal and pseudepigraphic works. Inscriptions employing the language include the Siloam Inscription from the eighth century B.C. and the Gezer Calendar from the tenth century B.C.

TRANSLATION.

1st line. "(Behold) the excavation! Now this had been the history of the excavation.   While the workmen were still lifting up

2nd „   " the axe, each towards his neighbour, and while three cubits still remained to (cut through), (each heard) the voice of the other who called

3rd „   " to his neighbour since there was an excess in the rock on the right hand and on (the left).   And on the day of the

4th „   " excavation the workmen struck, each to meet his neighbour, axe against axe, and there flowed

5th „   " the waters from the spring to the pool for a thousand two hundred cubits ; and . . . . .

6th „   " of a cubit was the height of the rock over the heads of the workmen."   [2 Kings xx., 20.   2 Chron. xxxii., 30].

The Siloam Inscription, with translation. It is one of the earliest documents available in Hebrew, found carved in the walls of Hezekiah's Tunnel. © MPS

Ancient Semitic Alphabets

(With modern Hebrew, in column at right, for comparison)

Inscr. of Dibon. 9th. cent. B.C. Gram. §2,2. §5,1.	Phoenician Coins and Inscript.	New-Pu-nic.	Old. Hebr. Coins and Gems.	Sama-ritan.	Aram.-Egyptian. 5th. — 1st. cent. B.C.	Palmyra Inscript. 1st cent. B.C. — 4th. cent. A.C.	Heb. Inscr. Christ's Time.	Square Char.	Raschi.	Modern Hebrew	
										א	'
										ב	b, bh
										ג	g, gh
										ד	d, dh
										ה	h
										ו	w
										ז	z
										ח	ch
										ט	ṭ
										י	y
										כ ך	k, kh
										ל	l
										מ ם	m
										נ ן	n
										ס	s
										ע	ʿ
										פ ף	p, ph
										צ ץ	ṣ
										ק	q
										ר	r
										שׁ	sh
										ת	t

From Davies-Mitchell, Student's Hebrew Lexicon.
See also article on WRITING.

General view of Hebron. The mosque in the center of the picture is built over the Cave of Machpelah, the tomb of Abraham and Sarah. © MPS

In large measure, the OT Hebrew must be self explanatory. However, the Ugaritic Ras Shamra tablets shed much light upon the meaning of the Hebrew Bible, and since the structure and vocabulary were so very similar in the various Semitic tongues, much cognate language help is available for the understanding of the language of the Israelites. The Greek translation of the OT, the LXX, is also of much value in interpretative study of Biblical Hebrew.

As the language encountered Aramaizing and Hellenizing influences in the half dozen centuries preceding the advent of Christ, its use as a spoken language became less and less. Some of the Dead Sea Scrolls were written in Hebrew, and Hebrew was the vehicle for the writing of such Jewish religious literature as the Mishnah and the Midrashim in the early part of the Christian era and in medieval times for Biblical commentaries and philosophical and literary works. In modern Israel, Hebrew has again become a living tongue.

The historical origins of the language are somewhat obscure but go back beyond 2000 B.C. The OT literature, written over a period of more than a thousand years, reveals a minimum of stylistic changes, although loan words and new ways of expression became more or less noticeable with the passing of years, especially after the Exile. It is also true that at a given time dialectical differences existed, a fact attested by the narrative in Judges 12, in which Ephraimites were unable to pronounce the "sh" of their neighbors to the south.

With its short sentences and simple coordinating conjunctions, ancient Hebrew lent itself well to the vivid expression of events. These features, together with parallelism and rhythm and special meanings and constructions made Hebrew poetry, as found in the Psalms and to a large extent in the Prophets, most expressive and strikingly effective.

Basic tools for the understanding of the language include the latest revisions of Gesenius' grammar and lexicon, and the lexicons of Koehler & Baumgartner and Davies-Mitchell, and the concordances of Mandelkern and Lisowsky.   B.L.G.

HEBRON (hē'brŏn, Heb. *hevrôn, league, confederacy*). 1. One of the oldest cities of the world, and one which has had several names at different times. It is located 19 miles SW of Jerusalem on the main road to Beer-sheba, and has one of the longest records for continuous occupation. Though lying in a shallow valley, it is about 3,000 feet above sea-level and 4,300 feet above the Dead Sea which lies a few miles E of Hebron. The hills about the city still bear choice grapes, and the Jewish people there make a fine wine. The brook of Eshcol from which the spies brought an immense cluster of grapes (Num. 13:22-24) ran quite near Hebron. Hebron's original name was Kiriath-arba, i.e. "fourfold city" (Josh. 14:15; 15:13).

Hebron is replete with historical interest. It was early a camping place for Abram, to which he removed his tent, and dwelt by the oaks of Mamre (Gen. 13:18 mistranslated in KJV "the plain of Mamre"). This was close to Hebron, and here Abram built an altar unto the Lord. The only land that Abram owned, though God had promised him Canaan (Gen. 15:18-21), was the field of Machpelah, which he purchased from the Hittites as a burial place for Sarah (Heb. 11:8-10; Gen. 23:17-20). In this cave Sarah and Abraham, later Isaac and Rebekah, then Jacob and Leah were buried. At the partition of Canaan after the partial conquest, Hebron and its environs were given to Caleb to conquer (Josh. 14:6-15), which he did (15:14-19); but later the city itself was given to the Kohathite Levites (I Chron. 6:55,56), though Caleb's descendants kept the suburban fields and villages. When David was king over Judah, but not yet over all Israel, his capital city was Hebron for seven and a half years, and there the elders of Israel anointed him king over all Israel. He removed the capital to Jerusalem, but when Absalom rebelled against his father, he made Hebron his headquarters and there prepared his coup-d'état (II Sam. 15:7-12).

2. Third son of Kohath, and so an uncle of Moses, Aaron and Miriam (Exod. 6:18). His descendants, 1,700 men of valor in the days of David,

had the responsibility for the Lord's business and for the service of the king west of Jordan (I Chron. 26:30).

3. A town in Asher (Josh. 19:28 KJV). ASV has "Ebron," but "Abdon" (Josh. 21:30, copied in I Chron. 6:74) is almost certainly the correct reading.

4. A descendant of Caleb, son of Hezron, son of Perez, son of Judah (I Chron. 2:42,43), not to be confused with Caleb the good spy, who was a distant cousin.

HEDGE, loose stone walls without mortar, or cut thorn branches or thorny bushes, common as "hedges" and "fences" in Palestine. The word can be rendered, *fence, wall* or *hedge*. The use of a hedge about a vine or tree was mainly for protection (Ps. 80:12). Figuratively, prophets should make up a hedge for the people's protection (Ezek. 13:5), and God is pictured as so doing (Mark 12:1) for His people. The very poor live in highways and hedges (Luke 14:23).

HEGAI or **HEGE** (hĕg'ā-ī, hē'gē), the eunuch employed by Xerxes the Great ("Ahasuerus") as keeper of the women in the king's harem (Esth. 2:3,8,15). Some think that "Hegai' 'is not a proper name but means "eunuch."

HEIFER, a young cow (Gen. 15:9; Deut. 21:3; I Sam. 16:2). Heifers were used in religious rites only in the ceremony of Deuteronomy 21:1-9.

HEIFER, RED (See Animals)

HEIR (See Inheritance)

HELAH (hē'là), one of the two wives of Ashur (ASV Ashhur), posthumous son of Hezron (I Chron. 4:5,7).

HELAM (hē'lăm, Heb. *hēlām*), a place in the Syrian desert E of the Jordan where David defeated the forces of Hadarezer, king of Aram-zobah (II Sam. 10:16,17). The exact location is unknown.

HELBAH (hĕl'bà, *a fertile region*), a town in the tribe of Asher from which the men of Israel failed to expel the Canaanites. Near the River Leontes in Lebanon (Judg. 1:31).

HELBON (hĕl'bŏn, *fertile*), a city of northern Syria, celebrated in ancient times for its wine (Ezek. 27:18). Some think that a village in the Anti-Lebanon about 13 miles NW of Damascus is intended.

HELDAI (hĕl'dā-ī). 1. The captain over 24,000 men whose duties were in the 12th month under David (I Chron. 27:15). Probably the same as Heled in I Chronicles 11:30 and as Heleb in II Samuel 23:29.

2. One of three noble Jews who brought gold and silver from Babylon, and who were to surrender the metal to Zechariah (Zech. 6:9-15) that he might make crowns for Joshua the high-priest. (The name is spelled "Helem" in 6:14).

HELEB (hē'lĕb), one of David's valiant men of war (II Sam. 23:29). See HELED and HELDAI.

HELED (hē'lĕd), a mighty man of David's army (I Chron. 11:30). See HELEB and HELDAI.

HELEK (hē'lĕk), the second son of Gilead of the tribe of Manasseh and head of a family (Num. 26: 30; Josh. 17:2).

HELEM (hē'lĕm, *health*). 1. A man of the tribe of Asher (I Chron. 7:35), called Hotham in verse 32.

2. An ambassador, mentioned only in Zechariah 6:14; but also certainly the same person as Heldai (Zech. 6:10).

HELEPH (hē'lĕf, *change*), an ancient village on the border of Naphtali (Josh. 19:33). Perhaps on the site now called Beitlif in Galilee.

HELEZ (hē'lĕz). 1. A man of Judah, of the family of Hezron, but also of Egyptian descent (I Chron. 2:39).

2. One of David's mighty leaders, called a "Paltite" in II Samuel 23:26, but "Pelonite" in I Chronicles 11:27; an Ephraimite (I Chron. 27:10).

HELI (hē'lī, Heb. *'ēlī*), the father of Joseph, the husband of Mary, in the genealogy of Jesus in Luke 3:23. According to another view, he is the father of Mary, the mother of Jesus, a view that is reached by punctuating the Gr. differently. See GENEALOGY OF JESUS CHRIST.

HELIOPOLIS (hē-lĭ-ŏp'ō-lĭs, Heb. *'ōn*, Gr. *Heliopolis, city of the sun*), a city near the S end of the Delta of the Nile, the site of a temple to the sun built by Amenophis I. It was a very old and holy city, with a learned school of priests. Joseph's father-in-law belonged to the priests of the Sun Temple (Gen. 41:45; 46:20). In the intertestamental period Onias built a Jewish Temple there. The modern site is the village El-Matariye.

HELKAI (hĕl'kā-ī, perhaps an abbr. of *Helkiah*), a priest of the Jews in the days of Joiakim (Neh. 12:15).

HELKATH (hĕl'kăth, Heb. *helqath, a field*), a town on the southern border of the tribe of Asher (Josh. 19:25) given to the Gershonite Levites (Josh. 21: 31). Later called Hukok (I Chron. 6:75). Site uncertain .

HELKATH HAZZURIM (hĕl'kăth hăz'ū-rĭm, *the field of the sharp knives*), a piece of ground near the pool of Gibeon where the men of Joab fought with an equal number of the men of Abner, and all 24 fell down slain (II Sam. 2:12-16).

HELL. The real existence of hell is irrefutably taught in Scripture as both a *place* of the wicked dead and a *condition* of retribution for unredeemed man.

No formal statement of immortality occurs in the Old Testament, yet it constantly alludes to the "cutting off" of the wicked from God. While the word, *Sheol*, does not pointedly refer to a definitive doctrine of endless retribution, but rather to a shadowy existence beyond the grave, it nevertheless reflects the belief in a future and continued existence. Translated by KJV and ERV as "hell," the word carries the connotation of doom, hopelessness and futility. "The wicked in a moment go down into Sheol" (Job. 21:13). "The wicked shall be turned into Sheol, and all the nations that forget God" (Ps. 9:17). "If I ascend up into heaven, thou art there; if I make my bed in Sheol, behold thou art there" (Ps. 139:8). "The way of life is above the wise, that he may depart from Sheol beneath" (Prov. 15:24). The etymology of the word is uncertain. It may be translated merely as "grave" or "abode of the dead," or it may be given the stronger connotation of "hell." However it may be translated, its meaning is clear — it represents the place of future retribution (Job 26:6), the abode of the wicked (Prov. 23:4, Job 21:30), a place of punishment (Prov. 15:11). It is inseparably associated with spiritual death (Ps. 89:48), and is contrasted with the destiny of the righteous (Ps. 17:15).

In the Inter-Testamental period, both apocryphal literature and Rabbinical teaching continued the development of the association of immortality and retribution until, during the New Testament times, two words were used: Hades (Gr. *hádes*) and Gehenna (Gr. *geénna*). *Gehenna*, used 13 times in the New Testament, and with but one exception (James 3:6) always by Christ, indisputably refers to the place of retributive suffering.

The word derives its meaning from the Hebrew, *ge-hinnom* (*the valley of Hinnom*) which was a pit into which refuse was dumped. A site which had long been contemptuously regarded in the Hebrew mind, as when Josiah dumped the filth of Jerusalem (II Kings 23:10) to be burned, and in which the bodies of executed criminals were tossed, it had become a technical term for unending torment, and is so used in Matthew 10:28 and Mark 9:43. *Hades*, used by the Septuagint translators for *Sheol*, and thus somewhat undefined in early usage, undeniably assumed definiteness of meaning by Christ's use of it in Matthew 11:23 (Luke 10:15), where it represents destruction, in Matthew 16:18, where it is synonymous with the kingdom of evil, and in Revelation 1:18, where it represents confinement in prison and is identified with death. In each of these cases, the reality of hell is established through Christ's reference to it.

The *nature* of hell is indicated by the repeated reference to everlasting punishment (Matt. 25: 46); everlasting fire (Matt. 18:8); everlasting chains (II Thess. 1:8); the eternal fire (Jude 7); the pit of the abyss (Rev. 9:2,11); outer darkness (Matt. 8:12); the wrath of God (Rom. 2:5); second death (Rev. 21:8); eternal destruction from the face of God (II Thess. 1:9); and eternal sin (Mark 3:29). While many of these terms are symbolic and descriptive, they connote real entities, about which existence there can be no doubt.

The *duration* of hell is explicitly indicated in the NT. The word "everlasting" (*aionios*) is derived from the verb *aion*, signifying an "age" or "duration." Scripture speaks of two *aions*, or ages: the present age and the age to come (Matt. 12:32; Mark 10:30; Luke 18:30; Eph. 1:21). The present age — this world — is always contrasted with the age to come as temporal, while the future age is to be endless. As the everlasting life of the believer is to be endless, just so the retributive aspect of hell refers to the future infinite age. In every reference in which *aiōnios* applies to the future punishment of the wicked, it indisputably denotes endless duration (Matt. 18:8; 25:41,46; Mark 3:29; II Thess. 1:9; Heb. 6:2; Jude 6).

Hell is, therefore, both a *condition* of retribution, and a *place* in which the retribution occurs. In both these aspects, the three basic ideas associated with the concept of hell are reflected: (1) absence of righteousness, (2) separation from God, and (3) judgment.

The absence of personal righteousness, with its correlative of the presence of personal unrighteousness, renders the individual unable to enter felicitude with the holy God (Mark 3:29). The eternal state of the wicked, therefore, will involve a separation from the presence of God (John 3: 36). The concept of judgment is heightened by the note of finality in the warnings against sin (Matt. 8:12). It is a judgment, however, against man's sinful nature — still unredeemed though Christ died — (Matt. 25:31-46) and is decisive and irreversible.

When all else has been said about hell, however, there is still the inescapable fact of Scripture — it will be a retributive judgment upon the *spirit* of man — the inner essence of his being. The severity of the judgment will be upon the fixed character of his essential nature — his soul, which will involve the eternal loss of exclusion from Christ's kingdom and fellowship with God.   C.B.B.

BIBLIOGRAPHY: H. Buis, *The Doctrine of Eternal Punishment* (Philadelphia: Presbyterian and Reformed Publishing Company) 1957; W. Shedd, "Hell," *Dogmatic Theology* (New York: Charles Scribners Sons) 1888.

HELLENISTS (hĕl'ĕn-ĭsts), non-Greeks who spoke Greek, a term used specially of Jews who made Greek their tongue, and with it often adopted Greek ideas and practices (Acts 6:1; 9:29). The KJV has Grecians, RSV Hellenists.

HELMET (See Arms, Armor)

HELON (hē'lôn, *valorous*), father of Eliab, a leading man of Zebulun at the first census (Num. 1:9).

HELPMEET, now often used as one word, meaning a helper, generally a wife; but in Genesis 2:18 it is two words. "I will make him a help, meet for him," i.e., suitable for or answering to him. It is often changed to "helpmate," which means the same.

HELPS. In the NT there are four lists of "gifts" which God has given to His Church (Rom. 12:6-8, I Cor. 12:7-11, 28-31, and Eph. 4:11,12) and these are not to be confused with the officers who are listed elsewhere. "Helps" are mentioned only in I Corinthians 12:28, and the Greek word occurs only here. It means *protector* or *assistant*, and probably refers to the ability to perform helpful works in a gracious manner.

HEMAM (hē'măm), a grandson of Seir the Horite (Gen. 36:22). "Homam" in I Chronicles 1:39.

HEMAN (hē'măn, Heb. *hêmān, faithful*). 1. A grandson of Judah through Zerah (I Chron. 2:6). He is listed as one of the most notable wise men, though Solomon was wiser.

2. The first of the three Levites whom David appointed to lead in the musical services (I Chron. 6:33). He was "the king's seer in the words of God to lift up the horn" (I Chron. 25:5) and had 14 sons and three daughters.

3. Psalm 88 is attributed to Heman the Ezrahite, and if "Ezrahite" means "Zerahite," as many think, he may be the same as 1. above.

HEMATH (hē'măth). In Amos 6:14 "Hemath" should be "Hamath" as in ASV. In I Chronicles 2:55 "Hemath" should be Hammath" as in ASV. He was the father of Rechabites (Jer. 35:2-18). See HAMATH.

HEMDAN (hĕm'dăn, Heb. *hemdān, pleasant*), an early Horite in the land of Seir, who discovered hot springs in the wilderness (Gen. 36:26). In I Chronicles 1:41 the Heb. text and RV have "Hamran," but KJV has "Amram." Hemdan is probably the original form.

HEMLOCK (See Plants)

HEM OF A GARMENT, the fringes or tassels on the borders of the Jewish outer garment (Num. 15:38,39) containing a thread of blue. The word "hem" (Exod. 28:33,34, 39:24-26) should be "skirt." Cf. ASV *in loco*. To "touch the hem (ASV "border") of his garment" (Matt. 9:20,21, 14:36) denoted a reverent approach, not daring to lay hold of Him, but having faith in the efficacy of His miraculous power.

HEN (Heb. *hēn, favor*), a son of Zephaniah (Zech. 6:14), but RV margin has "for the kindness of the son of Zephaniah," in which case the son's name disappears.

HEN (Gr. *órnis*), a general term for "bird," "fowl," etc. (Matt. 23:37; Luke 13:34).

HENA (hēn'a, Heb. *hēna'*), a city on the south bank of the Euphrates, about 180 miles NW of ancient Babylon. It was mentioned by Rabshakeh, along with four other cities whose gods could not save them from destruction by Sennacherib, as a proof that Jehovah could not save Jerusalem (II Kings 18:34, 19:13, Isa. 37:13).

HENADAD (hĕn'á-dåd, *favor of Hadad*), head of a family of Levites who helped Zerubbabel (Ezra 3:9), and who in the next century helped Nehemiah in building (Neh. 3:18,24).

HENOCH (See Enoch)

HEPHER (hē'fẽr, *pit, well*). 1. Head of the family of the Hepherites (Num. 26:32). His son Zelophehad had five daughters who were commanded to marry within their tribe so as not to alienate any of the tribal property of Manasseh to another tribe (Num. 27:1-8, 36:1-9).
2. A son of Ashhur (KJV Ashur), the founder of Tekoa (I Chron. 4:5,6).
3. One of David's mighty men (I Chron. 11:36) from Macherah, a place otherwise unmentioned and unknown.
4. A royal city in Canaan listed among the 31 which Joshua conquered (Josh. 12:17). The land of Hepher (I Kings 4:10) was SW of Jerusalem.

HEPHZIBAH (hĕf'zĭ-bà, Heb. *hephtsî-vâh, my delight is in her*). 1. Wife of King Hezekiah (II Kings 21:1) and mother of Manasseh.
2. A symbolical name given to Zion (Isa. 62:4).

HERB (See Plants)

HERD. Israel, before Joshua's time, like the Bedouin of today, was a nomadic people, and after the conquest of Canaan continued to be a pastoral people for the most part. For the property of such a people see Job 1:3 or 42:12. The herds consisted of the larger animals, as contrasted with the flocks of sheep, goats, etc. The cattle were used in plowing and threshing, and for sacrifice, but were not commonly fattened for food, though in contrast, see Ezekiel 39:18.

HERDMAN. Hebrew has three words rendered herdman in the Bible: *bôqēr, a cowherd* (Amos 7:14); *rō'eh,* a general term for any kind of herdman (Gen. 13:7,8; 26:20); *nōqēdh, one who spots or marks the sheep,* hence *a herdman* (Amos 1:1). Herdmen generally did not own the sheep; they were hirelings.

HERES (he'rez, *sun*). 1. A district around Aijalon from which the Amorites were not expelled (Judg. 1:35). The meaning is uncertain.
2. A place E of the Jordan from which Gideon returned after his defeat of Zebah and Zalmunna (Judg. 8:13).
3. An Egyptian city (Isa. 19:18). Undoubtedly Heliopolis.

HERESH (hē'resh, *dumb, silent*), a Levite who early returned from captivity (I Chron. 9:15).

HERESY (hâr'ĕ-sē, Gr. *haíresis,* from vb. *haíreo, to choose*). 1. A sect or faction, not necessarily representing a departure from orthodox doctrine, as "sect of Sadducees" (Acts 5:17), "sect of Nazarenes" (Acts 24:5). The Pharisees are called "the straitest sect" (Acts 26:5). Christianity is called a heresy in Acts 24:14; 28:22.
2. A doctrine or sect representing a departure from sound doctrine (II Pet. 2:1).

HERMAS (hûr'măs, Gr. *Hermás*), a Roman Christian (Rom. 16:14), not to be confused with the writer of the "Shepherd of Hermas" in the second century.

HERMES (hûr'mēz). 1. The Greek name which is rendered "Mercury" in Acts 14:12. He was one of the mythological gods of Greece and Rome, and messenger of the gods.
2. One to whom Paul sends greetings in Romans 16:14, of whom nothing else is known.

HERMOGENES (hûr'mŏj'ē-nēz, Gr. *Hermogénes, born of Hermes*), one of the professed Christians

in Asia (probably at Ephesus) who deserted Paul when he was in trouble (II Tim. 1:15).

HERMON (hûr'mŏn, Heb. *hermôn, sacred mountain*), the mountain that marks the southern terminus of the Anti-Lebanon range. A line drawn from Damascus to Tyre will pass through Mt. Hermon at its middle point, and will practically coincide with the northern boundary of Palestine. The ridge of Hermon is about 20 miles long. It has three peaks, two of them rising over 9,000 feet. Hermon has borne several names: the ancient Amorites called it "Shenir" or "Senir" (Deut. 3:9; cf. Ps. 29:6 and Ezek. 27:5, where it is called a source of fir trees for Tyre); the Sidonians called it "Sirion" (Deut. 3:9 though Ps. 29:6 would apparently separate them); the Arabs call it "Jebel-esh-Sheikh" or "Mountain of the old man" perhaps because of its white head, but more likely because of its dignity.
Hermon is awe-inspiring whether seen from the NE at Damascus, the W from Lebanon back of Sidon, the SW from Nazareth or the SE from Hauran. Our Lord's transfiguration almost certainly occurred on its slopes, for He was at Caesarea-Philippi just S of the mountain only a week before. Before the advent of modern refrigeration, both Damascus and the summer resorts on Mt. Lebanon obtained ice from Hermon, and so it was often called "Jebel-et-telj," i.e., "Ice-mountain." Hermon is once called "Sion" (Deut. 4:48) not to be confused with Zion in Jerusalem, which is "Sion" in the NT. A.B.F.

HEROD (hĕr'ŭd). When Pompey organized the East in 63 B.C., he appointed Hyrcanus, second of that name, to be the high-priestly ruler of an ethnarchy comprising Galilee, Samaria, Judaea, and Perea. One Antipater, an Idumaean was Hyrcanus' senior officer or vizier. Pompey's arrangements were modified by Gabinius in 57 B.C. by the reduction of Hyrcanus' authority and the division of the ethnarchy into autonomous communities. Notable services rendered at Alexandria to Julius Caesar in 48 B.C., led to the restoration of Hyrcanus' authority and the appointment (47 B.C.) of Antipater to the procuratorship of Judaea. Antipater had, in fact, been the leading spirit in the policy which won Caesar's favor, and Antipater used his advantage with an astuteness which foreshadowed the career of his son. Antipater persuaded the now aged Hyrcanus to appoint Phasael, Antipater's eldest son, to the prefecture of Jerusalem, and Herod, his second son, to the governorship of Galilee.
When Antipater was murdered in 43 B.C., his two sons succeeded to his position in Hyrcanus' court. It was the year after Julius Caesar's assassination, and jubilant that Caesar's plan for a decisive campaign on the vulnerable eastern frontier of Rome was shelved, the Parthians. the perennial military problem of the northeast, were restive. In 40 B.C. they penetrated Palestine, carried off Hyrcanus, and drove Phasael, also a captive, to a death of suicide. Herod eluded both military action and Parthian treachery. He withdrew from Jerusalem, shook off pursuit by clever rearguard skirmishing near Bethlehem, and escaped to Egypt. Outwitting Cleopatra, and reaching Rome through the perils of winter voyaging, Herod set his case before Octavian and Antony. It is a remarkable tribute to his charm, daring, political acumen, and consummate diplomacy, that he won the support of both triumvirs who were so soon to divide in disastrous rivalry. The whole remarkable story is told drily in the first book of Josephus' *Wars of the Jews.*

An awe-inspiring view of beautiful Mount Hermon, as viewed across the Sea of Galilee. © MPS

The thirteen years which lay between the assassination of Caesar, and the emergence of Octavian as the victorious Augustus, after Antony's defeat at Actium in 31 B.C., were a time of paralysis and uncertainty throughout the Roman world. Herod saw in such confusion the opportunity for decisive action. Landing at Acre in 39 B.C., with only the promise of Roman favor, Herod went to claim his kingdom, and to unseat the Parthian puppet, Antigonus. Palestine, with its hill-country, deserts, and fenced cities, called for a variety of military ability. Herod showed himself the able master of varied types of war. The two years of tireless activity which made him, by the age of thirty-six, the master of his inheritance, revealed all the facets of Herod's amazing personality. He was a ruthless fighter, but at the same time a cunning negotiator, a subtle diplomat, and an opportunist. He was able to restrain his Roman helpers and simultaneously circumvent the Jews. Between 39 and 37 B.C. Herod revealed those qualities, if qualities they may be called, which enabled him for thirty-four years to govern subjects who hated him, within the major framework of Roman imperial rule, to steer, as the task demanded, a safe course through political dilemma, and to pursue a dual policy without ruinous contradiction.

In 30 B.C. Herod succeeded in retaining the favor of Octavian, shared though that favor had been with the defeated rival, Antony. He was confirmed in his kingdom, and for the rest of his life never departed from the policy of supporting the emperor, and in all ways promoting his honor. Restored Samaria was called Sebaste, the Greek rendering of Augustus; Caesarea was built to form a harbor on the difficult open coast of Palestine, to provide Rome with a salutary bridgehead and base on the edge of a turbulent province, and to make a center of Caesar-worship in the land of the nationalistic and monotheistic Jews.

Ruins of Herod's summer palace at Samaria (Sebaste). JFW

Simultaneously Herod followed a policy of Hellenization, establishing games at Jerusalem, and adorning many of the Hellenistic cities of his domains. At the same time Herod sought to reconcile the Jews, who hated his pro-Roman and Hellenizing policies, and who never forgave his Edomite blood. During the great famine in Judaea and Samaria of 25 B.C., Herod spared no trouble or private expense to import Egyptian corn, and in the eighteenth year of his reign (20 B.C.) began the great Jerusalem temple, which was forty-three years under construction (John 2:20). Nothing he did served to win metropolitan Jewry. It was Herod's policy to crush the old aristocracy, married though he was to Mariamne, the heiress of the Hasmonaean house. He built up a nobility of service, drawing upon both Jews and Greeks. He sought subtly to channel messianic ambitions of the baser sort in his direction by encouraging the political party of the Herodians (Mark 3:6; 12:13 et al.), whose policy seems to have been the support of the royal house and a Hellenized society. Politically, this royalist group was descended from the old Hellenizing apostates whom Jason called Antiochians (II Macc. 9:9-14). They were probably Jews of the Dispersion, from whom Herod also recuited his subservient priesthood, and were Sadducees in religion. Such varied patronage and support produced checks and balances in the composite society of Herod's kingdom which made for stability of rule, but of course did nothing to reconcile the divided elements of the populace, metropolitan and Hellenistic Jews, Sadducees and Pharisees, people and hierarchy. It was only the common challenge of Christ which drew together such dissidents as Sadducee and Pharisee, and the Romans and the priests, just as it healed, according to a surprising footnote of Luke (23:12), a rift between Antipas and the procurator.

To manage a situation so complex and to survive, demanded uncommon ability, and an ordered realm. Of Herod's ability there is no doubt, and with his foreign mercenaries, his system of fortresses, and the centralized bureaucracy which he built in imitation of the Ptolemaic system, he gave Palestine order, and even opportunity for economic progress. At the same time Herod was a cruel and implacable tyrant. His family and private life was soiled and embittered by feuds, intrigue, and murder. The king's sister Salome seems to have been in league with Herod's son Antipater by Doris, his first consort, against Mariamne, daughter of Hycranus II, the king's favorite wife. Mariamne was put to death in 29 B.C., and her two sons, Alexander and Aristobulus, in 7 B.C. Antipater himself was put to death by Herod in the last days of his reign. He died in 4 B.C. The murder of the Innocents recorded in the Gospels falls within the context of his final madness. Josephus' grim picture (*Wars*, I:33:5) of the physical and mental degeneration of the aging king is detailed enough for diagnosis. It is the picture of an arteriosclerotic, the former athlete and "hard liver," increasingly prone to delusions of persecution, and uncontrollable outbursts of violence, the results of hypertension and a diseased brain.

Herod's will divided the kingdom. Archelaus, son of Malthace, a Samaritan woman, took Judaea and Idumaea, by far the choicest share. Herod Antipas, of the same mother, received Galilee and Peraea, and Philip, son of a Jewess named Cleopatra, took Ituraea, Trachonitis and associated districts in the northeast. Archelaus, who inherited his father's vices without his ability, took the title of king and bloodily quelled disorders which broke out in Jerusalem. The result was a wide uprising, which required the intervention of Varus, governor of Syria. It was at this time that the Holy Family returned from Egypt (Matt. 2:22): "But when Joseph heard that Archelaus was reigning as King over Judaea in the place of his father Herod, he was afraid to go there . . . but withdrew into Galilee and came to a town called Nazareth."

It was imperative for Archelaus to reach Rome, and secure from Augustus confirmation of his position, before the situation in Palestine could be presented in too lurid a light by his enemies. Archelaus' petition was opposed in person by Herod Antipas, who made much of Herod's testamentary incapacity, and by a Jewish embassy. Somewhat surprisingly, Augustus declared in favor of Archelaus, though he denied him the royal title. The incident provided the background for the Parable of the Pounds, related by Luke (19:11-27). Archelaus was the "nobleman" who went "to receive a kingdom," and the facts were no doubt brought to mind by the sight of the palace which Archelaus had built at Jericho, where the story was told. (Josephus. *Ant.* 17:13:1). It is a striking illustration of the fact that the incidental machinery of a parable is exempt from theological and moral significance. It is a canon of such exegesis that the main point only must be disengaged, and no significance attached to pictorial and background detail. Archelaus maintained his stupid and tyrannical reign for the ten years. In A.D. 6, a Jewish embassy finally secured his deposition and banishment to Gaul. Herod I first built the palace at Jericho. It was burned down at the time of his death, but rebuilt and restored by Archelaus. It was discovered and excavated in 1951. Judaea fell under procuratorial rule. Coponius, a Roman knight, was appointed governor (Josephus *B.J.* 2:8). A tax-census was the first administrative necessity, and this precipitated the revolt of Judas of Gamala, and the emergence of the Zealots as a sinister force in Palestinian politics.

Herod Antipas (the word is an abbreviation for Antipater) equalled his father's long reign. "That fox," Christ called the ruler of Galilee, and the name has reference to the Herodian cunning, the subtle diplomacy, and astute management of a difficult situation, which enabled Antipas to retain his puppet position and petty royal power until A.D. 39. It was probably some time before A.D. 23, that Herod Antipas met the evil genius of his latter years, the dynamic Herodias, wife of his half-brother Philip. This brother, who is not to be confused with the son of Cleopatra, the tetrarch of Ituraea, was the son of an unnamed wife of Herod I. Some have said that this woman, who was the daughter of Simon the high-priest, was another Mariamne, but it is difficult to establish this. Philip lived quietly in Rome, and it was here that Antipas met Herodias, Philip's niece and wife, daughter of Aristobulus, son of Herod I and Mariamne.

It is difficult to say who was primarily to blame for the notorious liaison which took back Herodias to Palestine as the *de facto* Queen of Antipas. She remained loyal to the tetrarch in his later misfortunes, though offered release by Caligula, and the immoral partnership of the twain seems to have been cemented by genuine physical attraction and community of temperament. But trouble dogged the union. Herod's rightful queen, daughter of Aretas, king of Nabataeans, heard of the liaison before the couple reached Palestine, and escaped first to the fortress of Machaerus, and thence

Herod's Gate in the Jerusalem city wall. © MPS

about A.D. 30. After Philip died in A.D. 34, she married her cousin Aristobulus, king of Chalcis, north of Abilene in the Anti-Lebanon hill-country.

Philip of Ituraea seems to have been the best of Herod's three surviving sons (Josephus, *Ant.* 17:2:4; B.J.II 9). His remote province insulated him from some of the problems of Jewry, but he seems in his own person to have been a man of generous mold and notable justice. He beautified the town of Caesarea Philippi, and marked his continuation of the Herodian pro-Roman policy by naming the northern Bethsaida Julias after Augustus' unfortunate daughter.

The deceased Philip's vacant tetrarchy was the first foothold of the third Herod to be mentioned in the NT (Acts 12:1). Herod Agrippa I, named after the able minister of Augustus, grandson of Herod I, son of Aristobulus, and brother of Herodias, had been brought up in Rome under the protection of Tiberius' favorite son, Drusus. He had all the Herodian charm and diplomatic subtlety, which explains how, as the boon companion of the mad Caligula, he was yet able to deter that prince from the final folly of setting up his statue in the Temple at Jerusalem (Jos. *Ant.* 18:8). Such an achievement demanded not only clever wits, but courage of no mean order. In A.D. 37, on Caligula's succession, Herod Agrippa was granted Philip's realm. To this was added Galilee and Peraea, on the exile of Antipas and Herodias. The malicious word in Rome had paid rich dividends. With his grandfather's subtlety, Agrippa knew how to survive a succession. When Caligula was assassinated in A.D. 41, Agrippa, who had played his cards with remarkable astuteness, remained in the favor of Claudius, Caligula's successor, who turned over to Agrippa's control the whole area of his grandfather's kingdom. He succeeded to such dignity, moreover, with the consent and the favor of the Jews. The old hostility to the Idumaean dynasty had vanished, and even the Pharisees were reconciled. Hence the gesture of favor in the first royal persecution of the Church. Luke's account (Acts 12:20-23) of the king's shocking death in his royal seat of Caesarea, is substantiated by Josephus' longer narrative (*Ant.* 19: 8:2). Josephus looked upon Herod with admira-

The remains of the third wall of Jerusalem, called Agrippa's Wall. © MPS

to her father's capital of Petra, before her returning husband could detain her. Herod therefore came home to find a troublesome frontier war on his lands. Hence the celebration of his birthday, the tragic feast described in the Gospels, at the stronghold of Machaerus. Josephus is authority for this. Hence, too, the death of John the Baptist, for here, after his denunciation of Herod's sin, the preacher of the wilderness had been incarcerated. The crime so dramatically contrived was the final turning point in Herod's life. Until then, according to a strange remark in the Second Gospel (Mark 6:20), there had been some faint aspiration for good: "Herod feared John, knowing that he was a just man and a holy, and he respected him; and when he heard him he did many things, and heard him gladly."

The campaign against Aretas ended disastrously. Antipas was forced to appeal to Rome for help, and the task was assigned to Vitellius, governor of Syria. The affair dragged on until A.D. 37, when Tiberius died. A prey to that uncertainty which was increasingly to attend changes in the Roman principate, Vitellius stayed his hand, and Antipas never won revenge. Two years later, Antipas fell. He had been trusted by Tiberius, who appreciated the tetrarch's continuation of his father's pro-Roman policy, to which the foundation of Tiberias on Galilee was a solid monument. Tiberius, in the last year of his principate (A.D. 36), had even used Herod as a mediator between Rome and Parthia. Presuming upon this notable imperial favor, and incited by Herodias, Herod petitioned Caius Caligula, Tiberius' successor, for the title of king. He was, however, deposed by that incalculable prince, on a suspicion of treasonable conduct, a charge levelled successfully by Herod Agrippa I, his nephew. Herodias accompanied the man she had ruined morally and politically into obscure exile. Salome her daughter, the dancer of the Machaerus feast, married her uncle Philip, tetrarch of Ituraea,

tion as the last great Jewish monarch, and the correspondence between the historian's account and Luke's unfavorable notice is remarkable. In both accounts the pomp and circumstance of Agrippa's royal estate is notable. Agrippa died in A.D. 44, and his eminence was therefore brief. Whether it would have long survived under a less indulgent prince, or under an imperial government which had already vetoed his proposal to fortify Jerusalem, is a matter which his early death left undecided. It is possible for modern medicine to diagnose the intestinal complaint described by Luke in the accepted terminology of his profession. A symptom is a visible, violent, and agonizing peristalsis. Luke uses a single adjective for the cause of death, admitting more readily this metaphorical significance than the English phrase "eaten of worms." Agrippa was only fifty-four years of age. After his death Palestine fell wholly under Roman rule, a take-over facilitated by the consolidation under Agrippa of the old Herodian domains. There was considerable disorder over the next four years.

Agrippa left a teen-age son, who was made by Claudius the king of Chalcis in A.D. 48. This was a Lebanese ethnarchy. In A.D. 53, the territory of Philip the tetrarch and Lysanias were added to this realm, together with an area on the western side of Galilee, including Tiberias. The appointment carried the title of King, so in 53 Agrippa became Agrippa II, last of the Herodian line. He appears only in the brilliantly told story of Acts 25, where, as Festus' guest, he heard the defense of Saint Paul. After the fashion of Eastern monarchies, Agrippa was married to his sister Bernice. Another sister was the wife of Antonius Felix, the procurator of Judaea, whom Festus succeeded. This young woman was named Drusa, after the Roman protector of Agrippa I, Drusus, son of Tiberius. Drusilla, the diminutive, was a pet-name. Probably in 53, Drusilla was married to Aziz of Emesa, a principality north of Syria, which included the city of Palmyra. In the following year, significantly after Claudius' death, she yielded to the solicitations of Felix, Claudius' freedman, and that emperor's notorious appointment to the procuratorship of Palestine. In October 54, she became Felix' third wife. It was probably the influence of Agrippa II and Bernice, working through a Jewish party in Rome which had obscure connections with Poppaea, wife of Nero, which secured the dismissal of Felix. Drusilla and her son Agrippa appear to have resided in Pompeii, and possibly perished in the eruption of Vesuvius in A.D. 79.

In the story of the examination of Saint Paul is seen a vivid and revealing picture of the deference Rome was prepared to pay to a puppet king, and indeed some of the respect which Rome undoubtedly owed to a remarkable royal house which had been a major bastion of Roman peace in the Middle East for three generations. In the king himself is seen a typical Herod of the better sort, royal, intelligent, pro-Roman, but vitally interested in Judaism, which, with live understanding, he saw to be the key to the history of his land.

With this event, which is difficult to date precisely, Agrippa and the Herodian line disappear from history. Festus died in A.D. 64. One brief reference in Josephus reveals that Agrippa lived on in the garrison town of Caesarea to see the vast ruin and destruction of his country in the Great Revolt of A.D. 66 to 70. So ended the Herods, an astonishingly able family, whose pro-Roman policy went far to postpone the inevitable clash between Rome and the Jews, and played, in consequence, an unwitting but significant part in holding the peace during the formative years of the Christian Church in Palestine. E.M.B.

HERODIANS (hĕ-rō'dĭ-ănz, Gr. *Herodianoi*), a party mentioned only three times (Matt. 22: 16; Mark 12:13; 3:6) as joining with the Pharisees to oppose Jesus. Nothing more is known about them than what the Gospels state. It appears that they were neither a religious sect nor a political party, but Jews who supported the dynasty of Herod, and therefore the rule of Rome. The first time they are referred to (Matt. 22:16) they join with the Pharisees to destroy Jesus; the second time (Mark 12:13) they try to trap Jesus by asking Him whether it is proper to pay tribute to Caesar.

HERODIAS (hĕ-rō'dĭ-ăs, Gr. *Herodiás*), wicked granddaughter of Herod the Great who married her uncle Philip, but his brother Antipas saw her at Rome, desired her and married her. John the Baptist reproved Herod Antipas for his immoral action (Luke 3:19,20) and was put in prison for his temerity (Matt. 14:3-12; Mark 6:14-29). This did not satisfy Herodias, so by a sordid scheme she secured the death of John. Later, Antipas was banished to Spain. Herodias accompanied him, and died there.

HERODION (hĕ-rō'dĭ-ŏn, Gr. *Herodíon*), a Christian at Rome, kinsman of Paul and recipient of his greeting (Rom. 16:11).

HERON (hĕr'ŏn, Heb. *'ănāphâh*), a bird mentioned only in Leviticus 11:19 and Deuteronomy 14:18, where they are listed among the birds Israelites could not eat. They were of three kinds — white, blue, and brown. Their wing-sweep was from 3½ to 5 feet. They lived principally on fish and reptiles, and could be found in abundance in the swamps of Lake Huleh, on the Jordan, the Kishon, and the seacoast of Palestine.

HESED (hē'sĕd, *mercy*), father of one of Solomon's officers (I Kings 4:10).

HESHBON (hĕsh'bŏn, Heb. *heshbôn, reckoning*), an ancient city of the Moabites lying nearly 20 miles E of the Jordan. Sihon, king of the Amorites in the days of Moses took this and the surrounding country from the Moabites, and Israel in turn took it from Sihon (Num. 21:21-31). Sihon's territory, of which Heshbon was the capital, reached northward from the Arnon to the Jabbok, at the strong border of the Ammonites. The tribe of Reuben asked Moses for this land as it was suitable for cattle, and Moses granted their request; so, three hundred years later

A view of the Heshbon (Hesban) area, east of the Jordan, with the city of Sihon toward the upper right. © MPS

(1260 B.C.) when the Ammonites made war against Israel, Jephthah taunted them (Judg. 11: 12-28) with the fact that their god Chemosh was not able to stand against Israel for all those centuries. Heshbon and its suburbs were given to the Levites (I Chron. 6:81). Isaiah's prophecy of doom upon Moab (Isa. 15:4; 16:8,9), describes the normal fertility of the land around Heshbon, and the fact that it had gotten back into the hands of Moab before Isaiah's time; and when Jeremiah, a century later pronounced his dooms, Heshbon was still standing, though to be judged of Jehovah (Jer. 48:2-35; 49:3). The city still stands, but it is a ruin. It is known as Hesbân.

HESHMON (hĕsh'mŏn), a town on the S boundary of Judah (Josh. 15:27).

HETH (hĕth, Heb. *hēth*), great-grandson of Noah through Ham and Canaan (Gen. 10:15) and progenitor of the great Hittite people. They are sometimes called "sons of Heth" (Gen. 23:3), "daughters of Heth" (Gen. 27:46), but generally "Hittites" i.e. "terrible." For many centuries their records, except as recorded in the Bible, were lost; but now they are well known to archaeologists and are reckoned with the Babylonians and the Egyptians as one of the great peoples of the time. See HITTITES.

HETHLON (hĕth'lŏn, Heb. *hethlôn*), a place NE of Tripoli, Syria and just N of Mt. Lebanon from which one passes into the great plain of Coelo-Syria to the entrance of Hamath (Ezek. 47:15; 48:1); mentioned as the beginning of the northern boundary of restored Israel. The exact location is unknown today.

HEXATEUCH (hĕk'sà-tūk), "the six-volumed book," a term invented to include the book of Joshua with the Pentateuch in a literary unit, on the assumption that its component parts were combined by a common editor.

HEZEKI (hĕz'ē-kī, Heb. *hizkî*), a Benjamite mentioned only in I Chronicles 8:17. ASV Hizki.

HEZEKIAH (hĕz'ē-kī'à. Heb. *hizqîyâh, Jehovah has strengthened*), king of Judah for 29 years, from c. 724 to 695 B.C. His story is told in II Kings 18-20, II Chronicles 29-32, and Isaiah 36-39. He lived in one of the great periods of human history. The first Olympiad from which the Greeks dated their history occurred in 776 B.C.; Rome was reputed to have been founded in 753 B.C. Assyria, though approaching its end, was still a mighty power; and Egypt, though weak, was still strong enough to oppose Assyria. Judah's position, on the main road between Egypt and Assyria, was a very precarious one. Hezekiah's grandfather Jotham reigned at Jerusalem (755-739 B.C.) when Hezekiah was a child, and though he was in some ways a good king, he allowed the people to sacrifice and burn incense in the high places. Because of Judah's growing apostasy, Jehovah permitted the Syrians and the Northern Kingdom to trouble Jerusalem. In Hezekiah's youth and early manhood, his weak and wicked father Ahaz was king. He went so far as to follow the abominable rites of the Moabites by burning children in the fire (II Chron. 28:3), and this in spite of the warnings of the Prophets Hosea, Micah, and Isaiah. It was at this time when Israel and Syria were threatening that God gave through Isaiah the famous "virgin-birth" prophecy (Isa. 7:14). For a while Hezekiah was associated in the government with his father, but because of his father's incapacitation he was made active ruler. He began his reign, at the age of 25, in troublous and threatening times. Some counselled with Egypt against Assyria; others

favored surrender to Assyria to save themselves from Egypt. Isaiah warned against trusting in foreign alliances. One of the first acts of Hezekiah was the cleansing and reopening of the temple, which his father had left closed and desecrated. After this was accomplished, the Passover feast was celebrated (II Chron. 30). The idolatrous altars and high places were destroyed.

From the fourth to the sixth year of Hezekiah's reign the Northern Kingdom was in trouble. Sargon finally destroyed Samaria and deported the people to Assyria. According to an Assyrian account, Sennacherib subjugated Judah (c. 715 B.C.). Hezekiah became ill, probably from a carbuncle, and almost died, but God granted him 15 years' extension of life (II Kings 20:1-11). After his recovery, Merodach-Baladan of Babylon sent an embassy ostensibly to congratulate him, but actually to persuade him to join a secret confederacy against the Assyrian power. Hezekiah, flattered by the attention he was being shown by the Babylonian ambassador, displayed to him his wealth, and was soundly rebuked by Isaiah (II Kings 20: 12-19). Assyria compelled Judah to pay heavy tribute, to obtain which Hezekiah even had to strip the plating from doors and pillars of the temple. Shortly after, Assyria decided to destroy Jerusalem, but God saved the city by sending a sudden plague which in one night killed 185,000 Assyrian soldiers. After Hezekiah's death, his son Manasseh succeeded him (II Kings 20:21).   A.B.F.

HEZION (hē'zĭ-ŏn, *vision*), father of Tab-rimmon and grandfather of Benhadad, king of Syria (I Kings 15:18).

HEZIR (hē'zēr, *swine*). 1. A priest in the 17th course of Aaronic priests (I Chron. 24:15).
2. One of the covenanters with Nehemiah in the revival (Neh. 10:20).

HEZRAI (hĕz'rā-ī), a Carmelite, one of David's heroes (II Sam. 23:35; RV has Hezro). In I Chronicles 11:37 both KJV and RV have Hezro.

HEZRO (See Hezrai)

HEZRON (hĕz'rŏn, *enclosure*). 1. A grandson of Judah through Perez (Gen. 46:12, etc.).
2. A son of Reuben (Gen. 46:9).
3. A place on the southern border of Judah (Josh. 15:3). Cf. HAZOR (3) which is the same place.

HIDDAI (hĭd'ā-ī), one of David's heroes (II Sam. 23:30). The same as Hurai of I Chronicles 11:32.

HIDDEKEL (hĭd'ē-kĕl, Heb. *hiddegel*), the Hebrew name of the Tigris river, one of the four rivers of Genesis 2:11-14. It was the eastern boundary of Mesopotamia and of Babylon and its bank seems to have been a resort of Daniel (Dan. 10:4).

HIEL (hī'ĕl, Heb. *hî'ēl*, probably, *God liveth*), a man of Bethel during the reign of Ahab who rebuilt Jericho and thereby brought upon himself and his sons the curse which Joshua had pronounced half a millennium before (I Kings 16:34; cf. Josh. 6:26).

HIERAPOLIS (hī'ēr-ăp'ō-lĭs, Gr. *Hierápolis, sacred city*), a city mentioned only in Colossians 4:13, in the territory of ancient Phrygia but in the NT period a part of the Roman province of Asia. It received its name from the fact that it was the seat of worship of important deities. The location was on the right bank of the Lycus about eight miles above its junction with the Maeander. Tradition connects the Apostle Philip with the church, and Papias, notable disciple of John the beloved, was born there. Great ruins survive.

HIEROGLYPHICS (See Writing)

HIGGAION (hĭ-gā′yŏn, Heb. *higgāyôn*), a musical term occurring in Psalm 9:16, probably referring to the "solemn sound" of harp music that was to be played at that point. In Psalm 92:3 it is rendered "solemn sound."

HIGH PLACES (Heb. *bāmâh, rāmâh, elevation*). It seems to be inherent in human nature to think of God as dwelling in the heights. From earliest times men have tended to choose high places for their worship, whether of God, or of the false gods which men have invented. In Canaan these high places had become the scenes of orgies and human sacrifice connected with the idolatrous worship of these imaginary gods; and so, when Israel entered the Promised Land they were told to be iconoclasts as well as conquerors. "Then ye shall drive out all the inhabitants of the land from before you, and destroy all their figured stones (KJV 'pictures') and destroy all their molten images, and demolish all their high places" (Num. 33:52). These figured stones bore upon themselves crude carvings, sometimes more or less like geometrical figures, or else talismans, or other signs presumably understood by the priests and used to mystify or terrorize the worshipers. Israel partly obeyed but largely failed in this work. In Judges 1:19-35 we read of the failures of eight different tribes to drive out the people of the land, and though "the people served Jehovah all the days of Joshua, and all the days of the elders" who outlived Joshua (Josh. 24:31; Judg. 2:7), they soon relapsed into idolatry, used the high places for the worship of Baalim, and "provoked Jehovah to anger."

Before God would use Gideon to drive out the Midianites (Judg. 6:25) Gideon had to throw down his father's altar to Baal and the image (*Asherah*) which was beside it. Before Solomon built the temple, there was a mixed condition of worship. The tent of meeting (i.e. the tabernacle) with most of its furniture was at the high place at Gibeon, several miles N of Jerusalem, though David had brought the ark to Jerusalem. Solomon went to the high place at Gibeon to offer sacrifice, and there God heard his prayer and granted him surpassing wisdom (II Chron. 1:1-13). Later some godly kings like Hezekiah (II Chron. 31:1) destroyed the high places, while others like Manasseh relapsed and rebuilt them (II Chron. 33:3). After Manasseh had been punished and had repented, he was restored to his throne, and resumed the temple worship, but the people "sacrificed still in the high places, but only unto Jehovah their God"

A view of the "high place" at Gezer, showing standing worship stones. PEF

(II Chron. 33:17). Through Manasseh's early influence, the people had gone so far into apostasy that they could not repent, but through the godliness of Josiah, especially after he had heard the law read (II Kings 22:8-20), the judgment was delayed till after the death of Josiah. His great "housecleaning" is described in II Kings 23:1-25. God's attitude toward the godly kings and toward the wicked ones like Ahab in the north and Ahaz and Manasseh in the south depended largely upon their attitude towards the high places.   A.B.F.

HIGH PRIEST (See Priest)

HILEN (hī′lĕn), a city of Judah assigned to the Levites (I Chron. 6:58); spelled Holon in Joshua 15:51; 21:15.

HILKIAH (hĭl-kī′à, Heb. *hilqîyâh, the portion of Jehovah*), the name of seven persons mostly priests in Israel: 1. The father of Eliakim who was manager of Hezekiah's household (II Kings 18:18).

2. A Merarite Levite (I Chron. 6:45).

3. Another Merarite, door-keeper in David's time (I Chron. 26:11).

4. The high priest in the days of Josiah, king of Judah. It was he who found the book of the Law while cleaning the temple (thought by many to have been the book of Deuteronomy) and sent it to Josiah (II Kings 22,23; II Chron. 34).

5. A priest who returned to Jerusalem with Zerubbabel 536 B.C. (Neh. 12:7).

6. The father of Jeremiah, dwelling at Anathoth (Jer. 1:1).

7. Father of Gemariah (Jer. 29:3), a priest who stood with Ezra at the Bible reading (Neh. 8:4).

HILL COUNTRY (Heb. *giv‘âh, har, ‘ôphel*), a term applied to any region of hills and valleys which could not quite be called mountainous, but in Scripture it generally applies to the higher part of Judaea (Luke 1:39,65) and in the OT to the southern part of Lebanon E of Sidon (Josh. 13:6). In Joshua 11:3, RV speaks of "the hill country" near Jerusalem where KJV has "mountains."

HILLEL (hĭl′ĕl, *he has praised*), the father of Abdon who judged Israel. He was from Pirathon, a hill-village in Ephraim.

HIN (See Weights and Measures)

HIND (See Animals)

HINGE, a contrivance which enables a movable part such as a door or a window to swing in its place, often used figuratively for something of cardinal importance. Ancient heavy doors swung upon "ball and socket" joints. In I Kings 7:50 it means the socket on which the doors turned. In Proverbs 26:14 the word is derived from a verb meaning to twist or to turn in pain or in laziness. Hinges as we know them today were unknown in ancient times.

HINNOM, VALLEY OF (hĭn′ŏm), more properly "the valley of the son of Hinnom," running southward from the Jaffa gate at the W side of Jerusalem, then turning eastward and running S of the city till it joined the valley of the Kidron. It was a part of the boundary between Judah on the S (Josh. 15:8) and Benjamin on the N (Josh. 18:16). No one knows anything of the "son of Hinnom" except that he lived before Joshua's time, and presumably owned the valley. It seems to have been a dumping ground and a place for burning. Here was Topheth (II Kings 23:10) where human sacrifices had been offered to Molech, and so it was later to be called "the valley of slaughter" (Jer. 19:6). The Hebrew name, transliterated into Greek *geenna* (or *gehenna*) becomes the word for "hell," used 11 times by our Lord and once by

Looking westward up the Valley of Hinnom, from the Hill of Offence above Siloam. Mount Zion is on the upper right. © MPS

James (3:6). Our Lord is speaking of the final destination of the wicked; and probably "the lake of fire" (Rev. 19:20; 20:10,14,15; 21:8) is a description of the same terrible place. That the mythological name "Tartarus" was also used is implied in II Peter 2:4, where Peter uses a verb derived from "Tartarus" to mean "to cast down to hell." See Gehenna.   A.B.F.

HIP AND THIGH, used only in Judges 15:8 to denote the thoroughness with which Samson slew the Philistines.

HIRAH (hī′rà), a "friend" of Judah, living at Adullam (Gen. 38:1,12,20) SW of Bethlehem.

HIRAM (hī′răm, Heb. *hîrām,* sometimes also *hûrām* and *hîrôm*). 1. King of Tyre in the reigns of David and of Solomon, with both of whom he was on friendly terms. His father was Abibaal. Hiram is first mentioned in II Samuel 5:11, almost at the beginning of his reign, when he sent messengers to David with cedar-trees, carpenters and masons who built David a house. The wood was floated in rafts down the coast to Joppa, and then brought overland to Jerusalem. Hiram, an admirer of David, after David's death sent an embassy to Solomon (I Kings 5:1), of which Solomon promptly took advantage and arranged that Hiram should send him timber of cedar and fir from Lebanon. It is evident that Tyre had the hegemony of Phoenicia at the time, for the Sidonians (I Kings 5:6) are spoken of as servants of Hiram; and the "stone-squarers" (I Kings 5:18 KJV) were men of Gebal (modern Jebail) N of Beirut.

A century later Sidon seems to have become more powerful, for Ethbaal, who is reckoned by the genealogists as great grandson of Hiram, is called "king of Sidon" (I Kings 16:31). Both Solomon and Hiram were Semites, and were keen businessmen. Solomon not only supplied Hiram with vast quantities of wheat and olive oil annually for food (I Kings 5:11), but he surrendered to Hiram 20 "cities" of Galilee (9:10-13). When Solomon had finished building the temple (seven years) and his own palace (thirteen years), Hiram journeyed to Galilee and was greatly dissatisfied when he surveyed the cities, and he nicknamed them "Cabul," a term of uncertain origin which

The monument of King Hiram at Tyre. © MPS

Josephus (*Ant.* 8:5:3) says means in the Phoenician tongue "not pleasing." Hiram and Solomon built a navy and supplied it with shipmen on the Red Sea. They made expeditions from Ezion-geber at the head of the Gulf of Aqabah southward to Ophir, whence they brought gold (I Kings 9:28). They had also a "navy of Tarshish" on the Mediterranean which brought to them from afar "gold and silver, ivory, apes and peacocks" (I Kings 10: 22). No definite record is found of his death. He had a daughter who became one of Solomon's "seven hundred" (I Kings 11:1,3).

2. A worker in brass whom Solomon brought from Tyre to assist in the building of the temple (I Kings 7:13,14,40-45; II Chron. 2:13,14; 4:11-16). His mother was a woman of the tribe of Dan, who had married first into the tribe of Naphtali, then later a Tyrian man. The expressions "of Huram, my father's" (II Chron. 2:13) and "Huram, his father" (II Chron. 4:16) are of uncertain meaning.

HIRELING, laborer who works for his wages. He was ordinarily to be paid at once: "In his day thou shalt give him his hire" (Deut. 24:15). Cf. the parable of the 11th hour laborers (Matt. 20:1-6); but service might be for a longer time as when Jacob worked seven years for each of his wives and six years for his flocks and herds, all of which were his hire (Gen. 29:15-20,27,28, 30:28-36). A hireling from outside Israel could not partake of the passover (Exod. 12:45).

HITTITES (hĭt'īts, Heb. *hittîm*), as also the Mesopotamians and Egyptians (II Kings 7:6) were one of the three great powers confronting early Israel. Once held to be unreliable, the Biblical portrayals of Hittite dominance were first substantiated by discoveries at Carchemish on the Euphrates in 1871 and then totally vindicated by Hugo Winckler's excavations at Khattusa (Boghaz-koy) in Turkey, 1906-07. Ten thousand tablets from this ancient Hittite capital served to confirm Joshua's description of the entire western Fertile Crescent as "land of the Hittites" (1:4).

The original Hittites, or "Hattians," sprang from Ham, through Canaan's second son Heth (Gen. 10:15, I Chron. 1:13), and became established along the Halys River in what is now central Turkey by the mid-third millennium B.C. The Hittite dress, of heavy coats and turned-up-toed shoes, reflect the rugged cold of this Anatolian plateau. From some time after 2200 B.C. the Hattians were overrun by a vigorous, Indo-European speaking people from the north, who became Heth's ruling class, while adopting the older and often immoral Hittite culture.

Ancient monuments depict the Hittites as a stocky people with promient noses, retreating foreheads, and thick lips. The Hittite strain became widely diffused throughout Palestine, along with that of the Hurrians, whose Aryan rulers had assumed the leadership of upper Mesopotamia at about this same time. Scripture thus regularly lists "Hittites" among the peoples of Canaan (Gen. 15:20, Exod. 3:8,17; even in first place, Deut. 7:1, 20:17). They were "the people of the land" (Gen. 23:7), especially in the central hills (Num. 13:29, Josh. 11:3). At Hebron, in 2029 B.C., Abraham purchased Machpelah from the Hittites (Gen. 23:3-20, 49:29-32, 50:13); 60 years later, Esau married Hittite (or Hurrian-Hivite) wives (26:34, 36:2), to the distress of Rebekah (27:46); with Israel's conquest of Canaan, despite the Mosaic ban (Deut. 20:17) Hittite unions became common (Judg. 3:5-6); and from Solomon to Ezra (I Kings

11:1, Ezra 9:1) such intermarriage continued. Ezekiel thus condemned his people's morals and race, by exclaiming, "Your mother was a Hittite, and your father an Amorite" (16:3,45).

The history of the main body of Turkish Hittites embraces the Old Kingdom (1850-1550 B.C.) and the New Empire (1450-1200), though all Hittite dates are approximate, their hieroglyphic inscriptions furnishing no king-lists with precise regnal years. Pitkhana of Kussara founded a major dynasty W of the Halys River about 1850 B.C. His son Anitta broke a rival coalition, took Khattusa itself, and subdued all Asia Minor. The dating of Anitta's son Tudkhaliya I at about 1750 B.C. renders improbable his proposed equation with Tidal, the opponent of Abraham (Gen. 14). Detailed Hittite history begins with the Syrian raids of Labarna I (1650). His grandson, Mursil I, then succeeded in capturing Aleppo in 1570, and 20 years later sacked Babylon itself. After his assassination, however, traditional Hittite feudalism reasserted itself against weaker successors. During the early 15th century, Egypt swept N to the Euphrates; and, upon Egyptian recession, the conquering Hebrews under Joshua overwhelmed the Palestinian Hittites (1406-1400 B.C.; Josh. 9:1, 11:3).

Meanwhile, Anatolia regained capable sovereigns (cf. Judg. 1:26), who capitalized upon the newly introduced horse-drawn war chariot (I Kings 10:29). Suppiluliuma (1385-1345), greatest of the New Empire monarchs, began his reign by instigating disorders within the nominally Egyptian states of Syro-Palestine (compare the contemporaneous raids of Cushan-rishathaim of Mesopotamia; Judg. 3:8). Eventually Suppiluliuma absorbed Hurrian Mitanni, extending his borders to Lebanon, and brought order to the entire west, securing Israel's 40 years of peace under Othniel (3:11). His son, Mursil II (1340-1310), inherited the most powerful monarchy of his time.

With the rise of the Nineteenth Dynasty in the 1320's, a revived Egypt challenged Hittite supremacy, leaving Moab free to oppress Israel (3:12-14). But after defeating the Hittites on the Orontes, Pharaoh Seti I came to terms with Mursil. The famous treaty of 1315 divided the Near East into spheres of influence: Syria and the north to Heth; Phoenicia, Canaan, and the south to Egypt. The stability that resulted is then reflected in Israel's 80 years of peace following upon the victories of Ehud and Shamgar (3:30-31). Shortly before the death of Muwatal (1310-1295), Rameses II aggressively broke his father's treaty. He survived a close but desperate struggle at Kadesh on the Orontes, against superior Hittite tactics; but years of indecisive fighting followed, and in 1279 Khattusil III (1290-1260) achieved a renewal of the former treaty. Its terms were strictly enforced for the next half-century. Hittite decay ensued. The last significant monarch, Khattusil's grandson Arnuwanda III (1230-1200), suffered famine and civil revolt. Finally, invading "sea-peoples" from the west, part of that general movement in which the Achaeans of Thessaly took Troy and Crete, overwhelmed Anatolia, burned Khattusa, and forever destroyed the Hittite Empire.

Hittite culture, however, survived for another half-millennium in the city-states of Syria to the S. King Toi of Hamath, 1000 B.C., supported David (II Sam. 8:9-10); and Hittite warriors served among his heroes (I Sam. 28:6; II Sam. 11:3, 23:39). Solomon reduced the Palestinian Hittites to bondservice (I Kings 9:20), but one of Ahab's major allies against Assyria at the battle of Qarqar in 853 was Irkhuleni of Hamath. The Hittite stronghold of Carchemish fell to the Assyrians only in 717 B.C. (cf. II Kings 19:13). Independency continually plagued the Hittites and their law codes exhibit mildness toward the feudal aristocracy. This indeed produced a commendable humanitarianism, in restricted death penalties and regard for womankind. But it also legitimatized serious moral laxity. In the service of their depraved mother-goddess of fertility, "Diana of the Ephesians" (Acts 19:24-35), the Hittites became guilty of "a bestiality of which we would gladly think them innocent" and which corrupted God's people Israel (Ezek. 16:44-45). J.B.P.

HIVITES (hī'vī'ts, Heb. *hiwwî*) one of the seven nations of the land of Canaan which Jehovah delivered into the hand of Joshua (Josh. 24:11) "the Amorite, and the Perizzite, and the Canaanite, and the Hittite, and the Girgashite, the Hivite and the Jebusite." They are generally named in conjunction with other tribes of the land. In the original table of the nations (Gen. 10) they are listed with the Canaanite descendants of Ham, Noah's youngest son. All of these differed characteristically from the Japhethites who moved westward to the Mediterranean, northward into northern Europe and eastward toward Persia and India. They differed also from the Semites who later occupied Mesopotamia, Palestine and Arabia. The word "Hivite" probably comes from a word meaning a "village of nomads" and they seem to have been located in diverse places. In the time of Jacob, the city of Shechem, in the middle of Palestine, was ruled by the son of Hamor, the Hivite, the prince of the land (Gen. 34:2). They seem to have been a peaceable commercial people (Gen. 34:21), though with Canaanite morals.

Later in Joshua's time, "the Hivite under Hermon in the land of Mizpah" is mentioned, locating them in the land E of the Sea of Galilee; and in Joshua 9:1,7 the people of Gibeon just a few miles N of Jerusalem are classified as "Hivites." This indefiniteness of locality (or at least variety of locality) plus the derivation of the word would make it seem that the Hivites were not a compact tribe, like the Jebusites of Jerusalem (Josh. 15:63) nor representatives of a great nation, like the Hittites, nor descendants of one person like the Moabites and the Ammonites (Gen. 19:37,38), but villagers moving from place to place as business or politics dictated. The latest reference to them is when Solomon raised a levy from their remnants to do task-work for him (II Chron. 8:7). Some scholars doubt whether they ever had a separate existence. There is a possibility that they were the same as the Horites. A.B.F.

HIZKIAH, HIZKIJAH (hĭz-kī'à, hĭz-kī'jà), found twice in KJV but in each case should be Hezekiah as in ASV. 1. The great-great-grandfather of Zephaniah (Zeph. 1:1) given to show his relationship with king Josiah.
2. One of the covenanters with Nehemiah (Neh. 10:17).

HOBAB (hō'băb, Heb. *hōvāv, beloved*), a person who is named only twice in the Bible. In Numbers 10:29 he is called "the son of Reuel, the Midianite, Moses' father-in-law" which would seem quite clearly to make him a brother of Zipporah (Exod. 18:2) and brother-in-law of Moses. In Judges 4:11 KJV speaks of "Hobab, the father-in-law of Moses" while ASV with more deference to logic reads "Hobab, the brother-in-law of Moses." It is true that the Hebrew word generally refers to one who gives his daughter in marriage, but words of

relationship are used loosely by the Orientals, and the whole story fits together better by making him Moses' brother-in-law. Moses pleaded with Hobab to serve with him as a guide to Israel in the wilderness, which the aged Jethro or Reuel could hardly have done, even if he desired to leave his work as the priest of Midian. Hobab at first refused, but finally consented (Num. 10:29; Judg. 1:16; 4:11).

HOBAH (hō'bà), a place N of Damascus to which Abram pursued the captors of his nephew Lot (Gen. 14:15).

HOD (hŏd, *majesty),* a man of the tribe of Asher (I Chron. 7:37).

HODAIAH (hō-dā'yà), a son of Elioenai, a descendant of the royal line of Judah. (I Chron. 3:24). ASV, RSV, Hodaviah.

HODAVIAH (hō'dà-vī'à). 1. A chief of the half tribe of Manasseh, E of Jordan (I Chron. 5:24).
2. The son of Hasenuah, a Benjamite (I Chron. 9:7).
3. A Levite and founder of the family of the Ben-hodaviah (Ezra 2:40). Also called Hodevah (Neh. 7:43) and Judah (Ezra 3:9).

HODESH (hō'dĕsh), a wife of Shaharaim, a Benjamite (I Chron. 8:9).

HODEVAH (See Hodaviah)

HODIAH (hō-dī'à), according to KJV (I Chron. 4:19), a "wife," but ASV, RSV show that Hodiah was a man who married the sister of Naham, and who was reckoned in the tribe of Judah. See Hodijah.

HODIJAH (hō-dī'jà). 1. A Levite of the time of Ezra and Nehemiah (Neh. 8:7; 9:5; 10:10, 13).
2. A chief of the people under Nehemiah (Neh. 10:18).

HOGLAH (hŏg'là), one of the five daughters of Zelophehad, a Manassite. Their father having no sons, a new law was made, permitting daughters to inherit, provided they did not marry outside the tribe (Num. 26:33; 27:1-11; 36:1-12; Josh. 17:3,4).

HOHAM (hō'hăm), an Amorite king of Hebron, who entered into league with other kings against Joshua; one of the five kings captured in the cave of Makkedah and put to death (Josh. 10:3).

HOLINESS, HOLY, usually translate words derived from a Heb. root *qadash* and Greek *hag-.* The basic meaning of *qadash* is *separateness, withdrawal.* It is first applied to God, and is early associated with ideas of purity and righteousness. Long before the prophetic period the ethical content is plain. Greek *hag-* is an equivalent of *qadash* and its history is similar. Beginning as an attribute of deity the *hag-* family of words developed two stems, one meaning "holy," the other "pure." The use of words of this family in the LXX to translate the *qadash* family resulted in a great development of their ethical sense, which was never clear in classical Greek. What became increasingly evident in the OT is overwhelmingly explicit in the NT: that holiness means the pure, loving nature of God, separate from evil, aggressively seeking to universalize itself; that this character inheres in places, times and institutions intimately associated with worship; and that it is to characterize human beings who have entered into personal relations with God.

The words "holiness, holy" do not occur in Genesis, though implied in the dread which the presence of God inspires (Gen. 28:16,17), but from Exodus 3:5 on, where God reveals His name and nature, holiness is constantly stressed. Only samples of the many Biblical references will be given. God is "glorious in holiness" (Exod. 15:11); He acts with "his holy arm" (Isa. 52:10); His words and promises are holy (Jer. 23:9; Ps. 105:42); His name is holy (Lev. 20:3; I Chron. 29:16); His Spirit is holy (Isa. 63:10; 11; Ps. 51:10, see separate article, HOLY SPIRIT). Places are made holy by God's special presence: His dwelling in heaven (Deut. 26:15); His manifestation on earth (Exod. 3:5; Josh 5:15); the tabernacle (Exod. 40:9); the temple (II Chron. 29:5,7); Jerusalem (Isa. 48:2); Zion (Obad. 17). Anything set apart for sacred uses was holy: the altars and other furniture of the tabernacle (Exod. 30:10,29; 29:37); animal sacrifices (Num. 18:17); food (Lev. 21:22); the tithe (Lev. 27:30); first fruits (Lev. 23:20; 19:24); anything consecrated (Exod. 28:38); the anointing oil and incense (Exod. 30:23-25,34-38). Persons connected with holy places and holy services were holy: priests (Lev. 21:1-6) and their garments (Exod. 28:2,4); Israel as a nation (Jer. 2:3); individually (Deut. 33:3); many things connected with Israel (I Chron. 16:29). Times given to worship were holy (Exod. 16:23; 20:8; 12:16; Isa. 58:13).

In classical Greek *hágios* was first applied to sanctuaries; in Hellenistic times, to gods; then to the Mysteries (of Dionysos, etc.). *Hágios* came into frequent use from Oriental religions in the Hellenistic period, which wide use explains its occurrence in the LXX as the equivalent of *qdsh*. In the NT the holiness of things is less prominent than that of persons. What in Isaiah 6:3 was a personal revelation to the prophet is proclaimed to all from heaven in Revelation 4:8, with power and glory. God is holy and true (Rev. 6:10). Jesus prays, "Holy Father" (John 17:11). I Peter 1:15 repeats the assertion of God's holiness and the exhortation to His people to be holy, of Leviticus 19:2. Jesus' disciples are to pray that the name of God may be treated as holy (Matt. 6:9; Luke 11:2). The holiness of Jesus Christ is specifically stressed. Evil spirits recognized Him as "the holy one of God" who has come to destroy them (Mark 1:24; Luke 4:34). Jesus is holy because of His wondrous birth (Luke 1:35). The Father "hath sanctified" Him, declared Him and made Him holy (John 10:36). He is "holy and true" Rev. 3:7). To the Jerusalem church Jesus is "the holy one" (Acts 3:14), the "holy child Jesus" (Acts 4:27,30), fulfilling the prophecy of Isaiah 42:1-4, quoted in Matthew 12:16-21. In Hebrews 9 Christ is the fulfillment of OT priesthood and sacrifice, in both of which capacities He must be holy (sanctified, Heb. 2:11). Holiness in connection with the Holy Spirit is treated in a separate article, HOLY SPIRIT.

The holiness of the Church is developed in the NT. As in the OT, Jerusalem is holy (Matt. 4:5; 27:53; Rev. 11:2), so is the temple (Matt. 24:15; Acts 6:13) and the new temple, the church; collectively (Eph. 2:21,22) and individually (I Cor. 3:16,17). Stephen refers to Mt. Sinai as "holy ground" (Acts 7:33) and Peter to the Mount of Transfiguration as "the Holy Mount (II Peter 1:18). The Scriptures are holy (Rom. 1:2; II Tim. 3:15). The law is holy (Rom. 7:12). Since the earthly holy place, priests, cult apparatus, sacrifices and services were holy, much more are the heavenly (Heb. 8:5). The Church is a holy nation (I Pet. 2:9; 1:16). The argument of Romans 11:11-32 rests the holiness of Gentile Christians on their growing out of the root (11:16) of Jesse (Rom. 15:12). Christ died for the Church in order to make it holy (Eph. 5:26; I Cor. 1:2, sanctified in Christ Jesus I Cor. 6:11). Gentile Christians are now "no more strangers and foreigners, but fellow-citizens with the Jewish Christian "saints" (holy ones, Eph. 2:19). Thus the Church as a whole, the local churches, and individual Christians, are holy, "called . . . saints" (Rom. 1:7; I Cor. 1:2; II Cor. 1:1; Eph. 1:1; Phil 1:1; Col. 1:2; "saints" translating *hágioi*, holy. The life of the individual Christian is to be a living, holy sacrifice (Rom. 12:1), not only through death (Phil. 2:17), but through life itself (Phil. 1:21-26). In the OT the sacrifice was a *thing*, separate from the offerer: in the NT it is the *offerer himself*. Holiness is equated with purity (Matt. 5:8; I Tim. 1:5; II Tim. 2:22; Tit. 1:15; Jas. 1:27; Matt. 23:26), a purity which in Acts 18;6; 20:26 is innocence . The means of purification is the truth of the Word of God (John 17:17). The "holy kiss," in the early churches, was a seal of holy fellowship (I Cor. 16:20; II Cor. 13:12; I Thess. 5:26). Holiness is prominent in the book of Revelation from 3:7 to 22:11.

Of other Hebrew and Greek words translated "holy," two must be mentioned. Heb. *hāsîdh* and its Greek equivalent *hósios* mean "good, kind, pious." *Hāsîdh* has many translations, *hósios* a few. Translated "holy," *hāsîdh* occurs in Deuteronomy 33:8; Psalms 16:10; 86:2; 89:19; 145:17. *Hósios* occurs in Acts 2:27; 13:35, quoting Psalm 16:10. It or derivatives are found in Luke 1:75; Ephesians 4:24; I Timothy 2:8; Titus 1:8; Hebrews 7:26; Revelation 15:4.

Summary: the idea of holiness originates in the revealed character of God, and is communicated to things, places, times and persons engaged in His service. Its ethical nature grows clearer as revelation unfolds, until the holiness of God the Father, Son and Holy Spirit, of the Church as a body, and of individual members of that body, fills the NT horizon. Holiness is interwoven with righteousness and purity. To seek holiness apart from the other qualities of a Christlike life, is to wander from the way of holiness itself.   E.R.

HOLON (hō'lŏn). 1. A city in the hill country of Judah (Josh. 15:51) assigned to the Levites (called Hilen [hī'lĕn], in I Chron. 6:58); Khirbet 'Alin.

2. A town probably in the plain of Moab near Medeba (Jer. 48:21), site unknown.

HOLY OF HOLIES (See Tabernacle)

HOLY GHOST (See Holy Spirit)

HOLY PLACE (See Tabernacle)

HOLY SPIRIT (Gr. *pneúma hágion*, in KJV of NT, Holy Ghost), the Third Person of the Triune Godhead (Matt. 28:19; II Cor. 13:14).

That the Holy Spirit is a power, an influence, is plain from Acts 1:8; that He is a Person, the NT makes clear in detail: He dwells with us (John 14:17), teaches and brings to remembrance (14:26), bears witness (15:26), convinces of sin (16:8), guides, speaks, declares (16:13,15), inspires the Scriptures and speaks through them Acts 1:16; II Pet. 1:21), spoke to Philip (Acts 8:29), calls ministers (13:2), sends out workers (13:4), forbids certain actions (16:6,7), intercedes (Rom. 8:26), etc. He has the attributes of personality: will (I Cor. 12:11), mind (Rom. 8:27), thought, knowledge, words (I Cor. 2:10-13), love (Rom. 15:30). The Holy Spirit can be treated as a Person: lied to and tempted (Acts 5:3,4,9), resisted (Acts 7:51), grieved (Eph. 4;30), outraged (Heb. 10:29 RSV), blasphemed against (Matt. 12:31). The Holy Spirit is God; equated with the Father and the Son (Matt. 28:19; II Cor. 13:14). Jesus speaks of Him as of His other self (John 14:16,17) whose presence with the disciples will be of greater advantage than His own (John 16:7). To have the Spirit of God is to have Christ (Rom. 8:9-12). God is Spirit (John 4:24) in essential nature, and sends His Holy Spirit to live and work in men (John 14:26; 16:7).

The Heb. and Greek words translated "Spirit" are *rûach* and *pneûma* respectively, both meaning literally "wind, breath." Both came to be used for the unseen reality of living beings, especially God and man. (For the meaning of "Holy" see article HOLINESS). Therefore breath and wind are symbols of the Holy Spirit (Gen. 2:7; Job 32:8; 33:4; Ezek. 37:9,10; John 20:22). Other symbols are: the dove (Matt. 3:16; Mark 1:10; Luke 3:22; John 1:32) oil (Luke 4:18; Acts 10:38; I John 2:20); fire for purification (Matt. 3:11; Luke 3:16; Acts 2:3,4); living water (John 7: 37-39; 4:14; Isa. 44:3); earnest or guarantee of all that God has in store for us (II Cor. 1:22; Eph. 1:13,14). In the OT the Spirit of God appears from the beginning (Gen. 1:2); "My Spirit" (Gen. 6:3); and the Spirit of God comes upon certain men for special purposes (e.g., Bezaleel, Exod. 31:3; some Judges, Judg. 3:10; 6:34; 11:29; David, I Sam. 16:13). This was temporary (e.g., Saul, I Sam. 10:10; 16:14); so David, repentant, prayed, "Take not the Holy Spirit from me" (Ps. 51:11). The Spirit of God is upon the Messiah (Isa. 11:2; 42:1; 61:1). God acts by His Spirit (Zech. 4:6).

In the Gospels as in the OT, the Holy Spirit comes upon certain persons for special reasons: John the Baptist and his parents (Luke 1:15,41, 67); Simeon (Luke 2:25-27); Jesus as a man (Matt. 1:18,20; 3:16; 4:1; Mark 1:8,10; Luke 1:35; 3:16,22; 4:1,14,18; John 1:32,33). Jesus promises the Holy Spirit in a new way to believers in Him (John 7:37-39, cf. 4:10-15); also as "the promise of the Father" in Luke 24:49; in detail, Acts 1:1-8. Jesus taught the nature and work of the Holy Spirit in John 14:16; 26; 15:26; 16:7-15). This work is: to dwell in the disciples as Comforter, Counselor, Advocate (Greek *paráklētos*); to teach all things; to recall what Jesus had said; to testify of Jesus; to reprove the world of sin, righteousness and judgment; to guide the disciples into all truth; not to speak of Himself, but only what He hears; to show the disciples things to come; to glorify Jesus by showing the things of Jesus to them. The evening of the Resurrection, Jesus "breathed on" the disciples (Thomas being absent) and "saith unto them, Receive ye the Holy Ghost" (John 20:22). This was not the complete enduement of the Holy Spirit which Jesus taught and promised, and which came to pass at Pentecost; but it was provisional, and enabled the disciples to persevere in prayer until the promised day.

At Pentecost a new phase of the revelation of God to men began (Acts 2); as new as that when the Word became flesh in the birth of Jesus. With the rushing of a mighty wind and the appearing of cloven tongues like fire, the disciples were all filled with the Holy Spirit, and spoke in foreign languages (listed in 2:9-11). The excitement drew a crowd of visitors to the feast, to whom Peter explained that the prophecy of Joel 2:28-32 was being fulfilled, in accordance with the salvation which Jesus of Nazareth had wrought in dying on the cross. Three thousand souls were added by baptism to the 120 disciples, and thus began the fellowship of apostolic teaching, of breaking of

bread and of prayer, which is the Church. When the first crisis which threatened the extinction of the early church was passed, again "they were all filled with the Holy Ghost" (Acts 4:31) binding them more closely together. When the first Gentiles were converted, the Holy Spirit was poured out on them and they spoke in tongues (Acts 10:44-48); likewise when Paul met a group of John the Baptist's disciples (Acts 19:1-7).

The NT is full of the work of the Holy Spirit in the lives of believers (Rom. 8:1-27): e.g., His gifts (I Cor. 12-14); that our "body is the temple of the Holy Ghost" (I Cor. 6:19); "the fruit of the Spirit" (Gal. 5:22,23). Being "filled with the Spirit" (Eph. 5:18) we shall experience Christ living within us (Rom. 8:9,10). As the heavenly Father is God, and His Son Jesus Christ is God, so the Holy Spirit is God. The Holy Spirit as well as the Son was active in creation; on occasion acts in His own Person in OT times; more intensively in the gospels; and in Acts and the epistles becomes the resident divine Agent in the Church and in its members. Teaching concerning the Holy Spirit has been both neglected and distorted, but the subject deserves careful attention as one reads the NT.   E.R.

HOMAM (hō'măm), son of Lotan and grandson of Seir (I Chron. 1:39). Also called Hemam (Gen. 36:22 KJV; Heman in ASV, RSV).

HOMER (See Weights and Measures)

HONEY (Heb. *devash*, Gr. *méli, honey*), at first rare (Gen. 43:11), found wild in clefts of the rocks (Deut. 32:13; Ps. 81:16), in the comb on the ground (I Sam. 14:25-43). Job 20:17 speaks of brooks of honey and butter, indicating abundance due to domestication of bees. Canaan is "a land flowing with milk and honey (from Exod. 3:8 to Ezek. 20:15). Assyria is so referred to (II Kings 18:32). Honey is a product of Palestine (Jer. 41:8; Ezek. 27:17). Samson ate wild honey found in the carcass of a lion (Judg. 14:8-18). Honey became a common food (II Sam. 17:29) even in times of scarcity (Isa. 7:15,22). No honey was put in a sacrifice but it was a first fruits offering (Lev. 2:11; II Chron. 31:5). Strained honey was kept in a jar or cruse (I Kings 14:3). Honey as food is recognized and recommended, but in moderation (Ezek. 16:13,19; Prov. 24:13; 25:16,27; 27:7). Honey is a standard of comparison for pleasant things, good or bad (S. of Sol. 4:11; 5:1; Prov. 16:24; 5:3; Ezek. 3:3; Rev. 10:9). John the Baptist ate honey (Matt. 3:4; Mark 1:6). The risen Jesus ate a honeycomb Luke 24:42 KJV. ASV, RSV omit "honeycomb").

HOOD (See Dress: Headdress)

HOOK, the translation of several Heb. words: 1. *'aghmôn, reed*, Job 41:2a, where a rope of rushes is meant (ASV, RSV). 2. *Wāw*, hook or *peg* of gold or silver, used to support the hangings of the tabernacle (Exod. 26:32,37; 27:10,17; 36:36,38; 38:10-19,28). 3. *Hah, hook, ring, fetter* (II Kings 19:28; Isa. 37:29; Ezek. 29:4; 38:4). 4. *Hakkâh, angle, hook, fishhook* (Job 41:1a RSV). 5. *Tsinnâh, thorn, hook* (Amos 4:2a). 6. *Shephattayîm, hook-shaped pegs, double hooks* (Ezek. 40:43). 7 *Fleshhook, mazlēgh,* probably a *small pitchfork with two or three tines,* (Exod. 27:3; RSV forks). 8. Pruning hook, *mazemērôth*, a sickle-shaped knife for pruning vines. 9. *Hôah, hook* (Job 41:2b RSV; KJV has "thorn," which is probably right). 10. The Greek word, occurring only once in the NT, is *ágkistron, fishing hook* (Matt. 17:27), a word as old as Homer (Odyssey 4:369).

HOOPOE (See Birds)

HOPE, with faith and love, is a gift of the Holy Spirit which abides, an essential characteristic of the Christian when prophecies, tongues and knowledge pass away (I Cor. 13:8,13). The Greek noun *elpis* and related verbs are translated "hope," but KJV has "faith" in Hebrews 10:23 and "trusted" in Ephesians 1:12. The Biblical concept of hope is not mere expectation and desire, as in Greek literature, but includes trust, confidence, refuge in God, the God of hope (Rom. 15:13). Christ in you is the hope of glory (Col. 1:27). All creation hopes for redemption (Rom. 8:19-25 RSV). Christ Jesus is our hope (I Tim. 1:1 RSV). Hope of eternal life is bound up with "that blessed hope, and the glorious appearing of . . . Jesus Christ" (Tit. 1:2; 2:13), which motivates purity (I John 3:3). Hope is linked with faith (Heb. 11:1). It depends on the resurrection of Christ (I Cor. 15:19). Hope is little spoken of in the Gospels, while Jesus is on earth, and in Revelation, where He is again present in His own person. The Acts and Epistles are full of this Christ-centered hope. The hope which animated Paul (Acts 26:6-8) was "the hope of Israel" (Acts 28: 20). In the OT "hope" translates a variety of Heb. words in KJV, which mean "confidence, trust, safety," etc., and are so translated in ASV, RSV. NT hope has deep roots in the OT.

E.R.

HOPHNI (hŏf'nī, Heb. *hophnî*), a son of Eli, the high priest and judge who proved unworthy of his sacred offices (I Sam. 1:3; 2:34; 4:4,17). Hophni is always associated with his brother Phinehas. The two were partners in evil practices and brought a curse upon their heads (I Sam. 2:34; 3:14). Both were slain at the battle of Aphek and this, coupled with the loss of the Ark, caused the death of Eli (I Sam. 4:17,18). Both sons disgraced their priestly office, in claiming and appropriating more than their share of the sacrifices (I Sam. 2:13-17), and in their immoral actions in the tabernacle (I Sam. 2:22; Amos 2:6-8).

HOR (hôr, Heb. *hōr, mountain*). 1. A conspicuous mountain, probably a day's march N or NE of Kadesh-barnea, where Aaron died and was buried (Num. 20:22-29; 33:37-41; Deut. 32:50), perhaps Jebel Maderah, a prominent, steep-sided white chalk hill. Hence Israel set out to march S toward the Red Sea (Num. 31:4), which fact renders possible the earlier identification with Jebel Neby Hārūn, SE of Kadesh-barnea, although this site is well within the borders of Edom in Mt. Seir, with which kingdom Israel had not yet made contact. 2. A mountain on the N border of the land given to the Israelites, between the Great Sea (Mediterranean) and the entrance of Hamath (Num. 34:7,8), variously identified, with no certainty as yet possible.

HORAM (hō'răm), a king of Gezer, defeated and slain by Joshua (Josh. 10:33).

HOREB (hō'rĕb, *drought, desert*), the mountain where Moses received his commission (Exod. 3:1); where he brought water out of the rock (Exod. 17:6); where the people stripped off their ornaments in token of repentance (Exod. 33:6); eleven days' journey from Kadesh-barnea (Deut. 1:2); mentioned also in Deuteronomy 1:6, 19; 4:10,15; 5:2; 9:8; 18:16; I Kings 8:9; II Chronicles 5:10; Psalm 106:19; Malachi 4:4, in connection with the journeys of Israel, the giving of the law, and events of the year in which the Israelites stayed nearby. Elijah fled hither (I Kings 19:8). It is geographically indistinguishable from Sinai.

HOREM (hō'rĕm, *consecrated)*, a fortified city in Naphtali, near Iron (Josh 19:38), unidentified.

HOR-HAGIDGAD (hôr'hă-gĭd'găd, *hollow* or *cavern of Gilgad*), an Israelite camp in the wilderness, between Bene-jaakan and Jotbathah (Num. 33:32, 33), called Gudgodah in Deuteronomy 10:7. See GUDGODAH.

HORI (hō'rī, *cave-dweller*). 1. A son of Seir, a Horite, and founder of the Horites (Gen. 36:22, 29,30; I Chron. 1:39).

2. A Simeonite whose son Shaphat was one of the spies (Num. 13:5).

HORIM (See Horites)

HORITE, HORIM (hō'rīt, hō'rĭm), a people found in Mount Seir as early as the time of Abraham, and conquered by Chedorlaomer and his allies (Gen. 14:6); the early inhabitants, before the Edomites dispossessed them and intermarried with them (Gen. 36:20-30; Deut. 2:12,22). Esau married the daughter of one of their chieftains, also called a Hivite (Gen. 36:2). The Hivites are thought to be identical with, or else confused with, the Horites (Gen. 34:2; Josh. 9:7), in which case the Horites lived as far N as Gibeon and Shechem in the time of Jacob's sons, and till the conquest under Joshua. The LXX makes this identification. The Horites are now commonly thought to be Hurrians, from the highlands of Media, who before the middle of the second millennium B.C. overspread the region from Media to the Mediterranean, forming, or being merged in, the kingdom of Mitanni, subsequently destroyed by the Hittites . The Horites of Palestine then would be enclaves of this once-conquering race left behind when their empire receded before the Hittite advance. The Hurrian nobles appear to have been Aryans, the peasants non-Aryans, whether Semites or other, perhaps Armenoids, is not settled. The Hurrian language is in process of being deciphered, so that further investigation should clear up a picture which is at present confused.

E.R.

Mount Hor (Jebal Harun), near Petra. On the summit is the tomb of Aaron. © MPS

HORMAH (hôr'mà, Heb. *hormâh, a devoted place*), perhaps Tell es-Sheriah, N of the road and about midway between Gaza and Beer-sheba. Here the disobedient Israelites were defeated by Amalekites and Canaanites (Num. 14:45; Deut. 1:44). In war with the king of Arad the place was taken by the Israelites, and given the name Hormah, meaning "devoted," because it was devoted to destruction (Num. 21:1-3). In the list of kings conquered by Joshua it appears with Arad (Josh. 12:14). Hormah was originally given to Judah (Josh. 15:30), but shortly after allotted to Simeon (Josh. 19:4), because the portion of the tribe of Judah was too large for them. Judges 1:17 relates that it was Judah and Simeon who subdued Zephath and renamed it Hormah. David sent part of the spoil of Ziklag to Hormah, as one of the cities of Judah (I Sam. 30:26-30), but Hormah was reckoned among the cities of Simeon "until the reign of David" (I Chron. 4:30).

HORN (Heb. and Aram. *qeren*, Gr. *kéras, an animal horn*). *Inkhorn* (Ezek. 9:2,3,11) is Heb. *qeseth*, translated "writing case" in RSV. In Joshua 6, Heb. *yôvēl*, from a root meaning "ram," a word which has puzzled interpreters. In the context here and elsewhere it appears to refer to the ram's horns which were blown on solemn occasions, and whose use gave rise to the term "Jubilee" for the 50th year of release, "the year of the ram's (horn), *Qeren* referred to the horn on the animal (Gen. 22:13); used as a musical instrument (Josh. 6:5; I Chron. 25:5, but RSV has "to exalt him"); or as a vessel to hold liquids (I Sam. 16:1,13; I Kings 1:39). Tusks are meant in Ezekiel 27:15, and so RSV).

The "horns of the altar" were of one piece with the frame of the altar of burnt offering, made of acacia wood overlaid with bronze (Exod. 27:2; cf. Ezek. 43:15); likewise the altar of incense (Exod. 30:2; 37:26; cf. Rev. 9:13), but overlaid with gold. Blood of sacrificial animals was on certain occasions put on the horns of both altars (Exod. 30:10; Lev. 4:7,18,25,30,34; 16:18; cf. Ezek. 43:20). To cut off its horns rendered an altar useless for religious purposes (Amos 3:14). A person seeking sanctuary might catch hold of the horns of the altar in the temple, but this did not save Adonijah (I Kings 1:50; 51; 2:28-34). Jeremiah felt that the sin of Judah was engraved on the horns of their altars (Jer. 17:1). The purpose of altar horns is in doubt. "Bind the sacrifice with cords, even unto the horns of the altar" (Ps. 118:27) is not thought to reflect the normal practice, and RSV translates "Bind the festal procession with branches, up to the horns of the altar." Horns represent aggressive force (Dan. 8:7 literally; I Kings 22:11; II Chron. 18:10 symbolically; Deut. 33:17; Ps. 22:21; 92:10; Zech. 1:18-21; Luke 1:69, etc., figuratively). Horns in Habakkuk 3:4 are translated "rays" in ASV, RSV, because of the context (light). Multiple horns on one animal denote successive nations or rulers (Dan. 7:7-24; 8:3-22; Rev. 13:1; 17:3-16), "7" with "horns" (Rev. 5:6; 12:3) indicates perfection of power, good or evil. The beast with two horns like a lamb, which spoke like a dragon (Rev. 13:11) suggests outward lamblikeness and inward wickedness.   E.R.

HORNET (See Insects)

HORONAIM (hôr-ŏ-nā'ĭm, *two hollows, caves* or *ravines*), a place in Moab, location uncertain (Isa. 15:5; Jer. 48:3,5,34).

HORONITE (hôr'ō-nīt), a designation of Sanballat (Neh. 2:10,19; 13:28), probably indicating Moabite origin (from Beth-horon or Horonaim).

HORSE (See Animals)

HORSE GATE, one of the gates of Jerusalem, between the Water Gate and the Sheep Gate; probably near the SE corner of the city (Neh. 3:28-32; Jer. 31:38-40). Here Athaliah was killed by order of Jehoiada the priest (II Kings 11:16; II Chron. 23:15).

HORSE LEECH (Heb. *'ălûqâh*), a carnivorous or bloodsucking worm which clings to the flesh. There is only one reference to it in the Bible (Prov. 30:15). The RVm substitutes *vampire*, a ghoul believed to haunt graves and suck human blood.

HOSAH (hō'sà, Heb. *hōsâh, refuge*). 1. A town on the N border of Asher, near Tyre; site uncertain (Josh. 19:29).

2. A Levite porter selected by David to be one of the first doorkeepers to the ark after its return (I Chron. 16:38; 26:10,11,16).

HOSANNA (hō-zăn'à, Heb. *hôsa'-nā'*, Gr. *hosanná, save now*), originally a prayer, "Save, now, pray" (Ps. 118:25), which had lost its primary meaning and became an exclamation of praise (Matt. 21:9,15; Mark 11:9,10; John 12:13). That it is transliterated instead of translated in three of the Gospels (Luke omits it) is evidence of the change of meaning. Not that the Heb. word no longer had any connection with salvation: the context, which is a reminiscence of Psalm 118:25,26, if not a direct quotation from or allusion to it, shows that in its application to God the Father and to Jesus, Hosanna was concerned with the Messianic salvation.

HOSEA (Heb. *hôshēa'*, Gr. *Oseé, salvation*). Of all the prophetic material contained in the Old Testament, the writings of Hosea were the only ones to emerge from the northern kingdom of Israel. This notable eighth century B.C. prophet lived during a period of great national anxiety. He was born during the reign of Jeroboam II (c. 786-746 B.C.), the last great king of Israel, and according to the superscription of his book (1:1) he exercised his prophetic ministry in Israel when Uzziah (c. 783-743 B.C.), Jotham (c. 742-735 B.C.), Ahaz (c. 735-715 B.C.) and Hezekiah (c. 715-686 B.C.) reigned in Judah. While Hosea made no mention of the events referred to in Isaiah 7:1 and II Kings 16:5, he certainly experienced the raids of the Assyrian ruler Tiglath-pileser III on Galilee and Transjordan in 733 B.C.

The time of Hosea was marked by great material prosperity. Under Jeroboam II the northern kingdom experienced a degree of economic and commercial development unknown since the early days of the united kingdom. The development of city life attracted many people from the agricultural pursuits which had formed the basis of the Israelite economy, and this presented serious problems at a later time. Characteristic of this period was the rise of successful middle-class businessmen, which was offset by the appearance of an urban proletariat. The latter came into being because of the wanton demands made by the luxury-loving upper classes upon the increasingly impoverished peasants and smallholders. As the latter succumbed to economic pressure they were compelled to abandon their property and seek whatever employment was available in urban centers. Thus there resulted an ominous social gap between the upper and lower classes, which was a serious portent for the future of the national economy.

While there is no reference to the occupation of

Beeri, father of Hosea, he may well have been a middle-class merchant, perhaps a baker. Hosea himself was an educated person, and probably hailed from a town in Ephraim or Manasseh. A man of profound spiritual vision, he was gifted with intellectual qualities which enabled him to comprehend the significance of those unhappy events which marked his domestic life and interpret them as a timely reminder of Divine love towards a wayward, sinful Israel.

Ever since the days of Joshua the religious life of the Israelites had been dominated by the influence of corrupt Canaanite worship. Archaeological discoveries in northern Syria have uncovered a great deal of information about the religion of the Canaanites, who had occupied Palestine from an early period (Gen. 12:6). This seductive worship had already gained a firm foothold in Israelite religious life before the Judges period, and by the time of Amos and Hosea Canaanite cult-worship had become the religion of the masses.

The deities chiefly venerated were the fertility god Baal (from a word meaning "lord," "master" or "husband") and his consort Anat (sometimes known as Asherah or Ashtoreth), a savage, sensual female. Both deities were often worshiped under the form of bulls and cows, so that when Jeroboam I set up two golden calves, one at Dan and the other at Bethel (I Kings 12:28), he was encouraging the people to indulge in the fertility religion of Canaan.

The cultic rites were celebrated several times each year, and were marked by drunkenness, ritual prostitution, acts of violence and indulgence in pagan forms of worship at the shrines. The widespread prevalence of cultic prostitution is evident from the fact that in Jeremiah's day, a century after the time of Hosea, prostitution flourished in the temple precincts (II Kings 23:7).

Hosea saw that this form of worship was the exact opposite of what God desired of His people. The emphasis of the Sinaitic covenant was upon the exclusive worship of Jehovah by a nation holy unto the Lord. However, the religious life of the covenant people had degenerated to the point of becoming identified with the shameless immoral worship of the pagan Canaanite deities. The emphasis upon unbridled sexual activity coupled with excessive indulgence in alcohol was sapping the vitality not only of the Canaanites but also of Israel. All this, carried out against a background of magic and pagan mythology, was vastly removed from the purity of worship contemplated in the Sinai covenant.

It was Hosea's primary duty to recall wayward Israel to its obligations under the agreement made at Sinai. On that occasion Israel had voluntarily made a pact with God which involved surrender, loyalty and obedience. As a result Israel had become God's son (11:1; cf. Exod. 4:22) by adoption and Divine grace. Of necessity the initiative had come from God. But Hosea saw that it was important to emphasize the free co-operative acceptance of that relationship by the Israelites. Hence he stressed that Israel was really God's bride (2:7,16,19) and employed the marriage metaphor to demonstrate the voluntary association of the Bride with her Divine Lover.

His own marital experience (chapters 1-3) was made a parable for all to see. He was commanded to marry a woman who would subsequently be unfaithful, to have children by her, and to give them symbolic names indicating Divine displeasure with Israel. After Gomer has pursued her paramours she was to be brought back and with patient love readmitted to his home, there to await in penitence and grief the time of restoration to full favor. This was a clear picture of wayward Israel in its relationship with God, and showed the unending faithfulness of the Almighty.

The remainder of the prophecy (chapters 4-14) is an indictment of Israel, delivered at various times from the later days of Jeroboam II up to about 730 B.C. The style of this section is vigorous, though the Hebrew text has suffered in transmission, making for difficulties in translation. The first three chapters have been regarded by some as allegorical, and though the book is generally held to be a unity, critical writers have maintained that interpolations and editorial material occur throughout the work.

ANALYSIS:
1-3 Hosea's unhappy marriage and its results.
4 The priests condone immorality.
5 Israel's sin will be punished unless she repents.
6 Israel's sin is thoroughgoing; her repentance halfhearted.
7 Inner depravity and outward decay.
8 The nearness of judgment.
9 The impending calamity.
10 Israel's guilt and punishment.
11 God pursues Israel with love.
12-14 An exhortation to repentance, with promised restoration. R.K.H.

HOSHAIAH (hō-shā′yà, Heb. *hôsha'yâh, Jehovah has saved*). 1. The man who led half the princes of Judah and walked behind the chorus at the dedication of the wall (Neh. 12:32).
2. The father of Jezaniah (Jer. 42:1) or Azariah (Jer. 43:2), who opposed Jeremiah after the fall of Jerusalem (Jer. 42:1-43:7, see ASV, RSV). If Jaazaniah of II Kings 25:23; Jeremiah 40:8 is the same Jezaniah, this Hoshaiah was a Maacathite.

HOSHAMA (hŏsh′à-mà), a son of Jeconiah or Jehoiachin, captive king of Judah (I Chron. 3:18).

HOSHEA (hō-shē′à, Heb. *hôshēa', salvation*). 1. Joshua's earlier name, changed by Moses (Num. 13:8,16 ASV, RSV; Deut. 32:44 RSV Joshua).
2. The son of Azaziah and prince of Ephraim in David's reign (I Chron. 27:20).
3. A son of Elah; the last king of the northern kingdom (II Kings 15:30; 17:1-6; 18:1-10).
4. A chief ruler under Nehemiah, who with others signed the covenant (Neh. 10:23).

HOSPITALITY (hŏs′pĭ-tăl′ĭ-tē, Gr. *philoxenía, loving strangers*). Although the word occurs but few times in the Bible (I Tim. 3:2; Tit. 1:8; I Pet. 4:9; Heb. 13:2 RSV), the idea appears as early as Abraham (Gen. 14:17-19). One might be entertaining angels unawares (Heb. 13:2) as Abraham did (Gen. 18), graciously inviting chance passers-by, having their feet washed, preparing fresh meat, having his wife bake bread (vss. 1-8), accompanying them when they left (v. 16). Lot entertained the same angels (Gen. 19). The extreme to which protection of a stranger might be carried is illustrated in verses 4-9. Rebekah showed kindness to Abraham's servant, giving him and his camels water, and receiving gold ornaments as a reward (Gen. 24:15-28). Laban seconded her hospitality (vss. 29-31). Jacob fared well in the same household (Gen. 29:1-14). Joseph's hospitality to his brothers had a purpose (Gen. 43:15-34). As a refugee, Moses found welcome with Reuel, after helping his daughters water their flocks (Exod. 2:13-22). Manoah entertained an angel (Judg. 13:2-23), combining hospitality with a burnt offering. The plight of a stranger in a city where only one

"Given to hospitality." © SPF

old man showed the ancient virtue of hospitality is told in Judges 19:11-28. Solomon entertained lavishly (I Kings 4:22); Ahasuerus (Esth. 1:2-8); Vashti (Esth. 1:9); Esther's dinners were private and purposeful (Esth. 5:4-8; 7:1-10). Jezebel fed 850 prophets (I Kings 18:19). The common people continued to entertain (I Sam. 28:21-25; II Kings 4:8-10). Nehemiah regularly entertained 150 (Neh. 5:17). The Law enjoined kindness to strangers (Lev. 19:33,34). Jesus exercised hospitality when He fed 5,000 (Matt. 14:15-21; Mark 6:35-44; Luke 9:12-17; John 6:4-13), 4,000 (Matt. 15:32-38; Mark 8:1-9); after the resurrection (John 21:4-13), and received hospitality from grudging Pharisees (Luke 7:36-50; 14:1-14); in a home at Bethany (Luke 10:38-42; Matt. 21:17; 26:6-13; Mark 14:3-9; John 12:1-8); from Zacchaeus, self-invited (Luke 19:5-10); for the Last Supper (Matt. 26:17-30; Mark 14:12-26; Luke 22:7-39; John 13:1-18:1); at Emmaus (Luke 24:29-32). Jesus taught hospitality in Luke 10:30-37 by the parable of the Good Samaritan, and told His disciples where they would and would not find it (Matt. 10:11-15; Luke 10:5-12). Apostles were entertained and churches begun in homes (Acts 1:13; 9:43; 10:1-48; 12:12; 16:15,34; 18:3,7; 20:8, 20; 21:8,16; 28:30; Rom. 16:5; I Cor. 16:19; Col. 4:15). The letters to Philemon, II and III John exhibit and exhort to hospitality. E.R.

HOST. In the OT: 1. Oftenest Heb. *tsāvā', army* (Gen. 21:22 RSV army); *angels* (Ps. 103:21; Josh. 5:14 RSV army; Dan. 8:11); *heavenly bodies* (Deut. 4:19); *creation* (Gen. 2:1); *God of hosts* (I Sam. 17:45). 2. Heb. *hayil, army* (Exod. 14:4).

3. Twice Heb. *hêl* (II Kings 18:17 ASV, RSV *army*; Obad. 20 RSV *army*). 4. Heb *mahaněh*, oftener translated "camp"; (Exod. 32:27 RSV *army*; Exod. 14:24). The above references are only samples.

Host occurs but four times in the NT: 1. Gr. *stratiá, army* (Luke 2:13 *angels*; Acts 7:42 *heavenly bodies as objects of worship*). 2. Gr. *xénos, guest*, also *host* (Rom. 16:23). 3. Gr. *pandoxeús, one who receives all comers* (Luke 10:35 RSV *innkeeper*).

HOSTAGE (Heb. *ben-ta'ăruvôth, son of pledges*). Jehoash (Joash), King of Israel, took hostages after his victory over Judah, to ensure that King Amaziah would keep the peace.

HOTHAM (hō'thăm), a son of Heber, of the family of Beriah. An Asherite (I Chron. 7:32). See also HOTHAN.

HOTHAN (hō'thăn), an Aroerite, whose two sons Shama and Jehiel were among David's heroes (I Chron. 11:44; ASV, RSV have Hotham).

HOTHIR (hō'thĕr), the 13th son of Henan, David's seer and singer. A Kohathite (I Chron. 25:4,28).

HOUGH (hŏk, Heb. *'āqar, to hamstring an animal*). In Genesis 49:6 ASV has "they hocked an ox," RSV "they hamstrung oxen," for KJV "they digged down a wall." God commanded Joshua to hough the horses of the Canaanites, and Joshua obeyed (Josh. 11:6,9, ASV hock, RSV hamstring). David houghed the horses of Hadadezer, King of Zobah (II Sam. 8:4; I Chron. 18:4, ASV hock, RSV hamstring). A cruel practice, justified only by extreme military necessity.

HOUR, found in the OT only in Daniel, Aramaic *she'ā', a brief time, a moment* (Dan. 3:6,15; 4:33; 5:5, where RSV has "immediately"). In 4:19, ASV has "a while," RSV "a long time." The day was divided into "degrees" (II Kings 20:9-11; Isa. 38:8, ASV, RSV "steps") on the dial of Ahaz. In the NT Greek *hóra, hour*, is often used of a point of time (e.g., Matt. 8:13). The day had 12 hours (John 11:9). The parable of the vineyard (Matt. 20:1-16) names the third, sixth, ninth and eleventh hours. As these are working hours, they obviously begin in the morning, and this is the Palestinian mode of reckoning. So in Acts 2:15, the third hour of the day; Acts 10:3,9, the ninth and sixth hours; Acts 23:23, the third hour of the night. Elapsed time is indicated (Luke 22:39, an hour; Gal. 2:5, RSV, a moment; Acts 5:7, three hours; 19:34, two hours). Once Gr. *árti, now*, is translated "this hour" in KJV (I Cor. 8:7, ASV now, RSV hitherto). In the accounts of the crucifixion, Mark 15:25 tells us that Jesus was crucified "the third hour." The supernatural darkness began at the sixth hour (Matt. 27:45,46; Mark 15:33,34; Luke 23:44-46) and lasted till the ninth hour. John 19:14-16 says that it was about the sixth hour when Pilate brought Jesus out to the people and delivered Him to be crucified. This raises the question whether John used the Palestinian reckoning of time. If so, he must have used "sixth hour" in a very general sense, for strictly the sixth hour was noon. John, writing in Ephesus late in the first century, may well have adopted the then current Roman reckoning which, like ours, numbers from midnight and from noon. John mentions the tenth hour (John 1:39); the sixth (4:6); seventh (4:52). In these cases 10 A.M., 6 P.M. and 7 P.M. respectively would be as appropriate as Palestinian reckoning 4 P.M., noon and 1 P.M. References in Revelation 9:15; 17:12; 18:10,17,19; and 8:1, half an hour, are to the brevity of a period of time. E.R.

HOUSE. In OT oftenest Heb. and Aramaic *bayith,
a dwelling place* (Gen. 12:15); occasionally *a
tent* (Gen. 27:15), usually of solid materials
(Exod. 12:7); or its inhabitants (Gen. 12:17);
or the family or race wherever dwelling (Exod. 2:
1), often translated "household" or "family"; the
tabernacle (Exod. 23:19; 34:26), or temple (I
Kings 5:3-7:1) as the house of God; a temple of
heathen gods (Judg. 16:23-30; I Sam. 31:9,10). It
might be a nomad tent (Gen. 14:13,14, cf. 18:1)
or a building (Gen. 19:2-11) in a city. God contrasts tent with house in II Samuel 7:6. Jacob even
called a place outdoors marked by a stone "the
house of God" (Gen. 28:17-22). In Psalm 83:12
KJV has houses, ASV habitations, RSV pastures,
for Heb. *nā'âh.* In Job 1:3 Heb. *'avudâh,* service,
is translated "household" in KJV and ASV, "servants" in RSV. In NT Greek *oikía, house,* refers to
a building (Matt. 2:11; 7:24-27) except Matthew
12:25; Mark 3:25; John 4:53 (RSV household);
I Corinthians 16:15 (RSV household), where the
inhabitants are meant. In John 14:2 "my Father's
house" is the dwelling of God in heaven. In Luke
2:49 "my Father's house" (ASV, RSV; KJV has
"my Father's business") translates Greek *toîs toû
patrós mou, the (affairs) of my Father.* In II Corinthians 5:1 the first house (RSV tent; Greek "tent-
house") is the physical body, the second house the
resurrection body. The related Greek *oîkos* also
refers to a building (Matt. 9:6,7, RSV home); but
often to its inhabitants (Luke 19:9; Acts 11:14,
RSV household); or to descendants (Matt. 10:6;
Luke 1:33); or the temple (Matt. 12:4).

We read of no shelters in Eden, for probably
none were needed in its mild climate; but Cain built
a city (Gen. 4:17), which could have been a tent-
city or a cave-city, in which probably houses were
built. After the Flood, Nimrod is credited with the
building of several cities (Gen. 10:10-12), where
archaeologists have uncovered the remains of early
houses. In Mesopotamia burned bricks joined with
bitumen were used in place of stone (Gen. 11:3).
Elaborate houses in Ur, of the period when Abraham lived there (Gen. 11:31) have been excavated. He abandoned these luxurious surroundings
to live in a tent (Gen. 12:8) in the land of promise.
Abraham found houses in Egypt (Gen. 12:15) at
least one for the Pharaoh. When Lot separated
from him, at first Lot moved his tent to Sodom
(Gen. 13:12), but later dwelt in a house (Gen.
19:2-11). There were many houses in the numerous cities of Canaan. Finally Lot took refuge in a
cave (Gen. 19:30). The house of Laban may well
have been a tent (Gen. 24:31,32; 29:13,14). When
Joseph arrived in Egypt he found houses there:
Potiphar's (Gen. 39:2-5); that of the captain of the
guard in the prison (Gen. 40:3); Joseph's own
house (Gen. 43:16-34; 44:14); Pharaoh's (Gen.
45:16). The law made provision in advance of the
settlement in Canaan for the cleansing of a stone
house in which there was leprosy (Lev. 14:33-55).
Israelite spies stayed in a house in Jericho (Josh.
2:1) with a roof where stalks of flax were dried
(2:6), with a window (2:15), the house being
built into the city wall (2:15).

After the conquest under Joshua, the Israelites
came increasingly to live in houses in the cities and
towns of Canaan; though some, like the Rechabites
(Jer. 35:7,10) continued to live in tents; and some
took refuge in caves in times of uncertainty (I
Kings 19:9). House walls were often of rough
stone as much as three feet thick; of unburned clay
brick (Job 4:19), sometimes protected with a cas-
ing of stone slabs. In larger buildings the stones

were squared, smoothed and pointed. In the ordinary small house, from the street one entered a
forecourt, with a covered portion on one side.
From the forecourt, doors opened into a living
room, with two small bedchambers beyond. When
the sons married, additions were made as space
permitted, by using the court, complicating the design. Especially on a hilly site, a large boulder
would be built into the corner to support the walls,
the most necessary stone being called the cornerstone (Isa. 28:16). The importance of dedicating
a new house (in earliest times by sacrifices) was
recognized by excusing a man from military duty
until he had done so (Deut. 20:5). The floor might
be leveled rock surface, more often beaten clay.
The rich might have a stone slab floor. Solomon's
temple had a floor of cypress boards (I Kings 6:
15). For doors there were square openings in the
wall with a stone or wood lintel, doorposts (Exod.
12:22,23; I Kings 6:31) and a stone threshold.
Doors might be of textiles, leather or rushes, but
wooden doors fastened by a bar were used early.
Stone sill and head-sockets indicate pivot hinges,
requiring sturdier construction of the door. A key
is referred to as early as Judges 3:25. Locks (S. of
Sol. 5:5) may have been bolts. Hearths were provided, but no chimney, the smoke escaping
through doors and windows. Braziers were also
used (Jer. 36:22 ASV, RSV). Windows were high,
small openings provided with covers like the doors,
for protection, and sometimes had lattices. Roofs
had beams with transverse rafters, covered with
brushwood and overlaid with mud mixed with
chopped straw. They were flat, and were beaten
and rolled. The roof was used for worship (II
Kings 23:12; Jer. 19:13; 32:29; Acts 10:9). Absalom pitched his tent on the roof for publicity (II
Sam. 16:22). Three thousand Philistines used the
roof of their temple as bleachers (Judg. 16:27),
illustrating its strength, while its weakness was
demonstrated when Samson pushed apart the middle pillars on which the structure depended. There

Well-preserved ruins of a house and courtyard at
ancient Ur of the Chaldees, birthplace of Abraham.
© MPS

The housetop was a popular place in Bible days.
© SPF

Important visitors at a modest home in Judea. © MPS

were outside stairs leading to the roof and its
"upper chamber." In some cases the "upper room"
may have been inside the house. In the living room
a raised brick platform ran across one side of the
room (in the Hellenistic period at least), sometimes with ducts to heat it, and on this the family
spread their bedding by night, or sat by day. In

Cross section of an Oriental house, with courtyard
and well. UANT

cold weather the cattle might be admitted to the
lower part of the living room of a poor family.

Palaces were much more elaborate (I Kings 7:
1-12). There is a sharp contrast between the humble homes of the common people and the luxurious
dwellings of kings and the very rich, in Egypt,
Mesopotamia, Palestine under the Hebrew monarchy and after, in Greece and Rome of the Hellenistic period. But a Christian community, many
of whose members were slaves, would be familiar
with the lavish contents of great houses (II Tim.
2:20). While Christians at first continued to worship in temple and synagogue, from the beginning
they met also in private homes (Acts 1:13; 2:2,
46). "The church in their house" is a well-established pattern in Paul's ministry (Rom. 16:5; I
Cor. 16:19; Col. 4:15; Philem. 2). Special buildings for Christian churches do not appear in the
NT. The family had been the religious unit from
the beginning of creation (Gen. 2:8); worship centered in the house, from tent to palace. Tabernacle and temple were "the house of God" and
of the larger family of God, the Chosen People.
So in the NT the house where a Christian family
lived welcomed other Christian brothers and sisters besides its own members to worship together,
and when the temple was destroyed and the synagogue closed to Christians, the church in the home
became the sole refuge of the believer, until special
buildings were erected. Thus to all the human associations of home which permeate a house are
added the sanctifying influences of the spiritual
life.   E.R.

HUKKOK (hŭk'ŏk), a border town of Naphtali, on
the waters of Merom, W of Chinnereth and Capernaum at the N end of the Sea of Galilee (Josh.
19:34). Modern Yāqûq.

HUKOK (See Helkath)

HUL (hŭl), the second son of Aram and grandson
of Shem. A descendant of Noah (Gen. 10:23).
Also called son of Shem (I Chron. 1:17).

HULDAH (hŭl'dà, Heb. *huldâh, weasel*), a prophetess in the reign of Josiah (II Kings 22:14-20; II
Chron. 34:22-28), the wife of Shallum, keeper of
the wardrobe, who dwelt in the Second Quarter
(ASV, RSV) of Jerusalem. When Hilkiah the
priest found the book of the law in the temple,

Josiah sent messengers to Huldah. She attested the genuineness of the book and prophesied ruin because of desertion of the law. Her message, accepted as from God, greatly influenced the reforms carried out by Josiah.

HUMANITY OF CHRIST (See Christ)

HUMILITY (Heb. *'ănāwâh*, Gr. *tapeinophrosúne*), humility and the related substantive ana verb, *humble*, translate several OT Heb. words, and the NT Greek *tapeíno*, family. The meaning shades off in various directions, but the central thought is freedom from pride, lowliness, meekness, modesty, mildness. There is a false humility (Col. 2:18. 23), properly rendered "self-abasement" in RSV. God humbles men to bring them to obedience (Deut. 8:2). To humble ourselves is a condition of God's favor (II Chron. 7:14) and His supreme requirement (Mic. 6:8). God dwells with the humble (Isa. 57:15). Humility is enjoined (Prov. 15: 33; 18:12; 22:4). To the Greeks humility was weak and despicable, but Jesus made it the cornerstone of character (Matt. 5:3,5; 18:4; 23:12; Luke 14: 11; 18:14). Jesus by His humility drew men to Himself (Matt. 11:28-30; John 13:1-20; Rev. 3: 20). Paul emphasized the humility of Jesus (Phil. 2:1-11; II Cor. 8:9); commanded us to be humble toward one another (Phil. 2:3,4; Rom. 12:10; I Cor. 13:4-6) and spoke of himself as an example (Acts 20:19). Peter exhorted to humility toward the brethren and toward God (I Pet. 5:5,6). The above and other passages show that humility is an effect of the action of God, circumstances, other people, ourselves, or of any or all of these upon our lives.   E.R.

HUMTAH (hŭm'tà), a town in the hill country of Judah near Hebron; unidentified (Josh. 15:54).

HUPHAM (hū'făm), a son of Benjamin and founder of a tribal family known as the Huphamites (Num. 26:39). Probably the same as Huppim in Genesis 46:21 and I Chronicles 7:12; and as Huram in I Chronicles 8:5.

HUPHAMITES (See Hupham)

HUPPAH (hŭp'à), a priest of the 13th course in David's time (I Chron. 24:13).

HUPPIM (hŭp'ĭm, Heb. *huppîm, coast people*), probably the same as Hupham, but the references leave his descent uncertain (Gen. 46:21; I Chron. 7:12,15).

HUR (hûr, Heb. *hûr, whiteness*). 1. One who, with Aaron, held up Moses' hands during a battle against Amalek, bringing victory to Israel (Exod. 17:10,12); appointed magistrate while Moses was on the mount (Exod. 24:14).
2. Grandfather of Bezaleel of the tribe of Judah, chief workman in the tabernacle (Exod. 31: 2; 35:30; 38:22; II Chron. 1:5). I Chronicles 2:19, 20 say that Caleb married Ephrath, who bore him Hur, grandfather of Bezaleel. In verse 50 KJV, ASV call Caleb son of Hur, first-born of Ephratah, but RSV divides the verse to remove the difficulty. In I Chronicles 4:1 Hur is named as a descendant of Judah, but in verse 4 he is called first-born of Ephratah, father of Bethlehem. Jewish tradition identifies Nos. 1 and 2, and calls him the husband of Miriam, Moses' sister.
3. One of five Midianite kings killed with Balaam (Num. 31:1-8); a leader of Midian and a prince of Sihon the Amorite king (Josh. 13:21).
4. In KJV, the father of one of 12 officers who supplied food for Solomon's household (I Kings 4:8); ASV, RSV treat "son of" (Heb. *bēn*) as part of a proper name, Ben-hur.
5. Father of Rephaiah, who helped Nehemiah

build the wall; ruler of half of Jerusalem (Neh. 3:9).

HURAI (hū'rā-ĭ, hū-rā'ĭ, hū'rī), one of David's heroes from the brooks of Gaash (I Chron. 11:32). Also called Hiddai (II Sam. 23:30).

HURAM (hū'răm, Heb. *hûrām, noble-born*). 1. A Benjamite, son of Bela (I Chron. 8:5). See Hupham.
2. The king of Tyre who aided Solomon (II Chron. 2:3,11,12). Usually called Hiram.
3. A Tyrian artificer sent to Solomon by No. 2 (II. Chron. 2:13; 4:11,16), ASV "of Huram my father's," margin, "even Huram my father" in 2:13; "Huram his father" in 4:16. RSV "Huramabi" in II Chronicles 2:13; 4:16. Elsewhere called Hiram.

HURI (hū'rī), the father of Abihail, a Gadite (I Chron. 5:14).

HURRIANS (See Horites)

HUSBANDMAN (hŭz'bănd-măn), a farmer, whether owner or tenant. The term is retained in ASV except Zechariah 13:5, "tiller of the ground," where Zechariah asserts that he is a farmer, not a professional prophet. The Heb. words mean "farmer, plowman, tiller of the soil," and RSV uses all three translations in the OT. King Uzziah loved farming (II Chron. 26:10). Farmers were left in the land when others were carried captive to Babylon (II Kings 25:12; Jer. 52:16). The farmers of Israel are promised peace, and those of Babylon destruction, in the restoration (Jer. 31: 24; 15:23). Joel 1:11 and Amos 5:6 predict suffering for farmers in the national disaster. Noah (Gen. 9:20), like Cain (Gen. 4:2), was a farmer. The NT Greek word *georgós* means *farmer, worker on the land*. In the Gospel parable (Matt. 21:33-41; Mark 12:1-9; Luke 20:9-16) the farmers are tenants in RSV. The right of the farmer to the first share of the crop is recognized (II Tim. 2:6). He is held up as an example of patience (James 5:7). In John 15:1, God is the vinedresser (RSV), as the context shows.

HUSBANDRY (See Occupations & Professions: Farmer)

HUSHAH (hū'shà), a son of Ezer, the son of Hur, a Judahite (I Chron. 4:4).

HUSHAI (hū'shī, hū'shā-ĭ), one of David's two leading men, an Archite (II Sam. 15:32,37; 16:16-18; 17:5-15; I Chron. 27:33) — the friend and counselor of David who overthrew the counsels of Ahithophel. The Archite clan occupied Ataroth, a border town of Ephraim (Josh. 16:2,7).

HUSHAM (hū'shăm), a king of Edom, who succeeded Jobab. He came from the land of Teman (Gen. 36:34,35; I Chron. 1:45,46).

HUSHATHITE, THE (hū'shăth-īt), the patronymic of Sibbecai, one of David's 30 heroes (II Sam. 21: 18; I Chron. 11:29; 20:4; 27:11) called Mebunnai in II Samuel 23:27.

HUSHIM (hū'shĭm). 1. The sons of Dan (Gen. 46: 23), called Shuham in Numbers 26:42.
2. The sons of Aher, a Benjamite (I Chron. 7: 12).
3. One of the two wives of Shaharaim (I Chron. 8:8,11).

HUSKS, Luke 15:16, the pods of the carob tree (so ASV margin; RSV "pods"). Greek *kerátia*, little horns, from their shape; *Caratonia siliqua*, a tree about 30 feet high, with a crown of like spread, which matures fruit in 30 years, and has glossy evergreen leaves and leathery leguminous pods with pea-like seeds embedded in a sweet pulp. A staple cattle food throughout the Mediterranean basin, the pods are eaten by the poor. Called "St. John's Bread" from a belief that carob pods rather than insects were the locusts which John the Baptist ate (Matt. 3:4; Mark 1:6).

HUZ (hŭz), the eldest son of Nahor and Milcah (Gen. 22:21; ASV, RSV Uz).

HUZZAB (hŭz'ăb, Heb. *hūtstsav*). It is disputed whether the word in Nahum 2:7 is to be taken as a noun or as a verb. If a noun (KJV; ASV margin), it may be an epithet of Nineveh or of its queen (and so RSV "its mistress"). If a verb, ASV text has "it is decreed." The LXX does not help. Moffatt and the Jewish version have "the queen"; Knox has "the warriors of Nineve(h)." Archaeology has as yet shed no light here.

HYACINTH (hī'à-sĭnth, Gr. *huákinthos*). 1. The name of a color, deep purple (Rev. 9:17); KJV has "jacinth."

2. In Revelation 21:20, where a precious stone is meant, RV has "sapphire."

HYENA (See Animals)

HYKSOS (hĭk'sōs, -sŏs, Egyptian *hik shasu, rulers of foreign lands*, or *of the lands of the nomads*), a West Semitic (Canaanite, Amorite) people who ruled an empire embracing Syria and Palestine; called the Shepherd Kings by the Egyptian historian Manetho. Around 1700 B.C. their use of a new weapon, the horse-drawn chariot, enabled them to conquer Egypt, where they ruled till about 1550 B.C. During their rule, which was more friendly to foreigners than were native Egyptian dynasties, Joseph came to Egypt and rose to be prime minister, bringing his father Jacob's family to dwell in Goshen, near the Hyksos capital at Avaris in the Delta. The Hyksos built great earthwork enclosures for their horses, and immense fortifications. Between 1600 and 1550 B.C. the Hyksos were driven out by a native Egyptian dynasty unfriendly to foreigners, and the capital restored to Thebes, its earlier location. From this time date the misfortunes of Jacob's rapidly increasing descendants, terminating only with their escape from Egypt.

HYMENAEUS (hī'mĕ-nē'ŭs, Gr. *Hyménaios, pertaining to Hymen, the god of marriage*), a professed Christian who had fallen into heresies, who tried to shipwreck the faith of true believers, and who was excommunicated by Paul (I Tim. 1:19,20; II Tim. 2:16-18).

HYMN (See Music)

HYPOCRISY (hĭ-pŏk'rĭ-sē). Hypocrite or hypocritical, in the OT, render words from a Heb. root *hnph, pollute*, correctly translated "profane, godless" in ASV, RSV (Isa. 32:6; 9:17; 10:6; 33:14; Job 8:13; 13:16; 15:34; 17:8; 20:5; 27:8; 34:30; 36:13; Prov. 11:9; Ps. 35:16). The LXX used Greek *hypokrínomai, act a part in a play; hypókrisis, hypocrisy; hypokrités, hypocrite*, which occur in the NT and are taken over in English (Matt. 6:2,5,16; 7:5; 15:7; 22:18; 23:13,15,23,25,27,28, 29; 24:51; Mark 7:6; 12:15; Luke 12:1,56; 13:15). In Galatians 2:13 KJV, ASV have "dissimulated . . . dissimulation," RSV "acted insincerely . . . insincerity." *Anypókritos, without hypocrisy* (Rom. 12:9; II Cor. 6:6; I Tim. 1:5; II Tim. 1:5; I Pet. 1:22 is usually rendered "sincere, genuine" in RSV. In Luke 20:20 the verb is translated "feign themselves." The thought in the NT lies close to the literal meaning "play-acting," with special reference to religion, "having a form of godliness, but denying the power thereof" (II Tim. 3:5), as Matthew 6:1-18; 23:13-36 plainly show.

HYSSOP (See Plants)

I

IBHAR (ĭb'hår, Heb. *yivhār, he chooses*), one of David's sons, born at Jerusalem (II Sam. 5:15; I Chron. 14:5).

IBLEAM (ĭb'lē-ăm, Heb. *yivle'ām*), a town in the territory of Issachar, given to the tribe of Manasseh (Josh. 17:11). The inhabitants, however, were not driven out and continued to live in the land (Judg. 1:27). Ahaziah, king of Judah, was slain near there when he fled from Jehu (II Kings 9:27). Zechariah, king of Israel, was killed there (II Kings 15:10, text of Lucian). It is generally identified with Bileam, a town of Manasseh given to the Levites (I Chron. 6:70). Ruins of the town remain.

IBNEIAH (ĭb-nī'yà, Heb. *yivneyâh, Jehovah builds*), a son of Jeroham, a chief man in the tribe of Benjamin in the first settlement in Jerusalem (I Chron. 9:8).

IBNIJAH (ĭb-nī'jà, Heb. *yivnîyâh, Jehovah builds up*), a Benjamite, father of Reuel (I Chron. 9:8).

IBRI (ĭb'rī, Heb. *'ivrî, a Hebrew*), a Merarite Levite, son of Jaaziah (I Chron. 24:27).

IBZAN (ĭb'zăn, Heb. *'ivtsān*), the tenth judge of Israel, who ruled for seven years. He was a native of Bethlehem (whether of Judah or Zebulun is not stated). He had 30 sons and 30 daughters (Judg. 12:8-10).

ICHABOD (ĭk'à-bŏd, Heb. *'îkhāvôdh, inglorious*), son of Phinehas, Eli's son, slain by the Philistines at the battle of Aphek when the ark was taken. Ichabod was born after his father's death, and was given this name by his mother on her death-bed because she felt that the "glory (had) departed from Israel" (I Sam. 4:19ff). His nephew Ahijah was one of those who remained with Saul and his men at Gibeah just before Jonathan attacked the Philistines (I Sam. 14:2ff).

ICONIUM (ī-cō'nī-ŭm, Gr. *Ikónion*), a city of Asia Minor, visited by Paul and Barnabas on Paul's first missionary journey after they had been expelled from Antioch in Pisidia, which lay on the W, and revisited by them on their return journey to Antioch (Acts 13:51ff). On his second missionary journey Paul with Silas stopped off at Iconium to read the letter sent out by the Jerusalem Council on the Judaizing question, and at nearby Lystra he took young Timothy with him as his associate (Acts 16:1-5). In II Timothy 3:11 Paul alludes to per-

Coins from Iconium (1st century B.C.). The one at left shows Zeus with scepter and thunderbolt; the one at right shows Athena Polias, goddess of the city, holding a serpent-entwined spear. UANT

secutions endured by him at Antioch, Iconium, and Lystra.

In the first century it was one of the chief cities in the southern part of the Roman province of Galatia. It was a city of immemorial antiquity, and was situated near the western end of a vast, level plain, with mountains a few miles towards the W, from which streams flowed which made it a veritable oasis. Two important trade-routes passed through it, and it was on the road leading to Ephesus and Rome. Geography makes it the natural capital of Lycaonia. Archaeological inscriptions found there in 1910 show that the Phrygian language was spoken there for two centuries after the time of Paul, although at neighboring Lystra the natives spoke the "speech of Lycaonia" (Acts 14:11). Hadrian made the city a Roman colony. The city has had a continuing history, and is now known as Konia, still the main trading center of the Lycaonian plain.   S.B.

IDBASH (ĭd'băsh, Heb. *yidbāsh, honey-sweet*), a man of Judah, one of the sons of the father of Etam (I Chron. 4:3).

IDDO (ĭd'ō), the English equivalent of several Jewish names: 1. [Heb. *yiddô*]. a. Son of Zechariah, and a captain of the half-tribe of Manasseh E of the Jordan, under David (I Chron. 27:21). b. One who had taken a foreign wife at the time of Ezra (Ezra 10:43).

2. [Heb. *'iddô*]. The head of a community of Nethinim at Casiphia who provided Ezra with Levites and Nethinim (Ezra 8:17).

3. [Heb. *yiddô, ye'dô, ye'dî*]. a. A Levite descended from Gershom; ancestor of Asaph (I Chron. 6:21). b. A seer and prophet, who wrote a book which was the Chronicler's source for the reign of Solomon and Jeroboam (II Chron. 9:29), and books about the deeds of Rehoboam (II Chron. 12:15) and of King Abijah (II Chron. 13:22). c. Father of Abinadab, a purveyor of Solomon at Mahanaim in Gilead (I Kings 4:14). d. Grandfather of the prophet Zechariah (Zech. 1:1,7; Ezra 5:1; 6:14).

IDOL (See Idolatry)

IDOLATRY (ĭ-dŏl'à-trē, Gr. *eidololatreía*). Idolatry in ancient times included two forms of departure from the true religion: the worship of false gods, whether by means of images or otherwise; and the worship of Jehovah by means of images. All the nations surrounding ancient Israel were idolatrous, although their idolatry assumed different forms. The early Semites of Mesopotamia worshiped mountains, springs, trees, and blocks of stone, in which the deity was supposed to be in some sense incarnate. A typical example of such wooden representations is the sacred pole, the idol of his clan, which Gideon destroyed (Judg. 6:25-32). The religion of the Egyptians centered mostly about the veneration of the sun and of the Nile, as sources of life. They also had a number of sacred animals: the bull, cow, cat, baboon, crocodile, etc. Some of the deities had human bodies and animal heads. Among the Canaanites, religion took on a very barbarous character. The chief gods were personifications of life and fertility. The gods had no moral character whatsoever, and worship of them carried with it demoralizing practices, including child sacrifice, prostitution, and snake-worship. Human and animal images of the deities were worshiped. The Israelites, on succeeding to the land, were commanded to destroy these idols (Exod. 23:24; 34:13; Num. 33:52; Deut. 7:5).

The word "idolatry," which occurs only once in the KJV (I Sam. 15:23), has no exact Hebrew

The "Baal of Lightning," from Ras Shamra, dated about 1800 B.C. LM

equivalent. There are, however, a number of Hebrew words which are rendered "idol" in the KJV. They all give expression to the loathing, contempt, and dread excited in godly men by idolatry. The terms are as follows. 1. *aven*, "emptiness," "nothingness"; that is, a vain, false, wicked thing (Isa. 66:3). 2. *emah,* "an object of horror or terror," referring either to the hideousness of the idols or the shameful character of their worship (Jer. 50:38). 3. *el,* the name of the supreme god of Canaan; used also as a neutral expression for any divinity (Isa. 57:5). 4. *elil,* "a thing of naught, cipher," resembling *aven* in meaning (Lev. 19:4; 26:1; I Chron. 16:26; etc.). 5. *miphletseth,* "a fright, a horror" (I Kings 15:13; II Chron. 15:16). 6. *semel,* "a likeness," "semblance" (II Chron. 33:7,15). 7. *atsab,* "a cause of grief" (I Sam. 31:9; I Chron. 10:9, etc.). 8. *etseb,* "a cause of grief" (Jer. 22:28). 9. *otseb,* "a cause of grief" (Isa. 48:5). 10. *tsir,* "a form," and hence an idol (Isa. 45:16). Besides the above words there are a number of others, not translated "idol," but referring to it which express the degradation associated with idolatry: *bosheth,* "shameful thing," applied to Baal and referring to the obscenity of his worship (Jer. 11:13; Hos. 9:10); *gillulim,* a term of contempt meaning "shapeless, dungy things" (Ezek. 4:2; Zeph. 1:17); *shikkuts,* "filth," referring especially to the obscene rites associated with idolatry (Ezek. 37:23; Nah. 3:6).

The first clear case of idolatry in the Bible is the account of Rachel's stealing her father's teraphim, which were images of household gods (Gen.

31:19). They were used in Babylonia. Without Jacob's knowledge, Rachel stole them from Laban and carried them with her to Canaan. During their long sojourn in Egypt, the Israelites defiled themselves with the idols of the land (Josh. 24:14; Ezek. 20:7). Moses defied these gods by smiting their symbols in the plagues of Egypt (Num. 33:4). In spite of the miracles of their redemption from Egypt, the Israelites insisted on having some visible shape with which to worship God, and at Sinai, while Moses was absent, they persuaded Aaron to make them a golden calf, an emblem of the productive power of nature with which they had become familiar in Egypt. The Second Commandment, forbidding man to make and bow down to images of any kind, was directed against idolatry (Exod. 20:4,5; Deut. 5:8,9). This sin seems to have been shunned until the period of the judges, when the nation was caught in its toils again.

The whole of Judges tells of successive apostasies, judgments, and repentances. The story of Micah in Judges 17,18 is an illustration of how idolatry was often combined with outward worship of Jehovah. It is significant that Jonathan, a Levite and a grandson of Moses, assumed the office of priest to the images of Micah, and that later he allowed himself to be persuaded by some Danites, who had stolen Micah's idol, to go with them as the priest of their tribe. He became the first of a line of priests to officiate at the shrine of the stolen idols all the time that the tabernacle was at Shiloh.

The prophet Samuel persuaded the people to repent of their sin and to renounce idolatry; but in Solomon's reign the king himself made compromises that affected disastrously the whole future of the kingdom. His wives brought their own heathen gods with them, and openly worshiped them. Rehoboam, Solomon's son by an Ammonite mother, continued the worst features of his father's idolatry (I Kings 14:22-24); while under Jeroboam a great and permanent schism was effected in the religion of Israel when he erected golden calves at Bethel and at Dan and had his people worship there instead of in Jerusalem. The kings that followed Jeroboam in the northern kingdom differed little from him. One of them, Ahab, to please his Zidonian queen Jezebel, built a temple and an altar to Baal in Samaria (I Kings 16:31-33); while she put to death as many prophets of Jehovah as she could find (I Kings 18:4-13). Henceforth Baal worship became identified with the kingdom of Israel, and no king ever rose up against it.

In the southern kingdom things went somewhat better. Hezekiah restored the temple services, which had been abandoned during his father's reign, but the change was only outward (II Chron. 28,29; Isa. 29:13). Not long before the destruction of Jerusalem by Babylonia, Josiah made a final effort to bring about a purer worship, but it did not last (II Chron. 34). Not even the Captivity cured the Jews of their idolatrous tendencies. When Ezra went to Jerusalem from Babylon, he found to his dismay that many Jews had married foreign wives and that the land was filled with abominations (Ezra 9:11). More than 200 years later, when Antioches Epiphanes tried to extirpate Judaism and Hellenize the Jews, many of them obeyed his command to offer sacrifices to idols, although his action led to the Maccabean war.

In the ritual of idol worship the chief elements were: offering burnt sacrifices (II Kings 5:17), burning incense in honor of the idol (I Kings 11:8), pouring out libations (Isa. 57:6), presenting tithes and the first-fruits of the land (Hos. 2:8),

A goddess with two horns, entertaining a worshiper, on a tablet from Bethshan, about 1300 B.C.   UMP

kissing the idol (I Kings 19:18), stretching out the hands to it in adoration, prostrating oneself before it, and sometimes cutting oneself with knives (I Kings 18:26,28). Some of these practices were analogous to the worship of Jehovah.

For an Israelite, idolatry was the most heinous of crimes. In the OT the relation between God and His covenant people is often represented as a marriage bond (Isa. 54:5; Jer. 3:14), and the worship of false gods was regarded as religious harlotry. The penalty was death (Exod. 22:20). To attempt to seduce others to false worship was a crime of equal enormity (Deut. 13:6-10). The God of Israel was a jealous God who brooked no rivals.

In the NT, references to idolatry are understandably few. The Maccabean war resulted in the Jews becoming fanatically opposed to the crass idolatry of OT times. The Jews were never again tempted to worship images or gods other than Jehovah. Jesus, however, warned that to make possessions central in life is also idolatry, and said, "Ye cannot serve God and mammon" (Matt. 6:24). Paul, in Romans 1:18-25, teaches that idolatry is not the first stage of religion, from which man by an evolutionary process emerges to monotheism, but is the result of deliberate religious apostasy. When man sins against the light of nature and refuses to worship the Creator revealed thereby, God as a punishment withdraws the light, and man then descends into the shameful absurdities of idolatry. Christians in apostolic times, many of whom were converted from heathenism, are repeatedly warned in the epistles of the NT to be on their guard against idolatry (I Cor. 5:10; Gal. 5:20; etc.). The OT conception of idolatry is widened to include anything that leads to the dethronement of God from the heart, as, for example, covetousness (Eph. 5:5; Col. 3:5).

A special problem arose for Christians in connection with meats offered to idols (Acts 15:29; I Cor. 8-10). Some of the meat sold in butcher shops had been bought from heathen temples. Should a Christian make careful inquiry about the meat he purchased, and would he countenance or indirectly support idolatry if he bought meat that had been offered to an idol? Or should a Christian invited to dinner by a friend ask before accepting whether he would be eating meat that had been offered to an idol? Many Christians had real qualms about eating such meat; while others, feeling themselves "strong" spiritually, were convinced that there was no harm in it at all. Paul does not take sides in the matter, but he urges against the latter that they should not be careless, for even though idols are nothing, they still are a tangible expression of demons who are back of them; and, moreover, Christians should never insist on their "rights," if such insistence will cause the weak to stumble. They should be governed by the law of love. In the last book of the Bible the Apostle John predicts a time of idolatrous apostasy in the last days, when the Beast and his image will be accorded divine honors (Rev. 9:20; 13:14). S.B.

IDUMAEA (ĭd′ū-mē-à, Gr. *pertaining to Edom*, in KJV of OT *Idumea*). the name used by the Greeks and Romans for the country of Edom (Mark 3:8). See EDOM.

IGAL (ī′găl, Heb. *yigh'āl, God redeems*). 1. One of the 12 spies sent by Moses to search out the land of Canaan (Num. 13:7).
2. One of David's heroes, the son of Nathan (II Sam. 23:36).
3. A son of Shemaiah, a descendant of King Jeconiah (I Chron. 3:22).

IGDALIAH (ĭg′dà-lī′à, Heb. *yighdalyāhû, Jehovah is great)*, father of the prophet Hanan (Jer. 35:4).

IGEAL ī′ge-ăl, Heb. *yigh'āl, God redeems*), a son of Shemaiah, of the Davidic line (I Chron. 3:22, RV Igal).

IIM (ī′ĭm, Heb. *'iyîm, heaps, ruins*). 1. A town in Judah near Edom (Josh. 15:29). The exact site is uncertain.
2. A town E of the Jordan (Num. 33:45).

IJE-ABARIM (ī′jē-ăb′à-rĭm, Heb. *'iyê hā-'ăvārîm, ruins of Abarim*), a halting place in the journeyings of Israel, said to be "in the border of Moab" (Num. 33:44). Exact site unknown.

IJON (ī′jŏn, Heb. *'iyôn, a ruin*), a town in the territory of Naphtali, captured by Ben-hadad, king of Syria, at the instigation of Asa (I Kings 15:20; II Chron. 16:4). Its inhabitants were subsequently carried into captivity by Tiglath-pileser in the reign of Pekah (II Kings 15:29). The site is located about eight miles NW of Banias.

IKKESH (ĭk′ĕsh, Heb. *'iqqēsh, crooked*), a man from Tekoa, father of Ira, one of David's heroes (II Sam. 23:26; I Chron. 11:28).

ILAI (ī′lā-ī, Heb. *'îlay*), one of David's mighty men (I Chron. 11:29); called Zalmon in II Samuel 23:28).

ILLYRICUM (ĭl-ĭr′ĭ-kŭm, Gr. *Illurikón*), a province of the Roman Empire, bounded on the N by Pannonia, on the E by Moesia, on the S by Macedonia, and on the W by the Adriatic Sea. The Alps run through it. The inhabitants, wild mountaineers and pirates, were conquered by the Romans in the third century B.C. In Romans 15:19 Paul, emphasizing the extent of his missionary activities, says that "from Jerusalem, and round about even unto Illyricum, I have fully preached the gospel of Christ." "Illyricum" in this verse probably means the Roman province, not the much wider area the name sometimes included. "Unto Illyricum" must mean up to the borders of Illyricum, although the preposition "unto" may be either exclusive or inclusive. Paul's preaching tour to the Illyrian frontier must be assigned to his third missionary journey, as his movements on his first visit to Macedonia are too carefully recorded to allow for a trip to the borders of Illyricum.

IMAGE (See Idolatry)

IMAGE, NEBUCHADNEZZAR'S. Nebuchadnezzar in his second year had a dream which none of his wise men could describe or interpret for him except Daniel, to whom God had revealed the secret of the dream in a night vision. The king's dream was of a huge image with a head of gold, the breast and arms of silver, the belly and thighs of brass, the legs of iron, and the feet of iron mixed with clay. A stone cut without hands fell on the feet and broke them in pieces, and then became a mountain, filling the whole earth. Each of the four principal parts of the image is interpreted to represent one of four successive empires. The head of gold represented Nebuchadnezzar's empire. The other three empires intended are not expressly indicated and it has been much disputed what they are. Among the various identification for the second empire that have been proposed are the Grecian, the Median, and the Medo-Persian. The third has been referred to Medo-Persia, Persia, Alexander, Greece, and Rome. The fourth has been thought to be Nabonidus and Belshazzar, Mohammed, Greece, Syria, the successors of Alexander, and Rome. The stone cut without hands represents the kingdom of God smiting and destroying the anti-theocratic powers of the world. The central truth of this chapter (Daniel 2) is that some day the kingdom of God will supersede all human empires. S.B.

IMAGE OF GOD. Two fundamental truths about man taught in Scripture are that he is created by God and that God made him in His own image. Man came into being as the result of special deliberation on the part of God. He is God's creature, and there is therefore an infinite qualitative difference between them; but he has been made like God in a way that the rest of creation is not. The passages in which it is expressly stated that man is made in God's image are Genesis 1:26,27; 5:1, 3; 9:6; I Corinthians 11:7; Ephesians 4:24; Colossians 3:10; and James 3:9. Psalm 8 should be added to these, although the phrase "image of God" is not used, for the creation narrative as it relates to man is given here in poetic form. Another passage where the idea is not directly stated but is implied is Acts 17:22-31 — Paul's address on Mars Hill. The words "image" and "likeness," used together in Genesis 1:26,27, do not differ essentially in meaning, but strengthen the idea that man uniquely reflects God. They are, moreover, used interchangeably elsewhere. The Scriptures do not specifically describe the nature of the image; consequently theologians differ in their views regarding it. Among the principal views are the following: God has a bodily form, and this serves as the pattern for the body of man; it consists in simple lordship over the animals; it refers to man's moral nature; it is his personality. Since it is unlikely that it consists in bodily form, for God is a spirit, it can only refer to spiritual qualities, in man's mental and moral attributes as a rational, self-conscious, self-determining creature, capable of obedience to moral law, and intended by God for fellowship with Himself. All this, of course, makes possible dominion over the animal world. The image of God is restored in the redemption of Christ (Eph. 4:24; Col. 3:10). S.B.

IMAGE WORSHIP (See Idol)

IMLAH (ĭm'là, Heb. *yimlâh, fulness*), the father of the prophet Micaiah, a prophet of the Lord in the days of Ahab (I Kings 22:8,9; II Chron. 18: 7,8).

IMMANUEL (ĭ-măn'ū-ĕl, Heb. *'immānû'ēl, God is with us*), the name of a child (occurring three times in the Bible: Isaiah 7:14; 8:8; Matt. 1:23) whose birth was foretold by Isaiah, and who was to be a sign to Ahaz, during the Syro-Ephraimitic war (Isa. 7). At this time, 753 B.C., Judah was threatened by the allied forces of Syria and Israel, who were trying to compel it to form an alliance with them against Assyria, whose king, Tiglath-pileser, was attempting to bring the whole of Western Asia under his sway. The prophet bade Ahaz remain confident and calm in Jehovah, and not to seek aid from Tiglath-pileser. To overcome the king's incredulity, he offered him a sign of anything in heaven or earth, but when the king evasively refused the offer, Isaiah, after bitterly chiding him for his lack of faith, proceeded to give him a sign, the sign of "Immanuel."

Isaiah's words have led to much controversy and have been variously interpreted, chiefly because of the indefinite terms of the prediction and the fact that there is no record of their fulfilment in any contemporary event. 1. The traditional Christian interpretation is that the emphasis should be laid upon the virgin birth of Immanuel, as Matthew does when he relates the birth of Jesus (1:22,23). Difficulties with this view are that the idea of a virgin birth is not unambiguously expressed and such an event could not serve the purpose of a sign to Ahaz, who expected a miracle to be performed in the immediate future. 2. Another explanation is that the event of the birth of the child is intended as a sign to Ahaz and nothing more. At the time of Judah's deliverance from Syria and Ephraim, some young mothers who then give birth to sons will spontaneously name them "Immanuel." Children bearing this name will be a sign to Ahaz of the truth of Isaiah's words concerning deliverance and judgment. 3. A third view, somewhat similar to the preceding one, is that Isaiah has a certain child in mind, the *almah* being his own wife, or one of Ahaz's wives, or perhaps someone else. Before its birth it will have experienced a great deliverance (vs. 14); before he has emerged from infancy, Syria and Ephraim will be no more (vs. 16); and later in his life Judah will be a country fit only for the pastoral life (vs. 15). 4. There are semi-Messianic interpretations, which apply the prophecy to a child of Isaiah's time and also to Jesus Christ. 5. Perhaps the most widely-held view in evangelical circles is that Isaiah has in mind the Messiah. When the prophet learns of

the king's cowardice, God for the first time gives to him a revelation of the true King, who would share the poverty and affliction of His people and whose character and work would entitle Him to the great names of Isaiah 9:6. In this interpretation the essential fact is that in the coming of Immanuel men will recognize the truth of the prophet's words. He would be Israel's deliverer and the government would rest upon His shoulder (9: 6). II Samuel 7:12 and Micah 5:3 show that the Messianic idea was prevalent in Judah at this time. S.B.

IMMER (ĭm'ēr, Heb. *'immēr*). 1. The ancestral head of the 16th course of priests. He lived in David's time (I Chron. 24:14). Descendants of his are mentioned in Ezra 2:37; 10:20; Nehemiah 3: 29; 7:40; 11:13.

2. A priest, in Jeremiah's time, the father of Pashur (Jer. 20:1). It is possible that he was a descendant of the Immer mentioned in 1.

3. A place in Babylonia, the home of a priestly family (Ezra 2:59).

IMMORTALITY (ĭm-ŏr-tăl'ĭ-tē, Gr. *athanasía, aphtharsía, áphthartos, incorruption*). The Biblical concept of immortality is not simply the survival of the soul after bodily death — the bare continued existence of the soul — but the self-conscious continuance of the whole person, body and soul together, in a state of blessedness, due to the redemption of Christ and the possession of "eternal life."

Belief in some sort of survival of the soul is practically universal, but in most cases the soul lives on in a joyless, shadowy state bearing only a ghostly resemblance to life on earth. The body is looked upon as a clog, happily sloughed off by the soul. The soul, moreover, is regarded as inherently indestructible, with neither beginning nor ending. In the Bible, however, only God possesses immortality "as an original, eternal, and necessary endowment." The soul's immortality is conferred upon it by God and is therefore contingent on His will.

A number of arguments have been adduced by philosophers for the soul's immortality, among the more important the following: 1. The fact that the belief is found among all races and nations points to its being a natural instinct, something involved in the very constitution of human nature; (2) the soul is immaterial in nature; physical dissolution, therefore, cannot destroy it; (3) human nature is endowed with rich capacities and possibilities which can never be fully developed in this life and which require a future existence so that they may come to full fruition; (4) there must be a future life in order that the moral order may be vindicated, for in this life much good goes unrewarded and much evil goes unpunished.

The above arguments are not absolutely demonstrable; they do no more than furnish a strong presumption in favor of immortality. For greater assurance on this matter we must rely on the authority of Scripture. The Bible, however, nowhere explicitly mentions the immortality of the soul, and never attempts to prove it in a formal way. Everywhere it assumes man's immortality as an undisputed postulate, in much the same way that it assumes the existence of God.

The OT teaches immortality, but not with the clarity of the NT, chiefly because God's revelation in Scripture is progressive and gradually increases in clearness. 1. Unlike animals, man is composed of body and soul, and is made in the image of God. He is constantly reminded that he is constituted for fellowship with God and that he is only a pilgrim on this earth. God has set eternity in his heart (Eccl. 3:11). 2. The dead in the OT descend into *Sheol* (*Hades*, in the Greek), a word which may be rendered in a number of ways, depending on the context: grave, state of death, underworld, or hell. In *Sheol* they are in a state of conscious existence. 3. Belief in immortality by OT Jews is obvious from the practice of necromancy, or consulting the dead, against which there are frequent warnings in the OT (Lev. 19:31; 20: 27; Deut. 18:11; Isa. 8:19; 29:4). 4. Jesus points out to the Sadducees that the doctrine of the resurrection of the dead is implicitly taught in the statement in Exodus 3:6, "I am the God of . . . Abraham, the God of Isaac, and the God of Jacob." It is explicitly taught in such passages as Job 19: 23-27; Psalm 16:9-11; 17:15; 49:15; 73:24; Isaiah 26:19; Daniel 12; Hosea 13:14. 5. Some OT passages speak confidently of enjoying communion with God after death (Job 19:25-27; Ps. 16:9-11; 17:15; 73:23,24,26).

The doctrine of immortality is found everywhere in the NT. 1. A future state for both righteous and wicked is clearly taught. The continued existence of believers appears from such passages as Matthew 10:28; Luke 23:43; John 11:25f; 14:3; II Corinthians 5:1. The survival of the wicked is made clear in Matthew 11:21-24; 12:41; Romans 2:5-11; II Corinthians 5:10. 2. There are passages which show that future existence implies the resurrection of the body. The bodily resurrection of believers is taught in Luke 20:35,36; John 5:25-29; I Corinthians 15; I Thessalonians 4:16; Philippians 3:21; and of unbelievers, in John 5:29; Acts 24:15; Revelation 20:12-15. Paul teaches that after death the soul is in an unclothed and therefore incomplete state until the resurrection. 3. The condition of believers in their state of immortality is not a bare endless existence, but a communion with God in eternal satisfaction and blessedness. Among the blessings of the eternal state are likeness to Christ, freedom from pain and sorrow, the service of God, and a vision of the divine glory.

Those who reject belief in the personal immortality of the soul usually try to substitute for it belief in some other form of immortality, such as racial immortality, immortality of commemoration, or immortality of influence.   S.B.

IMMUTABILITY (í-mū-tà-bĭl'í-tē, Gr. *ametáthetos, unchangeableness*), the perfection of God by which He is devoid of all change in essence, attributes, consciousness, will, and promises. No change is possible in God, because all change must be to better or worse, and God is absolute perfection. No cause for change in God exists, either in Himself or outside of Him. The immutability of God is clearly taught in such passages of Scripture as the following: "I am the Lord, I change not" (Mal. 3:6). He is "the Father of lights, with whom is no variableness, neither shadow of turning" (James 1:17). "The heavens shall perish, but thou shalt endure" (Ps. 102:26). "The counsel of the Lord standeth forever" (Ps. 33:11). The immutability of God must not be confounded with immobility, as if there were no movement in God. Immutability is consistent with constant activity and perfect freedom. God creates, performs miracles, sustains the universe, etc. When the Scriptures speak of His repenting, as in Jonah 3:10, "God repented of the evil that he had said that he would do unto them," one should remember that this is only an anthropomorphic way of speaking. God adapts His treatment of men to the variation of their actions and characters. When the righteous do wickedly, His holiness requires that His treatment of them must change.   S.B.

IMNA (ĭm'nà, Heb. *yimnā', He — God — keeps off,* i.e., *defends*), the ancestral head of a family of Asher (I Chron. 7:35).

IMNAH (ĭm'nà, Heb. *yimnâh, right hand,* or, *good fortune*). 1. Son of Asher and founder of a tribal family (Num. 26:44; I Chron. 7:30; Gen. 46:17). 2. A Levite, father of Kore, in the reign of Hezekiah (II Chron. 31:14).

IMPRECATORY PSALMS. A number of OT Psalms, especially Nos. 2, 37, 69, 79, 109, 139, and 143, contain expressions of an apparent vengeful attitude towards enemies which, for some people, constitute one of the "moral difficulties" of the OT. It is thought that the spirit of the imprecatory Psalms is morally not justifiable by the standard of the ethics of the NT. Such passages may cause less difficulty when it is observed that they are not dictated merely by private vindictiveness, but spring ultimately from zeal for God's cause, with which the psalmist identifies himself, and they show a willingness to leave vengeance in the hands of God. They show, moreover, a keen sense of the great conflict constantly going on between God and His enemies, a conflict then being waged between Israel as God's covenant people and the nations which threatened to destroy Israel. They show a spirit of righteous indignation, and spring from an aroused sense of justice.   S.B.

IMPUTATION (See Impute)

IMPUTE (ĭm-pūt', Heb. *hāshav*, Gr. *logízomai*), a word meaning to attribute something to a person, or reckoning something to the account of another. This sometimes takes place in a judicial manner, so that the thing imputed becomes a ground of reward or punishment. In the KJV the Heb. and Gr. words are also translated *to count, to account, to reckon, to esteem, to think.* The doctrine of imputation is frequently mentioned in the OT (Lev. 7:18; 17:4; II Sam. 19:19; Ps. 32:2) and the NT (Rom. 4:6-25; 5:13; II Cor. 5:19; James 2:23). It underlies the Scripture doctrines of Original Sin, Atonement, and Justification.

1. IMPUTATION OF ADAM'S SIN TO HIS POSTERITY. The story of the Fall, in Genesis 2 and 3, taken in connection with the subsequent history of the human race as recorded in the rest of the OT, implies that Adam's sin not only affected but was imputed to his posterity. This doctrine is more fully developed in the NT, especially in Romans 5:12-21, where Paul shows that it was by Adam's sin that death and sin entered the world and passed to all men. All men were condemned and made sinners in Adam.

2. IMPUTATION OF THE SIN OF MAN TO CHRIST. This is not expressly stated in the Bible, but is implied in those passages which affirm that Christ bore our sins and died in our stead. Isaiah 53 teaches that the Servant of Jehovah bore our iniquity, and God caused to fall on Him the iniquity of us all. Peter had this passage in mind when he wrote that Christ "his own self bare our sins in his body upon the tree" (I Pet. 2:24). The same thought is expressed in II Corinthians 5:21 where Paul says that Christ was "made to be sin on our behalf," and in Galatians 3:13, where it is said that Christ became "a curse for us." This truth is basic to the doctrine of the Atonement.

3. THE IMPUTATION OF CHRIST'S RIGHTEOUSNESS TO THE BELIEVER. This is the basis of Paul's doctrine of justification, a judicial act of God by which He declares righteous, on the ground of Christ's expiatory work and imputed righteousness, those who put their faith in Christ as their Saviour. The NT stresses that justification is absolutely free and

unmerited so far as the sinner is concerned (Rom. 3:24; 5:15; Gal. 5:4; Titus 3:7). The merits of Christ's suffering and obedience are imputed to the sinner and he is henceforth looked upon as just in God's sight. S.B.

IMRAH (ĭm'rà, Heb. *yimrâh, He [God] resists*), a descendant of Asher; son of Zophah (I Chron. 7:36).

IMRI (ĭm'rī, Heb. *'imrî*, contraction of *Amariah*).
1. A man of Judah, son of Bani (I Chron. 9:4).
2. The father of Zaccur, who helped in the rebuilding of the wall of Jerusalem after the Captivity (Neh. 3:2).

INCARNATION. The doctrine of the incarnation is taught or assumed throughout the Bible, and comes to explicit statement in such passages as John 1:14, "The Word became flesh and dwelt among us" (cf. I Tim. 3:16; Rom. 8:3). In NT usage "flesh," by metonymy, means "human nature." "Incarnation" is from the Latin, meaning "becoming flesh," that is, "becoming human." The doctrine of the incarnation teaches that the eternal Son of God (see TRINITY) became human, and that He did so without in any manner or degree diminishing His divine nature. A somewhat detailed statement of the incarnation is found in Philippians 2:5-11. Christ Jesus, "remaining (*hyparchōn*)" in the "form" of God, i.e. with all the essential attributes of God, took the "form" of a servant and died on the cross.

The virgin birth is necessary for our understanding of the incarnation. In the process of ordinary birth, a new personality begins. Jesus Christ did not begin to be when He was born. He is the eternal Son. The virgin birth was a miracle, wrought by the Holy Spirit, whereby the eternal Son of God "became flesh," i.e. took to Himself a genuine human nature, in addition to His eternal divine nature. It was a *virgin* birth, a miracle. The Holy Spirit has never been thought of as the father of Jesus. Jesus was not half man and half god like the Greek mythological heroes. He was fully God, the Second Person of the Trinity. "In Him dwells all the fullness of the Godhead in bodily form" (Col. 2:9). At the same time He became genuinely a man. To deny His genuine humanity is "the spirit of the Antichrist" (I John 4:2,3).

The Biblical data on the incarnation came to permanent doctrinal formulation at the council of Chalcedon, A.D. 451. That council declared that Christ was "born of the virgin Mary" and is "to be acknowledged in two natures, inconfusedly, unchangeably, indivisibly, inseparably . . . the property of each nature being preserved, and concurring in one Person . . ." This doctrine is concisely stated in the Westminster Shorter Catechism, Q. 21. "The only Redeemer of God's elect is the Lord Jesus Christ, who, being the eternal Son of God, became man, and so was, and continueth to be, God and man, in two distinct natures and one Person for ever."

The creed of Chalcedon was the culmination of more than three centuries of discussion in which the main stream of Christian thought eliminated a variety of false interpretations as follows: 1. The Gnostic Docetae, condemned in I John 4:2,3, denied the genuine humanity of Jesus, and taught that He only appeared to suffer. 2. The Ebionites in the second century denied His deity. 3. The Arians, condemned at Nicea, A.D. 325, denied that His divine nature was equal with the Father's. 4. The Apollinarians, condemned at Constantinople, A.D. 381, denied that He had a complete human nature. 5. The Nestorians, condemned at Ephesus, A.D. 431, admitted the two natures, but taught that He was two personalities. 6. The Eutychians, condemned at Chalcedon, A.D. 451, taught that the two natures were so united and so changed that He was neither genuinely divine nor genuinely human. 7. The Biblical doctrine of the incarnation formalized at Chalcedon, A.D. 451, as stated above, is the Christology of the true historical Church.

But we need an *understanding of the words* of our doctrine, not just a formula to repeat. First, the emphasis upon the unity of His personality means that He was, in Himself, in His *ego,* His nonmaterial self, the same numerical identity, the same person. The person who was God and with God "in the beginning" before the created universe, is the same person who sat wearily at the well of Sychar, the same person who said, "Father, forgive them," on the cross. Secondly, the distinction of His natures means, and has always meant to the Church, that Jesus is just as truly God as the Father and the Spirit are God, and at the same time, without confusion or contradiction, He is just as truly man as we are men. (His humanity as the "last Adam" is perfectly sinless, yet genuinely human as was Adam before the fall.)

In this second matter, we must remember that a "nature" in the Biblical usage, is not a substantive entity. A nature is not a personality in the sense in which we are speaking. *A nature is a complex of attributes.* Since man is made in the image of God (see Jesus' argument in John 10:34-38 as discussed in the article on TRINITY) it follows that for God the Son, without diminution of His divine attributes, to assume a genuine human complex of attributes, including a normal human body, involves no contradiction. J.O.B.

INCENSE (ĭn'sĕns), the KJV translation of two Hebrew words which were distinct in meaning at first, although later the second came to have virtually the same meaning as the first: *levônâh, frankincense,* and *qetōrâh, incense.* Incense was an aromatic substance made of gums and spices to be burned, especially in religious worship. It was compounded according to a definite prescription of stacte, onycha, galbanum, and pure frankincense in equal proportions, and was tempered with salt (Exod. 30:23f). It could not be made for ordinary purposes (Exod. 30:34-38; Lev. 10:1-7). Incense not properly compounded was rejected as "strange incense" (Exod. 30:9). The offering of incense was common in the religious ceremonies of nearly all ancient nations (Egyptians, Babylonians, Assyrians, Phoenicians, etc.), and was extensively used in the ritual of Israel.

A small

incense altar,

from Megiddo,

about 1000 B.C.

OIUC

The altar of incense was overlaid with pure gold, and was set in the Holy Place, near the veil that concealed the Holy of Holies. Originally, to burn it was the prerogative of the high priest, and he did so each morning when he dressed the lamps (Exod. 30:1-9). On the Day of Atonement he brought the incense within the veil and burned it in a censer in the Holy of Holies, so that the mercy seat was enveloped in a cloud of fragrant smoke (Lev. 16:12,13). The Korahites were punished with death for presuming to take it upon themselves to burn incense (Num. 16); the sons of Aaron died for offering it improperly (Lev. 10). By the time of Christ, incense was offered by ordinary priests, from among whom one was chosen by lot each morning and evening (Luke 1:9). The offering of incense was regarded as a solemn privilege. In offering of incense, fire was taken from the altar of burnt-offering and brought into the temple, where it was placed upon the altar of incense, and then the incense was emptied from a golden vessel upon the fire. When the priest entered the Holy Place with the incense, all the people were obliged to leave the temple. A profound silence was observed by them as they prayed outside (Luke 1:9,10). When the priest placed the incense on the fire, he bowed reverently towards the Holy of Holies, and retired slowly backwards, lest he alarm the congregation and cause them to fear that he had been struck dead for offering unworthily (Lev. 16:13).

The use of incense in the temple may have been partly a sanitary measure, since the smell of blood from the many animal sacrifices must have polluted the atmosphere, and the air would have to be fumigated; but it is largely explained by the love of the Oriental for sweet odors. Incense was often offered to those one wished to honor. For example, when Alexander the Great marched against Babylon, incense was offered on altars erected to him.

Incense was symbolical of the ascending prayer of the officiating high priest. The psalmist prayed, "Let my prayer be set forth before thee as incense" (Ps. 141:2). In Revelation 8:3-5 an angel burns incense on the golden altar, and smoke ascends with the prayer of saints. .   S.B.

INDIA (ĭn'dĭ-à, Heb. *hŏddû*, Gr. *Indiké*). The name occurs in the Bible only in Esther 1:1; 8:9, of the country which marked the eastern limit of the territory of Ahasuerus. The Hebrew word comes from the name of the Indus, *Hondu*, and refers not to the peninsula of Hindostan, but to the country adjoining the Indus, i.e. the Punjab, and perhaps also Scinde. Some have thought that this country is the Havilah of Genesis 2:11 and that the Indus is the Pishon. Many characteristic Indian products were known to the Israelites.

INFLAMMATION (See Diseases)

INHERITANCE (ĭn-hĕr'ĭ-tăns). The English word, in the OT, is a rendering of the Hebrew words *nahalâh, heleq, yerushshâh,* and *môrāshâh,* the last two being rare. The first occurs most often — almost 200 times, and is the common term for something inherited, an estate, a portion. A fundamental principle of Hebrew society was that real, as distinguished from personal, property belonged to the family rather than to the individual. This came from the idea that the land was given by God to His children, the people of Israel, and must remain in the family. The Mosaic Law directed that only the sons of a legal wife had the right of inheritance. The first-born son possessed the birthright, i.e., the right to a double portion of the

father's possession; and to him belonged the duty of maintaining the females of the family (Deut. 21:15-17). The other sons received equal shares. If there were no sons, the property went to the daughters (Num. 27:8), on the condition that they did not marry out of their own tribe (Num. 36:6ff). If the widow was left without children, the nearest of kin on her husband's side had the right of marrying her; and if he refused, the next of kin (Ruth 3:12,13). If no one married her, the inheritance remained with her until her death, and then reverted to the next of kin (Num. 27:9-11). An estate could not pass from one tribe to another. Since the land was so strictly tied up, testamentary dispositions were of course not needed. This strong feeling regarding family hereditary privileges was chiefly responsible for the Jews' taking such care to preserve the family genealogies.

"Inheritance" is not used in Scripture only to refer to inherited property. It is also used with a definitely theological significance. In the OT, at first it refers to the inheritance promised by God to Abraham and his descendants—the land of Canaan, "thy land, which thou hast given to my people for an inheritance" (I Kings 8:36; cf. Num. 34:2; Deut. 4:21,38; 12:9f; 15:4; Ps. 105:9-11; 47:4). The conquest of the land under the leadership of Joshua was by God's help, not by Israel's military prowess (Josh. 21:43-45). God directed the partitioning of the land among the tribes (Num. 26:52-56; Josh. 14:1-5; 18:4-9). Israel could continue to possess the land only on condition of faithfulness to God (Deut. 4:26ff; 11:8,9). Disobedience to God would result in the loss of the land, which could be recovered only by repentance and a new whole-hearted submission to God. (Isa. 57:13; 58:13f).

The idea finds a further expansion and spiritualization along two other directions. Israelites came to learn that Jehovah Himself was the inheritance of His people (Jer. 10:16) and of the individual believer (Ps. 16:5f; 73:26; 142:5), and that His inheritance is His elect, brought "out of Egypt to be unto him a people of inheritance" (Deut. 4:20). "For the Lord's portion is his people; Jacob is the lot of his inheritance" (Deut. 32:9). This conception was later broadened until Jehovah's inheritance is seen to include the Gentiles also (Isa. 19:25; 47:6; 63:17; Ps. 2:8).

The conception of inheritance is very prominent in the NT too, but now it is connected with the person and work of Christ, who is the heir by virtue of His being the Son (Mark 12:7; Heb. 1:2). Through Christ's redemptive work believers are sons of God by adoption and fellow-heirs with Christ (Rom. 8:17; Gal. 4:7). As a guarantee of this "eternal inheritance" (Heb. 9:15), Christ has given to them the Holy Spirit (Eph. 1:14). The Epistle to the Hebrews shows that as Israel in the Old Covenant received her inheritance from God, so in the New Covenant the New Israel receives an inheritance, only a better one. This inheritance, moreover, is not for Jews alone, but includes all true believers, including Gentiles (Eph. 3:6). The inheritance is the kingdom of God with all its blessings (Matt. 25:34; I Cor. 6:9; Gal. 5:21), both present and eschatological (Rom. 8:17-23; I Cor. 15:50; Heb. 11:13; I Pet. 1:3,4). It is wholly the gift of God's sovereign grace.   S.B.

INK (Heb. *deyô*, from a root meaning *slowly flowing*, Gr. *mélan, black*), any liquid used with pen or brush to form written characters. Mentioned once in the OT (Jer. 36:18), where Baruch says he wrote Jeremiah's prophecies "with ink." Hebrew ink was probably a lamp-black and gum, as is suggested by the "blotting out" of Exodus 32:33 and Numbers 5:23; but it is possible that in the course of Jewish history various inks were used. The word occurs three times in the NT (II Cor. 3:3; II John 12; III John 13). The NT books were written on papyrus, and the black ink used was made of vegetable soot mixed with gum and moistened as the writer needed it. The better black inks were made of nutgalls, sulphate of iron, and gum. The writing of MSS of the first century is remarkably well-preserved.

INN (Heb. *mālôn*, Gr. *pandocheíon, katáluma*). The Heb. word *mālôn* means a "night resting-place," and can apply to any place where there is encampment for the night, whether by caravans, individuals, or even armies. The presence of a building is not implied. It was originally very probably only a piece of level ground near a spring where carriers of merchandise could, with their animals, pass the night. Inns in the modern sense were not very necessary in primitive times, since travelers found hospitality the rule (Exod. 2:20; Judg. 19:15-21; II Kings 4:8; Acts 28:7; Heb. 13:2). We do not know when buildings were first used, but they would be needed early in the history of trade as a protection from inclement weather and in dangerous times and places. The "lodging place of wayfaring men" of Jeremiah 9:2 may have been such an establishment. An Oriental inn bore little resemblance to a hotel today. It was a mere shelter for man and beast. Like the modern "khan" or "caravanserai," it was a large quadrangular court into which admission was gained by a strong gateway. The more elaborate ones were almost as strong as a fortress. In the center of the court there was a well, and around the sides there were rooms and stalls. An upper story was reached by stairways. Travelers usually brought food for themselves and their animals.

Innkeepers in ancient times had a very bad reputation, and this, together with the Semitic spirit of hospitality, led Jews and Christians to recommend hospitality for the entertainment of strangers. One of the best-known inns in Palestine was half way between Jerusalem and Jericho (Luke 10:34). The Gr. word *katáluma*, used of the "upper room" where the Last Supper was held (Mark 14:14), and of the place in Bethlehem that turned away Joseph and Mary (Luke 2:7), was probably a room in a private house rather than in a public inn — corresponding to a spare room in a private

An inn, or caravanserai, with lodgings for travelers above, and stables for animals below. DV

The Good Samaritan Inn, on the Jerusalem-Jericho road. © MPS

house or in a village, probably that of a sheikh. The vast numbers who went to Jerusalem to attend the annual feasts were allowed to use such guest-chambers; and for this no payment was taken.   S.B.

INNOCENTS, SLAUGHTER OF, the murder, by Herod the Great, of all the male children in Bethlehem two years old and under, when the wise men failed to return and tell him where they found the infant Jesus.

I.N.R.I., the initials of the Latin superscription which Pilate had placed above the cross of Jesus in three languages (Greek, Hebrew, Latin). The Latin reads: IESUS NAZARENUS, REX IUDAEORUM, *Jesus of Nazareth, King of the Jews* (Matt. 27:37; Mark 15:26; Luke 23:38; John 19:19).

INSECTS OF THE BIBLE. Through the centuries, insects have been an important factor in the life and well-being of man. Over 600,000 described species of insects are known and there are many hundred thousand more undescribed species. The frequent mention of insects in Bible references indicates their prevalence throughout Bible lands and times.

Insects compose the class *Hexapoda* of the phylum *Arthropoda* which is the largest phylum of the animal kingdom. Arthropods are characterized by bodies composed of similar segments joined together, bearing jointed legs. Insects are the air-breathing arthropods with bodies in three distinct divisions: head, thorax, and abdomen. They have one pair of antennae, three pairs of legs and usually one or two pairs of wings in the adult stage.

Insects have two types of development. First, the complete metamorphosis consisting of four stages: egg, larva, pupa and adult. Flies have a complete metamorphosis, the larval stage being the legless maggot. Second, the incomplete or gradual metamorphosis consisting of the three stages: egg, nymph, and adult. The nymph through a series of molts passes into the adult stage. Grasshoppers have a gradual metamorphosis in which the nymphal form bears some resemblances to the adult.

The economic significance of insects is extensive. Their destructive influences include such dreaded diseases as malaria, typhoid, typhus and yellow fever, filariasis and bubonic plague of which they are the carriers or essential hosts of the causal organisms. Fernald estimates that "the loss of labor by sickness and death caused by malaria alone is at least 100 million dollars and by all insect-borne diseases is over 350 million dollars each year in the United States" (H. T. Fernald, *Applied Entomology,* McGraw-Hill, New York, 1935, p. 34). Studies also indicate that crop losses average annually 10 per cent and with insect outbreaks yields may be reduced to 20 or 30 per cent. Further, add to this loss the almost incalculable cost of all types of pest and disease control throughout the world.

Beneficial effects of insects are also to be listed. Some parasitic forms serve as vital predators upon insect pests. Valuable products secured from insects include honey, wax, shellac, silk, and various dyes. The estimated value of commercial products from insects is 125 million dollars annually in the United States. The flower-visiting habits of insects provide required means of pollination for many plants, including most of the fruit trees which could not produce seed apart from insect activity. Insects also serve as food for fish, birds, and mammals.

Many insects are mentioned in the Bible, especially in the Old Testament. This article discusses the various insects with the references, identification wherever possible, influence upon human welfare, and brief pertinent life history details.

I. Grasshoppers, Locusts, and Crickets.

The grasshopper is the most frequently mentioned insect of Scripture with many Hebrew words used. Edible locusts are listed in Leviticus 11:21,22 as the locust *chargōl,* bald locust *sal'ām* or edible winged leaper or consumer, the grasshopper, and the beetle which is a misnomer for cricket. The Talmud is quoted by Broadus indicating the characteristics for identifying edible locusts. In the East locusts are still eaten by the poor. "The heads, legs and wings being removed, they are boiled, stewed or roasted and sometimes dressed in butter. They are eaten both fresh, and dried, or salted" (John A. Broadus, *Commentary on the Gospel of Matthew,* American Baptist Publication Society, 1886, p. 37). The insects John the Baptist ate were locusts (Mark 1:6).

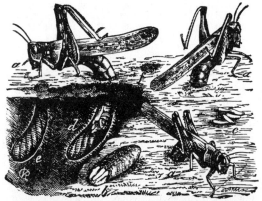

Locust laying eggs, with ovipository deep in the ground. (from Comstock **Intro. Entomology**).   © MPS

A swarm of locusts devouring herbage, as in the plague of locusts (Ex. 10, etc.) and the book of Joel. © MPS

The bristling locust, *yeleq,* is designated the palmerworm in Joel 1:4, and is also listed in Joel 2:25, Nahum 3:15,16; Psalms 105:34; Jeremiah 51:14,27 and other references. The name, grasshopper, *chāgāb,* the "coverer" is listed in Leviticus 11:22; Numbers 13:33; Ecclesiastes 12:5 and Isaiah 40:22. The term, locust, *'arbeh,* is the edible winged leaper mentioned in Exodus 10:4,12,13,14; Leviticus 11:22; II Chronicles 6:28, and many other references. The Hebrew word, *ts'lātsāl,* of Deuteronomy 28:42, and *gāzām* of Joel 1:4; 2:25; and Amos 4:9 also refer to locust. *Gāzām* in the latter reference is more properly translated "cutting locust" RSV rather than "palmerworm," KJV.

These insects belong to the order, *Orthoptera,* which includes cockroaches, mantids, walkingsticks, crickets, katydids, grasshoppers and locusts. Grasshoppers and locusts are included in the family *Locustidae,* a large family of most destructive insects from the earliest times. Comstock states, "It is to these insects that the term 'locust' is properly applied; for the locusts of which we read in the Bible, and in other books published in the older countries, are members of this family." (John Henry Comstock, *An Introduction to Entomology,* Comstock, New York, 1936, p. 253). Most species of locusts are non-migratory, but some which are small in size and countless in number "migrate in vast swarms, short or long distances, settling in grainfields, orchards, and other cultivated areas and often devastating everything before them" (E. O. Essig, *Insects of Western North America,* Macmillan, New York, 1926, p. 72). They are omnivorous feeders on all kinds of vegetable matter and become cannibalistic and carnivorous when natural food is lacking.

A plague of locusts in the Jordan Valley in 1959 is described, reminding us of the ravages prophesied in Scripture (Joel 1:4; Nah. 3:15; Rev. 9:3,7). *Eternity* magazine states, "Now the pests (locusts) are swarming into Jordan and Israel and there are ominous portents that the summer may see a fresh irruption from the inexhaustible breeding grounds of the desert locust in Arabia. A Desert Locust Survey has been founded on a permanent basis. The Food and Agricultural Organization of the United Nations is sponsor to an International Desert Locust Information Service which is maintained by the Anti-Locust Research Center in London" (*Eternity,* July 1959, "Plague of the Locusts," p. 33).

Female locusts lay eggs in the soil 30 to 60 together. These hatch in the spring into nymphs which after feeding extensively and passing through several molts mature into adults in the midsummer or fall and migrate in countless numbers great distances.

A fig tree at Jerusalem, in full leaf, before invasion of locusts. At right, the same tree fifteen minutes later, completely denuded of every leaf by a locust swarm. © MPS

Jerome in his commentary on Joel describes his own observation of locusts. "Even in our time we have seen troops of locusts cover the land of Judah. Then, when the shores of both seas were filled with heaps of dead locusts, which the waters had cast forth, their decay and stench became harmful to the extent of infecting the air and engendering disease for both animals and men (Jerome: *Commentary on Joel,* II, col. 25, col. 970).

II. Scale insects.

The scarlet color often mentioned in Scripture was made from the dried bodies of scale insects belonging to the order *Homoptera.* This order includes the cicadas, leaf-hoppers, aphids, scale bugs, tree-hoppers, white flies, and others. The scale insects are indirectly mentioned in the Bible. The two Hebrew words, *argvan* and *hokkinos* are translated "scarlet." *Argvan* occurs in Genesis 38: 28,30; Exodus 25:4f; Leviticus 14:4,6,51,52; Joshua 2:18,21. *Hokkinos* occurs in 2 Samuel 1:24; Proverbs 31:21; Song of Solomon 4:3. New Testament references also of interest include Matthew 27:28; Hebrews 9:19 and Revelation 17:3,4.

The scale insect of Scripture is *Coccus ilicis,* the host of which is the oak *Quercus coccifera,* common in Syria. It is called *kirmi* (Sanskrit), *kermes* (Arabic), and *karmil* (Hebrew) hence *carmin.* The family *Coccidae* includes these scale insects and also such familiar insects as mealy bugs, rose-scale, and San Jose scale. Many of the worst horticultural pests are of this family. The female is wingless and remains attached to the leaf. The young are deposited in a waxy material. The female dies and the body dries into a concave shell under which the young develop. These dried bodies when made into a powder produce the red dye.

The Cochineal Coccids have been cultivated in India, Spain and elsewhere for the purpose of gathering the females which are dried and ground into powder for dye. Aniline dyes now largely replace the insect dyes.

The lac-insect, *Tachardia lacca,* excretes a resinous substance useful as a source of shell-lac or shellac. The bodies are then used for lac-dye.

III. Moths and Butterflies.

The order *Lepidoptera* includes two groups of insects, moths and butterflies. Moths commonly called "millers" are nocturnal, with wings wrapped around the body or spread horizontally and usually thread-like antennae. Butterflies are daytime insects most of which fold wings vertically, and have clubbed antennae. There are over 9,000 species of Lepidopterous insects in America.

These insects develop through a complete metamorphosis. Larvae are *caterpillars* which are usually hairy. A cocoon is spun consisting of body hairs and silk or fragments of debris in which the pupal stage is passed. The larval forms of many moths and butterflies are serious chewing pests of field and orchard crops. These are not to be confused with the larval stage of many flies which are naked, legless maggots. Lepidopterous larvae vary greatly in form and appearance, usually cylindrical and provided with 10 to 16 legs, including six thoracic legs and four to ten abdominal prolegs which are shed with the last larval skin. Adults of this order are characterized by the apparently dust-like covering of the wings which is minute scales of regular and identifying shape.

The moth of Scripture is usually the familiar clothes moth of the large family, *Tineidae.* The moth ash is mentioned in Job 4:19; 13:28; 27:18; Psalm 39:11; Isaiah 50:9; 51:8; Hosea 5:12 and Matthew 6:19. From ancient times, the clothes moth has been a most destructive pest of valued fabrics and the symbol of the perishable.

The family *Tineidae* includes over 125 North American species, the clothes moth being among the most common. Three species are well-known: the naked clothes-moth, the larva of which spins some silk wherever it goes making neither case nor gallery; the case-bearing clothes-moth, the larva of which makes a case from pieces of its food material webbed together; and the tube-building clothes-moth or tapestry moth, the larva of which makes a long, winding gallery of silk mixed with cloth fragments.

Scale insects on an olive branch (from Comstock **Intro. Entomology**).

The adult flies at night laying eggs on woolen goods, furs, or feathers. The larvae hatch in about ten days and begin feeding immediately. Wool, hair, furs, skins, feathers, and dried animal matter all constitute suitable food material, which is often completely destroyed by holes made by the larval stage. The mature larvae pupate, after which the adults emerge, mate, and the females lay the eggs of the next generation.

Scripture also mentions silk garments (Prov. 31:22; Ezek. 16:10,13; Rev. 18:12). Silk is reeled from the cocoons of the silk worm pupae. Essig states that the Chinese or mulberry silkworm, *Bombyx mori Linn.*, is by far the most important commercial member of the insect world. The silkworm is native to Asia and has been domesticated so long as to require human care. It is the basis of large industries in Asiatic and European countries. Wing expanse of the adults measures 40-45 mm., and the caterpillar stage 45-55 mm. Larvae mature in 45 days and pupate in a thick oval white or yellow silken cocoon. Pupae are killed in the cocoons by heat or hot water and the raw silk is reeled for later use. White and black mulberry leaves are the preferred food of the larvae, although osage orange and even lettuce can be used to some extent. By procuring the silkworm eggs, larvae can be reared easily in confinement, using mulberry leaves. Special treatises on the subject should be secured before attempting the project.

The worm of Jonah 4:7 may have been a Lepidopterous larva. Such larvae are often voracious feeders, becoming very large before pupating and emerging as adults. Most of the references to worms in the Bible refer to the larvae of flies familiarly known as maggots.

IV. Flies.

All insects properly termed flies are included in the order *Diptera*. Comstock states that true flies are distinguished by a single pair of wings and a pair of halteres, thread-like clubbed appendages which are the second pair of wings and bear sense organs. This large order has 8,000 described species in North America distributed in over one thousand genera.

All types of crops are attacked by flies. Many species attack humans with most serious results. Malaria, yellow fever and filariasis are transmitted by flies.

Flies figured prominently in the plagues of Egypt. The third judgment of Exodus 8:16-19 termed "lice" (*kinnim*) was probably a sandfly capable of inflicting a painful sting, though identification is not certain. The fourth judgment of Exodus 8:20-32 termed "flies" is considered by many to be the mosquito from the Hebrew *arob*, meaning to suck.

Eggs of the mosquito are laid singly or in rafts on water or mud. The larvae are the "wrigglers" found in stagnant water which pupate and emerge into adult mosquitoes. Several diseases are caused by this insect. Certain species of the genus *Anopheles* transmit the parasites of malaria. The complex life-cycle of this unicellular parasite requires both the Anopheles mosquitoes and man. Upon biting an infected person, the malarial parasite is transferred to the alimentary canal of the mosquito where further stages occur. From the alimentary canal the organisms move to the body cavity of the mosquito and later to the salivary glands of the host from which they pass with saliva into the next person bitten. Hence, campaigns to eliminate mosquitoes are essential in eradication of malaria. Yellow fever, dengue fever and filari-

asis are also mosquito-born diseases. The parasitic worms causing filariasis increase in the blood stream causing severe stoppage of the lymphatic trunks of the body. Elephantiasis is one such disease. For detailed description of mosquito-caused diseases consult William A. Riley and Oskar A. Johannsen, *Medical Entomology*, New York: McGraw-Hill Book Company, Inc., 1938, p. 225.

Another fly not mentioned in the Bible but probably the cause of losses to olive crops is the olive fly. Frequent references are made to such losses (Deut. 28:40; Amos 4:9; Mic. 6:16; Hab. 3:17). The olive fly is a very serious pest to ripe olives in the Mediterranean region and also occurs in Northwest India on wild olives. The adult fly deposits eggs beneath the skin of ripening olives. A maggot hatches from the egg destroying the fruit.

In Acts 12:23 Herod is described as dying the horrible death of being eaten of worms. The screwworm is capable of such ravages. The adult female fly lays eggs on decaying animal matter and also in wounds, sores, nostrils and ears of men and cattle causing serious diseases. The following vivid description is quoted by Riley and Johannsen from Castellani and Chalmers: "Some days after a person suffering from a chronic catarrh, foul breath, or ozaena has slept in the open or has been attacked by a fly when riding or driving — i.e., when the hands are engaged — signs of severe catarrh appear, accompanied with inordinate sneezing and severe pain over the root of the nose or the frontal bone. Quickly the nose becomes swollen, and later the face also may swell, while examination of the nose may show the presence of the larvae. Left untreated, the patient rapidly becomes worse, and pus and blood are discharged from the nose, from which an offensive odor issues. Cough appears as well as fever, and often some delirium. If the patient lives long enough, the septum of the nose may fall in, the soft and hard palates may be pierced, the wall of the pharynx may be destroyed. By this time, however, the course of the disease will have become quite evident by the larvae dropping out of the nose; and if the patient continues to live, all the larvae may come away naturally" (William A. Riley and Oskar A. Johannsen, *Medical Entomolgy*, McGraw-Hill Book Company, Inc., New York, 1938, p. 385).

Several Bible verses speak of worms on dead bodies (Job 7:5; 17:14; 21:26; Isa. 14:11; 66:24). Mark 9:43-48 probably conveys the same repulsive phenomenon. The flesh-flies of the family *Sarcophagidae* lay eggs in the bodies of dead animals which hatch into maggots. These pass the entire larval period feeding on the decaying mass. Also the blow-flies of the family, *Calliphoridae* have very similar habits to the flesh-flies. They are the familiar noisy, large flies of shining greenish or bluish color. They serve the beneficial purpose of assisting in the decomposition of dead bodies.

V. Fleas.

Two Bible verses speak of the flea (I Sam. 24:14; 26:20). The flea (*par'osh*), belongs to the order *Siphonaptera*. The description given by Comstock is that of a small, wingless insect with body greatly laterally compressed. In I Samuel 24:14, David's reference to the flea is to indicate insignificance. The second reference seems to indicate the agility of the insect and difficulty of catching it. The flea illustrates this faculty with its body surface hard and smooth and its legs highly developed for jumping. Studies indicate that the human flea can jump 13 inches horizontally, and 7¾ inches vertically. Only with difficulty does one succeed in catching a flea, and having caught it, the task of killing it is still more difficult.

There are over 500 species of fleas and their distribution is very wide. They are abundant and offensive in the Orient and common in Palestine and Arabia. The bite is very irritating.

Bubonic plague of history is a flea-borne disease. It is spread by rats infected through fleas. In the 14th century, 25,000,000 deaths were caused by this disease. The simultaneous death of rats led to a study which proved the disease to be primarily a rodent disease conveyed to man by fleas. In 1665 the plague accounted for 68,596 deaths in London.

Eggs of fleas are scattered on floors of dwellings and sleeping-places of infested animals. Larvae are slender, worm-like creatures which feed on decaying particles of animal and vegetable matter. Fleas are parasitic only in the adult stage.

Dog-flea and its larva. Below, formicid ant (after Comstock).

VI. Ants and bees.

Ants. Two Bible verses speak of the ant (Prov. 6:6; 30:25). The industry and foresight of the ant are here eulogized. Studies of their habits reveal these characteristics dramatically true. Some ants raid other ant nests, carrying away captives for slaves. Over 100 kinds of ants raise fungi for food. In large numbers they climb trees cutting leaves which they drop to the ground for the "ground crew" to gather and drag to the colony for fungi-growing medium. Ants tending root-feeding aphids carry them to protective galleries, convey them to food sources, collect and store their eggs for winter, and in the spring take them to their food. Some ants tend aphids for the honeydew secreted. The honey-ants *Myrmecocystus,* are so called from the characteristic of individual workers serving as reservoirs for storing honey-dew gathered by other ants of the colony. These are called "repletes." They swallow sufficient honey-dew gathered by the others to distend their abdomens to a pea-sized sphere. Now incapable of locomotion, they remain quiet in the colony disgorging their honey-dew supply for nourishment to the others in time of need.

Typical ants belong to the subfamily *Formicinae,* including the carpenter ant, mound-building ant, blood-red slave-maker, harvesting ants, and many others. Most harvesting ants are found in arid regions of scant food supply and are therefore compelled to feed on seeds. Solomon's ants mentioned in Proverbs 6:6 and 30:25 are harvester ants. Species of harvester ants include the small harvester ant, acrobat ant, black harvester ant, agricultural ant, and the mound-building prairie ant. The prairie ant lives in large colonies surrounded by a cleared area 6 to 15 feet in diameter with mounds 4 to 12 inches high and 2 to 3 feet in diameter. Tunnels in the soil below the surface reach a depth of 9 feet.

Ants are all social insects. There are three castes: males, female or queen, and workers. Comstock states that the most important work on the subject is that of Professor W. M. Wheeler, *Ants, Their Structure, Development and Behavior,* 1910.

Bees. Hornets and yellow jackets belong to the family *Vespidae.* In Exodus 23:28; Deuteronomy 7:20 and Joshua 24:12 the hornet is mentioned as the means used by God to drive out the enemies of Israel. Hornets are medium-sized insects, mostly yellow and black in color, and build large and small paper nests mostly above ground, but also below. They feed on flies and are beneficial insects. They possess a severe sting, a pugnacious spirit, and fast flight thus making them a formidable opponent from which to flee.

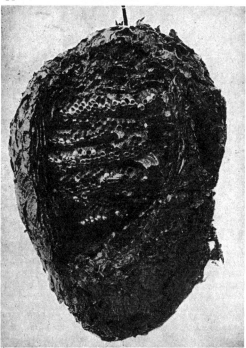

A nest of hornets (**Vespa**), exposing interior (from Comstock).

Several references in Scripture speak of bees (Deut. 1:44; Ps. 118:12; Isa. 7:18). Enemies are likened unto bees in their pursuing tactics and large numbers. Bees are very common in Palestine where the warm climate and abundance of flowers favor their increase.

The mention of a swarm of bees and honey in Judges 14:8 may refer to the honey-bee of commerce today. There is no evidence that the Hebrews cultivated honey-bees. The honey bee is a highly social insect living in colonies varying from 20,-000 to 50,000 individuals. The phrase "bee hive of activity" is a graphic picture, for the hive is the residence of these many thousands of individuals each with responsible activity. Within the hive is found the nursery for rearing larvae, the place of wax production for food storage, the processing of nectar for honey, the preparation of pollen for food and plant waxes for plastering. A continuing stream of bees depart and return throughout sunny daylight hours in ceaseless work for the hive. Food gathered in the hive includes honey which is made from nectar brought from flowers and elaborated in the honey sac of the workers and stored in the wax cells of the comb. Bee bread is also a food material for larvae consisting of pollen gathered from flowers and mixed with honey. Royal jelly is a highly nutritious material secreted mostly by young adult workers and fed to all very young larvae. It is the entire food of larvae destined to become queens, for the production of queens is a voluntary activity of the workers controlled by the use of this food material exclusively.

Periodically the old queen and a large number of workers and drones leave the hive in a swarm to establish a new hive leaving ample "personnel" to maintain the old hive. [The location of the new hive varies widely.]   W.M.W.

INSPIRATION. In the KJV of the Bible the word *inspiration* is used twice, in Job 32:8 to translate the Hebrew word *neshāmâh* (*breathe*) and in II Timothy 3:16, where it translates the Greek word *theópneustos*. The latter passage has given its meaning to the word *inspiration* as commonly applied to Scripture. Literally translated, *theópneustos* means *God-breathed*. The key to its meaning may be gleaned from the OT concept of the divine breathing as productive of effects which God Himself is immediately accomplishing by His own will and power (see Ps. 33:6). By this word, therefore, Paul is asserting that the written documents, called Holy Scripture, are a divine product.

Precisely the same idea is set forth in II Peter 1:19-21. In this passage the prophetic Word (i.e., Scripture) is contrasted with mere fables devised by human cunning. Scripture is more sure and trustworthy than the testimony of any eyewitness. The explanation for its unique authority lies in its origin. It was produced not as a merely human private interpretation of the truth, but by God's Spirit through the prophets.

In both II Timothy 3:16 and II Peter 1:19-21 the fact of the divine productivity (spiration rather than *in*spiration) of the "Holy Writings" is thus explicitly asserted. This divine (in)spiration is further confirmed by a host of NT passages. The authors of Scripture wrote in or by the Spirit (Mark 12:36). What the Scripture states is really what God has said (Heb. 3:7; Acts 4:25; and see especially Heb. 1:5ff). This is true irrespective of whether or not in the particular passage cited the words are ascribed to God or are the statements of the human author. In the mind of the NT writers any passage of Scripture was really "spoken" by God. Our Lord employed the same type of reference, attributing directly to God the authorship of Scripture (Matt. 19:4 and 5).

Because of the character of the God of truth who "inspired" (or produced) the Holy Scriptures, the result of "inspiration" is to constitute it as fully trustworthy and authoritative. Indeed, this absolute divine authority of Scripture, rather than its inspiration, is the great burden of Scriptural teaching about its own nature (see Pss. 19:7-14; and 119:89, 97, 113, 160; Zech. 7:12; Matt. 5: 17-19; Luke 16:17; John 10:34 and 35; I Thess. 2:13). Besides those passages directly teaching the authority of Scripture, such phrases as "It is written" (Luke 4:4,8,10; Matt. 21:13). "It (or He) says" (Rom. 9:15; Gal. 3:16), and "Scripture says" (Gal. 3:8; Rom. 9:17) — all clearly imply an absolute authority for the OT Scriptures.

These passages teaching the authority of Scripture indicate also the extent of inspiration. If the authority and trustworthiness of Scripture are com-plete, inspiration itself must also extend to all of Scripture. This completeness of inspiration and consequent authority of all Scripture is made explicit in such passages as Luke 24:25: "O, fools, and slow of heart to believe all that the prophets have spoken" (see also Matt. 5:17-19; Luke 16: 17; and John 10:34 and 35).

The inerrant and infallible inspiration of Scripture, though not exactly synonymous terms, are nevertheless both correctly applied to Scripture in order to indicate that inspiration and authority are complete. The word *inerrant* suggests that the Scriptures do not wander from the truth. *Infallible* is stronger, suggesting an incapability of wandering from the truth ("Do ye not therefore err, because ye know not the Scriptures?" (Mark 12:24).

The completeness of inspiration is further established by the fact that Scripture lacks altogether any principle for distinguishing between those parts of it which are inspired and thus possess binding authority, and supposedly uninspired parts which do not possess binding authority. The method of inspiration is never developed in the Scriptures, although the basic fact that Scripture is produced by the power of God working in and through the prophet indicates the mutual interworking of the divine and human hand. By pointing to a human author of Scripture (e.g. "David himself said by the Holy Spirit" — Mark 12:36; "Moses wrote" — Mark 12:19; and "Isaiah said" — John 12:39), by stating his purpose in the writing of a book (e.g. John 20:30 and 31 and Luke 1:1-4), and by acknowledging research in the preparation of the writing of Scripture (Luke 1:2 and 3), the Biblical authors make indubitably plain that the divine method of inspiration was not any process of dictation.

At this point great caution should be taken not to read into the Biblical idea of the origin of Scripture suggestions derived from the English word *inspiration* (or Latin *inspiratio*). The point of the Biblical teaching is never a divine heightening of the human powers of the prophet (though the Bible does not deny that in certain instances such may have taken place). Rather, by all those inconceivable means at the disposal of a sovereign God, the Holy Spirit used the writers of Scripture to produce through them the message that He wished to communicate to man. God's Spirit obviously did not need in every case to "inspire" (i.e. to raise to greater heights than ordinarily) a Micah or a Luke; rather God produced the writing He wished by His sovereign preparation and control of a man who could and freely would write just what God desired to be His divinely authoritative message to His people.

Biblical inspiration must be complemented by an interior illumination of the Holy Spirit (I Cor. 2: 14ff) in order to make that which God has given in the past really become His living, revealing Word today in the heart and mind of the believer. It is in this sense that the word *inspiration* is used in the Authorized translation of Job 32:8. In traditional theological terminology this latter work is generally referred to as the illumination of the Holy Spirit.

In summary, Biblical inspiration (as distinguished from illumination) may be defined as the work of the Holy Spirit by which, through the instrumentality of the personality and literary talents of its human authors, He constituted the words of the Bible in all of its several parts as His written word to men and therefore of divine authority and without error in the autographs.

K.S.K.

INTEREST (ĭn'tēr-ĕst, Heb. *neshekh, something bitten off, mashā', lending on interest,* Gr. *tókos, something produced by money*). In the OT there is no trace of any system of commercial credit. Large commercial loans were not made in ancient Israel. Only the poor borrowed, and they did it to obtain the necessities of life. The law of Moses forbade lending at interest to a fellow Israelite (Exod. 22: 25), but permitted charging interest to a foreigner (Deut. 23:20). A needy Israelite might sell himself as a servant (Lev. 25:39; II Kings 4:1). The prophets condemn the taking of interest as a heinous sin (Ezek. 18:8,13,17; Jer. 15:10). In the NT, references to interest occur in two parables — of the Pounds (Luke 19:23) and of the Talents (Matt. 25:27), and it is distinctly encouraged.

INTERMEDIATE STATE. The life of man is represented in Scripture as falling into three stages: first, the period from birth until death, which is life in the present world and in the natural body; second, life in the intermediate state, between death and the resurrection, which is life without the body; and, third, life in the resurrection body, which is the final and eternal state.

The Bible does not have a great deal to say regarding the intermediate state. Rather, it focuses attention on the second coming of Christ and the glories of heaven that will follow. For this reason, while such a state is generally acknowledged by Christians everywhere, there are differences of opinion regarding its nature: whether the soul is conscious or asleep, whether those who die unsaved have another chance in the next life, whether the wicked will be annihilated.

For the righteous the intermediate state is a time of rest and blessedness, holiness and happiness. The NT sometimes represents the state of death as a "sleeping" and the act of dying as a "falling asleep" (Matt. 9:24; John 9:4; 11:11; I Thess. 4:13,15; II Pet. 3:4), but this does not mean that the soul is unconscious until the resurrection, but that the dead person is like one asleep in not being alive to his surroundings. The story of the rich man and Lazarus represents the latter as conscious and blessed in Abraham's bosom (Luke 16:19-31). On the cross Jesus said to the penitent thief, "Today shalt thou be with me in Paradise" (Luke 23:43). John says, "Blessed are the dead which die in the Lord from henceforth: yea, saith the Spirit, that they may rest from their labors; and their works follow them" (Rev. 14:13). Paul says to the Corinthians that he is "willing rather to be absent from the body, and to be at home with the Lord" (II Cor. 5:8); and to the Philippians he writes that he has a "desire to depart and to be with Christ" (Phil. 1:23). But while the intermediate state is for believers a time of freedom from sin and pain, it is nevertheless also one of imperfection, or incompleteness. This is because the soul is without a body, which for man is an abnormal condition, and because Christ's rewards to His people for the labors of this life will not be given until His second coming. The blessings of the intermediate state are, as it were, only an earnest of the good things to come.

That the intermediate state involves conscious suffering for the unregenerate, is shown by the story of the rich man and Lazarus, in which the rich man finds himself in torment immediately upon dying, with his brothers still on earth (Luke 16:19-31).

Some scholars regard Sheol-Hades as a neutral place, neither heaven nor hell, where all men, good and bad, go and remain, either permanently or until some communal resurrection. Careful study shows, however, that the words are not always used in the same sense, but may, depending on the context, refer to the state of death, the grave, the place of departed souls, or hell. In the following passages Sheol refers to the place of punishment for the wicked: Deuteronomy 32:22; Job 21:13; Psalm 9:17; Proverbs 7:27.

The theory of "second probation," that those who die unsaved will have another chance for salvation in the next life, is based upon the erroneous principle that only the conscious rejection of Christ and His Gospel causes men to perish. Scripture, however, shows that men are already under God's condemnation when salvation is offered to them. The main Scriptural basis for this view is found in I Peter 3:19 and 4:6, which are understood to teach that Christ in the period between His death and resurrection preached to the spirits in Hades. But these passages may be interpreted quite differently, as any scholarly commentary shows. Scripture represents the state of the lost after death as a fixed state (Luke 16:19-31; John 8:21,24; II Cor. 5:10; 6:2; II Pet. 2:4,9; Jude 7-13). The final judgment is always represented as determined by things done in the body, not in the intermediate state (Matt. 7:22,23; 10:32,33; 25:34-36; II Cor. 5:9,10).

Annihilationism holds to the view that there is no conscious existence, if any existence at all, of the wicked after death. Support for it is found in those passages of Scripture which represent eternal life and immortality as a gift of God to those who believe in Christ (John 3:16; 10:27,28; 17:3; Rom. 2:7; 6:22,23; Gal. 6:8). The "death" and "destruction" with which sinners are threatened are interpreted to mean non-existence (Matt. 7:13; 10:28; John 3:16; Rom. 6:23; 8:13; II Thess. 1:9). Scripture, however, teaches that both saints and sinners exist forever (Eccl. 12:7; Matt. 25:46; Rev. 14:11; 20:10), and represents the punishment of the wicked as everlasting (Matt. 25:41,46; 18:8; Mark 9:43,44; Rev. 14:11; 20:10). The Greek word for "everlasting" (*aionios*) is used to describe both the blessings of the saved in heaven and the punishment of the lost.　　S.B.

IPHEDEIAH (ĭf-ĕ-dē'yà, Heb. *yiphdeyâh, Jehovah redeems*), a descendant of Benjamin (I Chron. 8:25).

IR (ĭr, Heb. *'îr, watcher*), the ancestral head of a clan of Benjamin. He belonged to the family of Bela (I Chron. 7:7,12).

IRA (ī'rà, Heb. *'irā'*). 1. A chief minister, or priest, in the time of David (II Sam. 20:26).

2. A son of Ikkesh, a Tekoite, one of David's mighty men (II Sam. 23:26; I Chron. 11:28).

3. An Ithrite, one of David's heroes (II Sam. 23:38; I Chron. 11:40).

IRAD (ī'răd, Heb. *'îrādh*), grandson of Cain and son of Enoch (Gen. 4:18).

IRAM (ī'răm, Heb. *'irām*), a chief of Edom (Gen. 36:43; I Chron. 1:54).

IR-HA-HERES (ĭr-hă-hē'rĕz, Heb. *'îr ha-heres*), a city of Egypt mentioned only in Isaiah 19:18, "In that day shall five cities in the land of Egypt speak the language of Canaan, and swear to the Lord of hosts; one shall be called, The city of destruction." The passage is difficult of exegesis because of the uncertainty of the text, and many interpretations have been given of it, especially in modern times. Many MSS and several versions read "City of the Sun," and some have thought that it refers to the city of Heliopolis in Egypt, called in the Bible

"On" (Gen. 41:50, etc.), a city of great importance in the religion of Egypt. This is the reading preferred by the RSV translators. The LXX reads "city of Righteousness." The Massoretic reading, "the city of destruction," seems to indicate that we have here not the name of a city, but merely a descriptive appellation of that city which should be destroyed. It is not possible to identify this city exactly.

IRI (ĭ'rī, Heb. *îrî*), a Benjamite of the family of Bela (I Chron. 7:7,12).

IRIJAH (ĭ-rī'jà, Heb. *yir'îyāyh, Jehovah sees*), a captain of the guard, who at the time of the Chaldean siege of Jerusalem, arrested Jeremiah, who was leaving the city at the gate of Benjamin, on suspicion of intending to desert to the enemy (Jer. 37:13).

IR-NAHASH (ĭr-nā'hăsh, Heb. *'îr nāhāsh*), a town of Judah of which Tehinnah is called the "father," probably meaning "founder" (I Chron. 4:12). The site is uncertain.

IRON (Heb. *barzel*, Gr. *síderos*). Tubal-cain, of the race of Cain, is described as "an instructor of every artificer in brass and iron" (Gen. 4:22). It used to be thought that the use of iron began very late, but modern archaeology shows that there was a knowledge of iron as early as the third millennium B.C. Remains of an iron blade dating c. 2700 B.C. have been found by the Oriental Institute at the University of Chicago at a site about 50 miles NE of Baghdad. A small steel axe from Ur and other early objects of iron have also been found. The fact that not more iron objects of an early period have been found is undoubtedly due to the fact that iron oxidizes quickly. Iron was not smelted in Egypt before 1300 B.C. The Taurus Mountains, the chief iron supply of Asia Minor, were for many years controlled by the Hittites. Iron began to come into general use in Palestine in the 13th century B.C. The Israelites in the period of the judges and the early monarchy envied and dreaded the iron furnaces of the Philistines, which gave the iron a tremendous superiority in arms. It·was both inconvenient and expensive for the Israelites to go to Philistia to get iron tools made or repaired (I Sam. 13:20). Lack of iron for farming implements, nails, and weapons for war kept the Israelites comparatively poor through the period of the judges. They could not drive the Canaanites out of the plains because the latter had chariots and weapons of iron (Josh. 17:18; Judg. 1:19; 4:2,3). Even in the time of Saul, his army had no swords or spears for battle, he and Jonathan alone possessing them (I Sam. 13:22). When the power of the Philistines was broken by Saul and David, the iron-smelting formula became public property, and the metal came to be widely used in Israel.

Iron ore was brought in by Tyrian traders, mainly from Spain, although it was also found in the Lebanon range (Jer. 11:4; Deut. 4:20; 8:9; I Kings 8:51) and probably Egypt (Deut. 4:20). The Jews seem to have learned the art of working in iron from the Phoenicians (II Chron. 2:14). The ore was reduced in furnaces built of stone; charcoal was used in them, and the fire was blown by bellows (Ezek. 22:20). Wrought iron, cast iron, and steel were made.

Iron was used in Bible times much as it is used today. Out of iron, blacksmiths in the Mosaic period made axes and other implements (Num. 35:16). We read that Og's bedstead was made of iron (Deut. 3:11), although some hold it was made of basalt, a black iron-like stone. In the time of Joshua and of the judges vessels were made of metal (Josh. 6:19,24). Later, of iron were made threshing instruments (Amos 1:3), harrows (II Sam. 12:31), axes (II Sam. 12:31; II Kings 6:6), other tools (I Kings 6:7), weapons (Num. 35:16; Job 20:24), armor (II Sam. 23:7), horns (I Kings 22:11), fetters (Ps. 105:18), chariots Josh. 17:16), yokes (Jer. 28:14), chisels (Job 19: 24; Jer. 17:1), sheets or plates (Ezek. 4:3), gods (Dan. 5:4), weights (I Sam. 17:7). Iron was among the materials gathered by David for the building of the temple (I Chron. 22:14,16; 29: 2,7). There are allusions to iron gates (Acts 12: 10), prison bars (Ps. 107:10,16; Isa. 10:34), nails or bolts (I Chron. 22:3). We read that when David captured the city of Rabbah, he set the inhabitants to laboring with saws, iron picks, and iron axes (II Sam. 12:31). There is a description of a smith at work in Ecclesiasticus 38:28.

The word *iron* is often used figuratively in Scripture. It is made to represent barrenness (Deut. 28:23), slavery ("yoke of iron," Deut. 28:48), captivity (Ps. 107:10), moral deterioration (Jer. 6:28), political strength (Dan. 2:33), fortitude ("iron pillar," Jer. 1:18), strength "bars of iron," Job 40:18), severity ("rod of iron," Ps. 2:9), destructive power ("iron teeth," Dan. 7:7), and affliction ("iron furnace," Deut. 4:20; Ezek. 22: 18-22). See MINERALS AND METALS.　　　S.B.

IRON (ī'rŏn, Heb. *yir'ŏn*), a fortified city in the territory of Naphtali (Josh 19:38). It is probably the present village of Yarun, ten miles W of Lake Huleh.

IRPEEL (ĭr'pī-ĕl, Heb. *yirpe'ēl, God heals*), a city of Benjamin (Josh. 18:27)); site uncertain, but probably near the ancient Gibeon.

IRRIGATION (ĭr-ĭ-gā'shŭn), a word for which there is no Hebrew or Greek equivalent in the Bible, although the use of irrigation for watering plants and trees is frequently implied (Eccl. 2:5,6; Isa. 58:11). There was less need of irrigation in Palestine and Syria than in Egypt and Babylonia. In Palestine it was necessary only in the summer.

IR-SHEMESH (ĭr-shē'měsh, Heb. *'îr shemesh, city of the sun*), a city of Dan (Josh. 19:41), the same as Beth-shemesh.

IRU (ī'rōō, Heb. *'îrû*), eldest son of Caleb (I Chron. 4:15); probably to be read *Ir*.

ISAAC (ī'zàk, Heb. *yitshāk, Gr. Isaák, one laughs*), the only son of Abraham by Sarah, and the second of three Hebrew patriarchs who were the progenitors of the Jewish race. He was born in the south country, probably Beer-sheba (Gen. 21:14,31), when Abraham was 100 and Sarah 90 years old (Gen. 17:17; 21:5). He was named Isaac because both Abraham and Sarah had laughed incredulously at the thought of having a child at their age (Gen. 17:17-19; 18:9-15; 21:6). His birth must be regarded as a miracle. It was 25 years after God had promised the childless Abraham and Sarah a son, that the promise was fulfilled. He is thus rightly called the child of promise, in contrast with Ishmael, who was born of Hagar, Sarah's maid, and Abraham. When he was eight days old, he was circumcised (Gen. 21:4). Fearing future jealousy and strife between the two boys when she observed Ishmael mocking Isaac, Sarah tried to persuade Abraham to cast out Hagar and Ishmael. Abraham was loath to do this because he loved the boy, and did so only when he received explicit direction from God, who said to him that his seed would be called in Isaac, but He would also make of Ishmael a nation (Gen. 21:9-13).

The next recorded event in the life of Isaac is connected with God's command to Abraham to offer him as a sacrifice on a mountain in the land of Moriah (Gen. 22). His exact age then is not stated, but he is described as a "lad," able to carry up the mountainside the wood for the burnt-offering. In this whole experience his filial acquiescence in his father's purpose, his unquestioning submission and obedience, stand out almost as remarkably as his father's faith. Bound upon the altar and about to be slain, his life was spared when an angel of the Lord interposed and substituted for him a ram, which was offered up in his stead. God's purpose in this great test of Abraham's faith is looked at in various ways, among the more important being the following: it is the last and culminating point in God's education of Abraham regarding the meaning of sacrificial obedience; it is a rebuke by God of the widespread heathen practice of sacrificing human beings; it is an object lesson to Abraham of the great sacrifice of the Messiah for the redemption of mankind.

Sarah died at Hebron when Isaac was 36 years old (Gen. 23:1). At the age of 40 he married Rebekah, a kinswoman from Mesopotamia (Gen. 24), but he and his wife were childless until, in answer to prayer, twin sons, Esau and Jacob, were born to them when he was 60 (Gen. 25:20,26). At a time of famine, God admonished him not to go down into Egypt, as he had thought of doing, but to remain in the promised land; and he pledged His word to be with him. He went to the Philistine city of Gerar, and there, fearing for his own life, he passed off his wife as his sister, as his father had done before him; and was justly rebuked by Abimelech the king for his duplicity (Gen. 26:10). He then pitched his camp in the valley of Gerar and became so prosperous as a wheat-grower and herdsman that the envious Philistines began a systematic, petty harassment by stopping up the wells which his father had dug and which he had opened again. Abimelech even advised him to leave the country in the interests of peace (Gen. 26). Isaac subsequently returned to Beersheba. There the Lord appeared to him at night and promised to bless him for his father's sake. Realizing that God was with him, Abimelech then came from Gerar to make overtures of peace, and the two men formally entered into a covenant (Gen. 26:26-31). Probably at a considerably later period, Esau, at the age of 40, brought grief of mind to Isaac and Rebekah by marrying two daughters of Caanan (Gen. 26:34,35).

The last prominent event in the life of Isaac is the blessing of his sons (Gen. 27). Esau, the elder, was his father's favorite, even though God had told him that the elder would serve the younger, while Rebekah's favorite was Jacob (Gen. 25:28). When he was over 100 years old, and dim of sight, and perhaps thinking that his end was near, he desired to bestow his last blessing upon his elder son; but through Rebekah's cunning and guile, Jacob the younger supplanted his brother, and the blessing of the birthright was bestowed upon him. To save Jacob from the murderous wrath of Esau, who determined to kill him after his father's death, Rebekah induced Isaac to send Jacob into Mesopotamia, that, after his own example, his son might take a wife from among his own kindred, and not imitate Esau by marriage with Canaanite women. Isaac invoked another blessing upon the head of Jacob and sent him away to Laban in Padan-aram (Gen. 27-28:5).

Isaac is mentioned only once more, when 20 years later, Jacob returned from his sojourn in

The site of ancient Gerar (Tell Jemmeh), as seen from the west. This was the birthplace of Isaac. © MPS

Mesopotamia, having, agreeably to his father's command, married into Laban's family. Jacob found the old man at Mamre in Hebron, and there Isaac died, 180 years old, and his two sons, Esau and Jacob, buried him (Gen. 35:27-29).

The NT refers to Isaac almost a score of times. His sacrifice by Abraham is twice mentioned, in Hebrews 11:17,18 and James 2:21, but while the submission of Isaac is referred to, the stress is upon the triumph of Abraham's faith. He is contrasted with Ishmael, as the child of promise and the progenitor of the children of promise (Rom. 9:7,10; Gal. 4:28; Heb. 11:18). In our Lord's argument with the Sadducees on the matter of resurrection, He represents him, although gathered to his people, as still living to God (Luke 20:37). In the Sermon on the Mount Jesus proclaimed that many would come from the E and the W to sit down with Abraham, Isaac, and Jacob in the kingdom of heaven.

Of the three patriarchs, Isaac was the least conspicuous, traveled the least, had the fewest extraordinary adventures, and lived the longest. He was free from violent passions; quiet, gentle, dutiful; less a man of action than of thought and suffering. His name is always joined in equal honor with Abraham and Jacob.   S.B.

ISAIAH. Little is known about the Prophet Isaiah except what his own words reveal. His name Isaiah (*Salvation of Jehovah*) is almost identical in meaning with Joshua (*Jehovah is salvation*) which appears in the NT as Jesus, the name of the Messiah whom Isaiah heralded. That his name played a formative role in his life is not improbable since it expresses the great theme of his prophetic ministry. His father, Amoz, may have been a person of prominence, since the prophet is so often called (13 times) "the son of Amoz," but nothing is known about him. Isaiah was married and had two children to whom he gave significant names (7:3; 8:3).

Period. Isaiah prophesied in four reigns, from Uzziah to Hezekiah (1:1). The first date given is the year of Uzziah's death (6:1), which probably occurred about 740 B.C. or several years later. The last historical event referred to is the death of Sennacherib (37:38) which occurred in 681 B.C. The most important events are the Syro-Ephraimitic war in the days of Ahaz (7:1-9), which Isaiah treated, despite its devastation (II Chron. 28:5-15), as almost insignificant compared with the far greater scourge. Assyria, which was so soon to follow (vss. 17-25). Assyria is the great enemy with which much of chapters 7-39 deals; and beyond it looms an even mightier foe, Babylon, whose downfall is foretold already in chapters 13-14 and is the great theme of 40-48. Over against these terrible instruments of divine judgment Isaiah pictures the Messianic hope, first in counseling unbelieving Ahaz, and repeatedly thereafter.

Analysis. The structure of Isaiah is, in its broad outlines, a simple one, but in its details it raises many problems. It may be briefly analyzed as follows:

I. Chapters 1-5, Introductory. Chapter 1 contains the "great arraignment." Like so many of Isaiah's utterances, it combines dire threatenings with urgent calls to repentance and gracious offers of forgiveness and blessing. It is followed by the promise of world redemption (2:1-5). Then come a series of threatening passages, including a detailed description of the finery of the women of Jerusalem as illustrating the sinful frivolity of the people as a whole. The land is likened to an unfruitful vineyard, which will soon become desolate. It concludes with a series of six woes which end in gloom: "and the light is darkened in the heavens thereof."

II. Chapter 6, The Temple Vision. Whether this represents the initial call of Isaiah has been much debated. If the woe pronounced on himself by the prophet is to be understood as the seventh woe, intended to show that the prophet was as conscious of his own sin as of the sin of his people, we may assume that this chapter stands in its proper place chronologically and that this vision came to him some time after he began to prophesy. But the question must remain unsettled. It is a vision of the Holy God; and "Holy One of Israel" becomes one of Isaiah's favorite titles for the Deity in whose name he speaks.

III. Chapters 7-12, the Book of Immanuel. This group of chapters belongs to the period of the Syro-Ephraimitic war (II Kings 16:1-20; II Chron. 28). In the midst of this time of peril, Isaiah utters the great prophecies regarding Immanuel (7: 14-16; 9:6f.; 11:1-10); and he concludes with a song of triumphant faith which ends with the assurance, "great is the Holy One of Israel in the midst of thee." Here again "woe" (10:1-4) and "threatening" (vss. 5-19) stand in vivid contrast with Messianic blessing (11:1-16).

IV. Chapters 13-23, Prophecies against the Nations. These are ten "burdens," i.e., weighty, solemn, and grievous utterances (Jer. 23:33f.) against nations which were or would be a menace to God's people: Babylon (13-14:27), Philistia (14:28-32), Moab (15-16), Damascus (17-18), Egypt (19-20), Babylon (21:1-10), Dumah (vss. 11-12), Arabia (vss. 13-17), Jerusalem (22), Tyre (23). Here prophecies regarding the near future (16:14; 21:16:cf.22:20 with 37:2) appear along with others which refer to a more distant (23:17) or a quite remote time. Thus the fall of Babylon is so certain that Israel is told the taunt-song it will sing "in that day" (14:4-20). Compare 21:6-10 which describes it as having already taken place, with 39:6 which speaks of the Babylonian Captivity as still future — a method of prophetic description frequently found in Isaiah. This group of prophecies is chiefly minatory, but it also contains wonderful promises of blessing. Israel's mightiest foes will share with her in the future blessedness (19:23-25).

V. Chapter 24 looks far into the future. It is world-embracing and may be called an *apocalypse*. The world judgment will be followed by songs of thanksgiving for divine blessing (26-26). A prophecy against Egypt follows (27). Then there are again six woes (28-34), the last being a frightful curse on Edom. This group also closes with a beautiful prophetic picture of future blessedness (35).

VI. Chapters 36-39, Historical (comp. parallel passages in Kings and Chronicles). They describe the blasphemous threats of Sennacherib against Jerusalem, Hezekiah's appeal to Isaiah who ridicules the invader, the flight and death of the blasphemer (36-37) — one of the most thrilling stories in the whole Bible. Probably Hezekiah's illness and the embassage of Merodach Baladan (38-39) took place during the reign of Sargon. If so, the arrangement is topical and intended to prepare for the prophecies of consolation which follow.

Chapters 40-66 have been called the **Book of Consolation.** The words "Comfort ye, comfort ye my people" are clearly intended to give Israel a comfort and hope not to be gathered from Hezekiah's words, which they immediately follow. These chapters fall into three parts as is suggested by the refrain-like words, "There is no peace, saith the Lord unto the wicked" (48:22; compare 57: 21) which have their terrible echo in Isaiah's final words (66:24).

Chapters 40-48 deal with the coming of Cyrus and the fall of Babylon as proof of the power of the God of Israel both to foretell and fulfill, in amazing contrast to the idols of the heathen which can do neither. The utter folly of idolatry is portrayed most vividly in 44:9-20 and 46:1-11. The last mention of Babylon, "Go ye forth from Babylon, flee ye from the Chaldeans" (48:20) is clearly to be thought of as describing flight from a doomed city, like the flight of Lot from Sodom. In the two remaining parts of the book there is no mention of either Assyria or Babylon except by way of reminiscence (52:4).

Chapters 49-57 form a logical and climactic sequel to the preceding group. The figure of the "servant" is common to both. The word occurs 20 times in chapters 40-53. Nine times he is called Israel, Jacob, or Jacob-Israel. Six times the Lord calls him "my servant." The title is used in three senses: of the servant as deaf and blind (42:18f.), sinful and needing redemption (44:22, cf.43:25); of the servant as faithful and as having a mission to Israel and the Gentiles (42:1-7; 49:1-6; 50:6-9); and finally of One who, Himself innocent, suffers for the sins of others (52:13-53:12). The first three of these four passages which are often called the "Servant Songs" can refer to the pious in Israel as sharing with their Lord in His mission of salvation. In the last the reference to the Messiah is "predominant and exclusive" (Alexander). This is one of the most precious chapters in the Bible. It speaks both of the humiliation of the Saviour and also of the glory which is to follow. The greatness of the salvation secured by the Ser-

The complete scroll of Isaiah, from the Dead Sea Scrolls, opened to chapter 40. The entire scroll consists of 17 sheets of parchment, sewn together (as seen at right), and measures 24 feet in length.
ASOR

vant is described in glowing terms and its worldwide scope is made clear in vss. 10-12 and again and again in the chapters which follow, especially 61:1-3.

Chapters 58-66 continue the same general theme which reaches its height in 66:1-3, a passage which foretells that day of which Jesus spoke to the woman of Samaria, when the true worshiper shall worship not in temples made with hands, but "in spirit and in truth" (John 4:21-24). Yet here again as constantly elsewhere warning and denunciation alternate with offers and assurances of blessing. Thus 65:17 which speaks of the "new heavens and the new earth" (cf. 66:22) follows a denunciation of those who practice abominations. And the book closes with a reference to the torments of the reprobate.

Principal Themes of Isaiah. Isaiah is preeminently the prophet of redemption. The greatness and majesty of God, His holiness and hatred of sin and the folly of idolatry, His grace and mercy and love, and the blessed rewards of obedience are constantly recurring themes. No wonder that the NT writers quote so often from Isaiah and that so much of Handel's *Messiah* is taken from it. Redeemer and saviour (save, salvation) are among his favorite words. It is significant that the words which describe the character of the promised Messiah (9:6) are frequently on his lips: wonderful (25:1; 28:29; 29:14), counsellor (19:17; 25:1; 28:29; 40:13f; 46:10), mighty God (30:29; 33:13; 40:17f, 26; 42:13; 49:20-26; 60:16), everlasting father (26:4; 40:28; 45:17; 55:3; 57:15; 60:19f.; 63:16; 64:8), a prince of peace (26:12; 45:7; 52:7; 53:5; 55:12; 57:19; 66:12). Isa-

iah has a deep appreciation of beauty and wonder of the world of nature (e.g., chap. 35). A striking figure which he uses repeatedly is the "highway" (11:16; 19:23; 33:8; 35:8; 36:2; 40:3; 49:11; 57:14; 62:10). All the barriers which separate nation from nation and delay the coming of the King to his kingdom will be removed and "the glory of the Lord shall be revealed and all flesh shall see it together" (40:5).

Importance. The importance of the book is indicated by the frequency with which it is quoted in the NT. Isaiah is quoted by name 21 times, slightly more than all the other writing prophets taken together; and there are many more allusions and quotations where his name is not given. He has been called the evangelist of the OT and many of the most precious verses in the Bible come to us from his lips. The fact that the Lord began His public ministry at Nazareth by reading from Chapter 61 and applying its prophetic words to Himself is significant of the place which this book has ever held in the Christian Church.

Unity. An article on Isaiah written today must deal with the unity of the book, since this has been vigorously assailed for nearly two centuries. The attack is not due to any discoveries that have been made, but to the new theory regarding prophecy which is widely prevalent today and which minimizes or denies prediction, declaring that the OT prophet spoke only to the men of his own time and not to future generations. This theory is refuted by the fact that the NT frequently quotes the words of the prophets, notably Isaiah, as fulfilled in the earthly life of Jesus Christ. In John 12:38-40 two quotations from this book are brought together, the one from 53:1, the other from 6:9f., and as if to make it quite clear that they have one and the same source, the evangelist adds: "These things said Isaiah, when he saw his glory and spake of him."

The main argument for a Second Isaiah is that Cyrus is referred to as one who has already entered upon his career of conquest (e.g., 41:1f.,25); and it is claimed that the writer of all or part of chapters 40-66 must have lived at the close of the Babylonian Captivity. It is to be noted, therefore, that the prophets, notably Isaiah, often spoke as if they were eye witnesses of the future events which they described. The viewpoint or situation of the one who penned Chapter 53 is Calvary. He describes the sufferings of the Servant as ended and depicts in glowing colors the glory which shall follow, yet the prophet cannot have lived at that time. He must have lived many years, even centuries, before the advent of the One whose death he so vividly portrays. Consequently, one must either hold that the prophet neither in 7-12 nor in 53 predicted the coming and work of the Messiah or that he could and did speak of future events, of the coming of Cyrus and of a greater than Cyrus, as if he were living in the glorious days of which he speaks with such delight. For those who accept the testimony of the Bible and hold that conception of predictive prophecy which it sets forth, the unity of Isaiah is not a discredited tradition but a well accredited fact.   O.T.A.

ISCAH (ĭs'kà, Heb. *yiskâh*), a daughter of Haran and sister of Milcah (Gen. 11:29). Identified by tradition with Sarah, Abraham's wife, but not with sufficient reason.

ISHBAH (ĭsh'bă, Heb. *yishbah*), a member of the tribe of Judah, the ancestor or head of the inhabitants of Eshtemoa (I Chron. 4:17).

ISHBAK (ĭsh'băk, Heb. *yishbāq*), a name in the list of sons of Abraham by Keturah (Gen. 25:2), the names probably representing tribes.

ISHBI-BENOB (ĭsh'bĭ-bē'nŏb, *Heb. yishbî venōv*), a giant slain by Abishai as he was about to kill David (II Sam. 21:16,17).

ISH-BOSHETH (ĭsh'bō'shĕth, Heb. *'îsh-bōsheth, man of shame*), the fourth son of Saul (II Sam. 2:8), originally called Eshbaal, "man of Baal," but for some reason subsequently changed. After the death of Saul and his three elder sons at the battle of Gilboa, where the Philistines won an overwhelming victory, he was proclaimed king over Israel by Abner, the captain of Saul's army, at Mahanaim (II Sam. 2:8ff.), while Judah proclaimed David as its king. Ish-bosheth was then about 40 years old, and reigned two years (II Sam. 2:8-10). He was not successful in the war which he waged with David to rule over all 12 tribes, but the war did not come to a close until Abner transferred his allegiance to David because of a serious charge made against him by Ish-bosheth (II Sam. 3:6ff.). Abner fulfilled David's condition to return to him Michal, his wife, before peace could be made. It was not, however, until Abner was murdered at Hebron that Ish-bosheth lost heart and gave up hope of retaining his power (II Sam. 4). Soon after, Ish-bosheth was murdered by his own captains, but David had the assassins put to death for their crime and buried Ish-bosheth in the grave of Abner at Hebron. Ish-bosheth's death ended the dynasty of Saul.

ISHI (ĭsh'ī, Heb. *'îshî, my husband*), a symbolic term, expressive of the ideal relation between Jehovah and Israel (Hos. 2:16).

ISHI (Heb. *yish'î, salutary*). 1. A man of Judah (I Chron. 2:31).

2. Another man of Judah (I Chron. 4:20).

3. A descendant of Simeon (I Chron. 4:42).

4. The head of a family of Manasseh (I Chron. 5:24).

ISHIAH (ĭ-shī'à, Heb. *yishshîyyâh, Jehovah forgets*). 1. A man of Issachar (I Chron. 7:3).

2. The head of a Levite family (I Chron. 24:21).

3. Another head of a Levite family (I Chron. 23:20, Jesiah in KJV).

4. One of David's men at Ziklag (I Chron. 12:6).

ISHIJAH (ĭ-shī'jà, Heb. *yishshîyâh*), a son of Harim, one of those induced by Ezra to put away their foreign wives (Ezra 10:31).

ISHMA (ĭsh'mà, Heb. *yishmā'*), the ancestral head of a clan of Judah; descended from Hur (I Chron. 4:3,4).

ISHMAEL (ĭsh'mā-ĕl, Heb. *yishmā'ēl, God hears*, Gr. *Ismaél*). 1. The son of Abraham by Hagar, the Egyptian maid of his wife Sarah. Sarah was barren (Gen. 16:1); and in accordance with the custom of the age she gave to Abraham her handmaid Hagar, an Egyptian, as his concubine, hoping that he might obtain a family by her. Abraham was then 86 years old, and had been in Canaan for ten years (Gen. 16:3). When Hagar saw that she had conceived, she began to despise her mistress, so that Sarah complained bitterly to Abraham, who told her that since Hagar was her slave, she could do anything she wanted with her. Sarah made things so difficult for her that she fled, and somewhere on the road to Egypt the angel of Jehovah met her and told her to return to her mistress and submit herself to her hands, and he encouraged her by the promise of a numerous seed. Ishmael was circumcised when he was 13 (Gen. 17:25). Abraham loved him, and even after God had promised him a son by Sarah, he fervently exclaimed, "O that Ishmael might live before thee!" (Gen. 17:18).

At the weaning of Isaac, the customary feast was made, when Ishmael, now a boy of 16, was seen by Sarah to be mocking. Jealous, and probably fearing future trouble if the boys were brought up together, Sarah tried to get Abraham to cast out Ishmael and his slave-mother, but this he was unwilling to do until he was encouraged to do so by God. Sent away with bread and a bottle of water, Ishmael and his mother wandered about in the wilderness of Beersheba, and when he became faint for thirst and was on the verge of death, she put him in the shade of a shrub and sat nearby, resignedly expecting his death. For the second time in her life, the angel of the Lord appeared to her. He directed her to some water and renewed His former promise of Ishmael's future greatness (Gen. 21:19,20). Ishmael grew up and became famous as an archer in the wilderness of Paran. He was married by his mother to an Egyptian wife. When Abraham died, he returned from exile to help Isaac to bury their father (Gen. 25:9). He became the father of 12 sons and a daughter, whom Esau took for his wife. He died at the age of 137 (Gen. 25:17). In Galatians 4:21-5:1 Paul expounds the narrative of Ishmael and Isaac allegorically. Hagar represents the old covenant, and Sarah, the new; while the rivalry between Ishmael and Isaac foreshadows the conflict in the early church between those who would cling to the ordinances of the Law, which must pass away, and those who realize that through the grace of Christ there is freedom from the Law.

2. A descendant of Jonathan (I Chron. 8:38; 9:44).

3. The father of Zebadiah, a ruler in the house of Judah in the reign of Jehoshaphat (II Chron. 19:11).

4. The son of Jehohanan. He helped Jehoiada to restore Jehoash to the throne of Judah (II Chron. 23:1).

5. The son of Nethaniah, a member of the royal house of David. After the capture of Palestine, Nebuchadnezzar left behind as governor of Judah a Jew called Gedaliah, who promised to protect all those Jews who would put themselves under his care. Among those who came was Ishmael, who, instigated by the king of the Ammonites, intended to assassinate the governor. Gedaliah was warned of Ishmael's treachery by some loyal captains, but paid no attention to the warning. About two months after the destruction of Jerusalem, Gedaliah and others with him were murdered at a banquet held in honor of Ishmael, who then attempted to flee to the Ammonite country with some captives he had with him, including the king's daughters. His pursuers overtook him at Gibeon; but while his captives were recovered, he and a few of his men succeeded in escaping to the king of Ammon (II Kings 25:25: Jer. 40:7-16; 41:1-18).

S.B.

ISHMAELITE (ĭsh′mā-ĕl-īt, Heb. *yishme′ēlîm*), a descendant of Ishmael, the son of Abraham and Hagar, whom Abraham sent away into the desert after the birth of Isaac (Gen. 21:14-21). The 12 sons of Ishmael, and his Egyptian wife, became princes and progenitors of as many tribes. They lived in camps in the desert of Northern Arabia, although occasionally some of them settled down, as the Nabateans. Mostly, however, they lived like Ishmael, "a wild man" of the desert (Gen. 16:12), and also like him they were famous for their skill with the bow. Joseph was sold by his brothers to some Ishmaelites (Gen. 37:25-28).

The word is apparently used in the OT in a wider sense, referring to the nomadic tribes of Northern Arabia generally (Gen. 37:28,36; Judg. 8:24). All Arabs, following Mohammed's example, claim descent from Ishmael.

ISHMAIAH (ĭsh-mā′yȧ, Heb. *yishma′yâh, Jehovah hears*). 1. A Gibeonite who joined David at Ziklag (I Chron. 12:4).

2. Chief of the Zebulunites in David's reign (I Chron. 27:19).

ISHMEELITE (See Ishmaelite)

ISHMERAI (ĭsh′mē-rī, Heb. *yishmeray, Jehovah keeps*), a Benjamite, son of Epaal, resident of Jerusalem (I Chron. 8:18).

ISHOD (ī′shŏd, Heb. *'îshehôdh, man of majesty*), a man from Manasseh whose mother was Hammoleketh (I Chron. 7:18).

ISHPAN (ĭsh′păn, Heb. *yishpān, he will hide*), descendant of Benjamin, son of Shashak (I Chron. 8:22).

ISHTAR (ĭsh′tăr), a Semitic goddess worshiped in Phoenicia, Canaan, Assyria, and Babylonia. Her name is spelled in various ways — Ashtoreth, Astarte, Ashtartu (in the Amarna letters), Ishtar (in Babylonia), etc. The name and cult of the goddess were derived from Babylonia, where she was the goddess of love and war. The chief seat of her worship in Babylonia was Erech, where prostitution was practiced in her name by bands of men and women. In Assyria the warlike side of the goddess was stressed, and immoral rites were not a part of her worship. In Canaan her warlike attri-

An Ishmaelite caravan halts at Dothan on its journey from Gilead to Egypt, reminiscent of Genesis 37:25-28.
© MPS

butes were dropped, and she became a moon-goddess and the consort of Baal. The Philistines worshipped her and built a temple for her at Ascalon. The immoral rites with which her worship was accompanied in Babylonia were transferred to Canaan (Deut. 23:18). As early as the times of Judges her cult had spread to the Hebrews (Judg. 2:13; 10:6). Solomon supported her worship (I Kings 11:5; II Kings 23:13), and the Hebrew women in Jeremiah's day gave her a high place in their worship (Jer. 44:17f).

Remains of the Ishtar Gate at Babylon, showing forms of animals embossed on the brick walls. © MPS

ISHTOB (ĭsh′tŏb, Heb. *'îsh tôv, the men of Tob*), a place in Palestine which supplied at least 12,000 soldiers to the Ammonites in their war with David (II Sam. 10:6,8).

ISHUAH (ĭsh′ū-à, Heb. *yishwâh, he will level*), the second son of Asher (Gen. 46:17; I Chron. 7:30).

ISHUAI (ĭsh′ū-ī, Heb. *yishwî, level*). 1. The third son of Asher, and founder of a tribal family (Num. 26:44, Jesuai in KJV).

2. A son of Saul (I Sam. 14:49, Ishui in KJV).

ISHUI (ĭsh′ū-ī). See Ishuai, of which Ishui is another spelling in the KJV.

ISLAND, ISLE. These words render the Hebrew *'î*, which has a much wider significance than the English words. Its root-meaning is supposed to be habitable land. 1. Dry land, as opposed to water (Isa. 42:15).

2. An island as usually understood (Jer. 2:10).

3. A coastland, whether belonging to continents or islands, as the coastland of Palestine and Phoenicia (Isa. 20:6), and the coasts and islands of Asia Minor and Greece (Gen. 10:5).

4. The farthest regions of the earth (Isa. 41:5; Zeph. 2:11). The Jews were not a maritime people, and consequently there are not many references to islands in the OT. Most of them are found in Isaiah, Jeremiah, and Ezekiel. In the NT a number of islands are mentioned in connection with the missionary journeys of the Apostle Paul, e.g. Cyprus, Crete, Lesbos, Samos, Samothrace, Chios, Melita, and Sicily. John was banished to the isle of Patmos for the sake of the Word of God. (Rev. 1:9).

ISMACHIAH (ĭs′mà-kī′à, Heb. *yismakhyâhû, Jehovah sustains*), an overseer connected with the temple in the reign of Hezekiah (II Chron. 31:13).

ISMAIAH (ĭs-mā′yà, Heb. *yishma'yâh, Jehovah hears*).1. A Gibeonite who joined David's forces at Ziklag (I Chron. 12:4).

2. A chief of Zebulunite forces in David's time (I Chron. 27:19).

ISPAH (ĭs′pà, Heb. *yishpâh, firm*), a Benjamite, son of Beriah (I Chron. 8:16).

ISRAEL (ĭz′rā-ĕl) is used in Scripture to designate: (a) an individual man, the son of Isaac (see Jacob); or (b) his descendants, the twelve tribes of the Hebrews; or (c) the ten northern tribes, led by Ephraim, as opposed to the southern, under Judah.

Before the year 2100 B.C., the God who directs all history chose the patriarch Abraham and called him out of Ur of the Chaldees (Gen. 11:31; Neh. 9:7). The Lord's redemptive purpose was to bring Abraham and his descendants into a saving (covenant) relationship with Himself (Gen. 17:7) and also to make of Abraham's seed a nation in Palestine (vs. 2) through which He would some day bring salvation to the entire world (12:3; 22:18). God accordingly blessed Abraham's grandson Jacob with many children. Furthermore, upon Jacob's return to Palestine in 1909 B.C., God "wrestled" with him and brought him to a point of total submission (32:25; Hos. 12:4). By thus yielding his life to God's purpose, Jacob achieved victory; and God changed his name to Israel, Hebrew *Yisrā'ēl*, which means, "He strives with God (and prevails)" (Gen. 32:28; 35:10). Jacob's twelve sons were thus, literally, the children of "Israel" 42:5; 45:21). Israel, however, was aware that God would build each of them into a numerous tribe (49:7,16). The term "children of Israel" came therefore to signify the whole body of God's chosen and saved people (32:32; 34:7). It included Jacob's grandchildren and all subsequent members of the household, as they proceeded to Egypt for a sojourn of 430 years, 1876-1446 B.C. (46:8; Exod. 1:7).

I. Mosaic Period. In the space of approximately ten generations, God increased Israel from a clan of several hundred (Gen. 14:14; 46:27) to a nation of almost 3,000,000 souls (Exod. 12:37; Num. 1:46), equipped with all the material and cultural advantages of Egypt (Exod. 2:10; 12:36; Acts 7:22). Their very increase, however, seems to have aroused the envy and fear, first of the land's foreign "Hyksos" rulers (Dynasties XV-XVI, about 1730-1580 B.C.) and then of the native Egyptian Empire that followed (Dyn. XVIII), Exodus 1:8-10. Israel was thus enslaved and compelled to erect certain Hyksos store-cities in the region of the eastern Delta (1:11; compare Gen. 15:13) and was threatened with total national destruction under the anti-Semitic policy of the Empire (Exod. 1:16). Moses (born 1527) was indeed befriended by an Egyptian princess, perhaps the one who was to become the famous queen, Hatshepsut; but even he was forced to flee Egypt during the reign of the great conqueror and oppressor, Thothmes III (dated 1501-1447 B.C.).

God, however, still remembered His covenant promises with Abraham (Exod. 2:24-25). At the death of the great Pharaoh (vs. 23) He appeared to Moses in a burning bush on Mt. Sinai and commissioned him to deliver the enslaved people (3:10). Moses accordingly returned to the Egyptian court, with the cry, "Thus saith Jehovah, 'Israel is My son, My first-born: and I have said unto thee, Let my son go that he may serve Me; or behold, I will slay thy son, thy first-born'" (4:22-23). The new monarch, Amenhetep II (1447-1421), had inherited the domineering qualities of his father; and he refused to heed the divine summons. Only after a series of ten miraculous plagues, climaxing in the death of all the first-born of Egypt (see Passover), was the hard-hearted Pharaoh compelled to yield to the Lord (12:31).

In the spring of 1446 B.C. the nation of Israel achieved their exodus from Egypt (12:37-40). This date has been reduced by a number of critical scholars to about 1290 B.C. Scripture, however, is explicit in placing the Exodus in the 480th year before the beginning of Solomon's Temple in 966 B.C. (I Kings 6:1); and the 15th century date is then confirmed by other scriptural testimonies (compare Judg. 11:26; Acts 13:19 ASV). Israel marched eastward from Goshen toward the Red Sea. But when the perfidious Pharaoh pursued

Lower portion of the stele of Pharaoh Merneptah, which contains the only direct contemporary reference to "Israel" in inscriptions of this period. The enlarged excerpt below is a detail of the name "Israel" from the tablet. CM

after the seemingly entrapped Hebrews (Exod. 14: 3), the Lord sent a strong east wind that blew back the waters of the Sea (vs. 21). Israel crossed, and then the Lord caused the waters to return so that the Egyptians were destroyed to the last man (Exod. 14:28; excepting the Pharaoh, who is not mentioned after vs. 10).

Israel reached Mt. Sinai at the commencement of summer, 1446 (19:1). At this point God extended the covenant offer of reconciliation that He had made with Abraham and Israel (Jacob, Gen. 28:13-15) so as to embrace the whole nation of the sons of Israel, promising, "Now therefore, if ye will obey My voice indeed, and keep My covenant, then ye shall be Mine own possession from among all peoples: for all the earth is Mine; and ye shall be unto Me a kingdom of priests, and a holy nation" (Exod. 19:5-6). God, on His part, provided the objective way of salvation by officially "adopting" Israel as His own sons and daughters (compare Exodus 4:22) on the basis of the atoning death that Jesus Christ, the unique Son of God, would some day suffer to redeem all of God's people (24:8; Heb. 9:15-22). For Israel's choice involved a universalistic goal, that they should become a "kingdom of priests," to bring salvation to others (compare Isa. 56:6-7). Israel, however, on their part were required to fulfill certain subjective conditions, so as to share in this testamental inheritance: "*If* ye will keep My covenant, then . . ." Basically, they must in faith commit themselves to God, to be His people. As Moses proclaimed, "Hear, oh Israel . . . thou shalt love the Lord thy God with all thy heart" (Deut. 6:4-5). God therefore provided Israel with His fundamental moral law, the Decalogue, or "ten commandments" (Exod. 20:3-17), together with elaborations in the various other codes of the Pentateuch. God also furnished them with His ceremonial law, to depict Israel's reconciliation with their heavenly Father (see for example Lev. 23:39-40) and to provide a symbolical way of forgiveness, should they transgress His moral requirements (see for example Lev. 6:1-3,6-7). The ceremonials, however, gained their true effectiveness because they foreshadowed, or typified, the ultimate redemptive work of Jesus Christ (Heb. 9:9-14,23-24).

In May of 1445 B.C. Israel broke up camp (Num. 10:11) and marched northeast to Kadesh, on the southern border of the promised land of Canaan. But after taking 40 days to spy out the land, all the tribal representatives except Caleb and Joshua reported unfavorably on attempting any conquest of Canaan: "The people that dwell in the land are strong, and the cities are fortified and very great" (13:28). Impetuous Israel thereupon refused to advance into the promised land and prayed for a return to Egypt (14:4). Moses' intercession did save them from immediate divine wrath; but the Lord still condemned them to wander for 40 years in the wilderness, one year for each day of spying, until that entire generation should fall by the way (14:32-34).

Israel's route of march, after an extended stay at Kadesh (Deut. 1:46), is described in Numbers 33; but the various camps cannot be identified, except that they are known to have passed through Ezion-geber at the head of the Gulf of Aqabah before a final return to Kadesh (vss. 35-36). This rough, nomadic existence forced the people into a life of dependence upon God, who tested them and yet at the same time cared for them, miraculously (Deut. 2:7; 8:2-4). This training-period was still marred by repeated "murmurings" and defections, such as the revolts of Korah, Dathan, and

Abiram (Num. 16-17). Even Moses, when producing water for the thirsty people, failed to credit God with the glory (20:10-11) and was therefore denied entrance into the promised land (vs. 12).

In the late summer of 1407 B.C. (20:28; 33:38), the advance of the Hebrews upon Canaan was resumed. The Edomites, however (a people descended from Israel's twin brother Esau), refused to allow kindred Israel to pass through their territories (20:21). The result was that they were compelled to double back to Ezion-geber on the Red Sea and go completely around the land of Edom, marching northward up "the king's highway" along the eastern border of Edom and Moab (21:4,22). Opposite the mid-point of the Dead Sea, Israel reached the territory of the Canaanitish kingdom of Sihon of Heshbon. But though Sihon refused to allow Israel further passage, it was actually God who had hardened the king's heart (Deut. 2:30): his very attack proved the occasion for his total overthrow and for Israel's occupation of the land of Gilead (Num. 21:24). Similar aggression by Og, king of Bashan, resulted in their acquisition of northern Transjordan as well (vs. 35); and, by the end of February, 1406, Israel was able to set up camp on the Plains of Moab, across the Jordan from Jericho (Deut. 1:3-5).

During the last month of Moses' life, God's great servant conducted a "numbering" or census of the people, which indicated a figure of over 600,000 fighting men, only slightly less than had taken part in the Exodus 40 years before (Num. 26:51, compare 1:46). Moses then acceded to the request of the tribes of Reuben, Gad, and half of Manasseh to settle in the conquered lands of Transjordan (Num. 32); and he provided for the division of western Canaan among the remaining tribes (33-34). At this time Balaam, who had been employed by the Moabites to curse Israel, uttered his famous blessings. The seer climaxed his oracles by predicting the future Messianic king, whose coming constituted the purpose of Israel: "I see Him, but not now; I behold Him, but not nigh: there shall come forth a star out of Jacob, and a sceptre shall arise out of Israel, and shall smite through the corners of Moab, and break down all the sons of tumult" (24:17). Moses then anointed Joshua as his successor (27:23), spoke his final two addresses, that constitute most of the book of Deuteronomy, Chapters 1-4 and 5-30, and ascended Mt. Pisgah to view the promised land. There Moses died and was buried by God's own hand (Deut. 34:5-6). He had been the founder of the Hebrew nation; "And there hath not arisen a prophet since in Israel like unto Moses, whom the Lord knew face to face" (vs. 10).

A "Moses'-eye-view" of the Promised Land, looking westward, as seen from Mount Nebo-Mount Pisgah. The Jerusalem area is on the horizon, just right of center, and the Bethlehem area to the left. Below, in the foreground, is the northern end of the Dead Sea. © MPS

Ruins of ancient Jericho of Joshua's day. The remains of the old city wall are seen along the right edge of the ruins. © MPS

II. The Conquest. At Joshua's accession, the land of Canaan lay providentially prepared for conquest by the Hebrews. Comprising nominally a part of the Egyptian empire, Canaan suffered the neglect of Amenhetep III (about 1412-1376), called "the magnificent," whose rule was one of luxury, military inactivity, and decay. Political organization within Palestine was that of many small city-states, impoverished by a century of Egyptian misrule, and deficient in cooperative defense. Canaanitish standards of living, however, were still superior to those of the invading Hebrews, a fact which was later to lend "cultural" appeal to their debased religion.

In the spring of 1406 the Jordan was in its annual flood-stage (Josh. 3:15). But Joshua anticipated a miracle of divine intervention (vs. 13), and the Lord did indeed open a gateway into Canaan. For "The waters which came down from above stood, and rose up in one heap, a great way off, at Adam," some 15 miles N of Jericho (vs. 16). Israel thus marched across the relatively dry river bed (compare 4:18), led by the ark of God's testament (3:16).

Joshua's war of conquest developed in three major campaigns: in central, southern, and northern Canaan. His first objective was the city of Jericho, to his immediate W in the Jordan Valley. But just as Israel was preparing to storm Jericho's walls, the Lord caused their collapse (Josh. 6:20); and Joshua proceeded to "devote" the city to God (vs. 21, ASVmg). Joshua ascended westward into Canaan's central ridge and, after an initial setback because of sin in the camp (7:20-21), seized the post of Ai. It seems to have served as an outer defense of the major city of Bethel (8:17), which surrendered without further resistance (12:16, compare Judg. 1:22). Joshua was thus able to assemble Israel at Shechem to reaffirm the Mosaic law (Josh. 8:33, per Deut. 27:11ff), having subdued all of central Canaan.

To the south, Gibeon next submitted and, by trickery, saved themselves from the destruction that God had decreed (Josh. 9:15; Deut. 7:2). Their action, however, provoked an alliance of five kings of the southern Amorites, under the headship of Jerusalem, which retaliated by laying siege to Gibeon (Josh. 10:5). Joshua, upon being informed, advanced by forced march to the relief of his clients (vs. 9); surprised the enemy; and, with divine aid, routed them westward down the Aijalon Valley. Israel then proceeded to ravage the whole of southern Palestine (10:28-42).

The northern Canaanites finally awoke to their danger and formed an offensive alliance under the leadership of Jabin, king of Hazor (Josh. 11:5). Joshua, however, attacked unexpectedly at the Waters of Merom, NE of Galilee, and completely routed the allied forces (vss. 7-8). Only Hazor was actually destroyed (vs. 13); but this triumph meant that within six years of the fall of Jericho (compare 14:10) all Canaan had come to lie at Joshua's feet (11:16). "So Jehovah gave unto Israel all the land which He sware unto their fathers . . . all came to pass" (21:43,45). The Canaanites had not yet lost their potential for resistance; and, indeed, what the Lord had sworn to Israel had been a gradual occupation of the land (Exod. 23:28-30; Deut. 7:22). Much still remained to be possessed (Josh. 13:1), but at this point Joshua was compelled by advancing age to divide the land among the 12 Hebrew tribes (Chapters 13-22). He then charged his people with faithfulness to Jehovah (24:15) and died.

III. The Judges. Moses had ordered the "devotion" (extermination) of the Canaanites (Deut. 7:2), both because of their long-standing immoralities (9:5; compare Gen. 9:22,25; 15:16) and because of their debasing religious influence upon God's people (Deut. 7:4; 12:31). In the years immediately following Joshua's death, Judah accordingly accomplished an initial capture of Jerusalem (Judg. 1:8; though the city was not held, vs. 21); and Ephraim and west-Manasseh slew the men of Bethel (vs. 25), which city had begun to reassert itself. But then came failure: Israel ceased to eradicate the Canaanites; no more cities were taken (vss. 27-34); and the tribe of Dan actually suffered eviction themselves (vs. 34). Tolerance of evil had to be rectified by national chastening (2:3).

The next three and one-half centuries were thus used of God to impress upon His people three major lessons. 1. The Lord's wrath at sin. For when Israel yielded to temptation, God would "deliver them over into the hands of their enemies round about, so that they could not any longer stand" (2:14). 2. God's mercy upon repentance. For the Lord would then "raise them up judges and save them out of the hand of their enemies" (2:18). 3. Man's total depravity. For "it came to pass, when the judge was dead, that they turned back and dealt more corruptly than their fathers" (2:19). The period of the 14 judges (12 in Judges, plus Eli and Samuel in I Samuel) thus demonstrates a repeated cycle of human sin, of servitude, or supplication, and then of salvation.

From about 1400 to 1250 B.C. the chief external forces that God employed for the execution of His providential dealings were the rival empires of the Hittites, N of Palestine, and of the Egyptians to the S. Neither of these powers was conscious of the way in which God was using them; but still, the years in which either succeeded in maintaining Palestinian law and order prove to be just the period that God had chosen for granting "rest" to Israel. Shubbiluliuma, for example, who took the throne of the Hittite New Kingdom in about 1385 B.C., fomented dissension among the Palestinian states that owed nominal allegiance to Amenhetep III and IV; and with this international intrigue coincides Israel's first oppression, by Cushan Rishathaim, an invader from Hittite-controlled Mesopotamia (Judg. 3:8). The underlying cause, however, lay in Israel's sin against the moral requirements of God's Sinaitic testament. (Compare the sordid events of Micah and the Danites and of the Benjamite outrage, Judg. 17-21, which belong to this period, 18:1; Josh. 19:47; 20:28). But when they "cried unto Jehovah, Jehovah raised up a saviour to the children of Israel, even Othniel, Caleb's younger brother" (3:9). The 40 years of peace that then followed correspond to the time of undisputed Hittite sway over Palestine, until some years after the death of Shubbiluliuma in about 1345.

Founded in the 1320's, however, the Nineteenth Dynasty began to reassert Egypt's territorial claims. But behind this international confusion lay the fact that "Israel again did that which was evil, and Jehovah strengthened Eglon the king of Moab [so that] the children of Israel served Eglon 18 years. But when they cried unto Jehovah, He raised them up a saviour, Ehud the Benjamite (Judg. 3: 12-15), and granted them eighty years of peace. This was the time, moreover, of the treaty of 1315 between Seti I of Egypt and Mursil II of Heth, who preserved order by dividing the Near East into respective spheres of influence. The treaty was then renewed in 1279, after a futile war of aggression by Rameses II, and was strictly enforced until the demise of the last great Hittite king, in about 1250.

Against the oppressive Canaanitish hand of Jabin II of Hazor (Judg. 4:2-3), God raised up the fourth of the judges, the woman Deborah. Her military commander, Barak, proceeded to muster the north-central tribes to the Valley of Esdraelon for war with Jabin's officer, Sisera. Then, "The stars in their courses fought against Sisera" (5:20, compare vs. 21): a divinely sent cloud-burst immobilized the powerful Canaanite chariotry, and Sisera himself was murdered in flight by a Kenite woman. The 40-year peace that followed Deborah's victory coincides with the strong rule of Rameses III at the turn of the century, the last great Pharaoh of the Nineteenth Dynasty.

Next came the nomadic Midianites and Amalekites out of the eastern desert to plunder sinful Israel (Judg. 6:2-6). In about 1175, however, the Lord answered the repentant prayers of His people and raised up Gideon with his chosen band of 300. "The sword of the Lord and of Gideon" then cleared Israel of the nomadic raiders (7:19-25; 8:10-12), as witnessed by the peaceful picture of Ruth 2-4 some 25 years later. The turmoil that resulted from the attempt of Gideon's son Abimelech to make himself king over Israel (Judg. 9) was rectified by the sixth and seventh judges, Tola and Jair (who must have overlapped, for no separate deliverance is ascribed to the latter, 10:1-5). But with their deaths in 1110 B.C. and the apostasy that subsequently arose, God delivered up His land to two simultaneous oppressions: that of the Ammonites in the east, and that of the Philistines in the west (10:7). After 18 years, eastern Israel was freed by Jephthah, the eighth judge (chap. 11), who was succeeded by three minor judges. Western Israel, however, remained subject to the rising power of the Philistines for a full 40 years (13:1),

until the advent of Samuel in 1070. This period must therefore embrace the activity of Eli (until about 1090, I Sam. 4:18), as well as the spectacular but politically ineffective exploits of Samson, the 12th and last judge of the Book of Judges (Chapters 13-16, to about 1075 B.C., 15:20).

These Philistines were a Hamitic people. But unlike the native Palestinians, who were descended from Ham's son Canaan, they traced their descent from an elder brother, Mizraim (Egypt), through Casluhim (Cyrene, Gen. 10:14) and Caphtor (Crete, Amos 9:7). Some of these "Minoan" peoples had settled along the Mediterranean coast of Palestine as early as 2100 B.C. (Gen. 21:32; 26:14; compare Deut. 2:23; Josh. 13:23). The very name Palestine, in fact, means the "Philistine land." But with the fall of Crete to barbarian invasion in 1200 B.C., "the remnant of the isle of Caphtor" (Jer. 47:4) came to reinforce the older Minoan settlements. Though driven back from Egypt by a crushing defeat at the hands of Rameses III in about 1196, these "sea peoples," by reason of their superior discipline and equipment (cf. Judg. 3:31; I Sam. 13:22; 17:5-6), were able to mount three oppressions, commencing respectively in 1110, 1055, and 1010 B.C., and thereby to threaten the very existence of Israel.

Their opening oppression climaxed in the first battle of Ebenezer (I Sam. 4) and resulted in the deaths of Eli and his sons, in the capture of the ark, and in the destruction of the Lord's house at Shiloh (see Jer. 7:14). God in His grace, however, raised up the Prophet Samuel, who ended the oppression by a God-given victory at the second battle of Ebenezer in about 1070 (Judg. 7). But later, as Samuel turned over many of his powers as judge to his corrupt sons (8:3), the Philistines returned with barbaric cruelty (compare 31:8-10; Judg. 16:25), seeking to crush disorganized Israel.

IV. The United Kingdom of Israel was precipitated by the demand of the people themselves. Despite God's directive that they be holy and separate (Lev. 20:26), they still wished to be "like all the nations" (I Sam. 8:5), with a human king to fight their battles (vs. 20), rather than God, acting through a theocratic judge (vs. 7). They conveniently forgot that it was faithlessness that brought them under attack in the first place. Still, their rebellion served to accomplish God's purpose (see Ps. 76:10); for He had long before decreed a kingdom in Israel over which Jesus the Messiah should some day reign (Gen. 49:10; Num. 24:17). The Lord accordingly authorized Samuel to anoint a king (I Sam. 8:22), and directed him to Saul of Benjamin (Chapter 9).

Saul's accession proceeded in three steps. He was first privately anointed by Samuel and filled with God's Spirit (10:10), then publicly selected at Mizpah (vs. 24), and at last popularly confirmed at Gilgal, after having delivered the town of Jabesh- gilead from Ammonite attack (Chapter 11). The primary concern of his 40 year reign (1050-1010 B.C., compare Acts 13:21) was the Philistines. These oppressors had already occupied much of his territory, and open war was provoked in 1048 (I Sam. 13:1 ASV) when one of their garrisons was destroyed by Saul's son Jonathan (vs. 3). In the ensuing battle at Michmash, Jonathan's personal bravery (14:14), plus the Philistines' own superstitious reaction to a heaven-sent earthquake (vss. 15,20), brought about their total defeat. Saul thus terminated the second oppression but, by his failure to submit to Samuel (13:8-9), suffered the rejection of his dynasty from the throne of Israel (vs. 14).

From his capital in Gibeah of Benjamin, Saul "did valiantly" and pushed back the enemies of Israel on every hand (14:47-48). In about 1025 B.C., however, having been ordered to destroy Israel's implacable enemies the Amalekites (15: 1-3; compare Exod. 17:14), Saul disobeyed and spared both the king and the best of the spoils, under pretext of making offerings to God (vs. 15). Samuel answered, "Behold, to obey is better than sacrifice" (vs. 22) and declared Saul's personal deposition from the kingship (vss. 23,28). Samuel then privately anointed David, a son of Jesse of Judah, as king over Israel (16:13). David was about 15 at the time (compare II Sam. 5:4); but, by God's providence, he gained rapid promotion at court, first as a minstrel (vss. 21-23) and then by his victory over the Philistine champion Goliath (Chapter 17). Even Saul's growing jealousy, which removed David from court to the dangers of battle, augmented the latter's popularity (vss. 27-30). Saul's overt hostility finally drove David and his followers into exile, first as outlaws in Judah (I Sam. 20-26) and then as vassals to the Philistine king of Gath (27-30). But while Saul was diverting his resources in the futile pursuit of David, the Philistines prepared for a third, all-out attack on Israel, 1010 B.C. David barely escaped engaging in war against his own people (29:4, compare vs. 8); and Saul, routed at Mt. Gilboa, committed suicide rather than suffer capture (31:4). Israel's sinful demand for a king had brought about its own punishment.

Having learned of the death of Saul, David moved to Hebron and was there proclaimed king over his own tribe of Judah (II Sam. 2:4). But despite David's diplomacy, the supporters of Saul set up his son, Ish-bosheth, over the northern and eastern tribes (vss. 7-8). Civil war followed, but David increasingly gained the upper hand (3:1). Finally, after the death of Ish-bosheth, the tribal representatives assembled to Hebron and anointed David as king over all Israel (1003 B.C.). The Philistines now realized that their vassal had gotten out of hand and that their own future depended upon prompt action. David, however, after an initial flight to his former outlaw retreat (5:17), rallied his devoted forces (compare 23:13-17); and, by two brilliant victories in the vicinity of Jerusalem (5:9-25), not simply terminated the last Philistine oppression but eventually incorporated Gath into his own territory and subdued the remaining Philistine states (I Chron. 18:1).

The time was ripe for the rise of a Hebrew empire. The Hittites had succumbed to barbarian invasion; the Twenty-first Dynasty of Egypt stagnated under the alternating rule of priests and merchants (1100 B.C. on); and Assyria, after having weakened others, was itself restrained by inactive kings. With Philistia broken, Israel remained free from foreign threat for 150 years. David's first strategic move was to capture Jerusalem from the Canaanites. Militarily, Mt. Zion constituted a splendid fortress (II Sam. 5:6,9); politically, the city afforded David a neutral capital between the recently hostile areas of Judah and northern Israel; and religiously, Zion's possession of the ark of God's testament (6:17) centered the people's spiritual hopes within its walls (Ps. 87). From about 1002 to 995 B.C. David then extended his power on every side, from the Euphrates River on the N (8:3) to the Red Sea on the S (vs. 14).

In Jerusalem David sought to construct a fitting "house" or temple for Jehovah. This ambition was denied him because of his excessive bloodshed

(I Chron. 22:8; compare II Sam. 8:2); but God's prophet did inform him, "Jehovah will make thee a house" (II Sam. 7:11). He explained, "When thou shalt sleep with thy fathers, I will set up thy seed after thee; and he shall build a house for My name." God's promise, moreover, extended beyond Solomon and climaxed in that One in whom Israel's ultimate purpose should be fulfilled, "And I will establish the throne of his kingdom for ever. I will be His [the Messiah's] Father, and He shall be My Son" (7:13-14; Heb. 1:5). The eternal Christ would indeed suffer a "testator's" death (Ps. 22:16-18), but would rise in power to give everlasting life to His own (Ps. 22:22,26; 16:10-11). Jesse's son thus experienced in his Davidic testament (Ps. 89:3; 132:12) fundamental clarifications of God's former redemptive revelation of Sinai; and he exclaimed in his psalms and other inspired writings,

"For is my house not so with God?
For He hath made with me an everlasting testament,
Ordered in all things and sure:
For it is all my salvation, though all His desire,
For will he not make it to sprout a branch?"

(II Sam. 23:5 Heb.). In his later life David became involved in sins of adultery and murder (II Sam. 11) and of failure to control his sons (13-14), and for this he received corresponding punishments (15-16, compare 12:10-12). The revolt of Absalom served also to intensify the antagonism between northern Israel and southern Judah (19: 41-43). But at his death in 970 B.C. David was able to commit to his son Solomon an empire that marked the peak of Israel's power.

Solomon, after a bloody accession (I Kings 2: 25,34,36), reigned in peace, culture, and luxury, experiencing only one military campaign in 40 years (II Chron. 8:3). He was further able to consummate a marriage alliance with the last Pharaoh of the Twenty-first Dynasty (I Kings 3:1). The king is most famous, however, for his unexcelled wisdom (4:31), which was achieved by humility before God (3:7-12), and through which he composed the inspired Proverbs, Ecclesiastes, and Song of Solomon, plus numerous other works (Pss. 72, 127; compare I Kings 4:32). His greatest undertaking was the Jerusalem temple, erected from 966 to 959 B.C. (I Kings 6) out of materials lavishly provided by David (I Chron. 22). Like the tabernacle before it, the temple symbolized the abiding presence of God with His people (I Kings 8:11).

But Solomon also engaged in a number of luxurious building projects of his own (7:1-12), so that despite his great commercial revenues (9:26-28, 10:14-15) indebtedness forced him to surrender territory (9:11-12) and to engage in excessive taxation and labor-conscription. Unrest grew throughout the empire; and, while the tribute continued during his lifetime (4:21), surrounding subject countries, such as Edom and Damascus, became increasingly independent (11:14,23). More serious was Solomon's spiritual failure, induced by wanton polygamy (vss. 1-8). "And Jehovah was angry . . . and said unto Solomon, 'Forasmuch as thou hast not kept My covenant, I will surely rend the kingdom from thee and will give it to thy servant . . out of the hand of thy son' "(vss. 9-12).

V. The Divided Kingdom. Early in 930 B.C. Solomon died and his son Rehoboam went to Shechem to be confirmed as king. The people, however, were led by Jeroboam of Ephraim to demand relief from Solomon's tyranny (I Kings 12:4); and

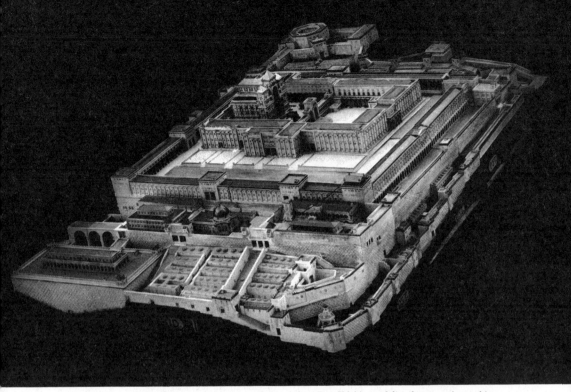

The majestic temple of Solomon and its environs (after Dr. Shick's model), the crowning achievement of the united Israelite kingdom of David and Solomon. © MPS

when Rehoboam spurned their pleas, the ten northern tribes seceded to form an independent kingdom of Israel. Underlying causes for the rupture include the geographical isolation of the tribes (compare the phrase, "to your tents," vs. 16) and their long-standing social tensions (II Sam. 2:7-9; 19:43). But the basic reason lay in God's decision to punish Solomon's apostasy (I Kings 11:31; 12: 15,24). Furthermore, while northern Israel possessed the advantages of size, fertility, and foreign trade-contacts, these very features diminished their devotion to Jehovah and His Word. Ephraim's spiritual laxness became immediately apparent, when Jeroboam introduced two golden calves, with sanctuaries at Dan and Bethel to rival Jerusalem (vs. 28). He did attempt to associate these images with the historic God of the Exodus; but they were still idols, "other gods" (14:9), and not mere pedestals for Jehovah's invisible presence. Each succeeding king of Israel likewise "walked in the way of Jeroboam, wherewith he made Israel to sin"; and the division thus served ultimately to separate the sinful Hebrews from the two faithful tribes of Judah and Benjamin: "For they are not all Israel that are of Israel [Jacob]" (Rom. 9:6).

The relations between Ephraim and Judah passed through seven stages. 1. Hostility marked their course for the first two generations. Initially, both kingdoms suffered from raids by Shishak, the energetic founder of Egypt's Twenty-second Dynasty (II Chron. 12:1-9). Later, Jeroboam advanced against Rehoboam's son Abijam (913-910 B.C.); but God granted a great victory to outnumbered Judah (II Chron. 13), "because they relied upon Jehovah the God of their fathers" (13: 18). Pious Asa (910-869) ended Twenty-second Dynasty threats by routing the hosts of Zerah the Cushite (Pharaoh Osorkon I?) at the turn of the century (14:9-15) and then led Judah in a re-

vival of faith in God's testament (15:12). But when faced by Ephraimite garrisons at Ramah, only six miles from Jerusalem, the king panicked and hired Benhadad of Damascus to divert the energies of Israel (16:1-4). God's prophet condemned Asa because he "relied on the king of Syria, and not on Jehovah" (vs. 7); and the precedent of Syrian intervention had serious consequences. King Omri (885-874) founded Samaria as the new capital of Ephraim; but Benhadad laid repeated siege to the city, and Omri's son Ahab was saved only by the grace of God (I Kings 20).

2. Asa's son Jehoshaphat made peace with Ahab (22:44). The allies, together with Benhadad, did manage to halt the westward advance of Shalmaneser III of Assyria at the bloody battle of Qarqar on the Orontes (853 B.C.). But Jehoshaphat had married his son to Athaliah, the Baal-worshiping daughter of Ahab and his Phoenician queen Jezebel, the persecutor of Elijah (I Kings 19:2); and such compromise could never be honored by God (II Chron. 19:2). Jehoshaphat was almost killed at the side of Ahab at Ramoth-gilead (I Kings 22:32-35). His joint commercial projects met with disaster (II Chron. 20:35-37). Moab succeeded in revolting from Ephraim (II Kings 1: 1) and Edom from Judah (8:22); and when Jehu executed God's sentence against the house of Ahab in Israel (841 B.C.), he slew Judah's young king with them (9:27). Athaliah then slaughtered her princely grandchildren and seized the throne in Jerusalem (11:1).

3. The years between 841 and 790 saw no major dealings between Israel and Judah because of Syrian domination over both kingdoms (see II Kings 8:12). Thus, even though Athaliah was slain in Jerusalem, the boy-king Joash suffered humiliating submission to Hazael of Damascus (12:17-18).

Detail of front panels of the Black Obelisk of Shalmanezer III, recording the tribute of King Jehu, son (i.e., successor) of Omri. It shows Jehu (top panel) bowing before the Assyrian king, and this is the only contemporary picture we have of any Israelite king. BM

Jehu fared even worse, rendering tribute to Shalmaneser in 841 and then, upon Assyria's departure, forfeiting his entire Transjordanian territory to Hazael. Only an Assyrian victory over Damascus shortly before 800 B.C. brought relief to Israel (13:5).

4. By 790 Amaziah of Judah had sufficiently recovered to reconquer Edom (14:7), but his success deceived him: he dared to challenge Jehoash of Israel (see vs. 10), and Jerusalem was rendered totally subservient to Ephraim until the death of Jehoash in 782.

5. Under the strong monarchs Jeroboam II in Israel and Uzziah in Judah, the two kingdoms lived for 30 years in mutual respect and peace. It was their "Indian summer": Egypt slumbered on under the Twenty-third Dynasty; Syria was broken by Assyria; and Assyria herself, now without aggressive leadership, could be swayed even by the contemporary Hebrew prophet Jonah (14:25). But beneath the outward prosperity lay moral corruption. Amos proclaimed impending judgment on "the day of Jehovah" (Amos 5:18). Hosea, too, warned of deportation to Assyria (Hos. 10:6); but with the abrogation of God's old testament with Israel, he anticipated a future, newer testament in which men would "know God" in truth, under "David [the Messiah] their King" (2:20; 3:5).

6. In 752 B.C. Jeroboam II's son was murdered, and Uzziah (Azariah) of Judah assumed the leadership of the western states against the rising power of Assyria. The general Pul, who became Tiglath-pileser III, was able in 743 to chronicle his defeat of "Azariah the Yaudaean"; and while Judah apparently escaped with little damage, Damascus and Israel, being farther N, were laid under heavy tribute (II Kings 15:19).

7. The Syrians and Ephraimites then united in reprisals against Ahaz, Judah's new but weak and faithless ruler (16:5; Isa. 7:1-2). Isaiah admonished him to trust in God and in Immanuel, the virgin-born Messiah (Isa. 7:3-14); but in 734 Ahaz submitted to Assyria for deliverance (II Kings 16:7). Edom and Philistia continued to plunder Judah (II Chron. 28:17-18) and may thus provide the background to Obadiah (see vs. 10) and Joel (3:4,19); but Ephraim's northern tribes were taken

captive by Tiglath-pileser in 733 (II Kings 15:29), and Damascus was destroyed (16:9). Shortly thereafter the energetic Twenty-fifth (Cushite) Dynasty rose to power in Egypt, and So (Shabaka?) incited Israel to a final revolt (17:4). Samaria fell to the Assyrians in 722 B.C. Sargon II (722-705) proceeded to deport 27,290 Ephraimites (17:6) and replaced them with foreign colonists, who produced the half-breed Samaritans (vss. 24-33). "Israel believed not in Jehovah their God and rejected His covenant . . . Therefore Jehovah removed them out of His sight: there was none left but Judah only" (vss. 14-15,18).

Hezekiah (725-796) meanwhile seized the opportunity to purify the Jerusalem temple (II Chron. 29) and to destroy the corrupt high places, whether outrightly pagan or claiming the name of Jehovah. His reform included even Israel, which was now helpless under Assyrian siege (31:1); and he invited Ephraimites and Judeans alike to the greatest passover since Solomon (Chapter 30). "Israel" came thus to be applied to God's faithful remnant, regardless of their previous citizenship (vs. 6; compare Ezra 9:1; 10:5). Hezekiah was warned by both Isaiah (30:1-7; 31:1-3) and Micah (1:9) to take no part in Shabaka's disastrous battle against Sargon in 720; and he managed to withdraw from the equally unsuccessful revolt of Ashdod in 711, which was sponsored by Egypt and Babylon (Isa. 20 and 39; compare 36:1). But with the accession of Sennacherib in 705, Hezekiah attempted to throw off the Assyrian yoke. Egypt, however, proved again to be a "broken reed" (II Kings 18:21): Shabaka was defeated at Eltekeh near Ekron in 701, and Sennacherib claims to have taken over 200,000 Jews captive (compare Isa. 43:5,14) and to have "shut up Hezekiah like a caged bird in Jerusalem." Hezekiah resubmitted (II Kings 18:14-16), but the false Sennacherib made further demands (vs. 17). God then rose to the defense of His chastened people (Isa. 37:6,21-35); and, when a relief army arrived under Shabaka's brother Tirhaka, it found the Assyrians smitten by the angel of the Lord (II Kings 19:9,35; compare the Egyptian legend of a plague of mice in the camp of Sennacherib, Herodotus, II,141). The event

A portion of the clay prism of Sennacherib wherein he boasts of victory over Hezekiah and the Jews. OIUC

ranks with the crossing of the Red Sea as one of the greatest examples of God's deliverance. Isaiah thus had a sound basis for comforting Israel (40: 1-2) and directing their hope to that day when God should fulfill His redemptive purpose among them (53:6).

The reign of Manasseh (696-641) was the longest and worst of Israel's history. He surrendered Hezekiah's dearly-bought freedom by resubmitting to Assyria; and he rebuilt the high places, served Baal with human sacrifice, and mimicked Assyrian star-worship (II Kings 21:2-9). Through imprisonment (after the Babylonian revolts of 652-648?), he experienced personal conversion (II Chron. 33:11-16); but it was too late to reform the people as a whole (vs. 17; compare II Kings 21:11,15; 23:26). God, however, was yet to raise up Josiah (639-608), the greatest of Israel's reformers. While still in his teens (627 B.C.) he responded to prophetic teaching such as Zephaniah's (1:14-17) and began actively to eliminate idolatry (II Chron. 34:3-7). At this point the barbaric Scythians erupted over the Near East; and the terror they inspired seems likewise to have turned men's hearts to God. (Compare Jeremiah's earliest sermons [6:22-26]). The Scythians were finally driven back by the newly-formed Twenty-sixth Dynasty in Egypt, but their devastations did serve to release Judah from foreign control for a full 20 years. Josiah used these last precious decades to establish the testamental faith once and for all among the pious. His reforms climaxed in 621 B.C. with the discovery of "the book of the law of Jehovah by the hand of Moses" (II Chron. 24:14), perhaps the chief sanctuary scroll of the Pentateuch (Deut. 31:25-26) that had been misplaced under Manasseh (compare II Chron. 35:3). Josiah and his people reconsecrated themselves "to perform the words of the testament that were written in this book" (34:31). He removed the high places (II Kings 23:8-9), including even Jeroboam's original altar at Bethel (v. 15), and kept the greatest passover since the days of the judges (II Chron. 35). "Like unto him there was no king before him that turned to Jehovah with all his heart, according to all the law of Moses" (II Kings 23:25).

In 612 B.C. Nineveh fell to the Medes and Babylonians, just as Nahum had prophesied (Nah. 3:18-19). The Medes then withdrew, but Egypt and Babylon arose to claim the spoils. Josiah intervened to oppose the advance of Pharaoh Necho II and was slain at Megiddo in 608 B.C. (II Chron. 35:20-24). Necho, however, was decisively defeated by the Babylonians at Carchemish in 605; and Nebuchadnezzar appropriated the formerly Assyrian territories (II Kings 24:7). Josiah's son Jehoiakim was threatened with deportation to Babylon (vs. 6); but only a few of the nobility, such as Daniel (Dan. 1:3), were actually taken captive at this time. The date does mark the commencement of Israel's predicted 70 years of captivity (Jer. 25:11-12). But while the prophet Habakkuk was admonishing his people to "live by faith" (Heb. 2:4), Jehoiakim reverted to the sins of his fathers (Jer. 22:13-19). He also rebelled against Babylon (II Kings 24:1); but he died in 598 B.C., and it was his son, with 10,000 of the leaders of Judah, who suffered the second deportation, when Jerusalem surrendered on March 16, 597 (24:10-16). Finally, Jehoiakim's brother Zedekiah yielded to the inducements of Pharaoh Hophra of the Twenty-sixth Dynasty and defied Nebuchadnezzar (compare Jer. 37:11). The Babylonians advanced, Hophra withdrew, and Jerusalem fell in 586. The city and temple were burned (II Kings 25:9), the walls were dismantled

(vs. 10), and most of the people were carried into exile in Babylon (vs. 11). A small, fourth deportation in 582 removed even some of the poor that were left (vs. 12, Jer. 52:30). Israel had "mocked the messengers of God and despised His words, until the wrath of Jehovah arose against His people, till there was no remedy" (II Chron. 36:16). But though the external kingdom of Israel had ceased to exist, it did so because it had accomplished its divine purpose. A remnant, albeit small, had been nurtured to the point of profiting from the fiery trial of Babylon (see Exile) so as to be ready for that ultimate day, when, "Behold, saith Jehovah, I will make a new testament with the house of Israel: and I will put My law in their inward parts, and in their heart will I write it; and I will be their God, and they shall be My people: . . . for I will forgive their iniquity, and their sin will I remember no more" (Jer. 31: 31-34; Heb. 8:6-13, 10:15-22, ASV). J.B.P.

ISRAELITE (See Israel)

ISSACHAR (ĭs′ă-kär, Heb. *yissākhār,* meaning uncertain). 1. The ninth son of Jacob and the fifth of Leah (Gen. 30:17,18; 35:23). Almost nothing is known of his personal history beyond his share in the common actions of the sons of Jacob. He had four sons, and with them went down with Jacob into Egypt (Gen. 46:13; Exod. 1:3). There he died and was buried. His descendants formed a tribe, consisting of five great tribal families (Num. 26:23,24).

Not much is known of the tribe. It lay S of Zebulun and Naphtali, and N of Manasseh; and was bounded on the E by the Jordan. It occupied the greater part of the very fertile plain of Esdraelon, which, however, was mostly held by the Canaanites. Along the S edge of the plain there were fortresses held by Manasseh. At the first census in the wilderness the tribe numbered 54,400 fighting men (Num. 1:28,29); at the second, 64,300 (Num. 26:25). In the days of David the figure had reached 87,000 (I Chron. 7:5). Igal, son of Joseph, was the spy from Issachar (Num. 13:7). Deborah and Barak belonged to it; and in Deborah's song (Judg. 5:15), the tribe is mentioned as having taken part in the battle against Sisera. One of the judges, Tola, belonged to it (Judg. 10:1); and so did two kings, Baasha and his son (I Kings 15:27). The princes of Issachar abandoned allegiance to Saul's family and accepted David as king of all Israel (I Chron. 12:32). Many men from the tribe attended Hezekiah's passover, although they belonged to the northern kingdom (II Chron. 30:18). The tribe is mentioned in Revelation 7:7, where we are told that 12,000 from Issachar were sealed.

2. A Korahite doorkeeper in the reign of David (I Chron. 26:5).

ISSHIAH (ĭs-shī′ă, Heb. *yishshîyāhû, Jehovah exists*). 1. A man of Issachar, a great-grandson of Tola (I Chron. 7:3, Ishiah in KJV).

2. One of those who came to David at Ziklag (I Chron. 12:6, Jesiah in KJV).

3. A Levite of the house of Rehabiah (I Chron. 24:21).

4. A Levite of the house of Uzziel (I Chron. 23:20; 24:25).

ISUAH (See Ishuah)

ISSUE (See Diseases: Miscellaneous Medical Disorders)

ISUI (See Ishui)

ITALIAN BAND. A cohort of volunteer Roman soldiers recruited in Italy and stationed in Caesarea when Peter preached the Gospel to Cornelius, who was a centurion in it (Acts 10:1). It consisted mostly of Italians who could not find service in the Praetorian Guard.

ITALY (ĭt'à-lĭ, Gr. *Italía*), the geographical term for the country of which Rome was the capital. Originally, it applied only to the extreme S of what is now Italy, the region now called Calabria, but gradually the application of the name was extended, until in the first century of our era it began to be used in the current sense. It is referred to four times in the NT. 1. In Acts 18:2 Aquila and Priscilla had just come from Italy because the Emperor Claudius had commanded all the Jews to leave Rome.

2. It is mentioned in Acts 27:1 as Paul's destination when he had appealed to Caesar; and in verse 6 Paul is put on board a ship of Alexandria sailing for Italy.

3. In Hebrews 13:24 Christians from Italy send their greetings along with those of the author of the epistle.

4. In Acts 10:1 it is mentioned as the country that gave its name to the cohort stationed at Caesarea, of which Cornelius was the centurion. Christianity was early introduced into Italy, but the time and circumstances are uncertain.

ITCH (See Diseases)

ITHAI (îth'à-ī, *îthay*), a Benjamite, one of David's chief men (I Chron. 11:31); called Ittai in the parallel passage II Samuel 23:29).

ITHAMAR (ĭth'à-màr, Heb. *ithāmār*), the youngest of the four sons of Aaron, the others being Eleazar, Nadab, and Abihu. Aaron and his sons were consecrated to the priesthood (Exod. 28:1), but Nadab and Abihu were put to death for offering strange fire (Lev. 10). During the wilderness wanderings he was the treasurer of the offerings for the tabernacle (Exod. 38:21) and superintendent of the Gershonites and Merarites (Num. 4:28,33). He founded a priestly family, to which Eli and his descendants belonged, and this continued after the Captivity (I Chron. 24:4-6; Ezra 8:2).

ITHIEL (ĭth'ĭ-ĕl, *îthî'ēl God is*). 1. One of two persons to whom Agur addressed his sayings Prov. 30:1).

2. A Benjamite (Neh. 11:7).

ITHMAH (ĭth'mà, Heb. *yithmâh, purity*), a Moabite, one of David's heroes (I Chron. 11:46).

ITHNAN (ĭth'năn, Heb. *yithnān*), a town in the S of Judah (Josh. 15:23). Not identified.

ITHRA (ĭth'rà, Heb. *yithrā', abundance*), the father of Amasa, commander of Absalom's rebel army. His mother was Abigail, David's sister (I Chron. 2:17, Jether in KJV). In II Samuel 17: 25 he is called an Israelite, but in I Chronicles 2: 17; I Kings 2:5,32 (Jether in KJV), an Ishmaelite.

ITHRAN (ĭth'răn, Heb. *yithrān, excellent*). 1. A Horite, son of Dishon (Gen. 36:26; I Chron. 1: 41).

2. A son of Zophah of the tribe of Asher (I Chron. 7:37).

ITHREAM (ĭth'rē-ăm, Heb. *yithre'ām*), the sixth son born to David at Hebron. His mother was Eglah (II Sam. 3:5; I Chron. 3:3).

ITHRITE (ĭth'rīt, Heb. *yithrî, excellence*), a family which lived at Kiriath-jearim (I Chron. 2:53). Two of David's heroes belonged to this family, Ira and Gareb (II Sam. 23:38; I Chron. 11:40).

ITTAH-KAZIN (ĭt'à-kā'zĭn, Heb. *'ittâh kātsîn*), a place on the border of Zebulun (Josh. 19:13). Exact site unknown.

ITTAI (ĭt'à-ī ,Heb. *'ittay*). 1. A son of Ribai, a Benjamite, one of David's 30 mighty men (II Sam. 23:29; I Chron. 11:31).

2. A native of Gath who left his native Philistine city and attached himself to David. He commanded 600 men. He was loyal to David through all vicissitudes. When Absalom rebelled against David, Ittai fled with the king and refused to return to Jerusalem, where, David told him, his interests lay. David made him a commander of a third part of his army, with Joab and Abishai; and in the battle that followed Absalom was killed (II Sam. 15:18-22; 18:2,5).

ITURAEA (ĭt'û-rē'à, Gr. *Itouraía, pertaining to Jetur*). This word is found only once in Scripture, in the description of Philip's territory, which the KJV renders, "of Ituraea and of the region of Trachonitis" (Luke 3:1). It was a region NE of Palestine, beyond the Jordan, and cannot now be exactly located. The Ituraeans were descended from Ishmael (Gen. 25:15), who had a son named Jetur, from whom the name Ituraea is derived. The Ituraeans were semi-nomads and famous archers, a lawless and predatory people. According to an ancient writer, David warred against them. It is not known when they moved from the desert to the mountains in the N. Until the fourth century A.D. there was no defined territory called Ituraea; only the ethnic name Ituraeans was used. In Luke 3:1, according to Ramsay, the word is an adjective. In 105 B.C. Aristobulus I conquered and annexed the kingdom to Judea. In 66 B.C. Pompey defeated its king, Ptolemaeus, who purchased immunity with a large sum of money. Lysanias, the son of Ptolemaeus, was put to death by Antony, who thereupon gave the tetrarchy to Cleopatra (36 B.C.). Later Augustus gave it to Herod the Great, and after his death it passed to his son Philip.

IVAH (ī'và, Heb. *'iwwâh*), a city, probably in Syria, captured by the Assyrians, according to the boast of Sennacherib's representative (II Kings 18:34; 19:13; Isa. 37:13).

IVORY (ī'vō-rĭ, Heb. *shēn*, Gr. *elephántos*). The word *shen* means a *tooth*, but it is also frequently used in the sense of *ivory*. The context always makes clear how it should be rendered. Ivory was brought to Palestine by both ship and caravan, and came from India. Solomon's throne was made of ivory (I Kings 10:18); and he imported large quantities of it. Amos denounces Israel for its luxuries, among them the use of ivory (Amos 3:15; 6:4). Even houses were overlaid with it (I Kings 22:39; Ps. 45:8).

IZCHAR (See Izhar)

IZHAR (ĭz'hàr, Heb. *yitshār, the shining one*). 1. A Levite, son of Kohath, whose descendants formed a tribal family (Exod. 6:18,19; Num. 3: 19; I Chron. 6:18,38).

2. A descendant of Judah, whose mother was Helah (I Chron. 4:7).

IZRAHIAH (ĭz'rà-hī'à, Heb. *yizrahyâh, Jehovah arises* or *shines*), a chief of the tribe of Issachar (I Chron. 7:3).

IZRAHITE (iz'ra-hit, Heb. *yizrâh, rising, shining*). Shamhuth, the captain of the fifth monthly course, is called an Izrahite (I Chron. 27:8). The name may be a corruption of "Zerahite," a descendant of Zerah of Judah.

IZRI (ĭz-rī, Heb. *yitsrî, creator, former*), a man of the "sons of Jeduthun," chief of one of the Levitical choirs (I Chron. 25:11). Called Zeri in verse 3.

J

JAAKAN (jā'à-kăn, Heb. *ya'ăqān*), a descendant of Esau (I Chron. 1:35-42, spelled *Jakan*). He was the son of Ezer, who was a Horite (Gen. 36: 20-27, spelled *Akan*). Israel rested in the land of Jaakan where there were wells (Beeroth) and Aaron was buried there (Deut. 10:6,7). In the report of Israel's wanderings the camp is called *Bene* (sons of) *Jaakan* (Num. 33:31,32).

JAAKOBAH (jā'à-kō'bà), a Simeonite prince. (I Chron. 4:36).

JAALA, JAALAH (jā'à-là, jā'à-là), a servant of Solomon whose children returned from Babylon. (Ezra 2:56).

JAALAM (jā'à-lăm), the second son of Esau by a Hivite woman. He became a duke in Edom (Gen. 36:2,5,18).

JAANAI (jā'à-nī), a son of Gad, who settled in Bashan near the heritage of Reuben (I Chron. 5:11,12).

JAARE-OREGIM (jā'à-rē-ôr'ē-jĭm, Heb. *ya'ărê-ōreghīm*), the father of Elhanan, who slew the giant brother of Goliath (II Sam. 21:19). The title *oregim* means weaver and seems to have been added by a scribe who confused the real name with the size of the giant's sword. Jaare also seems to be a scribal error, since the name is given in Chronicles as Jair (I Chron. 20:5). Most authorities agree that the name in Chronicles is correct.

JAASAU (jā'à-sāū, Heb. *ya'āsû*, RV has *Jaasu*, RVm Jaasai), one of a number of captives who married alien women but put them away upon demand of a council headed by Ezra (Ezra 10:16-19,37).

JAASIEL, JASIEL (jā-ā'sĭ-ĕl, jā'sĭ-ĕl, Heb. *ya'ăsî'ēl, God makes*), a son of Abner, of the tribe of Benjamin, a leader of Benjamites (I Chron. 27: 21) and valiant warrior (I Chron. 11:47).

JAAZANIAH (jā-ăz'à-nī'à, Heb. *ya'ăzanyāhû, ya'ăzanyah, Jehovah hears*). 1. A member of the tribe of Maacah whose land E of the Jordan was given to Manasseh (Josh. 13:7-11). He was captain under Gedaliah (II Kings 25:23). Jeremiah calls him Jezaniah (40:8, 42:1), and Azariah (43: 2). He joined a group who slew Gedaliah and then, contrary to advice from Jeremiah, led a band into Egypt (Jer. 43:1-7).

2. Jaazaniah was the son of a Rechabite named Jeremiah, and was among a group of refugees who refused to drink wine which Jeremiah offered (Jer. 35:1-11).

3. Another of the name was a leader in idolatrous worship which Ezekiel saw in a vision (8:10-12).

4. The son of Azur, one of a band of 25 men who led in wickedness and idolatry in Israel (Ezek. 11:1-3).

JAAZER, JAZER (jā'à-zêr, jā'zêr, Heb. *ya'ăzêr, helpful*), a stronghold E of the Jordan in a fertile area (Isa. 16:8-11). It was taken from the Amorites by Moses (Num. 21:32) and made a part of the heritage of Gad (Josh. 13:24,25). Later it was given to the Levites (Josh. 21:39). It was a grazing region (Num. 32:1-5) and a good place for vineyards (Jer. 48:32). Joab considered it important enough to be included in the census

(II Sam. 24:5). The city grew mighty men of valor during David's latter years (I Chron. 26: 31). Moab captured and despoiled the city (Isa. 16:8f) and later the Ammonites seized, ravaged and burned it (Josh. *Ant.* XII:8; 1). The Sea of Jazir (Jer. 48:32) may be identified today as Khirbet Jazzir, Sea of Salt N of the Dead Sea.

JAAZIAH (jā'àz-ī'à, Heb. *ya'ăzīyāhŭ, Jehovah strengthens*), a descendant of Levi; temple musician of David's time (I Chron. 24:26,27).

JAAZIEL (jā-ā'zĭ-ĕl, Heb. *ya'ăzî'ēl, God strengthens*), a temple musician (I Chron. 15:18), called Aziel in verse 20.

JABAL (jā'băl, Heb. *yāvāl*, meaning uncertain), a son of Lamech, who was the great-grandson of Cain (Gen. 4:19,20). He and his brothers, Jubal and Tubal, are credited with the origin of civilized society (Gen. 4:21,22).

JABBOK (jăb'ŏk, Heb. *yabbōq, flowing*), an important river E of the Jordan about halfway between the Dead Sea and the Sea of Galilee. It was the northern border of the Amorite king, Sihon, (Josh. 12:2) and was captured by the Hebrews after Sihon refused to let them cross his land (Num. 21:21-25). It was also the southern border of the kingdom of Og (Josh. 12:5). At a ford on the Jabbok, Jacob had his encounter with the angel, which resulted in his being given a new name (Gen. 32:22-30). The word for wrestle is *abbaq,* and may have given the Hebrew name to the stream, or an ancient fortress between Damascus and Mecca, Xarka, may have furnished the name. Its modern name is Ez-zerka, *river of blue.* It is shallow except during occasional rains, and its fords are easily crossed. Its basin is second in size of Jordan's eastern tributaries, only the Yarmuk to the north having a larger watershed. Its banks are covered with heavy vegetation, the portion near the Jordan being semi-tropical. It rises within 20 miles of the Jordan, but runs 60 miles, at first NE, then nearly due W in a great arc before turning SW to the Jordan. This unusual course accounts for the record in Numbers 21:24, the upper section being the boundary between Sihon and Ammon, and the arc the eastern boundary of Sihon's realm. J.D.F.

A scene in the gorge of the Jabbok River. SHH

JABESH (jā′bĕsh, Heb. *yavēsh, dry*). 1. Father of Shallum, who slew Zachariah and reigned instead for a month (II Kings 15:8-13).

2. A short term for Jabesh-Gilead (I Chron. 10:12), a town. See JABESH-GILEAD.

JABESH-GILEAD (jā′bĕsh-gĭl′ē-ăd, Heb. *yavēsh gil′ādh, dry*), the metropolis of the Gileadites (Jos. *Ant.* VI:5;1). It lay a night's journey across the Jordan from Beth-shan (I Sam. 31: 11,12). It was in the area given to the half tribe of Manasseh (Num. 32:33). When the citizens refused to attend the sacred assembly at Mizpeh, an army was sent to destroy them (Judg. 21:8-15). The city was not destroyed and grew again into power and wealth. During Saul's reign over Israel, Nahash, king of Ammon, besieged the city. Appealed to for a treaty, he proposed to grant peace if every able-bodied man would have his right eye put out. A seven-day truce was granted during which time Saul's help was enlisted. He sent pieces of slain oxen throughout his land, indicating what would happen to those who refused to help in his battle for Jabesh. His army defeated Nahash; the city was saved and the nation reunited (I Sam. 11:1-15). One of the purposes behind this military aid was to secure wives for Benjamites, since Israel had sworn never to allow Benjamites to marry their daughters (Judg. 21:1). Later, when Saul's forces had been routed by the Philistines and he and his sons slain, men of Jabesh-Gilead rescued their bodies, cremated them and buried the remains in Jabesh (I Sam. 31:1-13). Upon becoming king, David sent thanks for the act (II Sam. 2:4-6) and had the remains of Saul and Jonathan exhumed and interred in the tomb of Kish in the land of Benjamin (II Sam. 21:12-14).

It is probable that the stream Wady-Yabish received its name from the city. Al-Dair (ed Dair) is now thought to be the probable site of the ancient city. It was ten miles E of the Jordan and about 25 miles S of the Sea of Galilee. J.D.F.

JABEZ (jā′bĕz, Heb. *ya′bēts, to grieve*). 1. The head of a family in Judah (I Chron. 4:9). His offspring are listed as scribes and as Kenites (I Chron. 2:55). He was more honorable than his brethren (I Chron. 4:9). He made an earnest appeal for a blessing and it was granted (I Chron. 4:10). Zobebah (4:8) is probably another title for him.

2. Jabez was also an unidentified town in Judah in which scribes carried on their trade (I Chron. 2:55).

JABIN (jā′bĭn, Heb. *yāvîn, able to discern*). 1. A king of Hazor, the leading city in the northern part of Palestine (Josh. 11:1). When Joshua had succeeded in conquering the neighboring provinces and had massed his forces at Gilgal (Josh. 10:7), Jabin led in forming an alliance against him. These tribes occupied the area S of the Sea of Galilee (Josh. 11:1-4). Joshua was cowed by the great force thus gathered against him, but was assured of God that he could defeat them (Josh. 11:6). They joined battle with Jabin at the waters of Merom. He chased the enemy all the way to the coast at Zidon, leading city of Phoenicia (Josh. 11:8). Hazor was taken and Jabin slain (11:10).

2. Another king by the name of Jabin was a Canaanite who, after the death of Othniel, enslaved Israel, who were rescued by the strategy of Deborah (Judg. 4). He seems to have been only a puppet of Sisera, since he is not mentioned in the Song of Deborah recorded in Judges 5.

JABNEEL (jăb′nē-ĕl, Heb. *yavne′ēl, God causes to build*). 1. A town in the northern border of Judah, just S of Joppa (Josh. 15:11), modern Jab-

na. It is called Jabneh in II Chronicles 26:6. It belonged to the tribe of Dan. (Jos. *Ant.* vs. 2,3); Judas Maccabaeus captured it (II Macc. 12·8,9). It was freed by the emperor Pompey 62 B.C. Herod gave it to Salome, who in turn gave it to the wife of Augustus. Probably through her influence Augustus returned it to the Jews, 30 A.D. (Jos. *Ant.* XIII:2;2). After the fall of Jerusalem it became the seat of the Sanhedrin.

2. A frontier town of Naphtali (Josh. 19:33). Perhaps the same as Yemma, not far from Tiberias.

JABNEH (jăb′nĕ), the same as Jabneel 1.

JACHAN (jā′kă), a descendant of Gad (I Chron. 5:13).

JACHIN, JACHIN AND BOAZ (jā′kĭn, Heb. *yākhîn, he will set up*). 1. The fourth son of Simeon (Gen. 46:10, Jarib in I Chron. 4:24). Founder of the tribe of Jachanites (Num. 26:12).

2. One of the priests in Jerusalem during the captivity (Neh. 11:10). During David's reign he was leader of the twenty-first course of priests (I Chron. 24:17).

3. Jachin and Boaz were the names of two symbolic pillars in the porch of Solomon's temple, Jachin (speed) on the S and Boaz (power) on the N. They were designed by Hiram of Tyre (I Kings 7:13-22), hence of Phoenician origin. They were at first ornamental, but came to have a religious meaning, guarding the doors to the sacred halls.

JACINTH (jā′sĭnth, Gr. hyarinthos, *hyacinth*), one of the precious stones in the foundation of New Jerusalem (Rev. 21:20). A yellow gem, sometimes with a tinge of blue. Easily cut, it was used by the Greeks in making intaglios, by the Romans in making cameos. Hyacinth in RV. See MINERALS.

JACKAL (See Animals)

JACOB (jā′kŭb, Heb. *ya′ăqōv, supplanter*), one of the great names of history, a person about whom a multitude of traditions gathered and of whose record there is among scholars wide diversity of opinions.

1. The Background. Abraham had not long separated himself from the people of the Tigris-Euphrates Valley. Jacob's name was an old one among the Semitic people. As early as 2000 B.C. it occurs among writings of Hammurabi as *Yakibula*. That it was well-known among the Canaanites of pre-Abraham days is attested by records in the temple at Karnak. Among cities captured by Thotmes III are found two which are similar to the Hebrew word Joseph-el and Jakob-el. Jacob and Esau were children of faith, as was their father (Heb. 11:20). The continuing influence of Aramaean paganism which Abraham had left is seen in Rachel's act of taking her father's idols when Jacob was leaving the home of Laban (Gen. 31:19). From ancient Assyrian culture came the cunning and creative abilities which enabled Jacob to raise a family that shaped the destiny of the human race.

2. Birth and Youth (Gen. 25:19-26). At the age of 40 Isaac married Rebekah, a sister of his uncle Laban (vs. 20). In answer to prayer on behalf of his barren wife, she conceived twins (vs. 21). An unusual prenatal incident caused her to consult Jehovah who revealed to her the coming of the founders of two great nations (vs. 23). An ominous rivalry, begun in the womb, became visible during birth. Esau came first; Jacob followed at once, holding Esau by the heel, hence his name "tripper" or "supplanter" (vv. 25,26). Nothing is revealed about the childhood of the boys. Because of the ancient law of primogeniture, Isaac naturally favored the older son; but because, no doubt, of the revelation from God, Rebekah was partial to Jacob (vs. 28). Jacob's cunning was revealed in the way he induced Esau to sell his birthright (vss. 27-34).

3. Gain and Loss (Gen. 27:1-29:30). Isaac grew to be old and became blind. Knowing that his end was near, he desired to impart the paternal blessing. Esau was still the favorite son, so he asked him to prepare the favorite dish, after eating which he would pronounce the blessing (27:1-4). Rebekah overheard the request and took advantage of Isaac's blindness to further her plan to make Jacob first in every way. Jacob, as ambitious as his mother, joined in the plot. A dramatic scene is given in Genesis 27:6-45. Jacob, dressed to simulate Esau, was clad in his brother's robe, having skillfully applied goat skins to make his hands and neck hairy like his brother's. Rebekah made a savory dish which Jacob presented to his father. He deliberately told falsehoods: (1) "I am Esau"; (2) "God helped me secure the game with speed." Deceived by the odor of Esau's garments and pleased with the food, Isaac imparted the first-born's blessing to Jacob. Esau, upon learning of his brother's perfidy, wept and begged for another blessing which was granted (vss. 34-40). Rebekah, knowing of Esau's vow to kill Jacob, induced Isaac to send Jacob to Haran to choose a wife from the family of Laban (27:42-28:5).

En route to Haran, Jacob camped at Luz where he had a vision of a ladder, with angels ascending and descending. In his dream he had a promise from Jehovah both to inherit the land about him and to have a numerous progeny (28:10-15). He recognized that God had been with him, so named the place Bethel, "house of God" (28:16-19), and made a vow to tithe all his future possessions (vss. 20-22). He met Rachel at a well-side in Haran, watered her flock, revealed himself to her, and was soon at home with Laban (Gen. 29:1-14). His contract to serve seven years for Rachel ended after 14 years of indentured servitude (29:15-30).

4. The Offspring and Closing Years (Gen. 29:31-50:13). The conflict between Jacob and Esau had its counterpart in that between Leah and Rachel. Leah won favor from God and bore Reuben (*See! a son!*), Simeon (*God heard*), Levi (*Added*), and Judah (*Praise*—29:31-35). Rachel's desire for a son led her to give her maid to Jacob, and she bore Dan (*Judge*) and Naphthali (*Wrestling* — Gen. 30:1-8). Leah in turn gave her maid who bore Gad (*Troop*) and Asher (*Gladness*). She herself also bore Issachar (*Pay for hire*), Zebulun (*Abiding*), and finally Dinah (feminine for *Dan* or *Judge*). Rachel then bore a son, Joseph (*Adding*, 30:22-27). Then Jacob grew eager to return to his own land. After outwitting Laban in stock-breeding, he made his departure. Rachel, probably to insure her share in Laban's estate, stole the teraphim, or family gods, some small (Gen. 35:2,4), some large (I Sam. 19:13-17 marg.). Laban, learning of Jacob's flight, pursued and overtook him at Mount Gilead where they settled their difficulties by a covenant, sealed upon a memorial heap called Mizpeh or Watch tower (31:25-55).

At Mahanaim, Jacob met God, then sent messengers to Esau in Edom. They soon returned to report that Esau was near with a formidable force. Jacob went to Jehovah in prayer and received assurance that all would be well. Being alone that night, he wrestled with the angel of

Jacob's Well near Sychar, as it appeared for centuries, before it was glamorized and enshrined in marble. This is the well where Christ spoke to the Samaritan woman (John 4). © MPS

the Lord and secured a new name, Israel, or "Prince of God" (32:24-32). The meeting with Esau was emotion-packed (33:1-17) Jacob went to Shechem and bought land near Shalem on which he erected an altar named *El-elohe-Israel* "God is God of Israel" (33:18-20) Dinah was ravished at this place. To secure her marriage to Shechem, the men of Shalem submitted to circumcision (34:1-24), but while they were incapacitated by the operation Simeon and Levi slew them and pillaged the city (34:25-31). Jacob fled to Bethel. The 12th son, Benjamin, *son of my right hand*, was born and Rachel died (35:1-20). Jacob continued to dwell in Canaan where Joseph incurred the ill will of his brethren, was sold to Egyptians and became servant of Pharaoh's chief ruler. He saved the Hebrews (Gen. 37:1-47:31). Jacob's final act was to call his 12 sons about him, prophesy regarding the future of each one's offspring and bestow his parting blessing When he died, he was embalmed and taken by Joseph and a troop of Egyptian soldiers to Canaan and buried in the Cave of Machpelah (Gen. 49:1-50:13). J.D.F.

JACOB'S WELL. Modern *Bir Ya'kub* is doubtless the well mentioned in John 4:6 as the well of Jacob (*Pegè toú Iakób*). For more than 23 centuries Samaritans have believed that this is true. Jews likewise have believed the same in spite of the location of the well in Samaria. The ground mentioned by John had been purchased by Jacob (Gen. 33:19). The area was later wrested by force from the Amorites (Gen. 48:22). The well is near the base of Mt. Gerizim, whose bluffs may have inspired Jesus to say "this mountain" (John 4:21). A narrow opening four feet long led from the floor of the vault into the well which was dug through limestone. The depth has not been determined. One explorer in 670 A.D. claimed it was 240 feet. Another reported in 1697 that it was 105 feet. In 1861 a Major Anderson found it only 75 feet deep. For centuries tourists cast pebbles into it until Greek Catholics bought the site and put it under guard.

JADA (jā'dȧ, Heb. *yādhā', a wise one*), a son of Onam and grandson of Jerahmeel of Judah (1 Chron. 2:26,28).

JADAU (jā'dō, Heb. *yiddô*), an Israelite who married an alien woman during the captivity (Ezra 10:43).

JADDUA (jȧ-dū'ȧ, Heb. *yaddûa', known*). 1. An Israelite prince who had part in making the covenant after the return from Babylon (Neh. 10:21). 2. A son of Jonathan and great-grandson of Eliashib. He was among the priests who returned with Zerubbabel from Babylon (Neh. 12:11).

JADON (jā'dŏn, Heb. *yādhôn, he will plead*), one of the laborers who rebuilt the wall of Jerusalem under Nehemiah (Neh. 3:7).

JAEL (jā'ĕl, Heb. *yā'ēl, wild goat*), the wife of Heber the Kenite (Judg. 4:17). Sisera fled to Heber's tent when defeated by Barak (Judg. 4: 15,17). The perfidy of Jael in ignoring rules of hospitality becomes less heinous if seen in the light of war's long record of brutality. Being a woman she could not meet Sisera in combat, so resorted to cunning, slaying him with a weapon she had long since learned to use, a tent peg. That Deborah approved of her act (Judg. 5:24) only shows to what extremes a harassed people can be driven by a brutal foe. Jael's deed was considered an act of Israel, hence the manner in which Deborah gloated over it. No question is raised in the record about the moral nature of Jael's deed, nor is it attributed to divine leading, although the victory over Sisera was (Judg. 5:20).

JAGUR (jā'gêr, Heb. *yâghûr*), a town in the extreme S of the heritage of Judah (Josh. 15:21). Its site is unknown.

JAH (jȧ, Heb. *yāh*), a contraction of *Jahweh*. It is found in poetry, as in Psalms 68:4: 118:14, RSV marg., and is seen in such compound words as Isaiah, *Jah is saviour* and Abijah, *Jah is father.*

JAHATH (jā'hăth, Heb. *yahath,* perhaps *God will snatch up*). 1. A grandson of Judah (I Chron. 4: 1,2). 2. A great-grandson of Levi (I Chron. 6:16-20). 3. A chief among the Gershonite Levites (I Chron. 23:10,11). 4. Another Levite of the Izharite clan (I Chron. 24:22). 5. An overseer of construction during the restoration of the temple under Josiah (II Chron. 34: 8-12). He was a Merarite.

JAHAZ (jā'hăz), **JAHAZA** (jȧ-hā'zȧ), **JAHAZAH** (jȧ-hā'zȧ), a city in Reuben's heritage (Josh. 13: 18) in the land given to the Merarites (Josh. 21:34-36, Jahazah). The Moabite stone tells of a king of Israel who dwelt in Jahaz during a war with Mesha in which Mesha conquered. Later Israel captured the city, conquered Sihon and took the region (Num. 21:21-25). It was once a stronghold N of the Arnon river. Isaiah (15:4) and Jeremiah (48:20,21) call it a city of Moab.

JAHAZIAH (jȧ-hā'zĭ-ȧ, Heb. *yahzeyâh, God sees*), one of four who opposed Ezra's plan to rid Israel of alien wives married during the captivity (Ezra 10:15).

JAHAZIEL (jȧ-hā'zĭ-ĕl, Heb. *yahăzî'ēl, God sees*). 1. One of a band of ambidextrous warriors who aided David at Ziklag (I Chron. 12:1-4). 2. A priest who sounded the trumpet before the ark (I Chron. 16:6). 3. A son of Hebron and one of a host called by David to help build the temple (I Chron. 23: 2-20).

4. The chief bearer of the name was a descendant of Asaph. In a time of great peril he was led by the Holy Spirit to announce a victory when defeat seemed certain (II Chron. 20:14ff). Psalm 83 may have been written by him to commemorate the victory. 5. An ancestor of one of the families of the restoration (Ezra 8:5).

JAHDAI (jȧ'dā-ī), either a concubine or, more probably, a male descendant of Caleb (I Chron. 2:46,47).

JAHDIEL (jȧ'dĭ-ĕl, *God gives joy*), a mighty man, ancestral head of a Manassite clan (I Chron. 5: 24).

JAHDO (jȧ'dō), a Gadite, a son of Buz and a Gileadite of Jotham's day (I Chron. 5:14).

JAHLEEL (jȧ'lē-ĕl), a son of Zebulun (Gen. 46: 14); founder of the Jahleel clan (Num. 26:26).

JAHMAI (jȧ'mā-ī), a grandson of Issachar, a chieftain in his tribe (I Chron. 7:1,2).

JAHWEH (See God)

JAHZAH (jȧ'zȧ), a town given to Reuben (I Chron. 6:78).

JAHZEEL (jȧ'zē-ĕl), **JAHZIEL** (jȧ'zĭ-ĕl), a son of Naphthali (Gen. 46:24); Jaziel in I Chronicles 7:13.

JAHZERAH (jȧ'zĕ-rȧ), a priest of Israel (I Chron. 9:12), perhaps the same as Ahasai of Nehemiah 11:13.

JAIR (jā'ēr, Heb. *yā'îr, he enlightens*). 1. a son of Manasseh and a leading warrior in the conquest of Gilead by Moses (Num. 32:40,41). 2. One of the judges, a Gileadite who served 20 years (Judg. 10:3,4). 3. A Bethlehemite and the father of Elhanan who slew Goliath the Gittite (II Sam. 21:19 marg.). 4. The father of Mordecai (Esth. 2:5).

JAIRUS (jā'ĭ-rŭs, Gr. *Iáeiros*), a synagogue ruler whose child Jesus raised from death (Mark 5:22; Luke 8:41). The Gospel accounts vary somewhat in details, but all agree that a miracle occurred when the dead body lived again.

JAKAN (jā'kăn), a Horite (I Chron. 1:42). The same as *Akan* in Genesis 36:27, and *Jaakan* in Genesis 36:20,21,27; Deuteronomy 2:12, etc.

JAKEH (jā'kĕ, Heb. *yāqeh, very religious*), the father of Agur, a writer of proverbs (Prov. 30:1-27). Nothing is known about either Jakeh or Agur. "The prophecy" may mean prediction, burden, or oracle. The Hebrew word *ha-massa* is believed to mean *the Massaite.* "Jakeh the Massaite". would be a natural reading. (Gen. 25:14).

JAKIM (jā'kĭm, Heb. *yâkîm, God lifts*). 1. A son of Elpaal, a Benjamite (I Chron. 8:12,19). 2. Head of 12th course of priests (I Chron. 24: 12).

JALON (jā'lŏn), a son of Ezra, of the tribe of Judah (I Chron. 4:17).

JAMBRES (jăm'brēz), one of the magicians who opposed Moses before Pharaoh (II Tim. 3:8).

JAMES (Gr. *Iákobos*), the English form of Jacob. 1. James the son of Zebedee (Matt. 4:21; 10:2; Mark 1:19; 3:17) and Salome (cf. Matt. 27:56 with Mark 15:40), and the elder brother of the Apostle John (Matt. 17:1; Mark 3:17; 5:37; Acts 12:2), one of our Lord's earliest disciples (Matt. 4:21) and one of the apostles (Matt. 17:1; Mark 5:37; Luke 8:51; 9:28). It is possible that the brothers were cousins of Jesus, which may be why Salome asked special honors for them in the Messianic kingdom (Matt. 20:20). His home was probably in Capernaum. By occupation James and John were fishermen on the Sea of Galilee, in partnership with Peter and Andrew (Luke 5:10). Early in the ministry of Jesus the four were called by Jesus to leave their fishing to follow Him (Luke 5:10,11). From the reference to hired servants in the employ of Zebedee (Mark 1:20) and the mention of the fact that Salome was one of the women who ministered of their substance to Jesus and His company (Mark 15:41; Luke 8:3), it may be inferred that the family was one of some means. It is uncertain whether James was at one time a disciple of John the Baptist. He occupied a prominent place among the apostles, and, with Peter and John, became the special confidant of Jesus. Only these three apostles were with Jesus at the raising of Jairus' daughter (Mark 5:37), at the transfiguration (Matt. 17:1-8), and at the agony in the Garden of Gethsemane (Matt. 26:36-46). Soon after the transfiguration he and John received from Jesus the surname Boanerges, or sons of thunder, when they asked Jesus whether it was right for them to call down fire from heaven to consume the inhabitants of a Samaritan village that had refused Jesus and the apostles permission to pass through on their way to Jerusalem (Mark 3:17). The ambitious self-seeking of James and John in asking Jesus for a special place in the coming kingdom called forth the wrath of the other apostles (Mark 10:41). On Tuesday of Passion Week James was one of the four who asked Jesus the question concerning the last things (Mark 13: 3,4). He was also present when the risen Lord appeared to the disciples at the Sea of Tiberias (John 21:1-14). He was the first martyr among the apostles, being put to death by King Herod Agrippa I about the year A.D. 44, shortly before Herod's own death (Acts 12:2).

2. James the son of Alphaeus and one of the apostles of Christ (Matt. 10:3; Acts 1:13). Nothing more is known about him. He is usually identified with James the Little or the Less, the brother of Joses and son of Mary (Matt. 27:56; Mark 15:40). In Matthew 10:3 and Mark 3:18 he is coupled with Thaddaeus, and since Matthew or Levi is also called the son of Alphaeus (cf. Matt. 9:9; Mark 2:14), it is possible that he and James were brothers.

3. James, the Lord's brother (Matt. 13:55; Mark 6:3; Gal. 1:19). The exact relationship of the "brethren" to our Lord has long been disputed. Some think of them as His cousins; others, as His half-brothers, children of Joseph by a former marriage; others as the children of Joseph and Mary. They did not believe in Jesus during His ministry (John 7:5), but they did after His resurrection (Acts 1:14). The conversion of James apparently took place as a result of a special appearance of Jesus to him after the resurrection (I Cor. 15: 7). He early appears as the head of the church in Jerusalem (Acts 12:17; 21:18; Gal. 1:19; 2: 9,12). He probably took part in the election of Matthias to the vacant apostleship (Acts 1:15-25). Paul had an interview with him and Peter on his first visit to Jerusalem following his conversion (Gal. 1:19). On Peter's miraculous release from prison, soon after the death of James the brother of John, Peter went immediately to the house of Mary the mother of Mark and asked that the news of his deliverance might be sent to James and the brethren (Acts 12:17). When Paul visited Jerusalem for the second time after his conversion,

the leaders of the church, James, Peter, and John gave him their approval and told him that he and Barnabas should preach to the Gentiles, while they would minister to the Jews. At the Jerusalem council James acted as the head and supported Paul's position over against the Judaizers (Acts 14). Peter's inconsistency in regard to eating with Gentiles is explained by the arrival in Antioch of some who said they came from James (Gal. 2:11-14). He appears for the last time in the NT in Acts 21, where after Paul makes a report to him of his third missionary journey, he and the elders with him warn Paul of strong Jewish feeling against him, and advise him to join in a Nazirite vow which some members of their community have undertaken. He is usually regarded as the author of the Epistle of James. Josephus says that he was martyred by the Jewish High Priest soon after the death of Festus (*Antiq.* xx.9,1), about the year 62.

4. James, the father of the Apostle Judas (not Iscariot), referred to in Luke 6:16 and Acts 1:13. Nothing further is known of him.   S.B.

JAMES THE LESS (See James)

JAMES, EPISTLE OF. This epistle is among the last to become firmly established in the NT canon. While traces of it seem to be found in the writings of the Apostolic Fathers (90-155 A.D.), the oldest author to mention it by name is Origen (250 A.D.), who considers it canonical, although he is aware that its canonicity is not universally acknowledged. Eusebius (323 A.D.) lists it among the disputed books, but says it is read in most churches. In the East the church accepted it from a very early period, but in the West it was not received into the canon until the end of the fourth century.

The author of the epistle refers to himself as "James, a servant of God and of the Lord Jesus Christ" (1:1). The NT mentions four who bore the name of James: (1) the father of Judas the Apostle, not Iscariot (Luke 6:16), (2) the apostle, James the son of Alphaeus (Matt. 10:3), (3) the apostle, James the son of Zebedee and the brother of John (Matt. 4:21), (4) the brother of our Lord (Matt. 13:55; Gal. 1:19). The father of Judas the apostle is entirely unknown except for the mention of his relation to the apostle, and nothing is said of James the son of Alphaeus except that he was an apostle, so it is unlikely that either of these two men could have written the epistle. James the son of Zebedee was martyred about 44 A.D. (Acts 12:2), so he cannot be the author; and besides, the author of this epistle does not call himself an apostle, but describes himself merely as a servant. Tradition attributes the authorship of the epistle to James the brother of the Lord, who was favored with a special appearance of the risen Christ (I Cor. 15:7) and who from a very early date occupied a leading position in the church at Jerusalem (Acts 12:17; Gal. 1:19). Paul names him first among the three pillars of the church in Jerusalem he saw on his second visit there after his conversion (Gal. 2:9), and in Acts 15 he is described as the leader and chief spokesman of the Apostolic Council. All that is known of him shows that he was highly esteemed not only by Christians but by unbelieving Jews. According to Josephus he was put to death by the High Priest in the interregnum between the death of Festus and the arrival of his successor Albinus in 62 A.D.

All the characteristics of the epistle support the traditional attribution of it to James the brother of the Lord. The author speaks with the authority of one who knew he did not need to justify or defend his position. There is no more Jewish book in the NT than this epistle; and this is to be expected from a man whom both tradition and the rest of the NT show was distinguished by a greater attachment to the law of Moses than Paul. The whole of the epistle, moreover, bears a striking resemblance to the Sermon on the Mount both in the loftiness of its morality and in the simple grandeur of its expression.

The letter is addressed to "the twelve tribes which are scattered abroad." This ambiguous expression may be interpreted in a number of ways. 1. The Jews of the Diaspora in general, who were living throughout the Mediterranean world outside Palestine. This meaning is impossible, for the writer is addressing Christians (1:18,25; 2:1,12; 5:7-9). 2. The Jewish Christians of the Diaspora. 3. The Christian Church as the new people of God living far from their heavenly homeland. Early Christians regarded themselves as the true Israel (Gal. 6:16), the true circumcision (Phil. 3:3), and the seed of Abraham (Gal. 3:29; Rom. 4:16), so it would not be surprising if they also thought of themselves as "the twelve tribes." There is no doubt, however, that the epistle is intended for Jewish Christians, although its message is applicable to all Christians. Those to whom the author writes worship in synagogues (2:2), and the faults he attacks were characteristic of Jews: misuse of the tongue (3:2-12; 4:2,11), unkind judgments of one's neighbor (3:14; 4:11), the making of rash oaths (5:12), undue regard for wealth (2:1-13), etc. On the other hand, there is no mention of specifically pagan vices — idolatry, drunkenness, and impurity — against which Paul so often warns Gentile Christians. The object of the author is to rebuke and correct the error and sins into which his readers have fallen, and to encourage them in the heavy trials through which they were going.

The scholars who consider this epistle the work of James the brother of the Lord are not agreed on the date when it was written. Two views are held, one that it was composed shortly before the death of James, in the early sixties; the other, that it appeared in the middle forties, before the Apostolic Council. In favor of the early date are the striking simplicity of church organization and discipline, the fact that Christians still meet in the synagogue (2:2), and the general Judaic tone. All this is thought to suggest a time before Gentiles were admitted into the church in any large numbers. Scholars who prefer the later date say that the epistle gives evidence of a considerable lapse of time in the history of the Church, at least enough to allow for a declension of the spiritual fervor that characterized the church in early apostolic times. The readers are obviously not recent converts. The author has a position of long-established authority. The references to persecutions, moreover, fit a later date better than an early one.

The informal character of the epistle makes a logical analysis difficult. It is not a formal treatise, but a loosely juxtaposed series of exhortations, warnings, and instructions, all dealing with the moral and religious life. The author rules authoritatively on questions of church life and discipline which have been brought to his attention.

After the address (1:1), James first admonishes his readers on having a right attitude towards tribulations and temptations (1:2-18), and exhorts them to be doers and not merely hearers of the word of God (1:19-25). He forbids them to slight the poor and favor the rich (2:1-13), and shows them the insufficiency of faith without works (2: 14-26). He then warns them against the misuse

of the tongue (3:1-12), and sets forth the nature of true and false wisdom (3:13-18). He rebukes them for their avarice and concupiscence (4:1-12), and for making foolhardy plans for the future in business (4:13-17). The epistle closes with a warning to the godless rich (5:1-6), an exhortation to patience in suffering (5:7-12), a reminder of the power of prayer in every need (5:13-18), and a declaration of the joy of Christian service (5: 19,20).

The section on faith and works (2:14-26) is not a polemic against Paul's doctrine of justification by faith, but a rebuke of the prevalent Jewish notion that saving faith is mere intellectual assent to a set of doctrinal propositions. He points out that saving faith manifests itself in works, and that if the works are not there the genuineness of the faith may be questioned Paul and James are in perfect harmony in their views of the relationship of faith and works to salvation.   S.B.

JAMIN (jā'mĭn, Heb. *yāmîn, right hand*). 1. A son of Simeon (Gen. 46:10), or clan of Simeon (Num. 26:12).

2. A son of Ram of the tribe of Judah (I Chron. 2:3,27).

3. A teacher of the law under Ezra (Neh. 8:7).

JAMLECH (jăm'-lĕch, Heb. *yamlēkh, whom God makes king*), a prince of the tribe of Simeon (I Chron. 4:34).

JANNA (jăn'à, Gr. *Iannaí*), an ancestor of Jesus, fifth in line before Joseph (Luke 3:23,24).

JANNES (jăn'ēz, Gr. *Iannés*), a magician who withstood Moses and Aaron by duplicating some of their miracles. Paul, who was familiar with rabbinical traditions, named him along with Jambres as types of evil men of the last days (II Tim. 3:8).

JANOAH (jà-nō'à), **JANOHAH** (jà-nō'hà) in KJV of Joshua. 1. A town of Naphthali captured by Assyria (II Kings 15:29).

2. A town on the boundary line of Ephraim (Josh. 16:6,7).

JANUM (jā'nŭm), a town in the land of Judah, site unknown; part of heritage of Judah (Josh. 15:53 marg. Janus). Same as Janim.

JAPHETH (jā'fĕth, Heb. *yepheth, God will enlarge,* Gen. 9:27), a son of Noah. He was older than Shem (Gen. 10:21), but comes third in some lists of the three sons (Gen. 6:10; 9:18). Shem, however, is usually named first (Gen. 5:32; 11:10). Japheth and his wife were saved in the ark (Gen. 7:7); he aided Shem in covering the naked body of their drunken father (Gen. 9:20-27). He is the progenitor of the more remote northern peoples of southeastern Europe. That he was to occupy the tents of Shem is thought to refer to conquests of the Greeks who were descendants of Japheth. This he did during the days of Assyrian power. He had seven sons whose descendants occupied the isles of the Gentiles, Hellenes or Greeks (Gen. 10:5), an area including Asia Minor and upper Greece.

JAPHIA (jà-fī'à, Heb. *yāphîa', tall* or *may God make bright*). 1. A ruler of Lachish who joined a coalition against Joshua (Josh. 10:1-5). In a momentous battle in the Valley of Ajalon (vss. 12-14), the allies were defeated, the five kings fled and sought refuge in a cave which Joshua sealed up and left under guard while his forces pursued the enemy. Later he had the kings executed and buried in the cave (vss. 22-27).

2. A son of David born in Jerusalem (II Sam. 5:15; I Chron. 3:7).

3. A small city on the eastern border of Zebulun (Josh. 19:12). It has quite definitely been shown to be modern Yafa, a site not far from Nazareth.

JAPHLET (jăf'lĕt), a great grandson of Asher, or the name of a clan descended from Asher (I Chron. 7:32).

JAPHLETI (jăf'lē-tī), an ancient clan whose land was the western border of Joseph's heritage (Josh. 16:1-3). RV has Japhletite.

JAPHO (jā'fō), the Hebrew form of Joppa, a border town of Dan's inheritance (Josh. 19:46). See JOPPA.

JARAH (jā'rà, *honeycomb*), a descendant of Gibeon (I Chron. 9:42), called Jehoaddah of 8:36.

JAREB (jā'rĕb, Heb. *yārēv, contender*), an Assyrian king to whom Ephraim went for help (Hos. 5:13). The title is not found among Assyrian records, but this may be an earlier name of Sargon. It may be a term of derision, "king who is contentious."

JARED (jā'rĕd), the father of Enoch (Gen. 5:18-20).

JARESIAH (jăr'ē-sī'à), a son of Jerohan (I Chron. 8:27), of the tribe of Benjamin. RV has Jaareshiah.

JARHA (jär'hà), an Egyptian slave of Sheshan, a Jerahmeelite (I Chron. 2:34,35). Since Sheshan had no son, he gave Jarha his freedom so he could marry a daughter. Jewish sources claim him as a proselyte. That Ahlai (vs. 31) was the wife seems probable, although the name is masculine. Another idea is that Ahlai is the name given Jarha when he was set free.

JARIB (jā'rīb, *he strives*). 1. A son of Simeon, also called Jachin (I Chron. 4:24; Gen. 46:10 marg.).
2. A chief of returning captives, sent by Ezra to secure Levites to carry on the temple worship (Ezra 8:15-20).
3. One of the priests who had alien wives during the captivity, whom Ezra compelled to be put away (Ezra 10:18).

JARMUTH (jär'mŭth, Heb. *yarmûth, height*). 1. One of the numerous places included in the heritage of Judah (Josh. 15:35), which had been captured from its king, Piram, who was a member of the coalition called by the king of Jerusalem to oppose Joshua (Josh. 10:1-5). Ruins of the city have been found 16 miles W by S from Jerusalem. Walls and numerous wells show it to have been a stronghold — modern Khirbit el Yarmuk.
2. Another city of the name was given to the Gershonite Levites from the heritage of Issachar (Josh. 21:27-29), called Remeth (19:21), and Ramoth (I Chron. 6:73).

JAROAH (jà-rō'à), a chieftain of the tribe of Dan, living in land of Bashan (I Chron. 5:14).

JASHEN (jā'shĕn, *brilliant*), father of some of David's heroes (II Sam. 23:32). Confusion arises from I Chronicles 11:33f where his father is called Hashem, the Gizonite. This is evidently another spelling, which should be "Gunite."

JASHER, BOOK OF (jā'shêr, Jashar in RSV), quoted in Joshua 10:13, II Samuel 1:18, and in LXX of I Kings 8:53. This ancient book is thought to have been a collection of poetry, probably odes and psalms in praise of Israel's heroes and exploits. Many ideas about the book have been advanced: 1. It continued the Song of Deborah (Judg. 5). 2. It contained the book of the law. 3. It vanished during the Babylonian captivity. It was certainly a well-known bit of Hebrew literature.

JASHOBEAM (jà-shō'bē-ăm, Heb. *yāshōv'ām, the people return*). 1. One of the heroic men who went to Ziklag to aid David in his struggle with Saul (I Chron. 12:6). A Korahite.
2. One of David's chieftains who was a ruler of captains. He slew 300 during one battle (I Chron. 11:11, or 800, II Sam. 23:8). The LXX usually gives the name as Ishbaal. He is called Adino in II Samuel 23:8, Jashebassebet in margin. The difference in the report of the number slain has been explained by supposing that some scribe confused the words for three and eight when he copied the Samuel record. Jashobeam is supposed to have been one of the three who brought David water from the well of Bethlehem (I Chron. 11:15-19).
3. One who commanded a division of 24,000 men of Israel (I Chron. 27:2,3). This man could have been No. 2, in which case Hachmonite was an official title.

JASHUB (jā'shŭb, Heb. *yāshûv, he returns*). 1. A son or clan descended from Issachar (Num. 26:24). Genesis 46:13 has *Job* in the KJV. The LXX has Jashub in both passages.
2. Shear-Jashub, a son of Isaiah, who went to meet Ahaz (Isa. 7:3).
3. One of those who had married foreign wives (Ezra 10:29).

JASHUBI-LEHEM (jà-shoō'bī-lē'hĕm, Heb. *yāshuvî-lehem*), a word of doubtful meaning. Probably a man, a member of the tribe of Judah (I Chron. 4:22,23).

JASON (jā'sŭn, Gr. *Iáson, to heal*), a believer who sheltered Paul and Silas in Thessalonica (Acts 17:5-9). He was among those who sent greetings from Corinth to Rome (Rom. 16:21).

JATHNIEL (jăth'nĭ-ĕl), a son of Meshelemiah, a Korahite Levite and a temple porter (I Chron. 26:2); also a gate (threshold) guard (9:19).

JATTIR (jăt'êr), a large town in the hills of Judah (Josh. 15:20,48), given to the Levites (I Chron. 6:57). It was an important center (I Sam. 30:27). Modern Khirbet Attir is evidently its location.

JAVAN (jā'văn, Heb. *yāwān, Ionian*), a region settled by one of the sons of Japheth (Gen. 10:2). Javan was the name of this country to Ezekiel (27:11f), who saw it as an important trade center. So Javan (Greek, Ionia) came to be the name of Greece to the Hebrews. During the period 700-630 B.C. the Ionians carried on extensive trade in the Near East, hence all people of Greece were called Javan. When the Phoenicians developed their commerce, they often sold captives from Judah to the Greeks (Joel 3:4-6). These later became the agents of God's vengeance against Greece (Zech. 9:13). Note the contrast of "children of Greece" with "children of Sion." Critics have sought to show that Hebrews of pre-Exilic days were not familiar with the Ionians, but discoveries are proving that by Solomon's day the Hebrews had much trade with them.

JAVELIN (See Arms, Armor)

JAZER, JAAZER (jā'zêr), a city in Gilead E of the Jordan, having dependent villages (Num. 21:31, 32). Built by Gadites (Num. 32:34,35), it later became a Levitical city (Josh. 21:34-39). David found mighty men among her citizens (I Chron. 26:31).

JAZIZ (jā'zĭz), an overseer of the flocks of David (I Chron. 27:31).

JEALOUSY, WATER OF, the name given holy water which was used in determining the guilt or innocence of a wife accused by her husband of being untrue (Num. 5:11-25). The accuser brought his wife and made an offering; dust from the floor was put in the water which the woman drank after assenting to a curse on her body if guilty.

JEARIM (jē'à-rĭm), a hill on the northern border of Judah's heritage, with Chesalon, a village, on it (Josh. 15:10).

JEATERAI (jē-ăt'ē-rī), a Gershonite Levite, grandson of Iddo (I Chron. 6:21). RV has Jeatherai.

JEBERECHIAH (jē-bĕr'ē-kī'à), the father of Zechariah, a trusted scribe (Isa. 8:2).

JEBUS (jē'bŭs, Heb. *yevûs*), the name by which Jerusalem was known when it was in the possession of the Jebusites (Josh. 15:63; Judg. 19:10; I Chron. 11:4). Jebus was small in area compared with the size of Jerusalem in Solomon's time. David took the city from the Jebusites and made it the capital of Israel (II Sam. 5:1-9). Its citadel was the stronghold of Zion (I Chron. 11:5).

JEBUSITES (jĕb'ū-zīts, Heb. *yebûsi*), a Canaanite tribe, descended from Canaan according to the table of nations in Genesis 10, and dwelling in the land before the Israelite conquest (Gen. 10:15,16; 15:21; Exod. 3:8,17; 13:5; 23:23; 33:2; Deut. 7:1; 20:17; Josh. 3:10; 10:1-5; 12:8; 18:16; Judg. 1:8). Their king, Adonizedec, was one of the five who conspired against Gibeon and was slain by Joshua. The Jebusites long lived at the site of Jerusalem (which was called Jebus), and were not dislodged until David sent Joab and his men into the city (Josh. 15:8; Judg. 19:11). David then bought the threshing floor of Ornan (or Araunah) the Jebusite as a site for the temple, and this large flat rock where the altar of burnt offering stood is now supposed to be visible in the Dome of the Rock (Mount Moriah) at Jerusalem, q.v.

JECAMIAH, JEKAMIAH (jĕk'à-mī'à). 1. A descendant of Sheshan by a freed slave (I Chron. 2:34-41).
2. The fifth of seven sons of a king named Jeconiah (I Chron. 3:17,18).

JECOLIAH, JECHOLIAH (jĕk-ō-lī'à), mother of King Uzziah (II Chron. 26:3; II Kings 15:2).

JECONIAH (jĕk'ō-nī'à, Gr. *Iechonías*), a variant of Jehoiachin. He was the son of Jehoiakim and grandson of Josiah (I Chron. 3:15,17). He began to reign when 18 years of age, but after three months was captured by Nebuchadnezzar (II Kings 24:1-12). Contracted to Coniah (Jer. 22:24,28; 37:1).

JEDAIAH (jē-dā'yà, Heb. *yedha'yâh, Jehovah knows*), a common name among the descendants of Aaron and Levi. To distinguish among those bearing it is difficult. 1. A descendant of Simeon and the father of a prince (I Chron. 4:37,38).
2. A priest who returned with Zerubbabel and aided in rebuilding the walls of Jerusalem (Neh. 3:10; 12:6,19).
3. One of the priests whose names were entered in the book of the kings which held the genealogy of the Hebrew captives in Babylon (I Chron. 9:1-10). He received the second lot when the order of temple service was set up (I Chron. 24:7). By the time of the return from Babylon his family had grown to be very large (Ezra 2:1,36; Neh. 7:39).
4. Another priest among the captives, who was commissioned by Nehemiah to have part in the prophetic coronation of Joshua who was the son of Josedech, the high priest (Zech. 6:9-15).

JEDIAEL (jē-dī'à-ĕl, Heb. *yedhî'à'ēl, known of God*). 1. A son of Benjamin who became head of

a mighty clan (I Chron. 7:6,11). Since the name does not appear among the three sons named in I Chronicles 8:1, it is assumed by some scholars that he and Ashbel are the same. Whether he is the same Jediael who joined David's forces at Ziklag and helped swell the host that supported him against Saul (I Chron. 19-22) is uncertain.
2. Another valiant man in David's band (I Chron. 11:45), probably the same as No. 1.
3. Another Jediael was a temple doorkeeper, a descendant of Kore (I Chron. 26:1,2).

JEDIDAH (jē-dī'dà, *beloved*), mother of King Josiah (II Kings 22:1).

JEDIDIAH (jĕd'ī-dī'à, *beloved of Jehovah*). Either David or Bathsheba named their baby boy "Solomon," but because of Jehovah's love for the child, the prophet Nathan gave him this name (II Sam. 12:24,25).

JEDUTHUN (jē-dū'thŭn, Heb. *yedhûthûn, praise*), a Levite whom, with Heman and others, David set over the service of praise in the tabernacle (I Chron. 25:1-3). They with their children were to give thanks and sing, with harps and cymbals accompanying. This Jeduthun must have been aged in David's time for his sons and their sons are mentioned as serving. In I Chronicles 25:3 he is credited with six sons, of whom five are named and the sixth was probably Shimei of verse 17. Psalm 39 by David is dedicated to Jeduthun and Psalms 62 and 77 are "after the manner of Jeduthun."

JEEZER (jē-ē'zêr), head of a family in the tribe of Manasseh (Num. 26:30). The name is written Abiezer "father of help" in Joshua 17:2. He was an ancestor of Gideon (Judg. 6:11 ff). ASV has Iezer.

JEGAR-SAHADUTHA (jē'gàr-sā'hà-dū'thà, *heap of witness*), the name given by Laban to the "cairn of witness," called by Jacob *Galeed* (Gen. 31:47).

JEHALELEEL, JEHALELEL (jē-hăl'ē-lĕl), more correctly Jehallelel, as in ASV. 1. A descendant of Judah (I Chron. 4:16).
2. A Merarite Levite, father of one of the leaders in cleansing the temple in the days of Hezekiah (II Chron. 29:12).

JEHDEIAH (jē-dē'yà, *Jehovah will be glad*). 1. A direct descendant of Moses through Gershom in the days of David (I Chron. 24:20). His father is called Shubael in this passage but Shebuel in chapter 23:16 where he is called "the chief," i.e. of his family.
2. A man of the tribe of Zebulun whom David appointed to have charge of the asses which belonged to the king (I Chron. 27:30).

JEHEZEKEL (jē-hĕz'ē-kĕl, *God will strengthen*), a priest in David's time (I Chron. 24:16). *Jehezkel* in RV.

JEHIAH (jē-hī'à, *Jehovah lives*), one of the two doorkeepers for the ark in David's time (I Chron. 15:24).

JEHIEL (jē-hī'ĕl, *God lives*). 1. One of the players on psalteries set to high voices in David's time (I Chron. 15:18,20; 16:5).
2. A Gershonite Levite treasurer for Jehovah's house (I Chron. 23:8; 29:8).
3. A son of Hachmoni "the wise" who was with David's sons, probably as tutor (I Chron. 27:32).
4. A son of Jehoshaphat (II Chron. 21:2).
5. A descendant of Heman the singer in Hezekiah's time (II Chron. 29:14). ASV, RSV, Jehuel.
6. One of the overseers of the offerings brought to the temple under Hezekiah (II Chron. 31:13).
7. One of the rulers of the house of God in Josiah's time (II Chron. 35:8).

8. Father of Obadiah who came from captivity with 218 men in Ezra's day (Ezra 8:9).

9. Father of Shecaniah who in Ezra's time was the first to confess to having married a foreign wife and who proposed a covenant with God to put away these foreign wives and their children (Ezra 10:2).

10. One of the priests who confessed to having married a "strange" wife (Ezra 10:21).

JEHIELI (jē-hī'ĕ-lī), a Gershonite Levite in David's day (I Chron. 26:21,22); cf. Jehiel (I Chron. 23: 8).

JEHIZKIAH (jē'hĭz-kī'à, *Jehovah strengthens*), a son of Shallum, an Israelite in the days of Ahaz, king of Judah, who stood against the men of the north enslaving their brethren of Judah (II Chron. 28:12).

JEHOADAH (je-hō'à-dà), a descendant of King Saul through Jonathan (I Chron. 8:36). In ASV more correctly "Jehoaddah." In I Chronicles 9:42 he is called "Jarah," perhaps by error of a scribe.

JEHOADDAN (jē'hō-ăd'ăn), wife of King Joash of Judah and mother of Amaziah (II Chron. 25:1). In II Kings 14:2 ASV has Jehoaddin from a variant spelling.

JEHOAHAZ (jē-hō'à-hăz, Heb. *yehô'āhāz, Jehovah has grasped*). 1. The son and successor of Jehu, and 11th king of Israel. He is said to have reigned 17 years, c. 815-800 B.C. (II Kings 10:35; 13:1). Like his father, he maintained the calf-worship begun by Jeroboam; and as a result of his apostasy God permitted the Syrians to inflict heavy defeats upon his armed forces, until he had almost none left. His kingdom became involved in such awful straits that he in desperation called upon Jehovah for help. God answered his prayers after his death in the persons of his two successors, Jehoash and Jeroboam II, through whom Israel's ancient boundaries were restored. The life of Elisha extended through his reign. When he died he was succeeded by his son Jehoash (II Kings 13:2-9, 22-25).

2. King of Judah 608 B.C. He was the third son of Josiah, and upon his father's death he succeeded to the throne; but he reigned only three months, and was then deposed and taken in chains into Egypt by Pharaoh Necho, who had defeated Josiah in battle. The throne was given to Jehoahaz's elder brother (II Kings 23:30-45). He is also called Shallum (I Chron. 3:15; Jer. 22:10-12). He died in Egypt.

3. A variant form of the name of Ahaziah, king of Judah (II Chron. 21:17; cf. ch. 22:1).

4. The full name of Ahaz, king of Judah, according to an inscription of Tiglath-pileser III.   S.B.

JEHOASH, JOASH (jē-hō'ăsh, Heb. *yehô'āsh*; jō'ăsh, Heb. *yô'āsh*), a word of uncertain meaning, perhaps *Jehovah supports* or *whom Jehovah gave*. 1. A son of Becher and grandson of Benjamin, probably born soon after the descent into Egypt (I Chron. 7:8).

2. An early descendant of Judah through Shelah, who with his brother Saraph had dominion in Moab (I Chron. 4:22).

3. A descendant of Abiezer son of Manasseh (Josh. 17:2). Evidently his family had fallen upon hard times, for Gideon, his son, said "My family is the poorest in Manasseh, and I am the least in my father's house" (Judg. 6:15), but in spite of that Gideon could call upon ten of his servants for help (6:27). This Joash, though "Jehovah" was a part of his name, had succumbed to the polytheism around him and had built an altar to Baal; but when the men of his city demanded the death of Gideon for destroying the altar, Joash, truer to his family than to his god, stood by his son and said "Jerubbaal" i.e. "Let Baal plead!" This exclamation became a nickname for Gideon, whom many called "Jerubbaal" from that day forth. Gideon was later buried in Joash's sepulchre (Judg. 8:32).

4. The keeper of David's cellars of oil (I Chron. 27:28).

5. One of the brethren of King Saul who fell away to David while he was in voluntary exile at Ziklag and became one of the commanders of his forces (I Chron. 12:3).

6. A son of King Ahab who was ordered to imprison Micaiah the prophet and to feed him "with bread of affliction and with water of affliction" till Ahab would return to deal with him — but Ahab never returned and Joash presumably freed Micaiah (I Kings 22:26, copied in II Chron. 18:25,26).

7. King of Judah from 884-848 B.C. (II Kings 11-13; II Chron. 24,25). As an infant he was rescued from Athalia's massacre of the seed royal after the death of Ahaziah, in the revolt of Jehu (II Chron. 22:8,9). Jehosheba (II Kings 11:2) or Jehoshebeath (II Chron. 22:11,12), sister of king Ahaziah and wife of the priest Jehoiada, hid the baby Joash in the house of God for six years, after which Jehoiada showed him to the people and made a covenant with them. Joash became king, living a godly and useful life all the time that his uncle instructed him. See II Chronicles 24 and II Kings 12 for the details of his reign. He was succeeded by his son Amaziah.

8. The king of Israel from 848-832 B.C. (II Kings 13:10-13; 14:8-16; II Chron. 25:17-24). He was son of Jehoahaz, son of Jehu, and was father of Jeroboam II. These four comprised the dynasty of Jehu (II Kings 10:30,31). Joash, like the other kings of the north, was an idolater. See AHAZIAH, ATHALIAH, JEHU.

JEHOHANAN (je'hō-hā'năn, Heb. *yehôhānān, Jehovah is gracious*). 1. One of six brothers, doorkeepers of the tabernacle in David's time (I Chron. 26:3).

2. A military leader in Jehoshaphat's time (II Chron. 17:15).

3. Father of Ishmael who assisted Jehoiada (II Chron. 23:1).

4. One who had married a foreigner in Ezra's time (Ezra 10:28).

5. A priest and head of a "fathers' house" in the days of Joiakim the high priest (Neh. 12:13).

6. A priestly singer at the dedication of the new wall of Jerusalem, rebuilt by Nehemiah (Neh. 12:42). "Jehohanan" or "Johanan" is the origin of the name "John."

JEHOIACHIN (je-hoi'à-kĭn, Heb. *yehôyākhîn, Jehovah establishes*), next to the last king of Judah, reigning at Jerusalem three months and ten days (II Chron. 36:9) in the year 597 B.C. Jeremiah thrice calls him "Coniah" (22:24,28; 37:1); he is also called "Jeconiah" seven times; and in Matthew 1:11,12 the name is Hellenized to "Jechonias" in KJV.

Jehoiachin was born to Jehoiakim, and his wife Nehushta, during the reign of the godly Josiah, his grandfather. According to II Kings 24:8, he was 18 when he came to the throne, but II Chronicles 36:9 gives his age as eight. Probably an early scribe made a mistake of ten years in copying one of these two books. The evidence favors the record in II Kings, for Chapter 24:15 speaks of his wives, and he would hardly have been married at eight years of age. Jehoiakim displayed his contempt for the Word of God by cutting up and burning the prophecies of Jeremiah (Jer. 36:23,32) thereby adding to the curses which the Lord pronounced upon Jerusalem.

In Ezekiel 19:5-9, Jehoiachin is characterized as "a young lion, and he learned to catch the prey and devoured men." The prophet announced that the "young lion" would be taken to Babylon, which was literally fulfilled later. Although Jeremiah was prophesying with mighty power all through the youth of Jehoiachin, the influences of the palace were stronger than those of the prophet. Jehoiakim had been rapacious, violent and oppressive. He was "buried with the burial of an ass, drawn and cast forth beyond the gates of Jerusalem" (Jer. 22:13-19). In these sad conditions and under the threatening shadow of Nebuchadnezzar, Jehoiachin became king and in his three months of power, "he did that which was evil in the sight of Jehovah according to all that his father had done" (II Kings 24:9). "At the return of the year King Nebuchadnezzar sent, and brought him to Babylon" (II Chron. 36:10) where he remained a captive the rest of his life, though apparently in not too hard conditions. Nebuchadnezzar died 561 B.C. and his son Evil-merodach, who succeeded almost immediately, took Jehoiachin from prison and "spake kindly to him and exalted his throne above the throne of the (vassal) kings that were with him in Babylon and changed his prison garments." After these thirty-seven years of captivity (II Kings 25:27) Jehoiachin was given a daily allowance of food the rest of his life.   A.B.F.

JEHOIADA (jē-hoi′à-dà, Heb. *yehôyādhā′, Jehovah knows*). 1. Father of Benaiah, one of David's most faithful officers. He is mentioned 20 times, but only as the father of his more notable son, who was over the mercenary troops of David. He came from Kabzeel in Judah (II Sam. 20:23; 23:20; I Kings 1:38; etc.).

2. Grandson of the preceding (I Chron. 27:34). This Jehoiada was second counselor of David, immediately after Ahithophel, who later became a traitor.

3. A powerful descendant of Aaron who with 3,700 men came to David at Ziklag (I Chron. 12:27).

4. Son of Azariah (I Chron. 6:11) and brother of Amariah whom he succeeded as high priest. Jehoiada was a high-priest, a statesman, a man of God, by marriage a member of the royal family of Judah and, humanly speaking, the preserver of the Messianic line. He lived 130 years (II Chron. 24:15). He married Jehosheba (II Kings 11:2), otherwise called Jehoshebeath (II Chron. 22:11), and she bore him that Zechariah (II Chron. 24:20-22; Luke 11:51) who denounced the wickedness of the people that they stoned him at the commandment of Joash. When Joash was seven years old, Jehoiada prepared his coup d'état. He first revealed his plan to five of the captains of hundreds (II Chron. 23:1; II Kings 11:4) and showed them little Joash; then they went through Judah and gathered the Levites and the heads of loyal houses to Jerusalem, where Jehoiada again exhibited little Joash and started the new reign by anointing him. Athaliah appeared and they slew her, then Jehoiada made a covenant with the people to serve the Lord. During the early years of Joash's reign, he was under the instruction and guidance of the godly Jehoiada, the temple was repaired and Judah began again to prosper. Jehoiada was buried among the kings.   A.B.F.

JEHOIAKIM (jē-hoi′à-kĭm, Heb. *yehôyāqîm, Jehovah sets up*), second son of the godly Josiah, king of Judah. He was originally named "Eliakim" (*whom God sets up*). In 607 B.C. Pharaoh Necho of Egypt marched northward, intending to fight the king of Assyria at the river Euphrates. Josiah imprudently intercepted him and was mortally wounded at Megiddo near Mount Carmel. The people of Judah passed by Eliakim and made his youngest brother Shallum or Jehoahaz king after Josiah (I Chron. 3:15; II Chron. 36:1). Jehoahaz reigned for three months in Jerusalem, when Necho in displeasure bound Jehoahaz at Riblah in the north of Syria, then sent him to Egypt where he died. The king of Egypt next took Eliakim, elder half-brother of Jehoahaz, changed his name to Jehoiakim, put the land under heavy tribute and made Jehoiakim king over Jerusalem where he reigned from 607-597 B.C. Jehoiakim was an oppressive and thoroughly godless king (II Kings 23:36-24:7, II Chron. 36:4-8 and compare Jeremiah, chaps. 22-36). The prophecies of Jeremiah 22:1-23 were uttered (if all at one time) soon after the death of Josiah and the taking away of Jehoahaz (vss. 10-12) and describe the wrong-doing and oppression by Jehoiakim (vss. 13-23).

The prophet wrote at the direction of the Lord the dooms of Judah and the other nations. When the princes heard these words they let Jeremiah and his clerk Baruch hide themselves, then when the king heard the words of the book, he cut out the leaves which displeased him and burned them, with the result that the book of Jeremiah was rewritten and enlarged. Jehoiakim died in disgrace "buried with the burial of an ass" (Jer. 22:19).

JEHOIARIB, JOIARIB (jē-hoi′à-rĭb, joi′à-rĭb, Heb. *yehôyārîv, Jehovah will contend*). 1. A priest in the days of David who drew first place in the divine service (I Chron. 24:7).

2. One of the first priests to return from exile with Zerubbabel (I Chron. 9:10).

3. A man Ezra sent back to Babylon to bring them Levites to assist the priests, which they did (Ezra 8:16,17).

4. The son of Zechariah, son of a man of Shiloh but of the tribe of Judah. (Neh. 11:5).

5. A priest who returned with Zerubbabel (Neh. 11:10; 12:6).

JEHONADAB (jē-hŏn′à-dăb, Heb. *yehônādhāv, Jehovah is liberal*), also appears as *Jonadab* (jŏn′-à-dăb). 1. Son of David's brother Shimeah (II Sam. 13:3).

2. Son of Rechab, of the Kenite clan (I Chron. 2:55). He assisted Jehu in abolishing Baal-worship in Samaria (II Kings 10). In Jeremiah 35 he is called the "father" of the Rechabites, who derived from him their primitive simplicity of manners.

JEHONATHAN (jē-hŏn′à-thăn, Heb. *yehônāthān, Jehovah gave*), variant form of *Jonathan*. 1. One of the administrators of the property of David (I Chron. 27:25).

2. One of the teaching Levites appointed by the godly Jehoshaphat (II Chron. 17:8).

3. A priest in the days of Joiakim, high priest (Neh. 12:18).

JEHORAM (jē-hō′răm, Heb. *yehôrām, Jehovah is exalted*), often contracted to *Joram*. 1. Son of Jehoshaphat of Judah, Jehoram was associated with his father in the kingship for the last four or five years of Jehoshaphat's reign. He took complete charge at his father's death in 849 B.C. Jehoshaphat had seven sons, and in order that there might not be rivalry for the throne, he gave the younger ones great gifts of silver and gold and precious things, with fortified cities in the kingdom of Judah (II Chron. 21:2,3) but when Jehoram became the sole ruler, he slew his own brothers with the sword. Just as we can charge a good deal of the abominable behavior of Ahab to his strong-minded but diabolical consort Jezebel, so we can guess that Athaliah, daughter of Ahab and Jezebel, was back of most of Jehoram's wickedness. Jehoshaphat had been a godly man, but he had made one terrible error, that of joining affinity with Ahab (I Kings 22; II Chron. 18) and through this league, Jehoram had married the wicked Athaliah. As soon as his father died (900 B.C.) Jehoram began to slip into the idolatrous ways of the northern kingdom; but because of God's covenant with David (II Kings 8:19) and no doubt because of Jehoshaphat's goodness, God did not remove the kingdom from Jehoram's hand, but God did cause him to have real troubles. Edom revolted from under the rule of Judah. Libnah in Judah, a Levitical city far enough from Jerusalem to be somewhat independent, showed its abhorrence of Jehoram's deeds by revolting at the same time (II Kings 8:22). Meanwhile, the great prophet Elijah sent to Jehoram a letter of denunciation for his wickedness. God sent a plague upon Judah, especially upon the family of Jehoram. He suffered and died unlamented from a horrible disease. The Arabians or their associated forces slew all of Jehoram's sons (II Chron. 21:17) except Ahaziah, the youngest, who succeeded his father at his death.

2. Second son of Ahab and Jezebel, he succeeded his brother Ahaziah, who died childless, as king of Israel. He reigned for 12 years (853-840 B.C.).

Mesha, king of Moab, who had been rendering tribute to Israel (II Kings 3:4) rebelled after the death of Ahab, and Jehoram made war against him. Jehoram invited Jehoshaphat of Judah to assist him in the war (II Kings 3:7) and Jehoshaphat accepted the invitation. Jehoram was not as evil as his father Ahab had been, but like all the other kings of the north he clung to the idolatry which Jeroboam had set up in order to keep the northern people from going up to Jerusalem to worship at Solomon's Temple.. While Israel and Judah, with the help of Edom, were going against Mesha, water failed and they were in despair, but Elisha in deference to Jehoshaphat (II Kings 3:14-16) told the kings to dig ditches, which they did; water came, and the Moabites, at sunrise, seeing the reflection of the rising sun in the water, took it for blood, and hastened to the prey, only to be badly defeated. Jehoram came to his end, with all his family, at the hand of Jehu (II Kings 9) and Jehu succeeded to the throne.

3. A priest in the days of Jehoshaphat whom the king sent with a group of learned Levites to go through Judah and to teach the people the law of the Lord (II Chron. 17:8). A.B.F.

JEHOSHABEATH (jē'hō-shăb'ē-ăth, Heb. *yehôshav'ath, the oath of Jehovah*), the name of Jehosheba (*q.v.*) as it is found in II Chronicles 22:11.

JEHOSHAPHAT (jē-hŏsh'à-făt, Heb. *yehôshāphat, Jehovah is judge*), in KJV of NT *Josaphat*. 1. One of the seven priests who blew trumpets before the ark of the Lord in David's time (I Chron. 15:24, the Hebrew text and ASV here have *Joshaphat*).

2. Son of Ahilud, and recorder or chronicler in the time of David (II Sam. 8:16, etc.).

3. Son of Paruah, appointed by Solomon as officer of the commissariat over the tribe of Issa-

The Tomb of Jehoshaphat in the Valley of Jehoshaphat, otherwise known as the Kidron Valley, outside Jerusalem. © MPS

char (I Kings 4:17) He had to provide the household of the king with food one month of every year.

4. Son and successor of King Asa on the throne of Judah. He reigned for 25 years, including five years of rule with his father. He began to reign about 871 B.C. His mother was Azubah, the daughter of Shilhi. For the account of his reign, see I Kings 22; II Chronicles 17-20. Jehoshaphat was the second of the five kings of Judah who were outstanding for godliness, the later ones being Joash, Hezekiah and Josiah. He took away the high places and Asherim from Judah (II Chron. 17:6), though he apparently was not able to keep the people from using certain high places in worshiping the Lord (I Kings 22:43). Apparently one of the first men to sense the importance of religious education for the people, he sent out in the third year of his reign princes and priests and Levites to teach the people the law of the Lord. They went throughout the cities of Judah in this work (Chron. 17:7-9). Because of Jehoshaphat's godliness, "the fear of Jehovah" fell upon the surrounding nations and even the Philistines and the Arabians brought him tribute. With all this godliness, he seems, however, to have been lacking in spiritual discernment, for he made the great and almost fatal mistake of making affinity with the wicked King Ahab of the northern kingdom; so much so that his son Jehoram married Athaliah, who was almost as wicked as her mother Jezebel.

Ahab made a great show of hospitality to Jehoshaphat during a visit to Samaria and then asked him if he would be his ally in a campaign to recover Ramoth-Gilead. Jehoshaphat suggested that they first determine the will of God. Ahab agreed and asked his prophets for their advice, and they all prophesied good success for the venture. Jehoshaphat was not satisfied, and asked if there were not a real prophet of Jehovah present, and they sent for Micaiah, a man of God, whom Ahab hated. He told them the truth, that God had put a spirit of delusion in the minds of all the prophets, so that Ahab might be doomed. Ahab partly believed this, and arranged a trick, pretending to give Jehoshaphat the glory, but Ahab was slain. Jehoshaphat died at the age of 60, about the year 850 B.C. His son Jehoram succeeded to the throne.

5. The son of Nimshi, and father of Jehu who destroyed the house of Ahab (II Kings 9:2,14).

JEHOSHAPHAT, VALLEY OF (jē-hŏsh'à-făt, Heb. *yehôshāphāt, Jehovah judgeth*), a name used in Joel 3:2,12 as the scene where all nations shall be gathered by Jehovah for judgment. Since the fourth century the Kidron valley (*q.v.*) has been named the Valley of Jehoshaphat, but there is no real reason for believing that this is the spot referred to by Joel. He may have spoken of an ideal spot only. There is no evidence that any valley ever actually bore this name.

JEHOSHEBA (jē-hŏsh'ē-bà, Heb. *yehôsheva‘, Jehovah is an oath*), sister of King Ahaziah (II Kings 11:2) and daughter of King Jehoram and his wicked consort Athaliah, daughter of Jezebel. She married the high priest Jehoiada. When Athaliah usurped the throne and slew the seed royal, Jehosheba (called Jehoshebeath in II Chronicles 22:11), rescued the baby Joash, hid him with his nurse in a bedchamber in the temple, and preserved the Messianic line.

JEHOSHUA, JEHOSHUAH (jē-hosh'ū-à, *Jehovah saves*), a variant spelling for Joshua (Num. 13:16; I Chron. 7:27 KJV).

JEHOVAH (jē-hō'và), the English rendering of the Hebrew tetragram YHWH, one of the names of God (Exod. 17:15). Its original pronunciation is unknown. The Jews took seriously the third commandment "Thou shalt not take the name of Jehovah thy God in vain; for Jehovah will not hold him guiltless that taketh his name in vain" (Exod. 20:7) and so, to keep from speaking the holy name carelessly, around 300 B.C. they decided not to pronounce it at all; but whenever in reading they came to it they spoke the word *adhonai* which means "Lord." This usage was carried into the LXX where the sacred name is rendered "Kurios," i.e. LORD. Consequently in the KJV, LORD occurs instead of Jehovah, whereas ASV renders tne name "Jehovah." When the vowel points were added to the Hebrew consonantal text, the Massoretes (Jewish scribes) inserted into the Hebrew consonantal text the vowels for *adhonai*. The sacred name is derived from the verb "to be," and so implies that God is eternal ("Before Abraham was, I AM") and that he is the Absolute, i.e. the Uncaused One. The name "Jehovah" belongs especially to Him when He is dealing with His own, while "God" is used more when dealing with the Gentiles. See for instance II Chronicles 18:31 where "Jehoshaphat cried out and Jehovah helped him; and God moved them to depart from him."

There are ten combinations of the word "Jehovah" in the OT. Besides the five with which succeeding articles deal, are *Jehovah-ropheka*, "Jehovah that healeth thee" (Exod. 15:26); *Jehovah-meqaddeshkem*, "Jehovah who sanctifieth you" (Exod. 31:13); *Jehovah-tsabaoth*, "Jehovah of hosts" (I Sam. 1:3); *Jehovah-elyon*, "Jehovah Most High" (Ps. 7:17); and *Jehovah-roi*, "Jehovah, my Shepherd" (Ps. 23:1). See JEHOVAH JIREH, - NISSI, - SHALOM, - SHAMMAH, - TSIDKENU.

A.B.F.

JEHOVAH-JIREH (jē-hō'và-jī'rĕ, *Jehovah will provide*), the name given by Abraham to the place where God provided a ram instead of his son Isaac (Gen. 22:14).

JEHOVAH-NISSI (jē-hō'và-nĭs'ī, *Jehovah is my banner*), the name which Moses gave to an altar he built as a memorial of Israel's victory over the Amalekites at Rephidim (Exod. 17:15).

JEHOVAH-SHALOM (jē-hō'và-shā'lŏm, *Jehovah is peace*), the name Gideon gave to an altar he built at Ophra to commemorate the word spoken to him by the Lord, "Peace be unto thee" (Judg. 6:24).

JEHOVAH-SHAMMAH (jē-hō'và-shă'mà, *Jehovah is there*), the name of the heavenly Jerusalem as seen in the vision of Ezekiel (48:35 m).

JEHOVAH-TSIDKENU (jē-hō'và-tsĭd-kē'nū, *Jehovah is our righteousness*), the symbolic name given to the king who is to rule over restored Israel (Jer. 23:6), and to the state or capital (Jer. 33:16).

JEHOZABAD (jē-hŏz'à-băd, Heb. *yehôzāvādh, Jehovah has bestowed*). 1. A son of Shimrith, a Moabitess, who conspired against King Joash (II Chron. 24:26).

2. One of the eight sons of Obed-edom, a doorkeeper of the tabernacle in the days of David (I Chron. 26:4). Not to be confused with the Obed-edom of II Samuel 6:10-12.

3. A Benjamite in the days of King Jehoshaphat (II Chron. 17:18). He was commander of 180,000 soldiers prepared for war.

JEHOZADAK (jē-hŏz'à-dăk, Heb. *yehôtsādhāq, Jehovah is righteous*), the high priest of Israel through most of the Babylonian captivity (I Chron. 6:14,15). His father, Seraiah, was slain by the Babylonians (II Kings 25:18-21), and Jehozadak was taken into captivity. In Haggai and Zechariah, where he is six times referred to as father of Joshua, the high priest at the first return, KJV spells his name "Josedech," and in Ezra and Nehemiah, KJV and ASV referring to him in the same way five times, call him "Jozadak," a shortened form of *Jehozadak*.

JEHU (jē'hū, Heb. *yēhû', probably Jehovah is he*). 1. Son of Obed and father of Azariah, mentioned only in the genealogy of Elishama (I Chron. 2:38).

2. A Simeonite mentioned only in I Chronicles 4:35.

3. A Benjamite of Anathoth who joined David at Ziklag (I Chron. 12:3).

4. Son of Hanani and a prophet of Israel, who pronounced the curse of the Lord upon Baasha in almost the same words that had been used against Jeroboam (cf. I Kings 14:11; 16:4). Several years later he went out to denounce Jehoshaphat (II Chron. 19:1-3) for helping Ahab. Jehu wrote an account of the reign of Jehoshaphat which was inserted in the lost "book of the kings of Israel" (II Chron. 20:34).

5. Tenth king of Israel, and founder of its fourth dynasty. Son of Jehoshaphat, but more often called "son of Nimshi," perhaps because Nimshi, his grandfather, was better known than Jehoshaphat. Jehu appears first as a soldier in the service of Ahab (II Kings 9:25). Ahab and Jezebel were rejected for their crimes. God commanded Elijah to anoint Jehu king over Israel, a command which was fulfilled by Elisha, who sent a young prophet to Ramoth-Gilead, where Jehu was with his army, to carry out the command. Jehu was commissioned to smite the house of Ahab. When Jehu told his fellow officers that he had been so anointed, they proclaimed him king. Jehu sealed the city, that the news should not precede him, then he crossed the Jordan and drove impetuously as was his custom (II Kings 9:20) to Jezreel whither King Joram of Israel had gone after being wounded in battle with Hazael of Syria. Jehu denounced Joram and slew

him, and had his body thrown into the field of Naboth (II Kings 9:24-26); then he caused Ahaziah, king of Judah, to be killed, and his servants carried him up to Jerusalem for burial. He also slew Jezebel, and would have had her buried, but the dogs had eaten her. Jehu reigned in Samaria 28 years (c. 842-814 B.C.). He executed God's judgments upon the house of Ahab and tho oughly extirpated the worship of Baal, killing all worshipers whom he could collect, but he did not depart from the sins of Jeroboam. Because of his zeal for the Lord in the matter of Ahab's house, God allowed him to set up a dynasty which lasted just over 100 years (Jehu, Jehoahaz, Joram and Jeroboam II).   A.B.F.

JEHUBBAH (jē-hŭb′à), an Asherite (I Chron. 7: 34).

JEHUCAL (jē-hū′kăl, probably *Jehovah is able*), one whom King Zedekiah sent to Jeremiah, asking for prayers (Jer. 37:3). In Jeremiah 38:1, Jucal.

JEHUD (jē′hŭd), a town in the tribe of Dan, about seven miles nearly E of Joppa and near the modern Tel-Aviv (Josh. 19:45).

JEHUDI (jē-hū′dī, Heb. *yehûdhî, a Jew*), one who sat with the princes in Jehoiakim's court and who secured from Baruch the prophecies of Jeremiah and read them to the king (Jer. 36:14,21).

JEHUDIJAH (jē′hū-dī′jà, Heb. *yehudhîyâh, Jewess*), in I Chronicles 4:18 this word is written as a proper name, but in the Hebrew it has the definite article, and ASV properly translates it "the Jewess" to distinguish her from Bithiah, the Egyptian princess, who was the other wife of Mered.

JEHUSH (jē′hŭsh), a Benjamite of Saul's family (I Chron. 8:39). See JEUSH.

JEIEL (jē-ī′ĕl, Heb. *ye′î′ēl*, probably *God has gathered*). 1. A Reubenite (I Chron. 5:7).

2. A Benjamite of Gibeon (I Chron. 9:35).

3. Son of Hotham of Aroer and one of David's mighty men (I Chron. 11:44).

4. A harpist in the days of King David who also acted as gate-keeper of the tabernacle (I Chron. 15:18,21).

5. A Levite of the sons of Asaph (II Chron. 20: 14).

6. A scribe who acted as recorder of the military forces under Uzziah (II Chron. 26:11).

7. A chief of the Levites in the days of Josiah (II Chron. 35:9).

8. A husband of a foreign wife in Ezra's time (Ezra 10:43).

JEKABZEEL (jē-kăb′zē-ĕl, Heb. *yeqavtse′ēl, God gathers*), one of the places re-inhabited by the men of Judah (Neh. 11:25).

JEKAMEAM (jĕk′à-mē-ăm, Heb. *yeqam′ām, the kinsman will raise up*), the head of a Levitical house (I Chron. 23:19; 24:23).

JEKAMIAH (jĕk′à-mī′à, Heb. *yekamyâh, may Jehovah establish*). 1. A man from Judah, son of Shallum (I Chron. 2:41).

2. A son of King Jeconiah (Jehoiachin); in AV Jecamiah (I Chron. 3:18).

JEKUTHIEL (jē-kū′thĭ-ĕl, Heb. *yeqûthî′ēl, God will nourish*), a man of Judah, father of the inhabitants of Zanoah (I Chron. 4:18).

JEMIMA (jē-mī′mà, Heb. *yemîmâh, a dove*), the first of the three daughters born to Job after his restoration from affliction.

JEMUEL (jē-mū′ĕl, Heb. *yemû′ēl,* meaning unknown), a son of Simeon (Gen. 46:10; Exod. 6: 15). Called "Nemuel" in Numbers 26:12 and I Chronicles 4:24.

JEPHTHAH (jĕf′thà, Heb. *yiphtâh, opened* or *opener*),eighth judge of the Israelites, whose history is given in Judges 10:6-12:7. He was the son of Gilead, a Gileadite, and of a woman who was a harlot. Because of his illegitimacy, his brothers born in wedlock drove him from the paternal home and refused him any share in the inheritance. Their action was confirmed by the elders of Gilead. He fled to the land of Tob, probably a region in Syria or the Hauran. There he made a name for himself by his prowess and gathered about him a band of men without employment, like David's men (I Sam. 22:2). He must not be thought of as just a captain of a band of freebooters, for he was a God-fearing man, with a high sense of justice and of the sacredness of vows made to Jehovah. At the time of his expulsion by his brothers, Israel had been for many years under bondage to the Ammonites. In the course of time, when these oppressors of Israel were planning some new form of humiliation, the elders of Gilead offered to anyone who was willing to accept the office of captain the headship over all the inhabitants of Gilead. In their extremity, as no one volunteered, they went to Jephthah and pressed the office upon him. He accepted, and solemn vows were made before the Lord that all promises would be kept. On assuming the headship of Gilead, his first effort was to secure the cooperation of the tribe of Ephraim, one of the most influential of the tribes during the period of the judges, but he was refused their help. He then sent messengers to the king of the Ammonites, asking for the grounds of his hostile action and requesting that he desist; but the king refused to listen to reason. Endued with the Spirit of the Lord, Jephthah prepared for war, but before going out to battle he made a vow that if he were victorious he would offer to God as a burnt-offering whatever first came to him out of his house. He defeated his enemies with a very great slaughter and recovered 20 cities from them. The Ephraimites then came to him with the complaint that he had slighted them in the preparation for the Ammonite campaign, but he answered their false accusation and defeated them in battle. Forty-two thousand Ephraimites were slain. Jephthah judged Israel for six years. Samuel cited him as one proof of God's faithfulness in raising up deliverers for Israel in time of need (I Sam. 12:11). He is listed among the heroes of faith in the 11th chapter of Hebrews (vs. 32).

The great point of interest in his history is his vow (Judg. 11:29-40) and the way in which it was fulfilled. On his return home after the victory over the Ammonites, his own daughter was the first to meet him from his house. A man of the highest integrity, he knew that he could not go back on his vow to the Lord, and his daughter agreed with him. She asked only that she and her companions be allowed to go for two months to the mountains to bewail her virginity. When she returned to her father, he "did with her according to his vow which he had vowed: and he knew no man" (Judg. 11:39). After that she was lamented by the daughters of Israel four days every year.

How was the vow fulfilled? Did he actually sacrifice his daughter as a burnt offering, or did he redeem her with money and doom her to perpetual celibacy? The ancient Jewish authorities and the early Church fathers, as well as many in modern times, like Martin Luther, hold that she was actually sacrificed, as a first reading of the narrative suggests. It is said that Jephthah was either ignorant of the law against human sacrifices or that he flagrantly violated it. Those who hold the other

The birthplace of Jeremiah, the little village of Anathoth, northeast of Jerusalem. © MPS

view support it by saying that Jephthah's whole history, and especially his message to the king of the Ammonites, shows him to be a man well acquainted with the history of God's dealings with His people, as given in the law of Moses, and able to appreciate its bearing on his own age. His own words, and those of his daughter(Judg. 11:34,35), imply a knowledge of the Mosaic law as to vows (Num. 30:2; Deut. 23:23). A true worshiper of Jehovah could not regard human sacrifices with anything but abhorrence. Such a thing would be impossible of Jephthah, the chosen leader of God's people, all of whose dealings are thoroughly godly; who had just been filled with the Spirit of God to carry on his work; and whose faith is celebrated in Hebrews. Leviticus 27:1-8 contemplates the possibility of a man's vowing to give himself or some person of his household to the Lord, and makes provision for the redemption of such a person in money. We know too from the experience of Samuel that sometimes persons coming under a vow were handed over for the service of the sanctuary (I Sam. 1:11). It is therefore thought that Jephthah redeemed his daughter with money and gave her up to the service of the Lord as a perpetual virgin. That is the meaning of her request that she- be allowed to bewail her virginity for two months, and of the statement made in Judges 11:39, "and she knew no man." The fact is, however, that we cannot be absolutely certain of the mode of fulfilment of Jephthah's vow.   S.B.

JEPHUNNEH (jē-fŭn′ē, Heb. *yephunneh, it will be prepared*). 1. The father of Caleb, one of the 12 spies. He was from the tribe of Judah (Num. 13:6).

2. A son of Jether, an Asherite (I Chron. 7:38).

JERAH (jē′rà, Heb. *yerah, moon*), an Arabian tribe descended from Joktan (Gen. 10:26; I Chron. 1:20).

JERAHMEEL (jē-rà′mē-ĕl, Heb. *yerahme′ĕl, may God have compassion,* or *God pities*). 1. A descendant of Judah through Perez and Hezron (I Chron. 2:9,25-27,33,42).

2. A Merarite Levite, son of Kish, not Saul's father (I Chron. 24:29).

3. One of the three officers sent by King Jehoiakim to arrest Jeremiah and Baruch (Jer. 36:26). He was probably a royal prince, though not necessarily the son of a ruling prince.

JERASH (See Gerasa)

JERED (jē′rĕd, Heb. *yeredh, descent*). 1. Son of Mahalaleel (I Chron. 1:2).

2. A Judahite and father of the inhabitants of Gedor (I Chron. 4:18).

JEREMIAH (jĕr′ĕ-mī′à, Heb. *yirmeyâhû, Jehovah founds,* or perhaps, *exalts*), in KJV of NT "Jeremy" and "Jeremias" (Matt. 2:17; 16:14).

The Life of Jeremiah. Jeremiah was one of the greatest Hebrew prophets. He was born into a priestly family of Anathoth, a Benjamite town two and one-half miles NE of Jerusalem. His father was Hilkiah (1:1), not to be confused with the high priest Hilkiah mentioned in II Kings 22,23. Because of the autobiographical nature of his book, it is possible to understand his life, character and times better than those of any other Hebrew prophet.

Jeremiah was called to prophesy in the 13th year of King Josiah (626 B.C.), five years after the great revival of religion described in II Kings 23. This was a time of decision, great with both hope and foreboding. Looking back, we can know it as the last religious awakening in a series which only slowed down the idolatry and apostasy of the Hebrews, which apostasy finally plunged the nation into destruction. It was the time of the revival of the Babylonian empire. After the fall of the city of Nineveh in 612 B.C., the Assyrian empire disintegrated and Babylon for a little while again ruled the world under her vigorous leader Nebuchadnezzar, who sought to subdue the whole fertile crescent to himself. Nebuchadnezzar's design on Egypt inevitably included control of Palestine, and Jeremiah's lifetime saw the fall of the Hebrew commonwealth to Babylon. This fall was preceded by a generation of unrest and decline in Judah. Many solutions to her troubles were proposed, and at court pro-Egyptian and pro-Babylonian parties vied for favor with the policy makers. This situation of deepening crisis is the background without which Jeremiah and his book cannot be understood. Jeremiah's ministry continued through the reigns of five successive Judean kings, and saw the final destruction of Jerusalem in 587 B.C. The prophet died in Egypt, probably a few years after the city was destroyed.

Jeremiah's call is described in Chapter 1. The young priest pleads his youth (1:6) but God assures him that he will be strengthened for his task. At this time the theme of destruction from the North (i.e., from Babylon) is already introduced (1:13-15). This theme, that Judah would inevitably fall because of its apostasy, earned for the prophet the undying hostility of most of his contemporaries (even his fellowtownsmen, 11:21) and led to his being charged with treason (38:1-6) and to frequent imprisonments. Jeremiah's faithfulness to his call under the most difficult circumstances makes him a prime example of devotion to God at greatest personal sacrifice.

Undoubtedly Jeremiah supported Josiah's reform (11:1-8; 17:19-27), but as time went on he realized its inadequacy to stave off national disaster (3:10). Upon Josiah's unhappy death (609 B.C.) Jeremiah mourned Judah's last good king (II Chron. 35:25) and life became more difficult for him. Jehoahaz, son of Josiah, reigned only three months before he was deported to Egypt. Jeremiah said he would not return (22:10-12). Jehoiakim, the brother of Jehoahaz, succeeded him and reigned 11 years. A strong ruler and a very wicked man, he tried to do away with the prophet, and failing that, to silence him. In Jehoiakim's fourth year Jeremiah dictated the first edition of his prophecies to Baruch, which the king promptly destroyed (36). During this reign Jeremiah preached his great temple discourse (7-10), which led to a plot to kill him, from which he was saved only by the intervention of friendly nobles who were a remnant of Josiah's administration (26). There now also occurred the battle of Carchemish (46:1-12) in which Egypt was crushed (605 B.C.) by the Babylonian crown prince Nebuchadnezzar, who soon afterward became king of Babylon. Egypt's star quickly set, and Babylon entered her brief period of greatness. Judah was brought into the Babylonian orbit when Jerusalem fell to Nebuchadnezzar in 605 B.C. and a few Hebrews (Daniel among them) were deported to Babylon. Jehoiakim later rebelled against Babylon. Jeremiah opposed this strong-willed despot all his reign and predicted a violent death for him (22:13-19). It has been supposed that he fell in a palace coup.

Jehoiachin, son of Jehoiakim, succeeded him to the throne. Jeremiah called this king Coniah and Jechoniah (24:1; 27:20; 29:2). After he had reigned only three months, the Babylonians attacked Jerusalem and carried off Jehoiachin to Babylon (597 B.C.) as Jeremiah had predicted (22:24-30), together with many artisans and other important Jews.

In Jehoiachin's place Nebuchadrezzar appointed Zedekiah, who maintained a precarious position on the throne for 11 years. Although a weak character, he protected Jeremiah and asked his advice, which he was never able to carry out. Jeremiah advised submission to Babylon, but goaded by the nobles, Zedekiah rebelled and made an alliance with Egypt. Finally the Babylonians came again, determined to stamp out the rebellious Judean state. A long siege resulted, in which Jeremiah suffered greatly. He was accused of treason and thrown into a vile prison from which the king transferred him to the more pleasant court of the guard (37:11-21). Now that the judgment had come, the prophet spoke of a hopeful future for the nation (32,33). As the siege wore on, he was cast into a slimy cistern, where he would have perished had not Ebed-melech, a courtier, rescued him (38:6-13). Again to the court of the guard he was taken, until the city fell (38:28).

After a siege of a year and a half, Jerusalem was destroyed. Zedekiah was blinded and carried in chains to Babylon. For the events in Judah after the destruction of Jerusalem we are dependent almost exclusively on Jeremiah (40-45). The captors treated Jeremiah with kindness, giving him the choice of going to Babylon or remaining in Judah. He chose to stay behind with some of the common people who had been left in Judah when most of the Jews were deported. Gedaliah was made puppet governor over this little group. After civil unrest, in which Gedaliah was assassinated, the Jews fled to Egypt, forcing Jeremiah to accompany them. In Egypt, a very old man, he died.

The Man and His Message. Jeremiah was called to be a prophet at a most unhappy time. With the failure of Josiah's revival the final decline of the nation was under way. When he was called, it was intimated to Jeremiah that his message would be one of condemnation rather than salvation (1:10,18,19). Yet he was also given a message of hope (30:1-3,18-22; 31:1-14,23-40). Throughout his long ministry of more than 40 years his preaching reflected this theme of judgment. God had risen early and sent His servants, the prophets, but Israel would not hear (7:25; 44:4). Now the fate predicted for an apostate nation in Deuteronomy 28-30 was inevitable. Babylon would capture Judah, and it would be better for the people to surrender and so to save their lives.

This message, coming to men whose desperate nationalism was all they had to cling to, was com-

The beautiful Ain Farah gorge, probably the "Euphrates" of Jeremiah 13. © MPS

pletely rejected, and the bearer was rejected with his message. Jeremiah was regarded as a meddler and a traitor, and people, nobles and kings alternately tried to do him to death. Although he needed the love, sympathy and encouragement of a wife, he was not permitted to marry, and in this prohibition he became a sign that life as usual was soon to cease for Jerusalem (16:1-4). Because his book is full of autobiographical sections — Jeremiah's "Confessions" — Jeremiah's personality can be understood more clearly than that of any other prophet. These outpourings of the human spirit are some of the most poignant and pathetic statements of the tension of a man under divine imperative to be found anywhere in Scripture. The most important are listed below. They show us a Jeremiah who was retiring, sensitive and afraid of people's "faces," one we should consider singularly unfit for the work which was placed upon him. That he tenaciously clung to his assigned task through the succeeding years of rejection and persecution is both a tribute to the mettle of the man and to the grace of God, without which his personality would surely have gone to pieces.

Jeremiah's Confessions.

10:23,24	17:9-11,14-18
11:18-12:6	18:18-23
15:10-21	20:7-18

Jeremiah's penetrating understanding of the religious condition of his people is seen in his emphasis on the inner spiritual character of true religion. The external theocratic state will go, as will the temple and its ritual. Even Josiah's reform appears to have been a thing of the outward appearance — almost engineered by the king, an upsurge of nationalism more than a religious revival (3:10). The old covenant had failed; a new and better one will take its place and then God's law will be written on men's hearts (31:31-34). God will give His renewed people a heart to know Him (24:7). In this doctrine of the "new heart" Jeremiah unfolds the depth of human sin and predicts the intervention of divine grace (Heb. 8:1-9:28).

The Foe from the North. Throughout Jeremiah's sermons are references to a foe from the *north* who would devastate Judah and take her captive. Chapter 4 is typical of these oracles: The foe will destroy like a lion or a whirlwind and leave the land in desolation like the primeval chaos. Who is this destroying enemy? The fulfillment indicates that the northern foe was Babylon. Although Babylon is on the same latitude as Samaria, her invasions of Palestine always came from the north, as the desert which separates the two was impassable. The view that the Scythians are referred to as the northern foe in some places of the book seems not to be held so widely today as it once was, and may be rejected.

Sometimes (50:3,9,41; 51:48) north is used of the origin of the conquerors of Babylon. This use of the term is difficult to pin-point. The Persians, who were the principal captors of Babylon, came from the east. Probably here north has become an expression for the source of any trouble, arrived at because Israel's troubles for so long a time had come from that direction.

Other Jeremiahs. Six other Jeremiahs are briefly mentioned in the OT: a Benjamite and two Gadites who joined David at Ziklag (I Chron. 12:4,10,13), the head of a family in Manasseh (I Chron. 5:24), a native of Libnah and the father of Hamutal, wife of King Josiah and mother of Jehoahaz (II Kings 23:30,31), and the son of Habaziniah, a Rechabite (Jer. 35:3).   J.B.G.

JEREMIAH, BOOK OF.

The Composition of the Book. Jeremiah is a book of prophetic oracles, or sermons, together with much autobiographical and historical material which gives the background of these oracles. Many modern scholars believe that the book contains substantial parts by later writers whose point of view differed markedly from the prophet's. Believing that the critics have failed to prove their case for later editors, this article takes the traditional position that the oracles are essentially Jeremiah's, and that the narratives, if not dictated by the prophet (they are usually in the third person), were probably composed by Baruch.

While accepting the Jeremianic origin of the contents of the book, it is impossible to say how or when these materials were assembled in their present form. Plainly the book has gone through a number of editions, each succeeding one containing additional material. The story of the production of the first and second editions is told in Chapter 36. Baruch, the amanuensis of the prophet, wrote down certain judgment oracles of the prophet (we do not know the exact contents) at his dictation. This scroll was contemptuously burned by king Jehoiakim; whereupon the prophet dictated again to Baruch "all the words of the book which Jehoiakim king of Judah had burned in the fire, and there were added besides many like words" (36:32); i.e., a new and enlarged edition was produced. Obviously this was not our present book, which carries the history on for at least 20 more years. This account is of great interest in that it gives the only detailed OT description of the writing of a prophetic book. That Jeremiah should dictate to a secretary is normal for the times. Writing was a specialized skill, often restricted to a professional class. Learned men might be able to read but (like executives today) scorned to write. The document was probably written on a blank papyrus scroll imported from Egypt.

It has long been noted that the book of Jeremiah in the Greek translation of the OT called the Septuagint (made in Egypt before 132 B.C.) is about one-eighth shorter than the Hebrew book, from which our English translations have been made. Further, the Septuagint omits many of the repetitions which are contained in the Hebrew copy, and rearranges the material somewhat. Some scholars believe that the Greek Jeremiah was made from a different edition of the Hebrew text from our present received text. It is not now possible to arrive at any certain conclusion about the relationship of the Septuagint to the Hebrew text, nor to know how either version came to its present condition.

The material contained in Jeremiah's book is not arranged in chronological order. The outline given below indicates what seems to have been the purpose of the present arrangement — to set forth a group of oracles against the Jewish nation, then to record selected events in the prophet's ministry, then to give certain preachments of Jeremiah against foreign nations, and finally to tell the story of the fall of Jerusalem. The record of Jerusalem's fall had been given in Chapter 39; the somewhat different account at the end of the book (chap. 52) is practically identical with II Kings 24,25 and may have been added from that source to give a climactic conclusion to Jeremiah's oracles.

Outline.

I. JEREMIAH'S ORACLES AGAINST THE THEOCRACY, 1:1-25:38.
   A. The prophet's call, 1:1-19.
   B. Reproofs and admonitions, mostly from the time of Josiah, 2:1-20:18.
   C. Later prophecies, 21:1-25:38.

II. EVENTS IN THE LIFE OF JEREMIAH, 26:1-45:5.
   A. The temple sermon and Jeremiah's arrest, 26:1-24.
   B. The yoke of Babylon, 27:1-29:32.
   C. The book of consolation, 30:1-33:26.
   D. Some of Jeremiah's experiences before Jerusalem fell, 34:1-36:32.
   E. Jeremiah during the siege and destruction of Jerusalem, 37:1-39:18.
   F. The last years of Jeremiah, 40:1-45:5.

III. JEREMIAH'S ORACLES AGAINST FOREIGN NATIONS, 46:1-51:64.
   A. Against Egypt, 46:1-28.
   B. Against the Philistines, 47:1-7.
   C. Against Moab, 48:1-47.
   D. Against the Ammonites, 49:1-6.
   E. Against Edom, 49:7-22.
   F. Against Damascus, 49:23-27.
   G. Against Kedar and Hazor, 49:28-33.
   H. Against Elam, 49:34-39.
   I. Against Babylon, 50:1-51:64.

IV. APPENDIX: THE FALL OF JERUSALEM AND RELATED EVENTS, 52:1-34.

Chronological Order of the Book. In spite of the fact that the book is not at all in chronological order, it is possible to date many of its sections because they contain chronological notations. These sections are here listed with their dates.

1. In the Reign of Josiah.
   In the 13th year, chap. 1.
   Later in this reign, chaps. 2-6.
   Possibly much of chaps. 7-20 (except material specifically listed below) is to be dated to Josiah's reign.
2. In the Reign of Jehoahaz.
   None.

3. In the Reign of Jehoiakim.
Early in this reign, chap. 26 and probably 7: 1-8:3; 22:1-23.
In the fourth year, chaps. 25,36,45,46:1-12.
After the fourth year, chap. 35.
4. In the Reign of Jehoiachin.
22:24-30; possibly chap. 14.
5. In the Reign of Zedekiah.
In the beginning, chap. 24, 49:34-39.
In the fourth year, chaps. 27,28; 51:59-64.
In unnoted years, chaps. 21,29.
During the early part of the siege, chap. 34.
During the interruption of the siege, chap. 37.
During the resumption of the siege, chaps. 32, 33,38,39:15-18.
6. In Judah after the fall of Jerusalem, 39:1-4; 40:1-43:7.
7. In Egypt after Jeremiah was taken there, 43:8-44:30.

Jeremiah and the Lachish Letters. Lachish, in the Judean foothills, was one of a series of fortresses for the defense of Jerusalem against attack from the Mediterranean Plain. It was one of the last cities to fall to the Babylonians prior to the final taking and destruction of Jerusalem (34:7). An interesting light has been shed on these last hectic days of Judah's history by a discovery in the ruins of ancient Lachish. When the city was excavated (in 1932 through 1938) there were found in a guard room of the outer gate 21 letters written on broken pieces of pottery. They were written in the ancient Hebrew script with carbon iron ink at the time of Jeremiah, when Lachish was undergoing its final siege.

Many of these letters were written by a certain Hoshaiah, who was a military officer at some outpost near Lachish, to Yaosh, the commander of Lachish. Their language is very much like that of the book of Jeremiah. Hoshaiah is constantly defending himself to his superior. Could it be that he was under suspicion of being ready to go over to the Babylonians? Once he describes one of the princes in words almost like those which the princes use against Jeremiah (38:4). There is mention of "the prophet" whose message is "Beware." Is this a reference to Jeremiah? We cannot be sure. According to the book of Jeremiah, there were plenty of prophets in that troublous time. Another letter mentions the inability of Hoshaiah to see the smoke signals of Azekah, although those of Lachish are still visible. Perhaps Azekah had already fallen (34:7). Although the specific meaning of many of the references of these letters eludes us, they do throw a vivid light on the disturbed and fearful days just prior to the fall of the Judean kingdom, the days of Jeremiah. A translation of these letters may be found in *Ancient Near Eastern Texts Relating to the OT,* edited by James B. Pritchard, second edition, Princeton, 1955. J.B.G.

JEREMOTH (jĕr'ē-mŏth, Heb. *yerēmôth, swollen, thick*). 1. A Benjamite of the family of Becher (I Chron. 7:8).
2. Another Benjamite (I Chron. 8:14).
3. A Levite, family of Merari, house of Mushi (I Chron. 23:23; 24:30).
4. The head of the 15th course among the musicians in the reign of David (I Chron. 25:4,22).
5. A prince of Naphtali in David's reign (I Chron. 27:19).
6. Three men who consented to put away their foreign wives in the time of Ezra (Ezra 10:26, 27,29).

JERIAH (jē-rī'à, Heb. *yerîyāhû, Jehovah sees*), head of a Levitical house, the house of Hebron (I Chron. 23:19; 24:23; 26:31).

JERIBAI (jĕr'ĭ-bī, Heb. *yerîvay, Jehovah pleads*), a son of Elnaam, and one of David's mighty men (I Chron. 11:46).

JERICHO (jĕr'ĭ-kō, Heb. *yerēhô, yerîhô,* Gr. *Iereichó, moon city*).

The Site. Jericho, also called the city of palm trees (Deut. 34:3) is located five miles W of the Jordan and seven miles N of the Dead Sea, some 800 feet below sea level. Its climate is tropical, with great heat during the summer. In the winter it becomes a resort for people fleeing the colder weather of the Palestinian hill country. In ancient times date palm trees flourished here, and balsam, from which medicine was extracted, was the source of great income. Today there are many banana groves. The presence of springs of water makes the locality a green oasis in the middle of the dry Jordan rift area.

There are three Jerichos. The OT city was situated on a mound now called Tell es-Sultan, a mile NW of the modern town. NT Jericho is on a higher elevation nearby. Modern Jericho, called Er Riha by the Arabs, has a population of about 10,000 people of a very much mixed racial descent.

Outskirts of modern Jericho, the "City of Palm Trees." SHH

Jericho is probably the oldest city in the world. Its strategic site by a ford of the Jordan controlled the ancient trade routes from the East. After crossing the river these branched out, one going towards Bethel and Shechem in the north, another, westward to Jerusalem, and a third to Hebron in the south. Thus Jericho controlled the access to the hill country of Palestine from Transjordan.

Jericho in the Bible. Jericho first enters the Biblical story when it is captured by Joshua and the invading Hebrews as the opening wedge of their campaign to take Canaan (Josh. 6). The city's location made its capture the key to the invasion of the central hill country. It was regarded as a formidable obstacle by the Hebrews, requiring divine help to take it. After the two spies searched it (Josh. 2) Joshua led the Hebrew forces against the city, marching around it daily for six days. On the seventh day they circled it seven times, then stood and blew their trumpets and "the wall fell down flat, so that the people went up into the city every man straight before him, and they took the city" (Josh. 6:20). The city was devoted to God, totally destroyed and burned, except for metal objects found in it (Josh. 6:17-19). Only Rahab, who had cared for the spies, with her family, was saved (Josh. 6:22,23,25). Joshua placed

An aerial view of the mound of ancient Jericho (foreground) and the plain of Jericho, looking southward over the modern city. © MPS

a curse on the place, that it might not be rebuilt (Josh. 6:26). The site seems to have remained a ruin for centuries.

Jericho next becomes prominent when it is rebuilt by Hiel the Bethelite in the days of Ahab (c. 850 B.C.; I Kings 16:34). Evidently it again became an important place during the divided kingdom era. It is mentioned in connection with Elisha's ministry (II Kings 2:5,19; see also II Chron. 28:15; II Kings 25:5; Jer. 39:5; Ezra 2:34; Neh. 3:2; 7:36).

In the time of Christ, Jericho was an important place yielding a large revenue to the royal family. Since the road from the fords of the Jordan to Jerusalem passed through it, it became a stopping place for Galilean pilgrims to Jerusalem, who came south through Perea to avoid defilement by contact with the Samaritans. Thus Jesus passed through it on a number of occasions. Nearby are the supposed sites of His baptism (in the Jordan) and His temptation (the hill Quarantania, W of the city). Near the city Jesus healed Bartimaeus (Mark 10:46-52) and two other blind men (Matt. 20:29-34). Here occurred the conversion of Zacchaeus (Luke 19:1-10), one of the most graphic of the Gospel narratives. In the parable of the Good Samaritan (Luke 10:29-37) the traveler was attacked as he was going down from Jerusalem to Jericho, a winding road, often passing between crags, going through the desolate Judean wilderness, which was a frequent hiding place of criminals.

The Archaeology of Jericho. During the past 50 years there have been a number of excavations of Tell es-Sultan, OT Jericho. Between 1908 and 1910, the German scholars Sellin and Watzinger excavated there. A very important expedition, led by the British archaeologist John Garstang dug there from 1930 to 1936. The latest attempt to uncover ancient Jericho's secrets began in 1952, when the British School of Archaeology and the American School of Oriental Research in Jerusalem, under the leadership of Dr. Kathleen Kenyon excavated the tell. At the end of the 1957 season, this work was suspended.

The earliest evidence of settlement on this site is dated (by radiocarbon tests) to the seventh and sixth millennia B.C., when a pre-pottery neolithic town was built there. A surprisingly strong city wall, mud brick and stone houses, plastered floors with reed mats, and clay figurines of animals and the mother goddess show that the civilization was not crude. Of special interest from this period are several human skulls with the features modeled in clay and with shells for eyes, used possibly for cultic purposes. This in one of the oldest cities known to man — existing some 5,000 years before Abraham!

Of greatest interest to the Bible student is the evidence bearing on the overthrow of the city in the days of Joshua. About this (the late bronze age) city there has been dispute ever since Garstang's excavation, and Miss Kenyon's reports, which scholars had hoped would solve the mystery only accentuated the problem. Garstang believed that he had found ample evidence of Joshua's destruction of the late bronze age city, which he labeled "city D," and dated to the 15th century B.C. He found that this city had been surrounded by a double wall, which encircled the summit of the mound, the inner wall 12 feet thick and the outer six feet. These walls had been violently destroyed and had toppled down the slopes of the mound. Layers of ash and charcoal testified to the burning of the city by its captors, and great amounts of charred grain and other foodstuffs suggested the total destruction of which the Bible speaks. Not all of Garstang's fellow archaeologists accepted his reconstructions and the world of scholarship awaited Miss Kenyon's findings.

After seven seasons at Jericho, Miss Kenyon reports that virtually nothing remains of the Jericho of the period of Joshua (1500-1200 B.C.). The mound has suffered such denudation that almost all remains later than the third millennium B.C. have disappeared. The two walls which Garstang connected with his city D Miss Kenyon discovered to date from the third millennium, hundreds of years before the Exodus. Only a bit of pottery and possibly one building remain from the late bronze age. If there was once evidence of a great city of Jericho destroyed by Joshua, it has long since been eaten away by the elements. Much that has been written on this subject prior to 1952 — often written with the best intentions to "prove" the truth of the Bible — is now outmoded. Many scholars now believe that the Jericho of Joshua's day was little more than a fort.

It is unlikely that the problem of Jericho will ever be solved by further archaeological work. The many successive years of digging have left the tell in a mixed-up condition, and it may be that other cities mentioned in the conquest narrative in Joshua (e.g. Hazor) will now more readily yield their answers. In the meantime, the thoughtful Christian will not forget the mutability of scientific theories.

NT Jericho, Tulul Abu el-Alayiq, was excavated in 1950. Much of it had been built by Herod the Great as his winter capital. Here Herod died (4 B.C.). It was a magnificent Roman-style city, with pools, villas, a hippodrome and a theater. A great civic center, of the best Roman masonry, with a grand facade containing statuary niches, potted plants and a reflecting basin before it, bear witness to the grandeur of the international culture that was Palestine's during the time of Jesus.   J.B.G.

JERIMOTH (jĕr'ĭ-mŏth, Heb. *yerēmôth, thick, swollen*). 1. A Benjamite (I Chron. 7:7).

2. A Benjamite who joined David at Ziklag (I Chron. 12:5).

3. Son of David and father of Mahalath, the wife of Rehoboam (II Chron. 11:18).

4. A Levite, an overseer of the temple in the reign of Hezekiah (II Chron. 31:13).

5. A Levite musician in David's time (I Chron. 25:4).

6. A son of Mushi, a Merarite (I Chron. 24:30).

JERIOTH (jĕr'ĭ-ŏth, Heb. *yerî'ôth, tent curtains*), one of Caleb's wives (I Chron. 2:18).

JEROBOAM I (jĕr'ō-bō'ăm, Heb. *yārov'ām, the people contend,* or *the people become numerous*), son of Nebat, of the tribe of Ephraim, and of Zeruah, a widow (I Kings 11:26-40). He founded the kingdom of Israel when the nation was split following the death of Solomon. His father was an official under Solomon and came from the village of Zeredah in the Jordan. As a young man Jero-

Excavating the old city walls of ancient Jericho.
© MPS

boam showed such ability that Solomon put him in charge of the fortifications and public works at Jerusalem and made him overseer of the levy from the house of Joseph (I Kings 11:28). He, however, used his position to stir up disaffection against the government. This was not difficult to do, as the people were already filled with bitterness over the enforced labor and burdensome taxation imposed upon them by Solomon. One day as he was walking outside Jerusalem, he was met by the prophet Ahijah of Shiloh, who tore into 12 pieces a new mantle he wore and gave 10 of them to Jeroboam, informing him, moreover, that because of the idolatrous defection of Solomon's reign, the kingdom would be rent asunder, two of the tribes to remain with David's house, while Jeroboam would become the head of the other ten. He also told him that if as king he walked in the fear of the Lord and kept His commandments, the kingdom would be his and his descendants for many a year. When news of these happenings reached Solomon, he tried to kill Jeroboam, but he escaped to Egypt, where he was kindly received by Shishak, the pharaoh who succeeded (and, it is thought, dethroned) the pharaoh whose daughter Solomon had married. As soon as Solomon died, Jeroboam returned from Egypt, and when the people met at Shechem to proclaim Solomon's son Rehoboam king, they invited Jeroboam to come and take the lead in urging their grievances. As spokesman of the people, he urged that their burdens be alleviated, but the request was contemptuously rejected; whereupon the ten tribes revolted from the house of David and made Jeroboam their king. Thus Ahijah's prophecy that the ten tribes would form a separate kingdom with Jeroboam as king was fulfilled.

Although divinely set apart for his task, and raised to the throne with the approval of the people, Jeroboam nevertheless failed to rise to the greatness of his opportunities. The prophet had told him the conditions of success as a ruler, but it was not long before he began to depart from the counsels of the Lord. Afraid that if his people went annually to Jerusalem to worship, it would not be long before they would be won back to the house of David, he decided to establish centers of worship at the two extremities of his kingdom, Dan in the N and Bethel in the S. This was at variance with the law of Moses, according to which there was to be but one altar of burnt-offering and one place of meeting God. His disobedience became much greater when, in defiance of the commandment forbidding the worship of God by means of images, he set up a golden calf in each of the new sanctuaries and quoted to the people the words of Aaron, "Behold thy gods, O Israel, which brought thee up out of the land of Egypt" (I Kings 12:28). These radical changes involved the necessity of others. Since priests refused to serve at the new altars, he had to supply their place from such as could be had, "the lowest of the people." Furthermore, he made a house of high places, and ordained that the feast of tabernacles, which had been held in the seventh month, should henceforth be observed on the eighth. He, moreover, sometimes took it upon himself to minister in the priests' office. The mass of people conformed to the new religious ways. This was the "sin of Jeroboam the son of Nebat, wherewith he made Israel to sin" (I Kings 12:30; 16:26). He sacrificed the higher interests of religion to politics. To establish his throne firmly, he led the people into the immoralities of heathenism which led eventually to the destruction of the nation. The successive kings, with possibly one exception, supported this idolatrous worship until Israel fell.

Although Jeroboam made Israel to sin by introducing religious customs that conflicted radically with those taught by Moses, God gave him a solemn warning to give heed to his evil ways through an unnamed prophet who came to Bethel from Judah. One day — apparently the very day the altar was consecrated — as Jeroboam stood ministering at the altar, the man of God suddenly appeared before the king and foretold that the time would come when a member of the Davidic dynasty would desecrate that altar by burning men's bones upon it, a prophecy that was fulfilled in the time of Josiah. When the king heard these words, he pointed to the prophet and cried out, "Lay hold on him," whereupon the hand that was extended menacingly instantly withered and became useless, and the altar was rent in two so that the ashes spilled to the ground. The king then besought the prophet to pray that his hand might be restored to him. The prophet prayed and the hand was restored. He refused the king's invitation to go home with him to dine, saying that it was against the will of God, and then left for home. In spite of this terrible warning from God, Jeroboam continued on his evil way, so that God decided to cut off and destroy his house.

At a later date, exactly when is not clear, Jeroboam's eldest son fell seriously ill. The distracted father thought of Ahijah, now old and blind, and sent his queen to him in disguise to find out from him whether the child would live. The prophet saw through her disguise and told her not only that the child would die, but that the house of Jeroboam would be utterly destroyed by someone whom the Lord would raise up to be king of Israel.

There was desultory warfare between Jeroboam and Rehoboam (I Kings 15:6), and a great battle was fought between Jeroboam and Rehoboam's successor, Abijam, in which the army of Israel was thoroughly routed and defeated with great slaughter, and Bethel, only a few miles from Jerusalem, was captured by Abijam (I Kings 15:7). Jeroboam reigned for 22 years and was succeeded to the throne by his son Nadab.

For the people of Israel the reign of Jeroboam was a supreme political and religious calamity. The warfare between the two kingdoms inevitably brought weakness and prostration to both, leaving them open to outside attack. The introduction of the golden bulls led to the "baalization" of the religion of Jehovah. In about 200 years the moral and religious corruption of the people had gone so far that there was no more hope for them, and God brought in a heathen power to lead them into captivity.

S.B.

JEROBOAM II (jĕr-ō-bō′ăm, Heb. *yārov′ām, the people contend,* or *the people become numerous*), the son and successor of Jehoash, king of Isarel; fourth son of the dynasty of Jehu. He became king in Samaria c. 785 B.C., and reigned 41 years. He followed the example of Jeroboam I in keeping up the idolatrous worship of the golden calves (II Kings 14:23). In spite of this, his reign was outwardly flourishing. He ruled contemporaneously with Amaziah (II Kings 14:23) and Uzziah (II Kings 15:1), kings of Judah. He continued and brought to a successful conclusion the wars which his father had undertaken against Syria, and took their chief cities, Damascus and Hamath, which had once been subject to David, and also restored to Israel territory E of the Jordan from Lebanon to the Dead Sea (II Kings 14:25; Amos 6:14). Moab and Ammon, probably tributaries of Syria, were reconquered (Amos 1:13; 2:1-3).

All these successful wars brought much tribute to Jeroboam and his nobles. The wealthy had both winter and summer homes; some lived in houses of ivory; others in houses of hewn stone. There were many great houses. The prophet Amos, contemporary with Jeroboam in his later years, gives us a graphic description of a banqueting scene in which the perfumed guests lay upon silken cushions, eating the flesh of lambs and stall-fed calves, drinking wine from bowls, and singing songs to the music of viols. But side by side with this luxury there was also much poverty in the land. Twice the prophet says that the needy were sold for a pair of shoes (Amos 2:6; 8:6). No one, however, was grieved for the afflictions of the poor or was distressed for the corruption that prevailed in the land. Drunkenness, licentiousness, and oppression went unrebuked by the religious hierarchy.

Not that the land was devoid of religion. Worship went on not only at Dan and Bethel, but at subsidiary temples and altars at Gilgal and Beersheba (Amos 4:4; 5:5; 8:14), both places with long religious associations. Amos complains (5:21 ff) that ritual was substituted for righteousness, and that votaries prostrated themselves before altars clothed in garments taken in cruel pledge, and drank sacrificial wine bought with the money of those who were condemned (Amos 2:8).

During the reign of Jeroboam lived the prophets Hosea, Joel, Jonah, and Amos. Amos says that he was commanded by God to go to Bethel to testify against the whole proceedings there. He was to foretell the destruction of the sanctuaries of Israel, and of the house of Jeroboam with the sword (Amos 7:9). When Amaziah, the highpriest of Bethel, heard this denunciation, he sent a messenger to the king of Samaria with a report of a "conspiracy" of Amos and that Amos had declared, "Jeroboam shall die by the sword," which Amos had not done. There are some who regard this as a prophecy that was not fulfilled, as there is no evidence that the king died other than a natural death, for he was buried with his ancestors in state (II Kings 14:29) The probability, however, is that the high-priest, in order to inflame Jeroboam against him, gave the prophet's words an unwarranted twist.

In II Kings 14:25 we are told that the large extension of territory to Israel by Jeroboam was foretold by Jonah, the son of Amittai, the same prophet whose mission to Nineveh forms the subject of the Book of Jonah (1:1).

Jeroboam was succeeded on his death by his son Zechariah (II Kings 14:29), a weak king with whom the dynasty ended.   S.B.

JEROHAM (jē-rō'hăm, Heb. *jerōhām, may he be compassionate*, or *be pitied* (by God). 1. A Levite, the father of Elkanah, and grandfather of Samuel (I Sam. 1:1; I Chron. 6:27,34).

2. A Benjamite, whose sons were chief men and lived at Jerusalem (I Chron. 8:27). Probably identical with the following.

3. A Benjamite, father of Ibneiah who dwelt at Jerusalem (I Chron. 9:8).

4. Ancestor of a priest in Jerusalem (I Chron. 9:12; Neh. 11:12).

5. A Benjamite of Gedor, father of two of David's recruits at Ziklag (I Chron. 12:7).

6. Father of Azarel, chief of the tribe of Dan in the reign of David (I Chron. 27:22).

7. Father of Azariah, one of the captains who supported Jehoiada in overthrowing Queen Athaliah and putting Joash on the throne of Judah (II Chron. 23:1).

JERUBBAAL (See Gideon)

JERUBBESHETH (See Gideon)

JERUEL (jē-roō'ĕl, Heb. *jerû'ēl, founded by God*), a wilderness in Judah, "by the cliff of Ziz," in the vicinity of En-gedi, but its exact location is unknown. Jahaziel predicted that King Jehoshaphat should meet the hordes of Moabites and Ammonites there (II Chron. 20:16).

JERUSALEM, in the history of God's revelation to man in those Divine acts by which redemption has been accomplished, by far the most important site on this earth. It was the royal city, the capital of the only kingdom God has (thus far) established among men; here the temple was erected, and here alone, during the kingdom age, were sacrifices legitimately offered. This was the city of the prophets, as well as the kings of David's line. Here occurred the death, resurrection, and ascension of Jesus Christ, David's greater Son. Upon an assembled group in this city the Holy Spirit descended at Pentecost, giving birth to the Christian Church, and here the first great Church Council was held. Rightly did the chronicler refer to Jerusalem as the "city which Jehovah had chosen out of all the tribes of Israel to put his name there" (I Kings 14:21). Even the Roman historian Pliny, of the first century, referred to Jerusalem as "by far the most famous city of the ancient Orient" (H.N.V.14). This city has been the preeminent objective of the pilgrimages of devout men and women for over 2,000 years, and it was in an attempt to recover the Church of the Holy Sepulchre in Jerusalem that all the Crusades were organized.

No site in all the Scriptures receives such constant and exalted praise as Jerusalem. Concerning no place in the world have such promises

A first glimpse of Jerusalem, the "City of Peace," from the belfry of the Church of the Holy Sepulchre, looking out over the Dome of the Rock (mosque), and the Mount of Olives. © MPS

been made of ultimate glory and permanent peace. As George Adam Smith has well said, "Jerusalem felt His presence. She was assured of His love and as never another city on earth has been, of His travail for her worthiness of the destiny to which He had called her."

Names of the City. While the word *Jerusalem* is Semitic, it apparently was not a name given to the city for the first time by the Hebrew people. Far back in the time of the Tell-el-Amarna (1400 B.C.) letters, it was called *U-ru-sa-lim,* that is, a city of Salim, generally taken to mean "city of peace." In the Hebrew Bible, the word first appears in Joshua 10:1 where it is spelled *Yerushalayim.* In the Aramaic of Ezra 4:8,20,24,51, it is *Jerushlem.* In the records of Sennacherib, it is called *Ursalimu.* In the Syriac, it *is Urishlem;* in the LXX, it is *Hierousalem.* The Romans, at the time of Hadrian, 135 A.D., changed the name to *Aelia Capitolina.* For some hundreds of years now the Arabs have called the city *Al-Kuds al-Sharif,* which means the Sanctuary. There is no reason for insisting that Salem is to be taken as the name of a Canaanitic deity, that is, the city of the god Salem. Salem was probably the earlier name for the city, the name given to it in the memorable interview of Abraham with Melchizedek, the king of Salem (Gen. 14:18; Ps. 76:2). Because the very name of the city means *peace,* we are told that in this place, God Himself will give peace (Hag. 2:9). The children of God are exhorted to "pray for the peace of Jerusalem" (Ps. 122:6). Isaiah, at the end of his great series of prophecies, returns to the theme, "Thus saith Jehovah, behold, I will extend peace to her like a river" (Isa. 66:12). This word Salem is the basis of the Arabic greeting "Salam," and the Jewish greeting "Shalom," both meaning "peace be with you."

The Rabbis say there are 60 different names for Jerusalem in the Bible, a characteristic exaggeration, but truly there are a great number. Jerusalem itself occurs about 600 times in the OT, though it is not found in Job, Hosea, Jonah, Nahum, Habakkuk, and Haggai.

A general air view of the Jerusalem area, showing the Kidron Valley running around the city on the right, and the Valley of Hinnom on the left. Mount Moriah, the old temple area, now dominated by the huge mosque, the Dome of the Rock, is in right center, with the Garden of Gethsemane below it, outside the wall, to the right, in the Kidron Valley. © MPS

Jerusalem appears in the NT after the close of the Book of Acts rather infrequently, four times near the conclusion of the epistle to the Romans (15:17,25,26,31), once at the close of the first letter to the Corinthians (16:3), and again in the Galatian epistle (1:17,18 and 2:1). The most frequently used name for this city, apart from Jerusalem, of course, is *Zion,* which occurs over 100 times in the OT, beginning as early as II Kings 19:21, and found most frequently in the Book of Psalms and the prophecy of Isaiah (1:8; 4:4, 5; 62:11). Zion appears in the NT in some very interesting passages, which cannot be discussed here. Twice on the lips of our Lord (Matt. 21:5; John 12:15); twice in the epistle to the Romans, with spiritual significance (9:33 and 11:36); and similarly in I Peter 2:6 and Revelation 14:1. Jerusalem is often called in the historical books and once in the prophetical writings, "the city of David" (II Sam. 5:7, 9; 6:10-16; Neh. 3:15 and 12:37; Isa. 22:9, etc). This title is later, on one occasion, applied to Bethlehem (Luke 2:4, 11).

The greatest group of titles for this city are those which identify it as *the city of God.* It is called exactly this in the Psalms, as well as in the NT (Psa. 46:4; 48:1, 8; 87:3; Heb. 12:22; Rev. 3:12). It is also called the city of Jehovah (Isa. 60:14); the mountain of the Lord (Isa. 2:3 and 30:29); the mountain of Jehovah of hosts (Zech. 8:3); the holy mountain of Jehovah (Isa. 27:13; 66:20); Zion of the Holy One of Israel (Isa. 60:13). The Lord Himself refers to it, and to no other place, as "my city" (Isa. 45:13), or more often, "my holy mountain" (Isa. 11:9; 56:7; 57:13; 65:11, 25; 66:20). Because it is the city of God, where He has put His name, it is often re-

ferred to as the Holy City (Isa. 48:2; 52:1; Neh. 11:1-18), a title twice used by Matthew (in 4:5 and 27:53) and once of a future event by St. John (Rev. 11:2), and used in referring to our eternal heavenly home at the close of the Scriptures (Rev. 21:2; 22:19). Generally, the phrase, "the holy mountain," refers to this city (Ps. 48:1; Isa. 11:9; Dan. 11:45, etc.). Once it is given the beautiful name of Hephzibah, meaning "My delight is in her" (Isa. 62:4). Isaiah in one passage calls the city Ariel, the meaning of which is a very disputed matter (Isa. 29:1,2,7), a word that in itself means "Lion of God." At the beginning of his prophecy he gives two titles to the city in most radical contrast. He designates it, because of its wickedness, as Sodom and Gomorrah (1:10), but in the same passage, he promises that the day will come when it will be accurately called "the city of righteousness" (1:26).

The Site. Different from most cities that have witnessed great historical events over many successive centuries, Jerusalem has always remained on the same site. Specifically it is located 31° 46′ 45″ N lat., and 35° 13′ 25″ long. E of Greenwich. It is situated 33 miles E of the Mediterranean, and 14 miles W of the Dead Sea, at an elevation of 2,550 feet above sea level. Geologically speaking, the city rests upon three hills. The SE hill, the original city of the Jebusites, the city which David seized, later to be called Zion, occupied about eight to ten acres, and "was shaped somewhat like a gigantic human footprint about 1,250 feet long and 400 feet wide." The area of Megiddo in contrast was 30 acres. The northern hill was the one on which Solomon built the great temple, and his own palace, called Ophel. It is probable that Millo (II Sam. 5:9; I Kings 9:15f)

Section of the east city wall of Jerusalem — on the right, a part of the old Herodian wall, and to the left, the closed Golden Gate. © MPS

was "either a fortress guarding the northern approach to Ophel or a fill of rocks and dirt to shore up the wall at its most vulnerable point" (Gottwald). On the E of these two hills was a deep valley known as the Kidron. To the S of the city was another deep valley called the Hinnom. Down through the middle of the city, running from N to S, was a third valley, now built over, and only discernible by careful investigation of the contours of the rock level, called the Tyropoeon Valley. On the far side of the Western hill was the Valley of Gehenna, a continuation of Hinnom. These valleys today give no idea of their original depth, for debris has filled them up in some places to a depth of 50 to 60 feet. The city never occupied what could be called a large area. Even in the time of Herod the Great, the area within the walls was not more than a mile in length, nor more than five-eighths of a mile in width. The city was off the beaten path of the great caravan routes, and was not, as most larger world capitals, on a navigable river or on a large body of water. Its site, therefore, had an exclusiveness about it. On the other hand, being 19 miles N from Hebron, and 30 miles S of Samaria, it was centrally located to serve as the capital of the kingdom of Israel. Many travelers have testified to the fact that Jerusalem "from whatever direction it is approached, can be seen only when one has arrived in its immediate vicinity: a peculiarity which always brought a moment of pleasant surprise to travelers of bygone days" (J. Simmons).

Walls and Gates. The matter of Israel's gates and walls is complicated and has given rise to a great many technical disagreements, and can be discussed here only in a general way. Because of the deep valleys on the E, S and W of the city, it was only the northern side which could be more easily penetrated by an invading army. The walls on the E and W are built on the ridges of these valleys. There was probably in early days, a southern wall extending far below the present southern wall structure. The first northern wall extended from what is called the Jaffa Gate to the middle of the great temple area. The second northern wall began at the Jaffa Gate, extended northward and then curved to the east to the Tower of Antonia, just beyond the northern end of the Temple area. The modern wall extends N and then E from the northern end of the western wall to the northern end of the present eastern wall. There was a third north wall of which we have become aware only during the days of modern excavation. The walls of the city are more elaborately described

Above, the Golden Gate, now closed. Center, St. Stephen's Gate. Below, bringing sheep to market at the Damascus Gate. © MPS

in the book of Nehemiah than in any other place in the Bible. Beginning at the southeastern end of the early wall is the Dung Gate; moving northward one comes to the Fountain Gate; and then, nearly in the middle of the wall of the old temple area, the famous, now-closed, Golden Gate. Above this is Stephen's Gate. Turning west on the northern modern wall, we come to Herod's Gate, then the much-used Damascus Gate, and then toward the end of

The New Gate, the most westerly of the three gates on the north side of the city, opened during the Turkish administration in the 19th century. Below, a street scene just inside the Damascus Gate, the main gate in the northern wall. © MPS

this northern wall, the New Gate. If we turn left again at the western wall, we come to the last of the gates now in use, the Jaffa Gate, out from which the road proceeds to the Mediterranean. The present wall, though much of it is, no doubt, on the site of earlier walls, was built by Soliman II about 1540, extending for two and one-half miles, with an average height of 38 feet.

History. The early history of Jerusalem is wrapped in obscurity. Pottery from before 2000 B.C. has been found at Al Buqueia, SW of Jerusalem, though we are not acquainted with any names of individuals appearing at this site at such an early period. The first reference that we have to Jerusalem in secular annals is in the famous Tell-el-Amarna letters of the 14th century B.C., in which is some most interesting correspondence from the governor of this city, Abd-Khiba, addressed to the pharaoh of Egypt, complaining that his city is being threatened, and that the Egyptian government is not giving him the support he needs and expected. (These letters may be found in Pritchard's *NET* 487-488). We do, however, have a reference to the Jebusites, who are the ones who inhabited the city of Jebus, that is, Jerusalem, as early as the great ethnological passage in Genesis 10 (vss. 15-19). Actually, the first reference to Jerusalem as such is found in the story of the amazing interview of Abraham with Melchizedek, king of *Salem* (Gen. 14:17-24). Here is the first occurrence of the word "priest" in the Bible, and because Melchizedek was the "priest of God most high," we are compelled to believe that even before the nation Israel was founded, and perhaps 800 years before this site was taken by David, there was a witness to the true God at this place. While there is some difference of view on this point, many believe, and tradition is unanimous here, that the place of Abraham offering up Isaac at Mt. Moriah (Gen. 22:2; II Chron. 3:1) was the exact site on which, centuries later, the Temple of Solomon was built. Josephus himself affirms that Jerusalem was in existence during the days of Abraham (*Ant.* I X-2, VII XI-3).

The actual name Jerusalem occurs for the first time in Joshua 10:5, where we are told that the king of the city confederated with four other kings in a futile attempt to defeat Joshua. In the same book it is frankly confessed that the Israelites were unable to drive out the Jebusites (15:8, 63; 18:28). At the beginning of the book of Judges (1:7) it is stated, however, that the Israelites in an hour of victory had overwhelmed a large opposing force including Adoni-bezek and "brought him to Jerusalem," where he died. This would seem to imply that for a brief space the Israelites held part of this city, but were not able to keep it: "The children of Benjamin did not drive out the Jebusites that inhabited Jerusalem; but the Jebusites dwell with the children of Benjamin in Jerusalem unto this day" (Judg. 1:21).

Nothing is known of the history of Jerusalem, either from Biblical or non-Biblical writings, from the time of Joshua's death until the capture of this city by David (II Sam. 5:6-10; prob. 998 B.C.). No doubt the fortress which David took is that which later came to be called Zion, located on the SE hill, and outside of the present walls of the city. Kraeling estimates that the population of this city during David's time did not exceed 1,230, estimating it as 250 people per acre. Later David purchased "the threshing floor of Araunah, the Jebusite" (II Sam. 24:18; I Chron. 21:18-28) on which site the great Temple of Solomon later was erected. (See TEMPLE). Upon finishing the temple, Solomon then built a magnificent palace to the N of it, of which there is not the slightest vestige today.

With the death of Solomon, the glory of Israel, and so also the glory of Jerusalem, began to dim. In the fifth year of Rehoboam, 917 B.C., Shishak, king of Egypt, without any struggle whatever, coming up to Jerusalem, "took away the treasures of the house of Jehovah, and the treasures of the king's house; he even took away all: and he took away all the shields of gold which Solomon had made" (I Kings 14:26; II Chron. 12:9). This is the first of eight different plunderings of the Jerusalem Temple occurring within a little more than 300 years. Not only must its wealth have been fabulously great, but no doubt, in times of national prosperity, the more religiously inclined citizens of Judah would bestow new treasures upon the temple. Shortly thereafter, Asa (911-871 B.C.) bribed Ben-Hadad the king of Syria, by taking "all the silver and the gold that were left in the treasures of the house of Jehovah and the treasures of the king's house and delivered them into the hand of the servants of the Syrian king" (I Kings 15:18). Twice then, within a few years after Solomon's death, Judah's kings prevented an invasion of the city only by bribing her enemies with the treasures of the Lord's House. Again during the reign of Jehoram (850-843 B.C.), in an episode about which we know very little, the Arabians and the Philistines "carried away all the substance found in the king's house and his sons also and his wives" (II Chron. 21:16,17). For the fourth time within a century and a half after the death of Solomon, the temple treasures were used for bribing a threatening enemy, by Jehoash (837-800 B.C.), who "took all the hallowed things that Jehoshaphat and Jehoram and Ahaziah, his fathers, kings of Judah, had dedicated, and his own hallowed things, and all the gold that was found in the treasures of the house of Jehovah, and of the king's house, and sent it to Hazael, king of Syria: and he went away from Jerusalem" (II Kings 12:18). Thus far it is foreign kings that are bribed with these treasures, but the fifth occasion involved the King of Israel, Joash (801-786 B.C.). Coming up to Jerusalem, he broke down the western wall for a length of 600 feet, and then "took all the gold and silver, and all the vessels that were found in the house of Jehovah, and in the treasures of the king's house, and hostages also, and returned to Samaria" (II Kings 14:13,14; II Chron. 25:23).

One attack upon the city of Jerusalem failed in the reign of Ahaz (733-714 B.C.), when Rezin, the king of Syria, and Remaliah, the king of Israel, were repulsed in their attempt to seize the temple (II Kings 16:5). However, while Ahaz was still king, there came up to Jerusalem a mighty king of Assyria, Tiglath-pileser III (745-737 B.C.), to whom Ahaz took "a portion out of the house of Jehovah and out of the house of the king and of the princes, and gave it unto the king of Assyria." However, as the text informs us "It helped him not" (II Chron. 28:20,21).

In 701 B.C. occurred an event relating to Jerusalem's history to which the OT actually gives more space, with greater detail, than even to the destruction of Jerusalem by Nebuchadnezzar, namely, the threat of Sennacherib (704-681 B.C.), who cast one insult after another in the face of King Hezekiah (715-687 B.C., reminding him that he, Sennacherib, had already captured practically every city of Judah, and how could the king think Jerusalem would escape? But by divine intervention, with God's assurance that the king would this time be kept from invasion, Sennacherib's host suffered a mysterious blight and he returned to Assyria without fulfilling his threat (II Kings 18 and 19; II Chron. 32; Isa. 36). For Sennacherib's own account of this episode, see Pritchard's NET 287, 288).

Another century passes during which we know very little of Jerusalem's history. In 605 B.C., Nebuchadnezzar, King of Babylon, forced into submission Judah's king Jehoiakim. After three years, the king of Judah foolishly revolted and this brought Nebuchadnezzar back to the city for its final destruction. Within the last few years, Mr. Donald J. Wiseman of the British Museum has translated and published the hitherto unknown tablets, officially recording Nebuchadnezzar's military exploits. As Wiseman says, we "now know precisely for the first time" the exact date of Jerusalem's capitulation, March 16, 597 B.C. The destruction was on a wholesale scale. It is estimated that some 60,000 citizens were carried away to Babylon at this time, and, of course, the remaining treasures of the temple were also removed, to be restored again in the days of Ezra (II Kings 24:1-25:21; II Chron. 36:1-21 and Jer. 52). As Jeremiah vividly reminds us, "The kings of the earth believed not, neither all the inhabitants of the world, that the adversary and the enemy would enter into the gates of Jerusalem" (Lam. 4:12). "The history of the ruined city remains a blank until Cyrus" (Conder).

Though the post-exilic books of Ezra and Nehemiah are filled with details regarding Jerusalem, we can only mention the two main events they record. Under Zerubbabel, the rebuilding of the temple by permission of Darius I was begun in 538, though, due to many forms of opposition, it was not finished until 516 B.C. Some 60 years later, Nehemiah, cupbearer of the King of Persia, Artaxerxes I, successfully undertook the rebuilding of the walls of the city (Neh. 1-6), followed by a great revival under the leadership of Ezra (Neh. 8-9). The condition of the city however, even under these great leaders, was not one marked by prosperity; somehow it had lost its attractiveness for the Jews, necessitating a vigorous effort to bring people into the city who were living in areas surrounding it (Neh. 11:1). For the next 100 years, we again know very little of Jerusalem's history.

Upon the death of Alexander the Great, the rulers of Egypt and the South were known as Ptolemies, and those of Syria and the North as the Seleucidae. In 320 B.C., Jerusalem came under the rule of Ptolemy I Soter. One hundred years later, the city passed from the Ptolemies to the Seleucidae. In the year 199, but only for a year, Palestine and Jerusalem were recovered for Egypt by Scopas, the last time Egypt was to possess this city. In 198 the powerful Antiochus III (the Great) took the city, welcomed by the Jews, who were repaid for this service by the Syrian king's presenting treasures to the temple. Any hope, however, on the part of the Jews that this would be the beginning of happier days for them, was soon seen to be unjustified. For in the next generation there appeared (169-168 B.C.) the very type of Anti-Christ himself, Antiochus IV (Epiphanes), who desecrated the temple by sacrificing a pig on the altar, prohibited Jewish sacrifices, circumcision, and the observance of the Sabbath, and issuing a decree that any Jew found possessing a copy of the Holy Scriptures should be killed, and great was the slaughter. (See the opening chapters of the First Book of Maccabees).

The events that now follow must be referred to with the greatest brevity. In 165, Jerusalem was delivered from its bitter yoke by Judas Maccabaeus on the 25th of the month Chisle (our month of December). Ever since, this time of deliverance has been celebrated by the Jews as Hanukkah, or

Ancient Church of the Holy Sepulchre, originally founded in the 4th century A.D. The larger dome of this Greek Orthodox cathedral is supposedly built over the tomb of Christ. © MPS

the Feast of Lights. Two years later, Antiochus IV (Eupator) overthrew the walls and the temple, but soon thereafter the city again came into the hands of the Jewish authorities. But this did not mean peace. Jealousy and schism increased, until one of the Jewish leaders himself, Alexander Jannaeus, actually crucified 800 Pharisees!

The Romans now appear on the scene. The city was besieged in 65 B.C. by a Roman general, who, however, was ordered to desist, leaving the city open for the conquest by Pompey in 64 B.C., who destroyed Jerusalem's walls. The temple was again pillaged in 55 B.C. by Crassus. Fifteen years later the area was occupied by the Parthians. The hour had struck for the rise of that cruel but gifted ruler whose name will be prominent as the New Testament narrative opens, Herod the Great, made king of the Jews by Augustus in 40 B.C. He fought for the possession of the territory that had been given to him, but was not able to take Jerusalem until 37 B.C., after a siege of three months. Herod, like many other Romans,

Map of Jerusalem in New Testament times (20 B.C.-70 A.D.). UANT

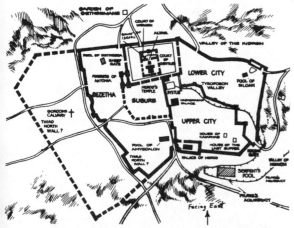

had a passion for erecting vast buildings, and out of this was born the determination to build what came to be known as Herod's Temple, probably the most significant structure ever to stand upon that holy site. He began its erection in 20 B.C., dying himself in 4 B.C., and not until 62 A.D. was the temple finished. In our Lord's day, it presented a spectacle before which even the disciples seem to stand in amazement (Matt. 24:1).

Entire books have been written, of course, on the single subject of Jesus and the city of Jerusalem. Here we can only summarize the relevant data. One is safe in saying that of the four Gospel writers, it is Luke who, though a Gentile, seems to have had the greatest interest in this city, so that the opening events of our Lord's life occurring here are exclusively in the third Gospel and many of the concluding events are here also alone recorded. We begin with the annunciation to Zacharias, a priest in the temple (Luke 1:5-22). Our Lord, when a babe, was taken up to Jerusalem for what is called His presentation (Luke 2:22-38). Luke alone records our Lord's visit to the city at the age of 12. The principal episodes down to the last year of our Lord's life are given exclusively by John. If we place the death of our Lord in A.D. 30, then in April A.D. 27, we have the first cleansing of the temple (John 2:13-25); on April 28 the healing of the man at the pool of Bethesda (John 5:1-47); on October 29 He goes up to Jerusalem at the time of the Feast of Tabernacles where we have a detailed record (John 7:2; 10:21); on December 29, He is in Jerusalem for the Feast of Dedication (Luke 10:38-42). Of course, as all know, the final week of our Lord's life was spent in and near the city (Matt. 27:1-27:66; Mark 11:1-15:47; Luke 19:29-23:56; John 12:12-19:42). Of the five appearances of our Lord on Easter Sunday, four of them are found only in Luke's Gospel (chap. 24). The sixth appearance in Jerusalem a week later is recorded only by John (20:26-29). In Jerusalem our Lord appeared to all the disciples (Acts 1:1-8 and Luke 24:49), and from the Mount of Olives nearby He ascended (Luke 24:50-53).

Our Lord made four principal statements about the city, all of them with a note of sadness. First of all, in stating that He must go up to Jerusalem He declared, "It cannot be that a prophet perish out of Jerusalem" (Luke 13:33). On Tuesday of Holy Week, He cried out, "O Jerusalem, Jerusalem, that killeth the prophets, and stoneth them that are sent unto her! how oft would I have gathered thy children together, even as a hen gathereth her chickens under her wings, and ye would not!" (Matt. 23:37). We are told by Luke that as He wept over the city. He said sadly, "If thou hadst known in this day, even thou, the things which belong unto peace! but now they are hid from thine eyes" (Luke 19:42). Finally, our Lord declared that the buildings of that city, and their very walls, would be thrown down, and that Jerusalem would be trodden down of the Gentiles until the times of the Gentiles are fulfilled (Matt. 24:2; Mark 13:2; Luke 21:24).

The Book of Acts opens with a group of the followers of Jesus meeting together in an Upper Room in Jerusalem, probably the place where the Lord's Supper was held, waiting for the fulfillment of the promise of Christ, that they might be endued with power from on high. The church is born in Jerusalem on the Day of Pentecost (Acts 2). The early persecutions occurred in that city toward these initial believers, and the Sanhedrin that condemned Christ was now confronted with the phenomenon of a growing company of the faithful of the crucified and risen Lord. In this city, the first great crisis of the Church was successfully faced in the first Council, deciding forever the question of salvation wholly by grace, apart from works (Acts 15). Years later in this same city, the Apostle Paul was arrested, mobbed in the temple and falsely accused (Acts 21 and 22).

The destruction of the city, after a siege of 143 days by Roman armies, under the leadership of Titus, while predicted in the Gospels, is not, strange to say, actually recorded anywhere in the NT. Before this dreadful event concluded, 600,000 Jews were slain and thousands more were led away into captivity. "Jerusalem has no history for 60 years after its destruction" (C. R. Conder). One futile and tragic attempt of the Jews to win freedom from the Romans, concentrated in the rebellion of A.D. 134, led by the false Messiah Bar Cochba, was overwhelmingly crushed, and what was left of the city was leveled to the ground,

even the foundations being plowed up. Two years later the Romans began the rebuilding of the city, now to be called Aelia Capitolina. From this new city, all Jews were strictly excluded for two centuries, until the reign of Constantine. In the early part of the fourth century, due to the fervent devotion of Helena, the mother of the emperor, concerning whom traditions soon multiplied regarding divine assistance given to her, leading to the discovery of the true cross, there was built the great Church of the Holy Sepulchre called Anastasis (the Greek word for resurrection). From now on, Jerusalem became increasingly the object of pilgrimages and of rich gifts. Jerome says, "It would be a long task to try to enumerate chronologically from the day of the ascension of our Lord until our own time, the bishops, martyrs, and doctors of the Church who came to Jerusalem, believing themselves to be deficient in religion, in science, and to possess only an imperfect standard of virtue until they had worshiped Christ on the very spot where the Gospel first shone from the gibbet."

For Jerusalem's subsequent history, we must give only the barest outline. What a tragic history still awaited this originally designated city of peace! In A.D. 614, a Persian general under King Chosroes II, seized the city and slaughtered 60,000 Christians, taking 35,000 more into slavery: "The devastation in and around the city was so vast that to this day the countryside has never fully recovered." Join-Lambert does not exaggerate in saying that this awful event "sounded the knell of Christian Jerusalem." In 628, Heraclius made peace with the son of the invader Chosroes, entering Jerusalem in triumph through the Golden Gate. In 637, the city capitulated to Omar the Caliph, who entered its precincts without bloodshed. In 688 the first Dome of the Rock was erected.

Mohammed, more or less acquainted with both the OT and NT, felt it was necessary to be in some way identified with this city, holy to both Jews and Christians, and Islam soon interpreted a passage in the Koran as implying that Mohammed was miraculously carried to Jerusalem and there divinely consecrated, a journey for which there is no real evidence whatever. In 969, Jerusalem fell under the power of the Shia'h Khalif of Egypt. In 1009, the Caliph Hakim, son of a Christian mother, began his devastating work in Jerusalem, by ordering the destruction of the Church of the Holy Sepulchre. By 1014 some 30,000 churches

The Jerusalem temple area today, as viewed from the Tower of Antonia. The scene is dominated by the lavish Moslem mosque, center, known as the Dome of the Rock, the original of which dates back to 688 A.D. © MPS

in Palestine had been burnt or pillaged! "The persecution stopped (1016) only when Hakim became convinced that he himself was divine." In 1077 a general of the Seljuk Turks drove out the Egyptians, slaughtering some 3,000 residing within the walls.

A new era, pitiful, sad, and shameful, now dawns for Jerusalem. In 1099, the Christian Army of the First Crusade encamped before this city, on June 7. The city was seized on July 14, and the awful slaughter pursued by these so-called Christian knights was something that the Moslem world has never forgotten or forgiven. For 80 years, the city knew no other enemy at her gates. There then came upon the stage of history the truly great Saladin, who, after his overwhelming victory in his battle with the Crusaders at the Horns of Hattin, encamped before the city September 20, 1187. He entered in on the second of October, enforcing strict orders that no force of violence and orgy of conquest should be engaged in by his soldiers such as the Christian Crusaders had engaged in almost a century before. By this act of mercy he put the Christians to shame. But the city was not to know peace. In 1229, it was regained by Frederick II, through negotiations. In 1244 it fell before the Kharezmian Tatars; in 1247 it was seized again by the Egyptians; in 1260 it was recaptured by the Tatars; in 1517 it was seized by the Ottoman Turks, who held it for four centuries. Passing over the (for us) inconsequential events of the next 400 years, we come down to the first World War. General Allenby of the British forces entered the city on foot, December 9, 1917, and on October 31 of the next year, the armistice was signed, when 400 years of Turkish misrule came to an end. "Thus again, after more than seven centuries, was Jerusalem entered by a Christian conqueror. Not a stone of the city had been injured. Not a soldier was allowed to enter the city except on duty, until all sacred spots had been placed under guards consisting of men of the religions to which such spots were respectively sacred" (H. O. Lock: *The Conquerors of Palestine,* London, 1920, p. 108).

On April 24, 1920, the mandate for Palestine and Transjordan was assigned to Great Britain, and for nearly 30 years, she suffered one reverse after another in her attempt to rule this country. On May 14, 1948, the British mandate terminated, and the National Council at Tel-Aviv proclaimed the State of Israel. There followed the bitter, often brutal war for Palestine, as a result of which nearly a million Arabs were driven from their homes. At this time there were about 100,000 Jews in the city of Jerusalem, about ten per cent of all that there were in Palestine. By the spring of the next year, Israel was recognized by 45 governments.

Until Israel's war for independence, the city within the walls for centuries had been divided into nearly four equal quarters: on the SE the Jewish quarter, on the SW the Armenian, in the NE, the largest of the four areas, was the Moslem quarter, and in the NW the Christian quarter. There are, of course, no Jews living within the walls of Jerusalem today.

It may be that we are on the threshold of some great archaeological discoveries in Jerusalem. The city has never yet been thoroughly explored archaeologically, because of the many sacred sites which cannot be disturbed, and the hereditary holdings of great numbers of families who would hesitate to give permission for excavation. However, the British School of Archaeology is now about to begin serious excavation at the Western Hill, in an

The reading of General Allenby's proclamation, ending 400 years of Turkish rule, December 11, 1917. The scene is at the entrance to the Tower of David, and General Allenby is just to the right of the gate, in the front row. © MPS

JERUSALEM TODAY

SCALE (feet)   0   500   1000

PRESENT
CITY WALL ▬▬▬▬

UANT

area destroyed during the War of Independence, and also near the north wall of the Church of the Holy Sepulchre, all under the able direction of Dr. Kathleen Kenyon, for years the Director of the excavations carried on at Jericho.

Population. In 1830 it was said by those visiting the city that there were not 100 Jews living within the walls. In 1838, there were but 3,000 Jews in Jerusalem, and only 11,000 in all Palestine. In 1872 there was a slight proportionate gain — of 21,000 in all of Palestine, 10,600 were in Jerusalem. By 1900 there was further gain — of a population in the city of 46,500, there were 29,-000 Jews, 8,500 Moslems and 9,000 Christians. In 1915 there were 50,000 Jews in the Holy City. Israel's War for Independence has radically altered this entire matter — in 1957, the old city, Jerusalem proper, had a population of 80,000, of whom *none* were Jews. The city of Jerusalem, Israel, to the N and W of the old city, in March, 1959, had a population of 156,000, with Tel Aviv-Jaffa far ahead, with 380,000. At that time the total population of Israel was 2,054,434.

Jerusalem in Prophecy. Though there are scores of prophecies in the Bible relating to cities, rivers, and nations, no Bible encyclopedia ever includes these matters in its articles on such geographical terms. Here it is possible to give only a bare summary of those pertaining to Jerusalem.

1. In Deuteronomy 12, though no name is mentioned, six times reference is made to the future place of the sanctuary, "the place which Jehovah your God shall choose" (See also I Kings 8:29, 48).

2. The promise that Sennacherib's attempt to capture the city would fail (Isa. 29:7; 30:19; 31:4, 5; II Kings 19:32-34).

3. Of the destruction of the city by Nebuchadnezzar (II Kings 22:16,17; 23:7; II Chron. 34:24,25;

Relief map of Jerusalem, showing the barbed wire barrier dividing the city into Israeli (west, left) and Arab (east, right) control. © MPS

Isa. 4:3-5; 10:11,12; 22:9-11; 32:13-15; 34:8; 39:6; 64:10,11; Jer. 4:1-6,22,23; 7:14,32,34; 9:11,19; 11:6; 11-13; 13:9,13,27; 15:5; 16:1-21; 17:24-27; 19:8, etc.; 21:5,6,9,10; 22:4-9; 35:17; 38:2,17-23; Ezek. 8:9; 24, etc.).

4. The desecration of the city by Antiochus Epiphanes (Dan. 8:11-14; 11:30-32).

5. The destruction of the city by the Romans, under Titus (Dan. 9:26; Luke 13:33-35; 19:41-44; 21:6,20,24; Matt. 24:2; Mark 13:2).

6. A prophecy concerning this city during the present age (Dan. 9:26; Zech. 12:3; Luke 21:24). (A very remarkable passage).

7. The Jewish people at the end of this age will return to Palestine, and this, of course, includes Jerusalem sometimes specifically designated (Joel 3:1; Isa .49:22,23 [probably]). This includes the erection of some kind of temple in the Holy City (Dan. 9:27; 12:11; Jer. 31:8,9; Isa. 55:11; 60:1-3; Matt. 24:15; Mark 13:14; II Thess. 2:3,4).

8. The episode of the two witnesses, to be martyred in this city (Rev. 11).

9. A final assault upon this city by the nations of the earth (Joel 3:9-12; Isa. 29:1-7, 31-34; Zech. 14:1-3).

10. A cleansing of the city of its spiritual uncleannesses (Isa. 1:25,26; 4:3,4; Joel 3:17; Zech. 14:20,21).

11. A city that will ultimately know, and permanently, the presence of the glory of God (Ezek. 43:1,2; Isa. 62:2); peace (Ps. 122:6-9; Isa. 60:17; 66:12); and joy (Ps. 53:6; Isa. 5:11).

12. To this city the nations of the earth will come for instruction and blessing (Isa. 2:2-4; Ps. 102:21,22).

Jerusalem as a Term of Spiritual Connotation. There is no doubt about it that even in the OT, Jerusalem, especially when referred to as Zion, sometimes was used to express spiritual rather than geographical or historical ideas. In the NT such interpretations are twice recognized by the Apostle Paul, who in that enigmatical passage speaks of "Jerusalem that is above is free, which is our mother" (Gal. 5:26), and the writer of the Epistle to the Hebrews, in a passage that is also fraught with difficulties, tells these Hebrew Christians that they have already "Come unto Mount Zion, and unto the city of the living God, the heavenly Jerusalem" (12:22). The exalted conception of the yet-to-come New Jerusalem, as set forth in the Apocalypse, is well known to everyone (Rev. 3:12; 21:2 ff.).

The greater Church Fathers, such as Jerome, Chrysostom, Augustine, etc., almost unanimously interpreted Zion of the Psalms and Prophets (this is not defending this exegesis) as references to the Church, see, e.g., their interpretations of Psalm 48, as collected in J. M. Neale and R. F. Littledale: *A Commentary on the Psalms: from Primitive and Mediaeval Writers* II. 136-150). Even the Crusaders merged earthly and heavenly ideas in their determination to repossess the Holy Sepulchre. (See Ray C. Petry: *Christian Eschatology and Social Thought*, N. Y., 1956, pp. 123-132).

In the 14th century, wholly divorced from the earthly site, Walter Hylton (d. 1396), an Augustinian canon of Thurgarten in Nottinghamshire, wrote the once widely-read mystical *Ladder of Perfection*, in which the progress of the soul in this life is likened to a pilgrimage to Jerusalem.

Above all is John Bunyan's (1628-1688) *The Holy City; or, The New Jerusalem,* which appeared in 1665, 13 years before the first part of the far more important *Pilgrim's Progress.* This is an allegorical treatment of Revelation 21:10-22:4

The Ecce Homo Arch on the Via Dolorosa, traditional site of Pilate's declaration, "Behold, the Man." © MPS

The hymn *Jerusalem My Happy Home*, of about the beginning of the 17th century, by an unknown author, in its original form extended to 26 stanzas of four lines each. It began to appear in English hymn books as early as 1693, and from then on some of its stanzas may be found in almost all of the major hymn books of the Church. (See Julian 580-583; H. Bonar: *New Jerusalem*, 1852, etc. The well-known *Jerusalem on High*, by Samuel Crossman (1624-1684) was first published in 1664. John Newton's (1725-1807) universally used *Glorious Things of Thee Are Spoken*, first appeared in 1779. The lesser known *Jerusalem, Jerusalem, enthroned once on high*, was published in 1827 by Reginald Heber (1783-1826). The anonymous *O Heavenly Jerusalem*, first appearing in the *Paris Brenary* of 1822, was translated by I. Williams in 1839. Samuel Johnson (1822-1882), an American, joint author with Samuel Longfellow of *A Book of Hymns for Public and Private Devotions* (1846) was the author of *City of God, how broad and fair* (1864). (In Julian's *Dictionary*, pp. 1381, 1382, are listed 43 hymns whose first lines begin with the word Jerusalem (or Hierusalem, and, pp. 1454, 1504, thirty beginning with the words Sion or Zion, some of which refer to identical hymns).

Jerusalem in Poetry. In addition to the poetic compositions that have entered into the hymns of the Christian Church, there are many poems centered upon the history, or the hope, or the typical significance of the Holy City. By far the most famous is the *Jerusalem Delivered* by the gifted, though tragedy-beset Italian poet, Torquato Tasso, 1581 (1544-1595), translated into English by Edward Fairfax in 1594, in which love stories are romantically interwoven in his imaginary presentation of the episodes of the First Crusade. Possibly the best known one written in English is *The Fall of Jerusalem*: A Dramatic Poem, by the great ecclesiastical historian Henry Hart Milman (London, 1820. Reprinted in his *Poetical Works*, London, 1839. Vol. I, pp. 1-114; and, in part, in Geo. A. Kohut: *A Hebrew Anthology*, Part II, pp. 985-1034.)

For many others, worthy and mediocre, see Elon Foster: *Cyclopaedia of Poetry*, second ser. New York, 1884, pp. 259-275; and Henry C. Fish: *Heaven in Song*, New York, 1874, pp. 137-171, 180-184, 228-231, with two renderings of J. M. Meyfart's *Jerusalem thou city fair and high*, pp. 182-184 and 499-501; and the 16th century poem, *O Mother Dear, Jerusalem!* extending to 31 stanzas of eight lines each. Quite a number of poems on the subject of Jerusalem not found elsewhere, are in a treasury of good things, *Lays of the Holy Land* (second ed. New York, 1871). Lord Byron wrote on the destruction of Jerusalem by Titus, beginning, "From the east hill that looks on thy once holy dome"; and Lord Tennyson also on the same tragic event, *The Fall of Jerusalem* in which are the lines, "Signs on earth and signs on high, Prophesied thy destiny." Kohut (Vol. I, pp. 474, 475), inserts a poem, "On Jerusalem," by Matthew A. Berk, and reprints Books X and XI from the *Judaid, On the Destruction of Jerusalem* (pp. 460-472), by Johnson Pierson.

(one wonders why he omitted 21:1-9), and his interpretations would be accepted by very few today. The Holy City here is "the gospel church, returning out of her long and anti-Christian captivity." Thus, "the building of this wall, that is here spoken of, it must be understood of the recovering again the purity of those doctrines, in which the Lord Jesus, with all his benefits, is found and made ours, for our everlasting defense and safety."

Jerusalem in Christian Hymns. As early as the sixth (or, possibly, the seventh) century, a great hymn was created by the Latin Church, known by its first two lines as *Urbs beata Hierusalem, dicta pacis visio*, translated by J. M. Neale (1851) as *Blessed City, heavenly Salem, Vision dear of peace and love* (for full discussion, see John Julian: *Dictionary of Hymnology*, pp. 1198-1200).

A notable hymn, *Jerusalem the Golden*, is a part of one of the most important compositions of the later Middle Ages, *De Contemptu Mundi*, of Bernard de Morlaix (of Cluny), of the 12th century. The entire poem extends to some 3,000 lines, and is devoted to the subject of the advent of Christ to judgment, with the purpose of persuading men to have only contempt for the world. It is from the section beginning *Hora novissima*, that the great hymn *Jerusalem the Golden* derives. (See Julian 532-534. The entire work is translated by Henry Preble, with extensive notes, in the *American Journal of Theology*, 1906, X, 72-101, 286-308, 496-516. There was a critical edition published by H. C. Hoskier, 1929. See also J .M. Neale: *The Rhythm of Bernard de Morlaix, Monk of Cluny*, on the *Celestial Country*, London, 1859. The canto beginning Urbs Syon indyta, forms our hymn known as *Hail Zion, City of Our God*).

From a 15th century manuscript comes a less familiar hymn, *Jerusalem luminosa*, beginning, in the English form, *Light's abode, Celestial Salem*. (See Julian 579, 580).

Jerusalem in Art. Cities, as such, have never been a major theme in painting, and Jerusalem is no exception. Of the 750 items mentioned in the American Bible Society's *The English Bible and British and American Art*, only one painting on Jerusalem is mentioned (the one by Eastlake). Of course, there are a number of paintings of episodes in the life of Christ that occurred in the Holy City,

Mount Zion, as viewed from the east. At top center is the bell tower of the Church of Domitian, supposedly built over the tomb of David, and in right center is the Church of St. Peter. © MPS

as *Christ before the Doctors in the Temple, the Crucifixion*, etc., but these do not emphasize the subject of the city as such.

There was a famous painting by Wilhelm von Kaulbach (1805-1874), The Destruction of Jerusalem, in the New Museum, Berlin, but it is not known where it might be today, since World War II. Also, on the same theme, one hung in the New Ponakothek, in Munich.

Sir C. L. Eastlake (1793-1866), president of the Royal Academy, and Director of the National Gallery, painted the well-known *Christ Lamenting over Jerusalem*; Thomas Seddon (1821-1856) who accompanied Holman Hunt to the Holy Land, 1853, devoted five months to his moving *Jerusalem and the Valley of Jehoshaphat* (see E. T. Cook: *Popular Handbook to the Tate Gallery*, L. 1898 pp. 51-55). A painting by Thomas Hovenden (1840-1895), *Jerusalem the Golden*, is in the Metropolitan Museum of Art; another, by F. E. Church (1826-1900), *Jerusalem from the Mount of Olives*, hangs in Cooper Union, New York City; and the *Jerusalem* of Kokoschka (1886-   ) hangs in the Detroit Institute of Arts.

Bibliography. The distinguished Dutch Biblical scholar, Dr. J. Simons, in his authoritative work mentioned below has well said, "The literature on the historical topography and archaeology of Jerusalem has assumed such proportions, that it may be considered a special province within the general science of Palestinology and is probably vaster than the combined literature on all other ancient Palestinian cities and sites" (p. 35, n. 3). For nearly half a century the great two-volume work by Dr. George Adam Smith: *Jerusalem* (L. 1907, 1908), was recognized as the best work covering the Biblical data, down to the destruction of 70 A.D. Much work has since been done, however, and for the Old Testament period, by far the most important work is the great quarto volume *Jerusalem in the Old Testament*, by J. Simons (Leiden, 1952, pp. XVI, 517, with 33 plates and 66 figures).

For volumes covering the history of the city to modern times, we must for the most part, still use such works as Besant and Palmer: *History of Jeru-*salem (L. 1888); C. R. Conder: *The City of Jerusalem* (L. 1909); Lionel Cust: *Jerusalem* (L. 1924), and especially the more recent work *Jerusalem*, by Michel Join-Lambert, Ĺ., N.Y., 1958). There are excellent sections still worth reading in Baedeker's *Syria and Palestine*, third ed., London. 1893, pp. 19-93.

For specific periods one may consult Bevan: *Jerusalem under the High Priests*; Lewis B. Paton: *Jerusalem in Bible Times*, L. 1908; Guy L. Strange: *Palestine Under the Moslems*, L. 1890; Selah Merrill: *Ancient Jerusalem*, N.Y. 1908; G. Frederick Owen: *Abraham to Allenby*, Grand Rapids, 1939.

For archaeological matters, one must consult the publications of the Palestine Exploration Fund, Bliss and Dickie's *Excavations at Jerusalem* (1898), and articles appearing in the *Annual* and *Bulletin* of the American School of Oriental Research; the *Journal of the Palestine Oriental Society*; the *Quarterly* of the Department of Antiquities in Palestine; the *Biblical Archaeologist*; and the *Israel Exploration Journal*.

There are some very worth-while articles on Jerusalem in a number of encyclopedias, e.g., by G. A. Smith, in *Encyclopedia Biblica* (II 1901, vols. 2408-2432); C. R. Conder, in Hastings' *Dictionary of the Bible* (1899; II, 584-601); E. W. G. Masterman: Hastings: *Dict. of Christ and the Gospels*, (I, 849-859); Jewish Encyclopedia (N.Y., 1904 Vii, 118-157); by E. W. G. Masterman, in *International Standard Bible Encyclopedia* (1915 III, 1595-1621); more recently, *Harper's Bible Dictionary*, (New York, 1952, pp. 314-321); and, in the newly published *Baker's Bible Atlas* (Grand Rapids, 1961).

A remarkable work, not too well known in our country, published in Jerusalem in 1954, is *Jerusalem the Saga of the Holy City*, by various Jewish scholars. This is a quarto volume, which, in addition to 76 pages of text, contains 6 maps and 23 plates. Here are, for example, a view of Jerusalem in 1483, 13" x 26", in colors, with 104 sites located; a reconstruction of the city of Herod, with 60 sites indicated; a contour map of the Old City, in colors, 24" x 29", etc.   W.M.S.

JERUSALEM, NEW, a name found twice in the Bible, Revelation 3:12 and Revelation 21:2. In both references the New Jerusalem is described as coming down out of heaven from God. In Revelation 21:2 it is also called "the holy city"; and in Revelation 21:10, "that great city, the holy Jerusalem." In Revelation 21:10-22:5 the city is described in material terms, as though it were literal. It is in the form of a cube, 1500 miles square; its walls are of jasper; its streets, of gold; the foundations of the walls are precious stones; its 12 gates are of pearls. For light it needs neither moon nor sun. A pure river of water of life flows through it; and in the midst of it there is the tree of life, whose leaves are for the healing of the nations.

Views on the nature of the city, whether it is literal or symbolic, and on when it comes into existence are legion. Hardly any two expositors fully agree, but, in general, there are two main views. Some hold that the city is a symbol of the ideal church as conceived in the purpose of God and to be fully realized in His own time. The Church, allegorically depicted by the city, is of course already in existence, but God's ideal for it will not be reached until the new age has been ushered in by the Lord's return. The great size of the city denotes that the church is capable of holding almost countless numbers. The fact that the city descends "out of heaven from God" means that it is the product of God's supernatural workmanship in the historic process of redemption. In support of this view is it said that in Revelation 21:9,10, when John is told that he would be shown the bride, the Lamb's wife, he is actually shown the New Jerusalem; and, moreover, as Jerusalem and Zion are often used for the inhabitants and faithful worshipers of Jehovah, so the new Jerusalem is symbolical of the church of God.

Those who look on the New Jerusalem as a literal city usually regard it as the eternal dwelling place of God — not as a special creation of God at the beginning of the Millennium, to be inhabited by the saints, first during the Millennium, and then, after the creation of the new heaven and new earth, throughout eternity. The city will, however, not be in sight during the Millennium, but will evidently be above the earthly Jerusalem. The saints in the city will have the privilege of seeing the face of God and of having His name upon their foreheads. Some expositors hold that the New Jerusalem as a literal city does not appear above Jerusalem during the Millennium: the description in Revelation 21:10-22:5 has reference to the eternal state.   S.B.

JERUSHA, JERUSHAH (jē-rōō'sha, Heb. *yerûsha', possessed,* i.e., *married*), the wife of Uzziah, king of Judah, and mother of Jotham, his successor (II Kings 15:33; II Chron. 27:1). Her father's name was Zadok (I Chron. 6:12).

JESAIAH, JESHAIAH (jē-sā'ya, jē-shā'ya, Heb. *yesha'yâh* and *yesha'yâhû, Jehovah saves*). 1. A son of Jeduthun, and a musician in David's reign; he became the ancestral head of one of the courses of musicians (I Chron. 25:3,15).
2. A Levite, son of Rehabiah and ancestor of Shelemoth, one of David's treasurers (I Chron. 26:25).
3. A son of Hananiah, and grandson of Zerubbabel (I Chron. 3:21).
4. A son of Athaliah and descendant of Elam; he returned from Babylon with Ezra (Ezra 8:7).
5. A descendant of Merari who returned with Ezra from Babylon (Ezra 8:19).
6. A Benjamite, the father of Ithiel (Neh. 11:7).

JESHANAH (jĕsh'a-na or jē-shā'na, Heb. *yeshānâh, old*), a town near Bethel, in Ephraim, captured by Abijah from the Northern Kingdom (II Chron. 13:19). It is probably the same as the Isanos of Josephus (*Ant.* XIV, xv, 12), and is represented by the modern 'Ain Sinia, 3¼ miles N of Bethel.

JESHARELAH (jĕsh'a-rē'la, Heb. *yesar'ēlâh,* meaning doubtful), the ancestral head of the seventh course of musicians (I Chron. 25:14), called Asarelah in Verse 2.

JESHEBEAB (jē-shĕb'ē-ăb, Heb. *yeshev'āv,* meaning uncertain), the ancestral head of the 14th course of priests (I Chron. 24:13).

JESHER (jē'shĕr, Heb. *yēsher, uprightness*), a son of Caleb (I Chron. 2:18).

JESHIMON (jē-shī'mŏn, Heb. *hayeshîmōn, a waste, a desert*). The word is often used as a common noun to refer to the desert of Sinai (Deut. 32:10; Ps. 78:40; 106:14; Isa. 43:19, etc.), and is usually translated "desert." Sometimes it is used as a geographical term, and probably refers to two different districts. 1. The "desert" in the Jordan Valley, NE of the Dead Sea, which was overlooked from Pisgah (Num. 21:20; 23:28). This is a bare, salty land without any vegetation.
2. The sterile plateau into which David retired before Saul. It was near Ziph and Maon, SE of Hebron. It refers to the eastern section of the Judean hills, which stretch toward the Dead Sea. For most of the year it is bare of vegetation. Its chalky hills have always been the home of outlaws (I Sam. 23:19,24; 26:1,3).

JESHISHAI (jē-shīsh'ā-ī, Heb. *yeshîshay, aged*), a Gadite, descended from Buz (I Chron. 5:14).

JESHOHAIAH (jĕsh-ō-hā'ya, Heb. *yeshôhāyâh,* meaning unknown), a prince in Simeon (I Chron. 4:36).

JESHUA, JESHUAH (jĕsh'ū-à, Heb. *yēshūa',* another form of Joshua, *Jehovah is salvation*). 1. A name used once for Joshua, the son of Nun (Neh. 8:17).
2. Name of the head of the ninth of the 24 courses of priests (I Chron. 24:11).
3. The name of a family of Pahath-moah, which returned with Zerubbabel from Babylon to Jerusalem (Ezra 2:6; Neh. 7:11).
4. A Levite in charge of the distribution of tithes in Hezekiah's time (II Chron. 31:15).
5. The high priest who returned with Zerubbabel (Ezra 2:2; Neh. 7:7, called "Joshua" in Haggai 1:1 and in Zech. 3:1ff). He helped to rebuild the altar (Ezra 3:2,8) and the house of God (Ezra 4:3; 5:2).
6. A Levitical family with oversight of the workmen in the temple (Ezra 2:40; 3:9; Neh. 7:43). It also assisted in explaining the Law to the people (Neh. 8:7), in leading in the worship (Neh. 9:4), and in sealing the covenant (Neh. 10:9). From the last passage, it appears that Jeshua was the son of Azaniah.
7. A post-Exilic town in the S of Judah (Neh. 11:26). It is identified with Tell es-Sa'weh and may be the same as the Shema of Joshua 15:26.

JESHURUN, JESURUN (jĕsh'ū-rŭn, jĕs'ū-rŭn, Heb. *yeshūrûn, upright one*), a poetical or ideal title of Israel. Except in Deuteronomy 32:15, where it is used in reproach of Israel, because it had departed from its moral ideal, it is always used as a title of honor (Deut. 33:5,26; Isa. 44:2).

JESIAH (jē-sī'a, Heb. *yishshîyâh*). I Chronicles 23:20. See ISSHIAH.

JESIMIEL (jē-sĭm'ĭ-ĕl, Heb. *yesîmi'ēl, God establishes*), a prince of Simeon (I Chron. 4:36).

JESSE (jĕs'ē, Heb. *yishay,* meaning uncertain), son of Obed, of the family of Perez. He was descended from Nahshon, chief of the tribe of Judah in the days of Moses, and was the grandson of Boaz, whose wife was Ruth the Moabitess (Ruth 4:18-22). From his descent and from the fact that when Saul pursued David he entrusted his parents to the care of the king of Moab (I Sam. 22:3,4), we can assume that he was the chief man of his village. He had eight sons, of whom the youngest was David (I Sam. 17:12-14), and two daughters, the latter being by a different wife from David's mother (I Chron. 2:16; cf. II Sam. 17:25). Jesse lived at Bethlehem, and probably had land outside the town wall, like Boaz. When Samuel went to Jesse to anoint a king from among his sons, neither of them at first discerned God's choice. Jesse had not even thought it worth while to call his youngest son to the feast (I Sam. 16:11). He is almost always mentioned in connection with his son David. After Saul had quarreled with David, he usually called him the son of Jesse (I Sam. 20:31; 22:7; 25:10), undoubtedly in derision of David's relatively humble origin. We are not told when Jesse died. The contrast between his small beginnings and future glory is brought out in Isaiah 11:1,10 and Micah 5:2.

JESUI (jĕs'ū-ī). 1. A son of Asher, and founder of a tribal family (Gen. 46:17; Num. 26:44; I Chron. 7:30).

2. A son of Saul (I Sam. 14:49).

JESUS, JESUS CHRIST (See Christ)

JETHER (jē'thêr, Heb. *yether, abundance, excellence*). 1. In Exodus 4:18 for Jethro, father-in-law of Moses (see KJVm).

2. Gideon's eldest son (Judg. 8:20,21), who was asked by his father to slay the captives, Zebah and Zalmunna, but he shrank from doing so, and thus they escaped the shame of dying at the hands of a boy.

3. The father of Amasa, Absalom's commander-in-chief (I Kings 2:5). According to I Chronicles 2:17, he was an Ishmaelite.

4. A descendant of Judah through Jerahmeel (I Chron. 2:32).

5. A Judahite, the son of Ezrah (I Chron. 4:17).

6. A man of Asher, apparently the same as Ithran, son of Zophah (cf. I Chron. 7:37 with vs. 38).

JETHETH (je'thĕth, Heb. *yethĕth,* meaning unknown), a clan chieftain of Edom (Gen. 36:40; I Chron. 1:51).

JETHLAH (jĕth'là, Heb. *yithlâh, a hanging* or *lofty place*), a town of Dan (Josh. 19:42), about three miles E of Yalo (Aijalon).

JETHRO (jĕth'rō, Heb. *yithrô, excellence*), a priest of Midian and father-in-law of Moses (Exod. 3:1). Reuel, which means friend of God, seems to have been his personal name (Exod. 2:18; 3:1), and Jethro, his honorary title. When Moses fled from Egypt to Midian, he was welcomed into the household of Jethro because of his kindness to the priest's seven daughters, whom he helped water their flocks. Moses married Zipporah, one of the daughters, and kept his father-in-law's flocks for about 40 years (Exod. 3:1,2). After the Lord commanded Moses to return to Egypt to deliver the enslaved Israelites, Jethro gave him permission to depart. Moses took with him his wife Zipporah and their two sons (Exod. 4:18-20), but later sent the three back temporarily to stay with Jethro. After the deliverance from Egypt, before the Israelites reached Sinai, Jethro came to see Moses, bringing back to him his daughter and her two sons (Exod. 18:1-7). We are told that he "rejoiced for all the

The Valley of Jethro, or Jethro's Pass, below Mount Sinai, showing the ancient monastery of St. Katherine, occupied for the last 1500 years by Greek Orthodox monks and containing a famous ancient library of scrolls, etc. © MPS

goodness which Jehovah had done to Israel," and offered a burnt offering to Jehovah. When he saw how occupied Moses was in deciding disputes among his people, he suggested the appointment of judges of various grades to help him dispose of cases of minor importance. Moses acted on his advice. Thereafter, Jethro returned to his own country.

JETUR (jē'têr, Heb. *yetûr,* meaning uncertain), a people descended from Ishmael (Gen. 25:15; I Chron. 1:31). The 2½ tribes warred against this clan (I Chron. 5:18f). They are the Itureans of NT times.

JEUEL (jē-ū'ĕl, Heb. *ye'û'ēl,* meaning unknown). 1. A man of Judah who with 690 of his clan lived at Jerusalem (I Chron. 9:6).

2. A Levite who took part in the reformation under Hezekiah (II Chron. 29:13).

3. A leader of Ezra's company (Ezra 8:13, Jeiel in KJV).

JEUSH (jē'ush, Heb. *ye'ûsh, he comes to help*). 1. A son of Esau by his wife Oholibamah (Gen. 36:5).

2. A Benjamite, son of Bilhan (I Chron. 7:10).

3. A Gershonite Levite (I Chron. 23:10,11).

4. A descendant of Jonathan (I Chron. 8:39, Jehush KJV).

5. A son of Rehoboam (II Chron. 11:19).

JEUZ (jē'ûz, Heb. *ye'ûts, he counsels*), a Benjamite, son of Shaharaim by his wife Hodesh (I Chron. 8:10).

JEW (Heb. *yehûdî,* Gr. *Ioudaíos,* Lat. *Iudaeus*). This word does not occur before the period of Jeremiah in OT literature. Originally it denoted one belonging to the tribe of Judah or to the two tribes of the Southern Kingdom (II Kings 16:6; 25:25), but later its meaning was extended, and it was applied to anyone of the Hebrew race who returned from the Captivity. As most of the exiles came from Judah, and as they were the main historical representatives of ancient Israel, the term Jew came finally to comprehend all of the Hebrew race throughout the world (Esth. 2:5; Matt. 2:2). As early as the days of Hezekiah the language of Judah was called Jewish. In the OT the adjective applies only to the Jews' language or speech (II Kings 18:26,28; Neh. 13:24; Isa. 36:11,13). In the Gospels "Jews" (always pl.) is the usual term for Israelites; and in the NT Jews (Israelites) and Gentiles are sometimes contrasted (Mark 7:3; John 2:6; Acts 10:28). Paul warns against "Jewish fables" in Titus 1:14, and speaks of the "Jews' religion" in Galatians 1:13,14.   S.B.

JEWEL, JEWELRY. Orientals are much more given to adorning themselves with jewelry than Occidentals. This was true in ancient times as well as now. There are consequently many allusions to jewelry in Scripture. Among the articles of jewelry in OT times were diadems, bracelets, necklaces, anklets, rings for the fingers, gold nets for the hair, pendants, head-tire gems, amulets and pendants with magical meanings, jeweled perfume and ointment boxes, and crescents for camels. Many were acquired as booty in war. Many were personal gifts, especially at betrothals. At the court of every king there were special quarters for goldsmiths, and silversmiths were a familiar sight in the silver markets of large cities. Jewelry was used not only for personal adornment and utility, but also for religious festivals. Custom required the use of rich, festal garments and a gorgeous display of jewelry when approaching the deity. When the worship was over, they were taken off. What became of all these jewels? Many were buried in the ground for safekeeping in time of war and were never recovered; others were carried away as booty by conquerors. A surprisingly large number have been unearthed.

Among the oldest jewels discovered in Bible lands are those found in 1927 by the archaeologist Sir Leonard Woolley in the Sumerian city of Ur, the heathen city which Abraham left for the Promised Land. In his excavations he found a hoard of jeweled wealth in the royal tombs, in which Queen Shub-ad, her husband, and her faithful court had been buried about 2500 B.C. Buried with the queen were 68 court ladies who in full regalia had walked alive into the tomb and had sat in orderly rows to die, thus showing their loyalty to her. In the royal tombs were found the queen's personal ornaments, including her diadem, a cape of polished gold and precious stones, rings, seals, earrings, amulets, and pins of gold. With the court ladies were found hair ribbons made of fine beaten gold. Ancient Sumerian artists were capable of producing filigree work with gold at least equal in delicacy with the best done by goldsmiths today.

Artist's reconstruction of a scene in the death pit, in the royal tombs of the city of Ur. UMP

The servant of Abraham, sent to Mesopotamia to find a bride for Isaac, gave to Rebekah after she had watered his camels an earring and two bracelets made of gold; and at her betrothal to Isaac gave her also jewels of silver and of gold, and to others in the family he also gave precious things (Gen. 24:22,30,53).

When the Israelites left Egypt with Moses, "they borrowed of the Egyptians jewels of silver, and jewels of gold" (Exod. 12:35). Not much later, while Moses was on Mount Sinai receiving the law, they took the golden earrings worn by men and women and gave them to Aaron to make a golden calf (Exod. 32:2-4). As evidence of their repentance, they were commanded by Moses to strip themselves of their ornaments (Exod. 33:4-6). For the building of the first tabernacle, the people contributed, at Moses' request, bracelets, earrings, rings, tablets, and jewels of gold (Exod. 35:22).

Exodus 39 gives a description of the official garments of the Jewish High Priest, worn when discharging his peculiar duties. They were gorgeous in their jeweled splendor. The robe of the ephod, a long, blue, sleeveless garment, was adorned below with a fringe of alternate pomegranates and bells of gold. Over the robe of the ephod there was worn the ephod, a shorter, richly-embroidered vestment intended for the front and back of the body. It was made of two parts clasped together at the shoulders by onyx stones. Over the ephod there was a breastplate, described as square, made of gold thread and fine twisted linen, set with four rows of precious stones, three in a row, each inscribed with the name of a tribe of Israel. The first row was a sardius, a topaz, and a carbuncle; the second, an emerald, a sapphire, and a diamond; the third, a ligure, an agate, and an amethyst; and the fourth, a beryl, an onyx, and a jasper. Each stone was set in a gold mounting. Golden chains and rings fastened the breastplate to the ephod of the priest at his shoulders and to the blue lacers of the woven bands. The miter was surmounted by a crown of pure gold, on which was attached a gold plate engraved with the words, "Holiness to the Lord."

In the period of the judges, Gideon, after turning down the offer of kingship, requested that every man cast into a spread garment all the gold earrings, crescents, necklaces, and camel chains captured from the Midianites. With these he made an ephod, which later became a snare to Israel when the people came to regard it idolatrously (Judg. 8:24-27).

Until about 1000 B.C. gold and silver were not common in Palestine, and even iron was so scarce that jewelry was made of it for kings. Archaeology has uncovered comparatively little indigenous Palestinian art. Fragments of jewelry that have been found in excavated palaces of kings is the work of imported artists. Such finds have been made at Megiddo, a fortress-city guarding the Plain of Esdraelon which was destroyed in the period of the judges.

David accumulated a large mass of jewels, mostly gotten in conquests against Syrians, Moabites, Ammonites, Amalekites, and Philistines. All these he dedicated to Jehovah (II Sam. 8:7,8) and passed on to Solomon for the building of the temple in Jerusalem. When his nobles saw what he was donating, they brought for the same purpose gold, silver, brass, and iron; and the common people added what they could (I Chron. 28). We are told that in the reign of Solomon gold was "not anything accounted of" (II Chron. 9:20), and silver was as abundant as stones around Jerusalem. The

Queen of Sheba brought to Solomon gold and precious stones. The throne of Solomon was overlaid with gold; the steps leading to it were of gold; his footstool was of gold; his drinking cups were all of gold; and "all the vessels of the house of the forest of Lebanon were of pure gold" (II Chron. 9:20). In the succeeding reigns of the kings of Judah and Israel both monarchs and people gave increasing regard to accumulations of jewelry. Repeatedly OT prophets warned the Israelites that apostasy would be punished with the loss of their gems (Ezek. 23:26).

A jeweled necklace, from Ras Shamra, with beads of gold, silver, amber and pearls, from about 1400 B.C. Above, a signet ring from Jericho, and below, an ear-ring from Megiddo. DV

Not a great deal is said about jewelry in the NT, and what is said is mostly condemnatory. Jesus twice mentioned jewels, in the parable of the pearl merchant and in the saying about casting pearls before swine. Paul exhorts Christian women not to rely for adornment upon "broidered hair, or gold, or pearls, or costly array" (I Tim. 2:9). James warns his readers not to give preference to a man who comes into their assembly with a gold ring and fine apparel, as though he were better than a poor man (James 2:2). In the Revelation of John the destruction of Babylon is described in terms of merchants who can no longer sell "merchandise of gold, and silver, and precious stones, and of pearls" (Rev. 18:12). The New Jerusalem is described in Revelation 21 as having a wall of jasper, and the foundations of the walls are garnished "with all manner of precious stones" (Rev. 21:19)—jasper, sapphire, chalcedony, emerald, sardonyx, sardius, chrysolyte, beryl, topaz,

chrysoprasus, jacinth, and amethyst — a list recalling the list of precious stones in the breastplate of the High Priest. S.B.

JEZANIAH (jĕz-à-nī'à, Heb. *yezanyāhû*, probably *Jehovah hears*), a captain of the forces, son of Hoshaiah, a Maacathite. He lived at the time of the fall of Jerusalem. II Kings 25:23; Jeremiah 40: 7,8; 42:1.

JEZEBEL (jĕz'ĕ-bĕl, Heb. *'îzevel*, meaning uncertain, perhaps *unexalted, unhusbanded*). 1. Daughter of Ethbaal, king of the Zidonians, and queen of Ahab, king of Israel (c. 874-853 B.C.) She had been brought up a zealous worshiper of Baal, and as the queen of Ahab she not only continued her ancestral religion, but tried to impose it upon the people of Israel. To please her, Ahab built a temple and an altar to Baal in Samaria (I Kings 16: 32). Four hundred fifty prophets of Baal ate at her table (I Kings 18:19). She slew all the prophets of Jehovah on whom she could lay her hands (I Kings 18:4-13). When she was told of the slaughter of the prophets of Baal by Elijah, she threatened his life, and he was obliged to flee. In II Kings 9:7 we are told that the slaying of Ahab's family was a punishment for the persecution of the prophets of Jehovah by Jezebel. Later, she secured Naboth's vineyard for Ahab by causing its owner to be judicially murdered (I Kings 21). When Elijah heard of this crime, he told Ahab that God's vengeance would fall upon him and that dogs would eat Jezebel's body by the wall of Jezreel. The prophecy was fulfilled when, 11 years after the death of Ahab, Jehu executed pitiless vengeance upon the royal household. Jezebel painted her face and attired her head, and standing at an open window taunted him for being his master's murderer. Jehu asked those who were on his side to throw her down, and this was unhesitatingly done by some eunuchs. Jehu drove over her body with his chariot, and her blood spattered the horses and the wall. Later he gave directions that she be buried, but it was found that dogs had left nothing of her but the skull, the feet, and the palms of the hands (II Kings 9:7,30-37).

2. In Revelation 2:20, in the letter to Thyatira, we read of "the woman Jezebel, who calleth herself a prophetess," and led some members of the Christian Church there to commit spiritual fornication. This may be a symbolic name, given because of a resemblance between her and the idolatrous wife of Ahab. S.B.

JEZER (jē'zēr, Heb. *yetser, form, purpose*), a son of Naphtali, and founder of a tribal family (Gen. 46:24; Num. 26:49; I Chron. 7:13).

JEZIAH (jē-zī'à, Heb. *yizzîyâh, Jehovah unites*), a faithful Jew of the family of Parosh who was one of those who put away their foreign wives (Ezra 10:25).

JEZIEL (jē'zĭ-ĕl, Heb. *yezû'êl,* meaning uncertain), a Benjamite, son of Azmaveth, who became one of David's recruits at Ziklag (I Chron. 12:3).

JEZLIAH (jĕz-lī'à, Heb. *yizlî'âh, Jehovah delivers*), a son of Elpaal, of the tribe of Benjamin (I Chron. 8:18).

JEZOAR (jē-zō'êr, Heb. *yitshār, the shining one*), a man of Judah, family of Hezron, son of Ashur (I Chron. 4:5-7).

JEZRAHIAH (jĕz-rà-hī'à, Heb. *yizrahyâh, Jehovah appears, or shines*). 1. A descendant of Issachar, family of Tola, and son of Uzzi (I Chron. 7:3).

2. The leader of the singing at the purification of the people in the time of Nehemiah (Neh. 12: 42).

The so-called Tower of Jezebel in the village of Jezreel (Zerin) on the Plain of Esdraelon. © MPS

JEZREEL (jĕz'rē-ĕl, jĕz'rēl, Heb. *yizre'e'l, God soweth*). 1. A city on the border of the territory of Issachar (Josh. 19:18), not far from Mount Gilboa. The Israelites made their camp near it before the battle of Gilboa (I Sam. 29:1), its people remaining faithful to the house of Saul. Abner set Ishbosheth over it among other places (II Sam. 2:9). Ahab built a palace there (I Kings 21:1), and his son Joram also lived there (II Kings 8:29). Naboth was a Jezreelite, and he was stoned outside the city for refusing to give up his vineyard to Ahab (I Kings 21). Jehu ordered that the heads of Ahab's 70 sons be placed in heaps at the gate of Jezreel (II Kings 10:1-11). Jezebel met her death by being thrown from a window of the palace in Jezreel, and it was there that her body was eaten by dogs (II Kings 9:30-35). Jezreel was the scene of the meetings between Elijah and Ahab (I Kings 21:17ff).

From the time of the Crusades the site of Jezreel has been identified with the modern village, Zer'in, on the northwestern spur of Gilboa, but this identification is now questioned because excavations have failed to reveal any evidence of Israelite occupation in ancient times. From Jezreel there was a splendid view of the plain reaching toward the Jordan (Josh. 17:16; Hos. 1:5). Throughout history it has been a battlefield of nations. In the OT the term "valley of Jezreel" is applied to this valley, and not to the great plain immediately N of Carmel which is better known as the Plain of Esdraelon or the Plain of Megiddo.

2. A town in the hill country of Judah from which David obtained his wife Ahinoam the Jezreelitess (I Sam. 25:43; 27:3).

3. A descendant of Judah (I Chron. 4:3).

4. A son of the prophet Hosea, so called because God had declared that He would avenge the blood of Jezreel on the house of Jehu (Hos. 1:4,5).

JIBSAM (jĭb'săm, Heb. *yivsām, fragrant*), a descendant of Issachar, family of Tolah (I Chron. 7:2).

JIDLAPH (jĭd'lăf, Heb. *yidhlāph*, perhaps *he weeps*), a son of Nahor and Milcah, and the ancestral head of a Nahorite clan (Gen. 22:22).

JIMNA (jĭm'nà, Heb. *yimnâh*, probably *good fortune*), a son of Asher (Num. 26:44).

JIPHTAH (jĭf'tà, Heb. *yiphtāh*), an unidentified town in the Shephelah of Judah. It is named with Libnah, Ether, and Ashan (Josh. 15:43).

JIPHTHAH-EL (jĭf'thà-ĕl, Heb. *yiphtah'ēl*), the valley of Iphthah-el lay on the N border of Zebulun (Josh. 19:14,27). It is probably to be identified with the modern Tell Jefat, nine miles NW of Nazareth.

JOAB (jō'ăb, Heb. *yô'āv, Jehovah is father*). 1. The second of the three sons of Zeruiah, the half-sister of David, the other two being Abishai and Asahel (II Sam. 8:16; I Chron. 2:16). He first appears in public life in the narrative of David's war with Ishbosheth for the throne left vacant by Saul's death. He was David's captain of the host, while Abner led the forces of Ishbosheth. When the two armies met, a tournament took place between 12 men from each side, followed by a general engagement in which, after Joab's men were routed, Asahel was killed in his pursuit of Abner (II Sam. 2:12-32). When Abner transferred his allegiance to David, Joab treacherously slew him, with the connivance of Abishai, for killing Asahel at the battle of Gibeon, although Abner had done so in self-defense. David declared himself innocent of this murder, and after composing a lament for Abner, commanded that there be a period of public mourning for the dead man (II Sam. 3:31). David pronounced a curse upon Joab and his descendants, but he did not bring him to justice, perhaps because he was politically too weak to do so.

Joab was made the commander of all David's armies as a reward for his being the first to enter the fortress on Mount Zion when that stronghold was assaulted. In the war against the Ammonites, which was declared when David's ambassadors to the king had been maltreated, Joab achieved a great victory, utterly routing the enemy (II Sam. 10:1-14; I Chron. 19:1-15); and after a resumption of this war he called for David to storm the town of Rabbah, which he himself had successfully besieged, in order that David might have the credit for the victory (II Sam. 11:1; 12:26-29). It was during this war that David got Joab to put Uriah in the forefront of a battle that he might be killed and David be free to marry Bathsheba (II Sam. 11:6-27).

Joab again attempted to have Absalom restored to royal favor after a three year banishment because of the murder of his brother Amnon. He arranged for a "wise woman" of Tekoa to bring to David an imaginary complaint about a son of hers who had killed his brother and whose life was now sought, a story paralleling David's own experience with Absalom. David saw in the story a rebuke of his own treatment of Absalom, and gave permission to Absalom to return to Jerusalem, although he was to remain in his own house and was not allowed to see his father (II Sam. 14:1-24). Joab resisted Absalom's attempts to get him to intercede with his father for a complete restoration, until his barley field was set on fire by the prince (II Sam. 14:28-33). Joab then got David to receive his son back into the royal home.

When Absalom revolted, he made Amasa, another nephew of David, general instead of Joab

(II Sam. 17:24f). Joab remained loyal to David, and when the king fled, pursued by Absalom, he led one of the three divisions of the royal forces and defeated the rebels. Informed that Absalom was caught in a tree by his hair, he first scolded his informer for not having killed him, and then himself killed the prince by thrusting three darts through his heart. When David gave vent to extravagant grief at the death of his rebel son, Joab sternly rebuked him (II Sam. 19:1-8).

On David's return to Jerusalem, Joab was replaced as captain of David's forces by Amasa. Shortly after this, Sheba, a Benjamite, led a revolt against David; and when Amasa took more time than was deemed necessary to prepare to quell it, David asked Abishai to take the field. Joab seems to have gone with him. The two met Amasa at Gibeon, and there Joab, on pretense of kissing his rival, slew him. He then assumed command of Amasa's men, besieged Sheba in Abel of Beth-maachah, and arranged with a woman of the city to deliver to him the head of Shebah. Thus ended the revolt.

Joab was opposed to David's suggestion of a census, but eventually carried it out, although he intentionally did the work imperfectly (II Sam. 24:1-9; I Chron. 21:1-6). He supported Adonijah in his claim to the throne, but deserted him on hearing that Solomon had been proclaimed king (I Kings 1:7,28-49). David on his deathbed made known that Joab should be brought to justice for the murders of Abner and of Amasa (I Kings 2:5). At the order of Solomon, Joab was slain as he clung to the horns of the altar in the court of the tabernacle. His slayer was Benaiah, chief of the bodyguard, who became his successor as head of the army. He was buried in his own house in the wilderness (I Kings 2:5,6,28-34).

2. Son of Seraiah and descendant of Kenaz of the tribe of Judah. He was father of the valley of Charashim, or valley of craftsmen (I Chron. 4:14).

3. Founder of a family of returned exiles (Ezra 2:6; 8:9; Neh. 7:11).

4. A village, apparently in Judah (I Chron. 2:54, RV). In the KJV the name is rendered "Ataroth, the house of Joab." S.B.

JOAH (jō′à, Heb. *yô′āh, Jehovah is brother*). 1. A son of Obed-edom (I Chron. 26:4).

2. A Levite, son of Zimmah and a descendant of Gershom (I Chron. 6:21). He may be the Levite who helped in the religious reformation under King Hezekiah (II Chron. 29:12).

3. Son of Asaph and recorder under King Hezekiah (II Kings 18:18,26; Isa. 36:3,11,22). He was one of the three men sent by Hezekiah to speak to the Assyrian envoys at the siege of Jerusalem.

4. Son of Joahaz and recorder under King Josiah (II Chron. 34:8).

JOAHAZ (jō′à-hăz, Heb. *yô′āhāz, Jehovah has grasped*), father of Joah, who was the recorder of King Josiah (II Chron. 34:8).

JOANNA (jō-ăn′à, Gr. *Ioána* or *Ioánna*). 1. The wife of Chuza, Herod's steward. She was one of the women "which had been healed of evil spirits and infirmities" who ministered to Jesus and His disciples of their substance during His Galilean ministry (Luke 8:2,3). Along with some other women, she accompanied Jesus from Galilee to Jerusalem. With them she prepared spices and ointments for His burial and went to the tomb with the intention of embalming the body of Jesus, and there received from the angels the message of the resurrection (Luke 23:55,56; 24:10).

2. An ancestor of Christ mentioned in Luke's genealogy (3:27). He lived about 500 B.C.

JOASH, I (jō′ăsh, Heb. *yô′āsh, Jehovah has given*), a shorter form of "Jehoash." 1. A man of Manasseh, and father of Gideon (Judg. 6:11,15). Although Gideon says that the family was the poorest in Manasseh, Joash was undoubtedly a man of substance, as Gideon was able to command ten servants to destroy the altar of Baal and the Asherah (Judg. 6:27,34). Even though the altar had been erected by Joash, he refused to hand over his son to punishment for the sacrilege, declaring that if Baal was really a god, he should avenge himself (Judg. 6:11-32).

2. A son of Ahab (I Kings 22:26; II Chron. 18:25). Ahab handed Micaiah the prophet over to the custody of Joash and Amon.

3. A Benjamite of Gibeah who joined David's recruits at Ziklag (I Chron. 12:3).

4. A man of Judah, family of Shelah (I Chron. 4:22).

5. Son of Ahaziah, king of Judah. When Joash was an infant, his father was murdered, and he too would have been slain along with the rest of the royal family, had not the late king's sister hidden him in the temple. In the seventh year he was brought out and crowned king. He reigned for 40 years. For the first part of his reign he was under the direction of the godly high priest, Jehoiada, but after the death of this wise and pious man, he led his people into idolatry. When Zechariah, the son of Jehoiada, denounced this apostasy, Joash had him murdered. After a long illness, he was slain in his bed by his servants for the murder of Zechariah (II Kings 12:20; II Chron. 24:25).

6. Son of Jehoahaz, king of Israel. He began to reign c. 800 B.C., and reigned 16 years. Although he worshiped the two calves at Bethel and Dan, he had a high regard for Elisha the prophet, who told him that he was to gain three victories over the Syrians. Amaziah, the king of Judah, forced him into a battle at Beth-shemesh, in which Joash was victorious. When he died, he was succeeded by his son, Jeroboam II.

JOASH, II (jō′ăsh, Heb. *yô′āsh, Jehovah has come to help*). 1. A Benjamite, family of Becher (I Chron. 7:8).

2. One of David's officers. He was in charge of the cellars of oil (I Chron. 27:28). S.B.

JOATHAM (jō′à-thăm, Gr. *Ioátham*), the KJV for RV "Jotham" (Matt. 1:9). He was a king of Judah, the son of Uzziah.

JOB (jōb, Heb. *′îyôv*, meaning uncertain). The formal kinship of Job is with eastern *hokmây* (wisdom) literature. Within the canon of the OT, the function of the wisdom books (cf. also Prov.,Eccl., and in a sense S. of Sol.) was to apply the foundational Mosaic revelation to the problems of human existence and conduct as they were being formulated in the philosophical circles of the world. A figure like Job, standing outside the Abrahamic-Mosaic administrations of the Covenant, was an ideal vehicle for Biblical wisdom doctrine, concerned as it was with the common ways and demands of God rather than His peculiarly theocratic government of Israel.

Even the approximate date of the anonymous author is uncertain. The events he narrates belong to the early patriarchal period, as is evident from features like Job's longevity, revelation by theophany outside the Abrahamic Covenant, the nomadic status of the Chaldeans, and early social and economic practices. But the question is: When was the Joban tradition transformed by the inspired author into the canonical book of Job?

Modern discussions of authorship and date are

perplexed by critical doubts concerning the unity of the book. Most widely suspected of being interpolations into an original poem are the prologue-epilogue, the wisdom hymn (chap. 28), the discourse of Elihu (chaps. 32-37), and parts at least of the Lord's discourses (chaps. 38-41). The LXX text of Job is about one-fifth shorter than the Massoretic but the LXX omissions exhibit an editorial pattern of reduction. The argument for interpolations, therefore, leans primarily on internal considerations — language, style, alleged inconsistencies of viewpoint. Conservative scholars, however, agree that the internal evidence points compellingly to the book's integrity, though they of course allow for corruption in textual details.

Dates have been assigned by 20th century critics all the way from the Mosaic to the Maccabean ages. The early extreme is obviated by the nature of the development of the OT canon; the late extreme, for one thing, by the discovery among the Dead Sea Scrolls of fragments of a Joban manuscript in old Hebrew script. The majority of negative critics favor an Exilic or post-Exilic date. Conservatives favor the pre-Exilic era, especially the Solomonic age because Biblical *ḥokmâ* flourished then, and there are close affinities in sentiment and expression between Job and Psalms (cf. Pss. 88, 89) and Proverbs produced at that time. The same evidence indicates an Israelite identity for the anonymous author, conceivably one of Solomon's wisdom coterie (cf. I Kings 4:29-34). The theory that he was an Edomite has found little support; that he was Egyptian, still less.

Outline:

I. DESOLATION: The Trial of Job's Wisdom. 1:1-2:10.

II. COMPLAINT: The Way of Wisdom Lost. 2:11-3:26.

III. JUDGMENT: The Way of Wisdom Darkened and Illuminated. 4:1-41:34.
   A. The Verdicts of Men. 4:1-37:24.
     1. First Cycle of Debate. 4:1-14:22.
     2. Second Cycle of Debate. 15:1-21:34.
     3. Third Cycle of Debate. 22:1-31:40.
     4. Ministry of Elihu. 32:1-37:24.
   B. The Voice of God. 38:1-41:34.

IV. CONFESSION: The Way of Wisdom Regained. 42:1-6.

V. RESTORATION: The Triumph of Job's Wisdom. 42:7-17.

Stylistic comparison of other ancient wisdom writings with Job reveals similarities but also Job's uniqueness. The dialogue form of Job is paralleled to an extent in Egyptian and Babylonian wisdom poetry, and the various individual literary genres employed in Job (psalms of lament and thanksgiving, proverb, covenant oath, etc.), were not novelties. Nevertheless, as a masterly blend of a remarkably rich variety of forms, within a historical framework, with exquisite lyric and dramatic qualities, and all devoted to didactic purpose, Job creates its own literary species. Of particular significance is the bracketing of the poetic dialogue within the prose (or better, semi-poetic) prologue and epilogue. This ABA structure is attested elsewhere (e.g., Code of Hammurabi, The Eloquent Peasant) and thus supports the book's integrity.

The Joban revelation is a reproclamation of the fundamental stipulation of the Covenant, a call for perfect consecration to the covenant Suzerain. This call is issued through a dramatization of a crisis in redemptive history. God challenges Satan to behold in Job the triumphing of divine grace.

This faithful servant epitomizes the fulfillment of God's evangelical decree, which even in its initial enunciation had taken the form of an imprecatory challenge to the tempter (Gen. 3:15). By proving under fierce temptation the genuineness of his devotion to God, Job is to vindicate the veracity of his God as the author of redemptive promise and His sovereignty in putting enmity between His people and Satan. Prostrated by well-nigh total bereavement, he utters doxology. While hopelessly despondent and protesting passionately against what he interprets as an unjust divine sentence upon him, it is still to God that Job turns and cries. And he repentantly commits himself anew to his Lord, although the Voice from the whirlwind has offered neither explanation of the mystery of his past sufferings nor promise of future restoration from his desolation. By following the covenant way, Job shows himself ready by God's grace, and contrary to Satan's insinuations, to serve his Lord for nought.

The particular purpose of Job as *ḥokmâ* is to articulate this covenant concept in terms of the current discussions of eastern sages, indicating the religious perspective which must inform the philosophical quest; in short, to point the direction for a true apologetic for the faith. The doctrine of God as incomprehensible Creator and sovereign Lord is offered, therefore, not only as the fundamental reality man must reckon with as a religious being serving God amid the historical tensions of this life, but also as the presupposition he must start with as a philosophical being bent on the interpretative adventure. This enterprise is illustrated by the debate of Job and his friends over the problem of theodicy, and the folly of the traditional methodology founded on human observation and speculation is portrayed by the silencing of the trio who represent it. The book of Job identifies the way of the covenant with the way of wisdom (cf. 28:28) and so brings philosophy under the authority of divine revelation.

No comprehensive answer is given to the problem of suffering since theodicy is not the book's major theme; nevertheless, considerable light is afforded. In addition to the prologue's contribution is that of Elihu, who traces the mystery to the principle of divine grace; sufferings are a sovereign gift, calling to repentance and life. Moreover, impressive assurance is given that God as a just and omnipotent covenant Lord will ultimately visit both the curses and blessings of the covenant on His subjects according to righteousness. Especially significant are the insights Job himself attains into the role God will play as his heavenly vindicator, redeeming his name from all calumnies and his life from the king of terrors. Job utters in raw faith what progressive revelation elaborates in the doctrines of the eschatological theophany, resurrection of the dead, and final redemptive judgment. This vision does not reveal the why of the particular sufferings of Job or any other believer, but it does present the servants of God with a framework of hope.
                     M.G.K.

JOBAB (jō′băb, Heb. *yôvāv, to call loudly, howl*).
1. An Arabian tribe descended from Joktan (Gen. 10:29; I Chron. 1:23).
2. The second king of Edom. He was the son of Zerah of Bozrah (Gen. 36:33; I Chron. 1:44,45).
3. A king of Madon. He joined the northern confederacy against Joshua, but he and his allies were thoroughly defeated at the waters of Merom (Josh. 11:1; 12:19).
4. A Benjamite (I Chron. 8:9).
5. A Benjamite (I Chron. 8:18).

JOCHEBED (jŏk′ĕ-bĕd, Heb. *yôkhevedh, Jehovah is glory*), daughter of Levi, wife of Amram and mother of Moses (Exod. 6:20; Num. 26:59). She was a sister of Kohath, Amram's father (Exod. 6:20).

JOED (jō′ĕd, Heb. *yô′ēdh, Jehovah is witness*), a Benjamite, descended from Jeshaiah (Neh. 11:7).

JOEL (jō′ĕl, Heb. *yô′ēl, Jehovah is God*).

1. **The Prophet.** Joel the son of Pethuel is the author of the second of the Minor Prophets books. Concerning the man, his life and times we know nothing. His name, meaning "The Lord (Yahweh) is God," was a common one, for a dozen other persons mentioned in the OT bear it (see below).

The Book. The book of Joel is without the customary dating formula used by the prophets (Hos. 1:1; Amos 1:1) and nowhere indicates the date either of the ministry of the prophet Joel or of the writing of the book. Indirect references throughout the book have been claimed in support of dates which have differed from each other by as much as half a millennium.

Scholars who follow the traditional viewpoint believe the book to be pre-Exilic, written perhaps during the reign of the boy king Joash (837-800 B.C.), for the following reasons: 1. The enemies of Judah which are mentioned, the Philistines and Phoenicians (3:4), Egypt and Edom (3:19) are those of the pre-exilic period (II Kings 8:20-22; II Chron. 21:16,17) rather than the Assyrians and Babylonians who later molested Judah. 2. Amos seems to be acquainted with Joel's prophecies (3: 16; cf. Amos 1:2; 3:18; cf. Amos 9:13). 3. The fact that the elders and priests are mentioned rather than the king would seem to point to the time of Joash's minority (II Kings 11:21). 4. The location of the book between two early prophets and its style, quite different from that of the post-Exilic prophets, have also been mentioned.

Many modern scholars believe the book to have been written much later, about 350 B.C. Others deny its unity and claim that the apocalyptic elements come from a time as late as 200 B.C. Thus it is claimed that Joel is the last OT prophetic book. Some arguments for the book's late date: 1. There is no reference to the northern kingdom, Israel. 2. The Greeks are mentioned in 3:6. This is believed by some to be a reference to the Seleucid line which ruled Palestine in the second century B.C. Even if the identification of the "Greeks" with the Seleucids is tenuous, it is felt that the Hebrews would hardly have known about the Greek people before the Exile. 3. References to the destruction of Jerusalem are detected in 3:1-3,17b. 4. Certain other arguments depend on a radical reconstruction of Israel's history and hardly need to be considered here.

The unity of the book may be taken for granted, since it is conceded by many radical critics today. The arguments for a late date are not too strong. In such a short book there need be no reference to the northern kingdom, and it is quite possible that the Hebrews may have known the Greeks at a time well before the Exile. It should be added that since the book makes no claim as to its date, this matter is not of primary importance. Locust plagues are frequent in the Near East and almost any such visitation would provide a background for this book.

The occasion of the book was a devastating locust plague. Those who have not experienced such a calamity can hardly appreciate its destruction. An article, with convincing photographic illustrations appeared in the *National Geographic*

A vineyard stripped of every leaf, and the branches left bare and white, within a matter of minutes during a locust plague. A similar devastation was part of the background of the book of Joel. © MPS

Magazine of December 1915, describing a locust attack on Jerusalem in that year. This description of a visitation similar to that which occasioned Joel's prophecy would provide an excellent background for understanding the book of Joel. The prophet, after describing the plague and its resulting chaos, urges the nation to repent of its sins and then goes on to predict a worse visitation, the future Day of the Lord.

Outline:

I. THE LOCUST PLAGUE AND ITS REMOVAL, 1:1-2:27.
   A. The plague of locusts, 1:1-20.
   B. The people urged to repent, 2:1-17.
   C. God pities and promises relief, 2:18-27.
II. THE FUTURE DAY OF THE LORD, 2:28-3:21.
   A. The Spirit of God to be poured out, 2:28-32.
   B. The judgment of the nations, 3:1-17.
   C. Blessing upon Israel following judgment, 3:18-21.

The book opens with a description of the locust plague in terms of a human army The locusts are *like* soldiers (2:7) and horses and chariots (2: 4,5). Once the figures of speech are understood to be such, the description is extremely vivid and entirely in keeping with the OT figurative language. The locusts are called a "northern army" (2:20). Although locust plagues in Palestine do not ordinarily come from the north, invasions of these insects from that direction are not unknown, the last having occurred in 1915. This calamity is called "the day of the Lord" (1:15; 2:1). Some commentators regard this term, in its every occurrence in the Bible, as eschatological — describing the future troubles which are to usher in the Messianic day, or referring to that day itself. If this is the case, then Joel's locust plague is a type or picture of the day of the Lord. On the other hand, while this expression is usually eschatological, there is no reason why it must always be so. The context determines meaning, and it would seem that here Joel was referring to the locust visitation as a day of the Lord's judgment and destruction. If this insect invasion, stripping the land of its verdure and making it like a desert, is a day of the Lord, how much worse will be the final divine visitation against a sinful world?

In the second chapter Joel continues to describe the plague and to urge repentance. The verbs in 2:1-11 should be rendered in the present tense, as in the RSV, for an event taking place in the prophet's own time is being described. Evidently the people responded to Joel's message, for a section follows (2:18-27) full of comfort and promise of the renewal of the land. Here, too, should be noticed the more accurate rendering of the verbs in the RSV.

The second major theme of Joel's prophecy is introduced in 2:28: after the present trouble will come the future day of the Lord, a time of great trouble for the nations when Israel will be vindicated and the Messianic age of peace brought in. This frequent theme of OT prophecy is here presented with emphasis on the outpouring of the Spirit of God which will begin it (2:28,29). Then terrifying portents will appear (2:30,31) and Judah and Jerusalem will be delivered and the nations judged (3:1-21).

Joel's greatest contribution to Christian thought is his teaching of the outpouring of the Holy Spirit "on all flesh" (2:28). This prophecy is quoted by Peter in his Pentecostal sermon (Acts 2:14-21). The Holy Spirit came upon men in OT times to enable them to serve God acceptably (Judg. 6:34; I Sam. 16:13) and certainly He was in the world and dwelling in the saints then as now, although they had very little consciousness of this fact. But in a special way the new age was to be one of the Spirit (Isa. 32:15; Zech. 12:10; John 7:39). All of God's people would now be priests and prophets, for the ideal stated when the law was given but never achieved would now become actual (Exod. 19:5,6; I Pet. 2:9,10).

Other Joels in the OT: 2. Samuel's firstborn son (I Sam. 8:2; I Chron. 6:33).

3. A Simeonite prince (I Chron. 4:35).

4. A Reubenite chief (I Chron. 5:4,8).

5. A Gadite chief (I Chron. 5:12).

6. An ancestor of Samuel, of the tribe of Levi (I Chron. 6:36).

7. A chief of Issachar (I Chron. 7:3).

8. One of David's mighty men (I Chron. 11:38).

9. A Levite (I Chron. 15:7,11,17; probably also mentioned in I Chron. 23:8; 26:22).

10. David's officer over half of Manasseh (I Chron. 27:20).

11. A Levite of Hezekiah's time (II Chron. 29:12).

12. A Jew who had married a foreign wife (Ezra 10:43).

13. A Benjamite overseer (Neh. 11:9). J.B.G.

JOELAH (jō-ē'là, Heb. yō'ē'lâh, perhaps let him help), a son of Jeroham of Gedor. He was one of David's recruits at Ziklag (I Chron. 12:7).

JOEZER (jō-ē'zēr, Heb. yō'ezer, Jehovah is help), one of David's recruits at Ziklag (I Chron. 12:6).

JOGBEHAH (jŏg'bē-à, Heb. yoghbehâh, lofty), a city in Gilead assigned to Gad (Num. 32:35; Judg. 8:11). It is represented today by Jubeihah, a village midway between Rabbath Ammon and es-Salt.

JOGLI (jŏg'lī, Heb. yoghlî, led into exile), father of Bukki, of the tribe of Dan (Num. 34:22).

JOHA (jō'hà, Heb. yôhā', meaning unknown). 1. A Benjamite, son of Beriah (I Chron. 8:16).

2. A Tizite, son of Shimri, and one of David's mighty men (I Chron. 11:45).

JOHANAN (jō-hā'năn, Heb. yôhānān, Jehovah has been gracious). 1. Son of Kareah, a captain who with his men submitted to Gedaliah, appointed by Nebuchadnezzar as governor over Judah (II Kings 25:22,23; Jer. 40:8,9). He warned Gedaliah of Ishmael's plot to murder him (Jer. 40:13,14); and when the governor paid no heed and was assassinated, he tried to avenge his death (Jer. 41:11-15). Against the advice of Jeremiah, he and other Jewish leaders led the remnant down into Egypt, taking Jeremiah with them.

2. The eldest son of King Josiah (I Chron. 3:15). He seems to have died young.

3. A son of Elioenai (I Chron. 3:24).

4. Father of the Azariah who was priest in Solomon's time (I Chron. 6:9,10).

5. A Benjamite recruit of David at Ziklag (I Chron. 12:4).

6. A Gadite recruit of David at Ziklag who was made a captain in David's army (I Chron. 12:12, 14).

7. An Ephraimite chief (II Chron. 28:12).

8. Son of Hakkatan, of the clan of Azgad. He was one of the men who accompanied Ezra from Babylon (Ezra 8:12).

9. Son of Tobiah, the Ammonite, who married a Jewess in the days of Nehemiah (Neh. 6:18).

10. Son of Eliashib. Ezra went to his chamber and, without food or drink, mourned for the sin of those who had contracted foreign marriages (Ezra 10:6).

11. A high priest, grandson of Eliashib (Neh. 12:22). The Jews at Elephantine appealed to him for help when their temple was destroyed in 411 B.C. (Elephantine Papyri). Josephus says that he killed his brother Jesus in the temple because he feared he might be superseded as high priest (Jos. Antiq. xi. 7,1).

JOHN (Gr. Ioánnes, from Heb. Yôhānān, Jehovah has been gracious), the name of five men in the NT, and of five others in the OT Apocrypha: 1. John the Baptist (q.v.).

2. The apostle, the son of Zebedee, and brother of James (see JOHN, THE APOSTLE).

3. John Mark (q.v.).

4. Father of Simon Peter (John 1:42; 21:15,17, called Jonas in KJV).

5. A relative of Annas the high priest who took part with Annas, Caiaphas, Alexander, and other kindred of Annas in calling Peter and John to account for their preaching about Jesus (Acts 4:6).

6. Father of Mattathias, who started the Maccabean revolt against the Syrians (I Macc. 2:1).

7. Eldest son of Mattathias. He was surnamed Gaddis, and slain by the children of Jambri (I Macc. 9:36).

8. Father of Eupolemus (I Macc. 8:17). He was sent on a mission to Rome to establish friendly relations (II Macc. 4:11).

9. John Hyrcanus, son of Simon, and nephew of Judas Maccabaeus. He was civil governor and high priest from 135 to 105 B.C. (I Macc. 13:53; 16:1).

10. One of the envoys sent to treat with Lysias (II Macc. 11:17).

JOHN, THE APOSTLE. The sources for the life of John are relatively meager. All that exists is what is found in the NT and what has been preserved by tradition. One can, therefore, give no more than a fragmentary account of his life. He was the son of Zebedee, and brother of James the apostle, who was put to death by Herod Agrippa I about A.D. 44 (Matt. 4:21; Acts 12,1,2). It may be reasonably inferred that his mother was Salome (cf. Matt. 27:56 with Mark 15:40) and that she was the sister of Mary, the mother of Jesus. Jesus and John would then have been cousins. The family lived in Galilee, probably at Bethsaida. The father and the two sons were fishermen on the Sea of Galilee (Mark 1:19,20). There are reasons for thinking that the family was not without some means. They had hired servants, and thus belonged to the employer class. Salome was one of the women who ministered to Jesus of their substance (Luke 8:3; Mark 15:40), and was also one of the women who bought spices and came to anoint the body of Jesus (Mark 16:1). The fact that John knew the high priest well enough to gain entrance to the court where Jesus was tried and could get permission for Peter to enter also suggests that the family was not exactly poor.

John is first introduced as a disciple of John the Baptist (John 1:35). He had therefore heeded the Baptist's call to repentance and baptism in preparation for the coming of the Messiah. How long he had been a follower of the Baptist is not known. In his Gospel he tells how he first met Jesus and became His disciple (1:35-39). One day as he stood with Andrew and John the Baptist, he heard his master say, as Jesus walked by, "Behold, the Lamb of God!" The two disciples of John immediately followed Jesus, and when they were asked what they wanted, they said they wanted to know where Jesus was staying. He invited them to come and see. Their stay changed their lives and was so memorable that many years later, when John wrote the story in his Gospel, he still remembered that it was about four o'clock in the afternoon. The next day he and some others accompanied Jesus to Galilee to attend a wedding feast at Cana (John 2:1-11). From Cana they went to Capernaum, and then down to Jerusalem, where Jesus cleansed the temple and had an interview with Nicodemus (John 2:13-3:21). John was with Jesus during His seven months' sojourn in the country of Judaea, calling the people to repentance and baptism. Since Jesus Himself did not baptize, he undoubtedly helped in the administration of the baptismal rite (John 4:2). When Jesus heard of the Baptist's arrest, He decided to return to Galilee. A probable factor in His leaving Judaea was His realization that the Jewish religious leaders were worried over the fact that He was acquiring an even larger following than the Baptist. On the way north, as they passed through Samaria, there occurred the incident of the Samaritan woman, so fully described in John 4. For a time after Jesus returned to Galilee His disciples seem to have returned to their normal occupations, but one day Jesus appeared by the Sea of Galilee and called Peter and Andrew, James and John from their fishing to be with Him constantly so that they might be trained to become fishers of men (Matt. 4:18-22; Mark 1:16-20; Luke 5:1-11). This was the second stage of discipleship in John's preparation for his life work. Some time later, he was chosen to the apostolate (Matt. 10:2-4; Mark 3:13-19; Luke 6:12-19). The list of the Twelve given in Mark's Gospel states that Jesus surnamed James and John, Boanerges, that is, Sons of Thunder, evidently because of the impetuosity of their temperament.

During the course of the Lord's ministry the experiences of John were common to all the apostles. There are, however, a few scenes in which he takes an important part. The Gospels make clear that he was one of the most prominent of the apostles, and his own Gospel makes clear that he was greatly loved by Jesus. He was one of the three apostles who were closest to Jesus, the other two being Peter and his own brother James. With the other two in the inner circle of the apostles, he was admitted to witness the raising of Jairus' daughter (Mark 5:37; Luke 8:51); the same three were chosen by Jesus to be present at the Transfiguration (Matt. 17:1; Mark 9:2; Luke 9:28); and they were nearest to Jesus during the agony in Gethsemane (Matt. 26:37; Mark 14:33). It was John who told Jesus that they had seen someone casting out devils in His name, and that they had forbidden him because he was not of their company (Mark 9:38; Luke 9:49). The two brothers, James and John, gave evidence of their impetuosity when they went to Jesus with their mother and requested that in the coming kingdom they be given places of honor above the others (Mark 10:35). On Tuesday of Passion Week John was among those who asked Jesus on the Mount of Olives when His prediction about the destruction of the temple would be fulfilled (Mark 13:3). He and Peter were sent by Jesus to make ready the Passover (Luke 22:8), and at the Passover feast he lay close to the breast of Jesus and asked who His betrayer would be (John 13:25). When Jesus was arrested, he fled, as did the other apostles (Matt. 26:56), but before long recovered enough courage to be present at the trial of Jesus; and, through his acquaintance with the high priest, secured entrance for Peter, too (John 18:16). He stood near the cross on which Jesus was nailed, and there received Jesus' commission to look after His mother (John 19:26). On the morning of the resurrection, when he and Peter were told by Mary Magdalene about the empty grave, together they went to see for themselves (John 20:2,3). In the account of the appearance of the risen Lord in Galilee the sons of Zebedee receive special mention, and it is John who first recognizes Jesus (John 21:1-7), and in the scene which follows, the impression is corrected that John should not die before the Lord's return. At the end of the chapter the truthfulness of the Gospel record is confirmed (21:20-24).

In the rest of the NT there are only a few scattered references to John. After the ascension of Jesus he remained in Jerusalem with the other apostles, praying and waiting for the coming of the Holy Spirit. In the Acts he appears with Peter in two important scenes. Soon after Pentecost they healed a man who had been lame from his birth, and while explaining the miracle to the astonished crowd gathered around them, they were arrested. The next day they were brought before the Sanhedrin, and after being warned not to preach about Jesus any more, they were released (Acts 4:1-22). Later, after the Gospel had been preached to the people of Samaria by Philip, Peter and John were sent by the apostles to Samaria, and they prayed and laid hands on the new converts that they might receive the Holy Spirit (Acts 8:14, 15). John's name is once mentioned in Paul's epistles — in Galatians 2:9, where Paul says that on his second visit to Jerusalem after his conversion he met and consulted with James (undoubtedly the Lord's brother), Peter, and John, who were pillars of the church and who gave him the right hand of fellowship. The only other mention of him in the NT is in Revelation 1:1,4,9, where the authorship of the book is ascribed to John.

Five books of the NT are attributed to him — the fourth Gospel, three epistles, and Revelation. The only one in which his name actually appears is the last. According to tradition, he spent his last years in Ephesus. Very likely the seven churches of Asia enjoyed his ministry. The Book of Revelation was written on the Isle of Patmos, where he was exiled for the Word of God and the testimony of Jesus (Rev. 1:9). Tradition says that he wrote the Gospel in Asia at the request of Christian friends, and that he agreed to do so only after the church had fasted and prayed about the matter for three days. He apparently died in Ephesus about the end of the century.

It is evident from all that we know of John that he was one of the greatest of the apostles. He is described as the disciple whom Jesus loved, no doubt because of his understanding of and love for his Lord. The defects of character with which he began his career as an apostle — an undue vehemence, intolerance, and selfish ambition — were in the course of time brought under control, until he became especially known for his gentleness and kindly love.   S.B.

The birthplace of John the Baptist, Ain Karim, in the hill country of Judea. The Monastery of John the Baptist, at left, supposedly marks the site of the home of Zacharias and Elizabeth. © MPS

JOHN THE BAPTIST, the immediate forerunner of Jesus, sent by God to prepare the way for the coming of the Messiah. John was of priestly descent on the side of both his parents. His father, Zacharias, was a priest of the course of Abija, while his mother, Elizabeth, belonged to the family of Aaron. They are described as being "righteous before God, walking in all the commandments of the Lord blameless" (Luke 1:6). He was born in a city of the hill country of southern Judaea, about six months before the birth of Jesus. His parents were then old. His birth had been foretold by an angel to Zacharias while he was serving in the temple. The angel told him that his prayer for a child would be answered and that his wife would give birth to a son who was to be named John and who was to prepare the way for the coming of the Messiah. About his childhood and youth we know only that he lived as a Nazirite in the desert and that he was filled with the Holy Spirit even from birth. It is thought by some that he was a member of a Jewish sect of monks called the Essenes, but there is no clear evidence that this was so.

His first public appearance is carefully dated by Luke (3:1,2), according to the way time was then reckoned. This was somewhere about A.D. 26 or 27. His early ministry was laid in the wilderness of Judaea and in the Jordan valley. The main theme of his preaching was the near approach of the Messianic age and the need of adequate spiritual preparation to be ready for it. His mission was to prepare the people for the advent of the Messiah so that when He made His appearance they would recognize and accept Him. His message did not harmonize with what many of his hearers expected, for while they looked for deliverance from and judgment upon the foreign oppressor, he said that the Messiah would separate the good from the bad and would cast into the fire any tree which did not bring forth good fruit. Many of the Jews, especially the Pharisees, thought that they would enter the kingdom of God automatically, simply because they were physically descended from Abraham, but John declared in no uncertain terms that this was not so at all. He called upon them to repent sincerely of their sins and to be baptized. The baptism by water which he administered signified a break with and cleansing from sin. His baptism was not something utterly new to the Jews; it had its roots in practices already familiar to them: in the various washings required by the Levitical law (Lev. 11-15), in the Messianic lustration foretold by the prophets (Jer. 33:8; Ezek. 36:25,26; Zech. 13:1), and in the proselyte baptism of the Jewish church. His baptism, however, differed essentially from these, in that while the Levitical washings brought restoration to a former condition, his baptism prepared for a new condition; the Jews baptized only Gentiles, but he called upon Jews to be baptized; and his baptism was a baptism of water only in preparation for the Messianic baptism of the Spirit anticipated by the prophets.

While the multitudes of common people flocked to the Jordan, Jesus also came to be baptized. Although Jesus and John were cousins, it appears that John did not know that Jesus was the Messiah until he saw the Holy Spirit descend upon Him at His baptism (John 1:32-34). When Jesus came to him for baptism, he saw that He had no sin of which to repent, and would have refused, had Jesus not insisted, saying that it was necessary for Him to fulfil all righteousness. Shortly after, John said to two of his disciples as they saw Jesus pass by, "Behold the Lamb of God, which taketh away the sin of the world" (John 1:29), and they left him to follow Jesus. He recognized the subordinate and temporary character of his own mission. For some unexplained reason, some of his disciples did not leave him to follow Jesus; and when some of them came to John with the complaint that all men were coming to Jesus, he said to them, "He must increase, but I must decrease" (John 3:30), and that he was not the Messiah, but only the forerunner of the Messiah. Little is known about John's training of his disciples beyond the fact that it included forms of prayer (Luke 11:1) and frequent fastings (Matt. 9:14); but he must also have taught them much concerning the Messiah and His work. The loyalty to him is shown in their concern over Jesus' overshadowing popularity, their refusal to abandon him in his imprisonment, the reverent care they gave his body after his death, and in the fact that 20 years later there were disciples of his, including Apollos, the learned Alexandrian Jew, in far-away Ephesus (Acts 19:1-7).

The exact time of John's imprisonment or the length of time he was in prison is not known. It is clear, however, that Jesus began His ministry in Galilee after John was put in prison and that he was in prison approximately seven months at the time he sent two of his disciples to Jesus to inquire whether He really was the Messiah. This inquiry seems strange in view of his previous signal testimonies, and is probably to be explained either in the interest of his disciples, who needed assurance that Jesus was really the Messiah, or in some misgivings of his own because the Messianic kingdom was not being ushered in as suddenly and as cataclysmically as he had expected, and perhaps because he thought he was being forgotten while others were being helped. When the two disciples returned to John, Jesus expressed Himself in the frankest appreciation of John, declaring him to be more than a prophet and God's messenger sent to prepare the way for Him (Matt. 11:10-19).

The Gospels tell that John met his death through the vindictiveness of Herodias, whose sin of living in adultery with Herod, John had denounced. Josephus, on the other hand, attributes John's death to Herod's jealousy of his great influence with the people. He also says that the destruction of Herod's army, in the war with his spurned wife's father-in-law, was regarded by the Jews as God's punishment upon him for the murder of John. Josephus undoubtedly gives, not the real reason, which he would not dare to give to the public, but the reason Herod chose that the public be given.   S.B.

The site of Machaerus, Herod's stronghold east of the Dead Sea, where John the Baptist was imprisoned and beheaded. © MPS

JOHN, EPISTLES OF.

The First Epistle of John is evidently written by the author of the fourth Gospel. The author does not give his name in either the Epistle or the Gospel, but the early church attributed both works to the Apostle John, and this attribution is supported by the internal evidence of both books. The writer of the Epistle speaks with authority, as an apostle would (1:2; 2:1; 4:6,14). He claims to have lived in personal contact with Christ and to have first-hand knowledge of the facts which underlie the Gospel message (1:1-3; 4:14). The tone and teaching of the letter are such as we should expect from the aged apostle, writing to his disciples a last message regarding the truths he had taught throughout his life. When the Gospel and the Epistle are compared, the conclusion is well-nigh irresistible that the two books are by the same person. There are striking resemblances in style, language, and thought. Among these resemblances are characteristic words used in a peculiar sense, like *life, light, darkness,* and *world*; characteristic expressions, like *eternal life, a new commandment,* and *abide in Christ*; and identical phrases, like *walketh in darkness,* and *that your joy may be full.* The divergencies, of which there are a few, are easily explainable on the basis of differences of purpose and of subject.

We cannot be sure whether the Epistle was written before or after the Gospel. Tradition says that the Gospel was written late in the life of John, towards the end of the first century. Evidences of a late date for the Epistle are that Christianity has been so long in existence that its precepts may be spoken of as an "old commandment" (I John 2:7) and signs that the Gnostic movement had begun, although it had not yet grown to its developed form.

The purpose of the author is to warn the readers against false teachers who are trying to mislead them, and to exhort them to hold fast to the Christian faith which they have received and to fulfill conscientiously the duties, especially brotherly love, which flow from it. Although he does not exactly describe the false doctrines which he attacks, there is no doubt that he has in mind the heresy of Gnosticism, with its docetic interpretation of the person of Christ and its antinomian view of morals. The false teachers are called Antichrists (2:18,22; 4:3). They claim a knowledge of God which is superior to that of ordinary Christians, but, John says, their claims are false (I John 2:4). They deny that Jesus is the Christ (2:22), the Son of God (4:15; 5:5), and that Jesus Christ has come in the flesh (4:2). They also impugn the fundamental moral teachings of the Church by their dualistic interpretation of existence, for, according to Gnosticism, sin is not moral opposition of the human personality to God, but a physical principle inherent in all matter.

Although the Epistle does not have the usual characteristics of the ancient Graeco-Roman epistle — salutation, final greetings, messages to individuals, etc., there is no doubt that it is a genuine epistle. Most likely it is a pastoral or circular letter addressed to the churches in the province of Asia, where the church was in danger of the errors that are warned against.

The plan of the Epistle is difficult to follow, and has been differently understood. Some fail to recognize any regular plan at all. Thoughts that are repeated again and again throughout the Epistle are the necessity of doing righteousness as an evidence of divine sonship, the necessity of love for the brethren by those who claim to love God, and believing that Jesus is the Christ come in the flesh.

The Second Epistle of John. Both the Second and Third Epistles of John are similar in words, style, ideas, and character to the First Epistle, and must have been written by the same author, who refers to himself simply as "the elder" (2:1; 3:1). Both are very brief, containing just the number of words which could conveniently be written on one sheet of papyrus. Although written to different people and for different purposes, there are striking resemblances of wording in them. The opening address is almost identical in both. In both Epistles the writer expresses joy in the spiritual progress of those to whom he writes, and does so in almost the same words. The conclusion in the Epistles is the same in both thought and words.

II John is addressed to "the elect lady and her children" (vs. 1). It is generally supposed that the reference is to a church and her spiritual children, although some hold that a particular individual named Kyria (Gr. for *lady*) is meant. The introductory greeting is followed by an exhortation to hold fast to the commandments which they had received, especially brotherly love, a warning against false teachers who deny that Christ is come in the flesh, and a prohibition against receiving them. The author concludes with a promise soon to visit them.

The Third Epistle of John. This is addressed to Gaius the wellbeloved, who is eulogized for walking in the truth and being hospitable to evangelists sent, apparently by John, to the church of which Gaius is a member. The author then censures another member of the church, the talkative, overbearing Diotrephes, who for some unexplained reason, probably jealousy, not only refused to receive the itinerant preachers, but did all he could to get the whole church to follow his course, even to the length of threatening excommunication for those who took a different view of their duty. The elder adds that he has written a letter to the church also, but apparently he has little hope that it will overcome the headstrong opposition of Diotrephes. He threatens a speedy visit to the church, when he will call Diotrephes to account for his bad conduct. There is in this Epistle no suggestion of a heretical tendency in the church.   S.B.

JOHN, THE GOSPEL OF.

Authorship, Date, Place. Never was there a book written that made higher claim for its "hero." To the Jesus of history, its author gives the most exalted titles. In fact, in the very opening verse he calls him *God*. This becomes even more remarkable when note is taken of the fact that the author describes himself as one who belongs to the same race, stock, and family as does Jesus, in fact as an eye-witness of the scenes which he so vividly portrays. No one knew Jesus better than he did. He walked with Him from day to day. He reclined on His bosom. He stood by His cross. He entered His tomb (John 13:25; 19:26; 20:8). Yet he does not shrink from proclaiming that this Jesus of history, whom he knew so well, was and is Himself God!

Tradition holds the Apostle John to be this author, and that "the-date-and-place" of authorship was sometime toward the close of the first century A.D., Asia Minor. This tradition can be traced back from Eusebius (the church-historian) at the beginning of the fourth century to Theophilus who flourished about A.D. 170-180. The major witnesses, besides Eusebius, are Origen, Clement of Alexandria, Tertullian, Irenaeus, the writer of the Muratorian Canon, and Theophilus. Irenaeus, one of the earliest of these witnesses, was a disciple of Polycarp, who, in turn, had been a disciple of the Apostle John. The inference would seem to be legitimate that this tradition can be traced back to the disciple whom Jesus loved. Moreover, because of his wide travels the witness of Irenaeus may be called a representative testimony, the firm conviction of the early church which this Greek church-father knew so well. In fact, the early writers (mentioned above) show us that in the last quarter of the second century the fourth Gospel was known and read throughout Christendom: in Africa, Asia Minor, Italy, Gaul, Syria, and that it was ascribed to the well-known Apostle John.

Among the witnesses that are even earlier, Justin Martyr (*Apology* I.61) quotes from John 3:3-5. He uses a number of expressions from this Gospel (see also his *Dialogue with Trypho,* chapter 105) His doctrine of the Logos presupposes acquaintance with the fourth Gospel, which his pupil Tatian included in his *Diatessaron* or *Harmony.* Ignatius, who went to his martyrdom about the year A.D. 110, alludes to John's Gospel again and again. See *Epistles of Ignatius, Short Recension.* Very significant also is the testimonial of the elders of Ephesus (John 21:24). The traditional belief regarding the authorship and date of the fourth Gospel has received strong confirmation in the discovery of a very early Gospel of John fragment of a papyrus codex, which seems to have originated in the Christian community of Middle Egypt. On the basis of solid evidence it has been established that this papyrus scrap belonged to a codex which circulated in that general region in the first part of the second century. On the recto this scrap has part of John 18:31-33, on the verso part of Verses 37-38. Now if this Gospel was already circulating in Middle Egypt in the early part of the second century, it must have been *composed* even earlier. From Ephesus, where according to tradition this Gospel was written, to Middle Egypt, where this codex circulated, is a long distance. This means, therefore, that the traditional view with respect to the date and composition of the fourth Gospel has at length been confirmed by archaeological evidence.

Internal evidence, moreover, is in line with tradition. The author was evidently a Jew, as his style, thorough acquaintance with the OT, and intimate knowledge of Jewish religious beliefs and customs indicates (John 2:13,17,23; 4:9,25; 5:1; 6:4,15; 7:2,27,37,38,42; 10:22,23,34,35; 11:38,44,49; 12:40, etc.). He was probably a Palestinian Jew, for he has a detailed knowledge of Palestinian topography (1:28; 2:1,12; 3:23; 4:11,20; 11:1,54; 12:21); particularly, of Jerusalem and its immediate vicinity (5:2; 9:7; 11:18; 18:1; 19:17); and of the temple (2:14,20; 8:2,20; 10:22,23; 18:1,20). Having been an eye-witness, he remembers the time and place where the events occurred (1:29,35,39; 2:1; 3:24; 4:6,40,52,53; 6:22; 7:14; 11:6; 12:1; 13:1, 2; 19:14,31; 20:1,19,26). He knows that Jesus was weary when He sat down by the well (4:6); remembers the very words spoken by the neighbors of the man born blind (9:8-10); saw the blood and water issuing from Jesus' pierced side (19:33-35); knows the servant of the high priest by name (18:10); and is acquainted with the high priest (18:15). So intimate and full is his knowledge of the actions, words, and feelings of the other disciples that he must have been one of the Twelve (1:35-42; 2:17,22; 4:27; 6:19; 12:16; 13:22-28; 18:15, 16; 20:2; 21:20-23). By a process of logical elimination it can easily be shown that the author was the Apostle John and could not have been any one of the others who composed the Twelve, for though he does not mention himself by name but calls himself "the disciple whom Jesus loved," he distinguishes himself from others whom he does mention by name (Simon Peter, 1:40,41,42,44, etc.; Andrew, 1:40,44; 6:8; 12:22; Philip, 1:43-46, etc.; Nathanael, 1:45-49; 21:2; Thomas, 11.16; 14: 5; 20:24-29; 21:2; Judas the Greater, 14:22; and Judas the Traitor, 6:71; 12:4; 13:2,26,29; 18:2, 3,5). Matthew's name can be eliminated for it is associated with another Gospel. So also can be the names of obscure disciples likes James the Less and Simon the Zealot. This leaves only the sons of Zebedee: James and John. But James died an early death (Acts 12), while this Gospel's author survived even Peter (who survived James). It is clearly evident from 21:19-24 that the author of the fourth Gospel was still alive and bearing witness when it first appeared (note present tense in Verse 24) though Peter had already gained the martyr's crown (Verse 19). The reasonable conclusion would surely seem to be that it was the Apostle John who wrote the fourth Gospel.

We are not saying that this external and internal evidence constitutes absolute proof. In the final analysis we accept it *by faith*, but a faith which is not foolish but takes account of the facts, namely, that toward the close of the first century A.D. (probably sometime between A.D. 80 and 98) at or near Ephesus the Apostle John wrote the fourth Gospel. Radical criticism has not been able to present any evidence whatever that demolishes this well-established position.

Purpose. The author states his purpose as follows: "Now Jesus, to be sure, in the presence of the disciples, also performed many other signs, that are not written in this book. But these are written in order that you may continue to believe that Jesus is the Christ, the Son of God, and in order that believing you may continue to have life in his name" (Ch. 20:30,31). The faith of believers was being undermined by the errors of men like Cerinthus, who taught that Jesus was not really God and that Christ had not actually come into the flesh (had not adopted human nature). The apostle, seeing this danger and being guided by the Holy Spirit, writes this Gospel in order that the Church may abide in the true faith. Thus, Irenaeus definitely states that John seeks by the proclamation of the Gospel to remove the error which Cerinthus was trying to spread (*Against Heresies* III.xi.1). According to Cerinthus, at baptism the *Christ* in the form of a dove had descended on Jesus, but this same *Christ* had left him again on the eve of his (Jesus') suffering. Hence, it was not really Christ who suffered and died and rose again but Jesus (*op. cit.* I.xxvi.1; III.iii.4). Over against this, John defends the thesis that Jesus Christ is *one*, and that this one divine and human Person came not only by water (baptism) but also by blood (suffering and death). For proof see John 19:34-37; cf. I John 5:6. From the very beginning, therefore, Jesus is Himself God. He adopts human nature into personal union with His divine and keeps it ("the Word became flesh," John 1:1,14). However, combating the error of Cerinthus was not John's *main* aim in writing this book. It was subsidiary to the aim already quoted from 20:30,31.

The readers for whom this Gospel was primarily intended (though in the final analysis it was composed for the Church of the entire NT period, cf. 17:20,21) were living in Ephesus and surroundings. They were Christians from the Gentiles mostly. This explains why the evangelist adds explanatory notes to some of his references to Jewish customs and conditions (2:6; 4:9; 7:2; 10:22; 18:28; 19:31,41,42). It also explains the circumstantial manner in which he locates places that were situated in Palestine (4:5; 5:2; 6:1; 11:1,18; 12:1,21).

Characteristics. In harmony with John's aim, as described above, this Gospel has the following characteristics:

1. It is emphatically the *spiritual* Gospel, whose aim is to show who Jesus is (and this with a definitely practical purpose, John 20:31). Hence, much of what is found in Matthew, Mark, and Luke (the Synoptics) is here omitted, and on the other hand much material is added, the type of material that brings into clear focus the glory of the Lord: His Messianic office and deity. (See John 2:11; 3:16; 4:25,26,29,42; 5:17,18; 6:40; 7:37,38; 8:36,46,51; 9:38; 10:30; 11:40; 13:3; 14:6; 17:3,5; 20:28). The miracles here recorded also emphasize this same thought.

2. In close connection with (1) is the fact that here it is not the kingdom (as in the other Gospels) but the King Himself upon whom the emphasis falls. This also accounts for the seven "I Am's" (6:35; 8:12; 10:9,11; 11:25; 14:6; and 15:5).

3. This Gospel, far more than the others, records Christ's work in Judea.

4. It is far more definite than are the others in indicating the time and place of the events that are related.

5. It abounds in non-parabolic teaching.

6. It dwells at great length on the events and discourses which belong to a period of less than twenty-four hours (Chapters 13-19).

7. It records with special emphasis the promise of the coming and work of the Holy Spirit (14:16,17,26; 15:26; 16:13,14).

8. Its style, especially in the Prologue, is rhythmic. The manner in which the clauses are co-ordinated, so that often a truth is stated first positively, then negatively or vice versa (1:3; 14:6; 15:5,6; 14:18; 15:16), and its careful balancing of sentences so that antithesis is followed by synthesis, brief and pithy clauses by longer sentences: all this makes this Gospel a very beautiful book.

Contents. The arrangement of John's Gospel is superb. First, we see the Word in His pre-incarnate glory, so that His condescending love in the salvation of sinners may be deeply appreciated. In His earthly ministry He reveals Himself to ever-widening circles (a few disciples, His mother and friends at Cana, to Jerusalem, "the land of Judea," Samaria, Galilee), but is rejected both in Jerusalem and in Galilee (Chapters 1-6; especially 5:18; 6:66). Nevertheless, He makes His tender appeal to sinners, that they may accept Him (Chapters 7-10; especially 7:37,38; 8:12,31-36; 10:7,18,27, 28). Meanwhile opposition grows into bitter resistance (7:20,49; 8:6,40,48-59; 9:22; 10:20,31, 39). Next, by two mighty deeds — the raising of Lazarus and the triumphal entry into Jerusalem — Jesus manifests Himself as the Messiah (Chapters 11 and 12). But though the Greeks seek Him (12:20-36), the Jews repulse Him (12:37-50). By way of contrast this rejection causes the anointing at Bethany to stand out in all its beauty (12:1-8). So He *turns* — and this is indeed a *turning-point* in this Gospel — to the inner circle, and tenderly instructs the Twelve in the Upper Room, first mainly by means of *example* (washing the feet of His disciples, Chapter 13), and then mainly by means of His *Word* (of *comfort*, Chapter 14; of *admonition*, Chapter 15; and of *prediction*, Chapter 16), and commits Himself, them, and all later generations of believers to His Father's care (Chapter 17). In His very death (Chapters 18 and 19) He overcomes the world and brings to completion the glorious work of redemption (19:30; cf. 12:30,31; 16:33), and by means of His resurrection and loving manifestations (to Mary Magdalene, the eleven, the ten, the seven, particularly Peter and John) He proves His majestic claims and reveals Himself as the proper object of abiding trust (Chapters 20 and 21, especially 20:30,31).

Outline:
Jesus, the Christ, the Son of God

I. DURING HIS PUBLIC MINISTRY
   A. Revealing Himself to ever-widening circles, *rejected*. (Chaps. 1-6)
   B. Making His tender appeal to sinners, *bitterly resisted* (Chaps. 7-10).
   C. Manifesting Himself as the Messiah by two mighty deeds, *repulsed* (Chaps. 11, 12).

II. DURING HIS PRIVATE MINISTRY
   A. Issuing and illustrating His new commandment (Chap. 13).
   B. Tenderly instructing His disciples and committing them to the Father's care (Chaps. 14-17).
   C. Dying as a substitute for His people (Chaps. 18, 19).
   D. Triumphing gloriously (Chaps. 20, 21).
                                                    W.H.

JOHN MARK (See Mark)

JOIADA (joi′à-dà, Heb. *yôyādhā′, Jehovah knows*).
1. A son of Paseah, one of those who repaired the walls of Jerusalem (Neh. 3:6; in KJV Jehoiada).
2. Son of Eliashib the high priest. One of his sons married the daughter of Sanballat, the governor of Samaria, and was therefore expelled from the priesthood by Nehemiah (Neh. 12:10; 13:28).

JOIAKIM (joi′à-kĭm, Heb. *yôyāqîm, Jehovah raises up*), son of Jeshua and father of Eliashib, the high priest (Neh. 12:10,12,26).

JOIARIB (joi′à-rĭb, Heb. *yôyārîv, Jehovah pleads*).
1. A "teacher" of Ezra's time (Ezra 8:16).
2. A Judahite, descended from a certain Zechariah (Neh. 11:5).
3. A chief of the priests who returned from Babylon with Zerubbabel (Neh. 12:6,7).

JOKDEAM (jŏk′dē-ăm, Heb. *yoqedh′ām*), a town in Judah, probably S of Hebron, named with Maon, Carmel, and Ziph (Josh. 15:56).

JOKIM (jō′kĭm, Heb. *yôqîm, Jehovah raises up*), a man of Judah descended from Shelah (I Chron. 4:22).

JOKMEAM (jŏk′mē-ăm, Heb. *yoqme′ām, let the people arise*), a town of Ephraim (I Chron. 6:68). It was assigned to the Kohathite Levites. The KJV in I Kings 4:12 wrongly has Jokneam.

JOKNEAM (jŏk′nē-ăm, Heb. *yoqne′ām*), a town on or near Mt. Carmel (Josh. 12:22). It was assigned to the Merarite Levites (Josh. 21:34). It was located on the S margin of the Plain of Esdraelon, about 15 miles NW of Jezreel.

JOKSHAN (jŏk′shăn, Heb. *yoqshān*, meaning unknown), son of Abraham and Keturah (Gen. 25: 2,3). From him descended Sheba and Dedan.

JOKTAN (jŏk′tăn, Heb. *yoqtān*, meaning unknown), a tribe descended from Shem through Eber and from whom 13 tribes of Arabia descended (Gen. 10:25,26,29; I Chron. 1:19,20,23).

JOKTHEEL (jŏk′thē-ĕl, Heb. *yoqethe′ēl*). 1. A town in the lowland of Judah. Site unknown (Josh. 15:38).
2. A name given by Amaziah, king of Judah, to a place in Edom which he conquered (II Kings 14:7). It is usually identified with Petra, the capital of Edom.

JONA (See Jonah, Jonas)

JONADAB (jŏn′à-dăb, Heb. *yehônādhāv, Jehovah is bounteous*). 1. Son of David's brother Shimeah (II Sam. 13:3). He planned for Amnon the sin against Tamar.

2. The son of Rechab (II Kings 10:15ff). After becoming head of his tribe he taught it to live in tents, live a nomadic life, and to refrain from wine; and this rule it kept, so that it became characteristic of it. He helped Jehu abolish Baal-worship in Samaria.

JONAH (jō′nà, Heb. *yônâh, dove*). 1. A prophet of Israel, the son of Amittai, and of the town of Gath-hepher in the tribe of Zebulun (II Kings 14: 25). He predicted the restoration of the land of Israel to its ancient boundaries through the efforts of Jeroboam II. The exact words of the prophet are not given, nor are we told the specific time when the prophecy was uttered; but it may be deemed certain that it was pronounced sometime before the conquests of Jeroboam, either about the commencement of the king's reign, or towards the close of the preceding reign. Jeroboam ruled over a period of 40 years (790-750 B.C.). When he ascended the throne, he found the kingdom weak because ever since the time of Jehu, his great-grandfather, the people had been forced to pay continual tribute to Assyria. He became the most powerful of all the monarchs who ever sat upon the throne of Samaria, capturing Hamath and Damascus and restoring to Israel all the territory it used to have from Hamath to the Dead Sea. The Prophet Hosea also prophesied in the time of Jeroboam, but it must have been only toward the very close of his reign, as his prophetic activity extended to the time of Hezekiah, 60 years away.

The identity of the prophet with the prophet of the Book of Jonah can not reasonably be doubted. Jonah 1:1 reads, "Now the word of the Lord came to Jonah the son of Amittai, saying." It is extremely unlikely that there were two prophets with the same name. While the author of the Book of Jonah does not identify himself, the likelihood is that he is the same as the book bearing his name. It is sometimes objected that he writes in the third person; but this is true of the OT prophets in general. In all probability the book was written not long after the events recorded, in the latter part of Jeroboam's reign.

The spirit and teaching of the Book of Jonah rank with the highest of the OT prophetical books. Not as much can be said for the prophet himself, who ranks low in the catalog of OT prophets. He was a proud, self-centered egotist: wilful, pouting, jealous, blood-thirsty; a good patriot and lover of Israel; without proper respect for God or love for his enemies.
2. Father of Simon Peter (Matt. 16:17; John 1:42; 21:15).

JONAH, BOOK OF, fifth in the order of the Minor Prophets. It differs from them in that while they for the most part contain prophetic discourses, with a minimum of narrative material, the Book of Jonah is mainly occupied with a story, and the prophetic message in it is almost incidental. The chapter divisions mark the natural divisions of the book: Chapter 1, Jonah's disobedience; Chapter 2, Jonah's prayer; Chapter 3, Jonah's preaching to the Ninevites; Chapter 4, Jonah's complaints. Chapter 1 begins with the account of Jonah's call to preach at Nineveh because of its great wickedness. Instead of obeying, he took a ship in the opposite direction, to Tarshish, probably in southwestern Spain. His disobedience undoubtedly arose from his fear that the Ninevites would heed his message and repent, and that God would forgive the city which had for many years grievously oppressed his own land. He was a narrow-minded patriot who feared that Assyria would some day destroy his own people; and he did not want to do anything which might contribute to that event. He was unwilling to be a foreign missionary to a people towards whom he could feel nothing but bitterness. In the sequel of the story he frankly gives the reason for refusing to obey God's command, "Therefore I fled before unto Tarshish: for I knew that thou art a gracious God, and merciful, slow to anger, and of great kindness, and repentest thee of the evil" (Jonah 4:2). During a violent storm at sea, the heathen sailors prayed to their own gods, who, they thought, must be offended with some person on board. They cast lots to discover the culprit, and when the lot fell on Jonah he confessed that he was fleeing "from the presence of the Lord," and volunteered to be thrown overboard for their sakes. This was done, and the storm subsided; whereupon the sailors offered a sacrifice to Jehovah.

Jehovah prepared a great fish to swallow Jonah. Surprised to find himself alive in the body of the fish, the prophet gave thanks to God and expressed the confident hope that he would ultimately be delivered. After three days and three nights the fish vomited him upon the dry land.

Commanded a second time to go to Nineveh, Jonah obeyed and delivered his message, "Yet forty days, and Nineveh shall be overthrown!" The effect of his message was undoubtedly greatly heightened by the story of his deliverance, which had either preceded him or been told by himself. The people of Nineveh repented in sackcloth and ashes, and God spared the city.

When Jonah learned that Nineveh was to be spared, he broke out into loud and bitter complaint, not because he felt discredited as a prophet on account of the failure of his prediction, but because he was sure that the sparing of Nineveh sealed the doom of his own country. By the withering of a gourd, the Lord taught the prophet that if a mean and perishable plant could come to have such value to him, how much greater should be the estimate put on the lives of thousands of children and cattle in the great city of Nineveh. These meant more to God than Jonah's gourd could ever mean to him.

The purpose of the book is primarily to teach that God's gracious purposes are not limited to Israel, but extend to the Gentile world. The author wishes to enlarge the sympathies of Israel, so that as God's missionaries they will lead the Gentiles to repentance and to God. The ready response of the Ninevites shows that the heathen are capable of genuine repentance. The Book of Jonah may be regarded as a great work on foreign missions. It anticipates the catholicity of the Gospel program of Jesus, and is the OT counterpart of John 3:16, "For God so loved the world."

The book is anonymous, and its authorship is in dispute. The traditional view is that the Prophet Jonah is the author, and his book is a record of his own experiences. A more recent view is that the book was written long after Jonah's time by some anonymous author, and that it is a work of fiction with a moral lesson. Among the chief arguments advanced for the second view are the following. 1. In the prayer ascribed to Jonah there are quotations from post-Exilic psalms (cf. Jonah 2:3 with Ps. 42:7; Jonah 2:5 with Ps. 69:1; Jonah 2:9 with Ps. 50:1). 2. The narrative is written throughout in the third person, with no indication that the prophet of the story was the writer. 3. There are in the book Aramaic linguistic features which are found in the late books. 4. From Jonah 3:3b it is inferred that Nineveh was a thing of the past (the city was destroyed in 612 B.C.). 5. The

The Yunis Mound, the traditional Tomb of Jonah in Nineveh, in Iraq, ancient Babylonia. © MPS

failure to give the name of the king of Assyria indicates that it was unknown to the author. These arguments, however, are very debatable, and therefore inconclusive.

The traditional view, that Jonah is the author and the story historically true, is supported by a number of considerations. 1. The book is written as a simple narrative, and was so regarded by both Jews and Christians until about a century ago. 2. There seems no doubt that our Lord thought of the story as history and taught it as such. On three different occasions He referred to Jonah (Matt. 12:38-41; 16:4; Luke 11:29-32), saying that as Jonah was three days and three nights in the body of the fish, so should the Son of Man be three days and three nights in the heart of the earth, and that the men of Nineveh repented at the preaching of Jonah, while His own contemporaries for the most part rejected His message. Some critics, taking refuge in the doctrine of the Kenosis (Phil. 2:5-8), set aside the teaching of Jesus on this point as erroneous; while others, holding to a doctrine of accommodation, think that Jesus did not consider it worth while to correct the wrong views of His contemporaries; but neither of these explanations harmonizes with a Biblical view of the person of Christ.

Most modern critical scholars in the last hundred years have regarded the book as a work of the imagination. Some call it a myth; others an allegory; others a parable; others a didactic story; etc. This interpretation avoids the miraculous elements in the story, which the critics find it impossible to accept; but it does not do justice to the fact that our Lord very evidently held to the historicity of the book.   S.B.

JONAN (jō'năn, Gr. *Ionán*, perhaps *Jehovah is gracious*), an ancestor of Jesus mentioned in the genealogy of Luke (3:30). He lived about 200 years after David.

JONAS (jō'năs, Heb. *yônâh*, Gr. *Ionás*). 1. The name given in Matthew 12:39-41; 16:4; Luke 11:29-32 KJV to the OT prophet Jonah.

2. The name given in John 21:15,16 KJV to the father of the Apostle Peter. In John 1:42 KJV he is called Jona.

JONATH ELEM RECHOKIM, UPON (jō'năth ē'lĕm rē-hō'kĭm, *the silent dove of them that are afar off*), probably the tune to the melody to which Psalm 56 was written.

JONATHAN (jŏn'à-thăn, Heb. *yehônāthān, yônā-thān, Jehovah has given*), a proper name met with from the time of the judges onwards. 1. A Levite, son or more distant descendant of Gershom, son of Moses (Judg. 18:30). For a time he lived in Bethlehem-judah, but left to become the priest of Micah in Ephraim. Some Danites, after stealing idolatrous images from the house of Micah, induced him to go with them and be their priest. At Laish he founded a priesthood which officiated at the shrine of the stolen idols "until the day of the captivity of the land" (Judg. 18:30).

2. Son of King Saul. See separate article, following.

3. Son of the high priest Abiathar. He helped David during Absalom's rebellion, and brought to Adonijah the news that Solomon had been crowned king (II Sam. 15:27,36; 17:17,20; I Kings 1:42, 43).

4. A son of Shimea, a nephew of David (II Sam. 21:21).

5. One of David's mighty men (II Sam. 23:32).

6. A Jerahmeelite (I Chron. 2:32,33).

7. A son of Uzziah, one of David's treasurers (I Chron. 27:25).

8. David's "uncle," a wise man and a scribe (I Chron. 27:32). He may be the same as "4" above.

9. The father of Ebed, a returned exile (Ezra 8:6).

10. A son of Asahel who opposed Ezra in the matter of foreign marriages (Ezra 10:15).

11. A priest, a son of Joiada, descended from Jeshua (Neh. 12:11).

12. A priest in the days of the high priest Joiakim (Neh. 12:14).

13. A Levite of the lineage of Asaph (Neh. 12:35).

14. A scribe in whose house Jeremiah was imprisoned (Jer. 37:15,20).

15. A son of Kareah, probably the same as "14" (Jer. 40:8).

16. Youngest son of the priest Mattathias (I Macc. 2:5; 9-13), who initiated the Maccabean revolt.

17. Son of Absalom (I Macc. 13:11).

18. A priest who offered prayer at the first sacrifice after the return from exile (II Macc. 1:23).

JONATHAN, the eldest son of Saul, the first king of Israel (I Sam. 14:49). He first comes upon the scene soon after his father was crowned king and gained an important victory over the Ammonites, who had been harassing the Israelites. Saul's army numbered 3000 men, a third of whom he placed under the command of Jonathan at Gibeah, while the rest he retained at his headquarters at Michmash. In the valley midway between the two camps, at a place called Geba, the Philistines established an outpost and forced Saul to evacuate and fall back on Gibeah and Gilgal with a greatly reduced army, now numbering only 600 men, the rest having fled in fear to hide in caves or having been pressed into the enemy's service. In spite of this, Jonathan, attended only by his armor-bearer, surprised the Philistine outpost at Geba and killed 20 men. The resulting panic spread to the main camp, and when Saul came to attack, he found the Philistines confusedly attacking one another, and soon the whole Philistine army was in headlong flight. In this rout, the only weapons the Israelites had were farming implements (I Sam. 13:20), Saul and Jonathan alone being armed with swords and spears. The victory would have been even more complete had not Saul superstitiously ordered the people to refrain from eating until the day was over (I Sam. 14:24). Ignorant of this

The gorge at Michmash, showing the rocks over which Jonathan and his armor bearer climbed, "upon hands and feet," during the war against the Philistines (I Sam. 14:4, 5, 13). © MPS

prohibition, Jonathan, in his hot pursuit of the enemy refreshed himself by eating wild honey. Saul would have had him put to death, but the people intervened. They recognized that, with the help of God, his energetic action had brought them to a mighty victory.

But great as were Jonathan's military qualities, he is best remembered as the friend of David. He exemplified all that is noblest in friendship — warmth of affection, unselfishness, helpfulness, and loyalty. His love for David began the day the two first met after the slaying of Goliath (I Sam. 18:1-4), and it remained steadfast despite Saul's suggestion that David would some day be king in their stead (I Sam. 20:31). When Jonathan first realized his father's animosity towards David, he interceded for his friend (I Sam. 19:1-7); and later, more than once, he risked his life for him. Once, Saul, angered by what he regarded as unfilial conduct, threw a javelin at him, as he had done several times at David. The last meeting of the two friends took place in the desert of Ziph, where Jonathan strengthened his friend in God (I Sam. 23:16). He could not take part in the proceedings of his father against his friend, who was forced to live in hiding and from whom he was separated for many years. His disinterestedness and willingness to surrender all claims to the throne for the sake of his friend gives evidence of a character that is unsurpassed. While always holding to his own opinion of David, he conformed as much as he could to his father's views and wishes, and presents a noble example of filial piety. There was one temporary estrangement between Saul and Jonathan, provoked when Saul impugned the honor of Jonathan's mother. Jonathan fell with Saul and his brothers on Mt. Gilboa in battle against the Philistines (I Sam. 31:2). Their bodies were hung on the walls of Beth-shan, but under cover of night the men of Jabesh-gilead, out of gratitude for what Saul had done for them at the beginning of his career, removed them and gave them honorable burial. One son, Mephibosheth, survived. David showed him kindness, and his posterity through him may be traced for several generations. Like their ancestors, they were famous soldiers, especially distinguished in the use of the bow (I Chron. 8:33ff; 9:40ff).   S.B.

JOPPA (jŏp'pà, Heb. *yāphô*, Gr. *Ióppe*), once in KJV Japho (Josh. 19:46), an ancient walled town on the coast of Palestine, about 35 miles from Jerusalem. It was allotted to Dan, but there is no evidence that the Israelites ever possessed it in pre-Exilic times. It is mentioned in the Amarna letters. It was the seaport for Jerusalem. Timber from the forests of Lebanon were floated from Tyre to Joppa for the building of the Temple of Solomon (II Chron. 2:16), and again when the temple was being rebuilt, after the return from the Babylonian Captivity (Ezra 3:7). It was then under Phoenician control. Jonah took a ship for Tarshish there when he fled from the presence of the Lord (Jonah 1:3). In Maccabean times the city was garrisoned by Syrians, but when some 200 Jews were treacherously drowned, after being induced to go aboard ships, Judas Maccabaeus in revenge set fire to the docks and the boats in the harbor, and slew the fugitives. In NT times Peter there raised Dorcas to life (Acts 9:36f), and on the roof of Simon the tanner's house he received the famous vision which taught him that the Gospel was intended for Jew and Gentile alike (Acts 10:1ff; 11:5ff). In the Jewish war of A.D. 66 the Romans killed 8,400 of its fanatical inhabitants. After that, pirates gained control of the city and preyed upon the shipping in the surrounding waters. Vespasian then captured and destroyed the city. Joppa, now called Jaffa, is built on a rocky ledge 116 feet high, at the edge of the sea. The harbor is poor because of rocks which abound in it. The city has a very picturesque setting.   S.B.

JORAH (jō'rà, Heb. *yôrâh*, meaning uncertain), a family which returned with Zerubbabel (Ezra 2: 18). It is called Hariph in Nehemiah 7:24.

JORAI (jō'rā-ī, Heb. *yôray, whom Jehovah teaches*), the ancestral head of a Gadite family (I Chron. 5:13).

JORAM (jō'răm, Heb. *yôrām, Jehovah is exalted*).
1. A son of Toi, king of Hamath, who congratulated David on his victory over Hadadezer (II Sam. 8:10).
2. A Levite (I Chron. 26:25).
3. Son of Ahab, king of Israel. He succeeded his brother, Ahaziah on the throne. The name is the same as Jehoram (II Kings 8:29).
4. Same as Jehoram, king of Judah (II Kings 8:21-24; 11:2; I Chron. 3:11; Matt. 1:8).
5. A priest sent by Jehoshaphat to instruct the people (II Chron. 17:8).

JORDAN RIVER, the only large flowing body of water in Palestine and, as such, it played a significant part in the history of Israel, as well as in the earlier days of our Lord's ministry. The word *Jordan* derives from a Hebrew word, *hayyardēn,* meaning "flowing downward," or "the descender," and one with any knowledge of its course can easily see the appropriateness of the name. Four rivers in Syria are recognized as the source of what later becomes the Jordan River proper. They are the Bareighit; the Hasbany, at the western foot of Mount Hermon, 24 miles long; the Leddan; and, the most famous of all, though the shortest, the Banias, five and a half miles long. On this last-

The modern city of Jaffa, ancient Joppa, on the Mediterranean coast. Through the centuries it has been the seaport for Jerusalem. © MPS

named river once stood the city of Paneas, where was the well-known grotto of the Greek god, Pan. Later this was called Caesarea Philippi, and here occurred the great confession of Simon Peter (Matt. 16:13). These rivers join and pour into Lake Huleh, 20 miles long and five miles wide, the surface of which is seven feet above sea level. In recent years this lake has been drained by Israeli settlers for farm land. The Jordan then descends for ten miles to the sea of Galilee, a beautiful body of water 12 miles long and from three to six miles wide, the surface of which is 696 feet below the level of the sea. From the place where the Jordan makes its exit from the Sea of Galilee, also called the Sea of Tiberias, to the place at which it enters the Dead Sea, is, in a straight line, a length of 70 miles. But the river itself, because of its serpentine curves, is 200 miles in length! As Professor Glueck has vividly said, "Squirming frantically, burrowing madly, seeking wildly to escape its fate, the Jordan course, from its crystal clear beginning, to its literally dark and bitter end, is a helpless race to a hopeless goal." The surface of the Dead Sea is 1292 feet below sea level. The Jordan River proper varies from 90 to 100 feet in width, and from three to ten feet in depth, but the gorge which it has cut out varies from four miles at the north to 14 miles near Jericho.

An aerial view showing the winding course of the Jordan River, looking northward. © MPS

Two views of the Jordan River: At left, looking downstream, showing abundant vegetation in the river gorge; at right, looking northward, showing the great overhanging marl cliffs, portions of which occasionally fall into the river, blocking and changing its course. © MPS

Though the largest river of Palestine, the Jordan differs from other great national rivers in the fact that, due to the presence of 27 rapids between the Sea of Galilee and the Dead Sea, it carries no traffic; and because of the swampy condition of part of this valley, the terrific heat in many places, and the presence of many wild animals, especially during Israel's history, no large city was ever built directly on the banks of the Jordan. These factors led George Adam Smith to say with his usual brilliance, "There may be something on the surface of another planet to match the Jordan Valley; there is nothing on this" (p. 468).

While the Jordan is never called by any other name in the Bible, it is once referred to as "The River of the Wilderness" (Amos 6:14) and "the pride of the Jordan" (Jer. 12:5; 49:19; 50:44 and Zech. 11:3).

The natural life found in the Jordan Valley has been carefully studied, some of it proving to be quite unique. Of the 30 species of fish found in this river, 16 are said to be found nowhere else; of the 45 species of birds observed in this tortuous valley, 23 are peculiar to this area. About 162 species of plants and trees have been identified here, of which 135 are African. These included the castor oil plant, the tamarisk, willows, poplars, and near Jericho, the oleander, etc. While it is true that no large city was actually ever built on the banks of this river, still there are some geographical terms that belong to this area. Beginning in the north at the time of our Lord's advent, there was an area called the Decapolis, a federation of ten Greek cities, nine on the eastern side of the Jordan, and mentioned once at the beginning of our Lord's ministry (Matt. 4:25). Another city in this group was Pella, not mentioned in the Bible, but according to tradition, the city to which the Christians fled at the time of the destruction of Jerusalem, A.D. 70.

Of the important rivers pouring into the Jordan, all are on the eastern side (no river emptying into the Jordan on the west is referred to in the OT). The first, four miles S of the Sea of Galilee, is the Yarmuk, not mentioned in the Bible. Here is located the great modern Rutenberg electric power plant. Below this river was the city of Beth-Shan, referred to in Joshua 17:16, the excavation of which has revealed a civilization going back to 3500 B.C. Later it was called Scythopolis. South of this site is Aenon where we are told that John the Baptist carried on some of his baptizing work (John 3:23). Not far from here may have been located the Brook Cherith, referred to in I Kings 17:2-7. The next important river, about midway between the Sea of Galilee and the Dead Sea, is the Jabbok, famous as the place where Jacob wrestled with the angel (Gen. 32:22), later designated as a boundary (Num. 21:24; Josh. 12:2, etc.). At the junction of this river with the Jordan was the site known as Adam, where the waters of the great river were held back at the time of Israel's crossing (Josh. 3:16).

Near the Dead Sea on the western side of the river, one mile E of Jericho, stood the city of Gilgal, where Israel set up 12 stones at the command of God (Josh. 4:19,20), a place that later became an important religious center (I Sam. 7:16 and 10:8).

By far the most important single event relating to the Jordan River in the entire history of Israel is the crossing on the part of the Israelites, after the death of Moses. Actually, this crossing is referred to, in anticipation, by Moses in the book of Deuteronomy 3:20,25,27. In reality, while the Jordan River is now and then referred to as a boundary, it was *not* a boundary for Israel, or even for the specific tribes, for Manasseh occupied a huge territory on both sides of the river. Nevertheless, Israel was told that until this river was crossed, and the territory on the western side possessed, she would not be occupying the land flowing with milk and honey (Num. 35:10; Deut. 3:20; 11:31; 31:13; Josh. 1:2, etc.). One might say that the Promised Land more generally refers to the territory on the western side of the Jordan than to all of the land occupied by Israel. The story of the crossing of the Jordan is given in detail in the third and fourth chapters of Joshua.

The Jordan is important in only one particular in the New Testament. It was here that John the Baptist carried on his ministry (Matt. 3:6; Mark 1:5; John 1:28 and 3:26), and thus in this river Jesus Himself was baptized (Matt. 3:13; Mark 1:9; Luke 4:1). No other event occurs in the New Testament directly relating to the Jordan River.

(References to our Lord's ministry on the far side of the Jordan (Matt. 19:1; Mark 10:1) only imply that the Lord did cross the river). In the statement relating to the closing days of our Lord's ministry, when escaping from those who would make Him King, He "resorted once more to the place beyond the Jordan, where John first baptized, and there He stayed" (John 10:40, Berkeley Version). When the early Church began its great missionary work, apart from the interview of Philip with the Ethiopian eunuch near Gaza, all the ministry of the apostles and early disciples, according to the New Testament, proceeded neither south into Egypt nor eastward toward Babylon, but northward into Syria and Asia Minor, and then westward to Greece, to Italy, and probably Spain. Nothing of any great historic importance has actually happened at the Jordan River since the baptism of our Lord. In fact, the Jordan Valley, from the Sea of Galilee to near Jericho, was practically unexplored until the 19th century.

The theme of the Jordan River in the ritual of the church and in its hymnology and poetry, has never been comprehensively surveyed. With the early church fathers, it was practically ignored. However, it was given an important place in the Coptic and Ethiopian prayers. The Ethiopian prayer for the consecration of baptismal water has the following significant typological references to the Jordan: "It is Thou, O Lord, who in the days of Joshua, the son of Nave, caused the powerful waves (of the Jordan) to flow back; it is Thou — who can withstand Thy sight! — who didst mark Thine acceptance of the sacrifice of Elias in the water by sending down fire from heaven; it is Thou who didst show by Eliseus the water of the generation of life, and who didst cause that Naaman should be purified by the water of the Jordan; Thou canst do all things and nothing is impossible to Thee. Give to this water the great gift of the Jordan, and may the Holy Spirit come down upon it." (The *Bible and the Liturgy* by Jean Danielou, Notre Dame, Indiana, 1956, p. 99. See especially the entire chapter here on "Types of Baptism," pages 99-113).

The most famous hymn in which the Jordan is a basic theme is the one by Charles Cuff (sometimes listed as Coffin (1676-1749), originally written in Latin, and published in the *Hymni Sacri*, as well as the *Paris Breviary*, both in 1736. It appears in almost all Anglican hymnals, as well as in many others. The first stanza is as follows:

> *On Jordan's bank the Baptist's cry*
> *Announces that the Lord is nigh;*
> *Awake and hearken, for he brings*
> *Glad tidings of the King of kings.*

Another famous hymn with the Jordan theme is by an English Baptist clergyman, Samuel Stennett (1727-1795), beginning with the famous clause, "On Jordan's stormy banks I stand." This was included in the famous *Sacred Songs and Solos* edited by Mr. Sankey. The first stanza is as follows:

> *On Jordan's stormy banks I stand,*
> *And cast a wistful eye*
> *To Canaan's fair and happy land,*
> *Where my possessions lie.*

Among other hymns in which the Jordan River appears, is the well-known "Guide Me, O Thou Great Jehovah," by William Williams, the third stanza of which contains the two lines, "When I tread the verge of Jordan . . . Land me safe on Canaan's side." The idea of passing through death for the Christian being compared with the crossing of the Jordan on the part of the Israelites cannot be said to be a very accurate interpretation of Israel's history at this point. Israel did not enter into a time of peace when she crossed the Jordan, but was ushered into a series of wars, many oppressions and defeats, followed by victories of more or less length, and ultimately ending in disaster and expulsion from the land.

It is significant that in our large volumes of famous quotations, the word Jordan does not even appear, and even the great *Oxford English Dictionary* passed by this word in its original publication though adding it in the later supplementary volume (1945).   W.M.S.

BIBLIOGRAPHY. The definitive work by the archaeologist, Dr. Nelson Glueck, *The River Jordan*, published in 1956 (with 114 full-page illustrations), renders all previous treatments of the subject comparatively inadequate. However, for other chapters, see George Adam Smith: *The Historical Geography of the Holy Land*, 26th ed., 1931, pages 467-496; Gustaf Dalman: *Sacred Sites and Ways*, 1935, pages 81-94; and the excellent article by Charles Warren in *Hastings Dictionary of the Bible*, II, 756-767. One may also still read with profit J. Macgregor's once widely circulated *Rob Roy On the Jordan* (1869).

A peaceful view on the Jordan, near the traditional site where John the Baptist carried on his ministry and baptized his converts. © MPS

JORIM (jō'rĭm, Gr. Ioreím, from Heb. yehôrām), an ancestor of Jesus in the genealogy of Luke (3:29).

JORKEAM (jôr'kē-ăm, Heb. yorqe'ām), a place inhabited by members of the family of Hezron and house of Caleb (I Chron. 2:44). It may be identical with "Jokdeam" of Joshua 15:56.

JOSABAD, JOZABAD (jŏs'à-băd, jŏz'à-băd, Heb. yôzāvādh, Jehovah has bestowed). 1. One of David's recruits at Ziklag (I Chron. 12:4).
2. Two Manassites who joined David at Ziklag (I Chron. 12:20).
3. A Levite overseer in Hezekiah's time (II Chron. 31:13).
4. A Levite, son of Jeshua (Ezra 8:33).
5. One of the priests who put away their foreign wives in the time of Ezra (Ezra 10:22).

JOSAPHAT (jŏs'à-făt, Gr. Iosaphát), KJV for Jehoshaphat in Matthew 1:8, the genealogy of Christ. An ancestor of Jesus.

JOSE (jō'sé, Gr. Iosé), KJV form for Jesus in Luke's genealogy (3:29).

JOSEDECH (jŏs'ĕ-dĕk, Heb. yehôtsādhāq, Jehovah is righteous), father of Jeshua the high priest (Ezra 3:2,8). He went into captivity under Nebuchadnezzar.

JOSEPH (jō'zĕf, Heb. yôsēph, may God add). 1. The eleventh of Jacob's 12 sons, and the firstborn son of Rachel, who said when he was born, "The Lord shall add to me another son," and therefore called his name Joseph (Gen. 30:24). He became the ancestor of the two northern tribes, Manasseh and Ephraim. The story of his birth is told in Genesis 30:22-24, and the story of the rest of his life in Genesis 37-50. He was born in Padan-aram when his father was 90 years old, and was his father's favorite child because he was Rachel's child and the son of his old age. The father's favoritism was shown in his getting for Joseph a coat of many colors, which was probably a token of rank indicating that it was his intention to make Joseph the head of the tribe; and it naturally aroused the envy of his elder brothers. Their ill will was increased when he somewhat imprudently told them two dreams he had which were suggestive of his future greatness and their subservience to him. When he was 17 years old, his father sent him to see how his brothers were doing at Shechem, where they were feeding their flocks; but when he arrived there, he found that they had gone on to Dothan, and he followed them thither. When they saw him coming, they planned to kill him, and thus make impossible the fulfilment of his dreams. Reuben, however, persuaded them not to kill him but to throw him alive into a pit, intending to rescue him later and restore him to his father. During a brief absence of Reuben, the brothers saw a caravan of Ishmaelites making their way to Egypt, and decided that instead of allowing Joseph to die in the well, they would sell him to these merchantmen. Joseph was sold. The brothers took his coat of many colors, besmeared it with the blood of a goat they had killed, and took it to Jacob, with the story that they had found the coat and assumed that their brother was dead, torn to pieces by some wild beast. The aged father, grief-stricken and disconsolate, mourned the loss of his son for many days.

In the meantime, Joseph was taken to Egypt by the Ishmaelites and sold in the slave market to an officer of the pharaoh, an Egyptian named Potiphar. The young slave proved himself to be so intelligent and trustworthy that his master soon entrusted to him all the affairs of his household, which prospered under Joseph's administration. But on the false accusations of Potiphar's wife, who had made improper advances, which he had rejected, Joseph was cast into prison, where he remained for years. God was with him, however, and the Providence that had previously saved his life now brought him to the favorable attention of the pharaoh. The prison keeper, finding that he could put implicit confidence in Joseph, committed to his charge the other prisoners. Among these were two of the pharaoh's officers, his chief butler and chief baker, who had been imprisoned for having offended the king. Joseph interpreted for them two dreams they had had; and three days later, on the king's birthday, as Joseph had foretold, the chief baker was hanged and the chief butler restored to his office (Gen. 40:5-23).

After two years, during which Joseph's circumstances remained unchanged — the chief butler having forgot his promise to mention him to the king—the pharaoh had two dreams which no one could interpret. They had to do with fat and lean kine, full and withered ears. The chief butler now remembered Joseph and told the king of Joseph's skill in interpreting dreams. Joseph was sent for. He told the pharaoh that both his dreams had the same meaning: seven years of plenty would be followed by seven years of famine, and suggested that preparation be made for the years of famine by storing up the surplus produce during the seven years of plenty against the years of famine. The king immediately made Joseph head of the royal granaries and invested him with authority of giving effect to his own proposal. As the head of a department of state, Joseph became one of the officials next in rank to the king (Gen. 41:39-44), and as a further mark of royal favor, he was given an Egyptian name and was married to the daughter of the priest of the great national temple of On. Joseph was now 30 years old. During the seven years of plenty he amassed corn in the granaries of every city, and his wife bore him two sons, Manasseh and Ephraim.

The famine that Joseph had predicted affected not only Egypt but all the known world, so that all countries came into Egypt to Joseph to buy corn. Joseph's brothers came too. They did not recognize him, but he knew them; and when they prostrated themselves before him he saw the fulfilment of the dreams which had aroused in them such intense jealousy. The crisis of the story is reached when Joseph, after testing their character in various ways, to see whether they had changed

The well at Dothan known as Joseph's Well. © MPS

for the better over the years, on their second visit made himself known to them, told them that he bore them no ill will for the wrong they had done him, and persuaded them and their father to settle in Egypt. The pharaohs then reigning in Egypt were probably members of the Hyksos dynasty, and were Semites, like Joseph; and they consequently cordially welcomed Jacob and his family to Egypt.

In the years that followed, Joseph brought about a permanent change in the Egyptian system of land-tenure, so that almost all the land became the property of the Pharaoh and the previous owners became his tenants. Jacob lived with Joseph in Egypt 17 years. Before he died, he adopted Joseph's two sons, putting them on the same level as his own sons in the division of the inheritance. Joseph lived to the age of 110. Before he died he expressed his confidence that God would some day bring the children of Israel back to Canaan, and solemnly directed that his bones be buried there. His wishes were carried out, and his bones were buried finally in Shechem, in the plot of ground bought there by Jacob. He became the ancestor of the two tribes Manasseh and Ephraim, the latter being the most powerful and important in northern Israel. He presents a noble ideal of character, remarkable for his gentleness, faithfulness to duty, magnanimity, and forgiving spirit, so that he is often regarded as an OT type of Christ.

2. The father of Igal of Issachar, one of the 12 spies (Num. 13:7).

3. A son of Asaph and head of a course of musicians in the reign of David (I Chron. 25:2,9).

4. A son of Bani, who had married a foreign wife and was induced by Ezra to put her away (Ezra 10:42).

5. A priest of the family of Shebaniah in the days of the high priest Joiakim (Neh. 12:14).

6. The name of three ancestors of Jesus according to the KJV (Luke 3:24,26,30); the name of two according to the RVs, which read "Josech" in Luke 3:26.

7. Son of Zacharias, defeated by Gorgias, c. 164 B.C., when he disobeyed the orders of Judas Maccabaeus about going into battle (I Macc. 5:18, 55-62).

8. The husband of Mary, the mother of Jesus (Matt. 1:16; Luke 3:23). He was a carpenter (Matt. 13:55) living in Nazareth (Luke 2:4). He was of Davidic descent (Matt. 1:20; Luke 2:4), the son of Heli (Luke 3:23) or Jacob (Matt. 1:16), and the supposed father of Jesus (Matt. 13:55; Luke 3:23; 4:22; John 1:45; 6:42). After learning that Mary was with child before marriage, he was minded to put her away "privily," but an angel assured him in a dream that the child to be born was conceived by the Holy Spirit, and he thereupon made her his wife (Matt. 1:18-25). When the emperor Augustus decreed that all the world should be enrolled in their ancestral homes, Joseph went with Mary to Bethlehem, and there Jesus was born. He was with Mary when the shepherds came to do homage to Jesus (Luke 2:8-20), and when, 40 days after His birth, Jesus was presented in the temple. Warned by the Lord in a dream that Herod was plotting the murder of the child, he fled with Mary and Jesus to Egypt (Matt. 2:13-19), returning to Nazareth after the death of Herod. Every year, at the Passover, he attended the feast in Jerusalem (Luke 2:41); and when Jesus was 12, he too went with Joseph and Mary. He undoubtedly taught Jesus the carpenter trade (Mark 6:3). It is likely that he was alive after the ministry of Jesus had well begun (Matt. 13:55), but as we do

Joseph's Tomb at the foot of Mount Ebal, on the "parcel of ground that Jacob gave to his son Joseph." © MPS

not hear of him in connection with the crucifixion, and as Jesus commended Mary to John at the crucifixion (John 19:26,27), it may be inferred that he had died prior to that event.

9. One of the brethren of Jesus, according to RV (Matt. 13:55). KJV has "Joses."

10. A Jew of Arimathaea, a place probably to the NW of Jerusalem. He is described as a rich man, a member of the Sanhedrin (Matt. 27:57; Mark 15:43), and a righteous man looking for the kingdom of God (Luke 23:50; Mark 15:43). A secret disciple of Jesus because of his fear of the Jews (John 19:38), he did not take part in the resolution of the Sanhedrin to put Jesus to death. After the crucifixion, he secured permission from Pilate to remove the body of Jesus from the cross, and laid it in his own newly-hewn tomb (Matt. 25:57-60; Luke 23:50-53; John 19:38).

11. A Christian called Barsabas, or son of Sabas, and surnamed Justus (Acts 1:23). He was one of those who had companied with Jesus and the apostles from the time of Jesus' baptism, and was one of the two candidates considered by the apostles as a replacement of Judas Iscariot. The lot fell upon Matthias (Acts 1:21,26).

12. The personal name of Barnabas (Acts 4:36; in KJV "Joses"). S.B.

JOSEPH BARSABAS (jō′sĕf bàr-sàb′ăs), an early disciple of Christ who became a candidate for the apostleship against Matthias (Acts 1:21,26), in order to fill the vacancy produced by the apostasy of Judas. Matthias was chosen. He may have been a brother of Judas, called Barsabbas (Acts 15:22).

JOSES (jō′sĕz, Gr. *Iosés*, a Gr. form of "Joseph"). 1. One of the brothers of Jesus (Mark 6:3). In Matthew 13:55 the Gr. is *Joseph*.

2. A name of Barnabas, for a time a co-worker of Paul (Acts 4:36). The Gr. has Joseph in this passage.

JOSHAH (jō′shà, Heb. *yôshâh*, Jehovah's gift), a descendant of Simeon, and the head of his family (I Chron. 4:34).

JOSHAPHAT (jŏsh′à-făt, Heb. *yôshâphât*, Jehovah has judged). 1. One of David's mighty men (I Chron. 11:43).

2. A priest and trumpeter in David's time (I Chron. 15:24, in KJV Jehoshaphat).

JOSHAVIAH (jŏsh′à-vī′à, Heb. *yôshawyâh*), son of Alnaam, one of David's mighty men (I Chron. 11:46).

JOSHBEKASHAH (jŏsh′bē-kā′shà), a son or descendant of Heman and a leader in music (I Chron. 25:4,24).

JOSHEB-BASSEBET (jŏ'shĕb-bă'sē-bĕt, *he that sitteth in the seat*, II Sam. 23:8), probably a corruption of Jashobeam, as in I Chronicles 11:11. One of David's mighty men. In ASV Josheb-basshebeth.

JOSHUA (jŏsh'ū-à), an Ephraimite, son of Nun (I Chron. 7:22-27), though born in Egyptian bondage, c. 1500 B.C., was named, significantly, Hoshea (Oshea), "salvation" (Num. 13:8; Deut. 32:44). Two months after Israel's exodus, 1446 B.C., he was appointed Moses' commander and successfully repulsed an Amalekite attack (Exod. 17:9). Moses changed Hoshea's name to Jehoshua *yehôshûa'*, "Jehovah is salvation" (Num. 13:16; I Chron. 7:27), or Joshua, later forms of which are Jeshua (*yēshûa'*, Neh. 8:17) and, in Greek, Jesus (*Iesoús*, Acts 7:45; Heb. 4:8); compare Matthew 1:21. Joshua attended Moses on Sinai (Exod. 24:13; 32:17) and guarded both his tent (33:11) and position (Num. 11:28). In 1445 B.C. he represented Ephraim in spying out Canaan. Joshua opposed the majority report, insisting that Israel, if faithful to God, could conquer Canaan, and almost suffered stoning (Num. 14:7-10). Subsequently, however, for having "wholly followed the Lord" (32:12), he not only escaped destruction (14:38) but also received assurance, unique to himself and Caleb (13:30; 14:24), of entering the Promised Land (14:30; 26:65).

In the spring of 1406 B.C., E of Jordan, God designated Joshua as Moses' successor (Num. 27:18). Moses charged him to faithfulness (Num. 27:23; Deut. 31:23), committed the "song of admonition" and other writings to him (Deut. 32:44; Exod. 17:14), counseled him on procedures (Num. 32:28; 34:17), and encouraged both new leader and people (Deut. 3:21; 31:3,7). God Himself warned Joshua of coming apostasy (31:14), but promised his successful accomplishment of the conquest (31:23; 1:38; 3:28).

Upon Moses' death, Joshua, as the oldest man in Israel, must have been in his nineties (contrast the octogenarian Caleb, Josh. 13:1; 14:7-11). Yet God assured him of victory, as he relied on the inspired Book of Moses (1:6-9). From this point onward, Joshua's history is that of Israel's occupation of Canaan. His personal actions, however, include making preparations (1:10-18), sending spies against Jericho (2:1,23-24), and then ordering Israel's advance across Jordan (3:1). His faith in anticipating its passage inaugurated a life of undiminishing esteem, similar even to that of Moses (3:7; 4:14; cf. liberalism's usually limiting Joshua to local Ephraimitic leadership, IB II: 546). West of Jordan, Joshua superintended Israel's rituals (5:2) and the construction of monuments for the faith of children yet to come (4:4-7). The theophany of "the Prince of Jehovah's host" (5:13-15 ASV) served as a dramatic sentence upon Jericho but also as a visible confirmation of Joshua's divine call, similar to the Angel of the Lord's appearance to Moses at the burning bush (Exod. 3:2-6). Joshua worshiped and then executed the God-directed siege (Josh. 6:2-6). He "devoted" (destroyed) Jericho (vs. 17), pronounced a curse on its rebuilding (vs. 26, I Kings 16:34), and achieved widespread recognition (vs. 27).

When the disobedience of Achan brought defeat at Ai, Joshua's prayer, his zeal for God's glory, and his enforcement of divine judgment (7:6-9,19, 25) compare favorably with his subsequent faithfulness to God's orders and exemplary execution of Ai's king (8:2,29; cf. 10:24-27,40-41). With central Palestine subdued, Joshua personally wrote

Moses' law on the stones at Ebal and then proclaimed this law to the whole Israelitish assembly (8:30-35). Though guilty of rashness with the Gibeonites, he later condemned these pagans to bondage (9:15,22-23,26-27); and the energy he displayed in forced marches and sudden attacks frustrated Canaanite counter-offensives in both south (10:9) and north (11:7). Basically it was Jehovah who fought for Israel, but even His prolonging of light for battle at Beth-horon (10:12-14) came in answer to Joshua's prayers (cf. Bernard Ramm, *Christian View of Science and Scripture*, Grand Rapids: Eerdmans, 1955, pp. 156-161, with J. B. Payne, *Bulletin E.T.S.* 3:4 [1960], 95-96). In six years (14:10), Joshua took the whole land, "leaving nothing undone of all that the Lord commanded Moses" (11:15,23).

Yet Moses had anticipated a gradual occupation (Exod. 23:28-30). God had left in Canaan many nations, subdued but still powerful, to prove His people (Josh. 13:2-6; Judg. 2:21-3:4); and Joshua could not achieve Israel's final "rest" (Heb. 4:8). Thus, because of his advanced age, he forthwith allotted Canaan to the tribes (Josh. 13:6-7; 14:1; 19:51). At Gilgal he confirmed Moses' Transjordanian settlement and assigned territory to Judah, including Caleb's portion at Hebron (14:13; 15:13), and to Ephraim and Manasseh (cf. 17:4), encouraging them to more effective conquest even while refusing to show them partiality (17:14-18). Later, at Shiloh, he exhorted the seven hesitant tribes, dispatched a commission on apportionment, and thus allotted the remaining lands (18:3,8-10), including cities of refuge and Levitical assignments (20-21). He himself requested and built Timnath-serah in Ephraim (19:49-51).

As death approached, Joshua first summoned Israel's leaders, urging them to faithfulness in conquest (23), and then assembled the tribal heads to Shechem, charging them to "choose this day whom ye will serve" (24:15). Having renewed their covenant with Jehovah, he inserted it in the book of God's law (24:25-26) and died at an age of 110 (24:29-30; Judg. 2:8-9). Throughout his days, and even thereafter, he maintained Israel in faithfulness to her Lord (Josh. 24:31; Judg. 1:1; 2:7). J.B.P.

JOSHUA, BOOK OF, stands sixth in Scripture, recording how Moses' successor, after whom the book is named, conquered Canaan, as promised (1:1; 24:31; see JOSHUA, above). But while Joshua commences "the historical books" in English (and Greek), it introduces "the prophets" in the original Hebrew canon of Law, Prophets, and Writings. These prophetical books include the "latter prophets," Isaiah-Malachi, but also the "former prophets" — Joshua, Judges, Samuel, and Kings — since Biblical prophets, as God's spokesmen (Exod. 7:1-2), enforced their messages both from the past and from the future. Joshua thus exemplifies historical "prophetic" preaching, in respect to authorship as well as content.

Joshua's prophetic author is not named; but his statements about the deaths of Joshua and his colleagues (Josh. 24:29,31), plus his allusions to Othniel, the migration of the Danites (15:17; 19:47), and the name Hormah (12:14; 15:30; 19:4) indicate his living after the rise of Israel's judges, c. 1380 (Judg. 1:12-13,17). At the same time, his designation of Jerusalem as Jebusite (Josh. 15:8, 63; 18:16,28) and his writing before its choice as the site of God's temple (9:27), require him to antedate David, 1000 B.C. (I Chron. 11:4-6; 22:1). His references, moreover, to Sidon rather than to Tyre as Phoenicia's leading city (11:8; 13:4-6;

19:28) suggest a date prior to 1200 B.C. Indeed, the writer must have been an eye-witness of the events he describes. For he speaks of the Lord's blocking Jordan, "until *we* were passed over" (5: 1, consonantal Hebrew text); he identifies Israel's previous generation by saying, "God would not show them the land, which . . . He would give *us*" (5:6); he says of the harlot Rahab, "She dwelleth in Israel even unto this day" (6:25); and after outlining their boundaries he addresses Judah directly, "This shall be your south coast" (15:4). Compare also his detailed narratives (2:3-22; 7: 16-26) and repeated use of pre-conquest place names (15:9,49,54). Since the writer follows Moses' deuteronomic style and seemingly had access to Joshua himself (cf. 5:13-15), a proposed author has been Phinehas, the son and successor of high-priest Eleazar, the son of Aaron, who ministered at Peor in 1406 (Num. 25:7-13; 31:6-8) and thereafter (Josh. 22:13-20; Judg. 20:28). Someone, then, of his standing composed the prophetical book of Joshua, approximately 1375 B.C.

"Almost all" (IB II:541) modern critics, however, attribute Joshua to four mutually contradictory source-documents, brought together over a millennium after Phinehas: not such authenticated sources as Joshua's own writings (24:26, plus other sections, cf. P. A. Fernandez, *Commentarius in Librum Josue*, Paris: P. Lethellieux, 1938, pp. 3-22) and the contemporary poetry (The Book of "the *yāshār* [Upright]," 10:13, an anthology of hero-songs, cf. David's later lament over Jonathan, II Sam. 1:18), but J.E.D.P. documents, as alleged by Wellhausen for the Mosaic writings (see PENTA-TEUCH), thus making Genesis-Joshua into a "hexateuch" (cf. Pfeiffer's elaborate analysis, *Introduction to the Old Testament*, New York: Harper, 1941, pp. 296-313; or John Bright's more cautious approach, which acknowledges the impossibility of tracing-out the "documents," even while insisting upon their existence, IB II:541; or Martin Noth's theory, *Das Buch Josua*, Tübingen: Mohr, 1938, of a complete, deuteronomic [non-Pentateuchal] history of Israel). In particular, the "E" and "D" records of conquest under Joshua are rejected in favor of the "earlier" "J" records, purportedly teaching a gradual occupation of Palestine by independent tribes (cf. Judg. 1; but contrast W. F. Albright's opposition to Noth and insistence upon Joshua's historicity, though dated in 1230 rather than 1400, BASOR 74 [1939], p. 23, and Bright's harmonizations, IB II:547-548). But while Joshua does fulfill God's former promises (Gen. 13:14-17; 15:13-20), Scripture knows nothing of a hexateuch. The Pentateuchal books of Moses are unique (Josh. 1:7-8; II Chron. 34:14; cf. Christ's own testimony, Luke 24:44), while Joshua forms a sequel to the Law (Josh. 24:26), though doubtless accepted upon completion as a "prophet," and fully canonical in "The Book" (I Sam. 10:25 ASVm).

The prophetical character of Joshua, moreover, affects content, in the book's two divisions: conquest (1-12), and settlement (13-24). The conquest embraces Israel's entrance into Canaan: Joshua's inauguration, the Jericho spies, crossing Jordan, and ceremonies (1-5:12); the conquest of the center: Jericho, Ai, and the assembly at Ebal (5:13-8); of the south: Gibeon, and the Jerusalem confederacy (9:10); and of the north: the Hazor confederacy, plus a summary (11-12). But since this took "a long time" (11:18; 1406-1400 B.C., 14: 10), the Biblical content limits itself to representative instances of rewarded faithfulness: "Be strong, and there shall not a man be able to stand before thee" (1:5-6; 11:23). Israel's settlement embraces

Joshua's territorial apportionments, at Gilgal (13-17), and Shiloh (18-19), including cities of refuge, Levitical towns, and Transjordan (20-22), and demonstrating how God "gave unto Israel all the land which He sware unto their fathers" (21:43). Then follow Joshua's two farewell addresses, enjoining upon Israel that response which prophecy ever elicits: "The Lord our God will we serve, and His voice will we obey" (24:24).   J.B.P.

JOSIAH (jō-zī'à, Heb. *yŏ'shîyāhû, Jehovah supports him*), son of Amon and Jedidah and the grandson of Manasseh, the son of Hezekiah. Josiah's reign on the Davidic throne for 31 years was the last surge of political independence and religious revival before the disintegration of the Southern Kingdom which ended with the destruction of Jerusalem in 586 B.C.

When palace slaves slew King Amon in 642 B.C. the eight-year-old Josiah was crowned king of Judah. While the boy-king grew to manhood, the imposing international influence of Assyria declined rapidly. Insurrections and rebellions in the East and the death of Ashurbanipal (c. 633 B.C.) provided an opportunity for a rising tide of nationalism in Judah. By 612 B.C. the coalition of Media under Cyaxares and Babylon under Nabopolassar converged on Nineveh to destroy Assyria's famous capital. Within three years the Babylonians had routed the last of the great Assyrian army. These decades gave Josiah the political advantage not only to assert Judah's independence but also extended its influence into the northern tribes — perhaps even kindling fond hopes of claiming the boundaries as established by David and Solomon.

Josiah's religious leadership ranks him with Jehoshaphat and Hezekiah as an outstanding righteous ruler. Gross idolatry — Baal altars, asherim, star and planetary worship. Moloch deity acknowledged in the sacrifice of children in the Hinnóm Valley, astrology, occultism, altars for worshiping the host of heaven in the temple court, and the shedding of innocent blood — all these permeated the land of Judah during the reign of Manasseh (686-642 B.C.), whose personal penitence and reform in all likelihood did not penetrate the kingdom of Judah sufficiently to reconstruct the religious pattern. Whatever reform had been affected by Manasseh after his release from captivity was countered by a reversion to idolatry under Amon. Josiah gradually reacted to these godless influences that permeated his kingdom (II Chron. 34). In the eighth year of his reign (c. 632 B.C.) he began to seek after God and four years later initiated reforms. Images, altars, and all manner of idolatrous practices were destroyed not only in Jerusalem and Judah but in the cities of Manasseh, Ephraim, Simeon, and as far north as Naphtali. At the same time offerings and contributions were collected throughout the nation for the restoration of the temple in Jerusalem which had been neglected for such a long period.

In the course of renovating the temple (622 B.C.) the book of the law was recovered. The reformation movement consequently was stimulated anew by the reading of this "book of the Law given by Moses." Not only had the reading and observance of the law been neglected in preceding decades, but it is possible that Manasseh even destroyed existing copies which were in circulation throughout the land of Judah. Huldah the prophetess warned the people of impending judgment awaiting them for their neglect of the law. Stirred by these developments Josiah led his nation in the observance of the Passover in a manner unprecedented in Judah's history.

With the king himself leading the reformation movement, changes in personnel occurred. Priests serving by royal appointment of former kings and dedicated to idol worship were removed from office. Josiah, however, made temple revenues available for their support. The religious climate established by Josiah must have provided favorable conditions for Jeremiah's ministry during the first 18 years of his ministry (627-609 B.C.), even though no references are made to the association of these great leaders in the historical records (II Kings 22-23 and II Chron. 34-35).

In 609 B.C. Josiah's leadership was abruptly ended. In an effort to interfere with Necho's plans to aid the Assyrians Josiah was fatally wounded at Megiddo. National and religious hopes vanished with the funeral of this 39-year-old king so that all Judah had reason to join Jeremiah in lamenting for Josiah. S.J.S.

JOSIBIAH (jŏs'ĭ-bī'à), a Simeonite mentioned only in I Chronicles 4:35. In ASV Joshibiah.

JOSIPHIAH (jŏs'ĭ-fī'à, Heb. *yôsiphyâh, Jehovah will increase*), the ancestor of 160 men who returned with Ezra from Babylon (Ezra 8:10).

JOT (jŏt), a corruption of *iote* (found in early editions of the KJV), an English transliteration of *iota,* the ninth letter of the Greek alphabet, which is the nearest equivalent of the Hebrew *yodh,* the smallest letter in the Hebrew alphabet and almost identical with our apostrophe sign, '. Used figuratively, the "jot" signifies something of apparently small moment. See Matthew 5:17,18.

JOTBAH (jŏt'bà, Heb. *yotbâh, pleasantness*), a Levitical city in Judah, just S of Hebron. Called Juttah in Joshua 15:55; 21:16. Mentioned in II Kings 21:19 as the home of the father-in-law of Jotham, king of Judah.

JOTBATH (jŏt'băth), Deuteronomy 10:7; see Jotbathah.

JOTBATHAH (jŏt'bà-thà, Heb. *yotbāthâh, pleasantness*), a place in the Wilderness of Paran in the peninsula of Sinai where Israel encamped (Num. 33:33,34; Deut. 10:7). Site unknown. In KJV once Jotbath (Deut. 10:7).

JOTHAM (jō'thăm, Heb. *yôthām, Jehovah is perfect*). 1. The youngest of the 70 sons of Gideon, and the speaker of the first Bible parable (Judg. 9:5-57). After the death of Gideon, Abimelech, an illegitimate son, got the men of Shechem behind him and desired to make himself a king over Israel. To that end he slew his half-brothers, all but Jotham, the youngest, who hid himself, and so escaped. When the Shechemites had made Abimelech king, Jotham spoke his notable parable of the trees and the bramble and pronounced a curse upon them and upon Abimelech.

2. A man of the tribe of Judah (I Chron. 2:47).

3. King of Judah. He was born a son of Uzziah, king of Judah. Uzziah had been for the most part a good and a powerful king, but his successes turned his head and he intruded into the priest's office (II Chron. 26:16). As a result, he was struck with leprosy, and Jotham acted as regent. Jotham began to reign just about the time when Isaiah began his great ministry (Isa. 6:1) and was probably influenced by that godly man, and perhaps by Hosea and Micah as well. He had victory over the Ammonites, who were forced to pay him heavy tribute, and he himself was a great builder, fortifying several places in Judah and building the upper gate of the temple. For his story see II Kings 15:32-38 and II Chronicles 27.

JOURNEY, SABBATH DAY'S, mentioned only in Acts 1:12, according to tradition, was 2,000 cubits, which would fit the description of the mount called Olivet as being a Sabbath day's journey from Jerusalem.

JOY. In the Word of God, joy is an attribute of Deity (Ps. 104:31), and is an important part of that ninefold "fruit of the Spirit" (Gal. 5:22,23) which He imparts to believers (Gal. 5:24). Joy is often equated with happiness, but the two are quite distinct. Happiness depends largely upon happenings: good health, congenial company, pleasant surroundings, etc. Happiness and unhappiness do not exist together; but joy and sorrow can and do. Our Lord was "a man of sorrows and acquainted with grief" (Isa. 53:3) but "for the joy that was set before him, endured the cross, despising the shame, and is set down at the right hand of the throne of God" (Heb. 12:2). Paul and Silas, scourged and imprisoned and with their feet in the stocks could hardly be described as "happy," but at midnight they sang praises to God (Acts 16:23-33) with such joy that God caused an earthquake, and not only delivered them but brought joy and salvation to the jailer's household. A.B.F.

JOZABAD (jŏz'à-băd, Heb. *yôzāvādh, Jehovah endows*). 1. A man from Gederah in Judah who joined David at Ziklag (I Chron. 12:4 but "Josabad" in KJV).

2. Two men of the tribe of Manasseh who also joined David (I Chron. 12:20).

3. One of the Levites whom Hezekiah appointed to be overseers in the house of God (II Chron. 31:13).

4. A chief Levite in the time of Josiah who gave large offerings of cattle to the Levites for passover offerings (II Chron. 35:9).

5. A Levite who assisted in the weighing of the gold and silver which Ezra and his companions had brought from Babylon as gifts for the house of God (Ezra 8:33).

6. A priest who had married a woman outside of Israel in the days of Ezra, and who gave his promise to put her away (Ezra 10:22).

7. A Levite who had committed the same offense (Ezra 10:23).

8. A Levite, who at the reading of the law in Nehemiah's reformation, translated from the Hebrew as it was read into the Aramaic so that the common people would understand (Neh. 8:7).

9. A chief Levite in Nehemiah's time who helped oversee the outward business of the temple (Neh. 11:16).

JOZACHAR (jŏz'à-kàr, Heb. *yôzāchār, whom Jehovah has remembered*), one of the two assassins of Joash, king of Judah. He was the son of an Ammonite woman named Shimeath (II Kings 12:20,21; II Chron. 24:26). In the second of these passages he is called Zabad, almost certainly by error of an early scribe. Jozacar in RV.

JOZADAK (jŏz'à-dăk, Heb. *yehôtsādhāq, Jehovah is righteous*), father of Jeshua the priest who returned with Zerubbabel (Ezra 3:2, etc.). Called Josedech in Haggai and Zechariah.

JUBAL (joo'băl, Heb. *yûvāl*), son of Lamech by his wife Adah. He was the inventor of the harp and pipe (Gen. 4:21).

JUBILEE (joo'bĭ-lē, Heb. *yôvēl, ram's horn, trumpet*; Gr. *iobelaios*). According to Leviticus 25, every 50th year in Israel was to be announced as a jubilee year. Three essential features characterized this year. First, liberty was proclaimed to all Israelites who were in bondage to any of their countrymen. The law provided that the price of slaves was to vary according to the proximity of the Jubilee Year. Second, there was to be a return of ancestral possessions to those who had been compelled to sell them because of poverty. This, of course, excluded the possibility of selling a piece of land permanently. This law applied to lands and houses outside of the walled cities, and also to the houses owned by Levites, whether in walled cities or not. As in the case of the price of slaves, the law made provision that the price of real property was to vary according to the proximity of the Jubilee Year. The third feature of this year was that it was to be a year of rest for the land. The land was to remain fallow, even though it had been so in the previous sabbatical year. The people were to live simply, on what the fields had produced in the sixth year and whatever grew spontaneously. It is impossible to say whether the Jewish people ever really observed the Jubilee Year.

S.B.

JUBILEES, BOOK OF, a Jewish apocalyptic book written in the inter-testamental period. It gives a history of the world from the creation to the giving of the law, and defends Pharisaical views as against liberal Hellenistic tendencies.

JUCAL (jōō'kăl, Heb. *yehûkhal, Jehovah is able*), one of the evil princes of Judah who put Jeremiah into prison for his prophecies (Jer. 38:1).

JUDA (See Judah)

JUDAEA (See Judea)

JUDAH (jōō'dà, Heb. *yehûdhâh, praised*). 1. The fourth son of Jacob; his mother was Leah (Gen. 29:35). Few details of his life are known. He saved Joseph's life by persuading his brothers to sell him to the Midianites at Dothan (Gen. 37:26-28.) His disgraceful actions recorded in Genesis 38 left a stain upon his memory. He gradually appears to have achieved leadership among his brothers (Gen. 43:3; 46:28; 49:8-12) and no doubt it was during his own lifetime that the rivalry among them arose which was much later to give rise to the division of the kingdom. Through his son Perez, Judah became an ancestor of David (Ruth 4:18-22) and of Jesus Christ (Matt. 1:3-16). The blessing of dying Jacob to Judah (Gen. 49:9, 10) is usually understood as being a Messianic prophecy.

2. Also the name of the Hebrew tribe descended from the man Judah described above. In the wilderness, the tribe camped to the E of the tabernacle, next to the Issachar tribe (Num. 2:3-5). Caleb, a hero among the Hebrew spies and captors of Canaan, was a member of this tribe (Num. 13:6; 34:19). Judah was one of the tribes which stood on Mt. Gerizim to bless the people at the ceremony of covenant renewal at Shechem (Deut. 27: 12). After Joshua's death, this tribe seems to have been first in occupying its allotted territory in the southern hill country of Canaan, even to occupying temporarily the city of Jerusalem (Judg. 1:1-20). Upon settling in Canaan, the tribe of Judah occupied the territory extending from the extreme southern point of the Dead Sea eastward to the Mediterranean, lying S of Kadesh Barnea. Its western boundary was the Mediterranean. On the N, the boundary began at the northern end of the Dead Sea and lay westward in a crooked line, running to the S of Jericho, and just S of Jerusalem (the valley of Hinnom, which was the southern boundary of this city was also the Judeans' northern line) and thence to the Mediterranean through Beth Shemesh and Timnah. Of course, the Dead Sea was the eastern boundary (Josh. 15).

Judah's was one of the largest tribal territories. From E to W it measured some 45 miles. The north-south dimension of that part fit for intensive habitation was about 50 miles, while if the Negev area, suited only for scattered dwelling was included, the length was 100 miles. Judah's territory consisted of three north-south belts of land: (1) the Judean hill country (Josh. 15:48), the eastern slopes of which were the wilderness of Judah; (2) the lowlands of Shephelah (Josh. 15:33), the low, rolling land where the hill country meets the plain, and (3) the plain near the Mediterranean sea. The southern part, near and S of Beer-sheba was called the Negev. Much of the tribe's land was hilly and rocky, but apart from the wilderness of Judah and the Negev, was well suited for pasture and for the cultivation of the grape and olive (Gen. 49:11,12). In ancient times the hills were terraced.

During the period of the rule of the judges, Judah tended to be separated from the rest of the Hebrew tribes, which lived to the N, by pagan people dwelling between them (Gibeonites, Josh. 9; Jebusites, Judg. 19:10-13), and also by rough and wild land, with deep east-west valleys to the N of Judah. The Simeonites, who lived in southern Judean cities tended to become assimilated into Judah and thus to lose their tribal identity.

Othniel, the judge who delivered the people from the domination of Mesopotamia, was a Judean (Judg. 3:8-11). The Philistine threat must have been especially troublesome to this tribe, for the Philistine plain, as it came to be called, was actually Judah's coastal plain land. The story of Ruth and Boaz, which centers in Bethlehem, occurs during the time of the judges and first brings the country town of Bethlehem into prominence in Hebrew history. Saul, whose reign brings the judges' period to an end, ruled over Judah, and it was the Judeans who first anointed their fellow tribesman, David, king at Hebron (II Sam. 2:1-4).

3. Judah is also the name of five individuals who are mentioned in Ezra-Nehemiah. Three were Levites (Ezra 3:9; Neh. 12:8; Ezra 10:23), one a Benjamite (Neh. 11:9) and the fifth probably a prince of Judah (Neh. 12:34). J.B.G.

JUDAH, KINGDOM OF.

1. The United Hebrew Kingdom. Saul, a Benjamite was Israel's first king (I Sam. 8-II Sam. 1). His reign was not a success, and when he died (about 1000 B.C.), a period of civil war broke out among the Hebrew tribes. Out of this chaos emerged David (II Sam. 1-I Kings 2), a member of the tribe of Judah, who founded the dynasty which continued to rule in Jerusalem until the destruction of the capital city by the Babylonians (587 B.C.). David and his son Solomon (I Kings 2-11) succeeded in unifying the Hebrew tribes and imposing their rule on the whole nation. During their reigns the Hebrews achieved national greatness and empire. When Solomon died, all of this came to an end; the greater part of the nation seceded from the Judean rule to form the northern kingdom of Israel. The Davidic dynasty continued to rule at Jerusalem over a small remnant of the nation. This remnant is called the kingdom of Judah.

2. Background of the Divided Kingdom. It must not be thought that the mere ineptitude of Rehoboam, Solomon's son (I Kings 12) caused the split of the Hebrew kingdom. Ever since their settlement in Canaan after the exodus from Egypt, the Israelite tribes had manifested a fierce independence of each other and a great reluctance to give up tribal sovereignty to a national head. On several occasions during the period of the judges (Judg. 8:1-3; 12:1-6; 20) strife and even open war broke out among the tribes. It would appear that the troubles in the period between the death of Saul and David's move of the capital to Jerusalem (II Sam. 2-4) amounted to a divided kingdom, with Judah (the southern center of power) adhering to David, but Israel (the Joseph tribes in central Palestine, and the northern tier of tribes) keeping aloof from David, seeking to establish Saul's son Ishbosheth as their king. Evidently they felt that accepting David's claims meant giving up too much local autonomy to the central government. After his capture of Jerusalem and the submission of all the tribes to him, David managed to keep the nation together by firm rule combined with a wise handling of explosive personalities. In the weakness of his old age, however, the centrifugal forces again asserted themselves (II Sam. 20). Solomon clamped on the nation a firm rule, assessing heavy taxes and forced labor. We infer that Judah was exempt from his most objectionable requirements, a condition hardly likely to please the ever restless Israelite tribes.

When Solomon died there already existed an Israelite government in exile, headed by Jeroboam, son of Nebat (I Kings 1:26-40). He returned to Palestine to confront Solomon's son Rehoboam with an ultimatum — "make the heavy yoke lighter or we will not serve you" (I Kings 12:1-11). Rehoboam, stubborn and inept, tried to assert force instead of making concessions, and Jeroboam split the kingdom by organizing a secession government in Israel, which ultimately (under Omri) was centered in the city of Samaria.

3. Resources and Organization of the Kingdom of Judah. Rehoboam continued to reign over a small southern region, mainly equal to the territory of Judah. Most of Benjamite territory appears to have gone with the northern rebels (I Kings 12:20), but Jerusalem, in the extreme south of Benjamin, stayed with Judah, because of the presence of Rehoboam's army there, and remained his capital. Thus the boundary between Judah and Israel must have run a few miles N of Jerusalem. All of southern Palestine (much of it desert) was held by Rehoboam. Even so, his territory was not more than half the size of the northern kingdom; his arable land, less than one-fourth as much as Israel's. Judah claimed suzerainty over Edom, and asserted it when she was able. Judah's population (estimated at 300,000) was about half that of Israel's. The northern kingdom had the best farm land and was favored with more rainfall than the south.

In spite of her small size Judah enjoyed certain advantages over Israel. Jerusalem, with its ancient heritage of the temple and its divinely ordained worship, together with the Davidic dynasty and the buildings and traditions of the strong Solomonic empire were hers. Her location in the southern hill country removed her somewhat from the ever increasing tempo of struggle for control of the road to Egypt by the Assyrians, which struggle was to eventuate in Israel's destruction. She tended to be a city state (no other Judean city could begin to compete with Jerusalem) with a homogeneous population and strong centralization of authority, thus avoiding the weakness of decentralization which characterized the northern kingdom. The continuing Davidic dynasty (Israel had nine dynasties during the reign of 19 kings) and a Levitic priesthood (attached to the Jerusalem temple) were sources of continuing strength.

4. The History of the Kingdom of Judah. It is difficult to isolate Judah's history. In the Biblical sources (the books of Kings and Chronicles) the accounts of Israel and Judah are intertwined, with Israel predominating. One gets the impression that Israel's story is dynamic and attractive, while Judah's existence (except for certain great periods) was conservative — essentially a "holding operation."

This article will not attempt to detail the events of the reigns of each of Judah's 19 kings. The student is referred to the articles in this dictionary on each of these kings for the details. The purpose of this article is rather to see the history as a whole. Judah's history from the death of Solomon to the fall of Jerusalem to the Babylonians may be divided into three periods.

a. Judah from the death of Solomon to the mid-eighth century, 922-742 B.C. During this period of nearly two centuries Judah and Israel lived side by side. For the first two generations the successive Judean kings fought against Israel, seeking to compel her to reunite with the South. Beginning with Jehoshaphat, however, they saw the impossibility of success in this attempt, for Israel was, if anything, more powerful than Judah. Jehoshaphat began a tradition of friendly cooperation with Israel, which, with few exceptions, characterized the Judean kings until the fall of Samaria left the South to carry on alone.

The split of the kingdom at the accession of Rehoboam has been described. Obviously, with this event the Hebrew empire raised by David and Solomon collapsed. Judah was now a second-rate power — a city state in the hills. As if to prove its degradation, Shishak, a soldier turned king of Egypt invaded Palestine seeking to revive the Egyptian empire. According to the Bible he badly looted Jerusalem; Shishak's own historical inscriptions at Karnak indicate that he sacked most of Palestine. Rehoboam's pathetic copper shields, a cheap imitation of the looted gold ones (I Kings 14:25-28) symbolize the condition of post-Solomonic Judah—the grandeur had departed.

Rehoboam and his son Abijah (Abijam) seem to have carried on Solomon's syncretistic tendencies; pagan rites flourished. Asa and Jehoshaphat instituted reforms aimed at purifying the worship of Yahweh of paganism. Jehoshaphat is known for the marriage of his son Jehoram to Athaliah, daughter of Ahab and Jezebel, of Israel, thus sealing his new policy of friendliness for the northern kingdom. This policy seems to have brought great prosperity to Judah, but also the threat that the baalism sponsored by Ahab in Israel might spread to the south.

Jehoram and Ahaziah were briefly succeeded by Athaliah, who was their wife and mother, respectively. She sought to stamp out all the Judean royal house and to make Baalism the worship of Judah. A palace-temple coup resulted in her death (837 B.C.), the restoration of the Davidic line in the person of Joash, the boy king, and the revival of the worship of Yahweh sponsored by Jehoiada the high priest.

Amaziah and Uzziah reigned during a great burst of political and economic prosperity, just before the coming of the Assyrian invasions and Israel's captivity. Judah and Israel occupy briefly much of the old Solomonic empire land. Increased trade brought home great wealth. Luxury (especially in Israel) was unprecedented. It was to the spiritually careless people of this time, at ease in Zion that the great eighth century prophets—Amos, Hosea, Jonah, Isaiah and Micah — came.

b. Judah during the period of the Assyrian Ascendancy, 742-687 B.C. In the third quarter of the eighth century an event occurred which was to influence all of succeeding history. The Assyrian empire, with its capital at Nineveh, moved westward in its effort to capture the civilized world. Ultimately Israel, located as she was on the road to Egypt, was destroyed by Assyria (722 B.C.) and Judah severely damaged.

King Ahaz first brought Judah into the Assyrian orbit when he called on her to relieve him from the attack of an anti-Assyrian coalition, Syria and Israel. Judah was saved, Damascus destroyed and part of Israel overrun by the Assyrians (733-732 B.C.), but at the cost of bringing Judah into the Assyrian orbit. There naturally followed spiritual subordination, and Ahaz introduced Assyrian religious practices into Jerusalem. This problem of imported paganism was to plague Judah until its fall. Late in Ahaz' reign the city of Samaria was destroyed and Israel's national existence brought to an end. Hezekiah, the pious son of Ahaz, sensing a weakening of Assyrian power, sought to throw off both the political and religious yoke of Assyria. Under him, Judah managed to survive the attacks of Sennacherib, although at fearful cost. Hezekiah reformed the national religion, purifying it of paganism. His treaty with the rising power of Babylon, a threat to Assyrian domination of Mesopotamia, although condemned by Isaiah, was another facet of his struggle to keep Judah free. The prophets Isaiah and Micah continue their ministry into this period. Certainly much of Hezekiah's success in religious reform was due to Isaiah's support.

c. The Last Century of the Kingdom of Judah, 687-587 B.C. During Judah's last century of national existence Palestine was the scene of intermittent warfare; empires clashed, fell and rose around her until finally she fell to the last Semitic world empire — Babylon. The destruction of the city of Nineveh (612 B.C.) spelled the fall of the Assyrian empire. It was replaced by the new Babylonian empire, of which Nebuchadnezzar was the militant head. Egypt still tried to play a part in the political struggle and her nearness to Palestine made her also a power to be reckoned with in Judah. Placed between great world powers, relying alternately upon each, but seldom (according to the prophets) on her God, Judah played a fateful, increasingly unsteady role until Jerusalem was destroyed and her people taken captive.

Manasseh, son of Hezekiah, through a long reign chose to submit again to Assyrian political and religious control. His grandson, Josiah, was the last good Hebrew king, and the last one whose reign saw anything like normal times in the Judean kingdom. Josiah's famous revival (621 B.C.), the most thorough-going in Judah's history, was aided by the rediscovery of the Mosaic law (probably Deuteronomy) in the temple. Josiah made a great effort to rid Judah of all paganism and to centralize all the worship of Yahweh at the Jerusalem temple. This meant rebellion against Assyria, which Josiah was able to carry out; in fact, it was during his reign that the Assyrian empire disintegrated. Josiah tragically lost his life trying to oppose the forces of the Egyptian Pharaoh Necho, who were crossing Palestine on their way to Syria to fight in the battles which marked the death throes of Assyria.

During Josiah's reign the young Jeremiah began his prophetic career, which extended into the period of the captivity. A sad man with a depressing message, Jeremiah predicted the fall of the nation because of her sins. Evidently Josiah's revival had done little to stop the downgrade trend.

Unsettled, fearful times followed Josiah's death. King Jehoiakim, a puppet of Egypt, was unworthy to follow his father Josiah. Jeremiah steadily opposed his easy trust that the temple would bring security. The Babylonians raided Jerusalem during his reign (605 B.C.). Finally the proud, wicked king was killed in a coup and his son Jehoiachin replaced him. After three months the Babylonians captured Jerusalem (597 B.C.) and took captive to Babylon many important persons, including the king. This was the beginning of the end. Babylon, having replaced Nineveh as the center of world power would dominate Judah until she destroyed her.

Zedekiah, another son of Josiah, was made regent in the place of captive Jehoiachin. He rebelled against Babylon, made a league with Egypt and so incurred the wrath of the Babylonians that they decided to destroy Jerusalem. After a bitter siege of a year and a half the city fell to Nebuchadnezzar and was destroyed, Zedekiah was blinded and carried to Babylon, and the great bulk of the population taken there with him (587 B.C.). Archaeologists have found that all of the cities of Judah were completely destroyed at this time. Thus ended the glorious kingdom of David and Solomon. Observers would have said that the Hebrew nation was annihilated, and indeed, the other nations conquered by the Assyrians and Babylonians did cease to exist. But the prophets proclaimed a better hope for the chosen people. "A remnant shall return" Isaiah had said, and in time this remnant, purged and returned, became the basis on which a new Israel would be built.   J.B.G.

JUDAISM (jōō′dā-ĭz'm), the religious system held by the Jews. Its teachings come from the OT, especially from the law of Moses as found from Exodus 20 through Deuteronomy; but also from the traditions of the elders (Mark 7:3-13), some of which our Lord condemned. The principal elements of Judaism include circumcision, a strict monotheism, an abhorrence of idolatry, and sabbath-keeping.

JUDAS, JUDA (jōō′dàs, jōō′dà, Heb. *yehûdhâh, praised,* Gr. *Ioúdas*). 1. An ancestor of our Lord. (Luke 3:30 ASV).

2. A Galilean insurrectionist (Acts 5:37). According to Gamaliel, this Judas perished and his followers were scattered.

3. One of the brothers of our Lord (Matt. 13:55). This Judas is almost certainly the "Jude" who wrote the epistle by that name.

4. An apostle of Jesus called "Judas of James" (Luke 6:16) rendered in KJV "Judas the brother of James," and in ASV "Judas, the son of James."

5. One who apparently had a guest-house or hostel in the street which was called Straight in the city of Damascus and with whom Paul lodged (Acts 9:11).

6. One of the leading brethren in the church at Jerusalem at the Council of Jerusalem (Acts 15:6-35). His surname "Barsabas" i.e. "son of Saba" hints that he *may* have been brother of Joseph Barsabas (Acts 1:23) "the Just" who was so highly regarded by the brethren before Pentecost that he was suggested as a substitute for Judas. Judas Barsabas was a preacher ("prophet," Acts 15:32) and with Silas, was entrusted with the decrees of the Council that they might be delivered safely to the Christians at Antioch.   A.B.F.

JUDAS ISCARIOT, the arch-traitor, who betrayed our Lord. He and his father Simon were both surnamed "Iscariot" (see John 6:71 in Greek and in

ASV). "Iscariot" is commonly thought to be from the Hebrew *Ish Kerioth*, i.e. "a man of Kerioth," and Kerioth is almost certainly in the south of Judah (Josh. 15:25). Nothing is known of his early life. He may have joined the disciples of Jesus from pure motives and probably showed evidence of business acumen and so was appointed as treasurer for the disciples (John 12:6; 13:29), but his hopes for a high place in an earthly kingdom of Jesus were dashed (John 6:66) and he became a thief. His indignation when Jesus was anointed at Bethany was hypocritical. His pretended zeal for the poor was really covetousness, and is so interpreted by John (12:6), though the disciples of Jesus apparently trusted him to the end (John 13:21-30). Jesus, however, was not deceived (John 6:64), but knew from the beginning who should betray him. It was only at the last supper that Jesus revealed that "one of you shall betray me" (John 6:71). Then Satan entered into Judas; Jesus dismissed him; and he went out to do the dastardly deed which he had already planned (Mark 14:10). He sold the Lord for thirty pieces of silver, betrayed him with a kiss, then in remorse threw down the money before the chief priests and elders (Matt. 27:3-10) and went out and committed suicide. Matthew (27:5) says he hanged himself, and Acts (1:18) says that falling headlong, he burst asunder. He is always mentioned last among the apostles.   A.B.F.

JUDAS BARSABAS (See Judas)

JUDAS OF GALILEE (See Judas)

JUDE (jōōd, Gr. *Ioúdas*), writer of the last of the epistles in the NT. Both James and Jude in the opening of their epistles show their Christian humility and their faith in the deity of Jesus by referring to themselves as "bond-servants" of Jesus Christ, rather than His brothers in the flesh. Beyond this we know of him from Scripture only that, like his brothers, he did not believe in Jesus during His earthly life (John 7:5), but became His follower after the resurrection (Acts 1:14). Hegesippus (c. 110-c. 180) says that two grandsons of his were brought before Domitian as descendants of David, but were dismissed as harmless peasants.

JUDE, EPISTLE OF. The author of the epistle gives his name as Jude or Judas, and calls himself a bondservant of Jesus Christ and brother of James (vs. 1). There is good evidence for believing that Jude and James were brothers of the Lord (Matt. 13:55; Mark 6:3), although neither refers to himself as such in his epistle. They were not apostles, and did not believe in Him until after the resurrection. Its destination is quite general: "To them that are called, beloved in God the Father, and kept for Jesus Christ" (vs. 1). It is not clear where he was when he wrote or precisely when he wrote. It could not, however, have been written later than A.D. 81, the year of the accession of the Roman emperor Domitian, as Hegesippus (c. 110-c. 180) says that two grandsons of Jude were brought before Domitian as descendants of David, but were dismissed as harmless peasants, and it is most likely that if Jude were still alive he would have been brought before the emperor. It could have been written as early as A.D. 64, if it was written before II Peter.

The occasion for the writing of the epistle was the appearance among Jude's readers of an alarming heresy with immoral tendencies, perhaps the Gnosticism rebuked elsewhere in the NT, and its aim was to save them from its inroads. How he had received information about this is not told, but it is obvious that he was deeply disturbed about

it. A striking feature of the book is the use made of apocalyptic literature. There is an almost exact quotation from the Book of Enoch (1:9) in Verses 14 and 15, and Verse 9 apparently refers to something recorded in the Assumption of Moses. The epistle also has echoes from the Testament of Moses.

The epistle bears a striking resemblance to II Peter 2-3:4 in the subjects treated, the illustrations used, and even in the language. Because of this it is generally held that one of the writers must have made use of the other, but there is no agreement about which came first. It is apparent, however, that in Peter the description of false teachers is predictive, whereas in Jude the false teachers are actually present; and, moreover, in Jude the false teachers are worse than in Peter. Both writers seem to have in view the same corrupt parties. It appears, therefore, that Peter's is the older writing.

After the introduction and the reason given for the writing of the epistle in Verses 1-4, Jude announces the condemnation in store for the false teachers (vss. 5-16). He then explains the duty of Christians in the circumstances (vss. 17-23), and ends with a doxolgy (vss. 24,25).

Because of its brevity it was not quoted by the earliest Church Fathers and apparently was not everywhere known in the church. Origen and Clement of Alexander (c. 200) say that in their day it was not universally received, and Eusebius (c. 325) says the same thing. The Muratorian Canon, however, dating c. 200, includes it among the books of Scripture, and it was undoubtedly part of the Christian canon for many, long before this. S.B.

JUDEA, JUDAEA (jōō-dē'ā, Heb. *yehûdhâh*, Gr. *Ioudaía*), a geographical term that first appears in the Bible in Ezra 5:8, where it designates a province of the Persian Empire. The land of Judea is also mentioned in the apocryphal books I Esdras (1:30) and I Maccabees (5:45; 7:10). Since most of the exiles who returned from the Babylonian exile belonged to the tribe of Judah, they came to be called Jews and their land Judea.

Under the Persian empire, Judea was a district administered by a governor who was usually a Jew (Hag. 1:14; 2:2). With the banishment of Archelaus, Judea became annexed to the Roman province of Syria; but its governors were procurators appointed by the Roman emperor. Their immediate superior was the proconsul of Syria, who ruled from Antioch (Luke 3:1). The official residence of the procurators was Caesarea. This was true during the ministry of Christ. Geographically, Judea was about 55 miles N to S, and the same distance E to W, extending from the Mediterranean to the Dead Sea, with its northern boundary at Joppa, and its southern a few miles S of Gaza and the southern portion of the Dead Sea. Its exact boundary was, however, never fixed. S.B.

JUDGE (Heb. *shôphēt*, Gr. *dikastés, krités*), a civil magistrate. In patriarchal times the judges were the heads of families and the elders of the tribes. Moses, on the advice of Jethro, organized the judiciary of Israel, assigning judges for groups of thousands, hundreds, fifties, and tens, while only the most important cases were brought before him (Exod. 18:13-26; Deut. 1:9-17). Samuel established an organized circuit court (I Sam. 7:16; 8:1). After the institution of the monarchy, cases were tried by the king in the palace gate (I Kings 7:7), but there were also local courts (I Chron. 23:4; 26:29). Jehoshaphat organized a supreme court at Jerusalem (II Chron. 19:5-8). The public could view the proceedings of the court (Exod. 18:13; Ruth 4:1,2). In criminal cases at least two witnesses were necessary (Deut. 19:15; Num. 35: 30). The prophets often complained about courts corrupted by bribery and false witnesses (Isa. 1:23; Amos 5:12; Micah 3:11).

JUDGES, THE.

1. The civil magistrate. In patriarchal times Hebrew life was organized around the family and clan. Heads of families ("patriarchs") and elders of the tribes were the judges (Gen. 38:24) and their authority was based on custom.

After the Exodus from Egypt, Moses (upon the advice of Jethro (Exod. 18:13-26), organized the nation into groups of thousands, hundreds, fifties and tens, within each tribe. Over each unit a qualified man was placed as judge, and only the most important cases were brought before Moses (Deut. 1:12-18; 21:2). Upon entering Canaan, a similar plan of local government was followed (Deut. 16: 18-20; 17:2-13; 19:15-20; Josh. 8:33; 23:2; 24:1; I Sam. 8:1). During the period of the judges the office assumed a very different character; this will be treated below.

When the monarchy was instituted, the king himself tried important cases (II Sam. 15:2; I Kings 3:9,28; 7:7; Prov. 20:8). David assigned Levites to the judicial office, and appointed 6000 as officers and judges (I Chron. 23:4; 26:29). According to II Chronicles 19:5-8, Jehoshaphat enlarged the judicial system of Judah with a kind of supreme court, made up of Levites, priests and heads of fathers' houses, at Jerusalem.

The prophets often complained bitterly that justice was corrupted by bribery and false witness (Isa. 1:23; 5:23; 10:1; Amos 5:12; 6:12; Mic. 3:11; 7:3). Kings were often unjust (I Kings 22: 26; II Kings 21:16; Jer. 36:26) and the case of Ahab's seizure of Naboth's vineyard (I Kings 21: 1-13) shows how far a king could go in getting his own way, in flagrant contradiction of law and custom, at least in the northern kingdom of Israel.

In OT times the judges' activities were not limited to what today would be considered judicial functions. Our present division of powers between the legislative, executive and judicial is a modern innovation. The word *judge* is often parallel to *king* (Ps. 2:10; 148:11; Isa. 33:22; 40:23; Amos 2:3). In several Semitic languages the term used in the Hebrew Bible for judge (*shōphēt*) is used for rulers of various kinds. This breadth of meaning attached to the term judge in ancient times leads to its extended use in the book of Judges.

2. The leaders during the period of the judges. From the time of the death of Joshua to the reign of Saul, Israel's first king, the principal leaders of the people were called judges. These men and their times are described in the book of Judges and in I Samuel 1-7. They were charismatic leaders; that is, they were raised up to be Israel's "saviors" by a special endowment of the Spirit of God. It is clear that they were judges only in the broadest sense of that term. In reality, they were principally military deliverers, raised up to save the people of Israel from oppressing foreign powers. Much general information about the period of the judges, together with a complete list of their names and the regions in which they ruled is given in the article, JUDGES, BOOK OF.

This discussion will be restricted to a consideration of the careers and times of the most important of the judges. The times were most distressing. The period was cruel, barbarous and bloody. The tribes, scattered in the hill country of Canaan, were divided into many separate enclaves. Even the tabernacle at Shiloh, which should have provided a religious unity, seems to have been generally neglected in favor of the local high places. Only an unusual crisis, such as the crime which brought on the Benjamite war (Judg. 19:1-30; 20:1) could bring the tribes to united action. It would appear that Judah in the south was unusually isolated from the other tribes.

The first judge mentioned in detail is Ehud, son of Gera (Judg. 3:12-30). A Benjamite, he is said to have been lefthanded, a serious defect in those superstitious times. Few if any of the judges are pictured as ideal individuals. The occasion of the raising up of Ehud was an oppression by Eglon, king of Moab, who with the Ammonites and Amalekites(all Transjordan herdsmen or nomads), occupied the region of Jericho ("the city of palm trees," 3:13). After 18 years of oppression, Ehud led a revolt by killing Eglon when he presented the tribute. The gory details of the deed fit well this violent period. With Ephraimite help Eglon took the fords of the Jordan and slew the Moabites as they sought to flee homeward. There followed an 80-year period of peace.

In the second detailed deliverance story (Judg. 4,5), the scene shifts from the lower Jordan valley to the valley of Jezreel and the Galilee hill country in northern Palestine. The oppressor is Jabin, king of Canaan, who reigned in Hazor, whose 900 chariots of iron must have struck terror into the Hebrew tribes still in the stone age (I Sam. 13: 19-22). The recent excavation of Hazor by Israeli scholars has underscored the importance of this Canaanite stronghold, probably the largest city in ancient Palestine. The deliverers were Deborah "the prophetess," surely the actual leader of the uprising, and Barak, son of Abinoam, a fearful man (4:8) who led the Hebrew army at Deborah's urging. The tribes of the Galilee hill country united for this battle, which was fought in the valley of Jezreel by the brook Kishon. Evidently a cloudburst upstream caused the Kishon to overflow onto the plains through which it flows, thus immobilizing the Canaanite chariots, upon which they depended (4:15; 5:20-22). The army of Jabin defeated, his general Sisera fled, only to be killed ignominiously by the woman Jael (4:17-22). Deborah's warlike song of praise (Judg. 5) is believed to be one of the oldest poems of the Bible, and is noted for its rough primitive vigor. A 40-year rest followed this deliverance.

The third great judge was Gideon (chaps. 6-8), the location of whose village of Ophrah is a matter of uncertainty. It was located somewhere W of the Jordan, probably in the region between Beth-Shan and Tabor. The oppressing Midianites, desert Bedouin from the Transjordan region, had crossed the Jordan, because of the internal weakness of the land, and were raiding in Palestine proper. Gideon is commonly remembered for his doubt and reluctance to take action (6:15,17,36-40; 7:10) but it should be noted that once he assumed command he proved a steady and effective soldier (6:25-27; 7:15-24). His ruse, carried out by a mere 300 companions, frightened the disorganized Bedouin from the valley of Jezreel into full retreat across the Jordan. Gideon promptly called the Ephraimites to take the Jordan fords, by doing which they destroyed the Midianites. Gideon appears to have established some form of regular rule over at least the region of the Jezreel valley during his lifetime. His importance can be gauged by his rather large domestic establishment (8:30). Adhering to the ancient ideal of charismatic leadership, he rejected the idea of setting up a dynasty (8:22,23). His rule is said to have lasted 40 years.

The story of Gideon's son Abimelech and his violent rule over the Shechem area in the central hill country is told in Judges 9. Abimelech is not called a judge and he appears more as a brigand or political-military adventurer than as a deliverer of Israel from an oppressing enemy. He died as he lived — his head crushed by a millstone; and finally killed by his armorbearer. Probably his career is described solely to give a feeling of the violent unsettled state of things during the times of the judges. If that is its purpose, it can be said to have succeeded.

Jephthah, a Transjordan chieftain, next appears (Judg. 11,12), as the deliverer of Gilead and Manasseh (northern Transjordan) from the oppression of the Ammonites — a pastoral people who pressured Manasseh from the south. He is chiefly remembered for his thoughtless vow (11:30,31). While authorities differ as to what was involved in it, it is not unlikely that the vow involved offering his daughter as a sacrifice to God in the event of victory over the Ammonites (11:34-39). If it be objected that this was completely out of keeping with Hebrew religious practice, it may be answered that this only shows the extent of the religious degradation of the Hebrews during this turbulent period.

The last of the great judges was Samson (Judg. 13-16) with whom the scene shifts to a different part of Palestine — the Philistine Plain. It is likely that Samson lived late in the judges period, at the time when a large invasion of the Palestinian seacoast was occurring. The invaders, sea peoples from the Aegean area, had been repulsed in their attempt to enter Egypt (by Ramses III) and had subsequently settled in what became known as the Philistine Plain. Samson lived in the Shephelah area which bordered that plain. He was dedicated to a life of Nazirite obedience before his birth. His life was the tragedy of one whose great potential was vitiated through the lack of self discipline.

Hardly a very religious person, Samson was known for his great strength. He thus became the Hebrews' champion against the Philistines, doubtless as the Philistine Goliath later did against the Hebrews. His failure to discipline his sensuous nature led him into three liaisons with Philistine women. Doubtless each was an instrument of the Philistine lords in their effort to subdue Samson.

We do not know that Samson ever led a Hebrew army against the Philistines. Rather, he made single-handed exploits in Philistine territory, a number of which are described (14:19; 15:4,5,8,15; 16:3). The story of Samson's subduing at the hand of Delilah is well known. Killing in his death more Philistines than he killed in his life (16:30), he became at the last a tragic figure. He had judged Israel 20 years.

Eli (I Sam. 1-4) and Samuel (I Sam. 2:12) are also called judges. Although they did do some of the work of the judges described above, it would seem better to regard them as priest and prophet respectively — transitional figures preparing the way for the monarchy.　　　J.B.G.

JUDGES, BOOK OF. The seventh book of the OT takes its name from the title of the men who ruled Israel during the period from Joshua to Samuel. They are called judges (shōphetîm, Judg. 2:16), their principal function being that of military deliverers to the oppressed Hebrews.

The book makes no clear claim to authorship or date of composition. Much of it appears to be very old. The Jebusites are referred to as still dwelling in Jerusalem (1:21). David's capture of Jerusalem about 1000 B.C. (II Sam. 5:6-10) brought this situation to an end. The Canaanites still dwelt in Gezer (1:29) which city first became Hebrew at the time of Solomon (I Kings 9:16). On the other hand, there are also references which cannot be understood except as written at a time well after that of the judges. The thematic "In those days there was no king in Israel: every man did that which was right in his own eyes" (17:6; 18:1; 19:1; 21:25) could not have been written before the reign of Saul; indeed, it would be unlikely until a time well after the institution of the monarchy, when the earlier chaotic days tended to be forgotten. The reference to the worship at Dan "until the day of the captivity of the land" (18:30) seems to be a reference to the conquest of Galilee by Tiglath-pileser III in 733 B.C. It would seem, then, that the book contains very old material which may well have been edited at a later date. It may be noted that recent scholarship, while holding to a later date for the final editing of the book, emphasizes the historicity of the narrative and its use as the major source for our understanding of the period of the judges.

It is difficult to date the historical period covered by the book of Judges. It appears to have ended about a generation before Saul became king; thus we may place the end of the book at about 1020 B.C. The date of the death of Joshua, with which the book opens, depends upon the date of the Exodus from Egypt, about which there is much dispute. Accordingly, some scholars date the beginning of the judges period at c. 1370-60 B.C.; others, at c. 1220-10 B.C.; still others, later. At first sight it would appear that the book itself gives the answer, for it states the duration of the judgeships of the various judges. A close examination of the text, however, reveals that most of the judges were local, not national in their influence, and it appears likely that their periods overlapped. Further, the frequency of the number 40 for the length of their office (3:11; 5:31; 8:28; 13:1; I Sam. 4:18) makes it appear likely that this figure is a round number for a generation and not to be taken exactly.

The purposes of the book of Judges are: 1. To bridge in some manner the historical gap between the death of Joshua and the inauguration of the monarchy. 2. To show the moral and political degradation of a people who neglected their religious heritage and compromised their faith with the surrounding paganism. 3. To show the need of the people for the unity and leadership by a strong central government in the person of a king.

In its structure, the book falls into three easily recognizable parts: (1) Introduction: the state of things at the death of Joshua, 1:1-2:10; (2) Main body: the judges' cycles, 2:11-16:31; (3) Appendix: life in Israel in the days of the judges, 17-21.

1. Introduction, 1:1-2:10. This section gives a description of the state of the conquest of Canaan when Joshua died. It is a record of incomplete success. The less desirable hill country had been taken, but the fertile plains and the cities were still largely in Canaanite hands. This description does not contradict the conquest story in the book of Joshua, which only claims that the Hebrew armies had "blitzkrieged" the whole land, while plainly stating that not all had been possessed (Josh. 13:1-6). It was one thing for the Hebrew armies to sweep through the land; it was quite another for the individuals and tribes of the Hebrews to dispossess the Canaanites from the land and settle there. This latter they failed to do. This failure meant that the Hebrews lived as neighbors with pagan Canaanites, and thus the way was prepared for the syncretism which so characterized the Hebrews during this period. Their culture and religion were often largely Canaanite and pagan. This is the reason for the moral and spiritual degradation of the Hebrew people during the period of the judges.

2. Main body of the book, 2:11-16:31. Here occur the stories of the judges, the cycles of failure, oppression and relief by a judge. The cycle is set forth in the abstract in 2:11-3:6. There follow the stories of the judges. It will be noted that these men were not principally civil magistrates. They were rather military deliverers, who led the people of Israel to freedom against their enemies, and seem frequently to have been singularly unfitted to be what we would today denominate *judges.* The judges, and that part of Israel which they served (when that can be known), are here listed. For a discussion of the principal judges, see article JUDGES, THE.

1. Othniel (3:7-11).
2. Ehud (3:12-30): Central Palestine and Transjordan.
3. Shamgar (3:31): Philistine plain.
4. Deborah and Barak (4, 5): Central Palestine and Galilee.
5. Gideon (6-8): Central Palestine and Transjordan.
6. Abimelech (9): Central Palestine. Abimelech is considered by many as merely an outlaw and not a judge.
7. Tola (10:1, 2): Central Palestine.
8. Jair (10:3-5): Transjordan.
9. Jephthah (10:6-12:7): Transjordan.
10. Ibzan (12:8-10): Southern Palestine.
11. Elon (12:11, 12): Northern Palestine.
12. Abdon (12:13-15): Central Palestine.
13. Samson (13-16): Philistine plain.

3. Appendix, 17-21. The events recorded here seem to have occurred, not after the judges mentioned in the main part of the book, but during their judgeships. They are relegated to the appendix probably because they are stories in their own right and if inserted in the main body would have marred the symmetry of the judge cycles there. These stories describe life during this turbulent near-pagan period, and give a frank and unvarnished description of the brutality and paganism with which Israel was contaminated because of her close association with her pagan Canaanite neighbors.

The Levite (17, 18) was a priest who could follow his religious practice anywhere. He was hired as a family chaplain and soothsayer, and his presence was certain to bring "good luck" (17:13). He evidently functioned with idols (18:20) and was quite willing to change situations if the change involved a better salary (18:19, 20). All of this is in direct contrast to the divine command concerning the priesthood in the Mosaic law.

The migration of the Danites (chap. 18) was necessitated by their failure to capture the territory assigned to them (Josh. 19:40-48; Judg. 1:34-36.) They then traveled to a northern valley, remote and defenseless, captured it and settled there. Thus originated the northern Dan, known in the expression, "From Dan to Beersheba."

The story of the Levite's concubine (chap. 19) casts a livid light on the brutality and beastliness of the times and introduces the war of the tribes against the Benjamites (20, 21). This is not the only intertribal war of the period (8:1-3; 12:1-6). In fact, it is clear that the loyalty of the Hebrews at this time was a merely tribal one, as is the case with the Bedouin until today. There was no real Hebrew nation; Israel was at best a very loose confederation of tribes around a central sanctuary, the tabernacle at Shiloh (18:31).

The cruelty and paganism of the stories of Judges are often a stumbling block to readers. It should not be imagined that the writer is approving of everything which he records. Rather, the book should be viewed as a story of the tragic judgment of God upon a people who failed to keep their heritage of true religious faith by assimilating far too much of their surrounding culture. The story of the Judges has been called "The struggle between faith and culture." In this struggle, faith lost.

All this should not close our eyes to the beauty of the book of Judges as literature. Many of the stories would rank high in any collection of the short stories of the world. Even in the most brutal passages there is an austere dignity. Sin is never reveled in; it is always held up to the gaze of horror. In the pungent words of Jotham (9:7-15), Judges has preserved almost the only fable in ancient Hebrew literature. The song of Deborah, much studied by recent scholars, has a sonorous quality and vivid narrative power. The narratives of the book are amazingly brief. The Hebrew literary artist was at his best when he crammed action and emotion into a few sentences. J.B.G.

JUDGMENT (jūj'měnt, Heb. *dhîn, mishpāt,* etc., Gr. *kríma, krísis,* etc.), a word found many times in the Bible, referring sometimes to the pronouncing of a formal opinion or decision by men, but more often to a calamity regarded as sent by God, by way of punishment, or a sentence of God as the judge of all. Among the more important judgments of God prior to the Exodus are those upon Adam, Eve, and the serpent after the fall, (Gen. 3) the Flood (Gen. 6:5), Sodom and Gomorrah (Gen. 18:20), and the confusion of tongues (Gen. 11:1-9). God brings judgment to His creatures when they rebel against His will.

In the OT the relationship between Jehovah and Israel is thought of under the form of a covenant. God says He will take care of His people and protect them from their enemies if they will be His people, living in accordance with His will. The history of Israel, beginning with the Exodus, is the story of a succession of judgments upon the enemies of God's people and upon His covenant nation when they flouted His will. The "day of Jehovah" becomes a day of punishment for all the unjust, even for those who boast of belonging to the people of the covenant (Isa. 2:12; Amos 5:18; Hos. 5:8). The purpose of the judgment of God's people is not their total destruction, but their purification. A remnant will survive, and this will be the nucleus of the new Israel (Amos 5:15). In the later prophets there are expressions of a hope of an ultimate victory of the divine Judge, of a final or last judgment. Here God's judgment is not thought of so much in terms of His intervention in history, but of a last judgment at the end of time of all men. Perhaps the clearest expression of this is found in Daniel 12:1-3, where the dead are described as being raised, some for everlasting life, others for shame and everlasting contempt.

In the NT the idea of judgment appears in both human and divine contexts. Jesus warns against uncharitable judgments (Matt. 7:1). Paul says that the spiritual man cannot be judged by unbelievers (I Cor. 2:15), and in Romans 14 and I Corinthians 8-10 he warns against judging those who are "weak" in the faith.

In the NT, judgment is one of the aspects of the coming of the kingdom of God. God's judgment, says John the Baptist, will fall upon those who do not make ready the way of the Lord (Luke 3:9). Jesus declares that some day He will come to judge both the living and the dead (Matt. 25:3lff).

In the NT, as in the OT, judgment is an aspect of the deliverance of believers (Luke 18:1-8; Rom. 12:19; II Thess. 1:5-10; Rev. 6:10). God is long-suffering in meting out judgment so that men may be able to come to repentance (Luke 13:6-9; Rom. 2:4; II Peter 2:9). The notion of judgment, when God will overthrow every resistance, both among evil spiritual powers (I Cor. 6:2, 3) and also among men (Matt. 25:31-46). This judgment will affect all men, because all are responsible to God according to the grace that has been granted them (Matt. 11:20-24; Luke 12:17ff; Rom. 2:12-16). This present world will be shaken and destroyed (Matt. 24:29, 35), and a new world will replace the present one (II Peter 3:13; Rev. 21:1). God will entrust the administration of this final judgment to His Son at His appearance in glory (Matt. 3:11, 12; John 5:22; Rom. 2:16, etc.). S.B.

JUDGMENT, DAY OF (See Judgment)

JUDGMENT HALL (Gr. *praitórion*), originally the tent or building where the general or governor held council. In John 18:28—19:9 KJV renders it "hall of judgment" or "judgment hall," whereas ASV uses the Latin term *praetorium*, but with "palace" in the margin. The term comes in again in the story of Paul at Caesarea (Acts 23:35), where it refers to the palace of Herod, used as the official residence by the propraetors Felix and Festus in their day. In Matthew 27:27 KJV renders the word "common hall"; and in Philippians 1:13 KJV has "palace," and ASV "praetorian guard," but with "praetorium" in the margin.

JUDGMENT SEAT (Gr. *béma, a raised place, platform, tribune*), the bench or seat where a judge sits to hear arguments and pleas and delivers sentence. Although the word is used principally in the NT in connection with the trials of Christ (Matt. 27:19, John 19:13) and of Paul (Acts 18:12), its principal theological interest is concerned with the judgment seat of Christ before which all believers will stand (Rom. 14:10, II Cor. 5:10).

JUDGMENT SEAT OF CHRIST (See Judgment)

JUDGMENT, THE LAST (See Judgment)

JUDGMENTS, THE (See Judgment)

JUDGMENTS OF GOD (See Judgment)

JUDITH (jōō'dĭth, Heb. fem. of *yehûdhî, Judean, Jew*). 1. One of the wives of Esau (Gen. 26:34) and daughter of Beeri the Hittite.
2. Heroine of the apocryphal book of Judith.

JULIA (jōōl'ya, Gr. *Ioulía*), an early Christian at Rome to whom Paul sent greetings (Rom. 16:15), perhaps the wife of Philologus.

JULIUS (jōōl'yŭs, Gr. *Ioúlios*), a Roman centurion of the Augustan band in whose care Paul was placed for the journey to Rome (Acts 27:1,3). He trusted Paul to go to his friends at Sidon, and he with his soldiers saved Paul's and their lives by frustrating the sailors' plot near Malta.

JUNIA, JUNIAS (jōō'nĭ-à, jōō'nĭ-ăs), a kinsman and fellow prisoner of Paul (Rom. 16:7). He had become a Christian before Paul's conversion (Rom. 16:7).

JUNIPER (See Plants)

JUPITER (jōō'pĭ-têr, Gr. *Zeús, páter*), the chief of the Roman gods. The Greeks called him "Zeus." The people of Lystra called Barnabas "Jupiter" and Paul "Mercury" (Acts 14:12, 13). In Acts 19:35 that "which fell down from Jupiter" was probably a meteorite which the Ephesians worshiped as an image of Diana. Jupiter was worshiped all over the Greek and Roman world.

JUSHAB-HESED (jōō'shăb-hē'sĕd, Heb. *yûshav hesedh, mercy has returned*), a son of Zerubbabel (I Chron. 3:20).

JUSTIFICATION (jŭs'tĭ-fĭ-kā'shŭn, Heb. *tsedheq, tsādhēq*, Gr. *dikaióo, to make valid, to absolve, to vindicate, to set right*). Justification may be defined as, "that judicial act of God, by which, on the basis of the meritorious work of Christ, imputed to the sinner and received by him through faith, He declares the sinner absolved from his sin, released from its penalty, and restored as righteous."

Representative Scriptures from which the doctrine is derived are Acts 13:38,39; Romans 3:24-26 and Romans 4:5-8, where justification is said to be an act of God in the life of the believer by which man is freed from the penalty of sin and identified with the life and nature of Christ in a positive application of grace.

The Nature of Justification. As a reversal of God's attitude toward the sinner because of his new relation in Christ, justification is: a *declarative* act, by which the sinner is *declared* to be free from guilt and the consequences of sin (Rom. 4:6-8; 5:18-19; 8:33-34; II Cor. 5:19-21); a *judicial* act in which the idea of judgment and salvation are combined to represent Christ fulfilling the law on behalf of the sinner (Rom. 3:26; 8:3; Gal. 3:13; II Cor. 5:21; I Pet. 3:18; Matt. 10:41 and I Tim. 1:9); a *remissive* act in which God actually remits the sin of man unto forgiveness (Rom. 4:5 and 6:7); and, a *restorative* act by which the forgiven sinner is restored to favor through the imputation of Christ's righteousness (Rom. 5:11; Gal. 3:6; I Cor. 1:30).

The major emphasis in justification is that it is an *act* of God. It is an act, however, from three perspectives: an act *in process of completion*, as a continuous operation of the work of Christ (Rom. 4:25; 5:18); an act *as already accomplished* in the completed work of Christ (Rom. 5:16-18 and I Tim. 3:16); and, at the same time, as a *state in Christ* to which the justified sinner is elevated (Rom. 8:10 and I Cor. 1:30).

The Essentials of Justification. Four basic essentials in the act of justification are taught by Scripture. Justification involves:

1. Remission of punishment, in which the justified believer is declared to be free of the demands of the law since they have been satisfied in Christ (Rom. 4:5) and is no longer exposed to the penalty of the law (Rom. 6:7). It is more than a pardon from sin, but a declaration by God that the sinner, though guilty, has had the fact of his guilt remitted in Christ.

2. Restoration to favor, in which the justified believer is declared to be personally righteous in Christ, and therefore accepted as being in Christ's righteousness. Mere acquittal or remission would leave the sinner in the position of a discharged criminal. Justification goes further in that it implies that God's treatment of the sinner is as if he had never sinned since he is now regarded as being personally righteous in Christ (Gal. 3:6). In this restoration there is not only acquittal, but approval; not only pardon, but promotion. Remission from sin is never separated from restoration to favor.

3. Imputed righteousness of God, which is granted the justified believer through Christ's presence in him. His salvation in Christ imparts the quality and character of Christ's righteousness to him (Rom. 3:25,26). Christ is made the Justifier through whom a new life is inaugurated in the believer (I Cor. 1:30). Paul uses the word righteousness to mean both the righteousness which acquits the sinner and the life-force which breaks the bondage of sin. Salvation can never be separated from the participational act of man in Christ, in which he is regarded judicially as having righteousness because the actual effect of righteousness has indeed come to him (Phil. 3:9; Rom. 3:22).

4. New legal standing before God in which, instead of being under the condemnation of sin, the justified believer stands before God in Christ. There has been an absolute interchange of position: Christ takes the place of the sinner, the place of curse (Gal. 3:13) being made sin in our behalf (II Cor. 5:21) and judged for our sin; while we stand in Christ's righteousness (Rom. 3:25) and are viewed as sons (Gal. 4:5).

The Grounds of Justification. The grounds upon which justification rests is the redeeming work of Christ's death. The inherent righteousness of Christ is the sole basis upon which God can justify the sinner (Rom. 3:24; 5:19; 8:1; 10:4; I Cor. 1:8; 6:11; II Cor. 5:1; and Phil. 3:9). It is this righteousness which, in being imputed to the justified believer, is the ground of his justification in that it declares him to have the same standing before God in personal holiness as Christ Himself (Titus 3:7).

The instrumental cause of justification is faith, as the response of the soul to God's redeeming grace (Rom. 3:28). Faith is the condition of justification not in that it is considered meritorious, but only as the condition by which the meritorious work of Christ is apprehended by man. The final ground of justification is the completed, finished, sufficient work of Christ atoning for man in His redeeming work upon the cross.   C.B.B.

Bibliography: G. C. Berkouwer, *Faith and Justification* (Grand Rapids: Eerdmans) 1954; J. Murray, *Redemption: Accomplished and Applied* (Grand Rapids: Eerdmans) 1955; A. H. Strong, *Systematic Theology* (Philadelphia: The Judson Press), Volume III; H. O. Wiley, *Christian Theology* (Beacon Hill Press) 1958, Volume II.

JUSTUS (jŭs'tŭs, Gr. *Ioústos, just*). 1. The surname of Joseph Barsabas, one of the two whom the "brethren" appointed as candidates for Judas' place among the Twelve (Acts 1:23-26).

2. The surname of Titus, of Corinth, with whom Paul lodged for a time (Acts 18:7).

3. The surname of Jesus, an early Hebrew Christian at Rome, evidently known to the Christians at Colosse (Col. 4:11).

JUTTAH (jŭt'à, Heb. *yuttâh, extended*), a town of the tribe of Judah, about five miles S of Hebron in the hill-country (Josh. 15:55; 21:16). It was later given to the family of Aaron as a priestly city. The same as Jotbah *q.v.* The place is now called Jutta.

K

KAB (See Cab, also Weights and Measures)

KABZEEL (kăb'zē-ĕl, Heb. *kavtse'ēl*, [*whom*] *God gathers*), a city in the south of Judah near the border of Edom (Josh. 15:21). It was the home of Benaiah (II Sam. 23:20), one of David's mighty men. In Nehemiah 11:25 it is called Jekabzeel. The site is unknown.

KADESH (kā'dĕsh, Heb. *qādhēsh*, from *qādhôsh, be holy*), also Kedesh, Josh. 15:23, or Kadesh-barnea, was also known in Biblical times as En-mishpat (cf. Gen. 14:7). Though there is some uncertainty concerning its modern identification, it is usually identified as 'Ain Qedeis, discovered by J. Rowlands in 1842 and rediscovered by H. C. Trumbull in 1881, in the Negev (cf. Gen. 20:1), about fifty miles south of Beersheba. This K. should not be confused with Kadesh on the Orontes, the site of the famous battle between Rameses III and the Hittites, presently identified as Tell Nebi Mend (this K. is not mentioned in the Bible, with the possible exception of II Sam. 24:6, LXX). The first Biblical reference to K. is Genesis 14:7, where it is equated with En-mishpat, one of the cities singled out in connection with the invasion by the four eastern kings. When Hagar fled from Sarah (Gen. 16:7), she was met by the angel of the Lord at Beer-lahai-roi, which was located between K. and Bered (Gen. 16:14). Later, Abraham went from Mamre toward the Negev and lived between K. and Shur (Gen. 20:1). The primary relationship of the Israelites to K. centers in the period of some years that they spent there during the exodus from Egypt (cf. Deut. 1:46; Num. 33:37-38; Deut. 2:14). From Horeb (Sinai), via Seir, it was an eleven-day journey to K. (Deut. 1:2). K. is described as being in the wilderness of Paran (Num. 13:26); it is also said to be in the wilderness of Zin (Num. 33:36; cf. Num. 20:1); Psalm 29:8 mentions "the wilderness of Kadesh." These references illustrate the overlapping of geographic territories whose precise limits are difficult to determine and indicate the character of K. as a border location. When the Israelites reached this place, Moses sent the twelve spies to scout southern

Possible site of Kadesh, or Kadesh-barnea, in the Negev north of Sinai. © MPS

Canaan (Num. 13:1,17,26; 32:8; Deut. 1:19-25; Josh. 14:6-7). Encouraged by the Lord to invade the land at that time, the people rebelled (Deut. 9: 23) and were sentenced to the delay in possessing the land (Num. 14:34). At K., Miriam died and was buried (Num. 20:1). It was in this area also that the waters of Meribah ("Contention") were located (Num. 20:2-13,24; Meribath-Kadesh, Num. 27:14; Deut. 32:51). It seems likely that while the Israelites were in this region they did not stay only at 'Ain Qedeis, which preserves the ancient name of K., but that they also availed themselves of nearby springs such as 'Ain Qudeirat and 'Ain Qoseimeh. K. was also on the west border of Edom and it was from K. that Moses sent emissaries to the king of Edom to request permission for Israel to pass through Edomite territory (Num. 20:14-16,22; cf. Judg. 11:16-17). The conquest of the southern section of Palestine by Joshua refers to an area from K. to Gaza (Josh. 10:41). K. also is named as marking the southern border of Judah (Josh. 15:3,23) and therefore the southern boundary of the land possessed by the Israelites (Num. 34:4; Ezek. 47:19; 48:28). C.E.D.

KADESH-BARNEA (See Kadesh)

KADMIEL (kăd'mĭ-ĕl Heb. *kadhmî'ēl, God is in front*), head of a family of Levites who returned with Zerubbabel (Ezra 2:40, Neh. 7:43). He helped in the rebuilding of the temple (Ezra 3:9). One of his family sealed the covenant (Nah. 10:9).

KADMONITES (kăd'mŏn-īts, Heb. *kadhmōnî, children of the East*), a very ancient tribe, one of the ten whose possessions God gave to the seed of Abraham. They lived somewhere between Egypt and the Euphrates (Gen. 15:18-21).

KAIN (kān, Heb. *kāyin, smith*). 1. A town in Judah, in KJV spelled Cain (Josh. 15:57).
2. A tribal name; KJV has "the Kenite" (Num. 24:22; Judg. 4:11). See Kenites.

KALLAI (kăl'ā-ī, Heb. *qallai, swift*), a high priest in the days of Joiakim (Neh. 12:20), of the family of Sallai.

The ruins of Kedesh Naphtali, one of the Cities of Refuge. © MPS

KAMON (See Camon)

KANAH (kā'na, Heb. *qānâh, reeds*). 1. A brook running from S of Shechem westward to the Mediterranean Sea. It formed a part of the boundary between the tribes of Ephraim and Manasseh (Josh. 16:8; 17:9).
2. A city near the boundary of the tribes of Asher (Josh. 19:28) probably modern Kana, about eight miles SE of Tyre.

KAREAH (ka-rē'a, Heb. *qārēah, bald*), father of Jonathan and Johanan, who warned Gedaliah the Babylonian governor of Judah of his danger (II Kings 25:23, where KJV has Careah; Jer. 40:8-43:5).

KARKA (kär'kå, Heb. *ha-qarqā'âh, ground*), a place on the southern boundary of Judah (Josh. 15:3). KJV has Karkaa.

KARKOR (kär'kôr, Heb. *qarqōr*), a place in the territory of the Ammonites where Zebah and Zalmunna were resting with the remains of the great army of the Midianites, and where Gideon overtook them and destroyed them (Judg. 8:10). Exact location unknown.

KARTAH (kär'tå, Heb. *qartâh, city*), a city in Zebulun given to the Merarite Levites in the days of Joshua (Josh. 21:34).

KARTAN (kär'tăn, Heb. *qartān*), a city in Naphtali given to the Gershonite Levites in Joshua's time (Josh. 21:32). Copied in I Chronicles 6:76 as Kiriathaim (KJV Kirjathaim), which means the same.

KATTATH (kăt'ăth, Heb. *kattath*), a town in Galilee given to Zebulun (Josh. 19:15). Perhaps the same as Kitron in Judges 1:30.

KEDAR (kē'dêr, Heb. *kēdhār,* probably either *mighty* or *dark*). 1. One of the 12 sons of Ishmael, son of Abram by Hagar (Gen. 25:13). These sons were called "princes." They helped originate the Arab peoples.
2. The tribe which descended from him, and their territory. They were for the most part nomads (Ps. 120:5, S. of Sol. 1:5), raising sheep (Isa. 60:7), but sometimes intruding into villages (Isa. 42:11). The "doom of Kedar" declared in Jeremiah 49:28-33) tells us something of their desert civilization and also of their terror when they learned that Nebuchadnezzar was coming against them. Their territory was in the northern part of the Arabian desert.

KEDEMAH (kĕd'ē-mà, Heb. *qēdhmâh, eastward*), son of Ishmael, head of a clan (Gen. 25:15).

KEDEMOTH (kĕd'ē-mŏth, Heb. *qedhēmôth, eastern parts*), a place E of the Jordan given to the tribe of Reuben (Num. 21:21-32, Deut. 2:26), later set apart for Merarite Levites with its suburbs (Josh. 21:37).

KEDESH (kē'dĕsh, Heb. *qedesh, sacred place*). 1. A city of the Canaanites conquered by Joshua in his northern campaign (Josh. 12:22), later given to the tribe of Naphtali (Josh. 19:37), appointed as a city of refuge (Josh. 20:7, 21:32) and bestowed upon the Gershonite Levites. Here Barak and Deborah assembled the hosts of Israel to fight against Sisera of the Canaanites (Judg. 4:6-10), and about 600 years later Tiglath-pileser, king of Assyria, conquered the land of Naphtali, including Kedesh and took their people to Assyria (II Kings 15:29).
2. A city in the tribe of Issachar, given to the Gershonite Levites (I Chron. 6:72).
3. A city in the very southern part of Judah near the border of Edom (Josh. 15:23).

KEDESH NAPHTALI (See Kedesh)

KEDRON (See Kidron)

KEHELATHAH (kĕ'hĕ-lā'thȧ, Heb. *kehēlāthāh, gathering*), a station in the wilderness of Paran where Israel encamped (Num. 33:22,23).

KEILAH (kē-ī'lȧ, Heb. *ke'îlâh*). 1. A city lying in the Shephelah (Josh. 15:44). It was threatened by the Philistines, but David rescued it (I Sam. 23: 1-13) and Abiathar the priest joined him there. The people of Keilah were ungrateful and David had to flee from there.

2. A man of Judah, descended from Caleb, son of Jephunneh (I Chron. 4:19).

KELAIAH (kē-lā'yȧ, Heb. *kēlāyâh*), also Kelita, a Levite who had taken a foreign wife in the days of Ezra and gave her up (Ezra 10:23).

KELITA (See Kelaiah)

KEMUEL (kĕm'ū-ĕl, Heb. *kemû'ēl*). 1. Son of Nahor and brother of Bethuel, therefore uncle of Laban and Rebekah (Gen. 22:21). Nahor had married his niece Milcah, daughter of Terah's oldest son Haran (Gen. 11:28) who had died before the family left Ur of the Chaldees. Kemuel had a son Aram.

2. A prince of the tribe of Ephraim appointed by Moses to help divide the land of Canaan (Num. 34:24).

3. Father of Hashabiah, a leading Levite in the days of David (I Chron. 27:17).

KENAN (kē'năn), a great-grandson of Adam (I Chron. 1:2). In KJV of Genesis 5:9-14 Cainan.

KENATH (kē'năth, Heb. *qenāth, possession*), a city of the Amorites in the region of Bashan in the kingdom of Og. In the last days of Moses, one Nobah, presumably of Manasseh, went and took it with its outlying villages and named it after himself (Num. 32:42). Later the two little kingdoms of Geshur and Aram, near Mt. Hermon, took Kenath along with the cities of Jair who had 23 cities in the land of Gilead (I Chron. 2:22,23). KJV apparently makes "Geshur and Aram" the direct objects instead of the subjects of the sentence, a possible but very unlikely rendering. Cf. ASV, which seems better.

KENAZ (kē'năz, *qenaz, hunting*). 1. A grandson of Esau through Eliphaz (Gen. 36:11,15). He and others are called "dukes" in KJV under the influence of English titles, and "chiefs" in ASV, but the Arab title "sheikh" would give a truer picture.

2. Father of Othniel (Josh. 15:17; Judg. 1:13; 3:9-11).

3. A grandson of Caleb through his son Elah (I Chron. 4:15), though the Hebrew seems ambiguous here. KJV reads "even Kenaz," and ASV, "and Kenaz," but neither is clear.

KENEZITE, KENIZZITE (kē'nĕz-īt, kē'nīz-īt, Heb. *qenizzî*), a patronymic name derived from Kenaz. One of the ten tribes of Canaan in the days of Abram, mentioned only in Genesis 15:19. No one knows who was the "Kenaz" from whom these Kenizzites were descended; and the tribe disappears from history with this mention. Some think that the Edomite tribe descended from Kenaz, grandson of Esau (Gen. 36:11,15) united at least in part with Israel because Caleb of the tribe of Judah (Josh. 14:6,14) is called the "son" of Jephunneh the Kenizzite.

KENITES (kē'nīts, Heb. *ha-qēnî, smith*). 1. One of the ten tribes of Canaan in the time of Abraham (Gen. 15:19), perhaps the same as those doomed by the prophecy of Balaam (Num. 24:21,22).

2. The descendants of Hobab, the brother-in-law of Moses (Judg. 4:11). Hobab visited Israel as they left Sinai and Moses invited him to come along with Israel and to act as a pathfinder (Num. 10: 29-32), which he did. His descendants were friendly with Israel; they went with Judah from Jericho (Judg. 1:16) and amalgamated with the tribe of Judah. Later, Heber the Kenite (Judg. 4:11) separated from the others and moved northward to Kedesh near the Sea of Galilee and made peace with Jabin, the king of Hazor. Heber's wife Jael, slew Sisera the Canaanite general, and so fulfilled Deborah's prophecy to Barak that a woman would get the honor for his victory (read Judg. 4). Later Saul, sent to destroy the Amalekites, gave friendly warning to the Kenites (I Sam. 15:6) to depart and save themselves, because of the kindness they had shown to Israel more than 500 years before. David told Achish, king of Gath (I Sam. 27:10), that he had raided the Kenites, but this was to deceive Achish.

KENIZZITES (See Kenezite)

KENOSIS (kē-nō'sĭs, Gr. *kénosis, from kenóo, he emptied himself, divested himself of his privileges*, Phil. 2:7). Apart from the context in Philippians, the verb has two main meanings: 1. *to make empty of content, to deprive of possession* or *property*; 2. *to ruin, destroy, come to nothing*.

Kenosis concerns what Christ did when he became man. In Philippians 2:6-8 Paul pictures Christ as existing in the form of God. He says that Christ did not count the being on an equality with God a prize to be taken advantage of or to be profited by. Rather, "he made himself of no reputation" (KJV), "he emptied himself" (ASV, RSV).

The idea that Christ emptied Himself has given rise to much theological speculation. Did Paul mean Christ emptied Himself of deity, that He ceased to be God? Certainly this is not what Paul meant. That would be self-annihilation and a complete transmutation of being. In the early 20th century some theologians insisted that Christ retained the divine attributes of holiness, love, and truth while emptying Himself of the attributes of omniscience, omnipotence, and omnipresence. A. H. Strong denied any such surrender of the characteristics of God. Because there were times that Christ did not show omniscience (see Matt. 24:36; Mark 13:32), Strong concluded that Christ did surrender the *independent exercise* of these attributes. From this point of view, Christ had, for example, omniscience when the Father granted to Him this quality. But all such speculation about attributes assumes that "empty himself" must be the meaning of *kenoo* in Philippians 2:7 and ignores the context.

A careful study of the context shows that a different translation is preferable. The pre-incarnate Christ is said to have existed or have been in the form of God. He did not regard His being on an equality with God as a prize to be used to His own advantage. Rather, *He deprived Himself by taking* (*or when He took*) *the form of a servant.* The question now must be asked: of what did He deprive Himself? He deprived Himself of the manner of living which He had with God before He became man. Behm shows how this is true when he says: "The form of God, in which the pre-existent Christ was, is nothing different than the divine 'glory'; the 'being in the form of God' of Paul corresponds perfectly with John 17:5: 'with the glory which I had with you before the world was' " (TWNT, IV, 759). By his own voluntary decision Christ deprived Himself of His manner of living, surrounded by glory. This manner of living He had always enjoyed with His Father. The form of God involved glory. The form of a slave involved humility. Christ did not cease to be God when He deprived Himself of divine glory. Neither has Christ ceased to be man because He is free from the humiliation of the servant. In depriving Himself of His pre-incarnate manner of living, involving the radiation of divine glory from His being, Christ made clear His complete awareness of all that redemption costs. Such a self-deprivation is described further in Philippians as a humbling of Himself (2:8), a becoming obedient even to the point of death. This is followed by God's exaltation of Christ with every being confessing that Jesus Christ is Lord to the glory of God the Father (Phil. 2: 11). Glory forsaken is forever reclaimed.

A.B.M.

KERCHIEF (See Dress)

KEREN-HAPPUCH (kĕr'ĕn-hăp'ŭk, *horn of antimony, i.e. beautifier*), the youngest daughter of Job, born to him after his release from the torments of Satan (Job 42:14,15).

KERIOTH (kĕr'ĭ-ŏth, Heb. *qerîyôth, cities*). 1. Kerioth-hezron (not "Kerioth and Hezron" as in KJV), a city in the south of Judah (Josh. 15:25); otherwise "Hazor." Said to have been about ten miles S of Hebron.

2. A city of Moab, and judging from Amos 2: 1-3 probably its capital in the eighth century B.C. In "the judgment of Moab" (Jer. 48) Moab is pictured as ruined because of its idolatry (vs. 13) and its pride (vs. 29) and Kerioth is pictured as under judgment from God (vss. 24,41). The city lay in what is now Jebel Druz, nearly S of Damascus and in high country.

KEROS (kē'rŏs), one of the Nethinim (temple servants), some of whose descendants returned with Zerubbabel (Ezra 2:44; Neh. 7:47).

KETTLE (Heb. *dûdh, a cooking vessel*), mentioned with pan, pot and caldron, and elsewhere translated by all these terms. Also a basket for carrying clay or bricks (I Sam. 2:14).

KETURAH (kĕ-tū'rà), Abraham's second wife (Gen. 25:1), married probably after the death of Sarah and marriage of Isaac (Gen. 24:67); but called his concubine (I Chron. 1:32; cf. Gen. 25: 6). She was the mother of six sons, ancestors of Arabian tribes (Gen. 25:2-6; I Chron. 1:33).

KEY (Heb. *maphtēah, opener*), an Oriental key was made of wood, with nails or wooden pegs to fit corresponding holes in the bolt which held the door fast (Judg. 3:25). Figuratively, a symbol of

Aerial view of the Kidron Valley, looking northward, and showing the Garden of Gethsemane between the road at center and the northeast portion of the Jerusalem city wall at left. © MPS

authority, carried on the shoulder (Isa. 22:20-22). Greek *kleís, something which shuts* (Luke 11:52); symbolic of the authority given to Peter (Matt. 16: 19), but which Jesus still retains (Rev. 1:18; 3:7); the key which keeps destructive forces (Rev. 9:1) and Satan (Rev. 20:1) in the bottomless pit.

KEZIA, KEZIAH (kĕ-zī'à), the second of three daughters of Job born after his great trial (Job 42:14). The name means "cassia."

KEZIZ (kē'zĭz), a valley near Beth-hoglah in Benjamin, KJV; a city, Emek-keziz (Josh. 18:21 ASV, RSV). Emek means valley. Location uncertain.

KIBROTH-HATTAAVAH (kĭb'rŏth-hă-tā'à-và, *the graves of lust or greed*), the next encampment of the Israelites after they left the wilderness of Sinai. Here they longed for flesh and gorged themselves on the quails God sent, dying of the resulting sickness. This explains the name (Num. 11:34,35; 33: 16,17; Deut. 9:22).

KIBZAIM (kĭb-zā'ĭm), a town in Ephraim, assigned to the Kohathite Levites (Josh. 21:22). Jokmean appears in its place in I Corinthians 6:68.

KID (See Animals: Goats)

KIDNEY (kĭd'nē, Heb. always in the pl. *kelāyôth*, Gr. *nephroí*). This organ, being surrounded by pure fat, was adapted to burning in sacrifice, when the whole animal was not burned (Exod. 29:13, 22; Lev. 3:4,10,15; 4:9; 7:4; 8:16,25; 9:10,19). Slaughter in a war which is a judgment of God is a sacrifice in which the kidneys figure (Isa. 34:6). "The finest of the wheat" ASV,RSV was called "fat of kidneys of wheat" KJV, ASV margin (Deut. 32:14). From their inaccessible location in the body, the kidneys were regarded as the seat of the emotions; KJV, ASV margin, *reins,* usually "heart" in ASV, RSV text (Job 19:27; Ps. 7:9; Jer. 11:20, etc.). Once RSV has "soul" (Prov. 23:16); ASV, RSV "inward parts" in Psalm 139:13. RSV has "kidneys" in Job 16:13, in a literal sense. In the NT, for KJV, ASV reins, RSV has "mind," parallel with "heart" (Rev. 2:23).

KIDRON (kĭd'rŏn, kĭ'drŏn, Heb. *qidhrôn,* Gr. *Kédron*), the valley along the E side of Jerusalem, in which is the Pool of Gihon, whose water was brought by an aqueduct into the Pools of Siloam within the walls. South of the city the Kidron joins the Valley of Hinnom near the Pool of En-rogel, and the united valley, Wâdi en-Nâr, runs down to the Dead Sea. Through the Kidron Valley runs a winter torrent, the Brook Kidron, dry much of the year. David's crossing of the Kidron (II Sam. 15:23) in his escape from his rebellious son Absalom, marked the decisive abandonment of his throne. When Solomon spared Shimei, he warned him that to cross the Kidron would bring him death (I Kings 2:37). Asa burned idols at the brook (I Kings 15:13; II Chron. 15:16); also Josiah (II Kings 23:4,6,12); Hezekiah (II Chron. 29:16; 30: 14). It is called "the brook" (II Chron. 32:4) which Hezekiah stopped, to deny the attacking Assyrians a water supply. Nehemiah went up it by night to view the state of the walls of Jerusalem (Neh. 2:15 KJV, ASV brook, RSV valley). Jeremiah mentions it in prophesying the permanent rebuilding of Jerusalem (Jer. 31:38-40). Our Lord crossed it on His way out of the city after the Last Supper, to reach the Garden of Gethsemane on the slopes of the Mount of Olives (John 18:1, KJV Cedron). He must often have looked across this valley "as he sat on the Mount of Olives" (e.g., Matt. 24:3; Mark 13:3) and crossed it on His triumphal entry to Jerusalem (Matt. 2:1-11; Mark 11:1-10; Luke 19:28-44; John 12:12-19). E.R.

KINAH (kī′nà), a city in the extreme south of Judah, near the border of Edom (Josh. 15:21,22), perhaps near Arad (Judg. 1:16); site uncertain.

KINE (See Animals: Cattle)

KING, a male ruler, usually hereditary, of a city, tribe or nation. Heb. *melekh* may mean *possessor*, stressing physical strength, or *counselor, decider*, stressing intellectual superiority. Some combinations of the two ideas probably was in the minds of most people, the latter predominating in better governed societies. Gr. *basileús*, is of obscure origin, but always denoted a ruler and leader of a people, city or state. Kings often had priestly functions in the maintenance of the religion of the group, though most of these were separated from the kingly office in the Heb. monarchy: the king was expected to further religion, but not to act as its priest. In the Orient, kings came to be regarded as divine beings: this was true of Egypt from the beginning; the idea was taken over by the Greek empire of Alexander and his successors, later by the Romans, after their empire came to include most of the East.

The earliest king mentioned in the Bible is Nimrod (Gen. 10:8-12), whose Mesopotamian kingdom was extensive. From this region came the kings who warred with kings of Canaan and were driven off by Abraham (Gen. 14). God promised Abraham (Gen. 17:6) and Jacob (Gen. 35:11) that kings should be among their descendants. There were city-kings such as Abimelech (Gen. 20:2), called king of the Philistines (Gen. 26:1, 8); kings of Edom (Gen. 36:31; I Chron. 1:43) before Israel had kings. Later the Edomites called their rulers dukes, chiefs or sheikhs. Kings of Egypt, the pharaohs, figure in the Egyptian period of Israelite history (Gen. 39-Exod. 14; Deut. 7:8; 11:3); also later when Egyptian influence was strong in Judah. Israel contacted many kings in their wanderings (Num. 20:14-33:40; Deut. 1:4-4:47; 7:24; 29:7; 31:4) and in Canaan (Josh. 2:2-24:12; Judg. 1:7-11:25; I Sam. 14:47; 15:8,20,32, Agag; 21:10,12; 22:4). These varied in power from headmen of towns to rulers of large areas.

It is reiterated that in the time of the judges there was no king in Israel (Judg. 17:6; 18:1; 19:1; 21:25); every man did that which was right in his own eyes. Moses had foreseen that the people would demand a king as a strong human ruler (Deut. 17:14,15; 28:36), not content with theocracy, but the direct rule of God over them (Deut. 33:5). Hannah looked forward to a time when there would be a God-appointed and anointed king of Israel (I Sam. 2:10). Israel, however, toward the end of Samuel's judgeship, was unwilling to wait for a Messianic King, and demanded one like all the nations (I Sam. 8:5,22; 19:19,24; 12:1-25; cf. Hos. 13:10). Samuel duly warned the people what to expect of a king, then selected Saul, whose choice they ratified. The reigns of Israelite kings are chronicled; Saul (I Sam. 12-31; I Chron. 10); David (II Sam.; I Kings 1; I Chron. 11-29); Solomon (I Kings 1-11; I Chron. 28-II Chron. 9); later kings of Israel and Judah (I Kings 12-II Kings 25; II Chron. 10:36). Ezra, Nehemiah and Esther deal with kings of Persia.

The prophets (especially Isa. 1-31; 36:1-39:7; Jer.; Lam.; Ezek.; Dan.) refer to kings of Judah and other nations. Job reflects that in death all are equal with kings (Job 3:14); that God debases kings (12:18); Eliphaz observes that trouble and anguish vanquish a man as does a king prepared for battle (Job 15:24); Bildad says that the wicked "is brought to the king of terrors" (Job 18:14); Job remembers that in prosperity he was like a king (29:25); Elihu thinks of the fear inspired by a king (Job 34:18); and sees that God sets Leviathan "a king over all the children of pride" (Job 41:34). Psalm 2 contrasts the Messianic king (vs. 6) with kings of the earth (vss. 2 and 10). Some references in Psalms are to human kings (Ps. 20:9; 21:1,7; 33:16; 63:11; 68:12,14,29; 72:10,11; 76:12; 89:27; 102:15; 105:14,20,30; 110:5; 119:46; 135:10,11; 136:17-20; 138:4; 144:10; 148:11; 149:8); some to God as King (Ps. 5:2; 10:16; 18:50; 145:1; 149:2, etc.). Psalm 24 acclaims the Lord as King of glory. Psalm 45 may have been a marriage-song for King Solomon, but its language well suits a messianic interpretation. Proverbs contains maxims for a king's conduct (e.g. Prov. 31:1-9). Ecclesiastes and the Song of Solomon view a king's life from the inside. Isaiah develops the concept of a messianic King (Isa. 32:1; 33:17) identified with the Lord (33:22; 42:21; 43:15; 44:6). Jeremiah refers to God as King (Jer. 8:19; 10:7,10; 46:18; 48:15; 51:57) and to the messianic King (23:5). Ezekiel 37:22,24 refers to the Davidic king of restored Israel whom the context shows to be messianic. The messianic King enters Jerusalem riding on a colt (Zech. 9:9); and God is King (Zech. 14:9,16,17; Mal. 1:14). Nebuchadnezzar praises the King of heaven (Dan. 4:37).

The Gospels speak of kings in general (Matt. 10:18; 11:8; 17:25; 18:23; 22:2,7,11,13; Mark 13:9; Luke 10:24; 14:31; 21:12; 22:25); Herod the Great (Matt. 2:1,3,9; Luke 1:5); Herod Antipas (Matt. 14:9; Mark 6:14,22-27); David (Matt. 1:6); the messianic King of the Jews (Matt. 2:2; 21:5; 25:34,40; 27:11,29,37,42; Mark 15:2,9,12,18,26, 32; Luke 19:38; 23:2,3,37,38; John 1:49; 6:15; 12:13,15; 18:37,39; 19:3-21); and God (Matt. 5:35). References in Acts are to earthly kings except 17:7, Jesus. A few references in the Epistles are to earthly kings; one is to God (I Tim. 1:17, cf. 6:15). In Revelation, besides earthly kings, reigning and prophesied, Jesus Christ is introduced as prince (ruler) of the kings of the earth (1:5), who made us kings (1:6; 5:10, ASV, RSV a kingdom; cf. I Pet. 2:9). The king of the apocalyptic locusts (Rev. 9:11) is the angel of the bottomless pit. God is King (Rev. 15:3) and the Lamb is King of kings (17:14). A king sits on a throne, holds a scepter (Ps. 45:6); wears a crown (II Kings 11:12); lives in a palace (I Chron. 29:1); rides in a royal chariot (I Sam. 8:11). From a few military and civil officers for city-kings and for Saul, the royal bureaucracy rapidly expanded (I Sam. 8:10-18) to the dimensions of David's (II Sam. 23:8-39; I Chron. 11:10,47) and Solomon's (I Kings 9:22; 4:1-28; II Chron. 8:9,10) establishments. Yet Solomon judged comparatively trivial cases (I Kings 3:16-28); Ahab shared the personal oversight of his cattle (I Kings 18:5,6). The Persian monarchy was a vast empire (Esth. 1:1). Kings frequently met death by assassination. Among God's chosen people a rightful king was designated by God and anointed by His representative (I Sam. 9:15,16; 16:1-13) with the approval of the people. He ruled by virtue of a covenant between God and His people, to which the king was a party (II Sam. 7). This covenant was extended and renewed as the basis of the NT Kingdom of God or of heaven, of which Jesus is sovereign until at the resurrection He delivers the Kingdom to His Father (I Cor. 15:24-28).

E.R.

KINGDOM OF GOD (Gr. *basileía toú theoú*). The word "kingdom" is capable of three different meanings: 1. the realm over which a monarch reigns; 2. the people over whom he reigns; 3. the actual reign or rule itself. In English, the third use of the word is archaic and therefore is not always given its rightful place in discussion of the term; but in Greek and Hebrew, this is the primary meaning.

All three meanings are found in the New Testament. 1. The Kingdom of God is sometimes the people of the Kingdom. In Revelation 5:10, the redeemed are a kingdom, not, however, because they are the people over whom God reigns but because they will share His reign. The same usage appears in Revelation 1:6.

2. The Kingdom of God is the realm in which God's reign is experienced. This realm is sometimes something present, sometimes future. It is a realm introduced after the ministry of John the Baptist into which men entered with violent determination (Luke 16:16). John did not stand within this new realm but only on its threshold; but so great are the blessings of God's Kingdom that the least in it is greater than John (Matt. 11:11). Jesus offered the Kingdom to Israel, for they were its proper heirs (Matt. 8:12); but the religious leaders, followed by most of the people, not only refused to enter its blessings but tried to prevent others from entering (Matt. 23:13). Nevertheless, many tax-collectors and harlots did enter the Kingdom (Matt. 21:31; see also Col. 1:13). In all of these verses, the Kingdom is a present realm where men may enjoy the blessings of God's rule.

Elsewhere the Kingdom is a future realm inaugurated by the return of Christ. The righteous will inherit this Kingdom (Matt. 25:34) and will shine like the sun in God's Kingdom (Matt. 13:43). Entrance into this future Kingdom is synonymous with entering the eternal life of the Age to Come (Matt. 19:16,23-30; Mark 10:30).

3. The kingdom is also God's reign or rule. *Basileia* is used of kings who have not received "royal power" (RSV) or "authority to rule as kings" (Rev. 17:12). Later, these kings give their "kingdoms," i.e., their authority, to the beast (Rev. 17:17). In Luke 19:12 a nobleman went into a distant country to receive the crown (*basileia*) that he might be king over his country.

This "abstract" meaning of kingdom is evident in many passages. Only those who "receive the kingdom of God," i.e., accept God's rule here and now, enter into the realm of its blessings in the future (Mark 10:15). When we seek God's Kingdom and righteousness, we seek for God's rule in our lives (Matt. 6:33).

However, God's Kingdom is not merely an abstract rule. The Kingdom is God's rule *dynamically* active to defeat evil and redeem sinners. I Corinthians 15:24-26 says that Christ must reign as King until He has destroyed (*katargeo*) all enemies, the last of which is death, and that He then will deliver the Kingdom to God. From this passage, we understand that the Kingdom of God is the dynamic rule of God manifested in Christ to destroy His (spiritual) enemies and to bring to men the blessings of God's reign.

The New Testament pictures three stages in the victory of God's Kingdom. Death is not finally destroyed until the end of the millennial reign of Christ (Rev. 20:14). Yet Christ has already destroyed (*katargeo*) death and brought life and immortality to light (II Tim. 1:10) through His death and resurrection.

Satan will be finally destroyed in the lake of fire at the end of the Millennium (Rev. 20:10); but at the beginning of the Millennium he is to be chained and locked in the bottomless pit (Rev. 20:1-3). Here are two future stages in the "destruction" of Satan; but there is yet a third. Christ became incarnate "that through death he might destroy (*katargeo*) him who has the power of death, that is, the devil. . . ." (Heb. 2:14,15).

This first defeat or "destruction" of Satan's power is reflected in Matthew 12. Jesus claimed that His ability to cast out demons was evidence that the Kingdom of God had come among men (Matt. 12:28). Furthermore, He said that no one could enter a strong man's house (Satan's realm) and despoil his goods (deliver demon-possessed men and women) "unless he first binds the strong man" (vs. 29). By this metaphor of binding, Jesus asserts that the Kingdom of God has come among men to break Satan's power and deliver men from satanic bondage.

Thus the Kingdom of God — His redemptive rule — has come into history in the person of Christ to break the power of death and Satan; it will come in power and glory with the return of Christ to complete the destruction of these enemies. Because of this present victory of God's Kingdom, we may enter the realm of its blessings in the present yet look forward to greater blessings when Christ comes again.

We may now define the Kingdom of God as the sovereign rule of God manifested in Christ to defeat His enemies, creating a people over whom He reigns, and issuing in a realm or realms in which the power of His reign is experienced.

The diversity of the New Testament data has led to diverse interpretations. 1. The **Old Liberal** interpretation of Harnack views the Kingdom as the essence of ideal religion and altogether a present subjective and spiritual reality, having to do with the individual soul and its relation to God. 2. **Consistent Eschatology.** Albert Schweitzer held that the Kingdom was in no sense a present spiritual reality. On the contrary, Jesus taught that (a) the Kingdom of God was altogether a future eschatological reality which would come by a miraculous inbreaking of God to terminate human history and establish the Kingdom; (b) and this apocalyptic Kingdom was to come immediately. Jesus' mission was to announce the imminent end of the world and to prepare men for the impending day of judgment. 3. **Realized Eschatology.** C. H. Dodd has reinterpreted eschatological terminology so that it no longer refers to the "last things" at the end of the Age but to the "ultimate" realities experienced in Christ. The Kingdom of God is the eternal which was broken into time in Christ. 4. **Inaugurated Eschatology** is a mediating view between Schweitzer and Dodd. The Kingdom of God is indeed being realized in the present, but there must also be an eschatological consummation. Many scholars follow Schweitzer in holding that Jesus expected an immediate end of the world, but modify His view by recognizing that in some sense the Kingdom was also present in the person of Jesus. They hold that Jesus was right in the basic structure but wrong in the time of the coming of the Kingdom.

In conservative circles, four views may be distinguished:

1. **Classical premillennialism** (the view set forth in this article) teaches that the Kingdom of God has to do primarily with redemption. The Kingdom was offered to Israel; but when it was

rejected, its blessings were given to "another nation" (Matt. 21:43), the Church (which is a "holy nation," I Pet. 2:9). The Kingdom now works in the world through the church, bringing to all who will receive it the blessings of God's rule. The return of Christ is necessary for the final defeat of the enemies of God's Kingdom and will involve two stages: the Millennium or thousand-year period when the glory of Christ's reign will be manifested in history and human society, and the Age to Come with its new heavens and new earth (Rev. 21:1; II Pet. 3:12-13). Israel, which is still a "holy people" (Rom. 11:16), is yet to be saved and brought into the blessings of the Kingdom, but in terms of New Testament redemption rather than the Old Testament economy. This view accepts the basic premise that the Old Testament prophecies are to be interpreted in terms of the New Testament teaching.

2. **Dispensational premillennialism** finds its definition of the Kingdom in the Old Testament. The Kingdom of God is theocratic, not soteriological. It is the earthly Davidic (millennial) Kingdom destined primarily for Israel. It does not have to do primarily with the Church nor with the redemptive blessings brought into the world by Christ but with the earthly national blessings promised to Israel. This view believes that God has two plans which must be kept separate: an earthly national plan for Israel and a spiritual redemptive plan for the Church. The Kingdom has to do with the former, not with the latter.

3. **Amillennialism** is a modification of classical premillennialism, accepting its basic definition and structure of the Kingdom but omitting the millennial stage. The Kingdom is God's redemptive rule in Christ working in the world through the Church which will come to its consummation with the Second Coming of Christ to inaugurate the Age to Come. Most amillennialists deny that Israel has any future but see the Church as the new Israel which has experienced the fulfillment of the Old Testament prophecies in spiritual terms.

4. **Postmillennialism** sees the Kingdom as the reign of God in Christ through the Church, destined to conquer all the world and to establish God's reign in all human society through the triumphant preaching of the Gospel. Only after this "Millennium" or Golden Age will Christ return for the final judgment, the resurrection of the dead to inaugurate the Age to Come.   G.E.L.

Bibliography:
Premillenial: George Eldon Ladd, *Crucial Questions About the Kingdom of God* (Grand Rapids: Eerdmans, 1957). This book contains references to the modern views cited above.
Dispensational: Alva J. McClain, *The Greatness of the Kingdom* (Grand Rapids: Zondervan, 1959).
Amillennial: L. Berkhof, *The Kingdom of God* (Grand Rapids: Eerdmans, 1951).
Postmillennial: Loraine Boettner, *The Millennium* (Grand Rapids: Baker Book House, 1959).

KINGDOM OF HEAVEN (See Kingdom of God)

KINGDOM OF ISRAEL (See Israel)

KINGDOM OF JUDAH (See Judah)

KINGS, I AND II, BOOKS OF. These are named in English, as in Hebrew, by subject-matter: four centuries of Israelitish kings, from David (his death in 930 B.C.) to Jehoiachin (in Babylon, after 561). They thus provide a sequel to the books of Samuel, which embrace the reigns of Saul and David. The LXX actually entitles I and II Samuel "Books A and B of the Kingdoms" (Latin Vulgate and KJV subtitle: "I and II Books of the Kings"), so that I and II Kings become, correspondingly "III and IV King(dom)s." Like Samuel, Kings was written as a unit but was divided in two at the time of the LXX translation, about 200 B.C. In the original Hebrew canon, moreover, of Law, Prophets, and Writings, Kings preceded Isaiah-Malachi as the concluding volume of the "former prophets," following Joshua, Judges, and Samuel. For though listed among the "historical books" in English (and Greek), these four works possess an essentially prophetic character (contrast the priestly volumes of Chronicles, which see), employing the events of past history as a vehicle for contemporary preaching (cf. Dan. 9:6). Thus, even as Isaiah scanned the future to motivate his people's obedience (1:19-20), so the anonymous author of Kings drove home lessons, born of previous disasters, "Because they obeyed not the voice of the LORD their God" (II Kings 18:12).

The date of composition is not specified; but the author refers repeatedly to conditions that remain "unto this day" (e.g., the presence of the ark within the temple, I Kings 8:8; cf. 9:21; 12:19), indicating that he wrote prior to the destruction of Judah in 586 B.C. (II Kings 8:22; 16:6; 17:41 are less definite.) Even had he drawn upon earlier sources (see below), an Exilic writer would hardly have penned such words. Threatening *predictions* of the Exile (I Kings 9:7-9; II Kings 20:17-18; 21:14; 22:19-20) fail to invalidate this conclusion. I Kings 4:24 indeed speaks of the western Fertile Crescent as "beyond the River Euphrates" (ASVm); but this phrase had become stereotyped during Assyrian times and does not require Babylonian composition. Numerous stylistic parallels exist between the sermonic portions of II Kings 17 and 21 and the writings of Jeremiah. The whole book, moreover, breathes the spirit of Josiah's Deuteronomic reform of 621 B.C. (C. F. Burney lists 51 verbal parallels, *Notes on the Hebrew Text of the Books of Kings,* Oxford: Clarendon, 1903, pp. xiii-xiv). The prophet Jeremiah may thus well have composed I and II Kings, in his youthful enthusiasm for the Josianic reformation (Jer. 11:1-8; cf. Isaiah's similar authorship of a biography of Uzziah, II Chron. 26:22).

Yet following the climactic eulogy of Josiah, "Like unto him was there no king before him, that turned to the LORD . . . according to all the law of Moses," II Kings 23:25b adds, "Neither *after him* arose there any like him." Verse 26 goes on to assume the Exile (as does 24:3-4); II Kings 25:6-7, 11,21, describes the Captivity; and 25:27-30, though without awareness of the return in 538 B.C., speaks of events in Babylon from 561 down to the death of Jehoiachin (Jer. 52:34). It would appear, therefore, that the final two and a half chapters of II Kings from 23:25b, plus the total years of Josiah's reign in 22:1) must have been added, in Babylon, over half a century after the earlier writing. Talmudic tradition attributes the entire work to Jeremiah (*Baba Bathra* 15a); but Jeremiah seems to have died in Egypt, shortly after 586 B.C. (Jer. 42-44). J. E. Steinmueller indeed follows the rabbinic tradition that Jeremiah, in his old age, might have been taken to Babylon by Nebuchadnezzar, after his campaign against Egypt in 568 B.C. (*A Companion to Scripture Studies,* New York: J. F. Wagner, 1941-3, II:98). A more plausible approach, however, would be to suggest a later Babylonian prophet, such as Ezekiel, to supplement Jeremiah's work (Ezekiel's dated prophecies extended only to 571 B.C. (29:17); but cf. his known dependence upon Jeremiah and the stylistic similarity of such sermons as 20:5-32).

In compiling the books of Kings, Jeremiah(?) and his successor utilized written sources: "The book of the acts of Solomon" (I Kings 11:41) and "The books of the chronicles of the kings of Israel" (14:19; 15:31, etc.) and "Judah" (14:29; 15:7, etc.). These chronicles (not to be confused with canonical Chronicles, written in post-Exilic (days) were probably based on court annals, but their contents went beyond what would have appeared in the official records (II Kings 15:15; 21:17). II Chronicles 32:32 thus refers to "the acts of Hezekiah," compiled by Isaiah and then incorporated into "the book of the kings of Judah and Israel" (cf. Isa. 36-38:8; 38:21-39:8, with II Kings 18:13,17-20:19). Other unidentified sources seemingly provided the detailed biographies of Elijah and Elisha (I Kings 17-II Kings 8:15), plus other prophetic narratives (cf. Robert H. Pfeiffer, *Introduction to the Old Testament*. New York: Harper, 1941, pp. 374-375).

Recognition of this "two-stage" composition, however, in no way condones the current negative criticism of Kings, divided throughout into conflicting strata (cf. IB, III:10) similar to those of "JEDP" in the Pentateuch (which see). The pre-Exilic stratum, such views allege, was produced by the same prophetic group that "discovered" Deuteronomy in 621 B.C. and is said to be characterized by a tolerance of pre-Solomonic high places (I Kings 3:4), by faith in the unconquerability of Judah (II Kings 8:19), and by antagonism against northern Israel (17:21-23). The Exilic stratum is then said to manifest opposite attitudes (I Kings 3:3; 9:6-9; 12:24; cf. *ibid.*, pp. 377-378, 410-412). But Solomon actually conducted legitimate worship at no high place or shrine outside of Jerusalem (I Kings 3:15) other than at Gibeon, where rested the Mosaic tabernacle (I Chron. 16:39; 21:29); the northern kingdom obviously possessed both commendable and evil features; and the preservation of Judah never appears as more than temporary (II Kings 20:19; 22:20).

The teachings of the books of Kings are, however, undeniably "deuteronomic." But since Deuteronomy-like phrases appear as frequently in the quoted words of David as they do in the author's own comments, an unprejudiced explanation must be sought, not in theories of wholesale Josianic forgeries, but rather in the fact of the Mosaic authenticity of Deuteronomy, upon which the lives and words of Judah's pious monarchs (cf. Josh. 1:7-8) were consciously patterned. For Kings constitutes more than bare history (cf. its relative neglect of the politically significant reigns of Omri and Jeroboam II), a key to its theological aims appearing in David's opening admonition: "Keep the charge of the LORD . . . as it is written in the law of Moses, that thou mayest prosper in all that thou doest" (I Kings 2:3; cf. 3:14; II Sam. 7:14b). Divine retribution is then traced through the history of Solomon (I Kings 1-11); of the divided kingdoms, treated synchronously (I Kings 12-II Kings 17; cf. IB III:6, "a better scheme than most"); and of surviving Judah (II Kings 18-25). History, accordingly, metes out punishment to sinful Israel (II Kings 17:7-23) and Judah (23:26-27; 24:1-4), but also rewards for the righteous in both north (I Kings 21:29) and south (II Kings 22:19-20) and extending hope even in exile (25:27-30). Some may disparage the validity of this doctrine (Pfeiffer, *op. cit.*, p. 381); but, while admitting that many human acts do not find *immediate* retribution, particularly now when God deals less directly with His people, evangelical Christianity yet proclaims as fundamental to the Gospel of redemption the holy theology of Kings, that whatsoever a man soweth that must he also reap.   J.B.P.

Bibliography:
Montgomery, James A., CC (Kings).
Payne, J. Barton, *An Outline of Hebrew History*. Grand Rapids: Baker, 1954, pp. 110-155.
Pfeiffer, Robert H., *Introduction to the Old Testament*. New York: Harper, 1941, pp. 374-412.
Thiele, Edwin R., *The Mysterious Numbers of the Hebrew Kings*. Univ. of Chicago Press, 1951.
Young, Edward J., *An Introduction to the Old Testament*. Grand Rapids: Eerdmans, 1960, pp. 200-214.

KING'S GARDEN, probably between the two walls of Jerusalem (II Kings 25:4; Jer. 39:4; 52:7), near the Pool of Siloam (Neh. 3:15).

KING'S HIGHWAY, the ancient N and S road E of the Jordan through Edom and Moab. Peaceable passage by this route was denied to the Israelites as they journeyed toward Canaan (Num. 20:17; 21:22). The road is still in use.

KING'S VALE, OR DALE, the Valley of Shaveh E of Jerusalem, where Abram met Melchizedek (Gen. 14:17); and Absalom set up his pillar (II Sam. 18:18).

KINSMAN (kĭnz'măn, *near relative*, Heb. *gōʾēl, one who has the right to redeem*). Boaz exercised such a right by marrying Ruth and purchasing the property of her first husband's father, a near relative (Ruth 2:20-4:14). In Ruth 2:1, Heb. *môdhaʿ, acquaintance*, the feminine form of which is used figuratively (Prov. 7:4, ASV *familiar friend*, RSV *intimate friend*). Once Heb. *qārôv, neighbor* (Ps. 38:11). Heb. *sheʾēr*, and its feminine form, *flesh*; of a relationship within which marriage would be incestuous (Lev. 18:12,13,17; also translated "kin" 18:6; 20:19; 21:2; in 25:49 RSV *kinsman*). Once used of a relative who can inherit (Num. 27:11). Once *gōʾēl* refers to one who can receive restitution for a wrong done to a dead relative (Num. 5:8). In the NT, Greek *suggenés, of the same race* (Luke 14:12; John 18:26; Acts 10:24; Rom. 9:3; 16:7,11,21; in Mark 6:4, kin). The NT meaning is always the broad one of undefined relationship. In the OT, kinsman translates Heb. words with three distinct ideas: one who has a right to redeem or avenge; one too closely related for marriage; a neighbor, friend or acquaintance.

KIR (kûr, kĭr, Heb. *qîr, inclosure, wall*), a place to which the Assyrians carried the inhabitants of Damascus captive (II Kings 16:9; Amos 1:5), and whence they were to be restored to Syria (Amos 9:7). In Isaiah 22:6 soldiers from Kir are associated with others from Elam, which may indicate the general direction in which to look for Kir. In Isaiah 15:1 Kir-haraseth is called Kir of Moab, a different Kir. Heb. *qîr* means "wall," hence Kir may refer to a walled town, or to an enclosure where prisoners were kept, and may not be a true proper name at all.

KIR OF MOAB (See Kir)

KIR-HARASETH (kŭr-hăr'ǎ-sĕth), El-Kerak, E of the S part of the Dead Sea. The name appears in various forms: Kir of Moab; Kir-haresh (-hā'rĕsh); Kir-hareseth (-hăr'ē-sĕth, -há-rē'sĕth); Kir-heres (-hē'rĕs, -rĕz). The name formerly was thought to mean "City of the Sun," but now is interpreted as "New City." It was the capital of Moab when Jehoram, king of Israel, made war on Mesha, king of Moab (II Kings 3:4-25) and devastated the country except for this city, which he besieged. When Mesha offered his son as a sacrifice on the wall, the siege was raised (25-27). Its later destruction is a subject for serious lamentation (Isa. 15:1; 16:7,11; Jer. 48:31,36).

KIRIATH, KIRJATH

KIRIATH, KIRJATH (kĭr'ĭ-ăth, kĭr'jăth, Heb. *qir-yath, a city*). The word occurs alone (Josh. 18: 28 KJV, ASV) where Kiriath-jearim (so RSV) is meant, and as part of other names identified with the same: Kiriath-arim (Ezra 2:25); Kiriath-baal (Josh. 15:60; 18:14). It is found in Kiriath-arba, Hebron (Gen. 23:2, etc.); of Kiriath-sannah (Josh. 15:49) and Kiriath-sepher (Josh. 15:15), both Debir; and in Kiriath-huzoth (Num. 22:39) an unknown place in Moab.

KIRIATHAIM, KIRJATHAIM (kĭr'ĭ-à-thā'ĭm, Heb. means *double city*). 1. A city in the uplands of Moab, given to Reuben who fortified it (Num. 32:37; Josh. 13:19). Later lost to Israel, it was a Moabite town again (Jer. 48:1,23; Ezek. 25:9). Around it were plains, Shaveh Kiriathaim (Gen. 14:5). East of the Dead Sea, a little S of Ataroth and E of Machaerus, el-Qereiyât.

2. A city of the Gershonite Levites in Naphtali (I Chron. 6:76); Kartan (Josh. 21:32). In N Galilee, SE or Tyre, el-Qureiyeh.

KIRIATH-SEPHER (See Kiriath)

KIRIOTH (See Kiriath)

KIRJATH (See Keriath)

KIRJATH-ARBA (See Kiriath)

KIRJATH-ARIM (See Keriath)

KIRJATH-BAAL (See Kiriath)

KIRJATH-HUZOTH (See Kiriath)

KIRJATH-JEARIM (kĭr'jăth-jē'à-rĭm, *city of woods*). With Gibeon, Chephirah, and Beeroth, one of four Gibeonite towns (Josh. 9:17), same as Baalah (15:9) and Kirjath-baal (15:60); a Canaanite high-place and center of Baal-worship, first assigned to Judah (15:60); at the SW corner of the boundary with Benjamin, to which it was later assigned (18:14,15,28). Men of Dan, seeking a new home, encamped W of it in Judah at Mahanneh-dan (Judg. 18:12). Here the men of Beth-shemesh brought the ark when it was returned by the Philistines (I Sam. 6:21; 7:1,2); here it remained 20 years; and hence David brought it up to Jerusalem (I Chron. 13:5,6; II Chron. 1:4; called Baale-judah in II Sam. 6:2). Men from Kirjath-jearim were among the returning exiles (Neh. 7: 29; called Kiriatharim in Ezra 2:25). Men of Kirjath-jearim were listed in the genealogies (I Chron. 2:50-53). The prophet Urijah, son of Shemaiah, came from Kirjath-jearim. It is thought to be Tell-el-Azhar; by others Abû Ghôsh. Its location must be sought with reference to the other places mentioned, and it must be a high elevation. The name means "city of thickets or of forests," probably sacred groves.

KIRJATH-SANNAH (See Kiriath)

KISH (kĭsh, Heb. *qîsh, bow, power*). 1. A Benjamite, a son of Abiel and father of Saul, Israel's first king (I Sam. 9:1,3; 10:11,21). Called Cis in KJV of Acts 13:21).

2. Son of Abi-gibeon, a Benjamite (I Chron. 8: 30; 9:36).

3. A Levite in David's time, of the family of Merari and the house of Mahli (I Chron. 23:21,22; 24:29).

4. A Levite and a Merarite who assisted in the cleansing of the temple in Hezekiah's time (II Chron. 29:12).

5. A Benjamite, ancestor of Mordecai, the cousin of Queen Esther (Esth. 2:5).

6. A city in Mesopotamia, a few miles E of Babylon; Tell el-Oheimir, excavated in recent times. Not named in the Bible.

Abu Gosh, the likely site of ancient Kirjath-jearim, once a Canaanite high place and center of Baal worship. © MPS

KISHI (kĭsh'ĭ), a Merarite Levite, ancestor of Ethan (I Chron. 6:44). Called Kushaiah in I Chronicles 15:17.

KISHION (kĭsh'ĭ-ŏn, kĭsh'yŏn), a city in the tribe of Issachar, given to the Gershonite Levites (Josh. 19:20; 21:28 KJV Kishon; in I Chron. 6:72 called Kedesh).

KISHON, KISON (kī'shŏn, kĭsh'ŏn, or kī'sŏn, kĭs'-ŏn, Heb. *qîshôn, curving*), a stream which flows from sources on Mt. Tabor and Mt. Gilboa westward through the Plain of Esdraelon or Valley of Jezreel, and enters the Bay of Acre N of Mt. Carmel. In winter it becomes a raging torrent, which subsides into pools which are soon drained off for irrigation, except that the last few miles are fed from the slopes of Mt. Carmel and by tributaries from the N. It is treacherous to cross except at fords carefully chosen. It may be the brook E of Jokneam (Josh. 19:11). Along the banks of the river Kishon, Deborah the prophetess and Barak led Israel to victory over the Canaanite hosts of Jabin, under their commander Sisera (Judg. 4 and 5). The heavily armed soldiers and chariots

Excavated remains of the ancient Ziggurat of Kish, in Babylonia, where evidences of an extensive flood layer were uncovered. It is considered to be one of the first ancient cities to be rebuilt after the Flood. © MPS

The Kishon River, before Mount Carmel. © MPS

which were not cut down by the pursuing Israelites were swept away by the torrent Kishon (Judg. 5: 21; Ps. 83:9 KJV Kison). After his contest with the priests of Baal on Mt. Carmel, Elijah had the priests brought down to the brook Kishon and killed there. The stream is now known as the Nahr el-Muqatta.

KISHON RIVER (See Kishon)

KISS (Heb. *nāshaq*, Gr. *philéo, phílema, kataphiléo*), a common greeting among male relatives (Gen. 29:13; 33:4; 45:15; Exod. 4:27; 18:7; II Sam. 14:33); male and female relatives (Gen. 29: 11; 31:28); in farewell (Gen. 31:55; Ruth 1:9,14) and before death (Gen. 50:1). The kiss had a more formal character in connection with a blessing (Gen. 27:26,27; 48:10) or the anointing of a king (I Sam. 10:1). Friends kissed (I Sam. 20:41; II Sam. 19:39). The act might be a pretense (II Sam. 15:5; 20:9; Prov. 27:6). Kissing was an act of worship toward heathen gods (I Kings 19:18,20; Job 31:27; Hos. 13:2). Righteousness and peace will "kiss" each other, i.e., will unite to bless restored Israel (Ps. 85:10). Kisses may be a lure to illicit love (Prov. 7:13). The kiss in Psalm 2:12 is one of homage to the King's Son. The same Heb. word *nāshaq* is translated "touched" (Ezek. 3:13) of the gentle contact of the wings of the living creatures. The kiss was generally given on the cheek, forehead or beard, though a kiss on the lips is indicated (Prov. 24:26) and is probable (in S. of Sol. 1:2; 8:1). In the NT, the Greek verb *philéo* is usually translated "love," but when associated with the strengthened form *kataphiléo*, kiss repeatedly, effusively, it is translated "kiss," and the noun *phílema* is always so rendered. Once Jesus' host did not give Him this customary greeting, but a sinful woman kissed His feet (Luke 7:38,45). The father kissed the returning prodigal (Luke 15:20). Judas kissed Jesus as a sign to the temple police (Matt. 26:48,49; Mark 14:44,45; Luke 22:47,48). The Ephesian elders kissed Paul in farewell (Acts 20: 37). The kiss was adopted as a formal greeting among believers; the holy kiss (Rom. 16:16; I Cor. 16:20; II Cor. 13:12; I Thess. 5:26 or kiss of charity or love (I Pet. 5:14); given by men to men and by women to women.   E.R.

KITE (See Birds)

KITHLISH (kĭth'lĭsh), a town in the lowland of the territory of Judah (Josh. 15:40); ASV, RSV, Chitlish (chĭt'lĭsh). Site unknown.

KITRON (kit'rŏn), a town in the territory of Zebulun, whose inhabitants that tribe did not drive out (Judg. 1:30).

KITTIM (kĭt'ĭm, Heb. *kittîm*). 1. Descendants of Javan (Gen. 10:4; I Chron. 1:7).

2. KJV Chittim, ASV Kittim. Where RSV has Cyprus, that island is probably meant (Isa. 23:1, 12; Jer. 2:10; Ezek. 27:6). Invasion from that direction was expected, to help topple the Assyrian empire. Where RSV retains Kittim, the word characterizes ships of Grecian pattern (Num. 24:24; Dan. 11:30), which roamed the Mediterranean very early. Many think that the reference in Daniel is to the Roman fleet; even so, the Romans owed much to Greek naval architecture.

KNEADING TROUGH, a dish in which dough was prepared to be made into bread. The plague of frogs infested them in Egypt (Exod. 8:3). The Israelites bound them, dough and all, in the bundles of clothing on their backs, when they escaped from Egypt (Exod. 12:34). Called "kneading bowls" in RSV. KJV has "store" for the same Heb. word, where ASV, RSV have "kneading trough" (Deut. 28:5,17).

KNEE (Heb. *berekh*, Gr. *gónu*). The first references are to taking on the knees in token of adoption (Gen. 30:3; 48:12; 50:23). The knees are equivalent to the lap (Judg. 16:19; Job 3:12; II Kings 4:20). Their strength or weakness is commented on (Job 4:14; Ps. 109:24; Heb. 12:12). Gideon rejected men who knelt to drink (Judg. 7:5,6). Diseased knees follow disobedience (Deut. 28:35). Knees smite together in fear (Nah. 2:10; Dan. 5:6). Daniel was set trembling on hands and knees (10:10). To bow the knee to Baal identified one as his worshiper (I Kings 19:18; Rom. 11:4). Kneeling expressed homage or worship (II Kings 1:13, to Elisha; Matt. 17:14; Mark 1:40; 10:17; Luke 5:8, to Jesus; I Kings 8:54; II Chron. 6:13; Ezra 9:3; Rom. 14:11 quoting Isa. 45:23; Eph. 3: 14; Phil. 2:10; Acts 7:60; 9:40; 20:36; 21:5, to God in prayer; notably Luke 22:41, Jesus in Gethsemane; Dan. 6:10 shows that kneeling in prayer was already a customary practice). Kneeling in mockery, Mark 15:19.

KNIFE, a sharp-edged cutting instrument. 1. Heb. *herev*, usually *sword*, occasionally some other tool with a cutting edge; *the flint knife used in circumcision* (Josh. 5:2,3), kept for religious purposes long after bronze and iron were introduced; the swords (so ASV margin, RSV text) with which priests of Baal cut themselves in their contest with Elijah (I Kings 18:28); *a sword* (ASV, RSV) *used as a razor* (Ezek. 5:1,2).

2. Heb. *ma'ăkheleth*, a knife used to carve sacrifices (Gen. 22:6,10; Judg. 19:29; figuratively, Prov. 30:14).

3. Heb. *sakkîn*, knife (Prov. 23:2).

4. Heb. *mahălāph*, Ezra 1:9; named among temple vessels taken from Jerusalem as spoils, and returned after the Exile, are "29 knives" (KJV, ASV) which RSV calls "censers." The meaning is uncertain. A penknife (Jer. 36:23) was used to sharpen reed pens. Knives were not used to eat with, meat being cut in small pieces before serving, and bread broken at the table. The Philistines had metal knives long before they came into general use in Israel (see I Sam. 13:19,22).

KNOP (nŏp). 1. Heb. *kaphtôr, capital* (Amos 9: 1; Zeph. 2:14 ASV, RSV; KJV *lintel*). A knob or bulb ornamenting the golden candlestick in the tabernacle (Exod. 25:31-36; 37:17-22, RSV capitals).

2. Heb. *pĕqā'îm*, ornaments carved of wood on the cedar walls of Solomon's Temple (I Kings 6:18); or of bronze on the laver (I Kings 7:24); shaped like gourds (so RSV text, ASV margin).

KOA (kō'à), a people E of the Tigris, between Elam and Media, named with the Babylonians, Chaldeans, Assyrians, Pekod and Shoa as about to invade Judah (Ezek. 23:23).

KOHATH, KOHATHITES (kō'hăth, -īts), second son of Levi (Gen. 46:11), ancestor of Moses (Exod. 6:16-20; Num. 3:17,19; I Chron. 6:1-3). His descendants, the Kohathites, one of three divisions of the Levites, comprised four families (Num. 3:17-20,27-31). They camped S of the tabernacle. Numbering 8,600, on duty, they cared for the ark, table, candlestick, altars and vessels of the sanctuary. These they carried on foot, no wagons being assigned them (Num. 7:8,9). Joshua allotted them 23 cities (Josh. 21:4,5). Under the monarchy they are prominent (I Chron. 23:13-20; 24:20-25), especially Heman in the service of song (I Chron. 6:33ff; 16:41ff; 25:1ff). They took part in the religious service the day before Jehoshaphat's victory over his allied enemies (II Chron. 20:19); and in Hezekiah's cleansing of the temple (II Chron. 29:12-19).

KOLAIAH (kō-lā'yà, Heb. *qôlāyâh, voice of Jehovah*). 1. A Benjamite who settled in Jerusalem after the Captivity (Neh. 11:7).

2. The father of the false prophet Ahab, who suffered death for his false prophecies (Jer. 29:21).

KORAH, KORAHITE (kō'rà, -īt, Heb. *qōrah*). 1. A son of Esau (Gen. 36:5,14,18; I Chron. 1:35).

2. A grandson of Esau, nephew of No. 1 (Gen. 36:16).

3. A descendant of Caleb (I Chron. 2:43).

4. A Levite from whom descended the Korahites, doorkeepers and musicians of tabernacle and temple (Exod. 6:24; I Chron. 6:22). The Korahites, KJV also Korhites, Korathites, appear in Exodus 6:24; Numbers 26:58; I Chronicles 9:19, 31; 12:6; 26:1; II Chronicles 20:19. The sons of Korah are named in the titles of Psalms 42, 44-49, 84, 85, 87, 88).

5. A son of Izhar and grandson of Kohath (Exod. 6:21,24; I Chron. 6:37; 9:19) who led a rebellion (Num. 16; 26:9-11; 27:3; Jude 11 KJV Core). Korah, with two companions, resisted the civil authority of Moses. For refusing to appear before him as commanded, Korah, Dathan and Abiram and their followers were swallowed up by the earth. Then 250 rebellious Levites were consumed by fire from the Lord, but the children of Korah were spared (Num. 26:11).

KORE (kō'rē). 1. A Korahite whose son, Shallum, was a tabernacle gatekeeper (I Chron. 9:19; 26:1,19).

2. A Levite, son of Imnah, set over the free will offerings in Hezekiah's time (II Chron. 31:14).

KOZ (kŏz). 1. A priest whose descendants returned from exile with Zerubbabel, but lost their position through inability to prove their descent (Ezra 2:61; Neh. 7:63 ASV, RSV Hakkoz).

2. Ancestor of Meremoth, who helped in the repair of the wall (Neh. 3:4,21 ASV, RSV Hakkoz). In the case of both men, the KJV rendering Koz results from the translators taking "Ha-" as the Heb. article, and not as part of the proper name.

KUSHAIAH (kū-shā'yà), a Levite of the family of Merari (I Chron. 15:17). Called Kishi in I Chronicles 6:44.

L

LAADAH (lā'à-dà), a man of Judah, of the family of Shelah (I Chron. 4:21), the progenitor of the inhabitants of Mareshah.

LAADAN (lā'à-dăn), Ladan in RV. 1. An Ephraimite, an ancestor of Joshua (I Chron. 7:26).

2. A Levite of the family of Gershon (I Chron. 23:7-9; 26:21), called Libni in I Chronicles 6:17.

LABAN (lā'băn, Heb. *lāvān, white*). 1. The nephew of Abraham who lived in Haran on a tributary of the Euphrates river in Mesopotamia. He belonged to that branch of the family of Terah (Abraham's father) which was derived from Abraham's brother Nahor and his niece Milcah (Gen. 22:20-24), and is first mentioned when Rebekah is introduced, as Rebekah's brother (Gen. 24:29). In ancient Semitic custom, the brother was the guardian of the sister, and thus Laban takes a prominent place in the story of Rebekah's leaving for Canaan to be Isaac's bride. His grasping nature is hinted at in Genesis 24:30,31, where his fulsome invitation to Abraham's servant follows immediately after his appraisal of the servant's expensively equipped party.

Laban's later history is interwoven with Jacob's (*q.v.*). When Jacob fled from the anger of his brother Esau, he settled in his uncle Laban's house in Haran and stayed there 20 years. The relationship between Laban and his nephew is an interesting one. Both appear as resourceful, often grasping men, each eager to best the other in every transaction. Even in the circumstances surrounding the marriage of Jacob to Laban's daughters Rachel and Leah (Gen. 29) this competition is evident. After Jacob had served 14 years for his brides, there followed six more years in Haran in which, according to Jacob's testimony Laban changed his wages ten times (31:41). The famous contract involving the speckled and spotted sheep (30:31-43) was evidently one of the ten.

At the end of the 20 years, Jacob quietly stole away from Laban, taking his now large family with him to Canaan (Gen. 31). Pursuing him, Laban overtook him in Gilead. After mutual protestations and incriminations, uncle and nephew parted, after erecting a "heap of witness" — a kind of dividing line — between them. Laban is here called "the Aramean" (Gen. 31:24 RSV) and he gives the heap an Aramaic name (Jegar-shadutha), while Jacob calls it by its Hebrew equivalent Galeed (Gen. 31:47), both meaning "heap of witness."

These Aramaic references are interesting guides in the quest for better understanding of the origins of the patriarchs. In an old confession the Hebrews were taught to say "A wandering Aramean was my father" (Deut. 26:5 RSV). It seems likely that the patriarchal ancestors of the Hebrews sprang from a mixed Semitic stock in northeast Mesopotamia, among which the Aramean was a prominent strain.

2. Laban is also the name of an unidentified place in the Plains of Moab, or perhaps in the Sinai peninsula (Deut. 1:1). J.B.G.

LABOR. The noun *labor* is today confined to the abstract use — the act of laboring (Gen. 31:42; Rom. 16:6). Formerly it expressed also the fruit of labor, as in Exodus 23:16, "When thou hast gathered in thy labors out of the field," or John 4:38, "Ye are entered into their labors." The word is also used of labor in childbirth (Gen. 35:16).

In Bible times there was no class of men known as "labor" in contrast with "management." All but a favored few labored, and hard work was looked on as the common lot of man and a result of the curse (Gen. 3:17-19), a bitter servitude. Slavery (*q.v.*) was commonly practiced in the Bible world; the conscription of freemen for labor on government building projects was practiced by Solomon (I Kings 5:13-17) and Asa (I Kings 15:22).

Although most workers in the simple culture of OT times were what we today would call "unskilled," there were certain skilled occupations. The potter (Jer. 18) has left behind him unnumbered examples of his skill. Some technology in the working of metals was known. Remains of smelting furnaces have been found. Stone masons, scribes (Ezek. 9:2; Jer. 36:2,4), dyers, weavers, and workers in precious stones and ivory carried on their work. But for the greater part life was simple, work arduous, hours long and wages small: "Yet is their strength labor and sorrow, for it is soon cut off, and we fly away" (Ps. 90:10). By NT times, things had changed, and the more complex civilization of the Roman world, with its skilled and more diversified occupations and better standards of living, had come to Palestine.   J.B.G.

LACE, mentioned in the English Bible four times (Exod. 28:28,37; 39:21,31), always a translation of the Hebrew *pāthîl* ("thread" or "cord"), the "lace of blue" was used to bind the high priest's breastplate to the ephod.

LACHISH (lā'kĭsh, Heb. *lākhîsh,* perhaps meaning "rough"), the name of a Canaanitish royal city and Judean border fortress, that occupied a strategic valley 25 miles SW of Jerusalem, the southernmost of the five that transect the Palestinian Shephelah, or piedmont, and communicate between Judah's central ridge and the coastal highway leading into Egypt. First equated with Tell el-Hesy, Lachish has now been identified by written evidence (see below) with Tell ed-Duweir, a 22-acre mound excavated by J. K. Starkey from 1932 until his death by violence in 1938.

Even before 3000 B.C. Lachish was inhabited by chalcolithic cave dwellers, but in about 2700 an early-bronze city was constructed on the virgin rock. Following a gap occasioned by invaders of calciform culture (c. 2300 B.C.), middle-bronze Lachish arose, exhibiting cultural and political ties with Middle Kingdom Egypt (2000-1780). This was succeeded by a Hyksos-type community, which provided Lachish with its first observable fortifications, including the characteristic dry moat, or fosse. An inscribed dagger, dated about 1650, furnishes one of the earliest examples of that acrophonic writing from which all modern alphabets derive, two centuries older than the Sinaitic or the five subsequent Lachish inscriptions (Olga Tufnell *et al., Lachish IV-Text,* New York: Oxford, 1958, pp. 127-128). After the expulsion of the Hyksos from Egypt and their defeat in Palestine (c. 1578-1573 B.C.), a late-bronze Canaanitish citadel rendered at least nominal allegiance to New Empire Egypt. Its king, Japhia, joined with Adonizedek of Jerusalem in a confederacy against Joshua, 1406 B.C. (Josh. 10:3), only to be defeated and executed (10:23-26,12:11). In Joshua's subsequent sweep through the southwest, Israel captured Lachish (reinforced by Gezer) and annihilated its inhabitants, in accordance with Moses' ban (10:31-

One of the famous Lachish Letters. This is No. 3.
© MPS

33, Deut. 7:2). Scripture contains no record, however, of its destruction (cf. Josh. 11:13); and, though assigned to Judah (15:39), Lachish must have suffered rapid Canaanitish reoccupation, for a late-bronze temple constructed in the former fosse exhibits little interruption in its use. A generation later, the Amarna letters criticize Lachish for furnishing supplies to the *Khabiru* (invaders which include the Hebrews; see Israel, sec. B) and for overthrowing the Egyptian prefect, Zimridi (Letters 287-288). Lachish was burned in about 1230 B.C. Some interpreters have attempted to associate this conflagration with Joshua's campaign (cf. Millar Burrows, *What Mean These Stones?,* New Haven: American School of Oriental Research, 1941, pp. 76-77); but the excavators themselves attribute its fall to the contemporaneous raids of Pharaoh Merneptah or to attacks by immigrating Philistines (Tufnell, *Lachish II,* 1940, pp. 23-24).

Lachish was fortified by Rehoboam, shortly after the division of the Hebrew kingdom in 930 B.C. (II Chron. 11:9); and it witnessed the murder of King Amaziah in 767 (25:27). The Prophet Micah condemned Lachish's chariots as "the beginning of Zion's sin," perhaps because of the city's use as a staging point for the extravagant importation of Egyptian horses (1:13; cf. I Kings 10:28-29, Deut. 17:16). In any event, Lachish was successfully besieged by Sennacherib in 701 (II Chron. 32:9); thither Hezekiah directed his submission (II Kings 18:14); and from it the Rabshakeh's troops marched against Jerusalem (18:17,19:8). Starkey's excavations demonstrate successive destructions of Lachish in 597 and 587 B.C., corresponding to Nebuchadnezzar's second and third attacks against Judah. From the final ashes were recovered 21 inscribed ostraca. Consisting primarily of communications from an outpost commander named Hoshaiah to his superior, Joash, at Lachish, they constitute our first truly personal, Palestinian docu-

Above, the mound at Lachish (Tell ed-Duweir), the north and northeast sides of the Tell. Below, excavation work in progress on the mound at Lachish. © MPS

ments. Letter IV mentions signal fires (cf. Jer. 6:1) and establishes Jeremiah's assertion that Lachish and Azekah were the last cities, before Jerusalem, to fall to Nebuchadnezzar (34:7); and letter VI speaks of a warning prophet (like Jeremiah himself) and of critics that "weakened the hands" of anti-Babylonian resistance (Jer. 38:4). Finally, in Nehemiah's day a resettled Lachish (Neh. 11:30) achieved the construction of a palace and Persian sun temple that are among the finest of the period (Burrows, *op. cit.*, p. 132). J.B.P.

LADDER, mentioned only once in the English Bible — Jacob's ladder between heaven and earth, seen in his Bethel dream (Gen. 28:12). The Hebrew term is *sullām,* properly "a staircase." Scaling ladders were frequently used in storming ancient cities. They are often pictured on the Assyrian and Egyptian monuments, and are mentioned in I Maccabees 5:30.

LAEL (lā′ĕl), a member of the family of Gershon, father of Eliasaph (Num. 3:24). Meaning "belonging to God," the name is almost unique in the OT. It is formed by the addition of the divine name "El" to the preposition "la."

LAHAD (lā′hăd), a Judahite family name (I Chron. 4:2).

LAHAI-ROI (See Beer-Lahai-Roi)

LAHMAM (là′măm, Heb. *lahmām*), a town in the Judean Shephelah (Josh. 15:40), possibly to be identified with modern el-Lahm, two and a half miles S of Beit Jibrin.

LAHMI (là′mĭ, Heb. *lahmî*), according to I Chronicles 20:5 the brother of the giant from Gath, who was slain by a certain Elhanan. In the parallel passage in II Samuel 21:9 the name Lahmi seems to have been corrupted to "Bethlehemite," Hebrew, *Bêth Hallahmî.*

LAISH (lā′ĭsh, Heb. *layish*). 1. A city in the upper Jordan valley, which was captured by the Danites and renamed Dan (Judg. 18:7,14,27,29). It is called Leshem in Joshua 19:47. Laish in Isaiah 10:30 (KJV) should be rendered Laishah (RSV) and is a town a little N of Jerusalem.

2. The father of Phalti or Phaltiel, a Benjamite, to whom Michal, David's wife, was given by Saul (I Sam. 25:44; II Sam. 3:15).

LAKUM, LAKKUM (lā′kŭm, lăk′ŭm), a town of Naphtali (Josh. 19:33), location unknown.

LAMB, a translation of several Hebrew words in the English Bible, most of them meaning the young of the sheep. One however (*sheh,* used in Exod. 12:3-6), refers to the young of either sheep or goats (cf. Exod. 12:5) and seems to include adult specimens at times.

The meat of lambs was considered a delicacy among the ancient Hebrews (Deut. 32:14; Amos 6:4; II Sam. 12:3-6). Meat was scarce among them, and the killing of a lamb would mark an important occasion. Lambs were used for sacrifices from the earliest times (Gen. 4:4; 22:7).

The lamb was a staple in the Mosaic sacrificial system. It was offered for the continual burnt offering each morning and evening (Exod. 29:38-42); on the Sabbath the number was doubled (Num. 28:9). On the first day of each month (Num. 28:11), during the seven days of the Passover (vss. 16, 19), at the feast of Weeks (vss. 26,27), Trumpets (29:1,2), on the Day of Atonement (vss. 7,8), and on the feast of Tabernacles (vss. 13-36) lambs were offered. The lamb was one of the sacrifices accepted for the ceremonial cleansing of a woman after childbirth (Lev. 12:6) or for the cleansing of a recovered leper (Lev. 14:10-18). Of unusual interest is the use of the lamb in the Passover ceremony (see Lamb of God). J.B.G

LAMB OF GOD, Jesus was called the Lamb of God by John the Baptist (John 1:29,36). The expression certainly emphasizes the redemptive character of the work of Christ. More than a score of times in the Revelation the lamb is used as a symbol of Christ, and in Christian art of the succeeding centuries the motif is continued, as it is also in the communion service of many churches in the words, "Lamb of God, Son of the Father, that takest away the sins of the world, have mercy upon us."

The OT is full of the lamb as a sacrificial victim (see lamb). Of special interest is the Passover lamb (Exod. 12:3-6) with the sacrifice of which deliverance from Egypt was achieved. This deliverance became in time a picture of redemption from sin (Luke 9:31; I Cor. 5:7). The substitutionary use of the unblemished lamb in sacrifice led to the idea of the Suffering Servant who as a lamb died in the place of sinners (Isa. 53:4-7).

LAME (See Diseases)

LAMECH (lā'mĕk, Heb. *lemekh*, meaning undetermined), the name of two men in the antediluvian records: 1. A son of Methusael (Gen. 4:18-24). This man, a descendant of Cain, had two wives, Adah and Zillah. Lamech's sons by Adah, Tubal and Jubal, founded the nomadic life and the musical arts; Lamech's son by Zillah, Tubal-cain, invented metalcrafts and instruments of war; Lamech also had a daughter Naamah, by Zillah. As far as the record reveals, this man was the first poet. His song (Gen. 4:23f) expresses every feature of Hebrew poetry (parallelism, poetic diction, etc.). This song, addressed to his wives, has been interpreted variously. Some hold that it is nothing less than a bombastic boast of revenge on any man who will dare to attack him while he is armed with the weapons forged by his son Tubal-cain. Others, with greater probability, maintain that Lamech, having already killed a man who attempted to murder him, is now claiming immunity on the ground that he acted in self-defense; thus, he logically asserts, his act will receive at the bar of justice a seventy-times-seven acquittal over Cain's cold-blooded murder of Abel.

2. The son of Methuselah (Gen. 5:28-31). This man, a descendant of Seth, became the father of Noah. His faith is attested by the name he gave his son, (Noah, meaning "rest") and by the hope of "comfort" (Gen. 5:29) that he anticipated in his son's life. Thus, basing his faith upon the promised deliverance from the Adamic curse (Gen. 3:14-19), he foresees, even if faintly, the coming of One of his seed (cf. I Chron. 1:3; Luke 3:36)

who will remove that curse (cf. Rom. 8:18-25). He died at the age of 777. W.B.

LAMENTATIONS. This book, entitled in most English versions *The Lamentations of Jeremiah*, is placed between Jeremiah and Ezekiel in the LXX, Vulgate, and the English Bible. In the Hebrew text, however, it occurred in the Sacred Writings as one of the Megilloth or "five scrolls," of which it is the third. Its Hebrew title *êkhâh* ("Oh, how") is derived from the word with which the book commences. The Talmud renamed the book *Qinoth* ("Lamentations" or "elegies") as a more accurate designation of its true contents. This approach was adopted in the LXX title *Thrénoi* ("Elegies") and the Threni ("Lamentations") of the Latin versions. The latter introduced the ascription of the work to Jeremiah, and this was followed by most English versions. Because of its position in the Megilloth, the Book of Lamentations is read in synagogue worship on the fast of the ninth of Ab, during the evening and morning services. This particular occasion commemorates the destruction of Jerusalem by Chaldean forces in 586 B.C., and again by the Roman armies under Titus in A.D. 70.

The book comprises five poems lamenting the desolation which had overtaken the Holy City in 586 B.C. The first four compositions are highly artificial in structure, consisting of acrostics based on the Hebrew alphabet. Each verse of Chapters 1 and 2 commences with a word whose initial consonant is successively one of the 22 letters of the Hebrew alphabet. A slight variation of the regular order occurs in 2:16-17, 3:47-48 and 4:16-17. The third chapter is peculiar in that a triple alphabetical arrangement is followed, so that all three lines in each stanza commence with the same letter. The fifth chapter is not an acrostic, although like the others it contains 22 stanzas, and is a prayer rather than an elegy. Alphabetical forms of this kind probably served as a useful stimulus to memory at a time when manuscripts were rare and costly.

Some writers have regarded the mechanical structure of most of the book as incompatible with the grief and sincere penitence of the writer. These two ideas need not be inconsistent, however, particularly if the book was composed with a view to consistent liturgical usage. From the manner in which it has survived among the Jews it may well be that this was the intention of the author. The elegiac meter which characterizes the poems was occasionally employed in the writings of the eighth century B.C. prophets in Jeremiah (9:19 f), Ezekiel (19) and some Psalms (e.g., 84,119).

Although in the Hebrew no name was attached to the book, the authorship was uniformly ascribed by ancient authorities to Jeremiah. The LXX added an introductory note stating that "Jeremiah lamented this lamentation over Jerusalem," but the traditional view of the authorship appears to be rooted in the elegy composed for the mourning-period of the deceased Josiah (c. 609 B.C.) Many modern critics have envisaged several authors at work in the book, or else have assumed that Baruch was responsible for the work in its final form. The reasons adduced include the fact that the physical circumstances of the prophet would make the work of composition rather difficult; that there are certain implicit contradictions between the prophecy of Jeremiah and the Book of Lamentations, and that some literary expressions characteristic of Jeremiah are lacking in Lamentations. Thus the thought of Lamentations 2:9 that God no longer reveals Himself in His prophets is

Lamps of Palestine, in series, from patriarchal times to the New Testament era. Note the progression from simple open-dish types (above) to "slipper" types (below), with hole in top for adding oil. © Andrews University

held to be inconsistent with the thought of Jeremiah. Similarly the reference in Lamentations 4:17 to the possibility of Egypt as a deliverer ill accords with the patriotism of the prophet (42:15-17; 43:12f., etc.).

On the other hand, most of the poems appear intimately connected with the calamity of the Exile. Chapters 2 and 4 indicate that the author personally witnessed the tragedy of 586 B.C., while the remainder of the book may have been written in Babylonia in the early captivity. It seems improbable that the final chapter was written in Jerusalem after the return from Exile, perhaps about 525 B.C., as has been suggested by some writers. The arguments for diversity of authorship do not seem particularly strong, though the possibility that the poems were recast in mnemonic form at a time subsequent to their original composition must not be overlooked. Until more decisive evidence is forthcoming, there seems little reason for questioning the substantial unity and traditional authorship of Lamentations.

The book bewails the siege and destruction of Jerusalem, and sorrows over the sufferings of the inhabitants during this time. It makes poignant confession of sin on behalf of the people and their leaders, acknowledges complete submission to the Divine will, and prays that God will once again favor and restore His people.

Analysis:
The fallen city admits its sin and the justice of Divine judgment. (Chapter 1,2).

Lamentation; reassertion of Divine mercy and judgment; prayer for Divine intervention. (Chaps. 3,4).

Further confession and prayers for mercy. (Chap. 5). R.K.H.

LAMP, an instrument used for artificial lighting. Lamps are frequently mentioned in Scripture but no description of their form and structure is given. Archaeology has recovered many specimens in a great variety of forms from the early simple shallow, saucer-like bowl with one side slightly pointed for the lighted wick, to the later closed bowl with only a hole on top to pour in the oil, a spout for the wick, and a handle to carry it. Lamps for domestic use were generally of terra-cotta or of bronze.

The KJV often uses "candle" and "candlestick" where "lamp" and "lampstand" would be more literal. The Hebrew *nēr is* generally rendered

"lamp," but "candle" nine times, while *lappîdh* is rendered "lamp" eight times, and "torch" and "firebrand" twice each. The Gr. *lampás* is rendered "lamp" seven times, "light" and "torch" once each, but *lýchnos,* properly "lamp," is rendered "candle" eight times and "light" six, but in ASV always "lamp."

The use of lamps is mentioned in connection with the golden candlestick in the tabernacle and the ten golden candlesticks in the temple (Exod. 25:37; I Kings 7:49; II Chron. 4:20; 13:11; Zech. 4:2). As shown from their usage, the "lamps" of Gideon's soldiers were doubtless torches. The common NT mention of lamps is in connection with their household usage (Matt. 5:15; Mark 4:21; Luke 8:16; 11:33; 15:8). Such lamps were generally placed on a "lampstand," usually a niche built into the wall. It appears that the Hebrews were accustomed to burn lamps overnight in their chambers, perhaps because of a dread of darkness, more likely to keep away prowlers. The use of oil-fed lamps in a marriage procession is mentioned in Matthew 25:1. Since such lamps contained only a few spoonfuls of oil, a reserve supply would be a necessity. The lighted lamp is also mentioned metaphorically to symbolize (1) God's Word (Ps. 119:105; II Pet. 1:19); (2) God's guidance (II Sam. 22:29; Ps. 18:28); (3) God's salvation (Isa. 62:1); (4) man's spirit (Prov. 20:27; (5) outward prosperity (Prov. 13:9); (6) a son as successor (I Kings 11:36; 15:4). D.E.H.

LANCE (See Arms, Armor)

LANDMARK (Heb. *gevûl*), an object used to mark the boundary of a field. Landmarks were frequently such movable objects as a stone or a post. Since a cunning and unscrupulous individual could take advantage of his neighbor by shifting the location of such boundary marks, thus robbing him of part of his means of support, such removal of landmarks was prohibited by the Mosaic law (Deut. 19:14; 27:17). Hebrew piety denounced the act (Prov. 22:28, 23:10) and it was considered equal to theft (Job 24:2).

LANE (Gr. rhýme), an alley of a city. Occurs once in Luke 14:21. The Greek word is elsewhere translated "street" (Matt. 6:2; Acts 9:11).

LANGUAGES. The first language spoken by the invading Israelitish tribes in Palestine was Hebrew, a Semitic tongue related to Phoenician, to the Canaanitish dialects of the tribes they dispossessed, and to the speech of Moab. The Tell-el-Amarna letters, and the inscription of Mesha, are evidence of this. Hebrew, over the first centuries of the occupation of Palestine, was both the literary and colloquial language. It remained the literary language permanently. In colloquial use it was replaced by Aramaic. The date of the change is difficult to determine with precision. Eliakim's request to the Rabshakeh (II Kings 18:26) to speak "in the Syrian language," which, as a common eastern language of diplomacy, the leaders understood, and not "in the Jews" language shows that Hebrew was still the Jewish vernacular in 713 B.C. Such was still the case as late as Nehemiah, two centuries later.

The next evidence is from the NT where phrases quoted in the Palestinian vernacular (e.g. *talitha cumi,* and the cry from the Cross) are undoubtedly Aramaic. Before Aramaic replaced Hebrew thus, it had, of course infiltrated its vocabulary. The other colloquial dialect of NT times was Greek, which also provided the literary language for the NT writings. It is the common dialect of Greek which is thus represented, that simplified and basic form which descended from Attic and became an alternative language in most of the Mediterranean basin, and especially in the kingdoms of Alexander's successors. Christ spoke Aramaic, but undoubtedly understood Greek, and read the Scriptures in classical Hebrew. Paul knew all three languages, and used them with equal facility, with the addition of Latin.   E.M.B.

LAODICEA (lā-ŏd'ĭ-sē'à, Gr. *Laodikía*), a wealthy city in Asia Minor founded by Antiochus II (261-246 B.C.), and head of the "circuit" of "the Seven Churches of Asia." The city lay on one of the great Asian trade routes, and this insured its great commercial prosperity. Laodicea was a leading banking center. In 51 B.C. Cicero, en route for his Cilician province, cashed drafts there. It was no doubt the rich banking firms which, in A.D. 60, financed the reconstruction of the city after the great earthquake which prostrated it. Laodicea refused the Senate's earthquake relief. She was "rich and increased with goods" and had "need of nothing" (Rev. 3:17). The Lycus valley produced a glossy black wool, the source of black cloaks and carpets, for which the city was famous. Laodicea was also the home of a medical school, and the manufacture of collyrium, a famous eyesalve. The scornful imagery of the apocalyptic letter to Laodicea is obviously based on these activities. It also has reference to the emetic qualities of the soda-laden warm water from nearby Hierapolis, whose thermal springs ran into the Maeander. Laodicea's water supply also came from Hierapolis, and Sir William Ramsay suggests that its vulnerability, together with the city's exposed position, and its easy wealth caused the growth in the community of that spirit of compromise and worldly-mindedness castigated in the Revelation. Under Diocletian, Laodicea, still prosperous, was made the chief city of the Province of Phrygia.   E.M.B.

LAODICEA, CHURCH AT (See Laodicea)

LAODICEANS, EPISTLE TO, mentioned by Paul in Colossians 4:16 in urging the Colossians to exchange epistles with the Laodiceans. An epistle written by the Laodiceans to Paul is ruled out by the context; "from" (*ek*) here denotes present locality, not origin. Views of its identity are: 1. The spurious "Epistle to the Laodiceans" found among the Pauline epistles in some Latin Mss. from the sixth to the 15th centuries. Its 20 verses, being phrases strung together from Philippians and Gal-

Ruins of the Phrygian city of Laodicea.   © SHH

atians, are a forgery with no heretical motive. 2. A Pauline letter to the Laodiceans now lost. This is not improbable; opponents hold it multiplies epistles unnecessarily. 3. Our Ephesians. This view is very probable if the encyclical view of Ephesians is accepted, and accounts for Marcion's title of it as "the epistle to the Laodiceans."

LAPPED, LAPPETH (lăpt, lăp'ĕth, Heb. *lāqaq, to lap, lick*). The Hebrew verb is used (1) to indicate alertness and alacrity (in the test of Gideon's army; Judg. 7:5,6,7); (2) to indicate disgust and loathsomeness (in the comparison between Naboth's death and Ahab's death; I Kings 21:19; 22:38).

LAPPIDOTH (lăp'ĭ-dŏth, Heb. *lappîdhôth, torches* or *lightning flashes*), the husband of Deborah the prophetess (Judg. 4:4).

LAPWING (See Birds)

LASCIVIOUSNESS (lă-sĭv'ĭ-ŭs-nĕs, Gr. *asélgeia*). The ASV translates *asélgeia* "lasciviousness" (Mark 7:22; II Cor. 12:21; Gal. 5:19; Eph. 4:19; I Pet. 4:3; II Pet. 2:18; Jude 4), "lascivious" (II Pet. 2:7), "lascivious doings" (II Pet. 2:2), "wantonness" (Rom. 13:13). RSV uses "licentiousness" or "licentious" throughout. *Aselgeia* designates shameless immorality, a characteristic sin of ancient society.

LASEA (là-sē'à), a small seaport town on the S coast of Crete, about five miles E of Fair Haven, listed by Luke (Acts 27:8) in the log of Paul's voyage to Rome. No other ancient writer mentions the place.

LASHA (lā'shà, Heb. *lāsha'*), a place near Sodom and Gomorrah mentioned in Genesis 10:19 to mark off the Canaanite territory. Jerome, following Jewish sources, equates it with Callirrhoë, famous for its warm springs. The exact place has not yet been identified.

LASHARON (lă-shā'rŏn, Heb. *lashshārôn,* probably *to Sharon*), a royal Canaanite town whose king was slain by Joshua (Josh. 12:18). Listed along with Aphek, it is probably identifiable as the ancient Sarona, located on the plateau 6½ miles SW of Tiberias.

LATCHET (lăch'ĕt;-ĭt, Heb. *serôk,* [*sandal-*]*thong,* Gr. *himás,* same meaning), the thong or strap, usually made of leather, by which the sandal was fastened to the foot. It is used figuratively to describe (1) the most insignificant possession (Gen. 14:23); (2) the efficiency of an invading army (Isa. 5:27); (3) the most menial kind of service (Mark 1:7; Luke 3:16; John 1:27; cf. Acts 13:25). In Acts 22:25 *himas* is used literally of the thongs by which the Roman soldiers tied up Paul.

LATIN (lăt'ĭn), the language of the Romans, and, in Palestine, used primarily by the Romans. The official superscription on the cross was written in Hebrew, Greek, and Latin (Luke 23:38; John 19: 20). The NT contains about 25 administrative and military Latin words translated into Greek.

LATTICE (lăt'ĭs). Latticework, made by crossing laths or other material across an opening, served a threefold purpose: (1) privacy (so that one might look out without being seen; (2) ventilation (so that the breeze might flow in without the sun's hot rays); (3) decoration (so that a house or public building might be architecturally more attractive), Judges 5:28; Proverbs 7:6; II Kings 1:2.

LAUGHTER (lȧf'tẽr). 1. Laughter's limitations: it cannot satisfy (Prov. 14:13; Eccl. 2:2; 7:3,6; 10: 19).

2. God's laughter: He laughs at His enemies (Ps. 2:4; 37:13; 59:8).

3. The believers' laughter: they sometimes laugh incredibly (Gen. 17:17; 18:12-15; 21:6); but they can laugh for real joy (Ps. 126:2; Luke 6:21) and at the wicked (Job 22:19; Ps. 52:6; Isa. 37:22).

4. The unbelievers' laughter: they laugh at Christ (Ps. 22:7; Matt. 9:24), at believers (Neh. 2:19; Job 12:4; Ps. 80:6), and at God's ordinances (II Chron. 30:10); but their laughter will vanish (Prov. 1:26; Luke 6:25; James 4:9).

LAVER (lā'vẽr, Heb. *kîyyôr, pot, basin,* Gr. *loutrón*), a vessel containing water, located between the altar and the door of the tabernacle, at which Jewish priests washed their hands and feet before ministering (Exod. 30:17-22). Solomon's temple had ten such lavers, used for animal sacrifices, and one "molten sea" for priestly ablutions (I Kings 7:23-47). These lavers were partly destroyed by Ahaz (II Kings 16:17); later the remains were carried to Babylon (II Kings 25:13; Jer. 52:17).

Undoubtedly the laver had typical meaning, signifying: (1) baptism as a cleansing from sin (cf. Acts 2:38; 22:16; I Cor. 6:11; Eph. 5:26; Titus 3:5; Heb. 10:22; I Pet. 3:20f); (2) the need of daily purification before approaching the Lord (cf. Ps. 24:3f; John 13:2-10; I John 1:7ff).

LAW. 1. The Terms of Scripture. Of Hebrew words, the one most frequent of occurrence, *tôrâh,* may refer to human instruction (Prov. 1:8), to divine instruction (Isa. 1:10), to a regulation (Lev. 7:7), to the law of Moses (I Kings 2:3) or to custom (II Sam. 7:19). Other words which may be so translated include *dâth, hôq, mitswâh* and *mishpat.* The common Greek word *nómos* is occasionally used of law(s) in the most general sense (Rom. 3:27) of a principle which governs one's actions (Rom. 7:23), of the Pentateuch (Gal. 3:10), and of other portions of Holy Scripture (as John 10: 34; I Cor. 14:21), but most often for the Mosaic law (Acts 15:5). English synonyms include *commandment, direction, judgment, ordinance, precept, statute* and *testimony.*

2. The Moral Law. It is plain from the Decalogue (Exod. 20:3-17; Deut. 5:7-21) that morality is not to be derived from human standards and the verdict of society but from God and His declarations and one's relationship of subordination to Him. Right and wrong are not determined by the voice of society but by the voice of God.

The Ten Commandments enunciate the broad principles of God's moral law. We are warranted in finding positive teaching as to the will of God for our lives in those commandments which are couched in the negative and for discerning admonition and prohibition in those framed as positive exhortations. The Commandments constitute the regulative core of revelation as to acceptable lines of human conduct.

The first table of the law was considered to express man's duty toward God (Exod. 20:3-11) and the second his duty toward his fellow men (Exod. 20:12-17). The NT would seem to follow this division in summarizing the law, for Jesus said that it demanded perfect love for God and love for one's neighbor comparable to that which one has for himself (Matt. 22:35-40).

Rather than setting aside the moral law, the NT reiterates its commands, develops more fully the germinal truths contained in it, and focuses attention upon the spirit of the law as over against merely the letter. So it is that Paul affirms there is but one God (Eph. 4:6) and cautions against idolatry both directly and indirectly (I Cor. 10: 14; Rom. 1:21ff). While the NT suggests an attitude toward the sabbath somewhat different from that of Jewish legalism (Mark 2:23-28) and comes to recognize the time of observance as the first day of the week (Acts 20:7; I Cor. 16:2), it preserves the observance as of divine institution and enriches its significance by associating with it Christ's resurrection. So also, the NT emphasizes the law of love (Rom. 13:8-10; Gal. 5:14; James 2:8) and selflessness and humility as representative of the mind of Christ (Phil. 2:3-8). Although the NT commandments are for the most part by positive exhortations rather than by warnings and prohibitions, the underlying principles are the same.

Scripture makes clear the function of the moral law. As the expression of the character and will of God, it set forth the only standard of righteousness acceptable to Him, but man was without power to conform to that perfect standard. The law made man aware of his sinfulness (Rom. 7: 7,13), condemned him as unrighteous (Rom. 7:9-11; Gal. 3:13; James 2:9) and, having removed any hope of salvation through his own righteousness, brought him to the place where he would cast himself upon the grace of God that he might trust only in the righteousness and merit of the atoning Saviour, Jesus Christ (Gal. 3:24).

Christians are free from the condemnation of the law (Rom. 8:2) since the righteousness of Him who kept the law perfectly and who vicariously paid the penalty for the transgression of the law on the part of His people has been imputed to them. However, the believer is not only declared righteous by God (Rom. 4:5,6) but is renewed in righteousness and is progressively sanctified as the Holy Spirit applies the Word in his life (II Cor. 5:21; Gal. 5:16ff; I Thess. 5:23). The goal of the Christian is conformity to the moral image of God as manifested to man by the Incarnate Son (Eph. 4:13). So it is that the Christian is under obligation to keep the moral law (cf. Matt. 5:19ff; Eph. 4:28; 5:3; 6:2; Col. 3:9; I Pet. 4:15), not as a condition of salvation, but that he might become more and more like his Father in heaven (Rom. 8:1-9; Eph. 4:13), and this because of love for the one who redeemed him (Rom. 13:8-10; I John 5:2,3).

3. Social Legislation. In the giving of the law at Sinai, Moses first communicated to the people the body of principles, the Ten Words, and then the applicatory precepts. Careful study of the individual statutes shows the specific commands to be rooted in the basic principles set forth in the Decalogue.

OT laws of judicial, civil or political nature are to be found in the block of legislative material known as the Book of the Covenant (Exod. 20:23-

23:33), in the so-called Holiness Code (Lev. 17-26) and here and there throughout most of the Book of Deuteronomy, especially in chapters 21-25.

Since man is inherently sinful and lawless, social life must come under regulations. So it was that in OT times both Jews and Gentiles found themselves subject to law. Nor was the civil legislation binding upon the covenant line too different from that of the heathen nations. The Code of Hammurabi has much in common with the laws promulgated under Moses, and other ancient statutes are found as well among non-Jews as in Israel. Basic principles of right and wrong are the same everywhere and for all people, reflecting the work of the Holy Spirit in the realm of common grace. The difference was that in the Israelite theocracy the laws regulating society were recognized as declared through God's prophets and with divine authority, whereas in other nations the authority behind the codes was the voice of tradition or the voice of the state.

A basic institution ordained of God, the family was necessarily governed in its many relationships by various regulations that it might be preserved from corruption and dissolution. There were many prescriptions regarding marriage itself (Exod. 21; 22; 34; Lev. 18; 21; Num. 5; 25; 30; Deut. 7; 21; 22; 24; 25; 27). Within the family, children were to honor and obey their parents (Exod. 20:12; Deut. 5:16; 21:18-21; 27:16). And since the family circle might include servants, slaves and strangers, there were laws pertaining to them (Exod. 12; 21; 22; Lev. 19; 22; 24; 25; Num. 9; 15; 35; Deut. 1; 12; 14; 15; 16; 23; 24; 27).

As might be expected, crimes against society were to be punished according to law. These might partake of a moral nature, such as sexual violations or perversions (Exod. 20-22; Lev. 18-20; Num. 5; Deut. 5; 22-25; 27). Again, they might have reference to crimes against individuals, either their persons (Gen. 9; Exod. 20-23; Lev. 19; 24; Num. 35; Deut. 5; 19; 21; 22; 24; 27) or their property (Exod. 20; 22; Lev. 6; 19; Deut. 5; 19; 23; 25; 27). Or, the offense might be one against the state (Exod. 20; 23; Lev. 19; Deut. 5; 16; 19; 27).

In addition to the laws already mentioned, other regulations governing property are to be found in Exod. 21-23; Lev. 6; 24; 25; Num. 27; 36; and Deut. 21; 22; 25.

OT legislation contained numerous stipulations pertaining to the operation of the state. Certain aspects of political organization were outlined (Exod. 22; Num. 1; 3; 4; 26; 33; Deut. 17; 23). Specifications were made regarding the army (Num. 1; 2; 10; 26; 31; Deut. 7; 11; 20; 21; 23; 24). Judicial prescriptions are set forth (Exod. 18; 20; 21; 23; Lev. 5; 19; Num. 35; Deut. 1; 4; 5; 16; 17; 19; 25; 27). And provision was made for bringing to the people a knowledge of the law (Deut. 6; 11; 27; 31; Josh. 8).

Many Israelite laws were laws of kindness. Even the treatment of animals was subject to regulation (Exod. 23; 34; Lev. 22; 25; Deut. 22; 25). The general commandment of love, whether for friends or strangers, was invoked (Exod. 23; Lev. 19; Deut. 10). The poor, unfortunate, lowly, defenseless and needy were to be treated humanely (Exod. 21-23; Lev. 19; 23; 25; Deut. 14-16; 21-27).

The prescriptions of the law were to the end that there might be peace and order, whether in the operations of the state, the family or in other spheres of human interrelations. The dignity of the individual was to be preserved. A high premium was set on selflessness and consideration of others.

God's wisdom and grace were manifest in the legislation given the Israelites through His servant Moses.

4. Religious Legislation. Embodied in the OT are many laws governing the worship of God. Some are very general in nature, having to do with purity of worship. Large numbers of the laws concern the sanctuary, its priesthood, and the rites and ceremonies connected with it and the covenant relationship between the Israelites and their God. Some consist of prescriptions pertaining to special occasions of the religious year.

Basic principles of worship are outlined in the first table of the Decalogue (Exod. 20:3-11). They are then worked out into detailed applicatory legislation. Because Jehovah is the only true God, exalted and holy, other gods so-called are not to be worshiped (Exod. 22; 23; 34; Deut. 5; 6; 8; 11; 17; 30), apostasy is a sin (Deut. 13:1-18), idolatry is forbidden (Exod. 20:23; 34; Lev. 19; 26; Deut. 4; 7; 12; 16; 27) and such occult arts as witchcraft, sorcery and divination are not to be practiced (Exod. 22; Lev. 18-20; Deut. 18). So also, blasphemy is not to be tolerated (Exod. 22; Lev. 18; 19; 24) and God's sabbath day is to be kept inviolate (Exod. 23; 31; 34; 35; Lev. 19; 26; Num. 15).

Since Jehovah is the only true God, His people are not only to study and keep His law (Lev. 18-20; 25; Num. 15; Deut. 4-8; 10; 11; 22; 26; 27; 30) but are to separate themselves from the heathen and their religious practices (Exod. 22; 23; 34; Lev. 18-20; Deut. 6; 7; 12; 14; 18). They are to be a holy nation (Exod. 19; 22; Lev. 19; 26; Deut. 7; 14; 18; 26; 28), and they are to give to God the allegiance, love, gratitude and obedient service due Him (Exod. 23; 34; Lev. 19; 25; Deut. 4-6; 8; 10; 11; 13; 14; 17; 30; 31).

On Mt. Sinai, God delineated in detail to Moses the pattern for the sanctuary (Exod. 25-27), and the tabernacle was built in conformity to that pattern (Exod. 35-38). Later, its essential features were reproduced in Solomon's temple (II Chron. 3; 4). The sanctuary was in a special sense the dwelling place of God among His people and spoke silently of God's fellowship with them (Exod. 25:8,22). As the place where God drew nigh to the people and they to Him, it was designed to remind them of the Lord — His splendor, His magnificence, His glory, His transcendence, His holiness, His presence, His mercy and forgiveness, His requirements of men, and His covenant headship. Through its structure and the regulations as to who might enter each part, God's holiness was emphasized.

The brazen altar spoke of sacrifice and therefore of the necessity of worship and atonement. As one approached the holy God, the laver was mute evidence of the fact that cleansing from defilement must first take place. The altar of incense pointed to the importance of adoration and praise (Isa. 6:3,4; Ps. 141:2). The table of shewbread suggested the need for dedication, and the golden candlestick perhaps indicated that the worshiper should reflect in his life the light which comes from God and which is ever to be associated with Him. These conclusions rest upon the assumption that the sanctuary furnishings in the outer court and in the Holy Place were for the purpose of instructing the OT worshiper how men should draw near to God in worship.

On the other hand, the symbolism of the Holiest Place may be thought of as speaking of God in His approach to men. Through the tables of law in the ark, through the ark's cover and through the cherubim betokening the presence of God, Jehovah said to His people, "I, God, am a spiritual Being here in your midst. My law accuses and condemns. Who can keep it? But I have provided a covering, a propitiation, an atonement. Despite sin, it is still possible for you to look forward to dwelling in my immediate presence." The veil testified that that time had not come, but the typology was unmistakable.

The worshiper might come only as far as the court. The ordinary priest could enter the Holy Place. Only the high priest might enter the Holy of Holies, and that but once a year. The symbolism was plain: It was not a light thing to seek acceptance in the presence of the holy God, but there was indeed a way of approach.

Through the system of OT sacrifices, the worshiper learned that through the offering of sacrifice God dealt with sin and granted forgiveness (Lev. 4: 20), that through the shedding of blood there was atonement of sin (Lev. 16;15,16), that the animal of the ceremony was reckoned as a substitute for the worshiper (Lev. 16:20-22), that the sacrifices were perhaps not the full and final answer to the sin problem (since they must continue to be offered), that sacrifice without obedience to God's revelation was of no value (Isa. 1:10-17), and that God's suffering servant was to be a guilt offering (Isa. 53:10). The Mosaic legislation prescribes the kinds of sacrifices and the details governing them: The whole burnt offering (Exod. 20; Lev. 1; 6; Deut. 12:27); the sin offering (Lev. 4-6; 8-10; Num. 15); the guilt offering (Lev. 5-7; 19; Num. 5); the peace offering (Lev. 3; 7; 19; 22). Also, the law had much to say about other offerings and sacrificial dues (Exod. 10; 13; 18; 22; 23; 29; 30; 34; Lev. 2; 3; 6; 14; 19; 22; 23; 27; Num. 3; 5; 6; 8; 15; 18; 19; 28; 30; 31; Deut. 12; 14-18; 23; 26).

Through the priesthood, men came to understand that the transcendent, holy God cannot be approached in a casual way by sinful men but only by a mediator representing both God and man, that the mediator must be emblematic of holiness and perfection, and that God deals with sin through the representative acts of the mediator. As to the concept of the priesthood, the focus of attention was narrowed from the whole nation (Exod. 19:6) to the priests and Levites and finally to one man, the high priest, whose acts on behalf of the people brought reconciliation. Laws pertaining to the priesthood are to be found in Exod. 28-30; 39; 40; Lev. 2; 5-8; 10; 16; 21-24; 27; Num. 3-6; 15; 18; 31. The law codes regulated ceremonial cleanliness not only as regards the priests but in reference to food (Exod. 12; 22; 23; 34; Lev. 3:7; 11; 17; 19; 20; 22; Deut. 12; 14; 15) and purification (Lev. 5; 11-15; 22; Num. 6; 19; 31; Deut. 21; 24).

The feasts and festivals had significance which was partly historical, partly merely symbolical, partly typical. The Passover was a reminder of physical deliverance from bondage in Egypt (Exod. 12:17; Deut. 16:1). Sacred history and prophecy frequently blend, and so the observance of the Passover might well have had this message: As God delivered, so He *will* deliver. The central sacrifice in this festival as in others spoke as did the daily and weekly sacrifices, and the unleavened bread and the meat and drink offerings pointed to the importance of a holy, fruitful life before God. As a harvest festival, Pentecost signified rejoicing and the place of thanksgiving to God in the life of the covenant participant (Deut. 16:9,10) especially in the light of the deliverance from Egypt (Deut. 16:12). Except for the significance of the

extra sacrifices, the Feast of Tabernacles (Exod. 23; Lev. 23; Num. 29; Deut. 16) may have been to the Jews little more than a reminder of God's love and care during the period of the nation's youth when the Jews wandered in the wilderness and were tested by deprivation that they might learn to trust in God and His provision. On the other hand, the Day of Atonement emphasized the need for the expiation of sin, the atoning nature of the blood sacrifice and the idea of substitution in relation to atonement.

The rite of circumcision symbolized the taking away of defilement that the individual might be rightly related to God and partaker of the covenant of grace.

The NT spells out the antitypes involved. As God's dwelling among His people was symbolized in the OT through the Garden of Eden, the tabernacle and the temple, so the New Covenant tells us that God as the Son "tabernacled among us" (John 1:14), that He indwells the individual believer (I Cor. 6:19) and the Church (II Cor. 6: 16), and that the final and everlasting dwelling place of God with man will be heaven itself (Heb. 9:24; Rev. 21:3).

In the New Dispensation, that which was symbolized by the Passover celebration and circumcision came to be represented and to be defined more clearly in the Lord's Supper and Christian baptism. The types and shadows of the ceremonial law gave way to antitypes.

The cross replaced the brazen altar. There was no longer a sanctuary laver but a "laver of regeneration" (Titus 3:5). "The prayers of the saints" (Rev. 5:8) took the place of the altar of incense. Dedicated lives came to be offered (Rom. 12:1,2) rather than symbolic shewbread, and good works produced by children of the light made unnecessary the golden candlestick. Instead of the mercy seat as a "propitiatory covering" (LXX translation of I Chron. 28:11), Christ became the propitiation for the sins of His people (Rom. 3:25; I John 2:2; 4:10), and man redeemed and in fellowship with God became the prophetic fulfillment of the symbolic cherubim, which were basically human in form (Ezek. 1:5; 10:21) and always associated with the presence of Jehovah (Gen. 3:24; Ps. 18: 10; Ezek. 1; 10; 28). The Lord Jesus was seen to be God's Passover Lamb (I Cor. 5:7), a perfect, all-sufficient sacrifice (Eph. 5:2; Heb. 7:27; 9:11-14). As *the* High Priest, Christ made reconciliation (Heb. 2:17) and lives to make intercession for His own (Heb. 7:25).

A covenant child, our Lord was related to the ceremonial law as shown by His circumcision (Luke 2:21) and His presence at the temple at the Passover feast (Luke 2:42). He instructed lepers to carry out the provisions of the law (Luke 17:14). He drove from the temple those who defiled it (Matt. 21:12,13). He and His disciples were accustomed to go to Jerusalem at feast time (John 7:37; 13:1,29).

Christ spoke negatively regarding the traditions of the Jews but not of the ceremonial law as set forth in the OT, yet He indicated that the time was coming when the ritual of the law would give place to spiritual worship (John 4:24).

In the transitional period after the cross, the resurrection and the ascension, conditions in each case determined whether the stipulations of the law should be observed. Paul might circumcise Timothy (Acts 16:3) but not Titus (Gal. 2:3,4). He could assure the Corinthians that circumcision in the flesh was not essential for salvation (I Cor. 2:2; 7:18,19) and, in writing to the Galatians, he

The traditional Tomb of Lazarus at Bethany. JFW

could argue strongly against the contentions of the Judaizers (Gal. 2:4ff; 5:1ff) in line with the decisions of the council at Jerusalem (Acts 15:4ff). The argument of the book of Hebrews is that the types and shadows of the ceremonial law have passed away with the coming of Christ, the perfect High Priest, who as the Lamb of God offered Himself on Golgotha that He might satisfy every demand of the law and purchase salvation for His people.

By means of the ceremonial law, God spoke in picture language of the salvation He was to effect through the life and death of the Incarnate Son. Of necessity, therefore, it was but imperfect and temporary. The social legislation governing Israel was designed for a particular culture at a given period of history and so it, too, was but for a time, yet the principles which underlay it are timeless and applicable to all generations. God's moral law is in force everywhere and at all times, for it is a reflection of His very being. It has never been abrogated, nor indeed can be. See MARRIAGE, TABERNACLE, PRIEST.   B.L.G.

LAW OF MOSES (See Law)

LAWGIVER (Heb. *mehōqēq,* Gen. 49:10; Num. 21:18; Deut. 33:21; Ps. 60:7; 108:8; Isa. 33:22; Gr. *nomothétes,* James 4:12). God is the only absolute lawgiver (James 4:12). Instrumentally, Moses bears this description (John 1:17; 7:19).

LAWYER (Gr. *nomikós, pertaining to law*), a term used to describe a class of men well versed in the oral and written law whose duty consisted in teaching young men and in deciding questions concerning the Law. The term is found in Matthew 22:35; Luke 7:30; 10:25; 11:45f, 52f; 14:3; Titus 3:9,13. (The best mss. omit it in Luke 11:45.) Tertullus, a Roman lawyer, presented the Jewish case against Paul (Acts 24:1ff).

LAYING ON OF HANDS (Gr. *Epíthesis cheirón*), an act pregnant with manifold implications. In the OT the act symbolizes (1) the parental bestowal of inheritance-rights (Gen. 48:14-20); (2) the gifts and rights of an office (Num. 27:18,23; Deut. 34:9); and (3) substitution, of an animal for one's guilt (Exod. 29:10,15,19; Lev. 1:4; 3:2,8,13; 4:4,15,24,29,33; 8:14,18,22; 16:21; cf. Gen. 22: 9-13), of a tribe for the firstborn of other tribes (Num. 8:10-13), of one's innocency for another's guilt (Lev. 24:13-16; Deut. 13:9; 17:7). In the NT the act symbolizes (1) the bestowal of blessings and benediction (Matt. 19:13,15; cf. Luke 24: 50); (2) the restoration of health (Matt. 9:18; Acts 9:12,17); (3) the reception of the Holy Spirit in baptism (Acts 8:17,19; 19:6); (4) the gifts and rights of an office (Acts 6:6; 13:3; I Tim. 4: 14; II Tim. 1:6).

LAZARUS (lăz'à-rŭs Lat. from Gr., for Heb. *Eleazar*). 1. Lazarus, the brother of Martha and Mary, who lived in Bethany. Lazarus, during Christ's absence, took sick and died; Christ, after some delay, returned and raised Lazarus from death (John 11:1-12:19). The following factors enhance the importance of this miracle: (1) the number of days (four) between death and resurrection (John 11: 39); (2) the number of witnesses involved (John 11:45; 12:17f); (3) the evident health of Lazarus after the event (John 12:1f,9); (4) the evidential significance of the event among the Jews (John 11: 53; 12:10f).

This miracle (1) illustrates Christ's sympathy (John 11:5,11,34f) and power (John 11:40ff); (2) manifests the purposiveness of His miracles (John 11:4,40; 20:31); (3) gives concreteness to Luke 16:30f; (4) affords opportunity for eschatological teaching (John 11:23-25); (5) precipitates the crucifixion (John 11:45-53; 12:9-19).

The silence of the Synoptics is explainable thus: (1) the miracle was outside their scope; (2) it was not the leading accusation brought against Christ (cf. Matt. 26:61-66); (3) it was indirectly confirmed by the "envy" they attribute to the Jews (Matt. 27:18); (4) it did not fit into their plan as a didactic purpose as it did in John's (John 20:31).

2. Lazarus, a beggar who died and went to Abraham's bosom (Luke 16:19-31). The story illustrates these truths: (1) destiny is settled at death; (2) no purgatory awaits the righteous; (3) man has sufficient warning now.

LEAF, used in a threefold manner in the Bible. 1. Leaf of a tree (Dan. 4:12,14,21; Ezek. 17:9). Here we find the semi-physical or semi-spiritual uses: (1) the insufficiency of man's righteousness (Gen. 3:7); (2) the fruitfulness of the restored earth (Gen. 8:11); (3) the sign of a distressed and nervous spirit (Lev. 26:36; Job 13:25); (4) the spiritual productivity of the righteous (Ps. 1:3; Prov. 11:28 ["branch"]; Jer. 17:8; (5) the spiritual unproductivity of the wicked (Isa. 1:30); (6) the completeness of God's judgment (Isa. 34:4; Jer. 8:13); (7) the frailty and evanescence of man (Isa. 64:6); (8) the blessings of Messianic times (Ezek. 47:12); (9) the unfruitfulness of Israel (Ezek. 17:9; Matt. 21:19; Mark 11:13); (10) the nearness of the eschatological judgment (Matt. 24: 32; Mark 13:28); (11) the glory of an earthly kingdom (Dan. 4:12,14,21); (12) the glory and fruitfulness of the heavenly kingdom (Rev. 22:2).

2. Leaf of a door. In I Kings 6:34 *tsēlà'* is thus used; and in Ezekiel 41:24 *deleth* is translated both by "doors" and by "leaves."

3. Leaf of a book. So *deleth* in Jeremiah 36:23.

LEAH (lē'à, Heb. *lē'âh,* meaning uncertain), Laban's daughter and Jacob's first (though not preferred) wife (Gen. 29:21-30); mother of Reuben, Simeon, Levi, Judah, Issachar, Zebulun, and Dinah, a daughter (Gen. 29:31-35; 30:17-21). Loyal to Jacob (Gen. 31:14-16), she returned with him to Canaan, where, at her death, she was buried in Machpelah (Gen. 49:31). Two of her sons (Levi and Judah) became progenitors of prominent tribes in Israel; and through Judah, Jesus Christ came (Gen. 49:10; Mic. 5:2; Matt. 2:6; Heb. 7:14; Rev. 5:5; cf. Ruth 4:11).

LEASING (lēz'ĭng, Heb. *kāzav, lie, falsehood*), now obsolete, it is found twice in AV (Ps. 4:2; 5:6). RSV has "falsehood" and "lies."

LEATHER (lĕth'êr, Heb. *'ôr, skin,* Gr. *dermátinos, made of skin*), designates the skin of certain animals after it has been specially treated. Those who performed this work as a trade were called tanners (Acts 10:32). Leather was a common article of clothing (Lev. 13:48; Heb. 11:37). However, John the Baptist (Matt. 3:4) and his prototype, Elijah (II Kings 1:8), are the only ones specifically mentioned as wearing "a girdle of leather." Leather was also used for armor, shoes, containers, and writing material.

LEAVEN (lĕv'ĕn, Heb. *se'ōr, hāmēts,* Gr. *zúme*). The answer to seven questions will cover most of the Biblical material. 1. Why was leaven so rigidly excluded from "meal offerings" (ASV) ["meat offerings" (AV)] in the Sinaitic legislation (Exod. 29:2,23,32; Lev. 2:1-16; 6:14-23; 7:9f; 8:2,26,31; 10:12; Num. 15:1-9,17-21; 18:9; cf. Exod. 23:18; 34:15)? The answer seems to lie in the fact that leaven, representing corruption, symbolizes evil.

2. Why was leaven permitted in certain other offerings (Exod. 23:15f; 34:22f; Lev. 2:11; 7:13f; 23:17f; Num. 15:20)? The answer seems to be this: leaven, a part of the daily food, is included in the offerings of thanks. Some hold that leaven here symbolizes the evil that still inheres in the worshiper.

3. Why was leaven excluded from the Passover (Exod. 12:14-20; 23:15; 34:18; Deut. 16:2-4)? The record seems to indicate Israel's haste in leaving Egypt prompted this exclusion (Exod. 12:11,39; Deut. 16:3). However, the Passover as a type of Christ must be taken into account here (cf. I Cor. 5:7f).

4. Does Lot's use of unleavened bread (Gen. 19:3) anticipate the symbolism of the Sinaitic legislation? Haste may have been the reason; but the latent symbolism of evil (as inconsistent with angels) cannot be entirely ruled out.

5. What does Amos 4:5 indicate? Simply this: the degenerate Northern Kingdom mixed the permitted (Lev. 7:13; 23:17) with the forbidden (Exod. 23:18; 34:25; Lev. 2:11).

6. What about the NT significance of leaven? Apart from Matthew 13:33 (see below) leaven symbolizes either Jewish legalism (Matt. 16:6,12; Gal. 5:9) or moral corruption (I Cor. 5:6ff).

7. What, then, about Matthew 13:33? This is a passage around which much controversy gathers. Some interpret leaven as symbolizing the final apostasy of the professing Church; others explain leaven as symbolizing the permeating effect of the Gospel in Christianizing the world. W.B.

LEBANON (lĕb'ȧnŏn, Heb. *levānôn, white*), a snowclad mountain range extending in a northeasterly direction for 100 miles along the Syrian coast, from Tyre to Arvad, and the country which bears its name. The name signifies the whiteness either of the fossil-bearing limestone cliffs or the snowy crests of this mountain system. Rising precipitously from the Mediterranean (Josh. 9:1), Lebanon proper averages 6000 feet above sea level (cf. the steep grades on the present Beirut-Damascus highway), with peaks reaching 10,200; but the elevation then drops to 2300 feet, for ten miles across the Orontes River valley, known as Coele (hollow) Syria. East of this "valley of Lebanon" (Josh. 11:17; 12:7), however, rises the Anti-Lebanon range, the southernmost promontory of which is Mt. Hermon, whose 9383-foot peak remains visible as far S as Jericho. Scripture speaks of Lebanon and Sirion (Anti-Lebanon, Ps. 29:6, = S(h)enir, Deut. 3:9, sometimes excluding Hermon, I Chron. 5:23, S. of Sol. 4:8), though "Lebanon" may designate both ranges (J. Simons, *The Geographical and Topographical Texts of the Old Testament,* Leiden: Brill, 1959, pp. 43,55-56; cf. LXX *Antilibanos,* in Deut. 1:7; 3:25; 11:24; Josh. 1:4; 9:1), or even Anti-Lebanon alone (Josh. 13:6), "Lebanon toward the sunrising" (13:5; Simons,

Typical terrain of Lebanon, showing the town of Bshirre in the valley, and the road to the cedars.
© MPS

The cedars of Lebanon. At left, typical specimen. Right, the cedar grove of Lebanon, the only remnant of the massive old cedars. © MPS

op. cit., pp. 112-113). The melting snow of these watersheds (Jer. 18:14; S. of Sol. 4:15) creates the Orontes, flowing northward; the Abana, watering Damascus to the E; the westward-flowing Leontes or Litany; and the Jordan, meandering southward through Palestine to the Dead Sea. Yet these same peaks desiccate the moisture-laden western winds, causing desert farther E.

Lebanon's southern slopes grade into the foothills of Galilee, "literally the casting forth of the roots of Lebanon" (George A. Smith on Hos. 14:5, *The Historical Geography of the Holy Land,* 19th ed.; London: Hodder & Stoughton, 1896, p. 417); and the gorge of the Litany marks out a natural northwestern boundary for Israel (Deut. 11:24; II Kings 19:23). Lebanon thus "lies properly outside the Holy Land" (*ibid.,* p. xvii); and, though included in God's promise, it was never totally occupied (Josh. 13:5; though cf. its eschatological possession, Ezek. 47:15,16; Simons, *op. cit.,* p. 102). Its isolated crags, however, supported watch towers (S. of Sol. 7:4) and refuge-points (Jer. 22:20,23) and came to symbolize the exalted status of Judah's royal house (Jer. 22:6; Ezek. 17:3).

Ancient Lebanon was heavily forested with varieties of budding foliage (Isa. 29:17; Nah. 1:4), including the Phoenician juniper, which resembles the cypress (I Kings 5:8; II Kings 19:23; ASVm), and other tall conifers (Ezek. 27:5; cf. KB, p. 85), but above all the great cedars of Lebanon (I Kings 4:33). Biblical poetry expatiates on the motion of their massive branches (Ps. 72:16); on the fragrance of their wood (S. of Sol. 3:6-9; cf. 4:11 and Hos. 14:6 where Lebanon means trees, *per* Isa. 10:34; 40:16); on their height, as symbolical of dignity or pride (S. of Sol. 5:15; Isa. 2:13); and on their growth and resistance to decay (Ps. 92:12). The psalmists' inspired thought thus advances to the corresponding greatness of the Creator, who both plants the cedars (Ps. 104:16) and shatters them by His voice (29:5). The Lebanons were famous also for choice wine (Hos. 14:7), for thorny plants, and for beasts such as the lion and leopard (II Kings 14:9; Isa. 40:16; S. of Sol. 4:8). "The glory of Lebanon" climaxes Isaiah's prophetic descriptions (35:2; 60:13).

Coastal Lebanon was early inhabited by Phoenicians (Josh. 13:5-6), skilled in the employment of its cedars for civil and marine construction (Ezek. 27:4-5), while its sparser inland population was Hivite (Judg. 3:3; Hermon, Josh. 11:3). The name Lebanon appears in ancient Ugaritic, Hittite, Egyptian, and Babylonian, its first Biblical mention being Mosaic, 1406 B.C. (Deut. 1:7). It

was cited in Jotham's fable against Shechem, c. 1130 (Judg. 9:15; cf. the reference to fire hazard), as well as in Jehoash's against Amaziah, over three centuries later (II Kings 14:9; II Chron. 25:18). King Solomon contracted with Hiram of Tyre for the use of Lebanon's cedars in the Jerusalem temple, 966-959 B.C. (I Kings 5:6-18; cf. Ezra 3:7, concerning the second temple also), 10,000 workers per month hewing the timbers and floating them in great rafts along the Mediterranean coast. Solomon likewise erected government buildings and palaces in his capital, including a hall and armory called "the house of the forest of Lebanon" from its rows of cedar pillars and paneling (I Kings 7:2-7; 10:17,21; ICC, pp. 162-165; cf. Isa. 22:8). The king's Lebanese building projects (cf. I Kings 10:27) led him to construction-work in Lebanon itself, at least portions of which came within his widespread domains (9:19; S. of Sol. 4:8). Subsequent advances by the pagan empires of antiquity furthered both the conquest and ruthless exploitation of Lebanon's resources (Isa. 33:9). Egyptians, Assyrians, and Greeks left their successive inscriptions at the mouth of the Dog River (Nahr el-Kelb); and Ezekiel compares the destruction of Assyria's king with the felling of cedars of Lebanon (31:3,15-16; cf. Zech. 11:1). Habakkuk bewails the violence done also by Babylon in cutting down these forest giants (2:17; cf. Isa. 14:8). By the days of Justinian (A.D. 527-565) the once extensive groves had suffered heavy depletion, and most of the remainder were destroyed during 1914-1919 to supply fuel for the Beirut-Damascus railway. Conservation projects, however, are now attempting reforestation.   J.B.P.

LEBAOTH (lĕ-bā′ŏth, Heb. *levā′ôth, lionesses*), a town in S part of Judah (Josh. 15:32) also called Beth-lebaoth (Josh. 19:6) and (probably) Beth-birei (I Chron. 4:31). Location otherwise unknown.

LEBBAEUS (lĕ-bē′ŭs, Gr. *Lebbaíos, hearty*), one of Christ's apostles who is also called Thaddaeus (Matt. 10:3; Mark 3:18) and Judas (Luke 6:16; Acts 1:13). John 14:22 distinguishes him from Judas Iscariot.

LEBONAH (lĕ-bō′nà, Heb. *levônâh, frankincense*), a town, mentioned only in Judges 21:19, N of Bethel on the highway between Shiloh and Shechem. It is now generally identified as the modern Lubban.

LECAH (lē′kà, Heb. *lēkhâh, walking*), a "son" of Er (I Chron. 4:21); probably the name of an unknown town.

LEEKS (See Plants)

LEES (lēz, Heb. *shemārîm,* pl. fr. *shemer, something preserved*), a word that describes that undisturbed and thick portion of wine that naturally falls to the bottom of the vat. The word is used figuratively throughout to express (1) the blessings of Messianic times (Isa. 25:6; cf. Isa. 55:1). (2) the spiritual lethargy and decadence of Moab (Jer. 48:11); (3) the indifference of Israelites to spiritual realities (Zeph. 1:12); (4) the bitterness and inevitability of God's wrath upon the wicked (Ps. 75:8 — "dregs").

LEFT (Heb. *semō'l, the left, semā'lî, on the left, sim'ēl, take the left,* Gr. *euónymos, of good name*). The word has a variety of connotations in the Bible: (1) simple direction (II Kings 23:8; Neh. 8:4); (2) geographic North (Gen. 14:15; Ezek. 16:46, RSV); (3) all directions (with "right") (Job 23:9); (4) the lesser blessing (Gen. 48:13-19); (5) weakness (Judg. 3:15,21), immaturity (Jonah 4:11), perversity (Eccl. 10:2), or evil (Matt. 25:33,41); (6) completion (with "right") (Ezek. 4:4,6); (7) special ability (I Chron. 12:2); (8) a woman's preference (S. of Sol. 2:6; 8:3).

LEGION (lē'jŭn, Gr. *legión,* or *legeón,* fr. Lat. *legio*), the largest single unit in the Roman army, including infantry and cavalry. A division of infantry at full strength consisted of about 6,000 Roman soldiers. Each division was divided into ten cohorts, and each cohort was further divided into six centuries. Each subdivision, as well as the larger whole, had its own officers and its own standards. The term "legion" in the NT represents a vast number (Matt. 26:53; Mark 5:9,15; Luke 8:30).

LEHABIM (lē-hā'bĭm, Heb. *lehāvîm,* meaning uncertain), the third son of Mizraim (Gen. 10:13; I Chron. 1:11). It is now generally believed that Lehabim and Lubim (II Chron. 12:3; 16:8; Nah. 3:9), otherwise known as Libyans (Jer. 46:9; Dan. 11:43) or the inhabitants of Libya (Ezek. 30:5; 38:5; Acts 2:10), represent the same ethnic group. Descendants of Ham, they occupied the N coast of Africa W of Egypt.

LEHI (lē'hī, Heb. *lehî, jawbone, cheek*), a place in Judah between the cliff Etam and Philistia, otherwise unknown, where Samson killed 1,000 Philistines with a jawbone (Judg. 15:9,14). Samson's exploit changed its name to Ramath-lehi ("the hill of the jawbone"; Judg. 15:19).

LEMUEL (lĕm'ū-ĕl, Heb. *lemū'ēl, devoted to God*), a king, otherwise unknown, to whom his mother taught the maxims in Proverbs 31:2-9. Though many identities have been proposed, the name undoubtedly describes Solomon (Prov. 31:1).

LENTILE, LENTIL (See Plants)

LEOPARD (See Animals)

LEPER (See Diseases)

LEPROSY (See Diseases)

LESHEM (lē'shĕm, Heb. *leshem, gem*), the original of Dan (Josh. 19:47), a city at extreme N of Palestine (I Sam. 3:20); variant of Laish.

LETTER. In general, "letter" designates (1) an alphabetical symbol (Gal. 6:11, ASV); (2) rudimentary education (John 7:15); (3) a written communication (see below); (4) the external (Rom. 2:27,29); (5) Jewish legalism (Rom. 7:6; II Cor. 3:6).

A letter as a means of communication served many purposes: (1) information and instruction (II Sam. 11:14f; Esth. 1:22; 3:13; 9:20-30; Jer. 29:1ff); (2) credential of authority (Ezra 7:11-28;

Neh. 2:7-9; Esth. 8:5,10ff; Acts 9:1ff; I Cor. 16:3; II Cor. 3:1); (3) means of propaganda and strife (I Kings 21:8-11; Ezra 4:7-24; Jer. 29:24-32); (4) forged counter-instruction (I Kings 21:8-11; II Thess. 2:2); (5) invitation (II Chron. 30:1-6); (6) cause of misunderstanding (II Kings 5:5-7; II Cor. 10:9-11) and concern (II Kings 19:14ff).

LETTUSHIM, LETUSHIM (lĕ-tū'shĭm, Heb. *letûshîm, sharpened*), the second son of Dedan (who was the grandson of Abraham by Keturah (Gen. 25:3). His descendants (probably) settled in North Arabia.

LEUMMIM (lē-ŭm'ĭm, Heb. *le'ummîm, peoples, nations*), mentioned only in Genesis 25:3 as third son of Dedan, who was a grandson of Abraham by Keturah. The plural name possibly points to some tribe that settled in Arabia — otherwise unknown.

LEVI (lē'vī, Heb. *lēwî, joined*). 1. Jacob's third son by Leah (Gen. 29:34; 35:23). Levi, born in Haran, accompanied his father on his return to Canaan. He joined his brothers in sinister plots against Joseph (Gen. 37:4,28); and, with them, eventually bowed before Joseph (Gen. 42:6). A predicted famine caused Jacob's entire family to migrate to Egypt, where Levi died at age 137 (Exod. 6:16). His three sons, Gershon, Kohath and Merari (Gen. 46:11), later became heads of families. (See Levites.) Three things merit attention. (1) His name. His mother named him "Levi" at birth with the hope that Jacob, his father, would now be "joined" to her (Gen. 29:34). (2) His nature. His part in the massacre of the Shechemites on account of Shechem's raping of Dinah, his sister, manifested his twofold nature: duplicity and righteous indignation (Gen. 34:25-31). (3) His potential nobility. Jacob, with death imminent, pronounced a curse upon Simeon and Levi because of their iniquitous deed at Shechem (cf. Gen. 34:25-31 with Gen. 45:5-7); but, because of holy zeal (divorced from murderous savagery; cf. Gen. 49:5ff) manifested at Sinai (Exod. 32:25-29) and in Phinehas (Num. 25:6-13), Levi's curse became a blessing (Deut. 33:8-11) to his descendants.

2 and 3. Ancestors of Jesus (Luke 3:24,29).

4. See MATTHEW.

LEVIATHAN (See Animals)

LEVIRATE MARRIAGE (lĕv'ĭ-rāt, lē'vĭ-, from Lat. *levir, a husband's brother*), an ancient custom, sanctioned by practice (Gen. 38:8ff) and by law (Deut. 25:5-10, which does not contradict Lev. 18:16; 20:21, where the participants are all alive), whereby a deceased man's brother or nearest male kin was required to marry his brother's widow and raise up seed in his brother's name. To repudiate this obligation meant public infamy. Ruth's marriage to Boaz recognized this law (Ruth 4:1-17). It also underlies the argument of the Sadducees in Matthew 22:23-33.

LEVITES (lē'vīts), the name given to the descendants of Levi. The relevant facts may be set forth thus:

I. Their Origin. Levi was the third son of Jacob by Leah (Gen. 29:34; 35:22-26). The Genesis record gives no intimation regarding the later greatness of the tribe bearing Levi's name. Such silence bears indirect testimony to the fact that the Genesis account, contrary to the theories of negative criticism, must have been written prior to the noble event that took place at Mt. Sinai (Exod. 32:25-29) which caused Levi's descendants to receive a special status in Israel. The Genesis record is thus free of any tendentious element with reference to Levi's later greatness as a tribe in Israel.

Furthermore, if the Genesis account had been written after the event on Mt. Sinai, as claimed by modern criticism, it is difficult to understand why the story of Levi's notorious deed at Shechem (Gen. 34:25-31) was still retained — especially if, as also claimed by modern criticism, the early "history" was written, subjectively, to reflect the later greatness of Israel. Let us remember also that Genesis closes with a curse upon Levi for his participation in the crime at Shechem (Gen. 49: 5-7). This curse, pronounced by dying Jacob, would be utterly inconsistent with the critical view that Genesis, written by multiple writers late in Israel's history, reflects the national prestige of later times. The conservative view, accepting the Bible history as a record of real events, is free of such problems.

II. Their Appointment. Several discernible factors undoubtedly influenced the selection of Levi's descendants for their special place in Israel's religion. 1. The divine selection of Moses and Aaron, who were descendants of Kohath, one of Levi's three sons (Exod. 2:1-10; 6:14-27; Num. 26:59), obviously conferred upon the Levites an honor that was recognized by the other tribes. 2. However, an event of transcending importance at Mt. Sinai (Exod. 32:25-29) gave to the Levites as a tribe their place of privilege and responsibility in God's plan. The event just referred to transmuted the curse of Jacob's prophecy (Gen. 49:5-7) into the blessing of Moses' prophecy (Deut. 33:8-11). 3. Moreover, this choice was undoubtedly confirmed by a very similar event when an individual Levite, Phinehas by name, stayed the plague that was about to decimate the Israelites (Num. 25:1-13). Thus the true record of history shows how the curse upon Levi the ancestor became, by the wonders of God's providence, a blessing to his descendants.

It will not be amiss to consider here some of the purposes served in the divine plan by the selection of the Levites for their special ministry in the worship of God's ancient people. 1. As just recounted, their selection and appointment were rewards for their faithfulness to the Lord in a time of moral declension (Exod. 32:25-29). 2. The doctrine of substitution was illustrated by the selection of this tribe, for, although God claimed the firstborn males of all the tribes on the basis of the death of the firstborn among the Egyptians (Exod. 13:11-16), God graciously allowed the Levites to become substitutes for their fellow-tribesmen (Num. 3:9,11-13,40f,45-51; 8:14-19). 3. The simplification of service would surely result from the selection of one tribe, for one such tribe, closely knit by blood and by ancestral prestige, would be more manageable than uncertain detachments from many tribes. 4. The law of the tithe enhanced the selection of the Levites, for, in a sense, this tribe was a tithe of all the tribes; and it was to this tribe that the tithe was paid (Num. 18:21-30; Deut. 18:1-8; Neh. 10:37-39; Heb. 7: 5,9). 5. Israel's separation from the nations was further intensified by the selection of one tribe that was separated from all the tribes and separated and purified unto the Lord (Num. 8:5-22). 6. Life as a sojourn without an inheritance here is illustrated by the fact that the Levites had no inheritance in Israel; the Lord alone was their inheritance (Num. 18:20-24; 26:62; Deut. 10:9; 12:12; 14:27).

III. Their Organization. A threefold organization is discernible: 1. The top echelon was occupied by Aaron and his sons; these alone were priests in the restricted sense. The priests belonged to the family of Kohath. 2. The middle echelon included all the other Kohathites who were not of Aaron's family; to them were given certain privileges in bearing the most sacred parts of the tabernacle (Num. 3:27-32; 4:4-15; 7:9). 3. The bottom echelon comprised all members of the families of Gershon and Merari; to them lesser duties were prescribed (Num. 3:21-26,33-37).

IV. Priests and Levites. The Mosaic legislation made a sharp distinction between the priests and non-priests or ordinary Levites. 1. The priests must belong to Aaron's family; the Levites belong to the larger family of Levi. A priest was a Levite; but a Levite was not necessarily a priest. 2. Priests were consecrated (Exod. 29:1-37; Lev. 8); Levites were purified (Num. 8:5-22). 3. Levites were considered a gift to Aaron and his sons (Num. 3:5-13; 8:19; 18:1-7). 4. The fundamental difference consisted of this: only the priest had the right to minister at the altar and to enter the most holy place (Exod. 28:1; 29:9; Num. 3:10,38; 4:15,19f; 18: 1-7; 25:10-13). The rebellion of Korah, a Kohathite (Num. 16:1), against the uniqueness of Aaron's priesthood illustrated, in the way the rebellion was subdued, the heinous nature of attempting to enter the priesthood without the necessary prerequisites (Num. 16). The choice of Aaron was further confirmed by the budding of his rod (Num. 17:1-11; Heb. 9:4).

V. Post-Mosaic Changes. NT typology (cf. Heb. 8-10), considers the Sinaitic legislation as the standard form. The post-Sinaitic activity of the Levites may be succinctly summarized thus: 1. In the settlement in Canaan the Levites were necessarily relieved of some of their duties; the tabernacle no longer needed transportation. It is doubtful if the Levites ever fully occupied all the 48 cities assigned to them and the priests. The episode in Judges 17:7-13 does not, as maintained by critics, represent the earliest information concerning the priesthood.

2. In David's time the provision of Numbers 7:1-9, being neglected, brought death to a Levite (I Chron. 13:7-10; 15:12-15). David introduced innovations in the age and service of the Levites (I Chron. 23-26). Certain Levites, particularly Asaph, became musicians and probably wrote some of the Psalms (I Chron. 6:39,43; 15:16ff; 16:4ff; 25:1-9; Pss. 50; 73-83).

3. In the disruption of the united kingdom many Levites from the Northern Kingdom sought political and religious asylum in Judah (II Chron. 11:13-16; 13:9-12; 15:9); but some Levites were evidently involved in the apostasy of the Northern Kingdom (Ezek. 44:10-15). The Levites, during this period, were still considered as teachers (II Chron. 17:8ff; 19:8; cf. Deut. 33:10).

4. The Exilic period brings before us the symbolism of Ezekiel: only the true Levites, sons of Zadok, ministered in the temple (Ezek. 43:19; 44:10-16; 48:11f)

5. In the post-Exilic period Levites did not return from Babylon in the same proportion as the priests (Ezra 2:36-42; Neh. 7:39-45). Later, a special effort was required to get the Levites to return (Ezra 8:15-19). They were still considered to be teachers (Ezra 8:15ff) and musicians (Ezra 2:40f; 3:10ff; Neh. 7:43f).

6. Only a few references to the Levites are found in the NT (Luke 10:32; John 1:19; Acts 4:36; Heb. 7:11). Two points merit a final word: first, Levi, seminally in Abraham, paid tithes to Melchizedek (Gen. 14:17-20), thus proving the superiority of Melchizedek's (i.e., Christ's) priesthood to Aaron's (Heb. 7:4-10); second, since the Leviti-

cal priesthood could not bring perfection, it was required that another priest, from a different tribe and a different order, arise (Heb. 7:11-17; cf. Gen. 49:10; Ps. 110). W.B.

LEVITICAL CITIES. The plan set forth in Numbers 35:1-8 (fulfilled in Joshua 21) gave the Levites 48 cities. This plan involved a threefold purpose: 1. such cities caused the Levites to be "scattered" in Israel and thus fulfilled Jacob's dying prophecy (Gen. 49:7;) (2). thus "scattered," they could carry out their teaching ministry better (Deut. 33: 10); (3) since six of their cities were to be "cities of refuge" (Num. 35:6), they would thereby become more accessible to those seeking legal protection (Deut. 19:1-3,7-10,17ff). Negative criticism finds three problems: (1) The Levites were given "no inheritance" in Israel (Num. 18:20). True, but these cities were a gift from the other tribes (Num. 35:2,4,6-8). (2) No substantial evidence exists in pre-Exilic history for such cities. True, but Israel also failed to carry out fully their Mosaic legislation (cf. II Chron. 35:18; 36:21). (3) Numbers 35:1-8 is only an ideal theory never realized until Ezekiel 48:8-14. Not so; Ezekiel's symbolic idealization is based upon Numbers 35: 1-8 (and Josh. 21), though not literally confined to the earlier legislation.

LEVITICUS (lĕ-vĭt'ĭ-kŭs, Gr. *Leveitikón, relating to the Levites*), the designation in the English Bible of the third book of the Pentateuch, derived from the Latin rendering (*Liber Leviticus*) of the Greek title *Leveitikón*. The Hebrew title merely consists of the first word of the text (*wayyiqrā'*), "and he called." The book is closely associated with Exodus and Numbers in historical continuity, but differs from them in that the purely historical element is subordinate to legal and ritual considerations. Although the emphasis in Leviticus is more on priests than Levites, the English title is not inappropriate, since the Jewish priesthood was essentially Levitical (cf. Heb. 7:11).

Leviticus enshrines the laws by which the religious and civil organization of the primitive theocracy in Canaan was to be regulated. At Sinai the Israelites had been incorporated into a special relationship with God, had been given the covenant laws, and provided with a tabernacle for worship. Leviticus contains much that is technical in nature and meant for the direction of the priesthood in the conduct of worship and the regulating of social life. Thus it is distinct from Deuteronomy which is in effect a popular exposition of Levitical law.

The composition of the book was universally ascribed by ancient tradition, both Jewish and Gentile, to Moses the lawgiver of Israel. During the Middle Ages a number of writers denied certain aspects of Mosaic authorship of the Pentateuch, but it was only during the 18th century that literary criticism seriously challenged the traditional view. The movement grew in the following century and reached its classic formulation under Wellhausen in A.D. 1877. Using a background of Hegelian evolutionary philosophy he reconstructed Israelite history, and on the basis of a documentary hypothesis for Pentateuchal origins he assigned Leviticus to a post-Exilic date along with other elements of the so-called "priestly code."

This view has been widely espoused by liberal scholars, and in its developed form holds that Leviticus was compiled by temple priests between 500 and 450 B.C., using earlier legislation such as the "holiness code" (Lev. 17-26) which is regarded as dating from about 650 B.C. Most criti-

cal writers, however, concede that Leviticus contains very much older material, such as the Azazel or scape-goat ritual in Chapter 16 and traditional historical narratives including the punishment of Aaron's sons (10:1-7) and the stoning of the blasphemer (24:10-14).

The literary criteria employed in assigning a late date to the bulk of Leviticus have been criticized continuously since the time of Wellhausen, and the number of scholars who find them very difficult to sustain is increasing gradually. This arises in part from a wider knowledge of the media of communication in antiquity, and also from historical and archaeological considerations. It is now known that if the techniques of compilation alleged by Wellhausen had actually been employed in the composition of Leviticus and the rest of the Pentateuch, it would have been unique in the literary annals of the ancient Near East. Archaeological discoveries have shown that in actual fact the Hebrews employed much the same literary methods as their neighbors, and that significant areas of Biblical literature are closely related in language and style to contemporary writings.

The historical evidence furnished by the canon of the Samaritan Pentateuch indicates a date for Leviticus much in advance of that suggested by critical scholars. According to II Kings 17:24-28, organized Samaritan worship began in the time of Esarhaddon (c. 681-669 B.C.). Since the Samaritans employed only the Pentateuch as their basis for doctrine and worship, it is reasonable to assume that it was in its final form by about the eighth century B.C. Archaeological discoveries in the Dead Sea caves uncovered a fragment of Leviticus written in the Phoenician script current in the seventh century B.C. If this is a genuine product of that period it alone will compel careful re-examination of the entire Wellhausen theory. Other fragments of Leviticus dated c. 100 B.C. were also found in the caves, and appeared to have come from a Samaritan manuscript.

Analysis: The first seven chapters of Leviticus give the detailed sacrificial procedures showing how the various kinds of burnt offerings, the meal offering, the sin and guilt offerings and other sacrifices avail for the removal of sin and defilement under the covenant. A subsequent liturgical section (8:1-10:20) described the consecration of Aaron and the priesthood, being followed by the designation of clean and unclean beasts and certain rules of hygiene (11:1-15:33) The ritual of the Day of Atonement occurs in Chapter 16, followed by a section (17:1-20:27) treating of sacrificial blood, ethical laws and penalties for transgressors. The theme of 21:1-24:23 is priestly holiness and the consecration of seasons, while the following chapter deals with the legislation surrounding the sabbatical and jubilee years. A concluding chapter outlines promises and threats (26: 1-46), while an appendix (27:1-34) treats of vows. Man as sinner, substitutionary atonement and divine holiness are prominent throughout Leviticus. R.K.H.

LEVY (lĕv'ē, Heb. *mas, tribute*), a tax or tribute to be rendered in service. It is used of the 30,000 free Israelites conscripted by Solomon for four months service a year in Lebanon (I Kings 5:13-14); also of the tribute labor imposed upon the surviving Canaanites (I Kings 9:21).

LIBATION, the pouring out of liquids, such as wine, water, oil, etc, but generally wine, as an offering to a deity. Libations were common among the heathen nations (Deut. 32:38). Drink-offerings accompanied many OT sacrifices (Exod. 29:40-41; Lev. 23:13,18,37; Num. 15:4-10,24; 28:7-10). In Timothy 4:6, Philippians 2:17 Paul pictures his death as a drink-offering.

LIBERTINES (Gr. *Libertínoi*), probably originally captive Jews brought to Rome by Pompey in 63 B.C., (Suet. *Tib.* 36; Tac. *Ann.* 2.85; Philo. *Leg. ad Gai.* 23) liberated subsequently, and repatriated to Palestine, where, presumably they built a synagogue still occupied by their descendants a century after Pompey's Palestinian campaign (Acts 6:9). These people would be Roman citizens. There seems to be some evidence for a synagogue of Libertines at Pompeii. There is no substance in the conjectural alternative explanation that the Libertines were natives of "Libertum" near Carthage. The place is unknown to history or geography. The explanation adopted goes back to Chrysostom.

LIBERTY, freedom, the opposite of servitude or bondage, whether physical, moral, or spiritual. The term is used of slaves or captives being set free from physical servitude or imprisonment (Lev. 25: 10; Jer. 34:8,15-17; Acts 26:23; Heb. 13:23), or the granting of certain privileges while in imprisonment (Acts 24:23; 27:3). In Ezekiel 46:17 reference is made to "the year of liberty," the year of jubilee. The term has a legal and moral tone in I Corinthians 7:39 in asserting the right of a widow to remarry. The special concern of Christianity is the spiritual liberty of believers in Christ. Found in union with Christ, it carries with it freedom from the ceremonial law (Gal. 5:1; 2:4) and must be valued and guarded. The essence of Christian liberty lies not in external freedom but in deliverance from the bondage of sin and its consequent inner corruption (John 8:34-36; Rom. 6: 20-22).

Spiritual liberty is the result of the Spirit's regenerating work, for His presence and work within produces liberty (II Cor. 3:17), giving a sense of freedom through a filial relation with God (Rom. 8:15-16). Godly men of the OT knew a measure of this spiritual liberty (Psa. 119:45), but the Gospel reveals and offers it in its fulness. Using the picture of Isaiah 61:1, Christ proclaimed this liberty to be the goal of His mission (Luke 4:18). Intimately related to practical holiness of life (Rom. 6:18-22), spiritual liberty never condones license. Believers are warned against abuse of this liberty in sinful indulgence (Gal. 5:13; I Pet. 2:16; II Pet. 2:19), and speech and conduct are to be judged by "the law of liberty" (James 2:12) which has taken the place of the ancient law. In regard to things not expressly commanded or forbidden, Christian liberty must be granted, allowing for the exercise of individual judgment and Christian conscience before God (I Cor. 10:29-31); but its use must be limited by considerations of love, expediency, and self-preservation, lest that liberty become a stumbling block to the weak (I Cor. 8:9). In Romans 8:21 "liberty" points to creation's future deliverance from decay and imperfection when God's children are glorified.   D.E.H.

LIBNAH (lĭb'nà, Heb. *livnâh, whiteness*). 1. A desert camp of Israel, the fifth station after leaving Sinai (Num. 33:20-21). Perhaps the same as Laban (Deut. 1:1); its location is unknown.
2. A Canaanite city, near Lachish, captured by Joshua (Josh. 10:29-32; 12:15) and named at the head of a group of nine cities in the lowland (15: 42-44). It was designated a Levitical city in Judah (Josh. 21:13; I Chron. 6:57). Simultaneously with Edom it revolted from Jehoram (II Kings 8:22; II Chron. 21:10). As a strong fortified center it

sustained the seige of Sennacherib for some time (II Kings 19:8; Isa. 37:8). It was the native city of Hamutal, the wife of King Josiah and mother of Jehoahaz and Zedekiah (II Kings 23:31; 24:18; Jer. 52:1). Archaeology has identified it with modern Tell es Safi, at the head of the valley of Elah.

LIBNI (lĭb'nī, Heb. *livnî, white*). 1. The first-named of the two sons of Gershon, the son of Levi (Exod. 6:17; Num. 3:17; I Chron. 6:17,20). He is also called Laadan or Ladan (I Chron. 23:7; 26:21).
2. A Levite, son of Mahli, son of Merari (I Chron. 6:29).

LIBNITES (lĭb'nītes), the descendants of Libni. the son of Gershon (Num. 3:21; 26:58).

LIBRARIES. Polycrates of Samos, and Pisistratus of Athens are the first recorded owners of libraries. Euripides owned books, and Socrates, according to Plato, had access to collections (Plato, *Apol.* 26d; *Philod.* 97b.98b). Strabo states that Aristotle collected books, and taught the kings of Egypt to build libraries. The setting up of the great library of Alexandria by the first two Ptolemies (367 to 283, 308 to 246 B.C.) was a major event in the history of literature. On a conservative estimate, it contained half a million volumes, and under its scholarly librarians founded library methodology, and became a center of Hellenistic learning. the great library of Pergamum in Asia Minor, founded by Eumenes II in the early second century before Christ, was probably half the size of the Alexandrian library, and not nearly so influential. Lucullus is the first recorded Roman to possess a library (Plat. *Luc.* 42). Atticus, the friend and correspondent of Cicero, and Cicero himself, had considerable collections of books. Caesar commissioned the scholar Varro to collect a library for him (Suet. *Iul.* 44). The statesman C. Asinius Pollio founded the first public library at Rome (Plin. H.N. 7.30; 35.2), and Augustus established two, notably one on the Palatine attached to the temple of Apollo. Greek and Latin collections in both of these imperial foundations appear to have been kept separate, and a hall or reading room without a rule of silence seems to have been a feature (Gell. 13.19). Eventually, with further foundations by the Flavian emperors, Roman libraries totaled 26. Seneca regarded a library as essential as a bathroom. An Epicurean's library was found at Herculaneum (in the 'Villa of the Papyri,' excavated two centuries ago). Paul appears to have prized a small collection of good books (II Tim. 4:13).   E.M.B.

LIBYA (lĭb′ĭ-à), the ancient Greek name for northern Africa W of Egypt. The Heb. is *Put* (Ezek. 30:5; 38:5; Jer. 46:9; Dan. 11:43), and so rendered in ASV, except Daniel 11:43. It was the country of the Lubim, descendants of Ham (Gen. 10:13). Cyrene was one of its cities (Acts 2:10).

LICE (See Insects)

LIEUTENANTS (Aram. *ăhashdarpenîm*), the official title of satraps or viceroys governing large provinces of the Persian empire as representatives of the sovereign. KJV has "lieutenants" in Ezra 8:36; Esther 3:12; 8:9; 9:3 and "princes" in Daniel 3:2,3,27; 6:1-7; "satraps" in ASV.

LIFE, a complex concept with varied shades of meaning, rendering several Heb. and Gr. terms. It may denote *physical* or natural life, whether animal (Gen. 1:20; 6:17; Rev. 8:9) or human (Lev. 17:14; Matt. 2:20; Luke 12:22, etc). It is the vital principle, or breath of life, which God imparted to man, making him a living soul (Gen. 2:7). This life is a precious gift and the taking of life is prohibited (Gen. 9:5; Exod. 20:13; Lev. 24:17). It is propagated through physical generation and is subject to physical death. It may signify the period of one's earthly existence, one's lifetime (Gen. 23:1; 25:7; Luke 16:25, etc), or the relations, activities, and experiences which make up life (Exod. 1:14; Deut. 32:47; Job 10:1; Luke 12:15). Occasionally it means one's manner of life (I Tim. 2:2; I John 2:16) or the means for sustaining life (Deut. 24:6; I John 3:17). But the primary concern of the Scriptures is *spiritual* or *eternal* life for man. It is the gift of God, mediated through faith in Jesus Christ (John 3:36; 5:24; Rom. 5:10; 6:23; I John 5:12; etc). It is not synonymous with endless existence, which is also true of the unsaved. It is qualitative, involving the impartation of a new nature (II Pet. 1:3-4). It is communicated to the believer in this life, resulting in fellowship with God in Christ, and is not interrupted by physical death (I Thess. 5:10). It will find its perfection and full reality of blessedness with God in the life to come (Rom. 2:7; II Cor. 5:4). As "the living God" (Deut. 5:26; Psa. 42:2; I Thess. 1:9; I Tim. 3:15), the eternal and self-existent One, God has *absolute* life in Himself (John 5:26) and is the source of all life (Ps. 36:9; John 1:4; 17:3; I John 1:1-2; 5:20). D.E.H.

LIFE, THE BOOK OF, a figurative expression denoting God's record of those who inherit eternal life (Phil 4:3; Rev. 3:5; 21:27). From *man's* point of view individuals may be blotted out (Ps. 69:28; Matt. 25:29), but from *God's* point of view it contains only the names of the elect which will not be blotted out (Rev. 3:5; 13:8; 17:8; 20:15).

LIGHT (Heb. *'ôr*, Gr. *phós*, and a number of other words), denotes natural light; also used figuratively. Scripture pictures the coming into existence of *natural* light through the sublime command of God ("let there be light" Gen. 1:3) as the initial step in the preparation of the world for vegetable and animal life. The origin and nature of light find their explanation in the nature and purpose of God Himself (I John 1:5). The possession of light is one of the most remarkable and valuable blessings of this earthly sphere, without which life as we know it could not exist. Scientific studies of the nature, properties, and effects of light have only enhanced its wonders. Its crucial importance for life early led to the worship of the sun, the great source of the world's light and heat (Job. 31:26-27), an idolatry condemned by Scripture (Lev. 26:30; Isa. 17:8 ASV).

Mention is also made of *artificial* lights as temporary substitutes for natural light, as the candlestick in the tabernacle (Exod. 25:6; Lev. 24:2) or lamps in the home (Matt. 5:15; Luke 15:8) or in church (Acts 20:8). Scripture mentions several instances of *miraculous* light: the light in the dwellings of the Israelites while the Egyptians were in thick darkness (Exod. 10:23); the pillar of fire which led the Israelites "all the night with a light of fire" (Ps. 78:14; Exod. 13:21; 14:20); the glistening brightness of Christ's garments at the transfiguration (Matt. 17:2); the light brighter than the noonday sun appearing to Saul on the road (Acts 9:3; 22:6; 26:13). Scripture uses light to portray *figuratively* various spiritual realities. Thus "God is light" (I John 1:5), "the Father of lights" (James 1:17), "dwelling in the light unapproachable" (I Tim. 6:16 ASV; Ps. 104:2). Jesus called Himself "the light of the world" (John 8:12; 9:5; 12:46). Zacharias and Simeon sang of His birth as the coming light (Luke 1:78-79; 2:32). In revealing God to men and giving spiritual light He is "the light of men" (John 1:4,9). Light is thus the appropriate symbol of spiritual illumination wrought by Christ through the indwelling Spirit (II Cor. 4:6; Eph. 5:14; I Peter 2:9; Ps. 36:9).

Since darkness is the symbol of sin, by contrast light is the figure of holiness and purity (Isa. 5:20; Rom. 13:12; I John 1:6-7; 2:9-11). It is also a general figure for that which tends to cheer or renders prosperous (Esth. 8:16; Job 30:26), hence especially of spiritual joy (Ps. 27:1; 97:11). The Word of God is symbolized as light (Ps. 119:105; Isa. 8:20). The figure is also applied to believers generally (Matt. 5:14; Eph. 5:8; Phil. 2:15), or to individuals, like John the Baptist (John 5:35). Finally, the figure is applied to the bliss of the heavenly state (Isa. 60:19; Col. 1:12; Rev. 21:23-24; 22:5). D.E.H.

LIGHTNING (Heb. *bārāq*, Gr. *astrapé*), a visible electric discharge between rain clouds or between a rain cloud and the earth, producing a thunderclap. In Palestine and Syria lightning is common during the heavy fall and spring rains. The lightning is generally accompanied by heavy rain, and at times by hail (Exod. 9:23-24). The Scriptures mention lightning as a manifestation of God's power, symbolizing His command of the forces of nature (Job 28:26; 38:35; Ps. 135:7; Zech. 10:1); lightnings are His instruments in bringing about the destruction of His opponents (Ps. 18:14; 144:6; Zech. 9:14-15). Lightning is used as a symbol of speed (Ezek. 1:14; Nah. 2:4; Zech. 9:14) and of dazzling brightness (Dan. 10:6; Matt. 28:3). In Matthew 24:27, Luke 17:24 Jesus uses the figure of lightning to indicate the unmistakable certainty of the fact that He will come again. In Luke 10:18 Jesus speaks of beholding Satan fallen as lightning, symbolic of a definite and terrific defeat.

LIGN-ALOES (See Plants)

LIGURE (See Minerals)

LIKHI (lĭk′hī), a Manassite of the family of Gilead, mentioned in I Chronicles 7:19 as the third son of Shemidah.

LILY (See Plants)

LINE, the rendering in KJV of six different Heb. words and one Gr. word. Usually the meaning is *a measuring line* (II Sam. 8:2; Ps. 78:55; Isa. 34:17; Jer. 31:39; Ezek. 47:3; Zech. 1:16; 2:1), or a cord or thread (Josh. 2:18,21; Ezek. 40:3). In Isaiah 44:13 it means either "pencil" (ASV) or a cutting instrument. In Psalm 16:6 it means "portion" as fixed by measurement; in 19:4 it signifies the sound made by a musical chord (cf. Rom. 10: 18). In Isaiah 28:10 "line upon line," etc. is the drunkard's sneer at the childishness of Isaiah's ceaseless chidings. In II Corinthians 10:16 "line" means a "province" or sphere worked by another.

LINEN, thread or cloth, prepared from the fiber of flax. The use of flax fiber for cloth and other purposes is very ancient, being traceable as far back as the Stone Age. Flax was cultivated in Mesopotamia, Assyria, and Egypt, and linen was well known in the ancient Biblical world. Ancient Egypt was noted for its fine linen and carried on a thriving export with neighboring nations. Flax was being cultivated in the tropical climate around Jericho at the time of the conquest (Josh. 2:6). Having learned the art in Egypt (Exod. 35:25), Hebrew women practiced the spinning and weaving of flax (Prov. 31:13,19). The house of Ashbea attained eminence as workers in linen (I Chron. 4: 21).

Linen is the rendering for several different Heb. and Gr. words. The Heb. *pīshteh* denotes the flax plant (Josh. 2:6; Judg. 15:14; Prov. 31:13; Isa. 19:9) or the material made from it (Lev. 13:47; Deut. 22:11; Jer. 13:1; Ezek. 44:17; etc.), as opposed to woolen material. *Shaatnēz* is used twice to signify a garment made of two sorts of thread, linen and woolen, which the Israelites were forbidden to wear (Lev. 19:19; Deut. 22:11). The term *badh,* used 23 times (Exod. 28:42; Lev. 6:10; I Sam. 2:18; Ezek. 9:2; etc.), means "linen cloth," with the subordinate ideas of white and fine. *Shēsh,* like the later term *bûts,* means "fine linen," the epithet "fine" being coupled with it by the translators to denote the finer quality of the linen. *Shēsh* is rendered "fine linen" 37 times and "silk" once (Prov. 31:22 KJV). Since its meaning is "whiteness" it may have included other materials besides linen. It is the equivalent of the Gr. *bússos,* "fine linen." The Heb. *sādhîn* denotes a wider undergarment of linen worn next to the body (Prov. 31:24; Isa. 3:23; "sheet" in Judg. 14:12,13 KJV) and is synonymous with the Gr. *sindón,* the term for the linen sheet in which the body of Jesus was wrapped (Matt. 27:59; Mark 15:46; Luke 23:53). In Mark 14:51f it is apparently simply a sheet which the young man had wrapped around his body. In John 19:40; 20:5ff; Luke 24:12 "linen clothes" is *othónion* (in pl.), linen bands, linen cloth torn into strips. In Revelation 15:6 KJV and ASV marg. the word is *línon,* a linen garment.

The Biblical references show varied uses of linen. For clothing it was preferred to cotton material in warm climates because of the sensation of coolness given by linen garments. Its use is frequently mentioned in connection with the garments of the Aaronic priests (Exod. 28:42; Lev. 6:10; I Sam. 22:18; etc.), their tunics, breeches, and headdress being exclusively of linen, and the girdle largely of it (Exod. 28:39; 39:27-29). It was also preferred by others for religious services, as the child Samuel (I Sam. 2:18), the Levitical singers in the temple (II Chron. 5:12), and even royal personages (II Sam. 6:14; I Chron. 15:27). Angels are described as dressed in it (Ezek. 9:2; 10:2; Dan. 10:5; 12:6), as also the host of the redeemed returning with Christ from heaven (Rev. 19:14). In Revelation 19:8 linen is used figuratively of the moral purity of the saints. Linen was also used for garments of distinction (Gen. 41:42; Esth. 8:15). Apparently linen garments of a coarser material were worn by men (Judg. 14:12f) and women (Prov. 31:22). But the use of fine linen for ordinary purposes was apparently a sign of luxury and extravagance (Isa. 3:23; Ezek. 16:10; Luke 16:19;

Rev. 18:12,16). Linen was also used for nets (Isa. 19:9), measuring lines (Ezek. 40:3), girdles (Jer. 13:1), and for fine hangings (Esth. 1:6). In NT times at least, linen was extensively used by the Jews for burial shrouds, as at the burial of Jesus (Matt. 27:59; Mark 15:46; Luke 23:53; John 19: 40; 20:5ff). Egyptian mummies were wrapped exclusively in linen sheets of vast proportions.

D.E.H.

LINTEL (Heb. *mashqôph, overhanging*), the horizontal beam, of stone or wood, forming the upper part of a doorway (Exod. 12:22,23, vs. 7 "the upper door post" "lintel" ASV), to be marked by the blood of the paschal lamb at the first Passover. See also I Kings 6:31 (Heb. *'ayīl,* "post or column"); Amos 9:1; Zephaniah 2:14 (*kaphtōr,* "capital of a column"; "capitals" in ASV).

LINUS (lī'nŭs), a Christian in Rome joining Paul in sending salutations to Timothy in II Timothy 4:21. According to Irenaeus (III.3.3)and Eusebius (*H.E.* III.2), he became the first bishop of Rome.

LION (See Animals)

LITTER, a portable couch or sedan, a palanquin, borne by men or animals. The word is used only in Isaiah 66:20, but in a compound form is rendered *covered* wagons" in Numbers 7:3.

LITTLE OWL (See Birds)

LIVER (Heb. *kāvēdh, heavy*), the heaviest of the viscera, both in weight and importance, mentioned 14 times in the OT. Usually the reference is to the bodily organ in connection with sacrificial instructions (Exod. 29:13,22; Lev. 3:4,10,15; 4:9; 7:4; etc.). Its use for purposes of divination was common among heathen nations (Ezek. 21:21), but the practice is not verified among the Jews. Being closely identified with the source and center of life, it is mentioned in depicting profound sorrow (Lam. 2:11), and its injury was equivalent to death (Prov. 7:22-23).

LIVING CREATURES, mentioned in Ezekiel 1:5-22; 3:13; 10:15-20 and Revelation 4:6-9 (KJV "beasts") and apparently identical with the cherubim. In the creation account "living creature" designates aquatic animals (Gen. 1:21), mammals (1:24), or any animal (2:19).

LIZARD (See Animals)

LO-AMMI (lō-ăm'ī, Heb. *lō'-'ammî, not my people*), the symbolic name given to Hosea's third child; it is transliterated "Lo-ammi" in Hosea 1: 9:a, but translated "not my people' 'in Hosea 1:9b, 10; 2:23. Originally applied to express the rejection of the Northern Kingdom in contrast to the election of Judah (Hos. 1:6f), the name prophetically and paradoxically (Hos. 1:11; 2:23) becomes the designation of the rejected Gentiles now, during Israel's present blindness (Rom. 11:25f), incorporated into the true Israel of God (Rom. 9:24-26; cf. Deut. 32:21; Isa. 65:1; Rom. 2:28f; 9:6ff; 10: 19f; I Pet. 2:9f).

LOCK, LOCKS. 1. A mechanical device for fastening a city gate or a door. The primitive locks used to fasten city gates consisted simply of heavy beams of wood, the ends of which were dropped into slots cut into the masonry of the gate (Neh. 3:3-15; ASV "the bolts and bars"; cf. Deut. 3:5; I Sam. 23:7; etc.). Used figuratively, their strengthening spoke of divine protection (Ps. 147:13), their burning of a country's invasion (Jer. 51:30; Nah. 3:13). To strengthen them, iron bars were used (I Kings 4: 13; Isa. 45:2). When used to lock house doors (Judg. 3:23,24) they were reduced in size and became flat bolts. Usually several sliding pins dropped into corresponding holes in the bar, requiring a key to release them. Keys varied in size, often being large enough to be carried on the shoulder (Isa. 22:22). To open the door from without, the key was inserted through a hole in the door; the hole might be big enough to admit the hand with the key (S. of Sol. 5:5). Fear of the Jews caused the disciples to lock the door (John 20:19, 26).

2. In reference to the hair of the head, "locks" renders several different Heb. words. In Numbers 6:5 the term indicates the unshorn and disheveled locks of the Nazarite; in Judges 16:13,19 the braided locks of the Nazarite Samson; in Ezekiel 8:3 a forelock of the prophet's hair; in Song of Solomon 5:2,11 the luxuriant locks of the Hebrew youth. In Song of Solomon 4:1; 6:7; Isaiah 47:2 "locks" is better rendered "veil" as in ASV.

D.E.H.

LOCUST (See Insects)

LOD (lŏd, Heb. *lôdh*), a town built by Shemed, a Benjamite (I Chron. 8:12); located in the shephelah or low hills in SW Palestine. This is the Lydda of the NT.

LO-DEBAR (lō'dē'bàr, Heb. *lô dhevār,* probably *without pasture*), a town in Gilead E of the Jordan, where Mephibosheth, Saul's grandson, lived in the house of Machir until summoned by David to eat at his table (II Sam. 9:1-13). Machir also supplied David's needs when David fled from Absalom to E Jordan (II Sam. 17:27ff). The town is otherwise unknown.

LODGE, a temporary shelter erected in a garden for a watchman guarding the ripening fruit (Isa. 1:8); it is of a more temporary nature than a watchtower. In relation to travelers, "a lodging" is a temporary place of sojourn for strangers (Acts 28:23; Philem. 22).

LOFT, the upper chamber or story of a building, used in KJV in I Kings 17:19 and Acts 20:9.

LOGIA, the Greek word for "sententious sayings" or "epigrams," employed in reference to the non-Biblical sayings of Christ, the latest collection of which is the so-called Gospel of Thomas discovered in 1945, and first made public in 1959. The Church has always been aware of sayings of Christ not included in the Gospels. Paul speaks of "the words of the Lord Jesus, how He said, It is more blessed to give than to receive" (Acts 20:35). The Moslems have retained some such sayings. An ode of the poet Nizami tells the story of the dead dog in the market place in whom none could find aught but horror and ugliness. "Pearls," said One standing hardby, "cannot rival the whiteness of his teeth." A mosque near Agra contains another Moslem memory of Christ. Among the arabesques is woven the logion: "Jesus, on whom be peace, said, The world is merely a bridge; ye are to pass over it, and not build your dwellings upon it." This saying may descend from Thomas, who, according to tradition, carried the Gospel to India. Its imagery may be based on the causeway of Tyre. The Codex Bezae inserts a logion after Verse 5 of Luke 6: "On the same day, seeing someone working on the sabbath, He said to him, Man, if you know what you are doing, blessed are you. If you do not know, you are accursed, and a transgressor of the law." Luke speaks of "many who have taken in hand to draw up a narrative," and tradition has it that Matthew, before he wrote his Gospel, made a collection of sayings of Christ. Many such collections were probably current, of which the *Gospel of Thomas* is one. De Joinville, the medieval French crusader and historian, tells of another. In his account of the Third Crusade, De Joinville tells of the visit of a monk on an embassy to the Lebanese sheik, "the Old Man of the Mountain." The monk reported that his host had a book called *The Words of the Lord unto Peter.* This was in A.D. 1248. In the closing years of the 19th century a sheet of such sayings was discovered among the papyri. It included two new and now well-known logia: "Thou hearest with one ear but the other thou hast closed"; "Whenever there are two they are not without God, and if one be alone anywhere I say that I am with him. Raise the stone, there thou shalt find me. Cleave the wood, and there I am." A second sheet was discovered in 1904. It contained the logion reminiscent of a saying of Plato: "Let him who seeks cease not till he finds, and when he finds he shall be astonished. Astonished he shall reach the Kingdom, and having· reached the Kingdom he shall rest." See AGRAPHA.

E.M.B.

LOGOS (Gr. *lógos*), a philosophical and theological term and concept that goes back to the Ionian philosopher Heraclitus (c. 500 B.C.), with whom it expressed the universal reason permeating the world, and finding self-consciousness in the mind of the philosophers. Stoicism adopted the term for a dynamic principle of reason operating in the world, and forming a medium of communion between God and man. The latter function becomes prominent in Philo, with whom the Logos is at once the Stoics' active, intelligent, world-principle, the thought in the divine mind, which was identical with the sum-total of Plato's "Forms" or "Ideas," and a mediator between God and the matter of His creation. For Philo, as indeed for his predecessors, the Logos is neither personal nor impersonal. It was vaguely equated with God's utterance (Gen. 1:3; Ps. 33:9), His "word" in such passages as Psalms 107:20; 147:15,18, and such expressions as "the angel of the covenant," and with "wisdom" in such personifications as those of Proverbs 8 and Wisdom of Solomon 9:15ff. It is possible that the Qumran community fused the same Hebrew and Hellenistic concepts into their doctrine of the spirit of truth, which, like the spirit of error, was a creature of God. The relevant passages in the "Rule of the Community" document do not admit of dogmatism.

In the New Testament the Logos appears principally in Johannine contexts (John 1:1ff; I John 1:1; Rev. 19:13), though Pauline references and the Epistle to the Hebrews might be added. Logos is imperfectly rendered by "Word," and it is not easy to apprehend the full content of the idea in its Judaeo-Hellenistic context. There can be no doubt that both John and Paul saw value in expressing Christian thought in the terminology of the day, a point appreciated by the early Church Fathers in their sometimes perilous development of the Logos doctrine. Significantly enough, John wrote his prologues at the end of the first century when the first signs of Gnostic error were discernible. In John's use of "Logos" we must certainly see that blending of Judaic and Hellenistic concepts which appeared in Philo's use of the term. From its Greek ancestry, etymological and philosophical, the Johannine word would contain the notion of reason, but also the active expression of reason on a divine and perfect plane. Hence the conception of the visible universe as an expression of God's reason, that reason being the force and agency of creation, the Word which said: "Let there be . . ." But John becomes entirely original and creative when he boldly equates this reason with God Himself, and simultaneously sees its incarnation in Christ. It seems likely that John, in this bold thought, brought to firmer expression in the terminology of Hellenistic thought a concept already expressed in Hebrews 1:2,3 and in I Corinthians 8:6; Colossians 1:15-17. In view of the Colossian heresy of angelic mediatorship the last context is significant.

E.M.B.

LOIN, the part of the body between the ribs and the hip bones. It is the place where the girdle was worn (Exod. 12:11; II Kings 1:8; Jer. 13:1; Matt. 3:4; etc.), and the sword was fastened (II Sam. 20:8). Pain and terror were reflected in weakness and shaking of the loins (Ps. 38:7; 66:11; 69:23; Jer. 30:6). Girding the loins with sackcloth was the sign of mourning (I Kings 20:32; Isa. 32:11; Jer. 48:37). As the place of the reproductive organs the loins are euphemistically named for the generative function (Gen. 35:11; I Kings 8:19; Acts 2:30; Heb. 7:5). Since Oriental garments were worn ungirded about the house, to gird up the loins signified preparation for vigorous action (Exod. 12:11; I Kings 18:46; Job 38:3; Prov. 31:17; Luke 12:35; I Pet. 1:13). To have the loins girded with truth signified strength in attachment to truth (Eph. 6:14; Isa. 11:5).

LOIS (lō'is, Gr. *Loís*), the maternal grandmother of Timothy. Commended by Paul for her faith (II Tim. 1:5), she apparently was associated with Eunice in the religious training of Timothy.

LOOKING-GLASS (See Mirror)

LORD, the rendering in the KJV for a variety of Heb. and Gr. terms. It is applied to both men and God and expresses varied degrees of honor, dignity, and majesty. In the Aramaic portion of Daniel (2:4-7:28) three words are rendered "lord": *rab* (2:10), *a chief, leader,* or *captain; rabrevān, magnate* or *prince,* of certain Babylonian nobles (4:36; 5:1,9,10,23; 6:17); *mārē', an exalted one,* of the king (4:19,24) and of God (2:47; 5:23). *Seren,* used only in Joshua, Judges, I Samuel and I Chronicles, always designates "the *lords* of the Philistines." *Sar* (Ezra 8:25), a title of nobility, means *a prince,* while *shālîsh* (II Kings 7:2,17,19) indicates an *officer of the third rank* (ASV "captain"). The familiar term Baal (Heb. *ba'al, master* or *owner*) is applied to heathen deities or to a man as husband; in Isaiah 16:8 "the *lords* of the heathen" denotes heathen princes invading Moab. The Heb. *'ādhōnay,* frequently rendered "lord" or "master," may be a term of respect (Gen. 23:11; 24:18), but its meaning of *owner* indicates one having absolute control, as an owner of slaves, or a king. As applied to God it denotes the owner and governor of the whole earth (Ps. 97:5; 114:7; Isa. 1:24). The term *'adōnai,* perhaps the pl. of *'ādhôn,* "the Lord," is always used where God is submissively and reverently addressed (Exod. 4:10; Josh. 7:8; Neh. 1:11; etc.). In the KJV *'ādhōnay* is printed as LORD while LORD in capitals represents Jehovah (Heb. YAHWEH, *the self-existent One*), the supreme name of God alone, which the Jews, due to their interpretation of Leviticus 24:16, avoided pronouncing and read *'ādhōnay* instead. In the ASV it is rendered "Jehovah," which the KJV has only in Exodus 6:3; Psalm 83:18; Isaiah 12:2; 26:4. Of the four Gr. terms rendered "lord," *megistánes* is used in Mark 6:21 and means (pl.) "great men, courtiers." *Rabboní,* "my Lord" (heightened form of Heb. *rab*), occurs in Mark 10:51 KJV and John 20:16 (transliterated). *Despótes,* implying absolute ownership or power, is rendered "Lord" in Luke 2:29; Acts 4:24; II Peter 2:1; Jude 4; Revelation 6:10. The prevailing Gr. term rendered "lord" is *kurios,*

The Church of the Lord's Prayer, on the Mount of Olives. © MPS

master or *owner,* one who has power or authority over some property (Matt. 20:8; Luke 10:2), animals (Luke 19:34), or persons (Matt. 13:27). It may be used as a term of respect (Matt. 21:30; John 4:15; 12:21). It is frequently used of God (Matt. 1:22; Mark 5:19; Acts 7:33; etc.) as well as of Jesus as Messiah who by His resurrection and ascension was exalted to lordship (Acts 2:36; Phil. 2:9-11; Rom. 1:4; 14:8). At times it is difficult to determine whether by "the Lord" the Father or the Son is meant (Acts 1:24; 9:31; 16:14; Rom. 14:11; I Cor. 4:19; II Thess. 3:16; etc.). D.E.H.

LORD'S DAY, the day especially associated with the Lord Jesus Christ. The expression occurs in the NT only in Revelation 1:10. The adj. *kyriakós,* translated "the Lord's," is a possessive and means "belonging to the Lord" — to Christ. It denotes a day consecrated to the Lord. Cf. the parallel expression "the Lord's Supper" (I Cor. 11:20). Some would equate it with the OT prophetic "day of the Lord," but clearly John is dating his vision and is not yet speaking of that prophetic day. The form of his expression marks a distinction between the prophetic "day of the Lord" (I Cor. 5:5; II Cor. 1:14; I Thess. 5:2) and the first day of the week on which Christ arose. It was the resurrection victory on that day which marked it as distinct and sacred to the Christian Church. The Gospel emphasis upon "the first day of the week" as the day of resurrection stresses its distinctiveness. On that day the risen Christ repeatedly appeared to His disciples (Luke 24:13-49; John 20:1-25), and again a week later (John 20:26). The Pentecostal outpouring apparently also came on that day. Acts 20:7 and I Corinthians 16:1-2 show that the early Church consecrated the day to worship and almsgiving (but not to earning). Sunday (the name is of pagan origin) as the day of special worship is a Christian institution and must be sharply distinguished from the OT sabbath. Nor were the OT sabbath regulations transferred to the Lord's Day as a "Christian sabbath." The sabbath related to the old creation (Exod. 20:8-11; 31:12-17; Heb. 4:4), while the Lord's Day commemorates the new creation in Christ Jesus. No "sabbath" observance was stipulated in the demands upon Gentile Christians in Acts 15:28-29. Some Jewish Christians continued to observe the sabbath and Jewish festivals, while some members of the primitive Church made no distinction between days (Rom. 14:5-6), but it was held to be a matter of liberty (Rom. 14:1), as long as the observance of a special day was not regarded as necessary for salvation (Gal. 4:10; Col. 2:16-17).   D.E.H.

LORD'S PRAYER, THE, properly "the Disciples' Prayer," since not prayed with but taught to them by Jesus (Matt. 6:9-13; Luke 11:2-4). In Luke, Jesus, at the request of a disciple, gives a modified form of His earlier spontaneous presentation in the Sermon on the Mount. The earlier form is fuller and is commonly used. As a pattern prayer it is unsurpassed for conciseness and fullness, delineating the proper approach and order in prayer. It directs the disciples, as members of God's family, reverently to pray to a personal Heavenly Father. The petitions are divided into two parts, the first three relating to God's interests. They are arranged in a descending scale, from Himself, through the manifestation of Himself in His kingdom (the coming Messianic kingdom), to the complete doing of His will by His subjects. Placing God's interest first, the disciple can pray for his own needs. The petitions, whether counted as three or four, are arranged in an ascending scale — from the supply of daily material needs to the ultimate deliverance from all evil. The doxology in Matthew, which constitues an affirmation of faith, is lacking in the leading MSS and is generally regarded as a scribal addition derived from ancient liturgical usage.

D.E.H.

The Last Supper, as portrayed by the famous painter, Leonardo da Vinci. EG

LORD'S SUPPER. The meaning of the Lord's Supper may be gained by viewing its origin and theological significance.

Its historical significance arises out of the context of its institution by Christ on the night of His betrayal, when, celebrating the Passover with His disciples "as they were eating, Jesus took bread, and blessed it, and brake it, and gave to the disciples and said, Take, eat; this is my body. And he took the cup, and gave thanks, and gave it to them, saying, Drink ye all of it; for this is my blood of the new testament, which is shed for many for the remission of sins" (Matt. 26:26-28; Mark 14:22-24; Luke 22:19-20).

Its theological significance arises out of the interpretation placed on it by the apostle Paul who wrote, "The cup of blessing which we bless, is it not the communion of the blood of Christ? The bread which we break, is it not the communion of the body of Christ? For we being many are one bread and one body: for we are all partakers of that one bread" (I Cor. 10:16-17 and I Cor. 11:23-28). Both the historical and theological significance constitute it as the basis of fellowship by which the assembled church commemorates the death and ressurrection of Christ as its source of spiritual life.

The table of the Lord is known in Scripture by many names, each of which is descriptive of an aspect of its nature. It is called the body and blood of Christ (Matt. 24:26,28); the communion of the body and blood of Christ (I Cor. 10:16); the bread and cup of the Lord (I Cor. 11:27); the breaking of bread (Acts 2:42 and 20:7) and as the Lord's Supper (I Cor. 11:20).

The meaning of the ordinance is suggested by these usages, as: the Eucharist (meaning "to give thanks"); the communion; a memorial feast in commemoration of Jesus' death; a sacrifice of praise; and the presence of Christ.

The Nature of the Lord's Supper. The nature of the Lord's Supper is delineated by two interpretations: the meaning of the "body" and "blood" of Christ; and, by the significance of its observance in the life of the believer.

Three major interpretations have been placed upon the meaning of Christ's reference to his body and blood: the Romanist doctrine of *transubstantiation*; the Lutheran doctrine of *consubstantiation*; and the Reformed doctrine of *symbolic commemoration*.

Romanists assert that the elements used in the ordinance are literally transubstantiated as the actual body and blood of Christ at each observance, and that as such, they constitute a true sacrifice as an offering for the sins of man. Since the elements have become the actual body and blood, they are said to have intrinsic sacramental value for all who partake, with immediate consequences of grace and merit.

The Lutheran doctrine of consubstantiation denies that the elements change, but asserts that the literal presence of Christ is present in, under, and with the elements so that Christ may be received sacramentally by those who observe the ordinance.

The doctrine of symbolic commemoration, advanced by Calvin, asserts that the term body and blood are not to be taken literally, but only symbolically, and that the observance of the ordinance is a commemoration of the death of Christ in which Christ is spiritually present. The Lord's Supper is, therefore, a perpetual memorial and seal of the covenanted grace of God, to be observed as a means of consecration and renewal of obedience to the will of God.

The significance of its observance in the life of the believer is, therefore, conditioned by the interpretations just mentioned. The doctrine of symbolic commemoration, held by most non-Lutheran Protestants since the Reformation, avows that its nature is twofold: in its symbolism; and, as a memorial feast.

The symbolism arises out of its application to the Christian life. It symbolizes the death of Christ for our sins, and our death to sin in Christ (I Cor. 11:26 and Rom. 6:1-13); the extension of Christ's death as the means of our righteousness (I Cor. 5:7); our participation in the death of Christ (I Cor. 10:16); the union between ourselves and Christ through his death (Rom. 6:4); and our expectant hope in Christ until He comes again (I Cor. 11:26).

The elements used suggest the symbolism. Bread, as a symbol of the body of Christ, suggests the staff of life, the very basis of life itself. The breaking of the bread suggests the breaking of Christ's life in redemptive sacrifice. Wine, as a symbol of the blood of Christ, suggests the pressing out of Christ's life, the bruising by divine wrath. Together they symbolize the sacrifice of the very life of Christ.

Its greatest significance, however, lies in its nature as a memorial feast. It is here that the believer interacts inwardly and spiritually with the grace of God displayed in the death of Christ. As he receives the elements, symbolic in their nature, he submits himself again to receive the merits of Christ's death, not as if it needs to be renewed periodically, but as a continual commemoration of the time when God's mercy drew him into grace and imparted Christ's righteousness to him. As a memorial to Christ's death it is a renewal of obedience to Christ's will — an acknowledgement again that his salvation is solely through the broken body and shed blood of Christ.

The Requirements of the Lord's Supper. Two requirements for participating in the Lord's Supper are specified in Scripture: that the communicant be regenerated by grace, and that he be walking a life consistent with commemorating the death of Christ.

Since the Supper symbolizes the inward experience of grace, only such persons as have participated in Christ's meritorious death can memorialize his death. Each communicant is required to examine his faith before participating (I Cor. 11:27-29).

Furthermore, the communicant must be living a life of obedience, refraining from deliberate sin, and intent upon a more intimate fellowship in Christ when he comes to the table, discerning the full meaning of his act in commemorating Christ's death in his life (I Cor. 11:28).

Though it is not specified in Scripture, it is more than probable that the early Church required baptism as a prerequisite, and that it should so be thought of as a qualification today.

The Administration of the Lord's Table. No form of administering the ordinance is specified in Scripture. Early practice by the apostolic Church suggests, however, that it was observed with some regularity and that it was the focal point of the worship of the Church.

The example of Christ constitutes the usual form among non-liturgical churches. Christ took the bread, blessed it, broke it and gave to His disciples. Hence the communicant is to receive the bread and cup and to partake of them. This reception symbolizes the participation in the communion with Christ of death to sin.

As the sharing of the bread and cup by Christ identified them in fellowship with His atoning ministry, so participating in the Lord's table identifies the communicant in fellowship with Christ, and with other believers.

Though there is no saving grace in the ordinance, there are some concomitant relationships existing in it. It depicts the total work of Christ in man's behalf, and captures in one act man's total response to this work. When the believer receives the elements he receives spiritual blessings in proportion to the faith he exercises in Christ. The commemorative aspect of the ordinance lies not in its nature, but within the heart of the believer. It is here that faith must be exercised, and here that the efficacy of the Lord's table lies. C.B.B.

Bibliography: Harold Fey, *The Lord's Supper: Seven Meanings* (New York: Harpers) 1959; Angus J. B. Higgins, *The Lord's Supper in the New Testament* (Naperville: Allenson) 1957.

LO-RUHAMAH (lō-rōō-hà′mà, Heb. *lô'-rūhāmâh, not pitied*), the symbolic name given to Hosea's daughter; it is transliterated "Lo-ruhamah" in Hosea 1:6,8, but translated "not have mercy" in Hosea 2:4,23. It would seem to be a lesser description of the people described in Hosea as Lo-ammi. See LO-AMMI.

LOT. 1. A means of deciding an issue or of determining the divine will in a matter. The use of the lot to determine doubtful matters is very old and the practice of casting lots was common among the nations of antiquity: Haman's efforts to determine a lucky day to exterminate the Jews (Esth. 3:7); the detection of guilty Jonah by the pagan mariners (Jonah 1:7); the gambling of the Roman soldiers for the garments of Jesus (Matt. 27:35). See also Joel 3:3; Nahum 3:10; Obadiah 11. Its use among the Jews, generally with religious intent, is mentioned in determining the scapegoat (Lev. 16:8); assigning the land of Palestine among the tribes (Num. 26:55; Josh. 18:10; Acts 13:19); selecting men for an expedition (Judg. 1:1-3; 20:9); detecting a guilty party (Josh. 7:14; I Sam. 14:40-42); selecting the first king (I Sam. 10:20-21); dividing the returned priests into 24 courses (I Chron. 24:3-19); determining the service of the priests in the temple worship (Luke 1:5-9). In none of these instances is there a direct statement of the method or methods used in casting lots (but cf. Prov. 16:33). It was held in religious esteem by the covenant people and its use to determine God's will was usually accompanied by prayer (Judg. 1:1-3; Acts 1:24-26). Many scholars think that Urim and Thummim were used as lots. Only in the choice of a successor to Judas (Acts 1:26) is the use of lots by Christ's followers mentioned. As a distinctly Jewish mode of seeking divine direction its use was appropriate for the occasion. With the coming of the Spirit at Pentecost to take direction of the affairs of the Church its use is never mentioned again.

2. That which is assigned by lot, as a *portion, share,* or *inheritance* (Deut. 32:9; Josh. 15:1; Ps. 105:11; 125:3; Isa. 17:14; Acts 8:21; 1:17 ASV marg.).   D.E.H.

LOT (lŏt, Heb. *lôt, envelope, covering*), Haran's son and Abraham's nephew (Gen. 11:31; 12:5). His life may be summarized under the following heads: (1) Departure and dependence. Lot's father died and left him his possessions; Lot now was willing to follow Abraham from Mesopotamia to Canaan, thence to Egypt, and back again to Canaan (Gen. 11:27-32; 12:5,10; 13:1). During this period there was unity and fellowship between the uncle and the nephew. (2) Decision and destiny. Due to a conflict between their herdsmen, Abraham suggested that his nephew choose another place. Lot, prompted by selfishness, chose the country in the environs of Sodom, a city that had already become notorious because of its wickedness (Gen. 13:5-13). This fatal choice determined his subsequent destiny. It was Abraham now who maintained the greater spiritual status (Gen. 13:14-18). (3) Devastation and deportation, Lot, then, in Sodom, was taken captive when Chedorlaomer and his confederates conquered the king of Sodom and his four allies (Gen. 14:1-12). Abraham, the separated and faithful one, pursued the enemies, and recaptured his nephew (Gen. 14:13-16). (4) Depravity and degeneration. Angels then visited Lot in Sodom to hasten his departure from the imminent doom decreed upon the wicked city. Though originally only a sojourner (Gen. 19:9), Lot acted like a citizen; he had imbibed their mores and standards. Look at his willingness to sacrifice his daughters' chastity (Gen. 19:8); his utter ineffectiveness in dealing with his sons-in-law (Gen. 19:14); his hesitation in leaving the doomed city (Gen. 19:15f); his unwillingness to leave the comforts of a city (Gen. 19:17-22). In spite of all these adverse things, Lot was, as the NT so plainly declares, a "righteous man" (II Pet. 2:7f); and, furthermore, his righteous soul was daily vexed with the "lawless deeds" (II Pet. 2:8, ASV) of Sodom's inhabitants. By implication, it seems that the term "godly" is also applied to Lot (II Pet. 2:9). (5) Dénouement and disgrace. Lot, because of fear, left Zoar and dwelt in a cave with his two daughters (Gen. 19:30), his wife already having become, because of unbelief, "a pillar of salt" (Gen. 19:17,26; Luke 17:29). In this cave one of the most unseemly scenes recorded in the Bible took place (Gen. 19:31-38). Made drunk by his daughters, Lot became the unwilling father of their sons, Moab and Ben-ammi, the progenitors of the Moabites and the Ammonites (Deut. 2:9,19; Ps. 83:8). Entirely unsupported is the critical view that maintains that this infamous incident in the cave was "created" by a later writer to justify the inferior position of the Moabites and the Ammonites in their relationship with Israel. The almost buried faith of Lot reappeared in Ruth, a Moabitess, the great-grandmother of David and thus a member of the Messianic line (Ruth 1:16-18; 4:13-21).

Lot's life illustrates many spiritual truths: (1) the degenerating influence of a selfish choice (Gen. 13:11f); (2) the effect of a wicked environment on one's family (Gen. 19); (3) retribution in one's children (Gen. 19:8,31ff); (4) God, the only true judge of a man's real state (II Pet. 2:7ff).   W.B.

A pillar of salt on Jebel Usdum (Hill of Sodom), the mountain of salt on the western shore of the Dead Sea. This pillar of salt is known as "Lot's Wife." © MPS

LOTAN (lō'tăn, Heb. *lôtān, a wrapping up*), the son of Seir, a Horite chief, father of Hori and Heman (Homan), (Gen. 36:20,22,29; I Chron. 1:38, 39).

LOVE (Heb. *'ahăvâh,* Gr. *agápe*), presented in Scripture as the very nature of God (I John 4:8,16) and the greatest of the Christian virtues (I Cor. 13: 13). It receives definition in Scripture only by a listing of its attributes (I Cor. 13:4-7). It lies at the very heart of Christianity, being essential to man's relations to God and man (Matt. 22:37-40; Mark 12:28-31; John 13:34-35). Jesus taught that upon it hang all the law and the prophets (Matt. 22:40). It is the fulfilment of the law, for its sense of obligation and desire for the welfare of the one loved impels it to carry out the demands of the law (Rom. 13:8-10). Love found its supreme expression in the self-sacrifice on Calvary (I John 4:10).

The Bible makes the unique revelation that God in His very nature and essence is love (I John 4:8, 16), Christianity being the only religion thus to present the Supreme Being. God not only loves, He *is* love. In this supreme attribute all the other attributes are harmonized. His own Son, Jesus Christ, is the unique object of this eternal love (John 17:24; Matt. 3:17; 17:5; Isa. 42:1). God loves the world as a whole (John 3:16), as well as every individual therein (Gal. 2:20), and that in spite of man's sinfulness and corruption (Rom. 5:8-10; Eph. 2:4-5). God's love for His creatures manifests itself in supplying all their needs (Acts 14:17), but supremely in the redemption wrought for them (Rom. 5:8; I John 4:9-10). Believers in Christ are the objects of His special love (John 16:27; 17:23), causing Him to deal in chastisement with them (Heb. 12:6-11), but they are assured that nothing can separate them from His unfathomable love in Christ (Rom. 8:31-39).

All human love, whether Godward or manward, has its source in God. Love in its true reality and power is seen only in the light of Calvary (I John 4:7-10). It is created in the believer by the Holy Spirit (Rom. 5:5; Gal. 5:22), prompting him to love both God and man (II Cor. 5:14-15; I John 4:20-21). Love finds its expression in service to our fellow-men (Gal. 5:13) and is the chief test of Christian discipleship (John 13:35; Luke 14:26; I John 3:14). Love is vitally related to faith; faith is basic (Heb. 11:6; John 6:29), but a faith that does not manifest itself in love both toward God and man is dead and worthless (James 2:17-26; Gal. 5:6,13). The Christian must love God supremely and his neighbor as himself (Matt. 22: 37-39). He must love his enemy as well as his brother (Matt. 5:43-48; Rom. 12:19-20; I John 3:14). Our love must be "without hypocrisy" (Rom. 12:9 ASV) and be "in deed and truth" (I John 3:18). Love is the bond uniting all the Christian virtues (Col. 3:14).   D.E.H.

LOVE FEAST (Gr. *agápe*), a common meal eaten by early Christians in connection with the Lord's Supper to express and deepen brotherly love. Although frequently mentioned in post-canonical literature, these feasts are mentioned in the NT only in Jude 12 ("feasts of charity" KJV) and the doubtful reading in II Peter 2:13 (ASV marg.). But the situation in I Corinthians 11:20-22, 33-34 makes it clear that they were observed in the Corinthian church. The mention of breaking bread as associated with, yet distinguished from, the eating of a meal in Acts 20:7-11 indicates the practice by the church in Troas. They doubtless trace back to the communal meals observed in the early Jerusalem Church (Acts 2:42-47; 4:35; 6:1). As implied by the situation in I Corinthians 11, these love feasts were observed before, but in connection with the Lord's Supper (perhaps after the relation between the first Lord's Supper and the Passover). Because of abuses, which already appeared in apostolic churches (I Cor. 11:23-29; Jude 12), they were separated from the Lord's Supper. They subsequently fell into disfavor and were ultimately forbidden to be held in churches, largely due to the growth of the sacerdotal view of the Eucharist which regarded the union of the two as sacrilegious. A few smaller Christian groups today observe them.   D.E.H.

LOVING-KINDNESS (Heb. *hesedh*), a term which denotes the kindness and mercy of God toward man in the OT. The KJV does not reveal the difference between the meaning of this Hebrew word when it is applied to God, and when to man. But ASV has carefully made this distinction translating it as "loving-kindness" when from God and "kindness" or "mercy" when merely human qualities are meant. This term does not occur in the NT, but the concept of "grace" covers about the same area of meaning.

LUBIM (lū'bĭm, Heb. *lûvîm*), a people who are always mentioned in conjunction with Egyptians or Ethiopians (II Chron. 12:3; 16:8; Nah. 3:9). (In Jeremiah 46:9 KJV has "Libyans" for *pût* in the Hebrew text; ASV has "Put"). They are believed to be the Libyans who inhabited the area directly W of Egypt along the northern coast of Africa, where modern Libya is situated. The Lehabim of Genesis 10:13 are regarded as the same people. These ancient Libyans are occasionally mentioned in the records of ancient Egypt, usually as enemies. But one reference shows Libyan troops assigned with Egyptian soldiers and others on an expedition to Phoenicia. (James B. Pritchard, Editor, *Ancient Near Eastern Texts Relating to the Old Testament*, Princeton University Press, 1950, p. 476). This no-

tice corresponds with the appearance of the Libyans in the Bible, where they are always associated with the Egyptians or Ethiopians in war. No doubt they served as vassals of Egypt.

LUCAS (lū'cǎs, Gr. *Loukás*), occurs only in KJV in Philemon 24. ASV has Luke here. See Luke.

LUCIFER (See Satan, Devil)

LUCIUS (lū'shĭ-ŭs, Gr. *Loúkios*). 1. A Christian from Cyrene ministering in the church at Antioch (Acts 13:1).
2. A kinsman of Paul who evidently was with him in Corinth when he wrote his epistle to Rome (Rom. 16:21).

LUD, LUDIM (lŭd, lū'dĭm, Heb. *lûdh, lûdhîm*), either one or two nations of antiquity. Lud was the son of Shem (Gen. 10:22; I Chron. 1:17). It is generally agreed that Lud was the kingdom of Lydia in Asia Minor. Ludim was the son of Mizraim (Egypt) (Gen. 10:13; I Chron. 1:11), which indicates an African country. Other Bible references are: Isaiah 66:19 "to Tarshish, Pul, and Lud that draw the bow, to Tubal and Javan, to the isles afar off" — indicates Lud was in the Mediterranean area. Jeremiah 46:9 in a prophecy against Egypt "Cush (Ethiopia) Put (Phut) that handle the shield; and the Ludim that handle and bend the bow" — shows an African location for Ludim. Ezekiel 27:10 in a prophecy against Tyre "Persia and Lud, and Put (Phut) were in thine army" — indicates Lud might be in Asia or Africa. Ezekiel 30:5 in a prophecy against Egypt "Ethiopia and Put (Phut) and Lud . . . in league with thee" — indicates an African setting for Lud. This interchanging of Ludim for Lud has caused some scholars to think they are the same people. If the Ludim were a different people in Africa just what nation they were has never been established.

LUHITH (lū'-hĭth, Heb. *lûhîth*), a town of Moab located on a slope (Isa. 15:5; Jer. 48:5).

LUKE (lūk, Gr. *Loukás*). According to the oldest extant list of NT writings, known from the name of its discoverer as the Muratorian Fragment, and dating from the latter half of the second century, Luke was the writer of the Third Gospel, and the Acts of the Apostles. From the latter book his association with Paul is established. In four passages of varying length the author of Acts writes in the first person (16:10-17; 20:5-15; 21:1-18; 27:1-28: 16). These so-called "we-sections" constitute the major portion of the extant biographical material on Luke. Apart from this he is mentioned three times in the NT (Col. 4:14; Philem. 24; II Tim. 4: 11). From the first reference it is evident that Luke was a physician; from the last, that he was with Paul some time after he disappears from view at the end of the Acts of the Apostles. The context of the Colossians reference also suggests that Luke was a Gentile and a proselyte.

It appears from Luke's own writings that he was a man of education and culture. He begins his Gospel with an elaborate paragraph which shows that he could write in the sophisticated tradition of the Hellenistic historians, and then lapses into a polished vernacular. He used this speech with vigor and effectiveness. He is an accurate and able historian, and has left some of the most powerful descriptive writing in the NT. His medical knowledge and his interest in seafaring are apparent from his writings. Beyond this is tradition and conjecture. Luke was not "Lucius of Cyrene" (Acts 13: 1), for Lucas is an abbreviation of Lucanus, as Silas for Silvanus, and Annas for Annanus. There is no solid support for the conjecture that Luke was one of "the Seventy" (Luke 10:1), one of the Greeks of John 12:20, or one of the two disciples of Emmaus (Luke 24:13). More certain evidence supports other conjectures and traditions. That he knew Mary is fairly clear from the earlier chapters of his Gospel, and the period of acquaintance may have been during Paul's incarceration at Caesarea. Eusebius and Jerome say that Luke was a Syrian of Antioch, and he does seem to have a close knowledge of the Antiochene church. On the other hand certain features of the story of Paul's visit to Philippi suggest that he had an intimate knowledge of that city and no little loyalty towards it. Here, too, on two occasions, he appears to have joined Paul's party. This has given grounds for the contention that Luke was a Macedonian. Tradition and conjecture could be reconciled if Luke was an Antiochene of Macedonian origin, who had studied at the medical school of Philippi, and spent significant years in Macedonia. Luke must have been a person of singular sweetness of character to earn the apostle's adjective "beloved" (Col. 4:14). He was obviously a man of outstanding loyalty, of unusual capacity for research, and the scholar's ability to strip away the irrelevant and dispensable detail. A bare tradition states that he suffered martyrdom in Greece.　　　　　　　　　　　　　　　E.M.B.

LUKE, GOSPEL OF. 1. Authenticity. The authenticity of the Third Gospel has not been successfully challenged. References are frequent in the second century (Justin, Polycarp, Papias, Hegesippus, Marcion, Heracleon, the Clementine Homilies, Theophilus of Antioch). It is probable that Clement alludes to it (A.D. 95). It is mentioned as the work of Luke by the Muratorian Fragment (A.D. 170) and by Irenaeus (A.D. 180). Such testimony continues into the third century (Clement of Alexandria, Tertullian, Origen). Such a mass of evidence is quite decisive.

2. Date. Uncertain, but can be confined to fairly narrow limits. The abrupt termination of the *Acts of the Apostles* suggests that the author did not long survive his friend and associate, Paul. Nor is it likely to have been written after the fall of Jerusalem in A.D. 70. The period of Paul's imprisonment in Caesarea saw Luke in Palestine, and this period (conjecturally A.D. 58-59) would presumably give abundant opportunity for the research which is evident in the record. Luke's Gospel is thus the latest of the synoptic Gospels.

3. Historiography. William Mitchell Ramsay's work on the *Acts of the Apostles* has established the right of Luke to rank as a first-rate historian in his own capacity. He was demonstrated to have maintained a consistent level of accuracy wherever detail could be objectively tested, and the vividness of narration so evident in the second work is visible also in the Gospel.

4. Style. Luke's preface is in the elaborated style of such among ancient historians, and demonstrates that Luke could write with facility in the literary tradition of his time. At 1:5 he moves into the easy vernacular which he employs for his whole narrative. His language is the common dialect, but used with grace and vigor, and with an educated man's skill in composition.

5. Peculiar features. Much incident and much teaching is peculiar to Luke's Gospel: (a) The Nativity section is fresh and different, and seems to point to direct contact with Mary herself. Especially to be noted is the story of the birth of John the Baptist, and the four psalms (1:46-55; 68-79; 2:14; 2:29-32) which form a striking link between

the hymnology of the Old Testament and the New. (b) The human genealogy (3:23-38) of Christ, traced to Adam, is chosen in accordance with the cosmopolitan flavor of the Gospel, and the writer's conception of his book as the first movement of the great historical process which took the faith from Bethlehem to Rome. (c) The childhood of Jesus. The incident in the temple (2:41-52) is peculiar to Luke, and also points to the probability that Mary was the chief authority. (d) Discourses and sayings together with associated incidents, especially those contained in the unique section (9:51 to 18:14). Matthew and Mark report some of the sayings from this section in different connections. No revision, correction, or contradiction is involved, for preachers and teachers inevitably repeat their words on different occasions. Luke's Beatitudes (6: 21-23) are an illustration. In Luke they were uttered "on a plain" (6:17), and were not associated with the discourse which contained the Lord's Prayer. The latter is associated with other teaching (11:6-28) which may have been omitted by Matthew from the discourse "on the mount." Chapters 7, 9, 10 contain incidents quite peculiar to Luke (the rejection by the Samaritans, and the Seventy). The discourses of 14:25-35; 17:1-10 are similarly unique. So is the visit to Zacchaeus (19), and important parabolic teaching (see [e] below). An interesting illustration of Luke's management of an incident similarly reported in the other three Gospels is the story of the banquet in the house of Simon the Pharisee, and its associated sayings and incidents (7:36-50. Cf. Matt. 26:6-13; Mark 14:3-9; John 11:2-12:1-8). (e) Parables and illustrative anecdote peculiar to Luke merit separate listing: the two debtors (7:41-43), the good Samaritan (10:30-37), the importunate neighbor (11:5-8), the rich fool (12:16-21), the barren fig-tree (13:6-9), the lost coin and the prodigal son (15:3-32), the unrighteous steward, and the rich fool and Lazarus (16:1-12,19-31), the wicked judge, and the Pharisee and the tax-gatherer (18:2-14), the pounds (19:13-27). (f) Miracles: the draught of fish (5:1-11), the widow's son (7:11-14), the sick woman (13:11-13), the sick man (14:2-6), the ten lepers (17:12-19), the healing of Malchus in Gethsemane (22:51). (g) In the closing chapters of the Gospel, the prayer on the Cross (23: 34), the penitent thief (23:39-43), the walk to Emmaus (24:13-35), and much of the Ascension story, is peculiar to Luke.

6. Special characteristics. Apart from material content there are special characteristics of Luke's approach which should be noted: (a) As in the *Acts of the Apostles,* he exalts womanhood, an emphasis natural enough if Luke was a Macedonian. Apart from the Nativity narratives, note in this regard 7:11-17; 8:1-3,48; 10:38-42; 13:16; 23:28. Luke alone mentions Anna, and tells the intimate story of Martha and Mary (10:38-42). He alone mentions the tender phraseology of 8:48; 13:16 and 23:28. (b) It is perhaps part of the universality of Luke's conception of the Christian message that he stresses the Lord's attitude towards the poor. Note: 6:20-25; 8:2,3; 12:16-21; 14:12-15; 16:13; 18:25. (b) The same notion of a universal evangel, natural in an associate of Paul, is found as vividly in his completion of John's Isaian quotation ("and all flesh shall see the salvation of God" 3:6), as in Acts 17:27. Note in the same connection the strain of racial tolerance. The tale of the good Samaritan, and the word of praise for the grateful Samaritan leper, illustrates this, as also do the rebukes of 9:49-56. (c) Luke also gives prominence to prayer. He speaks of the Lord's prayer at His baptism, after cleansing the leper, before calling the Twelve, on the Mount of Transfiguration, on the Cross, and at death. See also 11:8; 18:1; 21:36 and the two parables 11:5-13, and 18:1-8. (d) A kindliness of judgment pervades Luke's Gospel as was proper in one who was not himself an associate of the Twelve. Note his milder version of Peter's denial. The faults of the apostles are touched with gentle hand, for Luke was, after all, writing of the leaders of the Church. Note how the conversation on the leaven of the Pharisees and the ambitious request of James and John are, for example, omitted. Similarly the disciples in the garden slept "for sorrow" (22:45), and their flight in the hour of danger is not recorded. This tact throws light on the reserve which marks the educated man. Others had a right to record such things, and properly did so. With equal propriety Luke ordered his narrative differently.

7. **Sources.** Beyond the writer's own statement (1:2) that he collected his material from eyewitnesses, it is impossible to be dogmatic. From the first words of the Gospel it is evident that Luke had both written accounts and living witnesses to draw from. In parts he would appear to have followed Mark or Mark's authorities and tradition. Mary could have supplied the Nativity stories, and the unique material on the Passion and Resurrection had apostolic authority.   E.M.B.

LUNATIC (See Diseases)

LUTE (See Musical Instruments)

LUZ (lŭz, Heb. *lûz, turning aside*). 1. A town located on the N boundary of the area of the tribe of Benjamin (Josh. 16:2; 18:13). To this place Jacob came when fleeing from home. He slept there and God appeared to him in a dream. To commemorate the occasion Jacob changed the name of the town to Bethel (house of God) (Gen. 28:19). But the place continued to be called Luz down to the time of the Judges.

The village of Lydda, with the church of St. George at left. © MPS

2. A town in the land of the Hittites built by a man from Luz in Canaan (Judg. 1:26).

LYCAONIA (lĭk'ā-ō'nĭ-à, Gr. *Lykaonía*), a district in the central plain of Asia N of the Taurus range, in early Roman days a division (or *conuentus*) of the province of Cilicia. Trajan transferred it to Galatia, but it reverted largely to Cilicia under the boundary adjustments of Antoninus Pius. Iconium, an ancient foundation rich in history, was the administrative capital. The province generally was backward, the inhabitants still speaking a native tongue in the first century A.D. In Acts 14:6 it is implied that, in passing from Iconium to Lystra, a frontier was crossed, a statement once set down as an error of the historian. W. M. Ramsay demonstrated the accuracy of the passage from local inscriptions.   E.M.B.

LYCIA (lĭsh'ĭ-à, Gr. *Lykía*), a district on the coast of the southern bulge of western Asia Minor, forming the western shore of the Gulf of Adalia. A mountainous area, Lycia successfully maintained its independence against Croesus of Lydia, and was granted a measure of independence under the Persians. The Athenians established a brief foothold there in Cimon's day (468-446 B.C.), but Lycia reverted to Persian rule. Under Alexander's successors the area was part of Syria, but the Ptolemies of Egypt exercised brief authority in the third century. After the Roman overthrow of Syria, Lycia was placed briefly under Rhodes, a situation which was bitterly resented. Freed in 169 B.C., the region enjoyed comparative independence in the imperial system until Vespasian. Even then the forms of local administration were retained (see I Macc. 15:23; Acts 21:1,2; 27:5).

LYDDA (lĭd'à, Heb. *lôdh*, Gr. *Lýdda*), or Lod, lies some 30 miles NW of Jerusalem at the mouth of the Vale of Ajalon and at the head of the valley which runs down to Joppa, an old highway called the Valley of the Smiths in recollection of ancient Philistine supremacy in iron (I Sam. 13:19). On the edge of the Maritime Plain, Lydda was of some commercial importance, "a village not less than a city" in Josephus' phrase. After the Exile, the settlements of the returning Jews reached this point before meeting the resistance of the occupants of the plain (Ezra 2:33; Neh. 7:37). Sir George Adam Smith (*Historical Geography of the Holy Land*, pp. 161, 164) demonstrates that the local cult of St. George, venerated by both Christian and Moslem, may have mythological links with the Fish-God Dragon once worshiped in this area by the Philistines. The incident of Peter and Aeneas took place at Lydda (Acts 9:32-38).

LYDIA (lĭd'ĭ-à, Gr. *Lydía*), Paul's first convert in Europe. She resided in Philippi as a seller of the purple garments for which Thyatira, her native city, was famous. She was evidently well-to-do as she owned her house and had servants. She was "one who worshipped God," meaning a proselyte. She and other women, probably also proselytes, resorted to a place by a river for prayer. She came into contact with the Gospel when Paul and his company came there and spoke to these women, and she became a believer. After she and her household had been baptized, she constrained the group to come to her home to stay, which they did (Acts 16:14,15). Her home thus became the first church in Philippi (v.40).

As Lydia was from a city in the kingdom of Lydia, and her name was the common term to denote a woman from Lydia, some scholars have suggested that her personal name was unknown, or that she may be either Euodia or Syntyche mentioned in Philippians 4:2 by Paul as women who labored with him in the Gospel.

LYRE (See Musical Instruments)

LYSANIAS (lī-sā'nĭ-ăs, Gr. *Lysanías*), tetrarch of Abilene mentioned by Luke (3:1). The tetrarchy is a small region in the Lebanon. There is no satisfactory explanation of the inclusion of this obscure non-Jewish ruler in the dating list. Epigraphical evidence frees the historian from the old allegation that he confused the tetrarch with an earlier ruler (*see Expositor's Greek Testament, ad loc.*).

LYSIAS (lĭs'ĭ-ăs, Gr. *Lysías*). Claudius Lysias, of the Jerusalem garrison, tribune by rank, was probably one of the career men of the days of Pallas and Narcissus, the powerful freedmen and executive officers of the Emperor Claudius. Lysias was a Greek, as his second name shows. His first name was assumed when he secured Roman citizenship "at a great price" (Acts 22:28), no doubt by favor of one of the venal freedmen of the court. Paul was fortunate in the officer he encountered. Lysias was a vigorous and capable soldier.

LYSTRA (lĭs'trà, Gr. *Lýstron, Lýstrois*), a Roman colony of Augustus' foundation, with an aristocratic core of citizens with franchise, a group likely to honor the similar status of Paul. The community at large was not culturally advanced. In Lystra, W. M. Ramsay discovered an inscription dedicating a statue to Zeus and Hermes, two deities who were linked in a local cult explained by Ovid (*Met.* 8:620-724).

Philemon and Baucis, the legend ran, entertained the two gods unawares with hospitality which the rest of the community churlishly withheld. Hence the identification of Paul and Barnabas with the same two deities (Latinized by Vulgate and KJV into Jupiter and Mercury). At Isauria, far away, an inscription has been found to "Zeus before the gate"; hence probably the location of the proposed ceremony mentioned in Acts 14:13. Timothy was a native of Lystra (Acts 16:1). Its ruins are near the modern village of Katyn Serai.

E.M.B.

LXX (See Septuagint)

Coins from Lystra. The one at left shows the founder of Lystra tracing the limits of the new city with bull-and-cow-drawn plow. At right, the city god of Lystra, crowned with a crescent and with ears of corn in her hand, signifying prosperity. UANT

M

MAACAH, MAACHAH (mā'à-kà, Heb. *ma'ăkhâh, oppression*). 1. Son of Nahor, brother of Abraham, by his concubine Reumah (Gen. 22:24).

2. A wife of David and the daughter of Talmai, king of Geshur; she became the mother of Absalom (II Sam. 3:3, I Chron. 3:2).

3. The father of Achish, king of Gath, in Solomon's time (I Kings 2:39).

4. The favorite wife of Rehoboam, and the mother of Abijam (II Chron. 11:20-22). She is said to be the daughter of Absalom (vs.20; I Kings 15:2), but Absalom had only one daughter, whose name was Tamar (II Sam. 14:27). The mother of Abijam, Micaiah (Maacah), is said to be the daughter of Uriel of Gibeah (II Chron. 13:2); probably she was the granddaughter of Absalom. She outlived Abijam and was queen during the reign of her grandson, Asa, until he deposed her for making an idol (I Kings 15:10,13; II Chron. 15:16).

5. A concubine of Caleb, son of Hezron (I Chron. 2:48).

6. Sister of Huppim and Shuppim and wife of Machir, the son of Manasseh (I Chron. 7:14-16).

7. Wife of Jeiel, the founder of Gibeon (I Chron. 8:29; 9:35).

8. Father of Hanan, one of David's mighty men (I Chron. 11:43).

9. Father of Shephatiah, the overseer of the tribe of Simeon in David's reign (I Chron. 27:16).

MAACHAH (mā'à-kà, Heb. *ma'ăkhâh, oppression*), a small country on the edge of the Syrian desert N of Gilead (ASV Maachah). The Ammonites hired a thousand men of the king of this nation to assist them in fighting against David. In the battle the Ammonites and their helpers were put to rout and the Syrians fled (II Sam. 10:6-14). David defeated them and they became subservient to him (II Sam. 10:18-19).

MAACHATHI, MAACHATHITES (mà-ăk'a-thī, mā-ăk'à-thīts, Heb. *ma'ăkhāthî*), the people of the nation of Maachah, residing near the Geshurites in the region of Bashan. They were in the area taken by Jair, the son of Manasseh (Deut. 3:14), situated on the border of the kingdom of Og, king of Bashan (Josh. 12:5). The half tribe of Manasseh, and the tribes of Reuben and Gad were assigned among other adjacent areas, "Gilead and the border of the Geshurites and the Maacathites, and all Mount Hermon and all Bashan" (Josh. 13:11). The Israelites did not drive out the Maacathites or Geshurites, but dwelt with them (Josh. 13:13). The grandfather of Eliphelet, one of David's mighty men, was a Maacathite (II Sam. 23:34). After the fall of Jerusalem, among the men who came to Gedaliah, the Babylonian governor at Mizpeh, was Jaazaniah, the son of a Maacathite (II Kings 25:23; Jer. 40:8). Eshtemoa, the son of Hadiah, a descendant of Judah, was a Maacathite (I Chron. 4:19). These Maacathites were descendants of the people whom the Israelites did not expel.

MAADAI (mā'à-dā'ĭ, Heb. *ma'ădhay, ornaments*), son of Bani, one of the Israelites who married foreign women (Ezra 10:34).

MAADIAH (mā-à-dī'à, Heb. *ma'adhyâh, Jehovah is ornament*), one of the chiefs of the priests who returned from exile with Zerubbabel (Neh. 12:5).

MAAI (mā-ā'ī, Heb. *mā'ay, to be compassionate*), one of the sons of the priests who blew trumpets at the dedication of the wall of Jerusalem (Neh. 12:36).

MAALEH-ACRABBIM (mā'à-lĕ-à-krab'ĭm, *ascent of Akrabbim*), a section of the area assigned to the tribe of Judah (Josh. 15:3).

MAARATH (mā'a-răth, Heb. *ma'ărāth, a place naked of trees*), one of the cities in the territory of Judah, located near Hebron (Josh. 15:59).

MAASEIAH (mā'à-sē'yà, Heb. *ma'ăsēyāhû, work of Jehovah*). 1. One of the Levites appointed to play a psaltery in praise of God while the ark was brought up to Jerusalem (I Chron. 15:18,20).
2. One of the captains of hundreds, the son of Adaiah, whom Jehoiada, the priest, took in covenant with him to resist the usurpation by Athaliah of the throne of Judah (II Chron. 23:1).
3. An officer in the army of Uzziah, king of Judah (II Chron. 26:11).
4. A son of Ahaz, king of Judah, who was killed by Zichri, a mighty man of Ephraim during a war with Israel (II Chron. 28:7).
5. The governor of Jerusalem in Josiah's reign, one of the officials whom the king put in charge of repairing the temple (II Chron. 34:8).
6. One of the priests who had married a foreign woman (Ezra 10:18).
7. A priest of the family of Harim who took a foreign wife (Ezra 10:21).
8. A priest of the family of Passhur who took a foreign wife (Ezra 10:22).
9. A man of Israel of the family of Pahath Moab who took a foreign wife (Ezra 10:30).
10. The father of Azariah, a man who worked on the wall of Jerusalem near his house (Neh. 3:23).
11. One of the men who stood on the right side of Ezra as he read the law to the people (Neh. 8:4).
12. One of the men who explained the law to the people (Neh. 8:7).
13. One of the chiefs of the people who sealed the covenant with Nehemiah (Neh. 10:25). May be the same as No. 12.
14. One of the descendants of the son of Baruch of Perez who dwelt in Jerusalem (Neh. 11:5).
15. A Benjamite whose descendants dwelt in Jerusalem (Neh. 11:7).
16. A priest, one of those who blew a trumpet at the dedication of the wall of Jerusalem (Neh. 12:41).
17. Another priest who took part in this dedication of the wall (Neh. 12:42).
18. A priest whose son Zephaniah was one of the two men whom Zedekiah, king of Judah, sent to Jeremiah to ask him to inquire of the Lord for him (Jer. 21:1; 37:3).
19. The father of Zedekiah, a false prophet whom Jeremiah condemned (Jer. 29:21).
20. The keeper of the threshold of the temple in Jeremiah's time (Jer. 35:4).
21. An ancestor of Baruch (Jer. 32:12). ASV has Mahseiah.

MAASIAI (mā-às'ĭ-ī, Heb. *ma'say, work of Jehovah*), a priestly family which dwelt in Jerusalem after returning from exile (I Chron. 9:12).

MAATH (mā'āth, Gr. *Maáth, to be small*), an ancestor of Christ (Luke 3:26).

MAAZ (mā'ăz, Heb. *ma'ats, wrath*), son of Ram, the first born son of Jerahmeel (I Chron. 2:27).

MAAZIAH (mā-à-zī'à, Heb. *ma'azyâhû, consolation of Jehovah*). 1. A priest of the 24 sons of Eleazar and Ithamar, sons of Aaron, to whom was assigned the 24th lot to serve in the tabernacle (I Chron. 24:18).
2. A priest who sealed the covenant with Nehemiah (Neh. 10:8).

MACCABEES (măk'à-bēs, Gr. *Makkabaíai*), the name given to a Jewish family of Modin in the Shephelah, who initiated the Jewish revolt against the Hellenizing policy which the Seleucid Syrian king, Antiochus Epiphanes, was unwisely endeavoring to force through in Palestine.

The story is told in the two books of the Maccabees in the Apocrypha. The rising began in 168 B.C., when Mattathias, an aged priest, struck down a royal commissioner and an apostate Jew, who were about to offer heathen sacrifice in the town. Mattathias leveled the altar, and fled to the hills with his sons. To his standard rallied the Chasidim ('the Pious,' Gk. *Hasidaeans*). The old priest died after a few months of guerrilla warfare, and the same early fighting claimed two of his sons, Eleazar and John. The remaining three sons, Judas, Jonathan, and Simon, succeeded in turn to the leadership of the insurrection, and all left a deep mark on Jewish history.

Judas won the name of Maccabee, or "the Hammerer," and he was the only member of the family to whom the term was applied in the Apocrypha. It was later history which used it as a surname for all three brothers. Judas was a fine soldier and patriot, with a clear policy of Jewish independence and religious reconstruction. Raising and organizing a fighting force of Galileans, Judas

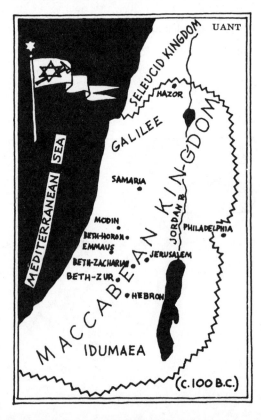

(C. 100 B.C.)

defeated major military expeditions sent against him in 166 and 165 B.C. In December of the latter year, Judas formally cleansed the temple of Syrian pollution and celebrated the occasion with a great festival. This festival became a permanent fixture, falling on December 25, and lasting eight days (I Macc. 4:52-59; II Macc. 10:6; John 10:22).

For the next 18 months, Judas campaigned E of Jordan, while Simon, his brother, collected the Jews who were scattered through Galilee into the comparative safety of Judaea. Judas at this point lost some of the support of the Chasidim, whose ambitions were largely fulfilled by the re-establishment of the temple services. Religious division, the perennial problem of all the Jewish struggles for independence, was thus responsible for a weakening of Judas' hand. Lysias, the Syrian general, whom Judas had signally defeated at Bethzur in the autumn of 165 B.C., gained his revenge at Beth-zacharias. Judas was routed, and the Syrian garrison still holding out in the citadel of Jerusalem was relieved. Lysias was in control of Syria during the brief reign of the minor, Antiochus Eupator, who succeeded Epiphanes in 163 B.C., and he was sensible enough to abandon Epiphanes' attack upon the religion of the Jews, for the much more effective political policy of patronage. He set up a puppet high-priest, Alcimus, who was accepted by the Chasidim. Judas was thus isolated, but on Lysias' withdrawal, marched against Alcimus. Demetrius I, who succeeded Eupator in 162 B.C., an able and decisive ruler, sent a force under Nicanor to put down this new rebellion. Defeated by Judas, Nicanor retired to Jerusalem, but foolishly drove "the Pious" into renewed support of the Maccabee by threatening reprisals against the temple. With the country again behind him, Judas defeated the Syrians at Adasa. Judas was now in control of the land, and negotiated a treaty with Rome, in the terms of which Rome ordered Demetrius I to withdraw from Palestine. Judas' move was a shrewd one, for since the Peace of Apamea (188 B.C.) Syria existed by Rome's sufferance, and Demetrius had spent his youth as a hostage in Rome. Time was against Judas, for ere the Senate's prohibition was delivered to the king, Judas was defeated and killed by the general Bacchides at Elasa (I Macc. 3-9:22). The international policy, illustrated by the approach to Rome, had again alienated the fickle Chasidim, and the withdrawal of support fatally weakened Judas' power of resistance, and led directly to his military defeat.

Jonathan succeeded his brother in 161 B.C., and the Maccabaean revolt reverted to the guerrilla warfare with which it had begun. Dynastic troubles in Syria, however played into Jonathan's hands. Alexander Balas, supported by Pergamum and Egypt, aspired to the Syrian throne, and both Demetrius and Alexander thought it expedient to secure the support of so determined a fighter as the second Maccabee. Demetrius offered the control of all military forces in Palestine, and the governorship of Jerusalem. Alexander added an offer of the high-priesthood. Jonathan chose Alexander, and thus became the founder of the Hasmonaean priesthood. By skilful support of Demetrius II, who dethroned Alexander, Jonathan maintained and strengthened his position. The difficulties of the later Seleucid empire served his purposes well. Jonathan was even able to extend his power over the maritime plain, to fortify Jerusalem and other strong-points in Judaea, and to enter into treaty relationships with Rome. An army revolt in 143

Remains of the Tombs of the Maccabees at Modin. © MPS

B.C. unseated Demetrius II, and the young son of Alexander was enthroned as Antiochus VI. Power was in the hands of the generals, one of whom, Tryphon, laid hold of Jonathan by treachery, and executed him (I Macc. 9:23-12:54).

Simon, the third brother, inherited this critical situation. Simon was an able diplomat, who carried on his brother's policy of profiting with some success by Syria's internal troubles. In 143 and 142 B.C. he succeeded in establishing the virtual political independence of Judaea. In 141 B.C., at a great assembly of princes, priests, and elders of the land, Simon was elected to be high-priest, military commander, and civil governor of the Jews, "for ever until there should arise a faithful prophet." The high-priesthood was thus rendered hereditary in the family of Simon. Simon re-established the treaty with Rome, which had proved a useful diplomatic advantage over Syria, which Rome watched with some care, and was not sorry to see embarrassed by her petty imperialism. Simon was murdered by his son-in-law at a banquet (I Macc. 13-16:16). His son, the celebrated John Hyrcanus, succeeded him, and held the inherited authority for 30 years before passing it on to his son Aristobulus, who assumed the royal title. The Hasmonaeans continued their dynasty till 34 B.C. when Herod and the Romans put down Antigonus, the last of Mattathias' line, but the Maccabees proper ended with Simon in 134 B.C.

The story as above outlined is told in two independent narratives written by authors of different emphases and abilities, the First and Second Books of the Maccabees. The first book is an honest piece of historical writing, detailing without adornment the events of a stirring struggle for freedom. The second book covers much of the same material, but slants the account in the direction of religious instruction and admonition. "By way of briefly characterizing the two authors of I and II Maccabees," writes Bruce M. Metzger, "it may be said that the former was a sober historian who wished to glorify Israel and its heroic Maccabaean leaders and that the latter was a moralizing theologian who wished to emphasize the immeasurable superiority of Judaism over heathenism." (*An Introduction to the Apocrypha*, p. 130). E.M.B.

MACEDONIA (măs'ē-dō'nĭ-à, Gr. *Makedonía*), the term is of varied import. Lying geographically between the Balkan highlands and the Greek peninsula, Macedonia was both a Greek kingdom and a Roman province. The kingdom, in its early centuries, occupied a quadrangle of territory which formed only the eastern half of the Roman provincial unit. The province extended from the Aegean to the Adriatic, with Illyricum to the NW, Thrace to the NE, and Achaea to the S. Culturally, Macedonia came under strong Athenian influence in the latter years of the fifth century before Christ, and in the first half of the fourth century, the period between Euripides, who emigrated to Macedonia in 408 or 407 B.C., and Aristotle, who came to Macedonia as tutor to Alexander in 343 or 342, after the death of Plato. The population was Indo-European, but of mixed tribal elements, of which the Dorian stock was probably a strong ingredient.

The history of the early kingdom is confused, and the tradition that Perdiccas I conquered the Macedonian plain in 640 B.C. probably marks the emergence of one dominant clan among an agglomeration of mountain tribes striving for the mastery of a significant area on an ancient invasion route. Until the reign of Philip II (359 to 336 B.C.), the kingdom was insignificant in Aegean history, and preoccupied with the continual tension of tribal war. By consolidation, conquest, pacification, and an enlightened policy of the Hellenization, carried out with the speed, precision, ruthlessness, and clear-headed determination which marked the man, Philip unified Macedonia, and finally conquered all Greece. The orations of Demosthenes, directed against the Macedonian menace, are poignant documents of this day of Athens' democratic decadence, and the upsurge of Macedonian power which was to extend Greek rule to the east. It was the army created by Philip which followed Alexander, his son, to the Ganges, and overthrew the Persian Empire.

The history of Macedonia from Hellenistic times to the Roman conquest and annexation (167 B.C.)

Entrance to the mosque over the Cave of Machpelah, at Hebron. © MPS

is undistinguished. Macedonia was the first part of Europe to receive Christianity (Phil. 4:15). The "man from Macedonia" of Paul's dream may have been Luke, who, if not a native of Philippi in Macedonia, was certainly long resident there (Acts 16:9ff). Paul was more than once in the province (Acts 19:21; 20:1-3; I Cor. 16:5; II Cor. 1:16). Macedonians were close to the Apostle; for example, Gaius and Aristarchus, Secundus, Sopater, and Epaphroditus (Acts 17:11; 20:4; Phil. 4:10-19; I Thess. 2:8,17-20; 3:10). The church in Macedonia was noted for its women leaders, a situation which reflects the wide emancipation of Macedonian women.   E.M.B.

MACHAERUS (mă-kē'rŭs, Gr. *Machairoús*), Herod's southernmost stronghold E of the Dead Sea, built by Alexander Janneus (90 B.C.?) (Jos. *Ant.* 14.5.2). "The second citadel of Judaea" (Plin. H.N. 5.16). The fort was on the border of Peraea, the tetrarchy of Herod Antipas. To the S lay the domains of Aretas, Herod's father-in-law, King of the Nabataeans. When Herod intrigued to replace the daughter of Aretas by Herodias, the former escaped from Machaerus to her father in the Arnon Valley, 12 miles to the S. In the subsequent troubles Herod occupied Machaerus with Herodias and Salome, and here John the Baptist died (Matt. 14:3ff). In the Great Rebellion Jewish zealots were starved out of Machaerus by the Romans and the fort was razed.   E.M.B.

MACHBANAI (măk'bà-nī, Heb. *makhbannay, clad with a cloak*), a Gadite who joined David's forces at Ziklag (I Chron. 12:13).

MACHBENAH (măk-bē'nà, Heb. *makhbēnâh, bond*), name of a place in Judah which occurs in the genealogical list of Caleb. It is from the same root as Cabban (I Chron. 2:49). ASV Machbena.

MACHI (mā'kī, Heb. *mākhî*), the father of Geuel, appointed from the tribe of Gad to be one of those who spied out the Promised Land (Num. 13:15).

MACHIR (mā'kĭr, Heb. *mākhîr, sold*). 1. The eldest son of Manasseh, son of Joseph. He married and had a family before the Israelites left Egypt (Gen. 50:23). By the time of the dividing up of the Promised Land, his descendants, the Machirites, were numerous and powerful. They conquered Gilead and settled there (Num. 32:39,40), except the family of Hepher which settled in Canaan (Josh. 17:3). So Machir is called the father of Gilead several times, and he is even said to have begotten Gilead (Num. 26:29. In Judges 5:14 Machir stands for Manasseh.

2. The son of Ammiel. David took Mephibosheth out of his house (II Sam. 9:4,5). This Machir was one of the men who brought refreshments to David as he fled from Absalom (II Sam. 17:27).

MACHNADEBAI (măk-năd'ē-bī), one of the men who married a foreign wife (Ezra 10:40).

MACHPELAH (măk-pē'là, Heb. *makhpēlâh, a doubling*), a field near Hebron which Abraham purchased from Ephron the Hittite for 400 shekels of silver in order to use a cave in it as a place of burial for Sarah (Gen. 23:19-20). Abraham (Gen. 25:9), Isaac, Rebekah, Leah, and Jacob (Gen. 50:13) were also buried there (Gen. 49:31). Its name may mean it was a double cave. A Moslem mosque stands over the cave of Machpelah today, and entrance into it is forbidden.

MADAI (măd'ā-ī, Heb. *mādhay, Media*), a people descended from Japheth (Gen. 10:2; I Chron. 1:5). They occupied the same area which Persia, modern Iran, does today. They were called the Medes.

MADIAN (See Midian)

MADMANNAH (măd-măn′-nà, Heb. *madhmannâh, dunghill*). 1. A town in southern Judah located about eight miles S of Kirjath-sepher (Josh. 15:31).

2. Grandson of Caleb (I Chron. 2:48,49).

MADMENAH (măd-mē′-nà, Heb. *madhmēnâh, dunghill*), a town in the tribe of Benjamin, evidently a little N of Jerusalem, but its location is uncertain (Isa. 10:31).

MADON (mā′dŏn, Heb. *mādhôn, contention*), a royal city of the Canaanites, whose king Jobab was defeated by Joshua (Josh. 11:1; 12:19). It was located near modern Hattin, about five miles E of the Sea of Galilee.

MAGBISH (măg′bĭsh, Heb. *maghbîsh, congregating*), name of either a man, the head of a family of which 156 persons returned with Zerubbabel from exile, or of a place to which these people belonged. The list contains names of both towns and persons (Ezra 2:30). It is listed in some atlases as a town, location unknown.

MAGDALA (măg′dà-là, Gr. *Magdalá*), a town on the NW shore of the Sea of Galilee, three miles N of Tiberias named only in the KJV rendering of Matthew 15:39. (ASV has more correct Magadan; Mark 8:10 the alternative Dalmanutha). It is identified mainly by the modern village of El Mejdel. Magdala may be Taricheae (Sir George Adam Smith, *Historical Geography of the Holy Land*, pp. 452, 453), one of the lost fishing towns of the lake. The town was the home or birthplace of Mary Magdalene.

MAGDALEN, MAGDALENE (See Mary)

MAGDIEL (mag′dĭ-ĕl, Heb. *maghdî'ēl, God is noble*), one of the chiefs of Edom (Gen. 36:43; I Chron. 1:54).

MAGI (mā′jī, Gr. *mágoi*). The magi were originally a religious caste among the Persians. Their devotion to astrology, divination, and the interpretation of dreams led to an extension in the meaning of the word, and by the first century the terms "magi" and "Chaldaean" were applied generally to fortune tellers and the exponents of esoteric religious cults throughout the Mediterranean world. Magus is, for example, the epithet of the charlatan Simon of Acts 8:9. The term is translated "sorcerer" in Acts 13:6,8. "The wise men from the east" of the Nativity story (Matt. 2) are often referred to as "the Magi." Nothing is known of their land of origin, but it is a likely theory that they came from Arabia Felix (Southern Arabia). Astrology was practiced there, and a tradition of Israelite Messianic expectation may have survived in the region since the days of the Queen of Sheba. Much early legend connects Southern Arabia with Solomon's Israel. Ancient report, linked to later astrological study, may have prompted the famous journey. This, of course, can be no more than speculation. The legend of "the Three Kings" is late and medieval. The old Arabian caravan routes enter Palestine "from the East." E.M.B.

MAGIC. Originally the word meant the science or art of the Magi, the Persian priestly caste, who, like the Levites, were devoted to the practice of religion. With the wide extension of the term "magus," the word magic, too, acquired broader significance. It came to mean all occult rituals or processes designed to influence or control the course of nature, to dominate men or circumstances by the alliance, aid, or use of supernatural powers, and generally to tap and to employ the forces of an unseen world. Divination, the art of

The village of Magdala and surrounding plain on the west coast of the Sea of Galilee. © MPS

forecasting the future with a view to avoiding its perils and pitfalls, might be included under the same classification. Its methods were frequently "magic." In lands ethnologically stratified, magic was often associated with the religion of a conquered or depressed class, or with imported faiths. Hence the frequency with which magic is found in the hands of foreign elements, and is secret in its practice and frequently under official ban as anti-social and illicit. Hence the stern prohibitions of the Bible against all forms of "wizardry" and "sorcery" (Exod. 22:18; Lev. 19:26; 20:27; Deut. 18:10,11). Hence, too, the security precautions surrounding the royal visit to "the witch of Endor" (II Sam. 28:7 *seq.*).

It was part of the advanced wisdom of the Mosaic code to show that active faith in a worthy deity, moral responsibility, and true religion, were not promoted by superstition and the practice of the occult, while genuine prophecy (in the wider sense of that word) was vitiated by such perversion. It was also realized that magic arts were part of the surrounding paganism from which it is the first preoccupation of the Old Testament to separate the Hebrew race. Magic, too, was widely

The well of the Magi on the Bethlehem-Jerusalem road. © MPS

practiced in Egypt (Exod. 7:11; 8:7,18,19; 9:11), and in Babylon (Dan. 1:20; 2:2). In both empires the craft and ritual of magic long antedated the Persian religious caste whose practices provided the later name. None the less, both before and after Moses, the intrusion of such unhealthy beliefs may be detected in Hebrew history. The incident of the mandrakes found by Reuben (Gen. 30:14) is a clear example, and perhaps, too, the obscure incident of Jacob's trickery with the rods "pilled with white strakes" at the water-hole (Gen. 30:37). It is not claimed in the record that the magic manipulation was the prime cause of the result. It is fairly evident that Jacob's empirical knowledge of animal genetics was determining the breeding trend, but he was remote from the lofty monotheism of his family, and the Euphrates valley towns were devoted to magic, hence the "teraphim" later in the story (Gen. 31:19. See also Judg. 17: 5; I Sam. 19:13; Ezek. 21:21-26; Zech. 10:2). These were household deities, crudely carved, like the Roman Lares and Penates. In popular religion their worship was a base addition to, or substitute for the worship of Jehovah. Similar in concept was the cult of the "baals" of the fields, whose corrupt worship in fertility rituals and sympathetic magic was fiercely castigated by the prophets for the obscene thing it was. In every revival of pure worship the teraphim were swept away with other forms of vicious paganism (e.g. II Kings 23:24).

References to magic practices are also found in the New Testament. The reference to the heathens' "vain repetitions" (Matt. 6:7; for example see I Kings 18:26 and Acts 19:28) may allude to the belief in the magic repetition of set formulae such as the Tibetan's meaningless *"om mani padme hum"* ("Hail to the jewel in the lotus flower"). Simon (Acts 8:9) and Elymas (Acts 13: 8) are spoken of as practicing "curious arts." There is evidence that this tribe of charlatans was widespread, and often in origin Jewish (e.g. "the Sons of Sceva" in Ephesus, Acts 19:14). The Emperor Tiberius had given much encouragement to "the Chaldaeans and soothsayers" by his belief in magic. Juvenal pictures the old prince in retirement on Capri "with his wizard mob" (*cum grege Chaldaeo*. Juv. 10.94). The Senate, indeed, had more than once banished them, but a Roman weakness for the caster of horoscopes and the purveyors of superstition always ensured the return of the magicians, whom Tacitus bitterly describes as "a tribe faithless to the powerful, deceitful to those who hope, which will ever be banned among us — and ever tolerated" (*Hist.* 1:22). Sergius Paulus, the governor of Cyprus, seems to have held his Jewish soothsayer with a light hand, and to have been quite convinced by the apostle's exposure of him. The story of the first Christian impact on the city of Ephesus reveals the tremendous influence of magic among the populace at large. With the spread of Christian doctrine, those who practiced "curious arts" brought their books of incantations of magic formulae to burn. The estimated price was "fifty thousand pieces of silver." The reference is probably to the silver denarius, one of which was the standard wage for a day's labor in the Palestine of the Gospels. The early Church, in general, did not dismiss magic as a delusion, but attributed its results to the work of malign and evil beings who were without power against a Christian. The Council of Ancyra (A.D. 315) first legislated against magic.   E.M.B.

MAGICIANS (See Magic)

MAGISTRATE (măj'ĭs-trāt, Heb. *shephat, judge*, Gr. *árchon, ruler, strategós, commander*). The word *shephat* is found only once (Ezra 7:25) when it is translated "magistrates." The term *archon* is only once rendered magistrate (Luke 12:58). The word *strategós* is translated "magistrates" five times (Acts 16:20,22,35,36,38), where it denotes the rulers of the city of Philippi, a Roman colony. These authorities were called *praetors* in Latin. They were the highest officials in the government of a colony and had the power of administration of justice in less important cases.

MAGNIFICAT (măg-nĭf'ĭ-kăt), the song of praise by Mary recorded in Luke 1:46-55. This name comes from its first word in the Vulgate version, *Magnificat mea anima* (my soul doth magnify). Mary spoke this song in response to the assurance from Elizabeth that God would surely fulfill the words of the Angel Gabriel that she would be the woman chosen to bring the Son of God into the world. The song resembles closely the poetry of the Old Testament; its similarity to Hannah's prayer in I Samuel 2:1-10 is very striking. There can be no doubt that Mary said these words; all the Greek manuscripts ascribe it to her, but three Latin manuscripts read Elizabeth instead of Mary in verse 46.

MAGOG (mā'gŏg, Heb. *māghôgh, land of Gog?*), a son of Japheth (Gen. 10:2; I Chron. 1:5); Josephus and Greek writers generally applied this name to the Scythians. Modern Christian writers indicate the Tartars of Russia and of southern Europe. The names of King Gog, "prince of Rosh, Meshech and Tubal" (Ezek. 38:2), resemble the modern Russia, Moscow, and Tobolsk. "The nations which are in the four corners of the earth, Gog and Magog" (Rev. 20:8) means all the ungodly nations of the earth who oppose the people of God.

MAGOR-MISSABIB (mā'gôr-mĭs'à-bĭb, *terror on every side*), the symbolic name which Jeremiah gave to Pashhur, the son of the priest Immer, who struck him (Jer. 20:3).

MAGPIASH (măg'pĭ-ăsh, Heb. *magpi'osh, moth killer*), a chief who sealed the covenant with Nehemiah (Neh. 10:20).

MAGUS, SIMON (See Simon)

MAHALAH (mà-hā'là, Heb. *mahlâh, disease*), a child, sex uncertain, probably a son, of Hammolecheth, sister of Machir, son of Manasseh (I Chron. 7:18). ASV Mahlah.

MAHALALEEL (mà-hā'là-lē'ĕl, Heb. *mahălal'ēl, praise of God*), the son of Kenan, who lived 895 years, and was the father of Jared (Gen. 5:12,13, 15,16,17; I Chron. 1:2; Luke 3:37). ASV Mahalalel.

MAHALATH (mā'hà-lăth, Heb. *mahălath, sickness*). 1. A daughter of Ishmael whom Esau took for his third wife (Gen. 28:9).

2. The first wife of Rehoboam; she was a granddaughter of David (II Chron. 11:18).

3. Musical term in the heading of Psalm 53 and 88.

MAHALI (mā'hà-lī, Heb. *mahlî, sick*), son of Merari, son of Levi (Exod. 6:19).

MAHANAIM (mā'hà-nā'ĭm, Heb. *mahănayim, two hosts*), a town so named by Jacob when he was met there by angels as he was returning from Padan-aram to Canaan (Gen. 32:2). This town was appointed a city of refuge, and was assigned to the Levites (Josh. 21:38; I Chron. 6:80). It was situated in Gilead E of the Jordan, on the boundary between Gad and Manasseh (Josh. 13: 26,30). After the death of Saul, Mahanaim was made the capital of Israel for a short time (II Sam. 2:8).

David, fleeing from Absalom, came to this place (II Sam. 19:32). Solomon's officer, Abinadab, was stationed in this city (I Kings 4:14).

Mahanaim is mentioned in an Egyptian inscription as one of the cities conquered by Sheshonk I (Shishak of the Bible). This occurred on his raid into Palestine mentioned in I Kings 14:25,26; II Chronicles 12:2,3. The exact location of Mahanaim has been much discussed, but still remains uncertain.

Song of Solomon 6:13 ASV refers to a dance called Mahanaim (in margin, "of two companies," KJV "of two armies"). James B. Pritchard, edit., *Ancient Near Eastern Texts Relating to the Old Testament*, Princeton University Press, 1950, p. 243. C.E.H.

MAHANEH-DAN (mā'hà-ně-dǎn, Heb. *mahănēh-dhān, camp of Dan*). 1. A place where Samson grew up and first began to be moved by the Spirit of Jehovah. It was situated between Zorah and Eshtaol (Judg. 13:25 KJV).
2. A place behind Kiriath-jearim where 600 men of war of the tribe of Dan encamped on their way to conquer Laish (Judg. 18:12). These both may be the same place though they seem to be several miles apart.

MAHARAI (mà-hăr'ā-ī, Heb. *mahăray, impetuous*), one of David's mighty men (II Sam. 23:28; I Chron. 11:30). He was the captain over 24,000 men to serve the king during the tenth month of the year. He was a Zerahite living in Netoph (I Chron. 27:13).

MAHATH (mā'hăth, Heb. *mahath, seizing*). 1. A Kohathite, an ancestor of Heman the singer (I Chron. 6:35).
2. One of the Levites who cleansed the temple in Hezekiah's reign (II Chron. 29:12). He was appointed one of the overseers of the dedicated things (II Chron. 31:13).

MAHAVITE (mā'hà-vīt, Heb. *mahăwĭm*), the family name of Eliel, one of David's warriors (I Chron. 11:46).

MAHAZIOTH (mà-hā'zĭ-ŏth, Heb. *mahăzî'ôth, visions*), a son of Heman who praised God in the temple in song and with instruments (I Chron. 25:4). He was given the 23rd lot to serve in song (I Chron. 25:30).

MAHER-SHALAL-HASH-BAZ (mā'hēr-shăl'ăl-hăsh'băz, *the spoil speeds, the prey hastens*). This phrase was written down by Isaiah and officially recorded as a witness by God's direction. Later when the prophet's second son was born the Lord told Isaiah to give him this phrase as a name. It was a sign that Samaria would be carried away before the child would be old enough to talk (Isa. 8:1,3).

MAHLAH (mà'là, Heb. *mahlâh, disease*). 1. Eldest daughter of Zelophehad of the tribe of Manasseh. This man had no sons but seven daughters, who obtained permission to inherit land as if they were sons, provided they married within the tribe (Num. 26:33; 27:1ff; Chapter 36; Josh. 17:3ff).
2. Daughter of Hammolocheth, the sister of Machir, son of Manasseh (I Chron. 7:18).

MAHLI (màh'lī, Heb. *mahlî, sick*). 1. Son of Merari, son of Levi, ancestor of the Mahlites (Exod. 6:19 KJV, Mahli; Num. 3:20; Ezra 8:18).
2. Son of Mushi (I Chron. 6:47; 23:23; 24:30).

MAHLITE (màh'līt, Heb. *mahlî*), a descendant of Mahli, son of Merari (Num. 3:33; 26:58). There was one case among them of a family of daughters marrying cousins (I Chron. 23:22).

MAHLON (mà'lŏn, Heb. *mahlôn, sick*), son of Elimelech. Married Ruth in Moab, leaving her a widow about ten years later (Ruth 1:2,5; 4:9,10).

MAHOL (mā'hŏl, Heb. *māhôl, dance*), father of Calcol and Darda, men famous for their wisdom, but not as wise as Solomon (I Kings 4:31).

MAID, MAIDEN. 1. Heb. *'āmâh, handmaiden, or female slave*, the property of her owners (Exod. 2:5; 21:20,26), and often a bondmaid (Lev. 25:44).
2. Heb. *bethûlâh, virgin*, a girl secluded and separated from intercourse with men. Often used with this meaning (Exod. 22:16; Judg. 19:24; Ps. 78:63; 148:12).
3. Heb. *na'ărâh, girl, maiden* (Exod. 2:5; Ruth 2:8,22,23; 3:2 and often).
4. Heb. *'almâh*, a girl of marriageable age, occurs only seven times (Gen. 24:43; Exod. 2:8; Ps. 68:25; S. of Sol. 1:3; 6:8; Prov. 30:19; Isa. 7:14).
5. Heb. *shiphhâh*, maid servant, a synonym of *āmâh*, maid (Gen. 16:2,3,5,6,8; 29:24,29; 30:9,10, 12,18, etc.). bondmaid (Lev. 19:20), bond woman (Deut. 26:68; II Chron. 28:10; Esth. 7:4), hand maid (Gen. 16:1; 25:12; 29:24,29 and often, maid servant (Gen. 12:16; 24:35; 30:43, etc.).

MAIL, COAT OF (See Armor)

MAIMED (See Diseases)

MAKAZ (mā'kăz, Heb. *māqats*), a town near Beth Shemesh where Solomon's supply officer, Bendeker, was stationed (I Kings 4:9).

MAKHELOTH (măk-hē'lŏth, Heb. *maqhēlōth*), a station where Israel encamped in the wilderness (Num. 33:25,26).

MAKKEDAH (măk-kē'dà, Heb. *maqqēdhâh, a place of shepherds*), a town near Libnah and Azekah conquered by Joshua. Five kings hid in a cave in this town and were killed and buried there (Josh. 10:16ff). The city was assigned to Judah (Josh. 15:41).

MAKTESH (măk'tēsh, Heb. *makhtēsh, mortar or hollow place resembling a mortar*), occurs only once and is left untranslated as the name of a place; location unknown (Zeph. 1:11).

MALACHI (măl'à-kī, Heb. *mal'ākhî, messenger of Jehovah* or *my messenger*), the name given to the last book of the OT, and it is also probably the name of the prophet whose oracles the book contains. The book's title reads: "The burden ('oracle' RSV) of the word of the Lord to Israel by Malachi" (1:1). Thus it would seem that the prophet's name was Malachi. *Malachi* is the Hebrew expression meaning "my messenger" and it is so translated in 3:1, where there is an obvious pun on the author's name. For this reason, some have supposed Malachi to be a title for the prophet, not his proper name. But since the prophetic books of the OT always begin with the stating of the prophet's name, it seems more likely that here, too, the name of the prophet is given. It is not unusual to have puns on the names of real people (Ezek. 3:8,9). Nothing more is known about the author of this book.

The book of Malachi is believed to be one of the latest of the OT books. Since no statement as to its date is made in the book, one must seek to determine this by the nature of its contents. It is clearly post-Exilic. The temple had been completed and sacrifices were being offered (1:7-10; 3:8). A Persian governor (the word for governor in 1:8 is a borrowed word, used for the Persian governors in Palestine in post-Exilic times) was ruling in Jerusalem. This indicates a date later than that of Haggai and Zechariah.

It is also clear that the early zeal for the rebuilding of the temple has now died out, and a situation of moral and religious declension has set in. The mixed marriages (2:10-12), failure to pay tithes (3:8-10) and offering of blemished sacrifices (1:6-14) are conditions not unlike those referred to in the times of Ezra and Nehemiah (Ezra 7-Neh. 13) and it would seem that Malachi's prophecy was given at about that time, or possibly shortly thereafter — about the middle or end of the fifth century B.C.

There are two principal themes in the book: 1) The sin and apostasy of the people of Israel, emphasized in chaps. 1,2; 2) The judgment that will come upon the faithless and the blessing in store for those who repent, predominating in chaps. 3,4. A more detailed analysis follows.

1. Title, 1:1.

2. An argument for the love of God towards Israel as shown in the contrasted experiences of Edom and Israel, 1:2-5.

3. A protest against the negligence of the priests in worship, 1:6-2:9.

4. A condemnation of those who divorce their wives and marry foreign women, 2:10-16.

5. An answer to those who complain that God is indifferent to injustice: a day of judgment is at hand, 2:17-3:5.

6. A rebuke for the neglect of tithes and offerings, 3:6-12.

7. A reply to doubters, and a promise to the faithful, 3:13-4:3.

8. A recall to the law and a prophecy of the coming of Elijah, 4:4-6.

Certain features are unique in this book:

1. The use of the rhetorical question and answer as a method of communication. This device begins most of the eight sections referred to above. It anticipates the later catechetical method of teaching.

2. Malachi contains prophetic and priestly interests. It has been called "Prophecy within the law." Generally the prophets exhibit little interest in sacrifices and ceremonial laws, preferring to stress the more inward aspects of religious life. Malachi, however, sees the people's apostasy manifested by their carelessness in the sacrificial offerings (1:6-14), the priests' neglect of their duties (2:1-9), and the failure of the people to pay their tithes and other offerings (3:7-12). This book is thus an antidote to the view commonly held today that the prophets did not believe in the necessity of the ritual law. They accepted the sacrificial system, but frequently protested against its abuse due to the people's failure to apprehend the necessity of inward faith and outward moral righteousness in addition to ritual cleanness.

3. The growing OT Messianic expectation is witnessed to in the announcement of God's "messenger of the covenant" by whose coming Israel will be purified and judged (3:1-5; cf. Matt. 11: 10), and of the Prophet Elijah who will announce the day of the Lord (4:5,6; cf. Matt. 17:9-13).

J.B.G.

MALCHAM, MALCAM (măl'kăm, Heb. *malkām*), in Zephaniah 1:5 supposed to refer to Milcom, an idol of the Moabites and Ammonites. But the same form in Amos 1:15 is translated *their king*. In Jeremiah 49:1 (ASV) it may also mean "their king," but in vs. 3 it means the idol.

MALCHIAH, MALCHIJAH (măl-kī'à, măl-kī'jà, Heb. *malkîyâh* [Jer. 38:6 only *malkîâ*] *my king is Jehovah*). 1. A Gershonite, the ancestor of Asaph the singer in David's time (I Chron. 6:40).

2. An ancestor of the priest Adaiah who returned from exile and lived in Jerusalem (I Chron. 9:12; Neh. 11:12).

3. A priest of David's time to whom was assigned the fifth lot of service (I Chron. 24:9).

4. An Israelite in the family of Parosh who had married a foreign woman (Ezra 10:25).

5. Another in the same family who did the same (Ezra 10:25).

6. A member of the family of Harin who was guilty of the same practice (Ezra 10:31).

7. A son of Harim who worked on the wall (Neh. 3:11), possibly the same as No. 6.

8. The son of Rechab, who repaired the dung gate of the wall (Neh. 3:14).

9. A goldsmith who worked on the wall (Neh. 3:31).

10. One of the men who stood on the left side of Ezra as he read the law to the people (Neh. 8:4).

11. One of those who sealed the covenant with Nehemiah (Neh. 10:3).

12. A priest who took part in the dedication of the wall (Neh. 12:42). May be same as No. 11.

13. Father of Pashur, messenger of the King Zedekiah to Jeremiah (Jer. 21:1) and who helped arrest the prophet (Jer. 38:1).

14. The son of King Zedekiah, and the owner of the dungeon into which Jeremiah was put (Jer. 38:6).

MALCHIEL (măl'kĭ-ĕl, Heb. *malkî'êl, God is my king*), son of Beriah, son of Asher (Gen. 46:17; Num. 26:45; I Chron. 7:31).

MALCHIJAH (See Malchiah)

MALCHIRAM (măl-kī'răm, Heb. *malkîrām, my king is high*), son of Jeconiah (I Chron. 3:18).

MALCHI-SHUA (măl-kĭ-shōō'à, Heb. *malkîshûa', king of aid*), third son of King Saul (I Sam. 14: 49; 31:2 [KJV Melchi-shua]; I Chron. 8:33; 9:39), killed by the Philistines (I Sam. 31:2; I Chron. 10:2).

MALCHUS (măl'kŭs, Gr. *Málchos*), a servant of the high priest whose ear Peter cut off with a sword during Christ's arrest (John 18:10).

MALEFACTOR (măl'ĕ-făk'têr, Gr. *kakopoiós, evil doer*), the term by which the Jewish leaders described Christ to Pilate (John 18:30). (ASV has "evil doer" here). *Kakoúrgos, malefactor,* the designation of the two thieves who were crucified with Christ (Luke 23:32,33,39).

MALELEEL (See Mahaleel)

MALLOTHI (măl'ō-thī, Heb. *mallôthî, I have uttered*), one of the sons of Heman, who with their father praised God with musical instruments. To him fell the 19th lot (I Chron. 25:4,26).

MALLOW (See Plants)

MALLUCH (măl'lŭk, Heb. *mallûkh, counselor*).

1. Ancestor of Ethan, a Levite, son of Merari (I Chron. 6:44).

2. Son of Bani, one of the men who married foreign women (Ezra 10:29).

3. Son of Harim, another man who took a foreign wife (Ezra 10:32).

4. A priest who sealed the covenant (Neh. 10: 4). He had come from Babylon under Zerubbabel (Neh. 12:2).

5. A chief of the people who sealed the covenant (Neh. 10:27).

MALTA (See Melita)

MAMMON (măm'ŭn, Gr. *mamonás, riches*), the Aramaic word for "riches." Christ used it as a life-goal opposed to God (Matt. 6:24; Luke 16: 13). Jesus also employed the word in the phrase "mammon of unrighteousness" (meaning "money") in commenting on His parable of the unjust steward (Luke 16:11,13).

MAMRE (măm′rē, Heb. *mamrē′, strength*). 1. An Amorite who was confederate with Abram (Gen. 14:13,24).

2. A place a few miles N of Hebron where oak trees grew. Abram dwelt by the "Oaks of Mamre" (KJV "plains of Mamre") (Gen. 13:18; 18:1). This place apparently derived its name from the Amorite above who lived there. The burial cave in the field of Machpelah is described as located before Mamre (Gen. 23:17,19; 25:9; 35:27; 49:30; 50:13). The modern name of the site is *Ramet el-Khalil*.

MAN (Heb. *'ādhām, 'îsh, 'ēnôsh, gibbôr,* Gr. *anér, ánthropos*). The English word "man" occurs in the Bible over 3000 times, represented chiefly in the original text by the five terms given above. The basic meaning of these words for "man" is different in each case, but many times they seemed to be used somewhat indiscriminately. *'Ādām* comes from the word *'ādāmâh* (*ground*, or *earth*); it means man as being of the earth, a human being. It occurs 460 times in the meaning of "man." It also means "red" or "ruddy." It is used to contrast man and God, "God created man in his own image" (Gen. 1:27). God said "no man shall see me and live" (Exod. 33:20); in the sense of a human being, "Man that is born of a woman is of few days and full of trouble" (Job. 14:1); "Cease ye from man whose breath is in his nostrils" (Isa. 2:22). *'Ish* is the most common word for "man" in the Old Testament. It occurs over 2000 times, meaning *a man, a husband, an individual.* "Therefore shall a man leave his father and mother and shall cleave unto his wife" (Gen. 2:24); "every man and woman whose heart made them willing" (Exod. 35:29); as an individual, "O deliver me from the deceitful man" (Ps. 43:1); "a man that hath friends must show himself friendly" (Prov. 18:24). *'Ēnôsh* occurs most frequently (480 times) in plural form *'anashîm,* as the plural of *'îsh.* In the singular form it emphasizes the inferiority or insignificance of man. It is chiefly found in the poetic books: "What is man that thou art mindful of him?" (Ps. 8:4); "as for man his days are as grass" (Ps. 103:15). *Gibbôr* means a mighty man, a hero. In its several forms it occurs over 150 times: "Gird up thy loins now like a man" (Job 38:3); "Go now ye that are men and serve the Lord" (Exod. 10:11); "a man's enemies are of his own house" (Micah 7:6).

A few other words are used a few times for "man"; *bēn,* son; *ba'al,* owner or master; *zākār,* male person; *nephesh,* soul; and *'āhād,* one. In the NT *anér* means a man as opposed to woman; a husband. It is used over 200 times: "but the woman is the glory of the man" (I Cor. 11:7); "Is it lawful for a man to put away his wife?" (Mark 10:2). *Ánthropos* is the common word for man in the New Testament, occurring over 550 times. It denotes a human being, man in the sense of a person: "Man shall not live by bread alone" (Matt. 4:4); "Blessed are ye when men shall hate you" (Luke 6:22); "he knew what was in man" (John 2:25). A few other Greek words are used sometimes for man: *tis* means *someone, a certain one,* it is used quite frequently; *árrhen, male; ársen, male,* and *téleios, fully grown.*

Paul, in his epistles, used certain terms to denote the spiritual condition of various persons. Old

These impressive ruins, at Ramet el-Khalil (Mamre), may date back and mark the site of the dwelling of the patriarch Abraham when he lived under the oaks at Mamre. © MPS

man (*palaiós ánthropos*) is the fleshly nature of a regenerated person (Rom. 6:6; Eph. 4:22; Col. 3: 9). New man (*kaínos ánthropos*) denotes the spiritual nature of the regenerated individual (Eph. 2: 15; 4:24). Natural man (*psychikós ánthropos*) means the man who has only natural life, an unregenerated man (I Cor. 2:14). Inner man (*éso ánthropos*) is the man within, the soul (Rom. 7:22; Eph. 3:16). Outward man (*éxo ánthropos*) means the man outside, that is, the body (II Cor. 4:16).

Man was brought into existence through creation by God (Gen. 1:27). His body is made of the dust of the ground and his soul of the breath of God (Gen. 2:7). Man is thus a soul with a body. Man also has a spirit (I Cor. 2:11), the moral nature which makes man religious, and gives him a conscience.

Science teaches, as does the Bible, that man is a single species (see Acts 17:26). He was created in God's image (Gen. 1:27). This likeness to the divine is personality plus the moral nature. Though man has a physical body similar to animals, his intellectual power and religious aspirations set him far above the beasts. Adam was created God-centered in his outlook. When he sinned, he became self-centered; the moral nature was perverted. So men ever since the fall of Adam have served themselves and practiced a corrupt religion. Redemption through faith in the blood of Christ turns the soul to be God-centered again and brings new life to the moral nature (II Cor. 5:17).   C.E.H.

MAN OF SIN (See Antichrist)

MAN, SON OF (Heb. *ben 'ādhām,* Gr. *ho huios toú anthrópou*). This phrase was used once by the Lord in addressing Daniel (Dan. 8:17) and over 80 times in addressing Ezekiel. This name is confined to these two prophets. There must have been a special reason for its use with them. Both of them were privileged to behold visions of God. Probably the Lord wanted to emphasize to them that they were, after all, only men of the earth, in spite of this privilege.

Daniel used this phrase to describe a personage whom he saw in a night vision. He beheld one like unto "a son of man" who received an everlasting kingdom with great glory (Dan. 7:13,14). The individual so described can only be Jesus Christ. The phrase "a son of man" means that this personage whom Daniel saw looked like a human being.

When the Son of God came down to earth as a man, mingling with people, He very significantly took this phrase as His designation of Himself. Often He put His statements about Himself into the third person form to give His teachings more force. Whenever He did this He used this phrase as a name for Himself. No doubt He took it from Daniel's prophecy. The Jews must have been familiar with this prophecy. Jesus, in assuming this title, was saying to the Jews, "I am the Son of man in that prophecy." This title emphasized His union with mankind. It was also a name no one would criticize. Christ could not call Himself the Son of God, or the Messiah. The Jews would not accept Him as such. But they did not object to the term, the Son of Man. But no one else ever called Him by that name.

Once this phrase occurs without the definite article simply "a son of man" (John 5:27 ASV). Jesus made the statement that He had been given authority to execute judgment because He was a son of man. That is, because of His experience as a man, living among men, He was qualified to judge man.   C.E.H.

MANAEN (măn'á-ĕn, Gr. *Manaén*, the Gr. form of the Heb. *Menahem, comforter*), a leader in the church at Antioch (Acts 13:1). He is designated as the foster-brother of Herod the tetrarch (Herod Antipas).

MANAHATH (măn'á-hăth, Heb. *mānahath, resting place*). 1. An Edomite, the son of Shobal (Gen. 36:23; I Chron. 1:40).
2. A town in Edom, site unknown (I Chron. 8:6).

MANAHETHITES (má-nā'hăth-īts, Heb. *mānahtî*). 1. Half of the Manahethites, (ASV has "half of the Menuhoth"), a Judean clan, descendants of Shobal, son of Caleb, the son of Hur (I Chron. 2:52).
2. Another group, "half of the Manhethites," descended from Salma, son of Caleb, the son of Hur (I Chron. 2:54). ASV Manahathites.

MANASSEH (mă-năs'sĕ, Heb. *menashsheh, one who forgets*). 1. The elder son of Joseph, born in Egypt (Gen. 41:51). Jacob claimed him and his younger brother Ephraim for his own sons, and when he blessed them he predicted Ephraim would be greater than Manasseh (Gen. 48:5,19). Manasseh had a son, Machir, and his descendants made up the tribe of Manasseh. According to I Chronicles 7:14 Manasseh also had another son, Asriel. But in Numbers 26:30 Asriel and his descendants are listed with the sons of Gilead, son of Machir. So probably I Chronicles 7:14 means Asriel was Manasseh's grandson.
2. King of Judah, and son of Hezekiah. He was only 12 years old when he came to the throne in 687 B.C. Evidently after the death of his father the orthodox party was considerably weakened. The group in power around the new king were for doing away with the religious reforms Hezekiah had made. Manasseh was too young to hinder them. He went along with them. No doubt the people had resented being deprived of the high places, and they rebuilt them the first chance they had after Hezekiah's death. But Manasseh went way beyond this restoration. Judah was a vassal of Assyria, and paid tribute every year. The young king must have been much more impressed by the power of Assyria than by the power of God. He became a fanatical idolater, bringing a whole host of heathen practices into his realm. He built altars to Baal, and made a symbol of Asherah. He worshiped and served the host of heaven — sun, moon, stars, and planets. He built altars to them in the courts of the temple. He also put a heathen altar in the temple, and later moved the Asherah symbol into this building which had been dedicated to the true God of Israel (II Kings 21:1-7). He also had horses and chariots given to the sun (II Kings 23:11).

Much of this idolatry came from Assyria and Babylon where there was widespread worship of the heavenly bodies. Heathen practices expressly forbidden were introduced into Judah by Manasseh. He made his son pass through the fire, which probably means he sacrificed him to Moloch the god of the Ammonites; he practiced soothsaying; he used enchantments or observed omens; he indulged in sorcery; he sponsored ghosts and familiar spirits, that is persons in touch with the spirit world (II Kings 21:6; II Chron. 33:6). He persecuted the pious people who were faithful to the Jehovah, the true God (II Kings 21:6). Jewish traditions says he sawed the prophet Isaiah asunder. All this evil influence set loose in Judah sealed her fate. The subsequent reformation of Josiah could not bring the people back to true worship again. Manasseh brought his country to ruin (Jer. 15:4).

As a vassal of Assyria this king must have been suspected of disloyalty because he was taken captive by the king of Assyria and carried to Babylon. After a time he was returned to his throne in Jerusalem again, and repented of his sins and tried to undo his evil work (II Chron. 33:10-13, 15-17). He also did some building (vs. 14).

Many critics refuse to believe that this episode in the life of Manasseh could be true. If he actually had been taken captive to Babylon he would never have been sent back, and someone else would have reigned in his place. But in the Assyrian records is a report of Necho, an Egyptian king who was carried captive to Nineveh and later sent back to his throne by Ashurbanipal (Rassam Cylinder, Column II, lines 5-19). This incident, which all critics accept, is almost a parallel case to Manasseh's experience. The Assyrian king could find no one else to take his place and made him swear to remain loyal to Assyria. Other Assyrian inscriptions prove Judah paid tribute to Assyria during Manasseh's reign. He is mentioned by name in them (Prism of Esar-haddon, Col. V 54-VI 1 and Cylinder C of Ashurbanipal Col. 1 lines 23-50). All these inscriptions mentioned were translated in *Ancient Near Eastern Texts Relating to the Old Testament*, Rassam Cylinder on page 295, Prism B of Esarhaddon on page 291, and Cylinder C of Ashurbanipal on page 294.
3. An intentional change of the name Moses (Judg. 18:30). Someone named Moses was priest of a brazen image at Dan, and since it was thought a disgrace for one with so honored a name to be guilty of such sacrilege, someone changed the name to Manasseh. This was easily done in Hebrew by the insertion of one letter in the name of Moses.
4. One of those who married foreign wives (Ezra 10:30).
5. Another of those who married foreign wives (Ezra 10:33).

The prism of Esar-haddon, King of Assyria, which contains historical records, including mention of Manasseh's captivity and tribute. UMP

MANASSEH, TRIBE OF, the descendants of Manasseh. This tribe contained 32,200 men of war, those over 20 years old, (Num. 1:34) before the Israelites marched from Sinai. When the tabernacle was finished and dedicated, each tribe through its leader presented an offering. Gamaliel, the son of Pedahzur, offered on the eighth day for Manasseh (Num. 7:54). In the order of march where the three sections of the Levites intermingled with the other tribes, Manasseh came in the 11th place (Num. 10:23). In the layout of the camp Manasseh was on the W side in the third division (Num. 2:20). Forty years later the new generation in Manasseh numbered 52,700 men of war (Num. 26:34). Before the Israelites crossed over the Jordan river into Canaan, half the tribe of Manasseh along with the tribes of Reuben and Gad chose land E of the river and Moses assigned it to them (Num. 32:33). The descendants of Machir, son of Manasseh, conquered Gilead and lived there. Jair also captured other towns (Num. 32: 39-41). The half tribe of Manasseh was given the north half of Gilead, all of Bashan, and the region of Argob (Deut. 3:13). This territory included 60 cities among which were Gilead, Ashtaroth and Edrei (Josh. 13:31). The rest of the tribe was given ten parts of land in Canaan including areas for Zelophehad's daughters (Josh. 17:1-6). This territory was situated between Ephraim on the S

and Asher, Zebulon, and Issachar on the N. Its eastern border was the Jordan river and on the W was the Mediterranean Sea (Josh. 17:7-10). Golan in the half tribe E of the Jordan was selected as one of the cities of refuge (Josh. 20:8). E of the river 13 cities of Manasseh were assigned to the Gershonites of the Levites, and W Manasseh furnished ten cities to the Kohathites of the Levites (Josh. 21:5,6). W Manasseh failed to drive the Canaanites out of the towns (Judg. 1:27). Gideon was of the tribe of Manasseh (Judg. 6:15), also Jair the Gileadite who judged Israel 22 years (Judg. 10:3). Jephthah came from Gilead in E Manasseh (Judg. 11:1). This half tribe, with Reuben and Gad, fell into idolatry and was later carried away into captivity by Assyria (I Chron. 5:25, 26) during Pekah's reign over Israel (II Kings 15: 29).

Manasseh joined David while he was a fugitive from Saul (I Chron. 12:19-22). When David was made king at Hebron, W Manasseh furnished 18,-000 soldiers, and E Manasseh with Reuben and Gad 120,000 (I Chron. 12:31,37). People from W Manasseh and Ephraim joined with Judah in making a covenant to seek Jehovah during the reign of Asa, king of Judah (I Chron. 15:9-15). Certain pious souls from W Manasseh joined in the passover service during Hezekiah's reign (II Chron. 30:10-22). When Josiah was king he destroyed idols and purged altars in Manasseh's territory as well as elsewhere (II Chron. 34:6). The people of Manasseh contributed to an offering for the repairing of the temple in Josiah's time (II Chron. 34:9).   C.E.H.

MANASSES (See Manasseh)

MANASSITES (mà-năs′ĭts, Heb. *menashshî, forgetting*), descendants of the oldest son of Joseph (Gen. 41:51). A tribe of noble standing which Gilead, under Jephtha, delivered from the Ephraimites by the password Shibboleth" (Judg. 12:4-6). Moses gave them a city of refuge in Bashan (Deut. 4:41-43). Because of evil under Jehu, God caused the Manassites to be cut off (II Kings 10: 31-33).

MANEH (See Weights and Measures)

MANGER (Gr. *phátne, a stall*). The word was made notable by Luke's account of the birth of Jesus. The LXX used *phátnē* for the Hebrew which is given in II Chronicles 32:28 as *stall* and in Job 39:9 as *crib* (see Prov. 14:4 and Isa. 1:3). Luke alone gives *phatnē* as the birthplace of Jesus. Justin Martyr wrote about 100 A.D. that the stall was in a cave adjoining an inn. The cavern was used for livestock. Since Justin lived only 40 miles from Bethlehem, his word may be reliable. It is more probable that stalls were arranged around a courtyard of an inn with guests rooms and balcony above. Either kind of stall would have provided privacy for Mary and the cradle for the infant Lord.

MANNA (Heb. *mān*, Gr. *mánna*), a special food provided for the Hebrews during the exodus from Egypt. The name is of uncertain meaning. The Heb. *man* is a question and added to *hu* would be "What is it?" On the other hand it may be an adaptation of the Egyptian *mennu,* food. Josephus and other ancient writers attribute the name to the question "Is it food?" which is in keeping with the wilderness setting. Just what it was has puzzled naturalists for ages. It came at night, resembling hoar frost, coming with the dew (Num. 11: 9), and may have collected in dewdrops (Exod. 16:4). It was white, of delicious flavor, and resembled seed of the coriander, a plant of the eastern Mediterranean area which was both tasty and nourishing (Exod. 16:31). That it came by miraculous means is shown by its nature, its time of coming, and its preservation over the sabbaths (Exod. 16:20-26; Deut. 8:3). Being seed-like in form it had to be ground (Num. 11:7,8). As soon as other food was available, the manna ceased (Josh. 5:12).

While many attempts have been made to explain the manna as a natural phenomenon, ancient Hebrew scholars knew it to be of supernatural origin (Wisd. 17:20). No known substance meets the description of this food. A tamarisk plant grows along the route of the Hebrews from Sinai, that exudes a sweet liquid which collects at night upon twigs and falls to the ground. After sunrise it disappears unless protected. But this plant produces the food for only a brief period each year. Other naturalists would identify it with a peculiar mossy plant which, when mature, is ground and mixed with honey. It, however, is not available for the entire year.

The Bible makes it certain that manna came as a temporary provision for the chosen people. The poet Asaph called it "corn from heaven" (Ps. 78:24). It was also bread from heaven (Ps. 105:40). Hebrew writers called it "angels' bread" (II Esd. 2:1; Wisd. 16:20). Jesus referring to Himself, used it as a metaphor (John 6:31-63). John called it spiritual food, meaning a hidden agent for spiritual sustenance for the risen saints (Rev. 2:17). J.D.F.

MANOAH (mà-nō'à, Heb. *mānôah, rest*), the father of Samson. Little is known about him except from the record in Judges 13, which states that he was of the tribe of Dan and was a good Hebrew who desired a son and heir. The appeal of his wife was answered by a visiting angel whose promise of a son was confirmed by a miracle during a sacrifice. He was a trustworthy parent, rearing Samson according to instructions. But he failed as a father so to indoctrinate his son as to make the idea of marrying a heathen woman abhorrent (Judges 14:1-11).

MANSIONS (Gr. *moné, an abiding place*), an expression that occurs only in John 14:2, where the plural is used. It is correctly rendered "abiding places," the plural form denoting the great extent of God's house as shown in Revelation 2:1.

MANSLAYER (Heb. *meratstsēah*, Gr. *androphónos*), a term used to describe a person who had killed another human being, whether by premeditation or accidentally or justifiably. Among the Israelites a manslayer could flee from an avenger of blood by taking asylum in a city of refuge (Num. 35:6,12) if the killing was not deliberate. There he was given a trial. If he was acquitted, he could stay in the city of refuge until the death of the high priest, after which he could return home (Num. 35:28). A deliberate murderer could find no protection in a city of refuge. If he tried it, he was immediately put to death (Exod. 21:14).

MANTLE, usually a large, sleeveless, outer garment, such as Elijah's (I Kings 19:18,19; II Kings 2:8,13,14), or such a garment with sleeves (Isa. 3:22).

MANUSCRIPTS, DEAD SEA (See Dead Sea Scrolls)

MAOCH (mā'ŏk, Heb. *mā'ôkh, a poor one*), father of Achish, a king of Gath (I Sam. 27:2). He protected David and his troop from Saul (I Sam. 29: 1-11).

MAON (mā'ŏn, Heb. *mā'ôn, habitation*). 1. A descendant of Caleb and father of Beth-zur, or perhaps the founder of this fortress near Bethlehem (I Chron. 2:42-45).

2. A town on an elevated plain south of Hebron. Around it lay an unpopulated region where David found refuge from Saul until the Philistines forced the king to cease pursuit. Because of this rescue, the hill was called Rock of Separation (I Sam. 23: 24-28, marg.). It was the home of Nabal and Abigail (I Sam. 25:1-3).

MAONITES (mā'ŏn-īts). Confusion exists regarding these enemies of Israel. They are named with others who were defeated by the Lord (Judg. 10: 11,12). They were called Mehunim and may have been from Arabia. Their descendants were among the temple servants of Ezra's day (Ezra 2:50). They came, no doubt, from the Arabian peninsula and were called Maonites because they grew strong on the Maon Plain.

MARA (mà'rà, Heb. *mārâh, bitter*), a name adopted by Naomi instead of her own, which meant pleasant or delightful (Ruth 1:20, marg.).

MARAH (mā'rà, Heb. *mārâh, bitterness*), a place about three days' journey from the Red Sea crossing, where the Hebrews found bitter water. When they complained, God showed Moses a plant whose foliage sweetened the water (Exod. 15:23-26).

MARALAH (măr'à-là, Heb. *mar'ălâh*), a city on the border of Zebulun's heritage (Josh. 19:10,11), about four miles from Nazareth. The location is not definitely known.

MARANATHA (mār'à-năth'à, Aramaic, *mārānā' 'āthāh, our Lord comes!*), an expression of greeting and encouragement as well as of triumphant faith, such as is shown in I Corinthians 16:22 RSV margin. That is to say, "Our Lord comes, regardless of man's enmity!" Paul put this word over against *anathema* (the curse) which befalls idolaters.

MARBLE (See Minerals)

MARCUS (màr'kŭs, Gr. *Márkos*), Roman name of a kinsman of Barnabas. He deserted Paul (Acts 13: 13) and later became a noted Christian worker (Acts 15:39; II Tim. 4:11).

MARESHAH (mà-rē'shà, Heb. *mārēshâh, a possession*). 1. The father of Hebron (I Chron. 2:42).

2. A grandson of Judah, more probably a town (I Chron. 4:21).

3. An important city of Judah, SW of Jerusalem (Josh. 15:44) which Rehoboam considered strategic and fortified (II Chron. 11:5-12). Good King Asa met a big Ethiopian army at Mareshah in the Valley of Zephathah and with divine aid overwhelmed it (II Chron. 14:9-15). Eliezer, a native of M. delivered a warning from God to wicked King Jehoshaphat for an unholy alliance with Ahaziah (II Chron. 20:35-37). It was a goodly city in Micah's day and he promised its people an heir (Mic. 1:15). Little of its record is found in the Bible. During the Maccabean period it was ravished by Judas Maccabeus (Jos. *Ant.* XII:8, 6). Hycranus, high priest about 130 B.C., captured it and compelled its citizens to adopt Jewish laws and customs (*Ant.* XII:9,1; X:2). It was strong enough to win special favors from Pompey (*Ant.* XIV:4,4), but when the Parthians invaded Judea, 40 B.C., the city fell and was destroyed. Discovery of some elaborate tombs about a mile S of modern Beit Jibrin confirmed the belief that El Sandagannah is its location.

MARI, an ancient city of the Euphrates Valley, discovered in 1933 as a result of work by grave diggers who uncovered a great statue. Excavations

A camel caravan pauses at the Springs of Moses (Ayoun Mousa), Biblical Marah (bitter water), where the Israelites stopped after crossing the Red Sea. © MPS

under the direction of André Parrot of the Louvre Museum resulted in rich finds, including some 20,-000 cuneiform tablets, translation of which has opened up new vistas into ancient Syrian civilization. The Mari kingdom was contemporary with Hammurabi of Babylon and the Amorite tribes of Canaan, ancestors of the Hebrews. They worshiped Ishtar, whose images, like those of Diana of the Ephesians (Acts 19:21-29), were numerous. Dagan, "king of the Country" was the chief male god. A palace, covering more than six acres has been partly exhumed from centuries-old layers of sand and rubble. It was built of mud brick, but so well constructed that some walls 15 feet high remain intact, while pottery drains are usable. Even baths were provided. The cuneiform of some tablets shows a close relationship to that of Ur of the Chaldees of Abraham's day. Some of them contain correspondence with Hammurabi. Much material remains to be deciphered and translated. It is expected that reliable information about the Amorites will be discovered. Falling a victim to the wiles of Hammurabi, the country was destroyed in the 32nd year of his reign.

MARK, a word is used in the KJV to translate words of varied meanings: (1) *'Ôth,* a special sign, a special brand. The *'ôth* of Cain (Gen. 4:15) is considered a brand of infamy, but was more probably a sign of the covenant to be protected against avengers. The marks which Paul bore were scars (*stigmata*) caused by the beatings which he had suffered (Gal. 6:17). (2) *Tāu',* a seal or sign of ownership. Ezekiel saw this symbol put upon the foreheads of a special people (9:4,6). In a similar way, the redeemed are to be protected in the last days (Rev. 7:2-8). *Tāw* appears in Job 31:35 and is rendered "signature" in the RSV. The illiterate man still makes his "mark" as a signature. (3) *Mattārā',* a target. Jonathan pretended to be shooting at a *mattārā'* (I Sam. 20:20). Job felt himself to be such a mark (16:12) and so did Jeremiah (Lam. 3:12). (4) *Qa'aqa',* a form of tattooing banned by the Lord (Lev. 19:28). (5) *Skopós,* a goal or end to be attained. Paul set his heart upon such a mark (Phil. 3:14). (6) *Cháragma,* a particular brand or characteristic, denoting the nature and rank of men. This mark of the beast is physical (Rev. 13:16).   J.D.F.

MARK, JOHN (Gr. *Márkos,* from Lat. *marcus, a large hammer;* Gr. *Ioánnes,* from Heb. *Yôhānān, Jehovah is gracious*), mentioned by name ten times in the New Testament. John was his Jewish name, Mark (Marcus) his Roman. In Acts he is twice 13:5,13) referred to simply as John, once (15:39) as Mark, and three times (12:12,25; 15:37) as "John, whose surname was Mark." In the epistles he is uniformly (four times) called simply Mark ("Marcus" three times in KJV).

The first allusion to John Mark may be in Mark 14:51,52. The most reasonable explanation for the passing mention of this incident is that it was a vivid personal memory in the mind of the author of the second Gospel.

The first definite reference is Acts 12:12. Peter,

when delivered from prison, went to the home of John Mark's mother, where many believers were praying for him. When Barnabas and Saul returned to Antioch from their famine visit at Jerusalem (Acts 11:27-30), they took along John Mark (Acts 12:25). This opened the opportunity for him to accompany them on their first missionary journey as an "attendant" (Acts 13:5, ASV).

The missionaries first evangelized the island of Cyprus. When they reached Perga in Pamphylia John returned home to Jerusalem. This decision was probably due to a mixture of homesickness, fear of perils in the mountainous country ahead, and displeasure that Paul had become the leader of the expedition (Acts 13:13, "Paul and his company"). Whatever his motive, Paul distrusted him and refused to take him on the second journey (Acts 15:37,38). The result was two missionary parties. Barnabas took Mark and revisited Cyprus, while Paul chose a new associate, Silas, and went overland to Asia Minor.

Mark next appears in Rome, where he is a fellow worker with Paul (Philem. 24). He is recommended by the apostle to the church at Colosse (Col. 4:10). Here he is called "sister's son to Barnabas" (KJV), but the proper sense of *anepsios* is "cousin" (ASV, RSV). That John Mark had fully reinstated himself with Paul is shown by the latter's statement in II Timothy 4:11: — "Take Mark, and bring him with thee; for he is useful to me for ministering." Peter refers to him as "Marcus my son" (I Pet. 5:13). This may be a mere expression of affection, or it may indicate that Mark was converted under Peter's ministry.

An early tradition says that Mark founded the church in Alexandria, Egypt, but this is uncertain.
R.E.

MARK, GOSPEL OF, is the shortest of the four Gospels. In comparison with Matthew and Luke it contains relatively little of the teachings of Jesus and nothing at all about his birth and childhood. Starting with the ministry of John the Baptist, it comes immediately to the public ministry of Christ, ending with His death and resurrection.

Authorship. On two points the tradition of the early church is unanimous: the Second Gospel was written by Mark and presents the preaching of Peter. Papias (c. A.D. 140) is quoted by Eusebius as saying: "And John the presbyter also said this, Mark being the interpreter of Peter, whatsoever he recorded he wrote with great accuracy . . . he was in company with Peter, who gave him such instruction as was necessary, but not to give a history of our Lord's discourses" (*Eccl. Hist.,* III, 39). This suggests that Mark has given us a summary of the message of Peter.

Justin Martyr (c. A.D. 150) quotes Mark 3:17 as from "Peter's Memoirs." Irenaeus (c. A.D. 185) writes that after the departure (*exodus*) of Peter and Paul from Rome, "Mark the disciple and interpreter of Peter, also transmitted to us in writing what had been preached by Peter" (*ibid.,* V, 8). Most scholars hold that "departure" means "death." Clement of Alexandria, however, affirms that the Gospel was written during Peter's lifetime. Here is his statement: "When Peter had proclaimed the word publicly at Rome, and declared the Gospel under the influence of the Spirit; as there was a great number present, they requested Mark . . . to reduce these things to writing, and that after composing the Gospel he gave it to those who requested it of him. Which when Peter understood, he directly neither hindered nor encouraged it" (*ibid.,* VI, 14). In spite of this minor confusion the early Fathers, including specifically Tertullian

(c. A.D. 200) and Origen (c. A.D. 230), unite in affirming that Mark's Gospel gives us the preaching of Peter. Such strong tradition can hardly be discounted, though some recent scholars have sought to do so. It may be remarked that the traditional authorship of the Second Gospel is accepted more universally today than is the case with any of the other three Gospels.

Date. Most scholars today place the writing of Mark between A.D. 65 and A.D. 70, shortly before the destruction of Jerusalem in the latter year (see B. H. Streeter, *The Four Gospels,* p. 499; C. H. Dodd, *About the Gospels,* p. 13; Vincent Taylor, *Mark,* p. 32). Conservatives commonly hold to a date in the 50's. The early dating was supported by Adolph Harnack (*Date of Acts and Synoptic Gospels,* pp. 126-133), and has recently been reasserted by Samuel Cartledge (*INT,* IX [1955], 187). Of course, if one accepts the tradition that Mark wrote after Peter's death, the later date would have to be adopted.

Place of Writing. About this there is little question. From the early Church — with the exception of Chrysostom — to the present it has been held that Mark's Gospel was written at Rome. Several distinctive features point in this direction. Mark uses ten Latin words, some of which do not occur elsewhere in the New Testament. He explains Jewish customs because he is writing to Gentiles. To his Roman readers he presents Jesus as the mighty conqueror and the suffering Servant of the Lord. Because of this purpose no genealogy is given, nor infancy narratives. These are found only in Matthew and Luke.

Character. In addition to those just mentioned, there are three main characteristics of this Gospel. The first is *rapidity of action.* The narrative moves quickly from one event to the next. This probably reflects the impulsive personality of Peter. Over 40 times we find that Greek word *euthys,* translated (KJV) as "immediately," "straightway," "forthwith." As Vincent aptly says: "His narrative runs" (*Word Studies,* I, 160). The second characteristic is *vividness of detail.* Mark often includes details omitted by the other Synoptics that make the narrative more alive. He gives special attention to the looks and gestures of Jesus. The third characteristic is *picturesqueness of description.* Mark's is pre-eminently the pictorial Gospel. He describes, for instance, the five thousand sitting on the green grass in "ranks" (lit., flower beds). Peter evidently was impressed with the striking scene of the groups of people in brightly colored Oriental garments of red and yellow sitting on the green hillside, and Mark has preserved the picture for us.

Mark's is the Gospel of action. Only one long message of Jesus is recorded, the Olivet Discourse (chap. 13). Mark includes 18 miracles of Jesus, about the same number as Matthew or Luke. In contrast he has only four of the parables, compared with 18 in Matthew and 19 in Luke.

Content. The period of preparation (1:1-13) for Jesus' public ministry is described very briefly. It consists of three items: the ministry of John the Baptist (1:1-8), the baptism of Jesus (1:9-11), and the temptation of Jesus (1:12,13). After only 13 verses of introduction — in contrast to 76 in Matthew and 183 in Luke — Mark plunges immediately into the public ministry of the Master.

First comes the great Galilean ministry (1:14-9:50). This is commonly thought to have lasted about a year and a half. It may be divided into three sections. The first period (1:4-3:12) was a time of great popularity. Jesus called four fishermen to follow Him — and later Levi — and engaged in a vigorous healing ministry. This was the time when large crowds thronged about Him.

In the second period (3:13-7:23) He appointed the 12 apostles and opposition began to show itself. The Pharisees clashed with Jesus over questions about sabbath observance and ceremonial cleansing. He healed the Gadarene demoniac and the woman with the issue of blood and raised Jairus' daughter. He sent out the twelve and fed the five thousand.

In the third period (7:24-9:50) Jesus gave more attention to His disciples. Three times He is described as withdrawing from the crowd to teach the disciples. After Peter's confession at Caesarea Philippi He began a new phase of teaching: predicting His passion.

The great Galilean ministry was followed by the briefer Perean ministry (10:1-52), and then by passion week (11:1-15:47) and the Resurrection (chap. 16).

Outline (Indicated under "Content").

Ending. A word must be said about the last 12 verses of Mark. The two oldest Greek manuscripts, Vaticanus and Sinaiticus (both fourth century), end the Gospel at 16:8. The usual ending in our English Bibles (16:9-20) is also omitted in the Sinaitic Syriac. The majority of scholars now agree that these last 12 verses are not a part of the original Gospel of Mark, although the matter is not settled conclusively.

Priority. Most scholars today favor the theory that Mark's Gospel was written first and was used by Matthew and Luke when they composed their Gospels. The fact is that about 95 per cent of Mark is found in Matthew and/or Luke. The freshness and vividness of Mark's language suggest it was written first. It should be noted, however, that this position is still being challenged.

Evaluation. In the early Church the Gospel of Mark received the least attention of any of the four. This is not true today. The importance of Mark as giving us the basic message of the primitive Church (cf. Acts 1:22; 2:22-24,36) is increasingly recognized. The theological, as well as historical, value of this Gospel is widely appreciated. It is the logical place to start one's study of the four Gospels.   R.E.

Bibliography:
Branscomb, B. Harvie. *The Gospel of Mark*, "The Moffatt New Testament Commentary." New York: Harper & Brothers, 1937; Earle, Ralph. *The Gospel According to Mark*, "The Evangelical Commentary." Grand Rapids: Zondervan Publishing House, 1957; Hunter, A. M. *Gospel According to St. Mark*, "Torch Bible Commentaries." London: SCM Press, 1948; Rawlinson, A. E. *St. Mark*, "Westminster Commentaries." London: Methuen & Co., 1925; Swift, C. E. Graham. "The Gospel According to Mark," *The New Bible Commentary*. Ed. F. Davidson. Grand Rapids: Wm. B. Eerdmans Publishing Co., 1953; Taylor, Vincent. *The Gospel According to St. Mark*. London: Macmillan & Co., 1952.

MARKET (Heb. *ma'ărāv, a place for trade*). The term also means things traded, hence should be rendered in Ezekiel 27:13,17,19 as merchandise. The NT word is *agorá*, the civic center in which people gathered for recreation (Matt. 11:16,17), where the unemployed loafed (Matt. 20:3,6), and where the proud paraded (Mark 12:38; Luke 11: 43). It was a courtroom (Acts 16:19) and also a forum (Acts 17:17). From a corner shop the market developed into a great urban multi-purpose center.

MAROTH (mā'rŏth, Heb. *mārôth*), a town probably in the plain W of Jerusalem. Her citizens waited for good when evil was dooming God's chosen ones (Mic. 1:12 RSV).

MARRIAGE is an intimate personal union to which a man and woman consent, consummated and continuously nourished by sexual intercourse, and perfected in a life-long partnership of mutual love and commitment. It is also a social institution regulated by the Word of God and by the laws and customs which a society develops to safeguard its own continuity and welfare.

Nature and Purpose. Marriage is an order of creation. The Creator made man and woman, displaying His full image only as both man and woman. Each is made for the other, their essential natures being complementary, and brought into oneness in marriage (Gen. 12:26f; Matt. 19:4-6).

Marriage is the sacrament of human society. Husband and wife both share and perpetuate their happiness in having and rearing a family within the sphere of their own love. Thus marriage is more than an end in itself; it is the means to ends outside the married couple. The unity of husband and wife is of God's creative will, for from Him come the love and grace which enable them to grow together in life comradeship, to beget children, and to fulfill their responsibilities toward their children and to society as a family unit. Husband and wife become one in relation to the community, so that through marriage a new social unit emerges.

Scripture itself says little about the purpose of marriage. The earliest creation narrative suggests unitive purpose ("one flesh"), while the second creation narrative suggests procreative ("be fruitful and multiply"). The NT mentions the unitive and analogical purpose, but not expressly the procreative. In the OT the procreative purpose is addressed once to mankind generally, three times to the patriarchs Noah and Jacob. This does not imply the procreative purpose is the chief end. The importance Jesus and Paul attach to Genesis 2:24 suggests that the establishment of the "one flesh" union is dominant. The great Pauline conception of marriage is unitive, the analogue of Christ's union with His church. Ephesians 5:25-33 is Paul's instruction on marriage, while I Corinthians 7 shows him as pastor-counselor in a specific situation where an improper marriage relation might endanger the Christian witness. Moreover, sexual intercourse has no exclusive connection with procreation, that being only its biological end. Intercourse implies the *possibility* of conception, the *certainty* of union in "one flesh."

Distinctly Christian marriage is one in which husband and wife covenant together with God and publicly witness their commitment not only to each other but together to Him, to the end that they

The market place was busy, and noisy with the shouts of buyers and sellers. KC © FC

shall in unity fulfill His purposes throughout life (I Cor. 7:39; cf. II Cor. 6:14). Marriage is contracted "in the Lord," received as a divine vocation, acknowledged with humility and thanksgiving, and sanctified by the Word of God and prayer (I Tim. 4:4-5).

Man is unique in that he can conceive of the future, and can relate the present to the future, even to the eternal. He lives in terms of a moral structure, and with meaningful interpersonal relations. He is the only creature that can have marriage instead of mating, for marriage involves commitment for the future and the confidence of permanence. Man also discerns his own loneliness and incompleteness (Gen. 2:18) and the possibility of the complementary nature of marriage, husband and wife each fulfilling that which is lacking in the other.

Sexual Fulfillment. Sex is holy, being the creation and gift of God. It is fulfilled only as regulated by the law of God in marriage. Man and woman were created to complement each other physically as in other ways, and to share together in God's creative process. Man alone can make sex moral, giving it a nonbiological meaning, and making it creative of personal and spiritual values. Thus man makes sex a function of the whole personality, combining it with love and fidelity. While sexuality alone permits the establishment of a relationship which is procreative, a couple's God-centered union permits them to establish a spiritually creative relationship through their sexuality. Human sexuality, then, has a dual purpose of communion and reproduction.

The exclusive sexual relation between husband and wife points to the exclusive commitment of total responsibility for each other. Sexual intercourse is an act of the whole self, a personal encounter. Spiritually, the act itself must be offered to God in intention and in thanksgiving, husband and wife acknowledging that God is the Author of their love. Sexual intimacy affords husband and wife a medium for mutual disclosures, the senses becoming a channel of communication for all that lies too deep for utterance and yet must somehow be told in order to fulfill the total mutuality of marriage. Such intercourse is pleasurable, not merely because there is sensual gratification, but because of what it expresses of the joyful oneness of husband and wife. While the sense of independence is diminished, that of individuality is fulfilled. The sexual communion speaks of a pervading possessiveness, each partner offering a precious gift to the other which has been exclusively preserved for that one alone.

The sexual union is sacramental in the sense that is an outward sign of an inner commitment of love which is recognized as a gift from God. The union is more than physical, for from it emerges a spiritual gift and knowledge. And it is not a mere fact of nature; hence man is not in bondage to it. Rather, sex is a divine gift within a divine vocation, marriage, and as such it is subject to man's freedom and moral responsibility toward God the Giver. Sexual intercourse is to be employed according to the purpose of the Giver. Such fulfillment is both the need and the right of husband and wife alike (I Cor. 7:4). It must be part of loving the other for what one is in himself, and for what their union means in its exclusiveness and permanence. It is a creative relationship through which a couple express the whole meaning and quality of their marriage.

Love and Fidelity. Marriage is the highest fulfillment of human friendship, filling every ideal of human intimacy and mutuality and loyalty. Sex and parenthood both can enrich marriage; neither is capable of sustaining marriage. Love alone gives meaning and inward validity to marriage and guarantees its integrity. Fidelity, not as an expression of obligation, but as an element of love, is necessary to successful marriage.

The requisite love is other-person centered, giving and renouncing for the sake of the well-being of the beloved rather than in expectation of return. It is expressed through service, not exploitation, and is the ground for the most meaningful sharing of which human personality is capable. Such love dissolves differences and barriers, while such identification does not destroy self but rather extends self in a new dimension. In love for Christ is to be found the bond of oneness, and the determinant of the quality and strength of love for each other. Forgiving love is a creative force within marriage, deriving its nature from the experience of Christ's forgiving love. It will act as mercy, i.e., forgiving when there seems no adequate reason to forgive, and as grace, i.e., freely given with no promises demanded. It is creative love, suffering to achieve a high spiritual end. Marriage is endowed with spiritual significance when each partner is enabled by love to transcend his own self-centeredness and identify himself with the well-being and concerns of the other.

More than love is the sense that marriage is a divine order which is binding. Fidelity truly exists when the feeling of love is absorbed into one's personal will. Commitment is twofold: to the beloved, and to the divine will. Indissolubility is the principle upon which one is free to commit himself unreservedly to the marriage, to share and to venture all with confidence of fulfillment.

Paul comprehends marriage obligations for the husband under the principle of love, its highest standard being the love of Christ for His Church (Col. 3:19; Eph. 5:25,28). Fidelity is required (I Cor. 6; I Thess. 4:3-7; Gal. 5:19; Heb. 13:4). Thus is established an openness of exchange in which there is no concealment nor sense of "thine and mine."

Equality of the wife is indicated in the creation narrative where she is called a "helpmeet" (Gen. 2:18). By contrast, the subordination of the wife is appropriate as punishment for her initiative in the original transgression (Gen. 3:16; I Cor. 11:9). The NT continues the concept with modifications. Complete mutuality is taught in Ephesians 5 and in I Corinthians 7:3. Spiritual dignity is equal. The wife's duties, however, are summed up not under the principle of love, but of obedience (Eph. 5:22; Col. 3:18; I Pet. 3:1). This subordination is that of responsibility and subsequently of authority. It is not that of compulsion or of fear, and originates in her freedom and in reciprocal love for her husband. She is subject to her husband as he himself is subject to Christ and rules her, not by self will, but as fulfilling the will of God. The husband will have the respect and subjection of his wife so long as she has his love and headship under Christ. His love creates its own response, even as the love of Christ creates a reciprocal love in the believer (I John 4:19).

Monogamy and Indissolubility. The total unity of persons in marriage, comprehended in the expression "one flesh," demands monogamy and indissolubility. One cannot relate in this way to more than one person at a time, nor with reserve as to the length of time. It is indissoluble as in the union between Christ and His church. It is monogamous as is the relationship of Christ to His one bride, the Church. Monogamy is represented in the prophets as symbolic of the union of God with Israel (Hos. 2:19; Jer. 3:14; 31:32; Isa. 54:5). In the NT the bridegroom is God in Christ (Matt. 9:15), the bride the spiritual Israel elect out of every nation (II Cor. 11:2; Eph. 5:23-32; Rev. 19:7). Monogamy is consistent with Christ's Golden Rule, for under polygamy other men were robbed and wives degraded. Polygamy is represented in the prophets as having its counterpart in idolatry. It made its first appearance in the lawless line of the Cainites (Gen. 4:23). The backslidings and calamities in the reigns of David and Solomon are attributed to the polygamy practiced (II Sam. 5:13; I Kings 11:1-3; Deut. 17:7). Monogamous marriage best stabilizes the sexual impulse and transforms it into a creative energy which contributes to the spiritual and societal life of man, has the better power to "domesticate" the sexual desire and build it into the total structure of human existence and purpose, and best promotes the slow growth of mutual understanding and sympathy essential for mutual completion and fulfillment in marriage. It best fosters the security of the familial conditions necessary to maturation of children.

Divorce. The Lord's teaching on divorce (Matt. 5:31-32; 19:3-9; Mark 10:2-12; Luke 16:18) gives adultery as the sole reason a man may put away his wife. While Matthew suggests it is adultery on the wife's part only, Mark implies the same right belongs also to the woman. The Lord allowed, but did not make divorce mandatory. Throughout Scripture sin is characterized as spiritual adultery (Hos. 2:2; Jer. 3:9; 13:27), the essence consisting in difference to God, or even hatred of Him, and the giving of affection to others (Hos. 2:5; Jer. 2:20; Ezek. 20:30). Persistence entails the casting away, of which divorce is emblematic (Hos. 2:1f; Jer. 2:35f).

Divorce was granted on a bill of divorcement in OT times according to the Law (Deut. 24:1-2).

A Jewish bill of divorcement. DV

Remarriage was clearly acceptable. There was little else for a divorced woman to do. Jesus' statement in Matthew 5:31-32 that divorce is not to be allowed save for unchastity is not found in Mark. It does seem to indicate the principle that if a marriage is destroyed by unfaithfulness, it can not be further destroyed by divorce. Jesus was being put to the test by a group of hostile Jews who believed that only a woman could commit adultery, and Jesus there points out that a man can commit adultery too. He does not go further into the matter.

The Scriptures teach the higher law of forgiveness (Hosea) even for the repentant adulterer. Paul speaks in I Corinthians 7:10-15 of a specific case involving a mixed marriage. He states that should an unbelieving mate depart, the believer is not bound, the meaning of which is controversial. Some teach that Paul here allows for remarriage of the so-called innocent party.   D.H.S.

Bibliography:
Design for Christian Marriage, Dwight H. Small, Revell, 1959; *The Mystery of Love and Marriage,* Derrick S. Bailey, Harpers, 1952; *A Christian Interpretation of Marriage,* Henry A. Bowman, Westminster, 1959.

MARROW, the heart of the bone (Job 21:24; Prov. 3:8; Heb. 4:12). Used figuratively of richness (Ps. 63:5) (fatness) and good things (Isa. 25:6).

MARSENA (măr-sē′nȧ, Heb. *marsenā′*), one of the counselors who advised King Ahasuerus to banish Queen Vashti for disobeying the imperial command (Esth. 1:10-14).

Atop Mars Hill at Athens.   JFW

MARS HILL (Gr. *Áreios págos, Hill of Ares*), a barren hill, 370 feet high, NW of the famous Acropolis in Athens. It was dedicated to Ares, the god of war. The elevated place became the seat of the Greek Council. Because of sudden interest in his message, Paul was taken there to clarify his mysterious teachings (Acts 17:16-34).

MARSH, swamp lands near the mouths of some rivers and at various places along the banks of the Jordan and of the Dead Sea. Cf. Ezek. 47:11.

MARTHA (mȧr′thȧ, Aram. *lady, mistress*), sister of Lazarus and Mary of Bethany. Luke mentions a visit of Jesus to the home of Martha at a certain village (10:38). It is inferred from this that the beloved friends of Jesus had resided in Galilee before going to Bethany. Another problem grows out of the connection between the name of Martha and that of Simon the Leper. Was Martha the widow of Simon? It is quite possible that she was and that the Bethany home had been inherited from him upon his death. Matthew 26:6-12 and Mark 14:3 may indicate this. It seems more natural to think of Martha as a near relative of Simon for whom she acted as hostess. The scriptural narrative reveals Jesus was an intimate friend of Martha, Mary, and Lazarus. The sisters knew of His ability to work miracles (John 11:3,5). He, no doubt, was a guest in their home during the last fateful days on earth (Matt. 21:17; Mark 11:1, 11). Martha was a careful hostess and was familiar enough with Jesus to complain to Him about her sister's conduct (Luke 10:38-42) and about His delay in coming when Lazarus was ill (John 11: 1-3,21). But she gave the Master an occasion for presenting the great statement about the resurrection, "I am the resurrection and the life" (John 11:25). J.D.F.

MARTYR (màr'têr, Gr. *martús, martúr, witness*). Because of its use in connection with Stephen (Acts 22:20) and others who died for Christ, the word came to mean one who paid the extreme price for fidelity to Christ. Antipas was a faithful witness (Rev. 2:13). The harlot, Babylon, was drunk with the blood of martyrs (Rev. 17:6).

MARY (mâr'ĭ, Gr. *María, Maríam*, from Heb. *miryām*). The name of at least five women in the NT.
1. Mary of Rome. A diligent worker in the church at Rome to whom Paul sent special greetings (Rom. 16:6).
2. The mother of John Mark. She lived in Jerusalem, where she had a house in which Christians met for prayer. It was to her home that Peter immediately went when he was miraculously released from prison by an angel (Acts 12:1-16). She may have been a woman of some means, as she had at least one servant, a girl named Rhoda (Acts 16:13). John Mark is described as being the cousin of Barnabas (Col. 4:10), but the exact relationship of Barnabas to Mary is unknown. Some scholars think the "upper room" in which Jesus observed the Lord's Supper was in her home, but there is no proof of this.
3. Mary of Bethany. The sister of Lazarus and Martha. She lived in Bethany (John 11:1), about a mile E of the Mount of Olives. Jesus commended her for being more interested in hearing Him than in providing a bounteous dinner (Luke 10:42). John relates that she joined with Martha in saying to Jesus after the death of Lazarus, "Lord, if thou hadst been here, my brother had not died" (11: 21). Afterward, a week before the last passover, when Jesus was a guest in the house of Simon the leper (Mark 14:3), she showed her devotion to Jesus by anointing His head and feet with costly ointment and wiping His feet with her hair (John 12:3). To those who complained of this as being wasteful, Jesus said that her act would always be remembered (Matt. 26:6-13; Mark 14:3-9). Jesus looked upon what she did as being an act of love and as a preparation, though perhaps unintentional, of His coming death (John 12:7-8).
4. Mary the mother of James and Joses. Uncertainty exists regarding this Mary. There is reason for thinking that she, the "other Mary" of Matthew 27:61, and the wife of Clopas were the same person. Little is known about her except that she was very probably among the company of women who served Jesus in Galilee (Luke 8:2,3). She was at the cross when Jesus died (Matt. 27: 56; Mark 15:40). She witnessed the burial of her Lord (Mark 15:47), came to the tomb to anoint His body (Mark 16:1), and fled when told by the angel that Jesus was not in the tomb (Mark 16:

8). A comparison of Matthew 28:1, Mark 16:1, and Luke 24:10 seems to make it certain that the mother of James and Joses was also the wife of Clopas. That Clopas (Cleopas, Luke 24:18) and Alphaeus (Matt. 10:3) were the same has not been proved.
5. Mary Magdalene. Her name probably indicates that she came from Magdala, on the SW coast of the Sea of Galilee. After Jesus cast seven demons out of her (Mark 16:9; Luke 8:2), she became a devoted disciple of His. There is no real ground for thinking that she had been a woman of immoral life before Jesus healed her. The only ground for thinking so is the fact that the first mention of her (Luke 8:2) comes immediately after the story of the sinful woman who anointed Jesus (Luke 7:36-50). She followed the body of Jesus to the grave (Matt. 27:61) and was the first to learn of the resurrection (Matt. 28:1-8; Mark 16:9; Luke 24:1,10). Nothing is known of her life after Christ's resurrection. J.D.F.

MARY THE VIRGIN. All the authentic information we have about Mary the Virgin is found in the NT. In the opinion of many scholars she was descended from David, because she was told that her Son should receive "the throne of his father David," also because Christ is described as being of "the seed of David according to the flesh" (Acts 2:30; Rom. 1:3; II Tim. 2:8); and again because it is thought by many that Luke's genealogy of Christ is through His mother. She appears in the following passages: the infancy narratives (Matt. 1,2; Luke 1,2); the wedding at Cana of Galilee (John 2:1-11); the episode of Matthew 12:46; Mark 3:21,31ff; Luke 8:19-21; the incident at the cross (John 19:25ff); and the scene in the Upper Room (Acts 1:14).

1. Mary in the Infancy Narratives (Matt. 1,2; Luke 1,2). The source of these narratives is not known, but it is more than likely that they came from Mary herself. She lived into the apostolic period, whereas Joseph seems to have died before the crucifixion of Jesus, for there is no mention of him after the incident of Jesus in the temple when He was twelve, and she could very well have told the story to the early leaders of the church, including Luke. She was the "kinswoman" of Elizabeth, the mother of John the Baptist (Luke 1:36), but the exact nature of this relationship is uncertain. Luke tells the story of Jesus' birth from Mary's standpoint, describing her maidenly fears (1:26f), her humble submission to the will of God (1:38), her paean of praise to God for the favor accorded her in being the mother of the Messiah (1:39-55). Matthew, on the other hand tells the story from the standpoint of Joseph, describing his reaction when he found she was with child, his determination to protect her from shame and contumely as much as possible, his obedience to God's command that he marry Mary, his taking her and Jesus to Egypt to escape the wrath of Herod. The two stories harmonize and dovetail perfectly.

Mary shows herself to be a woman with a quiet spirit, humble piety, self-control, and knowledge of the OT. She was not given to talking with others about the mysteries of her experience, but kept all these things hidden in her heart (Luke 2: 51). It is apparent that neither she nor Joseph fully understood her Son (Luke 2:50). In spite of their experiences with the supernatural in relation to Him, He was something of an enigma to them.

2. Mary at Cana of Galilee (John 2:1-11). In this episode Mary seems to have some intimation that Jesus possessed more than natural powers.

She may have needed some correction from Him regarding her notion about the use of those powers, but it is wrong to think that Jesus sharply rebuked her. It must be kept in mind that He actually did exercise His power by relieving an embarrassing situation, as she had suggested; and the word "woman" is the same word He used when on the cross He tenderly commended her to the beloved disciple (John 19:26). His words to her were a gentle suggestion that it was not for her or any other human being to determine His course of action, for that was entirely in the Father's hands.

3. The Episode of Matthew 12:46; Mark 3:21, 31ff; Luke 8:19-21. In this incident Jesus is informed, while teaching the multitudes, that His mother and brothers desire to see Him. The reason for this desire is not stated; but it appears from the context in Mark's account that they were concerned for His safety because of the bitter opposition of the authorities, who were accusing Him of casting out demons in the power of Beelzebub, and they wanted to induce Him to go into retirement for a time, until it was safe to teach in public again. Jesus' words, "For whosoever shall do the will of God, the same is my brother, and sister, and mother," are meant to teach that physical relationship to Him conveys no special privilege, no right of interference with Him, the same lesson that He taught on a later occasion, in Luke 11:27.

4. Mary at the Cross (John 19:25ff). In this incident we find Mary, who had come to Jerusalem for the Passover, watching with agony the crucifixion. Jesus shows His appreciation of the earthly filial relation by committing her to the trustworthy keeping of the apostle who was closest to Him.

5. The Scene in the Upper Room (Acts 1:14). After the resurrection and ascension of Jesus, Mary appears in the midst of the Christian community, engaged with them in prayer for the baptism of the Holy Spirit, but without any discernible pre-eminence among them. This is the last notice of her in Scripture. It is not known how or when she died.

After Mary's death many legends grew up around her name, but none of them are trustworthy. The craze for further particulars about her was partly satisfied by the writers of the Apocryphal Gospels. There is no direct evidence of prayer being offered to Mary during the first four centuries. Augustine was among the earliest of the Church Fathers who thought it possible that she had never committed actual sins, although he agreed that she shared the common corruption of humanity. This led eventually to the promulgation by the pope of the dogma of the Immaculate Conception of Mary in 1854. About the middle of the fifth century some Christian leaders, wishing to exalt her, began to vie with one another in inventing new phrases in her honor. With the development of the idea that the celibate and virgin state is morally superior to the married state, it was suggested that she was a perpetual virgin and that the "brothers" and "sisters" of Jesus mentioned in the Gospels were not her children at all, but were either Joseph's children by a prior marriage or were the cousins of Jesus. In 1950 the pope declared the dogma of the Assumption of Mary, that is, that Mary's body did not decompose in the grave, but was reunited by God to her soul soon after she died. Roman Catholic theologians now openly refer to Mary as the "Co-creator" and the "Co-redemptrix" of the race. None of these post-apostolic developments have any support in Scripture. S.B.

MASCHIL (mǎs′kĭl, Heb. *maskîl, attentive, intelligent*), a Hebrew word found in the titles of Psalms 32; 42; 44; 45; 52; 53; 54; 55; 74; 78; 88; 89; 142. The meaning of the word is not certain, but it is usually taken to mean an instructive or meditative ode.

MASH (Heb. *mash*), a son of Aram and grandson of Shem (Gen. 10:22,23). Called "Meshech" in I Chronicles 1:17.

MASHAL (mā′shăl), a village in Asher (Josh. 19:26), assigned to the Gershonite Levites (Josh. 21:30). Called "Misheal" in Joshua 19:26, and "Mishal" in Joshua 21:30. It was probably located in the plain S of Acre, but its exact location is unknown.

MASON (See Occupations and Professions)

MASREKAH (mǎs′rē-kà, Heb. *masrēqâh*, perhaps, *vineyard*), a place mentioned in the list of kings that reigned in Edom "before there reigned any king over the children of Israel" (Gen. 36:31). It was the royal city of Samlah, son of Hadad (Gen. 36:36; I Chron. 1:47). Its locality is unknown.

MASSA (mǎs′à, *burden*), a tribe descended from Ishmael (Gen. 25:14; I Chron. 1:30). The marginal reading of the heading to Proverbs 31 refers to Lemuel as king of Massa, but the reading is doubtful. The tribe lived in the Arabian desert near the Persian Gulf.

MASSAH (mǎs′à, *strife*), name given to the site of the rock in Horeb from which Moses drew water for the rebellious Hebrews (Exod. 17:1-7; Deut. 6:16; 9:22). The name is connected with Meribah (Deut. 33:8).

MASTER, a term used to render a dozen Hebrew and Greek words in the Bible: (1) *'ādhôn, ruler, lord* (Sir); often it denotes the master of a servant or slave (Gen. 24:9; 39:2; etc.); in the plural it usually is used only of God; (2) *sar, prince, chief* (I Chron. 15:27); (3) *ba'al, owner* (Exod. 22:8; Judg. 19:22; Isa. 1:3); (4) *'ûr* (Mal. 2:12); (5) *rav* (Jonah 1:6; Dan. 1:3; etc.); (6) *didáskalos, teacher* (Matt. 8:19; 9:11; etc.); (7) *despótes, sovereign master* (I Tim. 6:1; II Tim. 2:21); (8) *epistátes, overseer* (Luke 5:5; 8:24; 45; etc.); (9) *kathegetés, guide, leader* (Matt. 23:10); (10) *kúrios, lord*, used frequently of God or of Christ (Matt. 1:20,24); (11) *kubernétes, steersman, shipmaster* (Acts 27:11); (12) *rhabbí* (Matt. 26:25,49).

MATHUSALA (See Methuselah)

MATRED (mā′trěd, Heb. *matredh, expulsion*), the mother of Mehetabel, wife of king Hadar of Edom (Gen. 36:39), called Hadad in I Chronicles 1:50).

MATRI (mā′trī, Heb. *matrî, rainy*), head of a family of Benjamites from which Saul, son of Kish, was chosen by Samuel to be king of Israel (I Sam. 10:21).

MATTAN (mǎt′ǎn, Heb. *mattān, a gift*). 1. A priest of Baal. He was among those who were slain under Jehoiada when Queen Athaliah had made Baal-worship supplant the worship of Jehovah (II Kings 11:1-18). Following the slaughter of Athaliah, a new order was begun (II Chron. 23:16f).

2. Another man named Mattan was among the conspirators who, incensed by the prophecies of Jeremiah, cast him into a filthy dungeon from which he was rescued by order of King Zedekiah (Jer. 38:1-28).

MATTANAH (mǎt′à-nà, Heb. *mattānâh, a gift*), the name of one of the camps of Israel while en route to Canaan, probably the site of a good well (Num. 21:18).

MATTANIAH (măt′à-nī′à, Heb. *mattanyāhû, gift from Jehovah*). This was a common name among the Hebrews; ten men who bore it are found in the OT record: 1. A brother of Jehoiachin's father whom Nebuchadnezzar set in Jehoiachin's place as king, changing the name to Zedekiah, which means Jehovah is mighty (II Kings 24:17).

2. A descendant of Asaph and chief choir leader (Neh. 11:17; 12:8). He was also a watchman over the storehouse (Neh. 12:25).

3. A Levite whose descendant, Jehazael, was inspired to help King Jehoshaphat battle against invaders from Moab (II Chron. 20:14).

4. Son of Elam.

5. A son of Zattu.

6. A son of Pahath-Moab.

7. A son of Bani, here as 4-7, one of those who had to put away alien wives (Ezra 10:26,27,30,37).

8. The grandfather of Hanan who was one of the Levites whom Nehemiah placed in charge of the Levitical storehouse (Neh. 13:10-13).

9. A son of Heman who was among the musicians whom David appointed to prophesy with instruments of music. He became head of the ninth group of Levites to whom was assigned this duty. There were 288 of these musicians, all skilled men (I Chron. 25:4,5,7,16).

10. A descendant of Asaph and one who helped Hezekiah restore the temple worship.

MATTATHA (See Mattathah)

MATTATHAH (măt′à-thà, Heb. *mattattâh, gift of Jehovah*), a son of Hashum who was among the

Matthew was a tax collector at Capernaum. © SPF

Israelites who put away pagan wives under Ezra (Ezra 10:33).

MATTATHIAS (măt′à-thī′ăs, Gr. *Mattathías, gift of Jehovah*). 1. One of those who stood at Ezra's right hand as he read the law (Neh. 8:4).

2. The name borne by two ancestors of Christ (Luke 3:25,26).

3. A priest, founder of the Maccabee family (I Macc., ch. 2).

4. A captain in the army of Jonathan Maccabeus (I Macc. 11:70).

5. A son of Simon the high priest (I Macc. 16: 14-16).

6. An envoy sent by Nicanor to Judas Maccabeus (II Macc. 14:19).

MATTENAI (măt′ē-nā′ī, *mattenay, a gift from Jehovah*). 1. A priest of the restoration who was among a special class called "heads of fathers" (Neh. 12:12-19).

2. Two priests under Ezra who were among the host who put away alien wives (Ezra 10:33,37).

MATTHAN (măt′hăn, Gr. *Maththán, gift of God*), grandfather of Joseph, Mary's husband (Matt. 1:15).

MATTHAT (măt′thăt, Gr. *Matthát* and *Maththát, gift of God*), two men in the ancestry of Jesus mentioned in the genealogy of Luke (Luke 3:24, 29).

MATTHEW (math′ū, Gr. *Maththaíos*), son of Alphaeus (Mark 2:14), a tax collector (*telōnēs*), also called Levi (Mark 2:14; Luke 5:27) whom Jesus met at the tax office and called to be one of His disciples (Matt. 9:9; Mark 2:14; Luke 5:27). Since double names were common among the Jews, (e.g., Simon became Peter, Thomas was called Didymus, Bartholomew was probably also named Nathanael, and Saul became Paul), there can be little doubt that Levi and Matthew were one and the same person. Levi probably changed his name to Matthew ("gift of Yahweh," or if a late form of Amittai, "true") when he became a disciple of Jesus.

The readiness with which Matthew responded to Jesus' call seems to indicate that he had previously come into contact with Jesus and His teachings and had already decided to dedicate his life to His cause. That Jesus should have chosen a Jewish tax collector who was in the employ of the Roman government to become His disciple is indeed remarkable. Tax collectors were bitterly hated by their own countrymen and regarded as little more than quislings. However, Matthew's background and talents would be of great value to Jesus. As a tax collector he was skilled at writing and keeping records. In addition, he must have been a man of deep spiritual convictions. This is revealed by his concern for his former colleagues whom he invited to a dinner at his own house (Luke's account alone (5:29-32) makes it clear that it was Matthew's house, not Jesus'), Jesus being the honored guest. No doubt Matthew's purpose was to win these men to Christ. Apart from the mention of Matthew in the lists of the Apostles (Matt. 10:3; Mark 3:18; Acts 1:13), no further notices of him are found in the NT.

W.W.W.

MATTHEW, GOSPEL OF, in the early Church Matthew was the most highly valued and widely read of the four Gospels. This is revealed both by its position in the canon — it is found in first place in all the known lists of the Gospels except two, — and by its widespread citation, for it is by far the most often quoted Gospel in the Christian literature before A.D. 180. Among the reasons for this popularity two are particularly important:

1. The Gospel's apostolic authority. Matthew's name was associated with it from at least the early second century.

2. Its emphasis on Christ's teaching. A growing church needed the authoritative word of Christ both to instruct converts and to refute heresy.

Authorship. The First Gospel, as is the case with the other three, is anonymous. Nevertheless, the Church, from the early second century until the rise of modern critical studies, unanimously ascribed it to Matthew, one of the Twelve (Matt. 9:9; 10:3; Mark 3:18; Acts 1:13), also called Levi (Mark 2:14; Luke 5:27), a tax collector by occupation. The results of source criticism, in particular the evident dependence of Matthew on Mark's Gospel, have led many, but by no means all, Biblical scholars (Of the older school the German Protestants T. Zahn and A. Schlatter, and more recently the Roman Catholic scholars B. C. Butler, and L. Vaganay, in addition to the Episcopalian, P. Parker, have defended the traditional view) to abandon the Matthaean authorship. Why would an eye witness to the life of Christ, as Matthew most certainly was, depend so heavily on Mark's account? On the other hand, how does one account for the early and unanimous tradition of Matthew's authorship? The answer of the consensus of modern Biblical scholarship is that the First Gospel was ascribed to Matthew, not because he wrote it, but because he was the author of one of its sources, viz., a sayings source, usually referred to as Q (from the German, *Quelle*, "source").

Despite the results of source criticism strong arguments persist for the traditional view: 1. Matthew's occupation as a tax collector peculiarly qualified him to be the official recorder of the words and works of Jesus. His job accustomed him to note-taking and the keeping of records. Since shorthand was widely known in the ancient Hellenistic world, perhaps he kept a shorthand-notebook record of Jesus' activities and teachings. E. J. Goodspeed suggests that Jesus, after the practice of the prophets (cf. Isa. 8:16,17), may have called Matthew to become a disciple for the specific purpose of preserving for posterity a written account of His teachings (*Matthew Apostle and Evangelist*, Philadelphia: Winston, 1959, pp. 50-56).

2. There is good historical tradition that Matthew actually wrote Gospel material. This comes from Papias of Hierapolis as quoted by the church historian Eusebius: "Matthew wrote down the *Logia* in the Hebrew [i.e., Aramaic] language and everyone translated them as best he could" (*Church History*, III, xxxix, 16). Much uncertainty exists as to the meaning of this famous statement, but one of two explanations seems most likely: (a) the reference is to an Aramaic Gospel, written by Matthew prior to the Greek Gospel, for the Jewish-Christian community in Palestine; (b) Papias' statement refers to an Aramaic compilation of the sayings of our Lord made by Matthew for the instruction of Jewish converts.

In either case the Matthaean authorship of our present Greek Gospel is not excluded. If an Aramaic Gospel preceded our Matthew, the publication of the Greek edition completely superseded the Aramaic, since no fragment of an Aramaic Matthew remains. A Greek edition is more likely than a Greek translation, since the Greek Gospel does not, on the whole, give evidence of being a translation. If the second alternative is accepted, viz., that the *Logia* were a collection of our Lord's sayings, then it is possible that Matthew expanded these into a Greek Gospel. It is a significant fact that the so-called Q material, with which Matthew's *Logia* is most often associated, shows signs of being a translation from Aramaic.

It should further be noted that the Matthaean authorship of the First Gospel does not necessarily rule out its dependence upon Mark. Dr. G. E. Ladd well remarks: "If Matthew wrote a first edition of his Gospel in Aramaic for the Jewish-Christian community in Antioch and Mark wrote a Gospel in Rome embodying the Petrine tradition, it is entirely credible that when Matthew later produced a second edition in Greek, he made free use of the Petrine Gospel, thereby adding his own testimony to its authority and proving that the apostolic witness to Christ was not divided" (*More Light on the Synoptics, ChT*, March 2, 1959, p. 16).

3. It is more likely that the Gospel would have taken its name from the person who put it in its Greek dress than from the author of one of its sources. Dr. Goodspeed makes a strong case for this point (*op. cit., passim*). The Greeks were not interested so much in who was the authority behind the sources of a book as in who made the book available in the Greek language. In this respect it is significant that although Peter is certainly the source of Mark's Gospel, it was not called the Gospel of Peter but of Mark.

4. The unanimous Christian tradition is that Matthew wrote it.

Thus, although certainty eludes us, there are cogent reasons for holding to the traditional view that Matthew, the Apostle and eye witness to the events of Christ's life, wrote the First Gospel. If he used other sources, in particular Mark, he added his own apostolic witness to that of Peter's, and by so doing may have contributed to the alleviation of tensions between Gentile and Jewish Christianity.

Date and Place of Origin. We do not know precisely when Matthew was written. Its dependence upon Mark and its failure to mention the destruction of Jerusalem (especially in connection with Jesus' prediction of that event in chapter 24) suggest a date shortly before A.D. 70.

Antioch is the most likely place of origin. Early in the second century Ignatius of that city refers to Matthew as "the Gospel." Also, the Gentile-Jewish character of the Antioch church accords well with the contents of the book.

Characteristics:

1. Matthew is *par excellence* the *teaching* Gospel. In this respect it greatly supplements Mark which is more interested in what Jesus *did* than in what He *said*.

2. Matthew is the Gospel of the *Church*. He is the only evangelist who uses the word church at all (16:18; 18:17). The first occurrence is in Jesus' response to Peter's confession. Here its use is clearly anticipatory. In 18:17 the context is church discipline and seems to indicate not only the existence of a "church" but the emergence of problems within it.

3. Matthew is the Gospel of *fulfillment*. It is especially concerned with showing that Christianity is the fulfillment of the OT revelation. The many OT proof texts cited by the use of the formula "that it might be fulfilled," the emphasis on the Messiahship of Jesus, and the presentation of

Christianity as a new "law" all reveal this basic concern of the author. F. F. Bruce has pointed out that "in places he even implies that the experiences of Jesus recapitulate the experiences of the people of Israel in Old Testament times. Thus, just as the children of Israel went down into Egypt in their national infancy and came out of it at the Exodus, so Jesus in His infancy must also go down to Egypt and come out of it, that the words spoken of them in Hosea 11:1 might be fulfilled in His experience, too: 'Out of Egypt have I called my son' (Matt. 2:15)" (*The New Testament Documents*, Grand Rapids: Eerdmans, 1960, p. 41).

4. Matthew is the Gospel of the King. The genealogy of chapter one traces His lineage back to David; at His birth the magi come asking, "Where is he that is born King of the Jews?" (2:2); eight times the regal title "Son of David" is ascribed to Christ (1:1; 9:27; 12:23; 15:22; 20:30,31; 21:9,15); the triumphal entry clearly has kingly significance (21:1-11); in the Olivet Discourse Jesus prophesies His future kingly reign (25:31); Pilate asks, "Art thou the King of the Jews?" to which Jesus gives the tacit assent, "Thou sayest" (27:11); and over the cross the words are written, "This is Jesus the king of the Jews" (27:37). The climax comes at the very end of the Gospel when Jesus in the Great Commission declares: "All power is given unto me in heaven and on earth" (28:18). There can be no doubt that the author of this Gospel deliberately presents Jesus as the King.

Structure. The arrangement of the material reveals an artistic touch. The whole of the Gospel is woven around five great discourses: (1) 5-7; (2) 10; (3) 13; (4) 18; (5) 24,25, each of which concludes with the refrain, "And it came to pass when Jesus had ended these sayings ..." In each case the narrative portions appropriately lead up to the discourses. The Gospel has a fitting prologue (1,2) and a challenging epilogue (28:16-20).

Outline:
1. Prologue: the birth of the King (1,2).
2. Narrative: the preparation of the King (3,4).
3. First discourse: the law of the Kingdom (5-7).
4. Narrative: the power of the King (8,9).
5. Second discourse: the proclamation of the Kingdom (10).
6. Narrative: the rejection of the King (11,12).
7. Third discourse: the growth of the Kingdom (13).
8. Narrative: the mission of the King (14-17).
9. Fourth discourse: the fellowship of the Kingdom (18).
10. Narrative: the King goes to Jerusalem (19-23).
11. Fifth discourse: the consummation of the Kingdom (24,25).
12. Narrative: the death and resurrection of the King (26:1-28:15).
13. Epilogue: the great challenge of the Kingdom (28:16-20).

Bibliography. W. Barclay, *The Gospel of Matthew, Daily Study Bible*, 2 vols. Philadelphia: Westminster, 1959; F. F. Bruce, *The New Testament Documents*, Grand Rapids: Eerdmans, 1960; E. J. Goodspeed, *Matthew Apostle and Evangelist*, Philadelphia: Winston, 1959; F. W. Green, *The Gospel according to Saint Matthew, The Clarendon Bible*, Oxford: Clarendon Press, 1936.
W.W.W.

MATTHIAS (mă-thī'ăs, Gr. *Matthías* or *Maththías, gift of Jehovah*), the one chosen by lot after the death of Judas Iscariot to take his place among the twelve apostles (Acts 1:15-26). He had been numbered among the followers of Christ (Acts 1:21,22). Some number him among the seventy, as, for instance, Clement of Alexandria and Eusebius. Nothing certain is known of his career subsequent to his appointment.

MATTITHIAH (măt'ĭ-thī'à, Heb. *mattithyâh, gift of Jehovah*), there are at least four men bearing this name in the OT. Scholars differ somewhat as to their identification. 1. A Korahite Levite, born of Shallum, put in charge of the baked offerings of the temple after the Exile (I Chron. 9:31).

2. A Levite, the sixth son of Jeduthun, appointed by David to minister before the ark in music and thanksgiving (I Chron. 15:18,21; 16:5; 25:3,21). Some make the man in 16:5 a different person but probably this is unwarranted.

3. One of the sons of Nebo who, after the Exile, put away his Gentile wife (Ezra 10:43).

4. One who stood at the right hand of Ezra as he read the law to the people (Neh. 8:4). He could possibly be identified with Mattithiah of I Chronicles 9:31.

MATTOCK (măt'ŭk, Heb. *mahărēshâh* [I Sam. 13: 20,21]; *herob* [II Chron. 34:6 — only in the margin in the RV], *ma'dēr* [Isa. 7:25]), a single-headed pickaxe with a point on one side and a broad edge on the other for digging and cutting.

MAUL (Heb. *mēphîts, a breaker*), originally a hammer such as used by coppersmiths. Today it refers to any smashing weapon like those carried by most shepherds (Prov. 25:18).

MAW (Heb. *qēbâh*), one of the stomachs of a ruminating animal. It was greatly prized by the ancients and with the shoulder and cheeks became the priest's portion of the sacrificial victims (Deut. 18:3).

MAZZAROTH (See Astronomy)

MEADOW (mě'dō, Heb. *'āhû* [Gen. 41:2,18], *ma'arēh* [Judg. 20:33]), the first word, meaning "reeds," would make a meadow to be a place where reeds grow. The word comes from an Egyptian word meaning "marshy ground." The second word implies a portion of land without trees.

MEAH (mē'à, Heb. *mē'âh, hundred*), a tower between the sheep gate and the tower of Hananeel, being the most important point in this area on the Jerusalem wall. The origin of the name is unknown.

MEAL (Heb. *qemah* [Gen. 18:6]; *sōleth* [Lev. 2:1]; Gr. *áleuron* [Matt. 13:33]), the ground grain used for both food and sacrificial offerings. It typified Christ in His perfect humanity. It has a remote figurative use in such passages as Isaiah 47:2 and Hosea 8:7.

MEAL OFFERING (See Offerings)

MEALS in the Bible periods varied greatly in time of eating, diet and table customs. Generally two meals were served daily, although three were not uncommon. The time of these meals was not set like ours today. The first meal of the day could be served at any time from early morning until noon (Prov. 31:15; John 21:12,15). The rank and occupation of a person caused the time of the noon meal to vary. It came after the morning meal when the morning was completed (Mark 7:4) or when the noonday heat made work too difficult (Ruth 2:14). The evening meal was not served at any set time but came when the day's work ended. This was usually the principal meal of the Hebrews (Ruth 3:7), while the Egyptians served their main meal at noon (Gen. 43:16). Jesus fed the multitudes at the end of the day (Matt. 14:15; Mark 6:35; Luke 9:12).

The food of the orientals generally may be classified into three groups, vegetables, fruits and animal foods. Wheat, barley, millet, spelt, lentils, beans, cucumbers, onions, leeks, garlic, salt-wort, pods of the carob tree referred to as "husks," and wild gourds were all eaten by the orientals. The corn referred to in the Bible was wheat. The grain was often picked in the field, rubbed in the hands to separate it from the chaff and eaten raw (Luke 6:1). Sometimes it was crushed with mortar and pestle and made into a porridge or cakes (Num. 11:8; Prov. 27:22). More often the grain was ground between two stones. The grinding was usually done by women (Matt. 24:41) or by servants (Exod. 11:5; Judg. 16:21).

No meal was considered complete without bread. "Indeed, in a sense, it constituted the meal. For the blessing was spoken over the bread, and this was supposed to cover all the rest of the food that followed . . ." (Alfred Edersheim, *The Life and Times of Jesus the Messiah*, New York: Longmans, Green & Co., 1897, Vol. II, p. 206). Bread was both leavened and unleavened. Sometimes honey and oil were mixed into the dough as it was being made in the kneading-troughs or wooden bowls. In these times of poverty bread was made from beans, millet and spelt (Ezek. 4:9)." (H. I. Hester, *At Home With the Hebrews,* Missouri: The William Jewell Press, 1942, p. 22). Bread was usually eaten warm and seldom by itself, but was served with sour wine or meat gravy. (John 13:26; 21:13).

Spices, used freely as flavors, consisted of cummin or dill, mustard or mint. Salt also became an important item in the diet of these people.

Fruits grew in great abundance in Palestine and consisted of grapes, figs, olives, mulberries (Sycamore), pomegranates, oranges, lemons, melons, dates, almonds and walnuts. Grapes were eaten as fresh food and dried as raisins. They were the chief source of the wines, which were used both sweet and fermented. Olives were eaten as food as well as used to make olive oil. There were two kinds of figs, early (Isa. 28:4) and late (Jer. 8:13). The late figs were dried and pressed into cakes. Dates were used both raw and dried.

The bulk of the meat came from sheep, lambs, kids and fatted calves. Swine were eaten, but not by the Hebrews. Some game such as the hart, gazelle, goat, antelope and deer as well as doves, turtle-dove and quail formed part of the meat diet. Some eggs were used for food (Isa. 10:14), locusts and fish. The Hebrews used milk from cattle and goats for drinking. From this they made cheese and butter. Arabs drank the milk from camels. The cheese was made from curdled milk and after being salted and formed into small units was placed in the sun to dry. Some of this was later mixed with water to make a sour but cooling drink.

Knives, forks and spoons were not used in eating. Meat was cooked and placed with its gravy in a large dish on the table. The contents were taken either with the fingers or placed on bread and carried to the mouth. The hands were usually washed and a prayer was offered before the meal. The Egyptians sat at a small round table for their meals. The early Hebrews sat, knelt or squatted as they ate. "After the time of Amos (750 B.C.) it came to be the custom to recline at meals . . ."

(Ibid. p. 75). This was probably derived from the Persians and became the NT practice. Women were sometimes included and sometimes excluded at mealtime. Three generally lay on one couch. Thus the head of one was on the bosom of another (John 13:23-25). They reclined at the three sides of a rectangular table leaving the fourth side free for the servants to use in serving.

Food was cooked in a variety of ways over a fire made from charcoal (Prov. 26:21), sticks (I Kings 17:10), thorns (Isa. 33:12), or grass (Luke 12:28). Archaeology is throwing light increasingly on the variety of utensils used in preparing food.   H.Z.C.

MEARAH (mē-ā'rà, Heb. *me'ârâh, cave*), a town or district in NE Palestine belonging to the Zidonians (Josh. 13:4). It may exist today as the modern village, Mogheiriyeh.

MEASURE (See Weights and Measures)

MEAT (See Food)

MEAT OFFERING (See Offerings)

MEBUNNAI (mē-bŭn'ī, Heb. *mevunnay, well-built*), one of David's bodyguard (II Sam. 23:27) who slew a Philistine giant (II Sam. 21:18). Due to a scribal error the spelling of this name is quite varied.

MECHERATHITE (mē-kē'răth-īt, Heb. *mekhērā-thî, dweller in Mecharah*), a description of Hepher, one of David's mighty men (I Chron. 11:36). Perhaps the name should read, Maachathite (II Sam. 23:34).

MEDAD (mē'dăd, Heb. *mēdhādh, affectionate*), one of the 70 elders appointed to assist Moses in the government of the people (Num. 11:24-30). He, together with Eldad, empowered by the Spirit, remained in the camp and prophesied. Joshua attempted to hinder them but they were defended by Moses.

Supper in the guest chamber of an Arab village in an area north of Jerusalem. © MPS

MEDAN (mē′dăn, Heb. *medhān, strife*), a son of Abraham by Keturah (Gen. 25:2; I Chron. 1:32), brother of Midian and by some writers mistaken for him.

MEDEBA (mĕd′ē-bà, Heb. *mêdhevā', uncertain*), a city lying high in the grazing section of Moab E of the Jordan, and first referred to in Numbers 21:30. It is part of the section of land assigned to the tribe of Reuben (Josh. 13:9), and is remarkably level portion of land (Denis Baly, *The Geography of the Bible*, New York: Harper & Brothers, 1957, pp. 30,172). The claim to this land was often disputed by the Reubenites, Ammonites and the Moabites. "Reuben, however, soon vanished from the scene, swallowed up by the vengeful Moab, and after the time of Joshua the tribe is only mentioned three times," (Ibid. p. 236). The Ammonites united with the Syrians in a campaign against Joab and were successfully defeated (I Chron. 19:7). The Biblical records together with the testimony of the Moabite Stone shows that it was constantly changing hands (cf. I Chron. 19:7 with Isa. 15:2). From I Maccabees one reads how John, the son of Mattathias was murdered by Jambri of Medeba. Jonathan and Simon avenged this death by lying in ambush in a cave and slaughtering a marriage party of the Jambri that was passing by (I Macc. 9:36-42). Josephus shows that later the city was taken by Hyrcanus after the death of Antiochus (*Antiquities of the Jews* 13:9, section 1). Later on in Roman history it became a seat of one of the early bishops. Today the modern Arab village, Madeba, occupies the general area, but the ruins of the old civilization are much in evidence. Some archaeological work has been carried on here. In 1896 an ancient mosaic map of Palestine was discovered and while it is badly damaged, it has proven of real value.

Ancient Mosaic map of Palestine, dating back to the fifth century A.D., in the Greek Orthodox church in Madeba. © MPS

MEDES, MEDIA (mēdz, mē′dĭ-à, Heb. *mādhî, mādhay*), the inhabitants of the land of Media. The boundaries of this land have varied from time to time, but generally it was regarded as that land to the W and S of the Caspian Sea. It was bounded on the W by the Zagros mountains, on the N by the Araxes and Cyrus rivers, on the E by Hyrcania and the great Salt Desert, and on the S by Susiana or Elam. Josephus feels its name was derived from Madai, the son of Japhet (*Antiquities of the Jews*, 1:6, section 1). It is shaped like a parallelogram with its longest portion extending 600 miles and its greatest width about 250 miles,

thus making it a territory of approximately 150,000 square miles (George Rawlinson, *The Seven Great Monarchies*, New York: John B. Alden, Vol. II, 1885, pp. 3-4). It had many natural barriers, making its defense easy. Its water supply was scant, thus making much of the land arid and sterile, though some of its valleys were abundantly productive. Irrigation for the most part was impractical, for some of its rivers were salty while others had worn such deep canyons as to make their waters useless for this purpose. Its few towns were scattered, since its people preferred to live in small groups. Its climate was varied, with some extreme temperatures in both directions. Minerals were many and animals and birds were plentiful. Eventually these factors led to luxurious living, spelling the downfall of the empire. It became famous for its horses, and at one time paid a yearly tribute of 3,000 horses, plus 4,000 mules and almost 100,000 sheep.

The people of Media were warlike and skillful in their use of the bow. They were linked very closely in their background, linguistically and religiously, to the Persians whom they antedate by several centuries and with whom they eventually united. While their early worship was polytheistic, there were some monotheistic leanings that were very significant. Their worship was conducted by priests and consisted of hymns, sacrifices — bloody and unbloody — and ". . . a peculiar ceremony called that of Soma, in which an intoxicating liquor is offered to the gods, and then consumed by the priests who drink until they are drunken" (*Ibid*. p. 46). Their religion was a revolt against the nature worship about them. They believed in real spiritual intelligence divided into good and bad. At the head of the good beings was one supreme intelligence who was worshiped as supreme creator, preserver and governor of the universe. He was called Ahuro-Mazdo and was the source of all good. Later there developed a worship of heavenly bodies along with a Zoroastrian dualism.

The people were a strong power for a long period. Shalmaneser plundered several of their more important cities but "there seems to have been no attempt to set up anything like Assyrian rule over any portion of Media but only to secure tribute" (Robert W. Rogers, *A History of Babylonia & Assyria*, New York: Eaton & Mains, 1901, p. 87, 113). They continued strong and were a menace to Assyria's last king, Ashurbanipal (Joseph Swain, *The Ancient World*, New York: Vol. 1, Harper & Brothers, 1950, p. 178). After the death of Ashurbanipal, the Median king Cyaxares carried on an extensive campaign.

The more than twenty references to these people or their land in the Scriptures show their importance. II Kings refers to their cities (II Kings 17:6; 18:11), Esther tells of the binding character of their laws (Esth. 1:19), Isaiah and Daniel tell of their power against Babylon (Isa. 13:17; Dan. 5:28). The last Scriptural reference to them is in Acts 2:9 where representatives are in Jerusalem at the time of Pentecost. H.Z.C.

MEDIA (See Medes)

MEDIATION (See Mediator)

MEDIATOR (mē′dĭ-a′tẽr, Gr. *mesítes, a middle man*), one who brings about friendly relations between two or more estranged people. He corresponds to the umpire or "daysman" of Job 9:33 AV. As used in the NT *mesítes* refers to the official position of Jesus Christ as He is related to man. He is *mesítes, peacemaker*, between God and man (I Tim. 2:5). He is the agent by whom the new covenant between God and man is made efficacious (Heb. 8:6; 9:15; 12:24; II Cor. 5:18-21; Col. 1:21,22). Three facts regarding this divine ministry should be noted:

1. The Grounds of Mediation. Throughout the Bible the estrangement between man and God is repeatedly set forth. God is the moral ruler; man, His natural subject, has violated His laws, hence has gone away from God. All men are thus alienated (Rom. 3:23) because they refused to be led by the revelation which God made of Himself (Rom. 1:18-26). Three inescapable moral facts never cease to be realized by man, namely: the fact of a moral order, the fact of sin, and the fact that atonement must be provided to bring release from guilt. Since man cannot keep the law perfectly from birth until death, it is evident that he cannot be saved from the curse of sin by the law (Rom. 3:20; 8:3; John 7:19; Acts 13:39). The law, therefore, is the pedagogue, servant of God, who by making sinners aware of their estrangement from God, causes them to turn to Christ as mediator (Gal. 3:24,25).

2. Examples of Mediatorial Work. These can be found in the OT. Jonathan was intercessor for David before Saul (I Sam. 19:4). Abraham made intercession on behalf of Abimelech (Gen. 20), also Sodom (Gen. 18:23-33). Moses was mediator on behalf of Pharaoh (Exod. 8:8-13; 9:28-33) and for Israel (Exod. 33:12-17). Samuel was middleman when Israel was given a king (I Sam. 9:15-27), and when she became wicked (I Sam. 12:19).

3. Other Agents of Mediation. In addition to the intercessory work of such individuals as Moses, God dealt with Israel through other agents. Angels who acted as media through whom God's will was made known to man (Judg. 6:11; Gen. 22:15; 24:40; 32:1). Because of the tendency of unthinking worshipers to put the mediating angel in the place of the promised Messiah, later Jewish scholars refused to recognize angels as mediators. At times God appeared in human form (Dan. 8:17; Gen. 12:7; 17:1; 35:7,9). In some cases "angel of the Lord" seems to have been a manifestation of God, perhaps a temporary appearance of Messiah (Gen. 16:7; 13). As the revelation from God came to be more fully understood and the results of it more clearly seen, there came the priestly class between man and God (Lev. 1-7). With the development of this class there arose the elaborate ritualistic rules for worship whereby God set forth the requirements for making atonement. Leviticus 9-24 gives rules for special events, for healing diseases and for making atonement; chapter 25 establishes the holy days and seasons, and chapter 27 lists penalties for violation of the laws. From this elaborate ritual the priests and rabbis slowly developed a system of rules that separated man from God and made him feel wholly dependent upon the prelates for any and all contacts with God. So, as the priests degenerated, the people likewise became more wicked. During days of captivity, when priests were not always at hand to serve, the longing of the people for the Promised One increased. And when Jesus did come He broke down the middle wall of partition between sinful man and the offended God (Eph. 2:14).

J.D.F.

MEDICINE (See Diseases)

MEDITERRANEAN SEA (mĕd′ĭ-tĕ-rā′nē-ăn, Gr. *he thálassa, the sea*). This body of water was the only ocean known to the Hebrews, so by NT times

Two views of the Mediterranean shore. Above, the rugged coast of Phoenicia, showing the "Ladder of Tyre." Below, the beautiful beach at Alexandria. © MPS

was designated as *The Sea*. Smaller seas were named, as Dead (or Salt) Sea, Sea of Galilee. The Canaanites occupied the land from Jordan to the Sea (Num. 13:29). It marked the end of the Promised Land (Num. 34:5). Joshua located it as "the great sea toward the going down of the sun" (1:4). It was the utmost sea (Deut. 11:24) or hinder sea (Deut. 34:2 RSV). It was also known as the Sea of the Philistines (Exod. 23:31). "Sea of Joppa" (Ezra 3:7) should be "sea at Joppa." Cedar for the temple was shipped from Tyre to Joppa (II Chron. 2:16). This sea played a big part in NT days. On one occasion Jesus may have seen its waters (Mark 7:24). Paul's missionary tours took him across the eastern half. If he did set foot in Spain, he saw most of this inland ocean.

The sea was known and used by many early civilized people, and they had intercourse across Palestine with civilizations of the Tigris-Euphrates valley. At one time it had an open channel to the Red Sea. Drifting sands from the African desert and silt from the Nile River closed this and made a land route from Asia to Africa. The sea is 2,300 miles long and more than 1,000 miles across at its widest point. An elevated area once reached from upper Tunisia in Africa easterly to Sicily. This shallow area divides the sea into the Eastern or Levant and the western sea. Its northern shore is broken by the Grecian and the Italian peninsulas. Crete and Cyprus made havens for shippers of ancient days. Paul was on both islands during his journeys (Acts 13:4; 27:7).   J.D.F.

The Mound of Megiddo (Tell El Mutesellim), as seen from the Plain of Esdraelon, showing the excavation dump, a source of many important archaeological objects and data. © MPS

MEEKNESS (Heb. *'ănāwâh, suffering,* Gr. *praútes*), a quality often commended in Scripture. The meek (oppressed) are assured of divine help and ultimate victory (Ps. 22:26; 25:9; 37:11). Jesus was sent to minister to the oppressed (Isa. 11:4; 29:19; Zeph. 2:3; Ps. 45:4). Meekness is a fruit of the Spirit (Gal. 5:23). It is characteristic of Jesus (Matt. 11:29; II Cor. 10:1). Believers are commanded to be meek and to show a lowly spirit one to another (Eph. 4:2; Col. 3:12; Titus 3: 2). A teacher should be meek (II Tim. 2:25). Meekness is a mark of true discipleship (I Pet. 3: 15:). The word does not imply a weak, vacillating or supine nature.

MEGIDDO (mĕ-gĭd'ō, Heb. *meghiddô, meghiddôn*), a city situated on the Great Road, which linked Gaza and Damascus, and controlling the principal pass through the Carmel Range, connecting the coastal plain and the Plain of Esdraelon. The road was the channel for the flow of peaceful commerce and also the route by which the armies of antiquity marched. One of the best recorded and most interesting military operations of ancient times took place at M. when Thutmose III defeated an Asiatic coalition headed by the king of Kadesh. The importance of the city is reflected in the statement of the Egyptian king that the capture of M. was the capture of a thousand towns. The continuing practicality of the M. pass for the movement of troops is seen from its effective use in 1918 by Allenby, whose cavalry thus took the Turks by surprise. The first mention of M. in the Bible is in the list of kings defeated by Joshua W of the Jordan (Josh. 12:21). In the tribal allotments, M. was in the territory of Manasseh, but this tribe was unable to conquer M. and the other fortress cities which rimmed the plains of Esdraelon and Jezreel (Josh. 17:11; Judg. 1:27).

During the period of the judges, Israelite forces under Deborah and Barak annihilated the army of Sisera in a battle which raged in part "by the waters of Megiddo" (Judg. 5:19), the sources of the Kishon. Though the Biblical record does not relate the circumstances under which Israel finally took the city, there are indications of the greatness of M. during the Solomonic period. M. is listed among the cities in the charge of Baana, one of the 12 officers responsible in rotation for the monthly provisions of the king and his court (I Kings 4:12). It is also singled out as one of the cities to which Solomon assigned forced labor for construction (I Kings 9:15); the text speaks of store-cities and cities for chariots and horsemen (I Kings 9:19; cf. II Chron. 1:14; see below). In the coup of Jehu against Joram, king of Israel, the hard-driving Jehu killed the Israelite king with an arrow, as Joram fled in his chariot, and ordered the shooting of the Judean Ahaziah, who also was attempting to escape. Mortally wounded, Ahaziah went as far as M. and there died (II Kings 9:27). In 609 B.C. Necho of Egypt marched north to aid the Assyrian remnant at Carchemish; on his way he was opposed by Josiah, king of Judah. In the brief battle which ensued in the plain of Megiddo, Josiah was hit by the Egyptian archers and soon died (II Kings 23:29-30; II Chron. 35:20-27, esp. vs. 22).

There is but one reference to M. in the prophetical writings of the OT; Zechariah mentions a heathen mourning which took place in the plain of Esdraelon: "On that day the mourning in Jerusalem will be as great as the mourning for Hadadrimmon in the plain of Megiddo" (12:11, RSV). The single NT reference to M. is in Rev. 16:16, where the word Armageddon is compounded from the Heb. *har megiddôn,* "hill of Megiddo," at which place "the battle of that great day of God Almighty" (16:14) will be fought. The excavation of the mound of Megiddo has provided much information concerning the history and culture of the city and considerable illumination of the Biblical text. The modern name for the site is Tell el-Mutesellim, where the first archaeological work was done by G. Schumacher of the *Deutsche Orientgesellschaft* in 1903-1905.

In 1925 the Oriental Institute of the University of Chicago began a large-scale stratigraphic clearance of the entire mound and continued until 1939. When the work was halted, soundings had revealed 20 strata and the clearance had reached Stratum V. The more important discoveries include the city gate and wall, the governor's residence, and the stables of Stratum IV, the water system, the temples and palaces of earlier levels, and a remarkable find of ivories (early 12th cent. B.C., Stratum VII). Though there are questions concerning the date of Stratum IV, it usually is assigned to Solomonic times. The stables for at least 450 horses illustrate the statements of I Kings 9:15-19 and II Chron. 1:14. Evidence of similar structures had been found at Tell el-Hesi, Taanach, Gezer, and Tell el-Far'ah (Megiddo and Gezer are included among the cities in which Solomon engaged in building activities, I Kings 9:15,17). An interesting feature of Stratum IV is the use of three courses of hewn stone and a course of cedar beams, as described in the building processes of Solomon at Jerusalem (I Kings 7:12). The temples and shrines of the earlier levels and numerous cult objects from various periods shed light on the religious life of the city. Inscriptural material includes some Egyptian cartouches and titles; e.g., a fragment of a stela of Shishak (Sheshonk) appeared early in the work of the Oriental Institute. Schumacher found two seals with Heb. inscriptions, one reading "(Belonging) to Shema', servant of Jeroboam." Innumerable small objects also contribute to the knowledge of the art, daily life, and commercial relations of M. C.E.D.

MEGIDDON (See Megiddo)

MEHETABEL (mĕ-hĕt'á-bĕl, *God benefits*). 1. A daughter of Matred, wife of King Hadar (Gen. 36:39).
2. One who sought to betray Nehemiah (Neh. 6:10-13).

MEHIDA (mē-hī'dà, Heb. *mehîdhā', renowned*), ancestor and family name of some Nethinim (temple servants) who returned with Zerubbabel from Babylonia to Judah (Ezra 2:52; Neh. 7:54).

MEHIR (mē'hîr, Heb. *mehîr, price, hire*), a son of Chelub (I Chron. 4:11) and a descendant of Judah.

MEHOLATHITE (mē-hō'là-thīt, Heb. *mehôlāthî*), Gentile designation of Adriel to whom Saul married his daughter Merab (I Sam. 18:19; II Sam. 21:8). The place Abel-meholah was located in the Jordan valley near Beth-shan, the native place of Elisha (I Kings 19:16).

MEHUJAEL (mē-hū'já-ĕl, Heb. *mehûyā'ēl*), descendant of Cain through Enoch and Irad, and father of Methusael (Gen. 4:18).

MEHUMAN (mē-hū'măn, Heb. *mehûmān*), one of the eunuchs of Ahasuerus, king of Persia (Esth. 1:10).

MEJARKON (mē-jàr'kŏn, Heb. *mê hayarqôn*), a place in the tribe of Dan between Gath-rimmon and Rakkon (Josh. 19:46), probably not far from Joppa. The place has not been identified.

MEKONAH (mē-kō'nà, Heb. *mekhōnâh*), a town in the southern part of Judah near Ziklag, and inhabited after the Exile (Neh. 11:28).

MELATIAH (mĕl-à-tī'áh, Heb. *melatyâh*), a Gibeonite who helped to repair the walls of Jerusalem in the days of Nehemiah (3:7).

MELCHI (mĕl-kī, Gr. *Melcheí*), the name of two ancestors of Jesus through Mary, according to Luke's genealogy: (1) The son of Addi and father of Neri (Luke 3:28); and (2) the son of Janna and father of Levi (Luke 3:24).

MELCHIAH (See Malchiah)

MELCHISEDEC (See Melchizedek)

MELCHI-SHUA (mĕl'kī-shōō'à, Heb. *malkî-shûa'*), a son of King Saul slain with his brothers on Mount Gilboa (I Sam. 31:2). Malchi-shua in ARV).

MELCHIZEDEK, MELCHISEDEK (mĕl-kĭz'ĕ-dĕk, Heb. *malkî-tsedhek, king of righteousness*), a priest and king of Salem, which place is identified with Jerusalem. The reference in Genesis 14:18-20 is the first mention of this city in the OT.

Melchizedek went out to meet Abram after his return from the slaughter of Chedorlaomer and the kings who were with him in the Vale of Siddim. He presented Abram with bread and wine, and blessed him in the name of "God Most High, possessor of heaven and earth." Abram gave him "a tenth of all." The Hebrew word for "God" in this instance is the same as in such phrases as "God Almighty" (17:1), "the Everlasting God" (21:33), "God, the God of Israel" (33:20), and "God of Bethel" (35:7), and is the oldest Semitic designation for God. Melchizedek was thus a monotheist and worshipped essentially the same God as Abram, who recognized him as a priest.

He appears the next time in Psalm 110:4: "Thou art a priest for ever after the order of Melchizedek." This psalm is of special interest because Jesus referred to it (Matt. 22:41f; Mark 12:35f; Luke 20:41f) and it is regarded as one of the Messianic psalms. The ideal ruler of the Hebrew nation would be one who combined in his person the role of both priest and king.

The author of the Epistle to the Hebrews uses Melchizedek (Heb. 5-7) in his great argument where he shows forth Jesus Christ as the final and perfect revelation of God because in His person He is Son, and in His work He is Priest (Heb. 1:2-10:18). The author cites Psalm 110:4 indicating that Jesus' priesthood is of a different order from the Levitical "after the order of Melchizedek."

The author of Hebrews, looking back upon the history of his people, comes to the conclusion that the Levitical priesthood proved to be a failure in that it was incapable of securing victory over sin and full communion with God.

And so the author cites Psalm 110. The ideal priest must belong to "the order of Melchizedek." To the author, Christ was the fulfillment of this prophecy, for He came out of Judah, a tribe with no connection with the Levitical priesthood. While the claims of the old priesthood were based on genealogy, Christ's were displayed in His power of an endless life. The claim of Jesus to be the real fulfillment of the psalmist's prophecy rested upon the fact of His resurrection and the proof which it afforded that His life was indestructible. The psalmist had declared that the ideal high priest would be forever — and only one whose life could not be destroyed by death could be said to answer to the psalmist's ideal, a priest after "the order of Melchizedek." J.G.J.

MELEA (mē'lē-à, Gr. *Meleá*), an ancestor of Jesus through Mary, in Luke's genealogy (Luke 3:31).

MELECH (mē'lĕk, Heb. *melekh, king*), a son of Micah, a grandson of Mephibosheth or Meribbaal, and a great grandson of Jonathan, mentioned in the genealogy of Benjamin (I Chron. 8:35; 9:41).

MELICU (See Malluch)

MELITA (mĕl'ĭ-tà, Gr. *Melíte*), an island, now called Malta, situated in a strategically important position some 60 miles S of Sicily. It was colonized by the Phoenicians about 1000 B.C., and became part of the empire of Carthage some four centuries later. Rome acquired the island in 218 B.C., but the Carthaginian language continued to be spoken. Hence Luke's phrase "the barbarous people" (Acts 28:2), "barbarous," of course, being used in the Greek sense of "foreign-speaking." Melita was

The modern village of Memphis, in Egypt. Below, ruins of the ancient capital. © MPS

MEMBER (Heb. *yātsur*, Gr. *mélos*), a word usually denoting any feature or part of the body (Job 17:7; James 3:5). "The members" is equivalent with "the body" (Ps. 139:16). The word is also used figuratively by the body of Christ (I Cor. 12:12-17; Eph. 4:16).

MEMPHIS (mĕm'fĭs, Heb. *nōph, mōph*; Copt. *menphe, memphi*, Gr. *Mémphis*), The first capital of united Egypt (c. 3200 B.C.), was situated on the W bank of the Nile, about 20 miles S of modern Cairo. Legend ascribes the founding of the city to Menes, the traditional first king. The original name of the city was "The White Wall"; later it was called Men-nefer-Pepi, after the name of the pyramid of Pepi I of the Sixth Dynasty, and it is from this name that "Memphis" is derived. The chief god of M. was Ptah; also prominent at Memphis was the worship of the Apis bull, whose famous burial place, the Serapeum, is located just to the W, in the necropolis of Sakkarah. All of the Biblical references to M. are in the prophets. Hosea foretold a return of Israelites to Egypt and refers to M. (Hos. 9:6). After the murder of Gedaliah, a number of Jews fled from Palestine to Egypt (cf. Jer. 41:16-18) and M. is mentioned as a place of their residence (Jer. 44:1, Noph). Both Isaiah and Jeremiah had seen the results of an Egyptian-Judean alliance and refer to M. (Isa. 19:13, Noph; Jer. 2:16, Noph). Jeremiah prophesied that M. would become a ruin (cf. Jer. 46:13,19); Ezekiel declared that the Lord would "destroy the idols and put an end to images in M." (30:13) and spoke of coming distresses in that city (30:16). To-day there is little for the casual visitor to see in the Memphite ruins and only the colossus of Rameses II and the alabaster sphinx attract tourist attention.

C.E.D.

MEMUCAN (mē-mū'căn, Heb. *memûkhān*), one of the seven wise men at the Persian court who advised King Ahasuerus to punish Queen Vashti for her refusal to appear at the court festival (Esth. 1:13-22).

MENAHEM (mĕn'à-hĕm, Heb. *menahēm, comforted*), son of Gadi and king of Israel (II Kings 15:13-22) whose reign of ten years began by killing his predecessor Shallum. "He did that which was evil in the sight of the Lord." Through gifts, collected from his subjects, he bribed the Assyrian king Pul (Tilgath-pileser III) and was thereby able to retain his throne. In this restless period of the Northern Kingdom with sinful men usurping the throne time and again, Menahem was the only king who died a natural death. His son Pekahiah inherited the kingdom.

MENAN (mē'năn, Gr. *Menná*), an ancestor of Jesus through Mary in Luke's genealogy (3:31). Only the KJV has Menan; other versions have Menna.

MENE, MENE, TEKEL, UPHARSIN (mē'nē, mē'nē, tē'kĕl, ū-fär'sĭn), four Aramaic words which suddenly appeared on the walls of Belshazzar's banquet halls where the king "made a great feast to a thousand of his lords, and drank wine" (Dan. 5) out of the golden vessels taken by Nebuchadnezzar from the temple at Jerusalem after its capture in 586 B.C. (II Kings 25:14f). The king became terrified when he saw the writing. "The wise men of Babylon" failed to interpret the words and Daniel was called in on the suggestion of the queen to decipher the message.

A great deal of discussion has taken place regarding this writing both as to the original form of the inscription and to its interpretation. The

the scene of Paul's shipwreck. "Adria" (Acts 27:27) was not the Adriatic. This sea lay between Italy, Malta, Crete, and Greece, and may be geographically identified thus by references in Strabo (2:5:20), and Pausanias (5:25:3). The wind described in Acts 27:14 would thus drive a galley from Crete to Malta, if it is assumed that a cautious pilot would fight to keep the ship as far north as possible from the Syrtes quicksands (Acts 27:17). Acts 28:3 speaks of snakes in Melita. There are none there today.

E.M.B.

MELODY (See Music)

MELON (See Plants)

MELZAR (mĕl'zàr, Heb. *ha-meltsar, overseer*), a man in whose care Daniel and his three companions were committed by the chief of the eunuchs of Nebuchadnezzar (Dan. 1:11,16). The word occurs as a proper name only in the KJV. In other versions it is translated "steward." The exact function of the melzar is unknown.

words should seem to refer to three weights in common use: the "mina," the "shekel," and the "half-mina." Or they may be terms used in Mesopotamian counting houses: "numbered, numbered, weighed, and divisions." It is to be noted that *upharsin* in the inscription (5:25) becomes *peres* in the interpretation. The *u* is the connecting participle "and," while *pharsin* is the plural form of "Peres" which word naturally suggests the Persians.

What Daniel had to deliver as the message by the mysterious writer was the fact that "God had numbered" the days of the kingdom; the king had been "weighed in the balances and . . . found wanting"; his "kingdom is divided and given to the Medes and Persians." And there was not much time between interpretation and fulfillment, for "in that night Belshazzar the Chaldean king was slain."

J.G.J.

MENI (mē'nĭ, Heb. *menî, fate, destiny*), a word translated "number" in the KJV but in other versions "destiny" in connection with Isaiah's denunciation of the rebellious people (65:11). The word can hardly have the KJV meaning. More likely it refers to the god of "good luck," which people seemed to believe in instead of the God Isaiah proclaimed. There is a connection between "Fortune" (ARV) in the same verse (cf. Gen. 30:11, ARV).

MEONENIM (mē-ŏn'ē-nĭm, Heb. *me'ônenîm*), "Plain of Meonenim" (AV) or "the oak of Meonenim" (ARV), meaning "the augur's oak (or terebinth) of Meonenim" (ARV, mg). The place is unknown, perhaps named for an oracle tree, and mentioned only in Judges 9:37.

MEONOTHAI (mē-ŏn'ō-thī, Heb. *me'ônôthay, my dwelling*), a son of Othiel and father of Ophrah (I Chron. 4:13,14). He was a descendant of Judah through Caleb.

MEPHAATH (mĕf'ā-ăth, Heb. *mēpha'ath, splendor*), a town in the territory of Reuben (Josh. 13:18) and given to the Levitical family of Merari (21:37). At the time of Eusebius and Jerome a Roman garrison was stationed in this place.

MEPHIBOSHETH (mē-fĭb'ō-shĕth, Heb. *mephîvō-sheth*). This name appears also as Meribaal in the genealogical lists of I Chronicles 8:34 and 9:40. 1. A son of King Saul and his concubine Rizpah. Together with his brother and other men Mephibosheth was delivered to the Gibeonites to be hanged with David's consent (II Sam. 21:8).

2. A son of Jonathan and grandson of Saul. His name appears as Merib-baal in the genealogical lists (I Chron. 8:34 and 9:40). After the disaster at Mt. Gilboa where both Saul and Jonathan were slain in the battle against the Philistines (II Sam. 1:4; I Chron. 10:1-8) Mephibosheth as a child of five was carried by his nurse to Lodebar, E of the Jordan where they took refuge in the house of Maachir, the son of Ammiel (II Sam. 9:4).

Upon David's accession to the throne Mephibosheth was called back to Jerusalem, given his father's inheritance, and allowed to eat at the king's table for the rest of his life. Saul's servant Ziba was commanded to serve him. The servant, however, tried to ingratiate himself with David at the expense of his master (II Sam. 16:1-4) by representing Mephibosheth as a traitor. David did not fully believe the servant's story, for later he received Mephibosheth in a friendly manner (II Sam. 19:24-30).

Mephibosheth was the father of Mica (II Sam. 9:12), or Micah in I Chronicles 8:35.

MERAB (mē'răb, Heb. *mērav*, perhaps *increase*), the older daughter of King Saul, her sister being Michal. After David had killed Goliath, the women sang his praises (I Sam. 18:7) and aroused Saul's jealousy. Saul sought to have David killed by the Philistines and so promised him Merab as wife if he would fight valiantly; then gave Merab to another man; but Michal loved David, and to win her David killed 200 Philistines. In II Samuel 21:8 by an early copyist's error "Michal" is written for "Merab," as the context clearly shows. Merab's five sons were slain by the men of Gibeon.

MERAIAH (mē-rā'yà, *rebellious*), a priest of Israel in the time of Joiakim (Neh. 12:12).

MERAIOTH (mē-rā'yŏth, Heb. *merāyôth, rebellious*). 1. A high priest of Israel in the seventh generation from Aaron (I Chron. 6:6,7).

2. Another in the priestly line and ancestor of the great Hilkiah (I Chron. 9:11).

3. Ancestor of Helkai, a priest in the days of Joiakim the high priest (Neh. 12:15). This one may have been the same as "Meremoth" in Nehemiah 12:3. In the very ancient Hebrew script the names are quite similar.

MERARI (mē-ra'rī, Heb. *merārî, bitter*), the youngest son of Levi who of course was patriarch of the tribe of Levi. The high priesthood descended through Aaron, and the other Levites assisted in the divine service. The "Merarites" had the responsibility for the woodwork of the tabernacle in its journeys (Num. 3:17,33-37). Later, they had 12 cities in Reuben, Gad and Zebulun (Josh. 21:7, 34-40).

MERATHAIM (mĕr-à-thā'ĭm, *repeated rebellion*), a symbolic name for Babylon, used by Jeremiah (50:21) in his "doom of Babylon" in chapters 50 and 51.

MERCHANDISE, MERCHANT (See Commerce)

MERCURIUS (mĕr-kū'rĭ-ŭs, Gr. *Hermés*), in English, Mercury, according to Greek mythology son of Zeus or Jupiter and Maia, the oldest of the Pleiades. As messenger of the gods he had wings on his feet and was notable also for eloquence. The people of Lystra called Paul "Mercury" because he was the chief speaker, and called Barnabas Jupiter (Acts 14:12).

MERCURY (See Mercurius)

MERCY (Heb. *hesedh, kindness, raham, bowels, hānan, gracious,* Gr. *éleos, kindness, oiktirmós, compassion*). 1. Forbearance from inflicting punishment upon an adversary or a law-breaker.

2. That compassion which causes one to help the weak, the sick or the poor. Showing mercy is one of the cardinal virtues of a true Christian (James 2:1-13) and is one of the determinants of God's treatment to us. Christian mercy is a part of the "fruit of the Spirit" (Gal. 5:22,23), made up in part of love, long-suffering, gentleness and goodness. God's mercy toward sinful man was shown most clearly and fully in His giving of His beloved Son to die in our stead; and our Lord's mercy enabled Him to make willingly the awful sacrifice (Rom. 5:8).

MERCY SEAT (See Tabernacle)

MERED (mē'rĕd, *rebellion*), a descendant of Judah who married a daughter of one of the Pharaohs (I Chron. 4:17,18).

MEREMOTH (mĕr'ē-mŏth, Heb. *meremôth, elevations*). 1. A priest who returned from Babylon with Zerubbabel (Neh. 12:3). 2. One who returned with Ezra 457 B.C. and who weighed the silver and gold that had been brought back. He was son of Uriah, a priest of Israel (Ezra 8:33). He helped Nehemiah to rebuild the wall (Neh. 3:4,21). (These may be two persons.)

3. One who had taken a foreign wife (Ezra 10:36).

4. A priest who signed the covenant with Nehemiah (Neh. 10:5).

MERES (mē'rez, *worthy*), a Persian prince under Xerxes ("Ahasuerus") (Esth. 1:14).

MERIBAH (měr'ĭ-bà, Heb. *merîbâh, contention*).

1. A place near and to the NW of Sinai where Moses, at the command of Jehovah, struck the rock and water gushed out for the refreshment of the people (Exod. 17:1-7). Moses named the place "Massah," i.e., "tempting," and "Meribah" because of the striving of the children of Israel, and because they tempted Jehovah.

2. A place near Kadesh-barnea where the people again thirsted and where Jehovah commanded Moses to speak to the rock. Moses exceeded his instructions, and apparently wanting some of the credit for the miracle, he struck the rock, and water came forth (Num. 20:1-13). For this arrogance, Moses was forbidden to enter the Promised Land.

MERIB-BAAL (měr'ĭb-bā'ăl, *Baal contends*), son of Jonathan, the son of king Saul (I Chron. 8:34; 9:40). Possibly the same as Mephibosheth, *q.v.*

MERIB-BAAL-KADESH (See Meribah)

MERODACH (mē-rō'dăk, Heb. *merōdhākh*, Akkad *Marduk*), a Babylonian god.

MERODACH BALADAN (mē-rō'dăk-băl'á-dăn, *Marduk has given a son*), a king of Babylon called Berodach-baladan in II Kings 20:12. He was a strong, courageous leader of the Chaldeans, who lived in the marshes of southern Mesopotamia. In 722 B.C. he rebelled against the Assyrians, who had controlled Babylon for many years, and became king of Babylon. Sargon, king of Assyria, recognized him as Babylonian king in 721. He reigned 11 years. At about 712, Merodach Baladan sent an embassy to Hezekiah. While it came ostensibly to congratulate the Hebrew king on his recovery (II Kings 20:12-19; Isa. 39:1-8), the embassy really came to invite him to join in a confederacy with Babylon, Susiana, Phoenicia, Moab, Edom, Philistia and Egypt for a grand attack on the Assyrian empire. Sargon, getting wind of the plot, attacked and defeated his enemies individually. In 710 he took Babylon; in 709 Bit-Yakin (Merodach Baladan's home in southern Mesopotamia) fell and Merodach Baladan was captured. He managed to be reinstated in his princedom of Bit-Yakin. In 703 he briefly took Babylon and ruled there, but was again driven to Bit-Yakin by Sennacherib, Sargon's son and successor. Later he was obliged to flee the country and found refuge in Elam, while the Chaldeans were subjugated. Although Merodach Baladan had failed in his project to revive the power of the city of Babylon, the Chaldeans, whose chief he was, became from his days the dominant caste in Babylon (Dan. 2:2,10; 5:7; Ezra 5:12). J.B.G.

MEROM (mē'rŏm, Heb. *mērôm, a high place*), a district near the head-waters of the Jordan river, N of the Sea of Galilee. Most of it is high in comparison with the "waters of Merom" through which the Jordan flows and which is just about sea-level. In Bible times, the waters of Merom formed a small lake, but for a long time it was only a marsh which has recently been drained. Its only mention in Scripture is in Joshua 11:5,7 as the site of the great battle of Joshua's northern campaign in which he, with the help of God, greatly discomfited Jabin, king of Hazor, and his Canaanite allies. The men of the tribe of Dan, when searching for a more commodious land for the tribe (Judg. 18) passed through this region and described it as "very good" and "the land is large."

MERONOTHITE (mē-rŏn'à-thīt), an inhabitant of Meronoth, a region in Galilee which was given to the tribe of Naphtali. Its principal town was Shimron-meron which Joshua conquered (Josh. 11:1; 12:20). For two Meronothites see I Chronicles 27:30; Nehemiah 3:7.

MEROZ (mē'roz, Heb. *mērôz*), a place in Galilee not far from Nazareth; infamous because its inhabitants "came not to the help of Jehovah" when Deborah and Barak needed help against Jabin, king of Canaan. Judges 5:23 attributes its curse to the angel of Jehovah.

MESECH (See Meshech)

MESHA (mē'shà, Heb. *mēshā', měshā'*). 1. A place in southern Arabia which marks a boundary of the habitations of the early Semitic Arabs (Gen. 10:30).

2. A Benjamite mentioned only in I Chronicles 8:9. He was probably born in Moab. (These first two seem to have the root meaning "retreat," whereas the next two are spelled differently in Hebrew and mean "welfare.")

3. A fourth generation descendant of Judah through Perez, Hezron and Caleb (I Chron. 2:42).

4. A king of Moab in the days of Ahab, and his two sons who succeeded him, Ahaziah and Jehoram. From David's time (II Sam. 8:2) Moab had been more or less subject to Israel, and Mesha, who was a sheepmaster, had been obliged to pay a tremendous tribute (II Kings 3:4), but he rebelled against Ahaziah. Jehoram, with the help of Jehoshaphat of Judah, attacked and defeated him (II Kings 3:4-27). Mesha in desperation sacrificed his own son. For Mesha's account of the affair see article on MOABITE STONE.

MESHACH (mē'shăk, Heb. *mēshakh*), the heathen name given to Mishael, one of the four princes of Judah taken by Nebuchadnezzar to be trained in his palace as counselors to the king. These four had borne names containing the syllable "el" for "God" or "iah" for "Jehovah," but the names were changed to honor gods of Babylon (Dan. 1:3-7).

MESHECH (mē'shěk, Heb. *meshekh, tall*). 1. A son of Japheth in the "Table of the Nations" (Gen. 10:2) associated with Magog and Tubal and thought by many to have been progenitors of Russians and other Slavic peoples.

2. The people descended from the preceding. They are noted as traffickers with Tyre in slaves as well as vessels of brass (Ezek. 27:13), and in Ezekiel 38,39 they are prophesied as joining in a northern confederation against Israel and as to be destroyed upon the mountains of Israel. The leader of this northern group is called "Gog."

3. A grandson of Shem, written "Mash" in Genesis 10:23 but "Meshech" in I Chronicles 1:17.

4. A tribe mentioned in Psalm 120:5 with (or probably contrasted with) the tents of Kedar. Probably the same as No. 2 above.

MESHELEMIAH (mē-shěl'ē-mī'à), father of Zechariah, leading gatekeeper of the tent of meeting. He had seven sons (I Chron. 9:21; 26:1,2,9). Called "Shelemiah" in I Chronicles 26:14.

MESHEZABEEL (mē-shěz'à-bēl, *God delivers*). 1. Ancestor of Meshullam (Neh. 3:4).

2. A covenanter with Nehemiah (Neh. 10:21).

3. A descendant of Judah through Zerah (Neh. 11:24).

MESHILLEMITH (See Meshillemoth)

MESHILLEMOTH (mē-shǐl'ē-moth, *recompense*).
1. Father of Berechiah, a noble Ephraimite who helped to clothe and feed the captives from Judah and to restore them to their homes (II Chron. 28:12).
2. Priestly ancestor of Amashsai, who dwelt at Jerusalem in the Restoration (Neh. 11:13). Meshillemith (I Chron. 9:12) is another spelling of the same name.

MESHOBAB (mē-shō'băb, *restored*), a Simeonite in the days of Hezekiah, who with others defeated the Meunim at Gedor, near Hebron, and took their pasture land (I Chron. 4:34).

MESHULLAM (mē-shǔl'ăm, Heb. *meshullām, reconciled*), a very common name in the OT. 1. Grandfather of Shaphan, trusted scribe of Josiah (II Kings 22:3).
2. A son of Zerubbabel in the Jewish royal family (I Chron. 3:19).
3. A leading Gadite in the days of Jeroboam II (I Chron. 5:13).
4. A chief Benjamite in Jerusalem (I Chron. 8:17).
5. Father of Sallu, a Benjamite of Jerusalem after the captivity (I Chron. 9:7).
6. Another Benjamite of Jerusalem (I Chron. 9:8).
7. A priest in the high-priestly lines whose descendants dwelt at Jerusalem (I Chron. 9:11; Neh. 11:11).
8. Ancestor of another priest (I Chron. 9:12).
9. A Kohathite, overseer of repairing the temple in the days of Josiah (II Chron. 34:12).
10. A chief man who returned with Ezra 457 B.C. (Ezra 8:16).
11. One appointed by Ezra in the matter of doing away with foreign marriages (Ezra 10:15).
12. One of the offenders in this matter (Ezra 10:29).
13. One who rebuilt two portions of the wall, but was connected by marriage with Tobiah, a hinderer (Neh. 3:4,30; 6:18).
14. Another repairer (Neh. 3:6).
15. One who stood with Ezra in the revival (Neh. 8:4).
16. A priest who signed the covenant with Nehemiah (Neh. 10:7).
17. Another covenanter (Neh. 10:20).
18. A man of Benjamin whose descendants lived in Jerusalem c. 444 B.C. (Neh. 11:7).
19. A priest c. 470 B.C. (Neh. 12:13).
20. Possibly the same man (Neh. 12:33).
21. Another priest c. 470 B.C. (Neh. 12:16).
22. A Levite gatekeeper at the time (Neh. 12:25).

MESHULLEMETH (mē-shǔl'ē-měth, fem. of *Meshullam*), daughter of Haruz of Jotbah, who married King Manasseh of Judah and was mother of Amon who succeeded to the throne (II Kings 21:19).

MESOBAITE (mē-sō'bà-īt, perhaps *from Zobah*), in ASV more correctly Mezobaite, a patronymic referring to a place otherwise unknown and unheard of (I Chron. 11:47).

MESOPOTAMIA (měs'ō-pō-tā'mǐ-à, from Gr. *mésos, middle,* and *pótamos, river*), the name applied in particular to the area between the Tigris and Euphrates rivers, a region which in the Hebrew is called Aram, Aram-Naharaim, or Padan-Aram, along with various other names for locali-

ties or peoples of this region. In present day application the term is used of a territory practically coextensive with modern Iraq. There are indications of the latter usage in the NT, such as Acts 7:2 and possibly Acts 2:9 (see below). The English OT frequently translates *'aram naharayim,* "Aram of the two rivers," as "Mesopotamia." Genesis 24:10 states that the servant of Abraham "went to Mesopotamia, unto the city of Nahor." This is in the vicinity of the Khabur River and attempts have been made to localize Aram-Naharaim between the Euphrates and the Khabur. Balaam, the soothsayer hired by Balak, king of Moab, to curse the Israelites, came from Pethor "of Mesopotamia" (Deut. 23:4; for a nearer definition of his homeland, see Num. 22:5). In Judges 3:8,10 the oppressor of the Israelites, Cushan-Rishathaim, is called "king of Mesopotamia." This geographic reference indicates the area E of the Euphrates and some commentators have regarded this king as a foreign conqueror of this territory.

Early in the reign of David, Hanum, the king of the Ammonites insulted the ambassadors whom David sent to bring condolences to the new Ammonite king upon the death of his father. Fearing reprisals on David's part, the Ammonites hired "chariots and horsemen from Mesopotamia, from Aram-maacah, and from Zobah" (I Chron. 19:6). In the description of the events which followed, the hired allies are lumped together under the term "Syrians." "Syria" is the usual English rendering of the Heb. *aram.* Aram (Gen. 10:22,23; I Chron. 1:17) was the progenitor of the Arameans, or Syrians. Bethuel and Laban are called Syrians (Gen. 25:20; 31:20 *et al.*) and even Jacob is referred to as a "wandering Aramean" (Deut. 26:5, RSV) from his stay in Padan-Aram, a term is used in the Bible only in connection with Jacob and which the LXX gives as Mesopotamia or Mesopotamia-Syria. There is some uncertainty concerning the meaning of the word Padan; it has been suggested that it means "garden," "field," or "plain." There can be no doubt about the location of Padan-Aram, for it is associated with Haran (Gen. 28:10; 29:4) and therefore is in the same general area as Aram-Naharaim. The most important cities in the region were Haran, on the Balikh River, and Gozan (II Kings 17:6, prob. modern Tell Halaf) on the Khabur, both of these rivers are tributaries of the Euphrates. It was in this district that relatives of Abraham lived and it is of more than passing interest to note that the names of a number of individuals thus mentioned in the Biblical text are preserved in place-names from this very area.

Several significant archaeological and historical features are associated with this Mesopotamia region. Tell Halaf is the type site for the period of prehistory whose beautifully painted pottery appears from Assyria to Syria and the Mediterranean coast. To the SE on the Euphrates, was Mari (Tell Hariri), which was an important state of the Hammurabi age. Its king, Zimri Lim, had a palace of almost 300 rooms and also a library and archives of more than 20,000 clay tablets. A royal concern for divination is attested by the presence of clay liver models found in one of the palace rooms; hepatoscopy was an important Mesopotamian practice and its appearance here is instructive in relation to the determined effort made by the king of Moab to procure Balaam to curse the Israelites. Just before the time of the Amarna letters, this area was the seat of Mitanni, a powerful Hurrian (Horite) kingdom ruled by an Indo-European aristocracy. The king of Mitanni was involved in the official correspondence with Egypt found at el-

Amarna and shortly thereafter Mitanni was overwhelmed by the Hittite Subbiluliuma.

In the NT, the mention of Mesopotamia as one of the regions from which the Jews of the Diaspora had come to Jerusalem (Acts 2:9, "residents of Mesopotamia," RSV) probably has reference to that part of the Near East included in modern Iraq and may refer more particularly to the area near ancient Babylon. Stephen's allusion to the fact that the call of God came to Abraham, "while he was in Mesopotamia, before he lived in Haran" (Acts 7:2), definitely puts southern Iraq in Mesopotamia, for Abraham was then in the city of Ur (Gen. 11:31). The southern part of Mesopotamia, including Ur and a number of other city-states, was known as Sumer; the central section was called Akkad and later was named Babylonia, after the city of Babylon gained the ascendancy; the northern division, along with Tigris, was Assyria, the land of Asshur.   C.E.D.

MESS, any dish of food *sent* to the table (Gen. 43:34; II Sam. 11:8; Heb. 12:16).

MESSIAH (mĕ-sī′à), a word that represents the Hebrew *māshîah*, the Aramaic *meshîhā′*, and the Greek *Messías*. "Messias" (John 1:41; 4:25 KJV), is a transcription of the Greek word. Thus "Messiah" is a modification of the Greek form according to the Hebrew. The basic meaning of the word is "anointed one." Christ is the English form of the Greek *Christós* which means "anointed." The Septuagint uses *Christós* 40 times to translate the Hebrew *māshîah*. In ancient Israel both persons and things consecrated to sacred purposes were anointed by having oil poured over them. When the tabernacle was dedicated, the building, its various parts, and the holy vessels were anointed (Exod. 30:26-30; 40:9-11). Official persons were consecrated with oil. Sometimes prophets were anointed when they were consecrated (I Kings 19:16). The statement in Isaiah 61:1, "the Lord hath anointed me to preach good tidings," is an allusion to this practice. Priests were also anointed with oil for their office (Exod. 29:21; Lev. 8:30). The kings apparently were anointed regularly (I Sam. 9:16; 16:3; II Sam. 12:7; I Kings 1:34). The king was "the Lord's anointed" in a special sense. In the OT the primary significance of the expression "the Lord's anointed" refers to the earthly king who is reigning over the Lord's people. It is a reference to the king's close relationship to the Lord and to the sacral character of his position and person. The Israelites did not think of crowning a king but of anointing him when he was enthroned. The fact that he was anointed was the essential characteristic of the ruler.

Where the expressions "the Lord's anointed," "mine anointed," "thine anointed," etc., occur in the OT, the reference is not used as a technical designation of the Messiah, but refers to the king of the line of David, ruling in Jerusalem, and anointed by the Lord through the priest. It is noteworthy that Isaiah uses the term only once and then of the Persian Cyrus (Isa. 45:1). Later, the expression, "Son of David" was a synonym for "Messiah" (Mark 10:47f; Matt. 21:9). It is obvious that there must be some historical connection between the designations "the Lord's anointed," "mine anointed," "thine anointed," "the anointed one," and the title "Messiah." The term "Messiah" apparently is a later expression and is an abbreviation of the fuller title "the Lord's anointed." It shows that the Messiah of Israel's Messianic hope derived His name from the sacral title of the kings of David's line. With the possible exception of

Daniel 9:25,26 the title "Messiah" as a reference to Israel's eschatological king does not occur in the OT. It appears in this sense later in the NT and in the literature of Judaism. In the NT the Messiah is "the Christ," the Greek equivalent of the Hebrew *māshîah*.

Closely related to the eschatological character of the Messiah is His political significance. He is to destroy the world powers in an act of judgment, deliver Israel from her enemies, and restore her as a nation. The Messiah is the King of this future kingdom to whose political and religious domination the other nations will yield. His mission is the redemption of Israel and His dominion is universal. This is the clear picture of the Messiah in practically all of the OT passages which refer to Him. The Messiah will put an end to war, for he is the Prince of Peace, and He will rule righteously over His people. He Himself is righteous and is called the righteous Messiah or the Messiah of righteousness (Jer. 23:6). But this implies more than a just judgment and government of His people. The term "righteousness" when used in connection with the Messiah is inseparably related to salvation. The Messiah will establish the right of His people against any foe from without or from within. He will establish this salvation and maintain it in the face of all opposing forces. Righteousness and salvation are the same because the Messiah's righteousness is declared in His saving acts. Jewish writers have made much of this with reference to Malachi 4:2. At the same time it is frequently emphasized that by His righteousness the Messiah will establish justice and righteousness, in the ethical sense, in the land. Sin will be rooted out and Israel will become a holy people.

Perhaps the most profound spiritual work of the Messiah is seen in His position as the intermediary between God and the people by interceding for them. This is the Targum's interpretation of Isaiah 53, but this chapter is much more profound than the Jewish exegetes seemed to realize. It is true that the Targum on Isaiah identifies the Servant of the Lord with the Messiah, and that it uses this expression as a title of the Messiah, but His suffering is interpreted merely as the danger and anxiety which are His lot in this war with the ungodly. There is no real distinction here between the suffering of the Servant and the suffering to which the prophets of Israel were exposed in fulfilling their mission. But what is said of the suffering of the Servant of the Lord by Isaiah is infinitely more significant than this. In the suffering Servant the Messiah is seen making vicarious atonement through His passion and death which has a positive purpose in the plan of God for the salvation of sinful men. The Messiah, as the suffering Servant in a measure sums up the entire prophetic movement and constitutes a climax in OT prophecy.

The progress of prophetic revelation in history leads up to the idea of the innocent suffering Servant of God, who in the redemptive purpose of His death reconciles men to God. In the Messiah's sacrifice of Himself as an expiation for sin His priestly office is revealed to be combined with His work as prophet and king. The redemptive work of the Messiah includes the restoration of the paradise that existed in the beginning but was lost through the fall of Adam. There will be through the Messiah the establishment of the kingdom of the end time, the kingdom of God on earth, the restoration of Israel. As the Messiah was present from the first in the creation so He is also present as the central figure of the last events. He is declared to be the first-born of creation and also its end and goal of creation (John 1:1; Col. 1:15-17; Rev. 3:14).

The NT conception of the Messiah is developed directly from the teaching of the OT. The essential features of the OT picture of the Messiah are gathered up and transformed in the person of Jesus. He combined the idea of the suffering, dying, and glorified Servant of the Lord with that of the Son of Man who will return on the clouds of heaven. It is the Messiah, as the Son of Man, who will suffer, die, and rise again on the third day. It was "according to the Scriptures" that the Son of Man must suffer and die. But even though Jesus was victorious over death in His resurrection and ascension to the right hand of the Father, yet He did not reign in His full Messiahship in His righteous kingdom. Thus His ultimate victory was revealed to be in the future and consequently He must come again in power to establish His Messianic throne and kingdom. Jesus frequently used the phrase "The Son of Man" to express His interpretation of His nature and His part in the coming of God's kingdom. It seems that Jesus preferred this title in referring to Himself. He uses it primarily not to express His humanity. On the contrary, it is a proclamation of the paradox that He, who appears as an ordinary man, is at the same time the One in whom there are supernatural powers of the kingdom of God. It means that He who took upon Himself the form of a man will some day be revealed as "the Son of Man" with power and glory. The title, then, is an expression for the triumphant Messiah who comes on the clouds in the majesty of His exaltation.

The expression "the Son of Man" used of the Messiah reflects the general picture, in the NT of a more profound view of His person. The Messiah as the Son of Man is a pre-existent heavenly being. Long before Abraham, Jesus said, the Son of Man *was* (John 8:58; cf. John 17:5; Col. 1:17). The origin of creation is linked with the Messiah Jesus in various Scriptures (Col. 1:15-17; I Cor. 8: 6; II Cor. 8:9). It is also as pre-existent that Jesus is called "elect" (I Pet. 2:6). God had prepared Him to carry out His purpose in redemption and eschatological judgment. Furthermore, the Messiah is revealed to be the Son of Man in a unique sense (John 1:1; Rom. 1:4). Jesus affirms this in His conversation with the priests and elders. Jesus is asked "Are you the Messiah . . . Are you the Son of God?" (Mark 14:62; Matt. 26:63f; Luke 22: 67-70) and His claim is clear. As the Son of God, the Messiah possesses the power of God's authority. It is as the Son of God that the divine nature of the Messiah is supremely revealed.   A.C.S.

MESSIAS (See Messiah)

METALS (See Minerals of the Bible)

METEYARD (mēt′yàrd, Heb. *middâh*), an archaic word for "measures of length" (Lev. 19:35).

METHEG-AMMAH (mē′thĕg-ăm′à, *the bridle of the metropolis*), a town David took from the hands of the Philistines (Ii Sam. 8:1). KJV makes it seem like a proper noun, but cf. ASV.

METHUSAEL (mē-thū′sā′ĕl, more correctly Methushael as in ASV), father of the Cainite Lamech before the Flood (Gen. 4:18).

METHUSELAH (mē-thū′zĕ-là, Heb. *methûshelah, man of the javelin*), antediluvian Sethite, died at 969 years of age, in the very year of the Flood (Gen. 5:22-27). He was the son of Enoch and the father of Lamech (Gen. 5:21-27).

MEUNIM (mē-ū′nĭm, Heb. *me′ûnîm, the people of Maon*), an Arab city still existing S of the Dead Sea not far from the more famous Petra. They are listed among the tribes that Uzziah of Judah conquered. II Chronicles 26:7 in KJV calls them "Mehunims." Ezra 2:50, repeated in Nehemiah 7: 52, speaks of their descendants. The Masoretes say that "habitations" (I Chron. 4:41) should read "Meunim." Ezra counts them among the "Nethinim" or temple-servants at the return (Ezra 2:50).

MEZAHAB (mĕz′à-hăb, Heb. *mêzāhāv*), grandfather of Mehetabel who married Hadar, an Edomite king (Gen. 36:39; I Chron. 1:50).

MIAMIN (mī′à-mĭn, Heb. *mîyāmîn, from the right hand* i.e. *fortunate*). 1. One who had taken a foreign wife (Ezra 10:25).
2. A priest who returned with Zerubbabel (Neh. 12:5).
3. "Mijamin" *q.v.* in I Chronicles 24:9 and Nehemiah 10:7 is the same word in Hebrew.

MIBHAR (mĭb′hàr, Heb. *mivhār, choice*), one of David's mighty men (I Chron. 11:38), the son of Haggeri (ASV more correctly Hagri).

MIBSAM (mĭb′săm, Heb. *mivsām, sweet odor*, related to *Balsam*). 1. One of the 12 Ishmaelite patriarchs, corresponding to the 12 sons of Jacob (Gen. 25:13).
2. A grandson or great-grandson of Simeon, perhaps named after the preceding (I Chron. 4:25).

MIBZAR (mĭb′zàr, Heb. *mivtsār, a fortress*), one of the 11 "sheikhs" or chiefs, not "dukes," descended from Esau (Gen. 36:42).

MICAH (mī′kà, Heb. *mîkkâh*), short form of the name *Micaiah* (or *Michael*), meaning "Who is like Jehovah (or God)?" The name is applied to seven individuals in the OT: 1. An Ephraimite mentioned in Judges 18 and 19.
2. A Reubenite listed in I Chronicles 5:5.
3. A grandson of Jonathan (I Chron. 8:34; 9: 40).
4. A Levite (I Chron.,23:20).
5. The father of one of Josiah's officers who is called *Achbor* in II Kings 22:12, but *Abdon* in II Chronicles 34:20 (Hebrew text — the Syriac says *Abchor* and the Greek manuscripts vary).
6. The canonical prophet Micah, the Moresthite (Mic. 1:1 and Jer. 26:18).
7. The son of Imlah, (II Chron. 18:14) usually called Micaiah.

Of these men, only No. 1, the Ephraimite, calls for special comment. The sixth, Micah the prophet, is unknown to us apart from the book that bears his name (see MICAH, BOOK OF). On the last, the son of Imlah, see MICAIAH.

Micah, the name of the Ephraimite, may indeed be a shortened form of Michael, as names compounded with *El*, "God," are more common in the early times before the monarchy. The record of Micah is a sad tale of apostasy in the days of the Judges. It forms a kind of appendix to the history of the 12 judges (Judg. 1 to 16), a place which it occupies along with the narrative of the Benjamite war (Judg. 19 to 21) and, in old Hebrew lists, the book of Ruth, which was at one time appended to Judges and like the other two stories concerns Bethlehem-Judah.

Micah had stolen some money from his mother, but confessed and restored it. She declared she had already dedicated it for an idol for her son and proceeded to use 200 shekels of it (a little over five pounds) to make such an image. Thereupon Micah set up a private sanctuary and ordained one of his sons as priest. Later he ordained a wandering Levite of Bethlehem-Judah. His idolatry, though far from the Mosaic prescriptions, was in the name of Jehovah and he evidently felt that a Levite, especially this Levite as we shall see, would win greater sanctity for his idol shrine.

This incident is linked with the Danite migration. The tribe of Dan first inherited in the South. Feeling restricted, they later moved to the far North where they appear later (Josh. 19:47; I Kings 12:29, etc.). On the way, their spies noticed Micah's sanctuary ·and later the Danite army pillaged Micah's shrine, abducted his priest and set up the sanctuary for their own, while the tabernacle was in Shiloh. The name of Micah's priest was Jonathan, a descendant of Moses (called *Manasseh* in Judg. 18:30 by courtesy of the Jewish scribes to protect the reputation of Moses, but the "n" is an insertion above the line! The Greek and other versions read *Moses*!) Thus Micah is mentioned incidentally to the record of this early apostasy of the tribe of Dan.   R.L.H.

MICAH, BOOK OF, the fifth of the Minor Prophets, comes from the late 700's B.C. It predicts the fall of Samaria which occurred in 722, but concerns more especially the sins and dangers of Jerusalem in the days of Hezekiah around 700 B.C. As an outline will show, the message oscillates between condemnation for present sins and God's purpose of ultimate blessing for His people:

Outline:
I. Predicted desolation of Samaria and Jerusalem, 1:1-3:12.
II. Eventual blessings for Zion, 4:1-8.
III. Invasions and deliverance by the Davidic ruler, 4:9-5:15.
IV. Condemnations for sins, 6:1-7:6.
V. Eventual help from God, 7:7-20.

In the opening portion of the book, 1:1-3:12, God's judgment is first announced upon Samaria for her idolatry. Micah's interest seems to lie chiefly in Jerusalem, however, whose desolation is announced in 3:12 in very similar terms. Chapters 2 and 3 are a catalogue of Judah's sins. Oppression of the poor was a characteristic, but another basic factor was the refusal to hear God's prophets. As in Jeremiah's day, they preferred prophets who predicted peace (cf. 3:5 with Jer. 8:10,11; Ezek. 13:10). It is not improbable that Jeremiah and Ezekiel took their texts on this subject from Micah. At least, Micah's warning of 3:12 was well known in Jeremiah's day (Jer. 26:18). Jeremiah's friends quote these words verbatim ascribing them to the Micah of Hezekiah's time. Negative critics point out that Jeremiah quotes Micah as a prophet of *doom* and they conclude that every prediction of *hope* in Micah is not genuine. The conclusion seems far-fetched. Jeremiah's friends quoted only that part of the book which was applicable to their situation. This is no argument against the rest of the book.

The second section includes millennial verses which are practically identical with Isaiah 2:1-4. Many have questioned whether Micah quoted Isaiah, or vice versa or whether both quoted a common oracle. But Isaiah 2:1 calls this passage the word of Isaiah, which should decide the matter. Micah evidently uses Isaiah's promise and skilfully weaves it into his own composition.

The third section, 4:9-5:15, comes against the background of the wars of Hezekiah's day. The Assyrians carried captive 40 cities of Judah and received tribute from Hezekiah as Sennacherib himself tells us (cf. also, II Kings 18:13-16). But God delivered Jerusalem (II Kings 18:35). The "seven shepherds and eight principal men" of 5:5 prob-

ably is merely a symbolic numerical way of saying "one great deliverer" — a numerical device that can be paralleled in old Canaanite literature of Ugarit.

Yet in this section the captivity and return from Babylon are also predicted. Negative critics insist that similar passages in Isaiah 48:20; 45:28; etc.; are late and actually written after the events described. In their denial of supernatural prediction, they must also say that Micah 4:10 is late. But according to Isaiah 39:6 and also by Assyrian testimony, Babylon was a menace in Micah's own day and these verses are quite appropriate.

Against these dangers to Judah God holds out the Messianic hope, 5:2. The mention of Bethlehem Ephratah identifies the Messiah as of David's line (cf. Isa. 11:1; Jer. 23:5; Ezek. 37:24; etc.). The "thousands of Judah" is read the "princes of Judah" in Matthew 2:6 by using different (and probably correct) vowels on the Hebrew consonants. "Thou Bethlehem," is masculine and therefore is probably a direct reference to the Messiah from Bethlehem, for the gender would be feminine if only the city were addressed.

The condemnations of Section IV (6:1-7:6) include several references to the Pentateuch and other historical books (6:4; 6:5; 6:16. Cf. also 5:6 with Gen. 10:8,9). The response of 6:8 is famous. Some have argued that it teaches salvation apart from sacrifice. Actually, it is an allusion to Deuteronomy 10:12 and involves Israel's duty to obey *all* the Mosaic injunctions. Christ probably alludes to this verse in his condemnation of the formalistic Pharisees (Matt. 23:23).

The book closes with the prophet's declaration of faith in the ultimate fulfilment of God's covenant of blessing for Abraham (7:20).   R.L.H.

MICAIAH (mī-kā′yà, Heb. *mîkhāyāhû, who is like Jehovah?*), a true prophet of God, residing at Samaria the capital of the northern tribes of Israel c. 900 B.C. in the last days of Ahab, king of Israel and of Jehoshaphat, king of Judah. Jehoshaphat, though a man of God, made the mistake of making affinity with Ahab, the worst of all the kings of Israel. (Contrast II Chron. 17:3-6 with I Kings 16:30-33.) Ahab took advantage of Jehoshaphat's visit by asking his assistance in taking Ramoth-Gilead from the Syrians whose king Benhadad I had taken it from Ahab's father, Omri. Jehoshaphat, letting his courtesy overcome his good judgment, consented, asking only that the prophets be consulted. Four hundred of Ahab's false prophets said, "Go up, for God will deliver it into the hand of the king." (For the whole story, compare I Kings 22 with II Chronicles 18).

When Jehoshaphat showed his distrust in the prophets and asked if there was not a prophet of Jehovah beside, Ahab replied "There is yet one man, but I hate him; the same is Micaiah, the son of Imla." A messenger was sent to bring Micaiah, who was told to prophesy favorably, but Micaiah replied that he could speak only what God would give him. After replying frivolously to Ahab's question, the king demanded the truth, and Micaiah told him how the hosts of heaven had planned to ruin Ahab by putting a false spirit in the mouth of all his prophets. Micaiah, after being insulted by the false prophet Zedekiah, was sent back to the city to be imprisoned and fed the bread and water of affliction until the king should return to deal with him. Micaiah boldly told Ahab that if he returned at all, Micaiah was a false prophet. Since Ahab partly believed this prophecy, he contrived a clever trick to get Jehoshaphat slain in his place. With a show of generosity he proposed that Jehoshaphat wear his kingly robes in the battle, but Ahab would disguise himself like a common soldier. To make the story short, Jehoshaphat cried out and escaped, but a Syrian drew a bow at a venture and the arrow slew Ahab. A.B.F.

MICHA (mĭ'cà, Heb. *mîkhā'*, evidently, like Micah, an abb. of Micaiah, *Who is like Jehovah?*). 1. A grandson of Jonathan (II Sam. 9:12).
2. A Levite covenanter (Neh. 10:11).
3. Another Levite (Neh. 11:17).
4. Another (Neh. 11:22; Micah in I Chron. 9:15). These are uniformly Mica in ASV.

MICHAEL (mĭ'kĕl, Heb. *mîkhā'ēl, who is like God?*). 1. Father of Sethur, a spy from the tribe of Asher (Num. 13:13).
2. Two Gadites who dwelt in Bashan (I Chron. 5:13,14).
3. A Gershonite of the 11th generation, great-grandfather of Asaph, the singer (I Chron. 6:40).
4. A chief man of Issachar (I Chron. 7:3).
5. A Benjamite (I Chron. 8:16).
6. A captain of a thousand of Manasseh who joined David in Ziklag (I Chron. 12:20).
7. The father of Omri of Issachar, one of David's mighty men (I Chron. 27:18).
8. A prince of Judah, son of Jehoshaphat and brother of Jehoram, kings of Judah (II Chron. 21:2).
9. Father of Zebadiah, a chief Jew who returned with Ezra (Ezra 8:8).
10. Last, and by far the most famous, the archangel whose chief responsibility seems to have been the care of the Jewish people. Michael had a dispute with Satan himself (Jude 9).

MICHAH (See Micah, Micha)

MICHAIAH (mĭ-kā'yà, Heb. *mîkhāyāhû, who is like Jehovah?*). 1. Father of Achbor, whom King Josiah sent with others to Huldah the prophetess to inquire about the prophecy which had been read to him (II Kings 22:12-14).
2. A daughter of Uriel of Gibeah, who had married Tamar, daughter of Absalom. She was the wife of Rehoboam of Judah and mother of Abijah who succeeded to the throne. See also "Maacah" which is another spelling of the name (II Chron. 13:2).
3. A prince of Judah whom Jehoshaphat sent to teach the people (II Chron. 17:7).
4. Ancestor of a priest in Nehemiah's time, (Neh. 12:35).
5. A priest in Nehemiah's time (Neh. 12:41).
6. Grandson of Shaphan the scribe in Josiah's day who had brought the book of the law of the Lord to the king.
In ASV the name is Micaiah.

MICHAL (mĭ'kăl, Heb. *mîkhāl*, a contraction of *mîkhā'ēl, Michael*), the younger daughter of King Saul of Israel (I Sam. 14:49). Saul, insanely jealous of David, desired to kill him but found it impossible to do so by his own hands (I Sam. 18:11), so he tried trickery. He offered David his elder daughter Merab for his service against the Philistines, but changed his mind and gave her to another; then he learned that Michal loved David, so he offered her to David if he would give evidence of having slain 100 Philistines. He slew 200 and married Michal; but Saul hated him all the more. Once, when Saul sent to slay David, Michal helped him to escape (I Sam. 19:11-17), deceiving Saul's officers by putting an image in his bed, and thus giving him time to make good his escape. Though Michal truly loved David, she could not comprehend him, and so scoffed at him for rejoicing before the Lord (II Sam. 6:16-23). As a result, she never had a child.

MICHMAS, MICHMASH (mĭk'măs, mĭk'mash, Heb. *mikhmās, mikhmāsh, a hidden place*), a place in the ancient tribe of Benjamin about eight miles NE of Jerusalem. A notable battle occurred there between Israel and the Philistines in the reign of Saul (I Sam. 13,14). Michmash lay in the pass which goes eastward from Bethel and Ai down to Jericho, and at one place the pass was contained between two rocks, "Bozez" and "Seneh" (I Sam. 14:4). There Jonathan and his armor-bearer clambered up and started the victory over the Philistines, and there the British forces under General Allenby used the same strategy and won a victory over the Turks. In Isaiah 10:28, where the prophet is picturing with dramatic detail an advance of the Assyrian forces against Jerusalem, he mentions Michmash as the place where the invaders stored their baggage, hoping no doubt, to gather it on their return (Isa. 37:36). In the return from the captivity under Zerubbabel (Ezra 2:27; Neh. 7:31) 122 men of this place are mentioned, indicating that it was a fair-sized community at the time. Here Jonathan Maccabeus made his governmental headquarters for a time (I Maccabees 9:73).

The village of Michmash, site of historic battles in the history of Israel. © MPS

MICHMETHAH (mĭk'mē-thà, Heb. *mikhmethâh*), a landmark on the borders of Ephraim and Manasseh (Josh. 16:6 and 17:7). It was eastward of, but quite close to Shechem, and instead of being a town, it may have been, as its name implies, merely a "lurking place."

MICHRI (mĭk'rī, Heb. *mikhrî*), grandfather of Elah, a Benjamite in Jerusalem after the captivity (I Chron. 9:8).

MICHTAM (mĭk'tăm, Heb. *mikhtām*), a word of uncertain meaning found in the titles of six psalms of David (16, 56-60). The margin of KJV reads, "A golden Psalm." It very likely refers to a Psalm having to do with sin — its heinousness, atonement, or consequences.

MIDDIN (mĭd'ĭn, Heb. *middîn*), one of the six cities of Judah lying in the wilderness just W of the Dead Sea (Josh. 15:61).

MIDDLE WALL, a term taken from Ephesians 2: 14, probably a reference to the barrier which stood between the Court of the Gentiles and the Court of the Jews in the temple in Jerusalem. Gentiles were forbidden to cross it under pain of death. Paul uses it as a symbol of the legal partition between Gentile and Jew, and points out that it has been removed by Christ.

MIDIAN, MIDIANITES (mĭd'ĭ-ăn, -īts, Heb. *midhyān, midhānîm*). 1. A son of Abraham by Keturah (Gen. 25:1-6).

2. His descendants and the land which they claimed, lying mostly E of the Jordan and the Dead Sea, then southward through the Arabah and (in the time of Moses) including the southern and eastern parts of the peninsula of Sinai. In Genesis 37:25,36 a caravan of traders is called "Ishmaelites," then "Midianites," the former referring to their descent from Ishmael (Gen. 25: 12-18) and the later to their abode in the land of Midian. When Moses fled from Egypt 40 years before the Exodus (Exod. 2:15-21) he helped the daughters of Reuel (or Jethro) the priest of Midian, was invited to their encampment, and married Zipporah, the priest's daughter. Thus the descendants of Moses had Midianite as well as Levite descent. Jethro, though priest of Midian, acknowledged Jehovah the God of Israel as supreme (Exod. 18:11) but neither he nor his son Hobab, though very friendly to Moses, could bring himself to join Israel (Num. 10:29).

Toward the end of the life of Moses, Midian had apparently become confederate with Moab (Num. 22:4). Through the counsel of Balaam, the Midianite women and girls wrought much harm in Israel and God commanded Moses to smite the nation (Num. 25:16-18). Two hundred years later, in the days of Gideon, God delivered Israel into the hand of Midian for seven years (Judg. 6:1-6). They allowed the Israelites to plough and to sow the seed, but they (the Midianites) did the reaping. Gideon defeated them and slew their two kings Zebah and Zalmunna (Judg. 7:21). The names of these kings, and of the princes of Midian "Oreb" and "Zeeb" (Judg. 7:25) give us a picture of their civilization — Zebah — "a slaying" or "a sacrifice"; Zalmunna — "to whom shade is denied"; Oreb — "a raven"; and Zeeb — "a wolf."

Though nomads, they had in the time of Moses great wealth; not only 675,000 sheep, 72,000 beeves (ASV "oxen"), and 61,000 asses, but also gold, silver, brass, iron, tin and lead; all of which are mentioned in the booty taken by the men of Israel (Num. 31:22,32-34). The Midianites have long since disappeared from among mankind.

A.B.F.

MIGDAL-EL (mĭg'dăl-ĕl, *tower of God*), one of the 19 fortified cities of Naphtali (Josh. 19:38); thought by some to be the "Magdala" of Matthew 15:39.

MIGDAL-GAD (mĭg'dăl-găd, *tower of Gad*), a city of Judah when Joshua divided the land (Josh. 15: 37). Now probably Mejdal about 24 miles W of Hebron.

MIGDOL (mĭg'dŏl Heb. *mighdôl*). 1. A place just W of the former shallow bay at the N end of the Gulf of Suez, the westward arm of the Red Sea (Exod. 14:2; Num. 33:7). Close by, the Israelites made their last encampment in Egypt, and here Pharaoh thought that they were entrapped.

2. A place in the N of Egypt to which many Jews resorted in the days of Jeremiah, and where they even practiced idolatry in spite of the prophet's warnings (Jer. 44:1-14; 46:14).

MIGRON (mĭg'rŏn, Heb. *mighrôn, precipice*), a locality near Gibeah of Saul about seven miles NE of Jerusalem, in the tribe of Benjamin. Here Saul sat (I Sam. 14:2) under a pomegranate tree and here he made the headquarters of his little troop of about 600 men. In Isaiah 10:28 the prophet pictures the Assyrians as passing Migron as they approach to attack Jerusalem.

MIJAMIN (mĭj'à-mĭn, Heb. *mîyāmîn, from the right hand*). 1. A priest in David's time (I Chron. 24:9).

2. A priest who covenanted with Nehemiah (Neh. 10:7).

3. A priest who returned with Zerubbabel from Babylon (Neh. 12:5,7).

4. A man who put away his foreign wife (Ezra 10:25).

MIKLOTH (mĭk'lŏth, Heb. *miqlôth, rods*). 1. A Benjamite in Jerusalem after the Exile (I Chron. 8:32; 9:37,38).

2. A ruler of 24,000 men in the time of David (I Chron. 27:4).

MIKNEIAH (mĭk-nē'yà), a Levite harp player in David's time (I Chron. 15:18,21).

MILALAI (mĭ-à-lā'ī), a priest with a musical instrument in Nehemiah's celebration (Neh. 12:36).

MILCAH (mĭlkà, Heb. *milkâh, counsel*). 1. A daughter of Haran, Abram's youngest brother, who died at Ur of the Chaldees, and sister of Lot. She married her uncle Nahor and bore him eight children of whom one was Bethuel, father of Rebekah and Laban (Gen. 11:27-29; 22:20-23).

2. One of the five daughters, co-heiresses of Zelophehad, the Manassite. They had to marry within their tribe (Num. 36, esp. vs. 12).

MILCOM (See Moloch)

MILDEW, a pale fungus growth which discolors and spoils grains and fruits in warm damp weather. In Scripture it is always associated with "blasting" (Deut. 28:22; I Kings 8:37; Amos 4:9; Hag. 2:17).

MILE (See Weights and Measures)

MILETUS (mī-lē'tŭs, Gr. *Míletos*), in KJV once Miletune. According to Pausanias, Miletus, southernmost of the Greek cities of Asia Minor, was a Cretan foundation. According to Homer, it was occupied by "foreign-speaking" Carians who fought in the Trojan confederation. Possibly a short time after the Trojan War (12th century B.C.) Ionians seized the city. In the great age of Greek colonization (eighth to sixth century B.C.) Miletus planted many *emporia* right around the circle of the Black Sea, and the wealth of such foundations points to vigorous and expansive life in the metropolis. A similar conclusion may be drawn from the fact that Miletus maintained contact with Sybaris in Italy until the fall of that town in 510, and exerted some pressure on Egypt. Miletus must have exercised strong sea-power during these active centuries, and her military might is shown by the resistance she offered to the Lydian kings, and the privileged position accorded even by the greatest of those rulers, Croesus. When Croesus' kingdom fell to the Persians in 546 B.C., no attempt was made to reduce Miletus' independence. In 499 Miletus took the lead in precipitating the Ionian Revolt. In a naval engagement at Lade she suffered defeat, and the city was occupied by the Persians in 494. The disaster ended Miletus' long prosperity, until then damaged only by the factional strife which was endemic in all ancient Greek cities. The sixth century B.C. was the "floruit" of the Milesian savants, Thales, statesman, philosopher, physicist, and astronomer, Anaximander and Anaximenes, the physicists and astronomers, and Hecataeus, the geographer. Industry flourished, and Milesian woolen goods were famous. After Persia's defeat at Mycale in 479, Miletus regained her freedom, and joined the Delian League, Athens' security organization, leaving it in 412, in the day of Athens' decline and disaster, only to fall under Persia again. In the fourth century the city was under Caria, whence came her first founders. Aspasia, blue-stocking mistress of Pericles, Hippodamus, who planned the Piraeus, and Timotheus, the poet, belong to this second period of Milesian vigor. The rest of Miletus' history was undistinguished. A silting harbor, the common bane of that coast, ended her sea-power and sea-borne commerce. At the time of St. Paul's visit (Acts 20:15, 17) Miletus was a city of no great standing in the Roman province of Asia. The sea is now ten miles from the ancient site.   E.M.B.

MILK (See Food)

MILL (Heb. *rēheh*, Gr. *múlos, mulón*), an apparatus used to grind any edible grain — wheat, barley, oats, rye, etc. — into flour. It consists of two circular stones, the lower one having a slightly convex upper surface to help the drifting of the broken grain toward the outer edge whence it drops. It is made of a hard stone, which after being shaped, is scratched with curved furrows so as to multiply the cutting and grinding effects. The lower stone has a stout stick standing at its center, and the upper one (called the rider) has a hole at its center so that it can rotate around the stick, and a handle eight or ten inches from the center by which it is turned. Generally it is worked by two women, facing each other, and each grasping the handle to turn the rider. One woman feeds the grain in at the center of the rider and the other guides and brushes the products into a little pile. The process is very ancient, for we read of "the maid-servant that is behind the mill" in the days of Moses (Exod. 11:5) and the process was no doubt old at that remote time. Even the manna which fell in the wilderness was tough enough so that the people used to grind it in mills or beat it in mortars before cooking it (Num. 11:7,8).

It is altogether probable that men pounded grain before they thought of grinding it, and so the mortar is probably more ancient even than the mill. Because men depended upon flour for "the staff of life" and because they generally ground it only as needed, it was forbidden to take a mill in pledge (Deut. 24:6). In Jeremiah 25:10 "the sound of the mill-stone" is mentioned as a sign of happy prosperous life, but in Isaiah 47:2 the prophet taunts the proud and delicate women of Babylon with the thought that they will have to become slaves and labor at the mill. When the Philistines blinded Samson (Judg. 16:21) he had to grind in the prison-house, and this mill was probably a larger one ordinarily turned by a blinded ox or donkey. Abimelech, usurping "king" of Israel, was slain by a woman who dropped a millstone upon his head (Judg. 9:53) and our Lord prophesies that at His coming "two women shall be grinding at the mill: one shall be taken and the other is left" (Matt. 24:41). A millstone cast into the sea is a symbol of absolute destruction (Rev. 18:21).   A.B.F.

MILLENNIUM, the Latin word for "thousand years." It comes from Revelation 20:1-15 where

Above, women grinding grain at a handmill. Below, a primitive wheat mill in Babylonia (Iraq), probably of the type that the blinded Samson was forced to turn in the Philistine prison. © MPS

a certain period of a "thousand years" is mentioned six times. During this period (1) Satan is "bound" with a "great chain," "locked up" and "sealed" in "the abyss," so that he can not "deceive the nations"; (2) persons designated as "martyrs" who have been "beheaded," "live" and "reign with Christ."

The "living" of the beheaded persons is declared (by synecdoche) to be "the first resurrection," that is, the resurrection of "those that are Christ's" (I Cor. 15:23) in contrast with the "living" of "the rest of the dead." "The rest of the dead" did not "live" until the end of the millennial period. After this period all the rest of the dead, without exception, are raised to stand before the "great white throne" of God.

Paul predicts (Rom. 8:17-26) that this created earth will realize its "hope," and will be delivered from the corruption of the curse (Gen. 3:17,18) "unto the glorious liberty of the children of God," and that this period of blessedness for the created earth will come after "the apocalypse of the sons of God." The latter event takes place at the Lord's return, according to I John 3:2 and Colossians 3:4.

Peter explains (Acts 3:20,21) that Christ, as to his visible presence, will remain in heaven until "the times of restitution of all things."

The reigning of the saints with Christ after His second coming is several times predicted in the Lord's teachings. In His ministry "beyond Jordan" on the last journey to Jerusalem, He said, "ye which have followed with me, in the regeneration, when the Son of Man shall sit in the throne of his glory, ye also shall sit upon twelve thrones, judging the twelve tribes of Israel" (Matt. 19:28). He repeated the same promise in somewhat amplified form at the last supper (Luke 22:18,28-30). It is doubtless this and similar promises of Christ to which Paul refers in I Corinthians 6:2,3, and II Timothy 2:12.

The reigning of the saints with Christ is definitely subsequent to His second coming: Paul rebukes the arrogant Corinthians, "Ye have begun to reign without us! I wish that you had begun to reign [in reality], so that we should be reigning with you" (I Cor. 4:8, original translation). Similarly the Augsburg Confession (Art. 17) condemns the opinion "that before the resurrection of the dead the godly shall occupy the kingdom of the world . . ."

The parable of the wheat and the tares (Matt. 13:24-30,36-43) explicitly places the kingdom in which the righteous participate subsequent to the harvest at the end of the age.

The parable of the nobleman who went to receive a kingdom, and then returned to take possession of it (Luke 19:11-28) is even more explicit. Alford and others point out striking similarities to aspects of the affairs of Archelaus, son of Herod the Great, whose rule over Judea had to be granted from Rome. (See Josephus, *Antiq.* XVII 11, ff and 13, 1.) Christ is the "nobleman" whose visible presence is now withdrawn from this world. He has resumed His eternal place at the right hand of the Father (Ps. 110:1; Heb. 1:13). At the time appointed by the Father (Dan. 7:13,14; Acts 1:6,7) He will return visibly and reign (Rev. 11: 15,17). The words addressed to faithful servants, "have thou authority over ten cities" and "be thou also over five cities" (Luke 19:17,19) coincide with Christ's promises cited above.

The eternal sovereignty of Christ as co-eternal, con-substantial, and co-equal in the Triune Godhead, must not be confused with His temporal kingship for which we pray in the petition, "Thy kingdom come, thy will be done on earth as it is in heaven." The latter kingdom is a phase of His omnipotent rule which obviously has a beginning in future time.

Those who look for Christ's visible return preceding His millennial kingdom, that is, premillennialists, adhere to the grammatico-historical method of exegesis, taking propositional truth in its simplest sense, understanding statements as "literal" unless there is sound reason to believe them to be intended figuratively. On the other hand, there has always been a tendency to "spiritualize" or "demythologize" whatever seems unfamiliar, and the "interpretations" of the millennium are numberless. Those called post-millennialists hold that Christ will return after the millennium. Amillennialists deny that there will be a millennial reign on earth.

The "blessed hope" of the church in all generations (Titus 2:13, cf. I Thess. 4:17) is the imminent, glorious return of Christ.   J.O.B.

MILLET (See Plants)

MILLO (mĭl'ō, Heb. *millô', fullness*), a mound or rampart built up and filled in with earth and stones to raise the level. 1. An ancient fortification in or near Shechem. In Judges 9:6,20 "the house of Millo" mentioned three times probably means the inhabitants of this tower or fortification.

2. A place just N of Mt. Zion and outside the city of David, though it was inside the city of Jerusalem from Hezekiah's time and onward.

When David had taken Zion (II Sam. 5:7-9), he began to fill up Millo and to build thence inward toward Zion. Solomon later strengthened Millo (I Kings 9:15,24; 11:27), and Hezekiah, 300 years later, again strengthened Millo, this time against the Assyrians (II Chron. 32:5). Joash or Jehoash, righteous and godly king of Judah for 40 years, was the victim of a conspiracy of his servants against his life and it was at the house of Millo that they slew him (II Kings 12:20,21).

MINA (See Weights and Measures)

MIND, a word that renders a number of Hebrew and Greek nouns in Scripture. Among the more important are the Heb. *lebh, heart; nephesh, soul;* and the Gr. *noús* and *diánoia,* the former denoting the faculty of reflective consciousness, of moral thinking and knowing, while the latter means *meditation, reflection.* None of these words is used with any precision of meaning. In the NT the word "mind" frequently occurs in an ethical sense, as in Colossians 2:18 and Romans 7:25.

MINERALS OF THE BIBLE. The present science of mineralogy with its names and exact terminology is a young science coming later than physics, chemistry, astronomy, or mathematics. Mineralogy as a science certainly did not exist at the time the Bible was written. It is quite impossible to be certain in all cases that when a mineral name is used in the Bible, it is used with the same meaning as that attached in modern mineralogy. The gemstones or precious stones of the Bible are minerals with identities in a considerable state of uncertainty and confusion. There are of course a number of minerals that present no problems. Water is a mineral, the identity of which has always been certain. No one questions the meaning of gold, silver, and iron.

Mineralogists find it somewhat difficult to define the word mineral, but its scientific meaning can be clarified by the use of specific examples. A granite boulder belongs to the mineral kingdom as contrasted to the animal or vegetable kingdoms, but it is a rock and not a mineral. It is composed

Amid the granite cliffs of Sinai. © MPS

ɔf a number of minerals most of which are of microscopic size. The minerals in granite visible to the naked eye are the clear, glassy, particles of quartz, one or more of the white or pink feldspars, and the darker biotite or hornblende. Quartz is classified as a mineral, first because it was formed in nature, second it was not formed by plant or animal, third it has a uniform composition throughout the particle, and finally quartz always crystallizes in the hexagonal system of crystals. Quartz is always composed of 46.7 per cent silicon and 53.3 per cent oxygen. Extremely slight amounts of impurities may impart a wide variety of colors, thus resulting in precious stones with differing names, yellow quartz being false topaz or citrine, purple quartz being amethyst. Pure water-clear quartz is rock crystal. Yet these various precious stones crystallize in identical hexagonal forms. The chemist may make silicon dioxide in the laboratory having the same percentage of silicon and oxygen as that of natural quartz. But it is not a mineral. It does not pass the test of having been formed in nature unattended by man; it is referred to as a synthetic. Alcohol in dilute form was certainly known by the ancients, but cannot be considered a mineral since it can be traced back to the sugar occurring in grapes, thus a vegetable source. Whereas quartz has a very definite composition, this condition is not a rigorous requirement for all minerals. The biotite or black mica of granite is a mineral somewhat variable in composition. This mineral contains chiefly the elements hydrogen, potassium, magnesium iron, aluminum, silicon and oxygen. Hydrogen and potassium may replace each other in the crystal pattern; magnesium and iron may also interchange. The shape of the crystal remains essentially the same as does the general appearance.

The minerals will be grouped as follows:
A. Precious stones.
B. Metals.
C. Common minerals such as salt, sulfur, and water.

A. PRECIOUS STONES. As indicated in the introduction to the minerals, there is much uncertainty in the identification of specific minerals as precious stones of the Bible. In spite of this difficulty man's reaction to beauty and to the things that endure does not change. Thus we share with the ancients certain criteria in the evaluation of precious stones. There must be beauty in terms of color, transparency, luster, and brilliance. There must be some degree of durability, at least if the gem is to be worn or handled. Selenite, a clear crystalline variety of gypsum, may be beautiful, but it is so soft that it can easily be scratched by the thumb nail. We now use a scale of hardness used by Mohs, the rating depending on the ease or difficulty of scratching. On this scale the hardness of thumbnail is 2½.

The Mohs Scale of Hardness (H)

1. Talc	5. Apatite	9. Corundum
2. Gypsum	6. Orthoclase	10. Diamond
3. Calcite	7. Quartz	
4. Fluorite	8. Topaz	

The most precious of stones are those having a hardness of 7, 8, 9, and 10, all of which would easily scratch glass, which has a hardness of 5½ to 6. Many of the precious stones of the Bible belong to the quartz and chalcedony family with a hardness of 7. Emerald is a green beryl (H 7½ to 8); topaz has a hardness of 8; the ruby and sapphire, both forms of the mineral corundum, have a hardness of 9.

Replica of Aaron's Breastplate, with twelve precious stones. Courtesy American Baptist Assembly, Green Lake, Wisconsin. © ABA

There are four principal lists of minerals recorded in the Scriptures. They are as follows:

1. The 12 precious stones of Aaron's breastplate, each stone representing one of the tribes of Israel (Exod. 28:17-20; 39:10-13).

A replica of this breastplate was presented to the Baptist Assembly at Green Lake, Wisconsin, in 1960. The replica and the story of its making are fully described (*Aaron's Breastplate*, by A. Paul Davis, St. Louis, Mo.). It is to be noted that with the exception of amethyst, the ninth stone of the breastplate, not a single gem stone named according to modern usage carries the same name as that of the King James Version. This is defensible, because of the considerable lack of agreement among scholars, and because of the absolute necessity of making a selection if a replica is to be made.

2. The wisdom list of Job (Job 28:16-19). Listed are the precious onyx, the sapphire, crystal, coral, pearls, rubies and topaz.

3. The gems of the king of Tyre (Ezek. 28: 13). Listed are the sardius, topaz, diamond, beryl, onyx, jasper, sapphire, emerald, and carbuncle.

4. The Precious Stones of the Holy City (Rev. 21:18-21). There is a precious stone for each of twelve foundations.

The Precious Stone List

1. Adamant (ăd'à-mănt). (Also adamant stone). (Ezek. 3:9; Zech. 7:12). This is a reference to a very hard stone, "harder than flint." This could mean the hardest of all, diamond. But the ruby, the sapphire, or the less attractive forms of corundum with a hardness of 9 would also be exceedingly hard stones.

2. Agate (ăg'àt). (Exod. 28:19; 39:12; Isa. 54: 12; Ezek. 27:16). This member of the chalcedony family is described under chalcedony.

3. Amber (Ezek. 1:4,27; 8:2). The Hebrew word, *hashmal,* refers to the color of a bright fire. This would be some shade of yellow. Amber as we know it today is a fossil resin generally found on seacoasts or in alluvial soils. The characteristic color is yellow, with brown and red shades possible. Specimens in our museums often show entrapped beetles or other insects. It is such a mixture that it cannot properly be classified as a single mineral. It takes a high polish and has been valued for beads and other ornaments.

4. Amethyst (ăm′ē-thyst). (Exod. 28:19; 39:12; Rev. 21:20). A purple to blue-violet form of quartz. This is one of the loveliest forms of quartz and there is general agreement that the amethyst of the Bible is our present amethyst. Natural cubic crystals of fluorite in transparent blues and purples match amethyst for beauty, but this mineral has a hardness of only 4 and is easily split by the mere tap of the tip of a knife blade. Amethyst was the ninth stone of the breastplate and the twelfth of the foundations of the Holy City of Revelation. The museum in Denver, Colorado, has a magnificent display of clusters of amethyst crystals of priceless value. Amethyst was once thought to be an antidote for drunkenness.

5. Bdellium (dĕl′ĭ-ŭm). (Num. 11:7; Gen. 2:12). Bdellium today is a gum resin that comes from certain species of tree. What was the bdellium of Genesis and Numbers? In Genesis it is something associated with gold and the onyx stone. From this association one could assume it to be a precious stone. In Numbers, "the manna was as coriander seed, and the color thereof as the color of bdellium." A more literal translation of the latter phrase would be, "the eye thereof as the eye of bdellium." In Exodus 16:14 manna is compared with the hoar frost, and in Exodus 16:31, with white coriander seed. Milky quartz flecked with gold occurs today in many gold-mining districts of the world. Even today this milky-white quartz is cut and polished for gems as gold quartz. Under the circumstances it is quite probable that bdellium was white or milky quartz spotted with gold particles. At the same time one would assume that manna was white flecked with golden or yellow spots.

6. Beryl (bĕr′yl). (Exodus. 28:20; 39:13; Ezek. 1:16; 10:9; Dan. 10:6; Rev. 21:20). Beryl, a beryllium aluminum silicate, is now mined and valued as a source of the light metal, beryllium, a metal not known until 1828. A single crystal taken from a mine in the Black Hills of South Dakota weighed as much as 75 tons. Gem varieties include yellow or golden beryl, emerald which is a highly prized translucent to transparent sea-green stone, aquamarine which is blue, and Morganite a rose-red variety. Beryl was the tenth stone of the breastplate and the eighth of the foundations of the Holy City. This stone has been variously considered as a blue, a green, a yellow, or a red stone, possibly other than beryl as we know it.

7. Carbuncle (kär′bŭng-k′l) (Exod. 28:17; 39:10; Isa. 54:12; Ezek. 28:13). The third stone in the breastplate, the carbuncle, could have been any one of a series of red precious stones. The modern carbuncle is the almandite garnet, an iron aluminum silicate. Much of the garnet available is not clear enough, and sufficiently free of cracks, to be of gem quality, and is used for abrasives. Salida, Colorado, is well known for its unusually large-sized crystals.

8. Carnelian (See Sardius described under chalcedony) (Same as sard or sardius). This is the RSV translation of the first stone of the breastplate, and the sixth of the Holy City.

9. Chalcedony (kăl-sĕd′ō-nĭ) (Rev. 21:19) (Agate in RSV).

Quartz and chalcedony are both composed of silicon dioxide, but the chalcedony does not crystallize out in the bold hexagonal forms taken by quartz. Any crystalline character that the various forms of chalcedony have is that of microscopic size. The lighter colored varieties are named chalcedony in contrast to such names as carnelian, jasper, etc.

The following are some of the varieties of chalcedony:

a. Agate. Agate is chalcedony with colors unevenly distributed, often banded, with the bands being curved. Petrified wood is often a form of agate, in which the silicon dioxide has replaced the original wood. Agates are very widespread and variable and have become one of the most popular minerals for cutting and polishing. The moss agates found along the Yellowstone River from Glendive, Montana, to Yellowstone Park have become particularly well known. The "thunder eggs" of Idaho and Oregon may look like drab gray rounded stones, but when sawed in two with a diamond saw, they may reveal a center of lovely agate.

b. Carnelian, sard, or sardius. Carnelian is chalcedony with colors usually clear red to brownish red. Iron oxide imparts the color.

c. Chrysoprase. This is an apple-green variety of chalcedony.

d. Flint. This is usually a dull gray to black form, not prized or classified as a precious stone, but highly prized by primitive peoples for arrow heads, spear points, skinning knives, etc.

e. Jasper. Jasper pebbles may be picked up in many gravel deposits. The petrified wood of Arizona is largely jasper. Jasper is hard, opaque, takes a beautiful polish, and is sufficiently abundant so that it must have been used by ancient man as a gem stone. The chief colors are red, yellow, brown, and green, though it comes in many shades. Green jasper is also known as chrysoprase. The colors are largely due to iron oxide.

f. Onyx. Onyx is very similar to banded agates, except that the bands are flat. Specimens are usually cut and polished parallel to the layers. This enables cameo production. Objects of Mexican onyx, beautifully cut and polished and available in a number of Mexican border cities are really not onyx at all. The composition is calcium carbonate instead of silicon dioxide. A little hydrochloride acid added to Mexican Onyx will cause effervescence, whereas all the forms of silica react negatively. The onyx of the KJV is considered by some to be a beryl.

g. Sardonyx. A sardonyx is merely an onyx that includes layers of carnelian or sard.

10. Chrysolyte (krĭs′ō-līt) (Rev. 21:20). The seventh foundation of the Holy City is chrysolite, a yellow to greenish-yellow form of olivine. A green olivine is known as peridot. The mineral is a silicate of magnesium and iron. Even today most gem quality olivines come from an island in the Red Sea.

11. Coral (Job 28:18; Ezek. 27:16). When the writer of Job shows the priceless value of wisdom, he lists gold five times, silver once, and the precious stones, the precious onyx, the sapphire, the crystal, coral, pearls, rubies, and topaz, once each. Here must be named the most precious and valued of all metals and gems. Yet with these, man could not buy wisdom. Two of these, coral and pearl, are relatively soft and do not seem to belong to the company of hard, enduring and valuable gem stones named. One can defend the inclusion of pearl, since this was highly valued for its unique pearly luster, and for its rarity. But the inclusion of coral, which grows in the sea and is too soft to be ranked with precious stones, is more difficult to accept. It appears to be in the wrong company. But coral has been used for various ornaments, such as beads and necklaces. Other factors such as vogue, symbology, and even superstition, may attach value at certain periods in history.

In Ezekiel, coral is again associated with valued gems, sapphire, and agate.

12. Chrysoprasus (krĭs′ō-prāz) (Chrysoprase, RSV) (Rev. 21:20). The tenth foundation of the Holy City, chrysoprase may have been the apple-green form of chalcedony, sometimes called green jasper. A small percentage of nickel may account for the green color. Beads of genuine chrysoprase dating to 1500 B.C. have been taken from an Egyptian grave.

13. Crystal (Job 28:17; Ezek. 1:22; Rev. 4:6; 21:11; 22:1). The crystal of the Bible is something transparent and colorless, and valued as a gem stone. Clear quartz is the most logical choice for this. It is plentiful. It is remarkably brilliant and beautifully shaped even as it is found in nature. This of course does not rule out other transparent and colorless minerals such as topaz and diamond.

When modern science uses the word crystal, the meaning is completely different. A crystal is a substance bounded by flat faces, giving the specimen the form of a cube, an octahedron, etc. The shape of the crystal is characteristic of the substance and the outward form is not the result of cutting and polishing by man. Common table salt crystallizes out in the form of cubes.

14. Diamond (Exod. 28:18; 39:11; Jer. 17:1; Ezek. 28:13). The sixth stone of the breastplate. What was it? Almost surely not a diamond, for we have no evidence that the ancients ever cut diamonds. The reference in Jeremiah is to writing with a pen of iron having a diamond point. This pen could have been tipped with various hard minerals, capable of writing on very hard substances. (See Mohs scale of hardness in the introduction to precious stones.)

15. Emerald (Exod. 28:18; 39:11; Ezek. 27:16; 28:13; Rev. 4:3; 21:19). The emerald, the fourth gem of the breastplate and the fourth foundation of the Holy City, is indeed a stone worthy of such a high position. It is a lovely transparent to translucent deep green form of beryl, beryllium aluminum silicate.

There is no really good reason for trying to replace this emerald with a red stone such as a carbuncle or ruby. An emerald is a magnificent gemstone which was available to the Hebrews and it would be odd indeed if they did not prize it sufficiently to include it among the most precious. Until proof exists to the contrary, the emerald should be retained.

16. Jacinth (also hyacinth). (jā′sĭnth) (Rev. 9:17; 21:20). (Also Exod. 28:19; 39:12 RSV). Today the jacinth or hyacinth is the transparent red, yellow, orange, or brown form of the mineral zircon, zirconium orthosilicate. Occasionally the correspondingly colored garnets are given these same names. Agreement has not been reached whether this 11th foundation stone was a yellow or a blue stone. If a blue stone, it could have been the true sapphire which is blue, or the golden sapphire which is yellow. In either case this would make the stone a form of corundum, aluminum oxide, next to diamond in hardness. Acceptance of the word sapphire would then necessitate changing the second foundation stone. We no longer use the term ligure for a gem stone. The seventh stone of the breastplate in the KJV is ligure, translated jacinth in the RSV.

17. Jasper (Exod. 28:20; 39:13; Ezek. 28:13; Rev. 4:3; 21:11,18,19). The last stone of the breastplate and the first in the foundation of the Holy City, jasper is described under chalcedony. It should be noted in passing that one characteristic of jasper as we know the stone is its opaqueness. Were it not for the odd descriptions of the gold of the New Jerusalem as clear or transparent as glass, early translators probably would not have chosen the word jasper at this point. For in Revelation 21:11,18, jasper is described as clear as crystal.

18. Ligure (Jacinth RSV) (Exod. 28:19; 39:21). See Jacinth.

19. Onyx (ŏn′ĭks) (Gen. 2:12; Exod. 25:7; 28:20; 39:13; Job 28:16; Ezek. 28:13). See Chalcedony. This form of chalcedony was the 11th stone of the breastplate, and possibly the fifth foundation of the Holy City. It was abundantly available and is still highly prized.

20. Pearls (Job 28:18; Matt. 7:6; 13:45,46; I Tim. 2:9; Rev. 17:4; 18:12; 21:21). Pearls, like coral, develop in the sea by the abstraction of calcium carbonate from sea water. The pearl develops around a bit of foreign matter within the shells of oysters or mussels. Like coral it cannot be classed with the hard enduring precious stones. It is easily destroyed. A small amount of acid would convert it to nearly worthless calcium chloride, a water-soluble salt, and the gas carbon dioxide. The reference in Matthew 7:6 implies a fragile structure. Swine might step on rubies without harming them, but pearls would be completely crushed. They are not much harder than finger nail. The references to pearls are found almost exclusively in the New Testament, and there is no reason to doubt the identity of this precious stone.

21. Ruby (Job 28:18; Prov. 3:15; 8:11; 20:15; 31:10; Lam. 4:7). Corundum as a mineral usually occurs as a dull, unattractive but hard form of aluminum oxide, often crystallized in hexagonal forms. Corundum of a rich, clear red variety is the ruby, while the other colors of gem quality corundum account for the sapphires. The best source for good rubies is Burma. In the first four of the references above, rubies are used as a norm for evaluating wisdom. In the fifth, it is used for measuring the worth of a virtuous woman. In the last reference there is a very clear indication that this stone was red. What better selection can then be made than that made by the translators?

22. Sapphire (săf′īr) (Exod. 24:10; 28:18; 39:11; Job 28:6,16; Lam. 4:7; Isa. 54:11; Ezek. 1:26; 10:10; 28:13; Rev. 21:19). Sapphires, like rubies, belong to the corundum or aluminum oxide family, with a hardness of 9, or next to diamond. True sapphires are blue; others are colorless, yellow, or pink. The sapphire is listed as the fifth stone of the Holy City. It is generally agreed that our modern lazurite (Lapis lazuli) was called sapphire by the ancients. But we must remember that it is entirely possible that a variety of blue stones were termed sapphire. Lazurite does not seem to belong to the elite company of the most precious stones. For the greater part these most precious stones are noted for a rich purity of color which lazurite does not have. Lazurite is beautiful but usually is a considerable mixture of minerals, including pyrite, calcite, muscovite, pyroxene, etc. In hardness it is softer than glass. (H 5 to 5½.)

In three of the references given above, there is

a strong implication that the mineral referred to was blue (Exod. 24:10; Ezek. 1:26; 10:1).

In Lamentations sapphire is linked to ruby, the other highly prized form of corundum.

23. Sardius or sardine stone. Same as carnelian. (See carnelian and also varieties of chalcedony.) (Exod. 28:17; 39:10; Ezek. 28:13; Rev. 4:3; 21:20). A red variety of chalcedony. The first stone of the breastplate, and the sixth of the Holy City.

24. Sardonyx (Onyx in RSV) (Rev. 21:20). This stone is merely an onyx layered with red sard or carnelian. See Onyx and carnelian under chalcedony.

25. Topaz (Exod. 28:17; 39:10; Job 28:19; Ezek. 28:13; Rev. 21:20). The modern topaz is an aluminum fluoro hydroxy silicate with a hardness of 8, thus harder than the quartz and chalcedony groups. The most highly prized is the yellow topaz, but colorless, pink, blue, and green varieties occur as well.

This probably yellow topaz, the second stone of the breastplate, and the ninth of the Holy City, is interpreted by some as a yellow citrine, a form of quartz, or chrysolite. (See chrysolite.)

B. METALS. Of the 103 elements now known to man, 78 are metals. Of these only gold, silver, iron, copper, lead, tin, and mercury were known to the ancients. The brass of the KJV of the Bible was copper in some instances and bronze in others. Brass was the most modern alloy of copper and zinc, bronze being the copper-tin alloy. A metal is an element with a metallic luster; it is usually a good conductor of heat and electricity. A metal such as gold, silver, and copper may occur in nature as the free recognizable metal, or as is the case with most metals, it may occur in compound form, chemically united with other elements in such a way that the ore appears dull and non-metallic.

Metallurgy is the science of winning the metal from its ore and the subsequent refining and treating for adapting it to its many and varied uses. The earliest reference to a man skilled in iron and bronze work is that in Genesis 4:22, this man being Tubal-cain.

Archaeologists recognize a chalcolithic or copper-stone age (4500-3000 B.C.) preceding the bronze age (3000-1200 B.C.). The iron age (1200-300 B.C.) follows. There is, of course, much overlapping, and none of these ages have really ended. In fact, when one considers the tonnages used, it should be apparent that we are still living in the iron or steel age.

The metals of the Bible will be discussed in the following order: 1. Gold; 2. Silver; 3. Copper; 4. Iron; 5. Lead; 6. Tin; 7. Mercury (Quicksilver).

1. Gold. Gold was known and used freely and skilfully in the oldest of civilizations. A multitude of gold ornaments in excellent condition in the museums of the world amply verify this. The earliest evidence of gold mining is that of rock carvings of Egypt, showing the washing of gold sands and the subsequent melting of gold in a small furnace. This went back to at least 2500 B.C. (G. Wilkinson, *The Manners and Customs of the Ancient Egyptians*, London 2.137, 1874). Strabo (Geographia 3.2) describes the country of the Iberians (Spain) as full of metals, gold, silver, copper, and iron. He further tells of mining gold by digging for it in the usual way and also by washing for it (hydraulic mining). This he wrote approximately 60 B.C. Pliny the Elder was killed in 77 A.D. when Vesuvius erupted. He had written 37 books of natural history; in his 33rd he accurately describes the occurrence of placer gold in

Gold helmet of a prince of Ur, about 2500 B.C. It was hammered from one piece of metal. UMP

stream beds, including the finding of nuggets. In addition he describes hydraulic mining that would put recent operations to shame; claiming that a river was brought from a distance and from the heights, with enough fall to wash away whole mountain sides, leaving the gold in sluice baffles. Most surprising of all, Pliny describes in some detail the use of mercury to capture the gold from the ore by amalgamation. This method is definitely used today by such large and efficient operations as that of the Homestake gold mine in the Black Hills of South Dakota.

Gold is named very early in the Bible (Gen. 2:11,12). We are told that in the land of Havilah, in the vicinity of the Garden of Eden, there was gold, and further that the gold was good.

Why has man ever valued gold so highly? Why is gold good? Gold is good and highly prized because it is warmly beautiful. It is enduring, for it never rusts or dissolves away. It retains its beauty. Of the common acids, only a mixture of concentrated nitric and hydrochloric acids (aqua regia) will dissolve it. Strong acid alone will have no effect. Pliny mentions gold as the only metal unharmed by fire. In fact Pliny said each time it went through a fire it came out better or more refined than before. Gold is good because it is so adaptable to shaping. It can be melted without harm; it can be hammered to thin leaves, being extremely malleable. It may easily overlay large objects thus imparting beauty and protection to the whole. It may readily be alloyed with other metals with an improvement of the degree of hardness while still retaining the beauty of gold. In fact Pliny noted correctly that gold comes naturally alloyed with silver. Finally gold has been valued because of its scarcity. It seems reasonable to presume that if the core of the earth is largely iron that the free metals such as gold, platinum, and even cobalt and nickel have been largely lost to us by dissolving in this core.

Gold is also mentioned at the very end of the Bible in Revelation 21:15,18,21. Here the most precious of metals is envisioned as constituting the Holy City and its streets, gold transparent as glass. The reed used to measure the city was a golden reed.

In between the beginning and the end of the Bible are so many references to gold that one must use an extensive concordance if he wishes to find all these references. In the 37th chapter of Exodus is described the making of the ark of the covenant, the mercy seat, candle sticks, dishes, spoons, bowls, cherubim, vessels, a table, lamps, snuffers, snuff dishes, and an altar, all made of gold or overlaid with gold. The word gold is used 20 times in this chapter. The skilled craftsman was Bezaleel of the tribe of Judah.

Besides the items listed in Exodus 37, other items of gold are bracelets, bells, censers, crowns, calves, earrings, ephods, gods, girdles, hooks, jewels, rings, sceptres, shields, tongs, and shekels (coins). And this list is not completely exhaustive.

When the writer of Job in the 28th chapter raises the question of where wisdom should be found, he points out that wisdom is so priceless that gold, silver and precious stones could not buy it. It is a remarkable fact that gold is mentioned five times while each of the other most precious items is mentioned but once.

2. Silver. At the present time much more silver is obtained as a by-product of the refining of copper and lead than by mining native silver or silver ore. The methods used in this refining were not available to the Hebrews, since it requires the extensive use of electricity, cyanide, zinc and aluminum. However, silver is ten times as abundant in the crust of the earth as is gold, and much of it was mined by the ancients. Of silver, Pliny says, "Silver is only found in deep shafts, and raises no hopes of its existence by any signs, giving off no shining sparkles such as are seen in the case of gold." Pliny describes its use in making mirrors. He says, "The property of reflecting images is marvelous; it is generally agreed that it takes place owing to the repercussion of the air which is thrown back into the eyes."

The shekel and the talent of silver are terms much used, indicating a wide use of silver as a medium of exchange. At first this was done by weighing out the silver pieces. This is apparent in Job 28:15, "Neither shall silver be weighed for the price thereof." In the NT it is clear that regular coins were freely in use. For example in Matthew 22:19,20, a penny was brought to Jesus and He asked whose image and superscription was on it.

Silver was used in conjunction with gold because of its beauty. A great many references are to silver and gold. Only occasionally are the terms reversed as in Esther 1:6, "the beds were of gold and silver." Again when Christ sent out the Twelve, he commanded them to provide neither gold, nor silver, nor brass in their purses (Matt. 10:9).

Many objects made of silver are referred to in the Scriptures. The cup that Joseph had secreted in Benjamin's sack of food was a silver cup (Gen. 44:2). Sockets, hooks, gods, chargers, bowls, trumpets, candlesticks, basins, cords, and images were made of silver. Demetrius, the silversmith of Ephesus, made silver shrines for Diana (Acts 19:24). Jesus was betrayed for 30 pieces of silver (Matt. 26:15).

Silver is used also in a figurative or symbolic sense for something refined and pure, free from dross. "The words of the Lord are pure words; as silver tried in a furnace of earth, purified seven times" (Ps. 12:6).

3. Iron. In spite of the advance in the light metals such as aluminum, magnesium, and beryllium, we are still living in the iron age. No other metal rivals iron in the tonnage of products. The reason for this is that iron ores, chiefly the oxides and carbonates, are abundant in concentrated deposits, the

metal is easily won from the ore, and the metal may be varied in its properties over a very wide range. By removing impurities, by heat treatment, and by alloying, the strength, hardness, ductility, malleability, resistance to corrosion, appearance, and retention of temper may be varied.

Iron does occur free in nature, but on such a minute scale that it may be considered a curiosity. Terrestrial free iron is very likely secondary, having been formed from regular ores by hot carbon or carbon containing materials, a process which we carry out in a blast furnace. That ancient man found meteoric iron and shaped it to some use is clear. Iron beads taken from a grave in Egypt dating from about 4000 B.C. showed a nickel analysis corresponding favorably to that of meteorites. In fact, the Egyptians and those of other cultures referred to iron as the metal from heaven. In ancient religious literature the Egyptians claimed that the firmament of heaven was made of iron. An iron object dating to about 3000 B.C. was blasted out of the masonry at the top of the Great Pyramid at Gizeh and is now in the British Museum. No one knows who first discovered a way to make iron out of the abundant iron ore, by reducing it in a furnace with charcoal. This chemical reaction occurs so readily that the discovery was made in a dim undetermined past. One would conjecture it was made by accident. Frescoes dating about 1500 B.C. in certain Egyptian tombs show small furnaces with men operating bellows or mouth blowpipes. In essence this is still the principle of the blast furnace. The first reference to iron in the Bible is found in Genesis 4:22. Tubal-cain was a worker in brass and iron. In Deuteronomy 4:20, I Kings 8:51, and Jeremiah 11:4 there is ample evidence that the Hebrews were familiar with furnaces for making iron. The indication is strong that in Egypt as slaves they had to work at these fiery furnaces; their lot must have been extremely difficult. The smith with his forge was well known as shown in Isaiah 44:12 and 54:16. The Philistines made it very difficult for the Hebrews to occupy Palestine. They were skilled in iron and prevented the Jews from making their own tools and weapons, by not allowing a single smith in all the land. The Israelites were forced to go down to the Philistines to sharpen their shares, coulters, axes, and mattocks (I Sam. 13:19,20). But the great victories of David ended all this. With David's coming to power, iron became abundant. Iron is frequently named in the Scriptures, as are many tools and objects. One reason that these are not found in greater abundance is the fact that iron rusts too rapidly and thus returns to the earth. Additional items of iron not previously mentioned are as follows:

The bedstead of Og was made of iron (Deut. 3:11). Og was a giant and needed a strong bed and a big one, about 15 feet long and 7 feet wide.

The Israelites feared the Canaanites because they had chariots of iron (Josh. 17:16,18)

The spearhead of Goliath weighed 600 shekels (roughly 20 pounds) of iron (I Sam. 17:7).

There is ample evidence that many types of fetters and means of binding captives and slaves were made of iron. At times the term is, however used in a figurative sense (Ps. 2:9; 107:10; 149:8 Jer. 28:13,14).

Pliny in his 35th book of Natural History discusses iron, its occurrence and smelting at considerable length. He introduces this with the comment, "Iron serves as the best and the worst of the apparatus of life, inasmuch as with it we plough the ground, plant trees, trim the trees . . . with it we build houses and quarry rocks, and we employ it for all other useful purposes, but we likewise use it for wars and slaughter and brigandage." His further discourses are reminiscent of Isaiah 2:4 concerning beating swords into plowshares and spears into pruning hooks.

"Subdued in fire the stubborn metal lies;
One brawny smith the puffing bellows plies
And draws and blows reciprocating air;
Others to quench the hissing mass prepare;
With lifted arms they order every blow,
And chime their sounding hammers in a row;
With labored anvils Etna groans below,
Strongly they strike ; huge flakes of flames expire;
With tongs they turn the steel and vex it in the fire."
— From Virgil's Aeneid about 30 B.C.
(See Mellor Vol. XII, p. 497)

4. Copper. There are two metals that impart some shade of yellow or red to a coin, a statue, an ornament, or tool, namely copper and gold. If the object is of gold, it is readily recognized as such. Thus all other yellow metals or alloys have been variously named as copper, brass or bronze. In Deuteronomy 28:9 the KJV would have brass dug out of the hills. And in Job 28:2 brass is said to be molten out of the rock. In both these cases the correct translation is copper, for brass is a man-made alloy of chiefly copper and zinc. Two vessels of fine copper, precious as gold are referred to in Ezra 8:27. One reference to a coppersmith is found in II Timothy 4:14. In the KJV the word brass is used many times. In nearly all cases the word bronze should have been used. Bronze is an alloy of copper and tin. It is not impossible that there was a small amount of actual brass, but it is very unlikely. Copper ranks with the earliest metals known to man. It does occur as free copper, sometimes in enormous masses. The ores are extremely varied and plentiful. Pliny claimed that copper was first found on the island of Cyprus. Pliny also indicated that copper was sometimes alloyed with silver and gold and that Corinthian bronze was the most valued of all. It is quite logical to conclude that relatively pure copper was used by man before the copper tin alloy, bronze, ushered in the bronze age. An Egyptian dagger dating from about 4500 B.C. showed an analysis of nearly pure copper and no tin. Nails, knives, statuettes and other objects continued to be made of pure copper far into the bronze age. It is, however, reasonably certain that from about 3000 B.C. on, an increasing use of tin with copper resulting in an alloy, bronze, became the pattern for objects of metal. Many analyses of excavated bronze objects show this. Cyprus bronze usually had from two to four per cent tin. A Nineveh cup of 1000 B.C. tested over 18 per cent tin.

The earliest reference (KJV) to brass was that in Genesis 4:22. This was likely pure copper, though it may have been bronze. Whereas the 37th chapter of Exodus may be called the gold chapter, the 38th is the bronze and silver chapter. The KJV uses the words brass and brazen 15 times. Bronze is used to overlay many parts of the altar of burnt offering and the hangings of the court. Vessels, pots, shovels, fleshhooks, fire pans, grate, rings, and a laver are made of bronze. A partial list of copper or bronze objects includes the serpent made by Moses (Num. 21:9), the armor of Goliath consisting of helmet, coat of mail, greaves, and target (I Sam. 17:5,6), fetters of

Remains of King Solomon's copper smelters at Ezion-geber, on the Gulf of Aqabah. ASOR

bronze (II Kings 25:7), bronze cymbals (I Chron. 15:19), gates (Ps. 107:16; Isa. 54:2), and idols (Rev. 9:20).

Perhaps the most exciting discoveries yet made concerning ancient copper mining are those initiated by the combined efforts of the American School of Oriental Research at Jerusalem, the Hebrew Union College, of Cincinnati, and the Transjordan Department of Antiquities in the spring of 1934. From the southern tip of the Dead Sea to the northern tip of the Gulf of Aqabah, this gulf being the eastern arm of the Red Sea, is a great rift, no doubt the result of an ancient earthquake. This rift, the Wadi Arabah, is arid and desolate but heavily mineralized even to this day. It seems reasonably certain as the result of the study and excavations by successive expeditions (*The Other Side of the Jordan*, by Nelson Glueck, American School of Oriental Research, New Haven, Connecticut) that between the tenth and eighteenth centuries B.C., the Israelites as the result of numerous battles won this rich source of copper and iron. This flowered into a gigantic operation under King Solomon. Many furnaces with slag piles may still be seen up and down the Wadi Arabah. The largest operation of all was at the port city of Ezion-Geber.

5. Lead. Free metallic lead is an extreme rarity as a mineral. The chief ore is that of lead sulfide, Galena, which often occurs as bright glistening clusters of cubic crystals. The metal is readily obtained from the ore and was known long before it came into common use. The British Museum has a lead figure of Egyptian origin dating to about 3000 B.C. Lead plates and statuettes have been found in Egyptian tombs of 1200 B.C.

References to lead in the Scriptures are as follows:

The high density of lead is noted in Exodus 15:10. In Numbers 31:22 lead is listed along with gold, silver, brass, iron and tin. Its use for lettering in rock is noted in Job 19:24. Bellows were used in a furnace with melting of lead (Jer. 6:29). Lead is listed with silver, brass, iron and tin as melted in a furnace (Ezek. 22:18,20) and again with silver, iron, and tin as the riches traded in the fairs (Ezek. 27:12). See also Zechariah 5:7,8.

6. Tin. Tin is not an abundant element, very little of it being mined today in the United States. The chief ore is the oxide cassiterite, which has to be reduced in a furnace. Pliny may have confused tin with lead, stating that there were two kinds of lead, plumbum nigrum, black lead (lead), and plumbum album, a white lead (tin). Although a goodly percentage of tin is found in the many bronze objects collected, actual articles of tin are rare. Tools, vessels, cups, and the like were apparently not made of tin. Could it be that the ancients were aware of the tin plague or museum disease? When tin remains long exposed to a temperature of 65 degrees Fahrenheit or lower, the shiny white tin slowly changes to the allotropic gray form and crumbles to dust.

The references to tin in the Bible are few. They are as follows: Numbers 31:22; Isaiah 1:25; Ezekiel 22:18,20; 27:12.

7. Mercury (Quicksilver). This strange metal which is liquid was not even recognized with certainty as a metal until J. A. Braun froze it to a solid in 1759. In the early history of mercury it was thought to be a form of silver and this up to as late as the sixth century. Mercury has been reported found in a grave of the 16th or 15th century B.C. (Mellor). Aristotle (320 B.C.) in the fourth book of his Meteorologica explains that mercury or liquid silver contains water and air and thus refuses to solidify on cooling. Pliny frequently discusses mercury.

The chief ore of mercury is a bright red mineral, cinnabar, which is mercury sulfide. With it occurs sometimes the free liquid mercury. One could thus reason that ancient man could not miss the unusual heavy red mineral, and the unusual silvery liquid drops. Furthermore, all it takes to obtain the free liquid mercury from the red cinnabar is to heat the material in a current of air.

When a small drop of mercury is rubbed on a silver coin, it spreads out quickly, forming an amalgam with a bright silvery luster. This also happens with many other metals including lead, tin, and copper. It can be driven off again by mere heating. Pliny (33.99) notes that the argentum vivum found in veins of silver in round drops always liquid, will break vessels by penetrating them. He also noted that copper could be gilded by first coating with this argentum vivum and then putting on gold leaf. These observations refer to the amalgamating power of mercury.

The Hebrew word, *sig,* interpreted as dross, meaning the scum or refuse, usually thought of in connection with silver refining, is found in the following passages: Psalm 119:119; Proverbs 25: 4,5; 26:3; Isaiah 1:22,25; Ezekiel 22:18,19,20.

The Proverbs reference, "Burning lips and a wicked heart are like a potsherd covered with silver dross" (Prov. 26:23), is very strongly indicative of mercury or amalgam as the deceptive gloss on the worthless bauble. This type of deception must have been practiced. If so, it could also be "purged by fire," that is, the mercury could be distilled away, leaving the refined silver or other metal in the amalgam. Compare this with Christ's references to a cup clean on the outside and to the whited sepulchres (Matt. 23:25,27).

"Thy silver is become dross, thy wine mixed with water" (Isa. 1:22). Here again dross is something specific and reminiscent of Aristotle's conception that mercury was silver mixed with water and air. Pliny and Dioscorides both use terms for mercury that imply water-silver, clearly a result of its liquid character and silvery appearance.

Even the references in Ezekiel suggest the molten or liquid character of mercury. The house of Israel has become brass, tin, iron, and lead in the furnace; they have become dross. This could refer to their liquid character, while in the furnace.

C. THE COMMON MINERALS.

1. Alabaster (Matt. 26:7; Mark 14:3; Luke 7: 37). All of these references include an alabaster box used to contain a precious ointment. Modern alabaster is a form of gypsum, hydrated calcium sulfate. It is soft, having a hardness of 2 and may be scratched by the thumbnail. It is easily carved and many larger decorative articles like book ends, vases, and paper weights are made of this material. It is usually very light colored, but may be mottled or veined with various colors. The ancients may have used a calcite or aragonite mineral, resembling our modern alabaster in its ability to take a high polish and in its general appearance. A simple test with the thumbnail would distinguish between the two varieties. Calcite has a hardness of 3 and cannot be scratched with the thumbnail.

2. Brimstone (Sulfur) (Gen. 19:24; Deut. 29: 23; Job 18:15; Ps. 11:6; Ezek. 38:22; Isa. 30:33; 34:9; Luke 17:29; Rev. 9:17,18; 14:10; 19:20; 20:10; 21:8). It is generally agreed that the brimstone of the Bible is sulfur. In modern times most of our sulfur comes from deep deposits and is brought to the surface by hot water and compressed air. Sulfur deposits also occur in the vicinity of volcanoes. Hot gases such as sulfur dioxide and hydrogen sulfide are emitted, chemically react and deposit sulfur in the surrounding rock. In the vicinity of hot springs which in turn are the relics of previous volcanic action, sulfur deposits are found. When sulfur is burned, it burns with a blue flame forming a gas, sulfur dioxide, which is a poison and a bleaching agent. With moisture it forms sulfurous acid. In the Bible context brimstone is nearly always associated with fire and with punishment and devastation. No natural product readily available to the ancients would so completely symbolize the awful punishment meted out to the wicked. The flame is hot and the sulfur dioxide has a terrible suffocating stench, with the ability to lay waste and kill. To add to the horror, hot sulfur turns to a bubbling dark red and very sticky liquid.

3. Marble (I Chron. 29:2; Esth. 1:6; S. of Sol. 5:15; Rev. 18:12). Marble is recrystallized limestone, which is capable of being given a high polish. Limestone is somewhat impure calcium carbonate. A dolomitic marble contains a considerable amount of magnesium carbonate as well as the calcium compound. Marble is used for decorative purposes, for statuary, for pillars and walls of buildings. In two of the above references marble pillars are indicated. There is no reason to think that the marble

Sculptured marble columns of a heathen temple (Artemis) at Jerash, ancient Gerasa. © MPS

of the Bible was much different from the marble of modern times, except in the sense that marble from different quarries varies in color and texture.

4. Nitre (niter) (Prov. 25:20; Jer. 2:22). The niter of the Bible cannot be the niter of mineralogy today. The latter is potassium nitrate or saltpeter and would have no chemical action with the acetic acid of vinegar such as is indicated in Proverbs 25:20. Neither would it be of any value whatsoever in washing with soap (Jer. 2:22). The same could be said of soda niter or Chile saltpeter, which is sodium nitrate. The usual interpretation of the Biblical niter is that the material is sodium carbonate. This would form a gas with vinegar and effervesce freely. Furthermore sodium carbonate would be useful in washing with soap. In fact it is used today to make soap and also as a water softener. And finally it does occur as the natural mineral in arid regions, either in solution in salty seas or in the mud surrounding such seas.

5. Salt. Salt is extremely abundant; the evaporation of one cubic mile of sea water would leave approximately 140 million tons of salts most of which would be sodium chloride or common salt. The salt sea of the Bible was no doubt the Dead Sea. In most of the many references to salt, either the preservative property or else the savor it adds to food was the point of interest. Jesus in Matthew 5:13 states that the children of the kingdom are the salt of the earth. This implies both the preservative and the taste qualities of salt. How could salt lose its savor? It has been suggested by some that in time the stored salt would chemically react and be salt no more. This is highly improbable. Under the conditions the salt would remain salt. But it certainly was contaminated with other salts such as magnesium chloride or sulfate, which in turn would attract moisture. In due time enough salt might leach away, leaving a quality of salt behind which would be continuously poorer salt. The less soluble contaminants would be left behind. The container might then be emptied on a foot path where it could at least keep down some of the weeds.

6. Water. This is the most marvelous and exciting mineral of the Bible. Every modern textbook of mineralogy includes a section of the oxides of nature such as those of silicon, copper, iron, aluminum, etc. But hydrogen oxide heads the list. This extremely abundant and widespread mineral is found either as liquid, water, or the solid forms snow and ice. There are more references to this mineral than to any other in the Bible.

As a chemical material it is a most unusual compound, with unusual properties. When it freezes it expands so that ice floats. The chemist accounts for most of its odd properties by explaining that hydrogen bonds form between oxygen atoms holding particles together into a framework. Were it not for these hydrogen bonds, water would boil away at 150 degrees Fahrenheit below zero.

The excitement concerning this mineral as named in the Bible comes in its many uses and implications. What is man without water? With it thirst is quenched, a cup of cold water is given, Peter tries to walk on it, the shepherd leads his sheep beside it. It is the water of life; with it man is baptized. It is made to come out of a rock; there are water wells where many events take place. So one might continue with many more of the rich allusions to the happenings of the Old and New Testaments. G.R.M.

MINES, MINING, an occupation of man that is very ancient, for we read in the description of Eden and its surroundings before the Flood of "the land of Havilah, where there is gold: and the gold of that land is good" (Gen. 2:11,12); and in the account of the antediluvian Cainite patriarchs, Tubalcain was "the forger of every cutting instrument of brass and iron" (Gen. 4:22). In Job 28:1-11 "a mine for silver and a place for gold is mentioned"; the statement that "iron is taken out of

Specimens of salt formations of Jebel Usdum (Hill of Sodom) at the Dead Sea. The square in the center, at bottom, shows the natural form. When shattered, salt breaks down into perfect squares, in all sizes, down to microscopic cubes. The salt of the Dead Sea area, with its byproducts, constitutes one of the great natural mineral resources of Palestine. © MPS

While not often thought of as such, water is the greatest and most marvelous of mineral resources. Here is a waterfall in the land of Moab (Wady Zerka Main), a stream of boiling water from hot springs. © MPS

the earth and copper is molten out of the stone" is followed by a poetic account of a man digging a mine. In Sinai are very ancient copper mines, worked by the Egyptians as early as Dynasty IV (the great pyramid builders); and, at the head of the Gulf of Akaba, at Elath, are the remains of Solomon's blast furnaces for copper. At this locality there is a constant strong north wind, and through openings and conduits this wind was used to form a draft for the furnaces. The great development of metal working in Israel must have come between the time of King Saul and of Solomon. Compare I Samuel 13:19-22, where the Philistines are in the iron age which the Israelites had not yet reached, with the accomplishments of Solomon's time (I Kings 7:13-50) only about a century later.

The Greeks and the Romans considered mining and metal working as very ancient, for they pictured Hephaestus or Vulcan, son of Zeus or Jupiter, as a metal-worker, a sort of mythological "Tubal-cain." In the time of Moses, the Midianites had gold, silver, brass, iron, tin and lead (Neh. 31:22) and the Israelites knew how to cleanse them by fire; and Moses described the Promised Land as "a land whose stones are iron, and out of whose hills thou mayest dig brass (copper)" (Deut. 8:9). Although shafts have been found in the "valley of the cave" in Sinai, they do not penetrate far, and the reason is probably the inability of the ancients to ventilate their mines. The fact that the Midianites had tin in the days of Moses probably points to a very ancient penetration of the Phoenician ships through the Mediterranean and across to the S shore of Britain.   A.B.F.

MINGLED PEOPLE (Heb. *'ērev,* from *'ārav, to mix*). The same Heb. word is rendered "mixed multitude" in Exodus 12:38 and Nehemiah 13:3. In the former passage the reference is to non-Israelite people who left Egypt with the Israelites. In Jeremiah 25:20 and 50:37 the term is used as an expression of contempt for the mixed blood of certain of Israel's enemies. In Numbers 11:4 such a motley body seduced Israel to sin.

MINIAMIN (mĭn'yȧ-mĭn). 1. A Levite in Hezekiah's time (II Chron. 31:15).

2. Head of a family of priests in Nehemiah's time (Neh. 12:17).

3. A priest in the time of Nehemiah (Neh. 12:41). See Miamin and Mijamin, which have the same meaning.

MINISTER (Heb. *shārath, shārēth,* Gr. *diákonos, leitourgós, hyperétes*), originally a servant, though distinguished from a slave who may work against his will, and a hireling, who works for wages. Joshua, as a young man, was minister to Moses (Exod. 24:13) though in rank he was a prince of the tribe of Ephraim (Num. 13:8). As minister of Moses, he led the army of Israel against Amalek (Exod. 17:8-16) and was permitted to ascend Mt. Sinai with Moses. The queen of Sheba, visiting king Solomon, was amazed at the attendance (Hebrew "standing") of his ministers (I Kings 10:5). In the NT certain governmental officers are called "ministers of God's service" (Rom. 13:6). Another word, *hyperétes,* which originally meant "an under-rower" is also used for "minister": "And he closed the book and gave it back to the minister (ASV "attendant") and sat down" (Luke 4:20), and the same word is used of John Mark (Acts 13:5) as an attendant of Paul and Barnabas. God Himself, has His ministers, the angels (Ps. 103:21; 104:4 KJV), who praise Him and go about as His messengers. In Jeremiah 33:21,22 God calls the priests of Israel His ministers, and this usage of the word for priests or religious leaders has come over into the Christian Church. The Christian minister is not only a servant of God, but he should also make it his business to serve the local church to which he is attached; and lest this be thought to be a degradation of dignity, even our

A view inside Solomon's Quarries at Jerusalem. © MPS

Lord declared "For the Son of man came not to be ministered unto but to minister and to give his life a ransom for many" (Mark 10:45). The NT word *diákonos* i.e. "deacon" means "minister" and indicates the duty as well as the privilege of the office. "Deacon" should not be confused with "elder" or "presbyter." A.B.F.

MINNI (mĭn'ī, Heb. *minnî*), mentioned only in Jeremiah 51:27 as a kingdom associated with Ararat and Ashkenaz as instruments or agents for the destruction of the wicked Babylon. It was in what was later called Armenia and some think that the word "Armenia" is from *har-minnî*, i.e. the mountain of Minni. In 719 B.C., Sargon, king of Assyria defeated the Minni. The kingdom is little known and the known references to it are very scarce.

MINNITH (mĭn'ĭth, Heb. *minnîth*), a city of the Ammonites which Jephthah smote while overcoming this nation. It and Abelcheramim were the easternmost limit of Jephthah's victories (Judg. 11: 33). It lay four miles N of Heshbon in the tribe of Reuben. It was a source of wheat for the markets of Tyre (Ezek. 27:17).

MINSTREL, in the OT a player upon a stringed instrument; but in the NT a piper, or player upon a flute. David played his harp to quiet king Saul when the evil spirit was upon him (I Sam. 16:23), and Elisha called for a minstrel to play, perhaps to calm his own mind so that he could better receive a message from God (II Kings 3:15). In Matthew 9:23 we read of "minstrels" (ASV "flute-players") at a funeral.

MINT (See Plants)

MIPHKAD (mĭf'kăd, RV Hammiphkad), the name of one of the gates of Jerusalem, near the temple and the SE corner of the city (Neh. 3:31).

MIRACLES. The word "miracle" (Latin *miraculum*) literally means a marvelous event, or an event which causes wonder. Some of the more important Biblical words designating miracles are *thaúma*, "wonder"; *pele'* and *téras*, "portent"; *gevhûrâh* and *dúnamis*, "display of power"; *'ôth* and *semeíon*, "sign."

The usage of "miracle" in Christian theology includes, but goes beyond, the meanings of the ancient words. A miracle is (1) an extraordinary event, inexplicable in terms of ordinary natural forces; (2) an event which causes the observers to postulate a super-human personal cause; (3) an event which constitutes evidence (a "sign") of implications much wider than the event itself.

Negatively, miracles should be distinguished (1) from works of providence. We must recognize that in good usage "miracle" has a metaphorical or hyperbolical meaning. Every sunrise, every tree, every blade of grass is a "miracle." But works of providence are, for Christians, the ordinary works of God through secondary causes. Unbelievers generally deny the supernatural cause of such things.

On the contrary, in the Biblical events strictly regarded as miracles, the adversaries of faith acknowledged the supernatural character of what took place. After the healing of the man "lame from his mother's womb," the "rulers and elders and scribes" etc., "beholding the man that was healed standing with them . . . could say nothing against it." But they said, ". . . that a notable miracle hath been done by them is manifest to all them that dwell in Jerusalem, and we cannot deny it" (Acts 3:1-4:22). In the case of the miracle at Lystra (Acts 14:8-23) the pagans said, "The gods are come down to us in the likeness of men."

With reference to the resurrection of Christ, Paul could ask a Roman court of law to take cognizance of an indisputable, publicly attested fact, for, said he, "This thing was not done in a corner" (Acts 26:26).

Miracles are further to be distinguished (2) from the type of answers to prayer which do not constitute "signs," or demonstrative evidence for unbelievers. When Elijah prayed for fire on the altar of Jehovah (I Kings 18:17-46), God answered with a demonstrative miracle which convicted the priests of Baal. In the experience of Christians, however, there are numberless events, constantly recurring, in which those who know the Lord can see the hand of God at work, but in which there is not the demonstrative "sign" element. It is a great mistake for Christians to distort their reports of answered prayer so as to make out "sign" miracles where nothing comparable to the Biblical "signs" has occurred. God gives abundant evidence of His love and care without any exaggeration on our part.

Miracles of God should also be distinguished (3) from works of magic. In magic, the wonder worker himself possesses a formula which causes the alleged result. The alleged supernatural power is controlled by the performer. Compare Exodus 7:11; 8:7. In miracles of God, the results depend wholly upon the divine will, and the one who works the miracle is simply an agent for the Lord.

Miracles of God must be distinguished (4) from miracles of Satanic or demonic origin. Christ warned in his Olivet discourse, "There shall arise false Christs and false prophets, and shall show great signs and wonders, insomuch that, if it were possible, they shall deceive the very elect" (Matt. 24:24). Paul foretells of the Man of Sin "whose coming is after the working of Satan, with all power and signs and lying wonders" (II Thess. 2: 9; Cf. Rev. 13:14; 16:14; 19:20).

Miracles must also be distinguished (5) from mere exotic occurrences. There are many events in nature which excite wonder, but such matters are evidences of nothing but oddity. Genuine miracles are always "signs" which teach a lesson. Every miracle of God is a part of God's great integrated system of revealed truth.

Epochs. The majority of the miracles recorded in the Bible fall into three great epochs. First came the miracles of the Exodus: the burning bush, the ten plagues of Egypt, the numerous miracles between the parting of the Red Sea and the crossing of the Jordan, the fall of Jericho, and the battle of Gibeon. This first epoch of miracles came at a time of great spiritual depression. The people in slavery in Egypt had forgotten the name of Jehovah their God. Wholly by His grace God brought them out, amalgamated them into a nation at Sinai, and brought them into the Promised Land. In all subsequent history, God's people have looked back to the miracles of the Exodus as a type of divine salvation.

There followed, after the first epoch of miracles, a long period of decline under the judges, and then a revival of godly faith under David and Solomon. During all this time miracles were very few. God left not Himself without a witness, but the working of miracles was not His chosen method.

Then came a period of idolatrous compromise and "inclusive" religion. The names of Jehovah and Baal were hyphenated, and even the good king Jehoshaphat was badly mixed up with idolatrous Ahab (I Kings 21:25,26; 22). So God gave the second great epoch of miracles centering in the ministry of Elijah and Elisha. By mighty "signs" and works of His grace, God restored and confirmed His pure worship.

The miracle of Jonah and two notable miracles at the time of Isaiah (II Kings 19:35; 20:9-11) were of outstanding significance, as were two or three special miracles in the experience of Daniel. But from the epoch of miracles in the time of Elijah and Elisha until the time of Christ and the apostles miracles were again very few. God worked through the prophets, through the providential discipline of the Babylonian captivity and in other ways. Enough revelation had been given by the time of Malachi for the spiritual life of God's people until the time of the coming of Christ. God's faithful servants were sustained without demonstrative "sign" miracles.

The greatest epoch of miracles in all recorded history occurred in the ministry of Christ and His apostles. It was, in a way, a time of the lowest ebb of spirituality. At the Exodus God's people had forgotten His name. At the time of Elijah and Elisha they had hyphenated His name with the name of Baal. But at the time of Christ and His apostles God's people had made the divinely prescribed system of worship an idolatrous object to such an extent that they were steeped in self-righteousness and hypocrisy. They read the Torah diligently, but they read with a dark veil of hardness over their eyes and hearts. They were so "religious" in their pride that they crucified the Lord of glory. It was to this kind of world that God sent forth His Son.

Nearly 40 demonstrative "sign" miracles wrought by Christ are recorded in the Gospels; but these are selected by the writers from among a much larger number. John says, "Many other signs [miracles] truly did Jesus in the presence of his disciples which are not written in this book (John 20:30).

The ministry of the apostles after Christ's ascension began with the miracle of "languages" on the day of Pentecost. This miracle recurred until the church organization for this age was well established, and probably until the NT books were all put into circulation. There were numerous other demonstrative miracles. As the author of the Epistle to the Hebrews puts it, this "great salvation . . . at the first began to be spoken by the Lord, and was confirmed unto us by them that heard him; God also bearing them witness both with signs and wonders, and with divers miracles and gifts of the Holy Ghost according to his own will" (Heb. 2:3,4).

The Purpose of miracles is revelation and edification. After calling to the many unrecorded miracles of Christ, John adds, "But these are written that ye might believe that Jesus is the Christ, the Son of God; and that believing ye might have life through his name" (John 20:31). Christ several times expressed His purpose in working miracles. He rebuffed the mere desire to see the spectacular. "An evil and adulterous generation seeketh after a sign." This was not a complete rejection even of idle curiosity, for He followed His rebuke even with a powerful reference to Jonah as a type of His own resurrection (Matt. 12:39,40; cf. also Luke 23:8). To seek to see miracles is better than merely to seek free food (John 6:26). His miracles were evidence of the genuineness of His message. "The works which the Father hath given me to finish, the same works that I do, bear witness of me, that the Father hath sent me" (John

(5:36). He preferred that men would accept His message for its intrinsic worth, but to believe Him because of His miracles was not wrong. "If I do not do the works of my Father, do not believe me; but if I do, even though you do not believe me, believe the works, so that you may come to know and continue to realize, that the Father is in me and I am in the Father" (John 10:37,38 original translation).

The question of miracles today is disturbing to the faith of many. In the ancient church the Montanist party insisted that miracles and predictive prophecy must be perpetual gifts. Christ pointed out that miracles do not occur with any uniform regularity (Luke 4:25-27). In fact, if miracles were regular occurrences they would cease to be regarded as miracles. Paul's rules for the restriction of the use of foreign languages (I Cor. 14:) might be applied by analogy to all miracles. Evidently the miracle of languages which occurred on the day of Pentecost had been confused, in the minds of devout people in Corinth, with mere ecstatic meaningless ejaculations. Paul points out, "Languages are a sign not for believers, but for unbelievers." (vs. 22) And he commands that in Christian assemblies not more than two or, at the most, three, in turn, should be allowed to speak in a foreign language, and "if there be no translator, he [the one who wishes to speak in a "tongue"] must keep silent in the church" (Vss. 27,28). At the same time Paul does not forbid the language of untranslatable ejaculations in private (Vss. 2-5).

If Paul's restrictions were literally carried out in the modern church, making sure that the translator *diermeneutes* is a genuine translator, following known rules of grammar and syntax and vocabulary, the actual miracle of languages as it occurred on the day of Pentecost would never be interfered with. Rather it would be the better attested; but the counterfeit "miracle" would be eliminated.

If analogous methods were used in examining reports of alleged miracles, genuine miracles would never be hindered, but would be the better attested. At the same time delusions and exaggerations would be prevented.

Some have sought to account for the occurrence or non-occurrence of miracles on "dispensational" grounds. Such a view seems to have little basis. The period of time between Sinai and Calvary is recognized with general unanimity by dispensationalists as one uniform age of "Law." Yet this "dispensation" included the epoch of miracles under Elijah and Elisha, as well as long periods of which no miracles are recorded. To account for lack of miracles at the present time on dispensational grounds seems without scriptural or factual warrant.

From Bible history, and history since Bible times, the fact stands out that God does not choose to reveal Himself by demonstrative miracles at all times. On the contrary there have been long periods of history, even in Bible times, when God has not used miracles (except the "miracle of grace") in His dealings with His people.

It is a mistake to say that God cannot, or will not work demonstrative "sign" miracles in our day. It is, however, a reasonable opinion, not controvertible by any clearly attested facts, that God generally ceased to work through "sign" miracles when the NT was finished; and that it is His will that the "miracle of grace," the witness of the Spirit, answered prayer, and supremely, the written

Word, shall be the chief sources of knowledge of Himself for His people during this age. It should be clear to all that the most godly, sacrificial, competent ministers, missionaries, and laymen today do not experience demonstrative "sign" miracles. God gives demonstrative miracles when, for reasons known to himself, He chooses to do so.

A healthy mind, full of faith in God's power and in God's wisdom, without denying that "sign" miracles may occur when God so chooses, expects to learn foreign languages by regular processes of study and hard work. A healthy Christian mind expects to observe the ordinary principles of bodily health and sanitation, using such physical provisions of food, shelter, and medicine as divine providence may make available. In spreading the Gospel one does expect the convicting ministry of the Spirit and the evidence of transformed lives, but one does not expect, unless God should so choose, that the sudden healing of a man born with twisted feet and ankle bones, will gather a crowd to hear us preach the Word. He is prepared to serve the Lord, to experience wonderful answers to prayer, and to find that the Word does not return void, regardless of "signs and wonders."

Miracles are an absolutely essential element in Christianity. If Jesus Christ is not God manifest in the flesh, our faith is a silly myth. If He did not arise from the dead in bodily form, the grave being empty and His appearance being recognizable, then we are yet in our sins and of all men most miserable. (See the author's *Behold Him*, Zondervan 1937, for a presentation of the evidences of Christ's resurrection). If the miracle of grace is not verifiable, the transformation of the life of the one who puts his faith in Jesus as his Lord and Saviour, then our Christian Gospel is a miserable fraud.

The rational nature of miracles has been misconstrued by David Hume and those who have followed his positivistic methods. Miracles are not violations of natural law as Hume supposed; they are intelligent acts of a personal God. They are not erratic or exotic occurrences; they are reasonable parts and phases of a cosmic program of revelation and redemption. There is no greater logical problem in the act of God in raising the dead than there is in the act of a man in lifting his hand. We speak or signal to our children and our neighbors with appropriate gestures; and God reveals Himself and His plan for us by "signs" or by other means according to His will.

Christianity is indeed a "supernatural" faith, but the distinction between the natural and the supernatural is only a convenient classification of events. From the point of view of the Biblical writers it was perfectly natural for God to wrestle with Jacob, or to roll back the Red Sea, or to raise his Son from the dead.

Consistent, miracle believing, Christian theism is just as unified in rational thought, just as scientific in its attitude toward evidence and verification, as any laboratory technician who believes that natural law does not exclude intelligent purposeful personal causation.

The Bibliography of the subject of miracles is enormous. In the opinion of the writer the best work in the field is Benjamin B. Warfield, *Counterfeit Miracles*, New York, Scribners, 1918. An excellent classic is Archbishop Richard Chenevix Trench, *Notes On the Miracles of Our Lord*, reprinted by Baker, Grand Rapids, 1949. A work often referred to by writers in this field is A. B. Bruce, *The Miraculous Element in the Gospels*, Hodder and Stoughton, 1929. The evidence for the incarnation and the resurrection are summarized in J. O. Buswell, Jr., *Behold Him*, Zondervan, 1936. For the rejection of the supernatural in history, the "demythologizing" of New Testament, see Rudolph Bultmann, *Theology of the New Testament*, English translation, two volumes, Scribners, 1951, 1955. J.O.B.

MIRIAM (mĭr'ĭ-ăm, Heb. *miryām*, various suggested meanings), the daughter of Amram and Jochebed and the sister of Moses and Aaron (Num. 26:59; I Chron. 6:3). She showed concern and wisdom in behalf of her infant brother, Moses, when he was discovered in the Nile by the Egyptian princess (Exod. 2:4,7-8). Miriam first appears by name in Exodus 15:20, where she is called a prophetess and is identified as the sister of Aaron. After the passage of the sea, she led the Israelite women in dancing and instrumental accompaniment while she sang the song of praise and victory (Exod. 15: 20-21). In Numbers 12:1 M. and Aaron criticized Moses for his marriage to a Cushite woman. Because of this criticism, M. was punished by the Lord with leprosy (Num. 12:9), but upon the protest of Aaron (vs. 11) and the prayer of Moses (vs. 13), she was restored after a period of seven days, during which she was isolated from the camp and the march was delayed. Her case of leprosy is cited in Deuteronomy 24:9. M. died at Kadesh and was buried there (Num. 20:1). Micah refers to her along with her brothers as leaders whom the Lord provided to bring Israel out of the Egyptian bondage (Mic. 6:4). C.E.D.

MIRMA (mûr'mà, *fraud*), head of a father's house in Benjamin after the captivity (I Chron. 8:10).

MIRROR, any smooth or polished surface as of glass or of metal that forms images by reflecting light. As is seen in Exodus 38:8, the "looking-glasses" of the serving women were made of brass, and so could be used as material for the laver. Elihu in Job 37:18 speaks of the sky as resembling a molten looking-glass. He was, no doubt, thinking of the brightness of the sky as like that of polished metal. Of the inadequacy of these ancient mirrors

Ancient bronze mirrors with sculptured handles, from Egypt, of the type that Israelite women took with them on the Exodus.
© BM

as compared with modern ones, Paul reminds us (I Cor. 13:12) by saying that "now we see through a glass darkly." Paul does not mean that the mirror is transparent, but that the image is indistinct. James compares a hearer of the word who is not also a doer to "a man beholding his natural face in a glass" (James 1:23,24) and then forgetting what manner of man he was. In all these cases ASV uses "mirror" for "glass" or "looking-glass" which is of course better, because the material was metal, not glass.

MISGAB (mĭs'găb, Heb. *ha-misgāv, a lofty place*), a town in the high hills of Moab, possibly another name for Moab's capital (Jer. 48:1).

MISHAEL (mĭsh'ā-ĕl, Heb. *mîshā'ēl, who is what God is?*). 1. A cousin of Moses and Aaron, being son of Uzziel, son of Kohath (Exod. 6:22; Lev. 10:4). He helped dispose of the bodies of Nadab and Abihu whom the Lord had slain.

2. A man, presumably a Levite, who stood with Ezra at the reading of the law (Neh. 8:4).

3. A prince of Judah, taken captive by Nebuchadnezzar, who through his officer, changed his name to Meshach, a name of disputed, though undoubtedly heathen meaning. Mishael and his companions, Hananiah and Azariah, were thrust into a burning fiery furnace (Dan. 3:19-30) but came out unharmed, having had the fellowship of "one like a son of the gods."

MISHAL (mī'shăl, Heb. *mish'āl*), a Levitical city (Gershonite) in the tribe of Asher (Josh. 21:30); called "Misheal" in Joshua 19:26 and "Mashal" in I Chronicles 6:74.

MISHAM (mī'shăm), a Benjamite, builder of cities (I Chron. 8:12); son of Elpaal.

MISHEAL (See Mishal)

MISHMA (mĭsh'mà, Heb. *mishmā'*). 1. Son of Ishmael and a prince of the Ishmaelites (Gen. 25:14; I Chron. 1:30).

2. Progenitor of a large family of Simeonites through his descendant Shimei (I Chron. 4:25ff). They held their cities till David's time.

MISHMANNAH (mĭsh-măn'à, *fatness*), a mighty man of Gad, who joined David at Ziklag (I Chron. 12:10).

MISHRAITES (mĭsh'rā-īts), a family of Kiriath-jearim in Judah (I Chron. 2:53).

MISPERETH (mĭs'pē-reth), one who returned with Zerubbabel (Neh. 7:7), called "Mispar" in Ezra 2:2.

MISREPHOTH - MAIM (mĭs're-fŏth - mā'ĭm, *hot springs*), a town or a region near Sidon to which Joshua chased the kings of the North who had joined against him (Josh. 11:8; 13:6). Perhaps the same as Zarephath where Elijah lodged (I Kings 17:9,10), the "Sarepta" of Luke 4:26. On the coast between Sidon and Tyre.

MIST. 1. Steamy vapor rising from warm damp ground into a humid atmosphere (Gen. 2:6).

2. A blinding dimness of vision like that caused by cataracts (Acts 13:11).

3. A part of the description of false teachers in II Peter 2:17.

MITE (See Money)

MITER (See Dress, also Priesthood)

MITHCAH (mĭth'kà, *sweetness*), probably a sweet fountain in Arabia Petraea (Num. 33:28,29). In ASV, "Mithkah."

MITHNITE (mĭth-nīt), patronymic designation of Joshaphat, a mighty man of David (I Chron. 11:43).

Part of an altar to Mithras, the god of celestial light, whose cult was powerful in the Roman empire in the first two centuries A.D. © FRC

MITHRAISM, the cult of Mithras, a Persian sun-god, which reached Rome in or about A.D. 69, by the agency of the eastern legions who set up Vespasian as emperor (Tac. Kist. 3:24). It is possible that the cult was known in the capital a century before, but it was the latter half of the first century of the Christian era which saw its strong dissemination in the West, and indeed its notable challenge to Christianity. Based on the trials, sufferings, and exploits of Mithras, the cult appealed to soldiers; and two Mithraea on Hadrian's wall, one excavated in 1948 at Carrawburgh, and another still covered at Housesteads, reveal the popularity of Mithraism with the British legions. Professor Ian Richmond has established a sequence of destruction and rebuilding at Carrawburgh, which he interprets as indicative of the practice of Mithraism or Christianity at local headquarters. The same shrine has a place of ordeal under the altar, for the initiate advanced through various grades by way of physical suffering and endurance. The archaeologists on the same site were able to establish the fact that chickens and geese were eaten at the ritual feasts, and that pine-cones provided aromatic altar fuel. December 25 was the chief feast of Mithras, and in fixing on that date for Christmas, the early Church sought to overlay both the Mithraic festival and the Saturnalia. Christianity triumphed over Mithraism because of its written records of a historic Christ, and its associated body of doctrine adapted for preaching, evangelism, and the needs of every day. Christianity, too, was universal, excluding neither woman, child, nor slave. It preached salvation by faith and demanded no stern ordeals.   E.M.B.

MITHREDATH (mĭth're-dăth, Heb. *mithredhāth, given by Mithras*, i.e., *by the Sun*), the Persian name of two men: 1. The treasurer of Cyrus, king of Persia, who had charge of the vessels from the temple (Ezra 1:8).

2. An enemy of the Jews in the days of "Artaxerxes," i.e., Cambyses, son of Cyrus (Ezra 4:7). He and others slandered the Jews and stopped their work for a time.

MITYLENE (mĭt-ĭ-lē'nē, Gr. *Mutiléne*). The name is more properly spelled Mytilene. It was the chief city of Lesbos, a splendid port with a double harbor (Acts 20:14), and a center of Greek culture. It was the home of Sappho and Alcaeus, the early lyric poets, and a considerable maritime and colonizing power. Sigeum and Assos were Mitylene's

The traditional tomb of the prophet Samuel at Nebi Samwil may be seen on the horizon at center.
© MPS

foundations. Mitylene's history forms the usual checkered story of a Greek state too weak for independence, and torn between the demands of rival imperialists, Persia, Athens, Rome.

MIXED MULTITUDE. When Israel left Egypt at the Exodus, they were accompanied by a "mixed multitude" (Exod. 12:38), made up, no doubt, of people who had been deeply impressed by the plagues and who realized the powerlessness of the gods of Egypt. Though they went with Israel, their hearts were in Egypt as is seen in Numbers 11:4-6. In the revival after the return with Ezra and Nehemiah, Israel separated itself from a similar group of "camp-followers" (Neh. 13:3).

MIZAR (mī'zȧr, Heb. *har mits'ār, small*), a small peak in the neighborhood of the great Mt. Hermon (Ps. 42:6). The word may be a common noun, "a little hill."

MIZPAH (mĭz'pà, Heb. *mitspâh, mitspēh, watchtower, lookout-post*), as a common noun meaning "watchtower, guardpost" (*mitspēh*), is found in II Chronicles 20:24 and Isaiah 21:8. As a proper noun, it is used of: 1. An unidentified town in the territory of Judah (Josh. 15:38), in the vicinity of Lachish.

2. An unknown city in Moab (I Sam. 22:3), to which David went to confer with the king of Moab concerning a place of refuge for his parents while he was dodging the armies of Saul.

3. An unidentified region or valley mentioned in Joshua 11:3 (*mitspâh*), and 11:8.

4. A city in Gilead (Judg. 11:29; cf. Ramoth-mizpeh, Josh. 13:26).

5. A town in Benjamin (Josh. 18:26), tentatively identified as Tell en-Nashbeh (see below).

Mizpah is: (1) a town in Gilead (see above and Josh. 10:17), which may be associated with Genesis 31:49, where the name is given to a heap of stones set up as a memorial or witness between Jacob and Laban. This Gileadite city was also the home of Jephthah (Judg. 11:34); (2) most frequently Mizpah is the town of Benjamin (cf. 5 above).

At M. the Israelites gathered to consider the steps to be taken against Gibeah in the case of the atrocity related in Judges 19 (cf. Judg. 20:1,3; 21:1,5,8). M. was one of the cities closely associated with Samuel, for he made the circuit of Bethel, Gilgal, and M. and judged Israel in those places (I Sam. 7:16). At M. Israel came to meet with Samuel in repentance (I Sam. 7:5-16) and from there they went out to meet the attacking Philistines and to gain the victory which was celebrated by the setting up of the Ebenezer memorial, "between M. and Shen" (vs. 12). Asa, king of Judah, fortified M. with stones transported from the building venture of Baasha, king of Israel, at Ramah (I Kings 15:22; II Chron. 16:6). After the destruction of Jerusalem by Nebuchadnezzar in 587/6 B.C., Gedaliah was appointed governor of Judah. He located his headquarters at M. (II Kings 25:22-23; Jer. 40:5-12) and the Jews who remained in the land gathered to him there. Johanan, the son of Kareah, and the other military leaders came to M. and warned Gedaliah of a plot against his life by Ishmael, son of Nethaniah. Johanan volunteered to kill Ishmael, but Gedaliah rejected the offer (Jer. 40:16) and ignored the warning. Ishmael carried out his plot successfully, killing not only Gedaliah but also other Jews and Babylonian soldiers who were there (Jer. 41:1-3; II Kings 25:25). The following day a group of 80 men on a religious pilgrimage arrived from Shechem, Shiloh, and Samaria. Ishmael deceived the men, killed them, and threw them into a cistern, except for ten men who were able to buy their lives. The cistern which Ishmael filled with the slain was part of the defense system which Asa had made against Baasha of Israel (Jer. 41:9). Ishmael took captive the remainder of the people of M., but the captives made their escape when Johanan and others gave pursuit. The survivors then went to Egypt, contrary to the Lord's command (Jer. 41:17-42:22). M. also appears in the lists of rebuilders of the walls of Jerusalem (Neh. 3:7,15,19) and is mentioned by Hosea (5:1) in his rebuke of Israel.

C.E.P.

MIZPAR (mĭz′pȧr), a leading companion of Zerub-abel (Ezra 2:2). Called Mizpereth (ASV Misper-eth) in Nehemiah 7:7.

MIZPEH (See Mizpah)

MIZRAIM (mĭz′rā-ĭm, Heb. *mitsrayim,* form and derivation uncertain). 1. The second son of Ham (Gen. 10:6; I Chron. 1:8), is associated with north-eastern Africa, possibly along with his brothers, Cush and Phut. Some of the descendants of Miz-raim (Gen. 10:13-14; I Chron. 1:11-12) probably are also to be linked with this area.

2. The usual Hebrew word for "Egypt" and al-ways so translated in the RSV.

MIZZAH (mĭz′à, Heb. *mizzâh, terror*), a grandson of Esau through his wife Basemath and his son Reuel. Reckoned as one of the chiefs of Edom (Gen. 36:13,17).

MNASON (nā′sŏn, Gr. *Mnáson*), a well-to-do Cypriot who had a house in Jerusalem, and who furnished hospitality for Paul and his party on their return from the third missionary journey. He had been a Christian from the early days of the Church (Acts 21:16).

24,000 men. It was on Mt. Pisgah in the land of Moab, that Moses died.

Nearly a century after the conquest of Canaan Israel "served Eglon, the king of Moab eighteen years" (Judg. 3:12-14). Moab was able to gather the Ammonites and the Amalekites against Israel, but when the children of Israel repented and prayed, God raised up Ehud who slew Eglon and so subdued Moab (Judg. 3:30). There seems to have been considerable travel to and fro between Moab and Judah, for in the days of the judges Elimelech of Bethlehem took his family to Moab to sojourn during a famine; there his two sons married and died, and Ruth, the Moabitess re-turned with Naomi, married Boaz and became an ancestress of David. David, when in difficulty with King Saul, took his father and mother to the king of Moab for their protection (I Sam. 22:3,4). Later, Mesha (q.v.) king of Moab, rendered heavy trib-ute to Ahab, king of Israel (II Kings 3:4). After the death of Ahab, he rebelled, but Jehoram, king of Israel with Jehoshaphat of Judah thoroughly de-feated him and, so far as possible, ruined his land.

Evening light on the mountains of Moab, viewed from the wilderness of Judea, across the north end of the Dead Sea. © MPS

MOAB (mō′ăb, Heb. *mô′āv, seed*). 1. Grandson of Lot by incest with his elder daughter (Gen. 19:30-38).

2. The nation or people descended from Moab. They settled first at Ar, just E of the southern part of the Dead Sea and quite close to the site of the destroyed cities of the plain. Moses was com-manded of the Lord not to vex them when Israel passed through their vicinity on their way to the Promised Land. However, when Israel had well-nigh reached their destination and were encamped in the plains of Moab (Num. 22-24) Balak, sens-ing that he could not save himself from Israel by force of arms, hired Balaam to come and curse Israel. Balaam desired with all his heart to come; but after being rebuked by the voice of a dumb ass for his sin, he was permitted of God to proceed, but on condition that he would speak only what God gave him to speak. As a result, he prophetical-ly gave blessing to Israel four times as he had to do, but he evidently said to Balak and the Moabites and Midianites, "Though you cannot conquer Israel by force of arms, you can seduce them" so the Moabite girls entered the camp of Israel (Num. 31:16) and seduced the men (Num. 25:1-9). As a result, God sent a plague that took off

From that time on, Moab gradually declined in ac-cordance with the word of the Lord through His prophets. Amos 2:1-3 pronounces the death sen-tence upon Moab; Isaiah 15,16, "The burden of Moab" gives in much detail the coming destruction of Moab, and this was fulfilled by Shalmanezer of Assyria or by his successor Sargon. Isaiah puts his finger on the prevailing sin of Moab aside from his idolatry: "We have heard of the pride of Moab, that he is very proud; even of his arrogancy, and his pride and his wrath" (16:6) and Ezekiel and Jeremiah, a century and a half later complete the picture. Moab and Seir are to be punished for lik-ening the house of Judah to the other nations (Ezek. 25:8-11). Jeremiah (chap. 48) depicts both past and future judgments upon Moab and Zephaniah 2:8-11 foretells utter destruction upon Moab for its wicked pride.

3. The land of the Moabites. Moab was bounded on the W by the Dead Sea, on the E by the desert, on the N by the Arnon, and on the S by Edom. It is about 3,200 feet above the level of the sea, and is chiefly rolling country, well-adapted for pastur-age. Machaerus, the place where John the Baptist was imprisoned and lost his life, was in Moab.

A.B.F.

Replica of the famous Moabite Stone in the Palestine government museum. It was a monument erected by Mesha, king of Moab, and dates back to about 850 B.C.
© MPS

MOABITE STONE, THE, an inscribed stone found in Moab and recording Moabite history. In 1868, F. A. Klein, a German missionary employed by the Church Missionary Society (Church of England) while traveling through the territory formerly occupied by the tribe of Reuben, E of the Dead Sea, was informed by an Arab sheikh of a remarkable stone inscribed with writing, and lying at Dibon, near Mr. Klein's route. The stone was bluish basalt, neatly cut into a monument about four by two feet with its upper end curved, and a raised rim enclosing an inscription. Mr. Klein informed the authorities of the Berlin Museum, and meanwhile M. Ganneau of the French Consulate at Jerusalem and a Capt. Warren had made "squeezes" and so had secured roughly the material of the inscription. While the French and the Germans were bargaining with the Turks for the stone, the Arabs, with Oriental acuteness, argued that if the stone as a whole was of value it would be far more valuable if cut to pieces, so they built a fire around it, poured cold water over it, and so well-nigh destroyed it; and would have succeeded had not the gentleman above mentioned ascertained the inscription. The fragments of the stone were purchased, pieced together and are now in the Louvre in Paris. The writing consisted of 34 lines, written in the Moabite language (practically a dialect of the Hebrew) by Mesha, king of the Moabites in the time of Ahaziah and Jehoram, the sons of Ahab, and giving his side of the story recorded in part in II Kings 3. It reads, in part: "I, Mesha, king of Moab, made this monument to Chemosh to commemorate deliverance from Israel.

My father reigned over Moab thirty years, and I reigned after my father. Omri, king of Israel, oppressed Moab many days and his son after him. But I warred against the king of Israel, and drove him out, and took his cities, Medeba, Ataroth, Nebo and Jahaz, which he built while he waged war against me. I destroyed his cities, and devoted the spoil to Chemosh, and the women and girls to Ashtar. I built Qorhah with prisoners from Israel. In Beth-Diblathaim, I placed sheep-raisers." It seems strange that though Mesha names Omri who had long since died, he does not name his son Ahab, who reigned almost twice as long, and to whom Mesha had paid heavy tribute (II Kings 3: 4). Perhaps he hated his very name. Neither does he mention the sons of Ahab, Ahaziah and Jehoram, by name, though he warred against them. Probably he had the monument made before the time of his defeat by Jehoram and Jehoshaphat.

Though the inscription is almost in pure Hebrew, it was written in the old "round" letters, which were later superseded (some say in Ezra's time) by the "square" letters in which Hebrew is printed today. Very ancient Hebrew, and Arabic as well, were written practically without signs for vowel sounds, but the Moabite stone uses the *aleph, waw* and *yodh* not only as consonants but as vowels, and also uses the silent *he* at the end of the words, just as in the OT. Some have called the Moabite stone "the earliest important Hebrew inscription" though written in Moabite. Since Moab and Jacob were both descendants of Terah, it is not strange that their tongues should resemble one another.

A.B.F.

MOADIAH (See Maadiah)

MOLADAH (mŏl′à-dà, Heb. *môlādhâh, birth*), one of the cities mentioned in Joshua 15 and 19 in the lists both of Judah and of Simeon. It lies about ten miles E of Beer-sheba. Now called Khirbet-el-Milh. At the Restoration, Judah occupied it (Neh. 11:26).

MOLE (See Animals)

MOLID (mō′lid, *begetter*), an early member of the tribe of Judah, mentioned only in I Chronicles 2:29.

MOLOCH, MOLECH (mō′lŏk, mō′lĕk, Heb. *ha-mōlekh*), a heathen god worshiped especially by the Ammonites with gruesome orgies in which little ones were sacrificed. At least in some places an image of the god was heated and the bodies of children who had just been slain were placed in its arms. The worship of Moloch was known to the children of Israel before they entered Canaan, for Moses very sternly forbade its worship (Lev. 18: 21; 20:1-5). In spite of this prohibition, King Solomon, to please his numerous heathen wives, set up high places for Chemosh and for Moloch on Mount Olivet (I Kings 11:7), though its principal place of worship in and after Manasseh's time was the valley of the son of Hinnom (II Chron. 33:6), a place of such ill repute that "Gehenna," i.e., "the valley of Hinnom" became a type for hell (Matt. 5:29,30). The words "Moloch," "Molech," "Milcom" (I Kings 11:5), "Malcam" (Zeph. 1:5) are all variants of Heb. words meaning "the reigning one." Latter-day Jews often went from the sacrifices to Moloch into the house of the Lord to worship there (Ezek. 23:37-39) and this impiety was particularly offensive to Jehovah as it added insult to injury. Read Jeremiah 7:9-11; 19:4-13. Because of this heathen worship God gave the land of Israel over to the rule of its enemies for many years (Ps. 106:35-42).   A.B.F.

MOLTEN SEA (See Tabernacle)

MONEY. While "the love of money is the root of all evil" (I Tim. 6:10), the study of money, particularly of money mentioned in the Bible, is rich and rewarding. Not only did Jesus and the apostles admonish Christians about the use of money, they also used it themselves and brought it into their teaching. The early Christians used money in their daily lives just as Christians and churches do today. Translators of the Bible, however, have always had difficulty finding terms for the various kinds of money in the Bible which indicate the value or purchasing power in Bible times. Therefore, a knowledge of the nature and value of ancient money is very helpful to the Bible reader in understanding the Bible today.

Brief History of Money. Money in the sense of stamped coin did not exist, so far as is known, before 700 B.C. There was no coined money in Israel until after the Exile. Before this time exchange of values took place by *bartering,* by trading one thing for another without the exchange of money. This method was followed by the weight system, later by minted coins, paper money, until today we have the credit system by which one may live, buy, and sell without the use of money at all. Wealth is first mentioned in the Bible in connection with Abraham (Gen. 12:5), "And Abram took (from Ur to Canaan) Sarai his wife, and Lot his brother's son, and *all their substance that they had gathered"* (cf. 12:16,20). The three main items of wealth in the ancient world are listed in Genesis 13:2, and Abraham had all three: "And Abram was very rich in *cattle,* in *silver,* and in *gold.*" Among the Romans the word for money was *pecunia* which is derived from *pecus,* the Latin word for cow or cattle. Perfumes and ointments also had great value. Besides gold, the Wise Men brought frankincense and myrrh to worship the new-born King.

The Shekel. The first metal exchange was crude, often shapeless, and heavy so as to approximate the value of the item purchased in actual weight. The buyer usually weighed his "money" to the seller. The Jewish *shekel* was such a weight (*shekel* means "weight"). It was based on the Babylonian weight of exchange, generally of gold, silver, bronze and even iron. Among the Jews the shekel was used for the temple tax, poll tax, and for redemption from the priesthood (Exod. 30:11-16; 13:13; Num. 3:44-51). Since Jesus was a first-born Son not of the tribe of Levi, His parents redeemed Him from the priesthood (Luke 2:21ff) by payment of a shekel (really a half-shekel coin). In Jesus' day the shekel was not a weight but a coin with the value of a shekel, worth about a day's wages at the time. The shekel shown (see plate) is

such a redemption shekel. It is a genuine piece from the days of the Maccabees, 175-140 B.C., although some scholars believe it comes from the last revolt of the Jews against the Romans, 66-70 A.D. On the obverse (front) is a pot of manna (Exod. 16:33) with the legend (writing or inscription) "Shekel Israel." On the reverse (back) is Aaron's budding rod (Num. 17:8) with the legend in Hebrew letters, "Jesusalem the Holy." Other weights mentioned in the Bible are: *talent* (circle), *māneh* (part), *gērâh* (grain), and *beqa'* (half shekel). It required 3,000 shekels to equal one talent of silver, which reveals that the 10,000 talents the unmerciful servant (Matt. 18:23-25) owed his master was an overwhelming debt. The *pound* (Luke 19:13) is a translation of the old weight *mina* or *maneh* (Greek: *mna*). Since a talent was 60 minas, a mina equaled 50 shekels in Attic weight and 100 shekels in Old Testament weight, which means that in the parable the gift of the Lord to His people is a most precious gift, namely, the Gospel.

Jewish coins of fourth century B.C. © BM PEF

Beginning of the Coin System. The Hebrews were not the first people to use minted coins. Except for a few brief periods of independence, they were compelled to use the coinage of their pagan conquerors. Thus in the Bible we find a wide variety of coins — mainly Greek, Roman, and Jewish — all used by the same people. Most historians believe that the earliest money pieces were struck about 700 B.C. in the small kingdom of Lydia in Asia Minor. These early Lydian "coins" were simply crude pieces of metal cut into small lumps of a standard weight and stamped with official marks to guarantee the value. The Egyptians also developed such a system. Later the quality of the metal and the image on the coin indicated the worth in buying power, much like today. It is believed that the Jews first became acquainted with the coinage of the Babylonians and Persians during the Captivity and that they carried these coins with them when they returned to Palestine.

| OBVERSE | REVERSE | AMERICAN NICKEL |

Jewish Shekel. Perhaps struck by Simon Maccabeus about 140 B.C. (I Macc. 15:6). Pot of manna on the obverse and the flowering rod on the reverse. Note size as compared to an American nickel.

OBVERSE   REVERSE   AMERICAN DIME

Tetradrachma of Ephesus. Both the bee on the obverse and the stag (with palm tree) on the reverse were symbols of the goddess Diana of the Ephesians (Acts 19:28). The Greek letters E Ph beside the bee are abbreviation for "Ephesus."

OBVERSE   REVERSE   AMERICAN QUARTER

Tridrachma of Corinth. The goddess Athena is wearing a Corinthian helmet. An unusual coin because the head is on the reverse.

OBVERSE   REVERSE   AMERICAN HALF DOLLAR

Greek Tetradrachma, or Shekel of Tyre. Head of the god Melkarth on the obverse, and an eagle standing on the rudder of a ship on the reverse. The legend reads, "Tyre the Holy and Invincible."

Coins from Concordia Seminary
Museum, Springfield, Illinois.

The Drachma. After 330 B.C. the world-conquering Greeks developed the Persian and Babylonian coinage, and their own, into something of a fixed world system. Animals, natural objects, and the Greek gods were used as symbols on the coins. Each coin was made individually with hammer, punch, and die. The Greeks called these coins *drachmas* (*drachma* means "handful") of which there was a variety with about the same value. Later the terms drachma and shekel were used somewhat interchangeably. The "lost coin" (Luke 15:8) was a silver drachma equivalent to a Roman denarius, a day's wages. The temple or half-shekel tax (Matt. 17:24) was a *didrachma*. Another drachma was the *tridrachma* of Corinth, a silver coin about the size of our quarter with the head of Athena on one side and the winged horse Pegasus on the other. It was worth a day's pay and no doubt Paul earned it making tents and used it for payment of passage on ships during his journeys. A Greek coin Paul also may have "spent" is the now famous "bee coin," a silver *tetradrachma* of Ephesus dating back to 350 B.C. All these drachmas were about equal in value to the Jewish shekel.

The Stater. The coin Peter found in the fish's mouth was the Greek *statér* (Matt. 17:27). Since the temple tax was a half-shekel the stater would pay for two. Many authorities believe that the stater really was the tetradrachma of Antioch or Tyre since these coins were accepted at the temple. It is believed that the thirty pieces of silver (Matt. 26:15; 27:3-5) which bought the greatest betrayal in history were these large silver coins, tetradrachmas of either Tyre or Antioch from about 125 B.C. In Exodus 21:32 we read that 30 shekels was the price of a slave.

The Assarion. The Greek *assárion* is mentioned twice in the NT (Matt. 10:29; Luke 12:6): "Are not two sparrows sold for a *farthing* (*assárion*)?" In the Roman Empire this Greek coin was both small in size and in value, and the English translators simply translated "farthing," in a similar small coin with which the people in England would be familiar. Today we might say "two sparrows for a penny," or "two for a nickel."

Lepton and Kodrantes (Widow's Mite). During pre-Roman times under the Maccabees (175-140 B.C.) the Jews for the first time were allowed to issue money of their own. One such piece, as we have seen, was the shekel. Another piece was the *leptón*, a tiny bronze or copper coin, which we know as the "widow's mite," "And there came a certain poor widow, and she threw in two *mites* which make a farthing" (Mark 12:42; Luke 21:2; 12:59). *Leptón* was translated "mite" because it was the coin of least value among coins. Even the metal was inferior and deteriorated easily. This coin should really be the "penny" of the Bible, not the denarius. The coin illustrated was struck much later by John Hyrcanus II, Jewish High Priest and ruler, 69-40 B.C. In contrast to the coins of pagan rulers, the Jewish coins had pictures from religion and agriculture instead of gods and men, obeying the command. "You shall not make yourself a graven image, or any likeness" (Exod. 20:4). The English translators are confusing when they also render *kodrántes* with "farthing": "And she threw in two *mites* which make a *farthing* (*kodrántes*)." The *kodrántes* had twice the value of a "mite," something like that of a two-cent piece today. The *kodrántes* shown here is really a Roman coin made for the Jews.

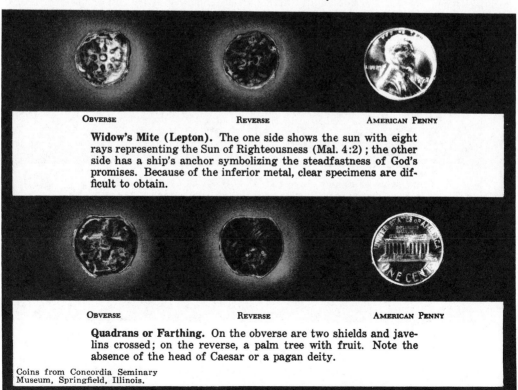

| OBVERSE | REVERSE | AMERICAN PENNY |

Widow's Mite (Lepton). The one side shows the sun with eight rays representing the Sun of Righteousness (Mal. 4:2); the other side has a ship's anchor symbolizing the steadfastness of God's promises. Because of the inferior metal, clear specimens are difficult to obtain.

| OBVERSE | REVERSE | AMERICAN PENNY |

Quadrans or Farthing. On the obverse are two shields and javelins crossed; on the reverse, a palm tree with fruit. Note the absence of the head of Caesar or a pagan deity.

Coins from Concordia Seminary Museum, Springfield, Illinois.

The Denarius. The most interesting coin of the Bible is the Roman *denarius* (Greek: *denárion*), known by collectors as the "penny" of the Bible because of this translation in the King James Version. This silver coin, which looks something like our dime, was the most common Roman coin during the days of Jesus and the apostles. Collectors have been able to obtain originals of all 12 Roman emperors (Augustus to Nerva) who reigned during the NT period, 4 B.C. to A.D. 100. There were also gold *denarii* but these were generally special issues and not nearly so numerous. The Romans as well as the Greeks struck mainly silver coins (alloys) and kept large government-owned silver mines throughout the empire, e.g., at Antioch and Ephesus. It is interesting to note that when Paul writes, "The love of money is the root of all evil," he really says in Greek, "The love of *silver* (*philargyría*) is the root of all evil" (I Tim. 6:10; cf. Luke 16:14; II Tim. 3:2).

The true value of the denarius may be seen in our Lord's parable of the laborers in the vineyard: "After agreeing with the laborers for a *penny* (Greek: *denárion*) a day he sent them into his vineyard" (Matt. 20:2,10). Sunday school teachers and children have always wondered why any man would toil all day and receive only a penny. Even those who worked but one hour deserved more than that. Was it because wages were so low? But if one remembers that in the Roman world the denarius represented a day's pay, the dilemma is solved. Army pay was also a denarius a day. For this reason it is misleading today to state, as Bible margins often do, that the denarius is worth "eighteen or twenty cents"; this is the value according to silver weight (pound sterling) but not according to buying power, which is the important thing. There is a relationship between "penny" and "denarius," however, which explains the translation. The English monetary system is based on the old Roman system. British symbols are: £-pounds; s-shillings; d-pence. The "d" for pence stands for the old denarius. The confusion began when "pence" became "penny" in our Bibles.

Similarly, in Jesus' parable of the unmerciful servant, we read: "But the same servant went out and found one of his fellow-servants which owed him an hundred *pence* (Greek: *denárion*)." This means that the amount the man owed was not a mere pittance, but a hundred days' wages; of course, it was insignificant compared to the 10,000 talents (30,000,000) *denarii*). Again, the lesson in good works taught in the parable of the Good Samaritan is greatly enhanced when we know the real value of a denarius. We read: "And on the morrow when he departed, he took out *two pence* (Greek: *denárion*), and gave them to the host, and said unto him, Take care of him; and whatsoever thou spendest more, when I come again, I will repay thee" (Luke 10:35). The fact that the Good Samaritan paid two days' wages and was willing to pay anything more over that amount to aid an unknown stranger, greatly enhances his love for his neighbor. In our day a gift of two ten-dollar bills to the Community Chest is not so much!

The denarius is mentioned in the miracle of feeding the five thousand (John 6): "Philip answered him, *Two hundred pennyworth* (*denarii*) of bread is not sufficient for them, that every one of them may take a little." If one assumes that the treasury of the group contained 200 *denarii*, then Jesus and His disciples dispensed more money to the needy than is generally recognized. Similar light is thrown on the generous act of Mary who anointed Jesus with the precious spikenard. In John 12:5 Judas is quoted as saying, "Why was not this ointment sold for *three hundred pence* (*denarii*), and given to the poor?" Considering the value of a denarius in Jesus' day, Mary's gift was truly great. Few could afford it today. Perhaps Judas would not have grumbled over the $60.00 usually stipulated as the cost of this nard (20c x 300), but it was the 300 days' wages which evoked this cold comment from the lover of silver. Incidentally, one can appreciate the severity of the famine represented by the black horse by knowing the value of a denarius (Rev. 6:5-6): "And he that sat on him had a pair of balances in his hand.

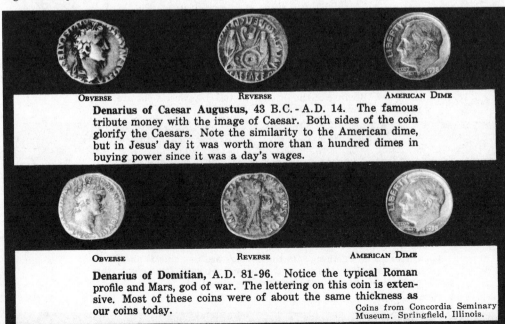

OBVERSE   REVERSE   AMERICAN DIME

Denarius of Caesar Augustus, 43 B.C. - A.D. 14. The famous tribute money with the image of Caesar. Both sides of the coin glorify the Caesars. Note the similarity to the American dime, but in Jesus' day it was worth more than a hundred dimes in buying power since it was a day's wages.

OBVERSE   REVERSE   AMERICAN DIME

Denarius of Domitian, A.D. 81-96. Notice the typical Roman profile and Mars, god of war. The lettering on this coin is extensive. Most of these coins were of about the same thickness as our coins today.

Coins from Concordia Seminary Museum, Springfield, Illinois.

And I heard a voice in the midst of the four beasts say, A measure (quart) of wheat for a penny (denarius), and three measures (quarts) of barley for a penny (denarius)."

The denarius was also the "tribute money" which the Romans imposed on the Jewish people. The story of the attempt of Jesus' enemies to trap Him in a treasonable statement (Matt. 22:15-22) tells us more about the denarius. "Is it lawful to give tribute to Caesar or not?" they asked. In answering, Jesus gave an example of early use of what we call visual aids. "Shew me the tribute money," He said. "And they brought unto him a penny (denarius)." He then asked them, "Whose is this image and superscription?" Since it was a denarius of Caesar, they answered, "Caesar's." The "image" on the denarius handed our Lord was the head of Caesar Augustus (43 B.C.-A.D.14), who issued the decree for the empire-wide census (Luke 2:1), or that of Tiberius Caesar reigning at the time, A.D. 14-39. Pictured is an original denarius, nearly 2000 years old, of the mighty Emperor Caesar Augustus. The obverse gives us the profile of this powerful Caesar. We note the typical Latin face and the head dress. From Nero's coins we can see that he was fat and pudgy. From the denarius came the idea of our American dime, one of which is pictured with Franklin Roosevelt's "image" in the same profile view. Caesar's name is spelled out entirely to the right of the head thus: CAESARAVGVSTVS. To the left of the head are the following Latin abbreviations, all run together: DIVIMPPATERPATRIAE. DIV means "divine"; IMP, "imperator"; PATER PATRIAE, Latin for "Father of His Country." On the reverse one sees the figures of two Caesars, and above and around the figures the Latin abbreviations: AVGVSPON- COSTRPGER. AVG is "Augustus"; PON, "Ponti- fex Maximus," religious ruler, or "Highest Priest"; COS, "consulship"; TRP, "Tribunica Potestate," Tribune power, civil head of the state. Below the images is the word CAESARES, Latin for "Cae- sars." From this coin alone one can discern that the Roman Emperor was an absolute monarch, head of both state and religion.

Photographs of a denarius of the Roman Em- peror Domitian have been included to illustrate how much "literature" is often found on the Ro- man coins. Domitian reigned at the end of the NT period, A.D. 81-96, and is no doubt the emperor who banished the Apostle John to Patmos. From the profile on the obverse one can assume that he was heavy in stature with a small face and deep-set eyes and large nose. The lengthy lettering, begin- ning below the image and proceeding clock-wise around the coin is as follows: IMP, "Imperator"; CAES, "Caesar", title of king, not his name; DOMIT, "Domitian", his given name (praeno- men); AUG. "Augustus," most distinctive title; GERM, "Germanicus" or German, hereditary title; PM, "pontifex maximus", head of the empire's re- ligion. TRP, "Tribunica potestate," supreme civil head, representative of the people. On the reverse is the image of Mars, god of war, holding a spear and a shield. When the nation was at peace he was pictured carrying an olive branch, but not in the days of Domitian. Around the image of Mars, reading left to right, are the words: IMP, "Imper- ator" or Emperor; XXII, means date of 90 A.D.; COS XVI, 16th consulship, about 90 A.D.; CENS PER, "Censor Perpetuus", another title of the chief of state, granted for lifetime, hence "perpet- ual." Seldom does one see so much said in so little space.

To study and handle these coins, some over 2000 years old, indeed brings one close to the people who lived in Bible days and helps to understand the times in which they lived. For instance, a study of the denarius reveals that this coin was not only to serve as a medium of exchange, but also to dis- seminate information and propaganda for the em- peror. Since there were no newspapers in those days, the government placed much information on its money, especially to glorify the emperor and to recite his deeds. The Roman emperors believed the people read the legends on the coins and went to much trouble to change them often, sometimes once a year. The coins also yield a good deal of historical information, i.e., the dates of the em- perors, and help to establish the historicity of the Bible.

The value of the coins fluctuated much in an- cient times. Therefore, it is often difficult to state the exact value of each coin. The government issued its money through money changers instead of banks and often the rate of exchange changed according to what a money changer was willing to give on a certain day. The denarius became much less in value after the second century.

Regarding the value of the Bible coins, it is generally misleading and confusing to give their value in pound sterling. For example, to state that a denarius is worth 20 cents may give the value in silver weight, but not the value in pur- chasing power which gives the true or real value of the coin, just as people have learned during these days of inflation in America. Bible translators will do greater service and reduce confusion by simply transliterating the Greek and Latin names for the coins (denarius, shekel, assarion, etc.), which the new RSV has attempted to do, and allow the Bible reader to interpret the value of the coins himself.

L.M.P.

MONEY CHANGER. In Judaea in NT times, Roman money was legal tender and so was used for ordinary purposes, but the priests taught the people that only Jewish currency was fit for wor- ship, so these men made a very profitable business for themselves. Having secured Jewish money from the priests, they sat in the court of the Gentiles and exchanged it (at a liberal profit for themselves) for Roman money, then would make another ex- change with the priests, no doubt making a profit at both ends. (See Matthew 21:12 with its parallel in Mark 11:15). Our Lord drove them out saying that they had made the Lord's house a den of rob- bers (KJV "a den of thieves").

The money changers. © SPF

MONOTHEISM (mŏn'ō-thē-ĭzm, from Gr. *mónos, one, théos, god*), the doctrine or belief that there is but one God. Atheism is the belief that there is no god; polytheism, that there is more than one god; monolatry, the worship of one god as supreme, without denying that there are other gods; and henotheism, belief in one god, though not to the exclusion of belief in others. There are three great monotheistic religions: Judaism, Christianity and Islam (Mohammedanism), the latter two having their origin in the first. According to the Bible, man was originally a monotheist. This has been denied by the school of comparative religion, which teaches that monotheism was a late development in human religious experience. According to it, the religion of Israel was not originally monotheistic; it gradually became so through the influence of the prophets. W. Schmidt, S. M. Zwemer, and others have shown, on the contrary, that polytheism was a late development. The Christian doctrine of the Trinity is not in conflict with the monotheism of the OT. There are intimations of the doctrine of the Trinity in the OT. Christ and the apostles, moreover, saw nothing incompatible between monotheism and the doctrine of the Trinity.   S.B.

MONSTERS (See Animals)

MONTH (See Calendar, Time)

MOON (See Astronomy)

MORASTHITE (mō-rās'thīt), an inhabitant of Moresheth, as was the prophet Micah (Mic. 1:1; Jer. 26:18). See MORESHETH-GATH.

MORDECAI (môr'dē-kī, Heb. *mordekhay*, from *Marduk*, chief god of Babylon). 1. A leader of the people of Judah during the return of Zerubbabel from exile (Ezra 2:2; Neh. 7:7).

2. The deliverer of the Jews in the book of Esther. He was a Benjamite who had been deported during the reign of Jehoiachin (Esth. 2:5, 6). He lived in Shushan (Susa) the Persian capital and brought up his cousin Esther, whose parents were dead (2:7). When Esther was taken into the royal harem, Mordecai forbade her to reveal her nationality (2:20); yet he remained in close connection with her. Mordecai discovered at the palace gate a plot against the king. By informing Esther of the plot, he secured the execution of the two eunuchs responsible (2:19-23). When Haman was made chief minister, Mordecai aroused his wrath by refusing to bow before him. To avenge the slight, Haman procured from the king a decree to destroy the Jews (chap. 3). Mordecai then sent Esther to the king to seek protection for her people (chap. 4). Haman meanwhile prepared a high gallows on which he planned to hang Mordecai (chap. 5). By a singular, almost humorous turn of events, Haman fell from favor and was hanged on the gallows he had prepared for Mordecai (chap. 7), Mordecai succeeded him as chief minister of the king (chap. 8). Thus the Persian officials everywhere assisted the Jews, who slew their enemies and instituted the feast of Purim to celebrate their deliverance (chap. 9). The book of Esther ends with an account of the fame and dignity of Mordecai (chap. 10). In the apocryphal additions to Esther, Mordecai is glorified still more. He is a favorite character in the Rabbinical literature as well.   J.B.G.

MOREH, HILL OF (mō'rě, Heb. *môreh, teacher*), mentioned only in Judge 7:1. Near this hill the Midianites were camped when Gideon attacked them. Although it cannot certainly be identified, most scholars believe the Hill of Moreh to be pres-

The Hill of Moreh and the Plain of Jezreel (Esdraelon). © MPS

ent-day Jebel Nabi Dahi, sometimes called the Little Hermon, to the NW of the Plain of Jezreel, about eight miles NW of Mt. Gilboa and one mile S of Nain.

MOREH, OAK OF (KJV, "Plain of Moreh"), mentioned in Genesis 12:6 as a place near Shechem where Abraham camped and erected an altar to the Lord. It was probably the tree under which Jacob later buried the amulets and idols his family had brought from Haran (Gen. 35:4). In Deuteronomy 11:30 the Oak of Moreh is mentioned as a landmark near Ebal and Gerizim. Sacred oaks have been known in Palestine from early times. Probably believed to be the abode of ancestral spirits by the Canaanites, they were thought to have oracular powers, and may have been tended by priests, as are cedars of Lebanon today.

MORESHETH-GATH (mō'rěsh-ĕth-găth, possession of Gath), a town mentioned only in Micah 1:14 in a group of places of the Judah-Philistine border area. Micah calls himself an inhabitant of Moresheth (1:1 RSV, cf. Jer. 26:18) — probably the same place. Gath may have been added to the name to indicate that this was the Moresheth which is near Gath. It may be identified with Tell ej-Judeideh, about five miles W. of Gath in the Shephelah.

MORIAH (mō-rī'à, Heb. *mōrîyâh*), a land or district where Abraham was told to offer up Isaac (Gen. 22:2). It was about a three days' journey from Beersheba where Abraham was living when given the command. Its location is not given. Jewish tradition has identified it with Jerusalem; Samaritan, with Mt. Gerizim. According to II Chronicles 3:1 Solomon built the temple on Mt. Moriah, where God had appeared to David (I Chron. 21:15-22:1). Whether this is the same Mt. Moriah mentioned in the account of Abraham is not certain.

MORNING SACRIFICE (See Offerings)

MORSEL, occurs once in the NT, where it means an "eating," i.e. one meal (Heb. 12:16).

MORTAL, MORTALITY, in the OT (only in Job 4:17) represents the Hebrew *'ěnôsh* (lit. "man"), translated "mortal man"; in the NT it is the translation of *thnetós* — subject to death (Rom. 8:11; I Cor. 15:53,54). Mortality occurs only in II Corinthians 5:4 and renders the same Greek word.

The Plain of Moreh (Shechem), Abraham's first stopping place in Palestine. © MPS

MORTAR. 1. A bowl-shaped vessel of stone or basalt rock in which grain, spices, etc., were crushed with the use of a pestle. The manna was so ground (Num. 11:8). Cf. Proverbs 27:22.

2. A substance (KJV mortar) used to bind bricks or stones together in a wall. Mud or clay was often used (Nah. 3:14); for better houses, a mortar of sand and lime. Some have thought that Ezekiel 13:10,11,14,15 refers to the latter, poorly mixed ("untempered" KJV). Recent scholars, however, believe the passage to refer to a whitewash (RSV) applied over a poorly made wall to disguise its weakness. In Babylon bitumen was used for mortar (Gen. 11:3 RSV). Many walls in Palestine were made by piling up large stones, using smaller stones, without mortar, to fill in the spaces between (cyclopean walls).

MOSAIC, a picture or design made by setting tiny squares or cones of varicolored marble, limestone or semiprecious stones in some medium such as bitumen or plaster to tell a story or to form a decoration. Mosaics are one of the most durable parts of ancient structures and often are the only surviving vestige. Mosaics have survived from ancient Sumer from as early as 2900 B.C. They were widely used in the early Christian and Byzantine buildings in Palestine, and remaining examples throw considerable light on ancient Biblical customs, as well as affording insight into early Christian beliefs and symbols.

Very famous is the fine mosaic picture-map of Jerusalem from the floor of a church in Madaba, probably from the sixth century AD. This is one of the earliest maps known from Palestine. The mosaics from the Arab palace at Khirbat al-Mafjar (near Jericho) are among the most beautiful known. Ancient Palestinian synagogues have yielded interesting designs and even pictorial art, as, e.g., the Beth Alpha synagogue, with its large circular representation of the zodiac, and the scene of Abraham sacrificing Isaac.   J.B.G.

MOSERAH (mō-sē′rȧ, *bond*), in KJV Mosera, an encampment of the Israelites in the wilderness near Bene-jaakan (Deut. 10:6 RSV). In Numbers 33:30 the plural form Moseroth is used as the name of the place. The site is unknown, but it was near Mt. Hor, by the border of Edom.

MOSES mō′zĕs, mō′zĭs, Heb. mōsheh, Egyp. mēs, *drawn out, born*), the national hero who delivered the Israelites from Egyptian slavery, established them as an independent nation, and prepared them for entrance into Canaan. Exact dates for the life of Moses are dependent upon the date of the Exodus. On the basis of an early date for the Exodus, c. 1440 B.C., Moses was born about 1520 B.C. (Merrill F. Unger, *Archaeology and the Old Testament,* Grand Rapids: Zondervan, 1954, pp. 140-152). Some scholars date the Exodus as late as 1225 B.C. (For a brief discussion and bibliography on various dates see Samuel J. Schultz, *The Old Testament Speaks,* New York: Harper, 1960, pp. 47-49).

Moses was born of Israelite parents in the land of Egypt. Perilous times prevailed. Not only were the Israelites enslaved, but a royal edict designed to keep them in subjection ordered the execution of all Israelite male children at birth. Hidden among the reeds near the river's bank, Moses was discovered by Pharaoh's daughter. So favorably was she disposed toward this Hebrew babe that she requested Moses' mother to nurse him until he was old enough to be taken to the royal court where he spent the first 40 years of his life.

Little is narrated in the Book of Exodus regarding the early period of the life of Moses. Stephen in his address to the Sanhedrin (Acts 7:22) asserts that Moses was not only instructed in the science and learning of the Egyptians but also was endowed with oratorical ability and distinctive leadership qualities. The court of Egypt provided educational facilities for royal heirs of tributary princes from city-states of the Syro-Palestinian territory subject to Egyptian pharaohs. Consequently Moses may have had classmates from as far N as the Euphrates River in his educational experiences in the Egyptian court.

Moses' first valiant attempt to aid his own people ended in failure. While trying to pacify two fellow Israelites he was reminded that he had killed an Egyptian. Fearing the vengeful hand of Pharaoh, Moses escaped to Midian where he spent a 40-year period in seclusion.

An ancient mosaic floor, representing loaves and fishes, commemorating the feeding of the five thousand. It is part of the floor of an ancient church near Bethsaida. © MPS

The traditional Hill of the Burning Bush, near Sinai.
© MPS

In the land of Midian Moses found favor in the home of a priest named Jethro (also known as *Reuel* in the Hebrew or *Reguel* in the Greek. In the course of time he married Jethro's daughter Zipporah. As shepherd of his father-in-law's flocks Moses gained a first-hand geographical knowledge of the territory surrounding the gulf of Aqaba. Little did he realize that through this area he would one day lead the great nation of Israel!

The call of Moses was indeed significant. Confronted with a bush afire he became conscious of a revelation of God, who commissioned him to deliver His people Israel from Egyptian bondage. Fully acquainted with Pharaoh's power, Moses was assured of divine support in contesting the authority of the ruler of Egypt. He furthermore anticipated the lack of confidence and the reluctance of the Israelites to accept him as a leader. To counter this God assured him that the great I AM was about to fulfill His promise made to the patriarchs to redeem Israel from bondage and settle them in the land of Canaan (Gen. 15:12-21). In addition two miraculous signs — Moses' staff which changed to a serpent and his hand which became leprous and later was healed — were provided as evidence for the verification of divine authority. Finally Moses was assured of Aaron's support in his divine commission to deliver the Israelites from the powerful clutch of the Pharaoh. Accompanied by his wife Zipporah and their two sons, Moses returned to the land of Egypt.

In a series of ten plagues Moses and Aaron countered Pharaoh's attempt to retain Israel in bondage. As a whole these plagues were directed against the gods of Egypt, demonstrating God's power to the Egyptians as well as to the Israelites. Pharaoh immediately expressed his attitude of resistance, retorting, "Who is the Lord, that I should obey his voice to let Israel go? I know not the Lord, neither will I let Israel go." As Pharaoh continued to resist, his heart was hardened. Finally the last plague brought judgment on all the gods of Egypt, as the first-born sons were slain throughout the land. Then Pharaoh complied with Moses' demand and allowed the Israelites to depart (For discussion of Pharaoh's hardened heart see J. P. Free, *Archaeology and Bible History* (5th ed., rev.; Wheaton: Scripture Press, 1956, pp. 93-94).

On the eve of Israel's dramatic departure the Passover feast was initially observed (Exod. 12). Each family unit that followed the simple instructions of slaying a year-old male lamb or goat and applied the blood to the doorposts and lintel of their home was passed by in the execution of this divine judgment. In lieu of death the first-born son in every Israelite family belonged to God. Immediately after partaking of this Passover meal consisting of meat, unleavened bread, and bitter herbs, the Israelites left Egypt. The annual observance of the Passover on the 14th day of Abib (later known as Nisan) was to remind each Israelite of the miraculous deliverance under Moses.

The exact route by which Moses led the Israelites, who numbered some 600,000 men, plus women and children, is difficult to ascertain. Succoth, Etham, Pi-hahiroth, Migdol, and Baalzephon are place names with imprecise meanings whose geographical identifications are uncertain. When the Israelites reached the Red Sea (Sea of Reeds) they were threatened by the Egyptian armies from the rear. As they appealed to Moses, divine protection was provided in the pillar of cloud that barred the Egyptians from overtaking them. In due time a strong east wind parted the waters for Israel's passage. When the Egyptian forces attempted to follow they were engulfed in a watery grave. Miriam, Moses' sister, led the Israelites in a song of victory.

Under divine direction Moses led Israel southward through the wilderness of Shur. At Marah bitter waters were sweetened, at Elim the Israelites were refreshed by 12 springs of water and 70 palm trees, and in the wilderness of Sin daily manna was supplied, solving the food problem for this great multitude throughout their years of desert wanderings until they reached the land of Canaan. At Rephidim Moses was commanded to strike the rock, which brought forth a gushing water supply for his people. Confronted by an Amalekite attack Moses prevailed in intercessory prayer with the support of Aaron and Hur, while Joshua led the armies of Israel in a victorious battle. In his administrative duties Moses appointed 70 elders to serve under him in accordance with Jethro's advice. In less than three months' journey from Egypt the Israelites settled in the environs of Mount Sinai (Horeb) where they remained for approximately one year.

In this wilderness encampment Moses became the great law giver through whom Israel's religion was revealed. As a representative for his people Moses received the law from God. This law constituted God's covenant with His newly delivered nation. In turn the congregation ratified this covenant (Exod. 20-24), which included the ten commandments commonly known as the decalogue. To enable the Israelites to worship their God properly Moses was given detailed instructions for the building and erection of the tabernacle. These plans were carefully executed under Moses' supervision. At the same time the Aaronic family, supported by the Levites, was designated for their priestly service and carefully equipped for their ministration (Exod. 25-40). Details concerning various sacrifices, laws for holy living, and the observance of feasts and seasons were set forth through Moses as God's prescription for His people Israel (Lev. 1-27). In this manner the Israelites were distinctively set apart from the religious and cultural pattern of Egypt and Canaan (Samuel J. Schultz, *op. cit.*, Chapter IV, "The Religion of Israel" pp. 56-74).

Moses also supervised the military census and organization of the Israelites during this encampment in the Sinaitic peninsula. The tabernacle with its court occupied the central position. Since the first-born of every Israelite family belonged to God by virtue of being spared during the last plague in Egypt, provision was now made for a Levite as a substitute. Consequently the Levites were placed immediately around the court, with Moses and the Aaronic family located at the east end before the entrance to the tabernacle. The other tribes were divided into four camps — each camp composed of three tribes — with the camp of Judah taking the place of leadership ahead of the priestly family.

Guidance and protection were provided for Moses and his people throughout this wilderness journey in the pillar of cloud and fire that was visible by day and night. Representing the presence of God with His people, this cloud first made its appearance in preventing the Egyptians from overtaking them (Exod. 13:21-22; 14:19-20). During Israel's encampment the cloud hovered over the tabernacle. Efficient human organization and responsible leadership provided the counterpart to the divine guidance conveyed by the cloud. Silver trumpets were used to assemble the leaders as well as to alert the people whenever divine indication was given en route. An efficient organization was in evidence whether Israel was encamped or journeying. Law and order prevailed throughout (Num. 1:1-10:10).

In an 11-day march northward from the Sinaitic peninsula to Kadesh, which was only about 40 miles SW of Beersheba, Moses not only encountered the murmurings of the multitude but was also severely criticized by Miriam and Aaron (Num. 11-12). The grumbling crowds who hankered for the fleshpots of Egypt were satiated to the point of intemperance when quails were supplied in excessive abundance. Aaron and Miriam were likewise humiliated when the latter was temporarily subjected to leprosy.

While at Kadesh, Moses sent out 12 representatives to spy out the land of Canaan. The majority report, given by ten spies, influenced the Israelites to demonstrate their unbelief. In open rebellion they threatened to stone Joshua and Caleb, the two spies who exercised faith and recommended that they should conquer and occupy the land promised to them. When God proposed to destroy the rebellious and unbelieving Israelites Moses magnanimously responded with intercession in behalf of his people. The final verdict involved all of the people who had been 20 years of age and older at the time of the exodus. They were doomed to die in the wilderness. Joshua and Caleb were the only exceptions.

Relatively little is recorded about Moses' leadership during the 38 years of wilderness wanderings (Num. 15-20). Not only was the political leadership of Moses challenged by Dathan and Abiram but Korah and his supporters contested the ecclesiastical position of Aaron and his family. In the course of these rebellions 14,000 people perished in divine judgment. Furthermore all Israel was given a miraculous sign when, among the 12 rods representing the tribes of Israel, Levi's rod produced buds, blossoms, and almonds. With Aaron's name inscribed on this rod the Aaronic priesthood was securely established.

The Israelites, denied permission to use the highway through the land of Edom, were led from Kadesh to the Plains of Moab by way of the Gulf of Aqaba. En route Moses himself forfeited entrance into the Promised Land when he struck the rock which he should have commanded to supply water for his people. When a scourge of serpents caused many murmuring Israelites to die, Moses erected a bronze serpent which offered healing to

At the summit of Mt. Sinai (Jebel Mousa), showing part of Moses' Chapel, also sometimes called the Chapel of Elijah. © MPS

all who turned to it in obedience. This historical incident was used by Jesus in explaining His own death on the cross and the simple principle of salvation involved (John 3:14-16).

When Moses by-passed Moab and led the Israelites into the Arnon Valley, he was confronted by two Amorite rulers — Sihon, king of Heshbon, and Og, king of Bashan. Israel defeated both kings and as a result claimed the territory E of the Jordan River which was later allotted to Reuben, Gad, and half of the tribe of Manasseh. With this Amorite threat removed, the Israelites settled temporarily in the Plains of Moab, N of the Arnon River.

Balak, king of Moab, was so disturbed about Israel's encampment near his people that he chose subtle designs to bring about the ruination of God's covenant people (Num. 22-25). He enticed Balaam, a prophet from Mesopotamia, with rewards of riches and honor, to curse Israel. Balaam accepted Balak's invitation. While en route he was vividly reminded by his donkey that he was limited in his oracles to speak only God's message. Although the Moabite leaders prepared offerings to provide an atmosphere for cursing, Balaam was restricted to blessings for Israel each time he spoke. God did not allow His chosen people to be cursed. When Balaam was dismissed his parting advice to the Moabites and Midianites was to seduce the Israelites into immorality and idolatry. Incurring divine wrath by accepting invitations to these heathen festivities, thousands of Israelites died in a plague and many guilty leaders were executed. Furthermore Moses led his people in a punitive war against the Midianites. In this battle Balaam, the son of Beor, was killed (Num. 31:16).

Moses once more ordered a military census. This was supervised by Eleazer, Aaron's son who had served as high priest since his father's death. The total count of Israel's military manpower was actually somewhat lower than it had been when they left Egypt (Num. 26:1-65). Joshua was appointed and consecrated as the successor to Moses. Inheritance problems and additional instructions for regular offerings, festivals and vows were carefully delineated (Num. 27-30). Reluctantly Moses granted permission to the Reubenites, Gadites, and some of the Manasseh tribe to settle E of the Jordan, exacting from them the promise to aid the rest of the nation in the conquest of the land beyond the river (Num. 32). Moses, anticipating Israel's successful occupation of the land of Canaan, admonished them to destroy the idolatrous inhabitants. He appointed 12 tribal leaders to divide the land among the tribes and instructed them

The famous statue of Moses, by Michelangelo, in the church of St. Peter at Rome. RTHPL

to provide 48 cities throughout Canaan for the Levites with adequate pasture area adjoining each city. Six of these Levitical cities were to be designated as cities of refuge where people might flee for safety in case of accidental bloodshed (Num. 34-35). Moses also provided solutions to inheritance problems when daughters inherited the family possessions (Num. 36).

The magnitude of Moses' character is clearly set forth in his farewell speeches to his beloved people. Even though he himself was denied participation in the conquest and occupation of the land, he coveted the best for the Israelites as they entered Canaan. His admonition to them is summed up in his addresses as given in the book of Deuteronomy. He reviewed the journey, beginning from Mount Horeb, where God had made a covenant with Israel. He pointed out especially the places where the Israelites had murmured, reminding them of their disobedience. Because of this attitude the generation that Moses had led out of Egypt was denied entrance into the land that God had promised them for a possession. With that as the background Moses warned them to be obedient. For their encouragement he pointed to the recent victories God had given them over the Amorites. This experience provided a reasonable basis for the hope of victory under the leadership of Joshua as they actually entered the land of Canaan (Deut. 1:1-4:43).

In his second speech (Deut. 4:44-28-68) Moses emphasized that love as well as obedience is essential for a wholesome relationship with God. The decalogue given at Mount Sinai was repeated. Whole-hearted love for God in daily life represented the basis for maintaining this covenant relationship in such a way that they could enjoy God's blessing. Consequently each generation was responsible for teaching the fear of the Lord their God to the next generation by precept and obedience. In this pattern of living they would be God's

holy people in practice. Faithfully Moses delineated many of the laws already given, admonishing the people to be true to God, warning them against idolatry, advising them in the administration of justice, and adding various civil and religious regulations. He concluded this speech with a list of curses and blessings which were to be read publicly to the entire congregation after they crossed the Jordan. In this manner he set before the Israelites the way of life and death. Moses provided a written record of the law as a guide for Israel.

At the close of Moses' career, Joshua, who had already been designated as Israel's leader, was ordained as successor to Moses. In a song (Deut. 32) Moses expressed his praise to God, recounting how God had delivered Israel and provided for them through the wilderness journey. Then, with the pronouncement of a blessing upon each tribe, Moses departed for Mount Nebo, where he was privileged to view the Promised Land before he died.   S.J.S.

MOSES, ASSUMPTION OF, an anonymous Jewish apocalyptic book, probably written early in the first century A.D. It is a prophecy of the future relating to Israel, put in the mouth of Moses and addressed to Joshua, patterned on the book of Deuteronomy. Many scholars, following Origen, believe that Jude's statement about Michael's contending with the devil for the body of Moses (Judge 9) is taken from the Assumption of Moses.

MOSES, LAW OF (See Law)

MOST HIGH, a name applied to God. It represents the Hebrew word 'ēl-'elyôn (Gen. 14:18,19,20,22; Ps. 7:17) which is translated "God Most High." The expression comes into the Greek of the NT as a part of the Semitic background inherited from the OT (Mark 5:7; Acts 7:48).

MOTE, a particle of dust or chaff, or a splinter of wood that might enter the eye. Used by Jesus (Matt. 7:3-5; Luke 6:41,42) in contrast with "beam" (KJV) or "log" (RSV) to rebuke officiousness in correcting small faults in others, while cherishing greater ones of our own.

MOTH (See Insects)

MOTHER (See Family, Marriage)

MOUNT, MOUNTAIN. *Hill, mount* and *mountain* are terms roughly synonymous in the English Bible. Much of Palestine is hilly or mountainous. These elevations are not dramatically high, but are old worn-down hills. A central hill country stretches from N to S in Palestine, attaining its greatest elevations in Galilee (nearly 4000 feet above sea level) and finally ending in the Negev in the S. Much of Transjordan is high plateau land, although in Syria N of Palestine this section reaches great height in Mt. Hermon (c. 9100 feet above sea level), which is snow covered throughout the year.

Many ancient peoples considered mountains as holy places. Mt. Sinai (Deut. 33:2; Judg. 5:4,5) and Mt. Zion (Ps. 68:16) were specially revered by the Hebrews as the places of God's revelation and abode. Mountains in Scripture are symbolic of eternity (Gen. 49:26) and of strength and stability, but God is more strong and stable than they (Ps. 97:5; 121:1,2 RSV; Isa. 40:12). They also portray the difficult obstacles of life, but God will overcome these mountains for His people (Isa. 49:11; Matt. 21:21).

"Mount" in several places in the KJV refers to the earthen mounds raised against the wall of a besieged city by an attacking army (Jer. 6:6; Ezek. 26:8).   J.B.G.

MOUNT OF BEATITUDES, the site of the Sermon on the Mount (Matt. 5-7; Luke 6:20-49) which contains the beatitudes is not identified in the Gospels. Tradition has identified it with Karn Hattin, near Capernaum, but with very little basis in fact. Like many of the sites of Jesus' ministry, its exact location is unknown.

MOUNT EPHRAIM (See Ephraim)

MOURN, MOURNING. The ancient Hebrews placed a much greater emphasis on external symbolic acts than do modern Western people, although people in the East today still carry on this respect for symbolic actions. Ceremonies for expressing grief at the death of a relative or upon any unhappy occasion are referred to frequently in the Bible. One reared in the modern Occident must be cautioned not to view these public expressions as hypocritical; they were a natural valid manifestation of grief in that culture.

The OT contains warnings against pagan mourning rites (Deut. 14:1,2; Lev. 19:27,28). Israelite priests were not allowed to take part in any mourning or other funeral ceremonies (Lev. 21:1-4,10, 11).

Upon receipt of bad news or in the presence of sudden calamity it was customary to rend the clothes (II Sam. 1:2) and to sprinkle earth or ashes upon the head (Josh. 7:6). Hair cloth ("sackcloth") was adopted as clothing (Isa. 22:12). We read of the covering of the head in mourning (Jer. 14:3), and also of the lips (Ezek. 24:17,22). Among those who habitually wore some covering on the head it was a sign of mourning to let the hair go loose (Lev. 10:6), which normally (like that of a Greek Orthodox priest in the Near East) would be coiled up.

A death in the household set in motion an elaborate ceremony of mourning which lasted a week or more. The members of the family and their friends gathered around the corpse and indulged in lamentations bordering on hysteria. The rites mentioned above were observed, but in a more abandoned form than for other mourning. William M. Thomson saw a ceremony of mourning carried out by the Arabs of Palestine a century ago. He described the three concentric circles of mourners, slowly marching, clapping their hands and chanting a funeral dirge. At times they stopped, and flinging their arms and handkerchiefs about in a wild frenzy, screamed and wailed like maniacs.

Professional mourners were often called in for a funeral (Jer. 9:17-22; Amos 5:16; Matt. 9:23). These were probably in earliest times to protect the living from the spirits of the departed, who were greatly feared. By Bible times, however, the mourning women were used merely as another manifestation of grief for the departed.

Jeremiah, the weeping prophet, made many references to mourning. He taught the mourning women their dirge (9:17-22), heard the land lament because of the destruction by the Babylonians (9:10; 12:4,11; 14:2; 23:10), mentioned Rachel's mourning (31:15,16). He urged Israel to mourn for its sins (4:8; 6:26; 7:29), and secretly mourned for the nation himself (9:1; 13:17).   J.B.G.

MOUSE (See Animals)

MOUTH. The principal Hebrew words for mouth are *peh,* translated "mouth," but also "language," "corner," "edge," "skirt," and any opening, such as of a well (Gen. 29:2), of a sack (Gen. 42:27), of a cave (Josh. 10:22), or of a grave (Ps. 141:7); and *hēkh,* translated "mouth" and "roof of the mouth" (i.e., palate, Job 29:10). In the NT *stóma*

is translated "mouth" except in the idiomatic "face to face" (lit. "mouth to mouth," II John 12; III John 14) and "edge (lit. mouth) of the sword" (Luke 21:24; Heb. 11:34).

The way in which the Bible constantly uses the organ of speech in the sense of "language" is a good example of the employment of the concrete for the abstract. Silence is the laying of the hand upon the mouth (Job 40:4), freedom of speech is the enlarged mouth (Eph. 6:19). So to receive a message is to have words put into the mouth (Jer. 1:9). Humiliation is the mouth laid in the dust (Lam. 3:29).

Finally, the mouth is personified; it is an independent agent. It brings freewill offerings (Ps. 119:108), God sets a watch before it (Ps. 141:3); it selects food (Prov. 15:14), uses a rod (Prov. 14:3), and has a sword (Rev. 19:15). This personification helped to contribute to the Jewish idea of the Angel of the Lord, the voice of the Lord, and prepared the way for the "word made flesh" (John 1:14).   J.B.G.

MOWING of the ripe grain was done in early Bible times with a short sickle made of pieces of sharp flint set in wood or even bone. As the Hebrews became more technologically advanced, sickles were made of metal — bronze, and then iron. The farmer grasped the grain with his left hand and lopped off the stalks fairly high up. They were then bound into sheaves and taken to the threshing floor. The king's mowings (Amos 7:1) were the portion of the spring harvest taken by the king as taxes. Only after the king's agents had taken the tax-grain could the owner mow the rest of his field. See AGRICULTURE.

MOZA (mō′zà, Heb. *môtsâh, sunrise*). 1. A man of Judah, of the family of Hezron, the house of Caleb (I Chron. 2:46).
2. A descendant of Jonathan (I Chron. 8:36, 37).

MOZAH (mō′zà, Heb. *môtsâh*), a town of Benjamin (Josh. 18:26). Its site is not certain; Qaloniyeh, about four and two-thirds miles NW of Jerusalem on the road to Jaffa, has been suggested.

MUFFLER (See Dress)

MULBERRY TREE (See Plants)

MULE (See Animals)

MUMMIFICATION (See Embalm)

MUPPIM (mŭp′ĭm, Heb. *muppîm*), a son or descendant of Benjamin (Gen. 46:21). He is also called Shupham (Num. 26:39) and Shuppim (I Chron. 7:12,15). Possibly the Shephuphan of I Chronicles 8:5 is the same person.

MURDER. From the days of Noah the Biblical penalty for murder was death: "Whoso sheddeth man's blood, by man shall his blood be shed" (Gen. 9:6). Throughout OT times, the ancient Semitic custom of the avenger of blood was followed: a murdered man's nearest relative (the *goel*) had the duty to pursue the slayer and kill him (Num. 35:19). Since in the practice of avenging blood in this fashion men failed to distinguish between murder and manslaughter, and thus vicious blood feuds would frequently arise, the Mosaic law provided for cities of refuge (Num. 35). To these cities a man pursued by the avenger of blood could flee. He would be admitted and tried; if judged guilty of murder he would be turned over to the avenger; if judged innocent he was afforded protection in this city from the avenger. It appears likely that the advent of the monarchy began a trend away from the ancient *goel* custom, for we find the king putting a murderer to death (I Kings 2:34) and also pardoning one (II Sam. 14:6-8).

In a murder trial, the agreeing testimony of at least two persons was necessary for conviction (Num. 35:30; Deut. 17:6). An animal known to be vicious had to be confined, and if it caused the death of anyone, the animal was destroyed and the owner held guilty of murder (Exod. 21:29,31).

The right as asylum in a holy place was not granted a murderer; he was dragged away even from the horns of the altar (Exod. 21:14; I Kings 2:28-34). No ransom could be accepted for a murderer (Num. 35:21). When a murder had been committed and the slayer could not be found, the people of the community nearest the place where the corpse was found were reckoned guilty. To clear them of guilt, the elders of this place would kill a heifer, wash their hands over it, state their innocency, and thus be judged clean (Deut. 21: 1-9). J.B.G.

MURRAIN (See Diseases)

MUSHI, MUSHITES (mū'shī, mū'shīts), a Levite, son of Merari, and the founder of a tribal family or "house," called the Mushites (Exod. 6:19; Num. 3:20; 26:58; I Chron. 6:19,47; 23:21,23; 24:26, 30).

MUSIC AND MUSICAL INSTRUMENTS OF THE BIBLE.

The Lyre (Heb. *kinnor*). Jewish historians ascribe the first use of musical instruments to the seventh generation after the creation of the world. Genesis 4:21 states that Jubal, son of Adah and Lamech, offspring of Methusael, son of Mehujael, son of Irad, son of Enoch, son of Cain, Adam and Eve's firstborn "was the father of all such as handle the harp (*kinnor*) and organ (*ugab*)." The *kinnor* was the famous instrument on which, later on, King David excelled, and which has erroneously been called "King David's harp." The *kinnor* was a stringed instrument, but it had no resonant body like the harp. It was a lyre, and whether its original form was square or triangular is not known due to the ancient commandment to refrain from the creation of images. No representation of musical instruments and no original Biblical melodies have come down to us. The *kinnor* was made of wood — David made it of *berosh*, but in I Kings 10:12 it is recorded that Solomon made some of almug for use in the temple. According to Flavius Josephus, the Jewish historian, the *kinnor* had ten strings which were plucked with a plectrum, and they were probably tuned pentatonically, without semitones, through two octaves.

The *kinnor* was used on joyous occasions; for instance, it is stated in Genesis 31:26-27: "And Laban said to Jacob, What hast thou done, that thou hast stolen away unawares to me, and carried away my daughters, as captives taken with the sword? Wherefore didst thou flee away secretly, and steal away from me; and didst not tell me, that I might have sent thee away with mirth, and with songs, with tabret, and with harp (*kinnor*)?" The Jews refused to play the *kinnor* during the Babylonian Exile. They suspended their *kinnorîm* on the willows; how could they "sing the Lord's song in a strange land?" (Ps. 137:4). The *kinnor* was gay, and when the prophets of old admonished the people, they threatened that the *kinnor*, the symbol of joy and happiness, would be silenced unless the people repented from their sins. The *kinnor* was one of the temple orchestra instruments and its tone is described as sweet, tender,

soft, and lyrical. I Chronicles 25:3 states that Jeduthun and his sons prophesied with a *kinnor;* and I Samuel 16:23 says about David and Saul: "And it came to pass . . . that David took a *kinnor,* and played with his hand: so Saul was refreshed, and was well, and the evil spirit departed from him." The *kinnor* was also a popular instrument among the more cultured classes in Israel.

The Pipe (Heb. *ugab*). The organ was the other instrument mentioned in Genesis 4:21. This instrument is not mentioned in the list of the musical instruments used in the temple and was not an organ, but rather a shepherd's pipe or flute. The only reference to *ugab* is in Job 21:12; 30:31 and in Psalm 150:4.

The Tambourine (Heb. *tof*). The two instruments mentioned in Genesis 31:27, to which reference was made earlier, were the tabret (*tupîm*) and the harp (*kinnor*). The form *tupîm* is the plural form of the Hebrew word *tof*. The *tof* was a small drum made of a wooden hoop and probably two skins, without any jingling contrivance like the modern tambourine. It was a rhythm-indicator, and used for dances and joyous occasions as well as religious celebrations. II Samuel 6:5 states that David employed the *tof* at the installation of the ark in Jerusalem. The *tof* is not listed among the musical instruments either of the First or Second Temple, despite its being mentioned three times in the Psalms: 81:2; 149:3; 150:4. The *tof* was played primarily by women: "And Miriam, the prophetess, the sister of Aaron, took a timbrel (*tof*) in her hand; and all the women went out after her with timbrels and with dances" (Exod. 15:20); Jephthah's unfortunate daughter "came out to meet him with timbrels and with dances" (Judg. 11:34); and the women of Israel coming to greet King Saul after David had slain Goliath, came "singing and dancing . . . with tabrets, with joy, and with instruments of musick" (I Sam. 18:6).

The Bell (Heb. *pa'amon*). In Exodus 28:33-35, where Jehovah prescribes the high priest's garments, he states: "And beneath upon the hem of it thou shalt make pomegranates of blue, and of purple, and of scarlet, round about the hem thereof; and bells of gold between them round about: A golden bell and a pomegranate, a golden bell and a pomegranate, upon the hem of the robe round about. And it shall be upon Aaron to minister: and his sound shall be heard when he goeth in unto the holy place before the Lord, and when he cometh out, that he die not." The little bells (*pa'amonim*) were either small bells or jingles. This custom typifies the ringing of the bell during the Roman Mass to call the attention of the worshipers to the sacred function in the sanctuary. Bells and jingles upon the hem of garments were found not only in Israel, but are used by many primitive tribes in worship.

The Shofar or *keren* (horn) is the only temple instrument still being used today in the synagogue. Originally, the *shofar* was a ram's horn without mouthpiece. It was used chiefly as a signal instrument in religious as well as in secular ceremonies. One single incident stands out in conjunction with the blowing of the *shofar*. This is recorded in Joshua 6:20: "So the people shouted when the priests blew with the trumpets (*shofar*): and it came to pass, when the people heard the sound of the trumpet, and the people shouted with a great shout, that the wall fell down flat, so that the people went up into the city, every man straight before him, and they took the city." Gideon the

A Rabbi blowing the Shofar to announce the New Year celebration. The Shofar is also sounded every Friday evening at sunset to begin the Sabbath. © MPS

Judge frightened his enemies, the Midianites, by the sound of the Lord's horn blown by 300 of his men (Judg. 7:16-22). The blowing of the *shofar* was even attributed to Jehovah Himself, in order to frighten His enemies and to gather the scattered remnant of Israel to His sanctuary. Thus, Zechariah says: "And the Lord God shall blow the trumpet (*shofar*). . . . The Lord of hosts shall defend them" (Zech. 9:14,15).

During the latter part of the period of the Second Temple, two types of *shofaroth* were in use: the curved (male) ram's horn and the straight (female) mountain goat's horn. The *Talmudian tractate Rosh-hoshana* 3:2-6 gives a detailed description of the *shofar*: "All shofars are valid save that of a cow. The *shofar* blown in the temple at the New Year was made from the horn of the mountain goat, straight, with its mouthpiece overlaid with gold. At the sides of them that blew the *shofar* were two priests that blew upon the silver trumpets. The *shofar* blew a long note and the trumpets a short note, since the duty of the day fell on the *shofar*. The *shofar* blown on New Year's Day was to remind God of his promise to Abraham, Isaac, and Jacob, and especially of Isaac's sacrifice and of the ram that substituted him (Gen. 22:13).

"The *shofars* blown on days of fasting were ram's horns, curved, with mouthpieces overlaid with silver. Between them were two priests who blew upon silver trumpets. The *shofar* blew a short note and the trumpets a long note, since the duty of the day fell on the trumpets. The Year of Jubilee is like to the New Year in the blowing of the *shofar*. Today, the sound of the *shofar* is to stir the hearts of the Jewish people to awe and reverence and to remind them of their duties to God. As a matter of fact, the Shofar Song is a simple but beautiful call to worship."

The Trumpet (Heb. *chatzotzera* or *hasora*). "And the Lord spake unto Moses, saying, Make thee two trumpets of silver; of a whole piece shalt thou make them: that thou mayest use them for the calling of the assembly, and for the journeying of the camps. . . . And if ye go to war in your land against the enemy that oppresseth you, then ye shall blow an alarm with the trumpets; and ye shall be remembered before the Lord your God, and ye shall be saved from your enemies. Also in the day of your gladness, and in your solemn days, and in the beginnings of your months, ye shall blow with the trumpets, over your burnt-offerings, and over the sacrifices of your peace-offerings; that they may be to you for a memorial before your God: I am the Lord your God" (Num. 10:1, 2, 9, 10).

Both the trumpets and the *shofar* were blown by priests and not Levites who were, so to speak, the professional musicians of the temple, and both these instruments served the same function of signaling.

Flavius Josephus has described the trumpet as a straight tube, "a little less than a cubit long," its mouthpiece wide and its body expanding into a bell-like ending. The form of the trumpet is still preserved on the Jewish coins of the latter part of the period of the Second Temple. And when, in 70 A.D., the Romans erected an arch for Emperor Titus after his conquest of Jerusalem, they depicted on it his triumphant return to Rome with the holy objects robbed from the temple, and among them a trumpet, which corresponds exactly to the description of Josephus.

Two of these silver trumpets were the minimum requirement for the temple service, and the maximum, 120. II Chronicles 5:12 states: "Also the Levites which were the singers, all of them of Asaph, of Heman, of Jeduthun, with their sons and their brethren, being arrayed in white linen, having cymbals and psalteries and harps, stood at the east end of the altar, and with them an hundred and twenty priests sounding with trumpets."

Copper and silver trumpets of the Egyptian pharaoh Tutankhamen. CM

The Harp (Heb. *nevel*). In I Samuel 10:5, Samuel the prophet tells the newly anointed King Saul that he would meet "a company of prophets coming down from the high place with a psaltery, and a tabret, and a pipe, and a harp (*nevel*), before them; and they shall prophesy." This is the first time the *nevel* is mentioned in the Bible. This large harp, like the lyre, was made of berosh and almug wood, but the harp had a resonant body. According to Josephus, the harp was played with the fingers and had 12 strings, in contrast to ten strings of the lyre, which was played with a plectrum.

These two instruments were the most important ones in the temple orchestra, and without which

The Blind Harper of Leiden, from the tomb of Patenemheb, dating from the Amarna period. ROL

no public religious ceremony could be held. The harp seems to have been a vertical, angular harp, larger in size, louder, and lower in pitch than the lyre. The harp is mentioned frequently in the Book of Psalms: 33:2; 57:8; 71:22; 81:2; 92:3; 108:2; 144:9; 150:3.

The harp was often used at secular festivities. Isaiah the prophet complains "And the harp, and the viol (*nevel*), the tabret, and pipe, and wine, are in their feasts: but they regard not the work of the Lord, neither consider the operation of his hands" (Isaiah 5:12). Amos the prophet writes: "Take thou away from me the noise of thy songs; for I will not hear the melody of thy viols (*nevels*)" (Amos 5:23). And in Amos 6:4-6, he prophesies woe to them that "lie on beds of ivory . . . and eat the lambs out of the flock . . . that chant to the sound of the viol (*nevel*) . . . that drink wine in bowls."

The Psaltery (Heb. *asor*). The harp (*nevel*) is often associated with the word psaltery (*asor* from *assara*, the Hebrew word for ten). The psaltery (*asor*) is mentioned twice in the Psalms in connection with the harp (*nevel*): Psalm 33:2 and 144:9; and with both harp (*nevel*) and lyre (*kinnor*), in Psalm 92:3.

It is generally accepted that this was a ten-stringed, rectangular zither. To the early Church Fathers this psaltery was symbolical: the ten strings, the Ten Commandments; and the four sides, the Gospels.

The Oboe (Heb. *halil* or *abub*). It is stated in I Kings 1:40, that after Zadok the priest had anointed Solomon "all the people came up after him, and the people piped with pipes (*halil*), and rejoiced with great joy, so that the earth rent with the sound of them." The pipe (*halil*) was a double reed instrument and is the Biblical equivalent of the modern oboe. It was probably a double pipe instrument, which pipes could be blown individually as well as simultaneously. There is no mention of this instrument as having been used in the services of the First Temple. In the Second Temple, two to 12 oboes (*halilim*) were used on 12 days of the year — at the first and second Passover sacrifice, on the first day of Passover, at the Feast of the Weeks, and in the eight days of

the Feast of the Tabernacles. The oboes were played at joyous festivities as well as mourning ceremonies. When Christ entered Jairus' home to restore life to his dead daughter, he found the funeral oboes in action. In Israel, even the poorest men hired at least two oboes for the funeral of their wives.

The Sistra or Rattle (Heb. *mnaamin*). II Samuel 6:5 states, "And David and all the house of Israel played before the Lord on all manner of instruments made of fir wood, even on harps, and on psalteries, and on timbrels, and on cornets (*mnaamin*), and on cymbals." In the KJV, this Hebrew word, "*mnaamin*," is translated cornets, which is incorrect. This actually refers to something which is to be shaken, probably the sistra, a rattle of Sumerian origin, which consists of a handle and a frame with jingling crossbars.

The Cymbals (Heb. *seslim* and *msiltayim*). The only permanent percussive instrument in the temple orchestra was the cymbal. In the Holy Scriptures, the use of cymbals is solely confined to religious ceremonies — the bringing back of the Ark from Kirjath-jearim (I Chron. 15:16, 19, 28); at the dedication of Solomon's Temple (II Chron. 5:13); at the restoration of worship by Hezekiah (II Chron. 29:25); at the laying of the foundation of the Second Temple (Ezra 3:10); and the dedication of the wall of Jerusalem (Neh. 12:27).

In Psalm 150, two types of cymbals are pointed out: "Praise him upon the loud cymbals: praise him upon the high sounding cymbals." The "loud cymbals" were of a larger diameter than the "high (pitch) sounding," and were two-handed cymbals. The high sounding cymbals were much smaller and played by one hand — the cymbals being attached to the thumb and the middle finger respectively.

In the time of David and Solomon, much stress was laid upon the cymbal and percussive instruments. The chief singer of David, Asaph, was a cymbal player (I Chron. 16:5). However, in the last century of the Second Temple the percussive instruments were restricted to one cymbal, which was used to mark pauses only, but not to participate while the singing and the playing were going on.

Although these temple instruments were definitely rhythmical in character, it is interesting to note that the rhythm of the melody was largely dependent on the innate rhythm of the words sung, for the content and the spirit of the words dominated the music. The singing and the playing of the instruments was not to perform or entertain or to elevate a lover of refined art, but rather to serve as a highly exalted form of speech. Rhythm proved important only in non-religious music, and the Jews also made a distinction between what they called spiritual music of the highly educated and the popular music of the masses.

The Organ (Heb. *magrepha*). The organ (*magrepha*) was perhaps a primitive pneumatic (wind) organ and an advanced form of the ancient "*ugab*" mentioned in Genesis 4:21, which has for centuries been wrongly translated "organ." The organ was constructed of a skin-covered box with ten holes and each of them able to produce "ten kinds of songs," so that the whole organ was able to produce 100 "kinds of songs." It was used solely as a signal instrument to call the priests and the Levites to their duties. Its tone was very strong, the Mishna tells us, perhaps a little exaggerated, that whenever the organ (*magrepha*) was played in the temple its sounds carried as far as Jericho.

Shalishim. I Samuel 18:6 states: "And it came to pass as they came, when David was returned from the slaughter of the Philistines, that the women came out of all cities of Israel, singing and dancing, to meet King Saul, with tabrets, with joy, and with instruments of music." This "instruments of music" has been the most disputed musical term of the Hebrew language. The Hebrew word "*shalishim*" is clearly connected with the Hebrew word that means "three," and many translators of the Bible have translated it as triangles, triangular harps, three-stringed lutes, and even three-stringed fiddles and a kind of pipe. Today, the word *shalishim* is generally regarded as referring to some dance form.

The Dance (*machol*) was considered an integral part of religious ceremonies in ancient Israel. This Hebrew word "*machol*" is found in the Holy Scriptures associated with the word *tof* or timbrel: "And Miriam the prophetess, the sister of Aaron, took a timbrel in her hand; and all the women went out after her with timbrels and with dances." (Exod. 15:20); and again, "Jephthah came to Mizpeh unto his house, and, behold, his daughter came out to meet him with timbrels and with dances. . . ." (Judg. 11:34). "David danced before the Lord with all his might. . . ." (II Sam. 6:14). Religious dancing fell into disuse in the Jerusalem Temple and it is mentioned only twice in the Psalms (149:3; 150:4). On the Feast of Tabernacles, at the celebration of "Water libation," prominent men would dance, displaying their artistic skill in throwing and catching burning torches. The custom, however, of procession around the sanctuary, or around the altar, on the Feast of Tabernacles was retained in the temple, accompanied with singing.

Finally, a word about the orchestral instruments of Nebuchadnezzar, king of Babylon, as described by Daniel: "That at what time ye hear the sound of the cornet, flute, harp, sackbut, psaltery, dulcimer, and all kinds of music, ye fall down and worship the golden image that Nebuchadnezzar the king hath set up" (Dan. 3:5). The Hebrew words for the above mentioned instruments would be: the *keren* (horn or trumpet), the *mashrokitha* (a pipe or a whistle), the *kathrus* (a lyre), the *sabka* (a kind of harp), the *psanterin* (a psaltery, a stringed instrument that was used to accompany the Psalms), the *sumphonia,* which means a combination of sounds, or just orchestra. "If we accept the Aramaic text of the Book of Daniel," says Curt Sachs, "the king's subjects heard the various instruments first singly and then all together, a performing custom of the orchestras of the East. The addition, 'all kinds of music,' may refer to drums and other percussion instruments. The people were thus instructed to wait for the horn signal, followed by solos of pipe, lyre, harp, and psaltery, after which the 'all kinds of music' (percussion instruments) would join the solo instruments in a *sumphonia* of sounds, which was the signal for them to fall down and worship the golden image."

The real meaning of the headings of the Psalms is still veiled in darkness. Whether they indicate the names of the instruments employed in accompanying the Psalms, or whether they refer to the tune to which they were sung, is still a problem for the musicologist. Curt Sachs made a comparison of moods of Psalms that have similar headings and found that the six *neginoth* Psalms (4, 54, 55, 61, 67, 76) are all prayers for escape, and that the three *gittith* Psalms (8, 81, 84) are joyful in character, and that the three *Jeduthun* Psalms (39, 62, 77) express a mood of resignation.

The word *selah,* which is found so frequently in the Psalms, is another word that has not been satisfactorily explained. Whether it means an interlude, a pause or cadence, is not known. Many scholars believe it indicates a musical interlude by the temple orchestra.

The history of Hebrew music, as well as the history of Israel's higher civilization in general and the organization of the musical service in the temple, began with King David's reign. To King David has been ascribed not only the creation and singing of the Psalms, but also the invention of musical instruments. II Chronicles 7:6 mentions "instruments of music of the Lord, which David the king had made to praise the Lord"; and according to I Chronicles 23:5, David himself said to the princes of Israel, to the priests and Levites, "four thousand praised the Lord with the instruments which I made to praise therewith."

King David chose the Levites to supply musicians for the Holy Temple. Out of the 30,000 who were employed at this time, the impressive number of 4,000 was selected for the musical service. I Chronicles 15:16 states: "And David spake to the chief of the Levites to appoint their brethren to be the singers with instruments of music, psalteries and harps and cymbals, sounding, by lifting up the voice with joy."

Years later, when King Solomon had finished all work for the temple and brought in all the things David his father had dedicated, the priest and the congregation of Israel assembled before the ark, and the musical service was begun by the Levites. I Chronicles 25:6-7 relates that the number of them with their brethren that were instructed in the songs of the Lord, "even all that were cunning," was two hundred fourscore and eight, and they were divided into 24 classes "under the hands of their fathers." On the day of the dedication of the temple, "the Levites which were the singers, all of them of Asaph, of Heman, of Jeduthun, with their sons and their brethren, being arrayed in white linen, having cymbals and psalteries and harps, stood at the east end of the altar, and with them an hundred and twenty priests sounding with trumpets: It came even to pass, as the trumpeters and singers were as one, to make one sound to be heard in praising and thanking the Lord; and when they lifted up their voice with trumpets and cymbals and instruments of music, and praised the Lord, saying, For he is good; for his mercy endureth for ever: that then the house was filled with a cloud, even the house of the Lord; so that the priests could not stand to minister by reason of the cloud; for the glory of the Lord had filled the house of God" (II Chron. 5:12-14). When the king and the people had offered their sacrifices, the Levites began to play, "and the priests sounded trumpets before them, and all Israel stood" (II Chron. 7:6).

In Solomon's Temple, the choir formed a distinct body. They were furnished homes and were on salary. Ezekiel says they had chambers between the walls and windows with southern views (Ezek. 40:44). The choir numbered 2,000 singers and was divided into two choirs. The Psalms, according to the Mishna, were sung antiphonally. The first examples in the Bible of antiphonal or responsorial singing are the songs of Moses and Miriam after the passage through the Red Sea (Exod. 15).

There were three forms after which the psalms and the prayers were rendered in the temple. First, the leader intoned the first half verse, whereupon the congregation repeated it. Then the leader sang each succeeding halfline, the congregation always repeating the same first halfline, which thus became a refrain throughout the entire psalm. Second, the leader sang a halfline at a time, and the congregation repeated what he had last sung. The third form was responsive in the real sense of the word — the leader would sing the whole first line, whereupon the congregation would respond with the second line of the verse. In ancient times, the people, in that they were primitive, would respond with but one word as refrain to laudations and supplications. Refrains such as *Amen, Halleluyah, Hoshiannah* (Oh, help!), *Anenu* (Answer us!), were mostly used in public worship. In later times we find a higher musical development of the people, as shown in their response with phrases as in Psalm 118:1-3 and Psalm 136.

The orchestra and the choir personnel were greatly reduced in the Second Temple. The orchestra consisted of a minimum of two harps and a maximum of six; minimum of nine lyres, maximum limitless; minimum of two oboes and a maximum of 12; and one cymbal. The Second Temple choir consisted of a minimum of 12 adult singers, maximum limitless. The singers, all male, were between 30 and 50 years of age. Five years of musical training was prerequisite to membership in the Second Temple choir. In addition to the male adults, sons of the Levites were permitted to participate in the choir "in order to add sweetness to the song."

The musical service in the temple at the time of Christ was essentially the same as that in King Solomon's Temple, with the exception of a few minor changes in certain forms of singing. There were two daily services in the temple — the morning and evening sacrifices. The morning sacrifice began with burning of incense on the golden altar within the Holy Place. The offering of incense took place before daybreak, and the priest upon whom the lot had fallen for the most honorable service in the daily ministry was alone in the Holy Place while burning the incense, and the congregation was praying without the gates of the temple at the time of incense offering. After this act followed the morning sacrifice. The president would direct one of the priests to ascend some pinnacle to see if it were time to kill the daily sacrifice. If the priest reported, "The morning shineth already," he was asked again, "Is the sky lit up as far as Hebron." If so, the president would order the lamb, which had been kept in readiness for four days, brought in. The elders who carried the keys now gave the order to open the gates of the temple. As the last great gate was opened a signal was given to the priests to blow three blasts on their silver trumpets, calling the Levites and the representatives of the people to their duties, and announcing to the city that the morning sacrifice was about to be offered. Immediately after this were the gates to the Holy Place opened to admit the priests who were to cleanse the candlesticks and the altar of incense. The opening of these great gates was actually the signal for slaying of the lamb without blemish. Following a prayer, the Ten Commandments were recited, which were followed by the Jewish Creed "Shema": "Hear, O Israel: The Lord our God is one Lord" (Deut. 6:4-9).

After the priestly benediction, which is taken from Numbers 6:24-26, the meal-offering was brought, and oil added to it. Having been previously salted, it was laid on the fire. Now the high priest's daily meal-offering was presented, which consisted of 12 cakes broken in halves. Twelve half-broken cakes were presented for the morning sacrifice and the other 12 for the evening sacrifice.

Finally came the drink offering, which consisted of wine poured at the foot of the altar.

With the sacrificial acts over, the *magrepha* (organ) was sounded, which was the signal for the priests to prostrate themselves, but to the Levites it marked the beginning of the musical service. Two priests would now take their stand at the right and left of the altar and blow their silver trumpets. After this, these two priests would approach the cymbal player and take their stand beside him, one on the right and one on the left. When given a sign with a flag by the president, this Levite sounded his cymbal, and this was the sign for the Levites to begin singing a part of the daily psalm, accompanied by instrumental music. Whenever they stopped singing the priests would again blow their trumpets and the people would again prostrate themselves. Not only psalms were sung but also parts of the Pentateuch. The Psalm of the day was sung in three sections and at the close of each the priests would blow three fanfares on their silver trumpets, a signal for the congregation to bow down and to worship the Lord.

The order of the Psalms in the daily service of the temple was as follows: On the first day of the week, Psalm 24: "The earth is the Lord's" in commemoration of the first day of creation. On the second day they sang Psalm 48: "Great is the Lord and greatly to be praised." On the third day, Psalm 82: "God standeth in the congregation of the mighty." On the fourth day, Psalm 94: "O Lord God, to whom vengeance belongeth." On the fifth day, Psalm 81: "Sing aloud unto God our strength." On the sixth day, Psalm 93: "The Lord reigneth." On the seventh day they sang Psalm 92: "It is a good thing to give thanks unto the Lord."

With the singing of the daily Psalm, the morning sacrifice came to a close. The evening sacrifice was identical with the morning sacrifice, with the exception that the incense offering took place after the evening sacrifice, at sunset. Thus they began and ended the day with prayer and praise, of which the burning of incense was symbolical.

L.G.O.

MUSTARD (See Plants)

MUTHLABBEN (mŭth'lăb'ĕn), an expression of doubtful meaning, occurring only in the title of Psalm 9. Probably it is the name of the tune to which the psalm was sung, just as in Christian hymnals tunes are named, e.g., "Old Hundredth."

MUZZLE. The Mosaic law forbade the muzzling of oxen when they were treading out the grain, i.e., threshing (Deut. 25:4). This was a simple, humane command, in accordance with the kindly spirit of much of the law. St. Paul makes a curious use of the injunction in I Corinthians 9:9 and I Timothy 5:18 where he quotes the command in support of his thesis: "The laborer deserves his wages" (RSV).

MYRA (mī'rà, Gr. *Mýra*), now Dembre, one of the southernmost ports of Asia Minor, and once the chief haven of Lycia. Hither Paul came on the "ship of Adramyttium" (Acts 27:5), the seaport on the Aegean opposite Lesbos, and the likeliest vessel to put the party into the westward flowing stream of traffic from Asia. There was an Alexandrian cornship in port to which they transferred. The vessel had chosen this northerly coasting route because of the lateness of the season. Some are, however, of the opinion that the Lycian coast was the regular shipping route from Egypt (e.g. W. M. Ramsay, *Saint Paul the Traveler and Roman Citizen*, p. 319).

MYRRH (See Plants)

MYRTLE (See Plants)

MYSIA (mĭsh'ĭ-à, Gr. *Mysía*), a district occupying the NW end of Asia Minor bounded (proceeding clockwise from the west) by the Aegean, the Hellespont (i.e. the Dardanelles), the Propontis (i.e. the Sea of Marmora), Bithynia, Phrygia, and Lydia. There were five areas: 1. Mysia Minor along the northern coast. 2. Mysia Major, the southeastern hinterland, with Pergamum as its chief city. 3. Troas, a geographical unit in the northwestern angle between Mt. Ida and the sea, the name deriving from the legend that it was under the rule of Troy, whose stronghold was a few miles inland at the entrance to the strait. It was a strategic area, a fact which no doubt accounted for the Achaean assault on Troy. It was also the scene of Alexander's first clash with the Persians (on the Granicus river). 4. Aeolis or Aeolia. This was the southern part of the western coast, a linguistic and ethnological, rather than a geographical unit. Near the end of the second millennium before Christ, Aeolian Greeks from Boeotia and Thessaly had migrated to this area by way of Lesbos and Tenedos. (The Troas was not occupied by Greeks until much later). Until the Persian conquest the political organization of this Hellenized district was a league of small city-states. 5. Teuthrania was the southwest angle between Temnus and the Lydian frontier. The aboriginal or early inhabitants of Mysia, the Mysi, had Tracian affinities and were probably, like the Trojans and the Hittites, an early wave of Indo-European invaders. The Hellespont made no fundamental racial division in early times.

From 280 B.C. Mysia formed part of the kingdom of Pergamum and fell to the Romans in 133 B.C. by the will and testament of Attalus III. It thereafter formed part of the province of Asia. The area was traversed by Paul on his second missionary journey (Acts 16:7,8), but no work was done. There is, however, evidence of very early church foundations. E.M.B.

MYSTERY (Gr. *mustérion*). The word *mystérion* occurs 28 times in the NT (including I Cor. 2:1 where it is present in the better MSS). Neither the word nor the idea is found in the OT. Rather, they came into the NT world from Greek paganism. Among the Greeks *mystery* meant not something obscure or incomprehensible, but a secret imparted only to the initiated, what is unknown until it is revealed. This word is connected with the mystery religions of Hellenistic times. These religions, very popular in the world of the first Christian century, consisted of secret rites and celebrations, which were only known to or practiced by those who had been initiated. There were many of them, the most famous being that of Eleusis, near Athens, associated with the worship of Demeter and her daughter Persephone. Other famous mysteries originated in Egypt. The mysteries appealed to the emotions rather than the intellect and offered to their devotees a mystical union with the deity, through death to life, thus securing for them a blessed immortality. Great symbolism characterized their secret ritual, climaxing in the initiation into the full secret of the cult.

Although occurring once in each of the synoptic Gospels and four times in Revelation, the chief use of mystery in the NT is by Paul. He, as an educated man of his day knew well the thought world of the pagans and accepted this term to indicate the fact that "his gospel" had been revealed to him by the risen Christ. This fact could best be made clear to his contemporaries by adopting the pagan term they all understood, pouring into it a special Christian meaning.

In a few passages, the term refers to a symbol, allegory or parable, which conceals its meaning from those who look only at the literal sense, but is the medium of revelation to those who have the key to its interpretation. So Revelation 1:20; 17:5,7; Mark 4:11; and Ephesians 5:32 where marriage is a mystery or symbol of Christ and the Church.

The more common meaning of mystery in the NT, Paul's usual use of the word, is that of a divine truth once hidden, but now revealed in the Gospel. A characteristic usage is Romans 16:25,26, ". . . my gospel and the preaching of Jesus Christ, according to the revelation of the mystery which was kept secret for long ages, but is now disclosed and through the prophetic writings is made known to all the nations . . ." (cf. Col. 1:26; Eph. 3:3-6). A mystery is thus *now* a revelation: Christian mysteries are revealed doctrines (Eph. 1:9; 3:3,5,10; 6:19; Col. 4:3,4; Rom. 16:26; I Tim. 3:16). Christianity, therefore, has no secret doctrines, as did the ancient mystery religions. To the worldly wise and prudent the Gospel is foolishness (Matt. 11:25; I Cor. 2:6-9); it is not uncommunicated to them, but they do not have the capacity to understand it (II Cor. 4:2-4). The Christian mystery, then, is God's world-embracing purpose of redemption through Christ (Rom. 16:25). J.B.G.

MYSTERY RELIGIONS, a term applied in the Greek, the Hellenistic, and the Roman world, to the cult of certain deities which involved a private ceremonial of initiation, and a reserved and secret ritual. They were probably survivals of earlier religions, maintaining themselves as secret societies after the introduction of the Olympian and other Indo-European deities, and ending after what seems a common social pattern, by winning their way with the conquering people. The deities with whose worship the Greek "mysteries" were principally connected, were Demeter, whose cult was organized into the ceremonials of Eleusis (*q.v.*), and Dionysus, whose predominantly female cult is strikingly illustrated by Euripides' play "The Bacchae" (see intro. to E. R. Dodd's edition 1960, and chapter 11 *The Male Characters of Euripides* by E.M. Blaiklock, Wellington N.Z. 1952). The worship of Demeter and Dionysus appears to have been in origin a nature worship, with a ritual symbolizing death and resurrection in a seasonal sequence, and a spiritual reference of this natural pattern to the experience of the soul.

Little is known about the rites of worship and initiation, for the initiates seem to have been faithful in the keeping of their vows of secrecy, but it is fairly certain that the worship had to do with notions of sin, ritual uncleanness, purification, regeneration, and spiritual preparation for another life. It is probable that their influence was widespread, and, on the whole, salutary in tranquility of spirit and uprightness of conduct. Besides the worship of the goddess and the god already named in connection with metropolitan Greece, there were other ancient deities whose cults can be properly named "mystery religions," for example, the worship of Orpheus, Adonis or Tammuz, Isis, and especially Mithras (*q.v.*). S. Angus (*The Mystery Religions and Christianity*, London, 1925) is of the opinion that the triumph of Christianity over the powerful rivalry of the mystery cults, and especially Mithraism, was due principally to its possession of a historic Person as the center of its faith. Paul adapted some of the vocabulary of the mystery cults to a Christian purpose, and his use of the word "mystery" for a truth revealed, but comprehended only by the "initiated," is a clear reference to them. E.M.B.

N

NAAM (nā'ăm, Heb. *na'am, pleasant*), a son of Caleb, and thus a descendant of Judah (I Chron. 4:15).

NAAMAH (nā'à-mà, Heb. *na'ămâh, pleasant*), the feminine of Naam, is the name of: 1. A daughter of Lamech and Zillah (Gen. 4:22). She was sister of Tubal-cain, "the forger of all instruments of bronze and iron."

2. A woman of Ammon, wife of Solomon, and mother of Rehoboam (I Kings 14:21,31) and as such the chief lady of the court.

3. A town mentioned in Joshua 15:41 as an inheritance of Judah. It was situated in the lowland, probably near Makkedah, although the site has not been identified. Some believe it was located where the modern Na'anah now is. There is no other mention of this place. In Job 2:11, etc., Zophar is called the Naamathite, but there is nothing else to connect him with this town.

NAAMAN (nā'à-măn, Heb. *na'ămān, pleasant*). 1. A son of Bela and grandson of Benjamin (Gen. 46:21). He was the eponymous ancestor of the Naamites (Num. 26:40).

2. The "commander of the army of the king of Syria" (II Kings 5:1-27). He was a courageous general in the continuous warfare existing in those days. To the successful story of his life, the Scriptures, however, add the pathetic phrase, "but he was a leper." This was a most dreadful disease at that time and meant ostracism and an untimely death.

A young girl, who had been taken captive in one of the Syrian raids into Israelitish territory, served Naaman's wife. One day she said to her mistress, "Would that my lord were with the prophet who is in Samaria! He would cure him of his leprosy" (5:3).

After a fruitless visit at the court of the king of Israel, Naaman finally goes to the prophet Elisha and is told to wash himself seven times in the River Jordan, a suggestion which is met with anger and contempt as Naaman recalls the clear waters of the rivers of Damascus which were "better than all the waters of Israel" (5:12).

Prevailed upon, however, by his servants to heed the prophet, Naaman "dipped himself seven times in the Jordan, according to the word of the man of God, and his flesh was restored like the flesh of a little child, and he was clean" (5:14), thus manifesting the power of God through his prophet. Naaman's cure led to his acceptance of the God of Israel as the only "God in all the earth."

The rest of the story as told in II Kings 5:15-19 shows how the people believed in henotheism — the belief that nations had their individual gods. Naaman wanted some of Israel's soil to take home so that he could worship Israel's God even if it was "in the house of Rimmon" where he had to worship in company with his king. (Rammon was the thundergod of the Assyrians.)

The great Omaiyid Mosque at Damascus, today the city's most magnificent structure is, according to tradition, built on the site of the temple of Rimmon where Naaman deposited his load of soil from Israel.

Remains of the house of Naaman the Leper in Damascus. © MPS

In Luke 4:27 Jesus referred to this incident in "the time of the prophet Elisha" when he spoke in the synagogue at Nazareth.   J.G.J.

NAAMATHITE (nā'à-mà-thīt, Heb. *na'ămāthî, a dweller in Naaman*), a gentilic noun with an article, applied to Zophar, one of Job's friends (Job 2:11; 11:1; 20:1; 42:9). The place was probably in N Arabia.

NAAMITES (nā'à-mīts, Heb. *ha-na'ămî*), patronymic name of a family descended from Naaman, Benjamin's grandson (Num. 26:40).

NAARAH (nā'à-rà, Heb. *na'ărâh, a girl*). 1. One of the wives of Ashhur, the father of Tekoa (I Chron. 4:5f).

2. A place on the border of Ephraim (Josh. 16:7).

NAARAI (nā'à-rī, Heb. *na'ăray*), the son of Ezbai (I Chron. 11:37), one of "the mighty men of the armies" in David's time.

NAARAN (nā'à-răn) Heb. *na'ărān*), one of the towns in the possession of the sons of Ephraim (I Chron. 7:28). In Joshua 16:7 the place is called Naarah.

NAARATH (See Naaran)

NAASHON, NAASSON (See Nahshon)

NABAL (nā'băl, Heb. *nāvāl, fool*), a rich sheepmaster of Maon in the southern highland of Judah. The vivid narrative in I Samuel 25:1-42 tells how he insulted David when the latter asked food for his men, who had protected Nabal's men and flocks; how his wife Abigail averted David's vengeance by her gifts and by wise words, and so won David's esteem. Abigail returned home to find Nabal feasting like a king. After he sobered, she told him, and his heart died within him, and he became as a stone, dying ten days later. Then David sought and won Abigail as his wife.

NABATEA, NABATEANS (năb′à-tē′ăn, Gr. *Nabataíoi*), an Arabian tribe named in the Apocrypha but not in the Bible, and important to Bible history. Between the sixth and fourth centuries B.C. they moved to Edom and Moab (as alluded to in Mal. 1:1-7; Obad. 1-7). In Hellenistic times they were a formidable foe to the Greek successors of Alexander the Great, their capital, Petra, being inaccessible and impregnable. While their king Aretas I befriended the early Maccabees, they were in conflict with the later Maccabees. By NT times their territory stretched from the Mediterranean Sea S of Gaza, and the Red Sea, to the Euphrates, including Damascus. They lost Damascus when the Romans came to the aid of the Jews against them, but later recovered it, so that their king Aretas IV controlled it when Paul was there (II Cor. 11:32). Aretas IV fought with the Romans against the Jews, and was victorious over Herod Antipas, who had divorced Aretas' daughter to marry Herodias. Nabatea was absorbed into the Roman province of Arabia, A.D. 106. The Nabateans, a nomadic people, influenced by Aramean, Hellenistic and Roman culture, developed skill in pottery, fine specimens of which have been recovered. The architecture of Petra, "the rose-red city," is remarkable; its religious high places, pillars and figures carved out of sandstone cliffs of a canyon is accessible only on foot or muleback. By 100 B.C. they developed water storage and irrigation systems in the highlands of Transjordan, the remains of which are still impressive. Yet the Nabateans in the Sinai peninsula and other outlying districts remained nomadic. They were traders between Egypt and Mesopotamia, dealing also in wares from India and China, both by caravan overland and by sea from a port on the Aqabah.

NABONIDAS, NABONIDUS (năb′ō-nī′dŭs), the last ruler of the Neo-Babylonian Empire, 556-539 B.C. His son Belshazzar (Dan. 5; 7:1; 8:1) was co-regent with him from the third year of his reign. His very existence was doubted until cuneiform tablets chronicling his reign were discovered and read. They record how he fled from Babylon when it was taken by the army of Cyrus king of Persia, Oct. 29, 539 B.C., how he returned and was arrested. His wife Nitocris, daughter of Nebuchadnezzar, died soon after, and was honored with an official five day period of mourning. No record of Nabonidus' death has yet been found.

NABOPOLASSAR (năb′ō-pō-lăs′âr), first ruler of the Neo-Babylonian Empire, 626-605 B.C. Allied with Medes and Scythians he overthrew the Assyrian Empire, destroying Nineveh in 612 B.C., as prophesied by Zephaniah 2:13-15 and Nahum. The destruction earlier prophesied by Jonah was averted by repentance (Jonah 3). When Pharaoh Necho came to aid the Assyrians, Josiah king of Judah opposed him and was killed at Megiddo (II Kings 23:29; II Chron. 35:20-27). Nabopolassar died in Babylon about the time his son Nebuchadnezzar II was engaged in the battle of Carchemish.

NABOTH (nā′bŏth, Heb. *nāvôth*), the Israelite who owned a vineyard beside the palace of King Ahab in Jezreel. The king coveted this land for a garden, but Naboth refused to sell or exchange his inheritance, which made Ahab "heavy and displeased" (I Kings 21:4). His wife Jezebel undertook to get it for him. She brought this about by having Naboth falsely accused of blasphemy and stoned to death (I Kings 21:7-14). When Ahab went to take possession of the vineyard, Elijah met him and pronounced judgment on Ahab and his family. For a repentant mood, temporary stay was granted (I

In the land of the Nabateans. At top is shown the rugged country around Petra, their fabulous capital. To right of center is a distant view of the temple Ed-Deir, carved in the rock cliff, and underneath this, in the second picture, is a close-up view of this temple. © MPS

Below, a view of El-Khazne, another temple carved in the rose-red rock of the capital city of Petra. © MPS

Kings 21:27-29), but after further warning by Micaiah the prophet, punishment fell on Ahab (I Kings 22:24-40) and on his son Joram and wife Jezebel (II Kings 9:25-37, where the vineyard is called "property, field, plot of ground," see KJV, ASV, RSV, showing that its use had been changed as Ahab purposed in I Kings 21:2).

NACHON, NACON (nā'kŏn, Heb. *nākhôn*), a Benjamite at whose threshing floor Uzzah was smitten for touching the ark (II Sam. 6:6). Also called Chidon in I Chronicles 13:9. Nacon in ASV, RSV.

NACHOR (nā'kôr), ASV, RSV Nahor, the grandfather of Abraham, in the genealogy of Jesus (Luke 3:34).

NADAB (nā'dăb, Heb. *nādhāv*). 1. Firstborn son of Aaron and Elisheba (Exod. 6:23; Num. 3:2; 26:60; I Chron. 6:3; 24:1). He accompanied Moses, Aaron, the 70 elders and his brother Abihu up Mt. Sinai, where they saw the God of Israel (Exod. 24:1,2,9-15). He and his father and brothers were appointed priests (Exod. 28:1). Nadab and Abihu offered "strange" (RSV unholy, i.e. unauthorized) fire in burning incense before the Lord. Fire from the Lord devoured them; they were buried, and no mourning permitted (Lev. 10:1-7; Num. 3:4; 26:61).
2. Great-grandson of Jerahmeel (I Chron. 2:26, 28,30).
3. A son of Jeiel the "father" of Gibeon (I Chron. 8:30; 9:36).
4. King of Israel for two years, succeeding his father Jeroboam I (I Kings 14:20; 15:25-31). His evil reign was ended by assassination at the hands of Baasha of Issachar who reigned in his stead. Thus ended the dynasty of Jeroboam, fulfilling the prophecy of Ahijah (I Kings 14:1-20).

NAGGAI, NAGGE (năg'ī, năg'ā-ī, năg'ē), an ancestor of Jesus Christ (Luke 3:25). KJV Nagge, ASV, RSV Naggai, both Greek forms of Heb. *Nogah.*

NAHALAL, NAHALLAL, NAHALOL (nā'hà-lăl, nā'hà-lŏl), a town in Zebulun whose inhabitants were not driven out but made tributary. Perhaps Tell en-Nahal, N of the River Kishon, NE of Mt. Carmel. In Joshua 19:15 KJV has Nahallal, ASV, RSV correctly Nahalal. All have Nahalal in Joshua 21:35, Nahalol in Judges 1:30.

NAHALIEL (nà-hā'lĭ-ĕl, nà-hăl'ĭ-ĕl), a valley between Mattanah and Bamoth where the Israelites camped on their way from the Arnon to Jericho (Num. 21:19). Perhaps Wadi Zerqâ Mā'in, which flows into the Dead Sea midway of its eastern side.

NAHAM (nā'hăm, Heb. *naham, comfort*), a descendant of Judah through Caleb. I Chronicles 4:19 KJV has "*his* wife Hodiah the sister of Naham," ASV, RSV "the wife of Hodiah, the sister of Naham."

NAHAMANI (nā'hà-mā'nĭ, nà-hăm'à-nī), one of the leaders of the people who returned from captivity with Zerubbabel (Neh. 7:6,7).

NAHARAI, NAHARI (nā'hà-rī), a Beerothite, Joab's armorbearer (II Sam. 23:37; I Chron, 11:39).

NAHASH (nā'hăsh, Heb. *nāhāsh*), probably from a root meaning *serpent* rather than from one meaning *oracle* or one meaning *copper*. 1. An Ammonite king whose harsh demands on the men of Jabesh-gilead led Saul to rally the Israelites against Nahash and to defeat him. This victory proved decisive in making Saul king (I Sam. 11:1,2; 12:12).
2. An Ammonite king whose son Hanun David befriended. Mistaking David's intentions, Hanun insulted David's messengers. David avenged the insult, and had no more trouble with the Ammonites (II Sam. 10; I Chron. 19). His son Shobi brought provisions to David during his flight from Absalom (II Sam. 17:27-29). 1 and 2 may be the same, though the length of time between the beginning of Saul's reign and the rebellion of Absalom in David's reign favors the view that 2 was a descendant of 1.
3. A parent of Abigail and Zeruiah (II Sam. 17:25). The state of the Heb. text baffles attempts to tell whether this Nahash was a man or a woman. I Chronicles 2:16 calls Jesse father of Abigail and Zeruiah. Either Nahash was their mother, or Nahash was an alternative name for Jesse, or the former husband of Jesse's wife. Nahash is a masculine name.

NAHATH (nā'hăth, Heb. *nahath*). 1. A son of Reul, son of Esau (Gen. 36:13,17; I Chron. 1:37).
2. A descendant of Levi, ancestor of Samuel (I Chron. 6:26); perhaps = Toah (I Chron. 6:34) and Tohu (I Sam. 1:1).
3. A Levite, overseer of offerings in the days of Hezekiah (II Chron. 31:13).

NAHBI (nà'bī), the representative from Naphtali among the spies sent out by Moses (Num. 13:14).

NAHOR (nā'hôr, Heb. *nāhôr*). 1. Son of Serug, father of Terah, grandfather of Abraham (Gen. 11:22-26; I Chron. 1:26,27).
2. Son of Terah and brother of Abraham (Gen. 11:26-29; 22:20,23; 24:15,24,47; 29:5; Josh. 24:2). The city of Nahor is in Mesopotamia (Gen. 24:10). The God of Nahor is the same God as the God of Abraham (Gen. 31:53). KJV has Nachor in Joshua 24:2 and Luke 3:34.

NAHSHON (nà'shŏn, Heb. *nahshôn*), the son of Amminadab (I Chron. 2:10,11); ancestor of David (Ruth 4:20); leader of the tribe of Judah on the march through the wilderness (Num. 1:7; 2:3; 10:14), and in presenting offerings at the dedication of the tabernacle (Num. 7:12,17). His sister Elisheba married Aaron (Exod. 6:23, KJV Naashon). He is named in the genealogies of Jesus Christ (Matt. 1:4; Luke 3:32, in both of which KJV has Naasson).

NAHUM, THE ELKOSHITE (nā'hŭm, Heb. *nahûm, compassionate*), the name is a shortened form of *Nehemiah.* Of Nahum and his city of Elkosh nothing is known outside of the book that bears his name. See Nahum, Book of.

NAHUM, BOOK OF. The short book of Nahum is largely a poem, a literary masterpiece, predicting the downfall of Nineveh, the capital of Assyria. Nineveh was conquered by the Babylonians, Medes, and Scythians in 612 B.C. Nahum declares that Nineveh will fall as did "populous No" (Thebes) which the Assyrians themselves had conquered in 663 B.C. The book therefore was written between 663 and 612. These were turbulent times. In 633 Assurbanipal, the last great king of Assyria, died. Soon Babylon rebelled and the Assyrian power rapidly dwindled. In Judah, the wicked Manasseh reigned until about 641, followed by Amon's two year reign and then the long reign of the good king Josiah (639-608). Perhaps it was in Josiah's days that Nahum prophesied the overthrow of the mighty nation that had so oppressed the Jews. At least, Zephaniah likewise prophesied in Josiah's time the overthrow of Nineveh (Zeph. 1:1; 2:13).

The book of Nahum is in two parts, first a poem concerning the greatness of God (1:2-15), then another and longer poem detailing the overthrow of Nineveh (2:1-3:19). The impassioned expressions of Nahum can be the better understood when we remember how Assyria had overthrown the Northern Kingdom of Israel in 722 B.C. and had later taken 40 cities of Judah captive, deporting over 200,000 people —according to Sennacherib's own boast in his royal annals (cf. II Kings 18:13). The cruelty of the Assyrians is almost beyond belief. Their policy seems to have been one of calculated terror. Their own pictures show captives staked to the ground and being skinned alive! No wonder Nahum exulted at the overthrow of the proud, rich, cruel empire of Assyria.

Some modern critics take issue with Nahum's theology, saying that such vengeful expressions are far from the spirit of the Gospel. Such views are usually based on a one-sided conception of New Testament teaching. In truth, God is merciful. Nahum recognizes this in a quotation from Exodus 34:6 (Nah. 1:3) — also in Nahum 1:7, "He knoweth them that trust in Him." Nahum also quotes from Isaiah the promise of good tidings of peace for his own (Neh. 1:15; Isa. 52:7). But for Nineveh the cup of iniquity was full. A century and a quarter earlier, Nineveh had repented at the preaching of Jonah. But the repentance was temporary and now a hundred years of savage cruelty and oppression of God's people must be paid for. Assyria, the pride of Tiglath-pileser, Sargon, Sennacherib, and Assurbanipal, must be laid in the graveyard of nations.

The poem of Nineveh's doom (2:1-3:19) is really quite remarkable. The figures of speech are bold, and in staccato fashion the strokes of war are given. The glamour of the attack with whip and prancing horses and flashing swords suddenly gives way to the picture of the innumerable corpses that mark Nineveh's defeat (3:2,3). If it was wrong for Nahum to rejoice at Nineveh's fall, what shall be said of the heavenly throng of Revelation 19:1-6? Inveterate sin must at last bring condign punishment. The death-knell of all opposition to the Gospel is here: "Behold I am against thee, saith the Lord of hosts" (Nah. 2:13; 3:5).　　R.L.H.

NAIL. 1. Heb. *tsippōren, finger-nail* (Deut. 21:12); Aram. *tephar, (Dan. 4:33; 7:19).*

2. Heb. *yathēdh, tent-pin* (Judg. 4:21,22; 5:26); *a peg driven in the wall to hang things on* (Ezra 9:8; Isa. 22:23-25), or *tent-peg* (Zech. 10:4).

3. Heb. *masmēr, nails of iron* (I Chron. 22:3) *and gold* (II Chron. 3:9; Isa. 41:7; Jer. 10:4) or either (Eccl. 12:11). Nails, pins and pegs were first of stone chips, wood, or bone, then copper or bronze, or in fine work, gold or silver.

4. Gr. *hélos,* used to nail Jesus' hands to the cross (John 20:25). Paul speaks of God nailing to the cross of Jesus the handwriting of the law which condemned us (Col. 2:14).

NAIN (*nā'ĭn,* Gr. *Naín*), modern Nein, a village of Galilee. Though unwalled, it had gates, near which Jesus raised a widow's son from death (Luke 7:11-17). The situation is beautiful, on the NW slope of the Hill of Moreh, known as Little Hermon. Eastward are ancient rock-hewn tombs. The view is wide, across plains NW to Mt. Carmel, N to the hills behind Nazareth, six miles away, NE past Mt. Tabor to the snowy heights of Mt. Hermon. S is Mt. Gilboa.

NAIOTH (*nā'ŏth,* -ōth, Heb. *nāyôth*), a place in or near Ramah of Benjamin, not far N of Jerusalem, where David stayed with Samuel during an early flight from Saul (I Sam. 19:18-20:1). It was the home of a band of prophets. When Saul pursued David thither, Saul himself was seized with the

spirit of prophecy, giving rise to the saying, "Is Saul also among the prophets?" Thus David escaped from Saul.

NAKED (nā'kĕd). The Heb. and Gr. words so translated mean: without any clothing (Gen. 2:25; 3:7-11; Isa. 20:2-4); poorly clad (Job 22:6; I Cor. 4:11; Matt. 25:36-44; James 2:15); without an outer garment (John 21:7). Often it is uncertain which meaning applies (II Chron. 28:15; Mark 14:51,52). RSV clears up some cases. There are also figurative senses: uncovered, open (Heb. 4:13); without the body (I Cor. 15:37; II Cor. 5:3,4); without preparation of the inner man (Rev. 3:17; 16:15). "Naked" is also a euphemism for parts of the body which should not be exposed (Lev.18:1-19) and for shameful acts (Gen. 9:22, 23).

NAME (Heb. *shem;* Gr. *onoma*). In Bible times the notion of "name" had a significance it does not have today, when it is usually an unmeaning personal label. A name was given only by a person in a position of authority (Gen. 2:19; II Kings 23:34), and signified that the person named was appointed to a particular position, function, or relationship (Gen. 35:18; II Sam. 12:25). The name given was often determined by some circumstance at the time of birth (Gen. 19:22); sometimes the name expressed a hope or a prophecy (Isa. 8:1-4; Hosea 1:4). Where a person gave his own name to another, it signified the joining of the two in very close unity, as when God gave His name to Israel (Deut. 28:9,10). To be baptized into someone's name therefore means to pass into new ownership (Matt. 28:19; Acts 8:16; I Cor. 1:13,15). In the Scriptures there is the closest possible relationship between a person and his name, the two being practically equivalent, so that to remove the name is to extinguish the person (Num. 27:4; Deut. 7:24). To forget God's name is to depart from Him (Jer. 23:27). The name, moreover, is the person as he has been revealed; for example, the "name of Jehovah" signifies Jehovah in the attributes He has manifested — holiness, power, love, etc. Often in the Bible the name signifies the presence of the person in the character revealed (I Kings 18:24). To be sent or to speak in someone's name signifies to carry his authority (Jer. 11:21; II Cor. 5:20). In later Jewish usage the name *Jehovah* was not pronounced in reading the Scriptures (cf. Wisdom 14:21), the name *Adhonai* ("my Lord") being substituted for it. To pray in the name of Jesus is to pray as His representatives on earth, in His Spirit and with His aim, and implies the closest union with Christ.　　S.B.

NAMES. By giving names, God enabled us to express relations of His creatures (Gen. 1:5,8,10; 2:11-14). Man named the beasts (Gen. 2:19,20), and woman (Gen. 2:23) by derivation. Her personal name is from her function as mother of all living (human) beings (Gen. 3:20). Cain's name is a pun on two Heb. words (Gen. 4:1). Seth is a reminder that God "appointed" him instead of Abel (Gen. 4:25). "Men began to call upon the name of the Lord" (Gen. 4:26) when they began to recognize Him by His revealed name, Jehovah (Yahweh). God changed the name of Abram to Abraham in view of his destiny (Gen. 17:5). Names in Genesis 10 are of individuals (Nimrod) or nations (Egypt=Mizraim; Jebusites, etc.) or eponymous ancestors or tribes descended from them. People were named for animals (Caleb, dog; Tabitha=Dorcas, gazelle), plants (Tamar, palmtree), precious things (Peninnah, coral or pearl), qualities (Hannah, grace; Ikkesh, perverse; Ira, watchful) or historical circumstances (Ichabod, the glory is departed), for relatives (Absalom named a daughter for his sister Tamar), etc.

The significance of the names of the tribes of Israel is brought out in Genesis 48 and 49. Men were distinguished as sons (ben, bar), women as daughters (bath) of their fathers (Benzoheth, Simon bar-Jona, Bathsheba). Names compounded with El (God) or Jeho-, -iah (Jehovah) became common. Jacob (Gen. 32:24-32) received the name Israel, prince with God, for Jacob, supplanter, and recognized God without learning His secret name. Prophets gave their children symbolic names (Isa. 8:1-4; Hos. 1:4-11). Messiah was given significant names: Immanuel, God with us; Jesus, Saviour (Isa. 7:14; Matt. 1:21,23; Luke 1:31). In His name (Acts 3:16) miracles are wrought, as He promised (John 14:13,14). When we act in Jesus' name we represent Him (Matt. 10:42). Place names are for natural features (Lebanon, white, because snow-capped; Bethsaida and Sidon from their fishing; Tirzah, pleasantness, for its beauty; etc.). By NT times both personal and family names were common (Simon bar-Jona) or descriptive phrases were added, as for the several Marys. Hybril or duplicate names occur in a bilingual culture: Bar (Heb.) -timeus (Greek); Saul (Heb.)=Paul (Roman); John (Heb.), Mark (Roman). Patriarchal times saw names as indicators of character, function or destiny. Soon names began to be given more hopefully than discriminatingly, until finally we are not sure whether the name tells us anything about the nature: was Philip a "lover of horses," or could Archippus ride them? The many genealogical tables in the Bible follow the practice of ancient historians, showing the importance of descent and of the relations thus established between individuals. E.R.

NANNAR (nàn'nàr), the name given at Ur to the Babylonian moon-god Sin.

NAOMI (nā'ō-mī, nā-ō'mĭ, Heb. *nā'ŏmî*), wife of Elimelech of Bethlehem. Bereft of husband and sons, she returned from a sojourn in Moab with her Moabite daughter-in-law Ruth, depressed that one whose name meant "pleasantness" might now appropriately be called "bitterness." She advised Ruth in the steps which led to Ruth's marriage to Boaz, and nursed Ruth's child (Ruth 1:1-4:22).

NAPHISH (nā'fĭsh, Heb. *nāphîsh*), a son of Ishmael whose clan was subdued by Reuben, Gad, and Manasseh (Gen. 25:15; I Chron. 1:31; 5:19). His descendants, temple servants, returned with Zerubbabel from exile (Ezra 2:50; Neh. 7:52; Nephisim, Nephushesim, etc.).

NAPHTALI (năf'tà-lī, Heb. *naphtālî*). 1. A son of Jacob. Naphtali was the second son of Bilhah, Rachel's handmaid. The name is a play on the word *pāthal* "fight," or "struggle." Of the patriarch himself practically nothing is known. He had four sons (Gen. 46:24). Jacob's blessing for this son is brief and noncommittal (Gen. 49:21).

2. The Tribe of Naphtali. Naphtali appears in the lists of Numbers as a tribe of moderate size. It furnished 53,400 soldiers at Kadesh Barnea (Num. 1:43) and 45,400 at the mustering of the troops across from Jericho (Num. 26:50). In the wilderness organization, Naphtali was supposed to encamp on the N side of the tabernacle under the standard of Dan, and this group of tribes brought up the rear in marching. Interestingly, they settled together in Canaan. Naphtali's prince Ahira gave the last offering for the dedication of the altar (Num. 7:78). Naphtali received the next to last lot in the final division of the land (Josh. 19:32-

39), but in many ways its inheritance was the best.

The territory of Naphtali, as nearly as we can tell, included the fertile scenic area just W of the Sea of Galilee and the sources of the Jordan. It reached from the lower limits of the Sea of Galilee almost up to a point opposite Mt. Hermon. On the W it reached half-way to the Mediterranean, being bounded by the tribe of Asher. The chief cities of Naphtali were Hazor, Chinnereth at the N end of the Sea of Galilee, and Kadesh Naphtali. The latter was the northernmost city of refuge in western Palestine.

Kadesh Naphtali was the home of Barak, and Naphtali figured largely in Deborah's conquest of Hazor (Judg. 5:18). It also assisted Gideon (Judg. 7:23). Naphtali is mentioned as one of Solomon's revenue districts (I Kings 4:15), and the collector was a son-in-law of the king.

Naphtali, lying exposed in the north, was conquered by Ben-hadad (I Kings 15:20) and was later deported after the first invasion of Tiglath-pileser about 733 B.C. (II Kings 15:29), who settled Gentiles in the territory. This event is mentioned in Isaiah 9:1 with a prediction of the Messiah who preached, as Matthew reminds us, in this same region of Galilee of the Gentiles in fulfillment of the ancient prophecy. R.L.H.

NAPHTUHIM (năf-tū'hĭm, năf'tū-hĭm, Heb. *naphtūhîm*), a "son" of Mizraim or (RSV) Egypt (Gen. 10:13; I Chron. 1:11). Naphtuhim being plural in form denotes a people. Their location has been sought inconclusively in various parts of Egypt.

NAPKIN (năp'kĭn, Gr. *soudárion*, Latin *sudarium*), a cloth for wiping off perspiration. In the parable of the pounds one man kept his pound in a napkin (Luke 19:20). The face of Lazarus was covered with one when he came forth from the tomb (John 11:44, RSV cloth). One had been on the head of Jesus when He was buried (John 20:7).

NARCISSUS (nàr-cĭs'ŭs, Gr. *Narkíssos*), a Roman whose household Paul greeted. The apostle's salutation is not addressed to Narcissus himself but to the members of his household. He may have been the favorite freedman of Claudius the emperor (Rom. 16:11).

NARD (See Plants, Spikenard)

NATHAN (nā'thăn, Heb. *nāthān, God has given*). 1. Prophet at the royal court in Jerusalem during the reign of David and the early years of Solomon. David consulted him regarding the building of the temple (II Sam. 7; I Chron. 17). Nathan at first approved, but that same night had a vision directing him to advise David to leave temple-building to the son who should succeed him. David humbly obeyed, expressing gratitude to God for blessings bestowed and others promised. Later Nathan rebuked David for adultery with Bathsheba (II Sam. 12:1-25). David earnestly repented. Its title links Psalm 51 with this incident. When Adonijah sought to supplant his aged father David as king, Nathan intervened through Bathsheba to secure the succession for her son Solomon (I Kings 1:8-53). Nathan wrote chronicles of the reign of David (I Chron. 29:29) and shared in writing the history of the reign of Solomon (II Chron. 9:29). He was associated with David and Gad the seer in arranging the musical services for the house of God (II Chron. 29:25).

2. A son of David, born to him after he began to reign in Jerusalem (II Sam. 5:14; I Chron. 14:4). His mother was Bathshua, daughter of Ammiel (I Chron. 3:5). He is named in the genealogy of Jesus Christ as son of David and father of Mattatha (Luke 3:31).

3. Nathan of Zobah, father of Igal, one of David's mighty men (II Sam. 23:36). He may be the same as Nathan the brother of Joel (I Chron. 11:38).

4. The two Nathans mentioned in I Kings 4:5 as fathers of Azariah and Zabud may be the same man, and identified with No. 1, the prophet. If Zabad (I Chron. 2:36) is the same as Zabud, his father Nathan may also be the prophet. In that case we know that the prophet's father was Attai, a descendant of Jerahmeel (I Chron. 2:25).

5. One of the leading men among those who returned from exile, whom Ezra sent on a mission (Ezra 8:16).

6. One of the returning exiles who had married a foreign wife, and who put her away (Ezra 10:39).

Zechariah 12:12 prophesies that the house of Nathan will join on the Day of the Lord in mourning over "him whom they have pierced." From the association with the house of David it would seem that the descendants of the prophet (No. 1) are meant (Zech. 12:10-14); but the descendants of David's son (No. 2) may be meant.

NATHANAEL (nȧ-thăn′ȧ-ĕl, Heb. *nethan′ēl, God has given*), one of the number of the 12 apostles introduced to Christ by Philip(John 1:45ff; 21:2). Nathanael was presumably of Cana of Galilee. The circumstances surrounding his calling are somewhat striking, since Christ praises his integrity upon their initial encounter, and demonstrates to Nathanael His own foreknowledge by reference to the fig tree. Evidently knowledge of the Scripture was considerable on the part of Nathanael, because of the rather amazing theological repartee, bordering on sacred pun, which was conducted between Christ and him (1:51). Nathanael is commonly identified as Bartholomew. The two names are used interchangeably by the Church fathers.

NATHAN-MELECH (nā′thăn-mē′lek, Heb. *nathan melekh, king's gift*), an officer to whom King Josiah remanded the horses "sacred to the sun" after burning the chariots in the fire (II Kings 23:11). The LXX styles him "Nathan, the king's eunuch."

NATIONS, the rendering of the Heb. *gôyim* (sing. *gôy*) which, however, is also rendered "Gentiles" and "heathen" and, a few times, refers to the Israelites, as in Genesis 12:2; Deuteronomy 32:28, etc. Ordinarily, it corresponds to the meaning of "Gentiles." The Gentiles were not sharply differentiated from the Israelites by the latter in OT times, but after the Babylonian exile, Gentiles were treated with scorn and hatred, and in NT times they were cursed if they even asked about divine things. The reason for this change in attitude was undoubtedly the awful sufferings the Israelites endured from the Gentiles between the time of the Exile and the time of Christ.

NATURAL. 1. In Deuteronomy 34:7 the word is the rendering of *lēah, moist, full of sap*, and has reference to physical vigor.

2. In the NT the word renders *phýsis*, meaning *belonging to nature*, as in Romans 1:26,27; II Peter 2:14; *according to nature*, as in Romans 11:21,24; *psychikós*, meaning *animal, sensuous*, as in I Corinthians 15:44 ("natural body"); and *unconverted*, as in I Corinthians 2:14 ("natural man"); and *génesis, origin, birth*, as in James 1:23 ("natural face").

NATURE, a word which in the KJV is found only in the NT where it renders *génesis* (James 3:6, "course of nature," meaning "the entire compass of one's life") and *phýsis, the inherent character of a person or thing* (Rom. 1:26; 2:14; 11:21-24;

I Cor. 11:14; Gal. 4:8), *by birth* (Rom. 2:27; Gal. 2:15; Eph. 2:3), *disposition* (II Pet. 1:4).

NAUGHTINESS (See Sin)

NAUM, NAHUM (nā′ŭm, nā′hŭm), one of the ancestors of Christ mentioned by the third evangelist (Luke 3:25).

NAVE (nāv), the hub of a wheel (I Kings 7:33).

NAVEL (nā′vĕl, Heb. *shōr*). Following the LXX, a different reading has been suggested in Proverbs 3:8: *she′ēr, muscle, body*. In Ezekiel the reading "navel" has been retained in the sense of the umbilical cord not being cut; a picture of an unwanted, untended babe (Ezek. 16:4).

NAVY (See Ships)

NAZARENE (năz′ȧ-rēn, Gr. *Nazarenós, Nazoraíos*). 1. A word derived from Nazareth, the home town of Christ. Jesus was often called a Nazarene. Used by His friends, it had a friendly meaning (Acts 2:22; 3:6; 10:38). Jesus applied the title to Himself (Acts 22:8). Used by His enemies, it was a title of scorn (Matt. 26:71; Mark 14:67). It is not altogether certain what Matthew intended in the words, "That it might be fulfilled which was spoken through the prophets, that he should be called a Nazarene" (Matt. 2:23). It is usually thought that he refers to Isaiah 11:1, where the Messiah is called *netser* or shoot out of the roots of Jesse. The name Nazareth was probably derived from the same root. Matthew sees a fulfillment of Isaiah's prophecy in the parents of Jesus taking up their residence in Nazareth.

2. In Acts 24:5 adherents of Christianity are called Nazarenes.

NAZARETH (năz′ȧ-rĕth, Gr. *Nazarét* and other forms), a town in lower Galilee belonging to the tribe of Zebulun, nowhere referred to in the OT, the home town of Mary and Joseph, the human parents of Jesus (Luke 1:26; 2:4). After the flight into Egypt to escape the ruthless hands of Herod the Great (Matt. 2:13ff), the holy family contemplated returning to Bethlehem of Judea. Hearing that none too propitious a change had occurred in the government, they withdrew to Nazareth in Galilee.

The rejection of Jesus Christ in the synagogue of Nazareth has been the cause of debate whether indeed there were two rejections or merely one. Though the matter will never be entirely settled, it seems as if there were two such experiences in the life of Christ. (Cf. Luke 4:16-30 with Mark 6:1-6 and Matt. 13:54-58.) The first occurred at the beginning of the ministry of Jesus. (Luke 4:14). The second transpired on the occasion of Christ's final visit to Nazareth (Matt. 13:54ff). The very exegetical structures of the stories appear to make their own demands for two incidents, as in the first (Lukan) account there arose such great hostility that the congregation actually attempted to take His life. In the second instance, a spirit of faithless apathy was the only noticeable reaction to His words. (Cf. Luke 4:29-31 with Matt. 13:57,58).

In regard to the city of Nazareth itself, the ancient site is located by the modern en-Natzirah, a Moslem village of about 10,000 inhabitants, on the most southern ranges of lower Galilee. Nazareth itself lies in a geographical basin so that not much of the surrounding countryside is in plain view. However, if one scales the edge of the basin, the sights of Esdraelon with its 20 battlefields and the place of Naboth's vineyard meet the eye. A distance of 30 miles can be observed in three direc-

A general view of Nazareth, as seen from the east. © MPS

The Nazareth Inscription, otherwise known as the Nazareth Decree, an Ordinance of Caesar, c. 50 A.D., now in the Louvre in Paris. LMP

tions. Unfortunately, however, the people of Nazareth had established a rather poor reputation in morals and religion. This is seen in Nathaniel's question: "Can any good come out of Nazareth?" (John 1:46).　　　　　　　　　　　　J.F.G.

NAZARETH DECREE, an inscription cut on a slab of white marble, sent in 1878 from Nazareth for the private collection of a German antiquarian named Froehner. It was not until 1930, when, on Froehner's death, the inscription found a place in the Cabinet de Médailles of the Louvre, that the historian Michel Rostovtzeff noticed its significance. The Abbé Cumont published the first description in 1932.

The decree runs: "Ordinance of Caesar. It is my pleasure that graves and tombs remain undisturbed in perpetuity for those who have made them for the cult of their ancestors, or children, or members of their house. If, however, any man lay information that another has either demolished them, or has in any other way extracted the buried, or has maliciously transferred them to other places in order to wrong them, or has displaced the sealing or other stones, against such a one I order that a trial be instituted, as in respect of the gods, so in regard to the cult of mortals. For it shall be much more obligatory to honor the buried. Let it be absolutely forbidden for anyone to disturb them. In the case of contravention I desire that the offender be sentenced to capital punishment on the charge of violation of sepulture."

Evidence suggests that the inscription falls within the decade which closed with A.D. 50. The central Roman government did not take over the administration of Galilee until the death of Agrippa in A.D. 44. This limits the date, in the opinion of competent scholarship, to five years under Claudius (e.g. vid. A. Momigliano, *The Emperor*

Claudius and His Achievement, 1932). It is possible to date the inscription rather more precisely. The *Acts of the Apostles,* confirmed by Orosius and Suetonius, the Roman historians, says that Claudius expelled the Jews from Rome (18:2). This was in A.D. 49. Suetonius adds that this was done "at the instigation of one Chrestos." The reference is obviously to Christ, and Suetonius' garbled account confuses two Greek words *christos* and *chrestos.*

Claudius was a learned man, misjudged by his contemporaries because of physical defects, probably due to the effects of what may possibly have been Parkinson's disease. His interest in continuing Augustus' religious policy led to a wide knowledge of the religions of the Empire, and would prompt investigation in the courts of any case involving cults or religious beliefs. Suetonius' phrase, and the act of expulsion, probably reflect the first impact of Christianity in Rome, disturbance in the ghetto, proceedings in the courts, and a review of the rabbis' complaints with a Christian apologia in reply, before the court with the Emperor on the bench. He hears the Pharisaic explanation of the empty tomb (Matt. 28:13), and Nazareth having recently fallen under central control, he proceeds to deal with the trouble on the spot. Inquiries are made in Palestine, and the local authority asks for directions. The result is a "rescript" or imperial ruling. Claudius wrote more than one long letter on religious matters (e.g. a notable letter to the Jews of Alexandria in A.D. 41). The decree set up at Nazareth was a quotation from such a communication, verbatim or adapted from a larger text.

E.M.B.

NAZIRITE, NAZARITE (năz'ĭ-rīt, năz'à-rīt, Heb. *nāzîr.* Connected with *nadhar, to vow,* hence, *people of the vow,* i.e. *dedicated* or *consecrated*). An Israelite who consecrated himself or herself and took a vow of separation and self-imposed abstinence for the purpose of some special service.

Origin. The question whether the concept of the Nazirite was indigenous to Israel has often been asked. It would appear that the practice of separation for religious purposes is very ancient and is shared by a number of peoples. In Israel, however, it assumed unique proportions. Its regulatory laws are laid down in Numbers 6:1-23. There were two different types of Nazirism, the temporary and the perpetual, of which the first type was far more common. In fact, we know only of three of the last class: Samson, Samuel and John the Baptist.

Distinguishing traits. The three principal marks which distinguished the Nazirite were: (1) a renunciation of wine and all products of the vine, including grapes; (2) prohibition of the use of the razor; (3) avoidance of contact with a dead body. It should be noted that he was not expected to withdraw from society, that is, to live a monastic type of life, nor to become a celibate. The question has been raised whether the Rechabites of Jeremiah 35 were included within the Nazirite classification. It appears, however, that the Rechabites had more the status of a (Hebrew) nomadic group, since they were not merely forbidden to drink wine, but also to refrain from owning real estate. They lived in tents (Jer. 35:7,10).

Nazirites in the NT. John the Baptist, the forerunner of Christ, was a Nazirite from birth (Luke 1:15). The connection between John the Baptist

and the Qumran community is rather tenuous, nor can it be proved that the men of Qumran were all Nazirites. The case of Paul and Naziritism has frequently called forth discussion. Though it can not be established that the Apostle assumed such a vow, it is certain that he did assume the expenses of those who did (Acts 21:23f). The court of Herod Agrippa supported a large number of Nazirites, according to Josephus.

Reasons for assuming the vow. The reasons for taking a Nazirite vow were numerous. A vow might be assumed before the birth of a child; by one in some sort of distress or trouble; by a woman suspected by her husband of unfaithfulness in their marriage relationship until the suspicion should be removed. Women and slaves could take vows only if sanctioned by their husbands or masters.

The period of time for the Nazirite vow was anywhere from 30 days to a whole lifetime. During the Maccabean days, a number of Jews became Nazirites as a matter of protest against the Hellenistic practices and demands of Antiochus Epiphanes.

Nazirites and the Prophets. There is only one clear-cut mention of the Nazirites by the prophets. The prophet Amos (2:11,12) voices a complaint of Jehovah against the children of Israel that He had given to Israel the prophets and the Nazirites as spiritual instructors and examples, but that the people had given wine to the Nazirites and had offered inducements to the prophets to refrain from prophesying. J.F.G.

NEAH (nē'à, Heb. *hanē'âh*), a town given by lot to the tribe of Zebulun (Josh. 19:13), possibly the same as the "Neiel" of vs. 27. Its exact location is unknown.

NEAPOLIS (nē-ăp'ō-lĭs, Gr. *Neápolis*), a town on the N shore of the Aegean Sea; the seaport of Philippi to which Paul and party sailed after seeing the "Man of Macedonia" at Troas (Acts 16:11, 12). Paul may have revisited Neapolis on his return trip to Jerusalem (Acts 20:3-5). The exact location of Neapolis is yet uncertain. However, on the basis of literary and archaeological evidences, it would appear that it is near Kavalla.

NEARIAH (nē'à-rī'à). 1. A descendant of David (I Chron. 3:22).

2. A descendant of Simeon (I Chron. 4:42). The LXX renders both occurrences as "Noadiah."

NEBAI (nē'bī), one of the signers of the covenant in the days of Nehemiah (Neh. 10:19).

NEBAIOTH, NEBAJOTH (nē-bā'yŏth, nē-bā'jŏth, Heb. *nevāyôth*). 1. The firstborn son of Ishmael, son of Abraham (Gen. 25:13; 28:9; 36:3; I Chron. 1:29).

2. Isaiah mentions Nebaioth as a tribe (Isa. 60:7). Some scholars regard Nebaioth as identical with the Nabataeans.

NEBALLAT (nē-băl'ăt), a Benjamite town occupied after the Exile, named along with Lod and Ono (Neh. 11:34). It is now Beit Nabala, four miles NE of Lydda.

NEBAT (nē'băt), the father of Jeroboam I, the first king of the northern confederacy after the great schism (I Kings 12:15).

NEBO (nē'bō, Heb. *nevô*, Assyr. *Nabu*). 1. A god of Babylonian mythology. The special seat of his worship was the Babylonian city of Borsippa. He receives mention by Isaiah (Isa. 46:1). Nebo was the god of science and learning. The thrust of Isaiah the prophet against him seems to be that Nebo himself, the imagined writer of the fate of all, is destined to go into captivity.

Mount Nebo, and the Springs of Moses. © MPS

2. The name of the mountain from which Moses beheld the Promised Land (Deut. 34:1ff).

3. A Moabite town near or on Mount Nebo (Num. 32:3).

4. A town mentioned immediately after Bethel and Ai (Ezra 2:29; Neh. 7:33).

NEBUCHADNEZZAR, NEBUCHADREZZAR (nĕb'ū-kăd-nĕz'êr, nĕb'ū-kăd-rĕz'êr), the great king of the Neo-Babylonian empire who reigned from 605 to 562 B.C. It was he who carried away Judah in the 70-year Babylonian captivity. He figures prominently in the books of Jeremiah, Ezekiel, Daniel, and the later chapters of Kings and Chronicles. Until recently, not many of Nebuchadnezzar's historical records had been found, though his building inscriptions are numerous. Now the publication by Wiseman of Nebuchadnezzar's chronicle fills in some of the gaps.

The name Nebuchadnezzar means "Nebo protect the boundary." The form Nebuchadrezzar is probably a minor variant. Cf. the variations Tiglath-pilneser (I Chron. 5:26; II Chron. 28:20) and Tiglath-pileser (II Kings 15:29). The appearance of the "n" may be an inner Hebrew phenomenon. Wilson and Young suggest that it is a rendition of the name assuming a variant etymology, "Nebo protect the servant." (R. D. Wilson, *A Scientific Investigation of the Old Testament*, rev. ed. by E. J. Young, Chicago: Moody Press, 1959, p. 68).

Nebuchadnezzar's father, Nabopolassar, seems to have been a general appointed by the Assyrian king. However, in the later years of Assyria he rebelled, and established himself as king of Babylon in 626. The rebellion increased and finally Nabopolassar with the Medes and Scythians conquered Nineveh, the Assyrian capital, in 612. The Medes and Babylonians divided the Assyrian empire and a treaty was probably sealed by the marriage of the Median princess to the Babylonian prince, Nebuchadnezzar. In 607 the crown prince Nebuchadnezzar joined his father in the battle with the remnants of the Assyrian power and their allies, the Egyptians. In 605, when his father was in his last illness, he decisively defeated the Egyptians at Carchemish. At this time Nebuchadnezzar took over all Syria and Palestine. Apparently Jehoiakim, king of Judah, who had been vassal to Egypt quickly did homage to Babylon and gave hostages (Dan. 1:1). Nebuchadnezzar at this time got news of his father's death and with a picked bodyguard he hastened home to secure his throne. On repeated occasions thereafter he struck toward the west. In about 602 B.C. Jehoiakim revolted (II Kings 24:1), probably with promise of Egyptian help, but was forced to submit. In 601, Nebuchadnezzar attacked Egypt itself but was defeated, as he frankly admits. Later, Pharaoh Hophra submitted to him. Again Jehoiakim rebelled, in 597, and Nebuchadnezzar called out his troops for another western expedition. Jehoiakim died either in a siege or by treachery (Jer. 22:18,19) and his son Jehoiachin ascended the throne. But he lasted only three months till the campaign was over, and he was taken as a hostage to Babylon where lived and finally was given relative freedom. Here the Biblical account (II Kings 25:27-30) is confirmed by discovery of the Weidner tablets (ANET p. 308).

Nebuchadnezzar installed Jehoiachin's uncle as puppet king, taking heavy tribute from Jerusalem. Ezekiel was among the captives of that expedition. Nebuchadnezzar's chronicle agrees with the Biblical account, telling how in 597 B.C. he "encamped against the city of Judah and on the second day of the month Adar (Mar. 15/16) he seized the city and captured the king. He appointed there a king of his own choice, received its heavy tribute and sent them to Babylon." (D. Wiseman, *Chronicles of the Chaldean Kings,* London: British Museum, 1956, p. 73). This discovery gives about the best authenticated date in the Old Testament.

In later years the Chronicle tells of repeated expeditions of Nebuchadnezzar toward the west to collect tribute and keep the satellite kingdoms in line. Unfortunately, the present tablets do not go beyond 593, so there is no record of the final and brutal devastation of Jerusalem in 586 B.C., when

Restoration of the Ishtar Gate and procession street of Babylon of Nebuchadnezzar. OIUC

Zedekiah revolted. The historical gap extends to
556 B.C. except for a brief account of a campaign
to southern Asia Minor by Neriglissar in 557.

Nebuchadnezzar is celebrated by the historians
of antiquity for the splendor of his building operations as well as for the brilliance of his military
exploits. Koldewey's excavations in Babylon illustrate the histories. Still impressive are the remains
of the Ishtar gate and the processional street lined
with facades of enameled brick bearing pictures
of gryphons. The temple of Esagila was famous,
as were also the ziggurat or temple tower and the
hanging gardens. These were regarded by the
Greeks as one of the wonders of the world, though
nothing certain of them has been excavated. According to legend, they were built for Nebuchadnezzar's wife, the Median princess Amytis who was
homesick for her mountains. Parrot, in a study of
the ziggurat, reconstructs it as a pyramidal tower,
298 feet square and rising in seven stages to a
height of 300 ft. (A. Parrot, *The Tower of Babel*,
London: SCM Press, 1955, pp. 46-51).

Our historical records are brief and could hardly
be expected to mention the incidents of Nebuchadnezzar's life detailed by Daniel. But there is nothing unreal in the dream of the vision of chapter 2
nor in the incident of the idol and the fiery furnace.
A similar practice seems to be referred to in Jeremiah 29:22. It has been pointed out that this incident is more suited to the Babylonian period than
the later Persian time, for the Persians worshiped
fire and would be less apt to use it for execution.

As to the madness of Nebuchadnezzar in Daniel
4, there is no historical account remaining for us,
but it must be remembered that much of Nebuchadnezzar's reign is an historical blank. Anything
could have happened. Among the Dead Sea Scrolls
has been found a fragment, the *Prayer of Nabonidus*, which refers to an illness of the king for seven
years which was healed by God after the testimony
of a Jewish magician. (J. T. Milik, *Ten Years of
Discovery in the Wilderness of Judea*, Naperville,
Ill.: Allenson, 1959, p. 36). Some now say that
this is the source of the legend which in Daniel
is misapplied to Nebuchadnezzar. This can hardly
be proved or denied from historical evidence. It
seems equally possible that the canonical record

A view of Nebuchadnezzar's Babylon, restored, according to Unger. OIUC

was duplicated and applied to the later king. Indeed, more than one king suffered from illness and
from mental distress — Assurbanipal and Cambyses may be mentioned. If truth is stranger than
fiction, both Nebuchadnezzar and Nabonidus may
have suffered in a somewhat similar way — the
similarities being emphasized in the latter prayer.
There is perhaps a bare possibilty that the names
are confused. Two rebels after the reign of Cambyses apparently took the name of Nebuchadnezzar (Wiseman, *op. cit.* p. 37). There is uncertainty as
to the name of Labynetus who mediated the Me-
dian-Lydian treaty of 585. Some think he was Nabonidus, some say Nebuchadnezzar (*ibid.* p. 39).

A brick from Babylon, 6th century B.C., inscribed
with the name and titles of Nebuchadnezzar, recording his restoration of the temples of the gods Marduk,
Nebo, etc. © BM

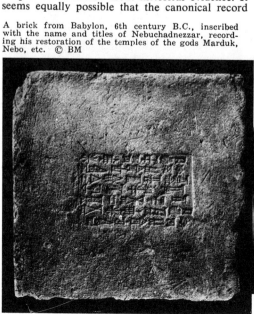

Ruins of the palace of Nebuchadnezzar at Babylon.
OIUC

Is it out of the question that Nabonidus also on occasion adopted the name Nebuchadnezzar? He had abundant precedent, but we have no positive evidence.

Of the death of Nebuchadnezzar we have no knowledge. He was succeeded by his son Evil-Merodach, then by his son-in-law, Neriglissar, for brief reigns. Nabonidus, who followed after the short reign of Labashi-Marduk, was perhaps related. There is some evidence that Nabonidus' mother was the daughter of Nebuchadnezzar by a second wife Nitocris. With the passing of the brilliant Nebuchadnezzar, however, the Neo-Babylonian empire soon crumbled and fell an easy prey to the Persians under Cyrus. R.L.H.

NEBUSHASBAN (nĕb'ū-shăs'băn, Akkad. *Nebo, save me*), an important officer in the army of Nebuchadnezzar at the time of the Babylonian siege of Jerusalem in 586 B.C. To his care another Babylonian official delivered the Prophet Jeremiah (Jer. 39:11-14).

NEBUZARADAN (nĕb'ū-zȧr-ā'dăn, Akkad. *Nebo has given seed*), Nebuchadnezzar's general when the Babylonians besieged Jerusalem (II Kings 25: 8,11,12,20; Jer. 52:12ff). The prophet Jeremiah was made the special charge and responsibility of Nebuzaradan (Jer. 39:11-14). Nebuzaradan bears the title the "Captain of the guard." After the fall of the city of Jerusalem in 586-85 B.C., Nebuzaradan was commissioned by Nebuchadnezzar to conduct the captives to Babylon. Before the appointment of Gedaliah (Jer. 40:5) Nebuzaradan was provisional governor of Palestine for the Babylonians. Nebuzaradan presented the option to Jeremiah to travel with him to Babylon or to remain in his own land (Jer. 40:1-6). The prophet chose to remain.

NECHO, NECHOH, NECCO (nē'kō, Heb. *par'ōh nekhōh* or *nechoh*), ruler of Egypt (609-595 B.C.), son of Psamtik I, famous in Greek history. Necho began his rule at a propitious time. The Assyrian Empire was falling and the Neo-Babylonian Empire was emerging. He thus was able to gain control over Syria until his humiliating defeat at the hands of Nebuchadnezzar at the battle of Carchemish. Of particular interest to the reader of the Bible is Josiah's defeat by Necho at the battle of Megiddo (II Kings 23:29; II Chron. 35:20ff). When Josiah died, Jehoahaz was made king, but Necho dethroned him and set up in his stead his brother, Jehoiakim (II Kings 23:29-34; II Chron. 35:20-36:4). In 605 B.C. he was badly defeated by Nebuchadnezzar at the battle of Carchemish, and lost all of his Asiatic possessions (II Kings 24:7).

NECK (Heb. *tsawwār, tsawwā'râh*, Gr. *nótos*), a term often used in Scripture with literal and figurative meanings. The bowed neck is often used as a symbol of submission, while the unbowed or "stiff neck" represents insubordination and disobedience (Exod. 32:9; Deut. 9:13; Ps. 75:5; Ezek. 2:4; Acts 7:51). It was a military custom for the conqueror to place his foot upon the neck of the vanquished (Josh. 10:24; Ps. 110:1; Rom. 16:20). "To shake off" or "to break the yoke" signifies to gain freedom. "To fall upon the neck" of a person is a common mode of salutation in the East and sometimes portrays great emotional stress (Luke 15:20; Acts 20:37; Gen. 46:29).

NECKLACE (Heb. *rāvîdh*), a chain worn as an ornament around the neck, and to which might be attached pendants (Isa. 3:19) or rings (Gen. 38: 25). The word is not found in the KJV, but such ornaments were very popular in ancient times.

NECROMANCER, NECROMANCY (nĕk'rō-măn-sēr, nĕk'rō-măn-sē). Necromancy was a form of witchcraft, and was considered as one of the "black" or diabolical arts. Etymologically, the term signifies conversing with the dead for purposes of consultation or divination. The Mosaic law sternly forbade such a practice (Deut. 18: 10,11). The most familiar case in the Bible is that of King Saul and the witch of Endor (I Sam. 28: 7-25). There are several quite legitimate interpretations of this admittedly difficult passage; perhaps the most feasible view is that God for His own purpose allowed Saul to converse with the deceased Samuel. See especially vs. 12 of this account.

NEDABAIAH (nĕd'ȧ-bī'ȧ), a descendant of King David (I Chron. 3:18).

NEEDLE'S EYE (Gr. *raphís*), found only in Christ's statement, "It is easier for a camel to go through the eye of a needle, than for a rich man to enter into the kingdom of God" (Matt. 19:24; Mark 10: 25; Luke 18:25). Jesus probably intended to teach that it is utterly absurd for a man bound up in his riches to expect to enter the kingdom of God. There is a rabbinical parallel, "an elephant through a needle's eye."

The Jaffa Gate in the wall of Jerusalem, showing the "Needle's Eye." Small doors such as this were common features of the gates of ancient cities; humans could pass through easily, but large animals, such as camels, had to be unloaded and kneel to get through, even then with difficulty. © MPS

NEEDLEWORK (Heb. *riqmâh, embroidery*), the art of working in with the needle various kinds of colored threads in cloth. The coverings of the ancient tabernacle in the wilderness were so embroidered. In Deborah's song, Sisera's mother imagines that he is collecting embroidered garments to bestow upon his ladies in waiting (Judg. 5:30). The king's daughter is regarded as clothed in clothing which has been embroidered (Ps. 45:14).

NEESING (nē'zĭng, Heb. *'ățîshâh, to sneeze* or *snort*). In Job 41:18 the crocodile is described as "neesing." This is Elizabethan English for "sneezing" or "snorting." It is hard to tell which the KJV translators intended here.

NEGEB (nĕg'ĕb, Heb. *neghev, dry*), the desert region lying to the south of Judea, and hence the term has acquired the double meaning of the "South," because of its direction from Judah or the "desert" because of its aridity. It came to refer to a definite geographical region, as when we read concerning Abraham that he journeyed from the South to Bethel (Gen. 13:1). Numbers 13:22 represents the 12 spies as spying out the land by way of the South. The Negeb is the probable site of Debir, a city of Judah c. 12 miles SW of Hebron.

The physical characteristics of the Negeb are that of rolling hills which abruptly terminate in the desert region. It is bounded on the E by the Dead Sea; on the W by the Mediterranean Sea. It is a land where the water supply is scarce, because of a very meager amount of rainfall in the summer months. At other seasons of the year, however, it is used by the nomads for pasturage. In this territory Hagar encountered the angel when she fled from the face of her mistress, Sarah (Gen. 16:7, 14). Here both Isaac and Jacob dwelt (Gen. 24:62; 37:1). This territory was part of the original territory of the Amalekites (Num. 13:29). On the basis of Joshua 19:1-9, the Negeb was allotted to the tribe of Simeon. However, in Joshua 15:20-31, it was given to the tribe of Judah. Many of David's exploits are described as happening in the Negeb, centering around Ziklag (I Sam. 27:5f). After Nebuchadnezzar sacked Jerusalem in 586-585 B.C., a group of Jews retreated to the Negeb, where they were harassed by the Edomites who sided with the Babylonians. Judas Maccabaeus expelled the Edomites in 164 B.C. John Hycranus compelled them to become Jews in 109 B.C.

NEGINAH (See Music)

NEHELAMITE (nē-hĕl'ȧ-mīt, Heb. *hanehĕlāmî*). Shemaiah, a false prophet, an adversary of Jeremiah, is styled a Nehelamite (Jer. 29:24,31,32). The place name Nehelam is not found in the OT.

NEHEMIAH (nē'hĕ-mī'ȧ, Heb. *nehemyâh, Jehovah has comforted*). 1. One of the leaders of the return under Zerubbabel (Ezra 2:2; Neh. 7:7).

2. The son of Azbuk, a prince of Beth-zur who helped repair the wall of Jerusalem (Neh. 3:16).

3. The son of Hachaliah and governor of the Persian province of Judah after 444 B.C. Of Nehemiah the son of Hachaliah little is known aside from what is in the book that bears his name. His times, however, are illuminated by the rather considerable material found in the Elephantine Papyri from Egypt which were written in the fifth century B.C. These papyri come from a military colony of Jews residing on an island up the Nile and are written in Hebrew. They include copies of letters to and from Jerusalem and Samaria. They name several men who are also mentioned in the book of Nehemiah.

Nehemiah was a "cupbearer" to King Artaxerxes (Neh. 1:11; 2:1). Inasmuch as some of the Elephantine papyri which are contemporary with Nehemiah are dated, we know that this Artaxerxes must be the first, called Longimanus, who ruled in 465-423 B.C. The title "cupbearer" clearly indicates a responsible office — not merely a domestic servant — for the king speaks to Nehemiah as an intimate and also indicates that he regards Nehemiah's journey to Jerusalem only as a kind of

The main street of Beersheba, chief city of the Negeb, and the desert beyond. The region is also known as the Negev, or the South. © MPS

vacation from official duties (2:4). Furthermore, the credentials given Nehemiah by the king and also the office of governor entrusted to him shows that the king looked upon him as a man of ability. That a captive Jew should attain to such an office need not surprise us when we remember the examples of Daniel, Esther, and others. Indeed some ancient courts made it a practice to train captive noble youths for service in the government (Dan. 1:4,5).

Nehemiah was an officer of the palace at Susa, but his heart was in Jerusalem. Word came to him from Hanani, one of his brothers, of the ruined condition of Jerusalem. Smitten with grief, Nehemiah sought the refuge of God's people — prayer — and God answered abundantly.

Hanani is called Nehemiah's brother in 1:2. In 7:2 a Hanani and Hananiah are both mentioned. It is possible that this verse means to equate the two forms of the name Hanani, calling Nehemiah's brother ruler of the palace at Jerusalem. It has been suggested that this Hanani is the same man mentioned in the Elephantine Papyri as an official who seems to have come into Egypt on a government mission. On one such trip Hanani learned about the sad state of affairs in Jerusalem and told Nehemiah (C. G. Tuland, *Hanani-Hananiah*, JBL, LXXVII, 157-161).

Only about 12 years earlier, in Artaxerxes' seventh year (457 B.C.), Ezra had gone back to Jerusalem with about 1,750 men, plus women and children (Ezra 8:1-20) and treasure worth a king's ransom (Ezra 8:26,27). But, if we refer Ezra 4:6-23 to the days of Ezra himself, it appears that his adversaries had persuaded the king to stop Ezra's efforts at rebuilding. The city, therefore, lay unrepaired, needing a new decree from the king. This permission Nehemiah providentially secured, thanks to his position at the court. Nehemiah therefore appeared at Jerusalem with a royal commission to continue the work that Ezra had begun.

Nehemiah was a man of ability, courage, and action. Arriving at Jerusalem, he first privately surveyed the scene of rubble (2:1-16), and encouraged the rulers at Jerusalem with his report of answered prayer and the granting of the king's new decree (2:18). Then he organized the community to carry out the effort of rebuilding the broken-down wall. Courageously and squarely he met the opposition of men like Sanballat, Tobiah, and Geshem (who are all now known from non-Biblical documents) and at last he saw the wall completed in the brief span of 52 days (6:15).

Nehemiah cooperated with Ezra in numerous reforms and especially in the public instruction in the law (chapter 8). However, he left for Persia, probably on official business, in 431 B.C. (13:6). Later he returned to Jerusalem, but for how long we do not know. Of the end of his life we know nothing. The Elephantine papyri indicate that a different man, Bagohi, was governor by 407 B.C.
R.L.H.

NEHEMIAH, BOOK OF. The Book of Nehemiah closes the history of the Biblical period. Closely allied to the Book of Ezra, it was attached to it in the old Jewish reckoning. It gives the history and reforms of Nehemiah the governor from 444 to about 420 B.C.

Outline:
I. Nehemiah returns to Jerusalem, 1:1 — 2:20.
II. Building despite opposition, 3:1 — 7:4.
III. Genealogy of the first returning exiles, 7:5-73 (= Ezra 2:2-70).
IV. The revival and covenant sealing, 8:1 — 10:39.
V. Dwellers at Jerusalem and genealogies, 11:1-12:26.
VI. Dedication of the walls, 12:27-47.
VII. Final reforms, 13:1-31.

Nehemiah's great work of restoring the wall of Jerusalem depended basically on securing permission from the king. Ezra had returned to Jerusalem with a sizable group of people and much gold and silver only a dozen years previously (see art. *Nehemiah*), but had been hindered in his work by adverse royal decrees secured by his adversaries. In God's providence, Nehemiah secured the return of royal favor.

The actual building of the wall was parceled out among different leaders. Various cities of the province of Judea gave contingents of workers and we can here learn something of the extent of Nehemiah's domain. The rapidity of building may have been due to preliminary work that Ezra might have accomplished. Most of the gates and sections of chapter 3 cannot be identified with assurance. Perhaps the wall enclosed only the eastern hill of Jerusalem.

The opposition to Nehemiah by Sanballat and others combined ridicule, threat, and craft. Sanballat is called the governor of Samaria in the Elephantine Papyri. He was apparently not anxious to see a rival province strengthened and there was religious antagonism as well to Nehemiah's strict reform program.

Internal difficulties also developed. The rich charged interest of one per cent (per month, apparently, 5:10) whereas the Mosaic law required outright charity to the poor. But against all opposition the wall was built by men who used both sword and trowel in the work of the Lord.

The genealogy of Nehemiah 7 is of interest, being a duplicate of that appearing in Ezra 2. There are unimportant differences between the lists such as is to be expected in the copying of detailed data like this. It is instructive to note that the record of Zerubbabel's returnees which Nehemiah used was a *written* record — not preserved by oral tradition as many have suggested was the method used for the passing on of Israel's histories.

Nehemiah's reform involved the teaching of Moses' law by Ezra and others at the feast of tabernacles (as commanded in Deut. 31:10). This led to the great prayer of confession of Nehemiah 9, redolent with quotations from and allusions to the Pentateuch. A covenant was solemnly sealed to walk in the law of the Lord as given by Moses (10:29).

Nehemiah's final reform included the removal of Tobiah from the temple precincts. Tobiah had entered through friendship with Eliashib the high priest while Nehemiah was back in Persia. Also a grandson of Eliashib had married Sanballat's daughter (13:28)! Evidently Eliashib was followed by his son Johanan in the reign of Darius II (423-404). This Johanan is mentioned in the Elephantine papyri as high priest in Jerusalem. His mention would indicate that Nehemiah's history continues till at least 423 B.C.
R.L.H.

NEHILOTH (nē'hĭ-lŏth), a musical term found in the title to the fifth Psalm. May mean "wind instrument."

NEHUM (nē'hŭm, Heb. *nehûm*), one of the 12 heads of Judah returning with Zerubbabel, also called Rehum (Ezra 2:2; Neh. 7:7).

NEHUSHTA (nē-hŭsh'tȧ, Heb. *nehushtā'*), the mother of King Jehoiachin of Judah. She was the daughter of Elnathan of Jerusalem (II Kings 24: 8). She was exiled with her son to Babylon (II Kings 24:12; Jer. 29:2).

NEHUSHTAN (nĕ-hŭsh'tăn, Heb. *nehushtān*, perhaps *brass serpent*), the name given to the serpent of brass surviving from the times of Moses, but destroyed by Hezekiah during his reforms because the Israelites had been making it an object of worship (II Kings 18:4).

NEIEL (nē-ī'ĕl), a boundary town between Zebulun and Asher (Josh. 19:27), may be the same as Neah (vs. 13).

NEIGHBOR (Heb. *rēa', 'āmîth, friend, qārôv, shākhēn,* Gr. *plesíon, near-by, geíton, inhabitant*). The duties and responsibilites of a man towards his neighbor are varied. In the OT, injunctions are given more in the negative than in the positive. The tenth commandment is directed towards the protection of the neighbor's property (Exod. 20: 17); the commandment immediately preceding, towards the protection of a neighbor's reputation (vs. 16). Cities of refuge were appointed for him who killed his neighbor accidentally (Deut. 19:4). The book of Proverbs is replete with admonitions concerning one's neighbor of which the following may be regarded as the epitome: "He that despiseth his neighbor sinneth" (Prov. 14:21). Due regard for one's neighbor is expressed in the great OT and NT precept, "Thou shalt love thy neighbor as thyself" (Lev. 19:18c; Matt. 19:19). The parable of the Good Samaritan (Luke 10:30-37) was given in answer to the question, "Who is my neighbor?" (vs. 29).

NEKEB (nē'kĕb, Heb. *neqev*), a town on the NW border of Naphtali (Josh. 19:33). Its site is uncertain.

NEKODA (nē-kō'dȧ), the head of a family of Nethinim who could not prove their Israelitish descent at the return from Babylon (Neh. 7:50,62; Ezra. 2:60).

NEMUEL (nĕm'ū-ĕl, Heb. *nemû'ēl*). 1. A Reubenite, brother of Dathan and Abiram who led the insurrection against Moses and Aaron (Num. 26:9).
2. A son of Simeon (Gen. 46:10; Num. 26:12; I Chron. 4:24), where variant "Jemuel" is used.

NEPHEG (nē'fĕg, Heb. *nephegh, sprout, shoot*). 1. Son of Izhar, brother of Korah, Dathan, and Abiram (Exod. 6:21).
2. A son of David (II Sam. 5:15; I Chron. 3:7; 14:6).

NEPHEW (Heb. *nekēdh*, Gr. *ékgonon*), a term found in the KJV four times, meaning grandson

(Judg. 12:14), descendant (Job 18:19; Isa. 14: 22), grandchild (I Tim. 5:4).

NEPHILIM (nĕf'ĭ-lĭm, Heb. *nephilim*), a term rendered "giants" in the KJV, describing certain of the antediluvians (Gen. 6:4) and aboriginal dwellers in Canaan (Num. 13:32,33), where they are identified with the Sons of Anak. Though no direct trace of a people of such abnormal stature has been discovered, there is ample evidence as to the underlying tradition. One should reject the view that they were angelic fallen beings (Deut. 1:28).

NEPHISH (See Naphish)

NEPHISHESIM (nē-fĭsh'ĕ-sĭm), a family of Nethinim (temple servants), perhaps originally from the tribe Naphish (Ezra 2:50; Neh. 7:52).

NEPHTHALIM (See Naphtali)

NEPHTOAH (nĕf-tō'à, Heb. *nephtôah, an opening*), a spring between Judah's and Benjamin's border (Josh. 15:9; 18:15). Identified as modern Lifta, a village two miles NW of Jerusalem.

NEPHUSIM (nē-fū'sĭm), a variant reading of Nephishesim, the head of a family of the Nethinim who returned from exile (Ezra. 2:50).

NER (nûr, Heb. *nēr, a lamp*). 1. Father of Abner (I Sam. 14:50; 26:14).
2. The grandfather of King Saul (I Chron. 8: 33. See II Sam. 8:12; I Kings 2:5,32).

NEREUS (nē'rūs, Gr. *Nereús*), a Roman Christian to whom the Apostle Paul extended greetings (Rom. 16:15). The name has been discovered on an inscription containing a listing of the emperor's servants. Whether this is the same Nereus is uncertain.

NERGAL (när'gàl, Heb. *nereghal*), a Babylonian deity of destruction and disaster, associated with the planet Mars (II Kings 17:30).

NERGAL-SHAREZER (när'gàl-shà-rē'zêr, Assyr. *nerghal sar-usar, may Nergal protect the prince*), the son-in-law of Nebuchadnezzar. Amil-Marduk, who succeeded Nebuchadnezzar as king, was assassinated by Nergal-Sharezer, who thereupon became king (Jer. 39:3-13).

NERI (nē'rī, Gr. *Neri*), a name listed in the ancestry of Jesus Christ, the grandfather of Zerubbabel (Luke 3:27). See NERIAH.

NERIAH (nē-rī'à, Heb. *nērîyâh, whose lamp is Jehovah*), the father of Seraiah and Baruch, the latter being the scribe of Jeremiah (Jer. 32:12,16, 36:4; 43:3). In Baruch 1:1, the Gr. form is given, *Nerias,* which Luke uses in abbreviated fashion as Neri (Luke 3:27).

NERIGLISSAR (See Nergal-Sharezer)

NERO (nē'rō, Gr. *Néron*), the fifth Roman emperor, born A.D. 37, commenced reign 54, died June 9th, 68. The original family name of Nero was Lucius Domitius Ahenobarbus, but after he was adopted into the Claudian gens by the Emperor Claudius, he assumed the name of Nero Claudius Caesar Germanicus. Nero's father was Enaeus Domitus Ahenobarbus, a man given to viciousness and vice. His mother was Agrippina, who cared little for her son's morals but was interested only in his temporal advancement.

The first years of Nero's reign were quite pacific and gave promise of good things to come. Nero himself could boast that not a single person had been unjustly executed throughout his extensive empire. During these "rational years" of Nero's administration, the Apostle Paul was brought before him as the regnant Caesar in compliance with

The Emperor Nero.

his own expressed appeal (Acts 25:10,11) c. A.D. 63. We can hardly do otherwise than infer that Paul was freed of all charges to continue his labors of evangelization.

Nero's marriage to Poppaea opened the second period of his reign. He killed his mother, his chief advisers Seneca and Burrus, and many of the nobility to secure their fortunes.

In A.D. 64 a large part of Rome was destroyed by fire. Whether or not Nero actually ordered the burning of the city is very controversial. However, justly or not, the finger of suspicion was pointed in Nero's direction. A scapegoat was provided in the Christians. Tacitus, who certainly cannot be accused of being called a Christian, bears testimony as to the severity of the sufferings inflicted upon them. "Their death was made a matter of sport; they were covered in wild beast's skins and torn to pieces by dogs; or were fastened to crosses and set on fire in order to serve as torches by night .. Nero had offered his gardens for the spectacle and gave an exhibition in his circus, mingling with the crowd in the guise of a charioteer or mounted on his chariot. Hence, ... there arose a feeling of pity, because it was felt that they were being sacrificed not for the common good, but to gratify the savagery of one man" (Tacitus, *Annals* XV, 44).

Nero's private life was a scandal. Surrendering himself to the basest of appetites, he indulged himself in the most evil forms of pleasure. Conspiracies and plots dogged the latter years of Nero. He was advised to destroy himself, but could not find the courage to do so. Learning that the Senate had decreed his death, his last cruel act was to put many of them to death. He finally died by his own hand in the summer of 68. Thus perished the last of the line of Julius Caesar. Both Paul and Peter suffered martyrdom under Nero.   J.F.G.

NEST (Heb. *qēn*, Gr. *nossiá* or *kataskénosis*). The nests of birds differ from species to species (Job 39:27; Jer. 49:16; Ps. 104:7). The first occurrence of the word *nest* in the Bible is in the parable of the prophet Balaam (Num. 24:21). In Deuteronomy 22:6, the law forbids one who happens to find a bird's nest with the mother and her brood from harming the mother bird. Among Semite people in general, it is viewed with extreme disfavor for anyone willfully to disturb a bird in the nest. Isaiah compares the despoiling of Israel by the Assyrians to the robbing of a bird's nest (Isa. 10:14; Matt. 8:20; Luke 9:58).

NETHANEEL (nĕ-thăn'ē-ĕl, Heb. *nethan'ēl, God has given*), the name of ten OT men: 1. The prince of Issachar just after the Exodus (Num. 1:8; 2:5, in ASV "Nethanel").

2. Son of Jesse and older brother of David (I Chron. 2:14).

3. One of the priests who played trumpets before the ark (I Chron. 15:24).

4. A Levitical scribe whose son Shemaiah was a recorder under David (I Chron. 24:6).

5. Fifth son of Obed-edom, appointed as one of the doorkeepers of the Tabernacle (1 Chron. 26:4).

6. A prince of Judah whom Jehoshaphat appointed to teach in Israel (II Chron. 17:7).

7. A wealthy Levite in Josiah's time (II Chron. 35:9).

8. A priest in Ezra's time who had taken a foreign wife (Ezra 10:22).

9. A priest and head of a household in the days of Joiakim c. 470 B.C. (Neh. 12:21).

10. A priestly musician in the days of Nehemiah (Neh. 12:36). Nathaniel of Cana of Galilee in the days of Jesus (John 1:45-49) had the same name, though in the Greek it is slightly changed.

NETHANIAH (nĕth'à-nī'a, Heb. *nethanyāhû, whom Jehovah gave*). 1. Father of Ishmael the assassin (Jer. 40:8-41:18).

2. A chief singer (I Chron. 25:2,12).

3. A teaching Levite (II Chron. 17:8).

4. Father of Jehudi whom the princes sent to Baruch for Jeremiah's book (Jer. 36:14).

NETHINIM (nĕth'ĭ-nĭm, Heb. *nethînîm, given ones*), a large group of temple servants, mentioned only in the later records of the OT. In a sense, all the Levites were "Nethinim" (Num. 8:19), for they were given by the Lord as a gift to Aaron and his sons for the divine service. At the conquest of Midian (Num. 31) the prey was divided between the warriors and the congregation and a fixed proportion was "given" for the Lord's service (vss. 40,42,47) of which 32 were "Nethinim" to the priests and 320 to the Levites in general. Later, when the men of Gibeon deceived Israel by claiming to have come a great distance (Josh. 9) they were allowed to live but were made "hewers of wood and drawers of water." The 392 descendants of these two groups, called "Nethinim" only in I Chronicles 9:2 and in Ezra and Nehemiah, came back with Israel after the Babylonian captivity (Ezra 2:43-58). At Ezra's return he lists 220 Nethinim (Ezra 8:20) and explains that David had appointed these for the service of the Levites.

NETOPHAH, NETOPHATHITES (nē-tō'fà, nē-tŏ'fa-thīt), a village of Judah and the inhabitants thereof. It lies about three miles S of Jerusalem and 3½ miles S of Bethlehem. The "villages of the Netophathites" (I Chron. 9:16, Neh. 12:28) were apparently given to, or inhabited by Levites, although Netophah is not mentioned in the earlier books. Several of David's men are named as from this place (II Sam. 23:28,29; I Chron. 2:54). Seraiah, the son of Tanhumeth the Netophathite, is mentioned (II Kings 25:23) among the slayers of Gedaliah, the governor.

NETTLE (See Plants)

NETWORK represents three distinct words in the Hebrew: 1. "Networks" (Isa. 19:9 KJV) is "white cloth," probably white linen as in ASV. 2. An ornamental carving or bas-relief upon the pillars of Solomon's temple (I Kings 7:18-42). 3. A Network of brass which served as a grate for the great altar of burnt-offerings at the tabernacle (Exod. 27:4, 38:4).

NEW BIRTH, the beginning of spiritual life in a believer (John 3:3,5,6; II Cor. 5:17; I Pet. 1:23). See REGENERATION.

NEW MOON (See Calendar, Feasts)

NEW TESTAMENT, a collection of 27 documents, the second part of the sacred Scriptures of the Christian Church, the first part being called by contrast the "Old Testament." In the name "New Testament," apparently first given to the collection in the second half of the second century, the word "testament" represents Greek *diathéke,* variously translated "testament," "settlement," "covenant," the last of these being on the whole the most satisfactory equivalent. The new covenant is the new order or dispensation inaugurated by the death of Jesus (compare His own reference to "the new covenant in my blood" in I Cor. 11:25); it was so called as fulfilling the promise made by God to His people in Jeremiah 31:31ff that He would "make a new covenant" with them whereby the desire and power to do His will would be implanted within them and all their past sins would be wiped out (cf. Heb. 8:6ff). By contrast with this covenant the earlier covenant established by God with Israel in Moses' day came to be known as the "old covenant" (cf. Heb. 8:13). The foundation documents of the new covenant inaugurated by Jesus are accordingly known as "the books of the new covenant (or testament)," the earlier Scriptures, which trace the history of the old dispensation, being known as "the books of the old covenant (or testament)" from the time of Melito of Sardis (A.D. 170) onwards ("the reading of the old covenant" in II Cor. 3:14 refers not to the sum-total of OT scripture but rather to the Mosaic law which formed the basis of that covenant).

Contents. In speaking of the books of the NT we must be clear whether we refer to the individual documents, or to the whole collection as such. The individual documents naturally existed before the collection, and some of them were grouped in smaller collections before they were ultimately gathered together in the NT collection. All, or nearly all, the individual documents belong to the first century A.D.; the NT as a collection made its appearance in the second century.

The order in which the 27 documents appear in our present-day NT is an order of subject-matter rather than a chronological order. First come the four Gospels—or rather the four records of the one and only Gospel — which narrate Jesus' ministry, death and resurrection. These are followed by the Acts of the Apostles, which takes up the Gospel story with Jesus' resurrection and shows how, over the next 30 years, Christianity spread along the road from Jerusalem to Rome. This book was originally written as the continuation of one of the four Gospels — Luke's. These five constitute the narrative section of the NT.

The next 21 documents take the form of letters written to communities or individuals. Of these 13 bear the name of Paul as writer, two the name of Peter, one of James, one of Jude (Judas). The others are anonymous. One of these, the Epistle to the Hebrews, is more properly described as a homily with an epistolary ending; its authorship remains a matter of guesswork to this day. The three which we know as the Epistles of John are so called not because they bear John's name but because from early times they have been closely associated with the Fourth Gospel (which, though itself anonymous, has from the first been known as John's). The first epistle is rather an exhortation in which the writer impresses on his readers

The opening page of the New Testament, the beginning of the Gospel of Matthew, from the Lindisfarne Gospels, a manuscript dating from A.D. 700. The handwritten notations are Anglo-Saxon. © BM

the practical implications of some of the leading themes of John's Gospel. In II and III John the writer refers to himself as "the elder."

The last book of the NT bears some features of the epistolary style, in that it is introduced by seven covering letters, addressed to seven churches in the Roman province of Asia; but for the most part it belongs to the class of literature called "apocalyptic," in which the outworking of God's purpose on earth is presented in the form of symbolical visions. Written probably when the Flavian dynasty ruled the Roman Empire (A.D. 69-96), its aim is to encourage the persecuted churches with the assurance that they are on the winning side; that Jesus, and not the Roman emperor, has won the victory which entitles Him to exercise sovereignty over the world and to control its destiny.

Order of Writing. While the four Gospels deal with events of the first 30 years of the Christian era, and the epistles belong to the remaining two-thirds of the first century, several of the epistles were in existence before even the earliest of the Gospels. With the possible exception of the Epistle of James, the earliest NT documents are those epistles which Paul wrote before his two years' detention in Rome (A.D. 60-62). This means that when one of the earlier Pauline epistles mentions an action or saying of Jesus, that mention is our earliest written account of it; thus, Paul's account of the institution of the Holy Communion (I Cor. 11:23ff) is earlier by some years than the account of it given in our oldest Gospel (Mark 14:22ff).

Jesus Himself wrote no book, but He gave His teaching to His disciples in a form which could be easily memorized, and enjoined them to teach others what they had learned from Him. And there is good reason to believe that one of the earliest Christian writings was a compilation of His teaching, arranged according to the chief subjects of which He treated, although this document has not been preserved in its original form but has been incorporated in some of the existing NT books.

The necessity for a written account of the story of Jesus was not felt acutely in the earlier years of the Christian mission. In those years, when there were so many eyewitnesses of the saving events who could testify to what they had seen and heard, their testimony was regarded as sufficient, and the Gospel story circulated far and wide by word of mouth. But even in those early years the necessity might and did arise for an apostle to give instruction in writing to people from whom he was separated at the time. For example, when Paul, during his missionary activity in Ephesus and the surrounding district, heard disturbing news of the state of affairs in the church which he had founded three or four years previously in Corinth, he was unable just then to visit Corinth in person, but sent his converts there a letter conveying much the same message as he would have given them orally had he been with them. Again, a few years later, during a brief stay in Corinth, he proposed to visit Rome in the near future, and thought it wise to prepare the Christians of that city, where he had never been before, for his coming; so he sent them a letter, in which he took the opportunity of making a full-length statement of the Gospel as he understood and preached it. In such "occasional" circumstances the NT epistles were first written. Yet the apostles were conscious that they expressed the mind of Christ, under the guidance of His Spirit, and so their letters are full of teaching, imparted to their first readers by apostolic authority, which retains its validity to the present time, and has by divine providence been preserved for our instruction.

The Gospels began to appear about the end of the first generation after the death and resurrection of Jesus. By that time the eyewitnesses were beginning to be removed by death, and the time must come when none of them would be left. It was desirable, therefore, that their testimony should be placed on permanent record so that those who survived them would not be at a disadvantage as compared with first-generation Christians. Around A.D. 60, then, we find Gospel writing first undertaken. Mark provides the Roman church with an account of Jesus' ministry, from His baptism to His resurrection, which we are told was based in large measure on the preaching of Peter. In the following years Matthew provides the churches of Syria and the neighborhood with an expanded account of the story of Jesus, in which His teaching is presented in systematic form; and Luke, Paul's companion and "beloved physician," having traced the course of events accurately from the beginning, sets himself to supply the "most excellent Theophilus" with an ordered narrative of Christian origins which not only relates "all that Jesus began both to do and to teach until the day in which he was received up" (Acts 1:1,2), but goes on to tell what He continued to do after He was received up, working by His Spirit in His apostles. Then, towards the end of the century, John retells the same story in such a way as to bring out its abiding and universal significance, so that his readers may apprehend the glory of Jesus as the Word became flesh, and by believing in Him may have life in His name. These four records are not biographies in the ordinary sense of the term; they are concerned rather to convey the apostolic witness to Jesus as Son of God and Saviour of the world.

The Gospel and Pauline Collections. For some time these four evangelic records circulated independently and locally, being valued, no doubt, by those for whom they were primarily written. But by the beginning of the second century they were gathered together and began to circulate as a fourfold Gospel-record throughout the Christian world. When this happened, Acts was detached from Luke's Gospel, to which it formed the sequel, and commenced a separate, but not insignificant, career of its own.

Paul's letters were preserved at first by the churches or individuals to whom they were sent; at least all that have come down to us were so preserved, for here and there in his surviving correspondence we find reference to a letter which was probably lost at a very early date (cf. I Cor. 5:9; Col. 4:16). But by the last decade of the first century there is evidence of a move to collect his available epistles and circulate them as a collection among the churches. Thus Clement of Rome, writing as secretary of his church to the church of Corinth about A.D. 95, can quote freely not only from Paul's Epistle to the Romans (which would naturally be available to him) but also from I Corinthians and possibly from one or two of his other epistles. What provided the stimulus for this move to collect Paul's letters, or who began to collect them, we can only speculate. Paul himself had encouraged some interchange of his letters (cf. Col. 4:16), and one or two of them were probably from the start general or circular letters, not intended for one single group of recipients.

By the early years of the second century, at any rate, a Pauline collection was in circulation — first a shorter collection of ten epistles, and then a larger collection of 13 (expanded by the inclusion of the three "Pastoral Epistles," those addressed to Timothy and Titus).

From the earliest days of such collections, the Pauline epistles appear to have been arranged mainly in descending order of length. That principle is still apparent in the arrangement most familiar today: Paul's letters to churches come before his letters to individuals, but within these two groups the letters are arranged so that the longest comes first and the shortest last. (One departure from the rule is that Galatians, which is slightly shorter than Ephesians, nevertheless precedes it, and has done so since the second century; certain theories have been propounded to explain this, bound up with the original purpose of Ephesians and Marcion's preference for Galatians.)

Canon of the New Testament. The circulation of two collections — the fourfold Gospel and the Pauline corpus — did not constitute a NT, but it represents a stage towards that goal. About A.D. 140 the Gnostic, Valentinus, according to Tertullian, accepted practically the whole NT as it was accepted later in the second century. It is not certain, however, whether Valentinus accepted the NT as a closed canon, or simply quoted as authoritative most of the documents which Tertullian acknowledged as making up the NT.

What chiefly stimulated the Church to define the NT limits more precisely was not the activity of the main Gnostic groups, but of Marcion. Marcion came to Rome about A.D. 140 from Asia Minor, where he had tried unsuccessfully to press his views on the church leaders. He rejected the OT completely, as revealing a different God from the God whom Jesus revealed as Father, and held that most of the writings which the Church accepted as authoritative were corrupted by Judaizers. He proposed a Christian canon comprising (1) "The Gospel" (an edition of Luke's Gospel edited in accordance with his own viewpoint) and (2) "The Apostle" (ten epistles of Paul, excluding

the Pastorals, similarly edited). Paul, in Marcion's eyes, was the only faithful apostle of Christ, all the others having Judaized; but even Paul's letters had been corrupted by Judaizers and required editing.

The publication of Marcion's canon — very much a closed list — was a challenge to the orthodox leaders. If they refused his canon, it was incumbent on them to define the canon which they accepted. They replied to his challenge by saying, in effect, that they did not reject the OT writings; they accepted them as Holy Scripture, following the example of Christ and the apostles. Along with them they accepted the NT writings — not one Gospel only, but four (one of the four being the authentic text of the Gospel which Marcion issued in a mutilated form); not ten epistles only of Paul, but 13; not epistles of Paul only, but of other apostolic men as well. They also accepted the Acts of the Apostles, and appreciated more than ever its crucial importance as the pivot of the NT. Acts links the fourfold Gospel with the apostolic writings because it provides the sequel to the former and the historical background to much of the latter. Moreover, it provides irrefutable evidence of the genuineness of Paul's apostleship. Tertullian and others were not slow to expose the folly of the Marcionites who asserted the exclusive apostleship of Paul while rejecting the one book which supplied independent testimony to his apostleship. Of course they had no alternative but to reject it, as it bore witness at the same time to the apostleship of Peter and others, whom the Marcionites repudiated. But the very fact that Acts attested the apostleship both of Paul and of Peter and his colleagues gave it all the greater value in the eyes of orthodox churchmen. From this time it came to be called "The Acts of the Apostles"; indeed one zealously anti-Marcionite document, the Muratorian list (c. A.D. 200), goes so far as to call it "The Acts of all the Apostles." That was a great exaggeration, but Acts does at least record something about most of the apostles or apostolic men to whom are ascribed the epistles which the orthodox churchmen accepted as authoritative.

Thus, from the second half of the second century onwards, the Church acknowledged a NT of the same general dimensions as ours. For a considerable time there was some questioning about a few of the books at the end of our NT, and claims were sometimes made for the recognition of books which did not ultimately retain a place within the collection. But after generations of debate about the few "disputed" books in relation to the majority of "acknowledged" books, we find the 27 documents which make up our New Testament today listed by Athanasius of Alexandria in A.D. 367, and not long afterwards by Jerome and Augustine in the West. These scholars were not imposing decisions of their own, but stating what was generally recognized. It is unhistorical to represent the limits of the NT as being due to the verdict of any church council. When first a church council did make a pronouncement on this subject (A.D. 393), it did no more than record the general consensus of the Church in east and west.

The invention of the codex, or leaf-form of book, made it possible for the NT writings, or indeed the whole Bible, to be bound together in one volume, as had not been possible with the older roll-form of book. The earliest comprehensive codices known to us belong to the fourth century; but already in the third century, and possibly even in the second, it was practicable to collect groups of NT books together in smaller codices. The Chester Beatty Biblical papyri include one codex of the four Gospels and Acts and one of the Pauline epistles and Hebrews.

Authority of the New Testament. The authority of the NT is not based on archaeological evidence or on any other line of comparative study. By such means we can confirm the historical setting of the record in the first Christian century, and provide ourselves with an illuminating commentary on it. The value of this should not be underestimated, but the essential authority of the NT derives from the authority of Christ, whether exercised in His own person or delegated to His apostles. The NT documents are the written deposit of the apostles' witness to Christ and of the teaching which they imparted in His name. When we emerge from the "tunnel" period which separates the apostolic age from the last quarter of the second century, we find the Church still very conscious of apostolic authority. The apostles are no longer there, but the apostolic faith is confessed, the apostolic fellowship is maintained, and apostolic church order is observed. We find, too, that the apostolic writings (whether penned directly by apostles or indirectly by "apostolic men") are available in the NT canon to serve as the Church's rule of faith and order — the criterion by which it may be determined whether doctrine or fellowship or anything else that claims to be apostolic really is so. And from those days to our own, it is the NT that, from time to time, has called Christians back to the ways of apostolic purity, to the truth as it is in Jesus. Reformation is not something that the Church needed once for all, in the 16th century; true "reformation according to the Word of God" is an abiding need of the Church. And where the NT is given its proper place in the Church's faith and life, true reformation goes on continually.

Not only in the works and words of Jesus during His earthly ministry, but in the continuing ministry which He has exercised since His exaltation, does He reveal God to men. Therefore not only the Gospels, which record the revelation given in the days of His flesh, but the other NT books, which record the further outworking of that revelation, are accepted by the Church as her normative foundation documents. The Holy Spirit, who came to make the significance of Jesus plain to His followers and to lead them into all the truth, still performs these services for us; and the NT writings are His primary instrument for their performance. How else could the Spirit take the things of Christ and declare them to us today if these writings were not available as a basis for Him to work on? The Spirit who was imparted in fullness to Jesus and who worked by the apostles is the Spirit under whose direction the Christians of the earliest centuries were enabled to recognize so clearly the documents which bore authoritative witness to Jesus; He is also the Spirit by whose illumination we in our day may appropriate that witness for our own and others' good.

In all this we do not ignore the place of the OT as an integral part of the Christian Scriptures. For the two Testaments are so organically interwoven that the authority of the one carries with it the authority of the other. If the OT records the divine promise, the New records its fulfilment; if the OT tells how the world was prepared over many centuries for the coming of Christ, the New tells how He came and what His coming brought about. If even the OT writings are able to make the reader "wise unto salvation through faith which is in Christ Jesus" and equip him thoroughly for

the service of God (II Tim. 3:15-17), how much more is this true of the NT writings! Our Lord's statement of the highest function of the former scriptures applies with at least equal force to those of the NT: "these are they which bear witness of me" (John 5:39).

Bibliography:
Merrill C. Tenney, *New Testament Survey* (Grand Rapids: Eerdmans, 1961); Alan Hugh McNeile, *An Introduction to the Study of the New Testament* (Oxford: Clarendon Press, 1953); Alexander Souter, *The Text and Canon of the New Testament* (London: Duckworth, 1954).

F.F.B.

THEOLOGY, THE NEW. The new (radical) theology is characterized chiefly by a departure from the neo-orthodoxy of Karl Barth and Emil Brunner which has dominated a segment of the theological scene during the past forty years. This article considers briefly three of the main expressions of this radicalism: Paul Tillich, Rudolf Bultmann and some of the proponents of the "God is dead" movement.

Paul Tillich (1886-1965) constructed a philosophical-theological system by accumulating a mass of historical, biographical and speculative data and arranging it by means of his "method of correlation" — philosophy (reason) asks the questions and theology (faith) gives the answers.

As an apologetic, Tillich's system begins with Being. In that no reality is more basic, all meaningful philosophies of life must start here. Being is Unconditional, all other realities are conditioned. Therefore, any statement made concerning Being, other than "God is Being," is symbolic. Symbols, such as the miracles, the Incarnation, the cross or the resurrection, participate in and point to the Unconditional, but in no way define it. To judge otherwise, would be to formulate an autonomous or a conditional god, which is idolatry.

Man is estranged from his ground of being. In Jesus as the Christ, however, he finds his way of salvation. Although existing under the conditions of man, Jesus as the Christ came under the control of His ground of being. Thus His way has become the way for all men. The way is through "ecstasy" — the supreme extension of man's ability to reason without doing violence to his rational powers. Acting concurrently with this (faith) rational exercise of man, is the "reaching down" of the Unconditional or the ground of man's being. Although the experience is always opaque, it is revelatory and satisfying to man's ultimate concern.

History is to be taken seriously, with culture providing the form which religion fills with content. Critical evaluation of the various philosophies and religions is possible by use of the Protestant principle. Positively, this principle constructs a system; negatively, it criticizes all systems including its own construction. In Tillich's judgment this principle will outlive all systems of religion or philosophies of life.

So massive in content and intricate in systemization is Tillich's theology, that all attempts to digest or summarize his thought should be viewed as pointers to rather than expressions of his thinking. A knowledge of his *Systematic Theology* (3 volumes) is essential for an understanding of his philosophy.

Rudolf Bultmann (1884-   ) is a German New Testament scholar who has developed a radical method of Biblical interpretation. The historical framework for the life of Jesus as found in the gospel records is the creation of the early church which best expresses her faith. Therefore, in order to find the basic Christian message (*Kerygma*) the records must be stripped of their historic (?) increments. That is to say, they must be demythologized.

Furthermore, it is not the reality of the experienced object that is important, but rather the immediate experience of consciousness. Consequently, the gospel message has meaning only when it brings meaning as an event to the individual through a decision made in faith. When the Bible speaks in this way, it is *kerygma;* when it speaks merely as history, it is *mythos.*

New Testament scholars of a more conservative bent have judged that Bultmann's abandonment of determining the historical Jesus has also disqualified him from formulating a Biblical Christology — a fundamental doctrine with historic Christianity.

Both Tillich and Bultmann contributed to the radical theologians who now constitute the "death of God" movement. However, some of the latter statements of Dietrich Bonhoeffer (1906-1945) point more directly to this radical theology.

Bonhoeffer was willing to abandon the definition of God as an individual reality in behalf of God as the ground of all being (Tillich); he also was willing to promote a secular Christianity. This meant the displacement of the old religious symbols (miracles, the cross, etc.) for new, more meaningful ones, understandable to the people outside the church. Furthermore, he believed that God was active in the world (without the help of the Church) and consequently the Church should react to its smallness and move out where the action is.

Bonhoeffer and his disciples have influenced many radical thinkers including: Bishop John A. T. Robinson, *(Honest to God);* William Hamilton, *(The New Essence of Christianity);* Paul van Buren, *(The Secular Meaning of the Gospel);* Harvey Cox, *(The Secular City);* Thomas J. J. Altizer, *(Radical Theology and the Death of God);* and Gabriel Vahanian, *(The Death of God; The Culture of Our Post-Christian Era).*

Basic to the more radical proponents of this movement is their insistence on the renunciation of the Transcendent God plus the Biblical symbols which they contend are no longer meaningful to contemporary man. This transference from an interest in the metaphysical to the pragmatic is interpreted as being expressive of the mature man. Man is reaching the apex of his existence; he no longer needs a god out there!

Although the ground from which this radical theology has sprung is fundamentally that of neo-orthodoxy with its existential, dialectic dimensions, it may be that future critical evaluations of this movement will judge it as basically a revival of the rational liberalism of the pre-Barthian era. Especially is this likely if liberalism is viewed as a mentality rather than a system of doctrine.

Bibliography:

The Systematic Theology of Paul Tillich by Alexander J. McKelway, John Knox Press, Richmond, Va., 200 pages, $5.50.

Creative Minds in Contemporary Theology, ed. by Philip Edgcumbe Hughes, Wm. B. Eerdmans Publishing Co., Grand Rapids, Mich., 488 pages, $6.95.

God Is Dead: The Anatomy of a Slogan, by Kenneth Hamilton, Wm. B. Eerdmans Publishing Co., 86 pages, $1.25.

NEW YEAR (See Feasts, Feast of Trumpets)

NEZIAH (nē-zī'à, *sincere*), one of the Nethinim whose descendants returned from captivity with Zerubbabel (Ezra 2:54; Neh. 7:56).

NEZIB (nē'zĭb, Heb. *netsîv*), a village mentioned only in Joshua 15:43, belonging to Judah and lying about 10 miles NW of Hebron. The word means "something set" and thus a "garrison." It retains today its name "Beit Nusib" i.e. "House of the garrison."

NIBHAZ (nĭb'hăz, Heb. *nivhaz*), a god, whose image in the form of a dog was made and worshiped by the Avites when the Samaritan race was being formed (II Kings 17:31).

NIBSHAN (nĭb'shăn, Heb. *nivshān*), a town in the S of Judah between Beersheba and the Dead Sea (Josh. 15:62).

NICANOR (nĭ-kā'nôr, Gr. *Nikánor*), one of the seven chosen by the church at Jerusalem to administer alms (Acts 6:5).

NICODEMUS (nĭk'ō-dē'mŭs, Gr. *Nikódemos, victor over the people*), a leading Pharisee, "a ruler of the Jews" and a member of the Sanhedrin. Perhaps from curiosity, and possibly under conviction, but certainly led of God, he came to Jesus by night (John 3:1-14). He must have thought of himself as quite condescending to address Jesus, the young man from Galilee, as "Rabbi," but Jesus, instead of being puffed up by the recognition, quickly put Nicodemus in his place by announcing the necessity of a new birth in order "to see the kingdom of God." Nicodemus did not then understand, but was deeply touched, though he had not yet the courage to stand out for the Lord. Later, when at the Feast of Tabernacles (John 7:25-44) the Jewish leaders were planning to kill Jesus, Nicodemus spoke up, though timidly, in the Sanhedrin, suggesting their injustice in condemning a man without a fair trial. After the death of Jesus, however, Nicodemus came boldly with Joseph of Arimathea (John 19:38-42), provided a rich store of spices for the embalmment, and assisted in the burial of the body. After that he is not mentioned in Scripture.

NICOLAITANS (nĭk'ō-lā'ĭ-tănz, Gr. *Nikolaitaí*), a group of persons whose works both the church at Ephesus and our Lord hated (Rev. 2:6) and whose doctrine was held by some in the Pergamene church (Rev. 2:15). Nothing else is surely known about them, but some have guessed that they were the followers of Nicolas of Antioch, one of the first so-called "deacons" (Acts 6:5), but there is no evidence for this. Their doctrine was similar to that of Balaam through whose influence the Israelites ate things sacrificed to idols and committed fornication (Rev. 2:14,15). A sect of Nicolaitans existed among the Gnostics in the third century, as is known from church fathers of the time (Irenaeus, Clement of Alexandria, Tertullian, etc.). It probably had its origin in the group condemned in Revelation.

NICOLAUS, NICOLAS (nĭk'ō-lā'ŭs, nĭk'ō-làs, Gr. *Nikólaos, conqueror of the people*), a "proselyte of Antioch" mentioned only in Acts 6:5 whom the church at Jerusalem very early chose to administer alms as one of the seven original "deacons." Being confused with the "Nicolaitans," (*q.v.*) many writers even in early times have accused him of originating this sect.

NICOPOLIS (nĭ-cŏp'ō-lĭs, Gr. *Nikópolis, city of victory*), an ancient city of Epirus situated on the Gulf of Actium, and founded by Augustus Caesar to celebrate his decisive victory over Mark Antony, 31 B.C. (In modern terms "on the Gulf of Arta" on the west coast of Greece.) When Paul wrote his epistle to Titus, in the interval between his first and his final imprisonment under Nero at Rome, he had determined to winter there (Titus 3:12).

NIGER (nī'jêr, Gr. *Níger, black*), a surname of Symeon, one of the five "prophets and teachers" of the church at Antioch who were led of the Lord to send forth Paul and Barnabas on the first missionary journey (Acts 13:1-3). Probably a Hebrew-Christian from North Africa.

NIGHT (See Time)

NIGHT HAWK (See Birds)

NILE (nīl, Gr. *Neílos,* meaning not certainly known), the main river, not only of Egypt, but of Africa as well, being exceeded in all the earth in length only by the Amazon and the Missouri-Mississippi rivers; and in the extent of the territory which it drains ranking sixth among the river systems of the world. The word "Nile" does not appear in the Heb. OT or in the KJV, strange to say, but in ASV we find it thrice in Isaiah 19:7 where KJV has "brooks." When we find in Scripture the words "the River," we can generally judge by the context whether the Nile, as in Genesis 41:1, or the Euphrates as in 31:21, is intended; though in Psalm 72:8 we may be in doubt. The common Bible name for the Nile is *ye'ôr*, an Egyptian word meaning "river" and almost always referring to the Nile, except in Daniel 12:5,6,7, where it clearly refers to the Tigris (cf. Dan. 10:4). The word "Shihor" (KJV "Sihor"), with the root meaning of "turbid," means the Nile in Isaiah 23:3; but in Joshua 13:3, I Chronicles 13:5, etc., where it marks the southwestern border of Canaan, it refers to the Wadi el Arish, a little channel that enters the Mediterranean about half way from the present Suez Canal to the southern end of the Dead Sea. The same stream is meant in Genesis 15:18 where we read "the river of Egypt."

The Nile issues forth from Lake Victoria on the Equator and flows northward nearly 2,500 miles to the Mediterranean. Of this, the northernmost 500 miles can be said to be in Egypt, from Assouan northward. The "White" Nile rises as above at the Equator and has a fairly even flow northward till it is joined by the "Blue" Nile at modern Khartoum in the Sudan. This stream and the other affluents which join the Nile from the E, rise in the mountains of Ethiopia and are fed by the torrential rains of the springtime. They fluctuate greatly, and provide the annual inundation which for thousands of years has flooded and fertilized lower Egypt. The ancient mythological belief was that the goddess Isis annually shed a tear into the upper Nile, thus causing the flood which is so great a blessing that Egypt has been called, from the time of Herodotus onward "the Gift of the Nile."

Near the end of June the water at Cairo and onward takes on a greenish tinge and an unpleasant taste, because of the vast multiplication of the algae, then about the beginning of July the life-giving inundation begins so that the delta region is overflowed and the stream deposits the rich gift of sediment brought down from the mountains. During an average year, the vast delta seems almost like a sea with islands protruding here and there. If the inundation is unusually deep, many houses are destroyed and loss ensues, while if it is much below the average level, famine follows. This failure of the inundation for seven successive years (Gen. 41) was used of God to work a great but peaceful revolution in Egypt in which Joseph bought up for the pharaoh practically all private property except that of the priests, and brought the Israelites into Egypt for a stay of several hundred years.

Through Upper Egypt, the Nile flows for many miles through high walls of sand and rock, with the desert encroaching on both sides, so that only by great efforts could the people irrigate a narrow strip of land, but from a point a few miles S of Cairo, the Nile divides, the Delta begins, and Lower Egypt (i.e. Northern Egypt) has long been one of the most fertile regions in the world.

From the days of Abraham, who as Abram, went down into Egypt (Gen. 12:10) till the infancy of our Lord Jesus Christ (Matt. 2:14) Egypt, and therefore the Nile, were well known by Israel and exerted a potent effect upon the civilization of Israel. In describing the Promised Land, Moses (Deut. 11:10-12) emphasized its difference from Egypt "where thou sowedst thy seed, and wateredst it with thy foot" (i.e. by irrigating furrows manipulated, and then altered from time to time by foot power); and the prosperity or poverty of Egypt at various periods was in proportion to the ingenuity and faithfulness of the people in spreading the water of the Nile upon their plants. The rise and fall of the Nile is very regular, but there have been times (e.g. 1877) when an unusually feeble flood led to widespread famine and many deaths. It was, no doubt, a series of these dry years in the days of Joseph which caused the seven years famine (Gen. 41) and which led, under God, to the descent into Egypt. Hundreds of years later, we find various references to the rivers of Egypt in the prophets: e.g. in Isaiah 7:18 we read that "Jehovah will hiss for the fly that is in the uttermost parts of the rivers of Egypt" and this hints at the prevalance of flies there, and even today the land seems full of them. In Isaiah 19:5 "the water shall fail from the sea, and the river shall be wasted and become dry" — "the sea" is a common title given to the Nile, which during the annual inundation must resemble a sea from parts of the Delta. In Isaiah 19:7 it is said that the meadows by the Nile and the sown fields of the Nile shall become dry and shall be driven away — and this has come to pass literally when the irrigating works have been neglected for a time. Strange to say, KJV renders *ye'ôr*, which plainly refers to the Nile, by the word "brooks" three times in this verse.   A.B.F.

NIMRAH (nĭm'rȧ, Heb. *nimrâh, limpid* or *flowing water*), a city in Gilead, assigned by Moses to the tribe of Gad (Num. 32:3) and cf. vs. 36 where it is called "Beth-nimrah" i.e. "house of limpid water." It lies about ten miles NE of Jericho. In Joshua 13:27 it is described as being "in the valley" and as a part of the former kingdom of Sihon, king of the Amorites whose capital was Heshbon.

NIMRIM (nĭm'rĭm, Heb. *nimrîm*), a place in Moab noted for its waters (Isa. 15:6; Jer. 48:34). It was probably SE of the Dead Sea.

NIMROD (nĭm'rŏd, Heb. *nimrôdh*). In the "Table of the Nations" (Gen. 10) many of the names seem to be those of cities, e.g. Sidon (vs. 15), countries, e.g. Canaan (vss. 6,15), or tribes, e.g. "Heth and the Jebusite," etc. (vss. 15-18), but Nimrod stands out clearly as an individual man, and a very interesting character. The beginning of his kingdom was in Babylonia, whence he moved northward and became the founder of Nineveh and other cities in or near Assyria. He became distinguished as a hunter, ruler, and builder. Many legends have grown up around the name of Nimrod, some claiming him to have been identical with "Ninus," an early Babylonian king or god. Again, some have associated Nimrod with the building of the Tower of Babel (Gen. 11:1-9). Others have identified him with the ancient king of Babylonia, Gilgamesh, but there is no proof that the two were identical.

Above, the mound of Nimrud (ancient Calah), once the capital of Assyria. Below, ruins of Birs Nimrud, with the mosque, the Shrine of Abraham, in the distance. © MPS

NIMRUD (nĭm'rŭd), ancient Calah in Assyria, founded by Nimrod, and scene of extensive excavations. See CALAH.

NIMSHI (nĭm'shĭ), the grandfather of Jehu whose coup-d'etat ended the rule of the house of Ahab (II Kings 9:2,14). Elsewhere Jehu is called "son of Nimshi" (I Kings 19:16).

NINEVEH, NINEVE (nĭn'ĕ-vĕ, Heb. *nînewēh*), one of the most ancient cities of the world, founded by Nimrod (Gen. 10:11,12), a great-grandson of Noah, and enduring till 612 B.C. Nineveh lay on the banks of the Tigris above its confluence with the Greater Zab, one of its chief tributaries, and nearly opposite the site of the modern Mosul in Iraq. It was for many years the capital of the great

Assyrian empire, and its fortunes ebbed and flowed with the long strife between Babylonia and Assyria. Of the two kingdoms, or empires, Babylonia was the more cultured but Assyria the more warlike. The kingdom over which Nineveh and its kings long ruled was N of Babylon and more in the hills, and these facts made more for warlikeness than the more sedentary culture of a warmer climate. Babylon was the more important from Abraham's time to David's; then from David's time to that of Hezekiah and Manasseh, Nineveh and its kings were paramount; then from the time of King Josiah and the prophets Jeremiah, Ezekiel, Habakkuk and Daniel, Babylon was again at the head.

Among the great rulers of Assyria might be mentioned Tiglath-pileser I, who made conquests about 1100 B.C., and Ashur-nasirpal and Shalmaneser III, who inaugurated a system of ruthless conquest and deportation of whole populations, which greatly increased the power of Assyria and the influence of Nineveh. It was this latter king (sometimes numbered as II instead of III) who defeated Hazael of Syria and boasted of receiving tribute from Jehu of Israel. The Assyrians, instead of numbering their years, named them from certain rulers; and lists of these "eponyms" have been found, but with a gap of 51 years around the beginning of the eighth century B.C., due, no doubt to some great calamity and/or the weakness of her kings. It was in this space of time that Jonah was sent of the Lord to warn the people of Nineveh, saying "Yet forty days and Nineveh shall be overthrown" (Jonah 3:4) but God gave Nineveh a respite for nearly 200 years. Esar-haddon, the great king of Assyria from 680-668 B.C., united Babylonia to Assyria and conquered lands as far away as Egypt (Isa. 19:4) and North Arabia. He was succeeded by his greater son Ashur-bani-pal (called by the Greeks "Sardanapalus"), who presided over Assyria in its brief climax of power and culture, but Nabopolassar of Babylon, who reigned from 625 to 605, freed it from Assyria and helped to bring about the destruction of Nineveh in 612 B.C. (Some date this destruction 606 B.C.) About 623 B.C., Cyaxares, king of the Medes, made his first attack on Nineveh, and this was probably the occasion of Nahum's prophecy. (His book is undated, but 3:8 speaks of No-amon in the past tense, and it was destroyed 663 B.C., and of Nineveh's destruction as future, so it must have been written about this time.

Ruins of ancient Nineveh, once the capital of Assyria. These ruins are near the banks of the Tigris, opposite modern Mosul in Iraq. OIUC

For many centuries the very location of Nineveh was forgotten, but it has been discovered and excavated (largely by Botta and Layard from 1843-'45), and among its buried ruins the great palace of Sargon, with its wonderful library of cuneiform inscriptions and its still striking wall ornamentation, has been exhumed. Because the name Sargon was omitted in some of the ancient lists of kings, some of the scholars scoffed (around 1840) at Isaiah 20:1, "when Sargon, king of Assyria sent him," saying in effect, "This is one of the errors of Isaiah, for we know that Sargon never did exist," and it is said that when Botta sent to Berlin some ancient bricks with the name Sargon baked into them, the "scholars" claimed that he forged the bricks! Nahum's reference (2:4) to chariots raging in the streets and rushing to and fro in the broadways of Nineveh does not prophesy automobile traffic, as some have tried to make out, but refers to the broad streets which distinguished Nineveh.

A.B.F.

NISAN (See Calendar)

NISROCH (nĭs'rŏk, Heb. *nisrōkh*), a god who was worshiped at Nineveh. In his temple Sennacherib was slain by his two sons Adrammelech and Sharezer after his return from his disastrous experience near Jerusalem (Isa. 37:36-38 repeated in II Kings 19:35-37). The name is not found elsewhere.

NITER (nī'têr, Heb. *nether*). Not the same as our present niter, but an impure mixture of washing and baking sodas found in deposits around the alkali lakes of Egypt. The references in Scripture are to its fizzing with vinegar and its use in cleansing (Prov. 25:20 "nitre," ASV "soda"). (Jer. 2:22, ASV, "lye").

NO (nō, Heb. *nō' 'āmôn, the city of the god Amon*), the great city and capital of Upper Egypt, lying on both sides of the Nile at the great semi-circular curve of the river about 400 miles S of Cairo. It was the capital of Egypt as early as the 11th century. Its tremendous ruins at Luxor and Karnak are among the world's wonders. Its fuller name was No-amon (Amon from a local god), but so similar to the Hebrew for "multitude" that the KJV mistranslates it. "The multitude of No" (Jer. 46:25) should be "Amon of No," as in ASV and "populous No" (Nah. 3:8) should be "No-amon." It was known to the classical writers under the name of Thebes. Its site is now occupied by some small villages on both sides of the Nile.

NOADIAH (nō'à-dī'à, Heb. *nô'adhyâh, with whom Jehovah meets*). 1. One of the Levites before whom the gold and silver vessels were weighed on the return to Jerusalem (Ezra 8:33).

2. A false prophetess, associated with Sanballat and Tobiah, who tried to terrorize Nehemiah, and against whom Nehemiah prayed (Neh. 6:14).

NOAH (nō'à, Heb. *nōah, rest*). 1. The son of Lamech and tenth in descent from Adam in the line of Seth (Gen. 5:28-29). He received this name because Lamech foresaw that through him God would comfort (Heb. *nâham*, same root as "Noah") the race and partially alleviate the effects of the Edenic curse. Noah was uniquely righteous (6:8-9; 7:1; Ezek. 14:14) in a totally corrupt age (Gen. 6:1-13). When he was 480 years old, 120 years before the Flood (6:3), he was warned of God that the world would be destroyed by water (Heb. 11:7). He was then given exact instructions for building the Ark (Gen. 6:14-16). While engaged in this colossal task, he warned men of the coming catastrophe, as a "preacher of righteousness" (II Pet. 2:5), while God in longsuffering waited

for men to repent (I Pet. 3:20). Noah's three sons, Shem, Ham, and Japheth, were not born until he was 500 years old (Gen. 5:32). One week before the Flood, God led Noah and his family into the Ark, and then, supernaturally directed, the animals "went in unto Noah into the ark, two and two of all flesh, wherein is the breath of life" (7:15). When all were safely inside, God shut the door (7:16).

The Flood came in Noah's 600th year, increased steadily for 40 days, maintained its mountain-covering depth for 110 more days, and then subsided sufficiently for Noah to disembark in the mountains of Ararat after another 221 days (see FLOOD OR DELUGE). During all this time, "God remembered Noah, and every living thing . . . in the ark" (8:1), implying that God did not leave the task of caring for these creatures entirely to Noah. To determine whether it was safe to disembark, Noah sent forth first a raven and then a dove at regular intervals (8:6-10). The freshly-plucked olive leaf proved to him that such sturdy plants had already begun to grow on the mountain heights. God commanded him to disembark, and Noah built an altar and offered clean beasts as burnt-offerings to God. The Lord then promised never to send another universal flood, confirming it with the rainbow sign (8:21-22; 9:9-17). God blessed Noah and his family and commanded them to multiply and fill the earth (9:1). Animals were henceforth to fear man and they were given to be food for man, except the blood (9:2-4). Human government was instituted by the provision of capital punishment for murderers (9:5-6). Among the things preserved in the Ark was sinful human nature. Noah became a husbandman, planted a vineyard, drank himself into a drunken stupor, and shamefully exposed himself in his tent (9:20-21). Ham, presumably led by his son Canaan, made fun of Noah. For this foul deed, Canaan was cursed and Ham received no blessing (9:25-27). On the other hand, Shem and Japheth showed due respect to their father (9:23) and received rich blessings for their descendants. Noah lived 350 years after the Flood, dying at the age of 950 (9:29).

In the Babylonian flood account (the Gilgamesh Epic), Noah's counterpart is Utnapishtim. He likewise received divine warnings of the Flood, built a huge ark, preserved human and animal life, sent out birds, and offered sacrifices. However, the

Gilgamesh seal of Utnapishtim. Below, digging below flood layer at Fara, Babylonia. UMP

gross polytheism and absurdities of the Babylonian account demonstrate that it suffered from a long oral transmission and that it did not influence Genesis in any way (cf. Merrill Unger, *Archaeology and the Old Testament*, Zondervan, 1954, pp. 46-71).

2. One of the five daughters of Zelophehad, of the tribe of Manasseh (Num. 26:33; 27:1; 36:11; Josh. 17:3), who received an inheritance in the land in their father's name, in spite of having no brothers. J.C.W.

NOB (nŏb, Heb. *nōv*), a town of the priests in the tribe of Benjamin just N of the city of Jerusalem. The language of Isaiah 10:32 would indicate that it was within sight of Jerusalem. In the time of King Saul the tabernacle stood here for a time, and David's visit to Ahimelech the priest (I Sam. 21) was the cause or at least the occasion for the complete destruction of the city by Saul (I Sam. 22:19). David, fleeing from Saul, asked for provision for his young men and for a sword, all of which the priest granted; but a mischief-maker, Doeg the Edomite, was a witness to the transaction and reported it to Saul, who in his insane hatred and jealousy of David, caused the priests to be slain and their city to be destroyed.

NOBAH (nō'bà, Heb. *nōvâh, barking*). 1. A man of Manasseh in the days of Moses, who in the conquest of the land of Bashan took the city of Kenath from the Amorites (Num. 32:42).

2. A town in the neighborhood of which Gideon finally defeated the Midianites and took their kings (Judg. 8:11).

NOBAI (See Nebai)

NOBLEMAN, one belonging to a king, *basilikós*, as in John 4:46-53, or one well born, *eugenós*, as in the parable of the pounds (Luke 19:12-27).

NOD (nŏd, Heb. *nôdh, wandering*), a district eastward from Eden to which Cain went in his wandering (Gen. 4:16). (Cf. Ps. 56:8, "my wanderings.")

NODAB (nō'dăb, Heb. *nôdhāv*), a tribe of Arabs, probably Ishmaelites E of the Jordan, early conquered by the two and a half tribes (I Chron. 5:19). Probably a patronymic name from an ancestor "Nodab," "noble."

NOE (See Noah)

NOGAH (nō'gà, Heb. *nōghah, brilliance*), a son of David born in Jerusalem (I Chron. 3:7; 14:6).

NOHAH (nō'hà, Heb. *nôhâh, rest*), the fourth among the ten sons of Benjamin (I Chron. 8:2), but not mentioned in Genesis 46:21.

NON (See Nun)

NOON (See Time)

NOPH (nŏf, Heb. *nōph*), better known as Memphis, a city on the W side of the Nile S of Cairo (Isa. 19:13; Jer. 2:16; 46:19).

NOPHAH (nō'fà, Heb. *nōphâh*), a city of Moab (Num. 21:30), site unknown.

NORTH. The word often occurs merely as a point of the compass, but there are many passages, especially in the prophets, where it refers to a particular country, usually Assyria or Babylonia (Jer. 3:18; 46:6; Ezek. 26:7; Zeph. 2:13). While Nineveh and Babylon were E of Jerusalem, they are usually referred to as "the north" because armies from there could not come across the desert, but had first to go to Northern Syria and then S. It is uncertain what country Ezekiel 38:6 refers to by "the north."

NOSE, NOSTRILS (Heb. *'aph, nehîrayim*). Because the nostrils quiver in anger, the word for nostril is rendered "anger," almost akin to "snorting" in 171 places; and this is used not only of Jacob (Gen. 27:45) but of Moses "the meekest of men" (Exod. 32:19) and even of the Lord (Num. 11:1,10). A tempestuous wind is described poetically as "the blast of thy nostrils" (Exod. 15:8; II Sam. 22:16), referring of course to God. A long nose was counted an element of beauty (S. of Sol. 7:4), and the nose was often decorated with a ring (Ezek. 16:12 ASV, cf. Isa. 3:21). A hook in the nose however was a means of subjection (Isa. 37:29).

NOSE JEWEL (See Dress)

NOVICE (nŏv'ĭs, Gr. *neóphytos, newly-planted*), used only in I Timothy 3:6 concerning the requirements for being a bishop. The Greek term from which we get "neophyte," i.e., "newly planted," refers to a recent convert.

NUMBERS. The Hebrews in ancient times used the common decimal system as a method of counting. There is no evidence that they used figures to denote numbers. Before the Exile they spelled the numbers out in full, as is seen in the present text of the Hebrew Scriptures, in the Siloam inscription, and on the Moabite stone. After the Exile some of the Jews employed such signs as were used among the Egyptians, the Aramaeans, and the Phoenicians — an upright line for 1, two such lines for 2, three for 3, etc., and special signs for 10, 20, 100. At least as far back as the reign of the Maccabean Simon (143-135 B.C.), they numbered the chapters and verses of the Hebrew Bible and expressed dates by employing the consonants of the Hebrew alphabet: *aleph* for 1, *beth* for 2, etc. The letters of the Greek alphabet were used in the same way.

Numbers were used conventionally and symbolically. Certain numbers and their multiples had sacred or symbolic significance: 3,4,7,10,12,40,70. For example, three expressed emphasis, as in "I will overturn, overturn, overturn it" (Ezek. 21:27). From early times seven was a sacred number among the Semites (Gen. 2:2; 4:24; 21:28). Ten was regarded as a complete number. Forty was often used as a round number (Exod. 24:18; I Kings 19:8; Jonah 3:4). Some of the higher numbers also seem sometimes to have been used as round numbers: 100 (Gen. 26:12; Lev. 26:8; II Sam. 24:3, etc.), 10,000 (Lev. 26:8; Deut. 32:30, etc.).

The later rabbis developed the theory that all numbers have secret meanings and all objects their fundamental numbers, and elaborate mathematical rules were devised to carry out these concepts. The system came to be known as gematria (a corruption of geometria). Some Bible students think that an example of this is found in Revelation 13:18, where the number of the beast is 666. It is thought that the context shows that the number was intended to be recognized as a definite person by those who knew how to interpret the book, while outsiders were left in the dark regarding his identity. S.B.

NUMBERS, BOOK OF, the fourth book of the Pentateuch, called *In the Wilderness* by the Jews after its first significant word. The Hebrew title is more meaningful than the English, for the book picks up the story of the wilderness wandering after the arrival at Sinai (Exod. 19), and tells the story of the Bedouin-like travels of Israel through all the 40 years of wandering.

The name *Numbers* comes from the Greek translation which gives a misleading impression of one of the features of the book. Both at the beginning (1:2-46) and near the end (26:2-51) the number of the Israelites is given — a little over 600,000 males above 20 years of age. The procedure sounds familiar to us. We call it a census. But the Biblical censuses were not just that. Israel was not merely interested in vital statistics. This was a count of the fighting force. Indeed, it probably was an actual mustering and organizing of the army. It is for this reason that the women, children, and Levites were not included. The numbering occurs twice because the army was called up twice for battle — first at the abortive attempt to invade the land at Kadesh-Barnea, and second at the end of the 40 years of wandering just before the conquest of Canaan.

Exception has been taken to the large number of Israelites — totaling an estimated two million. Some say the territory could not sustain so many people. This is true if the Israelites traveled as a closely-knit group seeking forage in a limited radius. But if they fanned out with their flocks over a wide area, they could sustain themselves as did the large Nabatean kingdom in the same area in Roman times. Furthermore, God specially and miraculously fed and sustained Israel. The size of the Israelite nation was surely great or Joshua would never have been able to conquer and occupy the land of Palestine as he clearly did. Large and well fortified cities were conquered in the area from Lachish in the S to Hazor 120 miles to the N, as well as the territory in all Trans-Jordan. Six hundred thousand men, not all active, would not have been too large a force to accomplish such a feat. David in later days of prosperity called up an army of 1,300,000 (II Sam. 24:9). David's numbers support the size of Joshua's army. Joshua's action explains the sinfulness of David's act. He was not merely taking a census either. He apparently was starting an unwarranted aggressive war.

The body of Numbers up to 10:11 gives additional legislation and the organization of the host. From 10:11 to 12:16 is recorded the march from Sinai to Kadesh-Barnea. Then comes the debacle at Kadesh recorded in chapters 13 and 14. The three leaders of this occasion, Joshua and Caleb, the believing spies, and Moses the intercessor are forever memorialized as among God's great men. Chapters 15 to 21:11 tell the story of repeated faithlessness on the part of the people. Apparently during much of the 40 years, according to Amos 5:25f and Joshua 5:2ff, the people wandered far away from God and even their national unity may have lapsed temporarily. The 40 years are treated very briefly.

From 21:11 on is given the conquest of Trans-Jordan and the preparations to enter the land. Sihon and Og of the northern territory were conquered in swift moves detailed more extensively in Deuteronomy. Then Numbers tells the very interesting story of Balaam, the hireling prophet who was supernaturally restrained from cursing Israel (22-24). These chapters are now studied with new interest because they appear to show a very early type of Hebrew. Final material includes the summary of the journeys (33), cities of refuge (35) and Joshua's installation (27).   R.L.H.

NUN (nŭn, Heb. *nûn*), a man of Ephraim and the father of Joshua (Exod. 33:11; Neh. 8:17). His descent is given in I Chronicles 7:25-27.

NURSE (See Occupations & Professions)

NUT (See Plants)

NYMPHAS (nĭm'făs, Gr. *nymphás*), member of a church in Laodicea, or Colossae, which met in his house (Col. 4:15). Paul sent him greetings.

O

OAK (See Plants)

OATH (ōth, Heb. *shevû'âh, 'ālâh,* Gr. *nórkos*), an appeal to God to witness the truth of a statement or of the binding character of a promise (Gen. 21:23; 31:53; Gal. 1:20; Heb. 6:16). Two varieties of the oath are found in the OT, a simple one for common use, and a more solemn one for cases of greater solemnity. Oaths played a very important part not only in legal and state affairs, but in the dealings of everyday life. A number of formulas were used in taking an oath, such as "the Lord be between thee and me forever" (I Sam. 20:23) and "as the Lord liveth" (I Sam. 14:39). Certain ceremonies were observed in taking an oath — in ordinary cases the raising of the hand toward heaven (Gen. 14:22; Deut. 32:40), in exceptional cases the putting of the hand under the thigh of him to whom the oath was taken (Gen. 24:2; 47:29). Sometimes one taking an oath slew an animal, divided it into two parts, and passed between the pieces (Gen. 15:8-18). Swearing was done by the life of the person addressed (I Sam. 1:26), by the life of the king (I Sam. 17:55), by one's own head (Matt. 5:34), by the angels, by the temple (Matt. 23:16), by Jerusalem (Matt. 5:35), and by God. It was forbidden to swear by a false god (Josh. 23:7). A virgin could take an oath if her father did not disallow it; and a married woman, if her husband permitted it. By the time of Christ the OT law regarding oaths (Exod. 22:11) was much perverted by the scribes, and our Lord therefore condemned indiscriminate and light taking of oaths, saying that men should be so transparently honest that oaths between persons are unnecessary. The lawfulness of oaths is recognized by the apostles, who called on God to witness to the truth of what they said (II Cor. 11:31; Gal. 1:20).

The Well of the Oath, set up by Abraham and Abimelech (Gen. 21). © MPS

OBADIAH (ō'bà-dī'à, Heb. *'ōvadhyâh, servant of Jehovah*), the name of several OT characters: 1. The governor of Ahab's household (I Kings 18: 3-16) who "feared Jehovah greatly" but who seemed to fear Ahab even more.

2. Head of a household of David's descendants (I Chron. 3:21).

3. A chief man of Issachar in David's time (I Chron. 7:3).

4. One of the six sons of Azel, a Benjamite (I Chron. 8:38 copied in 9:44).

5. A Levite who returned early from captivity (I Chron. 9:16) called "Abda" in Nehemiah 11: 17.

6. One of the martial Gadites who joined David in the wilderness (I Chron. 12:9).

7. Father of Ishmaiah, a prince of Zebulun in the days of David (I Chron. 27:19).

8. One of five princes of Judah whom Jehoshaphat sent out to teach the people of Judah the law of the Lord (II Chron. 17:7).

9. A Levite of the Merarite family, whom Josiah made an overseer of repairing the temple (II Chron. 34:12).

10. A Jew who led back 218 men in Ezra's return from captivity (Ezra 8:9).

11. A priestly covenanter with Nehemiah (Neh. 10:5).

12. A gate-keeper of Jerusalem in Nehemiah's time (Neh. 12:25).

13. The prophet who wrote the book of Obadiah.

OBADIAH, BOOK OF. The subject of the book is the destruction of Edom (vs. 1). From time immemorial Edom and the Edomites were hostile to Israel.

The book, like others of the Minor Prophets, is undated. The principal clue to the date of its writing is in verses 11,14. If "the day that thou stoodest on the other side" (vs. 11) alludes to the events of II Kings 8:20-22, II Chronicles 21:16-18, when the Edomites and others rebelled against King Jehoram early in the ninth century B.C., the book probably would be dated quite early; but if the reference is to Psalm 137:7, II Chronicles 36: 20, Ezekiel 25:13,14, the prophecy would be late; later than 586 B.C. The more likely view is that II Chronicles 28:16-18 is the apposite reference and that the time was late in the eighth century B.C., during the reign of Ahaz of Judah. At that time Edom and the Philistines were associated in warfare against Judah, and the names of the two nations are again coupled in Obadiah 19.

Verses 1-9 pronounce punishment upon Edom. Compare Jeremiah 49:7-22 with Obadiah 1-9. Apparently one of the two prophets made use of the other, or both made use of a common source which is no longer available.

In verses 10-14 Edom is arraigned for its guilt in standing with the enemies of Israel in the time when Judah and Jerusalem were in deep distress. In verses 12-14 the prophet exhorts Edom to quit its evil association with the enemies of Jerusalem. In verses 15,16 "the day of Jehovah" i.e. a time of awful judgment is proclaimed as being "near upon all the nations" and national annihilation is predicted for those peoples who fight against Jehovah — they "shall be as though they had not been." To this point in Obadiah, Jehovah has been addressing Edom in the second person singular, but in the closing paragraph, he speaks of a coming restoration of Israel when Zion shall be holy and God will use Israel as a flame to destroy Esau. The people of the Negeb (the southern part of Judah) are to possess the land of Edom; Israel

will greatly enlarge its borders (vss.19-21). The principal message of Obadiah to the peoples of today would seem to be the proclamation, not only of the danger of fighting against God, but also the peril of fighting His people. A.B.F.

OBAL (ō'băl), an early Arab, son of Joktan (Gen. 10:28), called Ebal in I Chronicles 1:22. Samaritan Pentateuch has "Ebal."

OBED (ō'běd, Heb. *'ōvēdh*, worshiper), the name of five OT men: 1. An early man of Judah, descended through Hezron and Jerahmeel (I Chron. 2:37,38).

2. One of the mighty men of David's army (I Chron. 11:47).

3. A Levitical gate-keeper of the tabernacle in David's time (I Chron. 26:7).

4. The father of one of the captains whom Jehoiada chose to help make Joash king (II Chron. 23:1).

5. If no names are omitted in the Messianic genealogy, the son of Boaz and Ruth and grandfather of David the king (Ruth 4:21,22 copied in I Chron. 2:12, Matt. 1:5, and Luke 3:32).

OBED-EDOM (ō'běd-ē'dŏm, Heb. *'ōvēdh-'ĕdhôm, one who serves Edom*). 1. A man of Gath into whose house David had the ark of God carried after "Perez-uzza" when God struck Uzza dead for touching the ark when the oxen stumbled (II Sam. 6:10-12, I Chron. 13:9-13). Obed-edom and his family revered the ark and God blessed them greatly. He probably is the same Obed-edom as the one in I Chronicles 26:4-8 who had eight sons and 72 early descendants.

2. One of the musical Levites (I Chron. 15: 18-24) who played a harp.

3. A son of Jeduthun who was a door-keeper of the tabernacle (I Chron. 16:38).

4. Perhaps the same as # 3, appointed with his sons over the treasury (I Chron. 26:15).

5. A descendant of # 4 who kept the treasury in Amaziah's time (II Chron. 25:24).

OBEDIENCE (Heb. *shāma'*, Gr. *hypakoé*). Man normally comes under five principal authorities which require obedience: first, as a child, his parents (Col. 3:20); then, in school, his teachers (Prov. 5:12,13); then in industry or business, his employers or masters (I Pet. 2:18); fourthly, the government (Rom. 13:1,2) and lastly and principally, God (Gen. 26:5 etc.). The supreme test of faith in God is obedience (I Sam. 28:18). He who obeys because he loves God, is very wise. Throughout the Bible obedience is linked to faith (Gen. 22:18; Rom. 1:5; I Peter 1:14). Christ Himself obeyed the Father (Phil. 2:8), giving to us the supreme example of obedience. Christians are called "children of obedience" (I Pet. 1:14).

OBEISANCE (ō-bā'săns, Heb. *shâhâh*), the act of bowing low or of prostrating one's self; whether before (1) God (Mic. 6:6), (2) a god (II Kings 5:18), (3) an earthly ruler (Gen. 42:6), or (4) in courtesy toward one's equals (Gen. 23:12). A careful distinction must be made between obeisance in courtesy and that which partakes of or borders on worship. The former is a mark of culture but the latter is a dreadful sin if directed to other than the true God (Exod. 20:4-6).

OBIL (ō'bĭl, *camel driver*), an Ishmaelite in the days of David who was put in charge of the king's camels (I Chron. 27:30).

OBLATION (See Offerings)

OBOTH (ō'bŏth, Heb. *'ōvōth, water-bags*), a place E of Moab, where Israel encamped (Num. 21: 10,11; 33:43).

OCCUPATIONS AND PROFESSIONS.

Apothecary, a compounder of drugs, oils and perfumes. More often the word could well be translated "perfumer." All large oriental towns had their perfumers' street. Their stock included anything fragrant in the form of loose powder, compressed cake, or essences in spirit, oil, or fat, as well as seeds, leaves and bark.

Perfumes were used in connection with the holy oil and incense of the tabernacle (Exod. 30:25,35; 37:29; II Chron. 16:14; Neh. 3:8). The ritual of Baal-worshipers (Isa. 57:9), and the embalming of the dead and rites of burial (Gen. 1:12; 16:14; Lk. 23:56) all used the perfume. The apothecary compounded and sold these sweet spices and anointing oils.

The frequent references in the OT to physicians and apothecaries indicate the high esteem in which the professions were held.

Artificer, a fabricator of any materials, as carpenter, smith, engraver, etc., (Gen. 4:22; Isa. 3:3). Especially workers skilled in metals, carving wood and plating it with gold, setting precious stones, and designing embroideries. From this word comes "artifacts," an archaeological term, meaning anything that was made or modified by human art or workmanship. Solomon procured many men of this class from Hiram, King of Tyre, when building the temple (I Chron. 29:5; II Chron. 34:11).

Author, the composer of a literary production. An authority on a statement or fact. Agur and Lemuel are referred to as having recorded "words" in the form of prophecy and wisdom (Prov. 30:1; 31:1).

Bakers, occupied a special street in Jerusalem (Jer. 27:21). The baking of bread is one of the chief household duties. But in the towns and principal villages, the larger oven of the regular baker is required. The superiority of this bread is implied in the Arabic proverb, "send your bread to the oven of the baker, though he should eat the half of it."

The modern oriental baker does not, as a rule, prepare the dough, but bakes what is sent to him for that purpose. A common sight is the baker's boy carrying on his head a tray of new bread for one house, and on his side a similar tray for another house. The dough is prepared by the house baker and sent to the public baker, who kneads it into flat cakes for his oven.

The oriental oven is a long, low stone vault, like half a railway engine boiler, with a stone pavement down the middle and a long narrow strip at each side for the firewood.

In addition to the home baker and the public baker was the royal baker, who baked for the king (Gen. 40:2).

The Hebrews made use of large stone jars, open at the mouth, about three feet high, with a fire inside for baking bread and cakes. As soon as the sides were sufficiently heated, the thin dough was applied to the outside, the opening at the top being closed. Sometimes wood was used for heating, but more often thorns and occasionally dry dung was used (Ezek. 4:12).

Kinds of ovens: 1. The bowl oven, the simplest form of oven, was used by ancients, and was made of clay, with a movable lid. The bowl was placed inverted upon small stones, and thus heated with dry dung heaped over and around it.

2. The jar oven, heated by grass or stubble, dry twigs or thorns (see above).

3. The pit oven, partly in the ground and partly built up of clay and plastered throughout, narrowing toward the top. The fire was kindled inside the oven.

Above, 1. A contemporary illustration of a royal Egyptian bakery. 2. Simplest form of baking, on a stone on an open fire. 3. Bowl oven. 4. A jar oven. 5. An oven with fire-pit below and baking space above. DV

Bakers delivering bread in Oriental fashion.

Barber. The barber may have originated in connection with the shaving of the head as part of a vow. The instruments of his work were probably, the razor, the basin, the mirror, and perhaps the scissors. He usually plied his trade in the open, on the street.

The word barber occurs but once in the Scriptures (Ezek. 5:1). However, great attention was paid to the hair and beard among the ancients. The barber must have been a well-known tradesman.

Beggar, one who lives from the alms of others. It was his regular business to solicit alms publicly, and even to go from door to door. Beggars are numerous in the East. They are usually "maimed, lame or blind" (Luke 14:13). The commonest and most pathetic form of infirmity is blindness. Some of these blind beggars are led by children and have regular places to station themselves.

The begging is sometimes only a simple statement of poverty, "I am poor," "I want a loaf of bread," or "give me the price of a loaf." But occasionally the expressive gesture of bringing the forefinger across the teeth and holding it up as a proof that there is absolutely no trace of food employed. It is "cleanness of teeth" (Amos 4:6).

Some of the beggars pose as sent of God. "I am your guest! I am God's guest! God will direct you! God will recompense you! God will preserve your children! God will prolong your days!" The beggars are thus the street-preachers of the E. Sometimes one finds entire families who beg for a meager living.

The beggars divide up the shops among them, and at the end of the week, they go around to get their allowance. Beggars are encouraged by a superstitious hope that alms given may atone for things obtained by cheating. Alms-giving has a high place among the religious virtues of the E.

Butler, an officer of considerable responsibility who attended Eastern monarchs. This officer is of very great antiquity, being mentioned in connection with the Egyptians, the Persians, the Assyrians and the Jewish rulers. The butler (also called cupbearer) was required to taste of the foods and wines before serving them, as a pledge that they were not poisoned (Gen. 40:1; Neh. 1:11). The butlers enjoyed the esteem and confidence of their royal masters.

Carpenter, a worker in wood; a builder. Joseph, the legal or foster father of Jesus, was a carpenter (Matt. 13:55); so also was Jesus (Mark 6:3). The work of carpenters is frequently mentioned in the Bible (Gen. 6:14; Exod. 37; Isa. 44:13). David employed Phoenician carpenters in building his palace (II Sam. 5:11; I Chron. 14:1).

The chief work of the carpenter was making roofs, doors, window-shutters, lattice-squares, divan frames for the houses, plows and yokes. Hence, Jesus knew yokes, as well as the various aspects of farm life; and could say "my yoke is easy and my burden is light." Along the coast there was a small industry of boat building.

Some of the tools used by the ancient Egyptians were the adze, saw, square, awl, hammer and gluepot (Jer 10:4; Exod. 21:6). The adze was their favorite implement. In ripping a board with the saw, the carpenter sat on the board and sawed away from himself (Isa. 44:13).

In its broadest sense, carpentry included an artificer in stone and metal, as well as wood.

Chamberlain, an officer employed to look after the personal affairs of a sovereign. Potiphar seems to have had such an officer (Gen. 39:1). This officer was introduced into the court by Solomon, and was sometimes referred to as "steward" (I Kings 4:6; 16:9; 18:3) or "governor."

His duties seem to have been to superintend the palace and attend to royal etiquette. This post later became one of special increasing influence, including the right of introduction to the king. He thus became the chief minister.

Erastus, the "chamberlain" of the city of Corinth, was one of those whose salutations to the Roman Christians were given (Rom. 16:23). The office was apparently that of public treasurer.

Clerk. The clerk or "town clerk" (Acts 19:35) was likely the city recorder. He was probably a magistrate of considerable authority and influence. He may have been mayor or the chief sovereign of the city. The clerk is often mentioned in Ephesian inscriptions.

The clerk may have been literally a temple-keeper, for this term, found on Ephesian coins struck about the time of Paul, originally signified a temple servant whose business it was to sweep out and decorate the temple, and ultimately grew to be an honorary title of towns in Asia Minor which were especially devoted to the service of any divinity and possessed a temple consecrated to that divinity.

Confectioner, a female perfumer or apothecary (I Sam. 8:13). When the orange-trees, violets and roses were in bloom, the women made scented waters which they kept in large, closely-sealed bottles for use in the summer as cooling syrup-drinks. These were presented to guests in tumblers of brass and silver trays. The king's confectionaries would be occupied with the preparation and mixing of such flavoring essences.

Coppersmith, a worker in any kind of metals. It is likely that Alexander was given this title because copper was so common in his day (II Tim. 4:14). The coppersmiths had a particular way of smelting the copper and iron. Their smelters were located so as to face the wind currents, thus using the natural winds to fan their fires sufficiently for smelting. King Solomon not only mined copper in the Arabah (S of the Dead Sea) and had it smelted at Ezion-geber, but enjoyed a thriving trade in this very useful metal (I Kings 7:45).

Counselor, an adviser in any matter, particularly the king's state adviser (II Sam. 15:12; I Chron. 27:33). Usually one of the chief men of

A Jewish carpenter's shop, such as one in which Jesus may have worked. KC © FC

the government (Job 3:14; 12:17). In the NT the name likely refers to a member of the Sanhedrin (Mark 15:43; Luke 23:50).

Doctor of the Law. Gamaliel was such a person (Acts 5:34,40). He kept and handed down the Cabala, or sacred laws as received from Mount Sinai. He was the 35th receiver of the traditions. This term may also have applied to the scribe in his practical administration of the law in the pronouncement of legal decisions.

Diviner, one who obtains or seems to obtain secret knowledge, particularly of the future, and is a pagan counterpart of prophecy. He stands in contrast to the prophet of the Lord, since he was believed to be inspired by demon power, and the Lord's prophet by the Spirit of God. Balaam was a heathen diviner but rose to the status of a bonafide prophet of the Lord, although he seems to have reverted back to paganism (Num. 22-24). Though the diviner is classed with the prophet, this does not mean an endorsement of divination.

Dyer. A Bible land society both wove and dyed its own textiles. The practice of dying textiles was in existence even before the time of Abraham. Dying vats and clay looms that were used as weights have been found in Lachish.

The dyer obtained his dye from various sources. The crimson was obtained from a worm or grub that feeds on the oak or other plants. Indigo was made from the rind of the pomegranate. The purple was made from the murex shell-fish found on the beach at the city of Acre. It was also found along the Phoenician coast N of Acre. Luke tells of Lydia, "a seller of purple, of the city of Thyatira" (Acts 16:14). Excavations have revealed that "a guild of dyers" existed in the vicinity of Thyatira.

Farmer. Farming had its beginning with the first man, Adam. Cain tilled the soil, and Abel was a livestock farmer, perhaps a shepherd. The early farm implements were very crude. The plow was a very crude affair, made of wood and having an iron share, small and shaped like a sword. Asses and oxen were used to pull the light plow, which had only one handle, except in cases where human beings were used in place of oxen.

When Israel entered the land of Canaan, farming took on a new aspect. Every seventh year the farmers allowed the ground to be idle. Whatever grew of itself was left to the poor, the stranger and the beasts of the field. To the Hebrews the terms "grain" and "corn" included almost every object of field culture. The farmers cultivated millet, spelt, various species of beans and peas, pepperwort, cummin, cucumbers, melons, flax and perhaps cotton. Farming was practiced by Cain, Noah, Elisha, David, Uzziah, and Solomon. Farmers were also called husbandmen, tillers of the ground, and laborers, and they were subject to certain laws.

Fisher. The Bible speaks of the fish of the Nile River and of the Mediterranean Sea. The frequent allusions to the art of fishing are in connection with the Sea of Galilee. The Israelites in the wilderness said: "We remember the fish, which we did eat in Egypt" (Num. 11:5). Several methods of fishing were practiced. 1. The casting-net, when the fisherman stood on the bank or waded breast-deep into the water, and skillfully threw the net which he had arranged on his arm into the water in front of him. It fell in the shape of a ring, and as the weights dragged it down, the net took the shape of a dome or cone and enclosed the fish. 2. The dragnet was used in herring and salmon fishing, with floats along the top of the weights to sink the net. It was usually operated from boats. 3. Hooks or angles were occasionally used. Fish were speared on the Mediterranean coast, being attracted to the surface by a moving torch. Night fishing was very common, especially on Galilee. In modern times Jewish fishing fleets operate along the Mediterranean coast and on Galilee. Shoals of fish are sometimes seen on the Sea of Galilee from the shore when the fishermen in the boat may not see them (John 21:4-6).

Fishermen mending their nets at early dawn on the shores of the Sea of Galilee. © MPS

Fullers at work. This is the wool-bleaching industry at Mosul, on the Tigris, in Iraq. © MPS

Fuller, one who washed or bleached clothing (II Kings 18:17; Isa. 7:3; 36:2). This is one of the oldest arts, and at an early period was comparatively perfect. Both men and women engaged in cleaning clothes and other materials. The fuller may have been a sub-division of the dyers. However, it consisted chiefly in cleaning and bleaching garments. The cleansing was done by treading or stamping the garments with the feet or with rods or sticks in containers of water. Alkaline, potash, niter and herbs were employed in the washing and bleaching process.

The fullers discovered a singular art of bleaching cloth white by the aid of alkali, soap, putrid urine, fumes of sulphur and the ashes of certain desert plants. Therefore, the fuller's shop was usually located outside the city where offensive odors could be avoided, the cloth could be trampled clean in a running stream, and the fuller then have room to spread the cloth out for drying. In Jerusalem the "fuller's field" was located near the conduit of the upper pool, which was in all probability in the Kidron Valley between Gihon (the present Virgin's Fountain), and the well En-rogel (Isa. 7:3).

Herdsman, a tender of oxen, sheep, goats and camels. The patriarchs were great herdsmen. The occupation was not inconsistent with state honors. David's herdsmen were among his chief officers of state (Gen. 13:7; 26:20; I Sam. 21:7; Amos 1:1; 7:14). In general, however, the herdsman was seldom the owner of the flock or herd which he tended.

The rich owners of herds placed them in charge of herdsmen, whose duty it was to protect them from wild beasts, to keep them from straying and to lead them to suitable pasture. The herdsmen usually carried a sharpened or metal-pointed goad, and a small bag or scrip for provisions. Their dress consisted of a long cloak. Their food was very simple, and they usually lived on what they could find. Their wages were given them in products of the herd.

Hunter. The hunter or fowler was one of the earliest occupations. It was originally a means of support, but later became a recreation. It was held in very high repute and was engaged in by all classes, but more frequently with royalty (Gen. 10:9; 27:3,5; I Sam. 26:20; Job 38:39; Prov. 6:5).

Three principal methods of hunting are mentioned in the Bible: 1. Shooting with the bow and arrows (Exod. 27:3). This method has been superseded by the fowling-piece. 2. Snaring by the spring net and cage, especially for birds, such as quail, partridge, and duck (Amos 3:5; Jer. 5:27). 3. Pits were covered with a net and brushwood for deer, foxes, wolves, bears, lions, etc. (Ps. 35:7; Isa. 24:18; 42:22).

Judge. The head of the house was considered the judge over his own household, even with life and death (Gen. 35:24). With the enlargement of the human family this power quite naturally passed to the heads of tribes and clans. After Israel came into the wilderness beyond Sinai, Moses found the responsibility of handling all the judicial matters too great. Upon the advice of his father-in-law, Jethro, he chose "able men, such as feared God, men of truth, hating covetousness" to handle these matters. There were to be judges over thousands and judges over hundreds and judges over fifties (Exod. 18:19-26). The more difficult cases were referred to Moses, and he turned such cases over to a higher court, with its seat at the place of sanctuary, and it was handled by priests and judges, the high priest being the supreme judge.

After coming into Canaan, judges sat at the gates of the cities (Deut. 16:18).

Lawyer, one who is conversant with the law. There were court lawyers and the synagogue lawyers (Matt. 22:35; Luke 7:30; 10:25; 11:45,46, 52; 14:3; Titus 3:13). The scribe functioned in the capacity of a lawyer in the pronouncement of legal decisions. (See Doctor of the Law.)

Magician, one who practiced superstitious ceremonies to hurt or to benefit mankind. The Hebrews were forbidden to consult magicians (Gen. 41:8; Exod. 7:11,22; Dan. 1:20; 2:2; 5:11; Acts 13:6, 8). Magic is of two kinds — natural or scientific and supernatural or spiritual. The first attributes its power to a deep, practical acquaintance with the power of nature. The second attributes its power to an acquaintance with celestial or infernal agencies.

There are many accounts of the use of magical art in the Scriptures. Before Israel left Egypt the magicians were called by Pharaoh to duplicate the works of God in converting the rod of Aaron into

Herdsmen tending their flocks on the Shepherds Fields near Bethlehem. © MPS

A judge being greeted in the market place. © SPF

a serpent. They were sometimes classified with the "wise men." In the interpretation of dreams and visions the magicians and soothsayers were called. The Chaldeans were particularly famous as magicians.

Mason, a worker in stone. Many of the most wonderful antiquities of the East were due to the work of the mason. Certain villages were famous for their masons. The farmers were usually skilful in building low terrace walls of undressed stone for the fields and vineyards. But buildings required a master mason.

The mason was acquainted with the proper kind of foundation. He knew how to lay the cornerstone. He knew how to select and lay the stones in the wall. His equipment consisted of the plumbline, the measuring reed, the leveling line, the hammer with the toothed edge for shaping stones, and a small basket for carrying off earth.

Musician. Since music was a very prominent art in Biblical times and played such an important part in the life of Israel, and their religious exercises and festivities, there was necessity for those who were apt in playing instruments, and in singing hymns and psalms. Hebrew music was primarily vocal, yet many of the Psalms have signs indicating that they were to be accompanied by musical instruments. The "chief musician" occurs in the titles of 54 of the Psalms. Asaph and his brothers were apparently the first to hold this position, and the office was probably hereditary in the family. Among the instruments used by the Hebrews were the cymbal, harp, organ, pipe, psaltery, sackbut and trumpets.

Nurse, one who looks after, tutors or guides another, as in a period of inexperience or sickness. In ancient times the nurse was an honorable person (II Sam. 4:4; II Kings 11:2). Most patriarchal families had a nurse or nurses. Rebekah's nurse went with her to Canaan, and was buried with great mourning (Gen. 24:59; 35:8). Foster fathers or mothers were sometimes referred to as nurses (Ruth 4:16; Isa. 49:23).

Physician, one who understands and practices medicine in the art of healing. The priests and prophets were expected to have some knowledge of medicine. In the days of Moses there were midwives and regular physicians who attended the Israelites (Exod. 21:19). They brought some knowledge of medicine with them from Egypt, whose physicians were celebrated in all antiquity. In the early stages of medical practice, attention was more frequently confined to surgical aid and external applications. Even down to a comparatively late period, outward maladies appear to have been the chief subjects of medical treatment among the Hebrews, although they were not entirely without remedies for internal and even mental disorders.

The medicines prescribed were salves, particular balms, plaster and poultices, oil-baths, mineral baths, etc. In Egypt the physicians aided in carrying out the elaborate preparations connected with embalming the body.

Plowman, one who used or held the plow. Husbandmen and plowmen were used synonymously in the Scriptures. The plowman was a farmer in general. The plow now used by Arabs in Palestine is lightly built, with the least possible skill or expense, and consists of two poles, which cross each other near the ground; the pole nearer the oxen is fastened to the yoke, while the other serves, the one end as the handle, the other as the plowshare. It is drawn by oxen, camels, cows or heifers. The operator of this instrument is a plowman.

Porter. The Biblical porter was a gate-keeper and not a burden-bearer (II Sam. 18:26; I Chron. 9:22). The Levites who had charge of the various entrances to the temple were called porters (I Chron. 9:17; 15:18; II Chron. 23:19). In some instances the same original word is rendered "doorkeeper" (I Chron. 15:23,24). A porter was stationed at the city gates, and among shepherds was responsible for keeping the doors of the sheepfold.

In David's time the porters of the temple, who were also guards, numbered 4,000 (I Chron. 23:5).

Potter. Although regarded as an inferior trade, it supplied a universal need, and potters lived in settlements in the lower city of Jerusalem (Jer. 18:2-4), in the neighborhood of Hebron and Beit Jibrin, where clay was plentiful and the royal potteries probably were situated (I Chron. 4:23).

There has been great demand for potters in the Orient. This is because copper vessels are so expensive, leather bottles are not suitable for some purposes and earthen vessels are so easily broken.

The maker of earthenware was one of the first manufacturers. The potter found the right kind of clay, prepared it by removing stones and other rough substances, shaped and made it into the vessel desired, baked and marketed it. If the vessel became marred in the making, it was "made over again another vessel." When one became broken after baking it was discarded, and thrown into "the potter's field."

The Hebrew potter, sitting at his work, turned the clay, which had first been kneaded with the feet, into all kinds of vessels on his wheels, which were generally of wood.

Preacher, one who heralds or proclaims, usually by delivering a discourse upon a text of Scripture. This method of presenting messages from God to man is as old as the human family. Noah is referred to as "a preacher of righteousness" (II Pet. 2:5). The prophets were given the responsibility of delivering messages of truth in song, in accusation and in rebuke, pleading and exhortation, prophecy and promise. The temple, the synagogue and the church has been designed chiefly as a place where the profession of preaching has been practiced, by man becoming the human channel through which God sent His messages.

Since the completion of the Bible, preaching has come to mean the giving out of the Word of God whether it be in prophesying, teaching, or preaching.

Priest, one who offers sacrifices, or presides over things relating to God. Previous to the Mosaic ritual, the offering of sacrifices pertained to private individuals. The father was the priest of his own family, and officiated at the domestic altar; being succeeded at death by his firstborn son. Possibly a more general priesthood existed, such as that exercised by Melchizedek.

When the Mosaic dispensation was introduced, a particular order of men was appointed to that special service (Exod. 28) with a very solemn and imposing ceremony. From that time, the offering of sacrifices was restricted, in the main, to those who were duly invested with the priestly office (II Chron. 26:18). All the posterity of Aaron were priests, except those who were disqualified by the special requirements laid down in the Mosaic law.

After the Captivity, those who could not prove their descent from Aaron lost their privileges as priests. The corruption of the priesthood, by making the office a means of amassing wealth and gaining political power, hastened the ruin of the Jewish nation. Christ is described in the NT as the firstborn king, the anointed, a priest after the order of Melchizedek (Heb. 7:8).

Prophet(-ess), a person who acts as the organ of divine communication with men, especially with regard to the future. The prophet differs from the priest in representing the divine side of this mediation, while the priest rather acts from the human side. The term "prophet" is an Anglicized Greek word, and literally denotes one who speaks for another or in another's name. The Hebrew term rendered "prophet" is thought by some to signify one elevated or excited, so as to pour forth animated oracles, or, according to others, a person imbued with the Spirit of God. Strictly speaking, a prophet is one to whom the knowledge of secret things is revealed, whether past (John 4:19), present (II Kings 5:26), or to come (Luke 1:76-79).

The wives of the prophets and also women who had the gift of prophecy were known as prophetesses. Among the prophetesses mentioned in the Bible are Miriam, Deborah, Huldah, Noadiah, and Anna.

Publican, an under-collector of Roman revenue. Of these there appear to have been two classes: 1. The "chief of the publicans" of whom Zacchaeus is an example. 2. The ordinary publican, the lowest class of the servants engaged in the collecting of the revenue, and of whom we have an instance in Levi, who was afterwards the Apostle Matthew.

The publicans were hated as the instruments by which the subjection of the Jews to the Roman emperor was perpetuated, and the paying of tribute was looked upon as a virtual acknowledgment of his sovereignty. They were noted for their imposition, rapine and extortion, to which they were tempted to oppress the people with illegal taxes that they might more quickly enrich themselves. The publicans of the NT were regarded as traitors and apostates, defiled by their frequent intercourse with the heathen, and willing tools of the oppressor. Hence, they were classed with sinners, harlots and the heathen (Matt. 9:11; 21:31; 18:17).

Rabbi, a title given by the Jews to the teachers of their law. It was also applied to Christ by His disciples and others (Matt. 23:7,8; John 1:38,49; 3:2,26; 6:25). The term Rabbi literally means "master" (John 1:38; 20:16). The use of the term cannot be verified before the time of Christ.

Recorder, an officer of high rank in the Jewish state, exercising the functions, not simply of an annalist, but of chancellor or president of the privy council (Isa. 36:3,22). He was not only the grand custodian of the public records, but kept the responsible registry of the current transactions of government (II Sam. 8:16; 20:24; II Kings 18:18).

In David's court, the recorder appears among the high officers of his household (II Sam. 8:16; 20:24). In Solomon's court, the recorder is associated with the three secretaries, and is mentioned last, probably as being their president (I Kings 4:3).

Robber, one who engages in theft and plunder. Ishmael, the Bedouin, became a "wild man" and a robber of trade (Gen. 16:12). Among the nomad tribes of the East it has been considered in the highest degree creditable.

The Mosaic Law strictly forbade robbery, as other wrongs against others and it was denounced in the Proverbs and by the prophets. The Prophet Hosea compares the apostate priests to "troops of robbers that wait for men." Robbery is frequently referred to in the Bible, and there are robbers in every age, but never is it commended.

Ruler, one who rules or governs, or who assists in carrying on a government. An honor often bestowed by kings on their subjects. Daniel was made ruler over the whole province of Babylon by Nebuchadnezzar for interpreting a dream; and again made third ruler of the kingdom after interpreting the writing upon the wall at the time of Belshazzar's great feast (Dan. 2:10,38; 5:7,16,29).

There was the ruler of the synagogue, the ruler of the treasures, or the chief treasurer, and the

The publicans were tax collectors and customs gatherers for the Romans. KC © FC

high priest who was considered the "ruler of the house of God" (I Chron. 9:11).

Sailor, one whose occupation is navigation, or the operation of ships. Particularly one who manipulates a ship with sails. Those that trade by the sea (Rev. 18:17).

Saleswoman, a woman who sells merchandise. Lydia, the "seller of purple" from Thyatira was a convert of the Apostle Paul at Philippi (Acts 16: 14,15,40).

Schoolmaster, one who exercised careful supervision over scholars, forming their manners, etc. Such person was considered stern and severe. The Mosaic Law is likened unto a "schoolmaster to bring us to Christ" (Gal. 3:24) because it awakens a consciousness of sin, and prepares the soul for an acceptance of Christ.

Scribe, persons employed to handle correspondence and to keep accounts. They were given a high place alongside the high priest. Hezekiah set up a body of men whose work it was to transcribe old records, or to put in writing what had been handed down orally (Prov. 25:1). The scribe came to be a student and interpreter of the law.

In the time of Christ, the scribes had attained great influence and power as a class, and were regarded with great respect. They were given the best places at feasts and the chief seats in the synagogues (Matt. 23:5; Luke 14:7).

Seer, one who is considered able to foresee things or events. A prophet (I Sam. 9:9) — "Beforetime in Israel, when a man went to enquire of God, thus he spake, Come and let us go to the *seer:* for he that is now called a prophet was beforetime called a *seer.*" Samuel identified himself as a seer (I Sam. 10:19). He is referred to as "the seer" who ordained David and Samuel (I Chron. 9:22).

Senators, the "elders of Israel" who formed one of the three classes represented in the Sanhedrin. The scribes and priests formed the other two classes (Acts 5:21). They were considered chief men or magistrates (Ps. 105:22). In other places this same Hebrew word is translated *elder.*

Sergeant, Roman lictors or officers who attended the chief magistrates when they appeared in public, and who inflicted the punishment that had been pronounced (Acts 16:35,38). They were literally "rod-holders."

Servant, sometimes applied to any one under the authority of another, and not necessarily a domestic or slave. In some passages of Scripture, the word properly means "young man" or "minister." It is applied to the relation of men to others occupying high position, as Eliezer, whose position in the household of Abraham compared with that of the prime minister (Gen. 15:2; 24:2).

Servitor, one who ministers to, or serves, but not in a menial capacity (II Kings 4:43). May be "one in waiting."

Sheepmaster, one who is both a shepherd and the owner of the sheep (II Kings 3:4). In some areas, the sheepmaster is one who owns a superior kind of sheep.

Sheep-Shearer, one who shears the sheep. When the wool is long and ready to "harvest," a sheep-shearing time is announced, and it is a great time of rejoicing (Gen. 38:12; II Sam. 13:23,24). This is a festival corresponding to our "harvest-home," usually marked by revelry and merry-making (Gen. 31:19).

Shepherds watching their flocks by night, on the Shepherds Fields near Bethlehem. © MPS

Shepherd, one employed in tending, feeding and guarding the sheep. Abel, Rachel and David were all keepers of sheep. The shepherd's equipment consisted of a scrip made of goat's skin with legs tied, and in which was placed food and other articles. He usually carried a sling to protect himself and the sheep against wild animals. He carried a rod (stick) about 30 inches long with a knob on one end. He had a staff that looked like our walking cane, usually with a crook on one end. He carried a flute made of reeds to entertain himself and to content his sheep. His cloak was used as bedding at night. He led his sheep, and knew them all by name, and they knew his voice. He saw that they were all safe in the fold at night.

Silversmith, a worker in silver (Acts 19:24). The most famous example of a silversmith was Demetrius, whose business was interfered with by the evangelistic work of the Apostle Paul.

Singer, a trained or professional vocalist. The Hebrew music was primarily vocal. Barzillai mentioned "singing men and singing women" (II Sam. 19:35). Solomon was a composer of songs, "A thousand and five" (I Kings 4:32). David's trained choir numbered 288.

Slave, a person held in bondage to another, having no freedom of action, his person and service being wholly under the control of his master or owner. Jewish slaves were of two classes — Hebrew and non-Hebrew — and both were protected by law. Hebrew slaves became such through poverty or debt, through theft and inability to repay, or in case of females, because they had been sold by their parents as maid-servants. Their slavery was the mildest form of bond-service.

At the time of Christ, slavery was established throughout the world and interwoven even by the wisest men as a normal state of society. But Christianity, by teaching the common creation and redemption of men and enjoining the law of kindness and love to all, first moderated the evils of slavery, then encouraged emancipation, and the ultimate extinction of the whole institution.

Smith, a workman in stone, wood or metal. The first smith mentioned in Scripture is Tubal-cain. So requisite was the trade of the smith in ancient warfare that conquerors removed them from a vanquished nation to more certainly disable it (Isa. 44:12; 54:16; Jer. 24:1).

Soldier, one engaged in military service, and receiving pay for his services. In the earlier times, every man above the age of 20 was a soldier (Num. 1:3); and each tribe formed a regiment, with its own banner and its own leader (Num. 2:2; 10: 14). Up until the time of David, the army consisted entirely of infantry (I Sam. 4:10; 15:4), the use of horses having been restrained by divine command (Deut. 17:16).

The Jews had experienced the great advantage to be obtained by chariots, both in their encounters with the Canaanites and at a later period with the Syrians, and hence much importance was eventually attached to them by the Hebrews.

Sorcerer, one who practiced the arts of the magicians by which he pretended to foretell events with the supposed assistance of evil spirits (Isa. 47:9,12; Acts 8:9,11). In its broader sense, a sorcerer is one who practices in the whole field of divinatory occultism.

Spinner, a person who used the distaff and the spindle in the making of thread from wool, flax or cotton. From the whirling spindle we get the word *spin.* From this also comes the "spinning wheel" (Prov. 31:19; Matt. 6:28).

Steward, one to whose care is committed the management of the household (Gen. 43:19; Luke 16:1). The term is also applied to ministers (I Cor. 4:1) and to Christians (I Pet. 4:10). The meaning of the word is different in Genesis 15:2 where it is rendered "he that shall be possessor" in the ASV.

Tanner, one who is skilled in dressing and preserving hides, or skins of animals. Among the ancient Jews, ceremonial uncleanness was attached to the occupation of the tanner, and hence he was obliged to pursue his calling outside the town. The tanneries of Joppa are now on the shore S of the city. Several circumstances confirm the tradition of the present "house of Simon" there (Acts 9:43; 10:6,32).

Taskmaster, one whose duty it is to assign tasks. An overseer or bond master (Exod. 1:11; 3:7; 5:6, 10,13,14). Pharaoh appointed taskmasters over the Hebrews to make their work hard and wearisome. He hoped by such oppression to break down their physical strength, and thereby to reduce their numerical growth, and also to crush their hope of ever gaining their liberty.

Tax Collector, Taxgatherer, one who collected or gathered a certain tax or revenue for the government. The publicans of the Roman Empire were engaged in this flourishing traffic. The farming out of import and export duties, excise on various commodities, and of the government tithe on produce, is universally practiced. A commercial company guarantees to the government a fixed sum for a certain tax or monopoly, and then directly or by further sub-letting proceeds to fix such a scale or charges as will ensure a profit by the transaction.

It has led to much oppression and injustice, and has fostered a feeling of hostility towards anything connected with the government. Zacchaeus was a tax collector (Luke 19:23).

Teacher, one who imparts instruction, and communicates knowledge of religious truth or other matters. "Doctors" or teachers are mentioned among divine gifts in Ephesians 4:11, where the Apostle seems to reckon them among the extraordinary donations of God and uses no mark of distinction or separation between "apostles" with which he begins, and "doctors" with which he ends. The latter doubtlessly refers to well-informed persons, to whom inquiring Christian converts might have recourse for removing their doubts and difficulties concerning Christian observances, the sacraments, and other rituals, and for receiving from

Tanners processing goatskins at a tannery at Hebron. These skins will become "bottles" for carrying water. © MPS

Scripture the demonstration that "this is the very Christ" and that the things relating to the Messiah were accomplished in Jesus.

Tent-maker, one skilled in making tents from hair or wool, or skins. The early patriarchs were largely tent-dwellers, and therefore had to have some knowledge in tent-making. In the NT times it was the custom to teach every Jewish boy some trade. Jesus was a carpenter, and Paul was a tent-maker. Paul practiced this trade in company with Aquila at Corinth (Acts 18:1-3).

Tetrarch, a ruler of the fourth part of a kingdom or province. This title is applied in the Bible to any petty ruler in the Roman empire. His authority was similar to that of a king, and that title was often given to him (Matt. 14:9).

Tiller, the greatest occupation of the Hebrews; tilling the soil, or cultivating the soil. This word is used synonymously with *husbandman.* A useful and honorable occupation (Gen. 9:20; Isa. 28:24-28). Christ used the word figuratively (John 15: 1) in parables and elsewhere to denote God's care for His people. Cain was a "tiller of the soil" (Gen. 4:2).

Times, Observer of, a phrase referring to those persons who had a superstitious regard for days that were supposed to be lucky or unlucky, as decided by astrology. Such people were condemned (Deut. 18:9-14). Such persons were supposed to be able to foretell political or physical changes by the motion of clouds.

Town Clerk, a keeper of the public records, who presided over public gatherings, and performed the duties of the chief magistrate when he was away. An official of great importance (Acts 19:35).

Treasurer, important officer in Oriental courts, probably having charge of the receipts and disbursements of the public treasury (Ezra 1:8; 7:21; Isa. 22:15). This title was given to the officer of state of great importance, and was considered superior to all others and was sometimes filled by the heir to the throne (II Chron. 26:21).

Watchman, one whose duty was to stand in the tower on the walls or at the gates of the city. They also patrolled the streets, and besides protecting the city and its inhabitants from violence, were required to call out the hours of the night (II Sam. 18:24-27; S. of Sol. 5:7; Isa. 21:11,12).

Weaver, one who was skilled in the making of cloth or rugs from spun thread or string. The art of weaving was probably learned from the Egyptians by the Israelites; and they seem to have made progress in it from their own resources, even before they entered Palestine. Weaving was for the most part in the hands of women, although there were also weavers among men. The stuffs woven were linen, flax, and wool (Exod. 35:35; Lev. 13: 48; I Chron. 11:23; Isa. 38:12).

Wizard, a "knowing or wise one." Witch was the name given to the woman and wizard the name given to the man who practiced witchcraft. There was a pretended communication with demons and spirits of the dead by means of which future events were revealed, diseases cured, evil spirits driven away, etc. It was severely denounced (Exod. 22: 18; Lev. 20:6; II Kings 9:22; Gal. 5:20).

Writer. The knowledge of writing was possessed by the Hebrews at a very early period. The materials on which they wrote were of various kinds. Tables of stone, metal, plaster, wax-covered frames, skins, paper made from bulrushes and fine parchment were used. The pens were also different to correspond with the writing material (Judg. 5: 14; Ps. 45:1; Ezek. 9:2). The prophets were often told to write, by the Lord, and may be considered writers (Rev. 1:11; 21:5).

Bibliography: Albert Bailey, *Daily Life in Bible Times;* George Barton, *Archaeology and the Bible;* John Calkin, *Historical Geography of Bible Lands;* James Freeman, *Handbook of Bible Manners and Customs;* Cunningham Geikie, *The Holy Land and the Bible,* Vol. 2; A. C. Haddad, *Palestine Speaks;* G. Robinson Lees, *Village Life in Palestine;* Lefferts A. Loetscher (Editor), *Twentieth Century Encyclopedia,* Vols. 1 & 2; George Mackie, *Bible Manners and Customs;* G. Frederick Owen, *Archaeology and the Bible;* George Adam Smith, *The Historical Geography of the Holy Land;* W. M. Thomson, *The Land and the Book,* Vol. 1.

H.P.H.

OCHRAN, OCRAN (ŏk'răn, Heb. *'ōkhrān*), father of Pagiel, prince of the tribe of Asher, appointed to assist in the first census of Israel (Num. 1:13; 7:72).

ODED (ō'dĕd, Heb. *'ôdhēdh, he has restored,* or *prophet*). 1. The father of Azariah the prophet.

2. A prophet in Samaria in the days of Ahaz, king of Judah (II Chron. 28:9-15). Pekah, king of the northern tribes, had taken captive 200,000 Jews, after slaying 120,000 valiant men of Judah, and as the captives and the spoil were being brought into Samaria Oded rebuked them and persuaded them to feed and clothe the captives and to return them to Judah. Oded strongly emphasized the wrath of God which had brought ruin to the Jews, and would ruin Israel also.

ODOR (ō'dẽr, Heb. *besem,* Gr. *osmé*), that which affects the sense of smell. In ASV the word refers to a pleasant or sweet odor, while an unpleasant one is called "ill savour" or "stench." The Levitical offerings which did not deal with sin were called offerings of sweet savor; and the incense also (Mal. 1:11) with its perfumed odor was acceptable to the Lord. The prayers of the saints (figuratively) are offerings of a sweet savor to the Lord (Rev. 5:8). Hypocrisy yields a stench (Amos 5:21).

OFFENSE (ŏ-fĕnś, Heb. *'āsham, hātā',* Gr. *skándalon*). The word is used in a variety of ways in Scripture, as it is in English: injury, hurt, damage,

A native weaver at work on his loom at Kifl, in Iraq. © MPS

occasion of sin, a stumbling block, an infraction of law, sin, transgression, state of being offended. In the NT it is often used in the sense of stumbling-block (Matt. 5:30; 11:6; 18:6; I Cor. 8:13, etc.). Throughout the NT there is warning by Christ and the apostles against doing anything that would turn anyone away from the faith.

OFFERINGS. The need for purification from sin or the desire of the worshiper to enter into fellowship with God underlay the prescription regarding the various kinds of offerings. They were derived from both the animal and vegetable kingdoms, and while they had certain elements in common with sacrificial rites in other nations, they were unique in many respects.

Sin offering, first mentioned at the consecration of Aaron (Exod. 29:10 seq.) was a special expiatory sacrifice. A bullock was killed before the bronze altar and on its projections (KJV *horns*) part of the sacrificial blood was smeared. The remainder was dashed against the base of the altar and the fat burned ceremonially. The flesh and skin were taken outside the tabernacle and burned separately. The law of the sin offering (Lev. 4:1-35; 6:24-30, etc.) provided for acts of unconscious transgression, mistakes or other inadvertencies. While cognizance was taken of differing circumstances and classes of offenders, no atonement could be made for deliberate rebellion against the covenant and its provisions (Num. 15: 30). The worshiper normally laid his hand on the head of the sin offering, symbolically designating it as his substitute in the sacrificial ritual. Poor people were permitted to offer two turtledoves or a small amount of fine flour. The flesh which remained after portions had been burned belonged to the priest, and was eaten in the sanctuary precincts (Lev. 5:13). A special sin offering for the nation took place annually on the Day of Atonement, in which a bullock and a goat were sacrificed and their blood ceremonially smeared on the mercy-seat. Another goat was driven into the wilderness after symbolic transfer of communal sin (Lev. 16:1-28).

Trespass offering (Lev. 5:14-6:7), or guilt offering, signified expiation and restitution, and availed for inadvert offenses, false swearing and improper dealings with a neighbor. By itself the offering made atonement towards God, but an additional one-fifth was required as a fine to compensate a neighbor adequately. The sacrificial ritual involved the slaughter of a ram, and was similar to that of the sin offering, although the imposition of hands and the sprinkling of blood in the holy place were not mentioned. Special offerings were required for the cleansing of a leper (Lev. 14:12-20) and a defiled Nazarite (Num. 6:12). All guilt offerings belonged to the priests, and were most sacred in character.

Peace offering symbolized right spiritual relations with God, and was among the earliest of the sacrificial offerings. The worshiper, if an ordinary Israelite, could bring a bullock, a lamb or a goat, male or female, and the ritual followed that of the sin-offering (Lev. 3:1-17). If the worshiper was a priest the fatty portions of the animal were removed and burned on the altar of God, while the blood was sprinkled at the base of the sacrificial altar. The ritual for a goat followed that laid down for a bullock.

Meal offering, or meat offering (KJV), was instituted when Aaron and his sons were consecrated (Exod. 29:41). It was forbidden to be offered on the altar of incense (Exod. 30:9), but was used when the tabernacle was completed (Exod. 40:29), and invariably accompanied the morning and evening burnt offerings. The ordinary Israelite was required to bring a mixture of fine flour, oil and frankincense, prepared in a variety of ways (Lev. 2:1-16), but without the addition of leaven or honey. All cereal offerings were to be seasoned with salt. The ritual for a priestly offerer required him to remove a token handful and burn it together with oil and frankincense as a memorial on the altar. What was left was most holy, and became priestly property.

Drink offerings, or libations, were common in the patriarchal period (Gen. 28:18; 35:14), and accompanied many of the sacrifices (Exod. 29: 40f). They could not be poured upon the golden altar of incense (Exod. 30:9), and were required as an accompaniment of all freewill and votive offerings (Num. 15:5 seq.), the continual burnt sacrifice (Num. 28:7f). sabbaths (Num. 28:9f) and other established feasts (Num. 28:14-31; 29: 6-39). The reference in Deuteronomy 32:38 indicates that drink offerings were common features of heathen cultic rituals. Oil and wine, used separately or as a mixture, constituted the normal libation.

Wave offering, heave offering. One part of the ritual associated with the peace offering involved the *wave* and *heave* offerings. Both were apparently initiated at the consecration of the Aaronic priesthood (Exod. 29:24-28). According to Leviticus 7:30-34, the worshiper was required to provide it from his own peace offering. When Aaron was consecrated, Moses placed the breast on the high priest's hands and waved the offering before the Lord. The portion was holy, and was a priestly prerequisite (Lev. 10:14f). The waving ritual applied also to the leper's male lamb (Lev. 14:12), the lamb of the guilt offering (Lev. 14:24), the sheaf of the firstfruits (Lev. 23:10-15), and the Nazarite's offering (Num. 6:19f). The Hebrew term implied a brandishing movement with the hands, symbolizing the presentation of the sacrificial portion to the deity and its return with approbation to God's priestly representative. Jewish interpreters state that in the wave ritual the priest

laid the portion on the hands of the offerer, placed his own beneath and then instituted a movement back and forth, up and down. If this description is correct, priest and worshiper were making the sign of the cross.

The heave offering comprised the right thigh, the choicest part of the animal usually reserved for the guest of honor at a feast (cf. I Sam. 9:24). One cake of the peace offering was also treated as a heave offering (Lev. 7:14). The sacred portions were to be eaten by the priests alone (Lev. 10: 14f). In Numbers 18:24 the Levites were promised a tithe of the Israelite heave offerings, and they in turn submitted a tithe of this to the priests (Num. 18:26-32). Deuteronomy 12:6,11 required all heave offerings to be eaten at the central sanctuary. Like the wave offering it was essentially sacred and belonged to the officiating priest. The Hebrew term comes from a root meaning "to be high," "to be exalted," which indicates a portion removed from a larger quantity rather than something "hurled" or "thrown." It was a token offering separated wholly to the service of God.

All offerings were related directly to covenantal religion, the basic principle of which was obedience. Each sacrifice was a reminder of human depravity and of divine provision for the helpless sinner. Without obedience and faith, however, the offerings were valueless.   R.K.H.

OFFICER, a holder of an official position. The word is used in a variety of senses: (1) one who has been set up over others (I Kings 4:7, etc.); (2) a eunuch, such as Oriental kings set in charge of their women and also of much of the routine business of the court (Gen. 37:36, etc.); (3) a writer or clerk (Exod. 5:6; Deut. 20:9, etc.); (4) a police officer or bailiff (Luke 12:58); (5) originally an assistant or under-ruler (Matt. 5:25).

OFFSCOURING (Heb. *sehî, refuse,* Gr. *perípsema, dirt*), a contemptuous word for sweepings, scrapings, filth, dung, etc. "Thou hast made us an offscouring and refuse" (Lam. 3:45); "the filth of the world, the offscouring of all things" (I Cor. 4:13).

OG (ŏg, Heb. *'ôgh*), Amorite king of Bashan (Deut. 31:4; Josh. 2:10; 13:21; I Kings 4:19). He was a man of gigantic stature, a physical characteristic of which there is strong evidence among the Canaanitish tribes. He held sway over 60 separate communities. Og's defeat before the invading Hebrews (Deut. 3:1-13) became proverbial, for it dispelled a legend of invincibility based upon the daunting appearance of some of the Canaanitish hoplites (Deut. 1:28). The tradition was long-lived (Ps. 135:11; 136:20). Og's territory was assigned in the partition of Palestine to Reuben, Gad, and the half-tribe Manasseh (Num. 32:33). The "bedstead of iron" preserved as a museum piece at Rabbah among the Amorites (Deut. 3:11) was possibly a sarcophagus cut from black basaltic rock. Iron was not common in Palestine at the time, the Iron Age having been introduced by the Philistines. To prepare a sarcophagus was common aristocratic practice.

OHAD (ō'hăd, Heb. *'ōhadh,* meaning unknown), the third son of Simeon (Gen. 46:10) and head of a clan in that tribe (Exod. 6:15).

OHEL (ō'hĕl, Heb. *ōhel, tent*), a son of Zerubbabel, a descendant of King Jehoiakim (I Chron. 3: 20).

OHOLAH, OHOLIBAH (ō-hō'là, ō-hŏl'ĭ-bà, Heb. *'ohŏlâh, 'ohŏlîvâh*), symbolic names for Samaria and for Jerusalem, pictured as harlots wandering off from God (Ezek. 23).

At left, Arab peasants harvesting the olive crop. At right, crushing olives with a large stone roller, preparatory to extracting the olive oil. © MPS

OIL (Heb. *shemen*, Gr. *élaion*), in the Bible almost always olive oil, perhaps the only exception being Esther 2:12, where it is oil of myrrh. The olives were sometimes beaten (Lev. 24:2), sometimes trodden (Mic. 6:15), but generally crushed in a mill designed for that purpose. The upper stone, instead of rubbing against the lower as in a flour mill, rolled upon it and so pressed out the oil. The wheel usually was turned by ox-power or donkey-power, the animal being blindfolded. Olive oil was not only a prime article of food, the bread being dipped in it, but it was used for cooking, for anointing, and for lighting. Oil was one of the principal ingredients in making soap (Jer. 2:22).

Anointing with oil was for three diverse purposes: wounded animals were anointed for the soothing and curative effects of the oil (Ps. 23:5); people anointed themselves with oil for its cosmetic value (Ps. 104:15); but most notably men were anointed as an official inauguration into high office. Priests (Exod. 28:41; 29:7), prophets, and kings (I Kings 19:15,16) were anointed and were called "messiahs" i.e., "anointed ones" (Lev. 4: 3,5,16; I Sam. 2:10; I Chron. 16:22). Anointing the head of a guest with oil was a mark of high courtesy (Luke 7:46). Oil is used also as a symbol for the Holy Spirit. Our Lord's Messiahship was not bestowed with the use of literal oil, but was evidenced when the Holy Spirit came down upon Him in the form of a dove at His baptism (Luke 3:22, etc.). Oil was also the prime source of light in dwellings and in the tabernacle. It was contained in little clay vessels so arranged that a wick lying in the oil was supported at one end, where the oil burned and furnished just about "one candle power" of light. A.B.F.

OIL TREE (See Plants)

OINTMENTS AND PERFUMES. The use of perfume in the form of ointment or impregnated oil was a Middle Eastern practice long before it spread to the Mediterranean world. In all probability it was originally used for ceremonial purposes, first religious then secular, and became a personal habit with the growing sophistication of society, and the need for deodorants in hot lands (Esth. 2:12; Prov. 7:17; 27:9; Isa. 57:9). So universal was the practice that its intermission was an accepted sign of mourning (Deut. 28:40; Ruth 3:3; II Sam. 14:2; Dan. 10:3; Amos 6:6; Mic. 6:15; etc.). The skin, as well as the hair, was thus perfumed and anointed (Ps. 104:15), and, especially on high occasions, the scented unguent was used with profusion (Ps. 133:2). Its use was also a courtesy to an honored guest (Luke 7:46). Among the directions listed for the service of the tabernacle are two prescribed "recipes," possibly Egyptian in form (Exod. 30:23-25; 34-36). It is to be noted that one recipe prescribes 750 ounces of solids in six quarts of oil. It is possible that the oil was pressed off when the scent of the aromatic gums was absorbed. The liquid would then be used as anointing oil, while the solid provided an incense. The process of manufacture is not clear, and the account takes for granted that "the art of the apothecary" (more correctly "perfumer") is commonly familiar to the reader (Exod. 30:25,35; Neh. 3:8; Eccl. 10:1). It is, however, clear enough that the compound was based on the aromatic gum of Arabian plants (indigenous especially in Arabia Felix in the south of the peninsula) and that the medium or base was some form of fat or oil (probably calves' fat and olive oil). In its later trade form the perfume was sometimes packed in alabaster boxes or flasks (Luke 7:37). Such ointment was heavily scented (John 12:3) and costly (John 12:5). E.M.B.

OLD GATE, at the NW corner of the city of Jerusalem in Nehemiah's time, near the present site of the Holy Sepulchre (Neh. 3:6). See also Nehemiah 12:39 for the celebration.

OLD TESTAMENT. The OT is composed of 39 books — 5 of law, 12 of history, 5 of poetry, 5 of major prophets, and 12 of minor prophets. The classification of our present Hebrew Bibles is different — 5 of law, 8 of prophets, and 11 of miscellaneous writings. These 24 in various combinations contain all of our 39 books. Neither of these classifications exhibits the fact that much of the Pentateuch is history, nor do they show the chronological relations of the books. A logical survey of the OT literature may approach the subject chronologically.

Before Abraham. The first 11 chapters of Genesis give a brief outline of major events from the creation to the origin of the Jewish people in Abraham. Genesis 1 is a majestic revelation of

God creating all the material and organic universe climaxing in man. This picture is not given in the categories of modern science and yet is in general agreement with much modern scientific theory. A prominent theory of today declares that all matter had a beginning in the distant but measurable past with a vast nuclear explosion, from which the universes have been differentiated. Creation of the universe or of man is not dated in Genesis. The creation of plants, animals and man is spread over six "days" or periods of indefinite length (called one "day" in 2:4). Genesis 2 and 3 detail the special creation of man and God's dealing with him in Eden. Man on probation fell into sin and the race was involved in sin and misery. God, however, promised a Redeemer (3:15) and instituted sacrifice as a type thereof.

The Flood. As men multiplied, sin increased and God sent a flood to destroy all mankind (chap. 6-8). Evidence is accumulating that about 8,000 B.C. some catastrophe associated with increased sedimentation on ocean floors overtook the earth with the last glaciation perhaps, and with the change of polar climates, which resulted in the destruction and freezing of great numbers of Siberian mammoths and other animals. Many widely separated cultures, including the old Babylonian, preserve legends of a great flood.

Early Genealogies. Pre-flood and post-flood genealogies are schematic and rather obviously incomplete, as are other Biblical genealogies. If Genesis 11:10-26 has no gaps, Shem would have outlived Abraham, which does not seem to be the Biblical picture. The dates of Noah and of Adam given in the margins of some Bibles assume the completeness of these lists and therefore are not valid.

Abraham and the Patriarchs. As sin again increased, God chose Abraham to found a new nation which God would protect, isolate to a degree, and through whom He would reveal Himself at last as Saviour. Abraham left polytheistic Mesopotamia and lived in Canaan where God instructed and blessed him, his son Isaac, and grandson Jacob. From Jacob came the 12 sons who fathered the tribes of Israel. The midpoint of Genesis, chap. 25, records the death of Abraham who lived in the Middle Bronze Age, about 1900 B.C. His characteristic was faith. To the sacrifices God now added infant circumcision as a sign of His covenant. Although circumcision was practiced elsewhere in antiquity, infant circumcision seems to have been unique. It was to be a sign both of the material and spiritual aspects of the covenant.

Bondage and Exodus (Exod. 1-19). Through providential circumstances of famine and through Joseph's exaltation, God took Jacob's family to Egypt for a period of growth. At first it was sheltered under Joseph's viziership. Later Israel was enslaved. God regarded the bitter bondage and through Moses delivered Israel by an outstretched hand. Ever since, Israel has remembered the deliverance from Pharaoh's army when the Lord brought them through the Red Sea (actually, one of the lakes through which the Suez Canal now passes). God led Israel to Mt. Sinai where the company of slaves became a nation under Moses, the great lawgiver, and where the Ten Commandments and other legislation were received.

The date of the Exodus has been much discussed. The Biblical data (I Kings 6:1; Judg. 11: 26; Acts 13:20) appears to favor a date of 1440

or 1400 (LXX) and a conquest of Palestine in the Amarna Age. Some of the archaeological evidence favors this, but some is interpreted to favor an invasion at about 1230 B.C. There was indeed a general desolation of Palestinean cities at that time, but was it by Joshua, or due to other conflicts in the troubled period at the beginning of the Iron Age? The cities of Palestine also changed hands in the Amarna Age — about 1360 B.C. — and this date of Joshua's conquest is preferable.

Israel's Law (Exod. 20 — Num. 10). At Sinai Israel encamped for one year. Here God revealed Himself and His commandments in majestic miracle. The Ten Comandments of Exodus 20 and Deuteronomy 5 summarize the eternal principles of man's duty to God and to his fellow men. The last 20 chapters of Exodus, except for the apostasy of the golden calf, which took place while Moses was on the mount, concern the building of the tabernacle. Leviticus mainly concerns the ceremonial worship of Israel — the offerings, feasts, and cleansings. The section Leviticus 18-22, however, also includes regulations for civil conduct of the nation, as does Exodus 21-23. Leviticus 11-15 includes laws of cleanliness which have a typical aspect. Their main purpose, however, seems to have been to protect Israel in her food, to protect from vermin by enjoining strict cleanliness, and to protect from contagion by instituting certain quarantines.

The Wilderness (Numbers 11-36). Numbers adds some laws to Leviticus, but mainly tells the story of the abortive attempt to invade Canaan from the S and the experiences during the 40 years of wilderness wanderings. The first numbering is not a mere census, but a mustering of the ranks for the invasion. In Numbers 14, Israel at Kadesh Barnea hears the reports of the spies and in little faith, fails to conquer. Condemned to wander, they live as nomads at the edge of the arable land in Sinai until the generation of wrath dies. Several of the rebellions of these years are given in Numbers. At the end of the book a new mustering of the people provides 600,000 fighting men for Joshua's army. These numbers seem large, but in those days they allowed for no exemptions from the army for physical or other reasons. The numbers compare favorably with David's manpower of 1,300,000 and Saul's army of 330,000 and the figures in Judges 20:2,15 of 426,000.

Deuteronomy. Moses before his death conquered trans-Jordan and allowed two and a half tribes to settle there. In Deuteronomy, Moses retells the story of this campaign and recounts much of the history and regulations of Exodus, Leviticus, and Numbers.

Job. The date of Job is uncertain. As it seems to speak of a time before the Levitical legislation, and names descendants of Uz, Buz, and others of Abraham's kin, it may be placed in the general time of Moses and in the area E of Palestine. It poses the problem of the suffering of the righteous and answers that the sovereign God has His own purposes for which He is not answerable to men. It suggests a further answer that apparent injustices in the treatment of men are to be adjusted in a future life.

The Conquest. Joshua's invasion of Canaan is detailed in the first half of his book, Chap. 1-12. In a whirlwind campaign, after the miracles of the crossing of Jordan and the fall of Jericho, he gained possession of the middle of the country. At Aijalon, he conquered the army of the southern confederacy and, thanks to the extended day of the battle, demolished the enemy before it took refuge in its cities. The deserted cities were then easily taken. Shortly, he turned N to Hazor and its confederates and won a signal victory, burning it to the ground. But Israel did not at once effectively occupy the area. The Canaanites reestablished themselves in many cities. Key fortresses like Bethshan, Megiddo, and Jerusalem never were subdued. The land was allocated to the tribes in the last half of the book of Joshua, but the period of the judges witnessed a varying battle with the Israelites restricted mainly to the central mountain section.

The Judges and Ruth. For some 350 years the Israelites lived disorganized and to an extent disunited. Frequently falling into apostasy, they were punished by God. Then a leader arose for military deliverance and often for spiritual reviving as well. Sketches of six of these twelve judgeships are given. The rest are barely named. The beautiful story of Ruth, the Moabite convert, belongs in this time.

The Early Monarchy. The last judge was Samuel. In his days Philistine expansion became a great threat to Israel. The sanctuary at Shiloh was destroyed, as excavations also attest, at about 1050. The nation was laid low. Yet under the leadership of four great men, Israel in 100 years attained its peak of greatness. Samuel, the first of these men, was a prophet of power. His preaching, prayers, and miracles led to an evangelical revival that was the basis for much of later successes. He was followed by Saul who was capable, but not good. Condemned in the records for his disobedience, he nevertheless seems to have made a real military contribution to Israel's unity. His army numbered 330,000 men. He gained important victories in the S and E and had some limited successes against the Philistines. His strength was sapped by disobedience to God and insane jealousy of David. He made a pitiable spectacle at the house of the witch of Endor before his final failure, in which he dragged down his fine son Jonathan and all Israel with him to defeat.

The Golden Age. David's history as king begins in II Samuel, which parallels I Chronicles after the first nine chapters of genealogies in the latter book. God had schooled David the hard way. Highly emotional, and consecrated to God as a child, he had gone through deep waters. Military lessons had come in repeated dangers as he was exiled by Saul. Faith was begotten and tested in adversity. At last, in God's time, He used this background to make David Israel's greatest conqueror, and best-loved poet, the founder of the royal house and re-establisher of Jehovah's worship. Family troubles resulting from the grievous sin with Bathsheba marred his later days, but the greatness of the man was shown in the depth of his repentance. He was a man after God's own heart.

In David's day, men would probably have honored him mostly for his military successes, his power and wealth, but actually, his greatest blessing to mankind has doubtless been his work in the establishing of psalmody. David composed at least half of the Psalms and arranged for the temple choirs and for Israel's liturgy. I Chronicles 15, 16, and 25 tell something of this work. Amos 6:5 mentions his lasting fame as an inventor of musical instruments. David's psalms of praise have lifted up the hearts of millions in godly worship. His psalms of trust in the midst of trouble have for centuries comforted them in sorrow and in despair. Psalm 23 is perhaps the best-loved of the

"He leadeth me," the Twenty-third Psalm. The Psalms of David are lasting glories of Israel's golden age. © MPS

OT. In the hour of death and in times of deliverance alike, it has expressed the faith of untold multitudes of God's people. Associated with David in song were the prophets Asaph, Heman, Jeduthun and others.

Solomon inherited David's vast kingdom which reached from the Euphrates in Syria to the border of Egypt and from the desert to the sea. To these large possessions Solomon added the natural resources of the copper mines S of the Dead Sea. He built a famous foundry at Ezion Geber, using the force of the prevailing winds to increase the temperature of his fires. For the first time man had harnessed the forces of nature in industrial processes. The products of his industry he exported in lucrative trade that drenched Jerusalem in opulence. His building program was extensive and is illustrated by many excavations, especially at Megiddo. It is best remembered in his construction of the temple, described in I Kings and II Chronicles. This remarkable building was so engineered that the stones were cut at a distance and the sound of a hammer was not heard on the spot. It was double the dimensions of the wilderness tabernacle and more lavishly adorned. Its two rooms repeated the tabernacle plan with the inner shrine, a suitable type of the holiness of God, unapproachable except through atoning blood. In the outer room the priests maintained the light of the seven-branched candelabra, symbolic of the Holy Spirit; the shewbread, typical of communion of man with God; and the altar of incense, representing the prayers of saints. The building was about 30 ft. high and wide, and 90 ft. long. A porch in front was also 30 ft. high (according to some texts) and the building was flanked on each side with three stories of rooms for priests' quarters and storage. In the front court was the great altar where Israel declared its faith that there is remission of sin through the blood of a substitute. Nearer the temple was the large and ornate laver or "sea" for the cleansing of sanctification. Near the end of his reign Solomon and his kingdom decayed. Solomon's many wives were probably not due to lust, but to his extensive political alliances. They proved his undoing, however. He had married these foreign wives (*outlandish women,* Neh. 13:26) and joined them to some extent in their heathen worship. For this compromise he was rejected.

Divided Monarchy to Ahab. Solomon's sins bore bitter fruit. Rehoboam attempted to maintain the old glory without returning to the old sources of power. God punished by allowing division. Jeroboam I took 10 tribes and established the Northern Kingdom about 920 B.C. Ahijah promised him God's blessing if he would do God's will, but for political reasons he at once broke with the worship of Jehovah at Jerusalem. He set up golden calves at Dan and Bethel in the N and S of his realm, instituted a new priesthood and counterfeit feasts. He thus sealed his doom. Following kings did not depart from Jeroboam's sins. In the next 200 years of its existence the Northern Kingdom had nine dynasties, many revolutions, and sank deeply into idolatry. The Southern Kingdom, Judah, had its troubles, but many of its kings like Asa, Jehoshaphat, Hezekiah, and Josiah were great and good men.

The N fell most deeply into the worship of the Baals of Phoenicia in the reign of Ahab. He was faced with the threat of the Assyrian empire expanding to the W. His policy was to form a western coalition. Thus he married Jezebel, daughter of the king of Tyre. He united with Jehoshaphat of Judah, marrying his daughter to Jehoshaphat's son. Politically, he was successful and his coalition at the battle of Qarqar in 854 stopped the Assyrians. The Assyrian records tells us that Ahab was their principal opponent.

Religiously, Ahab was a failure. The Bible, being more interested in character than in conquest, shows the unvarnished sins of Ahab and his queen Jezebel. At this time the great prophets Elijah and Elisha ministered in the N. Their deeds are graphically told in I Kings 17 to II Kings 13. Only a passing reference is made to them in Chronicles which is a book more interested in Judah. Elijah, the fearless prophet who stood alone on Mt. Carmel was one of two men in all history taken to heaven without death. Encouraged by Elisha, Jehu revolted, exterminated the dynasty of Ahab, slaughtered the devotees of Baal, and even killed Ahaziah of Jerusalem who was in Samaria at the time.

The Kingdoms to Hezekiah. For the chronology of the kingdoms, a reliable guide is E.R. Thiele, *Mysterious Numbers of the Hebrew Kings* (Chicago: Univ. of Chicago Press, 1951). The dynasty of Jehu began about 840 B.C. and lasted a century, its chief king being Jeroboam II, 793 to 753. The kings of Judah included some good men, but from about 740 to 722 both kingdoms were evil and felt the scourge of the great Assyrian monarchs, Tiglath-pileser, Shalmaneser, Sargon, and Sennacherib. This was the time of Isaiah and the first six Minor Prophets. Their messages in the N went unheeded and Samaria was destroyed in 722. In Judah there was a revival under Hezekiah and God wonderfully delivered him.

Isaiah and his Contemporaries. Hosea, Amos, and Micah prophesied especially to Israel, Obadiah and Joel to the Southern Kingdom. Jonah, the disobedient prophet, finally ministered in Nineveh. His experiences — miraculous, of course — in the fish's belly may well have affected his skin and compelled attention from the Ninevites. At least, the repentance of the Ninevites may well have delayed their invasion of Israel for a generation. It did not have lasting results in the Assyrian Empire. Amos and Micah give a forthright denunciation of the sins of the court and of the rich men of Israel. At the same time, Amos and Hosea, especially, denounce the idolatry of Bethel and of Samaria. Against the background of rebuke, these prophets announce Israel's and Judah's hope — the coming of the child from David's city, Bethlehem, and the re-establishing of the fallen tabernacle of David. To Isaiah, the evangelical prophet, it was given to condemn Ahaz for his idolatry, to encourage Hezekiah in his reforms, and to see beyond his day the threat of Babylon, the liberation of the exiles by Cyrus, and the coming of the Messiah in future suffering and glory. We think instinctively of the prediction of the virgin birth of Christ in Isaiah 7:14, of the atonement in chap. 53, and of the portrayal of the new Jerusalem in chap. 60.

Judah's Fall. The reforms of Hezekiah were engulfed in the long and wicked reign of his son Manasseh. Further decline followed in Amon's two years. Then in 640 the good king Josiah came to the throne. In his 13th year, Jeremiah began his ministry, and in five years more Josiah in a real revival invited all Judah and the remnant of Israel to a great passover. But, as reading of Jeremiah shows, the mass of the people were not changed. Josiah's successors reverted to type.

In 612 B.C. Babylon conquered Nineveh and the Assyrian government fled west. Egypt assisted Assyria, attempting to keep the old balance of power. On Egypt's first march N against Babylon, Josiah attempted to prevent Pharaoh Necho's passage at Megiddo and was killed. His son Jehoahaz succeeded him, but when Necho returned southward in three months, he took Jehoahaz to Egypt as a hostage and set his brother Jehoiakim on the throne. In 605 B.C. Nebuchadnezzar in his first year conquered the Assyrian and Egyptian forces at Carchemish on the Euphrates and proceeded S to Judah. He received Jehoiakim's submission and carried Daniel and others into captivity. In 597 Jehoiakim died, perhaps by assassination, and his son Jehoiachin took the throne, revolting against Babylon. Nebuchadnezzar came and on March 15, 597 (see tablets recently published by D. J. Wiseman) *Chronicles of Chaldaean Kings,* London: British Museum, 1956, p. 33) destroyed Jerusalem and took Ezekiel and others captive. He put a third son of Josiah, Zedekiah, on the throne. Zedekiah continued the wicked policies of the others. In 586 B.C. he too rebelled and Nebuchadnezzar returned in a final thrust, devastating Jerusalem and the cities of Judah. Palestine never fully recovered.

Nahum, Habakkuk, and Zephaniah were early contemporaries of Jeremiah. Nahum predicted the downfall of Nineveh. Habakkuk is famous for contrasting the wicked Babylonian invader with the just man who lives by faith.

Jeremiah first had a ministry to his people, rebuking them for sin and idolatry. The Assyrian and Babylonian gods had filtered into Judah until their idols were as numerous as the streets in Jerusalem. When some Jews had gone to Babylon, Jeremiah counseled the later kings to submit. Resistance was futile and would make it hard for those Jews already in exile. God would care for

The Mount of Olives, viewed from the east wall of Jerusalem, looking across the Kidron Valley. In the foreground is the Garden of Gethsemane. © MPS

Israel in captivity and in 70 years would bring them back (Jer. 25:11,12).

The Exile. For 70 years, from about 605 B.C. to about 538 B.C. the Jews were slaves in Babylon. Some Jews were left in Judah, and Jeremiah at first ministered to them. Many Jews had fled to Egypt and finally Jeremiah was taken to Egypt by some of these men. In Babylon God blessed the Jews and kept them in the faith through the witness of Ezekiel, Daniel and others.

Ezekiel prophesied to his people, being still greatly concerned with Jerusalem before its final fall. Like Jeremiah, he used many object lessons in his preaching. Finally (Ezek. 33) came the word that the city had fallen. Thereafter Ezekiel emphasized more the coming of the Davidic King Messiah. His final chapters picture in schematic form the re-establishment of the temple, a prophecy held by many to apply to millennial times. Daniel was a towering figure of those days. Beloved of God and vouchsafed many remarkable visions of the future times, he maintained his faith while an important figure at court. His prophecies accurately depict the future kingdoms of Medo-Persia, Greece, and Rome and tell both of Christ's first coming and His return. Christ's own designation for Himself, "Son of man," likely comes from this book. The book has been heavily attacked by criticism, but there is no good reason to deny the authorship by Daniel.

Post-Exilic Times. When Cyrus the Persian conquered Babylon, his policy was to allow captive peoples to go home. Thus he befriended the Jews. Ezra and Nehemiah tell about these returns. Haggai, Zechariah, and Malachi prophesied in this period. Zerubbabel led back the first contingent of about 50,000 men shortly after Cyrus gave them permission. His work is detailed in Ezra 1 to 6. He laid the foundation of the temple at once, but did not finish it till 516 under the prophesying of Haggai and Zechariah. A second contingent returned in 456 under Ezra, as is related in Ezra 7 to 10. Nehemiah returned with various royal pledges in 444 and these two together did much work in restoring Jerusalem. Nehemiah organized the work and carried through the rebuilding of the wall. Ezra, a ready scribe in the Law of Moses, instructed the people in the faith. Malachi, the final book of the OT, was written around 400 B.C. It reveals the problems of the day caused by insincerity among some of the priests themselves. But it also, like so many of the other prophets, pointed forward to Messianic times. The OT closes with the annunciation of the rise of a new and greater prophet in the spirit and power of Elijah who would precede the Messiah of Israel. R.L.H.

OLIVE (See Plants)

OLIVES, MOUNT OF (called Olivet in two KJV contexts: II Sam. 15:30; Acts 1:12).

1. Geographical. The feature is a flattened, rounded ridge with four identifiable summits, named from the olive groves which anciently covered it. It is of cretaceous limestone formation, something over a mile in length, and forms the highest level of the range of hills to the E of Jerusalem (Ezek. 11:23; Zech. 14:4), rising 250 feet higher than the Temple Mount, and to 2600 feet above sea level. Hence the supreme tactical significance of the Mount of Olives, demonstrated in the Roman siege of Jerusalem under Titus in A.D. 70. The Romans seem to have named the northern extension of the ridge "the Lookout," or Mount Scopus, for this very reason. It gave "a plain view of the great temple," according to Josephus (B.J. 5:2:2). The legions had a large camp on the Mount itself, which, as Josephus describes it in the same context, "lies over against the city on the E side, and is parted from it by a deep valley interposed between them." The valley is the so-called Valley of Jehoshaphat, through which flows the Kidron stream, encompassing the city in a slight curve to the E, before turning SE to flow down the long valley to the Dead Sea.

Near the foot of the Mount of Olives, on the western slope above the Kidron is the likely site of the Garden of Gethsemane. In NT times the whole area seems to have been a place of resort for those who sought relief from the heat of the crowded city streets. Dean Stanley called it the "park" of Jerusalem. In much earlier times it must have been heavily wooded, for when the Feast of the Tabernacles was restored in 445 B.C., Nehemiah commanded the people to "go forth into the mount and fetch olive branches, and pine branches, and myrtle branches, and branches of thick trees to make booths" (8:15). The palm fronds of Palm Sunday were also gathered there. Four summits are traditionally distinguished. Scopus has already been mentioned. R. A. S. Macalister (HDB p. 668) considers it erroneously named, and not the vantage-point to which Josephus refers. Second, there is the 'Viri Galilaei,' the Latin invocation of Acts 1:11 ("Ye men of Galilee"), and the reputed site of the Ascension. To the S, above the village of Silwan (old Siloam) is the so-called Mount of Offence. This vantage-point is separated from the rest of the mount by a deep cleft. It faces W along the line of Jerusalem's second valley, the Valley of the Sons of Hinnom or Gehenna. The eminence derives its name from the tradition that Solomon here built his altars to Chemosh, "the abomination of Moab," and to Moloch, "the abomination of the children of Ammon" (I Kings 11:7). The "offence" of this blatant paganism was purged by Josiah four and a half centuries later (II Kings 23:13). The Josian context adds Ashtoreth and Milcom to the "abominations" on the site.

The Hill of Offence, above the town of Siloam, viewed from across the Valley of Hinnom. © MPS

2. Historical. Historical associations have found incidental reference above, where their significance is inseparable from topography. The following points should be added. The ridge, besides being a tactical vantage point in war, was a peace time highway into Jerusalem. It was the route of David's flight from Absalom in the time of the palace rebellion (II Sam. 15:30; 16:1,13), and, significantly, was the route of Christ's approach for the triumphal entry on Palm Sunday, for it was there that the acclaiming multitude met Him. Hence, too, the prominence of the Mount in Josephus' account of the "Egyptian false prophet" and his 30,000 dupes (B.J. 2:13:5). "These he led round from the wilderness," the account runs, "to the mount which is called the Mount of Olives, and was ready to break into Jerusalem by force from that place." Here, it would appear, Felix met the rebels with his legionary force, and broke the revolt. The remaining OT reference to the Mount of Olives is the scene of the theophany of Zechariah 14:4, an obscure apocalyptic portion which awaits a clear explanation.

Historically the Mount of Olives finds its chief interest in NT times, where it is a locality intimately connected with the Jerusalem ministry of Christ. It is important here to distinguish authentic history from the thick accretions of legend and tradition. Christ's first sight of the city was from the summit of the Mount of Olives (Luke 19:41), and His visits to the home of Mary, Martha, and Lazarus in Bethany, must have taken Him frequently that way (Luke 21:37). The barren fig-tree of His striking object lesson on fruitless profession was probably on the slopes (Matt. 21:19). The Mount was also the scene of His apocalyptic utterance, inspired no doubt by the prospect of doomed Jerusalem from the mountainside (Matt. 24, 25). Gethsemane has already been mentioned as a locality somewhere on the Mount of Olives. The rest is wavering ecclesiastical tradition. Macalister remarks (HDB loc. cit.) that "the places pointed out have by no means remained unaltered through the Christian centuries, as becomes evident from a study of the writings of the pilgrims." He lists among the spurious sites, the tomb of the Virgin, the grotto of the Agony, one or both of the sites of the Garden, admitted though it is that it was somewhere on the Mount, the "footprint of Christ" in the chapel of the Ascension, the tomb of Huldah, the impossible site for Christ's lament over Jerusalem, the place where He taught the Lord's Prayer, and where the Apostles' creed was composed. This does not exhaust the list of legends. It has been the fate of Jerusalem to suffer thus from the pious, but not too scrupulous imagination of men. More authentic are a few archaeological remains, some Jewish and Christian tombs, and an interesting catacomb known as "the Tombs of the Prophets."   E.M.B.

OLYMPAS (ō-lĭm'păs, Gr. Olympás), a Christian in Rome to whom Paul sent greetings (Rom. 16:15).

OMAR (ō'màr, Heb. 'ômār), a grandson of Esau through his oldest son Eliphaz (Gen. 36:11,15).

OMEGA (ō-mē'gà), literally, big "O," last letter of the Greek alphabet, long o. In three contexts (Rev. 1:8; 21:6; 22:13) it is employed as a symbol of inclusiveness: ". . . Alpha and Omega, the beginning and the end, the first and the last."

OMER (See Weights and Measures)

OMNIPOTENCE (ŏm-nĭp'ō-tĕns), the attribute of God which describes His ability to do whatever He wills. God's will is limited by His nature, and He therefore cannot do anything contrary to His nature as God, such as to ignore sin, to sin, or to do something absurd or self-contradictory. God is not controlled by His power, but has complete control over it; otherwise He would not be a free being. To a certain extent, He has voluntarily limited Himself by the free will of His rational creatures. Although the word "omnipotence" is not found in the Bible, the Scriptures clearly teach the omnipotence of God (Job 42:2; Jer. 32:17; Matt. 19:26; Luke 1:37; Rev. 19:6).

OMNIPRESENCE (ŏm'nĭ-prĕz'ĕns), the attribute of God by virtue of which He fills the universe in all its parts and is present everywhere at once. Not a part, but the whole of God is present in every place. The Bible teaches the omnipresence of God (Ps. 139:7-12; Jer. 23:23,24; Acts 17:27, 28). This is true of all three members of the Trinity. They are so closely related that where one is the others can be said to be (John 14:9-11).

OMNISCIENCE (ŏm-nĭsh'ĕns), the attribute by which God perfectly and eternally knows all things which can be known, past, present, and future. God knows how best to attain to His desired ends. God's omniscience is clearly taught in Scripture (Prov. 15:11; Ps. 147:5; Isa. 46:10).

OMRI (ŏm'rē, Heb. *'omrî*). 1. Sixth king of Israel whose reign may be tentatively dated from 886 to 874 B.C. Omri, an able if unscrupulous soldier, and founder of a dynasty, is the first Hebrew monarch to be mentioned in non-Biblical records, and the fact may be some measure of his contemporary importance. It was not until 847 B.C. that Mesha included Omri's name in the inscription of the Moabite Stone, but it is a fact that Omri subdued Moab. It is of more significance that the Assyrian records after Omri's day frequently refer to northern Palestine as "the land of Humri" (the Assyrians spelled the name with an initial aspirate).

The brief but vivid account of Omri's somewhat sinister reign, and his military *coup d'état*, is told in I Kings 16:15-28. Omri was commander-in-chief under Elah, son of Baasha. When Elah was murdered by Zimri, Omri was proclaimed king by the army in the field, a pattern of events which was to become grimly familiar in the imperial history of Rome. The army was engaged, at the time, in siege of the stronghold of Gibbethon, a Levite town (Josh. 21:23) in the tribal territory of Dan (Josh. 19:44), which the Philistines appear to have held for a considerable period (I Kings 15:27; 16:15). Omri immediately raised the siege, marched on the royal capital of Tirzah, which does not appear to have been vigorously defended against him. Zimri committed suicide by burning the palace over his head. There was some opposition to the dominance of the military, for four years of civil war ensued, with half the populace supporting Tibni, son of Ginath, as king. Omri prevailed, and after a six-year reign at Tirzah, transferred the capital to Samaria, an eminently sensible move from the point of view of military security. Here Omri reigned for at least another six years. Samaria was named after Shemer, from whom Omri bought the hill-site (I Kings 16:24).

Omri is dismissed by the Hebrew historian as an evil influence (I Kings 16:25,26), and indeed, his marriage of Ahab, his son, to Jezebel, princess of Tyre, to cement, no doubt, a trade alliance, was fraught with most disastrous consequences, continuation, though it was, of Solomon's and David's Tyrian policy. The calf-worship of Jeroboam (I Kings 12:32) was continued at Bethel throughout

The ruins of Omri's Palace in Samaria. © MPS

the reign, and 140 years after his death, Micah is found denouncing "the statutes of Omri" (6:16). The palace of Omri has been excavated at Samaria, a series of open courts with rooms ranged round them. Omri died opportunely, one year before the first tentative thrust of the Assyrians towards the Mediterranean and Palestine. It was in 874 B.C. that Ashur-nazir-pal marched to "the Great Sea of the land of Amurru," and received tribute from the peoples of the coast. The Assyrian action is the preface to much misery.

2. A Benjamite, family of Becher (I Chron. 7:8).

3. A man of Judah, family of Perez (I Chron. 9:4).

4. A prince of the tribe of Issachar in David's reign (I Chron. 27:18).

ON (ŏn, Heb. *'ôn*). 1. A Delta city of Egypt, called by the Greeks Heliopolis (City of the Sun) and so rendered in the Septuagint (Gen. 41:45,50; 46:20). In Ezekiel 30:17 the name has been changed to "Aven" by misvocalization. "Aven" means "idolatry." It is called Bethshemesh in Jeremiah 43:13, a word of similar import. On is an Egyptian word signifying "light" or "sun," so the Greek and Hebrew names are fair translations. "Cleopatra's Needle" of Thames Embankment fame was originally one of the obelisks before the temple of the Sun at On, erected by Thothmes II (1503-1449 B.C.). On was founded at a very early date and was an important city long before the unification of Egypt. Herodotus' description of Egypt in his Second Book gives On (or Heliopolis) great attention. It was a nodal point of communication and a terminus of numerous caravan routes. In consequence it was the major center of commerce in northern Egypt. The priest of On, whose daughter Asenath became Joseph's wife, was thus a person of considerable importance. The worship of the Sun-god which was centered there had peculiar features which suggest Syrian influence. Ra was identified with Baal by Semites, and with Apollo by the Greeks. There must therefore have been a cosmopolitan element in the temple cult to match the atmosphere of a center of international trade. It is perhaps significant that On is named as the place of sojourn of the Holy Family after the flight into Egypt. Strabo the geographer describes the site

The Obelisk at Heliopolis (On), marking the site of the Temple of the Sun-god at On. © MPS

as almost deserted in early Roman times. His account was written just before the Christian era. It is still a ruin, the site of the famous temple being marked by one conspicuous obelisk, a monument set up by Sesostris I about 2000 B.C.

2. A Reubenite chief who took part in the rebellion of Korah (Num. 16:1). E.M.B.

ONAM (ō'năm, Heb. *'ônām, strong*). 1. Fifth son of Shobal, son of Seir the Horite (Gen. 36:23).

2. Great-great-grandson of Judah (I Chron. 2: 26,28).

ONAN (ō'năn, Heb. *'ônān, strong*), second son of Judah by a Canaanite wife, daughter of Shua. He refused to consummate a levirate marriage with Tamar, widow of his elder brother Er, who had been wicked, and so Jehovah slew him too, leaving Tamar twice a widow (Gen. 38:4-10).

ONESIMUS (ō-něs'ĭ-mŭs, Gr. *Onésimos, profitable*), probably a common nickname for a slave. Paul puns on the word in Philemon 11 and again in vs. 20. A plain reading of the letters to Philemon and the Colossian church leads to the conclusion that Onesimus was a slave of Philemon of Colossae who robbed his master, and made his way to Rome, the frequent goal of such fugitives, the "common cesspool of the world," as the aristocratic historian Sallust called the city (Cat. 37:5). Some Ephesian or Colossian in Rome, perhaps Aristarchus (Acts 27:2; Philem. 24; Col. 4:10-14), or Epaphras (Col. 1:7; 4:12,13; Philem. 23) seems to have recognized the man and brought him to Paul in his captivity. Onesimus became a Christian and was persuaded to return to his master. From the incident came the exquisite letter of Paul to Philemon, which demonstrates so vividly the social solvent which Christianity had brought into the world. It would appear that Onesimus left Rome in company with Tychicus, carrying the letter to Philemon, and also the Pauline communications to the Ephesian and Colossian churches.

Nothing more is known. The tradition that Onesimus became the martyr-bishop of Berea is of doubtful authenticity. E.M.B.

ONESIPHORUS (ŏn'ē-sĭf'ō-rŭs, Gr. *Onesíphoros, profit-bringer*), an Ephesian who ministered fearlessly to Paul at the time of the apostle's second captivity in Rome (II Tim. 1:16-18; 4:19). Paul's warm gratitude, and his care in the midst of his own distress to convey his greetings to the Ephesian family, is a light on his generous character, and further evidence of his capacity for commanding devotion. There are no valid grounds for concluding, as some scholars do, that Onesiphorus was dead at the time Paul wrote, much less to base upon the passage a doctrine of prayers for the dead. (See Guthrie, *The Pastoral Epistles, Tyndale NT Commentaries*, pp. 135, 136.) In the apocryphal *Acts of Paul and Thecla* an Onesiphorus appears as a man of Iconium. A man of the same name was martyred in Mysia between A.D. 102 and 114.

ONION (See Plants)

ONLY-BEGOTTEN, a title applied to our Lord by John (John 1:14,18; 3:16,18; I John 4:9) and once in Hebrews (11:17) connected with the doctrine of the "eternal generation of the Son of God" (cf. Ps. 2:7 with Acts 13:33; Heb. 1:5; 5:5).

ONO (ō'nō, Heb. *'ônô, strong*), a town ascribed to Benjamin in I Chronicles 8:12 because it was built by Shemed, a Benjamite, though in the territory originally assigned to the tribe of Dan. It lay in the plain, near the valley of craftsmen (Neh. 11: 35) and was about six miles SE of Joppa. Many of its men returned from captivity with Zerubbabel (Ezra 2:33), and the town was later inhabited by men of Benjamin (Neh. 11:35). Nehemiah refused an invitation thither (Neh. 6:2).

ONYCHA (ŏn'ĭ-kà, Heb. *sheḥēleth*), an ingredient of the sweet-smelling incense which Moses was directed to make (Exod. 30:34). It is supposed to have been the covering of a certain mussel found in India, which when burning emitted an odor resembling musk. Very costly. See INCENSE.

ONYX (See Minerals)

OPHEL (ō'fĕl, Heb. *ha-'ôphel, hill*), properly a hill, but when used with the definite article in Hebrew, it is rendered "Ophel" and refers to a part of Jerusalem. In II Kings 5:24 the word is rendered "tower" in the KJV and "hill" in the ASV, but no one knows the exact location. In Micah 4:8 it is rendered "stronghold" in the KJV, but the ASV has "the hill of the daughter of Zion," and probably refers to *the* Ophel of Jerusalem. In Isaiah

The Hill of Ophel, at the southeast corner of Jerusalem city wall, beyond which is the temple area. © MPS

32:14, the KJV has "forts," but the ASV, more accurately, "hill," and probably refers to Ophel. Ophel lies outside the wall of modern Jerusalem just S of the Mosque "el Aksa" and above the junction of the valleys of the Kidron and of the "son of Hinnom." Jotham, king of Judah, built much upon the wall of Ophel (II Chron. 27:3), and his great-grandson Manasseh further improved it (II Chron. 33:14), so that thenceforward it was inside the ancient city. In the restoration period it was principally a place of residence for the temple-servants, the Nethinim (Neh. 11:21).

OPHIR (ō'fêr, Heb. *'ôphîr*). 1. A son of Joktan, son of Eber (Gen. 10:29). Of Eber's two sons, Peleg became ancestor of the "Hebrews" thus named from Eber, but Joktan and his progeny moved into Arabia. The names in "the table of the nations" (Gen. 10) often indicate locations, and Ophir is placed between Sheba and Havilah, both of which were in southern Arabia.

2. The land occupied by the descendants of Ophir. In I Kings 9:28 it is mentioned as the source of much gold (cf. Gen. 2:11,12 where Ophir's neighbor Havilah is cited for its good gold). Ophir in Arabia was not only the source of gold, but it may have been a way-station for the "ships of Tarshish" coming westward from India, if the apes, ivory, and peacocks (I Kings 10:22), to say nothing of the almug trees (I Kings 10:11,12), had to come from India. These large ships which had made the round trip once in three years (I Kings 10:22) could have voyaged from the neighborhood of Goa on the west coast of India to Ophir, and thence up the Red Sea and the Gulf of Akaba to Ezion-geber (I Kings 9:26), keeping in sight or nearly in sight of land all of the way. Although many of the ancients, including Josephus (*Ant.* 8:6:4), thought of Ophir as being in India, the consensus of opinion today would place it as indicated above, in Arabia. Although gold is not mined there today, Ophir was famous for its gold from very early days (Job 22:24; 28:16).

OPHNI (ŏf'nī, Heb. *hā-'ophnî*), a city in the northern part of Benjamin, mentioned only in Joshua 18:24. It lay about 2½ miles NW of Bethel on one of the two main roads northward from Jerusalem to Samaria. Now called Jifneh.

OPHRAH (ŏf'rà, Heb. *'ophrâh, hind*). 1. A town in Benjamin (Josh. 18:23). Now called *Et-Taiyibah*. It lies on a conical hill about three miles NE of Bethel and probably is the "Ephraim" of John 11:54 to which our Lord retired when under persecution.

2. A town in the tribe of Manasseh (Judg. 6:24) pertaining to the Abi-ezrites, a family of that tribe. Here the Angel of Jehovah appeared, sitting under an oak tree, and talked with Gideon, commissioning him to deliver Israel from the Midianites, and here Gideon put the ephod to which the children of Israel bowed down.

3. A son of Meonothai, an early member of the tribe of Judah (I Chron. 4:14).

ORACLE (ŏr'à-k'l, Heb. *dāvar*, Gr. *lógion*). 1. An utterance supposedly coming from a deity and generally through an inspired medium. This is the classical usage, cf. "Sibylline Oracles."

2. In the Bible, an utterance from God. In II Samuel 16:23 we read that Ahitophel was so highly regarded before he turned traitor to David, that his words were considered as oracles from God.

3. In the ERV the word oracle is incorrectly used to render *devîr,* a term used to describe the

Holy of Holies in the temple (I Kings 6:5f). In heathen temples "oracle" was used to describe the room where the utterances were delivered by the oracle.

4. The OT was referred to as "living (KJV 'lively') oracles" (Acts 7:38), and in Hebrews 5:12 "the oracles of God" would include Christian teaching. Christians are told to speak as the oracles of God (I Pet. 4:11).

ORATOR. 1. Isaiah 3:3 (KJV) has "the eloquent orator," where ASV reads "the skilful enchanter" which is correct, for the word is derived from the verb for *charming serpents.*

2. A public speaker, especially an advocate. Acts 24:1 mentions "a certain orator, named Tertullus" whom the Jews employed to speak against Paul before Felix, not that they lacked eloquence, but because Tertullus, a Roman, could make the accusation in Latin, the language of the Roman courts.

ORDAIN, ORDINATION. In the KJV "to ordain" is the rendering of about 35 different Hebrew, Greek, and Latin words. The word has many shades of meaning, chiefly the following: (1) to set in order, arrange (Ps. 132:17; Isa. 30:33); (2) to bring into being (I Kings 12:32; Num. 28:6; Ps. 8:2,3); (3) to decree (Esth. 9:27; Acts 16:4; Rom. 7:10); (4) to set apart for an office or duty (Mark 3:14; John 15:16; Acts 14:23).

Ordination in the sense of setting aside officers of the Church for a certain work by the laying on of hands was practiced in apostolic times (I Tim. 4:14; II Tim. 1:6), but it is nowhere described or enjoined. No great emphasis was placed on this rite.

OREB AND ZEEB (ō'rĕb, zē'ĕb, Heb. *'ōrēv, ze'ēv, raven* and *wolf*), two princes of the Midianites in the days of Gideon. After Gideon's notable defeat of the Midianites, the Midianites who survived fled, and Gideon called upon the men of Manasseh to cut off the retreat at the crossings of the Jordan. Here they captured the two princes and beheaded them. The places of their deaths were named in their memory: Oreb died at the rock of Oreb and Zeeb at the wine-press of Zeeb (Judg. 7:24,25). Asaph, hundreds of years later, recalls these events in Psalm 83:11. The exact location of the killing is unknown.

OREB, ROCK OF (See Oreb and Zeeb)

OREN (ō'rĕn, Heb. *'ōren, cedar*), son of Jerahmeel, son of Hezron, son of Perez, son of Judah (I Chron. 2:25).

ORGAN (See Musical Instruments)

ORION (See Astronomy)

ORNAMENT (See Dress)

ORNAN (ôr'năn), a Jebusite prince (called Araunah in II Sam. 24:16ff, etc.) whose threshing-floor was purchased by David after a plague (I Chron. 21:15-25).

ORONTES (ō-rŏn'tēz), the chief river in Syria, almost 400 miles long, rises in the Anti-Lebanon range, at the height of almost 4000 feet, and flows N for the major portion of its course. It turns W round the northern end of the range at Antioch, and then bends SW to the sea. Its fertile valley forms the only extensive area in Syria-Palestine not broken by mountains where a powerful political unit might take shape. This geographical fact is evident in history. The Orontes valley was the scene of the campaign of Rameses II against the Hittites in 1288 B.C. The campaign, and the culminating battle of Kadesh on the river, form the

At the mouth of the Orontes, the chief river of Syria, not far from Ras Shamra (Ugarit), which lies just over the hills. © MPS

most publicized feat of ancient Egyptian arms. Juvenal, the Roman satirist, writing of the undesirable Syrian immigrants in Rome, uses the river as a metaphor for the whole province. "Long since," he writes, "has Syrian Orontes been a tributary of the Tiber" (3:62).   E.M.B.

ORPAH (ôr'på, Heb. *'orpâh, neck, i.e. stubbornness*), a Moabite woman whom Chilion, son of Elimelech and Naomi, married. She loved her mother-in-law, but kissed her goodbye and remained in Moab, while Ruth, Naomi's other daughter-in-law, clave to her (Ruth 1:4,14; 4: 9,10).

OSEE (See Hosea)

OSHEA (See Joshua)

OSNAPPAR (See Ashurbanipal)

OSPRAY (See Birds)

OSSIFRAGE (See Birds)

OSTIA (ôs'tyà), the port of Rome, on the Tiber mouth, some 16 miles from the city, traditionally founded by Ancus Marcius. Archaeological investigations have not yet confirmed dates earlier than 350 B.C. Ostia became a naval base during the Second Punic War, and continued to grow in commercial importance until the end of the second century of the Christian era. Evidence for a Christian community in Ostia can be traced with certainty as far back as A.D. 200. The ravages of Goth and Hun, and the appearance of endemic malaria made the site a desert.

OSTRAKA (ŏs'trà-kà), inscribed fragments of pottery (sing., ostrakon). In the ancient world handy writing material was rare, but potsherds, or broken pieces of earthenware, were abundant, hence the habit of writing brief memoranda or communications on such ready material. The surface holds the inscription well and some important ancient documents have come down to us in this form (e.g. the Lachish Letters). In ancient Athens the use of potsherds, or ostraka, for voting tablets in the peculiar Athenian process of relegation, led to the term "ostracise." The verb originally meant the writing on an ostrakon of the name of the person the voter wished thus to exile. Most of the ostraka from early Ptolemaic Egypt are tax-receipts. Later, orders, lists, brief letters, school exercises, magic formulae, and religious texts, both pagan and Christian, appear. A good deal about Egyptian Christianity has been deduced from this source. The material is scattered, most ostraka being recovered casually from rubbish-mounds or house-ruins.   E.M.B.

OSTRICH (See Birds)

OTHNI (ŏth'nī, Heb. *'othnî*, abbrev. of Othniel), son of Shemaiah, a doorkeeper of the tabernacle under David (I Chron. 26:7).

OTHNIEL (ŏth'nĭ-ĕl, Heb. *'othnî'ēl*), son of Kenaz, the brother of Caleb, who with Joshua had brought back a good report of the land of Canaan after spying it out. Caleb, in his old age at the division of the land, offered his daughter to any one who would take Debir, about ten miles to the SW of Hebron. His nephew Othniel took Debir and so acquired Achsah as wife (Josh. 15:13-19; Judg. 1: 11-15). Within 15 years after the death of Joshua, Israel fell off into apostasy and God delivered them into the hand of Cushanrishathaim (Judg. 3: 8-11), king of Mesopotamia. In their distress they prayed to the Lord, who raised up Othniel to deliver them. He was thus the first of the seven "judges" to deliver Israel from foreign oppression. He so restored Israel that a period of 40 years of peace set in. His son was Hathath (I Chron. 4:13).

OUCHES (ouch'ĕz, Heb. *mishbetsôth*). 1. Settings for precious stones on the high-priest's ephod (Exod. 28:11).

2. A rich texture inwrought with gold thread or wire (Ps. 45:13).

OVEN, a chamber which is heated so as to roast or to bake the food materials placed therein. There were three principal types. In Egypt there was in nearly every house an erection of clay built upon the house floor. In this, or on this, baking was done. In Palestine and Syria, a barrel-shaped hole in the ground is coated with clay and a quick hot fire of brambles or dry dung mixed with straw heats it. The dough, beaten very thin, is spread on the inside and almost immediately taken out, baked. In some places, a curved plate of iron is put over the sunken oven; but in cities the oven is a chamber of stone, from which the fire is raked when the oven is very hot, and into which the unbaked loaves are placed (Hos. 7:4-7). See also BREAD and OCCUPATIONS AND PROFESSIONS (BAKER).

OVERSEER, the rendering of several Hebrew and Greek words, each with its distinctive meaning: Heb. *pāqadh, inspector, overseer* (Gen. 39:4,5; II Chron. 34:12,17); *menatstsehîm, foreman* (II Chron. 2:18; 34:13); *shōtēr*, almost always *officer*; Gr. *epískopos, bishop, overseer* (Acts 20:28).

OWL (See Birds)

OWNER OF A SHIP. The phrase is found in Acts 27:11, where it says, "Nevertheless the centurion believed the master and the owner of the ship, more than those things which were spoken by Paul." A distinction is made between the master (*kybernétes*) and the owner (*naúkleros*). *Kubernétes* refers to the steersman, or pilot; while *naúkleros* refers to the sailing-master of a ship engaged in state service (although the word also means ship-owner). This was, however, a corn ship in imperial service, and would not be privately owned.

OX (See Animals, Cattle)

OX GOAD, a pointed stick used to urge the ox to further effort (Judg. 3:31). SEE GOAD.

OZEM (ō'zĕm, Heb. *'ōtsem*). 1. The sixth son of Jesse (I Chron. 2:15).

2. A son of Jerahmeel (I Chron. 2:25).

OZIAS (See Uzziah)

OZNI (ŏz'nī, Heb. *'oznî*), son of Gad and father of the Oznites (Num. 26:16).

P

PAARAI (pā'à-rī, Heb. *pa'ăray, devotee of Peor*), one of David's mighty men called "the Arbites" (II Sam. 23:35). He is called Naarai in I Chronicles 11:37.

PADAN-ARAM (pā'dăn-ā'răm, *plain of Aram*). The word originally, as shown by the cuneiform contract tablets, signified a unit of measuring. It is the home of Jacob's exile (Gen. 31:18), the home of Laban. Beyond much controversy, it is to be identified with Haran of the upper Euphrates Valley. It is also sometimes translated as simply "Mesopotamia." In Genesis 48:7, Padan only; RSV, Paddan-aram.

PADON (pā'dŏn, Heb. *pādhôn, redemption*), the name of one of the Nethinim who returned with Zerubbabel from Babylon (Ezra 2:44; Neh. 7:47).

PAGIEL (pā'gĭ-ĕl, Heb. *pagh'ĭ'ēl, a meeting with God*), the son of Ocran who was over the tribe of Asher (Num. 7:72).

PAHATH-MOAB (pā'hăth-mō'ăb, Heb. *pahath-mô'āv, governor of Moab*), a head of one of the chief houses of Judah. Part of the descendants of this man returned from Babylon with Zerubbabel (Ezra 2:6; Neh. 7:11) and another part returned with Ezra (Ezra 8:4). A son of Pahath-moab, Hashub, aided in repairing both the wall and tower of the furnaces (Neh. 3:11). He is one of the lay princes, whose name appears second in the signing of the sure covenant (Neh. 9:38; 10:14). His place in this list speaks of his importance. Eight of the sons of this man put away their strange wives (Ezra 10:30).

PAI (See Pau)

PAINTING THE EYES (See Dress)

PALACE (Heb. *'armôn, bîrâh, hēkhāl,* Gr. *aulé*), the dwelling place of an important official. Palaces are found all over the Biblical world. The science of archaeology has given much light on these ancient structures. Israel built many palaces and one finds frequent mention of them in the Scriptures. At Gezer the remains of a palace belonging to the period of Joshua's conquest have been found. It is thought to be the palace of Horam, king of Gezer, whom Joshua conquered (Josh. 10:33). Many of these old palaces were made of stone. This palace belongs to the group of palaces known as fortress palaces. They were sometimes the entrances to great tunnels. Some were constructed over important wells or springs of water which they controlled (Garrow Duncan, *Digging Up Biblical History*, Vol. I, London: Society for Promoting Christian Knowledge, 1931, pp. 38, 147-148).

The ruins of another palace at this site stem from a much later period. It is the Maccabean Palace and is thought to be the private headquarters of John Hyrcanus, the military governor (George Barton, *Archaeology and the Bible*, Philadelphia: American Sunday School Union, 1916, pp. 168-169).

W. F. Albright has excavated Saul's palace-fortress at Gibeah. Not much remains in order here, but enough to reveal the massive walls that once made up this structure (W. F. Albright, *The Archaeology of Palestine*, Baltimore: Penguin Books, 1956, pp. 120-121).

David had two palaces at different times in his ministry. The first was a simple one located at Hebron, but the second one was much more elaborate, built of cedar trees furnished by Hiram of Tyre and erected by workmen that Hiram supplied (II Sam. 5:11). Solomon's palace that came later was a much more lavish structure, judging from its description given in I Kings 7. It was about 150 feet by 75 feet in size, constructed mostly of cedar in the interior and of hand-hewn stones for the exterior. Some of the foundation stones were 15 feet long. Solomon's wealth together with the skilled Phoenician craftsmen must have produced a magnificent building. Nothing remains of this building today.

Remains of a palace have been found at Megiddo. Another palace has been discovered at Samaria and identified as belonging to Omri. The foundation of this palace is in the bedrock of that area. Most of these palaces are similar in style — a series of open courts with rooms grouped around them.

An ivory palace belonging to Ahab is mentioned in I Kings 22:39. For a long time scholars denied the truthfulness of this record, but the archaeologist has confirmed the report. It was a large edifice 300 feet long from N to S. Many of its walls were faced with white marble. Wall paneling, plaques and furniture have been uncovered, made of or adorned with ivory. Clarence Fisher, one of the excavators at Samaria, says that its name, "ivory palace," was probably derived from the ivory decorations as well as the marble-faced walls which resemble ivory (Barton, *op. cit.,* p. 168).

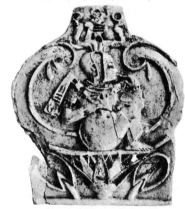

Two ivory panels from Samaria, probably decorative pieces from King Ahab's ivory palace. PAM

Later on in the history of Israel material prosperity produced a very great wickedness that led to murder even in these royal palaces of splendor. This was especially true in the time of Jeroboam II.

Probably the most famous palace in the NT period was the one belonging to Herod the Great. Josephus informs us that this structure was built in Jerusalem. Its rooms were of a very great height and adorned with all kinds of costly furniture (*Flavius Josephus, Complete Works,* translated by William Whiston, Grand Rapids: Kregel Publ., 1961, p. 385).

Besides these palaces of Palestine, there were many splendid structures in Mesopotamia in the Assyrian and Babylonian period. The remains of the great temple of Sargon II have been found at Khorsabad, 12 miles N of the site of old Nineveh. It was a mammoth structure covering 25 acres of land. Some of its walls were from nine to 16 feet thick. In the Oriental Institute Museum in Chicago one may see one of the stone bulls that once stood at the entrance of this palace. It is 16 feet long and 16 feet high, weighing 40 tons.

There are many other important palaces in Mesopotamia. One was that built by Nebuchadnezzar at Babylon, elaborately decorated. Another has been found on the Euphrates at Mari. This one has been quite well preserved and reveals paintings, offices, apartments and even a scribal school. Albright refers to it as one of the "show places of the world" (William F. Albright, *From the Stone Age to Christianity,* Baltimore: The John Hopkins Press, 1940, p. 111). This discovery was important for many reasons but especially because it ". . . revolutionized our idea of the development of Near-Eastern art in the early second millennium B.C." (Albright, *op. cit.,* p. 111).

Many famous palaces belonging to the pharaohs also have been found in Egypt. Perhaps the best known of these is the palace of Merneptah, from about 1230 B.C. Many of these were very elaborate structures.   H.Z.C.

PALAL (pā'lăl, Heb. *pālāl, he judges*), son of Uzai who helped in repairing the Jerusalem walls (Neh. 3:25).

PALESTINE (păl'ĕs-tīn, Heb. *pelesheth,* Gr. *Phylistieim, Allóphyloi*).

1. **Name.** The term "Palestine" occurs four times in the KJV (Exod. 15:14; Isa. 14:29,31; Joel 3:4). In all four contexts it refers to Philistia, the coastal strip in the southeastern littoral of the ·Mediterranean occupied by the Philistines, an Indo-European people from Crete. ERV renders "Philistia" in all cases. Philistia itself derives from the Hebrew term for the region *eres Pelistim,* "the land of the Philistines"; and "Philistine" was a native term of unknown origin and significance. Josephus uses *Palaistine* in the same restricted geographical sense (e.g. *Ant.* 1:6:2; 13:5:10). It is in Herodotus, the fifth century Greek historian, that the extension of the term to cover a wider area is first seen (2:104; 3:5,91:7:89). The name "Palestine" is therefore another example of the common phenomenon whereby a land or a people is named after the part or the division with which first contact is made. The Romans, for example, called the Hellenes *Graeci,* and the land of Hellas *Graecia,* after the minor tribe immediately opposite the heel of Italy. The French name for Germany, *Allemagne,* derives from the trans-Rhenane federation of the Allemanni. The Arabs call all Europeans "Franks." Herodotus derived his knowledge of Palestine from Egypt, and possibly popularizes the Egyptian nomenclature, which named the whole ill-defined area

to their north from the name of the occupants of the "Gaza Strip." A Philistine settlement had existed there since patriarchal times (Gen. 26). The older Semitic name was Canaan, a word of doubtful origin. According to Sir George A. Smith, the great geographer of Palestine, Canaan may mean "sunken" or "low land," and hence may have originally applied only to the coastal strip, as distinct from the highlands, extending then, after the fashion already noted, to wider geographic significance.

2. **Locality and Area.** The limits of Palestine in ancient times lack precise definition, save in the case of the second century Roman province of the name, whose boundaries may be fairly certainly drawn. The Leontes river (mod. Litani) is commonly regarded as the logical northern boundary, and the Wadi el 'Arish the natural frontier with Egypt. Political frontiers, ancient and modern, have not always respected these ideal boundaries. Even the limits poetically marked in the phrase "from Dan to Beersheba" do not correspond (Judg. 20:1). Dan was Laish, 30 miles due E of Tyre on the sources of the Jordan. Beersheba lay 150 miles to the S, as the crow flies, just where Palestine merges into the desert of the Negev. The "Promised Land" of Joshua 1:4 is geographically much more inclusive. The seacoast formed a definite enough western boundary, though from ancient Philistine to modern Egyptian, alien powers have always disputed possession of the fertile lowlands behind the coast. The deepening desert made a firm, if wavering boundary-line to the E. W of a line drawn down the Jordan valley, Palestine measures 6,000 square miles. If areas E of Jordan, from time to time counted part of Palestine, are also included, the total area is nearer 10,000 square miles. It is thus a little larger than the State of Vermont. It is remarked above that the distance from Dan to Beersheba is 150 miles. From W to E the distances are smaller still. In the N, from Acco to the Sea of Galilee, the distance is 28 miles. From Gaza to the Dead Sea in the S the distance is 54 miles.

3. **Climate.** In spite of its narrow limits, the varied configuration of Palestine produces great variety of climate. Thanks to the adjacent sea, the coastal plain, lying between latitudes 31 and 33, is temperate, with an average annual temperature of 57° at Joppa. Inland 34 miles, Jerusalem, thanks to its height of 2,600 feet registers an annual average of 63°, though with wider variations. Fifteen miles away at Jericho, 3,300 feet below Jerusalem, and 700 feet below sea level, tropical climate prevails with intense and enervating summer heat. A similar contrast marks the temperate climate round the Sea of Galilee, and the tropical heat round the Dead Sea. Prevailing winds are W or SW, and precipitate their moisture on the western slopes of the high country in a rainy season extending roughly from October to April. An occasional sirocco, or east wind, brings burning air from the great deserts of the hinterland (Job 1: 19; Jer. 18:17; Ezek. 17:10; 27:26). The southern desert, S of Beersheba, is a parched wilderness, at present the scene of some of the world's major experiments in "dry-farming." The chief climatic advantage is a heavy fall of dew. The "former rain" of the Biblical phrase (Joel 2:23) was the early part of the rainy season. This period is commonly followed by a time of heavy falls alternating with fine clear weather, until March or April, when the "latter rain" falls with immense advantage to the maturing crops before the dry season, the ripening, and the harvest.

4. Geography. (a) The coast. The coast of Palestine is a line which sweeps S, with a slight curve to the W, without break or indentation. North of Carmel is Phoenicia, where a great maritime nation found the means to use and tame the sea, but N of Carmel, significantly, the coast is more hospitable, and offers hope of haven for ships. Those who lived behind the stern, flat coast of Palestine necessarily found the sea a barrier (Josh. 1:4), and an image of violence and restlessness (Isa. 17:12,13). By the same token, they were agricultural rather than maritime. From Carmel S to the Nile Delta, the coastline is built of sandhills and low cliffs, without a sheltering off-shore island to form a roadstead, or a river-mouth to give a minimum protection from the sea. It is "a shelf for the casting of wreckage and the roosting of sea-birds" (G. A. Smith: *Historical Geography of the Holy Land*, p. 128). The currents are parallel with the coast, and still bear the silt of the Nile. The prevailing wind beats on the shore with ceaseless surf. No intruder, with the possible exception of the Philistines, has ever landed there. Palestine's invaders have followed the open roads of her N-S plains and valleys. For the same reason, artificial harbors anciently built on the coast, even Herod's fine port of Caesarea, have always been difficult to maintain. On the first relaxation of human effort, the sea has overwhelmed them. A recent survey of the coast has indicated that the lost ports of Palestine are likely to prove a fruitful field of under-water archaeological exploration. The makeshifts or artificial ports on the Mediterranean coast may be listed as follows: Dor was used as a port, but it was an open roadstead, and never in firm control of the Israelite authorities. Joppa was little better, save that some off-shore reefs broke the force of the Mediterranean swell, and offered a fair-weather port. First under Philistine, and later under Syrian control, Joppa fell to the Jews as a conquest of Simon Maccabaeus in 148 B.C. "To add to his reputation," runs the account, "he took Joppa for a harbor, and provided an access for the islands of the sea" (I Macc. 14:5). Simon found a considerable Greek population in the port, and was put to some trouble in occupying and fortifying it. After 85 years, during which the Syrians twice reoccupied the port, Pompey allotted it to Syria in his organization of the East (63 B.C.). In 47 Caesar returned it to the Jews, and Augustus made it part of the domains of Herod the Great. These historical vicissitudes illustrate the disadvantages of a littoral geographically so difficult. Ashkelon, the only Philistine city actually on the coast, and a foundation old enough to find mention in the Tell-el-Amarna letters, served also as a port, and archaeology may establish the presence of harbor works. Caesarea, Herod's ambitious foundation 20 miles S of modern Haifa, was an efficient port. Herod spent 12 years building not only a harbor but a city of some magnificence. Enormous blocks of stone formed a breakwater 200 feet wide in 20 fathoms of water, and made the only real harbor on the coast. Hence the Hebrew name *Leminah*, a Hebraic rendering of Greek *limen*, "a harbor." Associated harbor buildings, navigational aids, and a well-equipped town made Caesarea the natural seat for Roman authority in Palestine.

(b) The Maritime Plain. A coastal plain shaped like a long spear-point with its tip where Carmel thrusts to the sea is the main western geographical feature of Palestine. North of Carmel, the small plain of Acco or Acre, a detached section of the coastal plain, should be mentioned. S of Carmel,

Two views of the coastal region of Palestine: Above, fishermen off the coast of Caesarea, showing portions of ancient buildings which had fallen into the sea. Below, the busy port at Jaffa, ancient Joppa. © MPS

widening from eight miles to 12, and extending for 44 miles, is the Plain of Sharon, once an extensive oak-forest, well-watered, and bounded to the S by low hills. S again of this inconsiderable barrier, and similarly widening over the course of its whole 40 miles to the borders of Egypt, is the famous Plain of Philistia, after which the whole land was named. Marshes, the "Serbonian Bog" of Strabo, Diodorus, and Pliny, were found at the southern end of the Philistine plain. They were salt marshes behind the coastal dunes, and are mentioned because they were a breeding-ground of disease, which has played its part in history. Hereabouts Sennacherib's army was destroyed, perhaps by some devastating plague, sent, as Scripture says, by the angel of the Lord. Historical records, extending as far as Napoleon, refer to similar decimating attacks of pestilence among large bodies of men traversing this area. In spite, however, of the unhealthiness of the marshy strip, the coastal plain has always been a highway of commerce or aggression. By this path traveled the Egyptian conquerors seeking out their northern foes, the Hittites, Thothmes III, Ramses II, and Seti I. By this same path, and thence into the plain of Esdraelon, traveled Cambyses, Alexander, Pompey, Saladin, Napoleon, and Allenby. The plain forms the western blade of the Fertile Crescent, the grand highway between Africa, Asia, and Europe.

A relief map of Palestine, showing the deep rift of the Jordan valley, culminating in the Dead Sea, about 1300 feet below sea level. This is a reproduction of a map made by the Palestine Exploration Fund.   MPS

(c) The Uplands. The tumbled hill-country which forms the core or backbone of the land, is a continuation of the more clearly-defined Lebanon ranges to the N of Palestine. This extended mountain chain breaks up into confused hills in the desert of the S. Three divisions are to be distinguished: Galilee, Samaria, and Judah. Galilee is rugged, especially to the N, where a height of 4,000 feet above sea level is reached near Merom. The southern portion is less hilly, and might even be described as rolling land, arable, fertile, and temperate in climate. S of Galilee, the Valley of Jezreel, or the Plain of Esdraelon, cuts the range, the location of many important ancient towns, and an open highway to the N. The town of Megiddo controlled the pass into the Plain of Sharon. Since Mt. Carmel dominated the road along the coast, Megiddo was a place of paramount strategic importance. From the strife which, through the centuries, necessarily gathered around it, Har-Magedon, or "the Hill of Megiddo" became a symbol of the struggle of nations (Rev. 16:16). Two valleys from Esdraelon gave access to the Jordan. One passes between Tabor and Moreh, the other between Moreh and Gilboa. Here lay the best E-W traverse of the land. The Samaria hill-country forms the geographical heart of Palestine. The uplands rise in the N to 1,640 feet in Mount Gilboa, and throw up two conspicuous peaks of Ebal (3,077 feet above sea level), and Gerizim, a rather lower eminence. Fertile valleys intersect these high masses, and since the valley-floors are themselves of considerable altitude, the higher country has not the visible height or prominence which the sea level figures appear to indicate. The third division of the hill country is Judah. Here the summits are lower than in the region of Samaria, falling to 2,600 feet in Jerusalem, and touching their highest point, 3,370 feet near Hebron. This country forms a watershed which strains the moisture from the Mediterranean sea breezes. The eastern slopes, in consequence, deteriorate into the barren "wilderness of Judah," deeply intersected by the arid ravines which converge on the Dead Sea. This barren wasteland was the refuge of David in his outlaw days. Ordered life and agriculture concentrated on the W in the so-called "Shephelah," the sloping foothills and valley tongues which led up from the coastal plain into the Judaean hills. In sheltered folds of the hills, argiculture flourished, and fertility seeped down from the higher land. The Shephelah was disputed territory. In days of strength the Hebrew highlanders pressed down towards the plain. When the strength of the hill-men wavered or flagged, the Philistine lowlanders thrust up into the foothills. The Shephelah saw a pressure front between the Semitic claimants from the desert and the E, and the W. Fortresses such as Lachish, Debir, Libnah, Azekah, and Bethshemesh, were located in the Shephelah. To the S the Judean hill-country breaks up into the arid wilderness of the Negev. There is strong archaeological evidence for a considerable population in this area in the early centuries of the Christian era, made possible by efficient water conservation, irrigation systems, and the effective use, through rock-mulching, of the heavy fall of dew.

(d) The Jordan Valley. This depression, which contains the Jordan River and its associated sheets of water, is part of a huge split in the crust of the globe, a geological fault which extends N to form the valley between the two Lebanon ranges, and S of the Dead Sea, to form the arid

Above, the hill country around Nazareth and Mount Tabor. Below, the arid valley of the Arabah, mountains of Edom in the distance. © MPS

valley of the Arabah, the Gulf of Aqabah, and the African chain of lakes. The Jordan rises from multiple sources on the western slopes of Hermon, and becomes a distinctive stream a few miles N of the shallow reedy lake called Huleh today, Semechonitis by Josephus, and "the waters of Merom" in Joshua 11:5. The Canaanitish stronghold of Hazor lay a few miles to the SW. From its sources to Huleh, the Jordan drops 1,000 feet over a distance of 12 miles, and enters the lake seven feet above sea level. Over the 11 miles to the Sea of Galilee, it drops to 682 feet below sea level. From Galilee to the Dead Sea there is a further drop of 600 feet. Galilee is the OT *Chinnereth* or *Chinneroth* (Num. 34:11; Josh. 12:3), names echoed in the NT Gennesaret. John, writing for Gentile readers, calls the lake "the Sea of Tiberias" from the name of the town founded by Herod Antipas on the shore. Some of Palestine's most fertile soil is found around the shores, and the lake itself was the center of an extensive and vigorous fishing industry. Capernaum, Bethsaida, and perhaps Chorazin, were lakeside towns. So were Tiberias and Tarichea, neither of which is mentioned in the Gospels, unless the latter town is, in fact, Magdala. Bethsaida means "fishing-place," and Tarichea derives its name from a Greek word meaning "preserved fish." Both names therefore point to the lake's fishing industry. It is clear that the first disciples were called from an active and prosperous stratum of Galilean society. Flowing S from Galilee, through a wide-floored valley walled by cliffs, the Jordan follows a fantastically meandering course, taking 200 miles of winding stream to cover 65 miles measured in a straight line. Much of the valley floor is tangled vegetation, fed lushly by the periodic flood-waters of the river. It is this wilderness which Jeremiah calls "the swelling," or "the pride" of Jordan (12:5; 49:19). Fords are numerous. The river enters the Dead Sea near Jericho. This lake has no outflow and its water is therefore 25 per cent salt deposits, the raw material of a flourishing chemical industry recently established in the region of the lake. Two-thirds of the way down the eastern coast, W of Kir-hareseth in Moab, an irregular peninsula known as "the Tongue" projects into the sea. S of this peninsula the water is only a few feet deep, forming a large bay known anciently as "the Vale of Siddim" (Gen. 14:3). Here, it is thought, were situated the "cities of the plain" Sodom, Gomorrah, Admah, Zeboiim, and Zoar. About 2,000 B.C. a great catastrophe overwhelmed the area and depressed the ground level. Underwater archaeological exploration seems to confirm that Sodom and its associated towns perished in this cataclysm.

At the south end of the Dead Sea, evaporating pans to gather potash, part of a flourishing chemical industry. © MPS

(e) The Plateau of Transjordan. This is not part of modern Palestine, and was alien territory over much of ancient history. It was, however, intimately connected with Biblical history, and its geography relevant in consequence. N of the Yarmuk, a tributary of the Jordan S of the Sea of Galilee, is Bashan. Through this region in NT times curved the eastern members of the federation of ten cities known as the Decapolis. In its eastern quarter lay the Trachonitis of the Greeks (Luke 3:1), a tumbled waste of ancient volcanic stone, a natural defensive area, and part of the principality of Og of Bashan (Deut. 3:4). S of Bashan, and extending to the river, is Gilead. Jabbok whose banks were the scene of Jacob's contest (Gen. 33), rose near Rabbath-Ammon, the Philadelphia of the Decapolis, and irrigated a considerable territory. In the tribal settlement recorded in Numbers 32 and Joshua 12, Manasseh was allotted all Bashan in the N, Reuben the Moabite highlands in the S, and Gad the central land of

In the Bashan country, an area of fertile highland east of the Sea of Galilee. © MPS

Gilead. Hence the identification of Gad with Gilead in Judges 5:17. In Gilead was the Cherith, scene of Elijah's retreat, and David's refuge of Mahanaim. It was well-watered and wooded. S of Jabbok, down to the Arnon, which joins the Dead Sea, half-way down its eastern coast, the plateau becomes increasingly arid and desolate. This area contains the height of Nebo, the old land of Ammon. S of Arnon is Moab, a high plateau seldom controlled by Israel, and further S still is Edom, a region valuable for its minerable deposits, and first controlled and exploited by David and Solomon. It was possibly the iron of Edom, smelted in the considerable industrial district which had been developed just N of the Gulf of Aqabah, which enabled Israel to emerge from the Bronze Age, and meet the iron-using Philistines on their own terms. Petra, the strange rock of the desert trade-routes, was originally an Edomite stronghold. This survey of the form and shape of Palestine may appropriately conclude with an eloquent passage from Sir George Adam Smith: "There is no land at once so much a sanctuary and an observatory as Palestine: no land which, until its office was fulfilled, was so swept by the great forces of history, and was yet so capable of preserving one tribe in national continuity and growth: one tribe, learning and suffering and rising superior to the successive problems these forces presented to her, till upon the opportunity afforded by the last of them she launched with her results upon the world. It is the privilege of the student of the historical geography of Palestine, to follow all this process of development in detail. If a man can believe that there is no directing hand behind our universe and the history of our race, he will, of course, say that all this is the result of chance. But for most of us, only another conclusion is possible." (*Historical Geography of the Holy Land,* p. 112).

5. Animal Life. Besides the common domesticated animals of the ancient Middle East, the horse, ox, sheep, goat, camel, ass, mule, Palestine was the habitat of numerous predatory beasts, principally the lion, leopard, wolf, jackal, and fox. The hare, the coney (a species of rabbit), the wild boar, and the deer were also found. A concordance, under any of these heads, will show the variety of metaphor and imagery based on animal life, both tame animals and the "beasts of the field." The dog was considered almost a wild creature, and provides a term for uncleanness, treachery, and contempt. The dog of Palestine was a pariah and scavenger, and used in neither hunting nor shepherding, save for the doubtful reference of Job 30:1. The cryptic reference in Deuteronomy 23:18 probably has to do with homosexual prostitution (SEE ANIMALS). Song birds are rare, but scavenger and predatory fowl included the eagle, vulture, owl, hawk, and kite. The heron, bittern, osprey, partridge, peacock, dove, pigeon, quail, raven, stork, and sparrow were common, and find frequent reference in both Testaments (SEE BIRDS). Fish were plentiful, especially in Galilee, where the shoals were dense. The chief edible fish seem to have been carp. Bees, grasshoppers, and locusts were among the insects (SEE INSECTS). Palestine lies in the belt of territory subject to locust invasion, and the Book of Joel is striking evidence for the destructive visitation of such insect swarms.

6. Plant life. Flowers are abundant in spring, giving brilliant display for a brief period only. Hence their use as a symbol of the ephemeral nature of life (Job 14:2; Psalm 103:15). The "lilies of the field" (Matt. 6:28) may have been a comprehensive term covering anemones, irises and other blooms. The rose was probably the crocus (S. of Sol. 2:1; Isa. 35:1). Trees grow vigorously in Palestine under proper cultivation, but the forest coverage in ancient times is a matter for conjecture. It may safely be assumed that parts of Palestine must have been more heavily wooded in ancient times than in any other period. Invasion and the Turkish tax on trees combined over the centuries to destroy the arboreal flora of Palestine. On the other hand, Palestine is not an ideal region for major forest growth. Smith remarks: "The distribution of woodland may have been different (i.e. in ancient days) but the woods were what we find the characteristic Palestine wood still to be—open and scattered, the trees distinguished rather for thickness than for height, and little undergrowth when compared with a northern or a tropical forest. Here and there groves of larger trees, or solitary giants of their kind, may have stood conspicuous on the bare landscape" (*op. sup. cit.* p. 81). The chief varieties were the oak, including the evergreen ilex, the terebinth, the carob, and the box, which attains a height of 20 feet, some pines, cypresses, and plane trees by the water. The plane is probably the tree of Psalm 1, "planted by the rivers of water." Josephus mentions the walnut, and the sycamore is mentioned in Amos (7:14), Isaiah (9:9,10), and Luke (19:4). Smaller growth is formed of dwarf or scrub oak, dwarf wild olive, wild vine, juniper, and thorn. Such scrub often marks the abandoned sites of ancient cultivation. Oleanders sometimes line river-beds. The olive, the vine, the fig, and the date-palm were the chief fruit-bearing trees or plants of ancient Palestine, and balsam groves were farmed at Jericho. Corn crops were barley, wheat, and millet. Wheat grew in the broader valleys and plains, the best areas for its cultivation being Philistia and Esdraelon. Barley grew on the higher slopes, a less valued crop. It is significant that the apprehensive Midianite soldier saw Israel in his dream in the symbol of a barley-cake rolling disastrously from the hills (Judg. 7:13). Beans and lentils were the chief vegetables. Jacob's "pottage" (Gen. 25:30) was probably a variety of red beans or lentil. The land was poor in grass, pasturage, as Western countries know it being unknown. Hence the imagery of grass in reference to the brevity of life (Ps. 90:5-7; 103:15; Isa. 40:6).
(SEE PLANTS)   E.M.B.

PALLU, PALLUITE (păl'ū, păl'ū-īt, Heb. *pallû', distinguished, a descendant of Pallu*), Reuben's second son (Gen. 46:9). (See also Exod. 6:14; Num. 26:5,8; I Chron. 5:3). He was the founder of the Palluites (Num. 26:5).

PALMER WORM (Heb. *gāzām*), means "caterpillar," but the insect meant in the Heb. text is probably a kind of locust (Joel 1:4; 2:25; Amos 4:9).

PALM TREE (See Plants)

PALMYRA (See Tadmor)

PALSY (See Diseases)

PALTI (păl'tī, Heb. *paltî, delivered*). 1. One of the 12 spies, from the tribe of Benjamin (Num. 13:9). Once Phalti in KJV (I Sam. 25:44).
2. The man to whom Saul gave Michal, David's wife (I Sam. 25:44).

PALTIEL (păl'tĭ-ĕl, Heb. *paltî'ēl, God delivers*). 1. The son of Azzan from the tribe of Issachar (Num. 34:26).
2. Once Phaltiel in KJV (II Sam. 3:15), the same as Palti 2.

PALTITE (păl'tīt, Heb. *paltî, delivered*), the Gentile name of Helez, one of David's valiant men. Called the Pelonite (I Chron. 11:27; 27:10). Same as Palti.

PAMPHYLIA (păm-fĭl'ĭ-à, Gr. *Pamphylía*). At the time of St. Paul, Pamphilia was a small Roman province of southern Asia Minor extending along the Mediterranean coast 75 miles and 30 miles inland to the Taurus Mountains. It was surrounded by Pisidia on the N, Cilicia to the E, and Lycia to the SW. It never became an important province and its boundaries were often changed by sudden and arbitrary political decisions. The Emperor Claudius brought it into the Roman provincial system in the first century A.D.
The tiny country is first mentioned in the NT in Acts 2:10 where it is said that some of the people at Pentecost were from Phrygia and Pamphilia. The Apostle Paul visited the territory on his first missionary journey when he preached at Perga, its chief city (Acts 13:13; 14:24). At this point John Mark left the party and returned to Jerusalem (Acts 13:13; 15:38). Later, when Paul as a prisoner "sailed over the sea of Cilicia and Pamphilia" (Acts 27:5), he evidently crossed the Pamphilian Gulf. It is said that most of the inhabitants of Pamphilia were backward and illiterate. Christianity never flourished there as in other places of Asia Minor.

PANNAG (păn'ăg, Heb. *pannagh*, meaning uncertain), one of the articles of trade between Judah and Israel (Ezek. 27:17).

PAP (păp, Heb. *shadh*, Gr. *mastós, bulging*), an English word, now obsolete, that has been replaced by the word "breast" (Luke 11:27; Rev. 1:13).

PAPER (See Papyrus, Writing)

PAPHOS (pā'fŏs, Gr. *Páphos*), the capital city of Roman Cyprus, located at the extreme W end of this large island. The Paphos of the Bible is really New Paphos, a Roman city rebuilt by Augustus; the old Greek city of Paphos, dedicated to the worship of Aphrodite, lay ten miles to the S. In New Paphos Paul and Barnabas encountered the wiles of the Jewish sorcerer Elymas in the court of Sergius Paulus, the Roman governor. Paul's miracle of blinding the magician led to the conversion of Paulus (Acts 13:6-13). New Paphos is now known as Baffa.

The manufacture of papyrus was a flourishing business in Egypt, where baskets, sandals, boats and other articles were made of it. It was not unknown among the Hebrews (Job 8:11) and some believe that the ark of Moses was made of papyrus (Exod. 2:3). But the most common use of the product was for writing material, so much so that "papyrus" became the name for writing paper. The art of making papyrus goes back to 2,000 B.C. and it was the common writing material in the Greek and Roman worlds from 500 B.C. until A.D. 400, when vellum largely replaced it until the 15th century as paper and the printing press took over. There is little doubt that the New Testament books were written on papyrus (pl. *papyri*). The material was also called *chartes* in Greek and John no doubt wrote his Second Epistle on such paper (II John 12). For long books (rolls or scrolls) many pieces of papyrus were glued together and rolled up. Such a roll was called *biblos* or *biblion* from which our word Bible is derived (cf. Tim. 4:13; Rev. 10:10; Ezek. 2:9-10). The width of the roll varied from three to twelve inches and sometimes the roll got to be as long as 25 feet. Luke's Gospel is estimated at 30 feet, but II Thessalonians may have been only 18 inches long and short letters like *Jude* or *Philemon* were perhaps written on a single small sheet. The writer wrote in columns evenly spaced along the length of the roll and the reader read one column at a time, unrolling with one hand and rolling up with the other.

Papyrus, however, becomes brittle with age and easily decays, especially when damp. This is why the autographs of the New Testament writings have perished. They may also have been literally read to pieces and during persecution were deliberately destroyed. But thousands of ancient papyri have been found in the dry sands of Egypt and elsewhere. Our libraries contain large collections of both Biblical and secular papyri — Bible texts, legal documents, marriage contracts, letters, etc. Many of the New Testament papyri ante-date all other codices. Examples are the Rylands Papyrus, the famous Chester Beatty Papyri, and the more recent Bodmer Papyrus of the Gospel of John. They have added much to our knowledge of the Greek language and the text of the NT. L.M.P.

Bedouin women weaving papyrus mats for building tents or dwellings. © MPS

Above, papyrus plants growing at Lake Merom. Below, Bedouin women carrying bundles of papyrus, which are to be woven into mats. © MPS

PAPYRUS (pà-pī′rŭs, Gr. *papýros*), a plant-like reed or rush which grows in swamps and along rivers or lakes, often to the height of 12 feet with beautiful flowers at the top. The stalk is triangular in shape, something like a giant celery stalk. In ancient times it was found mainly along the Nile in Egypt but was also known in Palestine. For commercial use the stalk was cut into sections about a foot long and these pieces were then sliced lengthwise into thin strips which were shaped and squared and laid edge to edge to form a larger piece. Other strips were laid horizontally over these strips and both were pressed together, dried in the sun, scraped and rubbed until there emerged a smooth yellowish sheet much like our heavy wrapping paper, only thicker and heavier. The juice of the pith served as the glue but sometimes other paste was added.

A fragment of the famous Elephantine Papyri, mentioning Jewish priests and governors. There was a large Jewish community, and a temple built by Jews, at Elephantine, Egypt, at the time of Nehemiah. Below, a papyrus letter, rolled, tied and sealed. BM

PARABLE (păr′à-b′l, Gr. *parabolé, likeness*), derived from the Greek verb *parabállo*, composed of the preposition *para* meaning *beside* and the verb *bállo, to cast*. A parable is thus a comparison of two objects for the purpose of teaching.

Although the word properly belongs to the NT, being found there 46 times, it does occur 15 times in the OT. There it is the translation of the Hebrew *mashál*. It seems to be used in the OT in several senses. Sometimes it is a proverbial saying or byword (I Sam. 10:12; 24:14). In Numbers it is seen more as a prophetic figurative discourse (Num. 23:7,18,24). Ezekiel employs the word much as one would today with the idea of similitude or parable (Ezek. 17:2; 21:5; 24:3). Several writers treat the word as a poem (Num. 21:27-30; I Kings 5:12; Ps. 49:5; 78:2). The writer of the Proverbs thinks of it as a sentence that contains ethical wisdom (Prov. 10:1; 25:1). Finally it is associated with the riddle or dark saying (Ps. 49:4; Ezek. 17:2; 20:4-9). Five times the NT uses the Greek word *paroimía* for parable. This may be synonymous with *parabolé* or, as found in the Johannine writings, may refer to a didactic, symbolic or figurative utterance (John 10:6; 16:29).

There are a number of English words similar in meaning to the parable, and probably no one has been more definite and clear in distinguishing between these than Trench. Trench summarizes thus: "The parable differs from the fable, moving as it does in a spiritual world, and never transgressing the actual order of things natural — from the mythus, there being in the latter an unconscious blending of the deeper meaning with the outward symbol, the two remaining separate and separable in the parable — from the proverb, inasmuch as it is longer carried out, and not merely accidentally

and occasionally, but necessarily figurative —from the allegory, comparing as it does one thing *with* another, at the same time preserving them apart as an inner and outer, not transferring, as does the allegory, the properties and qualities and relations of one *to the other* (R. Trench, *Notes on the Parables*, pp. 15-16). The importance of definition is shown by Moulton when he says that, because of varied definition of a parable, scholars have counted 79, 71, 59, 39, 37, and 33 parables in the New Testament (W. J. Moulton, "Parable" in Hastings, *Dictionary of Christ and The Gospels*). See also Herbert Lockyer, *All the Parables of the Bible* (Zondervan, 1963).

In comparing the parable with the similar figures of speech, one must bear in mind that often the parable contains elements of these other figures. For instance, there are often elements in the parable that must be treated as allegorical. This does not justify giving the parable an allegorical interpretation.

While Christ did not invent the parable, it is significant that He is the only one who used them in the NT. At one time in His ministry it was His only method in speaking to the masses (Matt. 13:34). It is interesting to note when Christ began to use this methodology. So abrupt was the change in His form of teaching that His disciples asked Him why He did this (Matt. 13:10). In His reply one notes the value of this method of instruction. It was an effective method of revealing truth to the spiritual and ready mind and at the same time of concealing it from others (Matt. 13:11). Christ came as Israel's King and only after they had rejected Him did He employ this form of imparting spiritual truth. Those who had rejected Him were not to know the "mysteries of the kingdom of heaven" (Matt. 13:11).

In the discussion of the parable there is probably no area fraught with greater disagreement than the principle of interpretation. Ramm in discussing the rules for interpreting the parables notes four principles: "perspective, cultural, exegetical and doctrinal" (Bernard Ramm, *Protestant Biblical Interpretation*, Boston: W. A. Wilde Co., 1956, p. 257). Perspectively, one must understand the parables in their relation to Christology and God's kingdom. One must not overlook the cultural background in which our Lord lived and worked.

Parable of the day laborers (Matthew 20). © SPF

"The lost sheep." © MPS

Ramm shows four things that are involved in the exegetical principle: "(1) Determine the one central truth the parable is attempting to teach. . . . (2) Determine how much of the parable is interpreted by the Lord Himself. . . . (3) Determine whether there are any clues in the context concerning the parable's meaning. . . . (4) The comparative rule" (*Ibid.*, pp. 258-267).

The following classification of parables is adapted from A. B. Bruce, *The parabolic Teaching of Christ*, London: 1904, pp. 8ff:

I. Didactic Parables

A. Nature and Development of the Kingdom:
  1. The Sower (Matt. 13:3-8; Mark 4:4-8; Luke 8:5-8)
  2. The Tares (Matt. 13:24-30)
  3. The Mustard Seed (Matt. 13:31,32; Mark 4:3-32; Luke 13:18,19)
  4. The Leaven (Matt. 13:33; Luke 13:20,21)
  5. The Hidden Treasure (Matt. 13:44)
  6. The Pearl of Great Price (Matt. 13:45,46)
  7. The Drag Net (Matt. 13:47-50)
  8. The Blade, the Ear, and the Full Corn (Mark 4:26-29)
B. Service and Rewards:
  1. The Laborers in the Vineyard (Matt. 20:1-16)
  2. The Talents (Matt. 25:14-30)
  3. The Pounds (Luke 19:11-27)
  4. The Unprofitable Servants (Luke 17:7-10)
C. Prayer:
  1. The Friend at Midnight (Luke 11:5-8)
  2. The Unjust Judge (Luke 18:1-8)
D. Love for Neighbor:
  1. The Good Samaritan (Luke 10:30-37)
E. Humility:
  1. The Lowest Seat at the Feast (Luke 14:7-11)
  2. The Pharisee and the Publican (Luke 18:9-14)
F. Worldly Wealth:
  1. The Unjust Steward (Luke 16:1-9)
  2. The Rich Fool (Luke 12:16-21)
  3. The Great Supper (Luke 14:15-24)

II. Evangelic Parables

A. God's Love for the Lost:
  1. The Lost Sheep (Matt. 18:12-14; Luke 15:3-7)
  2. The Lost Coin (Luke 15:8-10)
  3. The Lost Son (Luke 15:11-32)
B. Gratitude of the Redeemed:
  1. The Two Debtors (Luke 7:41-43)

III. Prophetic and Judicial Parables

A. Watchfulness for Christ's Return:
  1. The Ten Virgins (Matt. 25:1-13)
  2. The Faithful and Unfaithful Servants (Matt. 24:45-51; Luke 12:42-48)
  3. The Watchful Porter (Mark 13:34-37)
B. Judgment on Israel and Within the Kingdom:
  1. The Two Sons (Matt. 21:28-32)
  2. The Wicked Husbandmen (Matt. 21:33-34; Mark 12:1-12; Luke 20:9-18)
  3. The Barren Fig Tree (Luke 13:6-9)
  4. The Marriage Feast of the King's Son (Matt. 22:1-14)
  5. The Unforgiving Servant (Matt. 18:23-25)
                   H.Z.C.

PARACLETE (păr'à-klēt, Gr. *parákletos*, literally *called to one's side*, hence *advocate*), one who pleads another's cause. It is used by Christ of the Holy Spirit in John's Gospel (14:16,26; 15:26; 16:7) and of Christ in I John 2:1. The rendering of the word in ERV is *Comforter* in the Gospel, and *Advocate* in the Epistle.

PARADISE (păr'à-dīz, Gr. *parádeisos, park*), a word of Persian origin, found only three times in Scripture (Luke 23:43; II Cor. 12:4; Rev. 2:7), referring in each case to heaven. There was a similar word in the Hebrew OT, *parades*, translated *forest* or *orchard* (Neh. 2:8; Eccl. 2:5; S. of Sol. 4:13). Scholars feel that it was introduced into the Greek language very early and Xenophon made it especially familiar.

The LXX uses the word 46 times and there it is applied to quite a wide category of places. It is used of the Adamic Eden (Gen. 2:15; 3:23); of the well watered plains of the Jordan that Lot envisioned (Gen. 13:10). Since it was used to describe gardens of beauty and splendor, one is not surprised to see the NT begin to use the term to refer to the place of spiritual bliss (Luke 23:43).

The exact location of paradise is uncertain. Paul uses it in II Corinthians 12:4 and identifies it with the third heaven. Ecclesiasticus 44:16 identifies paradise with heaven into which Enoch was translated. Christ's single use of the term seems to establish its location best for the believer, for He uses it as comfort for the dying thief.   H.Z.C.

PARAH (pā'rà, Heb. *pārāh, heifer*), a city in Benjamin's territory (Josh. 18:23) now identified as Farah, a short distance NE of Jerusalem.

PARALLELISM. This word is not found in the Bible, but is rightfully placed here since it refers to a unique aspect of OT Hebrew verse. Hebrew poetry is not characterized by either rhyme or meter, but by parallelisms. There are several forms, but four are most common: synonymous (Ps. 36:5), antithetic (Ps. 20:8), synthetic (Job 11:18), and climactic (Ps. 29:1).

PARALYSIS (See Diseases)

PARALYTIC (See Diseases)

PARAMOUR (păr'à-mŏor, Heb. *pilleghesh, a concubine*), a term used in Ezekiel 23:20 of a male lover, but rendered elsewhere by *concubine*.

PARAN (pā'răn, Heb. *pā'rān, ornamental*), a wilderness area first referred to in Genesis 14:6 as "El-Paran." Its boundaries seem to be uncertain; according to some authorities it may include the wilderness of Shur; according to others, the two have separate boundaries. It lies in the central area of the Sinaitic Peninsula. The four eastern kings passed up this region in their attempt to suppress the rebellion of their subjects (Gen. 14:6). It was the area in which Ishmael lived (Gen. 21:21). On two occasions after the Israelites left Mt. Sinai they camped in this wilderness (Num. 10:12; 12:16). When Moses commanded the spies to search the land of Canaan as God had commanded, they went up from the wilderness of Paran (Num. 13:3) and later returned to it (Num. 13:26). When David was grieved at the loss of Samuel, he resorted to Paran (I Sam. 25:1). Through Paran ran one of the main routes of that day, so that Hadad after revolting from King Solomon went through Paran in his flight to Egypt.

Twice in the Scriptures (Deut. 33:2; Hab. 3:3) Mount Paran is referred to. Two mountains are suggested as being identified as Mount Paran, but the rugged range of mountains W of the Gulf of Akaba seems to be the most logical site. H.Z.C.

PARBAR (pàr'bàr, Heb. *parbār, suburb*), a word apparently of Persian origin, and referring to some building on the W side of the temple area (I Chron. 26:18; II Kings 23:11).

PARCHED GROUND (Heb. *shārāv, a mirage*), a phrase used only once in the Scriptures (Isa. 35: 7). The ERV uses "glowing" here, referring doubtless to the strange movement of air just above dry, hot earth accompanied by mirages. The word here may be rendered "looming sand-waste" which is the Arabic name for mirage.

PARCHMENT (See Writing)

PARDON (Heb. *nāsa', sālah, kāphar, to lift, forgive, pardon, cover, expiate, cancel*). Pardon is distinctively an OT word and if all its forms are included it occurs only 20 times. However, it is so closely related to forgiveness and justification that the three are often taken together. The divine pardon offered to the sinner stands in sharp contrast to human pardon. God demands a righteous ground for His pardoning of the sinner, that can be found only in the atoning work of Christ at Calvary. In the OT the animal sacrifices had a typical significance and covered (*kāphar*) the believer's sin until it should finally be removed. Note Romans 3:25 in this connection. Pardon is one aspect of salvation. When Moses comes again into the presence of God after Israel's sin at Sinai, he prays for pardon (Exod. 34:9). Some sins could not be pardoned (I Sam. 15:25-26; II Kings 24:4), but for the one who met God's conditions pardon was offered in abundance (Isa. 55:7). H.Z.C.

PARENT (Gr. *goneús*), a distinctly NT word. Although our English word does not occur in the OT, there is much instruction there about the parent-child relation. Children were to honor their parents (Exod. 20:12) and obey and reverence them (Lev. 19:3; Deut. 5:16). Failure in these relations on the part of the child was a sin which could be punished by death (Deut. 21:18-21). The same high regard for parents is expected of children in the NT (Eph. 6:1; Col. 3:20). Parents were expected on the other hand to love their children, care and provide for them and not to provoke them to wrath (II Cor. 12:14; Eph. 6:4; Col. 3:21).

PARENTAL BLESSINGS were given much importance in OT times. Blessings from godly parents were prophetic of a child's future and assured him of success, whereas a parental curse was a severe loss (Gen. 27:4,12,27-29).

PARMASHTA (pàr-măsh'tà, Heb. *parmashtā', the very first*), one of the sons of Haman. He is listed as one of those slain by the Jews (Esth. 9:9).

PARMENAS (pàr'mē-năs, Gr. *Parmenás, constant*), one of the seven chosen to care for the daily distribution to the poor (Acts 6:5). Tradition tells of his martyrdom at Philippi.

PARNACH (pàr'năk, Heb. *parnākh*, meaning uncertain), the father of Elizaphan the prince of Zebulun (Num. 34:25).

PAROSH (pā'rŏsh, Heb. *par'ōsh, a flea*), one whose descendants returned to Babylon under Zerubbabel (Ezra 2:3; Neh. 7:8) and under Ezra (Ezra 8:3, *Pharosh* in KJV). One of their number, Pedaiah, helped rebuild the walls (Neh. 3:25).

PAROUSIA (pă-roō'sĭ-à, Gr. *parousía, presence, coming*), a word translated by both "coming" and "presence" in KJV. This is the word most frequently used in the NT of our Lord's return, and describes both the rapture and the return of Christ to the earth (I Cor. 15:23; I Thess. 4:15; Matt. 24:

3; I Thess. 3:13; II Pet. 1:16). Arndt and Gingrich show that the word, found in classical writings and in the apocryphal books as well as in the NT, has developed in two directions. It is used by false cults to express the coming of a hidden divinity and, on the other hand, has become the official term for the visit of a person of high rank. In view of the latter, the use of *parousia* in connection with the Lord's return is fitting. When it is translated "presence" it means the presence made possible by the coming of the individual. H.Z.C.

PARSHANDATHA (pàr'shăn-dā'thà, Heb. *parshandātha', inquisitive*), the eldest of Haman's sons (Esth. 9:7).

PARTHIANS (pàr'thĭ-ănz, Gr. *Párthoi*). Luke's geographical list of the people who were in Jerusalem on the day of Pentecost (Acts 2:9) is headed by "Parthians and Medes." By "Parthians" Luke no doubt meant all the Jews and proselytes who lived in the old Parthian Empire to the E, known today as Iran. The earliest dispersion of the ten tribes took place in the eastern countries. Later they were augmented by immigration and colonization so that by the first century A.D. the number of Jews in the eastern territories ran into millions.

There is only scant information about the early history of Parthia, a small country 120 x 300 miles, NW of old Persia and S of the Caspian Sea. Alexander subdued the people, and after the breakdown of his far-flung empire they fell under the rule of the Seleucids. After a successful revolt they soon became a rival power of Rome. Proud Roman Crassus was defeated and killed by them in 53 B.C. In 40 B.C. they seized Jerusalem. At one time their empire extended from the Tigris to India. Rome and Parthia learned to respect each other's power and there were many years of somewhat peaceful co-existence which extended through the first century A.D. Their success was due mainly to their unusual way of fighting. Almost all of their soldiers were mounted on horseback. They were excellent with the bow and arrow so that they have been described as "archers fighting on horseback." Known for their prowess in war, instead of the arts and sciences, they never developed a literature of their own. But it is certain that the apostles of our Lord preached the Gospel among them.

PARTITION, MIDDLE WALL OF. In Ephesians 2:14 Paul asserts that Christ has broken down the "middle wall of partition" which divided Jews and Gentiles, and has made of the two one new man. Paul probably has in mind a literal wall as a tangible symbol of the division between Jews and Gentiles — the wall in the temple area in Jerusalem separating the court of the Gentiles from the courts into which only Jews might enter. On this wall was a notice in Greek and Latin warning Gentiles to keep out on pain of death. In 1871 archaeologists who were excavating the site of the temple found a pillar with this inscription, "No man of another nation to enter within the fence and enclosure round the temple, and whoever is caught will have himself to blame that his death ensues." Paul himself almost lost his life in the temple enclosure when at the end of his third missionary journey his Jewish enemies accused him of bringing Trophimus the Ephesian past this barrier in the temple (Acts 21:29). S.B.

PARTRIDGE (See Birds)

PARUAH (pà-roō'à, Heb. *pārûah, blooming*), the father of Jehoshaphat employed by Solomon (I Kings 4:17).

PARVAIM (pàr-vā'ĭm, Heb. *parwāyim,* meaning uncertain), a place mentioned in II Chronicles 3:6 from which Solomon obtained gold for the temple.

PASACH (pā'săk, Heb. *pāsakh, to divide*), the son of Japhet who descended from Asher (I Chron. 7:33).

PASDAMMIM (păs'dăm'ĭm, Heb. *pasdamîm, place of bloodshed*), a place in Judah of encounter between David and the Philistines (I Chron. 11:13). It is called also "Ephesdammim" (I Sam. 17:1).

PASEAH (pà-sē'à, Heb. *pāsēah, lame*). 1. A son of Eshton (I Chron. 4:12).

2. The head of a family of Nethinim (Ezra 2:49; Neh. 7:51), one of whose descendants helped in the restoration of one of the gates of Jerusalem (Neh. 3:6).

PASHUR (păsh'hêr, Heb. *pashhûr*). 1. A priest, the son of Immer (Jer. 20:1), the "chief governor" in the Lord's house. Angered at the prophecies of Jeremiah, he placed him in stocks located near the house of the Lord. When released, Jeremiah told him that Jehovah had changed his name to Magor-missabib, meaning "terror on every side." Jeremiah also foretold Judah's future captivity by Babylon.

2. The priestly son of Melchiah who was one of the chief court princes during Zedekiah's reign. When Nebuchadnezzar was preparing for one of his attacks on Jerusalem, he was sent by the king to Jeremiah. Later he joined others in seeking to have Jeremiah put to death. In all probability he is the same person referred to in I Chronicles 9:12; Ezra 2:38; Nehemiah 7:41; 10:3; and 11:12.

3. The father of Gedaliah mentioned in Jeremiah 38:1 who aided in Jeremiah's imprisonment.

PASSAGE (Heb. *ma'avar, ford*), may refer to the ford of a river (Gen. 32:23), a mountain pass (I Sam. 13:23), or a crossing (Josh. 22:11).

PASSION OF CHRIST (See Christ, Jesus)

PASSOVER, FEAST OF (See Feasts)

PASTORAL EPISTLES. I. Authorship. The term "pastoral epistles," as a common title for I and II Timothy and Titus, dates from the early part of the 18th century. It is not exact. Though these letters do furnish worthwhile directions for pastors, the addressees were not pastors in the usual, present-day sense of that term. Rather, they were Paul's special envoys sent by him on specific missions and entrusted with concrete assignments according to the need of the hour. For biographical articles see TIMOTHY and TITUS.

In the 19th century F. Schleiermacher rejected the Pauline authorship of *one* of these epistles (I Timothy), and F. C. Baur of all *three.* Baur had many followers, and today this rejection is rather common. The grounds on which it is based are as follows:

1. Vocabulary. Difference in vocabulary between these three (I and II Timothy and Titus) and the other ten Pauline epistles (Romans, I and II Corinthians, etc.) must be admitted, but has often been exaggerated. Of words found in the three but not found in the ten *only* nine are common to the three. Detailed study, moreover, has shown that the Pastoral Epistles contain not one single word that was foreign to the age in which Paul lived and could not have been used by him. Besides, vocabulary always varies with the specific subject that is being discussed. Thus, in addressing Timothy and Titus, who were in need of good counsel with respect to their own task of imparting instruction, the frequent use of words belonging to

the word-family of *teaching* is certainly not surprising. Other factors which may have influenced the choice of words are: the character of the addressees, the apostle's age and environment, the progress of the Church with its ever-expanding vocabulary, and the not improbable use of secretaries.

2. Style. This argument is self-defeating, for candid examination of the actual facts clearly points to Paul as the author of these epistles. The three and the ten picture the same kind of person: one who is deeply interested in those whom he addresses, ascribing to God's sovereign grace whatever is good in himself and/or in the addressees, showing wonderful tact in counseling. Again, both the three and the ten were written by a person who is fond of *litotes* (cf. "not ashamed of the gospel" [Rom. 1:16], with "not ashamed of the testimony of our Lord" [II Tim. 1:8]), of enumerations (I Tim. 3:1-12; cf. Rom. 1:29-32), of play upon words (I Tim. 6:17; cf. Philemon 10,11), of appositional phrases (I Tim. 1:17; cf. Rom. 12:1), of expressions of personal unworthiness (I Tim. 1:13,15; cf. I Cor. 15:9), and of doxologies (I Tim. 1:17; cf. Rom. 11:36). When the three are compared with those sections of the ten that are comparable, it is clear that their style is definitely Pauline. Hence, many critics now grant that Paul wrote some but not all of their contents. But this theory does not go far enough in the right direction, for those who hold it are unable to show where the genuine material begins and the spurious ends. The acceptance, in some real sense, of Pauline authorship for the entire contents is the only theory that fits the facts.

3. Theology. It is claimed that grace is no longer in the center, and that there is here an over-emphasis on good works. The facts contradict this verdict. Is not grace the heart and center of such passages as I Timothy 1:14, II Timothy 1:9, and Titus 3:5? It is true that in these three epistles the *fruit* (good works) of faith is emphasized, but the reason is that the *nature* of faith and its *necessity* over against law-works had been fully set forth in the letters which preceded. The tree is first; then comes the fruit.

4. Marcionism. It is said that the Pastorals controvert second-century Marcionism (a heresy with erroneous views of Christ's person), hence cannot have been written by first-century Paul. The question is asked, "Does not I Timothy 6:20 refer to the very title of Marcion's book *Antitheses?*" This is shallow reasoning. Surely a merely verbal coincidence cannot prove any relationship between Marcion and Paul. What the author of I Timothy 6:20 has in mind is not Marcion's *contrast* between Christianity and Judaism but the *conflicting opinions* of those who speculated in Jewish genealogies. Other supposed allusions to second-century isms are equally far-fetched.

5. Ecclesiastical Organization. Do not the Pastorals reveal a marked advance in church-government, far beyond the time of Paul? Some reason that the three evidence the beginning of pyramidal organization, where *one bishop* (I Tim. 3:1,2; Titus 1:7) rules over *several presbyters* (Titus 1:5). In the Pastorals the terms *bishop* (overseer) and *presbyter* (elder) refer to the same individuals, as is proved by I Timothy 1:5-7 (cf. I Tim. 3:1-7; Phil 1:1; I Peter 5:1,2). With respect to age and dignity these men were called *presbyters;* with respect to the nature of their task they were called *overseers.* From very early times the Church had its *elders* (Acts 11:30; 14:23; cf. I

Thess. 5:12,13). It is also very natural that Paul, about to depart from this earthly realm, should specify certain qualifications for office, so that the Church might be guarded against the ravages of error, both doctrinal and moral.

6. Chronology. It is maintained that the book of Acts, which records Paul's story from his conversion to a Roman imprisonment that terminated in the apostle's execution, leaves no room for the Pastorals, which presuppose journeys not recorded in Acts. Acts points toward release, not execution (Acts 23:12-35; 28:21,30,31); so do Paul's prison-epistles (Phil. 1:25-27; 2:24; Philemon 22). Early writers—Clement of Rome, Eusebius—as well as later ones — Chrysostom, Jerome, etc. — bear witness to two Roman imprisonments with ample room for the writings of the Pastorals after the first of these two.

As to internal evidence, not only does the writer call himself *Paul, apostle*, but he also *describes* himself, and this description agrees with that of Paul in Acts. The letter-plan of the three, moreover, is similar to that of the ten. All the evidence, accordingly, favors the Pauline authorship of the Pastorals.

II. Background and Purpose.

1. Common to Timothy and Titus. Released from his first Roman imprisonment Paul, perhaps while on his way to Asia Minor, leaves Titus on the island of Crete to bring to completion the organization of its church(es) (Acts 2:11; Titus 1:5). At Ephesus Paul is joined by Timothy (back from Philippi? cf. Phil 2:19-23). On leaving for Macedonia Paul instructs Timothy to remain in Ephesus, which is sorely in need of his ministry (I Tim. 1:3,4). From Macedonia Paul writes a letter to Timothy in Ephesus (I Tim.) and one to Titus in Crete (Titus).

2. Further Background and Purpose of I Timothy. At Ephesus Judaizers are spreading strange and dangerous doctrines (I Tim. 1:4,7; 4: 7). Both men and women attend worship spiritually unprepared (I Tim. 2). To cope with that situation there is Timothy — *timid* Timothy. Letter's aim:

a. To impart guidance against error (cf. 1:3-11, 18-20; chap. 4; chap. 6). With this in mind proper organization is stressed: choosing the right kind of leaders (chap. 3, chap. 5).

b. To stress the need of proper preparation and conduct (for both men and women) with respect to public worship (chap. 2).

c. To bolster Timothy's spirit (I Tim. 4:14; 6: 12,20).

3. Further Background and Purpose of Titus. The reputation of the Cretans is poor. True sanctification is needed (2:11-14; 3:10). Gospel workers (such as Zenas and Apollos, whose itinerary includes Crete and who probably carry with them Paul's letter) must receive every assistance. As to Paul himself, having recently met Timothy, and the situation in Crete being critical, it is but natural that he wishes to have a face-to-face conference with Titus also.

Purpose of Paul's letter to Titus:

a. To stress the need of thorough *sanctification.*

b. To speed on their way Zenas the law-expert and Apollos the evangelist (3:13).

c. To urge Titus to meet Paul at Nicopolis (3: 12).

4. Background and Purpose of II Timothy. Emperor Nero, blamed for Rome's fearful conflagration (July, A.D. 64), in turn blames Christians, who suffer frightful persecution. Paul is imprisoned (second Roman imprisonment). He faces death (II Tim. 1:16,17; 2:9), Luke alone is with him. Others have left him, either on legitimate missions (Crescens, Titus) or by reason of having fallen in love with the present world. (Demas; 4:6-11). Meanwhile, soul-destroying error continues in Timothy's Ephesus (1:8; 2:3,12,14-18,23; 3:8:12). Letter's purpose, accordingly:

a. To urge Timothy to come to Rome as soon as possible in view of the apostle's impending departure from this life, and to bring with him Mark and Paul's cloak and books (4:6-22).

b. To admonish Timothy to cling to sound doctrine, defending it against all error (chap. 2; 4:1-5).

III. Contents.

I Timothy
Theme: The Apostle Paul, writing to Timothy, gives directions for the administration of the church.

Chapter 1
Paul salutes Timothy, and repeats his order that Timothy remain at Ephesus to combat the error of those who refuse to see their own sinful condition in the light of God's holy law, while pretending to be law-experts. By contrast, Paul thanks God for having made him, who regards himself as "chief of sinners," a minister of the gospel.

Chapter 2
Paul gives directions with respect to public worship. Prayers must be made in behalf of all men. Both the men and the women must come spiritually prepared.

Chapter 3
The apostle gives directions with respect to the offices and functions in the church.

Chapter 4
He warns against apostasy, and instructs Timothy how to deal with it.

Chapters 5 and 6
He gives directions with respect to certain definite groups and individuals: old(er) men, young(er) men, old(er) women, young(er) women, etc.

Titus
Theme: The Apostle Paul, writing to Titus, gives directions for the promotion of the spirit of sanctification:

Chapter 1
In congregational life. Well-qualified elders must be appointed in every town. Reason: Crete is not lacking in disreputable people who must be sternly rebuked.

Chapter 2
In family and individual life. All classes of individuals that compose the home-circle must conduct themselves so that by their life they adorn their doctrine. Reason: the grace of God has appeared to all unto sanctification and joyful expectation of the coming of "our great God and Saviour Jesus Christ."

Chapter 3
In social (i.e., public) life. Believers should be obedient to the authorities and kind to all men. Foolish questions should be shunned and persistently factious men should be rejected. Concluding directions with respect to kingdom travelers and believers in general.

II Timothy
Theme: Sound Doctrine.

Chapter 1
Hold on to it, as did Lois and Eunice; as I (Paul) do; and as did Onesiphorus.

Chapter 2

Teach it. This brings great reward, for the Gospel is glorious in its contents. Vain disputes serve no useful purpose.

Chapter 3

Abide in it, knowing that enemies will arise, and that it is based on the sacred writings.

Chapter 4

Preach it, in season, out of season. Remain faithful in view of the fact that I, Paul, am about to set sail.

Bibliography: Harrison, P. N., *The Problem of the Pastoral Epistles,* Oxford, Oxford University Press, 1921. Hendriksen, W., *Exposition of the Pastoral Epistles,* a volume in *New Testament Commentary,* Grand Rapids, Mich.: Baker Book House, 1957. A large section is devoted to the question of authorship (pp. 4-33; 377-381). Simpson, E. K., *The Pastoral Epistles,* Grand Rapids, Mich.: Wm. B. Eerdmans Pub. Co., 1954. W.H.

PATARA (păt′à-rà, Gr. *Pátara*), an ancient seaport of Lycia near the mouth of the Xanthus. Coins date from 440 B.C. There was an old oracle of Apollo situated in the town. Hence the poetic title for the god "Patareus" (Hor. Od. 3:4:64). The trade of the river-valley and its position on the Asia Minor coast gave the port its importance. It was convenient for ships running E before the prevailing autumn wind for Phoenicia or Egypt. For example, Paul made for Tyre in one stage from Patara (Acts 21:1,2).

PATHROS (păth′rŏs, Heb. *pathrôs*), mentioned five times in the OT prophets (Isa. 11:11; Jer. 44:1 and 15; Ezek. 29:14; 30:14) in connection with the repatriation of Jewish remnants. Pathros was Upper Egypt, the Egyptian "Pteres" or "Southland," extending from S of Memphis to the First Cataract. The division corresponds to two ancient kingdoms. There is papyrological evidence for settlements of Jews at Syene at the southern extremity of Pathros as early as 525 B.C. The "Pathrusim" of Genesis 10:14 seem to be the inhabitants of this territory.

PATHRUSIM (păth-rōō′sĭm, Heb. *pathrūsî, an inhabitant of Pathros*), Egyptians who, it is believed, came from Pathros, Egypt, from which their name is derived. They are descended from Mizraim (Gen. 10:13f; I Chron. 1:11f).

PATIENCE (Gr. *hypomoné* and *makrothymía*). Both of these Greek words are translated by our English word *patience,* but they are not exactly synonymous in meaning. *Hypomoné* is the quality of endurance under trials. Those possessing this virtue are free from cowardice or despondency. It is mainly an attitude of heart with respect to things. *Makrothymía, longsuffering,* is an attitude with respect to people. Longsuffering is listed in Galatians 5:22 as a fruit of the Spirit. Patience is a virtue that God prizes highly in man and seems to be best developed under trials (James 1:3-4; 5:11). Both terms are used of God (Rom. 2:4; 15:5; I Pet. 3:20), but as descriptive of His qualities seem always to apply to persons and never to things. H.Z.C.

PATMOS (Gr. *Pátmos*), a tiny wind-swept island of the Sporades group, lying off the coast of Asia Minor in the Aegean Sea about 28 miles S of Samos. It is only ten miles long and six miles wide at the broadest point, and its coastline is so irregular that it is only 25 sq. miles in area. Being of volcanic origin, it is rocky and almost treeless, with many volcanic hills rising as high as 800 feet. The harbor of Scala, the chief city, divides the islet, which is shaped like a horse's head, into two parts.

Few people would know of the island if it were not mentioned in the Bible. It was one of the many

On the Island of Patmos, a view from the monastery. © RTHPL

isolated places to which the Romans banished their exiles, and according to tradition the Emperor Domitian banished the Apostle John to this lonely place from Ephesus in 95 A.D. (Rev. 1:9). During the estimated 18 months spent there, he received the visions of the Lord now recorded in *The Revelation.* The cave or grotto near Scala in which John lived is still pointed out to travelers, as well as the Monastery of St. John above the city. During the middle ages the island was all but deserted but today has a population of 3,000 or more. It was under Turkish rule until 1912, when it passed into the hands of the Italians. Today it is known as Patino. L.M.P.

PATRIARCHS, PATRIARCHAL AGE. (Gr. *patriárches, the father of a family, tribe,* or *race*), a name given in the NT to those who founded the Hebrew race and nation. In the NT it is applied to Abraham (Heb. 7:4), the sons of Jacob (Acts 7:8,9), and David (Acts 2:29). The term is now commonly used to refer to the persons whose names appear in the genealogies and covenant-histories before the time of Moses (Gen. 5,11, histories of Noah, Abraham, Isaac, Jacob, etc.). In the patriarchal system the government of a clan was the right of the eldest lineal male. The patriarchal head was the priest of his own household.

While many scholars of the past have tended to regard the Biblical accounts in the patriarchal dispensation as legendary, recent archaeological discoveries have confirmed the truthfulness of the narratives and have thrown much light on customs of the time which had been somewhat puzzling, such as Abraham's taking Sarah's slave Hagar as a concubine, Abraham's making his steward Eliezer his heir, and Rachel's carrying away her father's household gods. Excavations at Ur, where Abraham lived, reveal it to have been a rich commercial center, with inhabitants of education and culture. S.B.

PATROBAS (păt′rō-bàs, Gr. *Patróbas*), a Roman Christian to whom Paul sent greetings (Rom. 16:14).

PAU (pā′ū, Heb. *pā′û, bleating*), the capital city of king Hadar of Edom (Gen. 36:39); written Pai in I Chronicles 1:50. It remains unidentified.

PAUL (Gr. *Paúlos*, from Latin *Paulis, little*), the great apostle to the Gentiles. The main Biblical urce for the life of Paul is The Acts of the Apostles, with important supplemental information from the Pauline Epistles. Allusions in the epistles make it clear that many events in his checkered and stirring career are unrecorded (cf. II Cor. 11: 24-28).

Names. His Hebrew name was Saul (Gr. *Saúlos*) and he is always so designated in Acts until his clash with Bar-Jesus at Paphos, where Luke writes, "But Saul, who is also *called* Paul" (13:9). Thereafter in Acts he is always called Paul. In his epistles the apostle always calls himself Paul. As a Roman citizen he doubtless bore both names from youth. His double name is implied in Luke's statement, "Saul, the one also Paul" (*Saulos ho kai Paulos*). It was a common practice among Jews of the dispersion. The change to the use of Paul is peculiarly appropriate at the time when he entered upon his position of leadership in bringing the Gospel to the Gentile world.

Background. Providentially, three elements of the world's life of that day, Greek culture, Roman citizenship, and Hebrew religion met in the apostle to the Gentiles. Paul was born near the beginning of the first century in the busy Graeco-Roman city of Tarsus, located at the NE corner of the Mediterranean Sea. A noted trading center, it was known for its manufacture of goats' hair cloth, and here the young Saul learned his trade of "tentmaking" (Acts 18:3). Tarsus had a famous university; although there is no evidence that Paul attended there, its influence must have made a definite impact on him, enabling him the better to understand prevailing life and views in the Roman Empire. He had the further privilege of being born a Roman citizen (Acts 22:28), though how his father had come to possess the coveted status is not known. Proud of the distinction and advantages thus conferred on him, Paul knew how to use that citizenship as a shield against injustice from local magistrates and to enhance the status of the Christian faith. His Gentile connections greatly aided him in bridging the chasm between the Gentile and the Jew. But of central significance was his strong Jewish heritage, being fundamental to all he was and became. He was never ashamed to acknowledge himself a Jew (Acts 21:39; 22:3), was justly proud of his Jewish background (11 Cor. 11:22), and retained a deep and abiding love for his brethren according to the flesh (Rom. 9:1-2; 10:1). Becoming a Christian meant no conscious departure on his part from the religious hopes of his people as embodied in the OT Scriptures (Acts 24:14-16; 26:6-7). This racial affinity with the Jews enabled Paul with great profit to begin his missionary labors in each city in the synagogue, for there he had the best prepared audience.

Born of purest Jewish blood (Phil. 3:5), the son of a Pharisee (Acts 23:6), Saul was cradled in orthodox Judaism. At the proper age, perhaps 13, he was sent to Jerusalem and completed his studies under the famous Gamaliel (Acts 22:3; 26:4-5). Being a superior, zealous student (Gal. 1:14), he absorbed not only the teaching of the OT but also the rabbinical learning of the scholars.

At his first appearance in Acts as "a young man" (7:58), probably at least 30 years old, he was already an acknowledged leader in Judaism. His active opposition to Christianity marked him as the natural leader of the persecution that arose upon the death of Stephen (7:58-8:3; 9:1-2). The persecutions described in 26:10-11 indicate his

The house of Ananias, near Straight Street, in Damascus (Acts 9:11). © MPS

fanatical devotion to Judaism. He was convinced that Christians were heretics and that the honor of Jehovah demanded their extermination (26:9). He acted in undoubting unbelief (I Tim. 1:13).

Conversion. The persecution was doubtless repugnant to his finer inner sensitivities, but Saul did not doubt the rightness of his course. The spread of Christians to foreign cities only increased his fury against them, causing him to extend the scope of his activities. As the persecutor, armed with authority from the high priest, was approaching Damascus, the transforming crisis in his life occurred. Only an acknowledgment of divine intervention can explain it. Repeatedly in his epistles Paul refers to it as the work of divine grace and power, transforming him and commissioning him as Christ's messenger (I Cor. 9:16-17; 15:10; Gal. 1:15-16; Eph. 3:7-9; I Tim. 1:12-16). The three accounts in Acts of the conversion are controlled by the immediate purpose of the narrator and supplement each other. Luke's own account (chap. 9) is historical, relating the event objectively, while the two accounts by Paul (chaps. 22, 26) stress those aspects appropriate to his immediate endeavor.

When the supernatural Being arresting him identified Himself as "Jesus whom thou persecutest," Saul at once saw the error of his way and surrendered instantaneously and completely. The three days of fasting in blindness were days of agonizing heartsearching and further dealing with the Lord. The ministry of Ananias of Damascus consummated the conversion experience, unfolded to Saul the divine commission, and opened the door to him to the Christian fellowship at Damascus. Later in reviewing his former life Paul clearly recognized how God had been preparing him for his future work (Gal. 1:15-16).

Early Activities. The new convert at once proclaimed the deity and Messiahship of Jesus in the Jewish synagogues of Damascus, truths that had seized his soul (9:20-22). Since the purpose of his coming was no secret, this action caused consternation among the Jews. Paul's visit to Arabia, mentioned in Galatians 1:17, seems best placed between Acts 9:22 and 23. There is no hint that its purpose was to preach; rather it seems that he felt it necessary to retire to rethink his beliefs in the light of the new revelation that had come to him. The length of the stay is not certain, but Paul came out of Arabia with the essentials of his theology fixed.

Upon returning to Damascus, his aggressive preaching forced him to flee the murderous fury of the Jews (Acts 9:23-25; Gal. 1:17; II Cor. 11: 32-33). Three years after his conversion Saul returned to Jerusalem with the intention of becoming acquainted with Peter (Gal. 1:18). The Jerusalem believers regarded him with cold suspicion, but the good offices of Barnabas secured his acceptance among them (Acts 9:26-28). His bold witness to the Hellenistic Jews aroused bitter hostility and cut the visit to 15 days (Gal. 1:18). Instructed by the Lord in a vision to leave (Acts 22:17-21), he agreed to be sent home to Tarsus (Acts 9:30), where he remained in obscurity for some years. Galatians 1:21-23 implies that he did some evangelistic work there, but we have no further details. Some think that many of the events of II Corinthians 11:24-26 must be placed here.

After the opening of the door of the gospel to the Gentiles in the house of Cornelius, a Gentile church was soon established in Syrian Antioch. Barnabas, who had been sent to superintend the revival, saw the need for assistance, remembered Saul's commission to the Gentiles, and brought him to Antioch. An aggressive teaching ministry "for a whole year" produced a profound impact on the city, resulting in the designation of the disciples as "Christians" (Acts 11:20-26). Informed by visiting prophets of an impending famine, the Antioch church raised a collection and sent it to the Jerusalem elders by Barnabas and Saul (11:27-30), marking Saul's second visit to Jerusalem since his conversion. Some scholars would equate this visit with Galatians 2:1-10, but Acts 11-12 reveals no traces as yet of such a serious conflict in the church about circumcision.

The old wall of Damascus, where St. Paul was let down in a basket (Acts 9:23-25). © MPS

Missionary Journeys. The work of Gentile foreign missions was inaugurated by the church at Antioch under the direction of the Holy Spirit in the sending forth of "Barnabas and Saul" (13:1-3).

The first missionary journey, begun apparently in the spring of A.D. 48, began with work among the Jews on Cyprus. Efforts at Paphos to gain the attention of the proconsul, Sergius Paulus, encountered the determined opposition of the sorcerer Elymas. Saul publicly exposed his diabolical character and the swift judgment that tell upon Elymas caused the amazed proconsul to "believe" (13:4-12). It was a signal victory of the Gospel.

After the events at Paphos Saul, henceforth called Paul in Acts, emerged as the recognized leader of the missionary party. Steps to carry the Gospel to untrodden regions were taken when the party sailed to Perga in Pamphylia on the southern shores of Asia Minor. Here their attendant, John Mark, cousin of Barnabas (Col. 4:10 A.S.V.), deserted them and returned to Jerusalem, an act which Paul regarded unjustified. Arriving at Pisidian Antioch, located in the province of Galatia, the missionaries found a ready opening in the Jewish synagogue. Paul's address to an audience composed of Jews and God-fearing Gentiles, his first recorded address in Acts, is reported at length by Luke as representative of his synagogue ministry (13:16-41). The message made a deep impression, and request was made for more the next sabbath. The large crowd, mainly of Gentiles, that flocked to the synagogue the following sabbath aroused the jealousy and fierce opposition of the Jewish leaders. In consequence Paul announced a turning to the Gentiles with their message. Gentiles formed the core of the church established in Pisidian Antioch (13:42-52). Jewish-inspired opposition forced the missionaries to depart for Iconium, SE of Antioch, where the results were duplicated and a flourishing church begun. Compelled to flee a threatened stoning at Iconium, the missionaries crossed into the ethnographic territory of Lycaonia, still within the province of Galatia, and began work at Lystra, which was apparently without a synagogue. The healing of a congenital cripple caused a pagan attempt to offer sacrifices to the missionaries as gods in human form. Paul's horrified protest (14:15-17), arresting the attempt, reveals his dealings with pagans who did not have the OT revelation. Timothy apparently was converted at this time. Fanatical agitators from Antioch and Iconium turned the disillusioned pagans against the missionaries and in the uproar Paul was stoned. Dragged out of the city, the unconscious apostle was left for dead, but as the disciples stood around him he regained consciousness, reentered the city, and the next day was able to make the trip to neighboring Derbe. After a fruitful and unmolested ministry there, the missionaries retraced their steps to instruct their converts and organize them into churches with responsible leaders (14:1-23). They returned to Syrian Antioch and reported how "God had opened a door of faith unto the Gentiles" (14: 27). That is a summary of Paul's philosophy of Gentile missions, salvation solely through faith in Christ.

The Jerusalem Conference (Acts 15; Gal. 2:1-10) arose out of the tension produced by the mass influx of the Gentiles into the church. This movement evoked the anxiety and opposition of the Pharisaic party in the church. Certain men from Judea came to Antioch and taught the brethren that unless they received circumcision they could not be saved. This demand, contrary to the Pauline doctrine of justification by faith, aroused sharp controversy and resulted in Paul, Barnabas, and certain others being sent to Jerusalem concerning this matter.

While some scholars reject the identification, it seems best to equate Galatians 2:1-10 with Acts 15. The differences are due to the differing standpoint of the two writers, Luke's account being historical, while Paul's was personal. In Acts there are apparently two public sessions, vss. 5 and 6, while Paul speaks of a private meeting with the Jerusalem leaders. After ample discussion of the problem, the conference repudiated the view of the Judaizers and refused to impose the law on Gentile believers, only requesting them to abstain from specific offensive practices. The decision was formulated in an epistle and sent to Antioch through Judas and Silas as official delegates.

Their position vindicated, Paul and Barnabas continued their ministry at Antioch. Apparently during this time the incident of Galatians 2:11-21 occurred. The Jerusalem conference left unmentioned the problem of the relation of Jewish believers to the law. As represented by James, Judaic Christians continued to observe the Mosaic law, not for salvation, but as a way of life, because they were *Jewish* believers. Peter's withdrawal from table fellowship with Gentiles, lest he offend those of the circumcision, led him into inconsistency which Paul recognized as undermining the status of the Gentile believer.

For the second missionary journey Paul and Barnabas separated because of their "sharp contention" concerning John Mark. Barnabas sailed to Cyprus with Mark, while Paul chose Silas and revisited the churches in Galatia (15:36-41). At Lystra Paul added young Timothy to the missionary party, having circumcised him to remove obstacles for work among the Jews. Negative leadings closed the door to missionary work in Asia and Bithynia, but at Troas the positive call to Macedonia was received (16:1-9). The use of "we" (16:10) reveals Luke's presence with the group that sailed for Macedonia. The vivid accounts of Lydia's conversion, the deliverance of the demon-possessed slave girl, the subtle charges against and imprisonment of Paul and Silas, the startling events that followed (16:11-40) bespeak the hand of an eye-witness. Paul's demands of the magistrates next morning established the dignity of the preachers and safeguarded the status of the young church.

Leaving Luke at Philippi, the missionaries next began an expository ministry in the synagogue at Thessalonica. With the synagogue soon closed to him, Paul apparently carried on a successful Gentile ministry there. A Jewish-instigated riot forced the missionaries to flee to Berea, where a fruitful ministry resulted among the "noble" Bereans. When the work there was interrupted by agitators from Thessalonica, Silas and Timothy remained, but Paul, the leader of the work, was brought to Athens by some brethren (17:1-15). From I Thessalonians 3:1-2 it appears that Timothy and Silas came to Athens as requested; Timothy was sent back to Thessalonica, and Silas apparently went back to Philippi (Phil. 4:15; II Cor. 11:9).

Stirred by the Athenian idolatry, Paul preached in the synagogue and daily in the market. Drawing the attention of the Athenian philosophers, he was requested to give a formal exposition of his teaching. His appearing on "Mars' Hill" was not a formal trial. His memorable speech before the pagan philosophers (17:22-31) is a masterpiece

A tablet on Mars Hill, Athens, commemorating Paul's sermon there. LO

of tact, insight, and condensation, but the contemptuous interruption at the mention of the resurrection prevented an elaboration of the further essentials of the Gospel. A few converts were made, but Paul regarded the mission at cultured, philosophical, sophisticated Athens with keen disappointment.

On the contrary, the work at Corinth, a city of commerce, wealth, squalor and gross immorality, proved to be a definite success, lasting 18 months (18:1-17). After finding employment at his trade with Aquila and Priscilla, recently expelled from Rome, Paul preached in the Corinthian synagogue. Apparently he was depressed from his experience at Athens, but the coming of Silas and Timothy lifted his spirits and a vigorous witness was begun (18:5). Timothy's report concerning the Thessalonians caused the writing of I Thessalonians. A few months later, because of further information from there, II Thessalonians was written. Unable to return to Thessalonica Paul wrote both letters to meet the needs of his converts. Some would also place the writing of Galatians at Corinth, but Galatians is capable of a wide range of dating within the Acts framework. A successful work among the Gentiles resulted in the formation of a large church, the majority of the members being from the lower levels of society (I Cor. 1:26). With the arrival of the new proconsul, Gallio, perhaps in May, A.D. 52, the Jews accused Paul of teaching an illegal religion, but the governor, declaring a religious controversy outside his jurisdiction, refused to judge the matter. His action in effect gave tacit governmental recognition to Christianity.

From Corinth Paul took Aquila and Priscilla with him as far as Ephesus, intending upon his return to continue the profitable partnership with them there. Refusing an invitation for further ministry in the Ephesian synagogue, Paul hurried to Judea. He apparently visited Jerusalem and then spent some time at Antioch (18:18-22).

Paul's departure from Antioch traditionally marks the beginning of the **third missionary journey.** It is convenient to retain the traditional designation, but it should be remembered that with the second journey Antioch ceased to be the center for Paul's activities.

Having strengthened the disciples in "the region of Galatia and Phrygia," Paul commenced a fruitful ministry at Ephesus, lasting nearly three years (19:1-41; 20:31). His work at Ephesus, one of the most influential cities of the E, placed Paul at the heart of Greco-Roman civilization. After three months of work in the synagogue, Paul launched an independent Gentile work, centering his daily preaching in the school of Tyrannus for a two-year period. The Ephesian ministry was marked by systematic teaching (20:18-21), extraordinary miracles (19:11-12), signal victory over the magical arts (19:13-19), and devastating inroads on the worship of Diana (19:23-27). Streams of people came to Ephesus for purposes of commerce, religion, or pleasure, where coming into contact with the Gospel many were converted and spread the message throughout the province (19:10). But the work was marked by constant and fierce opposition (20:19; I Cor. 15:32). The financially-prompted tumult led by Demetrius brought the work of Paul at Ephesus to a close (19:23-20:1).

While at Ephesus Paul inaugurated a collection among his Gentile churches for the saints in Judea (I Cor. 16:1-4). Since its delivery was to mark the close of his work in the E, Paul was making plans to visit Rome (Acts 19:21), intending from there to go to Spain (Rom. 15:22-29).

While at Ephesus Paul experienced anxieties due to various difficulties in the Corinthian church. In a letter now lost (I Cor. 5:9) he counseled them about their relations to pagan society. Perhaps he also made a brief visit to Corinth (II Cor. 12:14). The arrival of a delegation from Corinth with a letter from the church was the immediate occasion for the writing of I Corinthians (I Cor. 16:17,18; 7:1), wherein Paul dealt with the evils plaguing that church. Titus was sent to Corinth with plans for him to come to Paul at Troas. Paul found an open door at Troas, but anxiety because of the continued absence of Titus caused him to leave for Macedonia. The report of Titus, whom he met in Macedonia, relieved Paul's anxiety and was the immediate occasion for the writing of *II Corinthians* (II Cor. 2:12-13; 7:5-16), which was sent back to Corinth by Titus (II Cor. 8:6, 16-18). After "much exhortation" in Macedonia, Paul spent the three winter months in Corinth (Acts 20:2-3), where he wrote the Epistle to the Romans to prepare them for his coming visit and secure their support for his contemplated work in Spain (Rom. 15:22-29; 16:1,23).

The plan to take the collection to Jerusalem directly from Corinth was canceled because of a discovered plot on Paul's life; instead he went by way of Macedonia, leaving Philippi with Luke after the Passover (Acts 20:3-6). The church-elected companions in travel awaited them at Troas, where they spent a busy and eventful night (20:7-12). Hoping to reach Jerusalem for Pentecost, Paul called the Ephesian elders to meet him at Miletus. His farewell to them is marked by tender memories, earnest instructions, and searching premonitions concerning the future (20:18-35). The journey to Jerusalem was marked by repeated warnings to Paul of what awaited him there (21:1-16). Some interpreters hold that Paul blundered in persisting on going to Jerusalem in the face of these clear warnings, thus cutting short his missionary labors. Paul apparently interpreted the warnings not as prohibitions but as tests of his willingness to suffer for the cause of his Lord and the Church.

Paul the Prisoner. Although cordially received at Jerusalem by James and the elders, Paul's presence created tension in the church because of reports that he taught Jews in the dispersion to forsake Moses. To neutralize these reports they suggested to Paul a plan to prove that he had no aversion to a voluntary keeping of the law. Always anxious to avoid offense, Paul agreed to their proposal. The act of conciliation apparently satisfied the Judean believers but was the cause of Paul's arrest. Certain Jews from Asia, seeing him in the temple, created a tumult by falsely charging him with defiling the temple. Rescued from death at the hands of the Jewish mob by the Roman chiliarch and some soldiers, Paul proved his love for the Jews by securing permission to address them from the castle steps. They gave silent attention until he mentioned his commission to the Gentiles, when the riot broke out anew. A scourging, ordered to force information out of him, was avoided by Paul's mention of his Roman citizenship. Efforts by the chiliarch the next day to gain further information about Paul before the Sanhedrin proved futile. That night the Lord appeared to the discouraged apostle, commended his efforts at witnessing, and assured him that he would go to Rome. Informed of a plot to murder Paul, the chiliarch sent Paul to Caesarea under a large protective guard (23:17-23:35).

The trial before Felix at Caesarea made it clear to the governor that the charges against Paul were spurious but, unwilling to antagonize the Jews, he simply postponed a decision. Asked to expound the Christian faith before Felix and his Jewish wife, Drusilla, Paul courageously probed their consciences by preaching "of righteousness, and self-control, and the judgment to come." Terrified, Felix dismissed the preacher but later gave Paul opportunities to use bribery to secure his release. Felix after two years was summoned to Rome and left Paul an uncondemned prisoner (24:1-27).

With the coming of the new governor, Festus, the Jewish leaders renewed their efforts to secure Paul's condemnation. When it became clear to Paul that he could not expect justice from the new governor, he used his right as a Roman citizen and appealed his case to Caesar, thereby removing it from the jurisdiction of the lower courts (25:1-12). When Herod Agrippa II and his sister Bernice came to visit the new governor, Festus, perplexed about Paul's case, presented the matter to Agrippa, an acknowledged expert in Jewish affairs. The next day before his royal audience Paul delivered a masterly exposition of his position and used the occasion to seek to win Agrippa to Christ. Uncomfortable under Paul's efforts, Agrippa terminated the meeting, but frankly declared Paul's innocence to the governor (25:13-26:32).

Paul was sent to Rome, perhaps in the autumn of A.D. 60, under the escort of a centurion named Julius. Luke and Aristarchus accompanied him. Luke's detailed account of the voyage has the minuteness, picturesqueness, and accuracy of an alert eye-witness. Adverse weather delayed the progress of the ship. At Myra they transferred to an Alexandrian grain ship bound for Italy. Futile efforts to reach commodious winter quarters at Phoenix caused the ship to be caught in a typhonic storm for 14 days, ending in total wreck on the island of Malta. After three months on Malta, the journey to Rome was completed in another Alexandrian grain ship. Paul's treatment in Rome was lenient; he lived in his own hired house with a soldier guarding him. Permitted to receive all who

The Mamertine Prison, in Rome, where both Paul and Peter were imprisoned. At right, a tablet in Latin marking the site of these events. JFW

came, he was able to exercise an important ministry in Rome. The "Prison Epistles," Colossians, Philemon, Ephesians and Philippians, are abiding fruit of this period which afforded him opportunity to meditate and to write.

Closing Years. Acts leaves the question of Paul's release unanswered, but there is strong evidence for believing that he was released at the end of two years. The amicable attitude of the Roman government in Acts favors it, the Prison Epistles expect it, the Pastoral Epistles demand it, and tradition asserts it. Paul's subsequent activities must be inferred from scant references in the Pastorals. From their contents it seems clear that I Timothy and Titus were written before the outbreak of the Neronian persecution. After his release, perhaps in the spring of A.D. 63, Paul went east, visited Ephesus, stationing Timothy there when he left for Macedonia (I Tim. 1:3). He left Titus to complete missionary work on Crete, and in writing to him mentions plans to spend the winter at Nicopolis (1:5; 3:12). From Nicopolis he may have made the traditional visit to Spain, working there at the outbreak of the Neronian persecution in autumn of A.D. 64. II Timothy makes it clear that Paul is again a prisoner in Rome, kept in close confinement as a malefactor (1:16-17; 2:9). At his first appearing before the court he escaped immediate condemnation, but in writing to Timothy he has no hope of release (4:16-18,6-8). He was executed at Rome in late A.D. 66 or early 67. Tradition says he was beheaded on the Ostian Way.

Achievement and Character. Paul's achievements proclaim him as an unexcelled missionary statesman. His labors firmly planted churches in the strategic centers of Galatia, Asia, Macedonia, and Achaia, while his plans for work at Rome and in Spain reveal his imperial missionary strategy. His foresight led him to select and train strong young workers to carry on the work after him. Paul was supremely the interpreter of the Gospel of Jesus Christ, interpreted to the Gentile world through his labors and letters. It was primarily through his agency that the world-wide destiny of Christianity was established, liberated from the yoke of legalism. His epistolary writings, formulating, interpreting, and applying the essence of Christianity, are vital to Christian theology and practice. His theology was rooted in his own revolutionary experience with Christ. He saw man's inability to

attain to righteousness through his own efforts, but realized that God had provided a way of salvation, wholly out of grace and love, in Christ Jesus, available through faith in Him alone. He also saw that the Gospel made strenuous ethical demands upon the life and conduct of the believer. The essence of the Christian life for Paul was union with Christ; Him he loved and served, and yearned for His imminent return.

Physically, Paul did not present an imposing appearance, as is evident from II Corinthians 10:10. Tradition pictures him as being small of stature, having a decidedly Jewish physiognomy. That he possessed a rugged physical constitution seems plain from all the hardships and sufferings he underwent (II Cor. 11:23-27), as well as his ability, amid his spiritual anxieties, to earn his own living through manual labor. He endured more than most men could endure, yet he keenly felt his bodily frailty. Especially was he afflicted by "a thorn [or stake] in the flesh" (II Cor. 12:7). The exact nature of the affliction can only be conjectured; attempts at identification have varied widely. Whatever its precise nature, his feelings of weakness made him constantly dependent upon divine empowerment (II Chron. 12:10; Phil. 4:12-13).

The many-sided personality of the man is difficult to gather into one picture. He seems to embody polar extremes: bodily weakness and tremendous power, a keen intellect and profound mysticism, strongly attracting and furiously repelling men. Intellectually he was a man of outstanding ability, one of the world's great thinkers. He grasped truth at its full value and logically worked out its implications. But his subtlety of intellect was combined with practical good sense. He was a man of strict integrity, ever careful to maintain a good conscience. His life was characterized by a love of the truth which allowed no temporizing for the sake of expediency. Having understood his duty, he followed it unflinchingly, undeterred by possible consequences to himself. He was characterized by native zeal and ardor, giving himself wholly to his work. He was warm-hearted and affectionate, longing for and making strong friendships. He was humble, sincere, and sympathetic. He was by nature a religious man, and his religion, even as a Jew, much more as a Christian, dominated his life and activities. The secret of his unique career lay in his fervent nature as possessed and empowered by the Living Christ.   D.E.H.

PAULUS, SERGIUS (pô'lŭs, sûr'jĭ-ŭs, Gr. *Paúlos, Sérgios*). When Paul and Barnabas visited Paphos, the capital of Cyprus, on their first missionary journey, they were called before Sergius Paulus, the Roman proconsul (AV, "deputy"), because this man of understanding "desired to hear the word of God" (Acts 13:6-12). When Elymas, his court magician, attempted to turn him against the Gospel, Paul through a miracle struck him with blindness. The incident so affected Sergius Paulus that he "believed, being astonished at the doctrine of the Lord" (Acts 13:12). It is often said that Paul, then known as Saul of Tarsus, took his name from this first Gentile convert, but this may be only coincidence.

PAVEMENT, THE (Gr. *lithóstrotos, paved with stones*), the courtyard outside the Praetorium or palace in Jerusalem where Pilate passed public sentence on Jesus (John 19:13). Archaeologists believe it was either an area paved with large blocks of stone (4x3x2 ft.) laid in concrete, or a special mosaic. Some think it was "an elevated dais or tesselated pavement." (*Interpreter's Bible* Vol. 8, p. 774.) The meaning of *Gabbatha*, the Hebrew equivalent, is uncertain, although it has been traced to the Latin word for "platter" and perhaps referred to a paved court shaped like a dish or bowl. In II Chronicles 7:3 the term is used for the open court of Solomon's Temple.

PAVILION (pà-vĭl'yŭn, Heb. *sōkh* [Ps. 27:5], *sukkâh* [Ps. 31:20], *booth, tent*), a covered place in which a person may be kept hid. It is used chiefly to symbolize God's favor and protection provided for His children (Ps. 18:11). It grows out of the fact that to the eastern king's inner court or pavilion none has access except those to whom he gives permission.

PEACE (Heb. *shālôm, peace*, Gr. *eiréne, concord*), a frequent word in both testaments used in a variety of ways. In the OT times it was the usual word of greeting (Gen. 29:6). It is used also throughout the Bible to indicate a spirit of tranquillity and freedom from either inward or outward disturbance (Num. 6:26; I Kings 4:24; Acts 9:31). When nations enjoyed this, it was regarded as a gift from God (Lev. 26:6; Ps. 29:11). Perhaps its most frequent use in both testaments is to denote that spiritual tranquillity which all can enjoy when through faith in Christ they are brought into a right relation with God. There is the peace *with* God enjoyed by all truly regenerated persons (Rom. 5:1; Col. 1:20) and the peace *of* God enjoyed only by believers who meet its conditions (Phil. 4:6-7). Perhaps both aspects are implied in such passages as Isaiah 26:3 and John 14:27. Christ came to provide peace on earth (Luke 2:14), but this will not be realized fully until He returns again to effect it in person (Isa. 9:6-7; 11:6-9; Mic. 4:3). H.Z.C.

PEACE OFFERING (See Offerings)

PEACOCK (See Birds)

PEARL (Gr. *margarítes*). In the OT (Job 28:18, KJV), the RV and RSV have more correctly rendered the word "crystal." In the NT the word is used in several ways. It denotes the costly precious stone (I Tim. 2:9; Rev. 17:4). Pearls are accidental concretions formed within the bodies of certain mollusks, especially the *Avicula margaritifera* from the Indian Ocean and Persian Gulf.

The word has a figurative use in the NT. In Matthew 7:6 it is used to stand for spiritual truths which should not be cast before profane men who will not receive them. Christ is set forth in the parable of Matthew 13:45-46 as a merchant seeking the "pearl of great price," the Church. In the Book of Revelation the 12 gates of the New Jerusalem are each made from a pearl.

PEDAHEL (pĕd'à-hĕl, Heb. *pedhah'ēl, God delivers*), a prince of Naphtali appointed by Moses to apportion Palestine (Num. 34:28).

PEDAHZUR (pē-dà'zêr, Heb. *pedhāhtsûr, the rock*), a prince of the tribe of Manasseh, father of Gamaliel whom Moses appointed to aid in numbering the people (Num. 1:10; 2:20).

PEDAIAH (pē-dā'yà, Heb. *pedhāyāhû, Jehovah redeems*). 1. One from Rumah, father of Zedudah who was Josiah's wife and Jehoiakim's mother (II Kings 23:36).
2. Father of Zerubbabel, son of Jeconiah (I Chron. 3:18).
3. The father of Joel and ruler of western Manasseh under David (I Chron. 27:20).
4. One from the family of Parosh who aided in repairing the wall of Jerusalem (Neh. 3:25).
5. A Benjamite, father of Joed, Kolaiah's son (Neh. 11:7).
6. A Levite appointed by Nehemiah as one of the treasurers over the Lord's house (Neh. 13:13).

PEEP (Heb. *tsāphaph, to chirp*), a word describing the cry of a bird (Isa. 10:14) and the noise made by wizards uttering sounds that are supposed to come from the dead (Isa. 8:19).

PEKAH (pē'kà, Heb. *peqah, to open*), the son of Remaliah the 18th king of Israel. In the 52nd year of Uzziah, he usurped the throne by murdering his predecessor, Pekahiah. He began to reign about 734 B.C. and reigned for 20 years (II Kings 15:27). Incensed by the weakening of Israel under the leadership before him, caused by internal trouble and the heavy tribute paid to Assyria, he formed a league with the Gileadites to resist the encroachments of Assyria. To strengthen his position further and accomplish his purposes, he allied himself with Rezin of Damascus against Jotham, king of Judah (II Kings 15:37-38). The godly character of Jotham (II Chron. 27) probably delayed the realization of this plot until Jotham's son, Ahaz, was on the throne. The details of this campaign are recorded in two places in the OT (II Kings 16; II Chron. 28). Perhaps the most important thing about this struggle was that it occasioned the important prophecies of Isaiah 7-9. Finally Pekah became subject to the Assyrian power (II Kings 15:29) and a short time later was murdered by Hoshea. His sad epitaph is summarized in II Kings 15:28, "He did that which was evil in the sight of the Lord."

PEKAHIAH (pĕk'à-hī'à, Heb. *peqahyâh, Jehovah has opened*), Israel's 17th king, the son of Menahem. He was a wicked king, following the practices of idolatry formulated by Jeroboam (II Kings 15:24). There are some problems regarding the date of his reign caused by the statement in II Kings 15:23, "In the fiftieth year of Azariah." By dating the beginning of his reign 735 B.C. most of the date problem dissolves. After a brief reign of but two years, he was brutally murdered by Pekah and along with him the 50 Gileadites associated with him.

PEKOD (pē'kŏd, Heb. *peqôdh, visitation*), a name applied to an Aramaean tribe living to the E and near the mouth of the Tigris and forming part of the Chaldean empire in Ezekiel's day (Jer. 50:21; Ezek. 23:23).

PELAIAH (pē-lā'yà, Heb. *pelā'yâh, Jehovah is wonderful*), Elioenai's son from Judah's royal house (I Chron. 3:24). This name was given also to the Levite who aided Ezra in explaining the law (Neh. 8:7) and later sealed the covenant with Nehemiah (Neh. 10:10).

PELALIAH (pĕl'á-lī'á, Heb. *pelalyâh, Jehovah has judged*), the priestly father of Jeroham and son of Amzi who was a worker in the Lord's house (Neh. 11:12).

PELATIAH (pĕl'á-tī'á, Heb. *pelatyâh, Jehovah has delivered*). 1. Hananiah's son who descended from Salathiel from the family of David (I Chron. 3: 21). He was the grandson of Zerubbabel.

2. Ishi's son who headed a Simeonite group that helped rid the area of the Amalekites (I Chron. 4: 42) in Hezekiah's reign.

3. One of those who sealed the covenant with Nehemiah (Neh. 10:22).

4. One of the princes of the people, son of Benaiah (Ezek. 11:1) who along with others devised iniquity and gave wicked counsel in Jerusalem (Ezek. 11:2). Ezekiel was instructed to prophesy against them and while he was doing so Pelatiah fell dead (Ezek. 11:13).

PELEG (pē'lĕg, Heb. *pelegh, division*), one of the sons of Eber, brother of Joktan and the father of Rue (Gen. 10:25; 11:16-19; I Chron. 1:25). The reason for his name is that "in his days was the earth divided" (Gen. 10:25). This probably refers to the confounding of the language and the consequent scattering of the descendants of Noah (Gen. 11:1-9).

PELET (pē'lĕt, Heb. *pelet, deliverance*), Jahdai's son (I Chron. 2:47); also one of Azmaveth's sons from the tribe of Benjamin who joined David at Ziklag while he hid from Saul (I Chron. 12:3).

PELETH (pē'lĕth, Heb. *peleth, swiftness*). 1. The father of On, from the tribe of Reuben, who became a part of the conspiracy against Moses and Aaron (Num. 16:1).

2. A descendant of Jerahmeel through Onan (I Chron. 2:33).

PELETHITES (pĕl'ē-thīts, Heb. *pelēthî, courier*), a group who along with the Cherethites formed David's bodyguard. Perhaps, as the meaning of their name suggests, they were the ones who conveyed the king's messages to distant places.

PELICAN (See Birds)

PELLA (pĕl'á), a name that does not occur in the Bible, but is mentioned by Josephus as one of the towns of the district named Decapolis, or *Ten Cities*, by the Romans, which is mentioned in Matthew 4:25 and Mark 5:20; 7:31. Pella thus lay E of the Sea of Galilee in the mountains of Gilead. Josephus mentions Pella together with the towns of Gerasa, Gadara and Hippos in the same proximity. It is described as a flat fertile valley surrounded on all sides by a higher plain or plateau. Today it is full of old ruins, including an ancient Christian church. An interesting Biblical aspect of Pella is that it is supposed to have been one of the main refuge cities of the Christians during destruction of Jerusalem by the Romans (cf. Matt. 24:16). At the time of Christ the cities, which formed a city league originally formed by Pompey in 62 B.C., were Greek in culture and highly commercialized. See DECAPOLIS.

PELONITE (pĕl'ō-nīt, Heb. *pelônî, separates*), the title of two of David's mighty men, Helez and Ahijah (I Chron. 11:27,36). It is thought that this designation originated from their place of birth because of the reference in I Chronicles 27:10 that Helez was from Ephraim's tribe.

PEN (See Writing)

PENCE (See Money)

PENDANT (See Dress)

PENIEL, PENUEL (pē-nī'ĕl, pē-nū'ĕl, Heb. *penî'ēl, face of God*). 1. The spot where Jacob wrestled with the angel of God (Gen. 32:24-32). The exact location is unknown, though it was not far from Succoth and E of the Jordan.

2. Hur's son, the father of Gedor (I Chron. 4:4).

3. One of Shashah's sons (I Chron. 8:25).

PENINNAH (pē-nĭn'á, Heb. *peninnâh, coral*), one of Elkanah's wives, who bore children and taunted Hannah (I Sam. 1:2-7) while she was childless.

PENKNIFE, a small knife used to sharpen the pens or writing reeds of Jeremiah's day (Jer. 36:23).

PENNY (See Money)

PENTATEUCH, THE (pĕn'tá-tōōk, Heb. *tōrâh, law* or *teaching*). This is composed of five books: Genesis, Exodus, Leviticus, Numbers, and Deuteronomy. These books, whose canonicity has never been called into question by the Jews, Protestants, or Catholics head the list of the OT canon. As a literary unit they provide the background for the OT as well as the New.

Chronologically the Pentateuch covers the period of time from the creation to the end of the Mosaic era. Since the date for the creation of the universe is not given, it is impossible to ascertain the length of this entire era.

Genesis begins with an account of creation, but soon narrows its interest to the human race. Adam and Eve were entrusted with the responsibility of caring for the world about them, but forfeited their privilege through disobedience and sin. In subsequent generations all mankind became so wicked that the entire human race, except Noah and his family, was destroyed. When the new civilization degenerated, God chose to fulfill His promises of redemption through Abraham. From Adam to Abraham represents a long period of time for which the genealogical lists in Genesis 5 and 10 hardly serve as a time table.

The patriarchal era (Gen. 12-50), narrates the events of approximately four generations, namely those of Abraham, Isaac, Jacob, and Joseph. Scholars generally agree that Abraham lived during the 19th or 18th century B.C. — some dating him a century earlier and some considerably later. The contemporary culture of this period is much better known to us today through recent archaeological discoveries. In 1933 a French archaeologist, Andre Parrot, discovered the ruins of Mari, a city located on the Euphrates River. Here he found numerous temples, palaces, statues, and some 20,000 tablets which reflected the culture of the patriarchal era. Nuzu, a site E of Nineveh, excavated about 1925-1941, yielded several thousand documents which likewise provide numerous illustrations of customs that reflect the patriarchal pattern of living as portrayed in the Genesis record.

After the opening verses of Exodus the rest of the Pentateuch is chronologically confined to the lifetime of Moses. Consequently the deliverance of Israel from Egypt and their preparation for entrance into the land of Canaan is the prevailing theme. The historical core of these books is briefly outlined as follows:

Exodus 1-19, From Egypt to Mount Sinai
Exodus 19-Numbers 10, Encampment at Mount Sinai (approximately 1 year)
Numbers 10-21, Wilderness Wanderings (approximately 38 years)

Numbers 22-Deuteronomy 34, Encampment before Canaan (approximately one year)

The Mosaic law was given at Mount Sinai. As God's covenant people the Israelites were not to conform to the idolatrous practices of the Egyptians nor to the customs of the Canaanites whose land they were to conquer and possess. Israel's religion was a revealed religion. For nearly a year they were carefully instructed in the law and the covenant. A tabernacle was constructed and erected as the central place for the worship of God. Offerings and sacrifices were instituted to make atonement for their sins and for expression of their gratitude and devotion to God. The Aaronic family, supported by the Levites, was ordained to serve at the tabernacle in the ministration of divine worship. Feasts and seasons likewise were carefully prescribed for the Israelites so that they might worship and serve God as His distinctive people. After the entrance into Canaan was delayed for almost 40 years because of the unbelief of the Israelites, Moses reviewed the law for the younger generation. This review, plus timely instructions for the occupation of Palestine, is summarized in the Book of Deuteronomy.

For study purposes the Pentateuch lends itself to the following analysis:

I. The era of beginnings, Genesis 1:1-11:32.
    A. The account of creation, 1:1-2:25.
    B. Man's fall and its consequences, 3:1-6:10.
    C. The flood: God's judgment on man, 6:11-8:19.
    D. Man's new beginning, 8:20-11:32.

II. The patriarchal period, 12:1-50:26.
    A. The life of Abraham, 12:1-25:18.
    B. Isaac and Jacob, 25:19-36:43.
    C. Joseph, 37:1-50:26.

III. Emancipation of Israel, Exodus 1:1-19:2.
    A. Israel freed from slavery, 1:1-13:19.
    B. From Egypt to Mt. Sinai, 13:20-19:2.

IV. The religion of Israel, Exodus 19:3-Leviticus 27:34.
    A. God's covenant with Israel, Exodus 19:3-24:8.
    B. The place of worship, 24:9-40:38.
    C. Instructions for holy living, Leviticus 1:1-27:34.
       1. The offerings, 1:1-7:38.
       2. The priesthood, 8:1-10:20.
       3. Laws of purification, 11:1-15:33.
       4. Day of atonement, 16:1-34.
       5. Heathen customs forbidden, 17:1-18:30.
       6. Laws of holiness, 19:1-22:33.
       7. Feasts and seasons, 23:1-25:55.
       8. Conditions of God's blessings, 26:1-27:34.

V. Organization of Israel, Numbers 1:1-12:10.
    A. The numbering of Israel, 1:1-4:49.
    B. Camp regulations, 5:1-6:21.
    C. Religious life of Israel, 6:22-9:14.
    D. Provisions for guidance, 9:15-10:10.

VI. Wilderness wanderings, Numbers 10:11-22:1.
    A. From Mt. Sinai to Kadesh, 10:11-12:16.
    B. The Kadesh crisis, 13:1-14:45.
    C. The years of wandering, 15:1-19:22.
    D. From Kadesh to the Plains of Moab, 20:1-22:1.

VII. Instructions for entering Canaan, 22:2-36:13.
    A. Preservation of God's chosen people, 22:2-25:18.
    B. Preparation for conquest, 26:1-33:49.
    C. Anticipation of occupation, 33:50-36:13.

VIII. Retrospect and prospect, Deuteronomy 1:1-34:12.
    A. History and its significance, 1:1-4:43.
    B. The law and its significance, 4:44-28:68.
    C. Final preparation and farewell, 29:1-34:12.

The authorship of the Pentateuch has been a major concern of OT scholars for the last two centuries. According to the consensus of scholarship as developed since 1750, the Pentateuch was composed of four major documents, which actually reflected the historical conditions between Davidic and exilic times. These documents were then combined into one literary unit shortly before 400 B.C. This Graf-Wellhausen theory, as it is popularly known, has been somewhat modified in recent decades by regarding the Pentateuch as essentially Mosaic in that these documents were orally transmitted. This evolutionary historical approach often confuses the practice of Israel's religion with that which God had revealed to them through Moses.

The Pentateuch itself supports the view that Moses is essentially responsible for its authorship. References throughout the rest of the OT as well as the NT point to Moses as the author. Being personally involved as the deliverer and lawgiver of Israel, Moses was familiar with the developments as recorded in the last four books of the Pentateuch. Very likely he had many scribes to assist him in keeping a record of all the details that pertain to organization, geography, and history. Naturally it would have been his concern to leave a written copy of the law and a history of this unique experience of the Israelites before his departure. Especially was this in accord with his desire that they should carefully conform to the law in order that they might continually enjoy God's favor.

How Moses obtained the information recorded in the book of Genesis is not known. Since evidence of writing in the Ancient Near East dates back into the fourth millennium B.C., it is quite probable that the Patriarchs passed on some written records to their descendants. Oral tradition may have supplemented these sources. Some of the information, particularly the creation account, may have been imparted to Moses by divine revelation.

Moses was well qualified to write the Pentateuch. Trained in the court of Pharaoh he undoubtedly knew the Egyptian and Akkadian (Babylonian) languages in addition to his native Hebrew. Babylonian classics, civil administration, and military science may have been part of his curriculum. With this background and training plus the experience of leading Israel under divine guidance from Egyptian bondage to the borders of Canaan, Moses may have climaxed his career with the composition of the Pentateuch. Equally important was the divine enduement through which this literary production not only became the great Torah (law) for the Jewish nation but has been universally regarded as the introductory section to the Holy Scriptures.

                         S.J.S.

PENTECOST (pĕn'tĕ-kŏst, Gr. *pentecostē*). The word derives from the Greek for "the fiftieth day." It was the Jewish Feast of Weeks (Exod. 34:22; Deut. 16:9-11), variously called the Feast of Harvest (Exod. 23:16), or the Day of First-Fruits (Num. 28:26), which fell on the 50th day after the Feast of the Passover. The exact method by which the date was computed is a matter of some controversy.

Originally, the festival was the time when, with appropriate ritual and ceremony, the first-fruits of the corn-harvest, the last Palestinian crop to ripen, were formally dedicated. The festival cannot therefore have antedated the settlement in Palestine. Leviticus 23 prescribes the sacred nature of the holiday, and lists the appropriate sacrifices. Numbers 28 appears to be a supplementary list, prescribing offerings apart from those connected with the preservation of the ritual loaves. In later Jewish times, the feast developed into a commemoration of the giving of the Mosaic Law. To reinforce this function, the Rabbis taught that the Law was given 50 days after the Exodus, a tradition of which there is no trace in the OT, nor in the Jewish authorities, Philo and Josephus. It was the events of Acts 2 which transformed the Jewish festival into a Christian one. Some have seen a symbolic connection between the first-fruits of the ancient festival, and the "first-fruits" of the Christian dispensation. "Whitsunday" is therefore the 50th day after Easter Sunday. The names derives from the white garments of those seeking baptism at this festival, a practice of very ancient origin.

Of the events of Pentecost recorded in Acts 2, the "gift of tongues" requires consideration, for the claim to such a supernatural manifestation became, in the early decades of the 20th century, the most characteristic mark of religious groups which may be generally termed "Pentecostal." The nature of the "tongues" (Acts 2:4) is difficult to determine. The following points must be taken into account. First, those listed in Acts 2:9-11 were Jewish pilgrims from the synagogues of the Dispersion among the peoples named. They would all readily understand the two tongues of Palestine, Aramaic and Greek. The few foreign proselytes, who were no doubt of their number, would also be conversant with Greek, if not with Aramaic. No multiple "gift of tongues" in the literal sense of the phrase was therefore necessary, nor, if such an endowment was indeed given, as most commentators imply, did it long endure. Paul and Barnabas were clearly without knowledge of the tongue of Lystra (Acts 14:11-14), in spite of the fact that Paul says that he had "spoken with tongues" after the fashion discussed in I Corinthians 12 and 14 (cf. also Acts 10:46 and 19:6). It is generally assumed that the latter manifestation was a species of ecstatic utterance, which Paul tries to tone down, tolerate it though he does as a passing phase, and because, without specific direction, he hesitates to quench ardent spirits in the Church. Commentators vary strikingly. R. B. Rackham (*Acts of the Apostles*, p. 21) holds that Pentecost saw the glossolalia of Corinth, but that it was worship, not proclamation, that formed the subject of the message. Peter alone preached. Rackham admits that verses 8 and 11 require that some of the utterances should have been clothed in foreign words. In a polyglot world it is to be expected that such emotional and ecstatic speech would contain intrusions of alien vocabulary. F. F. Bruce (*The Acts of the Apostles*, p. 82) regards the phenomenon of Pentecost as a deliverance, under the urge of ecstatic emotion, from the pecularities of Galilaean speech and something different from the Corinthian experience, a purified or exalted utterance which removed dialectical barriers to understanding.

It seems reasonable, therefore, in view of the fact that, in a Greek and Aramaic-speaking audience, no immediately practicable purpose can be envisaged for a multiple employment of languages, to reject the view that alien tongues were used for the preaching of the new faith at Pentecost. The lack of any need for "interpreters" also makes it difficult to identify the situation with the one Paul sought to regulate in the Corinthian church. The "tongues" made for clarity; they did not destroy it for those who listened with sympathy. E.M.B.

PEOR (pē'ôr, Heb. *pe'ôr, opening*). 1. The name given to the mountain in Moab to the top of which King Balak led Balaam that he might see and curse Israel (Num. 23:28). It was a high peak near the town of Baal-Peor opposite the valley in which Israel camped (Deut. 3:29).

2. In Numbers 25:18; 31:16 and Joshua 22:17 Peor is used four times as a contraction for Baal-Peor.

3. Moses uses the term in two places (Num. 25:18; 31:16) to refer to the god of Baal-Peor.

PERAEA (pĕ-rē'á, Gr. *Peraía, Peraíos, Peraítes*), a word that does not occur in the Bible, but was used by Josephus and others to designate the small territory on the E side of the Jordan opposite old Judea and Samaria known in the Gospels as the land "beyond the Jordan" (*peran tou Iordanou*). For example, the words in Matthew 4:25 *apo tes Galilaias kai Ioudaias kai peran tou Iordanou* should be understood as "from Galilee and Judea *and Peraea,*" and is so listed on Bible maps (cf. Matt. 4:15; Mark 3:7-8). The curious statement in Matthew 19:1 which says that Jesus "departed from Galilee and came into *the coasts of Judea beyond Jordan*" must mean that Jesus went from Galilee to Judea by way of Peraea, the usual road the Jews took in order to avoid going through Samaria.

In the days of Jesus, Herod Antipas ruled the unfertile desert country together with Galilee; but after the Herods, at the time the Gospels were written, Peraea belonged to the larger province of Judea. It stretched from Pella in the N to Machaerus in the S. In the days of the Maccabees it was inhabited chiefly by Gentiles, but at the time of Christ it had a heavy Jewish population. Gadara may have been the capital. John baptized in Bethabara "beyond the Jordan," or in Peraea (John 1:28). Jesus did much of His teaching in Peraea (Mark 10:1-33) and made His final journey to Jerusalem from there (John 10:40; 11:54). Today it is part of the modern Kingdom of Jordan with the capital at Amman.

A view in Peraea, overlooking the Sea of Galilee, and showing remains of ancient theater at Gadara, the Peraean capital. © MPS

PERAZIM, MOUNT (pĕr'à-zĭm, Heb. *har perātsîm, mount of breaches*), usually identified with Baalperazim, where David obtained a victory over the Philistines (II Sam. 5:20; I Chron. 14:11).

PERDITION (pêr-dĭ'shun, Gr. *apóleia, perishing, destruction*). The idea of a loss or destruction predominates in the use of this word. In each of the eight uses of the English word in the NT (John 17:12; Phil. 1:28; II Thess. 2:3; I Tim. 6:9; Heb. 10:39; II Pet. 3:7; Rev. 17:8,11), the final state of the wicked is referred to. In popular usage men make this word a synonym for hell and eternal punishment.

PERDITION, SON OF (Gr. *huiós, tés apoleías*), a phrase used to designate two men of the NT. Christ uses it in referring to Judas Iscariot (John 17:12). Paul uses the same title in II Thessalonians 2:3, applying it to the "man of sin" who is the Antichrist. It is derived from the custom among the Hebrews of noting a certain trait or characteristic in a person and then referring to him as the son of that trait. The term, therefore, would designate these two men as being the complete devotees of all that "perdition" signified.

PEREA (See Peraea)

PERES (pē'rĕs, Aram. *peras, to split*), one of the words that was written by the hand on the wall for Belshazzar and interpreted by Daniel (Dan. 5:1-29). It is the singular of "upharsin" (Dan. 5:25) and interpreted in Daniel 5:28.

PERESH (pē'rĕsh, Heb. *peresh, dung*), Machir's son by his concubine, Maachah, the Aramite (I Chron. 7:14,16).

PEREZ (pē'rĕz, Heb. *perets, breach*), one of Judah's twin sons by his daughter-in-law, Tamar (Gen. 38:29). He is called also "Pharez" (Gen. 46:12; Num. 26:20,21).

PEREZ-UZZA (pē'rez-ŭz'à, Heb. *perets-'uzâh, the beach of Uzzah*). Uzzah was one who accompanied the ark on its journey from Kiriath-jearim. When the oxen stumbled, Uzzah, contrary to the command of God, took hold of the ark and died immediately. David, therefore, named the spot "Perez-uzzah" (II Sam. 6:8). It is perhaps to be identified with Khirbet el-Uz, "the ruins of Uzzah" located a short distance from Kirjath-jearim.

PERFECTION, PERFECT (Heb. *shālēm, tāmîm,* Gr. *téleios, teleiótes*). The most common OT term is *tāmîm,* whose basic meaning is close to the fundamental and etymological sense of the English word, "complete" or "finished." It is used for the ritually clean victim of sacrifice (Exod. 12:5), and for uprightness of character (Gen. 6:9; 17:1; Ps. 119:1). It is applied to the Law, and to God Himself. In the NT the commonest term is *teleios,* an adjective formed from the noun *telos, an end.* The metaphor involved suggests that perfection is the attainment of the end or aim of being, and is therefore a relative term to be understood within its context. Absolute perfection can therefore be an attribute of God alone. Hence the explanation of such apparent contradictions as Philippians 3:12 and 15. So, too, Matthew 5:48, command though it is, involves no impossibility. The Christian is enjoined to fulfill the functions of his being as God fulfills His, and the sermon in which the precept is embedded explains the mode and manner of such attainment. The concept of perfection which has been taught by some theologians and preachers has erred in neglecting the relativity of the term and such clear teaching as that of John (I John 1:8), James (3:2) and Paul (Phil. 3:12).

E.M.B.

PERFUME (Heb. *qetoreth, sweet smoke, incense,* a word rendered "perfume" in Exodus 30:35,37; Proverbs 27:9). There are many passages in the Bible that indicate the fondness for and use of perfume in Oriental countries. Perfumes had many uses in the Orient as the Bible indicates in many places. Spices were dried and mixed with resins and burned as incense at various occasions. In connection with the tabernacle worship, God revealed a special divine formula which could not be copied for personal use by the Hebrews apart from punishment (Exod. 30:7,8,34-38). These perfumes were prepared by men known as "apothecaries'" (Exod. 30:35; Eccl. 10:1).

Moses mentions one perfume to be made of pure myrrh, sweet cinnamon, sweet calamus, cassia and olive oil. It was to be used only as a holy anointing oil. Anyone who duplicated it would be cut off from his people (Exod 30:22-33).

Hebrews used perfumes for embalming their dead (John 19:38-40); for burning with the dead (II Chron. 16:14); for preparing a virgin to appear before the Persian king (Esth. 2:12-14); for preparing women for marriage (S. of Sol. 1:12-14); for setting a trap, by the harlot, for the innocent (Prov. 7:17). Special sweet-scented oils were used to anoint the bodies of those to whom respect was to be paid (Luke 7:37). When one wanted to mortify himself he would refrain from such oils (Dan. 10:3).

In the hot eastern countries perfumes became a sanitary necessity. They were used both to cover up bad odors which abounded in the Orient and to make life more enjoyable for all concerned.

Quite a large number of scents were used in the compounding of these perfumes. Perhaps the most frequently mentioned are frankincense (S. of Sol. 3:6) and myrrh (Ps. 45:8). For a list of plants and trees used in perfume making, see Winifred Walker, *All the Plants of the Bible,* New York: Harper, 1957.

H.Z.C.

PERGA (pûr'gà, Gr. *Pérge*), the chief city of old Pamphilia of Asia Minor located about 12 miles from Attalia on the River Cestris which formed an inland port. Paul and Barnabas passed through the city twice on the first missionary journey, both going and returning (Acts 13:13-14; 14:24-25). Here John Mark left the party and returned to Jerusalem. During Greek times a celebrated temple of Artemis, or Diana, was located in the vicinity which perhaps was the reason Christianity never flourished there as in other cities of Asia Minor. Today it is known as Murtana and the well-preserved ruins still reveal an immense theater holding about 13,000 people.

PERGAMUM, PERGAMOS (pûr'gà-mŭm, Gr. *Pérgamos*), a city of Mysia in the Caicus valley, 15 miles inland; in KJV, Pergamos. Royally situated in a commanding position, Pergamum was the capital until the last of the Pergamenian kings bequeathed his realm to Rome in 133 B.C. Pergamum became the chief town of the new province of Asia, and the site of the first temple of the Caesar-cult, erected to Rome and Augustus in 29 B.C. A second shrine was later dedicated to Trajan, and the multiplication of such honor marks the prestige of Pergamum in pagan Asia. The worship of Asklepios and Zeus were also endemic. The symbol of the former was a serpent, and Pausanias describes his cult image "with a staff in one hand and the other on the head of a serpent." Pergamenian coins illustrate the importance which the community attached to this cult. Caracalla is shown on one coin, saluting a serpent

An artist's reconstruction of the Acropolis at Pergamum, a cultural center of ancient Asia Minor.
© RTHPL

twined round a bending sapling. On the crag above Pergamum was a throne-like altar to Zeus now in the Berlin Museum (Rev. 2:13?). It commemorated a defeat of a Gallic inroad, and was decorated with a representation of the conflict of the gods and the giants, the latter shown as monsters with snake-like tails. Zeus, to deepen Christian horror at Pergamum's obsession with the serpent-image, was called in this connection, "Zeus the Saviour." It is natural that "Nicolaitanism" should flourish in a place where politics and paganism were so closely allied, and where pressure on Christians to compromise must have been heavy. Pergamum was an ancient seat of culture and possessed a library which rivaled Alexandria's. Parchment (*charta Pergamena*) was invented at Pergamum to free the library from Egypt's jealous ban on the export of papyrus. E.M.B.

PERIDA (pē-rī′dȧ, Heb. *perîdhā′, divided*), one of Solomon's servants (Neh. 7:57). Spelled "Peruda" in Ezra 2:55.

PERIZZITE (pâr′ĭ-zīt, Heb. *perizzî*). References in the Pentateuch, Joshua, and Judges make it clear that the Perizzites were a pre-Israelitish tribe or racial group of Palestine (Gen. 13:7; 34:30; Exod. 3:8,17; 23:23; 33:2; 34:11; Deut. 20:17; Josh. 3: 10; 24:11; Judg. 1:4). Apart from these well-defined Biblical references, the Perizzites seem to have left no other marks on history. No non-Biblical document mentions them. There is an etymological similarity between the word and the term for "dweller in an unwalled village," hence the suggestion that the Perizzites were Canaanitish argriculturists (or nomads) who were not a part of the ordered town and village communities of Palestine, but were not racially distinct. The suggestion is reasonable but cannot at this stage be proved. E.M.B.

PERJURY (pêr′jêr-ē), a word not found in our English Bible (KJV), but closely related to several Biblical words such as *oath* or *punishment*. Oaths were very common in the OT and frequent mention of them is made in the New. Oaths consisted of a promise made and an appeal to God for the ratification of it. Such oaths were considered binding promises, so that to break an oath was regarded as perjury as well as using falsehood under oath (Lev. 19:12; Ezek. 16:59).

PERSECUTION (pêr′sĕ-qū′shŭn), in its most common sense, signifies a particular course or period of systematic infliction of punishment or penalty for adherence to a particular religious belief. Oppression is to be distinguished from it. Pharaoh oppressed the Hebrews; so did Nebuchadnezzar. Daniel and Jeremiah were persecuted. Systematic persecution began with the Roman imperial government. Notably tolerant towards alien religious beliefs in general, the Romans clashed with the Christians over the formalities of Caesar-worship. In that fact, according to W. M. Ramsay, lies the prime significance of the persecutions. Persecution began as a social reaction, and became political later, a process which can be detected in the surviving documents (Acts of the Apostles; Tacitus' *Annals;* Pliny, *Epistles* X). The state's policy of repression was intermittent, and, as the evidence of Tertullian shows, was visibly daunted by the growing numbers of the Christians. A considerable body of literature has gathered round the difficult theme of the legal basis on which the authorities pursued their policy, and on the incidence and severity of the persecutions themselves. Disregarding Claudius' anti-semitism of A.D. 49 (Acts 18:2), in which the Christians were not distinguished from Jews, Nero must be regarded as the first persecutor. In A.D. 64 (Tacitus, *Annals* 15:38-44) this emperor used the small Christian community as scapegoats for a disastrous fire in Rome and the charge of incendiarism which was popularly leveled against him. Domitian's execution of Glabrio and Flavius Clemens in A.D. 95, and the exile of Domitilla for "atheism," and "going astray after the customs of the Jews" (Dio Cassius 67: 44), was probably anti-Christian action, an incident which strikingly reveals the vertical spread of Christianity by the end of the first century. Pliny's famous correspondence with Trajan in A.D. 112 (Pliny, *Epistles* 10:96,97) reveals the state more moderately but quite uncompromisingly in action. Trajan's policy, laid down for Pliny in Bithynia, was followed by Hadrian and Antoninus Pius (A.D. 117-161). Marcus Aurelius was guilty of a sharp persecution at Lyons (A.D. 117). At the close of the second century, with the death of Septimius Severus, a long period of peace followed, broken by Maximinus Thrax, Decius, and Valerian, but without widespread action or much determination. Diocletian continued a now established policy of toleration until A.D. 303 when, under the influence of Galerius, he initiated the last short but savage period of persecution, described by Lactantius and Eusebius. (The historical questions involved are dealt with in W. M. Ramsay, *The Church in the Roman Empire before A.D. 170;* E. G. Hardy, *Christianity and the Roman Government.* More briefly, the social background and historical significance are dealt with in Tyndale Lectures 1951 and 1959 by E. M. Blaiklock: *The Christian in Pagan Society* and *Rome in the New Testament*).   E.M.B.

PERSEPOLIS (pĕr-sĕp'ō-lĭs, Gr. *Persépolis*). This city, royal seat of the Achaemenid kings of Persia, lay 30 miles NE of modern Shiraz. It was founded by Darius I (521-486 B.C.), and archaeological investigation establishes the fact that this king leveled the rock-terrace and built the great hall of audience. Xerxes and Artaxerxes carried on the work, the Hall of the Hundred Pillars being attributed to the latter. The whole complex of palaces and public buildings was fortified. The bas-reliefs surviving in the ruins are among the best examples of Achaemenid art. The burial-place of the dynasty is nearby. Destruction dates from Alexander the Great, who took Persepolis, and burned and looted it as an act of warfare designed to break Persian resistance, in 331 B.C. There is some evidence that the fire was confined to the main palace (Diod. 17:71,72). Persepolis is mentioned in II Maccabees 9:2 in connection with an attempted raid by Antiochus Epiphanes (215-163 B.C.), an outrage defeated by strong local resistance. The reference suggests that Persepolis was still a rich and powerful city a century and a half after Alexander's vandalism.   E.M.B.

PERSEVERANCE (pûr-sĕ-vēr'ans, Gr. *proskartéresis*), a word found only once in the Bible (Eph. 6:18, KJV), where it is used in connection with prayer. The Bible has a number of other words that convey the same idea. For instance, *epimenein* in Acts 13:43 carries the idea of perseverance. This same thought is clearly the idea in Matthew 10:22 where the Latin uses the word *persevero*. Abraham persevered and this trait is expressed by the word *ekarteresen* (Heb. 11:27). Thus the idea of perseverance is certainly Biblical even though this English word is rare in our Bibles.

This word comes into use frequently in most theologies. The Calvinist believes the doctrine to be a Scriptural one and, therefore, defends it, while it is denied by the Arminian. Perhaps the most complete discussion of the subject in which both Calvinistic and Arminian positions are set forth and the Calvinistic idea is defended was written by John Owen. (*John Owen, Works of,* London: Richard Barnes, 1826, Vol. VI, pp. XXXI — 533; Vol. VII, pp. 2-324). Theologically considered the word signifies "that they whom God has regenerated and effectually called to a state of grace can neither totally nor finally fall away from that state, but shall certainly persevere therein to the end and be eternally saved" (Louis Berkhof, *Systematic Theology,* Grand Rapids: Wm. B. Eerdmans Publ. Co., 1941, p. 545). It is possible because the indwelling Spirit keeps those whom God has redeemed. Such passages as John 3:36; 5:24; 10:27-30; Philippians 1:6 are cited to support this.

The Arminian objects that the doctrine is contrary to Scripture (Luke 13:24; II Tim. 2:5; Col. 1:23; Heb. 6:4-6,11: II Tim. 2:17-18). Striving would be unnecessary if the saint could not lose his salvation. That it leads to immorality and that it is inconsistent with human freedom are both offered as objections.   H.Z.C.

PERSIA (pûr'zhà, Heb. *pāras,* Gr. *Persis*). As a geographical term Persia may be taken to mean the Iranian plateau, bounded by the Tigris valley on the W and S, the Indus valley on the E, and by the Armenian ranges and the Caspian Sea to the N, comprising in all something near one million

The ruins of Persepolis, a city established by Darius I and destroyed by Alexander the Great. OIUC

The great audience hall of Darius and Xerxes at Persepolis. OIUC

square miles. The plateau is high and saucer-shaped, rimmed by mountains rich in mineral wealth, but with wide tracts of arid desert in the interior. The land lies across the old road communications of Europe and Asia, a situation which has done much to determine Persia's ethnology and history. It is seldom possible to separate history and geography, and the term Persia has signified both less and more than the geographical and general meaning thus set forth. The original Persia was a small area N of the Persian Gulf, known as Persis, the modern Fars. It was a rugged area with desert on its maritime borders, its chief town known to the Greeks as Persepolis. The Medes lay to the N, Elam was on the W, and Carmania to the E. This small province was the original home of the Iranian tribe who finally dominated the whole country, and founded the vast Persian Empire, which at the time of its widest extent, stretched from the Aegean Sea, the Dardanelles, and the Bosporus, to the Indus River, and from N to S extended from the Black Sea, the Caucasus, the Caspian Sea, the Oxus and the Jaxartes, to the Gulf, the Indian Ocean, and the cataracts of the Nile. This was the imperial power described by Herodotus, which clashed with the Greeks at the beginning of the fifth century before Christ, and which Alexander overthrew a century and a half later. This, too, was the imperial Persia of the OT which rose on the ruins of Babylon, which is seen in the story of Esther, and which formed the background of the events described in the books of Ezra and Nehemiah.

The Persians belonged to the race or group of nations which spoke the hypothetical Indo-European language, so called and conjectured because most of the languages of Europe together with the Indic languages descended from it. The Iranian dialects formed a southern group. A common linguistic ancestry, and therefore, in all probability, a common homeland, can be demonstrated for all this group. Migrations during the third and second millennia before Christ, mainly W, E, and S, appear to have spread tribal groups who spoke a common language through the European peninsulas, into India, and the northern Middle East. The picture is complex. Britain itself, for example, experienced three waves of invasion, Celtic (itself multiple), Roman, and Teutonic (Angles, Saxons Danes). Infiltration into the Middle East was as tangled a process. Just as the inhabitants of an enclave by the Tiber, speaking a minor Italic dialect, imposed their will upon the whole of Italy, and began the process of historical evolution which produced the Roman Empire, so the Persians emerged to dominate the whole complex of the Iranian tribes, 12 in number according to Xenophon (Cyro. 1:2:5), 10 according to Herodotus (1:125). A ninth century Assyrian inscription mentions Parsua as a northern country adjoining Media. This may be the first historical reference to the Persians before their movement S into Anshan and Parsa, the Persis above mentioned. The Assyrians reference may catch the Iranian tribe in the process of its migration. In Persis, the Persians were at first subject to the power of their northern neighbors, the Medes, although Elam, encroaching from the W, tended to form a buffer state between them. If reasons are sought for historical processes, it could have been the stimulus of Elam which caused Persian expansion.

Through Elam, Persis had contact with the developed civilizations of the Euphrates Valley. On the other hand, it may have needed no more than the emergence of a masterful personality to initiate the process. Such a person was Cyrus, second of that name from the ruling family of the Achaemenids. Cyrus is the Latinized form of Greek Kuros, Persian Kurash. According to tradition (Herod. 1:107-130), Cyrus was related to Astyages, king of Medea. Rising against his relative, Cyrus threw off the Median hegemony and established the Persians as the dominant tribe in 549 B.C. Some form of governmental partnership appears to have been established, for Medes held privileged posts in the new administration. Cyrus then moved W to defeat the Lydian Empire of Croesus in 545 B.C. (Herod. 1:71ff), and S to defeat Nabonidus of Babylon in 538 B.C. The conquest of Lydia gave Cyrus Asia Minor; the overthrow of Babylon made him master of the Euphrates River plain, Assyria, Syria, and Palestine. Thus arose the greatest West Asian Empire of ancient times. It was indeed the first of the world's great imperial organizations, a foreshadowing of the system of Rome, beneficent and humane when set beside the Assyrian Empire in comparison, but too loosely held and geographically divided to survive. The conflict between Samaria and Jerusalem, depicted in the story of Nehemiah, is illustration of the indiscipline which could reign in remoter corners. Nehemiah was working by royal decree, and yet found his work hampered by armed interference. Ezra's fear (Ezra 8:22) suggests similar pockets of anarchy.

Cyrus' great empire was organized by him and by Darius (Dariavaush, 521-486 B.C.), who succeeded him, after a period of revolt and dynastic trouble. Coming to terms with geography, Cyrus and Darius sought to combine a measure of local autonomy with centralization in a supreme controlling power, a difficult task even where communications are swift and efficient. The empire was cut into provinces, each under the rule of a satrap, who might be a local ruler or a Persian noble. About the person of the satrap were military and civil officials directly responsible to the king, who also kept himself informed on local matters by means of his "eyes," or his itinerant inspectors. This was an attempt to check maladministration in the satrapies, and to anticipate such challenges to the royal power as that described by Xenophon in his *Anabasis*. All provinces were assessed for monetary and man-power contributions to the central treasury and armed forces. An attempt was wisely made to preserve efficient forms of local government, and Greek city-states on the Ionian seaboard still functioned with religion, language, and civic government intact. Inscriptions suggest that there were three official languages, Persian, Elamitic, and Babylonian. Darius further unified his empire by an efficient gold coinage, statehighways, and a postal system, arrangements which became famous for their usefulness. The four books of the OT in which Persia forms a background all illustrate the royal tendency to delegate special authority to individuals for specific tasks.

Cyrus and the Achaemenid kings were Zoroastrians, worshipers of Ahura Mazda, "the Wise Lord." The Magi of the Medes appear to have been reorganized by Cyrus into a Mazdaist priesthood. Zoroaster taught that Ahura Mazda, together with his holy spirit, wars against an evil spirit, Ahriman. There was an element of Messianism in the cult, for it taught that after the earthly life of a future Saviour, God will finally triumph over evil, and all souls pass over the "bridge of decision," and enjoy eternal bliss, though some must first go through a purgatory of fire. Zoroaster stressed truth and mercy. Isaiah 45:7 is supposed by some to be a reference to Zoroastrian religion. The context is a tribute to Cyrus, and in contrast with the crude paganism of other peoples, the Persian monotheism may have appeared to the Hebrews to contain elements of divine insight. The notable favor shown to the religion of Jehovah in the books of Ezra and Nehemiah may illustrate the same affinity from the other side. It will be useful in conclusion to list the Persian kings whose reigns have significance in OT history: 1. Cyrus, 538-529 B.C. II Chronicles 36: 22,23; Ezra 1 to 5 passim; Isaiah 44:28; 45:1; Daniel 1:21; 6:28; 10:1.

2. Cambyses, 529-522 B.C. Some have suggested that Cambyses is the mysterious Darius the Mede of Daniel 5:31; 6:9,25; 9:1; 11:1. Others regard this obscure person as Gobryas, governor of Media, who exercised authority for Cyrus in Babylon.

3. Gaumata, a usurper, held brief royal authority until put down by Darius 522-521 B.C.

4. Darius I (Hystaspis) 521-486 B.C., the great imperialist, whose sea-borne attack on Greece was defeated at Marathon in 490 B.C. He is known for his trilingual inscription at Behistun, famous in linguistic studies. This is the Darius mentioned by

Ezra under whose protection permission was given for the temple to be built.

5. Xerxes I (Ahasuerus) 486-465 B.C. This is the mad king who in a mighty combined operation sought to avenge Marathon, and whom the Greeks defeated at Salamis (480 B.C.) and Plataea (479 B.C.). The feast and assembly of Esther 1:3 is plausibly equated with Herodotus 7:8, while Esther 2:16 is a reference to the events of Herodotus 9:108,109.

6. Artaxerxes I (Longimanus), 464-424 B.C. It was this monarch who permitted Ezra to go to Jerusalem to restore the affairs of the Jewish community (Ezra 7 and 8), and who promoted the mission of his cup-bearer Nehemiah, 13 years later. (In Ezra 4 chronology is broken and it is a matter of some difficulty to identify and arrange events. The IVF Commentary (in loco) deals with the matter well). Nehemiah 2:1; 5:14; 13:6. Note: Darius the Persian (Neh. 12:22) is Codomannus, last king of Persia, overthrown by Alexander in 330 B.C.   E.M.B.

PERSIS (pûr'sĭs, Gr. *Persís, Persian*), a Christian woman at Rome greeted by Paul as "the beloved, who labored much in the Lord" (Rom. 16:12).

PERUDA (See Perida)

PESHITTA (pĕ-shēt'tà), or "simple" version, is the common name for the ancient Syriac (Aramaic) translation of the Bible. The OT was translated before the Christian era, no doubt by Jews who spoke Aramaic and lived in the countries E of Palestine. Syriac Christians rendered the NT during the early centuries of the Church, the standard version being that of Rabbula, bishop of Edessa in the fifth century. The Syriac Bible played an important role in the Christian missionary thrust into the countries of the Far East, including India.

PESTILENCE (pĕs'tĭlĕns, Heb. *dever*, Gr. *loimós*), a word frequently found in the OT to refer to any fatal epidemic often coming as the result of divine judgment (Exod. 5:3; Jer. 14:12). The word is used in the NT only by Christ (Matt. 24:7; Luke 21:11).

PESTLE (pĕs'l, Heb. *'ĕlî, lifted*), an instrument made either of wood or stone, rounded at the ends and used to grind in a mortar (Prov. 27:22).

PETER (pētêr, Gr. *Pétros, rock*), the most prominent of the 12 apostles in the Gospels and an outstanding leader in the early days of the Christian Church. His original name was Simon, a common Greek name, or more properly Symeon (Acts 15: 14), a popular Hebrew name.

Background. He was a native of Bethsaida (John 1:44), the son of a certain John (John 1: 42 ASV; 21:15-17 ASV), apparently an abbreviation for Jonah (Matt. 16:17). As a Jewish lad he received a normal elementary education. As a native of "Galilee of the Gentiles" he was able to converse in Greek, while his native Aramaic was marked with provincialisms of pronunciation and diction (Matt. 26:73). The evaluation by the Sanhedrin of Peter and John as "unlearned and ignorant men" (Acts 4:13) simply meant that they were unschooled in the rabbinical lore and were laymen. With his brother Andrew he followed the hardy occupation of a fisherman on the Sea of Galilee, being partners with Zebedee's sons, James and John (Luke 5:7). He was a married man (Mark 1:30; I Cor. 9:5) and at the time of Christ's Galilean ministry lived in Capernaum (Mark 1: 21,29).

Gospel period. Of the second period of his life, from his first encounter with Jesus until the ascension, the Gospels give a vivid picture. Simon attended the preaching ministry of John the Baptist at the Jordan and, like Andrew, probably became a personal disciple of John. When he was personally introduced to Jesus by his brother Andrew, Jesus on seeing him with prophetic insight remarked, "Thou art Simon the son of Jona: thou shalt be called Cephas" (John 1:42). That John translated the Aramaic *Kēphās* into Greek *Petros,* both meaning *rock,* indicates that it was not a proper name but rather a descriptive title (cf. "sons of thunder," Mark 3:17). The designation, afterwards more fully explained in its prophetic import (Matt. 16:18; Mark 3:16), came to be regarded as his personal name. (No other man in the NT bears the name Peter). After a period of companionship with Jesus during His early Judean ministry (John 1:42-4:43), Peter resumed his ordinary employment.

With the commencement of Christ's Galilean ministry, Peter and Andrew, with James and John, were called by Jesus to full time association with Him to be trained as "fishers of men" (Mark 1: 16-20; Luke 5:1-11). With the growth of the work, Jesus selected 12 of His followers to be His nearest companions for special training (Mark 3:13-19; Luke 6:12-16). In the lists of these 12 designated apostles (Luke 6:13), Peter is always named first (Mark 3:16-19; Luke 6:14-16; Matt. 10:2-4; Acts 1:13-14). His eminence among them was due to his being among the first chosen as well as his native aggressiveness as a natural leader. But the other disciples did not concede to Peter any authority over them, as is evident from their repeated arguments about greatness (Matt. 20:20-28; Mark 9:33-34; Luke 22:24-27). While He was with them, Jesus alone was recognized as their leader.

The development of an inner circle among the disciples is first seen when Jesus took Peter, James, and John with Him into the house of Jairus (Mark 5:37; Luke 8:51). The three were further privileged to witness the transfiguration (Matt. 17: 1; Mark 9:2; Luke 9:28) and the agony in the garden (Matt. 26:37; Mark 14:33). Even in this inner circle Peter usually stands in the foreground, but the Fourth Gospel indicates that his position of eminence was not exclusive.

Peter was the natural spokesman of the 12. When Christ's sermon on the Bread of Life produced a general defection among His followers, Peter spoke for the 12 in asserting their loyalty to Him (John 6:66-69). Again, at Caesarea Philippi, when Jesus asked the 12 their view of Him, Peter promptly replied, "Thou art the Christ, the Son of the living God" (Matt. 16:16). His confession of the Messiahship and Deity of our Lord expressed a divinely-given insight higher than the current view which regarded the Messiah only as a man exalted to the Messianic office (cf. Matt. 22:41-46). His confession elicited Christ's prompt commendation and the further assertion, "Thou art Peter, and upon this rock I will build my church" (Matt. 16:18). By his believing confession Peter has identified himself with Christ the true Rock (I Cor. 3:11; Isa. 28:16; I Pet. 2:4-5), thus fulfilling Christ's prediction concerning him (John 1: 42). He has thus become a rock (*petros*), and upon "this rock" (*petra*), composed of Peter and the other apostles joined by faith to Christ the chief corner stone (Eph. 2:20), Jesus announces that He will build His triumphant church.

The story in Acts historically interprets Peter's use of the keys in opening the doors of Christian

The courtyard of the house of Caiaphas, where a monk looks at a plaque representing a cock crowing, in remembrance of Peter's denial of his Lord. © MPS

opportunity at Pentecost (chap. 2), in Samaria (chap. 8), and to the Gentiles (chap. 10). The power of binding and loosing was not limited to Peter (Matt. 18:18; John 20:23). But Peter was also the spokesman in attempting to dissuade Jesus from His announced path of suffering, thus proving himself a "stumbling-block" (Matt. 16: 23; Mark 8:33).

Peter came into prominence in the Gospel story also in connection with the matter of the payment of the temple-tax (Matt. 17:24-27), his inquiry as to the limits on forgiveness (Matt. 18:21), and his reminder to Jesus that they had left all to follow Him (Matt. 19:27; Mark 10:28). During Passion Week his activities were prominent. He called Jesus' attention to the withered fig tree (Mark 11: 21), and with three others he asked Jesus concerning His prediction about the temple (Mark 13:3). With John he was commissioned to prepare for the Passover (Luke 22:8), objected to the Lord's washing his feet in the Upper Room, but impulsively swung to the opposite extreme when informed of the implications of his denial (John 13:1-11), beckoned to John to ask the identity of the betrayer (John 13:23-24), and stoutly contradicted Jesus when warned of his impending denials (Matt. 26:33-35; Mark 14:29-31; Luke 22: 31-34; John 13:37-38). In the garden, when chosen with James and John to watch with Jesus, he slept (Matt. 26:37-46; Mark 14:33-42). In fleshly zeal he sought to defend Jesus and received His rebuke (John 18:10-11). He fled with the other disciples when Jesus was bound, but anxious to see the end he followed afar, was admitted into the court of the high priest through John's action, and there shamefully denied his Lord in three rounds of denials (Matt. 26:58, 69-75; Mark 14:66-72; Luke 22:54-62; John 18:15-18, 25-27). The look of Jesus broke his heart and he went out and wept bitterly (Luke 22:61-62). That Peter witnessed the crucifixion is not stated (but cf. I Pet. 5:1).

On the resurrection morning he and John ran to the tomb of Jesus to investigate the report of Mary Magdalene (John 20:1-10). Somewhere during that day the risen Lord appeared to Peter (I Cor. 15:5). At His post-resurrection manifestation to seven at the Sea of Galilee, John was the first to recognize the Lord, but, typically, Peter was the first to act. Following the group breakfast, Christ tested Peter's love and formally restored him by the threefold commission to feed His sheep (John 21:1-23).

Early Church. The third period in Peter's life began with the ascension of Jesus. In the early days of the Church (Acts 1-12), Peter appeared as the spokesman of the apostolic group, but there is no hint that he assumed any authority not also exercised by the other apostles. He suggested the choice of another to fill the place of Judas (1:15-26), preached the Spirit-empowered sermon on Pentecost to the assembled Jews (2:14-40), and with John healed the lame man, the first apostolic miracle to arouse persecution (3:1-4:21). He was used to expose the sin of Ananias and Sapphira (5:1-12), was held in high esteem by the people during the miracle ministry in the church that followed (5:12-16), and spoke for the 12 when arraigned before the Sanhedrin (5:27-41). With John he was sent to Samaria where, through the laying on of hands, the Holy Spirit fell on the Samaritan believers and Peter exposed the unworthy motives of Simon (8:14-24). While on a tour through Judea Peter healed Aeneas and raised Dorcas from the dead (9:32-43). Through a divinely-given vision at Joppa Peter was prepared and commissioned to preach the Gospel to Cornelius at Caesarea, thus opening the door to the Gentiles (10:1-48). This brought upon him the criticism of the circumcision party in Jerusalem (11:1-18). During the persecution of the Church by Agrippa I in A.D. 44, Peter escaped death by a miraculous deliverance from prison (12:1-19).

Later life. With the opening of the door to the Gentiles and the spread of Christianity, Peter receded into the background and Paul became prominent as the apostle to the Gentiles. In the Acts narrative Peter is last mentioned in connection with the Jerusalem conference, where he championed the liberty of the Gentiles (15:6-29). The remaining NT references to Peter are scanty. Galatians 2:11-21 records a visit to Syrian Antioch where his inconsistent conduct evoked a public rebuke from Paul. From I Corinthians 9:5 it appears that Peter traveled widely, taking his wife with him, doubtless in Jewish evangelism (Gal. 2:9).

Nothing further is heard of Peter until the writing of the two epistles that bear his name, apparently written from Rome. In the first epistle, addressed to believers in five provinces in Asia Minor, the shepherd-heart of Peter sought to fortify the saints in their sufferings for Christ, while in the second he warns against dangers from within. A final NT reference to the closing years of Peter's life is found in John 21:18-19. John's interpretation of Christ's prediction makes it clear that the reference is to Peter's violent death. Beyond this the NT is silent about him.

Tradition uniformly asserts that Peter went to Rome, that he labored there, and there in his old age suffered martyrdom under Nero. The embellished tradition that he was bishop of Rome for 25 years is contrary to all NT evidence. He apparently came to Rome shortly after Paul's release from his first imprisonment there.

The roof of the house of Simon the Tanner in Jaffa, ancient Joppa, where Peter saw his vision. © MPS

Character. The character of Peter is one of the most vividly drawn and charming in the NT. His sheer humanness has made him one of the most beloved and winsome members of the apostolic band. He was eager, impulsive, energetic, self-confident, aggressive, and daring, but also unstable, fickle, weak, and cowardly. He was guided more by quick impulse than logical reasoning, and readily swayed from one extreme to the other. He was preeminently a man of action. His story exhibits the defects of his qualities as well as the tremendous capacities for good which he possessed. He was naturally forward and often rash, liable to instability and inconsistency, but his love for and associations with Christ moulded him into a man of stability, humility, and courageous service for God, becoming one of the noble pillars (Gal. 2:9) of the Church.   D.E.H.

PETER, FIRST EPISTLE OF, the keynote of the First Epistle of Peter is suffering, and the Christian method of meeting it. The writer endeavored to convey a message of hope to Christians who had been undergoing persecution, and who were succumbing to discouragement because they could find no redress. It contains a hortatory presentation of Christian truth, calculated to strengthen believers.

Authorship. Of the two epistles that bear the name of Peter, the first is better attested. Echoes of its phraseology appear as early as the epistle of Polycarp to the Philippians (c. 125), the Epistle of Barnabas (c. 135) and the writings of Justin Martyr (c. 150). The Second Epistle of Peter refers to a former epistle which probably means this one (II Pet. 3:1). It was unanimously accepted as Petrine by all of the fathers who mention it by name, beginning with Irenaeus (c. 170).

The internal structure reflects Peter's mind and life. The first main paragraph, "Blessed be the God and Father of our Lord Jesus Christ, who hath begotten us again unto a living hope by the resurrection of Jesus Christ from the dead (1:3) expresses the joy which Peter felt after the forgiveness bestowed on him by the risen Christ after the denial. The injunction to "feed (shepherd) the flock of God" (5:2) is almost identical in language with Jesus' commisson to him at the lake of Galilee (John 21:16). "Gird yourselves with humility" may be a reminiscence of the last supper, when Jesus girded Himself with a towel and washed the disciples' feet(John 13:4,5).

There are also some remarkable agreements between the vocabulary of I Peter and the speeches of Peter in Acts (I Pet. 1:17; Acts 10:34; I Pet. 1:21; Acts 2:32; 10:40,41; the quotation I Pet. 2:7, 8 with Acts 4:10,11).

Destination. The epistle was directed to members of the Dispersion located in the northern Roman provinces of Asia Minor which Paul did not visit, and which may have been evangelized by Peter between the Council of Jerusalem (A.D. 48) and the Neroian persecution at Rome (A.D. 64). There is some question whether the "Dispersion" should be taken literally as applying strictly to Jews, or whether it may be used figuratively of Gentiles, Christians who were scattered abroad. In favor of the former conclusion are one or two passages which seemingly indicate that the recipients were Jews (2:12; 3:6); on the other hand, "Gentiles" may be equivalent to "brethren," and the references to the ungodly past of these people (1:14; 4:3) do not seem to agree with the hypotheses that they were of Jewish descent. If Peter wrote this epistle from Rome, he may have been writing to refugees from the Neronian persecution who were converts from Judaism or proselytes who turned from Judaism to Christianity.

Date and Place. If the Silvanus (5:12) and Mark (5:13) were the same persons mentioned in Paul's epistles (I Thess. 1:1; II Cor. 1:19; Col. 4:10; II Tim. 4:11), I Peter must have been written subsequent to Silvanus' departure from Paul and prior to Mark's rejoining him. Silvanus was with Paul in Corinth in the early fifties, and Mark probably rejoined him just before his death, which took place about A.D. 65-67. Furthermore, I Peter bears traces of the influence of Paul's Epistle to the Romans and to the Ephesians in its structure and thought (cf. I Pet. 2:13; Rom. 13:1-4; I Pet. 2:18; Eph. 6:5; I Pet. 3:9; Rom. 12:17; I Pet. 5:5; Eph. 5:21) which would imply that it was written after A.D. 60. Probably I Peter was written about the year 64, when the status of Christians in the empire was very uncertain, and when persecution had already begun in Rome.

The place of writing is closely connected with the date. "Babylon" (5:13) may refer to the ancient city on the Euphrates, where there was a large Jewish settlement in Peter's day, or to a town in Egypt near Alexandria, where Mark traditionally ministered, or figuratively to Rome as the center of the pagan world (Rev. 17:5; 18:10). The second alternative need not be considered seriously, for the Egyptian Babylon was only a border fort. Opinion among commentators is divided between the other two opinions. In the absence of any strong tradition that Peter ever visited in the literal Babylon, it seems more likely that he wrote this epistle from Rome, shortly before his martyrdom. He would have had opportunity to find some of Paul's writings there and to have met Silvanus and Mark, both of whom were familiar to Paul.

Those who deny the Petrine authorship place the epistle in the early second century under the reign of Trajan (A.D. 96-117). Sir William Ramsay assigned it to the time of Domitian (A.D. 87-96), conceding that Peter might have been executed in the time of Vespasian or Domitian (c. A.D. 80).

Structure and Content. In general arrangement I Peter resembles closely the Pauline epistles, with a salutation, body, and conclusion. Its main subject is the Christian's behavior under the pressure of suffering, its key is the salvation which is to be revealed at the last time (1:5). The epistle may be outlined as follows:

    I. Introduction, 1:1,2
   II. The Nature of Salvation, 1:3-12
  III. The Experience of Salvation, 1:13-25
  IV. The Obligations of Salvation, 2:1-10
   V. The Ethics of Salvation, 2:11-3:12
  VI. The Confidence of Salvation, 3:13-4:11
 VII. The Behavior of the Saved under Suffering, 4:12-5:11
VIII. Concluding Salutations, 5:12-14

Bibliography: E. G. Selwyn, *The First Epistle of Peter*, London: Macmillan, 1946. Thomas, W. H. Griffith, *The Apostle Peter*, Grand Rapids, Mich.: W. B. Eerdmans Pub. Co., 1946.   M.C.T.

PETER, SECOND EPISTLE OF, is a general treatise, written to warn its readers of threatening apostasy. It purports to be written by Simon Peter and contains a definite allusion to a preceding letter (3:1).

Authorship. II Peter has the poorest external attestation of any book in the canon of the NT. It is not quoted directly by any of the fathers before Origen (c. 250), who affirms the Petrine authorship of the first epistle, but who seemed uncertain about the second, although he did not repudiate it. Eusebius, to whom we are indebted for quoting Origen's testimony, placed II Peter in the list of disputed writers. Its literary style and vocabulary differs from that of I Peter, and its close resemblance to the book of Jude has led some scholars to believe that it is a late copy or adaptation of that work. Numerous scholars have pronounced it spurious, and have relegated it to the middle of the second century.

On the other hand, the internal evidence favors Petrine authorship. It seems strange that if a forger knew First Peter, he could not have been more careful to copy its style exactly. The allusions to Peter's career agree with the existing records, and can best be explained as the testimony of an eye witness. They include the Transfiguration (1:17, 18), at which Peter was present (Matt. 17:1-8), and the Lord's prediction of his death (1:14; John 21:18,19). The Greek of the second epistle is more labored than that of the first, but if Peter did not have the aid of Silvanus in this work, as he did in the first epistle (I Pet. 5:12), he may have been forced to rely on his own writing. Doubtlessly he knew Greek, as most Galileans did, but he may not have been able to write it easily. II Peter reads more like a book which has been composed with the aid of a dictionary rather than by a man whose native tongue was Greek.

The allusion to the writings of "our beloved brother Paul" (3:15) confirms the impression that II Peter was written by someone who knew Paul personally and who treated him as an equal. A writer of the second century would have been more likely to say "the blessed apostle," for he would have regarded Paul with a greater veneration, and would thus have used a more elevated title.

There is, therefore, some reason for accepting the Epistle as Peter's. The relative silence of the early Church may be explained by the brevity of the epistle, which could have made it more susceptible to being overlooked or lost.

Date and Place. II Peter must have been written subsequent to the publication of at least some of Paul's letters, if not of the entire collection. It cannot, therefore, have been written before A.D. 60; but if Paul were living, or were still well known to the existing generation, it could not have been later than 70. Probably A.D. 67 is as satisfactory a date as can be established. The writer was anticipating speedy death (1:14), which may mean that the epistle was sent from Rome during the tense days of the Neronian persecution. There is no indication, however, that Peter had spent a long time in Rome. He may have labored there only at the conclusion of Paul's life between 63 and 67.

Destination and Occasion. The reference to a previous letter sent to the same group (3:1) connects this document with I Peter, which was written to the Christians of northern Asia Minor. Whereas the first epistle was an attempt to encourage a church threatened with official persecution and repression, the second epistle dealt with the peril of apostasy, which was even a greater threat. An influx of conscienceless agitators who repudiated the lordship of Christ (2:1) and whose attitude was haughty (2:10), licentious (2:13), adulterous (2:14), greedy (2:14), bombastic (2:18), and libertine (2:19) seemed imminent. Knowing that he would not be spared to keep control of the situation, Peter was writing to forestall this calamity and to warn the church of its danger.

Content and Outline. The key to this epistle is the word "know" or "knowledge," which occurs 16 times in the three chapters, six of which refer to the knowledge of Christ. This knowledge is not primarily academic, but is spiritual, arising from a growing experience of Christ (3:18). It produces peace and grace (1:2), fruitfulness (1:8), is the secret of freedom from defilement (2:20) and is the sphere of Christian growth (3:18). It may be that the false teachers were Gnostics, who stressed knowledge as the means of salvation, and that Peter sought to counteract their falsehoods by a positive presentation of true knowledge.

II Peter teaches definitely the inspiration of Scripture (1:19-21) and stresses the doctrine of the personal return of Christ, which was ridiculed by the false teachers (3:1-7). It concludes with an appeal for holy living, and with the promise of the new heavens and the new earth.

The following is a brief outline of the Epistle:

I. Salutation, 1:1
II. The Character of Spiritual Knowledge, 1:2-21
III. The Nature and Perils of Apostasy, 2:1-22
IV. The Doom of the Ungodly, 3:1-7
V. The Hope of Believers, 3:8-13
VI. Concluding Exhortation, 3:14-18.   M.C.T.

PETHAHIAH (pěth'à-hī'à, Heb. *pethahyâh, Jehovah opens up*). 1. The head priest of the 19th course of priests during David's reign (I Chron. 24:16).

2. A disobedient Levite who, in the time of Ezra, had married a foreign wife (Ezra 10:23). Most scholars identify him with the one mentioned in Nehemiah 9:5.

3. Meshezabeel's son who descended from Zearah from the tribe of Judah. He was the counselor for King Artaxerxes ". . . in all matters pertaining to the people" (Neh. 11:24).

PETHOR (pē'thôr, *pethôr*), mentioned twice in connection with the hireling prophet Balaam (Num. 22:5; Deut. 23:4). Both passages place Pethor in Mesopotamia on the Euphrates. There is a reference in an Assyrian inscription of Shalmaneser II to a place called Pitru on the Sagur near its confluence with the Euphrates. It cannot be

proved that Pitru is Pethor, but if such a reasonable inference is true, Pethor would appear to lie just W of Carchemish on the W bank of the Euphrates.

PETHUEL (pē-thū'ĕl, Heb. *pethû'ēl, God's opening*), the prophet Joel's father (Joel 1:1).

PETRA (pē'trà), translates *sela', meaning rock, cliff,* or *crag,* and, as a proper noun, seems to refer to one or two places in the OT (Judg. 1:36; II Kings 14:7; Isa. 16:1). No certain geographical identification is possible, although the second reference may be to the Petra of later history, the "rose-red city half as old as time," of Dean Burgon's sonnet, and capital city of the Nabataeans from the close of the fourth century before Christ until A.D. 105, when it became part of the Roman Empire. The town lies in a basin surrounded by mountains. The town's considerable ruins are not impressive, in spite of Burgon's oft-quoted eulogy the main curiosities of Petra being the narrow canyons which form its approaches, and the rock-hewn temples and tombs in the surrounding cliffs. Nothing is known of Petra's history before the Nabataeans took over in 312 B.C.   E.M.B.

Amid the rose-red rock canyons of Petra, fabled capital of the Nabateans. The El-Khazneh temple is carved in the rock cliff at right. © MPS

PEULETHAI, PEULTHAI (pē-ŭl'ē-thī, pē-ŭl'thī, *Jehovah is a reward*), a Levite who was Obededom's eighth son. He was a porter of the tabernacle in the time of David (I Chron. 26:5).

PHALEC (fā'lĕk, Gr. *Phalék*), a Greek form of the Hebrew *Peleg* (Luke 3:35).

PHALLU (See Pallu)

PHALTI (făl'tī, Heb. *paltî, delivered*). 1. The spy from Benjamin's tribe sent by Moses to search out Canaan (Num. 13:9).

2. Saul's son-in-law, called also "Phalti" (II Sam. married after Michal's husband, David, had been driven away (I Sam. 25:44). He is called "Phaltiel" in II Samuel 3:15,16.

PHALTIEL (făl'tĭ-ĕl, Heb. *paltî'ēl, God delivers*).
1. A prince of Issachar (Num. 34:26).
2. Saul's son-in-law called also "Phalti" (II Sam. 3:15).

PHANUEL (fà-nū'ĕl, Heb. *penû'ēl, face of God,* Gr. *phanouél*), the father of Anna the prophetess (Luke 2:36).

PHARAOH (fâr'ō, Heb. *par'ōh*). The government of Egypt, and ultimately the supreme monarch in whom all its powers were vested, was known as the "Great House," in Egyptian "Per-o," whence descends the term pharaoh. The recorded pharaohs of Egypt, 26 separate dynasties, extend from Menes, 3400 B.C. to Psamtik III, deposed at the Persian conquest in 525 B.C. The term pharaoh can be traced back to the Twenty-Second Dynasty (945-745 B.C.), since when it was commonly attached to the monarch's name. Thus "Pharaoh Necho," and "Pharaoh Hophra" are exact Hebrew renderings of the Egyptian title.

Pharaohs of Egypt are mentioned in the following OT contexts: 1. Genesis 12:10-20. The date of Abram's descent into Egypt must be in the early years of the second millennium B.C. Amenemhet I, according to Breasted's dating, was pharaoh from 2000-1970 B.C. There is no strong evidence that northern Egypt was already under the power of the Hyksos intruders at this time, plausible though it may seem to connect the patriarch's sojourn with the presence of racially related rulers. On the tomb of Khnumhotep at Beni Hassan, dating from the 20th century B.C., the visit of such a Semitic party is vividly portrayed.

2. Genesis 39 to 50 *passim*. It is reasonable to place the period of Joseph's (and Israel's) favor in Egypt in the times of the Hyksos invaders. These foreigners, which included Canaanitish and Semitic elements from Palestine, supplanted the weak rulers of the Thirteenth and Fourteenth Dynasties, and settled in the Delta and Lower Egypt, where they maintained their power for some two centuries. They were driven out in 1580 B.C.

3. Exodus 1 to 15 *passim*. Controversy surrounds the identity of the pharaoh of the Oppression, and the date of the Hebrew Exodus. One, to some extent, depends upon the other. John Garstang's excavations at Jericho in the early 1930's seemed to establish a date for the Hebrew storming of the city round the turn of the 14th century. This would postulate a date for the Exodus around 1440 B.C., and would identify Thutmose III as the Pharaoh of Oppression, and the famous princess Hatshepsut as Moses' protectress. The theory produces a neat pattern of dates, and the events of the Oppression through to the infiltration of the tribes into Palestine correspond very well with events of Egyptian history during the years 1580 to 1350 B.C., the period of the great Eighteenth Dynasty. Ahmose I would thus be the "pharaoh who knew not Joseph." Indeed, as the first native ruler after the expulsion of the hated Hyksos, he would be naturally hostile to the shepherd protégés of the old regime. The breakdown of Egyptian control in Palestine under Amenhotep IV (Ikhnaton), would also account for the comparative facility of the Hebrew conquest, and explain the "Habiru" references of the Tell-el-Amarna Letters.

Competent orthodox scholarship, however, not without backing from more recent work at Jericho,

The pharaohs of Egypt built great monuments in the form of obelisks, pyramids and temples. This is the famous obelisk of Queen Hatshepsut at Thebes. © MPS

still argues for the older dating, under which Seti I (1313-1292 B.C.) is regarded as the pharaoh of Exodus 1:8. Ramses II (1292-1225 B.C.), in whose reign the store-cities of Pitham and Ra'amses were completed, would thus fill the rôle of Pharaoh of the Oppression, and perhaps the Exodus (Exod. 1:11; 12:40). Ra'amses was the fort from which the great militarist Ramses II sought to control his Asiatic empire, and the war-base from which he marched to his great battle with the Hittites at Kadesh on the Orontes, the conflict depicted on the walls of the Ramesseum at Thebes. Those who thus identify the Pharaoh of the Oppression, point out that the Egyptian hold over Palestine slackened after Ramses' treaty with the Hittites, and that this weakening of policy allowed the fragmentation of the country from which the Hebrew incursion profited. Some more precisely date the Exodus in the reign of Ramses' son, Merneptah, mainly on the strength of the "Israel Stele," discovered by Flinders Petrie in 1896. This inscription, self dated in 'the third year of Merneptah' (1223 B.C.), tells of the pharaoh's victories in Canaan. One line runs: "Israel is devastated. Her seed is not" (or "Her crops are destroyed"). A natural reference from this statement might, however, be that Israel was already in settled possession of large tracts of Palestine. At this point the matter must, at the moment, be left.

4. I Chronicles 4:18 speaks of "the sons of Bithiah the daughter of the pharaoh, whom Mered married." No identification of this pharaoh is possible, and the name of the princess appears to be Hebraized.

5. I Kings 3:1; 9:16,24; 11:1. Solomon's reign may be reliably dated 961 to 922 B.C., which period corresponds with the reign of Pharaoh Sheshonk I (945 to 924 B.C.), the founders of the Twenty-Second Dynasty. Under this pharaoh Egypt's foreign policy again took on an aggressive

character, and at all such times it was Egypt's custom (not without illustration in recent events) to establish the safety of the northern approaches, virtually her only invasion route. Hence the policy of Thutmose III, Ramses II, Seti I, and Sheshonk. The dynastic alliance with Solomon, and the handing to his suzerainty of the city of Gezer, were part of the recurrent Egyptian plan to create a "glacis" or a defensive buffer in Palestine. The ruler who acted with such foresight and energy can hardly have been one of the feeble monarchs of the earlier dynasty. A further facet of the same policy is revealed by Pharaoh's befriending of Hadad of Edom (I Kings 11:14-22). Hadad was a useful weapon for possible employment against a recalcitrant Solomon, or against a hostile Palestine.

6. II Kings 18:21 and Isaiah 36:6 both mention the pharaoh of Sennacherib's day. He is "that broken reed of a staff, which will pierce the hand of any man who leans on it," says the Rabshakeh to the people of Jerusalem. The date is 701 B.C. Egypt was in the state of political disintegration and weakness pictured in Isaiah 19. Shabaka was pharaoh, the first monarch of the feeble Twenty-Fifth Dynasty. The army scraped together to face the Assyrian threat was a motley horde of mercenaries and ill-armed levies. Egyptian contingents had served in the past against Assyria, but this was the first time the two empires, that of the Tigris and that of the Nile, actually confronted each other. Sennacherib led in person. Shabaka entrusted his force to his nephew Taharka who, some 13 or 14 years later, became king of Ethiopia. Hence the title given in II Kings 19:9 by anticipation of events. The Assyrian rapidly dealt with Taharka's force, and was proceeding to overthrow Palestine and the strong pocket of resistance which he had left screened by a task-force in Jerusalem, when the famous plague which decimated his host fell upon him. This overwhelming catastrophe was the cause of the Assyrian retreat, and deliverance both for Palestine and Egypt.

7. II Kings 23:20-35. Pharaoh-Necho was the last of the pharaohs to endeavor to re-establish Egyptian authority in the northern approaches. He succeeded Psametik I, founder of the Twenty-

One of the many statues of Pharaoh Rameses II, who may have been the pharaoh of the Oppression, or of the Exodus. BM

Entrance of the great Temple of Amon at Karnak, Egypt. © MPS

Sixth Dynasty, in 609 B.C., and reigned until 593 B.C. Immediately upon his accession, taking advantage of the collapse of Nineveh, Necho drove N into Philistia. On the plain of Megiddo, where Egypt had won control of the land 900 years before, Necho routed and killed Josiah. He moved on to the Euphrates, unopposed by Nineveh, but not feeling strong enough to go against that stronghold. From Ribleh on the Orontes, three months after the battle at Megiddo, Necho deposed Jehoahaz, and sent him to die in Egypt. He placed Jehoiakim on the throne of Judah, and fixed a tribute for the conquered land. Two years later Necho's new empire fell before the attack of Babylon. Jeremiah refers to the event (37:7; 46:2).

8. Ezekiel 29:1. The date is 587 B.C., and the pharaoh referred to must therefore be Hophra, or Apries, in the first year of his rule. He reigned from 588 to 569 B.C. This was the pharaoh whose troops failed to relieve Jerusalem in 586 B.C., and whose weak action against Nebuchadnezzar's Babylon brilliantly vindicated the advice of Jeremiah. Egypt escaped the calamity which befell Palestine by prudent modification of her challenge. Preoccupied with Tyre, Nebuchadnezzar did not press the war against Egypt, and Apries brought his country its last flourish of prosperity before the land fell before the Persian conquest. See EGYPT.

E.M.B.

PHARES, PHAREZ (fā'rēz, Gr. *Pharés, breach*),
Judah's twin son by his daughter-in-law, Tamar
(Gen. 38:29; I Chron. 2:4). He had a large number of descendants (Ruth 4:12) who continued to
play a prominent role right up until the captivity
(I Chron. 27:3; Neh. 11:4,6). In a number of these
passages he is called "Perez."

PHARISEES (fâr'ĭ-sēz, Heb. *perûshûn*, Gr. *Phari-
saíoi*). Of the three prominent societies of Judaism
at the time of Christ — Pharisees, Sadducees and
Essenes — the Pharisees were by far the most influential. The origin of this most strict sect of the
Jews (Acts 26:5) is shrouded in some obscurity,
but it is believed the organization came out of the
Maccabean Revolt (165 B.C.). There was, however, a group of Jews resembling the Pharisees as
far back as the Babylonian Captivity.

The name "Pharisee," which in its Semitic form
means "the separated ones, separatists," first appears during the reign of John Hyrcanus (135
B.C.). Generally, the term is in the plural rather
than in the singular. They were also known as
chasidim, meaning "loved of God" or "loyal to
God." They were found everywhere in Palestine,
not only in Jerusalem, and even wore a distinguishing garb so as to be easily recognized. According to Josephus, their number at their zenith
of popularity was more than 6,000. Because of the
significant role the Pharisees played in the life of
the Lord and the Apostles, knowledge of the
character and teachings of this group is of great
importance for the understanding of the NT. They
are mentioned dozens of times, especially in the
Gospels, and often form the foil and fabric of the
works and words of Jesus.

Three facets or characteristics of the Jewish
nation contributed to the development of the Pharisees, or paradoxically, it may be said that the
Pharisees made these contributions to Judaism, so
that ultimately Pharisaism and Judaism became
almost synonymous. The first of these is Jewish
legalism, which began in earnest after the Babylonian Captivity. The temple worship and the
sacrifices had ceased and Judaism began to center
its activities in the Jewish Law and in the synagogue. The Pharisees studied the traditional exegesis of the Law and made it a part of Jewish thought.
The rise of the Jewish Scribes, who were closely
associated with the Pharisees, also gave great im-
petus to Jewish legalism. The Pharisees, who were
more of a fraternal order or religious society than
a sect, were the organized followers of these experts in interpreting the Scriptures; they formalized
the religion of the Scribes and placed it into
practice. This is why the Scribes and Pharisees are
often mentioned together in the NT. The Pharisees
were not the practical politicians like the more
liberal Sadducees, but were the religious leaders
of the Jews. The highest qualification for membership was strict adherence to the Law, oral or written. Josephus, a contemporary Jewish historian,
aptly describes them as "a body of Jews who profess to be more religious than the rest, and to explain the laws more precisely." A modern authority on Judaism, C. F. Moore, says, "the Pharisees
were a party whose endeavor it was to live in strict
accordance with the Law thus interpreted and
amplified by the study and exposition of the
Scribes, and the tradition of interpretation which
they had established, and to bring the people to a
similar conformity." (*Judaism in the First Centuries of the Christian Era*, p. 66). This familiar
characteristic of the Pharisees is well exemplified
in the NT concerning the sabbath (cf. John 9:16).

A concomitant and blood brother of Jewish
legalism was Jewish nationalism. Continued persecution and isolation crystallized this narrow
spirit. During the Captivity the Jews were a small
minority in a strange nation. The fierce persecution
of Antiochus Epiphanes (175-164 B.C.), who
made a bold attempt to Hellenize and assimilate
the Jews, only drew the Jewish people closer together. The Pharisees took the occasion to cultivate a national and religious consciousness which
has hardly been equaled.

A third contributing factor to Pharisaism was
the development and organization of the Jewish
religion itself after the Captivity and the Revolt.
Formulation and adaptation of Mosaic law by
Scribe and rabbi, increased tradition, and a more
rabid separatism from almost everything resulted
in almost a new religion much the opposite from
that handed down in the Covenant by the prophets.
Pharisaism epitomized this spirit. Especially did
they vehemently oppose all secularization of Judaism by the pagan Greek thought which penetrated Jewish life after the Alexandrian conquest.
They ferreted out and sought the death of any liberal or antinomian person, especially if he were a
fellow Jew. The Jewish ability to die for their
"religion" made the people all the more proud of
their traditions and law. This pride even developed
into a feeling of superiority over other nations and
people. The extreme separatism from the Samaritans, for example (John 4:9), which went far
beyond inter-marriage and social intercourse, came
from a superior feeling as well as religious emotion
and found its most extreme expression among the
Pharisees. They became a closely organized group,
very loyal to the society and to each other, but
separate from others, even their own people. They
pledged themselves to obey all facets of the traditions to the minutest detail and were sticklers for
ceremonial purity. They even vowed to pay tithes
of everything they possessed in addition to the
temple tax. They would not touch the carcass of a
dead animal or those who had come into contact
with such things. They had no association with
people who had been defiled through sickness. In
truth, they made life difficult for themselves and
bitter for others. They despised those whom they
did not consider their equals and were haughty
and arrogant because they believed they were the
only interpreters of God and His Word. It is only
natural that ultimately such a religion became only
a matter of externals and not of the heart, and that
God's grace was thought to come only from doing
the Law.

The doctrines of the Pharisees included predestination, or, as some have termed it, a teaching of special divine providence. They also laid
much stress on the immortality of the soul and
had a fundamental belief in spirit life, teachings
which usually caused much controversy when they
met the Sadducees who just as emphatically denied them (Acts 23:6-9). Being people of the
Law they believed in final reward for good works
and that the souls of the wicked were detained
forever under the earth, while those of the virtuous
rose again and even migrated into other bodies
(Josephus, *Antiq.* 18:1,3; Acts 23:8). They accepted the OT Scriptures and fostered the usual
Jewish Messianic hope which they gave a material
and nationalistic twist.

It was inevitable, in view of these factors, that
they bitterly opposed Jesus and His teachings. If
they despised the Herods and the Romans, they
hated Jesus' doctrine of equality and claims of
messiahship with equal fervor (John 9:16,22).

He in turn condemned both their theology and life of legalism. They often became a fertile background against which He taught God's free salvation by grace through His own death and resurrection. Clashes between Jesus and the Pharisees were frequent and bitter, as examples in the Gospels reveal: He calls them a generation of vipers and condemns them for impenitence (Matt. 3:7); condemns their work-righteousness (Matt. 5:20); upbraids their pride against others (Matt. 9:12; Luke 19:10); scorns their lovelessness on the sabbath (Matt. 12:2); rebukes them for not being baptized (Luke 7:30); teaches them regarding divorce (Matt. 19:3) and taxes (Mark 12:17); condemns them for their covetousness (Luke 16:14). The Pharisees, in turn, accused Jesus of blasphemy (Luke 5:21); of being in league with the devil (Matt. 9:34); of breaking the Law (Matt. 12:2); and often planned to destroy Him (Matt. 12:14). Jesus' longest and most scathing rebuke of the Pharisees is found in Matthew 23. Sample: "Woe unto you, scribes and Pharisees, hypocrites! for ye are like unto whited sepulchres, which indeed appear beautiful outward, but are within full of dead men's bones. and of all uncleanness" (Matt. 23:27).

The picture of the Pharisees painted by the NT is almost entirely black, but the discriminating Bible student should bear in mind that not everything about every Pharisee was bad. It is perhaps not just to say all Pharisees were self-righteous and hypocritical. Many Pharisees actually tried to promote true piety. What we know as Pharisaism from the NT was to some degree a degeneration of Pharisaism. Jesus condemned especially their ostentation, their hypocrisy, their salvation by works, their impenitence and lovelessness, not always Pharisees as such. Some of the Pharisees were members of the Christian movement in the beginning (Acts 6:7). Some of the great men of the NT were Pharisees — Nicodemus (John 3:1), Gamaliel (Acts 5:34), and Paul (Acts 26:5; Phil. 3:5). Paul does not speak the name "Pharisee" with great reproach but as a title of honor, for the Pharisees were highly respected by the masses of the Jewish people. When Paul says he was "in the matter of the Law, a 'Pharisee,'" (Phil. 3:5), he did not think of himself as a hypocrite but claims the highest degree of faithfulness to the Law. In similar manner, church leaders today might say, "We are the Pharisees." Much of modern scholarship, however, has cast the Pharisees into too favorable a light; when one reads our Lord's heated denunciation of Pharisaism in Matthew, chapter 23, where He specifically lists their sins, one has not only a true but a dark picture of Pharisaism as it was at the time of Christ. L.M.P.

PHAROSH (See Parosh)

PHARPAR (fàr'pàr, Heb. *parpar*). The scornful Naaman contrasted the silt-laden waters of the Jordan with "Abanah and Pharpar, the rivers of Damascus" (II Kings 5:12). Abanah is identified with the Barada. Pharpar is possibly the Awaj, a stream which rises E of Hermon, and one of whose sources is the Wadi Barbar. Naaman's remark does not necessarily mean that the river is close to Damascus.

PHARZITE (fàr'zīt, Heb. *perets*), a descendant of Pharez, son of Judah (Num. 26:20).

PHASEAH (See Paseah)

PHASELIS (fà-sē'lĭs, Gr. *Pháselis*), a Rhodian colony in Lycia dating from the seventh century B.C. It is mentioned in I Maccabees 15:23 as the recipient of a letter from the Romans on behalf of the Jews. The port was important as a stage on the great east-west trade-route between the Aegean and the East. Phaselis abetted the pirate fleets of the Cilician Zenicetes, and was captured and punished by the loss of its territory by Servilius Isauricus in 77 B.C.

PHASELUS (fà-sēl'ŭs), a Latinization of Phasael, alternatively Phasaelus, the son of Antipater the Idumaean, and brother of Herod I. He succeeded with his brother to the viziership of Hyrcanus II on Antipater's death, but lacking Herod's acumen was tricked by the Parthians, in their invasion of Palestine, and committed suicide in captivity in 40 B.C. Herod named one of the towers of his Jerusalem palace after him. The base survives under the so-called "tower of David" in modern Jerusalem.

PHEBE (See Phoebe)

PHENICE, PHOENIX (fē-nī'sē, fē'nĭks, Gr. *Phoiníke*), a town and harbor on the S coast of Crete (Acts 27:12). It has been identified with Loutro, the only harbor W of Fair Havens large enough to accommodate a galley as large as the vessel in the story. Some difficulty in this identification arises from the fact that Luke speaks of the harbor as "looking towards the south-west and north-west." Loutro faces E and the ERV resolves the difficulty by taking the text to mean "in the direction in which the south-west and north-west winds blow." There is no proof for this assumption. EGT lists and documents the authorities (vol. II, pp. 521, 522). (Note: Phenice is also used as a term for Phoenicia.)

PHICHOL (fi'köl, Heb. *pîkhōl*), the army captain belonging to Abimelech, who was the Philistine king of Gerah (Gen. 21:22,32; 26:26).

PHILADELPHIA (fĭl'à-dĕl'fĭ-à, Gr. *Philadelphía, brotherly love*), a Lydian city founded by Attalus II Philadelphus (159-138 B.C.). The king was so named from his devotion to his brother Eumenes, and the city perpetuated his title. Philadelphia was an outpost of Hellenism in native Anatolia. It lies under Mount Tmolus, in a wide vale which opens into the Hermus Valley, and along which the post-road ran. It is on a broad, low, easily defended hill, which explains Philadelphia's long stand against the Turks. The district is disastrously seismic, and the great earthquake of A.D. 17 ruined it completely. Placed right above the fault, Philadelphia was tormented by 20 years of recurrent quakes after the disaster of 17. Hence, says Ramsay, is derived the imagery of Revelation 3:12 ("a pillar," "go no more out," "a new name"). The "new name" is certainly a reference to the proposal to rename the city *Neocaesarea* in gratitude for Tiberius' generous earthquake relief. The district was vine-growing, and a center, in consequence, of Dionysiac worship. A Christian witness, in spite of Moslem invasion and pressure, was maintained in Philadelphia through medieval and into modern times. E.M.B.

PHILEMON (fī-lē'mŏn, Gr. *Philémon, loving*). Paul's epistle to Philemon dates, in all probability, from the period of his Roman imprisonment. Pauline authorship is not seriously disputed. It is addressed to "Philemon . . . Apphia . . . Archippus, and the church in your house." Apphia would be Philemon's wife, and Archippus, not improbably, his son. Archippus would appear to have been a person of some standing, but perhaps not notable for stability of character (Col. 4:17). It is to be noted that the Christian community was organized around a home, a practice of the early church. Many ancient churches were no doubt founded on the sites of homes where early Christians met. There is no evidence of church-building of any sort before the third century. The fourth century Christian chapel, recently discovered in the Roman villa of Lullingstone, Kent, England, is an illustration of the earlier practice. Justin Martyr provides similar evidence.

The occasion of the letter was the return of the runaway slave Onesimus to his master. There is a celebrated letter of the Roman writer, Pliny, on a similar subject, written perhaps 40 years later (Plin. *Ep.* 9.21). It is interesting to compare Pliny's language of humane generosity with Paul's language of brotherly affection. Pliny puts the plea for forgiveness on humanitarian and philosophical grounds; Paul founds all he has to say on Christian fellowship. He writes with exquisite tact and with words of praise before referring to obligation. The word "brother" comes like a friendly handclasp at the end of vs. 7; "for my son Onesimus," with curiously poignant appeal at the end of vs. 10. He is "Paul the ambassador" (the translation "aged" is certainly incorrect), and as such might speak of duty. An imperial legate had a right to speak for the emperor, and the analogy would not be lost on Philemon. Paul reminds Philemon that, in respect of bondage, his own position did not vary from that of the man for whom he pleaded. Onesimus was a fellow-bondsman and son. The Talmud said: "If one teaches the son of his neighbour the Law, this is the same as if he had begotten him." Paul has the rabbinical saying in mind. "Onesimus" means "useful," and the writer puns on the word in vs. 11, and proceeds immediately to point to the sacrifice he himself was making. Onesimus was "briefly parted" from Philemon, says Paul, and he proceeds strongly to hint that manumission might be the truest mark of brotherliness. With a closing touch of humor Paul gives Philemon his note of hand for aught the runaway owes, discounting, as he returns to seriousness, Philemon's own deep debt.

"Yes," Paul concludes, "I would have profit of you." He puns once more on Onesimus' name (*onaimen* is the verb). The remark is a further plea for Onesimus' freedom. The approach is characteristic of early Christianity. Slavery is never directly attacked as such, but principles are steadily inculcated which must prove fatal to the institution. To speak of brotherly love between master and slave ultimately renders slavery meaningless.

The letter ends on notes of intimacy. There was something truly Greek about Paul. The great Greek orators seldom placed the climax of their speech in the closing words. The oration closed on a minor note, designed to bring the excited audience back to normality and rest, and so it does here.

E.M.B.

PHILETUS (fĭ′lē′tŭs, Gr. *Phíletos, worthy of love*). Like several other men named in the Scriptures — Judas, Alexander, Demas, Hymenaeus — Philetus is remembered only for the evil he did. St. Paul alone mentions him as a false teacher in the church of Ephesus, who together with Hymenaeus, held that "the resurrection is past already" (II Tim. 2: 17), that is, he did not radically deny a doctrine of the resurrection but allegorized it into a spiritual awakening or conversion and not a bodily resurrection as St. Paul taught in I Corinthians 15.

PHILIP (See Herod)

PHILIP THE APOSTLE (fĭl′ĭp, Gr. *Phílippos, lover of horses*). In the lists of the apostles (cf. Matt. 10:3) the fifth in the list is called simply Philip, but the church has always called him "the Apostle" to distinguish him from Philip the Evangelist or Philip the Deacon (Acts 6:8). His home town was Bethsaida of Galilee and no doubt he was a close friend of Andrew and Peter who lived in the same fishing village (John 1:44). It is almost certain that he was first a disciple of John the Baptist, because Jesus called him directly near Bethany beyond the Jordan, where John was preaching (John 1:43). He is often characterized as being timid and retiring, but it is to be remembered that he brought Nathanael to Jesus (John 1:45). A more apt description appears to be that he was reluctant to believe wholeheartedly in the Kingdom and at times he seems to have had difficulty in grasping its meaning (John 14:8-14). This no doubt is why Jesus asked him the unusual question to arouse and test his faith before feeding the five thousand: "How are we to buy bread so that this people may eat?" (John 6:5-6). He served as something of a contact man for the Greeks and is familiarly known for bringing Gentiles to Jesus (John 12:20-23). The last information regarding Philip in the NT is found in Acts 1:13 where we are told that he was among the number of disciples in the upper chamber before Pentecost. His days after this are shrouded in legend and mystery, but the best tradition says that he did mission work in Asia Minor. The historian Eusebius says that he was a "great light of Asia" and that he was buried at Hierapolis.

L.M.P.

PHILIP THE EVANGELIST (fĭl′ĭp, Gr. *Phílippos, lover of horses*). Although the Church, beginning with the second century, often confused him with Philip the Apostle, this Philip's name does not occur in the Gospels, but his story is told in the Book of Acts. He was one of the famous seven deacons, said to be "men of good repute, full of the Spirit and of wisdom" (Acts 6:2). He is second in the list, following Stephen, the first Christian martyr (Acts 6:5), so he must have been well known in the early church. Since he was a Hellenist, that is, a Greek-speaking Jew, as a deacon he was to serve under the apostles (Acts 6:6) by taking care of the neglected Hellenist widows and of the poor in general in the Jerusalem church. But after the death of Stephen the persecutions scattered the Christians abroad and, due to the great need, the deacons became evangelists or Christian missionaries. They even performed signs and wonders among the people (Acts 8:39; 6:8). In Acts 8 it is said that Philip preached in Samaria with great success: "And the multitudes with one accord gave heed to what was said by Philip, when they heard him and saw the things which he did." He cast out devils and healed the paralytics and the lame just as the apostles did. Some of his converts were Simon the magician of Samaria (Acts 8:9-13) and the Ethiopian eunuch (Acts 8:26-40). Thus perhaps Philip was instrumental in introducing Christianity into Africa. Most of his labors seem to have been centered along the Mediterranean seaboard, where following the Lord's command, he preached to the Gentiles. It can easily be seen, therefore, why Paul dwelt at his home (Acts 21:8-9), since they had much in common. Philip was a forerunner of Paul in preaching to the Gentiles. In Acts 21 it is said that Philip had four unmarried daughters who were prophets. Little else is known of his later life. L.M.P.

Ruins of ancient Philippi. JFW

PHILIPPI (fĭ-lĭp'ī, Gr. *Phílippoi*), a Macedonian town in the plain E of Mount Pangaeus. It was a strategic foundation of Philip II, father of Alexander, in 358/7 B.C. The position dominated the road system of northern Greece; hence it became the center for the battle of 42 B.C. in which Antony defeated the tyrannicides, Brutus and Cassius. After Actium (31 B.C.), Octavian (the future Augustus), constituted the place a Roman colony, housing partisans of Antony whose presence was undesirable in Italy. There was a school of medicine in Philippi connected with one of those guilds of physicians which the followers of early Greek medicine scattered through the Hellenistic world. This adds point to the suggestion that Luke was a Philippian. There is a touch of pride in Luke's description of Philippi, "a city of Macedonia, the first of the district" (Acts 16:12 ASV). Amphipolis was, in fact, the capital. W. M. Ramsay comments: "Afterwards Philippi quite outstripped its rival; but it was at that time in such a position that Amphipolis was ranked first by general consent, Philippi first by its own consent. These cases of rivalry between two or even three cities for the dignity and title of "first" are familiar to every student of the history of the Greek cities. . . . The descriptive phrase is like a lightning-flash, revealing in startling clearness the whole situation to those whose eyes are trained to catch the character of Greek city history. . . ." (*St. Paul the Traveller and Roman Citizen*, pp. 206, 207). Philippi was the first European city to hear a Christian missionary, as far as the records go. Paul's choice of the locality throws light on the strategy of his evangelism. For an ancient description of the site see Appian 4:105-131.

E.M.B.

PHILIPPIANS (fĭ-lĭp'ĭ-ănz), one of the most personal of all the Apostle Paul's letters. It is written to "the saints in Christ Jesus who are at Philippi" (1:1).

The church at Philippi in ancient Macedonia was the first European church founded by Paul, and thus represents the first major penetration of the Gospel into Gentile territory (cf. Phil. 4:14-15). The events leading to the founding of the congregation are related in Acts 16:9-40. The great apostle, accompanied by his co-workers, Silas, Timothy and Luke, was on his Second Missionary Journey through Asia Minor. Forbidden by the Holy Spirit to preach in Asia and in Bithynia to the N, they made their way to Troas, farthest port of Asia on the Aegean Sea. In Troas, Paul received a vision from the Lord to take the Gospel to Europe. There stood a man in the night — a Greek of Macedonia who begged him: "Come over into Macedonia and help us" (Acts 16:9). Paul and his companions immediately answered this divine call and set sail for the nearest port — Neopolis of Philippi, named for Philip II of Macedon, the father of Alexander the Great.

Philippi had been thoroughly colonized by the Romans after 30 B.C. but the city was still more Greek in culture than Roman. Also the city was the first station on the Egnation Way and was the gateway to the East. Luke describes the city as follows: "And from thence to Philippi which is the chief city of that part of Macedonia, and a colony; and we were in that city abiding certain days" (Acts 16:12). It is not unusual, therefore, that Paul's first convert there was a merchant woman named Lydia, a seller of purple. Her whole household was baptized and became the nucleus of the new church (Acts 16:15). The remarkable conversion of the jailer with its accompanying miraculous events also took place in Philippi (Acts 16:25-34). There was, therefore, a very intimate relationship between the apostle and this church. No doubt this was true also because the congregation consisted mainly of Gentiles and Paul saw in them the real future of the church. They were poor, but the fruits of faith were abundant. On several occasions they collected funds for Paul and also aided him while in prison (Phil. 4:10-16). He visited this favorite congregation whenever possible. He has no rebuke for it in this letter. The members are his "joy and crown" (1:8).

Before 1900 it was universally accepted that the epistle to the Philippians was written at Rome where Paul was in prison after his Third Missionary Journey. In recent years, however, scholars have developed the hypothesis that it was written during Paul's imprisonment in Caesarea, but still more recently from the prison in Ephesus. The main reason for their hypotheses is that the old arguments for Roman authorship no longer fit the Roman situation alone. The problem of distance, the travels mentioned in Philippians itself, the similarity to the earlier epistles to Thessalonica, Galatia and Corinth make us believe it is more likely that the letter was written from Ephesus. Although no specific imprisonment of Paul is mentioned in Ephesians, it is possible Paul was in prison in Ephesus (cf. Corinthians 9:23; I Cor. 15:32).

Very few scholars — mostly extreme radicals — have said Paul did not write the letter. Today it is almost universally believed that the Apostle Paul is the author. Some scholars also believe the letter is made up of two or three smaller letters of Paul, but the best scholars now proclaim that the epistle is a single document, written wholly on one occasion.

The letter was occasioned by the gift of funds and clothing which Epaphroditus brought to Paul in prison. Paul took the opportunity to thank the Philippians for this and other favors. In doing so, as was his custom, Paul added practical Christian admonition to humility, joy and steadfastness, which a reading of the letter will reveal. The main emphasis is joy; the concept "rejoice" appears no less than 16 times in the letter. It also is a theological letter. The doctrines of the person and work of Christ, justification by faith, the second coming of Christ, etc., are found among the practical admonitions.

General outline of contents of the letter: *Chapter I:* Greetings and thanksgiving (1:1-11). Progress of the Gospel (1:12-20). On remaining in the world and working and suffering for Christ (1:21-30). *Chapter II:* Exhortation to humility based on the humiliation and exaltation of Christ (2:1-13). Exhortation to the Christian life (2:14-18). Personal remarks involving Timothy and Epaphroditus (2:19-30). *Chapter III:* Warning against false teachers (3:1-3). Paul's mighty confession of his faith (3:4-14). The Christian's hope of heaven (3:15-21). *Chapter IV:* "Rejoice in the Lord alway!" (4:1-7). Admonition to Christian virtues (4:8-13). Paul's confidence in Divine Providence (4:14-19). Final greeting (4:20-22).   L.M.P.

PHILISTINES (fĭ-lĭs'tēnz, Heb. *pelishtîm*), the name given to the people who inhabited the Philistine plain of Palestine during the greater part of OT times. The five cities of the Philistines were Ashdod, Gaza, Ashkelon, Gath and Ekron (Josh. 13:3; I Sam. 6:17). They were situated in the broad coastal plain of southern Palestine, except for Gath which is in the Shephelah or hill-country. Our word "Palestine" is derived from the term Philistine.

Origins. The origin of the Philistines is not completely known. They are said to have come from Caphtor (Jer. 47:4; Amos 9:7), which is believed to be a name for Crete, or perhaps for the island world of the Aegean area. It is clear that they had migrated to Canaan within historical times and that this migration was remembered by the Hebrews.

Most authorities connect the coming of the Philistines with certain political and ethnic movements in the eastern Mediterranean area in the late 13th and early 12th centuries B.C. Five groups of sea peoples left their homeland and moved southeastward at this time. They destroyed Ugarit (an ancient city-state in what is now Syria), and sought to invade Egypt, where they were repulsed by Raamses III in a great naval and land battle about 1191 B.C. Raamses on his monuments pictures these peoples as Europeans. Their pottery indicates that they came from the Greek islands, particularly Crete. The Philistines were one of these groups, and the Thekels another. After their repulse by the Egyptians, they invaded Canaan, the Philistines settling in what is now called the Philistine Plain, and the Thekels settling farther N, in the Sharon Plain.

What caused these people to leave their Aegean homeland and come to Canaan? There appears to have taken place at this time a great torrent of migration out of Europe, which swept through the Aegean world, Anatolia and northern Syria, destroying the Hittite empire and creating a situation of movement and folk wandering which was destined to change the ethnic makeup of the eastern Mediterranean world.

Civilization. The Philistines had a unique political organization. Their five city states were ruled by five "Lords of the Philistines" (Josh. 13:3; Judg. 16:5). The term "lord" is *seren* (always used in the plural, *serānîm*), a non-Semitic word probably to be equated with *tyrannos,* the Greek word denoting the ruler of a city state. The Philistine city states were certainly united in some sort of a confederation.

It is clear that the Philistines were more wealthy and more advanced in technology than their Hebrew neighbors. According to I Samuel 13:19-22 they had the knowledge of metal working, while the Hebrews did not. This monopoly the Philistines jealously guarded, forcing the Hebrews to come down to them even for agricultural implements, which they repaired at exorbitant cost (vs. 21 RSV). This situation has been confirmed by archaeology; the Philistines were in the iron age when they came to Palestine; the Hebrews attained to this level of advance only in the time of David. This technological superiority (the Philistines even had chariots, I Sam. 13:5) is the reason for the Philistines' military domination of the Hebrews so evident toward the end of the period of the Judges and in Saul's reign.

While the Philistines seem to have taught the Hebrews technology, the Hebrews and Canaanites influenced their Philistine neighbors in other ways. Soon after migrating to Canaan the Philistines seem to have adopted the Canaanite language and Semitic names. The Philistines worshiped the Semitic gods Dagon (Judg. 16:23; I Sam. 5:1-7), Astarte (I Sam. 31:10) and Baalzebub (II Kings 1:2,6,16). On the other hand, their non-Semitic origin is recalled in the epithet "uncircumcised" (Judg. 14:3) so frequently used of them in the Bible.

History. The book of Judges mentions the Philistines as a major contender against the Hebrews for the possession of Palestine. No doubt the tribes of Judah, Simeon and Dan felt the pressure most, for their lands were adjacent to the Philistines.

A panoramic view of the Plain of Sharon, the land of the Philistines, on the shore of the Mediterranean. © MPS

Ruins of Ashkelon, one of the five strong cities of the Philistines, on the edge of the Plain of Sharon. Note protruding pillars of an earlier day lodged in crumbled ruins on the Mediterranean coast. © MPS

The judge Shamgar fought them (3:31). A Philistine oppression is briefly mentioned in 10:6,7. The story of Samson, last of the deliverers mentioned in the book of Judges, is set in a violent struggle with the Philistines (13-16; note 14:4c; 15:11). Samson, a man of great strength but little self-discipline was finally snared by a Philistine spy, Delilah (16:4-21). No doubt the Danite migration (chap. 18) was occasioned by the Philistine pressure which kept the Danites from occupying the territory assigned them, and forced them to seek a more easily taken area. The book of I Samuel opens with the theme of Philistine oppression with which Judges closes. Eli's judgeship seems to have been characterized by Philistine domination (I Sam. 4-6). Samuel was able to see a measure of victory over them when he defeated them at the battle of Mizpah, and forced them to return to Israel certain cities they had taken from her (I Sam. 7:7-14). Saul's reign, although it began well, ended in complete defeat for the Hebrews, and the Philistines seem to have overrun most of Palestine W of the Jordan, even occupying Bethshan, at the eastern end of the valley of Jezreel (I Sam. 13: 5; 14:1-52; 17:1-58; 31:1-13).

During the latter part of the reign of Saul, David, the contender for the throne, fled for safety to the Philistines (I Sam. 21:10-15; 27:1-28:2; 29: 1-11), who gladly protected him, thinking thus to contribute to the weakness of the Hebrews. No doubt David learned from the Philistines many things he later used to advantage when he became king, including perhaps the technique for working iron.

Probably David remained a Philistine vassal during the 7½ years he reigned at Hebron (II Sam. 2:1-4). When at the end of this time he asserted his independence and united all Israel under his rule, he was immediately opposed by them, but in two battles decisively defeated them (II Sam. 5:17-25). From this time on, the Philistine grip was broken. In later campaigns (II Sam. 21:15-22; 23:9-17) David consistently bested them and it seems clear that from this time on the Philistines were confined to their own territory and were no longer a threat. It would seem that David had

peaceful relations with them at times, for his body-guards, the Cerethites and Pelethites appear to have been recruited from them (II Sam. 8:18; 15: 18).

After the death of Solomon and the division of the Hebrew kingdom the Philistines reasserted the independence they had lost to David and Solomon. Their cities appear to have engaged in commerce, for which their location certainly fitted them (Joel 3:4-8; Amos 1:6-8). Some of them paid tribute to Jehoshaphat, after whose death they raided Judah (II Chron. 17:11; 21:16,17). When the Assyrians later sought to control the road to Egypt, it is quite natural that the Philistines were frequently mentioned in their inscriptions, along with Israel and the other "Westlands" countries. Sargon (722-705 B.C.) captured the Philistine cities, deported some of the inhabitants and set over them an Assyrian governor. In the days of Hezekiah the Philistines played a great part in the revolt against Sennacherib. It appears that among them, as in Jerusalem, there were two political parties, one recommending submission to the world conquerors, the other urging a stubborn fight for freedom in union with their neighbors the Judeans.

Esarhaddon and Assurbanipal name Philistine tributaries as well as the Judean king Manasseh. The later struggles between Egypt and Assyria were the cause of great suffering to the Philistine cities, and practically close their history as strictly Philistinian. The cities did continue as predominantly non-Jewish centers, becoming Hellenistic cities in the Greek period.

Early Biblical Mention of the Philistines before the times of the Judges. Certain "Philistines" are mentioned in Genesis. The Philistine land is referred to (21:32,34). Abimelech king of Gerar is called "king of the Philistines" (26:1; cf. 26:14, 15). These references have often been regarded as anachronisms, since the Philistines appear not to have entered Canaan before the period of the judges. A more generous judgment has seen here a later revision of the text, bringing the proper names up-to-date. It is possible that a later editor, perhaps during the Hebrew kingdom, may have revised the proper names to make them meaningful in his time, thus introducing the term Philistine into Genesis (cf. also Exod. 13:17; 23:31; Josh. 13:2,3).

On the other hand, recent studies of the problem suggest another approach. Folk movements never are completed in one generation. It is not impossible that the great Philistine movement which entered Canaan during the judges period may have had a small precursor as early as the Patriarchal age. The army of Rameses III which repulsed invading Philistines in 1191 B.C., itself contained soldiers who are portrayed on the Egyptian monuments as Philistines. Evidently these had joined the Egyptian army as mercenaries at an earlier date. Further, pottery identified as Philistine has turned up in Palestinian excavations recently in layers earlier than those of the judges period. It also seems that the sea peoples invading Egypt came from land as well as sea, and Rameses III refers to "The Peleset (i.e. Philistines) [who] are hung up in their towns," implying that some of these troublesome people had already settled near by.

It therefore seems not impossible that some Philistines were settled in Gerar by the time of Isaac. They were not a large hostile group (as later), but a small settlement with which the patriarch had more or less friendly relations.

J.B.G.

PHILO JUDAEUS (fī'lō jōō-dē'ŭs), the Jewish scholar and philosopher, was born in Alexandria about 20 B.C. Alexandria had an old tradition of Jewish scholarship, and Philo sprang from a rich and priestly family. Few details are known of his life, save that in A.D. 39 he took part in an embassy to Rome to plead the case of the Jews whose religious privileges, previously wisely recognized by Rome, were menaced by the mad Caligula. The embassy is described by Philo in the *Legatio ad Caium*. Philo lived until A.D. 50 and was a prolific author. His writings include philosophical works, commentaries on the Pentateuch, and historical and apologetic works in the cosmopolitan tradition of Alexandrian Jewry, which had long sought to commend its literature to the Gentile world. Hence Philo's development of an allegorical interpretation of the Old Testament. His aim was to show that much of the philosophy of the Greeks had been anticipated by the Jews. He was also, like Paul of Tarsus, a citizen of two worlds, and sought to synthetize his own Hellenistic and Hebraic traditions. His doctrine of God most notably reveals this synthesis. His doctrine of the Logos is discussed above under its own heading. The Logos, in Philo's rendering of the Greek doctrine, was simultaneously the creative power which orders the universe, and also a species of mediator through whom men know God. John seems therefore to have had Philo's philosophy in mind when he wrote the first 18 verses of the Fourth Gospel, sharply personal though John's interpretation is. Others, too, were influenced by Philo's mysticism and principles of exegesis. Clement and Origen used his works, and the Latin Fathers generally following his methods of allegorical interpretation, established a tradition of exegesis which still finds favor in some quarters.   E.M.B.

PHILOLOGUS (fī-lŏl'ō-gŭs, Gr. *Philólogos, fond of learning*), a believer in Rome to whom Paul sent a salutation (Rom. 16:15).

PHILOSOPHY. The words "philosophy" (*love of wisdom*) and "philosopher" each occurs only once in the Bible, and that in a derogatory sense. Thayer (Lexicon p. 655) indicates that Greek usage connoted "zeal for, or skill in, any art or science." It is not genuine philosophy which Paul deprecates, but "philosophy and vain deceit, after the traditions of men, after the rudiments [i.e. idolatrous principles] of the world, and not after Christ" (Col. 2:8).

The same thought is expressed in the discussion of "wisdom" in I Corinthians (1:18-2:16; 3:18-21), where Paul not only emphasizes the inadequacy of worldly wisdom, but says, "we speak wisdom among the mature" (2:6), a "wisdom" based upon revelation. This is similar to the "wisdom" doctrine of Job, Ecclesiastes, certain psalms, and especially Proverbs. The book of Ecclesiastes, which teaches that "all is vanity under the sun," may be regarded as an answer to modern philosophical naturalism.

The "philosophers of the Epicureans and of the Stoics" (Acts 17:18) who led Paul to the Areopagus and heard him only part way through, are not to be taken as worthy or even serious representatives of those philosophies. Their superficiality is indicated in vs. 21. They "spent their time in nothing else but either to tell, or to hear some new thing."   J.O.B.

PHINEHAS (fīn'ē-ăs, Heb. *pînehās, mouth of brass*). 1. A son of Eleazar and grandson of Aaron (Exod. 6:25; I Chron. 6:4,50; 9:20; Ezra 7:5; 8:2), who slew Zimri and Cozbi at God's command

(Num. 25:6-15; Ps. 106:30). He conducted a successful embassy to the trans-Jordan tribes regarding the altar they had built (Josh. 22:13-34). These incidents evidence his great zeal and faithful service.

2. A son of Eli, unfaithful in his ministration of the priest's office (I Sam. 1:3; 2:12-17,22-25, 27-36; 3:11-13). He and his brother Hophni brought the ark into the camp of Israel in hope of its presence bringing victory against the Philistines, but the ark was taken and Hophni and Phinehas slain (I Sam. 4).

3. Father of the Eleazar who with other priests accounted for the valuables brought back to Jerusalem with the exiles returning from the Babylonian captivity (Ezra 8:32-34).

PHLEGON (flē'gŏn, flĕg'ŏn, Gr. *Phlégon, burning*), a believer in Rome to whom Paul sent a loving greeting (Rom. 16:14).

PHOEBE, PHEBE (fē'bē, Gr. *Phoíbe, pure*), a woman mentioned in the Scriptures only in Romans 16:1,2. She was one of the first deaconesses, if not the first, of the Christian Church, and was highly recommended by the Apostle Paul. In a single sentence Paul speaks of her Christian status ("sister"); of her position or office (*diákonos*); of her service record ("she has been a helper of many and of me also"); and of the importance of her work ("assist her in whatever matter she has need of"). Phoebe was serving as deaconess of the church at Cenchrea, port of Corinth, when Paul arrived there at the end of his third journey, and where he wrote his letter to the Romans. Either she was on her way to Rome to serve that church, or Paul entrusted her to carry this important epistle to the Roman Christians.

PHOENICIA, PHENICIA (fē-nĭsh'ĭ-à, Gr. *Phoiníke*), a strip of coastal territory between the Lebanon range, the uplands of Galilee, and the Mediterranean Sea, containing the trading-ports of the great maritime people which bore its name. Exact definition of boundaries is not possible, for the Phoenicians were associated with their cities rather than with their hinterland, after the fashion of the Greek colonies, and for analogous reasons. It can be said, however, that to the N Phoenicia never extended beyond Arvad or Arados, on the modern island of Ruad, 80 miles N of Sidon. The southern limits were Acco, modern Acre, just N of Carmel, and, according to the Egyptian papyrus which tells the story of Wen-Amon, Dor, just S of Carmel. The Semitic name for the land was Canaan, the "Kinachchi" or "Kinachna" of the Tell-el-Amarna letters, and the "Chna" of Phoenician coins. The name is of doubtful significance, but may mean "lowland," as distinct from the uplands parallel with the coast, which are a geographical feature of the eastern end of the Mediterranean. The term Phoenicia is from a Greek word meaning "dark red," but there is no clear reason why this was applied to the land. "Phoenix" in fact, may mean "dark red" because the Phoenicians were the discoverers of the crimson-purple dye derived from the murex shell-fish. "Phoenix" also means a date-palm, and there may be a clue in the fact that the palm is a symbol on Phoenician coins.

The Phoenicians were Semites who came to the Mediterranean as one ripple of the series of Semitic migrations which moved W and S round the Fertile Crescent during the second millennium B.C. Abraham was part of this historical process, but the movement brought major tribal elements, the Amorites, for example, to Palestine, the Kassite dynasty to Babylon, and the Hyksos to Egypt. The

Phoenicia, now and then. Above, modern Beirut, on St. George's Bay, with snow-clad Mount Sunnin in the distance. Below, ruins at Byblos, ancient Gebal, on the Phoenician coast. © MPS

tribes who occupied the coastal strip turned their attention to the sea because of the pressure on the agricultural lands in the narrow lowland strip, never more than 20 miles wide, behind them. A tradition of sea-faring may have accompanied the immigrants from the Persian Gulf, itself the first scene of human navigation and sea-borne trade. Such was the challenge and stimulus which made the Phoenicians the most notable sailors of the ancient world, and led to their feats of colonization, which spread their trading-posts round the African coast from Carthage westward, and established them in Spain and Sicily.

It is not known whether they built the towns which formed the centers of their power and trade, or whether, descending to the sea, they found the towns awaiting their occupation. According to Herodotus, who visited Tyre (2:44), the city was founded in 2755 B.C. He does not name the founders. Like that of the Greeks, the Phoenician civilization was organized round the city. That is why Phoenicia had no place in history as a political unit. It is Tyre and Sidon, and less frequently other cities, such as Acco and Dor, which appear in the record as units. Sidon was the most powerful and influential of the Phoenician cities. To Homer, Phoenicians were commonly Sidonians. Giving Telemachus a mixing bowl, King Menelaus of Sparta says: "Phaedimus the king of the Sidonians gave it to me. . . ." (Od. 6:618. Also ib. 15:118 and Il. 6:290). The OT uses the same nomenclature. "The gods of Sidon," Baal and Ashtaroth

(Judg. 10:6) were the gods of the Phoenicians generally (also Judg. 18:7; I Kings 5:6; 11:5 & 33; 16:31; II Kings 23:13). The reference to "Jezebel, daughter of Ethbaal, king of the Sidonians" (I Kings 16:31) is at first sight strange, for Ethbaal was king of Tyre. The explanation above given, that "Sidonian" had become a generic term for "Phoenician," is established, however, by the fact that Vergil, the Roman poet, who follows the legend that Dido, Queen of Carthage, was the daughter of Belus (= Ethbaal), king of Tyre (Aen. 1:621), calls Dido in the same context (ib. 613 cf. 678) "Sidonia Dido."

Phoenicia first appears in recorded history in the Egyptian account of the northern campaigns of Thutmose III. In his campaign against the Hittites of 1471 B.C., the pharaoh found it necessary to secure the Phoenician coastal strip as an essential avenue of communications. He punished severely the revolt of Arvad, the northernmost town of the Phoenicians, and went to considerable pains to organize the series of Phoenician ports as supply depots. Sporadically, as with the rest of the lands to the N, Egypt asserted or relaxed her authority. The Tell-el-Amarna letters show Phoenicia in the same state of disunity and internal rivalry as Palestine during the weak reign of the mystic Amenhotep IV. Seti I (1373-1292 B.C.) pushed his conquests as far as Acco and Tyre, Ramses II (1292-1225 B.C.) as far as Biruta (mod. Beirut). The whole coast revolted in the reign of Merneptah (1225-1215 B.C.), including Philistia, for the pharaoh boasts: "Plundered is Canaan with every evil."

Egyptian influence fluctuated over the next century, and when Ramses XII (1118-1090 B.C.) sent the priest Wen-Amon to buy cedar for his funeral barge, the Egyptian envoy was treated with the scan:est courtesy in Dor and Tyre. An entertaining papyrus tells his story. A century later found Hiram king of Tyre in alliance with David, a partnership which developed into a trade alliance in the days of Solomon. Solomon's fleet of "ships of Tarshish" at Ezion-geber on the Gulf of Aqabah seems to have been part of a combined trading venture whereby the Phoenicians used Solomon's port and piloted Solomon's ships to Southern Arabia and India (I Kings 10:22; II Chron. 9:21). If indeed "ivory, and apes, and peacocks" are Tamil words, Tarshish in these passages must be sought in the East rather than the West. The cargoes are certainly not Spanish.

With the division of the kingdom, Phoenicia became the neighbor and partner of the Northern Kingdom, while Judah lay across the communications with the Gulf of Aqabah and the Red Sea. Hence Ahab's alliance with Jezebel, the prosperity of the North (Ahab's "Ivory House"), and the sequence of events which led to Elijah's protest and the contest on Carmel. The Assyrians had dealings with Phoenicia. Ashur-nasir-pal (884-860 B.C.) imposed tribute on Tyre and Sidon after his thrust to the sea. Shalmaneser II added Arvad. Tiglath-pileser (745-727 B.C.) reasserted the Assyrian authority, which had lapsed. Shalmaneser IV (727-722 B.C.) unsuccessfully besieged Tyre for five years. Sennacherib (705-681 B.C.) besieged Sidon, and took tribute from Sidon and Acco, but left Tyre undisturbed. Tyre was a formidable task for a besieger. Ashur-banipal (668-626 B.C.) claimed to have reduced Tyre and Arvad, but by the end of the reign Phoenicia was free again, as Assyria lapsed into one of her phases of fatigue. Nebuchadnezzar (604-652 B.C.) invested Tyre for 13 years, and seems to have captured the city (Ezek. 26 to 29) or received its surrender on terms. Hence, probably, the pre-eminence of Sidon in Persian times. According to Diodorus and Herodotus, Sidon provided Xerxes with his best ships for the great raid on Greece. All the Phoenician cities submitted to Alexander after Issus (333 B.C.), except Tyre, which Alexander took after a vigorous siege of seven months. Under the Successors, the power of the Ptolemies of Egypt first extended far up the Phoenician coast, but after 197 B.C. the Seleucids of Syria controlled the land, until the whole area passed into Roman hands in 65 B.C. The reference to a "Syrophoenician woman" in Mark 7:26, reflects the fact of the century and a half of Syrian rule.

The Phoenician stock must by this time have been heavily diluted by emigrant blood, principally Greek. The whole area figured largely in the early evangelism of the Church (Acts 11:19; 15:3; 21:2). Phoenicia's achievement was principally in the realm of trade, and in her simplification and diffusion of the alphabet, as a tool and means, no doubt, of commercial intercourse. Ezekiel 27 and 28 give some notion of the extent and variety of Phoenician trade, but the Phoenicians did nothing to spread or communicate the knowledge, geographical and social, which their voyaging won. Tyre's colony at Carthage blockaded the Straits of Gilbraltar for many generations in an attempt to guard the western and Atlantic trade routes, and this secrecy was a Phoenician principle. The land made no contribution to art and literature, and its religious influence, heavily infected with the cruder fertility cults, was pernicious.   E.M.B.

PHRYGIA (frĭj'ĭ-à, Gr. *Phrygía*), in Bible times an inland province of SW Asia Minor. Its table lands which rose to 4,000 feet contained many cities and towns considerable in size and wealth. Most historians agree that the province included greater or lesser territory at different times and there is no common agreement on the boundaries since they shifted almost every generation. It seems that at one time it included a greater part of western Asia Minor. Then it was divided into Phrygia Major and Phrygia Minor; later the Romans even divided it into three parts. Some Bible students believe the term Phrygia is used loosely in the NT, as in the Book of Acts, and that it even included small provinces like Pisidia. In these days "Phrygia" meant an extensive territory which at times contributed territory to a number of different Roman provinces. It is thought to have this broader meaning in Acts 2:10 which speaks of devout Jews from Phrygia at Pentecost.

Whatever the exact extent of the province, it receives its renown mainly from Paul's missionary journeys. Paul and his co-workers visited the fertile territory which contained rich pastures for cattle and sheep and a heavy population needful of the Gospel during all three missionary journeys. If Phrygia is understood in its broader sense, Paul and Barnabas introduced Christianity into the province during the first journey (Acts 13:13 and 14:24). Acts 16:6 briefly describes the visit of Paul and Silas on the second journey in these words: "And they went through the region of Phrygia and Galatia, having been forbidden by the Holy Spirit to speak the word in Asia." On his third journey he quickly revisited the province on his way to Ephesus and Corinth (Acts 18:23): "After spending some time there (in Antioch) he departed and went from place to place through the region of Galatia and Phrygia, strengthening

all the disciples." Although a great deal of Christian activity took place in ancient Phrygia, with this reference it passes from the Biblical record.   L.M.P.

PHURAH, PURAH (fū'rà, Heb. *purâh, branch*), a servant of Gideon who went down with him to visit the host of Midian (Judg. 7:10,11; ASV, RSV Purah).

PHUT (fŭt, Heb. *pût*), third son of Ham (Gen. 10:6; I Chron. 1:8 Put, and so elsewhere in ASV, RSV). His descendants are not named. A comparison of translations of Heb. *pût* in KJV, ASV and RSV reveals the difficulty of locating Phut (Isa. 66:19; Jer. 46:9; Ezek. 27:10; 30:5; 38:5; Nah. 3:9). The question is partly textual, whether there is confusion between Put and Pul (Isa. 66:19), between Ludim and Lubim; partly etymological, whether the word is of Egyptian origin; partly involved in the location of lands with which Phut is associated. Some locate Phut W of Egypt on the North African coast; some in Nubia; others E of Somaliland, on both sides of the Red Sea, in both Africa and Asia. Genesis 10:6, which names Phut between two African lands, Cush (Ethiopia) and Mizraim (Egypt), and Asian Canaan, suggests the ambiguity, and no other reference removes it. The men of Phut were valued mercenary soldiers of Tyre (Ezek. 27:10) and Egypt (Jer. 46:9). They used shield (Jer. 46:9) and helmet (Ezek. 38:5), probably also the bow (Isa. 66:19). Possibly there were settlements of them in widely scattered places. Certainly they traveled far to fight.   E.R.

PHUVAH, PUA, PUAH (fū'và, pū'à, Heb. *pû'âh*).
1. The second son of Issachar (Gen. 46:13; Num. 26:23; I Chron. 7:1).
2. The father of Tola of the tribe of Issachar, who judged Israel after the death of Abimelech (Judg. 10:1).

PHYGELLUS (fĭ-jĕl'ŭs, Gr. *Phýgellos*). In his second letter to Timothy (1:15) Paul mentions by name Phygellus and Hermogenes as being among those Christians of Asia (western province of Asia Minor) who had turned away from the apostle. From the context (II Tim. 1:13-14) it may be assumed that the apostasy included the repudiation of Paul's doctrine. If we connect Phygellus with II Timothy 4:16 ("At my first answer no man stood with me") we may infer that he, being in Rome, forsook Paul's personal cause in the Roman courts at a crucial time when his testimony could have meant much for the future of the Church. Some scholars feel that Phygellus may also have been one of the leaders of a group of wayward Christians in Rome (Phil. 1:15-16).

PHYLACTERY (See Dress)

PHYSICIAN (See Occupations & Professions)

PI-BESETH (pī-bē'sĕth, Heb. *pî-veseth*), a city in the delta of Lower Egypt (Ezek. 30:17) near Aven (On or Heliopolis), on the western bank of the Pelusiae branch of the Nile. The names of Rameses II and of Shishak, conqueror of Rehoboam, are inscribed on the ruins. The red granite temple of the goddess Basht, admired by Herodotus, has been excavated, also a unique cemetery of cats sacred to Basht; buried, not mummified. Pi-beseth was occupied in the Fourth Dynasty of the Old Empire, the Middle Empire, Hyksos times, the New Empire to its end, and Roman times.

PICTURES (pĭk'tūrz), occurs three times in KJV. Numbers 33:52 ASV, RSV has "figured stones." Stone idols appear to be meant. In Proverbs 25: 11 ASV has "network", RSV "setting." Pleasing inlaid work in gold and silver seems to be the sense. In Isaiah 2:16 another word from the same Heb. root is translated "imagery" in ASV; margin "watchtowers." RSV has "beautiful craft," with a note, "Compare Gk: Heb. uncertain." The carved figureheads of ships, usually idolatrous symbols, may be intended. The Heb. root suggests something conspicuous, showy.

PIETY (pī'ĕ-tē), occurs once in KJV, ASV; RSV "religious duty." The phrase "show piety at home" refers primarily to reverence for parents; filial piety; but other uses of related Greek words broaden the sense to "godly behavior."

PIGEON (See Birds)

PI-HAHIROTH (pī'hȧ-hī'rŏth, Heb. *pî-ha-hîrôth*), the place in northeastern Egypt where the Israelites last camped before crossing the Red Sea. Here the Egyptian army overtook them (Exod. 14:2,9; Num. 33:7). Exact location unknown.

he was an illegitimate son of Tyrus, King of Mayence, who sent him to Rome as a hostage. In Rome, so the story goes, he committed murder and was then sent to Pontus of Asia Minor where he subdued a rebellious people, re-gained favor with Rome, and was awarded the governship of Judea. It is more probable that, like the sons of many prominent Romans, he was trained for governmental service and either because of his political astuteness or as a political plum he was given the hard task of governing the troublesome Jews by the Emperor Tiberius. The Romans had many such governors throughout the provinces, which was part of their success in local government. Judea had a succession of these smaller rulers before and after Pilate. Generally they were in charge of tax and financial matters, but governing Palestine was so difficult that the procurator there was directly responsible to the emperor and also had supreme judicial authority such as Pilate used regarding

An artist's restoration of the Ecce Homo Arch and the Gabbatha (pavement) at the Tower of Antonia in Jerusalem. This is the traditional site of Pilate's famous declaration, "Behold, the man!"
© MPS

PILATE (pī'lȧt, Gr. *Peilátos*), the 5th procurator, or governmental representative, of imperial Rome in Palestine at the time of Christ, holding this office A.D. 26 to 36. Whether it be considered an honor or a disgrace, he is the one man of all Roman officialdom who is named in the Apostles Creed — "suffered under Pontius Pilate." To Christians, therefore, he is known almost entirely for his cowardly weakness in the condemnation of Jesus to Roman crucifixion in A.D. 30. The four Gospels relate the sad but glorious story fully, especially the Gospel of John. Pilate is also mentioned in the Acts of the Apostles (3:13; 4:27; 13:28) and in I Timothy 6:13 where we are told that Jesus "before Pontius Pilate witnessed a good confession." His name *Pontius* was his family name, showing that he was descended from the Roman family or *gens* of *pontii,* while *Pilate* no doubt comes from the Latin *pilatus* meaning "one armed with a *pilum* or javelin."

Beyond this, little is known of his early or later years, since most of the secular references may be only legend and tradition, such as the story that

Christ. The territory included Judea, Samaria and old Idumea.

Most procurators disliked being stationed in a distant, difficult, dry outpost such as Judea. Pilate, however, seemed to enjoy tormenting the Jews, although, as it turned out, he was seldom a match for them. He never really understood them, as his frequent rash and capricious acts reveal. The Jewish historian Josephus tells us that he immediately offended the Jews by bringing the "outrageous" Roman standards into the Holy City. At another time he hung golden shields inscribed with the names and images of Roman deities in the temple itself. Once he even appropriated some of the temple tax to build an aqueduct. To this must be added the horrible incident mentioned in Luke 13:1 about "the Galileans whose blood Pilate had mingled with their sacrifices," meaning no doubt that Roman soldiers slew these men while sacrificing in the Holy Place. These fearful events seem to disagree with the role Pilate played in the trial of Jesus where he was as clay in the hands of the Jews, but this may be explained by the fact that his fear of the Jews increased because of their frequent complaints to Rome.

According to the custom, Pilate was in Jerusalem at the time to keep order during the feast. His usual headquarters were in Caesarea. After the Jews had condemned Jesus in their own courts, they brought Him to Pilate, no doubt residing in Herod's palace near the temple, early in the morning. It is surprising he gave them an ear so early in the day (John 18:28). From the beginning of the hearing he is torn between offending the Jews and condemning an innocent person, and he tries every device to set Jesus free apart from simply acquitting Him. He declares Jesus innocent after private interrogation; he sends Him to Herod; he has Jesus scourged, hoping this will suffice; finally he offers the Jews a choice between Jesus and a coarse insurrectionist. When he hears the words, "If thou let this man go, thou art not Caesar's friend," and "We have no king but Caesar!" he thinks of politics rather than justice and condemns an innocent man to crucifixion. Washing his hands only enhanced his guilt. Pilate is to be judged in the light of his times when one lived by the philosophy of self-aggrandizement and expediency.

Scripture is silent regarding the end of Pilate. According to Josephus, his political career came to an end six years later when he sent soldiers to Samaria to suppress a small harmless religious rebellion in which innocent men were killed. The Samaritans complained to Vitellius, legate of Syria, who sent Pilate to Rome. His friend Tiberius died while he was on his way to Rome and his name disappears from the official history of Rome. The historian Eusebius says that soon afterwards, "wearied with misfortunes," he took his own life. Various traditions conflict as to how and where Pilate killed himself. One familiar legend states that he was banished to Vienna; another that he sought solitude from politics on the mountain by Lake Lucerne, now known as Mt. Pilatus. After some years of despair and depression he is said to have plunged to his death into the lake from a precipice. L.M.P.

PILDASH (pĭl'dăsh, Heb. *pildash*), sixth son of Nahor, Abraham's brother (Gen. 22:22).

PILEHA (pĭl'ē-hà, Heb. *pilhā'*), one of those who, with Nehemiah, sealed the covenant (Neh. 10:24; ASV, RSV Pilha).

PILGRIM (pĭl'grĭm, Gr. *parepídemos, a sojourner in a strange place*). Hebrews 11:13-16 shows that the faithful sought a heavenly city and did not consider themselves permanently attached to earth. I Peter 2:11 exhorts Christians to purity because of this status. Pilgrims might be exiles (RSV), or voluntary sojourners in a foreign country.

PILGRIMAGE (pĭl'grĭ-mĭj, Heb. *māghôr, a place of sojourning*, or *the act of sojourning;* (see Exod. 6:4, ASV, RSV sojourning(s); Ps. 119:54). In Genesis 47:9 (ASV margin and RSV text, *sojourning,* a lifetime is meant. The Heb. root *ghûr* means "to dwell as a foreigner, newly come into a land in which he has no citizen rights, such as the original inhabitants possess." The Bible usage, whether the word is translated "pilgrimage" or otherwise, began with the wanderings of Abraham and his descendants, and later was applied to the status of a believer in the one true God, dwelling on an earth unfriendly to Him and to His people.

PILLAR (pĭl'êr), translates several Heb. words in the OT. Hezekiah's pillars (II Kings 18:16) are called doorposts in RSV and ASV margin; Heb. *'ōmenôth* from a root meaning *to stand firm*. The

Pillars have always played an important role in public and religious edifices. This is the restoration model of the great Hypostyle Hall at Karnak, Egypt, from a model at the Metropolitan Museum of Art, New York.

pillars for the house of the Lord (I Kings 10:12) are called *supports* in RSV; ASV margin "or, *a railing;* Heb. *a prop";* Heb. *mīse'ādh, a support.* More frequent are derivatives from the Heb. root *ntsb, to stand.* There is a religious element in the purpose and use of such pillars; stones set erect as memorials of a divine appearance in connection with the worship of the one true God (Gen. 28:18-22; 31:13; 35:14; Exod. 24:4; Hos. 3:4; 10:1, 2; Isa. 19:19). Stone pillars were set up in token of an agreement with religious sanctions between men (Gen. 31:43-52) in addition to a heap of stones raised by the parties. Rachel's grave was marked by a pillar (Gen. 35:20). Absalom in his lifetime erected a pillar to be his memorial (II Sam. 18:18). Lot's wife, looking back at the ruin of Sodom, became a pillar of salt (Gen. 19:26). In Judges 9:6 ASV margin has "garrison," but RSV like KJV has "pillar," though garrison is a possible meaning. Abimelech was made king either at a military strong-point, or by a religious ceremony at a consecrated pillar.

Standing stones used in idolatrous worship are referred to (Deut. 12:3) and are usually called images in KJV, where ASV margin has "obelisks" and ASV, RSV text "pillars" (Exod. 23:24; 34:13; Lev. 26:1; Deut. 7:5; 12:3; 16:22; I Kings 14:23; II Kings 17:10; 18:4; 23:14; II Chron. 14:3; 31:1; Mic. 5:13). In Ezekiel 26:11 KJV reads "garrisons," ASV, RSV "pillars," ASV margin "obelisks." The Heb. may mean either. Another common Heb. word for pillar, *'amûdh,* from a root "to stand," refers to the PILLAR OF CLOUD AND FIRE (see special article) which guided Israel in the wilderness; to pillars of shittim wood (KJV) or acacia (ASV, RSV) in the tabernacle (Exod. 26:32,37) or of bronze or material not named (Exod. 27:10-17; 36:36,38; 38:10-17,28; 39:33,40; 40:18; Num. 3:36,37; 4:31,32); to pillars of Solomon's Temple (I Kings 7:2-42; II Kings 25:13-17; I Chron. 18:8; II Chron. 3:15, 17; 4:12,13; Jer. 27:19; 52:17-22). Ezekiel 40:49; 42:6 speaks of the pillars of the new temple the prophet saw in vision. Samson broke down the Philistine temple at Gaza by pushing apart its supporting pillars (Judg. 16:25-29). Esther 1:6 refers to the marble pillars of the Persian king's palace. ASV margin has "or, on the platform" for the pillars by which Joash and Josiah stood (II Kings 11:14; 23:3). Solomon's litter or palanquin had pillars (RSV posts) of silver (S. of Sol. 3:10). Turning to figurative uses, columns (so RSV) of smoke (Judg. 20:40; — but the Heb. is *tîmer-ôth,* palm-trees, referring to the spreading tops, in

S. of Sol. 3:6; Joel 2:30). God promises to make Jeremiah an iron pillar (Jer. 1:18). A man's legs are compared to pillars of marble (S. of Sol. 5:15; ASV alabaster columns). The seven pillars of wisdom are mentioned but not defined (Prov. 9:1). The pillars of the earth (Job 9:6; Ps. 75:3) and of heaven (Job 26:11) need not be taken literally, since Job 26:7 states that God hangs the earth upon nothing. In Hannah's song (I Sam. 2:8) the Heb. is *mātsûq, molten pillars*. In the NT, Gr. *stýlos, pillar*, occurs figuratively, of God (I Tim. 3:15); of men (Gal. 2:9; Rev. 3:12); of an angel's legs (Rev. 10:1).   E.R.

PILLAR of cloud and fire. God guided Israel out of Egypt and through the wilderness by a pillar of cloud by day. This became a pillar of fire by night that they might travel by night in escaping from the Egyptian army (Exod. 13:21-22). When the Egyptians overtook the Israelites, the angel of the Lord removed this cloudy, fiery pillar from before them and placed it behind them as an effective camouflage (Exod. 14:19,20,24). The pillar of cloud stood over the tent of meeting outside the camp, whenever the Lord met Moses there (Exod. 33:7-11). The Lord came down for judgment in the cloud (Num. 12). Also in 14:13-35. God met Moses and Joshua in the cloud at the tent of meeting, to make arrangements for the succession when Moses was near death (Deut. 31:14-23). Psalm 99:7 reminds the people that God spoke to them in the pillar of cloud. When Ezra prays in the presence of the returning exiles at Jerusalem, he rehearses the way in which God led the people by the pillar of cloud and fire (Neh. 9:12,19). I Corinthians 10:1,2 speaks of the fathers being under the cloud, baptized unto Moses in the cloud. No natural phenomenon fits the Biblical description: the cloud and fire were divine manifestations, in a form sufficiently well-defined to be called a pillar.   E.R.

PILLOW (pǐl'ō). In Genesis 28:11,18, Heb. *mera'-ăshŏth, at the head*, refers to the stones Jacob set up, either under his head (ASV, RSV) or at his head for shelter during sleep outdoors. The same Heb. word is translated *bolster* in I Samuel 19:13, 16, in connection with *kevîr, a quilt* (ASV margin) or *fly-net thrown over the head*. In Ezekiel 13:18,20 the Heb. is *kesăthŏth, fillet, arm-band*, from a root "to bind, take captive." In modern Heb. it means *pillow, bolster, cushion*. RSV translates "bands," in conformity with the belief that the women sewed magic amulets on their arms. Only in Mark 4:38, Greek *proskephálaion, cushion for the head*, or any cushion (ASV, RSV), do we have an approach to the modern meaning. Here we probably have the pad on which a rower sat.

PILOT (pī'lŭt, Heb. *hŏvēl, sailor, rope-puller*), mentioned among the skilled craftsmen of Tyre (Ezek. 27:8,27,28,29).

PILTAI (pǐl'tī, Heb. *piltāy*), a priest, head of his father's house of Moadiah in the days of Joiakim (Neh. 12:17).

PIM (See Weights and Measures)

PIN (Heb. *yāthēdh*), a tent peg, usually of wood, sharpened at one end, shaped at the other for attaching the tent cord (Judg. 4:21; 5:26, KJV nail, ASV tent pin, RSV tent peg). The tent pins of the tabernacle (Exod. 35:18; 38:31; 39:40; Num. 3:37; 4:32) were of bronze (Exod. 27:19; 38:20). The pin of Judges 16:13,14 was a stick used for beating up the woof in the loom. Pins were used to hang things on (Ezek. 15:3), and this meaning occurs figuratively (Isa. 22:20-24 KJV, ASV nail, RSV peg; Ezra 9:8 KJV, ASV nail, RSV hold,

note, Heb. *nail* or *tent peg*). The same Heb. word is translated *stakes* in Isaiah 33:20; 54:2 where Zion is compared to a tent. In Deuteronomy 23:13 KJV has *paddle*, ASV margin, *shovel*, RSV *stick*, where a tool for digging is meant. The tent peg (KJV, ASV nail) like the corner stone assures support (Zech. 10:4 RSV). *Crisping pins* (Isa. 3:22 KJV), Heb. *hārîtîm*, were probably bags or purses (ASV satchels, RSV handbags).

PINE (See Plants)

PINNACLE (pǐn'á-k'l, pǐn'ǐ-k'l, Gr. *pterýgion*), anything shaped like a wing; on a building, a turret, battlement, pointed roof or peak. The pinnacle of the temple (Matt. 4:5; Luke 4:9) is the spot to which the devil conveyed Jesus, and whence he invited Him to cast Himself down. Many reasons have been advanced for various locations, but none is certain.

PINON (pī'nŏn, Heb. *pînōn*), a duke or chief of Edom, of the family of Esau (Gen. 36:40,41; I Chron. 1:52).

PIRAM (pī'răm, Heb. *pir'ām*), Canaanite king of Jarmuth, and one of those who joined Adoni-zedek against Gibeon, and who was killed there, either by Joshua or by hailstones (Josh. 10:1-11).

PIRATHON (pǐr'á-thŏn, Heb. *pir'āthôn*), a town of Ephraim in the hill country of the Amalekites, where Abdon, one of the judges, lived and was buried (Judg. 12:13-15). Benaiah also was from Pirathon (II Sam. 23:30; I Chron. 11:31; 27:14). Perhaps Pharathon, now Far'atā, W of Mt. Gerizim, S of Samaria.

PIRATHONITE (See Pirathon)

PISGAH (pǐz'ga, Heb. *ha-pisgâh*), a mountain on the NE shore of the Dead Sea; Râs es-Siâghah, slightly NW of Mt. Nebo. First mentioned in Numbers 21:20 as a peak in Moab looking down on Jeshimon (KJV) or the desert (ASV, RSV), on the route of the Israelites toward the Promised Land. Balak brought Balaam into the field of Zophim, to the top of Pisgah, where he built seven altars and tried to persuade Balaam to curse Israel (Num. 23:14). Ashdoth-pisgah (KJV) or the slopes of Pisgah (ASV, RSV text; ASV margin, springs) helps define the territory of the tribes settled E of the Jordan (Deut. 3:17). The springs (KJV text, ASV margin; ASV, RSV text, slopes) of Pisgah are named in bounding the same territory, as taken from the kings of the Amorites (Deut. 4:49). From the top of Mt. Pisgah Moses viewed the Land of Promise, which he was not permitted to enter (Deut. 3:27; 34:1). The latter verse either identifies or closely associates Mt. Pisgah with Mt. Nebo. The two peaks are near to one another, and the Heb. name, from a root meaning "pass through," means "cleft," probably referring to the shape of the mountain, either as sharply cut out, or as cleft in two peaks. The peak (head or top) of the mountain, and its slopes, and springs thereon, and a field near the top, figure in the Bible references.   E.R.

PISHON, PISON (pī'shŏn, Heb. *pîshôn*), KJV Pison, first of the four rivers of Eden, flowed around the whole land of Havilah. Conjectures as to its identification are almost as numerous as the rivers of southwestern Asia, and include the Persian Gulf thought of as a river, and even the Nile.

PISIDIA (pǐ-sǐd'ǐ-à, Gr. *Pisidía*), one of the small Roman provinces in southern Asia Minor just N of Pamphilia which lay along the coast. It was mountainous, but more densely populated than the rough coastal areas, especially because it contained the important city of Antioch. Because of this, Paul

Coins from Antioch of Pisidia: left, top, showing Roman standards, and at right, representing peace. Below, representing the gods of Antioch. UANT

visited the city twice. On his first journey (Acts 13:14-50) he preached a lengthy sermon in the synagogue, testifying of Christ. A week later "came almost the whole city together to hear the word of God" (vs. 44). Then the jealous Jews stirred up both the honorable women and the chief men of the city (vs. 50) and Paul and Barnabas were forced out of this greatest Pisidian city. On his second journey Paul revisited Pisidia and Antioch, going "throughout Pisidia confirming the souls of the disciples, and exhorting them to continue in the faith" (Acts 14:21-24).

PISON (See Pishon)

PISPA, PISPAH (pĭs′pà, Heb. *pispā'*), an Asherite, a son of Jether (I Chron. 7:38).

PIT (pĭt), represents several Heb. and two Greek words whose usages are not sharply distinguished. A pit may be a *bitumen deposit* (Gen. 14:10 so ASV margin; RSV); a *deep place*, natural or made by man (Matt. 12:11; Gen. 37:20-29; II Sam. 17:9; Exod. 21:33,34, etc.); often a *well* (Luke 14:5, so ASV, RSV) or *cistern* (Jer. 14:3 ASV, RSV; Isa. 30:14 ASV, RSV; Lev. 11:33 ASV, *earthen vessel*; RSV *cistern*, etc.). Pit stands also for *death*, the *grave*, or *Sheol* (Job 33:18; Isa. 14:15; Num. 16:30,33 ASV, RSV Sheol; Rev. 9:1,2).

PITCH (Heb. *zepheth, pitch*), either bitumen or a viscous, inflammable liquid associated with it, which was found in Mesopotamia and around the Dead Sea (Gen. 14:10 RSV); used to make vessels watertight (Exod. 2:3); Heb. *kōpher, pitch*, and cognate verb (Gen. 6:14). Also as a destructive agent (Isa. 34:9; cf. Gen. 19:24). As a verb, *pitch* renders several Heb. words also translated "encamp, set up" (ASV, RSV) and refers to placing tents, or the tabernacle (Gen. 12:8; 31:25; Exod. 17:1; Num. 1:51; Josh. 8:11, etc.); or other objects (Josh. 4:20); Gr. *pégnymi, fix* or *fasten in* (the ground).

PITCHER (Heb. *kadh*), an earthenware jar with one or two handles, ordinarily borne on the head or shoulder for carrying water (Gen. 24:14-20, 43-46 ASV, RSV *jar*). Jars empty of water once held lamps (Judg. 7:16-20 RSV, *jars*). To break one was so serious as to be a figure for death (Eccl. 12:6). KJV translates "barrel" (for meal) in I Kings 17:12-16; for water in I Kings 18:33. Once

Heb. *nevel,* an *earthen jar,* is rendered "pitchers" (Lam. 4:2 RSV, *earthen pitchers*). Gr. *kerámion* is an *earthenware vessel* or *jar* (Mark 14:13; Luke 22:10 RSV *jar*).

PITHOM (pī′thŏm, Heb. *pithōm*), a city in Egypt in the valley between the Nile and Lake Timsâh; perhaps Tell er-Retâbah; dedicated to the sun-god Atum; with Raamses to the N, one of the store-cities built by the slave-labor of the Israelites (Exod. 1:11) probably in the reign of Seti I or Rameses II (1319-1234 B.C.) Recent excavations at Tell Mashkûtah near Succoth have uncovered bricks made without straw in the upper layers; made with stubble and weeds pulled up by the roots on the middle level; and made with good, clean straw at the bottom of the walls. An inscription at Raamses relates that it was built with Semitic slave-labor from Asia. Whether Pithom is at Tell Mashkûtah or Tell er-Retâbah, it must be in the neighborhood, and the archaeological evidence mentioned above illustrates its construction by Israelite slaves. As a store-city on the frontier it held supplies of grain for military forces operating thence.

PITHON (pī′thŏn, Heb. *pîthôn*), a son of Micah and descendant of King Saul (I Chron. 8:35; 9:41).

PITY (pī′tē), a tender, considerate feeling for others, ranging from judicial clemency (Deut. 7:16, etc.) through kindness (Prov. 19:17; 28:8; Job 6:14) and mercy (Matt. 18:33) to compassion (Lam. 4:10). Pity may be mere regard for a thing (Jonah 4:10); for a thing deeply desired (Ezek. 24:21); or the concern of God for His holy name (Ezek. 36:21). Pity for one's children is of the essence of fatherhood, human or divine (Ps. 103:13); inherent in the redemptive activity of God (Isa. 63:9). The several Heb. words are translated variously in all versions, the translators being guided by the meaning in context rather than by the particular word used, for each has a wide range of connotation. In the NT three Gr. words occur once each: *eleéo, have pity* (Matt. 18:33); *eúsplangchnos, compassionate* (I Pet. 3:8, ASV, *tender hearted;* RSV, a tender heart); *polýsplangchnos, of great mercy* (James 5:11 RSV *mercy*) referring to God.

PLAGUE (See Diseases)

PLAGUES OF EGYPT, ten in number, these were the means by which God induced Pharaoh to let the Israelites leave Egypt. A series chiefly of natural phenomena, unusual in their severity, in that all occur within one year, in their accurate timing, in that Goshen and its people are spared some of them, and in the evidence of God's control over them, overcame the opposition of Pharaoh, discredited the gods of Egypt (the Nile and the sun), and defiled their temples.

1. **Water becomes blood** (Exod. 7:14-25). When the Nile is at flood in June, its water turns red from soil brought down from Ethiopia, but is still fit to drink, nor do fish die. But when the river is at its lowest, in May, the water is sometimes red, not fit to drink, and fish die. The Egyptians had to dig wells, into which river water would filter through sand. God directed Moses to lift up his rod at the right time. Once the time was disclosed, the Egyptian magicians could do likewise.

2. **Frogs** (Exod. 8:1-15). When the flood waters recede, frogs spawn in the marshes, and invade the dry land. God directed Moses to lift up his rod at such a time. This sign the Egyptian magicians also claimed to produce.

3. **Lice** (Exod. 8:16-19). What insect is meant is uncertain; RSV has "gnats," ASV margin, "sandflies or fleas." So many biting, stinging pests abound in Egypt that people might not be discriminating in naming them. The magicians failed, by their own admission, to reproduce this plague, and recognized in it "the finger of God," but Pharaoh would not listen to them.

4. **Flies** (Exod. 8:20-31). The rod is no longer mentioned. Swarms of flies came over Egypt in unusual density, to feed on dead frogs. God directed Moses as to the time. The magicians no longer compete with Moses. Now there is a differentiation between Goshen and the rest of Egypt. The Israelites, with higher notions of cleanliness, may have disposed of the dead frogs in their territory. Pharaoh tentatively offers to let the people go to sacrifice to their God, only in the land of Egypt (8:25). Moses protests that their sacrifice will be an animal which the Egyptians think it improper to sacrifice, and insists that they must go three days' journey into the wilderness. Pharaoh assents, provided they do not go far, and the plague is stayed at the intercession of Moses. The plague removed, Pharaoh again refuses to let the people go.

5. **The plague (RSV) of murrain (KJV) upon cattle** (Exod. 9:1-7). This is announced with a set time (tomorrow) for its occurrence. There is no record of its removal: presumably it wore itself out. The perhaps better cared for Israelite cattle are spared: evidence of God's favor and power.

6. **Boils (KJV), blains (ASV) or sores (RSV) upon man and beast** (Exod. 9:8-12). Moses was told to take ashes (ASV soot) from the furnace (RSV kiln) and sprinkle it in the air. Whether a symbolic act or the physical cause, the air over Egypt was filled with dust, and it became boils breaking out on man and beast. The magicians, still watching Moses, could not stand because of the boils. From the specific mention that the plague was upon "all the Egyptians" we may infer that the Israelites were not attacked. This plague was not recalled: presumably it wore itself out.

7. **Hail** (Exod. 9:13-35). God directs Moses to stretch forth his hand, and hail (which rarely occurs in Egypt) will descend in unusual violence. Egyptians who feared the word of the Lord — and after such displays of power there may have been many such —brought their cattle in out of the coming storm: those who did not, lost them to the violent hail. Only in Goshen there was no hail. The hand of God directed its local incidence. The season must have been January or February, for the flax was in the ear and the barley in bud (RSV) or in bloom (ASV: 9:31,32).

8. **Locusts** (Exod. 10:1-20). After seven plagues, even a frequently recurring one, such as locusts, is so dreaded that Pharaoh's servants use bold language in advising that the Israelites be let go (10: 7). Goshen is not spared this visitation. Still Pharaoh is obdurate.

9. **Darkness** (Exod. 10:21-29). A sand storm, accentuated by the dust-bowl condition of the land, and borne on the west wind which drove off the locusts, brought a tawny, choking darkness. The patience of God is at an end: Pharaoh will see the face of Moses no more. Three days the darkness lasted, but the children of Israel had light in their dwellings.

10. **Death of the first-born** (Exod. 11:1-12: 36). This final and convincing demonstration of God's power broke down the resistance of Pharaoh

long enough for the Israelites to escape. The Israelites are directed how to protect their first-born with the blood of the passover lamb, that they may not be slain along with those of the Egyptians. They "borrow" valuables of the Egyptians, and amid the lamentations of the latter are allowed to leave. Egypt has had enough. Even if the deaths were due to bubonic plague, as many think, the incidence upon the first-born alone is not thereby explained. Bubonic plague is said to take the strongest, but the first-born would not include all these. The character of this plague is clearly that of divine judgment upon incurable obstinacy.

The memory of the plagues was cultivated as a warning to Israel in later centuries (Ps. 78:43-51; 105:26:36; 135:8,9; Acts 7:36; 13:17; Heb. 11:28).   E.R.

PLAIN. 1. Heb. *'āvēl*, meadow (Judg. 11:33, see ASV margin).

2. Heb. *'ēlôn, terebinth* (Gen. 13:8, etc.), ASV *oak;* ASV margin and RSV *terebinth*.

3. Heb. *biq'âh, broad valley, plain* (Gen. 11: 2, etc., ASV, RSV *valley;* in Ezek. 3:22; Amos 1:5).

4. Heb. *kikkār, a round thing;* the plain of Jordan (Gen. 13:10-12, etc., RSV valley); the valley of Jericho (Deut. 34:3); the plain (Neh. 3:22 ASV margin, circuit); the plain around Jerusalem (Neh. 12:28 ASV margin, RSV circuit).

5. Heb. *mîshôr, a level place; the tableland* (so ASV margin, RSV) E of Jordan (Deut. 3:10, etc.); a plain as opposed to the hills (I Kings 20:23); tableland (ASV) as distinguished from the low country or Shephelah (II Chron. 26:10); a plain path (Ps. 27:11 RSV level); plain (Jer. 21:13; 48: 8,21 RSV tableland; Zech. 4:7).

6. Heb. *'ārāvāh, desert-plain, steppe;* of Moab (Num. 22:1, etc.); of Jordan near Jericho (Num. 31:12, etc.); the Arabah, the deep valley from the upper Jordan to the Persian Gulf (Deut. 1:1, etc.). By another reading of the text, ASV, RSV have "fords" in II Samuel 15:28; 17:16.

7. Heb. *shephēlâh, lowland;* usually the strip W of the mountains of Judea, ASV lowland, RSV Shephelah (I Chron. 27:28, etc.).

8. Greek *tópos pedinós, a level, flat place* (Luke 6:17 ASV, RSV a *level place*) which may have been on a mountain (Matt. 5:1) or elsewhere.

9. An adjective and adverb. Heb. *nākôah* (Prov. 8:9 RSV straight). Heb. *tām* (Gen. 25:27 ASV quiet, margin, harmless, Heb. *perfect;* RSV *quiet*): Jacob conformed. Gr. *órthos, straight, correct* (Mark 7:35 RSV plainly).

10. As verb. Heb. *bā'ar* (Hab. 2:2). Heb. *shavâh* (Isa. 28:25 ASV, RSV *leveled*). Heb. *sālal* (Prov. 15:19 ASV, a *highway;* RSV a *level highway*).

PLAISTER (See Plaster)

PLAITING (See Dress)

PLANE, a scraping tool used in shaping idol images (Isa. 44:13).

PLANE TREE (See Plants)

PLANTS OF THE BIBLE. The problems confronting the student of the plants of the Bible have long been perplexing ones. Even though difficult, however, few studies hold more fascination for the interested person. Only recently has the correct translation of many of the plants of the Testaments been accomplished. This critical analysis by botanical authorities has cleared away much of the earlier confused interpretation of the plant names included in such categories, for example, as spices, gums, incenses, brambles, and thorns.

Many names of plants growing in the Holy Land during Bible times present little or no difficulty for the translator, for they clearly refer to the plants or the close relatives of the plants that are growing now in our own temperate regions. The almond is an example of this. Others, however, still elude the systematist, their origins lost in antiquity.

Algum Tree, *Juniperus excelsa Bieb* (ălgŭm, Heb. *'algûmmîm*), now known as *Grecian juniper*, it reaches a height of 65 feet and is pyramidal in shape. It is abundant in the mountains of Lebanon and Gilead. The wood was eminently suitable for King Solomon's Temple (II Chron. 2:3,4,7-9).

Almond, *Amygdalus communis L.* (ā'mŭnd, Heb. *shākedh, to watch for*), belongs to the peach family and blooms very early; its pink blossoms appear before the leaves. It blooms prematurely when budded branches are placed in water in a warm place. The Israelites adopted the almond flowers with their sepals and petals (knops and flowers, Exod. 25:33-36) for the ornamentation of the cups of the golden candlesticks.

Almug Tree, *Pterocarpus santalinus L. F.* (ăl'mŭg, Heb. *'almûggîm, wrought wood*), a tree providing a sweet-scented timber which is black outside and inside a ruby red. It is a native of India and takes a high polish. It is known as red sandalwood. The wood is strong and so antiseptic that it is insecticidal. King Solomon's builders undoubtedly deliberately selected the wood of the almug tree for the pillars of the temple because of its specific qualities of strength, beauty, and long life (I Kings 10:11,12).

Aloes (OT), *Aquilaria agallocha Roxb* (ăl'ōz, Heb. *'āhālîm, aloes*), a large and spreading tree known as eagle wood or lign aloes. The inner wood of the tree, particularly when in a state of partial decay, is fragrant (Ps. 45:8).

Aloes (NT), *Aloe succatrina Lam* (ăl'ōz, Gr. *alóe*), a member of the lily family, this plant has a cluster of thick fleshy basal leaves which contain aloin, a substance which, dissolved in water and added to myrrh, was used by the ancients in their highly perfected art of embalming (John 19:38-40).

Amomum (Gr. *ámomum*), an odoriferous plant or seed used in preparing precious ointment (Rev. 18:13, not found in KJV). The exact species is not known. It grew in Armenia, Media, and Pontus, with seeds in clusters like grapes (Pliny, *Hist. Nat.* 12.28).

Anise, *Anethum graveolens L.* (ăn'ĭs, Gr. *ánethon, dill*), an annual, weedy umbellifer which grows like parsley and fennel. Wrongly translated anise, this plant was cultivated for its aromatic seeds, which records tell us were subject to tithe (Matt. 23:23).

Apple, *Prunus armeniaca L.* (ăp'l, Heb. *tappûah*). Much discussion has taken place over the "forbidden" fruit of the Garden of Eden (Gen. 3:3-13) as well as the true botanical nature of the "apple" in the numerous other references. The western "apple" did not thrive on the soils of ancient Palestine. Modern writers seem to concur in the opinion that the apricot is the only fruit meeting all the requirements of context. The apricot tree is a shade tree nearly 30 feet in height. Its fruit is regarded second only to the peach; its perfume strong and revitalizing.

Apples of Sodom, mentioned by Josephus (BJ, IV, 8.4), but it is uncertain what to what he refers.

An almond tree in blossom in Palestine. © MPS

Aspalathus, *Convolvulus floridus L. F.* (ăs-pălā'thŭs, Gr. *aspálathos*), a thorny, woody shrub bearing flowers similar to its morning glory-like relatives. Both the flowers and the wood are aromatic (Ecclesiasticus 24:15).

Balm (balsam), *Commiphora opobalsamum Engl.* (bàm, Heb. *tsŏrî, balsam*), the gum or thickened juice from the balsam trees believed to be the true balm of Gilead indigenous to Arabia (Ezek. 27:17).

Balm, *Balanites aegyptiaca (L) delile* (bàm, Gr. *resin* or *gum*, Heb. *tsŏrî*). The balm here recorded is the false balm of Gilead. It is the juice of a small tree growing in abundance around the Dead Sea. It was used as a healing salve (Jer. 51:8).

Barley, *Hordeum aistichon L.* (bàr'lē, Heb. *se'ōrâh, long hair,* Gr. *krithé*), a grain cultivated for man and beast from remotest antiquity. It is considered to be the most universally cultivated cereal. Barley bread was a staple food of the Hebrews and a symbol of poverty and scorn (Hos. 3:2). Barley corns were used by the Hebrews as a unit of measure.

Bay Tree (Green Bay Tree, q.v.)

Bdellium, *Commiphora africana (Arn.) Engl.* (dĕl'-ĭ-ŭm, Heb. *bedhōlah*), a tree that grew eastward of Persia. From its incised bark oozed a gum which when dry became transparent and wax-like and looked like a pearl (Num. 11:6,7).

Beans, *Vicia faba L.* (bēn, Heb. *pôl, bean*), the broad bean, extensively cultivated in Palestine. Dried ground beans were mixed in with grain flour to make bread (Ezek. 4:9). A staple article of diet for the poor of Palestine.

Bitter Herbs (Herbs, q.v.)

Box Tree, *Buxux longifolia Baiss* (Heb. *te'ashshûr, ashur wood*), a hardy evergreen forest tree of Lebanon and northern hills of Palestine. Because of the hardness of its wood it was used to provide inlays for cabinet work (Isa. 41:19; 60:13).

Bramble, *Rubus ulmifolius Scott* (brăm′b'l, Heb. *ātādh, bramble*), a strong growing bushlike plant with long, arching, stout, prickly stems. It is the blackberry bush of the European countrysides (Judg. 9:14,15).

Brier, *Ruscus aculeatus L.* (brī′ēr, Heb. *sillôn*), a prickly plant that is painful. A member of the lily family this small, evergreen shrub bears leaves reduced to small scales which enclose leaf-like branches with sharp apexes (Ezek. 28:24).

Bulrush, *Cyperus papyrus L.* (bŏŏl′rŭsh, Heb. *gōme′*), a tall, slender reed-like plant which formerly grew prolifically in and along the banks of the lower Nile. Papyrus provided the earliest known material for the making of paper which gets its name from the plant (Exod. 2:3).

Bush (Burning Bush), *Loranthus acaciae zucc.* (bŏŏsh, Heb. *seneh*), one of the many thorny acacias which in early times grew thickly over the Holy Land. When the berries of the mistletoe cover the bush, red, glowing, and transparent, they give the appearance of a burning bush (Ex. 3:2).

Camphire, *Lawsonia inermis L.* (kăm′fīr, Heb. *cōpher*), one of the earliest known of the spices and perfumes, and lauded by King Solomon for its beautiful fragrance. It is also the henna of the Arabs. The dried leaves of the henna crushed and made into a paste provide a violent yellow stain for the hair and beard. No relation to the camphor tree of Chinese origin. The camphire still luxuriates by the Dead Sea at Engedi (S. of Sol. 1:14).

Cassia, *Cinnamomum cassia Blume* (kăsh′ĭ-à, Heb. *kiddâh*), a fragrant tree resembling the cinnamon, though its bark is less delicate in taste and perfume. Its buds are used in place of cloves. The small leaves provide the medicine known as senna leaves (Exod. 30:22-25).

Cedar, *Juniperus oxycedrus L.* (sē′dēr, Heb. *'erez,* meaning undetermined), the brown-berried cedar or juniper of the mountains. It was the cedar that was used for sacrificial duty in the temple and by the priests at the altar (Num. 19:1, 2,6).

Cedar of Lebanon, *Cedrus libani Loud.* (Heb. *'erez,* derived from an old Arabic root meaning a *firmly-rooted, strong tree*), a magnificent evergreen often 120 feet high and 40 feet in girth. It exudes a fragrant gum or balsam. The wood does not quickly decay, nor is it eaten by insect larvae. It is of a warm red tone, solid and free from knots (Ezek. 31:3,5; Ps. 92:12).

Chestnut (plane tree), *Platanus orientalis L.* (chĕs′nŭt, Heb. *'armôn, peeling off, naked*), a stately tree thriving along the streams and rivers of the Holy Land. Each year the bark peels off, leaving the trunk and older branches smooth and yellowish-white (Gen. 30:37).

Cinnamon, *Cinnamomum zeylanicum Nees* (sĭn′à-mŭn, Heb. *qinnāmôn*), a tree about 20 feet high with stiff, evergreen leaves, native of Ceylon. Commercial cinnamon is obtained from the inner bark. The branches, one inch thick, are cut when this bark peels easily. Quills are produced when the cleaned inner bark dries around a thin rod (Exod. 30:23).

Cockle, *Agrostemma githago L.* (kŏk′l, Heb. *bo'shâh, stink*), a sturdy noxious weed introducing itself into wheat and barley fields. The seeds are poisonous if ground with flour (Job 31:40).

Coriander, *Coriandrum sativum L.* (kŏ′rĭ-ăn-dēr, Heb. *gadh*). The seeds of this plant in the carrot family are the size of a peppercorn. They have a sharp though pleasant aroma. Common in the Holy Land, the seeds were used for culinary and medicinal purposes (Exod. 16:31).

Corn (Wheat, q.v.)

Cotton, *Gossypium herbaceum L.* (kŏt′n, Heb. *karpas*). Like the hollyhock, cotton belongs to the mallow family. Only once is it mentioned in the Bible (Esth. 1:5,6 RSV). The clothing in which Egyptian mummies were wrapped was cotton fabric.

Cucumber, *Cucumis sativus L.* (kū′kŭm-bēr, Heb. *qishshū′îm*). The refreshing fruit of the cucumber vine was one delicacy the children of Israel constantly desired after leaving Egypt. It grew best along the banks of the Nile. Isaiah 1:8 records: "The daugher of Zion is left . . . as a lodge in a garden of cucumbers, as a besieged city." The lodge, a hut of four poles and walls of woven boughs, housed the watchman. In Hebrew a garden of cucumbers is *miqshâh.*

Cummin, *Cuminum cyminum L.* (kŭ′mĭn, Heb. *cammōn*). This plant is not found wild. It is the only species of its genus, and western Asia is its home. Its aromatic seeds are crushed and mixed with bread and added to the meat pot. The small tender seeds are harvested with a rod; if threshed otherwise, they would be ruined (Isa. 28:26,27).

Cypress, *Cupressus sempervirens var. horizontalis (Mill) Gord* (sī′prĕs, Heb. *tirzâh*), the true cypress with its hard, durable, reddish-hued wood. Authorities accept the statement that cypress wood was used to construct the ark (Isa. 44:14).

Desire (caper) *Capparis spinosa L.* (dē-zīr, Heb. *tapher*). This plant provided a much-needed appetite stimulant for the aging. It is the young pickled buds that give the "desire" of relish to the food. The fruit is inedible (Eccl. 12:5).

This great, venerable cedar of Lebanon is known as "God's Cedar." © MPS

Dove's Dung (Star of Bethlehem), *Ornithogalum umbellatum L.* (dō'vz dŭng, Heb. *divyônîm*), the bulb of the spring-blooming Star of Bethlehem. Dug up and dried, it can be eaten roasted or ground to flour and mixed with meal to make bread (II Kings 6:25).

Ebony, *Diospyros ebenaster Retz* (ĕb'ŭn-ē, Heb. *hovnîm,* ebony), a wood mentioned once in the Bible (Ezek. 27:15). It is hard, heavy and durable, and will take a glistening polish. This black heartwood of certain trees native to Ceylon and southern India, has long been used with native ivory to make inlaid objects.

Eelgrass, *Zostera marina L.* (ēēl'grăs, Heb. *sûph, weeds*), the marine eelgrass of tidal waters. It may grow out to a depth of 35 feet in the sea itself. Its three- to four-foot-long slimy, ribbon-like leaves lie in submerged masses, a menace to the off-shore diver who may become fouled in their coils (Jonah 2:5).

Elm (Turpentine Tree, q.v.)

Flag (Exod. 2:3,5; Bulrush, q.v. see; Job 8:11; Isa. 19:6, Rush, q.v.).

Fig, *Fiscus carica L.* (fĭg, Heb. *te'ēnâh, to spread out*), the first of the fruits to be recorded in the Bible (Gen. 3:6,7). It is a good shade tree (I Kings 4:25). The fruit often appears before the leaves. "Cakes of figs" and strings of dried figs were for eating when traveling (I Sam. 25:18).

Fir, *Pius halepensis Mill.* (fûr, Heb. *berôsh*). Translated "pine" by botanical authorities, the fir tree was an emblem of nobility and great stature. The largest of the pines on Mount Lebanon was the Aleppo Pine. Throughout the crusades there was an entire forest of these pines between Jerusalem and Bethlehem (Isa. 60:13,14).

Fitches, *Nigella sativa L.* (fĭch'ĕz, Heb. *ketsah*), or vetches, belong to the bean family, while the "fitches" of Isaiah 28:25-27 belong to the buttercup family and are called the "nutmeg flower" (unrelated to the cultivated nutmeg). Both cummin and nutmeg flower seeds are still harvested and threshed in the Holy Land as described by Isaiah. Its tiny, hot, and easily-removed seeds are sprinkled on food like pepper.

Flax, *Linum usitatissimum* (flăks, Heb. *pishtâh*), the plant used to make linen. The fibers from the stem of the plant are the most ancient of all textile fibers. Flax supplied the linen thread for the swaddling clothes of the infant Jesus, as well as in His burial wrappings (Luke 23:50,52,53).

Frankincense, *Boswellia thurifera Roxb.* (frăngk'ĭn-sĕns, Heb. *levōnâh*), a clear yellow resin that exudes from the incisions made in the bark of the frankincense tree and hardens into small yellow tears. The tree is native of northern India and Arabia (Matt. 2:10,11).

Galbanum, *Ferula galbaniflua* (găl'bá-nŭm, Heb. *helbenâh*), a gum resin excreted from the incised lower part of the stem of any one of the nine species of this genus *Ferula* growing as stout herbaceous perennials in the Holy Land. When the hardened tears of this resin are burned, the odor is pungent and pleasant (Exod. 30:34-36).

Gall, *Papaver somniferum* (gôl, Heb. *rō'sh*), the juice of the opium poppy. Opium is the dried juice that exudes from the incised capsules of the opium poppy. It induces a sleep so heavy that the person becomes insensible. The juice of this poppy was added to vinegar and offered to Jesus (Matt. 27:34).

Above, first and second figs. Below, a fig tree laden with first figs. © MPS

Garlick, *Allium sativum L.* (gàr'lĭk, Heb. *shûm*), one of the staple foods and an ingredient of many medicines. This bulbous plant grew in great abundance in Egypt. Small bulblets known as cloves of garlic grow around the main bulb. Numbers 11:5 is the only verse in the Bible mentioning the vegetables that were constantly missed by the Israelites during their journey toward the Promised Land.

Gourd, *Ricinus communis L.* (gôrd, Heb. *qîqāyôn, nauseous to the taste*), a large bush ten feet high with broad leaves. This is our castor bean. Castor oil is pressed from its seeds. This oil was not used medicinally by the Hebrews but as fuel for lamps and in their ceremonial rites. All true gourds are indigenous to tropical America so could not have been known in Palestine in Biblical times (Jonah 4:5-7).

Gourd (Wild Gourds, q.v.)

Grape (Vine, q.v.)

Green Bay Tree, *Laurus nobilis L.* (bā, Heb. *'zrāh*), a tree symbolic of wealth and wickedness (Ps. 37:35,36). The tree resembles a shrub, the young shoots sprouting from the ground around the parent stem. A perfumed oil is expressed from its evergreen leaves.

Hemlock, *Conium malculatum L.* (hĕm′lŏk, Heb. *rō'sh*), a tall and poisonous herbaceous plant which when injured emits a disagreeable odor. All parts of it, particularly the seeds, contain an oily substance known as caria. If taken internally by humans this irritant causes paralysis, convulsions and even death (Hos. 10:4).

Herbs, Bitter Herbs (ûrbs). Endive (*Cichorium endiva L.*), Common Chicory (*Cichorium intybus L.*), Garden Lettuce (*Sactuca sativa L.*), Water Cress (*Nasturtium officinale R. Br.*), Sorrel (*Rumex acetosella var. multifidus (L.) P. D. C. and Lam.*), and Dandelion (*Taraxacum officinale*), Heb. *merōrîm, bitter herbs*. These are the bitter herbs gathered fresh and eaten as a salad at the time of the Passover (Exod. 12:8; Num. 9:11).

Hyssop (NT), *Sorghum vulgare var. durra (Forsk) Dinsm.* (hĭs′ŭp, Lat. *hyssopus*), a sorghum cane reaching a height of over six feet. The seed is ground for meal and is known in Palestine as "Jerusalem corn." This is thought to be the hyssop of John 19:28,29. The "parched corn" received by Ruth from Boaz may have been the grain from this sorghum (Ruth 2:14).

Hyssop (OT), *Origanum maru var. aegypticum (L.) Dismn.* (Heb. *'ēzôv*), the Egyptian marjoram, a member of the mint family. The hairy stem of the much-branched inflorescence holds water very well, a characteristic identifying it with its place in the Passover rites (Exod. 12:21,22).

Juniper, *Retama raetam (Forsk.) Webb. and Berth* (jŏŏ′nĭ-pêr, Heb. *rōthem, to bind*), a plant wholly unrelated to the true juniper (Juniperus). A member of the pea family, the "flowering broom" as it is called, is a desert shrub. For centuries it has furnished shade for flocks and man and fuel for his fire (I Kings 19:3,4).

Leeks, *Alium porrum L.* (lēk, Heb. *hātsîr*), a robust bulbous plant of the lily family with rather succulent, broad leaves the bases of which are edible. The much desired small bulbs growing above ground are used in seasoning (Num. 11:5).

Lentil, *Lens esculenta Moench.* (lĕn′tĭl, Heb. *'ādhāshîm, to tend a flock*), a small trailing member of the pea family. Its seeds are used as a meal when dried and ground. When soaked and cooked, they made a nourishing meal known as "pottage" (Gen. 25:29,30,34).

Lilies (of the field), *Anemone Coronaria L.* (lĭl′ēz, Gr. *krínon*), thè plant of Luke 12:27. It is thought to be the anemone or windflower. Blooming from a bulb after the spring rains, its colorful blossoms carpet the plains and roadsides.

Lily, *Lilium Chalcedonicum L.* (lĭlē, Heb. *shôshān*), a true lily, its flowers a glowing red, the chalcedonicum lily grew in King Solomon's garden. It was a symbol of loveliness (S. of Sol. 5:13).

Lily (Water Lily, q.v.)

Locusts, *Ceratonia Siliqua L.* (lŏ′kŭst, Gr. *kerátion*), the fruit of the carob tree; accepted in the East as the food eaten by John the Baptist. It is known as St. John's bread. A member of the pea family, the carob tree produces peas in which the seeds are embedded in a flavorful, sweet and nutrious pulp (Matt. 3:4). Doubtless the pods of the carob (locust tree) were the "Husks" eaten by the prodigal son in Jesus' parable (Luke 15:16).

Mallows, *Atriplex halimus L.* (măl′ō, Heb. *mallûah, salty tasting plant*), most likely a species of

"Lilies of the field" (anemones) in the Jerusalem area. © MPS

salt bush or salt wort known as "sea purslane"; a robust bushy shrub related to spinach. Because of the implied saltiness from the Hebrew most authorities agree that these were not true mallows. It was a food of the poor (Job 30:1,3,4).

Mandrake, *Mandragora offinarum L.* (măn′drăk, Heb. *dûdhay*), a member of the potato family, the mandrake is also called "love-apple." The "apples," although insipid tasting and slightly poisonous, are much desired as an edible fruit. The mandrake root is large, sometimes resembling the human body in shape. It was used as a charm against the evil spirits and, as indicated by the story of Rachel and Leah, was credited with aphrodisiac qualities (Gen. 30:14-16).

Melon, (Watermelon), *Citrullus vulgaris Schrad.* (mĕl′ŭn, Heb. *'ăvattihîm*). Cultivated in Egypt since before recorded history, the fruits weighed as much as 50 pounds. Being abundant during the growing season, they were used by rich and poor alike for food, drink and medicine. The seeds were eaten after roasting. Some authorities believe that the reference to "melons" in Numbers 11:5 includes both watermelons and muskmelons, although the former had their origin in Africa and the latter in Asia.

Carob pods (locusts, or husks), known as St. John's Bread.

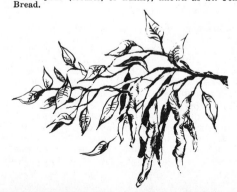

Millet (See Pannag)

Mint (Horse Mint or larger garden mint), *Mentha Longifolia L. Huds.* (mĭnt, Gr. *hedýosmon*). This pungent garden mint with the sharp-scented pennyroyal, and the refreshing peppermint added much to making the meat dishes of the Jews more palatable. These three varieties of mint grow in Palestine and are classified as lesser herbs. They are mentioned only in Matthew and Luke (Luke 11:42). All have medicinal value.

Mulberry Tree (mŭl'bĕr'ĭ, Heb. *bekhā'îm*). The Heb. word is the name of a tree (II Sam. 5:23,24; I Chron. 14:14,15) which cannot be identified.

Mustard, *Brassica nigra L. W. Koch* (mŭs'tērd, Gr. *sínapi*). A thick stemmed plant, under good conditions often growing higher than a man can reach. The field mustard was an important economic plant of the Holy Land. The leaves were used as "greens" and the seeds were either powdered or made into paste. The larger plants were the favorite haunts of the smaller birds (Matt. 13:31,32).

Myrrh (NT), *Commiphora myrrha (Nees) Engl.* (mûr, Heb. *mōr*), one of the most valuable of the gum resins. Either naturally or when the stems are injured, the gum oozes from the shrub-like tree. The pale yellow liquid gradually solidifies and turns dark red or even black. This aromatic gum was sold as a spice or medicine (Matt. 2:11; John 19:39,40).

Myrrh (OT), *Cistus creticus L.* (mûr, Heb. *lōt*), a small shrub known as the rockrose or "lot plant" which grows in rocks and sand in Palestine. It produces the perfumed gum which has been mistranslated "myrrh" in parts of the OT (Gen. 37:25,26,27). Not the true myrrh of the NT, q.v.

Myrtle, *Myrtus comminis L.* (mûr't'l, Heb. *hǎdhas, sweetness*), a large evergreen shrub with fragrant flowers and spicy-sweet scented leaves. All parts of the plant are somewhat perfumed. It has been used as a symbol of beauty and sweetness (Isa. 55:13). Out of its leafy twigs were made wreaths of acclaim and its boughs adorned the booths of the ancients at feast time (Zech. 1:7,8).

Nettle, *Acanthus spinosus L.* (nĕt'l, Heb. *hārûl*), a bushy plant of great size (Job 30:7) and of rapid growth. The acanthus grew as a common weed throughout the Holy Land (Zep. 2:9). Its leaf was carved in stone and became the basis of early Greek and Roman ornamental decoration.

Nuts (Walnut), *Juglans regia L.* (Heb. *ĕghôz*), our "English walnut," sometimes called Persian walnut. It is a native of Iran. Dye is obtained from the leaves and husk that covers the nut. The nuts are eaten, pressed to obtain a table oil or formed into oil cakes for the cattle. In Biblical times as now many gatherings were held under the spreading, shading branches of this beautiful tree (S. of Sol. 6:10,11).

Nuts (Pistachio), *Pistacia vera L.* (Heb. *bōtnîm*). Carried by Jacob's sons to Egypt, this nut known as the green almond has been in cultivation in the Holy Land for nearly 4,000 years. The nuts are borne in clusters. They are oval, containing two green edible halves covered by a reddish outer shell (Gen. 43:11).

Oak (Holly Oak), *Quercus ilex L.* (Heb. *'allôn*), a magnificent, long-lived tree growing usually alone and on high ground. Its leaves are holly-like; glossy green and spiny on the edges. The oak is the religious symbol of strength and long life (Gen. 35:8).

The Mustard Tree. © MPS

Oak (Valonia Oak), *Quercus aegllops L.* (Heb. *allôn*), one of the six species of oaks found in Palestine, the Valonia oak is not an evergreen. It grows in forests stands on the hillsides above the fertile valleys in Bashan. A black dye of commercial value is obtained from the acorn cups. The acorns are fed to the swine. Its insect galls contain allic acid and tannin from which ink is made (Zech. 11:2).

Oil Tree, *Elaeagnus angustifolia L.* (Heb. *'ets shemen*). Sometimes called "Jerusalem willow" or "Oleaster," this tree produces a fruit like a small olive from which may be pressed an inferior grade of medical oil. The fruits are edible but slightly bitter (Isa. 41:19).

Frankincense and Myrrh.

Olive branches loaded with fruit. © MPS

Olive, *Olea europaea L.* (ŏl'ĭv, Heb. *zayith*), an evergreen tree, the true olive. One tree could supply a family with fats. It flourishes only near the sea and under cultivation. The olives were beaten down with poles when ripe (black) and crushed by an upright stone wheel. The oil thus obtained was stored in vats. Oil for the temple lights was expressed specifically for that purpose (Exod. 27:20). Heated in lye to remove the bitter principle and soaked in brine, green olives were eaten with coarse brown bread (Hos. 14:6).

Arab peasants beating down olives, to harvest the crop. © MPS

Onion, *Allium cepa L.* (ŭn'yŭn, Heb. *betsel*), a bulbous plant mentioned only in Numbers 11:5. Both the inflated leaves and the bulbous underground base of this plant were universally used as food and have been cultivated since time immemorial.

Onycha, *Cistus ladaniferus L.* (ŏn'ĭ-kȧ, Heb. *shehēleth*), a rock rose like the OT Myrrh, q.v. It produces the gum known as labdanum. Late in the year this resin exudes from stems and leaves. It is spicy-aromatic and fragrant (Exod. 30:34,35, 36).

Palm (Date), *Phoenix dactylifera L.* (pȧm, Heb. *tāmār*), a tree with a single trunk. The crown of the date palm may be 100 feet above the ground. Its cultivation goes back at least 5,000 years. The fruit hangs in clusters below the leaves. A single inflorescence may have as many as 10,000 flowers. The leaves are woven into mats and the fibers provide thread and rigging for boats. The sap, after fermentation, becomes a liquor or vinegar (Num. 33:19).

Pannag (Millet), *Panicum miliaceum L.* (Heb. *pannagh*), a millet used to make a good grade of flour, its seeds being hard and white. One stalk may carry a thousand grains. The common people ate a mixture of wheat, barley, beans, lentils and pannag moistened with camel's milk and oil (Ezek. 4:9 and 27:17).

Parched Corn (Wheat, q.v.)

Pine Tree, *Abies cilicica L.* (Heb. *tidhhār*), the pine mentioned in Isaiah 60:1. It is the Cilician fir. (The fir is the pine; see FIR). This is a tall tree with wood that is easy to cut and tool.

Plane Tree (Chestnut, q.v.)

Pomegranate, *Punica granatum L.* (pŏm'grăn-ĭt, Heb. *rimmôn, apple with grains*), one of the trees grown in the hanging Gardens of Babylon. Its hard, thin-rinded, apple-shaped fruits contain many seeds, each in a pulp sack filled with a tangy, sweet amethyst-colored juice. Although a low shrub or small tree, giving little shade, its refreshing fruit more than compensated the tired traveler who rested under it (I Sam. 14:2). The pomegranate was used as a decorative model in building (I Kings 7:18,20) and in textile designs (Exod. 28:31,33, 34).

Poplar, *Populus Alba L.* (pŏp'lêr, Heb. *livneh*), a tall straight tree that sends out long shoots when young. It grows in the hills of Palestine. Young, fast-growing trees, growing from root buds are found in abundance about older "mother" trees.

Pulse (II Sam. 17:28, pŭls, Heb. *qālî* and Dan. 1:12,16; Heb. *zēr'ōnîm*). There is as yet no satisfactory identification of these Hebrew terms as they relate to our word pulse. Beans and lentils, both or either one probably were used as part of the ingredients of "pulse."

Reed, *Phragmites communis Trin.* (rēd, Heb. *'āghām, flowing together like water*), the plumed hollow-stemmed water plant found in the Holy Land by the sides of rivers and in standing waters (Job 40:21). It grows in clumps, its stalks reaching 12 feet in height. Reed pens were made from the canes.

Rie, Rye (Spelt), *Triticum aestivum var spilta L.* L. H. Bailey (rī, Heb. *kussemeth*), probably the "rie" of Exodus 9:32. It grows taller than wheat, yet will survive where other grasses will not thrive. Isaiah 28:24,25,26 makes it plain that the farmers of Israel knew of the ability of this grain to grow under adverse conditions.

At left, the crowning glory of a date palm tree loaded with fruit. At right, a pomegranate tree bearing fruit. © MPS

Rolling Thing (Rose of Jericho), *Anistatica hierochuntica L.* (Heb. *galgal*), the "rolling thing" of Isaiah 17:13 and the "wheel" of Psalm 83:13. In all probability these refer to the Palestinian tumbleweed, long known as the "holy resurrection flower." A member of the mustard family, the six inch-long stems of this annual lie in a circle flat on the ground until the seeds are mature; then the stems become dry and incurved, forming a globe. The wind finally breaks the dry tap root at ground level, rolling the plant over and over. Finally coming to rest, with the help of the rains, roots appear, the stems unroll and new shoots with leaves and flowers soon appear.

Rose (Narcissus), *Narcissus tazetta L.* (Heb. *hăvatstseleth*), a bulbous-rooted plant, most likely the yellow narcissus that grows wild and in abundance on the plain of Sharon. The "rose" of Isaiah 35:1.

Rose of Sharon, *Tulipa sharonensis Dinms.* (Heb. *hăvatstseleth*). A literal translation of the Hebrew word *hăvatstseleth* indicates a bulbous plant instead of a woody vine or shrub belonging to the genus *Rosa*. Botanists have concluded that the Sharon tulip found on sandy soil on the Sharon coastal plain is the "Rose of Sharon" of our Song of Solomon (S. of Sol. 2:1,2).

Rue, *Ruta graveolens L.* (rōō, Gr. *péganon*), mentioned only once in the Bible (Luke 11:42). Of the four varieties grown, the species *graveolens*, meaning "strong smelling," is the most common. It was relished for its peculiar though strong taste and was useful in cookery and medicine.

Rush (Flag), *Juncus effusus L.* (rŭsh, Heb. *'aghmôn*), known as the common soft or bog rush. There are 20 varieties of this grasslike plant growing in and along the water courses of Palestine. The Egyptian bulrush (Exod. 2:3) according to most commentators is cyperus papyrus; however, regarding the "rush," "reed," and "flag" referred to

in other portions of the OT (Job 8:11; Isa. 9:14; 9:6-15; 35:7), there is still much disagreement. All are related ecologically if not taxonomically.

Saffron, *Crocus sativus L.* (să'frŭn, Heb. *karkōm*), the stigmas of the autumn crocus, highly valued for their aromatic odor and their vivid orange dye used in food coloring. The plant grows from a bulb (S. of Sol. 4:14).

Scarlet, *Chermes ilicis on quercus coccifers L.* (skàr'lĕt, Heb. *shānî*), a lasting and rich scarlet dye produced by the Kermes insect (*Chermes ilicis*) which breeds in the soft down on the twigs of the Oak tree quercus Coccifera. This dye was used for the scarlet and crimson coloring of wool and linen thread in Bible times (II Chron. 3:14; Jer. 4:30; Heb. 9:19; Rev. 18:12).

Narcissus, possibly the "Rose of Sharon" of the Bible. © MPS

The shittah tree, or acacia, the source of the oft-mentioned shittim wood of the Bible, from which the Ark of the Tabernacle was built. © MPS

Shittah Tree, *Acacia seya L. Delile* (shĭt'à, Heb. *shittâh*), a gnarled, rough-barked, thorny tree of the pea family. The acacia or shittah tree of Isaiah 41:18 is mentioned only this once in the Bible, but its wood (shittim) is referred to many times. Shittim wood is insect repellent; a very beautiful close-grained wood, orange when cut, turning darker with age. It was used to fashion the Ark of the Tabernacle (Exod. 25:10). The shittah tree yields gum arabic and gum senegal.

Spicery (Spices, q.v.)

Spices, *Astragalus tragacantha L.* (spīs, Heb. *nekhō'th*). The word "spices" of II Chronicles 9:1 is an inaccurate translation of the word for thorny astragal or necath of the Bible. Its naturally-exuded gum is the gum tragacanth of commerce (Gen. 43:11; II Kings 20:13; Isa. 39:2; S. of Sol. 4:10, 14; 5:1,13; 6:2; 8:2,14).

Spikenard, *Nardostachys (Wall.) P. D.C. jatamansi* (spīk nērd, Heb. *nērd*). The rose-red, fragrant ointment made from the dried roots and woolly stems of the spikenard plant was a favorite perfume of the ancients. A precious ointment (Mark 14:3), it was and still is transported in an alabaster box to preserve its fragrance. Because it had to be imported from northern India, it was extremely yet understandably costly.

Stacte (Storax), *Styrax officinalis L.* (stăk'tē, Heb. *nātāph, a liquid drop*), a highly-perfumed gum resin that exudes from the incised bark of the storax tree, used in Biblical days as a component of the perfume formulated for use in the Holy Place (Exod. 30:34).

Strange Vine (Vine, q.v.)

Sweet Cane (Sugar Cane), *saccharum officinarum L.* (Heb. *qāneh*), a stout perennial resembling Indian corn, but growing to a height of 15 feet. The juice of the sweet cane mentioned in Isaiah 43:24, although not used at that time for sugar-making, was highly esteemed for sweetening foods and drinks and the pithy sweet stalks for chewing.

Sweet Cane (calamus, sweet calamus), *Andropogon aromaticus Roxb.* (Heb. *qāneh hattōv, the good cane*), the ginger-grass from northwestern and central India. It is called this because its bruised leaves give off a strong, spicy, aromatic scent and their pungent taste is like ginger (Jer. 6:20; Ezek. 27:19).

Sycamine, *Morus nigra L.* (sĭk'à-mĭn, Gr. *sykáminos*), the black mulberry tree. Botanists consider the leaves of this tree inferior to those of *Morus alba* the white mulberry as a food for the silk worms. It is, however, cultivated throughout Palestine for its delectable fruit (Luke 17:6).

Sycamore, *Ficus Sycomorus* (sĭk'àmôr, Heb. *shiqmâh*), the sycamore fig tree. A tree bearing fruit, like the ordinary fig, directly on the stem, but being of inferior quality. The wood is most durable (Amos 7:14; Luke 19:1,2,3,4).

Tares, *Lolium temulentum L.* (tärz, Gr. *zizánion*), the annual bearded darnel or rye grass that flourishes in wheat fields. It is difficult to tell it from wheat or rye until it heads. After harvest the wheat is fanned, then put through a sieve. The smaller darnel seeds left after fanning pass through the sieve leaving the wheat behind. The darnel is host to an ergot-like smut fungus which infects the seeds. The fungus is a serious poison if eaten by animals or man (Matt. 13:25).

Teil (Turpentine Tree, q.v.)

Thistles, *Silybum marianum L. Gaerth.* (thĭs''l, Heb. *dardar*, Gr. *tríbolos*), a prickly plant. There is rather uniform agreement that most of the references to "thistles" and "thorns" in both the Old and New Testaments are generic in character (II

The globe-thistle, one of the common "thistles" and "thorns" of Palestine. © MPS

Kings 14:9; II Chron. 25:18; Hos. 10:8; Matt. 7:16; 13:7; Heb. 6:8). Of the many thistles that grow in the Holy Land the Silybum or Mary's thistle and the true star-thistle *centaurea calcitrapa L.* are the commonest. Producing seeds in great numbers which are freely disseminated, the thistles are found in every part of Palestine.

Thorns (Crown of Thorns), *Paliurus spinachristi Mill.* (thôrn, Gr. *akántha*), the Christ-thorn. A straggling shrub growing from three to nine feet in height. Its pliable branches with their uneven stiff thorns (the longer ones straight and the shorter recurved) lent themselves to the platting of the "crown" or "wreath" made by the soldiers (Mark 15:17).

"The tares and the wheat." "Some seed fell among thorns." © MPS

Thorns, *Zizyphus spina-christi L.* (Gr. *akántha*), one of numerous and different spiny plants included under this generic term thorn. Zizyphus, above (Isa. 7:19 and 53:13; Matt. 7:16) and *Rhamnus palastine Boiss.*, the Palestine Buckthorn, (Gen. 3:18; Prov. 15:19; Isa. 33:12; Ps. 58:9 and Hos. 2:6) are the two "thorny" shrubs most widespread and well-known in Biblical times in Palestine. Both were planted as hedges and the latter used as fire wood under the meat pots.

Thyine Wood, *Tetraclinis articulata (Vahl) Masers* (thī'ĭn, Gr. *thýinos*), a small, slow-growing evergreen tree related to our arbor-vitae. A priceless commodity, thyine wood, mentioned only once in the Bible (Rev. 18:12), is rich in color, fine-grained, taking a high polish and almost indestructible. The tree, commonly said to be "worth its weight in gold," yields a resin known as "sandarac" which is used in making varnish and as an incense.

Turpentine Tree (Teil Tree), *Pistacia terebinthus var. palaestina (Boiss.) Post.* (tûr'pĕn-tīn, Heb. *'ēlâh, strong*), a thick-trunked, spreading tree of the hot, dry places. It usually grows as a solitary tree and casts a dense, cooling shade. When the bark is cut, a perfumed oily resin flows out. This is the cyprus turpentine of commerce (Isa. 6:13).

Vine (true), *Vitis vinifera L.* (Heb. *gephen*), the first plant to be recorded as cultivated in Biblical history. The grape, its origin lost in antiquity, grew first on the ground, over walls or on crude supports. Later it was trained on a trellis, and finally cultivated in vineyards. It was a symbol of fruitfulness and its harvesting a time of joyous festivity (Gen. 40:9-11; Deut. 8:8; Ps. 105:33; Zech. 3:10).

Vine (Strange Vine, Wild Grapes) (Isa. 5:2-4; Jer. 2:21). These two references seem to call for a plant that is closely related to the true vine in appearance in order to deceive the owner of the vineyard. A "wild" or unselected strain of the cultivated grape would be such a plant.

Vine (Wild Vine, Vine of Sodom, q.v.)

Vine of Sodom (Heb. *gephen sedhôm,* Deut. 32:23). It is uncertain what plant is intended.

Water Lily, *Nymphaea caerulea Sav.* (Heb. *shôshān*), a blue-flowered lily with floating leaf pads. Its seeds and rootstock are edible. The flowers served as a pattern in ornamental design (I Kings 7:19,22,26).

Weeds (Eelgrass, q.v.)

Wheat, *Triticum compositum L.* (Heb. *hittâh*), the most common cereal grain. This is the wheat of Joseph's time which bore seven ears in one stalk (Gen. 41:22). Wheat was planted in the winter by the Hebrews. Today as in the time of Jesus, certain varieties of wheat may yield 60 or even 100 grains to a head (Matt. 13:3-8). The heads roasted over fire constituted the parched corn of the OT (Lev. 23:14; Ruth 2:14; I Sam. 17:17 and 25:18).

Wild Gourd, *Citrullus colocynthis Schrad.* (gôrd, Heb. *paqqū'ōth-sādheh, to burst*), a vine resembling the cucumber, running wild over large areas in the Holy Land. When the orange-sized fruit is ripe, it bursts. The dry, powdery pulp is highly inflammable. The powdered pulp, when used as a medicine is a violent purgative (II Kings 4:38-40).

Willow (Aspen), *Populus euphratica Oliv.* (ăs'pĕn, Heb. *'ărābhîm*), the "willows" in Psalm 137:2. The trees inhabit the river and stream banks from Syria to Palestine, and especially the Jordan valley. They are now quite generally considered to be the Euphrates aspens. Their most interesting characteristic is their leaves; attached obliquely to the twigs by a flattened, weak petiole, they continually sway back and forth like "weeping and wailing women."

Willow, *Salix alba L.* (wĭl ō, Heb. *'ărābhîm*), a fast-growing tree found in moist places and on the margins of rivers and shallow streams. The "green withs" of Judges 16:7-9 and the "willows" of Job 40:22; Isaiah 15:7; 44:4 and Ezekiel 17:5 are generally thought by authorities to belong to the true Palestine willows of which there are four species.

Wormwood, *Artemisia judaica L.* (wûrm'woŏd, Heb. *la'ănâh*), a species related to our western sagebrush and the source of an essential oil obtained from the dried leaves and tops of the plant. Absinthe, a liqueur, the continuous use of which leads to mental deterioration and even death, derives its flavor from this oil (Lam. 3:15,19). The plant is a symbol of bitterness.

Bibliography: Hill, Albert F., *Economic Botany,* McGraw-Hill, New York, 1952. Moldenke, Harold N. and Alma L. Moldenke, *Plants of the Bible,* Chronica Botanica Co., Waltham, Mass., 1952. Schery, Robert W., *Plants for Man,* Prentice Hall, New York, 1952. Walker, Winifred, *All the Plants of the Bible,* Harper, New York, 1957. Youngken, H. W., *Pharmaceutical Botany,* Blakiston, Philadelphia, 1935.   J.L.L.

PLASTER (plăs'têr). The Egyptians plastered their stone buildings, even the finest granite, inside and out, to make a smooth surface for decoration. The poor used a mixture of clay and straw. On better buildings the first coat was gypsum and red clay or ashes, the finish coat slaked lime and white sand, sometimes with chopped straw. In Palestine and Syria, an outside clay coating would have to be renewed after the rainy season. Mortar was usually made with limestone, the process otherwise similar to that in Egypt. The Arabic word for mortar means "clay." Heb. *sîdh* (Deut. 27:2,4) means "to boil up," because of the action when water is poured on unslaked lime. *Gîr* (Dan. 5:5) means "burned in a kiln" (either lime or gypsum). *Tûah* (Lev. 14:42-48) means "to daub, smear."

PLASTER, MEDICINAL. In Isaiah 38:21 KJV, ASV) a cake of figs applied (RSV) to a boil.

PLEDGE, personal property of a debtor held to secure a payment (Gen. 38:17-26). Several synonymous Heb. words occur. The law of Moses was concerned with protection of the poor. If the pledge was an outer garment, it must be restored at sunset for a bed covering (Exod. 22:26-27; Deut. 24:12,13). The creditor was forbidden to enter his neighbor's house to take the pledge (Deut. 24:10,11). A handmill or its upper millstone might not be taken (Deut. 24:6), nor a widow's clothing (Deut. 24:17,18). Abuses of the pledge are censured (Job 22:6; 24:3,9; Amos 2:8; Hab. 2:6 ASV, RSV; "thick clay" in KJV mistranslates the Heb.) A wager is meant in II Kings 18:23 ASV margin, RSV; (Isa. 36:8). He who goes surety for strangers ought himself to be taken in pledge (Prov. 20:16; 27:13). The pledge David was to take from his brothers in exchange for cheeses may be a prearranged token (RSV) of their welfare (I Sam. 17:18). The pledge (ASV, RSV) in I Timothy 5:12 (KJV, ASV margin, faith) is the marriage troth (Greek *pístis, faith*).

PLEIADES (See Astronomy)

PLINY (plĭn'ē), Caius Plinius Caecilius Secundus, called "the Younger," to distinguish him from his learned uncle, lived from A.D. 61 to about A.D. 114. Pliny spent his youth under the guardianship of the distinguished soldier, Verginius Rufus, and was strongly influenced in all matters of literature and scholarship by his scientist uncle. Pliny passed through the ordered stages of the standard public career of a Roman aristocrat of the early Empire, survived Domitian, and as *consul suffectus* in A.D. 100, pronounced the customary oration of thanks to Trajan, later publishing the speech as the *Panegyricus,* a surviving work of no great merit. Pliny had a reputation as a lawyer, but his claim to fame in the modern world is his collection of ten volumes of literary letters. The epistles, exquisitely written, cover all manner of subjects, from the eruption of Vesuvius to the famous description of the Christian Church in Bithynia, a province which Pliny governed in A.D. 112, just before his death. Trajan's replies to his requests for instruction survive, and are important evidence for the official attitude towards the Christians (Ep. 10:96,97; Ramsay *The Church in the Roman Empire,* Ch. X).

E.M.B.

PLOWMAN (See Occupations & Professions)

PLOW, PLOUGH, a farming tool used to break up the ground for sowing. An ancient plow, as Heb. *harash* indicates, scratched the surface, but did not turn over the soil. It consisted of a forked stick, the trunk hitched to the animals which drew it, the branch braced and terminating in the share,

The typical forked-stick Palestinian plow. KC

which was at first the sharpened end of the branch, later a metal point. It was ordinarily drawn by a yoke of oxen (Job 1:14; Amos 6:12). Plowing with an ox and an ass yoked together was forbidden (Deut. 22:10), but this prohibition is not observed today. A man guided the plow with his left hand, goading the oxen and from time to time cleaning the share with the goad in his right, keeping his eyes front in order to make the furrow straight (Luke 9:62). Plowing done, the farmer sowed (Isa. 28:24-26 RSV). He who does not plow in autumn will have no harvest (Prov. 20:4 RSV). ASV, RSV have "lamp" for KJV, ASV margin "plowing" (Prov. 21:4). Amos 9:13 foretells a time when the soil will be so fertile that there need be no fallow interval between harvest and the next plowing. Then foreigners will plow for Israel (Isa. 61:5). Plowing indicates destruction (Jer. 26:18; Mic. 3:12). Hosea 10:11-13 contrasts plowing for righteous and for evil ends (see Job 4:8; Ps. 129: 3). Servants plowed (Luke 17:7). The plowman should plow in hope of a share of the crop (I Cor. 9:10). Elisha plowing with 12 yoke of oxen indicates his ability and the magnitude of his farming operations (I Kings 19:19). Samson calls the Philistines' badgering his betrothed to tell his riddle, "plowing with his heifer" (Judg. 14:18).

PLOWSHARE (plou'shâr, *the blade of a plow*), to beat swords into plowshares was symbolic of an age of peace (Isa. 2:4; Mic. 4:3); to beat plowshares into swords portended coming war (Joel 3:10).

PLUMB LINE (plŭm lĭn), a cord with a stone or metal weight, the plummet, tied to one end; used in testing whether a wall is perpendicular. Plumb line and plummet are used figuratively of God's action in testing the uprightness of His people (Amos 7:7-9; II Kings 21:13; Isa. 28:17).

POCHERETH (pŏk'ē-rĕth, pō'kĕ), a servant of Solomon whose descendants returned from exile with Zerubbabel (Ezra 2:57; Neh. 7:59).

POET (pō'ĕt, Gr. *poietés, a maker*). In Acts 17:28 Paul quotes from *Phaenomena,* 5, by the Greek poet Aratus (c. 270 B.C.) of Soli in Cilicia. A similar phrase occurs in the *Hymn to Zeus,* by the Stoic philosopher Cleanthes (300-220 B.C.), who taught at Athens. I Corinthians 15:32 may contain a quotation from Menander; Titus 1:12, from Epimenides. The poetic quality of many OT and NT passages entitles their authors to be called poets.

POETRY (pō'ĕt-rē). We recognize as poetry literature which has regular, rhythmically-patterned form and imaginatively concrete, emotionally charged substance. If the substance is lacking to the form, we call it verse; if the form is lacking to the substance, we call it poetic prose. All these terms are elastic: there is a wide range between what is readily recognized as poetry and what is obviously prose. The Greek conception of poetic form was so different from the Heb., and both from ours, that we must admit wide variation in our judgments as to what is poetry in the OT. Even in the Greek NT the influence of Hebrew poetry is so great, and the evidence for Greek poetic form so meager, that no hard and fast limits can be set to what is and what is not poetry. Former centuries had a feeling that to recognize a literary form such as poetry in any portion of Scripture was not consistent with due respect for its character as divine revelation. As Biblical criticism developed, there was a tendency to go to the other extreme, and to regard the Bible as "mere" literature. Yet there has been a growing recognition that for God and His patriarchs, prophets, and apostles to speak in poetic language, even in poetic form, does not derogate from the authority of the Bible as the Word of God. The growth of this feeling is illustrated by the fact that while the KJV is all in prose, the ASV prints a number of passages as poetry, and the RSV so prints a great many more. The Greek word poet means *maker, creator*: that God the Creator should be a poet is not surprising. Perhaps the wonder is, that more of the Bible is not in poetic form! In the NT we must remember that most of its human authors were Jews, to whom Greek was a second language. Luke the Gentile has more poetry than any other. Few men write poetry in any but their native language.

Poetry in the Bible has not in the past been so widely recognized because attention has been focused on the revelation of divine truth and its formulation in doctrine; the form of Heb. poetry is so different from ours that it is not easily recognized as such; through translation, the form has been lost. Secular poetry was not highly esteemed among the Hebrews (Isa. 5:12). That sacred poetry sometimes shared this ill repute may be inferred from Amos 6:5, though Amos may have referred only to David's musical compositions. Certainly the Psalms of David and of others were highly esteemed. Poetic prose has many examples (e.g., Gen. 1-3; Matt. 25:31-46; I Cor. 13). Hebrew poetry is marked by a distinctive vocabulary and syntax: some words and constructions occur only in poetry. Hebrew rhythm is irregular as compared with ours or the Greek. Greek rhythm is based on vowel length; ours on accent. Hebrew rhythm is based on the accented or tone syllables, and thus in a degree partakes of the characteristics of both, for tone implies length as well as stress. Since the vowel signs and the accented system in Hebrew are medieval and not ancient, we cannot be sure exactly what Hebrew poetry sounded like in OT times. A half-line usually has 2, 3 or 4 accents, a whole line 4 to 8. The lines are sometimes combined into stanzas or strophes (II Sam. 1:17-27). Rhyme is rare, but is believed to be present in a few cases (e.g., Gen. 4:23; 12:1-3; Judg. 16:23,24; Job 10:8-11; 16:12; Ps. 105; Isa. 27:3-5); alliteration (e.g. Ps. 6:8); assonance (e.g., Gen. 49:17; Exod. 14:14; Deut. 3:2). Refrains occur (e.g., Ps. 107; 136).

The most obvious feature of Hebrew poetic form is its parallelism. Many varieties have been distinguished, of which the three principal are:

synonymous, in which the meaning of both members is similar (e.g., Ps. 15:1; 24:1-3; I Sam. 18: 7); *antithetic,* in which the meanings of the members are opposed (Ps. 37:9; Prov. 10:1; 11:3); *synthetic,* in which noun corresponds to noun, verb to verb, and member to member, and each member adds something new (e.g., Ps. 19:8,9). Acrostic poems were favorites (e.g., Ps. 9,10; 34; 37; Prov. 31:10-31; Lam. 1-4). In Psalm 119 all the verses of each stanza of eight verses begin with the same letter of the Heb. alphabet. Mgr. Ronald Knox renders the acrostic psalms in English acrostics. Of the books always recognized as poetic, Psalms is a hymn book, containing songs suitable for public worship, and for private devotion; historical and other didactic poems. Proverbs is a collection of proverbs and other didactic poems. The Song of Solomon, at first glance appearing to be a secular love-cycle, has always been interpreted as an appropriate, rich and inspired expression of the love between the Messiah, Jesus Christ, and His Bride, the Church of OT and NT saints. Job is dramatic, though not technically a drama, and rises to ecstatic heights in God's address to Job (38-41). Didactic poetry and prose alternate in Ecclesiastes. Of the prophetic books, most of Isaiah is poetry; Jeremiah, except the historical sections; most of the minor prophets, except Haggai and Malachi. Of Jonah, only his prayer (2:2-9), and of Zechariah only 9:1-11:3,17; 13:7-9 are printed as poetry in RSV. Lamentations is poetry, 1-4 being acrostic, while in chapter 5 the singer's emotion may have become too intense to be confined in this artificial form. In Daniel there are poetic sections: 2:20-23, a psalm of praise; 4:3, praise; 4:34b,35, Nebuchadnezzar's praise of God; oddly, 6:26,27, Darius' decree; 7: 9,10,13,14, 23-27, apocalyptic. In Ezekiel, prose alternates with poetry.

Short poems (so printed in RSV) are embedded in the historical books, as follows: Adam to Eve (Gen. 2:23); God to the serpent, Adam and Eve (Gen. 3:14-19); Lamech to his wives (Gen. 4:23, 24); Noah about his sons (9:25-27); Melchizedek's blessing (14:19,20); God to Rebekah (25: 23); Isaac blesses Jacob (27:27-29); and Esau (27:39,40); Jacob blesses Joseph (48:15,16); and prophesies concerning his sons (49:2-27); the victory song of Moses (Exod. 15:1-18,21); the priestly blessing (Num. 6:24-26); a quotation from the Book of the Wars of the Lord (21:14,15); the song of the well (21:17,18); a ballad (21:27-30); Balaam's prophecies (23:7-10,18-24; 24:3-9,15-24); Moses' song (Deut. 32:1-43); and blessing of the people (33:2-29); the curse on a future rebuilder of Jericho (Josh. 6:26b); a quotation from the Book of Jasher (Josh. 10:12b,13a); the song of Deborah and Barak (Judg. 5); Samson's riddle, solution, and his answer (Judg. 14:14,18); his victory song (15:16); Hannah's song (I Sam. 2:1-10); a poem by Samuel (15:22,23); a women's song (18:7); David's lament over Jonathan (II Sam. 1:19-27); over Abner (3:33,34); his psalm (Ps. 18:2-50; 22:5-51); his last words (23:1-6); a quatrain by Solomon (I Kings 8:12,13); a popular song (12:16 = II Chron. 10:16); a prophetic poem by Isaiah (II Kings 19:21-28); a soldiers' song (I Chron. 12:18); a refrain (II Chron. 5: 13; 7:3b "for he is good, for his steadfast love endures for ever"); a snatch of song by Solomon (6:1b,2,41,42). The English reader and also the casual student of Hebrew will do well to content himself with appreciating the beauty of the poetic imagery in which so much of the OT is dressed, without trying to analyze the poetic form, for such analysis is a doubtful and uncertain work for experts, and has as little relation to appreciation and interpretation of the meaning, as botany has for the enjoyment of flowers. It is the thought within the form which edifies.

In the NT, easily recognizable poems are all in the Gospel according to Luke: the Magnificat of Mary (1:46b-55), adapted from Hannah's song (I Sam. 2:1-10); the prophecy of Zacharias (1: 68-79); the angels' Gloria in Excelsis (2:14); and the Nunc Dimittis of Simeon (2:29-32). All these are echoes of Hebrew poetry, sung by Hebrews. Snatches of Christian hymns are thought to be found in the epistles (Eph. 5:14; I Tim. 1:17; 3: 16; 6:16; II Tim. 4:18). Paul rises to heights of poetic eloquence (e.g., Rom. 8; 11:33-12:2; I Cor. 13; 15:25-57). James' letter is lyrical. The language of Jesus is poetic in the highest degree. The NT contains many quotations of OT poetry. But it is the elevated thought of the NT as of the OT and not the technical form, which gives us the feeling of poetry. Thus Bible language has lent itself admirably to the use of hymn writers in many languages, and to their native poetic forms. E.R.

POETS, PAGAN, QUOTATIONS FROM. New Testament quotations from pagan poets are confined to the writings and speeches of Paul. 1. Acts 17:28. Both Cleanthes (*q.v.*) and Aratus of Soli use the words quoted in the Areopagus address. They occur in Cleanthes' *Hymn to Zeus* and in Aratus' *Phaenomena*, a poem on astronomy. It is impossible to say who used the words first. It is possible that both writers were quoting Epimenides, the half-legendary Cretan poet and prophet of 500 B.C. (See E. M. Blaiklock, *Acts of the Apostles*, Tyndale Commentaries, p. 146). 2. Titus 1:12. "Liars, evil beasts, slow bellies" is a quotation from Epimenides, according to Clement of Alexandria. 3. Acts 17:27. "Feel after" may be an echo of *Odyssey* 9:416. The verb is used of the groping of the blinded Cyclops. 4. Acts 21:39. Paul's phrase "A citizen of no mean city" is an echo of a line of Euripides (*Ion* 8) applied to Athens. The Tarsians were probably in the habit of appropriating the quotation. 5. I Corinthians 15:33. "Evil communications corrupt good manners." The line is an iambic senarius from the poet of the New Comedy, Menander (342-291 B.C.). 6. In the Greek text, Hebrews 12:13 contains a hexameter, "every good and perfect gift," and Acts 23:5 an iambic senarius, "thou shalt not speak evil of the ruler of the people," which may indicate an unknown poetic source, or may be metrical accidents (e.g. in KJV: "Husbands love your wives, and be not bitter against them"; "Her ways are ways of pleasantness, and all her paths are peace"). E.M.B.

POISON (poi'z'n, Heb. *hēmâh, rō'sh*, Gr. *thymós, iós*), the venom of reptiles (Deut. 32:24,33; Job 20:16; Ps. 58:4; 140:3 = Rom. 3:13). James 3:8 may reflect a belief that the tongue conveyed the poison. Job 6:4 refers to poisoned arrows. Vegetable poisons also were known (Hos. 10:4 hemlock, RSV poisonous weeds; II Kings 4:39 wild gourds). The "deadly thing" of Mark 16:18 was a poisoned drink.

POLE (pōl, Heb. *nēs*), the standard (ASV) on which the brazen serpent was displayed that the people might look and live (Num. 21:8,9).

POLITARCH (pŏl'ĭ-tärk, Gr. *politárches*). The Acts of the Apostles twice refers to the city magistrates of Thessalonica as "politarchs" (Acts 17: 6 and 8). Since the term was unknown officially, it was once set down as a mistake of Luke. Sixteen epigraphical examples now exist in modern

Salonica, and one is located in the British Museum on a stone which once formed part of an archway. It was evidently a Macedonian term. It was Luke's general practice to use the term in commonest educated use. Hence he called the officials of Philippi "praetors," and an inscription has similarly established the fact that this was a courtesy title given to the magistrates of a Roman Colony.

POLL (pōl), as noun, Heb. *gulgōleth, skull, head*, a *unit for counting persons* (Num. 1:2-22 RSV, "head by head"; 3:47 RSV, "apiece"; I Chron. 23: 3,24 RSV omits poll). *Poll* as verb, Heb. *gāzaz, shear* (Mic. 1:16 ASV, RSV, "cut off hair") as sign of mourning; *gālah* (II Sam. 14:26 ASV, RSV, "cut the hair") *kāsam* (Ezek. 44:20 ASV, "cut off," RSV, "trim the hair").

POLLUTION (pŏ-lū'shŭn, Heb. *gā'al*, Gr. *alisgema*), may be from menstruation (Ezek. 22:10 ASV, RSV impurity); from food sacrificed to idols (Acts 15:20,29); from the evil in the world (II Pet. 2:20 ASV, RSV defilements). Imperfect offerings, brought with a wrong motive were polluted (Mal. 1:7-9). An altar was to be of unhewn stone: to cut was to pollute it (Exod. 20:25 RSV profane). Several Heb. and Greek words translated "pollute" refer to ceremonial or moral defilement, profanation, and uncleanness.

POLLUX (pŏl'ŭks, Gr. *Dióscouroi*), with Castor (Acts 28:11 KJV), one of the Dioscuri or Twin Brothers (ASV, RSV), sons of Zeus and patrons of sailors.

POLYGAMY (See Marriage)

POMEGRANATE (See Plants)

POMMEL (pŭm"l, Heb. *gullâh, basin, bowl*, II Chron. 4:12,13; I Kings 7:41,42), the bowl- or globe-shaped part of the capitals of the temple pillars.

PONTIUS PILATE (See Pilate)

PONTUS (pŏn'tŭs, Gr. *Póntos, sea*), a large province of northern Asia Minor which lay along the Black Sea (Pontus Euxinius). All the references to Pontus in the NT indicate that there were many Jews in the province. Jews from Pontus were in Jerusalem at the first Pentecost (Acts 2:9). Luke mentions in Acts 18:2 that a certain Christian Jew named Aquila was born in Pontus. So far as we know, Pontus and the other northern provinces were not evangelized by Paul. The Holy Spirit did not permit him to preach in Bithynia (Acts 16: 7). However, the Apostle Peter addresses his first letter to "the strangers (Jewish Christians) scattered throughout Pontus, etc." lending credence to the tradition that Peter preached in N Asia Minor rather than in Rome after Pentecost. In secular history, Pontus is noted for the dynasty of kings headed by the great Mithridates which ruled from 337 to 63 B.C.

POOL, a pocket of water, natural or artificial. Heb. *'ăgham, a marshy, reedy pond*, refers to natural depressions; by the Nile (Exod. 7:19; 8:5); in the wilderness (Ps. 107:35; 114:8 ASV, RSV); desolated Babylon (Isa. 14:23); the restored wilderness (Isa. 35:7; 41:18); dried up in judgment (Isa. 42: 15); for the sluices and ponds of Isaiah 19:10, ASV, RSV adopt entirely different readings of the text. Heb. *berēkhâh, pool*, from root "bless" refers to an artificial pool to conserve water for irrigation or drinking. Large ones were made by damming streams. Smaller ones were rectangular, wider than deep, to collect rain from the roofs or from the surface of the ground: similar to cylindrical pits or cisterns which served the same purpose. Water from springs was collected in masonry pools. All these were indeed blessings in a dry land. We read of the pool of Gibeon (II Sam. 2:13); of Hebron (4:12); of Samaria (I Kings 22:38); of Heshbon (S. of Sol. 7:4); of Shelah or Siloah (Neh. 3:15); the upper pool (II Kings 18:17; Isa. 7:3; 36:2); the pool Hezekiah made (II Kings 20:20); the lower pool (Isa. 22:9); the old pool (Isa. 22:11); the king's pool (Neh. 2:14); the pool "that was made" (Neh. 3:16, RSV, the artificial pool). Solomon made pools to water his forest nursery (Eccl. 2:6). Psalm 84:6 speaks of the rain filling pools (ASV has "blessings" here). Nineveh was of old like a pool (Nah. 2:8 KJV, ASV) or, being destroyed, like a pool whose waters have run out (RSV). Greek *kolymbéthra, pool, place for diving, swimming-bath*; the pool of Bethesda (John 5:2,4,7); of Siloam (John 9:7,11).

POOR (Heb. *'evyôn, dal, 'ānî, rûsh,* Gr. *ptochós*). God's love and care for the poor are central to His providence (Ps. 9:18; 12:5; Eccl. 5:8, etc.). He enjoins like consideration on us (Exod. 22:23, etc.). The Mosaic law has specific provisions for the benefit of the poor (Exod. 22:25-27; 23:11; Lev. 19:9,10,13,15; 25:6,25-30,39-42,47-54; Deut. 14:28,29; 15:12,13; 16:11-14; 24:10-15,17-22; 26:12,13; Ruth 2:1-7; Neh. 8:10). Israel as a nation was born out of deep poverty (Exod. 1:8-14; 2:7-10), and was never allowed to forget it (e.g., I Kings 8:50-53). If Israel met the conditions of God's covenant, there would be no poor among them, but God knew this would never be realized (Deut. 15:4-11). Wilful neglect leading to poverty is not condoned (Prov. 13:4-18, etc.). But national disasters brought it about that the poor became almost synonymous with the pious (e.g., Ps. 68:10; Isa. 41:17). Even in the early nomadic and later agricultural economy there were slaves and poor freemen; much more in the urban and commercial economy of the monarchy. The wrongs of the poor concern the prophets (e.g., Isa. 1:23; 10:1,2; Ezek. 34; Amos 2:6; 5:7; 8:6; Mic. 2:1,2; Hab. 3:14; Mal. 3:5).

At the outset of His ministry, Jesus, taking for His text Isaiah 61:1,2, presents as His first aim, "to preach the gospel to the poor." That physical poverty is meant is shown by the contrasts in Luke 6:20-26. Matthew 5:3 speaks of spiritual poverty. Jesus moved among the poor and humble. He associated Himself with them in His manner of living, His freedom from the encumbering cares of property (Matt. 8:20). He understood and appreciated the sacrificial giving of a poor widow (Mark 12:41-44). He recognized the continuing obligation toward the poor, as well as appreciating a unique expression of love toward Himself (Mark 14:7). The early church moves amidst the poor, who are not too poor to be concerned for one another's welfare (II Cor. 8:2-5,9-15), drawing inspiration from Christ's leaving heavenly riches for earthly poverty. The origin of the diaconate is linked with a special need (Acts 6:1-6). Those with property contributed to the common fund (Acts 2:45; 4:32-37). The Jerusalem Council asked Paul and Barnabas to remember the poor (Gal. 2:10). James has some sharp words about the relations of rich and poor (James 1:9-11; 2:1-13; 5:1-6).

POPLAR (See Plants)

PORATHA (pō-rā'tha, pŏr'a-tha), one of the sons of Haman the Agagite. He died with his brothers (Esth. 9:8).

PORCH (Heb. *'êlām, 'ūlām, porch*), in Solomon's temple (I Kings 6:3, etc.); in Solomon's palace (I Kings 7:6ff); in Ezekiel's new temple (Ezek. 40:7ff). RSV has vestibule. Heb. *misderôn, porch,*

colonnade (Judg. 3:23 RSV vestibule), before an upper room. Gr. *proaúlion, place before a court, vestibule* (Mark 14:68 RSV gateway, margin, ASV margin, forecourt). Gr. *pylón, gateway* (Matt. 26:71). Greek *stoá, roofed colonnade* (John 5:2), five porches at the pool of Bethesda; John 10:23; Acts 3:11; 5:12, all ASV margin, RSV portico). In every case an area with a roof supported by columns appears to be meant.

PORCIUS (See Festus)

PORTER (See Occupations & Professions)

PORTION (pôr'shŭn), a part, that is, less than the whole of anything; a share (Num. 31:30,47; as of food served to one person (Neh. 8:10,12; Dan. 1:5-16; 11:26; Jer. 51:33,34, see ASV, RSV; Deut. 18:8); of property acquired by gift (I Sam. 1:4,5) or by inheritance (Gen. 31:14; Josh. 17:14); a plot of ground (II Kings 9:10,36,37, RSV territory); destiny (Ps. 142:5; Job 20:29; 31:2; Lam. 3:24). Several Heb. and Gr. words are translated "portion," sometimes otherwise in ASV, RSV, and the shades of meaning are determined by the context. The most significant meaning appears in passages like Psalm 119:57, where one's relation to God and eternal wellbeing are involved.

POST (pōst, Heb. *mezûzâh, doorpost; rûts, to run; 'ayil, strength*). The first word represented the parts to the doorway of a building (I Kings 6:33). The last word is a post also, but has a larger use than door-posts. It was anything strong (Ezek. 40:14, 16). One of the most common uses of the word post is its reference to anyone who conveyed a message speedily. These were very early means of communication (Job 9:25). The first went by foot and later by horses. Royal messages were conveyed in this way (II Chron. 30:6,10).

POT, the translation of more than a dozen Hebrew and Greek words. Most of them referred to utensils for holding liquids, and solid substances such as grain and ashes. The Hebrew word *sir* was the most common pot used in cooking (II Kings 4:38; Jer. 1:13). It was also the vessel that held ashes (Exod. 27:3). Some of these vessels were made of metal and others of clay, and there were a great variety of sizes and shapes. Their chief NT use was for water or wine (John 2:6; Mark 7:4).

POTENTATE (pō'těn-tāt, Gr. *dynástes, mighty one*), a person with great power and authority (I Tim. 6:15). The Greek word is used of men in Luke 1:52 (KJV "the mighty") and Acts 8:27 (KJV "of great authority").

POTIPHAR (pŏt'ĭ-fêr, Heb. *pôtîphar, whom Re has given*), one of the pharaoh's officers mentioned in Genesis in connection with Joseph's sojourn in that land. He purchased Joseph from the Midianites, and made him head overseer over his house. When Joseph was falsely accused by the wife of Potiphar, he cast Joseph into prison (Gen. 39:1-20).

POTIPHERAH (pō-tĭf'êr-à, Heb. *pôtîphera', the one given by the sun-god*), the Egyptian priest of On whose daughter, Asenath, was given to Joseph for a wife (Gen. 41:45,50; 46:20).

POTSHERD (pŏt'shûrd, Heb. *heres*), a piece of earthenware. Job used a potsherd to scrape his body in his affliction (Job 2:8). Potsherds are referred to in other places in the Bible (Ps. 22:15; Prov. 26:23). There are many inscribed potsherds known as "ostraca" that furnish valuable information for the archaeologist.

The potter's shop. This Palestinian potter is using a foot-powered wheel, of the type used in Bible times. © MPS

POTTAGE (pŏt'ĭj, Heb. *nāzîdh, boiled*), a kind of thick broth made with vegetables and meat or suet. Jacob bought Esau's birthright for a mess of pottage (Gen. 25:29,30,34. See also II Kings 4:38-39).

POTTER (See Occupations & Professions)

POTTER'S FIELD (pŏt'êrz fēld, Gr. *Akeldamá*), the piece of ground which the priests bought with the money Judas received when he betrayed our Lord to be crucified (Matt. 27:7). It was used by the Jews as a burial plot in which to bury strangers. Judas is mentioned as the purchaser in Acts 1:18, but this is probably an idiomatic way of referring to a thing said to be done by the person whose action occasioned its transaction. This field is referred to in Acts 1:19 as "Aceldama" meaning "the field of blood." Alluding to the purchase of this field, Matthew refers to this transaction as fulfilling a prophecy spoken by "Jeremy the Prophet" (Matt. 27:9), though just what Matthew referred to here is not clear.

POTTER'S GATE, a gate in the wall of Jerusalem which is thought to be referred to by Jeremiah (Jer. 19:2). It may be the same gate that leads to the Valley of Hinnom or the Dung Gate.

POTTERY. Pottery making is one of the oldest crafts in Bible lands. James L. Kelso and J. Palin Thorley have termed pottery "the first synthetic to be discovered by mankind . . . an artificial stone produced by firing clay shapes to a temperature sufficiently high to change the physical and chemical properties of the original clay into a new substance with many of the characteristics of stone" ("Palestinian Pottery in Bible Times," BA, VIII (1945), 82). References, both literal and figurative, to the potter and his products occur throughout the Scriptures.

Pottery Production in Palestine. Let us follow Jeremiah down to the potter's house (Jer. 18:1-6). This "factory" was in the Valley of Hinnom near the Potsherd Gate (Jer. 19:2 RSV) and near the tower of the furnaces or pottery kilns (Neh. 3:11; 12:38). In addition to his workshop the potter (Heb. *yôtsēr*) needed a field (Matt. 27:7) for weathering the dry native clay-dust (*'āphār*) or wet stream-bank clay (*tît,* Nah. 3:14) and for mixing it with water and treading it by foot into potter's clay (*hōmer*), as in Isaiah 41:25. For cooking vessels, sand or crushed stone was added to temper the clay. In his house the potter kneaded the clay for several hours to remove all air bubbles. He could either build up a large vessel free-hand, using long sausage-like rolls of clay; or he could "throw" a ball of plastic clay on the center of a pivoted disc or dual stone wheel (*'obnāyim*) spun counter-clockwise by his hand or by his apprentice. By thrusting his forearm into the mass of wet clay he hollowed out the interior. The centrifugal force imparted to the spinning lump enabled the potter in a matter of minutes to form a vessel with only light pressure from his fingers. In mass production he pinched off (*qātsar,* Job 33:6b) the completed juglet from the cone of clay spinning on the wheel. Impurities in the clay or insufficient treading could mar the vessel on the wheel. The potter easily remedied this by reshaping the clay into a ball and making a less elegant object out of the former discard (Jer. 18:3,4).

After drying to a leathery consistency the vessel was replaced on the wheel for "turning," cutting and paring off excess clay as on a lathe. To fill the pores and beautify the vessel the potter could coat the pot with "slip," clay of the consistency of cream, often with a mineral color added. Next, he might burnish or rub the surface with a smooth stone to produce a sheen; or he might paint on a design. Finally, the jar was "fired" by heating it, usually between 700°C and 1050°C in an open fire or in a kiln. Firing was the most difficult art for the apprentice to master, and this skill was probably passed on from father to son as a trade secret. Such potters' installations have been found in a cave at Lachish (c. 1500 B.C.), within the Essene community center at Qumran, and by the Nabataean city of Avdat (Eboda) in the Negev.

God, who formed (*yātsar*) Adam from the dust (*'āphār,* Gen. 2:7), is likened to our Potter who fashions us according to His will (Job 10:8,9; 33:6; Isa. 29:16; 45:9; 64:8; Lam. 4:2; Rom. 9:20-23; II Tim. 2:20,21). He will smite the wicked as one smashes a piece of pottery (Ps. 2:9; Jer. 19:10,11; Rev. 2:27).

Historical Development of Pottery Styles in Palestine. Ceramic vessels, like clothing and automobiles, have been changing in fashion down through the centuries of human existence. Recognizing this fact, the Egyptologist Flinders Petrie in 1890 catalogued the sequence of broken pottery according to the varying shapes and decorations at Tell el-Hesi in southwestern Palestine. He succeeded in assigning rough absolute dates to several of his pottery periods by identifying certain wares with wares previously discovered in datable Egyptian tombs. Today when an archaeologist uncovers no more precise evidence (e.g. inscriptions on clay tablets, monuments, or coins), he depends on dominant pottery styles from an occupation level of an ancient city to furnish the clue to the date. On the second day of excavation in 1953 the Wheaton Archaeological Expedition verified that Dothan was settled in Joseph's time (Gen. 37:17) by unearthing orange and black burnished juglets and a double-handled juglet, exactly similar to Hyksos Age juglets found in the 1930's at Megiddo.

NEOLITHIC AGE — ?-4000 B.C. Pottery — all handmade — began to appear around 4500 B.C. But scores of generations before the first pottery at Jericho, people who practiced irrigation and constructed massive city fortifications settled the town. The vessels were either exceedingly coarse or else made with much finer clay, usually with painted decorations, and well-fired.

CHALCOLITHIC AGE — 4000-3100 B.C. At the time copper came into use the peculiar pottery styles included: swinging butter churns; jars with small "cord-eye" handles; cups with a long, tapering, spike-like "cornet" base; and ossuaries for human bones, made of pottery in the shape of miniature houses.

EARLY BRONZE AGE — 3100-2100 B.C. In this millennium potters began to use the stone disc tournette or turntable, predecessor of the potter's wheel. Characteristic EB features are: flat bottoms, hole-mouth pots, spouts on jars, inward-projecting bowl rims, ledge handles on water jugs, and bands of parallel, wavy, or criss-cross lines painted over the jar's surface.

MIDDLE BRONZE AGE I — 2100-1900 B.C. A transition period in pottery styles, these centuries saw the coming of Abraham to Palestine and an irruption of semi-nomadic Amorites from Syria who destroyed many towns and depopulated much of Canaan.

MIDDLE BRONZE AGE II — 1900-1550/1480 B.C. The Hyksos, descendants of the Amorites and native Canaanites, dominated Palestine in this era. Hazor was their chief city. They were already entering Egypt as merchants or Egyptian slaves in the 19th century when Jacob came to Goshen. Later they ruled in Egypt, 1730-1570 B.C. In the 19th century the fast-spinning potter's wheel revolutionized the industry in the Near East. Virtually all Middle Bronze II pottery was wheel-made. Distinctively Hyksos were the pear-shaped juglets with "button" base, double- or triple-strand handles, chalk-filled pinprick designs, and highly burnished vessels with orange or black slip. Bowls and jars with ring or disc bases were introduced in Palestine, as well as dipper flasks and chalices. Hyksos cities in southern Palestine fell before the pursuing Egyptians about 1550 B.C., whereas cities in northern Palestine remained in Hyksos hands until the campaigns of Thutmose III (c. 1480 B.C.).

LATE BRONZE AGE — 1500-1230 B.C. With the Hyksos power broken, numerous petty kings ruled in Canaan. The native pottery declined in gracefulness and technique as the prosperity slumped. Thus imported vessels from Cyprus are all the more striking: milk bowls with wishbone handle, and "bilbils," jugs with a metallic ring when tapped. From 1400 to 1230 B.C. Mycenaean pottery imports were common: stirrup vases, squat pyxis jars, and large craters with horizontal loop handles. While the nomadic Israelites invaded Canaan about 1400 B.C., they continued using wooden bowls, goatskins, and cloth sacks (Lev. 11:32) and produced little pottery until they could conquer a town and discard tents for more permanent houses.

IRON AGE I — 1230-925 B.C. In the latter time of the Judges, Israel was more settled and iron came into common use. Typical pottery objects were the traveler's water canteen, many-handled wine craters, and lamps with a thick, disc-like base. The decorative features are the most distinctive: hand burnishing and gaudy, painted designs, even on rims and handles. After 1150 B.C. Philistine painted-ware, very similar to late Mycenaean pottery elsewhere, is outstanding with its designs of swans pluming themselves, dolphins, spirals, loops, and maltese crosses. In Israel the period ended when Pharaoh Shishak destroyed many towns on his Palestinian campaign.

IRON AGE II — 925-586 B.C. During the Divided Monarchy the cities of Israel prospered materially and their potters excelled. Most helpful for dating

Finished pottery styles of the Hyksos period in Palestine. From Garstang, **The Story of Jericho.** © JBG

a town to this period are the ring-burnished water decanters; wheel burnishing on banquet bowls; twisted, ridged handles on storage jars; black perfume juglets; and the beautiful red, highly-burnished Samaria ware. Archaeologists have unearthed Hebrew writings in ink on potsherds, such as the seventy-odd Samaria ostraca from the palace of Jeroboam II and the 21 Lachish letters dated to 589/8 B.C. From Isaiah's time onward in Judah belong many inscribed handles of jars for wine, olive oil, or grain. In some cases, as on those found at Gibeon, the name of the owner of a vineyard was inscribed. On others the letters *lmlk* ("belonging to the king") appear together with the name of one of four cities, probably where royal potteries were established to make jars of the correct capacity for the payment of taxes in produce (cf. I Chron. 4:23 RSV). Nebuchadnezzar's devastating invasion produced a cultural void in Palestine for 50 years.

IRON AGE III — 538-333 B.C. During this Persian period locally made storage jars had pointed bases rather than the earlier rounded style. The lip of the lamp evolved into an elongated spout. The most distinctive pottery in the sixth century was imported Greek black-figured ware, and in the fifth, Greek red-figured ware. Coins, which began to appear in Palestine in the fifth century, aid the archaeologist in dating.

HELLENISTIC AGE — 333-63 B.C. Alexander's conquest began the Hellenization of Palestine. The double potter's wheel, with a large foot-power wheel to turn the thrower's wheel (*Ecclesiasticus* 38:29,30), was a Greek improvement. The ubiquitous Rhodian wine-jar handles, each stamped with the name of the potter or of the annual magistrate in Rhodes, immediately classify a stratum of an ancient town as Hellenistic.

ROMAN AGE — 63 B.C.-A.D 325. Pompey's capture of Jerusalem in 63 B.C. brought Palestine under Roman domination. Significant pottery styles are the beautiful red-glazed (terra sigillata) bowls and plates, jugs and pots with horizontally-corrugated surfaces, and the exquisitely painted, extremely thin Nabataean pottery from about 50 B.C. to A.D. 150.

Identification of Biblical Terms for Pottery Objects. The Hebrew and Greek words, about which there is some degree of understanding, are classified under several main groups:

A. Bowls, basins, and cups. The "cups" of Biblical times were usually small bowls without handles. Flat dinner plates were unknown, shallow bowls serving as platters and dishes.

1. *Kôs, potérion,* "cup," a small individual drinking bowl for water (II Sam. 12:3; Ps. 23:5; Matt. 10:42) or for wine (Prov. 23:31; Jer. 35:5; Matt. 26:27). It may be symbolic of one's destiny, whether it be of salvation (Ps. 16:5; 116:13) or of judgment and suffering (Isa. 51:17,22; Jer. 49: 12; Matt. 20:22; 26:39; Rev. 14:10).

2. *Tselōhîth.* Only in II Kings 2:20, this vessel must be an open, shallow bowl to hold salt, for salt would cake up in a cruse.

3. *Tsallahath.* Similar to #2, this may be the well-known ring-burnished bowl of Iron II. It had no handles to hang it up; hence it was turned over to dry (II Kings 21:13); it could be used by a

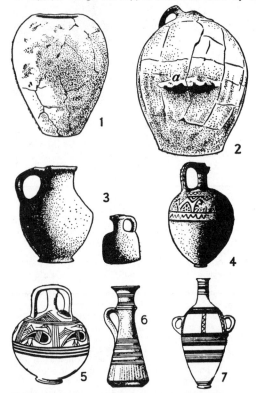

Pottery styles from Palestine. 1, 2. Large jars, from Jericho, Early Bronze Age. No. 2 has both loop and ledge handles, to facilitate balancing jar on the head. 3. Small jugs with handles, from Megiddo, Middle Bronze Age II. 4. Finely modeled egg-shaped jug, from Jericho, Hyksos style. 5. Decorated Philistine jug from Gezer. 6. Vase ornamented with rings, from Taanach, late Israelite. 7. Pitcher from Tell Zakariyeh (probably Azekah), Late Bronze Age. DV

sluggard both to cook and to contain his food. (Prov. 19:24; 26:15 — the word "bosom" should be "bowl").

4. *'Aggān* is a banquet bowl, ring- or spiral-burnished on the interior, with two or four handles, similar in size and purpose to our punch bowls (S. of Sol. 7:2). It is the word "cups" in Isaiah 22:24, able to be hung from the nail or peg in the tent-pole but large enough to help cause the peg to give way (see also *nēvel* on this verse).

5. *Sēphel* is probably an earlier style of #4, since the Arabic word for a large four-handled bowl in Palestinian villages today is *sifl.* Since it is called a "lordly bowl," Jael may have offered Sisera curded milk in one imported from Mycenae or Cyprus, decorated with painted designs and having pushed-up horizontal loop handles, holding from four to ten pints (Judg. 5:25). Or it may have been smaller and of the variety known as the Cypriote milk bowl with a wishbone handle, typical of LB II, and holding from one to three pints. Gideon used a similar bowl into which to squeeze the dew from his fleece (Judg. 6:38).

6. *Trúblion,* a large deep dish or bowl, either of metal or fine Roman sigillata pottery, from which all could take out food (Matt. 26:23).

7. *Niptér,* a basin or vessel for washing the hands and feet (John 13:5). In Iron Age II the Israelites had oval ceramic footbaths, about two feet long, with a raised footrest in the middle and drain-hole at the bottom of one side.

B. Cooking pots. Sherds of these common vessels are very numerous in excavated cities since every household needed several such pots. Because these vessels broke or cracked easily, they were often "despised," considered as the lowliest type of pottery; hence they seldom occur in tombs.

1. *Sir,* the wide-mouth, broad, round-bottom cooking pot, in Iron I handleless, in Iron II and later with two handles. The large diameter of its mouth permitted it to be used as a washpot (Ps. 60:8). It could be of great size, large enough to boil vegetables for all the sons of the prophets at Gilgal (II Kings 4:38). It was used by the Israelite slaves in Egypt (Exod. 16:3) and by the poor family whose only fuel was the thorn bush. (Eccl. 7:6; the word for "thorns" is *sîrîm,* thus a play on words).

2. *Pārûr* is a one- or two-handled cooking pot, deeper and with narrower mouth than the *sîr.* With one hand Gideon carried a *pārûr* containing broth, in the other hand carrying a basket containing bread and meat (Judg. 6:19). The Israelites boiled manna in a *pārûr* (Num. 11:8 ASV).

3. *Marhesheth* is a ceramic kettle used for deep-fat frying (Lev. 2:7; 7:9); the meal-offering cakes made in this vessel would be of the texture of our doughnuts.

4. *'Etsev,* the despised vessel of Jeremiah 22: 28, was probably a cooking pot, not an idol. Thus Coniah was a "big pot," about to be broken.

C. Jars. These include the large stationary jars for water (Arabic *zîr*), apparently not mentioned in the Bible, as well as the smaller jars for carrying water from well to house and for the storage of grain, of olive oil, and of wine.

1. *Kadh, hydría,* a jar 13 to 20 inches tall, with two handles, egg-shaped bottom, and a small mouth, used for carrying water on one's shoulder (I Kings 18:33; Eccl. 12:6; John 4:28). In Rebekah's day the flat-bottom, folded ledge-handle jar was in use in Palestine. For storing grain or meal the jar was often more cylindrical, with or without handles (I Kings 17:12ff — not a "barrel"!). The LB jars

used by Gideon's three hundred to conceal their torches must have had handles and must have been common and easily obtainable (Judg. 7:16ff).

2. *Nēvel* originally referred to a wineskin (I Sam. 1:24; 10:3; 25:18; II Sam. 16:1; Jer. 13:12); a prepared goatskin holds five to 12 gallons. In ceramics the *nēvel* is the storage jar used especially for wine, olive oil, and grain. It held approximately a *bath,* or about six gallons, and stood about two feet high. Since the *nēvel* had two handles, it was possible to hang it from a peg, but its weight might break the peg (Isa. 22:24). The men of Judah, recipients and containers of Jehovah's blessings as well as of His judgments, are likened to the *nēvel*: the breaking of a storage jar with its valued contents would be a household disaster (Isa. 30:14; Jer. 13:12; 48:12; Lam. 4:2).

A potter fashioning large storage jars. © MPS

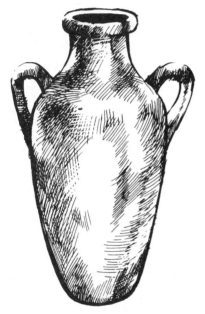

Large Palestinian water jar. UANT

3. *'Āsûk* in II Kings 4:2 is the typical Iron II jar for olive oil. It has three handles arranged at 90° around the mouth; the fourth quadrant has a funnel or spout probably "intended to hold the small dipper juglet used for taking oil from the jar. . . . Any drippings of oil from the juglet would go through the pierced spout back into the jar, or, in the unpierced variety, would be caught in the funnel" (J. W. Crowfoot, G. M. Crowfoot, Kathleen M. Kenyon, *The Objects from Samaria.* London: Palestine Exploration Fund, 1957, p. 193). Various sizes stand from six to 16 inches in height.

Decanters, flasks, and juglets.

1. *Baqbûq,* the handsome ring-burnished water decanter of Iron II. Its narrow neck causes a gurgling sound when the water is poured; hence its name. It came in graduated sizes from four to ten inches high. James L. Kelso says, "It is the most artistic and expensive member of the pitcher family. It was thus well-fitted to typify Jerusalem in Jeremiah's illustrated sermon (19:1-15). Its use was doubly significant since it had the narrowest neck of all pitchers and therefore could never be mended (19:11)" (*The Ceramic Vocabulary of the Old Testament,* New Haven: American Schools of Oriental Research, 1948, p. 17). Jeroboam I sent

to the prophet Ahijah a gift of honey in a *baqbûq* with other foods, a trifling gift from a king (I Kings 14:3).

2. *Tsappahath* is the two-handled traveler's flask or canteen so popular from LB until the middle of Iron II. "It was made of a lightly baked clay, which gives a certain porosity to the jar so that the air blowing on the moist surface of the canteen cools the water within. The mouth of the canteen is shaped both for drinking and for easy stoppering" (*Ibid.,* p. 30). See I Samuel 26:11ff; I Kings 19:6. In I Kings 17:12-16 this word is employed for the oil jar of the widow of Zarephath. While the porous clay of the canteen is ill-suited to contain oil, the widow was very poor and may have had to put her few vessels to unwonted uses; probably also she never had had a large supply of oil before this.

3. *Pak* is a small juglet for holding perfumed anointing oil (I Sam. 10:1; II Kings 9:1,3). In one or both of these cases the "vial" or "box" of KJV may have been a lovely Cypro-Phoenician juglet. Or it may have been the local blue-black hand-burnished juglet found in such quantities at Megiddo and Tell Beit Mirsim.

4. *Kerámion,* the one-handled ribbed water jug, eight to twelve inches high, by which Jesus' disciples were to identify the owner of the house with the upper room (Mark 14:13; Luke 22:10). Ordinarily only a woman would be seen carrying a jug of water into the city from the fountain.

E. Other vessels.

1. *Nēr,* the common pottery lamp burning olive oil. Basically the *nēr* in OT times was a small bowl or saucer; while the molded clay was still soft, the potter pinched in the rim at one section to hold the linen or flax wick (Isa. 42:3). Never more than a few inches in diameter, the lamp was suitable for carrying in the palm of the hand when walking (Ps. 119:105; Zeph. 1:12) or for placing in a niche in the wall of the house or cave-home. The Oriental feared darkness and left a lamp burning all night (Prov. 31:18); thus it was just as essential as the millstones for grinding grain (Jer. 25:10). The presence of a burning lamp with its light symbolized joy and peace (II Sam. 22:29); whereas the extinguishing of the lamp suggested utter gloom and desolation (Job 18:5,6; 21:17; Prov. 13:9; 20:20; 24:20). Since the ancient considered his life to be continued through his sons, his "light" was not put out if he had a son; thus the lamp also

The common slipper-type earthenware lamp of Bible times. BM

symbolized posterity (I Kings 11:36; 15:4; II Kings 8:19). In patriarchal times (MB I) the lamp sometimes had its rim pinched in four places. Some Israelite lamps had seven such pinched "wick-holders," undoubtedly reminiscent of the seven-branched golden candlestick or lampstand of the tabernacle and temple.

2. *Lampás* is also a hand-sized clay lamp but with considerable change in shape from the OT lamps. By the first century A.D. the pinched rim had given way to a nozzle for the wick. This type was carried by the ten virgins (Matt. 25:1-8), by the band led by Judas (John 18:3 Berkeley Version), and by the Christians congregating in an upper room in Troas (Acts 20:8). See LAMP.

3. *Lýchnos* is the lamp placed on a lampstand (*lychnía*) (Matt. 5:15; Luke 11:33-36).

4. *Menôrâh* usually refers to the golden lampstand in tabernacle and temple. But in II Kings 4:10 it probably refers to a pottery lamp of a different style from the *nēr*. Often discovered in Palestinian sites are "cup-and-saucer" lamps, a high cup in the center of a small bowl all made in one piece by the potter. Sometimes this style has been found in connection with shrines, serving a ritual purpose. Since the Shunammite couple considered Elisha a holy man of God, they chose a type of lamp appropriate for him.

5. *Tannûr, klíbanos,* refer chiefly to the common oven in every home, for baking flat bread (Lev. 2:4; 7:9a; Hos. 7:4-8). Like a hollow truncated cone, the *tannûr* was made of clay nearly an inch thick. The household oven varied from 1½ to 2½ feet in diameter, and often was plastered over with additional mud and potsherds on the outer surface. Placed over a depression in the courtyard floor, the oven was preheated by a smoky fire of grass, thorns, twigs, or stubble kindled inside it (Matt. 6:30; Mal. 4:1). The soot was then wiped off (Lam. 5:10) and the thin sheets of dough were slapped onto the concave inner surface of the oven and baked in a few seconds. A large cooking pot could be placed over the top opening, making the *tannûr* serve also as a stove (Lev. 11:35). When ten women could bake their pitifully small loaves in a single oven, then famine was stalking the land (Lev. 26:26).

6. *'Âh* is the small brazier for holding burning coals. King Jehoiakim's winter house may have had a metal brazier or a ceramic one (Jer. 36:22, 23).

7. *Mahăvath* must be the nearly flat disc-like baking tray or griddle mentioned in Leviticus 2:5; 6:14; 7:9; I Chronicles 23:29. Such pans, 12 to 14 inches in diameter, have holes punched or notched on the concave surface which is placed over the fire.

8. *Paropsís,* the side dish for relishes and other delicacies filled only by the extortion practiced by the scribes and Pharisees (Matt. 23:25,26, ASV).

J.R.

POUND (See Weights and Measures)

POWER (pou'êr, Heb. chiefly *hayil, kōah, 'ōz*). In the OT: of man (Gen. 31:29); military (I Chron. 20:1); official (Esth. 1:3); of Satan (Job 1:12); but chiefly of God (I Chron. 29:11; II Sam. 22:23; Isa. 40:29). In the NT: Gr. *dýnamis, power*; of men (Luke 1:17; Acts 3:12; I Cor. 4:19, 20); of God (Luke 1:35; 5:17; Rom. 1:16,20); as His Name (Matt. 26:64); of Christ (I Cor. 5: 4); of the Holy Spirit (Luke 4:14; Rom. 15:13, 19). Greek *exousía, authority*; of men (Acts 5:4; Rom. 9:21; 13:1-3; I Cor. 9:4-6; 11:10); of God the Father (Acts 1:7); of Christ (Matt. 9:6,8; 28: 18); of Satan (Acts 26:18). See ASV, RSV. Gr. words *ischýs* and *krátos* occur almost with the sense of *dýnamis.*

PRAETOR (prē'tôr). The word derives from the verb *praeire, to go before* or *to lead,* and designated originally the highest Roman magistrate. Hence the adjective *praetorius* in such expressions as *praetorium* for a provincial seat of government, and the *cohors praetoria* for the imperial guard. When the praetors of earlier days became known as consuls, the term *praetor* was applied to officials elected to administer justice. The usage may be traced back to 366 B.C. although there is some question whether a new office was created on or around that date, or whether the term represents a new division of functions. With Rome's acquisition of overseas provinces, there was an enlargement of praetorial activity, and the number of the officers increased to four in 227 B.C. to cover the administration of Sicily and Sardinia, and to six in 197 B.C. to cover Spain. Hence a resumption of military functions, earlier held by the consuls only, and a narrowing of the margin of superior authority between consul and praetor. The praetors played a major part as officers of justice in developing the corpus of Roman law. With the principate the office, though nominally in existence, declined in prestige, power and functions, until eventually it was an honorary sinecure. E.M.B.

PRAETORIAN GUARD (prē-tō'rĭ-ăn). The term "Praetorian Guard" does not actually occur in the Scriptures, but has been implied in the statements of Paul about the Praetorium and Caesar's household (Phil. 1:13 and 4:22), which have been viewed as the emperor's army garrison or bodyguard in Rome. Recently, however, scholars have discovered that "Caesar's house" refers not only to soldiers but to all those in government service, and this not confined to Rome but also in the provincial capitals as well. This gives the term a somewhat broader meaning and allows that Paul could have written the captivity letters while in prison in a city outside of Rome.

PRAETORIUM (prē-tō'rĭ-ŭm), also Pretorium, the Latin term for the Greek *praitórion* which among the Romans could refer to a number of things. Originally it meant the general's tent in the camp of an army station. Sometimes it referred to the military headquarters in Rome itself or in the provincial capitals. It also meant the staff of men in such an establishment or even the session of a planning council. In the Gospels (Matt. 27:27; Mark 15:16; John 18:28,33) it refers to the temporary palace or headquarters ("judgment hall") of the Roman governor or procurator while in Jerusalem, which was actually Herod's palace adjacent to the temple. Cf. Acts 23:35. It was the scene of the trial of Jesus before Pontius Pilate. No doubt the debated reference in Phil. 1:13 (cf. Phil. 4:22 "Caesar's household") means the headquarters of the emperor's bodyguard which modern research has shown could have been either in Rome or in some of the provincial capitals.

PRAISE (prāz), a broad term for words or deeds which exalt or honor men (Prov. 27:21), women (Prov. 31:30), heathen gods (Judg. 16:24) or God, especially in song (Exod. 15:11, RSV *glorious deeds*). Some of the Heb. and Greek words mean *thangsgiving, blessing, glory,* and are often so translated (II Chron. 7:3,6; Luke 1:64; John 9:24). Greek *areté, virtue,* occurs in I Peter 2:9, ASV *excellencies,* RSV *wonderful deeds.* We are to be the praise of God's glory (Eph. 1:6,12,14). The book of Psalms is filled with praise, increasing in intensity toward the end (Ps. 145-150). Psalms 113-118 are called the Hallel, the praises. Praise for redemption dominates the NT (Luke 2:13,14; Rev. 19:5-7).

PRAYER (Heb. *tephillâh,* Gr. *déesis, proseuché*). As an interesting aspect of comparative religion, prayer can be objectively, psychologically dissected, and historically studied; and unquestionably all of these approaches to it have a definite value. Our major interest, however, is with the concept and role of prayer in Biblical faith; prayer outside the revelational orbit will here be dealt with quite incidentally.

I. The Phenomenon of Prayer. Created in the image of God, man is incurably religious: "Atheists are made, not born." And because religion is universal and ineradicable, prayer is the same. Recognizing their dependence upon some higher order of reality, people everywhere seek a propitious relationship with that higher order no matter what their understanding of it may be — primitive or sophisticated, gross or spiritual, anthropomorphic or impersonal. People never outgrow their need for prayer any more than their need for air and food; prayer does not become anachronistic either culturally or chronologically. Living in a precarious world, surrounded by the vast and terrifying forces of nature, inescapably death-shadowed, people in their weakness, anguish, and need pray spontaneously. Especially in times of crisis is the instinctive nature of prayer disclosed (cf. Ps. 107:23-28).

While comparative religion documents the universality of prayer, the pages of the Bible also supply abundant evidence of this fact. Thus the priests of Baal cried unto their gods (I Kings 18:26-29); thus, too, among the learned idolators of Athens Paul found altars at every turn (Acts 17:15-23), mute witnesses of man's groping search for supernatural help and mercy. Poignant indeed is David's cry in Psalm 65:2.

Perhaps this universal phenomenon merely attests a universal illusion; perhaps there is no supernatural order, and hence human beings lift their hands to an empty sky. But the opposite hypothesis is equally as valid, more so indeed: prayer, we may boldly assert, attests the reality of a supernatural order upon which man ultimately depends and with which he was created to fellowship.

Yet though prayer is a universal phenomenon, it becomes unique and commanding in Biblical faith. So Friedrich Heiler writes in his remarkable study of this universal phenomenon, "Christianity, including the prophetic religion of the Old Testament is 'the peculiar home of personal prayer,' as Soderblom remarks, or it is, as Bousset says, simply, 'the religion of prayer,' that is, the religion in which prayer is the focus of personal piety. To be a Christian means to be one who prays. 'Thou then art not a Christian that art not a praying person' — such is the judgment of Bunyan. Luther

remarks in his homely way: 'As a shoemaker makes a shoe, and a tailor makes a coat, so ought a Christian to pray. Prayer is the daily business of a Christian.' To be sure, prayer is the essential utterance of all the religions of the world; it is not an exclusively Christian but a universally human phenomenon. But the personal *life of prayer,* free and living intercourse with God, has its native abode in Christianity as it has nowhere else in the entire history of religion" (Friedrich Heiler, *Prayer,* New York: Oxford University Press, 1932, p. 119).

And Biblical prayer, let it be borne in mind, is here and now the focus of our concern.

II. The Philosophy of Prayer. Scripture nowhere offers any *apologia* for prayer: it simply assumes the necessity and effectiveness of man's communication with God, provided certain conditions are met (cf. Section V. below, "The Principles of Prayer"). It does not argue, therefore, whether prayer is compatible with a system of law. In fact, it does not teach a reign of law; it teaches the sovereignty and activity of the living God in whose hands nature is like pliable clay. Consequently, it teaches that in answer to prayer God may produce events which a system of law left to itself could not and would not produce. And why, we may ask, is this incredible? Human will and intelligence constantly produce events in nature which nature left to itself could not and would not produce. Thus once we assume the reality of the living God, answered prayer becomes credible even in terms of modifying the natural order, to say nothing of modifying the psychological order (Prov. 21:1).

But even if the reality of the living God is assumed, a Person who is dynamic Will rather than static Intelligence, a Person who can be described in terms of anthropomorphic realism, must we not admit that the very idea of prayer implies a Deity whose mind can be changed? If God is all-wise, all-powerful, and all-good, prayer is apparently superfluous and futile. In His omnipotence He knows our needs, just as in His goodness and omnipotence He will certainly supply them. Moreover, He has assuredly mapped out from all eternity the entire course of things. Then why pray? The Bible does not debate these issues which emerge, obviously, from the paradoxical relationship between human responsibility and divine sovereignty. It asserts both sides of this paradox and leaves the riddle for future unraveling. Steadfastly, however, it presupposes that the relationship between God and man is genuinely interpersonal, not the relationship between impersonal automata but the relationship between Thou and I, Parent and child, Friend and friend, Master and servant, King and subject, Creator and creature. Hence it makes God's knowledge, power and goodness the very ground of petition (Matt. 6:32; 7:7-11). Hence, moreover, it makes prayer the channel of human creativity and causality in cooperation with the divine ordaining and over-ruling. Things are brought to pass only as man prays, and without his prayer some things do not occur (I Tim. 2:1-4), although of course the prayer, together with its answer and all of its outworking is embraced in God's eternal counsel.

Loyal to the teaching of Scripture, so doughty a Calvinist as Charles Haddon Spurgeon could say, "Prayer is able to prevail with Heaven and bend omnipotence to its desire." And Soren Kierkegaard could write in his diary, "The Archimedean point outside the world is the little chamber where a true suppliant prays in all sincerity — where he lifts the world off its hinges" (cf. Heiler, *op. cit.*, p. 279). Nor must we ignore this fact: according to the Bible prayer goes unanswered unless certain conditions, which we shall shortly examine, are met. Nothing could show more plainly that prayer is the farthest removed from pious pretense; it is no matter of spiritual gymnastics possessing only a reflex value psychologically. Quite the reverse. Biblically considered, it is a force, a *vera causa*, the efficacy of which depends upon a proper interpersonal relationship: Let Heiler once again sum up the case for us: "Because the man of today, entangled in the prejudices of a rationalistic philosophy, struggles against the primitive realism of frank and free prayer, he is inclined to see the ideal and essence of prayer in a vague, devotional mood and in aesthetic contemplation. But the essence of prayer is revealed with unquestionable clearness to penetrating psychological study, and it may be put thus: *to pray means to speak to and have intercourse with God,* as suppliant with judge, servant with master, child with father, bride with bridegroom. The severely non-rational character of religion nowhere makes so overwhelming an impression as in prayer. For modern thought, dominated by Copernicus and Kant, prayer is as great a stone of stumbling as it was for the enlightened philosophy of the Greeks. But a compromise between unsophisticated piety and a rational worldview obliterates the essential features of prayer, and the most living manifestation of religion withers into a lifeless abstraction. There are only two possibilities: either decisively to affirm prayer 'in its entirely non-rational character and with all its difficulties,' as Menegoz says, or to surrender genuine prayer and substitute for it adoration and devotion which resemble prayer. Every attempt to mingle the two conceptions violates psychological veracity" (*op. cit.,* p. 362).

III. The Practice of Prayer. As a many-faceted phenomenon, prayer must not be reduced merely to supplication, as is sometimes done. The immense sweep of Biblical teaching with respect to this phenomenon can scarcely be compressed into the single and rather crass category of "getting things from God," to quote the title of a once popular book by Charles A. Blanchard. Prayer, essentially, is *communion,* a desire to enter into conscious and intimate relationship with the Thou who is our life (Ps. 63:1-8; Ps. 73:25-26; Luke 6:12; I John 1:3). And the astonishing corollary of this truth is that God hungers for man's fellowship (Rev. 3:20). Prayer is also *adoration,* the praise of God because of His greatness and goodness. The Book of Psalms is a collection of man's loving, awe-inspired praise as, contemplating his Creator and Saviour, he is lost in wonder and amazement at the purity, pity, and power of the perfect Person. Again, prayer is *thanksgiving,* the outpouring of gratitude to God because of His grace, mercy, and lovingkindness. Psalm 103 is a classic expression of the emotion aroused by unmerited blessing. The entire Psalter, indeed, is full of such hymns. Once more, prayer is *confession* as sinful man acknowledges his guilty disobedience. David's penitential candor in Psalm 51 voices the common experience of transgression followed by grief-stricken remorse before God. Inevitably this kind of prayer becomes petition as the offender beseeches cleansing. In the words of Heiler, "Petition for the forgiveness of sins occupies a central position in prophetic prayer, while in mysticism it belongs to the periphery of the devotional life. The devout person seeks to be delivered from the feeling of guilt which oppresses him, from the crushing sense of his nothingness and powerlessness, which prevents him from meeting life in confidence and hope. Nothing but divine grace, freely bestowed, can transform the bitter self-condemnation to firm self-confidence, the trembling fear to peace and trust" (*op. cit.,* p. 243). Prayer, still further, then, is *petition,* a plea for personal help. Under the pressure of need man begs God for some specific favor. The legitimacy of petition is guaranteed by the very prayer which our Lord taught us to pray, in which we ask not only for pardon but likewise for bread and deliverance (Matt. 6:9-15). Paul is following his Master when he directs his converts to ask quite literally for anything (Phil. 4:6). Prayer, yet again, is *intercession* which we may define as petition on behalf of one's neighbor, entreaty for his good, his beatitude. Consider Paul's burden for Israel (Rom. 9:1-2; 10:1) in which egocentric interests are completely obliterated. Prayer, finally, is *submission.* As man abandons his own desires, he surrenders his will to God's will. This is prayer at its highest level, the antithesis of primitive magic which thinks that the supernatural may be coerced, wheedled, shamed, or bribed into doing man's will (cf. Heiler, *op. cit.,* pp. 32-35). When this level is reached, the instrumental use of the supernatural has been transcended by a faith which commits life unreservedly to the divine love, wisdom and power. The supreme illustration of such surrender is of course our Lord Jesus Christ who after His Gethsemane-struggle could say, "Not my will, but thine be done" (Luke 22:42). So when a worshiper practices prayer, he may be engaging in adoration, communion, thanksgiving, confession, petition, intercession, and submission.

Regardless of what kind of prayer he may be practicing, however, the pivotal factor is his attitude. Posture, language, place or time — none of these trifles matter. In all such respects the greatest liberty is permitted if only a man's heart is *en rapport* with God. In the Bible, accordingly, people pray kneeling (I Kings 8:54; Ezra 9:5; Dan. 6:10; Acts 20:36), standing (Jer. 18:20), sitting (II Sam. 7:18) or even lying prostrate (Matt. 26:39). They pray sometimes with hands uplifted (I Kings 8:22; Ps. 28:2; 134:2; I Tim. 2:8). They pray silently (I Sam. 1:13); they pray aloud (Ezek. 11:13); they pray alone (Mark 1:35; Matt. 6:6); they pray together (Ps. 35:18; Matt. 18:19; Acts 4:31); they pray at fixed times (Ps. 55:17; Dan. 6:10) or at any time (Luke 18:1); they pray everywhere (I Tim. 2:8) — in bed (Ps. 63:6), in open field (Gen. 24:11,12), in temple (II Kings 19:14)), at the riverside (Acts 16:13), on the seashore (Acts 21:5), or battlefield (I Sam. 7:5); they pray spontaneously (Matt. 6:7), they pray liturgically (e.g. Ps. 120-126); they pray, as we have observed, quite literally for everything (Phil. 4:6; Gen. 24:12-14; I Tim. 2:1-4).

The intensity, freedom and effectiveness of Biblical prayer may best be seen in the lives of its greatest personalities. Consider, for instance, the prayers of Moses (Exod. 32:11-13,31,32; 33:12-18; Num. 11:11-15; 14:13-19); Abraham (Gen. 18:22-33); Jacob (Gen. 32:24-30); Elijah (James 5:17-18); David (Ps. 3, 32, etc.); Solomon (II Chron. 1:7-12; 6:14-42); Hezekiah (II Kings 19:14-19; cf. Isa. 37:14-20); Ezra (9:5-15); Jeremiah (17:13-18; Lam. 5); Paul (Eph. 1:15-22; 3:14-19, etc.). Though these instances are rather arbitrarily selected, they nevertheless verify Heiler's conclusions. In Biblical faith and practice (1) prayer is carried on apart from sacrifice; (2) prayer is a matter of continuous intercourse with God;

(3) prayer is not only a human work or achievement; it is inspired, elicited, and energized by the Spirit of God; (4) prayer is a gift of power to be conscientiously desired, developed, and disciplined; (5) prayer is not a quest for mundane happiness but rather for divine fellowship and eternal salvation; (6) prayer is vastly more than petition and persuasion, it is "adoring reverence, wonder, ecstasy, yearning, desire, surrender, love, confidence, trust, resolve, resignation, serenity"; (7) prayer is in spirit and in truth, release from all limitations of place; the believing heart becomes God's temple (John 4:24; I Cor. 6:19-20) (cf. Heiler, *op. cit.,* pp. 105-115).

IV. The Pattern of Prayer. In this area of spiritual experience as in every area of relationship with God, Jesus Christ has left an unsurpassed and perfect example (I Pet. 2:21). Prayer occupied a place of singular importance in His own life and teaching. In time of decision and crisis He gave Himself to prayer. Thus our Lord prayed when He was baptized (Luke 3:21-22); when He chose His twelve apostles (Luke 6:12-13); when He was transfigured (Luke 9:29); when He was engaging in sustained and exhausting service (Mark 1:35-39); when He called forth Lazarus from the grave (John 11:41-42); when He was burdened for Simon Peter (Luke 22:31-32); when He faced betrayal, execution, and divine abandonment (Mark 14:32-42); when He thought of His disciples and their future ministry (John 17); and when He died (Luke 23:46).

But our Lord also prayed in times of joy (Luke 10:21), even as He prayed gratefully when food was served (Luke 22:17; John 6:11). Prayer, indeed, was so evidently the habit of our Saviour's life that His example aroused within His followers a longing for the same power and blessing (Luke 11:1). Every kind of prayer may be found in the Gospel record — communion, adoration, thanksgiving, petition, intercession, and submission; yes, every kind but one — confession. With that exception it may be said that our Lord's model prayer (Matt. 6:8-15), together with His parables and discourses on this subject, sprang from His own experience with the Father (Matt. 6:1-7; 18:21-33; Mark 11:22-26; Luke 7:3-4; 11:5-13; 18:1-8; John 14:13-14; 15:1-7; 16:24-26).

Now in His state of exaltation our Saviour functions as a Priest whose all-absorbing task is intercession (Heb. 7:25).

Questions concerning the necessity and value of prayer evaporate in the light of this Example. Philosophical and psychological difficulties are transcended as we follow the divine Pattern.

V. The Principles of Prayer. Undeniably, however, some requests are denied: fervent pleas do go unanswered — if we may ignore the contention that "No" and "Not yet" and "In some strange disguise" are divine answers equally as valid as "Yes." It is not merely that some of God's devoted servants have seasons when prayer seems to be unavailing (Ps. 88:13-14; Lam. 3:44; Hab. 1:2, 13); there are likewise cases where a repeated petition is refused for reasons which may be humanly opaque (II Chron. 12:7-9). Yet granting that some cases of unanswered prayer are at present inexplicable (I Cor. 13:12), there are other cases where the divine refusal can be accounted for by the suppliant's failure to obey the principles which govern effective intercession. The God-man relationship, we have previously asserted, is not that of automata; it is genuinely interpersonal. Hence, as in any I-Thou fellowship, certain conditions

Albrecht Durer's famous representation of prayer, "Praying Hands."

must be met. Assuming, then, that filial bond established by an acceptance of Jesus Christ as Saviour (Matt. 5:1-2; 6:8; Rom. 8:14-17; Gal. 3:23; cf. John 8:44), the following principles appear to be regulative. 1. Prayer avails only as it is made in faith (Heb. 11:6; Matt. 17:20; Mark 11:23-24; James 1:6). 2. Prayer avails only as it is made in the Name of Jesus (John 14:13; 15:16). This is scarcely reducible to a verbal formula thoughtlessly attached to any petition. No doubt it implies a trustful acknowledgment of our Saviour's person and work; but, in addition, this principle bespeaks an identification of purpose, a request to which Christ can affix His *imprimatur* because it is in harmony with His own concerns. 3. Prayer avails only as it is made in keeping with the will of God (I John 5:14-15). Hence sinful egocentricity precludes effectiveness in supplication (James 4:2-3). 4. Prayer avails only as it is made under the direction and dynamic of the Holy Spirit (Jude 20). This is not simply because of our tepid hearts; it is also because of our darkened minds. We are ignorant of God's will, and this ignorance must be dispelled (Matt. 20:22; John 4:10; Rom. 8:26-27). 5. Prayer avails only as it is made by a suppliant who has confessed and renounced sin (Ps. 66:18; Prov. 28:9; Isa. 59:1-2). 6. Prayer avails only as it is made by a forgiving heart; our Lord repeatedly indicates that unforgiveness is a fatal hindrance to effective intercession (Matt. 6:12-15; 18:21-35; Mark 11:25-26; cf. James 5:14-16). 7. Prayer avails only as it is made in a context of harmonious relationships on the human level (Matt. 5:23-24; 18:19; I Pet. 3:1-7). 8. Prayer avails only as it is made with importunity (Luke 11:5-8; 18:1-8), for persistence evidences genuine care, compassion, and concern. 9. Prayer avails only as it is made with concentration and intensity (James 5:16). This is one reason why our Lord teaches the need for detachment (Matt. 6:6; cf. Mark 1:35). This, too, is why He advises fasting (Mark 9:29; cf. Acts 13:1-3).

VI. The Profit of Prayer. Under the pressure of emotional and physical suffering Job skeptically inquired, "What is the Almighty, that we should serve him? and what profit should we have, if we pray unto him?" (Job 21:15). But prayer, obviously, is of incalculable profit. From the standpoint of human responsibility, it is the major element in the outworking of God's redemptive program (I Tim. 2:1-4). Besides this, prayer is the source of vision, power, creativity, and blessing in personal experience. Consequently, because of its profit, we are enjoined to give this ministry unquestioned priority (Luke 18:1; Eph. 6:18; Phil. 4:6; I Tim. 2:1; I Thess. 5:17). Neglect of prayer or indolence in prayer is nothing short of sin (I Sam. 12:23), since it impedes the operation of God's grace in man's life. V.C.G.

PREACHER, PREACHING (See Occupations & Professions)

PREDESTINATION (See Election)

PRESBYTERY (prĕz′bĭ-têr-ē, Gr. *presbytérion*), the Christian elders who formally recognized Timothy's spiritual gift (I Tim. 4:14, RSV *the elders*). The same Greek word occurs in Luke 22:66 (KJV, ASV *the elders,* RSV *the assembly of the elders*) and Acts 22:5 (KJV, ASV *the estate of the elders,* RSV *council of elders*) for the organized body of Jewish elders in Jerusalem.

PRESIDENTS (prĕz′ĭ-dĕnts, Heb. *sārekhîn, chief*). Administrative officers whose duties are not clearly defined. Three were placed by Darius over the 120 satraps in his kingdom and Daniel was one of the three (Dan. 6:2-7).

PRESS (Gr. *apothlíbo, to crowd* and *óchlos, a crowd*), words used in Mark 2:4 and Luke 8:19 in the sense of crowd.

PRESS FAT (prĕs′făt, Heb. *yeqev, a trough*), the vessel used to collect the liquid from pressed grapes (Hag. 2:16).

PRESS (oil or wine), a rendering of several Hebrew and Greek words used to refer to a device used for extracting liquids from certain fruits from which wines and oils were made. Some of these were small handmills while others were made of two large stones. One turned on the other by horses or mules so that the fruit was crushed between them.

PRICK (Heb. *sēkh, a thorn,* Gr. *kéntron, a goad*), any slender-pointed thing, like a thorn (Num. 33:55). The Greek expression is used of the spiritual goads of conviction against which Saul kicked before his conversion (Acts 9:5; 26:14).

PRIEST, PRIESTHOOD. The English word "priest" is derived from the Greek *presbýteros,* which means *elder,* and suggests the priestly function of counsel. The NT word for "priest," *hiereús,* related to *hierós, holy,* indicates one who is consecrated to and engaged in holy matters.

The Hebrew *kōhēn, priest,* is of uncertain origin, but seems originally to have meant a "seer," as well as one who has to do with divine things. The derivation of the words does not give much light on the Biblical usage. For practical Bible study we may simply say that a priest is a minister of any religion, whether heathen (Gen. 41:45; Acts 14:13) or Biblical (Matt. 8:4; I Pet. 2:5,9).

The history of the formal priesthood in Israel begins with the time of the Exodus. In the patriarchal times the heads of families offered sacrifices and intercessory prayers, and performed general religious functions, but there seems to have been no specialization and no separate priestly office, as there was among the Egyptians (Gen. 47:22, 26), and in the instance of Melchizedek (Gen. 14:18-20).

It is in Exodus 28 and 29 and Leviticus 8 that we have the record of the founding of the Aaronic order of priests. The choice of the tribe of Levi as the priestly tribe to serve as assistants to the Aaronic priests is recorded in Numbers 3 (see Exod. 32:26-29; Num. 8:16ff).

It is not possible in this article to go into technical historical and critical questions related to the OT priesthood. The reader who is interested in those matters will find extended discussions from a relatively conservative point of view in ISBE, HBD and in Oehler's *Old Testament Theology* (see index). The common critical view is given in R. H. Pfeiffer's *Int. to the OT,* 1941 (see "Priesthood," "Priestly Cities," and "Priestly Code" in the index, p. 913). Current critical opinion on the historical priesthood is reflected in the *Journal of Biblical Literature* for March 1961 in an article by Professor R. B. Y. Scott of Princeton University discussing the relationships between the priests, the prophets, and the wise men; and in the first article of a series by Professor Menahem Horan of the Hebrew University of Jerusalem on the ancient *Levitical Cities.*

Major attention must here be confined to the theological, devotional, and ethical implications of the Biblical idea of the priest and the priesthood.

The priesthood of Christ is the principal theme of the Epistle to the Hebrews. "Christ as our redeemer executeth the offices of a prophet, of a priest, and of a king, both in his estate of humiliation and exaltation" (*Westminster Shorter Catechism,* p. 23). The three offices of Christ are the subject of Chap. XV of Book II of Calvin's *Institutes.* The distinction of the offices, particularly the priestly, is not to be made rigidly, as though there were no overlapping; nevertheless the distinction has been found illuminating and profitable for an understanding of the Bible.

That Christ combines in Himself the three offices is a matter of special significance. After the establishment of the Aaronic priesthood, it was considered an offense in Israel for anyone not officially consecrated as a priest to offer formal ritual sacrifices. The rebellion of Korah (Num. 16) involved intrusion into the priesthood, even though he and his associates were Levites (vss. 8,9). King Saul was rebuked for a similar intrusion (I Sam. 13:18ff), and King Uzziah was smitten with leprosy for this offense (II Chron. 26:16ff).

The offices of prophet and priest might be combined in one person (John 11:49-52). Jeremiah was a member of a priestly family (Jer. 1:1). The offices of king and prophet might also be combined (Acts 2:29-31), but the kingly line of David was of the non-priestly tribe of Judah, and therefore no king of David's line could have been also a priest according to the Levitical law.

The NT writers make much of the fact that Jesus was "of the house and lineage of David" (Luke 2:4,5. Cf Mark 11:10; Matt. 21:9). How then could He be also a priest? The author of the Epistle to the Hebrews finds the scriptural answer in the order of Melchizedek (Heb. 6:10,20-7:17), who was Abraham's superior and both king and priest. This amplifies Zechariah's prophecy (6:13) that "the Branch" (cf. Isa. 4:2; Jer. 23:5,6) will be "A priest upon his throne."

The atonement of Christ was just as effective before the event as afterward. The highpriestly office of Christ did not begin at His incarnation; it was a fact known to David (Ps. 110:4) along with His sovereign lordship (vs. 1). His priesthood with reference to fallen humanity was established in the eternal decrees of God, and has been exercised in every age on behalf of God's elect. The Bible presents Christ, our Prophet, Priest and King, as a figure of cosmic proportions, whose work as our Redeemer has "neither beginning of days nor end of life."

The priestly ministry of Christ is introduced in the Epistle to the Hebrews 1:3 in the words, "when he had made a cleansing of sins." This is, of course, a reference to His death on the cross, regarded as an atoning sacrifice. But this act of sacrifice was not a mere symbol, as were all of the Aaronic priestly acts; it was of infinite intrinsic worth. He was "crowned with glory and honor for the purpose of suffering death, in order that by the grace of God he might taste of death [sufficiently for the offer of salvation] for every man" (2:9).

Christ's priesthood was in no sense contrary to the Aaronic order. It fulfilled all the soteriological significance of it. But the priesthood of Christ furnished the *substance* of which the Aaronic priesthood was only the shadow (Col. 2:17; Heb. 8:5) and symbol.

Examination of the wealth of detail in which the priesthood of Christ is said to complete and supersede the Aaronic priesthood, especially in Hebrews 5-10, would require an elaborate and extended thesis. All that is possible here is an attempt to clarify certain points of misunderstanding.

The tabernacle of which Christ is the High Priest is the entire cosmic scene of the redemption of God's elect. This was the "pattern" which Moses saw (Heb. 8:5), God's plan of salvation. It includes all the spiritual and temporal furniture of heaven and earth. The cross of Christ was the altar of sacrifice on which He offered Himself. When He gave up His life on the cross, the atonement was "finished" (John 19:30) once and for all (Heb. 7:27; 9:26) with absolutely nothing more for God or man to add to it. The meaning of Romans 4:25 is not that His resurrection added anything to our justification, but that, having died "on account of the trespasses" which we had committed, He was raised from the dead "on account of the justification" which He had fully accomplished in His death. His resurrection does not add to the atonement, but it proves that His death was a victory.

On the day of atonement in Levitical ritual (Lev. 16) the high priest had to go in and out past the veil, or curtain, which separated the holy of holies from the outer holy place. By this symbolism the Holy Spirit (Heb. 9:8,9) signifies that "the way of the sanctuaries was not yet made clear" while the Levitical mode of worship still had its proper standing. But when Jesus' body was broken on the cross, this symbolized the rending of the veil (Heb. 10:19-22) and the clear revealing of the way into the very presence of God (Matt. 27:51; Mark 15:38; Luke 23:45).

The notion that the atonement was not finished until Jesus presented His blood in some far distant sanctuary is entirely unscriptural. The atonement was finished on the cross in the immediate presence of God the Father. The "way of the sanctuaries" is now fully revealed. The veil is rent from top to bottom and no longer hides the "place of mercy."

True, the veil is once spoken of (Heb. 6:18-20; see also 4:14) as though it still cut off our view, but this is a different metaphor. It is not the "mercy seat" which is hidden in Hebrews 6:18-20, but the "hope which lies before us," the "unshakable kingdom" (Heb. 9:28; 12:26-29).

The present intercession of Christ is taught in Hebrews 7:25; Romans 8:34. (Cf. Rom. 8:26,27 for the intercession of the Holy Spirit.) But there is nothing in the Scripture to indicate an unfinished atonement or, as it were, an unfinished case in court. (The Adventist doctrine of "investigative judgment" is particularly erroneous. See Walter Martin's discussion of this doctrine in his valuable book on *Seventh Day Adventism*. Zondervan 1960). The NT word for intercession does not necessarily indicate any plea being offered. It suggests conferring over, or brooding over. Similarly the word "advocate" in I John 2:1 does not mean that our case is not completely settled. "Who is going to implead against the elect of God?" (Rom. 8:33.) Satan accuses, but he has no standing in court. The case is settled, the verdict is rendered. We are justified in Christ. Now our "Advocate," our great High Priest broods over us and counsels and guides.

The comparisons of different priesthoods in the epistle to the Hebrews are *not* between the religion of the OT and the "Churchianity" of this age. The comparisons are between the *outward form* of Judaism and the *reality* in Christ. Every argument against Judaism could be turned with equal logic against the outward forms of the church, if Christ be not the center of it all.

The priesthood of believers can be but briefly mentioned. Our church sacraments conducted by ordained ministers are analogous to those of the OT. They are but shadows, as worthless as "the blood of goats and bulls and the ashes of an heifer sprinkling the unclean" (Heb. 9:13), unless they are received by genuine faith in the atonement of Christ. No human being in any age could do more than shadow forth the atonement of Christ. (Ps. 49:7) "None of them can by any means redeem his brother, nor give to God a ransom for him."

All believers in all ages when mortal men exist are "a kingdom of priests" (Exod. 19:6; I Pet. 2:5,9; Rev. 20:6. The correct reading in Rev. 1:6 and 5:10 is not "kings" but "a kingdom" of priests). Paul in Romans 15:16; Philippians 2:17; II Timothy 4:6 uses symbols of priestly ritual with reference to his own ministry. We do not reign with Christ, i.e. we are not "kings," until He comes to reign (Matt. 19:28; Luke 22:18,28-30; cf. I Cor. 4:8) but we are priests as we bring the Word of God to men, and bring men to Christ. It is significant that the priestly function of believers continues through the millennial reign of Christ (Rev. 20:6), but not in the perfection of the new heavens and new earth (Rev. 21:4; 22:5) when mortality will have ended, and sin been completely eliminated. There will be no need for the priesthood of believers after the judgment of the Great White Throne. "Today" is the day of salvation (Heb. 3:13). J.O.B.

PRINCE, PRINCESS (prĭns, prĭn′-sĕs). A prince is a leader, an exalted person clothed with authority. A princess is the daughter or wife of a chief or king. Several Heb. and Greek words occur, the meaning varying with the context. There are princes of various nations (Matt. 20:25 ASV, RSV rulers); of (part of) the land of Canaan (Gen. 34:2); of Ishmael's descendants (Gen. 17:20; 25:16); of the Hittites (Gen. 23:6); of Egypt (Gen. 12:15); of the Philistines (I Sam. 18:30); of Persia (Esth. 1:3), called *satraps* in ASV, RSV of Daniel 3:2, etc.; of Babylon (Jer. 39:13 ASV, RSV *chief officers*); of Tyre (Ezek. 28:2); of the north (Ezek. 32:30); of Meshech and Tubal (Ezek. 38:2 ASV margin, *chief princes*). There were merchant princes in Tyre (Isa. 23:8). The heads of the tribes or of the congregation of Israel are princes (Num. 1:16 RSV *leaders*; Josh. 9:15 RSV *leaders*). David is called *prince* (I Kings 14:7 ASV margin, RSV *leader*), and he eulogizes Abner as a prince (II Sam. 3:38). The enemies of Jesus call Him Beelzebub, prince of the demons (Mark 3:22). The devil is the prince of this world (John 12:31 RSV ruler). Personal spiritual powers of evil are princes (I Cor. 2:6 ASV, RSV *rulers*; Eph. 2:2). Messiah is the prince (Dan. 9:25); of Peace (Isa. 9:6); of Life (Acts 3:15 ASV margin, RSV *Author*); of the kings of the earth (Rev. 1:5 ASV, RSV *ruler*). Bethlehem is called one of the princes of Judah (Matt. 2:6 RSV *rulers*) because the Davidic dynasty had its origin there.

Of princesses far less is said. Solomon had 700 princesses as wives, in contrast with 300 concubines (I Kings 11:3). Jerusalem is apostrophized as a princess (Lam. 1:1). A king's daughter (Ps. 45:9-12) a prince's daughter (S. of Sol. 7:1 RSV *queenly maiden*), and a daughter of a prince of Midian (Num. 25:18) are mentioned. The new name of Abraham's wife, Sarah, means princess (Gen. 17:15 ASV margin).

PRINCIPALITIES (prĭn'sĭ-păl'ĭ-tēz, Heb. *mera'ăshôth*, *headparts*, Gr. *arché*, *first*). The Hebrew word is found only in Jeremiah 13:18. Six times the NT uses the word in the English Bible to refer to powerful angels and demons (Rom. 8:38; Eph. 6:12).

PRINT, the translation of two Hebrew words and one Greek word, meaning a mark made by pressure. Moses forbade the Jews to make any cuttings or marks on the dead or living body (Lev. 19:28). Once the word is found in Job (Job 13:27). Twice John uses the word to refer to the print of the nails in Christ's hands (John 20:25).

PRISCA, PRISCILLA (prĭs'kȧ, Gr. *Príska*; prĭ-sĭl'ȧ, Gr. *Priskilla*). Priscilla (diminutive of *Prisca*, Rom. 16:3) was she was the wife of the Jewish Christian, Aquila, with whom she is always mentioned in the NT. They were tentmakers who seem to have migrated about the Mediterranean world teaching the Gospel wherever they went. Paul meets them in Corinth (Acts 18:2); they instruct Apollos in Ephesus (Acts 18:24-26); Paul sends them greetings in Rome (Rom. 16:3); and in I Corinthians 16:19 Paul speaks of them being in Ephesus again where they had a church in their house. In Romans 16:3-4 Paul not only lauds their service but their courage as well ("who for my life laid down their own necks"), and plainly states that all the churches owe them a debt of gratitude. From all the scriptural references one may easily infer that Prisca was a well-known and effective worker in the early church.

PRISON (prĭz'n), a place where persons suspected, accused, or convicted of crime are kept. Most Heb. and Greek words used have the idea of restraint. Joseph was cast into a pit while his brothers decided how to dispose of him (Gen. 37:22-28), and into the Egyptian king's prison, in the house of the captain of the guard (Gen. 39:20-40:7). Samson was confined in a Philistine prison at Gaza (Judg. 16:21,25). Prisoners taken in war were usually killed or enslaved (Num. 21:1 ASV, RSV captive; Isa. 20:4). Under the monarchy Micaiah the prophet was imprisoned (I Kings 22:27; II Chron. 18:26), where his food was bread and water. Jeremiah was threatened with prison (Jer. 29:26) including the stocks and shackles or collar (ASV, RSV), and subjected to long imprisonment (Jer. 32:2; 33:1) in the court of the guard in the king's house; again in a dungeon, whence he was transferred to the house of Jonathan the scribe, which had been made a prison (Jer. 37:14-21); then in a dungeon or cistern (RSV) in the prison (Jer. 38:6-28), whence Ebed-melech rescued him; restored to the court of the guard; and finally released (Jer. 39:14). Kings were imprisoned by conquerors (II Kings 17:4; 25:27,29; Jer. 52:11,33; Eccl. 4:14).

The pitiable state of those in prison is spoken of (Ps. 79:11; Isa. 14:17; 42:22; Lam. 3:34; Zech. 9:11), and their hope in God (Ps. 69:33; 102:20; 142:7; 146:7; Isa. 42:7). John the Baptist was imprisoned for criticizing a king's marriage (Matt. 4:12; 11:2; 14:3,10 and parallels); Peter and John for preaching about Jesus (Acts 4:3; 5:18-25); Peter was delivered by an angel (Acts 12:3-19). Paul led Christians to prison (Acts 8:3; 22:4; 26:10) and was himself often in prison (II Cor. 11:23); with Silas at Philippi (Acts 16:23-40); in Jerusalem (23:18); in Caesarea (25:27); on shipboard (27:1,42); under house arrest in his own rented dwelling (28:16,17,30). He refers to his imprisonment as for the Lord (Eph. 3:1; 4:1; Phil. 1:14,17; II Tim. 1:8; Philem. 9); to his fellow-prisoners (Rom. 16:7; Col. 4:10). Barabbas was released from prison in place of Jesus (Matt. 27:15,16 and parallels). Jesus refers to imprisonment on civil process, as for debt (Matt. 5:25; 18:30; Luke 12:58); to visiting those in prison (Matt. 25:36,39,43,44); and predicts that His followers will be put in prison during persecution (Luke 21:12; Rev. 2:10). Peter expresses willingness to go to prison with Jesus (Luke 22:33). Disobedient spirits are now in prison (I Pet. 3:19,20); Satan will be imprisoned during the Millennium (Rev. 20:7).   E.R.

PROCHORUS (prŏk'ō-rŭs), the third in the list of the first deacons (Acts 6:5) who were elected to take care of the Greek-speaking widows and probably the Christians stricken with poverty in Jerusalem.

PROCONSUL (prō'kŏn-sŭl, Gr. *anthýpatos*), a Roman official, generally of praetorian or consular rank, who served as deputy consul in the Roman provinces. The term of office was one year, although it could be longer in special instances, but the powers of the proconsul were unlimited in both the military and civil areas. Sergius Paulus, St. Paul's famous convert (Acts 13:7), and Gallio (Acts 18:12) were such officials mentioned in the Bible. They are often called "deputy" in the English Bible.

PROCURATOR (prō'kū-rā'têr), the Latin term for the Greek *hegemón*, which is translated "governor" in the KJV. Pilate, Felix and Festus were such governors in Palestine with headquarters in Caesarea. Generally the procurators were appointed directly by the emperor to govern the Roman provinces and were often subject to the imperial legate of a larger political area. It should be noted that Quirinius, "Governor of Syria" (Luke 2:2), was really not a procurator but an imperial legate of the larger province of Syria.

PROFANE (prō-fān', Heb. *hālal, to open* and Gr. *homologéo, to own before*). The basic idea seems to be to desecrate or defile. For one to do what he was not allowed to do in connection with holy things or places was to profane them. Such things as the altar, the sabbath, the sanctuary and God's name could all be profaned. Esau was called a profane person because he despised his birthright (Heb. 12:16). A godless or unholy person in the NT is called profane.

PROMISE (prŏm'ĭs, Heb. *dāvār, speaking, speech*; *dāvar, to speak*; *'āmar, to say*; *'ōmer, speech*; Gr. *epaggelía, promise*). In the OT there is no Heb. word corresponding to *promise*; the words *word, speak,* and *say* being used instead. In the NT, however, the word *promise* is often used, usually in the technical sense of God's design to visit His people redemptively in the person of His Son. This promise is first given in the *proto-evangelium* (Gen. 3: 15), is repeated to Abraham (Gen. 12:2,7, etc.), and to David that his house would continue on his throne (II Sam. 7:12,13,28), and is found repeatedly in the OT (Isa. 2:2-5; 4:2; 55:5, etc.). In the NT all these promises are regarded as having their fulfilment in Christ and His disciples (II Cor. 1: 20; Eph. 3:6). Jesus' promise of the Spirit was fulfilled at Pentecost. Paul makes clear that God's promises to Abraham's seed were meant not only for the circumcision but for all who have Abraham's faith (Rom. 4:13-16). In the NT there are many promises of blessing to believers, among them the kingdom (James 2:5), eternal life (I Tim. 4:8), Christ's coming (II Pet. 3:9).   S.B.

PROPHECY (See Prophets)

PROPHETS. Three Hebrew words are employed in the OT to designate the prophets, namely, *nāvî', rō'eh* and *hōzeh*. The last two words are participles, and may be rendered "seer." They are practically synonymous in meaning. The first term, *nāvî',* is difficult to explain etymologically, although various attempts have been made. The significance of these words, however, may be learned from their usage.

Each of the words designates one who is a spokesman for God. The usage of *navi'* is illustrated by Exodus 4:15,16 and 7:1. In these passages it is clearly taught that Moses stands in relation to the pharaoh as God. Between them is an intermediary, Aaron. Aaron is to speak to the pharaoh the words which Moses gives to him. "And he (i.e., Aaron) shall be thy spokesman unto the people: and he shall be, *even* he shall be to thee instead of a mouth, and thou shalt be to him instead of God" (Exod. 4:16). The man who can be designated a *nāvi',* then, is one who speaks forth for God.

The two words *rō'eh* and *hōzeh,* perhaps have primary reference to the fact that the person so designated sees the message which God gives him. This seeing is probably to be conceived as having taken place in a vision. At the same time, even these two words serve to designate a man who, having seen the message of God, declares that message. The Biblical emphasis throughout is practical. It is not the dark background of the mode of reception of the prophetic revelation that stands in the fore, but rather the deliverance of the message for God.

In the Greek language the term *prophetes* (a forth-teller) had a wider significance than did the Hebrew word. It signified one who spoke for the god and interpreted the god's will. He would interpret the message of the Delphic oracle (e.g., Herodotus 8:36,37) or expound the utterances of the *mantis*. At times the word might indicate those who kept or guarded the oracles. In the LXX the term merely serves as a translation of the Hebrew and does not have the broader connotations that adhere to it in the classical literature.

The Greek also employed the verb *manteuomai,* which might be used of prophesying but also of divining. It could also refer to consulting an oracle, and at times could have merely the significance of foreboding or presaging. Related to it is the noun *mantis* which could apply to a prophet, but also to a seer or diviner, one who obtained information by observing omens (cf. *Iliad* 1:106). The noun *manteia* could designate divination as such, the power of divination, oracular and obscure expressions, the method of divining and the seat of an oracle. In the LXX, Numbers 22:7, it even denotes the rewards of divination.

The Biblical prophet must be distinguished from the *prophetes* of the Greeks. The latter really acted as an interpreter for the muses and the oracles. The prophets, however, were not interpreters. They uttered the actual words which God had given to them, without any modification or interpretation upon their part. The Bible itself gives an accurate description of the function of the true prophet, ". . . and will put my words in his mouth; and he shall speak unto them all that I shall command him" (Deut. 18:18b). The words are placed in the prophet's mouth by God, i.e., they are revealed to the prophet, and then the prophet speaks unto the nation precisely what God has commanded him.

Position of the Prophet in the Old Testament Economy. The establishment of the prophetic institution was necessitated by the settlement of the nation Israel in the Land of Promise. In entering Canaan, Israel came with the precious possession of the law. This law, revealed by God at Mt. Sinai, laid the broad basis upon which the life of the people of God was to be built. The basic principles of divinely revealed ethics and morality are found in the Ten Commandments, and sundry rules for particular situations are expressed in the other laws. Upon this basis the life of the people of God was to be conducted.

At the same time this law was not adequate to meet all the situations that would arise when the period of Israel's nomadic wanderings should come to an end. This inadequacy was not due to any inherent weakness in the law itself, but simply to the fact that the law did not speak in detail upon every possible situation that should arise in Israel's life. There would be occasions when a specific revelation of God would be needed in order to show the nation the course which it should pursue. This needed revelation God would give to the people by means of His servants, the prophets.

When Israel was to enter Canaan, it would find a people that sought to learn the future and the will of the gods by the practice of various superstitions which the Bible calls abominations (Deut. 18:9). These abominations were being regularly and continually practiced by the inhabitants of Canaan, and there was a danger that the Israelites would be influenced by them and would themselves learn to do them. To offset this danger the Lord declared that He would raise up the prophets and that the Israelites were to hearken to the prophets and to obey them (Deut. 18:15). Scripture uses the singular, "prophet," but it is clear from the context that the reference is to a body of prophets.

The prophet whom the Lord will raise is said to be like Moses, and this similarity appears in that just as Moses was a mediator between God and the nation, so the prophet would serve as a mediator. At Horeb, when God appeared to the nation, the people trembled, and asked that Moses alone should speak to them. God commended Israel for their request, and announced that there would be a mediator, even the prophets. The prophets, then, served as mediators between God and the nation. Just as the priests represented the people before God, so the prophets represented God to the people.

In ancient Greece we have the god, the oracle, the prophet, and the people. The same seems to have been the case in the Mesopotamian countries also. In Israel, however, there was only one intermediary between God and the people, namely, the prophet. This arrangement was truly unique. One who heard the words of the prophet heard the very words of God Himself, and these words required implicit obedience.

In many nations of antiquity there were soothsayers or men who had visions. They represented a part of that web of superstition which covered the ancient world. The prophetic institution of Israel, however, according to the testimony of the Bible, was of divine origination. God Himself raised up this institution (Deut. 18:15-18), and it is this fact which distinguished the prophets from the soothsayers of the Homeric world, and from other so-called "prophets" of antiquity.

The Relation of the Prophets to Moses. Unique as was the prophetical body, it can properly be understood only as having served under Moses. Moses occupied a position of preeminence in the OT economy. He was faithful *in* all God's house as a servant, and so pointed forward to Christ who as a Son is faithful *over* God's house (Heb. 3:1-6). To the prophets God made Himself known in dreams and visions, and probably also in dark, enigmatic sayings. To Moses, however, God spoke clearly and distinctly, mouth to mouth, as a man speaks to his friend (Num. 12:1-8). A distinction in the method or manner of revelation thus appears with respect to Moses and the prophets. Moses was the leading figure of the Old Testament economy, and the prophets served under him. The revelations made to them were sometimes obscure and ambiguous, in that they were given in dreams and visions. It would follow therefore, that when the prophets spoke, they spoke in terms and forms of thought which were current in and which characterized the OT dispensation.

The entire Mosaic economy must be understood as a witness of the later-to-be-revealed NT economy. Moses and the prophets therefore were types of Christ and of His blessings. They witnessed, not to themselves, but to the "things to be spoken of" (Heb. 3:1-6). In speaking of the future salvation under Christ the prophets spoke sometimes in language that was not free from ambiguity, and the interpretation of their prophecies must depend upon a further revelation and in particular upon the NT.

It is sometimes said that the prophets were forthtellers and not foretellers. Such a disjunction, however, is not warranted. It is true that the prophets were forthtellers, speaking forth the message of the Lord. That message, however, sometimes had to do with past occurrences, as when the prophets often reminded the nation of how God had brought it out of the land of Egypt and given it Canaan for a possession. They also spoke of contemporary events, as witness the words of Isaiah with respect to the situation that confronted Ahaz (Isa. 7). At the same time, it must not be forgotten that the prophets also spoke of the future. They predicted future calamity to come upon the nation because of its refusal to repent for its sins, and they spoke also in language beautiful and mysterious of the coming of One who would save His people from their sins. The prophets truly were forthtellers, but they were foretellers as well, and the predictive element is extremely important for a proper understanding of the true nature of the prophets.

Classification of the Prophets. In the arrangement of the books in the Hebrew Old Testament there are three parts, the Law, the Prophets and the Writings. The division known as the Prophets is further subdivided into the former and the latter prophets. Under the first heading are included Joshua, Judges, I-II Samuel and I-II Kings. These books are anonymous, and their authors are not known. The authors, however, as the designation "former prophets" indicates, were men who held the prophetic office in ancient Israel. They wrote an interpretative history of the background of the period in which the great writing prophets lived and worked. Without this interpretative history it would be impossible to understand the work of the great prophets. The former prophets cover the period from Israel's entrance into the land of promise until the destruction of the theocracy under Nebuchadnezzar. It is with just this period that the writing prophets deal.

The latter prophets are also called writing prophets. They are the prophets who exercised so great a ministry in Israel — Isaiah, Jeremiah, Ezekiel and the Twelve. The designation "latter" does not necessarily have reference to historical chronology, but is simply a designation of those prophetical books which follow the "former" prophets in the Hebrew arrangement of the Old Testament.

The "latter" or "writing" prophets were not anonymous. The reason for this is that they were entrusted by God with the task and responsibility of addressing prophetical messages not only to the men of their own day but also to posterity. They must be accredited to their audience as genuine prophets, and for that reason their name is known to us. There were some prophets whose names we do not know, as, for example, the man who approached Eli and announced to him the downfall of his house. To us it is not necessary that the name of this man be known; it is enough that it was known to Eli. Those who received the messages of the prophets had sufficient evidence of their accreditation. To those first recipients of the messages the names were known; to us it is not necessary to possess similar information. The writing prophets, however, have uttered messages which are more relevant to us; they have spoken, for example, of the coming of the Messiah, and it is essential that we be assured that those who uttered such messages were truly accredited spokesmen of the Lord.

It must be noted, however, that the former and the latter prophets complemented one another. The "former" prophets set forth the history of a particular period in Israel's life; the "latter" or "writing" prophets interpret particular phases of that history. The one is necessary for the proper understanding of the other.

The Scripture does not say much as to the method in which the great "writing" prophets prepared their messages. The theory has been advanced by Herman Gunkel that the prophets were first of all oral preachers, and that they did not write their messages. The written books which we now possess, Gunkel argued, were the work of disciples of the prophets. From the example of Jeremiah, however, it would appear that the prophets did write down their messages. What the precise relationship between their spoken word and their written messages is it may be impossible for us fully to know. It could very well be that the prophets often spoke far more than they have written down. It could be that in many instances they enlarged upon their messages when they were delivering them orally, and that they made digests of these messages for writing.

With respect to the last 27 chapters of the book of Isaiah, for example, it may well be that these messages were never delivered orally. It is quite likely that the prophet, after retirement from active preaching and prophesying, went into solitude during the latter days of Hezekiah and wrote down the wondrous messages which concern the future destinies of the people of God and their deliverance from sin by the Servant of the Lord. It is quite possible also that some of the prophecies of Jeremiah are the results of intense polishing and reworking. These written messages need not in every instance have been identical with what had been delivered orally. What we have in the Scriptures is what the Spirit of God intended us to have.

Schools of the Prophets. After the people had entered the Promised Land there came a time when "every man did that which was right in his own eyes" (Judg. 21:25). It was evident that the nation must have a king, but the first requests for a king were made in a spirit and for a purpose that conflicted with what God intended the theocracy to be. The first king was not a man after God's own heart, but one who was sufficient unto himself. This was a time when there was danger not only from the idolatry of Canaan but also from the incursions of the Philistines. At this time, for the encouragement and spiritual welfare of the nation, there were raised up bands (*hevel*) of the prophets.

It is difficult to say what is intended by the word "band." Whether the groups of prophets so designated had a formal organization or not, one cannot tell. It may be that such groups were more or less loosely knit together, and that they served under Samuel. For that matter it cannot be positively asserted that Samuel was the founder of such groups, although such a supposition would seem to have much in its favor.

Following Samuel's death these prophetical bodies seem to have disappeared from the scene, and we hear no more of them until the times of Elijah and Elisha. During the days of these men groups of prophets again appear, although most likely they are not to be thought of as hereditary descendants of the bodies that existed under Samuel. The reason for this is that in Elijah's day they appear only in the northern kingdom. The theocracy had become divided, due to the schism introduced by Jeroboam the son of Nebat. There was now need for support against the worship of the Tyrian Baal as well as the calf worship of Dan and Bethel. Both Elijah and Elisha exercised a vigorous ministry in the N, but the government was opposed to them. They needed particular assistance, and this was found in the companies which now bear the designation "sons of the prophets." The phrase reveals the close and intimate association in which these men stood to the great prophets, Elijah and Elisha. After this period, however, they seem to die out, and we hear no more of them.

A page from the Book of Isaiah, 47:2 - 48:6, from the Dead Sea Scrolls. ASOR

The Prophets and the Temple. The regular worship of ancient Israel after the establishment of the monarchy was conducted in the temple located in Jerusalem. This worship was in the hands of priests, men who represented the nation before God. What was the relation in which the prophets stood to the temple worship? It used to be held, particularly by the school of Wellhausen, that the prophets and the priests were working in opposition one to another, that the priests represented a sacrificial type of worship, whereas the prophets were more concerned about ethics and behavior. It was even held that the prophets denied that God had ever required sacrifices, and this supposition was used to support the position of Wellhausen that the books of the Pentateuch in which sacrifices were enjoined were not composed until late in Israel's history, when the priestly religion had triumphed over the prophetical.

This reconstruction of Israel's history, once so dominant, is more and more losing ground. It is now being recognized, even by those who are very sympathetic to Wellhausen, that there was not, after all, such an antagonism between prophet and priest. In fact, some of the prophets, such as Jeremiah and Ezekiel, were themselves priests. Indeed, what the prophets were condemning, as a more careful and sober exegesis has shown, was not the sacrifices themselves, but the manner in which the sacrifices were offered (cf. Isa. 1:9-15). The sacrifices were truly an approach to God, but the worshiper must come with clean hands and a pure heart. Else the sacrifices in themselves, divorced from a proper attitude of humility and repentance upon the part of the worshiper, were nothing but vain oblations, and were not acceptable to the Lord.

If, then, the prophets were not condemning sacrifice in itself, what was the relation in which they actually stood to the worship of the temple? In recent years the opinion has become more and more widespread that the prophets were servants of the temple, and that they may even have received a salary and been in the employ of the temple. It is perhaps safest to say that this question cannot be answered positively one way or another. The prophets at times may have been officially connected with the temple; at times they may have been more or less on their own. It is difficult to say how they did earn their livelihood. The servant of Saul had suggested the giving of a small gift to Samuel in return for information as to the whereabouts of the lost asses of Saul's father (I Sam. 9:8). Possibly the prophets at times were dependent upon such small gifts and upon donations which they had obtained for services rendered. That they were actually officials in the employ of the temple is a matter upon which it is wisest not to speak dogmatically.

True and False Prophets. True religion has always been plagued by imitators. Alongside the faithful and true prophets of the Lord there were others, men who had not received a revelation from God. Jeremiah refused to have anything to do with these men. They were not true prophets, but men who deceived. There were those who claimed to have received messages from God, who as a matter of fact did not receive such messages.

Some of these false prophets may themselves have been sincere men who were deceived, but many of them doubtless were wicked men. Isaiah condemns them as drunken (28:7), and from the representations given in the Bible, it would seem that they were simply deluders, blind leaders of the blind. It was possible, however, for the devout Israelites to distinguish between messages uttered by true prophets and those spoken by the false. True prophets were accredited in that their prophecies were fulfilled (Deut. 18:20ff). When they spoke concerning the far distant future, their messages could be believed, inasmuch as their messages which concerned the present or immediate future would be fulfilled. Furthermore, they always spoke in the name of the Lord. False prophets, on the other hand, would find that their prophecies were not accredited or fulfilled. Hananiah, for example, predicted that the Exile would be of only two years' duration (Jer. 28:1ff). His prophecy would be shown to be false in that, when the two years had expired, the Exile would not be over. Thus, he would be generally discredited. Also, there were prophets who uttered prophecies in the name of other gods, and even accompanied their predictions with signs and miracles (Deut. 13:1-5). From such the people were to turn away. Also, it must be remembered that the true prophets actually did speak the Word of God, and God's people would recognize that Word. False prophecy is best conceived as a degeneration of the true.

Messianic Prophecy. Any proper estimation of the prophetic movement must take into account the following three factors. Prophecy was a continuous movement, extending over several centuries in Israel's history. There was nothing essentially similar to it anywhere in the ancient world. The prophets, during so many centuries, all claimed to be recipients of messages from Yahweh, the God of Israel, and to speak the messages which He had given to them. Lastly, in all these messages there runs a teleological element; the prophets spoke of a future deliverance to be wrought by the Messiah. It is this element of prophecy which we call "Messianic Prophecy."

The word "Messiah" is itself not of frequent occurrence in the Old Testament. It means "one who is anointed," and this anointing possesses an abiding character. The Messiah is a human individual who is to come to earth to perform a work of deliverance for God. He is also Himself a divine person, as appears from passages such as Isaiah 9:5,6. His coming to earth reveals the coming of the Lord. His coming is in connection with the supernatural, in that God is truly with Him. Furthermore, His coming represents the end of the age. It is to be in the "last days," and hence is eschatological. He is to come as a king, a descendant of David and is to reign on David's throne. Lastly, the purpose of His coming is to save His people from their sins. He is a Saviour, and is to bear the sins of His own that they may stand in right relation with God.

Messianic prophecy must be understood against the dark background of human sin. Man's disobedience in the garden of Eden had involved man in corruption of the heart and also in guilt before God. Man could not of his own efforts make himself right with God and hence it was necessary that God take the initiative. This God did in announcing that He would place enmity between the woman Eve and the serpent. God also announced the outcome of that enmity, in that the Seed of the woman would bruise the serpent's head (Gen. 3:15). This was the first definite announcement that the Messiah would come and that His work would be victorious.

All subsequent Messianic prophecy is based upon this mother promise. To Noah it was announced that the blessing of God would be with Shem, and hence among the descendants of Shem one must look for the Messiah. The promise is then narrowed down to Abraham and after him to Isaac. For a time it seemed that Abraham would have no son, and then Ishmael was born to Abraham's concubine. Yet the promise was not to be fulfilled through Ishmael, but through Isaac. After Isaac had been born, however, Abraham is commanded to slay him. Finally, when Abraham's faith is sufficiently tested, it is made clear that Isaac is after all the one through whom the Messiah is to come.

Of Isaac's two sons, Jacob is chosen and Esau rejected. Finally, Jacob calls his 12 sons about him and announces to them what will take place in the "latter days" (Gen. 49:1). In his prophecy he clearly points to the fact that Shiloh will come in Judah. Later, Balaam, a heathen soothsayer, also prophesies of the coming of a "Star out of Jacob, and a Sceptre shall arise out of Israel" (Num. 24: 17a). In Deuteronomy, in the passage in which the divine origin of the prophetic movement is revealed, we learn also of the Prophet to come, who was to be like Moses. Whereas in a certain sense, the entire prophetic body was like Moses, there was really only One who followed Moses, and that One was the Messiah.

In the books of Samuel (II Sam. 7) it is revealed that the throne of David is to be established permanently, and that a ruler on that throne will rule over an eternal kingdom. Upon the basis of this prophecy we are to understand many of the Psalms which speak of a King (e.g., Pss. 2, 45, 72, 110) and also many of the prophecies. The Messiah is to be the King of a kingdom that will never perish. This is taught by Isaiah, for example, who announces the supernatural birth of the Messiah and the government over which He is to rule. He is to be born of a virgin, and His supernatural birth is to be a sign to the people that God is truly with them. They need not fear before the growing power of Assyria. The Assyrian king will not destroy them nor render void the promises of God. They are to look to the King whom God will present to them. This king is the Messiah. His kingdom is to be eternal; it is to be built up in righteousness and justice, and it is to be the hope of the people.

Daniel also speaks of this kingdom as eternal. He contrasts it with the kingdoms of this world which are both temporal and local. These kingdoms, great and powerful as they are, will nevertheless pass away, and there will be erected a kingdom that will belong to a heavenly Figure, the One like a Son of Man. His kingdom alone will be universal and eternal, for He is the true Messiah. Stressing, as they do, the kingly work of the Messiah, many of these prophecies do not lay their emphasis upon the actual saving work which the Messiah was to perform.

There was a danger that the eyes of the people would be so attracted to the Messiah as a king that they might tend to think of Him only as a political figure. This danger became very real, and the Jews did more and more conceive of Him as merely One who was political, who would deliver them from the yoke of foreign oppressors.

To offset this danger it was necessary that the people know full well that the Messiah's work was truly to be spiritual in nature. Hence, in the latter portion of his book, Isaiah with remarkable lucidity speaks of what the Messiah will do to save His people. It is in these great "Servant" passages that we learn that the Messiah is to be a Saviour. He is set forth as one laden with griefs and sorrows, but they are not His own. They belong to His people, and He bears them in order that men may be free and may have the peace of God. The Messiah suffers and dies vicariously; that is the nature of His saving work, and that it is which Isaiah presents with such great vividness.

All the prophets were under Moses, and just as Moses was a type of Christ, so it may be said that the prophetical body as such, being under Moses, was also typical of the great Prophet to come. Although they did not understand the full depth of their messages, yet they were speaking of the coming salvation and so of Jesus Christ. Through them God spoke in "divers manners" and in "divers parts" unto the fathers. What is so remarkable is that, when their messages are taken as a whole and in their entirety, they form such a unified picture of the work of the Messiah.

We must guard against the view that there is merely a correspondence between what the prophets say and what occurred in the life of Jesus Christ. There was of course a correspondence, but to say no more than this is not to do justice to the situation. Jesus Christ did not merely find a correspondence between the utterances of the prophets and the events of His own life. Rather, the events of His life constituted the fulfillment of what the prophets had declared. It is this point upon which we must insist if we are to understand them properly. As was said of Isaiah, so we may say of the entire prophetic body, They saw Christ's day and spoke of Him.   E.J.Y.

CHRONOLOGICAL CHART OF THE PROPHETS

Northern Kingdom			Southern Kingdom		
Prophet	**King**		**Prophet**	**King**	
	Jeroboam	933-912			
	Nadab	912-911			
	Baasha	911-888			
	Elah	888-887			
	Zimri	887			
	Tibni	887-863			
	Omri	887-877			
ELIJAH	Ahab	876-854		Jehoshaphat	873-848
	Ahaziah	854-853		Jehoram	848-841
ELISHA	Jehoram	853-842		Ahaziah	841
	Jehu	842-815		Athaliah	841-835
	Jehoahaz	814-798	JOEL?	Jehoash	835-796
	Jehoash	798-793		Amaziah	796-767
JONAH	Jeroboam II	793-743	ISAIAH	Uzziah	767-740
AMOS	Zachariah	743	MICAH		
HOSEA	Shallum	743	OBADIAH?		
	Menahem	743-737			
	Pekahiah	737-736		Jotham	740-732
	Pekah	736-730		Ahaz	732-716
	Hoshea	730-722		Hezekiah	716-687
Fall of the Northern Kingdom					
			NAHUM?	Manasseh	687-643
				Amon	643-641
			JEREMIAH	Josiah	641-609
			HABAKKUK?		
			ZEPHANIAH?		
			The Exile	Jehoahaz	609
			DANIEL	Jehoiakim	609-598
				Jehoiachin	598-597
			EZEKIEL	Zedekiah	597-586
			The Restoration		
			ZECHARIAH	520	
			HAGGAI	520	
			MALACHI	432?	

PROPHETESS (Heb. *nevî'âh*, Gr. *prophétes*), a woman who exercised the prophetic gift in ancient Israel or in the early Christian church. In general, she would possess the charismatic gifts and powers characterizing the prophets themselves. There are at least four women bearing this designation in the OT: (1) Miriam, sister of Moses (Exod. 15:20); (2) Deborah (Judg. 4:4); (3) Huldah, (II Kings 22:14); (4) the unnamed wife of Isaiah, who bore him children with prophetic names (Isa. 8:3). In the NT, Philip the evangelist is said have had "four unmarried daughters who prophesied" (Acts 21:8, 9). After Pentecost, the differentiation between the sexes with regards to prophetic gifts was removed (Acts 2:19; cf. Joel 2:28). See PROPHECY, PROPHET, etc.

PROPITIATION (prō-pĭsh'ĭ-ā'shŭn). This is one of the semi-technical Biblical words which designate the Atonement, q.v. The English word "propitiation" is of Latin derivation, and signifies an objective "provision" for "pity," or mercy. This accurately translates the Greek word *hilastérion* (Rom. 3:25; Heb. 9:5. In Luke 18:13 and Heb. 2:17 a similar verb is used, and in I John 2:2; 4:10 a similar noun). *Hilastérion* in turn translates the Hebrew *kippōreth, mercy seat,* or the objective place of mercy, often referred to in the Pentateuch.

The NT committee of translators substituted "expiation" for "propitiation" in Romans 3:25 in the RSV, specifically because they would not admit an objective element in the atonement. (See the testimony of Rev. Joseph Bayly in *S. S. Times* for June 4, 1946, p. 194.) Although few English readers recognize the difference, "expiation" is more suggestive of a mere votive offering to gain favor, and substituting it for "propitiation" in Romans 3:25 opens the way to interpret that passage as though the atonement were a persuasive inducement offered to man, and not to God. In this translation both the lexicography of the word and the hermeneutics of the passage are violated. (See the significance of the noun ending "*-terion*" in A. T. Robertson's large *Grammar*, pp. 154, 157, 157n; and in Goodwin and Gulick *Greek Grammar*, p. 829.)

That the meaning of *hilastérion* (propitiation) in Romans 3:25 is "an objective provision for mercy," is borne out by the context. In vs. 24 we are said to be "justified by the *apolýtrosis* ('liberation procured by the payment of a ransom' [Thayer]) which is in Christ Jesus." This can only mean that our account, as sinners, before a holy God, is objectively settled. In vs. 26, this "propitiation . . . by His [Christ's] blood," this "vindication of His [God's] righteousness," is said to be directed to the purpose "that He might be just and the justifier of him which believeth in Jesus." In other words, the propitiation by the blood of Christ vindicates God's holy character as He justifies the sinner.

Without the propitiation, God would be saying, "Sin may be ignored." With the propitiation in the blood of Christ, God is saying "This is what your sin cost me, and I bore it in my Son, as I justified you."

In the OT ritual the climax of all is the sprinkling of blood on the "mercy seat" in the holy of holies on the day of atonement. How eminently appropriate that the LXX translators should use for this word "provision for (or place of) mercy," *hilastérion*, with which Paul later set forth the objective significance of the atonement of Christ! J.O.B.

PROSELYTE (prŏs'ĕ-līt). The Greek word *prosélytos* (from the verb *prosérchomai* which means

to "come unto") is the common LXX translation of the Hebrew word *gēr* which means a foreign resident. It is the word often rendered "stranger," as in the phrase "thy stranger that is within thy gates" (Exod. 20:10; Deut. 5:14). Before NT times the word had come to apply to a more limited group religiously and a more extended group geographically. In the NT and in the writings of Philo and Josephus the word designates a person of Gentile origin who had accepted the Jewish religion, whether living in Palestine or elsewhere.

The word occurs only four times in the NT:

1. In Jesus' denunciatory discourse, Matthew 23:1-39, one of His serious charges against the "scribes and Pharisees, hypocrites!" is, "ye compass sea and land to make one proselyte, and when he is made, ye make him twofold more the child of Gehenna than yourselves" (vs. 15). Rabbi Emil G. Hirsch, Ph.D. of the U. of Chicago, in the article on "Proselyte" in the *Jewish Encyclopedia* (Vol. X p. 221) mentions (but does not accept) the opinion that Matthew 23:15 "refers to an actual incident, the voyage of R. Gamaliel, R. Eliezer, G. Azariah, R. Joshua, and R. Akiba to Rome, where they converted Flavius Clemens, a nephew of Emperor Domitian." This is an anachronism, for this Flavius Clemens suffered martyrdom in A.D. 92 and his conversion to Christianity (not Judasim) must have been long after the words of Matthew 23:15 were uttered, and after the time of Rabbi Gamaliel. But the story, unreliable as it is, may illustrate the kind of evil political zeal which Jesus denounces.

At any rate, the words of Jesus do not condemn proselytes as such, nor call in question the sincerity of the majority of proselytes. It is hypocritical Pharisaism which is condemned here, and that alone.

The other three NT occurrences of the word "proselyte" are all in the book of Acts.

2. In the long list of places and peoples represented in Jerusalem on the day of Pentecost "Jews and proselytes" (Acts 2:10) are mentioned. There is, however, nothing whatever in the record to indicate any special attitude on the part of the proselytes in any way different from the rest of this Jewish crowd. That proselytes are mentioned in the manner they are, would indicate that they constituted a noticeable proportion of the multitude. There were thousands of pilgrims; there must have been hundreds of them who were proselytes. Of the 3,000 who were swept into the Christian movement that day, and the hundreds more who soon joined them, the probability is that there were many hundreds of proselytes.

3. When it came to the selection of the first diaconate (Acts 6:1-6) one of the seven was "Nicolas, a proselyte from Antioch" (vs. 5). Some think, from the names of the other six, that three of them were Greek-speaking Jews, to represent the Hellenists who had complained (vs. 1). Of this there is no certainty; but since one of the seven deacons was a proselyte, we may have some rough indication of the proportion of the proselytes in the early Jerusalem church.

4. After Paul's great sermon in the synagogue at Pisidian Antioch (Acts 13:14-41), we read that "many of the Jews and devout proselytes followed Paul and Barnabas, who, speaking to them, urged them to come and abide (*prosménein*) in the grace of God" (vs. 43). From this point on in the record we cannot distinguish the proselytes. "The Gentiles" came in great crowds, and "the Jews" became jealous and hostile (vss. 44-52).

Were all proselytes fully initiated Jews? Or did the term also include Gentile believers in God who had not accepted the initiatory rites, but who were associated with synagogue worship in varying degrees of fellowship? The opinion is prevalent, and is supported by Rabbi Hirsch (*op. cit.* 1903) that the phrase "proselyte of the gate," based upon such expressions as "thy stranger that is within thy gate" (Exod. 20:10; Deut. 5:14; 14:21) distinguished uncircumcised proselytes, i.e., those who had not fully identified themselves with the Jewish nation and religion.

On the other hand, Prof. F. C. Porter, Ph.D. of Yale, in the article on "Proselyte" in *Hastings Dictionary of the Bible,* 1902, (Vol. IV p. 135) says, "The phrase *'proselyte of the gate'* has nothing to do with the *seboumenoi tou Theou* [worshipers of God]. It is simply a late rabbinical title (after (Exod. 20:10; Deut. 5:14, etc.) for sojourners in Israel's land. . . . In distinction from these, the proselyte was called by the late Rabbis the *'Proselyte of righteousness'* while in the Mishna he is simply the *'gēr'.*" Porter thinks that in the time of the NT, Philo, and Josephus, there was only one class of proselytes, those who had gone all the way with the three initiatory steps, (1) circumcision of all the males of the family, (2) ceremonial washing or baptism for the women as well as the men, and, as long as the temple stood, (3) an offering. Others, he thinks, no matter how devout, were not called proselytes.

Much has been written on the details and technicalities of this question. The probability is that the first century Jews had no very fixed or rigid use of the term, and they differed among themselves.

The LXX version of Exodus 12:48 reads, "If any proselyte come to you to keep the passover, thou shalt circumcise all his males, and then he shall come to keep it, and he shall be as a native of the land. No uncircumcised [man] shall eat of it." In this instance, the proselyte as such is called a proselyte when he had not as yet accepted circumcision. Since the LXX was the Bible of the first century Jews outside of Palestine, it is hard to believe that the word *proselyte* for them referred exclusively to the fully initiated. The term must have included a multitude of non-initiated believers and inquirers as well as the fully initiated.

The fact is that Judaism up to the time of Christ was not the narrow racial national religion it is sometimes made out to be. There were evidently many Gentiles in the synagogue at Pisidian Antioch. Note, "Men of Israel *and ye that fear* God" (Acts 13:16); ". . . of the stock of Abraham *and whosoever among you feareth God*" (vs. 26); "Jews and devout proselytes" (vs. 43); "the *gentiles . . .* were glad" (vss. 47,48); ". . . Jews stirred up the *devout and honorable women*" (vs. 50). See also the references to those who *worshiped,* or *feared* God (Acts 10:2,7,22,35; 16:14; 17:4,17; 18:7); and study the instance of Cornelius (Acts 10:1-11:18) and Jesus' relations with the Roman centurion (Matt. 8:5-13; Luke 7:1-10).

Among the non-Israelitish recognized worshipers of the true God in the OT are Melchizedek, Job (the entire book is Gentile), Ruth, Rahab, Naaman, Uriah the Hittite, the Ninevites at the time of Jonah's preaching; the converts at the time of Esther (8:17). The "wise men from the East" are in the same category. The exclusivism of Ezra and Nehemiah was not to the contrary; it was the exclusion of idolatrous unbelief.

The subject of Israel's ancient mission among the Gentiles would require a far more extended study than is possible here. But, for example, Psalm 15; Isaiah 2:2-4; 44:5; Jeremiah 3:17; 4:2; 12:16; Zephaniah 3:9,10; Zechariah 8:20-23 are only a few of the OT passages indicating an evangelistic attitude toward the Gentiles.   J.O.B.

PROSTITUTE (prŏs'tĭ-tūt). The word occurs once in KJV (Lev. 19:29 ASV, RSV *harlot*), but also in ASV, RSV (Deut. 23:17, KJV *whore*). The idea is usually conveyed by "harlot" (Gen. 34:31; Matt. 21:31,32; Luke 15:30) or in KJV "whore" (Lev. 21:7). A famous example is Rahab (Josh. 2:1; Heb. 11:31; James 2:25). Israel, unfaithful to God, is called a harlot by the prophets (Isa. 1:21; Jer. 2:20; 3:1; Ezek. 16:15,16; Hos. 4:15). A special class of prostitutes performed sex acts in heathen worship; Heb. *kedēshâh,* a separated or "holy" woman (Deut. 23:17; Hos. 4:14). Tamar dressed herself like one of these (Gen. 38:15-24). The world-ruling city of Revelation 17 is called a whore (KJV) or harlot (ASV, RSV). Male prostitutes, KJV whoremongers, ASV fornicators, RSV immoral, are named (Eph. 5:5).

PROVENDER (prŏv'ĕn-dêr, Heb. *mispô'*), a term of rather wide meaning or usage, signifying *feed,* as grain or hay fed to cattle, horses and the like (Gen. 24:25,26; 42:27; Judg. 19:19,21). Sometimes, the feed was mixed with salt and fed to the younger animals (Isa. 30:24). The Bedouins of the deserts were especially anxious to provide rich pastureland, not only for its immediate use, but also for its future utilization for dried grain. Several other Hebrew words are employed, but they imply essentially the same thing.

PROVERB (prŏv'ûrb), a pithy saying, comparison or question; in OT usually Heb. *māshāl,* from a root meaning "represent, be like"; notably of Solomon's proverbs (I Kings 4:32; Prov. 1:1,6; 10:1; 25:1; Eccl. 12:9); others (I Sam. 10:12; 24:13; Ezek. 12:22,23; 16:44; 18:2,3). A man may become a proverb (Deut. 28:37); or Israel (I Kings 9:7; II Chron. 7:20); ASV, RSV have "byword" in Psalm 69:11; RSV in Jeremiah 24:9; ASV parable, RSV taunt in Isaiah 14:4. Numbers 21:27, a short poem (quoted in Jer. 48:45,46), RSV ascribes to "ballad singers." *Māshāl* is also translated *parable*; a few times *utter, speak, be like, compare.* Heb. *hîdhâh,* riddle, perplexing saying or question, is translated *proverb* once in KJV (Hab. 2:6, ASV margin, *riddle,* RSV *taunt*). It is also translated *riddle, dark saying, sentence, speech, hard saying.* In the NT, Greek *parabolé,* whose basic meaning is "comparison, placing side by side," is once translated *proverb* (Luke 4:23 KJV, RSV; parable in ASV). Usually it is translated *parable*; a few times *comparison,* or *figure.* Greek *paroimía,* also equivalent to Heb. *māshāl,* and to *mîdhâh,* means a saying of popular origin, ancient and widely known, accepted as obviously true (II Pet. 2:22). In John 16:25,29 ASV has *dark sayings,* margin, *parables*; RSV *figures.* A proverb is thought of as a short saying, a parable one somewhat longer, but the distinction is relative, and is not always observed by Bible writers. Comparison, using the concrete facts of life to represent its abstract principles, is the essential characteristic of both. A proverb may be a snatch of poetry, showing parallelism of structure; a sharp question; a pregnant sentence; a very brief story. Felicity of expression insures its long preservation and wide currency through oral transmission, even after it is fixed in literary, written form.   E.R.

PROVERBS, BOOK OF. The best representative of the so-called Wisdom literature of ancient Israel, the Book of Proverbs comprises 31 chapters of pithy statements on moral matters. Its text is "The fear of the Lord is the beginning of wisdom" (Prov. 1:7).

The headings in 1:1 and 10:1 claim a Solomonic authorship for the bulk of the book, and this claim, though often denied in recent days, has no objective evidence against it. Chapters 25-29 are said to be by Solomon, "copied out" by the men of Hezekiah. This obscure reference may refer to later collecting or editing of other Solomonic material. Of the authors Agur (chap. 30) and King Lemuel (chap. 31) we know nothing. They may even be poetic references to Solomon himself. Proverbs is mentioned in the apocryphal book of Ecclesiasticus (47:17), written about 180 B.C. Although the canonicity of Proverbs, Ezekiel, and a few other books was questioned by individual rabbis as late as in the council of Jamnia, A.D. 90, still it had long been accepted as authoritative Scripture, as the quotation in the Zadokite Document shows (col. 11, 1.19ff). It is quoted and alluded to several times in the NT.

An outline of the book should recognize the material and style of the composition. Damage has been done by some who find in the book merely a collection of ancient maxims for success — a kind of *Poor Richard's Almanac*. Actually the book is a compendium of moral instruction. It deals with sin and holiness. And the vehicle of instruction is a favorite Semitic device — teaching by contrast. The style of Proverbs with its pithy contrasts or more extended climactic poems can be paralleled in ancient literature in Egypt and Mesopotamia. The Hebrew author, however, has given instruction on life and holiness in the proverbial form. The case is similar in our Christian hymnody. We have abundant examples of secular poetry and melody combined in ordinary song. But Christian hymns use the vehicles of poetry and song to express distinctively Christian thought and experience.

Outline:
I. Introduction, 1:1-1:9.
II. Sin and righteousness personified and contrasted, 1:10-9:18.
III. Single-verse contrasts of sin and righteousness, 10:1-22:16.
IV. Miscellaneous and longer contrasts, 22:17-29:27.
V. Righteousness in poems of climax, 30:1-31:31.

The first section of the book begins (1:7) and ends (9:10) with the statement that the "fear of the Lord is the beginning of wisdom." It is obvious therefore that the wisdom extolled in Proverbs is not just a high degree of intelligence but a moral virtue. This is made plain in the first section by the contrasts involved. Wisdom is personified as a righteous woman, (8:1). This is natural because *wisdom* in Hebrew is a feminine noun. The foolish woman is presented as inviting men with identical words (9:4 and 16), but she invites them to sin. The harlot, who is given large place in this section, is typical of all sin. Murder and theft are the opposite of wisdom in chapter 1, but usually and forcefully the strange woman, the simple woman, the foolish woman — the harlot — is held up as the opposite of personified righteousness. Some find in wisdom, 8:22 a foreshadowing of Christ, but this is not sure. It is not so used in the NT.

In the major section, 10:1-22:16, the same contrast appears in single-verse aphorisms. Here the *personification* of sin and righteousness does not appear, but the same synonyms for virtue and vice are repeatedly used and should be understood as such. Perhaps the greatest error in interpreting the book comes from the tendency to quote these Proverbs as mere secular maxims instead of godly instruction. *Folly* here does not mean stupidity, just as *foolish woman* of 9:13 does not refer to an ignoramus. Both terms refer to sin. Through this whole section the terms *wisdom, understanding, integrity, knowledge*, etc. are synonymous terms referring to holiness. Their opposites, *fool, folly, simple, scorner, contentious, vain*, etc. refer to wickedness. In short, a *foolish son* is not a dullard, but a knave. A *contentious woman* is not merely argumentative, but downright evil. A *scorner* is not just supercilious, but is a wayward soul. The lack of context sometimes beclouds the interpretation. But occasionally a verse is partially repeated elsewhere where the variant form clarifies the meaning (cf. 27:15 and 21:19).

Section IV, 22:19-29:27, is more general, but uses the same vocabulary of morality. In this part are some special parallels with an Egyptian work entitled *The Wisdom of Amen-em-Opet*. The correspondences, however, do not invalidate the above claim that the author of Proverbs gives distinctive treatment to his theme.

The last section, 30:1-31:31, includes several climactic proverbs — four — which apparently emphasize the fourth point. Cf. 6:16-19 where among seven things the seventh is the climax. Here also is the famous final poem — an alphabetical poem — extolling the virtuous woman.   R.L.H.

PROVIDENCE. The universal providence of God is the basic assumption of all Scripture. As in English, the corresponding Hebrew and Greek words such as *rā'âh* (Gen. 22:8; I Sam. 16:1) and *problépon* (Heb. 11:40) in their contexts mean far more than mere foresight or foreknowledge. The meaning is "prearrangement." As used historically the theological term "providence" means nothing short of "the universal sovereign rule of God."

The definition in Q. 11 of the Westminster Shorter Catechism expresses the view of all Bible-believing Christians; "God's works of providence are, His most holy, wise, and powerful preserving and governing all His creatures, and all their actions." Divine providence is the out-working of the divine decrees, which are "the purpose of him who worketh all things after the council of his own will" (Eph. 1:11).

The Biblical doctrine of divine providence does not imply a mechanistic or fatalistic view of the processes of the world or of human life. In a more extended treatise on this subject, secondary causes, and the relation between human responsibility and divine sovereignty would have to be canvassed. For the present purposes it must suffice to quote what seem to the writer the best available brief creedal statements on these matters:

"Although, in relation to the foreknowledge, and decree of God, the first cause, all things come to pass immutably and infallibly, yet, by the same providence, He ordereth them to fall out according to the nature of second causes, either necessarily, freely, or contingently.

"[God's providence includes the permission of] all . . . sins of angels and men, and that not a bare permission, but such [permission] as hath joined with it a most wise and powerful bounding, and otherwise ordering and governing of them, in a manifold dispensation, to his holy ends; yet so as the sinfulness thereof proceedeth only from the creature, and not from God; who, being most holy and righteous, neither is nor can be the author or approver of sin" (Westminster Confession, Chap. V Paragraphs II and IV).

"Second causes" are the ordinary forces and events of nature which God usually employs to accomplish His purposes.

That God's providence includes His decree to permit sin should not seem strange or paradoxical. One of the good features of so-called "progressive education" is *learning by experience,* and this is based on the assumption that what *ought not to be* is *not* the same as what *ought not to be permitted.* One of the clearest Biblical illustrations of this principle is found in Joseph's words to his brethren in Genesis 50:20, "As for you, ye thought evil against me [they had sold him into slavery]; but God meant it unto good, to bring to pass as it is this day, to save much people alive."

It is customary to distinguish *special* providence from *general* providence. The former term refers to God's particular care over the life and activity of the believer. "We know that, in reference to those who love God, God works all things together for good" (Rom. 8:28 original tr.). "The steps of a good man are ordered by the Lord" (Ps. 37: 23; see Phil. 1:28). "Seek ye first the kingdom of God and 'his righteousness and all these things [daily needs] shall be added unto you" (Matt. 6: 23). The entire book of Job is devoted to the temporal sufferings of a godly man under divine providence. Hebrews 11:40 teaches that providence, for men of faith, includes something far better than experiences of this life.

General providence includes the government of the entire universe, but especially of the affairs of men. "Behold the heaven and the heaven of heavens is the Lord's thy God, the earth also with all that therein is" (Deut. 10:14); ". . . the Most High divided to the nations their inheritance; when he separated the sons of Adam he set the bounds of the people . . ." (Deut. 32:8; see also Neh. 9:6; Dan. 4:35).

Divine providence is presented as "upholding all things by his powerful word" (Heb. 1:3); ". . . he maketh his sun to rise upon the evil and the good, and sendeth rain on the just and on the unjust" (Matt. 5:45, see Ps. 68:9; Rom. 1:20; Acts 14:15-17. See Common Grace.)

Although God's grace is always offered to all men (Acts 10:34,35), yet the *main stream* of historical revelation and blessing for the world, through the instrumentality of Israel and the Church, is a principal theme of all Scripture (see Rom. 3:1,2; 9:3-6; 11:1; I Tim. 3:15; Acts 7:1-60; 13:16-43). To this end God sometimes moves in unrecognized events and processes (Isa. 40:1-5; 44:28-45:4).

Not only is the general course of nature sustained by God's providence, but the moral order and its logical consequences as well: "Whatsoever a man soweth, that shall he also reap. He that soweth to the flesh shall of the flesh reap corruption. He that soweth to the Spirit shall of the Spirit reap life everlasting" (Gal. 6:7,8). Divine providence sustaining the moral order is the principal theme of the book of Proverbs.

The distinction between God's immanent or natural action and His transcendent or supernatural action is of supreme importance in the understanding of the doctrine of providence. The reader should consult the article on MIRACLES. The case for Christianity depends entirely upon the miracles of the incarnation and the resurrection of

Christ. Nevertheless, as the article on miracles shows, godly faith has always existed in a world in which there are long periods of time, even in Bible history, in which God does not choose to give "signs" or display miracles as evidences. It is imperative that we learn to see the glory of God in the regular works of providence as well as in the miraculous.

Christian men of science sometimes complain that fundamentalists tend to invoke the supernatural whenever there are gaps in scientific knowledge, to the embarrassment of Christians when scientists fill in the gaps with well accredited facts. A mere "God of the Gaps" idea may be as harmful as mechanistic pantheism. The genuinely miraculous in Christianity is not dimmed but rather magnified, by recognition of God's providential faithfulness in the regular processes of nature. J.O.B.

PROVINCIA (prō-vĭn'sĭ-à), a word of doubtful etymology, signifies the sphere of duty of a magistrate. The "roads and forests of Italy" for example, were a *province,* supervised by the appropriate commissioner. With the gradual acquisition of the empire, spheres of magisterial duty signified increasingly the defense, organization, and government of overseas territories, and the word *province* acquired that geographical significance which became its prime Latin meaning, and its exclusive derived meaning. The provinces of Rome in this sense of the word were acquired over a period of more than three centuries. The first was Sicily (241 B.C.). The last were Britain, organized by Claudius, and Dacia, acquired by Trajan. Marcus Aurelius made a province out of Mesopotamia. Under the settlement of 27 B.C., all provinces were divided into two categories. First there were the imperial provinces, those which required a frontier army, and which, in consequence, were kept under the control of the emperor, who was commander-in-chief of all armed forces. Secondly there were the senatorial provinces, those which presented no major problems of military occupation or defense, and which were left in the control of the Senate. Imperial provinces were governed by the emperor's legati, or, in the case of smaller units like Judaea or Thrace, by procurators. The senatorial provinces were under proconsuls (e.g. the "deputy" (KJV) of Acts 13:7. Cyprus became a senatorial province in 22 B.C.). Egypt, a special case, was governed by a prefect. E.M.B.

PROVOCATION (prŏv'ō-kā'shŭn, Heb. *ka'as, mārâh*; Gr. *parazelóo, parorgízo*), any cause of God's anger at sin; the deeds of evil kings (I Kings 15:30; 21:22; II Kings 23:26); of Israel (Ezek. 20:28); of mockers (Job 17:2). In the prayer of repentance of the returned exiles (Neh. 9:18,26) the provocation (RSV *great blasphemies*) consisted in making the molten calf. In Psalm 95:8 ASV, RSV transliterate instead of translating Heb. *Meribah,* the geographical location named for the provocation when the Israelites demanded water, which Moses brought out of a rock (Exod. 17: 1-7; Num. 20:13,24; 27:14; Deut. 32:51; 33:8; Ps. 81:7), the waters of Meribah. The one NT passage in which (in KJV) *provocation* occurs (Heb. 3:8,15,16 RSV *rebellion*) relates to this incident. The verb *provoke* occasionally has a good sense, *to stir up* (Heb. 10:24).

PRUNING HOOK (Heb. *mazmerôth*), an agricultural tool used in the cultivation of the vine, with a sharp knife-like end for pruning (Isa. 2:4; Joel 3:10; Mic. 4:3).

"He leadeth me beside the still waters." The Twenty-third Psalm series. © MPS

PSALMS, THE BOOK OF, follows "the law" and "the prophets" in Hebrew (Luke 24:44), inaugurating the final division of the OT, called "the writings" (because of their heterogeneous, non-professionally prophetic authorship; see CANON). It is the longest book in the Bible. The majority of its chapters, moreover, are antedated only by Genesis-Ruth. But the basic reason why Psalms is more quoted by the NT and more revered by Christians than any other Old Testament book is found in its inspiring subject matter. Both for public worship — "the hymnbook of Solomon's temple" — and for individual devotional guidance, its 150 poems constitute the height of God-given literature.

I. Name. The Hebrew designation of Psalms is *Tehillim,* meaning "praises," a term that reflects much of the book's content (cf. Ps. 145, title). Its name in Latin and English Bibles, however, comes from the Greek, *Psalmoí,* which means "twangings [of harp strings]," and then, as a result, songs sung to the accompaniment of harps. This latter name originated in the LXX (cf. its NT authentication, Luke 20:42) and reflects the form of the book's poetry. The same is true of its alternate title, *Psalterion,* meaning "psaltery," and then, a collection of harp songs, from which comes the English term "Psalter."

II. Authorship. The Psalms, naturally enough, make no attempt within their respective poetic framework to elaborate the circumstances of their composition. But, as might indeed be expected, many of them do prefix explanatory titles in prose, indicating their authorship and occasion for writing, as well as poetic-type and musical direction (see below, Sections V and VI). Most commonly appears the phrase, Psalm of Moses (David, etc.). The Hebrew preposition rendered by the word "of" expresses authorship (cf. Hab. 3:1, "of Habakkuk the prophet") but also possession (Ps. 24:1a, "the Lord's") or dedication (Ps. 4, etc., RSV, "to the choirmaster"). But while "Psalm of David"

has sometimes been interpreted to mean merely "of Davidic character," or, "belonging to a collection entitled, *David,*" its actual usage in Scripture clearly indicates Davidic authorship (cf. Pss 7, 18). The book of Psalms thus assigns 73 of its chapters to David, two to Solomon (Pss. 72, 127), one each to the wise men Heman and Ethan (Pss. 88-89, cf. I Kings 4:31), one to Moses (Ps. 90), and 23 to the Levitical singing-clans of Asaph (Pss. 50, 73-83) and Korah (Pss. 42 (including 43), 44-49, 84-85, 87 — 88 concerns compilation; see below, Section IV. 49 remain anonymous.

Modern Biblical criticism consistently rejects the psalm titles as of little value (IB, IV, 8). One suspects, however, that such denials spring from an evolutionary bias, which refuses to admit as genuinely Davidic the advanced spiritual conceptions that Scripture thus assigns to an era 1000 years B.C. From the viewpoint of lower criticism, no reason exists for denying their authenticity within the text of the OT: All Hebrew MSS contain these titles; the earliest versions (such as the LXX) not only exhibit their translation but even misrepresent certain of their meanings, which had been lost in antiquity; and Hebrew Bibles regularly include them in the numbered verses of the inspired text (thus raising the verse numbers of many of the psalms by one or two digits). From the viewpoint of higher criticism, the exhaustive analysis of Robert Dick Wilson (PTR 24 (1926), 353-395) has demonstrated the compatibility of David's authorship with the content of each psalm attributed to him (cf. Ps. 44, once considered to be Maccabean, but equally comprehensible as from David's era, under military duress (H. C. Leupold, *Exposition of the Psalms,* Columbus, Ohio: Wartburg Press, 1959, pp. 344-345). Archeological research in Babylonia and Egypt has brought to light advanced hymnody centuries before Abraham; and the recovery of Canaanitish literature at Ugarit has furnished significant parallels to the Psalms, from the time of Moses. (cf. J. Patton, *Canaanite Parallels in the Book of Psalms,* Baltimore: Johns Hopkins Press, 1944, and the hesitancy of modern scholars to assign to later periods certain presumed Aramaisms in language, IB, IV,11). David himself is known to have enjoyed musical and literary endowments (I Sam. 16:16-18, Amos 6:5; cf. his acknowledged composition of II Sam. 1:19-27, etc.), to have exercised leadership in the development of Israel's liturgy (II Sam. 6:5,13; I Chron. 15-16,25; II Chron. 7:6, 29:30), and to have realized Spirit-born empowerment as "the sweet psalmist of Israel" (II Sam. 23:1-2; Mark 12:36; Acts 1:16, 2:30-31, 4:25; see DAVID). The NT

"He restoreth my soul." © MPS

repeatedly authenticates ascriptions to David: Pss. 16 (Acts 2:25), 32 (Rom. 4:6), 69 (Acts 1:16, Rom. 11:9), 110 (Luke 20:42, Acts 2:34). Certain of the anonymously-titled psalms are also recognized as of Davidic composition: Pss. 2 (Acts 4:25), 95 (Heb. 4:7, where "in David" = his person, not his book, as if Psalms were entirely his), 96, 105, and 106 (underlying David's words in I Chron. 16:8-36, though cf. HDB, IV,148). But it is significant that no psalm which claims *other* authorship, or contains later historical allusions (as Ps. 137, exilic) is ever attributed in Scripture to him.

III. Occasions. The titles of 14 of the Davidic psalms designate specific occasions of composition and contribute to a historical understanding of Scripture as follows (chronologically):

Ps. 59 (= I Sam. 19:11) sheds light on David's jealous associates (vs. 12)

56 (I Sam. 21:11) shows how David's fear at Gath led to faith (vs. 3)

34 (21:13) illumines God's subsequent goodness (vss. 6-8)

142 (22:1) depicts David at Adullam, persecuted (vs. 6)

52 (22:9) emphasizes Saul's wickedness (vs. 1)

54 (23:19) judges the Ziphites (vs. 3)

57 (24:3) concerns En-gedi, when Saul was caught in his own trap (vs. 6)

7 (24:9) introduces slanderous Cush (vss. 3,8 correspond to I Sam. 24:11-12)

18 (II Sam. 7:1) is repeated in II Samuel 22

60 (8:13-14) illumines the dangerous Edomitic campaign (vs. 10; I Kings 11:15)

51 (12:13-14) elaborates on David's guilt with Bath-sheba

3 (15:16) depicts David's faith vs. Absalom vs. 5)

63 (16:2) illumines the king's eastward flight vs. 11)

30 (II Sam. 24:25, cf. I Chron. 22:1) reviews David's sin prior to his dedication of the temple area (vss. 5-6)

Among the remaining psalms that express authorship, the 23 composed by Israel's singers exhibit widely separated backgrounds, since these Levitical clans continued active into post-Exilic times (Ezra 2:41). Most of them pertain to the Davidic or Solomonic periods. Psalm 83, however, suits the ministry of the Asphite Jahaziel in 852 B.C. (cf. vss. 5-8 with II Chron. 20:1-2,14), while Psalms 74, 79, and the concluding strophe of 88-89 were produced by Asaphites and Korahites who survived the destruction of Jerusalem in 586 B.C. (74:3,8-9; 79:1; 89:44). A few anonymous psalms stem from the Exile (137), from the return to Judah in 537 B.C. (107:2-3, 126:1), or from Nehemiah's rebuilding of Jerusalem's walls in 444 (147:13). Yet others that depict tragedy could as easily relate to the disorders of Absalom's revolt or to similar Davidic calamities (cf. Pss. 102:13-22, 106:41-47, with the critical caution of R. Laird Harris, in Carl F. H. Henry, ed., *The Biblical Expositor*, Philadelphia: Holman, 1960, II,49). Liberal scholars once spoke confidently of numerous Maccabean psalms (second century B.C.); but the discovery of the Dead Sea Scrolls, that date from this very period and contain manuscripts of both the canonical psalms and of the *Hôdhāyôth* (secondary psalmodic compositions), establishes the Persian era as the latest possible point for inspired psalmody (Frank M. Cross, *The Ancient Library of Qumran and Modern Biblical Studies,* Garden

"My cup runneth over." © MPS

City, N.Y.: Doubleday, 1958, p. 122). It reinforces the evangelical hypothesis of Ezra as the writer of I-II Chronicles (the last book in the Hebrew Bible) and as compiler of the entire Jewish canon, shortly after 424 B.C. (Darius II, mentioned in Neh. 12:22).

IV Compilation. Psalms is organized into five books: 1-41, 42-72, 73-89, 90-106, and 107-150; and, since the same psalm appears in more than one collection — e.g., Pss. 14 and part of 40 (Book I) as 53 and 70 (Book II), and the latter halves of 57 and 60 (Book II) as 108 (Book V) — it seems likely that each compilation experienced independent existence. Furthermore, since the last psalm of each collection was composed with terminal ascriptions that were designed for the book as a whole (41:13; 72:18-20; 89:52; 106:48, and the entire 150th Psalm for Book V), it appears that the origins of these five concluding psalms provide clues for the compilation of their respective books. Psalm 41 was written by David; and, since the remaining psalms of Book I are also attributed to him (except for Ps. 1, which constitutes the book's introduction; Ps. 10, which combines with 9 to form one continuous acrostic; and Ps. 33, which has no title), it would appear that David himself brought together this first collection. He further composed Psalm 106 (cf. I Chron. 16:34-36); so that Book IV, with its liturgical nature (contrast the more personal character of Pss. 1-41), must likewise be traced to David's own hand, prior to his death in 970 B.C. Books II-III exhibit more of a national interest (cf. their stress upon Elohim, God transcendent, rather than upon the Lord's personal name, Jehovah). King Solomon (d. 930 B.C.), who was responsible for the doxology of 72:18-20, thus becomes the historical compiler of Book II (his reference to "the prayers of David," 72:20, seems to be due to his father's having composed over half of the chapters that make up Pss. 42-72). Book III, however, was completed and

"Thou anointest my head with oil." © MPS

collected by unnamed Korahites soon after 586 B.C. (see above); for though the body of Psalms 88-89 was written by Solomon's Ezrahites, the title that is prefixed to both (cf. the inappropriateness of the description "song [joyful]" to Ps. 88 alone) designates the sons of Korah as its ultimate compilers (cf. its terminal strophe, 89:38-52, which they seem to have suffixed in the spirit of Ps. 88). Indeed, this third book includes several post-Solomonic and sixth century compositions; and, when combined with Books I-II, it constituted Israel's psalter of the Exile. Finally Book V, which parallels David's Book IV in liturgical interest but includes several post-Exilic (as well as early Davidic) psalms, came into being shortly after 537 B.C. It then remained for a Spirit-led scribe to bring Books IV and V into union with I-III, adding his own inspired composition of Psalms 146-150 as a grand halleluia for the entire Psalter. Since this last writing occurred in 444 B.C. (Ps. 147:13) at the time of Ezra's proclamation of the written law and reform of temple worship (Neh. 8-10), it may well be that Ezra himself executed the final compilation of the book (cf. Ezra 7:10).

V. Contents. Each of the 150 psalms exhibits the formal character of Hebrew poetry. This consists, not primarily in rhyme, or even rhythmic balance, but rather in a parallelism of thought, whereby succeeding phrases either repeat or in some way elaborate the previous line. The poems vary in content. Hermann Gunkel has proposed a number of categories, not all of which appear valid (see Section VI); but the following psalm-types do distinguish themselves, by subject or by their Hebrew titles. Certain portions (e.g., 34:11-16) exhibit a marked gnomic or wisdom character, much akin to Proverbs (cf. Pss. 37, 49, 73, 128, 133, and especially Solomon's Ps. 127). The title *Maschil*, "instructive"(?), which suggests a didactic or at least meditative quality, appears in 13 of the superscriptions. Included is the historical 78th Psalm (cf. the recited histories of Pss. 81, 105, 106). The title *Michtam*, "atoning"(?), introduces Psalms 16,56-60, perhaps because of reference to covered sins; and among David's most famous penitential psalms are the 32nd and 51st (cf. 38, 130, 143).

Most of the poems possess a lyric, singing quality and are entitled "psalm" (*mizmôr*, stringed accompaniment; 57 times) or "song" (*shîr*, joyful melody; 30 times). Their praises may be general Ps. 145) or specific (e.g., Pss. 19, 119, concerning God's revelation). The term *Shiggaion* (Ps. 7, Hab. 3:1), "dirge," suggests the emotion of grief and validates Gunkel's categories of both national and individual laments. Of related character are the imprecatory psalms. Such prayers for the overthrow of the ungodly, while never to displace the Christian's standard of love, yet constitute a necessary part of God's inspired Word. They describe God's abhorrence of sin (Pss. 101:8, 139:21), man's resignation of vengeance to God (37:8-9, 104:34-35), divine rather than personal vindication (83:3-5, 92:11-15), and heaven's ultimate triumph (125:4-5; or 109:6-19, predicting Judas, Acts 1:20. Cf. Chalmers Martin, "The Imprecations in the Psalms," PTR I. (1903), 537-553). Particular significance attaches to the 17 specifically Messianic psalms, in the whole or in parts of which Christ either is referred to in the third person (8:4-8; 72:6-17; 89:3-4, 28-29, 34-36; 109:6-19; 118:22; 132:11-12), is addressed in the second (45:6-7; 68:18; 102:25-27; 110), or speaks Himself in the first person (2; 16:10; 22; 40:6-8; 41:9b-c; 69:4, 21,25; 78:2).

VI Use. Psalm titles in Books I-III contain a number of musical terms in Hebrew. Some of these designate ancient melodies, to which the poems may have been sung: *Aijeleth Shahar*, "The doe of dawn" (Ps. 22); *Al-taschith*, "Do not destroy," probably a vintage-song (Pss. 57-59,75; cf. Isa. 65:8); *Jonath-elem-rechokim*, "Dove of distant trees" (Ps. 56); *Muth-labben*, "Death to the son" (9); *Shoshannim*, "Lilies" (45, 69); and *Shushaneduth*, "Lily of testimony" (60, 80). Others preserve musical instructions, much of the significance of which is now uncertain: *alamoth*, "maidens," treble"(?) (Ps. 46), perhaps contrasted with *sheminith*, "[lower] octave" (6, 12); *gittith*, "the instrument from Gath"? (8,81,84); *mahalath (leannoth)*, "grief (for afflicting)" (53,88); *neginoth*, "stringed instruments" (seven times, plus Hab. 3:19); *nehiloth*, "wind instruments" (Ps. 5); and *selah*, "lifting up" (71 times, not in titles but at the end of strophes; cf. 3:2,4,8), perhaps indicating a dramatic pause for musical effects (cf. *higgaion selah*, "meditation pause"(?) (9:16). A number of Israel's psalms had specific liturgical usage. The "songs of degrees" (Pss. 120-134) may have been chanted by pilgrims ascending to Jerusalem (cf. 121:1, 122:4). Psalm 92 was composed for sabbath use. The *Hallel* (113-118) accompanied the passover (cf. Matthew 26:30), and "The LORD reigneth (93-100) constitutes a liturgical series magnifying God's sovereignty. Gunkel, accordingly, proposes a category of "psalms for the enthronement of Yahweh." Sigmund Mowinckel even postulates an elaborate Hebrew new year's festival based on Babylonian analogies: the king, as Jehovah's "son," is said to have participated in various cult-dramas and processions, with a climactic reestablishment of God's kingship for another season. But while verses such as 24:7, "Lift up your heads, O ye gates . . . and the King of glory shall come in," probably do preserve references to David's historic procession to bring the ark of God into Jerusalem (II Sam. 6, cf. I Kings 8:6), Mowinckel's enthronement theory is both theologically unacceptable and historically unsupported (IB, IV,7; Harris, *op. cit.*, II,69).

Paralleling Mowinckel's stress upon cultic origins is a modern emphasis upon a collective rather than individualistic understanding and use of Psalms. Yet while certain of its poems do exhibit

"And I will dwell in the house of the Lord for ever." This is a view of Jerusalem from the Mount of Olives. © MPS

group expression (particularly among the pilgrim songs, 124,126, even when using "I," 129), others manifest distinctly individualistic consciousness (1, 21,112,127). The compilation embraces not simply the congregational hymnbook of Solomon's temple but also the devotional heart beat of men like David, who "strengthened himself [against the crowd] in Jehovah his God" (I Sam. 30:6 ARV). The richest blessings of the Psalms flow from its affirmations of personal faith, "The LORD is *my* shepherd; *I* shall not want" (23:1).

Bibliography: Harris, R. Laird, "Psalms," Carl F. H. Henry, ed., *The Biblical Expositor*. Philadelphia: Holman, 1960. II, 34-70. Johnson, A. R., "The Psalms," H. H. Rowley, ed., *The Old Testament and Modern Study*. Oxford: Clarendon, 1951. Leupold, H. C., *Exposition of the Psalms*. Columbus, Ohio: Wartburg Press, 1959. Paterson, John, *The Praises of Israel*. New York: Charles Scribner's Sons, 1950. Snaith, Norman H., *The Jewish New Year Festival*. London: Society for Promoting Christian Knowledge, 1947. Wilson, Robert Dick, "The Headings of the Psalms," PTR 24 (1926), 353-395. Young, Edward J., *An Introduction to the Old Testament*. Rev. ed.; Grand Rapids: Eerdmans, 1960. Pp. 307-327. J.B.P.

PSALMS OF SOLOMON. One of the pseudepigrapha, extant in Greek, apparently a translation from a Heb. original, consisting of 18 psalms in imitation of the canonical psalms, probably written between 64 and 46 B.C. They relate to the afflictions of the Jews of that period, and are significant for the light they shed on Jewish Messianic expectations.

PSALMODY (See Music)

PSALTER (See Music, Psalms)

PSALTERY (See Music, Psalms)

PSEUDEPIGRAPHA (sū'dē-pĭg'rá-fá), books not in the Heb. canon or the Apocrypha, ascribed to earlier authors; including *The Ascension of Isaiah, Assumption of Moses, Book of Enoch, Book of Jubilees, Greek Apocalypse of Baruch, Letters of Aristeas, III and IV Maccabees, Psalms of Solomon, Secrets of Enoch, Sibylline Oracles, Syriac Apocalypse of Baruch, Epistle of Baruch,* and *Testament of the Twelve Patriarchs.* They are important for their disclosure of Jewish ideas in the intertestamental period.

PTOLEMAIS (See Accho)

PTOLEMY (tŏl'ĕ-mē, Gr. Ptolemaíos), the common name of the 15 Macedonian kings of Egypt whose dynasty extended from the death of Alexander the Great in 323 B.C., to the murder of the young Caesarion, son of Julius Caesar and Cleopatra, at Octavian's orders in 30 B.C. The first Ptolemy, surnamed Soter, 367 to 282 B.C., was a distinguished officer of Alexander, became satrap of Egypt in 323 B.C., and, as one of the Diadochi, or "Successors" of Alexander, converted his command into a kingdom. As a successor of the pharaohs, Ptolemy I took over the ancient administration of Egypt, and especially the theory glimpsed in the OT story of Joseph, that the ruler owned the land. Hence a vast and ramified, highly centralized bureaucracy, which became a permanent feature of Ptolemaic rule, prepared the way for the Roman imperial administration of Egypt, and contrasted with the Hellenistic policies of the rival Seleucid regime.

A mass of papyrological evidence provides a detailed picture of state control in the Ptolemaic system. In passing, it may be mentioned that Ptolemy I wrote a history of Alexander, which is most unfortunately lost. The second Ptolemy, surnamed Philadelphus, 308 to 246 B.C., consolidated the organization of the land. He was responsible for much of its remarkable financial system, including the most highly developed banking system of ancient times, a rigid machinery of control in commerce and industry, and a nationalized, planned, and budgeted economy.

Ptolemy I, reproduced from a silver tetradrachma of the period (323-283 B.C.).

In the reign of Ptolemy II there first erupted the long rivalry with the Seleucids of Syria over the Palestinian frontier, with Antioch inheriting the old role of the Hittites and Assyrians, and Alexandria continuing the old pharaonic policy in the northern approaches. Ptolemy II also instituted the cult of the divine ruler, a simple enough graft on old indigenous beliefs, a preparatory factor for Caesar-worship. The great city of Alexandria grew apace during this reign. Ptolemy II built the amazing Pharos lighthouse outside the twin harbors, and the Museum, the most notable center of culture and literature in the ancient world. He established the famous library, and cut a canal from the Red Sea to the Nile. This was the Golden Age of Ptolemaic Egypt.

The next reign, that of Ptolemy III, surnamed Euergetes I, 288 to 221 B.C., saw the high tide of expansion and the first premonitory symptoms of decline. They were in full view under the fourth Ptolemy, surnamed Philopator, 244 to 205 B.C., whose reign saw some significant native uprisings, and the loss of Nubia for a generation. There followed a century of dynastic strife, palace intrigue, anarchic minorities, and decline, during which Egypt survived through the strength of its natural defenses and its strategic isolation rather than through the worth and enlightenment of its leadership. Ptolemy XI, surnamed Alexander II, 100 to 80 B.C., was the last of the male line of Ptolemy I. He was killed by rioting Alexandrians, notoriously an unruly populace.

Ptolemy XII, surnamed Auletes or the Fluteplayer, 116 to 51 B.C., fled to Rome in the face of Alexandrian lawlessness, and the restoration of the king to his tottering throne by Gabinius, at the Senate's orders, was Rome's first significant intervention in the land, which the Republic, no less than Napoleon nearly 19 centuries later, saw to be the strategic key to the Middle East. The wife of Ptolemy XIII was Cleopatra VII, the famous bearer of the name. Domestic, and consequently political and dynastic strife between husband and wife, led to Caesar's intervention, after his rival Pompey had met his death in Egypt. Ptolemy XIV was an insignificant brother of Cleopatra, Ptolemy XV her ill-fated son by Caesar.

The great achievement of the Ptolemies was Alexandria, with all that its immense cultural institutions signified in the ancient world. Alexandria was creative and conservative. It preserved much of the literature of Greece, and but for the plague of Islam, which engulfed the land, would have preserved more. It produced great writers and scientists. It fathered the Septuagint. It created 'Alexandrianism,' which meant much in the literature of Rome. Alexandria always stood apart from Egypt. It was a Greek city, and its peculiar contribution to Hellenism was the gift to history and civilization of the first Ptolemies.

E.M.B.

PUA (pū'à, Heb. *pû'âh*), another form of Puvah or Phuvah. A member of the family clan of Tola, of the tribe of Issachar. Num. 26:23.

PUAH, PUVAH (pū'à, pū'và), the name of one of the Hebrew midwives who refused to obey the edict of the Pharaoh to destroy the infant sons born of Hebrew women (Exod. 1:15-20).

PUBLICAN (See Occupations and Professions)

PUBLIUS (pŭb'lĭ-ŭs, Gr. *Póplios*), the chief person on the island of Malta (Melita) in the Mediterranean. He gave lodging and food to Paul and his companions after their shipwreck on the island's rocky coast. Paul also healed his father and many others (Acts 27:27-44; 28:7-10).

PUDENS (pū'dĕnz, Gr. *Poúdes, modest*), a Christian in the city of Rome who sends greetings to Timothy in Paul's last letter (II Tim. 4:21).

PUHITES (pū'hĭts, Heb. *pûthî, simple*) family descended from Caleb, residing in Kiriath-Jearim (I Chron. 2:50,53).

PUL (pŭl, pōol). 1. A king of Assyria, Tiglath-pileser III, who invaded Israel in the days of Menahem and was bribed to depart (II Kings 15:19), though he carried off captives (I Chron. 5:26).

2. A tribe or place in Africa, named between Tarshish and Lud (Isa. 66:19), conjectured to be Put.

PULPIT (pŭl'pit, Heb. *mighdôl*), a scaffolding, a platform, or a high object of any kind (Neh. 8:4), used primarily as a position from which to speak.

PULSE (See Plants)

PUNISHMENT (pŭn'ĭsh-mĕnt). Death was the punishment for striking or even reviling a parent (Exod. 21:15,17); blasphemy (Lev. 24:14,16,23); sabbath breaking (Num. 15:32-36); witchcraft Exod. 22:18); adultery (Lev. 20:10); rape (Deut. 22:25); incestuous or unnatural connection (Lev. 20:11,14,16); kidnaping (Exod. 21:16); idolatry (Lev. 20:2). Cutting off from the people is *ipso facto* excommunication or outlawry, forfeiture of the privileges of the covenant people (Lev. 18:29). The hand of God executed the sentence in some cases (Gen. 17:14; Lev. 23:30; 20:3; Num. 4:15,18,20). Capital punishment was by stoning (Deut. 22:24); burning (Lev. 20:14); the sword (Exod. 32:27); hanging: the hanged were accounted accursed, so were buried at evening, as the hanging body defiled the land (Gal. 3:13; II Sam. 21:6,9); strangulation (not in Scripture, but in rabbinical writings). Other punishments; sawing asunder (Heb. 11:37); cutting with iron harrows (II Sam. 12:31; RSV, labor with harrows, etc.); precipitation (Luke 4:29; II Chron. 25:12; stripes, only 40 allowed (Deut. 25:2,3), therefore only 39 given (II Cor. 11:24); the convict stripped to the waist, received them from a three-thonged whip, either lying on the ground (Deut. 25:2), or in a bent position tied to a pillar.

If the executioner exceeded the number he was punished. Punishment in kind (*lex talionis*) was a common principle (Exod. 21:23-25), also composition, restitution of the thing or its equivalent (Exod. 21:19,30). Slander of a wife's honor was punished by a fine and stripes (Deut. 22:18,19). Crucifixion was not practiced till Roman times. Punishment for sin is widely recognized in the Bible, and is in the hands of God (directly, Gen. 4:1-16; Lam. 3:37-39; 4:6; Zech. 14:19; indirectly, I Pet. 2:14; everlasting punishment (Matt. 25:46). See PRISON.   E.R.

PUNISHMENT, EVERLASTING. The fact of everlasting punishment, for those who reject God's love revealed in Christ, is plainly stated in Matthew 25:46, "These shall go away into everlasting punishment (*kolasin aionion*) but the righteous into life eternal (*zoen aionion*)." In this saying Jesus is speaking of persons who, by their attitude toward his "brethren" had given evidence of their rejection of himself (vs. 45).

The same doctrine is explicit in the OT in Daniel 12:2. (See discussion of this passage in the article on Resurrection.) Here it is predicted that those not raised "to everlasting life" will be raised "to shame and everlasting contempt."

In Matthew 25:46 one and the same Greek word *aionion* (translated "everlasting" in one instance and "eternal" in the other) applies to the destiny of both the saved and the lost. The same word is used in the LXX of Daniel 12:2, translating the Hebrew word *olam,* and applying to the destiny of both classifications of men. There are no stronger words in Hebrew or in Greek with which to express infinite time than those designating the duration of the punishment of the wicked.

The final place of everlasting punishment is called the "lake of fire" (Rev. 19:20; 20:10,14,15). This is also called "the second death" (Rev. 2:11; 20:6,14,15). In this connection it should be remembered that "death" in biblical usage *never* means extinction or non-existence. Always the word designates a relative state of existence. That "the second death" is a state of conscious existence is evident from Revelation 14:9-11; 20:10.

"Hell" is an Anglo-Saxon word the root meaning of which probably is "the hidden." This translates the probable root meaning of the Greek *Hades,* Hades, thought to be derived from *a, not,* and the root of *eidos, visible.* Consequently "Hell" and "Hades" both probably have the root meaning of "The unseen realm."

In the KJV "hell" translates *She'ol,* or Sheol in the OT, and this corresponds to the fact that LXX regularly renders *She'ol* as *Hades.* There are competent scholars who argue that in the OT *She'ol* always means the physical grave. On this point more study is needed.

In the NT, however, *Hades,* translated "Hell," occurs five times in contexts in which it could not mean the physical grave, and there are none of the remaining five passages (Matt. 11:23, parallel to Luke 10:15, these two obviously figurative; Matt. 16:18; Rev. 1:18; 6:8, the last also figurative) in which the context demands any other meaning than "the unseen realm where the souls of all the dead are."

In Acts 2:27,31, Peter, quoting Psalm 16:10, points out that Christ's soul did not remain in Hades. It is entirely contrary to all Biblical assumptions to think of the soul of a godly person as being in the physical grave. The thought of Christ's soul being in Hades while his body was in the grave is found in the Apostles' Creed, and is supported by His word, "Today shalt thou be

with me in Paradise" (Luke 23:43). See PARADISE.

Luke 16:19-31 gives considerable information about Hades, the invisible realm of the dead. The "rich man" is "in Hades," "in torments," and sees Lazarus "afar off" in the fellowship of Abraham (vs. 23), that is, in the part of Hades called "Paradise." But the "rich man" says, "I am tormented in this flame (vs. 24)," and he is told that he is separated from Paradise by "a great gulf" over which no man can pass, vs. 26." He is thus in that part of Hades which is 12 times (Matt. 5:22, 29,30; 10:28; 18:9; 23:15,33; Mark 9:43,45,47; Luke 12:5; James 3:6) called "Gehenna," and once (II Pet. 2:4) "Tartarus," for both of which, as well as for *Hades,* the KJV uses "Hell."

It is obvious that in Revelation 20:13,14, as well as in Acts 2:27,31 and Luke 16:23, discussed above, the word *Hades,* Hades, could not refer to the physical grave.

At the final resurrection Hades is to be completely emptied (Rev. 20:13). With the bulk of its remaining contents, i.e., those "not found written in the Book of Life," it will be "cast into the lake of fire" (Rev. 20:14,15).

The *reason* for eternal punishment is rejecting the love of God in Christ (John 3:18). "Light has come into the world, and men loved darkness rather than light" (John 3:19).

God has given men the free offer of the Gospel (John 3:16) and the convicting work of the Holy Spirit (John 16:8,9). Jesus described the act of rejecting this work of the Holy Spirit as being "guilty of eternal sin" (Mark 3:29).   J.O.B.

PUNITES (pū'nīts, Heb. *pûnî*), descendants of Puvah, of the tribe of Issachar (Num. 26:23; Gen. 46:13; I Chron. 7:1).

PUNON (pū'nŏn, Heb. *pûnōn*), a desert encampment of the Israelites marking the second stop after leaving Sinai (Num. 33:42,43). Eusebius identified it as being N of Petra, a penal colony where convicts were sent to mine copper, also called Phinon or Phainon. Eusebius is probably correct in his identification.

PUR (pūr, Heb. pl. *pûrîm, lots*), a Jewish festival celebrated on the 14th and 15th of the month Adar (Feb.-Mar.) commemorating the deliverance of the Hebrews from the plots of the wicked Haman in the post-Exilic period (Esth. 3:7; 9:26). So styled from the casting of the lot to determine the most expeditious time of Israel's mass murder.

PURA (See Phurah)

PURIFICATION (pūr'ĭ-fī-cā'shŭn). That the concept of purity was deep within the religio-social structure of the children of Israel since very early times will come as no surprise to the student of the Bible. The attitude of Jewry as a whole, and of the Pharisees as a class finds expression in Mark 7:3,4. Religious purity was both ceremonial and ethical. Under the Mosaic law, ceremonial purification was required for four acts: (1) the birth of a child, removed through circumcision (if male) and the isolation of the mother for a varying period (Lev. 12:2ff); (2) contact with a corpse; the offering of the red heifer is prescribed for the sacrifice of purification (Num. 19:1-10); (3) certain diseases, as leprosy (Lev. 13:8); (4) uncleanness due to a running sore (Lev. 15). Family purity was guarded through strict relations concerning sex (Lev. 20:1-21; Deut. 22:20, 21). In the NT though there is a transference from the outward to the inner; there is no relaxing of the basic requirements for purity itself (Matt. 5: 27f; 19:3-9; Mark 10:2-11; I Cor. 5:9-13; 6:18-20; 7:8ff).

PURPLE (pûr'p'l, Heb. *'argāmān*, Gr. *porphýra*). (Exod. 25:4; 26:36; 28:15; 35:6; Judg. 8:26; II Chron. 2:14; 3:14; Esth. 1:6; 8:15; S. of Sol. 3:10; Mark 15:17:20; Luke 16:19; Acts 16:4). Purple was a very costly dye extracted from the *marine mulex trunculus,* a marine mollusk, from which the Phoenicians were able to manufacture the dye. The shell was broken so that a small gland in the neck of the mollusk might be removed and crushed. The crushed gland gave out a milk-like fluid that turned purple or scarlet upon contact with the air. The shells of the mollusk from which purple is obtained can yet be seen strewn along the shore of Tyre and near the ancient dye-works of Athens and Pompei. Because of its extreme costliness, it became a mark of distinction to wear a robe of purple. In later times, ecclesiastical officials arrayed themselves in purple robes. In early times, royalty was so dressed. In very ancient times, the common people of the Sumerian civilization were forbidden on pain of punishment to wear the purple. The Saviour was dressed in mockery at His trial in a robe of purple (Mark 15:17). Lydia, Paul's first European convert, was a seller of purple (the purple dye) (Acts 16:14).

PURSE (Gr. *ballánion*), a rather finely finished leather pouch or bag which served as a "purse" in ancient times. The term translated "purse" in the KJV, Matthew 10:9, is the Gr. *zone* and refers to the Oriental girdle made of crude leather or woven camel's hair worn around the waist. Sometimes, these "girdles" were finely tooled, and contained "slots," in which gold and silver coins could be kept. If the "girdle" was made of cloth, then the money was placed within the folds themselves. Cf. Luke 10:4; 12:34.

PURTENANCE (pŭr'tĕ-năns, Heb. *qerev*), rendered "inwards" or "entrails" by the more recent versions (Lev. 1:9; 3:3; etc.).

PUT (pŭt, Heb. *pût*, Gr. *Phoúd*, variant from *Phoút*), the third son of Ham; as a nation, identi-

fied with Libya; the LXX renders Put as Phuge, "flight," in Nahum 3:9. Jeremiah identifies Put as being adept in the use of the shield (Jer. 46:9). Put has also been taken to signify Egypt.

PUTEOLI (pū-tē'ō-lē, Gr. *Potíoloi, little wells* or *springs*), a well-known seaport of Italy located in the Bay of Naples; it was the nearest harbor to Rome. It was the natural landing place for travelers from the East to Rome. In Acts 28:13-14 Luke reports that Paul landed there with the other prisoners when he was taken to Rome for trial. Paul and Luke and their party found Christian brethren there and enjoyed their hospitality for seven days before going on to Rome. The old ruins may still be seen in the northern part of the bay, including part of a pier Paul is supposed to have used. The modern name is Pozzuoli.

PUTIEL (pū'tĭ-ĕl, Heb. *pûtî'ēl*), the father-in-law of Eliezer, Aaron's son (Exod. 6:25).

PUVAH (See Phuvah)

PYGARG (See Animals)

PYRAMIDS (pēēr'à-mĭds), approximately 80 tombs with superstructures of pyramidal form still in existence from ancient Egypt. Many are in an extremely poor state of preservation, though their original form may be discerned. The Egyptian Old Kingdom, especially Dynasties 3-4 (about 2700 B.C.) was in a particular sense the Pyramid Age, for in that period it was customary for royalty to be interred in such a tomb. The largest and best preserved of the pyramids date from that time, including the well-known pyramids of Khufu (Cheops), Khafre (Chephren), and Menkaure (Mycerinos) at Giza. The pyramids of the Old Kingdom range geographically from Abu Roash in the N to Meidum in the S, on the W side of the Nile, in accordance with the theological concepts of the Egyptians.   C.E.D.

PYRRHUS (pĭr'ŭs, Gr. *Pýrros, fiery red*), the father of Sopater (Acts 20:4).

The famous pyramids of Egypt. At left, top, the great pyramid of Cheops at Gizeh (Giza), near Cairo, and left, bottom, the excavated Sphinx amid the pyramids. At right, near the top of the great pyramid of Cheops, showing the size of the stone blocks used in its construction. © MPS

Q

QUAIL (See Birds)

QUARANTANIA (kwŏr'ăn-tā'nĭ-à), the mountain where according to tradition Satan tempted Jesus to worship him (Matt. 4:8-10); Tell es-Sultân, a short distance W of OT Jericho.

QUARRIES (kwŏr'ēz, Heb. *pesîlim, graven images*). "The quarries" are mentioned in a doubtful passage in Judges 3:19,26. The marginal readings in KJV and ASV suggest "graven images," a rendering supported by the authority of the Septuagint and the Vulgate. Some piece of local nomenclature and a lost tradition are no doubt involved. Perhaps the place was a dump for discarded and roughly broken idols. Perhaps "sculptured stones" is the correct translation, and the reference to Joshua's stones of commemoration by Jordan. The word "quarry" occurs in another disputed passage at I Kings 6:7. RSV says, probably correctly, that the stones were dressed "at the quarry."

QUARTUS (kwôr'tŭs, Gr. *Koúartos*), a Christian man of Corinth whose greetings Paul sends to the church at Rome together with those of Gaius and Erastus (Rom. 16:23). No doubt he was a friend and assistant of Paul and a worker in the Corinthian church. There is an old tradition that he was originally one of the seventy disciples or missionaries Jesus sent out in Palestine (Luke 10:1).

QUATERNION (kwà-tẽr'nĭ-ŭn, Gr. *tetrádion*), a detachment of four men (Acts 12:4). The "four quaternions" to whom the prisoner was committed were the four patrols who took the four watches of the night. Two, no doubt, watched inside and two outside the guardhouse.

QUEEN. Dowager queens, or mothers of the monarch, are those who appear in the most influential roles in the Biblical records: 1. Jezebel, princess of Tyre who, during the 22 years of her husband Ahab's reign, and during the 13 years' rule of her sons Ahaziah and Joram, exercised a strong influence in favor of Phoenician pagan cults (I Kings 16:28-II Kings 9:37 *passim*). 2. Athaliah, daughter of Jezebel, and a similar character, was the wife of Jehoram of Judah, son of Jehoshaphat. On the accession of her son Ahaziah (not to be confused with Ahaziah of Israel, his uncle), Athaliah exercised a dominant authority and after Ahaziah's assassination held the throne alone, securing her position by dynastic massacre (II Kings 11). 3. Bathsheba, mother of Solomon, widow of David and Uriah, demonstrated her decisive character in the situation following the death of David (I Kings 1).

Foreign queens mentioned in the OT are: 1. Vashti, the deposed queen of Ahasuerus of Persia (Esth. 1). 2. Esther, the Jewess, her successor, a brave woman whose situation, nonetheless, violated the tenets of the Law and demonstrated the compromised position of those who took no part in the movements of restoration headed by Ezra and Nehemiah. 3. Balkis, legendary name of the Queen of Sheba (I Kings 10). 4. Nehemiah 2:6 and Daniel 5:10 refer to unnamed queens.

In the NT are: 1. Bernice, or Berenice, sister of Agrippa II, and wife of her uncle, Herod, king of Chalcis (Acts 25 and 26). 2. Drusilla, wife of King Azizus of Emesa, whom she deserted to become the third wife of Felix, procurator of Judaea. E.M.B.

QUEEN OF HEAVEN (Heb. *melekheth ha-shāmayim*). Some controversy surrounds the philology and significance of this title, but it seems best to regard it as the female deity to whom, with their families' aid and connivance, Hebrew women made offerings (Jer. 7:18; 44:17-25). The most likely identification is with Ashtoreth, goddess of love and fertility, synonymous with the Assyrian and Babylonian Ishtar, and the Roman Venus. The "wailing for Tammuz" was associated with her cult (Ezek. 8:14). Its ritual was the license and obscenity characteristic of the eastern fertility cults, ever a temptation to the Hebrews, and the chief objective of the prophets' attack on paganism. E.M.B.

QUICKSANDS (Gr. *Sýrtis*), occurs once in the NT (Acts 27:17) where it is used in a geographical sense. The "Syrtes" (plural) were shoals and shifting sands lying in the waters between Tunisia, Tripolitania, and Cyrenaica. The Syrtis Major, the area which the skipper of the Alexandrian grain-ship sought so desperately to avoid, formed the SE corner of the great oblong bay (i.e. the Gulf of Sidra) while the Syrtis Minor formed the westerly end (i.e. the Gulf of Gabes). Underwater archaeology has confirmed the evil reputation held by this North African bay as a graveyard of ships.

QUIRINIUS (kwĭ-rĭn'ĭ-ŭs, Gr. *Kyrénios*). The reference to this Roman governor in Luke 2:2 has raised some historical difficulties, and WH brackets it as a gloss. If Luke wrote the words, and he probably did, a historian of such proved accuracy is not likely to have made a major mistake. The task devolves upon the commentator to sort out the facts with due consciousness of the gaps in our historical material. It is known that Quirinius ("Cyrenius" is an Anglicized form of the Greek rendering of the name) was governor of Syria A.D. 6-9, that Judaea was incorporated at the time, and a census taken which caused the rebellion of Judas (Acts 5:37). Abundant papyrological evidence from Egypt has established the 14 year cycle of the census in that province, and fixes A.D. 20 as a census year. This fixes Quirinius' later census in A.D. 6, and demands 9 or 8 B.C. for an earlier occasion, or at least 7 or 6 B.C. if account be taken of political and practical impediments not apparent today. The difficulty then arises that Sentius Saturninus, and not Quirinius, was governing Syria from 9 to 7 B.C., and Quinctilius Varus from 6 to 4 B.C. A clue to a solution lies in an inscription which states that P. Sulpicius Quirinius governed Syria twice. W. M. Ramsay offers the best solution of this puzzle. He suggests that Quirinius was in control of the foreign relations of Syria during the war with the Cilician hill tribe of the Homonadenses in 6 B.C. This is consistent with the term used, and with Roman policy. An enrollment in Herod's kingdom would thus be supervised by him. (See Sir W. M. Ramsay's remarkable book, *Was Christ Born at Bethlehem?* esp. ch. XI.) The enrollment could have taken place in the autumn of 5 B.C., postponed thus by the dying Herod's devices of obstruction and procrastination. E.M.B.

QUOTATIONS FROM PAGAN POETS (See Poets, Pagan)

QURUN HATTIN (See Hattin, Horns of; Beatitudes, Mount of)

R

RA (See Re)

RAAMAH (rā'à-mà, Heb. *ra'mā'*), the fourth son of Cush and grandson of Ham (I Chron. 1:9); the father of Sheba and Dedan (Gen. 10:7; cf. I Chron. 1:9). The prophet Ezekiel identifies Raamah as one of the merchant tribes that traded in spices, gold and precious stones with Tyre (Ezek. 27:22).

RAAMIAH (rā'à-mī'à, Heb. *ra'amyâh, Jehovah has thundered*), one of the companions of Zerubbabel who returned with him to Jerusalem from the captivity (Neh. 7:7); called Reelaiah by Ezra (Ezra 2:2). The text may be corrupt at this point.

RAAMSES (rā-ăm'sēz, Heb. *ra'amsēs, Ra'mesēs*), a Hebrew place name derived from the Egyptian royal name Ramesses. In the OT it appears first as the name of the district of the Delta in which Jacob and his sons were settled by Joseph (Gen. 47:11). (The LXX also reads *Ramesse* for the second "Goshen" of the Hebrew (and English) text of Gen. 46:28). Raamses and Pithom are the names given in Exodus 1:11 for the two store cities the Israelites were forced to build for the Pharaoh of the Oppression. From Raamses the Israelites began their exodus from Egypt (Exod. 12:37; Num. 33:3,5). At present there is fairly general agreement that Raamses is to be identified with Avaris-Tanis-Zoan, the modern San el Hagar in the northeastern part of the Delta, an identification which has considerable bearing upon the interpretation of the exodus. C.E.D.

RABBAH, RABBATH (răb'à, Heb. *rabbâh*, Gr. *Rabbáth*; in KJV twice Rabbath [Deut. 3:11; Ezek. 21:20]). The full name is *rabbath benê 'ammôn*, Rabbah of the children of Ammon. The only city of the Ammonites to receive mention in Scripture; therefore we may conclude its importance. It is first mentioned in connection with the "bed" or sarcophagus of Og, King of Bashan (Deut. 3:11). Rabbah lay E of the Jordan, and was not assigned to the tribe of Gad at time of the division of the land (Josh. 13:2-5). It disappears from history following the days of Joshua until the days of David who sent an embassage of consolation to Hanun king of the Ammonites because of the death of his father. The Ammonite monarch grossly insulted the messengers of David (II Sam. 10:1-6). The next spring Rabbah was besieged by the army of David. The city capitulated when Joab captured the city's water-supply. The prophetic utterances against Rabbath-Ammon are of interest. Jeremiah (49:2f) utters imprecatory judgment against Milcom, the chief Ammonite deity. Ezekiel pictures Nebuchadnezzar as pausing at Rabbah to decide his further course of action (Ezek. 21:20f). Amos predicts a "fire being kindled in the wall of Rabbah" (Amos 1:14). It seems to have been at Rabbah that Baalis, king of the Ammonites, concocted the plot which was to cost Gedaliah, the provisional governor for the Babylonians, his life (Jer. 40:14f). Subsequently, Rabbah was captured by Ptolemy Philadelphus (285-247 B.C.), who changed its name to Philadelphia. It later became the seat of Christian Bishops. It is now known as Amman, the capital of the Hashemite kingdom of Jordan. J.F.G.

RABBATH-AMMON (See Rabbah)

RABBI (See Occupations and Professions)

RABBITH (răb'ĭth, Heb. *hārabbîth*), a town in the tribe of Issachar (Josh. 19:20). Identified by Knobel as Arabonheh at the southern tip of Mt. Gilboa and by Conder as Rama, eight miles S of Gilboa.

RABBONI (răb-bō'nī), a variant of *Rabbi*, the Heb. word for *Master*. The title used by Mary Magdalene to Jesus upon the resurrection morning (John 20:16). See Rabbi.

RAB-MAG (răb'măg, Heb. *rav māgh*), one of the Babylonian princes present at the capitulation of Jerusalem (Jer. 39:3). Same as Nergalsharezer (Jer. 39:3).

RABSARIS (răb'sà-rĭs, Heb. *rav-sārîs*), the title of an Assyrian and Babylonian official usually taken to be "chief eunuch," though Assyriologists have produced evidence for the reading "chief of the 'heads' (leaders, leading men)." The title appears in the Bible only in II Kings 18:17, where it is related that Sennacherib "sent the Tartan, the Rabsaris, and the Rabshakeh with a great army from Lachish to King Hezekiah at Jerusalem" (RSV) to effect the capitulation of that city to the Assyrians. The mission was unsuccessful, but was followed by another embassage, which also conveyed a letter to Hezekiah. Hezekiah took the matter to God in prayer and was encouraged by the word of the Lord as spoken by Isaiah. The angel of the Lord smote the Assyrian forces and Sennacherib returned to Nineveh (II Kings 19:35-36).

RABSHAKEH (răb'shà-kě, Heb. *ravshāqēh*), the title of an Assyrian official, with the meaning "chief cup-bearer" or "chief of the officers(?)" (II Kings 18:17,19,26-28,37; 19:4,8, and parallel, Isa. 36:2,4,11-13,22; 37:4,8). While Sennacherib was besieging Lachish, he sent his Rabshakeh to Jerusalem to deliver an ultimatum to that city. When representatives of Hezekiah protested that he should speak in Aramaic so that the people on the wall could not understand, he deliberately addressed his challenge to those onlookers and then left to join the Assyrian forces at Libnah.

RACA (rà'kà, Gr. *rhaká, empty, vain,* or *worthless fellow*), a term of contempt, signifying a depreciatory estimate of someone's intellectual endowment (Matt. 5:22).

RACE (Heb. *ōrah, mērôts,* Gr. *agón, stádiov,* most frequently, *a foot-race*). The clearest refs. are I Corinthians 9:24; Hebrews 12:1; II Timothy 4:7. Other passages may well allude to it (Rom. 9:16; Gal. 5:7; Phil. 2:16). The Greek race was one of a series of highly competitive games. It consisted of (a) the goal, a square pillar opposite the entrance to the course, marking the end of the track; (b) the herald, whose duty it was to announce the name and the country of each competitor, as well as the name and family of the victor; (c) the prize, the crown or wreath which was awarded the winner (cf. I Cor. 9:25; II Tim. 2:5); (d) the judges (II Tim. 4:8), where the Lord is viewed as the righteous Judge who bestows the wreath on those who have truly run well.

RACHAB (See Rahab)

RACHAL (rā'căl, Heb. *rākhāl*), a place in the Negev of Judah where David and his men roamed as fugitives as they were pursued by the relentless Saul (I Sam. 30:29). David sent spoil from Ziklag to some of its leading men.

RACHEL (rā'chěl, Heb. *rāhēl, ewe,* Gr. *Rhachél*), the wife of Jacob, the mother of Joseph and Benjamin (Gen. 29:6,16,18; 31, 30:1-9; cf. Jer. 31:

15; Matt. 2:18). Rachel was the younger daughter of Laban, the Aramaean (AV. "Syrian"), the brother of Rebekah, Jacob's mother (Gen. 28:2); thus Jacob and Rachel were full cousins. The circumstances under which Jacob met Rachel are interesting. Jacob had quarreled bitterly with his brother Esau over the latter's frustration in regard to the stolen blessing (Gen. 27:35ff). Accordingly, Jacob's mother, Rebekah, suggested that her son Jacob retire for a period, which she hopefully imagined would be brief, to the house of her brother Laban in Haran (Padan-Aram) (Gen. 27:43-45). Upon his arrival, struck by Rachel's beauty, Jacob immediately fell in love with her (Gen. 29:17,18). A contract was signed with Laban in terms of years of labor (the seven years being the usual period of indentured servants) at the expiration of which Rachel was to be Jacob's wife. In the light of the Nuzi tablets, much of the transactions between the two men becomes easier to understand, if not entirely justifiable by Christian mores. It would appear that according to Nuzian customs, Jacob became male heir, Laban at this time having no male heir of his own. He thus adopted Jacob as his son, giving him both Leah and her sister Rachel to wife. Thus arose the dispute over the right of the possession of the Teraphim, the household gods which Rachel concealed in the baggage as she, together with Jacob her husband, fled away (Gen. 31:30f). These household deities, about the size of a miniature doll, were regarded as indisputable evidence as to the rights and privileges of family ownership. Cf. Laban's indignant query, "Wherefore hast thou stolen my gods?" (Gen. 31:30). Jacob, after becoming prosperous, took his departure from the house of Laban (Gen. 31:21). One reason why the "face of Laban was not towards Jacob as it had been before," is that Laban by now seems to have sons of his own, who regarded Jacob as an interloper (Gen. 31:1). For some time, Rachel remained barren, bearing Jacob no children. The two children that Rachel bore to Jacob were Joseph (30:22), while yet in the house of Laban, and Benjamin after the return home. Rachel, however, died in childbirth with Benjamin (Gen. 35:16-19). This may partially show why Jacob favored the sons of his beloved Rachel above the sons of Leah. The character of Rachel varies between the very attractive and the unattractive. She partook of her family's traits of scheming and duplicity (Gen. 31:34). A believer in monotheism, she yet clung to the forms of polytheism. Jeremiah pictures her as rising from her grave to weep over the children who are being carried to Babylon, never to return (Jer. 31:15). The Apostle Matthew takes this as prophetic of the slaughter of the Innocents by Herod the great (Matt. 2:18).   J.F.G.

RADDAI (răd′ā-ī, Heb. *radday*), the fifth of the seven sons of Jesse, the father of David (I Chron. 2:14).

RAGAU (rā′gô, Gr. *Rhagaú*), the Greek form of Reu, an ancestor of Christ (Luke 3:35).

RAGUEL, REUEL (ră-gū′ĕl, Heb. *re′û′ēl*), the father-in-law of Moses (Num. 10:29), KJV Reuel (Exod. 2:18); a Midianite, also described as a Kenite (Judg. 4:11). It seems best to consider Hobab as Moses' brother-in-law and Jethro (Reuel, Raguel) as his father-in-law.

RAHAB (rā′hăb, Heb. *rāhāv, broad,* Gr. *Rháchab*). 1. A woman best known for her prominent role in the capture of Jericho during the days of Joshua (Josh. 2:1, etc. Matt. 1:5; Heb. 11:31; James 2:25). The spies sent by Joshua were received into

The so-called Tomb of Rachel near Bethlehem. © MPS

the house of Rahab prior to the siege of the city by the army of Israel. When the king of Jericho sent a posse of men in search of the spies, Rahab refused to betray their whereabouts. As a reward for her fidelity in this affair, she was promised by the two spies her own safety and the protection of her family, on condition of her continued loyalty and secrecy (Josh. 2:14-20). True to the promise that the spies had made to her, Joshua and his men spared Rahab after they had captured the city (Josh. 6:17). Jewish tradition has held Rahab in high honor, one tradition making her the wife of Joshua himself (Jew. Enc.).

According to Matthew's genealogy, she is not only one of the four women mentioned in the family tree of the Saviour, but also the mother of Boaz, the husband of Ruth, and the great-grandmother of King David (Matt. 1:5; Ruth 4:18-21). The author of Hebrews speaks of her as a shining example of faith (Heb. 11:31). James shows his appreciation of her as a person in whom faith was not merely "theological" but practical as well (James 2:5).

2. A mythical monster of the deep. In such passages as Job 9:13 and Psalm 89:10 the motif of the slaying of the dragon appears. In Isaiah 51:9 Jehovah's victory is complete because he has cut Rahab, the monster, to ribbons. This poetic symbolism has much in common with the Ras Shamra literature, and may be the prototype of legends like St. George and the Dragon. The RAHAB YASHAB (the "Rahab that sits still") of Isaiah 30:7 portrays the impotency of the monster of Egypt (symbolized by the crocodile) in the day of invasion.   J.F.G.

RAHAM (rā′hăm, Heb. *raham, pity, love*), son of Shema, father of Jorkeam (I Chron. 2:44).

RAHEL (See Rachel)

RAIMENT (See Dress)

RAIMENT, CHANGES OF (See Dress)

RAIN (Heb. *mātār, geshem, heavy rain; yôreh, former rain, malkôsh, latter rain,* Gr. *brécho, hyetós*). The word in the Scriptures is employed in both a literal and figurative sense. The amount of rainfall in Biblical countries varies greatly. In Egypt, for example, there is very little, if any rainfall, the land being dependent for water upon the Nile. In Syria and the land of Israel, however, the situation is the reverse, as the rainfall normally is abundant. The contrasting states of Egypt and the land of Israel's possession are brought out in Deuteronomy 11:10,11. Since the summer is very dry in Israel, the rainy seasons come in the spring (the "latter rains") and in the fall (the "former rains"). One can be almost certain that from c. 1 May to c. 15 October, no rain will fall. "The winter is past, the rain is over and gone" (S. of Sol. 2:11). Many people thus sleep on the roofs of the houses to escape the heat and to enjoy the cooling night breezes. The greatest amount of rain falls between November and February, tapering off till the coming of summer, and renewing itself the ensuing autumn. The latter or spring rains are considered such a natural blessing that they assume an eschatological significance (Zech. 10:1; Joel 2:23). The withholding of the rain at the proper season, particularly in the spring, was regarded as a most severe punishment indeed (I Kings 17:1-16; 18:18; Deut. 28:23,24), and in reverse order, the abundance of rain denoted the rich blessing of Jehovah upon His people (Deut. 28:12). Famine, one of the more tragic effects of the lack of rain, is also regarded as a token of the divine displeasure (II Sam. 21:1-14). In heathen concepts, Baal was conceived as the god of rain. This aids in explaining, but not justifying, the immoral practices of the fertility cults which believed that their sexual orgies would induce Baal to send rain. Elijah's contest upon Carmel was to prove the superiority of the God of Israel in the realm of the forces of nature.

RAINBOW (Heb. *qesheth, bow*). The Biblical interpretation of the rainbow is found in the story of Noah, with whom God entered into a covenant that never again would He send a universal deluge to destroy the whole inhabited earth (Gen. 9:8-17). This feature of the flood story is unique in that none of the accounts from Babylon, as the well-known Gilgamesh Epic, makes mention of the bow as the covenantal sign. Ezekiel compares the glory of God to that of a rainbow (Ezek. 1:28). John, as a prisoner on Patmos beheld the throne of God encircled by the rainbow (Rev. 4:3).

RAISINS (See Food)

RAKKATH (răk'ăth, Heb. *raqqath*), one of the fortified cities assigned to the tribe of Naphthali (Josh. 19:35). It is near the Sea of Galilee. There is some evidence that Tiberias was built upon the ruins of Rakkath.

RAM (See Animals, Sheep)

RAMA, RAMAH (rā'mà, Heb. *hārāmâh, height*).
1. Ramah-Arael, a city assigned by lot to the tribe of Naphthali, probably to be identified with the modern er-Rama, a large Christian village on the southern tier of the mountains of upper Galilee (Josh. 19:36).
2. Rhama-Ramah, a territory mentioned as forming the boundary of Asher (Josh. 19:29). It has been identified with Ramiyeh, a village some 13 miles SE of Tyre, and 12 miles E of the "Ladder of Tyre."
3. Ramah Iamah (or Ramah of Benjamin, and various other orthographic forms), a city assigned to the tribe of Benjamin, mentioned along with Gibeon and Beeroth; the headquarters of Deborah, judge of Israel during the days of the oppression of Sisera (Judg. 4:5). It was the home of the Levite whose concubine's flight and slaying brought about inter-tribal warfare (Judg. 20). At the time of the division of the kingdom, Ramah of Benjamin was destroyed, for we read that Baasha of Israel built it again to ward off his rival, Asa, king of Judah (I Kings 15:16,17). Ramah of Benjamin is mentioned in the "catalogue of doom" listing the cities about to be punished by the Assyrian king (Isa. 10:28-32).

Er-Ram, the probable site of Ramah, the birthplace of the prophet Samuel. © MPS

4. Ramah-Aramathaim, the hometown of Elkanah and Hannah, and the birthplace of the Prophet Samuel (I Sam. 1:19; 2:11). The text at this point bears evidence of having been corrupted, and various readings have been suggested, as, Ramathiam Zophim (KJV), "Aramathaim," etc. Later, Samuel made it the center of his circuit (I Sam. 7:16,17), and here he first became acquainted with King Saul (I Sam. 9:6ff). Here Israel demanded a king (I Sam. 8:4). Ramah of Benjamin: Samuel retired here after his final break with Saul (I Sam. 15:34); the place where David found refuge from the crazed king (I Sam. 19:18); the place marking the tomb of Samuel (I Sam. 25:1; 28:3). Its present site seems to be Er-Ram, NW of Jerusalem.
5. Ramah-of-the-south, see RAMATH-LEHI, below.

RAMATH-LEHI (rā'măth-lē'hī, Heb. *rāmath lehî*, the *hill* or *height of Lehi*), the place where Samson cast away the jawbone of an ass after the slaughter of the Philistines (Judg. 15:17). The hill may have received its name because of its real or fancied resemblance to a jawbone. Sometimes identified with the Wady-es Sarrar, not far from Timnath and Zorah, Samson's area of operation (Judg. 13:25; 14:1).

RAMATH-MIZPEH (rā'măth mĭz'pĕ, Heb. *rāmath-mitspeh, the heights,* or *the watchtower*), the northern boundary line of the tribe of Gad (Josh. 13: 26). It is probably the same place that marked the early sanctuary erected by Jacob and Laban as a witness (Gen. 31:46-48). It has the triple names of Mizpeh, Galeed, and Jegar-Sahadutha. Mizpeh implies the idea of watching, while the other two convey the thought of a cairn of stones set up as a witness between two contending parties. Probably Mizpeh is the same as Ramoth-Gilead, so famous in the subsequent history of Israel.

RAMATH (RAMAH) OF THE SOUTH (rā'măth, Heb. *rām'ôth neghev, Ramoth of the south*), a city in the southern sector of Judah which was allotted to the tribe of Simeon (Josh. 19:8 AV). It is understood to be the same as Baalath-beer by many, as well as identified with the Ramoth (pl.) to whose inhabitants David sent gifts which he had taken as spoil from the Amalekites (I Sam. 30:26). All proposed identification is tenuous.

RAMATHAIM-ZOPHIM (See Ramah)
RAMATHITE (See Ramah)

RAMESSES (râ-ăm'sēz, various other spellings,
e.g., Rameses, Ramses), the most common royal
name of Egyptian dynasties 19 and 20. Rameses I
was the founder of the Nineteenth Dynasty, but
the most illustrious of the bearers of this name
was his grandson, Rameses II. He was an ambitious
and imperious individual. He made a determined
effort to recover the Asiatic empire but his errors in
judgment in the Hittite encounter at Kadesh on the
Orontes eventuated in a stalemate which later produced an Egyptian-Hittite treaty. Rameses established his capital at Tanis, in the Delta, but his
building and rebuilding activities extended throughout the land and even beyond Egypt proper.
Among his impressive constructions are the completion of the hypostyle hall at Karnak and of his
father's funerary temple at Abydos; his own temple at Abydos; the forecourt and pylon of the
Luxor temple; the Ramesseum at the Theban necropolis; and Abu Simbel in Nubia. Extensive building operations were supplemented by his usurpa-
tions of monuments of his predecessors, a practice
which enhanced his reputation beyond his merits.
This, plus the presence in the OT of the name
Raamses for a city and district in the Delta,
brought about the acclamation of Rameses II as
the pharaoh of the Oppression, in spite of chronological complications with OT data. Among the
varying interpretations of the Exodus, this identification of Ramesses II is not widely held at present.
Ramesses III was the second king of the Twentieth
Dynasty; perhaps his most outstanding accomplishment was the repelling of an invasion of the Delta
by the Sea Peoples. His best-known construction is
his mortuary temple at Medinet Habu, not far from
the Ramesseum. At the end of his reign a serious
harem conspiracy occurred. The other eight kings
of this name, who followed in Dynasty 20, are relatively unimportant, though documents relating to
the tomb robberies in the Theban necropolis in the
reign of Ramesses IX are of interest. Though certain of these kings, such as Ramesses II and III,
must have had at least indirect influence on Israelite life, none of them is mentioned in the OT.

C.E.D.

RAMIAH (râ-mī'à, Heb. *ramyâh, Jah is set on
high*), a descendant of Parosh, mentioned in the
list of those who renounced their foreign wives at
the behest of Ezra (Ezra 10:25).

Es-Salt, ancient Ramoth-Gilead, now, next to the capital, Amman, the largest town in Jordan east of the
River Jordan. © MPS

A stele of Rameses II, eight feet high, with inscriptions, including a phrase claiming that he "built
Raamses with Asiatic Semitic (Hebrew) slaves." UMP

RAMOTH (rā'moth, Heb. *rāmôth, height*). 1. A
precious stone of uncertain variety (Job 28:18;
Ezek. 26:16).

2. An Israelite who after the Exile divorced his
Gentile wife at the urging of Ezra (Ezra 10:29).

3. One of the cities of refuge in the tribe of
Gad, elsewhere called Ramoth-Gilead (Josh. 20:
8; 21:38). It formed one of the administrative districts of Solomon over which Ben Geber was stationed (I Kings 4:13). It is perhaps best known
as the scene of the last battle of King Ahab. It
is identified as Tell Ramith in N Jordan (I Kings
22:1-37).

RAMS' HORNS (See Musical Instruments, Shofar)

RAMS' SKINS, the skins of the sheep tanned with oil used for outer clothing by the shepherds of the Near East. They were utilized as the exterior covering for the tabernacle (Exod. 25:5).

RANSOM (răn'sŭm, Heb. *kōpher, pidhyôn, gā'al*; Gr. *lýtron, antilýtron*), the price paid for the redemption of a slave (Lev. 19:20); a reparation paid for injury or damages (Exod. 22:10-12); a fee, fine, or heavy assessment laid upon a man as a substitute for his own life (Exod. 21:30). There was no ransom provided for the wilful murderer (Num. 35:31). In the NT the term signifies that redemptive price offered by Christ upon the cross for the salvation of His people (Mark 10:45; I Tim. 2:5).

RAPHA (rā'fà, Heb. *rāphā'*). 1. The last son of Benjamin (I Chron. 8:2).
2. A descendant of Saul through Jonathan (I Chron. 8:37).

RAPHU (rā'fū, Heb. *rāphû'*), father of Palti, one of the spies sent out to investigate the land of Canaan (Num. 13:9).

RAS SHAMRA (ràs shàm'rà, Arab. Fennel Head), the modern name of the mound which marks the site of the ancient city of Ugarit, located on the Syrian coast opposite the island of Cyprus. The city, with its port, Minet el Beida (White Harbor), was an important commercial center through which passed the trade of Syria and Mesopotamia with Egypt, Cyprus, and the Aegean area. Occasionally antiquities had been found here by local people, but in 1928 a peasant struck the roof of a buried tomb with his plow and made a discovery which attracted the attention of the authorities. In 1929 the French archaeologist C. F. A. Schaeffer began a series of excavations which have revealed much of the history of the site. Test shafts showed that there were five major strata, the earliest dating to the Neolithic period.

Ugarit was swept from the historical scene in about 1200 B.C., when the Sea Peoples overran the area. The city is mentioned in Egyptian historical inscriptions, in the Amarna Tablets (Akkadian), and in Hittite records. Its relations with Egypt were quite close during the Twelfth Dynasty and again in the time of Ramesses II. Ugarit was

An aerial view of Ras Shamra, ancient Ugarit, on the Syrian coast, showing excavations of the mound which have yielded the famous Ras Shamra tablets. ASOR

at the peak of its prosperity in the 15th-14th centuries B.C., and was destroyed by an earthquake in the mid-14th century. It recovered from this catastrophe, but was under Hittite and then Egyptian domination. Though the excavation of the mound has resulted in many significant finds, the most striking was that of a scribal school and library of clay tablets, adjoining the temple of Baal and dating from the Amarna Age. Various Near Eastern languages and scripts appeared at Ugarit, but the majority of the tablets used an unknown cuneiform script, which study showed to have an alphabet of some 30 signs. Credit for the work of decipherment goes to H. Bauer, E. Dhorme, and C. Virolleaud. The language, now called Ugaritic, was found to be of the Semitic family and closely related to Hebrew. The texts contain various types of writings: syllabaries and vocabularies; personal and diplomatic correspondence; business, legal, and governmental records; veterinary texts dealing with diagnosis and treatment of ailments of horses; and, most important, religious literature.

The myths and legends of Ugarit have provided valuable primary sources for the knowledge of Canaanite religion. These stories have been given modern titles, e.g., "The Loves and Wars and Baal and Anat," "The Birth of the Gods," "The Wedding of Nikkal and the Moon," "The Legend of Keret," "The Legend of Aqhat." At the head of the Ugaritic pantheon was El, who was also known as Father of Man, Creator of Creators, Bull El, etc. His consort was Asherah, a fertility goddess who was a stumblingblock to Israel. Ahab (I Kings 16:33) and Jezebel (I Kings 18:19) promoted her worship, and Manasseh even put her image in the temple (II Kings 21:7). Among the many offspring of El and Asherah was Dagon (Judg. 16:23; I Sam. 5), a grain god, whose son Baal was of great prominence. A god of rain and storm, Baal, whose proper name was Hadad (Thunderer), also figured in the fertility cycle. Baal was also called Aliyan Baal, Dagon's Son, Servant of El, Rider of Clouds, and Baal-Zebul (cf. I Kings 1; Matt. 12:24). In Israel, the priests of Baal lost an important contest with the prophet of God on Mt. Carmel (I Kings 18). Baal's sister and wife, the virgin 'Anat, goddess of love and fertility and goddess of war, is known in the OT as Astarte or Ashtoreth. In addition to these, numerous lesser divinities are named. The deities of Ugarit are often quite ungodly: El ordinarily is easy-going and easily influenced, but sometimes is rash and even immoral, as in his seduction and expulsion of two women. Baal mates with his sister and also with a heifer. 'Anat slaughters people and wades in blood and gore. This aspect of Canaanite religion occasioned the stern warning of the Lord to Israel concerning such worship.

The texts provide information concerning ritual and sacrifice and the temple plan, and recovered objects also contribute to an understanding of the religion and culture. The tablets and the OT elucidate each other; the Ugaritic texts have been used in OT textual criticism and have been helpful in Hebrew lexicography. Many interesting suggested relationships may be cited. Ugaritic practice illumines the Biblical prohibition against boiling a kid in its mother's milk (Exod. 23:19; 24:26; Deut. 14:21). A veterinary text refers to a poultice which has been cited as a parallel to Isaiah's prescription for king Hezekiah (II Kings 20:7; Isa. 38:21). The legend of Aqhat tells of a good and just king named Dan'el, whom some have sought to equate with the Daniel of Ezekiel 14:14,20; 12:3). The system of weights used at Ugarit was like that of Israel. These examples illustrate the type of information provided and discussion aroused by the investigation of the remains of this long-dead city.

C.E.D.

RASOR, RAZOR (rā′zêr, Heb. *ta′ar, môrâh*). The earliest razors were made of flint. Later they were made of bronze, and finally of steel. Joseph is said to have shaved himself before he was liberated from prison to stand before Pharaoh (Gen. 41: 14). This was no doubt due to deference to Egyptian, rather, than Hebrew custom, as the priests of Egypt shaved daily. The cutting of the beard by a priest of Israel was forbidden, presumably because of its affinity to pagan practices (Lev. 21: 5). The Nazarite was likewise forbidden the use of the razor as long as his vows were upon him (Num. 6:5).

RAVEN (See Birds)

RE, RA (rā), a masculine deity in the pantheon of the gods of Egypt, identified with the sun-god. He stands within the circle of the "creation-myths." Creation is viewed as a procreation on the part of the male and his female. The ancients, unlike the nation of Israel, drew no line of differentiation between the brute forces of nature and their deities. In fact, the elemental forces of nature were the deities, to whom were assigned personalized names. Re was thought to have engaged in a fierce battle against the dragon of chaos and darkness. The struggle was repeated yearly, or even daily in the ceremonial liturgy of Egypt. Yet life was not regarded in such tragic fashion as it was in Mesopotamia. Victory was always assured in the fullness and glory of the present order. The primeval hill upon which Re holds sway emerged from the floor of the ocean of chaos. Creation stems from the Sun. In later times, Re came to be referred to as Amen-Re, Osiris, and other such names. In the mystery religions, he was designated as a *Soter-Theos,* a "savior-god," a deity who rescues his people from death. The center of the worship of Re was Heliopolis, the ancient On. The ninth plague was in reality a judgment on Re, the Sun God (Exod. 12:21-23). Joseph, after being made food administrator of the land, married the daughter of the priest of On of the cult of Re (Gen. 41:45).

J.F.G.

REAIAH, REAIA (rē-ā′yà, Heb. *re′āyâh, Jah hath seen*). 1. The eponym of a Calebite family (I Chron. 4:2).

2. A Reubenite (I Chron. 5:5).

3. The family name of a company of Nethinim (Ezra 2:47; Neh. 7:50).

REAPING (Heb. *qātsar,* Gr. *therízo*). Reaping in ancient times consisted in either pulling up the grain by the roots, or cutting it with a sickle. The stalks were then bound into bundles and taken to the threshing floor. In Bible lands, cutting and binding are still practiced. The reaper sometimes wears pieces of cane on his fingers to prevent the sharp spears of wheat or the sickle from cutting him. Strict laws for reaping were imposed upon Israel (Lev. 19:9; 23:10; 25:11; Deut. 16:9). Samuel mentions that reaping will be a duty that the nation's newly-chosen king, Saul, will demand of them (I Sam. 8:12). The figurative usage of the term speaks of deeds that produce their own harvest (Prov. 22:8; Hos. 8:7; I Cor. 9:11; Gal. 6:7,8).

REBA (rē′bà, Heb. *reva′*), one of the five chieftains of Midian slain by Israel at the command of Moses (Num. 31:8; Josh. 13:21).

REBEKAH, REBECCA (rě-běk′à, Heb. *rivqâh,* Gr. *Rhebékka*), the daughter of Bethuel, her mother's name unrecorded. Her grandparents were Nahor and Milcah. She was the sister of Laban, the wife of Isaac, mother of Esau and Jacob, and first receives mention in the genealogy of Nahor, the brother of Abraham (Gen. 22:20-24).

It is in Haran, "the city of Nahor," where we are first introduced to Rebekah (Gen. 24). In this incident Eliezer, the servant of Abraham, is sent forth to seek a bride for Isaac. Rebekah, after listening to solicitations of the servant, decides to marry Isaac. In this story, the delineation of her character is winsome and attractive. In the story that follows, however, she is not only ambitious but grasping and rapacious. Though the object of her husband's love (Gen. 24:67), Rebekah bore him no children for 20 years. It was only after special intercession on the part of Isaac that God gave her the two famous children, Esau and Jacob. Although twins, Esau was reckoned as the firstborn and Jacob as the second. However, God told her "the elder shall serve the younger" (Gen. 25:23). Whether directly influenced by this predictive utterance or not, Jacob became his mother's favorite. This led her to perpetrate a cruel ruse upon the aged and blind Isaac. Disguised as his brother Esau, Jacob obtained the blessing (Gen. 27:5-17). When it became evident that Jacob and Esau could no longer live under the same roof, at her suggestion, Jacob fled from home to her relatives in Aram (Gen. 27:42-46). Rebekah never saw her son alive again. Outside of Genesis there is only one reference to her (Rom. 9:10-12).

RECAH, RECA (rē′kà, Heb. *rēchâh*), an unknown place in the tribe of Judah (I Chron. 4:12).

RECHAB (rē′kăb, Heb. *rēkhāv, horseman*). 1. One of the assassins of Ishbosheth, a son of Saul, who together with his brother Baanah entered the home of Ishbosheth while he was taking a rest at noon and slew him upon his own bed. They then decapitated him, and carried his head to David expecting to receive a reward, as the murder of Ishbosheth left David without a rival upon the throne of Israel. However, the reaction of the king was quite different from what they had anticipated, as he commanded them both to be executed (II Sam. 4: 5-11). They were Benjamites from Beeroth (4:5).

2. An early ancestor of the Kenite Tribe which later became identified with the tribe of Judah (I Chron. 2:55). Rechab was the founder of the order of the Rechabites. It was Jehonadab who rode with Jehu on the penal mission against the house of Ahab (II Kings 10:15ff). Jeremiah utilizes the example of the Rechabites and their obedience to their father to drink no wine as a method of sharply berating the nation for their lack of obedience to God (Jer. 35:1-19). The Rechabites, though thirsty, had refused to partake of the wine rather than break faith. The Israelites, though partakers of the divine blessings, had indeed broken the covenant (vss. 12-16). Thus the object-lesson is brought to completion.

RECONCILIATION (rěk′ŏn-sĭl-ĭ-ā′shŭn, Gr. *katallagé*). Reconciliation is a change of relationship between God and man based on the changed status of man through the redemptive work of Christ. Three aspects of this change are suggested by three words used for it in the New Testament.

1. A reconciliation of *persons* between whom there has existed a state of enmity. The Greek *katallasso* denotes an "exchange" which when applied to persons, suggests an exchange from enmity to fellowship. Reconciliation is therefore God

exercising grace toward man who is in enmity because of sin, establishing in Christ's redemptive work the basis of this changed relationship of persons (II Cor. 5:19). That this reconciliation is the burden of God is shown by Romans 5:10 where it is suggested that even while we were enemies, God reconciled us to Himself through the death of His Son.

This changed relationship, however, is possible only because of the changed status of man, not in God. God is never said to be reconciled to man, but man to God since it is man's sinfulness which creates the enmity (Col. 1:21; Rom. 8:7). This enmity precipitates God's wrath (Eph. 2:3,5) and judgment (II Cor. 5:10) which is allayed only through the reconciliation wrought through the death of Christ (Rom. 5:10) who knew no sin, but became sin for man that we might receive his righteousness as the basis of reconciliation.

2. A reconciliation of *condition* so that all basis of the enmity-relationship is removed and a complete basis of fellowship is established (II Cor. 5:18-20; Eph. 2:16). *Apokatallasso* denotes a "movement out of" and suggests that since man is redeemed through the righteousness of Christ he is redeemed out of his condition of unrighteousness and thus reconciled to God in this new relationship. The grace of God assures the reconciled man that the grace-basis replaces the sin-basis and that he is established before God in a new relationship.

3. A reconciliation arising out of the change in man *induced by the action of God. Katallagé* suggests that man is not reconciled merely because his relationship has changed, but because *God* has changed him through Christ so that he can be reconciled (Rom. 5:11; 11:15; II Cor. 5:18 and Eph. 2:5). Reconciliation arises therefore, out of God, through Christ, to man, so that not only may the barriers to fellowship existing in sinful man be removed, but the positive basis for fellowship may be established through the righteousness of Christ imputed to man.

The definitive basis for reconciliation rests both in what God does in annulling the effects of sin in man so that no enmity exists, and in what He does in creating a redeemed nature in man with which He can have fellowship. Reconciliation is always pre-eminently God working in man to change the basis of relationship. Yet, men are both given the ministry of reconciliation (II Cor. 5:18) and invited to be reconciled to God. From his position of being reconciled, as accomplished as fact, man is to turn to God to respond to the new relationship in faith and obedience.

Even though the sufficient ground of reconciliation is established in the completed redemptive work of Christ, reconciliation is the basis upon which the continued fellowship is established, "for if, when we were enemies, we were reconciled to God by the death of his Son, much more, being reconciled, we shall be saved by his life" (Rom. 5:10).   C.B.B.

RECORDER (See Occupations & Professions)

RED (Heb. *ādhōm*, Gr. *erythós*). The Hebrew word is a derivative of *dam* signifying *blood*; hence, a blood-like or a blood-red color. The adjective "red" is applied to the following items: (1) the badger skins dyed red which formed the outward covering for the Tabernacle (Exod. 25:5; 26:14; 35:7; etc.); (2) the color of certain animals (Num. 19:2; Zech. 1:8; 6:2; Rev. 6:4; 12:13); (3) the color of the human skin (Gen. 25:25; I Sam. 16:12); (4) redness of eyes (Gen. 49:12; Prov. 23:29); (5) red sores (Num. 12:10); (6) wine (Prov. 23:31; Isa.

27:2 AV); (7) water (II Kings 3:22); (8) pavement (Esth. 1:6); (9) the color of sin (Isa. 1:18); (10) the advancing foe against the city of Nineveh is depicted as bearing red or scarlet shields before him.

REDEEMED, REDEEMER (See Redemption)

REDEMPTION (rē-dĕmp'shŭn, Heb. *pāraq, to tear loose*, Gr. *lýtron, a ransom*). Rooted in the secular usage of the word, the NT doctrine of redemption draws its meaning from a parallel with the marketplace concept "to buy back," and thus describes the specific means by which the larger salvation concepts may be gained.

Its meaning is rooted in several words: *exagorazo, to buy out*, as the purchase of a slave for freedom, and is so used in Galatians 3:13 and 4:5; *lytróo, to release on receipt of a ransom*, as in Titus 2:14 of the work of Christ in redeeming men of iniquity; *lýtrosis, a deliverance*, as in Hebrews 9:12 of deliverance through Christ's death; and *apolýtrosis, a releasing from bondage on payment of a ransom*, as in Romans 3:24.

Originally restricted to its commercial usage, the word is used in the NT to contain both the idea of deliverance and the price of that deliverance, or ransom. Both ideas are in Romans 3:24 where it is asserted that man is freely justified by grace "through redemption that is in Christ Jesus"; in I Corinthians 6:20 where redemption is viewed as being "bought with a price"; and in Galatians 3:13 where Christ is said to have redeemed us "from the curse of the law being made a curse for us" (Eph. 1:7; I Pet. 1:18,19; Rev. 5:9).

Redemptiveness connotes deliverance from the enslavement of sin and release to a new freedom. This new freedom is presented in Scripture as always residing in Christ. Man is redeemed from sin to a new life in Christ (Rom. 6:4). This new life is not merely a life gained by being released from sin, but one which exists only in continual relation with Christ, gained through the positive implantation of Christ's righteousness to man.

The death of Christ is the redemptive price. His atoning sacrifice is the ransom paid for man's deliverance (John 3:17; Matt. 20:28; I Tim. 2:6). Moreover, His sacrifice is regarded as a substitute for man's bondage (John 11:50; Rom. 5:6,8; II Cor. 5:14,15,21; Mark 10:45). His death is both sacrificial and propitiatory, since it is in His death alone that man finds redemption.

The soteriological concept of redemption may be extended to three general areas. 1. It is closely associated with forgiveness, since man receives forgiveness through the redemptive price of Christ's death (Eph. 1:7; Col. 1:14); 2. It involves justification, since the deliverance achieved through redemption establishes man in a restored position of favor before God (Heb. 9:15). 3. It promises final deliverance from the power of sin at the coming of the Lord (Rom. 8:23; Eph. 4:30).

The fundamental idea of the word is a dual one: redemption *from* and redemption *to*. Redemption is from the law; from the penalty of the law; from sin; from Satan and from all evil. Redemption is to a new freedom from sin, a new relationship to God, and a new life in Christ.

Redemption to the new life in Christ is the basis of Christ's sacrificial death. The new life arises out of the new principle of life imparted to man (Rom. 6:4). Redemption to Christ is redemption to his life, his nature, his holiness. It is joining with him in his death and rising with him in the power of his resurrection glory. He has abolished the enmity between God and man by redeeming man out of

Moonlight on the Red Sea. "They that go down to the sea in ships, that do business in great waters; these see the works of the Lord, and His wonders in the deep" (Psalm 107:23, 24). © MPS

his sinful relationship, and establishing him in a new nature achieved through the efficacy of his death.

Redemption rests in Christ's satisfaction of the requirements for ransom. He took our sinful nature upon Himself in order that He might satisfy the demands of the Law by assuming our guilt. Voluntarily exercising His will so to do, He achieved the ransom within Himself in order that He might deliver us from the bondage of sin. "Christ also suffered for sins once, the righteous for the unrighteous, that he might bring us to God; being put to death in the flesh, but quickened in the spirit" I Peter 3:18.   C.B.B.

REDEMPTION OF LAND. In Hebrew society, any land which was forfeited through economic distress could be redeemed by the nearest of kin. If, however, there was no one to redeem it, the property still returned to its original owner in the year of Jubilee (Lev. 25:24-34).

RED HEIFER. The ashes of the red heifer were used for the removal of certain types of ceremonial uncleanness such as purification of the leper, or defilement incurred through contact with the dead (Num. 19:9; 20, 21).

RED SEA (Heb. *yam sûph*). Upon the occasion of the Exodus of the Israelites from Egypt "God led the people not by the way of the land of the Philistines, though that was near, . . . but God led them around by the way of the wilderness by the Red Sea" (Exod. 13:17,18). With Rameses as their point of departure (Exod. 12:37), the nation of liberated slaves marched across the eastern boundaries of the Land of Goshen towards a body of water, traditionally rendered as the "Red Sea." The site of Israel's encampment, however, previous to their crossing, is recorded as Pihahiroth, between

Migdol and the Sea. Hence, Israel took a southeasterly course to Succoth, about 32 miles away, and from there a road to Sinai which they most easily followed. Often the target of the critics, the route of the Exodus has now fairly well been established, as a long series of Egyptian fortifications along the route has actually been described by Pharaoh Seti I in his Karnak inscriptions in Upper Egypt. The "store chambers" of which the Biblical record speaks were actually discovered by Naville, not at Pithom, but at Succoth, c. nine miles E in the Wady Tumilat.

It is now quite evident that the "Red Sea" rendering is erroneous, as *Yam Sûph* should be rendered "Reed Sea" or "Marsh Sea." It is highly improbable that the northern arm of the Red Sea (the Gulf of Suez) is meant. There are no reeds in the Red Sea. In addition, the text implies that the *Yam Sûph* formed the barrier between the land of Egypt and the desert. If that which we think of as the Red Sea were intended, then Israel would have been obliged to cross a far greater territory in a far shorter span of time than the account actually indicates. Be it recalled that the Israelites as a nation of slaves resided in Goshen. Near the city of Rameses-Tanis (Goshen), there were two bodies of water, the "Waters of Horus" which is the same as Shihor, (Isa. 23:3; Jer. 2:18), and a body of water which the Egyptians themselves referred to as "Suph," called also the "papyrus marsh." This last mentioned "Sea of Reeds" or Lake Timsah is beyond reasonable doubt the body of water crossed by the fleeing Israelites, with the Egyptians in hot pursuit. This newer identification in no way mitigates nor militates against the miraculous deliverance of the people of God by supernatural means, nor does it dissipate the awful judgment which overtook the armies of Pharaoh.   J.F.G.

REED (rēd, Heb. *qāneh, 'āghammîm, 'āhû*; Gr. *kálamos*). A reed stalk was used as a measuring rod. In Babylonia six cubits made a reed or *qāneh*. Among the Israelites a reed came to denote a fixed length of six long cubits (Ezek. 40:5; 41:8). In Revelation 11:1 and 21:15,16 a reed is used to measure the temple and the holy city.

REED (See Plants)

REELAIAH (rē'ĕl-ā'yà, Heb. *re'ēlyâh*), one of the 12 heads of families returning with Zerubbabel after the captivity (Ezra 2:2; Neh. 7:7). Nehemiah renders the name "Raamiah." "Reelaiah" seems to be the preferred form.

REFINE, REFINER (See Occupations: Coppersmith)

REFUGE, CITIES OF (Heb. *'ārê hamiqlāt*, Gr. *póleis tón phygadeuteríon*), the six cities on either side of the Jordan which under the supervision of the Levites were set aside for the asylum of the accidental slayer. East of the Jordan, they were Bezer in the tribe of Benjamin, Ramoth-Gilead of Gad, Goian in Manasseh. West of the river, they were Hebron in Judah, Shechem in Ephraim, and Kedesh in Naphtali (Num. 35:6,14; Josh. 20: 7ff; 21:13; 27:32,38). The need for appointing cities of refuge arose because of the strong concept that it was one's duty to avenge the blood of his nearest slain relative even though the slaying was of an accidental nature. Therefore, these cities of refuge were designated until the accused could stand fair trial.

REGEM (rē'gĕm, Heb. *reghem*), a descendant of the house or clan of Caleb, son of Jadhai (I Chron. 2:47).

REGEM-MELECH (rēg'ĕm mĕlĕk, Heb. *reghem melekh*), one of a delegation sent to inquire of Zechariah concerning the propriety of the act of fasting (Zech. 7:2).

REGENERATION (rē-jĕn-êr-ā'shun, Gr. *palingenesía*). Regeneration has as its basic idea, "to be born again," or "to be restored." Though the word is actually used only twice in the NT (Matt. 19:28 and Titus 3:5), many synonymous passages suggest its basic meaning. Related terms are: born again (John 3:3,5,7); born of God (John 1:13; I John 3:9); quickened (Eph. 2:1,5); and renewed (Titus 3:5 and Rom. 12:2).

Regeneration is, therefore, the spiritual change wrought in the heart of man by an act of God in which his inherently sinful nature is changed and by which he is enabled to respond to God in faith.

This definition grows out of the nature of man's sinfulness. As long as man is in sin, he cannot believe in God. If he is to believe, he will do so only after God has initiated a change by which he may be released from the bondage of his will by sin. Regeneration is that act of God by which he is thus released, and from which he may exercise the dispositions of a freed nature.

Regeneration is basically, therefore, an act of God through the immediate agency of the Holy Spirit operative in man (Col. 2:13), originating in him a new dimension of moral life; a resurrection to new life in Christ. This new life is not merely a neutral state arising out of forgiveness of sin, but a positive implantation of Christ's righteousness in man, by which he is quickened (John 5:21), begotten (I John 5:1), a new creation (II Cor. 5:17) and a new life (Rom. 6:4).

Regeneration involves an illumination of the mind, a change in the will, and a renewed nature. It extends to the total nature of man, irrevocably altering his governing disposition, and restoring him to a true experiential knowledge in Christ.

It is a partaking of the divine nature (II Pet. 1:4), a principle of spiritual life implanted in the heart.

The efficient cause of regeneration is God (I John 3:9) acting in love through mercy (Eph. 2: 4,5) to secure the new life in man through the instrument of His word (I Pet. 1:23).

In regeneration, the soul is both passive and active: passive while it is still in bondage to sin, and active when it is released. The regenerating work of the Holy Spirit is not conditioned by a prior acquiescence of the soul, but when the soul is released from sin, regenerated, it voluntarily and spontaneously turns toward God in fellowship.

C.B.B.

REHABIAH (rē'hă-bī'à, Heb. *rehavyâh, rehavāhû, Jah is wide*), son of Eliezer, grandson of Moses (I Chron. 23:17; 24:21; 26:25).

REHOB (rē'hōb, Heb. *rehōv, broad*). 1. The northern limit to which the spies came as they searched out the land (Num. 13:21). It is mentioned in the wars of David against the Syrians (I Sam. 10:6). On the basis of Judges 18:28, Rehob and Beth-Rehob appear to be identical.

2. Two separate towns belonging to the tribe of Asher (Josh. 19:28; 19:30).

3. The father of Hadadezer, king of Aram, whose capital appears to have been Zobah, which David conquered in the battle on the banks of the Euphrates (II Sam. 8:3,12).

4. A Levite who was one of the co-signers of the covenant of Nehemiah (Neh. 10:11).

REHOBOAM (rē'hō-bō'ăm, Heb. *rehav'ām*), the son of Solomon and his successor on the throne of Israel. His mother was Naamah, an Ammonitess (I Kings 14:21). He was born about 975 B.C. and was 41 when he began to reign. He chose Shechem as the site of his inauguration. Solomon's wild extravagances and his vain ambition to make Israel the world power of his day led him to set up a tremendously expensive capital and a very elaborate harem. The importation of so many pagan women for his harem resulted in a spiritual debacle in Israel. The luxuries of his palace and the expenses of his diplomatic corps and of his vast building program resulted in burdensome taxation. The northern tribes turned to Jeroboam for leadership, to whom God had revealed that he was to rule ten of the tribes (I Kings 11:26-40). When the coronation had been set, Jeroboam was called home from Egypt, and through him an appeal was made to Rehoboam for easier taxes. The latter, however, heeding the advice of young men, refused to heed the appeal, with the result that Israel rebelled. When Adoram was sent to collect the tribute, he was slain and Rehoboam fled to Jerusalem (I Kings 12:16-19). Jeroboam was then made king of the ten tribes. Rehoboam raised an army from Judah and Benjamin, but was forbidden by God to attack (20-24). Jeroboam then fortified Shechem and Penuel, instituted pagan rites, and waged a relentless struggle against Rehoboam (I Kings 12:25-28; 14:29,30).

Rehoboam did not sit repining, but set to work to make his realm strong. Pagan high places were set up, and shrines throughout the land allowed abominable practices to be observed among the men (I Kings 14:22-24). Upon being dissuaded from attacking Israel, Rehoboam began to strengthen his land. He fortified Bethlehem, Gath, Lachish, Hebron and other cities, and made them ready to endure a siege by enemy forces. He gave refuge to priests and Levites whom Jeroboam had driven from Israel, and they brought wisdom and strength to his realm (II Chron. 11:5-17). The fortified cities were captured by King Shishak of Egypt. It is possible that Shishak's invasion resulted from Jeroboam's influence in Egypt, whither he had fled to escape Solomon's wrath (I Kings 11:40). Inscriptions in the temple at Karnak name 180 towns captured by Shishak, many of them being in the northern kingdom.

Rehoboam seems to have inherited his father's love for luxury and show, for he gathered a goodly harem and reared a large family (II Chron. 11:18-23). He had 18 wives and 60 concubines (30 according to Josephus. *Ant.* V:8; 1; 10; 1). He was not content with fortifying his land, but spent large sums upon ornate places of worship. He made Abijah, his son, his successor.   J.D.F.

REHOBOTH (rē-hō′bŏth, Heb. *rehōvôth, broad places*). 1. The name of a city built in Assyria by Ashur (Gen. 10:11). The home of Saul (Shaul in I Chron. 1:48), a king of Edom prior to the coming of a Hebrew Monarch (Gen. 36:31-37). Its location is not known.

2. A well dug by Isaac in the Valley of Gerar after Abimelech had driven him from the land of the Philistines (Gen. 26:9-22). Ruhaibah, near Beershebah, is the probable site, its ruins with numerous cisterns cut into solid rock indicating an ancient stronghold.

REHUM (rē′hŭm, Heb. *rehûm, beloved*). 1. A Hebrew who returned from captivity with Ezra (Ezra 2:2).

2. An officer of Artaxerxes' court who helped frame a report to his king, accusing the Jews of rebelling and warning him that to permit the completion of the job of restoring Jerusalem would result in the loss of these vassal people (Ezra 4:7-24).

3. A son of Bani who helped repair the walls of Jerusalem (Neh. 3:17).

4. One who signed the covenant with God after Israel had returned from captivity and had been so signally blessed (Neh. 10:25).

5. A priest among the host that went to Palestine with Zerubbabel (Neh. 12:3, KJV margin, *Hamm*).

REI (rē′ī, Heb. *rē′ī, friendly*), one who did not join Adonijah in his rebellion against David (I Kings 1:8).

REINS (rāns, Heb. *kilyâh*, Gr. *nephrós*), a word used to designate the inward parts. The kidneys were thought by the Israelites to be the seat of the emotions (Ps. 7:9; 26:2; Jer. 17:10; Job 19:27).

REKEM (rē′kĕm, Heb. *reqem, friendship*). 1. A king of Midian who was slain by order of Jah (Num. 31:1-8). He is called prince in Joshua 13:21.

2. A city belonging to Benjamin (Josh. 18:27), the location now unknown.

3. A son of Hebron and father of Shammai of the tribe of Judah (I Chron. 2:42-44).

RELIGION (Gr. *threskeía, outward expression of spiritual devotion*). The Latin *religare* means to hold back or restrain. It came to be applied to the services and ritual and rules by which faith in and devotion to deity were expressed. In the OT there is no word for religion. Fear (Ps. 2:11; Prov. 1:7) and worship (Ps. 5:7; 29:2; Deut. 4:19; 29:26) of God refer primarily to attitudes of the mind and acts of adoration, rather than to a ritual. *Threskeía* in the NT means outward expression of religion and the content of faith. James makes a

distinction between the sham and the reality of religious expression (1:26,27). Paul was loyal to his Hebrew religion before being converted (Acts 26:1-5). *Religious* in James 1:26 (*thréskos*) implies superstition.

REMALIAH (rĕm′à-lī′à, Heb. *remalyāhû, Jehovah adorns*), the father of King Pekah (II Kings 15:25).

REMETH (rē′mĕth, Heb. *remeth, height*), a city in the tribe of Issachar (Josh. 19:17-21); probably Ramoth of I Chronicles 6:73 and Jarmuth of Joshua 21:29.

REMMON (See Rimmon)

REMNANT, a rendering of different Hebrew words: *yether, what is left* (Deut. 3:11; 28:54); *she′ār, the remainder* (Ezra 3:8; Isa. 10:20; 11:16); *she′-ērîth, residue* (II Kings 19:31; Isa. 14:30). At first the word denoted a part of a family or clan left from slaughter, and later came to be applied to the spiritual kernel of the nation who would survive God's judgment and become the germ of the new people of God. Thus Micah saw the returning glory of Israel (2:12; 5:7). Zephaniah saw the triumph of this remnant (2:4-7), and so did Zechariah (8:1-8). Isaiah named a son She′ār Jashub which is "A remnant returns" (7:3).

REMON METHOAR (rĕm′ŏn-mĕth′ō-ȧr), a town on the border of the heritage of Zebulum (Josh. 19:13). See RIMMON.

REMPHAN (rĕm′făn), a pagan deity worshiped by the Israelites in the wilderness (Acts 7:37-50). It is probably a name for Chiun, or Saturn (Amos 5:26), a view supported by the LXX.

REPENTANCE (rē-pen′tans, Heb. *nāham, shûv*, Gr. *metanoéō, metamélomai*). The two Greek words translated "repent" in the English Bible suggest the basic meaning of the word. *Metanioa* (Acts 2:38; Rom. 2:4) connotes a *change of mind* with regard to sin, a sorrow for sin which primarily is intellectual in nature; while *metameleia* connotes a *change of soul*, a sorrow that leads to turning away from sin (Matt. 27:3; II Cor. 7:9,10).

The meaning of both words leads to defining repentance as that divinely wrought conviction of sin in the heart that the soul is guilty before God, and a resolute turning away from sin in which the sinner identifies himself with the gracious act of God in redeeming him. Repentance involves both a change of mind about sin, and a change of heart-attitude toward sin. It is at the time a renunciation of sin and an acceptance of the Holy Spirit's enablement to holy living.

Repentance may be viewed from both a divine and human perspective. God is said to be the author of repentance (Acts 4:31) in that it is through the regeneration wrought by the Holy Spirit that man is led to a consciousness of his sinfulness and to a rebellion against it as a principle of life. In his sinful nature, man cannot repent; however, through the illuminating work of the Holy Spirit he is led to see himself as a sinner in rebellion against God, and as evil in nature. Hence man's repentance is always preceded by God's illuminating activity.

Repentance is always conjoined with faith, however, and man must act, once illuminated by grace. Where there is true faith there will always be true repentance; and conversely, where there is not true repentance there can never be true faith.

Repentance is necessary to salvation. Jesus asserted that it was a necessary condition (Matt. 3:2,8; 4:17), while both Paul and Peter identified it with true salvation (Acts 20:21; II Pet. 3:9).

There are two aspects of repentance: the act of repenting, and the state of penitence. The act of repenting involves sorrow for both the fact of sin and the acts of sin in the life of the sinner. It precipitates decisive conviction of sin and resolution to change. The act of repentance, however, leads to the state of penitence in which the whole nature of man is changed so that he becomes identified with the grace of God, living in abhorrence of sin, with continual renunciation of it in his life.

Bibliography: W. D. Chamberlain, *The Meaning of Repentance* (Edinburgh: T & T Clark); G. B. Stevens, *Christian Doctrine of Salvation* (Edinburgh: T. & T. Clark).   C.B.B.

REPHAEL (rē'fā-ĕl, Heb. *rephā'ēl, God heals*), a son of Shamaiah who served as a tabernacle gatekeeper (I Chron. 26:7-12).

REPHAH (rē'fà, Heb. *rephah, a prop*), a grandson of Ephraim and a resident of Bethel (I Chron. 7:23-25).

REPHAIAH (rē-fā'yà, Heb. *rephāyâh, Jehovah heals*). 1. Descendant of David (I Chron. 3:21, *Rhesa* of Luke 3:27).

2. Son of Ishi, who helped defeat the Amalekites (I Chron. 4:42-43).

3. Grandson of Issachar and head of a clan (7:2).

4. Descendant of Jonathan (I Chron. 9:40-43).

5. Son of Hur, a builder (Neh. 3:9).

REPHAIM (rĕf'à-ĭm, Heb. *rephā'îm, mighty*), (in KJV twice Rephainer (Gen. 14:5; 15:20). The name of a giant people who lived in Canaan even before the time of Abraham (Gen. 14:5; 15:20). They are listed among Canaanites who were to be dispossessed (Gen. 15:20). They were like the Anakims in Deuteronomy 2:11,20. Og, king of Bashan, was a descendant of the Rephaim (Josh. 12:4; 13:12; 17:15 marg.).

REPHAIM, VALLEY OF (rĕf'à-ĭm, *vale of giants*). This was a fertile plain S of Jerusalem, three miles from Bethlehem. It was a productive area (Isa. 17:4,5), and thus was a prize for which the Philistines often fought. David twice defeated the Philistines in this valley (I Chron. 14:8-12; 14:16).

The Plain of Rephaim, south of Jerusalem, where David defeated the Philistines. This area is now built up with houses. © MPS

The luxurious palm grove at Wady Feiren, the Rephidim of the Israelite camp in the wilderness near Sinai. © MPS

REPHIDIM (rĕf'ĭ-dĭm, Heb. *rephîdhîm, plains*), a camping site of the Hebrews in the wilderness before they reached Sinai. There Moses struck a rock to secure water (Exod. 17:1-7; 19:2). At this place also occurred the battle with the Amalekites (Exod. 17:8-16). The camp of the Hebrews is supposed to have been at the present Wady Feiren. If so, it afforded ample protection against a surprise attack, its gateway into the vale being between rocky cliffs from one of which the water came. Archaeologists have found at this place evidence of a once fertile valley in which a strong city had been built.

REPROBATE (rĕp'rō-bāt, Gr. *adókimos*). The basic idea in reprobation is that of failing "to stand the test." *Adokimos,* (the negative of *dokimos,* meaning "to approve") connotes disapproval or rejection. When applied to man's relation to God it suggests moral corruption, unfitness, disqualification — all arising out of a lack of positive holiness. It is used in Romans 1:28 of a "reprobate (disapproved) mind"; in I Corinthians 9:27 of a "castaway body," and II Corinthians 13:5-7 of a "sinful nature." Other uses in II Timothy 3:8, Titus 1:16, etc., bear the same disapproval quality. Man in sin is reprobate, disqualified, disapproved, and rejected because he cannot "stand the test" of holiness. Only in Christ's righteousness may he be "approved."

RESEN (rē'sĕn, Heb. *resen, fortified place*), a town founded by Nimrod (Gen. 10:8-12) between Nineveh and Calah. Xenophon reports that Larissa was a strongly fortified city in this section and this may be the Resen of Scripture.

RESERVOIR (Heb. *miqwâh, a source of water*). Because most of western Asia was subject to periodic droughts, and because of frequent sieges, cities put great store by their waterworks. Some of the reservoirs and many private cisterns were hewn into solid rock. Some provided for abundant storage (Neh. 9:25 marg.). Uzziah helped his land by having many cisterns built (II Chron. 26:10). Elisha bade Israel to provide many special reservoirs (ditches) near Jerusalem (II Kings 3:12-17). It was considered wise for each home to have its own cistern (II Kings 18:31). Among the most famous reservoirs of Palestine were the pools of Solomon, 13 miles from the city (Eccl. 2:6). Water from these was conveyed to the city by aqueducts, some of which remain until today.

RESHEPH (rē'shĕf, *a flame*), a descendant of Ephraim (I Chron. 7:25). Nothing else is known about him.

REST (Heb. *nûah, menûhâh*, peace, quiet, Gr. *anápausis, katápausis*), a word of frequent occurrence in the Bible, in both Testaments. It is used of God as resting from His work (Gen. 2:2) and as having His rest in the temple (I Chron. 28:2). God commanded that the seventh day was to be one of rest (Exod. 16:23; 31:15) and that the land was to have its rest every seventh year (Lev. 25:4). God promised rest to the Israelites in the land of Canaan (Deut. 12:9). The word is sometimes used in the sense of trust and reliance (II Chron. 14:11). Christ offers rest of soul to those who come to Him (Matt. 11:28). Hebrews 4 says that God offers to His people a rest not enjoyed by those who died in the wilderness.

RESURRECTION (Gr. *anástasis, arising; egérsis, a raising*), a return to life subsequent to death. "The Bible . . . knows nothing of an abstract immortality of the soul, as the schools speak of it; nor is its Redemption a Redemption of the soul only, but of the body as well. It is a Redemption of man in his whole complex personality — body and soul together." So in the 1890's wrote James Orr, the great theologian of Glasgow. (*The Christian View of God and the World,* p. 196.) This distinctive fact has been noted by many competent exegetes and commentators, both before Orr's time and more recently. To deny the resurrection is, in Biblical thought, to deny any immortality worthy of the character of our faith in God (Matt. 22:31, 32; Mark 12:26,27; Luke 20:37,38). It is not that the soul does not exist in a disembodied state (see INTERMEDIATE STATE) between death and resurrection; but in the Biblical view, man in the intermediate state is incomplete, and awaits "the redemption of the body" (Rom. 8:23. See II Cor. 5:3ff and Rev. 6:9-11).

In the Old Testament the most explicit passage on the resurrection is Daniel 12:2. The KJV reads, "Many of them that sleep in the dust of the earth shall awake; some to everlasting life, and some to shame and everlasting contempt."

A clearer translation is suggested in the Jamieson Fausset and Brown *Commentary,* on the basis of data taken from Tregelles and supported by the Jewish commentators. The first two words of this text in Hebrew, *rabbim miyyeshene* literally mean "many from among the sleepers . . ." It is not correct, argues J. F. and B., to take "many" as equivalent to *hoi polloi* "the many" which often means "all." There is no article here in the Hebrew. The two words together indicate a distinction, "from among." It would have been very simple, if the writer had intended to indicate *all* the dead, for him to have omitted the preposition "from" and used *kol,* "all," or to have omitted *rabbim,* "many," and said, "Those who sleep . . ."

The word "some," used twice in this text, *elleh . . . elleh,* is preferably rendered "these . . . those." We therefore translate the verse as follows: "Many from among those who sleep in the dust of the earth will awake, these to everlasting life, but those [i.e. the rest of the dead, will awake] to shame and everlasting contempt." This clearer

translation throws light on Revelation 20:4-15 and other NT passages in which the predicted resurrection of the dead is divided into two distinct phases.

Isaiah predicts the resurrection of the righteous dead in no uncertain terms: "Thy dead men shall live; together with my dead body shall they arise. Awake and sing, ye that dwell in dust; for thy dew is as the dew of herbs, and the earth shall cast out the dead" (Isa. 26:19). Verse 14 of this chapter may be intended to indicate that the unrighteous will not be raised to enjoy the period of blessedness and expansion predicted in vs. 15. The distinction, however, is not as clear as in Daniel 12:2.

Isaiah 25:8a, "He will swallow up death in victory," is obscure in its OT context, but Paul (I Cor. 15:54. Cf. II Cor. 5:4b) interprets these words as pointing, not to resurrection, but to the sudden experience of being enveloped in immortality, that is, the "change" (I Cor. 15:51-53) to be experienced by the living saints at the "moment" of the "last trump."

A much discussed OT passage related to the doctrine of the resurrection is Job 19:23-27. It is regrettable that this inspiring confession of faith should have been made the subject of controversy, but such is the case. The crux of the difficulty is in the word *mibbesari,* which literally means "from my flesh" and is translated in the KJV, "in my flesh."

The preposition *min,* "from," is discussed in an article more than six and one half double column pages long in Brown, Driver, Briggs, our best Hebrew Lexicon. One section is devoted to the discussion of *min* as giving "the place out of which one looks."

Job's interest in the resurrection is evident from 14:13-15. In chapter 19 he is speaking of his resurrection when his Redeemer comes at the latter day to stand upon the earth. Jerome (340-420 A.D.) clearly so understood; and the Septuagint, although the text is obscure, certainly indicates that Job is referring to his future resurrection.

The translators of the ASV of 1901 were probably wrong in bringing in the highly questionable translation, "without my flesh." Their marginal reading "from my flesh," is strongly to be preferred. What Job literally said was, "Though, after my skin, [so diseased], they destroy this [body], yet from [the vantage point of] my flesh I shall see God." He then adds, in effect, "I myself shall see him with my very own eyes!"

Other OT references to resurrection are Psalm 16:9-11 (see Acts 2:25-28,31; 13:35; Ps. 17:15; 49:15). There are also many passages in which faith in the resurrection must be assumed in the background.

The question why there are not more and clearer resurrection passages in the Pentateuch and the historical books, must be met with facts as they stand in the progress of God's revelation. Not everything is revealed at once, yet every age has sufficient light for its spiritual life and fellowship with God. Contemporaneous heathen religions were permeated with fantastic notions of the future life. It is remarkable that the writers of Scripture maintained a simple faith in God without these heathen fantasies.

The non-canonical books of the ancient Judeo-Christian world contain much material on the resurrection which there is not space to discuss. The reader will find most of this material in R. H. Charles' *Apocrypha and Pseudepigrapha of the O. T.* Many exact references are given in the index in Vol. II under the heading "Resurrection."

In the New Testament the word *anastasis,* "resurrection," signifies the arising to life of dead bodies, or a dead body. There is one possible exception, Luke 2:34, though probably "resurrection" is the meaning here, too. In secular Greek the word may refer to any act of rising up or sitting up; but the theological interpretation of the word in the NT does not depend only upon its literal meaning, but upon the contexts in which it is found.

The doctrine of resurrection is stated clearly in its simplest form in Paul's words before the Roman law court presided over by Felix: "there will be a resurrection both of the just and of the unjust" (Acts 24:15). The most detailed statement of the doctrine of twofold resurrection is found in Revelation 20:4-15. (For the author's analysis of this passage see the article MILLENNIUM). In his article on "Resurrection" in ISBE, Burton Scott Easton said, "*Two* resurrections are found in Revelation 20:5,13 and quite possibly in I Thessalonians 4:16; I Corinthians 15:23,24. Hence the phrase, 'first resurrection.' "

In the words of Jesus the only clear allusion to a twofold resurrection is found in John 5:25,28,29. It must be remembered that John shares the cosmic perspective from which the eschatological complex began with the incarnation (see I John 2:18). As Dr. Geerhardus Vos (*Pauline Eschatology* pp. 36ff) has said, "The age to come [which began at the incarnation] was perceived to bear in its womb another age to come." In John 5:25 Jesus refers to the fact that He "now" exercises His power to raise the dead selectively, "they that hear will live." (Compare the resurrection of Lazarus, John 11, and of the son of the widow of Nain, Luke 7:11-17, as well as Matt. 27:50-53.) Verses 28 and 29 of John 5 refer to the future and allude to the distinction made in Daniel 12:2, which John explicates in Revelation 20:4-15.

Paul implies in I Thessalonians 4:16,17 that the dead who are not "in Christ" will not be raised at the same time with the redeemed. This is made more clear in I Corinthians 15:20-28. Verses 20-23 base the resurrection of the dead firmly upon the power of Christ as exhibited in his own resurrection (see RESURRECTION OF CHRIST), and state the substance of the later pronouncement before Felix (Acts 24:15). By the power of Christ all the dead will be raised.

With verse 23 Paul begins an enumeration of three "orders" of resurrection, one of which, the resurrection of Christ, is past. (1) *"aparche Christos,* Christ the firstfruits. (2) *epeita hoi tou Christou . . .,* afterwards those who are Christ's . . ." This second "order" of resurrection is 'said to take place "at his appearing, *parousia."* (3) *"eita to telos . . .,* then the end . . ." The "end" in this context follows the resurrection of "those who are Christ's." It includes the time when Christ "reigns" and subdues all His enemies. The last enemy, death itself is to be subdued. This must be regarded as taking place when all the rest of the dead without exception stand before the great white throne (Rev. 20:12ff). This final subduing of death is Paul's third "order" of resurrection.

Since Paul's first "order" is the resurrection of Christ, it is obvious that Paul's second and third "orders" of resurrection coincide with John's future "first resurrection" and his resurrection of "the rest of the dead" (Rev. 20:4-15).

The nature of the redeemed in the resurrection is not described in great detail, yet the Scripture does not leave us totally ignorant. We shall be corporeally "like his [Christ's] glorious body"

(Phil. 3:21. Cf. I John 3:2). It is enough to know that we shall be like our Lord.

This matter is discussed by Paul at length in I Corinthians 15:35-50. The numerical identity is the same. The corporeal identity which is "sown in corruption . . . sown in lack of honor . . . sown in weakness . . . sown a natural body . . ." is the same identity which is "raised in incorruption . . . raised in glory . . . raised in power . . . raised a spiritual body . . ."

But the numerical identity of the mortal body with the resurrection body has nothing to do with the disposition of the material particles which make up the body at the moment of death. Material particles are constantly changing in our mortal bodies without loss of bodily identity. The resurrection is simply a miracle.

It is essential to the Christian faith that Christ, like whom we shall be, arose from the dead "in the same body in which he suffered"; that the grave was empty and that His body of "flesh and bones" (Luke 24:39) was recognizable. Yet His body was "changed," "glorious," "spiritual," perfectly adapted as well for normal communications as for the free unencumbered activities of the spirit.

Our mortal body is "flesh and blood" (I Cor. 15:50) but not so the resurrection body. The marriage relationship in particular is a thing of the past for those who are raised from the dead as inheritors of the Kingdom (Luke 20:34-36; Cf. Mark 12:24, 25; Matt. 22:29,30).

The resurrection saints will participate with Christ in the government of the world (Matt. 19:28; Luke 22:28,29; I Cor. 6:2,3. See MILLENNIUM).

The moral implications of the doctrine of the resurrection of the body are sharply emphasized in I Corinthians 15:30-34. Why be concerned about carnality if the body is only a temporary shell? So argued the corrupt party in the Corinthian church. We are too "spiritual" to struggle against bodily appetites.

But Paul replies sharply, "Do not be deceived; evil associations corrupt good ethics. Sober up righteously and stop sinning. Some are shamefully ignorant of God. I speak to shame you" (vss. 33, 34; original translation). As Geerhardus Vos (*op. cit.* p. 61) "Eschatology . . . yields *ipso facto* a philosophy of history . . . and every philosophy of history bears in itself the seed of a theology . . . [which must bear] practical theological fruitage." If one denies the historical purposes of God in this created material world, including the implications to our bodily resurrection, Biblical ethics begin to be undermined. J.O.B.

RESURRECTION OF JESUS CHRIST. The Easter miracle is the heart of Christian faith: the NT, if anything, is even more resurrection-oriented than it is cross-centered. Indeed, it is the resurrection which interprets the cross and which therefore shapes the Church's theology as well as its worship and life. In the words of Floyd Filson, "The interpreting clue and the organizing fact of Biblical theology is the resurrection of Jesus" (*Jesus Christ The Risen Lord,* New York: Abingdon Press, 1956, p. 29). Both historically and theologically, A. Michael Ramsey insists, it is necessary to make the resurrection our standing place (*The Resurrection of Christ,* Philadelphia: The Westminster Press, 1946, pp. 9-10), recognizing that Christian faith is resurrection-faith and that Christian theism is resurrection-theism. The Christian God is not simply God, even the triune God: He is the God who raises the dead (Rom. 4:16-17; Eph. 1:19-20; I Pet. 1:21). Hence Christian faith *per se* is faith in the resurrection (Rom. 10:9), for the Easter miracle transforms the tragedy of the Cross into Gospel (I Cor. 15:3-4).

I. The Centrality of the Resurrection. A mere inventory of NT texts is sufficient to show that the resurrection must not be viewed as, in F. X. Durrwell's phrase, "a mere epilogue to Calvary." In our Lord's own teaching, for example, His resurrection is never divorced from His crucifixion. The atoning cross and the empty tomb form a redemptive complex (Matt. 16:21; Matt. 20:18-19; Mark 8:31; Mark 9:31; Mark 10:33-34; Luke 24:26; John 10:17-18). In the apostolic *kerygma* which figures so largely in the Book of Acts, the resurrection proves not only that the scandal of the cross is really God's saving deed, but also that Jesus is the true Messiah rather than a lying impostor (Acts 2:22-36; 3:12-18; 4:10; 5:29-32; 10:39-43; 13:19-37; 17:23-31). Peter's explicit witness to the resurrection is also stated in his First Epistle (1:3-5,21; 3:18-22). In all probability Peter's witness likewise forms the substance of the Marcan account. The testimony of the Johannine literature is somewhat limited but equally emphatic (John 11:25-26; 20-21; Rev. 1:18).

So frequently does Paul allude to the resurrection that McCheyne Edgar has every warrant for this conclusion: "The Pauline Gospel was preeminently that of a Risen Saviour" (*The Gospel of a Risen Saviour*, Edinburgh: T. & T. Clark, 1892, p. 69. Cf., e.g., Acts 13:19-37; 17:23-31; 26:8; Rom. 1:4; 4:25; 6:4-11; 7:4; 8:11,23; 14:9; I Cor. 15; II Cor. 1:9-10; 4:14; 5:14-15; 13:4; Gal. 1:4; Eph. 1:19-23; Phil. 3:10; Col. 1:18; 2:12; I Thess. 1:10; 4:14; 5:10; II Tim. 1:10; 2:8). Surely, then, Durrwell's appraisal of the Pauline Gospel is not exaggerated: "St. Paul more than anyone is the Apostle of the risen Lord; he is supremely the 'witness of the resurrection.' He has seen and heard Christ in His heavenly glory, and has seen and heard Him only thus. The Christ whom he met transcended the limitations of history; by His resurrection He was established in glory, and this was how the apostle knew Him in that first blinding experience of salvation. Consequently, his preaching was to be concerned less with recounting the words and deeds of Christ as handed down by tradition, than with trying to express his own realization of the risen Christ as the source of redemption. His Gospel is primarily this one fact, the resurrection of Christ from the dead; he sees Christ as the source of life, but it is the risen Christ that he sees" (F. X. Durrwell, *The Resurrection*, New York: Sheed and Ward, 1960, pp. 23-24).

Because of the prominence assigned to the resurrection in the NT, "it ought to occupy," William Milligan argues, "a far more important place than it generally does, alike in our theological systems and in our religious life" (*The Resurrection of Our Lord*, New York: The Macmillan Company, 1927, p. 232). Obviously his argument demands acquiescence.

II. The Theology of the Resurrection. All too often evangelicals seem excessively concerned with the evidential values and apologetic problems of the resurrection; in fact, with a few shining exceptions they have failed to emphasize properly its enormous implications for theology.

Christologically considered, the resurrection established Jesus as the Son of God with power. In Romans 1:4 does Paul simply mean that our Lord's deity was validated by the Easter miracle, or does he mean that, supernaturally raised up, the Son

of Mary entered upon that mode of existence which befits God's Son? Is Durrwell's Roman Catholic exegesis too far-fetched? "The Resurrection was not merely a coming back to life, but a birth into a new life which Christ did not have in his bodily humanity. . . . Born of the Virgin into the life of a son of man, on Easter day he was reborn into the life of the Son of God. Paul is not afraid of the notion of Christ's having a second birth. At Easter he interprets the Father as making that solemn statement, 'Thou art my Son; this day have I begotten thee.' (Acts xiii.33.) 'This day' starts at the first instant of Christ's existence (Rom. i.3; Phil. ii.6), but its high noon is at Easter. Following his birth into the world at Bethlehem, comes a new Christmas in a blaze of light" (*op. cit.*, p. 126). In any event, by virtue of His resurrection, Jesus became more than perfected Man, the prototype of glorified humanity (I Cor. 15:35-57; Phil. 3:20-21); He became even far more than the Destroyer of death (II Tim. 1:10; Rev. 1:18). By virtue of His resurrection Jesus was declared to be Lord and Christ (Acts 2:36), invested with universal power (Matt. 28:18). And in its NT use, as Filson points out, *kúrios* signifies "the Resurrection and Exaltation. . . . What do these references to Exaltation and lordship mean? They imply and result from the Resurrection. They recognize that for his earthly work Jesus has been uniquely honored by the Father. But this does not mean that Jesus is now taking a long heavenly vacation, without active interest in the life of the church. He has a central role in the continuing life of his people. As his position at the right hand of God implies, he acts with authority as God's supreme and central agent in the carrying out of God's will. The idea that once Easter is over, we are through with Jesus until the last judgment (if there is one), completely misunderstands NT faith and preaching. Jesus is the effective and active Lord of his church" (Filson, *op. cit.*, pp. 50-51). Thus by virtue of His resurrection, the despised Nazarene became Head of the Church (Eph. 1:19-23) and cosmic Sovereign, though His sovereignty is as yet *incognito* (Phil. 2:9-11). By virtue of His resurrection, He also became a life-giving Spirit (Acts 2:32-33; I Cor. 15:45). Milligan's comment on this point is insightful: "When, therefore, we apprehend in faith that Second Adam from whom the new life comes, it is with the Redeemer as One who not only died but who rose again that we have to do; and the Church of Christ felt this with that wonderful instinct of which it is difficult to speak as if it were less than inspiration. Why did her weekly day of worship not commemorate the Incarnation or the death upon the cross? Because neither was the beginning of her life. At neither of these points of His history was her Lord in a position to give her life. It was at His Resurrection that He became a 'life-giving spirit' — a spirit clothed with a body entirely conformed to His spiritual state, and able without let or hindrance to dispense itself to man in all the fulness of its heavenly power. In the Risen Christ, therefore, the new life of believers has its source" (Milligan, *op. cit.*, pp. 169-170).

By virtue of His resurrection, moreover, our Saviour entered upon His ministry as High Priest, presenting His own sacrificial blood to the Father, performing the functions of intercession (Rom. 8:34) and benediction. Though the Letter to the Hebrews contains only a single reference to the resurrection (13:20), the truth expressed in that single reference is nevertheless presupposed at every turn in the apostolic argument: the resur-

A panorama of the Garden Tomb enclosure, traditional site of Christ's burial, showing the tomb in the lower left corner of picture. © MPS

rected Christ is the Melchizedekian Priest. Again, by virtue of His resurrection, our Saviour was appointed Judge of the living and the dead (Acts 10: 42; 17:31). In sum, by virtue of His resurrection, Jesus is now perfected Man, seated at the right hand of the Majesty on high, victorious and vindicated, the Destroyer of death, a life-giving Spirit, the Saviour, Head, and Priest of His people, the world's future King and Judge.

Soteriologically considered, the resurrection is an integral part of the whole redemptive process. It is, to be sure, the sign of the Father's approbation, the miracle by which the Son's sacrifice is attested and accepted. But it is no mere *addendum* to Calvary, an idea which Milligan demolishes. On the cross, Jesus finished His work of passive obedience; there His submission to suffering and struggle came to an end. But very significantly in the NT salvation is never connected merely with the death of Christ; it is connected with His blood, the blood which as priest He now offers. A text like Hebrews 9:12-14 reveals irrefutably that "we must think of Christ's blood as living blood, and of the pardon of sin as only the initiatory result of His sacrifice of Himself. In short, through all Christ's offering we deal with life. Christ is 'a living sacrifice'; we are in Him, and sharing the blessings of His salvation, are also 'a living sacrifice' (Rom. xii.1). And the end and purpose of everything that is done is that we may be brought into loving fellowship with God, and into the holy life which such fellowship involves; 'for if the blood of goats and bulls, and the ashes of a heifer

sprinkling them that have been defiled, sanctify unto the cleanness of the flesh; how much more shall the blood of Christ, who through the eternal Spirit offered Himself without blemish unto God, cleanse your conscience from dead works to serve the living God?' (Heb. ix. 13,14)" (Milligan, *op. cit.,* pp. 283-284). Only a risen Lord can be a life-giving Spirit and therefore a Saviour. Only a risen Lord can be a Saviour because only a risen Lord, as Head and Priest of His people, can truly and fully save, carrying every member of His body with Him through death into glory by the power of His endless life.

Eschatologically considered, the resurrection is the pledge and pattern of a creation from which the ravages of sin have been sacrificially removed, a cosmos brought to its God-intended fulfillment. William Hordern is merely paraphrasing the NT when he writes concerning the resurrection: "It was the shattering of history by the creative act of God. It begins a new era for the universe, a decisive turning point for the human race. To men held in the grip of fear and futility, to men who see only the blind laws of nature grinding on their way, foredooming man to his fate; to men who see no hope for the future of mankind, the Resurrection proclaims the fact that there is a power at work in the world which is mightier than all the forces that crucified our Lord. The Resurrection is not just a personal survival of the man Jesus, a phenomenon to be studied by the Society of Psychical Research; it is a cosmic victory." (*A Layman's Guide to Protestant Theology,* New York: The

Part II of panorama of the Garden Tomb enclosure, showing Gordon's Calvary, traditional site of the crucifixion, in the background. © MPS

Macmillan Company, 1955, p. 205). The resurrection of Jesus is of course a guarantee that life continues after death (John 11:25-26; 14:19), as well as a guarantee of judgment to come (Acts 17:31). But the NT does not speak of an abstract, immaterial survival; it speaks of *bodily* resurrection, a life after death in which the total man participates. Thus the resurrected body of our Lord prophesies the nature of that future embodiment which believers will enjoy — a body recognizably the same (Luke 24:36-43; John 20:27), a body no longer subject to space-time limitations (Luke 24:31; John 20:19,26), a body changed and glorified (Matt. 22:30; I Cor. 6:13; 15:30-38,51), a body adapted to serve as the instrument of personality in a new dimension of existence.

Beyond the purely personal effects of the resurrection, however, lie its cosmic outworkings. Here the great and sufficient text is Romans 8:19-22. As Durrwell puts it in a memorable sentence, "The mystery of Easter will be imprinted on the universe" (*op. cit.,* p. 300).

III. The Historicity of the Resurrection. Granted that the disciples of Jesus believed Him to be alive after His passion — and virtually no scholar today denies that the early Church sprang from a sincere faith in the resurrection — what if that faith was sincerely mistaken? Then Paul's dolorous conclusions follow (I Cor. 15:17-19). To establish the factuality of the resurrection — insofar as the uniqueness of that event allows — is therefore a top-priority task in Christian apologetics.

Little time need be spent refuting the shopworn theories by which unbelief has sought to explain away the Easter miracle. The older criticism, whether deistic, agnostic, or atheistic, operated on the presupposition that we live in a closed universe, absolutely governed by a causal nexus which renders any divine inbreaking unthinkable. Thus it was driven to advance such untenable hypotheses as the *swoon* theory (on the cross Jesus passed into a death-like coma from which He revived in the coolness of the tomb), the *fraud* theory (the Jewish authorities were correct in alleging that the followers of Jesus had stolen His corpse), the *hallucination* theory (hope, faith, and love conspired *à la* Renan to create "appearances" which, while real to the disciples, were only illusions). Detailed refutation of these views is abundantly available. (Cf., e.g., the works by Milligan, Edgar, Ramsey, together with Frank Morison, *Who Moved the Stone?*, Doremus A. Hayes, *The Resurrection Fact,* and Arnold Lunn, *The Third Day*.)

More recent critics continue to operate on essentially the same presupposition even if they do so less blatantly. Adhering to theism in most instances, they recoil from the cross miracle of a bodily resurrection which leaves a tomb empty. Hastings Rashdall may serve as spokesman for this entire school of theology or, more correctly, philosophy. "The disappearance or absolute annihilation, the reanimation, or the sudden transformation into something not quite material and yet not quite spiritual, of a really dead body, would involve the violation of the best ascertained laws of physics, chemistry, and physiology. Were the testimony fifty times stronger than it is, any hypothesis would be more possible than that. But in the present state of our knowledge of the kind of causality which is discovered in the relation between mind and mind, or between mind and body, there is nothing to be said against the possibility of an appearance of Christ to His disciples which was a real, though supernormal psychological event, but which involved nothing which can properly be spoken of as a suspension of natural law" (From an unpublished essay quoted in Kirsopp Lake: *The Historical Evidence for the Resurrection of Jesus Christ,* New York: G. P. Putnam's Sons, 1907, pp. 268-269). That is why Kirsopp Lake personally advocates the hypothesis that the women who came to anoint the body of our Lord probably visited the wrong grave, coincidentally encountering a stranger from whom they fled. Lake candidly admits, however, that his hypothesis is indeed a hypothesis, a theory framed in keeping with his own conviction that a *quasi*-materialistic life after death is unthinkable. "The historical evidence is such that it can be fairly interpreted consistently with either of the two doctrinal positions . . . but it does not support either. The story of the empty tomb must be fought out on doctrinal, not on historical or critical grounds" (*op. cit.,* p. 253). For similar reasons Canon B. H. Streeter adopts the vision theory of Theodore Keim, who, repudiating the idea of hallucination, wrote in a

famous paragraph: "We find ourselves in the midst of impossibilities when we make the ordained of God to end, or when we leave the matter to the chance-play of visions, that he is awakened from the dead for the dead. The evidence that Jesus was alive, the *telegram from heaven,* was necessary after an earthly downfall which was unexampled and, in the childhood of the human race, would be convincing. The evidence that he was alive was therefore given by his own impulsion and by the will of God. The Christianity of today owes to this evidence, first its Lord and then its own existence: the latter, because it rejoices in Him, and because it sees its own future. . . . Thus, though much has fallen away, the faith-fortress of the resurrection of Jesus remains" (Quoted in Ramsey, *op. cit.,* p. 51). Streeter holds that the body of Jesus must have been removed by human agency and that, consequently, the tomb was actually empty. But in order to reassure the disciples God sent a *"telegram from heaven";* in other words, He granted a series of veritable appearances by the living Christ. Streeter further maintains that Jesus possibly revealed Himself to His disciples "in some form such as might be covered by Paul's phrase 'a spiritual body'; possibly through some psychological channel similar to that which explains the mysterious means of communication between persons commonly known as telepathy; or possibly in some way which we have at present no conception. On such a view the appearances to the disciples can only be called visions, if by visions we mean

A close-up view of the Garden Tomb, just below Gordon's Calvary, on the west side of Calvary. © MPS

something directly caused by the Lord Himself, veritably alive and personally in communion with them" ("The Historic Christ," *Foundations,* Seven Oxford Men, London: Macmillan and Co., Limited, 1913, p. 136). Emil Brunner also objects to the NT assertions regarding a bodily resurrection and a vacant tomb, though he holds fast to the "truth" or eschatological significance of the resurrection (*The Mediator,* Philadelphia: The Westminster Press, 1947, pp. 576-583. For an effective answer cf. G. R. Beasley-Murray *Christ Is Alive!,* pp. 15-18). The views of Karl Barth, Rudolph Bultmann, and John Knox are acutely analyzed in Richard R. Niebuhr's *Resurrection and Historical Reason.* It is Niebuhr's opinion that these theologians, however diverse their positions, are still enthralled by Immanuel Kant, "working . . . with conceptual tools fashioned by the father of modern philosophy. Hence Niebuhr charges that "So far as the basic problem of a positive attitude toward the Biblical history is concerned, there is no indication of a 'neo-orthodox' movement. Rather, the fundamental positions outlined by the nineteenth-century theologians continue to mold contemporary methodology" (Richard R. Niebuhr, *Resurrection and Historical Reason,* New York: Charles Scribner's Sons, 1957, p. 81). What Christianity requires, Niebuhr insists, is "a genuinely theological conception of history and historical reason" (*op. cit.,* p. 104). Into the subtleties of this debate it is unnecessary to enter now. Suffice it to say that there are no valid reasons for disbelieving the NT accounts of our Lord's resurrection (Twelve reasons for accepting the factuality of the Easter miracle are given by Samuel Zwemer, *The Glory of the Empty Tomb,* New York: Fleming H. Revell Company, 1947, pp. 43-44). On Christian presuppositions the Biblical evidence is more than adequate. Operating on their own presuppositions, evangelicals can say with Ramsey: "We would not use these presuppositions for the pressing of historical conclusions; but we would so bear them in mind as to avoid a sort of inhibition if the converging lines of evidence seem to point to a supernatural event at the climax of the story of Christ. Thus if the evidence is pointing us towards a Resurrection of an utterly unique sort we will not be incredulous, for the Christ is Himself a unique and transcendent fact in history. If the evidence is pointing us towards a miracle we will not be troubled, for the miracle will mean not only a breach of the laws that have been perceived in this world but a manifestation of the purpose of the creator of a new world and the redeemer of our own. And if the evidence is pointing us towards an act wherein spirit and body are strangely blended and exalted, our minds will have no terrors: for the message of the NT is pervaded through and through by the belief that the spiritual and the material are interwoven in the purpose of the Word-made-flesh. Why is it judged incredible with you, if God should raise the dead?" (*op. cit.,* pp. 57-58). V.C.G.

Interior of the Garden Tomb, supposedly the tomb from which Christ arose. © MPS

REU (rē'ū, Heb. *re'û, friendship*), the son of Peleg and a fifth generation son of Shem (Gen. 11:10-19). Peleg is called Phalec in Luke 3:35, and Reu is called Ragau.

REUBEN (rōō'bĕn, Heb. *re'ûvēn*, Gr. *Rhoubén, See a son!*), the eldest son of Jacob, born to him by Leah in Padan-aram (Gen. 29:32). Nothing is known about his early life, except that he brought mandrakes (*q.v.*) to his mother which she used in getting Jacob to give her another son (Gen. 30:14f). Reuben committed incest at Eder (Gen. 35:22). Either because of this sin, or out of innate weakness (Gen. 49:4) his tribe never rose to power. He delivered Joseph from death by warning his brothers against the results of such an act (Gen. 37:19-22; 42:22) and later offered his sons a surety for Benjamin (42:37). He took four sons into Egypt (Gen. 46:9). When Israel went from Egypt, he had 151,450 descendants (Num. 1:21, 2:16). Reubenites made a covenant with Moses in order to occupy the rich grazing lands of Gilead (Num. 32:1-33). That they kept the covenant is attested by the monument to Bohan, a descendant of Reuben (Josh. 15:6). When the other tribes were settled in Canaan, Reuben, Gad and half of Manasseh returned to Gilead and set up a great monument as a reminder of the unity of Israelites (Josh. 22). In protecting their flocks against marauding nomads they became a bold and skilled warlike people (I Chron. 5:1-19). They sent 120,-000 men to support King David (I Chron. 12:37). They were oppressed during Jehu's reign (II Kings 10:32,33). They were taken into captivity by Tiglath-pileser of Assyria (I Chron. 5:25,26).

REUBENITES (rōō'bĕn-īts), descendants of Reuben, son of Jacob. When Moses took the census in Midian, Reuben numbered 43,730 men of military age (Num. 26:1-7). They were joint possessors of Gilead and Bashan (Deut. 3:12; 29:8), and were praised by Moses for their fidelity (Josh. 22:1-6). They supported David against the Philistines (I Chron. 11:42; 12:37). Tiglath-pileser took them into the Assyrian captivity.

REUEL (rōō'ĕl, Heb. *re'û'ēl, God is friend*). 1. A son of Esau by Mashemath (Gen. 36:4,10).

2. A priest in Midian who gave Moses a daughter as wife (Exod. 2:16-22)), probably the same as Jethro (Exod. 3:1).

3. The father of Eliasaph (called Deuel in Num. 1:14; 7:42, etc.; Num. 2:14).

4. A Benjamite (I Chron. 9:8).

REUMAH (rōō'mà), a concubine of Nahor who was a brother of Abraham (Gen. 22:20-24).

REVELATION. The word "revelation" is of Latin derivation and means "unveiling." It is the translation of the Greek *apokalýpsis*. The last book of the Bible was named by its author *The Apocalypse* [Unveiling] *of Jesus Christ*, and the title (as also the same phrase in I Cor. 1:7; II Thess. 1:7; I Pet. 1:7,13) refers to the visible return of the Lord. But elsewhere the word almost always refers to the making known of truth in propositional or experiential form.

In Christian theology the doctrine of revelation is the doctrine of God's making Himself and relevant truths known to men. It is customary to divide the subject into "general" and "special" revelation. For purposes of this article, and contrary to custom, it seems best to discuss the latter first.

Special Revelation is found (1) in the person and work of Jesus Christ, and (2) in the Bible.

1. Christians hold that "God was in Christ reconciling the world to Himself" (II Cor. 5:19), not merely in the sense that Jesus was a man through whom God worked, but in the sense that "In him dwells all the fullness of deity (*theotes*) in bodily form" (Col. 2:9 my translation here and elsewhere if the KJV is not followed). He was "God manifest in the flesh" (I Tim. 3:16), the second person of the Trinity, coequal, coeternal, and consubstantial with the Father and the Spirit.

This being the case, it follows that Christians regard every act, every moment in the life of Jesus as revelatory. What He says, does, and experiences, God-in-the-flesh, says, does and experiences. The title "Word," *Logos* (John 1:1-18; Rev. 19:13), presents Him as the "rational expression" of God. He is the "visible presentation (*eikon*) of the invisible God" (Col. 1:15), "the [visible] stamp of His [God's] substance" *charakter tes hypostaseos autou* (Heb. 1:3). When Jesus said, "I and the Father are one" (John 10:30), He was not denying the numerical distinctions of the persons of the Trinity, but affirming the unity of the divine substance. When He said to Philip, "He that hath seen me hath seen the Father" (John 14:8,9), He indicated that, with reference to Philip's request, "Show us the Father," Jesus is Himself as full a "showing" as Philip could possibly comprehend.

The incarnation, Jesus Christ in history, is the point of the wedge in the Christian approach to the world. "God, who in many portions and many modes spoke of old to the fathers by the prophets, hath, at the end of these days, spoken to us by the Son" (Heb. 1:1,2). The Christian's God is not mythological or imaginary. He is revealed in a well-documented life in the flesh at a well-known juncture of time and place in history.

2. It is impossible in a brief article to enter into evidences that the Bible is divine revelation. Suffice it to say that for the faithful Church down through the centuries "the Bible is the Word of God, the only infallible rule of faith and practice." (See Gaussen's *Theopneustia*, James Orr's *The Bible Under Trial*, and especially Warfield's *Revelation and Inspiration*.)

That Christ and His apostles believed and taught that the Bible in its entirety is divine revelation is brought out by Warfield with overwhelming evidence. For example, Christ said, "The Scriptures cannot be broken" (John 10:35); and Paul said, "All Scripture is God-breathed" (II Tim. 3:16). Peter declares that "No Scripture ever came into being as a private release, nor was any [scriptural] prophecy ever brought by human volition, but men spoke from God, being carried along by the Holy Spirit" (II Pet. 1:20,21). For the writers of the NT, what the Scripture says, God says.

It may be argued that all the references cited in the last paragraph above apply to the OT. This is true, but there is abundant evidence that the NT writers claimed an equal authority. See, for example, II Thessalonians 3:6,14,16. Peter calls Paul's epistles "Scripture" (II Pet. 3:15,16); and Paul quotes a saying of Jesus' found in Matthew 10:10 and Luke 10:7 as Scripture (I Tim. 5:18).

On the nature of the Bible as revelation, the reader is invited to meditate. Peter refers to the prophetic Word as "more sure" than his own eyewitness experience of the transfiguration (II Pet. 1:16-19), and he says that to this Word, "you do well to devote yourselves, as to a light shining in a dark, squalid place."

General Revelation is found outside the Bible, and apart from Jesus Christ in the flesh, (1) in nature and (2) in the convicting work of the Holy Spirit. It is proper to consider general revelation after special revelation, because, while the Bible is just as truly a part of the human environment as any other book, and while Jesus is just as much a part of verifiable history (See the article on Resurrection) as Julius Caesar, yet it is in Christ and in the Bible that we find explicit propositional revelation. It is appropriate to begin with the propositional explicit in any inquiry, and to take up later the merely inferential.

1. Nature does not give propositional truth. It gives data from which inferences are reasonably drawn. Those who reject natural theistic evidences set these evidences off as though it were claimed that they are mathematical demonstrations. Thomas Aquinas, unsatisfactory as his formulations are, never claimed syllogistic cogency for his "proofs."

Psalms 8 and 19 (see Rom. 10:18) and many other Scriptures declare that there is divine revelation in nature. Inductive evidence may be good and sufficient evidence. Paul makes a vehement statement which assumes the force of natural revelation: "From the creation of the cosmos, God's invisible attributes, his eternal power and divine character (theiotes, not theotes as in Col. 2:9), known by the things [which he] made, are clearly seen, so that they [who turn from God] are inexcusable" (Rom. 1:20).

2. The promise of Christ that the Holy Spirit will convict the world of the sin of rejecting Him (John 16:8-11) does not indicate revelation of facts otherwise unknown, but it does emphasize a much neglected truth. Given the data of special revelation and of revelation in nature, the Holy Spirit, administering both the common grace and the special grace of God, does act upon the hearts and minds of men in convicting power, enabling them to see what they see (Matt. 13:13-15) and to comprehend what they hear, and enabling (Eph. 2:8; Phil. 2:13) God's elect to accept their Saviour. Thus Paul refers to his conversion (Gal. 1:15,16) as God's act of revealing His Son in Him. See also GOD.   J.O.B.

REVELATION, BOOK OF THE (Gr. *apocalýpsis, an unveiling*), sometimes called *The Apocalypse,* is the last book of the Bible and the only book of the NT that is exclusively prophetic in character. It belongs to the class of apocalyptic literature in which the divine message is conveyed by visions and dreams (see APOCALYPTIC LITERATURE). The title which the book itself assumes (1:1) may mean either "the revelation which Christ possesses and imparts," or "the unveiling of the person of Christ." Grammatically, the former is preferable, for this text states that God gave this disclosure to Christ that He might impart it to His servants.

The Author. Unlike many apocalyptic books which are either anonymous or published under a false name, Revelation is ascribed to John, evidently a well-known character among the churches of Asia Minor. He claimed to be a brother of those who were suffering persecution, and was called by one of the angels who imparted to him the vision of a "prophet."

The earliest definite historical reference to this Apocalypse appears in the works of Justin Martyr (c. A.D. 135), who, in alluding to the 20th chapter, said that John, one of the apostles of Christ, prophesied that those who believed in Christ would dwell in Jerusalem a thousand years. Irenaeus (A.D. 180) quoted Revelation five times, and named John as the author. Clement of Alexandria (c. A.D. 200) received the book as authentic Scripture, and the Muratorian Fragment (c. A.D. 170) lists it as a part of the accepted canon by the end of the second century.

Its relation to John, the son of Zebedee, was questioned by Dionysius of Alexandria (A.D. 231-265) on the grounds that the writer unhesitatingly declared his name, whereas the author of the Fourth Gospel did not do so, and that the vocabulary and style were utterly different from the Johannine Gospel and Epistle. He admitted that the Apocalypse was undoubtedly written by a man named John, but not by the beloved disciple. Eusebius, who quotes Dionysius at length, (*Historia Ecclesiae,* VII, 25) mentions both in the quotation and also in a discussion of his own (HE III, 39) that there were hints of two Johns in Ephesus, and intimates that one wrote the Gospel, and the other, Revelation. This view is not generally supported by the Fathers, nor does the internal evidence make it necessary. The second "John" is a shadowy figure, and cannot be identified with any of the known disciples of Jesus mentioned in the Gospels. The so-called grammatical mistakes are chiefly unidiomatic translations of Hebrew or Aramaic expressions, which would be impossible to render literally into Greek. The very nature of the visions made smooth writing difficult, for the seer was attempting to describe the indescribable. There are some positive likenesses to the accepted Johannine writings, such as the application of the term "Word of God" to Christ (19:13), the reference to the "water of life" (22:17), the concept of the "Lamb" (5:6). It is possible that John had the aid of an amanuensis in writing the Gospel and the Epistles, but that he was forced to transcribe immediately the visions that he had without the opportunity to reflect on them or to polish his expression.

Date and Place. There are two prevailing views regarding the date of the Apocalypse. The earlier date in the reign of Nero is favored by some because of the allusion to the temple in 11:1-2, which obviously refers to an early structure. Had the Apocalypse been written after A.D. 70, the temple in Jerusalem would not have been left standing. The number *666* in 13:18 has also been applied to Nero, for the total numerical value of the consonants of his name, if spelled NERON KESAR, will add up to 666 exactly. In the 18th chapter the allusion to the five kings that are fallen, one existing, and one yet to come, could refer to the fact that five emperors, Augustus, Tiberius, Caligula, Claudius, and Nero, had already passed away; another, perhaps Galba, was reigning, and would be followed shortly by still another (17:9-11). By this reasoning the Revelation would belong at the end of Nero's reign, when his mysterious suicide had given rise to the belief that he had merely quit the Empire to join the Parthians, with whom he would come to resume his throne later.

A second view, better substantiated by the early interpreters of the book, places it in the reign of Domitian (A.D. 81-96), almost at the close of the first century. Irenaeus (c. A.D. 180), Victorinus (c. A.D. 270), Eusebius (c. A.D. 328), and Jerome (c. A.D. 370) all agree on this date. It allows time for the growth of declension that is presupposed by the letters to the churches, and it fits better with the historical conditions of the Roman empire depicted in the symbolism.

The place of writing was the island of Patmos, where John had been exiled for his faith. Patmos was the site of a penal colony, where political prisoners were condemned to hard labor in the mines.

Destination. Revelation was addressed to seven churches of the Roman province of Asia, which occupied the western third of what is now Turkey. The cities where these churches were located were on the main roads running N and S, so that a messenger carrying these letters could move in a direct circuit from one to the other. There were other churches in Asia at the time when Revelation was written, but these seem to have been selected because they were representative of various types of need and of Christian experience. They have been variously interpreted to represent successive periods in the life of the Church, or as seven aspects of the total character of the Church. Undoubtedly they were actual historical groups known to the author.

Occasion. Revelation was written for the express purpose of declaring "the things which must shortly come to pass" (Rev. 1:1), in order that the evils in the churches might be corrected and that they might be prepared for the events that were about to confront them. The moral and social conditions of the empire were deteriorating, and Christians had already begun to feel the increasing pressure of paganism and the threat of persecution. The book of Revelation provided a new perspective on history by showing that the kingdom of Christ was eternal, and that it would ultimately be victorious over the kingdoms of the world.

Methods of Interpretation. There are four main schools of interpretation. The *Preterist* holds that Revelation is simply a picture of the conditions prevalent in the Roman empire of the late first century, cast in the form of vision and prophecy to conceal its meaning from hostile pagans. The *Historical* view contends that the book represents in symbolic form the entire course of Church history from the time of its writing to the final consummation, and that the mystical figures and actions described therein can be identified with human events in history. The *Futurist*, on the basis of the threefold division given in Revelation 1: 19, suggests that "the things which thou sawest" refer to the immediate environment of the seer and the vision of Christ (1:9-19), "the things which are" denote the churches of Asia, or the Church age, which they symbolize (2:1-3:22), and "the things which shall be hereafter" relate to those events which will attend the return of Christ and the establishment of the city of God. The *Idealist* or *Symbolic* school treats Revelation as purely a dramatic picture of the conflict of good and evil which persists in every age, but which cannot be applied exclusively to any particular historical period.

Structure and Content. Revelation contains four great visions, each of which is introduced by the phrase "in the spirit" (1:10; 4:2; 17:3; 21:10). Each of these visions locates the seer in a different place, each contains a distinctive picture of Christ, and each advances the action significantly toward its goal. The first vision (1:9-3:22) pictures Him as the critic of the churches, who commends their virtues and condemns their vices in the light of His virtues. The second vision (4:1-16:21) deals with the progressive series of seals, trumpets and bowls, which mark the judgment of God upon a world dominated by evil. The third vision (17:1-21:8) depicts the overthrow of evil society, religion, and government in the destruction of Babylon and the defeat of the beast and his armies by this victorious Christ. The last vision (21:9-22:5) is the establishment of the city of God, the eternal destiny of His people. The book closes with an exhortation to readiness for the return of Christ.

Outline:
Introduction: The Return of Christ 1:1-8
  I. Christ, the Critic of the Churches 1:9-3:22
  II. Christ, the Controller of Destiny 4:1-16:21
  III. Christ, the Conqueror of Evil 17:1-21:8
  IV. Christ, the Consummator of Hope 21:9-22:5
Epilogue: Appeal and Invitation 22:6-21

Bibliography: Smith, J. B., *A Revelation of Jesus Christ.* Scottdale, Pa.; Herald Press, 1961. Swete, H. B., *The Apocalypse of St. John.* London: Macmillan, 1911. Tenney, M. C., *Interpreting Revelation.* Grand Rapids, Mich.: Wm. B. Eerdmans Pub. Co., 1957. M.C.T.

REVELLING (Gr. *kómos, orgy*), a word used to designate any extreme intemperance and lustful indulgence, usually accompanying pagan worship. Paul lists it with murder as barring the way into the kingdom of God (Gal. 5:21), and Peter denounces it (I Pet. 4:3). The word is translated *riotous* in Romans 13:13 and *revel* in II Peter 2: 13 (RSV).

REVILE, REVILER, REVILING (Heb. *qālal*, Gr. *antiloidoréo, blaspheméo, loidoréo, oneidízo*), a word meaning to address with opprobrious or contumelious language; to reproach. Israelites were forbidden to revile their parents on pain of death (Exod. 21:17). Israel was reviled by Moab and Ammon (Zeph. 2:8). Jesus endured reviling on the cross (Mark 15:32). Revilers will have no part in the kingdom of God (I Cor. 6:10).

REVISED VERSIONS (See Bible, English version)

REWARD, a word rendering at least a dozen different Hebrew and Greek words with very similar meanings. In modern English the word means something given in recognition of a good act. In the ERV, however, it generally refers to something given, whether for a good or a bad act (Ps. 91:8; Jer. 40:5; Mic. 7:3; I Tim. 5:18).

REZEPH (rē'zĕf, Heb. *retseph, stronghold*), an important caravan center in ancient times. It was ravaged by Assyria during Hezekiah's reign (II Kings 19:8-12; Isa. 37:12). It may be the modern Rusafah, a few miles W of the Euphrates.

REZIA (rē-zī'á), a descendant of Asher (I Chron. 7:39); also Rizia.

REZIN (rē'zĭn, Heb. *retsîn*). 1. The last king of Syria to reign in Damascus. He was used to chasten Judah (II Kings 15:37). He restored Syrian cities 16:6), and the siege which he and Pekah undertook against Jerusalem led Isaiah to assure Judah by issuing the prophecy about the virgin birth of the Messiah (Isa. 7:4-16). To escape Rezin, Ahaz made an alliance with Tiglath-pileser, who invaded Israel, captured Damascus, slew Rezin and carried the Syrians into captivity (II Kings 16:9). Tiglath left many records of his conquests, some of which show Rezin (Rasuni in the tablets) to have been an important ruler. One tablet contains an account of his death, but it was lost after the English scholar Sir Henry Rawlinson had read it. After Rezin's death Syria never recovered her prestige.

2. Founder of a family of Nethinims, or temple servants, who are mentioned in I Chronicles 9:2; Ezra 2:43-48.

REZON (rē'zŏn, Heb. *rezôn, nobleman*), a citizen of Zobah, a small country NW of Damascus. Evidently a rebel, he took advantage of an invasion of Zobah by David and led a band of guerrillas to Damascus where he made himself king. Hadadezer, the rightful king, was overthrown by David, and Rezon met little opposition (I Kings 11:23-25). He must have been a wise ruler, for Syria soon became a strong nation. He made an alliance with Hadad of Edom and began to harass Israel whom he hated (vs. 25). He is almost certainly the same as Hezion mentioned in I Kings 15:18, although Hezion could have been his son. In either case, he founded a dynasty of strong Syrian rulers, among them being the noted Ben Hadad I and his son, Ben Hadad II.

RHEGIUM (rē'jĭ-ŭm, Gr. *Rhégion*), modern Reggio, was a Greek colony on the toe of Italy, founded in 712 B.C. Opposite Messana in Sicily, where the strait is only six miles wide, Rhegium was an important strategic point. As such it was the special object of Rome's care, and in consequence a loyal ally. The port was also a haven in extremely difficult water. Paul's ship, having tacked widely to make Rhegium, waited in the protection of the port for a favorable S wind to drive her through the currents of the strait on the course to Puteoli (Acts 28:13).

RHESA (rē'sà, Gr. *Rhesá*), the son of Zerubbabel, hence a scion of Solomon (Luke 3:27).

RHODA (rō'dà, Gr. *Rhóda, rose*), the name of the girl who answered the door in the very human story of Acts 12:13. She was a servant, probably a slave of Mary, John Mark's mother.

RHODES (rōdz, Gr. *Rhódos, rose*), a large island off the mainland of Caria, some 420 square miles in extent. Three city-states originally shared the island, but after internal tension and conflict with Athens which lasted from 411 to 407 B.C., a federal capital with the same name as the island was founded. Rhodes controlled a rich carrying trade, and after the opening of the E by Alexander, became the richest of all Greek communities, and able to maintain its independence under the Diadochi or "Successors" of Alexander. Rhodes, over this period, became a center of exchange and capital, and successfully policed the seas. Coming to terms with the rising power of Rome, Rhodes cooperated with the Republic against Philip V of Macedon, and Antiochus of Syria (201-197 B.C.). In the third Macedonian war Rhodes adopted a less helpful attitude, and in spite of the protests of Cato, preserved in one of the earliest samples of Latin oratory, the state was punished by economic reprisals. Rome in fact was seeking an excuse to cripple a rival to her growing eastern trade. The amputation of Rhodes' Carian and Lycian dependents, and the declaration of Delos as a free port ruined the community (166 B.C.). Loyalty to Rome in the war with Mithridates won back some of the mainland possessions, but Rhodes' glory was past, and when Paul called on his way from Troas to Caesarea (Acts 21:1), Rhodes was only a station on the trade routes, a free city, but little more than a provincial town. Rhodes was the center of a sun-cult, the famous colossus being a statue of Helios. See RODANIM.   E.M.B.

RIBAI (rī'bī), a Benjamite of Gibeah, father of Ittai (II Sam. 23:29), a mighty man (I Chron. 11:26,31).

RIBLAH (rĭb'là, Heb. *rivlâh*), the city at the head waters of the Orontes River was a stronghold for both Egyptians and Assyrians. Copious water ran from its springs; fertile lands, E and W, and timber lands in near-by Lebanon made it a coveted prize of war. When Pharaoh Necho captured Jerusalem about 600 B.C. he took King Jehoahaz, put Judah under tribute to Egypt, and led the king to Egypt where he died (II Kings 23:31-34). A few years later, Nebuchadnezzar, then at war with Egypt, captured Jeremiah and took King Zedekiah to Riblah as captive. There his sons were killed before him, his eyes were put out and he was taken in chains to Babylon (II Kings 25:6,7). Nebuchadnezzar then destroyed Jerusalem, and the chief

A 16th century artist's conception of the great Colossus of Rhodes, one of the seven wonders of the ancient world. It was of brass, more than 100 feet high, and spanned the harbor entrance. Erected about 288 B.C., it was wrecked by an earthquake about 224 B.C. © RTHPL

priests and temple guards were led to Riblah where, before the Jews were taken into captivity, they were slain (vss. 8:21). Riblah was on the E side of Ain, probably near Mt. Hermon (Num. 34:11).

RIDDLE (Heb. *hîdhâh*, from a root meaning *to bend* or *twist*, hence any artifice in speech, *a hidden saying, a proverb*). This is a form of language long used by man. The Queen of Sheba propounded to Solomon "hard questions," or riddles (I Kings 10:1; II Chron. 9:1). A classic example of the riddle is that propounded by Samson to entrap his enemies (Judg. 14:14, RSV). Samson's noted retort to the Philistines is also a riddle (Judg. 14:18b). Solomon became famous as an author of proverbs and riddles (I Kings 4:32). To know dark sayings is a mark of wisdom (Prov. 1:6). Riddle also refers to words of indefinite meaning, "dark speeches" (Num. 12:8; Ps. 49:4), "hard sentences" (Dan. 5:12), "taunting proverb" (Heb. 2:6). A NT riddle appears in Revelation 13:18, and another in I Corinthians 13:12, marg.

RIGHTEOUSNESS (Heb. *tsaddîq*, Gr. *dikaiosýne*, *the quality of rightness* or *justice*). One word root in the NT, *dik*, and a corresponding root in the OT, *tsedeq*, convey the essential idea of righteousness, or rightness. Some authorities say that the original meaning of *dik* is "upright"; others say "custom." The latter suggestion is doubtful. In any case the root meaning in Biblical Greek usage is "right," that is, right with reference to whatever norm is implied in the context.

In accordance with the meanings of noun endings (see noun suffixes in any good grammar) *dikaiosis* (Rom. 4:25; 5:18) speaks of the *act* of making right, or justification; *dikaiosýne* (Rom. 3:21-26 and elsewhere frequently) emphasizes the *status* of rightness, while *dikaioma* calls attention to the *result* of making right, either by legal enactment (Rom. 1:32; 8:4 and elsewhere), or by justification (Rom. 5:16,18; Rev. 19:8 and elsewhere). But these nouns are not always sharply distinguished.

In the most frequent and most important Biblical usage, righteousness is conceived as judged by the standard of God's holy law, which is derived from His holy character, and "summarily comprehended" in the decalogue (Exod. 20:1-17).

Throughout the Bible, mankind is considered to be corrupt and lacking in righteousness (Rom. 3: 23, etc.) on account of the representative, self-corrupting act of our original progenitor (Rom. 5: 12-21). Man is held to be totally incapable of making himself righteous (Rom. 3:19,20).

Only through the atoning work of Christ can man be given righteousness. (Isa. 54:17, "Their righteousness is of me, saith the Lord.")

This imparting of righteousness is in two distinguishable but inseparable phases. In justification by faith man is forensically made right with the demands of the law by the atonement of Christ (II Cor. 5:21). In sanctification he is progressively made righteous in character and conduct (I John 1:7-9). J.O.B.

RIMMON (rĭm'ŏn, Heb. *rimmôn, pomegranate*). 1. A city near Edom in the southern part of Judah's heritage (Josh. 15:32). It was often associated with Ain. Nehemiah called it En-rimmon (Neh. 11:29).

2. A noted rocky fortress not far from Gibeah was named Sela Rimmon, or Rimmon of the rocks (Judg. 20:45-47).

3. A Benjamite of the clan of the Beerothites. He had two sons who slew Ishbosheth, Jonathan's son, and took his head to David who, in great anger, had them slain (II Sam. 4:2-12).

4. A Syrian god was named Rimmon. After Naaman had been healed of his leprosy, he asked God's prophet for permission to accompany his king when he went to the temple of Rimmon to worship (II Kings 5:15-19).

5. A village of Simeon's heritage. It is listed next to Ain (I Chron. 4:32).

6. A city of Zebulun's heritage which was made a Levitical possession, going to the children of Merari (I Chron. 6:77).

RIMMON-METHOAR (rĭm'ŏn-mĕ'thō-àr, Heb. *rimmôn hamethō'ār*). This is evidently an error in translation. Rimmon was the place name, Methoar from a Hebrew word meaning "reaching out." It was part of the heritage of Judah (Josh. 19:13). Zebulun's land reached to it and may have included a suburb, hence the descriptive name.

RIMMON PAREZ (See Rimmon-Perez)

RIMMON-PEREZ (rĭm'ŏn pĕ'rĕz, *Parez* in KJV). It was the fourth camp of Israel after Sinai (Num. 33:16-19). Rimmon was a common place name, due to the abundance of pomegranates at the time in the Near East. Parez means cleft, so this was, no doubt, a valley into which entrance was made between cliffs.

RIMMON, ROCK OF, a natural fortress to which 600 Benjamites fled after escaping slaughter (Judg. 20:45,47; 21:13). It was identified by Robinson as a rocky area near Jeba or Gibeah, still bearing the name. Early Christian writers located it 15 Roman miles NW of Jerusalem.

RING (See Dress)

RING (Heb. *tabba'ath, to sink* or *stamp,* Gr. *daktýlios, pertaining to a finger*). This article of jewelry derived its Hebrew name from its use as a signet. It became the symbol of authority. The pharaoh gave a *tabba'ah* to Joseph (Gen. 41:42,43). King Ahasuerus gave one to Haman, the enemy of the Jews (Esth. 3:10). The prodigal's father placed a ring on the hand of his son (Luke 15:22). This was more than an ornament; it restored the son to authority in the household. The ring early became very valuable, as is shown by Isaiah's plaint (3:18-23). Originally the signet was worn on a chain or wire about the neck, but the need to safeguard it led to its being put on the hand. Earrings and nose rings were not called *tabba'ath*. The seal was an engraved stone, fastened to the ring (Exod. 28:11). Such rings have been found among Egyptian artifacts. That they were common during apostolic days is seen from James 2:2 where the Greek word *chrysodaktýlios,* means "ringed with gold" or wearing many rings.

RING-STREAKED (Heb. *'āqōdh, striped* or *notched*), mottled of color, characterizing Laban's sheep (Gen. 30:35; 31:8,12). Also ring-straked.

RINNAH (rĭn'à, Heb. *rinnâh*), a son of Shimon of Judah, called son of Hanan in LXX (I Chron. 4:20).

RIOT, translation of various words: Heb. *zālal, to squander in evil ways* (Prov. 23:20; 28:7); Gr. *asotía, waste* (Titus 1:6; I Pet. 4:4); *kómos, revelry* (Rom. 13:13); *tryphé, luxury* (II Pet. 2:13).

RIPHATH (rī'fáth, Heb. *rîphath*), a son of Gomer (Gen. 10:3; I Chron. 1:6 see marg.).

RISSAH (rĭs'à, Heb. *rissâh, ruins*), Israel's sixth camp after leaving Sinai (Num. 33:21). Its site is not known, but it was some 200 miles S of Jerusalem.

RITHMAH (rĭth'mà, Heb. *rithmâh, juniper*), the third camp of Israel from Sinai (Num. 33:18). Some authorities think this an error for Ramath of the South (Josh. 19:8).

RIVER. Of the dozen or so words rendered river in the Bible only three need be mentioned. 1. *Nāhār* (Gr. *potamós*) is used of the largest rivers known to the Israelites — the Tigris and Euphrates (Gen. 2:14), the Abana and Pharpar (II Kings 5:12), the Jordan (Mark 1:5), and the rivers of Ethiopia (Zeph. 3:10). The river or the great river usually refers to the Euphrates (Gen. 15:18; 31:21).

2. *Nahal* usually means a winter torrent the bed of which is dry in summer, but may refer to a perennial stream like the Jabbok (Deut. 2:37).

3. *Ye'ôr, a stream,* usually refers to the Nile and its mouths (Gen. 41:1; II Kings 19:24). Once it denotes the Tigris (Dan. 12:5-7).

RIVER OF EGYPT, a brook (RSV) on the SW border of Palestine flowing into the Mediterranean Sea (Gen. 15:18; Num. 34:5). Now Wadi el Arish.

RIZPAH (rĭz'pà, Heb. *ritspâh, hot stone*), a daughter of Aiah, a Horite (I Chron. 1:40, called Ajah in Gen. 36:24). Saul took her as a concubine (II Sam. 3:7a). Ishbosheth, a son of Saul, accused Abner, a cousin, of incest with her (II Sam. 3:7b). The accusation enraged Abner who transferred his allegiance from Saul to David (II Sam. 3:8-21). In his zeal to establish Israel, Saul had slain a host of Gibeonites, and as a result a serious famine had come to Israel. Upon consulting Gibeonites about restitution for the evil, David learned that only the death of Saul's sons would atone. Among those turned over to Gibeon were two sons by Rizpah (II Sam. 21:1-8). Because of Rizpah's devotion to her sons, David had the bones of her sons and those of Saul and Jonathan buried in the tomb of Saul's father, Kish (II Sam. 21:14).

ROADS. For a detailed and historical treatment of the roads of Palestine, Sir G. A. Smith's *Historical Geography of the Holy Land* may be consulted (esp. pp. 149-154, 263-283, 374, 375, 388-391, 425-430). To summarize: 1. The chief S-N traverse is the road via Pelusium, Rafia, and Gaza, and thence up the Maritime Plain, the ancient invasion route of Thutmose, Rameses, Sennacherib, Cambyses, Alexander, Pompey, Titus, Saladin, Napoleon and Allenby. Carmel closes the northern end. Passage was possible by a rough and exposed route on the seaward side, a path used by Richard Lion-Heart, and by Napoleon on his withdrawal, and known as *Les Detroits* by the Crusaders. On the landward side, Esdraelon, and thence Phoenicia, was reached by several low passes, chiefly those which run through Megiddo, and the route through the Valley of Dothan (Gen. 37:35). The latter route was used by those seeking Jordan and Damascus.

2. A more easterly traverse from Damascus S lay through the arid deserts and mountains E of the Jordan valley, through the tribal territories of Manasseh, Reuben and Gad, into Moab, and down the desert valley of the Arabah (Deut. 8: 15). This was the so-called King's Highway.

3. Lateral roads from the high country joined the N-S communications of the Maritime Plain, and provided alternative routes across Palestine to Syria and Damascus. One road ran from Gaza to Hebron. Another from Jerusalem ran through Lydda (Lod) to Joppa, with a loop to Emmaus, if that town may be properly located W of Jerusalem (Luke 24). This road was probably Paul's route to Caesarea (Acts 23), branching N at Lydda, and passing through Antipatris.

4. N-S routes inland were naturally not so numerous as those on the easy Maritime Plain. A road, however, ran up to Jerusalem from Hebron through Bethlehem, and continued N from Jerusalem to Samaria, forking at Sychar (John 4).

5. The roads from the E into Judaea cross miles of arid and difficult wilderness. There are roads from Jericho NW to Ai and Bethel, SW to Jerusalem, and SSW to the lower Kidron and Bethlehem. The first was Israel's invasion route, the second the road of Jesus' last journey to Jerusalem, the third probably the route of Naomi and Ruth. There are numerous minor roads W from Engedi and Masada.

6. The Negev desert lies across the southern approaches to Palestine, and thrusts the highways, as is indicated above, either W towards the level seacoast, or E into the Wadi Arabah. Solomon's cargoes from Ophir came, no doubt, by the Arabah route from Ezion-Geber on the Gulf of Akaba, cutting the corner of the Negev S and W of the Dead Sea, and reaching Jerusalem by way of Hebron.

7. "Galilee," writes Smith (*op. cit.,* p. 425) "is covered with roads to everywhere, roads from the harbors of the Phoenician coast to Samaria, Gilead, Hauran and Damascus; roads from Sharon to the valley of the Jordan . . . from Egypt to Assyria. They ran over Lower Galilee by its long parallel valleys, and even crossed the high plateau of Upper Galilee on the shortest direction from Tyre and Sidon to Damascus." The same authority analyzes their detailed routes and historical significance (pp. 425-430).

Sidelights: (a) Paul's conversion took place on one of two routes to Damascus. Paul joined either the road which struck east N of the Sea of Galilee, the main caravan route from Egypt, or, keeping a more northerly direction through Sychar, passed to Scythopolis, and S of the Sea of Galilee. (b) In traveling inland from Neapolis to Philippi, Paul traversed part of the famous *Via Egnatia,* whose western terminal was Dyrrachium. In proceeding N to Rome by way of Tres Tabernae, he was on the first of Roman roads, the ancient *Via Appia.* (c) Smith discusses "the desert Gaza" (Acts 8:26) which lay on the Ethiopian's southward journey. The roads of the Maritime plain avoided the dunes and drifting sand by an inland routing, and "desert Gaza" distinguished the ruined town of the Philis-

Above, a winding road in the Ain Fara Gorge. Below, an ancient Roman paved road near Antioch. © MPS

tines from the new port of the name, by which the Romans were seeking to provide a haven on the difficult coast. (d) Coming to Palestine from Samaria, or journeying back to Haran, Abraham, Eleazer, and Jacob followed old caravan and invasion routes of no clear definition round the westward horn of the Fertile Crescent. (e) None of the roads above listed were paved before Roman days. Smith (*op. cit.,* pp. 232, 626) mentions the remains of Roman road engineering in Palestine. (f) "The Way of the sea," (Isa. 9:1), the *Via Maris* of the Middle Ages was the route from Damascus to the Maritime Plain, the inner portion of the road from the Euphrates to the Nile, and applied equally to the alternative routes N and S of the Sea of Galilee.   E.M.B.

ROBBERY, illegal seizure of another's property. Early in Israel's history such a crime was forbidden by law (Lev. 19:13). In the days of the Judges it was unsafe to travel the highways because of robberies (Judg. 5:6) by highwaymen (Judg. 9: 25). Houses were built to resist robbers, who were often base enough to seize the money of orphans and widows (Isa. 10:2). Honor did not exist among thieves (Ezek. 39:10). So depraved had

Israel become by Hosea's day that companies of priests had turned to pillage (Hos. 6:9).

David warned against the lust for riches which resulted in robbery (Ps. 62:10). Isaiah wrote of God's hatred for this means of getting a burnt offering (61:8). Among vices of God's people listed by Ezekiel is robbery (22:29). Nahum accused Nineveh of being a center of numerous robberies (Nah. 3:1). Withholding tithes and offerings from God's storehouse was robbery of this kind (Mal. 3:8).

The prevalence of robbery during NT times is attested by the story of the Good Samaritan (Luke 10:30-37). Jesus warned against robbers who will enter the Christian fold (John 10:1). Heaven is the secure depository for those who expect treasures for the future (Matt. 6:19,20). Paul who knew his world as few men of his day knew it, was familiar with violent seizure by thieves (II Cor. 11:26). He also knew that Jesus' claim to equality with God was not one of illegal seizure (Phil. 2:6).

ROBE (See Dress)

ROBINSON'S ARCH is the portion of an arch which remains in the S part of the W exterior wall of the Haram esh-Sherif, or temple area, at Jerusalem. It is named for the Biblical scholar, Edward Robinson, who noted the stonework in 1838 and called attention to its significance in his *Biblical Researches*. These courses of stone begin some 39 feet from the SW corner of the enclosure wall and extend 51 feet along the wall. Robinson's recognition of their nature was based on the remark of a companion, and his acquaintance with the writings of Josephus led him to link this arch with the bridge to which the Jewish writer refers incidentally five times in his *Antiquities*. This bridge crossed the Tyropoeon Valley, joining the temple complex on Mt. Moriah with the Xystus, a kind

The spring of Robinson's Arch, in the Tyropean Valley at Jerusalem. © MPS

of gymnasium or assembly-place on Mt. Zion. Excavation in the valley by Charles Warren revealed the base of the pier of the arch and parts of the fallen arch itself, but further traces of a bridge at this point are lacking. Farther N along the wall is Wilson's Arch, which is almost completely preserved; here a crossing of the valley can be made out with some certainty. Since Josephus mentions four gates on the W side of the temple area, some associate the arches with these entrances and regard both arches as parts of bridges, but J. Simons and others judge that Robinson's Arch supported not a bridge but a balcony which provided a view of the valley and of the SW hill.   C.E.D.

ROBOAM (See Rehoboam)

ROCK (Heb. *sela'*, a cliff or *mass of stone; tsûr, a crag;* Gr. *pétra,* any *stone*). Horeb's rock which Moses was to strike (Exod. 17:6) was *tsûr,* that in Kadesh to which he was to speak was *sela'* (Num. 20:8). A *sela'* was often a natural fortress, as at Rimmon (Judg. 20:45,47). Sometimes it was a mountain (I Sam. 23:25,26). *Tsûr* in Numbers 23:9 means a craggy height. Both terms are used to refer to God: The Lord is my rock (II Sam. 22:2), my *sela'* and fortress (Ps. 18:2; 71:3). For their *tsûr* is not as our rock (Deut. 32:31). See also (Ps. 61:2; 62:3; 95:1). The NT use of *petra* was both literal and figurative. The *petra* gave security to the house (Matt. 7:24,25). The Lord's burial place had been cut into a *petra* (Mark 15:46). Jesus made a distinction between Simon the *petros* and the basic truth (*petra*) in Peter's confession, the truth upon which the *ekklesia* was to be built (Matt. 16:18). Believers are living stones builded into a spiritual house (I Pet. 2:5).

ROD (Heb. *maqqēl, matteh, shēvet,* Gr. *rhábdos*), originally a name given to a piece of tree limb used as a support or as a weapon. There is little difference between the word for rod and that for staff. The rod had varying uses in ancient times. Jacob used rods to change the color of Laban's goats and sheep (Gen. 30:37-41). Such rods became a symbol of authority (Jer. 48:17). Moses carried a rod when he returned to Egypt (Exod. 4:2,17,20; 7:9-20). Aaron's rod was used to bring lice upon Egypt (Exod. 8:16,17). Moses' rod, upheld, brought hail and lightning (Exod. 9:23), and locusts (10:13). It caused the sea to divide (14:16). He smote the rock at Horeb (17:5-7) with a rod, and at Kadesh (Num. 20). It was held aloft in Rephidim (Exod. 17:9-13). The rod, used at first as a weapon, came to be a sign of authority, hence a sceptre. To kill a servant with the rod was illegal (Exod. 21:20). The shepherd's rod was used in counting sheep (Lev. 27:32). God's anger was for Job a rod (Job 9:34). Chastisement was symbolized by the rod (Ps. 89:32; 125:3; Prov. 13:24; 22:15; 29:15). The coming of Christ was to be preceded by the rod (Mic. 5:1). Jesus is to win with a rod (sceptre, Ps. 2:9). Paul would use a rod if forced to do so (I Cor. 4:21). Aaron's budding rod was symbolic of Christ's eternal reign (Heb. 9:1-28). The victorious believer will rule with a rod (Rev. 2:27). The temple of God was measured with a rod-like reed (Rev. 11:1).

RODANIM (rŏd'à-nĭm), a tribe descended from Javan, a son of Japheth (I Chron. 1:5,7). Both here and in Genesis 10:4 the RV gives Dodanim, but the LXX gives Rodanim or Rodians, which rendering is supported by the RSV reading, "men of Rhodes" (Ezek. 27:15). Ezekiel's account of the trade by Dedan (KJV) would thus link that city with Rhodes. Records of trade between Rhodes and western Mediterranean ports date back to 700 B.C.

ROE, ROEBUCK (See Animals)

ROGELIM (rō'gē-lǐm), a thrifty community near Mahanaim. Its citizens took supplies to David's army (II Sam. 17:27,29), and led him across the Jordan (19:31).

ROHGAH (rō'gà), a descendant of Asher (I Chron. 7:34).

ROLL, a scroll, a literary work on papyrus or parchment rolled around a core or spool. The decree of Cyrus to restore the temple was a roll (Ezra 1:1), and Jeremiah wrote on such a roll (36:2). Books with pages did not come into use until the second century A.D. See WRITING.

ROLLER, anything that turns or revolves. Isaiah saw the confusion of wicked nations as a rolling thing before a hurricane (17:13).

ROMAMTI-EZER (rō-mǎm'tǐ-ē'zēr, *highest help*), one of the 12 sons of Heman who were set by David as temple musicians (I Chron. 25:4,31).

ROMAN EMPIRE. 1. Territorial. Considered as a territorial phenomenon, the Roman Empire was the result of a process of expansion which began in the sixth and seventh centuries before Christ. It was a process initiated by the pressure of a difficult environment, in a rapidly filling and not over-fertile peninsula, on a Latin-speaking community which occupied a strategically advantageous position on some low hills by the major ford over the Tiber. The main fortress and federation of this group of associated settlements was called Rome, probably an Etruscan name. The origin of the population was an amalgam of tribal elements welded into a dynamic unity on an enclave around the lower reaches of the river by the pressure of the Etruscans to the N, and the Italic hill-tribes of the highlands which formed their hinterland. Casting off the domination of Etruria in a conflict which found traditional consummation in the expulsion of the Tarquin kings in 509 B.C., Rome early began that search for a stable frontier which was to form the guiding motive of her history. That quest, with what Toynbee would call its successive challenge and response, took her step by step to the subjugation of the Italian peninsula, and the domination of its peoples — the Etruscans, whose culture and empire, Asiatic in origin, opportunely decayed in the fourth century before Christ; the Italic tribes, Oscan and Umbrian and related to the Romans, who occupied the highland spine of the peninsula with its associated plains; the Greeks, whose colonies, since the eighth century, had dotted the coast-line from Cumae to Tarentum; and finally the Celtic Gauls of northern Italy and the Po plain.

Italy was Roman to the Alps by the middle of the third century before Christ. This metropolitan empire was no sooner achieved than Rome clashed with Carthage, the great Phoenician commercial empire of the N African coast. The island of Sicily, half Greek, half Carthaginian, lay, a bridgehead and a temptation, between the continents, and became the scene of the first collision between two powers for whom the Western Mediterranean was proving too small a common sphere. Sixty years of intermittent war followed, from which Rome emerged victorious with her first provinces, Sicily, Sardinia, and Spain. An overseas empire thus visibly began, but defense and security were the motives as Rome moved into the sister peninsulas, first Spain and then Greece. In spite of the intrusion into later history of such figures as Caesar and Pompey, it may be fairly said that originally and generally Roman imperialism owed no inspiration to an Alexander, seeking conquest for motives

The Pillar of the Tenth Roman Legion, in the old city of Jerusalem. © MPS

of personal glory and mysticism, no Sennacherib or Nebuchadnezzar systematically building empires and concentrating the world's wealth in mighty capitals, no Cortes or Pizzaro in frank search of loot. Even in the second and first centuries before Christ, when the material advantages of Empire were manifestly corrupting the Republic's ruling class, expansion and conquest were still associated with the search for a defensible frontier and military security.

The eastward movement through Greece, Asia Minor, and the Middle East began in answer to Macedon's support of Carthage in the Second Punic War. It continued logically in the clash with imperial Syria, and found uneasy pause with Pompey's pacification and organization of the eastern Mediterranean completed in 63 B.C. The historic process of expansion was associated with the emergence of successive perils, and Rome's attempts to meet them. In similar fashion the drive to the E died out in the varied efforts to stabilize the Parthian frontier made from the days of Augustus to Trajan. The northward expansion through Gaul, which paused finally on the Rhine and the fortification lines of Northern Britain, was a process similarly motivated. If Pompey was the architect of the eastern Empire, Julius Caesar was the builder of the western, and although in that age of rival dynasts the personal ambitions of army commanders is an element which the historian cannot discount, it remains a fact that it was the uneasy memory in Italy of barbarian inroads from the unpacified northern hinterlands which provided impulse and first occasion for the conquest of Gaul and the associated islands across the Channel.

By the beginning of the Christian era the Roman Empire was reaching the limits of its expansion. It was the policy of Augustus to consolidate, but that policy was based upon a shrewd realization that the physical limit of Roman expansive energy was in sight. It is true that the sable frontier of long search was still elusive. Shocked by a major military disaster in A.D. 9, as the armies probed the difficult German forests towards the Elbe, Augustus had chosen the Rhine as a northern frontier. The Danube formed its logical eastward continuation. The Rhine-Danube line, which in general remained the limit of the Empire, was the longest riverline in Europe. Extensions beyond it, such as Dacia, were never completely integrated, and safer and more defensible alternatives were beyond physical reach. History was to demonstrate how difficult the Rhine-Danube line was to defend, and over it came final disaster. Spain, Gaul, and Britain formed stable enough buttresses in the W, while the southern marches rested on the Sahara, a desert frontier, and strategically the most stable of all. The E, with its vulnerable northern end, and the perennial problem of the Parthians, was never secured, and some of the imagery of the Apocalypse reflects the fear felt in the Middle East of the archer cavalry from over the Euphrates.

The NT came into being, and the early Church was established in an Empire which had organized and pacified a deep belt of territory round the Mediterranean basin, and western Europe. That area owed its security to Rome, a security achieved against notable dangers and grave disadvantages, and destined to endure for a vital three centuries. The same complex of territories owed to Rome a more stable government than much of it had ever known, and a community of life which went far to produce that fusion of Greece, and Rome, and of Palestine which formed the background and climate for the NT and subsequent Christendom.

2. **Politically,** the term Roman Empire is used in contradistinction to Roman Republic to describe the system of rule and government known as the principate. The year 31 B.C., the date of the Battle of Actium, is arbitrarily chosen as the dividing line. The contemporary observer was conscious of no change or transition. Such an observer saw the passing of a peril, and the prospect of peace after another violent bout of civil strife which had plagued a century of constitutional crises. Octavian, Julius Caesar's adoptive nephew, had defeated Antony, and when the victor drew into his hands the powers of the republican magistracies, concentrated in his person the offices and functions of ancient constitutional executives, and added thereto such marks of prestige as those which accompanied the title of "princeps," the appellation of "imperator," and the new name "Augustus," no one at the time, who observed merely the surface of events, saw aught but a continuation and an intensification of a policy which for 50 years had made a mockery of constitutional government. Extraordinary commands and special powers had long since prepared the way for the autocracy which emerged full-fledged with Augustus.

The constitutional breakdown from which the principate arose can be traced back for over a century. The Senate had ruled Rome, more by prestige than by clearly defined legal right to do so, in the great days of Rome's struggle with Carthage. A tight oligarchy, the great families whose members gave Rome her generals and administrators, ruled with a strength and a decisiveness the times demanded, and the land had no reason to regret their leadership. Rome emerged from the wars with Carthage, shaken but victorious, at the beginning of the second century before Christ. At the end of that century the ills which broke the Republic and led to the principate were in full view. The Senate whose leadership had sufficed for a compact city state, and had made shift to rule Italy,

proved, in fact, unequal to the task of governing an empire. Three problems were beyond their solution: the city mob, tool and instrument of a new breed of demagogues; the corruption in the dominant minority arising from the temptations of rule in conquered lands; and the power of the generals. All three were problems of empire. The urban proletariat had been built out of a decayed yeoman class ruined by changes in Italian land utilization following vast influx of capital from subjugated territories. The generals owed their power to the needs of distant defence and the military forces which new frontiers demanded. A vested interest was thus created, shared by soldiery and commander. Rome, throughout the next four centuries, was never to hear the last of it, and the only answer would have been the creation of a strong free middle class which the early acceptance of Christianity would have provided. Julius Caesar was the most notable of the military dynasts, and he died under the daggers of a frustrated Senate because he drove too ruthlessly towards the autocratic solution of the Senate's corruption and the Republic's breakdown. His adoptive nephew, Octavius, was a more subtle person. By a mixture of good fortune, astute diplomacy and a flair for picking colleagues, Octavius won power, but it was always power with a flavor of constitutional legality, and characterized by an ancient and accepted terminology. Octavius, later called by the honorary title Augustus, was "emperor" only in the sense that, as supreme commander, he alone had the right to the title "imperator" with which victorious generals had ever been saluted by their troops. To most men he was simply "princeps," or "prince," which meant simply "first citizen." His varied powers, functions and privileges nevertheless added up to autocracy. The system gave peace, and the world, especially the provinces, was prepared to barter a fiction of liberty for that.

The Roman Empire, using the word in the political sense of the term, was the governmental framework of the Roman Peace, that era of centralized government which held the Mediterranean world in comparative tranquillity for significant centuries. No wonder that the Eastern provinces, accustomed since the days of ancient despotism to the deification of rulers, early established the custom of worshiping the Emperor. The notion, justified in Rome itself by the myths of demigods and deified benefactors such as Hercules, gained currency through the writings of poets such as Horace and Vergil, who genuinely believed in the divine call of Augustus, and who, without a transcendent view of deity, saw no incongruity in ascribing divine attributes to a man of destiny. Such were the sinister beginnings of a cult which Rome chose as a cement of empire, and which led to the clash with the Church, whose early acceptance might have provided a more noble and effective bond.

Bibliography: For a general account: *A History of Rome Down to the Age of Constantine,* M. Cary, Macmillan, 1945; for the failure of the Republic and the rise of the principate: *The Roman Revolution,* R. Syme, Oxford, 1939.

E.M.B.

ROMANS, EPISTLE TO THE. The genuineness of the Epistle has never been seriously questioned by competent critics familiar with first century history. Although other NT epistles have been wrongly attacked as forgeries not written by the alleged authors, this epistle stands with Galatians and I and II Corinthians as one of the unassailable documents of early church history.

There can be no doubt that the author, Paul, formerly Saul of Tarsus (Acts 13:9), was a highly intellectual, rabbinically educated Jew (Gal. 1:14;

Acts 22:3) who had been intensely hostile to the Christian movement and had sought to destroy it (Gal. 1:13; I Cor. 15:9; Acts 8:1-3; 9:1,2). Even the critics who reject the supernatural cannot deny the extraordinary nature of the fact that this able enemy became the greatest exponent of the Christian faith and wrote the most powerful statements of Christian doctrine. The accounts of his conversion are given in Acts 9:3-19; 22:1-16; 26:9-18 and the event is alluded to in his writings (Gal. 1:15; I Cor. 15:8-10).

The literary unity of the last two chapters with the body of the epistle has been questioned. There are manuscripts which have the doxology of 16:25-27 at the end of chapter 14; some have it in both places. Yet none of the MSS lacks chapters 15 and 16, and there is no evidence that the epistle was ever circulated in a form in which it ended without its last two chapters.

It is not difficult for anyone who is familiar with letters of a theological and missionary nature to imagine how this inspiring doxology might appear out of its intended place in some copies.

This is a letter, not a treatise. It was not intended to be a formal literary product. In the midst of greetings from friends who were with the author as he wrote (16:21-23), Tertius, the scribe to whom the letter was dictated puts in his own personal greeting (16:22). Perhaps Paul was interrupted at vs. 21. As he stepped away, he said, "Tertius, put in your greeting while I attend to so and so." He returned in a moment and resumed his dictating. The people of the Bible were human beings under human circumstances, and the epistle means more to us because this is so.

Perhaps Paul composed this pericope, 16:25-27, at the end of his discussion of "judging and scandalizing," chapter 14. This little doxology is a compact paragraph, a unit in itself. It would fit in appropriately in a number of places.

The opening verses of chapter 15, on "the strong and the weak," are obviously related to the material in chapter 14. One pictures Paul resuming his work at 15:1 after an interruption. Tertius takes up his pen, and Paul says, "I must say more about the treatment of the weaker brother. The little paragraph of praise to God that we did last, is to go at the very end, after we have finished everything else." Tertius draws a line through it, and later faithfully copies it at the end.

The prayer at the end of chapter 15 is not to be taken as the conclusion of a letter. It is only the appropriate conclusion of a particular topic. Paul had been telling of his itinerary. He is deeply moved as he contemplates the perils of his impending visit to Jerusalem, and he strongly implores the prayers of the saints in Rome in respect to this matter (vss. 30-32). Quite naturally and spontaneously at this point he breaks into a prayer for them. The conclusions of Paul's letters always contain some striking use of the word "grace" (see II Thess. 3:17,18), a word not found here. Therefore the prayer of 15:33 should not be construed as a conclusion of a letter.

The main body of the letter ends at 16:20 with the words "The grace of our Lord Jesus Christ be with you. Amen." Verses 21 to 24 are intentionally a postscript. He has finished the personal greetings to people in Rome. Phebe, who is to take the letter to Rome, is nearly ready to begin her journey. Greetings from friends in Corinth, who may have assembled for a farewell, belong by themselves in a postscript, followed by another benediction (vs. 24). Then finally comes the exalted doxology (vss. 25-27).

A leaf from the Epistle of Paul to the Romans, from the Michigan Papyri P46 (Beatty-Michigan MS.), in the University of Michigan Library. UML

The peculiarities which have caused some to question the literary unity of the last two chapters with the main body of the epistle, give no ground whatever for questioning the epistle's genuineness. No forger or redactor would have left such matters open to question. The only reasonable explanation of the data is that the epistle is exactly what it purports to be, a personal letter from the Apostle Paul to the Church at Rome, which he was planning to visit.

The time of writing cannot here be discussed in detail. Suffice it to say that the epistle clearly places itself in the three month period (Acts 20:3) which Paul spent in Corinth just before going to Jerusalem. According to the best authorities in NT chronology this three month period was about Dec. 56 to Feb. 57.

Why the epistle was written is not a difficult question to answer. In the first place Paul was emphatic in his claim to be "the apostle of the Gentiles" (Rom. 11:13; 15:16; see also Gal. 2:7-9; Eph. 3:2-8; Acts 9:15; 22:15-21; 26:17-20,23), and Rome was the capital of the Gentile world. Paul was a Roman citizen and a visit to Rome was consistent with his regular mode of operation. He established churches in strategic centers and worked in major cities.

There was this difference, however. There was a church already existing at Rome, probably founded by local people who had heard the Gospel in their travels. It was Paul's peculiar policy to preach in hitherto unevangelized areas (Rom. 15:17-24; cf. also II Cor. 10:14-16). His proposed visit to Rome was not inconsistent, however, for (1) he had a contribution to make to their spiritual welfare (1:11-13), and (2) he planned to visit Rome on his way to evangelize Spain (Rom. 15:24).

He was asking the church in Rome to help him in this project. The structure of the epistle is built around Paul's travel plans.

There was a great theological reason for the writing of this epistle, a problem which had demanded the epistle to the Galatians at an earlier juncture in Paul's ministry. It concerned the relation of (1) the OT Scriptures, (2) contemporaneous pharisaic Judaism, and (3) the Gospel as implemented by the earthly work of Christ. It had been difficult for Peter to orient himself to the new day (Gal. 2:6-14 and ff); but he had made the transition (Acts 15:7-12; see also II Pet. 3:15,16). We may well marvel at Peter's humility and true vision when, in calling Paul's epistles "scripture," he certainly included Galatians, in which his own short sightedness is recalled.

It has been said that if Galatians is the "Magna Charta" of the Gospel, Romans is the "Constitution." The theological substance of this epistle had to be presented to the NT church, whether addressed to Rome or not, but there were circumstances in Rome which made it appropriate for Paul, in a relatively calm frame of mind, with time for fuller elaboration, and without having become personally involved in local affairs, as he had in Galatia, to expand the central doctrine of the epistle to the Galatians. Thus he explained his purpose in coming to Rome and the main purpose of his life ministry and message. There was friction and misunderstanding between Jewish and Gentile Christians in the Roman church. We know from the personal greetings at the end that it was a mixed church. The problem is reflected in almost every section of the epistle, but especially in chapters three, four, nine, ten and eleven. Both sides were stubborn. There was a moment, probably brief, even after Paul had reached Rome, when Mark and a certain Jesus Justus were the only Christian Jews in Rome who would cooperate with Paul (Col. 4:10,11). A clarification of the Gospel and its implications was needed.

The content and outline of this epistle must be understood from the point of view of Paul's total ministry and his particular travel plans. True, the *greatest* theme in the work is *justification by faith*. But this is *not an essay* on that subject. Much of the material simply does not fall under any subheading of that theme. This is a *letter* from the apostle to the Gentiles to the church in Rome, and the subject is *Why I Am Coming to Visit You.* Outlines which fail to see this viewpoint, and which seek to force the material into formal divisions as though this were an essay, are very likely to assign sub-topics and secondary sub-headings which do not fit. Some outlines are almost like "zoning" laws, forbidding the reader to find in certain sections material which certainly is there.

The following very simple outline is suggested. (The great doctrinal themes are discussed in articles on doctrinal topics.)

I. The Apostle Paul to the Christians in Rome. I am entrusted with a message which I must deliver to you; i.e., the Gospel in all its implications. (1:1-17).

II. (a) The Gentile world is wretchedly lost. (1: 18:32). This is true in spite of God's jus- 'ice toward attempted morality. (2:1-16).

   (b) The Jewish world is equally lost, in spite of all their privileges. (2:17-3:20).

III. Justification by Faith is my great message. (3: 21-5:21). There is no space for the wealth of sub-topics.

IV. Holy living in principle. (6:1-8:39).
V. God has not forgotten the Jews. (9:1-11:36).
VI. Details of Christian conduct. (12:1-15:13).
VII. (a) Travel plans. (15:14-33).
   (b) Personal to people in Rome. (16:1-20).
   (c) Personal from people in Corinth. 16: 21-23).
   (d) Doxology. (16:24-27).   J.O.B.

ROME. Of the Indo-European tribes who entered Italy, the Latins formed a separate branch, occupying an enclave round the Tiber mouth and the plain of Latium. They were surrounded, and indeed constricted, by the Etruscan empire in the N, the Greek maritime colonies in the S, and by related but hostile Italic tribes, who held the rest of the peninsula and the arc of hill-country, which fenced off the Latin plain. Hence arose a sense of unity imposed upon the Latin speaking communities, and the linking of their scattered groups into leagues and confederacies. Hence, too, the old need of lowlanders for defense to build stockaded retreats to which the plainsmen could retire with flocks and families, and to locate such forts on hills and outcrops of higher land. The habit may be illustrated from the acropolis of Troy to the Maori pass on Auckland's volcanic cones of precolonial days. In such wise Rome came into being. Vergil's idyllic picture of primitive Rome in the Eighth Book of his *Aeneid* is not far from the truth. The most ancient acropolis could have been the Palatine hill, where the stockade of one shepherd community was built.

But the Palatine was not the only eminence. The valley of the Tiber at the point is a deep trough, averaging a mile in width, cut into the soft tufa floor of the lower course of the river. The edges of this trench were anciently eroded by tributary streams, and thus, geologically speaking, was formed the famous group of hills with which the future city was always associated. They were the Capitol, the Palatine, and the Aventine, with the Caelian, Oppian, Esquiline, Viminal, and Quirinal as flat-topped spurs. Through the area the river forms an S-shaped curve. In the course of this curve the river shallows and forms an island. This point is the one practicable ford on the river between the sea and a very distant locality upstream. The Tiber tends to run narrow and deep. Geography thus played a dominant role in history. The group of hills and spurs were ultimately occupied by communities such as those whose ninth century traces have been discovered on the Esquiline and the Quirinal. The old habit of Latin federation gave them a sense of unity which was finally translated into common institutions and defense. Traffic across the Tiber ford necessarily concentrated at this point. Indeed all the trade between the Etruscan N and the Greek and Italian S perforce crossed the river there. The river valley was also a highway of commerce between the sea and the hills. Salt may have been the principal commodity carried that way. The group of hill settlements thus straddled Central Italy's main communications, and those who have held such positions of advantage have always grown rich and powerful. Perhaps a faint memory of the significance of the Tiber ford is embedded in the name *pontifex*, which appears to mean etymologically "bridgemaker."

Archaeological evidence suggests that the settlements had coalesced to form the original city by the sixth century B.C., for burials from the Palatine and Capitoline cemeteries, on the edge of the marshy bottom which was to be the Forum, cease at that time. The Cloaca Maxima, which drained these hollows, may have been commenced about this date. Synoecism, therefore, took place under the kings, whose rule in early Rome, encrusted though it is with legend, is established fact. The Wall of Servius made Rome into a considerable fortress, comparable with such hill-strongholds as Veii and Ardea. Over the period of the kings, and especially the Etruscan kings, whose rule closes the regal period of early Roman history, the city built the Pons Sublicius to replace the Tiber ford, developed the Campus Martius as a training-ground, concentrated business activities in the forum, and began to crowd the hills and hollows with houses and temples. Rome was probably a large populous city by the fourth century B.C. Valleys formed an irregular roading pattern which remained a feature through all history, and by the third century there is evidence of the great "insulae" or tenement houses, which were to become another characteristic feature of Rome, and which suggest the overcrowding, squalor, and slums of the early capital. It is difficult to obtain a clear picture of a city which has always been occupied, and whose accumulated building has limited archaeological investigation. Aqueducts, bridges, quays, temples, porticoes, the monuments of civic and of family pride, followed over the centuries. It is possible to trace great outbursts of building activity at certain periods. At the end of the second century B.C., the influx of capital from the beginnings of provincial exploitation promoted expansion. Sulla, who endeavored to reduce some of the central urban tangle to order, Pompey did much

to adorn the city, and Augustus boasted that he had "found the city built of brick and left it built of marble." Augustus set the fashion for two imperial centuries, and it is from the first and second centuries after Christ that most of the surviving ruins date: the great baths of Caracalla, Diocletian, and Constantine, for example, and, most famous of all, the Flavian Amphitheatre, called still by the medieval name of Colosseum.

A vivid picture of the perils and inconveniences of life in the great city at the turn of the first century of our era is found in the *Third Satire of Juvenal,* the rhetorical poem imitated in Johnson's *London.* In population the city of Rome probably passed the million mark at the beginning of the Christian era, and during the first century may have risen somewhat above this figure. It was a motley and cosmopolitan population. "Long since," Juvenal complained early in the second century, "Syrian Orontes has flowed into the Tiber," and he numbers the foreign rabble as one of the chief annoyances of urban life, to be ranked with traffic dangers, fire, and falling houses. In the third and fourth centuries, a time of urban decay all over the Empire, the city declined, and the population probably fell to something near half a million by the last days of the Western Empire.

It is possible roughly to estimate the proportion of Christians over the imperial centuries. In the Catacombs, ten generations of Christians are buried. It is difficult to reach an accurate estimate of the extent of these galleries in the tufa rock, or of the number of graves they contain. The lowest estimate of the length is 350 miles, the highest 600

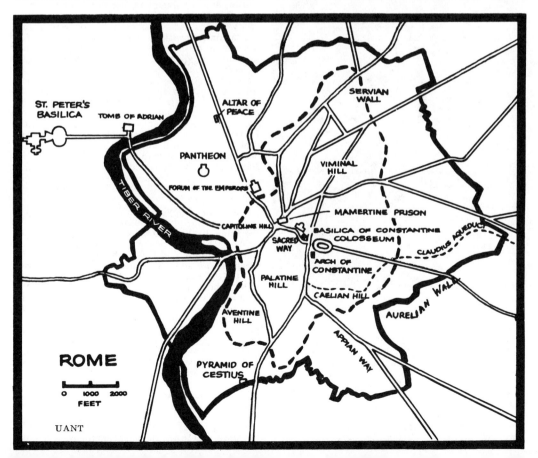

ROME

0   1000   2000
FEET

averaging is obviously bad statistical method, for the number of the Christian population would be smaller in the earlier and larger in the later centuries. But if the figure of 175,000 is taken to represent a middle point in the period, say about the middle of the third century after Christ, it becomes clear that Gibbon's well-known estimate is hopelessly awry. Gibbon suggested that, at this time, probably one twentieth of the population of the city were Christians. The most conservative estimate from the evidence of the Catacomb burials is that at least one fifth were Christians, and that probably the proportion was much larger.

Orr pointed out in his Morgan Lectures of some 65 years ago (*Neglected Factors in the History of the Early Church*) that the Catacombs also provide evidence of the vertical spread of Christianity in the imperial society of the capital, and likewise refuted Gibbon's statement that the Church was "almost entirely composed of the dregs of the populace." The case of Pomponia Graecina, for example, reported by Tacitus (*Ann.* 13:32), may be traced to the Catacombs, where De Rossi established the fact that the Crypt of Lucina was connected with the Pomponian gens, and suggested plausibly that Lucina may have been the Christian or baptismal name of Pomponia herself, who appears, from Tacitus' report, to have faced a domestic tribunal because of a Christian faith. If Pomponia was, in fact, a Christian, since she lived on into the principate of Domitian, she may have had part in two aristocratic conversions of which there is evidence — those of Flavius Clemens the consul, and of Domitilla, his wife. The former was the cousin, and the latter the niece of Domitian himself. Dio Cassius (67:44) informs us that these two were accused of "atheism," a common allegation against Christians, and of "going astray after the custom of the Jews." Flavius Clemens was put to death, and his wife banished. De Rossi appears to have established the fact that the illustrious pair were Christians. He discovered the crypt of Domitilla, and also an elegantly constructed "crypt of the Flavians." Harnack's contention that "an entire branch of the Flavian family embraced Christianity" thus seems established. Next to Domitian, Flavius Clemens and Domitilla held the highest rank in the Empire. Their two sons had even been designated by Domitian as his heirs. It seems, as James Orr remarked (*op. cit.* pp. 117 sqq), "almost as if, ere the last Apostle had quitted the scene of his labors, Christianity was about to mount the seat of Empire."

Rome, like Babylon, became a symbol of organized paganism and opposition to Christianity in the Bible. In the lurid imagery of the document of protest which closes the canon of the NT, John mingles Empire and City in his symbolism of sin. Chapters 17 and 18 of the Apocalypse envisage the fall of Rome. The former oracle, passionate, indeed shocking in its imagery, shows Rome like a woman of sin astride the seven hills, and polluting the world with her vice. The second of the two chapters reads like a Hebrew "taunt-song." It pictures, in imagery reminiscent of Ezekiel on Tyre, the galleys loading for Rome in some Eastern port. There was "merchandise of gold, and silver, and precious stones, and of pearls, and fine linen, and purple, and silk and scarlet and . . . vessels of ivory and . . . precious wood, and of brass, and iron, and marble, and cinnamon, and frankincense, beasts, and sheep, and horses, and chariots, and slaves, and souls of men." The climax is bitter, as the Seer pictures Ostia, the Tiber port of Rome, in the stark ruin in which it appears today, Rome un-

Scenes from ancient Rome. Above, ruins of the Forum, the Arch of Titus visible in the background at center. Below this are views of the Colosseum, exterior and interior. JFW and LO

miles. The lowest estimate of the burials is 1,175,-000, the highest 4,000,000. It is a pity that religious exclusivism prevents the final settlement of this question. At any rate, given a population averaging one million over the ten generations of the Church's witness, and this is rather high in view of the third and fourth century decline, we have on the first figure a Christian population averaging 175,000 per generation, and on the higher figure one averaging 400,000 per generation. Such

der the smoke of her burning, and the voice of gladness stilled.

The city appears once only in an historical context. Paul landed at Puteoli, probably traversed the Pontine Marshes by barge (Hor. *Sat.* 1:5:11-23), halted at Forum Appii (*ib.* 4), and pushed up the Appian Way through the village of Tres Tabernae, or Three Shops. Alerted by the little church of Puteoli (Acts 28:14,15) members of Rome's Christian community met Paul at both stopping places. On the evidence of the Nazareth Decree, it appears that a group had been established in Rome since the principate of Claudius in the late forties of the century. Paul would enter by the Capena Gate. His "hired house" (Acts 28:30) would be in some block of flats, an "insula."

E.M.B.

ROOM. 1. A chamber in a house (Acts 1:13).

2. In the KJV room is used in the sense of place or position in society (Matt. 23:6; Luke 14:7,8; 20:46). This meaning is now obsolete.

ROOT (Heb. *shōresh,* Gr. *rhíza*), usually used in a figurative sense. Judah was promised new roots after the captivity (II Kings 19:30; Isa. 37:31; see Rom. 15:12). The *roots* of the wicked shall not endure (Isa. 5:24). Jesus was the root of David (Isa. 11:1,10). The Messiah was to come from an unexpected *root* (Isa. 53:2). Daniel used the word in writing about Nebuchadnezzar whose roots (remnant of kingdom) would remain during his period of suffering for sin (Dan. 4:8-23). In the parable of the sower, the *roots* did not develop on or among stones (Matt. 13:20). The fig tree and its roots died (Mark 11:20). The source of spiritual life is in the *roots* (Rom. 11:17,18), even as the love of money is the *root* of evil (I Tim. 6:10).

ROPE (Heb. *hevel, line* or *cord, 'āvōth, a woven band,* Gr. *schoiníon, a cable*). Hushai counseled Absalom to have Israel bring *hevel* (strong cables), with which to pull into the river the city where David might take refuge (II Sam. 17:7-13). Sackcloth upon the body and a *hevel* about the head (I Kings 20:31,32) were symbols of deep servility (I Kings 20:31,32). In II Samuel 8:2 *hevel* is a line, as it was a small linear measure. Rahab used a *hevel* (rope) to let the spies over the wall of Jericho (Josh. 2:1-16). *'Āvōth* was used of the binding of Samson (Judg. 16:11,12). Isaiah used it in deriding Israel's efforts to pile up iniquity (5:18,19). Small ropes or cords were used to fasten the sacrificial animal to the altar (Ps. 118:27). In the NT *schoiníon* means either a cable made of bulrushes (Acts 27:32), or small ropes used to lead cattle (John 2:15).

ROSE (See Plants)

ROSETTA STONE, a damaged inscribed basalt slab, found accidentally at Fort St. Julien on the Rosetta branch of the Nile, near the city of Rosetta, by a French army work crew in 1799. Terms of the French surrender to the British gave the French finds to the victors and the Rosetta Stone was placed in the British Museum. The monument was originally set up in 196 B.C. as a formal decree of the Egyptian priesthood in honor of Ptolemy V (Epiphanes) with an identical text in three parts: hieroglyphic, demotic, and Greek. The parallel texts furnished the key for the decipherment of the Egyptian, with the proper names providing the basic clues for the achievement. Decipherment of the hieroglyphs was accomplished by Jean Francois Champollion in 1822. C.E.D.

ROSH (rŏsh, Heb. *rō'sh, head*). 1. A son of Benjamin who went to Egypt with Jacob and his sons (Gen. 46:21). He probably died without issue.

2. Head of three nations that are to invade Israel during the latter days (Ezek. 38:2,8). Gog is chief of Magog, Meshech, and Tubal (RSV). These tribes were from the far N, hence Rosh is probably Russia.

ROW, ROWERS (See Ship)

RUDDY (Heb. *'adhmônî, red*), a word used to refer to a red or fair complexion, in contrast to the dark skin of the Hebrews (I Sam. 16:12; 17:42; S. of Sol. 5:10).

RUDE (Gr. *idiótes, untrained, ignorant of rules*), used in II Corinthians 11:6 where Paul denies that his inability as a speaker indicates lack of knowledge of his subject. "I am not a technically trained orator" is the meaning.

RUDIMENTS (rōō'di-mĕnts, Gr. *stoicheía, the first principles or elements of anything*). The Greek word is found in the NT seven times, and the KJV renders it in three different ways: Galatians 4:3,9 and II Peter 3:10,12 "elements"; Colossians 2:8,20 "rudiments"; Hebrews 5:12 "first principles." In II Peter 3:10,12 it probably means the physical elements of the world. In Hebrews 5:12 the KJV rendering is correct. In Galatians 4:3,9 and Colossians 2:8,20 the reference is to rudimentary religious teachings, in this instance the ceremonial precepts of the worship of the Jews.

RUE (See Plants)

RUFUS (rōō'fŭs, Gr. *Rhoúphos*), the brother of Alexander and the son of Simon of Cyrene who bore the cross (Mark 15:21). A Rufus is also greeted by Paul in Romans 16:13; "Rufus, chosen in the Lord, and his mother and mine," is the Apostle's affectionate phrase. If the two references are to one man, it may be conjectured that Simon or Simon's widow became a Christian, and emigrated from Cyrene to Rome, this being the reason for Mark's cryptic reference. Mark was probably writing in Rome.

The Rosetta Stone, one of the most important archaeological finds in history, with identical inscriptions in 3 languages, Hieroglyphic, Demotic and Greek. BM

Gleaners in the fields of Boaz, near Bethlehem, a scene much like that in the Book of Ruth. © MPS

RUHAMAH (rōō-hà′mà, *to be pitied*), Hosea's daughter by Gomer (Hos. 2:1). The name at first given the child was Lo-ruhamah, "not to be pitied" (Hos. 1:6,8). God revealed to the prophet that she was to be symbolic of Israel, who would be fully pardoned (1:10,11).

RULER, a name used to translate several Hebrew and Greek words meaning *king, captain, exalted one, overlord, magistrate,* etc. 1. *Mōshēl,* a king or supervisor (Gen. 45:8; Prov. 23:1). 2. *Nāghîdh,* overseer (I Sam. 25:30; I Kings 1:35). 3. *Sar,* director or leader (Gen. 47:6; II Kings 11:4,19). 4. *Sāghān,* deputy (Ezra 9:2; Neh. 2:16 RSV marg). Other words occur in Daniel 3:2f; 5:29; in Deuteronomy 1:13; Isaiah 29:10; in II Samuel 6:21; Daniel 5:7.

In the NT the chief words are: 5. *árchon,* judge or magistrate (Acts 23:5; John 3:1). 6. *Archisuvágogos* is ruler of the synagogue (Mark 5:35). 7. In Ephesians 6:12 rulers of this world, *kosmokrátores,* are different from the ruler of the universe, *pantokrátōr.* 8. *Politárches,* mayor of a city (Acts 17:6,8). 9. *Architríklinos,* chief of a feast. John 2:9).

RUMAH (rōō′mà, Heb. *rûmâh, tall place*), the home of Pedaiah, whose daughter, Zebudah, bore Jehoiakim to Josiah of Judah. It is probably Arumah of Judges 9:41, Rumah in Joshua 15:52, LXX.

RUSH (See Plants)

RUTH (rōoth, Heb. *rûth*), a name found only in the book bearing the name. She was a Moabitess who married a son of Elimelech and Naomi of Bethlehem (Ruth 1:1-4). Her romance, resulting in her becoming an ancestor of the Messiah (Matt. 1:5), came during a famine in Israel during the days of the theocracy (1:1). Elimelech's two sons married Moabite women, whom they soon left widowed (1:5). When the three men died, Naomi returned to Judah (1:7). Ruth's decision to conform to the cus‛oms of the day, which made her a servant of the dead husband's family, won her lasting renown. God's hand guided Ruth into the field of Boaz (2:1-3). Returning home with much barley, Naomi knew she had found favor with her kinsman (2:20-23). Ruth was wise enough to obey Boaz and Naomi, with the result that Boaz, in keeping with Hebrew law (Deut. 25:5), took her to be his wife, after a nearer kinsman of Naomi had declined to do so (Ruth 4:6,13). Critics have maligned Ruth because of her lying at the feet of Boaz (3:1-5), being ignorant of the customs of the period. Naomi knew that this act was an appeal to Boaz to assume his obligations under law for her. In other words, it was a marriage proposal, and all that Boaz held sacred in manhood made him respond in honor.

RUTH, BOOK OF. The origin of this book has been a much-debated subject. From the time references in 1:1 it is certain that it was written many years after the period of the Hebrew theocracy. The reference to former times in Israel (4:7) indicates that it was of a later date than Deuteronomy. In the LXX, as well as the Vulgate, the book follows Judges in the OT canon, hence is rightly classed as a historical record. The primary purpose behind it was to present the link between Judah and the Gentile world in the ancestry of Jesus Christ (Matt. 1:5,6). Some scholars think it was only a romance written to justify the marriage of Jews with alien women. The author is unknown, but he could have been a post-Exilic scholar who objected to Ezra's rigid elimination of alien wives from among the returning captives (Ezra 9,10). Aside from its historical and genealogical contents, the book is of great merit because of its ethical teachings. Ruth's refusal to be free exalts the importance of safekeeping a moral obligation. She could not have known what would result from her decision. Her willingness to obey Naomi's instructions, as well as to be a menial laborer, emphasizes the message of the OT and of experience, that youth needs counsel from them who are more mature. Finally, the marriage ceremony shows that worthy people respect customs whose symbolism portrays basic commitments among men, e.g., the shoe as a sign of assuming another's obligations (4:7,8. See Deut. 25:5-10). J.D.F.

RYE (See Plants)

S

SABA, SABAEANS (să'bà, să-bē'ănz, Heb. *sevā', sevā'îm*, Gr. *Sabá*). The name Saba is mentioned in Genesis 10:7 and I Chronicles 1:9 as a son of Cush. In Isaiah 43:3 the name is coupled with Ethiopia, and in Psalm 72:10 with Sheba. In Isaiah 45:14 God says to Israel, "The labour of Egypt, and merchandise of Ethiopia and of the Sabeans, men of stature, shall come over unto thee, and they shall be thine." "Sabeans from the wilderness" are referred to in Ezekiel 23:42. Saba was situated between the Nile and the Atbara. It is a region about 400 miles long and 200 miles broad, and was known to the Hebrews as Cush. Strabo (xvi. 4, 8-10) says there was a harbor named Saba on the W coast of the Red Sea. Josephus (*Ant*, II, x, 2) identifies the Sabeans with the people of Saba in Upper Egypt, which he says Moses besieged and captured when in the service of the Egyptians. Another Sabaean race, mentioned in Genesis 10: 28; 25:3, was located in Arabia. They built a unique civilization and great empire. The Queen of Sheba who made a visit of state to the court of Solomon came from there.

SABACHTHANI (sà-băkh'thà-nē, Gr. *sabachthaneí*), a word in the utterance of Jesus on the cross, "My God, my God, why hast Thou forsaken me?" (Matt. 27:46, Mark 15:34). With some changes of form, the sentence is probably from Psalm 22:1.

SABAOTH, THE LORD OF (săb'à-ōth, Gr. *sabaóth, hosts*). The "Lord of Sabaoth" is the same as "Lord of hosts." The phrase is used in Romans 9:29 and in James 5:4. Its equivalent, the "Lord of hosts," is often found in the OT. It has sometimes been explained as meaning that Jehovah is the God of the armies of Israel, but more likely it means that all created agencies and forces are under the command and leadership of Jehovah. The title expresses Jehovah's great power.

SABBATH (săb'ath, Heb. *shabbāth*, Gr. *Sábbaton*, to *desist, cease, rest*), the weekly day of rest and worship of the Jews. The sabbath was instituted at creation. The story of creation (Gen. 1:1-2:3) closes with an account of God's hallowing of the seventh day, because on it He rested from His creative labors. We read, "And God blessed, and sanctified it: because that in it he rested from all his work which God created and made" (Gen. 2: 3). There is no distinct mention of the sabbath in Genesis, but a seven-day period is mentioned several times in connection with the Flood (Gen. 7:4,10; 8:10,12) and once in connection with Jacob's years at Haran (Gen. 29:27,28), showing that the hebdomadal division of time must have been known then.

There is no express mention of the sabbath before Exodus 16:21-30. In the wilderness of Sin, before the Israelites reached Mount Sinai, God gave them manna, a double supply being given on the sixth day of the week, in order that the seventh day might be kept as a day of rest from labor. Moses said to the people, "This is that which the Lord has said, Tomorrow is the rest of the holy sabbath unto the Lord: bake that which ye will bake today . . . and that which remaineth over lay up for you to be kept until the morning" (Exod. 16:23). Shortly afterward the Ten Commandments were given by Jehovah at Sinai (Exod. 20:1-17; 34:1-5). The fourth commandment enjoined Israel to observe the seventh day as a holy day on which no work should be done by man or beast. Everyone, including even the stranger within the gates, was to desist from all work and to keep the day holy. The reason given is that Jehovah rested on the seventh day and blessed and hallowed it. It is clear that God intended the day to be a blessing to man, both physically and spiritually. The sabbath is frequently mentioned in the Levitical legislation. It was to be kept a holy convocation for the worship of the Lord (Lev. 23:3), and was to remind the Israelites that God had sanctified them (Exod. 31: 13). Forty years later, Moses reminded the Israelites of God's command to observe the sabbath and told them that they were under special obligation to keep it because God had delivered them from bondage in Egypt (Deut. 5:15).

Various attempts have been made by OT critics to find a Babylonian origin for the Jewish sabbath. There is evidence that among the Babylonians certain things were to be avoided on the 7th, 14th, 19th, 21st, and 28th days of the month; but the 19th day breaks the sequence of 7's; and there is no question that the Hebrew sabbath is much older than this Babylonian observance. Among the Hebrews, moreover, the sabbath was associated with the idea of rest, worship, and divine favor, not certain taboos.

After the time of Moses the sabbath is mentioned sometimes in connection with the festival of the new moon (II Kings 4:23; Amos 8:5; Hosea 2:11; Isa. 1:13; Ezek. 46:3). The prophets always exalted the sabbath and found fault with the Israelites for the perfunctory observance of it. They made confession of Israel's sin in profaning the sabbath (Isa. 56;2,4; 58:13; Jer. 17:21-27; Ezek. 20:12-24).

The sanctity of the sabbath is shown by the offering upon it of two lambs, while only one was sacrificed on the other days of the week (Num. 28:9,19). The 12 loaves of shewbread were also presented on that day (Lev. 24:5-9; I Chron. 9: 32). A wilful sabbath-breaker was put to death (Num. 15:32-36). The Israelite could not even light a fire in his home on the sabbath. Psalm 92, expressing delight in the worship and works of Jehovah, was composed for the sabbath day. In the Persian period Nehemiah rebuked and took strong measures against those who disregarded the law of the sabbath by doing business on it (Neh. 10:31; 13:15-22).

With the development of the synagogue during the Exile, the sabbath became a day for worship and the study of the Law, as well as a day of rest. There are not many references to the sabbath in the apocryphal books. Antiochus Epiphanes tried to abolish it, along with other distinctively Jewish institutions (168 B.C.). At the beginning of the Maccabean war, Jewish soldiers allowed themselves to be massacred rather than profane the sabbath by fighting, even in self-defense. After 1,000 Jews were slaughtered in this way, they decided that in the future it would be permissible to defend themselves if attacked on the sacred day, but not to engage in offensive operations (I Macc. 2:31-41). It was not, however, considered allowable to destroy siege-works on the sabbath; and so Pompey was permitted to raise his mound and mount his battering rams against Jerusalem without interference from the Jews (Jos. *Antiq*. xiv. 4, 2 and 3).

During the period between Ezra and the Christian era the scribes formulated innumerable legal restrictions for the conduct of life under the law. Two whole treatises in the Talmud are devoted to the details of sabbath observance. One of these, the *Shabbath*, enumerates the following 39 principal classes of prohibited actions: sowing, plowing, reaping, gathering into sheaves, threshing, winnowing, cleansing, grinding, sifting, kneading, baking, shearing wool, washing it, beating it, dyeing it, spinning it, making a warp of it, making two cords, weaving two threads, separating two threads, making a knot, untying a knot, sewing two stitches, tearing to sew two stitches, catching a deer, killing, skinning, salting it, preparing its hide, scraping off its hair, cutting it up, writing two letters, blotting out for the purpose of writing two letters, building, pulling down, extinguishing, lighting a fire, beating with a hammer, and carrying from one property to another. Each of these chief enactments was further discussed and elaborated, so that actually there were several hundred things a conscientious, law-abiding Jew could not do on the sabbath. For example, the prohibition about tying a knot was much too general, and so it became necessary to state what kinds of knots were prohibited and what kind not. It was accordingly laid down that allowable knots were those that could be untied with one hand. A woman could tie up her undergarment, and the strings of her cap, those of her girdle, the straps of her shoes and sandals, of skins of wine and oil, of a pot with meat. She could tie a pail over the well with a girdle, but not with a rope. The prohibition regarding writing on the sabbath was further defined as follows: "He who writes two letters with his right or his left hand, whether of one kind or of two kinds, as also if they are written with different ink or are of different languages, is guilty. He even who should from forgetfulness write two letters is guilty, whether he has written them with ink or with paint, red chalk, India-rubber, vitriol, or anything which makes permanent marks. Also he who writes on two walls which form an angle, or on the two tablets of his account-book, so that they can be read together, is guilty. He who writes upon his body is guilty. If any one writes with dark fluid, with fruit juice, or in the dust on the road, in sand, or in anything in which writing does not remain, he is free. If any one writes with the wrong hand, with the foot, with the mouth, with the elbow; also if any one writes upon a letter of another piece of writing, or covers other writing" (*Shabbath* xii. 3-5). Jesus had things like this in mind when He said, "Woe unto you also, ye lawyers! for ye lade men with burdens grievous to be borne, and ye yourselves touch not the burdens with one of your fingers" (Luke 11:46).

Jesus came into conflict with the religious leaders of the Jews especially on two points: His claim to be the Messiah, and on the matter of sabbath observance. The rabbis regarded the sabbath as an end in itself, whereas Jesus taught that the sabbath was made for man's benefit, and that man's needs must take precedence over the law of the sabbath (Matt. 12:1-14; Mark 2:23-3:6; Luke 6:1-11; John 5:1-18). He Himself regularly attended worship in the synagogue on the sabbath (Luke 4:16).

The early Christians, most of whom were Jews, kept the seventh day as a sabbath, but since the resurrection of their Lord was the most blessed day in their lives, they began very early also to meet for worship on the first day of the week (Acts 2:1), and designated it as the Lord's day. Paul directed the Corinthian Christians to bring their weekly offering to the charities of the Church on the first day of the week (I Cor. 16:1,2). As the split between the Jews and Christians widened, the Christians came gradually to meet for worship only on the Lord's day and gave up the observance of the seventh day. S.B.

SABBATH, COVERT FOR THE, very obscure expression found in II Kings 16:18. Ahaz, king of Judah, turned from the house of the Lord for the king of Assyria "the covert for the sabbath that they built in the house, and the king's entry without." It appears to refer to some colonnade along which the king and his attendants could pass when he visited the temple on holy days. It is not mentioned in the description of the temple, and must have been added afterwards, and probably was richly adorned. It is not mentioned anywhere else.

SABBATH, MORROW AFTER THE, an expression of uncertain meaning found in Leviticus 23:11, where Moses instructs the Israelites that the priest was to wave a sheaf of the firstfruits of their harvests before the Lord "on the morrow after the sabbath." Some hold that the "sabbath" meant here was the ordinary weekly sabbath which fell during the seven days of the Passover. That was the view of the Sadducees of the time of Christ. The Pharisees, however, held, and many modern scholars agree with them, that the term sabbath here is not the weekly sabbath, but the first day of the Passover on whatever day of the week it might fall.

SABBATH, SECOND AFTER THE FIRST, an expression of uncertain meaning found in Luke 6:1. Scholars are not agreed as to its exact meaning. Many explanations have been suggested, of which the following may be mentioned. 1. The first sabbath of the second year in a sabbatical cycle of seven years.

2. The first sabbath after the second day of the Passover.

3. The first sabbath of the *ecclesiastical year*. The Jewish civil year began in Tisri (mid-September), while the ecclesiastical year began in Nisan (mid-March). In any case the time of the year was spring or early summer, as the mention of the ripe grain shows.

SABBATH DAY'S JOURNEY, used only in Acts 1:12, where it designates the distance between Mount Olivet and Jerusalem. A sabbath day's journey was a journey of limited extent which the scribes thought a Jew might travel on the sabbath without breaking the Law. Such a journey was 2,000 cubits (3,000 feet) from one's house or domicile, a distance derived from the statement found in Joshua 3:4 that there was to be that much distance between the ark and the people on their march. The rabbis, however, devised a way of increasing this distance without infringing the Law by depositing some food at the 2,000-cubit limit, before the sabbath, and declaring that spot a temporary residence.

SABBATICAL YEAR (See Feasts)

SABBEUS (să-bē'ŭs, Gr. *Sabbaías*), in I Esdras 9:32, the same as "Shemaiah" in Ezra 10:31.

SABTA, SABTAH (săb'tà, Heb. *savtā', savtâh*), the third son of Cush (Gen. 10:7; I Chron. 1:9). There was probably a place named Sabta in South Arabia, but its exact location is uncertain.

SABTECHA, SABTECHAH (săb'tē-kà, Heb. *savtekhā'*), the fifth-named of the sons of Cush in the genealogy of Genesis 10:5-7. His descendants probably lived in South Arabia.

SACAR (sā'kàr, Heb. *sākhār, wages*). 1. Father of Ahiam, a follower of David. He was a Hararite

(I Chron. 11:35). In II Samuel 23:33 the name is spelled "Sharar."

2. A son of Obed-edom (I Chron. 26:4).

SACKBUT (See Music)

SACKCLOTH (săk'klŏth). The English word is derived from the Hebrew *sak*, a course cloth, dark in color, usually made of goat's hair. It was worn by mourners (II Sam. 3:31; II Kings 19:1,2), often by prophets (Isa. 20:2; Rev. 11:3), and by captives (I Kings 20:31). Its exact shape is not known. Some think that originally it was a loin-cloth, which in prehistoric times was the only article of clothing worn by the ancestors of Israel, and which in later times was worn only as a religious duty. Others think it was like a corn-sack, with openings for the neck and arms. It was usually worn over another garment, but sometimes next to the skin (Jonah 3:6; I Kings 21:27; II Kings 6:30; Job 16:15; Isa. 32:11).

SACRAMENT (săk'ra-měnt), derived from the Latin *sacramentum*, which in classical times was used in two chief senses: as a technical legal term to denote the sum of money which the two parties to a suit deposited in a temple, of which the winner had his part returned, while the loser forfeited his to the temple treasury; as a technical military term to designate the oath of obedience of a soldier to his commander. In the Greek NT there is no word corresponding to "sacrament," nor do we find the word used in the earliest history of Christianity to refer to certain rites of the Church. Pliny the Younger (c. A.D. 112) uses the word in connection with Christianity in a famous letter in which he says that the Christians of Bithynia bound themselves "by a sacramentum to commit no kind of crime," but it is doubtful whether he uses the word with any special Christian meaning. The word *sacramentum* was used with a distinctively Christian meaning for the first time in the Old Latin Bible and in Tertullian (end of 2nd century). In the Old Latin and in the Vulgate it was employed to translate the Greek *mysterion*, "mystery" (e.g. Eph. 5:32; I Tim. 3:16; Rev. 1:20; 17:7). For a long time it was used not only to refer to religious rites, but to doctrines and facts.

Because of the absence of any defined sacramental concept in the early history of the church, the number of sacraments was not regarded as fixed. Baptism and the Lord's Supper were the chief. In the 12th century Hugo of St. Victor listed 30 sacraments that had been recognized by the church, while Gregory of Bergamo and Peter Lombard listed only seven: Baptism, Confirmation, the Eucharist, Penance, Extreme Unction, Orders, and Matrimony — a list adopted by Thomas Aquinas, and later by the Council of Trent. The number seven was supported by many fanciful arguments that seven is a sacred number. There is no NT authority for it, and it is a purely arbitrary figure. It is hard to see on what principle Baptism and the Lord's Supper, which were instituted by Christ, can be put in the same category with marriage, which is as old as the human race.

The Reformers saw in the NT sacraments three distinguishing marks: (1) they were instituted by Christ; (2) Christ commanded that they be observed by His followers; (3) they are visible symbols of divine acts. Since baptism and the Lord's Supper are the only rites for which such marks can be claimed, there can be only two sacraments. There is justification for classifying them under a common name because they are associated together in the NT (Acts 2:41,42; I Cor. 10:1-4).

Some modern critics challenge the claim that baptism and the Lord's Supper owe their origin to Christ, but a fair reading of the NT shows that these sacramental rites were universal in the Apostolic Church and that the apostles observed them because they were convinced that Christ had instituted them. They taught the Church to observe the things which Christ commanded (Matt. 28:20). Circumstances of great solemnity surrounded the institution of the sacraments by Christ. The Lord's Supper was appointed by Him upon the eve of His redemptive sacrifice, while baptism was commanded at the time of His ascension, for all who became His disciples.

These rites were regarded as ritual acts of faith and obedience towards God and as means appointed by Christ to bring the members of the Church into communion with His death and resurrection through the Holy Spirit (Matt. 28:19,20; I Cor. 11:23-27; Acts 2:38; Rom. 6:3-5; Col. 2; 11,12). They are symbolic rites setting forth the central truths of the Christian faith: death and resurrection with Christ and participation in the redemptive benefits of Christ's mediatorial death. They are visible enactments of the Gospel message that Christ lived, died, was raised from the dead, ascended to heaven, and will some day return, and that all this is for man's salvation. In the NT baptism is intimately connected with the following: the forgiveness of sin (Acts 2:38; 22:16; Eph. 5: 26; Titus 3:5); the gift of the Holy Spirit (Acts 2:38; I Cor. 12:13); union with Christ in His death and resurrection (Rom. 6:3-6; Col. 2:12); regeneration (John 3:5; Titus 3:5); entering into the relationship of sonship with God (Gal. 3: 26,27); belonging to the Church (Acts 2:41); and the gift of salvation (Mark 16:16). The Lord's Supper symbolizes Christ's death for the remission of sins (Matt. 26:28). It is a seal of the New Covenant in Christ's blood, an assurance of eternal life now, a promise of the Second Coming, a pledge of the eventual Messianic triumph. As means of grace the efficacy of the sacraments lies not in themselves as outward acts, but in the blessing of Christ through the Holy Spirit, and is conditioned by faith in the recipient.   S.B.

SACRIFICE (Heb. *zevah*, Gr. *thusía*), a religious act belonging to worship in which offering is made to God of some material object belonging to the offerer — this offering being consumed in the ceremony, in order to attain, restore, maintain, or celebrate friendly relations with the deity. The motives actuating the offerer may be varied, worthy or unworthy, and may express faith, repentance, adoration, or all of these together; but the main purpose of the sacrifice is to please the deity and to secure His favor.

Origin of Sacrifice. The origin of sacrifice is a matter of dispute. The question is, did sacrifice arise from the natural religious instinct of man, whether guided by the Spirit of God or not, or did it originate in a distinct divine appointment? Genesis records the first sacrifice, by Cain and Abel, but gives no account of the origin of the idea. The custom is clearly approved by God; and in the Mosaic Law it is adopted and elaborately developed. The view that the rite was initiated by an express command of God is based mainly on Genesis 4:4f, which states that Abel offered to God an acceptable sacrifice, and on Hebrews 11:4, where it is said that Abel's sacrifice was acceptable to God because of his faith. It is argued that Abel's faith was based upon a specific command of God in the past and that without such a divine command his sacrifice would have been mere superstition. Many who hold this view also say that the garments pro-

Above, the altar of sacrifice on the high place at Petra. SHH
Below, an altar rock for a heathen god at Baalbek, in Lebanon. JFW

vided by God to hide the nakedness of Adam and Eve must have come from an animal that was sacrificed and that in this sacrifice we have a type of the sacrifice of Christ to cover man's spiritual nakedness before God. While all this possibly may be deduced from Scripture, it is obviously not a necessary deduction.

Those who hold that sacrifice was devised by man, with or without direction by God's Spirit, as a means of satisfying the wants of his spiritual nature have advanced several theories. 1. The *gift* theory holds that sacrifices were originally presents to God which the offerer hoped would be received with pleasure and gratitude by the deity, who would then grant him favors. 2. The *table-bond* theory suggests that sacrifices were originally meals shared by the worshipers and the deity, with the purpose of knitting them together in a firmer bond of fellowship. 3. The *sacramental-communion* theory is a modification of the table-bond theory. The basis of it is the belief among some primitive peoples that animals share along with man in the divine nature. The worshiper actually eats the god, thus acquiring the physical, intellectual, and moral qualities which characterized the animal. 4. The *homage* theory holds that sacrifice originates not in man's sense of guilt, but in man's desire of expressing his homage to and dependence upon the deity. 5. The *expiatory* theory says that sacrifices are fundamentally piacular or atoning for sin. Conscious of his sin and of the punishment which it deserves, man substitutes an animal to endure the penalty due to himself, and so makes his peace with the deity.

738 **SACRIFICE**

Classification of Sacrifices. Sacrifices have been classified in a variety of ways, chiefly the follow- 1. Those on behalf of the whole congregation; and those on behalf of the individual. 2. Animal or bleeding sacrifices; and bloodless offerings. 3. Sacrifices assuming an undisturbed covenant relationship; and those intended to restore a relationship which has been disturbed. 4. Animal sacrifices; vegetable sacrifices; liquid and incense offerings. 5. Sacrifices made without the help of a priest; those made by a priest alone; and those made by a layman with the help of a priest. 6. Sacrifices which express homage to the deity; those designed to make atonement for sin; and peace offerings, to express or promote peaceful relations with the deity. 7. Self-dedicatory sacrifices; eucharistic sacrifices; and expiatory sacrifices. 8. Sacrifices in which the offering was wholly devoted to God; and sacrifices in which God received a portion, and the worshiper feasted on the remainder.

History of Sacrifice in OT Times. The sacrifices of Cain and Abel (Gen. 4:4f) show that the rite goes back almost to the beginnings of the human race. No priest was needed in their sacrifices, which were eucharistic and possibly expiatory. The sacrifice of Noah after the Flood (Gen. 8:20f), is called a burnt-offering, and is closely connected with the covenant of God described in Genesis 9:8-17. In the sacrifices of Abraham, several of which are mentioned (Gen. 1:7,8; 13:4,18; 15:4ff), he acted as his own priest, and made offerings to express his adoration of God and probably to atone for sin. In Genesis 22 he is shown by God that He does not desire human sacrifice, a common practice in those days. The patriarchs Isaac and Jacob regularly offered sacrifices (Gen. 26:25; 28:18; 31:54; 33:20; 35:7; 46:1). Job and his friends offered sacrifices (Job 1:5; 42:7-9), probably to atone for sin. The Israelites during their sojourn in Egypt no doubt were accustomed to animal sacrifices. It was to some such feast that Moses asked the pharaoh for permission to go in the wilderness (Exod. 3:18; 5:3ff; 7:16); and he requested herds and flocks for the feast to offer burnt-offerings and sacrifices (Exod. 10:24,25). The sacrifice of the Passover (Exod. 12:3-11) brings out forcibly the idea of salvation from death. Jethro, Moses' father-in-law, a priest, offered sacrifices on meeting Moses and the people (Exod. 18:12).

The establishment of the covenant between Israel and Jehovah was accompanied by solemn sacrifices. The foundation principle of this covenant was *obedience,* not sacrifices (Exod. 19:4-8). Sacrifices were incidental — aids to obedience, but valueless without it. The common altars were not abolished with the giving of the Covenant Code (Exod. 20:24ff), but continued to be used for centuries by Joshua, Gideon, Jephthah, Samuel, Saul, David, Elijah, and many others. They were perfectly legitimate and even necessary at least until the building of the temple in Jerusalem.

At the division of the kingdom in 931 B.C. golden calf worship was established at Dan and Bethel, with priests, altars, and ritual (I Kings 12:27f). High places, most of them very corrupt, were in use in both kingdoms until the time of the Exile, although occasionally attempts were made in the southern kingdom to remove them. With the destruction of the temple in Jerusalem in 586 B.C. the entire cultus was suspended, but on the return from the captivity an altar was built and sacrifices resumed. At the time of Nehemiah there existed a temple at Elephantine in Egypt, built by Jews, where a system of sacrifices was observed. Sacrifices were made in the temple in Jerusalem until its destruction by the Romans in A.D. 70. The Jews have offered none since then.

The Mosaic Sacrifices. Every offering had to be the honestly acquired property of the offerer (II Sam. 24:24). Sacrifices had value in the eyes of Jehovah only when they were made in acknowledgment of His sovereign majesty, expressed in obedience to Him, and with a sincere desire to enjoy His favor. The only animals allowed for sacrifice were oxen, sheep, goats, and pigeons. Wild animals and fish could not be offered. The produce of the field allowed for offerings was wine, oil, and corn, either in the ear or in the form of meal, dough, cakes, etc. Sacrifices were of two kinds: animal or bleeding, and vegetable or bloodless.

1. Animal Sacrifices. Both sexes were accepted for sacrifice, although for some sacrifices the male was prescribed. With one exception (Lev. 22:23), no animal with any sort of wound or defect could be offered (Lev. 22:21-24). The law enjoined that animals be at least eight days old (Lev. 22:27); and in some cases the age of the animal is specified (Lev. 9:3; 12:6; Num. 28:3,9,11). According to the later rabbis, animals more than three years old could not be sacrificed. There was no prescription of age or sex with regard to pigeons or turtle doves; but they were offered only by the poor as substitutes for other animals.

a. The Sin Offering (Lev. 4:1-35; 6:24-30). This was for sins unconsciously or unintentionally committed; sins committed intentionally, but with mitigating circumstances (Lev. 5:2,3; 12:6-8); certain kinds of ceremonial defilements (Lev. 5:2,3; 12:6-8); and sins deliberately committed but afterwards voluntarily confessed. For conscious and deliberate violations of the Law no atonement was possible, with some exceptions, for which provision was made in the guilt offerings. Capital crimes: the breaking of the law of the sabbath (Num. 15:32); adultery (Deut. 22:22,23); murder (Exod. 21:12); and sacrilege (Josh. 7:15) were punished with death. Sin-offerings were made for the whole congregation on all the feast days, and especially on the Day of Atonement. They were also offered on the occasion of the consecration of priests and Levites (Exod. 29:10-14,36). Every year, on the great Day of Atonement, sin-offerings were offered for the high-priest. With the exception of these important national occasions, the sin-offerings were presented only on occasions of special circumstances which demanded expiation of sin.

The costliness of the offering and the procedure to be followed depended upon the theocratic importance of the offender. For the high-priest a young bullock was the appointed offering (Lev. 4:3); for a prince it was a he-goat (Lev. 4:23); in ordinary cases a she-goat or a sheep was sufficient. The poor could offer two pigeons, and where even these were too much, a small portion of fine flour was substituted (Lev. 5:7,11).

In all other blood sacrifices the blood was simply poured around the altar; in this one the blood was sprinkled. If a member of the congregation made the offering, the blood was smeared upon the horns of the altar in the fore-court (Lev. 4:7,18, 25,30). When a sin-offering was for a priest or the whole congregation, the officiating priest took some of the blood of the sacrifice into the holy place and sprinkled it seven times before the veil of the sanctuary, and then smeared it on the horns of the altar of incense. The blood that was left had to be poured out at the base of the altar. After the blood was sprinkled, the fat portions of the animal were burned upon the altar. The remainder of the flesh was disposed of in two ways: in the case of sin-offerings of any of the congregation the flesh was eaten in the fore-court by the officiating priest and his sons; while in the case of sin-offerings for a priest or for the whole congregation, the whole animal was burned outside the camp in a clean place.

b. The Guilt Offering (Lev. 5:14-6:7). (In the KJV, the "trespass offering.") This was a special kind of sin-offering, and was offered for transgressions where restitution or other legal satisfaction could be made, or was made. When the rights of God or men were violated, the wrong had to be righted, the broken law honored, and the sin expiated by a guilt-offering. The offering, which was always a lamb, with one exception (Lev. 14:12), was made after the satisfaction required had been made. The ritual was the same as in the sin-offering, except that the blood was not sprinkled, but was poured over the surface of the altar. Its main purpose was to make expiation for dues withheld from God, like neglect to pay at the proper time what was due to the sanctuary; and from man, like robbery, failure to return a deposit, swearing falsely regarding anything lost, and seduction of a betrothed bond-maid. The sin-offering of a lamb made atonement to God. Restitution, with an additional one-fifth, made reparation to man.

c. The Burnt Offering (Lev. 1). The distinguishing mark of this offering was that it was wholly consumed on the altar; while in other animal sacrifices only the fat portions were burned. The purpose of the offering was propitiation; but with this idea was united another, the entire consecration of the worshiper to Jehovah. Because of the regularity and frequency with which it was offered, it was called the "continual" burnt-offering (Exod. 29:42); and because no part was left for human consumption, it was also called the "whole burnt-offering" (Ps. 51:19). This was the normal sacrifice of the Israelite in proper covenant relationship with

The Altar of Burnt Offering in Solomon's Temple once stood on this Rock of Moriah, which is now in the center of the mosque called the Dome of the Rock in the old temple area at Jerusalem. © MPS

God, and was the only sacrifice regularly appointed for the sanctuary service. It was offered every day, in the morning and in the evening. On ordinary days a yearling lamb was sacrificed; on the sabbath day two lambs were offered at morning and evening sacrifice (Num. 28:9,10). On other special feast days a larger number of animals was offered. There were also private burnt-offerings when a Nazirite fulfilled his vow or defiled himself (Num. 6), at the consecration of priests (Exod. 29:15), at the cleansing of lepers (Lev. 14:9), at the purification of women (Lev. 12:6), and for other ceremonial uncleanness (Lev. 15:15,30). This was the only sacrifice that a non-Israelite was permitted to offer (Lev. 17:8; 22:18,25).

d. The Peace Offerings (Lev. 3). These were called peace-offerings because they were offered by those who were at peace with God, to express gratitude and obligation to God, and fellowship with Him. They were not commanded to be offered at any set time, except Pentecost (Lev. 23:20), and were presented spontaneously as the feelings of the worshiper prompted (Lev. 19:5).

The ritual was the same as for the sin-offering, except that the blood was wholly poured upon the altar, as in the trespass-offering and burnt-offering. The fat was burned; the wave-breast and heave-leg were kept for the priests; and the rest of the flesh was eaten at the sanctuary by the sacrificer and his friends (Lev. 7:15f; Deut. 12:1,17f). A meat- and drink-offering always accompanied this sacrifice. This meal denoted the fellowship which existed between the worshiper and God, and was a symbol and pledge of friendship and peace with Him. There were three kinds of peace-offerings: praise-offerings, votive offerings, and free-will offerings. For all three classes oxen, sheep, and goats of either sex could be offered (Lev. 3:1,6,12). The animals had to be without blemish, except for the free-will offerings, where animals with too short or long a limb were allowed (Lev. 22:23). Peace-offerings were also offered on occasions of great public solemnity or rejoicing.

2. Vegetable or Bloodless Sacrifices. These were of two kinds, the meat-offerings (called "meal-offerings" in the ASV) and the drink-offerings. They were offered on the altar of the fore-court.

a. The Meat Offerings (Lev. 2:1-16; 6:14-18) were not animal offerings, as the name suggests, but offerings of fine flour, or of unleavened bread, cakes, wafers, or of ears of grain roasted, always with salt and, except in the sin-offering, with olive oil (Lev. 2:1,4,13,14; 5:11). They were sometimes accompanied by frankincense. Only a portion was consumed by fire on the altar; the rest was kept by the priests, who ate it in a holy place (Lev. 6:16; 10:12,13). The meal-offering accompanied the other offerings, except the sin-offering, on all important occasions (Lev. 7:11ff; Num. 15). It always followed the morning and evening burnt-offerings. The idea back of the meal-offering seems to have been that since people would not ordinarily eat meals consisting only of flesh, it would be wrong to offer only flesh to God.

b. The Drink Offerings were not independent offerings under the law, but were made only in connection with the meal-offering which accompanied all burnt-offerings and all peace-offerings which were Nazirite, votive, or freewill (Num. 6:17; 15:1-12). They did not accompany sin and trespass-offerings. The drink-offering consisted of wine, which was poured out upon the altar, probably upon the flesh of the sacrifice.

The High Priest in the Holy Place, before the Altar of Incense. At rear is the veil dividing the Holy Place from the Holy of Holies. At left is the seven-branched candlestick and accessories. At right, the Table of Shewbread. DV

Besides the above, three offerings were regularly made in the holy place: the 12 loaves of shewbread, renewed every Sabbath; the oil for the seven-branched candlestick, which was filled every morning; and the incense for the altar of incense, which was renewed every morning and evening. See also OFFERINGS. S.B.

SACRILEGE (săk'rĭ-lĕj). The expression "commit sacrilege" occurs in Romans 2:22 KJV as the translation of *hierosulein*, "rob temples" RV. The RV more exactly expresses the meaning of the Greek verb.

SADDLE (săd'l, Heb. *mercāv, a riding seat*). The verb *habhash*, "to bind on," is used of getting a beast (always an ass) for riding (Gen. 22:3; Num. 22:21; Judg. 19:10; II Sam. 16:1; 17:23; 19:26; I Kings 2:40; II Kings 4:24). Asses were not ridden with saddles. An ass carrying a heavy burden had a thick cushion on its back to relieve the pressure.

SADDUCEES (săd'yū-sēz, Gr. *Saddoukaíoi*), one of the religious parties which existed among the Jews in the days of Christ and the early Church, and which, while exercising comparatively little influence among the people, resisted the truth of the Gospel. Its origin is uncertain, but it is to be sought in the period in Jewish history between the restoration of the Jews to their own land (536 B.C.) and the Christian era. No evidence of Sadduceeism is to be found in Israel before the captivity.

The origin of the name of the sect is obscure. The root of the word means "to be righteous," and the word has sometimes been taken to be an adjective, "the righteous ones," but since the Sadducees were not particularly distinguished for their righteousness, it is unlikely that they got their name from this word. The probability is that the name is derived from some person named Zadok. The best-known Zadok in history was the Davidic high priest (II Sam. 8:17), from whom succeeding high priests claimed to descend. He himself was descended from Aaron through the line of Eleazar (I Chron. 24:3), and was instrumental in the return of the ark (II Sam. 15:24-29). The Prophet Ezekiel, in his description of the restored temple, says that because the sons of Zadok remained loyal to Jehovah when the Israelites went astray, they would be ministers in the new sanctuary (Ezek. 40:46; 44:15). Some scholars hold that the Sadducees trace their origin to this Zadok. Others, however, think that the name comes from another Zadok, a disciple of Antigonus of Socho (c. 250 B.C.), who taught that obedience to God should be absolutely disinterested, without expectation of future reward. This view goes back to an apocryphal legend in the Abot-de-Rabbi Nathan (c. 1000 A.D.). There is also the possibility that the name may be derived from some Zadok unknown to us.

The chief authorities for our knowledge of this sect are Josephus, the NT, and the Talmud. Josephus lays great stress upon the aristocratic nature of the Sadducees. He says, "They only gain the well-to-do; they have not the people on their side." They were the political party of the Jewish aristocratic priesthood from the time of the Maccabees to the final fall of the Jewish state. The Sadducees were priests, but not all priests were Sadducees. Josephus, for example, was a priest and a Pharisee. The likelihood is that the priestly party only gradually crystallized into the sect of the Sadducees. From the time of the Exile, the priesthood in general constituted the nobility of the Jewish people, and the high priest became an increasingly powerful figure. The priestly aristocracy became leaders in the Hellenizing movement that began with Alexander the Great. Because of their sympathy with the policy of Antiochus Epiphanes, they took no part in the Maccabean struggle, which was supported mainly by the Pharisees, a group of religious enthusiasts who opposed what they regarded as the religious deterioration of the Jewish nation. The high priesthood and the throne were united in a single person when, c. 143, B.C., Simon was recognized as both high priest and ruler of the Jews. This centralization of power led to a number of forms of reaction, especially from the Pharisees. Probably not theological at first, the Sadducees became so to defend their policies against the attacks of the Pharisees. Under the Romans, they became the party favorable to the government. As aristocrats, they were naturally very conservative, and were more interested in maintaining the political status quo than in the religious purity of the nation. Since they were satisfied with the present, they did not look forward to a future Messianic age. Not popular with the people, they nevertheless sometimes found it necessary to adopt the Pharisaic policy in order to win the popular support.

The Sadducees had a number of distinctive beliefs, contrasting strongly with those of the Pharisees:

1. They held only to the written Law, and rejected the traditions of the Pharisees. Josephus says: "The Pharisees have delivered to the people a great many observances by succession from their fathers, which are not written in the law of Moses; and for that reason it is that the Sadducees reject them, and say that we are to esteem those observances to be obligatory which are in the written Word, but are not to observe what are derived from the tradition of our forefathers. And concerning these things it is that great disputes and differences have risen among them" (Antiq. xiii.10,6). In other words, the Sadducees believed that the Word of God alone was the seat of religious authority. The Pharisees, on the contrary, believed that just as binding as the Law itself was the supposed oral tradition of the teachings of Moses and the rulings on the Law made by the scribes over the years. Some of the church fathers, notably Hippolytus, Origen, Jerome, and Tertullian, credited the Sad-

ducees with regarding the Pentateuch as alone canonical, but this is apparently an error, since Josephus does not mention this, and in the Talmud the Sadducees are introduced as drawing arguments from the other books of the OT in their own defense. It is unlikely, moreover, that the Sadducees would have been admitted to the Sanhedrin had this been true.

2. A second distinctive belief of the Sadducees was their denial of the resurrection of the body, personal immortality, and retribution in a future life. "The doctrine of the Sadducees," says Josephus, "is this, that souls die with the bodies" (Antiq. xviii.1,4); and again, "they also take away the belief of the immortal duration of the soul, and the punishments and rewards in Hades" (Jewish War, ii,i,14). According to the NT, the Sadducees denied the resurrection of the body (Matt. 22:23; Mark 12:18; Luke 20:27; Acts 4:1,2; 23:8), but it says nothing about their denial of immortality and future retribution.

3. According to Acts 23:8, the Sadducees denied the existence of angels and spirits. Seeing that they accepted the OT, in which supermundane spirits often appear, it is hard to understand their position on this subject. A number of factors may have been responsible for this: their general indifference to religion, their rationalistic temper, and the wild extravagances of the angelology and demonology of the Pharisees.

4. The Sadducees differed from both the Pharisees and the Essenes on the matter of divine predestination and the freedom of the human will. According to Josephus, the Essenes held that all things are fixed by God's unalterable decree; the Pharisees tried to combine predestination and free will; and the Sadducees threw aside all ideas of divine interposition in the government of the world. "They take away fate," says Josephus, "and say there is no such thing, and that the events of human affairs are not at its disposal, but they suppose that all our actions are in our own power, so that we are ourselves the causes of what is good, and receive what is evil from our own folly" (Antiq. xiii. 5,9; comp. also Jewish War, II.8,14). They felt no need of a divine providence to order their lives. They thought man is entirely the master of his own destiny and that the doing of good or evil is left entirely to man's free choice.

The Sadducees are mentioned by name in the NT only about a dozen times (Matt. 3:7; 16: 1,6,11f; 22:23,24; Mark 12:18; Luke 20:27; Acts 4:1; 5:17; 23:6-8); but it must be remembered that when mention is made of the chief priests, practically the same persons are referred to. They seem mostly to have ignored Jesus, at least in the early part of His ministry. Jesus directed His criticism against the Pharisees, although once He warned His disciples against the leaven of the Sadducees (Matt. 16:6,11). With the Pharisees, they asked Jesus to show them a sign from heaven (Matt. 16:1). They resented His action in cleansing the temple (Matt. 21:12f; Mark 11:15f; Luke 19:45f), and were filled with indignation at His claim of the Messianic title "son of David" (Matt. 21:15f). They tried to discredit Him in the eyes of the people and get Him in trouble with the Roman power by their questions as to His authority (Matt. 21:23), as to the resurrection (Matt. 22:23), and as to the lawfulness of paying tribute to Caesar (Luke 20:22). They joined the scribes and Pharisees in their attempt to destroy Him (Mark 11: 18; Luke 19:47). They sat in the Sanhedrin which condemned Him, and the chief priest who presided was a member of their party. In their opposition thev were probably most influenced by their fear that a Messianic movement led by Him would bring political ruin (John 11:49).

After the day of Pentecost the Sadducees were very active against the infant Church. Along with the priests and the captain of the temple they arrested Peter and John and put them in prison. A little later, they arrested all the apostles and took counsel to slay them (Acts 5:17,33). Their hostile attitude persisted throughout the rest of the Acts of the Apostles. There is no record of a Sadducee being admitted into the Christian Church. According to Josephus (Antiq. xx,9,1), they were responsible for the death of James, the brother of the Lord. With the destruction of Jerusalem in A.D. 70, the Sadducean party disappeared.   S.B.

SADOC (sā'dŏk). 1. An ancestor of Ezra (II Esdras 1:1).

2. Gr. *Sadók*. A descendant of Zerubbabel and ancestor of Jesus (Matt. 1:14).

SAFFRON (See Plants)

SAIL (See Ship)

SAILOR (See Occupations & Professions)

SAINT. In the KJV the word "saint" is used to translate two Hebrew words, *qādôsh* and *hasîdh*. The root idea of the first is separation. In a religious sense it means that which is separated or dedicated unto God, and therefore removed from secular use. The word is applied to people, places and things, as: the temple, vessels, garments, the city of Jerusalem, priests, etc. The root of the second word is personal holiness. The emphasis is on character. It has a strong ethical connotation. These words are used either in the plural or with a collective noun. The reason for this is that a person's standing before God is regarded as a matter of his belonging to a larger whole — the nation Israel or the Christian church — this larger whole standing in covenant relationship to God. In the Septuagint the word *hagioi* is used to refer to God's covenant people Israel. In the NT this word is transferred to the members of the Christian Church. The saints are the Church (I Cor. 1:2). The Church comprises people called out of the world by God's electing grace to be His own people. All who are in covenant relation with Him through repentance and faith in His Son are regarded as saints. Objectively, the saints are God's chosen and peculiar people, belonging exclusively to Him. Subjectively, they are separated from all defilement and sin and partake of God's own holiness. Throughout the Bible, but especially in the epistles of the NT, the saints are urged to live lives befitting their position (Eph. 4:1; Col. 1:10).   S.B.

SALA, SALAH (sā'là, Heb. *shelah, missile, petition*, Gr. *Salá*), a son of Arphaxad (Gen. 10: 24; 11:13ff; I Chron. 1:18,24; Luke 3:35-36).

SALAMIS (săl'à-mĭs, Gr. *Salamís*), a town on the E coast of Cyprus, founded, according to tradition, by Teucer, from the island of Salamis, off the coast of Greece. It possessed a good harbor and was a populous and flourishing town in the Hellenic and Roman periods. Paul and Barnabas preached the Gospel there in the synagogues of the Jews (Acts 13:5), showing that there was a large Jewish community in Salamis. Nothing is said of the duration or success of the visit. Paul did not return to Salamis, but Barnabas doubtless did on his second missionary journey (Acts 15:39), and according to tradition he was martyred there in the reign of Nero.

SALATHIEL (sà-lā'thĭ-ĕl, Gr. *Salathiél, I have asked God*), the son of Jeconiah, king of Judah,

and father of Zerubbabel, according to the genealogy in Matthew 1:12; while in the Lukan genealogy he appears as the father of Zerubbabel, indeed, but as the son of Neri (Luke 3:27). The apparent discrepancy in the genealogies is probably to be explained on the principle that Matthew gives the genealogy of Jesus according to the legal succession, while Luke gives it according to the actual succession or right of consanguinity. If the direct line failed in Jeconiah, because he had no son to succeed him, the right of succession went to Salathiel, a descendant of Nathan and the son of Neri, who, as being the legal heir to Jeconiah, was reckoned his son by Matthew.

SALCAH (săl'kà, Heb. *salekhâh*), a city on the extreme NE boundary of the kingdom of Bashan, near Edrei (Deut. 3:10; Josh. 12:5; 13:11). Og, king of Bashan, once ruled it, and undoubtedly it was included in the portion given to the half-tribe of Manasseh. It later became the N limit of the Gadites (I Chron. 5:11). It is now known as Salkhad.

SALCHAH (sal'kà), another spelling of Salcah, q.v.

SALEM (sā'lĕm, Heb. *shālēm, peace*), the name of the city of which Melchizedek was king (Gen. 14: 18; Heb. 7:1,2). Josephus (*Ant.* I,X,2) says that Jewish writers generally regarded it as a synonym of Jerusalem. It is apparently so regarded in Psalm 76:2.

SALIM (sā'lĭm, Gr. *Saleím*), a place referred to in John 3:23 as near Aenon, where John was baptizing. A comparison of John 1:28; 3:26; 10:40 shows that it must have been W of the Jordan, but its exact location is unknown.

SALLAI (săl'ā-ī, Heb. *sallay*). 1. Chief of a family of Benjamites who lived at Jerusalem (Neh. 11:8).

2. The name of a priestly family (Neh. 12:20), called "Sallu" in verse 7.

SALLU (See Sallai)

SALMA (săl'mà, Heb. *salmā', strength*), a son of Caleb, son of Hur, and father of Bethlehem (I Chron. 2:51; 2:54).

SALMON (săl'mŏn, Heb. *salmôn, clothing*), the father of Boaz the husband of Ruth, and grandfather of Jesse, father of David (Ruth 4:20,21; I Chron. 2:11; Matt. 1:4,5; Luke 3:32).

SALMONE (săl-mō'nē, Gr. *Salmóne*), a promontory forming the E extremity of the isle of Crete. Paul sailed near it on his way to Rome (Acts 27: 7). It is now known as Cape Sidero.

SALOME (sà-lō'mē, Gr. *Salóme*, fem. of Solomon). 1. The wife of Zebedee, and mother of James and John (cf. Matt. 27:56 with Mark 15:40; 16:1). She was one of the women who companied with Jesus in Galilee to minister to Him (Mark 15:40, 41). She was present at the crucifixion of Jesus, and was among those who at Easter morning came to the tomb to anoint the dead body of their Lord (Mark 16:1).

2. The daughter of Herodias, and the grandniece of Herod Antipas, whose dancing before Herod pleased him so much that as a reward she obtained the head of John the Baptist (Matt. 14:3-11; Mark 6:17-28). Her name is not given in the Gospels. For her name see Jos. *Antiq.* xviii. 5,4.

SALT was used in ancient times, as it is today, for seasoning and preserving food. Salt of a poor quality was found in great abundance on the shore of the Dead Sea, where it was gathered after the salty water had evaporated. It was also cut from the neighboring salt cliffs. On the sea coast the inhabitants filled holes in rocks with sea water and then collected the salt when the water had evaporated. In the N part of Palestine salt was probably purchased from Phoenician traders. Salt was also used as an antiseptic in medicine. Newborn babies were always bathed and rubbed with salt (Ezek. 16:4). The law required the use of salt with offerings of all kinds (Lev. 2:13; Ezek. 43:24). Sometimes captured cities were doomed to utter destruction by sowing the ground with salt. Abimelech did this to Shechem (Judg. 9:45). In Numbers 18:19 and II Chronicles 13:5 a "covenant of salt" is mentioned. To this day it is true among the Arabs that to eat of a person's salt, or to partake of his hospitality, is regarded as a token of amity and brings one under his protection. In Scripture the word salt is often used in a figurative sense. It typifies barrenness and sterility (Deut. 29:23; Jer. 17:6). Jesus calls His true disciples "the salt of the earth" (Matt. 5:13; Mark 9:50; Luke 14:34). Salt is used to describe wholesome character and speech (Mark 9:50; Col. 4:6). James says it is as incongruous for the same mouth to utter blessings and cursings as for a fountain to yield both sweet and salt water (James 3:11). (See Minerals)   S.B.

SALT, CITY OF, a city in the wilderness of Judah, not far from the Dead Sea. It is mentioned as being between Nibshan and Engedi (Josh. 15:62). Its exact site is uncertain.

SALT, COVENANT OF, a covenant of permanent and perpetual obligation. Since salt was a necessary part of the daily diet, and salt was always used in sacrifices to Jehovah (Lev. 2:13), it was not long before men saw a connection between salt and covenant making. To "eat salt with" a person meant to share his hospitality. When covenants were made, they were usually confirmed with sacrificial meals, and salt was always present. Numbers 18:19 says that offerings to Jehovah were to be "a covenant of salt for ever before Jehovah."

SALT SEA (See Dead Sea)

SALT, VALLEY OF, a valley in which great victories were won over the Edomites, first by the army of David (II Sam. 8:13), and later by Amaziah, king of Judah (II Kings 14:7; II Chron. 25:11). It was between Jerusalem and Edom, but its exact site is uncertain.

SALU (sā′lū, Heb. *sālû′*), a prince of the tribe of Simeon, and the father of Zimri who was slain by Phinehas (Num. 25:14; I Macc. 2:26).

SALUTATION (săl-ū-tā′shŭn, Gr. *aspasmós*), a greeting given either orally (Luke 1:29,41,44) or in writing (I Cor. 16:21; Col. 4:18; II Thess. 3:17). Greetings in the Bible sometimes included acts as well as words: a profound obeisance or prostration, a kissing of the hand, kneeling, falling upon the neck of another, embracings. Every situation in life had its own salutation: the return of a friend from a journey, the birth of a son, a marriage, wearing new clothes, dining, the appeals of a beggar, etc. Among the more common salutations on meeting were the following: "Blessed be thou of the Lord" (Gen. 43:29); "The Lord be with thee" (Ruth 2:4); "Peace be unto thee" (Luke 24:36); "Hail!" (Matt. 26:49). Monarchs were saluted with the words, "Let the king live for ever" (I Kings 1:31; Neh. 2:3). The Pharisees especially liked salutations in public places (Matt. 23:7; Mark 12:38). Because salutations were usually so time-consuming, when Jesus sent out the Seventy, He forbade salutations by the way (Luke 10:4). Salutations were given at partings as well as at

meetings. "Go in peace," or "Farewell" (I Sam. 1:17; 20:42; II Sam. 15:9; Mark 5:34). Epistolary salutations were more brief and direct. The salutations of Paul's epistles are usually elaborate and of rich spiritual fulness.   S.B.

SALVATION (săl-vā′shŭn, Heb. *yeshû′âh*, Gr. *sotérion*). In the Bible the word "salvation" is not necessarily a technical theological term, but simply denotes "deliverance" from almost any kind of evil, whether material or spiritual. Theologically, however, it denotes (1) the whole process by which man is delivered from all that interferes with the enjoyment of God's highest blessings, (2) the actual enjoyment of those blessings.

The root idea in salvation is *deliverance* from some danger or evil. This deliverance may be from defeat in battle (Exod. 15:2), trouble (Ps. 34:6), enemies (II Sam. 3:10), violence (II Sam. 22:3), reproach (Ps. 57:3), exile (Ps. 106:47), death (Ps. 6:4), sin (Ezek. 36:29). The outstanding instance of divine salvation in the early history of Israel was the deliverance from Egypt. Since it is God who provides the deliverance, He is often spoken of as Saviour (Isa. 43:3,11; Jer. 14:8), a title which in the NT is usually applied to Jesus Christ. In the OT salvation is at first thought of as deliverance from present evil in a temporal and material sense, but with the deepening sense of moral evil, salvation acquires a profound ethical meaning. At first the conception of salvation is primarily national, but gradually the prophetic horizon broadens and salvation is seen to include Gentiles as well as Jews (Isa. 49:5,6; 55:1-5). There is also increasing stress upon the individual. Salvation is not necessarily for the nation as a whole, but for the righteous remnant. It includes, moreover, deliverance from sin itself as well as from the various evils which are the consequence of sin (Ps. 51; Jer. 31:31-34; Ezek. 36:25-29). With the development of the Messianic idea the word salvation comes to be used in the technical theological sense of the deliverance, especially from sin, to be brought in with the Messianic age.

In the OT, complete trust in God was the most important of the human conditions for salvation. Next in importance, and following naturally from the first, was obedience to God's moral law as expressed in the various codes of law. God, however, was not satisfied with a mere legalistic fulfilment of the letter of the law. Forgiveness of sins was conditioned upon repentance. Most sins also required a ritual sacrifice as part of the act of repentance.

In the teaching of Jesus, salvation is often used to denote deliverance from trouble, like illness (Matt. 9:22), but it usually means deliverance from sin through entrance upon a new divine life. It is a present experience, although its complete fulfilment is eschatological. To the Pharisees of His day, salvation was a reward given to the man who perfectly lived up to the requirements of the law; but Jesus says that He came to seek the lost (Luke 19:10) and that salvation is through faith in Him, the incarnate Son of God (John 3:16).

The central theme of the entire apostolic age is the salvation brought by Jesus. Salvation is represented primarily as deliverance from sin. The whole NT lays stress upon the sufferings and death of Christ as mediating salvation (Eph. 2:13-18). As in the teaching of Jesus, salvation throughout the NT is regarded as a present experience, but it is eschatological as well. Indeed, the blessings of salvation the believer has now are only a foretaste of what are to be his in the coming age, after Christ

A first glimpse of the city of Samaria, from the Shechem road. © MPS

comes. The salvation Christ brings is not merely deliverance from future punishment, but also from sin as a present power (Rom. 6). It includes all the redemptive blessings we have in Christ, chiefly conversion, regeneration, justification, adoption, sanctification, and glorification. It provides a solution for the whole problem of sin, in all its many aspects. Through union with Christ, the believer has died to sin (Rom. 6:2), has crucified the flesh — or corrupt human nature (Gal. 5:24), and has become a new creature (II Cor. 5:17). He is free from the law (Rom. 6:14; 7:6) and has exchanged the bondage of its requirements for the freedom of the new man in Christ (Col. 2:14; Gal. 5:1,13, 18). The reception of the deliverance is made possible by faith, which involves not mere mental assent to certain doctrinal propositions, but repentance and whole-hearted commitment to Christ as Saviour and Lord (Rom. 3:28; Eph. 2:8). On the divine side, the ultimate cause of salvation is the divine mercy. It is entirely undeserved, and is by God's grace alone. So far as the possibility of receiving it is concerned, salvation is available to all men (John 3:16; I Tim. 4:10). In some sense, the doctrine of salvation extends beyond man so as to affect the universe. Eventually all things are to be subjected unto the Son (I Cor. 15:28), and all things in heaven and on earth will be summed up in Christ (Eph. 1:10). No foe will remain to dispute Christ's authority or in any way mar the glories of His eternal kingdom. Even the physical universe will be redeemed.

See also ADOPTION, CONVERSION, JUSTIFICATION, REGENERATION, SANCTIFICATION. S.B.

SAMARIA (sà-mâr'ĭ-à, Heb. shōmerôn, Gr. Samáreia). The country of Samaria occupied a rough square of some 40 miles N and S by 35 E and W. It was the territory occupied by the ten tribes led by Jeroboam, extending roughly from Bethel to Dan, and from the Mediterranean to Syria and Ammon. The frontiers are somewhat blurred, whether a geographical or a political definition is attempted. Sir George Adam Smith, after careful geographical and historical analysis, concludes: ". . . the southern frontier of Samaria gradually receded from the Vale of Ajalon to the Wady Isher and 'Akrabbeh. The northern was more fixed, and lay from the Mediterranean to Jordan, along the S edge of Esdraelon, by the foot of Carmel and Gilboa. If Carmel is shut off, the edge of Sharon may be taken as the western boundary; the eastern was Jordan . . ." (*Historical Geography of the Holy Land*, pp. 324, 325. Pp. 249-256 for detailed description). The earliest name for this section of the Palestinian uplands was Mount Ephraim (Josh. 17:15; 19:50; Judg. 3:27; 4:5 etc).

Viewed from the sea, the area does, in fact, present the appearance of a unit, a compact "massif." The western flank, generally poor country, falls away from the summits in a slope more gradual than that of the Judaean highlands. Access is easy, and little history gathered round slopes so indefensible and sterile. Over the divide, the one conspicuous pass is that in which Shechem lies, between Mounts Ebal and Gerizim. It crosses the range and merges into a valley swinging S to Jordan, dividing the eastern flank of Mount Ephraim into two portions, a close-piled bulwark of high country to the S, and an open series of broad valleys to the N. "Plains, meadows, and spacious vales" (Sir George Adam Smith, *op. cit.* p. 327) are a remarkable feature within this highland mass, providing both gentle access ("the out-goings of Mount Ephraim" of Josh. 17:18), and secluded pasture-lands within. Hence the trend of Samaria's history. The country was too open for successful defense. Hence, too, the frequency with which the chariot is mentioned in the annals of the northern kingdom, and the ease with which surrounding paganism poured into the life of the northern tribes.

It will be convenient to deal with the major centers of the land separately:

1. Shechem. Samaria is the "heart-land" of Palestine, and Shechem the geographical center of the whole country, and the hub of early Israelite history. Shechem lay in a fertile vale between Ebal and Gerizim, near modern Nablus (i.e. Neapolis, or New Town, Vespasian's foundation to replace the shattered Jewish town). It was the favorite pasturage of the patriarchs (Gen. 12:6; 33:18,19; 37:12,13), whither Joseph's bones were later borne (Josh. 24:32). There are few details in the record of the Hebrew infiltration of this area. Events ran true to the geography of the land, and the Canaanites offered little active resistance. Two opposing amphitheaters across the vale of Shechem were the scene of the great assemblies of Joshua 8 and 24. Judges 9 gives a vivid impression of the fertility of the valley. Its abundant food and verdure are woven with the grim story of Gideon's son. Shechem was the obvious site of the capital, after the lamentable division of the land, but Shechem was no fortress, as Jeroboam soon decided. He removed the royal seat to Tirzah (I Kings 14:17), a policy maintained by his immediate successors (I Kings 15:33; 16:6). The next usurper, Omri, who was a competent soldier, was not satisfied, and chose the site of Samaria.

Two views of the land of Samaria. At left, the Plain of the Maidens, near Shiloh (Judges 21:19-21). At right, looking north from Mount Gerizim, looking toward ancient Shechem, at left, Sychar in upper center, and Jacob's Well at right. Jacob's Well was the scene of Christ's conversation with the woman of Samaria. © MPS

2. . Samaria. It is sometimes a matter of difficulty in reading the later chapters of the records of the Kings, and some passages in the prophets, to decide whether Samaria refers to the land, or to Omri's foundation. In the NT it is sometimes equally difficult to decide. Luke 17:11 and John 4:4 refer to the district. In Acts 8:5-25 either meaning is possible, and Moffatt's rendering of vs. 5, "a town in Samaria," is quite legitimate. Samaria, or Shomeron, meant "Watch Tower," and so Omri intended his fortress to be. It commanded a wide prospect, and lay back from the center of the land towards the sea, a feature favored by a dynasty which made much of its Phoenician alliance. It took the Assyrians three years (723 to 721 B.C.) to reduce the fortress. Ahab and Jezebel, his Phoenician bride, established in Samaria a tradition of luxury, vice, and paganism, against which Amos, Micah, Isaiah, and Hosea raised their protest. The Assyrian conquest brought the utter doom which the prophets had predicted. The inhabitants were deported in mass to Assyria, and the dismantled stronghold repopulated by Assyrian settlers brought in to replace them. In 331 B.C., after a punitive massacre by Alexander the Great, a body of Macedonian colonists were also introduced. As Samaria had fitted the Phoenician policy

of Ahab, so too it was conveniently situated for the pro-Roman activities of Herod. As a place of residence it was conveniently linked with the port of Caesarea, which Herod built. The town of Sebaste, however, Herod's foundation, occupied only a portion of the eastern part of Samaria's ancient site. Here Herod married and murdered Mariamne, and sent to death his two sons.

3. Sychar and Jacob's Well. Until the middle of the last century (e.g. Dean Alford in his Greek Testament), Sychar of John 4:5 was commonly identified with Shechem. More recent opinion favors the Arab village of El-Askar. Smith devotes Chapter XVIII of his monumental work to the vexed question. It is impossible to be quite certain of the locality of either Sychar or the Well. The tradition of the Well is not OT, and the present cluttered site has no stronger claim to authenticity than many of the other holy places of Palestine.

4. Shiloh. This is probably the Arab village of Seilun 12 miles S of Shechem. Judges 21:19 pinpoints the place, and if Lebonah is indeed the modern Lubbar, the site of Shiloh is identified with some certainty. The locality appears as a sacred site for the "tent of meeting" in Joshua 18:1,9,10; Judges 21:19. The religious function of Shiloh was

At left, ruins of the old city gate of Samaria (II Kings 7:18). At right, ruins of the Grand Colonnade. © MPS

Amid the excavations at Bethel, walls of a house dating back to the time of Joshua. © MPS

preserved for some three to four centuries (I Sam. 4:4). Samuel served as a child at Shiloh, and it is notable that the "tent of meeting" had become by his time a permanent building (I Sam. 1:9; 3:15). The disaster and discredit which fell on Eli's family may have led to the abandonment of Shiloh as a religious center. At any rate it ceased to function thus about this time, and Psalm 78:60-62 and Jeremiah 7:12,14 may indicate that the Philistines overran it.

Bethel. This town, on the southern frontier of the district of Samaria, was a famous religious locality. It is mentioned 65 times in Scripture. It was the scene of Jacob's dream, the imagery of which may have been based on accounts of a Sumerian ziggurat, and to which Christ obliquely refers in John 1:51. Bethel was already a sanctuary when the land was divided, and Jeroboam used it as a holy place to displace the religious authority of Jerusalem. Here the king set up one of his golden calves, and established his idolatrous priesthood (I Kings 12:28). First an unnamed prophet from Judah (I Kings 13:1-3), and then the fiery Amos, attacked this worship. Hosea also spoke against the Bethel cult, and the prophecies of all three were fulfilled when Josiah of Judah destroyed the pagan altars (II Kings 23:15,16). The southern locality of Bethel, on an unstable frontier, made it peculiarly susceptible to such a punitive invasion. Amos 8 indicates that Bethel was a busy market-town, a function likely to develop at the junction of several important highways. Bethel is a few miles from Ai, and since archeological investigations have established the fact that Ai was destroyed about 2200 B.C., while Bethel provides much evidence of destruction in Joshua's time, it has been plausibly suggested that Bethel bore the name Ai at the time of the invasion. The Troas of the NT and ancient Troy are much further apart. E.M.B.

SAMARITAN PENTATEUCH (See Samaritans)

SAMARITANS (sà-măr'ĭ-tăns, Heb. *shōmerōnîm,* Gr. *Samareítai*). The word may signify, according to context: (1) the inhabitants of Samaria (the region rather than the town; *e.g.* II Kings 17:26; Matthew 10:5; Luke 9:52; 10:33; 17:16; John 4:9,30,40; Acts 8:25); (2) the sect which derived its name from Samaria, a term of contempt with

the Jews (John 8:48); (3) since the seventeenth century, "a good Samaritan" (Luke 10:33) has signified a generous benefactor.

Racially the Samaritans are difficult to identify. In 721 B.C. Sargon of Assyria destroyed Samaria. On the walls of the royal palace at Dur-Sarraku (Khorsabad), he recorded the fact, and his subsequent policy of depopulation, deportation, and reestablishment: "In my first year of reign . . . the people of Samaria . . . to the number of 27,290 I carried away . . . The city I rebuilt — I made it greater than it was before. People of lands which I had conquered I settled therein. My tartan I placed over them as governor." It seems clear that the policy of deportation applied particularly to Samaria as a city and not as a region. Jeremiah 41:5 for example, seems to imply that a remnant of true Israelites remained in Shechem, Shiloh, and Samaria a century later; so a substratum, or admixture, of the Hebrew stock in the later composite population must be assumed. The newcomers from the N may be presumed to have intermarried with the Israelite remnant, and ultimately the population took the general name of Samaritans.

The completeness of the devastation left by the Assyrian invasion is evident from the infestation by wild beasts of which the immigrants complained (II Kings 17). Superstitiously, the intruders concluded that "the god of the land" was angry at their presence and their ignorance of His propitiatory rites. They sent to the Assyrian monarch and asked him to select a priest from among the deportees to instruct them in the necessary ritual of worship. The king (it was Esarhaddon) acceded to the request, and some instruction in the faith of Jehovah penetrated the stricken district. It was a mixed religion which resulted. "They feared Jehovah," we read, "and served their own gods." Josiah's reforms crossed the border at Bethel, and seem to have extended into the northern districts. There was little indeed, to prevent their infiltration. Religious revival was not the sort of military penetration which invited Assyrian attention (II Kings 23:15; II Chronicles 34:6,7). The measure of purification, which may be presumed to have taken place in the Samaritan religion about this time, did not, however, reconcile Samaritan and Jew racially.

A Samaritan chief priest leads his congregation in prayer during a Samaritan Passover Feast on Mount Gerizim. © MPS

A Samaritan chief priest with an ancient scroll, in the Samaritan synagogue, Shechem. © MPS

After the return from captivity, enmity became inveterate between the Samaritans and the Jewish remnant of Ezra and Nehemiah. On the strength of their worship of Jehovah "since the days of Esarhaddon" (Ezra 4:2), the Samaritans sought a share in the rebuilding of the temple in Jerusalem, but were firmly rebuffed, hence the policy of obstruction from Sanballat of Samaria which was a serious hindrance to Nehemiah's work (Neh. 2:10,19; 4,6). Sanballat's son-in-law was Manasseh, grandson of the Jewish high-priest, and Nehemiah's drive for racial purity led to the expulsion of this young man from Jerusalem. By his emigration with a considerable band of dissident Jews to Samaria, the rift between the peoples, politically and religiously, was made permanent. Manasseh persuaded the Samaritans, according to tradition, to abandon many of their idolatrous practices, and with Sanballat's building on Mount Gerizim of a schismatic temple for his son-in-law, the sect of the Samaritans was established. It was from this time too, that Samaria became a refuge for malcontent Jews, with the consequent use of "Samaritan" as a term of abuse for a dissident rebel (John 8:48). John Hyrcanus destroyed the temple on Gerizim along with the city in 109 B.C. When Herod provided another temple in 25 B.C., the Samaritans refused to use it, continuing to worship on the mount (John 4:20,21).

Founded as it was before the rise of the great prophetic tradition, the religion of the Samaritans was based on the Pentateuch alone. Their position was held with some firmness, and Josephus mentions a disputation before Ptolemy Philometor on the question which the Samaritan woman poses in John 4:20, which resulted in the death, according to the rules of the debate, of the defeated Samaritan advocates. Christ's firm answer (*loc. cit. vss.* 21-23) stressed the incompleteness of the Samaritan tradition, its inadequate revelation, and the common transience of the cherished beliefs of both Samaritan and Jew. The greatness of Christ is shown in the story, for at no time had the bitterness between Samaritan and Jew been greater. At one Passover during the governorship of Coponius (A.D. 6-9), when, according to annual custom, the gates of the temple were opened at midnight, some Samaritans had intruded and polluted the holy place by scattering human bones in the porches. Samaritans were thereafter excluded from the services (Jos., *Antiq.* 18:2:2). They were cursed in the temple. Their food was considered unclean, even as swine's flesh. The whole situation narrated in John 4 is therefore remarkable, the buying of food in Sychar, the conversation at Jacob's Well, and the subsequent evangelization of the area. (See also Acts 8:5-25). It is a magnificent illustration of the emancipation which Christianity was to bring to those grown immobile in the bondage of Judaistic prejudice.   E.M.B.

SAMGARNEBO (săm′gȧr-nēb′bō, Heb. *samgarnevô, be gracious, Nebo*), one of Nebuchadnezzar's chief army officers who entered Jerusalem (Jer. 39:3).

SAMLAH (săm′là, Heb. *samlâh, a garment*), one of the kings of Edom. He was a native of Masrekah, and reigned before the Israelites had kings (Gen. 36:36,37; I Chron. 1:47,48).

SAMOS (sā′mŏs, Gr. *Sámos, height),* an island off western Asia Minor colonized by Ionians in the 11th century B.C., notable for metal-work, woollen products, and probably utility pottery, though it is not certain that "Samian ware" necessarily implied a large native industry of this sort. Samos joined the Ionian revolt but was treated generously by the Persians, fought for Xerxes at Salamis, but later joined the Athenian confederacy. With typical fickleness she deserted this, and the revolt was crushed by Pericles himself (441 B.C.). Thenceforward cooperation was loyal, and the Samians were given the citizenship by a grateful Athens after Aegospotami in 405 B.C. Samos was occupied by Lysander in the next year and regained by Athens only in 365 B.C. Samos produced the moralists and poets Aesop, Ibycus, and Anacreon, and the astronomer Conon. Paul touched at Samos on his last voyage to Jerusalem (Acts 20:15).
          E.M.B.

SAMOTHRACE (săm′ō-thrās, Gr. *Samothráke, Samos of Thrake),* an island in the NE Aegean, mountainous and rising to over 5,000 feet. Its population was Samian, and it was associated with the Athenian maritime confederacies. Samothrace was the home of the mystery cult of the Cabiri, twin gods of Phrygian or Phoenician origin, which was in wide vogue during the Hellenistic age, and included Roman notables among its initiates. Paul called here on his first voyage to Europe (Acts 16:11).

SAMSON (săm′sŭn, Heb. *shimshôn,* probably *little sun,* Gr. *Sampsón,* Lat. and Eng. *Samson),* one of the judges of Israel, perhaps the last before Samuel. The story of his life is told in Judges 13-16. He was an Israelite of the tribe of Dan, the son of Manoah.

Zorah, where he was born, was about half way between Jerusalem and the Mediterranean, along the coast of which the Philistines lived. His birth was announced by the angel of the Lord beforehand to his mother, who was barren. The angel told her that she would have a son, that this son should be a Nazirite from his birth, and that the Lord should begin to use him to deliver Israel out of the hand of the Philistines. Nazirites were under special vow to God to restrain their carnal nature, thus showing the people generally that if they would receive God's blessing they must deny and govern themselves and be faithful to their vows of consecration as God's covenant people. The preternatural strength that Samson exhibited at various times in his career was not his because he was a natural giant, but because the Spirit of the Lord came upon him to accomplish great deeds.

At the time of his birth the Israelites had been in bondage to the Philistines for 40 years because they had done evil in the sight of the Lord. After his birth "the child grew, and the Lord blessed him. And the Spirit of the Lord began to move him at times in the camp of Dan between Zorah and Eshtaol" (Judg. 13:24,25). But almost from the beginning of his career he showed one conspicuous weakness, which was ultimately to wreck him: he was a slave to passion. He insisted, against the objections of his parents, on marrying a Philistine woman of Timnath, which was not far from Zorah. At the wedding feast he propounded to the guests a riddle, wagering that if they guessed it he would give them 30 changes of raiment. By threatening the life of his bride, they compelled her to obtain the answer from him. When he found he had been tricked, in revenge he killed 30 Philistines of Askelon and gave his guests their garments, thus fulfilling his wager. He went home without his wife, giving the impression that he had forsaken her. When, later, he returned to her, he found that her father had given her in marriage to someone else, and was offered her sister in her stead. In revenge, Samson caught 300 jackals, and sent them into the Philistine fields of corn in pairs with burning torches tied between their tails. The Philistines retaliated by burning his wife and her father.

This act of vengeance only provoked another and a greater from himself. He smote them hip and thigh with a great slaughter, and took up his abode on the top of a rock called Etam. The Philistines invaded Judah and demanded the surrender of their arch-enemy. Samson agreed to allow the Israelites to deliver him into the hands of the Philistines, but on the way he broke the cords that bound him, and seizing the jawbone of an ass he killed with it 1,000 men. With this great feat Samson clearly established his title to the position of a judge in Israel. The historian says in this connection, "And he judged Israel in the days of the Philistines twenty years" (Judg. 15:20). The expression "in the days of the Philistines" implies that the ascendancy of the Philistines was not destroyed but only kept in check by the prowess of Samson.

Samson next went down to Gaza, a Philistine stronghold, and yielded to the solicitations of a harlot. When it became known that he was in the city, the Philistines laid a trap for him; but at midnight Samson arose, took the doors of the gate of the city, and the two posts, and carried them a quarter of a mile to the top of the hill before Hebron. God in His mercy continued to give him supernatural strength notwithstanding his evil actions.

Continuing his life of vicious self-indulgence, Samson before long became enamored of another Philistine woman, named Delilah, through whom he lost his physical power. The Philistine leaders bribed her with a large sum of money to betray him into their hands. By their direction she begged him to tell her in what his great strength lay. Three times he gave her deceitful answers, but at last he gave in to her importunities and revealed that if only his hair were cut he would be like other men. She lulled him into a profound sleep; his hair was cut; and when he awoke and heard her derisive cry, "The Philistines be upon thee Samson," he found that, not merely his strength, but also God had departed from him. Now at the mercy of his

The so-called Cave of Samson, at the Rock Etam. © MPS

enemies, he was bound with chains, his eyes were put out, and he was sent to grind in the prisonhouse of Gaza.

How long Samson continued in this state of shameful bondage is unknown — perhaps some weeks or even months. On the occasion of a great feast to the God Dagon, his captors resolved to make sport of him by making him play the buffoon before the assembled multitude. The temple of Dagon was filled with people — with 3,000 on the roof to watch the sport. Meanwhile, his hair had grown again, and with his returning strength he longed to be avenged on his enemies for at least one of his two blinded eyes (Judg. 16:28). He asked the lad who attended him to allow him to rest between the two pillars on which the building was supported. Taking hold of them, he prayed that God would help him once more; and with a mighty effort he moved the pillars from their position and brought down the roof, burying with himself a large number of Philistines in its ruins. In this dying act he slew more than he had slain in his life.

With all of his failings he is listed with the heroes of faith in Hebrews 11 (vs 32). By faith in God's gift and calling, he received strength to do the wonders he performed. In his life too often animal passion ruled. He was without real self-control; and accordingly he wrought no permanent deliverance for Israel.   S.B.

SAMUEL (săm'ū-ĕl, Heb. *shemû'ēl, name of God,* or *his name is El*; some grammarians prefer a derivation from *yishma' ' El, God hears;* others associate the name with *sha'al, to ask,* on the basis of I Sam. 1:20). Samuel is often called the last of the judges (cf. I Sam. 7:6,15-17) and the first of the prophets (3:20; Acts 3:24; 13:20). He was the son of Elkanah and Hannah, of Ramathaimzophim in the hill country of Ephraim. The account of the events associated with the birth of Samuel indicates that his parents were a devoted and devout couple. Hannah's childlessness led her to pour out her complaint and supplication to God in bitterness of heart; but she trusted God to provide the answer and promised to give to the Lord the son she had requested. When Samuel was born, she kept her promise; as soon as the child was weaned she took him to Shiloh and presented him to Eli. Then she praised the Lord in prayer (usually called her "Song," 2:1-10). Samuel grew up in the Lord's house and ministered to the Lord (2:11; 3:1) and each year when his parents came to sacrifice at Shiloh, his mother brought a little robe for Samuel. Spiritually and morally, the times were bad. The sons of Eli were unworthy representatives of the priestly office. In their greed they violated the laws of offering (2:12-17); they also engaged in immoral acts with the women who served at the entrance of the tent of meeting (2:22). Though Eli remonstrated with them, he was not firm enough and the Lord declared that He would punish him (2:27-36).

Under such circumstances there was little communion with God, but the Lord called to Samuel in the night and revealed to him the impending doom of Eli's house. The Lord blessed Samuel and "let none of his words fall to the ground" (2:19), so that all Israel knew that Samuel was a prophet of the Lord. Eli died upon receiving the news of the death of his sons and the capture of the Ark of the Covenant in a Philistine victory over Israel. Some time after the return of the Ark to Israel, Samuel challenged the people to put away foreign gods and to serve the Lord only (7:3). When the Philistines threatened the Israelite gathering at Mizpah, Samuel interceded for Israel and the Lord answered with thunder against the enemy. The Philistines were routed and Samuel set up a memorial stone which he called Ebenezer ("Stone of help," 7:12).

Samuel, judge and priest, made his home at Ramah, where he administered justice and also built an altar. He went on circuit to Bethel, Gilgal, and Mizpah (7:15). In his old age he appointed his sons, Joel and Abijah (cf. I Chron. 6:28), as judges in Beersheba, but the people protested that his sons did not walk in his ways but took bribes and perverted justice. The people requested a king to rule them, "like all the nations" (8:6). Samuel was displeased by their demand, but the Lord told him to grant their request and to warn them concerning the ways of a king. Samuel was now brought into acquaintance with Saul the son of Kish, who was searching for his father's lost asses. About to give up, Saul was encouraged by his servant to confer with Samuel, of whom he said, "There is a man of God in this city, and he is a man that is held in honor; all that he says comes true" (9:6 RSV). In I Samuel 9, Samuel is called a "seer" (ro'eh) rather than a "prophet" (nabi'), "for he who is now called a prophet was formerly called a seer" (vs. 9). God had revealed to Samuel that Saul was to come to see him; at the conclusion of this first meeting, Samuel secretly anointed Saul as king (10:1) and foretold some confirmatory signs, which came to pass as predicted (10:1-13). Samuel then called an assembly of Israel at Mizpah and the choice of Saul was confirmed by lot. Samuel related to the people the rights and duties of a king and wrote these in a scroll which was placed in the sanctuary (lit., "before the Lord," 10:25). After Saul's victory over the Ammonites, Samuel again convened Israel and Saul's kingship was confirmed at Gilgal. Samuel was now advanced in years and retired from public life in favor of the king. In his address to Israel he reviewed the Lord's

dealings with them and reminded them of their duty to serve God. He called on the Lord to bear witness to the words of His prophet by sending a thunderstorm, though it was the season of wheat harvest. The Lord sent the storm, and "all the people greatly feared the Lord and Samuel" (12:18). They requested Samuel to intercede for them and he replied with a significant statement on responsibility and intercession.

Samuel next appears in conflict with Saul; a national crisis had arisen with a Philistine threat and Saul summoned the people to Gilgal. When Samuel was late in coming to make offerings, Saul presumed to make them himself. Samuel accused Saul of foolishness and disobedience and said that Saul's kingdom would not continue. Samuel then went to Gibeah and Saul engaged in a victorious battle with the Philistines. After Saul's success, Samuel commissioned him to annihilate the Amalekites (chap. 15). In this expedition Saul again showed incomplete obedience; Samuel reminded him of the necessity of absolute obedience and told him God had rejected him to remain as king. This was the last official meeting of Samuel and Saul (15:35); Samuel returned to Ramah and grieved over Saul. The Lord appointed Samuel to serve again as "kingmaker" and sent him to Bethlehem to anoint the young shepherd, David, as Saul's successor (cf. I Chron. 11:3). Later, in flight from Saul, David took refuge on one occasion with Samuel in Naioth of Ramah (19:18), where Samuel was head of a group of prophets. When Saul came after David, the Spirit of God came upon Saul and he prophesied before Samuel (19:23-24). II Chronicles provides additional information concerning Samuel's part in the organization and conduct of the service of God. David and Samuel installed the gatekeepers of the tent of meeting (I Chron. 9:22). Samuel also dedicated gifts for the house of the Lord (I Chron. 26:28). Samuel was diligent in the Lord's service and it is noted that he kept the feast of the passover in a memorable way (II Chron. 35:18). Samuel was also a writer (cf. I Sam. 10:25); he is credited with "the Chronicles of Samuel the Seer" (I Chron. 29:29). Jewish tradition also ascribed to him the writing of the Biblical books which bear his name. Samuel died while Saul was still king and was buried by solemn assembly of the people at Ramah (I Sam. 25:1).

Samuel's last message to Saul came upon the occasion of Saul's recourse to the spirit-medium of Endor on the eve of Saul's death on Mt. Gilboa. Samuel is mentioned in several other OT books and is recognized as a man of prayer. In Psalm 99:6 it is said that he was "among those who called on His name." The intercession of Samuel is cited in Jeremiah 15:1. In the NT he is referred to by Peter (Acts 3:24) as one who foretold the events of NT times; Paul mentions him in a sermon at Antioch of Pisidia (Acts 13:20). In Hebrews 11:32 he is listed among those whose faith pleased God.

From the standpoint of modern research, a number of the places named in the OT in connection with Samuel have been identified and some have been excavated. Among those at which archaeological work has been done are Shiloh (Tell Seilun), Mizpah (Tell en-Nasbeh?), Gibeah (Tell el Ful), and Bethel (Beitin). Tradition also associates with Samuel the site called Nebi Samwil ("prophet Samuel"), which has also been suggested as the site of Mizpah.   C.E.D.

Fragments of a scroll of the Book of Samuel found among the Dead Sea Scrolls. PAM

SAMUEL, BOOKS OF. The books are named after Samuel, the outstanding figure of the early section. Originally there was only one book of Samuel, but the LXX divided it into two. The division was followed by the Latin versions and made its appearance in the Hebrew text in Daniel Bomberg's first edition (1516-1517). In the LXX the books of Samuel and the books of Kings are called I-IV "Books of Kingdoms"; the Vulgate numbers them similarly but names them "Books of Kings." The title Samuel, which appears in Hebrew manuscripts, is followed in most English translations.

Authorship and date. There is little external or internal evidence as to the authorship of Samuel. Jewish tradition ascribes the work to the Prophet Samuel: "Samuel wrote the book which bears his name and the Book of Judges and Ruth" (*Baba Bathra*, 14b), but it also raised the problem relating to Samuel's death, which is recorded in I Samuel 25:1. All of the events of I Samuel 25-31 and II Samuel occurred after Samuel's death. The statement of I Samuel 27:6, "Ziklag has belonged to the kings of Judah to this day" (RSV), is taken by some to demand a date in the divided kingdom; others insist that this need not be later than the end of the reign of David. Samuel was a writer and certainly his writing was used in the composition of these books. I Chronicles 29:29 refers to "the Chronicles of Samuel the seer," "the Chronicles of Nathan the prophet," and "the Chronicles of Gad the seer." Since David's death is not included in our books of Samuel, it has been thought probable that they were written before that event. Another suggestion is that some Judean prophet wrote the books shortly after the division of the kingdom, writing by inspiration and using sources such as those mentioned above. By liberal scholars, Samuel is regarded as a composite of at least two sources, early and late, similar to the so-called J and E sources of the Pentateuch. The earlier is dated to Solomonic times and centers around Saul and David; the later, of the eighth century, deals with Samuel; their union is assigned to a date about a century after that. O. Eissfeldt isolates three sources, which he labels L, J, and E. This division into "documents" stands on traditional

liberal bases: duplicates, contradictions, and differences in style and viewpoint. For detailed discussion, one must refer to the books on introduction and to the commentaries. In general it may be noted that alleged duplicates are records of separate but similar events, of the same incident from different viewpoints, or of references to previously recorded happenings. Supposed contradictions may often be harmonized by close examination of the text and context. Differences in style and point of view need not indicate multiple authorship, but may reflect various purposes in the writing of a single author. As usual in theories of composite authorship, the redactor or editor must bear a heavy load of mixed credit and blame. Positively, the unity of Samuel is attested by the following: (1) the orderly and consistent plan of the work; (2) the interrelations of parts of the books, as noted by Driver; (3) uniformity of language throughout. The unity of II Samuel is generally recognized. Additional light on the text of Samuel may be supplied by the Qumran materials.

Content. Outline (after Pfeiffer). (1) Shiloh and Samuel, I Samuel 1:1-7:1; (2) Samuel and Saul, 7:2-15:35; (3) Saul and David, I Samuel 16-31; II Samuel 1; (4) David as king of Judah, II Samuel 2-4; (5) David as king of all Israel, II Samuel 5-24. 1. The book begins with Hannah's distress, her supplication, and the answer in the form of Samuel's birth. The song of Hannah shows relationships to both the Magnificat (Luke 1:46-55) and the prophecy of Zechariah (Luke 1:68-79). Samuel's childhood was spent at Shiloh; here the Lord spoke to him and revealed the future of the priestly line of Eli. The battle with the Philistines resulted in a Philistine victory, the capture of the ark, and the death of Eli. A source of trouble in Philistia, the ark was sent back to Israel. 2. When the people requested a king, Samuel remonstrated with them but was directed by the Lord to grant their request. Saul was brought to Samuel and secretly anointed as king. This selection was later confirmed by lot at an assembly of all Israel at Mizpah. Saul's first impressive act, the rescue of Jabesh-Gilead from the besieging Ammonites, led to his confirmation as king of Gilgal. Samuel now retired from active public life (chap. 12) though he continued to serve as adviser to the king. Incomplete obedience brought about Saul's rejection from the kingship. 3. The youthful David was designated as Saul's successor and secretly anointed by Samuel. David became Saul's court musician and later served king and country well by slaying Goliath in single combat. On this occasion Saul inquired concerning David's family, so that Jesse too could be rewarded (cf. 17:24). David now became a close friend of Jonathan, Saul's son, but Saul was now both jealous and afraid of David, and his hostility soon produced open attempts upon David's life. David was forced to flee, and the pursuit by Saul, though intermittent, was not concluded until the Philistines swept the Israelites before them on Mt. Gilboa and Saul and his sons perished. David mourned their passing in an eloquent elegy (II Sam. 1). 4. David reigned as king of Judah in Hebron for 7½ years. Overtures were made to unite all Israel under his leadership. 5. These efforts were crowned with success and David wisely took Jerusalem and made it his new capital, for since it had been in Jebusite hands it had had no definite affiliation with Judah or the northern tribes. David continued to build the kingdom and the Lord announced to him the perpetuity of his dynasty (II Sam. 7). Though David conquered his enemies and was gracious to Jonathan's son, he was overcome by temptation in the idleness of semi-retirement. The affair with Bathsheba led to bitter heartache and also to sincere repentance on the part of the king. Circumstances in the royal family brought about the rebellion of Absalom, which again saw David in flight for his life. The killing of Absalom ended the revolt but increased David's sorrow. Restored to Jerusalem, David had to deal promptly with the short-lived revolt of Sheba. II Samuel ends with a summary of battles with the Philistines, David's praise of the Lord (chap. 22; 23:2-7), the listing of his mighty men, and the catastrophe of the census (chap. 24).

Purpose. The purpose of all OT history is clearly stated in the NT (Rom. 15:4; I Cor. 10:11): to serve as warning, instruction, and encouragement. More specifically, the books of Samuel present the establishment of the kingship in Israel. In preserving the account of Samuel, the judge and prophet, the books mark the transition from judgeship to monarchy, since Samuel filled the prophetic office and administered the divine induction into office of Israel's first two kings.   C.E.D.

SANBALLAT (săn-băl'ăt, Heb. *sanvallat*, Assyr. *Sin-uballit, the god Sin has given life*), a Horonite; that is, a man of Beth-horon. He was a very influential Samaritan who tried unsuccessfully to defeat Nehemiah's plans for rebuilding the walls of Jerusalem (Neh. 4:1ff). He then plotted with others to invite Nehemiah to a conference at Ono in order to assassinate him, but Nehemiah saw through his stratagem and refused to come. When this device failed, he tried vainly to intimidate the Jewish governor (Neh. 6:5-14). Sanballat's daughter married into the family of Eliashib, the high priest at the time of the annulment of the mixed marriages forbidden by the Law (Neh. 13:28), but her husband refused to forsake her, and went with her to Shechem, where he became the high priest of a new temple built by his father-in-law on Gerizim. Sanballat's name is mentioned in some interesting papyri letters found at the end of the 19th century in Egypt. He was then the governor of Samaria.

SANCTIFICATION (săngk-tĭ-fĭ-kā'shŭn, Gr. *hagiasmós*, a *separation, setting apart*). While the noun does not occur in the OT, the verb "to sanctify" (Heb. *qādhash*), appears frequently. Its meaning is not primarily ethical but formal, its fundamental force being to separate from the world and consecrate to God. To sanctify anything is to declare that it belongs to God. It may refer to persons, places, days and seasons, and objects used for worship. Among objects sanctified to Jehovah in the OT are the first-born of Israel (Exod. 13:2), the Levites (Num. 3:12), the priests and the tent of meeting (Exod. 29:44), the altar (Exod. 29:36), the offering (Exod. 29:27), the Sabbath (Neh. 13:19-22), the nation of Israel as a whole (Exod. 19:5,6), a man's house or his field (Lev. 27:14, 16). To sanctify Jehovah means to put Him in a category by Himself, to acknowledge Him as God, to recognize Him as supreme, sovereign, with a unique claim on all of His creation. When Christ sanctifies Himself (John 17:19), He means that He consecrates Himself to His mediatorial work as Redeemer. The word "saint" comes from the same root and means "a sanctified one" — one who belongs to Christ. This formal meaning appears in I Corinthians 7:12-14, where the unbelieving husband is said to be sanctified by the wife, meaning not that he is different in moral character, but stands in a certain privileged relation to God.

In an ethical sense sanctification means the progressive conformation of the believer into the image of Christ, or the process by which the life is made morally holy. The transformation of the believer's life and character follows naturally from his consecration to a God who is morally perfect. Now that we belong to Christ we are to live to Him (Eph. 4:1; Col. 3:1-4; I Thess. 5:10). God has made a twofold provision for the believer's sanctification: the redemptive work of Christ and the work of the indwelling Holy Spirit. Sanctification has its beginning when a person becomes a Christian. God then, in regeneration, implants a new life in man, and gives to him the Holy Spirit, who makes real in his experience that for which Christ died for him at Calvary. It is in Romans 6-8 that we have the most extended teaching in the Bible on the ground and experimental outworking of sanctification. In a sense it is a gift, as is every part of salvation, but it must be daily appropriated through the moral surrender of our life to God. It is not momentary and instantaneous, but a life-long process, completed only when we see Christ. See HOLINESS.   S.B.

SANCTUARY (săngk'tū-â-rē, Heb. *miqdāsh*, Gr. *hágion, holy place*), refers almost exclusively to the tabernacle or temple. God's sanctuary was His established earthly abode, the place where He chose to dwell among His people. Psalm 114:2 says that "Judah was his sanctuary, and Israel his dominion." God Himself is a sanctuary for His people (Isa. 8:14; Ezek. 11:19). The word is used particularly of the holy of holies, whether of the tabernacle or temple. When it is used in the plural, it usually denotes idolatrous shrines, or high places, which Israelites who compromised with heathenism sometimes built (Amos 7:9). A sanctuary was also a place of asylum, the horns of the altar especially being regarded as inviolable (cf. I Kings 2:28f). In the NT the word is used only in the Epistle to the Hebrews (8:2; 9:1,2; 13:11), where the author makes clear that the earthly sanctuary was only a type of the true sanctuary which is in heaven, of which Christ is the high priest, and in which He offers Himself as a sacrifice (Heb. 10:1-18).   S.B.

SAND (Heb. *hôl*, Gr. *ámmos*), a rock material formed of loose grains of small size formed as the result of weathering and decomposition of various kinds of rocks. It is found in abundance in deserts, in the sea, and on the shores of large bodies of water. The writers of the Bible were very familiar with it, and they often refer to it as a symbol of (1) numberlessness, vastness, (2) weight, (3) instability. The descendants of Abraham were numberless (Gen. 22:17; Jer. 33:22; Rom. 9:27; Heb. 11:12); as were also the enemies of Israel (Josh. 11:4; Judg. 7:12; I Sam. 13:5). Joseph accumulated grain as the sand of the sea (Gen. 41:49). God gave to Solomon understanding and largeness of heart as the sand on the seashore (I Kings 4:29). The thoughts of God, says the Psalmist, "are more in number than the sand" (Ps. 139:18). Job says that if his grief were weighed it would be heavier than the sand of the sea (Job 6:3). A house built on sand symbolizes a life not built on the teachings of Jesus (Matt. 7:26).

SANDAL (See Dress)

SANHEDRIM, SANHEDRIN (săn'hē-drĭm, săn'hē-drĭn, Talmudic Heb. transcription of the Gr. *synédrion, a council*), the highest Jewish tribunal during the Greek and Roman periods, often mentioned in the NT, where the Greek name is always in the

English version translated "council." The Talmud connects the Sanhedrin with Moses' 70 elders, then with the alleged Great Synagogue of Ezra's time; but the truth is that the origin of the Sanhedrin is unknown, and there is no historical evidence for its existence before the Greek period. During the reign of the Hellenistic kings Palestine was practically under home rule, and was governed by an aristocratic council of elders which was presided over by the hereditary high priest. The council was called *Gerousia*, which always signifies an aristocratic body. This later developed into the Sanhedrin. During most of the Roman period the internal government of the country was practically in its hands, and its influence was recognized even in the Diaspora (Acts 9:2; 22:5; 26:12). After the death of Herod the Great, however, during the reign of Archelaus and the Roman procurators, the civil authority of the Sanhedrin was probably restricted to Judaea proper, which is very likely the reason why it had no judicial authority over our Lord so long as He remained in Galilee. The Sanhedrin was abolished after the destruction of Jerusalem (A.D. 70). A new court was indeed established bearing the name "Sanhedrin," but it differed in essential features from the older body. It had no political authority, and was composed exclusively of rabbis, whose decisions had only a theoretical importance.

The Sanhedrin was composed of 70 members, plus the president, who was the high priest. Nothing is known as to the way in which vacancies were filled. The members probably held office for life, and successors were very likely appointed either by the existing members themselves or by the supreme political authorities (Herod and the Romans). Since only pure-blooded Jews were eligible for the office of judge in a criminal court, the same principle was probably followed in the case of the Sanhedrin. New members were formally admitted by the ceremony of the laying on of hands.

The members of the Sanhedrin were drawn from the three classes named in Matthew 16:21; 27:41; Mark 8:31; 11:27; 14:43,53; 15:1; Luke 9:22; 22:26: "the chief priests, with the scribes and the elders." By the chief priests is meant the acting high priest, those who had been high priests, and members of the privileged families from which the high priests were taken. The sacerdotal aristocracy were the leading persons in the community, and they were the chief members of the Sanhedrin. The scribes formed the Pharisaic element in the Sanhedrin, although not all Pharisees were professional scribes. The elders were the tribal and family heads of the people and priesthood. They were, for the most part, the secular nobility of Jerusalem. The president bore the honorable title of "prince." Besides the president, there were also a vice-president, called the "head or father of the house of judgment"; and another important official, whose business it was, in all probability, to assist in the declaration of the law. There were also two or three secretaries, and other subordinate officials, of which "constables" (Matt. 5:25) and "servants of the high priest" (Matt. 26:51; Mark 14:47; John 18:10) are mentioned in the NT. According to Josephus, in the time of Christ the Sanhedrin was formally led by the Sadducean high priests, but practically ruled by the Pharisees, who were immensely popular with the people (*Ant.* XVIII,1.4). The Pharisees were more and more represented in the Sanhedrin as they grew in importance.

A hearing before the Sanhedrin. © SPF

In the time of Christ the Sanhedrin exercised not only civil jurisdiction, according to Jewish law, but also, in some degree, criminal. It could deal with all those judicial matters and measures of an administrative character which could not be competently handled by lower courts, or which the Roman procurator had not specially reserved for himself. It was the final court of appeal for all questions connected with the Mosaic law. It could order arrests by its own officers of justice (Matt. 26:47; Mark 14:43; Acts 4:3; 5:17f; 9:2). It was also the final court of appeal from all inferior courts. It alone had the right of judging in matters affecting a whole tribe, of determining questions of peace or war, of trying the high priest or one of its own body. It pronounced upon the claims of prophets and upon charges of blasphemy. The king himself could be summoned to its bar; and Josephus relates that even Herod did not dare to disobey its summons (*Ant.* xiv.9.4). It had the right of capital punishment until about 40 years before the destruction of Jerusalem. After that it could still pass, but it could not execute, a sentence of death without the confirmation of the Roman procurator. That is why our Lord had to be tried not only before the Sanhedrin but also before Pilate (John 18:31,32). But for this, He would have been put to death in some other way than by crucifixion, for crucifixion was not a Jewish mode of punishment. The stoning of Stephen (Acts 7:57f) without the approval of the procurator was an illegal act — a lynching. In the case of one offense the Sanhedrin could put to death, on its own authority, even a Roman citizen, namely, when a Gentile passed the gate which divided the court of the Jews from that of the Gentiles (cf. Acts 21:28), but even this was subject to the procurator's revision of the capital sentence. The Roman authority was, however, always absolute, and the procurator or the tribune of the garrison could direct the Sanhedrin to investigate some matter, and could remove a prisoner from its jurisdiction, as was done in the case of Paul (Acts 22:30; 23:23f).

The Sanhedrin at first met in "the hall of hewn stones," one of the buildings connected with the temple. Later, the place of meeting was somewhere in the court of the Gentiles, although they were not confined to it. They could meet on any day except the Sabbath and holy days, and they met from the time of the offering of the daily morning sacrifice till that of the evening sacrifice. The meetings were conducted according to strict rules and were enlivened by stirring debates. Twenty-three members formed a quorum. While a bare majority might acquit, a majority of two was necessary to secure condemnation, although if all 71 members were present, a majority of one was decisive on either side. To avoid any hasty condemnation, where life was involved judgment was passed the same day only when it was a judgment of acquittal. If it was a judgment of condemnation, it might not be passed till the day after. For this reason, cases involving capital punishment were not tried on a Friday or on any day before a feast. A herald went before the condemned one as he was led to execution, and cried out: "So-and-so has been found guilty of death. If anyone knows anything to clear him, let him come forward and declare it."

S.B.

The tomb of Sarah in the Cave of Machpelah mosque in Hebron. © MPS

SANSANNAH (săn-săn'à, Heb. *sansannâh, a palm branch*), a town in the S of Judah (Josh. 15:31), identical with Hazar-susah, a town of Simeon (Josh. 19:5), and almost certainly the same as Hazar-susim (I Chron. 4:31). The site is not exactly identified.

SAPH (săf, Heb. *saph, a basin, threshold*), a Philistine giant, one of the four champions of the race of Rapha who was slain by one of David's heroes (II Sam. 21:18; I Chron. 20:4).

SAPHIR (sā'fẽr, Heb. *shāphîr, glittering*), one of a group of towns mentioned in Micah 1:10-15, which, because of its association with Gath, Achzib (of Judah), and Mareshah, was most likely in SW Palestine.

SAPPHIRA (să-fī'rà, *shappîrā', an Aramaic word meaning *beautiful*), the wife of Ananias who with her husband was struck dead because they both lied to God (Acts 5:1-10).

SAPPHIRE (See Minerals)

SARA, SARAH, SARAI (sâr'à, Heb. *sāray, sārâh,* Gr. *Sára. Sárah* means *princess;* the meaning of Sarai is doubtful). 1. The wife of Abraham, first mentioned in Genesis 11:29. She was ten years younger than Abraham, and was married to him in Ur of the Chaldees (Gen. 11:29-31). According to Genesis 20:12, she was Abraham's half-sister, the daughter of his father, but not of his mother. Marriage with half-sisters was not uncommon in ancient times. Her name was originally Sarai. She was about 65 years old when Abraham left Ur for Haran. Later, she accompanied Abraham into Egypt, and was there passed off by him as his sister because he feared the Egyptians might

kill him if they knew she was his wife. Years later, Abraham did the same thing at the court of Abimelech, king of Gerar (Gen. 20:1-18). In each instance grievous wrong was averted only by God's intervention, and Abraham was rebuked by the pagan rulers for his lack of candor. Still childless at the age of 75, she induced Abraham to take her handmaid Hagar as a concubine. According to the laws of the time, a son born of this woman would be regarded as the son and heir of Abraham and Sarah. When Hagar conceived, she treated her mistress with such insolence that Sarah drove her from the house. Hagar, however, returned at God's behest, submitted herself to her mistress, and gave birth to Ishmael. Afterward, when Sarai was about 90, God promised her a son; her name was changed to Sarah; and a year later, Isaac, the child of promise, was born (Gen. 17:15-27). It was during this period that Abraham almost brought upon himself dishonor and ruin by lying about Sarah to Abimelech, king of Gerar. A few years later, at a great feast celebrating the weaning of Isaac, Sarah observed Ishmael mocking her son, and peremptorily demanded the expulsion of Hagar and Ishmael (Gen. 21). Abraham reluctantly acceded, after God had instructed him to do so. Sarah died at Kiriath-arba (Hebron) at the age of 127, and was buried in the cave of Machpelah, which Abraham purchased as a family sepulchre (Gen. 23:1,2). Sarah is mentioned again in the OT only in Isaiah 51:2, where she is referred to as the mother of the chosen race. In the NT she is mentioned in Romans 4:19; 9:9; Galatians 4:21-5:1; Hebrews 11:11; and I Peter 3:6.

2. The daughter of Raguel, the wife of Tobias (Tobit 3:7,17).

S.B.

SARAPH (sā'răf, Heb. *sărāph, noble one*), a descendant of Judah. At one time he was a ruler in Moab (I Chron. 4:22).

SARDINE (See Mineral)

SARDIS (sàr'dĭs, Gr. *Sárdeis*), the chief city of Lydia, under a fortified spur of Mount Tmolus in the Hermus valley, near the junction of the roads from central Asia Minor, Ephesus, Smyrna, and Pergamum, capital of Lydia under Croesus, and seat of the governor after the Persian conquest. Sardis was famous for arts and crafts, and was the first center to mint gold and silver coinage. So wealthy were the Lydian kings, that Croesus became a legend for riches, and it was said that the sands of the Pactolus were golden. Croesus also became a legend for pride and presumptuous arrogance, when his attack on Persia led to the fall of Sardis and the eclipse of his kingdom. The capture of the great citadel by surprise attack by Cyrus and his Persians in 549 B.C., and three centuries later by the Romans, may have provided the imagery for John's warning in Revelation 3:3. The great earthquake of A.D. 17 ruined Sardis physically and financially. The Romans contributed 10,-000,000 sesterces in relief, an indication of the damage done, but the city never recovered.

Standing pillars of ruins of great temple of Artemis at Sardis. At left, a small Christian church. SHH

SARDITE (sàr'dīt), a name given to the descendants of Sered (Gen. 46:14; Num. 26:26).

SARDIUS, SARDONYX (See Minerals)

SAREPTA (sà-rĕp'tà, Gr. *Sárepta*), the name in Luke 4:26 (KJV) for the town of Zarephath, where Elijah lived with a widow and her son (I Kings 17:9,10). The RSV renders it Zarephath.

A relief portrait of Sargon II of Assyria, in stone, eight feet high, found at Khorsabad. BM

SARGON (sàr'gŏn, Heb. *sargôn, the constituted king*). 1. **Sargon I** was a famous king of early Babylon who founded an empire which extended to the Mediterranean (2400 B.C.). He is not referred to in the Bible. The story is told that he (like Moses) had been put by his mother into an ark of bulrushes in the river, there to be rescued, in the case of Sargon, by Akki the irrigator.

2. **Sargon II** (722-705 B.C.) was an Assyrian king who is mentioned by name in the Bible only in Isaiah 20:1. He was a usurper, perhaps of royal blood. Shalmaneser V, his predecessor, besieged Samaria in 724 B.C. During the siege Shalmaneser died (722), and in 721 the city fell to Sargon. It is strange that the Bible does not mention him in the story of Samaria's fall (II Kings 17:1-6). Some authorities believe that Sargon did not become king until after the city fell. However, Sargon claims to have captured Samaria, and a certain ambiguity in II Kings 17:6 allows for a new, although unnamed, Assyrian monarch there.

Above, excavation of Sargon's throne room at Khorsabad. Below, the base of Sargon's throne. OIUC

Soon after Sargon came to the throne, the Babylonians, assisted by the Elamites, revolted against him and were with difficulty subdued. According to Sargon's inscriptions the remnant of the Israelites at Samaria, who had been put under an Assyrian governor, revolted, along with other Syrian and Palestinian provinces (720 B.C.). This revolt Sargon quickly suppressed. At this time he also defeated the Egyptian ruler So, who had come to the aid of rebelling Gaza (II Kings 17:4).

Later Sargon captured Carchemish, the great Hittite city (717 B.C.), thus precipitating the fall of the Hittite empire. He also mentions placing Arab tribes as colonists in Samaria. Sargon claims on his inscriptions to have subdued Judah. Evidently Judah became more or less involved in a rebellion against Assyria, led by Ashdod. This Philistine city was captured by the Assyrians and reorganized as an Assyrian province (711 B.C.; cf. Isa. 20:1), and Judah was subdued but not harmed. Hezekiah was later to revolt against Sargon's son Sennacherib.

Sargon built a new palace and royal city ten miles NE of Nineveh, which he called Dur-sharrukin (Sargonsburg), the ruins of which are called Khorsabad. He was murdered in 705 B.C. and succeeded by his son Sennacherib.   J.B.G.

SARID (sā'rĭd, Heb. *sārîdh, survivor*), a village on the boundary of Zebulun (Josh. 19:10,12), probably modern Tell Shadud, N of Megiddo.

SARON (See Sharon)

SARSECHIM (sàr'sē-kĭm, Heb. *sarsekhîm*), one of Nebuchadnezzar's princes who entered Jerusalem when it fell (Jer. 39:3). The name is difficult to identify. Many scholars believe that it (together with the Nebo of the previous word) represents Nebushazban (cf. Jer. 39:13), a good Babylonian name. This person's title was Rabmag (i.e., a court official).

SARUCH (See Serug)

SATAN (sā'tăn, Heb. *sātān*, Gr. *Satán* or *Satanás, an adversary*), the chief of the fallen spirits, the grand adversary of God and man. Without the article the Heb. word is used in a general sense to denote some one who is an opponent, an adversary; thus, the angel who stood in Balaam's way (Num. 22:22); David as a possible opponent in battle (I Sam. 29:4); a political adversary (I Kings 11:14). With the definite article prefixed it is a proper noun in Job 1-2, Zechariah 3:1-2, designating Satan as a personality. In Psalm 109:6 the article is lacking, and reference may be to a human adversary (cf. ASV "an adversary"), but it is generally conceded that in I Chronicles 21:1 the word is a proper name without the article. The teaching concerning evil and a personal devil finds its full presentation only in the NT. In the NT the term Satan, transliterated from the Heb., always designates the personal Satan (but cf. Matt. 16:23; Mark 8:33). This malignant foe is known in the NT by a number of other names and descriptive designations. He is frequently called "the devil" (Gr. *diábolos*), meaning the slanderer (Matt. 4:1; Luke 4:2; John 8:44; Eph. 6:11; Rev. 12:12; etc.). ("Devils" in KJV and ERV is properly "demons"). Other titles or descriptive designations applied to him are "Abaddon" or "Apollyon" (Rev. 9:11); "Accuser of the brethren" (Rev. 12:10); "Adversary," Gr. *antídikos* (I Pet. 5:8); "Beelzebub" (Matt. 12: 24); "Belial" (II Cor. 6:15); "the deceiver of the whole world" (Rev. 12:9); "the great dragon" (Rev. 12:9); "the evil one" (Matt. 13:19,38; I John 2:13; 5:19); "the father of lies" (John 8: 44); "the god of this world" (II Cor. 4:4); "a murderer" (John 8:44); "the old serpent" (Rev. 12:9); "the prince of this world" (John 12:31; 14: 30); "the prince of the powers of the air" (Eph. 2:2); "the tempter" (Matt. 4:5; I Thess. 3:5).

These varied designations indicate the dignity and character of Satan. In the book of Job he is pictured as mixing with the sons of God (angels) in their appearing before God, although by his moral nature not one of them. Jude 9 pictures him as a formidable foe to Michael the archangel. While clearly very powerful and clever, he is not an independent rival of God but is definitely subordinate, able to go only as far as God permits (Job 1:12; 2:6; Luke 22:31). Christ gives a fundamental description of his moral nature in calling him "the evil one" (Matt. 13:19,38). Moral evil is his basic attribute; he is the very embodiment of evil. Christ's words in John 8:44 give the fullest statement of Satan's moral character: "He was a murderer from the beginning, and abode not in the truth, because there is no truth in him. When he speaketh a lie, he speaketh of his own: for he is a liar, and the father of it." I John 3:8 asserts that "the devil sinneth from the beginning." As a murderer, liar, sinner, evil is the very environment and inherent nature of the devil.

The origin of Satan is not explicitly asserted in Scripture, but the statement that he "abode not in the truth" (John 8:44) implies that he is a fallen being, while I Timothy 3:6 indicates that he fell under God's condemnation due to ambitious pride. While many theologians refuse to apply the far-reaching prophecies in Isaiah 14:12-14 and Ezekiel 28:12-15 to Satan, contending that these passages are strictly addressed to the kings of Babylon and Tyre respectively, conservative scholars generally hold that they contain a clear revelation of Satan's origin. These profound prophecies seem clearly to go much beyond any earthly ruler and harmonize with the scriptural picture of Satan's close relations with world governments (Dan. 10:13; Eph. 6:12; John 12:31). These passages picture Satan's pre-fall splendor as well as his apostasy through pride and self-exaltation against God. A consuming passion of Satan is to be worshiped (Matt. 4:9; Isa. 14:14; Rev. 13:4,15; I Cor. 10:20). In his fall Satan drew a vast number of lesser celestial creatures with him (Rev. 12:4).

Satan is the ruler of a powerful kingdom standing in opposition to the kingdom of God (Matt. 12:26; Luke 11:18). He exercises authority in two different realms. He is the head of a vast, compact organization of spirit-beings, "his angels" (Matt. 25:41). As "the prince of the power of the air" (Eph. 2:2), he skillfully directs an organized host of wicked spirits in the heavenlies who do his bidding (Eph. 6:12). Acts 10:38 makes it clear that the outburst of demonic activities during the ministry of Jesus was Satan-inspired. Satan is not omnipresent, but through his subordinates he makes his influence practically world-wide. He also exercises domination over the world of lost humanity. He is "the prince of this world" (John 12:31; 14:30; 16:11), the evil world-system which he has organized upon his own principles (II Cor. 4:3-4; Col. 1:13; I John 2:15-17). That "the whole world lieth in the evil one" (I John 5:19 ASV) indicates that the world is in the grip of and passively yielded to the power of the devil. This power over men he holds by virtue of usurpation.

Animated by an unrelenting hatred against God and all goodness, Satan is engaged in a world-wide and age-long struggle against God, ever seeking to defeat the divine plans of grace toward mankind and to seduce men to evil and their ruin. As "the deceiver of the whole world" (Rev. 12:9), his primary method is that of deception — about himself, his purpose, his activities, his coming defeat. Satan was the seducer of Adam and Eve (Gen. 3:1-7; II Cor. 11:3); he insinuated to God that Job served Him only for what he got out of it (Job 1:9); he stood up against Israel (I Chron. 21:1) and God's high priest (Zech. 3:1-2). Under divinely imposed limitations he may be instrumental in causing physical affliction or financial loss (Job 1:11-22; 2:4-7; Luke 13:16; II Cor. 12:7). He snatches away the Word of God sown in the hearts of the unsaved (Matt. 13:19), sows his counterfeit Christians among the sons of the kingdom (Matt. 13:25, 38-39), blinds the minds of men to the Gospel (II Cor. 4:3-4), and induces them to accept his lie (II Thess. 2:9-10). Often he transforms himself into "an angel of light" by presenting his apostles of falsehood as messengers of truth (II Cor. 11:13-15). He clashes in fierce conflict with the saints (Eph. 6:11-18), is ever alert to attempt to destroy them (I Pet. 5:8), and hinders the work of God's servants (I Thess. 2:18). Certain members of the church who were expelled are said to have been delivered to Satan, but with the design to produce their reformation, not their destruction (I Cor. 5:5; I Tim. 1:20).

Although Satan was judged in the cross (John 13:31-33), he is still permitted to carry on the conflict, often with startling success. But his revealed doom is sure. He now has a sphere of activities in the heavenlies (Eph. 6:12); he will be cast down to the earth and will cause great woe because of his wrath, which he will exercise through "the beast" (Rev. 12:7-12; 13:2-8; II Thess. 2:9). With Christ's return to earth he will be incarcerated in the bottomless pit for 1000 years; when again released for a season he will again attempt to deceive the nations but will be cast into the "lake of fire,"

prepared for him and his angels (Matt 25:41), to suffer eternal doom with those he deceived (Rev. 20:1-3, 7-10). D.E.H.

SATRAP (sā′trăp), the official title of the viceroy who in the Persian empire ruled several small provinces combined as one government. Each of these provinces had its own governor. In Ezra 8:36 and Esther 3:12 the term is translated *lieutenants* in KJV, but *satraps* in RSV. In Daniel 3:2; 6:1, the KJV renders it *princes;* the RSV, *satraps.*

SATYR (sāt′ẽr), a word that represents the Hebrew word *sā'ir* which is used to describe the wild animals or demons which should dance among the ruins of Babylon (Isa. 13:21, quoted in Rev. 18:2) and of the Edomite cities (Isa. 34:14). In Leviticus 17:7 and II Chronicles 11:15 (RSV) it denotes an object of idolatrous worship.

SAUL (sôl, Heb. *shā'ûl, asked of God*), the first king of Israel, a son of Kish, of the tribe of Benjamin, a handsome man a head taller than his fellow Israelites. He is introduced in I Samuel 9, after the people had requested Samuel for a king (chap. 8). Saul and Samuel met for the first time when Saul was searching for some lost asses of his father. Greeted by Samuel with compliments, Saul replied with becoming humility (9:21; cf. Judges 6:15). Before Saul left, Samuel secretly anointed him as king of Israel, as the Lord had directed. God gave Saul a changed heart (10:9) and Saul prophesied among a group of prophets who met him on his way home.

The choice of Saul as king was confirmed by lot at an assembly of Israel convened by Samuel at Mizpah, but the bashful young man was in hiding and had to be brought before the people. In spite of his manly appearance he was ridiculed by some riffraff, "but he held his peace" (10:27). His forbearance was supplemented by compassion and decision in his rescue of Jabesh-Gilead from the threat of the Ammonites (chap. 11). The lowly nature of the young kingdom is demonstrated by the fact that the king earned his livelihood as a dirt-farmer. When the message arrived from the besieged city, Saul was returning from the field behind the oxen (11:5). The king's summons to the people, in the form of pieces of a dismembered yoke of oxen, galvanized Israel into a unified response (11:7; cf. Judges 19:29).

After the deliverance of the city, Saul showed his generosity by insisting that his earlier detractors should not be punished. A military crisis with the Philistines revealed flaws in the character of Saul. When Samuel delayed in coming to make offering before battle, Saul presumed to present the offering himself. He thus showed himself to be only a superficially spiritual individual and attempted to justify his behavior with hollow excuses. For this action the kingdom was to be taken from him (13:13-14). On the human side, we are reminded of the pressure of the situation: the great superiority of the Philistines in number (13:5), attitude (13:6-7), and equipment (13:19-23). The Philistines had a monopoly of the metal industry; they limited smiths to Philistine territory and charged the Israelites high rates for the sharpening of tools. At the time of battle only Saul and Jonathan among the Israelites had sword or spear. The Philistines were routed in spite of Saul's bad judgment in denying food to the Israelites at a time when they most needed strength. Saul fought valiantly and successfully against all the enemies of Israel (14:47-48); though he was a brave leader he was not a good soldier, for he was not aware of the necessity of absolute obedience. The affair of the Amalekites, though a military success, was a spiritual failure; covetousness led to incomplete obedience and again Saul tried to vindicate himself by lies and religious excuses which Samuel set aside with the significant statement on the importance of obedience (15:22). Saul then returned to his house in "Gibeah of Saul," marked by the modern Tell el Ful, "the mound of the beans." Excavation has revealed the fortress-palace of Saul; of modest size, it was built with the practical strength and utility of casemate walls.

David enters the narrative in I Samuel 16; he was anointed by Samuel as future king and was introduced to court life by appointment as court musician to play the lyre for Saul when the king was tormented by an evil spirit. After David defeated Goliath, David was again presented before Saul and was heralded by the women of Israel as a greater hero than Saul. Jealousy, hatred, and fear led Saul to direct and indirect attempts against David's life (18:10-11; 18:21; 19:1,11) and resulted in the hide-and-seek chase which twice drove David into Philistine territory (21:10; 27:1 ff.). The unsuspecting aid given to David by the priests of Nob moved Saul to slaughter the priests and to annihilate the city (22:17-19). Saul's life was spared by David on two occasions, at Engedi (24:1-7) and in the wilderness of Ziph (26:6-12). The eve of Saul's final battle found the king consulting the witch of Endor and receiving from the deceased prophet Samuel the message of his fate. The next day Saul and his sons died in the battle on Mt. Gilboa. The Philistines decapitated Saul and took his remains to Bethshan, where they placed his armor in the temple of Ashtaroth (I Sam. 31:10), his head in the temple of Dagon (I Chron. 10:10), and his body on the city-wall. Excavation at this site (Tell el Husn) showed two temples of this period. The N. temple was identified by a hieroglyphic inscription as the temple of 'Antit ('Anat), which is a form of Astarte or Ashtaroth. The S. temple had no identification but probably is the "house of Dagon." The men of Jabesh-Gilead remembered Saul's concern for them; in gratitude they recovered his body and the bodies of his sons from the walls of Bethshan, gave them honorable burial at Jabesh, and fasted in mourning. David also, when he heard the report, went into mourning and expressed his grief in the elegy of II Samuel 1:19-27.　　　　　C.E.D.

The ruin mound at Bethshan. © MPS

SAVIOUR (sāv'yôr, Gr. *sotér, saviour, deliverer, preserver*), one who saves, delivers, or preserves from any evil or danger, whether physical or spiritual, temporal or eternal. A basic OT concept is that "God is the deliverer of His people"; it is emphatically declared that man cannot save himself and that Jehovah alone is the Saviour (Ps. 44.3,7; Isa. 43:11; 45:21; 60:16; Jer. 14:8; Hos. 13:4). The Heb. term rendered "saviour" is a participle, rather than a noun, indicating that the Hebrews did not think of this as an official title of God but rather as a descriptive term of His activity. In the OT the term is not applied to the Messiah; He receives salvation from God (Ps. 28:8; 144:10; II Sam. 22:51), but He comes to offer salvation to all (Zech. 9:9; Isa. 49:6,8; etc.). The term is also applied to men who are used as the instruments of God's deliverance (Judg. 3:9, 15 ASV; II Kings 13:5; Neh. 9:27; Obad. 21).

The Greeks applied the title *sotér* (Saviour) to their gods; it was also used of philosophers (e.g., Epicurus), or rulers (e.g. Ptolemy I; Nero), or men who had conferred signal benefits upon their country. But in the NT it is a strictly religious term and is never applied to a mere man. It is used of both God the Father and Christ the Son. God the Father is Saviour, for He is the author of our salvation which He provided through Christ (Luke 1:47; I Tim. 1:1; 2:3; 4:10; Titus 1:3; 2:10; 3:4; Jude 25). Saviour is pre-eminently the title of the Son (Titus 1:4; 2:13; 3:6; II Tim. 1:10; II Pet. 1:1,11; 2:20; 3:2,18; I John 4:10). At His birth the angel announced Him as "a Saviour, who is Christ the Lord" (Luke 2:11). His mission to save His people from their sins was announced before His birth (Matt. 1:21) and was stated by Jesus as the aim of His coming (Luke 19:10). The salvation which He wrought is for all mankind and He is "the Saviour of the world" (I John 4:14; John 4:42). Those who are saved are brought into a spiritual union with Christ as members of His body, hence He is called "the Saviour of the body" (i.e., the Church) (Eph. 5:23). In Titus 2:10 it is implied that Christian salvation extends also to the ethical ephere, since "the doctrine of God our Saviour" is urged as an incentive to holy living. Believers await a future work of Christ as Saviour when He shall come again to consummate our salvation in the transformation of our bodies (Phil. 3:20).　　　　　D.E.H.

SAVOR, SAVOUR (sā'vôr, Heb. *rēah*, Gr. *osmé*), the translation of Hebrew and Greek words meaning *taste* (Matt. 5:13, Luke 14:34) or, more often, *smell*, whether stench (Joel 2:20) or a pleasant smell. In the latter case it is in the OT usually qualified by the word sweet, and is used to refer to a sacrifice which God was pleased to accept. Thus, "The Lord smelled the sweet savor" (Gen. 8:21, cf. Num. 15:3). In the NT the word is used metaphorically to refer to the incense burnt in a victor's triumphal procession (II Cor. 2:14), to Christ's obedience to God (Eph. 5:2), or to the Christian's sacrifice of obedience to God (II Cor. 2:15, Phil. 4:18).

SAVORY MEAT, the meals made by Jacob and Esau for their father Isaac prior to receiving his blessing. They are called savory food in the RSV (Gen. 27:4,9,14,17,31). Meat in the KJV frequently means the more general term food. Said to have been made of venison (game, RSV, Gen. 27:3), this meal was a favorite of Isaac's (27:4), and thus a fitting preparation for his giving the blessing.

SAW. Probably the earliest saws were made of flint, with serrated edges, mounted in a frame. Other saws were like knives, of bronze or iron. Small handsaws were like ours today, but the teeth were shaped in the other direction, so that the worker did not shove, but pulled against the wood. Large western handsaws were unknown in Bible times. Palestinian carpenters probably sat on the floor and held the wood between their toes, which became as skillful as extra hands.

Stone was sawed as well as wood (I Kings 7:9). Saws used in the construction of the pyramids and other great buildings of Egypt were made of bronze and had one handle. The Assyrians used a double-handled saw. When Scripture says that David put his war captives "under saws" (II Sam. 12:31, cf. I Chron. 20:3), it probably means that "he set them to labor with saws" (RSV).

Hebrews 11:37 speaks of martyrs who were "sawn asunder." Jewish tradition (in the *Martyrdom of Isaiah,* a pseudepigraphical book) states that the prophet Isaiah was sawn asunder by a wooden saw by Manasseh. Perhaps the reference in Hebrews is to this event.   J.B.G.

SCAB (See Diseases, Skin)

SCAFFOLD (Heb. *kiyyôr*). Solomon knelt on a "brazen scaffold" when he dedicated the temple (II Chron. 6:13). The RSV translates the expression "a bronze platform."

SCALE. 1. Only fish having fins and scales were permitted as food for the Hebrews (Lev. 11:9-12). The Greek word *lepís* means *rind, husk, flake* and is used to describe St. Paul's recovery from temporary blindness: "There fell from his eyes as it were scales, and he received his sight" (Acts 9:18). Probably literal scales are not meant.

2. Scales as an instrument for weighing are referred to in Isaiah 40:12 and Proverbs 16:11 (balance, KJV). A simple balance is here meant. The weights used in these scales were, obviously, handmade and never uniform, hence the constant temptation to use "divers weights . . . and a false balance" (Prov. 20:23).

SCALL (See Diseases, Skin)

SCAPEGOAT (Heb. *'ăzā'zēl*), a term that occurs only in Leviticus 16:8,10,26 and has been interpreted quite variously. It is used to refer to the second of two goats for which lots were cast on the Day of Atonement. The first was sacrificed as a sin offering (16:9), but the second "for the scapegoat" (16:26) had the people's sins transferred to it by prayer and imposition of hands, and was then taken into the wilderness.

The Hebrew term translated *scapegoat* is thought to be related to an Arabic word meaning *remove;* thus it is often translated *removal* (i.e., scapegoat). The actual meaning of the term and its use in the context of Leviticus 16 are very uncertain.

Some authorities regard the term to be the name of the solitary place to which the goat was taken. This does not seem very likely. Others (as KJV) regard it as a qualifying word for goat — i.e., the goat which removes the guilt of the people, the scapegoat. Some scholars see in the word the name of a personal being — a demon of the wilderness or a fallen angel who seduces men to evil (as in the *Book of Enoch*), or an epithet applied to the devil.

A parallel to the scapegoat may be seen in the Scriptures. In the ritual for a recovered leper, the living bird was released in the country to carry the evil away and the leper declared clean (Lev. 14:6). In the Babylonian New Year's day festival a similar rite was practiced, when a slain sheep was taken away and thrown into the river, its bearers being regarded as unclean (cf. Lev. 16:26). Certainly the general idea of the scapegoat is clear: guilty Israel's sin had been removed and forgotten by God.   J.B.G.

SCARLET. The Hebrew and Greek words usually translated scarlet in the Bible are *shānî* and *kókkinos,* from the latter of which is derived the English cochineal. In Daniel 5:7,16,29 the Aramaic word for purple has been rendered scarlet. The color was probably a bright rich crimson. It was obtained from the eggs of the insect (*coccus ilicis*) called *kirmiz* by the Arabs, from which is derived the English word *crimson.* This insect abounds on the holm oak trees in Palestine.

Scarlet cloth was used for the hangings of the tabernacle (Exod. 25:4; Num. 4:8) and for the high priest's vestments (Exod. 39:1). Scarlet stuff was used for the cleansing of the recovered leper (Lev. 14:4) and in other ceremonies of purification (Num. 19:6). Its significance in this connection is unknown. Royal or expensive apparel was of scarlet (II Sam. 1:24; Prov. 31:21; Lam. 4:5; Matt. 27:28; Rev. 17:4; 18:12,16). It appears to have been used to mark thread or rope (Gen. 38: 28,30; Josh. 2:18,21), and the lips of the bride in Song of Solomon are likened to scarlet thread (4:3). Sins are "as scarlet" (Isa. 1:18); this may be the origin of the custom of using the term red or scarlet to denote things sinful, still in vogue today.   J.B.G.

SCARLET (See Plants)

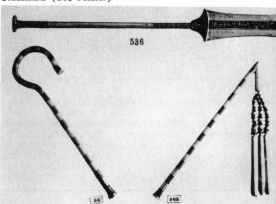

Baton, scepter and flail — all symbols of royal authority — from the tomb of Tutankhamen, in the Cairo Museum. The baton is gold-covered and jewelled; the scepter is of gold and blue glass; the flail of gilted wood, green glass and carnelian. SHH

SCEPTER (sĕp'têr, Heb. *shēvet;* Gr. *rhábdos*), a rod held in the hands of kings as a token of authority. The Hebrew *shēvet* is the word for *rod* or *club,* and is used of an ordinary rod (II Sam. 7:14), a shepherd's crook (Ps. 23:4), or the staff of a marshal (as RSV translates Judg. 5:14 — evidently the "writer" there mustered the troops), as well as of the symbol of authority.

This staff-scepter might be used for protection (II Sam. 23:21; Ps. 23:4) or for punishment (Isa. 10:24; 30:31). When dying Jacob blessed his son Judah and promised him the royal leadership in words which Christians understand as a Messianic prediction, it was the scepter which denoted the royal prerogative (Gen. 49:10). So, frequently the scepter indicates sovereignty in general, perhaps even conquest (Num. 24:17; Isa. 14:5; Amos 1:5,8; Zech. 10:11). God's kingship is also represented thus (Ps. 45:6).

The use of the scepter by an oriental monarch is illustrated by the story of king Ahasuerus, who held it out to Esther as a mark of favor. She touched the top of it, perhaps as an act of homage, or possibly to indicate a desire to be heard (Esth. 5:1,2). The scepter of Ahasuerus was of gold; Ezekiel refers to scepters made from vine branches (19:11,14). When Christ was mocked as a king, a reed was placed in His hand for a scepter (Matt. 27:29). J.B.G.

SCEVA (sē'và, Gr. *Skeuá*), a Jew, who was a chief priest living in Ephesus, whose seven sons were exorcists (Acts 19:14-17). There were only synagogues in Asia Minor, so he could not have been an officiating high priest. The Jews, although scattered throughout the Roman world, remembered their ancestry, and priests were probably then as now singled out for honor in the synagogue. A demon-possessed man overpowered the sons of this Sceva, and they fled the house naked and wounded.

SCHISM (sĭz'm, Gr. *schísma, a rent or division*), so rendered in NT only in I Corinthians 12:25; of a garment rendered "rent" (Matt. 9:16; Mark 2:21); of a crowd "division" (John 7:43; 9:16; 10:19), and "divisions" in I Corinthians 1:10; 11:18. The reference here is not to doctrinal heresy but to dissensions which threaten disruption.

SCHOOL, a place or institution devoted to teaching and learning. The word "school" occurs in our Bible only in Acts 19:9 where the reference is to the lecture-hall of Tyrannus, apparently a Greek teacher of rhetoric or philosophy, but the references to teachers and teaching are numerous in both Testaments. The OT stresses the duty and importance of religious teaching and training. Hebrew appreciation of the nature and value of the teaching function is evident from the fact that ten different Heb. verbs are rendered "teach" in our KJV. Yet significantly the Mosaic legislation contains no commands requiring the establishment of schools for formal religious instruction. Hebrew education was mainly domestic and continued to be so until after the return from the Babylonian captivity.

The home was the first and most effective agency for religious training. During the nomadic life of the patriarchs, education was purely a domestic activity, and the parents were the teachers. God called Abraham as the father of the chosen people and put upon him the responsibility to train his children and his household to walk in the ways of the Lord (Gen. 18:19; cf. Ps. 78:5-7). The reference in Genesis 14:14 to Abram's "trained men" implies a definite training program supervised by him. The varied commands in Deuteronomy to teach the children clearly imply domestic education (4:9; 6:7-9; 11:19; 32:46). Proverbs 22:6 is an exhortation encouraging the importance of parental instruction. The training was imparted primarily through conversation, example, and imitation; it utilized effectively the interest aroused by actual life-situations, such as the Passover, the redemption of the first-born, family rites, etc. (Exod. 12:26-27; 13:14-16). The well-known talent of the East for story telling would also be used in the vital transmission of religious truth and faith to the children. While all teaching was religiously oriented, reading, writing, and elementary arithmetic were taught. The command to the Israelites to write the precepts of the law upon their doorposts and gates (Deut. 6:9; 11:20) and upon great plastered stones in the land (27:2-8) implies a general ability among the people at the time to read and write.

Instruction in the home. A Jewish scribe in Jerusalem teaching his son the precepts of the Torah. ©MPS

The older people had opportunity to receive religious instruction from the priests and Levites (Lev. 10:10-11), who could be found at the sanctuary or in Levitical cities. Every seventh year, at the feast of Tabernacles, the law was read publicly for the instruction of the assembled people (Deut. 31:10-13). The priests and Levites, supported by the offerings of the people, were to be the religious teachers of the nation, but it seems clear that this aspect of their work was not consistently maintained. Only during the revival under King Jehoshaphat does one read of the priests and Levites fulfilling their calling to teach the people all the ordinances of the Law (II Chron. 17:7-9). The ineffective teaching ministry of a corrupt priesthood was supplemented by the service of the prophets, the first of whom was Samuel. To make his reform permanent and effective Samuel instituted a school of the prophets at Ramah (I Sam. 19:19-20). Later such schools flourished at Bethel (II Kings 2:3), Jericho (2:5), Gilgal (4:38), and elsewhere (6:1). Living in colonies under a leader, these "sons of the prophets" formed a religious training center, their chief study being the law and its interpretation. They became teachers and preachers who denounced national, family, and personal sins (I Kings 20:35-42; II Kings 17:13). Not all the students in these schools possessed the predictive gift, nor were all the prophets of Israel students in such schools (Amos 7:14-15). The preaching of God's prophets, rebuking, instructing, and announcing the future purposes of God, spread religious knowledge and stimulated spiritual life. Professional teachers were employed in the homes of the wealthy (II Sam. 12:25; II Kings 10:5; Isa. 49:23). The sages, or "men of wisdom," were apparently informal, self-appointed teachers, instructors in practical philosophy, the spiritual descendants of the great Solomon (Ps. 119:99; Prov. 5:13; 13:20). But there is no positive evidence that special rooms or buildings for school purposes were yet used, although the thought is not excluded.

With the return of the Jews from the Babylonian captivity there came a renewed emphasis upon religious instruction. Regular teaching was carried on during the days of Ezra and Nehemiah, the Levites being the teachers of the people (Neh 8:7-9; Ezra 7:10). Ezra the priest, described as "a ready scribe in the law of Moses" (Ezra 7:6), made the study and teaching of the law his chief concern. With the cessation of prophecy in Israel the study of the law became a matter of scholastic learning. Gradually there arose a class of men who came to be known as the scribes or lawyers, men whose chief employment was the study and interpretations of the law and who handed down interpretations as to its application to the practical duties of life. At first the scribes restricted their educational activities to adults, and the education of the children remained in the home.

The synagogue, which has a prominent place in post-exile Jewish life, apparently had its origin during the Babylonian captivity. When the exiled people were deprived of their temple and its services, they found it helpful to gather for the reading of the Scriptures and prayer. Upon their return to the land the synagogue spread rapidly and developed into an important educational agency. The synagogue services with their lections from the law and the prophets and the sermonic "exhortation" (Luke 4:17-21; Acts 13:15-16; 15:21), made their educational contribution to the religious life of the people. Regarded chiefly as places of teaching (never of sacrifice), they became associated with the development of an elementary school system among the Jews. Even before the days of Jesus synagogues, with schools for the young, were to be found in every important Jewish community.

A class in a synagogue school. KC © FC

The synagogue "attendant" (Luke 4:20) generally served as teacher; if there were more than 25 students an assistant was provided. Reading, writing, and arithmetic were taught as a means to an end. Since the primary aim of education was religious, the OT furnished the subject matter of instruction. Memorization had a prominent place, with emphasis on catechizing, drill, and review. Discipline was strict, the cane was kept available, but undue severity was not condoned. Students seeking training beyond that given in the synagogue schools turned to eminent scribes for further instruction. This was given partly in their homes, and partly in the synagogues or the temple porticoes. The instruction was devoted to the rabbinical interpretation of the law and its applications to life. Such advanced theological training Saul of Tarsus received in Jerusalem "at the feet of Gamaliel" (Acts 22:3).

Jesus was much more than a teacher, but He was first of all a teacher and was recognized as such by His contemporaries. Although unauthorized by the Jewish authorities, as a God-sent teacher He was constantly engaged in teaching the people. He generally employed the methods of the rabbis but poured into His teaching an authority that challenged and held His audiences. In selecting and training the twelve He became a teacher of teachers. He commissioned His followers to carry out a world-wide teaching ministry (Matt. 28:19-20). Teaching was an important phase of the work of the early Church in Jerusalem (Acts 2:42; 4:1-2; 5:21,28). The work of Barnabas and Saul at Antioch was essentially a teaching ministry (Acts 11:26). Paul the Apostle, preeminent as missionary and evangelist, was a peripatetic teacher, teaching in public assemblies, by personal contact, and by his epistles. He thought of himself as "a teacher of the Gentiles" (I Tim. 2:7). The NT places emphasis upon the teaching function in the Christian Church. "Pastor-teachers" (Eph. 4:11) were recognized as Christ's gift to His Church. Teaching was regarded as an essential function of the pastor (I Tim. 3:2). Unofficial or volunteer teachers also had an important part in the work of the church (James 3:1; Rom. 12:7). The author of Hebrews insisted that all believers should mature spiritually so that they could become teachers (5:12). Much unofficial Christian teaching was carried on by members in their homes (Acts 18:26; Titus 2:3-4). In NT times the Christian churches assembled in the homes of members (Rom. 16:3-5; I Cor. 16:19; Col. 4:15; Philem. 2). By the end of the first century the educational work of the Church came to be systematically developed. The Church Fathers were foremost in all educational matters and did much to develop and promote education, the chief handmaid of the Church. D.E.H.

SCIENCE, rendering of Heb. *maddā'* in Daniel 1:4 and Gr. *gnósis* in I Timothy 6:20 KJV, both meaning *knowledge.* Daniel 1:4 is literally "understanding knowledge or thought." In I Timothy 6:20 the reference is to that professed knowledge which sets itself up in contradiction to the truth of the Gospel. The word does not have its modern connotation.

SCOFF (Heb. *qālas, to scoff at, mock, deride,* rendered "mock" in II Kings 2:23, Ezekiel 22:5, Habakkuk 1:10.

SCOFFER (Gr. *empaíktes, one who scoffs or mocks*), one playing with trifles, hence one who derides, mocks (II Pet. 3:3, "mocker" in ASV; so rendered in Jude 18).

SCORPION (skôr'pĭ-ŏn, Heb. *'aqrab,* Gr. *skorpios*), an insect of the arachnid (spider-like) type, with claws that give it the appearance of a miniature lobster. Its tail bears a stinger with which it poisons its victim, and it is therefore described as a creature to be feared (Deut. 8:15; Ezek. 2:6; Luke 10:19, 11:12; Rev. 9:5,10). Several kinds are common in the desert areas of Palestine, where they hide underneath stones. The punishment with scorpions which King Rehoboam threatened (I Kings 12:11; II Chron. 10:11) likely referred to whips or scourges, q.v.

The scorpion of the Palestine desert. The stinger is at the tip of the tail. © MPS

SCOURGE (skûrj, Heb. generally *shût, to whip, lash, scourge; shôt,* a *whip, scourge;* Gr. *mastigóo,* to *whip, flog, scourge; mástix,* a *whip, lash; phragellóo,* to *flog, scourge,* as a public punishment of the condemned), the act or the instrument used to inflict severe pain by beating. Scourging, well known in the East, was familiar to the Hebrews from Egypt. The Mosaic law authorized the beating of a culprit, apparently with a rod, but limited to 40 the strokes given the prostrate victim (Deut. 25:3). Leviticus 19:20 does not impose true scourging (*biqqoreth,* rendered "punished" in ASV, expresses an investigation). I Kings 12:11, 14 apparently refers to true scourging. It was later legalized among the Jews and a three-thonged whip was used, but the legal limitation was observed (II Cor. 11:24). It was administered by local synagogue authorities (Matt. 10:17; Acts 22:19) or by the Sanhedrin (Acts 5:40).

Among the Romans either rods were used (Acts 16:22; II Cor. 11:25) or whips, the thongs of which were weighted with jagged pieces of bone or metal to make the blow more effective (Matt. 27:26; Mark 15:15; John 19:1). It was used to wrest confessions and secrets from its victims (Acts 22:24). The number of blows was left to the whim of the commanding officer. Its victims, tied to a stake with back bared to the tormentors, generally fainted from the resultant lacerations, or even died. It was forbidden to Roman citizens (Acts 22:25), being generally reserved for slaves or those condemned to death.

Scourge is used figuratively for "affliction" in Joshua 23:13; Job 5:21; 9:23; Isaiah 10:26; 28:15, 18. Note the mixed metaphors in Isaiah 28:15.

D.E.H.

SCREECH OWL (See Birds)

SCRIBES (See Occupations and Professions)

SCRIBES, JEWISH, a class of learned men who made the systematic study of the law and its exposition their professional occupation. In the NT they are generally called "scribes" (Gr. *grammateis, experts versed in the law; scribes*), corresponding to the Heb. *sopherim.* They are also called "lawyers" (Gr. *nomikoi, legal experts, jurists;* Matt. 22:35; Luke 7:30; 10:25; 11:45; 14:3) and "doctors of the law" (Gr. *nomodidaskaloi, teachers of the law;* Luke 5:17; Acts 5:34). They are prominent in the Gospels, often associated with the Pharisees (Matt. 5:20; 12:38; 15.1; 23:2,13, etc.; Mark 7:5; Luke 5:21,30; 6:7; 11:53; 15:2; John 8:3). But they are also mentioned alone and were not necessarily Pharisees (Matt. 9:3; Mark 2:6; 3:22; 9:14; Luke 20:39). The Pharisees were a religious party, while the scribes held an office. The double designation distinguishes them from the Pharisees, but the majority of the scribes belonged to the Pharisee party which recognized the legal interpretations of the scribes. Certain expressions imply that the Sadducees also had their scribes (Mark 2:16 ASV; Luke 5:30 ASV; Acts 23:9).

The powerful position of the scribes in the NT was the result of a long development. The scribes of pre-exilic days were public writers, governmental secretaries, and copiers of the law and other documents (II Sam. 8:17; 20:25; I Kings 4:3; II Kings 12:10; Jer. 8:8; 36:18; Prov. 25:1). The distinctive nature of the office of the scribe first comes into view with Ezra, who set himself to the task of teaching the law to the returning exiles (Ezra 7:6, 10-11, 21). At first this naturally fell to the priests (Neh. 8), but gradually there arose a separate group of professional students who devoted themselves to the preservation, transcription, and exposition of the law. When during the Hellenistic period the upper priests became largely tainted with paganism, the scribes became the zealous defenders of the law and the true teachers of the common people. By NT times they held undisputed sway as the recognized exponents of the law and the revered representatives of Judaism. They received the deep respect of the people, as indicated in the honorable term *rabbi,* meaning "my master, or teacher." Proudly they claimed the positions of first rank, sought the public acclaim of the masses, and dressed in long robes like the nobility (Matt. 23:5-7; Mark 12:38-39; Luke 11:43; 20:46). They demanded from their disciples utmost reverence, claiming an honor surpassing that due to parents. To facilitate discussion and the exchange of opinions, the scribes lived in communities, the main seat of their activity being Jerusalem (Matt. 15:1; Mark 3:22), but they were also found in Galilee (Luke 5:17), and even in the dispersion.

Accepting the law as the basis for the regulation of all of life, they made it their primary task to study, interpret, and expound that law as the rule for daily life. The lack of details in the law they filled up through the gradual development of an extensive and complicated system of teaching intended to safeguard the sanctity of the law. By their practice of making "a fence about the law" they added to its actual requirements, thus loading the people with "burdens grievous to be borne" (Luke 11:46; Matt. 23:4). Their diligent search of the OT for recondite meanings they felt was meritorious and entitled them to eternal life (John 5:39). This vast and complicated mass of scribal teaching, known as "the tradition of the elders" (Matt. 15:2-6; Mark 7:1-13), was orally transmitted and required prolonged study to master. In their desire to know the law the common people readily turned to the legal experts as teach-

Statue of an ancient Egyptian scribe of pre-Mosaic age, in the Metropolitan Museum, New York.

ers. They taught in the synagogues, and trained their pupils in their scribal lore. All higher instruction, if not all instruction of the day, was in their hands. Because of their legal knowledge the scribes were often called upon to serve as judges in Jewish courts. They constituted an important element in the membership of the Sanhedrin (Matt. 26:57; Mark 14:43; 15:1; Luke 22:66; Acts 4:5). Since the scribes functioned as judges and the law prohibited judges from receiving presents or bribes (Exod. 23:8; Deut. 16:19), they were obliged to make their living some other way. Most of them, like Paul (Acts 18:3), followed some trade even though their activity as scribe was primary. But apparently this principle was strictly observed only in connection with their judicial, not their instructional, activities. Christ's denunciation of their greed makes it obvious that while they professed to offer instruction gratuitously they had indirect ways of securing their fees (Mark 12:40; Luke 20:47).

Because Jesus refused to be bound by the scribal accretions to the law (John 5:10-18; Mark 7:1-13), the scribes soon fiercely opposed Him. Throughout His ministry they were His most watchful and determined opponents (Mark 2:16; Luke 5:30; 15:2). Their hypocrisy and unrelenting hatred drew forth Christ's devastating denunciation of them as recorded in Matthew 23. They played an important part in the death of Jesus (Matt. 26:57; 27:41; Mark 15:1,31; Luke 22:66; 23:10), also in the persecution of the early Church (Acts 4:5; 6:12). Not all the scribes were wholly bad, for Nicodemus and Gamaliel were scribes, but as a whole they were marked by spiritual corruption and were the very quintessence of Pharisaism.   D.E.H.

An old Samaritan scroll on display in a synagogue. © MPS

A Samaritan scribe penning a manuscript. © MPS

SCRIP (See Dress)

SCRIPTS (See Writing)

SCRIPTURE (See Bible, Canon, Old Testament, New Testament)

SCROLL. The scroll or roll was the usual form of the book in the Bible world. It had been used in Egypt from very early times, made of papyrus, the paper-like tissue made from the reeds growing along the Nile. The "roll of the book" (*megillath-sephĕr,* "scroll," RSV, Jer. 36:2) was the Hebrew name for a scroll. The one referred to in this passage in Jeremiah was made of papyrus — one of leather could hardly have been burned in an open brazier. The papyrus for making scrolls was imported from Egypt. Several sheets were glued together to make a scroll of the desired length, which was then rolled on rods so that the beginning of the scroll was on the right and the end on the left (the Hebrews wrote from right to left). The writing was in columns. In the story of the destruction of Jeremiah's scroll, as the successive columns (Jer. 36:23 RSV, not "leaves" as in KJV) were read, the king cut them off and burned them.

A library or royal archives is called a house of rolls (Ezra 6:1). Ezekiel is commanded to eat a scroll (2:9-3:3), no doubt in a vision.

As time went on, perhaps after the Exile, the Hebrews began to write important works on scrolls of smoothed skins of animals. Such rolls would last much longer than those of paper. The first scroll of Isaiah from Qumran (the Dead Sea Scrolls") was written on 17 pieces of skin of different sizes, sewn together at their edges, and in one place glued together as well. This scroll is a little more than ten inches wide and when unrolled is 24 feet long. It contains 54 columns of text. These skins are of leather, but in later times the skins were treated in a special way and called parchment, which was whiter, and in general made a more attractive appearance than did regularly tanned leather.

The Jews were extremely careful in the preparation of scrolls of the Scriptures. Only the skins of

The remains of an ancient Samaritan scroll. © MPS

clean animals could be used. To the present day the scroll is the form of the book used in the reading of the Scriptures in the synagogue.

The book-form or codex was introduced for private MSS in the second century A.D., and soon took over as a far more convenient form of the book, except in the synagogue. The famous fourth century MSS of the Greek Bible (Sinaiticus, Vaticanus) are in the codex form.

There were different ways of dividing the books of the Bible on the scrolls; either a separate scroll was taken for each book or several books were written on one scroll. "The Twelve" is the Hebrew name for the twelve Minor Prophets, since all were written on one scroll. To write the whole OT on one scroll would be almost impossible.

Among the awful portents of the day of judgment, it is said that "the heavens shall be rolled together as a scroll" (Isa. 34:4). J.B.G.

SCROLLS, DEAD SEA (See Dead Sea Scrolls)

SCULPTURE (See Art)

SCURVY (See Diseases, Skin)

SCYTHIAN (sĭth'ĭ-ăn, Gr. *hoi Skýthai*), the name is used by classical writers as a general term for the barbarians of the steppes. In common parlance it was a term for the savage and uncivilized (Col. 3:11). Scythia was the name given by the Greeks to an ill-defined area between the Carpathians and the Don, the western portion of which included the black earth wheatlands of the modern Ukraine. The steppe-land was wide open to nomadic invasion, and the Indo-European tribes who occupied it in the seventh century B.C. are those to whom most properly the term Scythian is applied. There must have been a considerable "folk-wandering" about this time, because Scythians appeared in upper Mesopotamia and Syria between 650 and 620 B.C. and another force reached the middle Danube. South Russia, to speak in modern geographical terms, was firmly occupied. The nomads were formidable soldiers, swift archer-cavalry versed in the tactics of desert warfare and mobile strategy. By a "scorched-earth" policy and by their elusive defense they frustrated an attack of Darius in 512 B.C., and similarly beat off Alexander's general Zopyrion in 325 B.C. They exploited the labor of the earlier inhabitants, and were considerable exporters of wheat to the Greek Black Sea colonies. Greek pottery and metal work were taken in exchange, and the tombs of the chiefs have produced a rich profusion of such articles. The Celts and Samaritans seem to have displaced the Scythians in the last three centuries before Christ. E.M.B.

SEA (Heb. *yām*, Gr. *thálassa*). In the Bible the term is used in several ways. 1. The ocean, the gathering of the waters at the creation, is called sea (Gen. 1:10; Pss. 8:8; 24:2).

2. Almost any body of water, salt or fresh, is called sea. The Mediterranean (Acts 10:6), the sea of Galilee (Matt. 4:18; Num. 34:11), the Dead Sea (Deut. 3:17), the Red Sea (Exod. 13:18; 14:2) are referred to in Scripture. Obviously, not all of these would be called seas by us. Galilee is a lake, being only about 12½ by 7½ miles in size, but it is often called a sea.

3. Even rivers may, in poetic language, be called a sea: the Nile (Isa. 18:2; 19:5), and the Euphrates (Isa. 21:1).

4. The basin in Solomon's temple was called a sea (see SEA, BRAZEN).

The ancient Hebrews were not a sea people. The sea in the Bible becomes a symbol of restlessness, instability and sin (Isa. 57:20; Jer. 49:23; James 1:6; Jude 13; Rev. 13:1).

SEA, BRAZEN, the great basin in Solomon's temple where the priests washed their hands and feet preparatory to temple ministry (I Kings 7:23-26; II Chron. 4:2-6). It was made of brass which David had taken in war (I Chron. 18:8), and stood between the altar and the holy place. It was round, ten cubits (18 feet) in diameter and five cubits (7½ feet) in height and held 2,000

Replica of Solomon's Brazen Sea in the Temple. BA

Impression of Hebrew Royal Seal from Beth Zur in Judea, from the time of Judas Maccabaeus. © MPS

baths (possibly 12,000 gallons, I Kings 7:23,26). It stood upon 12 brass oxen, in four groups of three each, facing the four directions of the compass. When Nebuchadnezzar captured Jerusalem he broke the basin to pieces and took them to Babylon (II Kings 25:13,16; Jer. 27:19-22).

SEA OF GLASS. In the vision of heaven in the Revelation, a glassy sea is seen before the throne of God (Rev. 4:6; 15:2). It is translucent, "like unto crystal." Nearby stand the victorious singing saints. The sea symbolizes God's purity and holiness, and also the victory of the redeemed hosts who have crossed it.

SEA OF JAZER (Heb. *yām ya'zēr*). No such sea is known. Jazer was a town in Gilead. The only mention of the sea of Jazer (Jer. 48:32) is probably a scribal error, and the city of Jazer is meant (cf. RSV).

SEA MEW (See Birds, Cuckoo)

SEA MONSTER (Heb. *tannîn*), any great fish of the sea (Gen. 1:21; Job 7:12; in KJV *whale*).

SEASON (See Time, Calendar)

SEAT (Heb. *môshāv, sheveth, kissē', tekhûnâh,* Gr. *kathédra, thrónos*), a place or thing upon which one sits, as a chair or stool (I Sam. 20:18; Judg. 3:20). Often (especially when it represents the Greek word *thronos*) it means throne (Luke 1:52; Rev. 2:13; 4:4; 11:16; 13:2; 16:10). It is used also of the exalted position occupied by men of rank or influence (Matt. 23:2; Ps. 1:1). Jesus reproached some of the men of his day for preferring the chief seats in the synagogue (Matt. 23:6; Mark 12:39; Luke 11:43; 20:46). These were special seats set in front of the reader's platform, facing the congregation, reserved for those held in honor. The great synagogue in Alexandria had 71 such seats, which were occupied by members of the great Council of that city.

SEBA (sē'bà, Heb. *sevā'*, Gr. *Sabá*), a people descended from Cush (Gen. 10:7) who lived in southern Arabia. Seba is a dialectical variation of Sheba. The people of Seba were called Sabeans.

SEBAT (sē'bắt, Heb. *shevāt*), the 11th month of the Hebrew year (Zech. 1:7), spelled Shebat in RSV. It corresponded to our February. See YEAR.

SECACAH (sē-kā'kà, Heb. *sekhākhâh*), a village in the wilderness of Judah (Josh. 15:61), whose location is unknown.

SECHU (sē'kŭ, Heb. *sēkhû*), a village near Samuel's town of Ramah (I Sam. 19:22), probably in the direction of Gibeah (vs. 9). The name is spelled Secu in RSV.

SEAL (Heb. *hôthām,* seal, signet; *tabb'ath,* signet-ring; *hātham,* to seal; Gr. *sphragízo, katasphragízomai,* to seal). 1. Literal sense. A device bearing a design, a name or some other words so made that it can impart an impression in relief upon a soft substance like clay or wax. When the clay or wax hardens, it permanently bears the impression of the seal. The discovery by archaeologists of thousands of seals reveals that their use goes back to the 4th millennium B.C. and that they were used throughout the ancient civilized world from Mesopotamia to Rome. They were made of a variety of hard substances like limestone, metal, and all kinds of precious stones. Originally they took the form of a cylinder with a hole from end to end for a cord to pass through, but this was gradually superseded by the scarab (beetle-shaped). Some were carried by cords hung from the neck or waist; many were cone-shaped, and were kept in boxes; but most were made into finger-rings. Every person of any standing had a seal. The best ones were engraved by skilled seal-cutters and were real works of art. A great variety of designs was represented on them — deities, people, animals, birds, fish, plants, and combinations of these. Many of them bore inscriptions giving the name of the owner or of his overlord, and his profession or office. Many seals with Biblical names have been found — among them Hananiah. Azariah, Menahem, Micaiah, Jotham, Nehemiah and Gedaliah. Excavations in Palestine have produced hundreds of jar-handles bearing seal impressions, some with the place of manufacture and personal names (perhaps of the potter).

Scarabs of the Seventeenth Century B.C., from Garstang, **The Story of Jericho.**

Seals were used for a number of purposes. (1) As a mark of authenticity and authority to letters, royal commands, etc. (I Kings 21:8; Esth. 3:12; 8:8,10). (2) As a mark of the formal ratification of a transaction or covenant, as when Jeremiah's friends witnessed his purchase of a piece of property (Jer. 32:11-14) and the chief men of Jerusalem set their seal to a written covenant to keep its laws (Neh. 9:38; 10:1). (3) As a means of protecting books and other documents so that they would not be tampered with (Jer. 32:14; Rev. 5: 2,5,9; 6:1,3). (4) As a proof of deputed authority and power (Gen. 41:42; Esth. 3:10; 8:2). (5) As a means of sealing closed doors so as to keep out unauthorized persons (Dan. 6:17; Matt. 27:66; Rev. 20:3). Usually doors were sealed by stretching a cord across them and then sealing the cord. (6) As an official mark of ownership, like the seals on jar-handles and jar-stoppers.

Detail

of seal

A typical seal on a jar handle, the seal impression of Eliakim, steward of King Jehoiachin, from Tell Beit-Mirsim, from about 587 B.C. © MPS

Impressions of cylinder seals from Mesopotamia. The one above shows gods in battle with a seven-headed dragon; the one below depicts Ea, god of wisdom. OIUC UMP

2. Figurative sense. Scripture often uses the term metaphorically to betoken authentication, confirmation, ownership, evidence, or security. God does not forget sin, but stores it up against the sinner, under a seal (Deut. 32:34; Job 14:17). Prophecies that are intended to be kept secret for a time are bound with a seal (Dan. 12:4,9; Rev. 5:1ff; 10:4). Paul speaks of having sealed the offering of the Gentiles for the saints in Jerusalem (Rom. 15:28). This may have been literal, thus guaranteeing his honesty, or it may denote Paul's approval of the Gentile gift. The word has the sense of authentication in I Corinthians 9:2, where Paul describes his converts at Corinth as the "seal" placed by Christ on his work — the proof or vindication of his apostleship. The circumcision of Abraham is described as an outward ratification by God of the righteousness of faith which he had already received before he was circumcised (Rom. 4:11). Believers are said to be "sealed with the promised Holy Spirit" (Eph. 1:13), as an owner sets his seal on his property; and the same thought is conveyed in the words, "in whom you were sealed for the day of redemption" (Eph. 4: 30). God marks off His own by putting His seal on their foreheads (Rev. 7:2-4).   S.B.

SECOND COMING OF CHRIST, THE, one of the most prominent doctrines in Scripture. In the NT alone it is referred to over 300 times. The night before His crucifixion Jesus told the apostles that He would come again (John 14:3), and at the time of His ascension two angels appeared to the apostles, saying that He would come back in the same manner as they had seen Him go (Acts 1:11). The NT shows that thenceforward His coming was the "blessed hope" of His people (Titus 2:13). There is a great difference of opinion as to what is meant by the Lord's return. Some regard it as the coming of the Holy Spirit on the day of Pentecost, or the coming of Christ into the heart at conversion, or Christ's coming in judgment at the destruction of Jerusalem in A.D. 70, or Christ's coming for the believer at death, or Christ's coming for the conversion of the world. Careful examination of the Scriptures referring to the second coming makes it clear, however, that His coming will be personal, bodily, and visible. For example, the coming of the Holy Spirit at Pentecost cannot be what is meant because the Acts and the Epistles show that long after the day of Pentecost the Church was still looking for the fulfillment of Christ's promise that He would come again. Christ Himself, moreover, clearly distinguished between death and His coming (John 21:23). The coming of Christ is the climax and culmination of His redemptive work, when the Church will be completed, and the Lord will usher in that Kingdom which will eventually result in God being all in all (Rom. 8:19-23; I Cor 15:23-28; Eph. 1:14). See also CHRIST.   S.B.

SECT (sĕkt, Gr. *haíresis, sect, party, school*), of schools of philosophy; in NT of religious parties: the Sadducees (Acts 5:17), the Pharisees (15:5; 26:5), the Christians (24:5; 28:22). Also in 24:14 ASV ("heresy" in KJV).

SECUNDUS (sē-kŭn'dŭs, Gr. *Sékoundos,* a name of Latin origin, meaning *second*), a Thessalonian Christian, otherwise unknown, who with several others had preceded Paul to Troas (Acts 20:4). If one of the delegates entrusted with the collection, he probably accompanied Paul to Jerusalem (Acts 24:17; II Cor. 8:23; Rom. 15:25-26).

SECURITY, the theological teaching which maintains the certain continuation of the salvation of those who are saved; also known as the perseverance of the saints. Its advocates appeal to the promises of Scripture, such as John 10:28; Romans 8:38-39; Philippians 1:6; II Thessalonians 3:3; I Peter 1:5. They maintain that since salvation is God's work, the regenerate must be ultimately saved or God's purpose and work would come to naught, and that the very nature of eternal life forbids the thought of its not being eternal. But the opponents reply by pointing to the numerous passages of warning, such as I Corinthians 9:27; Galatians 5:2-4; Hebrews 4:4-6; 10:31-35; II Peter 2:20-22; Ezekiel 3:20; 33:13,18; etc.; that the promises appealed to by the advocates are really conditional (cf. "they" and "I" in John 10:27-29); that Scripture teaches the necessity of human striving (Luke 13:24; Col. 1:29; II Tim. 2:5); that this teaching ignores the fact of human free will and disregards the realities of human experience. Both positions are held by devout, sincere, and godly believers. Extremes on either side have produced confusion and conflict. A third approach would recognize that Scripture gives both serious warnings and clear promises to the saved, that both should be accepted at face value, and that one should humbly acknowledge that he cannot completely rationalize the relation of the human and the divine in the salvation of the believer. D.E.H.

SEDUCER (sē-dūs'êr, Gr. *góes, wailer, howler*), a cheat, a false teacher, a deceiver, perhaps through the use of magical arts (II Tim. 3:13; "impostor" in ASV).

SEED (Heb. *zera',* Gr. *spérma, spóros*). There is a threefold usage of this word in Scripture. 1. *Agricultural.* The farmer held his seed in his upturned garment, casting it out as he walked. Grain was sown in the early winter, after the first rains. Christ's parable of the sower is well known (Mark 4:1-20; Luke 8:5-15). Land was measured by the amount of seed which could be sown on it (Lev. 27:16). The wilderness was "land not sown" (Jer. 2:2).

2. *Physiological.* "Seed of copulation" (RSV, "emission of semen") is a frequent expression in the Hebrew laws of cleanness (Lev. 15:16ff). The NT speaks of Christians as having been begotten by God — "of incorruptible seed" (I Pet. 1:23; I John 3:9).

3. *Figurative.* Here seed means descendants (Gen. 13:16) or genealogy (Ezra 2:59; Neh. 7:61), or a class of people ("seed of evildoers," Isa. 1:4). "The holy seed" (Isa. 6:13; Ezra 9:2) is a special designation of the people of Israel. St. Paul's use of *seed* (in contrast to "seeds") in Galatians 3:16 had for its purpose a proof that the promises to Abraham were realized in Christ. This is an example of rabbinical exegesis, used by the apostle against his rabbinical adversaries. J.B.G.

SEEDTIME (See Agriculture)

SEER (See Occupations)

SEGUB (sē'gŭb, Heb. *seghûv*). 1. The younger son of Heil. He died when his father set up the gates of Jericho, which he was then building (I Kings 16:34). Thus the curse pronounced by Joshua (Josh. 6:26) was fulfilled. Some regard Segub's death as an example of infant sacrifice, but this is not clear from the account.

2. Son of Hezron by a daughter of Machir (I Chron. 2:21,22).

SEIR (sē'ēr, Heb. *sē'îr*). Seir the Horite (Gen. 36: 20; I Chron. 1:38) was the ancestor of the inhabitants of the land of Seir.

SEIR, LAND OF and MOUNT (sē'ēr, Heb. *sē'îr*). 1. The Land of Seir and Mt. Seir are alternate names for the region occupied by the descendants of Edom or Esau. Originally called the land of Seir (Gen. 32:3; 36:20,21,30; Num. 24:18), it was later called Edom. It is a mountainous and extremely rugged country, about 100 miles long, extending S from Moab on both sides of the Arabah or the great depression connecting the southern part of the Dead Sea with the Gulf of Akabah (Gen. 14:6; Deut. 2:1,12; Josh. 15:1; Judg. 11:17, 18; I Kings 9:26). The summit of Mt. Seir rises about 3500 feet above the adjacent Arabah. The land is very rocky and not nearly so fertile as Palestine (cf. Mal. 1:2-4). Yet it had fields, vineyards, wells, and a N-S highway ran through it, as it does through the region today (Num. 20:17,19). Sela was the Edomite capital in the days of the Hebrew monarchy; later the place was called Petra. Bozrah and Teman were important places. In the Greek period the name of the land was modified to Idumea.

Two views from Mount Seir: The theater at Petra, ancient Sela, the Edomite capital, and below, the great circular ceremonial court before the Temple of Ed Deir. © MPS

Seir, the land and the mount: Two views, showing at left the Wadi Sayyaga, with the Wadi Mousa torrent bed and the Khubta range in the distance. At right, the great rock El-Biyara, at Petra (ancient Sela) on which the Edomite capital stood. © MPS

Esau made his home in Mt. Seir, and his descendants dispossessed the Horites (Deut. 2:12; Josh. 24:4), the original inhabitants (Gen. 14:6). A remnant of the Amalekites took refuge in these mountain fastnesses, but were finally destroyed by the Simeonites (I Chron. 4:42,43). The term Seir is also used collectively for the people who lived in Mt. Seir (Ezek. 25:8).

2. Another region called Seir is a ridge on the border of the territory of Judah W of Kirjath-jearim (Josh. 15:10), generally identified with the rocky point on which the village of Saris stands, southwest of Kirjath-jearim.　　　　J.B.G.

SEIRAH, SEIRATH (sē-ī′rà, sē-ī′răth), a place in Mt. Ephraim, probably in the SE part, to which Ehud escaped after murdering Eglon (Judg. 3:26).

SELA (sē′là, Heb. *sela'*, Gr. *pétra*), a place in Edom taken by King Ahaziah (II Kings 14:7). It is probably also referred to in II Chronicles 25:12; Isaiah 42:11 and Obadiah 3 where in each case the KJV translates "rock." The second reference the RSV translates "Sela." It seems to be the place made famous in Greek times by the name Petra, the capital of the Nabateans.

SELAH (sē′là, Heb. *sālal, to lift up*), a term occurring 71 times in the Psalms, and also in Habakkuk 3:3,9,13. The meaning of selah is unknown. It is generally believed that its usage was that of a musical or liturgical sign. The LXX seems to understand it as a direction to the orchestra — "lift up," i.e., play the instruments while the singers are silent. The Jewish Targums and St. Jerome render it "for ever," but there is no support for this. Jacob of Edessa (A.D. 640-708) compared it to the Amen sung by the Christians after the Gloria. Perhaps selah was used in a similar way, as a signal for the singing of some sort of doxology or benediction after psalms or parts of psalms divided for liturgical use. It will be noted that the word usually occurs at a place where a very significant statement has been made, making that a good place for a break or pause. It is believed that selah was introduced during the late Persian period.

SELA-HAMMAHLEKOTH (sē′là-hă-mà′lē-kŏth), a cliff in the wilderness of Maon. It was called Sela-hammahlekoth ("rock of divisions or escapes") because there David eluded Saul (I Sam.

23:28). About eight miles NE of Maon there is a great gorge called Wadi Malaki, impassable except by making a detour of many miles; this is probably the place.

SELED (sē′lĕd, Heb. *seledh*), a man of Judah of the family of Jarahmeel (I Chron. 2:30).

SELEUCIA (sē-lū′shĭ-à, Gr. *Seleukía*). The Seleucia of the NT was founded in 300 B.C. by Seleucus I Nicator, to provide a seaport for Syrian Antioch which lay some 16 miles inland. It lay near the mouth of the Orontes, and was a naval base in Roman imperial times. It was the port of departure for Paul and Barnabas on their first journey (Acts 13:4). This city is to be distinguished from the Seleucia on the Tigris founded by the same monarch 12 years earlier.

SELEUCIDS (sĕ-lū′sĭds, Gr. *Séleukos*). The Seleucids took their name from Seleucus, a cavalry officer of Alexander. He was one of the Diadochi, or "Successors," the name given to those remarkable military personalities who successfully partitioned Alexander's empire after his death. By 312 B.C., after some vicissitudes, Seleucus had established himself in command of Babylonia, Susiana, and Media, and from this date his dynasty and era can be conveniently reckoned. By 301 B.C. he was master of Syria, and forthwith founded Antioch and Seleucia to express the westward aspiration of his kingdom, and to balance Seleucia on the Tigris, its eastern bastion. The Seleucids, who commonly bore the name of the founder of the dynasty or of his son Antiochus, were the true heirs of Alexander. Their borders fluctuated with the give and take of strife on the eastern frontiers, and with the Ptolemies, who inherited the pharaohs' sensitivity to Palestine, but for over two centuries and more of independent rule the Seleucids held the major portion of Alexander's realms. Their empire was frequently termed Syria from the portion fronting the NE corner of the Mediterranean, which was their seat and center, and where they sought to establish an eastern Macedonia. In others ways, too, they followed Alexander's policy. The Ptolemies in Egypt took over the pharaonic system, and sought to be the pharaohs' successors in rule, government, and dignity. The Seleucids sought to Hellenize their domains, to mingle immigrant Greeks with Asiatics. In such wise was the stage set for Paul of Tarsus, heir of two cultures, and for the Greek New Testament. The clash between the Seleucids and the Jews, which precipitated the Maccabaean revolt, must be set to the debit side of this Hellenizing policy. The Greek cities, which the Seleucids founded all over their empire, were in general a civilizing force which prepared the way for the fruitful mingling of Palestine, Greece, and Rome, and hence for Europe as we know it in the West. Greek life and thought took root in the Middle East, and penetrated far into Asia. Royal authority, for all the democratic constitution of their Greek foundations, was shaped by the Seleucids on the Oriental model favored by Alexander. The Seleucid monarchy proved, in consequence, one of the political influences which prepared the eastern half of the Roman Empire for the deification of the Emperor, and the imperial cult which meant so much in the history of the early Church, and helped to precipitate the damaging contest between the Christians and the State. E.M.B.

SELVEDGE (sĕl'vĕj, Heb. *qātsâh*). The "self-edge" was the edge of each of the two curtains (which were themselves each composed of five parts), which together covered the boards of the sanctuary of the tabernacle. They were coupled at the selvedge by 50 loops of blue connected by clasps with 50 others on the opposite side (Exod. 26:4; 36:11).

SEM (See Shem)

SEMACHIAH (sĕm'à-kī'à, *Jehovah has sustained*), a Levite, a descendant of the doorkeeper Obededom (I Chron. 26:7).

SEMEI (sĕm'ē-ī, Gr. *Semeí*). 1. One of those who put away their "strange wives" (I Esdras 9:33), probably the same as Shimei in Ezra 10:33.
2. The KJV form of Semein (Luke 3:26).

SEMEIN (sĕm'ē-ĭn, Gr. *Semeeín*), an ancestor of Christ, who lived after the time of Zerubbabel (Luke 3:26).

SEMITES (sĕm'īts). The term Semite is derived from Noah's son Shem (Gen. 9:18,19; 10:21-31), and is used to identify a diverse group of ancient peoples whose languages are related, belonging to the Semitic family of languages. It is not certain that since these Semitic peoples spoke related languages, they themselves were related in blood. But since it is impossible now to gain a more accurate knowledge of the relationship of ancient peoples, this obvious connection in language is of some use.

The world of the Semites, in ancient historical times, was the Fertile Crescent, that green land which begins in southern Babylonia in the E, and includes Mesopotamia, Syria and Palestine, ending at the border of Egypt in the W. It is hemmed in by mountains, seas, and deserts. Strangely enough, one of the latter, the great Arabian desert, appears to have been the original homeland of the Semites. From earliest times there have been irruptions from this desert into the Fertile Crescent, bringing new strength to the Semitic civilizations. We can name some of the principal irruptions: the Amorites, the Canaanites, the Arameans, the Nabateans, and the Arabs. The last of these, under Mohammed's leadership, brought a new religion and later a great empire to a considerable part of the Asia-Africa-Europe continent.

The principal Semitic peoples of ancient times were:

1. The Akkadians — the Babylonians and Assyrians who lived in Mesopotamia and spoke a common language. From c. 2350 B.C. to 538 B.C. these gifted, vigorous people dominated Mesopotamia. Several times they produced empires which ruled the ancient world. Their Akkadian language, written on clay by means of cuneiform signs, was for more than a millennium the *lingua franca* of the world of that time. The cities of Ur, Babylon and Nineveh, rulers such as Sargon I, Shalmaneser III and V and Sennacherib, Hammurabi the law codifier (who though an Amorite ruled a Babylonian empire) and Assurbanipal the library builder testify to the greatness of the Akkadian civilization.

2. The Arameans. Principally traders and catalysts of culture rather than its creators, the Aramean speaking people lived in Syria from c. 1700 B.C. to the time of Christ, although their political power ceased some centuries earlier. Damascus, Aleppo, Hama, and Zobah were their cities. Their language supplanted Akkadian as the world language and was adopted by the Jews after their return from exile. It became the language of the Talmud, and half of the book of Daniel is written in Aramaic. It was through the Aramaic language that the Semitic civilization was given to the Greeks and Romans. Syriac (a form of Aramaic) was an important language in the early church. Today there are still a few Aramaic speaking islands of culture in the Middle East.

3. The Canaanites. This term is used to designate a number of peoples who lived in southern Syria (including Palestine) in ancient times. Even the Hebrews can be considered a Canaanite group. Although we still know very little about the Canaanites before the coming of the Hebrews, the recent finds at Ugarit are shedding light on their culture. The Edomites, Ammonites, and Moabites were Canaanites. It appears that the Canaanites invented the alphabet. The Hebrews seem to have borrowed the Canaanite language and culture, and made it their own. The Phoenicians were a Canaanite people, pushed up into the Lebanon littoral, who took to the sea, and became the first people to dominate the Mediterranean and make it their common highway (1200-400 B.C.).

4. The Arabs. Little is known about the inhabitants of Arabia prior to Mohammed. The great contributions of the Arabs after the coming of Islam lie beyond the scope of this work.

5. The Ethiopians. Across the Red Sea from southern Arabia, the Ethiopians had a flourishing Semitic civilization from 500 B.C. to the time of Mohammed. J.B.G.

SENAAH (sē-nā'à, Heb. *senā'âh*), the descendants of Senaah (sometimes spelled Hassenaah, with the Hebrew definite article attached) were a part of the company returning from captivity with Zerubbabel (Ezra 2:35; Neh. 7:38). They rebuilt the fish gate of Jerusalem (Neh. 3:3). The name may also refer to a place (unknown).

SENATE (sĕn'ăt, Gr. *gerousía, a council of elders*), mentioned in Acts 5:21; not a body different from the "council" (Sanhedrin) but a more precise equivalent indicating its dignity as composed of old men.

SENATOR (See Occupations & Professions)

SENEH (sē'nĕ, Heb. *seneh*), the name of the southern of two great cliffs between which ran the gorge of Michmash. Jonathan and his armorbearer passed here on their way to surprise the Philistine garrison (I Sam. 14:4,5). Located 3½ miles SE of Michmash.

SENIR (sē'nĭr, Heb. *senîr*), the Amorite name of Mt. Hermon (Deut. 3:9; S. of Sol. 4:8), a source of fir timber (Ezek. 27:5). Twice spelled Shenir in KJV.

One of the famous clay prisms of Sennacherib, the Taylor Prism in the British Museum, describing Sennacherib's military operations, including his invasion of Palestine in 701 B.C. BM

SENNACHERIB (sĕ-năk'êr-ĭb, Heb. *sanhērîv, Assyr. Sin-ahe-irba, Sin* (moon-god) *multiplied brothers*), an Assyrian king (705-681 B.C.), the son and successor of Sargon II (722-705 B.C.). He restored the capital to Nineveh, on the E bank of the Tigris, opposite the present city of Mosul. It is represented today by the mounds Kuyunjik and Nebi Yunus ("prophet Jonah"); Kuyunjik was dug in part by Layard and the palace of Sennacherib was found. Sennacherib constructed palaces, temples, city-walls, and a water system, including the aqueduct of Jerwan (cf. building inscriptions, D. D. Luckenbill, *Ancient Records of Assyria and Babylonia.* Chicago: University of Chicago Press, 1927, II, pp. 362-483; hereafter *ARAB*). He was an able soldier and it is in this capacity in which he is best remembered. Upon his succession to the the throne he found it necessary to deal with revolts throughout the empire. Exasperated by the repeated intrigues of Babylon and its king, Merodach-baladan, he finally reduced the city to ruins in 689 B.C. In the W there was like rebellion; among the rebels was Hezekiah of Judah. On his

third campaign, 701 B.C., Sennacherib marched west to settle those difficulties. The accounts of his campaigns were recorded on clay prisms, among which are the Taylor Prism (British Museum) and the Oriental Institute Prism, which include the Assyrian version of the conflict with Hezekiah. Sennacherib took Sidon and moved south, receiving tribute and capturing Ashkelon, Beth-Dagon, Joppa, and other Palestinian cities (*ARAB*, II, p. 239). At Eltekeh (cf. Josh. 19:44; 21:23) he defeated a coalition of Palestinians, plus some Egyptian forces. Hezekiah had taken Padi, king of Ekron, who was allied with Sennacherib, and made him a captive (*ARAB,* II, p. 240). Sennacherib now seized Ekron and restored Padi to his throne. He did not take Jerusalem, but he boasted that he shut up Hezekiah "like a bird in a cage." The OT gives three records of this invasion and its results (II Kings 18:13-19:17; II Chron. 32:1-22; Isa. 36:1-37:38).

It was in the 14th year of Hezekiah that Sennacherib came against Judah and took all of its fortified cities. Hezekiah offered to pay tribute and had to strip the temple of its treasures to make payment. The Assyrian sent his officers to Jerusalem to deliver an ultimatum concerning capitulation. At this time Sennacherib was besieging Lachish, which he took, and then moved against Libnah. The reliefs of the palace of Sennacherib at Kuyunjik depicted the capture of Lachish. When Sennacherib heard that Tirhakah king of Egypt was coming against him, he sent a second message to Hezekiah. Hezekiah made this a matter for prayer and the prophet Isaiah brought him God's assurance of deliverance. Tirhakah was involved in the coalition defeated by Sennacherib; Egypt of that period was correctly evaluated by the Assyrian spokesman as "a broken reed" (II Kings 18:21; Isa. 36:6). The Bible relates that Jerusalem was delivered by the Lord, who sent His angel to smite the Assyrian armies and thus forced Sennacherib to retire to his homeland (II Kings 19:35-36; II Chron. 32:21; Isa. 37:36-37). Various naturalistic explanations of this incident have been attempted. Herodotus preserves a story of an Assyrian defeat occasioned by a plague of mice, which consumed the equipment of the armies and left them helpless before their enemies; some have associated the mice with the carrying of some disease-plague.

Back in Nineveh, Sennacherib was assassinated by two of his sons in 681 B.C. (II Kings 19:37; Isa. 37:38) in an effort to upset the succession

Stone relief from Nineveh showing Sennacherib, King of Assyria, sitting upon his throne receiving spoils from the city of Lachish. BM

which he had decreed for Esarhaddon, but Esarhaddon was equal to the situation and gained the throne. The Assyrian account of the Judean campaign follows: "As to Hezekiah, the Jew, he did not submit to my yoke, I laid siege to 46 of his strong cities, walled forts and to the countless small villages in their vicinity, and conquered (them) by means of well-stamped (earth-) ramps, and battering-rams brought (thus) near (to the walls) (combined with) the attack by foot-soldiers, (using) mines, breeches (sic) as well as sapper work. I drove out (of them) 200,150 people, young and old, male and female, horses, mules, donkeys, camels, big and small cattle, beyond counting, and considered (them) booty. Himself I made a prisoner in Jerusalem, his royal residence, like a bird in a cage. I surrounded him with earthwork in order to molest those who were leaving his city's gate. . . . Hezekiah himself, . . ., did send me later, to Nineveh, my lordly city, together with 30 talents of gold, 800 talents of silver . . . his (own) daughters, concubines, male and female musicians. In order to deliver the tribute and to do obeisance as a slave he sent his (personal) messenger." (A. Leo Oppenheim, in J. B. Pritchard, *Ancient Near Eastern Texts Relating to the Old Testament.* 2nd ed. Princeton, N. J.: Princeton University Press, 1955, p. 288. Cf. *ARAB,* II, p. 240). C.E.D.

SENSUAL (sĕn'shū-ăl, Gr. *psychikós, pertaining to the soul*), having the nature and characteristics of the soul, i.e., the natural life which men have in common with brutes; of the physical body (I Cor. 15:44); of one dominated by the self-life with its carnal desires (Jude 19; I Cor. 2:14); of the sensual wisdom characterizing the unregenerated mind (James 3:15).

SENUAH (See Hasenuah)

SEORIM (sē-ō'rĭm, Heb. *se'ōrîm*), a descendant of Aaron; one of the courses or subdivisons of the priests in the time of David (I Chron. 24:1-8).

SEPHAR (sē'fär, Heb. *sephārâh*), the eastern limit of the territory of the sons of Joktan (Gen. 10:30). This may be equated with the Arabic Zafar, the name of two towns in southern Arabia.

SEPHARAD (sē-fā'răd, Heb. *sephārādh*), the place of captivity of certain people of Jerusalem (Obad. 20). Its location is uncertain; perhaps it is to be identified with Shaparda, which Sargon II, who exiled Israelites to the cities of the Medes, and claims to have conquered Judah, mentions as a district of southwestern Media. Among the Jews of the post-Biblical period the term was used to refer to Spain.

SEPHARVAIM, SEPHARVITE (sĕf'är-vā'ĭm, sē'-fär-vīt), the place from which the Assyrians brought colonists to live in Samaria (II Kings 17:24,31). The inhabitants of the place were called Sepharvites. The place is also referred to in the Rabshakeh's threatening speech to Jerusalem (II Kings 18:34; 19:13) as a place conquered by the Assyrian armies. Formerly Sepharvaim was identified with Sippar in Babylonia, but recently scholars have tended to reject that theory and have identified it with the Sibraim of Ezekiel 47:16, a place located in the region of Hamath.

SEPTUAGINT (sĕp'tū-à-jĭnt), the first and most important of a number of ancient translations of the Hebrew OT into Greek. Little is certainly known about it, for our information is frequently based on ancient traditions of doubtful authenticity, and scholars are divided in their judgments both concerning its origin and its usefulness in textual criticism.

The story of the origin of the Septuagint is told in the *Letter of Aristeas,* a pseudepigraphical book written in the second half of the second century B.C. It states that Ptolemy II (called Philadelphus, the king of Egypt, 285-247 B.C.) wished to have a translation of the Jewish Law for his famous library in Alexandria. At his request, the high priest Eleazer of Jerusalem sent 72 men, six from each tribe, to Egypt with a scroll of the Law. In 72 days, they translated one section each from this scroll, and afterwards decided on the wording together. So the version was called Septuagint (the translation of the 70, abbreviated LXX). Later writers elaborated on this story to the effect that the 72 had translated the whole OT (not the Pentateuch only), each independently of the other, in seclusion. The exact agreement of the 72 copies proved the work's inspiration.

What is the truth of this story? It is generally agreed that the Pentateuch was translated from Hebrew into Greek in Egypt at about the time of Ptolemy II, say 280 B.C. The rest of the OT was done at a later date. Most scholars believe the whole to have been finished by 180 B.C., although some scholars (notably Kahle) disagree, and believe that the LXX never contained more than the Pentateuch until the Christians took it over and added the rest of the OT books much later.

It seems most likely that the LXX originated not by the desire of Ptolemy II (although the project may have had his approval), but out of the need of the Alexandrian Jews. Alexandria of the third century B.C. was a large city with a great Jewish population. These Jews were Greek speaking, having long since forgotten their own language. The vigorous Jewish intellectual life of Alexandria (exemplified by Philo Judaeus a later century) would demand the Torah in Greek, just as an earlier generation of Jews made Targums of the OT in the Aramaic language.

The fact that the LXX was not made all at once is plain by the unevenness of its character. Some parts, e.g., the Pentateuch, are a rather literal and accurate translation of the Hebrew text. Other books, as I, II Samuel, differ greatly from the Masoretic Text (our present Hebrew Bible). Recent finds at Qumran ("The Dead Sea Scrolls") include a Hebrew MS of Samuel whose text seems very close to the LXX of this book. The LXX Daniel was such a free paraphrase that it was set aside in favor of a later translation made by Theodotion. The LXX Jeremiah is one-seventh, and the LXX Job is about one-fourth shorter than the Masoretic Text. The LXX, then, is not one book, but a collection of translations of the OT produced by Jews of the Diaspora.

The LXX came to have great authority among the non-Palestinian Jews. Its use in the synagogues of the Diaspora made it one of the most important missionary aids. Probably it was the first work of substantial size ever to be translated into another language. Now the Greeks could read the divine revelation in their own tongue. When the NT quotes from the OT, as it frequently does, the form of the quotation often follows the LXX.

The early Christian Church, built largely on converts from the synagogues of the Greek-speaking world, took over the LXX as their Bible. Their use of it, to prove to the Jews that Jesus was the Messiah, caused a change in the Jews' attitude toward it. Soon after A.D. 100, the Jews completely gave up the LXX and it became a Christian book. The Jews sponsored new translations of the OT, those by Aquila, Symmachus, and Theodotion being best known.

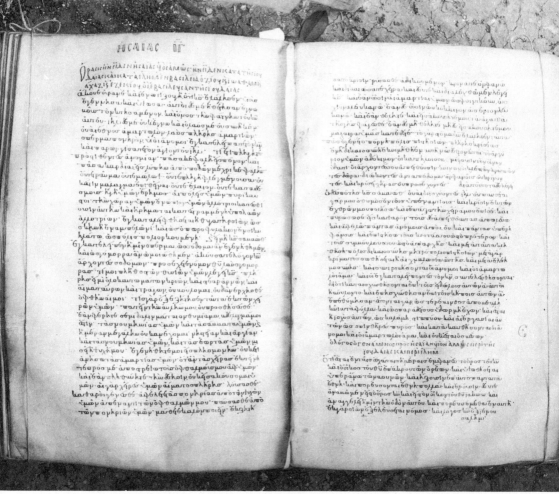

A manuscript page of the Book of Isaiah, from the ninth century A.D., in the Greek of the Septuagint (LXX). This volume is in the Greek library at Jerusalem. © MPS

Our oldest copies of the LXX today are from the three great Greek MSS of the Bible from the fourth and fifth centuries A.D. — Sinaiticus, Vaticanus, and Alexandrinus. It is quite plain that these represent a LXX which has had a long textual history, and that it is now impossible to say to what extent these copies agree with the original translation made some 600 or 700 years before. Origen (died c. A.D. 250) sensed the problem of many divergent readings in the MSS in his day, and sought to produce a resultant text in his *Hexapla*. The textual criticism of the LXX is a difficult task, on which the last word remains to be said.

The LXX is of use in two ways to Biblical studies today:

1. It is a valuable witness to the understanding of the OT in pre-Christian days. As such it is frequently the originator of an exegetical tradition still followed. When, e.g., the majority of English Old Testaments render the covenant name for God (in Hebrew *YHWH*) by "LORD," they are merely following the lead of the LXX, which rendered the word by the Greek *kyrios* — "Lord." Another example of the LXX's influence on subsequent translations is its rendering of the Hebrew *'ĕlōhîm* (God) by *aggeloi* ("angels"), e.g., in Psalm 8:5. The writer of the Hebrews epistle (2:7) followed the LXX here, as did the KJV: "a little lower than the angels." Most modern translators prefer to translate *'ĕlōhîm* literally, as, e.g., the RSV: "little less than God."

2. The LXX is a very important tool for use in the science of textual criticism — the attempt to bring to light the original text of the Bible. In quite a few cases the Masoretic Text and the LXX do not agree. A person knowing neither of the original languages can sense the difference by comparing Amos 9:11,12 with Acts 15:16,17. James quotes Amos, and his quotation agrees in general with the LXX, which is quite different from the Masoretic Text. Of course, the great majority of the differences between the two are inconsequential; the Amos-Acts passage was cited because the difference there is of some consequence for the meaning of the passage. Another example is Psalm 22:16, where the Hebrew Bible "like a lion my hands and my feet" is rendered "they pierced my hands and my feet" in the English Bibles, following the LXX. Often when the Hebrew text is difficult (as in the last example) modern translators correct the text by using the easier-to-explain readings of the LXX. To what extent this adherence to the easier reading is justified is not easy to say. A recent trend of thought among Biblical scholars is to question the correctness of these easier LXX readings and to seek by etymological study to make sense of the more difficult reading in the Masoretic Text. In spite of these problems, it can be said that the LXX is an eloquent witness to the accuracy with which the OT has come down to us from ancient days.

J.B.G.

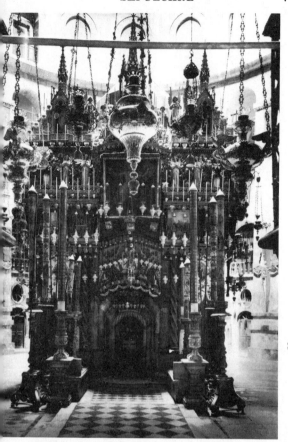

Interior of the Church of the Holy Sepulchre in Jerusalem, supposedly the site of the tomb of Jesus.
© MPS

SEPULCHRE (See Tomb)

SEPULCHRE, CHURCH OF THE HOLY, the church professedly covering the tomb where Jesus was buried. Tradition points to its identification by Helena, mother of Constantine, in A.D. 325. Constantine built an elaborate church on the site, dedicated in A.D. 335. The authenticity of the site is much disputed. The destruction of Jerusalem in A.D. 70 and its more complete devastation in A.D. 135 make the certainty of the identification questionable. According to Scripture the crucifixion and burial took place outside the city wall (John 19: 20; Matt. 28:11; Heb. 13:12). Many authorities seriously doubt that the traditional site was outside the city wall. It is very difficult (but not impossible) to plot the course of the wall so as to exclude the traditional site. Actually no remains of a city wall following such a course have been found. Discovery of remains of an apparently first-century wall N of the supposed line of the third wall, begun by Agrippa I in A.D. 41, suggests that the present wall is the true second wall and that the traditional second wall excluding the Holy Sepulcher never existed. This would place the site within the city. But authorities are not agreed as to the true significance of the discovery. The traditional site has its strong defenders and vigorous opponents. Demonstrable proof of the location of the actual tomb is lacking.   D.E.H.

SERAH (sē'rà, Heb. *serah*), a daughter of Asher (Gen. 46:17; I Chron. 7:30). Once spelled Sarah (Num. 26:46).

SERAIAH (sē-rā'yà, Heb. *serāyāhû*). 1. A son of Kenaz (I Chron. 4:13).

2. A scribe who held office under David (II Sam. 8:17).

3. A Simeonite, son of Asiel (I Chron. 4:35).

4. One of the men sent to arrest Jeremiah and Baruch (Jer. 36:26).

5. The high priest when Nebuchadnezzar captured Jerusalem. He was put to death by Nebuchadnezzar at Riblah (II Kings 25:18-21; Jer. 52: 24-27). He was the father of Jehozadak, who was taken into captivity, and the grandfather of Jeshua, the high priest under Zerubbabel at the return from exile. He may also be the Seraiah named as an ancestor of Ezra (I Chron. 6:14,15; Ezra 3:2; 7:1).

6. The son of Neriah, a quartermaster (RSV), carried to Babylon when Jerusalem fell (Jer. 51: 59-64).

7. The son of Tanhumeth, from the town of Netophah (II Kings 25:23; Jer. 40:8).

8. A priest, the third in the list of those who returned from Babylon to Jerusalem with Zerubbabel (Ezra 2:2; Neh. 7:7, where he is called Azariah; 12:1), and third also in the record of those who sealed the covenant binding all Jews not to take foreign wives (Neh. 10:2). He became governor of the temple when it was rebuilt (Neh. 11:11). He is mentioned (as Azariah) also in I Chronicles 9:11.

SERAPHIM (sĕr'à-fĭm, Heb. *serāphîm*), called in the KJV seraphims (*-im* is the Hebrew plural ending; hence the *s* is superfluous) were celestial beings whom Isaiah saw standing before the enthroned Lord when he was called to the prophetic ministry (Isa. 6:2,3,6,7). This is the only mention of these creatures in the Bible. They seem to be comparable to the four living creatures of Ezekiel 1:5-25 and Revelation 4:6-8.

The word seraphim means "burning ones." The same word is used to describe the serpents in the wilderness (Num. 21:6,8); some commentators have concluded that the seraphim of Isaiah's vision were serpentine in form. This is not correct. Actually, like the cherubim (*q.v.*) and the living creatures, they belong to an order of unearthly beings attending the throne of God. They were seen by Isaiah as having the hands, faces and voices of men and stood upright; they had three pairs of wings. It has been suggested that they symbolized lightning. Certainly their posture (their faces and feet covered by their wings) was one of worship and adoration before God, contributing to the sense of awe and reverence in His presence.   J.B.G.

SERAPIS (sĕ-rā'pĭs), a highly venerated Graeco-Egyptian god. His worship was introduced into Egypt under the Ptolemies with the transfer of his statue to Alexandria and the cult was accepted by the people as the anthropomorphic equivalent of the Egyptian divinities Osiris and Apis. The worship of this god soon won a wide acceptance in the Hellenic world, spread to Rome, and ultimately became one of the leading cults of the west. He is not mentioned in Scripture, but being worshiped at Corinth he must be included among the so-called "gods many" mentioned by Paul (I Cor. 8:5).

SERED (sē'rĕd, Heb. *seredh*), a son of Zebulun (Gen. 46:14; Num. 26:26), and founder of a tribal family.

SERGEANT (See Occupations & Professions)

SERGIUS PAULUS (sûr'jĭ-ŭs pô'lŭs, Gr. *Sérgios Paúlos*), the Roman proconsul (KJV "deputy") of Cyprus, a senatorial province from 22 B.C. He was "a prudent man," one possessed of intelligence and discretion; in his desire to know the truth he had come under the evil influence of Bar-Jesus but revealed his prudence in requesting to hear the missionaries, in Cyprus on the first journey. Deeply impressed by what he saw and heard, the proconsul "believed," which most naturally means that he became a Christian (Acts 13:7-12).

SERMON ON THE MOUNT, the first of six extended discourses of Jesus given in the Gospel of Matthew, covering chapters five, six and seven. The others are (2) the mission of the twelve (Matt. 9:35-11:1); (3) the parables by the sea (13:1-52); (4) on humility (chapter 18); (5) denouncing hypocrisy (chapter 23); (6) on eschatology (chapters 24 and 25).

Some of these discourses are given in Mark and Luke in the same situations as in Matthew, but always in shorter form. Much of the teaching material which Matthew gives in these long discourses is given also by Mark and Luke, with close verbal similarity, but in fragments in other settings than Matthew's.

These facts have caused critical students to question, in greater or less degree, the integrity of Matthew's record of the Lord's teaching ministry. Some relatively conservative scholars have held that Matthew's six great discourses of Jesus were built up by Matthew from scattered materials.

It is obviously impossible in this short article to give an answer in detail, but it can be stated that there is no sound reason to doubt that Matthew's account of the discourses of Jesus is true and reliable.

The nature of Jesus' itinerant ministry to shifting crowds was such that He must have repeated similar material a great many times under a great variety of circumstances. Moreover, in any one extended session of His teaching, there were interruptions, questions, arguments, digressions.

The word "sermon" is misleading to the modern mind. Matthew does not say that Jesus arose, entered the pulpit, and delivered a sermon which He had formally prepared in a quiet library! The crowds were following Him (Matt. 5:1; Luke 6:17) to see His miracles. He went up the mountain a little way so that His immediate followers would be nearer than the rest (Matt. 5:1); and then He came down with them to a level place (Luke 6:17), still in "the mountain." Presently He sat down and began to teach, with special attention to the disciples who were near.

The Biblical writers, of course, used no quotation marks, and the modern reader must understand that they do not claim to give quotations word for word. Neither do they claim to give all that was said on any occasion. They do claim that their words are a true presentation of the substance quoted.

Let the reader allow his imagination to picture the giving of the first beatitude, for example. Jesus says, "Blessed are you poor people." A dull person interrupts, "How can that be? We're in want." Jesus replies, "God's kingdom is yours (Luke 6:20) [if you will have it], but more important, — Blessed are they who feel their spiritual poverty, for the kingdom of heaven is theirs." (Matt. 5:3).

The "sermon," then, is a student's (Matthew's) report of a class lecture and discussion, and should be studied in that light. Luke's account is to be understood as based upon another student's notebook (See Luke 1:1-4 for Luke's sources of information). The fact that there are digressions from a formal outline (Matt. 5:25,26,29,30, etc.) is evidence of the genuineness of the record. What teach-

The view from Jebel Hattin (Horns of Hattin), looking out over the Sea of Galilee. This is the traditional site of the Sermon on the Mount, and it is generally known as the Mount of Beatitudes. © MPS

er in touch with the minds of his class is ever able to avoid digressions from the outline he had in mind?

This mode of regarding the matter does not in any way contradict the inspired truthfulness of the Gospel record as it stands.

It is remarkable what unity and order of thought is evident in the sermon on the mount. There is no space for a detailed analytical outline, which the careful reader can profitably make for himself. Is the teaching of Jesus literally applicable to human beings in this world? The meek do not now inherit the earth (5:5) and public or national non-resistance leads to slavery.

If we take the teaching of Jesus in the same reasonably flexible way in which He obviously intended it, the way in which He interpreted the ten commandments (Matt. 12:4,5,11,12, etc.), the way of the heart rather than of mere outward conduct (Matt. 5:22,28), there is not a word which we need not heed today. We should be willing to take a slap in the face. This is not to say that we must stand by and see the innocent suffer lawless injury. Jesus did not contradict the principle that those responsible for law enforcement must bear "the sword" (Rom. 13:1-5) and that "not in vain." The sermon on the mount is Christ's instruction to us for godly living in the present world.   J.O.B.

SERPENT (See Animals, Reptiles)

SERUG (sē'rŭg, Heb. *serûgh*, meaning uncertain), a descendant of Shem; son of Reu and great-grandfather of Abraham (Gen. 11:20,22f; I Chron. 1: 26). In KJV of Luke 3:35 he is called Saruch (Gr., *seroúch*); ASV and RSV have Serug. He is thus in the Messianic line. *Saurgi,* a city of Harran district mentioned in Assyrian texts, probably was named after him. He lived 230 years.

SERVANT (See Occupations & Professions)

SERVANT OF JEHOVAH, a term applied in the OT to the patriarchs (Exod. 32-13), Moses (Num. 12:7f), Joshua (Judg. 2:8), David (II Sam. 7:5-29), the prophets (Zech. 1:6), and others. It is chiefly used, however, as a title for the Messiah in Isaiah 40 — 66 (esp. in 42:1-9; 49:1-13; 50:4-11; 52:13 — 53:12). The Servant is the same person previously described in 7:14; 9:6f; 11:1-5; he is also identified as "the Branch" (cf. 4:2; 11:1; 53:2 with Jer. 23:5f; 33:15; Zech. 3:8; 6:12f). The NT applies the Servant-passages to Christ (42:1-4 is quoted as fulfilled in Matt. 12:18-21; and 52:13 — 53:12 is quoted in Matt. 8:17; Luke 22:37; John 12:38; Acts 8:32f; Rom. 10:16; cf. also John 1:29; Rom. 8:34; Heb. 9:28; I Pet. 2:21-25). The Servant's mission is fulfilled only in Christ: election (42:1; 49:7; I Pet. 2:4,6), birth (49:1; 53:2; Luke 1:31-35), anointing (42:1; 48:16; 59:21; 61:1; Matt. 3:16; Luke 4:18f), ministry (49:8-13; Acts 10:36-43), rejection (49:4,7; 53:1-3; Acts 3:13-18), obedience (50:4-7; Phil. 2:7f), new covenant (42:6; 49:8; 55:3; Matt. 26:26-29), vicarious death (53:4-12; I Pet. 2:22-25), resurrection (53:10-12; Acts 2:24-36), salvation offered (49:8; 61:2; Luke 24:46-49), mission to Gentiles (42:1,6f; 49:6,12; 60:3,9; Matt. 28:18-20), glorification and intercession (49:3; 53:12; Acts 2:33-36; Phil. 2:6-11; Heb. 7:24f).   **W.B.**

SERVICE. The word rendered "service" in KJV is chiefly the Hebrew noun *'avôdhâh* (*labor; service*), which is used in a wide variety of meanings: (1) the use of the earth (I Chron. 27:26 ["tillage"]; Ps. 104:14); (2) inferior or menial work ("servile work" — Lev. 23:7f, 21, 25, 35f); (3) work rendered as a slave (Exod. 1:14; 2:23 ["bondage"]; (4) a stipulated work-agreement between two persons for a definite period (Gen. 29:27; 30:26; Hos. 12:12); (5) military employment (I Chron. 26:30; Ezek. 29:18); (6) work connected with the construction or repair of the tabernacle or temple (Exod. 36:1,3,5; 30:32; I Chron. 28:20f; 29:7; II Chron. 34:13); (7) the performance of a ritual or ordinance (Exod. 12:25f; 13:5; Josh. 22:27; II Chron. 35:16); (8) chiefly, work as a ministration performed publicly by priests and Levites (Num. 3:6ff; 4:4-49; 8:11-26; 16:9; 18:4-7, 21-31; I Chron. 23:27f,32). Levitical and priestly service was God-ordained (Num. 18:7; I Chron. 24:19; 28:12f), orderly (I Chron. 24:3, 19; II Chron. 8:14; 29:35; 31:2; 35:10), manifold (I Chron. 23:28,32; 25:1,6), limited (Num. 8:24-26), and rewarded (Num. 18:21,24,31).

KJV renders the following words "service" in the NT: *diakonia* (*attendance; ministering* — Luke 10:40; Rom. 15:31; II Cor. 11:8; Rev. 2:19); *douleuo* (*to serve* [*as a slave*] — Gal. 4:8; Eph. 6:7; I Tim. 6:2); *latreia* (*ministration* — John 16:2; Rom. 9:4; 12:1; Heb. 9:1,6); *latreuo* (*to minister* — Heb. 9:9); *leitourgia* (*public ministration* — II Cor. 9:12; Phil. 2:17,30) (B. F. Westcott, *The Epistle to the Hebrews*, London: Macmillan and Co., 1889, pp. 230-232).   **W.B.**

SERVITOR (See Occupations & Professions)

SETH (sĕth, Heb. *shēth* [so KJV in Num. 24:17; I Chron. 1:1], see below). 1. Adam's third son; father of Enos (Gen. 4:25f; 5:3-8). His name (meaning "appointed," i.e., "substituted") signifies· that he was considered a "substitute" for Abel (4:25). His birth recalled man's tragic loss of the divine image (5:1f). He became the founder of the line of faith (4:26; Luke 3:38).

2. The Moabites (Num. 24:17). [Sheth, see ASV].

SETHUR (sē'thẽr, Heb. *sethûr, hidden*), son of Michael, a representative prince of the tribe of Asher sent by Moses, at Jehovah's command, to spy out Canaan (Num. 13:2f,13).

SEVENEH (sē-vē'nĕ, Heb. *sewēnēh*, meaning uncertain), mentioned in Ezekiel 29:10, 30:6. It is rendered Syene in the KJV. This is the Hebrew reading of an Egyptian town located on the first cataract of the Nile, known today as Aswan. Here the Jews, during the control of the Persians, erected a temple in which they worshiped Jehovah.

SEVENTY, THE, Disciples of our Lord. The mission of the Seventy (mentioned only in Luke 10:1-20) probably represents a rehearsal of responsibilities and conditions that the disciples would meet after Christ's departure. Note the following parallels with Acts: (1) the mission of others outside the Twelve (Luke 10:1; Acts 8:1,4); (2) the inclusion of the Gentiles (Luke 10:8; Acts 10:17); (3) the kingdom of God proclaimed (Luke 10:9, 11; Acts 8:12); (4) the reception (Luke 10:5-9; Acts 2:41f) and rejection (Luke 10:10ff; Acts 7:54-60) of the Gospel; (5) triumph over demonic powers (Luke 10:17ff; Acts 16:16ff); (6) joy of discipleship (Luke 10:17; Acts 5:41).

SEVENTY WEEKS, THE, a name applied to Daniel 9:24-27, a prophecy that presumably, in contrast to the general prophecies in Daniel 2 and 7, pin-points the exact time within the fourth kingdom when the Messiah shall appear. Practically all agree that the "weeks" designate 490 years. The prophecy is (1) divided: the successive periods are described as 7,62,1; (2) dated: its *terminus a quo* ("from" — 9:25) and its *terminus ad quem* ("unto" — 9:25); (3) determinative: its purposes regard Israel (9:24), redemption (9:24), the Messiah (9:24,26f), the sacrifices (9:27), Jerusalem (9:25,26f). (4) debated (see below). Three main views are held: (1) the *critical,* that the "prophecy" (written by a pseudo-Daniel in 165 B.C.) synchronizes (inaccurately) with the history between 586 B.C. (Jerusalem's fall) and 164 B.C. (Antiochus); (2) the *dispensational,* that the 69th week terminated at the crucifixion, leaving the 70th (with the present age intervening as a "great parenthesis") to be fulfilled in the Great Tribulation; (3) the *conservative,* or *traditional,* that the 70th week was introduced by Christ's baptism and bisected (3½ years) by His death, thus causing the sacrifices to cease (9:27).   **W.B.**

SEVEN WORDS FROM THE CROSS. These words of Christ were probably uttered in the following order: (1) Before the darkness: "Father, forgive them," etc. (Luke 23:34); "Verily I say unto thee," etc. (Luke 23:43); "Woman, behold ·thy son," (John 19:26f). (2) During the darkness: "My God, my God," (Matt. 27:46; Mark 15:34). (3) After the darkness: "I thirst" (John 19:28, fulfilling Ps. 69:21); "It is finished" (John 19:30); "Father, into thy hands" (Luke 23:46, quoting Ps. 31:5). These seven words may be described as: (1) propitiatory — "Father, forgive"; (2) promissory — "Today thou shalt be with me in paradise"; (3) provisionary — "Woman, behold thy son"; (4) protestatory — "My God, my God, why didst thou forsake me?" (Matt. 27:46, ASV mg.); (5) peremptory — "I thirst"; (6) proclamatory — "It is finished"; (7) pacificatory — "Father, into thy hands I commend my spirit." Theologically, these words, in the order given above, illustrate (1) divine forgiveness; (2) assurance of immortality; (3) good works; (4) the awfulness of Christ's death; (5) the true humanity of Christ; (6) the perfection of Christ's atonement; (7) the divine complacency.

SHAALABBIN (shā'ă-lăb'ĭn, Heb. *sha'ălabbîn,* prob. *haunt of foxes*; cf. Judg. 15:4), a town listed in Joshua 19:42 between Ir-shemesh and Aijalon as assigned to the Danites. See SHAALBIM.

SHAALBIM (shā-ăl'bĭm, Heb. *sha'albîm*), a town won by the Danites from the Amorites with the help of the Ephraimites (Judg. 1:35). In Solomon's time a representative from this town was appointed as commissary officer (I Kings 4:9). "Eliahba the Shaalbonite" (II Sam. 23:32; I Chron. 11:33), one of David's special guards, came from this town (Shaalbon = Shaalbim). Some have identified Shaalbim (Shaalbon, Shaalabin) with modern Selbit, a town in central Palestine. See SHAALABBIN.

SHAALBONITE (See Shaalbim)

SHAAPH (shā'ăf, Heb. *sha'aph,* meaning uncertain). 1. The sixth in a list of sons of Jahdai (I Chron. 2:47).

2. A scion of Caleb by Maachah, a concubine. This man became the progenitor of the inhabitants of Madmannah (I Chron. 2:49; cf. Josh. 15:31).

SHAARAIM (shā'ă-rā'ĭm, Heb. *sha'ărayim, two gates* [so rendered in LXX of I Sam. 17:52]; KJV [incorrectly] Sharaim in Josh. 15:36). 1. A town belonging to Judah in the Shephelah or "low country" (Josh. 15:36); mentioned elsewhere only in I Samuel 17:52.

2. A town belonging to Simeon (I Chron. 4:31); listed as Sharuhen in Joshua 19:6 and Shilhim in Joshua 15:32.

SHAASHGAZ (shā-ăsh'găz, Heb. *sha'ashgāz*); a chamberlain (or eunuch) in charge of "the second house" of concubines belonging to King Ahasuerus (Xerxes); Esther was entrusted to his care (Esth. 2:14).

SHABBETHAI (shăb'ĕ-thī, Heb. *shabbethay, Sabbath-born*), a Levite of Ezra's time who is mentioned as a participant in the foreign-wives controversy (Ezra 10:15, ASV; cf. mg.), as an interpreter of the Law (Neh. 8:7f) and as a chief Levite over the temple (Neh. 11:16).

SHACHIA (shà-kī'à, Heb. *sākheyâh,* probably *Jehovah has hedged about*), son of Shaharaim, a Benjamite (I Chron. 8:10).

SHADDAI (shăd'ī, Heb. *shadday,* exact meaning still uncertain, although KJV's *Almighty* probably approximates basic idea), a title for God found 48 times in the OT. Appearing first in Genesis 17:1 (cf. 35:11; Exod. 6:2f) as a self-designation of God, it is subsequently used by Isaac (Gen. 28:3), Jacob (43:14; 48:3; 49:25), Balaam (Num. 24:4, 16), Job (31 times), Naomi (Ruth 1:20f), David (Ps. 68:14; 91:1), and the prophets (Isa. 13:6; Ezek. 1:24; 10:5; Joel 1:15). Rightly understood, Exodus 6:2f does not support the critical view that El Shaddai (or Elohim) was God's exclusive name in the pre-Mosaic revelation.

SHADOW, a word used literally, figuratively, and theologically. Literally, of a mountain (Judg. 9:36), tree (Dan. 4:12; Hos. 4:13; Mark 4:32), dial (II Kings 20:9-11), booth (Jonah 4:5), gourd (Jonah 4:6), a person (Acts 5:15); figuratively, of life's shortness (I Chron. 29:15; Job 8:9; Ps. 102:11), of protection (either good, as in Ps. 17:8; 36:7; 91:1; or evil, as in Isa. 30:3; Jer. 48:45), of the Messiah's blessings (Isa. 4:6; 32:2; 49:2; 51:16), of death (either physical, as in Job 10:21f; Ps. 23:4; 107:10,14; or spiritual, as in Isa. 9:2; Matt. 4:16; Luke 1:79); and theologically as follows: (1) of God's unchangeableness (James 1:17); (2) of the typical nature of the OT (Col. 2:17; Heb. 8:5; 10:1), illustrated in these facts: the OT prefigures in outline the NT substance; the OT

represents externally (in rites and ceremonies) what the NT fulfills internally; the OT saints, nevertheless, could, by faith, comprehend the inner reality of the shadow; the NT, therefore, fulfills and abolishes the OT shadow; the NT saints, however, can still draw from the shadow spiritual instruction; and, finally, even NT saints, with the shadow and the substance, still await the full day of spiritual understanding (I Cor. 13:12). W.B.

SHADRACH (shā'drăk, Heb. *shadhrakh,* meaning uncertain), the Babylonian name given to Hananiah, one of the Hebrew youths committed to the prince of the eunuch (Dan. 1:3,7).

SHAFT, found in KJV only in Isaiah 49:2 (Heb. *hêts, arrow*) and in Exodus 25:31; 37:17; Numbers 8:4 (all Heb. *yārēk, thigh, loin, side, base*). In the latter passages it represents the shank of the golden candelabrum; in Isaiah 49:2 it is used in a Messianic sense.

SHAGE (shā'ge, Heb. *shāghē', wandering*), a Hararite ("the mountaineer"), father of Jonathan and one of David's mighty men (I Chron. 11:34; however, the text here is uncertain; cf. II Sam. 23:11,33).

SHAHARAIM (shā'hà-rā'ĭm, Heb. *shahărayim, double dawn*), a Benjamite who, in the land of Moab, had three wives (Hushim, Baara, Hodesh) and nine sons, who became heads of families (I Chron. 8:8-11). The text of vs. 8 is uncertain.

SHAHAZIMAH (shā'hà-zī'mà, Heb. *shahătsûmâh, toward the heights*), a town in Issachar between Tabor and the Jordan (Josh. 19:22). In ASV *Shahazumah.*

SHALEM (shā'lĕm, Heb. *shālēm, safe*), a place mentioned in Genesis 33:18 (KJV); however, most modern scholars (see ASV *in peace* and RSV *safely*) take the Hebrew to express the manner of Jacob's return to Shechem.

SHALIM, LAND OF (shā'lĭm, Heb. *sha'ălîm, district of foxes*), a region, probably near the N boundary of Benjamin's territory, traversed by Saul in search of his father's asses (I Sam. 9:4). ASV *Shaalim.*

SHALISHAH (shà-lī'shà, Heb. *shālishâh, a third part*), a district through which Saul went in search of his father's lost asses (I Sam. 9:4); identified by some with *Baal-shalishah* (II Kings 4:42). KJV *Shalisha.*

SHALLECHETH, THE GATE OF (shăl'ĕ-kĕth), the name of the W gate of Solomon's Temple assigned by lots to Shuppim and Hosah, Levitical porters (I Chron. 26:13-16). Some suppose that the offal of the temple was "cast" through this gate.

SHALLUM, SHALLUN (shăl'ŭm, shăl'ŭn, Heb. *shallûm* or *shallûn, recompense*), a name (*Shallum*) applied to all of the following except the last (*Shallun*): 1. The youngest son of Naphtali (I Chron. 7:13 = Shillem in Gen. 46:24 and Num. 26:48f).

2. The son of Shaul and grandson of Simeon (I Chron. 4:25; cf. Gen. 46:10; Exod. 6:15; Num. 26:12f).

3. The son of Sisamai and father of Jekamiah (I Chron. 2:40f).

4. Son of Kore and chief of the gate-keepers (I Chron. 9:17,19,31; Ezra 2:42; 10:24; Neh. 7:45 = Meshelemiah of I Chron. 26:1 and Shelemiah of I Chron. 26:14). Some hold, however, that I Chronicles 7:13 identifies a different person.

5. Son of Zadok and father of Hilkiah (I Chron. 6:12f); ancestor of Ezra (Ezra 7:1f = Meshullam of I Chron. 9:11 and Neh. 11:11).

6. A king of Israel who, having slain Zechariah, reigned in his place for one month; then he himself was slain by Menahem (II Kings 15:10-15).

7. The father of Jehizkiah and an Ephraimite chief (II Chron. 28:12).

8. Son of Tikvah and husband of the prophetess Huldah; custodian of the sacerdotal wardrobe (II Kings 22:14; II Chron. 34:22; perhaps = Jer. 32:7 [Jeremiah's uncle]; see 10 below).

9. A king of Judah, son of Josiah (I Chron. 3:15; Jer. 22:11); better known as Johoahaz II (II Kings 23:30f,34; II Chron. 36:1).

10. Uncle of Jeremiah (Jer. 32:7; see 8 above).

11. Father of Maaseiah (Jer. 35:4; cf. 52:24).

12. One of the Levitical porters who was compelled to divorce his foreign wife (Ezra 10:24).

13. A son of Bani who was compelled to divorce his foreign wife (Ezra 10:42).

14. The son of Hallohesh; a ruler who, with his daughters, helped to build the walls of Jerusalem (Neh. 3:12).

15. Shallun, son of Col-hozeh; ruler of the Mizpah-district; a builder of the walls of Jerusalem (Neh. 3:15).

SHALMAI (shăl′mī, Heb. *shalmay* in Ezra 2:46, but *salmay* in Neh. 7:48; ASV and RSV have *Salmai* in Neh. 7:48), the ancestral head of the Nethinim family that returned with Zerubbabel (Ezra 2:46; Neh. 7:48).

SHALMAN (shăl′măn, Heb. *shalman*), mentioned only in Hosea 10:14. The person (Shalman) and place (Beth-arbel) are now unknown. The ancient versions differ considerably. The two most likely theories: (1) a contraction of Shalmaneser; (2) the Moabite king Salmanu, mentioned in the inscriptions of Tiglath-pileser.

SHALMANESER (shăl′măn-ē′zêr, Heb. *shalman′-eser* = Assyr. *Sulman-asaridu*, [God] *Sulman is chief*), the title of five Assyrian kings, only one of whom is directly mentioned in the OT; another one is important because he refers to an Israelitish king.

1. Shalmaneser III (859-824 B.C.), son of Ashurnasirpal; the first Assyrian king who, as far as the records reveal, had political and military contacts with a king of the Northern Kingdom of Israel. Although Shalmaneser III is not mentioned as such in the Biblical narrative (I Kings 16:29-22:40; II Chron. 18:1-34), yet his Monolith Inscription in the British Museum recounts a coalition, composed principally of Syria [Hadadezer = Benhadad] and of Israel ["Ahab, the Israelite"], that he met and presumably defeated at Karkar, N of Hamath in the Orontes Valley, in 853 B.C. Ahab, according to this inscription, contributed 2,000 chariots and 10,000 troops in the battle against Shalmaneser. As indicated above, no record of this event is found in the contemporary Biblical data. The reference to Ahab in a non-Biblical archaeological source adds substantial weight to the trustworthiness of the OT record.

2. Shalmaneser V (726-722 B.C.), son of Tiglath-pileser (who died in 727 B.C.); the only Assyrian king named Shalmaneser in the OT history (unless Shalman, in Hos. 10:14, be a contraction of Shalmaneser). There are two references to him: (1) II Kings 17:3-5, which recounts how, first, Shalmaneser received tribute from Hoshea, the last king of the Northern Kingdom; then, after Hoshea had formed an alliance with So, king of Egypt, Shalmaneser, returning to Palestine in a more extensive campaign, imprisoned Hoshea and besieged Samaria for three years. The prophet Hosea, a contemporary of Hoshea's turbulent reign, often speaks out against entanglements with either As-

An engraved bronze band from a palace gate of Shalmaneser III of Assyria, showing a battle scene above, and tribute being paid to the victorious king in the lower panel. BA

syria or Egypt (Hos. 5:13; 7:11; 8:9; 12:1); (2) II Kings 18:9-11, which agrees in essential details with the previous passage (II Kings 17:3-5), but also synchronizes the siege and fall of Samaria with the ruling house of Jerusalem (Hezekiah). Since Sargon (mentioned only in Isa. 20:1 in ancient literature before the advent of modern discoveries) was, according to his own testimony, the conqueror of Samaria in 722/721 B.C.), the Biblical record implicitly agrees, for it says: (1) "the king of Assyria took Samaria" (II Kings 17:6); and (2) "they took it" (II Kings 18:10) — in neither case actually affirming that Shalmaneser was the one who took the city. There is a possible allusion to Shalmaneser V in "King Jareb" (i.e., "the champion king"), which Hosea uses as a humorous or sarcastic reference to some Assyrian king (Hos. 5:13; 10:6). W.B.

SHAMA (shā′mà, Heb. *shāmā′*, He [God] has heard), a son of Hotham, the Aroerite; one of David's mighty men (I Chron. 11:44).

SHAMARIAH (See Shemariah)

SHAMBLES (Gr. *mákellon*, from the Lat. *macellum, meat market* [so RSV]). Paul, answering a question of conscience regarding meat sold in the *makellon*, instructs the Corinthian Christians to eat such meat without further inquiry as to its use in pagan sacrifices. The essential nature of the meat as food has not been affected (cf. I Tim. 4:4); but this liberty must not endanger a weaker brother's conscience (I Cor. 10:23-33).

SHAME, SHAMEFACEDNESS (Heb. *bosheth*, Gr. *aischýne*, Gr. *aidós*). This subject has many aspects: subjective (Gen. 2:25; 3:7) or objective (Jer. 11:13; Hos. 9:10); positive (Prov. 19:26; 28:7) or negative (Prov. 10:5; Rom. 1:16; I John 2:28); literal (Exod. 32:25) or figurative (Rev. 3:18; 16:15); individual (Gen. 38:23) or national (Judg. 18:7; Isa. 30:3-5); removable (Isa. 54:4) or unremovable (Jer. 23:40); loved (Hos. 4:18, ASV) or hated (Eph. 5:12); punitive (Isa. 47:3; Ezek. 16:51-54; 44:12) or commendatory (I Sam. 20:30-34; II Sam. 6:20; 13:11-14); now (Heb. 6:6) or future (Ezek. 32:24f; Dan. 12:2); human (Ps. 119:31) or divine (Ps. 69:7-9; 89:45; Isa. 50:6; Heb. 12:2); due to something natural (II Sam. 19:1-5; I Cor. 11:6,14) or something unnatural (II Sam. 13:11-14; Phil. 3:19). "Shamefacedness" in I Timothy 2:9 denotes sexual modesty.

SHAMED (shā′mĕd, Heb. *shāmedh, destruction*; however, many MSS. read *shāmer, watcher*; ASV has *Shemed*), the third-named son of Elpaal; builder of Ono and Lod (I Chron. 8:12).

SHAMER (shā'mêr, Heb. *shemer, guard*). 1. A descendant of Levi; father of Bani (I Chron. 6:46).

2. Son of Heber and head of an Asherite clan (I Chron. 7:32; Heb. *Shômer* [so KJV]); same as *Shamer* (Heb. *Shāmer*) in vs. 34. Numerous variations exist in Heb. MSS. See also SHEMED (I Chron. 8:12) and SHEMER (I Kings 16:24).

SHAMGAR (shăm'gàr, Heb. *shamgar*), son of Anath; slayer of 600 Philistines (Judg. 3:31; cf. I Sam. 13:19-22). He is listed between Ehud and Barak; but no definite years are assigned to his judgeship. Since Beth-anath belonged to the tribe of Naphtali (Josh. 19:38; Judg. 1:33), and since this tribe was prominent in the contemporary struggle against the Canaanite king Jabin (Judg. 4:6,10; 5:18), it is probable that Shamgar was also a member of this tribe. Israel had been commanded to exterminate the inhabitants of Canaan completely (Exod. 23:31-33; Deut. 7:1-5; 20:16-18); but Israel had disobeyed this divine command (Judg. 1:27-36); therefore, these unsubdued Canaanites had now become a snare to the Israelites. In fact, the situation was now somewhat reversed: Israel was cowed and disarmed, surreptitiously using the "byways" (Judg. 5:5f). In this chaotic condition Shamgar slew 600 Philistines, using only an oxgoad as his weapon. He thus prepared the way for the greater deliverance of Israel under Deborah and Barak.

SHAMHUTH (shăm'hŭth, Heb. *shamhûth, desolation*), an Izrahite; the fifth divisional commander, for the fifth month of the year, in David's organization of his army (I Chron. 27:8, RSV); probably the same person as Shammah the Harodite (II Sam. 23:25) and Shammoth the Harorite (I Chron. 11:27).

SHAMIR (shā'mêr, Heb. *shāmîr, a sharp point*). 1. A town allotted to Judah (Josh. 15:48); now usually identified with the ruin Sōmerak, about 13 miles SW of Hebron.

2. A town in Mount Ephraim; the residence and burial-place of Tola, one of the judges (Judg. 10: 1f). Its identification is still uncertain. The residence of Tola, an Issacharian, in a city of Ephraim has been explained as due either to the turbulent condition of Issachar's territory or to the fact that Issachar had cities within Ephraim.

3. A Levite, son of Micah; a temple-attendant (I Chron. 24:24).

SHAMMA (shăm'à, Heb. *shammā', astonishment* or *desolation*), one of the 11 sons of Zophah; a descendant of Asher (I Chron. 7:37).

SHAMMAH (shăm'à, Heb. *shammâ, waste*). 1. The son of Reuel and grandson of Esau; an Edomite chief (Gen. 36:13,17; I Chron. 1:37).

2. The third son of Jesse and brother of David (I Sam. 16:9; 17:13); also called Shimea (I Chron. 20:7), Shimeah (II Sam. 13:3,32) and Shimei (II Sam. 21:21). He was one of the seven sons of Jesse rejected before the choice of David as king (I Sam. 16:1-13). He fought, with his two older brothers, in Saul's warfare against the Philistines (I Sam. 17:13-19,22f). He was the father of Jonadab (II Sam. 13:3,32) and of Jonathan, whose victory over a Philistine giant is especially noted (II Sam. 21:21f).

3. One of David's three mightiest men, the son of Agee (II Sam. 23:11 = Shage in I Chron. 11: 34). His single-handed victory over the Philistines (II Sam. 23:11f), his loyalty to David in the cave of Adullam (II Sam. 23:13), and his heroic deed in David's behalf (II Sam. 23:15-17) are especially noted concerning him. A comparison of I Chronicles 11:12 with II Samuel 23:11,33 makes it ap-

pear evident that Shammah's name (as one of the three mightiest) has been accidentally omitted from the former passage.

4. One of David's mighty men (II Sam. 23:33); also called Shammoth (pl. of Shammah) (I Chron. 11:27) and Shamhuth (I Chron. 27:8). Some consider him the same person as 3.

SHAMMAI (shăm'ā-ī, Heb. *shammay,* contraction of *shema'yâ, Jehovah has heard*), the name of three descendants of Judah: 1. A son of Onam, who was the son of Jerahmeel by Atarah; father of Nadab and Abishur (I Chron. 2:28,32).

2. A son of Redem and father of Maon (I Chron. 2:44f); a descendant of "Caleb the brother of Jerahmeel" (I Chron. 2:42).

3. A descendant of Ezrah [so Heb. and ASV; AV has Ezra] (I Chron. 4:17f). The text here is extremely ambiguous and uncertain; probably, by a transposition, Shammai was the son of Mered by Bithiah, Pharaoh's daughter (I Chron. 4:18).

SHAMMOTH (shăm'ŏth, Heb. *shammôth, desolation*), one of David's mighty men of war (I Chron. 11:27); apparently the same as Shammah (II Sam. 23:25) and Shamhuth (I Chron. 27:8).

SHAMMUA (shă-mū'à, Heb. *shammû'a, heard* or *renowned*). 1. The son of Zaccur, a spy, representing the tribe of Reuben, sent out to spy out the land of Canaan (Num. 13:4).

2. A son of David by Bath-sheba; brother of Solomon (II Sam. 5:14 [KJV has Shammuah]; I Chron. 14:4), or Shimea (I Chron. 3:5).

3. A Levite; father of Abda (or Obadiah) (Neh. 11:17 = Shemaiah in I Chron. 9:16).

4. The representative of the priestly family of Bilgah (I Chron. 24:14; Neh. 12:5,18 = Bilgai in Neh. 10:8); a priest, whose father returned with Zerubbabel (Neh. 12:1-7), officiating in the high priesthood of Joiakim (Neh. 12:12).

SHAMMUAH (shă-mū'à, Heb. *shammû'a*), son of David (II Sam. 5:14 = Shammua in I Chron. 14: 4 [KJV] and Shimea in I Chron. 3:5 [KJV]).

SHAMSHERAI (shăm'shē-rī, Heb. *shamsheray,* [?] *sunlike*), the first named of six sons of Jeroham; a Benjamite (I Chron. 8:26).

SHAPHAM (shā'făm, Heb. *shāphām*), a Gadite who lived in Bashan, second in authority in the time of Jotham (I Chron. 5:12).

SHAPHAN (shā'făn, Heb. *shāphām, hyrax* or *rock rabbit*), the faithful scribe during Josiah's reign (II Kings 22:3-20; II Chron. 34:8-28). The record cites four responsibilities that he faithfully performed: (1) his oversight of the finances of the repairs of the temple (II Chron. 34:8-13,16f); (2) his transmission of the newly discovered law-book to Josiah (II Chron. 34:14f); (3) his reading of this book before Josiah (II Chron. 34:18); (4) his mission, with others, to carry Josiah's message to the prophetess Huldah (II Chron. 34:20-28). Shaphan's faith is seen in the names he gave his sons: Ahikam (*my brother has risen up*); Gemariah (*Jehovah has accomplished*); Elasah (*God has made*); Jaazaniah (*Jehovah hearkens*). Shaphan's faith is seen in his son's lives: Ahikam, who accompanied his father on the mission to Huldah (II Chron. 34: 20ff) and later became Jeremiah's protector (Jer. 26:24); Elasah, who, with others, transmitted Jeremiah's message to exiles in Babylon (Jer. 29:1-3); Gemariah, who resisted destructive attempts against Jeremiah's writings (Jer. 36:10,12,25); but Jaazaniah did not possess his father's faith (Ezek. 8:11). Two sons of Ahikam, however, continued their grandfather's faith: Micaiah (Jer. 36:11-13) and Gedaliah (Jer. 39:14; 40:5f,9,11f; 43:6).

A pastoral scene on the Plain of Sharon. © MPS

SHAPHAT (shā'făt, Heb. *shāphāt, he has judged*).
1. The son of Hori, who was chosen from the
tribe of Simeon to spy out the land of Canaan
(Num. 13:5).

2. The father of Elisha the prophet (I Kings 19:
16,19; II Kings 3:11; 6:31).

3. A Gadite chief in Bashan (I Chron. 5:12).

4. The son of Adlai, one of David's herdsmen (I
Chron. 27:29).

5. The last named son of Shemaiah, a descendant of the royal line of David (I Chron. 3:22).
(Shemaiah's sons are here said to be six in number; but the fact that only five are actually named
shows that one name has been lost in the process
of the transmission of the text.)   W.B.

SHAPHER (shā'fēr, Heb. *shepher* [ASV more correctly renders *Shepher*], *beauty*), the name of a
mountain between Kehelathah and Haradah at
which the Israelites encamped in their wilderness
wanderings (Num. 33:23). It is otherwise unknown
and unidentified.

SHAPHIR (See Saphir)

SHARAI (shà-rā'ī, Heb. *shārāy*), a "son" of Bani;
mentioned in a list of men who, at Ezra's command, divorced their foreign wives (Ezra 10:10,
40,44).

SHARAIM (shà-rā'ĭm, Heb. *sha'ărayim, two gates*),
a town in Judah (Josh. 15:36, AV); see *Shaaraim*.

SHARAR (shā'rêr, Aram. *shārār, firm*), the father
of Ahiam the Hararite; one of David's mighty men
(II Sam. 23:33 = Sacar in I Chron. 11:35).

SHARE (Heb. *maharesheth, plowshare*), an agricultural instrument mentioned only in I Samuel
13:20 [LXX has "a reaping-hook"; other versions
differ considerably].

SHAREZER (shà-rē'zêr, Heb. *sar'etser*, Assyr.
Shar-usur, protect the king), 1. A son of the As-
syrian king Sennacherib, who, with his brother
Adrammelech, slew his father (II Kings 19:37 =
Isa. 37:38).

2. A contemporary of Zechariah the prophet
and member of a delegation sent from Bethel to
Jerusalem (Zech. 7:2 = *Sherezer* in KJV).

SHARON (shăr'ŭn, Heb. *shārôn* [always with definite article except in I Chron. 5:16], *plain*). 1. The
coastal plain between Joppa and Mount Carmel, a
place proverbial in ancient times for its fertility,
pasturage and beauty (I Chron. 27:29; S. of Sol.
2:1; Isa. 35:2); the location of such towns as
Dor, Lydda (Acts 9:35), Joppa, Caesarea and Antipatris.

2. The suburbs (ASVm "pasture lands") of
Sharon possessed by the tribe of Gad (I Chron.
5:16).

3. Lassharon q.v. (Josh. 12:18).

4. Figuratively, (a) of man's state of regenerancy
— fruitfulness and glory (Isa. 35:2); (b) of man's
eternal state — of peace for evermore (Isa. 65:
10,17).

SHARONITE (shăr'ŭn-īt, Heb. *shārônî, of Sharon*),
a description applied to Shitrai, David's chief
herdsman in the plain of Sharon; the only Sharonite mentioned in the Bible (I Chron. 27:29).

SHARUHEN (shà-rōō'hĕn, Heb. *shārûḥen*), an ancient town in SW Palestine, S of Gaza and W of
Beersheba; assigned to the tribe of Simeon within
Judah's territory (Josh. 19:6; cf. Gen. 49:7); apparently the same as Silhim (Josh. 15:32) and
Shaarim (I Chron. 4:31). See *Shaarim*. Now identified with Tell el-Fār'ah.

SHASHAI (shā'shī, Heb. *shāshay, whitish* or *noble*), a "son" of Bani; listed among those men
who, at Ezra's command, divorced their foreign
wives (Ezra 10:40).

SHASHAK (shā'shăk, Heb. *shāshaq*), a Benjamite,
son of Beriah (I Chron. 8:14f); father of 11 sons
(I Chron. 8:22-25).

SHAUL, SHAULITES (shā'ŭl, shā'ŭ-līts, Heb.
shā'ûl, asked [of Jehovah]; *shā'ûlî, of Shaul*). 1.
The sixth in a list of eight kings that ruled over
Edom (Gen. 36:37f [Saul in AV] = I Chron. 1:
48f).

2. A son of Simeon (Gen. 46:10; Exod. 6:15;
Num. 26:13; I Chron. 4:24). He is called "the son
of a Canaanitish woman" (Gen. 46:10; Exod. 6:

15). Thus the *Shaulites* (Num. 26:13), who descended from him, were of mixed blood.

3. A descendant of Levi; son of Uzziah; ancestor of Samuel (I Chron. 6:24 = Joel in vs. 36).

SHAVEH, VALLEY OF (shā′vě, Heb. *shāwēh, a plain*), also called "the king's dale"; a place near Salem (i.e., Jerusalem [Ps. 76:2]), where, after rescuing his nephew Lot, Abraham met the king of Sodom (Gen. 14:17). Identified by some as the same place where Absalom erected a memorial to himself (II Sam. 18:18).

SHAVEH-KIRIATHAIM (shā′vě-kĭr′ yà-thā′ĭm, Heb. *shāwēh qiryāthayim, the plain of Kiriathaim* [i.e., "twin cities"]), a plain where Chedorlaomer smote the Emim (Gen. 14:5), probably located on the E of the Dead Sea (cf. Num. 32:37).

SHAVING. The act of shaving is represented by the Hebrew words *gāzaz, to shear* (used of animals except in Job 1:20 [of man's head]; Jer. 7:29 [fig., of Jerusalem]; Mic. 1:16 [of a woman's, i.e., Jerusalem's, hair]; Nah. 1:12 ["cut down" = destruction by the Assyrians; cf. Isa. 7:20 below]), *gālaḥ* (used only of human shaving; in KJV = *poll*" [II Sam. 14:26], *shave, shave off, be shaven*), *'avar ta'ar, to cause a razor to pass over* (as in Num. 6:5; 8:7); and by the Greek word *xyrao* (only in I Cor. 11:5f; Acts 21:24 in NT). The priests (Lev. 21:5; Ezek. 44:20) and the Nazirites (Num. 6:5; cf. I Sam. 1:11) among the Israelites were prohibited from shaving; furthermore, the Hebrews as a people, in contrast to surrounding nations, generally accepted the beard as a sign of dignity (cf. II Sam. 10:4f). Shaving had these connotations: (1) an act of contrition (Job 1:20); (2) an accommodation to a custom (Gen. 41:14; cf. I Cor. 11:5f); (3) an act of consecration for Levites (Num. 6:9; 8:7); (4) an act of cleansing for lepers (Lev. 14:8f; 13:32ff); (5) an act completing a vow (Num. 6:18; Acts 18:18; 21:24); (6) an act of commitment of a captive woman (Deut. 21:12); (7) an act of conspiracy against a man's Nazirite vow (Judg. 16:19); (8) an act of contempt (II Sam. 10:4 = I Chron. 19:4); (9) an act, fig. expressed, of cleansing a corrupt nation (Isa. 7:20; cf. 1:16; 6:5; and II Kings 18:13ff).

SHAVSHA (shăv′shà, Heb. *shawshā'*), David's secretary of state (I Chron. 18:16 = *Shisha* in I Kings 4:3 = *Seraiah* in II Sam. 8:17 = *Sheva* in II Sam. 20:25).

SHEAF (Heb. *'ălummâh, 'ōmer, 'āmîr*). The sheaf was a handful of grain left behind the reaper (Jer. 9:22, RSV), gathered and bound usually by children or women (Ruth 2:7,15) in a joyous mood (Ps. 126:6; 129:7f). Thus stacked they became dry and inflammable (Zech. 12:6; cf. Judg. 15:1-5, ASV); but they were beautiful sights (S. of Sol. 7: 2). A donkey (Neh. 13:15) or a heavily loaded cart (Amos 2:13) bore these bundles to the threshing-floor (Ruth 3:6f; Mic. 4:12). Some sheaves, however, were left behind for the poor (Deut. 24: 19; cf. Ruth 2:7,15; Job 24:10). The sheaf of the first-fruit (Lev. 23:10-15; cf. II Chron. 31:5-10) typically represents: (1) Christians, as representatives of a larger harvest (Rom. 16:5; I Cor. 16: 15; James 1:18), possessed by the Spirit (Rom. 8:23), and dedicated to God (Rev. 14:1-5); (2) Christ, as an evidence of the believer's later resurrection (I Cor. 15:20,23).

SHEAL (shē′ăl, Heb. *she'āl, asking*), a "son" of Bani; listed among those who divorced their foreign wives (Ezra 10:29).

SHEALTIEL (shē′ăl-tĭ-ĕl, Heb. *she'altî'ēl, I have asked God*), the father of Zerubbabel (Ezra 3:2, 8; 5:2; Neh. 12:1; Hag. 1:1,12,14; 2:2,23 = *Salathiel* in I Chron. 3:17; Matt. 1:12; Luke 3:27). The apparent discrepancy between I Chronicles 3: 17 and Luke 3:27 and the other passages cited is explained by the supposition that the childless Sheatiel adopted Zerubbabel, the son of his brother Pedaiah, as his legal son.

SHEARIAH (shē′à-rī′à, Heb. *she'aryâh, Jehovah esteems*), one of the sons of Azel; a descendant of Jonathan (I Chron. 8:38; 9:44).

SHEARING HOUSE (Heb. *bêth 'ēqedh hārō'îm, house of binding of the shepherds,* i.e., *binding-house of the shepherds*), the place between Jezreel and Samaria where Jehu met and slaughtered 42 unsuspecting members of the royal house of Ahaziah, king of Judah, while they were on their way, apparently ignorant of Jehu's revolt, to Ahaziah, who was visiting Joram, the wounded king of Israel (II Kings 10:12-14). The corpses were cast into a pit (Heb. *bôr*; cf. its use in Gen. 37:24; Jer. 41:7,9). A possible identification of *Bêth-'ēqedh hārō'îm,* is *Kufr Ra'i,* the *Ra'i* supposedly preserving the Heb. word for "shepherds (*rô'îm*).

SHEAR-JASHUB (shē′àr-jà′shŭb, Heb. *she'ār yā-shûv, a remnant shall return*), the symbolic name of Isaiah's oldest son (Isa. 7:3; 8:18). The symbolism is reflected in the historic return from Babylon and is fulfilled in the spiritual return to the Lord at Messiah's advent (Isa. 1:9; 4:3f; 10:20-23; 65:8f; Rom. 11:5f,16-29).

SHEBA (shē′bà, Heb. *shevā', seven, an oath*). 1. A chief of a Gadite family (I Chron. 5:13).

2. A town allotted to Simeon (Josh. 19:2). Some suppose it to be a corruption of Shema (cf. LXX and Josh. 15:26); others, in view of its absence in I Chronicles 4:28, which gives a similar summation (cf. Josh. 19:2-6), suppose either that it is a variant form of Beer-sheba (see ASV) or that it has been accidentally introduced by the process known as dittography.

3. The son of Birchi, a Benjamite. Motivated by jealousy over the rising power of the Tribe of Judah, as represented by David, Sheba inspired a short-lived insurrection against the kingship of David. Finally cornered by Joab in Abel-beth-maachah, Sheba met an unexpected end when the inhabitants of Abel-beth-maachah, at the behest of a wise woman, threw Sheba's head over the town's wall and thus pacified the wrath of Joab and brought the rebellion to an inglorious end. As a result, David's rule over all Israel was considerably strengthened (II Sam. 20).

4. A son of Raamah, son of Cush (Gen. 10:7; I Chron. 1:9).

5. A son of Joktan; grandson of Eber (Gen. 10:28; I Chron. 1:22); the probable founder of the kingdom of the Sabeans (Sheba) in S. Arabia (see below).

6. The oldest son of Jokshan, Abraham's son by Keturah (Gen. 25:3; I Chron. 1:32). It is probable that this man's descendants, by intermarriage or otherwise, finally became identified with the descendants of 4 and 5; together they constitute what is called the kingdom of Sheba or the Sabeans. These people, known particularly by the Queen of Sheba and her illustrious visit to King Solomon (I Kings 10:1-13; II Chron. 9:1-12; Matt. 12:42), are pictured in the Bible as traders in precious stones and incense (Isa. 60:6; Jer. 6:20; Ezek. 27: 22; 38:13) and in slaves (Job 1:15; Joel 3:8).

SHEBAH (shē'bȧ, Heb. *shiv'âh, seven* or *oath*), the name of a well which the servants of Isaac dug. The town Beer-sheba, i.e. "well of the oath" is so called from this well (Gen. 26:31-33 but cf. 21: 28-31.

SHEBAM (shē'băm, Heb. *sevām, sweet smell*), a town in Reuben (Num. 32:3) called also "Shibmah" (Num. 32:38). ASV "Sebam" and "Sibmah" are more acceptable. E of the Dead Sea, but exact location unknown. Cf. Isaiah 16:8,9.

SHEBANIAH (shĕb'ȧ-nī'ȧ, Heb. *shevanyâh*, meaning uncertain). 1. One of seven priests appointed to blow trumpets before the ark of the covenant when it was brought to Jerusalem (I Chron. 15:24).
2. One of the Levites who led the people in praising God in Nehemiah's time and later signed the covenant with him (Neh. 9:4,5; 10:10).
3. Another Levite who was among the covenanters (Neh. 10:12).
4. A priest who was among the covenanters (Neh. 10:4).
5. The head of a family of priests who served in the days of the high priest Joiakim (Neh. 12:14).

SHEBARIM (shĕb'ȧ-rĭm, Heb. *shevārîm, breaches*, or ASV margin *quarries*), a place to which the men of Ai chased the soldiers of Israel (Josh. 7:5).

SHEBAT (See Sebat)

SHEBER (shē'bêr, Heb. *shever*), son of Caleb (not the famous spy) by his concubine Maachah (I Chron. 2:48).

SHEBNA (shĕb'nȧ, Heb. *shevnā'*). 1. Steward of Hezekiah (Isa. 22:15-21) who, in pride, had made a sepulchre for himself. For his pride, the Lord predicted that he would toss him like a ball into a far country where he would die, and his place would be taken by the godly Eliakim (Isa. 22:22, Rev. 3:7).
2. A scribe, also in Hezekiah's time, who went out with others to face the Rabshakeh, the emissary of Sennacherib (Isa. 36:3-37:2, II Kings 18).

SHEBUEL (shē-bū'ĕl, Heb. *shevū'ēl*). 1. A chief Levite in the time of David, descended from Moses through his son Gershom (I Chron. 23:16; 26:24), placed over the treasures. In I Chronicles 24:20 "Shubael."
2. One of the sons of Heman, chief musician in David's service of praise (I Chron. 25:4), also called Shubael in 25:20. Heman had 14 sons and three daughters, all in the choir.

SHECANIAH, SHECHANIAH (shĕk-ȧ-nī'ȧ, Heb. *shekhanyâh, dweller with Jehovah*). 1. Head of the tenth of the 24 courses of priests in the days of David. The priests had so multiplied that David divided them thus, giving two-thirds of the courses to descendants of Eleazar and one-third to descendants of Ithamar, the sons of Aaron (I Chron. 24:11).
2. An almoner of Hezekiah for the priests in their cities (II Chron. 31:15), the priests deriving their support principally from the oblations of the people.
3. A descendant of David in the time of the Restoration, and head of a house (I Chron. 3:21,22).
4. A descendant of Parosh, whose descendant Zechariah returned with Ezra leading 150 men (Ezra 8:3).
5. A son of Jehaziel (Ezra 8:5) who led back 300 men.
6. A son of Jehiel, one of the sons of Elam, who first made confession to Ezra of having married foreign women, and who proposed that a covenant be made and that the foreign wives and children be put away (Ezra 10:2-4).

7. The keeper of the E gate of Jerusalem in the time of Nehemiah. His son Shemaiah was one who helped repair the wall (Neh. 3:29).
8. Son of Arah, and father-in-law to Tobiah, the notorious foe of Nehemiah at the time of the rebuilding of the walls of Jerusalem (Neh. 6:18). The fact that he had given his daughter to Tobiah the Ammonite was proof of his unworthiness.
9. One of the chiefs of the priests who returned with Zerubbabel (Neh. 12:3).

SHECHEM (shē'kĕm, Heb. *shekhem, shoulder*), a personal name and the name of a district and city in the hill-country of Ephraim in N central Palestine. The city makes its initial appearance in Biblical history as the first place in Canaan to be mentioned in connection with Abram's arrival in the land. Here the Lord appeared to Abram and promised the land to his descendants; Abraham responded with the building of an altar (Gen. 12: 6-7). When Jacob returned from Paddan-Aram he settled down at Shechem and purchased land from the sons of Hamor (Gen. 33:18-19; Josh. 24:32). In Genesis 33-34 it is seen that Shechem was the name of the city and also of the prince of the city. It appears that the names Shechem and Hamor are hereditary names or perhaps a kind of title (cf. Judg. 9:28). While Jacob was at Shechem the unfortunate incident of Dinah occurred and Simeon and Levi, her full brothers, exacted drastic revenge on the city (Gen. 34). It was at Shechem that the brothers of Joseph were herding Jacob's flock when Joseph was sent to check on their welfare (Gen. 37:12-14). The city is not referred to again until the listing of the tribal divisions of the land after the conquest (Josh. 17:7); Shechem was in the territory allotted to Ephraim. It was selected by Joshua as one of the cities of refuge (Josh. 20:7; 21:21; I Chron. 6:67). Here Joshua gave his farewell address (Josh. 24:1) and made a covenant with the people (vs. 25). Joseph was buried in the plot of ground which his father Jacob had purchased here (Josh. 24:32).

One of the interesting personages in the kaleidoscopic history of Judges, Abimelech, the son of Gideon and a concubine, is closely associated with Shechem. Abimelech conspired with his mother's relatives to kill all the other sons of Gideon and to have himself made king of Shechem (Judg. 9: 6). Trouble developed between Abimelech and the people of Shechem; a conspiracy against Abimelech was revealed to him by the ruler of the city. In the fighting which followed, Abimelech took the city and completely destroyed it. When a number of people took final refuge in the stronghold of the temple of Baal-berith or El-berith, Abimelech gathered fuel and fired the stronghold, so that about 1000 persons perished in the conflagration (9:46-49). After the death of Solomon, his son Rehoboam went to Shechem to be made king by all Israel (I Kings 12:1; II Chron. 10:1); when the principles of his prospective administration were challenged by Jeroboam, Rehoboam followed the disastrous advice of his impetuous, youthful counselors and thus caused the rupture of the kingdom. Jeroboam became king of ten tribes and "built Shechem in the hill country of Ephraim" (I Kings 12:25) as his captital. The city is mentioned in parallel passages in the Psalms (Psa. 60:6; 108:7) and is named in a list of prophetic condemnations against Israel (Hosea 6:9). After the destruction of Jerusalem, men from Shechem and other cities came to Mizpah to be under the protection of Gedaliah and there were deceived and slain by Ishmael (Jer. 44:5ff.). The city is not certainly

A view of modern Shechem and Mount Gerizim. © MPS

mentioned again in the Bible, but the conversation of Jesus and the Samaritan woman (John 4) occurred in this vicinity. It has been suggested that the Sychar (usually identified as modern Askar) of John 4:5 should be read Sychem (Shechem; cf. Acts 7:16), with the Old Syriac Gospels. In A.D. 72 the city was rebuilt as Flavia Neapolis, from which the name of the present village of Nablus is derived.

The name Shechem occurs in historical records and other sources outside Palestine. It is mentioned as a city captured by Senusert III of Egypt (19th century B.C.) and appears in the Egyptian cursing texts of about the same time. "The mountain of Shechem" is referred to incidentally in a satirical letter of the 19th Dynasty. Shechem also figures in the Amarna Letters; its ruler, Lab'ayu, and his sons are accused of acting against Egypt, though he protests that he is devotedly loyal to the pharaoh. The site of the ancient city is Tell Balatah, just E of Nablus. The tell has a mixed archeological history: E. Sellin began work here in 1913 and resumed it in 1926. In 1928 G. Welter succeeded him as director; in 1934 the seventh and final campaign of the German archeologists was in charge of H. Steckeweh, whose labors are of particular value because the previous work had shown inadequate handling of both pottery, chronology and stratigraphy. In spite of limitations, the work produced some important results. In the first campaign a triple gate of Middle Bronze date was found in the NW section of the city; nearby, unearthed in 1926, was a large temple which has been identified as the temple of Baal-berith. In 1926 the eastern gate of the city was

found, along with part of the city-wall. Middle Bronze Shechem had a fine battered (sloping) wall of cyclopean masonry, found standing to a maximum height of 10 meters, with some of its stones over two meters long. Hyksos type fortifications also occur at Shechem, with ramparts of beaten earth (terre pisée). Several cuneiform tablets of the Amarna age add to the store of written materials from Palestine. In 1934 a limestone plaque bearing a representation of a serpent goddess and an inscription in alphabetic script was found. The most recent work at Balatah is that of the Drew-McCormick Expedition (1956-   ), with G. Ernest Wright as director. The first two seasons (1956, 1957) were devoted to a study of the fortifications and of the temple area. In 1960 work was continued on the temple and the palace underlying it and the expedition set for its objective the recovering of the stratigraphy of the city in a residential complex. It is of great interest that the excavators conclude that the temple of Baal-berith (Judges 9:4), "the house of Millo" (9:6), and the "tower" (9:46 ff.) are designations of the same temple-citadel structure. It is significant for the chronology of Judges that it appears that the events of Judges 9 are to be dated to the first half of the 12th century. Considerable work for the future is outlined by staff members of the expedition.   C.E.D.

SHECHINAH (See Shekinah)

SHEDEUR (shĕd'ē-êr, Heb. *shedhê'ûr, caster forth of light*), a Reubenite, the father of Elizur, prince of Reuben (Num. 1:5; 2:10; 7:30; 10:18).

SHEEP (See Animals)

A sheepfold built of rough stone walls. DV

SHEEPCOTE, SHEEPFOLD (Heb. *gedhērâh, mikhlâh, mishpethayin, nāweh;* Gr. *aulé*), an enclosure intended for the protection of sheep and also to keep them from wandering out and getting lost. These folds were simple walled enclosures, usually without roofs, with the walls covered with thorns to keep out robbers. Several flocks would usually pass the night in one fold under the care of a shepherd who guarded the door. Each shepherd knew his own sheep and was known by them.

SHEEP GATE (Heb. *sha'ar ha-tsō'n*), a gate of Jerusalem mentioned in Nehemiah 3:1,32; 12:39. It was probably near the NE corner of the wall as Nehemiah built it, but about one-fourth mile inward from the present NE corner of the wall.

SHEEP MARKET, not mentioned in the Greek NT but possibly implied in John 5:2. The Greek simply means something that pertains to the sheep.

SHEEPMASTER (See Occupations & Professions)

SHEEP-SHEARER (See Occupations & Professions)

SHEERAH (See Sherah)

SHEET, a large piece of linen (Acts 10:11; 11:5). The word used indicates the material rather than its use. In Judges 14:12,13 "sheets" in KJV probably means "linen undergarments," though ASV has merely "linen garments." Cf. Proverbs 31:24.

SHEHARIAH (shē-ha-rī'a, Heb. *sheharyâh*), one of the sons of Jeroham, a Benjamite (I Chron. 8:26) listed among the early inhabitants of Jerusalem after the captivity.

SHEKEL (See Money)

SHEKINAH (shē-kī'na, Heb. *shekhînâh, dwelling of God*), a word, though not occurring in the Bible, that is employed by some Jews and by Christians to describe the visible presence of Jehovah. It is alluded to in such places as Isaiah 60:2 by the phrase "his glory" and in Romans 9:4 by the phrase "the glory." Moses calls this the "cloud" in Exodus 14:19. Its first appearance occurred for a twofold purpose when Israel was being led by Moses out of Egypt. It hid the Israelites from the pursuing Egyptians and lighted the way at night for Israel (Exod. 13:21; 14:19-20). To the Egyptians it was a cloud of darkness, but to Israel a cloud of light. It later covered Sinai when God spoke with Moses (Exod. 24:15-18), filled the tabernacle (Exod. 40: 34;35), guided Israel (Exod. 40:36-38), filled Solomon's temple (II Chron. 7:1) and was frequently seen in connection with Christ's ministry in the NT (Matt. 17:5; Acts 1:9).

H.Z.C.

SHELAH, SHELANITE (shē'la, Heb. *shēlâh,* Gr. *Sála;* Heb. *shē'la-nīt, sprout*). 1. Son of Arpachshad and father of Eber among the early Semites (Gen. 10:24); written Salah in KJV, and Sala in Luke 3:35 KJV.

2. From another root meaning a petition, the third son of Judah (Gen. 38:5-26). The Shelanites were named from him. (Num. 26:20).

SHELEMIAH (shěl-ě-mī'a, Heb. *shelemyâh,* Gr. *Selemiá, friend of Jehovah*). 1. Door-keeper at the E side of the house of God in David's time (I Chron. 26:14). In the previous verses of this chapter, he is called Meshelemiah.

2. The son of Cushi and grandfather of Jehudi whom the princes of Jehoiakim sent to Baruch, Jeremiah's secretary (Jer. 36:14).

3. One of the three whom Jehoiakim sent to arrest Baruch and Jeremiah, the prophet (Jer. 36: 26).

4. The father of Jehucal or Jucal whom Zedekiah sent to Jeremiah to ask his prayers (Jer. 37:3, cf. 38:1).

5. Son of Hananiah and father of Irijah, a captain of the ward who arrested Jeremiah on a false charge as Jeremiah was about to leave Jerusalem (Jer. 37:13).

6. Two men of the family of Bani in the days of Ezra who had taken foreign wives and who were compelled to give them up in order to purify Israel (Ezra 10:39,41).

7. Father of Hananiah, a repairer of the wall (Neh. 3:30).

8. A priestly treasurer in Nehemiah's day (Neh. 13:13).

SHELEPH (shē'lěf, Heb. *shāleph*), a son of Joktan and head of an Arab tribe named for him (Gen. 10:26).

SHELESH (shē'lěsh, Heb. *shēlesh*), son of Helem, an early descendant of Asher, son of Jacob (I Chron. 7:35).

SHELOMI (shē-lo'mī, Heb. *shelōmî, at peace*), father of Ahihud, a prince of the tribe of Asher whom the Lord appointed to help divide the land (Num. 34:27).

SHELOMITH, SHELOMOTH (shē-lō'mĭth, shē-lō'mŏth, Heb. *shelōmîth, shelōmôth, peaceful*). 1. A daughter of Dibri of the tribe of Dan, in the days of Moses. She had married an Egyptian and their half-breed son was executed for blasphemy (Lev. 24:10-12,23).

2. A chief Kohathite Levite and a cousin of Miriam, Aaron and Moses (I Chron. 23:18).

3. A leading Gershonite Levite in David's time (I Chron. 23:9).

4. A descendant of Moses through his son Eliezer (I Chron. 26:25). David set him and his brethren over the things which were set apart to Jehovah to maintain his house.

5. A son or daughter of Rehoboam, king of Judah (II Chron. 11:20), and therefore brother or sister of King Abijah of Judah.

6. Daughter of Zerubbabel (not the great Zerubbabel who led back the Jews at the behest of Cyprus, but his cousin, both named "Zerubbabel" i.e. "born in Babylon") and sister of Meshullam and Hananiah (I Chron. 3:19).

7. Ancestor of a family of 160 men who returned with Ezra in 457 B.C. (Ezra 8:10). LXX has "of the sons of Bani, Shelomith, the son of Josiphiah," while the Hebrew text followed by the English is obscure.

SHELUMIEL (shē-lū'mĭ-ĕl, Heb. *shelumî'ēl, God is peace*), a chief Simeonite in the days of Moses who helped take the census and who presented an oblation for Simeon (Num. 1:6; 7:36).

SHEM (shěm, Heb. *shēm,* Gr. *sém, name, fame*), second son of Noah, and progenitor of the Semitic race, was born 98 years before the Flood (Gen. 11:10) and lived six hundred years, outliving his descendants for nine generations excepting Eber and Abraham. In the racial prophecy which Noah made after the event of his drunkenness (Gen. 9:25-27), he mentions "Jehovah, God of Shem." The three great monotheistic religions, Judaism, Christianity and Islam, all had Semitic origins, and Noah added concerning Japheth that his descendants would "dwell in the tents of Shem," indicating that the Aryan peoples to a large extent have derived their civilization from the Semites. In the "Table of the nations" (Gen. 10) Shem is given five sons, of whom Arpachshad (KJV "Arphaxad") was clearly an individual and the others are peoples or progenitors of peoples: e.g., "Lud" refers to the Lydians in Asia Minor, "Elam" points to the Elamites who lived E of the Tigris river; "Aram" means the Aramaeans or Syrians who lived in Syria and Mesopotamia and "Asshur" is Assyria. Scoffers pointed out a century ago that "Asshur" is mentioned also in the Hamite list (10:11), but archaeologists have found Hamitic artifacts under Semitic ruins of Assyrian cities. Shem, Ham and Japheth probably differed only as brothers do, but their descendants are quite distinct.   A.B.F.

SHEMA (shē′mà, Heb. *shemā′, fame, rumor*). 1. A town in the southern part of Judah (Josh. 15:26).

2. Son of Hebron of the descendants of Caleb in Judah, and father of Raham (I Chron. 2:44).

3. Son of Joel and father of Azaz in the genealogy of the Reubenites (I Chron. 5:8).

4. A Benjamite, head of a father's house in Benjamin who lived at Aijalon and put to flight the inhabitants of Gath (I Chron. 8:13).

5. One who stood at the right hand of Ezra in the revival in Jerusalem when Ezra read the book of the law to the people (Neh. 8:4).

6. "Shema" is the Hebrew name for Deuteronomy 6:4, probably the most often quoted verse in the Bible, as every good Jew repeats it several times every day — "Hear, O Israel: the Lord our God is one Lord."

SHEMAAH (shē-mā′à, *shemā′âh, fame*), a man of Gibeah of Benjamin whose two sons helped David at Ziklag (I Chron. 12:3).

SHEMAIAH (shē-mā′yà, Heb. *shem′yâh, Jehovah has heard*). 1. A prince among the families of the tribe of Simeon (I Chron. 4:37).

2. A Reubenite, son of Joel (I Chron. 5:4), possibly the same as Shema of verse 8.

3. A chief Levite of the sons of Elizaphan in the days of David (I Chron. 15:8,11).

4. A Levite scribe in the days of David; son of Nethaneel, who recorded the courses of the priests (I Chron. 24:6).

5. Also in David's time, the first-born son of Obed-edom and father of mighty men among the door-keepers of the house of God (I Chron. 26: 4,6,7).

6. A brave prophet of God who forbade Rehoboam, king of Judah, to go against the house of Israel in the N (I Kings 12:22-24). Shemaiah later wrote a biography of Rehoboam which has been lost (II Chron. 12:15).

7. A descendant of David, related to the Messianic line (I Chron. 3:22) and the father of five or six sons.

8. A Merarite Levite in the days of Nehemiah, who dwelt in Jerusalem (I Chron. 9:14; Neh. 12: 18).

9. A Levite, son of Galal and a descendant of Elkanah, mentioned among the first inhabitants who returned from exile (I Chron. 9:16). In Nehemiah 11:17 he is called "Shammua."

10. A Levite whom King Jehoshaphat sent to teach in the towns of Judah (II Chron. 17:8).

11. One of the Levites who cleansed the temple in the days of Hezekiah (II Chron. 29:14).

12. A Levite who was appointed to assist in the distribution of food to the cities of the priests in the days of Hezekiah (II Chron. 31:15).

13. A chief Levite in the days of Josiah who assisted in the great passover (II Chron. 35:9).

14. A leader of the Levites who returned with Ezra (Ezra 8:13).

15. One whom Ezra sent back for ministers (Ezra 8:16), possibly the same as the preceding.

16. A son of the priests, who had married a foreign wife (Ezra 10:21).

17. Another, guilty of the same sin (Ezra 10: 31).

18. Son of Shecaniah, keeper of the E gate of Jerusalem, who helped rebuild the wall (Neh. 3: 29).

19. One who tried to intimidate Nehemiah (Neh. 6:10).

20. A priest who signed the covenant (Neh. 10:8).

21. A priest or Levite who returned with Zerubbabel (Neh. 12:6).

22. A musical priest in the days of Nehemiah (Neh. 12:36).

23. A priest who assisted in the celebration of the completing of the wall, possibly the same as the preceding (Neh. 12:42).

24. The father of Uriah the prophet, whom Jehoiakim, king of Judah slew for prophesying against the sins of Jerusalem (Jer. 26:20).

25. A false prophet who fought against Jeremiah to his own hurt and therefore was not to see God's blessing nor to leave any seed (Jer. 29:24-32).

26. The father of Delaiah, one of the princes in the days of Jehoiakim, who heard the words of the prophet (Jer. 36:12).

SHEMARIAH (shĕm-à-rī′à, Heb. *shemaryâh, Jehovah keeps*). 1. One of the mighty men of Benjamin who joined David while he was at Ziklag (I Chron. 12:5).

2. A son of Rehoboam, king of Judah by his cousin Mahalath, a granddaughter of David (II Chron. 11:19).

3. One of the family of Harim who married a foreign wife and was compelled by Ezra to put her away (Ezra 10:32).

4. One of the sons of Bani who had been likewise guilty (Ezra 10:41). In KJV (II Chron. 11: 19) sometimes spelled Shamariah.

SHEMEBER (shĕm-ē′bĕr, Heb. *shem′ever*), king of Zeboiim, a city in the vicinity of the Dead Sea in the time of Abraham (Gen. 14:2). He rebelled against Chedorlaomer of Elam.

SHEMER (shē′mĕr, Heb. *shemer, guard*), owner of a hill in central Palestine which Omri, king of Israel, bought and fortified and named after its former owner, Samaria (I Kings 16:24). Shamar in KJV of Chronicles.

SHEMIDA, SHEMIDAH (shē-mī′dà, Heb. *shemîdhā′*), an early member of the tribe of Manasseh through Gilead, and therefore inheriting land E of the Jordan (Num. 26:32, Josh. 17:2). He had four sons (I Chron. 7:19).

SHEMIDAITES (shē-mī′dà-īts, Heb. *shemîdhā′*), the family descended from Shemida *q.v.* (Num. 26:32; Josh. 17:2), belonging to the half-tribe of Manasseh.

SHEMINITH (shĕm′ĭ-nĭth, *eighth*, i.e. the octave, and meaning the lower octave), a musical term. The harps tuned to the "sheminith" were to be used with men's voices (I Chron. 15:21, titles tor Pss. 6 and 12).

SHEMIRAMOTH (shĕ-mĭr'a-mŏth, Heb. *shemîrāmôth*). 1. One of the second degree Levites under David, for music (I Chron. 15:18,20).

2. One of the teaching Levites appointed by King Jehoshaphat to teach in Judah (II Chron. 17:8).

SHEMUEL (shĕ-mū'ĕl, Heb. *shemû'ēl, name of God*), the same as Samuel in Hebrew. 1. A Simeonite, divider of Canaan under Joshua (Num. 34:20).

2. Samuel, here spelled Shemuel in KJV (I Chron. 6:33).

3. The head of a house in Issachar (I Chron. 7:2).

SHEN (shĕn, Heb. *ha-shēn, tooth* or *pointed rock*), a sharp rock a short distance W of Jerusalem near which Samuel set up the monument of victory which he called "Ebenezer" (I Sam. 7:12).

SHENAZAR (shē-năz'ȧr, Heb. *shen'atsar*), a son of Jeconiah, i.e. Jehoiachin, son of Jehoiakim, born in captivity (I Chron. 3:18). ASV has it more correctly Shenazzar.

SHENIR (shē'nēr, Heb. *senîr, shenîr*), the Amorite name for Mount Hermon, a place of fir trees (Ezek. 27:5), one of the limits of the half-tribe Manasseh (I Chron. 5:23). KJV, Deuteronomy 3:9 and Song of Solomon have "Shenir," but the Hebrew and ASV have uniformly "Senir."

SHEOL (shē'ōl, Heb. *she'ôl*), the OT name for the place of departed souls, corresponding to the NT word "Hades." The word occurs 65 times in the Hebrew OT and is rendered in KJV 31 times "hell," 31 times "grave," and three times "pit." The reason for this variety of translation is that "hell" is ordinarily thought of as a place of punishment, and so "grave" is substituted when the reference is to the souls of good men; e.g., Jacob said that he would go down into the "grave" mourning for his son (Gen. 37:35), and Job prayed "Oh that thou wouldest hide me in the grave" (Job 14:13). In ASV, the word is not translated but merely transliterated "Sheol," without any attempt to theorize as to its meaning. Sheol is represented as being inside the earth. Numbers 16:30,33 pictures the earth opening and swallowing up Korah and his company so that they went down alive into Sheol. Amos 9:2-4 names five places in which the enemies of Jehovah might attempt to hide from him, but from whence he would bring them. Though the original sense may refer merely to a hollow place, it is quite commonly thought of as a place of punishment; e.g. "The wicked shall be turned into Sheol (Ps. 9:17), and certainly of severe discomfort (Ps. 116:3), "The pains of Sheol gat hold upon me," though the Messianic prophecy of Psalm 16:10, "For thou wilt not leave my soul to Sheol," quoted in the first Christian sermon (Acts 2:27), certainly could not refer to punishment. A large part of the confusion of thought concerning Sheol arises from the invisibility of the soul. Since it is difficult to conceive the idea of space in connection with invisible beings, Sheol often means the place or state of the soul between death and resurrection when the soul will be joined with a spiritual body (I Cor. 15:42-49). The clearest indication of different conditions in Sheol is in our Lord's parable of the rich man and Lazarus (Luke 16:19-31), where the rich man is pictured as in torment, while Lazarus was in "Abraham's bosom." A.B.F.

SHEPHAM (shē'făm, Heb. *shephām, nakedness*), a place in the NE of Canaan, near the Sea of Galilee (Num. 34:10,11).

SHEPHATIAH (shĕf'a-tī'à, Heb. *shephatyâh, Jehovah is judge*). 1. The fifth son of David, born at Hebron to his wife Abital (II Sam. 3:4).

2. Son of Reuel and father of Meshullam, dwelling in Jerusalem soon after the return from captivity (I Chron. 9:8).

3. One of the mighty men who joined David at Ziklag (I Chron. 12:5).

4. Son of Maacah, a Simeonite prince ruling his tribe in the days of David (I Chron. 27:16).

5. One of the seven sons of Jehoshaphat, king of Judah (II Chron. 21:2).

6. Founder of a family with 372 descendants who returned with Zerubbabel (Ezra 2:4).

7. One of the children of Solomon's servants whose descendants returned with Zerubbabel (Ezra 2:57).

8. One whose descendant Zebadiah returned with Ezra (Ezra 8:8). This may have been the same Shephatiah as the preceding.

9. Son of Mahalaleel whose descendant Athaiah dwelt at Jerusalem soon after the walls had been rebuilt (Neh. 11:4).

10. One of the men of Zedekiah who desired that Jeremiah be put to death for prophesying (Jer. 38:1).

SHEPHELAH, THE (shē-fē'là, Heb. *ha-shephēlâh*, Gr. *sephelá, saphelá, low country*). The word does not occur in the English Bible but the Hebrew has it 19 times, rendered in KJV "low country" or "low plain" four times, "plain" three times, "vale" five times, and "valley" seven times, but in ASV uniformly "lowland." It represents the undulating country between the mountains of Judah and the maritime plain S of the plain of Sharon, extending through the country of Philistia along the Mediterranean. In Joshua 12:8 it is one of the six geographical sections of the promised land W of Jordan. It had an abundance of sycamore trees (I Kings 10:27). Its limestone hills were from 500 to 800 feet high. In the valleys good crops were grown, especially grapes. Samson's exploits took place there, and David hid there from Saul.

SHEPHER (See Shapher)

SHEPHERD (See Occupations & Professions)

SHEPHI, SHEPHO (shē'fī, shē'fō, *barrenness*), one of the early descendants of Seir, the Horite (Gen. 36:23; I Chron. 1:40). "Shepho" in Genesis, "Shephi" in I Chronicles.

SHEPHUPHAN (shē-fū'făm, Heb. *shephûphān*), a grandson of Benjamin through Bela his firstborn (I Chron. 8:5). The name appears in Genesis 46:21 as "Muppim" and in I Chronicles 7:12,15; 26:16 as "Shuppim."

SHERAH (shē'rà, Heb. *she'ĕrâh*), a daughter or a granddaughter of Ephraim and apparently a powerful woman, for she built or fortified three villages (I Chron. 7:24 cf. II Chron. 8:5).

SHERD (See Potsherd, Ostraka)

SHEREBIAH (shĕr-ē-bī'à, Heb. *sherēvyâh*). 1. One of the chief priests who were brought from Casiphia to join Ezra on his return to Jerusalem, to whom Ezra entrusted treasures for the temple (Ezra 8:18,24), who translated the reading of the Law into Aramaic for the people (Neh. 8:7), and who confessed the sins of Israel (Neh. 9:4).

2. A covenanter with Nehemiah (Neh. 10:12).

3. A Levite who returned with Zerubbabel (Neh. 12:8).

4. A chief Levite in the days of Eliashib (Neh. 12:24).

SHERESH (shē'rĕsh, Heb. *shāresh*), a grandson of Manasseh through Machir (I Chron. 7:16) and the ancestor of Manassites living in Gilead.

SHEREZER (shĕ-rē'zēr, Heb. *sar'etser*), a man sent from Bethel to Jerusalem to ask the priests whether the days of mourning should be continued (Zech. 7:2).

SHESHACH (shē'shăk, Heb. *shēshakh*), in the opinion of many, a cryptogram for "Babel" formed by reversing the letters of the alphabet. When the prophet first used this device (Jer. 25:26) it was the first year of Nebuchadnezzar and it would have been folly openly to predict the doom of Babylon. When he later used it (Jer. 51:41), Israel was in captivity, Jerusalem had long been in ruins, and the use of the word with its explanation as Babylon could do no harm.

SHESHAI (shē'shī, Heb. *shēshay*), one of the sons of Anak, giants whom the spies feared (Num. 13: 22), but whom Caleb drove out (Josh. 15:14) and Judah destroyed (Judg. 1:10).

SHESHAN (shē'shan, Heb. *shēshān*), an early descendant of Judah through Perez, Hezron and Jerahmeel (I Chron. 2:31,34) who gave his daughter as wife to an Egyptian servant Jarha (I Chron. 2:35-41).

SHESHBAZZAR (shĕsh-băz'ĕr, Heb. *sheshbatstsar*), a prince of the Jews when Cyrus made a decree permitting the Jews to go back to Jerusalem to rebuild the house of God. He was made governor, was given the sacred vessels of the temple which had been taken at the captivity, and helped lay the foundation of the temple (Ezra 1:8,11; 5: 14,16). He may be the same as Zerubbabel.

SHETH (shĕth, Heb. *shēth, compensation*). 1. The name given by Eve to her third son (I Chron. 1:1).
2. An unknown race mentioned in Balaam's parable (Num. 24:17).

SHETHAR (shē'thàr, Heb. *shēthar*), one of the seven princes of Persia and Media who "saw the king's face" in the days of Xerxes (Esth. 1:14).

SHETHAR-BOZENAI, SHETHAR-BOZNAI (shē'thàr-bŏz'ē-nī, shē'thàr-bŏz'nī), a Persian official who tried to prevent the Jews from building the temple and complained to the king (Ezra 5: 3,6).

SHEVA (shē'và, Heb. *shewā'*). 1. David's scribe or secretary (II Sam. 20:25), perhaps the same as "Seraiah" in 8:17).
2. Son of Caleb (probably not the famous spy) by his concubine Maacah (I Chron. 2:49).

SHEWBREAD, SHOWBREAD (See Tabernacle)

SHIBAH (shī'bà, Heb. *shiv'âh*), the well from which Beer-sheba was named (Gen. 26:33). In KJV the name is written "Shebah."

SHIBBOLETH (shĭb'bō-lĕth, Heb. *shibbōleth, an ear of grain* or *a stream*), a word which was differently pronounced on the two sides of the Jordan, and so was used by the men of Gilead under Jephthah as a test to determine whether the speaker was of Ephraim or not (Judg. 12:5,6).

SHIBMAH, SIBMAH (shĭb'mà, Heb. *shivmâh*), a city taken by the tribe of Reuben from the Moabites (Num. 32:38).

SHICRON, SHIKKERON (shĭk'rŏn, Heb. *shikkerôn*), a town W of Jerusalem on the northern border of Judah (Josh. 15:11). ASV Shikkeron.

SHIELD (See Armor)

SHIGGAION (shĭ-gā'yŏn, Heb. *shiggāyôn*), a musical term found in the heading of Psalm 7. It may refer to a dithyramb, or rhapsody.

SHIGIONOTH (shĭg-ĭ-ō'noth), plural of Shiggaion. The heading of Habakkuk's lovely psalm (Hab. 3:1).

SHIHON, SHION (shī'ŏn, Heb. *shî'ôn*), a town on the border of Issachar (Josh. 19:19), a few miles W of the S end of the Sea of Galilee, near Nazareth. ASV Shion.

SHIHOR, SIHOR (shī'hôr, Heb. *shîhôr*). At least three views have been held regarding Shihor (usually Sihor in KJV): (1) it refers to the Nile; (2) it refers to a stream which separated Egypt from Palestine; (3) it refers to a canal, with waters drawn from the Nile, on the border between Egypt and Palestine. See Joshua 13:3; I Chronicles 13:5; Isaiah 23:3; Jeremiah 2:18.

SHIHOR-LIBNATH (shī'hôr-lĭb'năth, Heb. *shîhôr livnāth*), a small stream flowing into the Mediterranean Sea on the southern border of Asher (Josh. 19:26). Perhaps the Belus near Acre, from the sand of which glass was made.

SHIKKERON (See Shicron)

SHILHI (shĭl'hī, Heb. *shilhî*), father-in-law of Jehoshaphat, king of Judah (I Kings 22:42).

SHILHIM (shĭl'hĭm, Heb. *shilhîm*), a town in the S of Judah in Joshua's time (Josh. 15:32).

SHILLEM, SHILLEMITE (shĭl'ĕm, shĭl'ĕm-īt), the fourth son of Naphtali (Gen. 46:24) and the family descended from him (Num. 26:49). In I Chronicles 7:13 he is called Shallum.

SHILOAH (See Siloam)

SHILOH (shī'lō, Heb. *shîlōh*), the person referred to in the prophecy of Jacob in Genesis 49:10, "The sceptre shall not depart from Judah, nor the ruler's staff from between his feet, until Shiloh come." This has been interpreted in many different ways. The ASVm has " 'Till he come to Shiloh, having the obedience of the peoples,' Or, acc. to Syr., 'Till he come whose it is,' etc." The RSV has "until he comes to whom it belongs; and to him shall be the obedience of the peoples." The principal interpretations are the following:
1. The passage is Messianic. The difficulty of this interpretation is that nowhere else in the OT is Shiloh found as a personal name, and none of the ancient MSS apply the word personally to the Messiah. This application is not older than the 16th century (apart from a fanciful passage in the Talmud).
2. Shiloh refers to the town in central Palestine where Joshua placed the tabernacle after the conquest of Canaan (Josh. 18:1), and the reading, "Till he comes to Shiloh," is favored.
3. Shiloh is not regarded as a proper name at all. It is thought to be a compound word meaning "whose it is." This is apparently the reading presupposed in the LXX, the Peshitta, and the Jewish Targums, and seems to be alluded to in Ezekiel 21: 27, "until he come whose right it is." The passage has a Messianic reference if this reading is adopted.
S.B.

SHILOH (shī'lō, Heb. *shîlōh*), a city in the tribe of Ephraim, about 12 miles N and E of Bethel and about the same distance S of Sychar where Jacob's well was, just E of the highway from Bethel to Shechem (Judg. 21:19). It stood on an isolated hill which could easily be defended either against the Canaanites from the N or the Philistines from the SW. Here the children of Israel under Joshua assembled after the first phases of the conquest of Canaan and set up the tabernacle, thus making Shiloh the capital city of Canaan under the theocracy. Here the tabernacle remained till in the days of Samuel, about 400 years later, the ark was removed in a battle with the Philistines (I Sam. 4: 3) and began its wanderings which lasted almost to the days of Solomon's temple, which was built

The site of Shiloh, the Tell, or mound, in the middle foreground, and excavations at upper left. © MPS

to receive it. From Shiloh the men of Benjamin, by Israel's permission, kidnaped wives after the Benjamite war under the priesthood of Phinehas, the grandson of Aaron, and to Shiloh the godly Elkanah and his wife repaired before the birth of Samuel (I Sam. 1:3). Here the boy Samuel received his call from God (3:20,21).

From the time of the removal of the ark, Shiloh gradually lost its importance, and especially when David made Jerusalem the capital of the kingdom of Israel. This loss of importance was principally because God "forsook the tabernacle of Shiloh, the tent which he placed among men" (Ps. 78:60). During the reign of King Saul, Israel's first king, and especially during his war with the Philistines, Ahijah, great-grandson of Eli, was high priest of Israel wearing the sacred ephod at Shiloh (I Sam. 14:3). After the division of the kingdom, though the ark and the temple were at Jerusalem, and though Jeroboam, the apostate king, had set up centers of worship at Dan and at Bethel, another Ahijah, prophet of the Lord, was still at Shiloh, representing God before the true men of God in the northern kingdom, and to him Jeroboam sent to inquire about his sick son (I Kings 14), and here Ahijah pronounced the doom of Jeroboam's house (I Kings 14:13).

In the days of Jeremiah, Shiloh was a ruin (Jer. 7:12,14), though there were some men there after the destruction of Jerusalem (Jer. 41:5). The modern name for the place of Shiloh is Seilun.

A.B.F.

SHILONI, SHILONITE (shĭ-lō'nĭ, shī'lō-nīt, Heb. *shîlōnî*). 1. An inhabitant of Shiloh. The one most often mentioned is Ahijah, the Shilonite (I Kings 11:29; II Chron. 9:29).

2. Ancestor of Maaseiah, one of the Jewish princes who dwelt in Jerusalem under Nehemiah (Neh. 11:5).

SHILSHAH (shĭl'shà, Heb. *shilshâh*), one of the 11 sons of Zophah, an early member of the tribe of Asher (I Chron. 7:37).

SHIMEA (shĭm'ē-à, Heb. *shim'ā'*). 1. A brother of David whose son slew a giant of Gath (I Chron. 20:7).

2. Son of David and Bathsheba ("Bathshua") born in Jerusalem (I Chron. 3:5).

3. A Merarite Levite (I Chron. 6:30).

4. A Gershonite Levite, grandfather of Asaph who stood with Heman in the service of sacred song under David.

No. 1 is probably the same as "Shimma" (I Chron. 2:13 KJV), "Shamma" (I Sam. 16:9), "Shimeah" (II Sam. 21:21 KJV), and "Shimei" (*ibid.* ASV). The name is spelled three ways in the Hebrew, five ways in the English.

SHIMEAH (shĭm'ē-à, Heb. *shim'ā'*). 1. Brother of David (II Sam. 13:3).

2. A son of Mikloth a Benjamite (I Chron. 8:32) who lived at Jerusalem. In 9:38 his name is written "Shimeam."

SHIMEAM (See Shimeah)

SHIMEATH (shĭm'ē-ăth, Heb. *shim'ath, fame*), an Ammonitess, whose son Zabad (II Chron. 24:26) or Jozacar (II Kings 12:21) helped to assassinate King Joash of Judah.

SHIMEATHITES (shĭm'ē-ăth-īts, Heb. *shim'āthîm*), one of the three families of scribes that dwelt at Jabez in Judah (I Chron. 2:55). They were Kenites related to the Rechabites.

SHIMEI (shĭm'ē-ī, Heb. *shim'î, famous*). 1. A son of Gershon and head of a Levite family. Spelled Shimi in KJV (Exod. 6:17).

2. A Gershonite Levite in the days of David, and head of one of the courses of Levites (I Chron. 23:7-10).

3. One of David's mighty men who remained faithful in Adonijah's attempted usurpation of the throne (I Kings 1:8).

4. One of Solomon's purveyors of food who was over Benjamin (I Kings 4:18).

5. The grandson of Jehoiachin, or, as he was later called, Jeconiah (I Chron. 3:19).

6. A Simeonite, father of 22 children (I Chron. 4:26,27).

7. An early Reubenite, son of Gog and father of Micah (I Chron. 5:4).

8. An early Merarite Levite, cousin once removed of Moses and Aaron (I Chron. 6:29).

9. The head of a father's house in Judah (I Chron. 8:21), spelled Shimhi in KJV.

10. The head of one of the 24 courses of musical Levites, who with his 12 sons and brethren made up the tenth course (I Chron. 25:17).

11. A man of Ramah, whom David set over the vineyards (I Chron. 27:27).

12. One of the descendants of Heman, the singer, who helped in the house-cleaning of the temple under Hezekiah (II Chron. 29:14).

13. A Levite, treasurer over the oblations and tithes in Hezekiah's time (II Chron. 31:12,13).

14. One of the Levites who had married a foreign woman in Ezra's time (Ezra 10:23).

15. One of the family of Hashum who had married a foreign woman in Ezra's time (Ezra 10:33).

16. One of the family of Bani who had done the same (Ezra 10:38).

17. Son of Kish and grandfather of Mordecai the Jew who brought up Esther (Esth. 2:5).

18. A representative of a leading family who in the final restoration of Israel will weep in contrition when they look upon him whom they have pierced (Zech. 12:13).

19. A Benjamite of the house of Saul, and son of Gera who cursed David in the day when he

was fleeing from Absalom his son, and cast stones at David. David refused to let his cousin Abishai slay him (II Sam. 16:5-14). When David was returning, victorious, Shimei prayed for forgiveness and David pardoned him (II Sam. 19:16-23), but when Solomon sat upon the throne (I Kings 2:36-46) he first confined him to Jerusalem, then executed him for disobedience.

SHIMEON (shĭm'ē-ŭn, Heb. *shim'ôn, hearing*), one of the family of Harin in Ezra's time who had married a foreign wife (Ezra 10:31).

SHIMHI (See Shimei)

SHIMI (See Shimei)

SHIMITE (shĭm'īt), a member of the family descended from Shimei (Num. 3:21 KJV; ASV Shimeites).

SHIMMA (shĭm'à, Heb. *shammâh*), the third son of Jesse (I Chron. 2:13 KJV), also called Shammah (I Sam. 16:9).

SHIMON (shī'mŏn, Heb. *shîmôn*), head of a family in the tribe of Judah (I Chron. 4:20).

SHIMRATH (shĭm'răth, Heb. *shimrăth, watch*), one of the sons of Shimei in the tribe of Benjamin (I Chron. 8:21).

SHIMRI (shĭm'rī, Heb. *shimrî*). 1. Son of Shemaiah and head of a father's house in the tribe of Simeon (I Chron. 4:37).

2. Father of Jediael and Joha, two of David's mighty men (I Chron. 11:45).

3. A son of Hosah of the Merarite Levites, whom, although he was not the first-born, Hosah made chief of his 13 kinsmen. Spelled Simri in KJV (I Chron. 26:10).

4. A Levite who assisted in cleansing the temple (II Chron. 29:13).

SHIMRITH (shĭm'rĭth, Heb. *shimrîth, watchful*), a Moabitess, mother of Jehozabad who helped to slay Joash, king of Judah (II Chron. 24:26); also called Shomer (II Kings 12:21).

SHIMROM, SHIMRON (shĭm'rŏm, shĭm'rŏn, Heb. *shimrôn, a guard*). 1. The fourth son of Issachar, son of Jacob (Gen. 46:13). In I Chronicles 7:1 KJV has Shimrom.

2. A town in the northern part of Canaan whose king united with Jabin, king of Hazor, to fight against Joshua and the Israelites (Josh. 11:1ff). In Joshua 19:15 it is mentioned among the cities given in the division of the land to the tribe of Zebulun. In Joshua 12:20, among the conquests of Joshua, it is called Shimron-Meron.

SHIMRON-MERON (shĭm'rŏn-mē'rŏn), a town listed among the 34 victories of Joshua in the conquest of Canaan (Josh. 12:20).

SHIMSHAI (shĭm'shī, Heb. *shimshay, sunny*), a scribe among the enemies of the Jews who had been hindering the attempts to rebuild the temple (Ezra 4:8).

SHINAB (shī'năb, Heb. *shin'āv*), king of Admah, one of the Canaanite cities which later was destroyed with Sodom (Gen. 14:2).

SHINAR (shī'nàr, Heb. *shin'ar*), the region containing the cities of Babel, Erech (cf. modern Iraq), Accad, and Calneh, Genesis 10:10, the locations of which, except Accad, are unknown. Accad may have been the Agade known to archaeologists as the capital chosen by Sargon I, ancient king of Babylon. Shinar lay on the alluvial plain of Babylonia and for many centuries was perhaps the most fertile region on earth. Herodotus speaks of two-hundred-fold yields of grain there. Genesis 11:1-9 speaks of the early post-diluvians traveling E and finding a plain in the land of Shinar where they

started to build a tower. In the days of Abraham, Amraphel, king of Shinar, invaded Canaan (Gen. 14:1); Nebuchadnezzar was ruler of the land of Shinar, Daniel 1:2, and it is mentioned in prophecy (Isa. 11:1; Zech. 5:11).

SHION (shī'ŏn, Heb. *shî'ôn, overturning*), a town in Issachar, perhaps about three miles NW of Mt. Tabor (Josh. 19:19). KJV Shihon.

SHIPHI (shī'fī, Heb. *shiph'î*), father of Ziza, a prince in one of the families of Simeon (I Chron. 4:37).

SHIPHMITE (shĭf'mīt, Heb. *shephām*), the patronymic of Zabdi who was over the increase of the vineyards under David (I Chron. 27:27). Probably from Shepham in Judah.

SHIPHRAH (shĭf'rà, Heb. *shiphrâh, beauty*}, one of the Hebrew midwives who risked their lives to save the Hebrew boy babies (Exod. 1:15-21).

SHIPHTAN (shĭf'tăn, Heb. *shiphtān, judicial*), father of Kemuel, a prince of Ephraim, whom Joshua appointed to help divide the land (Num. 34:24).

SHIPS (Heb. *'ŏnîyâh, tsî, sephînâh*; Gr. *ploíon, ploiárion, naús, skáphe*). Ships and navigation find only a small place in the OT. The Hebrews were an agricultural people, and the Phoenicians and Philistines, over long periods, separated them from a coastline which was itself harborless and difficult. In Judges 5:17 there is cryptic reference to some experience of ships in the case of the two tribes of Asher and Dan, but Hebrew sea-faring in general was second-hand. The Phoenicians, confined to their coastal-strip, and with the timber resources of the Lebanon range in their hinterland, were prompted by geography to exploit the sea, and became, in the process, the great navigators of the ancient world; hence the symbolic vessel with ivory benches and embroidered purple sails of Ezekiel's metaphor in his denunciation of Tyre (Ezek. 27:4-11). Solomon's fleet at Ezion-geber (I Kings 9 and 10) was composed of Phoenician ships and manned by Phoenician crews. Jehoshaphat's later attempt to revive the trade ended in shipwreck, due, no doubt, to inexperienced Hebrew handling of the ships. The "ships of Tarshish" mentioned in this connection and elsewhere (e.g. Isa. 2:16), were probably sturdy vessels built, in the first instance, for the commerce with Tartessus in Spain, the term thereafter being applied, like "China clipper" and "East Indiamen," to vessels generally used for arduous and distant voyaging. Solomon's southern fleet, for example, traded to Ophir, and, if the cargoes are an indication, to Southern India as well (I Kings 10:22).

It is certain that the Phoenicians penetrated to Cornwall for tin, and to the Canaries. They probably used the trireme, the useful vessel with three banks of oars, which was a Phoenician invention. Remaining OT references are few and commonly poetic. Psalm 107:23-27 speaks of the terrors of a storm at sea, and Psalm 104:26 briefly mentions ships. Isaiah 18:2 speaks of the boats or rafts built of bound bundles of papyrus, which are sometimes depicted in Egyptian murals, and Daniel 11:30 refers to warships from Cyprus (Chittim or Kittim). In NT times the shipping of the Mediterranean was principally Greek and Roman. The Romans maintained war-fleets of triremes and quinqueremes ("three-oared" and "five-oared" ships). How the rowers on these vessels were arranged has been much debated, and the view that there were three banks of benches is now generally rejected. It is probable that the benches had a forward slant, and that each rower pulled an individual oar sitting three (or five in the case of of the quinquereme) to a bench. The warship (or "long ship," as it was sometimes called) was not designed for heavy loads, but for speed and maneuverability. Hence the frequency of shipwreck, and sometimes mass disaster, in Roman naval history. The great artists in the naval use of the trireme were the Athenians, whose admiral Phormion (c. 440-428 B.C.) developed the tactics which kept the Athenians supreme at sea until the Syracusans invented the ramming devices which struck Athenian naval power a fatal blow in the Great Harbor (413 B.C.). Merchant ships were more heavily built, and were designed to stay at sea for long periods in all weathers, and to carry considerable cargoes.

The classic passage is Acts 27 which contains Luke's brilliant account of the voyage and wreck of the Alexandrian grain-ship. These vessels were of considerable size. There were 276 people aboard the ship on which Paul and Luke traveled (Acts 27:37). Josephus states that he traveled to Rome on a ship with no less than 600 aboard (*Vita* 3). The Alexandrian grain-ship, Isis, of the second century A.D. measured 140 by 36 feet, and would be rated at 3250 tons burden. No doubt these were exceptional vessels, and the average merchant ship was probably in the vicinity of 100 tons. Paul's ship may have been on a northern route because of the lateness of the season (Acts 27:6), though Ramsay is of the opinion that this was the regular route from Egypt to Rome (*St. Paul the Traveller,* p. 319). There was a particularly dangerous period for autumn navigation, extending, according to Vegetius (De Re.Mil. 4:39), from mid-September to mid-November. Paul's voyage fell within this period. The story illustrates the difficulty of handling the ancient sailing ship in adverse winds. From Myra, on the extreme southern point of Asia Minor, the ship was proceeding west to Cnidus, a port at the SW extremity of Asia Minor. A wind off the shore drove the vessel S, and the shipmaster was compelled to seek shelter under the lee of the 140-mile-long island of Crete (27:7). Fair Havens, where the ship found refuge was (and is) a little more than half way along this coast, just E of the part where the island rises into a group of lofty mountains. Funnelled down from these highlands (27:14), the NE wind drove them S from the "more commodious" harbor of Phenice, over 23 miles of turbulent sea, to the off-shore

A warship (galley) drawn from a bronze coin of Ascalon, dated A.D. 72. UANT

A typical sailing and fishing boat of the Middle East. © MPS

island of Clauda. The brief advantage of the island's protection was used to haul in the boat, which was being towed water-logged behind (27:16). To the S lay the Syrtes, ancient graveyard of ships, as modern underwater archeology has strikingly revealed. Hence the battle to maintain a westerly course, aided by a veering of the wind to the E, as the cyclonic disturbance shifted its center. At this point (27:17) they "used helps, undergirding the ship." These tautened cables, employed to bind the straining timbers against the stress of the sea and the leverage of the loaded mast, are mentioned elsewhere in ancient literature. "See you not," says Horace, writing metaphorically of the laboring ship of state (*Od*. 1:14), "that the side is stripped of oars, the masts crippled by the rushing southwest wind, the yard-arms groaning, and that without ropes the hull can scarcely bear the too peremptory sea." (See also Plato *Rep.* 10:616c). It is possible that the hull was "undergirded" by strong ropes, but that an extension of the cables above deck formed a network which could be twisted to tautness. It is probable that the "tackling," which was thrown overboard, was the rigging and the long spar on which the main-sail depended, a device likely to become unmanageable during a storm. The ship on which Paul continued his voyage from Malta to the grain-port of Puteoli, had "the sign" of Castor and Pollux (28:11). The Great Twin Brethren were the patrons of ship-men, and had special care of storm-bound ships (Hor. *Od*. 1:12:27-32). The account in Acts 27 also tells of soundings for depth (27:28) and the bracing of the ship by a system of compensatory anchors (27:29). This is the purport of the metaphor in Hebrews 6:19. James 3:4 refers to the rudder paddles.

The "boats" of the Sea of Galilee, which figure in the Gospels, were sturdy fisher-craft or the barges of local lake-side trade. They comfortably contained a dozen men, but an unusual draught of fish was an embarrassment (Luke 5:7). It is not known what wood was used for the boats of Galilee, but Theophrastus says that sea-going ships were constructed from larch, cypress, and fir (Hist. Pl.5:7).

E.M.B.

SHISHA (shī'shȧ, Heb. *shîshā'*), the father of two of Solomon's secretaries; Elihoreph and Ahijah (I Kings 4:3), thought by some to be identical with Seraiah (II Sam. 8:17), Sheva (II Sam. 20:25 and Shavsha (I Chron. 18:16).

SHISHAK (shī'shăk, Heb. *shîshaq,* Egyp. *Sheshonk*), an Egyptian king, the founder of the 22nd or Libyan dynasty. He was from a Libyan family which for some generations had been situated at Herakleopolis in the Fayyum. Libyan mercenaries were common in the Egyptian army in the 21st dynasty and some of them rose to positions of rank. The weakness of Egypt during much of the 20th-21st Dynasties ironically permitted the Libyan-Egyptian Sheshonk to seize control of Egypt some two centuries after Rameses III had decisively defeated the Libyans. Shishak I located his capital at Bubastis (Pi-beseth, Ezek. 30:7) in the eastern Delta. To secure the succession of his newly founded dynasty he married his son to the daughter of the last king of the 21st dynasty. Shishak was a vigorous leader, who inaugurated an aggressive foreign policy and attempted to recover the lost Asiatic empire by force of arms. In the fifth year of Rehoboam, king of Judah, c. 926 B.C., he marched on Palestine, reaching as far N as Megiddo and Bethshan and E into Transjordan.

Earlier in his reign he had provided asylum to the Israelite Jeroboam, who had fled to Egypt to escape the wrath of Solomon (I Kings 11:40). With Jeroboam on the northern throne, Shishak showed no favoritism, but impartially overran both Judah and Israel. Jerusalem was a victim of this campaign and the temple was looted of its treasures (I Kings 14:25-26; II Chron. 12:1-9). At Megiddo a badly damaged stela of Shishak was found by the Oriental Institute of the University of Chicago. In Egypt the record of the campaign was carved on the S exterior wall of the temple of Karnak, just E of the Bubastite Portal. He is depicted in the traditional attitude of smiting his enemies, here Asiatics, and the god Amon is shown leading before the king a total of 156 captives in ten lines, each prisoner representing a conquered Palestinian town. The captives are portrayed in stylized form, an oval containing the name of the city surmounted by the head, shoulders, and pinioned arms of the victim. Many of the names which can be read and identified occur in the OT. Among them are Megiddo, Taanach, Shunem, Beth-shean, Ajalon, Beth-horon, Gibeon, and Socoh. The interesting place name, "Field of Abraham," appears in this list. The undisturbed burial of Shishak I was found at Bubastis (Tanis) by P. Montet in 1938-1939. Though his dynasty endured for roughly 200 years, internal conflict, stagnation, and incapability kept it at, or below, the level of mediocrity.

C.E.D.

SHITRAI (shĭt'rī, Heb. *shitray*), a Sharonite, placed by David over the flocks that fed in Sharon (I Chron. 27:29).

SHITTAH TREE (See Plants)

SHITTIM (shĭt'ĭm, Heb. *ha-shittîm*), the name of the wood which comes from the acacia tree, mentioned 26 times in connection with the tabernacle and its furniture (Exod. 25-38). The wood is hard, fine-grained, yellowish-brown in color but turns nearly black with age. It exudes a gum called "acacia-gum" or "gum-arabic." SEE PLANTS.

SHITTIM (place), a contraction of Abel-shittim, i.e. "meadow of acacias," the last stop of Israel in the wilderness before crossing the Jordan into the promised land (Num. 25:1; 33:49). There Balaam tried to curse Israel but had to bless instead, and

A portion of the relief of Pharaoh Shishak I, from the wall of the temple at Karnak, depicting conquered Palestinian captives. © MPS

there he told Balak how to seduce the men of Israel (Mic. 6:5; Num. 22:1; 25:3). From there Joshua sent the two spies to Jericho (Josh. 2:1) and thence Israel departed to cross the Jordan (Josh. 3:1). Used perhaps symbolically for a place which, in the future, Jehovah will richly bless (Joel 3:18).

SHIZA shī'zȧ, Heb. *shîzā'*), a man of Reuben, father of Adina, one of David's mighty men (I Chron. 11:42).

SHOA (shō'ȧ, Heb. *shōa', rich*), though written in the English versions as though a country or province, it is probably (with Pekod and Koa) to be taken as a description of Israel's great enemy, the Chaldeans (Ezek. 23:23).

SHOBAB (shō'băb, Heb. *shôvāv*). 1. A grandson of Hezron of Judah through Caleb (I Chron. 2:18).

2. A son of David born in Jerusalem (I Chron. 3:5).

SHOBACH (shō'băk, Heb. *shôvakh*), the general of the Syrian army under Hadarezer, king of Zobah, defeated by David (II Sam. 10:16-18). In I Chronicles 19:16, Shophach.

SHOBAI (shō'bī, Heb. *shovāy*), a gatekeeper of the temple, some of whose descendants returned with Zerubbabel (Ezra 2:42; Neh. 7:45).

SHOBAL (shō'băl, Heb. *shôvāl*). 1. One of the sons of Seir the Horite, very early inhabitant of what was later Edom (Gen. 36:20,23). These Horites or Hurrians were expelled and destroyed by the Edomites, descendants of Esau (Deut. 2:12). Shobal is listed as one of the chiefs of the Horites (Gen. 36:29).

2. An early Ephrathite of the sons of Caleb (not the spy), an ancestor or founder of Kiriath-jearim (I Chron. 2:50,52; Josh. 15:9).

3. A grandson of Judah and father of Reaiah (I Chron. 4:1,2).

SHOBEK (shō'bĕk, Heb. *shôvēq*), one of the 44 chiefs of the Jewish people who covenanted with Nehemiah to keep the law of Jehovah (Neh. 10: 24).

SHOBI (shō'bī, Heb. *shōvî*), a prince of the Ammonites, son of Nahash and probably brother of Hanun (II Sam. 17:27).

SHOCHO (shō'kō, Heb. *sôkhōh*), a city in Judah, built by Rehoboam (II Chron. 11:7). ASV here has Soco, KJV Shoco.

SHOE (See Dress)

SHOE LATCHET (See Dress)

SHOFAR (See Music, Musical Instruments)

SHOHAM (shō'hăm, Heb. *shōham*), a Merarite Levite in the days of David (I Chron. 24:27).

SHOMER (shō'mêr, Heb. *shōmēr, keeper, watcher*). 1. The father of Jehozabad, one of the conspirators against Joash of Judah, who slew him because of the blood of the sons of Jehoiada the priest (II Kings 12:20,21; II Chron. 24:25,26).

2. A great-grandson of Asher, through Beriah and Heber (I Chron. 7:32). In verse 34 he is called Shemer (ASV) and Shamer (KJV).

SHOPHACH (shō'făk, Heb. *shôvakh*), general of the Syrians, whom David slew (I Chron. 19:16, 18). In II Samuel 10:16, Shobach.

SHOPHAN (shō'făn, Heb. *shôphān*), the second half of the name of Atroth-shophan, a city of the tribe of Gad (Num. 32:35).

SHOPHAR (See Music, Musical Instruments)

SHORE, the land where it meets the sea, represented by five words in Scripture: 1. *hôph*, that which is washed by the sea (Judg. 5:17; Jer. 47:7).

2. *qātseh*, the end or extremity (Josh. 15:2), referring to the Dead Sea.

3. *sāphâh*, the lip or edge (Gen. 22:17), the sand which is on the sea-shore.

4. *cheílos*, the same idea in Greek (Heb. 11:12).

5. *aigialós*, in the ministry of our Lord in Galilee, the multitude stood on the shore and Jesus sat in a boat so that all could see and hear without thronging Him (Matt. 13:2). After His resurrection, Jesus stood on the shore while the disciples were fruitlessly fishing to hide their sorrow and perplexity (John 21:4), and in Acts 27:39 the bank of a wide creek is called a shore.

SHOSHANNIM (shō-shăn'ĭm, *lilies*), found in the titles of Psalms 45,69,80 and in Ps. 60 in the singular. Perhaps lily-shaped musical instruments, perhaps the name of spring-songs.

SHOULDER (Heb. *shekhem, kathēph, zeroa' shôq*; Gr. *ómos, brachíon*), a word often used in both a literal and figurative sense. When a man of Israel offered an ox or a sheep, the shoulder went to the officiating priest as a part of his portion (Deut. 18:8). The shoulder pieces of the ephod, the sacred garment of the high priest, were to bear onyx stones on which were graven the names of the tribes (Exod. 28:1-12), thus indicating that the priest bore a heavy responsibility for the people; and similarly, a ruler bears upon his shoulders the weight of the government (Isa. 9:6). Although in traveling, the sections of the tabernacle could be carried in wagons, the priests had to carry the

sacred furniture upon their shoulders (Num. 7:6-9), much as Jehovah is pictured as bearing his beloved upon his shoulders (Deut. 33:12), and as the good shepherd bears the lost sheep when he finds it (Luke 15:5). In much of the east, the "water-works" consist of wells, to which the maidservants resort to draw water, and whence they bear it on their shoulders (Gen. 21:14) in large jars; and even wellborn maidens carried water thus (Gen. 24:15). "To pull away the shoulder" (Zech. 7:11) is to refuse to obey, and to "thrust with the shoulder" (Ezek. 34:21) is insolence.   A.B.F.

SHOULDER PIECE (Heb. *kathēph*). That part of the ephod in which the front and the back were joined together so as to make the garment to be of one piece (Exod. 28:7,8).

2. The piece of meat which is taken from the shoulder of the beast (Ezek. 24:4).

SHOVEL (Heb. *rahath, ya', yāthēdh*), a tool used for clearing out ashes etc. from the altar (Exod. 27:3, II Chron. 4:11 etc.), for sanitary purposes (Deut. 23:13), or for winnowing (Isa. 30:24).

SHOWBREAD, SHEWBREAD (See Tabernacle)

SHRINE (Gr. *naós*), a dwelling for a god (Acts 19:24), used only once in the English versions, but the same Gr. word *naós* is used about 44 times and translated *temple*. (Acts 17:24, I Cor. 3:16).

SHROUD (Heb. *hōresh*), generally the dress for the dead, but also a bough (Ezek. 31:3) where KJV has " a shadowing shroud," but ASV has "a forest-like shade."

SHRUB (See Plants)

SHUA (shoo'a, Heb. *shua', prosperity*). 1. A Canaanite whose daughter became Judah's wife (Gen. 38:2,12). The KJV incorrectly spells this *shuah*. 2. The daughter of Heber who was the grandson of Asher (I Chron. 7:32).

SHUAH (shoo'ah, Heb. *shûah, depression*). 1. A son of Abraham by Keturah (Gen. 25:2; I Chron. 1:32).

2. (See Shua No. 1).

3. Chelub's brother (I Chron. 4:11). Some MSS read "Son of." This name is another form of "Caleb" and is doubtless used to distinguish him from Caleb, the son of Hegron and Caleb, son of Jephunneh.

SHUAL (shoo'al, Heb. *shû'āl, fox*). 1. One of the 11 sons of Zophat from the tribe of Asher (I Chron. 7:36).

2. I Samuel 13:17 refers to the "Land of Shual." It is named as one of the places invaded by one of the marauding tribes of Philistines. It probably lies a few miles NE of Bethel.

SHUBAEL (shoo'bā-ĕl, *shuvā'ēl, captive*). a name given to two Levites (I Chron. 24:20; 25:20). They are also referred to as Shebuel.

SHUHAM, SHUHAMITE (shoo'hăm, shoo'hăm-īt, Heb. *shûhām*), the son of Dan (Num. 26:42; Gen. 46:23), called also "Hushim." Dan's descendants are called "Shuhamites."

SHUHITE (shoo'hīt, Heb. *shûhî, a native of Shuah*), a term describing one of Job's friends by the name of Bildad (Job 2:11; 8:1; 18:1; 25:1; 42:9). It is very likely that this term refers back to Abraham's son by Keturah named Shuah. From him came a tribe of Arabs that dwelt near to Uz, the birthplace of Job (Job 1:1; 2:11). The exact location of this tribe is not certainly known, but it is likely that these people dwelt in the far northern area W of the Euphrates. If they were near Uz, as Job 2:11 indicates, this would place Uz in this region rather than farther S as is commonly done.

SHULAMITE (shōō′lăm- īt, Heb. *shunammîth, peaceful*), a title applied to a young woman in the Song of Solomon 6:13. There is some difference of opinion as to the origin of this term. It is not unlikely that it is a feminine form of Solomon. Both the RV and RSV have more correctly spelled this word Shulammite. If this word is the same word as "Shunammite," as the LXX rendering would imply, then it could be derived from the town of Shunem. See SHUNAMMITE, SHUNEM.

SHUMATHITES (shōō′măth-īts, Heb. *shumāthî, garlic*), a family of Kirjath-jearim (I Chron. 2:53).

SHUNAMMITE (shōō′năm-īt, Heb. *shunammîth, a native of Shunem*). 1. An unnamed woman whose son Elisha raised from the dead (II Kings 4:12). This woman had made her home available to the prophet when in this area. Later on, God used Elisha to save her from impending death (II Kings 8:1-6).

2. This word is applied also to David's nurse, Abishag (I Kings 1:3; 2:17-22).

SHUNEM (shōō′nĕm, Heb. *shûnēm*), a place belonging to the tribe of Issachar (Josh. 19:18). Here the Philistines encamped before they fought at Gilboa (I Sam. 28:4). Here lived David's nurse, Abishag (I Kings 1:3). Shunem was also the home of the woman who befriended Elisha whose son he restored (II Kings 4:8-37). It lies in a very rich section of Palestine a short distance N of Jezreel at the foot of "Little Hermon." A valuable spring of water doubtlessly attracted the Philistines to choose it as a camp site.

SHUNI, SHUNITE (shōō′nī, shōō′nīt, Heb. *shûnî*), the son of Gad who founded a group known as Shunites (Gen. 46:16; Num. 26:15).

SHUPHAM, SHUPHAMITE (shōō′fam, shōō′fămīt, Heb. *shûphām*), a son of Benjamin and founder of the group known as "Shuphamites" (Num. 26:39). He is probably to be identified with the person "Shephuphan" (I Chron. 8:5).

SHUPPIM (shŭ′pĭm, Heb. *shuppîm*). 1. A Benjamite (I Chron. 7:12,15).

2. One of the two who had charge of the gate of the temple, Shallecheth (I Chron. 26:16), a Levite.

SHUR (shŏōr, Heb. *shûr, wall*), a locality S of Palestine and E of Egypt. It was in this region that the angel of the Lord found Hagar when she fled from Sarah (Gen. 16:7-14). Abraham too dwelt in this territory at one time (Gen. 20:1).

SHUSHAN (shōō′shăn, Heb. *shûshan*), a city of the Babylonians probably named from the lilies that grow in this region in large numbers. It was famous in Biblical history as one of the capitals of the Persian empire (Neh. 1:1; Esth. 1:2; Dan. 8:2) during the time of Darius the Great. Here also Persian kings came to reside for the winter, and Daniel had the vision mentioned in Daniel 8:2. The Greeks called this place "Susa." It was located in the fertile valley on the left bank of the Choaspes River called Ulai in Daniel 8:2,16. It enjoyed a very delightful climate. Many Jews lived here and became prominent in the affairs of the city as the Books of Esther and Nehemiah show. From this city was sent the group who replaced those removed from Samaria (Ezra 4:9).

In the last part of the 19th century the French carried on extensive excavations at Shushan directed by Dieulafoy. This archaeological effort uncovered the great palace of King Xerxes (486-465 B.C.) in which Queen Esther lived.

The village of Shunem (Sulem) on the edge of the Plain of Esdraelon. © MPS

SHUTHELAH, SHUTHALHITE (shōō-thē′là, shōō-thăl′hīt, Heb. *shûthalhî*). 1. One of the three sons of Ephraim (Num. 26:35-36). His descendants are called "Shuthalhites" and are given in I Chronicles 7:20-21.

2. The sixth person descending from Shuthelah is also called by his name. I Chronicles 7:21 mentions his father as Zabad and reveals that he is the father of Ezer and Elead.

SHUTTLE (shŭ′tl, Heb. *'eregh*), a word used as a figure of the quick passing of life (Job 7:6). Job says that his days pass as swiftly as the rapidly moving shuttle of the weaver.

SIA (sī′à, Heb. *sî'ā', assembly*), a leader of the Nethinim whose descendants returned with Zerubbabel (Neh. 7:47). Spelled Siaha in Ezra 2:44.

SIBBECAI, SIBBECHAI (sīb′ē-kī, sīb′ē-kī, Heb. *sibbekhay*), a captain of several thousand men in David's army. He is usually designated as "The Hushathite" (II Sam. 21:18; I Chron. 11:29; 20:4; 27:11). He found a place among the mighty men of David chiefly for his victory over the Philistine Saph (II Sam. 21:18).

SIBBOLETH (See Shibboleth)

SIBMAH (sīb′mà, Heb. *sevām*), a town located on the E of the Jordan and belonging originally to Moab. It was finally taken by the Amorites led by King Sihon (Num. 21:26). Later it was captured by and given to the tribe of Reuben (Josh. 13:19). Most scholars feel it is to be identified with Shebam (Num. 32:3) or Shibmah (32:38). It was famous for its luxurious vines and fruits (Isa. 16:8; Jer. 48:32).

SIBRAIM (sīb-rā′īm, Heb. *sivrayim*), a point marking Palestine's northern boundary between Damascus and Hamath (Ezek. 47:16).

SICHEM (sī′kĕm, Heb. *shekhem*), the same as Shechem.

Sidon on the Mediterranean. At left, the harbor and old Crusaders' Fort.
At right, an air view of the city and the seafront.   PB   MPS

SICILY (sĭs'ĭ-lē), the triangular island lying off the toe of Italy was colonized in prehistoric times by a tribe closely related to those in the enclave round the mouth of the Tiber who became the Roman people. The W and S of the island was colonized from the eighth century B.C. onwards by the Carthaginians (themselves Phoenician colonists from Tyre), and the E and N by the Greeks. Colonization in both cases was by the building of "emporia," or seacoast towns, designed to exploit the hinterland. Centuries of tension and strife between the Greeks and Carthaginians ended with the intervention of Rome in the middle of the third century B.C. The western Mediterranean was too small for two first class powers, and Rome and Carthage both looked upon Sicily as a bridgehead. Hence the firmness with which Rome took advantage of factional strife at Messana to invade the island. The end of the Punic wars saw Sicily a Roman province.

SICK, SICKNESS (See Diseases)

SICKLE (sĭk'l, Heb. *hermēsh, a reaping hook, maggāl, a reaping hook;* Gr. *drépanon, a tool used for cutting grain*). The earlier sickles varied in size, shape, and in the material from which they were made. The earliest type seems to have been constructed of wood. It resembled our modern scythes, though smaller, and its cutting edge was made of flint. Later sickles were constructed of metal. These were used mostly for cutting grain, but on occasions they were used for pruning. Mark and John use the sickle in a figurative sense as the instrument of God's judgment (Mark 4:29; Rev. 14:14,16ff).

SIDDIM, VALE OF (sĭd'ĭm, Heb. *'ēmeq hasiddîm, the valley of the fields*), a place mentioned in Genesis 14:3-8 as the battle-ground where Chedorlaomer and his allies met the kings of Sodom and other nearby cities. In the time of Abraham it must have been a place of great fertility, since it was chosen by Lot because of its productivity (Gen. 13:10). From Genesis 14:3,10 it seems to have been near to the Dead Sea and full of slime pits. In the past some scholars have placed it at the N end of the Dead Sea. The general view today, however, is that Siddim was located at the southern end of the Dead Sea. Because of the wickedness of the inhabitants of this area, God judged the locality many years ago in the days of Abraham. Its cities were completely destroyed and probably much of this territory was inundated by the waters of the Dead Sea.   H.Z.C.

SIDON (sī'dŏn, Heb. *tsîdhôn*, Gr. *Sidón*), a Phoenician city midway between Berytus (Beirut) and Tyre. Small offshore islands made an excellent port. In ancient times they seem to have been linked by moles. Sidon appears in the OT as the chief city of Phoenicia, and the name was applied frequently to the whole nation (Gen. 10:15; Judg. 10:12). The city seems to have been a center of trade and enterprise. Homer, whose text dates from the eighth century before Christ, speaks of Sidon's artistic metal work ("A mixing bowl of silver, chased; six measures it held, and in beauty it was far the best in all the earth, for artificers of Sidon wrought it cunningly, and men of the Phoenicians brought it over the misty sea" (*Iliad* 23: 743-748). The *Odyssey* 4.613-619 speaks of a similar cup "lipped with gold"). Purple dyeing and glass blowing were also Sidonian industries. By an odd chance, the crimson dye which Sidonian inventors found how to extract from the murex shellfish, was called after the name of the other great Phoenician town, "Tyrian purple."

The art of glass blowing was discovered in the first century B.C. at Sidon, and the names of a number of Sidonian glass-blowers have been recovered from surviving samples of their art. Sidon shared fully in the seafaring, commercial, and colonizing enterprises of the Phoenician people. The last-named activity extended, according to tradition, as far as Malta. Outside the OT, Sidon finds its first mention in ancient documents in the Amarna Letters, which reveal Prince Zimrida of Sidon contesting Egyptian lordship of the coastal strip, the main area which the Phoenicians aspired to rule. Similar advantage was taken of a period of Egyptian withdrawal and decline, in the period of Sidonian expansion which followed the death of Rameses II. It was at this time that Sidon came into conflict over Dor with the other occupants of coastal Palestine, the Philistines. Israel suffered from the same burst of activity (Judg. 1:31; 10: 12). By and large, the history of Sidon followed the course of that of all Phoenicia. In common with the rest of the lands of the Middle East, Sidon fell under the power in turn of Assyria, Babylon, Persia, Greece, and Rome. Brief-lived patterns of alliance (Jer. 27:3), periods of independence, parley, subjection, ill-advised revolt, destruction, and renaissance, were the common lot of the smaller lands of the region amid the rise and fall of the great empires. Sidon had a bad name in Scripture as a hot-bed of Phoenician idolatry (Isa. 23; Ezek.

28), and of Gentile materialism (Matt. 11:21,22). The neighborhood of Sidon, not more than 50 miles from Nazareth, was visited by Christ (Matt. 15:21; Mark 7:24-31), and Sidonians resorted to Him (Mark 3:8; Luke 6:17). Sidon was a residence of Christian disciples, and a port of call of Paul (Acts 27:3). E.M.B.

SIEGE (See War)

SIEVE (sĭv, Heb. *kevārâh, netted, nāphâh, a sieve*), a utensil used by the eastern people to sift grains. Some of the Egyptian sieves were made of strings or reeds. Those constructed of string were used for finer work whereas those made from reeds were used for sifting coarser material. It is used in the Bible in a figurative sense in both passages where the word occurs (Isa. 30:28; Amos 9:9).

SIGN (Heb. *'ôth, a signal, môphēth, a miracle, omen;* Gr. *semeíon, an indication*). In Scripture this word generally refers to something addressed to the senses to attest the existence of a divine power. Miracles in the Old Testament were often signs (Exod. 4:8; 8:23). Several specific things were given as signs, such as the rainbow (Gen. 9: 12-13); some of the feasts (Exod. 13:9); the sabbath (Exod. 31:13); and circumcision (Rom. 4: 11). Often extraordinary events were given as a sign to insure faith or demonstrate authority. When Moses would not believe God, his rod was turned into a serpent and his hand became leprous as signs of God's divine commission (Exod. 4:1-8). Sometimes future events were given as present signs, as in the case of Ahaz (Isa. 7:14). When Christ was born, the place of His birth and His dress were to be signs of His identity to the shepherds. When the Scribes and the Pharisees asked Jesus for a sign, He assured them that no sign was to be given them except the sign of Jonah, whose experience in the fish was to portray Christ's burial and resurrection. Revelation tells that before Christ returns there will be signs in the heavens, in the stars, moon and sun. H.Z.C.

SIGNET (See Seal)

SIHON (sī'hŏn, Heb. *sîhôn*), a king of the Amorites who became prominent chiefly because of his opposition to Israel on their journey from Egypt to Palestine. His capital in the land E of the Jordan River was Heshbon. Prior to Israel's journey the Amorites under his leadership had driven out the Moabites from this section of land and had taken over this territory. God permitted him to dispossess the Moabites, but when he led the attack against Israel, he was killed and his forces scattered (Num. 21:21-24; Deut. 1:4,20,24-30). His capital was taken and the territory given to Israel. This episode is often referred to as a reminder to Israel of what God had done for them and became a source of encouragement to them (Deut. 3:2). When Jephthah was judge of Israel, the Moabites came and demanded that Israel return this land to them (Judg. 11:12-13). However, Jephthah reminded them that Sihon had seized this property and God had given it to them and, therefore, neither they nor the Ammonites had any right to it.

SIHOR (sī'hôr, Heb. *shîhôr, turbid*), a body of water mentioned in connection with Egypt (Josh. 13: 3; Isa. 23:3; Jer. 2:18). It is correctly spelled "Shihor." Its identity is uncertain, some thinking it is the Nile River, while others think it is Brook of Egypt, the modern Wady-el-'Arish.

SILAS (sī'lăs, probably the Aramaic form of Saul, *asked*), a name occurring only in the book of Acts, where it identifies a prominent member of the Jerusalem church (Acts 15:22,32) and a Roman citizen (Acts 16:37), who was sent by the church with Paul and Barnabas to deliver the letter which was formulated by the Jerusalem council to the church at Antioch (Acts 15:22,23). After spending some time at Antioch, Silas returned to Jerusalem. When Paul fell out with Barnabas, he turned for help on his so-called second missionary journey to Silas, whose ministry he no doubt had closely observed at Antioch. Little is said of Silas in Luke's account. He was with Paul at Philippi and shared both in the beating and imprisonment there. When Paul left Berea for Athens, Silas and Timothy were left behind. Apparently Timothy rejoined Paul only at Athens, while Silas stayed on in Macedonia. He, along with Timothy, who had returned to Thessalonica, rejoined Paul at Corinth (Acts 18:5).

Although no further references to the name Silas occur in the NT, it is almost certain that Silvanus is the same person. He joins Paul in the salutation of both I and II Thessalonians (1:1), and is mentioned by Paul in his second letter to the Corinthians with reference to the preaching of Christ at Corinth (II Cor. 1:19). Silvanus also appears as the amanuensis of Peter (I Pet. 5:12). W.W.W.

SILK (Heb. *meshî, drawn,* Gr. *sérikon, silken*), a word mentioned four times in the Bible (Prov. 31: 22; Ezek. 16:10,13; Rev. 18:12). It is doubtful if the OT passages refer to silk as we know it, but Revelation 18:12 does. The Greek word is *sér,* the Greek name for China, from which silk came.

SILLA (sĭl'à, Heb. *sillā', embankment*), an unknown place in the valley below Millo (II Kings 12:20).

SILOAH, SHILOAH (See Siloam)

SILOAM (sĭ-lō'ăm, Gr. *Siloám*), a reservoir located within the city walls of Jerusalem at the S end of the Tyropoean Valley. II Kings 20:20 states that Hezekiah "made the pool and the conduit and brought water into the city," and II Chronicles 32:30 that he "closed the upper outlet of the waters of Gihon and directed them down to the west side of the city of David." These words undoubtedly refer to the conduit leading from the intermittent Spring of Gihon (Jerusalem's most impor-

Entrance to the Siloam Tunnel (Hezekiah's) at the Spring of Gihon (Virgin's Fountain), at the northern end of the tunnel. © MPS

The Pool of Siloam at the southern end of Hezekiah's Tunnel, in the Kidron Valley. © MPS

tant water supply) through the rock Ophel to the reservoir called the Pool of Siloam. The earliest knowledge of this tunnel dates back to 1838 when it was explored by the American traveler and scholar Edward Robinson and his missionary friend Eli Smith. They first attempted to crawl through the tunnel from the Siloam end, but soon found that they were not suitably dressed to crawl through the narrow passage. Three days later, dressed only in a wide pair of Arab drawers, they entered the tunnel from the Spring of Gihon end, and advancing much of the way on their hands and knees and sometimes flat on their stomachs, went the full distance. They measured the tunnel and found it to be 1750 feet in length.

The tunnel is full of twists and turns. The straight line distance from the Spring Gihon to the Pool of Siloam is only 762 feet, less than half the length of the tunnel. Why it follows such a circuitous route has never been adequately explained. Grollenberg suggests that it may have been "to avoid at all costs any interference with the royal tombs, which were quite deeply hewn into the rock on the eastern slope of Ophel" (*Atlas of the Bible*, New York: Nelson, 1956, p. 93).

In 1867 Captain Charles Warren also explored the tunnel, but neither he nor Robinson and Smith before him, noticed the inscription on the wall of the tunnel near the Siloam end. This was discovered in 1880 by a native boy who, while wading in the tunnel, slipped and fell into the water. When he looked up he noticed the inscription. The boy reported his discovery to his teacher, Herr Conrad Schick, who made the information available to scholars. The inscription was deciphered by A. H. Sayce, with the help of others. It consists of six lines written in Old Hebrew (Canaanite) with prong-like characters. The first half of the inscription is missing, but what remains reads as follows: "[. . . when] (the tunnel) was driven through: — while [. . .] (were) still [. . .] axe(s), each man toward his fellow, and while there were still three cubits to be cut through, [there was heard] the voice of a man calling to his fellow, for there was an *overlap* in the rock on the right [and on the left]. And when the tunnel was driven through, the quarrymen hewed (the rock), each man toward his fellow, axe against axe; and the water flowed from the spring toward the reservoir for 1,200 cubits, and the height of the rock above the head(s) of the quarrymen was 100 cubits" (*Ancient Near Eastern Texts* ed. James B. Prichard, Princeton University Press, 1955, p. 321).

The importance of the Siloam inscription can scarcely be overestimated. Not only does it give a fascinating account of the building of the tunnel, but as G. Ernest Wright says it "has for many years been the most important monumental piece of writing in Israelite Palestine, and other Hebrew inscriptions have been dated by comparing the shapes of letters with it" (*Biblical Archaeology*, Philadelphia: Westminster Press, 1957, p. 169).

The Siloam Inscription, in early Hebrew monumental script, dating about 700 B.C. Removed from the walls of the Siloam Tunnel, it is now in the museum at Istanbul, Turkey. © MPS

In 1890 a vandal entered the tunnel and cut the inscription out of the rock. It was subsequently found in several pieces in the possession of a Greek in Jerusalem who claimed he had purchased it from an Arab. The Turkish officials seized the pieces and removed them to Istanbul where they are today.

The Siloam tunnel was not the only conduit which had been built to bring water from the Spring of Gihon into Jerusalem. At least two others preceded it, but neither was adequately protected against enemy attack. It was probably to one of these former conduits that Isaiah referred in the words, "the waters of Shiloah that flow gently" (Isa. 8:6).

It was to the pool of Siloam that Jesus sent the blind man with the command, "Go, wash" (John 9:7). He obeyed, and came back seeing. W.W.W.

SILOAM, TOWER OF (sĭ-lō'ăm), a tower which was probably part of the ancient system of fortifications on the walls of the city of Jerusalem near the pool of Siloam. The collapse of this tower and the resulting death of 18 persons (were they workmen employed on the aqueduct that Pilate was building? Cf. Jos. *BJ,* II, ix, 4) is cited by Jesus (Luke 13:4). Apparently the accident was well known to His hearers, but is not mentioned elsewhere.

SILOAM, VILLAGE OF (sĭ-lō'ăm). There is no mention of a village by this name in the Bible. However, on the rocky slope across the valley E of the Spring Gihon (see *Siloam,* above) is a rocky slope on which is situated the modern village of Silwan (Siloam). At this site an inscription over the door of a tomb, discovered at the end of the 19th century but only recently deciphered by Professor N. Avigad, indicates that the tomb may have belonged to Shebna, an official during Hezekiah's time (cf. Isa. 22:15,16).

SILVANUS (See Silas)

SILVER (See Minerals)

SILVERSMITH (See Artificer under Occupations and Professions)

SIMEON (sĭm'ē-ŭn, Heb. *shim'ôn,* Gr. *Symeón*). 1. The second son of Jacob by Leah (Gen. 29:33). He and his brother Levi massacred the Hivites living in Shechem because of an injury done to their sister Dinah (Gen. 34:24-31).

2. The tribe of which Simeon, the son of Jacob, became the founder. He had six sons, all but one of whom founded tribal families. At the distribution of the land of Canaan the extreme S of Canaan was assigned to this tribe. Eventually most of the tribe disappeared.

3. An ancestor of Jesus (Luke 3:30).

4. A righteous and devout man to whom the Holy Spirit revealed that he would not die until he had seen the Messiah. When the infant Jesus was brought into the temple, he took Him into his arms and praised God (Luke 2:25,34).

5. Simon Peter (Acts 15:14). See PETER.

6. One of the Christian leaders in the church at Antioch, surnamed Niger, who set apart Paul and Barnabas for their missionary work (Acts 13:1,2). Nothing more is known of him.

SIMEONITE, a member of the tribe of Simeon; see above 2.

SIMILITUDE (sĭ-mĭl'ĭ-tūd, Heb. *temûnâh, likeness; demûth, pattern; tavnîth, model;* Gr. *homoiótes, homoíoma, homoíosis, resemblance*). The first word is found four times in the OT (Num. 12:8; Deut. 4:12,15,16), and some form of the divine manifestation seems to be intended. The second word is probably best translated by "pattern," as

II Chronicles 4:3 reveals. The third word seems to convey a resemblance of that which it represents (Ps. 106:20; 144:12). The last three words, all derived from the verb *homoióo,* have the idea of something that is like or similar to another thing (Rom. 5:14; Heb. 7:15; James 3:9). While all three words are found in the LXX, the second of these is used to translate all three of the Hebrew words.

SIMON (sī'mŭn, Gr. *Símon, hearing*). 1. The son of Jonas, and brother of Andrew, a fisherman who became a disciple and apostle of Christ. He was surnamed Peter, "stone," and Cephas, Aramaic for "rock" (Matt. 4:18; 16:17,18, etc.). See PETER.

2. Another disciple of Jesus called the "Cananaean," a member of the party later called "the Zealots" (Matt. 10:4; Mark 3:18). The word does not mean "inhabitant of Cana." Luke properly translates the Hebrew by *zealot* (Luke 6:15; Acts 1:13).

3. A leper of Bethany in whose house Jesus' head was anointed (Matt. 26:6; Mark 14:3).

4. A brother of the Lord (Matt. 13:55; Mark 6:3).

5. A man from Cyrene, father of Alexander and Rufus, who was compelled to carry the cross of Jesus (Matt. 27:32; Mark 15:21; Luke 23:26).

6. A Pharisee in whose house Jesus' feet were anointed by the sinful woman (Luke 7:40,43,44).

7. Judas Iscariot's father (John 6:71; 12:4; 13: 2,26).

8. Simon Magus, a sorcerer at Samaria, with great power and influence among the people (Acts 8:9-13). He "believed" as the result of Philip's preaching there, although the real nature of his faith is not clear, as his subsequent action reveals. He undoubtedly was especially impressed by the operation of divine power in Philip, a power which exceeded his own. After being baptized he continued with Philip, hoping, no doubt, to learn more of this power. Subsequently Peter and John were sent from the Jerusalem church to Samaria to pray for the new converts and to lay hands on them with a view to their receiving the Holy Spirit. When Simon saw that the Spirit was given by the laying on of hands he tried to buy this power for himself from the apostles. His request called forth a blistering rebuke by Peter (Acts 8:14-24).

In post-apostolic Christian literature Simon Magus plays a prominent role. He was thought by Irenaeus *(Against Heresies,* I, 23) to be the founder of Gnosticism and the eponymous leader of the sect of the Simonians. According to Justin Martyr *(Apology,* I, 26), he went to Rome during the reign of Claudius, and the *Acts of Peter* relates how he led Roman Christians astray by his false teachings. He is particularly prominent in the pseudo-Clementine *Recognitions* and *Homilies* where he appears as the arch-opponent of Peter. The relationship between this Simon and the one in Acts is not clear. The actual founder of the sect of the Simonians may have been confused early in the Church with the Simon of Acts.

9. A tanner who lived at Joppa with whom Peter stayed "for many days" (Acts 9:43; 10:6,17, 32). W.W.W.

SIMON MACCABEUS (sī'mŭn măk'à-bē-ŭs), the second son of the priest Mattathias. He was surnamed Thassi, and was the elder brother of Judas Maccabeus. With his father and brothers he fought against the Syrians. At his father's death, he was made the adviser of the family. Eventually, as the last surviving member of the family, he succeeded in defeating the Syrians. He was acknowledged by the Jews as high priest, captain and leader, and was authorized to wear the purple. In 135 B.C. he was murdered by his son-in-law while visiting the cities of his dominion.

SIMON MAGUS (See Simon)

SIMPLE (Heb. *pethî, silly,* Gr. *ákakos, akéraios, harmless*). The basic idea of the word in the OT is "easily influenced" (Ps. 19:7; 119:130; Prov. 7: 7). The two uses of the word in the NT (Rom. 16: 18,19) carry the idea of being harmless or guileless.

SIMRI (sĭ'mrī, Heb. *shimrî*), a son of the Levite, Hosah. David appointed him as doorkeeper in the temple. While not the firstborn, he was made head of his tribe (I Chron. 26:10).

SIN (Heb. *hāttā'th, missing; pesha', transgression; 'awôn, perversion; ra', evil in disposition; resha', impiety;* Gr. *hamartía, missing the mark; parábasis, transgression; adikía, unrighteousness; asébeia; impiety; anomía, contempt and violation of law; ponería, depravity; epithumía, lust*). According to the Bible, the first sin in the universe was an act of free will in which the creature deliberately, responsibly and with adequate understanding of the issues, chose to corrupt the holy, godly character with which God originally endowed His creation.

There is definite indication in the Bible that mankind is not the only order of created personal beings among whom sin has become an actuality. In Jude, verse six, there is reference to "the angels that did not keep their own realm (*arche*) but left their proper dwelling." The parallel verse, II Peter 2:4, speaks of "the angels that sinned."

The Biblical writers assume that Satan is the chief of the fallen angels. In I John 3:8 we read, ". . . the devil sins from the beginning." From I Timothy 3:6, it is suggested that Satan's root or basic sin was pride. The words of Jesus are more explicit, "He [the Devil] was a murderer from the beginning. He did not take his stand in the truth; [this is evident] because truth is not in him. When he speaks falsehood he speaks out of his own things for he is a falsifier and the father of falsehood" (John 8:44).

Jesus' statement that the Devil is, from the beginning, a murderer and a falsifier is probably based upon the fact that by falsehood Satan brought about the fall of man, in which man (1) became liable to physical death, (2) became liable to eternal punishment, "the second death," and (3) became spiritually dead, that is, alienated from fellowship with God (Gen. 3).

There are expositors who hold that, aside from the above rather clear references to the fall of Satan, the prophetic denunciations of Babylon (Isa. 13: and 14:, especially 14:12-14) and of the King of Tyre (Ezek. 28:1-19, especially vss. 12-19) contain references to Satan's original status and his fall. We must reject "double meaning" exegesis, but it is not unreasonable to hold that certain sentences in these prophecies may contain analogies which would throw light upon Satan's probable original status and fall.

The statements are not very full, but yet the Biblical account of the primeval origin of sin is clear enough: Sin first became actual in an order of personal beings who are not a race (Matt. 22: 30; Mark 12:25; Luke 20:35,36). They do not have racial solidarity or racial representative responsibility. This order of beings, presumably having fully adequate understanding of the holy character of God and of God's impartation of His holy character to His creatures, were endowed with the power of ethical spiritual choice. Some of these

beings, including Satan as the chief, deliberately chose to corrupt their God-given holy character, and chose further to spread their corruption as widely as possible in God's creation. Their sin was the act of a group of individuals as individuals and does not involve the "federal" or representative principle. Since their sin was, we suppose, a deliberate act with fully adequate understanding, it is analogous to the fully conscious and responsible act, subsequent to conviction by the Holy Spirit, in which act Jesus said that the sinner is "guilty of eternal sin" (Mark 3:29). In other words, they sinned without remedy.

The original human sin is very simply recorded in the third chapter of Genesis, and its implications for mankind are expounded in Romans 5: 12-21. Man was created with a holy, godly nature, in fellowship with God. He was placed in an environment which was "all very good." He was then tempted by Satan, and he deliberately chose the path of self-corruption and enmity against God.

Unlike the angels, mankind is not a mere aggregate of individuals. Man is a race with group solidarity, and representative responsibility. The representative principle governs all of human life. Just as every American must say, "I signed the Declaration of Independence in 1776," or "I declared war Dec. 7, 1941," similarly, every descendant of Adam must say, "I became a wicked corrupt sinner in the garden of Eden; and I crucified the Lord of Glory at Calvary. My representatives did it, and the action was mine."

The nature of sin is suggested by the nature of the origin of sin in the universe, and the nature of the original sin of the human race. "Sin is any want of conformity unto, or transgression of, the law of God" (*Westminster Shorter Catechism*. Cf. I John 3:4).

The Biblical view of sin, however, does not depend wholly upon the concept of law, for the Biblical writers appeal to the holy character of God as the basis of the law. "Ye shall be holy for I, Jehovah, your God, am holy" (Lev. 19:2), is the constant presupposition. It was the revelation of the holy character of God (Isa. 6:1-6) which caused Isaiah to recognize his own sinful corruption. Thus sin is not only violation of the divine law, which is an expression of God's will; more profoundly, it is violation of the expression of God's holy character. It is corruption of the goodness which God originally imparted to His creatures; especially is it the corruption of the godliness with which God originally endowed man when He created him in His own image.

Sin may then be defined ultimately as anything in the creature which does not express, or which is contrary to, the holy character of the Creator. Sin then is not merely what we do, but what we *are.* There is sin in our race and in our nature.

The remedy for sin, according to the Biblical view (Rom. 5:12ff), is based equally upon the representative principle. In the time of world war II one might have repudiated the act of Congress in declaring war. He would then have been moved to a concentration camp. Tojo would have been his representative and Pearl Harbor would have been his deed.

Reversing the figure, the believer says, I repudiate my sin and I accept the One who died at Calvary as my representative. In Him, I died for my sins. My only hope is His substitutionary atonement, for He bore my sin "in His own body on the tree" (I Pet. 2:24). J.O.B.

A shepherd and his flock before the rugged slopes of Jebel Musa and Ras Safsaf, the traditional and most probable site of Mount Sinai, or Horeb. © MPS

SIN (Heb. *sîn, clay*), an Egyptian city mentioned only in Ezekiel 30:15,16, called by the Greeks "Pelusium," lying on the eastern arm of the Nile River. Ezekiel refers to it as "the stronghold of Egypt (Ezek. 30:15). A wall was built on the S, and with the sea on the N and impassable swamps on the other sides the city was practically impregnable. Since Thebes and Sin were at the opposite ends of Egypt, mentioning these two cities as Ezekiel does implies God's judgment falling upon the entire land of Egypt.

SIN, WILDERNESS OF, a wilderness through which the Israelites passed between Elim and Mt. Sinai (Exod. 16:1; 17:1; Num. 33:11,12). It is probably to be identified with Debbet er-Ramleh, a sandy tract in the interior of the peninsula of Sinai at the foot of Jebel et-Tih, but the coastal plain of el-Markhah has also been suggested. The fixing of its position depends upon the location of Mt. Sinai, on the exact site of which scholars are in disagreement.

SIN OFFERING (See Offerings)

SINA (See Sinai)

In the Wilderness of Sin. © MPS

SINAI (sī'nī, Heb.. *sînay,* meaning uncertain), a word used in three senses in the Old Testament:

1. It is applied to a peninsula which lay to the south of the Wilderness of Paran between the Gulf of Aqabah and Suez on the E and W respectively. This peninsula has a triangular shape and is 150 miles wide at the N and 250 miles long. Some of the Egyptian dynasties claimed this region as some of their most valued area. They carried on mining operations for turquoise, iron and copper, and much of their red granite and pink gneiss came from this locality.

2. It is applied to a wilderness, the "Wilderness of Sinai" (Exod. 19:1). It is the place where Israel came in the third month after they left Egypt. It may be used loosely as a synonym for the Sinaitic Peninsula but probably technically does not embrace as much territory.

3. Finally, there is the mountain often referred to as Mount Sinai (Exod. 19:20), or Horeb. It was on this mountain that God met and talked with Moses and gave him the law (Exod. 19:3). There has been much debate over the exact location of Mount Sinai. There are four possible sites: (1) Mount Serbal, on Wadi Feiran. A serious objection to this identification, however, is that there is no plain large enough in the neighborhood to offer camping ground for a large host; (2) Jebel Musa (Mountain of Moses) and Ras Safsaf, a short ridge with two peaks, one with an altitude of 6,540 feet and the other 7,363 feet. St. Catherine's Monastery, a monastery of Greek monks, is located at the foot of Jebel Musa; (3) Jebel Hellal, a 2,000 foot elevation 30 miles S of El-a'Arish; and (4) Mount Seir, on the edge of the Arabah. The only later visit to the mount recorded in Scripture is Elijah's when he fled from Jezebel (I Kings 19:8).   H.Z.C.

SINEW (sī'nū, Heb. *gîdh, sinew*), the tendons and sinews of the body (Gen. 32:32; Job. 40:17; Ezek 37:6-8). It is used once in a figurative sense (Isa. 48:4).

SINGING (See Song; Music)

SINGLE EYE (Gr. *ophthalmós haploús, a healthy eye*), an eye that is clear, sound, and healthy, with the connotation *generous* (Matt. 6:22; Luke 11: 34).

SINIM (sī'nĭm, Heb. *sînîm*), a country cited in a prophecy by Isaiah (49:12) to illustrate God's promise that the dispersed Israelites would some day be gathered from the farthest regions of the earth. It is obviously not W or N, since both are mentioned in the prophecy. It must, therefore, be S or E, and apparently very far away. The most widely held view is that China is meant, either because some Israelites were already living there or would live there. There is evidence that the Jews traded with the Chinese as early as the third century B.C.   H.Z.C.

SINITES (sī'nīts, Heb. *sînî*), a tribe descended from Canaan (Gen. 10:17; I Chron. 1:15). No definite identification is possible.

SION, MOUNT (sī'ŭn, Heb. *sî'ôn, lofty*, Gr. *Seón*), one of the varied designations by which Mount Hermon is referred to (Deut. 4:48).

SIPHMOTH (sĭ'fmŏth, Heb. *siphmôth*), a place in the southern part of Judah to which David often came (I Sam. 30:28). The site has not been positively identified.

SIPPAI (sĭp'ī, Heb. *saph*), a man, known also as Saph, descended from the giants. He was slain at Geser by Sibbechai (I Chron. 20:4).

SIRACH, SON OF (sī'răk, Gr. *Sirách*), the supposed author of the Apocryphal book of Ecclesiasticus. He calls himself "Jesus, the Son of Sirach the Jerusalemite." He wrote about 190-170 B.C.

SIRAH (sī'rà, Heb. *sirâh*), a well mentioned in II Samuel 3:26. It is probably 'Ain Sarah which is located about a mile N of old Hebron.

SIRION (sĭr'ĭ-ŏn, Heb. *siryôn, coat of mail*), a name given to Mt. Hermon by the Zidonians (Deut. 3:9). It is called Shirion in Psalm 29:6.

SISMAI, SISAMAI (sĭs'mī, sĭs'à-mī, Heb. *sismay*), a son of Eleasah from the tribe of Judah. One who descended from Sheshan's daughter (I Chron. 2:40).

SISERA (sĭs'êr-à, Heb. *sîserā'*). 1. A man employed by Jabin, king of Hazor, as the captain in his army. In Judges, chapters four and five, we have the account of the battle which was carried on between Sisera and Barak. Sisera was a thorn in Israel's side for 20 years, waging war against them with 900 iron chariots (Judg. 4:2-3). Finally, Deborah the prophetess, who judged Israel at that time, urged Barak under the direction of God to unite his forces and go against Sisera. She assured him that God would deliver him into Barak's hands. He agreed, if Deborah would go with him, and she gave her consent. These two armies met in battle on the plain at the foot of Mount Tabor (Judg. 4:14). The forces of Sisera were killed or scattered and Sisera fled on foot, taking refuge in the tent of Jael, the wife of Heber, the Kenite. Here he was killed by Jael while he slept in her tent. The remarkable victory was celebrated by the song of Deborah.

2. The name Sisera is found again in the names of the Nethinim (Ezra 2:53; Neh. 7:55) who returned from captivity under Zerubbabel's leadership. See BARAK, DEBORAH.

SISTER (Heb. *'āhôth*, Gr. *adelphé*), a word used in both Hebrew and Greek with varying ideas. In the OT it is used of females having the same parents, having but one parent in common, a kinswoman and a woman of the same country (Gen. 20:12; Num. 25:18; Lev. 18:9; Job 42:11). In the NT it is used of girls belonging to the same family or just to blood relatives (Matt. 13:56; Mark 6:3; Luke 10:39). It also has a figurative sense as seen in several places in the Bible (Ezek. 16:45; 23:11; Rom. 16:1; II John 13).

SITNAH (sĭt'nà, Heb. *sitnâh, hostility*), the name given to the second well dug by Isaac (Gen. 26: 21), suggesting a contest between the Israelites and the people of Gerah.

SIVAN (sē-vàn', Heb. *sîwān*), the name given to the third month of the Hebrew sacred year which is the ninth month of the civil year (Esth. 8:9). See CALENDAR.

SKIN (Heb. *'ôr, naked, geledh, smooth, bāsār, flesh*, Gr. *dérma, skin*). One of the very common words in the OT, *'ôr* is used of both animal skin (Gen. 3: 21; 27:16; Jer. 13:23) and human skin (Exod. 34: 35; Lev. 13:2; and Job 7:5). *Geledh* is found only once in the Bible (Job 16:15) describing the action of Job putting sackcloth on his body. This was a tight-fitting garment expressive of mourning and perhaps suggests the sad condition of Job's physical appearance. *Bāsār* is the most common word used for human flesh (Gen. 2:21; II Kings 4:34; Prov. 14:30) and for the flesh of animals (Lev. 7:15).

Skins of animals were used as bottles both for water and for wine. They formed many useful articles of clothing. Various kinds formed the protection for the tabernacle in the wilderness. Ezekiel tells of shoes being made from skins (Ezek. 16:10).

The word is also used figuratively in several places (Job 2:4; 19:20). The two Greek words are used only three times in the NT and in each case speak of articles of clothing.

SKIRT (See Dress)

SKULL (See Golgotha)

SKY (Heb. *shahaq, vapor*), a word found only in the plural in the Bible (Ps. 18:11; Isa. 45:8). The word refers sometimes to the clouds and other times to the firmament. At least once it is used figuratively (Deut. 33:26).

SLANDER (Heb. *dibbâh, slander*, Gr. *diábolos, slanderer*), a malicious utterance designed to hurt or defame the person about whom it is uttered. The Scriptures frequently warn against it (Lev. 19:16; Ezek. 22:9; Eph. 4:31; Col. 3:8; James 4: 11).

SLAVE, SLAVERY (Heb. *'evedh, servant, slave*, Gr. *dóulos, bondslave, servant*). While the Hebrew and Greek words are very common in the Bible, the English word *slave* is found but twice (Jer. 2: 14; Rev. 18:13), and the word *slavery* does not occur at all in the KJV, because both the Hebrew and the Greek word involved are more often rendered "servant."

Among the Hebrews, slaves could be acquired in a number of ways: as prisoners of war (Num. 31:7-9); by purchase (Lev. 25:44); by gift (Gen. 29:24); by accepting a person in lieu of a debt (Lev. 25:39); by birth from slaves already possessed (Exod. 21:4); by arrest if the thief had nothing to pay for the object stolen (Exod. 22:2-3); and by the voluntary decision of the person wanting to be a slave (Exod. 21:6). Slaves among the

Hebrews were more kindly treated than slaves among other nations, since the Mosaic Law laid down rules governing their treatment. They could gain their freedom in a number of ways (Exod. 21:2-27; Lev. 25:25ff; Deut. 15:12-23). Slavery continued in NT times, but the love of Christ seemed to militate against its continued existence (Eph. 6:5-9; Gal. 3:28).

SLEEP (Heb. *shēnâh, yāshēn, shākhav,* Gr. *hýpnos*), a word used in a number of ways in the Bible. Its most natural use is to refer to physical rest (I Sam. 26:7; Jonah 1:5-6). Most cases of physical sleep were natural ones, but some were supernaturally imposed to accomplish a divine purpose (Gen. 2:21; 15:12). Believers' rest in sleep is considered a gift from God (Ps. 127:2).

Methods of sleep varied usually with the social status of the people. The most common bed was simply a mat (Matt. 9:6). No special bed clothes were provided in this case, but those worn in the day were used (Exod. 22:26-27). Wealthy people had more elaborate beds variously constructed (Deut. 3:11; I Sam. 19:13).

Sleep is also used figuratively in the Bible, sometimes referring to those who are spiritually indolent (Matt. 25:5; Rom. 13:11) and to indicate the death of the believer (I Cor. 11:30; I Thess. 4:13).

SLIME (Heb. *hēmār, boiling up, zepheth, flowing*). Perhaps the two most common uses of this substance are found in Genesis 11:3 and Exodus 2:3. Probably it resembled asphalt and was used as a cement for bricks as well as for water-proofing. It is thought to be derived from natural gas and petroleum through a process of oxidation. In early Biblical history it seemed to be plentiful in the area around the Dead Sea.

SLIP (Heb. *zemôrâh, pruned*), a cutting from a plant. It is used but once in the Bible (Isa. 17:10).

SLOTHFUL (Heb. *ātsal, indolent; remiyyâh, treachery; rāphâh, slack;* Gr. *nothrós, sluggish; oknerós, indolent*). The combined idea from these words is that of a person who is undependable because of his laziness.

SLOW (Heb. *kāvēdh, heavy; 'erekh, to make long;* Gr. *bradýs, dull; árgos, inactive*). Moses says he is slow of speech (Exod. 4:10). This does not refer to any particular defect but simply to the fact that his words did not come readily. "Long-suffering" would almost be a synonym of *'erekh* as seen in many OT passages (Neh. 9:17; Ps. 103:8; 145:8). It always has a reference to the passions in the OT. The Greek words are found only three times in the NT (Luke 24:25; Titus 1:12; James 1:19).

SLUGGARD (See Slothful)

SMITH (See Occupations & Professions)

SMYRNA (smîr'nà, Gr. *Smýrna*), a port on the W coast of Asia Minor at the head of the gulf into which the Hermus debouches, a well protected harbor, and the natural terminal of a great inland trade-route up the Hermus valley. Smyrna's early history was checkered. It was destroyed by the Lydians in 627 B.C., and for three centuries was little more than a village. It was refounded in the middle of the fourth century before Christ, after Alexander's capture of Sardis, and rapidly became the chief city of Asia. Smyrna was shrewd enough to mark the rising star of Rome. A common danger, the aggression of Antiochus the Great of Syria, had united the two states at the end of the third century before Christ, and the bond formed in the face of the eastern peril remained unbroken. Smyrna was, indeed, the handiest of bridgeheads, a use-

Two views of Smyrna, on the coast of Asia Minor. Above, standing pillars of the ancient Forum; below, a view over the city. SHH

ful Roman counterpoise in Aegean waters to the naval power of Rhodes. It was to this ancient alliance, which Smyrna referred in A.D. 26, when the city petitioned Tiberius to allow the community to build a temple to his deity (Tac. *Ann.* 4.56). The permission was granted, and Smyrna built the second Asian temple to the Emperor. The city had worshiped Rome as a spiritual power since 195 B.C.; hence Smyrna's historical pride in her Caesar-cult. Smyrna was famous for science, medicine, and the majesty of its buildings. Apollonius of Tyana refers to her "crown of porticoes," a circle of beautiful public buildings which ringed the summit of Mount Pagos like a diadem; hence John's reference (Rev. 2:10). Polycarp, Smyrna's martyred bishop of A.D. 155, had been a disciple of John.   E.M.B.

SNARE (Heb. *pah, a spring net;* Gr. *pagís, trap; bróchos, a noose*), a device for catching both birds (Ps. 124:7) and animals. The words are employed often in the Bible in a figurative sense. "Snares of death" is a phrase used often to imply anything that might destroy (Ps. 91:3; 141:9). The word also is used in a variety of ways to point out things God's people should avoid: heathen gods (Deut. 7:16); the ephod Gideon made (Judg. 8:27); false prophets (Hos. 9:8); and riches (I Tim. 6:9).

SNOUT (Heb. *'aph, nostril*), the long, projecting nose of a beast, as of a pig. In Proverbs 11:22 a woman without discretion is compared to a jewel of gold in the swine's snout.

SNOW (Heb. *shelegh, white; telagh, white;* Gr. *chión*). Snow is common in the hill country of Palestine. It never becomes very deep and it is not uncommon to have winters without any. The tops of the high mountains are covered with snow most of the year and this becomes the source of much of the water there. It is stored in caves in the mountains in the winter for cooling beverages and for refrigerating purposes in the summer.

The Bible often refers to snow in a figurative sense. "Time of snow" seems to be a figure representing a winter day (II Sam. 23:20) and "fear of snow" is a similar phrase representing cold (Prov. 31:21). It is a symbol of the highest purity and stands for the condition of the redeemed soul (Isa. 1:18; Ps. 51:7); and the righteousness of the believer (Rev. 19:8). It symbolizes whiteness and purity (Matt. 28:3; Rev. 1:14). It describes the whiteness of the leper (II Kings 5:27). H.Z.C.

SNUFF (Heb. *sha'aph, to inhale; naphah, to blow at*). The first Hebrew word expresses the practice of wild asses who pant for wind like the dragons in view of the heat (Jer. 14:6). Malachi uses the second Hebrew word in a symbolic sense to express contempt for God's sacrifices (Mal. 1:13).

SO (Heb. *sô'*), the name of a king of Egypt, mentioned in II Kings 17:4 as king in the days of Ahaz, king of Judah, and Hoshea, king of Israel. Hoshea made an alliance with So, bringing down the wrath of Assyria upon Israel (II Kings 17:5). It is difficult to identify him. He is either the king mentioned in Herodotus by the name of Sabaeo, or he is to be identified with *Sib'e* who, in 720 B.C., because of his alliance with the king of Gaza, Hanun, had to fight with Sargon, by whom he was defeated.

SOAP (Heb. *bōrîth*). Soap in a modern sense was unknown in OT times. Even today it is not used in some parts of Syria. Clothes, cooking utensils, and even the body were cleansed with the ashes of certain plants containing alkali (e.g., soapwort, glasswort, and saltwort). This cleansing material is referred to in Jeremiah 2:22 and Malachi 3:2.

SOCHO, SOCOCH, SOCOH (sō'kō, Heb. *sōk-hōh, branches*). 1. One of the cities given to the tribe of Judah (Josh. 15:35). Later on King Rehoboam strengthened this city after the northern tribes had revolted (II Chron. 11:7). From this city Solomon drew his supplies (I Kings 4:10). It is identified with Khirbet Shuweikeh.

2. About ten miles SW of Hebron lies another city by this name (Josh. 15:48).

SOCKET (See Tabernacle)

SODI (sō'dī, Heb. *sôdhî*), the father of the Israelite spy representing the tribe of Zebulun (Num. 13:10).

SODOM (sŏd'ŭm, Heb. *sedhōm,* Gr. *Sódoma*), one of the so-called "Cities of the Plain," the others being Admah, Gomorrah, Zeboiim, and Zoar. The site of "the Plain" has been variously conjectured. A purple passage in Sir George Adam Smith runs: "Though the glare of this catastrophe burns still, the ruins of it have entirely disappeared, and there remains in the valley no authentic trace of the names it has torn and scattered to infamy across the world" (*Hist. Geog. of the Holy Land*, pp. 504, 505). Little more can be said, though recently the suggestion has been revived that "the Plain" is the shallow southern end of the Dead Sea, and that the waters cover the remains. Underwater archaeology may or may not confirm this assertion which appears first to have been made by Thomson in his 19th century classic, *The Land and the Book*.

Above, Jebel Usdum, the so-called Hill of Sodom, at the southern end of the Dead Sea. Below, ruins at Tel Ghassul, one of the supposed sites of Sodom in Trans-Jordan, excavated by Jesuits. © MPS

An area round the northern end of the Dead Sea was later favored, mainly on the grounds that this region only is fully within the range of vision from Bethel, from which vantage point Lot made his fatal choice (Gen. 13:10-12). The southern end is shut off by the high country round Engedi. Abraham's field of view from a point E of Hebron, from which he looked in the morning towards Sodom and Gomorrah (Gen. 19:28), may lead to the same conclusion. Reply might be made that what the patriarch saw was the column of smoke from whatever form of catastrophe destroyed the whole area. Attempts have been made to pin-point the site by a reconstruction of the invasion-route of the raid described in Genesis 14. According to II Chronicles 20:2 Hazazon-tamar is Engedi, half-way up the western shore of the Dead Sea. If the invaders, circling the sea from the S, clashed with the Amorites here, then they must have continued N to capture Sodom, and not returned upon their tracks. But could not the Hazazon-tamar of Genesis 14 be the Tamar of Ezekiel 47:19 to the SW of the water? Zoar can be located on the Moabite shore from Isaiah 15:5 and Jeremiah 48:34, and at the southern end of the sea from Josephus (*B.J.* 4:8:4), but Deuteronomy 34:3 assumes that the town was visible from Pisgah. Perhaps there were two towns of the name. The conclusion is that, failing conclusive archaeological evidence, the Cities of the Plain must be listed as lost. Sodom, on account of the story of Genesis 19, became a name for vice, infamy, and judgment (Isa. 1:9 and 10; 3:9; Jer. 23:14; Lam. 4:6; Ezek. 16:46, 48,49,53,55; Amos 4:11; Zeph. 2:9; Matt. 10:15; Luke 17:29; Rom. 9:29; II Pet. 2:6; Jude 7; Rev. 11:8). Hence the KJV term in Deuteronomy 23:17; I Kings 14:24, and elsewhere. It was the theme of judgment on iniquity which was in the mind of the Jew or Christian who, some time before the eruption of A.D. 79, scribbled on a wall in Pompeii "Sodoma Gomorra."   E.M.B.

SODOMA (See Sodom)

SODOMITE (See Sodomy)

SODOMY (sŏd′ŭm-ĕ, Heb. *qādhēsh, a male temple prostitute*). A sodomite was one who practiced that unnatural vice for which Sodom became noted (Gen. 19:5). Though not named as such it is referred to in Romans 1:27. God strictly forbade this practice (Deut. 23:17). Usually the practice was in connection with heathen worship, and its presence was a sign of departure from the Lord (I Kings 14:24). Both Asa (I Kings 15:12) and Jehoshaphat took measures against this sin (I Kings 22:46), but its practice continued, until in the days of Josiah it was being practiced in Jehovah's house (II Kings 23:7).

SOLDER (sŏ′dêr, Heb. *deveq, joint*), a metallic substance used to join metals together (Isa. 41:7).

SOLDIER (See Occupations & Professions, also Warfare)

SOLOMON (sŏl′ō-mŭn, Heb. *shelōmōh, peaceable*), the third and last king of united Israel. He built the kingdom to its greatest geographical extension and material prosperity. Though a very intelligent man, Solomon in his later years lost his spiritual discernment and for the sake of political advantage and voluptuous living succumbed to apostasy. His policies of oppression and luxury brought the kingdom to the verge of dissolution, and when his son Rehoboam came to the throne the actual split of the kingdom occurred. Solomon was the second son of David and Bathsheba, the former wife of Uriah the Hittite. When he was born, the Lord loved him, so that the child was also called Jedidiah, "beloved of the Lord" (II Sam. 12:24-25). He did not enter into the history of Israel until in David's advanced old age, when a conspiracy attempted to make Adonijah, the son of David and Haggith, king. Nathan and Bathsheba quickly collaborated to persuade David of the seriousness of the situation, and David had Solomon anointed king at Gihon by Zadok the priest while the conspirators were still gathered at En-rogel. As David's death drew near, he gave Solomon practical advice as to faithfulness to God, the building of the temple, and the stability of the dynasty. Solomon had to deal harshly with Adonijah and his followers when they continued to plot against him. Adonijah and Joab were put to death and Abiathar the priest was expelled from the priesthood. Solomon made Benaiah head of the army and Zadok became priest in Abiathar's stead. David had also told Solomon to kill Shimei, who had cursed David at the time of Absalom's revolt; this was done by Solomon, after placing Shimei on a probation which Shimei violated.

Solomon now began a series of marriage alliances which were his eventual undoing. He married the daughter of the king of Egypt, who had sufficient power to capture Gezer and to present it as a dowry to his daughter. Early in his reign he loved the Lord; he sacrificed at the great high place of Gibeon, where the tabernacle was located; here he offered a thousand burnt offerings. That night at Gibeon the Lord appeared to him in a dream and told him to make a request of Him of whatever he desired. Solomon chose above all else understanding and discernment. God was pleased with this choice and granted his request and also gave him riches and honor. A demonstration of this gift came upon his return to Jerusalem, where his decision in the case of two harlots caused the people to see that God's wisdom was in the king. He was an efficient administrator: each department had its appointed officers and the country was divided into 12 districts, different from the tribal divisions, each responsible for the provisions of the royal household for a month of the year. The corvée was in operation against the descendants of subjugated peoples and with taxation and conscription Israel began to see some of the evils of monarchy against which Samuel had warned (I Sam. 8:11ff), though during the reign of Solomon "Judah and Israel were as many as the sand of the sea; they ate and drank and were happy" (I Kings 4:20 RSV). The kingdom extended from the Euphrates in the N to the border of Egypt in the SW.

Solomon was a wise and learned man; it is stated that his wisdom was greater than that of the wise men of the East and of Egypt. He was expert in botany and zoology; he was a writer, credited with 3,000 proverbs and 1,005 songs; he is named the author of the Song of Songs, his greatest song (Song of Solomon 1:1), the book of Proverbs (Prov. 1:1), Ecclesiastes (Eccl. 1:1,12); and two Psalms (cf. titles, Pss. 72, 127). His fame was widespread and people came from afar to hear him. He made an alliance with Hiram king of Tyre, who had been a friend of David. This relationship was of great advantage to him, who now undertook a tremendous building program, particularly that of the temple in Jerusalem on Mt. Moriah. He contracted with Hiram for the supply of cedar and cypress wood and arranged for Phoenician builders to supplement the Israelite corvée. A chronological reference is supplied in I Kings 6:1, which states that the year that construction of the temple was begun numbered the fourth year of Solomon and the 480th year after the Exodus from Egypt. David had wanted to build the temple, but the Lord reserved that privilege for Solomon (II Sam. 7:13; I Chron. 17:4-6,12; 22:6-11; 28:6); nevertheless, Solomon got the complete plan of the structure from his father (I Chron. 28:11-19). David had also gathered much building material, especially precious metals and other costly commodities, and had taken freewill offerings for the building of the temple (I Kings 7:51; I Chron. 22:2-5; 29:1-19). A description of the temple is given in some detail (I Kings 6:2-36). It is said incidentally that "he built the inner court with three courses of hewn stone and one course of cedar beams" (vs. 36; cf. 7:12). The archaeologists of the Oriental Institute of the University of Chicago found at Megiddo evidence of the use of this technique in the Solomonic level.

Inside Solomon's Quarries, under the old city of Jerusalem. © MPS

A partial reconstruction of Solomon's Stables at Megiddo, showing clearly, at right, the posts to which the horses were tied. OIUC

The temple was finished in seven years and Solomon's palace was 13 years in building. The latter consisted of various houses or halls: the House of the Forest of Lebanon; the Hall of Pillars; the Hall of the Throne (also the Hall of Judgment); his royal quarters; and a palace for his Egyptian wife. A great amount of bronze was used for ornamental work, for architectural features such as the two large pillars of the temple vestibule, and for decorative and functional articles, such as the altar, the molten sea, and all sorts of utensils and implements used in the temple service. This part of the project was the responsibility of a craftsman, Hiram of Tyre (I Kings 7:14 RSV; cf. II Chron. 2:13-14). Much of the copper used for these purposes probably came from mines worked by the Israelites. It is only in comparatively recent years that the great mining and smelting enterprises of Solomon have become known, for they are not referred to in the Bible. In his explorations in the Negev, Glueck found that the area was of much importance in Solomonic times. Many towns were built and fortified and a number of copper mines were worked and the preliminary processing done nearby. Exploration led to the identification of Tell el Kheleifeh as Ezion-geber (proposed earlier by F. Frank). Excavation here brought to light the remains of an industrial town, with blast furnaces utilizing the prevailing winds to operate on the principle of the Bessemer forced-air draft.

When the temple was completed, an impressive dedication service was held. The Ark of the Covenant was brought up from Zion by the priests and was placed in the Holy of Holies. Solomon blessed the people, and made a heartfelt prayer of dedication. Sacrifices were made and fire from heaven consumed them. Finally, a great feast was held. The Lord appeared to Solomon again, as at Gibeon; He had heard his supplication and now promised to establish his heirs as He had promised to do for David, if he and his descendants remained faithful to the Lord. After the celebration of the dedication, Solomon settled accounts with Hiram king of Tyre. Solomon gave him 20 cities in the land of Galilee, but when Hiram inspected them and was not satisfied, he also paid him 120 talents of gold. Solomon's work of building extended throughout the land, with labor provided by a forced levy of the descendants of the people Israel did not annihilate at the time of the conquest. He built at Gezer, Hazor, Megiddo, Upper Beth-horon, Lower Beth-horon, Baalath, Tadmor

in the wilderness, and in Lebanon. He did additional building at Jerusalem. He made store-cities and cities for his chariots and cavalry throughout the domain. No longer need Israel fear for lack of armaments. Solomon had 1400 chariots and 12,000 horsemen (II Chron. 1:14); he also had 4,000 stalls for horses (II Chron. 9:25). Stables for at least 450 horses were found at Megiddo: similar stables were excavated at Gezer, Taanach, Tell el Hesi, and Tell el Far'ah. He also engaged in a profitable trade in chariots and horses between Egypt and the Hittites. His commercial interests led him to the sea; since the Mediterranean coast afforded no good harborage in the area held by him, he made his port at Ezion-geber near Eloth on the Gulf of Akabah of the Red Sea. Again he was assisted by Hiram, who provided Phoenician seamen (II Chron. 8:18).

The rulers were enriched by this trade with the East; Ophir was a source of gold, "almug (algum) wood," and precious stones. Solomon's ships also went to Tarshish with the Phoenician fleet and brought back all sorts of exotic things. Tremendous wealth thus came to Solomon by commerce, mining, tribute (I Kings 4:21), and gifts from visitors (10:25). Among the most distinguished of these visitors was the queen of Sheba. Women were a serious weakness of Solomon; not only did he make many political alliances through marriage, but he "loved many foreign women" (I Kings 11:1) and he "clung to these in love" (vs. 2). God had warned that such marriages would lead to apostasy; the harem of Solomon held a collection of some 700 wives and 300 concubines; and "his wives turned away his heart after other gods; and his heart was not wholly true after the Lord his God" (vs. 4 RSV). He built places of worship for the false gods to satisfy his heathen wives. The Lord was angered at Solomon's failure to keep His explicit commands and announced to him the rift in the kingdom which was to take place in the reign of his son.

The rule of Solomon had been quite peaceful, but trouble was brewing. Hadad the Edomite, who as a child had survived a raid by David and had escaped to Egypt, now returned to plague him. In Syria Rezon was made king at Damascus and became an enemy of Israel. In Israel a capable young man, Jeroboam the son of Nebat, was informed by the Prophet Ahijah that he would become ruler of 10 tribes of Israel. Solomon attempted to kill Jeroboam, but Jeroboam took refuge in Egypt until the death of Solomon. The signs of the impending division of the kingdom were evident; when he died in 930 B.C. and his son Rehoboam became king, the break soon became a reality. Other historical records of Solomon's reign cited in the Bible include "the book of the acts of Solomon" (I Kings 11:41), "the history of Nathan the prophet," "the prophecy of Ahijah the Shilonite," and "the visions of Iddo the seer concerning Jeroboam the son of Nebat" (II Chron. 9:29 RSV). A great temporal ruler, possessing every natural advantage, almost inconceivably wealthy in material splendor, learning, and experience, Solomon was nevertheless a disappointment. Though he began so well, the tragedy of his gradual apostasy had more disastrous results than the infamous scandal of his father, who sincerely repented and was a man after the Lord's own heart.   C.E.D.

SOLOMON, SONG OF (Heb. *shîr ha-shîrîm*) is unique among Biblical books, for its story centers in the joys and distresses of the love relationship between a man and a woman.

Name. The Hebrew name, "The Song of Songs," is taken from 1:1, which introduces the book as "the song of songs which is Solomon's." This use of the Hebrew superlative makes the book the best of the 1,005 songs of Solomon (I Kings 4:32) or perhaps the greatest of all songs.

Authorship and date. There is considerable range of opinion as to the authorship and date of the book. R. Pfeiffer concludes that the Song of Songs is "an anthology of erotic poems," of c. 250 B.C., using the language as the sole criterion for the date. The frequent use of Aramaic forms and words and the presence of names of foreign products, a Persian word, and a Greek word are taken as evidence for a late date. On the other hand, it has been pointed out that these usages are not inconsistent with Solomonic authorship. In view of the extensive commerce and widespread diplomatic relations of Solomon, the presence of foreign terms, especially for articles imported or imitated from foreign sources, is to be expected. The use of Aramaic is no indication of date and may also be accounted for by the northern origin of the Shulammite. The book ascribes its authorship to Solomon and there are lines of evidence which agree with this ascription. The book has relationships with other writings attributed to Solomon. The author's acquaintance with plants and animals is reminiscent of Solomon (I Kings 4:33). The mention of "a mare of Pharaoh's chariots" (1:9, RSV) accords with Solomon's engaging in horse-trading with Egypt and with his being married to a daughter of the pharaoh. The lover is called "the king" (1:4) and there are other indications of his royal interests, in addition to references to Solomon by name. The place-names range throughout Palestine and thus fit well with an origin predating the divided kingdom.

Content. Though the book is difficult of analysis, the divisions of Delitzsch are often followed. (1) The mutual admiration of the lovers, 1:2-2:7; (2) Growth in love, 2:8-3:5; (3) The marriage, 3:6-5:1; (4) Longing of the wife for her absent husband, 5:2-6:9; (5) The beauty of the Shulammite bride, 6:10-8:4; (6) The wonder of love, 8:5-8:14.

Interpretation. There is great diversity and much overlapping among interpretations of the Song of Solomon. Various views are: 1. Allegorical, 2. Typical, 3. Literal, 4. Dramatic, 5. Erotic-literary, 6. Liturgical, and 7. Didactic-moral.

1. The Allegorical view may be Jewish, Christian, or a combination of these. The first regards the Song as descriptive of the love of God and His people Israel; the second discerns the love of Christ and the Church or the individual believer. Usually this view denies or ignores the historicity of the events described. Hippolytus and Origen introduced this interpretation into the church and this has been the popular or prevailing position, along with the Typical view. Arguments in its favor include: (1) It explains the inclusion of the book in the canon. (2) It harmonizes with the Biblical use of marriage as an illustration of the Lord's relationship to His people. Against these are argued: (1) Other reasons may be advanced for its presence among the canonical books. (2) Elsewhere the figure of the marriage relationship is made the basis for specific teaching. (3) Nothing in the book itself vitiates its historicity. (4) The necessity of interpreting details leads to fanciful and absurd interpretations.

2. The Typical interpretation combines literal and allegorical views, maintaining both the historicity and the spiritualizing of the book. It is reasoned in support of this view: (1) The superlative of the title connotes spiritual meaning. (2) Solomon is a type of Christ; (3) marriage also is a type (cf. above). Against these are urged: (1) Spiritual value does not demand typology. (2) The definition and application of "type" are debatable.

3. The Literal view is that the book presents actual history and nothing more.

4. The Dramatic interpretation regards the Song as a drama based on the marriage of Solomon to a Shulammite girl. Here may be included the Shepherd-hypothesis (Jacobi, Ewald, et al), which proposes a triangle of Solomon, the girl, and her shepherd-betrothed. On this hypothesis, the girl refuses the blandishments of the king and remains true to her shepherd. The book is not labeled drama, which was not a widely used Hebrew literary form. If the book were merely a drama, its presence in the canon is not explained.

5. The Erotic-literary view (Eissfeldt, Pfeiffer) is that the book is simply a collection of love-songs.

6. The Liturgical view regards the Song as borrowed pagan liturgy associated with fertility-cults. It is inconceivable that a work of such an origin should be in the canon.

7. The Didactic-moral interpretation holds that the book presents the purity and wonder of true love. It regards the book as history and also agrees that the love portrayed does direct us to the greater love of Christ, in accordance with the history of Christian interpretation. The purpose of the Song of Solomon, therefore, is to teach the holiness and beauty of the marriage-love relationship which God Himself ordained.   C.E.D.

SOLOMON'S POOLS, three in number, were located a short distance from Jerusalem and were fed by two chief sources, surface water and springs. Cleverly engineered aqueducts carried water from the desired spring to the pools. From these pools the water was conveyed by the same means to the wells under the temple area (Eccl. 2:6).

In the summer of 1962, Solomon's Pools were again in the news, when a severe drought made necessary an emergency pipeline from a big new well at Hebron, to alleviate Jerusalem's water shortage. The 18 miles of pipe, furnished by the United States Agency for International Development, was laid within a matter of days, and the water was pumped into the ancient reservoirs, Solomon's Pools, eight miles S of Jerusalem (*Time,* Aug. 17, 1962).

Solomon's Pools, the finest of the three pools, south of Jerusalem. © MPS

SOLOMON'S PORCH, a magnificent colonnade built by Solomon on the E side of the temple area. Christ and the apostles walked in it (John 10:23; Acts 3:11; 5:12).

SOLOMON'S SERVANTS (Heb. *'avedhê shelō-mōh*). The descendants of Solomon's servants are named among those returning from Babylon to Jerusalem under Zerubbabel (Ezra 2:55,58; Neh. 7:57,60; 11:3). In the days of Solomon some were appointed to care for certain temple duties, and these being descendants of these servants, presumably carried on the same kind of duties. Whether they were Levites or non-Israelitish people is not known.

SOLOMON'S TEMPLE (See Temple)

SON (Heb. *bēn*, Gr. *huiós*), a word which has quite a variety of meanings in the Bible. Genetically the Hebrew word expresses any human offspring regardless of sex (Gen. 3:16). In genealogical records the word "son" is often a general term expressing descendants (Dan. 5:22). Many times, of course, the word means a person, usually a male, who was the direct child of a given father (Gen. 9:19; 16:15).

Another very common Biblical use of this word is in connection with another following word to express something about the individual or individual's described. Perhaps the most familiar usage of this kind is the two titles used of our Lord, "Son of man" and "Son of God." "Son of perdition" is used ot Judas. Sometimes groups are thus designated (I Thess. 5:5). Genesis 6:4 speaks of the "sons of God," and Deuteronomy 13:13 "sons of Belial."

Closely allied to this use is still another in which the word "son" indicates relationship in a certain group. Believers in the OT are often called "sons of God" (Deut. 14:1), and believers in the NT have the same designation (I John 3:2). The word is sometimes used to indicate membership in a guild or profession (II Kings 2:3,5; Neh. 3:8).

H.Z.C.

SON OF GOD. The key text for a proper understanding of the words "Son of God," as applied to Jesus, is John 5:18b. ". . . he said that God was his own Father, making himself equal with God." The same thought is frequently emphasized. Cf. "that all men should honor the Son just as they honor the Father" (John 5:23 original tr.). In John 10:30ff Jesus' words "I and the Father are one" touched off violent opposition. His adversaries said ". . . we stone you . . . for blasphemy, even because you, being a man, make yourself out to be God" (vs. 33). Jesus answered ". . . why do you say to him whom the Father sanctified and sent into the world, 'You blaspheme,' because I said, 'I am the Son of God?' " (vs. 36). The words "Son of God" were clearly understood in the Jewish setting as meaning "God," or "equal with God."

It is not denied that the words in other contexts may have other meanings. (See SONS OF GOD, CHILDREN OF GOD.) But deity is implied in the words as applied to Jesus.

This fact doubtless stems from the Hebrew usage in which, when the context did not in any way indicate derivation of being, the words "son of . . ." meant "of the order of . . .," as the sons of the prophets, of the apothecaries, of the goldsmiths, of the singers (Neh. 3:8,31; 12:28).

With this usage in mind, it is easy to see how Jesus' contemporaries in Palestine took His claim to be the Son of God as a claim to be of the order of God, that is, "equal with God," or "God."

It is suggested (contrary to common opinion) that "Son of God" as applied to Jesus *never* has reference to the derivation, or "eternal generation," of His being, but the words simply designate His eternal, co-equal and consubstantial deity.

1. All references to His being sent forth from the Father (like His saying "the Father is greater than I" John 14:28) point to His particular temporal activity and function in the divine economy, not in any way to His eternal and essential being.

2. The word *monogenes*, wrongly translated "only begotten," is not from *gennao*, "to beget," but from *genos*, "kind." It means "the only one of his kind," or "unique." The French Bible correctly reads "*son Fils unique,*" "his unique Son."

3. There can be no doubt that the prophetic words "Thou art my Son; this day have I begotten Thee," in Psalm 2:7 refer to Christ. But to refer these words to the "eternal generation" of His being, or to any actual generation in time, would involve all manner of contradictions and inconsistencies. The words must be taken as declaratory of a previously existing fact.

The speaker in the psalm is a king and he speaks as of his coronation day. This verse is quoted by Paul in Acts 13:30 in connection with the evidential nature of Christ's resurrection. Again it is quoted in Hebrews 1:5; 5:5. In the former instance the author seems to associate the text with Christ's second coming. We are reminded of the heavenly announcement of Christ's Sonship on the occasion of His baptism (Matt. 3:17; Mark 1:11; Luke 3:22; cf. John 1:32-34), in His transfiguration (Matt. 17:5; Mark 9:7; Luke 9:35; II Pet. 1:17,18); and the similar voice from heaven during His public teaching (John 12:28). On all these occasions, and in any phase of the ministry of Christ in time, especially in any phase of his exaltation, the Father declares and acknowledges His eternal Son. We must therefore take the words "this day have I begotten thee" as a figurative expression, meaning, "on this occasion I reveal and declare thy Sonship."

4. It is a very common opinion among Bible-believing scholars that the phrase "Son of God" refers in some instances to the virgin birth of Christ. To the present writer this opinion seems doubtful. It is true that Christ took human nature and entered this world at Bethlehem by the miracle of the virgin birth. He was "conceived by the Holy Ghost, born of the virgin Mary" literally. But this was not the origin of His personality and did not make Him the Son of God. The Scripture is very explicit that the miracle by which the eternal Son of God "became flesh" was wrought by the Holy Spirit, the third Person of the Trinity. Yet never in the history of Christianity, never in orthodox or heretical literature, never has any group of people who claimed to believe the NT spoken or thought of the Holy Spirit as the father of Jesus. His birth was a miracle and in the absolute sense of the word, a *virgin* birth.

There is indeed one statement, Luke 1:35b, which seems to stand to the contrary. In English it reads, "therefore also that holy thing which shall be born of thee shall be called the Son of God." This reading is certainly possible, even probable according to the *textus receptus* as it was punctuated before Hort. However, Westcott and Hort's reading and punctuation, supported also by Nestle's margin, points in the direction of the following translation, "therefore also that which is born shall be called holy; the Son of God." The meaning of the verse is the answer to the question, How can the "Son of the Highest" (vs. 32) be sinlessly born, i.e. Mary's question of vs. 34. The answer is that by the miraculous protection of the Holy Spirit, that which is to be born will be "holy," free from any taint of sin, as the Son of God must be. Thus the virgin birth is not the ground and reason of the title Son of God, but the supernatural protection of the Holy Spirit is the ground of the sinlessness, holiness, of the virgin birth.

5. There should be extensive and thorough research into the history of the doctrine of the "eternal generation of the Son." It arose in Christian theology to negate the Arian error that there ever was a time when the Son was not. Origen made "eternal generation" a kind of Platonic subordinationism. His views, and the pre-Nicene views of Eusebius were repudiated by the orthodox church. In Athanasian theology, "eternal generation" is simply a firm denial of Arianism and nothing more. Now that we know that *monogenes* is not related to *gennao* ("to beget") but simply means "unique," we have a clearer view of the absolute deity of Christ than was possible in the fourth century.

Son of God, as a title of Jesus, thus refers exclusively to His co-equality, co-eternity, con-substantiality with the Father and the Spirit in the eternal Triune Godhead. J.O.B.

SON OF MAN. In Hebrew usage the phrase "son of . . ." frequently meant "of the order of. . . ." (See SON OF GOD.) "Son of man" seems to mean essentially, *man,* a distinct member *of the order of humanity.* It is applied to Ezekiel repeatedly (Ezek. 2:1,3,8ff), and to Daniel once (8:17).

The one OT usage which colors all NT use of the phrase as applied to Christ is Daniel 7:13,14, "I saw in the night visions, and behold one like the Son of Man came with the clouds of heaven, and came to the Ancient of days, and they brought him near before him. And there was given him dominion, and glory, and a kingdom, that all people, nations, and languages, should serve him. His dominion is an everlasting dominion, which shall not pass away, and his kingdom that which shall not be destroyed."

That Jesus identified Himself as the Son of man in this sense is clear from His words when on trial before the Jewish authorities: "You will see the Son of man sitting at the right hand of power; and coming with the clouds of heaven" (Mark 14:62. Cf. Matt. 26:64; Luke 22:69). Jesus here preceded the quotation from Daniel 7:13,14 by a phrase from Psalm 110:1. The Son of man sitting at the right hand of God, as referred to in the NT (see esp. Acts 2:34,35; Heb. 1:13; 10:12,13), points to His awaiting in heaven (Acts 3:21) the time of His appointment to take the earth as His visible kingdom. He is now, as to His visible presence, like the nobleman in the far country (Luke 19:11-27). The parable alludes to Archelaus who went to Rome to be appointed king in Herod's realm and to come back and rule. At the time appointed by the Father, Jesus will come as the heavenly Son of man to rule the world. Thus Jesus, before the Jewish authorities, distinguishes two future stages in the doings of the Son of Man (1) His resuming His seat in heaven, and (2) His coming again to reign.

In the Olivet discourse Jesus predicted (Matt. 24:27; cf. Luke 17:24) that His return as the heavenly Son of man would be instantaneously visible everywhere like a flash of lightning. Further, He identified this coming as the heavenly Son of man with the prophecy of Zechariah 12:10-14, which contains the significant words, "they shall look upon me whom they have pierced." In Matthew 24:30 Jesus says, "And at that time will be seen the sign of the Son of man in heaven. And at that time 'all the tribes of the land will mourn' [cf. Zech. chapter 27] and they will see 'the Son of man coming upon the clouds of heaven' [Dan. 7:13] with power and great glory."

A little earlier in His ministry Jesus has said, "Truly I tell you that you who have followed with me [in my trials, Luke 22:28,29], in the regeneration when the Son of man sits upon his glorious throne, you will sit upon twelve thrones judging the twelve tribes of Israel" (Matt. 19:27,28).

Warfield says, "Whenever, in the Apocalyptic literature we meet the figure of the Son of Man, it is transcendentally conceived. When our Lord Himself derived from it His favorite self-designation of Son of Man, He took it over in a transcendental sense; and meant by applying it to Himself to present Himself as a heavenly Being who had come forth from heaven and descended to earth on a mission of mercy to lost men." (Warfield, *Christology and Criticism,* pp. 46f; reprint from *Prin. Theol. Rev.* XIV 1916.)

Although Son of Man, as Jesus uses the term, always refers to Himself as the *One* who is coming again to rule the world, this does not mean that everything He says of the Son of Man is eschatological. He adopts the title with its eschatological implications, and applies it to Himself in any and all situations. Since His incarnation He *is* that Son of Man. Thus He asked, as Matthew (16:13) records His question, "Who do men say the Son of Man is?"

Liberal writers on the "Life of Christ" from Reimarus (1694-1768) to Albert Schweitzer have made the great mistake of construing Matthew 10:23b eschatologically, and arguing that Jesus when He gave instructions to the twelve for their mission did not yet regard Himself as the heavenly Son of Man. Liberals generally picture Jesus as sitting down to wait for the Son of man to come in the clouds, suffering great disappointment, and finally deciding that He must Himself be the Son of Man. (See Schweitzer *Quest* p. 335. Edwin Lewis *NH and NE* pp. 131f.)

The context should have prevented this error. In Matthew's record (8:20; 9:6) Jesus had previously been familiarly designating Himself as Son of Man in the presence of His disciples. When He said (10:23b), "You will not finish with the cities of Israel until the Son of Man comes," they understood His plan to come where they were preaching, as given in Matthew 11:1 (cf. Luke 10:1). "When Jesus had finished instructing his twelve disciples he departed thence to teach and preach in their [the disciples'] cities." Chapter 11 records Jesus' ministry as He follows up the twelve, and in chapter 12 they are all together again.

The title Son of Man as used by Jesus to apply to Himself is found some 78 times in the Gospels. (Cf. also Acts 7:56; Rev. 1:13; 14:14). In all circumstances it designates Him as the God-Man. J.O.B.

SONG (Heb. *shîr, shîrâh*). Singing played a prominent part in the worship and national life of the Hebrews. The first song in the Bible was sung by Lamech (Gen. 4:23-24). It was not uncommon for the Jews to compose a song celebrating some special victory or religious experience that was significant (Exod. 15). The Psalter has been designated "The Song Book of Israel" and it contains many kinds of songs. The music to which these songs were sung has been lost, but it was undoubtedly similar to that of the Arabs today — plaintive, limited in compass, and marked by emphasis in rhythm.

Paul urges believers to sing (Eph. 5:19; Col. 3:16). The book of Revelation speaks often of heavenly singing (Rev. 5:9; 14:3).

SONG OF DEGREES (See Music)

SONG OF SONGS (See Solomon, Song of)

SONG OF THE THREE HEBREW CHILDREN, an addition to the book of Daniel found in the OT Apocrypha. It consists of 68 verses and in the LXX and Vulgate follows Daniel 3:23 and forms an integral part of that chapter. It is one of three additions to Daniel found in the Apocrypha. The author of the Song is unknown; the date of writing is about 164 B.C.; and the language is Greek. It is a hymn of praise, and has practically nothing to do with the sufferings of the three young men.

SONS OF GOD, CHILDREN OF GOD. The words here discussed may refer metaphorically to any personal creatures of God. In Job 1:6; 2:1; 38:7; angelic beings are designated. In speaking of the inappropriateness of worshiping idols (Acts 17:28) Paul quotes Aratus, "we also are his offspring," thus applying the concept to the entire human race. Compare Luke 3:38; "Adam was the son of God."

The meaning of "sons of God" (*benê-hā-'ĕlōhîm*), occurring twice in Genesis 6:1-4 is much disputed. The meaning of "giants" (*hannephilîm*) and of "mighty men . . . of renown" (*haggibbōrîm . . . hashshēm*) is involved in the question.

It is possible here only to summarize the opinion which is presented as preferable: 1. The term "mighty men . . . of renown" explains the word "giants." Neither term indicates anything demonic or mythological, but both should be understood in their simple literal meaning, even as in modern English. (See I Chron. 11:10,24; Num. 13:33; and see "giant" in Webster's dictionary.) 2. The statement of Genesis 6:4, taken simply and literally, informs the reader that such giants of old, mighty men of renown, were born of normal human marriage. In other words, they were not demonic beings. 3. "Sons of God," here as often elsewhere, simply means human beings with special emphasis upon man's nature as created in the image of God. 4. There is nothing essentially wicked in men selecting beautiful wives. The words translated "of [literally, from among] all which they chose," do not properly suggest any excess or even polygamy, but rather discriminating selection, choice from among those who were eligible. 5. The fact that the context condemns gross universal wickedness (vss. 5-7 and possibly also vs. 3) does not prove that vss. 1,2,4 designate anything in itself wicked, or abnormal. In fact "mighty men of renown" is rather likely to point to outstanding good men among evil men.

It is reasonable therefore to hold that "sons of God" in Genesis 6:1-4 is a normal reference to men created in the image of God. The most important scriptural use of "sons" or "children of God" is that which designates the regenerate as distinct from the unregenerate. The teaching that all men are, in this sense, spiritually children of God is very objectionable. Jesus said, "If God were your father, ye would love me . . . Ye are of your father the Devil . . . He that is of God heareth God's words" (John 8:41-47). John said, "In this the children of God are manifested, and the children of the Devil . . ." (I John 3:10). God's appeal to humanity is an offer of spiritual sonship (II Cor. 6:17-7:1). Paul develops this theme (Rom.

8:14-19) and looks forward to "the apocalypse of the Sons of God" (vs. 19. Cf. Col. 3:4; I John 3:2).

J.O.B.

SONS OF THE PROPHETS, a title given to members of prophetic guilds or schools. Samuel was the head of a company of prophets at Ramah (I Sam. 7:17; 28:3), and 200 years later Elijah and Elisha were presidents of similar groups. They were men endowed with the prophetic gift (I Sam. 10: 10; 19:20-23) who gathered around God's great leader for common worship, united prayer, religious fellowship and instruction of the people (I Sam. 10:5,10; II Kings 4:38,40; 6:1-7; 9:1). In the times of Elijah and Elisha they formed a comparatively large company (II Kings 2:7,16) and lived together at Bethel, Jericho, and Gilgal (II Kings 2:3,5; 4:38).

SOOTHSAYER, SOOTHSAYING, one claiming or thought to possess the power to foretell future events (Josh. 13:22; Jer. 27:9), interpret dreams (Dan. 4:7), and reveal secrets (Dan. 2:27).

SOP (Gr. *psomíon, a morsel of bread*), a thin wafer used to dip food from a common platter (John 13:26). Using the sop had long been common among the Hebrews (Ruth 2:14; Prov. 17:1).

SOPATER (sō'pà-têr, Gr. *Sópatros*), son of Pyrrhus who accompanied the apostle Paul on his last journey from Corinth to Jerusalem (Acts 20:4). He was a Christian from the church at Berea and is the same as Sosipater who joins with Timothy, Lucius and Jason in sending greetings to the church at Rome (Rom. 16:21).

SOPHORETH (sō'fē-rĕth, Heb. *sōphereth*), one of Solomon's servants who was among the captives to return to Jerusalem with Zerubbabel (Ezra 2: 55).

SORCERER, SORCERY (Heb. *kashshāph, kāshaph*; Gr. *mágos*), one who claimed to have supernatural power or knowledge. He often used magic potions and was considered to be in league with evil forces. The practice of sorcery was widespread in ancient times (Exod. 7:11), and was regarded an evil practice for Israel (Isa. 47:9; Mal. 3:5). Practice of the occult arts was prevalent in NT days. Simon of Samaria used sorcery, but was converted under Philip (Acts 8:9-13), and Paul and Barnabas found a sorcerer in Paphos (Acts 13:8-11).

SORE (See Diseases)

SOREK (sō'rĕk, Heb. *sôrēq, vineyard*), a valley which extends from near Jerusalem to the Mediterranean Sea about eight and one-half miles S of Joppa. It was in this valley that Samson found Delilah (Judg. 16:4). It was a fertile area in which vineyards flourished. Today it produces rich harvests of grains. A modern railroad follows the valley to Jerusalem. In OT times a highway ran along the same route. It was over this road that the Ark was conveyed after it had been taken from the Philistines (I Sam. 6:10-14). There the Philistines suffered a great defeat at the hands of the Israelites (I Sam. 7:3-14). It is doubtless Wadi es-Sarar.

SOSIPATER (See Sopater)

SOSTHENES (sŏs'thĕ-nēz, Gr. *Sosthénes*), the apparent successor of Crispus, the ruler of the synagogue at Corinth. During Paul's first visit in that city, Sosthenes was beaten by the crowd in the presence of Gallio, the Roman proconsul of Achaia (Acts 18:17). No reason is given for this action, but it is likely that they took "advantage of the snub which the proconsul had administered to the leaders of the Jewish community" to vent their anti-Semitic sentiment (F. F. Bruce, *The Book of Acts,* Grand Rapids: Eerdmans, 1956, p. 375). It is quite possible that he subsequently became a Christian, for a Sosthenes joins Paul in the salutation of I Corinthians. If this is not the Sosthenes of Acts 18, he is otherwise unknown in the NT.

SOTAI (sō'tī, Heb. *sōtay*), one of the servants of Solomon who returned from captivity under Zerubbabel (Ezra 2:55; Neh. 7:57).

SOUL (Heb. *nephesh*, Gr. *psyché*), the word commonly used in the Bible to designate the non-material ego of man in its ordinary relationships with earthly and physical things. It is one of a number of psychological nouns, all designating the same non-material self, but each in a different functional relationship. Thus, the "mind" (*nous*) is the self in its rational functions. Again "mind" (*phronema*) is the self as deeply contemplating. "Heart" (*kardia*) is the self as manifesting a complex of attitudes. "Will" (*thelesis*) is the self as choosing and deciding. "Spirit" (*pneuma*) is the self when thought of apart from earthly connections. When the blessed dead in heaven are spoken of as having been put to a martyr's death, they are called "souls" (Rev. 6:9). When there is no reference to their former bodily experience, they are called "spirits" (Heb. 12:23).

These functional names of the ego are not used with technical discrimination. They often overlap. The difference between man and beast is not that man has a soul or spirit (Gen. 1:20; 7:15; Eccl. 3:21), but that man is created in the image of God, whereas the beast is not.

The above remarks assume dichotomy, that is, that there are only two substantive entities which make up the whole man (1) the body, which at death returns to dust, awaiting the resurrection, and (2) the non-material self which, if regenerate, goes to paradise or heaven; if not, to the abode of the wicked dead. There are many, however, who hold to a trichotomous view, arguing that "soul" and "spirit" are two distinct substantive entities, and the body, a third. They cite I Thessalonians 5: 23; I Corinthians 15:44; Hebrews 4:12 for evidence.

Modern non-Christian psychology ignores or denies the existence of the soul as a substantive entity. The "self" is usually spoken of as a mere behavior pattern, a conscious*ness,* but not a being which is conscious.

It should be held that, in this created world, whenever movement in space occurs, there is something which moves; and similarly, whenever consciousness occurs, there is something, the soul or mind, which is conscious.   J.O.B.

SOUTH, the translation of various Heb. words in the KJV. They refer to a compass point, a country, or a general direction. The most common Hebrew word (*neghev, a dry region*) refers primarily to an indefinite area lying between Palestine and Egypt. Abram journeyed toward the South (Gen. 12:9). He went to the South when returning from Egypt (Gen. 13:1). David conquered the South (I Sam. 27:8-12), and so did the Philistines (II Chron. 28:18). Ramoth was in this area (I Sam. 30:27 RSV). Isaac dwelt here when he met Rebekah (Gen. 24:62-67). The Hebrews were commanded to conquer the South (Deut. 1:7). Judah's heritage extended from the Dead Sea, across the South, to the confluence of the River of Egypt and the Great Sea (Josh 15:1-47). Caleb gave a portion of the South to his daughter Achsah as her dowry when she was given to the hero, Othniel (Judg. 1:15).

This region extended from the lower end of the Dead Sea SW to Kadesh-Barnea, thence NW along the River of Egypt to the Mediterranean, its boundaries being somewhat indefinite in the semi-desert regions. Its name, "a dry region," does not indicate a desert; it probably arose because it had a less ample supply of water than Judah had. In it the Hebrews found Amelekites (Num. 13:29) Jerahmeelites (I Sam. 27:10) and other tribes whom they either exterminated or absorbed.
J.D.F.

SOVEREIGNTY of GOD. The word "sovereign," although it does not occur in any form in the English Bible, yet conveys the oft-repeated Scriptural thought of the supreme authority of God. He is called "[*Pantokrator*] Almighty" (II Cor. 6:18 and nine times in Rev.); "the blessed and only Potentate [*Dynastes*], the King of Kings and Lord of Lords" (I Tim. 6:15). He "worketh all things after the counsel of his own will" (Eph. 1:11). His sovereignty follows logically from the doctrine that he is God, Creator and Ruler of the universe.

The sovereignty of God is sometimes presented in the Bible as an unanalyzed ultimate. "Nay but, O man, who art thou that repliest against God? Shall the thing formed say to him that formed it, Why hast thou made me thus? Hath not the potter power over the clay, of the same lump to make one vessel unto honor, and another unto dishonor [i.e. to suffer dishonor]?" (Rom. 9:20,21; See Isa. 45:9. Cf. Ps. 115:3; Dan. 4:35; and many similar passages). God is not subject to any power or any abstract rule or law which could be conceived as superior to or other than Himself.

Yet the Scripture is equally emphatic that God's character is immutably holy and just and good. "He cannot deny himself" (II Tim. 2:12). "It is impossible for God to lie" (Heb. 6:18; cf. Titus 1:2). A man of faith may rightly stand before Jehovah, and plead, "Shall not the judge of all the earth do right?" (Gen. 19:25). "His mercy endureth forever" is an oft recurring phrase (Ps. 136). He assures His people of His eternal self-consistency: "I am the LORD, I change not; therefore ye sons of Jacob are not consumed" (Mal. 3:6).

The inscrutable sovereignty of God is manifested, not so much in the punishment of the reprobate as in the salvation of His people. In His holy character He must logically punish moral evil. (See SIN) But His sovereignty is most marvelously revealed in that He has graciously elected to save a people from their sin and from its consequences.   J.O.B.

SOWER, SOWING (See Agriculture)

SPAIN (Gr. *Spanía*), the westernmost peninsula of Europe, populated basically by an Indo-European stock allied to the Celts. The land was early noticed by the Phoenicians who established a major emporium at Tartessus. The Carthaginians inherited the Phoenician interest in Spain, and New Carthage (Cartagena) was developed by Hannibal as his base against Italy in the Second Punic War. Spain, in consequence, became a theatre of conflict in this clash of nations, and with the victory of Rome remained in Roman hands. It was not until the time of Augustus that the peninsula was finally pacified and organized. It was rapidly Romanized. Trajan, Hadrian, and Theodosius I, among the emperors, were Spaniards; among men of letters, the two Senecas, Lucan, Columella, Quintilian, Martial, and Prudentius came from Spain. Paul's projected visit (Rom. 15:24) was clearly in line with his evident policy to capture for the Church the nodal points and principal bastions of empire. E.M.B.

SPAN (See Weights and Measures)

SPARROW (See Birds)

SPECKLED (Heb. *nāqōdh, mottled in color*), a word used to denote varied colors of beasts. The most familiar example of its use is in Genesis 30: 25-43 where Jacob applied his knowledge of selective breeding of livestock in order to collect from Laban what he considered a fair wage.

SPICE (Heb. *besem, bōsem, sammîm, nekhō'th, reqah;* Gr. *ároma, ámomon*), anything having a pleasant odor, usually herbs. The principal Heb. word (*besem, sweet-scented*) refers to any aromatic vegetable compound, such as myrrh, cinnamon, cassia and so forth (Exod. 30:23,24). Spices were often mixed with oil to make them more durable and easily applied (Exod. 30:25, 35:8). Spices played an important part in worship throughout the Near East (Exod. 25:1-6). In the temple, Levites were keepers of spices (I Chron. 9:29). A rare spice (*bōsem, creating desire*) is indicated in the Song of Solomon 5:13; 6:2. In Genesis 37:25 and 43:11 spices, or spicery, mean treasure. Hezekiah revealed to spies of Babylon the temple treasures, including rich spices, and was rebuked by Isaiah (II Kings 20:12-18). Spices were used in preparing the body of Jesus for burial (John 19:40). Some were brought to the tomb after Jesus had risen (Mark 16:1).   J.D.F.

SPIES (Heb. *rāgal, to travel by foot*). The custom of sending secret agents to discover facts about an enemy is age-old. The Heb. word for a spy is suggested by the secrecy with which he did his work— he went stealthily. Joseph accused his brothers of being spies (Gen. 42). Joshua sent spies to Jericho (Josh. 6:23). David sent them to see if Saul was with his army at Hachilah (I Sam. 26:1-4). Absalom put secret agents throughout Israel to seize power when notified he had become king (II Sam. 15:7-10). Priests and scribes sent spies to entrap Jesus (Luke 20:20).

SPIKENARD (See Plants)

SPINDLE (Heb. *kîshôr, shaft*), an implement, 8 to 12 inches long, used in spinning. The rope of carded fiber or wool was attached to one end and the spindle rotated by hand. Thus the thread was twisted. In Egypt both men and women did spinning, but among the Hebrews only women did the work (Exod. 35:25; Prov. 31:19).

SPINNING (See Occupations & Professions)

SPIRIT (Heb. *rûach, breath, spirit;* Gr. *pneúma, wind, spirit*), one of the Biblical nouns (see list of such nouns, and also the trichotomist view, in the article on SOUL) denoting the non-material ego in special relationships. The self is generally called "spirit" in contexts where its bodily, emotional, and intellectual aspects are not prominent, but where the direct relationship of the individual to God is the point of emphasis.

A typical instance is Romans 8:15b,16, which would be better translated, "In that we cry . . . 'Father,' the Spirit himself bears witness with our *spirit* that we are children of God." The martyrs in heaven are called "souls" when there is special reference to the brutal form of their death (Rev. 6:9). But in the exalted description of the heavenly goal which lies before the church (Heb. 12:22-24), the blessed dead are referred to as "the spirits of just men made perfect."

In modern non-Christian culture the Biblical personal meaning of "spirit" is commonly denied. The Biblical word "spirit" has an impersonal mean-

ing in both Hebrew and Greek, as it has in English. See the expression "the spirit of slumber" in Romans 11:8; and "the spirit of deep sleep" in Isaiah 29:10. The context must show whether the meaning is personal or impersonal. Usually there is no doubt.

The same Hebrew and Greek words translated "spirit" can also mean "wind" or "breath." In at least one passage (John 3:8) the interpretation is doubtful, but this verse would much better be translated, "The Spirit breathes where he chooses. You hear his voice, but you do not know where he comes from nor where he goes. So everyone is born who is born from the Spirit." This brings out the sovereign grace of God in regeneration. In the context the word *pneuma* clearly designates the Holy Spirit, who is a non-material person. (See John 4:24, "God is a Spirit," and cf. GOD).

J.O.B.

SPIRIT, HOLY (See Holy Spirit)

SPIRITS IN PRISON. The words under consideration occur in I Peter 3:18-20, and the same thought is suggested in I Peter 4:6. On the basis of a superficial reading of these texts, a doctrine of a *limbus patrum*, or borderland place of confinement of the patriarchs who died before the time of Christ, has grown up. In support of this view it is held that Ephesians 4:8ff. teaches that, at His ascension, Christ took the patriarchs from this limbus to heaven. Matthew 27:52,53 is somehow made to fit in with this theory, and the phrase, "He descended into Hades" in the Apostles Creed is also brought in.

In this brief article the sound opinion in which Calvin (Institutes II, XVI, IX), Charles Hodge (Systematic Theology Vol. II pp. 616-625) A.T. Robertson (Word Pictures Vol. VI. pp. 115ff), Warfield (quoted by Robertson) generally (though not in every detail) agree, can only be summarized. 1. "Quickened by the Spirit" (I Pet. 3:18) refers to Christ's resurrection (Rom. 8:11), not to His disembodied state. 2. The time when Christ, in the Spirit, "went and preached" (vs 19) was when the longsuffering of God waited in the days of Noah" (vs 20. Cf. I Pet. 1:11; II Pet. 2:5). 3. The "spirits in prison" (vss. 19,20) are those who, in the days of Noah, refused Noah's message, and are now, as Peter writes, in the Tartarus (II Pet. 2:4) part of Hades. 4. I Peter 4:6 means "This is why the Gospel was preached [of old (cf. Gal. 3:8)] to [those who are now] dead, so that they might be judged as men [now] in the flesh [are to be judged], and might live according to God by the Spirit."

There is nowhere in Scripture any warrant for the doctrine of a chance to hear the Gospel after death.   J.O.B.

SPIRITUAL GIFTS (Gr. *charísmata*). The word is used in the NT to refer to extraordinary gifts of the Spirit given to Christians to equip them for the service of the Church. Several lists of such gifts are given (Rom. 12:6-8; I Cor. 12:4-11, 28-30; cf. Eph. 4:7-12). They may be broadly divided into two categories, those connected with the ministry of the word of God, and those connected with the ministry of practical service.

In the first group belong *apostleship,* involving the proclamation of the Word of the Gospel to the unbelieving world; *prophecy,* the ministry of the word to the believing Church, including rarely the prediction of a future event; *discerning of spirits,* the ability to discern between false and true prophets and apostles; *teaching,* including the word of knowledge and the word of wisdom; *tongues; and interpretation of tongues.*

In the second group belong *working of miracles* such as exorcism and raising the dead; *gifts of healings; ruling* and *governments*, that is, knowing how wisely to direct the affairs of the Church; and *helps*, such as being of assistance to the weak, as in the office of deacon.   S.B.

SPIT, SPITTLE, SPITTING (Heb. *yāraq, rōq;* Gr. *ptúo*). Spitting in the face indicated gross insult (Num. 12:14; Deut. 25:9). Spittle allowed to run on the beard means to drool (I Sam. 21:13). The Gr. word for spit evidently arose because of the peculiar sound made in spitting, *ptúo*. Jesus used spittle in curing blind eyes in Bethsaiada (Mark 8:23) and put spittle upon a mute tongue in Decapolis (Mark 7:33). Jesus was insulted during His trial by being spat upon (Matt. 26:67; Mark 14:65).   J.D.F.

SPOIL (Heb. *bizzâh, meshissâh, shōd, shālāl;* Gr. *harpagé, skýlon*), the plunder taken from the enemy in war; pillage; booty; loot. The spoils of war were divided equally between those who went into battle and those who were left behind in camp (Num. 31:27; Josh. 22:8; I Sam. 30:24). Parts were given to the Levites and to the Lord (Num. 31:28,30). Under the monarchy, the king received part of the spoils (II Kings 14:14; I Chron. 18:7,11).

SPOKES (Heb. *hishshūrîm*), rods connecting the rim of a wheel with the hub. In the temple there were ten lavers or basins made of bronze (I Kings 7:27-33), apparently for the washing of sacrifices. They were set on bases of elaborate design moving upon wheels. The spokes were part of these wheels.

SPONGE (See Animals)

SPOT (Heb. *mûm*, Gr. *spílos*). The Heb. word denotes a blemish on the face (S. of Sol. 4:7; Job 11:15). It is also rendered "blemish" (Lev. 24:19f) and "blot" (Prov. 9:7). The Gr. word is used figuratively of a stain of sin (II Pet. 3:14; Jude 23).

SPOUSE (See Marriage)

SPREAD, SPREADING (Heb. *pāras, to disperse,* Gr. *strónnymi*), to scatter, strew, or disperse, as in "spread abroad" (Isa. 34:3; Matt. 21:8; Mark 1:28).

SPRINKLING (Heb. *zāraq, nāzâh;* Gr. *rhantízein*). Sprinkling of blood, water, and oil formed a very important part of the act of sacrifice. In the account of the forming of the covenant between Jehovah and Israel (Exod. 24:6-8), half the blood was sprinkled on the altar and the rest on the people. When Aaron and his sons were consecrated, some blood was sprinkled on the altar and some on Aaron and his sons and on their garments. In the various offerings — burnt, peace, sin — blood was always sprinkled. Sprinkling was sometimes done in handfuls, sometimes with the finger, and sometimes with a sprinkler — a bunch of hyssop fastened to a cedar rod.

STABLE (Heb. *naweh, a fold*), a building, tent, or enclosure in which to lodge and feed animals (Ezek. 25:5).

STACHYS (stā'kĭs, Gr. *Stáchys, head of grain*), a Roman Christian to whom Paul sent a greeting (Rom. 16:9).

STACTE (stăk'tē, Heb. *nātāph, a drop*), a rare ointment used as an ingredient of the sacred perfume to be used in the tabernacle worship (Exod. 30:34,38), very probably myrrh.

STAFF, STAVES (See Rod)

STAIRS (Heb. *maălâh,* Gr. *anabathmós*). The name was given to steps leading to an upper chamber

(I Kings 6:8; Mark 14:15; Acts 9:37). Stairs led up to the city of David (Neh. 12:37), to the porch of the gate to Jerusalem (Ezek. 40:6), and to the altar on its east side (Ezek. 43:17). Since stone steps have not been found among ruins in Palestine, it is supposed that stairs in ancient times were made of wood.

STAKE (Heb. *yāthēdh*), a tent-pin or tent-pole (Exod. 27:19; Isa. 33:20; 54:2).

STALL (Heb. *marbēq, 'āvas, 'urvâh, repheth, 'ēvūs,* Gr. *phátne*), a place for the care of livestock. One kind was not enclosed, often being a thatched or tented shelter, at times a fattening place (Amos 6:4; Mal. 4:2). In winter, horses were kept in barns in which each had its fenced room. Solomon's barns provided stalls for 4,000 horses (II Chron. 9:25, 40,000 in I Kings 4:26). The stall where Christ was born was a feeding place, usually connected with an inn (Luke 13:15).

STAR (See Astronomy)

STAR OF THE WISE MEN (See Astronomy)

STATURE (Heb. *middâh, measure,* and *qômâh, standing up;* Gr. *helikía, greatness*). The giant of Gath was of great stature (II Sam. 21:20), as were the sons of Anak (Num. 13:32,33), and the Sabaens (Isa. 45:14). God does not regard stature in size as a primary asset for leadership (I Sam. 16:7; Isa. 10:33). Jesus grew in stature (Luke 2:52). Zacchaeus was short in stature (Luke 19:3). One's height (stature) cannot be increased by wishing (Matt. 6:27; Luke 12:25).

STEEL (See Minerals: Iron)

STELE (stē'lē, Gr. *stéle, an erect block or shaft*). The custom of erecting stone markers, usually upright narrow slabs, prevailed among ancient Egyptians. They were placed in tombs and public buildings where they honored people of high estate. The Hebrews do not seem to have adopted the custom, probably because it was felt they violated the Fourth Commandment (Exod. 20:4). A noted stele showing a Moabite victory over Israel was found in Bethshan in 1868. The Grecian stele was the forerunner of modern gravestones.

STEPHANAS (stĕf'à-năs, Gr. *Stephanás, crown*), a Christian at Corinth, whose household were Paul's first converts in Achaia (I Cor. 16:15). Paul had not only won them to Christ, but they also were among the few at Corinth whom he had personally baptized (I Cor. 1:16). Subsequently, they had rendered invaluable service to the Church (I Cor. 16:15). Stephanas himself had come to Paul at Ephesus along with Fortunatus and Achaicus (I Cor. 16:17). It is thought that they may have delivered the letter which was sent by the Corinthian church to Paul.

STEPHEN (stē'vĕn, Gr. *Stephanós, crown*), one of the seven appointed to look after the daily distribution to the poor in the early church (Acts 6:1-6). The need for such men arose out of the complaint of the Hellenists (i.e., Greek-speaking Jews) that their widows were not receiving a fair share of this relief. Stephen, described as "a man full of faith and of the Holy Spirit" (Acts 6:5), and six others were elected by the church and consecrated by the apostles in order to insure an equitable distribution.

Stephen's ministry was not, however, limited to providing for the poor. He did "great wonders and signs among the people" (Acts 6:8). While this probably brought him into great favor with the people generally, another aspect of his ministry engaged him in bitterest conflict with the adherents of Judaism. He taught in the synagogue of

The Greek Orthodox Chapel of St. Stephen, at the lower right hand corner of the picture, marks the traditional spot of the stoning of the first Christian martyr (Acts 7:58, 59). Hence the name, St. Stephen's Gate, is applied to the gate in the east city wall of Jerusalem close by. The large church in the center of the picture is the Basilica of Gethsemane, and above this, on the lower slope of the Mount of Olives, is the Church of Mary Magdalene. © MPS

the Libertines (i.e., freedmen) and there debated with *Diaspora* Jews from Cyrene, Alexandria, Cilicia and Asia. When it was evident that they could not refute Stephen's arguments in open debate, these Jews hired informers to misrepresent his arguments. They went around proclaiming, "We have heard him speak blasphemous words against this holy place, and the law: For we have heard him say, that this Jesus of Nazareth shall destroy this place, and shall change the customs which Moses delivered us" (Acts 6:13,14). These accusations were such that the council could be assured of the support of the people of Jerusalem. Since they were largely dependent upon the temple for their livelihood, any threat to it constituted a threat to them.

Acts 7 records Stephen's remarkable *apologia* before the council. F. F. Bruce rightly points out that it was "not a speech for the defense in the forensic sense of the term. Such a speech as this was by no means calculated to secure an acquittal before the Sanhedrin. It is rather a defense of pure Christianity as God's appointed way of worship" (*The Book of Acts, NINTC*, Grand Rapids: Eerdmans, 1956, p. 141). Stephen's exclamation at the close of his speech is particularly important to a proper understanding of it: "Behold, I see the heavens opened, and the Son of man standing on the right hand of God" (Acts 7:56). This is the only occurrence of the title "Son of Man" in the NT on the lips of anyone other than Jesus Himself. It reveals that *"Stephen grasped and asserted the more-than-Jewish-Messianic sense in which the office and significance of Jesus in religious history were to be understood. . . . Whereas the Jewish nationalists were holding to the permanence of*

their national historical privilege, and even the 'Hebrew' Christians gathered around the Apostles were, with all of their new Messianic faith, idealizing the sacred institutions of the past, . . . Stephen saw that the Messiah was on the throne of the Universe. The Son of Man, spoken of by Daniel the prophet, had arrived in the presence of God, and had received from God 'dominion, and glory, and a kingdom, that all peoples, nations, and languages should serve him' " (William Manson, *The Epistle to the Hebrews*, London: Hodder and Stoughton, 1951, pp. 31,32).

Such radical thinking was too much for the listening Sanhedrin. "They cried out with a loud voice and stopped their ears . . . and cast him out of the city, and stoned him," and the witnesses, whose responsibility it was to cast the first stones (cf. Deut. 17:7), laid their clothes at Saul's feet (Acts 7:57,58).   W.W.W.

STEWARD (See Occupations & Professions)

STOCK, STOCKS. 1. The bole of a tree was a stock and was worshiped by apostate Israel (Isa. 44:19; Jer. 2:27; Hos. 4:12).

2. A family (Lev. 25:47; Isa. 40:24; Acts 13:26; Phil. 3:5). Children of the stock of Abraham were appealed to by Paul in Antioch (Acts 13:26). He was proud of being of the Hebrew stock (Phil. 3:5).

3. An instrument of punishment. There were various kinds. One was a machine by which the body was twisted into an unnatural position and thus made to endure excruciating agony (Jer. 20:2,3). Madmen, posing as prophets, were put on the rack (Jer. 29:26). Paul and Silas were put in stocks to make sure they did not escape from prison in Philippi (Acts 16:24).

STOICISM (stō'ĭ-sĭzm). Though the influence of Stoicism upon the NT writers was apparently next to negligible (cf. Morton Scott Enslin, *The Ethics of Paul,* pp. 14-44), this school of philosophy is of interest to Bible readers because of the apostle's encounter with it in Athens (Acts 17:18). Boasting a galaxy of distinguished exponents, both Greek and Roman — e.g. Zeno, Cleanthes, Seneca, Cicero, Epictetus, and Marcus Aurelius—Stoicism was a system of pantheistic monism. It held that fire is the ultimate substance with God, the active principle of the cosmos, permeating everything as a sort of soul. Nature, it taught, is a hierarchical unity controlled by the universal Logos, an impersonal reason at once immanent and divine. As participant in the Logos, man is also participant in deity. Indeed, the true essence of humanity is *nous* or mind, the capacity to understand the rational order veiled by phenomena. As a logos-being, man can perceive and assent to the determinism which makes all events necessary and which therefore reduces evil to mere appearance. By assenting to this determinism — indifferently called fate or providence — man is able to live in harmony with nature. Hence the Stoic ethic is egocentrically negative. Nothing lies within man's power except imagination, desire, and emotion; thus by cultivating not alone detachment from the world outside him but also mastery over his reactions to the world's impingement upon himself, the philosopher achieves freedom, happiness, and self-sufficiency. Impressively noble and lofty when practiced by, say, a Marcus Aurelius, Stoicism was aristocratic and austere, rigorously excluding pity, denying pardon, and suppressing genuine feeling. Its view of sin was hopelessly shallow, since it did not think in terms of obedience to a personal God. Sin was simply an error of judgment, easily rectified by a change of opinion. But among its virtues were cosmopolitanism and egalitarianism. Whatever his position or handicap, any man, Stoicism affirmed, even a slave like Epictetus, can be inwardly free. Moreover, as partakers of a common rational nature, men everywhere are subject to the same law. Implicit in Stoicism, accordingly, was the idea of a universal morality rooted in the universal Logos.   V.C.G.

STONE (Heb. *'even,* Gr. *líthos*). Upon entering Canaan, the Hebrews, who had made bricks in Egypt (Exod. 5:7), readily turned to the abundant supply of stones, both from quarries and from stream beds. Limestone (Isa. 27:9), gravel (Lam. 3:16), and stones rounded by water in streams (I Sam. 17:40; Job 14:19), were abundant.

Large flat slabs were used as covers for wells (Gen. 29:2-10), doors for caves (Josh. 10:18), and for burial caves (Matt. 27:60). Stones were also used as landmarks (II Sam. 20:8). The stones mentioned in Deuteronomy 19:14; 27:17 and Proverbs 22:28 were boundary stones (see Josh. 15:6; I Kings 1:9). Great stones were used in the foundation of the temple (I Kings 6:7). The palace for the pharaoh's daughter was of costly stones (I Kings 7:8-12). One may today see samples of Israelite stone work in the Wailing Wall of Jerusalem. A stone from the city wall is 14 feet long and three and three-quarter feet square. Remains of quarries in many places of the land show how widespread the use of stone was in ancient times.

Stones were used in setting up altars and memorials. These were of various kinds: cairns, tables, steles or upright slabs, and circular areas enclosed by rocks. After Joshua had led the Hebrews over Jordan he set up a cairn composed of 12 stones taken from the river's bed by representatives of the 12 tribes (Josh. 4:1-9). Jacob set up a cairn to commemorate his experience at Bethel (Gen. 28:18). His contract with Laban was sealed by a stele (Gen. 31:45-46). The miraculous victory over the Philistines called for a memorial (I Sam. 7:5-12). A cairn was placed over one who was executed by stoning, as were the king of Ai (Josh. 8:29), and Absalom (II Sam. 18:17,18). Joshua's last official act was to erect a memorial to Israel's covenant with God (Josh. 24:26-28).

Stone weapons were frequently used by the Israelites. The familiar story of David's victory over the giant of Gath reveals the skill of one who had mastered the use of the sling (I Sam. 17). Among David's warriors were some who could sling stones (I Chron. 12:2). King Uzziah included in his arsenal stones for slingers and for catapults (II Chron. 26:14,15). Stones were used in individual conflict (Exod. 21:18; Num. 35:17-23). Certain crimes were punished by stoning (Lev. 20:2,27; 24:23).

The transition from using an object or a rite in worship to making it an object of worship is never difficult. So Israel was prone to worship stones. Among other pagan evils Isaiah found libations being offered to river stones (57:3-7). The law prohibited any such use of stones (Lev. 26:1).

An illustration of the use of stones as objects in heathen worship. This is the Temple of Obelisks at ancient Gebal, the Biblical name for what is now Byblos on the Phoenician coast. SHH

Figurative uses of stone are frequent in Heb. writings: Egyptians sank like stones (Exod. 15:5); God's arm could make His enemies still as stones (Exod. 15:16); Nabal's fear petrified him (I Sam. 25:37); Job spoke of ice as stone (38:30). God has power to change stony hearts into flesh (Matt. 3:9). The hard heart is like stone (Ezek. 11:19). The new name given Simon (*Petros, a little stone*) was bestowed by the Master as an indication of the character which this apostle would have in the days ahead (John 1:42). God is the stone of Israel (Gen. 49:24; Dan. 2:34). The messianic kingdom is a stone which will crush the kingdoms of men (Dan. 2:34; Matt. 21:44). Jesus Christ is the stone which the builders rejected (Ps. 118:22; Matt. 21:42). Paul presented Jesus as the chief cornerstone of the new dispensation (Eph. 2:20-22). Believers are living stones in God's temple (I Pet. 2:5-8). J.D.F.

STONES, PRECIOUS (See Minerals)

STONING, the ordinary form of capital punishment prescribed by Hebrew law. Stoning was the penalty for blasphemy (Lev. 24:16), idolatry (Deut. 13:6-10), desecration of the sabbath (Num. 15:32-36), human sacrifice (Lev. 20:2), and occultism (Lev. 20:27). Achan and his family were stoned because of his perfidy to Israel (Josh. 7:16-26). Jesus rebuked Jerusalem for stoning the prophets (Matt. 23:37; Luke 13:34). Stephen was stoned (Acts 7:58,59). The execution took place outside the city (Lev. 24:14; I Kings 21:10,13; Acts 7:58).

STOOL, a three or four-legged seat, long known among men. The Shunammite woman put one in Elisha's room (II Kings 4:10). A stool of peculiar form was used in Egypt for women in childbirth (Exod. 1:16).

STORE CITIES, supply depots for provisions and arms. Solomon built some in a region given to his Egyptian wife by Pharaoh (I Kings 9:15-19; II Chron. 8:4-6). Some were captured by Ben-hadad (II Chron. 16:4) and restored by Jehoshaphat (II Chron. 17:12).

STOREHOUSE, a place for keeping treasures, supplies, and equipment. Obedience to Jehovah was rewarded with full storehouses (Deut. 28:8; Mal. 3:10). David built a storehouse and thus prepared an abundant supply of materials for the temple (I Chron. 29:16). The temple storehouse was a vital part of equipment needed in Hebrew worship (II Chron. 31:10).

STORK (See Birds)

STOVE, in Palestine, usually made of clay. Some were small portable fireplaces, burning charcoal. Others were built outside the house and were heated with dry sticks, grass, and even dung. The hearth mentioned in Jeremiah 36:22 was a bronze heater. Only the well-to-do could afford a brazier. For cooking, the stove was molded so as to hold the pot or pan above the fire bowl through which air passed from vents at the bottom. The fire by which Peter warmed himself during the trial of Jesus was probably in a brazier (Mark 14:67).

STRAIGHT STREET, a name given to any route extending in a straight course across a city. Most streets were narrow and crooked. The avenue across Damascus, 100 feet wide with a walk along each side, was called Straight (Acts 9:11).

STRAKES, an older English word for "streaks" (Gen. 30:37; Lev. 14:37).

STRANGER (Heb. *gēr, sojourner* or *stranger; tôshāv, sojourner; nokhrî, ben nēkhar, foreigner; zār,*

stranger). A *gēr* or *tôshāv* was a foreigner who put himself under the protection of Israel and of Israel's God, who submitted to many requirements of the law of Israel, and who was therefore given certain privileges not accorded to the *nokhrî* and the *zār,* who were also called strangers. The *gēr* was allowed to rest on the Sabbath and was supposed to be treated kindly (Exod. 20:10; 22:21; 23:9,12). He was classed with the Levite, the fatherless, and the widow (Deut. 14:21,29; 16:11; 26:11-13). He offered sacrifices to Jehovah, and was expected to observe various ceremonial and other requirements (Lev. 17:10ff; 18:26; 20:2; 24:16:22). The *nokhrî* was a foreigner who did not have cultus-fellowship with Israel, since his allegiance was claimed by another people and another deity. He was forbidden to enter the sanctuary (Ezek. 44:7-9); interest could be exacted from him (Deut. 15:3; 23:20). The *zār* was not necessarily a foreigner. The meaning of the word may be determined from its context. It is often used of foreigners as people entirely different from, or even hostile to, Israel (Isa. 1:7; Ezek. 11:9).

STRANGLE (Heb. *hānaq,* Gr. *pnígo, to choke*), to deprive of life by choking, and so without bloodshed. Israelites were forbidden to eat flesh from strangled animals because it contained the blood (Lev. 17:12). At the Jerusalem council even Jewish Christians were forbidden to eat such meat, lest they offend the Jews (Acts 15:20).

STREAM OF EGYPT (See River of Egypt)

STRIKER (Gr. *pléktes*), *a pugnacious person* (I Tim. 3:3; Titus 1:7).

STRINGED INSTRUMENTS (See Music)

STRIPES (Heb. *nākâh,* Gr. *plegé*). Scourging by lashing was a common form of punishment in ancient times. The Jewish law authorized it for certain ecclesiastical offenses (Deut. 25:2,3). Among the Jews a scourge consisting of three thongs was employed, and the number of stripes varied from a few up to 39. When scourging took place in the synagogue, it was done by the overseer, but the Sanhedrin also administered such punishment

A stove of baked clay, 3 feet high, from Taanach, with decorated sides, and holes for draft intake. DV

(Acts 5:40). Roman scourges had pieces of metal or bones attached to the lashes. The victim was stripped to the waist and bound in a stooping position. The body was horribly lacerated so that often even the entrails were exposed.

STRONG DRINK (See Wine)

STUBBLE (Heb. *qāsh, teven*; Gr. *kaláme*), the stalks of grain left after reaping. Usually about half of the stem remained in the field. When the Hebrews made brick in Egypt, they had to gather this rather than use the straw from threshing floors which had previously been provided (Exod. 5:10-14). The word became a simile for wayward Israel (Isa. 47:14).

STUMBLING BLOCK (Heb. *mikshôl*, Gr. *skándalon*), a term referring to anything that causes a person to trip or fall. In a figurative sense it means a cause of material or spiritual ruin. Israel's iniquity and idolatry were a stumbling block to her (Ezek. 14:3,4; Jer. 18:15). Paul urged Christians not to put a stumbling block in the way of a brother (Rom. 14:13; I Cor. 8:9). Jesus, as preached by Paul (Rom. 9:32), was a stumbling block to the Jews (I Cor. 1:23).

SUAH (sū'à, Heb. *sûah*), one of the descendants of Asher (I Chron. 7:36).

SUBURB (Heb. *migrāsh, open land*), lands near cities used for pasturage of animals (Josh. 21:2,42; Ezek. 45:2).

SUCCOTH (sŭk'ŏth, Heb. *sukkôth, booths* or *huts*). 1. A place E of the Jordan at which Jacob built a house for himself and booths for his animals after his return from Mesopotamia (Judg. 8:4,5; Gen. 32:22). It was in the valley of the Jordan, near Zarethan (I Kings 7:46), and was assigned to the Gadites (Josh. 13:27). Gideon punished the town severely for its refusal to assist him when he pursued Zebah and Zalmunna (Judg. 8:5-16). The site has not been identified.
2. The first station of the Hebrews on leaving Rameses (Exod. 12:37; 13:20; Num. 33:5). The exact position is unknown.

SUCCOTH BENOTH (sŭk'ŏth bē'nŏth, Heb. *sukkôth benôth*), a pagan god whose image was worshiped in Samaria after Assyria had captured it and put foreign rulers over it (II Kings 17:24-30). It may be a title of Marduk, the tutelary deity of Babylon.

SUCHATHITES (sū'kăth-īts), a native or inhabitant of Sucah or Socah (I Chron. 2:55). The site is unknown.

SUETONIUS (swē-tō'nĭ-ŭs). Gaius Suetonius Tranquillus lived from about A.D. 69 to A.D 140. He was a friend of Pliny (*Ep.* 3.8), practiced law, and was briefly secretary to Hadrian. He was a voluminous writer, and his *Lives of the Caesars,* his major surviving work, gives him a secure, if minor, place in Roman literature. His reference to the expulsion of the Jews under Claudius, following trouble in the Roman ghetto, "at the instigation of one Chrestos," is an almost certain reference to the Church (See Acts 18:2; Suetonius, *Claudius* 25:4; Arnaldo Momigliano, *The Emperor Claudius and His Achievement* [1932]).   E.M.B.

SUKKIIM (sŭk'ĭ-ĭm, Heb. *sukkîyîm*), a tribe of people whose warriors joined Shishak of Egypt when he invaded Judah. Their identity is uncertain.

SUKKOTH (See Feasts)

SULPHUR (See Minerals)

SUMER (sū'mêr), one of the two political divisions, Sumer and Akkad, originally comprising Babylonia. Its principal cities were Nippur, Adab, Lagash, Umma, Larsa, Erech, Ur and Eridu, most of which were on or near the Euphrates.

SUN (Heb. *shemesh, server; ôr, luminary; hammâh, hot body; heres, blistering;* Gr. *hélios, sun*). The beneficent nature of the sun was known among the Hebrews. Sun, moon and stars determine times and seasons (Gen. 1:14; Jer. 31:35). Night and day were caused by the sun (Gen. 1:5). Since the location of the sun determined the extent of heat and light, the day was divided accordingly. Mid-morning was when the sun grew hot (I Sam. 11:9); noon was when it was brightest (Gen. 43:16); beyond noon the heat waned and it was the cool of the day (Gen. 3:8). Times and seasons were controlled by the "ordinances of heaven" (Job 38:33; Ps. 119:91). The sun also determined directions. The rising of the sun became E (Isa. 45:6); the going down of the sun (Ps. 50:1) became W. The left hand or darker quarter was N, and the right hand or brighter quarter S (Gen. 13:14; Job 37:17; Ezek. 40:24). The sun also made it possible for man to survive, for it produced fruits (Deut. 33:14). Poetic fancies arose about the sun. It is like a bridegroom (Ps. 19:4,5), stands in his house (Hab. 3:11), is ever watchful (Ps. 19:6b), dependable (Ps. 72:5), and tells of God's continuing care (Ps. 84:11). The problem of astronomy created by the standing sun (Josh. 10:13) and the returning sun dial (II Kings 20:11; Isa. 38:8) will be answered when the full story of time has been learned by man.   J.D.F.

The great Temple of Horus, a god of the Day, or the Sun, at Edfu, in Egypt. © MPS

SUN, WORSHIP OF. The worship of the sun has found varied forms as far apart as the cult of Apollo in Greece and the religion of the Mayas and Incas in the American continent. Egypt, however, in the ancient world, was its special home. Breasted writes: "In a land where a clear sky prevailed, and rain was seldom seen, the incessant splendor of the sun was an insistent fact, which gave him the highest place in the thought and daily life of the people" (*History of Egypt,* pp. 58,59). The center of such worship was On, or Heliopolis, a city in the Delta. Here the sun was called Re, the solar orb. Atum was the dying sun, tottering to the west. As Kephri, the sun was a youth rising with vigor. In the reign of Amenhotep IV, or Ikhnaton, a purified form of sun-worship was introduced. Reviving an old name for the sun, Aton, and identifying the deity with Re, the pharaoh, who was something of a religious genius, endeavored to bring his people to a more spiritual form of worship, a project which involved a fierce contest with the Amon hierarchy of Thebes, a battle won by the priests with the ruler's death. The beautiful psalm to the sun written by the pharaoh bears striking resemblance to Psalm 104 of the Hebrew Psalter, and throws vivid light on a remarkable religious leader, and the most interesting religious movement in Egyptian history. (See Chapter XVIII in J. H. Breasted, *op. cit.*)

E.M.B.

SUNDAY. The name Sunday is derived from pagan sources. Dividing the calendar into seven-day weeks was the work of Babylonian astrologers. From them the plan went into Egypt, where the days were named for planets, one for the sun. By 250 A.D. this method of reckoning time had become well established throughout the civilized world. (Cassius, *Hist. of Rome,* 37:18). After Christianity had been planted in northern Europe, the Teutonic people substituted the names of their gods for Egyptian titles, so we have Tiwes-day (Tuesday), 'Woden's Day (Wednesday) and Thor's Day (Thursday). But the first day continued to be called Sun's Day, largely because Emperor Constantine by royal decree in 321 made it *Solis Day,* day of the sun.

No doubt Abraham learned about the seven-day week while in Ur. The revelation given to Moses about the order followed in creation (Gen. 1) confirmed the teachings of Abraham. The sabbath thus became a vital part of the seven-day week. Jesus, by His example, led the Jewish converts to continue to observe the sabbath (Matt. 12:9; 13:54; Mark 6:2; Luke 4:16; John 6:59). But He also distinguished between the ritual-bound sabbath of the Jews and the day which God had sanctified for the welfare of man. He said He is the lord of the sabbath (Matt. 12:1-8). He healed the sick on the sabbath (Matt. 12:10-13). Slavery to sabbatical regulations is not the will of God (Mark 2:27,28). In places where the Jews were numerous, their refusal to concede that one can be saved apart from observance of the Hebrew ritual, led to grave controversy within the ranks of Christians, especially those in Antioch. From 200 A.D. on we find no mention by the church fathers of the observance of the seventh day as the time for Christian worship.

After the resurrection, which occurred on the first day of the week (Luke 24:1; John 20:1), the disciples of Jesus quite naturally met on that day to celebrate the event. Jesus endorsed their choice by some special appearances on that day (Mark 16:9; John 20:19). The disciples in Troas worshiped on the first day (Acts 20:7). In his first letter to the Corinthians Paul admonished them to lay by in store as God had prospered them, doing it week by week on the first day (I Cor. 16:2). Since the Greeks had no seven-day week at the time, one must infer that Paul had already let the Corinthians know that the first day is the Christian sabbath. That he nowhere mentions the seventh day as a day for worship is evidence that it had

been supplanted by the first day. The term Lord's Day occurs only in Revelation 1:10 and is a natural adaptation of a Roman custom of calling the first day of the month "Emperor's Day." By 150 A.D. the designation had been accepted throughout the Christian world. As the stronger Hebrew Christian churches declined in influence, the tendency to observe the Hebrew sabbath slowly passed.

The early Christian writers confirm the fact that the first day was taken as the Christian day of worship, and subsequently history proves that it supplanted the Heb. sabbath, even among the converts from Judaism. Justin Martyr, who lived during the second century, wrote of the Lord's Day services. Ignatius, bishop of Antioch about 110 A.D., claimed that the day had supplanted the Jewish sabbath. The Epistle of Barnabas, written in the second century, likewise supports the view that the Lord's Day had become the day for stated worship of Christians. The Roman historian, Pliny, wrote in 112 A.D. to Emperor Trajan, telling him how Christians in Bithynia met on a certain day before dawn to sing hymns to Christ as God. The *Didache,* or *Teachings of the Apostles,* gives a command for believers to come together on the Lord's Day. Undoubtedly Jewish persecution caused Christian Jews to abandon meeting in the synagogues on the sabbath. Eventually, they met only on the Lord's Day to worship their Lord.

J.D.F.

SUPERSCRIPTION (sū'pêr-skrĭp'shŭn, Gr. *epigraphé, an inscription* [so RSV]). 1. The wording on coins (Matt. 22:20; Mark 12:16; Luke 20:24).

2. The words painted on a board which was attached to the cross (Mark 15:26; Luke 23:38). The Roman custom was to have such a board, naming the crime of which the condemned man was accused, carried before him to the place of execution. John 19:19,20 call it a title (Greek, *títlos*). Matthew 27:37 says that Jesus' accusation, written, was set over His head. Each evangelist gives the wording as it impressed him, John the most fully, or perhaps it appeared in a slightly different form in each of the three languages in which it was written.

SUPERSTITIOUS (sū'pêr-stĭsh'ŭs). In Acts 17:22 Paul calls the Athenians *deisidaimonésterous,* which KJV translates, *too superstitious;* ASV margin, *somewhat superstitious;* ASV, RSV, *very religious.* The Greek word is neutral and applies to any religion, good or bad. The comparative form used means "more religious than most people." This would be the sense in which Paul used it; he would not deliberately antagonize his hearers.

SUPH, SUPHAH (sōof, Heb. *sûph*). KJV has "the Red Sea" for both names. Suph (Deut. 1:1 ASV, RSV) is the place in front of which Moses repeated the law to Israel. Suphah (Num. 21:14 ASV, RSV) is also E of Jordan. Neither place can be identified.

SUPPER, LORD'S (See Lord's Supper)

SUPPLICATION (See Prayer)

SURETY, SURETYSHIP (shoŏr'tē, -ĕ-tē, -shĭp). 1. In the phrase of "of a surety," meaning "surely," as the translation of various words (Gen. 15:13; 18:13; 26:9; Acts 12:11).

2. Relating to the giving of a pledge and a promise to give or do something if another fails; signified by "striking hands." Thus Judah remains in prison as surety that Benjamin will come to Joseph (Gen. 43:9; 44:32). Becoming surety for either a foreigner or a neighbor is consistently condemned in Proverbs (6:1-5; 11:15; 17:18; 20:16;

22:26; 27:13), as periling the assets and the peace of mind of the surety. Job, unable to find any human being to give him the needed assurance, asks God to be his surety (Job 17:3). Hezekiah follows his example (Isa. 38:14); also the psalmist (Ps. 119:122). Jesus, by His incarnation, life, death, resurrection and ascension became the surety for the performance of all the promises of God relating to salvation and assurance in the new and better covenant (Heb. 7:22).   E.R.

SURFEITING (sûr'fĕt-ĭng, Gr. *kraipále, a drinking-bout*), over-indulgence of food or drink; intoxication; a drunken headache (Luke 21:34). *Dissipation* is a good rendering (RSV).

SUSA (See Shushan)

SUSANCHITES (sū-săn'kīts, Heb. *shûshānekhāyē'*), colonists planted in Samaria by the Assyrians when they deported the Israelites (Ezra 4:9,10), ASV *Shushanchites*; RSV *the men of Susa, that is, the Elamites*). They came from Susa or Shushan in Elam.

SUSANNA (sū-zăn'a, Heb. *shôshannâh*, Gr. *Sousánna, lily*). 1. One of the women who went with Jesus and the Twelve on their missionary journeys, and provided for them out of their means (Luke 8:1-3).
    2. The heroine of *The History of Susanna*, in the OT Apocrypha. See APOCRYPHA.

SUSI (sū'sī, Heb. *sûsî*), a Manassite, father of Gaddi, one of the 12 men sent to spy out the land (Num. 13:11).

SWADDLING BAND (Heb. *hăthullâh*, Gr. *spárgana*), bands of cloth in which a new born baby was wrapped. The child was placed diagonally on a square piece of cloth which was folded over the infant's feet and sides. Around this bundle swaddling bands were wound. Mary herself wrapped the baby Jesus in swaddling bands (Luke 2:7,12). For a figurative use, see Job 38:9.

SWALLOW (See Birds)

SWAN (See Birds)

SWEAR (See Oath)

SWEAT (Heb. *zē'âh*, Gr. *hidrós*). After the Fall, God tells Adam that he will now have to work hard enough to cause sweat, in order to get his food (Gen. 3:19). Priests in the future temple are not to wear anything that causes sweat (Ezek. 44:18). During Christ's agony in Gethsemane "his sweat became as it were great drops of blood falling down upon the ground" (Luke 22:44).

SWEAT, BLOODY, a physical manifestation of the agony of Jesus in Gethsemane (Luke 22:44). Since Luke is believed to have been a physician, his language has been subjected to closest scrutiny. He does not say that the sweat became blood, but that it became "as it were" or "like" great drops of blood. He is not identifying, but comparing the sweat with blood. The Greek word *thrómboi*, translated "great drops," elsewhere means "clots," and is used of clots of blood, curds of milk, nipples, elevated places; all solid matter. Nevertheless, the point should not be stressed: drops, however thick, of sweat are here meant. Ancient and modern medicine know cases of blood extravasated from the capillaries mingling with and coloring the sweat, under severe stress of emotion.

SWELLING (swĕl'ĭng, Heb. *ga'awâh*), usually translated "pride," but in Psalm 46:3 refers to the tumult of a stormy sea. Heb. *gā'ôn*, (elsewhere translated *pride, excellency, majesty, pomp, arrogancy*, in Jeremiah 12:5; 49:19; 50:44); Zech. 11:3 KJV *pride of Jordan*; RSV always *jungle of*

The Village of Sychar, in Samaria, near Jacob's Well. In the background is Mount Gerizim. © MPS

the Jordan, refers to the dense thickets infested by wild beasts, difficult and dangerous to penetrate, along the banks of the Jordan. Greek *physíosis* (II Cor. 12:20, RSV *conceit*) means "pride, being puffed up." Gr. *hypérogkos* (II Pet. 2:18 RSV, *loud boasts of folly;* Jude 16 RSV, *loud-mouthed boasters*) means *swelled up, talking big.*

SWINE (See Animals)

SYCAMINE (See Plants)

SYCAMORE, SYCOMORE (See Plants)

SYCHAR (sī'kär, Gr. *Sychár*), a village of Samaria located near Jacob's well, where Jesus met the Samaritan woman (John 4:5). It was situated on the main road that led from Jerusalem through Samaria to Galilee. No mention is made of it in the OT, but there is a Suchar or Sichar referred to in the rabbinical writings (cf. *SBK*, II, 432, 433). Sychar is most often identified with the modern Askar, although the identification is not certain. It is situated close to Shechem (with which it has often been incorrectly identified) and on the eastern slope of Mount Ebal. The site which by continuous tradition has been identified with Jacob's well lies about half a mile to the S. In Jesus' day Sychar was only a small village.

SYCHEM (See Shechem)

SYENE (sī-ē'nē, Heb. *sevēnēh*), an Egyptian city, identified as present-day Aswan, at the First Cataract of the Nile, on the E bank of the river, opposite the island of Elephantine, which is well-known to Biblical students from the Aramaic papyri found there. During much of the history of Egypt this area marked the effective southern boundary of Egypt. The name Syene appears but twice in the OT (Ezek. 29:10; 30:16), both times in prophecies against Egypt and in geographic designations of the extent of Egyptian territory, from Migdol in the N to Syene in the S.

SYMBOL, that which stands for or represents something else; a visible sign or representation of an idea or quality or of another object. Symbolism in its religious application means that an object, animal, action, form or words or whatever else is involved has a deeper spiritual meaning than a simple literal interpretation might suggest. A symbol, unlike a type, is usually not prefigurative but rather represents something which already exists. The Passover, however, was both symbolical and typical, and the symbolic actions of the OT prophets were often predictive in nature.

Interpretation of Symbols. The literature of all the peoples of the world contains symbols. Symbolism was particularly attractive to the oriental mind. Thus the Bible contains many symbols. Some parts of Scripture, of course, contain more (viz., the prophetic literature and apocalyptic books) than others. The interpretation of these symbols presents a formidable problem to the student of the Word of God.

Symbols and their meanings arise out of the culture of the peoples that use them. The more remote and obscure the culture the more difficult the interpretation of the symbols. Bernard Ramm suggests the following general rules for the interpretation of symbols:

1. *Those symbols interpreted by the Scriptures are the foundation for all further studies in symbolism.* The Book of Revelation interprets many of its symbols, e.g., the bowls of incense are the prayers of the saints (5:8), the great dragon is Satan (12:9), the waters are peoples, multitudes, nations and tongues (17:15). When the Bible interprets its own symbols we are on sure ground and can often find the same symbols used elsewhere in Scripture in the same or at least similar ways.

2. *If the symbol is not interpreted:* a. Investigate the *context* thoroughly. b. By means of a concordance check other passages which use the same symbol and see if such cross references will give the clue. c. Sometimes the nature of the symbol is a clue to its meaning (although the temptation to read the meanings of our culture into these symbols must be resisted). d. Sometimes comparative studies of Semitic culture reveal the meaning of a symbol.

3. *Beware of double imagery in symbols.* Not all symbols in the Bible have one and only one meaning. The lion is a symbol for both Christ ("the Lion of the tribe of Judah") and for the Devil (I Pet. 5:8). Some entities have more than one symbol to represent them, i.e., Christ is represented by the lion, lamb and branch, and the Holy Spirit by water, oil, wind and the dove (*Protestant Biblical Interpretation*, Boston: Wilde, 1956, pp. 214, 215).

Symbolism of Numbers. It is evident that certain numbers in the Bible have symbolical significance. The following are particularly important: *Seven*, probably the most important number in Scripture (it occurs about 600 times), has been called the sacred number *par excellence*. In the literature of ancient Babylonia it is the number of totality or completeness. To speak of the seven gods is to speak of all the gods. This seems to be its primary symbolical meaning in Scripture (cf. the seven creative days in Gen. 1), although M. S. Terry thinks that it symbolizes "some mystical union of God with the world, and accordingly, may be called the sacred number of the covenant between God and his creation" (*Biblical Hermeneutics*, Grand Rapids: Zondervan, 2 ed., n. d., p. 382). The Book of Revelation makes frequent use of the number seven. There are seven churches (1:4), spirits (1:4), candlesticks (1:12,13), stars (1:16), lamps (4:5), seals (5:1; 8:1), horns and

eyes (5:6), trumpets (8:2), thunders (10:3), heads of the great dragon (12:3), angels with plagues (15:1), vials (15:7), heads of the beast (13:1), mountains (17:9) and kings (17:10). *Three* appears to be symbolical of "several," "a few," "some," although at times it means "many" or "enough." Terry thinks that it is the number of divine fulness in unity (*ibid.*, p. 381). The three persons of the Trinity particularly suggest this symbolical meaning. *Four* in the Bible seems to stand for completeness, especially in relation to range or extent. Thus there are four winds (Jer. 49:36; Ezek. 37:9), four directions, four corners of a house (Job 1:19), of the land of Israel (Ezek. 7:2) and of the whole earth (Isa. 11:12). *Ten*, since it is the basis of the decimal system, is also a significant number. In the Bible it is often a round number of indefinite magnitude. *Twelve* seems to be the mystical number of the people of God. The twelve tribes, twelve apostles, and the twelve thousand times twelve thousand sealed in the Book of Revelation bear out this symbolical meaning. *Forty* is the round number for a generation and also appears to be symbolical of a period of judgment (cf. the forty days of the flood, the forty years of wilderness wandering, and the forty days and nights of Jesus' temptation).

Of special interest is the mysterious number 666 in the Book of Revelation (13:18). This may be an example of Jewish *Gematria*, i.e., the art of attaching values to names according to the combined numerical value of the letters composing them. The numerical value of *Neron Kaesar* in Hebrew is 666. However, M. Tenney points out that "the usual spelling of Caesar must be changed in order to fit the explanation — a device which makes the interpretation dependent upon it at least suspicious" (*Interpreting Revelation*, Grand Rapids: Eerdmans, 1957, p. 19).

Symbolism of Colors. Since color differentiations were not as exact in the ancient world as they are in modern times, it is difficult to identify Biblical colors precisely. As an example, Ramm cites the use of the Latin word *purpureus* which "was used to describe snow, the swan, the foam of the sea, a rose, a beautiful human eye, and purple objects" (*op. cit.*, p. 218). Particularly difficult are the Hebrew words translated blue, purple, and scarlet. No unanimity of opinion exists among Biblical scholars with regard to the symbolical meaning of colors. Much care must be taken, therefore, in seeking to assign symbolic meanings to colors. The following are suggestions: *White*, the color of light, is a symbol of purity, holiness and righteousness (Rev. 7:14). *Blue* is difficult, but perhaps Terry is right when he says that "blue, as the color of the heaven, reflected in the sea, would naturally suggest that which is heavenly, holy and divine" (*op. cit.*, p. 393). Scarlet, since it was most often the dress of kings, is regarded as symbolic of royalty. *Black*, the opposite of white, would naturally be associated with evil, such as famine (Rev. 6:5,6) or mourning (Jer. 14:2). *Red* is symbolic of bloodshed and war (Rev. 6:4; 12:3).

Symbolic Actions. Not only objects, names, numbers and colors are symbolic in Scripture, but actions too may be symbolic. Symbolic actions often are prefigurative and are especially associated with the Old Testament prophets. H. L. Ellison points out that "behind these actions lie the deep convictions of more primitive men that words and actions are significant, and that by doing something similar to what you prophesy, you are helping forward the fulfilment and making it more certain" (*Ezekiel, the Man and His Message,* Grand Rapids: Eerdmans, 1956, p. 32). Ellison does not mean that the prophets necessarily believed this but that it made their message more impressive. Such symbolical actions by the prophets are found as early as Samuel's day. When Saul took hold of Samuel's robe and tore it, this was understood by Samuel to be symbolic of the tearing away of Saul's kingdom (I Sam. 15:27,28). By tearing his garment into 12 pieces Ahijah symbolized the break-up of the kingdom of Solomon (I Kings 11:29,30; cf. also II Kings 13:14-19; 22:11). Symbolic action is especially frequent in the prophecies of Jeremiah and Ezekiel. Jeremiah's smashing of the pot before the elders of the people and the senior priests in the Valley of Benhinnom was clearly understood by the people, as their subsequent reaction shows. Symbolic action was involved in Ezekiel's call to the prophetic office when the Lord commanded him to eat the scroll, inscribed on the front and back with words of lamentation and mourning and woe (Ezek. 2:9, 10). Ezekiel was not only thereby informed of the content of his message but the importance of assimilating the same. Many of Ezekiel's symbolic actions were calculated to gain a hearing of the message God had given him to proclaim. This was particularly true of his drawing on the brick of the siege of Jerusalem (Ezek. 4:1-4). Ellison pointedly remarks, "We can easily understand . . . the excitement in Tel-Abib as the news went round that Ezekiel, who had not been seen outside the house for days, was acting in a way calculated to bring disaster to Jerusalem" (*ibid.,* p. 33).

Jesus also used symbolical actions to convey spiritual truth. While all the Gospels attest to our Lord's symbolical actions, the author of the fourth Gospel places special stress on them. He calls Jesus' miracles signs (*semaia*). Tenney has pointed out that the verb form of this word (*semainein*) "evidently meant a kind of communication that is neither plain statement nor an attempt at concealment. It is figurative, symbolic, or imaginative, and is intended to convey truth by picture rather than definition" (*op. cit.,* p. 186). When in the Fourth Gospel Jesus multiplies the loaves, this is symbolic of the fact that He is Himself the Bread of Life (John 6). The blind man healed is symbolic of Christ as the Light of the World (John 9), and Lazarus raised from the dead is symbolic of Jesus as the Resurrection and the Life (John 11).

Bibliography. Bernard Ramm, *Protestant Biblical Interpretation,* Boston: W. A. Wilde Company, 1956, pp. 213-219; Milton S. Terry, *Biblical Hermeneutics,* Grand Rapids: Zondervan, n. d., pp. 347-395. W.W.W.

SYMEON (See Simeon)

SYNAGOGUE (Gr. *synagogé, place of assembly*), a Jewish institution for the reading and exposition of the Holy Scriptures, which originated perhaps as early as the Babylonian exile. It is supposed that the synagogue had its precursor in the spontaneous gatherings of the Jewish people in the lands of the exile on their day of rest and also on special feast days. Since religion stood at the very center of Jewish existence, these gatherings naturally took on a religious significance. The Jews of the exile needed mutual encouragement in the faithful practice of their religion and in the hope of a restoration to the land. These they sought and found in spontaneous assemblies which proved to be of such religious value that they quickly spread throughout the lands of the dispersion. G. F. Moore thinks that elements of the later synagogue service orig-

Ruins of the Synagogue at Capernaum (Tell Hum), partially restored. The site is probably the same as where Jesus taught, although the ruins of this limestone building are of a later date. © MPS

Above, artist's restoration of building. UANT

inated in the things which would have been most natural for the people to do and say under such circumstances (*Judaism,* Cambridge: Harvard University Press, 1927, I, 283).

No specific mention of a synagogue occurs in pre-Christian writings with the possible exception of Psalm 74:8: "They have burned up all the synagogues ["meeting places" RSV] of God in the land." This is a late psalm, possibly belonging to the Persian era.

From about the second century B.C. onward, the sect of the Pharisees assumed a leading role in the synagogues. It was an institution peculiarly adapted to achieve their ends. "Through it, more perhaps than by any other means, they gained the hold upon the mass of the people which enabled them to come out victorious from their conflicts with John Hyrcanus and Alexander Jannaeus and to establish such power as Josephus ascribes to them" (Moore, *ibid.,* II, 287).

By NT times the synagogue was a firmly established institution among the Jews, who considered it to be an ancient institution, as the words of James in Acts 15:21 show: "For from early generations Moses has had in every city those who preach him, for he is read every sabbath in the synagogues" (RSV). Josephus, Philo and later Judaism traced the synagogue back to Moses. While this, of course, has no historical validity, it does reveal that Judasim regarded the synagogue as one of its basic institutions.

In the first Christian century synagogues could be found everywhere in the Hellenistic world where there were sufficient Jews to maintain one. In large Jewish centers there might be numbers of them. However, the 480 synagogues claimed by the Jerusalem Talmud (*Megillah* 73 d) for Jerusalem must be taken with a grain of salt!

Purpose. The chief purpose of the synagogue was not public worship but instruction in the Holy Scriptures. The very nature of Judaism, a religion of revelation, demanded such an institution to survive. For the Jews "it was not to be imagined that a man or a people could be righteous without knowing God's holy character, and what was right in his eyes and what was wrong. And if God had revealed these things, plainly revelation was the place to go to learn them" (Moore, *ibid.*, I, 282). All of the rabbis emphasized the importance of knowing the Law. Hillel taught: "An ignorant man cannot be truly pious" (*Aboth,* ii, 5) and "The more teaching of the law, the more life; the more school, the more wisdom; the more counsel the more reasonable action. He who gains a knowledge of the law gains life in the world to come" (*Aboth,* ii, 14). The destiny of both the nation and the individual was dependent on the knowledge of the Law. It was the explicit purpose of the synagogue to educate the whole people in the Law.

How effectively the synagogue, along with the school, fulfilled this purpose is to be seen (1) from the survival of Judaism, especially in the *diaspora* despite the pressures of pagan influences; (2) from the thorough Judaistic nature of Galilee in the first century which in the time of Simon Maccabeus was largely pagan; and (3) from the knowledge of the Scriptures which the Apostle Paul assumes of his hearers in the Hellenistic synagogues.

Officials. Although there might be more in some of the larger synagogues, there were always at least two officials. The Ruler of the Synagogue (Heb. *ro'sh ha-keneseth;* Gr. *archisynagogos*) was probably elected by the elders of the congregation. He was responsible for (1) the building and property; (2) the general oversight of the public worship, including the maintenance of order (cf. Luke 13:14); (3) the appointing of persons to read the Scriptures and to pray; and (4) the inviting of strangers to address the congregation (Acts 13:15). Generally there was only one ruler for each synagogue, but some synagogues had more (Acts 13:15).

The Minister or Attendant (Heb. *hazzān;* Gr. *hyperetes,* cf. Luke 4:20) was a paid officer whose special duty was the care of the synagogue building and its furniture, in particular the rolls of Scripture. During the worship it was the *hazzān* who brought forth the roll from the chest and handed it to the appointed reader. He also returned it to its proper place at the conclusion of the reading (Luke 4:20). He had numerous other duties which included the instruction of children in reading, the administration of scourgings, and the blowing of three blasts on the trumpet from the roof of the synagogue to announce the beginning and end of the sabbath. Since his work was closely associated with the synagogue building and its equipment, he sometimes lived under its roof.

Building and Furniture. Synagogue buildings varied greatly. They were usually built of stone and lay N and S with the entrance at the S end. Their size and elegance were largely determined by the numerical strength and prosperity of the Jewish communities in which they were built. The principal items of furniture were (1) a chest in which the rolls of Scripture were kept, wrapped in linen cloth; (2) a platform or elevated place on which a reading desk stood; (3) lamps and candelabra, trombones and trumpets and (4) benches on which the worshipers sat.

Worship. The congregation was divided, the men on one side and the women on the other. The more prominent members took the front seats. The service began with the recitation of the Jewish confession of faith, the *Shema'*: "Hear, O Israel, the Lord our God, the Lord is One, and thou shalt love the Lord thy God with all thy heart, and with all thy soul, and with all thy might" (Deut. 6:4, 5). This was both preceded and followed by thanksgivings, two before and one after the morning *Shema',* and two both before and after the evening *Shema'.* The first of the two which preceded both morning and evening *Shema'* reads: "Blessed art thou, O Lord our God, King of the world, former of light and creator of darkness, author of welfare (peace), and creator of all things."

After the *Shema'* came the prayer (*Tefillah*). The Ruler of the Synagogue could call upon any adult male of the congregation to say this prayer. The person praying usually stood before the chest of the rolls of Scripture. The oldest form of the *Tefillah* consisted of a series of ascriptions or petitions each of which ended in the benedictory response: "Blessed art thou, O Lord," etc. About the close of the first century an arrangement was made in which there were 18 of these prayers, from which the name "The Eighteen" (*Shemoneh 'Esreh*) was derived, a name which was maintained even when a 19th prayer was added. Prayers 1-3 were in praise of God; 4-16 were petitions; and 17-19 were thanksgivings. On sabbaths and festival days only the first three and last three were recited. A single prayer was substituted for the intervening 13 petitions, so that the total prayer consisted of seven parts. On New Year's, however, three prayers were substituted for the 13.

Ruins of ancient synagogue uncovered in 1962 at Ostia, the old Roman port city 15 miles SW of Rome, which archaeologists now believe date back to the First Century A.D. © Keystone Photo.

An artist's representation of a service in a synagogue of Bible times. The reader is reading from a scroll of the Scriptures. KC © FC

The Scripture lesson which followed the *Tefillah* could be read by any member of the congregation, even children. The only exception was that at the feast of Purim a minor was not allowed to read the book of Esther. If priests or Levites were present in the worship service, they were given precedence. The readers usually stood while reading (cf. Luke 4:16).

Prescribed lessons out of the Pentateuch for special sabbaths were established early. For other sabbaths the reader himself chose the passage, but subsequently all the Pentateuchal readings became fixed. Sections, called *sedarim,* were established in order to complete the reading of the Pentateuch within a prescribed time. Babylonian Jews divided the Pentateuch into 154 sections and thus completed reading it in three years, whereas Palestinian Jews read it through once every year.

A lesson from the prophets immediately followed the reading from the Pentateuch. This custom is mentioned as early as the Mishnah, and was practiced in NT times. When Jesus came to His home town, Nazareth, and entered the synagogue, He stood up to read (Luke 4:16ff). The book of the Prophet Isaiah was given to Him, and when He opened the book, He read. It is not clear from this account whether or not Jesus Himself chose the portion. He may have, because the readings from the prophets were not fixed and either the ruler of the synagogue or the reader could choose them. The prophetical lessons were usually considerably shorter than those from the Pentateuch and have been likened to texts rather than Scripture lessons. Translations often accompanied both readings. In Palestine, where the Scriptures were read in Hebrew, an extemporaneous and free translation accompanied in Aramaic, one verse at a time for the Law, three at a time for the prophets.

The sermon followed the reading from the prophets (cf. Acts 13:15 where it is called a "word of exhortation," *logos parakleseos*). That this was an important part of the synagogue service is revealed by the many references to teaching in the synagogue in the NT (Matt. 4:23; Mark 1:21; 6:2; Luke 4:15; 6:6; 13:10; John 6:59; 18:20). The preacher usually sat (Luke 4:20), but the Acts account has Paul standing (13:16). No single individual was appointed to do the preaching. Any competent worshiper might be invited by the ruler to bring the sermon for the day (Luke 4:16,17; Acts 13:15). The importance of the "freedom of the synagogue," as this custom was called, to the propagation of the Gospel can scarcely be overemphasized. Jesus constantly went into the synagogues to teach, and everywhere Paul went he searched out the synagogue. This was not only that he might preach the "good news" to his fellow countrymen but also to reach the God-fearers (*hoi sebomenoi, hoi phoboumenoi*). These were Gentiles who had become disillusioned with the old pagan religions and were attracted to Judaism because of its high ethical morality and its monotheistic faith. They were not proselytes. Certain requirements in order to attain that status, particularly circumcision, kept them out. But they were interested observers. Some even kept the Jewish holy days, observed eating regulations and were tolerably conversant with the synagogue prayers and scripture lessons. These God-fearers proved to to be ready recipients of the Gospel, and it was primarily to reach them that Paul often used the "freedom of the synagogue" to preach Christ.

The worship in the synagogue closed with a blessing which had to be pronounced by a priest and to which the congregation responded with an "Amen." If no priest was present, a prayer was substituted for the blessing.

The form of worship of the synagogue was adopted by both the Christian and Muslim religions, and that form in its general outline is to be found today in their places of worship.

Bibliography. Israel Abrahams, "The Freedom of the Synagogue," *Studies in Pharisaism and the Gospels,* First Series, pp. 1-17. Cambridge: University Press, 1917; G. F. Moore, *Judaism,* Vol. I, pp. 281-307. Cambridge: Harvard University Press, 1937; Emil Schürer, *A History of the Jewish People in the Time of Jesus Christ,* Second division, Vol. II, pp. 44-89, Edinburgh: T. & T. Clark, 1885. W.W.W.

SYNAGOGUE, MEN OF THE GREAT, a council of 120 men, supposedly originating at the time of Ezra, to which Jewish tradition attributed the origination and authoritative promulgation of many ordinances and regulations. Among the many functions ascribed to them were the completion of the collection of sacred books by the addition of Ezekiel, Daniel, Esther and the Twelve, minor alterations of the OT text, the authorization of the observance of the Feast of Purim and the days on which it was to be kept, and the setting up of the curriculum of study in the three main branches of Jewish learning, Midrash, Halakah, and Haggadah. One of its latest members is said to have been Simon the Just (c. 200 B.C.). Much doubt exists about the reliability of these traditions, and some scholars deny the existence of any such council at all.   W.W.W.

SYNOPTIC PROBLEM (See Gospels)

SYNTICHE, SYNTYCHE (sĭn'tĭ-chē, Gr. *Syntúche, fortunate*), a prominent woman member of the church at Philippi who was having a disagreement with a fellow lady Christian, Euodias. Paul, in his letter to that church, entreats these two women "to agree in the Lord" (Phil. 4:2).

SYRACUSE (sĭr'à-kūs, Gr. *Syrákousai*), a town on the E coast of Sicily. Syracuse was the most important and prosperous Greek city on the island. It boasted two splendid harbors which contributed substantially to its material prosperity. Corinthian and Dorian Greeks, led by Archias, founded the city in 734 B.C. The Athenians, at the height of their power (413) tried to take the city, but were completely routed. In 212 B.C. Syracuse passed under the control of Rome.

The Alexandrian ship in which Paul sailed from Malta to Puteoli put in at Syracuse for three days (Acts 28:12). Whether or not Paul went ashore during this time is not stated in the Acts account.

SYRIA (sĭr'ĭ-à, Heb. *'ărām*, Gr. *Syría*). An abbreviation of Assyria or possibly from the Babylonian *Suri*, the name of a district in N Mesopotamia. Herodotus first applied the name Syria to the territory occupied by the Aramaeans, but this name was not popularized until the Hellenistic period. In the Hebrew Bible it is called 'Aram, after the Aramaeans, nomads from the Syro-Arabian desert who occupied the area in the 12th century B.C.

Location and Area. The territory of Syria varied considerably, often had vague boundaries and really never constituted a political unit. Generally speaking, it included the area S of the Taurus Mountains, N of Galilee and Bashan, W of the Arabian desert and E of the Mediterranean. This was a territory approximately 300 miles N to S and 50-150 miles E to W. The chief cities were Damascus, Antioch, Hama, Biblos, Aleppo, Palmyra and Carchemish.

Topography. Two mountain ranges, both running N and S, constitute the most prominent topographical features. The eastern range includes Mt. Hermon (over 9,000 ft. high), and the western Mt. Casius and the Lebanon. Between these two ranges is the high plain called Coele Syria watered by the Jordan, Leontes, and Orontes Rivers. To the E of Hermon flow the Abana and the Pharpar, while in the N of Syria there are tributaries of the Euphrates. The many rivers and good soil made Syria generally more prosperous than her neighbor to the S.

History. In the earliest period of its history Syria was dominated by Amorites, Hittites, Mitanni and especially Egyptians. When, however, the sea peoples invaded Syria from the N in the 12th century, an opportunity was afforded the Semitic Aramaean tribesmen of the desert to abandon their nomadic way of life and settle in the best areas of Syria. They had actually begun to infiltrate this area before the 12th century, but had not had the opportunity to establish themselves.

The Aramaeans at the time of David and Solomon were divided into a number of small kingdoms, the principal ones being: Aram of Damascus, Aram of Zobah, Aram-maacah, Aram of Beth-rehob and Aram-haharaim. The strongest of these was Zobah, whose king Hadadezer David defeated in battle along with the Syrians of Damascus who came to Hadadezer's aid (II Sam. 8:3-7). David also subdued Aram-maacah (I Chron. 19:6-19), Aram of Beth-rehob (II Sam. 10:6) and Aram-naharaim ("Aram of the rivers," usually translated "Mesopotamia" in the RSV, I Chron. 19:6).

Solomon was unable to hold David's gains in Syria, and the political and military weakness in Israel caused by the disruption afforded the Syrian kingdoms, particularly Damascus, opportunity to further strengthen themselves.

Asa, king of Judah (911-876) appealed to Syria for help against Baasha, king of Israel (909-886). This resulted in an invasion by Benhadad I, king of Damascus, of the northern kingdom (I Kings 15:16-21).

Omri (885-874) of Israel, being faced with the growing power of Syria, strategically consummated an alliance with the Phoenicians by the marriage of his son Ahab to Jezebel, daughter of Ethbaal, king of the Sidonians (I Kings 16:31). Twice during Ahab's reign (374-853) the Syrians under Benhadad I tried to invade Israel. but were put to flight first at Samaria (I Kings 20:1-21) and the following year at Aphek (I Kings 20:26-34). Three years of peace with Syria followed. Then Ahab, in alliance with Jehoshaphat of Judah, made an attempt to recover Ramoth-Gilead and was killed on the field of battle.

Jehoram of Israel (852-841) allied himself with Ahaziah (852) to war against Benhadad's successor, Hazael, and was wounded in battle at Ramoth-Gilead (II Kings 8:28,29).

During Jehu's reign (841-814) Hazael captured the area E of the Jordan (II Kings 10:32,33), and during the reign of Jehu's son, Jehoahaz (814-798), completely overran Israel and took numbers of its cities. These were retaken by Jehoash (798-782) from Hazael's successor, Benhadad II (II Kings 13:25). The successes of Jehoash were continued by his son, Jeroboam II (782-753), who recovered all of the cities which had been taken by the Syrians from Israel over the years. He even successfully reduced Damascus (II Kings 14:25-28).

Nothing is known of Syria from about 773 until the accession of Rezin in 750. During this time the Assyrian threat which had been present already for a considerable time was becoming progressively more real. To meet it, Rezin of Damascus and Pekah of Israel (740-732) formed a military alliance. In 735 or 736 they attacked Jerusalem (II Kings 16:5; Isa. 7:1) either to eliminate Judah as a possible foe or to force her into their coalition. Judah's king, Ahaz (735-715), had just come to the throne. He panicked, and despite the Prophet Isaiah's warnings, sent for help from Assyria (Isa. 7:1,25). This apparently was just the excuse Tiglathpileser III needed to invade Syria-Palestine. He captured the Israelite cities in the territories of Dan and Naphtali (II Kings 15:29) and took the people captive to Assyria. He then turned his at-

Ruins of the Temple of the Sun in Palmyra, one of the chief ancient cities of Syria. The name in Hebrew was Tadmor, q.v. © MPS

tention to Damascus and in 732 subdued the city and brought an end to the Aramaean state, something his predecessors had tried vainly to accomplish for over 50 years.

In subsequent years the Chaldeans and Egyptians fought over Syria and with the rise of the Persians it passed into their hands. The Battle of Issus (331) brought Syria under the control of Alexander the Great. At his death it became the most important part of the Seleucid kingdom, which included large areas to the E, including Babylon. By the close of the second century Syria, with Antioch as its capital, was all that was left of the kingdom of the Seleucidae. In 64 B.C. the Romans made it a province and increased its area to include all the territory from Egypt to the Taurus Mountains, and from the Mediterranean to the Euphrates.

Syria played a prominent part in the early Church. It was at Antioch that the followers of Jesus were first called Christians (Acts 11:26). Paul was converted in Syria on the road to Damascus (Acts 9:1-9) and was commissioned with Barnabas by the Antioch church to take the Gospel to the Gentiles (Acts 13:1-3).   W.W.W.

SYRIA MAACHAH (See Maachah)

SYRIAC, the Syrian tongue or language, the KJV terms for the Hebrew, *'ărāmîth*, "Aramaic" or the "Aramean language" (II Kings 18:26; Ezra 4:7; Isa. 36:11; Dan. 2:4). Syriac is Eastern Aramaic and the literary language of the Christian Syrians. Early Syriac versions of the Bible are important for textual study.

SYRIAC VERSIONS (See Texts and Versions)

SYRIAN (sĭr'ĭ-ăn, Heb. *'ărām,* Gr. *Sýroi*). 1. The language of Syria; Aramaic (II Kings 18:26; Ezra 4:7; Isa. 36:11; Dan. 2:4 KJV, Syriac).

2. The people of Syria (II Sam. 8:5, etc.); in earlier times, broadly the Arameans (Gen. 25:20; 28:5; Deut. 26:5).

SYROPHOENICIAN (sī'rō-fē-nĭsh'ăn, sĭr'ō-, Gr. *Syrophoínissa*), an inhabitant of the region near Tyre and Sidon, modern Lebanon. A Greek-speaking Canaanite woman, native of this region, though a Gentile, by persistence and humility won from Jesus healing for her daughter (Mark 7:26; cf. Matt. 15:22).

SYRTIS (sûr'tĭs, Gr. *Sýrtis*). The Syrtes (pl.) were the banks of quicksand off the coast of Libya. The Greater Syrtis was located W of the Cyrene. When the northeaster hit the ship on which Paul was traveling, the sailors feared lest they were being driven on to this great shoal of quicksand (Acts 27:17).

T

TAANACH (tā'à-năk, Heb. *ta'anak*), a fortified city of Canaan, whose king was defeated by Joshua, but which was not occupied by the Israelites until later, when it was held by Manasseh (Judg. 1:27, 5:19; Josh. 12:21, 17:11; I Chron. 7:29). Mentioned in the El Amarna letters and other Egyptian records. A ruin mound remains.

TAANATH-SHILOH (tā'à-năth-shī'lō, Heb. *ta'ănath shilōh, approach to Shiloh*), a town on the NE border of the heritage of Ephraim (Josh. 16:6). It was about ten miles E of Shechem and the same distance W of the Jordan River. Several large cisterns and ruins SE of Nablus are supposed to mark the site of the town.

TABBAOTH (tă-bā'ŏth, Heb. *tabbā'ôth, rings*), a family of temple servants who returned to Jerusalem under Zerubbabel (Ezra 2:43; Neh. 7:46).

TABBATH (tăb'ăth, Heb. *tabbāth*), a place named in tracing the route of flight of the Midianites and their allies after Gideon's 300 defeated them (Judg. 7:22). If the current identification with a site E of the Jordan between Jabesh-gilead and Succoth is correct, the army must have crossed the Jordan in their flight.

TABEAL, TABEEL (tā'bē-ăl, tā'bē-ĕl). 1. Father of one of the allied kings whom Rezin of Damascus and Pekah of Israel attempted to make their puppet king of Israel (Isa. 7:6 KJV Tabeal; ASV, RSV Tabeel).

2. An official in Samaria who complained to Artaxerxes about the activity of the Jews (Ezra 4:7, all versions Tabeel).

TABERAH (tăb'ē-rà, Heb. *tav'ērâh, burning*), a place in the wilderness where the fire of the Lord burned some outlying parts of the camp of Israel as punishment for their complaining (Num. 11:1-3; Deut. 9:22). Probably three days' journey from Sinai (Num. 10:33); site unidentified.

TABERNACLE (Heb. *'ōhel, mô'ēdh, tent of meeting; mishkān, dwelling;* Gr. *skené, tent*). The religious vitality of the Hebrews and the resilience of their social and political organization in the time of Joshua would indicate that the period of the wilderness wanderings was the truly creative era from which all that was best in subsequent Israelite history and religion took its rise. Under the dynamic spiritual leadership of Moses the children of Israel came to worship a cosmic deity whose virility contrasted sharply with the capricious decadent gods of ancient Near Eastern religion. The God of Sinai revealed Himself as a supremely moral being whose leadership extended over the whole earth. He was the only true God, and He desired to enter into a special spiritual relationship with Israel as a means of His self-expression in the world.

Since this relationship demanded the undivided worship of the Israelites, it was of supreme importance for a ritual tradition to be established in the wilderness so that Israel could engage in regular spiritual communion with her God. The nomadic nature of the sojourn in the Sinai peninsula precluded the building of a permanent shrine for worship. The only alternative was a portable sanctuary which would embody all that was necessary for the worship of Jehovah under nomadic conditions, and which could also serve as a prototype of a subsequent permanent building.

Such tent-shrines were by no means unknown in the ancient world. An early writer (c. 700 B.C.) spoke of a primitive Phoenician structure which was apparently placed on a cart and pulled by oxen. In pre-Islamic times the *qubbah* or miniature red leather tent with a dome-shaped top was used for carrying the idols and cultic objects of the tribe. Some *qubbahs* were large enough to erect upon the ground, while others were smaller and were mounted upon the backs of camels. Such tents were credited with the power of guiding the tribe in its journeys, and in time of war were particularly valuable for the degree of protection which they afforded. The *qubbah* possessed an innate sanctity which was only slightly inferior to that of the sacred cultic objects which it housed. It was used as a rallying point, a place of worship, and a locale for the giving of oracles. Since the majority of tents in antiquity were dark in color, the fact that the sacred shrine was a conspicuous red (cf. Exod. 25:5) indicates a religious tradition which reaches back to remote antiquity. Other forms of portable tent-shrines have been preserved on basreliefs, notably one from the time of Rameses II (c. 1301-1234 B.C.) which shows the tent of the divine king placed in the center of the Egyptian military camp. Another from the Roman period at Palmyra in Syria depicts a small domed tent erected on the back of a camel.

At Sinai, Moses was given a divine revelation concerning the nature, construction and furnishings of the tabernacle (Exod. 25:40). The work was carried out by Bezaleel, Oholiab and their workmen, and when the task was accomplished the tent was covered by a cloud which enshrouded the divine glory (Exod. 40:34).

The descriptions of the tabernacle in Exodus 26-27 and 35-38 make it clear that the structure was a portable shrine. Particularly characteristic of its desert origins are the tent curtains, the covering of red leather, and the acacia wood used during the construction. While it is possible to be reasonably certain about the ground plan of the Mosaic tabernacle, there are a number of problems connected with the terminology used in relation to the structure itself. The tabernacle stood in an outer enclosure or court, described in Exodus 27:9-18 and 38:9-20. Taking the ancient Hebrew cubit to indicate a linear measure of 18 inches, the dimensions of the enclosure were 150 feet in length and 75 feet in width. The sides were covered with curtains made from finely-woven linen. They were about seven feet long and were fastened at the top by hooks and at the bottom by silver clasps to 60 supporting pillars of bronze, placed at intervals of some seven feet. The enclosure thus formed was uninterrupted apart from an opening in the E wall which was screened by linen curtains embroidered in red, purple and blue. These hangings were about 30 feet wide, while those at either side of the entrance were a little over 20 feet wide. The pillars had capitals (KJV "chapiters") overlaid with silver, and were set in bases (KJV "sockets") of bronze. They were held in position by bronze pins (Exod. 27:19; 38:20).

Within this open court the various types of sacrificial offerings were presented and the public acts of worship took place. Near the center was situated the great altar of burnt offering made from acacia wood overlaid with bronze (Exod. 27:1-8), measuring nearly eight feet square and about five feet in height. Its corner projections were known as the "horns" of the altar. The various sacrificial implements associated with this altar were also made of bronze. A fire which had been miraculously kindled burned continuously on the altar, and was tended by the priests (Lev. 6:12; 9:24). Almost in the center of the court was the bronze laver which was used by the priests for ritual ablutions (Exod. 30:17-21).

To the W end of the enclosure, parallel to the long walls, stood the tabernacle itself. A rectangular structure about 45 feet by 15 feet, it was divided into two parts, a holy place and a most holy place. The basic constructional material was acacia wood, easily obtainable in the Sinai peninsula, fashioned into 48 "boards" some 15 feet in height and a little over two feet in width, overlaid with gold. The KJV "board" (*qerashim*) should be rendered "frame," since the same word is found on a Canaanite tablet describing the "throne room" (i.e., a trellis pavilion) of the deity El. When the vertical arms (*yadhoth*) were joined to the acacia frames the same general effect would be produced. The resultant structure would be light in weight yet sufficiently sturdy for ritual purposes. The base of the trellis was set in a silver fixture, and the whole was held together by horizontal bars at the top, middle, and bottom.

The completed structure was divided into two compartments by a curtain on which cherubim were embroidered in red, purple, and blue, and which was suspended on four acacia supports. The outermost of these two areas was known as the holy place, and was about 30 feet by 15 feet in area. The innermost part of the tabernacle, the "holy of holies" or most holy place was 15 feet square. The entrance to the tabernacle was screened by embroidered curtains supported by five acacia pillars overlaid with gold.

The wooden framework of the tabernacle was adorned by ten linen curtains (Exod. 26:1-7), embroidered and decorated with figures of cherubim. It measured about 40 feet in length and six feet in width, being joined in groups of five to make two large curtains. These were then fastened together by means of loops and golden clasps (KJV "taches") to form one long curtain 60 feet long and 42 feet wide. This was draped over the tabernacle proper in such a way that the embroidery was visible from the inside only through the apertures of the trellis work. Three protective coverings were placed over these curtains. The first was made of goat's hair and measured 45 feet long and six feet wide; the second consisted of red-dyed rams' hides, while the third was made of *tahash*-leather (KJV "badger's skins"). Much speculation has centered upon the latter term, and it appears to be connected etymologically with an early Egyptian word *tj-h-s*, used technically of treating or processing leather. Thus the Hebrew would imply a specially finished covering of leather.

The information furnished in Exodus makes it difficult to decide whether the tabernacle proper had a flat, somewhat sagging drapery roof, or one which was tent-like in shape with a ridge-pole and a sloping roof. Present day models of the tabernacle vary in their interpretation of this question. Historically speaking, if the influence of the desert-tent was predominant there may well have been some peak or apex to the structure. If, however, the tabernacle had anything in common with the design of contemporary Phoenician shrines, a flat roof would probably result.

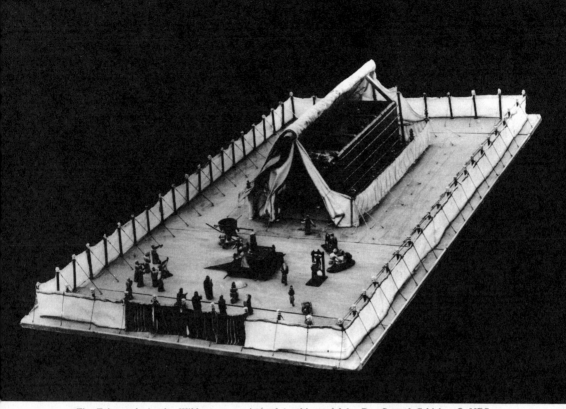

The Tabernacle in the Wilderness as pictured in this model by Dr. Conrad Schick. © MPS

Exodus 25:10-40 described the furniture of the sanctuary. The holy place, or outer chamber of the tabernacle, contained a table of showbread, a small acacia-wood structure overlaid with gold measuring three feet in length, 18 inches in breadth and a little over two feet in height. According to Leviticus 24:5-9, 12 cakes were placed on this table, along with dishes, incense bowls and flagons of gold. The bread was renewed each week, and was placed in two heaps upon the table. Nearby stood the elaborately-wrought *menorah* or seven-branched candlestick of pure gold. A carefully-executed floral motif was a feature of its design, and associated with the candlestick were golden snuffers. The furnishings of the holy place were completed by the addition of a gold-covered altar of incense, about 18 inches square and three feet in height. Like the great bronze altar it had projections on each corner, and like the table of showbread had golden rings and gold-covered stave to enable it to be moved readily.

The furniture of the innermost shrine, the most holy place, consisted entirely of the ark of the covenant. This was a small, box-like structure of acacia wood whose length was just under four feet, while the breadth and height were slightly above two feet. It was covered on the inside and outside with sheet gold, and had golden rings and staves like the table of showbread and the altar of incense. The lid of the ark, the "mercy seat," was covered with solid gold. On each end was a golden cherub whose wings stretched towards the center of the lid. The precise appearance of the cherubim is a matter of some uncertainty, but in the OT they were generally represented as winged creatures having feet and hands. Some ivory panels unearthed at Samaria depict a composite figure having a human face, a four-legged animal body and two elaborate, conspicuous wings.

The ark was the meeting place of God and His people through Moses, and contained the tablets of the law (Exod. 25:16,22). According to Hebrews 9:4 a pot of manna and Aaron's rod were also placed in the ark. An elaborately-worked veil separated the most holy place from the outer compartment of the tabernacle, and when the Israelites journeyed from place to place the sacred ark was secluded from view by being wrapped in this curtain. Consequently the ark was normally seen only by the high priest, and that on very special ceremonial occasions.

In the tabernacle all the sacrifices and acts of public worship enjoined by the law were undertaken. A wealth of detail surrounds the legislation for sacrificial offerings in the Mosaic code, but for practical purposes they could be divided into two groups, animal and vegetable. Flour, cakes, parched corn, and libations of wine for the drink-offerings constituted the normal vegetable sacrifices, and were frequently offered in conjunction with the thanksgivings made by fire (Lev. 4:10-21; Num. 15:11; 28:7-15). Acceptable animals were unblemished oxen, sheep and goats, not under eight days old and normally not older than three years (cf. Judg. 6:25). In cases of poverty doves could be offered as a sacrifice (Exod. 12:5; Lev. 5:7; 9:3f), but fishes were not acceptable. Human sacrifice was explicitly prohibited (Lev. 18:21; 20:25). Salt, an emblem of purity, was employed in conjunction with both the vegetable and slain offerings. The sacrifices were normally presented to the officiating priests in the outer court of the sanctuary, but on occasions were offered elsewhere (Judg. 2:5; I Sam. 7:17, etc.). In all sacrifices it was necessary for the worshiper to present himself in a condition of ritual purity (Exod. 19:14). In animal sacrifices he then identified himself with his offering by laying his hand upon it and dedicating it to the purposes of atonement through vicarious sacrifice. Afterwards the blood was sprinkled near the altar and the tabernacle proper. When worshipers partook of a sacrifice in the form of a meal, the idea of communion with God was enhanced. On the Day of Atonement the nation's collective sins of inadvertence were forgiven, and on that occasion only the high priest entered the most holy place.

According to Exodus 40:2,17 the tabernacle was set up at Sinai at the beginning of the second year, fourteen days before the passover celebration of the first anniversary of the Exodus. When the structure was dismantled during the wanderings, the ark and the two altars were carried by the sons of Kohath, a Levite. The remainder of the tabernacle was transported in six covered wagons drawn by two oxen (Num. 7:3 seq.).

For over 35 years during the wilderness period the tabernacle stood at Kadesh, during which time the ordinary sacrifices were apparently not offered consistently (cf. Amos 5:25). Apart from the comment that the ark preceded the Israelites when on the march (Num. 10:33-36), little is said of the tabernacle during the sojourn in the Sinai peninsula.

Under Joshua the first site of the tabernacle in Canaan was probably at Gilgal (Josh. 4:19), though there is no direct mention of this. Probably an early location was at Shechem, where the desert covenant was renewed (Josh. 8:30-35). During the lifetime of Joshua the tabernacle was settled in Shiloh, in Ephraimite territory, to avoid disputes and jealousy on the part of the tribes. Perhaps the degree of permanence associated with this site led to the designation of the structure by the term "temple" (I Sam. 1:9; 3:3). This may indicate that the fabric of the original tabernacle had become worse for wear, and that it had been replaced by a more substantial building. Whatever may have been the case, Shiloh was the central sanctuary until the ark was captured by the victorious Philistines after the battle of Ebenezer (c. 1050 B.C.).

The subsequent history of the tabernacle is somewhat obscure. Saul established it at Nob, close to his home in Gibeah, but after he massacred the priests (I Sam. 22:11ff) the tabernacle was transferred to Gibeon (I Chron. 16:39; 21:29), perhaps by Saul himself.

When David wished to institute tabernacle religion in his capital city of Jerusalem, he prepared a place for the ark and pitched a tent in the tradition of the Gibeon tabernacle (II Sam. 6:17ff). The ark was brought from Kirjath-jearim and subsequently lodged in the Davidic tabernacle with due ceremony. This act climaxed David's plan to give the security and legitimacy of religious sanction to his newly-established monarchy. The altar of the tabernacle at Gibeon was used for sacrificial worship until the time of Solomon, when both it and the Davidic tabernacle were superseded by the building of the temple. The new edifice incorporated all that remained of earlier tabernacle worship (I Kings 8:4) and at that point the history of the tabernacle terminated.

Some of the archaic technical terms associated with the tabernacle call for comment. The designation 'ôhĕl mō'ĕdh (Exod. 33:7 et al) or "tent of meeting" was first applied to a structure which antedated the tabernacle proper. It was pitched outside the camp, and Joshua was its sole attendant (Exod. 33:11) in the absence of a regularized priesthood. It was a place of revelation, where the people met with God. The word mō'ĕdh has been discovered in an Egyptian document dated c. 1100 B.C., referring to an assembly of the citizens of Byblus. The term occurs again in Isaiah 14:13, where the reference is to the assembly of the gods in the remote northern regions, a popular theme in pagan Canaanite writings. The "tent of meeting" or "tabernacle of the congregation" referred to in Exodus 33 is apparently an interim structure, based on the pattern of a simple desert shrine. It combined political and social functions with the religious revelations given by God to His covenant assembly.

The word mishkan, commonly used to designate the tabernacle, is related to the ordinary Canaanite word for "dwelling-place," and meant originally a tent, thus reflecting the nomadic background of tabernacle worship. A related verb, shakhan (KJV "dwell"), is used of God being "tabernacled" with His people (Exod. 25:8; 29:45 et al). This usage is found in a number of ancient Semitic writings and means "to encamp." The sense is that of God's revealing Himself on earth in the midst of His chosen people. This is clearly distinguished from the use of the verb yashav, "to dwell" "inhabit," which is only used of God dwelling in heaven. This subtle distinction was noted by the Apostle John when he recorded that the word became flesh (i.e., a body) and dwelt (eskenósen, literally, was tabernacled) amongst us (John 1:14). The doctrine of the shekinah glory, which grew up in the intertestamental period, was also related to the words shakhan and mishkan, denoting a local manifestation of Divine glory.

A degree of symbolism was naturally attached by the Hebrews to various aspects of the tabernacle. The structure typified God dwelling with His people (Exod. 25:8), while the ark of the covenant spoke particularly of His presence and forgiving love. The 12 cakes of showbread represented the Twelve Tribes dedicated to divine service. The menorah typified Israel as a people called to be the children of light (cf. Matt. 5:14ff), and the ascending incense symbolized the act of prayer (cf. Rev. 5:8; 8:3). The writer of Hebrews interpreted the tabernacle proper in terms of its twofold division typifying the earthly and heavenly aspects of Christ's ministry. The old tabernacle was but a shadow of the true ideal (Heb. 8:5; 10:1), the latter being pitched by God, not man (8:2). The language of Ephesians 5:2 is distinctly reminiscent of Levitical sacrificial terminology, and the Evangelists were sufficiently impressed by the symbolism of the rent veil to point out that Christ had opened up for all a way into the most holy place. In the early Church and in later times more elaborate, sometimes even fanciful, interpretations were imposed upon the structure and ritual of the tabernacle.   R.K.H.

TABITHA (tăb'ĭ-thà, Aram. Tabeithá; Gr. Dorcás, meaning, in Greece, a roe, in Syria and Africa, a gazelle), the name of a Christian woman disciple who lived in Joppa and made clothing to give to poor widows. When she died, Peter was summoned, and he raised her from death (Acts 9:36-43).

TABLE (Heb. lûah, Gr. pláx, writing tablet). The law was engraved on stone tablets (Exod. 24:12; II Cor. 3:3; Heb. 9:4). Of undefined material (Isa. 30:8; Hab. 2:2; Luke 1:63 Gr. pinakídion). Figuratively of the heart (Prov. 3:3; 7:3; Jer. 17:1). Heb. mēsav (S. of Sol. 1:12 RSV) and Gr. klíne (Mark 7:4 see ASV, RSV note) mean "couch." Heb. shuleban, originally a leather mat spread on the ground (Ps. 23:5; 78:19); the table of the shewbread (Exod. 25:23, etc.; Heb. 9:2 Gr. trá-

Mount Tabor, in Galilee, the traditional Mount of Transfiguration. © MPS

peza) made of acacia wood overlaid with gold. Kings, queens and governors had dining tables (I Sam. 20:29; I Kings 18:19; Neh. 5:17); also private persons (I Kings 4:10; Job 36:16). Psalm 128:5 is an attractive picture of a family table. Gr. *trápeza*, a four-legged table, is used of dining tables (Luke 22:21; 30; Acts 6:2). To eat under the table was for dogs and the despised (Judg. 1: 7; Matt. 15:27; Luke 16:21). Moneychangers used tables (Matt. 21:12, etc.). Communion is served from the Lord's table (I Cor. 10:21).   E.R.

TABLE OF SHEWBREAD (See Tabernacle)

TABLES OF THE LAW, stone tablets on which Moses wrote the ten commandments (Exod. 24:3, 4a,12; 31:18; Deut. 4:13; 5:22). It is said that God wrote them with His finger, though He dictated them to Moses. When Moses came down from the mountain and saw the worship of the golden calf, he threw down the tablets, breaking them (Exod. 32:15; 19; Deut. 9:9-17; 10:1-5). At God's command, Moses again went up the mountain with two new tablets, and wrote the law anew (Exod. 34: 1-4,27-29). Though God said "I will write," He also said to Moses, "Write these words." Moses put these tablets in the ark (Deut. 10:5) where they were in the time of Solomon (I Kings 8:9 = II Chron. 5:10). They are referred to in the NT (II Cor. 3:3; Heb. 9:4).

TABLET (See Dress)

TABOR (ta′bêr). 1. A mountain in Galilee where the borders of Issachar, Zebulun and Naphtali meet (Josh. 19:22). On its slopes Barak gathered 10,000 men of Naphtali and Zebulun (Judg. 4:6, 12,14; 5:18) including contingents from some other tribes (5:13-15), to fight against Sisera and the Canaanite army at Megiddo. Here Zeba and Zalmunna, kings of Midian, killed Gideon's brothers (8:18,19). This commanding height was long a sanctuary of idolatrous orgies (Hos. 5:1). Mt. Tabor is E of Nazareth, SW of the Sea of Galilee, NE of the plain of Esdraelon. From its summit, 1843 feet above sea level, the Hill of Moreh rises to the S, with Mt. Gilboa beyond. To the N, beyond the N Galilean hills, rises Mt. Hermon, with which it is linked in Psalm 89:12. With Carmel it is compared to the mass of Nebuchadnezzar's advance against Egypt (Jer. 46:18). An-

cient tradition places the Transfiguration here, although it is far from Caesarea Philippi, and can be called "exceeding high" only because of the extensive view. But six days would have sufficed to make the journey from Caesarea Philippi to Mt. Tabor (Matt. 16:13; 17:1 and parallels), hence the identification is not impossible. A recently built Franciscan church, monastery and hostel, perpetuating the tradition, now crown the summit.

2. The plain of Tabor, or (ASV, RSV) oak of Tabor (I Sam. 10:3). Samuel told Saul he would meet men bearing gifts here, as a sign of God's favor. Geographical notes in the context (9:5-10: 10) have led to the opinion that this oak cannot have been on Mt. Tabor, in which case its site is uncertain. Anciently and until recently Mt. Tabor was heavily forested. The oak or terebinth (ASV margin) might have been a well-known sacred tree or grove.

3. A Levite city of the sons of Merari, in Zebulun (I Chron. 6:77). Some identify it with the village of Dabareh or Dabrittha, modern Debûriyeh, on the western slope of Mt. Tabor, whose name may perpetuate the memory of the prophetess and judge, Deborah, or Judges 4 and 5.   E.R.

TABRET (See Musical Instruments)

TABRIMMON, TABRIMON (tăb-rĭm′ŏn), son of Hezion and the father of Benhadad, king of Syria (I Kings 15:18). Tabrimon in KJV.

TACHE (tăch, Heb. *qerāsîm, a clasp*), a clasp of gold, to couple the cloth curtains of the tabernacle (Exod. 26:6; 36:13); of bronze, to couple the goat's hair curtains (26:11; 36:18). The veil hung from the clasps in a manner not explained (26:33). Taches (RSV, *hooks*) are associated with the frame of the tabernacle (35:11; 39:33). In all other references ASV, RSV have "clasps."

TACHMONITE, TACHEMONITE (tăk′mō-nīt, Heb. *tahkemōnî*), the family of David's chief captain (II Sam. 23:8) who sat in the gate (KJV) or Josheb-basshebeth (ASV, RSV); the same as Jashobeam, a Hachmonite (I Chron. 11:11). The text of both verses is difficult.

TACKLING (Heb. *hevel, rope*, Gr. *skeué, equipment, ship's tackle*), refers either to the hawsers (Isa. 33:23) or furniture (Acts 27:19) of a ship.

General view of Roman ruins at Tadmor, near Damascus in Syria. The Roman name for the city was Palmyra. © MPS

TADMOR (tăd'môr, Heb. *tadhmōr*), a city in the desert NE of Damascus. In patriarchal times a much-traveled road ran through it from Damascus N to Haran. When Israel was in Egypt, a caravan route already ran eastward from Qatna to the Euphrates. Solomon either built a new city close by, or rebuilt the old, after his conquest of Hamath-zobah (II Chron. 8:4). The context (8:3-6) mentions Solomon's building projects in various parts of his dominion. In the parallel passage in I Kings 9:18 KJV, Tadmor is spoken of as "in the wilderness, in the land." ASV has Tamar, RSV "Tamir in the wilderness, in the land of Judah." The Heb. consonantal text has *tmr*, which should represent Tamar; but which is pointed with the vowel signs of Tadmor; and so it was traditionally read. The context in I Kings 9:15-19 also speaks of many places throughout Solomon's kingdom, though in a different order (from II Chron. 8:3-6), so that it is possible that the two Tadmors are identical. If so, the added "of Judah" in RSV must be rejected. There are textual variants which would yield either "in the wilderness of Aram (Syria)" or "In the wilderness of the South (Negev)" instead of "in the wilderness, in the land" in I Kings 9:18. In NT times and later Tadmor or Tudmur became Palmyra, city of palm trees, a magnificent and wealthy city on the caravan route eastward from Emesa to Babylon and to Dura. Excavations reveal impressive Roman ruins. Palmyra enjoyed its greatest fame and prosperity under its Roman-appointed king Odenatus and his widow Zenobia, who made herself queen and defied the Romans. The ruins include Corinthian columns and a temple to the sun.   E.R.

[T]AHAN, TAHANITE (tā'hăn-īt, Heb. *tahan*). 1. A son of Ephraim and founder of a tribal family (Num. 26:35).

2. A descendant of the same family in the fourth generation (I Chron. 7:25).

[T]AHAPANES, TAHPANHES (tà-hăp'à-nēz, Heb. *'ahpanhēs*), a fortress city at the eastern edge of [t]he Nile Delta, on the eastern border of Egypt, on an old caravan road to Palestine and beyond; early a Greek settlement, by them named Daphnae, perpetuated in the modern Tell Defenneh. Jeremiah saw it as powerful enough to break "the crown" of Judah. Hither Jews fled after the fall of Jerusalem (Jer. 2:16 KJV Tahapanes, ASV, RSV Tahpanhes; 43:1-7). Here Jeremiah (43:8-11; 44:1; 46:14) prophesied its destruction; Ezekiel also (30:18, Tehaphnehes). During their century it was a city of trade and the manufacture of pottery and jewelry. Excavations have uncovered ruins of this period.

TAHASH (tā'hăsh, Heb. *tahash*), a son of Reumah, concubine of Nahor, Abraham's brother (Gen. 22: 24 KJV, Thahash).

TAHATH (tā'hăth, Heb. *tahath, below*). 1. A Kohathite Levite, son of Assir and father of Uriel (I Chron. 6:24,37).

2. Son of Bered, grandson of Shuthelah the son of Ephraim (I Chron. 7:20). Also the name of the 24th station of Israel from Egypt, and the 11th from Sinai (Num. 33:26,27).

TAHPENES (tà'pēn-ēz, Heb. *tahpenês*), the Egyptian queen who brought up Genubath, the son of her sister and of Hadad, the Edomite adversary of David and Solomon (I Kings 11:14-22).

TAHREA (tà'rē-à, Heb. *tahrēa'*), a grandson of Mephibosheth, son of Micah, and so a descendant of Saul through Jonathan (I Chron. 9:41; called Tarea in 8:35).

TAHTIM-HODSHI (tà'tĭm-hŏd'shī), a town at the northern limit of David's census (II Sam. 24:22). RSV, following a Septuagint reading, translates "to Kadesh in the land of the Hittites." Kadesh on the Orontes was the southern Hittite capital.

TALE, in KJV renders several Heb. and Gr. words which in ASV, RSV are translated according to their different meanings: a sigh (Ps. 90:9); number (Exod. 5:8,18); count (I Chron. 9:28); slander (Ezek. 22:9); idle talk (Luke 24:11).

TALEBEARING, slander, forbidden in the law (Lev. 19:16, see RSV); reproved in Proverbs 11:

13; 20:9, RSV *gossiping*). A word meaning "whisperer" (so ASV, RSV) is used in Proverbs 18:8; 26:20,22. (See also I Tim. 5:13.)

TALITHA CUMI (tă-lē'thả kŏŏ'mē), the Aramaic words which Jesus spoke when He raised Jairus' 12-year-old daughter from death (Mark 5:41). They are intimate and endearing, and might be rendered, "Little lamb, get up."

TALMAI (tăl'mī, -mā-ī, Heb. *talmay*). 1. A son of Anak in Hebron and probably the founder of the family of the Anakim, driven from Hebron by Caleb (Num. 13:22; Josh. 15:14; Judg. 1:10).
2. A king of Geshur, whose daughter Maacah was one of David's wives and Absalom's mother (II Sam. 3:3; 13:37; I Chron. 3:2).

TALMON (tăl'mŏn, Heb. *talmôn*), a Levite porter and founder of a tribal family, members of which returned with Zerubbabel and served as porters in the new temple (I Chron. 9:17; Ezra 2:42; Neh. 7:45; 11:19; 12:25).

TALMUD (tăl'mŭd), a collection of Jewish writings of the early Christian centuries. There is a Palestinian Talmud, and a later, more authoritative, much longer Babylonian Talmud. Each consists of Mishnah and Gemara. Mishnah grew out of oral tradition, whose origin is obscure. The Mosaic Law did not cover all the needs of a developing society, and the defect was supplied by oral rabbinical decisions. When, to preserve these, they came to be written down, a further need was felt for a commentary on them. This function the Gemara fulfils. The scope of the Talmud may be seen in the titles of the six parts of the Mishnah: Seeds, relating to Agriculture; Feasts; Women and Marriage; Civil and Criminal Law; Sacrifices; Clean and Unclean Things and their Purification.

TAMAH (tā'mả, Heb. *temah*), the children of Tamah (Neh. 7:55) or Thamah (Ezra 2:53) were Nethinim or temple-servants (RSV) who returned from exile with Zerubbabel. ASV, RSV Temah.

TAMAR (tā'mêr, Heb. *tāmār, palm tree*). 1. The wife of Er; then Levirate wife of Onan; by whom, after the death of Onan, her father-in-law Judah had twin sons, Perez and Zerah (Gen. 38). She is remembered in Ruth 4:12, in the genealogy in I Chronicles 2:4, and her name is recorded as that of one of the women in the ancestral line of Jesus (Matt. 1:3 KJV Thamar).
2. A daughter of David and sister of Absalom, whom her half-brother Amon violated (II Sam. 13:1-33).
3. The daughter of Absalom (II Sam. 14:27).
4. A place at the SE corner of the boundary of the future Holy Land as described in Ezekiel's vision (Ezek. 47:18,19; 48:28).
5. A city in Syria, more commonly known as Tadmor, later Palmyra. See TADMOR.

TAMIR (See Tadmor)

TAMMUZ (tăm'ŭz, Heb. *tammûz*), a fertility god widely worshiped in Mesopotamia, Syria, and Palestine; equivalent to Osiris in Egypt and Adonis of the Greeks. His consort was the goddess Ishtar (Astarte or Ashtoreth). Their cult involved licentious rites. Tammuz was supposed to have been killed by a wild boar, while shepherding his flocks. His wife rescued him from the underworld. His death was taken to represent the onset of winter. The long dry season was broken by spring rains when he came to life again. The fourth month of the Babylonian and later Jewish calendar was named for him (June-July). The only mention of him in the Bible occurs in connection with the custom of women mourning for Tammuz (Ezek. 8:14),

which, being observed at the very gate of the temple of the true God, seemed to the prophet one of the most abominable idolatries. His Greek name Adonis is derived from the Phoenician and Hebrew word for "Lord."

TANACH (See Taanach)

TANHUMETH (tăn-hū'mĕth, Heb. *tanhūmeth*), a Netophathite and father of Seraiah, one of the Hebrew captains who joined Gedaliah at Mizpah (II Kings 25:23; Jer. 40:8).

TANIS (See Zoar)

TANNER, TANNING (See Occupations and Professions)

TAPHATH (tā'făth, Heb. *tāphath*), Solomon's daughter, wife of the son of Abinadab, Solomon's commissariat officer in Dor (I Kings 4:11).

TAPPUAH (tă-pū'ả, Heb. *tappûah*). 1. A city whose king Joshua conquered (Josh. 12:17); in the lowland or shephelah of Judah (15:34); location uncertain.
2. A town on the boundary of Ephraim (Josh. 16:8); "The land of Tappuah belonged to Manasseh, but the town of Tappuah on the border of Manasseh belonged to the sons of Ephraim" (Josh. 17:8 RSV). Its spring, En-tappuah, was on the boundary of Manasseh (17:7). Modern Sheikh Abū Zarad.
3. One of the sons or descendants of Hebron (I Chron. 2:43). Beth-tappuah in the hill country of Judah (Josh. 15:53) may have been his home.

TARAH (tā'rả, Heb. *terah*), a stage in Israel's march between Tahath and Mithcah (Num. 33: 27,28 ASV, RSV Terah).

TARALAH (tăr'ả-là, Heb. *tar'ălâh*), a city of Benjamin between Irpeel and Zelah (Josh. 18:27). Exact location unknown.

TAREA (tā'rē-ả, Heb. *ta'ărēa'*), a descendant of King Saul (I Chron. 8:35), written Tahrea in I Chronicles 9:41.

TARES (See Plants)

TARPELITES (tàr'pĕl-īts, Heb. *tarpelāyē'*), the people of a nation from whom the "great and noble Osnappar" transported into the region around Samaria many colonists (Ezra 4:10). KJV has "Asnapper." He was probably Esar-haddon (Ezra 4: 2) or a general under him.

TARSHISH (tàr'shĭsh, Heb. *tarshîsh*). 1. A son of Javan, great-grandson of Noah (Gen. 10:4), and presumably progenitor of a Mediterranean people, as most of these names in the "Table of the Nations" refer not only to individuals but to the people descended from them.
2. A place, presumably in the western Mediterranean region, conjecturally identified by many with Tartessus, an ancient city located on the Atlantic coast of Spain but long lost. Jonah fled to it (Jonah 1:3).
3. "Ships of Tarshish" seems to refer to large ships of the kind and size that were used in the Tarshish trade, for Solomon had "ships of Tarshish" going from Ezion-geber through the Red Sea and on to India, making the round trip in three years (I Kings 10:22).
4. A great-grandson of Benjamin (I Chron. 7: 10).
5. One of the seven princes of Persia and Media who stood in the presence of Xerxes (Esth. 1:14).

TARSUS (tàr'sŭs, Gr. *Tarsós*), a city of Cilicia, the capital of the province from A.D. 72, and the birthplace and early residence of the Apostle Paul, a fact which he himself notes with civic pride (Acts

A street scene in Tarsus, Paul's native city, in Asia Minor. JFW

21:39), echoing a line of Euripides (*Ion* 8) applied to Athens, which the Tarsians appear to have appropriated. The city stood on the Cilician plain, a little above sea-level, and some ten miles inland. The Cydnus provided an exit to the sea, and in ancient times the river course was equipped with artificial dock and harbor facilities. Tarsus was an ancient city, the seat of a provincial governor when Persia ruled, and, in the days of the Greek Syrian kings, the center of a lumbering and linen industry. Acts 18:3 probably refers to an associated skill, the manufacture of a rough goat-hair cloth, known from the same province as "cilicium." During the first century before Christ the city was the home of a philosophical school, a university town, where the intellectual atmosphere was colored by Greek thought.

Tarsus stood, like Alexandria, at a confluence of East and West. The wisdom of the Greeks and the world-order of Rome, mingled with the good and ill of Oriental mysticism, were deep in its consciousness. A keen-minded Jew, born and bred at Tarsus, would draw the best from more than one world. The Jews had been in Tarsus since Antiochus Epiphanes' refoundation in 171 B.C., and Paul belonged to a minority which had held the Roman citizenship probably since Pompey's organization of the East (66-62 B.C.). E.M.B.

Coins from Tarsus. At left, showing the goddess of the city. At right, showing Apollo atop a column, with Perseus and a city god worshiping beside the altar. UANT

TARTAK (tàr'tăk, Heb. *tartāq*), a god worshiped by the Avvites, a people of Assyria who were transplanted from their land to Samaria after its fall to Assyria (II Kings 17:31).

TARTAN (tàr'tăn, Heb. *tartān*), a commander-in-chief of the Assyrian army (Isa. 20:1; II Kings 18:17). A title, not a proper name.

TASKMASTERS (See Occupations & Professions)

TATTENAI, TATNAI (tăt'ĕ-nī, tăt'nī, Heb. *tattenay*), a Persian governor of the territory W of the Jordan who was ordered to assist the Jews in the rebuilding of the temple (Ezra 5:3,6; 6:6,13).

TAVERN (See Inn)

TAVERNS, THREE, the place where the Christian brethren of Rome met Paul (Acts 28:15), near or at Appii Forum, about 33 miles SE of Rome.

TAXES, charges imposed by governments, either political or ecclesiastical, upon the persons or the properties of their members or subjects. In the nomadic period, taxes were unknown to the Hebrews. Voluntary presents were given to chieftains in return for protection. The conquered Canaanites were forced to render labor (Josh. 16:10; 17:13; Judg. 1:28-35). Under the theocracy of Israel every man paid a poll-tax of a half shekel for the support of the tabernacle worship (Exod. 30:13; 38:25,26), and this was the only fixed impost. It was equal for rich and poor (Exod. 30:15). Under the kings, as Samuel had warned the people (I Sam. 8:11-18), heavy taxes were imposed. They amounted to a tithe of the crops and of the flocks besides the forced military and other services which would be imposed. In the days of Solomon, because of his great building program (the magnificent temple, the king's palaces, thousands of stables for chariot-horses, the navy, etc.) the burden of taxes was made so oppressive that the northern tribes rebelled at his death (I Kings 12).

During the days of the divided kingdom Menahem (II Kings 15:19,20) bribed the Assyrian king with a thousand talents of silver to support him, and he raised this from the rich men of his kingdom. Similarly Hoshea (II Kings 17:3) paid heavy tribute to Assyria and on refusing further to pay he lost his kingdom. Later, Pharaoh Necho of Egypt put Judah under heavy tribute, and Jehoiakim oppressively taxed Judah (II Kings 23:33, 35). Under the Persian domination, "tribute, custom or toll" (Ezra 4:13) were forms of taxation, though Artaxerxes exempted "priests, Levites," etc. (Ezra 7:23,24). The Ptolemies, the Seleucidae, and later the Romans, all adopted the very cruel but efficient method of "farming out the taxes," each officer extorting more than his share from those under him, and thus adding to the Jewish hatred of the publicans, among whom were at one time Matthew and Zacchaeus, both converts later. A.B.F.

TEACHER, TEACHING (See Occupations & Professions, School, Synagogue)

TEBAH (tē'bà, Heb. *tevah*), a nephew of Abraham, born to Nahor by his concubine Reumah (Gen. 22:24).

TEBALIAH (tĕb-à-lī'à, Heb. *tevalyāhû*), a son of Hosah, a Merarite Levite, a gate-keeper of the tabernacle under David (I Chron. 26:11).

TEBETH (See Calendar)

TEETH (Heb. *shēn*, Gr. *odoús*). Isaiah 41:15 tells of "a sharp threshing instrument having teeth," literally "possessor of sharp edges," a figure referring to Israel as God's instrument of judgment upon the nations. In Psalm 58:6 "great teeth," literally "biters," could refer either to teeth or jaws. In Proverbs 30:14 "jaw teeth as knives" is clearly figurative, referring to the oppressors of the poor, and the same word in Joel 1:6, "the jaw-teeth of a lioness," is hyperbole, describing the very destructive habits of the locust. In none of the preceding instances is the ordinary word for tooth used. Some of the more frequent uses of the common words are illustrated in the following passages: Genesis 49:12 "his teeth white with milk" probably refers to the purity and holiness of the Messiah; "tooth for tooth" (Exod. 21:24) is of course literal; gnashing with the teeth can be a token of anger (Job 16:9) or of remorse (Matt. 8:12 and several other references to the suffering of the wicked after death) or of contemptuous rage (Lam. 2:16; Acts 7:54). Proverbs 10:26 provides a hint, if one is needed, that the ancients did not have good dental care. Song of Solomon 4:2 speaks of the beauty of teeth.   A.B.F.

TEHINNAH (tē-hĭn′à, Heb. *tehinnâh, entreaty*), son of Eshton of Judah, "father of the city of Na-hash" (I Chron. 4:12).

TEIL TREE (See Plants)

TEKEL (tĕ′kĕl, Heb. *teqēl*), part of the curse of Belshazzar, who was weighed in the balances and found wanting (Dan. 5:25). It means "weighed," from the same root as "shekel" which was a weight long before it was a coin.

TEKOA, TEKOAH, TEKOITE (tĕ-kō′à -ĭt, Heb. *teqôa', tekô'âh*), a city of Judah or an inhabitant thereof. Tekoa lay 12 miles S of Jerusalem and the same distance NE of Hebron. It was fortified by Rehoboam (II Chron. 11:6). Previous to this, Joab, David's cousin and general, had sent to Tekoa for a "wise woman" and intrigued with her to persuade David to bring back Absalom. The prophet Amos describes himself as "among the herdsmen of Tekoa" (Amos 1:1) and later as a "dresser of sycomore-trees" (7:14) and this gives us a hint as to the civilization of the city and surrounding country. Jeremiah warns Judah of the approaching danger from the N (Jer. 6:1). Ruins of the place survive in Takū′a.   A.B.F.

TEL-ABIB (tĕl′à′bĭb, Heb. *tēl 'āvîv*), a place by the river Chebar in Babylonia where Ezekiel visited and ministered to the Jewish exiles (Ezek. 3:15). Not to be confused with the modern city Tel-aviv in Palestine.

TELAH (tē′là, Heb. *telah, fracture*), an early Ephraimite (I Chron. 7:25).

TELAIM (tē-lā′ĭm, Heb. *ha-telā′îm, lambs*), the place where Saul mustered his army against Amalek (I Sam. 15:4); possibly the same as Telem (Josh. 15:24) in Judah. See TELEM.

TELASSAR (tē-lăs′ẽr, Heb. *tela'ssār*), a place mentioned by the Rabshakeh of Assyria as inhabited by the children of Eden, whose gods could not deliver them from the Assyrian kings (Isa. 37:12). It has not been identified.

TELEM (tē′lĕm, Heb. *telem*). 1. A city of Judah near the border of Edom (Josh. 15:24).
2. A porter who put away his foreign wife after the return from captivity (Ezra 10:24).

TEL-HARESHA, TEL-HARSA (tĕl′hà-rē′shà, tĕl′-hàr′sà, Heb. *tēl-harshā'*), a place in Babylonia from which certain people who returned to Jerusalem with Zerubbabel had difficulty in proving that they were truly Israelites (Ezra 2:59; Neh. 7:61).

In the Wilderness of Tekoah, northeast of Hebron. © MPS

TELL (Arabic, Heb. *tēl*), a mound or heap of ruins which marks the site of an ancient city and is composed of accumulated occupational debris, usually covering a number of archeological or historical periods and showing numerous building levels or strata. Ordinarily, city sites were selected in association with certain natural features, such as a spring or other convenient water supply, a hill or similar defense advantage, or trade routes determined by local geography. In the course of the history of a town, many rebuildings would be necessitated because of destruction by war, earthquake, fire, neglect, or like causes. In the Bible, the fact that a city had become only a mound is often regarded as a result of judgment. Deuteronomy 13:16 prescribes that an apostatizing city should be destroyed and reduced to a tell. Joshua executed judgment upon Ai when he burned it and "made it forever a heap of ruins" (Josh. 18:28, RSV). Jeremiah prophesied that Rabbah of Ammon would become "a desolate mound" (49:2, RSV). In harmony with this is the declaration of Jeremiah that in the restoration of the land of Israel "the city shall be rebuilt upon its mound" (30:18, RSV). Joshua 11:13 states that in the northern campaign Joshua did not destroy any of "the cities that stood upon their mounds" (RSV), except Ai (here the KJV missed the point of the text, translating, "the cities that stood still in their strength"). The term *tel* also appears as an element in place-names of living towns; see Ezekiel 3:15; Ezra 2:59; and Nehemiah 7:61.   C.E.D.

TELL EL AMARNA (tĕl-ĕl-à-mär′nà), or more accurately, simply *El Amarna,* is the modern name for Akhetaton, the city built as the capital of Egypt by Akhnaton (Amenhotep IV, c. 1387-1366 B.C.), as a result of his break with the priests of Amon at Thebes. Both the city and the religious innovations of the king did not long survive his reign.

A Tell El Amarna letter, from a city governor in Palestine, appealing to the Egyptian pharaoh for help. BM

Of great historical importance are the clay tablets (more than 350) accidentally discovered here by a peasant woman in 1887. These tablets, written in cuneiform and addressed to Amenhotep III and Amenhotep IV, mainly represent the official correspondence from the petty rulers of Palestine-Syria, but also include letters from the kings of Mitanni, Assyria, and Babylonia. The princes of Palestine-Syria complain of intrigues and of incursions of outsiders and request the sending of Egyptian troops. Among the invaders are the Habiru, whose relationship to the Hebrews, or Israelites, and the Exodus has been much discussed. C.E.D.

TEL-MELAH (těl-mē'là, Heb. *tēl-melah, hill of salt*), a Babylonian town, probably on the low salty district not far N of the Persian Gulf (Ezra 2:59; Neh. 7:61).

TEMA (tē'mà, Heb. *têmā'*). 1. One of the 12 sons of Ishmael and progenitor of a tribe (Gen. 25:12-16).
2. A place at the northern edge of the Arabian desert where the above tribe lived (Job 6:18-20; Isa. 21:14; Jer. 25:23).

TEMAH (See Tamah)

TEMAN (tē'măn, Heb. *têmān, on the right*), i.e. toward the south). 1. A grandson of Esau through Eliphaz (Gen. 36:11,15).
2. An Edomite chief probably not the same as #1 above (Gen. 36:42).
3. A city in the northeastern part of Edom, noted at one time for the wisdom of its people (Jer. 49:7).

TEMANI (těm'à-nī), an inhabitant of Teman (Gen. 36:34).

TEMENI (těm'ě-nī, Heb. *têmenî*), a son of Ashhur (I Chron. 4:6).

TEMPERANCE (Gr. *egkráteia, nephálios, sóphron*). The prime meaning is self-control (Acts 24:25; Gal. 5:23; II Pet. 1:6; I Cor. 9:25). It is not limited to abstinence from liquor. In Acts 24:25 the reference is to chastity. In I Timothy 3:2,11; Titus 2:2 it is the opposite of "drunken."

TEMPLE (Heb. *hêkhāl, bayith,* Gr. *hierón, naós*), the name given to the complex of buildings in Jerusalem which was the center of the sacrificial cult for the Hebrews. This ritual of sacrifices was the central external service of the ancient people of God, and the unifying factor of their religion, at least in OT times. By the time of Christ, the importance of the temple was somewhat lessened because of the place of the local synagogue in Jewish life.

Three temples stood successively on Mt. Moriah (II Chron. 3:1) in Jerusalem. This site is today called the Haram esh-Sherif and is a Muslim holy place. The first temple was built by Solomon, the second by Zerubbabel and the Jews who returned from the Babylonian exile. The third temple, which was in use in the days of Jesus, was begun and largely built by Herod the Great.

Most ancient religions had temples. Indeed, the Canaanite temples found at Megiddo and Hazor are not unlike that of the Hebrews in ground plan. The Jerusalem temple was distinctive in that it contained no idol in the inner sanctum, but only a box (called the ark) containing the two tables of the law, with the worshiping cherubim above.

The central place of the temple in the religious life of ancient Israel is reflected throughout the Bible. The Psalms abound in references to it (42:4; 66:13; 84:1-4; 122:1,9; 132:5,7-8,13-17). The temple was the object of religious aspiration (23:6; 27:4,5). Pilgrimage to the temple brought the people of Israel from the ends of the earth (Ps. 122:1-4; Acts 2:5-11). The visit of Jesus to the temple at the age of 12 is well-known (Luke 2:41-51). Later He exercised some of His ministry there (Matt. 26:55; Luke 19:45; John 7:28,37; 10:23). The early Jerusalem Christians also worshiped there until the break between Israel and the Church became final (Acts 3:1; 5:12,42; 21:26-34).

Solomon's Temple. The great economic and cultural development of the Hebrews during the reigns of David and Solomon led to the desire to build a temple. The tabernacle, the previous sacrificial center (Exod. 35-40), was a simple and impermanent structure brought to Palestine by the Hebrews from their desert wanderings. It was natural enough that David should wish "God's house" to be as grand as his own (II Sam. 7:2). David, however, was not permitted to undertake the construction of this "house" (II Sam. 7:5-7; I Chron. 22:8). He did prepare for it, both in plans and materials (I Chron. 22:1-19; 28:1-29:9) and more especially by arranging its liturgical service (I Chron. 23:1-26:19).

There are no known remains of Solomon's temple. It is clear that it was patterned after the tabernacle, but was much more complex and ornate. The Phoenicians, who were more advanced culturally than the Hebrews, played a great part in the design and construction of the temple. Recently, archeologists have discovered remains in Phoenicia and Syria which have increased our understanding of the details and motifs of the temple at Jerusalem. Especially useful is the temple found at Tell Tainat in Syria, which was built at about the same time as Solomon's. Its architectural details are believed to be the best guide extant today in reconstructing the details of Solomon's temple. Much of this information is to be found in an article by Paul L. Garber, "Reconstructing Solomon's Temple" (BA vol. xiv:1: May 1951), and in a model of the temple made by E. G. Howland (based on Garber's research) pictured in this arti-

An aerial view of the temple area, atop Mount Moriah, as it appears today, now the Haram-esh-Sherif Mosque, the Dome of the Rock. A large part of the old city of Jerusalem is included in the view, and in the right foreground is the Kidron Valley and the Garden of Gethsemane (at the extreme lower right). © MPS

cle. This model is probably a much more authentic reconstruction than the famous one made by Schick in the last century.

The temple was noted for lavish beauty of detail rather than for great size. It was accessible only to the priests; the lay Israelites came to it, but never entered it. Seven years were required to complete the temple, which was dedicated in Solomon's 11th year, c. 950 B.C. (I Kings 6:38), and destroyed when the Babylonians burned Jerusalem in 587 B.C.

The temple was a prefabricated building. It was made of limestone finished at the quarries (I Kings 6:7) in or near Jerusalem. When the stones were brought to the building site they were built into the wall according to plan. From this arose the tradition of the rejected cornerstone (Ps. 118:22; I Pet. 2:6-8). The stone walls were covered with paneling of Lebanon cedar wood, probably finished by skilled Phoenician craftsmen (I Kings 5:6; 6: 15,18). The main descriptions of Solomon's temple are found in I Kings 5:1-9:25 and II Chronicles 2:1-7:22. While many details are uncertain, what can be known of the building with fair certainty is here given.

The temple consisted of three sections: 1. The *Ulam* or porch through which the temple proper was entered. 2. The *Hekhal* or Holy Place, which was lighted by clerestory windows (I Kings 6:4). Its dimensions were 30 feet wide, 60 feet long and 45 feet high. It was paneled with cedar, with gold inlay to relieve the wooden monotony and to give the impression of grandeur. 3. The *Devir* or Holy of Holies (II Chron. 3:8-13), the inner sanctum, a 30 foot cube, windowless and overlaid with gold. The floor was raised and the cubicle was reached by steps from the *Hekhal*. Here God especially manifested His presence by the Shekinah glory cloud.

The temple was built on a nine-foot high platform, which was reached by ten steps, a dramatic approach for religious processions. On this platform, before the entrance to the *Ulam,* stood two pillars, called Jachin and Boaz (I Kings 7:15-22). Possibly these names are the first words of inscriptions carved upon the pillars. Just behind them, doors led to the *Ulam* or porch, a kind of antechamber to the *Hekhal.* The cypress doors were carved with cherubim, palm trees and open flowers inlaid with gold, (I Kings 6:18,32,35). These motifs are frequently found in ancient Near Eastern temple structures.

The *Hekhal* contained ten golden lampstands (I Kings 7:49, not "candlesticks," as in KJV). A lampstand from Herod's temple is pictured on the Arch of Titus in Rome, where it is being carried away by the Roman soldiers after the destruction of Jerusalem in 70 A.D. Twelve tables held the 12 loaves of shewbread ("bread of the presence"). The incense altar (I Kings 7:48), with horns, stood near the entrance of the *Devir.*

The *Devir* contained two guardian cherubim, made of olive wood and adorned with gold. A number of archeological remains lead to the conclusion that these were winged sphinxes, with a lion's body, human face and great wings. They symbolized the majestic presence of God. On the floor beneath them stood the ark of the covenant, the box overlaid with gold, its lid called the mercy seat, upon which the atoning blood was sprinkled on the Day of Atonement (Lev. 16:14,15).

At both sides and at the rear of the temple were built three-storied storage rooms. They were not as high as the central structure and thus the light from the clerestory windows supplied illumination for the *Hekhal.* This clerestory feature would appear to have been an ancestor of the same window arrangement of the medieval cathedrals (recessed

The Howland-Garber model of Solomon's Temple. Front and cross-section. © EGH

window-walls rising above the lower wings or aisle portions). In the chambers around the sanctuary was kept the immense temple treasury (I Kings 7:51).

In the courtyard before the temple stood two objects intimately connected with the temple worship: the sacrificial altar and the laver or molten sea. The altar of burnt offering was the central object in the sacrificial service. It was made of brass (II Chron. 4:1) and probably stood on the great rock which is today covered by the Dome of the Rock on the Haram esh-Sherif.

South of the altar stood the copper alloy laver or molten sea (I Kings 7:23-26; II Chron. 4:2-6). This mammoth cast "sea" was made in the Jordan Valley where clay suitable for molding the metal was to be found. It was 3½ inches thick, about 15 feet in diameter and 7½ feet high, and stood on the backs of 12 bulls, three facing in each direction. Similar animal supports for thrones are known to have existed among Israel's neighbors. The bull was the Canaanite symbol of fertility and associated with Baal (Hadad), the god of rain. The presence of this motif in Solomon's temple suggests that more syncretism may have taken place in the Hebrew religion than is at first evident when one reads the Bible. Some scholars have doubted whether this immense reservoir with a capacity estimated at 10,000 gallons could have practicably been used for the ceremonial washing, especially since ten small lavers are mentioned (II Chron. 4:6), and think that its main purpose was to symbolize that water or the sea is the source of life. The Babylonians broke up and carried off this amazing example of ancient metal casting (II Kings 25:13).

The temple did not stand alone; it was one of a number of royal buildings constructed by Solomon in the new section of Jerusalem, just N of the old city of David. Solomon's own palace, another for the pharaoh's daughter, the House of the Forest of Lebanon, the Hall of Pillars, and the Hall of the Throne (I Kings 7:1-8) were others in this government quarter. Viewed in this context, the temple appears like a royal chapel. The temple was dedicated by Solomon himself. His prayer on that occasion (I Kings 8:22-61) shows a great religious spirit reaching out even to including the pagan nations in the worship of Yahweh.

Above, the Rock Moriah as seen from the dome in the Dome of the Rock mosque, shown below, which stands on the site of the temples of Solomon and Herod. © MPS

Dr. Conrad Schick's famous model of Solomon's Temple. Compare with Howland-Garber opposite. © MPS

Certain changes doubtless took place in the temple during the Hebrew kingdom. Pagan idolatry was occasionally introduced (II Kings 16:10-18; 21:4-9; Ezek. 8:3-18). Pious kings reformed, refurbished and rededicated it (II Chron. 29:3-31; 34:8-33). Foreign kings raided it (I Kings 14:25,26; II Kings 12:18; 14:14; 18:15,16). When Jerusalem finally fell to the Babylonians in 587 B.C., the temple along with the rest of the city was destroyed and its valuable contents carried to Babylon (II Kings 25:8,9, 13-17).

Ezekiel's Temple. Ezekiel the prophet was also a priest. In the early part of his book he predicts that God will judge His idolatrous people by withdrawing His presence from Jerusalem, leaving it to the Gentiles to desolate. But the latter part of the book predicts the reversal of this. Judah and Israel reunited will be regathered. The climax of this vision is the prophet's description of the restored temple of God, with the living waters proceeding from it and the people of God dwelling around it (40-48). *Yahweh Shammah,* "The Lord is there" is the key to this vision; God will yet again dwell among His people. The temple here described is an ideal construction, both like and unlike Solomon's; none ever existed like it and it is difficult to see how any such temple could ever be built.

Differing views have been held concerning the meaning of this temple vision. Those interpreters who look for a very literal fulfillment of the prophecies believe that this temple will be a part of the millennial kingdom, a great world center of the worship of God, located at Jerusalem. The sacrifices mentioned (43:18-27) are regarded as commemorative in nature — looking back to Christ's perfect sacrifice rather than forward to it, as did the OT sacrifices.

Other scholars argue that this description can hardly be taken literally. They maintain that the Hebrews epistle states that the sacrificial system prefigured Christ, and now that His perfect sacrifice has been made, the imperfect types are done away (Heb. 7:11-10:39). John in the Revelation (21:9-22:5) appears to use Ezekiel's temple vision, but he writes not of a millennial temple but of the eternal glory of the church, Thus these interpreters understand Ezekiel's temple as a highly figurative foreshadowing of the new and holy temple of the Lord which is the body of Christ (Eph. 2:11-3:6).

The Restoration Temple of Zerubbabel. The return of the Jews from Babylonian exile (in 538 B.C.), made possible by the decree of Cyrus, was a small and unpromising one. The returnees were few in number and their resources were so meager as to need frequent strengthening from the Jews who remained in Babylon. The temple they built is a good example of this. When the foundation was laid, the old men, who had seen the "first house" (Solomon's temple), wept for sorrow (Hag. 2:3), but the young men, who had been born in exile, shouted for joy (Ezra 3:12). Like most of the reconstruction in that first century of the Second Commonwealth, the temple must have been modest indeed.

Soon after the return, the community began to rebuild the temple. Jeshua the high priest and Zerubbabel the governor were the leaders of the movement. Many difficulties kept the builders from completing the temple until 515 B.C. At that time they were urged on in the work by the prophets Haggai and Zechariah and the building was finished. No description of this temple exists. Its dimensions were probably the same as Solomon's, but much less ornate and expensive.

The Holy Place of the new temple seems to have had a curtain at its front. It had one lampstand, a golden altar of incense and a table of shewbread. Another curtain separated the *Hekhal* from the Holy of Holies. According to Josephus, the Holy of Holies was empty. Evidently the ark had been destroyed in 587 and was never replaced. A single slab of stone marked its place. The Babylonian Talmud asserts that five things were lacking in the new temple: the ark, the sacred fire, the Shekinah, the Holy Spirit, and the Urim and Thummim.

No doubt the temple was repaired and beautified many times in the succeeding centuries, but of this we have no information. Our next knowledge of it comes from the days of Antiochus Epiphanes. In 168 B.C. this Syrian king sought to stamp out the Hebrew religion, robbed the temple of its furniture and desecrated it, forcing the High Priest to sacrifice swine upon its altar. This action precipitated the Maccabean revolt. In 165 the Jews, led by the Maccabees, recaptured, cleansed and rededicated the temple. I Maccabees 4:44-46 tells how they replaced the stone altar of burnt offering with stones that had not been defiled, meanwhile saving the old stones "until there should come a prophet to give an answer concerning them." The story of the rededication of the temple and the miraculous supply of oil for the lamps is perpetuated in the Jewish festival of Hanukkah.

Judas Maccabaeus at this time fortified the temple with walls and towers, making it the citadel of Jerusalem. Sometime during the next century a bridge was built across the Tyropoeon Valley connecting the temple with the Hasmonean palace. The Hasmoneans (a later name for the Maccabees) were both high priests and kings and by this bridge they sought to make the temple easier to defend. All of this points up the fact that the Second Commonwealth period was one of uneasy peace at best, and that the temple henceforth was to be both the religious and military center of the Jews, until, in A.D. 70, the temple fell and the Jews lost both the religious life as they had always known it, and their fatherland as well.

In 63 B.C. the Roman general Pompey captured Jerusalem and took the temple after a hard struggle, breaking down the Hasmonean bridge. Although Pompey did not harm the temple, the Roman consul Crassus plundered it of all its gold nine years later.

The magnificent Herodian temple, as reconstructed in the model of Dr. Conrad Schick. The building, ⌐f gleaming white marble, took tens of years to complete, was really finished only a few years before the destruction of Jerusalem. © MPS

Herod's Temple. Our sources of information concerning Herod's Temple are Josephus the Jewish historian, who flourished about A.D. 70, and who was a priest, and the tract *Middoth* of the Mishnah written at least a century after the destruction of the temple. Neither can be used uncritically, and many details of the Herodian building and service remain uncertain.

Herod the Great (37-4 B.C.) was an indefatigable builder. Many cities and heathen temples had been rebuilt by him and it was natural that he should wish to show his own grandeur by making the modest restoration temple larger, more complex, and much more beautiful. Other motives probably moved him, especially his desire to ingratiate himself with the more religious Jews, who resented his Idumean origin and friendliness with the Romans.

Herod began his work in his 18th year (20-19 B.C.). The Jews were afraid that the work would interrupt the temple service, but Herod went to great lengths to prevent this, rebuilding the old structure piecemeal, never stopping the ritual observances, until an entirely new temple came into being. Since only priests could enter the temple and the inner court, one thousand of them were the masons and the carpenters for that inner area. The "house" itself was finished in a year and a half; eight years were spent on the surrounding buildings and courts which were not finally completed until A.D. 64. The Jews said to Jesus that the temple had been 46 years in building (John 2:20); more than 30 more years were to pass before it was really finished, then only to be destroyed. All speak of the grandeur of the building, which was of white marble, its eastern front covered with plates of gold, which reflected the rays of the rising sun.

The temple area was probably equivalent to the modern Haram esh-Sherif, except that the N end of the Haram was the location of the fortress Antonia. This area, twice as large as that on which Zerubbabel's temple was situated was artificially built up by underground arches (the present

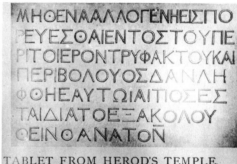

"Solomon's Stables") and fill held in by retaining walls (the Wailing Wall is a part of Herod's western retaining wall). The area, some 26 acres in size, was surrounded by a high wall. Gates on each side led into it, but the principal gates were in the S and W walls, leading in from the city. The eastern gate may have been the Beautiful Gate (Acts 3:2,10) perhaps located where the Golden Gate stands today. Around the inside of the walls ran porches. The finest one was on the S side — the Royal Porch — having four rows of dazzling white marble columns in the Corinthian style, 162 columns in all. The eastern porch was called Solomon's (John 10:23; Acts 3:11; 5:12). During the feasts the Roman guards used to walk on the roofs of the porches to see that order was kept.

Near the NW corner of the temple area was located the fortress Antonia. It dominated the temple and was the headquarters of the guard so often needed to keep the peace. From the stairs which led from the temple precincts to Antonia, Paul delivered his sermon (Acts 21:31-22:21) after having been rescued by the guard from the mob.

Entering the temple area one came to four successive walled courts which surrounded the temple, each more exclusive than the one outside it. The first was the Court of the Gentiles. It was not holy ground and non-Jews were permitted there. Here buying and selling went on; it was here that Jesus cleansed the temple (John 2:14-17). Within the Court of the Gentiles were situated the temple and inner courts, built on a platform 22 feet above the floor of the outer court. Stairways led up to this platform. A stone wall surrounded it, on which wall were placed stones with inscriptions in Greek and Latin forbidding non-Jews from entering on pain of death. Several of these stones have been found (cf. Acts 21:26-28).

On the platform was the inner court. It was the temple precinct and holy ground. Only the covenant people could enter here. It was surrounded by a high wall and against the inner side of this wall were built storage chambers and colonnades. Ritual paraphernalia was kept in some of the chambers and the Sanhedrin is believed to have met in one of them. The inner court was divided into two unequal parts by a cross wall running N and S. The eastern and smaller area was the Women's Court. Here women as well as men were permitted and here were located 13 chests like inverted trumpets, into which offerings for the expenses of the temple services were placed. In this place the poor widow was commended by Jesus when she gave her two copper coins (Mark 12:41-44). For reasons of ceremonial purity only men were allowed in the western area, which contained in its center the temple proper. Around the temple was the Court of the Priests which contained the altar of burnt offering and the laver. Around the Priests' Court was the Court of Israel, accessible to all Jewish males. Here the men gathered when the service was being carried on, to pray and to observe the offering of the sacrifices (Luke 1:10).

In the center of these many courts within courts stood the temple itself, raised 12 steps above the Court of the Priests. Perhaps the forbidding inaccessibleness of the sanctuary is in Paul's mind when he says that Christ "has broken down the dividing wall of hostility" to bring the Gentiles into the fellowship of the people of God (Eph. 2:14).

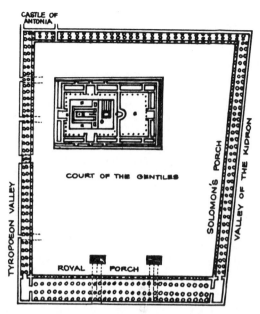

Ground plan of the Temple of Herod, looking northward. UANT

The temple had a porch facing the E, 100 cubits in length and breadth, and 20 cubits deep. It projected 15 cubits beyond the sides of the temple proper, for the temple was only 70 cubits wide. Above the entrance to the porch (which had no door) Herod had placed a golden eagle, which as a Roman emblem (and an unclean bird!) was most distasteful to the Jews. Shortly before his death it was destroyed. In front of the doorway to the *Hekhal* or holy place hung a beautifully colored Babylonian curtain or veil. The inner area of the *Hekhal* was 40 cubits long, 20 cubits broad and 60 cubits high, and it contained the altar of incense in the middle, the table of shewbread on the N, and the lampstand on the S. Only the officiating priests could enter this room, to bring in the incense morning and evening, to trim the lamps daily, and to replace the shewbread every sabbath.

Between the *Hekhal* and the *Devir* or holiest place hung two curtains, with a cubit's space between them. On the Day of Atonement the high priest entered the *Devir* with his censer by going to the S side, passing between the curtains to the N side, and thus emerging into the holiest place. The Gospels refer to these as one veil, which was rent at

A close-up aerial view of the temple area today, as seen from the east. The old fortress, Tower of Antonia, is in the extreme upper right-hand corner. © MPS

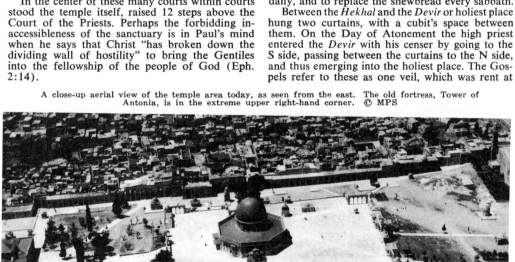

the time of Jesus' crucifixion (Matt. 27:51; Mark 15:38; Luke 23:45). The *Devir* was empty and entered by the high priest once a year, upon the Day of Atonement.

An upper room, 40 cubits high, covered the two chambers of the temple. From this room workmen were let down in boxes to effect needed repairs. Probably this was to avoid needless walking through the sacred house. As in Solomon's, so in Herod's temple, there were storerooms along the sides, except for the front or E, where the porch stood. These were used for storage and for the residence of officiating priests. No natural light came into this temple from roof or windows. It depended on the lamps for its light.

In front of the temple, in the Courtyard of the Priests, stood the altar of burnt offering. It is believed that this altar stood on the great rock which is covered today by the building called the Dome of the Rock on the Haram esh-Sherif. It was made of unhewn stones. There was a fire burning on the altar always. At the SW corner was located a drainage channel for the blood to the Kidron Valley. N of the altar were 24 rings affixed to the ground. To these were tied the sacrificial victims, and there they were killed by slitting the throat. Still further to the N were pillars with iron hooks on which the carcasses were hung for dressing. If this reminds the modern reader of a butcher shop rather than a place of worship, he should remember that this antithesis would have been meaningless in the Biblical world. Not only did the priests live by eating many of the sacrificial victims, but any slaying of an animal for food anywhere was considered a kind of religious act — a sacrifice — and certain rituals were prescribed.

South of the sacrificial altar was the bronze laver or washbasin, where the priests washed their hands and feet. The water was supplied by pipes from the temple spring.

The temple was burned when Jerusalem fell to the Roman armies in August, A.D. 70. Pictures on the triumphal arch of Titus in Rome show the soldiers carrying off the temple furniture as loot. This destruction made complete and final the break between the Temple and the Church and thus helped to establish the Church as a religion completely separate from Israel. The early Christians saw in this forced cessation of the Jewish ritual a proof of the validity of Christ's claims to be the Redeemer foreshadowed by the OT ceremonial law.

Relief on the Arch of Titus in Rome, showing soldiers carrying off the golden lampstand of the temple, as booty. SHH

In the NT the term *temple* is used figuratively in a number of ways. Jesus spoke of the temple of His body (John 2:19,21). The individual believer is a temple (I Cor. 6:19). So also is the Church, but this temple, unlike the earthly one, is equally accessible to all believers (Heb. 6:19; 10:20), now freed by Christ from the ritual limitations of the Old Covenant (Eph. 2:14). The book of Hebrews (especially chaps. 7-10) in great fulness expounds on Christ as the fulfiller of the typology of the temple and its ritual. The culmination of this idea of the "better covenant" is seen in the New Jerusalem where "I saw no temple in the city, for its temple is the Lord God the Almighty and the Lamb" (Rev. 21:22).   J.B.G.

TEMPTATION (Heb. *massâh*, Gr. *peirasmós, trial, proof*). It is essential that a distinction be drawn immediatey between the two antithetical ideas which are embraced within this concept. On the one hand, temptation signifies any attempt to entice into evil; on the other hand, temptation indicates a testing which aims at spiritual good. Unless these two meanings are kept in view, the positive as over against the negative aspect, confusion inevitably results.

In its negative significance, that of enticement to perpetrate evil, temptation in Biblical teaching is traceable to Satan, the malignant being who stands opposed to the divine purposes. The very embodiment of evil — intelligence and will devoid of any morality — Satan is the ultimate source of all desire and action contrary to the holy love of God. Designated the Tempter in Matthew 4:3 and I Thessalonians 3:5 (cf. I Cor. 7:5), his mode of operation is vividly described in Genesis 3, which supplies, typologically and historically, the analogue of our Lord's temptation experience. Employing the serpent as his tool, Satan skillfully undermines man's fidelity to God (I Tim. 2:14-15). Taste, sight, and sinful egoism are utilized to bring about apostasy. "And when the woman saw that the tree was good for food, and that it was pleasant to the eyes, and a tree to be desired to make one wise, she took of the fruit thereof, and did eat, and gave also unto her husband with her; and he did eat" (Gen. 3:6). Obviously, the eating of the forbidden fruit only externalizes the internal apostasy which has preceded the overt act. Here, then, in this aboriginal drama the devices of the Tempter are fully revealed — the lust of the flesh, the lust of the eyes, and the pride of life, as the apostle calls them (I Jn. 2:16). These are Satan's basic stratagems (Eph. 6:11) which he deploys with endless variation. These same stratagems were deployed against our Lord on the threshold of His ministry. In Matthew's account (cf. 4:1-11) the Tempter suggested that Jesus make stones into bread; but the lust of the flesh was resisted. The Tempter next suggested that Jesus cast Himself down from a pinnacle of the temple and be miraculously delivered, thus dazzling the multitude by a sheer wonder; but the lust of the eyes was resisted. Finally, the Tempter suggested that Jesus gain the world and its glory by abandoning His Father and becoming the Devil's accomplice; but the pride of life was resisted. Never once did Jesus waver in His allegiance to God. He refused to sign any declaration of independence; He refused to prostitute His power to selfish ends. Triumphantly He ran the whole gamut of evil enticement. Hence the author of the Epistle to the Hebrews declares that our Saviour was "in all points tempted like as we are, yet without sin" (4:15). And that same author declares that, because of His triumph over temptation, Jesus "is able to succour them that are tempted" (2:18).

In the struggle with temptation one must, consequently, bear in mind that the human agents who entice to evil are only dupes and instruments, almost invariably aware of their deepest motivation (Deut. 13:6; Eph. 2:2; 5:6). He must remember, too, that the temptation is almost invariably camouflaged: evil artfully masquerades as good, appropriating the highest levels of life, and religion especially, for its own malignant purposes (II Cor. 11:14). One must also remember that as fallen creatures men have susceptibility to sin which neither Adam nor the Second Adam had (James 1:14). They must likewise recognize their own frailty and pray, "Lead us not into temptation" (Matt. 6:13). Resolutely they must shun any situation in which they may become the objects of Satanic enticement. Yet in our frailty there is comfort in Paul's assurance, "There hath no temptation taken you but such as is common to man: but God is faithful, who will not suffer you to be tempted above that ye are able; but will with the temptation also make a way to escape, that ye may be able to bear it" (I Cor. 10:13).

The positive significance of temptation is that of testing with the intent of creating spiritual good: it is *proving* with a view to *approving* or *improving* and occasionally *reproving*. Thus God, who as Holy Love can never be the source of evil in any form (James 1:13), tested Abraham (Gen. 22:1). Thus God tested Job, who exclaimed, "But he knoweth the way that I take; when he hath tried me, I shall come forth as gold" (Job 23:10). Thus God still tests His people (I Pet. 1:7; 4:12-13; James 1:2,12). But He tests, even sometimes severely and painfully, only for purposes of reproving and improving (Deut. 8:2-3; 13:3; Judg. 2:20-23; I Cor. 11:32; Heb. 12:4-11) or for purposes of approving. The divine intention in testing is plainly stated in Deuteronomy 8:16.

In a moral universe where conflict rages between the Creator and His adversary, an order characterized by freedom, sin, and faith, even redeemed man must expect to live in spiritual tension (Acts 14:22; Heb. 10:32-34). After all, Jesus Christ did, and the servant is not above his Lord. But by the illumination of Scripture and the enablement of the Holy Spirit (Luke 4:1-13), the servant too can experience blessing and victory after — and in the very throes of — struggle.

The traditional literature on this subject has been greatly enriched by C. S. Lewis: *The Screwtape Letters;* Helmut Thielicke: *Between God and Satan;* and Dietrich Bonhoeffer: *Temptation.*

V.C.G.

TENONS (tĕn'ŭn, Heb. *yādh*, hand), small projections at the lower ends of the tabernacle boards to sink into sockets to hold the boards in place (Exod. 26:17 etc.).

TENT (Heb. *'ōhel*, Gr. *skené*), a temporary dwelling generally made of strong goat's-hair cloth stretched over poles and held in place by cords reaching out to stakes driven into the ground. It is the typical dwelling of nomadic peoples. Tents are of various shapes — round and tapering, flat and oblong. All of the belongings of a nomadic family could normally be carried on one pack animal. A sheikh would, of course, have several tents. The word tent is often used to refer to a habitation generally (Gen. 9:27; I Kings 8:66; Job 8:22; Ps. 84:10), and it is often used figuratively (Isa. 13:20; 54:2; Jer. 10:20).

TENT OF MEETING (See Tabernacle)

The Mount of Temptation (Quarantinia), supposedly the site of Satan's tempting of Jesus. The brook in the foreground flows from Elisha's Fountain. © MPS

TERAH (tē'rà, Heb. *terah*). 1. Son of Nahor (Gen. 11:24-32), lived at Ur of the Chaldees and was an idolater (Josh. 24:2). When God called Abram out of Ur with its civilized idolatry, Terah went as far as Haran in Mesopotamia where he and his family remained till Terah died at 205 years of age; then Abram with his family and his nephew Lot proceeded to Canaan.

2. A wilderness camp of the Israelites (Num. 33:27,28).

TERAPHIM (tĕr'à-phēm, Heb. root and meaning dubious), a term used of a kind of household idol and means of divination. In Genesis 31:19 the teraphim of Laban were stolen by Rachel; these were small enough to be concealed in a camel-saddle (vss. 34-35). They were a valuable possession, for their ownership involved the inheritance of the property of Laban, as is illustrated by the Nuzi tablets. In I Samuel 19:13-16 Michal, by placing such an object in David's bed, deceived Saul's messengers into thinking that David was there but was too ill to receive visitors. This idol resembled a man in size and appearance sufficiently well to make the ruse temporarily effective.

Two kinds of tents: A Bedouin dwelling tent made of papyrus mats, and below, Bedouins holding court in a chief's tent in the Beersheba area. © MPS

Teraphim, or household idols, of the type that Rachel stole from Laban. These are from Nuzi. BA

In the time of the judges, Micah had teraphim among the religious articles of his household shrine (Judges 17:5); these furnishings were coveted and seized by the Danites (18:14-20). In the spiritual revival under King Josiah the teraphim and other "abominations" in Judah and Jerusalem were put away (II Kings 23:24). Zechariah asserted that "the teraphim utter nonsense" (Zech. 10:2, RSV). Hosea prophesied that "the children of Israel shall dwell many days without king or prince, without sacrifice or pillar, without ephod or teraphim" (Hosea 3:4, RSV). Ezekiel included the consultation of teraphim among the divination practices of the king of Babylon preceding the destruction of Jerusalem (Ezek. 21:21).   C.E.D.

TERESH (tē'rĕsh, Heb. *teresh*), a chamberlain of Xerxes ("Ahasuerus") of Persia who attempted to assassinate his master but was discovered by Mordecai and thwarted (Esth. 2:21).

TERRACE (Heb. *mesillâh*), one of a series of steps which Solomon made of algum trees as an approach to the temple (II Chron. 9:11).

TERROR, in ordinary usage, means extreme fear or dread; or sometimes, the one who causes such agitation. The word renders about a dozen Hebrew and Greek words which are rendered also by such words as "dread," "fear," "horror," "terribleness," "ruin," etc. Characteristic are Psalm 55:4, "the terrors of death"; Genesis 35:5, "the terror of God was upon the cities," II Corinthians 5:11, "knowing therefore the terror of the Lord, we persuade men."

TERTIUS (tûr'shĭ-ŭs, Gr. *Tértios*), the scribe or amanuensis of Paul, the writer, at the Apostle's dictation of the Epistle to the Romans. He added a personal salutation (16:22).

TERTULLUS (têr-tŭl'ŭs, Gr. *Tértyllos*), a diminutive of Tertius. It was the name borne by the professional advocate employed by the Jews to state their case against Paul before Felix, the procurator of Judaea (Acts 24:1). A few words only of Tertullus' elaborate oration are given, but enough to reveal the nature of his rhetoric and the character of his accusation. It is not unlikely that the orator was a Roman, for there is a Latin ring about some of his phrases as they appear in Luke's Greek, and his name, of course, is Latin, though this does not necessarily fix his nationality. He was obviously trained in the arts of contemporary rhetoric, and what impressed Luke was his elaborate exordium. Such a subterfuge, wrote Calvin, is "a sign of bad faith." It is rather a traditional courtesy, and the device, albeit purged of mendacity and sycophancy, is to be distinguished also in the opening gambit of Paul's reply (Acts 24:10). E.M.B.

TESTAMENT, a word that occurs several times in the NT as a translation of the Greek *diathéke,* more accurately rendered "covenant." It is true that the Greek word signifies a testamentary disposition, but the NT usually appears to use the Greek word in the meaning rather of its cognate *synthéke,* which accurately renders the OT *berith,* a binding agreement or contract between man and man, or man and God. The earliest account of the institution of the Lord's Supper contains the words: "This cup is the new covenant (testament) in my blood" (I Cor. 11:25). The reference is to Exodus 24:8. A new relation between God and man was thereby created. The imagery in Hebrews 9:15-20 takes in the further notion of a testamentary disposition, operative only after the death of the testator. Hence the Revisers' preference in vss. 16, 17 for the word "testament."   E.M.B.

TESTAMENTS OF THE TWELVE PROPHETS, an apocryphal document that claims to report the last words of the 12 sons of Jacob. It is probably a second century production concocted of traditional material, and containing Christian interpolations. Each patriarch is represented as dealing with the particular vice or virtue which attaches to him in the historical record, and as speaking in elaborate description of judgments and rewards. The work has survived in Greek and Armenian versions. It is obviously inspired by Jacob's commission to his sons from his deathbed (Gen. 49).
                E.M.B.

TESTIMONY, generally "a solemn affirmation to establish some fact" and commonly, among Christians, the statement of one's Christian experience. In Scripture, it usually refers to that which was placed in the ark of the covenant (Exod. 25:21), or to the Word of God (Ps. 119:14,88,99, etc.). In Mark 6:11 shaking off the dust of the feet in leaving an unfriendly city was to be considered as a testimony against it.

TETRARCH (See Occupations & Professions)

TEXTS AND VERSIONS (OLD TESTAMENT). The OT is a book of sacred literature for Jews and Christians, and has no rival in quality or scope of influence among other sacred writings of the world today. It is the focal unit of Judaism and the foundation of Christianity's sacred literature. In Jesus' time it was called "The Scriptures," though Jesus himself often referred to it by its divisional terminology. On the day of His resurrection Jesus declared to the men on the road to Emmaus, "that everything written about me in the law of Moses and the prophets and the psalms must be fulfilled" (Luke 24:44). It was also the Bible of Peter, Stephen, Philip, Paul, and the other early Christians (Acts 2:7; 8:13).

I. Origin of the Old Testament

A. General Discussion: The OT today consists of 39 books, identical with those of the Hebrew Bible, which has a different arrangement. Customary divisions of the English version are Historic, with 17 books: Poetic, with five; and Prophetic (major and minor), with 17. The Hebrew Bible was divided under Law (*Torah*), comprising the Pentateuch; Prophets (*Neviim*): Kings, and Later Prophets, Isaiah, Jeremiah, Ezekiel, and the Twelve Minor Prophets; and Writings (*Kethuvim*), including the eleven remaining books. With certain combinations the Hebrew OT numbered only 24 books. Josephus reduced the number to 22 by further combinations.

B. Canonization: The final confirmation of the books of the Law, the Prophets, and the Writings as exclusively canonical by Jewish scholars cannot be placed later than 400, 200, and 100 B.C. respectively. However, the writing and adoption by consensus doubtless antedated these dates by centuries. Since some contemporary writings were accepted and some rejected during the periods of the above mentioned tripartite divisions, some basis for discrimination was necessary. The critical term for this process is "Canon," derived from the Greek word *Kanon*, "rod," which came from the Hebrew and Old Babylonian words for "reed," meaning "measure." There were no canonical decrees governing selection, but Scriptural authority seems to have been derived from usage by devout Jews, and any pronouncements of measuring methods were only confirmations thereof. Some critics think that the formation of the Canon began in 621 B.C. during Josiah's reign and ended in the Council of Jamnia, A.D. 90. Actually the Council only confirmed the established authority of the books composing our present OT, recognized and accepted before the time of Jesus. The need for some criterion, however, for standardization to insure protection and preservation of holy writ was doubtless long in the minds of the rabbis. Probably the first to sense keenly this need were the scribes, the *Sopherim,* who elaborated a theory of inspiration. They said that inspiration belonged to the prophetic office, and the range of prophetic activity began with Moses and ceased with Ezra (though according to rabbinical writings it ended in the time of Alexander the Great). According to these limitations, any writings before Moses or after the prophets would automatically be apocryphal. Consequently the books of the OT were all inspired writings of men chosen of God, and spanning a period of approximately a thousand years, embraced within the traditional dates of 1450-444 B.C.

C. Authorship. Evidences of authorship and transmission of the respective books of the OT are negligible. The traditional view of authorship, as preserved in the Talmud, has basic validity. "Moses wrote his own book and the section concerning Balaam (Num. 22:2-25:9) and Job. Joshua wrote his own book and (the last) eight verses of the Torah. Samuel wrote his own book and Judges and Ruth. David wrote the Book of Psalms, incorporating the productions of ten elders: Adam (139), Melchizedek (110), Abraham (89), Moses (90), Heman (88), Jeduthun (39, 62, 77), Asaph (50, 73-83), and the three sons of Korah (42, 44-49, 84, 85, 87). Jeremiah wrote his own book and the Book of Kings and Lamentations. Hezekiah and his company wrote Isaiah, Proverbs, the Song of Songs, and Koheleth. The men of the Great Synagogue wrote Ezekiel, the Twelve, Daniel and Esther. Ezra wrote his own book and the genealogies of the Book of Chronicles, including his own" (MHSM ch. II).

Internal and external evidences combine to give a provisional view of Biblical authorship. The cultural development of the Hebrews in correlation with that of their contemporaries may be seen through the eyes of the archeologists. First however, the Scriptural record should be reviewed.

Belief in special revelation to the authors of the OT, of divinely inspired and directed writers, has textual bases. In the Pentateuch numerous claims are made to Moses' divine commission and written contributions. "Jehovah spake unto Moses" occurs again and again in Leviticus. The earliest reference to writing in the Bible is Exodus (17:14), where "The Lord said to Moses, 'Write this

as a memorial in a book' "; and in 24:4 "Moses wrote all the words of the Lord" (Cf. 34:28). In Numbers 33:2 (RSV) the record states that "Moses wrote down their starting places, stage by stage." Deuteronomy 31, verse 9 states that "Moses wrote this law," verse 24 concludes that "Moses had finished writing the words of this law in a Book." Other evidences showing that Moses is the substantial author of the Pentateuch are found in several books of the OT and in the Gospels (Josh. 1:7f; Judg. 3:4; II Chron. 25:4; Ezra 6:18; 7:6; Mal. 4:4; Matt. 8:4; Mark 7:10; 10:5; Luke 20:37; John 5:45-47; 7:19).

In Exodus 24:7 concerning Moses, "Then he took the book of the covenant, and read it in the hearing of the people." The Book of the Covenant (Exod. 20-23) is probably the oldest writing in the OT. It is the nucleus around which the framework of the Pentateuch was built.

II. Texts

A. Fragmentary Scripts. No autograph texts of any Old Testament writing are known to exist today, but the textual critic tries with all available means to reconstruct texts as nearly like the originals as possible. Until 1947, when the Dead Sea Scrolls were discovered, the earliest complete extant manuscripts of the Hebrew Bible were dated about A.D. 1000. There were, however, fragmentary evidences of considerable value, brought to light from time to time by archeologists, contributing to the validity of the Bible claims.

B. The art of writing was known as early as 3,000 B.C. among the old civilizations of the Near East. Temple inscriptions, the Code of Hammurabi, and the Gilgamesh Epic, with accounts of Creation, original sin, and the Flood, antedate Moses by several centuries. Numerous examples of early writing exist to support the claim that Moses, who "was instructed in all the wisdom of the Egyptians," (Acts 7:22), could have and did write the passages claimed for him in the Bible.

C. Antecedents of the Hebrew language may be found in Old Phoenicia, a land on the Mediterranean coast N of Palestine settled by an early wave of Semites. These precocious seafaring people are accredited with giving the world its first alphabet. As early as the sixteenth century B.C. evidences of a Hebrew-Phoenician alphabet are found, from which a standardized script emerged about the tenth century B.C. This is the cursive script, in which the Old Hebrew was written, and that employed for the original writing of the OT books. This script was replaced by the Hebrew-Aramaic square script probably a century before Christ. However, since the Samaritan Pentateuch is in the Old cursive script, the square letters must not have been used until after the schism between Judea and Samaria about 432 B.C. (Neh. 13:28). Modern scholarship dates the Samaritan Pentateuch at 128 or 122 B.C. Furthermore, the transition seems not to have preceded the Septuagint, though the Aramaic square letters were in use centuries before by the Jews in Egypt. Seemingly, the square Aramaic script was gradually adopted by the Jews after the Exile (536-538 B.C.), and used latest in sacred writing. The letter from 'Arsha.ı (c. 410 B.C.), Egypt, is non-Biblical, and is written in the square Hebrew letters. Jesus' reference to the "jot" in the law indicates this type of script in Biblical use in his time (Matt. 5:18).

Other writings discovered in Phoenicia have had valuable bearing on Hebrew philology. Excavations in a mound at Ras Shamra, ancient Ugarit, unearthed a small temple with a library under-

Portion of the scroll of the Book of Isaiah from the Dead Sea Scrolls. PG

The Hebrew Bible is the work of many authors over a period of more than a thousand years, roughly between the fifteenth and fifth centuries B.C. As it grew in size it also grew in sacredness and authority for the Jews.

F. Preservation of the Texts. Two obvious factors have militated against the preservation of autograph writings and archaic texts. First, when transcriptions were made onto new scrolls, the old deteriorating ones were destroyed lest they fall into the hands of profane and unscrupulous men. Second, attempts were made at different times by the enemies of the Jews to destroy their sacred literature. Antiochus Epiphanes (c. 167 B.C.) burned all the copies he could find, and many rolls were destroyed during the Roman wars (c. A.D. 70).

Another hazard of the Scriptures, which threatened accurate transmission, was the repeated copying by hand. Scribal errors and explanatory marginal notes doubtless resulted in slight deviations from the original, but the fidelity of the copyist is amazing. Ezra and his school of scribes, the Great Synagogue, and subsequent rabbinical schools and priests and scribes worked diligently to perpetuate the original Scriptures. It was the Masoretic scholars who devised the present vowel system and accentual marks. Before this the consonantal Hebrew Scripture was not vocalized. Chapter divisions came much later, appearing first in the Vulgate, A.D. 1227 or 1248, and transferred to the Hebrew Bible about 1440. Verses were marked in the Vulgate as early as 1558.

G. The Dead Sea Scrolls. In 1947 some Palestinian herdsmen accidentally stumbled onto a cave in the Judean hills that proved to be a veritable treasure house of ancient scriptures. Thereupon the announcement of the Dead Sea Scrolls was acclaimed by Biblical scholars as the greatest manuscript discovery in modern times. From this and other caves by the Wadi Qumran, NW of the Dead Sea, came a hoard of OT parchments dated 200 B.C. to the first century A.D.

The first major find comprised four scrolls. One of the first documents was a copy of the Book of Isaiah in Hebrew, and another a copy of the first two chapters of the book of Habakkuk in Hebrew, with added commentary. Later discoveries yielded fragments with portions of other Biblical books in Hebrew. The Deuteronomy fragments were written in archaic script. Altogether, the manuscript fragments constitute over 400 books, a few almost intact, and more than 40,000 fragments. Ninety of these books were parts of the Bible, with every OT book except Esther being represented among them.

These scrolls are of great critical value on the basis of such factors as antiquity and authenticity. The scroll of Isaiah A is dated near 200 B.C., while that of Ecclesiastes and the fragments of Exodus and Samuel are estimated by some to be as old as 250 and 225 B.C. respectively.

One valuable contribution of the Dead Sea Scrolls is to provide a critical basis for the study of the three main lines of transmission by which the text of the Old Testament has come down to us. The first of these, and probably the most trustworthy, is the Massoretic Hebrew text of the eighth and ninth century A.D.; the second is the Greek Septuagint; and the third is the Samaritan Pentateuch. The respective forms of Hebrew texts which were the antecedents of these three families seem now to have been varying types of texts current among the people of Israel in general in the clos-

neath. Among the finds were tablets containing script of only 27 different characters. This proved to be archaic Hebrew, dated about 1400 B.C., hence one of the earliest alphabetic writings yet known. Another important discovery on the Phoenician coast was made at Byblos, Old Testament Gebal (Ezek. 27:9). It was a remarkable alphabetical inscription on the Ahirams sarcophagus, dated about 100 B.C. Byblos is the name from which our term Bible is derived.

D. Fragments of the Hebrew Language. From Palestine, the mound of Old Lachish (Josh. 10:31f) yielded a bowl, a jar, and a dagger containing brief inscriptions in alphabetic script, similar to that found in Sinai, and dating probably between 1750 and 1550 B.C. Similar characters inscribed in ink on a potsherd were found at Beth-shemesh from about the tenth century B.C. Twenty-one letters found at Lachish consisted of broken pieces of pottery on which were inscribed archaic Hebrew by a military commander during the invasion of Nebuchadnezzar in 588 B.C. To these may be added fragmentary inscriptions from the Gezer Calendar, c. 900 B.C.; Moabite Stone, c. 800; Siloam Tunnel, c. 700; and numerous others. Prior to the discovery of the Dead Sea Scrolls, the small sheet known as the Nash Papyrus, dated second to first century B.C., was our earliest Biblical Hebrew document. It contains the Ten Commandments and the Shema' (Deut. 6:4).

E. The Bible in the Hebrew Language. The OT was originally written in Hebrew, with the exception of a few chapters and verses in the later books. These were written in Aramaic, a kindred language, and are found in Daniel 2:4 to 7:28; Ezra 4:8 to 6:18; 7:12-26; and Jeremiah 10:11.

The Scriptures were written on animal skins, called vellum or parchment, or on papyrus. Papyrus comes from a water plant of that name from the marshes of the Nile. The glutinous pith was sliced and the stripes laid at right angles and pressed together, making a very smooth and durable paper.

ing centuries of the Second Jewish Commonwealth, and in no sense sectarian. It may be that the Masoretic text was derived from a Babylonian recension, the Septuagint from Egyptian Hebrew, and the Samaritan from a Palestinian text, but it seems obvious that all were used in Judea.

III. Versions of the Old Testament

A. Greek Versions.

1. The Septuagint, whose value can hardly be over estimated, was in popular use in Jesus' time and is often quoted by NT writers. It is a translation of Hebrew into Greek by Jewish scholars in Alexandria, Egypt. The Pentateuch was translated about 250 B.C. and the entire OT completed a hundred years later. The term "Septuagint" is the Latin word for seventy, the number of rabbis who did the translating, probably under orders of Ptolemy Philadelphus. The Greek employed was not the classical idiom but rather anticipated that of the NT, the *Koine*. It was designed to preserve the old religion among the dispersed Jews in a language they commonly used. The oldest extant fragments of the Septuagint today are from a papyrus roll of Deuteronomy, dated about 150 B.C., found on an Egyptian mummy, and now in the John Rylands Library, Manchester, England.

2. Other Greek Versions. Three Greek translations from the Hebrew were made in the second century A.D., but only fragments of them have survived. Aquila, a proselyte Jew, made a very literal translation which became the official Greek version for the Jews. Theodotion, a Christian of Pontus, made a translation between A.D. 180 and 192 which seemed to be partially a revision of the Septuagint. It was a free rendering of the idiomatic Greek and became popular in the early Christian churches. About A.D. 200 Symmachus faithfully translated the Hebrew into good smooth Greek though somewhat paraphrastic. Jerome's commentary on these versions was that, "Aquila translates word for word, Symmachus follows the sense, and Theodotion differs slightly from the Septuagint."

3. The Hexapla was a translation and six-column arrangement by Origen in Caesarea about A.D. 240. This was a kind of harmony of the translations of Aquila, Theodotion, Symmachus, and the Septuagint. It became the authoritative Greek OT for some churches. Only fragments of this work remain.

4. Several Greek manuscripts containing excerpts from the OT have been discovered. The oldest were written on papyrus, and those after the fourth century on vellum. The script of the latter is in "uncials," capital letters written separately, used generally from the third to the tenth century A.D., and in "cursives," from about the ninth to the sixteenth century A.D.

A papyrus manuscript of the minor prophets, in uncials, dated the latter part of the third century A.D., was found in Egypt and is now in the Freer collection, Washington, D.C.

B, *Codex Vaticanus,* dated about the middle of the fourth century A.D., contains most of OT and NT. It is in the Vatican Library where it was known as early as the fifteenth century.

ℵ (*or Aleph*), Codex Sinaiticus, contains a limited fragment of the OT of equal age with B. It was discovered in 1844 by Tischendorf in the Monastery of St. Catherine at Mt. Sinai, and placed in the royal library at St. Petersburg (Leningrad). It was later purchased from the Soviet Government and placed in the British Museum in 1933.

A, *Codex Alexandrinus,* a manuscript in uncials dated in the fifth century A.D., was a gift to King

Page from the Septuagint, Codex B (Codex Vaticanus), dated Fourth Century A.D., now in the Vatican library at Rome. RTHPL

James I and brought to England later in 1628, and placed in the British Museum.

C. *Codex Ephraemi,* contains 64 leaves of the Old Testament dated from the fifth century, and is now in the Bibliothèque Nationale in Paris.

B. Aramaic Versions. The Targums were probably oral translations of the Hebrew Scriptures into Aramaic after the later replaced the Hebrew as the spoken language of the Jews. The Targums contain religious instructions along with interpretations which accompanied the reading of scrip-

A page from the Septuagint, Codex A (Codex Alexandrinus), dated First Century A.D., now in the British Museum. RTHPL

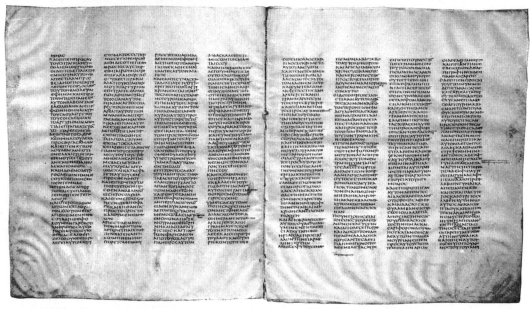

Two pages of the Gospel of Luke, from the Codex Sinaiticus, from Sinai, Fourth Century A.D. The script is in Greek, in uncial letters, on vellum. Photo about 1/6 actual size. BM

ture in the synagogues. Compare Jesus in the synagogue at Nazareth (Luke 4:16-27). Besides the Targum of Jonathan on the Prophets, there are three on the Pentateuch, all of which were put into written form from about the first to the ninth century A.D. The three are the Onkelos (Babylonian), the Jerusalem Targum, and the Fragmentary Palestinian Targum.

C. Syriac Versions. The Peshitta is the Syriac Bible of the Old Testament translated in the second or third century A.D. for the benefit of Christians whose language was Syriac. Many manuscripts survive. The earliest date known on any manuscript of the Bible is found on one containing Genesis, Exodus, Numbers, and Deuteronomy, in the British Museum, and corresponding to A.D. 464.

D. Latin Versions.

1. The Old Latin versions probably originated among the Latin-speaking Jews of Carthage and were adopted by the Christians. An entire Bible in "Old Latin" circulated in Carthage by A.D. 250. There were a variety of Latin versions before Jerome's day, representing three types of Old Latin text: African, European, and Italian.

2. The Vulgate was produced by the scholarly Jerome in a cave in Bethlehem adjacent to what he believed was the Grotto of the Nativity. Jerome translated directly from the Hebrew with references to the Septuagint and Origen's Hexapla. He was commissioned in A.D. 382 by Pope Damasus to make an official revision of the Old Latin Bible. His work was completed in A.D. 405. The Vulgate is a creditable work, though not an infallibly accurate translation of the original text. Rather, it was an interpretation of thought put into idiomatic, graceful Latin. It was virtually without a rival for a thousand years. The Douay Version, translated from the Vulgate, is the authorized Roman Catholic Bible in English.

E. Other Eastern Versions. The Coptic versions were made for Christians in Egypt in the second or third century A.D. The Ethiopic version was made in the fourth or fifth century. The Gothic

version was prepared by Ulfilas about A.D. 350. The Armenian version, beautiful and accurate, was made for Christians of eastern Asia Minor about A.D. 400. A twin to the latter was the Georgian version of the fifth or sixth century. The Slavonic version of the ninth century is preserved in the oldest manuscript of the whole Bible in existence today. It is dated 1499, and known as Codex Gennadius, now in Moscow. The Arabic version, necessitated by the Arabic conquests of the 7th and 8th centuries, was begun by Saadya in the tenth century.

These ancient versions aid the critic in trying to restore the original text and in interpretations. For data on English versions, see BIBLE, ENGLISH VERSIONS.   G.B.F.

TEXTS AND VERSIONS (NEW TESTAMENT). The Bible, and especially the NT, occupies a place which is unique in the literature of ancient times, and not least so in respect to the history of its transmission through the centuries. No other ancient writing approaches it in the number of copies which were made of it from the time it was written until the age of printing; its existing mss. approach the date of its origin far more closely than do the mss. of almost any other piece of ancient literature; and the NT (with the OT) stands virtually alone in the literature of antiquity as a work which was translated into other languages. In the beginning, of course, there was no "New Testament" as a single volume. The individual books were written over a period of years and afterwards were gradually brought together.

1. The Greek Manuscripts. What did a book of the NT look like when it was first written? Its language was Greek. There doubtless were both written and oral records, probably both in Aramaic and in Greek, which lay behind our Gospels. Proof is lacking, however, that any of the NT books as such were originally written in Aramaic.

An original copy of a NT book was probably written on papyrus sheets, either folded into a codex, which is the modern book form, or possibly on a papyrus roll. It was long thought that the earliest copies of the NT books were written in roll form, since this was the regular form for both the OT and for literary writings of the period. However, even the very oldest NT papyrus mss. or fragments which are now known are from the codex form, not the roll. Although the codex form was used for notes, rough drafts of an author's work, etc., the early Christians were pioneers in using the codex form for "literary" purposes—i.e., for copies of books of the NT and perhaps for the originals of some of the NT books. The codex was far better suited for ready reference to passages and was generally easier to use than the roll.

The style of the Greek letters in the original of a NT book may have been one of two in common use. Literary works of the period were written in "uncial" or "majuscule" letters, rounded capitals, the letters not connected to each other. A "cursive" or "minuscule" hand, in which the letters were connected somewhat as in English longhand writing, was used for personal letters, business receipts, and other non-literary materials. The Greek mss. were written with no separation between words. This was not merely in order to save space, because the size of the letters in many mss. indicates that space was not necessarily an important consideration. It was simply an accepted custom. Latin mss. similarly do not separate words, but Hebrew mss. do. The originals of Paul's letters may therefore have been written in the cursive hand as being simply private correspondence; the Gospels would probably have been originally written in uncial letters. Of course, when the Pauline letters began to be copied and recopied they would be thought of as public writings and would doubtless soon be copied in uncial letters. All of the earliest known mss. of the NT are written in uncial letters.

The first three centuries are the period of the use of papyrus as a writing material. Sheets were made from thin strips of the papyrus reed, which grew along the Nile and in a very few other places in the Mediterranean world. The strips were laid side by side, with a second layer placed on top at right angles to the first layer. Pounded together and dried in the sun, these sheets made very serviceable material to receive writing from a reed pen. In a roll, the side which normally received the writing was the side on which the strips were horizontal. In the codex form, both sides would be used, but the "verso," with the strips vertical, would give the writer more difficulty than the "recto."

At the beginning of the fourth century a notable change occurred in the production of NT mss., when vellum or parchment began to displace papyrus as a writing material. The use of tanned skins to receive writing had long been known and was the material commonly used for the Hebrew OT. Vellum and parchment, however, are skins which have been treated with lime and made into a thin material with a smooth, firm writing surface. The term "vellum" was applied to the finer skins of calf, kid, or lamb, and "parchment" (from Pergamene, a city prominent in its manufacture) to ordinary skins; but the two terms are now used synonymously. A few papyrus mss. of the NT from the fifth and sixth centuries are known; but apparently papyrus was quickly displaced by the far more durable parchment, and the fourth century may be called the beginning of the parchment period of NT mss., a period which lasted until the introduction of paper as a writing material in the 14th century.

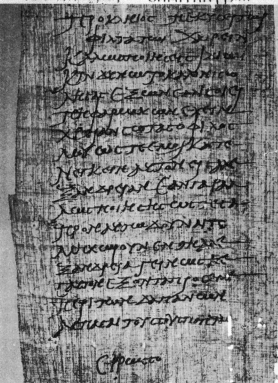

Above, a portion of the Gospel of John from the Codex Sinaiticus, in uncial letters. Compare with the semi-cursive writing of a private letter on papyrus, below, dated First Century A.D. BM

In the ninth century another significant development occurred, with the development of the cursive style of handwriting into a literary hand called "minuscule." By the end of the tenth century the uncial hand had been completely displaced by the minuscule, which remained the regular style of writing until the invention of printing.

In addition to the mss. containing a continuous NT text, many mss. of lectionaries from these centuries have survived. These are mss. which contain NT passages organized for reading on particular days.

We may summarize as follows: from the first to the fourth centuries, NT mss. were written in uncial letters on papyrus; from the fourth to the tenth, in uncial letters on vellum; from the tenth to the 14th, in minuscule letters on vellum; from the 14th to the invention of printing in the 15th century, in minuscule letters on paper.

Almost 70 papyrus mss. and fragments are known, about 250 uncial mss., 2500 cursive mss., and 1600 lectionaries. Papyri are designated by "P" and a superscript number (e.g., P66). Uncials are designated by capital letters of the English and Greek alphabets plus the Hebrew letter *Aleph*, so far as these letters permit; but all uncials are also designated by a number with a zero prefixed (e.g., 047). Cursives are designated by a number only (e.g., 565), and lectionaries by a number with a lower-case letter "l" prefixed and sometimes italicized (e.g., *l*299).

2. Variant Readings. While these paleographical developments were taking place, there were other developments concerning the text written on these mss. Since copies were made individually by hand, mistakes and changes inevitably occurred—omissions, additions, changes of words, word order, and spelling—usually unintentionally made, but sometimes intentionally to clarify, explain, or to avoid a doctrinal misunderstanding. In the mss. now known there are thousands of these "variants." The vast majority, however, make no difference in meaning; and the application of accepted principles of textual criticism make it possible to determine the original form of the text for all practical purposes although not to verbal perfection. No fundamental Christian doctrine is left in doubt by any textual variant.

These variants, moreover, tended to group themselves into companies. A ms. would tend to contain the errors of the ms. from which it was copied; and as mss. were carried to various cities and lands, and copies would tend to be made from mss. at hand, the mss. of a given region would tend to contain a similar group of variants, and these would be somewhat different from the variants of mss. in another region. Scholars recognize at least three of these "text types," as they are called, from the fifth century and earlier: "Alexandrian," "Caesarean," and "Western" — names which are only partially significant geographically. After the official recognition of Christianity in the fourth century, with more opportunity to compare mss., these "local texts" were gradually displaced by a type of text which tended to smooth out rough constructions, harmonize parallel passages, and to make for ease of understanding. This text-type, known as "Byzantine," was dominant by the eighth century. It remained the accepted text, becoming known as the "Textus Receptus" after the invention of printing, and was the text which principally underlay the King James version. It was not until the latter part of the 19th century that textual scholarship brought about a return to the older text-types.

3. Patristic Quotations. If every ms. of the NT itself were destroyed, the NT could virtually be reconstructed from another significant source, viz., the thousands of quotations of NT passages in the writings of the ancient Church Fathers, principally in Greek, Latin, and Syriac. These quotations must be consulted with care, as they were often given from memory or simply as a scriptural allusion and hence not verbally exact. Yet many are textually reliable; and these are valuable, because readings quoted by a particular Church Father can usually be assumed to have been current during that Father's lifetime and in the region of his activity.

4. Ancient Versions. In the case of most ancient writings, when the mss. in the original language of the work have been consulted, the limits of the field have been reached. The Bible, especially the NT, is therefore virtually unique in ancient literature in this respect; for not only was it translated into other languages in the earliest centuries of its history, but these translations are sufficiently accurate to be of help in textual criticism in determining the original text of the NT. Of course, no original mss. of these ancient translations remain, and the copies which are known must first be examined to determine the original text of the translation. However, certain types of Greek variants would not be reflected in certain versions (e.g., the presence or absence of a definite article in Greek would not normally be reflected in Latin, as Latin has no definite article); but in many respects the versions are useful, not least in helping to show the regions in which certain textual readings were current.

The NT must have been translated into Latin, the official language of the Roman Empire, very shortly after the books were written and certainly before the second century had passed. The 40 or so extant mss. of this Old Latin differ extensively among themselves, and it is not clear whether they represent one or several translations. As a result of these variations, in 382 Pope Damasus commissioned Jerome to undertake a revision of the Latin Bible. In the NT Jerome worked cautiously, making changes only where he felt they were absolutely necessary. This revision, the Latin Vulgate, became the official Bible of the Western Church and remains the official Roman Catholic Bible. Probably 8,000 mss. are in existence.

Syriac, a dialect related to Aramaic, which was spoken in lands around Palestine, likewise received the NT during the second century. The first such translation seems to have been either the original, or a translation of a Greek original, of a continuous Gospel account known as the Diatessaron (meaning "through the four"), constructed by combining elements from all four Gospels. It was composed about 160 by Tatian and seems to have been the Syriac Gospel in common use for over a century. There was also made, however, perhaps in the second century, a translation of the four Gospels, known as the Old Syriac, which is now known in two mss., the Sinaitic and the Curetonian.

The Syriac which is still the standard version is the Peshitta (meaning "simple"), translated in the fifth century, perhaps by Rabbula, bishop of Edessa. Some 250 mss. are known, none of which contain II Peter, II and III John, Jude, or Revelation. The Peshitta was revised in 508 by authority of Philoxenus, bishop of Mabbog. It is thought by some that this Philoxenian version still exists in or is related to the current Syriac text of the four books named above which were not in the original Peshitta but are now printed in the Syriac NT. The Philoxenian was in turn revised in 616 by Thomas of Harkel. The Harklean Syriac is so extremely literal to the Greek that it even violates Syriac idiom at times to follow the Greek. It is likewise characterized by numerous marginal alternative readings, often in Greek. About 50 mss. of this version are known.

The Palestinian Syriac version was made about the sixth century. It exists in fragmentary mss., including some lectionary material. The so-called Karkaphensian Syriac, which has sometimes been named as a version, is in fact only a collection of Scripture passages accompanied by notes on spelling and pronunciation.

Likewise significant in textual criticism are the two principal versions of Egypt. The earlier of these is the Sahidic, the dialect of southern Egypt,

At left, the Theater of Dionysus at Athens, reputed to be the oldest theater in the world.
At right, the Theater of Dionysus at Pergamum. JFW & SHH

which probably received its NT in the third century. It exists in numerous but fragmentary mss. The Bohairic, the dialect of Alexandria and the Nile delta, was more literary, and later displaced the other dialects to become the current Coptic. About 100 mss. of the Bohairic NT are known. Fragments exist of versions in three other Egyptian dialects: Fayumic, Middle Egyptian, and Akhmimic.

The Gothic version, translated very accurately from the Greek by the Gothic Bishop Ulfilas, dates from the fourth century and is the earliest version representing the Byzantine text-type.

The Armenian version originated about 400, the work of Mesrop and Sahak, using an alphabet created by Mesrop. The version was probably made from Syriac. A revision was made a century or two later. Many mss. of the Armenian version are known but only one is earlier than the tenth century.

Christianity became established in Georgia in the fourth century, and the Georgian version of the NT probably was in existence before the middle of the fifth century, apparently translated from Armenian. A thorough revision, based on Greek mss., was made about the 11th century.

The Ethiopic version originated about 600, perhaps translated from Syriac rather than Greek. About 100 mss. are extant, but the earliest is from the 13th century.

The NT was translated into Arabic by about the seventh century. Several translations were made at various periods from the Syriac, Greek, Coptic, and Latin.

The Persian exists in two versions, the earlier made from the Peshitta and the later from Greek. They are later than the Arabic, the exact date unknown.

The Slavonic version originated in the ninth century, the work of Cyril and Methodius, who translated from Greek into the Macedo-Bulgarian dialect, using an alphabet created by Cyril. This version is only partially extant.

Other translations were made from time to time, but they have virtually no significance for textual study, and are more appropriately dealt with under the subject of Bible translations.   J.H.G.

THADDAEUS (thă-dē′ŭs, Gr. *Thaddaíos*), one of the 12 apostles, mentioned only in two of the four lists (Matt. 10:3; Mark 3:18). The other two lists (Luke 6:14-16 and Acts 1:13) omit this name but insert instead Jude, son of or possibly brother of James. In the first list KJV has "Lebbaeus whose surname was Thaddaeus" but "Lebbaeus" is omitted in the two best manuscripts (Sinaitic and Vatican). Nothing is certainly known beyond the first two references above. At one time a spurious "Gospel of Thaddaeus" was in existence.

THAHASH (See Tahash)

THAMAH (See Tamah)

THAMAR (See Tamar)

THANK OFFERING (See Offerings)

THARA (See Terah)

THARSHISH (See Tarshish)

THEATER. In spite of a rudimentary dramatic structure discernible in the Book of Job and the Song of Songs, Israel produced no drama, and had therefore no theaters. The name "theater" is Greek, a noun derived from the Greek *theaomai*, "to view," or "to look upon." The Greek theater, and the Roman theater which followed it, were therefore structures designed to seat the viewers at a dramatic representation. Usually the theater was an open-air structure, a semicircle of stone seats built into the side of a hill, and seating up to five or six thousand people. The seats were cut concentrically, and at the foot of the auditorium a semicircular piece of level pavement provided the "orchestra" or the place where the chorus, indispensable adjunct of all Greek dramas, and the actors performed. In the more primitive theaters a tent backed the diameter of this semicircle, into which the actors retired to change their masks, and by implication, their roles. (There were only three actors in a Greek tragedy, but a longer list of *dramatis personae*.) On the tent was painted a rough representation of trees, or a temple, or a house, to indicate that the scene of action was town or country and so on. The Greek for "tent" is *skené*, hence "scenery" in the dramatic sense. Surviving Greek theaters are acoustically remarkable. Theaters were commonly used for public gatherings, since they were likely to provide the largest places of assembly in the city; hence the use of the only theater mentioned in the NT (Acts 19:29), that of Ephesus. The ruins of this theater, a most imposing structure, seating 25,000 people, have been excavated. Roman theaters tended to be more elaborate than those of the Greeks, contained a more finished stage, and, perhaps in conformity with the needs of a severer climate, were at least in part roofed over.   E.M.B.

Two views of Thebes (Karnak) on the Nile, Egypt. Above, a portal before the Temple of Khonsu, showing the typical inward slope of perpendicular lines characteristic of ancient Egyptian architecture. Below, the obelisk at the entrance to the Temple of Luxor at Thebes. © MPS

THEBES (thēbz, Heb. *nō', nō' 'āmôn,* from Egyp. *niwt, town, village*), the capital of Egypt during the imperial splendor of the Eighteenth Dynasty. Situated on the E bank of the Nile, the ancient city is represented today by the ruins of Karnak and Luxor, while across the river is the great necropolis of royalty and nobles as well as the remains of funerary temples and a workmen's village. Thebes was the cult center of the god Amon and the Heb. *nō' 'āmôn* is derived from the Egyp. "town of Amon." In Jeremiah 46:25 the Lord declares that He is "bringing judgment upon Amon of Thebes." Ezekiel 30 states that the Lord "will execute acts of judgment upon Thebes" (vs. 14) and will "cut off the multitude of Thebes" (vs. 15); "Thebes shall be breached" (vs. 16, RSV). Nahum used the calamity of Thebes as an object lesson for Nineveh (Nahum 3:8ff).   C.E.D.

THEBEZ (thē'bĕz, Heb. *tēvēts*), a city in the tribe of Ephraim approximately half-way from Beth-Shean to Shechem. It is mentioned only in connection with the death of Abimelech, son of Gideon, who wanted to be king (Judg. 9:50; II Sam. 11:21). Abimelech had taken the city except for a central tower, from the top of which a woman dropped a millstone upon him, thus causing his death. It is now called Tubas.

THELASAR (thē-lā'sêr), the spelling in II Kings 19:12 (KJV) for Telassar, *q.v.* Located in Mesopotamia.

THEOCRACY (thē-ŏk'rà-sē, Gr. *theokratía*), a government in which God Himself is the ruler. The best and perhaps the only illustration among nations is Israel from the time that God redeemed them from the power of the pharaoh by drying the Red Sea (Exod. 15:13; 19:5,6) and gave them His law at Mt. Sinai, till the time that Samuel acceded to their demand, "Now make us a king to judge us like all the nations" (I Sam. 8:5). During this period, God ruled through Moses (Exod. 19-Deut. 34), then through Joshua (Josh.) and finally through "judges" whom he raised up from time to time to deliver His people. From the human standpoint, the power was largely in the hands of the priests, who acted on the basis of laws issued by God, in whom were united all the powers of the state — legislative, executive and judicial. Such a government was, of course, possible only because of God's special revelation of Himself to the nation.   A.B.F.

THEOPHANY, a visible appearance of God, generally in human form. In the early days of humanity, before men had the written Word, before the incarnation, and before the Holy Spirit had come to make His abode in human hearts, God sometimes appeared and talked with men. Before man sinned, he walked and talked with God, but after sin entered, Adam and his wife hid when they heard the voice of the Lord God (Gen. 3:8). God spoke to Cain (Gen. 4); Enoch and Noah "walked with God" (Gen. 5:24; 6:9), and He gave Noah detailed instructions concerning the ark and the flood. One of the loveliest and most instructive of the theophanies is found in Genesis 18. From Abraham's time on, theophanies generally occurred when men were asleep as in the Bethel vision of Jacob (Gen. 28:10-17) and others, but God addressed Moses "face to face" (Exod. 33:11). There is good reason to think that theophanies before the incarnation of Christ were visible manifestations of the pre-incarnate Son of God. It is to be noticed that theophanies ceased with the incarnation of our Lord.   A.B.F.

THEOPHILUS (thē-ŏf'ĭ-lŭs, Gr. *Theóphilos*). It is reasonable to suppose that Theophilus, to whom Luke dedicated both his Gospel (1:3), and the Acts (1:1), was a real person. The title "most excellent" demands this, while the name and title together suggest a person of equestrian rank who became a Christian convert. Theophilus is most probably a baptismal name (see W. M. Ramsay, *St. Paul the Traveller and Roman Citizen*, pp. 388, 389). Nothing is known of the man. He was certainly not Seneca, as one rash conjecture would have it. It is impossible to decide whether he was pure Roman, Greek, or Jew, or whether the omission in Acts of the honorable title employed in the Gospel, indicates a deepening friendship when the second book was dedicated, the abandonment of office, or dismissal for Christian profession.

E.M.B.

THESSALONIANS, EPISTLES TO THE. With the possible exception of Galatians, I and II Thessalonians are the earliest letters surviving from the correspondence of Paul. They were written to the church in Thessalonica which was founded by Paul on his second journey en route from Philippi to Achaia. His preaching of Jesus as the Messiah aroused such violent controversy in the synagogue at Thessalonica that the opposing Jewish faction brought him before the city magistrates, charging him with fomenting insurrection against Caesar (Acts 17:5-9). Paul's friends were placed under bond for his good behavior, and to protect their own security, they sent him away from the city. He proceeded to Berea, and after a short stay, interrupted by a fanatical group of Jews from Thessalonica, he went on to Athens, leaving Silas and Timothy to continue the preaching (17:10-14). From Athens he sent back instructions that they should join him as quickly as possible (17:15). According to I Thessalonians they did so, and it is possible that he sent Timothy back again to encourage the Thessalonians while he continued at Athens (I Thess. 3:2). In the meantime, Paul moved to Corinth, and there Timothy found him when he returned with news of the growth of the Thessalonian church (3:6; Acts 18:5). The first Epistle was prompted by Timothy's report.

I Thessalonians

Authenticity. There can be little doubt of the genuineness of this epistle. Ignatius (*Ephesians* X) and the *Shepherd of Hermas* (*Visions* III, ix, 10) both contain passages that may have been taken from it, and it is listed in the canon of Marcion (A.D. 140). Irenaeus (c. A.D. 180) quotes it by name (*Against Heresies* V, vi, i); Tertullian attributes it to "the apostle" (*On the Resurrection of the Flesh* XXIV); and his contemporary, Clement of Alexandria, ascribed it directly to Paul (*Instructor* I, v). As noted above, the autobiographical allusions in I Thessalonians correspond well with the data on the life of Paul given in Acts. Furthermore, no forger of the second century would have been likely to stress the imminency of the coming of Christ as Paul did.

Date and Place. Paul's stay both in Thessalonica and in Athens was brief, and he probably arrived in Corinth about A.D. 50. According to the narrative in Acts, Paul had begun his ministry there while working at the tentmaker's trade with Aquila and Priscilla (Acts 18:1-3). When Silas and Timothy rejoined him after their stay in Macedonia they brought funds which enabled him to stop working and to devote his entire time to evangelism (Acts 18:5; II Cor. 11:9). Shortly afterward the Jewish opposition to Paul's preaching became

so violent that he was forced out of the synagogue. About a year and a half later he was haled before the tribunal of Gallio, the Roman proconsul (18:12). Gallio had taken office only a short time previously, in A.D. 51 or 52. The first epistle, then, must have been written at Corinth about a year prior to that date, in A.D. 50 or 51.

Occasion. Timothy brought a report concerning the problems of the church, with which Paul dealt in this letter. Some of his Jewish enemies had attacked his character, putting him under obligation to defend himself (2:1-6,10,14-16). A few of the converts were still influenced by the lax morality of the paganism from which they had so recently emerged and in which they had to live (4:3-7). Some of the church members had died, causing the rest to worry whether their departed friends would share in the return of Christ (4:13). Still others, anticipating the Second Advent, had given up all regular employment and were idly waiting for the Lord to appear (4:9-12). The epistle was intended to encourage the Thessalonians' growth as Christians and to settle the questions that were troubling them.

Outline and Content, I Thessalonians

I. The Conversion of the Thessalonians 1:1-10

II. The Ministry of Paul 2:1-3:13
    A. In Founding the Church 2:1-20
    B. In Concern for the Church 3:1-13

III. The Problems of the Church 4:1-13
    A. Moral Instruction 4:1-12
    B. The Lord's Coming 4:13-5:11
    C. Ethical Duties 5:12-22

IV. Conclusion 5:23-28

I Thessalonians is a friendly personal letter. The persecution in Thessalonica and the uncertainty concerning the coming of Christ which Paul had preached had disturbed the believers. Paul devoted the first half of his letter to reviewing his relationship with them in order to counteract the attacks of his enemies. The body of teaching in the second half of the letter dealt with sexual immorality, by insisting on standards of holiness. The chief doctrinal topic was the second coming of Christ. Paul assured his readers that those who had died would not perish, but that they would be resurrected at the return of Christ. In company with the living believers, who would be translated, all would enter into eternal fellowship with Christ (4:13-18). Since the exact time of the return was not known, they were urged to be watchful, that they might not be taken unawares.

The walls of ancient Thessalonica. GL

The Arch of Galerius at Thessalonica. GL

II Thessalonians

Authenticity. The genuineness of II Thessalonians has been challenged because of its difference from I Thessalonians. The warning of signs preceding the day of the Lord (II Thess. 2:1-3) in contrast to a sudden and unannounced appearing (I Thess. 5:1-3); the teaching on the "man of sin" (II Thess. 2:3-9), unique in the Pauline epistles; and the generally more somber tone of the whole epistle have been alleged as reasons for rejecting the Pauline authorship. None of these is convincing, for the two epistles deal with two different aspects of the same general subject, and bear so many resemblances to each other that they are clearly related.

Early evidence for the acceptance of II Thessalonians is almost as full as for that of I Thessalonians. Shadowy references to it appear in the *Didache* (xvi), Ignatius (*Romans* X), and possibly Polycarp (*Philippians* xi). Justin Martyr (A.D. 140) quotes II Thessalonians unmistakably in his *Dialogue with Trypho* (cx). Irenaeus (A.D. 170) mentions it definitely as one of the epistles of Paul in *Against Heresies* (III, vii, 2), as does Clement of Alexandria (*Stromalia* V, iii).

Date and Place. The second epistle was probably sent from Corinth in A.D. 51, not more than a few months after the first epistle. Since Silas and Timothy were still with Paul, it is likely that no great interval elapsed between the writing of the two.

Occasion. Evidently the Thessalonian Christians had been disturbed by the arrival of an epistle purporting to come from Paul, which he had not authorized (II Thess. 2:2). Some of them were suffering harsh persecution (1:4,5); others were apprehensive that the last day was about to arrive (2:2); and there were still a few who were idle and disorderly (3:6-12). The second epistle serves to clarify further the problems of the first epistle, and to confirm the confidence of the readers.

Outline and Content, II Thessalonians

I. Salutation 1:1,2

II. Encouragement in Persecution 1:3-12

III. The Signs of the Day of Christ 2:1-17
    A. Warning of False Rumors 2:1,2
    B. The Apostasy 2:3
    C. The Revelation of the Man of Sin 2:4-12
    D. The Preservation of God's People 2:13-17

IV. Spiritual Counsel 3:1-15

V. Conclusion 3:16-18

Whereas the first epistle heralded the resurrection of the righteous dead and the restoration of the living at the return of Christ, the second epistle described the apostasy preceding the coming of Christ to judgment. Paul stated that the "mystery of iniquity" was already at work, and that its climax would be reached with the removal of the "hinderer" (II Thess. 2:6,7), who has been variously identified with the Holy Spirit, the power of the Roman empire, and with the preaching of Paul himself. With the disappearance of any spiritual restraint, the "man of sin" will be revealed, who will (2:3-10) deceive all men and will be energized by the power of Satan himself.

In view of this prospect, Paul exhorted the Thessalonians to retain their faith and to improve their conduct. He spoke even more vehemently to those who persisted in idleness (3:6-12), recommending that the Christians withdraw fellowship from them.

M.C.T.

THESSALONICA (thĕs′à-lō-nī′kà, Gr. *Thessaloníke*), a Macedonian town founded by Cassander, Alexander's officer, who took control of Greece after Alexander's death in 332 B.C. Thessalonica was probably founded towards the end of the century by consolidating small towns at the head of the Thermaic Gulf. It dominated the junction of the northern trade-route and the road from the Adriatic to Byzantium, which later became the Via Egnatia. Its comparatively sheltered roadstead

Greek inscription from a Roman arch at Thessalonica, mentioning "politarchs" (city officials) as in Acts 17:6-9. BM

made it the chief port of Macedonia, after Pella yielded to the silting which was the perennial problem of Greek harbors. It was a fortress which withstood a Roman siege, surrendering only after the battle of Pydna sealed Rome's victory in the Macedonian Wars. In 146 B.C. it became the capital of the Roman province and was Pompey's base a century later in the Civil War with Julius Caesar. Prolific coinage suggests a high level of prosperity. The population included a large Roman element, and a Jewish colony. Paul visited Thessalonica after Philippi, and appears to have worked among a composite group, comprising the Jews of the synagogue and Greek proselytes among whom were some ladies of high social standing. There was a high degree of emancipation among the women of Macedonia. In Acts 17:6 and 8, the officials of the town are called in the original "politarchs." Its use was once dismissed as a mistake of the historian because it was a term unknown elsewhere. Sixteen epigraphical examples now exist in modern Salonica, and one is located in the British Museum. It was evidently a Macedonian term, and Luke's use of it was in line with his habit of using accepted terminology.   E.M.B.

THEUDAS (thū′dàs, Gr. *Theudás*). Josephus (*Ant.* 20:5:1) mentions a Theudas who led a considerable revolt in A.D. 44 or 45. This cannot have been the Theudas of Gamaliel's speech, which was made some ten years earlier. To suggest that Luke used Josephus, and confused Theudas and Judas (Acts 5:36,37), reversing their chronological order, is to disregard Luke's customary accuracy. There is little correspondence between Luke's definite "four hundred" and Josephus' account of a more extensive rebellion. It is quite possible that the reference in Josephus was rather an interpolation from Acts. There could have been more than one Theudas and our knowledge of the history of the province is far too sketchy to dispute this clear possibility. W. M. Ramsay writes: "The period is very obscure; Josephus is practically our only authority. He does not allude or profess to allude, to every little disturbance on the banks of the Jordan . . ." (*Was Christ Born at Bethlehem?* pp. 258, 259). Indeed "no testimony could be stronger than that of Josephus himself to the fact that at the time of the Advent Judaea was full of tumults and seditions and pretenders of all kinds" (EGT 2:158). The movements of Theudas and Judas were probably associated, and both took place in the time of Quirinius.   E.M.B.

THIEF, THIEVES (Heb. *gannāv, steal*; Gr. *kléptes, lestés, thief*). The word is used for anyone who appropriates someone else's property, including petty thieves and highwaymen (Luke 10:30; John 12:6). Under the law of Moses, thieves who were caught were expected to restore twice the amount stolen. The thieves with Jesus on their crosses must have been robbers or brigands, judging by the severity of the punishment and the fact that one of them acknowledged that the death penalty imposed upon them was just (Luke 23:41).

THIGH (Heb. *yarekh, shôq*, Gr. *merós*), the upper part of the leg in man; or of a rear leg in a quadruped. To put one's hand under the thigh of another, was to enhance the sacredness of an oath (Gen. 24:2,9; 47:29). To "smite hip and thigh" (Judg. 15:8) implied not only slaughter but slaughter with extreme violence. When the Angel of Jehovah wrestled with Jacob, so that Jacob might know the weakness of his human strength, he touched the hollow of Jacob's thigh and threw it

out of joint at the hip; thus making him change from struggling to clinging, and when he thus changed, God changed him from Jacob "a supplanter" to Israel "a prince with God" (Gen. 32: 24-32); and remembering this event the Israelites "eat not the sinew of the hip which is upon the hollow of the thigh." In Oriental feasts, the shoulder or the thigh of the meat is often placed before an honored guest (cf. I Sam. 9:23,24) and he has the privilege of sharing it with those near him at the feast. The thigh was the place for a man to gird his sword (Judg. 3:16). To smite upon the thigh is a sign of amazement or of great shame (Jer. 31:9; Ezek. 21:12).   A.B.F.

THIMNATHAH (thĭm′nà-thà, Heb. *timnâthâh*), occurs only in Joshua 19:43 (KJV). Properly "Timnah" as elsewhere and in ASV here. See TIMNAH.

THISTLE (See Plants)

THOMAS (tŏm′às, Gr. *Thomás*, from Aram. *te'oma*, twin), one of the 12 apostles (Matt. 10:3). He was also called "Didymus" or "the Twin" (cf. John 11: 16; 20:24; 21:2). The Gospel of John gives the most information about him. When the other apostles tried to dissuade Jesus from going to Bethany to heal Lazarus because of the danger involved from hostile Jews, Thomas said to them, "Let us also go, that we may die with him" (John 11:16). Shortly before the Passion, Thomas asked, "Lord, we know not whither thou goest; how know we the way?" (John 14:1-6). Thomas was not with the other apostles when Jesus presented Himself to them on the evening of the Resurrection, and told them later that he could not believe in resurrection (John 20:24,25). Eight days later he was with the apostles when Jesus appeared to them again, and he exclaimed "My Lord and my God" (John 20: 26-29). He was with the six other disciples when Jesus appeared to them at the Sea of Galilee (John 21:1-8) and was with the rest of the apostles in the upper room at Jerusalem after the ascension (Acts 1:13). According to tradition he afterward labored in Parthia, Persia, and India. A place near Madras is called St. Thomas' Mount.   S.B.

THOMAS, GOSPEL OF. This was the major item in a jar of papyri discovered at Naj Hamadi between Cairo and Luxor in 1945. It took some 14 years for the knowledge of the find to reach the West. Some inkling of the Gospel of Thomas had emerged in 1903 from a papyrus discovered by Grenfell and Hunt. The Naj Hamadi document is a collection of one hundred and fourteen sayings of Christ in the form of isolated dicta or brief conversations, some known, some entirely new, the whole work being ascribed to the apostle Thomas. Some of the sayings are inconsiderable and without the edge and patina so characteristic of the Biblical utterances of Christ. Others, on the contrary, are both fresh and pungent, and may well represent a genuine tradition. Consider a few illustrations of the latter sort: "Jesus said: Whoever is near me is near the fire, and whoever is far from me is far from the kingdom." The words coincide with more than one warning of the inevitability of persecution, and the consistent claim that discipleship was the path to God. Again: "They said to Him: Come and let us pray today and let us fast. But Jesus said: which then is the sin I have committed, or in what have I been vanquished?" In the Fourth Gospel the words occur: "Which of you convicts me of sin?" Again: "Jesus said: Become passersby." The words are in tune with a saying of Christ preserved in the arabesques of a Moslem mosque: "Life is a bridge. You pass over it but build no houses on it." The meaning, of course, is that the wise and good avoid entanglements and too great involvement in material things. Such sayings have a ring of authenticity. So do such words as the new Beatitude: "Blessed is the man who suffers. He finds life." And the reproach to the Pharisees, catching up a simile of the Greeks which is still in common usage: "Woe to them, for they are like a dog sleeping in a manger of oxen, for neither does he eat nor allow the oxen to eat." The collection is dated A.D. 140 and it is not perhaps surprising that some well-known sayings have become somewhat worn and altered. Compare, for example, the parable of the Sower and the Seed in the canonical Gospels with the attenuated version in the Gospel of Thomas: "See the sower went out, he filled his hand, he threw. Some seed fell on the road, the birds came, they gathered them. Others fell on the rock, and did not strike root in the earth, and did not produce ears. Others fell in the thorns. They choked the seed and the worm ate them. Others fell on the good earth, and brought forth good fruit. It bore sixty per measure, and one hundred and twenty per measure." This is obviously a different tradition held no doubt by a Christian community in Egypt, perhaps a remnant who escaped from Jerusalem before A.D. 70 to live in some measure of isolation in a foreign land. Thomas may, in fact, have been the author of their original document.   E.M.B.

THORN (See Plants)

THORN IN THE FLESH, Paul's description of a physical ailment which afflicted him and from which he prayed to be relieved (II Cor. 12:7). Some hold that there are hints that it was ophthalmia. Paul generally dictated his epistles, but signed them with his own hand (II Thess. 3:17; I Cor. 16:21). He wrote the end of Galatians with his own hand, but apologized for the large handwriting (Gal. 6:11). Not "how large a letter" as in KJV, but "with how large letters" as in ASV. His affliction was apparently not only painful but disfiguring. The Galatians did not despise him for it, and would have plucked out their own eyes and given them to the apostle, were it possible (Gal. 4:13-15). He says he was unable to recognize the high priest (Acts 23:5). Ramsay thought it was some form of recurring malarial fever.
                                                        A.B.F.

THOUSAND (Heb. *eleph*, Gr. *chílioi*), frequently used hyperbolically for a very large but indefinite number, or as the division of a tribe (Num. 31:5; Josh. 22:14). The word was also used as the subdivision of the tribe which was known technically as "a father's house" (Num: 1:2,4,16; Judg. 6:15; I Sam. 10:19,21).

THOUSAND YEARS (See Millennium)

THRACE (thrās, Gr. *Thrakía*), a kingdom and later a Roman province, in SE Europe, E of Macedonia. The name does not appear in the canonical books, but II Maccabees 12:35 mentions an unnamed Thracian horseman who rescued Gorgias, the governor of Jamnia, from possible Jewish capture.

THREE HOLY CHILDREN, SONG OF (See Apocrypha)

THREE TAVERNS (Lat. *Tres Tabernae*). This village, which may be rendered "Three Shops," was a stopping place on the Via Appia, some 33 miles from Rome, at the junction of the road from Antium, near modern Cisterna. It was a place of some importance (Acts 28:15; Cic. *Ad Att.* 2:12).

Bringing in the sheaves to the threshing floor of an Arab village. © MPS

THRESHING (Heb. *dûsh*, to trample out; *hāvat*, to beat out or off; *dārakh*, to tread; Gr. *aloáo*, to tread down). It was performed in two ways: (1) by beating the sheaves with a rod or flail; (2) by trampling them under the feet of oxen that pulled a wooden sled around the threshing floor (Isa. 28: 27). Threshing was done out-of-doors on a hard surface of ground. The word also had a figurative use (Isa. 21:10; 41:15; Mic. 4:12,13; I Cor. 9:10). See AGRICULTURE, FARMING.

THRESHING FLOOR (Heb. *gōren*, Gr. *hálon*), the place where grain was threshed. Usually clay soil was packed to a hard smooth surface. Sheaves of grain were spread on the floor and trampled by oxen which usually drew crude wooden sleds with notched rims (Deut. 25:4; Isa. 28:27; I Cor. 9: 9). A shovel and fan were used in winnowing the grain (Isa. 30:24). Since robbers would visit the floor at threshing time (I Sam. 23:1), the laborers slept there (Ruth 3:4-7). Threshing floors were often on hills where the night winds could more easily blow away the chaff.

THRESHOLD (Heb. *saph*, threshold, entrance; *miphtān*, threshold, sill), the piece of wood or stone which lies below the bottom of a door, and has to be crossed on entering a house. The sill of a doorway, hence the entrance to a building.

THRONE (Heb. *kissē'*, Gr. *thrónos*), a chair of state occupied by one in authority or of high position, like a high priest, judge, governor, or king (Gen. 41:40; II Sam. 3:10; Neh. 3:7; Ps. 122:5; Jer. 1: 15; Matt. 19:28). Solomon's throne was an elaborate one (I Kings 10:18-20; II Chron. 9:17-19). For ages the throne has been a symbol of authority, exalted position, majesty (Ps. 9:7; 45:6; 94:20; Prov. 16:12).

THUMB, either the great toe of the foot or the thumb of the hand. The Heb. word *bōhen*, followed by a modifying term, indicates which is meant (Exod. 29:20; Lev. 8:23; 14:14). To cut off these members was to handicap a victim and brand him. A son of Reuben was named Thumb (*bōhen*) (Josh. 15:6).

THUMMIM (See Urim and Thummim)

THUNDER (Heb. *ra'am, qôl,* Gr. *bronté*), the noise that follows a lightning discharge. In Palestine it was a rare phenomenon during summer months, so if it did occur it was considered a sign of divine displeasure (I Sam. 12:17). So unusual was it in summer that it was likened to snow in that season (Prov. 26:1). A spectacular electrical storm accompanied the plague of hail in Egypt (Exod. 9: 22-26). Such a display was seen at Sinai (Exod. 19:16-18). Thunder operates according to natural law (Job 28:26; 38:25). Hebrews considered thunder to be a revelation of God's power (Job 37:2-5; 40:9; Ps. 18:13; 29:2-9; Isa. 30:30), and it represented God's anger and chastening (I Sam. 2:10).

THUNDER, SONS OF (*huioí brontés*), the title given James and John by Jesus (Mark 3:17) apparently because of their bold and sometimes rash natures (Luke 9:54; Matt. 20:20-23).

THUTMOSE (also Tuthmosis, Thotmes), does not appear in the Bible, but is a common personal name and one of the great royal names of Egypt, given to four kings of the eighteenth dynasty. The outstanding Thutmose was Thutmose III, one of the greatest military leaders and administrators of antiquity. Thutmose I made a military expedition beyond the Euphrates and also extended the southern boundary to the Third Cataract. He did some building at Karnak; one of his obelisks still stands there. Thutmose II married his half-sister, Hatshepsut, and their daughter became the wife of Thutmose III. Hatshepsut was regent for a period after the death of Thutmose II and even had herself proclaimed "king"; upon her death, Thutmose

The top of the obelisk of Thutmose III at Karnak, also known as the obelisk of Queen Hatshepsut. OIUC

III burst from obscurity and attempted to eliminate all references to this aunt and mother-in-law. He began his 17 expeditions to Palestine-Syria with a brilliantly strategic victory over an Asiatic coalition at Megiddo. He reached beyond the Euphrates and set up a stele beside that left by his grandfather (Thutmose I). An ardent sportsman, Thutmose III here engaged in a great elephant hunt. He was also active in the S and pushed the boundary to Gebel Barkal, just below the Fourth Cataract.

The records of his expeditions are preserved in his annals at Karnak. The tribute gained from his successes greatly enriched the priesthood of Amon at Thebes, while the influx of foreign products and peoples effected a cosmopolitanism which eventually contributed to the breakdown of the empire that had been built in large measure by the abilities of Thutmose III. In building activity he is credited with constructions at Karnak: the hall of the annals; building intended to conceal the obelisks of Hatshepsut; the Sixth Pylon; the Seventh Pylon; and the Festival Hall to the E. On the W bank at Thebes, he built at Medinet Habu, and to the N erected a mortuary temple which has not survived. He also built temples at other sites in Egypt and Nubia. For various reasons Thutmose III has been endorsed as the pharaoh of the Oppression, and his successor, Amenhotep II, as the pharaoh of the Exodus. Though this is an attractive hypothesis in many respects, it is burdened with difficulties and the identity of those pharaohs is still problematic. Thutmose IV, the son of Amenhotep II, is the last of the kings of this name. The Dream Stele, which still stands between the forelegs of the Sphinx at Giza, relates how he came to the throne.   C.E.D.

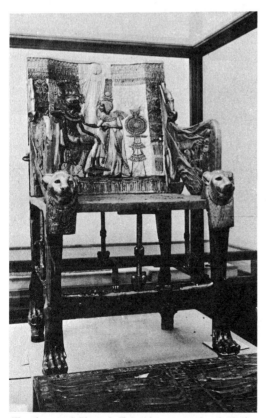

The throne of Pharaoh Tutankhamen, made of wood overlaid with gold, and with jeweled inlays, in the Cairo Museum.

THYATIRA (thī'à-tī'rà, Gr. *Thyáteira*), a city in the province of Asia, on the boundary of Lydia and Mysia. Thyatira has no illustrious history, and is scarcely mentioned by ancient writers. Coinage suggests that, lying as it did on a great highway linking two river valleys, Thyatira was a garrison town over long centuries. Its ancient Anatolian deity was a warlike figure armed with a battle-axe and mounted on a charger. An odd coin or two shows a female deity wearing a battlemented crown. The city was a center of commerce, and the records preserve references to more trade-guilds than those listed for any other Asian city. Lydia, whom Paul met in Philippi, was a Thyatiran seller of "turkey red," the product of the madder-root (Acts 16: 14). It is curious to find another woman, nicknamed after the princess who sealed Ahab's trading partnership with the Phoenicians, leading a party of compromise in the Thyatiran church (Rev. 2:20,21). Necessity for guild membership in a trading community must have strengthened temptation to compromise. Thyatira played no significant part in the later history of the Church.   E.M.B.

TIAMAT (tī'à-măt), a mythical monster in the Babylonian-Assyrian creation story (*Enûma elish*), which is primarily an epic honoring the god Marduk. When Tiamat threatened the gods, Marduk, as their champion, defeated and killed her. He then split her into two parts, from which he made the heavens and the earth. Some scholars have seen a reflection of Tiamat in the Hebrew *tehom*, "the deep," but differences between the terms in form, meaning, and usage have been demonstrated by A. Heidel and others.

TIBERIAS (tī-bē'rĭ-ăs, Gr. *Tiberiás*), a city of Herod Antipas, built between the years A.D. 16 and 22 on the western shore of the Sea of Galilee, or the Sea of Tiberias, as John, writing for non-Jewish readers, calls the lake (John 6:1; 21:1). It was named, of course, after the reigning emperor, Tiberius, reflecting the pro-Roman policy consistently followed by the Herods. The city is said to have occupied the site of Rakkath, an old town of Naphtali, and since Rakkath means "strip" or "coast," this may have been the case. Jewish rumor said Tiberias was built over a graveyard, and the place was therefore dubbed unclean (Josephus. *Ant.* 18:2:3). Macalister is of the opinion that this proves that no earlier city occupied the site (HDB p. 934), but Herod could easily have included the burial-place of Rakkath in his larger foundation. Herod built ambitiously. The ruins indicate a wall three miles long. There were a palace, a forum, and a great synagogue, for the foundation illustrated strikingly the dual Herodian policy, which sought to combine pro-Roman loyalty with effective patronage of the Jews. Jewish boycott, however, compelled Herod to populate his new town with the lowest elements of the land. Defended by its strong acropolis, Tiberias survived the passing of the other lakeside towns. Saladin, who took Tiberias in 1187, was unable to reduce the citadel until after Hattin. The hot springs and baths lay S of the city wall. Their healthful nature is mentioned by the Elder Pliny (H.N. 5:15), and a coin of Tiberias of Trajan's day shows a figure of Hygeia (Health) feeding a serpent (sign of Aesculapius, god of healing) as she sits on a rock over a spring.   E.M.B.

TIBERIAS, SEA OF (See Sea of Galilee)

TIBERIUS (tī-bēr'ĭ-ŭs, Gr. *Tibérios*). Tiberius Julius Caesar Augustus succeeded to the principate on the death of Augustus in A.D. 14, becoming thus the second Roman emperor. He was born in 42 B.C., son of the Empress Livia, wife of Augustus, by her first husband, Tiberius Claudius Nero. He had a distinguished military career in the East and in Germany, and, in the absence of direct heirs to Augustus, was the logical successor. Augustus, however, did not like Tiberius, and Tiberius, over many years, was the passive witness of several attempts to bypass his claims and his abilities. The experience of disapproval and rejection no doubt contributed to the dourness, secretiveness, ambiguity, and suspicious preoccupations which marred the years of Tiberius' power. A morbid fear of disloyalty led to the heavy incidence of treason trials which were a feature of the Roman principate under its worst incumbents. There is no evidence that Tiberius was unduly tyrannous, but aristocrats, and writers of their number, blamed the prince for features of later tyranny, and for manifold precedents

The seafront at the modern town of Tiberias, on the shores of the Sea of Galilee. © MPS

Tiberius Caesar. **JHK**

for oppression. This, added to the natural unpopularity of a reticent and lonely man, left Tiberius with a reputation which modern scholarship, discounting Tacitus' brilliant and bitter account, has been at some pains to rehabilitate. Tiberius had great ability and some measure of magnanimity; for, in spite of many unhappy memories, he sought loyally to continue Augustus' policy, foreign and domestic. The rumors of senile debauchery on Capri can be listed with the slanders of earlier years, though there is some evidence of mental disturbance in the later period of the principate. Tiberius died on March 16, A.D. 37. He was the reigning emperor at the time of Christ's death.

E.M.B.

TIBHATH (tĭb'hăth, Heb. *tivhath*), a city in the kingdom of Zobah, E of the Anti-Lebanon Mountains. David captured it from Hadarezer, and sent its treasures to Jerusalem (I Chron. 18:7-9, Betah of II Sam. 8:8).

TIBNI (tĭb'nī, Heb. *tivnî*), a son of Ginath. When Zimri died, he was an unsuccessful competitor for the throne of Israel with Omri (I Kings 16:15-21). Nothing else is known about him.

TIDAL (tī'dăl, Heb. *tidh'āl*), an unidentified king, mentioned only in Genesis 14:1,9, where he is called "king of Goiim" ("nations," KJV) and is allied with three other kings, with Chedorlaomer, king of Elam, as the leader (see 14:5,17). Invading westward, they defeated the kings of the cities of the plain and took plunder and captives, including Lot. Abraham routed the coalition in a night raid, recovered the goods, and rescued the captives (14:15-16).

TIGLATH-PILESER (tĭg'lăth-pĭ-lē'zêr, Assyr. *Tukulti-apil-esharra*, Heb. *tiglath-pil'eser, tilleghath-pilne'ser*), a famous name among Assyrian kings. Tiglath-pileser I (1114-1074 B.C.) was a conqueror whose campaigns extended northward to the vicinity of Lake Van and westward to the Mediterranean. His annals tell of his efforts to establish a world empire, but his reign was followed by several centuries in which Assyria was weak. In 745 a usurper took the Assyrian throne and assumed the name Tiglath-pileser. Tiglath-pileser III (745-727) injected new vigor into the Assyrian empire, which

had suffered another decline after a resurgence of power in the ninth century. He engaged in campaigns to E and W and was recognized as king even in Babylon, where he was known as Pulu, from which comes the Biblical name Pul, by which he is referred to in II Kings 15:19 and I Chronicles 5:26. His annals list Azariah of Judah among the kings from whom he received tribute; the OT does not relate this account. (See D.D. Luckenbill, *Ancient Records of Assyria and Babylonia,* Chicago: University of Chicago Press, 1926-27, I, p. 770; hereafter *ARAB.*) The annals also mention tribute from Menahem of Samaria, who bought him off (II Kings 15:19-20, RSV: "Pul the king of Assyria came against the land; and Menahem gave Pul a thousand talents of silver, that he might help him to confirm his hold of the royal power. . . . So the king of Assyria turned back, and did not stay there in the land." Cf. *ARAB,* I, pp. 772, 815).

During the reign of the Judean king Ahaz, Pekah of Israel and Rezin of Syria moved against Judah. Ahaz secured the help of Tiglath-pileser (II Kings 16:5-8), who captured Damascus, deported its people, and killed Rezin. He took a number of Israelite cities and exiled the inhabitants to Assyria (II Kings 15:29; cf. *ARAB,* I, p. 816: "the land of Bit Humria (= house of Omri = Israel) . . . all its people, together with their goods I carried off to Assyria."). He was also responsible for the deportation of Transjordanian Israelites, whom he brought to "Halah, Habor, Hara, and the river Gozan" (I Chron. 5:6,26). The transfer of peoples to foreign areas was a practical policy which he designed to reduce the possibility of revolts in conquered regions (cf. *ARAB,* I, pp. 770, 772, 777). Ahaz also requested military aid from him because of invasions by Edomites and Philistines; he "gave tribute to the king of Assyria; but it did not help him" (II Chron. 28:20-21; cf. *ARAB,* I, p. 801).

C.E.D.

A relief showing Tiglath-pileser III, king of Assyria 745-727 B.C., in his war chariot. Tablet from Nimrud. **BM**

An aerial view of the Tigris River, showing groves of countless palm trees fringing the river's banks. This area is close to Bagdad, capital of Iraq. © MPS

TIGRIS (tī′grĭs, Assyr. *Idiglat, arrow,* Heb. *hidde-qel*), one of the two great rivers of the Mesopotamian area. It originates in the Taurus Mountains of Armenia; in its 1,150 miles it receives three principal tributaries from the E, the Great Zab, the Little Zab, and the Diyala. It is difficult for navigation, since for some months it is very shallow, yet is subject to flooding and during the rainy season ranges outside its banks. In antiquity the Tigris and the Euphrates entered the Persian Gulf by separate mouths, but today the Tigris joins the Euphrates at Kurna to form the Shatt el-Arab. The rivers of Iran also have been an important factor in the formation of the delta. Through what was Assyria and Babylonia the Tigris flows past famous cities, living and dead: Mosul, on the W bank, looks across the river to the mounds of Nineveh; farther downstream are Asshur, Samarra, and Baghdad. In the Bible the Tigris is mentioned with the Euphrates and two other streams as rivers which watered the garden of Eden (Gen. 2:14). Daniel 10:4 states that it was while the prophet "was standing on the bank of the great river, that is, the Tigris" (RSV), that he saw the vision he subsequently recorded.　　　　　　　　C.E.D.

TIKVAH (tĭk′và, Heb. *tiqwah*). 1. The father-in-law of the prophetess Huldah, the wife of Shallum (II Kings 22:8-14).

2. During the reforms under Ezra a son of another Tikvah was a chief leader (Ezra 10:9-15).

TIKVATH (See Tikvah)

TILE (Heb. *levēnâh, brick,* Gr. *kéramos*). Ancient writing was done with a stilus on blocks of soft clay, which varied in size according to need. Ezekiel used such a tile in drawing a prophetic picture of the doom awaiting Jerusalem (Ezek. 4:1-8). When a permanent record was desired the inscribed tile was baked in a furnace. So skilled were scribes of the day that many of their tiles remain in perfect condition after 3,000 years. Roofing tiles are mentioned in Luke 5:19 and Mark 2:4.

TILGATH-PILNESER (See Tiglath-Pileser)

TILING (Gr. *kéramos*), used only in Luke 5:19, where the reference is apparently to clay roofing — tiles with which the roof was covered. Clay tiles were not commonly used as roofing material for houses in Palestine, roofs usually being covered with a mixture of clay and straw. It may be that Luke uses the expression "through the tiles" to mean "through the roof," without reference to the material used for the roof.

TILON (tī′lŏn, Heb. *tîlôn*), one of the sons of Shimon (I Chron. 4:1,20), a descendant of Judah.

TIMBREL (See Musical Instruments)

TIME. The history of the development of various measurements for time, and the making of instruments for determining them, is an interesting one. Before the days of Abraham, the Chaldeans had set up a system of days and seasons, and had divided the periods of darkness and light into parts. Their seven-day week had been accepted by Egyptians before the day of Moses. Day and night were determined by the sun. The week, no doubt, was determined by the phases of the moon. The month was based upon the recurrence of the new moon. Thus the new moon was the sign of a new month. In order to provide in the calendar for the extra days of the solar year over the 12 lunar months, the Jews added an intercalary month. They had no way of determining an absolute solar year, so the extra month was added every third year, with adjustments to provide seven extra months each 19 years. It was added after the spring equinox, hence was called a second Adar (the preceding month being Adar). This method of keeping the lunar and the solar years synchronized was probably learned by the Israelites during the Babylonian captivity. For ages, years were not numbered consecutively as we number them, but were counted from some outstanding event, such as the founding of Rome (*ab urbe condita*). Hebrews had a civil year which began at the vernal equinox, after the custom of Babylon, and a sacred year which began with the harvest or seventh month (Lev. 25: 8,9). They divided the year into two seasons, seed-time or wet cold season, winter; and harvest, summer (Gen. 8:22; 45:6; Exod. 34:21; Prov. 10:5).

The Hebrew word for day (*yom*) means period of daylight, or a period of 24 hours. We have no way of knowing how the period was determined before the solar system was completed (Gen. 1: 14-19). The Roman day began at midnight and had 12 hours (John 11:9). The Heb. day was reckoned from sunset. There was the cool of the day (Gen. 3:8) or twilight (Job 24:15). Mid-morning was when the sun had become hot (I Sam. 11:9). Noon was the heat of the day (Gen. 18: 1). Night was divided into watches, so that the length of each varied with changing seasons. The first watch came about 9:30 p.m. Midnight was the middle watch (Judg. 7:19). Morning watch began about 9:30 a.m. (Exod. 14:24). It was called cockcrow in NT times (Matt. 26:34; Mark 13: 35). The watch was so named because of the changing of watchmen and was not a very definite period (Ps. 90:4; 119:148; Jer. 51:12). Roman influence caused a revision of the watches, so in the days of Christ there were four divisions of the night (Matt. 14:25; Mark 6:48), these being approximately 9:30 p.m., midnight, 2:30, and 5:00 a.m.

In the Scriptures the words translated *time* have varied connotations. Temporal existence is "my time" (Ps. 89:47, called "my life" in Job 7:7). A period allotted for a special object, task, or cause was its time (Eccl. 3:1; 8:6). A special period of life was "a time," as a period of conception (Gen. 18:10,14) and the days of pregnancy (I Sam. 1:20); any special feast or celebration (Ps. 81:3); an occasion for the consummation of divine plans (Job 24:1; Jer. 2:27; John 7:6,8; I Tim. 6:15; Acts 3:21; Rom. 8:22,23); a time for showing affection (Eccl. 3:8; Ezek. 16:8). The dispensation of grace is the time of salvation (Ps. 69:13; Isa. 49:8; II Cor. 6:2).

Ancient people had no method of reckoning long periods of time. The Greeks did develop the idea of eras, or connected time elements. The Olympian era dated from 766 B.C.; the Seleucid era from 312 B.C. Their year began on January 1. In Asia Minor the year began with the autumnal equinox. It is, therefore, difficult to determine any precise date for events occurring during NT days. Luke's dating of events (1:5; 2:1,2; 3:1) when John the Baptist began his ministry is the only definite fact upon which to determine the times of Jesus with any certainty.

The Hebrews used great and well-known events like the Exodus, the Babylonian Exile, the building of the temple, the earthquake (Amos 1:1) as fixed points for indicating the time of other events. In the Maccabean age the beginning of the Seleucid era (312 B.C.) became a starting-point. J.D.F.

TIMES, OBSERVER OF (See Occupations and Professions)

TIMEUS, TIMAEUS (tĭ-mē'ŭs, Gr. *Timaiós*), the father of a blind man whose eyes Jesus opened (Mark 10:46-52), the name Bartemaeus meaning "son of Timaeus."

TIMNA (tĭm'nà, Heb. *timna', holding in check*). 1. A concubine of Esau's son Eliphaz (Gen. 36:12).
2. Horite woman, sister of Lotan, who was a son of Seir (Gen. 36:22).
3. A chief or clan descended from Esau (Gen. 36:40, spelled Timnah).
4. A son of Eliphaz (I Chron. 1:36). (There is some uncertainty regarding the above.)

The Hill of Timnah, now called Tibnah, which site figured in the story of Samson. © MPS

TIMNAH (tĭm'nà, Heb. *timnâh*). In KJV eight times Timnath (Gen. 38:12-14; Judg. 14:1-5), once Thimnathah (Josh. 19:43). 1. A town on the border of Judah (Josh. 15:10), later given to the tribe of Dan (Josh. 19:43). Its site is at Tibnah, c. three miles SW of Beth-Shemesh.
2. A town in the hill country of Judah (Josh. 15:57). Its exact location is uncertain.
3. Probably a town in Edom (Gen. 36:12,22,40; I Chron. 1:39,51).

TIMNATH (See Timnah)

TIMNATH-HERES (See Timnath-Serah)

TIMNATH-SERAH (tĭm'năth-hē'rēz, Heb. *timnath serah*), the same as Timnath-heres (Judg. 2:9). It was a village in Ephraim which Joshua requested as an inheritance (Josh. 19:50), which he rebuilt, and where his remains were buried (Josh. 24:30). It is probably Tibnah, 12 miles NE of Lydda.

TIMNITE (tĭm'nīt, Heb. *timnî*), a native of Timnah whose daughter was married to Samson (Judg. 15: 3-6).

TIMON (tī'mŏn, Gr. *Tímon*), one of the seven chosen by the church in Jerusalem to relieve the apostles of having to look after the poor (Acts 6:5).

TIMOTHEUS (See Timothy)

TIMOTHY (tĭm'ō-thē, Gr. *Timótheos, honoring God*), Paul's spiritual child (I Tim. 1:2; II Tim. 1:2), later the apostle's fellow-traveler and official representative. His character was a blend of amiability and faithfulness in spite of natural timidity. Paul loved Timothy and admired his outstanding personality-traits. One must read Philippians 2:19-22 to know how highly the apostle esteemed this young friend. None of Paul's companions is mentioned as often and is with him as constantly as is Timothy. That this relationship was of an enduring nature is clear from II Timothy 4:9,21. Paul knew that he could count on Timothy. He was the kind of person who in spite of his youth — he was Paul's junior by several years (I Tim. 4:12), his natural reserve and timidity (I Cor. 16:10; II Tim. 1:7), and his frequent ailments (I Tim. 5:23), was willing to leave his home to accompany the apostle on dangerous journeys, to be sent on difficult errands, and to remain to the very end Christ's faithful servant.

In the popular mind the distinction between Timothy and Titus is not always clear. Both of these men were Paul's worthy fellow-workers. The difference, however, is as follows. Titus was more of a leader; Timothy, more of a follower. Titus was resourceful, a man of initiative in a good cause. One finds in him something of the aggressiveness of Paul. (See the article on *Titus.*) Timothy, on the other hand, was shy, reserved. Nevertheless, he was ever obedient, cooperative. He manifested this complete willingness even when he was required to do things which ran counter to his natural shyness.

Timothy is first mentioned in Acts 16:1, from which passage it may be inferred that he was an inhabitant of Lystra (cf. Acts 20:4). He was the offspring of a mixed marriage: a Greek pagan father and a devout Jewish mother, Eunice (Acts 16:1; II Tim. 1:5). From the days of his childhood Timothy had been instructed in the sacred writings of the OT (II Tim. 3:15). In the manner of devout Israelites his grandmother Lois and mother Eunice had nurtured him (II Tim. 1:5). Then came Paul who taught this devout family that Jesus Christ is the fulfilment of the OT. First grandmother Lois and mother Eunice accepted the Christ, then, as a result of their cooperation with Paul, Timothy also did so (II Tim. 1:5). This took place on Paul's first missionary journey. Hence Timothy knew about the persecutions and sufferings which the missionaries (Paul and Barnabas) had experienced on that first journey (II Tim. 3:11), that is, even before Timothy had joined Paul in active missionary labor. When, on the second journey, Paul and Silas came to Derbe and Lystra, Timothy became an active member of the group. Paul took Timothy and circumcised him. Here it must be remembered that Timothy's mother was a Jewess. The case with him was different, therefore, from that of Titus. Timothy's case was not a test case to determine upon what basis Gentiles would be allowed to enter the church. In all probability it was also at this time that by the elders of the local church Timothy was ordained to his new task, Paul himself taking part in this solemn laying on of hands (I Tim. 4:14; II Tim. 1:6).

Timothy then accompanied the missionaries by crossing over into Europe: Philippi, Thessalonica. He also helped the others in the next place to which they came, Berea. Here he and Silas were left behind to give spiritual support to the infant church, while Paul himself went on to Athens (Acts 17:10-15). At Paul's request Timothy a little later left Berea and found the apostle while the latter was still at Athens. Afterward he was sent back to Thessalonica for the purpose of strengthening the brothers there (I Thess. 3:1,2). After Paul had left Athens and had begun his labors in Corinth, both Silas and Timothy rejoined the apostle (Acts 18:1,5). At Corinth Timothy worked with Paul. On the third missionary journey Timothy was again with the apostle during the lengthy Ephesus ministry. From there he was sent to Macedonia and to Corinth (Acts 19:21,22; I Cor. 4:17; 16:10). When Paul arrived in Macedonia, Timothy rejoined him (II Cor. 1:1). Afterward he accompanied the apostle to Corinth (Rom. 16:21) was with him on the return to Macedonia (Acts 20:3,4), and was waiting for him at Troas (Acts 20:5). He was probably also with Paul in Jerusalem (I Cor. 16:3). During Paul's first imprisonment at Rome the two were again in close contact (Phil. 1:1; Col. 1:1; Philem. 1:1). When the apostle expected to be released shortly, he told the Philippians that he expected to send Timothy to them soon (Phil. 2:19).

Timothy is next found in Ephesus, where the apostle has joined him. Paul, on leaving, asked Timothy to remain at this place (I Tim. 1:3). While there, Timothy one day received a letter from Paul, the letter which we now call I Timothy. Later another letter arrived in which Paul, writing from Rome as a prisoner facing death, urged his friend to come to him before winter (II Tim. 4:9, 21). Whether the two ever actually saw each other's face again is not recorded. That Timothy tried to see the apostle is certain. See TITUS.

W.H.

TIMOTHY, EPISTLES TO (See Pastoral Epistles)

TINKLING, the sound of small bells worn by women on a chain fastened to anklets. The picture in Isaiah 3:16 is that of affected pose and short, jerky steps which jingled the chain and bells. I Corinthians 13:1 should be rendered "clanging cymbals."

TIPHSAH (tĭf'sà, Heb. *tiphsah*). 1. A town on the northern border of Solomon's kingdom (I Kings 4: 24). It was an important city on the Euphrates River where the caravan route from Egypt and Syria passed en route to countries to the East. Greek and Roman records give it Thapsaeus and indicate that it was strongly fortified. Xenophon tells how Cyrus II crossed the river at this ford (Anab. 1: 4:2).

2. A town, apparently not far from Tirzah, the inhabitants of which were massacred by Menahem (II Kings 15:16). It was on the Jordan, and is possibly modern Tappuah.

TIRAS (tĭ'răs, Heb. *tîras*), youngest son of Japheth (Gen. 10:2; I Chron. 1:5). He is not mentioned elsewhere. Josephus (Ant. 1:6; 1) held with other ancients that he was founder of the Thracians. Modern scholars do not agree, but make him founder of a race of pirates called *Tursenich* who once plied the Aegean Sea. The name Thrusa has been found among Egyptian records, which indicates that they invaded the land during the reign of Merneptah about 1250 B.C.

TIRATHITE (tĭ'răth-ît, Heb. *tîr'āthîm*), a member of a family of scribes from Tirah who lived in Jabeth (I Chron. 2:55).

TIRE (Heb. *pe'ēr, headdress*), an ornamental headdress (Ezek. 24:17,23) worn by Aaron (Exod. 39:28; KJV bonnet), women (Isa. 3:20; KJV bonnet), and bridegrooms (Isa. 61:10; KJV ornaments).

TIRHAKAH (tûr'hà-kà, Heb. *tirhāqâh*), an Egyptian king, the third and last king of the twenty-fifth or Ethiopian dynasty. He was the son of Piankhi, whose capital was at Napata, just below the Fourth Cataract. This Nubian kingdom was quite Egyptian in character, and late in the eighth century Piankhi conquered all of Egypt. There was much confusion in the Egyptian political situation, as described in Isaiah 19, and Isaiah saw the danger of relying on Egypt. Tirhakah was commander of the ·army of Shabaka, his uncle and first king of Dyn. 25, and led the Egyptian armies in their initial conflict with Assyria. II Kings 19:9 and Isaiah 37:9 state that Sennacherib, while besieging Judean cities, heard that Tirhakah was coming against him. Sennacherib was successful against Tirhakah, but the loss of his troops forced him back to Assyria (I Kings 19:35-36; Isa. 37:36-37). Becoming king about 689, Tirhakah enjoyed a respite from the Assyrian threat for some years, but was defeated by Esarhaddon and later by Assurbanipal; he was driven S, where he retained rule of Upper Egypt.

C.E.D.

TIRHANAH (tûr′hà-nà, Heb. *tirhanâh*), a son of Caleb by his concubine Maacah (I Chron. 2:48).

TIRIA (tĭr′ĭ-à, Heb. *tireyā′*), a son of Jehaleleel (I Chron. 4:16).

TIRSHATHA (tûr-shā′thà, Heb. *tirshāthā′, revered*), the Persian title of the governor of Judah under the Persians. Zerubbabel (Ezra 2:63; Neh. 7:65,70), and Nehemiah (Neh. 8:9; 10:1) bore the title.

TIRZAH (tûr′zà, Heb. *tirtsâh*). 1. The youngest daughter of Zelopehad (Num. 26:33; Josh. 17:3).
2. A town six miles E of Samaria captured by Joshua (Josh. 12:24). It must have been noted for its beauty, since Solomon compared his beautiful Shulamite woman to the beauty of Tirzah (Song 6:4). With the division of the kingdom after the death of Solomon, it became the capital of the northern kingdom (I Kings 14:17). In it reigned Baasha (15:21-33), his son Elah, and Zimri (16:6-15). Omri defeated Tibni and, since Zimri had destroyed the palace in Tirzah (vs. 18) moved the capital to Damascus (vss. 23,24). While Uzziah ruled in Judah, Menahem of Tirzah conspired against Shallum of Israel, slew him, and began a ten-year wicked reign (II Kings 15:16-18). It is probably to be identified with Tell el-Far′ah about seven miles NE of Nablus. J.D.F.

TISHBITE (tĭsh′bīt, Heb. *tishbî*). Elijah is mentioned as a Tishbite in I Kings 17:1. The RSV gives a good reading, "Elijah the Tishbite of Tishbeh in Gilead." The place has been identified, with some probability, with the modern el-Istib, a little W of Mahanaim.

TITHE (tīth, Heb. *ma'ăsēr*, Gr. *dekáte, the tenth*). Just when and where the idea arose of making the tenth the rate for paying tribute to rulers and of offering gifts as a religious duty cannot be determined. History reveals that it existed in Babylon in ancient times, also in Persia and Egypt, even in China. It is quite certain that Abraham knew of it when he migrated from Ur (Gen. 14:17-20). Since Melchizedek was a priest of the Most High, it is certain that by Abraham's day the giving of tithes had been recognized as a holy deed (see Heb. 7:4). Dividing the spoils of war with rulers and religious leaders was widespread (I Macc. 10:31). Samuel warned Israel that the king whom they were demanding would exact tithes of their grain and flocks (I Sam. 8:10-18). When Jacob made his covenant with God at Bethel it included payment of tithes (Gen. 28:16-22).

It was a long time before definite legal requirements were set upon tithing, hence customs in paying it varied. At first the tither was entitled to share his tithe with the Levites (Deut. 14:22,23). After the Levitical code had been completed, tithes belonged exclusively to the Levites (Num. 18:21). If a Hebrew lived too far from the temple to make taking his tithes practicable, he could sell them and use the money gained to buy substitutes at the temple (Deut. 14:24-26). This permit eventually led to gross abuses by priests (Matt. 21:12,13; Mark 11:15-17). Tithed animals were shared with the Levites (Deut. 15:19,20).

The methods developed for paying the tithes and for their use became somewhat complicated, when to the tithes of the first fruits (Prov. 3:9) were added the firstlings of the flocks (Exod. 13:12,13). Then when the Levitical system was established, provision for the upkeep of the sons of Levi was made by tithes (Num. 18:21-24). A penalty of 20 percent of the tithe was exacted from one who sold his tithes and refused to use the money to pay for a substitute (Lev. 27:31). The Levites in turn gave a tenth to provide for the priests (Num. 18: 25-32). The temple was the place to which tithes were taken (Deut. 12:5-12). One could not partake of his tithes at home, but only when delivered at the temple (Deut. 12:17,18).

To make sure that no deceit would be practiced regarding tithing, each Hebrew was compelled to make a declaration of honesty before the Lord (Deut. 26:13-15). In taking the tithe of the flocks every tenth animal that passed under the rod, regardless of its kind, was taken; no substitution was allowed (Lev. 27:32,33). Was there only one tithe each year or was the third-year tithe an extra one? Confusion exists about this, even among Hebrew scholars themselves. As the needs for funds increased with the expansion of the temple service, a third-year tithe, all for the use of the Levites and those in need was exacted. It seems probable that the increase of temple expenses, due to the number of priests and Levites, made it necessary to impose extra tithes. According to Josephus, even a third tithe was collected (Ant. IV:4;3; VIII:8;22). Malachi (3:8-10) railed at the Jews for refusing to bring their tithes to the temple storehouse. This did not apply to money but to grains, animals, and fowls, money being deposited in the treasury box (Luke 21:1-4).

By the time of Christ, Roman rule had greatly affected the economic life of Judea, hence it was difficult for people to tithe. But that the laws regarding the tenth were still observed is shown by the fact that the Pharisees tithed even the herbs that were used in seasoning food (Matt. 23:23; Luke 11:42). J.D.F.

TITTLE (tĭt′l, Gr. *keraía, a horn*), a small, horn-shaped mark used to indicate accent in Hebrew (Matt. 5:18; Luke 16:17). In Matthew 5:18 it is used with *jot* (Gr. *iota*) to denote a minute requirement of the law.

TITUS (tī′tŭs, Gr. *Títos*), a convert, friend, and helper of Paul (Titus 1:4), in the NT mentioned only in Paul's epistles, especially in II Corinthians. He was a Greek, a son of Gentile parents (Gal. 2:3). After his conversion he accompanied Paul to Jerusalem, where Paul rejected the demand of the Judaists that Titus be circumcised. Hence, Titus became a person of significance for the principle of Gentile-admission to the Church solely on the basis of faith in Christ. During Paul's third missionary journey Titus was assigned missions to Corinth to solve its vexing problems (I Cor. 1-6; II Cor. 2:13; 7:5-16) and to encourage material assistance to the needy at Jerusalem (II Cor. 8). Much later Titus was in Crete, left behind there by Paul to organize its churches (Titus 1:4,5). He was requested to meet Paul at Nicopolis (Titus 3: 12). Titus was consecrated, courageous, resourceful. He knew how to handle the quarrelsome Corinthians, the mendacious Cretans, and the pugnacious Dalmatians (II Tim. 4:10). W.H.

TITUS, EPISTLE TO (See Pastoral Epistles)

TITUS, FLAVIUS VESPASIANUS. Born A.D. 39, the son of the future emperor Vespasian, Titus served in Germany and Britain before proceeding to Palestine as a legate on his father's staff. When Vespasian emerged from the troubled events of A.D. 69 as the successful claimant for the principate, Titus inherited the Jewish war, which he concluded in A.D. 70 by his capture of Jerusalem. On his return to Rome, Titus was associated with his father's government and marked out thus for the succession. He succeeded to the principate on Vespasian's death in A.D. 79. Good-looking, intelligent, open-handed, and the darling of the troops,

Titus was a popular emperor during the two brief years of his principate. Despite the advantage of Vespasian's carefully hoarded wealth, had he not died prematurely in A.D. 81, he might have proved financially incapable of continuing the easy course of generosity which was an element in his popularity. Titus completed the Colosseum. The great eruption of Vesuvius (Aug. 24, 79) occurred at the beginning of Titus' reign. In the latter years of Vespasian, Titus was notorious for his liaison with Bernice, sister of Agrippa II, who listened to Paul's defense at Caesarea (Acts 15:13). E.M.B.

TITUS JUSTUS (See Justus)

TIZITE (tĭ′zīt, Heb. *ha-tîtsî*), the designation of Toha, one of the valiant men of David's army (I Chron. 11:45).

TOAH (tō′à, Heb. *tôah*), an ancestor of Samuel (I Chron. 6:34, Nahath in vs. 26). He is called Tohu in I Samuel 1:1.

TOB (tŏb, Heb. *tôv*), a fertile district in Syria, extending NE from Gilead. Jephtha, a mighty man of Gilead, took refuge in Tob (Judg. 11:1-3). When Israel was beset by Ammonites, the elders in Gilead begged him to return and take charge of their army (Judg. 11:4-11). When Ammon was being overcome by David, 12,000 men of Tob were hired by David against him (II Sam. 10:6,8).

TOB-ADONIJAH (tŏb-ăd-ō-nī′jà, *tôv 'ădhônîyâh, Jehovah is good*), a Levite, sent by Jehoshaphat to teach the law to Judah (II Chron. 17:7-9).

TOBIAH, TOBAJAH (tō-bī′à, tō-bī′jà, Heb. *tôvîyâh, Jehovah is good*). 1. One of the Levites whom Jehoshaphat sent to teach the law in Judah (II Chron. 17:7-9).

2. A family among the exiles who returned to Jerusalem under Zerubbabel, who were not able to provide proofs of being Israelites (Ezra 2:59, 60; Neh. 7:61,62).

3. An Ammonite, half Jew, who with Sanballat tried to hinder Nehemiah in repairing Jerusalem (Neh. 2:10,19). Prior to the coming of Nehemiah, Tobiah had connived with a priest named Elisha, and made himself private quarters in the temple. Nehemiah dispossessed him (Neh. 13:4ff).

4. One of the exiles who returned to Jerusalem bringing gold and silver from Babylon from which Zechariah was instructed to make a crown for the high priest (Zech. 6:9-15).

TOBIT, BOOK OF (See Apocrypha)

TOCHEN (tō′kĕn, Heb. *tōkhen, a measure*), a town included in the heritage of Simeon (I Chron. 4: 32).

TOGARMAH (tō-gà′mà, Heb. *tôgharmâh*), a man who appears in two genealogies (Gen. 10:3; I Chron. 1:6) as a son of Gomer, who is a descendant of Japheth. Ezekiel 27:14 states that Beth-togarmah traded "horses, war horses, and mules" (RSV) for Tyrian wares. Later the prophet lists among the forces of Gog: "Beth-togarmah from the uttermost parts of the north with all his hordes" (Ezek. 38:6, RSV). Togarmah is found in the Hittite texts from Boghaz Koi and some Assyriologists equate Togarmah with Til-Garimmu, a province between the Euphrates River and the Antitaurus Mountains. It would appear, however, that the prophet may refer to a people or nation more distant from Palestine.   C.E.D.

TOHU, an ancestor of Samuel (I Sam. 1:1). See NAHATH 2.

TOI (tō′ē, Heb. *tō′û*), king of Hamath who congratulated David for his victory over their common foe, Hadadezer, king of Zobah (II Sam. 8:9-11).

TOKEN (Heb. *'ôth, sign, token;* Gr. *éndeigma, éndeixis, sússemon, semeíon*), a word which in the OT is used practically synonymously with *sign* (Exod. 13:9,16). In Numbers 17:10 and Joshua 2:12 it means a memorial of something past. In the NT the word is self-explanatory (Mark 14:44; Phil. 1:28; II Thess. 1:5; 3:17).

TOLA (tō′là, Heb. *tôlā'*). 1. One of Issachar's sons who migrated to Egypt under Jacob and founded a tribal family (Gen. 46:1-13).

2. Son of Puah, of the tribe of Issachar, who judged Israel 23 years (Judg. 10:1,2).

TOLAD (tō′lăd, Heb. *tôladh*), a city occupied by sons of Simeon (I Chron. 4:29).

TOMB (Gr. *táphos*). The word tomb is used rather loosely. It may mean a chamber, vault or crypt, either under ground or above. It may refer to a pretentious burying place on a special site. It may be a bee-hive structure wherein many bodies can be placed. In general, any burying place is a tomb.

The so-called Tombs of the Judges, near Jerusalem. Top view is the outside entrance, and below, the interior, showing crypts, or loculi. The character of architecture and decoration indicate a much later date than the time of the Judges. © MPS

The Hebrews were not impressed by the tombs of Egypt, hence their burials remained simple, most burying sites being unmarked. Some kings were interred in a vault in Jerusalem, the "sepulchre of their fathers" or of David (II Sam. 2:32; Neh. 2:3). Just where this burial place was located has not been determined.

Tombs of NT times were either caves or else were dug into stone cliffs. Since only grave clothes are mentioned in connection with tombs, it seems certain that the Jews used neither caskets nor sarcophagi. Tombs carried no inscriptions, no paintings. Embalming, learned in Egypt (Gen. 50:2), was soon a lost art (John 11:39). A general opening gave access to vaults which opened upon ledges to provide support for the stone doors. The door to such a grave weighed from one to three tons, hence the miracle of its being rolled away (Luke 24:2; John 20:1). J.D.F.

An ossuary from a Jewish tomb at Jerusalem. These stone boxes held the bones of deceased when room was required for new burials in the tombs. Large numbers of these ossuaries date from the time of Jesus and the Apostles. UANT

TONGS (Heb. *melqāhayim*). In the Heb. the word usually means snuffers, and is used with snuffdish (Exod. 25:38; Num. 4:9); in Isaiah 6:6 it is *tongs*. In I Kings 7:49 and II Chronicles 4:21 it could be either. In Isaiah 44:12 (RSV) it is correctly rendered *axe*.

TONGUE (Heb. *lāshôn*, Gr. *glóssa*). 1. An organ of the body, used by Gideon's men in drinking (Judg. 7:5; see also Zech. 14:12; Mark 7:33; Ps. 68:23; Rev. 16:10).

2. An organ of speech (Job 27:4; Ps. 35:28; Prov. 15:2; Mark 7:35).

3. A language or dialect (Gen. 10:5,20; Deut. 28:49; Esth. 1:22, tr. language in the KJV, Dan. 1:4; Acts 1:19; 2:8; 10:46).

4. A people or race having a common language (Isa. 66:18; Dan. 3:4; Rev. 5:9; 10:11, note the repetition, "peoples, nations, tongues").

5. The figurative uses of the word are interesting. The tongue can be sharpened, i.e. made to utter caustic words (Ps. 64:3; 140:3). It is a sharp sword (Ps. 57:4). It is a soft tongue when it uses quieting language (Prov. 25:15). Ranting is a rage of tongues (Ps. 31:20; Hos. 7:16). It is the pen of an eager writer (Ps. 45:1), a shrewd antagonist (Ps. 52:2). The tongue of the just is a treasure (Prov. 10:20; 12:18), and a mark of wisdom (Isa. 50:4). It is like a bow (Jer. 9:3), an arrow (Jer. 9:8), and a lash (Jer. 18:18). The miracle at Pentecost had cloven tongues (Acts 2:3). The tongue is little but can do great things (James 3:5,8). In Acts 1:19; 2:8; 21:40; 22:2, etc., the original word is *dialektos, dialect,* which is rendered *language* in the KJV.

A well-preserved tomb, with a rolling stone at the entrance, near Kirjath-jearim. © MPS

TONGUES, CONFUSION OF. The Tower of Babel presents an answer to an otherwise insoluble mystery, and a revelation regarding God's anger against human vanity and disobedience. That there was originally a common language among men becomes more certain as linguistic research progresses. Many theories have arisen to account for the sudden confusion of tongues at Babel. One is that the whole account is a myth, adapted by Moses to account for the varied speeches which he knew. Another attributes the confusion to a slow change in speech caused by an ancient population explosion resulting in widely scattered peoples who, having no written language, soon developed various forms of speech. But for one to whom miracles exist only to the finite mind, it is easy to understand the account in Genesis 11:1-9, for He who designed the media of speech could have, in an instant, made such modifications in these media as to have caused the confusion. J.D.F.

TONGUES OF FIRE, one of the phenomena which occurred at the outpouring of the Holy Spirit on the day of Pentecost. "Tongues parting asunder like as fire . . . sat upon each one of them" (Acts 2:3 ASV) as they were all filled with the Holy Spirit. The tongues of fire were symbolic of the Holy Spirit who came in power on the Church.

TONGUES, GIFT OF, a spiritual gift mentioned in Mark 16:17; Acts 2:1-13; 10:44-46; 19:6; I Corinthians 12,14. The gift appeared on the day of Pentecost with the outpouring of the Holy Spirit on the assembled believers (Acts 2:1-13). The *external* phenomena heralding the Spirit's coming were followed by the *internal* filling of all those assembled. The immediate result was that they "began to speak with other tongues." "Began" implies that the phenomenon recorded was now first imparted and that it was afterwards repeated (cf. Acts 8:17-18; 10:44-46; 19:6). The context makes it clear that "other tongues" means languages different from their own, and by implication, previously unknown to the speakers, for the amazement of the crowd, coming from many lands, was caused by the fact that *Galileans* could speak these varied languages. Under His control they spoke "as the Spirit gave them utterance"; the utterances were *praise* to God (2:11; 10:46). The gift was not designed merely to facilitate the preaching of the Gospel; the message in vss. 14-36 was not delivered in more than one language. There is no *express* NT instance of this gift being used to evangelize others. (At Lystra Paul and Barnabas preached in Greek, not the native Lycaonian which they did not understand). The gift of tongues on Pentecost was a direct witness to God's presence and work in their midst. While the gift came upon all those assembled when the Spirit was poured out (vs. 4), there is no indication that the 3,000 converts at Pentecost received the gift.

It is not stated that the Samaritans received this gift when the Spirit was imparted to them, but the request of Simon to buy the power to bestow the Spirit indicates that some *external* manifestation did result (Acts 8:14-19). The Pentecostal phenomenon clearly appeared again when the Holy Spirit was poured out upon the Gentiles in the house of Cornelius (Acts 10:44-46). Here again it served as a miraculous token of the divine approval and acceptance of these Gentile believers (11:15-17; 15:7-9). The appearing of the phenomenon in connection with the 12 disciples at Ephesus (Acts 19:6), who dispensationally stood before Pentecost, marked the full incorporation of this group into the Church and authenticated Paul's teaching.

The gift of tongues is mentioned by Paul as one of the spiritual gifts so richly bestowed upon the Corinthian believers. Their reaction to this gift drew forth Paul's discussion of the varied gifts. They are enumerated, compared, and evaluated by their usefulness to the Church. Twice he lists the gifts and places tongues and their interpretation at the very bottom of the scale (12:8-10,28-30), thus rebuking their improper evaluation of this spectacular gift. He emphasized the comparative value of tongues and prophecy by insisting that "five words" intelligibly spoken in the church were of more value than "ten thousand words in a tongue" not understood (14:19). Paul felt it necessary to regulate the use of tongues in their assembly; the ideal place for their exercise was in private (14:28). He insisted that not more than two or three speak in tongues, and that in turn, and one interpret; no one was to speak in tongues if no interpreter was present (14:27-28). Their use was not prohibited (14:39), but intelligent preaching in understandable words was vastly superior. He further insisted that women were not to speak in such meetings (14:34).

Two views are held as to the exact nature of the Corinthian "tongues." One view holds that they were foreign languages which the speakers were miraculously enabled to speak without having previously learned them. This view is demanded by Acts 2:1-13, unless it is admitted that the two phenomena are quite distinct. That they were intelligible utterances is urged from the fact that they could be interpreted and were the vehicle of prayer, praise, and thanksgiving (I Cor. 14:14-17). Modern commentators generally hold that the Corinthian tongues were not identical with the Pentecostal tongues, but were ecstatic outbursts of prayer and praise in which the utterances often

became abnormal and incoherent and the connection with the speaker's own conscious intellectual activity was suspended. It is held that the utterances were incomprehensible to the speaker as well as to the audience (14:14) and that the resultant edification was emotional only (14:4). But 14:4 may only mean that his understanding was "unfruitful" to others. Its advocates further hold that this view is indicated in the fact that interpretation was likewise a special gift (12:10). From 14:27-28 it is clear that this speaking in tongues was not uncontrollable: it was very different from the religious frenzy which marked some heathen rites in which the worshiper lost control both of reason and the power of will. Any manifestation of tongues which is not under the control of the speaker is thereby suspect (14:32).   D.E.H.

TOOLS. In the Bible a variety of tools used by the ancients are mentioned. These may be grouped into various categories: 1. Cutting tools: knife (Gen. 22:6,10; Judg. 19:29); saw (Isa. 10:15); sickle (Joel 3:13); axe (Deut. 19:5; 20:19); reaping hook (Isa. 44:12); pruning hook (Isa. 2:4; 18:5).

2. Boring tools: the aul (Exod. 21:6; Deut. 15:17).

3. Forks and shovels (I Sam. 13:21; I Kings 7:40,45); tongs (Exod. 25:38).

4. Carpentry tools: hammer (Judg. 5:26); plane (Isa. 44:13); plummet (Amos 7:8); level (II Kings 21:13).

5. Drawing tools: stylus (Isa. 44:13); compass (Isa. 44:13).

6. Measuring tools: line (I Kings 7:23; II Kings 21:13); measuring reed (Ezek. 40:3-8; Rev. 11:1).

7. Tilling tools: ploughshare (I Sam. 13:20,21); mattock (I Sam. 13:20,21).

8. Metal-working tools: anvil (Isa. 41:7); file (I Sam. 13:21).

9. Stone-working tools: chisel (Exod. 20:25); saw (I Kings 7:9).

TOOTH (Heb. *shēn, tooth, ivory*; Gr. *odoús, tooth*). These words are used to denote human teeth in Numbers 11:33, also in the following passages: in the law of retaliation, "a tooth for a tooth" (Exod. 21:24; Lev. 24:20; Deut. 19:21; Matt. 5:38; cf. Exod. 21:27); in the common expression: "gnashing of the teeth," in cruel hatred (Job 16:9; Ps. 35:16; 37:12; Lam. 2:16; Acts 7:54), or in anguish and despair (Ps. 112:10; Matt. 8:12; 13:42; 22:13; 24:15; 25:30; Luke 13:28); once gnashing the teeth is mentioned as due to epilepsy (Mark 9:18; ASV "grinding"); Proverbs 10:26 refers to the effect of acid on teeth.

A number of references mention the teeth of animals: of unspecified beasts (Deut. 32:24); of young lions (Job 4:10); of leviathan, probably a crocodile (Job 41:14); two prophetic visions reveal symbolic beasts with teeth: a bear (Dan. 7:5), a terrible beast (Dan. 7:7,19), locusts with teeth like lions' (Rev. 9:8).

The teeth are used in a variety of figurative expressions: Jeremiah and Ezekiel cite a proverb of the people, "the fathers have eaten sour grapes and the children's teeth are set on edge" (Jer. 31:29; Ezek. 18:2), meaning that the children were suffering on account of the sins of their fathers, but the Lord changed this proverb to read: "every man that eateth sour grapes, his teeth shall be set on edge" (Jer. 31:30); a prophetic passage mentions "teeth white with milk" as part of the description of abundant prosperity (Gen. 49:12); the teeth are used to depict evil people, the teeth standing for the person: the unrighteous (Job 29:17), enemies (Ps. 3:7), the wicked (Ps. 124:6), false prophets

(Mic. 3:5), an oppressor (Zech. 9:7); conquered Judah has had her teeth broken (Lam. 3:16); metaphorical uses: teeth like spears and arrows (Ps. 57:4), misplaced confidence is like a broken tooth (Prov. 25:19), teeth as swords (Prov. 30: 14), teeth like freshly-washed sheep (S. of Sol. 4: 2; 6:6); teeth as the weapons of a nation (Joel 1:6); other statements: take his flesh in his teeth, meaning taking his own life (Job 13:14), escaped by the skin of his teeth meaning a narrow escape (Job 19:20), cleanness of teeth, meaning a famine (Amos 4:6).   C.E.H.

TOPHEL (tō'phĕl, Heb. *tōphel, lime, cement*), a place in the wilderness where Moses addressed the Israelites (Deut. 1:1). It is identified by some with modern *el-Tafeleh*, 15 miles SE of the Dead Sea.

TOPHET, TOPETH (tō'phĕt KJV, tō'phĕth ASV, Heb. *tōpheth*), an area in the valley of Hinnom where human sacrifices were made to Molech (Jer. 7:31; II Kings 23:10). It is first mentioned by Isaiah who declared that a Topheth, a place of burning, was prepared by the Lord for the king of Assyria (30:33). Jeremiah predicted that the name of the place would be changed to the valley of slaughter because of the many people who would be killed there (Jer. 7:32,33; 19:6). Josiah defiled this place so that it no longer could be used for idolatrous practices (II Kings 23:10).

TORAH (tō'rà, Heb. *tôrâh, direction, instruction, law*), the common Hebrew word for "law," so rendered over 200 times in the OT. It is used for human instruction, but it usually expresses divine law. So *tôrâh* is direction and guidance from God. Its emphasis is on the purpose of the guidance rather than the origin of it. But authoritative direction means law, thus *tôrâh* is the law of God. Other words cover special kinds of laws such as *judgments* and *statutes*; *tôrâh* is the overall term, the supreme law. Probably, for this reason the entire Pentateuch became known as the Torah. This section of the OT is constantly referred to in the Scriptures as the "law of Moses" or the "law of the Lord." Torah even became the name of the entire Jewish Scriptures. Jesus, cited Psalm 82:6 as part of the law (John 10:34).

The division of the Hebrew Scriptures into the Law (*tôrâh*), the Prophets, and the Writings comes from ancient times. The Samaritans have had only the Pentateuch for their Scripture since ancient times. Perhaps that means that only these five books of Moses were in the sacred canon when the Samaritans began their separate worship. The Torah was divided into 154 sections for usage in the synagogue services. It was read through, a section at a time, in three years.   C.E.H.

TORMENTOR (Gr. *basanistés, torturer*). This word occurs only in the NT (Matt. 18:34) where the unforgiving debtor is delivered to tormentors, probably meaning the jailers.

TOU (tō'ōō, Heb. *tō'û*), king of Hamath who sent presents to David for conquering their common enemy Hadarezer of Zobah (I Chron. 18:9,10). In II Samuel 8:9,10 this name is Toi. See TOI.

TOW (Heb. *ne'ōreth*), the coarse and broken part of flax ready for spinning. In the OT it is used as an example of easily inflammable material (Judg. 16:9; Isa. 1:31).

TOWEL (Gr. *léntion, linen cloth, towel*), a word occurring only in John 13:4,5 where Jesus wrapped Himself in a towel and wiped the disciples' feet with it.

TOWER (Heb. *mighdāl, mighdōl, bāhan, misgāv, pinnâh;* Gr. *pýrgos*), a lofty structure used for pur-

An orthodox Jewish scribe in Jerusalem transcribing the Torah on parchment. © MPS

poses of protection or attack: to defend a city wall, particularly at a gate or a corner in the wall (II Chron. 14:7; 26:9); to protect flocks and herds and to safeguard roads (II Kings 17:9; II Chron. 26:10; 27:4); to observe and to attack a city (Isa. 23:13; to protect a vineyard (Matt. 21:33).

TOWN, the translation of several words used in the OT: *bānôth,* literally *daughters,* always in the plural, the towns surrounding a city. Cities listed as having towns are: Heshbon, Jazer (Num. 21: 25,32 ASV [KJV has "villages"]), Ekron, Ashdod (Josh. 15:45-47), Bethshean, Ibleam, Dor, Endor, Taanach, Megiddo (Josh. 17:11; Judg. 1:27), Areor (Judg. 11:26), Jair, Kenath (I Chron. 2:23), Bethel, Gezer, Shechem, Azzah (I Chron. 7:28), Ono, Lod (I Chron. 8:12), Gath (I Chron. 18:1), Jeshanah, Ephron (II Chron. 13:19), Soco, Timnah, Ginzo (II Chron. 28:18 ASV [KJV "villages"]), Kiriath-arba, Dibon, Jekabzeel, Beersheba, Meconah, Azekah (Neh. 11:25-30 ASV, KJV "villages"). All the "daughters" of these cities were small towns without walls: *hawwôth, village, tent village* (Num. 32:41; Josh. 13:30; I Kings 4:13; I Chron. 2:23), sometimes in compound names — Havoth-jair (ASV Havvoth-jair) (Deut. 3:14; Judg. 10:4). These villages may have been the dwelling places of nomads, that is, tent dwellings; *hātsēr, settled abode, village* (Gen. 25:16 KJV [ASV "village"]). This village was of the Ishmaelites, probably a movable one made up of tents, but this word usually means villages without walls around them; *'îr, city,* the common Hebrew word for "city," translated "town" especially where the context indicates an unwalled town (Deut. 3:5 unwalled, I Sam. 16:4 KJV [ASV "city"]); (I Sam. 23:7) town with gates and bars (I Sam. 27:5 KJV [ASV "city"]), unwalled (Jer. 19:15; Hab. 2:12); *qîr, wall,* once translated "town" (Josh. 2:15; ASV omits); *perāzôth, open region, hamlet* (Zech. 2:4 KJV [ASV "villages"]). This word denotes villages in the open country in contrast to those located in the mountains.

The NT has only one word which means "town": *komó-polis,* which denotes a community larger than a village but smaller than a city; it occurs only once (Mark 1:38). Another word: *komé, village,* is rendered "town" ten times in KJV: (Matt. 10: 11; Mark 8:23,26,27; Luke 5:17; 9:6,12; John 7: 42; 11:1,30). The ASV translates "village" in all three cases.

TOWN CLERK (See Occupations and Professions)

TRACHONITIS (trăk-ō-nī'tĭs, Gr. *Trachonítis, rough region*), a volcanic region SE of Damascus. It has been identified by inscriptions and is mentioned in Luke 3:1 as a tetrarchy of Philip. The "Rough Region" is still known to the Arabs as "the Refuge" or "the fortress of Allah." It has been likened to "a tempest in stone," or a black, petrified sea. The "region of Argob" (Deut. 3:4), part of the realm of Og of Bashan, probably included this wild infertile part. Josephus, writing in the first century, speaks of the predatory nature of the people of Trachonitis (*Ant.* 16:9:1, 10:1). Trajan in A.D. 106 made it part of the new province of Arabia, based on Bosra.   E.M.B.

TRADE AND TRAVEL. I. Trade in the Old Testament. Abraham came from a trading port, Ur of the Chaldees, which stood in those days at the head of the Persian Gulf, on whose waters man first learned deep-sea navigation. Pottery from Ur has been identified in the ruins of Mohenjo-Daro on the Indus, and Ur was no doubt a trading-station between the sea-borne commerce of the Gulf and the Arabian Sea, and the caravan routes of the Euphrates Valley. The most negotiable route between East and West ran this way. The fact that Abraham was rich in gold and silver, wrought and unwrought, as well as in the nomad wealth of flocks and herds (Gen. 13:2; 24:22,53) is indication of the wealth of his birth-place, and of the commerce which no doubt existed between the desert and the town. The middlemen of this early commerce in the Middle East were the people of the desert.

Egypt, from earliest times, had been a great trading nation. A famous wall painting tells pictorially the story of the exploratory trading expedition sent by Princess Hatshepsut to Punt, on the Somali coast, 14 centuries before Christ, and an interesting papyrus speaks of Wen-Amon's quest for fine cedar on the Lebanese shore, three centuries later. Hatshepsut's venture had been a quest for myrrh trees, for the embalming practices of the Egyptians needed vast imports of spices and incense. Arabia Felix owed its name to the myrrh and frankincense produced there, and the bulk of this commerce followed the caravan routes NW through the Arabian peninsula with Egypt as the chief market. Slave-trading formed a profitable side-line, and it is significant that Joseph was sold to a company of Ishmaelites carrying myrrh into Egypt (Gen. 37:25). The rich imports of the land were balanced by an export trade in corn, and by tribute-money from the neighboring spheres of Egyptian dominance. It is recorded that corn was paid for in weighed silver (Gen. 41:57; 42:3,25, 35; 43:11; 1·2:21). Egypt was a heavy importer of precious stones and metals, some of which must have been of Indian origin brought up the Red Sea, and through the canal which was periodically open between the head of that waterway and the Nile. Egyptian monuments speak of similar commerce with the North, and with the Minoan thalassocracy of Crete, the Keftiu of the records.

The first organized commerce of the Hebrew people was under Solomon, whose farsighted trad-

ing ventures were inspired by the Phoenician mercantile cities of Tyre and Sidon. It is possible that the building of the temple first made the Phoenicians aware of the market to be found in their own hinterland, and of the profit to be gained from a partnership with the people who dominated the land route to the Gulf of Akaba. Cedar for the architectural projects of David and Solomon was collected at Tyre from the lumbermen in the ranges, and rafted down to Joppa, a distance of 74 miles. It was then hauled 32 miles up to Jerusalem (I Kings 5:6,9; II Chron. 2:16). The partnership thus begun was extended in a joint commerce out of Ezion-Geber at the head of ¦the Gulf of Akaba, down the Red Sea to Ophir and India. Hiram, king of Tyre, supplied the pilots (I Kings 9:27,28; 10:11). Ophir was, in all probability, in southern Arabia, but the cargoes mentioned in I Kings 10:22 suggests a trading connection with India. A larger type of vessel was used in this ocean-going commerce, the "ships of Tarshish" mentioned in the verse. Tarshish was probably Tartessos in Spain and for such distant and exacting voyaging the Phoenicians had developed a sturdy type of vessel called by this name. An "Indiaman" or a "China clipper" in the days of more recent sail, did not necessarily journey to the lands embedded in the title. They were types of reliable ocean craft. Similarly the Egyptians called the Phoenician galleys engaged on the Cretan run "Keftiu ships." The text quoted seems to imply that Solomon's traders were speedily throwing off the tutelage of Tyre and venturing forth on their own account. Phoenicia was supplied from Judaea with wheat, honey, oil, and balm (I Kings 5:11).

The interchange of such primary produce can even be traced into NT times (Acts 12:20). Tyrian traders brought fish into Jerusalem and distressed Nehemiah by their sabbath trading (Neh. 13:16). The timber trade, too, continued into post-captivity days, and Ezra was constrained to make arrangements similar to those of Solomon to secure his supplies of Lebanese timber (I Kings 5:6,9; II Chron. 2:16; Ezra 3:7). Oil was also exported to Egypt (Hos. 12:1), and a small domestic export trade in woven goods from Judaea seems to be implied in Proverbs 31:24.

When the Hebrew monarchy fell apart after Solomon's death, it is possible that an interesting commercial situation may have arisen. Israel, the northern kingdom, must have inherited the profitable but seductive alliance with the Phoenician trading towns. Jezebel, daughter of the prince of Sidon, was a seal on this partnership. The southern kingdom, however, lay across communications with Akaba and the Red Sea, and there is every evidence that Judah had reverted, after Solomon, to an agricultural economy with nothing more than petty trading. Apart from a half-hearted attempt by Jehoshaphat to revive it (I Kings 22:48), the eastern trade seems to have vanished with the king who inspired and ordered it. It may have been at this time that the Phoenicians, denied the covenient route down the Red Sea, discovered the sea route to India by way of the Cape of Good Hope. A passage in Herodotus (4:42) seems to imply that the intrepid traders succeeded in this amazing achievement. The prosperity of the Phoenician cities certainly continued, and Ezekiel 27 is an eloquent record of the wide and tireless trading activity of Tyre. Ahab's prosperity is also vouched for by the archeologists' confirmation of the king's "ivory house" (I Kings 22:39).

The commercial consequences of the break with Baal-worship, and the death of Jezebel, is an in-

Trade and travel of early Bible days is typified by this view of a camel caravan crossing the Euphrates River on a pontoon bridge near Kufa, in Iraq. © MPS

teresting speculation. Tyre, without great difficulty, could strangle the economic life of Israel. Tyre's dependence on the hinterland for primary produce would provide a strong deterrent, but there is no doubt that the choice on Carmel with which Elijah confronted the people involved economic, as well as theological considerations. The Hebrew kingdoms from this time onward fell into the background as far as commerce was concerned. The captivity brought vast depopulation, and restored Israel was a largely agricultural economy. Internal interchange of goods was vigorous enough from earliest times, and provisions in the Law lay stress on fairness of dealing, and honesty in weights and measures (Lev. 19:35-36; Deut. 25:13-16). The petty trading of the temple, castigated by Christ, was a sample of the seamier side of this internal commerce, but the foreign trade which provoked investment (vid. Moffatt on Eccl. 11:1: "Trust your goods far and wide at sea . . . take shares in several ventures . . .") and brought great wealth, was no more. Palestine at the close of the OT, and in the time of Christ, was a poor land.

II. Trade in the New Testament. Trade and commerce have small place in the Gospels. The people of Palestine were aware of the activities of merchant and of trader, for such parables as those of the talents, and the merchant who found a "pearl of great price" were obviously meant to be understood by those to whom they were addressed. Trade, in the wider sense of the word, all through NT times, was supremely in the hands of Rome and of Italy. There was a growing interference of the State in matters of commerce. The legal machinery by which a "mark in hand or head" could prevent the non-conformist from buying or selling (Rev. 13:16,17) was early apparent.

The foreign trade of the Empire was extensive and varied and one-sided, too, in important cases, for the hoards of Roman coins commonly found in India are an indication of perilously unbalanced trade and great leakage of bullion. Latin and Greek words in early Irish, German, Iranian and even in Indian and Mongolian tongues, suggest the influence of trade. Archeology, especially on the South Indian coast, has a similar word to say. Roman merchants were ubiquitous. There was a Roman market at Delphi outside the sacred precincts, for the prosecution of trade in amulets and souvenirs, and this was probably typical of Italian enterprise abroad wherever crowds were gathered for purposes sacred or profane. From the second century a Roman city stood on Delos, the Aegean center of the slave-trade, and when Mithridates in 88 B.C. massacred the Italian residents of Asia Minor and the surrounding coasts, 25,000 fell in Delos alone out of a total of 100,000, mostly traders and the agents of commerce.

Rome itself was a vast market, and a grim satiric chapter in Revelation (18), constructed after the fashion of an OT taunt-song, and partly in imitation of Ezekiel 27, speaks of the wealth and volume of the capital's trade and the disruption of the world's economy at the fall and passing of a market so rich. Roman trade extended far beyond the boundaries of the Empire. It is certain that merchants from Italy carried their goods into unsubdued Germany, Scandinavia, India, and perhaps China. All this activity sprang from Rome's dominance, the peace which she widely policed, and the absence of political frontiers. There was reason in the merchants' lament imagined in the chapter quoted. Petronius' Trimalchio, the "nouveau riche" of the *Satiricon,* could make fortunes and lose them, and make them over again. And of Augustus the merchants said that "through him they sailed the seas in safety, through him they could make their wealth, through him they were happy." The fascinating account of the last journey of Paul to Rome, first in a tramp-ship from Adramyttium and then in an Alexandrian freighter, probably under charter to the Roman government for the transport of Egyptian corn to the capital, gives a first-hand picture of the hazards of trade, and of the navigation, the ships, and the management of Mediterranean commerce.

Of the commodities of export trade information is not copious. Oysters came to Rome from Britain in barrels of sea-water. The tin-trade of Cornwall, first exploited by the Phoenicians, doubtless continued under Rome. Northern Gaul seems to have had the rudiments of an exporting textile industry, and Gaul certainly exported Samian pottery. Underwater archeology on wrecked ships has revealed that large cargoes of wine were carried. A monogram device of a double S in a trident seems to indicate that one such freighter, wrecked near Marseilles, was the property of a shipowner domiciled at Delos, one Severus Sestius. On the subject of mass production for such trade there is little information, and none on the business organization involved. Certain localities, however, became famous for special commodities, and the commerce implied was no doubt in the hands of specialist traders working a market of their own choice and creation. Lydia, for example (Acts 16:14), "a seller of purple of the city of Thyatira" in Asia Minor was found at Philippi in Macedonia in pursuit of her trade. Corinthian bronze, and the Cilician cloth which was the raw-material of Paul's "tent-making," were probably distributed, locally or abroad, by similar private enterprise (Acts 18: 3). The imagery of John's apocalyptic letter to Laodicea (Rev. 3:14-18) is based partly on the trade and industry of the rich Asian town. An important item of trade in Ephesus, now that the harbor was silting and the port losing its trade and prosperity to Smyrna, was the manufacture of silver shrines of Artemis to sell to the pilgrims and tourists who visited the famous temple.

Ramsay's illuminating researches established the fact of a Laodicean trade in valuable wool garments of various kinds. Glossy black fleeces were produced in this district and the neighboring Colossae by some system of cross-breeding, the genetic effects of which were apparent in the Anatolian flocks of the area until comparatively recent times. There is also evidence of a Laodicean eyesalve, based probably on the thermal mud of the nearby Hierapolis. Hence the taunt in the letter about "white garments," and the anointing of the eyes of the spirit with a more effective medicament. Another of the seven churches of the Apocalypse was a center of trade and commerce. More trade guilds are named in the records of Thyatira than in those of any other Asian city. Lydia, the Thyatiran "seller of purple," was mentioned above, and there are records in inscriptions of wool-workers, linen-workers, dyers, leatherworkers, tanners, potters, bakers, slave-dealers, and bronze-smiths. Lydia's trade possibly fell under the category of the dyers. They brewed a red dye, perhaps the modern Turkey red, from the madder root, which grows abundantly in the district. This "purple" was nearer in color to scarlet than blue, and Lydia's presence in Macedonia, 500 miles away, suggests that the commodity was an important export. It is curious to note in this connection that John uses the figure of Jezebel, the ancient seal and symbol of a compromising trade

alliance with the pagan world, as a description of a "Nicolaitan" of Thyatira, whose fault may have been some spiritually damaging mode of trade relationship with the surrounding pagan world.

The guilds were a major source of difficulty with Christians who sought to work out that mode of intercourse with the secular world around them by which livelihood could be guarded with a conscience intact. The guilds or collegia are mentioned in the story of Ephesus in Acts 19 as a source of organized opposition to the preaching of Christianity. The guilds were not trade unions in the modern sense of the word. Their functions were primarily social, and they covered all trades and professions. Records exist of guilds of bankers, doctors, architects, producers of linen and woolen goods, workers in metal, stone, or clay, builders, carpenters, farmers, fishers, bakers, pastrycooks, embalmers, and transport workers. Like the modern Rotary Club the guilds satisfied the need for social intercourse, but in the close-knit society of the ancient world they exercised a function, and demonstrated an influence, unlike that of any comparable organization today.

Ephesus saw the guild of the silver smiths and allied trades exert pressure on authority and public opinion enough to check the free activities of Paul in the city. The famous letter of Pliny (Ep. 10.96), in which the repression of vigorous Christian activity in Bithynia in A.D. 112 is vividly described, is fairly clear indication that the guild of the butchers, alarmed at the falling-off in sales of sacrificial meat, was the ally of the pagan priesthoods in rousing the official persecution of the thriving church. Nor was it easy for a Christian to prosper in his trade or business if he went out of his way to demonstrate his unsociability by refraining from membership of the appropriate guild, or participation in its activities. Since those activities included periodical feasts in the temple of the god or goddess whose patronage was traditionally acknowledged by the trade or calling concerned, what was the faithful Christian to do? Hence the activities of the "Nicolaitans," the "followers of Balaam," and of "Jezebel" of Thyatira, castigated by Jude, Peter and John. The simple functions and operations of trade and commerce may thus have proved a source of embarrassment, controversy and division in the early church.

III. Travel. Trade implied travel and many of the great journeys of the ancient world were made in the pursuit of commerce and remain unrecorded. Those who pioneered the trade routes from the Euphrates and the Persian Gulf to the Indus civilization and Ceylon must have been intrepid voyagers. The blazing of the "amber route" from Italy to the Baltic coast, the "incense routes" from Arabia Felix through Petra to Palestine, or the Phoenician seaways to Cornwall and the West African coast, not to mention the circumnavigation of the Continent, must have been by experienced and determined travelers. All this voyaging was in the interests of ultimate commercial gain. But there were other motives:

A. Colonization. Motivated first by the pressure of increasing population on the limited resources of the Greek homeland, Greek colonies spread round the coasts of the Mediterranean and Black Sea, unbroken save for the length of African littoral from the Gulf of Syrtis Major westwards. These colonies, like the "factories" of the East India Company were places of trade as well as of settlement, and the population often remained distinctive and apart from the natives of the area.

Communication was maintained between colony and metropolis and this intercourse was a major occasion of ancient travel. Motives similar to that which sent Abraham's steward to the homeland in search of a bride for Isaac, kept people moving over such routes of folk-migration.

B. Exploration. Curiosity and desire for knowledge have always been important objects for human wandering. Curiosity accounted for the journey of the Queen of Sheba to visit Solomon (I Kings 10), and if the Magi, as their gifts imply, also came from Arabia Felix, it was the same southeastern caravan route which, in a nobler curiosity, brought the Nativity visitors to Bethlehem. Curiosity, with historical ends in view, had been the travel-motive of the Greek Herodotus in the fifth century before Christ. His journeyings covered a wider area even than those of Paul. Exploration was organized by Hatshepsut around the Somali coast, by Alexander around Arabia, and by Nero up the Nile. Trade and conquest were the motives in mind. Less complex was the journey of the daring party from the Bay of Tripoli who, according to Herodotus (4.174), crossed the Sahara, discovered the pygmies, and first saw the Niger.

C. Migration. Great folk movements fill all ancient history from neolithic times onward, and the Bible mentions directly and indirectly, instances of such mass travel. Abraham left Ur by the northwestern caravan routes which followed the Fertile Crescent in a great curve up the Euphrates Valley and around into Canaan. The same route continued down the Jordan Valley and by the coast road into Egypt, or by way of the Arabah into the Sinai triangle or Egypt. It was along this southern route that Jacob's family journeyed on their various movements into and out of Egypt.

The nomad movements of the Israelites after the Egyptian captivity form a record of mass migration like the "folk-wanderings" of the Indo-European tribes which peopled Europe and determined the character of Iranian and Indian ethnology in the second millennium before Christ. When Abraham's tribe moved into Palestine, a colony from Crete was already established on "the Gaza Strip." After the fall of Crete at an undetermined date towards the close of the second millennium before Christ, this movement assumed much more massive shape. A sudden influx of refugees would account for the aggressive imperialism of the Philistines in the time of Saul and David. The movements of conquest and deportation might find a place under this head. It was a policy of Assyria, and of Babylon, its successor, to transfer large masses of subject populations and such travel, arduous and enforced though it was, occasioned much movement geographically. There was some freedom of intercourse between the deportees and those who remained behind, as might be illustrated both from the Books of Nehemiah and Ezra, and from the apocryphal Book of Tobit.

D. Pilgrimage. Religious centers like Jerusalem have always been an occasion of travel. The Gospels mention the annual influx from Galilee into Jerusalem, and the story of the Crucifixion speaks of one Simon from Cyrene in Libya, who was present in the Holy City as a pilgrim. Paul (Acts 20:16) was anxious to be in Jerusalem in time for Pentecost, and was prepared to travel from Greece for the purpose.

E. Preaching. The exigencies of preaching and teaching caused widespread travel in both Greek and Roman times, and this, of course, is most strikingly illustrated in the well-defined and admirably recorded journeys of Paul. The apostle was only one of many. It is traditionally believed that Thomas traveled to India, and a large Christian group in that sub-continent is traditionally believed to have descended from his original foundation. Apollos (Acts 18:24-28) had moved about, no doubt on teaching missions, between Alexandria, Corinth, and Ephesus. The Emperor Claudius, in a stern communication to the Jews of Alexandria, speaks of trouble-makers who had journeyed to the delta town by sea from Syria, and it is likely that this is the first reference in secular literature to the widespread missionary travels of early Christian preachers. Acts 11:19 and 28:15 similarly refer to such unrecorded travelers. It is likely that their journeys were very extensive. The tradition, for example, that Joseph of Arimathea traveled to Glastonbury in Britain, may not be history, but the story could have arisen only in a world which took for granted the widest and most distant traveling.

F. Business. Search of a livelihood, as distinct from the pursuance of trade, took thousands on long journeys in the ancient world. Juvenal, at the end of the first century, complains that the Orontes had long since flowed into the Tiber, that the city had become so cosmopolitan that native merit could find no place, and that the needy and the bad from the ends of the earth had sought refuge there. The inhabitants of the Roman ghetto were Jews whose business had brought them from Palestine and the many provincial centers of the Dispersion, and such uprooted groups were not necessarily static.

G. Service. There were Roman soldiers who had traveled the whole world, and the story of Paul's journey to Rome is an illustration of an official journey of a centurion with an armed escort, engaged on a long and highly responsible courier task. In OT times we find Abraham's steward undertaking a long journey at his master's express command, Tobit acting as Medish agent for the King of Assyria, and Nehemiah adroitly turning a cherished personal project into a royal commission with the travel privileges and facilities such a task conferred.

H. Exile. Moses' flight into Midian was an early instance of a journey undertaken to escape from justice, and more formal banishment was an accepted penalty in ancient penology. After the troubles in the ghetto, associated, if the Nazareth Decree is rightly interpreted, with the first Christian preaching in Rome, Claudius banished all the Jews of the capital (Acts 18:2), and Aquila and Priscilla are found in Corinth. It is interesting to note that Aquila had come originally from Pontus in Asia Minor.

Travel was not without its hazards, and Paul, in an eloquent passage (II Cor. 11:25-27) which finds confirmation in more than one ancient writer, speaks of the perils of road and seaway. Luke's superbly told story of the voyage and wreck of the Alexandrian grainship is further illustration. In NT times, however, travel was rather safer by land than it has been at most periods of history.

Roads were the great contribution of the Romans to Mediterranean civilization, and roads promoted the rapid movement of travelers, and contributed substantially to their safety by facilitating the rapid movement of troops and aiding pacification. The Persians had invented a swift postal system, but it was used mainly for official communications, and no engineering of any major importance was involved. Persia and Babylon relied upon the corvée

Travel in Biblical days was often beset by roadside dangers and lawlessness. © SPF

and local labor for the opening of highways, and the imagery of Isaiah 40:3,4 is based on the call to such contributions of manpower. The Romans, on the other hand, formed and planned their roads, engineered them boldly, and for the most part paved them. Hence a major contribution to rapid travel. In NT times, in spite of the continuing dangers listed by Paul from his own experience, the roading system was speeding up travel, and the Roman Peace was quelling lawlessness.

Regular passenger services by land or sea were unknown, and there is no evidence that the pattern of procedure changed from OT times to New. "Jonah," the records runs (Jonah 1:3), "rose up to flee to Tarshish . . . and went down to Joppa and found a ship going to Tarshish. So he paid the fare thereof and went down into it to go with them to Tarshish." Nine centuries after the approximate date of Jonah's flight a similar record reads: "And we sailed over the sea of Cilicia and Pamphylia and came to Myra a city of Lycia. And there the centurion found a ship of Alexandria sailing to Italy. And he put us therein" (Acts 27:5,6). Travelers evidently made their own arrangements, attached themselves to official parties, accompanied caravans, and coordinated their movements with those of trade and commerce.

The relative convenience of travel by land and sea cannot be estimated. In Claudius' communication to the Alexandrians it is expressly stated that the troublesome envoys who came from Syria came by sea. A perfectly good land route south from Palestine existed, for the Ethiopian eunuch of Queen Candace was using it and riding in a chariot. On the other hand, the centurion in charge of Paul disembarked his party at Puteoli and proceeded to Rome probably via the canal through the Pontine Marshes and certainly via the Via Appia, the route described by the poet Horace who negotiated it a century before. Why Paul decided (Acts 20:13) to go afoot across the base of Cape Lectum by the Roman road to Assos in Mysia is difficult to explain, unless it was because he sought privacy for meditation impossible aboard the crowded ship. Discomfort must have been the common lot of travelers by sea. E.M.B.

TRADE GUILDS or *collegia,* are first mentioned in *The Acts of the Apostles,* chapter 19, as a base of organized opposition to the Christian Church. These societies were not trade unions in the modern sense. Their functions were primarily social. Records exist of guilds of bakers, bankers, doctors, architects, producers of linen and woolen goods, dyers, workers in metal and stone, or clay, builders, carpenters, farmers, pastrycooks, barbers, embalmers, and transport workers. Their ramifications extended to such convivial groups as the "Late Sleepers" and "Late Drinkers" who left their record in the graffiti of Pompeii. "No other age," wrote Dill (*Roman Society from Nero to Marcus Aurelius,* pp. 267, 271) "felt a greater craving for some form of social life, greater than the family and narrower than the State" and the *collegia* satisfied the need of the humble for the pleasures of social intercourse, and the dignity of self-expression. It was the guild of the silversmiths and associated trades which, adroitly led, forced Paul to withdraw from Ephesus. It was, it appears, the guild of the butchers which precipitated the persecution of A.D. 112 in Bithynia (vid. s.v. Pliny). The guild banquets, with associated worship of the patron deity, and the compromising fellowship involved, were probably the problem of I Corinthians. The attempt of certain groups to work out a form of compromise, so essential to the social comfort, and indeed livelihood of many Christians, led to the strong reproaches of Jude, II Peter, and Revelation 2 and 3. E.M.B.

TRADITION (trȧ-dĭ'shŭn, Gr. *parádosis, a giving over,* by word of mouth or in writing). This term does not occur in the Heb. OT. There are three types of tradition mentioned in the NT. First, the most common use, is the kind of tradition handed down by the Jewish fathers or elders which constituted the oral law, regarded by many of the Jews as of equal authority with the revealed law of Moses. Indeed, the Pharisees tended to make these traditions of even greater authority than the Scriptures (Matt. 15:2f; Mark 7:3f). The Pharisees were incensed at Christ because He disregarded their traditions and also permitted His disciples to do so. A classic example of their traditions is recorded in the Gospels (Matt. 15:2-6; Mark 7:1-13).

Paul refers to his former zeal for the traditions of his fathers (Gal. 1:14). Josephus says "that the Pharisees have delivered to the people a great many observances by succession from their fathers which are not written in the law of Moses" (Ant. XIII 10 6).

The second type of tradition is mentioned in Colossians 2:8. Some scholars hold that this verse refers to Judaistic heresies, but the emphasis seems to be upon the *human,* not necessarily Jewish, origin of these teachings.

The third type of tradition is the Gospel truths that the Apostle Paul taught. He uses the word three times (I Cor. 11:2 ASV [KJV "ordinances"]; II Thess. 2:15; 3:6). The meaning of this kind of tradition is "instruction." Paul had taught the believers in Corinth and Thessalonica the doctrines of the Gospel and he urged them to keep these instructions in mind. C.E.H.

TRAIN. 1. Heb. *hayil,* army, a much used word which has the meaning of a train or retinue of a monarch, as in the case of the Queen of Sheba (I Kings 10:2).

2. Heb. *shûl, skirt* of a robe; this word, in regard to the Lord whom Isaiah saw in his vision, is best rendered "train," as it has been in our versions (Isa. 6:1).

3. *Hānak, to train up*, used in Proverbs 22:6 in regard to rearing a child.

4. Gr. *sophronízo, to discipline*, occurs once in the NT (Titus 2:4); translated in KJV "teach," changed in ASV to "train."

TRAJAN (trā'jăn). Marcus Ulpius Traianus held the principate from A.D. 98 to 117. Born in Spain in A.D. 53, Trajan was adopted by Nerva as his heir in A.D. 97, after a distinguished military career. The choice of the able and popular Spanish-born soldier was a wise one. Trajan began his principate by dealing firmly with the growing menace of the Roman garrison, the Praetorian Guard, and succeeded in conciliating the senatorial class, of whose loyalty and regard Pliny's fulsome *Panegyric* is a document. Trajan proved an able financial organizer and a vigorous builder. A large program of public works was financed largely from the loot of the Dacian war. The principate was marked by wide military activity on the Danube, the Parthian, and the African frontiers. During Trajan's principate, in fact, the Empire reached its widest extent, and stood confidently on frontiers held more firmly than ever before or after that time. Provincial administration was economical, strict, humane, and progressive. A volume of correspondence between Trajan and Pliny, who was governor of Bithynia just before his death, survives, and an interesting reply on the problem of the Christians in the province illustrates strikingly the desire of the emperor to combine firmness with humanity in his legislation (Pliny *Ep.* 10:79). Conscious of an imperial mission Trajan sought, as few other emperors did so urgently and sincerely, to found a rule of "Felicitas, Securitas, Aequitas, Justitia." He bore, no doubt, too heavy a personal burden, and decided too much from Rome, but the tradition he endeavored to found was a noble one, and shows the Empire at its best, not unconscious of a duty to mankind. E.M.B.

TRANCE (Gr. *ékstasis, a throwing of the mind out of its normal state*), a mental state in which the senses are partially or wholly suspended and the person is unconscious of his environment while he contemplates some extraordinary object. Peter describes a trance he had in which he saw a vision of unclean animals, and heard a voice bidding him kill and eat them because God had cleansed them (Acts 10:9-16). Paul relates how he fell into a trance while praying in the temple and saw the Lord telling him to leave Jerusalem and go to the Gentiles (Acts 22:17-21). There are other similar experiences recorded in the Scriptures which are not called trances but must have been such. Balaam, son of Beor, in his third and fourth prophecies said he saw the vision of the Almighty as he fell down with his eyes open (Num. 24:4,16). Isaiah saw a vision of the Lord's glory and heard Him call him to be His prophet (Isa. 6:1-13). Also, Ezekiel's visions (Ezek. 8-11; 40-48) must have been given in a trance. In the NT, John, on the island of Patmos, saw the vision of the revelation of Christ (Rev. 4-22). Probably in the case of every vision recorded in the Bible which came to a person while he was awake, that individual was in a trance during the time he beheld it. C.E.H.

TRANSFIGURATION, the name given to that singular event recorded in all the Synoptic Gospels (Matt. 17:1-8; Mark 9:2-8; Luke 9:28-36) when Jesus was visibly glorified in the presence of three select disciples. The name is derived from the Latin term used to translate the Gr. *metamorphóō,* meaning "to change into another form." The accounts portray the transformation as outwardly visible and consisting in an actual physical change in the body of Jesus: "the fashion of his countenance was altered" (Luke 9:29), "his face did shine as the sun" (Matt. 17:2), while "his garments became glistening, exceeding white" (Mark 9:3), having a dazzling supernatural whiteness. The glory was not caused by the falling of a heavenly light upon Him from without but by the flashing forth of the radiant splendor within. He had passed into a higher state of existence, His body assuming properties of the resurrection body.

The place is simply identified as "a high mountain apart" (Mark 9:2). Tradition has identified it with Mt. Tabor, but because of its distance from Caesarea Philippi and the fortification on it at that time, a spur of Mt. Hermon seems more probable. Jebel Jermuk has also been suggested. It was witnessed by Peter, James, and John, and occurred while Jesus "was praying" (Luke 9:29). The natural simplicity of the accounts and their sober insistence upon its detailed features powerfully testify to the reality of the event. Its historical reality is attested by the Apostle Peter (II Pet. 1:16-18).

While recorded without interpretation, the uniform dating as being "after six days" (Matthew and Mark) or inclusively "about eight days after these sayings" (Luke), clearly sets the transfiguration in the context of the crucial events at Caesarea Philippi, Peter's confession and Christ's announcement of His coming death. The experience gave encouragement to Jesus setting His face to the cross. To the shocked disciples it confirmed the necessity of the cross through the conversation of the heavenly visitors about Christ's coming "decease" (Gr. *exodus,* Luke 9:31) as well as the divine endorsement upon Christ's teaching. It inseparably linked the suffering with the glory. It was the crowning with glory of the perfect human life of Jesus, God's stamp of approval upon His sinless humanity. The divine approval established His fitness to be our Sinbearer on the cross. It was also an entry for Jesus into the glory in which He would reign, thus constituting a typical manifestation of the King coming in His kingdom (Matt. 16:28). D.E.H.

TRANSGRESSION (trăns-grĕ'shŭn, Heb. *pesha', rebellion, transgression*; Gr. *parábasis, transgression*), the breaking of a law (Prov. 17:11; Rom. 4:15).

TRANSJORDAN, TRANS-JORDAN (trăns-jôr'dăn), a country included today in the Hashemite Kingdom of the Jordan, which is bordered on the W by Israel, on the N by Syria, on the E by Iraq, and on the S by Egypt and Saudi Arabia. In the OT there is no one name given to this area, though the expressions, "this side of the Jordan" and "the other side of the Jordan," appear frequently, their usage depending on the actual or idealized situation of the speaker. Various sections of Transjordan are called by national or ethnic names. The region is essentially a plateau, and ranges from about 2,000 to 3,000 feet in elevation. Opposite the N end of the Dead Sea, Mt. Nebo, from whose heights Moses viewed the Land of Promise (Deut. 34:1-3), rises to 2,664 feet.

Nelson Glueck made extensive surveys of the archeological sites of Transjordan; the results indicate flourishing civilizations at three main periods: (1) c. 2300-1900 B.C.; (2) c. 1200-700 B.C.; and

Two views of the Transjordan area. Above, ruins of the Salkhad Castle in the Druze Mountains of Bashan, northeast of the Sea of Galilee. Below, ruins of the Roman theater at Jerash, ancient Gerasa, chief city of the Decapolis. © MPS

(3) c. 100 B.C.-A.D. 600 (Nabatean-Byzantine). Rich deposits of iron and copper have been found in the S (Deut. 8:9), and ancient mines and smelting furnaces have been discovered. E of the Jordan and in Edom to the S was a road the OT calls "the King's Highway," which probably marks the route taken by the eastern kings of Genesis 14. In Numbers 20:17 this road is mentioned as the passageway along which the Israelites requested permission of Edom to traverse its territory. The king of Edom denied this permission and Israel was forced to skirt the region. Edom was in the southern part, S of the Wadi el-Hesa (the brook Zered; see Num. 21:12; Deut. 5:13-14), with its capital at Sela ("the Rock" Petra). This region is also called Seir in the OT (see Deut. 2:4,22). It was here that the copper mines were found; at Ezion-Geber (Tell el-Kheleifeh) Glueck excavated the now-famous smelting center of Solomon. Solomon also used Ezion-Geber as a port (I Kings 9:26-28; II Chron. 8:17-18). Edom was important also because it controlled the trade routes between Arabia and Syria. The Nabateans developed a powerful kingdom (c. 100 B.C.-A.D. 100) with Petra as their capital; during NT times their dominion extended to Damascus (II Cor. 11:32).

Adjoining Edom on the N was Moab; at an earlier period Moab extended farther N, but at the time of the Exodus the Arnon River (Wadi el-Mojib) formed the boundary between Moab and the Amorites (Num. 21:13,26). It was to Moab that Elimelech and Naomi went during the famine in Judah (Ruth 1:1). It was also a place of refuge to which David took his parents while he was dodging Saul (I Sam. 22:3-4). The importance of

Moab as a grazing land is indicated by II Kings 3:4; the Moabite view of the conflict between Israel and Mesha of Moab is given by the Moabite Stone, which was found at Dibon in 1868. Between the Arnon and Yarmuk Rivers was Gilead, which was the land of the Amorite king Sihon, whom the Israelites defeated (Num. 21:21-26; Deut. 2:26-37; Josh. 12:12, etc.). This territory was given to the tribes of Reuben and Gad (Deut. 3; Josh. 13). David fled to this region at the time of the rebellion of Absalom (II Sam. 17:22,24,26). A number of the cities of the Decapolis, a confederation of independent Hellenized cities, were located in this area. E of Gilead and the Jabbok River (Nahr ez-Zerka) was the country of the Ammonites, with their capital at Rabbath-Ammon. The northernmost division of Transjordan was Bashan, whose precise northern limits are not certain. Its Amorite king, Og, was also bested by the Israelites (Num. 21:23-35; Deut. 3:1-11; Josh. 12:4-5, etc.). Bashan was allotted to the one-half tribe of Manasseh (Deut. 3; Josh. 13).   C.E.D.

TRANSLATE (trăns'lāt, Heb. *'āvar, to transfer;* Gr. *metáthesis, a transfer, methístemi, to remove from one place to another*). The Hebrew word is rendered once as "translate," "to translate the kingdom from the house of Saul" (II Sam. 3:10 KJV, ASV has "transfer"). The Greek words occur in Hebrews 11:5, "By faith Enoch was translated that he should not see death; and he was not found, because God translated him: for he hath had witness borne to him that before his translation he had been well pleasing to God" ASV. *Methístemi* is also found in Colossians 1:13 where the believer is described as passing from the kingdom of darkness into that of light.

TRANSPORTATION (See Trade and Travel)

TRAVAIL (trăv'āl). In the OT the word *yalādh, to bear a child,* is used a few times for literal travail (Gen. 35:16; 38:27; I Sam. 4:19), and many times figuratively. Also figuratively for toil or trouble *hûl, anguish* (Isa. 23:4; 54:1; 66:7,8); *hālāh, to be weak or sick* (Jer. 4:31); *'āmāl, toil* (Eccl. 4:4,6; Isa. 53:11); *'invan, occupation, task* only in Ecclesiastes (1:13; 2:23,26; 3:10; 4:8; 5:14); *hābal, writhe, twist* (Ps. 7:14; S. of Sol. 8:5 ASV); *telā'âh, weariness, hardship* (Exod. 18:8; Num. 20:14; Lam. 3:5).

In the NT the following words occur: *odíno* (Rev. 12:2) of a figurative woman; (Gal. 4:19,27) *sense of care and concern; odín* (Matt. 24:8 and Mark 13:8 ASV; Acts 2:24, *pains or pangs;* I Thess. 5:3); *syndíno* (Rom. 8:22); *tíkto, bring forth a child* (John 16:21); *móchthos, hard labor, toil* (II Cor. 11:27 ASV; I Thess. 2:9; II Thess. 3:8).

TRAVEL (See Trade and Travel)

TREASURE, a word that signifies a collection of objects of value, including stores of provisions (e.g. Jer. 41:8, where RSV renders "stores"). See Ezekiel 28:4, and Daniel 11:43. In Job 38:22 and Psalm 135:7 the word rendered "treasures" in the former case (KJV), and "treasuries" in the latter, appears correctly as "storehouses" in RSV. The "treasure cities" of Exodus 1:11 were arsenals and depots for provisions (cf. Gen. 41:48,56). A similar confusion between the precious store, and the place of its storing, occurs in the NT. For example Matthew 2:11 and 19:21 refer to the store of precious things, but Matthew 12:35 obviously to the storehouse. In Acts 8:27 both notions are incorporated. The word *gáza'* is a Persian word, and is used only in this place in the NT. In Matthew

27:6 the word is Hebrew. They cannot put the polluted silver into the *korbanas,* the sacred treasury, into which the *corban* gifts were paid. This seems to be distinguished from the *gazophylákion,* the "treasury" of the temple, into which general offerings were cast (Mark 12:41; Luke 21:1). This was simply a collection-box. John 8:20 means that Jesus was teaching in the colonnade, where boxes were placed for the convenient reception of gifts. The metaphorical meaning of treasure is a more common figure of speech in the OT than in the NT (Exod. 19:5; Deut. 28:12; Ps. 17:14; Matt. 13: 44; Luke 12:21; II Cor. 4:7). The last reference is to practices such as those illustrated by the Dead Sea Scrolls, the preservation of precious possessions in earthenware jars, sealed for safety.

E.M.B.

TREASURER (See Occupations and Professions)

TREE (Heb. *'ēts, tree, wood;* Gr. *déndron, tree, xýlon, timber, wood, tree*). Palestine in ancient times must have been extensively wooded as there are over 300 references to trees and wood in the Bible. Also over 25 different kinds of trees have been identified as having grown in the Holy Land. Most of the wooded areas in Palestine have been cut down.

Trees identified with holy places were permitted to flourish. Trees venerated by heathen people who believed gods inhabited them. Sacrifices were often offered under trees (Deut. 12:2; I Kings 14:23, etc.). The Hebrews were forbidden to plant a tree near a sacred altar (Deut. 16:21). Trees identified places (Gen. 12:6; Deut. 11:30, etc.; "plain" KJV, "oak" ASV). Tree limbs were used in celebrating the Feast of Tabernacles (Lev. 23: 40). Jesus used the fruit bearing of trees as an illustration of believers' fruit bearing (Matt. 7:16-19). See PLANTS.

C.E.H.

TREE OF KNOWLEDGE, a special tree in the garden of Eden, set apart by the Lord as an instrument to test the obedience of Adam and Eve (Gen. 2: 9,17). It must have been a real tree since the test was real, by real people, and with real results. Its fruit probably was not much different from that of the other trees from which they ate. The sin in eating its fruit did not lie in the tree but in the disobedience of the persons who ate.

The phrase "to know good and evil" is used in other places: infants do not know good and evil (Deut. 1:39); nor does an old man of failing mind (II Sam. 19:35); but a king does know good and evil (I Kings 3:9); as do angels (II Sam. 14:17) and God Himself (Gen. 3:5,22).

C.E.H.

TREE OF LIFE, was another special tree in the garden of Eden, (Gen. 2:9; 3:22). This tree appears again in Revelation 22:2 as a fruit-bearing tree with leaves. It will have healing in its leaves (Rev. 22:2). The phrase "tree of life" in Proverbs 3:18; 11:30; 13:12; 15:4 is figurative for an exhilarating experience.

TRENCH, the rendering in KJV of two Hebrew words *hēl* and *ma'gāl,* translated "trench" (II Sam. 20:15; I Sam. 26:5,7; 17:20), but which mean "rampart" and "intrenchment"; ASV has "the place of the wagons" for *ma'gāl.* A third word *te'ālâh, trench,* occurs in I Kings 18:32,35,38; a Greek word *chárax, palisade,* occurs in Luke 19:43.

TRESPASS (trĕs'păs, Heb. *'ashām,* Gr. *paráptoma*), the violation of the rights of others, whether of God or of man. In Jewish law, acknowledged violation of a man's rights required restoration, plus one-fifth of the amount or value of the thing involved, and the presentation of a trespass offering.

Unintentional trespass against God, when the guilty person became aware of it, required a trespass offering to remove guilt. Trespasses against us must be forgiven by us because God has forgiven our trespasses.

TRESPASS OFFERING (See Offerings)

TRES TABERNAE (See Three Taverns)

TRIAL OF JESUS, the tumultuous proceedings before the Jewish and Roman authorities resulting in His crucifixion. All four Gospels record at least part of the twofold trial (Matt. 26:57-27:31; Mark 14:53-15:20; Luke 22:54-23:25; John 18:12-19: 16), but because of the brief and selective nature of their narratives the precise chronological order of events is not always certain. It is clear that both parts of the trial were marked by great irregularities, but the Gospel writers never assert that this or that in the trial was illegal, for they wrote not as lawyers but as witnesses.

Following His arrest in Gethsemane, Jesus was at once taken before the Jewish authorities in Jerusalem. John alone tells us that He was first brought before the ex-high priest Annas, who conducted a preliminary examination by questioning Jesus about His disciples and teaching. With dignity Jesus reminded him of its illegality, only to be basely struck by an attendant (18:12-14, 19-23). Meanwhile the Sanhedrin members had assembled in the palace of Caiaphas, the president of the Sanhedrin, for an illegal night session. To them Annas sent Jesus in fetters (John 18:24 ASV). The attempt to convict Jesus through false witnesses collected and instructed by the Sanhedrin failed because of their contradictory testimony (Matt. 26:59-61; Mark 14:55-59). Before their charges Jesus maintained a dignified silence, even when blustering Caiaphas demanded an answer (Matt. 26:62), thus denying the validity of the process. Aware that their case had collapsed, Caiaphas brushed aside the witnesses and put Jesus under oath to tell the court "whether thou be the Christ, the Son of God" (Matt. 26:63). The answer, in forced self-incrimination, was used to condemn Jesus for blasphemy (Matt. 26:64-66; Mark 14:61-64). The session broke up in disorder, with indignities being heaped upon Jesus (Matt. 26:67-68; Mark 14:65; Luke 22: 63-65). After dawn the Sanhedrin assembled in its council chamber and re-enacted a pretense at a trial by questioning Jesus on His messianic claims and deity (Luke 22:66-71). This meeting was held to give a semblance of legality to the condemnation.

Since the Romans had deprived the Sanhedrin of the power of capital punishment, it was necessary to secure a confirmatory death-sentence from the Roman governor, who found it expedient to be in Jerusalem during the Passover seasons. Accordingly "the whole company" (Luke 23:1) in formal procession brought Jesus, bound, to Pilate. When asked their charges, they indicated that they wanted him simply to sanction their condemnation of Jesus without a full trial (John 18:29-32). Upon Pilate's insistence three charges were advanced (Luke 23:2). The charge of treason alone Pilate deemed worthy of investigation. When Jesus explained to him the nature of His kingdom, Pilate concluded that Jesus was harmless and announced a verdict of acquittal (John 18:33-38). This verdict should have ended the trial, but it only evoked a torrent of further charges against Jesus by the Jews, charges which Jesus refused to answer to Pilate's surprise (Matt. 27:12-14). Having learned that He was a Galilean, Pilate decided to be rid of the unpleasant task by sending Jesus to Herod Antipas, also present for the Passover, on the plea that He belonged to Herod's jurisdiction. When Jesus refused to amuse Herod with a miracle, maintaining complete silence toward him, Herod mocked Him and returned Him to Pilate uncondemned (Luke 23:2-12).

With the return of Jesus, Pilate realized that he must handle the case. Summoning the chief priests "and the people," he reviewed the case to prove the innocence of Jesus but weakly proposed a compromise by offering to scourge Jesus before releasing Him (Luke 23:13-16). When the multitude requested the customary release of one prisoner (Mark 15:8), Pilate offered them the choice between the notorious Barabbas and Jesus (Matt. 27:17). He hoped that the crowd would choose Jesus, thus overruling the chief priests. Before the vote was taken Pilate received an impressive warning from his wife (Matt. 27:19-21). Meanwhile the Jewish leaders persuaded the people to vote for Barabbas. When asked their choice the people shouted for Barabbas, demanding that Jesus be crucified (Matt. 27:20-21; Luke 23:18-19). Further remonstrance by Pilate proved useless (Luke 23:20-22).

According to John's Gospel, as a last resort to avoid His crucifixion, Pilate had Jesus scourged, allowing the soldiers to stage a mock coronation, and then brought out the pathetic figure before the people, hoping that the punishment would satisfy them. It only intensified their shouts for His crucifixion (19:1-6). A new charge, that Jesus made Himself the Son of God, aroused the superstitious fears of Pilate, causing further futile efforts to release Him (19:7-12). Using their last weapon, the Jewish leaders threatened to report Pilate to Caesar if he released Jesus (19:12). This threat, because of Pilate's grievous maladministration, broke all further resistance in the vacillating governor. To his last appeal whether he should crucify their king, the Jews gave the blasphemous answer that they had no king but Caesar (19:15). When Pilate sought to absolve himself of the guilt of Christ's death by publicly washing his hands, the people voluntarily accepted the responsibility (Matt. 27:24-26). Keenly conscious of the gross miscarriage of justice, Pilate yielded by releasing Barabbas and sentencing Jesus to the cross. See CHRIST, JESUS. D.E.H.

TRIBE, TRIBES (Heb. *matteh, rod, staff, tribe; shĕvĕt, rod, scepter, tribe;* Gr. *phylé, tribe*). With two exceptions (Isa. 19:13; Matt. 24:30) these words always denote the tribes of Israel. A tribal group comprised all the individuals descended from the same ancestor. In the case of the Hebrews, each tribe was made up of all the persons descended from one of the sons of the patriarch Jacob. The clan was composed of kinsmen on the father's side. The leaders of the tribes are called "princes" or *rulers* (Exod. 34:31), *heads* (Num. 1:16), or *chiefs* (Gen. 36:15ff).

The 12 tribes of Israel (the name of Jacob [Gen. 32:28]) were first mentioned by Jacob in prophecy (Gen. 49:16,28). While the Hebrews were in Egypt they were grouped according to their fathers' houses (Exod. 6:14). After they left Egypt the whole company was conceived of as the 12 tribes of Israel (Exod. 24:4). The 12 sons of Jacob were Reuben, Simeon, Levi, Judah, Zebulun, Issachar, Dan, Gad, Asher, Naphtali, Joseph, and Benjamin. Although they all had a common father, they had four mothers, Leah and Rachel, who were full wives, and Bilhah and Zilpah, who were concubines. The tribes were called by these names. On

Representations of two of the twelve precious stones, with tribal emblems, from the replica of Aaron's Breastplate at the American Baptist Assembly, Green Lake, Wisconsin. Above is that of the tribe of Reuben (blood-red jasper) and below, that of Levi (emerald). © APD, ABA

the breastplate of the high priest were 12 precious stones arranged in four rows; each stone had the name of a tribe engraved on it (Exod. 28:21,29; 39:14).

When the Israelites were numbered to find out the number of the men of war in each group, the tribe of Levi was left out of this census because the Lord selected them to take care of the keeping and transporting of the tabernacle and its furniture (Num. 1). The whole encampment of Israelites at Sinai was organized and each tribe assigned its place in which to march and to camp (Num. 2).

The leadership of Judah among the tribes was prophesied by Jacob (Gen. 49:10), and this tribe was assigned first place in the order of marching (Num. 2:3; 10:14). Judah also was the first tribe to offer an oblation after the setting up of the tabernacle (Num. 7:12).

The withdrawal of the Levites from the group of tribes left 11 of them. In the list of leaders from each tribe who were to take the census, the children of Joseph are represented as divided between the tribe of Ephraim, and the tribe of Manasseh (Num. 1:10).

Before the Israelites entered the Promised Land two tribes, Reuben and Gad, and half of Manasseh chose to settle on the E side of the Jordan (Num. 32:33). After the land of Canaan was subdued, the land was divided among the nine and a half tribes (Josh. chaps. 15-19). Judah was given the first lot, and received the largest area of territory (Josh. 15:1-62). The tribe of Simeon was assigned territory within Judah (Josh. 19:1). Judah had all the land W of the Dead Sea and S to Kadesh-barnea. N of her were Dan and Benjamin. Ephraim was next to them, Manasseh (half tribe) was next;

then Issachar, Zebulun, Naphtali and Asher were situated N of the valley of Jezreel E of the Sea of Galilee and extended northward to the Lebanon Mountains. Part of the tribe of Dan went N and seized some territory just S of Mount Hermon, thus being the farthest N of all Israelites (Judg. chap. 18).

During the period of the Judges in Israel the tribes were each one a law unto themselves. The Judges' leadership was sectional. When David became king over the whole land the 12 tribes were unified. Jerusalem was conquered and made the capital of the country. There Solomon built the temple. The Lord chose this city as the one place out of all the tribes of Israel where He would put His name (II Chron. 12:13). David appointed a captain over each tribe (I Chron. 27:16-22). He also took a census of the tribes (II Sam. 24:2). Later, when Elijah, in the contest with the prophets of Baal on Mount Carmel, built an altar, he used 12 stones to represent the 12 tribes of Israel (I Kings 18:31).

The unity of the tribes had a tendency to be disrupted into two factions. After the death of Saul, David reigned over only Judah at first (II Sam. 2:4), and did not become king of all the tribes until later (II Sam. 5:3). After the death of Solomon this same division occurred again, Judah and Benjamin became one nation, the kingdom of Judah, and all the area N of them became another nation, the kingdom of Israel (I Kings 12:20). This division continued until both kingdoms went into captivity, Israel in 721 B.C. to Assyria and Judah in 586 B.C. to Babylon. These catastrophes wiped out tribal distinctions. The tribes are not mentioned by name again except in the devotional literature of the Psalms and in prophecy.

Jesus says that the apostles of Christ will sit on 12 thrones judging the 12 tribes of Israel (Matt. 19:28; Luke 22:30). The holy city, the New Jerusalem, will have 12 gates, each bearing the name of one of the tribes of Israel (Rev. 21:21).

C.E.H.

TRIBULATION, GREAT TRIBULATION (trĭb-ū-lā′shŭn, Heb. *tsar, narrow;* Gr. *thlípsis, pressure*). The Hebrew word has a large variety of meanings in the OT, but usually refers to trouble of a general sort (Job 28:33; Ps. 13:4). Likewise the Greek word refers to tribulation of a general sort (Matt. 13:21; John 16:33). Sometimes this suffering is just the natural part of one's life (Rom. 12:12; James 1:27), while at other times it is looked upon as a definite punishment or chastening from the Lord for misbehavior (Rom. 2:9).

The Great Tribulation is a definite period of suffering sent from God upon the earth to accomplish several purposes. According to premillennial eschatology it precedes the millennial reign of Christ. Postmillennial theology places it at the end of the thousand-year reign of Christ. Amillennial theology places it just before the new heavens and the new earth are brought in. This period of suffering will be unlike any other period in the past or future (Dan. 12:1; Matt. 24:21). H.Z.C.

TRIBUTE (Heb. *mas, forced laborers; middâh, tribute, toll;* Gr. *kénsos, tax, census; phóros, tax, burden*). The Heb. word *mas* is incorrectly rendered "tribute," since it means "forced laborers, labor gang." Solomon had a force of taskworkers consisting of 30,000 men, raised by levy upon the people (I Kings 5:13; 9:15,21). David had had a labor gang too (I Kings 4:6; 5:13). Conquered populations were often compelled to render forced

labor (Deut. 20:11; Josh. 16:10). In NT times the *kénsos* was an annual tax levied on persons, houses, or lands paid to a prince or civil governor on behalf of the Roman treasury. The *phóros* was a tax paid by agriculturists. Customs (*téle*) were collected by the publicans.

TRINITY. The Biblical doctrine of the Trinity is most distinctly expressed in the words of Christ in the "Great Commission" (Matt. 28:18-20), ". . . baptizing them in the name of the Father and of the Son and of the Holy Ghost . . ." There are many other clear indications of the Trinity. See, for example, the apostolic benediction (II Cor. 13:14). The doctrinal formalization of the Biblical data on the Trinity is satisfactorily worded in the Westminster Shorter Catechism, questions 5 and 6: " 'Are there more Gods than one?' There is but one only, the living and true God. 'How many persons are there in the Godhead?' There are three persons in the Godhead, the Father, the Son, and the Holy Ghost; and these three are one God, the same in substance, equal in power and glory."

It is important to realize that the doctrine of the Trinity has not been given to the Church by speculative thought. It is not an *a priori* concept, nor in any sense derived from "pure reason." This doctrine has come from the data of historical revelation. In the process of history God has revealed Himself as one God, subsisting in three Persons. God as revealed in the Bible is not a simple undifferentiated Subject; but His being is in three objectively distinguished Subjects.

The unity of the Godhead is unanimously attested throughout the entire range of the Judeo-Christian sources (cf. Deut. 6:4,5; Isa. 44:6-8; 45:21-23; I Cor. 8:5,6).

That the being of God is complex, in the sense of objectively distinguished Subjects, is a basic presupposition of many OT passages. Psalm 110:1, "Jehovah saith unto my Lord, Sit thou at my right hand until I make thine enemies thy footstool." See the comment of Jesus on this verse (Matt. 22:41-45 and parallels in Mark and Luke). See also Hebrews 1:13; 10:12,13. For other OT passages implying personal distinctions in the Godhead see Warfield, *Biblical Doctrines*, pp. 139ff and other standard extended works on the Trinity, especially Charles Hodge, *Systematic Theology* Vol. I, Chapters VII and VIII.

That the Jewish mind in NT times saw no problem in the personal distinctions in the being of God is a remarkable fact. It was the idea of God *in the flesh* to which they objected. "Thou, *being a man*, makest thyself God" (John 10:33). They sought to kill him because He, a man, "called God his own Father, making himself equal with God" (John 5:18).

That the concept "Son of God," meaning "equal with God," was well defined in the Jewish mind was doubtless due to such OT passages as Psalm 2:6,7. Never did the NT Christians have to meet the objection that there could not be a Son of God equal with God. What Christ and the NT Christians had to meet was the thought that the Son of God could not humble Himself to become a man. This is the argument which Jesus meets in John 10:34-36. He quotes Psalm 82:6 to show that, since man is made in the image of God, the nature of man and the nature of God are not contradictory. The claim that He is the Son of God *might* be true; it is *not necessarily* blasphemy. Then He appeals to the *evidence* (vss. 37, 38) to show that His claim *is* true.

When the NT Christians apply to Jesus OT passages which relate to Jehovah (Rom. 10:13 quoting Joel 2:32; Rom. 14:10,11 quoting Isa. 45:23), they reflect the OT presupposition that the Messiah would be Jehovah, sent by Jehovah (Jer. 23:5,6; 33:14-16), and they show no awareness of controversy on this latter point. It was not the Jewish mind of the first century which stumbled at the personal distinctions in the Godhead.

The personal deity of the Holy Spirit seems to have been assumed in the horizons of NT Christianity without the least opposition. There was no obstacle to this assumption such as the humiliation of Jesus was to the acceptance of His deity. The Holy Spirit of God, sent forth by God, is frequently referred to in the OT (Ps. 51:11; Isa. 63: 10,11; Hag. 2:5. Cf. W. H. Griffith Thomas *The Holy Spirit of God*, Ch. II). The uncontroverted assumption of the personal deity of the Holy Spirit is illustrated in Peter's words addressed to Ananias, "Why hath Satan filled thy heart to lie to the Holy Spirit . . . Thou has not lied unto men but unto God" (Acts 5:3,4).

That the persons, Father, Son, and Holy Spirit are not merely modes of one Person, as Sabellians hold, is evidenced by the prayer life of Jesus (cf. John 17) in which He speaks objectively to the Father; by the Father's witness to the Son (Mark 1:11; 8:7 and parallels; John 12:28,29); and by numerous objective references to the Holy Spirit (John 15:26; 16:7-15).

The data of revelation, then, established in the minds of NT Christians four convictions: 1. God is One. 2. Jesus is God. 3. The Holy Spirit is God. 4. The three Persons are Subject and Object, "I and Thou," each to the others.

With these convictions well attested by the early apologists and church fathers, the council of Nicea, 325 A.D., brought the Biblical data to focus in a doctrinal expression to which Bible-believing Christians have rather consistently adhered.

Spiritual and philosophical values in the doctrine can only be mentioned. 1. Only in terms of the Trinity, including infinite Subject-Object relationships, can we conceive of the eternal existence of God before the creation of the finite universe. 2. Only in terms of the Trinity can we conceive of God's redemptive program: The Father gave the Son (John 3:16); the Son gave Himself (Gal. 2: 20); "through the eternal Spirit" He "offered Himself" (Heb. 9:14). 3. The revelation of the Eternal Son illuminates our finite sonship in the "household" of God (Rom. 8:16,29; I John 3:1,2; 17:21, 22). J.O.B.

TRIUMPH (Gr. *thriambeúo, to lead in triumph*). In the OT the eight Heb. words for triumph all are used with reference to God — in praise and prayer to or in discussion concerning God. Paul uses the word twice in his epistles (II Cor. 2:14; Col. 2:15). In Roman times a triumph was a magnificent procession in honor of a victorious general, the highest military honor he could obtain. He entered the city in a chariot, preceded by the senate and magistrates, musicians, the spoils of his victory, and the captives in chains. Sacrifices were made to Jupiter and incense burned by the priests. It was undoubtedly such a triumphal procession that Paul had in mind when he wrote, "thanks be unto God, who always leadeth us to triumph in Christ" (II Cor. 2:14).

TROAS (trō'ăs, Gr. *Troás*), a name applied both to a region and a city. 1. The region is the NW corner of Asia Minor, in the district of Mysia, and the Roman province of Asia, fronting the Aegean and the entrance to the Dardanelles, and backed by the Ida massif. In the Troad or Troas, Alexander first defeated the Persians, in the Battle of the Granicus, repeating in recorded history the earlier clash of E and W in the Greek siege of Troy.

2. The city was Alexandria Troas, some ten miles from the ruins of ancient Troy at Hissarlik, and founded by Lysimachus in 300 B.C. on the site of the earlier Antigoneia. Troas was a Roman colony in Augustus' day, and one of the most important cities of NW Asia. It was a port of call on the trade-route between Macedonia and Asia (Acts 16:8; 20:5; II Cor. 2:12). Considerable ruins remain. E.M.B.

TROGYLLIUM (trō-jĭl'ĭ-ŭm, Gr. *Trogýllion*). The phrase in which Trogyllium is mentioned in Acts 20:15 is the occasion of some textual difficulty, but there is no geographical objection to its retention. (W. M. Ramsay discusses the question in his *Church in the Roman Empire*, p. 155). Trogyllium is a slender promontory thrusting SW from the Asian mainland N of Miletus, and overlapping the eastern extension of Samos. The narrow strait forms a protected roadstead in which a small coasting vessel would naturally await suitable wind conditions on the last lap to Miletus.

TROPHIMUS (trŏf'ĭ-mŭs, Gr. *Tróphimos, nourishing*), a Gentile Christian of Ephesus (Acts 21:29) and companion of Paul. He was one of the companions-in-travel, apparently the chosen delegates of the churches to bear the collection (II Cor. 8: 19ff), mentioned in Acts 20:4. In Jerusalem he was the innocent cause of the tumult resulting in Paul's imprisonment when hostile Asian Jews hastily *supposed* that Paul had illegally introduced him into the temple itself (Acts 21:29). He is conjectured to be one of the two brethren sent to Corinth with Titus to complete the collection (II Cor. 8: 18-22). Shortly before his final Roman imprisonment Paul left Trophimus sick at Miletus (II Tim. 4:20).

TRUTH. The word "truth," *alétheia* in the NT, and a variety of words, chiefly *'emeth* in the OT, always connotes (1) the interrelated consistency of statements and their correspondence with the facts of reality, and (2) the facts themselves. The former may be called propositional truth, and the latter, ontological truth.

The Biblical usage of the word has rich suggestive meanings which go beyond the literal connotations. When Moses (Exod. 18:21) refers to "able men, such as fear God, *men of truth*, hating covetousness," there is suggested an integration of character, and adherence of virtue, a kind of reliability, which includes and goes beyond the literal meaning to include those aspects of personal behavior which seem to be implied by the love of truth. The concept of truth is assumed to be derived from the character of God, and is the exact opposite of the concept of lying. "It is impossible for God to lie" (Heb. 6:18. Cf. Titus 1:2; II Tim. 2:13).

Jesus prayed, "Sanctify them in thy truth; thy word is truth" (John 17:17). And He promised, "If ye continue in my word, then are ye my disciples indeed, and ye shall know the *truth* and the *truth* shall make you free" (John 8:31b,32). In such sayings, "*the* truth" means the most important truth, that is, the Gospel of the grace of God.

Perhaps the saddest scene in the Bible (John 18: 37,38) is that in which Pilate asks Jesus, "What is truth?" and does not even wait for an answer. Jesus had just said, "To this end was I born, and for this cause came I into the world, that I should bear witness unto *the truth*. Everyone that is *of the truth* heareth my voice." Jesus' words refer not merely 'to truth, but to *the truth*. Pilate's question omits the article, and expresses skepticism, not merely as to the Gospel, but as to the very concept of truth.

The Gospel invitation to "believe" is always based upon the assumption that the evidence is sufficient, and that it is a moral question whether one will *accept* the grace of God in Christ. Those who disbelieve the Gospel are morally reprehensible in the sight of God (John 3:18,19,36; II Thess. 2:10-12). Christ is *the truth*, as the sun is *the light*. Those who turn away from Christ, it is assumed, do so wilfully, and culpably.   J.O.B.

TRYPHENA (trĭ-fē'nà, Gr. *Trýphaina, dainty*), a Christian woman who lived in Rome and was known to Paul. He asked the Roman believers to greet her and Tryphosa, her close relative (Rom. 16:12). This name has been found on inscriptions of name plates in the burial places of the servants of the royal household of Rome from the time of Paul.

TRYPHOSA (See Tryphena)

TUBAL (tū'-bàl, Heb. *tûval*), a tribe descended from Japheth (Gen. 10:2). It is mentioned with Javan (Isa. 66:19) as trading in the markets of Tyre. The Libareni or Libarenoi of the classical writers are the descendants of Tubal.

TUNIC (See Dress)

TURBAN (See Dress)

TURTLE (See Birds)

TURTLEDOVE (See Birds)

TWELVE, THE (See Apostles)

TYCHICUS (tĭk'ĭ-kŭs, Gr. *Týchikos, fortuitous*), an Asian Christian and close friend and valued helper of Paul. First mentioned in Acts 20:4, he is described as being "of Asia," perhaps a native of Ephesus. As one of the delegates chosen by the churches to bear the collection (II Cor. 8:19ff), he apparently went all the way to Jerusalem with Paul. He was with Paul during the first Roman imprisonment and carried the letters to the Ephesians (Eph. 6:21) and the Colossians (Col. 4:7-9), being delegated to report to them concerning Paul. Onesimus, returning to his master, accompanied him (Col. 4:7-9; Philem.). Paul told Titus that he would send either Artemas or Tychicus to replace him for the difficult work on Crete (Titus 3:12). Tychicus was with Paul during his second Roman imprisonment and was sent to Ephesus by him (II Tim. 4:12), perhaps as bearer of the letter to replace Timothy. Tychicus was a man distinguished for integrity and fidelity; he held the affection and confidence of Paul as an able worker in the service of Christ (Col. 4:7).   D.E.H.

TYRANNUS (tĭ-răn'ŭs, Gr. *Týrannos, tyrant*). According to the commonly accepted text of Acts 19:9, Paul, at Ephesus, taught in the afternoon in "the school of a certain Tyrannus," which, since instruction was commonly given in the morning (Martial 9:68; 12:57; Juv. 7:222-6), would be vacant for his use later in the day. If this reading is correct, Tyrannus was a living Ephesian schoolmaster. If another well-supported reading is followed, the text would run, "in the school of Tyrannus." This could indicate a public building traditionally named thus, or a school founded by Tyrannus. The name was common enough. W. M. Ramsay discusses the question in *The Church in the Roman Empire*, p. 152 and *St. Paul the Traveller and Roman Citizen*, p. 271.

A general view of Tyre, with entrance to its harbor, on the Mediterranean Coast of ancient Phoenicia.
© MPS

TYRE (tīr, Heb. *tsôr, a rock*, Gr. *Týros*), a Phoenician port S of Sidon and N of Carmel. Phoenicia itself is a coastal strip backed by mountains, and Tyre was further defended by rocky promontories (one of them the famous "Ladder of Tyre"), which effectively hampered invasion. Herodotus dates the foundation as early as 2740 B.C.; Josephus, as late as 1217 B.C. Isaiah (23:2,12) implies that Tyre was a colony of Sidon, and Homer's mention of "Sidonian wares," without reference to Tyre, seems to confirm the greater antiquity of the former city. The Tell-el-Amarna letters, apparently refuting Josephus' date, contain an appeal from the ruler of Tyre, dated 1430 B.C., imploring help from Amenhotep IV against the invading Habiri. Joshua assigned Tyre to Asher, but in all probability the city was not occupied (Josh. 19:29; II Sam. 24:7).

An obscure period of some four centuries follows, from which the record emerges with the name of Hiram, friend of David. This able monarch seems to have rebuilt and fortified Tyre, taking within its ambit nearby islands, and providing the city with two harbors. The trade of Tyre at this time included the exploitation of the cedar forests of the Lebanon range. "Tyrian purple," the product of the murex shellfish, was also a famous export. The cedar forests also provided material for the famous Phoenician galleys, and, accepting the challenge of the sea which was the one road to wealth for the narrow little land, the Tyrians, like the rest of their kinsfolk, ranged far and wide in quest of the precious shellfish, and the metals in which they traded. The copper of Cyprus, the silver of Spain, and the tin of Cornwall, were carried in Tyrian ships. Under Solomon, who inherited the partnership with Hiram, the Hebrews participated in Tyrian commerce, provided a southern port at Ezion-geber on the gulf of Akaba, and shared the trade with Ophir and the East. It was probably the loss of this southern outlet to the Red Sea and the East which stimulated the Tyrian exploration of the coast of Africa, and led ultimately to the circumnavigation of the continent. Dynastic troubles followed Hiram's death. One Ethbaal emerged victorious after the assassination of his brother. It was Ethbaal's daughter Jezebel who became Ahab's notorious queen (I Kings 16:31). Renewed troubles after Ethbaal's death led to the emigration of Elissa, the Dido of Vergil's Aeneid IV, and to the foundation of Carthage.

During the 200 years of Assyrian aggression, Tyre suffered with the rest of the Middle East, but owing to the strength of her position and her sea-power, maintained a measure of independence over much of the troubled era. She broke free from Nineveh a generation before that last stronghold of the Assyrians fell (606 B.C.). These years were the greatest years of Tyrian glory. Ezekiel's account (27,28), set though it is in a context of de-nunciation and prophecy of ruin, gives a vivid picture of the power and wealth of the great trading port. Ruin came. Babylon succeeded Assyria, and although Tyre seems successfully to have resisted the long siege of Nebuchadnezzar, the strain of her resistance to Babylon, and the damage to her commerce, brought the city to poverty. She fell into the power of Egypt briefly, and then became a dependency of Babylon, a status she held until Babylon fell to Persia. Persia inherited Babylon's rule. We read of an order of Cyrus II to Tyre to supply cedar for the restoration of the temple in Jerusalem (Ezra 3:7). Cambyses II conscripted a Tyrian fleet against Egypt, and Tyrian ships fought on the Persian side against the Greeks at Salamis. In 332 B.C., in the course of his conquest of the East, Alexander appeared before Tyre. The island stronghold closed her gates, and Alexander was forced to build a causeway, and after long months of frustration and vast penetration, take the city by costly storming. Tyre was broken, and the cause-way still remains, a place, as Ezekiel foretold, on which fishermen might dry their nets (26:5,14; 47:10). Tyre made a measure of political recovery, and for a period functioned as a republic. She struck an early treaty with Rome, and her inde-pendence was respected until 20 B.C. when Au-gustus withdrew it. Remaining history is without significance.   E.M.B.

TYROPEON VALLEY (See Jerusalem)

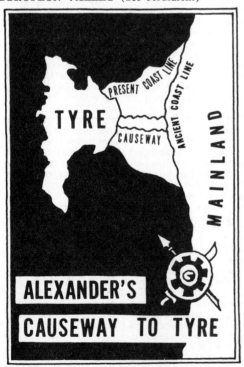

ALEXANDER'S
CAUSEWAY TO TYRE

Fishermen today dry their nets where Alexander the Great once built a causeway to conquer Tyre. UANT & SHH

U

UCAL (ū′kăl, Heb. *'ūkhāl*), a word of uncertain meaning found in Proverbs 30:1, regarded as a proper noun by many interpreters. If this is the correct interpretation, it is the name of one of two men to whom Augur addresses his proverbs. Others regard the word as a verb, and render it "I am faint."

UEL (ū′ĕl, Heb. *'û'ēl, will of God*), one of Bani's sons whom Ezra mentions as having taken foreign wives (Ezra 10:34).

UGARIT (ū′gȧ-rĭt), a word not found in the Bible but closely related to its history. It is the name of an ancient city on the North Syrian coast, 40 miles SW of Antioch; also called Ras Shamra. It was a great commercial and religious center. It was founded in the Early Bronze period and was de-stroyed about 1200 B.C. It was discovered by chance in 1928 and considered one of the great archeological finds of the 20th century. The ex-cavations took place between 1929 and 1939, re-sulting in the discovery of many objects of great archeological value, including hundreds of tablets known as "The Ras Shamra Tablets." The con-tributions from this city are unusually important for several reasons. First, they forever silence the old argument that Moses could not have written the Pentateuch because writing was unknown at such an early period. Then too, since they date from the 15th and 14th centuries B.C., they throw a flood of light on the culture and religion of this period. The moral depravity of the Canaanites which these tablets reveal confirms the justice of God in commanding the Israelites to obliterate these cults of Canaan.   H.Z.C.

UKNAZ (ŭk′năz, Heb. *ûqenaz*), Jephunneh's son (I Chron. 4:15). KJV has "even Kenaz"; RV has "and Kenaz." The text is probably corrupt.

ULAI (ū′lī, Heb. *'ûlāy*, meaning uncertain), a river which Daniel mentions twice (8:2,16). It ran through the province of Elam, and flowed through Susa.

ULAM (ū′lăm, Heb. *'ûlām*). 1. A son of Sheresh from the tribe of Manasseh (I Chron. 7:16,17).

2. A descendant of the Benjamite, Eshek. His two illustrious sons were known as "mighty men of valor" (I Chron. 8:39-40).

ULLA (ŭ'là, Heb. *'ullā'*, meaning unknown), one of Asher's descendants who became the father of three distinguished men of the tribe (I Chron. 7:39).

UMMAH (ŭm'à, Heb. *'ummâh, association*), one of the cities belonging to the tribe of Asher (Josh. 19:30). Unless it is to be identified with the modern "Akka," which is at best a mere guess, no other identification is known.

UNCIAL LETTERS (See Texts, Writing)

UNCIRCUMCISED (ŭn-sûr'kŭm-sīzd, Heb. *'ārēl,* Gr. *akrobystía*), a word used in both Old and New Testaments in several ways. Literally it refers to one who has not submitted to the Jewish rite of circumcision. Figuratively, it is used for the heathen (Judg. 14:3; Rom. 4:9). In a similar sense it is used of the heart (Lev. 24:26); the ear (Jer. 6:10).

UNCLE (Heb. *dôdh, beloved*), a word used in the OT denoting any kinsman on the father's side (Lev. 10:4; Amos 6:10).

UNCLEAN, UNCLEANNESS (Heb. *tūm'âh, uncleanness, defilement; niddâh, separation, impurity; 'erwâh, 'erwath dāvār, unclean things; tamē', defiled, filed; tāmē', to make or declare unclean;* Gr. *akatharsía; miasmós, pollution; akáthartos, unclean; koinóo, to defile; miaíno, to defile; molýno, to make filthy; spilóo; phtheíro, to corrupt*).

Sin arose very early in the history of mankind and brought about changes in both the physical life of man and his spiritual life as well. It has greatly affected the entire universe, making the terms "clean" and "unclean" very common in the thinking of mankind from the earliest times. These words have been factors in determining their diets, friends, and habits, in fact, their entire deportment. These words took on new meaning when God began to call the nation Israel into being. They fall largely into two main divisions: spiritual or moral uncleanness and ceremonial uncleanness.

Some have felt that there is a relation between the forbidden foods of other nations and those which Jehovah forbade to Israel. This could be true, but it does not take away from the fact that the Biblical laws on unclean foods came directly from God. Israel's restricted foods were, unlike those of some other nations, all pertaining to meats. Leviticus, chapter 11, is explicit in declaring the clean from the unclean in animals (Lev. 11:1-8, 26-28); sea creatures (Lev. 11:9-12); birds (Lev. 11:13-25); and creeping things (Lev. 11:29-38). Nothing that died of itself was fit for their food nor were they to eat anything strangled. Blood was a forbidden part of their diet. Animals that did not chew the cud and part the hoof; fish that did not have both fins and scales; birds that were birds of prey or had unclean habits; and insects that did not have legs above the feet for leaping were for Israel unclean.

Certain kinds of uncleanness among the Israelites were connected with death. A dead person, regardless of the cause of his death, made anyone who touched him unclean (Num. 19:22). Likewise anything he touched (Num. 19:22) or the enclosure in which he died was made unclean (Num. 19:14). Provisions were made for the cleansing of the unclean in this class by sprinkling his body with the ashes of a red heifer on the third and seventh days (Num. 11:17-19). Anyone touching the carcass of an animal became unclean and could only be cleansed by the washing of his clothes in water (Lev. 11:24-28). Certain types of creeping things that died made anything they touched unclean.

Some objects thus touched could be cleansed by washing while others had to be destroyed (Lev. 11:29-37).

Leprosy, being a type of sin, was looked upon as unclean whether it was in people, houses, or clothing. God required the person pronounced leprous by the priest to identify himself in a prescribed manner and to separate himself from the rest of the people. Any time anyone drew near to him he was to cry "Unclean, unclean." Since this disease was also very contagious, detailed instructions are given for dealing with it (Lev. 13-15).

Whatever the seminal fluid that issued from the body touched became unclean. This applied also to certain other kinds of issues (Lev. 15:1-18). Issues from women rendered them as well as the things they touched unclean (Lev. 15:19-33). Regulations for the cleansing of such persons or things were carefully laid down in the two passages above. According to the Law childbirth made a woman unclean and this uncleanness lasted for different periods of time depending on whether the child was a male or female. In this case too, special instructions were given for cleansing (Lev. 13).

In the NT one notes the cumbersome systems of defilement developed by the Scribes and Pharisees, which Jesus condemned. Most of the OT regulations passed away with the passing of the Law and when the matter was discussed at the Apostolic Council only four restrictions were placed upon the new believers (Acts 15:28-29). From the Cross on, uncleanness was moral, not ceremonial.

                      H.Z.C.

UNCTION (ŭngk'shŭn, Gr. *chrísma, anointing*), the act of anointing, in the KJV found only in I John 2:20. In I John 2:27 the Greek is translated "anointing."

UNDEFILED (Heb. *tām, perfect;* Gr. *amíantos, unsullied*), any person or thing not tainted with moral evil (Ps. 119:1; Heb. 7:26; 13:4; I Pet. 1:4).

UNDERSETTERS (*kāthēph, shoulder*), a word used of the supports of the laver in Solomon's temple (I Kings 7:30,34).

UNICORN (See Animals)

UNITY (Heb. *yāhadh, unitedness;* Gr. *henótes, oneness*), used in the OT in the sense of togetherness of persons (Gen. 13:6); fellowship (Judg. 19:6); praise (Ps. 34:3); or of animals (Isa. 11:6-7). The NT word bespeaks the unity of faith that binds together the people of God (Eph. 4:13).

UNKNOWN GOD (Gr. *ágnostos theós*). These words occur only in Acts 17:23. When Paul came into Athens on his second missionary journey he found the city "wholly given to idolatry." While disputing with the Jews in their synagogues and market places, he was asked by the philosophers concerning his faith. On Mars Hill Paul began his message by saying, "I found an altar with this inscription, *To the unknown God*" (Acts 17:23). This was probably a votive altar erected by some worshiper who did not know what god to thank for some benefit he had received. Using this as a starting point, Paul preached the true God unto them. Altars erected to unknown gods were common in Athens.

UNKNOWN TONGUE (Gr. *glósse, tongue*), an expression found in the KJV but not in the Greek or the ERV (I Cor. 14:2,4,13,14,19,27). It refers to the charismatic gift of speaking in tongues.

UNLEARNED, a word rendering a number of Greek words in the NT: (1) *agrámmatos, illiterate,* in Acts 4:13 meaning "lacking technical rabbinical instruction"; (2) *amathés, ignorant, uninstructed* (II Pet. 3:16); (3) *apaídeutos, an uneducated person;* (4) *idiótes, private person, non-professional* (I Cor. 14:16,23f).

UNLEAVENED (Heb. *matstsâh, sweet;* Gr. *ázymos*), a word often found in both Testaments, usually in a literal but sometimes in a figurative sense. When used literally, it refers to bread unmixed with leaven or to the Passover Feast, when only unleavened bread could be used. When used figuratively it means "unmixed" (I Cor. 5:7,8).

UNLEAVENED BREAD, bread that was made without any fermented dough. It was eaten at the Passover Feast (Exod. 12:8).

UNLEAVENED BREAD, FEAST OF (See Feasts)

UNNI (un'ī, Heb. *'unnî,* meaning unknown). 1. One of the Levites whom David appointed to play in connection with the tabernacle service (I Chron. 15:18,20).

2. Another Levite employed in the music service of the temple following the captivity (Neh. 12:9). "Unno" is the corrected spelling.

UNPARDONABLE SIN, not a phrase used in the Bible, but the usual way of referring to the blasphemy against the Holy Spirit (Matt. 12:31-32; Mark 3:28-29; Luke 12:10). There is much difference of opinion as to the meaning of this sin, but it probably refers to the sin of decisively and finally rejecting the testimony of the Holy Spirit regarding the person and work of Jesus Christ.

UNTEMPERED MORTAR (Heb. *tāphēl*), mortar made of clay instead of slaked lime. It was smeared on the walls of houses made of small stones or mud bricks so as to prolong the life of the building. Ezekiel uses the term symbolically to refer to the flimsiness of the work of the false prophets.

UPHARSIN(ū-fàr'sĭn, Heb. *ûpharsîn, and divided*), one of the words found written on the wall at Belshazzar's feast (Dan. 5:24-28). It probably means "divisions" or "divided." See Mene, Mene, Tekel, Upharsin.

UPHAZ (ū'făz, Heb. *'ûphāz,* meaning unknown), a word used of the famous gold-producing region mentioned in Jeremiah 10:9 and Daniel 10:5. Its location is still unknown. Perhaps "Ophir" or "and fine gold" should be read instead.

An excavated schoolroom at Ur, from the time of Abraham. UMP

The stele of Ur-Nammu, builder of the great ziggurat temple at Ur, which project this limestone slab (5 x 10 ft.) commemorates. The king is shown in prayer at the top, and in the panel below he is shown receiving orders from the goddess Ningal and the god Nannar, to build them a temple. UMP

UPPER CHAMBER, UPPER ROOM (Heb. *'ăliyâh, lofty;* Gr. *anógeon, a room upstairs; hyperóon, upper*), a room frequently built on the roofs of houses and used in summer because it was cooler than the regular living quarters (Mark 14:15; Luke 22:12; Acts 1:13; 20:8). One of these was the scene of our Lord's last supper (Luke 22:12).

UR (ûr, Heb. *'ûr, flame*), the father of Eliphal, one of David's mighty men (I Chron. 11:35).

UR OF THE CHALDEES, the early home of Abraham, mentioned in Genesis 11:28,31; 15:7; I Chronicles 11:35; and in Nehemiah 9:7. Through extensive archeological excavations it is now known that this city was located in southern Mesopotamia, about 140 miles SE of the site of old Babylon. The most extensive archeological work has been done by C. Leonard Woolley between 1922 and 1934.

Education was well developed at Ur, for a school was found there with its array of clay tablets. Students learned to read, write, and do varied forms of arithmetic. Further studies have revealed the fact that commerce was well developed and that ships came into Ur from the Persian Gulf bringing diorite and alabaster used in statue making, copper ore, ivory, gold and hard woods.

Ruins of the great ziggurat temple at Ur. For an idea of size, see the Bedouin figures in right foreground. © MPS

Much light has been shed on the worship and religious life of Abraham's day. Nanna was the moon-god worshiped there. The temple, ziggurat, and other buildings used in connection with the worship of this pagan deity have been found. Evidences of worship in the homes of that day are revealed by idols found in private niches in the home walls.

From this city of idolatry God called Abraham and sent him by promise to the land of Canaan.

H.Z.C.

URBANE (ûr′bān, Gr. *Ourbanós, polite*), a Roman Christian to whom Paul sent greetings (Rom. 16:9).

URI (ū′rī, Heb. *'ûrî, fiery*). 1. The father of Bezaleel (Exod. 31:2; 35:30; 38:22; I Chron. 2:20; II Chron. 1:5).

2. The father of Geber, one of the 12 provision officers of Solomon (I Kings 4:19).

3. A porter of the temple who put away his foreign wife (Ezra 10:24).

URIAH, URIAS (ū-rī′à, ū-rī′ăs, Heb. *'ûrîyâh, Jehovah is light*). 1. A Hittite, the husband of Bathsheba (II Sam. 11:3). The fact that he had married a Hebrew wife, his Hebrew name, and his loyalty and devotion as a soldier (II Sam. 11:11) all indicate that he probably was a worshiper of Jehovah. After David had committed adultery with Bathsheba, he recalled Uriah from the battle and sent him to his house, trying thus to hide his sin. When Uriah refused to do violence to his religion, David sent him back to the war with special instructions for Joab to place him in the thick of the fight that he might die. When he was finally killed, David took Bathsheba for his own wife.

2. A priest during the kingship of Ahaz. He was one of "the faithful witnesses" (Isa. 8:2) taken by the king to record the matter concerning Maher-shalalhashbaz. It also seems highly probable that he was the one who executed the king's command to build an Assyrian altar in the temple which was to be used for sacrifice (II Kings 16:10-16).

3. A priest who aided Ezra in carrying on his ministry (Neh. 8:4). He may be the Uriah referred to as the father of Meremoth (Ezra 8:33; Neh. 3:4,21).

H.Z.C.

Below, two more views of the ruins at Ur, the Temple of Ningal at bottom. © MPS SHH

URIEL (ū'rĭ-ĕl, Heb. *'ûrî'ēl, God is light*). 1. A Levite, the son of Tahash and father of Uzziah from the family of Kohath (I Chron. 6:24).

2. A chief of the Kohathites (I Chron. 15:5,11). With his 120 brethren he assisted in bringing the ark from the house of Obed-Edom.

3. The father of Michaiah, wife of Rehoboam. He was from the land of Gibeah (II Chron. 13:2).

URIJAH (ū-rī'jà, Heb. *'ûrîyâh, Jehovah is light*). 1. A prophet, the son of Shemaiah of Kirjath-jearim. He predicted the destruction of Judah (Jer. 26:20). When the king, angry at his predictions, sought to put him to death, he fled to Egypt, but he was apprehended by the king and slain (Jer. 26:21-23).

2. The KJV refers to Uriah by this name (II Kings 16:10 and Neh. 3:4,21). For a discussion of these see under Uriah numbers 2 and 3 respectively.

UTHAI (ū'thī, Heb. *'ûthay, meaning uncertain*). 1. A descendant of Judah who lived in Jerusalem after the Babylonian captivity (I Chron. 9:4).

2. One of the sons of Bigvai who returned with Ezra (Ezra 8:14).

UZ (ŭz, Heb. *'ûts, meaning uncertain*). 1. One of Nahor's sons by Milcah (Gen. 22:21). He is called "Huz" (KJV).

2. One of the sons of Aram (Gen. 10:23), the grandson of Shem (I Chron. 1:17).

3. One of the sons of Dishan (Gen. 36:28).

4. The country in which Job lived (Job 1:1). This country is referred to also twice by Jeremiah (Jer. 25:20; Lam. 4:21). There are quite a few details given in the Scripture by which this land can be identified. Eliphaz, one of Job's friends, came from Teman located in Idumea. Uz was exposed to attacks by the Chaldeans and Sabeans

Replicas of Urim and Thummim, from Aaron's Breastplate. (See Minerals) © APD & ABA

URIM AND THUMMIM (ū'rĭm and thŭm'ĭm, Heb. *hā'ûrîm wehatûmmîm, lights and perfections*), objects not specifically described, perhaps stones, placed in the breastplate of the high priest which he wore when he went into the presence of the Lord and by which he ascertained the will of God in any important matter affecting the nation (Exod. 28:30; Lev. 8:8). It is uncertain what they were or what they looked like, or how they were used. One theory is that they were used as the lot and cast like dice, the manner of their fall somehow revealing the Lord's will (I Sam. 10:19-22; 14:37-42). Another theory is that they served as a symbol of the high priest's authority to seek counsel of Jehovah, God's will being revealed to him through inner illumination.

They are first mentioned in Scripture with no explanations (Exod. 28:30) making certain that Israel was already familiar with them. They seemed to form a necessary part of the equipment of the high priest, for they were passed on from Aaron to Eleazar (Num. 20:28). The last reference to them in the Scripture is in Nehemiah 7:65.

USURY (Heb. *neshekh, interest; nāshakh, to bite, to lend on interest; nāshâh, to remove; nash', lead astray*; Gr. *tókos, interest on money*). God gave specific instructions to Israel with regard to interest on money loaned. Any money that a Jew lent to his brother was to be without interest (Exod. 22:25; Deut. 23:19). Money could, however, be lent to a stranger with interest (Deut. 23:20). The main purpose for lending money among the Israelites was for the relief of the poor for which, according to law, no interest was to be demanded (Lev. 25:35-36). During Israel's time in Babylon many abuses arose regarding the lending of money (Ezek. 18:8,17). Because of this, Nehemiah, after the return from exile, took measures to have this practice stopped (Neh. 5:10-12).

In the NT reasonable rates of interest received for money loaned is never condemned. It was a common practice in the days of our Lord, and is referred to in the parable of the talents. The meaning of the English word *usury* has changed in recent centuries. While it once meant simply the charging of interest on money loaned, it has now come to mean excessive interest. H.Z.C.

(Job 1:15,17). Then it must have been located near a city at the gate of which Job sat. It must also have been good pasture land, for Job had extensive herds of cattle (Job 1:3; 42:12). Delitzsch accepts the tradition that places Uz in Hauran, the scriptural land of Bashan not far from the Sea of Galilee. Others place it in the north Arabian desert about 200 miles E of Petra. H.Z.C.

UZAI (ū'zī, Heb. *'ûzay, meaning unknown*), the father of Palal who aided Nehemiah in rebuilding the walls of Jerusalem (Neh. 3:25).

UZAL (ū'zăl, Heb. *'ûzâl, meaning uncertain*), a Shemite, the sixth son of Joktan (Gen. 10:27; I Chron. 1:21). He founded Uzal, the capital of Yemen, probably now the same as Sanaa.

UZZA (ŭz'à, Heb. *'uzzâh, strength*). 1. The son of Shimei who became the father of Shimea (I Chron. 6:29).

2. The eldest son of Ehud (I Chron. 8:7).

3. The caretaker of, owner of, or one in whose memory a garden was named in which Manasseh and his son, Amon, were buried (II Kings 21:18, 26).

4. One whose children returned under Zerubbabel (Ezra 2:49; Neh. 7:51).

UZZA, GARDEN OF, a garden mentioned in II Kings 21:18,26. Manasseh and his son Amon were buried here.

UZZAH (ŭz'à, Heb. *'uzzâh, strength*). One of Abinadab's sons from Kirjath-jearim. He was one of those who accompanied the ark of the Lord when it was being brought from Kirjath-jearim to Jerusalem. The ark was being drawn on a cart pulled by oxen and when something happened causing the ark to shake, Uzzah took hold of it, thus displeasing the Lord. As a result, he met instant death (II Sam. 6:3-8; I Chron. 13:6-11).

UZZEN-SHERAH (ŭz'ĕn-shē'ē-rà, Heb. *'uzzēn-she'erâh, plat of Sherah*), a town built by Ephraim's daughter Sheerah (I Chron. 7:24).

UZZI (ŭz'ī, Heb. *'uzzî, strong*). 1. One of Aaron's descendants who became the father of Zerahiah (I Chron. 6:5,51; Ezra 7:4).

2. Tola's son from the family of Issachar (I Chron. 7:2,3).

3. Bela's son from the tribe of Benjamin (I Chron. 7:7).

4. Another Benjamite, the father of Elah who returned to Jerusalem from the captivity (I Chron. 9:8).

5. The son of Bani living at Jerusalem and an overseer of the Levites (Neh. 11:22).

6. A priest in the family of Jedaiah (Neh. 12:19).

UZZIA (ŭ-zī′à, Heb. *'uzzîyā'*, strength), one of David's mighty men who was from Ashtaroth (I Chron. 11:24).

UZZIAH (ŭ-zī′à, Heb. *'uzzîyāh, Jehovah is strength*). 1. Uzziah, also called Azariah, the son of Amaziah. At the age of 16 he became Judah's 10th king (II Kings 14:21), and ruled 52 years. He came to the throne at a difficult time. His father, because of a military failure, had been slain (II Kings 14:19). Uzziah was the people's choice as his successor (II Kings 14:21). He undertook, very early in his career, an expedition against his father's enemies, and won battles against the Edomites, Philistines, Arabians, and the Mehunims (II Kings 14:22; II Chron. 26:1-7). He strengthened his kingdom (II Chron. 26:2), and made many improvements on his home front (II Chron. 26:9-10). He possessed real ability at organization (II Chron. 26:11-15). The report of his strength spread as far as Egypt (II Chron. 26:8).

In spite of these successes, he strayed far from the Lord at the end of his life. Apparently as long as the Prophet Zechariah lived, his influence was great on the king and "as long as he sought the Lord, God made him to prosper" (II Chron. 26:5). However, when he became strong, pride filled his heart, and going into the temple he determined to burn incense unto the Lord, a duty to be performed only by the priest. The chief priest, Azariah, with 80 priests went into the temple to reason with him, but he would not listen. Because of his self will, God struck him with leprosy which stayed with him until his death (II Chron. 26:16-21).

2. A Levite descended from Kohath (I Chron. 6:24).

3. The father of a certain Jehonathan in David's time (I Chron. 27:25).

4. One of the sons of Harim who put away his foreign wife when admonished by Ezra the priest (Ezra 10:16-21).

5. The father of Athaiah who came to Jerusalem after the Exile (Neh. 11:4).

UZZIEL, UZZIELITE (ŭ-zī′ĕl, ŭ-zī′ĕl-īt, Heb. *'uzzî'ēl, God is strength*). 1. A Levite, son of Kohath (Exod. 6:18,22; Lev. 10:4; Num. 3:19,30; I Chron. 6:2,18).

2. A captain in the days of Hezekiah from the tribe of Simeon, son of Ishi (I Chron. 4:42).

3. One of Bela's sons and head of a Benjamite family (I Chron. 7:7).

4. One of David's musicians, a son of Heman (I Chron. 25:4).

5. One of the sons of Jeduthun, a Levite, who, heeding King Hezekiah's commandment, assisted in cleansing the temple (II Chron. 29:14-19).

6. The son of Harhaiah, a goldsmith, who aided Nehemiah in repairing the walls of Jerusalem (Neh. 3:8).

Anyone who descended from Uzziel, the Levite, was known as a Uzzielite. This group is referred to in several places (Num. 3:27; I Chron. 26:23; 15:10). During David's day Amminadáb was their chief, and those whom he led numbered 112 (I Chron. 15:9).

V

VAGABOND (Heb. *nûdh, to wander*), a word used in the curse pronounced upon Cain (Gen. 4:12, 14). The plural form is found in the imprecatory prayer in Psalm 109:10. The sorcerers mentioned in Acts 19:13 as "vagabond Jews" were professional exorcists.

VAJEZATHA (và-jĕz′à-thà, Heb. *wayzāthā', son of the atmosphere*), one of the ten sons of Haman who was hung by the Jews in Shushan (Esth. 9:9).

VALE, VALLEY. 1. *Gaye', a gorge.* The word is used to describe the place of Moses' burial (Deut. 34:6), the valley of Hinnom (Josh. 15:8; 18:16; II Kings 23:10; Jer. 7:31), a valley of salt (II Sam. 8:13; I Chron. 18:12; II Chron. 25:11), the valley of Hamon-gog (Ezek. 39:11,15), and the great valley formed when Christ returns to the earth to rule (Zech. 14:4-5).

2. *Nahal, receiving,* today often translated *wady.* It refers to a valley that is the bed of a brook or river which can be filled quickly by rain, which often happens in the climate of Palestine (Gen. 26:19; Num. 13:23; Josh. 12:1).

3. *'Ēmeq, a deep place.* This term describes a number of places such as: Valley of Achor (Josh. 7:24); Valley of Ajalon (Josh. 10:12); of Gibeon (Isa. 28:21); of Hebron (Gen. 37:14); of Jehoshaphat (Joel 3:2); of Jezreel (Josh. 17:16).

4. *Biq'âh, a split,* a plain between two hills or mountains and in that sense a valley (Deut. 11:11; 34:3; Josh. 11:17).

5. *Shephēlâh, lowland.* It is in reality not a valley, but the low lying hills that stretch from Israel's coast up to the mountains (Josh. 10:40; Jer. 32:44).

6. Gr. *pháragx,* a ravine (Luke 3:5).

VALLEY GATE (Heb. *sha'ar haggay', gate of the Gai*), a gate mentioned in Nehemiah 2:13; 3:13; 12:31,38. There is disagreement as to whether it was in the SW or NW corner of the city.

VANIAH (và-nī′à, Heb. *wanyâh,* meaning unknown), a son of Bani who in response to Ezra's request gave up his Gentile wife (Ezra 10:36).

VANITY (Heb. *hevel, 'āwen, shāw'*; Gr. *kenós, mataiótes*), a word occurring almost 100 times in the KJV, but never in the sense of conceit or undue self-esteem. It means emptiness, evanescence, worthlessness, futility, and is applied to things that are empty or worthless, such as the fruitlessness of human endeavors, the worthlessness of idolatry, and the futility of wickedness. It appears most often (37 times) in the Book of Ecclesiastes. Man's natural life is vanity (Job 7:3; Ps. 39:5,6, etc.). All idolatry is vanity and consequently unprofitable (I Sam. 12:21; II Kings 17:15; Isa. 41:29; 44:9). The proclamation of false prophets is vanity (Jer. 23:16; Ezek. 13:1-23; Zech. 10:2). In the NT the word occurs only three times (Eph. 4:17; II Pet. 2:18; Rom. 8:20). In the KJV the word is sometimes used for one of the Hebrew words which mean iniquity (Job 15:35; Ps. 10:7; Prov. 22:8).
S.B.

VASHNI (văsh′nī, Heb. *washnî, weak*), the name of the firstborn of Samuel, according to I Chronicles 6:28. This presents a problem, since Samuel's firstborn was Joel and his second Abijah (I Sam. 8:2). The likelihood is that the Hebrew text is corrupt and that *washnî* should be translated "and the second," the name of the first son being accidentally omitted by some copyist.

VASHTI (văsh′tī, Heb. *washtî, beautiful woman,* from the Persian), Xerxes' queen whom he divorced because of her refusal to show herself to the king's guests at a feast and whose place was taken by Esther (Esth. 1:11).

VEIL (See Dress, Temple)

VEIN (Heb. *môtsā′, source*), a word found only in Job 28:1 KJV, "a vein for the silver." The RV "mine" probably conveys the meaning of the Hebrew more accurately. The Hebrew word, however, is found 27 times with a much broader meaning than is indicated in the passage in Job (Num. 30:12; Deut. 8:3; Ps. 19:6).

VENGEANCE (Heb. *nāqam, to grudge*), any punishment meted out in the sense of retribution. The word is used in both a bad sense (Judg. 15:7) and a good sense (Jer. 11:20; 20:12). Three Greek words are used for this English term in the NT (KJV): *díke* is twice rendered *vengeance* (Acts 23:4 and Jude 1:7), in both cases in the sense of punishment for wrong done; *ekdíkesis* is used in much the same sense (Heb. 10:30; Luke 18:7; Rom. 12:19; II Thess. 1:8); *orgé*, meaning "impulse," is used especially of God in punishing evil in man (Matt. 3:7; John 3:36; Rom. 1:18; Col. 3:6; Rev. 6:16, 17).

VENISON (Heb. *tsayidh, tsēdhâh, game of any kind*), properly the flesh of the deer, but as used in Genesis 25:28 and 27:5ff it could mean any game taken in hunting.

VERMILION (Heb. *shāshār*), a red pigment used for painting walls of palaces (Jer. 22:14) and for coloring the exotic clothing of the Chaldeans (Ezek. 23:14).

VERSIONS OF THE SCRIPTURES (See Bible, also Texts and Versions)

VESSEL (Heb. *kelî*, Gr. *skeúos*), any material thing or object which may be used for any purpose, whether it be a tool, implement, weapon, or receptacle. The KJV translates them 146 times by "vessel," but by an almost equal number of times by other terms, including "armor," "artillery," "bag," "carriage," "furniture," "instrument," "jewel," "pot," "sack," "stuff," "thing," "wares," "weapon." The RSV uses "utensils" rather than "vessels" where the context shows that a hollow utensil is meant. Hosea 13:15 has "pleasant vessels" in the KJV; this is more correctly rendered by "precious thing" in the RSV. In Romans 9:20-24 and II Timothy 2:20,21 the term is applied to persons, and in II Corinthians 4:7 it means the person as an instrument of God's will. The "weaker vessel" of I Peter 3:7 is "weaker sex" in the RSV. In I Thessalonians 4:4 "vessel" is used figuratively for either a man's own body or for his wife, more likely the latter.

VESTRY (Heb. *meltāhâh*), a place where royal or ceremonial vestments were kept (II Kings 10:22).

VESTURE, an archaic word denoting dress which in the KJV is used to render a number of Hebrew and Greek words: Heb. *beghedh, cloak, garment, covering* (Gen. 41:42); *kesûth, a covering* (Deut. 22:12); *levûsh, clothing, dress, attire* (Ps. 22:18; 102:26); Gr. *himátion, an outer garment* (Rev. 19:13,16); *himatismós, dress, apparel* (Matt. 27:35); *peribólaion, what is thrown around one* (Heb. 1:12).

Along the Via Dolorosa (the "sorrowful way") in Jerusalem. © MPS

VIA DOLOROSA, "the sorrowful way," the traditional route which our Lord traveled on the day of His crucifixion from the judgment seat of Pilate (Matt. 27:26,31; Mark 15:20; Luke 22:25; John 19:16) to the place of His crucifixion on Mount Calvary (Matt. 27:33; Mark 15:22; Luke 23:33; John 19:18). Nothing is surely known of the exact location of Pilate's judgment hall. Jerusalem was destroyed by the Romans under Titus (A.D. 70), and again at the rebellion of Bar Cochbar (A.D. 135), when it was so thoroughly demolished that the very marks of the ancient streets were obliterated. By monkish tradition, the "fourteen stations of the cross" are marked in the modern city, and also are denoted by pictures or images in many churches and private homes as helps to devotion. The stations are as follows: (1) Christ is condemned to die in Pilate's hall; (2) He receives the cross; (3) He falls under its weight; (4) He meets his mother; (5) Simon of Cyrene is forced to bear the cross (Matt. 27:32; Mark 15:21; Luke 23:26); (6) His face is wiped by Veronica; (7) He falls again; (8) He meets the women of Jerusalem (Luke 23:28-31); (9) His third fall; (10) He is stripped of His garments (cf. Matt. 27:35); (11) He is nailed to the cross (Matt. 27:35, etc.); (12) He dies (Matt. 27:50; Mark 15:37; Luke 23:46; John 19:30); (13) His body is taken down (Matt. 27:59; Mark 15:46; Luke 23:53; John 19:40); (14) and it is laid in the tomb (Matt. 27:60; Mark 15:46; Luke 23:53; John 19:41,42).   A.B.F.

VIAL (Heb. *pakh*, from a root meaning *to pour*, Gr. *phiále*), a flask or bottle (I Sam. 10:1), rendered "box" in II Kings 9:1,3 KJV, but "vial" in ASV. In Revelation 5:8, 21:9 "vial" represents a shallow bowl or basin.

VICTUAL (See Food)

Walls and watchtowers amid the terraced vineyards of Palestine. © MPS

VILLAGE. Villages were usually grouped around a fortified town to which the people could flee in time of war. Generally they were unwalled, but in northern Syria even today an agricultural village is often surrounded by a wall, sometimes coinciding with the backs of houses which face inward, and the farmers walk out daily to their fields, some at quite a distance from the village. In the OT, the word frequently renders the Hebrew *bath,* i.e. "daughter," as in II Chronicles 28:18 three times "with the villages thereof" (ASV "towns"). The usual OT word (*hātsēr*) signifies an enclosure (Josh. 13:23,28) and is frequently compounded to name a particular village e.g. Hazar-addar (Num. 34:4), Hazar-gaddah (Josh. 15:27), Hazar-susah (Josh. 19:5) and its plural may represent a group of hamlets ("Hazeroth" Num. 11:35). Another frequent root-word is from the verb *kāphār,* signifying shelter or protection, e.g. "Capernaum" i.e. "Village of Nahum."

VINE (See Plants)

VINEGAR (Heb. *hōmets,* Gr. *óxos*), with us, generally a sour fluid obtained by fermentation of cider, but in Bible times from wine. The Nazirite was to abstain from drinking it (Num. 6:3), and it was used as a condiment on bread (Ruth 2:14). Its action on the teeth (Prov. 10:26) and its fizzing with soda (Prov. 25:20) are mentioned by Solomon. Our Lord, upon the cross, was offered vinegar (ASV "wine") mixed with gall or with myrrh (Matt. 27:34, cf. Mark 15:23) in fulfillment of Psalm 69:21, but He refused it. Later He was offered on a sponge a mixture of water and vinegar (Matt. 27:48), a drink very popular among the poor and used by Roman soldiers when in camp.

VINE, VINEYARD (Heb. *gephen,* usually the cultivated grapevine; *sōrēq,* dark grapes; *nāzîr,* undressed vine; Gr. *ámpelos, staphylé, bótrys*). The common grapevine is mentioned throughout Scripture, often in a figurative sense. It was grown in ancient Egypt and in Canaan prior to the time of Abraham (Gen. 14:18; Num. 13:20,24). The mountain regions of Judaea and Samaria, largely unsuited for cereals, were well adapted for vine growing. A vineyard was usually surrounded with a protecting wall of stones or thorny hedges to keep out destructive animals (Num. 22:24; Ps. 80:8-13; Prov. 24:30,31; Isa. 5:5). A part of every vineyard was a tower for the watchman, a winepress hollowed out of a flat rock, and a vat into which the wine flowed from the winepress (Isa. 1:8; 5:1-7; Matt. 21:33-41). The vine branches were usually allowed to lie along the ground or to fall over the terraces, but sometimes they were raised above the ground with sticks or supported on poles to form a bower.

Vines required constant care to keep them productive. Hence they were pruned every spring, and the ground was ploughed and kept free of weeds. Pruned branches were gathered and burned (John 15:6). During the harvest season watchmen were stationed in the towers, and sometimes the whole family of the owner took their residence in booths as a protection against thieves. The harvest season was always one of special happiness. The treaders of the winepress shouted and sang as they trod the grapes (Judg. 9:27; Isa. 16:10; Jer. 25:30; 48:33). The gleanings were left to the poor (Lev. 19:10; Deut. 24:21; Judg. 8:2). The wine was stored in new goatskin bags (Matt. 9:17) or in large pottery containers. Every seventh year the vines were allowed to lie fallow (Exod. 23:11; Lev. 25:3).

Grapes were an important part of the diet of the Hebrews. A part of the harvest was preserved in the form of raisin cakes (I Sam. 25:18). Grapes were also their only source of sugar. The juice of the grapes was drunk fresh and fermented.

Figuratively, the vine symbolized prosperity and peace among the ancient Hebrews (I Kings 4:25; Mic. 4:4; Zech. 3:10). The vine also symbolized the chosen people, who instead of producing outstanding fruit yielded only wild grapes.

A Palestinian vinedresser pruning the grapevines in the spring. © MPS

Below, an Arab peasant girl picking grapes in a vineyard of Ephraim. © MPS

A number of parables of Jesus relate to vines and culture (Luke 13:6-9; Matt. 20:1-6; Matt. 9: 17; Matt. 21:28-32; Matt. 21:33). Jesus referred to Himself as the only true vine with whom His disciples are in organic union (John 15).   S.B.

VINEYARDS, PLAIN OF THE, so translated in Judges 11:33 (KJV) but transliterated "Abel-cheramim" in ASV. A village of the Ammonites E of the Jordan.

VIPER (See Animals)

VIRGIN. This word renders three Heb. and Gr. terms: 1. *bethûlâh,* from a root meaning "to separate," is the technical term for "virgin," a young unmarried woman (Gen. 24:16; Exod. 22: 16f; II Sam. 13:2). It is also used figuratively to personify a city or a state (Isa. 23:12; 47:1; Amos 5:2).

2. *'almâh, mature,* used of a young woman of marriageable age, whether married or not (Gen. 24:43; S. of Sol. 1:3; 6:8; Isa. 7:14, etc.). Only the context can give it the force "virgin".

3. *parthénos,* used in the LXX chiefly as the rendering of *bethûlâh* (of *'almâh* in Gen. 24:43 and Isa. 7:14). In the NT it is the usual Gr. word for "virgin" (Matt. 1:23, etc.), but in Revelation 14:4 it is used of men, with the emphasis on the idea of chastity.   S.B.

VIRGIN BIRTH. Christendom in the Apostles' Creed confesses that its Lord and Saviour was "conceived by the Holy Ghost, born of the Virgin Mary." This formulation of faith, going back to the second century, is based upon two NT passages, Matthew 1:18-25 and Luke 1:26-2:7. The Matthean account is apparently derived from an Antiochean source, the Lukan from a Palestinian; it seems, however, that ultimately the Matthean version came from Joseph, the Lukan from Mary. These two accounts are the only NT passages which deal explicitly with the birth of Jesus. In their monographs on this subject both Orr and Machen have shown by exhaustive analysis that these accounts are first century documents which have been transmitted in unimpeachable integrity; because textual interpolation or corruption is ruled out, this miracle must be accepted as a valid element in the apostolic witness. Though independent, the accounts are complementary; moreover, while they alone definitely teach the doctrine of the Virgin Birth, other NT writings either presuppose that doctrine or are at least completely congruous with it. The two Evangelists affirm this miracle flatly as a matter of history. They represent no arguments to support it; they draw no conclusions from it. They simply state it as an event of indisputable reality. No slightest evidence of apologetic concern can be detected in their narratives. Hence critics of the doctrine are totally unjustified in dismissing it as a piece of illegitimate rationalization, an attempt to support the mystery of the incarnation by a biological wonder.

The Virgin Birth means that Jesus Christ entered into the stream of human life without the mediation of an earthly father, born not as a result of sexual intercourse but as a result of supernatural "overshadowing." To view the Holy Spirit as a male substitute, a sort of apotheosized husband, as Karl Barth puts it, is to miss the central point of this immaterial conception. There was no union, no impregnation; any idea of such a relationship between Creator and creature was quite literally unthinkable to the Jewish mind. Justin Martyr has therefore admirably expressed the Biblical teaching in his comment on Isaiah 7:14, "The words, 'Behold the virgin shall conceive,' signify that the virgin conceived without intercourse; for if she had had intercourse with anyone whatever, she would no longer be a virgin. But the power of God coming upon the virgin overshadowed her and caused her to conceive though she was a virgin. . . . Accordingly, the Spirit and the power which was from God must be understood as nothing else than the Logos, who also is the firstborn of God, as Moses the aforementioned prophet declared; and this, coming upon the virgin and overshadowing her, caused her to be with child not by intercourse but by power" (quoted by Machen, *The Virgin Birth of Christ*, p. 334).

From a strictly theological perspective, the Virgin Birth has weighty significance. For one thing, it attests the omnipotent grace and creative freedom of God as He inaugurates a new order of redemption by a miracle pure and simple, a miracle which breaks in upon and shatters the old order of sin. Barth in particular emphasizes "the miracle of Christmas" as a demonstration of the Father's saving sovereignty (*Church Dogmatics*, Vol. I, Pt. 2, pp. 186, 191, 192). Again, the Virgin Birth signifies and establishes an organic connection with mankind, on the one hand, and a radical discontinuity with it, on the other. How else could the double requirement of soteriology, simultaneous connection and discontinuity, be achieved? Once more, the Virgin Birth reveals the heavenly origin and unique status of the Messiah's Person. Orr, for example, vigorously contends that the sinlessness of Jesus, His pre-existence, and his role as the Second Adam require the Virgin Birth: Jesus was a spiritual miracle whose entrance into the human race necessitated a physical miracle (*The Virgin Birth of Christ*, pp. 200ff).

Yet few Scriptural miracles have been more impugned and controverted. Thus Walter Horton declares that "a very solid contingent of leading Protestant thinkers now accept the orthodox doctrine of the Incarnation while admitting their perplexity over the evidence for the Virgin Birth" (*Christian Theology: An Ecumenical Approach*, pp. 198-199). Ferré asserts that "it is pious adulation and should honestly be accepted as creative myth to adorn history's most significant Event" (*Christ and the Christian*, p. 215). The reasons for this attitude are apparently threefold. First, the Virgin Birth is *factually* suspect: De Wolf marshals the arguments on this score (*A Theology of the Living Church*, pp. 230-232), but Orr and Machen, and more recently Barth (*op. cit.*, pp. 174-176), rebut the critical case effectively. Second, the doctrine is *polemically* hazardous. Horton in particular highlights the propensity of Roman Catholic dogmaticians to build a vast structure of Mariology, an inverted pyramid resting upon the apex of the Virgin Birth (*op. cit.*, pp. 199-203). But surely there is no need of throwing out the baby of revelational truth with the bathwater of extravagant superstition. Third, the doctrine is *theologically* pernicious. Ferré especially is afraid that the Virgin Birth implies a subtle Docetism. "If the Virgin Birth in any way endows Jesus with a predetermined sinlessness or, even more, with some initial presence of God which sets Him off essentially from normal human beings, then the Son of God never took on our human nature. Then we have, in fact, no real doctrine of the Incarnation as the full union of God's and man's nature" (*op. cit.*, p. 104). But Ferré's charge is more than masterfully answered by Barth who maintains "the rightness and importance" of the Virgin Birth theologically (*op. cit.*, pp. 177ff).

If the actuality of the Christmas miracle is denied, how can the origin of this dogma be accounted for? How did this particular belief concerning Jesus Christ ever arise? Allegedly the notion of a Virgin Birth was inspired by OT prophecy or borrowed from paganism. But neither theory is viable, as Machen and Orr have shown. Was the doctrine of the Virgin Birth inspired perhaps by Isaiah 7:14? The Jews never applied that particular passage to the Messiah. Isaiah does indeed predict the Virgin Birth; nevertheless the Jews did not interpret his prediction Messianically. Machen's verdict is judicious: "The *actual* interpretation of that prophecy which was prevalent among the Jews in the first century after Christ was, unless all indications fail, as far as possible from finding in the prophecy any prediction of the virgin birth of the Messiah" (*op. cit.*, p. 293). Was this notion, then, derived from some pagan source? Let Harnack's magisterial statement suffice: "The oldest Christianity strictly refrained from everything polytheistic and heathen . . . the unreasonable method of collecting from the mythology of all peoples parallels for original Church traditions, whether historical reports or legends, is valueless . . . the Greek or Oriental mythology I should leave entirely out of account; for there is no occasion to suppose that the Gentile congregations in the time up to the middle of the second century adopted, despite their fixed principle, popular mythical representations" (quoted by Orr, *op. cit.*, p. 176). But if the doctrine of the Virgin Birth was derived from neither Judaism nor paganism, how did it arise? It arose because it was grounded in a miraculous fact to which Matthew and Luke bear witness. Thus, though it may be readily acknowledged that the Virgin Birth does not occupy a major place in the *kerygma* as do the Incarnation and the Resurrection, nevertheless it ought not to be expunged from the great symbols of the faith; it must not be reduced to, in Horton's phrase, "an optional, second-rank position." Involved in its unfeigned acceptance are the issues of orthodox Christology, revelational authority, and of course Biblical infallibility. That is why Barth, himself no believer in verbal inspiration, insists that the Church is not at liberty "to convert the doctrine of the Virgin Birth into an option for specially strong or for specially weak souls. The Church knew well what it was doing when it posted this doctrine on guard, as it were, at the door of the mystery of Christmas. It can never be in favor of anyone thinking he can hurry past this guard. It will remind him that he is walking along a private road at his own cost and risk" (*op. cit.*, p. 181). In short, faith in the miracle of the Virgin Birth still serves as a convenient touchstone of faith in the mystery of God enfleshed.

In defense and explication of the Virgin Birth, cf. James Orr, *The Virgin Birth of Christ*, 1907; J. Gresham Machen, *The Virgin Birth of Jesus Christ*, 1932; Karl Barth, *Church Dogmatics*, Vol. I, Pt. 2, E. T., 1956; Alan Richardson, *An Introduction to the Theology of the New Testament*, 1958; J. S. K. Reid, "Virgin Birth," *A Theological Word Book of the Bible*, ed. Alan Richardson, 1950.

For a mediating position, c. Walter Marshall Horton, *Christian Theology: An Ecumenical Approach*, 1955.

For a negative evaluation, cf. L. Harold De Wolf, *A Theology of the Living Church*, 1953; Nels F. S. Ferré, *Christ and the Christian*, 1958; Emil Brunner, *The Mediator*, E. T., 1947.

V.C.G.

VIRTUE (Heb. *hayil, strength, ability,* often involving moral worth; Gr. *areté,* any excellence of a person or a thing; *dýnamis, power, influence*). The phrase, "a virtuous woman" (Ruth 3:11; Prov. 12:4; 31:10,29), is literally "a woman of ability." Sometimes the word is used in its Old English sense of "power" (Mark 5:30; Luke 6:19; 8:46) and "strength" (II Cor. 12:9; Heb. 11:11).

VISION (Heb. *hāzôn, hizzāyôn, mar'âh*; Gr. *hórama, optasía*). It is impossible to draw a sharp line of demarcation between dreams and visions. The various Heb. and Gr. words for this word all come from roots having to do with seeing. Visions in the Bible were for the most part given to individuals, and were not apprehended by their companions. Through them God revealed to the seers truth in pictorial form. They came under various circumstances, in men's waking hours (Dan. 10:7; Acts 9:7); by day (Acts 10:3) or by night (Gen. 46:2). In the OT both "writing" and "non-writing" prophets were recipients of visions (Isa. 1:1; Obad. 1; Nah. 1:1; II Sam. 7:17; I Kings 22:12-19; II Chron. 9:29). With perhaps one exception (Num. 24:4) they were given only to holy men in the service of God, and those of a revelatory nature were always recognized as coming from God. In the NT, Luke especially manifests great interest in visions (Luke 1:22; Acts 9:10; 10:3; 10:10ff; 18:9). Biblical visions concerned both immediate situations (Gen. 15:1f; Acts 12:7) and more distant ones connected with the development of the kingdom of God, as may be seen in the writings of Isaiah, Ezekiel, Hosea, Micah, Daniel, and John. In the OT false prophets feigned visions and were denounced by Jeremiah (14:14; 23:16) and Ezekiel (13:7).   S.B.

VISITATION (Heb. *pekuddâh,* Gr. *episkopé*), a divine visit for the purpose of rewarding or punishing people for their deeds (Jer. 10:15; Luke 19:44; I Pet. 2:12).

VOPHSI (vŏf'sī, Heb. *wopsî*), a man of Naphtali, one of the spies whom Moses sent to Canaan (Num. 13:14).

VOW (Heb. *nedher,* Gr. *euché*), a voluntary promise to God to perform some service or do something pleasing to Him, in return for some hoped for benefits (Gen. 28:20-22; Lev. 27:2,8; Num. 30; Judg. 11:30); or to abstain from certain things (Num. 30:3). In the OT vows were never regarded as a religious duty (Deut. 23:22), but once made they were considered as sacred and binding (Deut. 23:21-23; Judg. 11:35; Eccl. 5:4; Ps. 66:13). Fathers could veto vows made by their daughters; and husbands could veto their wives' vows; but if a husband did not veto a wife's vow, and then caused her to break it, the blame was his, not hers (Num. 30). A vow had to be uttered to be binding (Deut. 23:23). Almost anything — people, possessions, one's self — except what was already the Lord's or was an abomination to the Lord (Deut. 23:18), could be vowed, and all these things could be redeemed with money, with their value to be determined by a priest. Houses, lands, and unclean animals that were added to make up the redemption money. In the NT Jesus mentions vows only to condemn the abuse of them (Matt. 15:4-6; Mark 7:10-13). Paul's vow in Acts 18:18 was probably a temporary Nazirite vow.   S.B.

VULGATE (See Texts and Versions)

VULTURE (See Birds)

W

WADI (wá'dē), a valley which forms the bed of a stream during the winter, but which dries up in the hot season (Gen. 26:19). The word is Arabic, and does not appear in the Bible, but Palestine contains hundreds of these "wadis." Sometimes "wady."

WAFERS (Heb. *rāqîq, tsappîhith*), thin cakes. The word in Exodus 16:31 emphasizes the thinness, while that in Exodus 29:2 indicates the process of beating which rendered the cakes thin. The same word is rendered "cakes" in I Chronicles 23:29 KJV.

WAGES (Heb. *hinnām, maskōreth, pe'ullâh, sākhar,* Gr. *misthós, opsónion*), pay given for labor, generally reckoned by the day, and distinguished from fees paid for professional service or salaries which may be paid by the month or the year. In civilizations where slavery is a regular institution, the servant or slave necessarily received his living, but not much more, except when the master was kind and loving and made the servant practically a member of the family. The earliest mention of wages is in the bargaining between Laban and his nephew Jacob (Gen. 29). It is implicit in the narrative that he must also have received his living during those 14 years: then he labored for another six years, receiving as his wages considerable herds and flocks (Gen. 29,30). Pharaoh's daughter promised wages to the mother of Moses to act as his nurse (Exod. 2:5-9). In the Mosaic law, a hired servant must be paid at the end of the day (Lev. 19:13; Deut. 24:14,15), thus implying a "hand to mouth" existence. The same sort of poverty is in the parable of the 11th hour laborers (Matt. 20:1-16), but too much emphasis should not be put upon the supposed value of the *denarion,* for whether "a penny" as in KJV or "a shilling" as in the ASV, the fact remains that the laborer, and presumably his family, could live on it. Mercenary soldiers were advised by John the Baptist to "be content with your wages" (Luke 3:14). The idea of wages is spiritualized in "the wages of sin is death" (Rom. 6:23), where it is contrasted with "the gift of God — eternal life in Christ Jesus our Lord." Paul speaks of his gifts from churches at Philippi as "wages" (II Cor. 11:8; cf. Phil. 4:15-18), and though he earned his living with his hands, he teaches the right of the laborer to his hire (I Tim. 5:18).   A.B.F.

WAGON (Heb. *'āghālâh,* from *'aghal, to be round, to roll*), a vehicle with wheels (usually two) used for carrying goods as well as persons. Ancient wagons were crude, with wheels made of wood. They were covered or uncovered, usually drawn by oxen, but sometimes horses. Wagons are first mentioned in Genesis 45:19-46:5 when Pharaoh sent wagons to help move Jacob and his family. Covered wagons, each drawn by two oxen, were used for moving the tabernacle (Num. 7:3-9), but not the sacred furniture, which was carried on the shoulders of priests.

WAIL (Heb. *mispēdh, nehî,* Gr. *alalázo, penthéo*). In ancient funeral processions wailing relatives, often accompanied by hired female (sometimes male) mourners and musicians, preceded the body to the grave (Jer. 9:17f; Amos 5:16; Matt. 9:23).

The famous Jewish Wailing Wall in Jerusalem. © MPS

WALK, as a verb renders more than a dozen Hebrew and Greek words. To walk is used hundreds of times, generally literally but often figuratively (Ps. 1:1). In the NT epistles the word is used uniformly in the figurative sense and refers to the whole manner of life and conduct (Eph. 2:2,10; 5:2,8,15) and the observance of laws or customs (Acts 21:21).

WALL. In ancient times all over the East the walls of houses were built of crude or sunbaked brick. Stone was used only in certain few localities where it was plentiful. In Chaldea stone was entirely absent; in Assyria it was so rare that it was used only as an accessory. In Palestine houses were constructed of crude brick, although sometimes wood, mud-brick, and stone were used in alternate layers. In Egypt houses were built of crude brick mixed with chopped straw. Every ancient city had enormous walls surrounding it, sometimes containing chambers inside. There still exist some of the stones in the wall of the temple enclosure at Jerusalem. They measure 30 feet long, eight feet wide, and three and a half feet high, weighing over 80 tons. Josephus tells of stones in the temple of Solomon 60 feet long.

WAR (Heb. *milhāmâh,* from *laham, to fight;* Gr. *pólemos*). Every phase of Israel's life, including her warfare, was bound up with her God. War therefore had religious significance. It was customary for priests to accompany Israel's armies into battle (Deut. 20:1-4). Campaigns were begun and engagements entered into with sacrificial rites (I Sam. 7:8-10; 13:9), and after consulting the oracle (Judg. 20:18ff; I Sam. 14:37; 23:2; 28:6; 30:8). Prophets were sometimes asked for guidance before a campaign (I Kings 22:5; II Kings 3:11).

The blowing of a trumpet throughout the land announced the call to arms (Judg. 3:27; I Sam. 13:3; II Sam. 15:10), and priests sounded an alarm with trumpets (II Chron. 13:12-16). Weapons included slings, spears, javelins, bows and arrows, swords, and battering-rams. Strategical movements included the ambush (Josh. 8:3ff); the feint (Judg. 20:20ff); the flank movement (II Sam. 5:22f); the surprise attack (Josh. 11:1f); the raid (I Chron. 14:9); the foray (II Sam. 3:22); and foraging to secure supplies (II Sam. 23:11). Sometimes when opposing armies were drawn up in battle array, champions from each side fought one another (I Sam. 17). Armies engaged in hand to hand combat. Victorious armies pillaged the camp of the enemy, robbed the dead (Judg. 8:24-26; I Sam. 31:9; II Chron. 20:25), and often killed or mutilated prisoners (Josh. 8:23,29; 10:22-27; Judg. 1:6), although prisoners were usually sold into slavery. Booty was divided equally between those who had taken part in the battle and those who had been left behind in camp (Num. 31:27; Josh. 22:8; I Sam. 30:24f), but some of the spoils were reserved for the Levites and for the Lord (Num. 31:28,30).

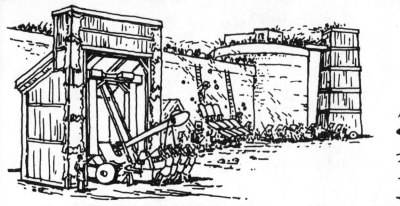

At left, artist's conception of Romans storming a city during a siege, using a catapult. At right, one of Alexander's siege towers (hele-poleis), as high as a 20-story building. UANT

When a city was besieged, the besiegers cast up huge mounds of earth against the walls from which battering-rams were brought into play against the walls (II Sam. 20:15; Ezek. 4:2). The besieged tried to drive off the enemy by throwing darts and stones and shooting arrows at them from the walls. Captured cities were often completely destroyed, and victory was celebrated with song and dance (Exod. 15:1-21; Judg. 5; I Sam. 18:6).

Jesus accepted war as an inevitable part of the present sinful world order (Matt. 24:6), but warned that those who take the sword must perish by it (Matt. 26:52). In the epistles the Christian is said to be a soldier (II Tim. 2:3; I Pet. 2:11). The Apocalypse uses the figure of battle and war to describe the final triumph of Christ over Satan (Rev. 16:14-16; 17:14; 19:14).   S.B.

WASHING (Heb. *rāhats, kāvas*, Gr. *nípto, loúo, loutrón*). Frequent bathing was necessary in the warm climate of the East. In Egypt, Syria, and Palestine people washed the dust from their feet when they entered a house (Gen. 18:4; John 13:10). Ceremonial defilement was removed by bathing the body and washing the raiment (Lev. 14:8; Num. 19:7-8). The priests washed their hands and feet before entering the sanctuary or offering a sacrifice (Exod. 30:19-21). In the time of Christ the Jews did much ceremonial washing of hands before eating (Mark 7:3,4), and used public baths like the Greeks and Romans.

WATCH (Heb. *'ashmurâh, 'ashmōreth*, Gr. *phylaké*), a man or group of men set to guard a city. Nehemiah, when building the walls of Jerusalem, set a watch day and night against his enemies (4:9) and after the walls were completed, he set watches near the gate (7:3). Even today, when the crops are ripening in the fields and vineyards in the East, one may see watchmen on guard day and night. The temporary shelters set up by the watchmen in fields are alluded to in Isaiah 1:8, for they are deserted as soon as the crops have been gathered. Metaphorically, David prays "Set a watch, (a restraint) O Jehovah, before my mouth, Keep the door of my lips" (Ps. 141:3). The Latin word *custodia*, transliterated into Greek, is used thrice (Matt. 27:25,26; 28:11) for the Roman watch that was set to guard our Lord's tomb.   A.B.F.

WATCHES OF THE NIGHT, the divisions into which the 12 hours of the night were divided. The Jews had a threefold division (Judg. 7:19), while the Romans had four watches (Mark 6:48).

WATCHMAN (Heb. *tsôpheh, shōmēr*, Gr. *phýlax, terós*), one who guards a city or the headquarters of an army (I Sam. 14:16; II Sam. 18:24-27). Such watchmen were set on city walls or on hilltops (Jer. 31:6). God's prophets and preachers should also be His watchmen to warn His people (Isa. 21:6).

A typical vineyard watchtower near Taibeh, in ancient Ephraim. © MPS

In Jesus' day, ceremonial hand-washing among the Jews had degenerated into an empty ritual. UANT

Shepherds on the night watch observing the stars. © MPS

WATER (Heb. *mayim*, Gr. *hýdor*). Because of the scarcity of water in Palestine, it is much appreciated there. For its people absence of water is very serious (I Kings 17:1ff; Jer. 14:3; Joel 1:20), and rain is a sign of God's favor. The rivers of Palestine are mostly small and have little if any water in summer. Consequently it depends upon rain as its source of water. This supplies springs and fountains. Cisterns are a necessity for the storing of water, and this if stored too long becomes filthy and a menace to health. In the summer there is no rain, so that vegetation is dependent upon the heavy dews. Irrigation is carried on where there is sufficient water. When water was scarce, as during a time of siege, it had to be rationed. Drinking water, carried in goatskins, was often sold in the streets. Wells and pools, although comparatively scarce, are often mentioned in the Bible (Gen. 21: 19; 24:11; John 4:6; 9:7). Water was used not only for refreshment, but for ceremonial washings before meals and in the Jewish temple-ceremony (Lev. 11:32; 16:4; Num. 19:7). The Bible uses it as a symbol of the cleansing of the soul from sin (Ezek. 16:4,9; 36:25; John 3:5; Eph. 5:26; Heb. 10:22; I John 5:6,8).   S.B.

WATER OF BITTERNESS, or, as in KJV, "the bitter water that causeth the curse" (Num. 5:12-31), water, mingled with dust from the floor of the sanctuary, which a woman suspected of carnal sin was asked to drink — a sort of "trial by ordeal" but ordered of the Lord. If she were guilty, her body would swell and her "thigh fall away," a statement possibly meaning dire disorder of the generative organs. If she were innocent, the water had no effect.

WATER OF JEALOUSY (See Water of Bitterness)

WATER OF SEPARATION, or, as in ASV, "water for impurity" (Num. 19:9,13,20,21; 31:23). Water for the removal of impurity (Num. 19:9,13,20, 21; 31:23).

WATERPOT (Gr. *hydría*), earthen jars for carrying or holding water, either for drinking (John 4: 28) or for purifying purposes (John 2:6f). The latter were large, holding 18 to 20 gallons each.

WATERSPOUT (Heb. *tsinnôr*), mentioned only in Psalm 42:7 where ASV has "waterfall." It is used of a large rush of water sent by God, perhaps great floods of rain.

WAVE OFFERING (See Offerings)

WAY. There are about 25 Heb. and Gr. words rendered "way" in the Bible. It is often used metaphorically to describe the conduct or manner of life, whether of God or of man (Exod. 32:8; Deut. 5:33; Job 16:22). In the NT, God's plan of salvation is called "the way of the Lord" (Matt. 3:3, etc.). The term is also used to mean Christianity or Judaism (Acts 9:2; 19:9; 22:4).

WAYFARING MAN (Heb. *'ōrēah, 'āvar 'ōrah, hālakhderekh*), one who walks the roads; a traveler (Judg. 19:17; II Sam. 12:4; Isa. 33:8; 35:8).

WEALTH (Heb. *hôn, hayil, nekhāsîm,* Gr. *euporía*), abundance of possessions whether material, social or spiritual. In the nomadic civilization of the early Hebrews, wealth consisted largely of flocks and herds, silver and gold, brass, iron and clothing (Josh. 22:8). In the days of Job, his sons had houses, but their wealth consisted largely of camels, asses, flocks and herds and "a very great household" (Job 1:3), no doubt implying many servants. From the beginning of Israel, God taught His people that He was the giver of their wealth

A Bedouin woman weaving, in her tent near Beersheba. © MPS

(Deut. 8:18): "For it is he that giveth thee power to get wealth." He taught them to be liberal: "There is that scattereth and yet increaseth, and there is which withholdeth more than is meet, but it tendeth to poverty" (Prov. 11:24). NT teaching goes even further: "Let no man seek his own, but every man another's good" (I Cor. 10:24). A careless reading of the Bible gives some the impression that in OT times wealth always went with godliness (Ps. 112:3), that poverty was for the wicked (Prov. 13:18), whereas in NT times blessings are only of a spiritual nature. Cf. Matthew 6:19-33 where good provision is promised to those of a single eye for God's glory and who lay up treasures in heaven.   A.B.F.

WEAN, WEANING (Heb. *gāmal, to complete, wean*). To wean is to accustom a child to depend upon other food than its mother's milk. In the East, weaning is often deferred for as much as three years (I Sam. 1:22; 2:11). The weaning of a child was celebrated by a feast (Gen. 21:8) and with an offering (I Sam. 1:24).

WEASEL (See Animals)

WEAPON (See Arms, Armor)

WEATHER. There is no Heb. word corresponding to "weather." The temperature in Palestine varies from that at the top of Hermon (9,000 feet above sea-level) where there is snow on the ground the year around to the oppressive heat of the region near Jericho (1,300 feet below sea-level). The temperature of much of Palestine is comparable to that of California, and so oranges, lemons, and olives are profuse on the coastal plains, figs and grapes a little higher, and most of the hill country is suitable for barley and other crops which mature quickly in a semi-arid climate. From about

mid-November to mid-January much rain falls, the "former rain" of Scripture (Jer. 5:24). In late March, if the land is favored, comes the "latter rain" (Joel 2:23), thus assuring good crops. If the latter rain fails, much of the harvest is lost. The Bible clearly teaches that, at least in OT times, there was a close relationship between the spiritual condition of the people and the weather (I Kings 8:35,36; Joel 1:17-20). Sin brought physical punishment in dearth, plagues of insects and storms. In the highlands, as at Jerusalem, it became quite cold in winter (Ezra 10:9,13), especially since the houses were very inadequately heated (Jer. 36:22). One who has lived on the coast of the Mediterranean soon learns to predict weather conditions by looking out over the sea. When the water looks like bright metallic blue, and the horizon is very sharp, he knows that the wind is from the N and he predicts clear, cool weather (Job 37:9,22; read 36:24-38:37). When sea and sky seem to blend together, he predicts pleasant warm weather. The occasional hot sirocco is like the breath of an oven.   A.B.F.

WEAVING (Heb. *'āragh*), the uniting of threads by crossing each other to produce cloth. The art of weaving is well-nigh universal, even among primitive peoples, and its beginnings are lost in the mists of antiquity. Job complained, "My days are swifter than a weaver's shuttle" (7:6), showing that he not only knew of weaving, but that the art had progressed to the point where the weaver's hands were swift in passing the shuttle to and fro. Jabal, an antediluvian, is called "the father of such as dwell in tents and have cattle" (Gen. 4:20), implying that the weaving of tents and the taming of cattle had their beginnings nearly at the same time. Weaving, as a fine art, was in the case

of Bezalel and Oholiab an enduement from God
(Exod. 35:30-35), and their woven work for the
tabernacle, the curtains and veils may have surpassed in beauty anything previously known in
cloth. Damascus, one of the oldest cities of the
world, was long known for its woven work, and
"damask" with its beautifully woven figures takes
its name from that city. The lovely acrostic poem
on the virtuous woman (Prov. 31:10-31) pictures
her as acquainted with the work of spinning and
weaving, as well as the work of dressmaking; but
the heavier work of weaving tentcloth was often
done by men. Acts 18:2,3 mentions Paul, with
Aquila and his wife Priscilla, as tent-makers. The
Oriental tents were generally woven of goats' hair
made so well as to be well-nigh water proof and
so strong as to last for a lifetime. In the "doom of
Egypt" (Isa. 19) the weavers of both linen and
cotton cloth are spoken of as "confounded" (vs.
9), indicating the importance of weaving to the
economy of Egypt in her prosperity. In Hezekiah's
description of his despair in the days of his sickness (Isa. 38:10-18) he speaks of God as cutting
off his life as a weaver cuts the thrum when his
work is complete (vs. 12). Isaiah speaks of the
wicked as weaving the spider's web (59:5), thus
indicating the futility of their efforts, and II Kings
23:7 speaks with horror of "the women that wove
hangings for the Asherah." A giant had a spear
like a weaver's beam (I Chron. 11:23). A.B.F.

WEDDING (Gr. *gámos*). Marriage customs in the
Bible center around the two events of betrothal
and wedding. The wedding itself did not include
a religious ceremony, although it is probable that
the betrothal was ratified by an oath (Ezek. 16:8;
Mal. 2:14); and after the Exile written contracts
were drawn up and sealed. On the day of the wedding the bride dressed in white, elaborately embroidered robes, bedecked herself with jewels (Isa.
61:10), and put on a veil (Gen. 24:65) and a
garland. The bridegroom, attended by friends and
accompanied by musicians and singers, went to
the bride's house (Matt. 25:7); and then after
receiving her from her parents with their blessing
he conducted the whole party back to his own
house. On the way other friends of the bride and

A wedding procession of Bible times. © SPF

groom joined the party, and there was much music
and dancing (Ps. 45:15). A feast was held at the
bridegroom's house. Later in the evening the bride's
parents escorted her to the nuptial chamber (Gen.
29:23), while he was led there by his friends or the
bride's parents. The next day the festivities were
resumed and continued for one or two weeks (Gen.
29:27; Judg. 14:12). The wedding festivities included much music and joking.   S.B.

Bedouin bridesmaids at a wedding, in the Transjordan region. © MPS

An Arab peasant measuring wheat. "Good measure, pressed down and shaken together and running over" (Luke 6:38). © MPS

WEDGE (Heb. *lāshôn zāhāv, tongue of gold*). The word occurs only in Joshua 7:21,24, where the word *lashon*, "tongue," indicates the shape. Its occurrence in Isaiah 13:12 is an error. Cf. ASV which properly renders the adjective as "pure."

WEEDS (See Plants)

WEEK (See Calendar)

WEEKS, FEAST OF (See Feasts)

WEIGHTS AND MEASURES. The modern reader of the Scriptures lives in a world dominated by the scientific method and the reign of "fact" — measurable fact. Meat is weighed in pounds and ounces on scales checked periodically by a bureau of weights and measures. Exact measurements in miles and fractions thereof state the distance between places. Liquids are measured exactly, from the contents of an oil tanker to that of a hypodermic needle. Such exact measurements cannot be expected in the Bible. The ancient Hebrew lived in a different kind of a world. The lack (for most of Biblical times) of a strong, paternalistic central government, the simple life of self-sufficient country folk, and the frequent influence of foreign nations whose standards differed from the Hebrews help to account for the lack of consistent and specific measurements. One must be content with round numbers in the study of the weights and measures of the Bible.

Our information is gained from two sources — written and archeological. Written sources include the Bible and other ancient books such as the works of Josephus, Herodotus, the Talmud, and references in classical literature. Archeological information is uncovered by the excavator in the lands of the Bible — labeled weight-stones, jars, and other objects which will be mentioned in this article, which attempts a synthesis of the information from all the sources.

Measures of Length. Hebrew measures of length arose (as did the English foot) from the simple estimating of distance in terms of the body. Farmers today measure the height of horses by hands. The ancient Hebrews used the terms *pace* (about a yard), *cubit* (the length of the forearm), *span* (of a hand; about half a cubit), *palm* (handbreath; about ⅓ of a span), and *finger* (about ¼ of a palm). In Egypt a similar system was used.

The ordinary *cubit* is equivalent to about 17½ or 18 inches today; it is once referred to as "the cubit of a man" — i.e. the distance which might be measured by a man's forearm (Deut. 3:11; "the common cubit," RSV). There was a longer cubit, just as we today have a land mile (5280 ft.) and a nautical mile (6080 ft). Ezekiel mentions a "long cubit" which he equates with a cubit and a handbreadth (40:5; 43:13 RSV), roughly equivalent to 20½ inches. The Egyptians had two cubits of about the same length (about 17½ and 20½ inches). The usual cubit in the Bible is the shorter one. The longer cubit is used in Ezekiel's measurements and possibly in Solomon's temple (II Chron. 3:3 may be a reference to it). The chart below shows the equivalences.

The Common Cubit

	equals	inches
Finger		¾
Palm	4 fingers	3
Span	3 palms	9
Cubit	2 spans	18

The length of Hezekiah's water tunnel underneath Jerusalem is stated by the inscription in the tunnel to be 1200 cubits. The tunnel is 1749 feet long according to the most reliable measurement. The cubit length thus arrived at is 17.49 inches. This does not mean that the cubit in Hezekiah's time was 17.49 inches long. The figure of 1200 cubits is a round number, nor is it certain at what point the ancient measuring of the tunnel began. The Siloam inscription indicates only that our approximate length for the cubit — a little less than 18 inches — is not too far off, which is as positive a conclusion as can be hoped for under the circumstances.

Confirmatory evidence for this length of the cubit is also seen in the fact that many ancient buildings have been found upon excavation to be measurable in terms of a cubit of about 17½ inches, or in reeds equivalent to six such cubits.

Some other terms of measurement in the Bible are the *reed*, the *gōmedh*, and the *fathom*. The *reed*, mainly an instrument for measuring rather than a unit of measurement, was six cubits long (Ezek. 40:5). The term *gōmedh*, which occurs only in Judges 3:16 and is translated "cubit," is thought by present scholars to refer to a shorter distance — ⅔ of a cubit at most — for a dagger rather than a sword is referred to. The *fathom* (armstretch; Acts 27:28) was about six feet.

Measurements of Distance and Area. In OT times distance was usually measured by the length of time necessary to traverse it. Thus we read of "three days journey" (Gen. 30:36) and "seven days journey" (Gen. 31:23). In the NT these terms are used: stadium ("furlong" KJV, Luke 24:13; John 6:19), about 606 feet. Mile (Matt. 5:41), about 4860 feet. About the Sabbath day's journey there is some uncertainty. The term, used to indicate the distance one might walk without breaking the Sabbath law, seems to have been an elastic one. Josephus calls it five stadia in one place and six in another, which would make it equal 3000 or 3600

Above, Hebrew liquid measures, and below, Hebrew dry measures, on display in the museum of the Hospice of Notre Dame deFrance at Jerusalem. © MPS

feet. This is about the distance from Jerusalem to the Mount of Olives (Acts 1:12).

Land measurements were indicated in terms of the area which a team of oxen could plow in one day (I Sam. 14:14). This is the meaning of "acres" in Isaiah 5:10, where the Hebrew is *semedh* — "yoke (of oxen)." In Mesopotamia this area equaled 2/5 of an acre. Elsewhere area was stated as that part of a field which could be seeded with barley in one day (Lev. 27:16).

Measures of Capacity. Our uncertainty about the units of capacity is understandable when one considers the origin of these terms. They seem to have arisen from common household pots (all handmade locally), or from the farmer's estimate of the carrying ability of man or beast. The *hin* was a pot and the *ephah* a basket (both words are of Egyptian origin). The *omer* was a sheaf and the *homer* a donkey load. The word *bath* means "daughter"; could this jar be the one the daughters carried home from the well (Gen. 24:15)?

The student of the English Bible will have diffi-culty in following this discussion in his Bible because of the untechnical character of his translation. Many of the terms mentioned below are translated "measure" in quite a few places in the standard English versions. The best way to discover to which unit the Hebrew or Greek text refers is to use a comprehensive concordance (such as Strong's or Young's), where the Hebrew and Greek terms are clearly distinguished.

The *bath* was the standard liquid measure in OT times. Its value is a matter of dispute. At present scholars regard it as equal to about six US gallons, rather than 10 gallons as formerly. The finding of fragments of large jars, inscribed "bath of the king" (perhaps an attempt to standardize the bath for use in tax payments) or simply "bath" have helped to bring about this reduction in size. Unfortunately, these jars cannot be completely restored, hence there is still some uncertainty. Subdivisions of the bath are hin (1/6 bath) and log (1/12 hin).

The liquid measures of NT times are difficult to equate with those of the OT. The English "measure" may equal a *kōr*, as in Luke 16:7, or a *bath*, as in Luke 16:6. The *firkin* of John 2:6 (KJV) held about 10.3 US gallons.

The *homer* was the standard dry measure of the OT. Homer means "donkey," and therefore a donkey-load, or about 6¼ bushels. It is to be equated with the *cor*. The *ephah* (about 3/5 bushel) is the dry opposite of the liquid measure *bath* (Ezek. 45:10). The *lethekh* is mentioned only in Hosea 3:2 and is probably given its correct value in the KJV, which translates it "half homer."

Three smaller dry measures are: the *se'âh*, about 1/5 bushel; the *'ōmer*, 4 dry pints; the *'issārôn* ("tenth deal," KJV, "tenth measure," RSV), evidently equivalent to the *omer*; and the *cab*, a little more than two dry pints. It must be added that modern authorities differ greatly as to the value of the dry measures, some inclining toward a substantially higher value for each. The system followed here is substantially that of R. B. Y. Scott in the article referred to at the end of this subject.

NT dry measures are: *bushel* (Matt. 5:15), about 7½ dry quarts or slightly less than ½ US bushel; *measure* ("quart" RSV), about 1 dry quart; *pot* (Mark 7:4), about 1 dry pint.

Weights. It must be remembered that coinage was not used in Palestine until after the Exile. Ezra 2:69 is probably the first mention of coined money in the Bible ("drams," KJV, "daries," RSV). During most of OT times, barter (Gen. 30:27-34; 31:8; II Kings 3:4) or precious metal weighed out was the means of exchange. The *shekel* is a weight in the OT, not a coin (Ezek. 4:10), and the verb *shāqal* means "to weigh out," as in Jeremiah 32:10. Simple balance scales were used, and stones of certain weight (often shekels) were used to determine the weight of the silver or gold involved in the transaction. Proverbs 16:11 reads literally

SOME BIBLICAL MEASURES

	Liquid			Dry	
Hebrew term	equals	US liquid measures	Hebrew term	equals	US dry measures
log		2/3 pint			
			cab		2+ pints
			omer	1 4/5 cabs	4 pints
hin	12 logs	1 gal.			
			se'â	3 1/3 omers	1/5 bushel
bath	6 hins	6 gals. ==ephah	3 se'âs	3/5 bushel
cor	10 baths	60 gals. ==homer	10 ephahs or 100 omers	6 1/4 bushels

A Hebrew talent weight on view in the Museum of St. Anne in Jerusalem. © MPS

"The stones (English Bible 'weights') in the bag." In the Canaanite poem (found at Ras Shamra in Syria) describing the wedding of Nikkal and the Moon, occurs a description of the weighing of the marriage price, a good illustration of an ancient business transaction:

Her father sets the beam of the balances
Her mother, the trays of the balances
Her brothers arrange the ingots(?)
Her sisters (attend) to the stones of the balances
(77:34-39).

In addition to the Biblical references to weights, quite a few stone weight-pieces (especially shekels) have been found in the excavations in Palestine, many of them labeled. There is a certain amount of disparity among these. Some have speculated that this is graphic evidence for the necessity of the prophetic indictment of the dishonest merchants who "make the ephah small and the shekel great, and deal deceitfully with false balances" (Amos 8:5 RSV). While this explanation is not to be ruled out completely, it must never be forgotten that life in ancient Palestine was simple, rural and predominantly agricultural. Most of the time there was no strong central government, and certainly no bureau of weights and measures. To some extent, the period of David and Solomon is an exception to this. David seems to have had a "king's weight" (II Sam. 14:26). That standardization which controls every aspect of modern life and makes modern men so much alike in all their ways was almost completely lacking. In the summer of 1958 the writer of this article found farmers in eastern Jordan selling grapes and melons by simple balance scales, with roughly cut stones for weights. No doubt such simple arrangements usually sufficed in Bible times. Estimates of values of ancient weights must therefore be rather general, and figures taken to two decimal places represent a futile attempt to reduce ancient men to the monotony of modern uniformity.

The Hebrews used a modified sexagesimal system of weights modeled on that of the Babylonians. The *shekel* (called by the Babylonians *shiqlu*) was the basic unit. Fifty shekels equaled a *maneh* (or *mina*; Babylonian *manû*), and 60 manehs a *talent* (Hebrew *kikkār*; Babylonian *biltu*). A *shekel* was made up of 20 *gerahs*. A *bekah* was half a shekel.

The Babylonians had 60 shekels in their maneh, but from Exodus 38:25,26 it appears that the Hebrew maneh consisted of only 50. Half a shekel

was paid by 603,550 men, and totaled 100 talents and 1,775 shekels, which means that the talent here equaled 3,000 shekels. Since the talent was almost always 60 manehs, the maneh here equals 50 shekels. Ezekiel uses a different system, with 60 shekels to the maneh (45:12).

When one attempts to define the shekel in terms of presently understood weights the difficulties are formidable. One of the best recent treatments of the problem is R. B. Y. Scott's (see Bibliography at end of article), which takes into account the many stone weights found in Palestine and computes values in great detail. The weight-pieces discovered vary greatly. In addition to the double standard mentioned above and the generally unregimented way of ancient Israelite life, the standards themselves may have tended to depreciate, as standards do. The influence of foreign systems may also have been a disturbing factor. The larger weights seem to indicate smaller shekel units than do the smaller weights.

The *beqa'* or *half shekel* is the only weight the name of which is mentioned both in the OT and on discovered weights, and of which the relationship to the shekel is given (Exod. 38:26). Several stone weights have been found with the Hebrew consonants BQ' (*beqa'*) cut on them, weighing on an average about 6 grams (actual weights vary from 5.8 to 6.65 gm.). One thing these *beqa'* weights indicated: the shekel weighed about 12 grams. Therefore the numerous stones bearing a symbol resembling a figure 8 with an open loop, weighing about 12 grams, must be shekel weights. This symbol seems to be a representation of a tied bundle of lump silver (see illustration).

Scott concludes that there were three standards for a shekel: the temple shekel of 10 grams (about .35 oz.), the common or commercial shekel of about 11½ grams (.4 oz.), and a "heavy" shekel of about 13 grams (.45 oz.). The last of these was probably used in weighing some special commodity.

Certain recent excavations have yielded weights inscribed *pim*, weighing about 2/3 of a shekel. Thus the name of another unit of Hebrew weight is recovered and light is shed on a difficult statement in I Samuel 13:21. This verse contains the word *pim*, which was unknown elsewhere and believed to be a textual corruption. Now that *pim* is known to be the name of a weight, the RSV is able to give an improved translation, which indicates that the Philistines, to keep the Hebrews in subjection, made it difficult for the Hebrews to get iron implements and probably overcharged them for repairing them.

The Common Shekel

Name	Comparative value	Value today
talent	60 minehs	75.5 lbs.
mineh	50 shekels	20 oz.
shekel	2 beqa's	.4 oz.
bekah	10 gerahs	88 gr.
gerah		9 gr.

Few weights are mentioned in the NT. *Talent* and *pound* in Luke 19:13-25 are sums of money. *Pound* in John 12:3 and 19:39 represents another Greek word, *litra*, a weight of some 7/10 pound avoirdupois.

Bibliography. The best nontechnical treatments of this subject are "Weights and Measures of the Bible," by R. B. Y. Scott, BA:xxii:2, May 1959, pp. 22-40, and "Chronology, Metrology, Etc.," by Georges Augustin Barrois, IB, vol. I, New York, 1952, pp. 142-164.   J.B.G.

Wells are extremely important in the arid regions of Palestine. At left is a busy scene at a desert well. At right, a large goatskin bucket is being drawn up by a pulley and camel power. © MPS

WELL (Heb. *be'ēr,* Gr. *phréar*), a pit or hole dug in the earth down to the water-table, i.e., the level at which the ground is permanently saturated with water. For purposes of safety as well as permanence, the well is generally surrounded by a wall of stone, and in the case of some famous wells, like that of Jacob at Sychar (John 4) the walls were beautifully constructed with dressed stone. A well is generally to be distinguished from a cistern (Jer. 2:13), which is merely for storing water, a spring, which is found at the surface of the ground, and a fountain, from which the water is actively flowing (Josh. 15:9).

WEST (Heb. *yām, sea; māvô', setting of the sun; ma'ārāv, west;* Gr. *dysmé*). *Yam,* sea, is the Heb. word usually used for "west," because the Mediterranean Sea lies to the W of Palestine. The word is sometimes used figuratively with "east" to denote great distance (Ps. 103:12).

WHALE (See Animals)

WHEAT (See Plants)

WHEEL (Heb. *'ôphan, galgal, gilgal, 'ovnayim, pa'am,* Gr. *trochós*), probably at first just a disk of wood cut from a log, but quite early developed into something resembling the modern device. When the Egyptians with their chariots pursued the Israelites at the Red Sea (Exod. 14:24,25), the Lord took off their chariot wheels. In I Kings 7: 30-33 where the bases of the great "sea" of Solomon's temple are described, reference is made to wheels with their axle-trees, their naves, spokes and felloes, showing that by Solomon's time (c. 1000 B.C.) the wheel was quite developed and was similar to modern wagonwheels. Cart-wheels were used for threshing some kinds of grain, but not cummin (Isa. 28:27). The word for "potter's wheel" means literally "two stones" (Jer. 18:3). In ancient times two circular stone disks were joined by a short shaft, and so spun. Today, the shaft is longer and the wheels are of wood.

WHELP (Heb. *gūr* or *gôr*), one of the young of a dog or a beast of prey; a cub. In the Bible the term is always used figuratively (Gen. 49:9; Deut. 33: 22; Jer. 51:38; Nah. 2:11,12).

WHIP (Heb. *shôt*), an instrument of punishment or inciting to work; generally a lash attached to a handle. Used figuratively by Rehoboam of his father (I Kings 12:14).

WHIRLWIND (Heb. *sûphâh, se'ārâh, sa'ar*), in Biblical usage does not exactly conform to our modern idea of a violent whirling as at the vortex of a tornado; but rather emphasizes the idea of being tossed about. These Hebrew words are often rendered "storm" or "tempest," which is a more accurate translation; and they are used figuratively of swift and terrible destruction (Prov. 1:27; Isa. 5:28; Jer. 4:13; Hos. 8:7). Elijah was carried to heaven by a whirlwind (II Kings 2:1,11).

WHORE (Heb. *zānâh,* Gr. *pórne*), a woman who habitually commits adultery or fornication, especially for hire; a prostitute, harlot. It is noteworthy that in a very large proportion of cases, the word is used for idolatry. The two words "adultery" and "idolatry" can be identically defined as "taking the love which belongs to one and giving it to another." In the former case, the one wronged is the wife or husband who has been deserted; in the latter it is God. The practice of selling daughters into whoredom was not unknown in Israel (Lev. 19: 29), but was forbidden of the Lord. Whoredom was a capital crime (Gen. 38:24).

The wooden wheels of an ancient pre-flood chariot, excavated at Kish, near Babylon. CNHM

WIDOW (Heb. *'almānâh*, Gr. *chéra*). Widows in the OT are regarded as being under God's special care (Ps. 68:5; 146:9; Prov. 15:25). From early times they wore a distinctive garb. The Hebrews were commanded to treat them with special consideration and they were punished if they did otherwise (Exod. 22:22; Deut. 14:29; Isa. 1:17; Jer. 7:6). The church looked after poor widows in apostolic times (Acts 6:1; James 1:27). Paul gives instructions to Timothy about the care of widows by the church (I Tim. 5:4); but only those were taken care of who were at least 60 years of age, had been married only once, and had a reputation for good works (vs. 9,10). In the second and third centuries there was an order of widows in the church. Its members looked after the women of the congregation. This order was abolished by the synod of Laodicea, A.D. 364.   S.B.

WIFE (See Family, Marriage)

WILD VINE OR GRAPE (See Plants, Vine)

WILDERNESS. In Scripture this word refers either to a barren desert or to an uncultivated region suitable for pasturage and occupied by nomads. (1) The most common Heb. word rendered "wilderness" is *midhbār, a place for the driving of cattle* (Num. 14:33; Judg. 1:16; Deut. 2:8). The word may refer to grassy pastures (Ps. 65:12; Joel 2:22) or a waste of rock and sand (Deut. 32:10; Job 38:26); (2) *yeshîmôn;* sometimes rendered as a proper name "Yeshimon" in the KJV (Num. 21:20) refers to a dry or riverless region (Isa. 43:19,20); (3) *'ărāvâh, arid, barren* (Isa. 33:9; 51:3) when used with the definite article denotes the plain of the Jordan and Dead Sea (Ezek. 47:8; II Sam. 2:29) and is rendered "Arabah" in the RV; (4) *tsiyyâh, land of drought* (Hos. 2:3); (5) *tohû, empty waste* (Job. 6:18; 12:24; Ps. 107:40) refers to barren deserts; (6) Gr. *éremos,* a word which like *midhbār* above is used with considerable latitude (Matt. 14:13; Heb. 11:38).

WILLOW (See Plants)

WILLOWS, BROOK OF THE, a brook on the boundary of Moab (Isa. 15:7); generally identified with the Zered (Wâdi el-Hesā) which flows into the southern end of the Dead Sea and forms the boundary between Edom and Moab.

WILLS, or testaments, are statements, oral or written in form, to which law courts give effect, by which property may be disposed of after death. Covenants between living persons might be bilateral, each party making promises, or unilateral, an agreement by one party which the other may accept or reject, but may not alter. Wills grew out of the latter. In early times among the Hebrews as elsewhere, property descended according to laws of inheritance without wills. The only distinct Bible reference to a will is in Hebrews 9:16, 17, and the meaning of this is disputed. The context (9:11-22) seems to assimilate the testament to a unilateral covenant of God with His people: Greek *diathéke* always primarily meant a will, but was used in the LXX for Heb. *berîth, covenant.* The fact that here an instrument effective only after the death of the one who made it is in question, justifies RSV in translating it as "will."

WINDOW (See House)

WINDS are important in the Bible, both literally and figuratively. God causes them, He created them (Gen. 8:1; Exod. 13:10; Num. 11:31; Ps. 107:25; 135:7; 147:18; Jer. 10:13=51:16; Jonah 1:4). The four winds are limits of distance or direction (Jer. 49:36; Ezek. 37:9; Dan. 7:2; 8:8; 11:4;

Zech. 2:6; Matt. 24:31=Mark 13:27; Rev. 7:1). Of the cardinal directions, the east wind is most frequently mentioned (Exod. 10:13; 14:21; Job 15:2; Ps. 48:7; Isa. 27:8; Jer. 18:17; Ezek. 17:10; 19:12; 27:26; Hos. 12:1; 13:15; Jonah 4:8; Gen. 41:6,23,27; Job 27:21; 38:14; Ps. 78:26; Hab. 1:9). It is stormy, wrecks ships, withers growing things. The north wind brings rain (Prov. 25:23), is refreshing (S. of Sol. 4:16) or stormy (Ezek. 1:4). The south wind is gentle, helps growth (S. of Sol. 4:16; Ps. 78:26; Job 37:17). The west wind blew away the plague of locusts (Exod. 10:19). Winds figure in notable storms (I Kings 18:45; 19:11; Job 1:9; Matt. 8:26,27=Mark 4:35,37, 39,41=Luke 8:23-25; Matt. 14:24,30,32=Mark 6:48,51=John 6:18; Acts 27:4,7,14,15). In Acts 27:13; 28:13 the south wind (Gr. *nótos*), in 27:12 the northwest wind (*chóros*) and the southwest wind (*líps*) are named; in 27:14 the northeaster (RSV), Gr. *eurakúlon*. Whirlwinds are mentioned several times. Wind blows chaff (Ps. 1:4; 35:5; 83:13; Isa. 17:14; 41:16; Jer. 13:24; Dan. 2:35; Job 21:18); fulfils God's commands (Ps. 148:8; 104:4 RSV); reveals weakness, transitoriness, worthlessness (Job 7:7; 15:2; 30:15,22; 6:26; 8:2; Ps. 18:42; 78:39; 103:16; Prov. 11:29; 25:14; 27:16; 30:4; Eccl. 5:16; 11:4; Isa. 7:2; 26:18; 41:8; 57:13; 64:6; Jer. 5:11; 22:22; 49:32); clears the sky (Job 37:21); drives ships (James 3:4). Elisha promises water not brought by wind (II Kings 3:17). God rides on the wings of the wind (II Sam. 22:11=Ps. 18:10; 104:3). The circulation of the wind is recognized (Eccl. 1:6). Wind has a drying effect (Isa. 11:15; Jer. 4:11,12). Princes are to be a hiding place from the wind (Isa. 32:2). An observation of animal life (Jer. 2:24; 14:16 RSV). Ezekiel scattered hair to symbolize scattering of the people (Ezek. 5:2,10,12; 12:14; 17:21). Strong, destructive winds (Jer. 51:1; Ezek. 13:11,13; Hos. 4:19; 13:15). A proverbial expression: "sow the wind, reap the whirlwind" (Hos. 8:7). The weight of the wind (Job 28:25). Believers are warned against evil winds of false doctrine (Eph. 4:4; Jude 12). Stars will fall like figs shaken from a tree by the wind (Rev. 6:13). Wind moved the wings of women carrying an ephah (Zech. 5:9). Wind in Heb. is usually *rûah,* translated also *breath, spirit,* etc.; in Gr. *ánemos,* always *wind.* Once each, Gr. *pneúma,* breath, wind, spirit (John 3:8); *pnoé, breath* (Acts 2:2); the verb *pnéo, blow* (Acts 27:40).   E.R.

WINE. Several Heb. words occur, of which two are frequent. *Yayin,* wine; as a common drink (Gen. 14:18); as a drink-offering (Lev. 23:13); intoxicating (Gen. 9:21); figuratively, of wisdom (Prov. 9:2,5), of wrath (Jer. 25:15), of love (S. of Sol. 1:2; 4:10). *Tîrôsh, must, fresh* or *sweet wine;* with approval (Gen. 27:28; Judg. 9:13; II Kings 18:32; Zech. 9:17); once with disapproval (Hos. 4:11). Priests were forbidden to drink wine on duty (Lev. 10:9; Ezek. 44:21). Nazirites were not even to touch grapes while under a vow (Num. 6:5,20; Judg. 13:4-14; Luke 1:15). Abuse of wine is condemned in Proverbs (4:17-31:6), also in the prophets (Isa. 5:11), but God offers wine of His Word (Isa. 55:1). In the NT, Gr. *oínos, wine;* once *gleúkos,* new, sweet wine; or grape juice; which may imply that the disciples, known to drink only unfermented grape juice, in their exuberant enthusiasm appeared intoxicated. New wine fermenting would burst old wineskins (Matt. 9:17). Jesus refused the wine offered Him on the cross because it was drugged (Mark 15:25). Jesus contrasts Himself with John the Baptist (Luke 7:33,

34) as one who ate and drank with others. In OT times wine was not diluted. Before NT times, the Hellenistic practice of mixing it with much water was common in Palestine. Wine was a disinfectant (Luke 10:34) and medicine (I Tim. 5:23). It is right for a Christian not to drink wine, if it causes his brother to stumble (Rom. 14:21). Men (I Tim. 3:8) and women (Titus 2:3) church officers were warned against over-indulgence. Jesus made water into wine at Cana (John 2:2-11).

Means for preserving grape-juice were well known: Cato, *De Agri Cultura* CXX has this recipe: "If you wish to have must (grape-juice) all year, put grape-juice in an amphora and seal the cork with pitch; sink it in a fishpond. After 30 days take it out. It will be grape-juice for a whole year." At the Last Supper Jesus spoke of "the fruit of the vine" (Matt. 26:29), as in the Passover liturgy; it may be a studied avoidance of the term wine, indicating that the drink was unfermented, as the bread was unleavened. Whatever use Jesus or others made of wine is no proof that its use in our tense age is wise. The Bible gives more space to the danger than to the benefit of wine.   E.R.

Treading grapes in a winepress. UANT

WINEPRESS, Heb. *gath* (Judg. 6:11; Neh. 13:15; Isa. 63:2,3), Gr. *lenós* (Matt. 21:33), *a trough,* usually of stone, cement-lined, from which juice flowed through a hole near the bottom into a vat (Heb. *yeqev;* Num. 18:27,30; Judg. 7:25; Isa. 5:2; Gr. *hypolénion,* Mark 12:1). The grapes were pressed by men treading them, holding to ropes suspended overhead. The process is compared to the execution of the wrath of God (Lam. 1:15; Rev. 14:19,20; 19:15).

WINESKIN (See Bottles)

WING (Heb. *kānāph,* Gr. *ptéryx*). Birds (Lev. 1:17); cherubim (I Kings 6:24) or "living creatures" (Ezek. 16; 10:5; Rev. 4:8) have wings. Migration is suggested in Job 39:26. The most significant Bible uses of wings are figurative: wings of the wind (Ps. 18:10); to seek rest (Ps. 55:6); refuge in God (Ps. 17:8; 91:4); emblem of prosperity (Ps. 68:13; vanishing, Prov. 23:5); rays of the rising sun (Ps. 139:9; Mal. 4:2); renewed strength (Isa. 40:31); compassion (Matt. 23:37). Note two symbolic women (Zech. 5:9; cf. Rev. 12:4).

WINNOW (See Farming)

The King's Winepresses, north of Jerusalem. This landmark is the farthest north mentioned in connection with the measuring line of the city of Jerusalem (Zech. 14:10; Jer. 31:40). © MPS

WINTER, Heb. *hōreph, harvest-time, autumn;* and the cold, rainy season following (Gen. 8:22; Ps. 74:17; Zech. 14:8); verb "to winter" (Isa. 18:6). Heb. *sethāw, winter* (S. of Sol. 2:11). Gr. *cheimón, winter;* the cold, stormy season (Matt. 24:20; Mark 13:18; John 10:22; II Tim. 4:21) and related verbs (Acts 27:12; 28:11; I Cor. 16:6; Titus 3:12).

WINTERHOUSE (Heb. *bēth ha-hōreph*). Kings and the wealthy had separate residences for the hot and cold seasons (Amos 3:15). King Jehoiakim had a fire in the brazier in his winterhouse (Jer. 36:20).

WISDOM. The commonest OT words for wisdom are Heb. *hākham* and related forms; Gr. *sophía.* In God, the infinite, perfect comprehension of all that is or might be (Rom. 11:33-36). In man, an eminently practical attribute, including technical skill (Exod. 28:3, RSV an able mind); military prowess (Isa. 10:13); shrewdness for questionable ends (I Kings 2:6). Wisdom is shown in getting desired ends by effective means. Men of the world are often wiser in their generation than the children of light (Luke 16:8). Yet God is the source of wisdom as of power, and wisdom is given to men through the fear of the Lord (Ps. 111:10; Job 28:28). The wisdom of Solomon was far-ranging in statecraft (I Kings 10:23,24), understanding of human nature (I Kings 3:16-25), in natural history, literature, and popular proverbs (I Kings 4:29-34). Wisdom is personified (Prov. 8) in terms related to the concept of the Word in John 1:1-18, and became one of the names of God the Father and the Son, the Holy Spirit being the Spirit of Wisdom.

Wisdom Literature in the OT consists of Proverbs, Ecclesiastes and Job, with Psalms 19, 37, 104, 107, 147, 148 and short passages in other books; in the OT Apocrypha, Ecclesiasticus and Wisdom of Solomon. Heb. wisdom was not all religious: it dealt, as in Proverbs, with everyday conduct in business, family and social relations, elementary morality. Ecclesiastes ranges farther afield to consider the ultimate value of life. Wise men, unlike prophets, claimed no special inspiration. They exercised no priestly functions, and were not, like the scribes, devoted exclusively to the study of the sacred writings. Eventually wise men and scribes coalesced into one class. With worsening political conditions and a deepening sense of moral problems in the period of the prophets and later kings, men came to despise worldly wisdom as irreligious and as characteristic of the heathen, who might be superior in secular culture, but were inferior from a moral and religious point of view (Isa. 10:12-19). Wisdom is bound up with doing the

A camel caravan nearing Bethlehem from the East, a picture reminiscent of the visit of the Wise Men. © MPS

will of the Lord (Deut. 4:6); to forsake His Word is to forfeit one's wisdom (Jer. 8:8,9). Though wisdom literature often seems to equate right with advantage (profit, Eccl. 1:5), there is clear evidence of the controlling hand and moral interest of God in human affairs. The sayings of Jesus, largely proverbial and parabolical, are the crown of Biblical wisdom. Paul calls Jesus "the wisdom of God" (I Cor. 1:24,30), and says that in Him all the treasures of wisdom are hidden (Col. 2:3). When Paul compares the wisdom of men with the wisdom of God (I Cor. 2), he is thinking of the former as that of Greek philosophers rather than OT Biblical wisdom. James' letter is wisdom literature at its best, a clear mirror of the teaching of Jesus.   E.R.

WISDOM OF JESUS, SON OF SIRACH (See Apocrypha)

WISDOM OF SOLOMON (See Apocrypha)

WISE MEN. The name is often applied to men of understanding and skill in ordinary affairs (Prov. 1:5; Job 15:2; Ps. 49:10; Eccl. 2:4; I Cor. 1:26; 10:15; James 3:13); to Solomon superlatively (I Kings 2:9; 5:7; II Chron. 2:12); there are wise ladies (Judg. 5:29) or court women (II Sam. 14:2; 20:16). In a more specialized sense in Israel, the builders of the tabernacle (Exod. 34:8); the leaders of the tribes (Deut. 1:13,15). Wise, understanding, experienced older men came to be recognized as a distinct class, widely esteemed by the discerning. In heathen nations the wise men, grouped with and identified as magicians, sorcerers, enchanters, astrologers, Chaldeans, appear in Egypt (Gen. 41:

8; Exod. 7:11), Babylon (Dan. 2:12-5:15), and Persia (Esth. 1:13, men "who knew the times' RSV; 6:13 Haman's friends). The wise men of Matthew 2:1-16, the Magi, Gr. *magoi,* are shadowy figures, except for this one incident. *Magoi* originally referred to the Median priestly caste in Persia, who were both religious leaders and philosophical teachers. While this meaning continued throughout Greek history, the word developed the further meaning, any "possessors of supernatural knowledge and power." From this the descent to "magician" was easy, and thence to "deceiver," still with a religious reference. This development was aided by confusion of the word *magos,* borrowed from Persian, with another Greek word. *maganon,* always associated with charms and sorceries. Among the Jews, rabbinic literature applies the name to both magicians and Persian priests. In Philo it refers to a man something less than truly religious or philosophical. In the LXX, *magoi* are linked with "astrologers, sorcerers and Chaldeans" (Dan. 2:1). The clues to the meaning Matthew intended are the facts that the wise men are from the East, that is, Mesopotamia, Persia, or possibly farther E; and that they followed a star; that is, they were astrologers. Astrology was more respectable in ancient times than it is today. It was inextricably mixed with astronomy. Theirs was both the best science of the day, and the purest religion outside of the most spiritual strain of Judaism. Legend says there were three, gives them names and countries of origin, mounts them on camels. We know only that there were at least two, and that they came from the East.   E.R.

WITCH, a woman, in early England, also a man, in league with evil spirits. Heb. *kāshaph, to practice sorcery,* is sometimes so translated in ASV, often in RSV (Exod. 22:18; Deut. 18:10; II Chron. 33:6; II Kings 9:22; Mic. 5:12; Nah. 3:4 ASV charms). Heb. *qesem, divination,* is once translated "witchcraft" (I Sam. 15:23 KJV, ASV) otherwise "divination." Greek *pharmakeía* (Gal. 5:20 ASV, RSV sorcery) means the use of drugs, charms or magic words. In Acts 8:9,11, "bewitch" renders Greek *exístemi, to amaze;* in Galatians 3:1, Greek *baskaíno, to use the evil eye on one.* The famous witch of Endor (I Sam. 28:7-25) is not called a witch in the Bible; KJV, ASV "a woman that hath a familiar spirit," RSV "a woman who is a medium." By whatever name, all such practices are strongly condemned (Exod. 22:18; Deut. 18:9-14; I Sam. 28:3,9; II Kings 23:24; Isa. 8:19; Acts 19:18,19).

WITHE (wĭth, wīth, Heb. *yether, bowstring, cord*), a strong, flexible willow or other twig. The "green withes" with which Samson was bound (Judg. 16:7-9) were probably new (ASV margin) or fresh (RSV) bowstrings.

WITHERED HAND (See Diseases)

WITNESS (Heb. *'ēdh* and related forms; Gr. *mártys* and related words and combinations), one who may be called to testify to an event at which he was present. Things may be witnesses; a heap of stones (Gen. 31:44-52), as a sign that God witnessed Jacob and Laban's covenant; a song (Deut. 31:19-21); the Law (Deut. 31:26); an altar (Josh. 22:27-34); a stone which has "heard" God speak (Josh. 24:27); an altar and a pillar on the border of Egypt (Isa. 19:20). Bearing false witness is condemned (Exod. 20:16; 23:2; Deut. 5:20) and punished as for the crime of which one accused another (Deut. 19:16-18). True and false witnesses are contrasted (Prov. 14:5). Two or three witnesses were required in legal proceedings (Deut. 19:15; Matt. 18:16; II Cor. 13:1; I Tim. 5:19; Heb. 10:28). Jeremiah (32:6-25,44) describes the use of witnesses in a conveyance of real property. The tabernacle of witness or testimony (Num. 17:7,8; 10:2; II Chron. 24:6) was so named because in it was the witness of God's presence, the tables of the Law and the Shekinah. God is called upon as a witness (Gen. 31:50; Job 16:19; Jer. 29:23; 42:5; Mic. 1:2; Mal. 3:5; Rom. 1:9; I Thess. 2:5, 10). On solemn occasions men acknowledged themselves witnesses (Josh. 24:22; Ruth 4:9-11). God called His people His witnesses (Isa. 43:10, 12; 44:8; Luke 24:48; Acts 1:8) and the apostles acknowledged themselves to be such (Acts 2:32; 3:15; 5:32; 10:39,41; I Thess. 2:10). Peter thought that Judas must be replaced as a witness (Acts 1:22). Paul had a special appointment as witness (Acts 22:15; 26:16). He reminds Timothy of many witnesses (I Tim. 6:12; II Tim. 2:2). Peter exhorts as a witness of the sufferings of Christ (I Pet. 5:1). John calls Jesus Christ the "faithful witness" (Rev. 1:5; 3:14). The cloud of witnesses (Heb. 12:1) resemble the crowd of spectators at athletic games.

E.R.

WITNESS OF THE SPIRIT. "When we cry, 'Abba! Father!' it is the Spirit himself bearing witness with our spirit that we are children of God" (Rom. 8:15b,16). Verses 17-27 develop the work of the Holy Spirit in and for us in consequence of this new, intimate, filial relationship to God. The origin of this witness in the work of Christ, and its operation in the believer, is further spelled out in I John 5:6-13. The content of the witness of the Spirit appears in John 14:16,17,26; 15:26; 16:7-15; Romans 5:5; I Corinthians 2 and wherever the work of the Holy Spirit in relation to the believer is spoken of. The Spirit witnesses through Scripture (Heb. 10:15-18), sometimes expressly on particular subjects (I Tim. 4:1; Acts 20:23). The witness of the

A man adds a "witness stone" to the pile, known in Arabic as "Shawahid." This scene is in the valley of the River Jabbok (Wadi Zerka Main). © MPS

The village well is the daily gathering place of the women of the town, a place to exchange news and gossip. © MPS

Spirit, though direct, immediate and personal, is always in harmony with the written Word: we are to test the spirits, for many spirits other than the Spirit of God seek to get our attention (I John 4:1-6). This is the test: the Spirit of God witnesses to the incarnate humanity of God's only-begotten Son. The Holy Spirit talks about Jesus, not about Himself (John 16:13-15).   E.R.

WIZARD (wĭz′êrd, Heb. *yidde′ōnî, one who knows*), a male or female magician or sorcerer; one acquainted with the secrets of the unseen world, or an intimate acquaintance of soothsayers (Lev. 19: 31; 20:6,27; Deut. 18:11; I Sam. 28:3,9; II Kings 21:6; 23:24; II Chron. 33:6; Isa. 8:19; 19:3).

WOLF (See Animals)

WOMAN (Heb. *'ishshâh*, Gr. *gýné*). Genesis (1: 26,27) asserts the full humanity of woman. The special account of her creation (Gen. 2:18-24) emphasizes woman's superiority to all lower animals; man's need of her as helper; her intimate relationship to him as part of his inmost being; and the indissoluble nature of marriage. Though many OT women were shadowy, subordinate figures, the patriarchal wives Sarah, Rebekah and Rachel were outstanding; likewise Moses' sister Miriam (Exod. 2:1-9; 15:21; Num. 12). In the period of the Judges Deborah exercised unusual leadership (Judg. 4,5) and the Moabitess Ruth became a chaste blessing to Israel. Hannah (I Sam. 1:1-2:11) illustrates both the despair of a childless woman and the grace of godly motherhood. The advice of Lemuel's mother to her son (Prov. 31) pictures the tireless life of woman in even a prosperous family. Queens good and bad, and evil women of lesser degree are frankly portrayed in the Bible. The ancient world was a man's world: such prominence as women attained was achieved by force of character; sometimes, as in the case of Esther, aided by circumstances not of her seeking. The teaching of Jesus stressed the original nature of marriage, the obligation of purity toward women (Matt. 5:27-32). His example in healing (Matt. 9:18-26) and social intercourse (Luke 10: 38-42) reinforced His words. The Gospel of Luke

is full of evidence of Jesus' understanding of and sympathy with women, which set a pattern for normal Christian living. Godly women were influential in Jesus' background: Elizabeth, mother of His forerunner (Luke 1); the Virgin Mary; Anna (Luke 2:36-38); the sinner of Luke 7:36-40: Mary Magdalene; Martha and Mary of Bethany; the women who accompanied the disciples on missionary journeys and who provided for them out of their means (Luke 8:3 RSV). Women remained at the crucifixion until the burial, and were first at the empty tomb. Between the Ascension and Pentecost women joined the men in prayer (Acts 1:14). The disciples met in the house of Mary, mother of John Mark in Jerusalem (Acts 12:12). Women were the first converts in Europe, including the prosperous business woman Lydia at Philippi (Acts 16:13-15). Phoebe, a deaconess, and many other women are greeted in Romans 16. Paul (I Cor. 11:2-16; 14:34,35) urges subordination for women, in the immoral atmosphere of Corinth, but exalts her as a type of the Church, the Bride of Christ (Eph. 5:21-33). He sets high standards for the wives of church officers, and for women in official position (I Tim. 3:11; Titus 2: 3-5). I Peter 3:1-6 urges a subordinate but noble role for married women. To evaluate Bible teaching with regard to women, it is necessary to consider carefully all the pertinent material, and to hold firmly to the normative and authoritative character of the words, deeds and attitude of Jesus Christ.   E.R.

Women of Palestine today — the young and the old. These are from the South country, near Beersheba. At left, a young woman carrying a water jar on her head and her baby boy in her arms. At right, an elderly Bedouin woman spinning yarn. © MPS

WOOL (Heb. *tsemer*, Gr. *érion*), the fleece of sheep and some other animals. A first fruit to the priests (Deut. 18:4). Israelites were forbidden to wear mixed woolen and linen stuff (Deut. 22:11). It symbolizes purity (Isa. 1:18), "as wool," restored to its original undyed whiteness. It was woven into cloth from which woolen garments were made. It was used principally for the outside garments. Snow is compared to it (Ps. 147:16).

WORD, WORD OF THE LORD. Of several Heb. words translated "word" the commonest is *dāvār, a thing said*. Greek *lógos, a thing to be said*, stresses the thought in the mind of the speaker; *rhéma, the thing said, the expression;* but the choice is often one of emphasis rather than of meaning. *Lógos* is used of Jesus as the Revelation of God (John 1:1; I John 1:1; Rev. 19:13; Heb. 1:2). He is the supreme and definitive Word or Revelation of God. Before He came into the world, the Word of God came to men through patriarchs (Gen. 15:1), through the lawgiver Moses (Exod. 4:30; 20:1), and through prophets (Num. 22:38; II Kings 7:1; Isa. 1:10; Jer. 1:2). The Word of the Lord is creative (Ps. 33:6; Gen. 1:3,6,9,11,14,20,24,26; Heb. 11:3). The Word of God is sure (Ps. 119:89; Isa. 40:8) forever, and cannot be broken (John 10:35). Words are distinguished from power (I Cor. 4:20; I Thess. 1:5) and from deeds (Mal. 2:17; I Cor. 4:20; I John 3:18), for the Word of God is to be done as well as heard and talked about (James 1:22-25).

WORLD. The Biblical meanings are best described under the several Heb. and Gr. words. Heb. *'erets, earth, land, country, ground*, is rendered "world" when speaking of the kingdoms of the world (Isa. 23:17; Jer. 23:26). Heb. *hedhel* occurs once (Isa. 38:11 and is thought to mean "land of cessation" (of earthly existence), i.e., Sheol. Heb. *heledh, short duration* (Ps. 17:14; 49:1) refers to the ephemeral character of life. Heb. *'ôlām, long duration*, past or future (usually translated "ever," etc.) always referring to time: ASV, RSV "eternity" (Eccl. 3:11), RSV "eternity" (Isa. 45:17), ASV, RSV "of old" (Isa. 64:4). The commonest Heb. word for world is *tēvēl, the habitable earth*, the earth as made for man, often parallel and synonymous with "earth."

In the NT, Greek *gé*, earth, land, ground, country, is rendered "world" once in KJV (Rev. 13:3 ASV, RSV *earth*). Greek *aión* and derivatives developed in meaning from "life-force, lifetime" to "age, period of time, eternity." Where KJV has "world," ASV sometimes, margin usually, RSV, have "age, forever, of old" or the like. Present and future are contrasted (Matt. 13:22; Mark 10:30; Luke 18:30; 20:34,35; Eph. 1:21). *Aión* and derivatives primarily refer to limited but long periods of time; also, especially in phrases where the word is repeated, to endless time, eternity. Greek *oikouméne* is first geographical (the inhabited earth: Matt. 24:14; Luke 4:5; 21:26; Acts 17:31; Rom. 10:18; Heb. 1:6); then cultural (the Hellenistic world: Acts 19:27); then political (the Roman Empire: Luke 2:1; Acts 11:28; 24:5); though a first century man felt them practically coëxtensive (Rev. 3:10; 12:9; 16:14). ASV margin has "inhabited earth" in all cases. Hebrews 2:5 uses *oikouméne* of the world to come. Greek *kósmos* and derivatives range over the meanings "order, beauty, world, universe," never losing their connotation of harmony and beauty. *Kósmos* is a favorite word with John, used of Jesus as Creator (John 1:10; 17:5), Redeemer (1:29; 3:16,17; 4:42; 6:35,51; 12:47; I John 2:2; 4:9,14), Light of the world (John 1:9; 3:19; 8:12; 9:5; 12:46), Prophet (6:14), He that cometh, Christ (11:27), Judge (9:39; 12:31; 16:11). The contrast between Jesus and His disciples on the one hand, and the world on the other, is drawn in John 8:23; 14:17-22; 15:18, 19; 17:9; 18:36, and often in I John. John 17 is rich in references to the relation of believers to the world, considered as a fallen universe hostile to God. In the epistles the ethical meaning prevails

(e.g., I Cor. 1:20-28). Other uses are: "since the world began" (John 9:35); the sun as the light of the world (11:9); the prince of this world (14:30). Heb. cosmology is not tied in with the concept "world" so much as with "heaven and earth" (Gen. 1:1), which embraces the God-oriented universe of sun, moon, planets, stars and earth, with the abode of God above and Sheol beneath. The Heb. words for "world" refer either to the earth itself, or as formed for and inhabited by man. Greek cosmology must be reckoned with in the use of such terms as *aión* and *kósmos* in the LXX and in the NT. *Aión* denotes the temporal or durative aspect of that which exists; *kósmos* the ordered arrangement, though disordered by sin, of all that is, except God. The *kósmos* includes angels, spiritual principalities and powers, men, beasts, earth, heavenly bodies, Hades. In the NT, *kósmos* commonly refers to man and his affairs, especially in an evil sense, over against the new life in Christ, the kingdom of God, the Body of Christ, the Church. As God is in the world but not of it, so are we: God's mode of being penetrates without mixture the world's mode of being. A physical analogy would be the penetration of iron by magnetism, or of copper by electricity. Cf. John 17:14-18.   E. R.

WORM (See Insects)

WORMWOOD (See Plants)

WORSHIP (Heb. *shāhâh, bow down, prostrate*, Gr. *proskynéo, to prostrate, do obeisance to*), the honor, reverence, and homage paid to superior beings or powers, whether men, angels, or God. The English word means "worthship," and denotes the worthiness of the individual receiving the special honor due to his worth. While the word is used of men, it is especially used of the divine honors paid to a deity, whether of the heathen religions or the true and living God.

When given to God, worship involves an acknowledgement of Divine perfections. It may express itself in the form of direct address, as in adoration or thanksgiving, or in service to God; and may be private or public, involving a cultus. Worship presupposes that God is, that He can be known by man, and that His perfections set Him far above man.

In the Bible public worship is found in four stages of development. The first is the somewhat primitive mode practiced until the building of the Temple. During this time no sharp line was drawn between private and public worship. In the second stage it became highly organized in the Temple ritual, which indeed had its origin in the Tabernacle set up in the wilderness. It was led by the priests assisted by the Levites, and included a complex ritual and system of sacrifices. The third stage was that of the synagogue, which began during the Exile. This greatly differed from worship in the Temple. Whereas the latter was centralized in Jerusalem, the former was found wherever there were Jews. In the synagogues, however, the emphasis was more upon instruction than upon worship, although the latter was not neglected. The fourth stage was that of the early Christian churches. Jewish Christians continued, as long as they were permitted, to worship in the Temple and in the synagogue, although for them the whole ceremonial and sacrificial system ended with the death and resurrection of Jesus. Public Christian worship developed along the lines of the synagogue. It appears that from the first, Christians met in homes for private brotherhood meetings, and the time was the Lord's Day (John 20:19,26; Acts 20:7; I Cor. 16:2). Christian public worship consisted of preaching (Acts 20:7; I Cor. 14:19), reading of Scripture (James 1:22; Col. 4:16), prayer (I Cor. 14:14-16), singing (Eph. 5:19; Col. 3:16), baptism and the Lord's Supper (Acts 2:41; I Cor. 11: 18-34), and almsgiving (I Cor. 16:1,2). Sometimes there were also prophesyings and tongues. S.B.

WRATH, the translation of many Heb. and Gr. words, and ranges widely in tone, intensity and effects (Ps. 85:4; II Chron. 26:19; Esth. 1:12; Gen. 27:25; Matt. 2:16). The first display of human wrath recorded in the Bible (Gen. 4:5-6) is followed by many more frank accounts of disaster wrought by the wrath of man, which never works the righteousness of God (James 1:20) and is never more than tolerated (Eph. 4:26; Ps. 37:8; Rom. 12:19). The wrath of God, just, pure and holy, is dreadful to evildoers (Num. 11:1-10; Heb. 10:26-31), yet God is slow to anger and eager to forgive (Ps. 103: 8,9) and so should we be (Eph. 4:31,32). Less frequently mentioned in the NT than in the OT, the wrath of God is no less terrible, most so as the wrath of the Lamb (Rev. 6:16; John 1:29), and abides on him who does not obey the Son of God (John 3:36).

WRESTLE, Heb. *pāthal,* root meaning "twist" (Gen. 30:8); of Rachel's wrestling (emotional and vocal rather than literal) with Leah, which led Rachel to name her handmaid's son Naphtali, *my wrestlings.* Heb. *'āvaq, get dusty, wrestle* (Gen. 32:24,25); of Jacob's wrestling with the angel (physical effect, the dislocation of Jacob's thigh). Greek *pále, wrestling;* later any kind of fighting; used (Eph. 6:12) of the Christian's spiritual conflict with the powers of evil.

WRITING. The earliest forms of writing were not phonetic but pictographic. That is to say, the ideas were recorded by means of pictures or sense-symbols, rather than by sound-symbols such as are used in most modern languages today. Primitive man resorted to a picture of the idea he wished to represent, rather than using any type of sign to show how the word in question was to be pronounced. Thus the circle of the sun-disk might indicate either the sun itself (in Egyptian the word *re',* in Sumerian *ud*) or else the word "day" (in Egyptian *heru,* in Sumerian *u* or *ud*) as the span of time during which the sun would shine. The concept of "man" was conveyed in Egyptian by the picture of a man sitting with one leg curled under him and the other bent with the knee upright. This figure would be accompanied by a single vertical stroke to indicate that only one man was involved, or by more strokes according to the number of men referred to. In Sumerian the idea of man (*lu*) was conveyed by a triangular head and a turnip-shaped torso; at first it stood up on end, facing right, but later it lay flat on its back facing upward (for all Sumerian signs underwent a 90-degree shift in direction from vertical to horizontal sometime between 3000 and 2500 B.C.). This earliest stage in writing was marked by the use of the pure *ideogram.* (This same principle was operative in primitive Chinese, which developed a system of sign-language that has endured to the present day; nearly all of its basic characters or "radicals" represent pictures of the type of object being referred to. This picture may or may not be accompanied by other strokes which indicate the sound-value of the word.)

The next stage in the history of writing was the introduction of the *phonogram,* or the type of sign which indicates a sound. At first this was achieved by the *rebus* principle, that is, by the use of objects which have a name sounding like the sound of the

Limestone tablet from Kish, near Babylon, containing one of the earliest Sumerian inscriptions with pictographic script, c. 3000 B.C.   BM

word which the writer wishes to convey, even though the meaning of the object portrayed is entirely different. Thus in English *rebus* one may indicate that a man became *pale* with fear by drawing a picture of a *pail.* Similarly in Egyptian the sign for "duck" could also represent "son," because in both cases the word was pronounced *sa.* The Sumerian city of Girsu was spelled by a picture of a dagger (*gir*) followed by a piece of hide or skin (*su*).

Both in Sumerian and Egyptian there was a very early development of this rebus principle, so that the writing system became equipped with a large number of signs which could convey syllabic sounds, independent of meaning, and thus furnish building-blocks for words of two or more syllables. Naturally the number of signs necessary to indicate all possible syllables which could occur in the spoken language was very numerous indeed. Both Egyptian and Sumerian writing retained both ideograms and syllabic phonograms right to the end of their history. Both of them also used signs known as *determinatives* which had no sound value at all, but which simply indicated the class of object referred to. In Sumerian the name of a city would often be preceded by the sign for "city" (even though it was not to be pronounced aloud as a separate word); similarly a star (standing for *dingir* or "god") would precede the name of any deity. Or else these determinatives would follow the rest of the word, rather than preceding it; thus the Sumerian name of Babylon was written *ka-dingir-ra* KI. *Ka* was an ideogram for "gate," *dingir* was an ideogram for "god," *ra* was a phonogram indicating that *dingir* ended in an *r* sound and was followed by the genitive particle *-a(k)*; the final *KI* was the sign for "earth" or "land," and served simply as a determinative.

Observe that in this last example the Sumerian name for Babylon (or Babylonia) meant "The Gate of God." When the Semitic-speaking Akkadians and Babylonians conquered the Mesopotamian valley, they took over the writing-system of the Sumerians and adapted it to their own language. In some cases they took the Sumerian ideograms and gave them the pronunciation of the word in their own language. Thus the Babylonian for "gate" was *babum* ("gate of" being pronounced *bab*); the word for "god" was *ilu* (in the genitive *ili*). Hence the very same signs which the Sumerians pronounced as *ka-dingirrak* the Babylonians pronounced as *bab-ili* (which came into Hebrew as *Babel*). Operating upon this principle the Babylonians contrived ways of expressing all the necessary sounds in their own language. They would either use the Sumerian phonograms to express the same sound in Akkadian (the language spoken by the Babylonians and Assyrians), or else they would assign new sound-values to them. Thus the Sumerian word for "wood" or "tree" was *gish* and was written by four wedges forming a rectangle; the corresponding Akkadian word was *isu*. Hence in Akkadian the sign could furnish the phonetic syllable *gish* (as it did in Sumerian) or else the syllable *is* (derived from the Akkadian word), as for example in the word *is-su-ru* "bird." Thus it was by ingenious adaptation that the Sumerian system of writing was taken over by a nation speaking an entirely different language and employed — still in the mixed ideographic and phonographic form — to give written expression to their Semitic tongue. Incidentally, if Abraham's family was residing in Ur back in the Twentieth Century B.C., this would have coincided with the brilliant Sumerian culture that flourished under the Third

Dynasty of Ur. Quite possibly he would have learned to speak Sumerian and also to read it, and it is quite possible that this was the only type of writing with which he had any acquaintance, except for that period when he lived in Egypt.

The Egyptian system of writing — at least in its monumental form — remained in an artistic pictorial form from its earliest rise about 3000 B.C. until its slow demise in the Roman period, 3200 years later. Its characters never degenerated into combinations of wedges bearing little resemblance to the original pictographs, as was the case in Sumerian and Akkadian. Of course Egyptian was also (at least as early as the Sixth Dynasty) written in a cursive, hieratic form, especially in business documents, correspondence, and secular literature. But apart from esthetic considerations, Egyptian writing developed peculiarities of its own which were quite foreign to the Sumerian-Akkadian system. In the first place, it recorded only the consonants of the spoken language, not its vowels. Some of these consonants were like the so-called vowel-letters of Hebrew, Aramaic and Arabic; that is, the *aleph* or glottal catch, the *y* indicating a neighboring *i* sound, and the *w* indicating a *u* sound before it. On the other hand, the transcriptions of Egyptian names into Akkadian cuneiform and into Greek furnish important evidence as to how Egyptian was vocalized, and these transcriptions do not come out to any consistent pattern of correspondence with these Egyptian "vowel-letters." Neither is there any standard relationship between them and their descendants in the Coptic language (which was written in the Greek alphabet and preserved the form of Egyptian as it was spoken in the early Christian centuries). And so it must be recognized that Egyptian hieroglyphic is essentially as consonantal as were the Semitic languages which used the Phoenician alphabet.

A second noteworthy contrast between Egyptian and Sumerian is that it developed genuine alphabetic signs, as well as two-consonant (or three-consonant) syllabic signs. Therefore to the Egyptians goes the credit for being the first to develop an alphabetic system of writing. However they did

Portion of an Egyptian hieroglyphic inscription, with translation (after Pfeiffer).

This shows how cuneiform writing was done on a clay tablet, with a stylus. Below the inscription the soft clay has been impressed with a pictorial seal. BA ASOR

not see any need of abandoning their ideograms, determinative signs and syllabic characters just because they had alphabetic letters; and so they simply employed all four types of sign in the writing out of their language. Even the more cursive, shorthand type of writing referred to above as *hieratic* introduced virtually no changes in this complicated and cumbersome system; it simply enabled the scribe to write out his four kinds of hieroglyphic signs with a fair degree of rapidity. The same was true of a still more cursive and simplified form of hieratic known as *demotic,* used after 1000 B.C. Not until Egypt was conquered by Alexander the Great (about 332 B.C.) did the influence of a foreign system of writing become decisive upon Egyptian conservatism. By the third century A.D. (the period of the earliest Coptic glosses in the Oxyrynchus Papyri) the Egyptians were writing out their vernacular, vowels and all, in the letters of the Greek alphabet, to which they soon added seven more alphabetic signs of their own invention, to represent sounds not found in Greek.

The fact that the Egyptians did develop a full set of alphabetic signs has led some scholars to conclude that the most primitive form of the so-called "Phoenician" alphabet consisted of modifications of various Egyptian consonantal or syllabic signs. This was a reasonable inference, perhaps, but no convincing list of correspondences could be made up by even the most ingenious advocates of this theory. The true origin of the "Phoenician" alphabet is to be sought rather in the alphabetic hieroglyphs of the Sinaitic Inscriptions of Serabit el-Khadim (written some time between 1900 and 1500 B.C. — for the scholars' estimates vary). These signs are tabulated on Plate A (according to R.H. Pfeiffer's analysis of them). Since they were inscribed by Semitic miners in the employ of Egypt, and since these documents are found side by side with Egyptian hieroglyphic inscriptions (on statues dedicated to the goddess Hathor), it is fair to conclude that these miners got the idea for their alphabet from the Egyptians themselves. But instead of resorting to ideograms and syllabic signs,

PROTO-SINAITIC ALPHABET (ca. 1700 B.C.)		OLD PHOENICIAN ALPHAB (ca. 1200 B.C.)	
ʾ (ʾaleph)			āleph (ox)
b			bēt (house)
g			gimel
d			dālet (door)
h			hē
w			wāw (hook)
z			zajin
ḥ			ḥēt
ṭ			ṭēt
y			jōd (hand)
k			kaph (open hand)
l			lāmed
m			mēm (water)
n			nun (fish-snake)
s			samekh (fish)
ʿ (ʾajin)			ʾajin (eye)
ṣ			ṣādē
p			pē (mouth)
q			qōph
r			rēš (head)
š			šīn (tooth)
t			tāw (mark)

PLATE A

they contented themselves with alphabetic symbols chosen on the basis of *acrophony*. That is to say, the first sound of the name of the object represented conveyed the alphabetic unit intended. In Egyptian a sign for "hand" was used as the alphabetic sign for *d*, since the word for "hand" was *dert*. Following this principle, the Semitic miner chose the picture of a hand extended as a sign for *y* (since the word for "hand" was *yadu* in his language). The head of an ox was used for the sound of *aleph* (the glottal catch) because the word for "ox" was *'alpu* (a name which was preserved in the later Heb. *aleph* and in the still later Greek *alpha*). Interestingly enough, this particular letter has been quite well preserved from 1900 B.C. until the present, for if our capital A is turned upside down, it bears a fairly close similarity to that ancient Sinaitic sign for *aleph*, the ox's head.

During the ensuing centuries this Sinaitic type of script (or modifications of it) was cultivated in Canaan, for household objects like daggers, rings, ewers, pots and plaques have been found with short inscriptions, mostly of very uncertain interpretation. But a totally different form of alphabetic writing assumed great importance during this period (1800-1400 B.C.), namely the cuneiform alphabet associated with Ras-shamra or Ugarit. Unlike the cuneiform of Babylonia and Assyria, this kind of cuneiform represented an alphabet of about 29 or 30 characters, all of them consonantal (except that

A cuneiform tablet, with a list of Assyrian kings. © Andrews University SHH

three of them indicated the type of vowel occurring after *aleph*, whether *a, i* (or *e*) or *u*). This very early dialect of Canaanite (for Ugaritic is much closer to Biblical Hebrew than to any other known Semitic language) contained several consonants not appearing in any of the Northwest Semitic scripts, in some cases sounds still preserved only in Arabic (such as rough *heth, z* as in Arabic *nazara* "to see," *th* as in *thalāthun* "three"), and others apparently different from any sound found in Arabic (such as *zh* like the English *s* in *pleasure*). The shapes of the characters formed by these wedges bear no consistent similarity to the signs either of Sinaitic letters or of the Akkadian syllabary. They are very simple in structure and seem to have no pictographic origin whatever. This type of alphabet flourished not only at Ugarit but also in more southerly localities as well. But after the violent destruction of Ras Shamra in the 15th century, the use of the Ugaritic alphabet seems to have declined in favor of the Phoenician.

Several so-called Proto-phoenician inscriptions have been discovered in Palestinian localities such as Gezer, Lachish and Shechem, exhibiting forms which could be transitional between the Sinaitic and the authentic Phoenician of the 11th century B.C. Unfortunately, however, these short lines of writing do not fall into a consistent pattern and they cannot be deciphered with real certainty. As to the earliest Phoenician inscriptions, those of Shaphatbaal and Ahiram found at Gebal (Byblos) on the coast north of Sidon, there is still much dispute as to the time when they were written. The inscription on the sarcophagus of King Ahiram is dated by various authorities from before 1250 to as late as 1000 B.C. (the later date being advocated by Dunand, who maintained that the Shaphatbaal inscription was centuries earlier — cf. Driver p. 104, Février pp. 206-27). Here we have the 22-letter alphabet which is to hold the stage from then on in all the Northwest Semitic languages (Phoenician, Hebrew, Moabite, Aramaic and Syriac). The early form of it appears in the right-hand column of Plate A, as well as in the leftmost column of Plate B. It can be easily seen from Plate B how closely related to it were all the forms of the alphabet used in Jerusalem in Hezekiah's time (second column), in Carthage (where a dialect of Phoenician was spoken) 400 years later,

North Semitic Alphabets

Phoenician - Hebrew			Aramaic		Palmyrene Syriac		Square Hebrew	
Old			North	Egyptian				Modern
Phoenician 1100 BC	Jerusalem (c 700 BC)	Carthage (c 300 BC)	Syria (c 750 BC)	Papyri (c 400 BC)	Palmyra (137 AD)	Estrangelo (c 500 AD)	Inscriptions (100-400 AD)	Print
𐤀	𐤀 𐤀	𐤀𐤀𐤀	𐤀	𐤀 𐤀	א	ܐ	ܐܐܐܐ	א
𐤁	𐤁 𐤁	𐤁	𐤁	𐤁𐤁	ב	ܒ	בבב	ב
𐤂	𐤂	𐤂	٨ ٨	𐤂	٨	ܓ	٨	ג
𐤃	𐤃	𐤃	𐤃	𐤃	٩	ܕ	٦٦٦	ד
𐤄	𐤄𐤄	𐤄	𐤄	𐤄𐤄	𐤄	ܗ	ח ח	ה
𐤅	𐤅	𐤅	𐤅	𐤅	?	ܘ	?١١	ו
𐤆	𐤆	𐤆𐤆	I z	𐤆𐤆	I	٠	١٢	ז
𐤇	𐤇𐤇	𐤇𐤇	𐤇𐤇	𐤇𐤇	𐤇	٠	ܚܢܚ	ח
𐤈		𐤈𐤈	𐤈𐤈𐤈	𐤈 𐤈	G	ﯼ	٥ ٥	ט
𐤉	١ ٢	ما ما ما	𐤉	𐤉	? ?	،	١١٠٠	י
𐤊	𐤊𐤊	𐤊𐤊	𐤊	𐤊	ܟ ܟ	٦	٦٦٦	ך כ
𐤋	𐤋𐤋	𐤋٦𐤋	𐤋	𐤋𐤋𐤋	٤	ܠ	٥٥	ל
𐤌	𐤌	𐤌𐤌	𐤌	𐤌𐤌	ܡ	ܡ	ܟܟܟ	ם מ
𐤍	𐤍	𐤍	𐤍	𐤍𐤍	٥٥	ܢ	٥١١	ן נ
𐤎	𐤎𐤎	𐤎𐤎	𐤎	𐤎	٥٥	٠	٦٦٦	ס
𐤏	٥	٥ ٥	٥	٥٥٥	𐤏	٨	٨٨	ע
𐤐	𐤐	٠١١	𐤐	٢	٦٦٥	٥	١١	ף פ
𐤑		٢ ٢	٢	٢٢	٨	٨	٢٢	ץ צ
𐤒	𐤒 𐤒	𐤒	٢	𐤒𐤒𐤒	٦	٠	ܩܩܩ	ק
𐤓	𐤓	𐤓	𐤓	𐤓	٢٢	٠	٦٦	ר
w	w	ساسا	w	٠	V	٠	ܟܘܘ	ש
x +	x	٦٦٦	xX	٨	٦	٨	ח ח	ת

PLATE B

and in Aramaic-speaking Syria in the time of Amos. The earliest Israelite document which has survived in this script is the Gezer Calendar of about 900 B.C. or a few decades earlier. It is a small limestone tablet inscribed with the irregular hand of a schoolboy and containing a list of the successive phases of the agricultural year from season to season. The discovery of this schoolboy's exercise witnesses to the extent of literacy in the reign of Solomon. Unfortunately we have no documents from an earlier period to serve as a reliable guide, but it is most likely that Moses used a Proto-phoenician type of script rather than any kind of cuneiform (although the use of Akkadian cuneiform for international correspondence is well attested for the time of Joshua in Palestine). Even in the Tell el-Amarna correspondence, consisting of letters in Akkadian addressed by Canaanite princes to the Egyptian court, there were numerous glosses (or explanatory synonyms) in Canaanite or Hebrew, written out in Akkadian cuneiform syllabic signs. Hence this type of writing would also have been known to Moses and available to him. (See article, HEBREW LANGUAGE)

The next important Hebrew inscription after the Gezer Calendar was the Siloam Inscription, incised on the wall of the underground tunnel dug through to the Pool of Siloam in preparation (probably) for the siege of Jerusalem by Sennacherib in 701 B.C. Here we see a trend toward the more freely flowing style of manuscript writing, rather than the stern angularity of monumental style. In particular some of the long-tailed letters (like *mem*, *nun* and *kaph*) curve with a bottom swoop to the left. Examples of the rapid brush-stroked type of script are furnished by the Samaritan Ostraca of about 770 B.C. (containing tax-receipts paid to the government of Jeroboam II) and the Lachish Ostraca of 588 B.C. These last consist of letters written by the captain of a Jewish outpost to Yaosh, commander of Zedekiah's troops in Lachish. Here the letters are formed in a very compressed or flattened form, but are still of essentially the same pattern as the old Phoenician. For some time after the Babylonian Exile this Paleo-Hebrew script (as it is called) was retained for some types of text, such as the books of the Pentateuch, for fragments of Leviticus and Exodus have been discovered in the Qumran Caves, dating from the late fourth century (according to the estimate of some scholars). The Samaritan sect, which originated from the schism of 535 (when Zerubbabel refused to allow the Samaritan heretics to participate in rebuilding the temple at Jerusalem) for some reason developed a special form of this Paleo-Hebrew script all their own, and retained it for all their religious literature down through the time of the Moslem conquest, and even to this day. Palaeo-Hebrew was employed on Jewish coinage of the Maccabean period (second century B.C.) and also of the First and Second Revolts (67-70 A.D. and 132-135 A.D., respectively). By and large the Aramaic-speaking peoples of Damascus, Hamath and parts north used the same style of alphabet, although with minor regional peculiarities.

The so-called Square Hebrew character seems to have developed first on Aramaic soil, possibly during the sixth century. Yet early examples of this script are regrettably sparse and it remains impossible to trace its rise and development very much prior to the second century B.C. At all events it does not seem to have derived from the epistolary cursive of the Elephantine Papyri (400 B.C.) a set of legal documents and letters written in Aramaic by Jewish mercenaries stationed on an island near the southern border of Egypt. As can be seen from the fifth column in Plate B, it was an extremely cursive script, but still bore stronger affinity to the Palaeo-Hebrew than to the Square Hebrew of the Dead Sea Caves. A monumental form of Square Hebrew is exhibited in the eighth column of the same plate, but this dates from a much later period. For examples of the type of Square Hebrew used by the scribes of the Maccabean (Qumran) period, see TEXTS, VERSIONS, O.T.

It is important to observe that the Greeks received their alphabet from the Phoenicians and Aramaeans, perhaps through contact with their merchants. (Through the investigations of Michael Ventris and his co-laborers it has now been quite well established that Cretan Linear B, used in Crete during the latter half of the Second Millennium B.C., consisted of a syllabary somewhat similar to the syllabic writing anciently employed on the island of Cyprus. It was an independent invention, so far as we know, and has no relation to any system of writing employed in the Semitic Near East. The inscriptions themselves were written in a sort of Mycenean dialect of Greek. But these constituted an isolated development without any lasting influence upon later times). Apart from these special developments in Crete and Cyprus, the Hellenic tribal groups found written expression for their languages through the Phoenician alphabet, which supplied the first 22 letters of the Greek alphabet (i.e. *alpha* through *tau*). Those Semitic letters which expressed sounds not employed by the Greeks were adapted to express vowels. The glottal catch, *aleph*, was used to convey the sound *a*; the soft *h*-sound of the Semitic *hē* was redesigned for the Greek *e*; the rough aspirate of the Semitic *heth* was employed by the Western Greeks to express their soft aspirate (the English *h*), but by the Ionians to convey the long *e* sound (pronounced like French *e*-acute). The Athenians at first followed the Western practice, using *epsilon* to express long *e* as well as short *e*, but later adopted the Ionic employment of the *H* as *ēta*, using the broken halves of aspirate-H to express the rough breathing (equivalent to *h*) and the smooth breathing (which was without sound). The Semitic *y* of *yodh* was simplified to a single vertical stroke as the letter *i* or *iota*, while the guttural Semitic *'ayin* was adapted to express the sound of *o* (at first either long *o* or short, but later specialized as short *o* or *omicron*). From the Semitic *waw* or *w* the Greeks of the West used one form to express the *w*-sound; as such it resembled a modern *F*. The other form of *waw*, that shaped like a *Y*, was employed to express the *u*-sound (later modified in pronunciation to a French *u* or German *ü*). Besides this last-mentioned letter, the *üpsilon*, the Greeks added four more letters, the *phi* (at first pronounced like *ph* in "uphill," but later sounded like *f*); the *khi* (at first pronounced like *kh* in "workhouse," but later pronounced like German or Scotch *ch*); *psi*, which rendered the consonant-cluster *p-s* as in "capsule"; and *omega*, a modification of *omicron* designed to express long *o* only. This, then, was the writing medium which in the providence of God came to be used to convey the redeeming message of the NT Scriptures. From the Western form of the Greek alphabet the Romans derived their Latin alphabet, omitting from it those letters used by the Eastern Greeks which were unnecessary to express the sounds of the Latin tongue. This, then, is the alphabet which has descended to us at the present day, ultimately derived from the Semites of the Holy Land. G.L.A.

Ruins, possibly of the palace of Xerxes (Ahasuerus) at Susa, ancient Shushan. This is very likely the place of the great banquet of the Book of Esther, and where Queen Esther lived. (The modern building on the horizon is an archaeological expedition headquarters.) SHH

X

XERXES (zûrk′sēz, Gr. *Xérxes*, meaning unknown), king of the Persian Empire from 486-465 B.C. He is the same as Ahasuerus, mentioned in the books of Ezra, Esther, and Daniel. The main support for this identification is to be found in the linguistic equivalence of the names, and a close similarity has been noted between the character of Xerxes and the character of the king of the Persians portrayed in the book of Esther. There are also historical correlations. Thus, the feast which was held in the third year of the reign of Ahasuerus at Shushan (Esth. 1:3) corresponds to an assembly held by Xerxes in his third year in preparation for the invasion of Greece. Herodotus states that Xerxes, following his defeat at Salamis and Plataea, consoled himself in his seventh year with the pleasures of the harem (Herodotus IX, 108). This parallels the Biblical account which relates that Ahasuerus replaced Vashti by marrying Esther in his seventh year (Esth. 2:16) after gathering all the fair young virgins to Shushan.

Below, detail of Crown Prince Xerxes standing behind his father, King Darius, on the throne. This is from the stone relief at Persepolis, shown in excavation scene at right. OIUC

Y

YAHWEH (See God, also YHWH below)

YARMUK, WADI EL. This word, though not found in the Bible itself, is the name given to one of the three important streams to the SE of the Sea of Galilee. Located six miles to the SE of this sea, it contributes large quantities of water to the Jordan. It is now the site of a large hydro-electric plant. It marked the southern boundary of the ancient kingdom of Bashan.

YARN (värn, Heb. *miqweh*), the KJV translation of the Hebrew word which occurs in I Kings 10:28 and II Chronicles 1:16. In each of these cases "linen yarn" seems to convey the wrong meaning. It is correctly rendered in the RSV by the proper name "Kue," the old Assyrian name given to Cilicia, the land located in the southeastern portion of Asia Minor.

YEAR (See Calendar)

YHWH. This is not in reality a word, but is known as the "tetragrammaton," the four consonants standing for the ancient Hebrew name for God commonly referred to as "Jehovah" or "Yahweh." The original Hebrew text was not vocalized. YHWH was considered too sacred to pronounce; so *'adonai* (*my Lord*) was substituted in reading. When eventually a vowel system was invented, since the Hebrews had forgotten how to pronounce YHWH, they substituted the vowels for *'adonai*, making "Jehovah," a form first attested at the beginning of the 12th century A.D.

YODH (See Jot)

YOKE (Heb. *môtâh, an oxbow; 'ôl, a yoke; tsemedh, yoke of oxen, an acre,* i.e., as much land as a yoke of oxen could plow in a day; Gr. *zeúgos, a team* and *zygós, yoke*). In the literal sense, a bar of wood so constructed as to unite two animals, usually oxen, enabling them to work in the fields. Drawing loads and pulling instruments used in farming, such as the plow, were the two chief works the yoke made possible. Archeological studies have shown that the yoke was variously constructed in different periods of history. It was commonly used all over the ancient world. Also used figuratively in the sense of servitude (Jer. 27,28) and "the law of God."

YOKEFELLOW (Gr. *sýnzygos, yoked together*), a common word among Greek writers referring to those united by close bonds, as in marriage, labor, etc. It is found only once in the NT (Phil. 4:3) and the meaning here is not clear. Some feel that Paul refers here to a fellow worker; others think the word is a proper noun, Sunzugos.

YOM KIPPUR (See Feasts)

Z

ZAANAIM (zā'à-nā'ĭm, Heb. text uncertain), a word found only in Judges 4:11, but it is probably the same place referred to as Zaanannim in Joshua 19:33. This place was located on Naphtali's southern border near to the spot where Sisera lost his life at the hands of Heber the Kenite. It is the same as the modern Khan et-Tujjar, located about three miles NE of Mount Tabor.

ZAANAN (za à-năn, Heb. *tsa'ănān*), a place mentioned by Micah (1:11) in the Shephelah of Judah. The place has never been certainly identified, but it may be Zenan.

ZAANANNIM (See Zaanaim)

ZAAVAN (zā'à-văn, Heb. *za'āwān, not quiet*), one of the three sons of Ezer (Gen. 36:27; I Chron. 1:42).

ZABAD (zā'băd, Heb. *zāvādh, Jehovah has given*). 1. The son of Nathan, who was the son of Attai, who was the son of Ahlai. Hence this man is called the son of Nathan (I Chron. 2:36) and the son of Ahlai (I Chron. 11:41). Note also I Chronicles 2:31-37.

2. One from the tribe of Ephraim, son of Tahath (I Chron. 7:21).

3. The son of Shimeath, the Ammonitess. He conspired against King Joash and was later killed by Amaziah (II Chron. 24:26; cf. 25:3-4).

4-6. Three Israelites are given this name, all of them sons of Zattu (Ezra 10:27), Hashum (Ezra 10:33), and Nebo (Ezra 10:43) respectively. In response to Ezra's plea after the captivity, they put away their Gentile wives.

ZABBAI (zăb'à-ī, Heb. *zabbay,* meaning unknown). 1. One of the sons of Bebai who put away his foreign wife at the request of Ezra (Ezra 10:28).

2. The father of Baruch (Neh. 3:20).

ZABBUD (zăb'ŭd, Heb. *zabbûdh, given*), the son of Bigvai who accompanied Ezra to Jerusalem from Babylon (Ezra 8:14).

ZABDI (zăb'dī, Heb. *zavdî, he (God) has given*). 1. Achan's grandfather, from the tribe of Judah. His father's name was Zerah (Josh. 7:1,17).

2. Son of Shimei from the tribe of Benjamin (I Chron. 8:19).

3. One of the officers of David listed as having charge of the wine cellars (I Chron. 27:27). He is called "the Shiphmite."

4. One of the ancestors of Mattaniah, who aided in worship in the days of Nehemiah (Neh. 11:17).

ZABDIEL (zăb'dĭ-ĕl, Heb. *zavdî'el, God has given*). 1. The father of Jashobeam (I Chron. 27:2).

2. A temple overseer (Neh. 11:14).

3. An Arabian who, after beheading Alexander Balas, sent his head to Ptolemy (I Macc. 11:17).

ZABUD (zā'bŭd, Heb. *zāvûdh, bestowed*), the son of Nathan; a principal officer of Solomon and his best friend (I Kings 4:5).

ZABULON (See Zebulun)

ZACCAI (zăk'à-ī, Heb. *zakkay*), the ancestral head of a post-Exilic family whose 760 descendants returned to Jerusalem with Zerubbabel (Neh. 7:14 and Ezra 2:9).

ZACCHAEUS (ză-kē'ŭs, Gr. *Zakchaíos,* from the Hebrew *zakkay, pure*), a publican, referred to only in Luke, who resided at Jericho. He is described as a "chief" publican, and therefore had charge of collecting taxes. When Jesus was passing through Jericho on one occasion, Zacchaeus became very desirous of seeing Him, and being small in stature, climbed a tree to accomplish his mission. He must have been quite surprised, therefore, when Jesus paused in His journey beneath this very tree and, looking up, urged Zacchaeus to come down, for He had decided to abide at his house (Luke 19:5). With joy he made haste to comply. The salvation he experienced that day was evident because of his change of life (Luke 19:8).

ZACCUR (zăk'ûr, Heb. *zakkûr, remembered*). 1. The father of the Reubenite spy, Shammua (Num. 13:4).

2. The son of Hamuel, a Simeonite (I Chron. 4:26), Zacchur in AV.

3. One of the sons of Merari (I Chron. 24:27).

4. One of the sons of Asaph set apart by David for musical service (I Chron. 25:1-2; Neh. 12:35).

5. The son of Imri who aided in rebuilding the wall of Jerusalem (Neh. 3:2).

6. One of those who, with Nehemiah, sealed the covenant (Neh. 10:12).

7. One of the treasurers, father of Hanan (Neh. 13:13).

ZACCHUR (See Zaccur)

ZACHARIAH (zăk'à-rī'à, Heb. *zekharyâh, Jehovah has remembered*), the 14th king of Israel, the son of Jeroboam II. In fulfillment of II Kings 10:30, he was the last of the house of Jehu. After a brief reign of six months, he was slain by Shallum, his successor (II Kings 15:8-10).

ZACHARIAS (zăk'à-rī'ás, Gr. *Zacharías, Jehovah has remembered*). 1. The name of the father of John the Baptist (Luke 1:5). He was a priest of the course of Abijah who was childless in his old age. Both he and his wife were righteous, and while Zacharias was performing his services in the temple, an angel appeared and reported to him that he was to have a son whom he was to name John. Because of doubt, he was stricken dumb until his son was named, at which time his speech was restored (Luke 1:67-69).

2. The son of Barachias, mentioned in Matthew 23:35 and in Luke 11:51, by Christ as having been slain between the altar and the temple. His true identity has not been fully determined.

ZACHER (zā'kêr, Heb. *zākher, memorial*), one of Jehiel's sons (I Chron. 8:31; 9:37).

ZADOK (zā'dŏk, Heb. *tsādhōq, righteous*). 1. The most familiar Bible character bearing this name is the son of Ahitub. He was a priest in the time of David (II Sam. 8:17), and came to minister to David in Hebron after the death of King Saul (I Chron. 12:23-28). After the death of Uzza, David called Zadok and asked him to assist, as a Levite, in bringing the ark into its prepared place in Jerusalem (I Chron. 15:11-13). So faithful was he to David that he accompanied him with the ark when he fled from Jerusalem at the rebellion of Absalom and abode with him until commanded by David to return to Jerusalem to act for him as a spy (II Sam. 15:24-36; 17:15,17-21).

His continued loyalty was further seen when, at the end of David's life, Adonijah aspired to be king. He followed out the instructions of King David and anointed Solomon, David's son, king in

Gihon (I Kings 1:8-45). His loyalty was not forgotten even after David's death, for Solomon favored him by making him the high priest, demoting Abiathar who had been sharing this role with him (I Kings 2:26-35).

2. The son of another Ahitub who is the father of Shallum (I Chron. 6:12).

3. Jerusha's father (II Kings 15:33; II Chron. 27:1).

4. The son of Baana who aided in the construction of the wall at Jerusalem in the time of Nehemiah (Neh. 3:4). He is also probably one of those listed as signers of the covenant with Nehemiah (Neh. 10:21), especially since in both of these instances his name follows the name of Meshezabeel.

5. The son of Immer, another priest who also shared in the labor of rebuilding the Jerusalem walls under Nehemiah (Neh. 3:29).

6. One appointed by Nehemiah to be a scribe (Neh. 13:13). There is probably nothing to hinder this scribe from being also one of the two wall-builders mentioned.

ZAHAM (zā'hăm, Heb. *zāham, odious fool*), Rehoboam's youngest son (II Chron. 11:19).

ZAIR (zā'ĭr, Heb. *tsā'îr, small*), a village somewhere E of the Dead Sea in Idumea, which to date has not been identified for certain, where Joram smote the Edomites (II Kings 8:21).

ZALAPH (zā'lăf, Heb. *tsālāph, caper-plant*), the father of Hanun who aided Nehemiah in repairing the Jerusalem walls (Neh. 3:30).

ZALMON (zăl'mōn, Heb. *tsalmôn, dark*). 1. A Benjamite who was one of David's mighty men (II Sam. 23:28). He is also called "Ilai" (I Chron. 11: 29), and in both passages "The Ahohite."

2. A forest near Shechem (Judg. 9:48) from which wood was taken by Abimelech in the destruction of Shechem. Its identity has not been determined with certainty.

ZALMONAH (zăl-mō'nà, Heb. *tsalmônâh, gloomy*), one of the places in the wilderness where Israel camped. It lay SE of Edom.

ZALMUNNA (zăl-mŭn'à, Heb. *tsalmunnā', deprived of shade*), one of the two kings of Midian whom Gideon captured and killed during his bold raid on the Midianites (Judg. 8:4-21; Ps. 83:11).

ZAMZUMMIM (zăm-zŭm'ĭm, Heb. *zamzummîm, murmurers*), a name found only in Deuteronomy 2:20. It is used of the race of giants, called Rephaim (II Sam. 5:18,22), who lived in a spot E of the Jordan. Later on the Ammonites captured them and occupied their land. They are described as "a people, great, and many, and tall" (Deut. 2:21). They may be the same as the Zuzims (Gen. 14:5).

ZANOAH (zà-nō'à, Heb. *zānôah, rejected*). 1. A town located in the low-lying hills of Judah (Josh. 15:34). After the Babylonian captivity some Jews returned to live there (Neh. 11:30), and assisted in the rebuilding of the walls of Jerusalem (Neh. 3:13). It has been identified with Khirbet Zanu', and is situated 10 miles W of Jerusalem.

2. A town located in the mountains of Judah (Josh. 15:56) 10 or 12 miles SW of Hebron. It was built or rebuilt by Jekuthiel who is called its "father" (I Chron. 4:18). It is identified with Zenuta.

ZAPHENATH-PANEAH (zăf'ē-năth-pà-nē'à, Heb. *tsaphenath-pa'ăneah, the one who furnishes the sustenance of the land*), the name given to Joseph by the pharaoh on the occasion of his promotion for showing the pharaoh the meaning of his dream (Gen. 41:45).

ZAPHON (zā'fŏn, Heb. *tsáphôn, north*), a territory E of the Jordan allotted by Moses to Gad (Josh. 13:27). It is the modern Amateh.

ZARA (zā'rà, Gr. *Zará*, meaning unknown), the Greek for the Hebrew Zerah, mentioned in the ancestry of Christ (Matt. 1:3).

ZAREAH (See Zorah)

ZAREATHITE (See Zorah)

ZARED (See Zered)

ZAREDA (See Zarethan)

ZAREPHATH (zăr'ē-făth, Heb. *tsárephath, refinement*), an OT town remembered chiefly because Elijah resided here during the latter half of the famine caused by the drought (I Kings 17:9ff). Its Greek equivalent "Sarepta" is mentioned in Luke 4:26, where it is described as being in the land of Sidon. Here God miraculously sustained the prophet through the widow. Ruins of the ancient town survive S of the modern village of Sarafand, about 8 miles S of Sidon, 14 miles N of Tyre.

The town of Sarafand, ancient Zarephath (Sarepta) on the Mediterranean coast. SHH

ZARETHAN (zăr'ē-thăn, Heb. *tsārethān*), a place near Beth-shean and Adam mentioned in connection with Israel's crossing of the Jordan (Josh. 3:16); spelled Zaretan in KJV. Bronze castings for the temple were made there (I Kings 7:46). In II Chronicles 4:17 the name is given as Zeredah. Its exact site has not been ascertained.

ZARETH-SHAHAR (zā'rĕth-shā'hàr, Heb. *tsereth hashahar, the glory of dawn*), a city located in the land belonging to Reuben "in the mount of the valley" (Josh. 13:19). It has not been identified.

ZARHITES, THE (zàr'hĭts, Heb. *zarhî, those who shine*), members of the tribe of Judah descended from Judah's son, Zerah (Num. 26:13,20; Josh. 7: 17; I Chron. 27:11,13).

ZARTANAH (zàr-tā'nà, Heb. *tsarethanâh*), a place referred to only in I Kings 4:12 as a means of locating Bethshean. Its location is uncertain.

ZARTHAN (zàr'thăn, Heb. *tsărethăn*, meaning uncertain). 1. A place between Succoth and Zarthan where Hiram cast the copper vessels of the temple which he gave to King Solomon (I Kings 7:46). The clay soil in this area was the reason for choosing this place (I Kings 7:45-46). It is called "Zeredathah" in II Chronicles 4:17.

2. Another place by this name is cited in connection with the passage of the children of Israel across the Jordan. It is used as a means of locating the city of Adam (Josh. 3:16).

ZATTHU (See Zattu)

ZATTU (ză'tū, Heb. *zattû'*), head of a large family of children (Ezra 2:8; Neh. 7:13) who returned with Zerubbabel to Jerusalem from the Babylonian captivity and signed the covenant with Nehemiah (Neh. 10:14). Several of his children were among those who put away their Gentile wives (Ezra 10:27).

ZAVAN (See Zaavan)

ZAZA (zā'zà, Heb. *zāzā'*), a Jerahmelite (I Chron. 2:33).

ZEALOT (zĕl'ŭt, Gr. *zelotés, zealous one*), a member of a Jewish patriotic party started in the time of Cyrenius to resist Roman aggression. According to Josephus (BJ, IV, iii, 9; v,1; VII, viii,1), the Zealots resorted to violence and assassination in their hatred of the Romans, their fanatical violence eventually provoking the Roman war. Simon the Zealot was distinguished from Simon Peter by this epithet (Luke 6:15; Acts 1:13).

ZEBADIAH (zĕb'à-dī'à, Heb. *zevadhyâhû, Jehovah has bestowed*). 1. A descendant of Benjamin through Beriah (I Chron. 8:15).

2. Another Benjamite descending from the line of Elpaal (I Chron. 8:17).

3. A Benjamite who joined David at Ziklag to assist him in his defense from Saul. He used bows and arrows as well as stones and was just as adept with his left as with his right hand. He descended through Jeroham of Gedor (I Chron. 12:1-7).

4. One of the Korahite door keepers of David's time, son of Meshelemiah (I Chron. 26:2).

5. One of the officers of David's army, son of Joab's brother, Asahel (I Chron. 27:7).

6. A Levite sent by King Jehoshaphat to teach the law to the residents of Judah (II Chron. 17:8).

7. Ishmael's son who was head of the house of Judah in all matters that pertained to King Jehoshaphat (II Chron. 19:11).

8. One of those who returned with Ezra from Babylon to Jerusalem with 80 men. He was the son of Michael (Ezra 8:8).

9. A priest who had married a foreign wife after the return from the Babylonian captivity. He was a son of Immer (Ezra 10:20).

ZEBAH (zē'bà, Heb. *zevah, sacrifice*), one of the two kings of Midian whom Gideon overthrew, the other being Zalmunna (Judg. 8:10,12; Ps. 83: 11). The Ephraimites had destroyed the large majority of the Midianites, 120,000 warriors (Judg. 8:10), but these two kings escaped. Gideon captured them and completely routed the rest. Having heard their personal confession that they had killed some of the Israelites (Judg. 8:18-19), he ordered them slain. The son to whom this command was given, being but a youth, refused, and when these kings asked Gideon to kill them, he did so (Judg. 8:19-21).

ZEBAIM (zē-bā'ĭm, Heb. *tsebayim, gazelles*), the native dwelling place of Solomon's slaves, "sons of Pochereth" who returned with Zerubbabel (Ezra 2:57; Neh. 7:59).

ZEBEDEE (zĕb'ĕ-dē, Gr. *Zebedaíos*, meaning uncertain), a fisherman on the Sea of Galilee (Mark 1:20), the father of James and John (Matt. 4:21; Mark 1:19). He was the husband of Salome and in all probability lived in the vicinity of Bethsaida (Matt. 27:56; Mark 15:40). Because of Mark's reference to his hired servants, one would judge him to be a man of means and influence (Mark 1:20). Our only glimpse of him in the Bible is with his sons in their boat mending their nets (Matt. 4:21,22; Mark 1:19-20).

ZEBINA (zē-bī'nà, Heb. *zevîna', purchased*), a descendant of Nebo who put away his strange wife after the captivity (Ezra 10:43).

ZEBOIIM, ZEBOIM (zē-boi'ĭm, zēbō'ĭm, Heb. *tsevō'îm, gazelles, hyena*). 1. One of the five cities in the vale of Siddim that God destroyed with Sodom and Gomorrah (Gen. 10:19; 14:2,8; Deut. 29:23; Hos. 11:8).

2. A ravine in Benjamin not far from Michmash (I Sam. 13:18; Neh. 11:34).

ZEBOIM, VALLEY OF (zē-bō'ĭm, Heb. *tsevō'îm, hyena*), see under ZEBOIIM, No. 2.

ZEBUDAH (zē-bū'dà, Heb. *zevûdhâh, given*), Josiah's wife, the daughter of Pedaiah, the mother of Jehoiakim the king (II Kings 23:36).

ZEBUL (zē'bŭl, Heb. *zevul, dwelling*), one who, under Abimelech, ruled the city of Shechem (Judg. 9:28,30,38). He aided in the overthrow of the enemy led by Gaal and acted as adviser to Abimelech in behalf of the affairs of Shechem.

ZEBULONITE (See Zebulun)

ZEBULUN (zĕb'ū-lŭn, Heb. *zevûlûn, habitation*). 1. The sixth and last son that Leah produced through Jacob, her tenth, was named Zebulun (Gen. 30:19-20). Three sons were born to him in the land of his birth (Gen. 46:14). Aside from this, little is recorded in the Scripture of his personal history.

2. One of the 12 tribes of Israel springing from Zebulun. When God asked Moses to number the able-bodied men at Sinai, the tribe of Zebulun had 57,400 (Num. 1:31). The place assigned to this tribe at this period was on the E side of the tabernacle with the standard of Judah (Num. 2:7). While the exact boundaries of Zebulun's territory are unknown, its portion lay between the Sea of Galilee and the Mediterranean. This area included many points at which Christ later carried on His ministry, and Matthew records that He thus fulfilled the ancient prophecy of Isaiah (Isa. 9:1-2; Matt. 4:12-16).

3. The city of Zebulun was located in the tribe of Asher between Bethdagon and the valley of Jiphthahel (Josh. 19:27).

ZEBULUNITE (See Zebulun)

ZECHARIAH (zĕk'à-rī'à, Heb. *zekharyâhû, Jehovah remembers*). 1. A Reubenite chief (I Chron. 5:7).

2. A Korhite, son of Meshelemiah who is described as "a porter of the door of the tabernacle of the congregation" (I Chron. 9:21), and as "a wise counsellor" (I Chron. 26:2,14).

3. A Benjamite, son of Jehiel, brother of Kish (I Chron. 9:37).

4. A Levitical doorkeeper in the time of David (I Chron. 15:17-18) appointed to play with psalteries (I Chron. 15:20; 16:5).

5. One of the Davidic priests who was used as a trumpeter to help in bringing the ark from the house of Obededom back to Jerusalem (I Chron. 15:24).

6. A Levite from Uzziel, son of Isshiah (I Chron. 24:25).

7. A Merarite in David's day, son of Hosah (I Chron. 26:11).

8. A Manassite in the time of David. He was the chief of his tribe and the father of Iddo (I Chron. 27:21).

9. One of the princes whom Jehoshaphat sent to teach in the cities of Judah (II Chron. 17:7).

10. The father of the Prophet Jahaziel, son of Benaiah (II Chron. 20:14).

11. The third son of Jehoshaphat whom Jehoram killed (II Chron. 21:2-4).

12. A son of Jehoiada, the high priest, who lived in the days of King Joash of Judah. Acting in some official capacity, he sought to check the rising tide of idolatry. A conspiracy was formed against him and, on the king's orders, he was stoned (II Chron. 24:20-22).

13. A prophet whose good influence on King Uzziah was outstanding (II Chron. 26:5).

14. The father of Abijah. Perhaps "Abijah" should be "Abi," thus making him Hezekiah's grandfather through Abi, Hezekiah's mother (II Chron. 29:1).

15. A Levite, the son of Asaph, who in King Hezekiah's day assisted in the purification of the temple (II Chron. 29:13).

16. A Kohathite, from among the Levites, who was one of the overseers who faithfully assisted in the repair of the temple in the days of King Josiah (II Chron. 34:12).

17. One of the temple rulers in the time of King Josiah (II Chron. 35:8).

18. One "of the sons of Parosh" who with 150 men returned to Jerusalem with Ezra (Ezra 8:3).

19. The son of Bebai who returned with Ezra (Ezra 8:11).

20. One of those who stood by Ezra as he read the law to the people (Neh. 8:4); a chief whom he had summoned by the river Ahava, and with whom he entered into counsel (Ezra 8:15-16).

21. A son of Elam who at Ezra's suggestion, divorced his Gentile wife (Ezra 10:26).

22. One from the tribe of Judah, son of Amariah, who dwelt in Jerusalem (Neh. 11:4).

23. "The son of the Shilonite" dwelling at Jerusalem (Neh. 11:5).

24. The son of Pashhur, who with others aided in the work at Jerusalem after the captivity (Neh. 11:12).

25. Son of Iddo, one of the priests in the days of Joiakim (Neh. 12:8,16). This man may possibly be identical with the author of the book of Zechariah mentioned in both Ezra 5:1 and in 6:14.

26. A priest, the son of Jonathan, one of the trumpeters at the dedication of the wall at Jerusalem under the leadership of Ezra and Nehemiah (Neh. 12:35,41).

27. The son of Jeberechiah, contemporary of Isaiah. He was found faithful in the ministry of recording (Isa. 8:1-2).

28. The next to the last of the 12 minor prophets. He came from a line of priests, being the son of Berechiah and grandson of Iddo (Zech. 1:1). He was a prophet as well as a priest (Zech. 1:7). He returned from the Babylonian captivity to Jerusalem under the leadership of Zerubbabel. It was during the eighth month of the second year of the Persian king, Darius, that he began his prophetic ministry (Zech. 1:1). He was contemporary with Haggai, beginning his ministry just two months after the latter prophet.

ZECHARIAH, BOOK OF. 1. Historical Background. Zechariah was the grandson of Iddo, the head of one of the priestly families that returned from the Exile (Neh. 12:4,16). Twenty years after the return, the temple still lay a blackened ruin, and the discouraged people did not see how it could be restored. At this critical moment God raised up the prophets Haggai and Zechariah to encourage the Jews to rebuild the temple. The prophecies of the two men were delivered almost at the same time. Haggai appeared first, in August 520 B.C., and within a month after his appeal

was made the foundation of the temple was laid. Soon after, Zechariah uttered his first prophecy (Zech. 1:1-6). Haggai finished his recorded prophecies the same year. The following year Zechariah gave a message consisting of eight symbolic visions, with an appendix (1:7-6:15). Two years later he gave a third message in answer to an inquiry by the men of Bethel regarding the observance of a fast. The two prophecies found in chapters 9-14 are not dated, and were probably given at a much later period.

2. Contents. I. Chapters 1-8. Messages delivered on three separate occasions.

A. 1:1-6. A general introduction.

B. A series of eight symbolic night-visions, followed by a coronation scene. 1:7-6:15. These visions were intended to encourage the Israelites to complete the temple.

1. The horsemen among the myrtle trees. They patrol the earth for the Lord and bring Him tidings from all parts of the earth. 1:8-17. The purpose of the vision is to assure the Israelites of God's special care for and interest in them.

2. The four horns and the four smiths (1:18-21), teaching that Israel's enemies are now destroyed and there is no longer any opposition to the building of God's house.

3. The man with a measuring line (chap. 2), teaching that Jerusalem will expand till it outgrows its walls, and God will be its best defense.

4. Joshua, the high priest, clad in filthy garments which represent the sins of himself and the people is cleansed and given charge of the temple. He is a type of the Messiah-Branch to come who will take away all iniquity. Chap. 3.

5. A seven-branched candlestick fed by two olive trees, teaching that the people of God will receive God's grace through their spiritual and temporal leaders, through whose efforts the prosperity of the nation will be accomplished. Chap. 4.

6. A flying roll (5:1-4), teaching that the land shall be purified from wickedness when the temple is built and God's law taught.

7. A woman (typifying the besetting sins of Israel) is carried off in an ephah-measure to the land of Babylon (5:5-11), teaching that God not only forgives the sins of His people, but carries them away from their land.

8. Four war-chariots go forth to protect God's people (6:1-8), teaching God's protective providence.

These visions are followed by a scene in which a party of Jews have just come from Babylon with silver and gold for the temple. Zechariah is instructed to take part of it and make a crown for the high priest, a type of the Messiah-Branch who is to be both Priest and King to His people.

C. Chapters 7 and 8 were spoken two years later than the series of visions described above, and represent Zechariah's answer to questions put to him by certain visitors as to whether the fasts observed in memory of the destruction of Jerusalem should still be kept. The reply is No; for God demands not fasts, but observance of moral laws. God has come to dwell with His people; and even the heathen will desire to worship God in Jerusalem.

II. Chapters 9-14. This is made up of two distinct prophecies, without dates.

A. Chaps. 9-11. God will visit the nations in judgment and His people in mercy. The Prince of Peace will come and confound the evil shepherds, but He will be rejected by the flock, and they will consequently again experience suffering.

B. Chaps. 12-14. A prophecy describing the victories of the new age and the coming day of the Lord. Three apocalyptic pictures are presented. 1. Jerusalem will be saved from a siege by her enemies by the intervention of Jehovah. 2. A remnant of Israel shall be saved. 3. The nations will come to Jerusalem to share in the joyous Feast of Tabernacles, and all will enjoy the blessings of God's kingdom.

3. Unity of the Book. Many scholars hold that chapters 9-14 are not the work of Zechariah and therefore are not a part of his prophecy. Some suggest a pre-Exilic date; others, a post-Zecharian, as late as 160 B.C. The main arguments against Zechariah's authorship are the difference in atmosphere between 1-8 and 9-14, the reference to Greece as an important power in 9:13, and the supposed derogatory reference to prophecy in chap. 13. The first objection may be answered by the likelihood that the two sections of the prophecy were given at widely-separated times — the second when Zechariah was an old man; the second, by the realization that Greece is mentioned long before the time of Zechariah in Isaiah 66:19 and Ezekiel 27:13,19, and in Zechariah's time was a source of trouble to Persia; and the third, by the realization that it would be impossible for a prophet to belittle prophecy. According to Jewish tradition, these prophecies were written by Zechariah himself, and this is corroborated by internal evidence. It is difficult to see how the makers of the OT canon added these chapters to Zechariah's work if he had nothing to do with them. S.B.

ZEDAD (zē'dăd, Heb. *tsedhādhâh, a siding*), a city located on the ideal northern boundary of Palestine (Num. 34:8; Ezek. 47:15).

ZEDEKIAH (zĕd'ē-kī'à, Heb. *tsidhqîyāhû, Jehovah is righteous*). 1. The son of Chanaanah, the leader and voice for the 400 prophets whom Ahab consulted to learn the outcome of his proposed expedition against Ramoth-gilead. In reply to Ahab's question, Zedekiah said that Ahab would be successful in winning a victory over the Syrians. Apparently these were all false prophets, judging from the question raised by Jehoshaphat: "Is there not here a prophet of the Lord besides . . .?" (I Kings 22:7). When the true prophet was finally called and asked as to the outcome of this planned battle, he revealed the truth and was consequently struck by Zedekiah (I Kings 22:19-24; II Chron. 18:10).

2. The last king of Judah, son of Josiah and Hamutal (II Kings 24:18). Because of the wickedness of Judah, God finally brought on the predicted Babylonian captivity. Nebuchadnezzar came to Jerusalem, took Judah's king, Jehoiachin, to Babylon and made Mattaniah, whose name he changed to Zedekiah, king in his stead. Having taken away the men of influence from Judah, he felt the remaining Jews would be easily subdued (Ezek. 17:11-14). Zedekiah, however, rebelled against the king of Babylon, and as a result, he was taken by Nebuchadnezzar and bound. His sons were killed before his eyes and his own eyes put out. He was then taken to Babylon where he died (II Kings 24,25). Because of his evil he was permitted only 11 years of reign, many details of which are given in Jeremiah chaps. 34-37.

3. The son of Jeconiah (I Chron. 3:16).

4. The son of Maaseiah. He was a false prophet who carried on his ruinous work among those who had been deported to Babylon. He was singled out by Jeremiah and publicly denounced for having prophesied lies. His death by being "roasted in

the fire" was foretold by Jeremiah as a warning to the rest (Jer. 29:21-23).

5. The son of Hananiah. He was a prince of Israel in the reign of Jehoiakim (Jer. 36:12).

6. A high official who sealed the renewed covenant (Neh. 10:1).

ZEEB (zē'ĕb, Heb. *ze'ev, wolf*), one of the two princes of Midian slain by Gideon's men at a winepress named for him (Judg. 7:25ff).

ZELAH (zē'là, Heb. *tsēla'*), a town in Benjamin probably close to Jerusalem (Josh. 18:28). Here David reinterred the bones of Saul and Jonathan in the family sepulchre which had belonged to Kish (II Sam. 21:14). "Zela" (ASV) is closer to the Hebrew.

ZELEK (zē'lĕk, Heb. *tseleq, a fissure*), an Ammonite who served in David's inner circle of mighty men (II Sam. 23:37; I Chron. 11:39).

ZELOPHEHAD (zē-lō'fē-hăd, Heb. *tselophādh*, meaning unknown), a Manassite who died in the wilderness leaving five daughters but no sons; and in the division of the land, they begged a share in the inheritance (Num. 27:1-11). This Jehovah granted, and when their tribesmen feared that their property might be alienated from the tribe by marriage (Num. 36:1-12) he commanded that they should marry only within their tribe, and this became a general law regarding heiresses.

ZELOTES (See Zealot)

ZELZAH (zĕl'zà, Heb. *tseltsah*), a town in the southern border of Benjamin near Rachel's tomb (Gen. 35:19,20; 48:7; I Sam. 10:2).

ZEMARAIM (zĕm'à-rā'ĭm, Heb. *tsemārayim*). 1. An ancient town allotted to the tribe of Benjamin, about four miles N of Jericho in the Arabah, and long since merely a ruin (Josh. 18:22).

2. A mountain in the hill country of Ephraim upon which King Abijah stood and rebuked Jeroboam and Israel for their rebellion against Judah and for their idolatry (II Chron. 13:4ff). Though Jeroboam's army was twice the size of Abijah's, God gave the victory.

ZEMARITES (zĕm'à-rīts, Heb. *ha-tsemārî*), a tribe of Canaanites mentioned in the "table of the nations" (Gen. 10:18) in the Hamite list between the Arvadites and the Hamathites. The site was probably modern Sumra, on the coast between Arvad and Tripolis.

ZEMIRA (zē-mī'rà, Heb. *zemîrâh*), a grandson of Benjamin through his son Becher (I Chron. 7:8).

ZENAN (zē'năn, Heb. *tsenān, tsa'ănān*), a place in the lowland of Judah (Josh. 15:37), the same as Zaanan *q.v.* See Micah 1:11.

ZENAS (zē'nàs, Gr. *Zenás*), a Christian lawyer in Crete whom Paul asked to be sent to him, with Apollos, in Nicopolis (Titus 3:13).

ZEPHANIAH (zĕf'à-nī'à, Heb. *tsephanyâh, hidden of Jehovah*). 1. An ancestor of the prophet Samuel (I Chron. 6:36).

2. Author of the book of Zephaniah and very probably related to the kings of Judah as follows (Zeph. 1:1): Amariah and King Manasseh were brothers, Gedaliah and King Amon were cousins, Cushi and King Josiah were second cousins, and Zephaniah was third cousin of the three kings Jehoahaz, Jehoiakim and Zechariah; thus putting the prophet into familiar relationship with the court, to which his message seems to be specially directed (e.g. 1:8). His principal work seems to have been early in Josiah's reign, like that of his contemporaries Nahum and Habakkuk and before the greater prophecies of his other contemporary, Jeremiah.

3. A priest, son of Maaseiah, whom Zedekiah sent to inquire of Jeremiah (II Kings 25:18-21; Jer. 21:1). The Babylonian captain of the guard took him to Riblah where Nebuchadnezzar had him slain.

4. Father of a Josiah in the days of Darius to whom God sent the Prophet Zechariah with a message of comfort and encouragement (Zech. 6:9-15).

ZEPHANIAH, BOOK OF, the ninth of the Minor Prophets and the last before the Seventy Years' Captivity of Judah. Zephaniah's ministry was probably aided by his social position, as he was very probably related to the kings of the day, and he certainly was fearless in his denunciation of the evils of his time. He was hopeful in his outlook, for though he dreaded the horrors of the Day of Jehovah which he saw fast approaching, he could look beyond and rejoice in the Restoration message. The prophecy is dated in 1:1 in the reign of Josiah, that is, between 639 and 608 B.C.

The book divides naturally into 14 paragraphs (12 in ASV) as follows: 1. Title, author, and date (1:1). 2. Apostates to be destroyed (1:2-6), including the idolatrous priests. 3. Announcement of the great "Day of Jehovah" (1:7-13). 4. The Day of Jehovah described (1:14-18). 5. A plea for repentance (2:1-3). 6. Philistia to be destroyed (2:4,5). 7. The Philistine coast will some day belong to Israel (2:6,7). 8. Moab and the Ammonites denounced for their pride (2:8-11). 9. Ruin predicted from Ethiopia to Assyria (2:12-15). 10. Woe also to rebellious Jerusalem (3:1-7). 11. The judgment of the nations (3:8). 12. Restoration of Israel promised (3:9-11). 13. A remnant to be blessed (3:12,13). 14. Jehovah in the midst of Zion (3:14-20).   A.B.F.

ZEPHATH (zē'făth, Heb. *tephath, watch-tower*), a Canaanite city about 22 miles SW of the southern end of the Dead Sea, in the territory later occupied by the tribe of Simeon. It was utterly destroyed in the time of the Conquest by the tribes of Judah and Simeon and renamed "Hormah," i.e. "devoted to God" in the sense of being laid waste (Judg. 1:17). Cf. "Hormah" in Numbers 21:3 for the use of the word.

ZEPHATHAH (zěf'à-thà, Heb. *tsephāthâh, watch-tower*), a valley near Mareshah in the western part of Judah, where King Asa met the hosts of Zerah the Ethiopian, and where, in answer to prayer, God gave a great victory to Judah (II Chron. 14:9-12).

ZEPHI (zē'fī, Heb. *tsephî, watchtower*), a grandson of Esau through Eliphaz (I Chron. 1:36); in Genesis 36:11,15, "Zepho."

ZEPHO (See Zephi)

ZEPHON (zē'fŏn, Heb. *tsephôn, watching*), a Gadite from whom the family of Zephonites descended (Num. 26:15). In Genesis 46:16 he is called "Ziphion."

ZEPHONITES (See Zepho)

ZER (zêr, Heb. *tsēr*), a fenced city, NW of the Lake of Galilee, given in Joshua's time to the tribe of Naphtali (Josh. 19:35).

ZERAH (zē'rà, Heb. *zerah, rising*). 1. One of twin sons born to Judah (Gen. 38:30). Of him came the Zarhite family of Numbers 26:20 (ASV "Zerahites"). He was great-grandfather of Achan, "the Troubler of Israel" (Josh. 7).

2. A cousin of the preceding; son of Simeon (Num. 26:13) and head of another Zarhite family.

3. A Gershonite Levite of the sixth generation (I Chron. 6:21).

4. Another Gershonite Levite, but later (I Chron. 6:41).

5. A grandson of Esau through Reuel, son of Basemath (Gen. 36:13). He was a chief (Gen. 36:17 in KJV "duke").

6. Father of Jobab, the second of the early kings of Edom (Gen. 36:33). He lived at Bozrah several miles S of the Dead Sea.

7. A king of Ethiopia (II Chron. 14:9) in the latter part of the tenth century B.C. who invaded Judah with an immense army during the reign of Asa, but Asa prayed and the Lord smote the Ethiopians and gave Asa victory.

ZERAHIAH (zěr-à-hī'à, Heb. *zerahyâh, Jehovah is risen*). 1. A Levite in the ancestry of Ezra (I Chron. 6:6,51).

2. A leader of 200 men who returned with Ezra (Ezra 8:4).

ZERED (zē'rĕd, Heb. *zeredh*), a valley running north-westward on the border between Moab and Edom and debouching at the southern end of the Dead Sea; also the brook which follows the valley. A camping place of Israel at the end of their long wanderings (Num. 21:12, KJV Zared; Deut. 2:13, 14). In Isaiah 15:7 it is called "the brook of the willows"; in Amos 6:14 the "river of the wilderness."

ZEREDA (zěr-ē'dà, Heb. *tserēdhah*), the birthplace of Jeroboam of Ephraim (I Kings 11:26). ASV properly has Zeredah. Metal work for the temple was cast there. It was located somewhere in the Jordan valley, but the exact site is unknown.

ZEREDATHAH (See Zarthan)

ZERERATH (zěr'ĕ-răth, Heb. *tserērāthâh*), a part of the valley of Jezreel to which the Midianites fled from Gideon (Judg. 7:22). ASV has "Zererah," but some MSS of the Hebrew have "Zeredah" which is more probably correct.

ZERESH (zē'rĕsh, Heb. *zeresh, golden*), the wife of Haman the Agagite, the enemy of the Jews, who advised him to build a gallows for Mordecai, but later saw her error (Esth. 5:10,14; 6:13). Her name is Persian.

ZERETH (zē'rĕth, Heb. *tsereth, splendor* (?)), an early descendant of Judah through Helah, second wife of Ashhur (I Chron. 4:7).

ZERI (zē'rī, Heb. *tserî*), one of the sons of Jeduthun in the days of David, who with harp and voice praised the Lord (I Chron. 25:3); perhaps the same as Izri, vs. 11.

ZEROR (zē'rôr, Heb. *tserôr*), a Benjamite, great-grandfather of King Saul (I Sam. 9:1).

ZERQA (zêr'kà), a wadi running westward to the Jordan and corresponding to the ancient river Jabbok. Also "Zerka." See JABBOK.

ZERUAH (zê-rōō'à, Heb. *tserû'âh, leprous*), the widow of Nebat, father of Jeroboam of Israel (I Kings 11:26).

ZERUBBABEL (zě-rŭb'à-běl, Heb. *zerubbāvel, shoot of Babylon*), the son of Shealtiel and the grandson of King Jehoiachin (Ezra 3:2; Hag. 1:1; Matt. 1:12). In I Chronicles 3:19 he is declared to be the son of Pedaiah, Shealtiel's brother. The explanation for this apparent discrepancy is very likely that Shealtiel died without issue; and either his nephew was his legal heir and therefore called his son (Exod. 2:10) or else Pedaiah married his brother's widow and thus Zerubbabel became Shealtiel's son by levirate law (Deut. 25:5-10). He was heir to the throne of Judah (I Chron. 3:17-19) and is listed in the genealogy of our Lord (Matt. 1:13; Luke 3:27).

When Cyrus allowed the Jews to return to their own land, he appointed Zerubbabel governor of the colony (Ezra 1:8,11; 5:14). Joshua the high priest was the religious leader. When they reached Jerusalem, they first set up the altar of burnt offerings, then they proceeded to lay the foundation of the new temple. Soon, however, opposition arose. The adversaries of the Jews made an apparently friendly offer of assistance (Ezra 4), but Zerubbabel and the other leaders rebuffed them; whereupon they wrote to the king and succeeded in stopping the work during the reigns of Cambyses (the "Ahasuerus" of Ezra 4:6) and the pseudo-Smerdis (the "Artaxerxes" of Ezra 4:7ff). In 520 B.C. the work was resumed and completed four years later. A great celebration was held at the dedication of the new temple (Zech. 6:16-22), and so far as the record tells, the work of Zerubbabel was complete. It is not known when he died.

ZERUIAH (zêr'ōō-ī'à, Heb. *tserûyâh*), sister of David and mother of Joab, Abishai and Asahel. She was probably not a daughter of Jesse, but a daughter of David's mother by an earlier marriage with Nahash (II Sam. 17:25).

ZETHAM (zē'thăm, Heb. *zethām, olive tree*), a Gershonite Levite in David's time. He was son of Ladan (I Chron. 23:8), or, according to 26:22, his grandson through Jehieli. KJV calls his father "Laadan."

ZETHAN (zē'thăn, Heb. *zethān, olive tree*), a Benjamite, son of Jediael (I Chron. 7:10).

ZETHAR (zē'thàr, Heb. *zēthar*), one of the seven chamberlains of Xerxes (Ahasuerus, Esth. 1:10).

ZEUS (zūs, Gr. *Zeús*), the chief of the Olympian gods, corresponding to the Roman Jupiter (see Acts 14:12,13; 19:35). His ancestry was as follows: Chaos, a heterogenous mass containing all the seeds of nature produced Gaea (Earth) who in turn produced Uranus (Heaven) and married him. Among their numerous progeny were Cronos (Saturn) who married his sister Rhea and they became "Father and mother of the gods." Chief of their children was Zeus, head of the Olympian gods and by various marriages and illicit unions the father of most of the greater gods of the Greek pantheon. One of the crowning insults which Antiochus Epiphanes, king of Syria 176-164 B.C., offered to the Jews was his dedication of the temple at Jerusalem to Zeus (II Macc. 6). A.B.F.

ZIA (zī'à, Heb. *zia'*), an early Gadite (I Chron. 5:13).

ZIBA (zī'bà, Heb. *tsîvā', tsivā', a plant*), a servant or slave of King Saul (II Sam. 9:2). He had 15 sons and 20 servants. David, desiring to show kindness to the house of his departed friend, Jonathan, appointed Ziba to work for Mephibosheth, Jonathan's crippled son. When David was in trouble, Ziba offered him service (II Sam. 19), but ascribed treachery to his master Mephibosheth. David thereupon gave Ziba his master's property; but later (19: 24-30) when Mephibosheth declared his innocence, David altered the decree.

ZIBEON (zĭb'ē-ŭn, Heb. *tsiv'ôn, hyena*), a Hivite, grandfather of Oholibama, a wife of Esau (Gen. 36:2,14). The text should probably be amended to "Horite."

ZIBIA (zĭb'ĭ-à, Heb. *tsivyā', gazelle*), an early descendant of Benjamin (I Chron. 8:9).

ZIBIAH (zĭb'ĭ-à, Heb. *tsivyâh, gazelle*), a woman of Beersheba who married King Ahaziah and was mother of Joash, king of Judah (II Kings 12:1; II Chron. 24:1).

ZIDDIM (zĭd'ĭm, Heb. *ha-tsiddîm, sides*), a fortified city in Naphtali (Josh. 19:35), perhaps less than one-half mile N of the Horns of Hattin, W of the Sea of Galilee.

ZIDKIJAH (See Zedekiah)

ZIDON (zī'dŏn, Heb. *tsîdhôn, a fishery*), the ancient Phoenician city in the Lebanon. In the KJV usually Zidon in the OT, and always Sidon in the NT. It was a Canaanite city (Gen. 10:15,19), 22 miles N of Tyre. Homer often mentions it, but never Tyre. It was near Zebulun (Gen. 49:13); and Asher reached it (Josh. 19:28), although the Asherites never expelled its inhabitants (Judg. 1:31). Baal and Ashtoreth, a goddess of fertility, were its chief gods (I Kings 11:5,33; II Kings 23:13). The father of Jezebel was a king of Sidon (I Kings 16: 31). It has a checkered history, times of great prosperity alternating with periods when the city was under foreign control; and more than once it was destroyed. In 64 B.C. it passed to the Romans. People from Tyre came to hear Jesus preach in Galilee (Mark 3:8; Luke 6:17), and once Jesus visited the city (Matt. 15:21; Mark 7:24,31). Paul stopped off there (Acts 27:3). One of the most ancient of cities, it still survives in the modern Saida, on the NW slope of a small promontory jutting out into the sea.   S.B.

Artist's restoration of the great altar of Zeus at Pergamum. The temples of Athena Polias and Augustus are in the background. RTHPL

ZIDONIANS (See Zidon)

ZIF (zĭf, Heb. *ziw*), the second month of the old Hebrew calendar, corresponding to Iyyar in the later Jewish calendar (I Kings 6:1,37).

ZIGGURAT (zĭg′ōō-răt, Assyr-Bab. *zigquratu,* from the verb *zaqaru,* meaning *to be high* or *raised up*; hence the top of a mountain, or a staged tower). A temple tower of the Babylonians, consisting of a lofty structure in the form of a pyramid, built in successive stages, with staircases on the outside, and a shrine at the top. These structures are the most characteristic feature of temple architecture in Mesopotamia, and the locations of more than two dozen are known today. The oldest one known is at Uruk in Mesopotamia. It measured 140 by 150 feet and stood about 30 feet high. At the top was the shrine, 65 feet long, 50 feet wide, and built about a narrow court. It was made of packed clay strengthened with layers of asphalt and unburnt bricks. The ziggurat at Ur was 200 feet long, 150 feet wide, and some 70 feet high. The inside was made of unbaked brick; the outside consisted of about eight feet of baked brick set in bitumen. The Stele of Ur-Nammu is a contemporary record of the building of this ziggurat. The tower of Babel was a ziggurat (Gen. 11:1-9).   S.B.

ZIHA (zī′hà, Heb. *tsîhā′*). 1. Head of a family of temple servants, "Nethinim," who returned to Jerusalem with Zerubbabel (Ezra 2:43; Neh. 7:46).

2. A ruler of the Nethinim in Ophel in the days of Nehemiah (Neh. 11:21).

ZIKLAG (zĭk′lăg, Heb. *tsiqelagh*), a city in the south of Palestine, given to Judah in Joshua's day (Josh. 15:31) but subsequently given to or shared by Simeon (Josh. 19:5). Later it was ruled by the Philistines; Achish, king of Gath, assigned it to David and his men who were fleeing from Saul (I Sam. 27:1-7). During their occupation of the city, David offered to go with Achish against Saul, but the Philistines sent him back, and on reaching Ziklag he found that the Amalekites had raided it, burned it and had carried off the women and children. David recovered his property, returned to Ziklag and from there began to recruit men of Judah to take his side when they would be needed. Later Ziklag became the property of the kings of Judah till the captivity.

ZIKRI (zĭk′rī, Heb. *zikhrî*). 1. A Levite, first cousin of Aaron and Moses (Exod. 6:21).

2. A Benjamite of the family of Shemei or Shema (KJV Shimhi) (I Chron. 8:19, cf. vs. 13, 21).

3. Another Benjamite, son of Shashak (I Chron. 8:23).

4. Still another Benjamite, son of Jeroham (I Chron. 8:27). All these mentioned were heads of "fathers' houses" and so of some renown in their day.

5. A Levite ancestor of Mattaniah who returned from captivity (I Chron. 9:15, but called "Zabdi" in Nehemiah 11:17).

6. A descendant of Eliezer, younger son of Moses, in the days of King David (I Chron. 26:25).

7. The father of Eliezer, ruler of the tribe of Reuben in David's time (I Chron. 27:16).

8. Father of Amasiah, the leader of 200,000 men of valor of Judah in the time of Jehoshaphat (II Chron. 17:16).

9. Father of Elishaphat who covenanted with Jehoiada to put Joash on the throne (II Chron. 23:1).

One of the most famous ziggurats, or temple towers, of the ancient world was the ziggurat at Ur, of which these ruins remain. SHH

10. A mighty man of Ephraim who, in Pekah's war against Judah, killed the son of Ahaz and other leaders (II Chron. 28:7).

11. Father of Joel, the overseer of the Benjamites under Nehemiah (Neh. 11:9).

12. Head of a fathers' house of priests in the days of Nehemiah 12:17, a descendant of Abijah.

ZILLAH (zĭl′à, Heb. *tsillâh, shadow*), one of the two wives of the Cainite Lamech, the first known polygamist; and mother of Tubal-cain the patriarch of all workers in brass and iron (Gen. 4:19-22).

ZILPAH (zĭl′pà, Heb. *zilpâh,* meaning uncertain), handmaid of Leah, given to her by her father Laban, and later through Jacob, the mother of Gad and Asher (Gen. 29:24; 30:9-13).

ZILTHAI (zĭl′thī, Heb. *tsillethay, shadow of Jehovah*). 1. An early Benjamite, and descended from Shema (I Chron. 8:20; in ASV Zillethai).

2. Captain of a thousand of the tribe of Manasseh who joined David at Ziklag (I Chron. 12:20).

ZIMMAH (zĭm′à, Heb. *zimmâh*), a Gershonite Levite (I Chron. 6:20,42,43; and perhaps II Chron. 29:12).

ZIMRAN (zĭm′răn, Heb. *zimrān*), a son of Abraham and Keturah (Gen. 25:2; I Chron. 1:32).

ZIMRI (zĭm′rī, Heb. *zimrî*). 1. A prince of the tribe of Simeon who shamelessly brought a Midianite woman into the camp of Israel to commit adultery with her, even while God was dealing with Israel for its sin in this way (Num. 25:14). Phinehas, grandson of Aaron, slew the two of them.

2. The fifth king of the northern kingdom. He had been captain of half the chariots of his master Elah (I Kings 16:9-20). He assassinated Elah, who was in a drunken condition, and reigned for seven days, when he himself was besieged by Omri, and committed suicide by burning the king's house over himself. His capital was at Tirzah in the hills of Samaria and his "reign" was short, wicked and inglorious.

3. Son of Zerah, and grandson of Judah (I Chron. 2:6), possibly the same as the Zabdi of Joshua 7:1.

4. Son of Jehoaddah or Jarah of the tribe of Benjamin and father of Moza (I Chron. 8:36; 9:42).

5. An unknown tribe in the East (Jer. 25:25), but apparently important because its kings were listed with the kings of Elam and of the Medes.

Jerusalem, as seen from the south across the Valley of Hinnom. © MPS

ZIN (zĭn, Heb. *tsin*), a wilderness the Israelites traversed on their way to Canaan. It was close to the borders of Canaan (Num. 13:21) and included Kadesh-barnea within its bounds (Num. 20:1; 27: 14; 33:36). Edom bordered it on the E, Judah on the SE (Josh. 15:1-3), and the wilderness of Paran on the S. It was not the same as the wilderness of Sin, Zin and Sin being quite different Hebrew words.

ZINA (zī'nà, Heb. *zîzâh*), a Levite of the family of Gershom (I Chron. 23:10). The correct spelling is Zizah, as in verse 11.

ZION (zī'ŭn, Heb. *tsîyôn,* Gr. *Sión,* meaning of word uncertain, but probably *citadel*), one of the hills on which Jerusalem stood. It is first mentioned in the OT as a Jebusite fortress (II Sam. 5:6-9). David captured it and called it the city of David. At this time the citadel stood on the long ridge running S of the temple, although not all scholars are agreed on this. This location is near the only known spring; it is suitable for defense; its size is about that of other fortified towns; archeological remains show that it was inhabited long before David's time; and certain Bible references (I Kings 8:1; II Chron. 5:2; 32:30; 33:14) indicate that this was the original Zion. David brought the Ark to Zion, and the hill henceforth became sacred (II Sam. 6:10-12). When Solomon later removed the Ark to the temple on nearby Mount Moriah, the name Zion was extended to take in the temple (Isa. 8:18; 18:7; 24:23; Joel 3:17; Micah 4:7). Zion came to be used for the whole of Jerusalem (II Kings 19:21; Ps. 48; 69:35; 133:3; Isa. 1:8, etc.). The name is frequently used figuratively for the Jewish Church and polity (Ps. 126:1; 129:5; Isa. 33:14; 34:8; 49:14; 52:8) and for heaven (Heb. 12:22; cf. Rev. 14:1).   S.B.

The so-called Citadel of Zion towering above the Jerusalem city wall. © MPS

Atop the walls, or ramparts, of Zion, adjoining the temple area at Jerusalem. © MPS

ZIOR (zī′ôr, Heb. *tsî′ōr, smallness*), a town in the S of the Promised Land given to Judah in the days of Joshua (Josh. 15:54). It was probably near Hebron.

ZIPH (zĭf, Heb. *zīph,* meaning unknown). 1. A city in the Negeb "toward the border of Edom" given to the tribe of Judah in Joshua's division of the land. Probably about four miles S by E from Hebron.

2. The wilderness named from #1 which was in the southern part of Jeshimon, and where David hid from Saul till the Ziphites betrayed him (I Sam. 23:14-24; 26:1,2).

3. A city in the western part of Judah which Rehoboam fortified (II Chron. 11:8).

4. Possibly the same as #1 though mentioned separately in Joshua 15:55.

5. A Calebite family name (I Chron. 2:42).

6. A son of Jehallelel of the tribe of Judah (I Chron. 4:16). In KJV his father is Jehaleleel.

ZIPHAH (zī′fà, Heb. *zīphâh,* fem. of *ziph*), one of the sons of Jehaleleel (I Chron. 4:16).

ZIPHIMS (See Ziphites)

ZIPHION (See Zephon)

ZIPHITES (zĭf′īts, Heb. *zîphî*), the inhabitants of Ziph, whether the town or the wilderness surrounding it (I Sam. 23:14-23; 26:1-5). Twice, apparently, David, being pursued by King Saul, hid in their vicinity and each time the Ziphites, though of David's tribe, told Saul of his location. They seemed to think it best to support the reigning king than to be kind to David, whom they considered a rebel.

ZIPHRON (zĭf′rŏn, Heb. *ziphrôn*), a place on the ideal northern border of the land of Canaan. It is mentioned between Zedad and Hazar-enan and is probably not far from the city of Homs (Num. 34:9;

ZIPPOR (zĭp′ôr, Heb. *tsippôr, bird*), the father of Balak, king of Moab, and apparently of the Midianites (Num. 22:3,4).

ZIPPORAH (zĭ-pō′rà, Heb. *tsippōrâh, bird,* fem. of *Zippor*), daughter of Jethro or Reuel, the priest of Midian, who became the first wife of Moses (Exod. 2:21). She was the mother of Gershom and of Eliezer (Exod. 18:1-6). Apparently Moses sent her back to her father during the stirring times connected with the Exodus, though she had at least started to Egypt with him (cf. Exod. 4:20; 18:2).

ZITHRI (zĭth′rī, Heb. *sithrî, my protection*), a Kohathite Levite, first cousin of Aaron and Moses (Exod. 6:22). Sithri in ASV.

ZIV (See Zif)

ZIZ (zĭz, Heb. *tsîts, shining*), a cliff mentioned only in II Chronicles 20:16, which stood near the W side of the Red Sea on the way from Engedi to Tekoa. A great horde of Moabites, Ammonites and apparently some Syrians had assembled against Judah at Engedi. When Jehoshaphat heard of their approach, he feared, but being a godly man he prayed, and God through a prophet cheered him and told him where to find the enemy, "at the ascent (KJV "cliff") of Ziz," and that they would not need to fight, "for Jehovah is with you." Trusting the Lord, Jehoshaphat set his musicians *before* the army, and when "they began to sing and to praise," the Lord dispersed the enemy, and the Jews gathered the spoil.

ZIZA (zī′zà, Heb. *zîzā′, abundance*). 1. Son of Shiphi (KJV "Ziphi") a Simeonite who with others, in the days of King Hezekiah, drove out the ancient inhabitants of Gedor, SW of Bethlehem, and took their land for pasture (I Chron. 4:37-41).

2. A son of Rehoboam and brother of Abijah, kings of Judah (II Chron. 11:20). His mother was Maacah (KJV Maachah), the favorite wife of his father.

ZIZAH (zī′zà, Heb. *zîzâh*), second son of Shimei, a leading Gershonite Levite in the days of David (I Chron. 23:11). Called Zina in the preceding verse.

ZOAN (zō′ăn, Heb. *tsō′an*), an ancient Egyptian city, built seven years later than Hebron (Num. 13:22) on the E part of the Delta. The first kings of Dynasty XII made it their capital; the Hyksos fortified it and changed the name to Avaris. When the Hyksos were driven out, the city was neglected, but it was re-established by Sethi I. The Egyptian god Seth had a center of worship there. Moses met the pharaoh at Zoan (Ps. 78:12,43). Isaiah and Ezekiel refer to it as an important city (Isa. 19:11,13; Ezek. 30:14). For a time the Assyrians were in control of it. The Greeks called it "Tanis." Eventually it was superseded by the new city of Alexandria. Extensive ruins survive near the modern village of San (i.e., Zoan), about 18 miles SE of Damietta.

ZOAR (zō′êr, Heb. *tsō′ar, little*), an ancient Canaanite city now probably under the waters of the bay at the SE part of the Dead Sea. Formerly called "Bela" (Gen. 14:2), it was saved from immediate destruction with Sodom and Gomorrah in answer to the prayer of Lot, "is it not a little one?" (Gen. 19:20-22). When Moses stood on Mt. Pisgah to view the Promised Land, Zoar was at the southern limit of his view (Deut. 34:3). In the "Doom of Moab" (Isa. 15) the fleeing Moabites were to go to Zoar (vs. 5) and in its later doom (Jer. 48:34) we read again of Zoar. During the Middle Ages it was an important point between Elath and Jerusalem.

ZOBA, ZOBAH (zō′bà, Heb. *tsôvâh*), a region in central Syria, sometimes under one king (II Sam. 8:3), but in its first occurrence (I Sam. 14:47) we

At Zorah, the home of Samson, overlooking the Plain of Sharon, the area of Samson's exploits. © MPS

read that Saul of Israel fought against the kings of Zobah, which may indicate more than one kingdom, or possibly successive kings. The kings of Zobah were persistent enemies of Israel, not only fighting against Saul, but against David (II Sam. 8) and Solomon. Solomon prevailed against Hamath-zobah (II Chron. 8:3) and we hear no more of this kingdom. The servants of Hadadezer in the days of David had shields of gold (II Sam. 8:3-12) and a large army all of which David captured. Later the Ammonites, in warring against David, hired mercenary troops from Zobah, and these too were badly defeated (II Sam. 10). It lay between Hamath and Damascus. Zoba in Hebrew and KJV.

ZOBEBAH (zō-bē'bȧ, Heb. *tsōvēvâh*), a Judahite name referring either to a place, person, or a clan (I Chron. 4:8).

ZOHAR (zō'hȧr, Heb. *tsōhar*). 1. A noble Hittite, father of Ephron from whom Abraham purchased the field of Machpelah where he buried the body of Sarah in a cave (Gen. 23:8; 25:9).

2. A son of Simeon, second son of Jacob (Gen. 46:10; Exod. 6:15), called "Zerah" in Numbers 26:13 and I Chronicles 4:24.

3. A man of Judah (I Chron. 4:7).

ZOHELETH (zō'hē-lĕth, Heb. *zōheleth, serpent*) a stone beside En-rogel where Adonijah, fourth son of David, and older than Solomon, gathered his conspirators before David's death, slaying sheep

and oxen, in order to make himself king at or before the death of his father. The plot was revealed to David, who caused Solomon to be anointed and thus the plot was foiled (I Kings 1, esp. vs. 9). Its exact site is unknown.

ZOHETH (zō'hĕth, Heb. *zohēth*), son of Ishi, a Judahite (I Chron. 4:20).

ZOPHAH (zō'fȧ, Heb. *tsōphah*), an Asherite, son of Helem (I Chron. 7:35,36).

ZOPHAI (zō'fī, Heb. *tsōphay*), an ancestor of Samuel the prophet (I Chron. 6:26; called "Zuph" in vs. 35).

ZOPHAR (zō'fêr, Heb. *tsōphar*), one of Job's friends who came to comfort him in his affliction (Job 2:11).

ZOPHIM (zō'fīm, Heb. *tsōphîm, watchers*), a field near the top of Pisgah (Num. 23:14). The exact site is unknown.

ZORAH (zō'ra, Heb. *tsorâh*), a city about 15 miles W of Jerusalem on the borders of Judah and Dan (Josh. 15:33; 19:41), the home of Manoah, father of Samson (Judg. 13:2). Samson was buried near there (Judg. 16:31). From Zorah the Danites sent spies to seek a new home for their tribe (Judg. 18:2).

ZORATHITES (zō'ra-thīts, Heb. *tsor'āthî*), the inhabitants of Zorah (I Chron. 2:53 — KJV has Zoreathites; 4:2).

ZOREAH (See Zorah)

ZORITES (zō'rīts, Heb. *tsor'î*). In I Chronicles 2: 54 "Zorathites" should probably be read; otherwise the reference is to a man of some unknown place.

ZOROBABEL (See Zerubbabel)

ZUAR (zū'êr, Heb. *tsû'ār, small*), the father of Nethaneel of the tribe of Issachar, who was a prince of his tribe (Num. 1:8; 2:5).

ZUPH (zŭf, Heb. *tsûph, honeycomb*). 1. An ancestor of the Prophet Samuel. He was a Levite descended from Kohath (I Chron. 6:35). Called "Zophai" in I Chronicles 6:26.

2. A district in Benjamin, near its northern border (I Sam. 9:5). Location unknown.

ZUR (zûr, Heb. *tsûr, rock*). 1. One of the five kings of the Midianites slain by Israel (Num. 25:15; 31:8. Cozbi, his daughter, was slain by Phinehas, grandson of Aaron.

2. An inhabitant of Gibeon in Benjamin; son of Jeiel (I Chron. 8:30,33).

ZURIEL (zū'rĭ-ĕl, Heb. *tsûrî'ēl, whose rock is God*), son of Abihail, prince of the Merarite Levites in the wilderness (Num. 3:35).

ZURISHADDAI (zū'rĭ-shăd'ī, Heb. *tsûrîshadday, whose rock is the Almighty*), father of Shelumiel, head of the tribe of Simeon in the wilderness (Num. 1:6; 2:12; 7:36,41; 10:19).

ZUZIM (zū'zĭm, Heb. *zûzîm*), a primitive race of giants, smitten by Chedorlaomer and his allies at an unknown place called Ham, E of the Jordan, in the days of Abraham (Gen. 14:5); erroneously called "Zuzims" in the KJV.

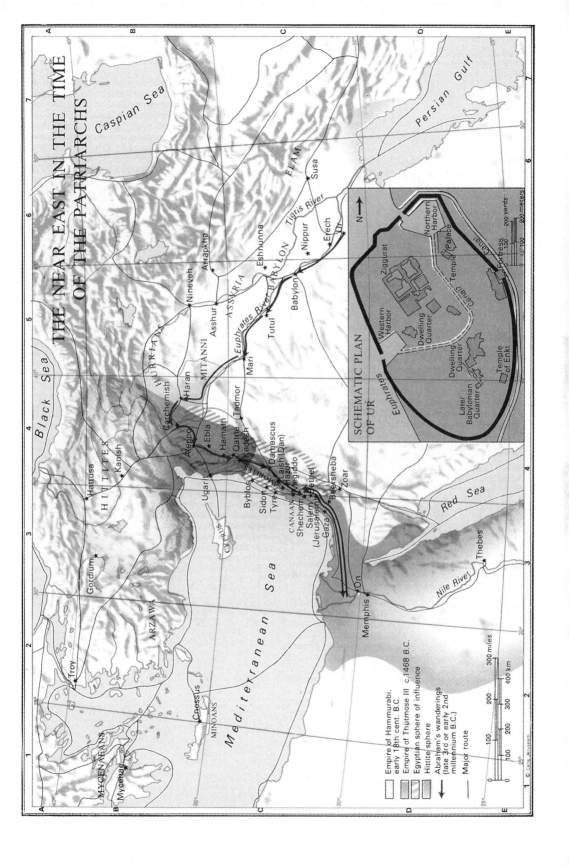

THE NEAR EAST IN THE TIME OF THE PATRIARCHS

Caspian Sea

Persian Gulf

Black Sea

ELAM

Susa

ARRAPKHA

Arrapkha

Nineveh

HURRIANS

ASSYRIA

Asshur

Nippur

Babylon

Erech

MITANNI

Euphrates River

Tutul

Tigris River

Eshnunna

BABYLON

Haran

Mari

Carchemish

Tadmor

Hamath

HITTITES

Kanish

Qatna

Aleppo

Ebla

Kadesh

Damascus

Hattusa

Ugarit

Laish (Dan)

Byblos

Hazor

Sidon

Megiddo

Gordium

Tyre

Shechem

ARZAWA

Bethel

Salem (Jerusalem)

CANAAN

Beersheba

Gaza

Zoar

Troy

On

MYCENAEANS

CYPRUS

Mycenae

MINOANS

Memphis

Mediterranean Sea

Cnossus

Red Sea

Nile River

Thebes

SCHEMATIC PLAN OF UR

N

Euphrates

Ziggurat

Northern Harbor

Palace

Temple

Western Harbor

Dwelling Quarter

Canal

Fortress

Dwelling Quarter

Temple of Enki

Later Babylonian Quarter

100   200 yards

100   200 meters

Empire of Hammurabi, early 18th cent. B.C.

Empire of Thutmose III, c.1468 B.C.

Egyptian sphere of influence

Hittite sphere

Abraham's wanderings (late 3rd or early 2nd millennium B.C.)

Major route

300 miles

400 km

© Carta, Jerusalem

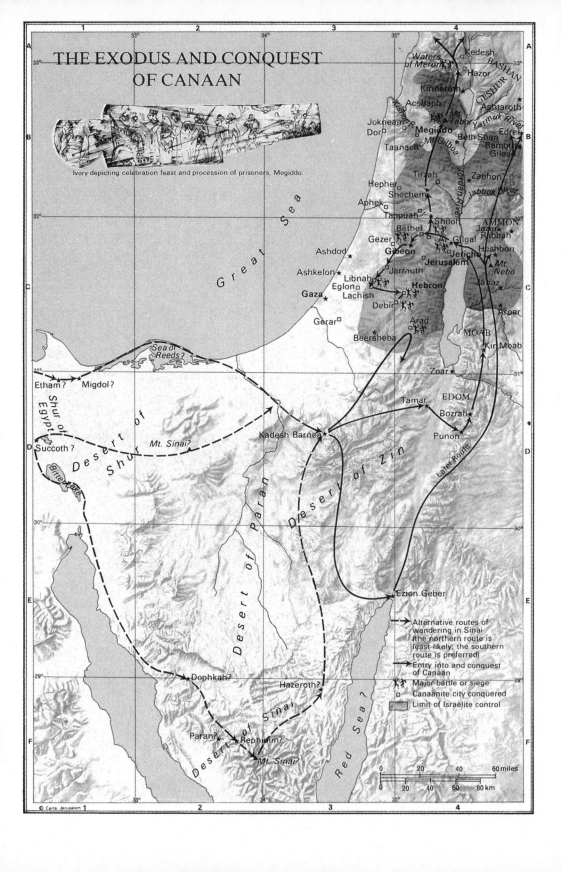

THE EXODUS AND CONQUEST
OF CANAAN

Ivory depicting celebration feast and procession of prisoners, Megiddo.

Great Sea

Waters of Merom
Kedesh
BASHAN
Hazor
Kinnereth
Acshaph
Ashtaroth
GESHUR
Jokneam
Mt. Tabor
Megiddo
Yarmuk River
Edrei
Dor
Mt. Gilboa
Beth Shan
Ramoth
Taanach
Gilead
Tirzah
Zaphon
Hepher
Jabbok River
Shechem
Aphek
Tappuah
Shiloh
AMMON
Bethel
Jazer
Rabbah
Gezer
Ai
Gilgal
Heshbon
Ashdod
Gibeon
Jericho
Ashkelon
Jerusalem
Libnah
Jarmuth
Hebron
Eglon
Gaza
Lachish
Jahaz
Debir
Aroer
Gerar
Arad
MOAB
Beersheba
Kir Moab
Zoar
Tamar
EDOM
Etham?
Migdol?
Bozrah
Shur of Egypt
Punon
Succoth?
Desert of Shur
Mt. Sinai?
Kadesh Barnea
Bitter Lake
Desert of Paran
Desert of Zin
Later Route
Sea of Reeds?
Ezion Geber

Alternative routes of wandering in Sinai (the northern route is least likely; the southern route is preferred)
Entry into and conquest of Canaan
Major battle or siege
Canaanite city conquered
Limit of Israelite control

Dophkah?
Hazeroth?
Desert of Sinai
Paran?
Rephidim?
Mt. Sinai?
Red Sea?

0   20   40   60 miles
0 20 40 60 80 km

© Carta, Jerusalem

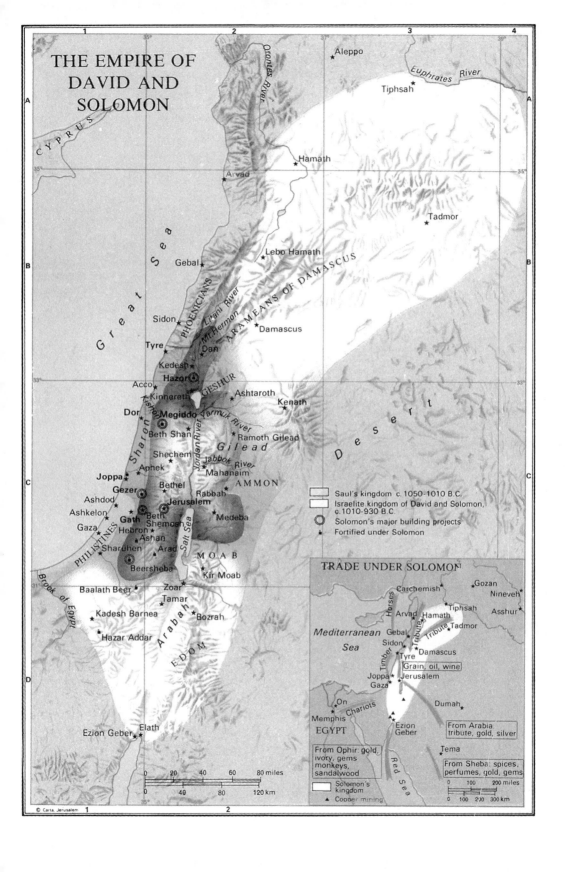

THE EMPIRE OF DAVID AND SOLOMON

CYPRUS

Otrontes River

Aleppo

Euphrates River

Tiphsah

Great Sea

Hamath

Arvad

Tadmor

Lebo Hamath

Gebal

PHOENICIANS

Litani River

Mt. Hermon

ARAMEANS OF DAMASCUS

Sidon

Damascus

Tyre

Dan

Kedesh

Acco

Hazor

GESHUR

Ashtaroth

Kishon River

Kinnereth

Kenath

Dor

Megiddo

Yarmuk River

Beth Shan

Jordan River

Ramoth Gilead

Gilead

Shechem

Jabbok River

Aphek

Mahanaim

Desert

Joppa

Bethel

AMMON

Gezer

Jerusalem

Rabbah

Ashdod

Beth

Medeba

Ashkelon

Gath

Shemesh

Gaza

Hebron

Ashan

PHILISTINES

Sharuhen

Arad

Salt Sea

Beersheba

M O A B

Kir Moab

Baalath Beer

Zoar

Tamar

Brook of Egypt

Kadesh Barnea

Bozrah

Hazar Addar

Arabah

E D O M

Ezion Geber

Elath

- ☐ Saul's kingdom c. 1050-1010 B.C.
- ☐ Israelite kingdom of David and Solomon, c.1010-930 B.C.
- ◎ Solomon's major building projects
- ★ Fortified under Solomon

TRADE UNDER SOLOMON

Carchemish

Gozan

Nineveh

Horses

Arvad

Tiphsah

Asshur

Mediterranean Sea

Hamath

Tadmor

Tribute

Tribute

Gebal

Sidon

Damascus

Timber

Tyre

Grain, oil, wine

Joppa

Jerusalem

Gaza

Dumah

On

Chariots

Memphis

EGYPT

Ezion Geber

From Arabia: tribute, gold, silver

Tema

From Ophir: gold, ivory, gems, monkeys, sandalwood

Red Sea

From Sheba: spices, perfumes, gold, gems

☐ Solomon's kingdom

▲ Copper mining

0   20   40   60   80 miles

0   40   80   120 km

0   100   200 miles

0   100   200   300 km

© Carta, Jerusalem

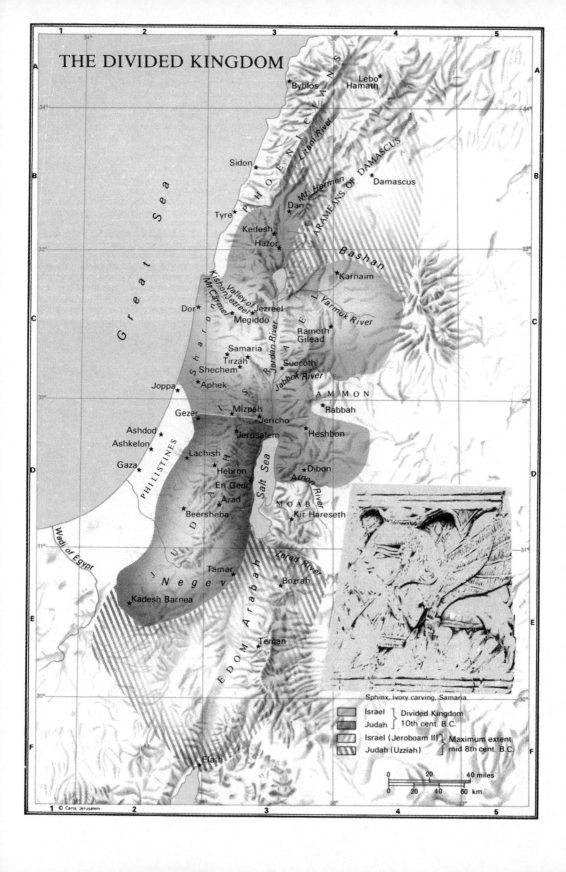

THE DIVIDED KINGDOM

Byblos

Lebo Hamath

PHOENICIANS

Litani River

Sidon

Mt. Hermon

Damascus

ARAMEANS OF DAMASCUS

Tyre

Dan

Kedesh

Hazor

Bashan

Karnaim

Dor

Valley of Jezreel

Mt. Carmel

Kishon River

Jezreel

L. Yarmuk River

Megiddo

Ramoth Gilead

Sharon

Samaria

Jordan River

Succoth

Tirzah

Shechem

Jabbok River

Joppa

Aphek

AMMON

Gezer

Mizpah

Rabbah

Ashdod

Jericho

Ashkelon

Jerusalem

Heshbon

PHILISTINES

Lachish

Gaza

Dibon

Hebron

Salt Sea

Arnon River

En Gedi

JUDAH

Arad

MOAB

Beersheba

Kir Hareseth

Wadi of Egypt

Zered River

Tamar

Bozrah

Negev

Kadesh Barnea

EDOM

Arabah

Teman

Sphinx, ivory carving, Samaria.

	Israel	⎫ Divided Kingdom
	Judah	⎭ 10th cent. B.C.
	Israel (Jeroboam III)	⎫ Maximum extent
	Judah (Uzziah)	⎭ mid 8th cent. B.C.

Elath

0   20   40 miles

0   20   40   60 km

© Carta, Jerusalem

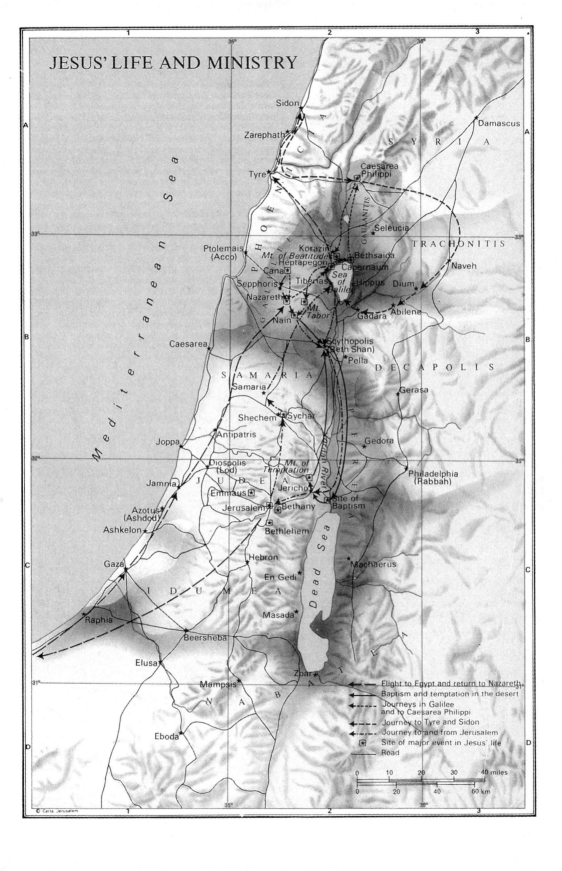

JESUS' LIFE AND MINISTRY

Sidon

Zarephath

Damascus

Tyre

Caesarea
Philippi

Mediterranean Sea

Seleucia

S Y R I A

P H O E N I C I A

G A U L A N I T I S

T R A C H O N I T I S

Ptolemais
(Acco)

Korazin
Mt. of Beatitudes
Heptapegon
Cana
Bethsaida
Capernaum
Sea
of
Galilee
Tiberias
Hippus
Naveh
Dium

G A L I L E E

Sepphoris
Nazareth
Nain
Mt. Tabor
Gadara
Abilene

Caesarea

Scythopolis
(Beth Shan)
Pella

D E C A P O L I S

S A M A R I A

Samaria
Gerasa

Shechem
Sychar

Antipatris
Gedora

Joppa
P E R E A

Diospolis
(Lod)
*Mt. of
Temptation*
Jericho
Philadelphia
(Rabbah)

Jamnia
J U D E A
Emmaus
Jerusalem
Bethany
Site of
Baptism

Azotus
(Ashdod)
Bethlehem

Ashkelon

Gaza
Hebron
Machaerus

I D U M E A
En Gedi

Dead Sea

Raphia
Masada

Beersheba

Elusa

Zoar
Mampsis
N A B A T E A

Eboda

Jordan River

| | 0 | 10 | 20 | 30 | 40 miles |
| | 0 | 20 | 40 | 60 km |

Flight to Egypt and return to Nazareth
Baptism and temptation in the desert
Journeys in Galilee
and to Caesarea Philippi
Journey to Tyre and Sidon
Journey to and from Jerusalem
Site of major event in Jesus' life
Road

© Carta, Jerusalem

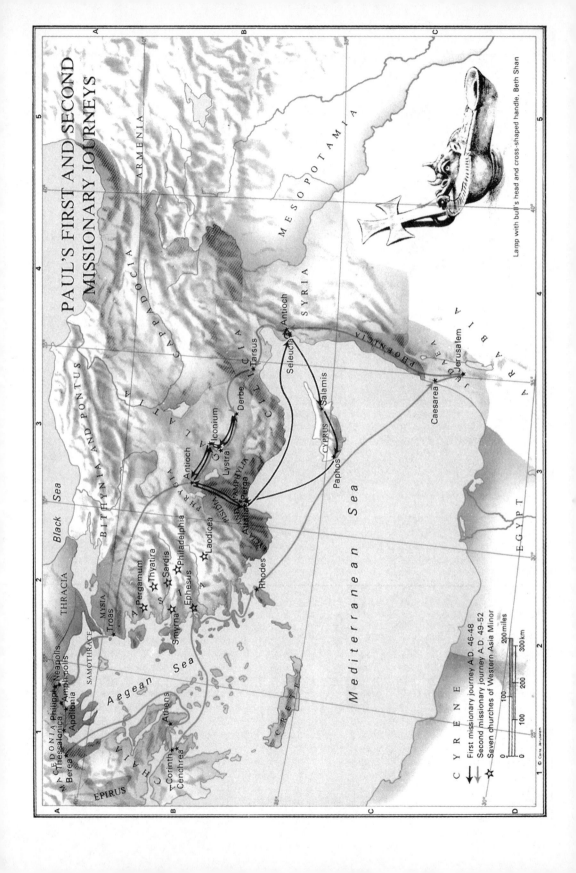

PAUL'S FIRST AND SECOND MISSIONARY JOURNEYS

Lamp with bull's head and cross-shaped handle, Beth Shan

First missionary journey A.D. 46-48
Second missionary journey A.D. 49-52
Seven churches of Western Asia Minor

ARMENIA

CAPPADOCIA

MESOPOTAMIA

SYRIA

Antioch

Seleucia

Tarsus

CILICIA

Salamis

CYPRUS

Paphos

Caesarea

JUDEA

Jerusalem

PHOENICIA

ARABIA

EGYPT

CYRENE

Mediterranean Sea

Derbe

Iconium

Antioch

Lystra

PISIDIA

PAMPHYLIA

Perga

Attalia

Laodicea

Philadelphia

Rhodes

CRETE

Ephesus

Smyrna

Sardis

Thyatira

Pergamum

Troas

MYSIA

SAMOTHRACE

THRACIA

BITHYNIA AND PONTUS

GALATIA

PHRYGIA

Black Sea

Aegean Sea

Athens

Corinth

Cenchrea

ACHAIA

EPIRUS

MACEDONIA

Philippi

Neapolis

Amphipolis

Apollonia

Thessalonica

Berea

0   100   200miles
0   100   200   300km

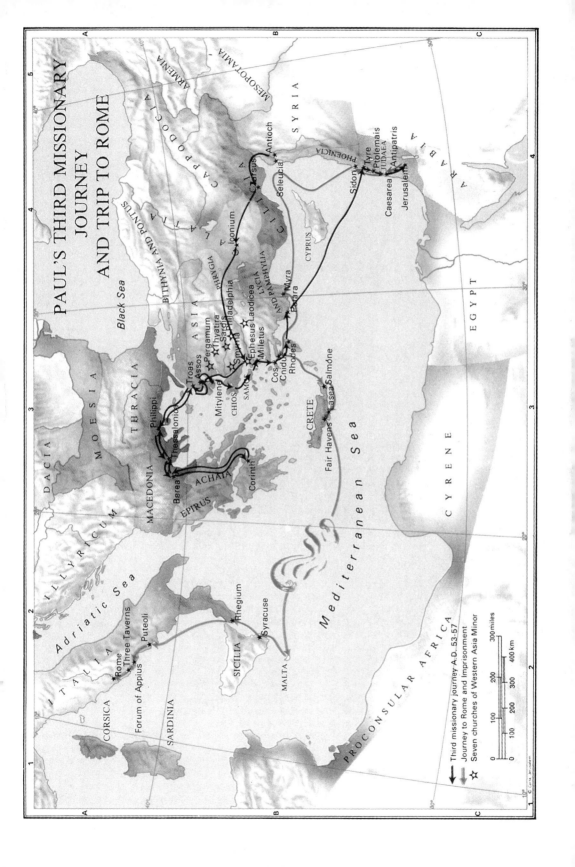

PAUL'S THIRD MISSIONARY
JOURNEY
AND TRIP TO ROME

Black Sea

Mediterranean Sea

Adriatic Sea

ARMENIA

MESOPOTAMIA

CAPPADOCIA

BITHYNIA AND PONTUS

GALATIA

SYRIA

Antioch
Tarsus
Seleucia
CILICIA
PHOENICIA
Sidon
Tyre
Ptolemais
IUDAEA
Caesarea
Antipatris
Jerusalem
ARABIA

CYPRUS

Iconium
PHRYGIA
ASIA
Pergamum
Thyatira
Sardis
Philadelphia
Laodicea
Ephesus
Smyrna
Miletus
LYCIA
AND PAMPHYLIA
Myra
Patara
Cos
Cnidus
Rhodes
SAMOS
CHIOS
Mitylene
Troas
Assos

THRACIA
MOESIA
Philippi
Thessalonica
Berea
MACEDONIA
EPIRUS
ACHAIA
Corinth

CRETE
Lasea Salmone
Fair Havens

DACIA
ILLYRICUM

ITALIA
Rome
Three Taverns
Forum of Appius
Puteoli
CORSICA
SARDINIA
SICILIA
Rhegium
Syracuse
MALTA

CYRENE

EGYPT

PROCONSULAR AFRICA

→ Third missionary journey A.D. 53–57
→ Journey to Rome and Imprisonment
★ Seven churches of Western Asia Minor

300 miles
400 km
0   100   200   300
0   100   200

© Carta, Jerusalem

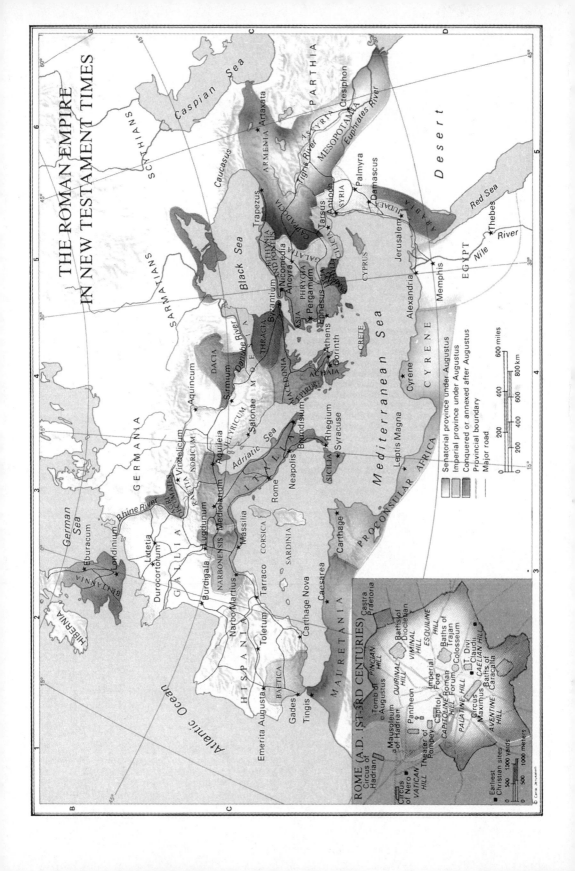

THE ROMAN EMPIRE
IN NEW TESTAMENT TIMES

German Sea

Atlantic Ocean

BRITANNIA

HIBERNIA

Eburacum

Londinium

Durocortorum

Lutetia

Burdigala

Narbo Martius

GALLIA

Lugdunum

VINDELICIA

Emerita Augusta

Toletum

HISPANIA

BAETICA

Gades

Tingis

Carthage Nova

Tarraco

CORSICA

SARDINIA

MAURETANIA

Caesarea

Carthage

PROCONSULAR AFRICA

SARMATIANS

Caspian Sea

SCYTHIANS

GERMANIA

Rhine River

Vindelicum

NORICUM

RAETIA

Aquincum

DACIA

Danube River

Sirmium

ILLYRICUM

PANNONIA

Salonae

Aquileia

Mediolanum

Rome

Neapolis

ITALIA

Brundisium

Rhegium

Syracuse

SICILIA

Massilia

Adriatic Sea

Leptis Magna

Mediterranean Sea

CYRENE

Cyrene

Caucasus

ARMENIA

Artaxata

PARTHIA

Ctesiphon

ASSYRIA

MESOPOTAMIA

Tigris River

Euphrates River

CAPPADOCIA

Trapezus

Black Sea

Byzantium

THRACIA

MOESIA

MACEDONIA

EPIRUS

ACHAIA

Athens

Corinth

CRETE

Salonae

BITHYNIA
AND PONTUS

Nicomedia

Ancyra

GALATIA

PHRYGIA

Pergamum

ASIA

Ephesus

LYCIA

CILICIA

Tarsus

CYPRUS

Antioch

SYRIA

Palmyra

Damascus

JUDEA

Jerusalem

ARABIA

Desert

Red Sea

Thebes

Nile River

EGYPT

Memphis

Alexandria

Senatorial province under Augustus

Imperial province under Augustus

Conquered or annexed after Augustus

Provincial boundary

Major road

| 0 | 200 | 400 | 600 miles |
| 0 | 200 | 400 | 600 | 800 km |

ROME (A.D. 1ST-3RD CENTURIES)

Castra
Praetoria

Tomb of
Augustus

PINCIAN
HILL

Baths of
Diocletian

QUIRINAL
HILL

VIMINAL
HILL

ESQUILINE
HILL

Mausoleum
of Hadrian

Pantheon

Theater of
Pompey

Capitol

CAPITOLINE
HILL

Imperial
Fora

Roman
Forum

Baths of
Trajan

Colosseum

T. Divi
Claudii

CAELIAN HILL

PALATINE HILL

Circus
Maximus

AVENTINE
HILL

Baths of
Caracalla

Circus
of Nero

VATICAN
HILL

■ Earliest
Christian sites

| 0 | 500 | 1000 yards |
| 0 | 500 | 1000 meters |

© Carta, Jerusalem

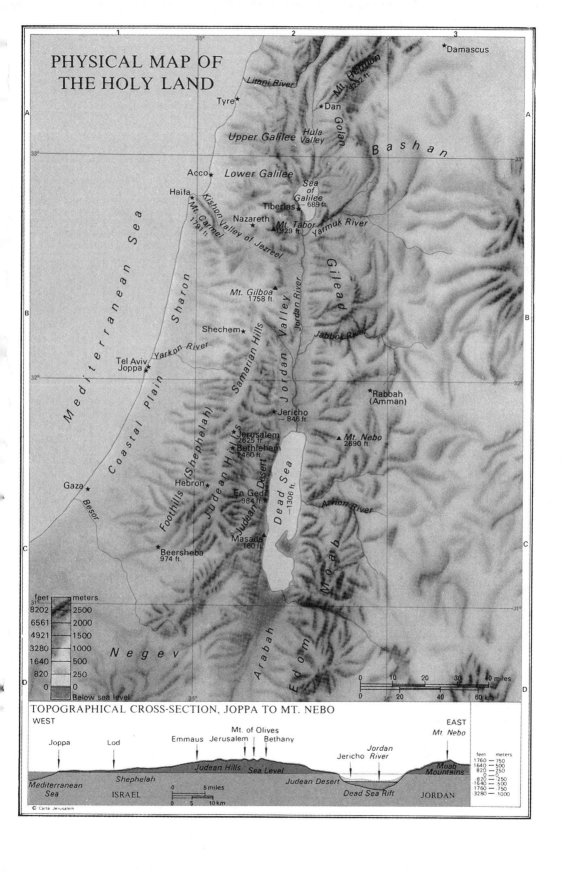

PHYSICAL MAP OF THE HOLY LAND

★Damascus

Litani River

Mt. Hermon
9232 ft.

Tyre★

★Dan

Upper Galilee

Hula Valley

Golan

B a s h a n

Acco★ Lower Galilee

Haifa★

Sea of Galilee
-689 ft.

Kishon Valley

Mt. Carmel
1791 ft.

Tiberias★

Nazareth★ Mt. Tabor
1929 ft.

Valley of Jezreel

Yarmuk River

M e d i t e r r a n e a n   S e a

Sharon

Gilead

Mt. Gilboa
1758 ft.

Jordan Valley

Jordan River

Shechem★

Jabbok River

Yarkon River

Samarian Hills

Tel Aviv
Joppa★

★Rabbah
(Amman)

Coastal Plain

Jericho★
-846 ft.

★Mt. Nebo
2690 ft.

Foothills (Shephelah)

Jerusalem★
2625 ft.
Bethlehem★
2460 ft.

Judean Desert

Judean Hills

Gaza★

Besor

Hebron★

En Gedi
-984 ft.

Dead Sea
-1306 ft.

Arnon River

Masada
160 ft.

Moab

Beersheba
974 ft.

feet   meters
8202 — 2500
6561 — 2000
4921 — 1500
3280 — 1000
1640 — 500
820 — 250
0 — 0
Below sea level

N e g e v

Arabah

Edom

0   10   20   30   40 miles
0   20   40   60 km

TOPOGRAPHICAL CROSS-SECTION, JOPPA TO MT. NEBO

WEST

EAST
Mt. Nebo

Joppa   Lod

Emmaus Jerusalem
Mt. of Olives
Bethany

Jericho Jordan River

Judean Hills   Sea Level

Moab Mountains

feet   meters
1760 — 750
1640 — 500
820 — 250
0 — 0
820 — -250
1640 — -500
1760 — -750
3280 — -1000

Mediterranean Sea

Shephelah

Judean Desert

Dead Sea Rift

ISRAEL

0   5 miles
0   5   10 km

JORDAN

© Carta, Jerusalem

Also in the Zondervan Classic

When you want to understand what the Bible says —

Matthew Henry's Commentary

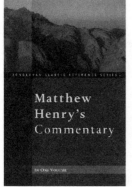

This one-volume edition of the classic devotional commentary preserves the best of Matthew Henry in his own words, giving a new generation of Bible students the wealth of exposition and comment, metaphors, analogies, and illustrations that has made *Matthew Henry's Commentary* a mainstay for almost three centuries.

As relevant today as ever, *Matthew Henry's Commentary* is of incomparable insight and written on a highly devotional level. Nothing has been added nor has there been any paraphrasing or altering of the original. Over 650,000 copies in print!

> *One of the great theological classics of English literature.*
> • F. F. Bruce, general editor,
> *New International Bible Commentary*
> ISBN: 0-310-26010-8

Jamieson, Fausset, & Brown's Commentary

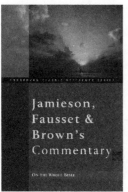

The revered 1870s classic commentary in one volume. Brief verse-by-verse exposition on the biblical text will add depth to your scriptural understanding.

> *It contains so great a variety of information that if a man had no other exposition he would find himself at no great cost if he possessed this and used it diligently. I have of it a very high opinion...and I consult it continually.*
> • Charles H. Spurgeon
> ISBN: 0-310-26570-3

ZondervanReference is committed to publishing outstanding books and software that help you better understand the Bible. Our contemporary reference tools and time-tested classics contain the most reliable and accessible evangelical scholarship supporting the NIV and traditional Bible translations. Depend on ZondervanReference when you want to know more about the Bible.

Reference Series

When you want to find something in the Bible —

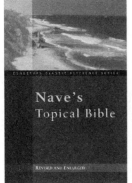

Nave's Topical Bible

When you use the *Nave's Topical Bible* you will find it an invaluable tool in understanding the Bible and in applying the great Bible truths to your life. It is arranged by topic and provides over 6,000 entries with more than 100,000 Scripture references (most of them with complete Bible text).

Use the *Nave's Topical Bible* to

• Study what the Bible says on abortion, salvation, suicide, praise, and more than 6,000 other topics.
• Find Bible references on more than 20,000 subjects.
• Find definitions of all persons, places, objects, and events in the Bible
• Find information about archaeological discoveries
• Develop sermon outlines
• Prepare Sunday school lessons
• Enhance devotional reading

> *Outside the Bible, this is the book that I depend on more than any other. Certainly there has been no book that has helped me more in my study.*
> • Billy Graham
> ISBN: 0-310-33710-0

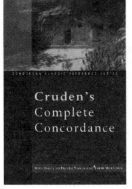

Cruden's Complete Concordance

First published in 1737, *Cruden's Complete Concordance* has long been considered the most practical and usable concordance on the market. It includes more than 200,000 references to Scripture in both the King James Version and the Revised Version. It also includes an index to all the key words of the Bible.

> *Next to the Bible I would advise you to get* Cruden's Concordance!
> • D. L. Moody
> ISBN: 0-310-22920-0

Available at your local Christian bookstore.

ZondervanPublishingHouse
Grand Rapids, Michigan
http://www.zondervan.com

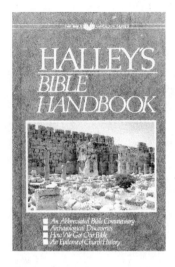